40th
ANNIVERSARY EDITION

CAMRA's GOOD BEER GUIDE

2013

D0453232

Edited by Roger Protz

Project Co-ordinator Emma Haines
Assistant Editors Ione Brown, Katie Hunt, Simon Tuite
Head of Publishing Simon Hall

BOOKS

Contents

The Pubs

The Breweries

Holding on to Hard-Won Victory   674
Celebrate by all means... but don't forget to campaign
A word from our sponsor: Society of Independent Brewers

Indexes & Further Information

Noble Beers get the Bullet   937
How much loved ales are being killed

Special thanks to 140,000 CAMRA members who carried out research for the pub entries; the Campaign's Regional Directors and Area Organisers, who co-ordinated the pub entries; Paul Moorhouse for assembling the beer tasting notes; Rick Pickup and Steve Westby for advising on new breweries; John Duffy for updating Irish breweries information; Warren Wordsworth and members of CAMRA's Norwich & Norfolk branch for their help with the pub crawl feature; Michael Slaughter for advising on heritage pubs; Tom Whitaker for his four-course meal feature; the publicans, breweries and others who kindly contributed their photographs; and CAMRA's National Executive for their support.

Thanks also to the following at CAMRA head office: Chief Executive Mike Benner; Marketing and Public Affairs: Lauren Anderson, Claire Cain, Sam Hargreaves, Jon Howard, Tony Jerome, Chris Lewis, Jonathan Mail, Jay Norton, Emily Ryans, Gregory Rycroft; What's Brewing/ BEER: Tom Stainer, Claire-Michelle Taverner-Pearson; Administration: Steven Brooks, Gillian Dale, Cressida Feiler, Gary Ranson, Nicky Shipp; Membership Services: Caroline Clerembeaux, John Cottrell, Catrin Davies, Gary Fowler; Finance and Branch Support: Robert Ferguson, Anita Gibson, Liz McGlynn, Malcolm Harding; Warehouse: Neil Cox, Steve Powell, Barnaby Smith, Ron Stocks.

Photo credits: [Key: t = top; b = bottom; c=centre; l = left; r = right] Front cover: Brian North; p7(t): WPA Pool/Getty Images; (b): Cath Harries; p10 (tr): Ewan Munro/Flickr; (tl): Adrian Tierney-Jones; (cr): Andrew Fogg/Flickr; (bl): Mike Forsyth/Flickr; (br): Cath Harries; pp12–15: Cath Harries; p16(l): Ascot Racecourse/RPM; pp16–17: Richard Brooks; p17(t): Jonas Smith; p21: Greene King; pp22–25: Cath Harries; p27: Nick Otley; p32: Cath Harries; p671: Cath Harries; p927: Tom Stainer; p929 (tl): Andrew Head/Flickr; (tr): Nigel Mullender; (bl): Mike Cattell/Flickr; (br): Bob Steel; p930 (all except tr): Kath Harries; (tr): George Gimber; p931 (tr): Warren Wordsworth; p932 (bl): calflier001/Flickr; p933 (bl): Helge Nareid; p939: Apple Inc.

Production: Cover design: Dale Tomlinson; colour pages design: Keith Holmes, Thames Street Studio; database, typesetting and indexes: AMA Dataset; pubs section maps: David and Morag Perrot, PerroCarto; map p15, Mark Walker, MW Digital Graphics; Photoshop work: James Hall.

Printed and bound in the UK by William Clowes, Beccles, Suffolk.

Published by the Campaign for Real Ale Ltd, 230 Hatfield Road, St Albans, Herts, AL1 4LW.
www.camra.org.uk
© Campaign for Real Ale 2012/2013.
All rights reserved. ISBN 978-1-85249-290-8

Disclaimer: Every effort has been made to ensure the contents of this guide are correct at the time of printing. Nevertheless, the Publisher cannot be held responsible for any errors or omissions, or for changes in any details given, or for the consequences of any reliance on the information provided by the same. This does not affect your statutory rights. It is inevitable that some pubs and breweries will change their character during the currency of the Guide.

All of the papers used in this book are recyclable and made from wood grown in managed, sustainable forests. They are manufactured at mills certified to ISO 14001 and/or EMAS.

PEFC
BMT-PEFC-0826

About the Good Beer Guide

Celebrating 40 editions!

The guide that led the way in introducing consumers to the best pubs and beer

Forty years in the life of any guide book would be cause for celebration but in the case of the *Good Beer Guide* we can raise a collective tankard and salute a remarkable achievement: a book that underscores a dogged consumer determination to save and revive Britain's unique beer style – real ale.

The *Good Beer Guide* has always been more than a pub guide. Pubs are the central core, the essential outlets for real ale. But the *Good Beer Guide* has always worn both belt and braces, with its Breweries section complementing the pub listings by detailing all the U.K. producers of cask beer and their ales.

This 40th edition looks back to the early days of the Guide but the main thrust is about the present day. As well as listing some 4,500 of the finest outlets for real ale and the ever-growing number of breweries, we also look at the modern threats to the pub and good beer: see the Introduction on pages 6–7. But this year we can allow an element of nostalgia, for the way the Guide is compiled today bears little relation to the methods used by the pioneers in the early 1970s.

Charting a real ale revival

As the interview with the first editors of the Guide on pages 8–9 shows, the early editions were put together when CAMRA was only a nascent organisation and pub surveys were conducted by a mere handful of enthusiasts in their spare time.

It was a different world. Real ale was in retreat under the onslaught of giant national breweries – the infamous 'Big Six' – determined to foist fizzy keg beers on the drinking public. Pubs were losing their hand pumps and independent breweries were closing. The brewery listings in the first Guide ran to just two pages. Today, the Breweries section is a book in its own right, with more than 200 pages detailing an astonishing 1,025 breweries. In 1974 (when the first professionally-produced edition of the Guide

was published), the terms 'micro-brewery' and 'pubco' were unheard of. The explosion of small breweries lay in the future and most pubs were 'tied houses' owned and controlled by breweries with no possibility of 'guest beers'. Consumer choice was restricted and those breweries that still produced real ale had limited portfolios of mild, bitter and best bitter.

To monitor all of Britain's breweries today, CAMRA cannot rely on scraps of information from friends and acquaintances as in the early days of the Guide – keeping apace with them all is a significant challenge. So, each brewery has a CAMRA liaison officer and he or she will regularly visit their breweries and check on the beers being produced before reporting the information to a constantly updated database.

This provides the basis for the Breweries section of the Guide. As soon as a new brewery comes on stream, a liaison officer will be appointed to make sure the Guide is fully updated every year and readers are aware of the increased choice of beers available.

The 1974 Guide with the current edition

Democratically selected entries

The way in which pubs are chosen is equally meticulous. It's far removed from the early days of the Guide when a handful of dedicated volunteers would search – more in hope than expectation – for pubs serving real ale just off the Great North Road and stopping short at Hadrian's Wall. The *Good Beer Guide* is unique in the way in which pubs are chosen. The entire 140,000-plus membership is encouraged to be involved and those members who cannot be active or attend regular meetings are invited to recommend pubs via e-mail or branch websites.

Regular inspections

The entries in most pub guides are chosen either by small editorial teams or by members of the public, whose recommendations are not necessarily checked. On the other hand, every pub that appears in this Guide has been visited regularly, often weekly, by CAMRA members. We offer full entries, with no unchecked 'lucky dip' sections of pubs sent in at random.

Keeping up to date

The Campaign has more than 200 branches. Each branch surveys the pubs in its area and monitors not only the quality of the cask beer in each one but also watches for changes of ownership or management which could affect the range of ale on offer and its overall quality.

The way in which entries are compiled changes constantly. The early editions of the Guide were compiled with the aid of notebooks and pens. But within the past decade there has been a major switch from paper to modern technology. Many members now go to pubs armed with laptop or tablet computers to conduct their surveys. The information they glean is compiled on a national database from which the entries in the Guide are produced. Together with the breweries database, CAMRA and the Guide share an unrivalled electronic storehouse of information about pubs and breweries nationwide.

There is a cynical saying in the publishing world that 'all guide books are out of date as soon as they appear'. That's not the case with the *Good Beer Guide*. Thanks to modern technology, the Guide is checked and re-checked many times before publication and both pub and brewery entries can be amended or deleted at a late date.

It's not only about quality beer

The changes are profound, but the driving force of the Guide – beer quality – has not changed over 40 editions. The Guide takes account of the history and architecture of pubs and such important aspects as food, accommodation, family and disabled facilities, gardens, special events such as mini-beer festivals, and even the standard of the toilets. But from 1974 to today, it has been our belief that if a publican looks after the real ales

in the cellar then the quality of the other facilities will most likely be of an equally high standard.

One difference between the early Guides and this 40th edition is the amount of information given about each pub. In 1974, pub descriptions were short, sparse or even non-existent. Today, CAMRA volunteers are called on to be minor essayists, describing in detail all aspects of the pubs they choose. We know from the feedback we receive that users of the Guide want full and reliable information about pubs before embarking on journeys to visit them.

Town & country pubs

Also, users want a good spread of pubs. Unlike some guides that concentrate on rural pubs, we recognise that most people live in towns and cities and expect a good selection of pubs in those areas. But we don't neglect suburban and country pubs: on the contrary, CAMRA campaigns for the survival of rural pubs that are often vital hubs of their isolated communities.

We are at pains to ensure that all areas of the country are covered. Each county or region has an allocation of pubs based on a scientific calculation of its population, number of licensed premises and level of tourism among other factors. As a result, the Guide's reach is unparalleled.

Still proudly independent

Finally, unlike many of our competitors, **all of our pub entries are free**. CAMRA is a proudly independent organisation and we do not charge pub owners to appear in the *Good Beer Guide*. CAMRA is a broad church and the Guide reflects that by choosing pubs across a wide spectrum that will appeal to people from all walks of life.

Methods may have changed, but the *Good Beer Guide* of yesterday and today remains committed to the simple pleasure of enjoying a good pint in a pleasant pub. With justifiable pride, we celebrate 40 editions of bibulous endeavour and salute the pioneers who made the Guide possible.

 **Reader updates & feedback**

🍺 All CAMRA members can vote for the quality of beer in pubs by using the National Beer Scoring Scheme. The scheme uses a 0–5 scale that can be submitted online. For more information go to **www.beer-scoring.org.uk**.

🍺 You can keep you copy of the Guide up to date by visiting the *Good Beer Guide* area of the CAMRA website: **www.camra.org.uk/gbg**. Click on 'Updates to GBG 2013' where you will find information about changes to pubs and breweries.

🍺 The Guide is keen to hear from readers. If you wish to recommend a pub or feel that one you have visited fell below expectations, then we would like to know. Please use the Readers' Recommendations and Have Your Say forms at the back of the book or contact the editor at **camrabgeditor@camra.org.uk**.

Introduction

Campaign to support your local pub!

The real ale boom could go into reverse unless consumers do more to prevent the cull of community locals

The bald figures are astonishing: there are now 1,008 breweries operating in Britain, the biggest number since the 1940s. CAMRA membership stands at more than 140,000, the highest in the Campaign's 42-year history. The growth in both brewery numbers and CAMRA membership shows no signs of slowing.

And while around 12 pubs a week are closing, the rate of closure is slowing. There are encouraging signs that people are returning to pubs not only to enjoy good beer but also because they recognise them as an important community resource that needs to be supported.

The revival of real ale is nothing short of miraculous. Until recently, the real ale sector was seriously under-promoted by the brewing industry. The big money went on advertising lager and nitro-keg beers. Cask beer became almost an underground drink, sought out with the aid of this Guide, local CAMRA guides, and websites and blogs devoted to the subject.

But now, real ale has put its head above the parapet. Wells & Young's has advertised its premium cask beer, Bombardier, on television for several years, using the actor Rik Mayall, and in 2012 it introduced a new series of TV slots for the beer. In the same year, Greene King launched a TV campaign for its IPA that cost a reputed £4 million. The advertisement was filmed in a real pub and the presentation promoted both cask beer and the pleasures of the local.

Most significantly, these promotions are seen not only on mainstream television but also on the 'blokeish' channel Dave, and on such social media as YouTube, Facebook and Twitter. Greene King and W&Y have done their research and know that real ale is no longer confined to people inhabiting that ancient cliché of woolly jumpers and Hush Puppies. As even the most casual visitor to a CAMRA beer festival will see, cask beer today is being enjoyed with relish by people usually dubbed 'the lager generation'.

The statistics underscore the trend. In 2012, total beer sales were down by 3.7% on the previous year while the ale sector declined by 5%. But most of ale's decline was accounted for by a decline in nitro-keg sales. Cask real ale was down by a mere 0.3% and was easily the best performer in the total beer market, where lager declined by 2.9%.

Real ale's strong performance in a declining market is the all the more remarkable when you consider the giant roadblocks that stand in its way. Taxation is the major obstacle. British brewers suffer from punitive rates of duty. Duty in the U.K. accounts for 40% of all the beer taxes within the European Union but the British consume only 13% of the beer produced in the EU. Only Finland has a higher rate of beer tax than Britain and as there are five million Finns compared to 62 million Britons, the British exchequer's income from beer is the highest in Europe.

Duty increased by 42% between 2008 and 2012. The problem has been made worse by the 'duty escalator' introduced by the last Labour Chancellor, Alistair Darling, and continued by his Conservative successor, George Osborne.

Big River in Brough is one of over 150 new breweries listed in this year's Guide

Wells & Young's has poured money into promoting Bombardier, including a high-profile campaign starring actor Rik Mayall

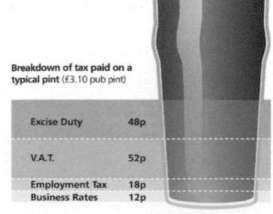

Breakdown of tax paid on a typical pint (£3.10 pub pint)

Excise Duty	48p
V.A.T.	52p
Employment Tax	18p
Business Rates	12p

Over $^2/_5$ of the price of the average pint is taken in tax

When the coalition came to office it promised to be a pub-friendly government. Yet, like its predecessor, it has done nothing to support the pub nor has it taken steps to tackle the market-distorting power of the supermarkets. Between 2009 and 2012, 4,500 pubs closed – half of them while the coalition has been in office. The rate of closure may be slowing, but pubs – many of them vital hubs of their communities – will continue to close unless they receive support from the government.

It is vital for the government to introduce measures to control the supermarkets and support pubs. If not, then the real ale revival will hit the buffers. Cask beer can be sold only in pubs – a beer that comes to fruition in its cask was designed specifically for the pub trade. If pub numbers continue to decline, sales of real ale will fall and small breweries without pub estates will inevitably go out of business.

David Cameron promised that his would be a pub-friendly government. Pubs are still waiting to see any signs of government support

The *Good Beer Guide* urges the government to introduce the following measures:

☐ Scrap the beer duty escalator that penalises beer sales in pubs: publicans don't enjoy the deep discounts offered by brewers to supermarkets.

☐ Follow the Scottish government and introduce minimum pricing for alcohol, which would not affect beer prices in pubs but would increase supermarket prices. Minimum prices must include production costs as well as duty and VAT. This would lead to the price of a supermarket pint increasing by between 35 and 40 pence, dramatically closing the gap between the on-trade and the off-trade.

☐ Tighten planning laws to stop viable pubs being closed and turned into fast-food outlets, betting shops or private houses. Central and local government should work together to save the pub as a vital community asset.

☐ Encourage people to use their pubs. One way to tackle alcohol abuse and the impact on the NHS is to laud the pub as a licensed and controlled environment where beer can be enjoyed sensibly and moderately.

CAMRA is campaigning to scrap the beer 'duty escalator'

The Guide asks its readers to support these demands by writing to their MPs and to consider the following suggestions:

● When a viable community pub is threatened with closure, contact your local CAMRA branch (**www.camra.org.uk/branches**) and join any campaign to save the pub by running it as a co-operative or with local shareholders.

● Support local breweries and CAMRA's LocAle scheme. Try a range of real ale in pubs: drink 'outside the box'.

● Support CAMRA's Community Pubs Month in April 2013: see **www.communitypubsmonth.org.uk** for full details.

The pub and real ale are rooted in Britain's history and heritage. Let us use our consumer power and voice to make sure they survive for future generations to enjoy.

CAMRA's successful LocAle scheme promotes pubs stocking locally-brewed beer

Looking Back Over 40 Years
The Guide, and beer, have come a long way

Since the Campaign for Real Ale was formed in 1971 to challenge the terminal decline of real ale, both the *Good Beer Guide* and real ale have seen enormous changes. Here, we look at the very early days of the Guide, revisit a classic article from a past edition and showcase seven remarkable pubs which have featured in every edition.

The first professionally-produced edition of the *Good Beer Guide* in 1974 was almost the last. The printers, John Waddington, threatened to withdraw the book from publication as they claimed it contained a gross libel of the giant London brewer Watney. The brewery list at the back of the 96-page guide advised drinkers to avoid the creator of Red Barrel keg beer 'like the plague'.

Michael Hardman and Graham Lees, two of the founding members of CAMRA, were journalists and they leaked the story to the press. Next day, the papers were packed with news about the Guide and its description of Watney. Hardman quickly met with Waddington's and the result was a compromise: the Watney's entry was amended to read 'avoid at all costs', the book was duly printed and quickly sold out.

CAMRA had good reason to thank Waddington's, as the young Campaign lacked the funds to produce a guide. In an emergency meeting held in October 1972, Graham Lees suggested one way of raising funds would be to sell a printed list of pubs that sold real ale. The following month, a hurriedly produced, loose-leafed *Good Beer Guide* listing was printed and went on limited sale. The next edition was to be a more professional and commercial production, and a proper book. Waddington's Beric Watson, a keen cask beer drinker, offered to print the guide and take the financial risk. John Hanscomb was appointed to edit it. With that important amendment to the brewery section, the book appeared in 1974, priced 75 pence, and it's been in annual production ever since.

'It's a wonder it ever happened,' says Michael Hardman, production editor for the 1974 Guide. 'There was a complete lack of knowledge about pubs serving real ale and CAMRA had no effective branch structure.'

With the exception of Young's Brewery in south London, breweries refused to give CAMRA information about their beers, pubs or free trade accounts. The Brewers' Society, the industry's umbrella organisation, told the Campaign, in

Michael Hardman and John Hanscomb – pioneer editors of the 1974 *Good Beer Guide*.

Hardman's phrase, 'to bugger off'. 'We had no idea about the strengths of beer and the brewers refused to disclose them.'

'We went through a learning process,' John Hanscomb recalls. 'We found there were many people with the knowledge we lacked, such as Tom Linfoot, who became assistant editor. Andrew Cunningham knew a great deal about beer, and Chris Hutt was researching a book about pubs.'

The key man was Frank Baillie, author of the *Beer Drinker's Companion* (1973), who is described by Hardman as 'God'. Baillie's book was the first to give beer lovers information about the country's breweries and their beers. He generously made his information available to the *Good Beer Guide* and Hardman and Hanscomb added their own comments as their knowledge grew.

A list of breweries was important but what beer lovers also needed was information about where they could find cask beer. The 'Big Six' national brewers owned half the country's pubs and were flooding them with heavily-promoted pressurised beers. As a result, handpumps disappeared like the snows of winter.

Graham Lees was running the office of a local newspaper in St Albans. He spotted a letter in the paper complaining about the lack of good beer in the city. When Hardman and Lees investigated, they found that all Whitbread's pubs had lost their handpumps, replaced by founts for Flower's Keg. At a time when St Albans had more than 60 pubs, only one, McMullen's Farriers Arms, sold real ale.

The choice of pubs was hit-and-miss. With only a handful of CAMRA branches set up, Hardman and Hanscomb had to rely on their own research and they were limited by the fact they had full-time jobs to attend to. Hanscomb admits his choice in Huntingdonshire was confined to visiting pubs just off the A1. But that county, with seven entries, fared better than Scotland, which was not represented at all in the first Guide.

By the time the 1975 edition of the Guide was compiled, CAMRA branches had sprung up all over the country and a national organisation was beginning to take shape. But coverage of some areas remained patchy. Michael Hardman set out to survey Cornwall with graphic designer John Simpson.

'We packed a small tent in the back of the car in case of emergencies,' Hardman says. 'It was a wise precaution. One day, we couldn't find a B&B and by the time we left the last pub on our list, it was dark. We drove down a narrow road, turned in to a field, put the tent up and went to sleep.'

They were woken at dawn by a sound, Hardman says, like several helicopters hovering overhead. When he looked through the flap, he discovered they had put the tent up a few feet from the main Cornwall-to-London railway line.

The first real edition of the Guide was nearly axed because of an alleged libel. The next might never have appeared if the editor had been mown down by an express train from Truro to Paddington but, thankfully, the Guide survived to become the bible for beer and pub lovers over four decades.

A classic article from the archives

For the 1989 edition of the Guide, the renowned beer writer Michael Jackson contributed an article called 'But I don't like beer...' It was aimed at lager drinkers and could have gone badly wrong, seen as sarcastic and patronising. But Michael was pitch-perfect and wrote a minor masterpiece. These extracts from the piece are our tribute to a great writer who frequently wrote for the Guide and who died in 2007.

'But I don't like beer...'

Lager has its place. Let us not be niggardly; it has its places. There are at least three of them: Czechoslovakia, if you would like to try the golden-coloured, dry, flowery style of lager that was first made in the

Michael Jackson

town of Pilsen, Bohemia; or Vienna, if you think you might prefer a fuller-coloured, spicier, lager; or Bavaria, if your taste could run to a lager that is sweetly malty and sometimes in the original, dark brown style.

I drink Ersatzenbräu. That's German.

German-ish. It's brewed under licence in a place you thought was nothing more sinister than a missile silo, at a convenient intersection of trucking routes between three major centres of population.

It's refreshing. That's really why I drink it.

Ever tried Fuller's Chiswick Bitter in London? Or Jennings in Cumbria?

Those are beers. I don't like beer.

Lager is beer, too. Ale is a British (and Belgian) style.

Ale? You mean Bitter?

Mild Ale, Bitter Ale, Brown Ale, Pale Ale, Light Ale, Heavy Ale, Old Ale, Barley Wine. Not to mention Porter and Stout.

Let's go to a pub. Where do we start?

Gently. We begin with something low in alcohol but full of fruity flavour. We will head for Hertfordshire to try some of the wonderfully complex pale Mild brewed by the McMullen brewery. After that, go to the real Mild Ale regions: the West Midlands and Manchester.

You've persuaded me. Where can we get a good pint of Bitter?

Depends on what takes your fancy. For a really dry, hoppy Bitter, let's stay in the South: Shepherd Neame's brewery at Faversham is set among the hop gardens of East Kent that grow the Goldings, the world's most aromatic ale hop. Young's and Fuller's in London both make hoppy Bitters. For really dry, fruity Bitter, the splendidly tart Greene King of Bury St Edmunds; the more complex, salty Adnams from Southwold. For creamy Bitter, Yorkshire and the adjoining counties: Tetley's, Timothy Taylor and Samuel Smith's of Yorkshire. Across the Durham border, Strongarm from Cameron's.

For firm-bodied, acidic Bitter, the North-west. The malty-dry Lees; the deceptively soft Hydes; the austere Holt's; the gentle, subtle Robinson's; all from Greater Manchester. For really chewy Bitter, Wales: the big, rounded Bitter from Felinfoel; the dry, profound Special Ale from Brain's.

What about Pale Ale, then?

Certainly, we'll have to go to Burton for that. We'll have elegant Marston's Pedigree in the pub, as an aperitif, and take home a bottle of sedimented Worthington's White Shield to have with our roast beef dinner.

What about Scotland?

Full-bodied, warming ales – especially the strong, Export style from Belhaven and Maclay's. Or a beautifully clean and malty, extra strong 90 Shilling from Caledonian, a magnificent brewery that has regained its independence. Its 90 Shilling is a classic pale Scotch ale, the beer world's answer to a Lowland malt. Traquair House is the classic Scotch Ale. Oaky-tasting from its fermentation in wood and almost 'Chateau-bottled'.

What would a man in a bar in Bordeaux think of comparisons with French wine?

He'd drink his bottle of Traquair House and toast the Auld Alliance. That's what he'd do.

The Magnificent Seven!

The *Good Beer Guide* salutes pubs that have been in every edition

There's an extra-special cause for celebration with the publication of the 40th edition of the *Good Beer Guide*, for seven pubs have appeared in every edition. It's a remarkable tribute to the publicans of these pubs who have maintained an exemplary standard of beer over all those years. The pubs are:

Buckingham Arms, 62 Petty France, London SW1 (see p302)
This tall, imposing building has small leaded windows on the ground floor and a pub sign depicting George Villiers, the first Duke of Buckingham in the 16th century. The long room inside is almost a corridor, served by an equally long bar that dispenses Young's and Wells' beers. The pub dates from the 1840s and has been a Young's house since 1930.

New Inn, The Hill, Kilmington, Devon (see p123)
The thatched and whitewashed New Inn dates from the early 19th century. Its survival in the Guide is all the more remarkable as it was rebuilt following a devastating fire in 2004. But landlords Brian and Denise Jenkins were swiftly manning the pumps again with the help of Palmer's of Bridport, whose ales grace the bar. The New Inn has a skittle alley that helps make it a vibrant part of village life.

Queen's Head, Newton, Cambridgeshire (see p64)
The Queen's was saved from closure in the 1960s by the Short family and has remained in their hands ever since. When David and Juliet Short retire, their son Rob will take over. The Queen's has two bars, ancient timbers, stoves, settles, old photos and prints on the walls, and the ancient pub game of Devil Among the Tailors. Adnams' ales are served straight from the cask.

Roscoe Head, 24 Roscoe Street, Liverpool (see p340)

The Roscoe is a traditional side-street local named after William Roscoe, an 18th-century poet and biographer. It has several small rooms and a snug, and has been in the same family's hands for more than 20 years. The current landlady, Carol Ross, took over when her parents retired. Carol bases her success on offering a good range of beers – Jennings, Tetley and guest ales – along with good pub fare and no intrusive juke boxes or fruit machines.

Square & Compass, Worth Matravers, Dorset (see p140)
This ancient ale house takes its name from the tools used by miners excavating the local Purbeck stone. It's been in the hands of the Newman family since 1907 and current owner Charlie Newman has no intention of modernising the pub. There's no bar – beer comes straight from the cask behind a hatch. There are two comfortable rooms with benches and fires in winter. In good weather, you can sit outside, sample Palmer's ale or Charlie's home-made cider.

Star, Netherton, Northumberland (see p372)
'It's like stepping into someone's home,' is the common response of visitors to this fine old building dating from 1788. There's a simple room with settles, a stove, and the pub's many awards displayed on the walls. It's been run by the Morton family since 1917 and Vera Morton-Wilson, the present incumbent, is the grand-daughter of the publicans who arrived in pony and trap to take over the place. Beer is served through a hatch and comes from a cellar where a stone gantry keeps it cool and in immaculate condition.

Star Tavern, 6 Belgrave Mews West, London SW1 (see p301)
This Grade II-listed Fuller's house was built in 1848 for the servants and tradesmen who supplied the great houses of Belgrave Square. In the 1960s it was the haunt of a 'demi-monde' of dodgy spivs, gangsters and minor celebrities but today it attracts a more respectable crowd who enjoy the excellent beer and good food in the big, airy rooms downstairs with comfortable benches, and a smaller overspill room up narrow stairs.

CAMRA's Pub of the Year

Pub saved from closure now judged best in Britain

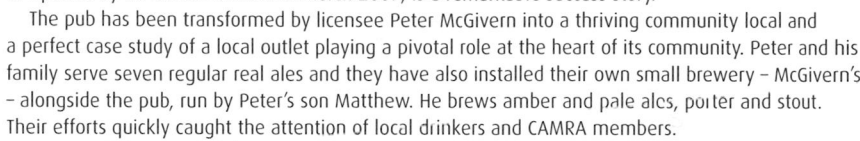

The Bridge End Inn in Ruabon, North-East Wales, has been named CAMRA's National Pub of the Year.

An old coaching inn on the road from England to Wrexham, the Bridge End Inn (see p594) enters CAMRA's history books as the first ever Welsh pub to win its National Pub of the Year competition and, having only been re-opened by its current owners in March 2009, is a remarkable success story.

The pub has been transformed by licensee Peter McGivern into a thriving community local and a perfect case study of a local outlet playing a pivotal role at the heart of its community. Peter and his family serve seven regular real ales and they have also installed their own small brewery – McGivern's – alongside the pub, run by Peter's son Matthew. He brews amber and pale ales, porter and stout. Their efforts quickly caught the attention of local drinkers and CAMRA members.

Peter said: 'We are delighted with this national award, particularly as we were told when first taking on the pub that there was little demand for real ale in the area. Through a lot of passion and hard work for what we do, we've enjoyed great success in a short space of time, which couldn't have been achieved without the support of family, close friends, staff and customers. We're not focused on food – it's a place where visitors can pay us a visit and sample a range of traditional beers'.

CAMRA's Pub of the Year competition analyses all the criteria that make a good pub, including the quality and choice of real ale, atmosphere, decor, facilities, customer service and value. The competition is initially judged by CAMRA's 140,000-plus members in regional competitions. Sixteen winners then battle it out to reach the final stages. Look out for the ♥ symbol against pub entries in the Guide and see 'Award winning pubs' on pages 928–933.

The runners-up were:

Engineers Arms, High Street, Henlow, Bedfordshire (see p39)
A lively two-bar pub with 10 handpumps offering a wide range of beers, and five ciders and perries. It's decorated with pictures of local history, sports stars and brewery memorabilia.

Front, Custom House Quay, Falmouth, Cornwall (see p81)
A small, cellar-style pub with a low, vaulted ceiling focuses on Cornish beers. It's a popular student haunt and has regular live entertainment, including folk and shanty singers. The range of guest beers add to the appeal.

Swan with Two Necks, Main Street, Pendleton, Lancashire (see p245)
The Swan is a true local with a friendly, relaxed atmosphere and home-cooked food. It's been run by the Dilworth family for 25 years and they concentrate on serving beer from local breweries, along with cider. Rosie the pub cat is thought to be the oldest feline in the country.

Norwich Pub Crawl

The 'City of Ale' has a fine choice of places to drink

Norwich calls itself 'City of Ale' and supporters claim it's the best place in the country to drink cask beer. It would be churlish to disagree, for Norfolk's capital has made a spirited recovery from the dog days of the 1970s when it was dubbed a beer desert by CAMRA.

The first edition of the *Good Beer Guide* listed just one pub in the city. Today there are 16 entries (on pages 354–355) and many more clamour for inclusion. In 2011 a festival called City of Ale ran for 10 days in May and June, supported by brewers, publicans and CAMRA members. Pubs and breweries displayed banners promoting the event while a special bus took supporters on a tour of the city's beery delights. The festival was backed by local press, radio and TV.

The event was repeated in 2012 with even greater support from 30 breweries in Norwich and Norfolk and 60 pubs in and around the city. City of Ale will be held again in 2013 from 30 May to 10 June (cityofale.org.uk). The event celebrates the rebirth of cask beer in Norwich and the revival of pubs serving it. Norwich will also be host to the 2013 CAMRA Members' Weekend and AGM, which will see CAMRA members from around the country flock to the city and St Andrew's & Blackfriars Hall to enjoy the ales on offer.

The city has come a long way since it suffered at the hands of the London brewer Watney. In 1966, the company bought and eventually shut three large commercial breweries in Norwich and closed hundreds of 'unviable' pubs in urban and rural areas, destroying many isolated communities in its wake.

If nature abhors a vacuum, it also dislikes pubs without good beer. This pub crawl cannot be comprehensive as a result of the vast number of outlets now serving real ale. It points visitors in the direction of a few pubs with fascinating stories and a good range of beer: for greater choice see the pubs listed in the Norwich section.

1 The **Gardeners Arms**, 2-8 Timber Hill, is a short stroll from the train station to the castle area. If you get lost, don't ask for the pub by that name as it's known to all and sundry as 'the Murderers'. The breathtakingly ancient

Gardeners Arms – also known as the Murderers

building, with beamed ceilings, standing timbers, higgledy-piggledy rooms and wobbly floors, dates from the 17th century and has been a pub since 1841. The nickname stems from a grisly murder in 1895, when a former cavalryman, Frank Miles, killed his estranged wife, Milly, the daughter of the landlady. Miles worked for Morgan's, one of the breweries put to death by Watney some 70 years later. Miles was spared the gallows as the result of a petition signed by 22,000 people, who claimed he had suffered 'extreme provocation'.

What owner Phil Cutter doesn't know about pubs and beer can be written on the back of the proverbial postage stamp. He started work in the Murderers aged 15 and has been there for 24 years. He's peppered the pub with newspaper front pages reporting other horrible murders, including the activities of the notorious Kray Gang in London and the assassination of John F Kennedy. Where ale is concerned, Adnams Bitter and Woodforde's Wherry are regulars and they are kept company by an ever-changing choice of guests from micro-breweries in East Anglia and further afield. Phil is a driving force behind City of Ale and when the event is running he turns one area of the pub into a small beer festival, with a host of ales served by gravity. In short, the Gardeners Arms is a fine place to murder a pint.

2 The **Trafford Arms**, 61 Grove Road, has suffered more than just the occasional murder. It was bombed by the Luftwaffe during World War Two: there are photos on the wall showing the extent of the damage. Today, it has an open-plan interior, with one area set aside for diners.

The Trafford Arms sells local and national beers

But beer is the key to the pub's success and a large L-shaped bar groans under the banks of handpumps offering Adnams and Wherry as staples along with a rare visitor to these parts, Tetley Bitter. Guest beers may include Meantime and Oakham. There's always a dark beer available, such as Greene King Mild.

The Trafford Arms is run by Chris Higgins, who was Sheriff of Norwich in 2001 and 2012 and, in full medieval attire, opened the first City of Ale festival. The name of the pub suggests a Manchester connection but Chris is keen to point out that the aristocratic Trafford family came from Norwich, though it had links to the North-west. The Trafford family arms are engraved on a mirror in the pub.

3 The **Fat Cat**, 49 West End Street, is a Norwich institution, one of the most popular outlets for cask beer in the country. It has twice won CAMRA's National Pub of the Year award, in 1998 and 2004, testimony to its devotion to the real ale cause. It was opened in 1991 by Colin Keatley, who has since added the Shed in Lawson Road, complete with the Fat Cat micro-brewery, and then in 2012 the Fat Cat & Canary in Thorpe Road, near the train station. It's handily placed for Norwich City football stadium where the local team, in their bright yellow and green kit, are nicknamed the Canaries.

The Fat Cat dates from the late 19th century and is an ale house, pure and simple. Twelve

The Fat Cat is a keen supporter of LocAle

handpumps dispense a dazzling array of cask beers and there are also genuine Continental lagers and Belgian specialities: all the beers on tap are chalked on boards above the bar. A window gives a view of the ground-floor store, showing all the beers on stillage. The Fat Cat beers include Meow Mild, Cougar, Honey Cat and Best Bitter and they are joined by ales from Adnams, Elgood's, Oakham, Stonehenge and Timothy Taylor – but the range is liable to constant change.

You can sit in the Fat Cat, with its bare boards and half wood-panelled walls, and learn the history of brewing in Norwich. The pub is packed with memorabilia, including old posters for beers from the three long-defunct local breweries, Bullard's, Morgan's and Steward & Patteson. There's even a poster for Watney's Sparkling Ale, which proves the old saying that all that glisters is not gold.

The colourful and renowned Fat Cat

4 The **White Lion**, 73 Oak Street, has a modern facade that belies an older interior. The building dates from 1558 and was once a much smaller, one-room ale house. It became a Bullard's pub in the 19th century and was later extended by the simple device of buying the hairdresser's next door. It closed in 2003 and re-opened in 2008, owned by the Milton Brewery of Cambridgeshire through a sister company, Individual Pubs. There's an excellent offering of cask beers, but the White Lion is best known as a cider pub and has been named Cider Pub of the Year by the local CAMRA branch. If you enjoy the juice of the apple and the pear, there are no fewer than 36 ciders and perries to choose from.

Ale and 36 ciders and perries at the White Lion

The beer range includes a number of Milton brews, including Justinian, Pegasus and Sparta, topped up by ales from Buntingford, Dark Star and Potton. Pint in hand, you can wonder through the three bars, from the small front room with a tiled floor, leather settees and chairs, into a large back bar where darts and bar billiards are played, and a third room with settles and beams. As well as beer and cider, the White Lion has rapidly established a good reputation for food: vegetarians are well catered for.

The revived King's Head is a vibrant free house

The revival of good beer and pubs in Norwich is enshrined in the **King's Head**, 42 Magdalen Street. It was a bikers' pub for many years, closed for 18 months and became almost derelict. It took a further 18 months to refurbish it and enable it to become a vibrant free house. The design is Victorian though, as with many buildings in Norwich, it could be older and some parts of the exterior suggest it could have been a coaching inn. Its main claim to fame is that it refuses to sell a single drop of keg beer or lager and it's also free of televisions and piped music. It's a brave stance to take in this modern world, but it has paid dividends.

It has two linked bars. The small, cheery, intimate front bar has six handpumps, a tiled floor, open fire and a useful map of the city. The back bar is spacious, with wooden settles, a bar billiard table in common with the White Lion, the pub is in the local bar billiards league

– and many old photos of the area. There are eight pumps in this room and both bars are dedicated to beers from East of England breweries. Winter's provides a house beer, King's Head Bitter, and further contributions come from Elgood's, Elmtree, Fat Cat, Grain, Green Jack, Panther and Woodforde's.

King's Head beer menu

The final pub on the crawl has so much history attached that an entire book could be devoted to it. **Ketts Tavern**, 29 Ketts Hill, stands alongside Mousehold Heath, scene of a great rebellion in the 16th century. The present pub dates from 1832 but it's thought there has been an inn on the site for 300 years or more. First, the history. In 1549 Robert Kett and 20,000 agricultural labourers camped on Mousehold Heath before marching on the city in a protest against land enclosures. They broke through the city walls and defeated an army of 15,000. It took a second attack by the Earl of Warwick's forces to vanquish Kett's army: Kett was subsequently hanged in Norwich.

Ketts Tavern sells Norfolk Square ales

His portrait is on the inn sign of this whitewashed, cottage-style pub. Inside, there's a modern conservatory extension, but the original interior is a delightful ramble of areas, with free-standing timbers, bare boards, low ceilings, settles and an inglenook. Beers come from the Norfolk Square Brewery in Great Yarmouth but they are re-badged Norwich Bear for the pub. The range of beers includes Pooh Bear, Norwich Bear Classic, Legend, Perfect Day and Platinum Blonde.

Home-cooked food is available lunchtimes. In the evening curries can be ordered from an

Indian takeaway. The pub is decorated with Norwich City FC memorabilia as it's a favourite watering hole for fans. The Norwich City Football ground is only a short walk away, beyond the station.

From Ketts Tavern you can stroll back to the train station, 10 minutes away, down Riverside Road, which runs alongside the River Wensum where many brightly-painted boats are moored.

The friendly Ketts Tavern

And if you still have a thirst, the new Fat Cat & Canary, 101 Thorpe Road is up and running close to the station.

It's run, of course, by the indefatigable Colin Keatley, and is modelled on the original Norwich Fat Cat. It sells the full range of Fat Cat beers brewed in the city along with ales from Crouch Vale, Oakham and other independents.

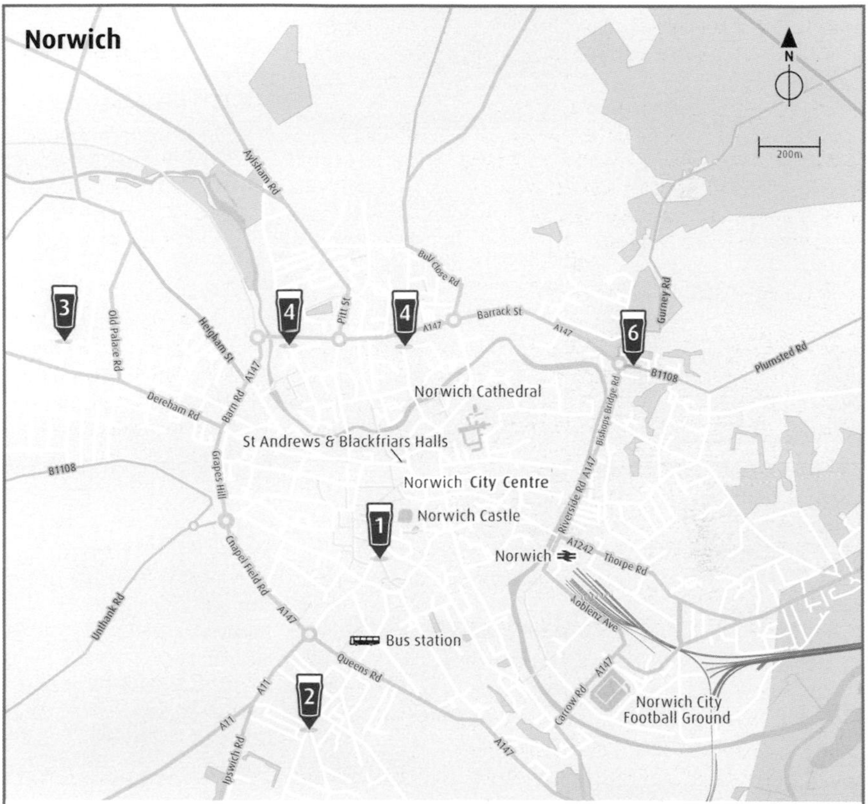

Norwich

Pub information

1. Gardeners Arms
2-8 Timberhill, NR1 3LB
☼ 10-11.30 (1.30am Fri & Sat); 12-10.30 Sun
☎ (01603) 621447
⊕ themurderers.co.uk

2. Trafford Arms
61 Grove Road, NR1 3RL
☼ 11-11 (11.30 Fri & Sat); 12-10.30 Sun
☎ (01603) 628466
⊕ traffordarms.co.uk

3. Fat Cat
49 West End Street, NR2 4NA
☼ 12-11 (midnight Thu-Sat)
☎ (01603) 624364
⊕ fatcatpub.co.uk

4. White Lion
73 Oak Street, NR3 3AQ
☼ 12-11 (10.30 Sun)
☎ (01603) 632333
⊕ individualpubs.co.uk/whitelion

5. King's Head
42 Magdalen Street, NR3 1JE
☼ 12-midnight (11 Sun)
☎ (01603) 620468
⊕ kingsheadnorwich.com

6. Ketts Tavern
29 Ketts Hill, NR1 4EX
☼ 3-11.30; 12-midnight Fri & Sat; 12-11 Sun
☎ (01603) 449654
⊕ norwichbear.co.uk

CAMRA Beer Festivals

THE CAMPAIGN FOR REAL ALE'S BEER FESTIVALS are magnificent shop windows for cask ale and they give drinkers the opportunity to sample beers from independent brewers rare to particular localities. Beer festivals are enormous fun: many offer good food and live entertainment, and – where possible – facilities for families. Some seasonal festivals specialise in spring, summer, autumn and winter ales. Festivals range in size from small local events to large regional ones. CAMRA holds two national festivals, the National Winter Ales Festival in January, and the Great British Beer Festival in August; the latter features around 500 beers.

The festivals listed are those planned for 2013. For up-to-date information, visit the CAMRA website **www.camra.org.uk** and click on 'CAMRA Near You'. By joining CAMRA – there's a form on page 944 – you will receive the Campaign's monthly newspaper *What's Brewing*, which lists every festival on a month-by-month basis. Dates listed are liable to change: check with the website or *What's Brewing*.

JANUARY
National Winter Ales –
Manchester
Atherton – Bent & Bongs Beer
  Bash
Cambridge – Winter
Colchester – Winter
Ely – Winter
Exeter – Winter
Newark – Winter
Salisbury – Winter

FEBRUARY
Battersea
Chappel – Winter
Chelmsford – Winter
Chesterfield
Derby – Winter
Dorchester
Dover – White Cliffs Winter
Fleetwood
Gosport – Winter
Hucknall
Jersey – Winter
Liverpool
Luton
Pendle

Redditch
Stockton – Ale & Arty
Tewkesbury – Winter

MARCH
Bradford
Bristol
Burton
Darlington – Spring
Hitchin
Hove – Sussex
Leeds
Leicester
London Drinker
Loughborough
Manchester – MOSI
St Neots – Booze on the Ouse
Thanet
Walsall
Whitehaven
Wigan
Winchester

APRIL
Barnsley
Bexley
Bury St Edmunds – East Anglian
Chippenham
Coventry
Doncaster
Farnham
Glenrothes – Kingdom of Fife
Larbert – Falkirk
Maldon
Mansfield
New Mills
Newcastle-upon-Tyne
Paisley
Skipton

MAY
Banbury
Cambridge
Clitheroe

Colchester
Dewsbury
Halifax
Kidderminster
Kingston
Lincoln
Macclesfield
Newark
Newport (Gwent)
Northampton – Delapre Abbey
Reading
Stockport
Stourbridge
Stratford-Upon-Avon
Wolverhampton
Yapton

JUNE
Aberdeen
Braintree
Bromsgrove
Cardiff – Great Welsh
Chappel Cider Festival
Edinburgh – Scottish
Gibberd Garden – Harlow
Greater Manchester Cider and
  Perry Festival
Lewes – South Downs
Rugby
Salisbury
Southampton
St Ives (Cornwall)
Tenterden – Kent & East Sussex
  Railway
Thurrock
Woodchurch – Rare Breeds

JULY
Ardingly
Bishops Stortford
Canterbury – Kent
Chelmsford
Chorlton
Ealing

Derby
Devizes
Hereford – Beer on the Wye
Plymouth
Rochford – South East Essex
  Cider Festival
Stafford
Stowmarket
Winchcombe – Cotswold
Windsor
Woodcote – Steam Fair
Wykefest – Wyke Regis

AUGUST
Great British – London
Clacton
Grantham
Harbury
Ipswich
Morecambe
Overton – Hampshire
  (provisional)
Peterborough
Swansea
Watnall – Moorgreen
Worcester

SEPTEMBER
Bridgnorth – Severn Valley
Carmarthen
Chappel
Durham
East Malling (Kent)
Erewash Valley (Long Eaton)
Faversham – Hop
Hinckley
Jersey
Keighley
Letchworth
Lytham
Melton Mowbray
Minehead (West Somerset
  Railway)

Nantwich
Newton Abbot
North Cotswolds – Moreton-in-
  Marsh
Northwich (provisional)
Ripley – Derbyshire
St Albans
St Helens
Scunthorpe
St Ives (Cambs) – Booze
  on the Ouse
Tamworth
Ulverston
York

OCTOBER
Alloa
Ascot (provisional)
Barnsley
Basingstoke – Hampshire
  Octoberfest
Bath
Bedford
Birkenhead
Birmingham
Cambridge – Octoberfest
Carlisle
Chester
Chesterfield – Market
Eastbourne
Egremont, Cumbria
Falmouth
Gainsborough
Huddersfield – Oktoberfest

Kendal
Long Eaton
Louth
Milton Keynes
Norwich
Nottingham
Oxford
Quorn – Octoberfest
Redhill
Richmond (N Yorks.)
Sheffield
Solihull
South Woodham Ferrers –
  South Essex
Southport
Stoke-on-Trent –
  Potteries
Sunderland
Swindon
Thanet – Cider
Troon – Ayrshire
Twickenham
Wallington
Watford
Weymouth
Woolston – Southampton
Worthing

NOVEMBER
Belfast
Dudley
Heathrow
Poole
Rochford
Saltburn
Shrewsbury
Wakefield
Wantage
Woking

DECEMBER
Harwich
London – Pig's Ear

Cask Marque
Join the 'World's Biggest Ale Trail'

Following the success of the CaskFinder smartphone app which recognises your location and shows you the nearest Cask Marque pubs, Cask Marque have now launched the World's Biggest Ale Trail. All 8,000-plus accredited pubs are part of an ale trail covering the whole of Britain and even parts of Europe!

What is Cask Marque?

Cask Marque is a not-for-profit organisation formed in 1997 to promote cask beer and, in particular, beer quality. We have 45 assessors, mainly brewers, making over 20,000 visits to pubs a year to check the quality of the beer they serve. When assessing a pint, our assessors are meticulous, and consider temperature, appearance, aroma and taste. If any one beer fails our tests the pub will fail the whole inspection. So, seeing a Cask Marque plaque outside a pub provides consumers with the reassurance that they can expect a great pint.

There are now over 8,000 pubs in the U.K. who proudly display the Cask Marque plaque, and while they receive a minimum of two unannounced visits a year to check their beer quality, having CAMRA members provide feedback at other times of the year is invaluable. Please continue to tell us about your beer experiences in Cask Marque pubs, both good and bad, via **info@cask-marque.co.uk**

The world's biggest ale trail

By using the new ale trail feature on our CaskFinder app, users can join in an ale trail of all 8,000-plus Cask Marque accredited pubs.

It is very easy to participate:

- If you already have the free CaskFinder app, then all you need to do is click on the ale trail button.
- If not, then search for **CaskFinder** on either the iTunes app store (iPhones) or the Play Store (Android phones).

Once you have filled in the very short registration form then you are ready to go. Each time you visit a Cask Marque pub, look for the framed Cask Marque certificate and scan the QR code. Each code is unique to the pub and will record your visit. You can see a list of the pubs you have visited.

Prizes are awarded as follows:

- 25 pubs visited – Cask Marque fridge magnet and bottle opener.
- 50 pubs visited – Cask Marque polo shirt.
- 100 pubs visited – become a Cask Marque ambassador and we will work together to promote quality beer and quality pubs.

As well as the Ale Trail, the CaskFinder app also has many other great features:

- Information on beer festivals – both official CAMRA and local pub festivals.
- Cyclops beer tasting notes for over 1,200 beers.
- A growing list of brewers and their key beers.
- A beer blog from beer writer Pete Brown.
- Updated information about which beers are on sale in individual pubs.
- Consumer beer ratings – results are on our website in the 'beer info' section.

The app is used over 50,000 times a month so why not give it a go? To find out more look at our short video by doing a web search for "**You Tube CaskFinder**"

New website 'beer search'

Following feedback from CAMRA members, we have improved the pub search on our website. It is now much easier to find Cask Marque pubs all over Britain and we now have a unique 'beer search' feature. Using the data gathered from all of our pub visits, consumers can now see what beers the pubs were serving last time we visited. Although this data is from a given moment in time, it gives users of our website an idea of the range of beers that individual pubs are serving and indicates whether they are serious about their beer offering. Users can also search for a particular beer they might like and see if there are any pubs nearby which have stocked it.

The list of beers on the site is powered by the **www.Cyclopsbeer.co.uk** database which provides simple descriptions of beers. Any missing beers are due to the fact that the beers have not been through the accreditation process. Send an email to **info@cask-marque.co.uk** and we will encourage the brewer to get involved. Check out the beer search at **www.cask-marque. co.uk/pubs**

What else do we do?

We are also the industry's leading trainer in how to handle beer, delivering over 400 courses a year and have now trained over 12,500 people.

We champion cask ale by working closely with other organisations such as CAMRA, Independent Family Brewers of Britain, British Guild of Beer Writers and the Beer Academy.

We are also a shareholder as are CAMRA in Cyclops which gives each cask beer a simple beer tasting note. This is then used to inform both bar staff and consumers of beer flavours. Look out for Cyclops tasting notes on barrel ends at beer festivals, or indeed if you are involved in running a beer festival go online and print off your own barrel end with the beer description and pricing for $1/3$, $1/2$ and pints.

Again working with CAMRA we both promote Cask Ale Week which is held in the first week of October each year. This is an event to celebrate cask beer and the British pub, both of which are inextricably linked. Register your interest and see what is happening at **www.caskaleweek.co.uk**

Through the Beer Academy we are also promoting a course on how to judge beer which is very useful for any CAMRA members who are involved in beer competitions. Further information can be found on **www.beeracademy.co.uk**

Cask Marque training manager Annabel Smith inspects another perfect pint

Cask Marque in America

Cask Marque recently launched in the United States with a trial in Pennsylvania. Working closely with Wells & Young's, Fuller's, Marston's and Greene King we are developing a similar Cask Marque accreditation scheme. Although important, in America our remit is not just about the quality of beer in the glass but also about getting brewers and retailers to understand what is cask ale.

There are many micro-breweries in America and each of them is the equivalent size to one of our larger regional brewers. Cask ale is becoming increasingly popular but from a very low base and we want to inform drinkers about the values attached to cask ale and help develop more interest in this beer category.

To find out more about Cask Marque visit our website on **www.cask-marque.co.uk** and we hope you will join with us in championing beer quality in the glass to make sure you get served the perfect pint, every time.

Cask Marque and Cyclops

The unparalleled levels of choice and diversity of beers now on offer require significantly more customer guidance than was ever the case when we were merely deciding which was our favourite bitter or mild.

Cyclops has been developed as a simplified and accessible flavour-profiling system designed to de-mystify the taste of beer and provide just such orientation. It is increasingly seen on bottle labels, pump clips, websites and phone apps to assist navigation through what might otherwise be a bewildering minefield of decision-making.

Cask Marque is proud to be a partner in Cyclops, along with SIBA, the IFBB and CAMRA, and is keen to encourage its industry-wide use as a common scheme.

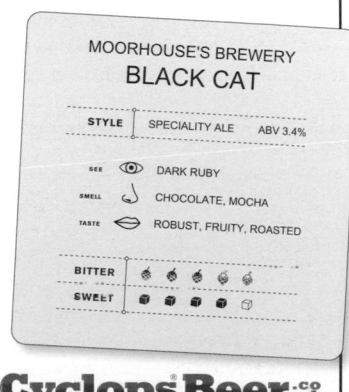

MOORHOUSE'S BREWERY
BLACK CAT

STYLE	SPECIALITY ALE	ABV 3.4%
SEE	DARK RUBY	
SMELL	CHOCOLATE, MOCHA	
TASTE	ROBUST, FRUITY, ROASTED	

BITTER	🍺 🍺 🍺 🍺 🍺 🍺
SWEET	🍺 🍺 🍺 🍺 🍺 🍺

Cyclops Beer.co.uk

Beer Trends

Strong beers under the hammer from new tax regime

The key beer trend in the past year has involved duty – the tax on beer. The changes introduced will affect both the taste of beer and the long-term future of some treasured British beer styles.

Thornbridge St Petersburg hit by HSBD beer tax

To encourage moderate consumption, the government reduced by 50% the duty on beers with strengths of between 1.2% and 2.8% ABV. This decreases the price of a pint of 2.8% beer by around 18 pence. Until the new duty rate was introduced, there were few beers rated at 2.8% or less as many brewers consider it difficult to create taste with so little malt and alcohol.

Fuller's 2.8% Mighty Atom

The take-up has not been spectacular. Fuller's introduced Mighty Atom and Greene King launched Tolly English Ale, both cask beers at 2.8%. But most of the new beers brewed to a low strength have been either variations of existing global lagers that had little flavour in their original form, or bottled beers.

In a tasting of a dozen low-strength beers – bottle, cask and keg – by the trade paper the *Publican's Morning Advertiser*, the judges were less than enthusiastic. Greene King's Tolly received some praise for being 'quite hoppy' and 'close to the real thing' but top marks in the ale category went to dark bottled beers brewed by Harveys and JW Lees. If the new sector is to have some impact then it would seem that darker ales, with roasted grain character, are likely to be the most popular.

Tax penalises the bold

There has been a disturbing change at the other end of the scale. Beers of 7.5% ABV or higher – which include some of the most exceptional, complex beers produced – have been placed in a tax bracket known as Higher Strength Beer Duty (HSBD). The duty increase amounts to 25% on the price of a pint and is pro rata, starting at 80.18 pence and rising to 100.22 pence on a beer of 12%. The government claims it has 'park bench

drinkers' in mind – consumers of extra-strength lagers. But the new rates could have a serious impact on such styles as IPA, old ales, barley wines and imperial stouts – styles that have enjoyed a considerable recovery in recent years and are increasingly competing with wine as drinks to be enjoyed with food. Miles Jenner, head brewer at Harveys, who brews the bottle-conditioned Imperial Extra Double Stout at 9%, says: 'I serve it instead of port with the cheese course and treat it with the same respect. It's a long way removed from two cans of Special Brew on a park bench.'

There are some two dozen beers listed in this Guide that will qualify for the new, higher rate of duty. They include Abbeydale's Last Rites, Robinson's Old Tom and Thornbridge St Petersburg Imperial Russian Stout. Thornbridge has already said it will reduce the strength of St Petersburg to avoid the duty trap. If consumers turn against strong beers on the grounds of cost, existing beers could be either reduced in strength or axed while other brewers will be deterred from producing beers that fall foul of HSBD.

Finding new flavours

One encouraging trend has been the growing fascination with the different aromas and flavours imparted by hops. Many British brewers are looking to hops from other countries for inspiration. Fuller's has always been faithful to English hops, but in 2012 it introduced a new draught beer, Wild River (4.5%), inspired by the American craft brewing movement and its intensely hoppy beers. Using pale malt only, Wild River is hopped with four American varieties, Cascade, Chinook, Liberty and Willamette. The result is a beer with a massive citrus hit of grapefruit, orange peel and fresh lemons along with a quinine-like bitterness.

But English hops are not being overlooked. Westerham Brewery, in the heart of the English hop fields, introduced a new cask beer called Spirit of Kent (4%) in which brewer Robert Wicks uses nine all-English varieties: Bramling Cross, Finchcock's, First Gold, Goldings, Northdown, Pilgrim, Progress, Sovereign and Whitbread Goldings Variety.

Which are best, American or English hops? Let battle commence.

All About Ale
The best beer comes naturally

Brewers call real ale 'cask-conditioned beer', a term that neatly sums up why this style is different from all other forms of beer. Cask beer has deep roots in Britain. In the 19th century, as the lager revolution spread from central Europe to most other parts of the world, Britain remained loyal to beer made in a time-honoured fashion that requires skill, commitment and even passion.

Most beer – lager as well as ale – is filtered, often pasteurised, and run into sealed containers called kegs in the brewery. When it reaches the pub or bar, it's served by applied gas pressure, either carbon dioxide or nitrogen or a mix of both.

Real ale on the other hand is a natural, living product. It's neither filtered nor pasteurised and reaches the peak of perfection in its cask in the pub cellar. It's possible – and legal – to produce something called 'beer' made with rice, maize and corn syrup, and flavoured with green juice squeezed from pulverised hops. But cask beer brewers turn their backs on such practices and prefer instead to use the finest malting barley and hops in their natural state. They may blend in darker malts and other grains, such as wheat or oats, but they avoid the cheap adjuncts used by the producers of global brands.

This insistence on quality chimes with the requirements of consumers who are concerned about how and where food and drink are made. Thanks to the work of malting companies and farmers, it's possible to trace where barley and hops are grown, even to the precise field where they are harvested. CAMRA's LocAle scheme, which encourages publicans to source some of their beers from breweries within a 30-mile radius, reduces carbon footprints. It's this insistence on locally-grown ingredients and beer brewed close to pubs that gives real ale a special appeal to the 'green generation'.

The critical difference between real ale and other types of beer is found at the brewery gate. While keg beer is finished and ready to be served, cask beer has yet to end its journey.

Before it leaves the brewery, additional hops and special brewing sugar may be added to casks to encourage a further fermentation and to increase hop aroma and flavour. In the pub cellar, each cask is 'stillaged' on its belly on a cradle. A tap is knocked through the bung at the flat end of the cask while a peg, called a spile, is driven into a hole called the shive on top. The peg, made of porous wood, allows excess carbon dioxide to escape as the beer undergoes a secondary fermentation. As the beer has not been filtered, it retains yeast that attacks the remaining sugars in the beer. After a day, the porous peg is replaced by a hard one that keeps the remaining CO_2 inside the cask to give the finished beer a natural sparkle in the glass: the beer is said to have 'good condition'.

Meanwhile, isinglass finings added in the brewery start a natural chemical reaction that draws yeast cells and protein to the foot of the cask. When the publican or cellar manager is satisfied – by drawing a sample from the cask – that the beer has 'dropped bright', plastic tubes called lines are attached to a tap in the bung and the beer is ready to be served. The familiar handpump on the bar operates a beer engine or suction pump that draws beer from cellar to bar. In some pubs, the beer is served 'by gravity' – direct from the cask.

Real ale should be served cool: 'warm British beer' is a myth. Cask beer should be delivered to the bar at a cellar temperature of 11-13°C. Some summer beers and golden ales are served cooler at 9-10°C. The beer in your glass should be rich in malt and hop aromas and flavours, naturally made and naturally served.

On the next three pages you can follow the brewing process in a modern small artisan brewery, Pitfield in Essex

Micro-brewing on an Essex farm

Pitfield puts the emphasis on organic grain for a range of beers

Pitfield brewery in Essex wouldn't win an award in a Small is Beautiful competition. In common with many microbreweries, it's squeezed into a compact building, with vessels almost on top of one another. In the case of Pitfield, it's in an old grain store on a farm a few miles from Epping.

The brewery may be minuscule but it has grown from its original site in Islington, North London, where it was crammed into one side of the Beer Shop, a major retailer of British and imported beer run by Martin Kemp. The space was so tiny that the brewing vessels were designed along the lines of a Russian doll, with each vessel removed from its companions as it finished its part in the brewing process.

Hops give both aroma and flavour to beer as well as bitterness. Pitfield use varieties from the United States, central Europe and New Zealand for its wide range of beers and styles.

Pitfield proved you can win top awards for beer from the most unlikely sources, for in 1987 the brewery's Dark Star ale, against stiff competition from national and regional giants, won the coveted Champion Beer of Britain title at the Great British Beer Festival. Almost 20 years later, Martin packed his brewing kit into a Transit van in 2006 and moved to Ashlyns Farm. Martin is dedicated to organic production and by 2000 he had converted all his beers to organic recipes, using malts and hops produced without fertilisers and pesticides. He nailed his colours to the mast with a golden ale called Eco Warrior: no messing with Martin.

He had the good fortune to find a base on a farm surrounded by 25 acres of organically-grown barley in ravishing countryside: he avoided the industrial estates that are home to many small breweries. But barley has to be transformed into malt before it can be used for brewing and Martin sources his supply from Warminster Maltings in Wiltshire, a specialist firm that offers a 'grain to glass' service. It buys barley from named farmers and can trace the crop back to individual fields. This means that brewers who worked well with a particular batch of malting barley can order it from the same farm the following year.

Malted barley is the essential ingredient in brewing. Pitfield use barley from Warminster Maltings, where the best quality grain is spread on heated floors and allowed to germinate before roasting in a kiln.

Warminster leads the way in supplying England's finest variety of malting barley, Maris Otter, and it's also a major provider of organically-grown grain. Malt arrives at Pitfield as crushed grain.

Bigger breweries have their own mills but in smaller plants, where space is at a premium, the maltster will do that essential work for the brewer.

Martin now spends most of his time selling and delivering beer, and brewing is in the hands of Andy Skene, a Canadian from Toronto. With a dozen regular beers and a raft of seasonals brews, Andy has a wide range of grains at his disposal, including pale, crystal, caramel, chocolate and Munich malts, along with wheat and oats. Andy is brewing to recipes devised by Martin back in his London days. He has a dual passion: organic ingredients and reviving old beer styles. His range includes Dark Mild, Shoreditch Stout, 1850 London Porter, 1837 India Pale Ale and 1792 Imperial Stout. The mild, porter and

Pitfield brewer Andy Skene empties the mashing vessel after the start of the brewing process. During mashing, pure water and grain are heated, causing starch in the grain to turn into sugar.

stouts require dark grains for colour and flavour. And with a portfolio ranging from lager, through golden, IPA, red ale to the darker styles, Martin and Andy need to add a wide variety of hops.

The hops are supplied by Charles Faram of Malvern in Worcestershire, a company that has been supplying hops to brewers since the 19th century. For decades it concentrated on such English varieties as Fuggles and Goldings but in recent years it has widened its range and now offers hops from central Europe, North America and New Zealand, including organic varieties. With such a large range of beers, Andy and Martin need an equally large choice of hops to give each brew a distinctive character. The hop sacks at Pitfield include such English varieties as Challenger, First Gold, Fuggles, Goldings, Pilgrim and Sovereign with German Hersbrucker and Sapphire, New Zealand Hallertau and American Cascade. Each variety will add its distinctive floral, grassy, herbal, piny, spicy, peppery and resinous note to the beers.

The sugary liquid 'wort' from the mashing vessel is next boiled with hops in a copper. At the end of the boil, the hopped wort is pumped to a cooler: the boiling liquid must be reduced in temperature before fermentation.

Once Andy has his supplies of malts and hops he is ready to brew. Next he needs water or 'liquor' as it's known to brewers. Pitfield's liquor comes from the Essex main water supply. It's similar to London water, rich in calcium carbonate, which is ideally suited to brewing dark beers and explains why, centuries ago, London was the major producer of dark mild, porter and stout. This type of liquor, conversely, is not ideal for making pale beers, and Andy and Martin 'Burtonise' the water when they're producing IPA and similar styles. This means adding such sulphates as gypsum and magnesium to replicate the famous brewing water of Burton-on-Trent.

With limited space, Andy heats the liquor in the copper and, when it reaches the required temperature of 65°C, transfers it to the mash tun. Everything is done by hand and next Andy shovels a blend of the required grains into the vessel and thoroughly mixes them with hot liquor. The mash lasts for around one and a quarter hours and during that time enzymes in the malt – natural chemical time bombs – convert the starch into a special type of brewing sugar: maltose.

When the mash is finished and Andy calculates there has been a good conversion of starch to sugar, the sweet, biscuity extract known as wort is transferred to the copper, where it's vigorously boiled with hops. The hops are added at different stages during the copper boil, which lasts for close to one and a half hours. Depending on the recipe and the degree of hop character and bitterness required, the hops are added at the start of the boil, midway through and just before the end. The final addition of hops is vital, as some of the plant's aroma has been distilled and lost to the atmosphere – this is known as 'the angels' share'.

Andy adds liquid yeast to a fermenting vessel. Yeast performs the magic of the brewing process by attacking the sugars in the hopped wort and creating both alcohol and natural CO_2... plus delicious aromas.

Pitfield can produce five barrels of beer at a time. The original Islington kit, with just one fermenting vessel, has been augmented by two additional fermenters. The liquid from the copper – called hopped wort – is cooled and transferred to the fermenters for its date with destiny with brewers' yeast. Martin uses a blend of two yeast cultures, Nottingham Ale and S04. In common with Andy,

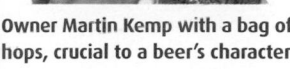

Owner Martin Kemp with a bag of hops, crucial to a beer's character

Once fermentation is under way, a 'rocky head' of yeast and protein protects the fermenting liquid from oxidisation and infection, which would create unpleasant flavours in the finished beer.

Nottingham yeast originates in Canada and is specially formulated for microbrewers. Unlike most ale yeast cultures, which create a thick carpet of foam and protein during fermentation, Nottingham does its work with a minimum of head creation, enabling the maximum amount of liquid to fill the fermenting vessels.

Fermentation lasts for four days and during that time the yeast voraciously attacks the maltose, creating alcohol and carbon dioxide. Andy then skims off the yeast and collects it for further brews. The young beer is then racked into casks or bottles, primed with a careful measure of yeast and brewing sugar to ensure a good secondary fermentation. The cask beer then matures for several days before being delivered to pubs – the bottled beer might mature for much longer. A maturation period is necessary to purge the beer of rough alcohols and to develop the beer's flavour.

Pitfield's beers are accredited by the Soil Association and the bottled versions and some cask versions are suitable for

After fermentation has ended, much of the beer is racked into casks where it conditions for several days before being delivered to pubs.

vegetarians and vegans (available from **www. pitfieldbeershop. co.uk**). Andy and Martin, in common with their colleagues throughout the micro movement, are the face of modern brewing – producing beer with passion, commitment, the best ingredients and a reverence for Britain's brewing heritage.

A lot of Pitfield's beer is also bottled: an important part of their business.

Beer appreciation

Beer is sometimes dismissed as a simple drink to quench the thirst, lacking distinctive flavours, while a major vocabulary has been built around the aromas and palate of wine. Yet beer – especially the type of beer found in these pages – is just as complex as wine and deserves greater appreciation.

It could be argued that beer is *more* complex than wine as it relies on two vastly different ingredients for its character – grain and hops – as well as pure water and yeast. It's the balance and interaction of malt and hops that makes beer such a fascinating member of the alcohol family. Even when two beers carry the same stylistic label, such as pale ale, bitter, stout or barley wine, they will vary widely in their aromas and palates as a result of the malts and hops used.

The aim of this section is to describe many of the characteristics found in beer and its many styles, and to decipher some of the terms used in the tasting notes found in the Breweries section at the back of the Guide – terms that pinpoint the character of individual beers.

Grain

Barley is the main grain used in brewing. Its robust character delivers rich, biscuit flavours and blends well with hops. Before it can be used in brewing, it goes through a malting process that turns starch into fermentable sugar or maltose. The colour of the malt depends on the malting temperature. All beer, even the darkest stout, is made predominantly from pale malt, as this has the highest level of natural enzymes that finish the conversion of starch to sugar in the brewery. When a beer is made from pale malt only, its aroma and flavour is often described as being similar to Horlicks. When malt is roasted or 'kilned' at a low temperature, as with lager malt, a sweet, honey note can be detected: lager malt is often used in golden ales.

Depending on the malting temperatures, darker malts come in a number of forms: amber, brown, black and chocolate. Unmalted roasted barley is often used in stouts for both colour and a bitter, roast character. Crystal malt, made in a similar fashion to toffee, cannot be fermented, but it adds toffee, nutty and fruity – raisin and sultana – flavours. A butterscotch note is the result of the creation of a natural by-product of fermentation known as diacetyl.

Other grains used in cask beer include wheat – and even 'wheat beers' are a blend of malted barley and wheat – and oats, which give a creamy character to stouts and porter, in Scotland in particular. Specialist brewing sugars also add colour and flavour.

Malt, other grains and sugar deliver characteristics ranging from pale honey through fresh bread, wholemeal biscuits, caramel, vanilla, burnt fruits, to coffee, liquorice, molasses, cocoa in dark ales and stouts, with fresh tobacco and smoked grain in old ales and barley wines. While tart and tangy fruit comes from hops (see below) other fruit characteristics are the result of fermentation and the creation of 'esters': banana and pineapple are familiar beer esters.

Hops

Hops are renowned for giving bitterness to beer and balancing the sweetness of malt. But hops – described as 'the grapes of brewing' by one leading British artisan brewer – come in many forms. Much of the 'fruitiness' and spiciness described in beers in tasting notes come from hops. English varieties, such as Fuggles and Goldings that date from the 18th and 19th centuries, contribute peppery and spicy notes. A more intense bitterness comes from modern varieties such as Challenger, Northdown and Target, while Bramling Cross delivers a pronounced 'jammy' fruitiness. New 'hedgerow' varieties, such as First Gold, that grow to only half the height of conventional plants, have a good punch of bitterness allied to tart citrus notes.

Many British brewers use the more floral, herbal and grassy notes from hops grown in Germany, the Czech Republic and Slovenia. But in recent years many microbrewers, entranced by developments in the United States, have added American hops to their portfolios. As a result of the summer heat found in the main hop-growing states of Oregon and Washington, such varieties as Amarillo, Cascade, Chinook, Citra, Liberty and Willamette deliver intense citrus and other fruit flavours, powerfully reminiscent of orange, grapefruit, lemon, melon, passion fruit and peach. They have to be used with great skill by the brewer to avoid the citrus element becoming too dominant and masking malt flavours.

Water and yeast

Even the strongest beer has 93% water in its make-up, 'brewing liquor', as it's known professionally, plays a key role in the brewing process. While the water in a famous lager-brewing city such as Pilsen is virtually free from minerals, the waters of the Trent Valley in

England, the historic home of pale ale, are rich in gypsum and magnesium. These salts act as flavour enhancers, emphasising the malt and hop character of beer, and they also encourage powerful yeast activity during fermentation.

All brewers of pale ale and bitter 'Burtonise' their water with the addition of mineral salts. London, once famous for its dark beers – mild, porter and stout – has water with a strong carbonate content that brings out the full, rich character of dark malts. Brewing water, whether it comes from springs, wells or the public supply, is carefully cleaned before it's used in the brewery.

Yeast not only turns malt sugars into alcohol during fermentation but also contributes to the flavour of beer. Yeast is a single-cell micro-organism or fungus that grows and reproduces itself by feeding on the sugars present in the fermenting vessel. It also picks up and retains the flavours created by the entire brewing process. As a result, brewers treat their yeast cultures like gold dust. They refrigerate them and also deposit samples in a national yeast bank from where they can get fresh supplies if they should suffer a bacterial infection in the brewery. If a brewer changes his or her yeast strain, the character of the beer will also change.

Sampling

The skill of the brewer and the ingredients used come to fruition in the glass of beer in your hand. Gently swirl the liquid to release the aroma or 'nose' and appreciate the malt, hop and fruit notes that emerge. Allow the beer to trickle slowly over the tongue, which picks up bitterness, sweetness and salt, and enjoy the palate or 'mouthfeel' as the beer coats the inside of the cheeks. Finally, appreciate the 'finish' or aftertaste as the beer trickles down the back of the throat. Depending on the style, in the finish you will find further malt character, ranging from light juicy malt through roast notes, chocolate or coffee, along with hop bitterness and citrus fruit. *Above all – enjoy!*

Beer is a complex drink, available in a wide spectrum of colours and different flavours

Beer Heaven at the Dinner Table

Top chef Tom Whitaker designs a four-course meal with ale

The path walked by those who match food and wine is well-trodden. Beer and food matching, on the other hand, is a new art, but one that makes sense at a time of a resurgence in breweries and brewing. Food and beer pairings are naturally subjective: I'll try not to be too specific in my choices but give you a more general guide to what might work well. We'll look at four different main types of beers: porters/stouts, IPAs, golden ales and milds. I have constructed a four-course meal, with each course geared towards one of these four general categories.

The starter. When designing a menu, most chefs will try to create harmony in the dishes they choose, in order to allow the diner to appreciate all the elements of the meal. On this basis, a good place to start for me is with golden or summer ale. These beers tend to be lighter in style, with more pronounced citrus notes and not so hop heavy.

So what to pair? I looked for something predominantly summery as a dish. The first ingredients that spring to mind are courgettes – with their flowers if possible – fennel, artichokes, broad beans and peas. Even a little light spicing would lend itself to this style of ale.

A butter-based sauce such as hollandaise also matches wonderfully. The reason for this is that the relatively high citrus element to these ales cuts though the butter and provides real balance. Also, an array of fresh garden herbs such as dill, tarragon or chives would complement the above ingredients and remain harmonious with the ale. In terms of meat, I'd say veal or poultry such as high-grade chicken or guinea fowl.

The fish course in some ways is the most difficult course to match but I tend to err on the side of boldness here and I've chosen mild ale. Modern milds tend to be quite dark but in flavour are what the term suggests – relatively mild with a malty tonality. If you select your fish carefully and are willing to experiment I think the match can really work. I'd be tempted by something that matches well with ingredients that I naturally associate with mild, such as mushrooms, ham, figs and potato, with such grains as flax and spelt. If I were constructing a dish with these things in mind I'd look at sea bass, black bream or turbot, all of which have a pronounced flavour and will not be overawed by the ale.

Octopus would also be a great match for mild. Its texture and flavour are really consistent with those of a good mild, but shell fish would also work, especially crab – possibly a spelt risotto of white and brown crab with deep fried octopus shavings.

The main course is usually the big event and is the most dominant in terms of its flavours. In choosing a beer for such a course the choice for me would be an IPA. I'm referring to the new-style IPAs produced today that tend to be rich and hoppy in flavour with a high alcohol content.

The type of dish I'd be looking at serving with an IPA would be something robust and woody and predominantly English in style so I'm thinking truffles, wild mushrooms, asparagus, pumpkin and swede, with herbs such a thyme and rosemary. Also toasted seeds such as pumpkin and sunflower would work really well.

In terms of the meat, I think IPA is built for game: pheasant and roe deer would work really well but for me two game birds really stand out: squab pigeon and early season grouse. Just simply pan fried or roasted and served with any of the above

Worthington's White Shield is a classic IPA – Tom's choice of beer style for his main course

would work really well. Try making some stuffing using a bit of black pudding to go with it. (And while I shouldn't advocate the consumption of booze at such an hour, a pint of IPA with black pudding and duck eggs for breakfast has to be one of my all time favourites!)

For vegetarians, a roasted squash or two would work well – something with a nutty flavour, such as an acorn squash. I would roast the slices of squash and then grate some Parmesan and add mustard on top of the slices and pop them under the grill until nicely coloured.

Finally, dessert. Some people might not want to move on to a porter style ale at the end of the meal but if you look at the flavours that generally occur in such ales – coffee, malt and that slightly burnt edge – they actually lend themselves beautifully to many desserts.

The dessert that first springs to mind is caramelised rice pudding with cinnamon and prunes. I salt the caramel before I torch it and it's this saltiness that I believe really matches a porter. Another great match for this is ice cream. My colleague and Master Chef Tim Anderson

made some insanely good ice cream for an event we did for BrewDog in Scotland. The ice cream was malted miso and it was awesome, especially served with a porter-style beer.

A porter and ice cream float is a thing of pure indulgence: just make sure it's good ice cream. I think pastry is a killer with stouts. Try something like *tarte tatin* with milk and honey ice cream and a pint of the dark stuff.

This is by no means the last word on the subject but if you're planning to do a bit of beer and food matching in the future, you won't go too far wrong with some of the above ideas. One of my pet-hates about wine matching is the rules that govern what you should and shouldn't match. It's down to personality and taste and I would recommend that you don't limit yourself to any pre-conceived ideas of what goes best with what. Many of the great flavour combinations were discovered simply by people doing what convention said they shouldn't.

Tom Whitaker was a 2011 Masterchef finalist and is an exponent of British food and ingredients.

Welsh wizardry from the valleys

The Bunch of Grapes, the flagship pub of the Otley brewery in Pontypridd (page 574), has built a reputation for pairing beer and food that goes far beyond South Wales. People travel considerable distances to sup the brewery's range of delicious beers and to choose from the superb food cooked by head chef Sebastien Vanoni and his staff.

Nick Otley, who runs the brewery with his brothers Charlie and Matthew, is a trained chef as well as a brewer: his family has run pubs in South Wales for many years and Nick has learned all the skills of bar, kitchen and brewery. He joins

forces with Sebastien to conjure beer and food matches for both the regular menus at the Bunch of Grapes, and for special events, which included a wine versus beer dinner in 2001 that attracted national media attention.

Nick and Sebastien responded in mouth-watering style to a challenge from the *Good Beer Guide* to prepare a series of special dishes paired with their beers, several of which have won major awards. O1 was Champion Golden Ale of Britain in 2008, and O2, O4 and O-Garden have all won top prizes in the Champion Beer of Wales competition.

Suggested Otley beer and food pairings:

Marinated beetroot and Cardiff-grown tomato bruschetta with basil oil and crumbled Perl-las cheese, paired with O3 Boss bitter.

Pan-fried cockles, laver bread, leeks and home-made cured pancetta on fried bread and charred lemon, paired with O4 Colomb-O golden ale hopped with American Columbus.

Pan-fried garden herb marinated sea-reared trout, courgette fritters, crab, cockles and lemon broth paired with Otley Thai Bo crystal wheat beer flavoured with lemongrass and lime leaf.

Otley braised rabbit with charred courgette, pomme paille [similar to rosti] and Talgarth black pudding matched with O1 golden ale, which was also used to braise the rabbit.

Toasted Bara-brith [fruit bread] with Penderyn whisky ice cream, clotted cream and Dark O Stout syrup, matched with O6 Porter, a dark beer flavoured with coffee and chocolate.

Britain's Classic Beer Styles

IN THE WORLD OF BEER, Britain is best known for the style known as bitter which, in the 20th century, developed from the pale ales first brewed in Victorian times. But there is far more to British beer than bitter. Older styles have reappeared while the likes of golden ale, fruit beer and wheat beer have been fashioned in recent years to give further choice to drinkers. In this briefing, **Roger Protz** gives an indication of some of the great beers available in British pubs and recommends some of his favourite versions of each style.

PORTER & STOUT

Porter was a London beer that created the first commercial brewing industry in the world in the early 18th century. Porter started life as a brown beer and became darker when new technology made it possible to roast grain at higher temperatures to obtain greater colour and flavour. The strongest version of porter was dubbed stout porter or stout for short. The name porter was the result of the beer's popularity with the large number of porters working the streets, markets and docks of 18th-century London.

Porter and stout were exported to the rest of the British Isles and, as a result, Arthur Guinness built his own porter brewery in Dublin. During World War One, when the British government prevented brewers from using heavily-roasted malts in order to divert energy to the arms industry, Guinness and other Irish brewers came to dominate the market. In recent years, porter and stout have made a spirited comeback in both Britain and the United States, with brewers digging deep in to old recipe books to create genuine versions of the style from the 18th and 19th centuries.

Look for a jet-black colour with a hint of ruby around the edge of the glass. Expect a dark and roasted malt character, with raisin and sultana fruit, espresso or cappuccino coffee, liquorice and molasses. The beer should have deep hop bitterness to balance the richness of malt and fruit.

ROGER'S ROUND
PITFIELD
1792 IMPERIAL STOUT
TITANIC STOUT
WICKWAR STATION PORTER

MILD

Mild was once the most popular style of beer in Britain but it was overtaken by bitter in the 1950s. It was developed in the 18th and 19th centuries as a less aggressively bitter style of beer than porter and stout, and was primarily drunk by industrial and agricultural workers to refresh them after long hours of arduous labour. Early milds were much stronger that modern interpretations, which tend to fall in the 3% to 3.5% category, though Rudgate's Dark Ruby Mild at 4.4% is more in keeping with earlier strengths. Mild is usually dark brown in colour, due to the use of well-roasted malts or roasted barley, but there are paler versions such as Banks's Mild, Timothy Taylor's Golden Best and McMullen's AK. Look for rich malty aromas and flavours, with hints of dark fruit, chocolate, coffee and caramel, with a gentle underpinning of hop bitterness.

ROGER'S ROUND
HIGHLANDER
DARK MUNRO
HOBSON'S MILD
MIGHTY OAK
OSCAR WILDE
VALE BLACK SWAN

OLD ALE

Old ale is another style from the 18th century, stored for months or even years in wooden vessels where the beer picked up some lactic sourness from wild yeasts and tannins in the wood. As a result of the sour taste, it was dubbed 'stale' by drinkers and the beer was one of the components of the early blended porters. In recent years, old ale has made a return to popularity, primarily due to the popularity of Theakston's Old Peculier and Gale's Prize Old Ale. Contrary to expectation, old ales do not have to be especially strong and can be no more than 4% alcohol. Neither do they have to be dark: old ale can be pale and bursting with lush malt, tart fruit and spicy hops. Darker versions will have a more profound malt character, with powerful hints of roasted grain, dark fruit, polished leather and fresh tobacco. The hallmark of the style is a lengthy period of maturation, often in bottle rather than cask.

ROGER'S ROUND
BALLARD'S WASSAIL
KING'S OLD ALE
LEES MOONRAKER

BARLEY WINE

Barley wine dates from the 18th and 19th centuries when England was often at war with France and it was the duty of patriots, usually from the upper classes, to drink ale rather that French claret. Barley wine had to be strong – often between 10% and 12% – and was stored for as long as 18 months or two years. The biggest-selling barley wine for many years was Whitbread's 10.9% Gold Label, now available only in cans. Fuller's Vintage Ale (8.5%) is a bottle-conditioned version of its Golden Pride and is brewed with different varieties of malts and hops every year. Expect massive sweet malt and ripe fruit of the pear drop, orange and lemon type, with darker fruits, chocolate and coffee if darker malts are used. Hop rates are generous and produce bitterness and peppery, grassy and floral notes.

> **ROGER'S ROUND**
> KELTEK
> BEHEADED
> OTLEY O8
> WOODFORDE'S
> HEADCRACKER

IPA

India Pale Ale changed the face of brewing in the 19th century. The new technologies of the industrial revolution enabled brewers to use pale malts to fashion beers that were pale bronze in colour. First brewed in London and Burton-on-Trent for the colonial trade, IPAs were strong in alcohol and high in hops to keep them in good condition during long sea journeys. IPA's life span was brief, driven out of the colonies by German lager. But the style has made a spirited recovery in recent years, brewed with great passion in both Britain and the U.S. In Chicago, Goose Island's IPA is arguably the finest American interpretation of the style while in Britain Marston's Old Empire and Meantime's IPA are just two modern versions of the style arousing new interest. Look for a big peppery hop aroma and palate balanced by juicy malt and tart citrus fruit.

> **ROGER'S ROUND**
> ACORN IPA
> FULLER'S
> BENGAL LANCER
> LITTLE VALLEY
> PYTHON IPA
> ST AUSTELL
> PROPER JOB

BURTON ALE

As the name suggests, the origins of Burton Ale lie in Burton-on-Trent, but the style became so popular in the 18th and 19th centuries that most brewers had 'a Burton' in their portfolio and the expression 'gone for a Burton' entered the English language. Bass at one time had six different versions of the beer, ranging from 6% to 11.5%: the stronger versions were exported to Russia and the Baltic States.

In the 20th century, Burton was overtaken in popularity by pale ale and bitter but it was revived with great success in the late 1970s with the launch of Ind Coope Draught Burton Ale. But when Allied Breweries broke up, the beer moved first to Tetley's in Leeds and then J W Lees in Manchester, where it's brewed in small batches but is worth seeking out: it's based on the recipe for a once-famous bottled beer, Double Diamond Export. Other Burton Ales exist under different names today: Young's Winter Warmer was originally called Burton. Bass No 1, brewed occasionally, is called a barley wine but is in fact the last remaining version of a Bass Burton Ale. Look for a bright amber colour, a rich malty and fruity character underscored by a solid resinous and piny hop note.

> **ROGER'S ROUND**
> BRUNSWICK OLD
> ACCIDENTAL
> IND COOPE
> BURTON ALE
> TOWER GONE
> FOR A BURTON
> YOUNG'S WINTER
> WARMER

PALE ALE

The success of IPA in the colonial trade led to a demand for beer of a similar colour and character in Britain. IPA, with its heavy hopping, was considered too bitter for the domestic market, and brewers responded with a beer dubbed pale ale that was lower in both alcohol and hops. Pale ale was known as 'the beer of the railway age', transported round the country from Burton-on-Trent by the new railway system. Brewers from London, Liverpool and Manchester built breweries in Burton to make use of the local, mineral-rich water to make their own versions of pale ale. From the early years of the 20th century, bitter began to overtake pale ale in popularity and as a result pale ale became mainly a bottled product. A true pale ale should be different to bitter, identical to IPA in colour and brewed without the addition of coloured malts. It should have a spicy, resinous aroma and palate, with biscuity malt and tart citrus fruit. Many beers are called bitter today but are in fact pale ale, Marston's Pedigree being a case in point.

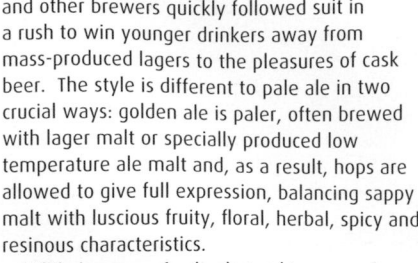

ROGER'S ROUND

ADNAMS
GHOST SHIP
BLACK HOLE
SUPERNOVA
CAMDEN PALE ALE
DARK STAR
AMERICAN PALE ALE

BITTER

Towards the end of the 19th century, brewers built large estates of tied pubs and they moved away from beers stored for months or years and developed 'running beers' that could be served after a few days of conditioning in the pub cellar. Bitter was a new type of running beer: it was a member of the pale ale family but was generally deep bronze or copper in colour due to the use of slightly darker malts, such as crystal, that gave the beer fullness of palate. Best is a stronger version of bitter but there is considerable crossover. Bitter falls into the 3.4% to 3.9% band, while best bitter is 4% upwards, though a number of brewers dub their ordinary bitters 'best'. A further development of bitter comes in the shape of extra or special strong bitter of 5% or more: Fuller's ESB and Greene King Abbot being well-known examples. With ordinary bitter, look for spicy, peppery and grassy hop character, a powerful bitterness, tangy fruit and juicy/nutty malt.

With best and strong bitters, malt and fruit character will tend to dominate but hop aroma and bitterness are still crucial to the style, often achieved by 'late hopping' in the brewery or by adding hops to casks before filling.

ROGER'S ROUND

ELGOOD'S
CAMBRIDGE BITTER
HAWKSHEAD BITTER
KELHAM ISLAND
PRIDE OF SHEFFIELD
TRIPLE FFF
ALTON'S PRIDE

GOLDEN ALE

Golden ales have become so popular, with brewers of all sizes producing them, that they now have their own category in the Champion Beer of Britain competition. Exmoor Gold and Hop Back Summer Lightning launched the trend in the early 1980s

and other brewers quickly followed suit in a rush to win younger drinkers away from mass-produced lagers to the pleasures of cask beer. The style is different to pale ale in two crucial ways: golden ale is paler, often brewed with lager malt or specially produced low temperature ale malt and, as a result, hops are allowed to give full expression, balancing sappy malt with luscious fruity, floral, herbal, spicy and resinous characteristics.

While brewers of pale ale tend to use such traditional English hops as Fuggles and Goldings, imported hops from North America, the Czech Republic, Germany, Slovenia and New Zealand give radically different hop notes to golden ale. As a result, golden ales offer a new and exciting drinking experience. They are often served colder than draught bitter and some brewers, such as Fuller's, have installed special cooling devices attached to beer engines to ensure the beer reaches the glass at an acceptably refreshing temperature.

ROGER'S ROUND

CUMBRIAN
LEGENDARY
LOWESWATER GOLD
HOLDEN'S
GOLDEN GLOW
OAKHAM
INFERNO

WHEAT BEER

Wheat beer is a style closely associated with Bavaria and Belgium and the popularity of the style in Britain has encouraged many brewers to add wheat beer to the portfolios. The title is something of a misnomer as all 'wheat beers' are a blend of malted barley as well as wheat, as the latter grain is difficult to brew with and needs the addition of barley, which acts as a natural filter during the mashing stage. But wheat, if used with special strains of yeast developed for brewing the style, gives distinctive aromas and flavours, such as clove, banana and bubblegum that make it a complex and refreshing beer. The Belgian version of wheat beer often has the addition of herbs and spices, such as milled coriander seeds and orange peel – a habit that dates back to medieval times.

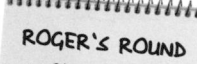

ROGER'S ROUND

O'HANLON'S
GOLDBLADE
LITTLE VALLEY
HEBDEN'S WHEAT
SULWATH
SOLWAY MIST

FRUIT/SPECIALITY BEERS

Brewers have become restless in recent years in their quest for new flavours that will help them reach a wider and more appreciative audience for their beers. The popularity in Britain of Belgian fruit beers has not gone unnoticed and now many home-grown brewers are using fruit in their beer. Others have gone the extra mile and add honey, herbs, heather, spices, and even spirit – brandy and rum feature in a number of speciality beers. It's important to dispel the belief that fruit and honey beers are sweet: both fruit and honey add new dimensions to the brewing process and are highly fermentable, with the result that beers that use the likes of cherries or raspberry are dry and quenching rather than cloying.

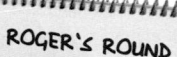

ROGER'S ROUND

AMBER CHOCOLATE
ORANGE STOUT

OTLEY O GARDEN

WILLIAMS BROS
SEVEN GIRAFFES

SCOTTISH BEERS

Historically, Scottish beers tend to be darker, sweeter and less heavily hopped that beers south of the border: a reflection of a colder climate where hops don't grow and beer needs to be nourishing.

The classic traditional styles are Light, Heavy and Export, which are not dissimilar to mild, bitter and IPA. They are also often known as 60, 70 and 80 Shilling Ales from a 19th-century method of invoicing beers according to their strength. A 'Wee Heavy' or 90 Shilling Ale, now rare, is the Scottish equivalent of barley wine. Many of the newer brewers in Scotland produce beers that are lighter in colour and with more generous hop rates.

ROGER'S ROUND

FYNE
HIGHLANDER

STEWART
80/-

WILLIAMS
BROS 80/-

Only accept perfect pints

Remember, you're the consumer, forking out a high price for beer, so don't be afraid to take your pint back to the bar if:

- It's either too cold or too warm. Cask beer should be cool, not cold – but bear in mind that some golden ales are meant to be served at a lower temperature than milds and bitters. At the other end of the spectrum, it's a myth that real ale should be served at room temperature. Warm beer tastes bad, as the temperature creates unpleasant off flavours. If your beer smells of acetone, vinegar or stale bread, take it back.

- The pint has no head, is totally flat and out of condition.

- It's not only flat but hazy and has yeast particles or protein floating in the liquid.

If you get the response 'Real ale is meant to be warm and cloudy', invite the publican to join the 21st century. If the offending pub has a Cask Marque plaque, get in touch with Cask Marque. Otherwise, let us know at the *Good Beer Guide* – **camragbgeditor@camra.org.uk**.

And please go back to the bar if you are served a short measure – less than a pint (or half-pint) of liquid in the glass. Drinkers lose millions of pounds a year as a result of short measures. It's an outrageous rip-off. CAMRA beer festivals serve beer in over-size glasses that ensure drinkers always get the amount of beer they have paid for. Most pub owners refuse to use over-size glasses, preferring brim-measure glasses that allow them consistently to serve short measures. It's a scandal. Don't put up with it.

CAMRA's Beers of the Year

THE BEERS LISTED BELOW are CAMRA'S Beers of the Year. They were short-listed for the 2012 Champion Beer of Britain competition, held at the Great British Beer Festival in August, or the Champion Winter Beer of Britain Competition, held in January that year. Each beer was found by a panel of trained CAMRA judges to be consistently outstanding in its category and they all receive a 🍺 against their entry in the Breweries section. In the Champion Beer of Britain finals, the best beers from each category in both competitions are judged together to decide the overall national winner. For the full results, visit **www.camra.org.uk/cbob**.

BEST BITTERS

Ashover, Hydro
Bank Top, Flat Cap
Bathams, Best Bitter
Bowman, Quiver Bitter
Cairngorm, Stag
Fyne, Maverick
Great Oakley, Wot's Ocurring
Green Jack, Trawlerboys Best Bitter
Kelham Island, Pride of Sheffield
Milk Street, Funky Monkey
Milton, Pegasus
Oakwell, Senior Bitter
Otter, Otter Amber
Purple Moose, Glaslyn Ale
Salopian, Hop Twister
Sandstone, Post Mistress
Surrey Hills, Shere Drop
Thwaites, Lancaster Bomber

BITTERS

Bryncelyn, Holly Hop
Deeside, Nechtan
Orkney, Raven Ale
Purity, Pure Gold
Purple Moose, Snowdonia Ale
Salopian, Shropshire Gold
Acorn, Barnsley Bitter
Adnams, Southwold Bitter
Barngates, Cat Nap
Branscombe Vale, Branoc
DarkTribe, Sternwheeler
Flowerpots, Bitter
Fuller's, Gales' Seafarers Ale
Fulstow, Fulstow Common
Green Jack, Excelsior
Hawkshead, Bitter
High House Farm, Auld Hemp
Tintagel, Castle Gold

BARLEY WINES & STRONG OLD ALES

Abbeydale, Last Rites
Coniston, No. 9 Barley Wine
Goachers, Old 1066 Ale
Heart of Wales, High as a Kite
Isle of Skye, Cuillin Beast
Kinver, Over the Edge
Moor, Old Freddy Walker
Oakham, Attila
Thornbridge, Halcyon

GOLDEN ALES

Adnams, Explorer
Cumbrian Legendary Ales, Langdale

Dark Star, American Pale Ale
Goose Eye, Chinook Blonde
Great Oakley, Marching In
Highland, Orkney Best
Hobsons, Town Crier
Otley, Colombo
Skinner, Cornish Knocker

MILDS

Batmans, Dark Mild
Bushys, Ruby 1874 Mild
Driftwood, Blackheads Mild
Highland, Dark Munro
Hobsons, Hobsons Mild
Rhymney, Dark
Rudgate, Ruby Mild
Son of Sid, Muck Cart Mild
Triple FFF, Pressed Rat & Warthog

OLD ALES & STRONG MILDS

Beowulf, Dark Raven
Bragdy'r Nant, Mwnci Nell
Brunswick, Black Sabbath
Chalk Hill, Flintknappers
Driftwood, Alfie's Revenge
Hesket Newmarket,
   Old Carrock
Isle of Skye, Black Cuillin
Palmers, Tally Ho!
Theakston, Old Peculier

PORTERS

Batemans, Salem Porter
Blythe, Johnsons
Conwy, Telford Porter
Elland, 1872
Hammerpot, Bottle
   Wreck Porter
Hawkshead, Brodie's Prime
Nethergate, Old Growler
Sulwath, Black Galloway
Wickwar, Station Porter

SPECIALITY BEERS

Atlas, Wayfarer IPA
Burton Bridge, Bramble Stout
Dunham Massey, Chocolate
   Cherry Mild
Little Valley, Hebden's Wheat
Milestone, Raspberry
   Wheat Beer
Nethergate, Umbel Magna
O'Hanlon's, Original Port Stout
Otley, O Garden
Windsor & Eton, Conqueror

STOUTS

Acorn, Gorlovka
Ascot Ales, Anastasia's Exile Stout
Beartown, Polar Eclipse
Brunswick, Father Mike's Dark
   Rich Ruby
Cairngorn, Black Gold
Cambridge Moonshine,
   Black Hole
Heart of Wales, Welsh Black
Titanic, Stout
Wessex, Russian Stoat

STRONG BITTERS

Dark Star, Festival
Fat Cat, Marmalade Cat
Highland, Orkney IPA
Moorhouse's, Pendle Witches Brew
Mordue, Radgie Gadgie
O'Hanlon's, Stormstay
Rhymney, Export Ale
Salopian, Golden Thread
Thornbridge, Jaipur IPA

REAL ALE IN A BOTTLE

Draycott, Buckden Ruby Bitter
Beeston, Norfolk Black
Spire, 80/-
Thornbridge, Saint Petersburg
   Imperial Russian Stout
Dark Star, Imperial Stout
Fuller's, 1845
Great Gable, Yewbarrow
Marble, Chocolate
Stewart, Embra
Tryst, Bla'than
St Austell, Proper Job
O'Hanlon's, Port Stout
Wye Valley, DG Wholesome Stout
Molson Coors, Worthington's
   White Shield
Durham, Evensong
Little Valley, Ginger Pale Ale

CHAMPION WINTER BEER OF BRITAIN 2012
Driftwood,
Alfie's Revenge

CHAMPION BEER OF BRITAIN 2012
Coniston, No. 9
Barley Wine

The Pubs

Cambridge Blue, Cambridge (p59

NORTHERN
ISLES

SHETLAND

HIGHLANDS
&
WESTERN ISLES

ABERDEEN
& GRAMPIAN

TAYSIDE

ARGYLL &
THE ISLES

LOCH LOMOND,
STIRLING
& THE
TROSSACHS

FIFE

EDINBURGH & LOTHIANS

GREATER
GLASGOW &
CLYDE VALLEY

BORDERS

AYRSHIRE
& ARRAN

DUMFRIES &
GALLOWAY

NORTHERN
IRELAND

ISLE OF
MAN

MERSEYSIDE

NW
WALES

NE
WALES

CHESHIRE

LANCASHIRE

GREATER
MANCHESTER

NORTHUMBER-
LAND

TYNE &
WEAR

CUMBRIA

DURHAM

NORTH
YORKSHIRE

WEST
YORKS

EAST
YORKS

SOUTH
YORKS

DERBYSHIRE

STAFFORD-
SHIRE

NOTTINGHAM-
SHIRE

LINCOLN-
SHIRE

SHROPSHIRE

WEST
MIDLANDS

LEICESTERSHIRE
& RUTLAND

MID
WALES

WORCESTER-
SHIRE

WARWICK-
SHIRE

NORTHAMPTON-
SHIRE

CAMBRIDGE-
SHIRE

NORFOLK

SUFFOLK

HEREFORD-
SHIRE

GWENT

WEST
WALES

GLAMORGAN

GLOUCS &
BRISTOL

OXFORD-
SHIRE

BEDFORD-
SHIRE

BUCKINGHAM-
SHIRE

HERTFORD-
SHIRE

ESSEX

GREATER
LONDON

BERKSHIRE

WILTSHIRE

SURREY

KENT

SOMERSET

HAMPSHIRE

WEST
SUSSEX

EAST
SUSSEX

DEVON

DORSET

ISLE OF
WIGHT

CORNWALL

CHANNEL
ISLANDS

England

BEDFORDSHIRE

Ampthill

Albion 🍷 🄻
36 Dunstable Street, MK45 2JT TL033377
✪ 11.30-11 (midnight Fri & Sat); 12-10.30 Sun
☎ (01525) 634857
**B&T Shefford Bitter, Golden Fox, Dragon Slayer;
Everards Tiger Best Bitter; guest beers** Ⓗ
A proper, narrow-fronted Victorian pub with one
large bar and 12 handpumps serving a range of
local B&T beers as well as Everards Tiger and eight
constantly changing ales mainly from
microbreweries. Three real ciders or perries are
available. Beer and cider festivals are held at least
annually. Filled rolls are on offer at lunchtimes.
There is a meeting room, and patio garden outside.
Dogs are welcome. English music night features
once a month on a Wednesday. Local CAMRA
County Pub of the Year 2012. ⌂☆❀🗎♣👣🚏

Old Sun ✪
87 Dunstable Street, MK45 2NQ TL034379
✪ 12-midnight (12.30am Fri & Sat; 11.30 Sun)
☎ (01525) 405466
**Adnams Southwold Bitter; Fuller's London Pride;
Sharp's Doom Bar** Ⓗ
Picturesque and popular two-bar pub serving at
least three ales plus a real cider. Real fires add to
the cosy feel in winter. A large rear garden with
covered decking, and seating in front of the pub,
make this a pleasant outdoor venue in the summer
months. There is a games room for pool and darts

with its own serving hatch. Various local interest
groups meet here throughout the year. A function
room is available. ⌂☆❀🗎♣👣P🚏

Ossory Inn
9 Arthur Street, MK45 2QQ TL034377
✪ 12-11; 10.30-midnight Fri & Sat; 10.30-11
Sun ☎ 07711 000628
Greene King IPA; guest beers Ⓗ
An unpretentious and welcoming no-nonsense,
back-street, two-bar pub of the best kind. Two
guest ales are served alongside the regular IPA. A
beer festival is usually held here at Easter with the
ales served on gravity direct from the cooled cellar.
Real cider is occasionally available. Bar food is
available all day every day, with wholesome and
hearty breakfasts cooked Friday to Sunday
especially popular with the locals. There is TV, pool
and darts in the main bar and a quiet and
comfortable separate lounge. Dogs welcome.
☆◑🖲♣

Bedford

Bedford Arms ✪
2 Bromham Road, MK40 2QA (opp HM Prison)
✪ 12-midnight ☎ (01234) 214656
∰ thebedfordarmsbedford.co.uk
**Wells Bombardier; Young's Bitter, Special; guest
beers** Ⓗ
A Charles Wells Speciality Beer House offering
changing guest beers in addition to three regular

Wells & Young's ales. The guest cider also changes regularly. Burgers, home-made chilli and pies are available on Thursday and Friday evenings and noon-10pm at weekends. There is live jazz on Monday evenings and Sunday afternoons, local bands on Sunday evenings, traditional music on the first Thursday of the month and a book club on the second Thursday. ✿❶⇌🅱️♨️⚑

Cricketers Arms 🍷 🅛
35 Goldington Road, MK40 3LH (on A4280 near rugby ground)
✪ 5 (7 Sun)-11 ☎ (01234) 303958 ⊕ cricketersarms.co.uk
Adnams Southwold Bitter; guest beers 🄷
Small, friendly, one-bar pub near Bedford Blues rugby ground, popular with fans of the game and very busy on match days. It opens at noon on Saturdays for Blues home games. Live rugby is shown (terrestrial TV only) and the pub also opens early for live Six Nations games. Guest beers include brews from local SIBA breweries. There is a covered, heated courtyard for smokers and drinkers. Local CAMRA Pub of the Year 2012. ✿🅱️(5)⚑

Devonshire Arms 🅛 ✔
32 Dudley Street, MK40 3TB (1 mile E of town centre S of A4280)
✪ 5 (12 Fri & Sat)-11; 12-10.30 Sun ☎ (01234) 359329
⊕ devonshirearmsbedford.co.uk
Courage Directors; Wells Eagle IPA; Young's London Gold; guest beers 🄷
Pleasant Victorian two-bar local in a quiet residential area east of the town centre. Guest beers may be from various breweries, and the pub is a supporter of LocAle. Pub festivals are held in May and December. The front bar has bare floorboards and an open fire, while the carpeted rear bar is a more traditional saloon. The private rear garden has a heated gazebo for smokers, and a non-smoking lawn area. A good range of wines is sold by the glass or bottle. Local CAMRA Most Improved Pub 2012. 🔔Q✿🅱️(4)⚑

Three Cups
45 Newnham Street, MK40 3JR (200yds S of A4280 near rugby ground)
✪ 11-11; 12-10.30 Sun ☎ (01234) 352153
Greene King IPA, Abbot; H&H Bitter; guest beers 🄷
Five minutes from the town centre and close to the rugby ground, this 1770s pub with old-style wood panelling feels like a welcoming village inn. A popular lunchtime menu is available with a wide range of food served in generous portions and a roast on Sunday. The pleasant garden has a heated smoking shelter. Dogs are welcome in the public bar and garden. Quiz night is Tuesday. Local CAMRA Pub of the Year 2009. Q✿❶🅱️(4,5,7)♣P⚑

Wellington Arms 🅛
40-42 Wellington Street, MK40 2JX (off A6 N of town centre)
✪ 12-11 (10.30 Sun) ☎ (01234) 308033
Adnams Southwold Bitter; B&T Two Brewers; guest beers 🄷
Award-winning, street-corner local operated by B&T brewery, offering a wide range of regional and microbrewery beers, plus Westons cider (and perry in summer) from 14 handpumps. A good selection of draught and bottled Belgian and other imported beers is also available. The courtyard is partly covered for drinkers and smokers. A friendly pub with a mixed clientele, it can get very busy on Friday and Saturday evenings. Filled rolls are available weekday lunchtimes. Local CAMRA Pub of the Year 2010. ✿♨️⚑

White Horse 🅛 ✔
84 Newnham Avenue, MK41 9PX (on A5140 just S of A4280)
✪ 10 (12 Sun)-11 ☎ (01234) 409306
⊕ whitehorsebedford.co.uk
Wells Eagle IPA, Bombardier; guest beers 🄷
Large, single-bar suburban pub a mile east of the town centre. Good-value food is available, with a Sunday roast and regular themed and charity evenings. Breakfast is available Monday to Saturday. Quiz nights are Sunday and Tuesday, while Monday is open-mic night. The pub has won several brewery and local business awards. A May Day weekend local beer, food and talent festival, and a November beer and banger festival are held each year. Check the website for monthly events. ✿❶🅱️(4)P⚑

Biggleswade

Golden Pheasant 🅛 ✔
71 High Street, SG18 0JH
✪ 12-11.30 (midnight Fri); 11-midnight Sat; 1-11.30 Sun
☎ (01767) 313653 ⊕ goldenpheasantpub.co.uk
Courage Directors; Wells Eagle IPA; guest beers 🄷
This cosy town-centre pub, just five minutes' walk from the bus and train station, was the first of the Charles Wells Speciality Beer Houses. The entrance from the street leads into the single bar area, which has low ceilings and oak beams. No electronic distractions ensure that conversation takes centre stage. Outside, there is sheltered seating on the large patio at the rear. Four rotating guest ales often come from small breweries. Quiz and cribbage evenings are popular, and live music features occasionally. ✿⇌🅱️♨️⚑

Stratton House Hotel 🅛
London Road, SG18 8ED
✪ 10-midnight ☎ (01767) 312442
⊕ strattonhouse-hotel.com
St Austell Landlord's Choice; guest beers 🄷
The comfortable front bar is popular with all ages, providing armchairs, settees and table seating. Additionally there is a small patio outside. The St Austell-brewed house ale is keenly priced. Three guest beers often include a stout or porter. A springtime beer festival is gaining in popularity and usually features some ales from far-flung parts of the UK. Fortnightly quizzes are held and Wi-Fi access is free – password on request. ✿🛏️❶🅱️P⚑

Wheatsheaf ✔
5 Lawrence Road, SG18 0LS
✪ 11-4, 7-11.30; 11-midnight Fri & Sat; 12-11 Sun
☎ (01767) 222220
Greene King IPA; guest beer 🄷
Sport dominates the conversation and the TV in this friendly single-room pub, built in 1873, which also offers regular games of darts, cribbage and

dominoes. The landlord and landlady have run the pub for 23 years and were awarded the Greene King national Quality in Glass prize in 2005. They continue to maintain the same exceptional standards. Slightly off the beaten track, the Wheatsheaf is well-worth the short walk from the High Street. There is a pleasant garden at the rear. ⊛≈♣⌐

Bolnhurst

Plough Ⓛ

Kimbolton Road, MK44 2EX (on B660 S of village) TL088587

✪ closed Mon; 12-3, 6.30-11 (not Sun eve)

☎ (01234) 376274 ⊕ bolnhurst.com

Beer range varies Ⓗ

Award-winning pub restaurant with roots dating back to Tudor times, offering excellent food and beer, and good service. The main bar features a wood-burning stove, and a second room is set aside for diners and functions. Up to three real ales, often from local microbreweries, are selected to complement the food. Outside is a large garden with decking beside a small pond. The pub is closed from Christmas until the second week of January each year. ⋈Q⊛Ⓓ♿P

Clophill

Stone Jug

10 Back Street, MK45 4BY (off A6 at N end of village) TL083381

✪ 12-3.30, 6-11; 12-11 Fri & Sat; 12-10.30 Sun

☎ (01525) 860526

B&T Shefford Bitter; guest beers Ⓗ

Originally three 16th-century cottages, this popular village local has an L-shaped bar that serves two drinking areas and a family/function room. Excellent home-made lunches are available Tuesday to Saturday. The four guest beers are often from local breweries. Picnic benches at the front and a rear patio garden offer space for outdoor drinking in fine weather. Parking can be difficult at busy times. A former local CAMRA Pub of the Year. Q⌸⊛Ⓓ⌐(44,81)♣♥P⌐

Cople

Five Bells

1 Northill Road, MK44 3TU

✪ 12-2.30, 4.30-11.30; 12-midnight Sat; 12-11.30 Sun

☎ (01234) 831330 ⊕ fivebellscople.com

Greene King XX Mild, IPA; guest beers Ⓗ

A 17th-century building with colour-washed rough cast walls over a timber frame, listed for its special architectural and historic interest. The main bar has low beams and a side room with an even lower ceiling. There is a second smaller bar that can be used for functions and a small room at the back for dining. A large garden opens onto fields at the rear. The guest beer is from Greene King. No food Sunday or Monday evenings. ⋈⊛Ⓓ♿⌐(74)P⌐

Dunstable

Gary Cooper ✪

Grove Park, LU5 4GP TL019223

✪ 9am (8am Sun)-midnight; 9am-2am Fri; 8am-2am Sat

☎ (01582) 471452

Fuller's London Pride; Greene King Abbot; Ruddles Best Bitter; guest beers Ⓗ

Modern, spacious, high-ceilinged bar/pub with a friendly atmosphere situated in the town centre opposite the local park. A varying selection of ales and a real cider or perry from Westons are served along with all-day food. Steak night, curry night and Sunday roasts all feature. There is a variety of seating inside with a covered smoking area outside. The bar is child-friendly with easy disabled access but no dogs are allowed. A range of continental beers and fine teas and coffees are available. ⊛Ⓓ♿⌐♥⌐

Globe Ⓛ

43 Winfield Street, LU6 1LS (off High Street North opp old grammar school) TL012222

✪ 12-11 (midnight Fri & Sat; 10.30 Sun) ☎ (01582) 512300

⊕ globe-pub.co.uk

B&T Two Brewers, Shefford Bitter, Black Dragon Mild, Dunstable Giant, Edwin Taylor's Extra Stout; guest beers Ⓗ

Popular beer destination and community local where 13 handpumps boast a good range of regular B&T beers, five ever-changing microbrewery beers, real cider and perry. More than 20 Belgian beers are also available. Bare boards, bar stools, breweriana and a famous plank at the end of the bar create a traditional town pub atmosphere buzzing with conversation. On Tuesday nights the back room hosts The Globe Acoustic Session. Dog- (and people-) friendly. Local CAMRA Pub of the Year 2009/10. Q⊛♿♣♥⌐

Pheasant Ⓛ

208 West Street, LU6 1NX TL013217

✪ 12-11; 10.30am-midnight Fri & Sat ☎ (01582) 662706

Courage Directors; Sharp's Doom Bar; guest beers Ⓗ

Family-run free house situated a short walk west of the busier part of town. Six handpumps dispense the regular beers plus continually rotating guests, often from microbreweries. 'Flights' of three thirds are available to enable full range tasting. The large rear Sports bar has pool and darts, and doubles as a popular function room catering for up to 150 people. Live sporting events are screened here regularly and in the more traditional front bar. There is a heated front patio for smokers. ⊛⌸Ⓓ⌐♣P⌐

Victoria Ⓛ

69 West Street, LU6 1ST TL017217

✪ 11-12.30am (1am Fri & Sat); 12-midnight Sun

☎ (01582) 662682

Tring Victoria Bitter; guest beers Ⓗ

Popular town-centre pub that usually offers four ales including a house beer, Victoria Bitter, from Tring Brewery. The varying guest ales are from micro and regional breweries, with one sold at a reduced rate on weekdays. Good value food is available until early evening Monday to Saturday and Sunday lunchtimes. Darts, dominoes and crib are popular and televised sport features in the bar. Beer festivals are held several times a year. There is a separate function room available. ⊛⌸Ⓓ⌐(61)♣⌐

Dunton

March Hare Ⓛ

34 High Street, SG18 8RN

✪ 6-11 (11.30 Fri); 12-11.30 Sat; 12-10.30 Sun

☎ (01767) 448093 ⊕ duntonvillage.org.uk/pub/home.htm

Beer range varies Ⓗ

Reopened in 2010 by a CAMRA husband and wife team, this restored village pub is now an integral part of the community. Three or four excellent ales, usually including one from Buntingford, complement the local Dunton cider. The home-brew award-winning landlord plans to open a microbrewery in the near future. Although there is no regular menu, there are themed food nights, and parties and buffets can be catered for on request. Folk music features on the first Tuesday of the month. ▲Q❀❄(188)♣♠

Eversholt

Green Man
Church End, MK17 9DU SP984325
🕐 12-2.30 (not Mon), 6-11; 5-11 Fri; 12-11 Sat; 12-6 Sun
☎ (01525) 288111 ⊕ greenmanevershott.com
Sharp's Doom Bar; guest beers Ⓗ
Genuine free house with modern flagstone floors and exposed brick fireplaces, conveniently located near the tourist attractions of Woburn. Good-quality food, including an award-winning Sunday lunch, is served in the bar or restaurant. There is a large patio and garden, which is the location for the annual beer festival held over the May bank holiday weekend. Two varying guest ales, possibly including one from a local brewery, are usually available. ▲❀❄◑♠P⅃

Everton

Thornton Arms
1 Potton Road, SG19 2LD
🕐 12-2.30, 6-11; 12-11 Sat; 12-10.30 Sun ☎ (01767) 681149
⊕ the-thornton-arms.co.uk
Beer range varies Ⓗ
Built in 1852, this three-room pub is the first stop-off when travelling the Greensand Ridge Walk from east to west. The front entrance leads directly to the bar. To the right is a restaurant area with popular Sunday lunches and Friday steak nights; to the left, a games room with TV and electronic machines is well supported by darts, pool and cribbage teams. One beer is usually from the Wells & Young's range, three others are mostly from regional and national breweries. ❀◑❄(188)♣P⅃

Flitton

Jolly Coopers Ⓛ
Wardhedges, MK45 5ED TL067358
🕐 12-3 (not Mon), 5.30-11.30; 12-midnight Sat; 12-10.30 Sun
☎ (01525) 860626
Wells Eagle IPA; guest beers Ⓗ
Two ever-changing and varied guest ales are served alongside the regular Eagle. Situated in the quiet hamlet of Wardhedges at the east end of Flitton, the pub is ideally placed for some very pleasant walks in the countryside. Traditional British food is served in the bar and separate restaurant, with a choice of menus. There is a large garden to the rear and a patio with spectacular floral displays in the summer months. Dogs are welcome in the bar. ▲❀❄◑&♣P⅃

Great Barford

Anchor Inn ✔
High Street, MK44 3LF (by river bridge 1 mile S of village centre) TL134517

🕐 12-3, 6.30 (6 Fri)-11; 12-11 Sat; 12-4, 6.30-10.30 Sun
☎ (01234) 870364 ⊕ anchoringreatbarford.co.uk
Young's Bitter, Special; guest beers Ⓗ
Busy local inn next to the church, overlooking the River Great Ouse. At least two guest beers are usually available from an extensive range offered by the pub company. Good home-cooked food is served in the bar and restaurant, as well as a fine selection of wines. The pub is popular with river users in the summer. Occasional themed nights are hosted, mainly during the winter months. Three rooms are available for B&B. ▲Q🛏◑&❄(27)P⅃

Harlington

Old Sun
34 Sundon Road, LU5 6LS TL037303
🕐 12-midnight (1am Fri & Sat; 10.30 Sun) ☎ (01525) 877330
⊕ theoldsunharlington.com
St Austell Tribute; Thwaites Wainwright; guest beers Ⓗ
This traditional, half-timbered building dating back to the 1740s has been a pub since 1785. There are two separate bars with a side room and outdoor seating plus a children's play area. Two or more varying guest ales are available, and at least two beer festivals are held throughout year. Food is served from a varied menu in the evenings. The pub is situated in a popular commuter village and is a short walk from the rail station. ▲❀❄◑⇌❄(X42)♣P⅃

Henlow

Engineers Arms ❦ Ⓛ ✔
68 High Street, SG16 6AA
🕐 12-midnight (1am Fri & Sat) ☎ (01462) 812284
⊕ engineersarms.co.uk
Beer range varies Ⓗ
A finalist in CAMRA's National Pub of the Year awards in 2012, this friendly pub has up to 10 handpumps dispensing an ever-changing range and style of beers, together with five ciders and a perry. The main room, whose walls feature pictures dedicated to sports stars, has wide-screen TVs. The front bar has books, brewery memorabilia and pictures illustrating local history. Occasional live music and disco evenings are held plus regular poker sessions. An October beer festival features over 100 real ales. ▲❀❄◭▲❄(71/72,82)♣♠⅃

Kempston

Duke ✔
10 Woburn Road, MK42 7QA
🕐 12-11 (midnight Fri & Sat) ☎ (01234) 857201
Wells Eagle IPA, Bombardier Ⓗ
A large community pub which can be found just south of the main shopping street and close to residential and light industrial areas. An L-shaped bar separates the large lounge from a games area with a pool table, and there is a big screen for sports. At the rear is a beer garden and children are welcome. ❀◑&❄(1,2,53)♣P⅃

Half Moon ✔
108 High Street, MK42 7BN
🕐 12-3, 6 (5 Fri)-11.30; 12-11 Sat & Sun ☎ (01234) 852464
Courage Best Bitter; Wells Eagle IPA Ⓗ
Well-supported community pub with a comfortable lounge bar and a public bar with games. The venue hosts a number of sports teams playing in local

leagues. The large garden, which includes a children's play area, is busy in good weather. The Great Ouse a short distance away offers popular riverside walks. No food is available on Sunday and evening meals need to be booked in advance. ⚇⚘⟐⚆⚅⊟(1,53,68)♣P⚊

Leighton Buzzard

Golden Bell ✅
4-6 Church Square, LU7 1AE TL920250
⚙ 10-11 (midnight Fri & Sat); 11-11 Sun ☎ (01525) 373330
⊕ thegoldenbell.co.uk
St Austell Tribute; Wychwood Hobgoblin; guest beers Ⓗ
Welcoming, lively pub with four handpumps dispensing two regular and two constantly changing guests. Beer can be drawn on gravity directly from the cask if requested. The building originally housed stonemasons erecting the nearby 13th-century church. The single bar has a low-beamed ceiling and a comfy area with sofas. Live sporting events are shown on four large TVs. Traditional pub grub includes Market Day roast dinners on Tuesdays, Saturdays and Sundays. The beer garden has a TV. ⚘⟐⇌⊟♣P⚊

Swan Hotel ✅
High Street, LU7 1EA TL921250
⚙ 7am-midnight (11.30 Sun) ☎ (01525) 380170
Fuller's London Pride; Greene King Abbot; Ruddles Best Bitter; guest beers Ⓗ
A town centre landmark, this 400-year-old coaching inn, with its 18th-century façade, was given a tasteful and sensitive renovation by Wetherspoon in 2011. With good-value food and 39 guest rooms, the Swan is busy and bustling for much of the week. The friendly and efficient staff operate one long bar serving two rooms, a conservatory and a courtyard. Guest beers often come from local microbreweries and real cider is available. Events include occasional Meet the Brewer evenings. ⚇Q⚘⚄⟐⚅⚊⚊

Luton

Bricklayers Arms ✅
16-18 High Town Road, LU2 0DD TL093217
⚙ 12-11 Mon; 12-2.30, 5-11 Tue-Thu; 12-midnight Fri & Sat; 12-10.30 Sun ☎ (01582) 611017
⊕ bricklayersarmsluton.co.uk
Batemans XB; guest beers Ⓗ
Five busy handpumps serve ever-changing guest beers, often including a mild and an Oakham brew, and three draught Belgian beers are also available. This officially 'quirky' town-centre pub has been run by the same landlady for the past 25 years. It is popular with Hatters fans on match days, and has a TV in both bars showing football and other sporting events. Quiz night is Monday. Lunchtime bar meals are served Monday to Saturday. ⚘⟐⇌(Luton)♣P⚊

English Rose
46 Old Bedford Road, LU2 7PA TL090219
⚙ 12-11 ☎ (01582) 723889 ⊕ englishroseluton.co.uk
Beer range varies Ⓗ
Popular, family-run, town local with a friendly village-pub atmosphere. Four frequently changing guest beers are chosen from a range of breweries nationwide – 500 different ales were served in 2011. A cider or perry from Mr Whiteheads or

Westons is also available. Quiz night on Tuesday is a highlight. The pub garden is probably the best in town, catering for smokers and non-smokers in four specially designed heated huts. An annual beer festival is held each June, as well as a rolling Christmas beer festival throughout December. ⚘⟐⚅⇌⊟(24,25)⬤⚊

London Hatter ✅
46 Park Street, LU1 3ET TL094210
⚙ 8-midnight (1am Fri & Sat) ☎ (01582) 390920
Fuller's London Pride, ESB; Greene King Abbot; Ruddles Best Bitter; guest beers Ⓗ
Wetherspoon pub opened in 2011 in a former nightclub at the university end of the town. A local ale often features on the guest handpumps, normally fairly strong as favoured by the manager. Real cider and/or perry are usually available. The pub's smart interior caters more for dining than partying and local history features heavily in pictures adorning the walls. ⚇⟐⚅⇌⚊

Wigmore Arms Ⓛ ✅
Wigmore Lane, LU2 8AD TL121224
⚙ 11-11 (1am Fri; 10.30 Sun); 10-midnight Sat
☎ (01582) 417343
Greene King IPA; Wells Bombardier; guest beers Ⓗ
Lively and large two-bar modern pub in a residential area of Luton next to Asda supermarket. Beer festivals are held in April and October each year. There is a comfortable lounge with a dining area where food is served all day every day. The sports bar has two large HD screens and 3D TV showing sports TV and the Luton Town channel. Live music features on the last Saturday of the month. ⟐⚅⚆♣P

Moggerhanger

Guinea
Bedford Road, MK44 3RG
⚙ 11.30-11; 12-10 Sun ☎ (01767) 640388
⊕ guineamoggerhanger.co.uk
Courage Directors; Wells Eagle IPA; guest beers Ⓗ
Large 18th-century village pub with a log fire and beamed ceilings in a prominent position on the main road in the centre of the village. There is a garden at the front and a car park at the side and rear. The main bar has a spacious drinking area and an area beyond for diners. A second bar has a skittles table and dartboard. Up to two guest beers are supplied by Charles Wells. ⚘⟐⚅⚆⊟(73,188)♣P⚊

Potton

Rising Sun Ⓛ ✅
11 Everton Road, SG19 2PA
⚙ 12-3, 6-midnight; 12-midnight Sat & Sun
☎ (01767) 260231
Wells Eagle IPA; guest beers Ⓗ
The ground floor has low walls, wooden beams and features a covered well. There is a separate games room with a pool table and upstairs is a quiet function room and roof-top terrace. The eight handpumps offer a wide range of well-kept ales, often including a second one from Wells & Young's and one from Oakham, plus a Welsh cider. Beer festivals are held during the early May and late August bank holiday weekends. Good-value food is served daily until 9.30pm. ⚘⟐⊟(188/190)♣⬤⚊

Pulloxhill

Cross Keys Ⓛ ✅
13 High Street, MK45 5HB TL063341
🕓 12-3, 5-11 (6-10.30 Sun) ☎ (01525) 712442
Adnams Broadside; Wells Eagle IPA; guest beer Ⓗ
A rare gem of a proper village community pub, run by the same family for over 41 years. The attractive, half-timbered building dates back to 1640. The back bar doubles as a large function room, which is used by various local interest groups. Busy at meal times, the pub serves a traditional English menu. Regular events include quiz nights and live music, with jazz every Sunday evening. The large garden caters for all sorts including archers and campers. Q✿⊕▷&▲🚗♣P⁻

Renhold

Polhill Arms
25 Wilden Road, MK41 0JP (at Salph End) TL083527
🕓 12-3, 5-11; 12-11 Fri & Sat; 12-10.30 Sun
☎ (01234) 771398 ⊕ polhillarms.co.uk
Greene King IPA; Morland Old Speckled Hen; guest beers Ⓗ
One-bar, family-friendly village local with a welcoming atmosphere and large garden, play area and restaurant. An interesting collection of pub and brewery artefacts is on view. Traditional pub food is served as well as fish and chips and a choice of pizzas (not Sun eve). Live entertainment and quiz nights feature regularly, and darts and skittles are played. Two guest beers are usually available, with Olde Trip a popular choice. 🏚✿⊕▷🚗(27,151)♣P⁻

Salford

Red Lion Hotel Ⓛ
Wavendon Road, MK17 8AZ (2 miles N of M1 jct 13) SP934389
🕓 11 (12 Sun)-2.30, 6-11 ☎ (01908) 583117
⊕ redlionhotel.eu
Wells Eagle IPA, Bombardier Ⓗ
Friendly, traditional country hotel serving a fine choice of home-cooked food in the bar and restaurant. The cosy bar is heated by an open fire in winter and offers a selection of interesting board games. The large garden includes a covered area and a secure children's playground. Six rooms are available for overnight accommodation. 🏚Q🛏✿🍴⊕▷🚗&♣P⁻

Sandy

Sir William Peel Ⓛ ✅
39 High Street, SG19 1AG (opp church)
🕓 12 (11 Sat)-midnight; 12-10.30 Sun ☎ (01767) 680607
⊕ sirwilliampeel.webs.com
Batemans XB; guest beers Ⓗ
Popular open-plan free house with comfortable seating, set between the railway station and bus stops. Choose between Batemans XB, three rotating guest ales and several real ciders. The spring Beer Festival also includes up to 10 ciders. No food is served except the landlady's Sunday cheeseboard, but you are welcome to bring in a take-away meal. Regular quizzes and occasionally local musicians engage in 'Peel Jam'. The pub is home to Sir William Peel FC and is dog-friendly – biscuits provided! ✿⇌🚗(73,188/190)♦P⁻

Shefford

Brewery Tap
14 North Bridge Street, SG17 5DH
🕓 11.30-11; 12-10.30 Sun ☎ (01462) 628448
B&T Shefford Bitter, Dunstable Giant, Dragonslayer; Everards Tiger Best Bitter; guest beers Ⓗ
The Tap was rescued by the nearby B&T Brewery in 1996. Primarily a drinkers' pub, it offers four regular beers and one weekly guest ale. The open-plan interior, featuring a display of breweriana, is divided into two distinct areas, plus a family room at the rear, all served from the same bar. Pies and filled rolls are available at lunchtime. The rear patio garden is heated on cool evenings. Car park access is through an archway next to the pub. 🛏✿🚗(71,72)♣P⁻

Souldrop

Bedford Arms Ⓛ
High Street, MK44 1EY (½ mile W of A6) SP987617
🕓 closed Mon; 12-3, 6-11; 12-midnight Fri & Sat; 12-11 Sun
☎ (01234) 781384
Black Sheep Best Bitter; Greene King IPA; Phipps NBC Red Star; guest beers Ⓗ
Large village pub created partly from a 17th-century hop and ale house. Guest beers are often from local microbreweries. The welcoming restaurant has a central, open fireplace and serves traditional pub favourites prepared to order, with daily specials and a roast lunch on Sunday (no food Sun eve). A large games room with skittles runs off the main bar. The spacious garden and play area are popular with families in summer. Local CAMRA Pub of the Year 2011. 🏚✿⊕▷🚗(125)♣P⁻

Stevington

Royal George
8-10 Silver Street, MK43 7QP
🕓 12-2 (not Wed), 5-11; 12-11 Sat & Sun ☎ (01234) 822184
Wells Eagle IPA; guest beers Ⓗ
A friendly community pub created from two old houses joined together. London commuters will appreciate the hanging straps over the bar. Two Westons real ciders or perry are served from the cellar. Good-value lunches include sandwiches, baguettes and bacon, egg and chips. Live bands play occasionally at weekends. A key to the restored 18th-century Stevington windmill east of the village centre may be borrowed for a small deposit. 🏚✿⊕▷🚗(26)♣♦P⁻

Studham

Red Lion
Church Road, LU6 2QA TL022158
🕓 12-2.30, 5-11; 12-11.30 Fri & Sat; 12-10.30 Sun
☎ (01582) 872530 ⊕ theredlion-studham.co.uk
Adnams Southwold Bitter; Fuller's London Pride; Greene King IPA; guest beers Ⓗ
Ideally situated in the centre of the village adjacent to a wildlife common and in the middle of a network of countryside footpaths, this pub is the focal point of the local community. With Whipsnade Zoo only a couple of miles away, it is the perfect place to rest by the log fire after a long day at the zoo. See the blackboard for the latest guest ales. 🏚Q🛏✿⊕▷🚗&🚗(X31)P⁻

Tebworth

Queen's Head 🄻
The Lane, LU7 9QB TL991268
⬡ 12-3 (not Sun-Wed), 6 (7 Sat)-11 ☎ (01525) 874101
Adnams Broadside; Courage Directors 🄶; Wells Eagle
IPA 🄷; seasonal beers 🄶
This traditional village pub with old-style public bar
and saloon warmed by open fires has been in
every edition of the Guide since 1975. One
handpump features in each bar with two more ales
served straight from the cask. With 30 years under
the present landlord, renowned for his old-style
banter and verbal riposte, this is a pub that
welcomes all – a real trip back in time with no airs
or graces. Live music is hosted every Friday. Dog-
friendly with a large garden. No food is served.
🏚Q🏡😊🄴🅗♣P🖢

Toddington

Oddfellows Arms
2 Conger Lane, LU5 6BP TL010289
⬡ 5-11 (midnight Fri); 12-midnight Sat; 12-11 Sun
☎ (01525) 872021
Adnams Broadside; Fuller's London Pride; guest
beers 🄷
Attractive 15th-century pub facing the village
green with a heavily beamed and brassed bar
featuring a vast collection of pump clips, and a
games room with a pool table. Westons Old Rosie,
and often a guest cider or perry, are available, as
well as a good range of bottled ciders. Beer
festivals are held in the spring and autumn. The
patio garden is popular in summer and has a
shelter for smokers. 🏚🏡🅗🖥♣🐾🖢

Totternhoe

Cross Keys
201 Castle Hill Road, LU6 2DA SP979218
⬡ 11.30-3, 5-10 (11 Wed); 11.30-11 Thu-Sat; 11.30-10 Sun
☎ (01525) 220424
Adnams Broadside; Greene King IPA; guest beers 🄷
A great place to relax and unwind, this attractive
thatched, Grade II-listed building dating from 1433
has a glorious damson orchard and sweeping views
over Ivinghoe Beacon and the Vale of Aylesbury.
Guest beers rotate weekly from a list chosen by the
locals. In the warmer months basket meals and
barbecues are available in the garden. Dogs are
welcome in the public bar.
Q🐕🏡🅗🖥(61,71)♣P🖢

Whipsnade

Old Hunters Lodge
The Crossroads, LU6 2LN TL014181
⬡ 11.30-2.30 (3 Sat), 5.30-11; 12-11 Sun ☎ (01582) 872228
⊕ old-hunters.com
Greene King IPA, Abbot; guest beers 🄷
The closest inn to Whipsnade Zoo, this 15th-century
thatched house, packed with original features, is
one of the oldest buildings in the village. There is a
comfortable bar manned by friendly staff where
you can sit and enjoy a pint, good conversation and
good bar food, plus a separate à la carte restaurant.
The inn is ideally located to explore the many
attractions the area has to offer. Regular Friday
theme nights are held during the year.
🏚Q🏡🅗🖥(X31)P

Wingfield

Plough
Tebworth Road, LU7 9QH TL002263
⬡ 12-3, 5.30-midnight; 12-midnight Sat; 12-11 Sun
☎ (01525) 873077 ⊕ theploughinn.com
Fuller's London Pride, ESB; Gale's Seafarers Ale, HSB;
guest beers 🄷
Charming thatched village inn dating from the 17th
century, decorated with paintings of rural scenes
and ploughs. Beware the low beams! Good home-
cooked food is served daily except Sunday evening
when a fortnightly quiz is held. There are tables
outside at the front, and to the rear is a
conservatory and prize-winning garden,
illuminated at night in the summer. Heated
umbrellas are provided for smokers.
🏚Q🏡🅗🖥(68)♣P🖢

Wootton

Chequers 🄻
Hall End, MK43 9HP (small hamlet on NW edge of
village) SP001457
⬡ 12-3, 6-11; 12-11 Sat & Sun ☎ (01234) 765005
⊕ chequersinnwootton.co.uk
Wells Eagle IPA; guest beers 🄷
Originally a farmhouse, this handsome old inn
retains a wealth of heavy wooden beams and
period features. A free house, it offers a wide
range of guest beers largely from local small
breweries. An interesting, quality menu is served
in the restaurant and good-value bar food is
available throughout the pub (no food Sun eve).
The large, pleasant garden is popular in fine
weather and is used to host fun events and the
occasional beer festival. 🏚Q🏡🅗🖥(68)♣P🖢

Beer not brandy

Before brandy, which has now become common and sold in every little alehouse, came to
England in such quantities as it now doth, we drank good strong beer and ale, and all
laborious people (which are the greater part of the kingdom), their bodies requiring after
hard labour some strong drink to refresh them, did therefore every morning and evening
used to drink a pot of ale or a flagon of strong beer, which greatly helped the promotion
of our grains and did them no great prejudice; it hindereth not their work, neither did it
take away their senses nor cost them much money, whereas the prohibition of brandy
would prevent the destruction of his majesty's subjects, many of whom have been killed
by drinking thereof, if not agreeing with their constitution.
Petition to the House of Commons, 1673

Great British Pubs

Adrian Tierney-Jones

NEW TITLE

CAMRA'S
GREAT BRITISH PUBS

Adrian Tierney-Jones

CAMPAIGN FOR REAL ALE

Unmissable pubs • Perfect pints • Favourite destinations

Great British Pubs is a celebration of the British pub. This fully illustrated and practical book presents the pub as an ultimate destination – featuring pubs everyone should seek out and make a visit to. It recommends a selection of the very best pubs in various different categories, as chosen by leading beer writer Adrian Tierney-Jones. Every kind of pub is represented, with full-colour photography helping to show-case a host of excellent pubs from the seaside to the city and from the historic to the ultra-modern. Articles on beer brewing, cider making, classic pub food recipes, traditional pub games and various other aspects of pub life are included to help the reader truly appreciate what makes a pub 'great'.

£14.99   ISBN 978-1-85249-265-6   CAMRA members' price £12.99   296 pages

For this and other books on beer and pubs visit the CAMRA bookshop at
www.camra.org.uk/books

BERKSHIRE

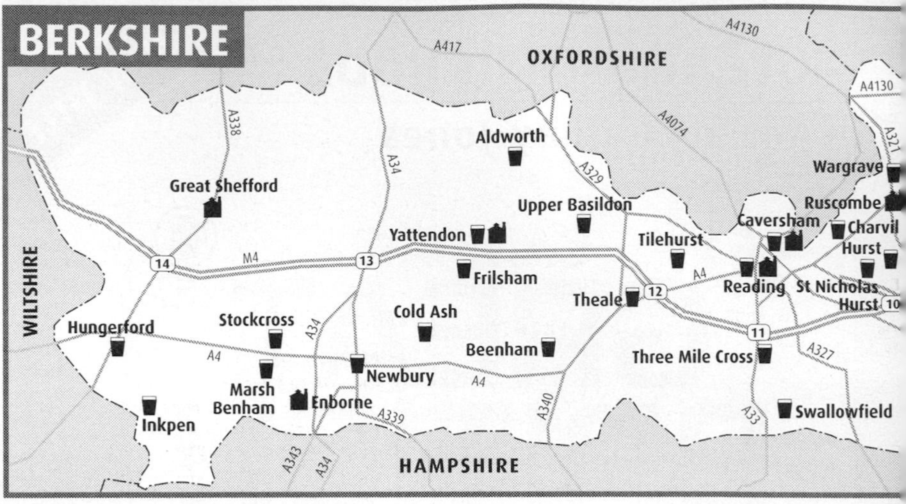

Aldworth

Bell Inn ★ 𝕃

Bell Lane, RG8 9SE (off B4009) SU555796
✪ closed Mon; 11-3, 6-11; 12-3, 7-10.30 Sun
☎ (01635) 578272
Arkell's 3B, Kingsdown; West Berkshire Maggs' Mild, Good Old Boy, seasonal beers Ⓗ
A former CAMRA National, Regional and Branch Pub of the Year, this popular inn is an enduring entry in the Guide. A classic rural gem, it features a timeless interior and a capacious garden for hot days. With more than 250 years of history, it is now in the fifth generation of ownership. A wide range of delicious hot rolls and soups is served. Draught local ciders are increasingly popular.
⌂Q❀◐♣●P

Beenham

Six Bells 𝕃

The Green, RG7 5NX SU585688
✪ 12-2.30 (not Mon & Tue), 6-11; 12-3, 6.30-11 Sat; 12-3, 6.30-10.30 Sun ☎ (0118) 971 3368 ⊕ thesixbells.co.uk
Fuller's London Pride; guest beers Ⓗ
A welcoming and comfortable two-bar village local which offers two guest beers from smaller local breweries alongside London Pride. It also serves highly regarded home-cooked food. Four bedrooms offer accommodation, and there are conference facilities. After a meal, or with your pint, you can enjoy a range of board games in front of open fires or in the conservatory.
⌂Q❀◐♿🚌(104)♣P

Binfield

Jack o' Newbury 𝕃

Terrace Road North, RG42 5PH SU845718
✪ 11-3, 5.30-11; 12-3, 7-10.30 Sun ☎ (01344) 454881
⊕ jackofnewbury.co.uk
Loddon Hoppit; West Berkshire Good Old Boy; guest beers Ⓗ
To the north of Binfield, this family-run free house offers a friendly welcome. A range of beers is available, many from local microbreweries, as well as occasional real cider. Binfield Best (3.9%) is the house beer. A traditional skittle alley is in a separate building and can be hired for private events. No food Sunday and Monday evenings.
⌂Q❀◐🚌(151)♣P⁵̶

Victoria Arms ✔

Terrace Road North, RG42 5JA SU842713
✪ 11.30-11 (midnight Fri & Sat); 12-11 Sun
☎ (01344) 483856
Fuller's Discovery, London Pride, ESB; Gale's HSB; guest beers Ⓗ
Compact, vibrant village local with rooms converging around a central serving area overlooked by a huge bottle collection displayed among the roof beams. The bar is dominated by two TV screens often showing different events, but between times provides a peaceful retreat. A decent selection of bar meals is offered plus a daily specials board. There is a large, covered, heated patio and a pleasant beer garden. Families are welcome. Quiz night is Sunday. A long-standing Guide entry. ⌂❀◐♿🚌(53,153)P⁵̶

Bracknell

Old Manor 🏆 𝕃 ✔

Grenville Place, RG12 1BP (on inner ring road)
✪ 8-midnight (1am Fri & Sat) ☎ (01344) 304490
Greene King Abbot; Ruddles Best Bitter; guest beers Ⓗ
Built in the Tudor era, this charming Wetherspoon pub stands out in a 1960s new town. Its two bars offer a total of six guest beers, plus the popular Old Rosie Scrumpy cider and Broadoak Perry. Steak and curry nights feature during the week, with a wide-ranging menu of pub food served until 10pm. A 10-minute walk from Bracknell rail station. Local CAMRA Pub of the Year 2012. Q❀◐♿⇌🚌●P⁵̶

Caversham

Baron Cadogan 𝕃 ✔

22-24 Prospect Street, RG4 8JG
✪ 9-11 (midnight Fri & Sat; 10.30 Sun) ☎ (0118) 948 1078
Greene King Abbot; Loddon Cadogan's Gold; Ruddles Best Bitter; guest beers Ⓗ
Unmistakably a Wetherspoon, though smaller than most, the Baron is a five-minute stroll from the River Thames at Caversham Bridge. Converted from

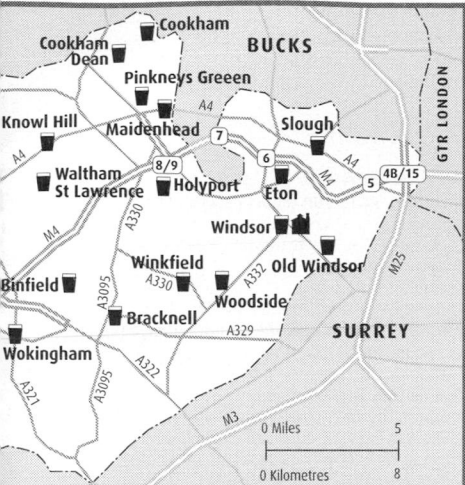

a former Co-op store in 1997, this open-plan pub is popular for food as well as its six handpumps. Regular Cadogan's Gold (4.4%) is locally brewed by Loddon – its Ferryman's Gold rebadged. Real cider, usually Westons, is also available. There is disability access from the public car park at the rear in Chester Street. Q◑&⊟(2,22,24)●⁺⁻

Charvil

Lands End
Park Lane, RG10 0UE SU778746
☼ 12-3, 6-11; 12-10.30 Sun ☎ (0118) 934 0700
Brakspear Bitter; guest beers Ⓗ
Brakspear pub next to a ford crossing the River Loddon, which can be impassable after heavy rain. To avoid the ford, approach from either the Woodley or Charvil directions, rather than on the road from Hurst. The large back garden has views of the river, and appropriately the pub has angling décor. The large room overlooking the back garden is used during busy periods. Dogs in garden only.
ਠ⊛◑&P

Cold Ash

Castle Inn Ⓛ ✓
Cold Ash Hill, RG18 9PS SU511697
☼ 11.30-11.30 (midnight Fri & Sat); 12-11 Sun
☎ (01635) 863232 ⊕ thecastleatcoldash.co.uk
Courage Best Bitter; Fuller's London Pride; guest beers Ⓗ
Welcoming 19th-century inn that has been in the same family for 18 years. Known for its good food, it serves a popular pensioners' weekday lunch, and offers cream teas in the summer months. As well as its regular ales it serves a locally brewed beer from West Berkshire Brewery and two other guest beers. Monday is quiz night (no meals served) and a meat raffle is held on Friday.
ਔ⊛◑⊟(101)♣P⁺⁻

Cookham

Bounty Ⓛ
Riverside, SL8 5RG (over railway bridge from Bourne End station or walk along Cookham towpath) SU890871

☼ 12-11 (closed Mon-Fri; 12-dusk Sat & Sun winter)
☎ (01628) 520056
Rebellion IPA, Mutiny; guest beer Ⓗ
Located on the National Trust's Cockmarsh between Cookham village and Bourne End, this quirky, characterful pub is only accessible on foot or by boat. Summer weekends can be busy. The boat-shaped bar is packed with nautical knick-knacks and daft jokes. Bar billiards can be played while listening to '60s music. Live events are held throughout the summer including theatre. The kitchen closes at 8pm. Note the reduced winter opening hours. ਔਠ⊛◑≉(Bourne End)♣⁺⁻

Cookham Dean

Jolly Farmer Ⓛ
Church Road, SL6 9PD
☼ 11.30-11 (11.45 Fri); 12-10.30 Sun ☎ (01628) 482905
⊕ jollyfarmercookhamdean.co.uk
Brakspear Bitter; Courage Best Bitter; guest beers Ⓗ
Eighteenth-century village pub opposite the Norman church and owned by the village since 1987. It has two bars – the cosy adults-only bar, and the larger Dean bar for families, diners and drinkers, with a real log fire in winter. Dogs are welcome. The three guest beers always include a LocAle. Outside is a large beer garden and children's play area. A number of beer festivals are held throughout the year. ਔQਠ⊛◑⊟(M1)♣P

Eton

Watermans Arms Ⓛ ✓
Brocas Street, SL4 6BW (short walk from Eton Bridge)
☼ 12-11 (11.30 Wed & Thu; midnight Fri & Sat)
☎ (01753) 861001 ⊕ watermans-eton.com
Beer range varies Ⓗ
A building has been on this site since the mid-16th century, and it went through various guises before becoming a public house, including a workhouse and a temporary mortuary during the plague. A horseshoe-shaped bar greets you on entry and a small area to the side with comfortable sofas provides space to relax. A large function room to the rear is available to hire. Local ales are always available. Dog-friendly.
ਔ⊛◑≉(Windsor & Eton Riverside)⊟(60)

Frilsham

Pot Kiln Ⓛ
Yattendon to Bucklebury Road, RG18 0XX (on unnamed road between Yattendon and Bucklebury) SU552732
☼ 12-2.30, 6-10.30; closed Tue; 12-11 Sat; 12-9.30 Sun
☎ (01635) 201366 ⊕ potkiln.org
West Berkshire Mr Chubb's Lunchtime Bitter, Brick Kiln Bitter, seasonal beers; guest beer Ⓗ
A delightful pub in remote, unspoilt countryside. The bar is small, cosy and welcoming, complemented by picturesque gardens.

INDEPENDENT BREWERIES

Binghams Ruscombe
Butts Great Shefford
Two Bridges Caversham (brewing suspended)
Two Cocks Enborne (NEW)
West Berkshire Yattendon
Windsor & Eton Windsor
Zerodegrees Reading

Handpumps dispense three beers from the nearby West Berkshire Brewery including Brick Kiln Bitter, the fourth is from a regional micro. Bar food is available. A restaurant adjoins the bar, run by TV chef Mike Robinson, who has owned the pub since 2005. The location makes this a convenient stop-off for walkers and cyclists, especially at weekends. ♛Q✿◑◗⊟♣P

Holyport

White Hart ✔

Moneyrow Green, SL6 2ND (½ mile S of village) SU890770

✪ 12-11 (10 Sun) ☎ (01628) 621460

🌐 thewhitehartholyport.co.uk

Greene King IPA; Morland Old Speckled Hen; guest beers 🄷

Two-bar pub where the wood-panelled lounge features leather sofas and log fires in winter. The larger public bar has wooden flooring, a TV and traditional pub games including bar billiards. Food is available every day except Monday. Music and quiz nights are held regularly. Outside is a large, fenced beer garden with a pétanque pitch and children's play area. ♛✿◑◗🚌(6a)♣P⚐–

Hungerford

Hungerford Club 🄻 ✔

3 The Croft, RG17 0HY (on foot via Church Lane, by road via Church St and Croft Rd) SU336686

✪ 11-3, 7-11 (10.30 Sun) ☎ (01488) 682357

🌐 hungerford-club.co.uk

Fuller's London Pride; West Berkshire Maggs' Mild; guest beers 🄷

Welcoming social club that is home to tennis and bowls club members. The popularity of snooker, billiards and indoor games is reflected by the full trophy cabinet. The club overlooks a quiet green between the high street and the church. The TV is switched on for major sporting events. Filled rolls are available Saturday lunchtimes. Show this Guide or CAMRA membership card for entry. ✿⇌🚌♣P⚐–

Hurst

Castle 🄻

Church Hill, RG10 0SJ

✪ 12-3, 5.30 (5 Sat)-11; 12-10 Sun ☎ (0118) 934 0034

🌐 castlehurst.co.uk

Binghams Twyford Tipple; guest beers 🄷

Classic village pub enjoying a spectacular resurgence since the lease was handed back by Greene King to the local church opposite. Parts of the building date back to the 10th century. The local bowling green is at the rear of the pub; W G Grace is said to have played here. It does good pub food, sourced locally whenever possible. ♛Q🐎✿◑◗⊟🚌(129)P

Inkpen

Crown & Garter 🄻

Inkpen Common, RG17 9QR SU378639

✪ 12-3 (not Mon & Tue), 5.30-11; 12-5, 7-10.30 Sun

☎ (01488) 668325 🌐 crownandgarter.co.uk

Fuller's London Pride; Two Cocks Gibbet Ale; West Berkshire Good Old Boy 🄷

Former coaching inn that has recently received a full refurbishment. Enjoy a delicious meal in the dining area or relax in the bar by a wood-burning stove while enjoying a pint of the exclusively brewed Gibbet Ale. Outside at the rear is a large, mature garden. En-suite accommodation is available. ♛Q✿🛏◑◗♿🚌(13)♣P⚐–🍺

Knowl Hill

Bird in Hand 🄻

Bath Road, RG10 9UP (on A4 between Reading and Maidenhead) SU820792

✪ 11-11; 12-10.30 Sun ☎ (01628) 826622

🌐 birdinhand.co.uk

Beer range varies 🄷

Fourteenth century countryside inn with five ales that come from across the country, including at least one from a local brewery such as Binghams, Vale or Ascot (see the website for current beers). Real cider is available during the summer. Food is served in the dining room or in front of an open fire in the bar area. Regular events hosted throughout the year including beer festivals and barbecues. ♛Q🐎✿🛏◑◗🚌(127,239)🍎P⚐–

Maidenhead

Greyhound 🄻 ✔

92-96 Queen Street, SL6 1HZ

✪ 8am-midnight (1am Fri & Sat) ☎ (01628) 779410

Fuller's London Pride; Greene King Abbot; Loddon Hoppit; guest beers 🄷

A large Wetherspoon bar located a short walk from Maidenhead station, named after the original Greyhound in the high street, which burned down in 1735. LocAle-accredited, guest beers come from local micros. Westons Old Rosie and Vintage ciders are stocked. The large open-plan bar has a family area and a smaller room at the front. A quiet pub during the week, with music on Friday and Saturday nights. ◑◗⇌🚌🍎⚐–

Maidenhead Conservative Club ✔

32 York Road, SL6 1SF

✪ 11-11 (11.45 Fri & Sat); 12-11 Sun ☎ (01628) 620579

🌐 maidenheadconclub.co.uk

Fuller's London Pride, seasonal beers; guest beers 🄷

Friendly real ale outlet close to the station. Two guest ales from independent breweries are available, along with a selection of bottle-conditioned beers. Hot meals are served weekday lunchtimes. Crib and darts nights are held during the week. A public car park is 100 yards away. A CAMRA membership card allows entry for a minimal fee. 🐎◑♿⇌🚌♣P⚐–

Marsh Benham

Red House 🄻

RG20 8LY (off A4 at Marsh Benham sign, 400yds on left) SU428675

✪ 11-11.30; 12-10 Sun ☎ (01635) 582017

🌐 theredhousepub.com

West Berkshire Mr Chubb's Lunchtime Bitter, Good Old Boy; guest beer 🄷

Rural pub approximately five minutes' walk from the canal. Food is available all day, made with ingredients locally sourced by Laurent Lebeau, the head chef, who has owned the pub since 2010. Beers are sourced from local microbreweries including Butts and Two Cocks. The pub is closed just two days a year, Christmas and for the staff party. ♛✿♿P⚐–

Newbury

Lock, Stock & Barrel ✅
104 Northbrook Street, RG14 1AA SU471672
☼ 11-11 (midnight Fri & Sat); 12-10.30 Sun
☎ (01635) 580550
Fuller's Discovery, London Pride, ESB, seasonal beers Ⓗ
Popular and welcoming canalside pub, close to the town bridge and local amenities. It has fine views of the locks and nearby St Nicolas Church. Food is served all day until 9pm (8pm Sun), and live music plays on Sunday afternoons. A Fuller's seasonal beer and a guest from either Butts or West Berkshire breweries supplement the regular ales. The L-shaped bar is stylish and comfortably furnished. A roof terrace and plenty of outside seating provide the perfect setting for a fine day.
❀❀⏾◐⅃≢⊟⊷

Old Windsor

Jolly Gardeners ✅
92-94 St Luke's Road, SL4 2QJ
☼ 12-11 (midnight Thu, Fri & Sat; 10.30 Sun)
☎ (01753) 830215 ⊕ jollygardeners.com
Courage Best Bitter; Wells Bombardier Ⓗ
A friendly locals' pub run by a landlord who is fastidious about the quality of his beer A horseshoe-shaped bar serves a single area with a cosy fire in winter. Outside, a covered and heated area is provided for smokers on the patio garden. Darts is played and sports shown. Reasonably priced food is served weekday lunchtimes, and Sunday roasts are a highlight (1-4pm).
∰❀⏾◐⊟(71)P⅃⊷

Pinkneys Green

Stag & Hounds 🄻
1 Lee Lane, SL6 6NU
☼ 11-11; 12-10.30 Sun ☎ (01628) 630268
Rebellion seasonal beer; guest beers Ⓗ
This free house on the edge of the NT-owned green has Rebellion's monthly offering, four other frequently changing guest ales and Thatchers cider. One of its two rooms has table seating for good-value meals (no food Sun eve or Mon). A function room hosts a family-friendly Sunday carvery and beer festivals, one on the second weekend of May when Carters Steam Fair visits the green. There is a large garden and a heated shelter for smokers. Wednesday is quiz night. Well-behaved dogs are welcome. Q❀☙❀⏾◐⅁⊟(5,8)⊷P⅃⊷

Reading

Alehouse 🄻
2 Broad Street, RG1 2BH
☼ 11-11; 12-10.30 Sun ☎ (0118) 950 8119
⊕ hobgoblinreading.co.uk
Beer range varies Ⓗ
Formerly known as the Hobgoblin, this is the perfect escape from the travails of a hard day's work or shopping. The front room is full of character and friendly banter, and the back room is divided into several booths for a more intimate setting. Thousands of pump clips adorn the walls and ceiling, and all manner of real ales including three from West Berkshire Brewery, plus cider and perry, can be found on the bar. The only pub in Reading that sells mead. ❀≢⊟⊷⅃⊷☐

Back of Beyond ✅
104-108 King's Road, RG1 3BY
☼ 9-midnight ☎ (0118) 959 5906
Courage Best Bitter; Fuller's London Pride; Greene King Abbot; Ruddles Best Bitter; guest beers Ⓗ
Wetherspoon pub standing on the site of a ginger beer factory, later used as a Salvation Army barracks, claiming to take its name from its location on the edge of Reading's town centre. It has the usual JDW mixture of tables, chairs and booths, and its long rectangular lounge stretches back to look out on the Kennet & Avon Canal. Prints of old Reading adorn the walls and there is a good sized outdoor seating area to the rear. Q❀⏾◐⅃≢⊟⊷⅃

Foresters Arms 🄻
79-81 Brunswick Street, RG1 6NY
☼ 4 (12 Sun)-11; 12-midnight Fri & Sat ☎ (0118) 376 9128
Beer range varies Ⓗ
A popular two-roomed backstreet local retaining much of its original layout – the two bars are connected by a rare side corridor. A change in ownership a few years ago has brought welcome improvements. Enjoy the refurbished garden on a sunny day with live chickens in attendance, or try some of Tucci's Italian-themed cuisine in the rear bar. Quiz night is alternate Mondays; folk night is the second Friday of the month.
∰❀⏾◐⅁⊟≢(West)⊟♣⊷⅃

Nag's Head 🍷 🄻
5 Russell Street, RG1 7XD
☼ 12-11; 11-midnight Fri & Sat ☎ (0118) 957 4649
⊕ nagsheadreading.com
Beer range varies Ⓗ
A recent deal with the pubco owner has completely removed the tie on beer and cider here. This pub has been transformed over the past five years into a thriving destination venue for the ale and cider drinker. Run by a small group of family and friends, quality and choice of beer is at the forefront. Local CAMRA Pub of the Year 2011.
∰❀⏾◐≢(West)⊟♣⊷P⅃

Retreat 🄻
8 St John's Street, RG1 4EH
☼ 4.30-11; 12-11.30 Fri & Sat; 12-11 Sun ☎ (0118) 957 1593
⊕ retreatpub.co.uk
Harveys Sussex Best Bitter; Loddon Ferryman's Gold; Sharp's Cornish Coaster, Doom Bar; guest beers Ⓗ
Tucked away down a terraced side street, this friendly community pub can be tricky to find but is worth seeking out. A large range of real ale, cider and bottled foreign beers is skilfully squeezed into the small bar. In the back room there is a regular schedule of live music, beer festivals, talks and raffles, including annual pickled onion and mince pie competitions. Truly a retreat in the heart of Reading, the pub attracts a diverse range of customers, and dogs are welcome.
⊟(17,190)♣⊷⅃

Zerodegrees 🄻
9 Bridge Street, RG1 2LR
☼ 12-midnight (11 Sun) ☎ (0118) 959 7959
⊕ zerodegrees.co.uk/location-reading.html
Zerodegrees Wheat Ale, Pale Ale, Black Lager, Pilsner, seasonal beers Ⓟ
Near the Oracle shopping centre, Zerodegrees brews its range of beers on site and, with the brewery incorporated into the architecture of the bar, makes for a unique drinking experience. This is a great place to introduce new drinkers to the

benefits of real ale who might otherwise be put off by a more traditional pub setting. The beer is served chilled, but when allowed to warm the full flavours and aromas come through. ⊛⬤❶⬤♿⇌⬛⬚

St Nicholas Hurst

Wheelwrights Arms ⊘

Davis Way, RG10 0TR (off B3030 opp entrance to Dinton Pastures) SU790725

⊛ 11.30-3, 5.30-11; 11.30-11 Sat; 12-10.30 Sun
☎ (0118) 934 4100 ⊕ thewheelwrightsarms.co.uk

Wadworth Henry's IPA, Horizon, 6X, Bishops Tipple, seasonal beers; guest beers Ⓟ

Formerly an 18th-century wheelwright's shop, this vibrant village pub has two bars with low beams, flagstone floors and a great open fireplace, plus a separate dining area. A fine selection of Wadworth beers is always on handpump. Families are welcome, children until 8.30pm, but there is no children's menu. Newspapers are provided and there is ample outdoor seating, some covered and heated. The smokers' area is separate from the gardens. ⌂⊛❶⬤♿⇌(Winnersh)⬛(128)⬤Ｐ⬚

Slough

Moon & Spoon 🅛 ⊘

86 High Street, SL1 1EL

⊛ 8am-midnight ☎ (01753) 531650

Greene King Abbot; Ruddles Best Bitter; guest beers Ⓗ

Large Wetherspoon shop conversion popular with a wide cross-section of the community. The decor is plush and at the entrance is an eye-catching sculpture comprising 1148 spoons. The pub has a long modern bar with zoned sections, including a family dining area and private booths. Regular steak, curry and ale nights are hosted. Four guest beers are usually on offer, including a LocAle, along with a choice of real cider. Food is served 8am-10pm, with CAMRA members receiving a 20 per cent discount. Q⊛❶⬤♿⇌⬛⬤⬚

Rose & Crown

312 High Street, SL1 1NB (E end of High Street)

⊛ 11am-midnight; 12-12.30am Sun ☎ (01753) 521114

Beer range varies Ⓗ

This attractive Grade II-listed Regency two-bar inn is the oldest pub on the High Street and makes a pleasant contrast to its taller and more modern surroundings. Two beers are usually available, often sourced from Northumberland, along with a real cider. Entertainment includes regular quiz nights and TV sports events. The pub hosts the annual Slough conker championship in October. ⊛⬚⇌⬛♣⬤⬚

Stockcross

Lord Lyon 🅛 ⊘

Ermin Street, RG20 8LL SU437685

⊛ 12-3, 5-11; 12-10.30 Sun ☎ (01488) 608366
⊕ lordlyon.co.uk

Arkell's Wiltshire Gold, Moonlight, Kingsdown Ⓗ

Conveniently situated three miles from Newbury centre and one mile from the A34 bypass, this rambling Victorian building was originally built for workers on the nearby Benyon estate and is named after the 1855 Derby winner. Now owned by Arkell's Brewery, it offers more upmarket food than the usual pub grub. Recently five en-suite

bedrooms have been added. Voted CAMRA Community Pub of the Year for the Branch in 2011, and for Berkshire in 2012. ⌂⊛⬤❶⬛(4)♣⬤Ｐ⬚

Rising Sun 🅛

Ermin Street, RG20 8LG SU433686

⊛ 12-3 (not Mon), 5-11; 12-midnight Sat summer (closed Mon; 12-3, 6-11 winter); 12-10.30 Sun ☎ (01488) 608131
⊕ therisingsunatstockcross.co.uk

West Berkshire Mr Chubb's Lunchtime Bitter, Good Old Boy, Dr Hexter's Healer, seasonal beer Ⓗ

Welcoming, traditional village pub located just three miles to the west of Newbury. West Berkshire Brewery's only tied house, two guest ales and a real cider from Tutts Clump supplement the regular ales. A wide range of quality home-made food is served at all sessions. There is an enclosed beer garden situated at the rear of the pub. Well-behaved dogs on leads are welcome. Live acoustic music plays every Sunday evening. ⌂Q⊛❶⬛(4)♣⬤Ｐ

Swallowfield

Crown

The Street, RG7 1QZ

⊛ 12-3 (not Mon), 5.30-11; 12-midnight Fri & Sat; 12-11 Sun
☎ (0118) 988 3260 ⊕ thecrownswallowfield.co.uk

Beer range varies Ⓗ

An early 18th-century building, the large L-shaped main bar is supplemented by two smaller rooms, with images and maps of old Swallowfield adorning the walls. Traditional pub grub using locally sourced meats is recommended (no food Sun eve). Two ales are usually available, often including a local brew. Community focused and child-/dog-/walker-friendly, it has a beer garden to the rear. ⊛❶⬛(72,82,82k)Ｐ

Theale

Red Lion ⊘

5 Church Street, RG7 5BU

⊛ 12-3, 5-11; 12-11 Fri & Sat; 12-7 Sun ☎ (0118) 930 2394
⊕ redliontheale.co.uk

Beer range varies Ⓗ

Friendly, classic pub with a single open-plan bar, providing separate areas to eat or drink in comfort, play darts or sit at the bar chatting to the friendly staff and locals. Three beers are on handpump, chosen from the Punch Taverns Finest Cask scheme, and Fuller's London Pride is a firm favourite. Good quality home-cooked food is available weekday lunchtimes. A traditional skittle alley and function room are available for hire. ⊛❶⇌⬛♣Ｐ⬚

Three Mile Cross

Swan 🅛

Basingstoke Road, RG7 1AT (just S of M4 jct 11)

⊛ 11-11 (3 Sun); 12-3, 7-11 Sat ☎ (0118) 988 3674
⊕ theswan-3mx.co.uk

Fuller's London Pride; Loddon Hoppit; Taylor Best Bitter, Landlord; Wadworth 6X Ⓗ

A former coaching inn on the London-Portsmouth stagecoach route. The interior is split into two rooms with an open fireplace. Outside is a pleasant rear patio garden where dogs are welcome. Hearty home-cooked food is served lunchtimes and evenings until 9.30pm. As the closest pub to the Madejski Stadium, supporters of Reading FC and

London Irish can be found here in numbers on match days. A rare southern outlet for Timothy Taylor ales. ᏮQ🕸🍺🍴🚲🖵(72,82,82k)♣P

Tilehurst

Fox & Hounds 🅛
116 City Road, RG31 5SB
✪ 11.30-2.30, 4.30-11 Mon & Tue; 11.30-11 Wed-Sat; 12-10.30 Sun ☎ (0118) 942 2982
⊕ foxandhounds-tilehurst.co.uk
Courage Best Bitter; Sharp's Doom Bar; guest beers 🅗
There are three areas in the pub, each with a different character. The main bar bustles with locals and has darts and quiz machines. To the right is a quieter seating area for those contemplating their lot and finally there is a newly built conservatory for relaxed dining. Occasional beer festivals are held in a marquee in the garden. A senior citizens' meal deal is available 11.30-2pm Monday-Thursday. ⏰🕸🍴🚲🖵(33A)♣P🍺

Royal Oak ✓
69 Westwood Glen, RG31 5NW
✪ 2 (12 Sun)-11; 12-midnight Fri & Sat ☎ (0118) 941 6056
⊕ theroyaloak-tilehurst.co.uk
Beer range varies 🅗
Approached up a steep driveway, the Royal Oak has a long history, more of which is being uncovered by the current licensees. Originating as a drovers' inn, it has a window that was once used to hold a candle to show the pub was open. Ales are sourced from Punch's Finest Cask scheme. 🕸🖵(16,33)P🍺

Upper Basildon

Red Lion 🅛
Aldworth Road, RG8 8NG SU597761
✪ 11-3, 5-11; 12-10.30 Sun ☎ (01491) 671234
⊕ theredlionupperbasildon.co.uk
West Berkshire Good Old Boy; guest beers 🅗
Now the only pub in the village, the Red Lion is popular with locals and equally welcoming to drinkers and diners. The historic core has been sympathetically extended to include a separate restaurant area, and the good-quality food ranges from basic to posh. Three changing guest beer handpumps often feature a local ale in addition to Good Old Boy. All can enjoy the large garden. Ꮾ🕸🍴🖵(133)P

Waltham St Lawrence

Bell 🅛
The Street, RG10 0JJ (opp church) SU830769
✪ 12-3, 5-11; 12-11 Sat; 12-10.30 Sun ☎ (0118) 934 1788
⊕ thebellwalthamstlawrence.co.uk
Binghams Twyford Tipple; guest beers 🅗
The Bell is a village pub that dates back to the 14th century. Real ale is at its heart, with five beers ranging from the resident Twyford Tipple brewed by Binghams only three miles away, to those from further afield. The good food is all prepared on-site including the home-made pork pies if you are a bit peckish. Dog-friendly throughout. ᏮQ⏰🕸🍴🚲🖵(4,4C)🐕

Wargrave

Wargrave & District Snooker Club
Woodclyffe Hostel, Church Street, RG10 8EP (behind library in Woodclyffe Hostel)
✪ 7-11; closed Sat & Sun ☎ (0118) 940 3184
Beer range varies 🅗
A little real ale gem run by volunteers. With one beer always on and one waiting, usually sourced from microbreweries, the wall covered with CAMRA awards bears testament to continuous beer quality. The club offers three full-sized snooker tables and a bar area with comfortable seating and bar billiards, darts, cards, games and TV. Show this Guide or your CAMRA membership card to gain free entry (£3 guest fee to use a snooker table). ♿≅🖵(850)♣

Windsor

Carpenters Arms ✓
4 Market Street, SL4 1PB
✪ 11-11 (midnight Fri & Sat) ☎ (01753) 863739
Beer range varies 🅗
A previous local CAMRA Pub of the Year, in a narrow cobbled street close to the castle; the interior is on several levels. The front windows contain images of the tools of the trade which gives the pub its name. A mosaic on the front step reminds us of the long gone Ashley Brewery. There is an ever-changing selection of six ales, usually including one from Cornwall and one from Scotland. 🕸🍴≅(Windsor & Eton Central)🖵(71,702)

Horse & Groom 🅛 ✓
4 Castle Hill, SL4 1PD
✪ 10-11 (midnight Thu-Sat) ☎ (01753) 830172
⊕ windsorpubco.co.uk
Taylor Landlord; Windsor & Eton Guardsman, Conqueror 🅗
Small and cosy pub situated next door to Windsor Castle and extremely popular with visiting tourists. An ale house was recorded on this site in the early 18th century – the inn was formerly called the Rose & Crown. Local ales from Windsor are always available and food is sourced from the Windsor Farm Shop. Ꮾ🕸🍴≅(Windsor & Eton Central)🖵(71,702)

Two Brewers
34 Park Street, SL4 1LB
✪ 11.30-11 (11.30 Fri & Sat); 12-11 Sun ☎ (01753) 855426
⊕ twobrewerswindsor.co.uk
Fuller's London Pride; St Austell Tribute; Sharp's Doom Bar 🅗
Cosy, wood-panelled, 17th-century inn, close to the Cambridge Gate entrance to Windsor Great Park. Popular with locals and tourists alike, it is advisable to book a table to sample the tapas or main menu (no food Sun eve). Dogs are welcome but, due to its small size, children are not allowed inside the pub. However, there are seats at the front if weather permits. ᏮQ🕸🍴≅(Windsor & Eton Central)🖵(71,702)

Vansittart Arms 🅛 ✓
105 Vansittart Road, SL4 5DD
✪ 12-11 (11.30 Thu; midnight Fri & Sat) ☎ (01753) 865988
⊕ fullers.co.uk
Fuller's Discovery, London Pride, ESB, seasonal beers 🅗

Popular Fuller's pub that is a Guide regular. There are two distinct areas to the main bar, and a pool room to the rear with a small library for book swaps. Sport is keenly followed, with rugby usually taking priority. The large garden is ideal for summer barbecues and there is also occasional live music. A covered, heated area accommodates smokers.
ᄊ⊛◑⇌(Windsor & Eton Central)◻(71,702)⅄

Winkfield

Old Hatchet ✪
Hatchet Lane, Cranbourne, SL4 2EE (on A330 2 miles NW of Ascot) SU 923714
✪ 11.30-11; 12-10.30 Sun ☎ (01344) 899911
Fuller's London Pride, ESB; Gale's HSB Ⓗ
A lovely, traditional pub that dates back to the 16th century. Originally it was cottages belonging to two local woodmen and, during its transformation to the fine pub it is today, many of the original features have been retained. Together with the great service and exciting menu of freshly prepared food using locally sourced produce, the Old Hatchet is a wonderful retreat. Families are welcome and the Sunday roasts (served until 7.30pm) are highly recommended.
ᄊ⊛◑ὲ◻(191)P⅄

Wokingham

Crispin Ⓛ
45 Denmark Street, RG40 2AY (near town hall)
✪ 12-11 (11.30 Fri & Sat; 10.30 Sun) ☎ (0118) 978 0309
Courage Best Bitter; guest beers Ⓗ
Said to be one of the oldest inns in Wokingham, this local pub is situated in the heart of the town. A friendly little hostelry, it offers four different real ales including local brews from Vale, Binghams and Loddon. No food is served but in the evening you can bring in your own takeaway. Charity events are hosted and beer festivals held in the garden area, which has seating and a smoking area. Free Wi-Fi.
ᄊQ⊛⇌◻(190)♣♠⅄

Hope & Anchor ✪
Station Road, RG40 2AD (at jct with Shute End)
✪ 12-11 (midnight Fri; 1am Sat; 10 Sun) ☎ (0118) 978 0918
⊕ the-hope.net
Brakspear Bitter; Wychwood Hobgoblin; guest beers Ⓗ
Seventeenth-century inn with low wood beams constructed from former ships' timbers. Run by Canadians Reid and Hattie, it has been revitalised as a busy town-centre venue. Popular live music plays every Saturday night. The garden has a heated smoking area and a summer barbecue. Good home-cooked pub food is served (not Sun eve) and three en-suite letting rooms are available. Guest beers are usually from the Marston's range. ⊛⌖◑ὲ⇌◻♣⅄

Olde Leathern Bottel ✪
221 Barkham Road, RG41 4BY SU 795678
✪ 11-11 (11.30 Fri & Sat); 12-10.30 Sun ☎ (0118) 978 4222
Brains SA; Fuller's London Pride; Sharp's Doom Bar Ⓗ
Situated about a mile from the centre of Wokingham, this 17th-century Chef & Brewer pub, refurbished in 2012, will appeal to diners and drinkers alike. The interior features original wood beams, working fireplaces, a range of many dining areas, and a bar adorned with five handpumps

dispensing a choice of real ales. Good food is served all day and there is a large patio area outside. ᄊ⊛◑ὲ◻(144)P⅄

Ship Inn ✪
104 Peach Street, RG40 1XH (on A329)
✪ 11.30-11 (midnight Thu-Sat); 12-11 Sun
☎ (0118) 978 0389
Fuller's Discovery, London Pride, ESB, seasonal beers; Gale's HSB Ⓗ
A friendly former coaching inn with a good mixed clientele, large TVs in both bars are a big draw for all sports fans. Outside is a covered, heated patio area with a TV. Good, wholesome food is served lunchtimes and evenings (all day at the weekend), with a daily specials board. Sunday is quiz night and free Wi-Fi is available. ᄊ⊛◑⌖⇌◻P⅄

Victoria Arms Ⓛ
1 Easthampstead Road, RG40 2EH
✪ 12-11 (midnight Fri & Sat); 12-10.30 Sun
☎ (0118) 978 3023
Beer range varies Ⓗ
Single-bar pub in the town centre with a dual personality. During the working day it is a quiet refuge in which to enjoy a leisurely pint, with leather furnishings and a real fire in winter. However, the pub comes alive for sporting events, with satellite TV, including Saturday 3pm Premier League football. Two changing guest beers are on tap, including a LocAle and often Timothy Taylor's Landlord. There is a separate area for darts. Pay & Display car park nearby. ᄊ◑◻♣⅄

Woodside

Duke of Edinburgh ✪
Woodside Road, SL4 2DP (towards Ascot end of the road running through hamlet of Woodside) SU928709
✪ 11-11; 12-6.30 Sun ☎ (01344) 882736
⊕ thedukeofedinburgh.com
Arkell's 2B, 3B, Moonlight, Kingsdown Ⓗ
Licensees Nick and Annie have run this splendid Arkell's tied house since 1998, earning them a CAMRA long-service award. The Duke combines a friendly bar area with a restaurant that has a reputation for excellent food. The landlord is a big football fan, and he occasionally hosts charity football evenings with Chelsea FC legend Ron 'Chopper' Harris. Outside is a covered and heated smoking area. ᄊ⊛◑ὲP⅄

Yattendon

Royal Oak ♈ Ⓛ
The Square, RG18 0UF SU 552745
✪ 11-11; 12-10.30 Sun ☎ (01635) 201325
⊕ royaloakyattendon.co.uk
West Berkshire Mr Chubb's Lunchtime Bitter, Good Old Boy, seasonal beer; guest beer Ⓗ
Situated in this well-preserved village, the Georgian façade hides a pub many centuries older. Renowned for its excellent locally sourced food, the bars are decorated with photos and illustrations of local life, and there are also a number of rooms that can be hired for private functions. There is seating in front of the pub and in the splendid garden; in the winter there are up to three roaring log fires. The pub has close links with nearby West Berkshire Brewery. ᄊ⊛⌖◑P⅄⊡

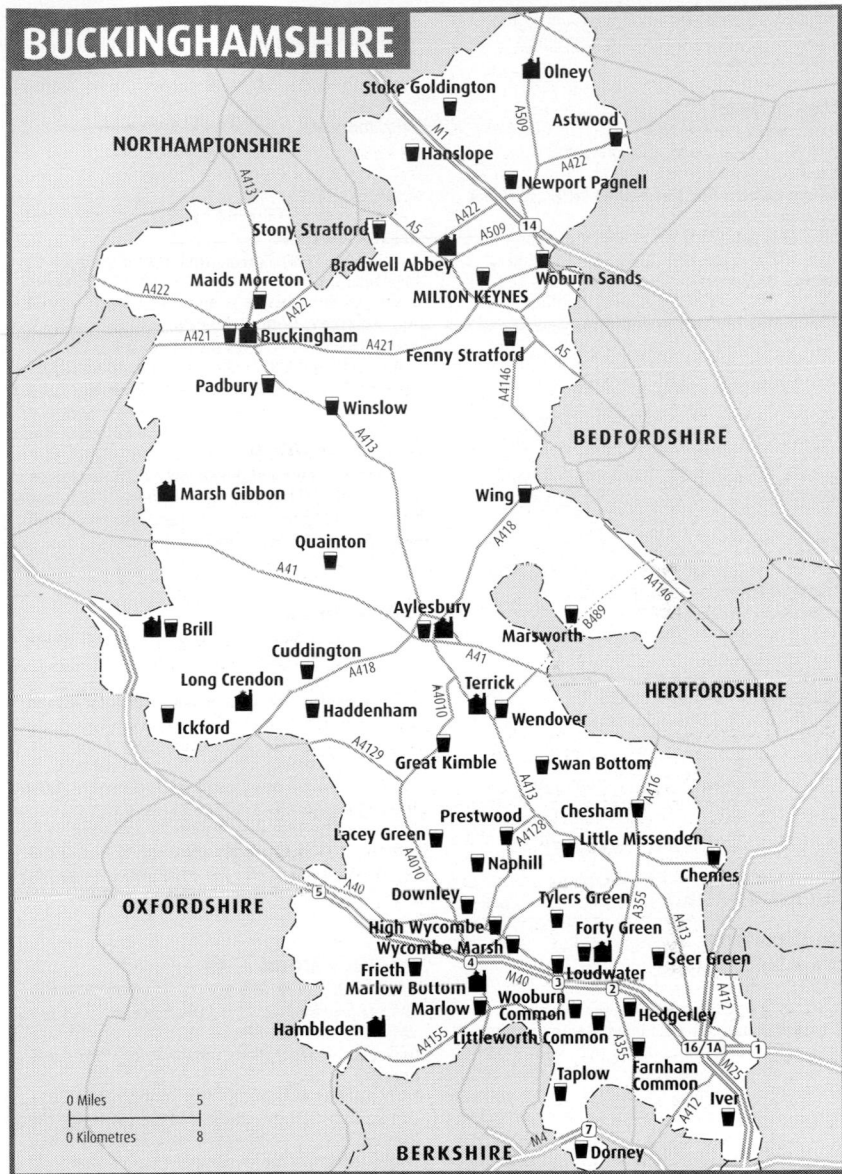

BUCKINGHAMSHIRE

Olney
Stoke Goldington
Astwood
NORTHAMPTONSHIRE
Hanslope
Newport Pagnell
Stony Stratford
Maids Moreton
Bradwell Abbey
Woburn Sands
MILTON KEYNES
Buckingham
Fenny Stratford
Padbury
Winslow
Marsh Gibbon
Wing
BEDFORDSHIRE
Quainton
Aylesbury
Brill
Marsworth
Cuddington
Terrick
HERTFORDSHIRE
Long Crendon
Wendover
Haddenham
Ickford
Great Kimble
Swan Bottom
Prestwood
Chesham
Lacey Green
Little Missenden
Naphill
Chenies
OXFORDSHIRE
Downley
Tylers Green
High Wycombe
Forty Green
Seer Green
Wycombe Marsh
Frieth
Loudwater
Marlow Bottom
Wooburn
Hedgerley
Marlow
Common
Hambleden
Littleworth Common
Taplow
Farnham
Common
Iver
Dorney
BERKSHIRE

0 Miles 5
0 Kilometres 8

Astwood

Old Swan

8 Main Road, MK16 9JS (off A422)
☺ closed Mon; 11-3, 6-11; 12-3 Sun ☎ (01234) 391351
⊕ oldswanastwood.co.uk
Beer range varies Ⓗ
Situated in a village just off the northern Milton Keynes-Bedford road, this delightful thatched free house dates from the 17th century. The pub has a superb reputation for high-quality food, with fresh fish a speciality on the menu (booking is a must). A large blue china collection and an impressive display of water jugs adorn the walls and ceiling. Up to three changing beers are on handpump, with regulars from Fuller's or Wells & Young's.
🏚Q⊛🛈ঌ🖃(40)P⅃⚊

Aylesbury

Hop Pole Ⓛ

83 Bicester Road, HP19 9AZ
☺ 12 (4 Mon)-11; 12-midnight Fri & Sat; 12-10.30 Sun
☎ (01296) 482129 ⊕ hop-pole.co.uk
Vale Best Bitter, seasonal beers; guest beers Ⓗ
'Aylesbury's Permanent Beer Festival' now has its own brewery. The Aylesbury Brewhouse was opened in December 2011, bringing brewing back to the town after nearly 75 years. Its weekly brews are sold in the pub and brewery shop, but may not last very long! The Hop Pole is also Vale's flagship pub, stocking its beers alongside myriad ales from other microbreweries. Two beer festivals are held at Easter and in October when the choice is more than doubled from the usual 10 beers available. A

friendly welcome and good food add to the attraction. Dogs on a lead are welcome.
❀◗💻🚆(2,16)🌸🏃

King's Head L
Market Square, HP20 2RW
❂ 11-11; 12-10.30 Sun ☎ (01296) 718812
⊕ farmersbar.co.uk
Chiltern Chiltern Ale, Beechwood Bitter, seasonal beers; guest beer Ⓗ
The oldest courtyard inn in England, dating back to 1455, the Farmers' Bar at the King's Head is situated in Market Square, close to bus and rail stations. The pub offers a quiet, comfortable, relaxed environment in which to enjoy beer from Buckinghamshire's oldest microbrewery. The food on offer is freshly sourced from local suppliers and often incorporates local ales. Following a recent policy change, children are now allowed in the pub, but only when accompanying adults for a meal. Events throughout the year include beer festivals, Chiltern beer challenges and food and beer-matching sessions. Q❀◗🐕⬅🚆🏃

Brill

Pheasant L
39 Windmill Street, HP18 9TG
❂ 12-11 (midnight Fri & Sat) ☎ (01844) 239370
⊕ thepheasant.co.uk
St Austell Tribute; Vale seasonal beer; guest beer Ⓗ
Refurbished to a high standard, the Pheasant provides a wonderful welcoming atmosphere in which to enjoy its fine ales. The garden allows drinkers a superb view over five counties and the famous Brill windmill. A warm fire provides a friendly welcome in the winter months and there is a good range of home-cooked food. A guest beer is available at the weekend. 🏠❀🚗◗🐕🏃

Buckingham

Woolpack ✅
57 Well Street, MK18 1EP
❂ 11-11 (midnight Fri & Sat); 12-10.30 Sun
☎ (01280) 817972 ⊕ buckinghamwoolpack.co.uk
St Austell Tribute; Sharp's Doom Bar; guest beers Ⓗ
Busy, attractively modernised pub, with a garden backing onto the River Ouse near the town centre. The Woolpack upholds the market town tradition of early opening. Its four pumps serve two regular beers and, depending on the season, one or two guests from the SIBA list. Beer festivals are held on the Whit and August bank holidays. The food is good and varied, and children are welcome in the large back room. Parking nearby can be a challenge. 🏠🚲❀◗🐕🚆(32,X5)🌸🏃

Chenies

Red Lion L
Latimer Road, WD3 6ED (off A404 between Chorleywood and Little Chalfont) TQ021980
❂ 11-2.30, 5.30-11; 12-3, 6.30-10.30 Sun ☎ (01923) 282722
⊕ redlionchenies.co.uk
Rebellion Lion Pride; Vale Best Bitter; Wadworth 6X; guest beer Ⓗ
Country free house dating from the 16th century, run by the same landlord and lady for 25 years. The three areas near the bar are lined with bench seats and festooned with old village photographs and brass plaques. The Lion's Den dining room is

situated to the rear. A range of menus is available, with home-made pies a speciality. Walkers (minus muddy boots) and well-behaved dogs are welcome; under 14s in dining area only. There is road-side patio seating and a disabled entrance near the small rear car park. Q❀◗🐕♿P

Chesham

Black Cat ✅
Lycrome Road, Lye Green, HP5 3LF (off A416) SP977034
❂ 11-2.30, 5 (7.30 Mon)-11; 12-11 Sat & Sun
☎ (01494) 773966 ⊕ blackcatchesham.co.uk
Taylor Landlord; Young's Bitter; guest beer Ⓗ
Cosy single-roomed pub, first licensed in 1828, crammed with interesting black cat memorabilia. A large room to the rear is home to two dartboards and also caters as an extended dining area. Good, generously portioned pub food is available at breakfast, lunch and dinner times. All the tables in the main bar feature a different novelty condiment set. A large garden and smokers' hut are to the rear. 🏠Q❀◗🐕🚆(52)🌸P🏃

Black Horse L ✅
The Vale, HP5 3NS (2 miles N of Chesham) SP964046
❂ 12-3, 6-11; 12-11 Sat; 12-6 Sun ☎ (01494) 784656
⊕ black-horse-inn.co.uk
Fuller's London Pride; Tring Side Pocket for a Toad; guest beer Ⓗ
Situated in a valley, the surrounding countryside is the perfect setting for this 500-year-old pub. Inside, there are low beams to be aware of. During the winter months a log fire burns in the inglenook fireplace. The pub is dog-friendly and there is free internet access for your laptop. Up to two guest beers and three ciders are available. Sunday hours may be extended in the summer. 🏠Q❀◗🐕P

Queen's Head L ✅
120 Church Street, HP5 1JD (in old town) SP956013
❂ 12-11 (midnight Thu & Fri); 11-midnight Sat; 11-10.30 Sun
☎ (01494) 778690
Brakspear Bitter; Fuller's London Pride, ESB; guest beer Ⓗ
Local CAMRA Pub of the Year runner-up in 2011, this traditional inn is situated in the old town. There are two bars, a comfortable saloon and a classic public retaining many original fittings. Thai food is served in both bars and the upstairs restaurant. Once a year customers take part in a charity cycle ride, the 'Tour de Pednor'; there are also mini beer and cider festivals throughout the year.
🏠Q❀◗🐕⬅⊖🌸P🏃

INDEPENDENT BREWERIES

Aylesbury Aylesbury (NEW)
Britannia Forty Green (NEW)
Buckingham Buckingham (NEW)
Chiltern Terrick
Concrete Cow Bradwell Abbey
Hopping Mad Olney
Old Luxters Hambleden
Oxfordshire Ales Marsh Gibbon
Rebellion Marlow Bottom
Vale Brill
XT Long Crendon (NEW)

Cuddington

Crown ✓
Spurt Street, HP18 0BB
🕓 12-3, 6-11; 12-11 Sun ☎ (01844) 292222
🌐 thecrowncuddington.co.uk
Adnams Southwold Bitter; Fuller's London Pride, seasonal beers Ⓗ
Delightful, cosy, traditional village pub full of welcoming ambience. Fuller's beers are served from the single long oak bar beneath a low ceiling. Customers are just as welcome to drop in for a chat and a pint as for a Michelin Guide meal. Fish and chip Friday, pie and pudding Thursday and curry night Wednesday all feature locally sourced produce. The charming Midsomer Murders frequented village of Cuddington is also famous for its wychert walls and summer fête.
🏚Q🌣❶🚃(110)P½⊖

Dorney

Palmer Arms
Village Road, SL4 6QW
🕓 11-11; 12-10.30 Sun ☎ (01628) 666612
🌐 thepalmerarms.com
Greene King IPA, Abbot; guest beer Ⓗ
Large pub based in a small village close to Eton Rowing Lake and the Jubilee River, popular with locals, businessmen and diners who come for the good quality food and relaxed atmosphere. Families are welcome and there is a well-hidden children's play area in the garden. The publicans are keen on promoting real ales and often hold beer festivals with live music. Guest ales come from the Greene King list. 🌣❶&P½⊖

Downley

De Spencer Arms ✓
The Common, HP13 5YQ (across common from the village) SU849959
🕓 12-11 (midnight Fri & Sat; 10.30 Sun) ☎ (01494) 535317
🌐 ledespencersarms.co.uk
Fuller's London Pride; Gale's Seafarers Ale, seasonal beers; guest beer Ⓗ
A flint pub on Downley Common with a warm, friendly atmosphere, open fire, rustic beams and stone-flagged floor. Serving traditional home-cooked food, good real ales and wines, the pub is popular with walkers and cyclists (dogs are welcome too). Wednesday is quiz night and you can keep up to date with forthcoming music, beer and food events on the website. This Fuller's Master Cellarman pub serves two guest ales alongside the regular beers. 🏚Q🌣❶🚃(31)P½⊖

Farnham Common

Emperor ✓
Blackpond Lane, SL2 3EG SU959842
🕓 12-11 (midnight Fri & Sat); 12-10.30 Sun
☎ (01753) 643006 🌐 theemperorpub.co.uk
Beer range varies Ⓗ
The four handpumps in this country pub and restaurant dispense an ever-changing selection from the Enterprise and SIBA ranges. The interior, featuring soft modern furnishings and lighting, belies to some extent the fact that this is a very old establishment. Originally thought to be the Brickmakers, it was certainly the King of Prussia in 1906 (as can be seen from a photo in the bar) and in 1917 became the Emperor of India. Later, it reverted again to the King of Prussia before becoming just the Emperor in recent years.
🏚🌣❶🚃(X74)P½⊖

Forty Green

Royal Standard of England
Forty Green Road, HP9 1XT (off Beaconsfield to Penn Road at Knotty Green) SU923919
🕓 11-11; 12-10.30 Sun ☎ (01494) 673382 🌐 rsoe.co.uk
Brakspear Bitter; Chiltern Ale; Marston's Pedigree; Rebellion Mild, IPA; guest beer Ⓗ
Historic hostelry with a fascinating pedigree, well-worth a detour. A barrel-shaped wooden partition wall/notice board leads to rooms containing log fires or cast iron stoves. Architecture and furniture is mixed rustic with hops adorning bar areas. The food is of exemplary standard and bottled beers are sourced from craft breweries. Orchard Pig Farm Pressed Cider is stocked. Bekonscot Model Village is close to Beaconsfield railway station, two miles away. This area is a walkers' paradise.
🏚Q🌣❶🐾P½⊖

Frieth

Prince Albert
Fingest Road, RG9 6PY
🕓 11-11; 12-10.30 Sun ☎ (01494) 881683
Brakspear Bitter; guest beers Ⓗ
A friendly welcome awaits you at this charming traditional country local. Sited a stone's throw from Frieth village, the pub is well-worth seeking out for its cosy aura. The small bar area boasts a log fire in winter and leads either way to further rooms and seating. The beer garden offers secluded summer family drinking. Evening meals are served Friday and Saturday only. Regular quiz nights and folk evenings are hosted. 🏚Q🌣❶P½⊖

Great Kimble

Swan
Grove Lane, HP17 9TR
🕓 12-3, 5.30-11 (7-10.30 Sun) ☎ (01844) 275288
Adnams Southwold Bitter; St Austell Tribute; guest beer Ⓗ
The Swan is a welcoming free house located on the village green at the hub of its local community. The pub, which was formerly two 18th-century cottages, has a separate public bar with a warming fire in the colder months. It is in a popular area for walkers, at the foot of the Chilterns and with the Aylesbury Ring and North Bucks Way trails passing close by. 🏚Q🌣🛏❶🍴🐾P

Haddenham

Rising Sun Ⓛ
9 Thame Road, HP17 8EN
🕓 11-2, 5-midnight; 12-1am Fri & Sat; 12-11 Sun
☎ (01844) 291744
Vale Best Bitter; Rebellion Smuggler; XT 3 Ⓗ**; guest beers** Ⓖ
The 'Risey' is a mini-mecca for LocAles and guest beers for the discerning members of 'Compost Corner', other regulars and visiting darts and pool teams. The opening of two new breweries means there are now four within seven miles. All ales are served straight from the cask, with a continual churn of new and different beers supported by

many firm old favourites such as Vale VPA and Gravitas. Local bands perform live monthly and a suntrap garden provides a safe haven for kids. ✿&🚋(280)'-

Hanslope

Watts Arms 🏆 🗓 ✅
Castlethorpe Road, MK19 7LG
✪ 12-11 (10.30 Sun) ☎ (01908) 510246
⊕ thewattsarms.co.uk
Wells Eagle IPA; guest beers 🖽
Situated in the heart of the village of Hanslope, this is a traditional British inn where you will always find a warm welcome on walking through the door. The publican is a real ale enthusiast and offers an ever-changing beer range. A great place to relax with a pint, the bar is warmed by an open fire on cold days. Fresh, home-cooked dishes including bangers and mash and hand-battered fish are served lunchtimes and evenings until 9pm. Local CAMRA Pub of the Year 2012.
🏚Q✿◑🍽(33)♣P'-

Hedgerley

White Horse 🏆 🗓
Village Lane, SL2 3UY (in old village)
✪ 11-2.30, 5-11; 11-11 Sat; 12-10.30 Sun ☎ (01753) 643225
Rebellion IPA; guest beers 🗓
A winner of many CAMRA awards, this village local offers an impressive range of up to eight real ales. Beers come from breweries all over the country, including those newly opened, making this a mecca for ale enthusiasts. A draught Belgian beer is also available, and three real ciders complement the ales all year round. This classic pub has a well-tended garden, which hosts regular bank holiday beer festivals. The heated, covered patio provides additional seating at busy times.
🏚Q✿◑🖼♣♠P'-

High Wycombe

Belle Vue ✅
45 Gordon Road, HP13 6EQ (100yds from train station, platform 3 exit)
✪ 12-11 (midnight Fri; 1am Sat; 10.30 Sun)
☎ (01494) 524728 ⊕ thebv.co.uk
Beer range varies 🖽
The pub is all that remains of a row of terraced houses. It is next to the railway but on the other side of the line from the station entrance – the quickest route from the station is via an underpass footway. There are six ales on handpump from the Punch portfolio. The ciders are from Westons and are on gravity dispense. This pub has become one of Wycombe's main venues for live music, with regular bands and open jam sessions.
🏚✿≈🍽(31,33)♣♠

Bootlegger 🗓 ✅
3 Amersham Hill, HP13 6NQ (opp station)
✪ 4.30-11 (midnight Wed & Thu), 12-1am Fri & Sat; 12-11 Sun ☎ (01494) 525457 ⊕ thebootleggerpub.co.uk
Rebellion IPA, seasonal beers; guest beers 🖽
The Bootlegger has a modern, relaxed feel, a varied and friendly clientele, and a welcoming landlord who is knowledgeable and enthusiastic about his beers. There are seven real ales, usually including three from Rebellion, one or two from other local microbreweries, and the rest from

national microbreweries. More than 300 bottled beers are available from around the world, including British real ale in a bottle, Belgian Trappist ales and American craft beers. A beer-lovers' paradise in the heart of High Wycombe.
✿≈🚋

Ickford

Rising Sun ✅
36 Worminghall Road, HP18 9JD
✪ 12-2.30, 4-11; 12-11 Sat & Sun ☎ (01844) 339238
⊕ risingsunickford.com
Adnams Southwold Bitter, Broadside; Black Sheep Best Bitter; guest beers 🖽
Classic family-run pub, popular with locals and visitors. Dating from the 15th century, with many oak beams and a welcoming open log fire in winter, it hosts local events, live music and games including crib, quizzes and Aunt Sally. Excellent, traditional home-cooked food is served. Outside is a large beer garden with a children's play area and a heated and covered smoking space. Close to the Oxford Way, it attracts ramblers and cyclists. Dogs on leads are welcome. 🏚Q✿◑🍽(110)♣P'-

Iver

Bull ✅
7 High Street, SL0 9ND
✪ 12-midnight (1am Fri & Sat; 10.30 Sun) ☎ (01753) 651115
⊕ thebullinn-iver.co.uk
Brakspear Bitter; Fuller's London Pride; Wadworth 6X; guest beer 🖽
An early Victorian village local where you can still see the bull motifs in the leaded windows. The public bar has a pool table and two dartboards. A quiz night is held on alternate Sundays and occasional live music evenings are hosted. Traditional pub food is reasonably priced and served lunchtimes and evenings (no food Sun). A heated and covered decking area is provided for smokers. Three reasonably priced bedrooms are available. 🛏◑🖼(58,583)♣P'-

Lacey Green

Black Horse
Main Road, HP27 0QU
✪ 11-3 (not Mon), 5-11; 11-11 Thu; 11-midnight Fri; 12-midnight Sat; 12-11 Sun ☎ (01844) 345195
⊕ blackhorse-pub.co.uk
Brakspear Bitter; guest beers 🖽
A real village pub offering a cosy, friendly atmosphere, located in the heart of the Chilterns. Excellent home-cooked, freshly prepared food includes traditional Sunday lunch (children under six eat free). Four draught ales are on offer, three of them changing every two weeks, plus a good selection of bottled beers and one regularly changing real cider. Walkers, cyclists and children are welcome and there is a play area in the garden. Full English breakfast is served Tuesday to Saturday from 9am. Q✿◑&🍽(300)♣♠P'-

Whip 🗓
Pink Road, HP27 0PG
✪ 11-11; 12-10.30 Sun ☎ (01844) 344060 ⊕ whipinn.co.uk
Beer range varies 🖽
High on the Chiltern Way and popular with ale aficionados, ramblers and cyclists, this pub is renowned for its variety of ales. It now has six

handpumps and serves more than 800 brews per annum, split equally between local ales, new ales to the pub and micro- and national-brewery beers. Two real ciders are also stocked. There is an attractive enclosed garden overlooking the Lacey Green windmill. An excellent range of reasonably priced bar food is also available.
🏚Q✿🌀💷🍺(300)♣💙P⌐

Little Missenden

Crown Inn
HP7 0RD (off A413, between Amersham and Gt Missenden) SU924989
✪ 11-2.30, 6-11; 12-3, 7-10.30 Sun ☎ (01494) 862571
⊕ the-crown-little-missenden.co.uk
Beer range varies Ⓗ
A real ale success story, this pub has featured in the Guide for over 30 years and it is easy to see why. Four real ales are usually on handpump, including one from the Rebellion Brewery – it is wise to check with the pub first to see which beers the landlord is offering his locals. Accommodation is now available in a converted barn.
🏚Q✿🛏🌀💷(177)P⌐

Littleworth Common

Blackwood Arms
Common Lane, SL1 8PP SU937863
✪ closed Mon; 12-11; 12-9.30 (7 winter) Sun
☎ (01753) 645672 ⊕ theblackwoodarms.net
Brakspear Bitter; Wychwood Hobgoblin; guest beers Ⓗ
Small but perfectly formed Victorian country pub brought back to life by an enthusiastic couple after a long period of closure. Close to Burnham Beeches and serving good traditional pub food, it attracts walkers and diners. An attractive garden with plenty of seating is well-used in warmer weather. In addition to the two regular ales there are two or three seasonal ales from the Marston's range plus one ale free of tie. Dog- and horse-friendly – hay provided. 🏚Q✿🌀P⌐

Loudwater

Derehams Inn
5 Derehams Lane, HP10 9RH (off A40 from jct 3 of M40)
✪ 11.30-3, 5.30-11; 11.30-midnight Fri & Sat; 12-10.30 Sun
☎ (01494) 530965 ⊕ derehamsinn.co.uk
Fuller's London Pride; guest beers Ⓗ
Traditional pub with a friendly atmosphere tucked away north of the main A40. The clientele is mostly local plus passing business at lunchtimes. Five handpumps serve the real ale, supporting breweries such as Loddon, Cottage and Binghams. The July beer festival started in 2007 and has now become a major draw. Many pub games feature here including darts, cribbage, pool, dominoes and a weekly quiz night. There is a classic car meeting once a month. 🏚Q✿🌀💷♣P⌐

Maids Moreton

Wheatsheaf Ⓛ
Main Street, MK18 1QR (off A413 Buckingham-Towcester road)
✪ closed Mon, 12-3, 6-11; 12-11 Sat; 12-6 Sun
☎ (01280) 815433
Beer range varies Ⓗ

Characterful, atmospheric, thatched village pub on the fringe of Buckingham, full of nooks and crannies and old-world charm. It has been sympathetically extended and has a modern dining conservatory where children are welcome. Booking is advisable for meals. Close to National Trust Stowe Landscape Gardens and Silverstone Circuit.
🏚Q✿🌀💷(32)P⌐

Marlow

Duke of Cambridge Ⓛ
19 Queens Road, SL7 2PS
✪ 11-11 (midnight Fri & Sat); 10-midnight Sun
☎ (01628) 488555
Rebellion IPA, seasonal beers; guest beer Ⓗ
Single-roomed, unpretentious locals' local, a short walk from the town centre. Two Rebellion ales are supplemented by an alternating guest beer, often a stout or porter. A true community pub, boasting a darts and two cribbage teams, patrons also participate in a monthly catering competition and the occasional quiz. Sea fishing and horse racing excursions are annual events. Fish and chip suppers are hosted on Wednesdays and roast lunches are popular on Sundays. Smokers are treated to sheltered seating. 🏚✿🌀♿💷(800,850)♣⌐

Three Horseshoes Ⓛ
Burroughs Grove Hill, SL7 3RA (on High Wycombe-Marlow Bottom road)
✪ 11.30-3, 5-11; 11.30-11 Fri & Sat; 12-5, 7-10.30 Sun
☎ (01628) 483109
Rebellion Mild, IPA, Smuggler, Mutiny, seasonal beers Ⓗ
A large, open-plan pub a short bus ride from both High Wycombe and Marlow. The extensive specials board, open fires and pleasant garden mean that this pub is popular with diners. Drinkers are made welcome too (as are well-behaved children and dogs), and the close proximity of the Rebellion Beer Co means that the six Rebellion ales on offer are always in good condition.
🏚Q✿🌀💷(800,850)P

Marsworth

Red Lion Ⓛ 💚
90 Vicarage Road, HP23 4LU (opp church) SP919146
✪ 11-3, 5-11; 11-11 Sat; 12-10.30 Sun ☎ (01296) 668366
Fuller's London Pride; guest beers Ⓗ
A beer-oriented 17th-century village pub supplying the full local experience in every way. Divided into three areas with an open fire, it feels cosy and complete. The main area keeps a public-bar feel; there is a side games area, and another with easy chairs. Good-value food is served in generous portions. Five beers are available, mostly local brews, with Vale and Rebellion featuring heavily, plus local Millwhites cider and others. Popular and rightly so, it's a real ale gem close to the Grand Union Canal. 🏚Q⛲✿🌀♿💷(61)♣💙P⌐

Milton Keynes: Central

Wetherspoons 💚
201 Midsummer Boulevard, MK9 1EA
✪ 9-midnight (1am Fri & Sat) ☎ (01908) 606074
Greene King Abbot; Ruddles Best Bitter; guest beers Ⓗ
Wetherspoons is a long-standing entry in the Guide. Guest beers are sourced directly from micros

such as Concrete Cow, Great Oakley and Potton, and are promoted alongside meal deals such as Tuesday grills and Thursday curries. The pub wholeheartedly participates in company beer festivals. Staff will remove sparklers if asked. Westons cider is served. There is a covered, heated patio for smokers. Q⊛◖◐ᓂ⇌(Central)🚌🐶⌐

Milton Keynes: Fenny Stratford

Red Lion
11 Lock View Lane, MK1 1BY (off Simpson Road)
❂ 12-11 (midnight Fri & Sat); 12-10.30 Sun
☎ (01908) 372317
Beer range varies Ⓗ
The Grade II-listed exterior reflects this small lockside pub's canal history. It is a gem of a local, renowned for friendly conversation and regularly changing seasonal ales, contrasting in strength and style. TV screens show sports. The garden is the perfect place to sit and watch the efforts of narrowboat crews negotiating the lock. MK Dons' football stadium is less than a mile away.
🏔⊛ᓂ⇌🚌(18)🐝🐶P⌐

Milton Keynes: Stony Stratford

White Horse
49 High Street, MK11 1AA
❂ 12-midnight (11 Sun) ☎ (01908) 567082
∰ rockinghorsenights.com
Beer range varies Ⓗ
Said to be the oldest pub in the town, with records dating back to 1540, this is a no-frills venue with live football on TV and darts played in the back room. Live music also features, with blues or folk on Thursday night and rock on Saturday. Two beers are served from local micros including B&T, Great Oakley, Nobby's and Vale. 🏠ᓂ🚌(5,5A)🐝P

Naphill

Black Lion
Woodland Drive, HP14 4SH
❂ 11 (12 Sun)-11 ☎ (01494) 563176 ∰ blacklionnaphill.com
Rebellion IPA; Sharp's Doom Bar; guest beers Ⓗ
The Black Lion is a family-friendly local, popular with walkers and cyclists, in the heart of the Chilterns. Recently refurbished with a lot of work done by the locals, the pub is comfortable and welcoming to drinkers and diners alike. Four cask ales are always available, including two regularly changing guests from local breweries, notably Rebellion, as well as others from further afield. Excellent pub food is served, made with the best local produce. Sightings of red kites are a regular feature from the large garden.
🏔⊛◖◐ᓂ🚌(300)🐝🐶P⌐

Wheel
100 Main Road, HP14 4QA
❂ 12 (4.30 Mon)-11; 12-10.30 Sun ☎ (01494) 562210
∰ thewheelnaphill.com
Greene King Abbot; Ruddles Best Bitter; guest beers Ⓗ
Chilterns pub popular with locals, walkers and cyclists, and dog- and family-friendly too. It has a large front garden, ideal for families in summer, a quieter courtyard to the rear, and a warm inviting atmosphere during the cold winter months. Food is served lunchtimes and evenings in the bars and a recently extended dining room. Four real ales are

always available – two regulars and two regularly changing guests, from both national breweries and independent micros. 🏔⊛◖◐ᓂ🚌(300)🐝🐶P⌐

Newport Pagnell

Cannon Ⓛ
50 High Street, MK16 8AQ
❂ 11-11 (midnight Fri & Sat); 12-11 Sun ☎ (01908) 211495
Banks's Bitter; Marston's Pedigree; guest beers Ⓗ
Now in its 16th consecutive year in the Guide, the Cannon deserves its reputation for well-kept, keenly priced real ale. Very much a drinkers' pub, its four pumps dispense Marston's beers and local ales. Look out for military memorabilia and intriguing bric-a-brac in display cases above the bar and on the walls. There are two heated smoking areas outside, and a function room for hire. Access to the car park is from Union Street behind the pub.
🏔Q⊛🚌(1,2,24)P⌐

Rose & Crown Ⓛ
61 Silver Street, MK16 0EG
❂ closed Mon; 11-11 ☎ (01908) 611685
∰ roseandcrown.eu
Wells Eagle IPA; Young's Special; guest beer Ⓗ
Friendly back-street hostelry with strong local loyalty. The pub has a modern feel to it with a well-lit cosy lounge bar and traditional public bar with a pool table. Beers are from the Wells and Young's stable, with an occasional guest from its list. During November and December the pub holds a German-style Christmas market in the car park. In summer there are barbecues in the garden.
⊛ᓂ🚌(1,2,24)🐝⌐

Padbury

New Inn Ⓥ
Winslow Road, MK18 2AW (on A413 Buckingham-Aylesbury road)
❂ 5-11; closed Wed; 12-2.30, 5-midnight Fri; 11-midnight Sat; 11-10 Sun ☎ (01280) 813173
Beer range varies Ⓗ
Family-run for 65 years, this traditional village pub and restaurant has been lovingly refurbished to appeal to all ages. Three handpumps serve an ever-changing selection of real ales, often local. A log-burning stove and an open fire enhance the welcoming and friendly atmosphere. Excellent fresh food is served including vegetarian options and traditional Sunday roasts. The pub hosts a monthly quiz night and occasional themed evenings and live music events. Outside is a lovely garden with seating. Local CAMRA Pub of the Year 2011. 🏔Q⊛◖◐ᓂ🚌(60)🐝P⌐

Prestwood

Green Man Ⓥ
2 High Street, HP16 9EB (on A4128 near Great Missenden)
❂ 12-midnight (1am Fri & Sat); 12-10.30 Sun
☎ (01494) 890074
Greene King IPA; guest beers Ⓗ
Snug local with two interconnecting bars, with darts, crib and dominoes players among its clientele, and dog-friendly. Outside is a patio with seating and a garden mainly to the rear. Late afternoon commuters regularly drop by to sample a wide selection of tasty beers from the pub company's portfolio and indulge in idle persiflage.

Great Missenden, one mile away, is where the Roald Dahl museum nestles in a narrow high street surrounded by eclectic shops. ﾶ❀🖳(45,48)♣P⅃

Quainton

George & Dragon 🗓 ✅
The Green, HP22 4AR
✪ 12-2.30, 5-11; 12-11 Wed-Sun summer (closed Mon; 12-2.30, 5-11; 12-11 Sat; 12-3, 6-10.30 Sun winter)
☎ (01296) 655436 ⊕ georgeanddragonquainton.co.uk
Hook Norton Hooky Bitter; Oxfordshire Triple B; Vale Best Bitter; guest beers Ⓗ
Delightful local on the village green overlooked by a working windmill. Two guest ales often include a mild, stout or porter. Real cider is available in summer. Biannual beer festivals with steam engines are held on the village green in conjunction with the nearby Buckinghamshire Steam Railway Centre. An extensive range of food is available with vegetarian and children's choices. Post Office facilities are in the bar on Wednesdays 2-4pm. The freehold was bought in February 2012. ﾶQ❀◑🖳(16)♣●P⅃

Seer Green

Jolly Cricketers 🗓 ✅
24 Chalfont Road, HP9 2YG SU966919
✪ 12 (5 Mon)-11.30; 12-midnight Fri & Sat; 12-10.30 Sun
☎ (01494) 676308 ⊕ thejollycricketers.co.uk
Fuller's London Pride; guest beers Ⓗ
Everything a village pub should be, this multi-award winning hostelry at the heart of the Seer Green community serves good food and offers a warm welcome to both families and dogs. London Pride is a fixture and other local beers are regularly rotated; draught cider is also available. The landlord aims to increase his stock of bottled beers over the next year. ﾶQ❀◑⬒Å≈🖳(305)♣●P⅃

Stoke Goldington

Lamb 🗓
16-20 High Street, MK16 8NR
✪ 12-2.30 (not Mon), 5-11; 12-11 Sat; 12-7 Sun
☎ (01908) 551233 ⊕ thelambstokegoldington.com
Beer range varies Ⓗ
This excellent village free house is very much the hub of the local community. Five handpumps offer ales from micros such as Frog Island and Tring, as well as a Westons cider. Northamptonshire skittles and darts teams are based here. Run by the Porritts since 2000, the pub hosts occasional live music events and, in September, a jazz and blues festival. Good genuinely home-cooked food is available – popular Sunday lunches are served until 5pm. ﾶ❀◑⬒🖳(37)♣●P⅃

Swan Bottom

Old Swan 🗓 ✅
Swan Lane, The Lee, HP16 9NU SP902055
✪ 6-9 Mon; 12-3, 6-11; 12-11 Fri & Sat; 12-7 Sun
☎ (01494) 837239 ⊕ theoldswanpub.co.uk
Brakspear Bitter; Chiltern Chiltern Ale; Sharp's Doom Bar Ⓗ
Family-run well-established ale house with a distinct view of its place in this outlying hamlet. The balance between the food and the beer areas is carefully maintained to give a true country pub

experience. Three beers are served in this characterful, beamed old world gem. It is a favourite with people who still like a cosy and welcoming pub, good beer and good food sensibly priced. Hours are tuned to help give it a fighting chance. No food Sunday evenings, Mondays or Tuesday evenings. ﾶ❀◑●P⅃

Taplow

Oak & Saw 🗓
Rectory Road, SL6 0ET
✪ 12-11 (midnight Fri); 12-10.30 Sun ☎ (01628) 604074
⊕ oakandsaw.co.uk
Brakspear Bitter; Fuller's London Pride; Rebellion seasonal beer Ⓗ
Situated opposite the village green and church in a chocolate box setting, this pub really is the village hub. It offers three beers, including a Rebellion monthly guest. Food is served all day every day except Sunday and Monday evenings – specials include Wednesday pizza night and Saturday steak night. Sunday is quiz night. The pub also runs a fish and chips takeaway service. There is a small garden at the rear with a covered, heated shelter. ﾶ❀◑≈🖳(53,75)P⅃

Tylers Green

Horse & Jockey ✅
Church Road, HP10 8EG (left at church at top of Hammersley Lane)
✪ 12-3, 5-11; 12-midnight Fri & Sat; 12-10.30 Sun
☎ (01494) 815963 ⊕ horseandjockeytylersgreen.co.uk
Adnams Southwold Bitter; Black Sheep Best Bitter; Fuller's London Pride; Greene King Abbot; Sharp's Doom Bar; guest beer Ⓗ
Opened as an inn in 1821, this Chilterns village pub retains the ambience of a 'proper' local – the U-shaped room has an area for darts on the right and dining tables on the left. There are five regular ales and one guest, with tasting notes displayed above the bar; two real ciders are also now on offer. Food is served lunchtimes and evenings, with pensioners' lunches and specials nights a feature. Ramblers are welcome too. ﾶQ❀◑🖳(31)♣●P⅃

Wendover

King & Queen
17 South Street, HP22 6EF
✪ 8am-11 (12.30am Fri & Sat); 8am-10.30 Sun
☎ (01296) 623272
St Austell Tribute; Sharp's Doom Bar; Young's Bitter Ⓗ
Welcoming pub found just off the High Street with a strong community feel. Three rooms cater for all, with space for a group get-together or a quiet drink, and there is also a separate restaurant. Food is highly recommended and ranges from the usual pub fare to the occasional more fancy dish. Breakfast is served 8-9am. A pleasant fireplace allows walkers to warm their feet after a rewarding walk in the nearby Chiltern Hills. Aylesbury Vale District Council Village Pub of the Year 2011. ﾶQ⇖❀◑⬒⬥≈🖳♣●P⅃

Pack Horse
29 Tring Road, HP22 6NR
✪ 12-11 (midnight Fri & Sat; 10.30 Sun) ☎ (01296) 622075
Fuller's London Pride; Gale's Seafarers Ale, seasonal beers; guest beer Ⓗ

Small, friendly village pub dating from 1769 and situated at the end of a terrace of thatched buildings known as Anne Boleyn cottages. On the Ridgeway Path, it has been owned by the same family for 49 years – the family also runs the White Swan, another Fuller's pub in the village which deserves a visit. The wall above the bar is decorated with RAF squadron badges, denoting connections with nearby RAF Halton. The pub runs men's and women's darts, dominoes and cribbage teams. ≈🖼♣♯

Wing

Queen's Head
9 High Street, LU7 0NS
🌣 11.30-11; 12-10.30 Sun ☎ (01296) 688268
🌐 thequeensheadwing.co.uk
Courage Directors; Wells Bombardier; Young's Bitter; guest beers 🅷
Set in the middle of the village, this welcoming local has gone from strength to strength. Since landlady Denise Redding arrived in 2004 it has won awards from Aylesbury Council and Cask Marque, and become a regular in this Guide. Log fires, comfortable sofas and a snug add to the ambience. The freehold was bought in 2009 and since then the pub has been largely refurbished. Guest ales are from micros including Tring, Slater's and Vale. 🏚🌣🄳🖼(150)♣P♯

Winslow

Nags Head
39 Sheep Street, MK18 3HL
🌣 6-11.30 (1.30am Fri & Sat); 12-4.30, 7-11 Sun
☎ (01296) 712037
Hook Norton Hooky Bitter; Shepherd Neame Spitfire; Tetley Bitter 🅷
The front window of this Grade II-listed pub boasts a startlingly lifelike waxwork called Eric, while the bar area is decorated with a massive collection of souvenir teaspoons. Pictures of sporting and country scenes adorn the walls of this characterful hostelry. There is a pool table in a raised area at the back, and a covered smoking area and beer garden outside. 🏚🌣🖼(60)♣P♯

Woburn Sands

Station Hotel
146 Station Road, MK17 8SG

🌣 9am-midnight (1am Fri & Sat); 10-10 Sun
☎ (01908) 582495
Sharp's Doom Bar; guest beers 🅷
As its name suggests, this pub stands by Woburn Sands railway station and crossing. Three handpumps dispense a varying choice of ale, and a wide range of reasonably priced food is served including an enormous 'build your own' all-day breakfast from 9am. A fascinating assortment of railway memorabilia is displayed on the walls and bar of the main area where sport is shown on several TVs; the smaller rear bar serves the pool room. 🌣🄳🄳≈🖼(17,300)♣P♯

Wooburn Common

Royal Standard
Wooburn Common Road, HP10 0JS (follow signs to Odds Farm) SU923876
🌣 12-11 (10.30 Sun) ☎ (01628) 521121
Dark Star seasonal beers; Hop Back Summer Lightning; St Austell Tribute 🅷; guest beers 🅶
Ever-popular semi-rural pub with a congenial ambience in the bar, catering for diners and discerning drinkers alike. Ten real ales, five direct from the cask, alongside real cider, make this venue an important flagship pub in the area. There is always at least one dark beer on offer, either a stout, porter or dark mild. Two beer festivals are held annually during the spring bank holiday weekend and in October. A former local CAMRA Pub of the Year. 🏚Q🌣🄳🄳♠P♯

Wycombe Marsh

General Havelock
114 Kingsmead Road, HP11 1HZ (N of M40)
🌣 12-2.30, 5.30-11; 12-11 Fri & Sat; 12-10.30 Sun
☎ (01494) 520391
Fuller's London Pride, ESB; Gale's Seafarers Ale, seasonal beers; guest beer 🅷
A regular entry in the Guide, appealing to all ages. The interior is adorned with an eclectic selection of knick-knacks. Situated to the south of the Kingsmead playing fields, it has been run by the same family since Fuller's bought it. There are always six beers available on the handpumps, including a non-Fuller's guest. Meals are served lunchtimes only (no food Sat). The garden is a peaceful haven in the summer. 🏚🌣🄳🖼(35)♣P♯

Spores for thought

Yeast is a fungus, a single cell plant that can convert a sugary liquid into equal proportions of alcohol and carbon dioxide. There are two basic types of yeast used in brewing, one for ale and one for lager. It is often said that ale is produced by 'top fermentation' and lager by 'bottom fermentation'. While it is true that during ale fermentation a thick blanket of yeast head and protein is created on top of the liquid while only a thin slick appears on top of fermenting lager, the descriptions are seriously misleading. Yeast works at all levels of the sugar-rich liquid in order to turn malt sugars into alcohol. If yeast worked only at the top or bottom of the liquid, a substantial proportion of sugar would not be fermented. Ale is fermented at a high temperature, lager at a much lower one. The furious speed of ale fermentation creates the yeast head and with it the rich, fruity aromas and flavours that are typical of the style. It is more accurate to describe the ale method as 'warm fermentation' and the lager one as 'cold fermentation'.

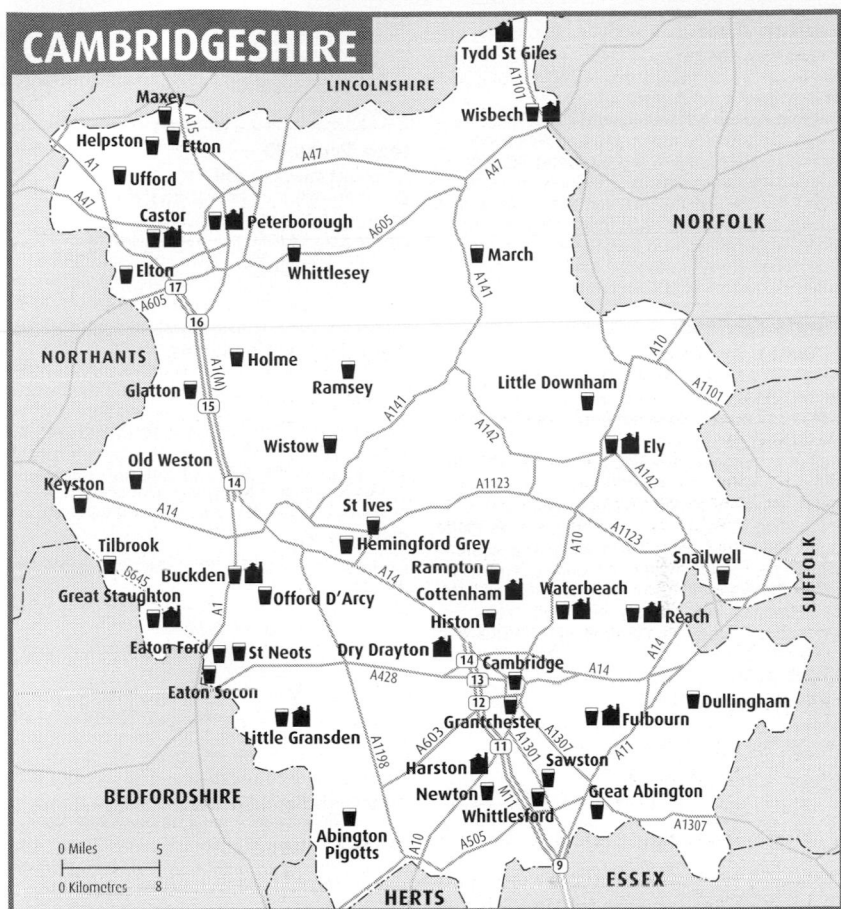

CAMBRIDGESHIRE

Abington Pigotts

Pig & Abbot ♈
High Street, SG8 0SD (off A505 through Litlington)
TL306444
☼ 12-3, 6-11; 12-11 Sat; 12-10.30 Sun ☎ (01763) 853515
⊕ pigandabbot.co.uk
Adnams Southwold Bitter; Fuller's London Pride; guest beers H
Located in a surprisingly remote part of the south Cambridgeshire countryside, this Queen Anne period pub extends a warm welcome. The interior has exposed oak beams and a large inglenook with a wood-burning stove. A comfortable restaurant offers traditional home-made pub food, specialising in fresh fish and chips, steak and kidney puddings and pies. Two guest beers are stocked, often including a beer from Woodforde's or Timothy Taylor. Local CAMRA Pub of the Year 2012. ♨Q✿◑P

Buckden

Lion Hotel
High Street, PE19 5XA
☼ 11-11; 12-10.30 Sun ☎ (01480) 810313
⊕ thelionbuckden.com
Adnams Southwold Bitter, seasonal beer; guest beer H

Grade II-listed village inn dating back to the 15th century. The building was originally the kitchen and dining area for the adjacent monastery. The lounge has a large open fire and retains the impressive original carved wood-beam ceiling. The bar and lounge area are popular meeting places for locals and visitors. Beers include Adnams Gunhill or Old when in season. ♨Q✿🚲◑🅿♿🚃(65,66)P♭☗

Cambridge

Cambridge Blue Ⓛ
85 Gwydir Street, CB1 2LG
☼ 12 (11 Sat)-11; 12-10.30 Sun ☎ (01223) 471680
⊕ the-cambridgeblue.co.uk
Elgood Black Dog; Nethergate Augustinian Ale; Woodforde's Wherry H; **guest beers** H/G
Busy, recently extended community pub with a surprisingly large garden for this part of town. The interior is decorated with breweriana and pump clips from the hundreds of different beers served each year – which come either from the pumps or are fetched from the taproom. A huge selection of bottled beers is available, plus several German and Belgian beers on draught. Ciders, perries and mead are also stocked. Impressive beer festivals are held four times a year. Wholesome home-cooked food is served all day. Local CAMRA Pub of the Year 2011. ♨Q🐕✿◑🍴🚲🚃(2)♣♿♭

59

Carlton Arms ⓛ

Carlton Way, CB4 2BY

❂ 12-11.30 (midnight Fri & Sat) ☎ (01223) 367422

⊕ thecarltonarmscambridge.co.uk

Oakham Bishops Farewell; guest beers Ⓖ

Large two-roomed community pub, reopened in July 2011 after a fire. It has a comfortable lounge with a large area available for diners, while the public bar offers darts, pool and skittles. Outside is a large patio which is ideal for warmer weather. Good, reasonably priced food is served. The wide beer range always includes a mild, and a range of ciders is stocked. ⊛◖Ⓓ 🍴🚃(1)♣♠🚶

Castle Inn

38 Castle Street, CB3 0AJ

❂ 11.30-3, 5-11; 11.30-11.30 Fri & Sat; 12-11 Sun

☎ (01223) 353194 ⊕ thecastleinncambridge.com

Adnams Southwold Bitter, Explorer, Broadside; Purity Mad Goose; guest beers Ⓗ

Adnams' most westerly tied house, the Castle offers a great selection of the brewery's own beers, including seasonals, plus a range of interesting changing guests. There is a wide range of drinking areas across two floors plus a suntrap garden next to the mound of the long-demolished castle. Excellent food is served every session – the Castleburgers are especially renowned. The landlord was Barry Wom in the Rutles. 🏚Q⊛◖Ⓓ🚃🚃

Champion of the Thames

68 King Street, CB1 1LN

❂ 11-11 (midnight Fri & Sat; 10.30 Sun) ☎ (01223) 352043

Greene King IPA, Abbot; guest beer Ⓗ

Small, two-roomed city-centre pub with a truly friendly atmosphere. It is one of four remaining pubs on the infamous King Street Run pub crawl, which historically involved a pint in each of eight pubs. The oarsman in the pub's name is commemorated in the fine etched windows. Both bars are wood-panelled with Victorian counters and bar backs, fixed benches and a part-glazed partition between the rooms. Opening hours may vary in winter. 🏚Q⊛🍴🚃♣🚶

Devonshire Arms 🍷 ⓛ

1 Devonshire Road, CB1 2BH

❂ 11-11 (midnight Fri & Sat); 12-10.30 Sun

☎ (01223) 316610 ⊕ individualpubs.co.uk/devonshire

Milton Minotaur, Pegasus; guest beers Ⓗ

Rescued from decline by the local Milton Brewery, its first pub in Cambridge has been impressively renovated with front and rear drinking areas offering a mixture of wooden booths and larger tables. Up to five Milton beers are available along with guests, a real cider and a fine selection of Belgian bottled beers. Good-quality food is on offer every session. A wood-burning stove warms the back room in winter. Local CAMRA Pub of the Year 2012. 🏚Q⊛◖Ⓓ🚃🚃(2)♠🚶

Elm Tree ⓛ

16a Orchard Street, CB1 1JT

❂ 11-11; 12-10.30 Sun ☎ (01223) 502632

⊕ theelmtreecambridge.co.uk

B&T Shefford Bitter, Black Dragon Mild, Edwin Taylor's Extra Stout; Wells Eagle IPA; guest beers Ⓗ

Quiet, relaxed back-street pub decorated with brewery memorabilia and quirky bric-a-brac. Ten handpumps dispense lovingly tended ales from B&T, Wells & Young's and myriad micros, plus ciders and perries. To complement the draught beer offering there is a large menu of bottled Belgian and other foreign beers, with occasional beer tastings. Interesting snacks are served at lunchtimes. Occasional music gigs – mainly folk and blues – and story-telling evenings are hosted. ◖🍴🚃(2)♣♠🚶

Free Press ✔

7 Prospect Row, CB1 1DU

❂ 12-2.30, 6-11; 12-11 Fri & Sat; 12-3, 7-10.30 Sun

☎ (01223) 368337 ⊕ freepresspub.com

Greene King XX Mild, IPA, Abbot; guest beers Ⓗ

Intimate, friendly pub serving high-quality food and great beer, including the rare XX Mild. Guests are from Greene King's seasonal and guest lists. An inn for 120 years, it nearly closed as part of the Kite redevelopment in the 1970s when the interior was reduced to a shell. Most of what you see now is a loving reconstruction, though the tiny snug was part of the original pub. It is named after a temperance movement newspaper that lasted for just one edition! Behind the pub is an intimate walled garden. Children and dogs are welcome. 🏚Q🐾⊛◖Ⓓ🚃(2)♣🚶🚸

Geldart ✔

1 Ainsworth Street, CB1 2PF (off Mill Road via Kingston St & Sturton St)

❂ closed Mon; 5-11.30 (1am Fri); 12-1am Sat; 12-11.30 Sun

☎ (01223) 314264 ⊕ the-geldart.co.uk

Caledonian Deuchars IPA; St Austell Tribute; Young's Special; guest beers Ⓗ

Large back-street corner pub within walking distance of the railway station, with two separate bar areas. Five changing guest beers come from Punch Finest Cask and SIBA Direct. The real ale bar also offers a good selection of malt whiskies and rums. Home-made food includes hot rock – where diners cook their own meat on a volcanic stone. Regular live music is hosted, from folk to jazz (see website for details) and functions can be catered for. Free internet and Wi-Fi access. 🏚🐾⊛◖Ⓓ🍴🚃🚶

Kingston Arms ⓛ ✔

33 Kingston Street, CB1 2NU

❂ 12-3, 5-11; 12-midnight Fri & Sat; 12-11 Sun

☎ (01223) 319414 ⊕ kingston-arms.co.uk

Crouch Vale Brewers Gold; Elgood's Black Dog; Oakham Bishops Farewell; Taylor Landlord; Thornbridge Jaipur IPA; guest beers Ⓗ

Classic side-street pub just off Mill Road. Eleven handpumps serve regular and ever-changing guest beers, with additional pumps for a changing local cider and Broadoak Perry. A large selection of Belgian and other bottled beers is stocked and monthly beer festivals are held in the warmer

INDEPENDENT BREWERIES

BlackBar Harston (NEW)
Cambridge Moonshine Fulbourn
Castor Castor
Devil's Dyke Reach
Draycott Buckden
Elgood's Wisbech
Fellows Cottenham
Hereward Ely
Lord Conrad's Dry Drayton
Milton Waterbeach
Oakham Peterborough
Red Great Staughton (NEW)
Son of Sid Little Gransden
Tydd Steam Tydd Saint Giles

months. The walled garden has canopies and heaters, making it popular all year round. Award-winning food is available at all sessions. The Recession Options menu offers beer and food at bargain prices and CAMRA members receive a 20p discount per pint. ⌾Q☸❍▷⇌➍(2)♣●♨

Live & Let Live 🅛
40 Mawson Road, CB1 2EA
☼ 11.30-2.30, 5.30 (6 Sat)-11; 12-3, 7-11 Sun
☎ (01223) 460261 ⊕ the-live.co.uk
Nethergate Umbel Ale; guest beers ⒣
Wood panelling and railway and beer memorabilia add to the atmosphere at this discreet street-corner local just off Mill Road. Seven handpumps present an array of ever-changing guest beers ranging from session bitters to strong ales, generally including a dark beer. The eighth handpump dispenses locally produced Cassells cider. There is an outstanding collection of rums from around the world, and occasional rum festivals take place. Food is restricted to snacks – the pork pies and Scotch eggs are excellent. Q⇌➍(2)♣●⟊

Maypole 🅛 ✅
20a Portugal Place, CB5 8AF
☼ 11.30-midnight (1am Fri & Sat); 12-11.30 Sun
☎ (01223) 352999 ⊕ maypolefreehouse.co.uk
Buntingford Highwayman; Crouch Vale Amarillo; Woodforde's Wherry; guest beers ⒣
The Castiglione family, who have run this city-centre pub for over 30 years, bought the freehold from Punch Taverns in 2009. It has since become a showcase for quality microbrewery beers, many of them local. This earned bar manager Vincent the local CAMRA branch's first Real Ale Champion award in 2010. The interior comprises two rooms either side of the bar plus a large upstairs function room. A pleasant suntrap patio provides covered space for smokers. The food offering focuses on home-cooked Italian dishes. Buntingford Maypole (ABV 3.8%) is the hoppy golden house beer.
☸❍⊟&➍(1,2)●♨

Pickerel ✅
30 Magdalene Street, CB3 0AF
☼ 12-11 (midnight Fri-Sun) ☎ (01223) 851634
Theakston Old Peculier; Woodforde's Wherry, Nelson's Revenge; guest beers ⒣
One of several claimants to be the oldest pub in Cambridge. Whether true or not, the interior has been much altered, with only portions of the internal walls remaining from what must have once been a warren of little rooms. However, there is still a good variety of drinking spaces and some genuinely old features including roof beams and a fireplace. Two guest beers change constantly and interesting brews often materialise. Food is served until 8pm every day. ⌾☸❍▷⊟(1,2)♨

St Radegund 🅛
127 King Street, CB1 1LD
☼ 5 (12 Sat & Sun)-11 ☎ (01223) 311794
⊕ radegund.org.uk
Beer range varies ⒣
The smallest pub in Cambridge, this unique free house is very traditional, with a selection of up to eight real ales, mostly from local breweries, including several from Milton. The interior is packed with mementos, from steam railway photos to sporting memorabilia. This is also the base of the infamous Hash House Harriers and has its own sports teams, including rowing and cricket.

The rain check tree enables you to buy a drink for someone not currently present. Occasional background music is not intrusive. Q⊟●

Castor

Prince of Wales Feathers 🅛
38 Peterborough Road, PE5 7AL
☼ 12-11.30 (1am Fri & Sat); 12-midnight Sun
☎ (01733) 380222 ⊕ princeofwalesfeathers.co.uk
Adnams Broadside; Woodforde's Wherry; guest beers ⒣
Attractive 17th-century stone-built inn with a central bar serving a number of areas including one for dining and another with deeply set sofas for watching Sky Sports. The busy village pub has five real ales at all times including one from the local Castor Ales. Lunches are served daily, evening meals weekdays only. There is an active social calendar including an annual beer festival in May. Games are played, including dominoes and shove-ha'penny. Live music is hosted every Saturday and a quiz on Sunday. ⌾☸❍⊟(402,404)♣●♨

Dullingham

Boot
18 Brinkley Road, CB8 9UW
☼ 11.30-2.30, 5-11; 11.30-11.30 Sat; 11.30-10.30 Sun
☎ (01638) 507327 ⊕ the-boot.biz
Adnams Southwold Bitter, Broadside; guest beers ⒣
Traditional village inn which Greene King tried to close as unviable in 2000. Rescued by a villager, it is now a vibrant and welcoming community local where something is always going on. The pub is home to darts, crib and pétanque teams, and features regular live music plus beer festivals twice a year. Simple, good value grub is served lunchtimes only (not Sun). Children are welcome until 8pm. ⌾☸❍♣P♨

Eaton Ford

Barley Mow ✅
27 Crosshall Road, PE19 7AB
☼ 11.30-11 (midnight Thu & Fri); 12-midnight Sat; 12-11 Sun
☎ (01480) 474435 ⊕ barleysneots.co.uk
Greene King IPA, Abbot ⒣
What makes this simple one-bar pub special, other than the excellent beer, is the customers. The Barley Mow is a true community venue with a wide variety of activities focused on the regulars. The bar decor is a mix of plaster, brick and wood panels, with a long bar dominating the centre of the room. Photos of past social events adorn the walls, some dating back to the early part of the last century. ⇴☸❍⊟(X5)♣P♨

Eaton Socon

Rivermill Tavern 🅛
School Lane, PE19 8GW
☼ 12-11 (midnight Fri) ☎ (01480) 219612
⊕ rivermilltavern.co.uk
Adnams Broadside; Greene King IPA; guest beers ⒣
This popular riverside pub on the Great Ouse was converted from a flour mill, with a galleried area above the bar. There is an extensive, varied menu, served all day at the weekend. Live music is provided on Tuesday and Friday evenings and a quiz takes place on Sunday evening. Up to three guest beers are stocked from independent

breweries. The patio offers splendid views of the river and marina. Moorings are available.
ॐ❀❍▲♨(X5)♣P⦄

Waggon & Horses ✅
Great North Road, PE19 8EF
✪ 12-3, 5-11; 12-11 Fri & Sat; 12-10 Sun ☎ (01480) 386373
Adnams Broadside; Woodforde's Wherry ⓗ
Traditional village pub dating from the 1700s with a large open inglenook fireplace and many exposed oak timbers and beams. The area of the pub close to the entrance functions as a bar, and the area beyond the fireplace as a restaurant.
⋈Qॐ❀❍♨(X5)P

Elton

Crown Inn Ⓛ ✅
8 Duck Street, PE8 6RQ (off B671 into Middle St, follow brown signs)
✪ 12 (5 Mon)-11 ☎ (01832) 280232 ⊕ thecrowninn.org
Grainstore Phipps IPA; Greene King IPA; guest beers ⓗ
Stone-built 16th-century thatched pub in the heart of the village overlooking the green, largely rebuilt in 1845 following a major fire. Five ales are usually on offer including the house beer, Golden Crown Ale, brewed by Tydd Steam, plus an ever-changing real cider. An open mic night is held on the third Monday of the month and a beer festival hosted in May. No bar food is served Saturday evening or Sunday. Five-star B&B accommodation is available.
⋈❀🛏❍♨(X4,24)♣P⦄

Ely

Fountain
1 Silver Street, CB7 4JF (on Barton Sq nr King's School)
✪ 5-11; 12-2, 6-11 Sat; 12-2, 7-10.30 Sun ☎ (01353) 663122
Fuller's London Pride; Woodforde's Wherry ⓗ
A street-corner pub opposite the Porta (monastic gatehouse), with a single bar that spans two distinct drinking areas. A variety of furnishings includes a barber's chair and an array of antler horns and taxidermy, and there are drawings, historic photos and paintings by local artists. The large, open log fireplace is a warm welcome in winter. Two changing guest ales often include a beer from Adnams. ⋈Q⇌

Townhouse Pub Ⓛ ✅
60-64 Market Street, CB7 4LS (near Ely Museum)
TL5410680446
✪ 11-11 (1.30am Fri & Sat); 12-11 Sun ☎ (01353) 664338
⊕ thetownhousepub.co.uk
Beer range varies ⓗ
Located in the city centre, this newly renovated Georgian Grade II-listed town house is now a popular modern bar with an airy conservatory and enclosed garden. A member of Oakham Ales Oakadamy, three changing ales and local Pickled Pig cider are always available. At least one beer is always on offer at a discounted price 5-7pm weekdays and 7-9pm weekends. Live music plays from 9pm on Friday and Saturday and a quiz is hosted on Sunday. An annual beer festival is held in July. Children are welcome. ❀❍⦄

Etton

Golden Pheasant ✅
1 Main Road, PE6 7DA

✪ 11.30-3, 4.30-11; 11.30-midnight Fri & Sat; 11.30-11 Sun
☎ (01733) 252387 ⊕ thegoldenpheasant.net
Castle Rock Harvest Pale; guest beers ⓗ
Former Georgian farmhouse and Grade II-listed building comprising a bar with dining area, separate restaurant and an extensive outside space including a marquee. There are four handpumps with ales changing constantly on three. The pub hosts numerous events each year (see the website for details) including beer festivals with over 25 ales, live music and firework displays. A CAMRA Gold Award winner in 2010. ⋈Q❀❍&♣♠P⦄

Fulbourn

Six Bells
9 High Street, CB21 5DH
✪ 11-3, 6-midnight; 11.30-midnight Fri-Sun
☎ (01223) 880244 ⊕ thesixbellsfulbourn.com
Adnams Southwold Bitter, Broadside; Greene King IPA; Woodforde's Wherry; guest beers ⓗ
Gloriously traditional thatched village pub, previously a coaching inn. The main bar has low ceilings, a real fire and many cosy corners. Good locally sourced and home-cooked food is served in the bar and separate dining room (no food Sun or Mon evening). The function room hosts a trad jazz club on the first and third Wednesdays of the month. A cheerful, and often cheeky, reception is guaranteed. ⋈ॐ❀❍🍴&♨(1)♣♠P⦄

Glatton

Addison Arms Ⓛ
Sawtry Road, PE28 5RZ
✪ 12-2.30, 5.30-11; 12-3, 7-10.30 Sun ☎ (01487) 830410
⊕ addisonarms.co.uk
Digfield Shacklebush; Grainstore Ten Fifty; guest beers ⓗ
Built at the start of the 18th century, the pub is named after the playwright and politician Joseph Addison (co-founder of The Spectator) who was a relative of the first landlord. Four real ales are offered, with a focus on local breweries including Oakham and Tydd Steam. Good food including daily specials is prepared from fresh locally sourced supplies. There is a thriving Sunday night quiz.
⋈Q❀❍🍴♨(47)♣♠P⦄

Grantchester

Blue Ball Inn
57 Broadway, CB3 9NQ
✪ 2-11; 12-midnight Sat; 12-10 Sun ☎ (01223) 840679
Adnams Southwold Bitter; guest beer ⓗ
Small, authentic local built in 1893 and retaining its original two-bar layout and many old fittings (including the landlord). No lager, no TV, no children – good beer, good conversation and traditional pub games are the order of the day. The piano is still played and there is live music every Thursday. At the back is a small walled garden with a heated 'smokeatorium'. Try your hand at ringing the bull. Dogs welcome. The name commemorates a balloon flight. ⋈Q❀♣⦄

Green Man Ⓛ ✅
59 High Street, CB3 9NF
✪ 11-11 ☎ (01223) 844669
⊕ thegreenmangrantchester.co.uk
Beer range varies Ⓖ

Dating back 500 years, this single-bar pub complete with oak beams has an extensive garden leading towards the River Cam. Run by real ale enthusiasts since reopening in December 2009, beers are sourced from regionals and micros, including local breweries, and regular beer festivals are held. Good home-made food made with local ingredients is served lunchtimes and evenings and all day at the weekend. A separate restaurant area caters for wedding receptions and parties. ₳Q⌂❄◑➌(18)♠P⌐

Great Abington

Three Tuns
75 High Street, CB21 6AB TL534488
✪ 12-2, 6-11; 12-11 Sat; 12-10.30 Sun ☎ (01223) 891467
⊕ thethreetuns-greatabington.co.uk
Greene King IPA; guest beers Ⓗ
Compact 16th-century two-bar free house opposite the village cricket green. It has a small dining room and a slightly larger main bar, both with wood floors and panelling. There is an outdoor area at the front of the pub. The changing beer range includes local ales, often from Woodforde's and Nethergate. An excellent Thai menu is offered. Accommodation is provided in five en-suite bedrooms. ₳❄✍◑➌Ⓓ♿➌(13)P⌐

Great Staughton

Snooty Tavern Ⓛ
12 The Green, PE19 5DG
✪ 12-3, 6-11; 12-10.30 Sun ☎ (01480) 860336
⊕ thesnootytavern.co.uk
Beer range varies Ⓗ
Open-plan pub in a light airy bistro style, with quarry-tiled floor. Meals are served lunchtimes and evenings, all day Sunday, with an à la carte menu, set menu, and blackboard specials. Typically three guest beers are available, usually including one from Buntingford, Oakham or Potton, and others from small independent brewers. ₳❄◑➌(156)P

Helpston

Blue Bell Ⓛ ✔
10 Woodgate, PE6 7ED
✪ 11.30-2.30 (3 Sat), 5 (6 Sat)-11; 12-10 Sun
☎ (01733) 252394
Grainstore John Clare; guest beers Ⓗ
Stone-built 17th-century village pub with traditional values. The wood-panelled bar is popular with locals and an extension into the old cellar has provided a dining area and cosy snug. The 18th-century poet John Clare, known as the peasant poet, was a pot boy here. Three guest beers usually include a mild, and a traditional cider is added in the summer. Good-value food is served lunchtime and evenings. The pub runs a crib team and has a pool table. ₳Q⌂❄◑➌Ⓓ♿➌(201)♣P⌐

Hemingford Grey

Cock Ⓛ
47 High Street, PE28 9BJ (off A14 SE of Huntingdon)
✪ 11.30-3, 6-11; 12-4, 6.30-10.30 Sun ☎ (01480) 463609
⊕ cambscuisine.com
Brewsters Hophead; Great Oakley Wagtail; guest beers Ⓗ
This award-winning village pub and restaurant has featured in more than 10 consecutive editions of

the Guide. The cosy bar area is popular with locals and diners alike who enjoy the well-kept locally sourced beers, as well as real Cromwell cider produced in the village. The separate restaurant features an extensive fish board, meat, game and excellent home-made sausages (booking essential at all times). During the summer, occasional beer festivals are held in the beer garden. ₳Q❄◑➌Ⓓ♿Å➌(5)♠P⌐

Histon

Boot Inn ✔
1 High Street, CB24 9LG 106317
✪ 11.30-3, 6-11; 11.30-midnight Fri & Sat; 12-9.30 Sun
☎ (01223) 566446
St Austell Tribute; Wells Bombardier; Woodforde's Wherry; guest beer Ⓗ
Village local with two bars, one small and intimate, the other large and with a covered patio beyond. There is also a dining room which doubles as a meeting place for a variety of local groups and is a venue for music sessions. Sport is shown on TV. Lunches, including Sunday roasts, are served all week. There are always four draught beers on tap, with the guest taken from the Finest Cask or SIBA lists. ₳❄◑Ⓓ♿➌♣P⌐

Red Lion
27 High Street, CB24 9JD
✪ 10.30-11 (midnight Fri); 12-11 Sun ☎ (01223) 564437
Batemans XB; Mighty Oak Captain Bob; Oakham Bishops Farewell; Theakston Lightfoot; Tring Blonde; guest beers Ⓗ
The two bars of this free house are adorned with a wonderful collection of breweriana and historical photos. Two changing guest beers and three Belgian beers on draught are complemented by a huge range of bottled Belgian and German beers plus draught cider and perry. Food is served every lunchtime and monthly themed food nights are popular. Two beer festivals are held annually – an Easter aperitif, then the main event in September. The infamous guided bus stops within half a mile. ₳❄◑➌➌(8)♣♠P

Holme

Admiral Wells Ⓛ
41 Station Road, PE7 3PH (jct of B660 and Yaxley Rd)
✪ 11-2.30, 5-11; 11-11 Sat; 11-10.30 Sun ☎ (01487) 800748
⊕ theadmiralwells.co.uk
Adnams Southwold Bitter; Digfield Shacklebush; Marston's Pedigree; Oakham JHB; guest beers Ⓗ
Victorian inn named after one of Nelson's pall bearers. It has two drinking areas and a function room at the rear. Next to the old Holme railway station, the walls are adorned with photographs from the steam railway days. Up to seven real ales and a cider are usually available and the pub serves excellent food. Quiz night is Tuesday. ₳Q⌂❄◑➌Ⓓ♿♣♠P⌐

Keyston

Pheasant Ⓛ
Village Loop, PE28 0RE (on B663, 1 mile S of A14, E of Thrapston)
✪ closed Mon; 12-3; 6-11; 12-4 Sun ☎ (01832) 710241
⊕ thepheasant-keyston.co.uk
Adnams Southwold Bitter, Broadside; guest beer Ⓗ

The village is named after Ketil's Stone, probably an Anglo-Saxon boundary marker. The pub offers high quality food, fine wines and well-kept cask ales. There is a splendid lounge bar and three dining areas include the Garden Room in a rear extension overlooking the herb garden. One regularly changing guest beer is offered – local microbreweries usually feature. One of the few pubs to feature in the first issue of the Guide in 1974. ♨Q☞✿◑P

Little Downham

Plough
106 Main Street, CB6 2SX (W end of village)
✪ 12-3 (not Mon), 6-11; 12-midnight Fri & Sat; 12-3, 6-10.30 Sun ☎ (01353) 698297
Greene King IPA; guest beers Ⓗ
Early Victorian Grade II-listed pub that retains much of its historic charm and character. This is a popular village watering-hole with up to three cask beers and an occasional local cider. Thai food is on offer, including a take-away service. The pub stays open all day at weekends, if busy, and children are welcome until 9pm. A popular spot for local folk dancers. ♨✿◑♣♠≞

Little Gransden

Chequers Ⓛ
71 Main Road, SG19 3DW
✪ 12-2, 7-11; 12-11 Fri & Sat; 12-6, 7-10.30 Sun
☎ (01767) 677348 ∰ sonofsid.co.uk
Beer range varies Ⓗ
Village pub, owned and run by the same family for more than 60 years. The unspoilt middle bar, with its wooden bench seating and roaring fire, is a favorite spot to pick up on the local gossip. The pub's Son of Sid brewhouse brews for the pub and local beer festivals. Fish and chips are a highlight on Friday night (booking essential). Real cider is usually available. Winner of numerous CAMRA awards. ♨Q✿⊟(18A)♠P≞

March

Rose & Crown Ⓛ
41 St Peters Road, PE15 9NA
✪ 12-11 (midnight Fri & Sat) ☎ (01354) 652077
Oakham JHB; guest beer Ⓗ
A traditional community pub dating back 150 years with low-beamed ceilings in both rooms and a real fire. Up to six real ales are on handpump, mainly from micros, with an Oakham ale and often a West Country beer. A beer festival is held at Easter and real cider is stocked. Good-quality food is served lunchtimes and evenings. Occasional live music plays on Saturdays. ♨Q✿◑⊟(X9,33)♠≞

Ship Inn Ⓛ
1 Nene Parade, PE15 8TD (off High St)
✪ 12-midnight (1am Fri & Sat) ☎ (01354) 607878
Oakham JHB; Woodforde's Wherry; guest beers Ⓗ
Grade-II listed, this thatched riverside establishment is one of the town's oldest pubs, built in 1680. A refit in 2010 saw the pub reopen as a free house. It has a small separate games room and extensive boat moorings are available.
✿⊟(33,35,X9)♣♠

Maxey

Blue Bell Ⓛ
High Street, PE6 9EE
✪ 5.30 (1 Sat)-11; 12-11 (12-4.30, 7.30-11 winter) Sun
☎ (01788) 348182 ∰ maxeyvillage.co.uk/facilities/blue-bell-pub/
Abbeydale Absolution; Fuller's London Pride, ESB; guest beers Ⓗ
The long, narrow interior has the main bar at the front with a log fire, stuffed birds and fish. A smaller bar is decorated with fishing photographs. Nine real ales are usually available including one from Oakham Ales. At the heart of the village, the pub is a meeting place for several groups including birdwatchers and golfers. Former CAMRA Community Pub of the Year and local Pub of the Year. ♨Q✿✪≞

Newton

Queen's Head
CB22 7PG
✪ 11.30-2.30, 6-11; 12-2.30, 7-10.30 Sun ☎ (01223) 870436
Adnams Southwold Bitter, Broadside; guest beers Ⓖ
This village local is one of a handful across the country to have appeared in every edition of the Guide. The list of landlords since 1729 has just 18 entries, their names displayed on the wall in the simply furnished but timeless public bar. The cosy lounge has a welcoming fire in the colder months. Simple but excellent food centres on soup and sandwiches. Guest beers are Adnams seasonals. ♨Q◁⊟⊟♣♠P

Offord D'Arcy

Horseshoe Ⓛ
90 High Street, PE19 5RH (on Godmanchester to St Neots road)
✪ 12-2.30, 5-11; 12-11.30 Fri & Sat; 12-10.30 Sun
☎ (01480) 810293 ∰ thehorseshoeinn.biz
Adnams Southwold Bitter; Oakham JHB; Potton Shannon IPA Ⓗ
Family-run free house, in a building dating from 1626. It actively supports beers from local breweries, including microbreweries, and the chef offers a quality menu featuring fresh locally sourced produce. There are two bars with a separate dining area – the snug, or village bar, has a TV. Outside is a family garden with children's play area. ♨✿✿◑⊟♿⊟(65)P≞

Old Weston

Swan
Main Street, PE28 5LL (on B660, N of A14)
✪ 6.30-11; 12-2.30, 7-11 Sat; 12-3.30, 7-10.30 Sun
☎ (01832) 293400
Greene King Abbot; Taylor Landlord; guest beer Ⓗ
Originally dating from the 16th century, at the end of the 19th century the pub had its own brewery. There is a central bar with a large inglenook, a dining area and a games section offering hood skittles and pool. At weekends a varied menu of traditional pub food is available, including home-made puddings. ♨Q✿◑♣P

Peterborough

Brewery Tap Ⓛ
80 Westgate, PE1 2AA

☼ 12-11 (late Fri & Sat) ☎ (01733) 358500
⊕ oakham-ales.co.uk/brewerytap
Oakham JHB, Citra, Inferno, Bishops Farewell; guest beers Ⓗ
Reputed to be the largest brewpub in Europe, housed in a 1930s former Labour Exchange. A smaller craft brewery can be seen through large windows, where limited editions of beers are brewed. Up to 12 ales are on offer, mainly from the Oakham range. The bar's modern design incorporates a mezzanine area and some brewing artefacts. Authentic Thai food is served. There is entertainment on Friday and Saturday evenings. Handy for bus and rail stations. ◖◗≠🚃

Burghley Club Ⓛ
7 Burghley Road, PE1 2QA (½ mile from city centre)
☼ 12-2.30; 5-11; 12-1am Fri & Sat; 12-11 Sun
☎ (01733) 896989 ⊕ theburghleyclub.com
Hopshackle Special Bitter; guest beers Ⓗ
A welcome addition to the north side of the city. The interior is divided into several areas with a small separate room at the front and a function room upstairs. A pool table, dartboard and TV are at one end. Up to five beers are served, mainly from local and country-wide micros. Snacks are available at lunchtimes and a roast lunch on Sunday. Visiting CAMRA members are admitted on production of a membership card. Q◖&≠🚃(1)♣🐾P▰

Charters Ⓛ
Town Bridge, PE1 1EH (down steps at Town Bridge)
☼ 12-11 (late Fri & Sat); 12-10.30 Sun ☎ (01733) 315700
⊕ oakhamales.com/charters
Oakham JHB, Citra, Inferno, Bishops Farewell; guest beers Ⓗ/Ⓖ
Moored on the River Nene, Charters is a converted Dutch grain barge from circa 1907. The upper deck houses an oriental restaurant and food is available in the bar. Outside is a large garden with a marquee, bar and landing stage for boats. Up to 12 ales are on offer plus Belgian bottled beers. The pub gets very busy on football days. Music and poetry nights are hosted. ⊛◖◗≠🚃♣🐾P▰

Coalheavers Arms
5 Park Street, Woodston, PE2 9BH
☼ 12-2 (Thu only), 5-11; 12-11 Fri & Sat; 12-10.30 Sun
☎ (01733) 565664 ⊕ individualpubs.co.uk/coalheavers
Milton Bombers Drop, Justinian, Sparta; guest beers Ⓗ
Friendly one-roomed back-street local dating back to 1850s. The beers are mainly from Milton – Bombers Drop is the house beer – with up to four guests. Traditional cider and Belgian bottled beers are also stocked, and an English unpasteurised lager. Fresh rolls are served on Friday and home-made jumbo Scotch eggs are available all week. The large garden is popular in summer and hosts beer festivals in spring and autumn. Busy on football match days. On Sunday evening there is a free quiz. Q⊛🚃♣🐾▰🎇

Draper's Arms Ⓛ ✔
29-31 Cowgate, PE1 1LZ
☼ 9-midnight (1am Fri & Sat) ☎ (01733) 847570
Courage Directors; Greene King Abbot; Ruddles Best Bitter; guest beers Ⓗ
Armstrong's drapers started life in 1899. Converted in 2005 by Wetherspoon, 10 handpumps serve the regular and ever-changing guest ales including beers from Oakham Ales and other local breweries, and a traditional cider. The interior is split into

intimate spaces by wood-panelled dividers. Good-value food is served all day and regular beer and wine festivals are hosted. Quiz night is Wednesday. Q◖◗&≠🚃🐾

Hand & Heart ★ Ⓛ
12 Highbury Street, Millfield, PE1 3BE
☼ 3 (11 Fri-Sun)-11; 12-10.30 Sun ☎ (01733) 564653
Beer range varies Ⓗ/Ⓖ
One of Britain's Real Heritage Pubs, this unspoilt 1930s back-street pub has the main bar to the front and a quiet room to the rear connected by a drinking corridor. The bar has five handpumps often offering hard-to-find real ales. The large garden has a separate bar that is used at least twice a year for beer festivals and a large wooden stage for live music. Local CAMRA Pub of the Year 2010. ♨Q⊛🚷🚃(1)♣▰

Ostrich Ⓛ
17 North Street, PE1 2RA
☼ 11-11 (1am Fri & Sat); 12-11 Sun ☎ (01733) 746370
Oakham Ales JHB; guest beers Ⓗ
In 2009 the Ostrich reopened after a major refurbishment. The one-roomed pub with a U-shaped bar is decorated with pictures and posters about the pub, bygone breweries and famous acts that have appeared in the city. There is an area for playing darts. Five handpumps serve regularly changing beers, many from local breweries, and a real cider. A small enclosed patio is at the rear. Live music plays most weekends. ⊛◖◗&≠🚃♣🐾▰

Ploughman Ⓛ
Staniland Way, Werrington, PE4 6NA
☼ 2 (12 Sun)-11; 12-midnight Fri & Sat ☎ (01733) 327696
Beer range varies Ⓗ
Once a pub with no real ale, this rejuvenated community establishment now has five handpumps serving beers from local breweries as well as from far and wide. An annual beer festival is held the first week in July. It hosts darts and pool teams, holds regular poker nights and is well-known for its charity events. Live music plays at weekends. It was local CAMRA Pub of the Year in 2011. ⊛🚷🚃(1,406,413)♣P▰

Rampton

Black Horse
6 High Street, CB24 8QE
☼ closed Mon; 6 (12 Sun)-11; 12-3, 6-midnight Sat
☎ (01954) 251867
Wells Eagle IPA; guest beers Ⓗ
Formerly a Greene King pub, the Black Horse has been a free house for some years now. At least one of the guest beers is likely to be a local ale. Beers can be bought in third-of-a-pint tasting glasses. The interior comprises two bars separated by an archway and both are smart and comfortable. Home-made food is available most evenings and Sunday lunchtime, with the pies particularly recommended. ♨Q🐾⊛◖&♣P▰

Ramsey

Railway
132 Great Whyte, PE26 1HS
☼ 12-midnight (2am Fri & Sat) ☎ (01487) 812597
Greene King Abbot; Thwaites Lancaster Bomber; Woodforde's Wherry; guest beer Ⓗ

Red brick 1930s pub that is largely intact with two rooms, each with a real fire, separated by a central bar. A friendly community hostelry serving good-quality real ale, it was awarded a local CAMRA Gold Award in 2011. The trophy case in the bar has awards dating back to the 1930s. Live music features on Saturdays. Handy for the nearby marina in the summer months. ⚒Q✿⊞&⊟(31)♣P

Reach

Dyke's End 🅛
8 Fair Green, CB25 0JD
✪ 12-2 (not Mon), 6-11; 12-11 Sat & Sun ☎ (01638) 743816
⊕ dykesend.co.uk
Adnams Broadside; Devil's Dyke Bitter; Thwaites Wainwright; guest beer ℍ
Quintessential village pub saved from closure by a group of villagers and now privately owned by a local with a passion for good beer and real food. The attached Devil's Dyke microbrewery was set up in 2007 and one or two beers are usually available in the pub. The interior comprises a food-free tap room, bar and attractive cosy restaurant serving freshly prepared home-cooked meals (no food Sun eve or Mon). Photos and art of local interest adorn the walls while the idyllic garden overlooks the village green. ⚒Q✿⊕&⊟♣P

St Ives

Floods Tavern 🅛
27 The Broadway, PE27 5BX
✪ 12-11 (midnight Thu-Sun) ☎ (01480) 700676
Elgood's Cambridge Bitter; guest beers ℍ
An Elgood's house, the pub has recently been given a stylish contemporary revamp and new menu. Three Elgood's real ales are served. The bar area features a real fire and TV screens for football. A riverside garden provides free moorings, idyllic views of the historic St Ives river bridge and Holt Island nature reserve, plus an outdoor cocktail bar, music stage and large outdoor screen for occasional sporting events. Evenings feature karaoke on alternate Thursdays and live music on Fridays (usually acoustic) and Saturdays. ⚒✿⊕⊟♣⚑

St Neots

Olde Sun
11 Huntingdon Street, PE19 1BL
✪ 12-11 ☎ (01480) 216863
Woodforde's Wherry; guest beers ℍ
Low-beamed traditional town-centre pub with two large inglenook fireplaces. At the front are three bar areas, to the rear a dining space and secluded patio. The zoned jukebox allows for quiet areas for conversation, and there is a bar billiards table. Six handpumps offer a constantly changing range from independent breweries. Good home-cooked food is served, with a menu of traditional pub food and blackboard specials. Meals are served lunchtimes and Tuesday to Thursday evenings. ⚒✿⊕♣⚑

Pig 'n' Falcon 🅛
9 New Street, PE19 1AE (behind Barretts department store)
✪ 10am-midnight (1am Thu; 2am Fri & Sat); 11am-midnight Sun ☎ 07951 785678 ⊕ pignfalcon.co.uk
Greene King IPA, Abbot; Oakham Inferno, Citra; Potbelly Best ℍ**; guest beers** 🅖

Town-centre free house with up to 10 real ales and four real ciders, focusing on microbreweries and unusual beers including milds, porters and stouts. It also offers a good range of bottled ciders and British and foreign bottled beers, including Draycott beers from the local Buckden brewery. Four beer festivals are held each year. Regular live blues and rock nights are hosted. Outside is a large, imaginative covered and heated garden. Local CAMRA Cider Pub of the Year 2012. CAMRA members receive a discount. ✿≠⊟(X5)♣●⚑ 🗗

Sawston

Black Bull 🅛
98 High Street, CB22 3HJ
✪ 5-10.30 (11.30 Fri); closed Tue; 11-11.30 Sat; 12-9.30 Sun ☎ (01223) 835726 ⊕ blackbullsawston.com
Milton Pegasus; guest beers ℍ
Rescued from closure a couple of years back, this traditional family-run hostelry offers the best choice of cask ales in Sawston including locally brewed beers – Buntingford ales often appear. It is also the oldest pub in the village – the Grade II-listed building dating from 1545 – hence the wealth of wooden beams, open fires and wonky walls. ⚒✿⊕≠(Whittlesford Parkway)🗗P⚑

Snailwell

George & Dragon
31 The Street, CB8 7LX (off A142 between Soham and Newmarket) TL6427667716
✪ 12-11 (8 Mon & Tue; midnight Wed); 12-7 Sun
☎ (01638) 577241 ⊕ thegeorgeanddragonsnailwell.co.uk
Fuller's London Pride; Wells Bombardier; guest beer ℍ
A welcoming village pub off the beaten track, popular with the local community for its good food. One guest beer is usually available. Pétanque is played in the large garden which has the River Snail flowing past at the bottom. Live music weekends are hosted in the summer. Children are welcome and evening hours may be extended if the pub is busy. ⚒✿⊕♣P

Tilbrook

White Horse 🅛 ✔
High Street, PE28 0JP
✪ 12 (5.30 Mon)-11 ☎ (01480) 860764
⊕ whitehorsetilbrook.com
Wells Eagle IPA; Young's Bitter; Wells Bombardier; guest beer ℍ
Two-roomed village pub dating in parts back to 1735, surrounded by large gardens and open fields. The public bar is furnished with sofas and bar stools and provides darts and hood skittles. There is a large lounge and bright conservatory with further seating. Traditional locally sourced food is served until 9pm (3pm Sun). The garden has swings and slides for children, and a petting zoo featuring ducks, chickens, goats and a goose. Look for the artistic photos in the Ladies and Gents. ♿✿⊕⊞⊟(150)♣P⚑🗗

Ufford

White Hart 🅛
Main Street, PE9 3BH
✪ 12-11 (midnight Fri & Sat); 12-9 (6 winter) Sun
☎ (01780) 740250 ⊕ whitehartufford.co.uk

Adnams Southwold Bitter H
Stone-built 16th-century village local comprising a public bar to the front, restaurant to the rear and an orangery to the side, leading to a separate function room. Behind the pub is a large car park, a number of outbuildings, a patio, large beer garden with tables and children's play area. There are six individually styled en-suite bedrooms. Traditional English fare using locally sourced ingredients is available throughout the day.
🅐Q🏮🛏�•🍴🛏♣♠P🏃

Waterbeach

Sun Inn ✅
Chapel Street, CB25 9HR
🕐 5-11; 12-midnight Fri-Sun ☎ (01223) 861254
🌐 thesun-waterbeach.co.uk
Adnams Broadside; Woodforde's Wherry; guest beer H
With a philosophy of 'good beer, good food, good music', this village local goes from strength to strength. The small, cosy lounge is dominated by a huge fireplace while the simply-appointed public, with its wood-block floor, is always lively. Behind the bar is a small meeting room and upstairs a function room hosts regular gigs. A changing guest beer comes from Punch's Finest Cask range. Football matches on Sky Sports are shown. Beer and music festivals feature on May and August bank holiday weekends. The Sunday roast is popular. No food Monday or Sunday evenings.
🅐🏮�🛏�•🍴🛏♣♠

Whittlesey

Boat L
2 Ramsey Road, PE7 1DR
🕐 4 (11 Fri-Sun)-midnight ☎ (01733) 202488
🌐 theboatuk.com
Elgood's Black Dog, Cambridge Bitter, Golden Newt, seasonal beers; guest beers G
This 11th-century inn is mentioned in the Domesday Book. It attracts locals, anglers and visitors, who all receive a warm welcome. The lounge has an unusual boat-shaped bar and hosts a whisky club that meet on the first Friday of every month. Up to five traditional ciders and perries supplement the real ales that are all served direct from the cask. Live music plays on Saturday evening. Outside is a pétanque terrain. Good-value accommodation is offered.
🚱🏮🛏🌕🍴🛏(31,33)♣●P🏃

George Hotel L ✅
10 Market Street, PE7 1AB
🕐 7-midnight (1am Fri & Sat) ☎ (01733) 359970
Courage Directors; Fuller's London Pride; Greene King Abbot; Ruddles Best Bitter; guest beers H
Built in the late 1700s, the building underwent significant alterations in the mid-19th century and became a Grade II-listed building in 1974. Once a popular locals' haunt with a basic bar and comfortable lounge, it was closed and unloved until it was refurbished and reopened by JD Wetherspoon in 2010. Now a favourite locally, offering a large selection of real ales – up to 10 at any one time – and Wetherspoon's decent food menu, at affordable prices.
🅐Q🌕Ⅱ🍴🛏(31,32,33)●P🏃

Letter B 🏆 ♛ L ✅
53-57 Church Street, PE7 1DE
🕐 5-11; 3.30-midnight Fri; 12-midnight Sat; 12-11 Sun
☎ (01733) 206975 🌐 theletterbpublichouse.co.uk
Adnams Southwold Bitter; Oakham Inferno; Tydd Steam Barn Ale; guest beers H
Popular with locals and new visitors alike, this is a 200-year-old traditional pub near the town centre. It hosts a beer festival in the spring and is home to the Gruftons, a local group dedicated to good real ale. The B&B accommodation is both good value and popular. A free house, the Letter B always has a good selection of real ales and a good range of real ciders. Local CAMRA Pub of the Year 2012.
Q🏮🛏🌕🍴🛏(31,32,33)♣●🏃

Whittlesford

Bees in the Wall
36 North Rd, CB22 4NZ TL467486
🕐 12-2.30 (not Mon), 6-11; 12-3, 7-10.30 Sun
☎ (01223) 834289
Taylor Landlord; guest beers H
Situated on the village's northern edge, this pub really does have bees in one wall. The public bar oozes atmosphere, especially with the fire blazing, and tends to be where the locals gather. Diners favour the long split-level lounge which opens onto a patio, huge paddock-style garden and the pub's own wood. Two guest beers are usually stocked. Evening meals are served Wednesday to Saturday only. The pub may stay open all day during the summer. 🅐Q🏮🌕Ⅱ🍴♣P🏃

Wisbech

Red Lion L
32 North Brink, PE13 1JR
🕐 11.30-3, 6-11; 12-3, 7-11 Sat; 12-11 Sun
☎ (01945) 582022
Elgood's Black Dog, Cambridge Bitter, Pageant; guest beer H
The nearest Elgood's pub to the brewery, the Red Lion is comfortable, with a pleasant, relaxed atmosphere. Drinkers and diners alike are well-catered for, with quality ales and excellent food including many home-cooked specials served seven days a week. Children are welcome. Wheelchair access is from the rear, where the outdoor drinking area is popular on sunny days.
Q🌕Ⅱ🍴🛏(X1)P🏃

Wistow

Three Horseshoes
Mill Road, PE28 2QQ
🕐 6-10 Mon; 12-3, 6-11; 12-10 Sat; 12-4 Sun
☎ (01487) 822270
Adnams Southwold Bitter, Broadside H
Traditional multi-roomed brick and thatch 18th-century pub opposite the village church with a strong local following and passing trade. Thought to have always been a pub, the building has evolved over time (part of the building used to be a blacksmith's). Traditional pub food is served daily and at least two real ales are always available, with occasional guests in summer. A quiz is held once a month. Families are welcome to use both bars. Outside is a covered smoking area.
🅐🚱🌕Ⅱ🛏🍴🛏(30)♣P🏃

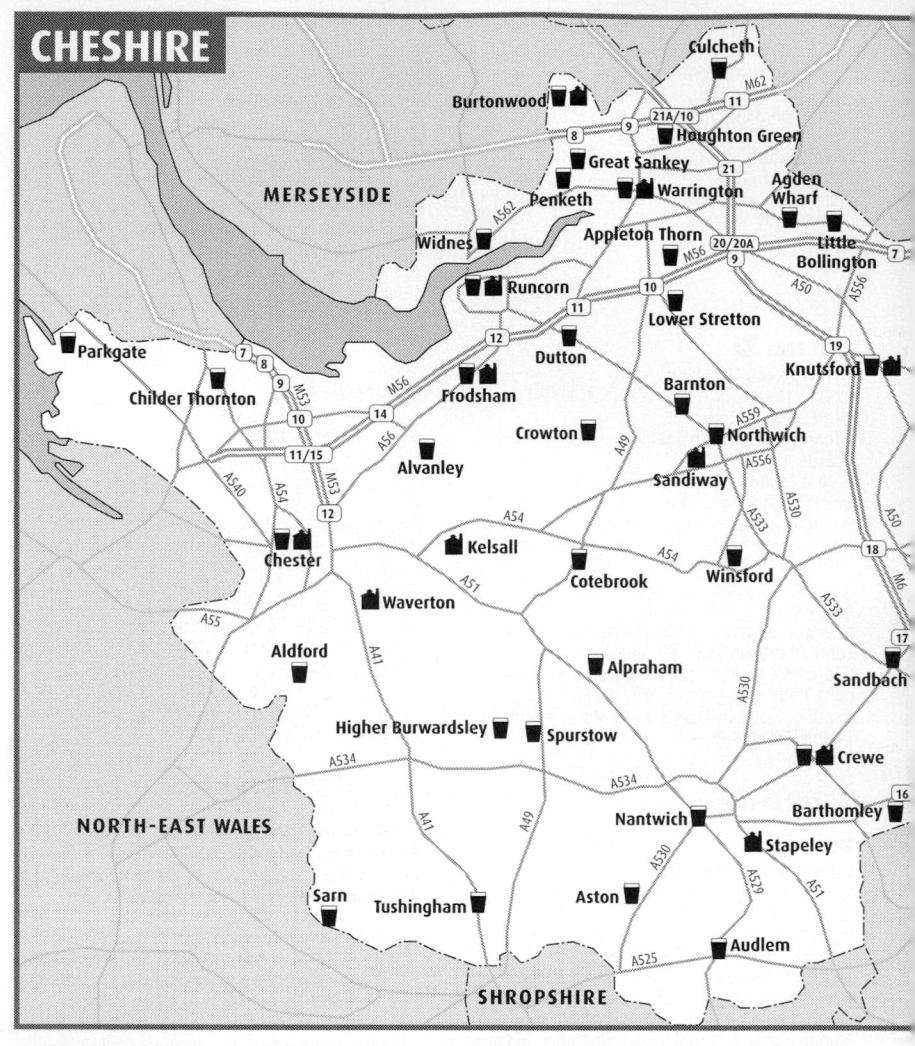

CHESHIRE

MERSEYSIDE

NORTH-EAST WALES

SHROPSHIRE

Culcheth
Burtonwood
Houghton Green
Great Sankey
Penketh
Warrington
Agden Wharf
Appleton Thorn
Little Bollington
Widnes
Runcorn
Lower Stretton
Parkgate
Dutton
Knutsford
Childer Thornton
Barnton
Frodsham
Northwich
Crowton
Sandiway
Alvanley
Kelsall
Chester
Cotebrook
Winsford
Waverton
Aldford
Alpraham
Sandbach
Higher Burwardsley
Spurstow
Crewe
Barthomley
Nantwich
Stapeley
Sarn
Tushingham
Aston
Audlem

Agden Wharf

Barn Owl ⅃

Warrington Lane, WA13 0SW (off A56) SJ707872
🕑 12-11 ☎ (01925) 752020 ⊕ thebarnowlinn.co.uk
Marston's Burton Bitter, Pedigree; guest beers Ⓗ
With a range of up to five guest ales sourced
mainly from micros complementing the two
regular beers, the Barn Owl is as renowned for its
ales as for its food. Freshly-cooked food made with
mainly local produce means the pub is especially
busy at meal times. Set in open countryside by the
Bridgewater Canal, the large single room
complements the canalside patio area offering
views across the countryside. Occasional live music
is played. ⊛❶&♣P⅃

Alderley Edge

Alderley Edge Sports & Social Club ⅃

Stevens Street, SK9 7NL
🕑 12-2.30, 6-midnight; 7-11 Sun ☎ (01625) 585506
Beer range varies Ⓗ

Three good-value real ales feature at this rare
outlet in the UK's champagne capital. Two LocAles
sourced within 15 miles often include a beer from
Storm Brewing plus traditional cider. Facilities
include full-size snooker tables, a county-class
bowling green and Sky Sports, and a simple food
menu is available. A beer festival is held in July.
Entry is £1 for non-members or show your CAMRA
membership card or copy of the Guide to come in
for free. Please knock on the door! ❧❶⇌🖼♣

Aldford

Grosvenor Arms ⅃

Chester Road, CH3 6HJ (on B5130)
🕑 11.30-11; 12-10.30 Sun ☎ (01244) 620228
⊕ grosvenorarms-aldford.co.uk
Beer range varies Ⓗ
Large, stylish Victorian free house, known far and
wide for its imaginative food menu. The lively
wooden bar is surrounded by quieter areas
adorned with library books and multitudinous
pictures and drawings. A pleasant conservatory
leads to an outside terrace and lawn with picnic

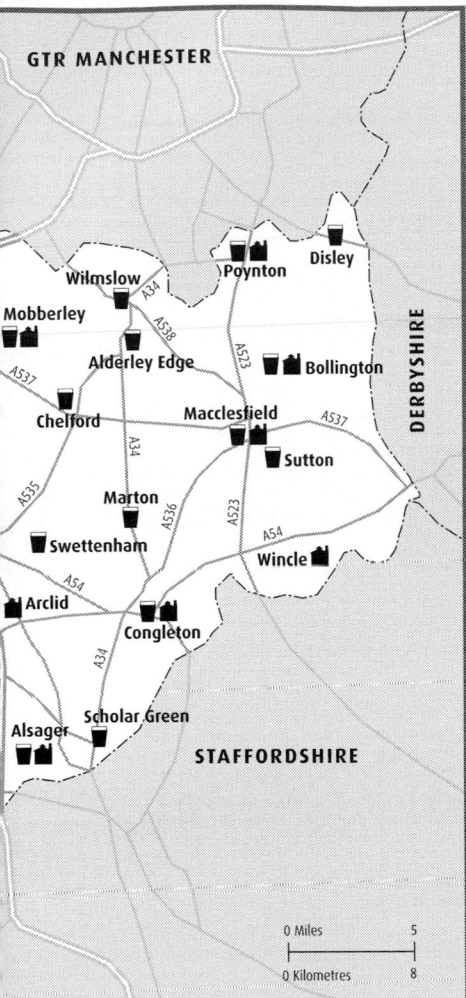

GTR MANCHESTER

Wilmslow · Poynton · Disley

Mobberley

Alderley Edge · Bollington

Chelford · Macclesfield

Sutton

Marton

Swettenham · Wincle

Arclid · Congleton

Scholar Green

Alsager

STAFFORDSHIRE

DERBYSHIRE

0 Miles 5
0 Kilometres 8

---

tables. A covered, heated area caters for smokers. Six changing beers are on sale, including a house beer from Phoenix, and a good range of wines and malt whiskies. Q❀❄◐⎶&⎶(C56)P℄

Alpraham

Travellers Rest ★ 🅛
Chester Road, CW6 9JA (on A51 at N end of village) SJ578598
🕐 6.30-11; 12-5, 6-11 Sat; 12-3, 7-10.30 Sun
☎ (01829) 260523
Tetley Bitter; Weetwood Eastgate 🅷
Close to the Shropshire Union Canal, this genuine rural free house has been owned and run by the same family for more than 100 years. One of Britain's Real Heritage Pubs, the cosy inn is always a delight to visit. The four rooms and their furnishings reflect an era when people had time to sit, sup, talk and relax. Visitors, locals, walkers, cyclists and passing motorists are always made to feel at home. No food is served. Note the limited opening times. Q❀❄⎶(84)♣P℄

Alsager

Lodge 🍷 🅛
88 Crewe Road, ST7 2LX
🕐 4 (3 Sun)-11; 1-midnight Fri & Sat ☎ (01270) 873669
Beer range varies 🅷
Large two-roomed pub, offering a changing range of ales, often sourced from microbreweries and including ales from its own on-site brewery, Goodall's. Three draught ciders and a selection of bottled beers are also stocked, and a beer festival is held at Easter. Baps and wraps are available at all times. The garden is popular in summer. The pub is well-served by public transport, and there is a public car park to the rear. 🚌❀◐&⎶⎶(20)♦

Alvanley

White Lion 🅛 ✅
Manley Road, WA6 9DD SJ497740
🕐 12-11 (10.30 Sun) ☎ (01928) 722949
🌐 whitelionalvanley.co.uk
Hartleys XB; Robinson's Dark 1892, seasonal beers 🅷
A recent internal refurbishment by Robinson's has made the White Lion almost unrecognisable from its previous incarnation – and as well as a new and more modern layout, the pub now bustles with life. Once part of a farm, it continues its diverse activity today with the operation of an on-site coal supply business. The food is excellent, with extensive specials boards dotted around the room. So successful is the pub that the car park is often full at weekends. 🚌Q❀◐♦P℄

Appleton Thorn

Appleton Thorn Village Hall
Stretton Road, WA4 4RT SJ637838
🕐 closed Mon-Wed; 7.30-11; 1-4, 7.30-10.30 Sun
☎ (01925) 261187 🌐 appletonthornvillagehall.co.uk
Beer range varies 🅷
The hub of the community, the Village Hall, previous CAMRA national finalist and local CAMRA Club of the Year 2012, has a comfortable lounge and a larger bar/function room served from a central bar. The function room hosts quizzes, live music and the annual beer festival in October. On the bar are up to seven beers from regional and microbreweries, plus up to eight ciders/perries. Light lunches are served on Sunday 1-3pm. Q❀&⎶(10,10X)♣♦P🍺

Aston

Bhurtpore Inn 🅛
Wrenbury Road, CW5 8DQ (¼ mile NW from A530 Nantwich-Whitchurch road) SJ610469
🕐 12-2.30, 6.30-11.30; 12-midnight Fri & Sat; 12-11 Sun
☎ (01270) 780917 🌐 bhurtpore.co.uk
Beer range varies 🅷
This popular, friendly, genuine real ale cornucopia at the heart of the local community has featured in every issue of the Guide since 1992. Eleven handpumps deliver a wonderful choice, frequently including LocAle. There will always be three premium and three session beers, one strong and a mild or porter/stout available, with beers from Hobsons at Cleobury Mortimer ever popular. The July beer festival is a must. An excellent range of home-cooked, locally sourced food is available – curries a speciality.
🚌Q❀◐&▲⎷(Wrenbury)⎶(72)♣♦P℄

Audlem

Lord Combermere ⓛ ✅

The Square, CW3 0AQ (opp St James' Church)
☺ 12-12.30am ☎ (01270) 812277
⊕ thelordcombermere.co.uk
Greene King IPA; Wells Bombardier; Taylor Landlord; guest beers Ⓗ
Friendly local with polite and helpful staff in the middle of Audlem. Open plan with a central bar, vestiges of the pub's 18th-century origins remain. Entertainment includes a Tuesday quiz night and the pub hosts a beer festival over the August bank holiday. Good home-cooked food is served daily from a varied range, including a full gluten-free menu. Popular with ramblers and canal users.
Ⓜ✿ⓓ♿◨(73)♠P⅃

Barnton

Barnton Cricket Club ⓛ

Broomsedge, Townfield Lane, CW8 4QL (200yds from A533 via Stoneheyes Lane) SJ631757
☺ 6.30 (12 (4 winter) Sat)-midnight (11.30 Mon; 11 Wed); 12-11 Sun ☎ (01606) 77702 ⊕ barntoncc.co.uk
Hydes Manchester's Finest; Theakston Best Bitter; Thwaites Nutty Black; guest beers Ⓗ
A finalist in the national CAMRA Club of the Year competition in 2011, this club is a beacon for real ale in an otherwise keg-only village. Sports feature heavily here with on-site squash courts as well as the main cricket pitch. The club has been awarded Clubmark accreditation from the England & Wales Cricket Board. A popular beer festival is held, usually in November. Food is available Monday, Thursday, Friday and Saturday evenings and Sunday lunchtime. ✿ⓓ♿◨(4)♣P⅃

Barthomley

White Lion ★ ✅

Audley Road, CW2 5PG (jct of Audley Road and Radway Green Rd) SJ767524
☺ 11.30-11; 12-10.30 Sun ☎ (01270) 882242
⊕ whitelionbarthomley.com
Jennings Cumberland Ale, Cocker Hoop, Snecklifter; Mansfield Cask Ale; Marston's Burton Bitter Ⓗ
Classic rural gem occupying an idyllic position in the centre of the village next to the church and stream. The 15th-century thatched, black and white timbered pub has an unchanging interior with two main rooms and an upstairs function room, each with wood panelling, tiled floors and simple, rustic furniture. There is a patio area and tables outside to sit in the sun and enjoy the tranquil surroundings. Wychwood Hobgoblin is occasionally available. ⓂQ✿ⓓP⅃

Bollington

Cock & Pheasant ⓛ ✅

15 Bollington Road, SK10 5EJ
☺ 11.30-11 (midnight Fri & Sat); 12-11 Sun
☎ (01625) 573289
Copper Dragon Golden Pippin; Storm Brewing Bosley Cloud; Tetley Bitter; guest beers Ⓗ
Large, popular pub on the main road entering Bollington, dating from 1756. Low ceilings and a stone-flagged floor make for a cosy bar, with a separate secluded dining area. Well-kept cask ales complement good food from a well-balanced menu served every day until 9pm. A conservatory,

patio and children's play area cater for all, and the bus stop is right outside the front door. A regular outlet for local breweries Storm and Wincle.
☗✿ⓓ♿◨(10,392)♣P⅃

Poachers Inn ⓛ

95 Ingersley Road, SK10 5RE
☺ 12-2 (not Mon), 5.30-11; 12-11 Sun ☎ (01625) 572086
⊕ thepoachers.org
Storm Brewing Desert Storm; Weetwood Old Dog; guest beers Ⓗ
Welcoming family-run free house near the Gritstone Way. The interior is divided into comfortable seating areas, with a warming coal fire in winter, and an outside suntrap garden for summer. Five handpumps enthusiastically promote local breweries including nearby Happy Valley. Belgian beers are available in bottles. Good-value, home-prepared food is available and events include Wednesday pie night and monthly quiz nights for local charities. Local CAMRA Pub of the Year 2010, the pub has featured in the Guide for more than 10 years. Ⓜ☗✿ⓓ◨(10,392)P⅃

Vale Inn ⓛ ✅

29-31 Adlington Road, SK10 5JT
☺ 12-2.30, 5-11; 12-11 Sat; 12-10.30 Sun ☎ (01625) 575147
⊕ valeinn.co.uk
Beer range varies Ⓗ
The brewery tap for the nearby Bollington Brewing Company, this 1860s single-room family-run free house features three to five of its beers plus one or two guests, also from local breweries. Seasonal mini beer festivals are hosted and excellent home-cooked food is available. The pub is popular with the local community as well as walkers and bikers using the nearby canal and Middlewood Way footpath. It sponsors the local Bollington cricket team and games can be watched from the beer garden. A former local CAMRA Pub of the Year.
Ⓜ☗✿ⓓ◨(10,392)♠P⅃日

INDEPENDENT BREWERIES

4Ts Runcorn/Warrington
Beartown Congleton
Blue Ball Runcorn
Bollington Bollington
Borough Arms Crewe
Burtonwood Burtonwood
Coach House Warrington
DB Runcorn
Frodsham Frodsham
Front Row Congleton (NEW)
Goodall's Alsager
Happy Valley Bollington
Merlin Arclid
Mobberley Mobberley (NEW)
Northern Sandiway
Norton Runcorn
Offbeat Crewe
Pied Bull Chester
RedWillow Macclesfield
Spitting Feathers Waverton
Storm Macclesfield
Tatton Knutsford
Tipsy Angel Warrington
Weetwood Kelsall
Wincle Wincle
Woodlands Stapeley
Worth Poynton

Burtonwood

Fiddle i' th' Bag
Alder Lane, WA5 4BJ SJ584929
✪ 12-3, 4.45-11; 12-11 Sat & Sun ☎ (01925) 225442
Beer range varies Ⓗ
On a country lane close to Alder Root Golf Club and the site of the Burtonwood USAF base. Space is limited inside, as every spare inch is full of curiosities, oddities and World War II memorabilia. Two rooms are dedicated to drinkers to chat to the enthusiastic staff and explore what seems to be a cross between pub and museum. Two further rooms are set aside for diners to enjoy the excellent food. A central bar serves up to three guest beers. Q✿❂❍☒(329)P

Chelford

Egerton Arms ♛ Ⓛ
Knutsford Road, SK11 9BB
✪ 12-11 (10.30 Sun) ☎ (01625) 861366
⊕ chelfordegertonarms.co.uk
Copper Dragon Golden Pippin; Wells Bombardier; guest beers Ⓗ
Free house comprising a large single room on three levels, with rustic decor, low lighting and candles on tables giving a measure of intimacy. There is also a small games room to the rear and a garden, barbecue and smoking area beyond that. The pub is child-friendly with a playground outside and dogs are permitted within limited areas. Food is available all day every day (booking advisable at weekends). ♨❧✿❍⚇☒(27A)P⚑

Chester

Bear & Billet
94 Lower Bridge Street, CH1 1RU (near Old Dee Bridge)
✪ 12-11 (11.30 Thu; 12.30am Fri & Sat) ☎ (01244) 311886
⊕ bearandbillet.com
Okells Bitter, IPA; guest beers Ⓗ
A fine historic building dating from 1664, retaining much of the original woodwork, both inside and out. The ground floor bar with heavy wood furnishings is divided into three areas with an open fire and plasma TV. There is a dining area on the first floor and a function room on the third floor. Outside is a small yard with tables for warmer weather. Up to six guest beers and an extensive range of continental beers are available. There are special mid-week food offers. ♨✿❍⚇☒❀⚑

Brewery Tap ♛ Ⓛ
52-54 Lower Bridge Street, CH1 1RU
✪ 12-11 (10.30 Sun) ☎ (01244) 340999 ⊕ the-tap.co.uk
Beer range varies Ⓗ
Situated on the first floor of a former Jacobean banqueting hall, the pub is reached via steps from the street. The large room has stone floors, high ceilings and tapestries, creating a terrific ambience. A comprehensive, frequently changing list of real ales from micros, many local, complements the Spitting Feathers house beers, giving drinkers a wide choice. The real cider is usually from Wales. Inventive, freshly prepared food is served. A gem not to be missed. Q❍☒❀

Carlton Tavern ✅
1 Hartington Street, Handbridge, CH4 7BN
✪ 4-11.30 (midnight Fri); 12-midnight Sat; 12-10.30 Sun
☎ (01244) 674821
Hydes Original Bitter, seasonal beers; guest beers Ⓗ

Traditional pub in a residential area, enthusiastically managed and presented by a knowledgeable licensee and staff. Recently redecorated throughout to a high standard, the lounge and separate bar are both served from a central facility. The bar has a pool table, darts and other pub games, plus a large TV for sport. The Hydes beers are complemented by a changing ale mainly from a local micro. Beer festivals are held with a good variety of guest ales. ♨Q✿☒❧✦⚑⚏

Cellar
19-21 City Road, CH1 3AE
✪ 4-midnight; 12-2.30am Fri & Sat; 12-midnight Sun
☎ (01244) 318950 ⊕ thecellarchester.co.uk
Beer range varies Ⓗ
Despite its name, the public bar is a square space at street level. Sparse and random furniture includes high tables and stools, and there is plenty of standing space which fills up on live music nights: Wednesday, Friday and Saturday. Two TV screens show sport. The cellar itself has its own bar and is available for private parties. Three handpumps serve a changing range of ales and a wide selection of foreign beers is available. A simple menu is offered in the evenings. ❍❀☒

Mill Hotel Ⓛ
Milton Street, CH1 3NF (by canal E of inner ring road A51/A56 jct)
✪ 12-midnight (10.30 Sun) ☎ (01244) 350035
⊕ millhotel.com
Coach House Mill Premium; Copper Dragon Golden Pippin; Phoenix Corn Mill; guest beers Ⓗ
City-centre hotel housed in a former corn mill alongside the Shropshire Union Canal and dating from 1830. A large range of real ales is served from over a dozen handpumps in the single bar, including a guest mild and a guest real cider. Three plasma screens show sports. Food ranges from bar snacks to full restaurant fare. Outside, a small drinking and smoking area overlooks the canal. ✿❍⚇❀✦P⚑

Old Harkers Arms Ⓛ
1 Russell Street, CH3 5AL (down steps off City Road to canal towpath) SJ412666
✪ 11.30-11; 12-10.30 Sun ☎ (01244) 344525
⊕ harkersarms-chester.co.uk
Brunning & Price Original; Weetwood Cheshire Cat; guest beers Ⓗ
Upmarket pub converted from the ground floor of a former Victorian canalside warehouse. Timber flooring, traditional wooden furniture and cast iron pillars reflect its former use. Blackboards list the real ales with tasting notes – nine beers are usually available including a selection of bitters, stouts, milds and porters, many from local breweries. Ciders are listed separately and dispensed from the cellar. Food is served all day (booking advised for the busy weekend period). There is seating outside with views of the canal. Q✿❍⚇❀☒❀

Pied Bull Ⓛ
57 Northgate Street, CH1 2HQ
✪ 10-11 (midnight Fri & Sat) ☎ (01244) 325829
⊕ piedbull.co.uk
Adnams Broadside; guest beers Ⓗ
Characterful pub close to the city centre and cathedral, one of Chester's oldest hosteries. The owner and manager have transformed the beer offering from the bland to the eclectic. A wide range of ales, many from local microbreweries, is

now complemented by beers from the pub's own cellar brewery. Beer festivals are held every six months. Good-quality pub food is served throughout the day. ⌂⏹🍴♿♪⏏

Telford's Warehouse 🄻
Tower Wharf, CH1 4EZ (off Raymond Street)
✪ 12-11 (1am Wed; 12.30am Thu; 2am Fri & Sat); 12-1am Sun ☎ (01244) 390090 ⏣ telfordswarehousechester.com
Thwaites Original; Weetwood Cheshire Cat; guest beers Ⓗ
Converted warehouse with large picture windows overlooking the Shropshire Union Canal basin. An industrial crane dominates the bar area and changing artwork adorns the walls. The downstairs bar is open for live music evenings and the Wednesday salsa sessions. A restaurant on the first floor serves high-quality food and there is an outside drinking area next to the canal. Admission charges apply after 10pm at weekends and during some live events. Check the website for beer festival details. ❀⏹🍴⊟P⏏

Childer Thornton

White Lion ✪
New Road, CH66 5PU (off A41 between Great Sutton and Hooton)
✪ 11.30-11.30 (11 Mon) ☎ (0151) 339 3402
Thwaites Original, Bomber, Wainwright; guest beer Ⓗ
Excellent old village pub dating back to 1724 with the original inglenook fireplace in the bar. A friendly locals' atmosphere welcomes you in three cosy rooms where good-value bar meals are served. There are pleasant outdoor drinking areas at both the front and back of the pub. ⌂❀⏹🍴⊟P⏏

Congleton

Congleton Leisure Centre
Worrall Street, CW12 1DT
✪ 7-10.30; closed Sat & Sun ☎ (01270) 387717
Beer range varies Ⓗ
Municipal leisure centre bar open to all, not just those participating in sporting activities. Ales usually include one from Copper Dragon plus one or two more from microbreweries. Popular beer festivals are held in March and October with a range of 20 ales plus a couple of real ciders. The venue has a welcoming atmosphere, with local CAMRA newsletters by the bar and an array of pump clips on the walls. Five minutes' walk from the bus station. ♿⊟P

Counting House ✪
18 Swan Bank, CW12 1AH
✪ 8-midnight (1am Fri & Sat) ☎ (01260) 272654
Greene King Abbot; Ruddles Best Bitter; Shepherd Neame Spitfire; guest beer Ⓗ
Enjoy a pint in a former bank vault at this much-improved Wetherspoon town-centre bank conversion with a typical open-plan layout. Regular beer festivals and local and regional beers feature strongly, particularly from Beartown and Titanic. CAMRA members receive a 20 per cent discount on food, making the meals even more competitive. ⌂❀⏹🍴♿⊟P⏏

Lord Mountbatten 🄻
70 Mill Street, CW12 1AG (off Mountbatten Way)
✪ 12 (4 Mon-Thu) midnight ☎ (07811) 199902
Beer range varies Ⓗ

This is the Congleton pub with the widest range of constantly changing beers from microbreweries. The range is dispensed through six handpumps plus one cider pump. New breweries are given an outlet here, which they lose if the second brew does not match up. The focus is clearly on the beer offering, with rugby and football on TV coming an (important but) poor second. The owner manages and runs the pub and is happy to advise on local beers. ⌂Q❀❀⏹🍴♿⊟♣●P⏏

Queen's Head Hotel 🄻
Park Lane, CW12 3DE
✪ 12-midnight (1am Fri & Sat) ☎ (01260) 272546
⏣ queensheadpub.org.uk
Draught Bass; Joule's Bitter; guest beers Ⓗ
Probably the most improved pub in town. The beer quality is tip-top and with eight handpumps there is an even mix between regular ales and microbreweries' beers. Meals are cooked to order and available lunchtimes and evenings. The bar staff are knowledgeable and friendly. The gardens have been re-landscaped with the addition of a boules court – probably the only one in Cheshire. ⌂❀❀⌂⏹🍴♿⊟(99)♣●P⏏

Cotebrook

Fox & Barrel 🄻
Foxbank, CW6 9DZ SJ573659
✪ 12-11 (10.30 Sun) ☎ (01829) 760529
⏣ foxandbarrel.co.uk
Caledonian Deuchars IPA; Weetwood Eastgate Ale; guest beers Ⓗ
Friendly country pub with a welcoming, relaxed atmosphere and helpful staff. Dating from 1730, it was sensitively refurbished in traditional style several years ago. A central bar serves a number of rooms and alcoves, with dining and drinking throughout. Guest beers come from local breweries as well as further afield. Food is served all day until 9.30pm (9pm Sun). Outside is a terraced area and beer garden. ⌂Q❀⏹P

Crewe

Angel
2 Victoria Centre, CW1 2PU (below street level in Victoria Centre)
✪ 10-7 (10 Fri & Sat); closed Sun ☎ (01270) 212003
Oakwell Barnsley Bitter Ⓗ
Basement pub accessed by stairs from the main shopping area in the town centre. It is close to the bus station and a short bus ride or 20-minute walk from the railway station. A raised seating area overlooks the bar and pool table. A rare outlet for Oakwell Barnsley Bitter, both the beer and lunchtime home-cooked food are excellent value. The pub may close early on quiet evenings. ⏹≠⊟♣

Borough Arms 🄻
33 Earle Street, CW1 2BG (on Earle Street Bridge) SJ707557
✪ 5 (12 Fri & Sat)-11; 12-10.30 Sun ☎ (01270) 254999
⏣ borougharmscrewe.co.uk
Beer range varies Ⓗ
Friendly, popular free house near the town centre. A split-level single bar serves three distinct drinking areas. A further large room downstairs leads to a sheltered, walled beer garden. The absence of pool, music and gaming machines

encourages earnest conversation, and dominoes matches are played. Nine handpumps serve a wide range of ales, mainly from small and microbrewers. Pale, hoppier beers are the mainstay here, but darker beers make regular appearances. Home to the Borough Arms Brewery. Q ⶁ❀⊞(14)♣⌐☐

Hops ⓛ
8-10 Prince Albert Street, CW1 2DF
✪ 11 (5 Mon)-11.30; 12-11.30 Sun ☎ (01270) 211100
Townhouse Enigma; guest beers Ⓗ
Friendly, family-run free house, voted local CAMRA Pub of the Year 2011, in a quiet part of the town centre. It has a comfortable downstairs bar, more seating on the first floor, and outside space for fine weather. The Townhouse house beer is joined by four guest ales, usually from local microbreweries. A comprehensive range of Belgian beers, bottled and draught, is always available. Lunchtime meals are served Wednesday to Saturday. CAMRA members are offered a discount on real ale on Monday night. Q❀◑&≠⊞♣♠P

Crowton

Hare & Hounds ✔
Station Road, CW8 2RN SJ578745
✪ 12-3 (not Tue), 5 (7 Sat & Sun)-11 ☎ (01928) 788851
⊕ harenhounds.co.uk
Greene King IPA; guest beers Ⓗ
Cosy, friendly pub with three linked rooms. In winter there are warm open fires with free toast and forks on Tuesday evenings. A variety of changing guest beers is chosen from the Punch list. The annual Easter duck race on the garden stream raises £3,000 for local charities. Joe the landlord is easily spotted as he'll be wearing his chef's uniform. For the hardy smoker there is a covered table outside with space heating. No food Mondays or Tuesdays. ⚌Q❀◑➠⊞(48)P⌐

Culcheth

Cherry Tree ⓛ ✔
35 Common Lane, WA3 4EX (on B5207, 400yds from A574)
✪ 11-11 (midnight Fri & Sat); 12-11 Sun ☎ (01925) 762624
Greene King Abbot; Tetley Bitter; guest beers Ⓗ
Large open-plan pub with an emphasis on dining, offering a good choice of excellent-value food, served all day until 9.30pm. Three changing guest beers include at least one from a local brewery. Popular with families and sports fans for 3D TV, it hosts a quiz on Wednesday and discos on Fridays and Saturdays. The impressive covered smokers' area has a tree growing through the middle. There is a public car park at the rear – the ticket price will be refunded at the bar. ❀◑&⊞(19,28,28A)P⌐

Disley

White Lion ⓛ ✔
135 Buxton Road, SK12 2HA
✪ 11.30 (6.30 Mon)-11 (12.30am Fri & Sat); 12-11 Sun
☎ (01663) 762800 ⊕ whitelion-disley.co.uk
Buxton Moor Top; guest beers Ⓗ
Large pub on the A6 towards the easterly end of the village. It offers eight real ales; six are constantly changing beers from SIBA member microbreweries. The contemporary, largely open-plan interior has a separate dog room with

blankets, water bowls and canine dinners. A comprehensive and varied food menu is served all day until 9pm (no food Mon). Quiz night is Thursday and live entertainment is hosted on the last Saturday of the month. A short walk from Peak Forest Canal (bridge 26). ⚌❀◑➠⊞(199)P

Dutton

Tunnel Top ⓛ
Northwich Road, WA4 4JY
✪ 12-11 ☎ (01928) 718181 ⊕ tunneltop.co.uk
Beer range varies Ⓗ
Saved from closure in 2010, this pub has gone from strength to strength thanks to the dedication of Moira and Kevin. Specialising in beers from local breweries, regulars include Coach House and Frodsham. The pub was the first outlet for the Runcorn-based Norton Brewery, a brewing initiative run by adults with disabilities. Sports fans can watch their game on the giant 8ft screen in the separate pavilion bar. Food is also sourced locally and served in the restaurant. ⚌❀◑&P⌐

Frodsham

Helter Skelter ⓛ
31 Church Street, WA6 6PN SJ518777
✪ 11-11 (11.30 Fri & Sat); 12-10.30 Sun ☎ (01928) 733361
⊕ helterskelter-frodsham.co.uk
Weetwood Best Bitter; guest beers Ⓗ
Friendly and popular, this large single-room pub has eight handpumps serving the always-available Weetwood Best Bitter together with an ever-changing mix of local and new micro beers plus real ciders and perries. Food is available every day in the ground-floor bar and upstairs restaurant. Local CAMRA Pub of the Year and Cider Pub of the Year in 2011. ◑➠⊞(48,X30)♠⌐☐

Great Sankey

Chapel House
380 Liverpool Road, WA5 1RU
✪ 4 (3 Fri; 12 Sat & Sun)-midnight ☎ (01925) 488860
Beer range varies Ⓗ
Welcoming community pub with lively conversation from all age groups rising above the background music. It retains a traditional feel with a large lounge divided into two areas and a smaller bar. Four handpumps dispense beers from Timothy Taylor and Black Sheep accompanied by guest beers usually from microbreweries. Wednesday is pie night when football is screened in the smaller lounge. Outside is a delightful Mediterranean-style walled patio area full of flowers and a separate smokers' shelter. ❀⊞➠(Sankey)⊞(14,15)P⌐

Higher Burwardsley

Pheasant Inn ⓛ
Barracks Lane, CH3 9PF (off A41, follow Candle Workshop signs) SJ523566
✪ 11-11; 12-10.30 Sun ☎ (01829) 770434
⊕ thepheasantinn.co.uk
Weetwood Best, Eastgate, Old Dog; guest beers Ⓗ
Charming country inn nestling among the Peckforton Hills and ideally situated for hikers walking the Sandstone Trail or for visitors to the nearby Candle Workshops. The emphasis is on quality local ales and wholesome food prepared from fresh, locally sourced products. The guest ale

is from a Cheshire microbrewery. Outside seating offers magnificent views over the Cheshire Plain towards the Clwydian Hills. Accommodation is in 12 en-suite rooms. ⚑Q✿☕🍴⏰♿P

Houghton Green

Millhouse ⃝

Ballater Drive, WA2 0LX SJ623915
✿ 12-11 (11.30 Tue & Thu; midnight Fri & Sat)
☎ (01925) 831189
Holt Mild, IPA, Bitter; guest beers ⃞
Built in the 1980s to cater for the expanding new estates of North Warrington, this large two-roomed open-plan pub is a popular community local. It has a spacious bar/games room with darts, pool and 3D TV, and a large lounge where a quiz takes place on Tuesday and Thursday nights, and live music on Saturday. Food is served until 8pm (6pm Sun). ✿🍴🍽♿🚃(23,26)♣P⏚

Plough ⃝ ✓

Mill Lane, WA2 0SU (off Delph Lane) SJ622918
✿ 11.30-11 (11.30 Thu & Sat; midnight Fri); 12-11 Sun
☎ (01925) 815409
Moorhouse's Pride of Pendle; Thwaites Wainwright; Wells Bombardier; guest beers ⃞
Nestling in a cul-de-sac on the edge of north Warrington, this pub is popular for both beer and food. It offers up to five changing guest beers with a focus on local brewers such as Weetwood. The modern, open-plan interior complements the pub's 1774 origins. A large outdoor drinking/dining area is a further attraction. Food is served until 10pm (9pm Sun). Quiz night is Thursday with an occasional mega quiz on Saturday. Children are welcome until 9pm. ✿🍴♿🚃(23,26)P

Knutsford

Lord Eldon ⃝

27 Tatton Street, WA16 6AD
✿ 11-11 (midnight Thu-Sat); 12-10.30 Sun
☎ (01565) 652261
Tetley Bitter; guest beers ⃞
This 300-year-old pub with sundial and hanging baskets has a surprisingly spacious interior, with a large bar area with a real fire and three separate rooms leading from it. At the rear is a pleasant beer garden. Live music features twice a week, open mic on Thursday and live bands on Saturday. One of the guest ales is usually from a local brewery. ⚑Q🐕✿🍴☕♣⏚

Little Bollington

Swan with Two Nicks ⃝

Park Lane, WA14 4TJ (off A56)
✿ 12-11 (10.30 Sun) ☎ (0161) 928 2914
Black Sheep Best Bitter; Greene King Abbot; Taylor Landlord; guest beers ⃞
Welcoming country pub on the fringes of the Dunham Massey National Trust property. The interior is rustic and comprises several rooms with a central bar. Local beers feature on the seven beer engines, four usually from Dunham Massey Brewery. The house beer, Swan With Two Nicks, is from Coach House. There is a varied food offering including gluten-free dishes served in the pub and restaurant, available all day until 9pm (8pm Sun). Handy for canal boaters, and dogs are welcome. ⚑🐕✿🍴☕🚃(5,37,38)P⏚

Lower Stretton

Ring o' Bells

Northwich Road, WA4 4NZ SJ622818
✿ 12-2.30 (not Mon; 3.30 Thu), 5.30 (5 Thu)-11; 12-3.30, 5-midnight Fri; 6-11 Sat; 12-4, 7-10.30 Sun
☎ (01925) 730556
Tetley Bitter; Fuller's London Pride; guest beer ⃞
A traditional, unspoilt village local, just as pubs used to be – no music or games machines, just conversation and banter. The main room, served by a single bar, leads to two smaller rooms for quieter drinking. A quiz night is held on the first and third Mondays of the month when the pub gets very busy. Closed Monday and Saturday lunchtimes. ⚑Q✿🚃(45,46)♣P⏚

Macclesfield

Baths Hotel ⃝

40 Green Street, SK10 1JH
✿ 12-11 (midnight Fri & Sat; 10.30 Sun) ☎ (01625) 262884
🌐 bathshotel.com
Bowland Sawley Tempted; Taylor Landlord; guest beers ⃞
Friendly corner terrace pub situated just out of the town centre but within easy walk of the bus and rail stations. Now one of a growing number of free houses in the town, four handpumps supply two regular beers from Bowland and Tim Taylor and two guests, often LocAle, giving a good mixed range. Specials include pie and a pint on Monday and curry night on Wednesday. Comfy seating areas and real fires make for a relaxed feel. ⚑🐕✿≒🚃♣⏚

Dolphin ⃝

76 Windmill Street, SK11 7HS
✿ 5 (12 Sat)-11; 12-10.30 Sun ☎ (01625) 616179
Robinson's 1892, Dizzy Blonde, Unicorn, seasonal beers ⃞
Traditional family-run local pub close to a playing field and handy for the nearby canal locks. There is a large lounge area with an open fire in winter, a public bar and a small snug room useful for meetings. Five handpumps offer a range of beers including Old Tom in winter months and the Robinson's seasonal at all times. Local CAMRA Pub of the Year 2011. ⚑Q🐕✿♿🚃♣

Park Tavern ⃝ ✓

158 Park Lane, SK11 6UB
✿ 4 (12 Sat & Sun)-11 ☎ (01625) 667846
🌐 park-tavern.co.uk
Beer range varies ⃞
Typical town-centre pub built in 1825 with a large bar area and a separate panelled room. Renovated in a modern style and reopened by Bollington Brewing Company in 2011, it is now a free house. With five Bollington beers on the bar plus one guest and two real ciders, this has rapidly become a must-visit pub in Macclesfield. Curry nights are Wednesday and Thursday, and traditional roast lunch is served Sunday 12-6pm. 🐕✿♿≒🚃⏚

Treacle Tap ⃝

43 Sunderland Street, SK11 6JL
✿ 12-11 (midnight Thu-Sat) ☎ (01625) 615938
🌐 thetreacletap.co.uk
Beer range varies ⃞
Opened in late 2010, this pub is already a favourite, winning the local CAMRA Pub of the Season award in 2011. The narrow building has a

boarded floor, simple wooden tables and chairs, and a bar at the rear. One of the best pubs in the area for local beer, it serves three varying LocAles. Excellent pies are available all day. Acoustic music features on Sunday afternoons. Q☎◐≠🖾

Waters Green Tavern 🅛
96 Waters Green, SK11 6LH
🕑 12-3, 5.30 (7 Sat)-11; 12-3, 7-10.30 Sun
☎ (01625) 422653
Beer range varies Ⓗ
Award-winning pub close to both rail and bus stations – making it an ideal waiting room. Recently renovated, it is now a free house, although the pub still trades on its core strengths of beer quality and a welcoming atmosphere. Great-value home-cooked food is served lunchtimes (no food Sun). A choice of up to seven beers is offered from the north-west and beyond. ♨☺◐≠🖾♣👜🚲

Wharf 🅛
107 Brook Street, SK11 7AW
🕑 4 (12 Sat & Sun)-midnight ☎ (01625) 261879
🌐 the-wharf-macc.co.uk
Otter Bitter; guest beers Ⓗ
To the front is a lounge area with comfortable seating and a real stove in a fireplace surrounded by shelves with books and games. Behind the bar is an open wood-floored area with space for darts, pool, a TV and live music on Friday evenings. The three guest beers usually include a LocAle as well as others from further afield. A wide range of British and foreign bottles is also available. ♨☻☺≠🖾♣👜🚲

Marton

Davenport 🅛
Congleton Road, SK11 9HF
🕑 12-3 (not Mon), 6-11; 12-midnight Fri-Sun
☎ (01260) 224269 🌐 thedavenportarms.co.uk
Courage Directors; Theakston Black Bull; guest beers Ⓗ
A rural restaurant/pub, its reputation for food does not affect its ability to maintain superb quality real ale. As well as the regular real ales, the proprietors are keen to offer new beers from the rapidly expanding number of microbreweries. The staff are friendly and knowledgeable and the proprietors are always on hand for a chat. Recommended for that trip to the country. ♨Q☻☺◐♿🚲

Mobberley

Bull's Head 🅛 ✅
Mill Lane, WA16 7HX
🕑 12-11 (midnight Fri & Sat; 10.30 Sun) ☎ (01565) 873395
🌐 thebullsheadpub.co.uk
Weetwood 1812 Overture, Bull's Head Bitter, Mobberley Wobbly; guest beers Ⓗ
Excellent country inn whose cobbled frontage is a promise of the delights of the traditional decor within. Six Cheshire beers are part of the ethos of the pub, with the house beers brewed by Weetwood. The handpumps have tasting notes and tasters are offered to help you decide. Much of the good freshly cooked food is locally sourced. ♨☻☺◐🖾(88)♣👜🚲

Nantwich

Globe 🅛
100 Audlem Road, CW5 7EA (S of town centre)
🕑 12-11.30 (11 Sun) ☎ (01270) 623374
🌐 theglobenantwich.co.uk
Woodlands Globe Bitter, Drummer, Light Oak, Oak Beauty, Bitter, Generals Tipple Ⓗ
Nantwich brewery Woodlands acquired and totally refurbished its first tied house in 2007 to serve as the brewery tap. Ten handpumps usually offer the full range and seasonal specials, plus an additional guest beer sourced elsewhere. There is a comfortable bar and a large restaurant area where excellent home-cooked meals are served until 9pm (8pm Sun). This is a friendly local with occasional live music, TV for sporting events and other community activities. Wi-Fi is available on request. ♨☺◐≠🖾(73)P🚲

Northwich

Penny Black 🍷 🅛 ✅
110 Witton Street, CW9 5AB SJ661740
🕑 8-11 (midnight Thu; 1am Fri & Sat) ☎ (01606) 42029
Greene King Abbot; Ruddles Best Bitter; Tetley Bitter; guest beers Ⓗ
Wetherspoon has done an excellent job in bringing this Grade II-listed former post office, dating from 1914, back to life. LocAle accredited, Cheshire-brewed beers are often to be found on the bar as well as at least one darker beer (mild, stout or porter). Large and mainly open plan inside, TVs screen news channels with subtitles throughout the day. Free Wi-Fi is available. The car park is behind the pub off Meadow Street immediately after the Royal Mail sorting office. Local CAMRA Pub of the Year 2012. Q☻☺◐♿≠🖾(1,45,289)👜P🚲

Parkgate

Boat House
1 The Parade, CH64 6RN
🕑 12-11 (10.30 Sun) ☎ (0151) 336 4187
🌐 theboathouseparkgate.co.uk
Greene King Old Speckled Hen; Theakston Best Bitter; Weetwood Eastgate Ale; guest beer Ⓗ
Attractive half-timbered building on the Dee Estuary overlooking an RSPB nature reserve. Beware occasional high tides that lap right up to the pub walls. A folk club meets upstairs on the last Thursday of the month and a jazz group plays on Tuesday evening. Freshly prepared food is served in the bar area until 6pm and the restaurant is open until 9.30pm (9pm Sun). A haven for nature lovers, good beer and food fans alike. Two guest beers include at least one from Brimstage. Q☺◐♿🖾(272,487)P

Red Lion
The Parade, CH64 6SB
🕑 10.30-11; 12-10.30 Sun ☎ (0151) 336 1548
Courage Best Bitter; Tetley Bitter; Wychwood Hobgoblin Ⓗ
A traditional lounge and bar offering superb views of the Welsh hills across the Dee estuary and marsh (famous for bird life), with local numbers swelled by many summer promenaders. The pub has a lively cricket and Rugby Union following, and drinkers have the choice of joining in with match day festivities or retreating to the quiet of the secluded walled garden, which may be hired for functions. Q◐🖾(272,487)♣

Penketh

Ferry Tavern
Station Road, WA5 2UJ (across railway and canal from end of Station Rd) SJ563866
🍺 12-3, 5.30-11 (midnight Fri); 12-midnight Sat; 12-10.30 Sun ☎ (01925) 791117 ⊕ theferrytavern.com
Jennings Cumberland Ale; Ruddles County; Taylor Landlord; guest beers Ⓗ
Lying between the River Mersey and the St Helens Canal, the Ferry was first licensed in 1762. A single bar serves up to three guest ales plus three regular beers and a large selection of whiskies. To the right of the bar, a quiet lounge features photographs and information about the pub's 250 year history, mostly compiled by present licensee Andy. With the Transpennine Trail nearby, it is a popular stop-off for walkers and cyclists. ᴍQ🕸🍴🚆(32)🐾P

Poynton

Poynton British Legion Ⓛ
St George's Road West, SK12 1JY (off A523)
🍺 12-11 (midnight Fri & Sat); 12-10.30 Sun
☎ (01625) 873 120 ⊕ poyntonlegionclub.co.uk
Beer range varies Ⓗ
Spacious private members' club offering a minimum of four handpulled beers, two from the on-site Worth Brewery and two from micros. A comfortable and quiet lounge drinking area is complemented by a public bar area with two snooker tables and a large-screen TV. A function room and bowling green are available for hire. Monthly folk, quiz and jazz nights are hosted. For free entry show a CAMRA membership card or a copy of this Guide. 🕸🍴🚆♿≠♣🐾P⅃

Runcorn

Prospect 🍸 Ⓛ
Weston Road, Weston Village, WA7 4LD
🍺 12-11 (10.30 Sun) ☎ (01928) 561280
⊕ folkattheprospect.co.uk
Adnams Broadside; Taylor Landlord Ⓗ
A welcome return to the Guide for this traditional two-room pub on the outskirts of the village, serving a range of beers from three handpumps. This is the meeting place for a well-established local folk scene. The lounge area is decorated with pictures of the locality in times gone by, while the bar area has a more unusual decor featuring vinyl 45s and LPs. No food on Sunday evening. ᴍ🕸🍴🚆♿🚆(3A,3C)🐾P⅃

Sandbach

Lower Chequer Ⓛ
Crown Bank, CW11 1FW
🍺 12 (6 Mon-Wed; 5 Thu)-11 summer; 1 (6 Mon-Wed, 5 Thu)-11 winter; 12 (1 winter)-10.30 Sun ☎ 07932 943977
Beer range varies Ⓗ
A warm welcome is assured from the award-winning licensees who have rejuvenated this black and white timbered pub set back on the cobbled square. Dating from 1570, the interior has two rooms and outside there is seating to the front and a marquee and patio to the rear. Six real ales on offer, all from small breweries, with Beartown Kodiak Gold a regular plus other local and regional ales. A porter, mild or stout is always available as well as a cider and a perry. Q🕸🚆(38)🐾P⅃

Sarn

Queen's Head Ⓛ
Sarn Road, SY14 7LN (off B5069 Threapwood Road) SJ440447
🍺 closed Mon; 6-midnight; 12-11 Sun ☎ (01948) 770244
⊕ queensheadsarn.co.uk
Marston's Burton Bitter; Taylor Golden Best; guest beer Ⓗ
Village inn known locally as the Sarn, its covered outdoor patio is adjacent to a converted water mill on Wych Brook which marks the boundary of the Welsh border. Excellent-value home-cooked meals are served in the dining room while drinkers congregate in the convivial lounge. There is also a small games room. The guest beer is usually from a local microbrewery and the pub provides a rare outlet for Taylor's light mild. ᴍQ🕸🍴🚆♿🅰♣P⅃

Scholar Green

Rising Sun ✅
Station Road, ST7 3JT (off A34)
🍺 12-3, 5-11.30; 9.30-midnight Fri; 12-midnight Sat & Sun
☎ (01782) 776235 ⊕ risingsuncheshire.co.uk
Jennings Cocker Hoop; Marston's Burton Bitter, Pedigree Ⓗ
Welcoming pub nestling next to fields on the edge of the village, with a fine view up to Mow Cop. There is a comfortable seating area with a real fire around a central bar, with a wood-beamed ceiling adding to the homely feel. The landlord makes good use of the Marston's range, with two seasonal guest ales, often one from Ringwood, always available. A full range of good-value meals is served in the bar and adjoining restaurant. ᴍ🕸🍴♣P⅃

Spurstow

Yew Tree Ⓛ
Long Lane, CW6 9RD (E of A49 Bunbury)
🍺 12-11; 11-10.30 Sun ☎ 01829 260274
⊕ theyewtreebunbury.com
Merlin Merlin's Gold; Stonehouse Station Bitter; guest beers Ⓗ
Handsome, 19th-century village pub, the interior features real fires, old beams and a large circular bar. At least six real ales are on offer, including the two house beers. It offers an excellent menu with freshly made, locally sourced food from a seasonal menu. Numerous special events are hosted throughout the year. ᴍQ🕸🍴P

Sutton

Church House Ⓛ ✅
Church Lane, SK11 0DS
🍺 12-midnight ☎ (01260) 252436
Banks's Bitter; Black Sheep Best Bitter; Robinson's Unicorn; guest beer Ⓗ
A friendly pub frequented by a large number of locals, in a good position on the road to Langley village. It is also popular with walkers and cyclists as they explore nearby Macclesfield Forest. There are two regular cask ales plus three guests, mostly local, as well as draught cider on tap. It has three seating areas and a real fire. Families and dogs are welcome and there is a children's play area. Good home-cooked food is served daily. ᴍ🛏🕸🍴♿🅰(14)🐾P⅃

Sutton Hall [L]
Bullocks Lane, SK11 0HE
� 11.30-11; 12-10.30 Sun ☎ (01260) 253211
🌐 suttonhall.co.uk
Brunning & Price Original Bitter; Flowers Original; guest beers [H]
Splendid 480-year-old manor house set in its own grounds, close to the Macclesfield canal. Tastefully refurbished by Brunning & Price, it won the 2010 CAMRA National Pub Design Refurbishment Award. It is notable for its many secluded areas, snug, library and seven dining spaces. While there is a strong food focus, with an excellent menu, drinkers are most welcome to enjoy one of the five real ales on offer, often from local breweries. Complemented by lovely gardens, this is a real gem. ▲Q🏠🕭🕪🍺🚗P🖰

Swettenham

Swettenham Arms [L] ✅
Swettenham Village, Nr Congleton, CW12 2LF
🌍 12-11 ☎ (01477) 571284 🌐 swettenhamarms.co.uk
Beartown Kodiak Gold; Hydes Original; Sharp's Doom Bar; Taylor Landlord; guest beers [H]
Restaurant/pub offering a good mix of beers from national brewers and local microbreweries on six handpumps. Its beer policy includes active participation from its regulars regarding beer choice. Food is available throughout the day but there is plenty of room for those wishing to drink and not eat. The pub is adjacent to Sir Bernard Lovell's arboretum and good walking country.
▲🏠🕭🕪🍺🖰P🖰

Tushingham

Blue Bell Inn [L]
SY13 4QS (signed Bell o' t' Hill from A41) MR522455
🌍 closed Mon; 12-2, 6-11; 12-3, 7-11 Sun ☎ (01948) 662172
🌐 bluebellinn.net
Oakham JHB; Salopian Shropshire Gold; guest beers [H]
Magnificent timber-framed 17th-century pub with plenty of atmosphere. A cobbled front leads to an ancient front door. One wall in the dining room reveals part of the original wattle and daub. Well-behaved dogs are welcome. Four caravan pitches are available in the paddock.
▲Q🏠🕭🕪A♣P🖰

Warrington

Albion [L]
94 Battersby Lane, WA2 7EG (200yds N of A57/A49 jct)
🌍 12-midnight (1am Fri & Sat; 11 Sun) ☎ (01925) 231820
Beer range varies [H]
A large and imposing Victorian frontage bearing the initials of the previous ownership gives way to a more contemporary interior. The pub supports sports teams, a folk club and community activity, and hosts occasional live music. Beer festivals are held in May, August, October and over the Christmas period. No food Monday and Tuesday, evening meals Wednesday to Friday only. Local CAMRA Cider Pub of the Year 2012.
🕭🕪🚆🚋≈(Central)🚗♣🖰🖰⊟

Lower Angel [L]
27 Buttermarket Street, WA1 2LY
🌍 11-11 (midnight Sat); 12-4 Sun ☎ (01925) 653326
🌐 lowerangel.co.uk
Tetley Bitter; Tipsy Angel Mild; guest beers [H]
Small unspoilt Victorian gem, still decorated in Walkers of Warrington livery, with a friendly welcome for visitors. The two-roomed pub in the town centre has a traditional vault and lounge, and a new beer garden overlooking the Tipsy Angel Brewery. The main outlet for a growing range of Tipsy Angel brews, many produced to authentic Walkers recipes, there are eight handpumps dispensing an ever-changing range. The vault has a top shelf of more than 70 malt whiskies, many extremely rare. 🕭🚆≈(Central)🚗🖰

Tavern [L]
25 Church Street, WA1 2SS
🌍 2 (12 Sun)-11; 12-11.30 Fri & Sat ☎ 07789 151610
Beer range varies [H]
A regular Guide entry and main outlet for 4T's beers, the Tavern offers up to eight beers from micros and regional brewers far and wide. At the weekend four more real ales are usually available in the Tavern Music Bar next door. The single-room pub regularly features sport, particularly football and Rugby League, on several TV screens. A covered rear area with a TV is provided for smokers. A range of whiskies plus bottled Belgian beer is also available. 🕭≈(Central)🚗♣🖰

Widnes

Premier ✅
Albert Road, WA8 6JS (5 mins walk from Albert Square shopping precinct)
🌍 9am-midnight ☎ (0151) 422 4920
Greene King Abbot; Ruddles Best Bitter; Marston's Pedigree [H]
Typically spacious Wetherspoon conversion of a former cinema that closed in the 1960s. On the edge of the shopping area of Widnes, parking is difficult, but there is ample parking in the town centre. 🕪🚆🖰

Wilmslow

Bollin Fee [L] ✅
6-12 Swan Street, SK9 1HE
🌍 9-midnight (1am Thu; 2am Fri & Sat) ☎ (01625) 441850
Greene King Abbot; Ruddles Best Bitter; guest beer [H]
Recently refurbished Wetherspoon bar in the town centre and handy for the railway station. The beer range varies, with frequent guests from local breweries, and a popular beer festival is held the first week of every month. Weekend nights can be very busy. Outside, there are two beer gardens, both with smoking areas. Sky Freeview channels and free Wi Fi access are available.
Q🏠🕭🕪🚆≈🚗🖰

Winsford

Queen's Arms ✅
Dene Drive, CW7 1AT
🌍 9-midnight (1am Fri & Sat) ☎ (01606) 595350
Greene King Abbot; Ruddles Best Bitter; guest beers [H]
Classic Wetherspoon close to the Winsford Cross shopping centre and Asda store. It has TV screens at both ends of the bar room with the sound usually muted. There are comfortable seating and dining areas, a patio to the front and a roof terrace providing fresh air in the summer and, for the more hardy, winter. 🕭🕪🚗🖰

CORNWALL

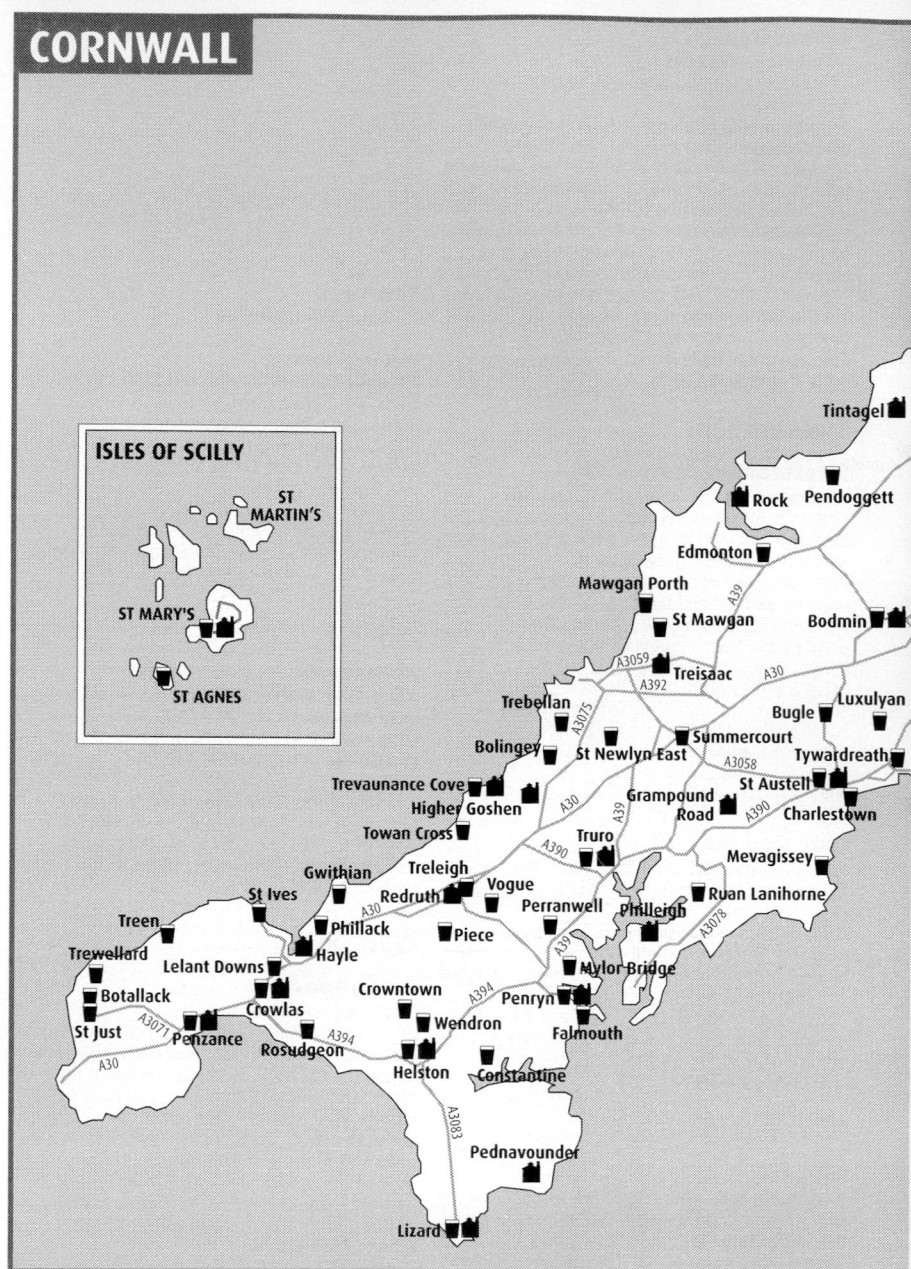

ISLES OF SCILLY

ST MARTIN'S

ST MARY'S

ST AGNES

Tintagel

Rock   Pendoggett

Edmonton

Mawgan Porth

St Mawgan   Bodmin

Treisaac

Trebellan   Bugle   Luxulyan

Bolingey   St Newlyn East   Summercourt   Tywardreath

Trevaunance Cove   Grampound   St Austell

Higher Goshen   Road   Charlestown

Towan Cross   Truro

Gwithian   Treleigh   Mevagissey

St Ives   Redruth   Vogue   Ruan Lanihorne

Treen   Perranwell   Philleigh

Trewellard   Phillack   Piece

Lelant Downs   Hayle

Botallack   Mylor Bridge

St Just   Crowlas   Crowntown   Penryn

Penzance   Rosudgeon   Wendron   Falmouth

Helston   Constantine

Pednavounder

Lizard

Altarnun

Rising Sun Inn ⃝

PL15 7SN (1 mile off A30, N of Five Lanes) SX216824

🕐 12-2.30, 5.30-11; 12-11 Sat; 12-10.30 Sun
☎ (01566) 86636 🌐 therisingsuninn.co.uk

Penpont St Nonna's, Cornish Gold; guest beers Ⓗ
Isolated, characterful, 16th-century building, a
community pub for 150 years, extending a warm,
friendly welcome. It offers up to four ales from the
local Penpont Brewery, two guest beers and real
cider from Skinner's. Open fires, slate floor,
beamed ceilings, old pictures and antique guns on

the walls all contribute to the atmosphere.
Deceptively spacious with a separate restaurant, it
also has a large patio and grassed area for outdoor
games including pétanque. Food is home cooked
using locally sourced produce. Children and dogs
are welcome. ⌂Q☞♨⌬♿♦▲♣☂Ⓟ⌐

Blisland

Blisland Inn ⃝

The Green, PL30 4JF (off A30 N of Bodmin)
🕐 11.30-11; 12-10.30 Sun ☎ (01208) 850739
Beer range varies Ⓗ/Ⓖ

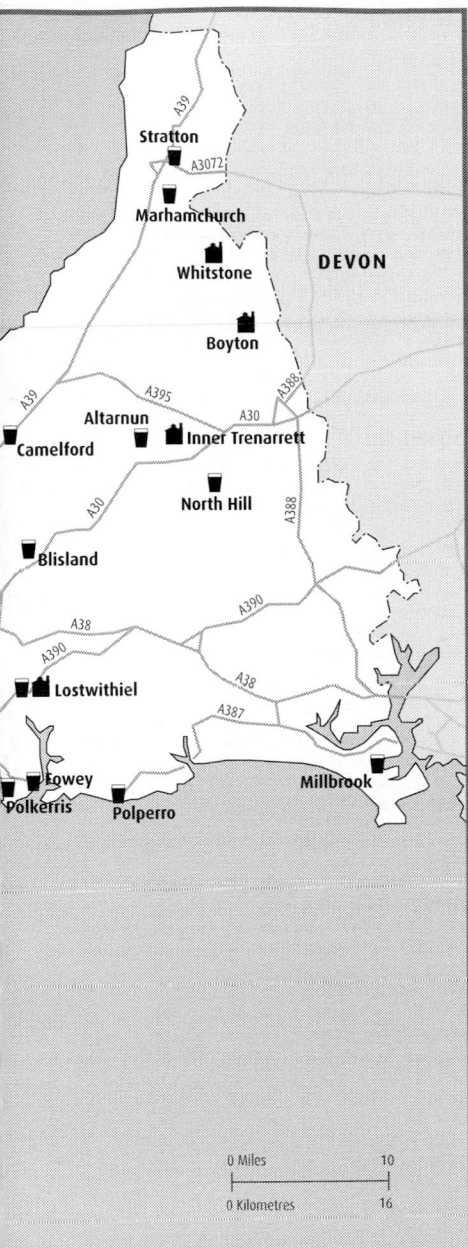

Set in an idyllic location on the green, the Blisland has so far served around 3,000 different real ales. Six or seven changing beers and real ciders, including more unusual varieties, are always available. Excellent freshly prepared food uses local produce. A friendly community inn, the pub is popular with walkers and cyclists. Well behaved children and dogs welcome. Q ⑤ ✿ ⓓ ⊞ ▲ ⊒ ♠ ⌐

Bodmin

Chapel an Gansblydhen L ✔
Fore Street, PL31 2HR SX068670

✿ 9-midnight ☎ (01208) 261730
Greene King Abbot; Ruddles Best Bitter; guest beers ⊞
This busy town-centre pub has been beautifully converted from a former Methodist chapel, with many original features restored and retained. The management is keen to support Cornish breweries and offers a good range of local and national ales and ciders. The pub pioneered the Wetherspoon Ale Club which meets every Wednesday and includes events such as Meet the Brewer visits, tutored tastings and 'guess the beer' competitions. Two beer festivals and a real cider festival are held annually. ⋒ Q ✿ ⓓ ⓺ ▲ ♠ ⌐

Masons Arms L
5-7 Higher Bore Street, PL31 1JS (top of town centre)
✿ 12-11.30 (11 Sun) ☎ (01208) 77442
Sharp's Doom Bar, Own; guest beers ⊞
Historic traditional two-bar free house, close to the Camel Trail. At least three ales are always on offer, with the emphasis on local Cornish breweries. Darts and dominoes are played and regular entertainment includes a quiz night on Tuesday, morris men on Thursday and a folk night on Friday. Two well-supported beer festivals are held each year. Wi-Fi is available. ⋒ Q ⑤ ✿ ⓺ ♣ P ⌐

Bolingey

Bolingey Inn L ✔
Penwartha Road, TR6 0DH SW763532
✿ 11-midnight (1am Fri & Sat); 12-11 Sun ☎ (01872) 571626
Sharp's Doom Bar; guest beers ⊞
There is always a warm welcome from the licensees at this quaint two-roomed village inn, with four beers on handpump from local breweries or the Punch Taverns current guest beer range. Two annual beer festivals maintain the interest. Substantial home-cooked meals are available. Worth seeking out, the pub is a short but well-hidden distance from the brighter lights of Perranporth and its excellent golden beach. The car park is small, but daytime buses are a short walk away. ⋒ Q ✿ ⓓ ▲ ⊒ (587) ♣ P ⌐

Botallack

Queen's Arms L
St Just, TR19 7QG (off B3306) SW368328
✿ 12-11.30 (12.30am Fri & Sat) ☎ (01736) 788318
⊕ queensarms-botallack.co.uk
Skinner's Heligan Honey; guest beers ⊞
A genuine welcome awaits at this charming family-run free house, situated in the heart of Penwith's copper and tin mining country and popular with coastal path walkers. The cosy single bar features an open fire and several distinct drinking and dining areas, with a family room at the rear; the homely decor depicts old local mining scenes. Up to four ales are available, usually from Cornish microbreweries, and good-quality food is served. An annual September beer festival is held. ⋒ Q ⑤ ✿ ⌂ ⓓ ▲ ⊒ (10,507) P ⌐

Bugle

Bugle Inn L ✔
57 Fore Street, PL26 8PB (on A391) SX015589
✿ 10-midnight (10.30 Sun) ☎ (01726) 850307
⊕ bugleinn.co.uk
St Austell Dartmoor Best, Trelawny, Tribute ⊞

Situated in the heart of clay country, this family-run village-centre pub is lively and welcoming. The comfortable, spacious interior accommodates a Z-shaped bar and dining room featuring open fires and an interesting collection of carved coconuts and witch effigies. Hearty meals including breakfast are available all day. With five en-suite rooms, this family-friendly pub provides an ideal base for visiting the nearby Eden Project. The pub is named for the sound of the horn of passing stagecoaches. ▲Q✿🚑◁◐)▲⇌🚃(529)♣P⌐

Camelford

Masons Arms
11 Market Place, PL32 9PB (on A39) SX106837
✪ 11-midnight ☎ (01840) 213309
St Austell Trelawny, Tribute, Proper Job 🅗
Family-friendly, unpretentious two-room town pub with open stone walls and low beamed ceilings, over 300 years old and popular with locals. The public is floored with tiles and wood, the lounge has a flagstone floor, and the pub is decorated with many interesting knick-knacks such as long-vanished domestic products, old toys and glass bottles suspended from the beams. Home-cooked meals include a selection of fresh fish. The spacious beer garden overlooks an early stage of the River Camel. Children and dogs on leads are welcome. ▲Q✿🚑◁◐)🖴🛆🚃(510,584,594)♣⌐

Charlestown

Harbourside Inn 🅛 ✅
Charlestown Road, PL25 3NJ (on harbour front) SX029516
✪ 11-11 (midnight Fri & Sat); 12-11 Sun ☎ (01726) 76955
⊕ pierhousehotel.com/harbourside_inn_in_cornwall.htm
Draught Bass; St Austell Tribute; Sharp's Doom Bar, Special; Skinner's Betty Stogs, Cornish Knocker 🅗
The old double doors of this former harbourside warehouse have been replaced by an extensive glass frontage, offering views of the tall ships moored in the harbour. The single-bar, split-level interior features exposed stonework and mixed slate and wood flooring, and wooden furnishings throughout. Up to seven ales are offered even in mid-winter, and good value locally sourced food is served throughout the day. Live music plays on Saturday evenings and there is a big-screen TV for sports fans. ✿🚑◁◐)▲🚃(525)♣⌐

Constantine

Trengilly Wartha Inn 🅛
Nancenoy, TR11 5RP (off B329 near Constantine) SW732283
✪ 11-3, 6-midnight; 12-midnight Sat & Sun
☎ (01326) 340332 ⊕ trengilly.co.uk
Beer range varies 🅗
Friendly, versatile, converted farmhouse, hidden down a pretty, steeply-wooded valley – its name means 'settlement above the trees'. It has a bar, snug and restaurant, with a conservatory extension serving as a family room. Up to three real ales are offered, mainly from Cornish breweries. Winner of many awards, the Trengilly's main emphasis is on fresh food – its wide-ranging and imaginative menu is prepared where possible with local produce, and summer barbecues are a highlight. Accommodation is above the pub or in garden rooms. ▲Q🌣🚑◁◐)♣P⌐

Crowlas

Star Inn 🅛
TR20 8DX (on A30 just E of Penzance)
✪ 11.30-11; 12-10.30 Sun ☎ (01736) 740375
Penzance Crowlas Bitter, Potion No 9; guest beers 🅗
Local CAMRA Pub of the Year for two years running, this red-brick roadside village free house is an ale drinker's paradise. The single long bar is festooned with handpumps, dispensing beers from the pub's microbrewery. There is a raised seating area to the right, and a pool table. A real locals' pub, beer quality reigns supreme and conversation abounds – no music, TV or noisy machines. Best to come by bus (stop nearby), as you will linger a while. Q✿🚃(17,18)P⌐

Crowntown

Crown Inn
TR13 0AD (on B3303 between Camborne and Helston) SW637309
✪ 5.30-11; 7-10.30 Sun ☎ (01326) 565538
⊕ crownlodges.co.uk
Beer range varies 🅗
Spacious granite community pub, once a Trevarno estate hunting lodge and about 250 years old. There are several distinct drinking areas, a dining area (with old Gothic arched doorway), and a separate space for the pool table. The varied choice of beers is mainly but not exclusively Cornish, dispensed by gravity straight from the cellar despite the array of four handpumps. The real cider is from Westons. An interesting collection of beer mats and tankards festoons the beams. Accommodation is in four en-suite lodges. ✿🚑◐)🖧♣🖤P⌐

Edmonton

Quarryman Inn 🅛
PL27 7JA (off A39 near Royal Cornwall Showground) SW965727
✪ 12-11 ☎ (01208) 816444
Beer range varies 🅗

Conversation and banter thrive in this characterful and convivial free house, where mobile phone usage is prohibited. Frequented by locals and tourists alike, the quiet, comfortable interior divides into public bar and lounge with dining area. Local art features among the somewhat eclectic decor. An ever-changing beer menu offers up to four quality ales and the excellent meals feature locally sourced produce. A diversion to this ever-popular gem of a pub close to the county showground well rewards the effort.
ᗰQ❀☗♨◑❄❖♿☷(510,555,594)♣●P╘╴

Falmouth

Chain Locker ✪
Lower Quay Hill, TR11 3HH (off Arwenack St) SW811326
❂ 11-11 (midnight Sat); 12-11 Sun ☎ (01326) 311085
Sharp's Doom Bar, Special; Skinner's Heligan Honey, Cornish Knocker Ⓗ; guest beer Ⓗ/Ⓖ
Harbourside pub tucked down a side street, overlooking Custom House Quay. The main bar is on split levels, with a rectangular near-island bar, and several distinct drinking areas. Subdued lighting, wooden floors, maritime bric-a-brac and a collection of ships' wheels in the ceiling add to the atmosphere of this old pub, long a favourite with visiting sailors of all nations. The secondary Shipwrights Bar opens in summer and on special occasions. Food is served all day, families welcome. Westons Old Rosie is the real cider.
❀◑≢(Town)☷♣●╘╴

Front ♈ Ⓛ
Custom House Quay, TR11 3JT (behind Trago Mills) SW811325
❂ 11-11.30 (midnight Fri & Sat); 11-11 Sun
☎ (01326) 212168 ⊕ thefrontfalmouth.co.uk
Beer range varies Ⓗ/Ⓖ
A little gem of a pub with a bare wood floor, low vaulted ceiling and dark interior, popular with students, locals and holidaymakers. The bar offers several hand-pulled beers, while a separate stillage dispenses beers straight from the cask – a mix of brews from Skinner's and other microbreweries both local and out of county. A selection of ciders and alcoholic ginger beer is also on offer. No food is served but you can bring your own. Finalist CAMRA National Pub of the Year in 2011. ❀≢(Town)☷●

Seven Stars ★
The Moor, TR11 3QA
❂ 11-3 (4 Fri & Sat), 6-11; 12-3, 7-10.30 Sun
☎ (01326) 312111
Draught Bass; Sharp's Special; Skinner's Cornish Knocker; guest beers Ⓖ
Grade II-listed, unspoilt town-centre drinkers' pub, family run and handed down from generation to generation. The interior comprises a narrow tap room to the front, a quieter snug to the rear, and corridor with the original 'bottle and jug' hatch. Note the eclectic collection of key fobs and mobile phones nailed to the beams – be warned! No food, but you may eat your own on benches outside.
Q❀☗≢(Town)☷╘╴

Fowey

Galleon Inn
12 Fore Street, PL23 1AQ

❂ 10 (12 Sun)-11 (midnight summer) ☎ (01726) 833014
⊕ galleon-inn.co.uk
Sharp's Cornish Coaster, Doom Bar; guest beers Ⓗ
Riverside pub in the town centre dating back 400 years, reached off Fore Street through a glass-covered corridor with a colourful marine life mural. The only free house in Fowey, it features mainly Cornish real ales and boasts delightful harbour views from the modernised main bar and conservatory dining area. Tables outside overlook the water and there is a heated, sheltered courtyard. A wide range of meals is available daily. Accommodation is en suite, with some rooms offering river views. ᗰQ❀☗♨◑❄☷(25,524)╘╴

Gwithian

Red River Inn Ⓛ
1 Prosper Hill, TR27 5BW SW586411
❂ closed Mon winter; 12-2, 5.30-11; 12-11 Sat & Sun
☎ (01736) 753223 ⊕ red-river-inn.co.uk
Sharp's Own; guest beers Ⓗ
Community-oriented, family-friendly free house, worth seeking out near the sand dunes of Hayle Towans. The quiet, relaxing single-bar interior, with separate dining areas, has wooden flooring, panelling and a wood-burning stove. Freshly cooked food is available daily. Two beers are always Cornish, served alongside up to three changing guest ales. Occasional beer festivals are held. The name refers to the nearby river which once ran red with waste from the area's mines.
ᗰQ❀◑❄⬥☷(515,547)♣P╘╴

Helston

Blue Anchor
50 Coinagehall Street, TR13 8EL SW658274
❂ 10.30-midnight (11 Sun) ☎ (01326) 562821
⊕ spingoales.com
Blue Anchor Spingo Jubilee IPA, Middle, Special, seasonal beer Ⓗ
More than 600 years old, this is one of the oldest brewpubs in Britain. The pub has changed little over the years and maintains much of its original character, with two small bars to the right and a sitting room to the left, all with worn granite floors. At the rear is a skittle alley and partly covered garden and barbecue, both with bars. Note the anchor on the thatched roof. Regular live entertainment, beer festivals and charity events are hosted throughout the year.
Q⍾❀☗☷(2,34)♣╘╴

Lelant Downs

Watermill Inn Ⓛ
Old Coach Road, TR27 6LQ (off A3074, on secondary St Ives road) SW541364
❂ 12-11 ☎ (01736) 757912
Sharp's Doom Bar; Skinner's Betty Stogs; guest beer Ⓗ
Standing in beautiful surroundings near Lelant Saltings station, this 18th-century former mill house is now a family-friendly two-storey free house offering three local ales. The original working watermill complete with millstones features downstairs in the traditionally styled single bar, separated into drinking and dining areas where bar meals are served. Upstairs, the former mill loft functions as a stylish evenings-only restaurant. Two beer festivals are held annually in

the extensive beer garden which straddles the mill stream. Live music plays on Friday nights.
♨Q❀◑⛺⇌(Saltings)🚌(14,17)P⚟

Lizard

Witch Ball

TR12 7NJ SW704125
⏲ 12 (5 Mon-Wed)-11 winter; 12-11 (midnight Sat) summer; 12-11 Sun ☎ (01326) 290662 🌐 witchball.co.uk
St Austell Dartmoor Best Bitter, Tribute; guest beer 🄷
Originally a 15th-century cottage, this is now a cosy family- and dog-friendly pub with bar, snug and dining room. Situated in the picturesque, remote Lizard village, it is the most southerly pub in mainland Britain, handy for the South West Coastal Path. The guest beer may be Cornish Chough Witch Ball or something from Sharp's or Skinner's. Good meals are available March to January, with seafood the speciality. A beer festival is held in August. Closing time varies in winter.
♨Q🐴❀◑♿⛺🚌(37)♣⚟

Lostwithiel

Globe Inn 🄻

3 North Street, PL22 0EG SX105598
⏲ 12-2.30, 6-11; 12-midnight Fri & Sat ☎ (01208) 872501
🌐 globeinn.com
Sharp's Doom Bar; Skinner's Betty Stogs; guest beers 🄷
Cosy 13th-century pub close to the railway station and medieval bridge, nestling in the narrow streets of this former stannary town. An interesting, somewhat rambling old building, it accommodates a single bar encompassing several drinking and dining areas, with an intimate restaurant and sheltered suntrap patio to the rear. The beer range includes up to two guests, mainly from microbreweries. The extensive home-cooked menu uses seasonal local produce, offering fish and game specialities. All accommodation is en suite. ♨Q❀🛏◑⛺⇌♣⚟

Luxulyan

King's Arms ✔

Bridges, PL30 5EF (4½ miles N of St Austell) SX048580
⏲ 10-midnight Mar-Oct; 11-11 (midnight Fri & Sat) Nov-Feb; 11.30-midnight Sun ☎ (01726) 850202
St Austell Trelawny, Tribute, HSD, seasonal beer 🄷
Granite inn, known locally as Bridges, with one large L-shaped room divided into drinking and dining areas in what were once the public bar and lounge, and a skittle alley in an outbuilding. The pub offers breakfast from 8.30am to noon in summer, and a take-away service. Nearby are the beautiful Luxulyan Valley, famous for its wildlife and industrial archaeology, and the Eden Project. The King's Arms is a stop on the Atlantic Coast Line Rail Ale Trail. Q❀◑♿⛺⇌🚌(523)♣P⚟

Marhamchurch

Buller's Arms Hotel 🄻 ✔

EX23 0HB (off A39 south of Bude) SS225036
⏲ 11-11 (midnight Fri & Sat) ☎ (01288) 361277
🌐 bullersarms.co.uk
Greene King Abbot; Tintagel Castle Gold; guest beers 🄷
Popular village centre pub and hotel with a spacious, L-shaped bar, beamed ceilings and a slate-flagged floor. The main Hunters Bar is well-appointed and doubles as a dining area, with a games area at one end of the room. One guest ale is always available, alternating between Skinner's Betty Stogs and Sharp's Doom Bar; another appears in summer. General Buller's Gold, the house beer, is Castle Gold rebadged. The pub has a reputation for good food and features regular live weekend entertainment. ♨Q❀🛏◑♿⛺🚌(518)♣P⚟

Mawgan Porth

Merrymoor 🄻 ✔

TR8 4BA (beside B3276 coast road)
⏲ 10-11.30 ☎ (01637) 860258 🌐 merrymoorinn.com
St Austell Tribute; Sharp's Doom Bar, Own; guest beers 🄷
Atmospheric pub run by the same family since 1961. The spacious main bar with its picture windows overlooking the sandy beach just 50 yards away is supplemented by a separate family room and large beer garden. Locally sourced food is cooked on the premises, with a carvery on Sundays. This pub is at the heart of the local community and raises large sums for charity every year. There is ample parking and accommodation in seven en-suite rooms.
Q🐴❀🛏◑♿⛺🚌(556)P⚟

Mevagissey

Fountain Inn ✔

3 Cliff Street, PL26 6QH
⏲ 12-midnight ☎ (01726) 842320
St Austell Dartmoor Best Bitter, Tribute, HSD 🄷
Friendly two-bar 15th-century inn near the harbour, with slate floors, stone walls and low beamed ceilings. The decor includes historic photographs and illustrations of old Mevagissey. The Smugglers Bar once housed a pilchard press – a glass plate in the floor covers the pit where the fish oil was collected, which also served as a store for contraband. The varied menu offers a range of home-cooked dishes. Nearby buses run to St Austell and the Lost Gardens of Heligan.
♨Q🛏◑⚓🚌(26,526)♣

Millbrook

Devon & Cornwall ✔

West Street, PL10 1AA (near B3247) SX422520
⏲ 12 (3 Mon-Thu)-11 ☎ (01752) 822320
Courage Directors; Otter Bitter; guest beer 🄷
Tucked away in Cornwall's 'forgotten corner', this convivial single-bar local is in the village centre. The seating area at one end of the L-shaped bar is warmed with an open fire and furnished comfortably with a mix of sofas, benches and chairs; at the other end, a partly-screened space is available for more private dining and drinking. Essentially a locals' pub, visitors are nonetheless warmly welcomed, with conversation the main entertainment. Cooked meals are served (not Mon or winter weekday lunchtimes).
Q❀🛏◑⛺🚌(81)♣⚟

Mylor Bridge

Lemon Arms ✔

Lemon Hill, TR11 5NA (off A393 at Penryn) SW804362
⏲ 11-3, 6.30-11; 12-3, 7-11 Sun ☎ (01326) 373666
St Austell Trelawny, Tribute, Proper Job 🄷

There has been a hostelry on this site since 1765. Once called the Griffin Inn, it became the Red Lion in 1829 and took its present name in 1837. A friendly one-bar pub in the centre of the village, it is home to local sports teams. Good home-cooked food is available (booking for the popular Sunday lunches is advisable). Families with children are made most welcome. Daytime buses run from Falmouth and Truro during the week.
ﾙ✿◑🖳(500)♣P⅃–

North Hill

Racehorse Inn
PL15 7PG (off B3254) SX273766
✪ 12-3, 6.30-11 ☎ (01566) 786916
⊕ theracehorseinn-cornwall.co.uk
St Austell Tribute; Sharp's Doom Bar; Tintagel Gull Rock, seasonal beer ℍ
Delightfully situated at the foot of Hawk's Tor in the heart of beautiful Cornish countryside, the Racehorse is a welcoming community pub, popular with locals and walkers alike. Formerly the village school, it is believed to be over 300 years old. It has a large single bar with distinct drinking areas separated by a wooden screen, and a separate restaurant, or you can eat in the bar. Excellent home-cooked food features locally sourced ingredients. Winter opening hours vary.
ﾙQ✿🖂◑🕭♣P⅃–🕯

Pendoggett

Cornish Arms 🅛
St Kew, PL30 3HH (on B3314) SX024794
✪ 11-11 (11-2, 5-11 Mon-Fri winter) ☎ (01208) 880263
⊕ cornisharms.com
Sharp's Doom Bar, PSB; guest beer ℍ
Picturesque family-run free house, welcoming and family friendly. Full of charm and character, the atmospheric interior comprises a main bar, snug, two drinking and dining areas and a restaurant. Quiet and cosy, the flagstoned floors, open beams, wooden panels, open fire, partitions and furnishings reflect the pub's origins as a 16th-century coaching inn. Caricatures of locals adorn the walls, and a handbell collection hangs over the bar. English and Thai cuisines are offered, with Thai banquets held monthly. ﾙQ✿🖂◑ⅈ♣●P⅃–

Penryn

Seven Stars
73 The Terrace, TR10 8EL SW784344
✪ 11 (12 Sun)-11 ☎ (01326) 373573
Blue Anchor Spingo Middle; Skinner's Betty Stogs, Heligan Honey; guest beers ℍ
The nearest thing Penryn has to an ale house, this single-bar town pub is run by a jovial Dutchman. Decorated with foreign cash, postcards and beer-related clippings, the spacious interior has a raised, comfortably furnished drinking annexe at the rear, dominated by a huge ship's wheel. The pub is home to the Penryn Community Theatre, who entertain with plays and pantos. A piano is available for competent pianists and occasional live music is performed. The Skinner's beer selection may vary and Press Gang cider is available.
ﾙ✿🛪🖳●⅃–

Penzance

Admiral Benbow
46 Chapel Street, TR18 4AF SW473301
✪ 11-11; 12-10.30 Sun ☎ (01736) 363448
St Austell Proper Job; Sharp's Doom Bar; guest beer ℍ
A short walk from the town centre takes you to this quirky but cosy low-ceilinged pub with its many nooks, crannies and separate drinking areas. The narrow frontage and bar area belie its Tardis-like interior, which extends way back and includes the Wreck Bar upstairs. Extensive nautical bric-a-brac is mostly salvaged from wrecks over the past 400 years. The St Austell ale may vary, with one Cornish guest beer offered in the busier summer months. Good, well-priced food is available. ◑🕭🖳●⅃–

Crown Inn
Victoria Square, TR18 2EP SW474305
✪ 12-midnight (12.30am Fri & Sat) ☎ (01736) 351070
⊕ thecrownpenzance.co.uk
Cornish Crown Bitter; Otter Ale; Skinner's Heligan Honey ℍ
Close to the bus and railway stations, and brewery tap for the Cornish Crown Brewery, this small, traditional community pub offers a relaxing atmosphere. Tucked away behind the main shopping street, the pub has a tidily furnished single bar with upholstered window seats and huge mirror covering one wall, and a cosy two-table snug at the rear. Three real ales are available including one from the Crown's own portfolio and one from Skinner's. Food is served Wednesday to Saturday, with Sunday roast. ﾙQ✿◑ⅈ🛪🖳♣–

First & Last Inn
24 Alverton Road, TR18 4TN SW470301
✪ 10.30-11; 12-10.30 Sun ☎ (01736) 364095
Beer range varies ℍ
A 10-minute-walk from the centre of Penzance, this Victorian establishment once called Mr Tonkin's Alehouse is now a two-bar town pub. Bare wood floors and part-wooden walls adorned with old pictures of the area add to its character. Up to five ales are mainly from Cornish and up-country microbreweries. The pub is popular with locals, full of lively chat and the occasional live band. There is a seating/dining area in the right-hand bar (no food Mon or Sat). Q✿◑🖾🛪🖳(5,6,512)♣

Perranwell

Royal Oak 🅛
TR3 7PX
✪ 11-3, 6-11; 12-3, 7-10.30 Sun ☎ (01872) 863175
Skinner's Betty Stogs; guest beers ℍ
At first sight this looks more of a restaurant than a pub, but do not be put off. Although food is important here, this 18th-century cottage-style inn is also a thriving village hub where drinkers are made welcome, the small bar area becoming quite crowded in the evenings. As well as quality food and wine (bookings advisable), the beers are also an attraction; at least two handpumps dispense Cornish brews, which may vary. On the Maritime Line rail ale trail. Q✿◑🛪🖳(82,500,543)P⅃–

Phillack

Bucket of Blood ✅
14 Churchtown Road, TR27 5AE SW563383

✪ 11-2.30 (not Mon-Wed winter), 5.30 (6 winter)-11 (midnight Fri & Sat); 12-4, 5.30 (7 winter)-11 Sun ☎ (01736) 752378 ⊕ bucketofblood.co.uk
St Austell Dartmoor Best Bitter, Black Prince, HSD Ⓗ
Gory legend (involving a well and a body) explains the name of this haunted old pub near the dunes of Hayle Towans. The single bar hosts a pool table at one end and a cosy drinking and dining area at the other, with settles and an old fireplace. A mural depicting St Ives Bay overlooks the pool table. 'Familiarity breeds contempt' written on one of the low beams is a warning rather than a proverb! The pub is dog-friendly. No food November-Easter.
🅼✿🅒🄳Å♣P⅃—

Piece

Countryman Inn
TR16 6SG (on Four Lanes-Pool road) SW679398
✪ 11-11 (midnight Sat); 12-11 Sun ☎ (01209) 215960
Greene King Old Speckled Hen; Sharp's Doom Bar; Skinner's Betty Stogs, Heligan Honey; Theakston Old Peculier; guest beers Ⓗ
A former miners' shop near the distinctive landmark of Carn Brea, residents of nearby towns are irresistibly drawn to this popular pub for its mix of good beer and entertainment. An array of nine handpumps offers a fairly static beer range, although the Skinner's beers may vary. Entertainment, in the larger of the two bars, includes live groups, karaoke, quizzes and a charity auction on Sunday lunchtime. Good-value pub grub is available all day. 🅼✿🅒🄳🖢Å🚃(442)♣P⅃—

Polkerris

Rashleigh Inn Ⓛ
PL24 2TL (off A3082 Par-Fowey road) SX094522
✪ 11-11; 12-10.30 Sun ☎ (01726) 813991
⊕ rashleighinnpolkerris.co.uk
Otter Bitter; Skinner's Betty Stogs; Taylor Landlord; guest beers Ⓗ
Former 18th-century pilchard boathouse in a one-time fishing hamlet, beside a secluded beach near the Saint's Way footpath. Now a family-run free house, its atmospheric interior features exposed stonework, beamed ceilings, open fires, comfortable furnishings and a splendid slate-topped bar. In summer, up to six ales may be available. Piano-accompanied singalongs are held on Saturday evenings. Dogs on leads are allowed in the bar. A sheltered terrace affords panoramic views of St Austell Bay. 🅼Q✿🅒🄳Å♣P⅃—

Polperro

Blue Peter Inn Ⓛ
Quay Road, PL13 2QZ SX210509
✪ 8.30-11 (10.30 Sun) ☎ (01503) 272743
⊕ thebluepeterinn.co.uk
Beer range varies Ⓗ
Named after the naval flag, this friendly inn is reached via a flight of steps near the quay, and is the only pub with a sea view in the village. It offers up to five real ales in summer, mainly from Cornwall and the South West, with cider from Cornish Orchards, and a varied menu of home-cooked dishes including breakfast. Low beams and wooden floors are decorated with unusual souvenirs, breweriana and work by local artists. The pub is popular with visitors, locals, fishermen – and their dogs. 🅼🅒🄳Å🚃(573)♣🖢

Crumplehorn Inn Ⓛ
The Old Mill, PL13 2RJ (at end of A387) SX205515
✪ 11-11; 12-10.30 Sun ☎ (01503) 272348
⊕ crumplehorn-inn.co.uk
St Austell Tribute; guest beers Ⓗ
Once a mill and mentioned in the Domesday Book, this 14th-century inn at the village entrance has a fine working waterwheel outside. Inside, the split-level bar is divided into three comfortable areas with flagstone floors and low ceilings. Guest beers are usually Cornish, and the menu features locally caught fish. A spacious outdoor patio by the millstream offers large umbrellas for protection from the sun. B&B and self-catering accommodation are available. In summer catch the milk float tram down to the harbour.
🅼Q✿🚪🅒🄳Å🚃(573)♣

Rosudgeon

Falmouth Packet Ⓛ
TR20 9QE (on A394 Penzance-Helston road) SW558296
✪ 12-2.30, 6-11; 12-11 Fri-Sun ☎ (01736) 762240
⊕ falmouthpacketinn.co.uk
Penzance Jolly Farmer, Tater Du; guest beers Ⓗ
This vibrant family-run free house enjoys a growing reputation for fine ales and excellent cuisine. The open fire, exposed stonework, slate floors and wooden furnishings add character to the quiet single-bar interior, which divides into drinking and dining areas. Comfortable throughout, an adjoining conservatory provides additional drinking/dining space, as does the patio garden, weather permitting. Up to two guest beers feature alongside the exclusive regular Penzance ales. The real cider is from Skreach. Local produce is sourced for an imaginative menu. A two-bedroomed holiday let is available.
🅼Q✿🚪🅒🄳🖢Å🚃(2, 2A)🖢P⅃—

Ruan Lanihorne

King's Head Inn Ⓛ
TR2 5NX (off A3078 at Tregony) SW895420
✪ closed Mon Easter-Oct; 12-2.30, 6-11; 12-2.30, 6-11 (12-4 winter) Sun ☎ (01872) 501263 ⊕ kingsheadruan.co.uk
Skinner's Betty Stogs, Cornish Knocker Ⓗ
Situated within the Roseland Peninsula, this delightful, traditional, family-run free house enjoys a burgeoning reputation for fine ales and superb meals. The quiet, characterful, homely interior accommodates two dining areas and the bar, offering up to four Skinner's ales including the house beer, Kings Ruan. A cosy ambience is created by the open fires, comfortable furnishings and rural decor. An adjacent sun terrace and quaint sunken garden offer a picturesque setting for alfresco dining and drinking. 🅼Q✿🅒🄳ÅP⅃—

St Agnes: Isles of Scilly

Turk's Head
TR22 0PL (close to landing stage) SV884085
✪ 11-4.30, 7-11 (11-11 Jul & Aug); 12-4.30, 7-10.30 (12-11 Jul & Aug) Sun ☎ (01720) 422434
St Austell Tribute; guest beers Ⓗ
The island's only pub, with a traditionally styled beamed interior and outdoor drinking areas unrivalled for their stunning scenery. Hours may vary according to boat times, but the jetty is nearby and you can watch your boat approaching from the bar. Summer evening boats run from St Mary's to

sample the ale and food. The Tribute is sold as house beer Turk's Ale, and up to two guest ales are usually Cornish. Order lunchtime pasties early! Phone to check winter opening times. ☎❀⑪♦▲♣

St Austell

Rann Wartha Ⓛ ✅
9 Biddick's Court, PL25 5EW
❀9am-midnight ☎ (01726) 222940
Ruddles Best Bitter; Greene King Abbot; guest beers Ⓗ
Popular town-centre Wetherspoon appealing to all ages and families, offering a varying selection of beers including Cornish brews. The bar is L-shaped, with a quiet area for family meals. Walls are extensively decorated with pictures of local historic people and the area's clay industry. The pub's Cornish name means Higher Quarter, relating to its position in the town. There is excellent disabled access, with a ramp, lift, wide main door and lift to the toilets. Parking is in the adjacent public car park. ▲Q❀⑪♿☵☲⌐

St Ives

Castle Inn
Fore Street, TR26 1AB
❀11 (12 winter & Sun)-11 ☎ (01736) 796833
Beer range varies Ⓗ
In the town centre, this pub is thought to have once formed part of the Union Castle shipping line offices. There is always a Skinner's beer or two here, and a number of guest ales (up to seven in summer), dispensed either by gravity or handpump. The comfortable single bar is characterful, with numerous nautical artefacts depicting the past. A busy pub with broad-based local support, its atmosphere is relaxing and welcoming. Good pub grub is available, though the emphasis here is more on the beer. Cider is from Cornish Orchards. Q⑪☵☲♣

St Just

Star Inn ✅
1 Fore Street, TR19 7LL SW371314
❀11.30-midnight (11.30 Sun) ☎ (01736) 788767
⊕ thestarinn-stjust.co.uk
St Austell Dartmoor Best Bitter, Tribute, Proper Job, seasonal beer Ⓗ
Reputedly the oldest pub in town, this 18th-century granite inn is a proper drinkers' pub, a timeless place, where conversation and singing abound. Long associations with mining and the sea are reflected in the atmospheric single-bar interior. Wooden furnishings and an open fire add character and warmth, as do Celtic flags adorn the beamed ceiling. Up to five St Austell ales are served, but no food. A separate snug functions as a family room. Live music features on Monday and Saturday nights. ▲Q❀♿▲☲(10,300,504)♣⌐

St Mary's: Isles of Scilly

Old Town Inn
Old Town, TR21 0NN (on A3112) SV915103
❀12 (5 winter)-11; 12-11 Sat; 12-10.30 Sun
☎ (01720) 422301 ⊕ oldtowninn.co.uk
Ales of Scilly Scuppered; Sharp's Doom Bar; guest beer Ⓗ

Modern and roomy pub lying just below the airport, a 20-minute stroll from Hugh Town. Wood panelling and flooring dominate the two bars. The front bar is for day-to-day drinking; the bar to the rear is a dual-purpose dining and function room. Offering occasional live entertainment, the pub is home to the Islands Folk Club. Good locally sourced, home-cooked food is served daily (no food Mon-Wed winter), and includes take-away pizzas and curries. Beer festivals are held twice yearly, in June and September. ▲❀☵⑪♿P

St Mawgan

Falcon Inn Ⓛ ✅
TR8 4EP (near Newquay airport) SW873658
❀11-3, 5-11 (5.30-midnight Fri & Sat) winter; 11-11 Sun & summer ☎ (01637) 860225 ⊕ thefalconinnstmawgan.co.uk
St Austell Trelawny, Tribute, HSD; guest beer Ⓗ
Although close to Newquay Airport, this charming family-friendly 16th-century inn in the village centre affords a quiet retreat. Nestling in the unspoilt Lanherne Valley, the picturesque pub is the hub of local activities. The quiet single bar interior has a cosy relaxed atmosphere, with decor reflecting country life. Excellent home-cooked meals are served in the bar and separate dining room. The extensive well-kept gardens provide an ideal setting for alfresco dining and drinking. Quality accommodation is also available.
▲Q❀☵▲⑪▲☲(556)♣P⌐

St Newlyn East

Pheasant Inn
Churchtown, TR8 5LJ
❀12-3, 6-midnight winter; 12-midnight Fri, Sat & summer; 12-11 Sun ☎ (01872) 510237
St Austell Tribute; Sharp's Doom Bar, Own; Skinner's Betty Stogs Ⓗ
A genuine two-bar local at the heart of village life, the Pheasant is frequented by a mix of customers. Darts, euchre and football teams are supported by an enthusiastic landlord who promotes real ale choice and holds an annual beer festival in November. The menu includes locally sourced produce wherever possible – the local butcher supplies his own Cornish meat. There is a large car park to the rear via a narrow access. Regular buses run during the week. ▲❀⑪☲(585,586)♣P⌐

Stratton

King's Arms Ⓛ ✅
Howells Road, EX23 9BX (off A39) SS228065
❀12-11 ☎ (01288) 352396
Sharp's Doom Bar; Tintagel Cornwall's Pride; guest beers Ⓗ
A must for visitors to Bude, this unspoilt 17th-century gem of a pub offers a real ale range unusual for the area. Its history is apparent as soon as you enter, with old flagstone floors of Delabole slate among many original features. The four beers are usually from Cornish and Devonian microbreweries, and a draught cider appears in summer. The pub name reflects Stratton's Civil War loyalties – the battle of Stamford Hill took place near here in 1643.
▲Q❀☵⑪☐♿☲(128,519,576)♣♥P

Summercourt

London Inn

1 School Road, TR8 5EA (off A30) SW888561
✪ 12-3, 5 (6 Fri & Sat)-midnight summer; 12-2.30 (not Mon-Thu), 5 (6 Fri & Sat)-midnight winter; 12-3, 7-midnight Sun ☎ (01872) 510281
Beer range varies Ⓗ
Former 17th-century coaching inn, now a lively family-friendly free house, where bonhomie and a genuine welcome are assured. Quality is guaranteed with traditional home-cooked food and an ever-changing beer menu, with two or three Cornish or up-country brews on offer. Wooden screens divide the spacious single bar interior into drinking and dining areas. The eclectic decor features coach lamps and wooden furnishings. Conversation and jocular banter dominate, creating a warm, jovial ambience – well worth a visit.
🏚Q✿◑▶ Å🚱(527,597)♣P⚊

Towan Cross

Victory Inn Ⓛ

Mount Hawke, TR4 8BN SW706484
✪ 12-midnight ☎ (01209) 890359
⊕ thevictoryinncornwall.co.uk
St Austell Tribute; Skinner's Betty Stogs, Kiss Me Harder; guest beer Ⓗ
Situated high on the cliffs above Porthtowan, this large, convivial, family-run free house enjoys extensive sea views. A traditional local, it has an open-plan, single-bar interior and is quiet and comfortable, with separate dining areas where an interesting good-quality menu is available. An adjoining conservatory doubles either as a family or dining room. There is also a large beer garden, ample parking and camping facilities. Guest ales are generally local, mainly from Skinner's. Truro-Porthtowan buses stop outside.
🐾✿◑ & Å🚱(304)♣P⚊

Trebellan

Smugglers' Den Inn Ⓛ ✓

TR8 5PY (off Cubert road from A3075) SW783574
✪ 11-11 summer; 12-3, 6-11 Thu-Sat winter; 12-11 Sun
☎ (01637) 830209 ⊕ thesmugglersden.co.uk
Beer range varies Ⓗ
Picture-postcard thatched pub in an idyllic setting, at the bottom of narrow country lanes but fortunately well-signposted. Popular for dining winter or summer, its beer range is always interesting, mainly sourced from local breweries. Beams, paved yards and open fires add to the atmosphere, as do the occasional folk or jazz evenings and quiz nights. There is a nearby caravan site, and local buses stop at the top of the (rather hilly) lane. A May Day weekend ale and pie festival is held. 🏚Q✿◑▶ Å🚱(585,587)P⚊

Treen (Zennor)

Gurnard's Head Ⓛ

TR26 3DE (on B3306 north coast road) SW436376
✪ 10-11.30 ☎ (01736) 796928 ⊕ gurnardshead.co.uk
St Austell Tribute; Skinner's Betty Stogs, Heligan Honey Ⓗ
Impressive, characterful free house named after the nearby headland. Its burgeoning reputation for fine ale and excellent food draws custom from near and far. An expansive wood-floored interior accommodates a single bar, cosy snug and stylish dining room. Local art is on display alongside open fires, wooden furnishings and comfy sofas. The Skreach Cider is locally produced. An extensive menu changes daily, reflecting availability of local produce. One Skinner's brew may vary.
🏚Q✿✉◑ & Å🚱(300,507,508)♣P⚊

Treleigh

Treleigh Arms Ⓛ

TR16 4AY (beside old Redruth bypass) SW703436
✪ 11-3, 5-11; 11-11 Fri-Sun ☎ (01209) 315095
⊕ treleigharms.org.uk/tarms/
Draught Bass; Sharp's Doom Bar; Skinner's Betty Stogs; guest beer Ⓗ
Stone-built roadside free house with a warm welcome, conveniently situated a short drive from the A30. With a comfortable interior featuring exposed stone walls and a wood-burning stove, the pub attracts a good mix of locals and diners. The cosy and relaxing ambience is not spoilt by TV or jukebox. The quality food menu is sometimes boosted when the Royle Treleigh Yacht Club holds a gastronomic evening (no boat required). The garden includes a pétanque pitch. Dogs are welcome. 🏚Q✿◑🚱(445)♣P⚊

Trevaunance Cove

Driftwood Spars Ⓛ ✓

Quay Road, TR5 0RT (signed from St Agnes Peterville) SW721513
✪ 11-11 (1am Fri & Sat) ☎ (01872) 552428
⊕ driftwoodspars.com
Driftwood Blue Hills Bitter, Red Mission, Lou's Brew; guest beers Ⓗ
An outstanding, popular and vibrant coastal free house and brewpub, this establishment goes from strength to strength. At the forefront of real ale promotion, up to eight ales are always on offer, and beer festivals are held every March and May. The historic granite building accommodates three different bars, a sea-view dining room and sun terrace. An imaginative menu features local seasonal produce. Outside are two separate beer gardens and ample parking. Entertainment includes live music and occasional live theatre. Real cider is from Skreach.
🏚Q✿✉◑ ⊕ & Å🚱♣P⚊

Trewellard

Trewellard Arms Ⓛ

Trewellard Road, TR19 7TA (on B3318/B3306 jct) SW377338
✪ 12-11 (midnight Sat & Sun) ☎ (01736) 788634
Beer range varies Ⓗ
A thriving family-run free house, the pub is family-friendly and welcoming. Formerly the nearby Geevor mine owner's residence, its cosy interior accommodates a spacious open-beamed single bar, pleasant restaurant and secluded cellar seating area. Comfortable throughout, open fires enhance its homely atmosphere. Up to six ales are on offer from an ever-changing beer menu, a mixture of Cornish and other South West beers. Good-value home-cooked food is served. Outside is a patio beer garden and car park with ample space, and access is easy by bus.
🏚Q✿◑▶ Å🚱(10,300,507)♣P⚊

Truro

City Inn L
Pydar Street, TR1 3SP (N side of city centre, through railway arch) SW822452
☼ 12-11.30 (12.30am Fri & Sat) ☎ (01872) 272623
Sharp's Doom Bar; Skinner's Betty Stogs; Courage Best Bitter; guest beer Ⓗ
Just after the railway viaduct near the city centre, this community-focused two-bar pub has the feel of a village local. The welcoming, traditional, wood-beamed interior includes a comfortable lounge with several drinking areas displaying an impressive collection of water jugs, and a sports-oriented back bar with a large TV screen. The sun-trap rear beer garden is fun for train watchers. Good-value meals are served. Occasional beer festivals are held as well as charity events including the annual conker and hogs pudding championships. Q❀✿◑⊞≠☷♣⅃

White Hart (Crab & Ale House) ✪
25 New Bridge Street, TR1 2AA
☼ 11-11 (1am Fri & Sat); 12-10.30 Sun ☎ (01872) 277294
Greene King IPA; Morland Old Speckled Hen; St Austell Tribute; Sharp's Doom Bar; guest beer Ⓗ
Truro's oldest inn first opened in 1802 as the White Hart (the name is on the frontage). Rebranding as the Crab & Ale House in reality changed little at this timeless old local. Handy for shops and the cathedral, the small city-centre local caters for all tastes, with good lunchtime food and quality beer – the single guest ale changes weekly and is often from a Cornish brewery. Entered down a step, the cosy single bar is decorated with nautical bric-a-brac. Q◑⅃≠⊞♣⅃

Tywardreath

New Inn
Fore Street, PL24 2QP SX086543
☼ 12-11 ☎ (01726) 813901
Draught Bass Ⓖ; **St Austell Trelawny, Tribute, Proper Job** Ⓗ, **seasonal beer** Ⓖ
Built in 1752 by mine owners, this classic local is the hub of village life. Many functions are held in its large, secluded garden, including morris dancing; electronic amusements are confined to the back room. Good conversation is the entertainment here, except on Cornish song nights. This St Austell house is covenanted to sell Bass in perpetuity and is their only pub to serve it by gravity. Look out for the brass token slot on the bar once used by miners.
🏠Q☾✿❀⅃&ⱡ≠(Par)⊞(25,524)♣P⅃

Vogue

Star Inn
St Day, TR16 5NP (on Redruth-St Day road) SW724424
☼ 12-midnight (1am Fri & Sat); 11-11 Sun
☎ (01209) 820242 ⊕ starinnvogue.biz
Beer range varies Ⓗ
Roadside pub with a welcoming atmosphere where darts, euchre and karaoke provide regular entertainment. The centre of the local community, lunchtimes are popular with pre-school families and pensioners for good-value home-cooked meals. Sunday lunchers are advised to book early as the pub may be busy. Outside, the boules pitch hosts matches. One Skinner's beer is usually available, accompanied by brews from other Cornish microbreweries. An annual beer festival takes place 10 weeks after Easter.
🏠❀◑ⱡ⊞(43)♣●P⅃

Wendron

New Inn L
TR13 0EA (on B3297 Helston-Redruth road) SW310678
☼ 12-3, 6-11 (7-10.30 Sun) ☎ (01326) 572683
St Austell Tribute; Skinner's Betty Stogs; guest beer Ⓗ
A welcoming and cosy village pub with a bar on the left and separate dining room on the right, accessed from the main door or through the bar. The character has changed little over the years, with an interesting carving of the Four Horsemen of the Apocalypse above the fireplace. The two local ales may vary occasionally, the third is ever-changing and usually from a microbrewery. An attractive specials menu is prepared by the landlady and her daughter. Q❀◑➊⊞(2A,34)♣P⅃

Witch Ball, Lizard (Photo: Chris Sapey)

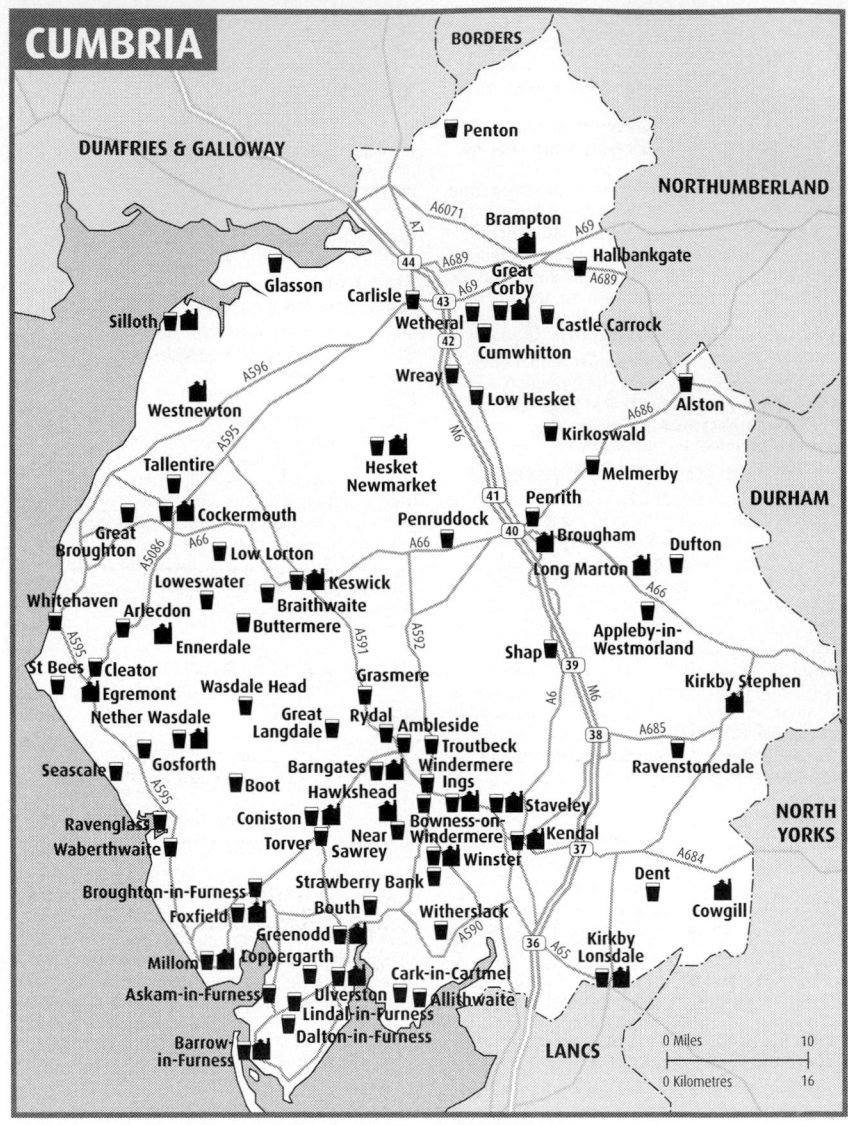

CUMBRIA

BORDERS

Penton

DUMFRIES & GALLOWAY

NORTHUMBERLAND

Brampton

Great Corby

Hallbankgate

Glasson

Carlisle

Wetheral

Castle Carrock

Silloth

Cumwhitton

Wreay

Low Hesket

Alston

Westnewton

Kirkoswald

Melmerby

DURHAM

Tallentire

Hesket Newmarket

Penrith

Cockermouth

Penruddock

Brougham

Dufton

Great Broughton

Low Lorton

Long Marton

Loweswater

Keswick

Whitehaven

Braithwaite

Appleby-in-Westmorland

Arlecdon

Buttermere

St Bees

Ennerdale

Shap

Kirkby Stephen

Cleator

Wasdale Head

Grasmere

Egremont

Great Langdale

Rydal

Ambleside

Nether Wasdale

Troutbeck

Ravenstonedale

Seascale

Gosforth

Windermere

Ings

NORTH YORKS

Boot

Barngates

Ravenglass

Coniston

Hawkshead

Staveley

Waberthwaite

Torver

Near Sawrey

Bowness-on-Windermere

Kendal

Winster

Dent

Broughton-in-Furness

Strawberry Bank

Cowgill

Foxfield

Bouth

Witherslack

Greenodd

Millom

Coppergarth

Kirkby Lonsdale

Cark-in-Cartmel

Askam-in-Furness

Ulverston

Allithwaite

Lindal-in-Furness

Barrow-in-Furness

Dalton-in-Furness

LANCS

| 0 Miles | 10 |
| 0 Kilometres | 16 |

Allithwaite

Pheasant Inn L

Flookburgh Road, LA11 7RQ

☼ 12-11 (midnight Thu-Sat) ☎ (01539) 532239
⊕ thepheasantinnallithwaite.co.uk

Thwaites Original; guest beers Ⓗ

Free house catering to locals and tourists alike, extensively refurbished in 2011 to a high standard incorporating an extension with stunning views over Humphrey Head to Morecambe Bay. One of the walks described in CAMRA's Lake District Pub Walks starts at Kents Bank station and visits here. The four changing guest beers are from local breweries. The emphasis is very much on good-quality and good-value food, but there is a separate bar area with open fires, where dogs are welcome if on a lead. There is a pub quiz on Thursday nights.
♨Q♣❶&Å⇌(Kents Bank)🚌(530,532)P⅃

Alston

Cumberland Inn L

Townfoot, CA9 3HX

☼ 12-11 ☎ (01434) 381875 ⊕ cumberlandinnalston.com

Yates Bitter; guest beers Ⓗ

A family-run 19th-century inn overlooking the South Tyne River. Close to the Coast-to-Coast cycle route and Pennine Way, it is an ideal base to explore the highest market town in England. Cumbrian beers are served alongside Northumbrian Ales and beers from further afield. Old Rosie and occasional Cumbrian ciders and perry are also stocked. Local CAMRA Pub of the Year 2009-2011. ♨Q♣❀⇌❶&Å🚌(680)●P⅃

Ambleside

Queens Hotel ✓

Market Place, LA22 9BU

🕏 10-11.45 (12.45am Fri & Sat); 11-11.45 Sun
☎ (015394) 32206 ⊕ queenshotelambleside.com
Coniston Bluebird; Cumbrian Legendary Loweswater Gold; Hawkshead Windermere Pale Ale; Jennings Cumberland Ale; Yates Bitter ⊞
Town-centre Cask Marque-accredited hotel with a large bar and dining area, and the separate Victoria's Restaurant on the ground floor as well as a cellar bar beneath. It is popular with locals and visitors for the quality of the beers and its location in the centre of the Lake District. Buses run to several villages and towns with tourist attractions and fine walking opportunities. ❀⌑◑⊟(555)♣⌐

Appleby-in-Westmorland

Golden Ball
4 High Wiend, CA16 6RD (off Boroughgate)
🕏 11 (12 Sun)-midnight ☎ (01768) 351493
Marston's Burton Bitter; guest beers ⊞
A traditional side-street pub where CAMRA members receive a discount. As you walk in there is a lounge and a public bar with a TV and an excellent rock and blues jukebox. Both bars are served from a central back to back bar counter with up to six real ales. As well as a strong local following, the pub attracts visitors, including railway enthusiasts using the Settle to Carlisle line. The patio has a large covered area and leads to the garden with a children's play area.
❀⌑◱⇌⊟(563)♣⌐

Midland Hotel
25 Clifford Street, CA16 6TS (opp railway station)
🕏 closed Mon; 11.30 (5 Tue & Wed)-11 ☎ (01768) 351524
⊕ themidlandhotelappleby.co.uk
Beer range varies ⊞
Set in the beautiful Eden Valley between the Lake District and Yorkshire National Parks, the Midland is adjacent to Appleby Station, which is on the Settle Carlisle Railway. The hotel has been extensively refurbished, with the bar area, accommodation and garden improved. The new decor has a modern feel, which is contrasted by up to three handpumps dispensing LocAles from Cumbria and offerings from interesting microbreweries throughout the country. Real cider or perry is regularly available.
🏠❀⌑◑⇌♣P⌐

Arlecdon

Hound
Parks Road, CA26 3XE
🕏 11.30 (11 Sun)-11 ☎ (01946) 862162
Jennings Bitter ⊞
The attention of passers-by is always grabbed by the railway carriage in the pub garden. This is the pub's Orchid Restaurant, an ex-Southampton boat train carriage, where opulence abounds. The pub itself is community-centred, with a darts team and a weekly quiz. It is an open-plan pub, but still has many original features, including bare stone walls and wooden beams. ❀◗♿P⌐

Askam-in-Furness

London House ⓛ
Duddon Road, LA16 7FB
🕏 closed Mon & Tue; 7-midnight Wed; 4-midnight Thu; 3-1am Fri & Sat; 3-10.30 Sun ☎ (01229) 463838
Cumbria Legendary Loweswater Gold; guest beer ⊞

Friendly family-run village pub popular with locals and visitors from the nearby caravan site and golf course. The main bar area has a real wood-burning stove; there are two other rooms, one with a pool table. TV is available for sporting events, mainly Rugby League. The friendly landlord has worked hard to promote real ale in a village that was formerly a desert for well-kept beer.
🏠❀♿⚓⇌🚐(7)♣⌐

Barngates

Drunken Duck Inn ⓛ
LA22 0NG (signed off the B5286 Hawkshead to Ambleside road) NY351013
🕏 11.30-11; 12-10.30 Sun ☎ (01539) 436347
⊕ drunkenduckinn.co.uk
Beer range varies ⊞
Home of Barngates Brewery, the Duck always serves four of the 10 beers brewed here and brewery tours can be arranged. The bar has been extensively renovated to create a pleasing mix of local and modern styles. Lunchtime bar meals and the à la carte menu available in the dining-room in the evening are of an exceptionally high standard. The outside seating area at the front offers magnificent views of the fells to the north-east.
🏠Q❀⌑◑P⌐

Barrow-in-Furness

Queen's Arms ⓛ
Biggar Village, LA14 3YG
🕏 closed Mon; 6-11.30 Tue; 12-10.30 Wed & Thu; 12-midnight Fri & Sat; 12-10.30 Sun ☎ (01229) 471880
⊕ thequeensarmsbiggar.co.uk
Barngates Red Bull Terrier; Hawkshead Lakeland Gold; Ulverston Laughing Gravy ⊞

INDEPENDENT BREWERIES

Abraham Thompson Barrow-in-Furness
Barngates Barngates
Beckstones Millom
Blackbeck Egremont
Bowness Bay Winster (NEW)
Coniston Coniston
Cumberland Great Corby
Cumbrian Legendary Hawkshead
Dent Cowgill
Derwent Silloth
Eden Brougham (NEW)
Ennerdale Ennerdale
Foxfield Foxfield
Geltsdale Brampton
Great Gable Egremont
Greenodd Greenodd
Hardknott Millom
Hawkshead Staveley
Hesket Newmarket Hesket Newmarket
Jennings (Marston's) Cockermouth
Kendal Kendal (NEW)
Keswick Keswick
Kirkby Lonsdale Kirkby Lonsdale
Nine Standards Kirkby Stephen
Strands Nether Wasdale
Stringers Ulverston
Tirril Long Marton
Ulverston Ulverston
Watermill Ings
Winster Valley Winster
Yates Westnewton

Nestled in the ancient village of Biggar, the Queen's Arms has risen like a phoenix from the ashes, sporting a substantial revamp while retaining its character and style. Several draught beers are served and there is always a warm welcome. The pub boasts a variety of events including Arts & Crafts, book clubs, and live music on Tuesday and Saturday. Beer festivals are planned. ᴹQ❀❄⇔❱♥P🛈

Boot

Brook House Inn ▯

CA19 1TG (200yds from Dalegarth station)
✪ 11-11 ☎ (01946) 723288 ⊕ brookhouseinn.co.uk
Cumbrian Legendary Langdale; Hawkshead Bitter; guest beers ▣
Deep in the western fells, with picturesque scenery and majestic peaks, this is a haven of quality food and real ale, serving up to seven beers in summer, with guest ales usually from Yates and Barngates. It is run by a dedicated family who, with two other local pubs, instigate their June beer festival, when the valley throngs with real ale lovers enjoying up to 100 beers, entertained by local morris dancers. Local CAMRA Pub of the Year 2010. ᴹQ❄❀❄⇔❱ Å⇌(Dalegarth)♣♥P🛈

Woolpack Inn ▯

Hardknott Pass, Eskdale, CA19 1TH (just over 1 mile from Dalegarth terminus of La'l Ratty) NY191100
✪ 8am-1am (closed 5-27 December) ☎ (019467) 23230
⊕ woolpack.co.uk
Jennings Cumberland Ale ▣
Two years' enthusiastic refurbishment has imaginatively preserved the inn's 16th-century character. The large walkers' and family bar, cosy with wood-burning stove in winter, combines tradition with bistro chic. The inn lies at the foot of the steep Hardknott Pass; completing the 19-mile Woolpack walk over the highest local peaks earns a free pint reward; there is an interesting and varied range of beer. Food is Eskdale-sourced if possible. Pizzas from the Italian wood-fired oven are an added attraction. ᴹQ❄❀❄⇔❱ ⬦Å♣♥P

Bouth

White Hart ▯ ✅

LA12 8JB (off A590, 6 miles NE of Ulverston)
✪ 12-11 (10.30 Sun) ☎ (01229) 861229
⊕ whitehart-lakedistrict.co.uk
Black Sheep Best Bitter; Coniston Bluebird; Jennings Cumberland Ale ▣
A 17th-century inn with old farming and hunting implements adorning the walls, and horse brasses and hops on beams. Slate-flagged floors and a wood-burning stove add to the atmosphere. A high standard of food is on offer using locally sourced ingredients and can be served in the bar, upstairs dining area, or on the terrace. In addition to a regular beer from Ulverston Brewery, guest ales come from local breweries. Magnificent views of the Rusland Valley and Coniston Old Man are a 20-minute walk away. ᴹ❄❀❄⇔❱⬦Å♥P🛈

Bowness-on-Windermere

Royal Oak

Brantfell Road, LA23 3EG
✪ 11-midnight (11 Sun) ☎ (01539) 443970
⊕ royaloak-windermere.co.uk

Coniston Bluebird; Jennings Cocker Hoop, Cumberland Ale; Taylor Landlord; Tetley Bitter ▣
Pleasant pub popular with locals and tourists, situated at the end of the Dales Way. Four to five real ales are on handpump throughout the year, with several local ales always available. It has a compact main bar with several smaller areas including a raised-level games room. There are lots of photographs and glasses adorning the walls and shelves, including local boxing mementos. Several local sports organisations frequent the pub, while local fundraising events are commonplace throughout the year. ᴹ❀❄⇔❱(599,618)♣P🛈

Braithwaite

Middle Ruddings Country Inn ▯

CA12 5RY (just off A66 at Braithwaite)
✪ 10.30-11 ☎ (01768) 778436 ⊕ middle-ruddings.co.uk
Beer range varies ▣
Situated in a village just off the A66 with great views of Skiddaw, it is well worth making a detour from the main road to visit this local. It has three handpumps and only sells Cumbrian ales – selected by the landlord who visits the breweries before taking the beers. The place is family run and family friendly, with children and dogs welcome. The restaurant also promotes local produce. The service is exceptional.
ᴹQ❄❀❄⇔❱Å⌷(X5,74,74A)♥P🛈

Broughton-in-Furness

Manor Arms ▯

The Square, LA20 6HY
✪ 12-11.30 (midnight Fri & Sat; 11 Sun) ☎ (01229) 716286
⊕ manorarmsthesquare.co.uk
Copper Dragon Golden Pippin; Yates Bitter; guest beers ▣
An outstanding venue, where the Varty family has celebrated over 20 years of ownership, which flies the flag for real ale in this popular Cumbrian village. Winner of numerous CAMRA awards, it has made it to the latter stages of the National Pub of the Year three times. The beer range promotes independent breweries and the eight handpumps are in themselves a mini beer festival. If you want to try real ale, this is the place. ᴹQ⇔⌷(7)♣♥🛈

Buttermere

Fish

CA13 9XA
✪ opening hours vary; closed 4 Jan-mid Feb
☎ (07687) 70253 ⊕ fishinnbuttermere.co.uk
Beer range varies ▣
The Fish has been an inn since the 17th century. In the 18th century it was the home of The Maid of Buttermere, whose father was landlord. Famed for her beauty, she featured in Wordsworth's Prelude. Today the comfortable bar is traditional but very welcoming, and specialises in offering beers from a range of Cumbrian breweries. Buttermere is within a five-minute stroll of the pub, making it ideal for easy walks around the lake. Phone to check opening times.
ᴹQ❀❄⇔❱⌷(77,77a)P

Cark-in-Cartmel

Engine Inn ▯

LA11 7NZ (3 miles W of Grange-over-Sands)

✪ 11.30-1am (midnight Sun) ☎ (01539) 558341
⊕ engineinn.co.uk
Beer range varies Ⓗ
Run by a family who are enthusiastic CAMRA members, this 17th-century inn, 300 yards from the railway station, is an excellent ending to the walk from Grange described in CAMRA's Lake District Pub Walks. Beers from the Punch Taverns range are supplemented by ales from local breweries. The pub (with five en-suite rooms), is named after a former mill engine in the village. It was extensively and tastefully refurbished in 2010, retaining the separate restaurant and games room. ⏴❀⌑◑&▲≒⛗(530,532)♣♠P⌐

Carlisle

Crown & Thistle
53 Church Street, Stanwix, CA3 9DS
✪ 10-midnight (11 Sun) ☎ (01228) 528191
Greene King IPA; guest beers Ⓗ
A real locals' old-fashioned boozer, refurbished and with a separate bar and lounge. Outside is a smoking area with further seating which is well used on hot summer days. Strong support for the city football team ensures it gets busy after a home game. Darts, dominoes, whist and on, on Thursday, a popular quiz night attract a varied mix of customers. Horse racing and other sports feature on the TVs, which are not left on longer than necessary. ❀⛗⛗(76,62)♣♠⌐

King's Head ♈ Ⓛ
Fisher Street, CA3 8RF (behind old town hall)
✪ 10-11 (midnight Fri); 11-midnight Sat; 12-11 Sun
☎ (01228) 533797 ⊕ kingsheadcarlisle.co.uk
Yates Bitter; guest beers Ⓗ
A pub that has won many CAMRA awards and rates as one of the oldest in Carlisle. Pictures of old Carlisle adorn the walls inside, and outside is an explanation of why Carlisle is not in the Domesday Book. Local brews are among the three guest beers, and take-away beer cartons are available. The Lanes shopping centre, the castle and cathedral are nearby. Good-value meals are served at lunchtime. The covered smoking area to the back has a large TV and barbecue for parties. No children allowed. Local CAMRA Pub of the Year 2012. ❀◑≒♣♠⌐

Linton Holme Ⓛ
82 Lindisfarne Street, CA1 2NB (E off London Road beside old tram sheds)
✪ 5 (4 Fri; 12 Sat)-11; 12-10.30 Sun ☎ (01228) 532637
Yates Bitter; guest beer Ⓗ
Former hotel retaining many original features including tiled mosaic floors, etched windows and a wonderful marble pillar outside. It is situated in a quiet residential area and well worth making the effort to seek out. Inside, a variety of rooms all open out to a bar area where there is a large pool table. Guest ales are frequently from microbreweries. TVs show sporting events and regular darts, pool and quiz nights are held. Toasties are available during opening hours. Local CAMRA award winner. ⏴❀⛗(76)♣⌐

Spinners Arms
Cummersdale Road, Cummersdale, CA2 6BD (1 mile W of Carlisle off B5299)
✪ 6 (12 Sat & Sun)-midnight ☎ (01228) 532928
⊕ thespinnersarms.org.uk
Beer range varies Ⓗ
Cosy family-friendly refurbished hostelry with unique animal-decorated gutters and a welcoming real fire. It is situated under half a mile from Carlisle's south-western boundary, close to the Cumbrian Way and National Cycle Route 7, which run alongside the River Caldew. A good variety of guest ales from Cumbrian and northern microbreweries is stocked. There is regular live music, and Irish music sessions every second and fourth Wednesday. Lunches are served Saturday and Sunday only, and evening bar meals 6-9pm (not Tue). Children (until 9pm) and well-behaved dogs are welcome. ⏴❀⌑◑&⛗⛗(75)♣⌐

Woodrow Wilson Ⓛ ✔
48 Botchergate, CA1 1QS
✪ 7am-midnight (12.30am Fri & Sat) ☎ (01228) 819942
Greene King Abbot; Jennings Sneck Lifter; Marston's Pedigree; Ruddles Best Bitter; guest beers Ⓗ
Wetherspoon pub in a refurbished Co-op building named after the former US president, who was born in Carlisle. Up to 12 handpumps offer the largest range of real ales in Carlisle, usually including many LocAle beers. Food is available all day till 10pm. At the rear there is a spacious heated patio for smokers. Children are welcome in some areas until 8pm. It is five minutes' walk from the railway station and city centre. Q❀◑&≒⛗♠P⌐

Castle Carrock

Duke of Cumberland Ⓛ
CA8 9LU
✪ 12-11.30 (midnight Fri & Sat) ☎ (01228) 670341
⊕ thedukeofcumberlandinn.com
Geltsdale Cold Fell; guest beers Ⓗ
With so many pubs closing, it was pleasing to see the Duke reopening in 2009, and it is now successfully re-established. Located at the foot of the Northern Pennines, it is ideally located for outdoor activity enthusiasts who can enjoy real ale from the local Geltsdale Brewery and sample the home-made food for which it has a growing reputation. The layout separates the games/TV area from the dining area. ⏴❀◑&♣P

Cleator

Brook ♈ Ⓛ
Trumpet Terrace, CA23 3DX (on A5086 between Cleator Moor and Egremont) NY021140
✪ 11-midnight (1am Fri & Sat); 12-midnight Sun
☎ (01946) 811635
Taylor Landlord; Yates Golden Ale; guest beers Ⓗ
A small pub with a big atmosphere. A real fire and lighting provided by candles and fairy lights make for a cosy but quirky feel. It is very community-centred – regulars' birthdays are chalked up on the notice board – but it is not cliquey. The food is very popular and booking is advised. Local CAMRA Pub of the Year in 2011 and 2012.
⏴◑⛗(22,31,31A)♣♠⌐

Cockermouth

1761
Market Place, CA13 9NH
✪ 4.30 (12 Sat)-11.30; 1-11.30 Sun ☎ (01900) 829282
⊕ bar1761.co.uk
Yates Bitter Ⓗ
Historic pub dating from 1761, this hostelry has been refurbished into an open-plan bar but still

retains period features. Two guest beers are constantly rotated, one of which is usually Cumbrian. A range of board games is available. ✿🖳(X4,X5,600)♣🍴

Castle Bar 🅛

14 Market Place, CA13 9NQ
✪ 11-11.30 (12.30am Sat); 11.30-11 Sun ☎ (01900) 829904
Jennings Bitter, Cumberland Ale 🅗
Large vibrant bar spread over three floors. Football and other sports are shown in all rooms. There is a dedicated upstairs restaurant, but food is served throughout the building. Three bar rooms are downstairs, with period features, including a large stone spiral staircase. ◑🖳

Coniston

Black Bull Inn 🅛

Yewdale Road, LA21 8DU
✪ 11-11 (10.30 Sun) ☎ (01539) 441335
⊕ blackbullconiston.co.uk
Coniston Oliver's Light Ale, Bluebird Bitter, Bluebird XB, Old Man Ale, Special Oatmeal Stout, Blacksmiths Ale 🅗
A 16th-century coaching inn that serves good food in traditional and comfortable surroundings and is the tap house for the on-site Coniston Brewing Company. The spacious bar and lounge, with beamed ceilings and tasteful decor, are always well-frequented by tourists in this hugely popular area. The outside seating area is perfect for the summer months, in this spectacular location near Coniston Old Man.
🏚Q🕭🛏🍴◑♿🖳(X12,505)●P🍴

Sun Hotel 🅛

LA21 8HQ (up the Walna Scar road from the village)
✪ 12-11.30 ☎ (01539) 441248 ⊕ thesunconiston.com
Coniston Bluebird; Copper Dragon Golden Pippin; Hawkshead Bitter; guest beers 🅗
Take the Walna Scar road up from Coniston village, or down from Coniston Old Man, to visit this 16th-century pub and hotel. The recently refurbished dual-level bar area has atmosphere and character, with slate flooring and abundant exposed beams, all heated by a large open range. The slate-topped bar offers up to eight cask ales, mostly from local brewers. The conservatory and terrace complete the picture, with delightful views over the garden and the village. 🏚✿🛏◑♿🖳(X12,505)P🍴

Cumwhitton

Pheasant Inn 🅛 ✔

CA8 9EX (4 miles SE of A69 at Warwick Bridge)
✪ closed Mon; 6-11 (10.30 Sun) ☎ (01228) 560102
⊕ pheasantinncumwhitton.co.uk
Geltsdale Pheasant Ale; guest beers 🅗
Partly dating from the 17th century, this pub has a well-deserved reputation for excellent food using fresh local ingredients, but retains that good pub welcome for the thirsty visitor in for a pint. There are three handpumps for real ale, including Pheasant Ale supplied by Geltsdale Brewery from nearby Brampton. The venue has won several CAMRA awards, proudly displayed in the bar alongside a water jug collection. Quiz nights are held every second week. Closed Mondays and open evenings only all other days. 🏚✿🛏♿P

Dalton-in-Furness

Brown Cow 🅛

Goose Green, LA15 8LQ (just off A590)
✪ 11.30-midnight ☎ (01229) 462553
⊕ browncowinndalton.co.uk
Black Sheep Best Bitter; guest beers 🅗
A warm and friendly atmosphere awaits visitors to this 400-year-old coaching house, which has retained many original features including beams, brasses, local prints and an open fire. A winner of many awards for its five real ales, the pub also serves excellent food from a full and varied menu. Meals can be enjoyed in the large dining room or, on warmer days, on the charming patio with heating and lighting. 🏚Q✿🛏◑≉🖳(6)P🍴

Dent

George & Dragon 🅛 ✔

Main Street, LA10 5QL
✪ 11 (12 Sun)-11 ☎ (01539) 625256
⊕ thegeorgeanddragondent.co.uk
Dent Ale, Golden Fleece, Station Porter, Aviator, Rambrau, Ramsbottom 🅗
The Dent Brewery tap showcases all its own beers. Set in the cobbled main street of this attractive village, it is a friendly, two-bar local welcoming walkers, cyclists and dogs. A games room with pool table is off the front bar and a restaurant offering a good variety of meals is down a flight of stairs. Extensive mahogany panelling is adorned with brewery memorabilia and awards for the pub and brewery. Served by the local bus on Wednesday and Saturday. 🏚Q🕭✿🛏◑🖽🖳(564)♣●P

Dufton

Stag Inn

CA16 6DB (3 miles NE of Appleby-in-Westmorland) NY689253
✪ 12-3 (not Mon), 6-11; 12-midnight Sat; 12-10.30 Sun
☎ (01768) 351608 ⊕ thestagdufton.co.uk
Black Sheep Best Bitter; guest beers 🅗
A genuine local beside the village green; the front door (which opens outwards) is approached by a paved patio. The bar has an operational kitchen range and a dining area. The rear lounge gives access to the garden and impressive fell views. Good-value meals using local produce are served. A local beer festival is held in August. The pub is set in a good walking area, with the Pennine Way passing close by. 🏚Q✿🛏◑♣P🍴

Foxfield

Prince of Wales 🅛

LA20 6BX (opp station)
✪ closed Mon & Tue; 2.45 (12 Fri & Sat)-11; 12-10.30 Sun
☎ (01229) 716238 ⊕ princeofwalesfoxfield.co.uk
Beer range varies 🅗
Honoured among CAMRA's Top 40 Campaigners, Stuart and Lynda are testament to what can be achieved through passion and hard work in this gem of a pub. The guest beers come from the pub's two house breweries – Foxfield and Tigertops – plus breweries throughout the country. Beers will always include a mild. Frequent beer and cider festivals throughout the year are an added bonus. A discount on B&B is offered to CAMRA members. Bus and rail stops outside.
🏚Q✿🛏♿≉🖳(7)♣●P🍴🍺

Glasson

Highland Laddie Ⓛ
Water Street, CA7 5DT (9 miles NW of Carlisle off B5307)
⊙ 12-midnight (1am Fri & Sat) ☎ (01697) 351839
⊕ highlandladdieinnglasson.co.uk
Jennings Best Bitter, Cocker Hoop; guest beer Ⓗ
Popular village local situated on the Hadrian's Wall route, close to the Solway Firth and a bird reserve. Meetings are held in the pub for the fishermen who follow the ancient occupation of haaf net fishing, unique to the Solway. Food is served every day lunchtimes and evenings. Two LocAles are available in winter with the addition of a guest beer, often from the Marston's range, in summer. A Real Ale and Haaf Netting festival is held annually in the summer. ꩜Q☺◑⊕⅃Ả⎚(93)♣

Gosforth

Gosforth Hall Inn
Wasdale Road, CA20 1AZ (from A595 follow road signed to Wasdale. Adjacent to St Mary's church) NY071037
⊙ 3 (12 Sat)-11 ☎ (01946) 725322 ⊕ gosforthhallinn.co.uk
Yates Golden Ale; guest beers Ⓗ
Regular beers include those from Hawkshead, Keswick and Yates. The wider portfolio is taken mainly from the north-west, particularly Cumbria. Gosforth Hall is a mid-17th-century Grade II-listed building. The original kitchen, now the lounge, features the widest spanning sandstone hearth in England. Accommodation is in 13 newly built and sympathetically designed rooms fitted out to a very high standard. Rod's pies famously satisfy the heartiest of hungers acquired walking the Lakeland fells.
꩜Q☜☺➱◑⊕⎚(6,X6)♣P⁵⌐⎕

Horse & Groom
Eskdale Road, CA20 1JA NY073034
⊙ 11-11; 12-10.30 Sun ☎ (019467) 25254
⊕ horsegroom.co.uk
Great Gable Burnmoor Pale Ale, Bitter, Wastwater Gold, Wry'nose, Yewbarrow Ⓗ
A recently and comfortably refurbished village pub, it is now the main outlet for the Great Gable Brewery and its CAMRA award-winning beers. Guest and seasonal beers can be interesting. Gosforth gives easy access to the spectacular Wasdale and Eskdale valleys with great walking and climbing, and you can get lots of advice from the experienced landlord.
꩜Q☜☺➱◑⊕⎚(6,X6)♣P⁵⌐

Grasmere

Dale Lodge Hotel (Tweedies Bar) ✅
Langdale Road, LA22 9SW
⊙ 12-11 (midnight Thu-Sun) ☎ (01539) 435300
⊕ dalelodgehotel.co.uk
Theakston Old Peculier; guest beers Ⓗ
The bar area has been enlarged by moving the bar counter back to include a former games room, and the pub is one of the few outlets for real cider in the lakes. The excellent choice of changing beers remains, and the wood-burning winter stove still manages to keep drinkers warm. Better than average meals are served in the bar. The large lawned grounds have ample seating. The Grasmere Guzzler beer festival, including a hog roast, is held each September. ꩜☺➱◑⊕⎚(555,599)♣●P⁵⌐

Great Broughton

Punchbowl Inn Ⓛ
19 Main Street, CA13 0YJ
⊙ 12-4 (3 Sun), 7-11 ☎ (01900) 824708
Jennings Bitter; guest beers Ⓗ
Classic village pub that is full of character and characters, not least the landlord himself. The venue dates from the 17th century, with beams, an open fire and an almost antique jukebox. Welcoming and friendly, it attracts locals and visitors alike – a true village pub. The guest ale can never be anticipated, which is part of the fun of going in. ꩜Q⎚(58)♣P

Great Corby

Corby Bridge Inn
CA4 8LL (2 miles S of the A69 at Warwick Bridge)
⊙ 3 (12 Sat & Sun)-11 ☎ (01228) 560221
⊕ corbybridgeinn.org.uk
Thwaites Wainwright, Bomber; guest beer Ⓗ
A short walk from Wetheral railway station across a spectacular viaduct over the River Eden leads to this lovely village pub. Set in a listed building but modernised a few years ago, it retains its original character. Four handpumps greet the visitor on entry, with an L-shaped room to the right and two further rooms to the left, all open plan. The furthest room contains both pool and darts. Meals are available Thursday-Saturday evenings and Sunday lunchtime. ꩜☺➱◑⅃≒(Wetheral)♣P⁵⌐

Great Langdale

Old Dungeon Ghyll Hotel
LA22 9JY (over bridge at end of B5343)
⊙ 11-11 (10.30 Sun) ☎ (01539) 437272 ⊕ odg.co.uk
Black Sheep Best Bitter, Ale; Jennings Cumberland Ale; Theakston Old Peculier; Yates Bitter; guest beers Ⓗ
Converted from a cowshed in the late 1940s, this pub is now a haven for walkers and climbers, offering a friendly welcome to those in muddy boots and waterproofs. The fire in the old range is much appreciated in winter, while impressive surrounding fell views can be enjoyed from the patio benches. An excellent range of Cumbrian beers is complemented by good home-cooked pub food. Meals in the hotel need to be booked in advance. ꩜Q☺➱◑Ẩ⎚(516)●P⁵⌐

Greenodd

Ship Inn Ⓛ
Main Street, LA12 7QZ
⊙ closed Mon; 6-11 (midnight Sat); 12-10.30 Sun
☎ (07782) 655294
Beer range varies Ⓗ
The tap house for Greenodd Brewery. A traditional village inn, the Ship was completely refurbished in 2012, opening up the bar area. A horseshoe bar serves the main open plan area, which has slate floors, wooden beams and open fires. There is a quiet room through the back and a games room upstairs. A good mix of locals can usually be found putting the world to rights, and visitors are made welcome. ꩜⎚(X12)♣P⌐

Hallbankgate

Belted Will 🗄

CA8 2NJ (on A689 Alston road 4 miles E of Brampton)
⚙ 5 (12 Sat & Sun)-midnight ☎ (01697) 746236
⊕ beltedwill.co.uk
Caledonian Deuchars IPA; Theakston XB; guest beer 🖽
The intriguing name (nickname of the 16th-century
Lord William Howard from nearby Naworth Castle)
is not all that attracts people here, as a warm
welcome is assured from mine hosts Stephen and
Alyson. Set in what was once an industrialised
area, not now apparent, the pub has a strong local
community spirit. Its peaceful location at the foot
of the North Pennines lends itself to all manner of
outdoor activities, including cycling, golfing,
fishing, pony trekking, bird watching (RSPB) and
walking. 🛏🏵🖂🛈🗄🚻🅿🚃(680)♣🚭

Hesket Newmarket

Old Crown 🗄 ✅

Main Street, CA7 8JG
⚙ 12-3 (not Mon-Thu), 5.30-11; 5.30-10.30 Sun
☎ (01697) 478288 ⊕ theoldcrownpub.co.uk
**Hesket Newmarket Skiddaw Special Bitter, Haystacks,
Hellvellyn Gold, Black Sail Stout, High Pike Bitter,
Catbells Pale Ale** 🖽
On the edge of the northern Lakeland Fells, this
pub is at the centre of village life. It is owned as a
co-operative by the local community, who are
dedicated to maintaining its original character. The
pub offers the full range of Hesket Newmarket
beers from the brewery located at the rear, with
new brews being tried out in the pub. Brewery
tours can be arranged by contacting the venue. A
firm favourite of Prince Charles and Sir Chris
Bonington. 🛏Q🏵🛈🗄🅰♣🚭

Ings

Watermill Inn 🗄

LA8 9PY (turn off A591 by church)
⚙ 12-11 (10.30 Sun) ☎ (01539) 821309
⊕ lakelandpub.co.uk
**Theakston Old Peculier; Watermill Collie Wobbles, A
Bit'er Ruff, Isle of Dogs, Wruff Night; guest beers** 🖽
Friendly, family-owned inn and brewery that has
deservedly won many awards during its 21-year
history. The excellent range and quality continues
and now includes eight Watermill beers brewed on
site, with a new brewery and accommodation
extension in progress. Two separate bars are
served by a central counter, and viewing windows
look into both the cellar and brewery. A wide
selection of meals is served daily until 9pm, and
dogs are provided with biscuits and water.
🛏Q🏵🖂🛈🚻🚃(555)♣🚭🅿🚭🗄

Kendal

Alexanders 🗄

Castle Green Lane, LA9 6RG
⚙ 12-11 ☎ (01539) 797017
Beer range varies 🖽
Set in the grounds of the Castle Green Hotel (a
former electricity board regional headquarters),
Alexanders occupies an older barn/stable block
and, as a free house, offers up to four different
Cumbrian beers, often including Coniston, Dent and
Hawkshead. A large conservatory provides
comfortable seating, dining facilities and fine views

over the extensive pub and hotel grounds, Kendal
castle ruins and the distant fells.
Q🏵🖂🛈🗄♿🚃♣🅿🚭

Burgundy's Wine Bar

19 Lowther Street, LA9 4DH
⚙ closed Mon; 11.30-3.30 (not Tue & Wed), 6.30-midnight;
11-midnight Sat; 7-11 Sun ☎ (01539) 733803
⊕ burgundyswinebar.co.uk
Beer range varies 🖽
Multi-level, town-centre bar, with a separate
entrance to the brewhouse. It offers a fine
selection of real ales – some brewed on site – as
well as an above-average range of continental
lagers, both draught and bottled. The street-level
bar area has bench seating, upstairs is a mezzanine
floor with tables and chairs and access to a patio,
while downstairs is another room with access to
the rear alleyway. The Cumbria Beer Challenge is
hosted here prior to Easter each year.
🏵🚃(41,555)🚭🚭

Riflemans Arms ✅

4 Greenside, LA9 4LD
⚙ 6.30 (4.30 Fri)-midnight; 12-midnight Sat & Sun
☎ (01539) 723224
Tetley Bitter; guest beers 🖽
A recently refurbished pub with fantastic pictures
of the Lakeland fells around the walls, featuring
walking and climbing groups. This dog-friendly pub
is pleasantly quiet with no jukebox, which gives it
a sociable, community pub feel, and it gets
involved with local events. It is located in a historic
part of Kendal, up the hill from the town centre.
Popular live folk music takes place on Thursday
evenings with free refreshments, and there is a
Sunday night quiz. A separate room has a pool
table and dartboard. Q🚃(44,48)♣

Keswick

Dog & Gun 🗄 ✅

2 Lake Road, CA12 5BT (off Market Place)
⚙ 12-11 ☎ (01768) 773463
Theakston Old Peculier; guest beers 🖽
Busy town-centre pub popular with locals and
tourists. A changing selection of six real ales is on
offer, five from Cumbrian breweries, including two
from the nearby Keswick Brewing Company. The
pub retains many original features, including a
stone floor and low ceiling. Bar meals are served
all day; Hungarian goulash is a house special. Food
is also provided for well-behaved dogs. Quiz night
is Thursday, with proceeds going to the Keswick
Mountain Rescue Team. 🛏Q🛈🅰🚃(X4,X5,73)

Kirkby Lonsdale

Orange Tree 🗄 ✅

9 Fairbank, LA6 2BD
⚙ 12-11 (midnight Sat) ☎ (01524) 271716
⊕ theorangetreehotel.co.uk
**Kirkby Lonsdale Ruskin's Bitter, Radical Red,
Monumental Blonde, Jubilee Stout; guest beer** 🖽
This family-run, buzzing town-centre pub is the
Kirkby Lonsdale Brewery tap. A central bar has
three varying beers from the brewery and two
local microbrewery ales on at any one time.
Around the bar there are several cosy seating areas
and a larger area where electric knick-knacks, old
photos and rugby mementos abound. There is a
separate dining room to the rear, and hearty meals

are produced from ingredients sourced from the excellent shops in town. CAMRA members receive a discount. ▲🍴◑ ▲🖼(567)♣♠

Kirkoswald

Fetherston Arms 🅛
CA10 1DQ
🌐 6 (5 Thu & Fri)-11; 12-midnight Sat & Sun
☎ (01768) 898284 ⏏ fetherstonarms.co.uk
Black Sheep Best Bitter; guest beers 🅗
Comparatively new to the pub scene, the Fethers was once a small private hotel, then a restaurant, before incorporating the adjacent buildings to become a pub in its own right after the closure of the nearby Black Bull. Its commitment to real ale is borne out by the beer festival it regularly organises, bringing in enthusiasts from a wide area. It is situated in the centre of this historic village opposite the now defunct cobbled market square. ▲🌀🍴◑ ▲🖼♣♠

Lindal-in-Furness

Railway Inn 🅛
London Road, LA12 0LL
🌐 4 (5 Thu)-11; 3-midnight Fri & Sat; 12-7 Sun
☎ (01229) 462889
Beer range varies 🅗
A welcoming open-plan, single-room pub with a beamed ceiling and slate floor. At one end is a comfortable lounge area around a stone fireplace and open fire. Adding to the character is a centrally positioned bar made from old church pews, with up to four handpumps active, and a local beer always available. With the exception of Saturday lunchtime and Monday evening, food is served lunchtimes and evenings every day (booking advisable). Visitors are also welcome at the quiz night on Thursday. ▲🌀◑🖼(6,6A)⁵⁻

Loppergarth

Wellington 🅛
Main Street, LA12 0JL (1 mile from A590 between Lindal and Pennington) SD260772
🌐 6-midnight (1am Fri & Sat) ☎ (01229) 582388
Beer range varies 🅗
Superb village local one mile from the A590. Four handpumps serve local beers, including from Foxfield. The central bar has four distinct areas and a large games room. There is no jukebox or fruit machine, just games, books and good conversation. A buy-and-return library operates in aid of local charities. Wood-burning stoves in the bar and family room make this a cosy pub. A popular quiz takes place on alternate Saturdays, and darts teams play here. The TV is usually on. Dogs on leads welcome. ▲🌀🍴♣♠⁵⁻

Low Hesket

Rose & Crown 🅛
Low Hesket, CA4 0HG (next to A6 in village)
🌐 6 (9 Mon)-midnight; 12-2, 6-11.30 Sun ☎ (01697) 473346
Jennings Bitter, seasonal beers; guest beers 🅗
A venue that was originally a coaching inn, dating from 1750. The modern restaurant extension features railway-themed memorabilia and a tree growing inside. The public bar continues the transport feel with pictures of road vehicles, and some of the seats are from a vintage bus. Locally

sourced food is a feature and Friday night is steak night. There are occasional seasonal beers from the Marston's range. The place is home to a team in the local darts league. Closed lunchtimes except Sundays. ▲Q🌀◑🍴🖼(104,130,134)♣P⁵⁻

Low Lorton

Wheatsheaf Inn
CA13 9UW (in village, on B5289)
🌐 11.30-11 ☎ (01900) 85199 ⏏ wheatsheafinnlorton.co.uk
Jennings Bitter, Cumberland Ale, Cocker Hoop, Sneck Lifter, seasonal beers 🅗
Three miles south of Cockermouth, with panoramic views of some of the finest Lakeland fells. The inn has a superb choice of real ales from the Jennings Brewery including every one of the monthly ales. Guests include some of the more obscure beers on the Marston's list. Two roaring open fires welcome locals and visitors alike. There is a quiz on Wednesday, and fresh fish on Thursday and Friday. Outside are extensive grounds and an enclosed beer garden. ▲Q🍃🌀◑🍴🖼(77,77a)♣P⁵⁻

Loweswater

Kirkstile Inn
CA13 0RU (off B5289, 5 miles from Cockermouth via Lorton) NY140210
🌐 10-11 (10.30 Sun) ☎ (01900) 85219 ⏏ kirkstile.com
Cumbrian Legendary Melbreak Bitter, Langdale, Grasmoor Dark Ale, Loweswater Gold; Yates Bitter 🅗
Sitting below Melbreak, this inn nestles between Loweswater and Crummock Water. The 17th-century hostelry has low ceilings and stone walls. It is the tap for the Cumbrian Legendary Ales brewery, with six handpumps. The guest beer is usually Yates but occasionally changes. Oversized glasses are used. Food is offered, and the pub can be busy with diners during peak times. A past local CAMRA Pub of the Year. ▲Q🍃🌀🍴◑🅙P🖰

Melmerby

Shepherds Inn 🅛
CA10 1HF (9 miles from Penrith on the A686)
🌐 12 (5 Mon-Thu winter)-11; 12-11 (10.30 winter) Sun
☎ (01768) 881741 ⏏ shepherdsinnmelmerby.co.uk
Tirril Old Faithful; guest beers 🅗
The original red sandstone pub dates back to 1789 but later incorporated an adjacent barn, resulting in differing floor levels. The main bar is on the lower level but this too has a raised area, usually used for food but also darts. Up to four guest beers are available depending on the season, many of them local. Melmerby is an attractive village ideally situated to catch travellers on the scenic route from the north-east to the Lakes. ▲🌀◑🅙▲♣P⁵⁻

Millom

Punch Bowl 🅛
The Green, LA18 5HJ (½ mile from Green Road station) SD179847
🌐 5 (10am Fri), 3-1am Sat; 12-11.30 Sun
☎ (01229) 779585
Yates Bitter; guest beers 🅗
Sitting on the A5093, the Punch Bowl is a thriving community pub with up to nine handpumps serving local beers from Beckstones and Yates breweries alongside ales from far and wide. It holds its own beer festival in the summer and is

also a venue for the popular Broughton Festival of Beer, held each autumn. The open-plan bar area has real fires. On a bus route and a pleasant walk down a quiet road from the railway station. ⛽Q✿≢(Green Road)🚌(7)🚲P½–🏠

Near Sawrey

Tower Bank Arms 🅛

LA22 0LF (on B5285 6 miles S of Ambleside) SD370956
✪ 11-11 Mon-Sat (closed 2.30-5.30 Mon-Fri winter); 12-10.30 Sun ☎ (01539) 436334 ⊕ towerbankarms.co.uk
Cumbrian Legendary Loweswater Gold; Hawkshead Bitter, Brodie's Prime; guest beer 🅗
All the features of a traditional 17th-century Lakeland inn are to be found here: slate floor, oak beams and a cooking range housing an open fire. Set in a beautiful rural location next to Hill Top, the former home of Beatrix Potter (which is open to the public), it can be very busy at holiday times. Food is served in the bar and restaurant. All beers are sourced locally. Children are welcome, as are dogs, but not in the restaurant. ⛽Q✿≡🍴🚲🚲P

Nether Wasdale

Strands 🅛

CA20 1ET NY125039
✪ 11-11; 12-10.30 Sun ☎ (01946) 726237
⊕ strandshotel.co.uk
Strands Responsibly, Brown Bitter, Errmmm..., T'Errmmm-inator 🅗
The Strands showcases the beers of the experimental brewer, who also runs the pub. Three distinct areas each offer a real fire and easy seating in a relaxed atmosphere. The menu is interesting and fresh local ingredients are used. Free Wi-Fi is available. ⛽Q♿✿≡🍴ÅP½

Penrith

Agricultural Hotel 🅛 ✔

Castlegate, CA11 7JE (close to railway station)
✪ 11-11; 12-10.30 Sun ☎ (01768) 862622
⊕ the-agricultural-hotel.co.uk
Jennings Bitter, Cumberland Ale, Sneck Lifter; guest beers 🅗
The hotel is built from local sandstone and the bar and dining room are open plan, with steps from one to the other. There is also a small reception area. It has a Victorian shuttered bar of sash screens with five handpumps selling Jennings and guest beers. Food is served in the large dining area, as well as in the bar at quiet times. Very convenient for the railway station and nearby bus stops. ⛽Q✿≡🍴♿≢🚌🚲P½–

Royal

92 Wilson Row, CA11 7PZ
✪ 12-midnight ☎ (01768) 862670
Beer range varies 🅗
Traditional pub on the edge of the town centre with tiled walls and lots of mellow wood. It has three separate areas served by one bar. Two handpumps operate with beers from all over the UK, but often featuring beers from local Cumbrian brewers. It is home to darts, dominoes and pool teams, who play in local leagues. There is full sports TV coverage. Live music sessions with a broad appeal are held on Sunday afternoons outwith the football season. Lunchtime food Saturday and Sunday only. ♿≢🚌(104)🚲

Penruddock

Herdwick Inn 🅛

CA11 0QU (at jct 40 M6 take A66 W for Keswick; right turn after 6 miles) NY426276
✪ 12-2.30, 5.30-11; 12-midnight Sat; 12-10.30 Sun
☎ (01768) 483007 ⊕ herdwickinn.com
Jennings Bitter, Cumberland Ale; guest beer 🅗
A charming 18th-century pub named after the hardy breed of Cumbrian sheep. Situated north of the A66 between Penrith and Keswick, it is all that a traditional village pub should be and more. Original oak beams, open fireplaces and local stone walls add to the character of this CAMRA award-winner. The Herdwick includes a bar, games room, large garden and restaurant with excellent food. Close to the Coast-to-Coast cycle route, the inn has secure cycle storage. Accommodation is recommended. ⛽✿≢🍴Å🚌(X4,X5,105)🚲P½–

Penton

Bridge Inn

CA6 5QB (on B6318 about 4 miles E of Canonbie) NY43757655
✪ 5-midnight ☎ (01228) 577041
Beer range varies 🅗
A warm welcome is to be found at this most northerly real ale pub in Cumbria. Accommodation is available and is used by fishermen coming to try their luck in the nearby Border Esk, famed for its game fishing. Three handpumps dispense a range of ales from local breweries such as Geltsdale, Hesket Newmarket and Cumberland. Food is served Wednesday to Sunday in the separate dining area. There is also a games room. Be aware that the pub is only open during the evenings. ⛽Q≡🚲P

Ravenglass

Ratty Arms

The Ratty Arms, CA18 1SN (through mainline station or village car park)
✪ 11-midnight Mon-Sat summer; 11-3, 5-midnight; 12-midnight Sat & Sun winter ☎ (01229) 717676
Ennerdale Blonde; Jennings Cumberland Ale; Theakston Best Bitter; Yates Golden Ale 🅗
A railway-themed pub deservedly popular with locals and tourists. It occupies the former station building at the junction of the main line and the La'al Ratty; this narrow-gauge steam train runs deep into Upper Eskdale, with more good pubs, high fells and Roman remains to explore. Local attractions are Muncaster Castle, a Roman bathhouse, and an impressive estuary, rich in wildlife. Guest beers are often from Ennerdale Brewery. Excellent good-value food is served all day. ⛽Q✿🍴♿Å≢🚌(6)P½–

Ravenstonedale

Black Swan Inn 🍷 🅛 ✔

CA17 4NG (village signed off A685)
✪ 8.30am-11 (1am Fri & Sat); 11-midnight Sun
☎ (01539) 623204 ⊕ blackswanhotel.com
Black Sheep Best Bitter; John Smith's Bitter; guest beers 🅗
An excellent example of a pub as the hub of the community, situated in a conservation area between the Lake District and the Yorkshire Dales. Combining a Cask Marque-accredited outlet with

the village shop, offering local produce, the bar serves up to five real ales, including two locals. It has a TV, and the lounge has adjoining dining rooms where locally sourced food is served. Across the road is a well-maintained garden complete with stream. An annual beer and music event is held. ♨Q❀🚲🍴◑🍽🔥🚌(564,569)♣P

Rydal

Glen Rothay Hotel (Badger Bar) 🄻
LA22 9LR
❀ 11-11; 11-10.30 Sun ☎ (01539) 434500
🌐 theglenrothay.co.uk
Beer range varies Ⓗ
Roadside inn dating from 1624 and especially popular with walkers. There is a warming log fire in the main bar, where owners with dogs are welcome. The five beers on offer are mainly Cumbrian, reflecting the importance placed here on the environment. The separate Oak Room has a fireplace with a superb overmantel. A well-appointed dining room looks out over Rydal Water. CAMRA members receive a discount.
♨Q❀🍴◑🚌(555,599)♣P🏕

St Bees

Manor House ✅
11-12 Main Street, CA27 0DE
❀ 11-11 (10.30 Sun) ☎ (01946) 820587
Jennings Bitter Ⓗ
At the start of the Coast-to-Coast walk, this pub is popular with locals and visitors alike. There are two bar rooms: one, with a wooden floor, has a pool table, dartboard, jukebox and TV to show sports. The other is more of a lounge, and is where food is served of an evening.
❀🍴◑🍽🔥🚉🚌(20,X6)P

Seascale

Calder House Hotel
The Banks, CA20 1QP
❀ 12-2, 5.30-11; 12-2 winter Sun ☎ (01946) 728538
🌐 calderhouse.co.uk
Jennings Bitter Ⓗ
Well appointed Victorian building, the interior retains many attractive features and memorabilia, echoing its past as as fashionable girls' school. Now, its attractions are the adjacent 18-hole golf course, the Cumbrian coastal walk, and cycle routes. It also provides access to the Western Lakes and views across the extensive sandy beaches and Irish Sea to the Isle of Man. Guest beers are often from Cumbrian Legendary Ales brewery and Lancashire's Cross Bay.
♨Q🛏❀🍴◑🍽🔥🅰🚉🚌(6,X6)♣P

Shap

Greyhound Hotel
Main Street, CA10 3PW (on A6)
❀ 11-11 ☎ (01931) 716474 🌐 greyhoundshap.co.uk
Black Sheep Best Bitter; Taylor Landlord; guest beers Ⓗ
A famous Westmorland hostelry dating back to 1680, with panoramic views of the Lake District fells. The revolving front door leads into a spacious bar/dining area served from an L-shaped counter with handpumps on both sides, dispensing up to eight beers. Most of the food is locally sourced.

Popular with walkers using the nearby Coast-to-Coast walk or visiting Shap Abbey and Haweswater. ♨🛏❀🍴◑🍽🔥🅰♣🐕P🏕

Silloth

Albion 🄻
Eden Street, CA7 4AS
❀ 3 (7 Mon)-11 (4.30-11 winter); 2-midnight Fri; 12-midnight Sat & Sun ☎ (01697) 331321
Derwent Parsons Pledge; Tetley Mild Ⓗ
Traditional one-bar pub with a separate family room containing a pool table and TV, well-supported by friendly locals and summer visitors. Pictures of old Silloth decorate the walls along with two models of whaling trawlers. There are numerous photos celebrating the Isle of Man TT races; the local motorcycle club meets here on the first Sunday of each month and welcomes visitors. The nearby Derwent Brewery often tries out new beers at this hostelry. A holiday cottage is available next door. ♨🛏❀🍴🅰🚌(38,60,71)♣🏕

Staveley

Beer Hall 🄻 ✅
Mill Yard, LA8 9LR
❀ 12-6 (5 Mon); 12-11 Fri & Sat; 12-8 Sun ☎ (01539) 825260
🌐 hawksheadbrewery.co.uk
Hawkshead Bitter, Red, Lakeland Gold, Brodie's Prime, Windermere Pale Ale, seasonal beers Ⓗ
The brewery tap to the next door brewery, the building has two storeys: upstairs there are comfy sofas while downstairs solid wooden furniture enhances the bar. The food menu has been developed to complement Hawkshead beers. Spring and summer beer festivals are held, with up to 52 beers to sample. The beer shop has a fantastic display of bottled Hawkshead and foreign beers. CAMRA members and train users get a 10 per cent discount, and there is a loyalty card scheme. Q❀◑🍽🚉🚌(555)♣P

Eagle & Child 🄻
Kendal Road, LA8 9LP
❀ 11-11; 12-10.30 Sun ☎ (01539) 821320
🌐 eaglechildinn.co.uk
Hawkshead Bitter; guest beers Ⓗ
In winter there are roaring log fires to keep you warm and in summer riverside tables and a garden to enjoy. The pub has an interesting range of artefacts around the walls. Regular beer festivals are held in a marquee next to the River Kent, complementing the range of beers in the pub. There are great lunchtime food deals and an entertaining Thursday evening quiz, which make this a popular pub with locals and visitors alike.
♨❀🍴◑🚉🚌(555)🐕P🏕

Strawberry Bank

Masons Arms 🄻 ✅
Cartmel Fell, LA11 6NW SD413895
❀ 11.30-11; 12-10.30 Sun ☎ (01539) 568486
🌐 strawberrybank.com
Hawkshead Bitter, Lakeland Gold; Thwaites Wainwright; guest beers Ⓗ
Owned by the Individual Inns group, this picturesque pub is set on a hillside, with spectacular views across the Winster Valley. Two solid fuel ranges and three seating areas provide a cosy atmosphere in winter, while the outdoor

seating and dining area is an idyllic location on a warm sunny day. Dogs are welcome in the garden only. The pub is popular with walkers and the local community alike. ᴁQ➎☺❀ᗄⅉ♣P⅄

Tallentire

Bush Inn

CA13 0PT
☼ closed Mon; 6-midnight; 12-2, 7-11.30 Sun
☎ (01900) 823707
Robinson's Dizzy Blonde Ⓗ
Pleasantly decorated but airy and not over fussy, this venue represents a good mix of the modern and traditional. It is noted for the quality of both its beer and food. The interesting selection of guest beers usually features a Robinson's. Charming small village setting, with an unassuming exterior. ᴁQ❀ⅉᗄ(58)♣P

Torver

Church House Inn Ⓛ

LA21 8AZ (2 miles SW of Coniston near jct of A593/A5084) SD285942
☼ 12-midnight ☎ (01539) 441282
⊕ churchhouseinntorver.com
Barngates Tag Lag; Coniston Bluebird; Cumbrian Legendary Loweswater Gold; guest beers Ⓗ
Offering good-quality food in the bar and dining room, and a friendly welcome, this unspoilt 14th-century inn features low beams, flagged floors and a magnificent open fire. It is a welcome sight whether you have just walked up Coniston Old Man or simply come in search of a fine pint (there are up to five to choose from) and a bit of craic with the locals. Occasional live folk music plays at weekends. The garden boasts a fine view of the surrounding fells. ᴁQ❀ᗄⅉ♿Åᗄ(X12)♣P⅄

Troutbeck

Mortal Man Inn

LA23 1PL (4 miles from Windermere just off A592)
☼ 10.30-midnight ☎ (015394) 33193
⊕ themortalman.co.uk
Hesket Newmarket Loughrigg; Jennings Cumberland Ale Ⓗ
Lovely unspoilt pub offering a real welcome for walkers, with two rooms and a large beer garden enjoying superb views of the Troutbeck Valley and Windermere. Three Cumbrian beers are available during the winter months, with more during the busier periods; the house beer, Sally Birkett's Ale, is brewed by Hawkshead. Oak beams are predominant throughout the pub, where a good selection of meals is served. There is a quiz night every Wednesday and a popular folk night on a Sunday. ᴁ❀ᗄⅉ♿Å♣P⅄

Ulverston

Devonshire Arms Ⓛ

Braddyll Terrace, Victoria Road, LA12 0DH
☼ 4 (3 Thu & Fri)-11; 12-midnight Sat; 12-11 Sun
☎ (01229) 582537
Beer range varies Ⓗ
Situated between bus and train stations (adjacent to the railway bridge), the Dev is a large single-room pub. Distinct areas are formed by the use of comfortable bench seating. Two TVs show major sporting events, and there is a jukebox, as well as

pool, darts and dominoes. This is a real locals' pub, where all are welcome. Six handpumps serve superb ales from near and far. A beer festival is held on the May Day weekend. ❀Å⇌ᗄ♣P⅄

Mill Ⓛ

Mill Street, LA12 7EB
☼ 11-11 (1am Fri & Sat); 11-10.30 Sun ☎ (01229) 581384
⊕ mill-at-ulverston.co.uk
Lancaster Amber, Blond, Black, Red; guest beers Ⓗ
With a town-centre location near the top end of King Street, the Mill has an interesting and characterful layout over the various floors, centred around a restored original waterwheel. The main bar has eight handpulls, dispensing four guest beers alongside the Lancaster Brewery range. There is a first floor outdoor patio area with seating, and picnic tables to the front. Quality food is deservedly popular, served in the bar and an upstairs restaurant (booking recommended). Live music plays and the pub holds occasional beer festivals. ❀ⅉ♿Å⇌ᗄ⅄

Stan Laurel Inn Ⓛ

The Ellers, LA12 0AB
☼ 7-midnight Mon; 12-2.30, 6-midnight; 12-midnight Sun
☎ (01229) 582814 ⊕ thestanlaurel.co.uk
Thwaites Original; guest beers Ⓗ
Just off the centre of Stan Laurel's home town, the Stan offers a warm welcome to locals and visitors alike. Six handpulls serve a variety of mainly locally brewed beers. Excellent-value quality food is available throughout the week (no food Mon). Adjacent to the bar is a large room with pool and darts and a smaller room primarily used by diners. In winter a log-burning stove adds to the pub's comfortable ambience. Well-behaved dogs are welcome. ❀ᗄⅉ♿Å⇌ᗄ♣P⅄

Swan Inn ♈ Ⓛ

Swan Street, LA12 7JX
☼ 3.30-11; 12-midnight Fri & Sat; 12-11 Sun
☎ (01229) 582519
Hawkshead Lakeland Gold; Yates Bitter; guest beers Ⓗ
Easily accessed, just off the town centre, the Swan offers up to 10 real ales, many rare for the area, sourced from near and far, encompassing all styles and strengths. A single bar serves three drinking areas, one with a real fire. Tuesday is quiz night, and there is regular live music including an open mic session on Wednesday. The popular Oktoberfest and Easter beer festivals take place in a large marquee in the garden, with all beers on handpull. ᴁ❀♿Å⇌ᗄ(6,6A,X35)♣●⅄☗

Waberthwaite

Brown Cow Ⓛ

LA19 5YJ (on A595) SD106932
☼ 11.30-1am; 12-midnight Sun ☎ (01229) 717243
⊕ thebrowncowinn.com
Hawkshead Bitter; Lancaster Amber; Moorhouse Pride of Pendle Ⓗ
Popular 100-year-old Cumbrian village pub offering up to seven interesting and frequently changing real ales, usually from Cumbrian and north Lancashire breweries, and always a cider. Meals use locally sourced food. There is occasional live music, regular quiz nights, and annual beer festivals in June and October. The Western Fells and Eskmeals nature reserve are close by. ᴁ➎❀ᗄⅉ♿Åᗄ(6X)♣●⅄☗

Wasdale Head

Wasdale Head Inn Ⓛ

CA20 1EX SD186087

☼ 11-11; 12-10.30 Sun ☎ (019467) 726229 ⊕ wasdale.com

Great Gable Iron Awe, Yewbarrow Ⓗ

Iconic climbers' pub/hotel in a superb location. The Climbers Bar supplies cask ale, hot drinks and pub food all day to meet the needs of walkers and climbers. Dirty boots and dogs are welcome, the staff helpful and cheerful. The manager is a keen supporter of real ale and he sources most beers locally, usually including beers from Great Gable Brewing. ♨Q❀❄◑Ⓓ✢❺ÅP

Wetheral

Wheatsheaf Ⓛ ✔

CA4 8HD

☼ 12-midnight ☎ (01228) 560686

Cumberland Corby Bitter; Geltsdale Cold Fell; guest beers Ⓗ

The Wheatsheaf is situated a short walk up the hill from the village green in this picturesque village on the banks of the River Eden. This venue, originally three separate rooms, now knocked into one, with a central bar, is very much a local and supported by those living nearby, especially when TV sport is on. The two regular beers are from the two nearest breweries to the pub. There is a beer garden and ample parking. An innovative website does justice to the pub. ♨❀◑Ɒ≈⊟(75)♣P↳

Whitehaven

Tavern Ⓛ

18 Tangier Street, CA28 7UX

☼ 12-midnight (2am Fri & Sat) ☎ (01946) 728283

Beer range varies Ⓗ

Popular pub with friendly staff, where dogs are welcome. The pub is close to the harbour and marina and only a short walk from the railway station, bus stop and public car park. It was closed for three years following a fire, but reopened in 2009 after a complete refurbishment, while keeping many of its original features such as the stone-flagged floor, spiral staircase and well. It has a wood-burning stove, games room and upstairs bar. The randomness of the guest beers is one of the main draws of the pub. ♨⊞≈⊟♣●↳

Windermere

Elleray Hotel ✔

2-6 Cross Street, LA23 1AE (200yds from railway station)

☼ 12-11 (midnight Fri & Sat) ☎ (01539) 488464 ⊕ elleraywindermere.co.uk

Copper Dragon Golden Pippin; Cumbrian Legendary Loweswater Gold; Jennings Cumberland Ale; guest beers Ⓗ

A friendly pub popular with both locals and visitors, it has a large main bar area and separate

restaurant offering good-quality food at reasonable prices. Up to five real ales are usually available throughout the year, with a stronger ale during the winter months; members receive a discount on their beer. The large patio to the rear is a suntrap in summer. Live music is performed most weekends, and an acoustic session is held on the first Tuesday of the month. ♨❀❄◑Ⓓ❺≈⊟↳

Winster

Brown Horse Inn Ⓛ

LA23 3NR (on A5074)

☼ 12-11 ☎ (01359) 443443 ⊕ thebrownhorseinn.co.uk

Winster Valley Best Bitter, Chaser, Hurdler, Old School Bitter; guest beers Ⓗ

Traditional rural pub with its own microbrewery, where the four handpumps serve mainly their own beers. The pub comprises a main bar with open beams, large tables and a log fire, and a separate restaurant area, but meals are served throughout the day in both areas. Local eggs and potatoes are available to buy over the bar. Beware: the brewery's Lakes Lager is keg. The outside seating area offers spectacular views of the surrounding countryside. Q❀❄◑Ⓓ❺P↳

Witherslack

Derby Arms Hotel Ⓛ

LA11 6RN (just off A590)

☼ 12-3, 6-midnight; 12-midnight Fri-Sun ☎ (01539) 552207 ⊕ thederbyarms.co.uk

Cumberland Corby Ale; Hawkshead Bitter; Thwaites Wainwright Ⓗ

Part of the same group as the Strickland Arms at Sizergh, this pub was reopened, after several years of closure, by the Witherslack Community Land Trust, and remains very much a community hub. A large room with open fires is straight inside the front door, and there is more dining space in the adjoining rooms, with a snug and games room at the rear. The house beer, Jolly Boys Outing, is brewed by the Cumbrian Legendary Ales brewery. ♨Q❄◑Ⓓ✢❺⊟(X35)♣P↳

Wreay

Plough Inn Ⓛ

Wreay, CA4 0RL (5 miles S of Carlisle, W of A6, 3 miles from jct 42 of the M6) NY436490

☼ closed Mon & winter Tue; 12-2.30 (not Tue), 6-11; 6-11 Sun ☎ (01697) 475770 ⊕ wreayplough.co.uk

Cumberland Corby Ale; guest beers Ⓗ

Five miles from the centre of Carlisle in a small, peaceful village, this pub is a real gem. Dating from 1786, the venue continues to be the traditional meeting place for the village guardians, the 12 men of Wreay – look for the display of their clay pipes. With a reputation for excellent food – locally sourced where possible – it is on two levels, with the main entrance and bar on the ground floor and dining tables down a few steps. ❀◑Ⓓ❺P

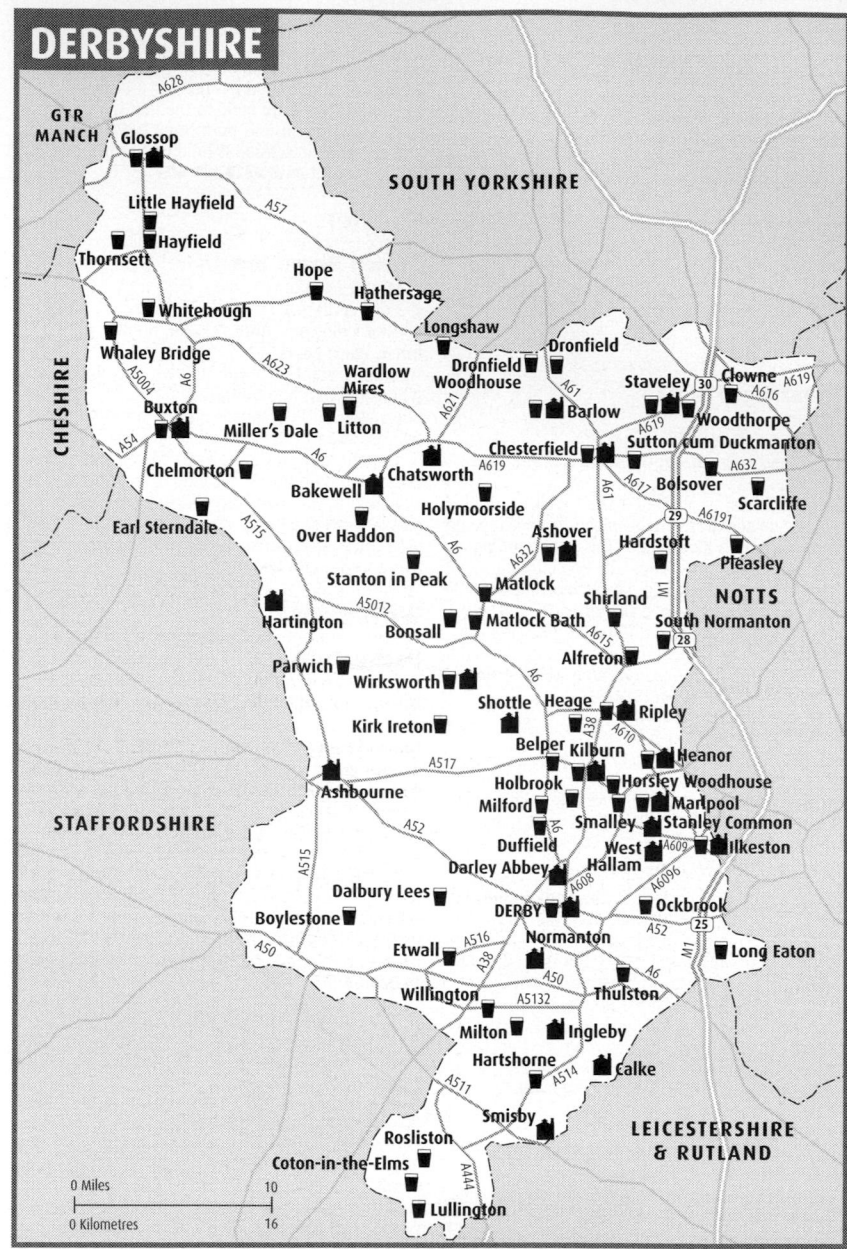

DERBYSHIRE

Alfreton

King Alfred L ✅

58 High Street, DE55 7BE

⏰ 10-midnight (12.30am Fri & Sat); 12-11 Sun
☎ (01773) 833274 ⊕ kingalfredalfreton.co.uk

Castle Rock Harvest Pale; Fuller's London Pride; guest beers Ⓗ

Landmark 1930s brewers' Tudor pub in the main shopping street. Within, two interconnecting rooms with exposed brick walls are adorned with old brewery signage. The arch-shaped bar has an area in front that doubles as a dance floor at weekends, when a vibrant atmosphere prevails courtesy of the disc jockey who plies his trade from 7.30pm. The five guest beers are augmented by Westons Old Rosie traditional cider. The bus station and Alfreton Town's football ground are not far away. ◖♣Pᔕ

Ashover

Old Poets' Corner L

Butts Road, S45 0EW (downhill from church)
⏰ 12-11 ☎ (01246) 590888 ⊕ oldpoets.co.uk

Ashover Light Rale, Poets Tipple; guest beers Ⓗ

The home of Ashover Brewery, this mock-Tudor building has a warm, welcoming atmosphere, with open fires, candle-lit tables and hop-strewn beams. Choose from 10 handpumps, including regular Ashover beers, along with a range of guest ales, six traditional ciders, draught and bottled Belgian beers, and country wines. Entertainment includes live music, a weekly quiz, folk evenings and three beer festivals a year. Dogs are welcome. ⚞Q☺☕🚃◑🚃♿🅰🚃(63,64)♣🚻P⌐

Barlow

Hare & Hounds 🅛
Commonside Road, S18 7SJ (from B6051, turn up hill at Commonside Road)
☀ 12 (11 Sat)-11.30; 12-10.30 Sun ☎ (0114) 289 0464
Barlow Brewery Heath Robinson, Three Valleys IPA; guest beers 🅷
Friendly, traditional village pub with three rooms around a central bar, plus a separate games room. The tap for Barlow Brewery, this pub has a strong community feel, though all are made welcome. In summer, Barlow Brewery's Carnival Ale is very popular. Views over the village to the countryside can be enjoyed from the back room. A tiny terrace area with colourful window boxes and planters is to the front of the pub. The landlord has been here for over 30 years. ⚞☺🚃🚃(89,89A)♣P

Belper

George & Dragon
117 Bridge Street, DE56 1BA
☀ 11-11.30; 12-10.30 Sun ☎ (01773) 880210
Draught Bass, East Mill Bitter; Greene King Abbot; Shottle Gold; guest beers 🅷
A fine Georgian former coaching inn with an attractive portico on the town's historic main thoroughfare and close to the famous East Mill. A deep, open-plan interior has unusual airline-style seating in the back area that was rescued from the old Derby Rugby Club. Belper Town Football Club, the beautiful river gardens and world heritage visitors' centre are nearby. The pub's car park and skittle alley to the rear are accessed through the archway. East Mill Bitter is brewed by Tower. ⚞☺≈♣🚻P⌐

Bolsover

Blue Bell
57 High Street, S44 6HF
☀ 12-3.30, 5-midnight; 12-3, 7-midnight Sun
☎ (01246) 823508 ⊕ bolsover.uk.com
Marston's Burton Bitter; Wychwood Hobgoblin; guest beers 🅷
Situated 200 yards from Bolsover Castle and built in 1749, this historic pub still retains many of its original features. Speak nicely to the landlord and he will show you the old stable and coachman's quarters. This venue is a traditional two-roomed pub where you can rediscover the art of conversation. The panoramic view from the beer garden is spectacular, and excellent food is served lunchtimes and evenings. Q🏃☺◑🚃🚃♣P⌐

Fidlers Rest 🅛
Craggs Road, S44 6BQ (just off A632, Bolsover Hill)
☀ 5 (12 Sat & Sun)-11 ☎ (01246) 828300
Beer range varies 🅷
Built as a private residence in 1812 by Peter Fidler, the famous explorer who mapped the Canadian wilderness for the Hudson Bay Company. Guest

beers are sourced mainly from local micros plus regular ales from Northumbria and Yorkshire. The modern interior has fine views over Bolsover Castle and the Peak District. Q☺🚃♣⌐

Bonsall

Barley Mow 🅛
The Dale, DE4 2AY
☀ closed Mon; 6-11; 12-midnight Sat; 12-10.30 Sun
☎ (01629) 825685 ⊕ barleymowbonsall.co.uk
Beer range varies 🅷
Tucked away in the south-west of the village in an area popular with walkers – Limestone Way passes close by – this quirky one-roomed pub offers a varied range of ales from near and far, as well as real ciders. The world hen racing championship is held here in August and the enthusiastic owners also offer regular music nights, which vary from folk to rock. Limited bus service from Cromford to Bonsall. ⚞Q☺◑🅰🚃(M2)♣🚻P⊟

Boylestone

Rose & Crown
New Road, DE6 5AA (off A515 between Sudbury and Cubley) SK176356
☀ 4.30-11; 11-midnight Sat; 12-11 Sun ☎ (01332) 330518
Marston's Pedigree 🅷
Many original features remain in this attractive village pub built in the 17th century. There are four

drinking areas, each with its own character, and the main bar is dominated by a welcoming, large real fire in winter. The pub has a very loyal following in the village, but visitors are made welcome. Renowned for its Pedigree, an occasional guest beer may also be seen. A separate modern restaurant attached to the pub is now open Thursday-Sunday. ⚑Q✿♣▲♣P²⌐

Buxton

Ramsay's Bar ✓
Buckingham Hotel, 1 Burlington Road, SK17 9AS
🕓 5 (4 Sat & Sun)-midnight ☎ (01298) 70481
⊕ buckinghamhotel.co.uk
Thornbridge Kipling; guest beers Ⓗ
A large public bar and adjoining lounge that are part of the Buckingham Hotel, and offer one of the best ranges of microbrewery beers in the area (six in summer, four in winter). Some ales are discounted during the happy hour – up to 8pm (10pm Sun & Mon). The TV plays silently except for the occasional football match. The outdoor smoking area is heated. ✿⛟◑ᴖ▲⇌➣P

Swan
40 High Street, SK17 6HB
🕓 11-1am ☎ (01298) 23278
Morland Old Speckled Hen; Storm seasonal beer; Tetley Bitter; guest beers Ⓗ
A hostelry that prides itself on being a drinkers' pub, with a friendly, welcoming atmosphere. Three rooms surround a central bar, and major sports matches are shown on TV, otherwise background music plays. There is always a Storm beer from nearby Macclesfield on handpump, and the pub has thriving darts and dominoes teams. Quiz night is Thursday. There is a small patio outside. ✿⛟⇌➣♣P

Wye Bridge House ✓
Fairfield Road, SK17 7DJ
🕓 8-midnight (1am Fri & Sat) ☎ (01298) 70932
Greene King Abbot; Marston's Pedigree; Ruddles Best Bitter; guest beers Ⓗ
Wetherspoon pub with a deserved reputation for serving an excellent selection of beers from local micros (usually three to five) in addition to two real ciders. The decor is modern, with a low ceiling, and a quieter area away from the bar. The substantial front patio is the best outdoor drinking area in Buxton. The place can be busy early evening. TVs play silently, and there are no sports channels. Parking nearby is limited. Q✿◑ᴖ⇌➣♣

Chelmorton

Church Inn ✓
Main Street, SK17 9SL
🕓 12-3.30, 6-11; 12-midnight Fri-Sun ☎ (01298) 85319
Adnams Southwold Bitter; Marston's Burton Bitter, Pedigree; guest beers Ⓗ
Set in beautiful surroundings opposite the local church, this traditional village pub caters for both locals and walkers. The main room is laid out for dining and good home-cooked food is on offer; however, a cosy pub atmosphere is maintained, with a low ceiling and real fire. Guest beers are usually from local micros. Parking is available at the end of the road in front of the pub and there is a patio area outside. Monday is quiz night. ⚑Q✿⛟◑▲♣

Chesterfield

Chesterfield Arms ♛ ⓛ
Newbold Road, S41 7PH
🕓 12-11 ☎ (01246) 236634
Everards Sunchaser; Fuller's London Pride; Leatherbritches CAD, Bounder; guest beers Ⓗ
A real ale emporium, this welcoming, family-run pub offers a selection of 10 beers – often from micros – augmented by six ciders and country wines. Oak-clad walls, open fires and hop-strewn beams create a relaxing ambience. A log-burning stove heats the barn area, open weekends, serving an extra six real ales. Monday is pie and peas night, quiz night is Wednesday and curry night Thursday. Lunch is available daily. Live music plays on the last Thursday of the month. Local CAMRA Pub of the Year 2012. ⚑✿➣(10)♣P²⌐

Derby Tup ⓛ
387 Sheffield Road, Whittington Moor, S41 8LS
🕓 12-3 (not Tue), 5-11; 12-midnight Fri & Sat; 12-11 Sun
☎ (01246) 454316
Castle Rock Harvest Pale, Screech Owl; Taylor Landlord; guest beers Ⓗ
Ten handpumps offer beers from local breweries as well as from further afield. A stout or porter is usually available, as well as Westons Old Rosie. The venue has a public bar with a real fire, a variety of wooden settles, and etched glass windows dating from its original incarnation as the Brunswick Hotel. There is also a small snug. Handily situated for the new Chesterfield B2net football stadium. ⚑Q⛟➣(43,50)♣

Market
95 New Square, S40 1AH (N side of marketplace)
🕓 11 (12 Sun)-11 ☎ (01246) 273641 ⊕ themarketpub.co.uk
Greene King Abbot; Kelham Island Easy Rider; Taylor Landlord; guest beers Ⓗ
Popular, friendly, town-centre pub serving up to eight real ales, often including a dark beer. Several small beer festivals are held throughout the year and a wide range of malt whiskies is available. Excellent food is served lunchtimes and early evenings Monday to Saturday, together with Sunday lunches. Quiz night on Thursday and live music on Sunday evening are additional attractions. Occasional events include whisky tasting, wine tasting and gourmet evenings. There is a small patio outside. ✿◑⇌➣♣²⌐

Rose & Crown ⓛ
104 Old Road, Brampton, S40 2QT
🕓 12-11 (midnight Fri & Sat) ☎ (01246) 563750
⊕ roseandcrownbrampton.co.uk
Brampton Golden Bud, Best, Wasp Nest, seasonal beers; Everards Tiger Best Bitter; guest beers Ⓗ
Everards' Project William's triumphant renovation of a run-down local enabled the Brampton Brewery to open its first tied house. A compact snug provides room for groups, while the main room has plenty of quiet corners. Memorabilia from the original brewery festoon the walls. Good-value food is served, including award-winning local produce. Quiz night is Tuesday, with a music quiz on the last Sunday of the month. A rear drinking area can be accessed through the pub, and free Wi-Fi is available. ⚑✿◑⇌➣(170)♣♣P²⌐

Spa Lane Vaults ⓛ ✓
34 St Marys Gate, S41 7TH
🕓 8-11 (midnight Thu-Sat) ☎ (01246) 246300

Beer range varies ⊞
The smaller and quieter of the two Wetherspoon pubs in the town, although it can be busy at the weekend and on club evenings. Across the road from Chesterfield's Crooked Spire, a brewers' Tudor exterior hides an Art Deco-influenced interior. Music, sport, TV and games machines feature. A multi-level patio area is popular in summer months. The beer range constantly changes. Free Wi-Fi available. 🌣🏠⊕◗≠🖾🌢'—

Tramway Tavern Ⓛ
192 Chatsworth Road, Brampton, S40 2AT
⊛ 4-11 Mon-Thu; 12-midnight Fri & Sat; 12-11 Sun
☎ (01246) 200111
Brampton Golden Bud, Best, seasonal beers; guest beers ⊞
Situated on the Brampton Mile, this is the Brampton Brewery tap. There are eight handpulls on the bar, four Brampton beers, one Everards and three changing guests. Quiz night is on Monday, with monthly music jam night on Sunday. A selection of Belgian and world beers is available, along with traditional ciders and perries. One area is dedicated to pictures and history of the old tram service that once passed by its doorway. There is an outdoor courtyard to the rear. Free Wi-Fi available. 🏠🏠🖾🌢'—

Clowne

Clowne Community Centre Ⓛ
Recreation Close, Villa Park, S43 4PL
⊛ 7-11 ☎ (01246) 819546
Beer range varies ⊞
A council-run community centre widely used by the locals for functions. The Rock & Blues Club has live bands every Sunday, and there is a popular quiz night on Tuesday with free food. The place is well cared for and the atmosphere is relaxed and friendly. Its first beer festival, last year, was very successful, with good attendance. Three changing guest beers are served. Ample car parking is available. Q🌣🏠⊕♿🖾(53,77,79)P'—🎁

Coton-in-the-Elms

Black Horse
17 Burton Road, DE12 8HJ (centre of village) SK246152
⊛ 4-11 (midnight Fri); 1-midnight Sat; 12-10.30 Sun
☎ (01283) 762947 ⊕ theblackhorsederbyshire.co.uk
Draught Bass; Joule's Original Pale Ale; Marston's Pedigree; guest beer ⊞
This Guide regular of some 30 years ago was revived in 2009 as a lively and popular free house after more than a decade of neglect. Tastefully renovated with extensive use of wood, the bright and airy main room is divided into bar and lounge areas by glass-topped wood partitions. A separate small snug, served through a hatch, features a bar billiards table. The guest beer is often sourced from a local microbrewery. Real cider is Woody's. Quiz night is Tuesday, and there is occasional live music Sundays. 🏠🏠🖾(22,813)♣🌢'—

Dalbury Lees

Black Cow
The Green, DE6 5BE SK265372
⊛ 12-3, 5-11; 12-midnight Sat & Sun ☎ (01332) 824297
⊕ theblackcow.co.uk
Marston's Pedigree; guest beers ⊞

Friendly pub next to the village green. There is a single open-plan drinking area leading to a games room housing a pool table. Separate modern dining areas have been created for diners sampling the restaurant-style menu. There is a small garden and outside patio area. Walkers and cyclists are actively encouraged. An annual beer festival is held in the summer, and the pub also has a small shop for essentials and newspapers. 🏠◗♣P'—

Derby

Alexandra Hotel Ⓛ
203 Siddals Road, DE1 2QE
⊛ 12-11 (midnight Fri); 11-midnight Sat ☎ (01332) 293993
⊕ alexandrahotelderby.co.uk
Castle Rock Harvest Pale, seasonal beers; guest beers ⊞
Named after the Danish princess who married the Prince of Wales (later Edward VII) in 1863, the Alex was originally called the Midland Coffee House. Long a Shipstones house and now with Castle Rock, it serves a range of six to eight guest ales from microbreweries near and far. The bar is adorned with railway memorabilia, the lounge with breweriana, both linked by a central bar. The pub was the birthplace of Derby CAMRA in 1974. 🏠Q🏠🛏⊕♿≠🖾♣P'—

Babington Arms ✔
11-13 Babington Lane, DE1 1TA
⊛ 8-11 (midnight Fri & Sat) ☎ (01332) 383647
Greene King Abbot; Marston's Burton Bitter, Pedigree; Ruddles Best Bitter; guest beers ⊞
Probably the best Wetherspoon in the country, the pub has won the company's prestigious Cask Ale Pub of the Year and local CAMRA City Pub of the Year twice. It showcases an amazing range of 18 beers on handpump, listed on a TV screen, and holds regular themed brewery weekends. The pub stands in the former grounds of Babington House, whose owners' plot led to the downfall of Mary Queen of Scots. Displays feature the former Grand Theatre that stands next door. Q◗♿🖾🌢

Brunswick Inn Ⓛ
1 Railway Terrace, DE1 2RU
⊛ 11-11; 12-10.30 Sun ☎ (01332) 290677
Brunswick White Feather, Triple Hop, Second Brew, Railway Porter, Father Mike's Dark Rich Ruby; Everards Beacon ⊞
Originally part of the railway village, the pub was closed in 1974 and fell into disrepair. Rescued and restored, it opened as Derby's first multiple choice real ale house in 1987. A purpose-built brewery was added in 1991, and it has since become one of the best-known free houses in the country. Although owned by Everards, its range of up to 16 real ales includes at least six from the in-house brewery. Busy on Derby County match days. 🏠Q🌣🏠⊕♿≠🖾♣🌢'—

Coach & Horses ✔
Mansfield Road, DE1 3RF
⊛ 12-midnight (1am Sat) ☎ (01332) 258901
Draught Bass; guest beers ⊞
Arts and Crafts Edwardian-style corner house in Little Chester, the oldest part of Derby, dating back to Roman times. Focused on the local community, there is a games room for pool and darts, and events include popular Sunday night quizzes, support for local charities and a book exchange. Draught Bass is served, plus two SIBA cask ales.

Live music is featured on bank holidays with a larger range of beers. A discount is available for card-carrying CAMRA members. ⚑🏠🍴(H1,9)♣P🚻

Exeter Arms 🅛

13 Exeter Place, DE1 2EU
✪ 11-11 (11.30 Fri; midnight Sat); 12-10 Sun
☎ (01332) 605323 ⊕ exeterarms.co.uk
Dancing Duck Ay Up, Nice Weather, 22, Gold; Marston's Pedigree; guest beers �,

Dancing Duck Brewery's first pub features a small bar with open fire, partitioned lounges and a wooden-settled snug with an old-fashioned range to the side. Live music features on Wednesday and Saturday and its secluded rear garden houses a stable-type bar that operates in summer with live music outside. One of the last of the old home-brew pubs in the city, it is perhaps fitting that one of Derby's newer breweries now runs this truly iconic pub. 🏚🏠🍴♣🍴🚻

Falstaff Tavern 🅛

74 Silverhill Road, DE23 6UJ
✪ 12-11 (midnight Fri & Sat) ☎ (01332) 342902
⊕ falstaffbrewery.co.uk
Falstaff Fistful of Hops, Phoenix, Smiling Assassin, seasonal beer ⏰

A 20-minute walk from the city centre rewards you with this atmospheric and reputedly haunted free house. Originally a coaching inn before the surrounding area was built up, it is now the Falstaff Brewery tap, making it the best real ale house in Normanton. The curved bar has a small lounge on one side where Offiler's Brewery memorabilia is displayed. Other collectables can be viewed throughout the games room and second bar room. 🏚🏠🍴🍴♣🍴🚻

Five Lamps 🍸 🅛 ✅

25 Duffield Road, DE1 3BH
✪ 12-11 (midnight Fri & Sat) ☎ (01332) 348730
⊕ fivelampsderby.co.uk
Buxton Kinder Downfall; Derby Five Lamps Ale; Everards Tiger Best Bitter; Peak Ales Chatsworth Gold; Whim Hartington Bitter; guest beers ⏰

Since it reopened in 2010, the pub has gone from strength to strength thanks to the dedication of the licensees and staff, which culminated in local CAMRA Pub of the Year 2012. Eleven handpumps showcase many local ales from breweries such as Peak, Buxton, Muirhouse and Whim. The Lamps is essentially open plan but with many little nooks and crannies to give it a homely feel. It has been tastefully refurbished with wood panelling and leather seating in traditional style. Q🏠🍴🍴🍴♣P🚻

Flowerpot 🅛

23-25 King Street, DE1 3DZ
✪ 11-11 (midnight Fri & Sat); 12-11 Sun ☎ (01332) 204955
⊕ the-flowerpot-pub.co.uk
Blue Monkey seasonal beers; Oakham Bishops Farewell; Whim Hartington IPA; guest beers ⏰/G

Dating from around 1800 but much expanded from its original premises, this pub reaches back from the small, roadside frontage and divides into several interlinking rooms. One room provides the stage for regular live bands and another has a glass cellar wall, revealing rows of stillaged firkins, which can be seen from the bar and from the road outside. Eight real ales are usually available and it is now the home of the Black Iris Brewery. Q🏠🍴🍴🍴♣🚻

Horse & Groom

48 Elms Street, DE1 3HN
✪ 12-11 ☎ (01332) 384775 ⊕ horseandgroomderby.co.uk
Draught Bass; guest beers ⏰

In the city's old West End, the pub dates from around 1850. A complete refurbishment has restored the building back to a thriving community local, with ladies' and gents' darts teams and two pool teams. The regular Bass is accompanied by three changing guests, often from Thornbridge, Ossett or Whim. There is regular live music at the weekend, jazz on the last Wednesday of the month, and a folk and blue-grass jamming session every Sunday evening. 🏠🍴♣🚻

Mr Grundy's Tavern 🅛

36 Ashbourne Road, DE22 3AD
✪ 11 (12 Sat)-11; 12-10.30 Sun ☎ (01332) 340279
⊕ mrgrundystavern.info
Draught Bass; Marston's Pedigree; Mr Grundy's Trenchfoot, No Man's Land, Coffin Nail; guest beers ⏰

The public bar within the Grade II-listed Georgian House Hotel serves up to 10 real ales, including many from the on-site brewery, Mr Grundy's. Named after a World War I veteran, the theme continues in the naming of the beers. The pub also supports LocAle. Wood-panelled throughout, the bar area features breweriana, film memorabilia, an unusual collection of hats and an old red telephone box. Outdoors is a large covered area and beer garden. No evening meals Sunday. 🏚🏠🛏🍴🍴(28,29)P🚻

Old Silk Mill 🅛

19 Full Street, DE1 3AF
✪ 11-midnight (11.30 Mon); 12-11 Sun
Castle Rock Harvest Pale ⏰**; Draught Bass** G**; Oakham Bishops Farewell; Purity Mad Goose** ⏰**; guest beers** ⏰/G

An amazing transformation into a traditional ale house won the Mill local CAMRA Pub of the Year in 2011. Two traditional ciders and nine real ales are served, increasing to 11 or more at the weekends when the rear John Lombe Bar offers beers from the cask. Two comfortable rooms feature real fires, with live music on Tuesday, Thursday and Sunday. Built in 1928 to replace an older inn nearby, it is close to the birthplace of the Industrial Revolution. 🏚🍴

Olde Dolphin Inne ★ ✅

5a Queen Street, DE1 3DL
✪ 10.30-midnight; 12-11 Sun ☎ (01332) 267711
⊕ freespace.virgin.net/dmh.derby/dolphin
Adnams Southwold Bitter; Draught Bass; Greene King Abbot; Taylor Landlord; guest beers ⏰

This is the oldest and most picturesque surviving pub in the city centre. The building dates back to 1530, though the Tudor-style façade dates from 1912. The warm, cosy and characterful interior comprises a bar, snug and two lounges, plus an upstairs steak bar. It has an extensive outside drinking area. The house beer, Dolphin 1530AD, is from Nottingham Brewery. There is a music quiz on Tuesday and a general knowledge quiz on Sunday. 🏚Q🏠🍴🍴

Peacock Inn

87 Nottingham Road, DE1 3QS
✪ 11-11 (midnight Thu-Sat); 12-10.30 Sun
☎ (01332) 603362

Leatherbritches Peacock Pale Ale; Marston's Pedigree; Oakham Bishops Farewell Ⓗ; Sarah Hughes Dark Ruby Ⓖ; Whim Arbor Light Ⓗ; guest beers Ⓗ/Ⓖ
Attractive 18th-century stone-built roadside pub that used to be a staging post on the main coach road out of Derby, which ran alongside the now filled-in old Derby Canal. Two rooms on different levels are divided by a central bar and consist of wooden floors, stove burners, photos of old Derby and Derby County memorabilia. Up to nine real ales and two ciders/perries feature; beer festivals are held in the large, covered garden area to the rear. Q✿❀⊞❀↰

Rowditch Inn
246 Uttoxeter New Road, DE22 3LL
✿ 12-2 (Sat & Sun only), 7-11 ☎ (01332) 343123
Marston's Pedigree; guest beer Ⓗ
Plain-fronted but warmly welcoming roadside hostelry with an unexpectedly deep interior, dividing into two drinking areas and a small snug. The rear garden is a positive haven in warmer weather. Pump clips adorning the walls of the bar are evidence of the myriad guest ales. The output of the pub's brewery is almost exclusively consumed on the premises. A pianist plays on the first and third Saturdays of the month. Worth the walk or bus out of the city centre. ▲✿❀⊞♣↰

Station Inn ✅
12 Midland Road, DE1 2SN
✿ 11.30-2.30, 6-11; 11 30-11 Fri & Sat; 12-3, 7-10.30 Sun
☎ (01332) 608014
Caledonian Deuchars IPA Ⓗ; **Draught Bass** Ⓖ; **Marston's Pedigree; Wells Bombardier; guest beer** Ⓗ
This immaculately kept city pub with its ornate frontage (by Charrington & Co) is convenient for the railway station and some of Derby's best Indian restaurants. Behind the bar and pool room is a large function room used by various organisations, including CAMRA. The landlord chairs the local Pub Watch scheme, and is renowned for his award-winning cellar and excellent Bass from the jug. Opening hours may be restricted when Derby County is playing at home. ⇌⊞♣

Dronfield

Coach & Horses Ⓛ
Sheffield Road, S18 2GD
✿ 5-10 Mon; 12-11 (midnight Fri & Sat); 12-10.30 Sun
☎ (01246) 413269
Thornbridge Jaipur IPA, seasonal beers Ⓗ
Roadside pub north of the town centre, with one comfortably furnished open-plan room. It is owned by Sheffield FC, the world's oldest football club, founded in 1857, whose ground is adjacent, but operated by Thornbridge Brewery. There are up to five Thornbridge beers available on a rotating basis, usually including the latest specials. Bar snacks are served every day until late. Regular live music takes place, including an acoustic night every Monday. Q✿❀⊃⇌⊞♣❀P↰

Three Tuns Ⓛ
135 Cemetery Road, S18 1XX
✿ 12-11 (midnight Fri & Sat) ☎ (01246) 410556
Spire Whiter Shade of Pale, Dark Side of the Moon, seasonal beers; guest beers Ⓗ
Built in 1938 by Stones Brewery as one of several multi-roomed brewers' Tudor roadhouses in the area; in 2011 it was acquired by Spire Brewery, refurbished and renamed. The 14 handpumps

showcase a changing range of six Spire beers, together with six guest beers and two real ciders. The menu features simple good-value food with quality ingredients. Home-made pizzas cooked in a wood-fired oven in the outdoor drinking area are sometimes available. Live music features periodically. ✿❀⊃⟐⇌⊞(43,44,44A)♣❀P↰─▯

Dronfield Woodhouse

Jolly Farmer ✅
Pentland Road, S18 8ZQ
✿ 12-midnight (1am Fri & Sat) ☎ (01246) 418018
Black Sheep Best Bitter; Taylor Landlord; Tetley Bitter; guest beers Ⓗ
Community pub built on a large housing estate in 1976 by Shipstones, and turned into a themed ale house in the 1990s. The cask beers are stillaged in a glass-fronted cellar behind the bar. The pub is open plan but has distinct areas, including a tap room with a pool table and a raised dining area. Two guest beers feature, usually from small independents, and a beer festival is held in November. ✿❀⊃⟐⇌⊞(43,89)♣P↰

Duffield

Pattenmakers Arms ✅
4 Crown Street, DE56 4EY
✿ 12-2, 5-midnight; 12-midnight Fri & Sat; 12-4, 7-midnight Sun ☎ (01332) 842844 ⊕ pattenmakersarms.co.uk
Draught Bass Ⓗ; **Marston's Pedigree; Taylor Landlord; guest beer** Ⓗ
A pleasant Edwardian pub – motto: Enter a stranger and leave as a friend – tucked away behind the main road. A traditional, welcoming and customer-focused local, it has retained much of its original character, with quarry-tiled and parquet floors and stained/etched glass windows. Skittles, darts, dominoes and quiz teams meet, and there are Sunday quizzes and weekend meat raffles. Good-value wholesome food is served every lunchtime, and breakfast from 10am on Saturday. Ecclesbourne Valley Heritage Railway is close by. ✿⟐⇌⊞♣❀P↰

Earl Sterndale

Quiet Woman
SK17 0BU (off B5053)
✿ 12-3 (4 Sat; 5 Sun), 7-11 ☎ (01298) 83211
Jennings Dark Mild; Marston's Burton Bitter; guest beer Ⓗ
Unspoilt local, set in the heart of the Peak District National Park, opposite the church and village green. Inside, a low-beamed room has a real fire on the left and a small bar to the right. There is a separate games room with a pool table. Local fresh eggs and traditional pork pies can be purchased at the bar. The pub offers its own selection of naturally conditioned bottled beers brewed by Leek Brewery. ▲Q✦✿▲⊞(442)♣P

Etwall

Spread Eagle
28 Main Street, DE65 6LP
✿ 12-11.30 (12.30am Fri & Sat) ☎ (01283) 735224
Draught Bass; Marston's Pedigree; guest beer Ⓗ
Modern free house popular with locals of all ages. It comprises a large single room with a central horseshoe bar. The traditional bar area boasts low,

leather-enclosed beams, two TVs, a dartboard and pool table. Local league pool games are played regularly. The lounge has comfortable seating and old photographs of the surrounding area. Outdoor seating at the front is popular in summer. Up to five real ales are featured, including those from local microbreweries. ✿🖼(V1,V2)♣P

Glossop

Crown Inn ★
142 Victoria Street, SK13 8JF (on Hayfield Road out of town centre)
✿ 5 (12 Fri & Sat)-11; 12-10.30 Sun ☎ (01457) 862824
Samuel Smith OBB Ⓗ
End-of-terrace local, a few minutes from the town centre and Glossop station, built in 1846 and the only Smith's house in the High Peak area since 1977. An attractive curved bar serves two side snugs, each with real fires in winter, and a pool/ games room. Old pictures of Glossop's past add to the traditional character. Prices are keen and Smith's bottled beers are also available. An enclosed outdoor drinking area is provided in the rear yard. ▲Q✿&≈🖼♣゚

Globe Ⓛ
144 High Street West, SK13 8HJ
✿ closed Tue; 5-1am (2am Fri & Sat); 1-midnight Sun
☎ (01457) 852417
Globe Amber, Blondie, Toby Porter, Comet, Imperial Stout, seasonal beers Ⓗ
Cosy local at the lower end of the High Street. The brewery for this brewpub is located in a small rear outbuilding off the beer garden. In addition to the selection of Globe ales, guest beers are often available, as are two real ciders, all on handpump. There is a lively music scene in the pub on Mondays, and live bands perform in the upstairs function room at weekends; quiz night is Wednesday. A reputation for good-value enterprising vegan food has been established, including home-made ice cream. Q✿🌶≈🖼🍴゚

Star Inn ✅
2 Howard Street, SK13 7DD (next to railway station)
✿ 2 (4 Mon & Tue)-11; 2-midnight Fri; 12-midnight Sat; 12-10.30 Sun ☎ (01457) 853072
Black Sheep Best Bitter; guest beers Ⓗ
Highly respected town-centre local run by long-standing CAMRA members. Guest beers are sourced from SIBA breweries and Old Rosie cider is a regular – all available on handpump. Locally produced ciders are sometimes also on offer and occasionally a pork pie competition is held. Pictures of bygone Glossop, wooden floors, and a rear tap room served by a hatch all add to the traditional atmosphere. Regular beer and cider festivals are held throughout the year. 🍴≈🖼(61,64,202)🍴P゚

Hardstoft

Shoulder at Hardstoft Ⓛ ✅
S45 8AE
✿ 11-11 ☎ (01246) 850276 ⊕ thefamousshoulder.co.uk
Greene King Abbot; Peak Ales Bakewell Best; Thornbridge Brewery Jaipur IPA; guest beers Ⓗ
Friendly, welcoming staff greet you at this 300-year-old local country pub only 10 minutes from junction 29 of the M1. Log fires and relaxing surroundings are provided for you to enjoy one of

five local real ales on the bar, with locally sourced food available. Located on the Five Pits Trail (from Tibshelf to Grassmoor), it welcomes walkers, cyclists and dogs, with four letting rooms and an excellent beer garden. ▲Q🌶✿🍴《Ⓓ&▲🖼P゚🛏

Hartshorne

Admiral Rodney Inn ♈
65 Main Street, DE11 7ES (on A514)
✿ 6-11.30; 5.30-midnight Fri; 12-2, 4-11.30 Sat; 12-midnight Sun ☎ (01283) 216482
Marston's Pedigree; guest beers Ⓗ
Traditional village pub dating back to the early 19th-century, but substantially rebuilt in 1959, and more recently refurbished to provide an open-plan L-shaped drinking area, retaining the original oak beams in the former snug. A small raised area behind the bar is served through a hatch. Up to four guest beers are available, usually from SIBA members. The Cheese Society meets here monthly on a Monday evening. The grounds include a cricket pitch, the pub remaining open during Saturday afternoon matches. ▲Q✿&🖼(61)♣P゚

Hathersage

Millstone Inn Ⓛ
Sheffield Road, S32 1DA (on A6187 E of village)
✿ 11.30-11; 12-10.30 Sun ☎ (01433) 650258
⊕ millstoneinn.co.uk
Black Sheep Best Bitter; Taylor Landlord; guest beers Ⓗ
Originally built to serve the nearby millstone quarry, and now popular with walkers and climbers as well as diners. A large pub, it has separate seating and dining areas either side of a central bar, and an extensive outdoor area, partly covered. The guest beers are from local breweries, and a quiz night is held on Fridays. Meals are served all day every day, with an extensive range of sausages available. ▲Q✿🍴《Ⓓ&🖼(272)♣P゚

Hayfield

Royal Hotel
Market Street, SK22 2EP
✿ 12-11 ☎ (01663) 742721 ⊕ theroyalhayfield.co.uk
Thwaites Original Bitter; guest beers Ⓗ
An imposing stone pub near the church, cricket ground and River Sett. The interior boasts original oak panels and pews that create a relaxing atmosphere, with real fires in winter. Several guest beers from local micros are always available and an annual beer festival is hosted in October. A restaurant and function room complete the facilities. The village is the base for many leisure activities in the Dark Peak area and was also the birthplace of Arthur Lowe, the immortal Captain Mainwaring in Dad's Army. ▲Q✿🍴《Ⓓ&▲🖼P゚

Heage

Black Boy
Old Road, DE56 2BN
✿ 11.30-11 ☎ (01773) 856799
Marston's Pedigree; guest beers Ⓗ
Friendly, family-run, stone-built free house in the heart of a village renowned for its restored six-sailed windmill. The comfortable two-roomed bar with coal fire attracts local trade, particularly on

Monday and Wednesday quiz evenings, which offer a free, home-made supper. A separate restaurant serves home-cooked food all day including vegetarian and fresh fish menus. A changing guest beer and traditional cider complement Black Boy Bitter, the house beer from Marston's. ⋈Q❀◑▯⊟(62)●P♪⌐

Heanor

Red Lion L ✅
2 Derby Road, DE75 7QG
❂ 9am-midnight ☎ (01773) 533767
Greene King Abbot; Ruddles Best Bitter; guest beers H
A Grade II-listed building, this Wetherspoon pub is in a good location just off the town centre and near the main bus routes. It is Cask Marque-accredited, with friendly, helpful staff serving four rapidly changing guest beers, usually from microbreweries, and one real cider alongside the regulars. The large, open-plan layout has three distinct drinking sections including a designated family area where food is served all day. There is good disabled access and outside is a patio area, partially covered for smokers. ⥽❀◑♿⊟●♪⌐

Holbrook

Dead Poets Inn
38 Chapel Street, DE56 0TQ
❂ 12-2.30, 5-11; 12-11 Fri & Sat; 12-10.30 Sun
☎ (01332) 780301
Draught Bass; Greene King Abbot; Marston's Pedigree G**; guest beers** H
Built in 1800 and formerly known as the Cross Keys, the pub has undergone a remarkable transformation to create an inn with a real medieval feel within. There is a delightful snug and the main bar has high-backed pews, stone-flagged floors, a real fire and inglenook. Around 25 guest beers feature during the week (six at any one time), usually including at least one from Abbeydale and Whim breweries. A great destination in summer and winter. ⋈Q❀◑⊟(71,138)●P♪⌐

Holymoorside

Lamb
16 Loads Road, S42 7EU SK339694
❂ 5 (4 Fri)-11; 12-3, 7-11 Sat & Sun ☎ (01246) 566167
Theakston Black Bull; guest beers H
Traditional locals' pub, unspoilt by progress, with a mixed clientele where all are welcome, including dogs and walkers (but take your boots off before going in). The public bar is warmed by a real open fire. Outside there is a paved outdoor drinking area that is ideal for warm summer evenings. A frequent winner of local CAMRA awards, with up to five guest beers. ⋈Q❀⊟(84)♣P

Hope

Cheshire Cheese L ✅
Edale Road, S33 6ZF SK170841
❂ closed winter Mon; 12-3, 6-midnight; 12-midnight Sat; 12-midnight (7 winter) Sun ☎ (01433) 620381
⊕ thecheshirecheeseinn.co.uk
Bradfield Farmers Blonde; Lees Bitter; Peak Ales Swift Nick; guest beers H

Cosy inn dating from 1578 with an open-plan bar area and a smaller room at a lower level that was probably originally used to house animals, but nowadays is a dining area (food available lunch, and eves except Sun). It is situated in walking country but parking is limited and the road outside narrow. Outdoor activities can be arranged by the pub. There are four double/twin rooms for B&B. ⋈Q❀⇄◑▯ÅP

Horsley Woodhouse

Old Oak Inn
176 Main Street, DE7 6AW (on A609)
❂ 4 (3 Thu & Fri)-11; 12-11 Sat; 12-10.30 Sun
☎ (01332) 881299
Bottle Brook seasonal beers; Leadmill seasonal beers; guest beers H
Flagship of the Leadmill Brewery, featuring a mouthwatering variety of its beers, plus a couple of guests. This traditional pub boasts four rooms of differing character, some with open fires. At weekends drinkers can enjoy the RuRAD bar – effectively a mini beer festival offering gravity dispensed ales from craft brewers near and far, alongside the familiar Leadmill and Bottle Brook beers. Homely, welcoming, and excellent value for money, this roadside tavern enjoys extensive views. ⋈Q⥽❀⊟♣●P

Ilkeston

Dewdrop Inn 🏆 L
24 Station Street, DE7 5TE (50yds from A6096 by railway bridge)
❂ 11-11; 12-10.30 Sun ☎ (0115) 9329684
Castle Rock Harvest Pale; Oakham Bishops Farewell; Thornbridge Kipling; guest beers H
Popular Victorian pub on the outskirts of town, the birthplace of Erewash Valley CAMRA. Under new management, the fine range of ales is sourced from microbreweries and is complemented by two ciders. The bar features a pool table and an oldies jukebox, while the lounge is renowned for its real fire and piano. Children are welcome in the front room, which doubles as a small function room. Cobs are made freshly to order. The rear yard has a covered smoking area. ⋈Q⥽❀⊟(27)♣●♪⌐

Spanish Bar
76 South Street, DE7 5QJ
❂ 10-11 (midnight Fri & Sat); 11-11 Sun ☎ (0115) 9308666
Whim Hartington IPA; guest beers H
Popular town-centre free house converted from two shops, served by major bus routes. The five real ales, usually from micros, are complemented by two real ciders. The long bar has a comfy seating area with a logburner. A second room is opened up for busy periods, including the Tuesday quiz night, darts and dominoes. Sports events are shown on the large-screen TV. The delightful rear garden houses a skittle alley and a heated, covered smoking area. Local CAMRA Pub of the Year 2010. ⋈❀⊟●♪⌐

Kilburn

Hunter Arms 🏆 L
Church Street, DE56 0LU
❂ 12-11 (midnight Fri & Sat) ☎ (01332) 781518
Oakham Bishops Farewell; guest beers H

Named after the owners of nearby Kilburn Hall when the pub was built in 1879, it was rescued from closure in 2009, and has won the local CAMRA Pub of the Year award in 2011 and 2012. The pub has a pleasant, opened-out interior with open fire, TV and free Wi-Fi. Four guest beers are sourced from smaller breweries, often featuring Thornbridge, Blue Monkey and Dancing Duck. Food is served Tuesday to Saturday only. Additional beers are available at weekends in the Old Slaughterhouse bar. ♨❀❀◑➡♣P

Kirk Ireton

Barley Mow Inn
Main Street, DE6 3JP (off B5023) SK266501
❀ 12-2, 7-11 (10.30 Sun) ☎ (01335) 370306
Whim Hartington IPA; guest beers Ⓖ
Set in a charming village overlooking the Ecclesbourne Valley, this tall, gabled Jacobean building houses an old-fashioned, down-to-earth pub, of the type that is increasingly hard to find. Several interconnecting rooms of different character have low beams, mullioned windows and well-worn woodwork, and there is a welcoming open fire in the main bar. A small serving hatch reveals a stillage with up to six gravity beers. Local CAMRA Pub of the Year runner-up in 2012. ♨Q❀❀⟷⊟♣●

Little Hayfield

Lantern Pike ✪
45 Glossop Road, SK22 2NG
❀ 12-3 (not Mon), 5-11; 12-11 Sat & Sun ☎ (01663) 747590
⊕ lanternpikeinn.co.uk
Taylor Landlord; guest beer Ⓗ
Picturesque ivy-clad pub nestling in a small hamlet within the Dark Peak area. The comfortable, traditional lounge bar, with a real fire in winter, connects to separate dining areas. Coronation Street originator Tony Warren once lived nearby and wrote some of the first episodes of the soap while in the pub (see photos and letter on display). There are superb views from the rear patio. Hikers welcome; it is approximately 10 minutes' walk from Hayfield. ♨❀❀⟷◑⊟(61)P⌐

Litton

Red Lion Ⓛ ✪
Church Lane, SK17 8QU SK163753
❀ 12-11 (midnight Fri & Sat; 10.30 Sun) ☎ (01298) 871458
⊕ theredlionlitton.co.uk
Abbeydale Absolution; Oakwell Barnsley Bitter; guest beers Ⓗ
Nestling on the green and the only pub in the village, the Red Lion is a welcome refuge for locals and visitors alike. There is a large fireplace serving several rooms off a central passageway, and the guest beers are often LocAle. Not to be missed is the annual Wakes Week at the end of June, with events including well dressing on the village green. Food is available all day every day.
♨Q❀◑⊟(65,66)♣⌐

Long Eaton

Barge Inn Ⓛ ✪
177 Tamworth Road, NG10 1DH
❀ 12-11.30 (1am Fri & Sat) ☎ (0115) 9725559
Copper Dragon Golden Pippin; guest beers Ⓗ

Spacious one-room pub with a single central bar serving up to six beers, usually from microbreweries. There is a separate area for pool and darts, a large upstairs function room, and a skittle alley outside. A lively, friendly place, it has three TV screens and holds regular live entertainment. Although it stands on a busy main road, the tree-lined Erewash canal, with moorings, is clearly visible from the front patio. Buses stop regularly outside. Dogs are welcome. ❀≒⊟♣P⌐

Stumble Inn Ⓛ
37 Tamworth Road, NG10 1JF
❀ 12 (2 Mon-Wed)-midnight ☎ (0115) 9724529
⊕ thestumbleinn.co.uk
Full Mash EPA; guest beers Ⓗ
During its short life, the Stumble has really established itself on the real ale scene in Long Eaton. Many local microbreweries are represented here, and along with the well-established late summer beer festival, the variety and range continue to expand. As a winner of local CAMRA awards and along with its own sports and pub games teams, it is now firmly part of the local community. A bus stop almost at the door makes this pub easily accessible. ♨❀≒⊟(R15)♣●⌐

Twitchel Inn Ⓛ ✪
Howitt Street, NG10 1ED (off pedestrian high street)
❀ 8am-midnight ☎ (0115) 9722197
Greene King Abbot; Marston's Pedigree; Ruddles Best Bitter; guest beers Ⓗ
Down a narrow side street, or twitchel, this pub is one of the smaller Wetherspoon's, using the tried and tested style of a large open-plan space and a partly raised drinking area containing many small cubicles. Fancy ceiling windows feature the pub's industrial heritage. The usual beer and food menus prevail, but real ale fans can put in requests for their favourite brews. On Sundays card-carrying CAMRA members can benefit from discounts on both beer and food. ◑&⊟(15)●

Longshaw

Grouse Inn
S11 7TZ (on A625) SK258779
❀ 12-3, 6-11; 12-11 Sat & Sun ☎ (01433) 630423
Banks's Bitter; Caledonian Deuchars IPA; Marston's Pedigree; guest beer Ⓗ
In the same family since 1965, this free house stands in isolation on bleak moorland south-west of Sheffield, and is deservedly popular with walkers and climbers. There are some fine photographs of nearby gritstone edges, as well as a collection of international bank notes on display. The comfortable lounge is situated at the front, with a smaller room to the rear separated by a conservatory. Lunch and evening (not Mon) meals are available, with food served all day on Sunday. ♨Q❀❀◑♣P

Lullington

Colvile Arms
Main Street, DE12 8EG
❀ 6-11; 12-3, 7-10.30 Sun ☎ (01827) 373212
Draught Bass; Marston's Pedigree; guest beer Ⓗ
Leased from the Lullington Estate, the seat of the Colvile family until the early 1900s, this popular 18th-century free house is at the heart of an

attractive hamlet at the southern tip of the county. The public bar comprises an adjoining hallway and snug, each featuring high-backed settles with wood panelling. The bar and a comfortable lounge are on opposite sides of a central serving area. A second lounge/function room overlooks the beer garden and lawn. ✿⊞♣P≒

Marlpool

Queen's Head 🄻
1 Breach Road, DE75 7NJ
✪ 11-midnight ☎ (01773) 768015
Beer range varies Ⓗ/Ⓖ
The multi-roomed interior of this tastefully restored local is free from any electronic distraction. Conversation often centres around the huge range of beers that frequently features Castle Rock, Thornbridge and Whim. A dark beer is always available alongside a multitude of ciders, some locally produced. Barbecues are often held in the outside drinking area at the front, while the rear area contains a covered space for smokers with an open fire. Well-behaved dogs welcome.
🚲Q✿🅗🚍(23,20)🍴P≒

Matlock

Thorntree
48 Jackson Road, DE4 3JQ
✪ 12-2 (not Mon), 6-11; 12-2.30, 5-midnight Fri; 12-midnight Sat; 12-11 Sun ☎ (01623) 580295
⊕ thorntreeatmatlock.co.uk
Draught Bass; Ruddles Best Bitter; Taylor Landlord Ⓗ
Perched high on the hill on the north side of Matlock, this two-roomed tavern is little altered and enjoys excellent views from the delightful patio over the town and along the Derwent Valley. A compact pub, popular with office workers at lunchtime, where food is served Tuesday-Friday lunchtimes, and Sundays. Evening meals are available Wednesday (pie night) and Thursday.
Q✿🅒🚍(M1)

Matlock Bath

Temple Hotel 🄻
Temple Walk, DE4 3PG (off A6)
✪ 4-10.30; 12-11.30 Sat; 12-10 Sun ☎ (01629) 583911
⊕ templehotel.co.uk
Blue Monkey Evolution; Leatherbritches Hairy Helmet; guest beers Ⓗ
Historic Georgian hotel with a public bar, high above the hustle and bustle of the Matlock Bath riverside promenade, affording splendid views across the Derwent Valley. Tourist attractions close by include the cable car rides and Peak District Mining Museum. Past visitors include Lord Byron, who etched a poem on a window. The landlord focuses on beers from Derbyshire microbreweries, with up to three from Thornbridge, Blue Monkey and Leatherbritches often featuring.
🚲✿🅒🅘🚍(6)♣P

Milford

King William IV
The Bridge, DE56 0RR
✪ 5 (12 Sat)-11.30; 12.30-11 Sun ☎ (01332) 840842
Greene King Abbot; Marston's Pedigree; Taylor Landlord; guest beers Ⓗ

Heading north on the A6, this stone-built Georgian inn, dramatically situated at the foot of sandstone cliffs, hoves into view. Within, an open fire at one end of the elongated bar adds to the ambience of the cosy, candlelit interior in the winter. Period furniture and quarry tiled flooring are from the same period as the building, which has three en-suite letting rooms. On-street parking is available on the adjacent Makeney Road. Milford is one of the Derwent Valley world heritage sites. Old Rosie traditional cider is served. 🚲🅒♣🍴

Miller's Dale

Angler's Rest 🍷 🄻 ✅
SK17 8SN (on B6049) SK142734
✪ 12-3, 6.30-11; 12-11 Sun; 12-10 Sun ☎ (01298) 871323
⊕ theanglersrest.co.uk
Adnams Southwold Bitter; Storm Silk of Amnesia; guest beers Ⓗ
Ivy-clad pub on the banks of the River Wye dating from 1753 and handy for the spectacular walk along the Monsal Trail. It is a multi-room pub including a cosy lounge with a real fire and a comfortable dining room. Walking boots and dogs are welcome in the hikers' bar. Good traditional pub food is served daily, and the guest beers are mostly LocAle. Accommodation is in a self-catering apartment. 🚲Q✿🅒🅘⊞🅰(65,66)♣P

Milton

Swan Inn
Main Street, DE65 6EF SK321263
✪ 11-5, 6-11; 12-10.30 Sun ☎ (01283) 703188
Marston's Pedigree; Sharp's Doom Bar; guest beer Ⓗ
This freehouse has been run since 2001 by licensees Stella and Roger who serve highly-praised ale including at least one guest beer, often from a local micro brewery. Excellent home-cooked food is on offer and the pub has mini beer festivals. There is a fine display of railway memorabilia in the bar. The pub is well worth a visit despite being a mile and a half east of Repton, its nearest village and bus route. 🚲✿🅘⊞🅖♣P≒

Ockbrook

Royal Oak 🄻
55 Green Lane, DE72 3SE
✪ 11.30-2.30 (3 Sat), 5.30 (6 Sat)-11 (11.30 Fri & Sat); 12-4, 6-11 Sun ☎ (01332) 662378
Draught Bass; guest beers Ⓗ
Run by the same family since coronation year, the pub seems little changed, and each of the six rooms preserves its own character. Varying guest beers include some from local breweries; beer festivals are held in May and October. Excellent home-cooked food is served every lunchtime and Monday to Friday evenings (no food Tue). Regular events include live music and other community activities. There are two pleasant gardens and a large function room. Local CAMRA Country Pub of the Year 2011 and 2012. Q✿🅘🅖♣🍴P≒

Over Haddon

Lathkil Hotel 🄻
DE45 1JE (signed in village) SK206665
✪ 11-3, 6-11 Mon; 11-11; 12-10.30 Sun ☎ (01629) 812501
⊕ lathkil.co.uk

Everards Tiger Best Bitter; Whim Hartington Bitter; guest beers H
The pub overlooks a masterpiece of Peak District scenery, marvellous in any weather. Walking in, one side is an old-fashioned bar with a real fire and oak beams, while superb home-cooked meals are served in the larger room opposite. A covered beer garden is the perfect place to while away summer evenings with a pint. Well-equipped rooms are available for staying over; dogs are welcome in the bar and walkers should take off their boots at the door. ⚒Q♿🅿🍴◑➌⊟🄿⅃🗢🛡

Parwich

Sycamore Inn
DE6 1QL (near church) SK187543
🕒 12-2, 7 (6 Thu & Fri)-11; 12-11 Sat & Sun
☎ (01335) 390212
Robinson's Double Hop, seasonal beers H
Attractive pub named after nearby cottages, situated in a small, remote Peak District village next to the green, duck pond and church. It is at the heart of village life, and includes the shop. Staff and locals alike welcome visitors. There are separate rooms for pool and darts; dominoes is also played. Three Robinson's beers are usually on offer, regular and seasonal, and Old Tom is available from September to April. A holiday cottage is availble nearby. ⚒Q♿◑➌⊟Å♣🄿

Pleasley

Nag's Head ✔
Chesterfield Road North, NG19 7PA (400yds off A617 at Pleasley)
🕒 5 (4 Fri)-midnight; 12-midnight Sat & Sun
☎ (01623) 810235
Greene King XX Mild; H&H Bitter H
Bob and Sue have run this family-friendly pub for the past 12 years. Two regular and two guest beers from the Greene King range are always available. The pub boasts Cask Marque accreditation, six table tennis teams, pool table, darts and dominoes. There is a separate beer garden and children's' play area. The pub has several rooms, one with an open fire – and, if you are lucky – crumpets. A function room is available for hire, and regular charity events are held. ⚒🏠♿⊟(50)♣🄿⅃

Ripley

Red Lion Ⓛ ✔
Market Place, DE5 3BS
🕒 8-midnight (1am Fri & Sat) ☎ (01773) 512875
Greene King Abbot; Marston's Pedigree; Ruddles Best Bitter; guest beers H
Dating from the 1960s, this former home brewery house faces the fine Victorian town hall, and is at the hub of a vibrant, well-pubbed market town. The large, open-plan interior is frequently buzzing, especially on weekend evenings. Outside there is a pleasant patio area that overlooks the parish church. A comprehensive selection of seven guest beers should satisfy the most ardent ale enthusiast, with Derventio and Thornbridge breweries often featured. You have to pay to use the adjoining car park. Westons Old Rosie cider is served.
Q♿◑♿⊟🄿⅃

Talbot Taphouse Ⓛ
1 Butterley Hill, DE5 3LT
🕒 5-11; 12-11.30 Fri & Sat; 12-11 Sun ☎ (01773) 742626
Amber Ales Amber Blonde, Barnes Wallis, Imperial IPA, Original Stout, seasonal beers; guest beers H
The eye-catching Amber Ales Brewery tap occupies a flat-iron site, and is handily situated between the town centre and Midland Railway heritage centre. Renovated in 2009, the Victorian former Shipstones house is blissfully free of electronic accoutrements, with the traditional games of bar billiards and table skittles holding sway. Innovation in brewing is the name of the game here, with experimental brews frequently featured, and beer safaris are organised by the nearby brewery. CAMRA members enjoy discounted prices on Amber Ales products.
Q⊟(91,92)♣🍴🄿

Thorntree Inn
161 Church Street, Waingroves, DE5 9TE
🕒 5-11; 3-11.30 Fri; 12-11.30 Sat; 12-10.30 Sun
☎ (01773) 513351 🌐 thorntreewaingroves.co.uk
Beer range varies H
The pub's name greets you on the superb mosaic floor tiling to the entrance of this cosy village local in a quiet backwater of Ripley. Distinct drinking areas warmed by an open fire, and a separate function room, make for a pleasant ambience. Six handpulls often feature Woodlands and locally brewed Leadmill and Bottle Brook breweries. Traditional cider is from Westons. Dogs and families are welcome. Quiz night is Wednesday. No food available Tuesday and Wednesday evenings.
⚒Q♿♿◑⊟(1A)♣🍴🄿⅃

Rosliston

Bull's Head
Burton Road, DE12 8JU (NW edge of village) SK242168
🕒 12-3, 7-11 ☎ (01283) 761705
Draught Bass; Marston's Pedigree H
Late 19th-century brick-built free house with a comfortable public bar and smart, cosy lounge, both featuring open fires and beamed ceilings, plus a large function room in a converted stable block. A collection of china bulls is displayed behind the bar, and interesting encased models of a Burton union brewing system can be found in both the public bar and the function room. The National Forest Forestry Centre is about half a mile away.
⚒◑⊟Å🚗⊟(22,813)♣🄿

Scarcliffe

Horse & Groom
Rotherham Road, S44 6ST (B6417 Bolsover-Shirebrook road) SK490687
🕒 12-midnight ☎ (01246) 823152
Black Sheep Best Bitter; Greene King Abbot; Stones Bitter; Wells Bombardier; guest beers H
More than 500 years old and now managed by the daughter of the owner, this genuine family-run free house offers up to seven real ales. The pub has featured in this Guide for 14 years and an impressive array of CAMRA awards indicates the care and attention the family gives to the real ales. The lounge bar is mobile-free, with a large open fire. Hot food is not served but locally made pork pies must be tried. Accommodation is sometimes available, but booking is essential.
⚒Q♿🍴♿Å🚗⊟(53,82)♣🄿⅃

Shirland

Shoulder of Mutton
Hallfieldgate Lane, DE55 6AA (on B6013, Wessington-Shirland crossroads) SK393582
✪ 5 (7 Tue; 4.30 Thu)-11; 11-11.30 Fri & Sat; 11-10.30 Sun
☎ (01773) 834992
Beer range varies Ⓗ
Eclectic 16th-century traditional drinking den, nestling on the edge of Amber Valley. The beer garden offers spectacular views and sunsets. A true free house where real people enjoy real ale from small breweries, there is no beer list on the wall because the ales change daily. The regulars are drawn from far and wide, fuelling the unique, easy atmosphere created by the irrepressible landlord and landlady. Dogs and hikers are welcome. Check out the teacups. 🏚Q🕸♿🖰♣P⚊

Smalley

Bell Ⓛ ✔
35 Main Road, DE7 6EF (on A608) SK407445
✪ 11.30-2.30, 5-11; 11.30-11 Fri & Sat; 12-11 Sun
☎ (01332) 880635 ⊕ thebellsmalley.co.uk
Adnams Broadside; Castle Rock Harvest Pale; Marston's Pedigree; Whim Hartington Bitter; guest beers Ⓗ
This mid-19th-century inn has three rooms in which brewing and other memorabilia adorn the walls, as well as a large attractive garden. A drinkers' pub, it serves four regular beers plus guests, but is also renowned for food, with a good and varied menu including daily home-made specials (no food Sun eves). Accommodation is in converted stables. Weekday opening hours may be extended in the summer. Q🕸🛏◑🖰🖰(H1)P⚊

South Normanton

Devonshire Arms ▼ Ⓛ
137 Market Street, DE55 2AA
✪ 12-midnight ☎ (01773) 810748
⊕ the-devonshire-arms.co.uk
Sarah Hughes Dark Ruby; guest beers Ⓗ
Genuine free house offering four reasonably priced real ales and Westons traditional cider. Home-cooked meals are served every day except Sunday, when a popular carvery is available (booking is strongly advised). Vegetarians, vegans and coeliacs are all catered for, and daily specials are offered. Sky Sports and ESPN are shown on three large-screen TVs. Local CAMRA Pub of the Year 2008-2012. 🐕🕸◑♿🖰(9.1,9.2)♣🖰P⚊

Stanton in Peak

Flying Childers ▼
Main Road, DE4 2LW (off B6056 Bakewell-Ashbourne road) SK240643
✪ 12-3 (2 Mon & Tue), 7-11 ☎ (01629) 636333
Wells Bombardier; guest beers Ⓗ
Created from four cottages during the 18th century, this is an unspoilt pub named after a famous racehorse owned by the Duke of Devonshire. In the centre of the village near the historic Stanton Moor and Nine Ladies stone circle, it is popular with tourists, walkers and locals alike. Both rooms are welcoming, with real fires, and there is a pleasant beer garden to the rear. Home-made soup and snacks are available lunchtimes. The guest beers change regularly. 🏚Q🕸🖰▲🖰P

Staveley

All Inn Ⓛ
Lowgates, S43 3TX (on A619)
✪ 4.30-11.30; 1-1am Sat; 1-11.30 Sun ☎ (01246) 473303
Beer range varies Ⓗ
Formerly the Smiths Arms, renamed after refurbishment, with a central bar flanked by a smart lounge area. This family-run, friendly local has a function room. Theme nights, live music and beer festivals all feature here. There is a sports bar with wide-screen TV, pool and cards. Usually there are two beers from the nearby Raw Brewing on the bar, plus two guests from other micros. Bar snacks are available. 🕸♿🖰♣🖰P⚊

Sutton cum Duckmanton

Arkwright Arms Ⓛ
Chesterfield Road, S44 5JG (A632 between Chesterfield and Bolsover)
✪ 12 (12.30am Fri) ☎ (01246) 232053
⊕ arkwrightarms.co.uk
Beer range varies Ⓗ
There is always a warm welcome at this brewers' Tudor-fronted free house, with three rooms all made cosy by open fires. An excellent range of guest ales, many from local micros, is complemented by 10 ciders and two perries. Beer festivals are held at Easter and on bank holidays, with mini events throughout the year. Quality food is served lunchtimes and evenings. A winner of numerous CAMRA awards, including East Midlands Cider Pub of the Year 2011 and Chesterfield Pub of the Year 2011. 🏚🕸◑🖰🖰(81,82,83)♣🖰P⚊

Thornsett

Printer's Arms
Thornsett, Birch Vale, SK22 1AZ
✪ 4.30-11; 12-midnight Sat; 12-11 Sun ☎ (01663) 744650
Beer range varies Ⓗ
Small stone-built pub substantially refurbished in 2010 resulting in a significantly enlarged open-plan interior with flag floors throughout. Three handpumps usually serve two varying beers from Storm Brewery and a further guest beer, often from one of the local micros. A small pool and darts area sits adjacent to the lounge bar, and TVs provide sports coverage in all areas. A small outdoor front patio offers views across the Sett Valley and there is an outdoor children's play area opposite. 🏚🕸🖰(62)

Thulston

Harrington Arms Ⓛ
4 Grove Close, DE72 3EY (off B5010)
✪ 11.30-3 (not Mon), 5-11; 11-midnight Fri & Sat; 12-10.30 Sun ☎ (01332) 571798
Draught Bass; Tollgate Earl's Ale; guest beers Ⓗ
Two former cottages, brightly lit after dark, have been smartly modernised without losing their cottage feel. This free house has low beamed ceilings, wooden-clad interior walls, open fires in winter, and a pleasant garden. Regular beer festivals are held and the adjoining restaurant serves good food. Elvaston Castle Country Park, former estate to the Earls of Harrington (hence the house beer's name) is nearby. Bass is served on gravity from the jug, on request. Guest beers are usually LocAle. 🏚🕸◑▲🖰♣🖰P⚊

Wardlow Mires

Three Stags' Heads ★
SK17 8RW (A623/B6465 jct) SK180756
✪ closed Mon-Thu; 7-11 Fri; 11-11 Sat; 12-10.30 Sun
☎ (01298) 872268
Abbeydale Brimstone, Deception, Absolution, Black Lurcher H

A quaint 300-year-old pub with two small rooms, stone-flagged floors and low ceilings. Unspoilt, it is one of the few pubs in the area recognised by CAMRA as one of Britain's Real Heritage Pubs. An ancient range warms the bar and the house dogs; the house beer, Black Lurcher, is named after a former resident. The food is locally sourced, with game a speciality. A severe rebuke awaits those wanting draught lager, but imported bottled lagers are available. ⚌Q✪◑♠A♣☝P'⸚

Whaley Bridge

Shepherd's Arms
7 Old Road, SK23 7HR
✪ 3 (12 Sat; 2 Sun)-midnight ☎ (01663) 732384
Marston's Burton Bitter, Pedigree; guest beers H

Attractive, whitewashed, stone-built pub that has been preserved unspoilt, conveying the feel of the farmhouse it once was. The unchanged taproom is a delight, with open fire, flagged floor and scrubbed table tops. Additionally, there is a comfortable lounge, and guest beers are selected from the Marston's range. ⚌Q✪⊞⇌☷(199)♣P'⸚

Whitehough

Old Hall Inn ♟ ℒ ✪
SK23 6EJ (⅓ mile off B6062)
✪ 12-midnight ☎ (01663) 750529 ⊕ old-hall-inn.co.uk
Marston's Burton Bitter; guest beers H

Nestling in an attractive hamlet, this 16th-century inn was the 2010 winner of local CAMRA Pub of the Year, and of the Great British Pub award for best cask pub in the region for the past two years. Eight handpulled local ales, with regulars from Thornbridge, are served, and local produce is used throughout the popular menu. The adjacent 14th-century Whitehough Hall, with minstrels' gallery, is used for dining and accessed directly from the inn. Popular beer festivals take place on the third weekend in September and the last weekend in February. ✪⚑◑♠A⇌(Chinley)☷(189,190)☝P'⸚

Willington

Green Man ✪
1 Canal Bridge, DE65 6BQ
✪ 11.30-11 (11.30 Wed & Thu; midnight Fri & Sat); 12-11 Sun
☎ (01283) 702377
Draught Bass; Marston's Pedigree; guest beers H

An attractive two-roomed pub at the heart of the village, dating back to the start of the 18th century. This local features oak beams throughout, along with traditional bench seating. A picture gallery of local landmarks can be found in the lounge, while a large child-friendly rear garden is complemented by tables and chairs at the front during the summer months. Live music sessions are held regularly and good home-cooked food is served daily (no food Sun eve). ✪◑⊞⇌☷(V3)♣☝P'⸚

Wirksworth

Royal Oak ℒ
North End, DE4 4FG (off B5035)
✪ 8-11.30 (midnight Fri & Sat); 12-3, 8-11 Sun
☎ (01629) 823000
Draught Bass; Taylor Landlord; Whim Hartington IPA; guest beers H

Excellent, ultra-traditional local in a stone terrace near the marketplace, highlighted at night by rows of fairy lights. The bar features old pictures of local interest and there is also a pool room and smoking grotto. The Oak enjoys a long-standing reputation for Draught Bass, and always has five ales to choose from, including a LocAle. The Ecclesbourne Valley Railway visitor attraction is close by, and this former lead mining town is an architectural gem with much to interest the historian. Q☷(6.1)'⸚

Woodthorpe

Albert Inn
Woodthorpe Road, S43 3BZ
✪ 5 (12 Sat)-11; 12-10.30 Sun ☎ (01246) 472634
Wells Bombardier; guest beers H

Friendly and welcoming community pub with a roaring log fire and a relaxed atmosphere. There are three changing guest beers on handpump, and various pub games can be found in the spacious main room. A separate function room is available for hire. Delicious home-cooked food is served Thursday and Friday evenings, with vegetarian options, together with Sunday lunches of generous portions. ⚌✪♠&☷♣☝P'⸚

Kitchen of an inn

In the evening we reached a village where I had determined to pass the night. As we drove into the great gateway of the inn, I saw on one side the light of a rousing kitchen fire beaming through a window. I entered, and admired for the hundredth time that picture of convenience, neatness, and broad honest enjoyment, the kitchen of an English inn. It was of spacious dimension, hung around by copper and tin vessels, highly polished, and decorated here and there with a Christmas green. Hams, tongues, and flitches of bacon were suspended from the ceiling; a smoke-jack made its ceaseless clanking behind the fireplace, and a clock ticked in one corner. A well-scoured deal table extended along one side of the kitchen, with a cold round of beef, and other hearty viands upon it, over which two foaming tankards of ale seemed mounting guard. Travellers of inferior order were preparing to attack this stout repast, while others sat smoking or gossiping over their ale, on two high-backed oaken settles beside the fire.

Washington Irving, Travelling at Christmas, 1884

Lake District Pub Walks

Bob Steel

Lake District Pub Walks is a practical, pocket-sized, traveller's guide to some of the best walking and best pubs in the Lake District. The walks are grouped geographically around tourist hubs with plenty of accommodation, making the book ideal for visitors to the Lakes. The book is fully illustrated with clear Ordnance Survey mapping and written directions to help readers navigate the routes. There is also useful information about local transport and accommodation and features which explore some of the region's fascinating historical and literary heritage as well as its thriving brewing scene. The book is a companion volume to CAMRA's popular *Edinburgh Pub Walks*, *Peak District Pub Walks*, *London Pub Walks* and *South East Pub Walks*.

£9.99   ISBN 978-1-85249-271-7   CAMRA members' price £7.99   160 pages

For this and other books on beer and pubs visit the CAMRA bookshop at www.camra.org.uk/books

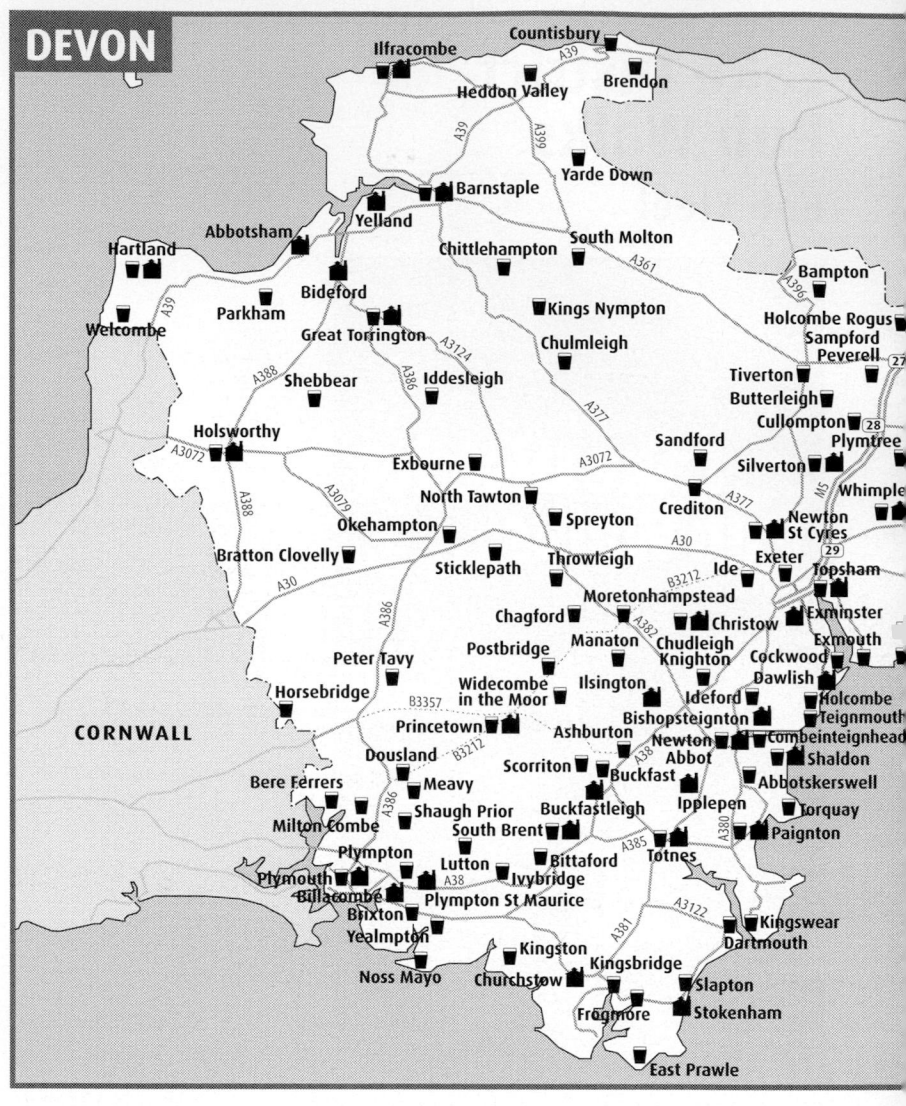

DEVON

Abbotskerswell

Court Farm Inn
Wilton Way, TQ12 5PG
🕐 11-11 (midnight Fri & Sat); 12-11 Sun ☎ (01626) 361866
🌐 courtfarminn.co.uk
Draught Bass; Otter Ale; St Austell Tribute; guest beers Ⓗ
Seventeenth-century Devon longhouse situated next to the parish church and converted into a pub in 1972. The attractive interior has exposed stone walls, flagged floors and beamed ceilings. Popular with locals and visitors, the lounge is mainly used by diners who can choose from a varies menu, including specials, while the bar hosts pool and darts matches. An upstairs room is available for meetings. The pub also claims to have a ghost – the Lady in Grey – who is said to pop by from time to time to enjoy a nightcap. The large garden at the front has a covered and heated area for smokers. Wedding receptions and functions are catered for.
🏵️🌗🍴🖿🚟(177)♣P🏵️

Ashburton

Dartmoor Lodge 🅛 ✅
Peartree Cross, TQ13 7JW (just off A38 at Peartee jct)
🕐 11-11; 12-10.30 Sun ☎ (01364) 652232
🌐 dartmoorlodge.co.uk
Butcombe Bitter; Dartmoor Jail Ale; guest beers Ⓗ
A good selection of local real ales is served at this 24-bedroom roadside hotel on the edge of the Dartmoor National Park and the town of Ashburton. There is a friendly and comfortable atmosphere in the oak-beamed bar and restaurant area which, in winter, has a welcoming log fire. Good-quality local food is served all day every day in both the bar and restaurant. The location makes it an ideal base for walkers, cyclists and canoeists, and rooms are available for meetings. Ashton Still cider is sold.
🏨Q🌗🏵️🍴🛏🚻⅃♿🅰🚟(X38,88)🍴P🏵️

Exeter Inn 🅛
26 West Street, TQ13 7DU (on main road through Ashburton opp church)

A historic 15th-century Devon longhouse, with small flagstone-floored rooms and logburners. All are served from a central bar displaying the six-barrel stillage as a focal point, from which the ales are dispensed by gravity. Guests beers are usually from Cotleigh or Exmoor breweries. Food is served lunchtimes and evenings all week. The 12 bedrooms are all en-suite, with TV and Wi-Fi. Situated in the upper reaches of the Exe Valley, the pub is popular with walkers and tourists to Devon and Exmoor. A top-quality, friendly hostelry.
🛏Q↻💢👁🍽🍚🍺🕛(398)P№

Swan
Station Road, EX16 9NG
⚙ 5-11 (not Mon); 12-midnight Sat; 12-10.30 Sun
☎ (01398) 332248 🌐 theswan.co
Red Rock Devon Storm; guest beers Ⓔ
The Swan is the oldest pub in Bampton and was the original lodgings for the masons and craftsmen who were hired to enlarge the nearby church. The pub has recently been renovated, with solid oak fittings, polished wood tables and boarded flooring giving it a wine bar feel. The large fireplace contains the original bread oven from 1450. The two guest beers are always from south west breweries. Set in an area well known for its hunting, fishing and shooting, the pub is popular with ramblers and cyclists. A large public car park, on the site of the old railway station, is close by.
🛏Q↻💢👁🍽🍚🍺(398)

Barnstaple

Panniers Ⓛ ✅
33-34 Boutport Street, EX31 1RX (opp Queen's Theatre and 200yds from bus terminus)

⚙ 11-2.30, 5-11 (midnight Fri & Sat); 12-3, 7-10.30 Sun
☎ (01364) 652013
Dartmoor IPA; guest beer Ⓔ
The oldest pub in Ashburton, built in 1131, with additions in the 17th century. A friendly local that originally housed the workers constructing the nearby church, it was used by Sir Francis Drake on his journeys to London. There are seated drinking areas either side of the entrance hallway in the main bar, which is L-shaped, rustic and wood-panelled, with a canopy. There is a smaller bar at the rear served via a small hatch and counter. Ashridge cider is on sale. Q👁🍺🕛(X38,88)♣🐕№

Bampton

Exeter Inn Ⓛ ✅
Tiverton Road, EX16 9DY (on A396 roundabout jct with B3190)
⚙ 12-11 ☎ (01398) 331345 🌐 the-exeter-inn.co.uk
Cotleigh Tawny Owl; Exmoor Ale; guest beers Ⓖ

INDEPENDENT BREWERIES

Barum Barnstaple
Bays Paignton
Beer Engine Newton St Cyres
Blackawton Ilsington (brewing suspended)
Branscombe Vale Branscombe
Bridgetown Totnes
Clearwater Great Torrington
Country Life Abbotsham
Dartmoor Princetown
Devon Yelland (NEW)
Devon Earth Buckfastleigh
Exe Valley Silverton
Exeter Exminster
Forge Hartland
Garage Plympton St Maurice (NEW)
Gidley's Christow
Holsworthy Holsworthy
Hunter's Ipplepen
Isca (Gargoyles) Dawlish
Jollyboat Bideford
O'Hanlon's Whimple
Otter Luppitt
Plymouth Plymouth (NEW)
Quercus Churchstow
Red Rock Bishopsteignton
Ringmore Shaldon
South Hams Stokenham
Summerskills Billacombe
Teignworthy Newton Abbot
Topsham Topsham
Union South Brent
Wizard Ilfracombe

✪ 7-11 (midnight Fri & Sat) ☎ (01271) 329720
Greene King Abbot; Ruddles Best Bitter; guest beers ⊞
Popular town-centre Wetherspoon's with an unrivalled selection of real ales in the area, many from local microbreweries, plus cider from Westons. The split-level interior offers several distinct seating areas with a small area for families. An exclusive beer festival for Devon CAMRA branches is held every February/March. On one weekend in four as a trial, the manager is selling all real ales from just one brewer. The rear garden area is a suntrap and offers covered and heated seating. ➰❀🌀&🖫🚲♦�

Reform Inn ⓁL
Reform Street, Pilton, EX31 1PD
✪ 11.30-11 (midnight Fri & Sat); 12-11 Sun
☎ (01271) 323164
Barum Original, seasonal beers ⊞
Well-established, popular community local and brewery tap for Barum Brewery, whose beers dominate here. From the main road, look above roof level for the pub sign to locate it. The skittle alley is the setting for the annual Green Man beer festival in July, and other regular beer festivals are held during the year. Music is played in the public bar, with open mic sessions every Monday and bands on alternate Fridays. The lounge bar is quieter. ❀🌀🖫(1,2,3)♣℄

Beer

Dolphin Hotel ⓁL ✅
Fore Street, EX12 3EQ
✪ 10-midnight (1am Fri & Sat) ☎ (01297) 20068
⊕ dolphinhotelbeer.co.uk
Fuller's London Pride; Skinner's Betty Stogs ⊞
A Grade II-listed hotel in the village centre, with 22 en-suite rooms. The Lounge Bar (closed 3-6 daily) is a comfortable hotel bar, while the Long Bar is the public bar, with lower prices, and attracts a strong local following. Each has one guest beer in winter and two in summer. Meals are served in both bars and in the restaurant, every lunchtime and evening. There is fortnightly live music. Dogs and families are welcome.
🏨🐾❀🚑🌀🍴&🖫(X53,899)♣♦P℄

Bere Ferrers

Olde Plough ⓁL
Fore Street, PL20 7JG (close to the church and river)
✪ 11-3, 6-11; 11-11 Sun ☎ (01822) 840358
Sharp's Doom Bar; guest beers ⊞
A 16th-century village inn with outstanding views over the River Tavy from the beer garden and only a 15-minute walk from the station on the picturesque Tamar Valley Line station. Inside, there are flagstone floors, exposed stonework walls, beamed ceilings, real fires and a welcoming atmosphere popular with locals and visitors alike. Live music, acoustic nights and jam sessions feature along with fish and chip suppers and curry nights. Guest beers are generally from breweries in Devon and Cornwall. 🏨🐾❀🌀🚲♣℄

Bittaford

Horse & Groom ⓁL
Exeter Road, PL21 0EL
✪ 12-11 (midnight Fri & Sat) ☎ (01752) 892358

Beer range varies ⊞
Previously sited on the opposite side of the main road, this 1930s community pub features one large bar, and is decorated with historic photos of the area taken from the former Moorhaven Hospital which overlooks the village. The house beer, Albion, is brewed by Hunter's, with the three guest beers regularly from Bays, Dartmoor and Hunter's. Thatchers dry cider is sold, with Ashridge cider in summer. Beer and cider festivals are held, supporting local charities. Beer tapas are available: three one-third pints of beer. CAMRA members receive a discount. 🏨❀🌀🚲🖫(X38,X80)♣♦P℄

Bratton Clovelly

Clovelly Inn ⓁL ✅
EX20 4JZ (between A30 and A3079) SX464919
✪ 12-3, 6-midnight; 12-midnight Sat & Sun
☎ (01837) 871447
Dartmoor Legend, Jail Ale; St Austell Dartmoor Best Bitter ⊞
On the north-western edge of Dartmoor National Park, this traditional 18th-century village pub features an oak fireplace lintel inscribed 1789. The main bar has a large wood-burning stove along with two separate dining areas and a games room. During summer the beers are joined by Sam's Medium cider from Winkleigh. Booking is advisable for mealtimes, particularly in the evenings. Well-behaved dogs are welcome. A Norman church nearby has rare 17th-century wall paintings on display. 🏨🐾🌀🖫(633)♣♦P℄

Brendon

Staghunters Inn ⓁL
Lynton, EX35 6PS (1 mile S of A39) SS768482
✪ 12-11 ☎ (01598) 741222 ⊕ staghunters.com
Beer range varies ⊞
Family-run hotel deep in the valley at Brendon. Built on the site of an old abbey, it is popular with walkers and those pursuing other outdoor activities. Up to five different real ales are available, with the emphasis on West Country brewers. Cider is mainly from Palmerhayes. A wide range of traditional, locally sourced food is available to suit all pockets. Dogs are welcome and allowed to stay in the accommodation with owners overnight for a nominal charge. ❀🚑🌀P℄

Brixton

Foxhound ♈ ⓁL
Kingsbridge Road, PL8 2AH SX554522
✪ 11-11 (midnight Fri & Sat); 12-11 Sun ☎ (01752) 880271
⊕ foxhoundinn.co.uk
Courage Best Bitter; guest beers ⊞
An 18th-century former coaching house in a rural village just east of Plymouth, popular with locals and well served by a frequent daytime bus service. The pub has two separate bars with a lounge and small restaurant. Traditional English meals are made using locally sourced ingredients including meat from a nearby National Trust farm. Ales from local breweries feature regularly. A monthly quiz night is held, as are curry nights. Local CAMRA Country Pub of the Year 2011, and Pub of the Year 2012. 🏨Q❀🌀🚲🖫(93,94)♣♦P℄

Buckfast

Abbey Inn ✪
30 Buckfast Road, TQ11 0EA (off A38; follow signs to Buckfast Abbey)
🕑 10.30-midnight ☎ (01364) 642343
🌐 theabbeyinn-buckfast.co.uk
St Austell Trelawney, Tribute, Proper Job Ⓗ
Close to the famous Buckfast Abbey, the pub is set in beautiful surroundings next to the River Dart within Dartmoor National Park. It has an outside terrace with seating and views overlooking the river, including glimpses of the abbey. Inside, the warm and welcoming oak-panelled bar is spacious, with traditional furniture and a wooden floor. The large dining room serves an excellent range of food and there any many visitor attractions within close vicinity of the pub. Accommodation is available. ⚄Q✿❀☎◖▲₪(X38,88)P⅄

Budleigh Salterton

Salterton Arms ✪
22 Chapel Street, EX9 6LX
🕑 11-11.30; 12-11 Sun ☎ (01395) 445048
Otter Ale; St Austell Dartmoor Best Bitter; guest beers Ⓗ
A welcoming traditional local pub, clean and tidy with a new decor with wooden and Cotswold stone floors; children are allowed on the premises. There is a good choice of two regular ales from the Otter and St Austell breweries, plus two guest beers. Food is served downstairs, as well as in a separate restaurant upstairs; darts and euchre players are welcome. ⚄Q◖❀₪(157,357)♣●

Butterleigh

Butterleigh Inn Ⓛ
The Green, EX15 1PN (opp church)
🕑 12-2.30 (not Mon), 6-11 (midnight Fri & Sat); 12-3 Sun ☎ (01884) 855433
Cotleigh Tawny Owl; Dartmoor IPA; Otter Ale; guest beers Ⓗ
Excellent country pub in a small quaint village, this splendid 17th-century Devon cob building is full of character. Lunchtimes tend to be quieter, catering for a mature clientele, but it is busier in the evenings and at weekends when a mix of generations creates a great atmosphere with diverse conversation. There is always a choice of four real ales, including two LocAle. Drink inside or outside, with lovely surroundings either way. Popular home-made food and a Sunday carvery feature, using locally sourced ingredients. ⚄Q❀❀☎◖❁♣●P⅄

Chagford

Sandy Park Inn Ⓛ
Sandy Park, TQ13 8JW (on A382 Moretonhampstead-Whiddon Down road)
🕑 12-11 (10.30 Sun) ☎ (01647) 433267
🌐 sandyparkinn.co.uk
Dartmoor Jail Ale; Otter Bitter Ⓗ; guest beers Ⓗ/Ⓖ
Thatched free house, thought to be 17th century. The main bar has a large open fireplace, ancient beams, stone floor and high-backed wooden bench seating. Beyond is a small snug. Another bar becomes an intimate restaurant at weekends, serving home-cooked food (no food Mon eve). Castle Drogo (NT), Fingle Bridge and Chagford

Village are nearby. A covered smoking den is next to the large garden. There is a small car park at the front of the pub. Guest beers are from local brewers. ⚄❀☎◖₪(173,178)P⅄

Chittlehampton

Bell Inn Ⓛ
The Square, EX37 9QL (opp church) SS636245
🕑 11-3, 6-midnight; 11-midnight Sat; 12-11 Sun ☎ (01769) 540368 🌐 thebellatchittlehampton.co.uk
Beer range varies Ⓗ/Ⓖ
Popular village local that has been in the same family for more than 30 years. Before entering, note the etched window commemorating its local CAMRA Pub of the Year win in 2007. As well as the varying selection of ales on handpump, more may be available on gravity – check the blackboard on the right-hand side of the bar. There are two patios, a conservatory, and an orchard which is home to alpacas. Well-behaved children and dogs are welcome. ❀☎◖❁▲♣●⅄

Christow

Teign House Inn Ⓛ
Teign Valley Road, EX6 7PL (on B3193)
🕑 12-3 (not Wed winter), 5-11.30; 12-11.30 Sat & Sun ☎ (01647) 252286 🌐 teignhouseinn.co.uk
Dartmoor Jail Ale; Otter Amber; Palmers Best; guest beers Ⓗ
Welcoming, atmospheric country pub, with beams and a warming log fire. A real part of the community, this pub enjoys strong local support. The sizeable garden attracts the families of locals and visitors alike, while an adjoining field has space for caravans and campers. A beer festival with as many as 30 beers is held on the second weekend in July. Great pub food is served, all home-cooked, with a popular Sunday carvery. The landlord is an ardent supporter of local breweries. Local CAMRA Pub of the Year 2010. ⚄Q❀◖❁▲₪(360)♣P⅄

Chudleigh Knighton

Anchor
Plymouth Road, TQ13 0EN
🕑 3 (12 Sat)-11; 12-10.30 Sun ☎ (01626) 852366
Beer range varies Ⓗ
A 15th-century building on the old Plymouth road and formerly a coaching inn, with the rear stables now the skittle alley. Entry is via a narrow porch into a gem of a largely unspoilt public bar, with low beams and photographs of the old village, including the now defunct Teign Valley railway. Another larger bar has a magnificent fire and leads out to the smokers' gazebo and hidden garden. Three handpumps dispense Devon beers, usually from Dartmoor and Teignworthy breweries. ⚄Q❀❁₪(39,182)⅄

Chulmleigh

Old Court House
South Molton Street, EX18 7BW (200yds N of town centre)
🕑 11.30-midnight ☎ (01769) 580045
🌐 oldcourthouseinn.co.uk
Exmoor Ale; Butcombe Bitter; guest beers Ⓗ
Grade II-listed historic local with three handpumps and real cider from Thatchers. The fire and a

friendly dog both add to the warm welcome in the main bar, and there is a separate restaurant. A quiz night each Thursday supports local charities, and a folk night is held on the second Tuesday in every month. A wall in one of the bedrooms still bears the coat of arms that marks the time Charles I stayed here in 1634. ▲▦☸☎◑☐▦(377)♣●⚊

Clayhidon

Half Moon Inn
EX15 3TJ
✿ 12-3, 6-11 (not Mon); 12-3, 7-10.30 (summer only) Sun
☎ (01823) 680291 ⊕ halfmoondevon.co.uk
Otter Bitter; guest beers Ⓗ
Traditional country inn, set in the Blackdown Hills near the Somerset border, with spectacular views over the Culm Valley. It was probably built originally as a cottage in the 13th century for stonemasons while they built the nearby church. Fresh locally sourced food is on the menu, with themed evening menus, pie night on Tuesday, and a fish and chips eat-in or take-away option on Friday nights. Live musical entertainment takes place on Wednesdays. Two guest beers are available and a beer festival is held each May. ▲☸◑▲♣●P⚊

Cockwood

Anchor Inn Ⓛ ✪
EX6 8RA (just off the A379, outside Starcross, next to Cockwood harbour) SX976807
✿ 11-11 (10.30 Sun) ☎ (01626) 890203 or 891203
⊕ anchorinncockwood.com
Otter Bitter, Ale; St Austell Tribute; guest beers Ⓗ
On picturesque Cockwood harbour, this 450-year-old inn and former seaman's mission has many old settles, timber panelling, low beams and snugs, with an impressive display of old nautical memorabilia throughout. It has an award-winning extensive seafood menu, especially featuring mussel dishes. Haunted by a friendly ghost and his dog, this is a really atmospheric Devon gem. Starcross station is a mile away and the no. 2 bus stops just across the harbour. Close to the main GWR line, it is a steam train spotters' paradise. ▲Q☸◑♿▲▦(2)♣P⚊

Ship Inn ✪
Church Road, EX6 8RA (just off the A379, outside Starcross, close to Cockwood harbour) SX975806
✿ 11-11; 12-10.30 Sun ☎ (01626) 890373
Exmoor Ale; St Austell Tribute, Proper Job; Sharp's Doom Bar; guest beer Ⓗ
A busy pub close to the picturesque harbour at Cockwood, offering a choice of four regular ales as well as three rotating ciders. Popular with drinkers and diners, the excellent food menu includes a varied selection of locally caught fish. It has a large beer garden with views of the estuary and a roaring log fire for the winter. Starcross station is a mile away and the bus stop is only a short walk. ▲Q☸◑▲⇌(Starcross)▦(2)♣●P⚊

Colyton

Kingfisher Inn ✪
Dolphin Street, EX24 6NA
✿ 11-3, 6-11 (midnight Fri); 11-11 Sat; 12-10.30 (6 winter) Sun ☎ (01297) 552476 ⊕ kingfisherinn.co.uk

Sharp's Doom Bar; Skinner's Betty Stogs; guest beers Ⓗ
A traditional 16th-century stone and timber pub close to the centre of this delightful small town, with a public car park nearby, and a tram that connects to the town of Seaton. A separate restaurant at the rear serves locally sourced good-value food. Themed food events take place once a month, and skittles, darts, crib and boules are regularly played at this friendly pub. Families and dogs are welcome. One or two guest beers are served, usually from the West Country. ☸◑▲▦(20,885)♣⚊

Combeinteignhead

Wild Goose Ⓛ
Shaldon Road, TQ12 4RA
✿ 9-3, 5.30-11 (midnight Thu & Fri); 9-3, 7-11 Sun
☎ (01626) 872241
Courage Best Bitter; Hunter's Black Jack; Sharp's Doom Bar; guest beers Ⓗ
A welcoming 17th-century beamed and cosy village pub, restaurant and shop. Two real fires, fresh locally sourced food, and a varied range of beers are all part of the attraction. An excellent selection of continental beers is available. Fish and chip suppers on Tuesday are popular, as are the Friday night music and Saturday quizzes. The cider is Sandford Orchard. An attractive garden abuts a 14th-century church. Two holiday cottages are available to rent. ▲Q☸◑◑♣●P⚊

Countisbury

Blue Ball Inn Ⓛ ✪
Countisbury Hill, EX35 6NE (1½ mile E of Lynmouth) SS747496
✿ 9-11 ☎ (01598) 741263 ⊕ blueballinn.com
Clearwater Real Smiler, Proper Ansome; St Austell Tribute; guest beers Ⓗ
Old coaching inn open every day of the year, with low ceilings, blackened beams and a large 13th-century inglenook fire near the bar. Four real ales are available including one guest. Food is served all day from an extensive menu either in the bar or the large dining area. Outside there is a spacious patio area with the car park opposite. Ideal for walkers and other followers of outdoor pursuits, and dog-friendly. A beer festival is held every November. ▲Q☸◑◑▦(300,401)P

Crediton

Crediton Inn Ⓛ
28A Mill Street, EX17 1EZ (near A377 and station)
✿ 10-11; 12-3, 7-10.30 Sun ☎ (01363) 772882
⊕ crediton-inn.co.uk
O'Hanlon's Yellow Hammer; guest beers Ⓗ
The framed deeds date this inn to 1878, with windows etched with the ancient town seal. This genuine free house is well-supported by the locals. The handpumps have increased to 10, served by local breweries, with an ale festival in November. The skittle alley doubles as a function room. Good home-cooked food is served at weekends, with snacks and renowned Scotch eggs available at other times. The bubbly owner is the longest-serving landlady in Crediton, having worked here for 32 years. ▲☸◑⇌▦(50,51,315)♣P⚊

Cullompton

Pony & Trap L ✓
10 Exeter Hill, EX15 1DJ (on B3181 S of town)
✪ 12-2, 5-11.30; 12-5, 8-11 Sun ☎ (01884) 34182
⊕ ponyandtrapcullompton.co.uk
Dartmoor IPA, Jail Ale; Otter Bitter; guest beers H
Traditional local with a good atmosphere and a mixed clientele. The smart interior with a logburner is cosy in winter, and flowers on the bar and ornaments give a homely feel. There are always five real ales available, and food is served Tuesday-Sunday lunchtimes, and evenings on request in advance. Outside, there is a garden and seating area. As for games, darts, skittles, shove-ha'penny, bar skittles and shut the box are all available.
🏚Q✿⊕🖵(1)♣⅃

Culmstock

Culm Valley Inn
EX15 3JJ
✪ 12-3, 6-11; 11-11 Fri & Sat; 12-10.30 Sun
☎ (01884) 840354
Beer range varies G
A 300-year-old village inn by a medieval bridge on the River Culm, with at least six changing real ales from small breweries at any one time, rising to 10 at weekends, all served by gravity from the cellar room behind the bar. Bollhayes and Tricky ciders are also available. A rustic bar area leads through to another side room, then on to the award-winning restaurant. There is a beer festival every end of May bank holiday weekend. Dogs are welcome. 🏚Q✿🚮⊕♣🐕P

Dartmouth

Cherub Inn
13 Higher Street, TQ6 9RB
✪ 11-11 Fri, Sat & summer; 11.30-2.30, 5.30-11 winter; 11 (12 winter)-10.30 Sun ☎ (01803) 832571
⊕ the-cherub.co.uk
Otter Bitter; St Austell Tribute, Proper Job; Sharp's Doom Bar; guest beers H
A wonderful Grade II-listed building, formerly a merchant's residence and reputedly the oldest in Dartmouth. Here you will find one small and cosy bar with ship's timbers and leaded light windows. A steep and twisting staircase leads to the first floor restaurant. Five handpumps dispense a variety of West Country beers; the Cherub bitter is brewed by Otter. Q⊕🖵(X81,93)

Royal Castle Hotel
The Quay, TQ6 9PS
✪ 9-11 ☎ (01803) 833033 ⊕ royalcastle.co.uk
Dartmoor Jail Ale; Otter Amber; Sharp's Doom Bar; guest beers H
A building with a wonderful exterior occupying a dominant position over the inner harbour and close to the pontoon where the ferry passengers disembark. The Galleon bar is cosy and welcoming to both regulars and visitors, and has a busy food trade under beamed ceilings, surrounded by esoteric artefacts including guns, swords and a stuffed fish. The Harbour bar is contemporary and quieter. The gentlemen's convenience is both unusual and dazzling. Beers come from the West Country. 🏚Q🚮⊕♿🖵(X81,93)

Dousland

Burrator Inn L ✓
PL20 6NP
✪ 11-11; 11-12.30am Sat; 12-11 Sun ☎ (01822) 853121
⊕ theburratorinn.com
Dartmoor IPA, Jail Ale; St Austell Tribute; Sharp's Doom Bar H
Substantial pub on the road between Yelverton, Burrator Reservoir and Princetown. Inside there is a large bar area with space for a pool table and two dartboards, along with various other rooms including a separate dining room. Food is served all day. Outside there is ample parking and a garden incorporating a children's play area. A beer festival is held annually in September, and a Sunday quiz night, live music and other entertainment feature regularly. 🏚Q✿🚮⊕♿♣P⅃

East Budleigh

Sir Walter Raleigh L
22 High Street, EX9 7ED (off B3178 opp Hayes Lane)
✪ 12-3, 6-11 (7-10.30 Sun) ☎ (01395) 442510
Otter Ale; Sharp's Doom Bar; guest beers H
Set in the middle of the delightful village of East Budleigh, the birthplace of Sir Walter Raleigh, this is a truly welcoming 16th-century country inn. Good-quality pub food is served lunchtimes and evenings, and normally there are four real ales to choose from. Originally two cottages, it was then converted into a Jacobean-style pub. The original wooden beams have been retained throughout the two different areas. This gem is well worth a visit for good quality real ale. Q✿⊕🖵(157)⅃

East Prawle

Pig's Nose Inn L
TQ7 2BY SX781365
✪ 12-2.30, 7-11 (closed Sun & Mon winter)
☎ (01548) 511209 ⊕ pigsnoseinn.co.uk
Otter Bitter G; **South Hams Devon Pride** H, **Eddystone** G; **guest beers** H
An old three-roomed smugglers' inn on the village green in an area that attracts birdwatchers and coastal walkers. Gravity beers are stored on a specially made rack behind the bar. It has twice won the local CAMRA Pub of the Year award. Home-cooked, locally sourced food is served. Children and dogs are welcome and even have their own menus. The maritime-themed interior is cluttered with objects, children's games and knitting for adults. There are occasional live music events in a hall adjoining the pub.
🏚🌳✿⊕▲♣🐕⅃

Exbourne

Red Lion Inn L ✓
High Street, EX20 3RY (200yds N of jct with A386)
SS602017
✪ 12-11 ☎ (01837) 851551
Dartmoor Legend; St Austell Tribute; Sharp's Own; guest beers G
A popular 16th-century village local that does not sell any draught lager, only bottles. Casks are set at one end of the L-shaped bar, with Sam's dry and medium ciders from Winkleigh. Good-value locally sourced food is served daily until 9.30pm in the adjacent cosy dining area. An offset room contains a pool table and TV. Well-behaved children and

dogs are welcome. Three beer festivals are held during the year, one with a popular Christmas pantomime. ⚏Q🕏🕏🕏🕏P

Exeter

Great Western Hotel L
St David's Station Approach, EX4 4NU
🕏 10-midnight (1am Fri & Sat) ☎ (01392) 274039
🌐 greatwesternhotel.co.uk
Branscombe Vale Branoc; Dartmoor Jail Ale;
O'Hanlon's Flagship, Port Stout; RCH Pitchfork, PG
Steam Ⓗ
Featuring probably the largest range of real ales in the city (at least eight at any one time), this is a traditional railway hotel with a good community spirit, twice winner of local CAMRA Pub of the Year. Meals are served in the bars and Brunel restaurant. Fairly priced home-cooked food comes from a varied menu, with curry nights, steak nights and a Sunday carvery to impress diners. Children and dogs are welcome. Q🕏🕏🕏🕏(St David's)🕏(H)

Imperial L ✅
New North Road, EX4 4AH
🕏 8-midnight (1am Fri & Sat) ☎ (01392) 434050
Greene King Abbot; Ruddles Best Bitter; guest
beers Ⓗ
Large Wetherspoon pub close to the university, Central and St David's railway stations, with buses passing close by. It has a large sunny garden with plenty of tables and seating. Ten beers are usually available including Abbot and Ruddles plus guest ales often from local breweries. Westons provides a real cider. Good-value food is served all day. The building is interesting architecturally, and features an attractive orangery. Wetherspoon's beer festivals are held, plus some showcasing local breweries.
Q🕏🕏🕏🕏(St David's/Central)🕏(D,50)🕏P

Mill on the Exe ✅
Bonhay Road, EX4 3AB
🕏 10.30-11 ☎ (01392) 214464 🌐 millontheexe.co.uk
St Austell Dartmoor Best Bitter, Tribute, Proper Job Ⓗ
Beautiful riverside pub just a few minutes' walk from the city centre and St David's railway station. It has two bars over two floors, each boasting four handpumps with St Austell brews, seasonal and guest ales. Quality home-cooked food is served from noon to 9pm every day. The large garden has stunning views of Blackaller Weir. Children and dogs are welcome, and there is a large car park.
⚏🕏🕏🕏🕏(St David's)🕏P🕏

North Bridge Inn L
11 St David's Hill, Iron Bridge, EX4 3RG
🕏 2-11 (9 Sun) ☎ (01392) 200253
Fremington IPA; guest beers Ⓗ
A welcoming modern local with traditional values. Food is served on Sunday, known as Lazy Lunch. It has four draught ale pumps; as soon as a cask runs out, another goes on in its place. The beers come from O'Hanlon's, Moor, Yeovil Ales, Dartmoor Brewery, Jollyboat and the Beer Engine. The landlady is keen to stay with local suppliers and serves award-winning Sandford Orchards ciders; she mulls her own in winter. Open mic is every Wednesday, live events take place every Friday, and jazz features once a month.
⚏🕏🕏(Central/St David's)🕏🕏🕏

Old Fire House L
50 New North Road, EX4 4EP
🕏 12-2am (3am Fri & Sat; 1am Sun) ☎ (01392) 277279
Beer range varies Ⓖ
Popular city-centre pub serving good-value food lunchtimes and evenings as well as late-night pizzas. Up to eight ales are available on gravity including beers from Otter and Teignworthy breweries, and four real ciders; regulars include Sam's, Sunnybrook, Autumn Mix and Sandford. Ale and cider festivals are held every bank holiday, and there is live music every Friday and Saturday evening. The pub is close to Exeter High Street, bus stops and Central railway station.
🕏🕏🕏🕏(Central)🕏🕏🕏

Exmouth

First & Last Inn L
10 Church Street, EX8 1PE (off B3178 Rolle St)
🕏 11-11 (11.30 Sat); 12-10.30 Sun ☎ (01395) 263275
Courage Directors; Otter Ale Ⓗ; guest beers Ⓗ/Ⓖ
Victorian pub near the town centre, with a public car park opposite, a genuine free house, much enlarged by the present owners. It provides three distinct drinking areas, and an outside patio area with heated awnings. Games include pool and darts, and there is a skittle alley. Televised sport is prominent in the pub. Well-behaved dogs are welcome. Two or three guest beers are sold, usually from the West Country, and the cider is Thatchers Dry. The pub has air conditioning.
🕏🕏🕏🕏(57,157)🕏🕏🕏

Grapevine
2 Victoria Road, EX8 1DL (just beyond Lloyds/TSB bank)
🕏 9-11 (midnight Fri & Sat; 5 Sun) ☎ (01395) 222556
🌐 grapevineexmouth.com
Beer range varies Ⓗ
The Grapevine opened in late 2010 as a bistro pub. Located centrally just off the pedestrianised Strand area, it is earning a reputation for being the place to go in Exmouth for dining and drinking. Free of tie, the licensee buys ale from breweries at a radius of up to 50 miles and takes the full beer range from each brewery. He also has plans to brew his own in 2013. 🕏🕏🕏🕏🕏(57,97)🕏🕏

Holly Tree ✅
161 Withycombe Village Road, EX8 3AN
🕏 11 (12 Sun)-midnight ☎ (01395) 273440
Draught Bass; Greene King Abbot; St Austell Proper
Job, HSD; Wells Bombardier; guest beers Ⓗ
A popular traditional inn that concentrates on serving good beer. There are two darts, four pool and two euchre teams, and Sunday is quiz night. A pub much supported by the local community, beer and conversation predominate. Dogs are welcome at all times, and families until 7pm. Outside there is a covered smoking area, plus two separate seating areas. This is a warm, comfortable and friendly local. The cider is Taunton Traditional.
🕏🕏🕏(97)🕏🕏🕏

Powder Monkey L ✅
2-2a The Parade, EX8 1RJ
🕏 8am-midnight (1am Fri & Sat) ☎ (01395) 280090
Greene King Abbot; Ruddles Best Bitter; guest
beers Ⓗ
A Wetherspoon pub named after Nancy Perriam, whose sewing skills earned her a berth in the navy where she also acted as a powder monkey. (A

powder monkey was naval slang for boys and girls who filled shells and cartridges with gunpowder on board ships of war.) Nancy lived in nearby Tower Street. The building was converted from local newspaper offices. The bar is adjacent to the central seating area, with a number of rooms off it. ▟Q☆❶❺⇆🚍(57)●ᵌ⌐

Frogmore

Globe Ⓛ
TQ7 2NR
✪ 11.30-3, 5.30-11; 12-3, 6-10.30 Sun ☎ (01548) 531351
⊕ theglobeinn.co.uk
Otter Ale; Skinner's Betty Stogs; South Hams Eddystone Ⓗ
A spacious pub that is accessible by car, bus or boat – the tidal Frogmore Creek has been enhanced by a pontoon and the place is popular with locals and visitors alike. Meals and snacks are served every day (not Mon lunch winter). Folk music evenings feature on the first Tuesday and third Thursday of the month. A recently refurbished terraced garden provides outdoor seating. B&B is available, as is takeaway food. ▟➢☆❺❶🚍(93)♣P⌐

Great Torrington

Black Horse Inn
High Street, EX38 8HN
✪ 11-11 (11.30 Fri & Sat); 12-11 Sun ☎ (01805) 622121
⊕ blackhorsedevon.co.uk
Courage Best Bitter; guest beers Ⓗ
Originally a 16th-century coaching inn that was used by Hopton and Fairfax during the Civil War Battle of Torrington in 1646, it is run by a local family and has a distinctive frontage with its white wall and dark framed leaded light windows. The interior is rich with traditional oak beams and panels, and purports to have a resident ghost. Up to four real ales are available along with great-value bar food or a full dining experience in the restaurant. Q❺❶

Royal Exchange Ⓛ
86 New Street, EX38 8BT
✪ 12-2.30 (not Mon & Tue), 5-midnight; 12-midnight Fri-Sun
☎ (01805) 623395
Forge IPA, Litehouse Ⓗ**; guest beers** Ⓖ
Friendly, welcoming 17th-century main-street local. The principal bar has low beams, two handpumps, and serves guest ales on gravity and Westons Scrumpy. The lower-level side bar contains darts, pool and a TV, leading to the rear restaurant that doubles as a function or family room. Good-quality food is available every day until 9pm, and Wednesday curry night is very popular. Children and dogs are welcome. A popular three-day music and beer festival is held every year in late May/early June. ▟➢☆❶🚍(70,71,315)♣●ᵌ⌐

Hartland

Anchor Inn Ⓛ
Fore Street, EX39 6BD
✪ closed Tue; 12-3, 6-11 Mon & Wed; 12-11 Thu-Sat; 12-4, 6-10.30 Sun ☎ (01237) 441414
⊕ theanchorinnhartland.co.uk
Forge Litehouse; guest beers Ⓗ
A 16th-century former coaching inn and now the brewery tap for the award-winning Forge Brewery

just around the corner. The main bar serves up to four real ales and has a pool table and fire. The other is a cosy lounge bar. The restaurant, which can also be used for functions and entertainment, serves excellent home-cooked food using local produce where possible. The patio area is covered and heated, and has views of the local countryside. Well-behaved dogs welcome.
▟☆🏠❶❺🅿🚍(319,519)♣P⌐

Heddon Valley

Hunters Inn Ⓛ
EX31 4PY (signposted from A399) SS655483
✪ 10-11 ☎ (01598) 763230 ⊕ thehuntersinn.net
Exmoor Ale, Hart, Gold, Stag, Beast; guest beers Ⓗ
Popular, large, renovated inn in a picturesque valley where peacocks are allowed to wander freely. Several real ales are available, along with Sam's Medium cider from Winkleigh. Spectacular views of the surrounding valley are plentiful and the footpath to Heddons Mouth is nearby. It is easy to see why walkers, hikers, cyclists, families with children and dog owners are attracted here. A popular three-day beer and music festival is held in the rear garden area in early September.
▟Q☆🏠❶⛰🅿♣●P

Holcombe

Smugglers Inn Ⓛ
27 Teignmouth Road, EX7 0LA (on A379 between Dawlish and Teignmouth)
✪ 11-11; 12-10.30 Sun ☎ (01626) 862301
⊕ thesmugglersinn.net
Dartmoor Legend; Teignworthy Reel Ale; guest beers Ⓗ
This roadside free house with resident proprietors and lovely coastal views has an excellent reputation for food. The carvery is a particular attraction, available noon to 9pm. The bar area has a wood-burning stove, and there are two regular Devon-brewed ales plus variable guests. The outside area is popular all year round, with a separate smokers' canopy. Regular entertainment and quizzes are hosted. There is a large car park, and buses pass the door. ▟☆❶⛰🅿(2)P⌐

Holcombe Rogus

Prince of Wales
TA21 0PN
✪ 12-3 (not Mon), 5.30-11 (midnight Fri); 12-midnight Sat; 12-10 Sun ☎ (01823) 672070
Otter Bitter; Sharp's Doom Bar; guest beers Ⓗ
A 17th-century country pub lying close to the Grand Western Canal and the Somerset border. The area is popular with walkers and cyclists. Inside, the bar features unusual cash register handpumps. Home-cooked food, including vegetarian options and a carvery on Sundays, is served. A large log-burning stove warms the pub in winter. There is a darts area, shove-ha'penny and dominoes. Live music features regularly and a beer festival is held in September. The attractive walled garden is popular in summer. Regular themed food nights are hosted. ▟☆❶⇆(Tiverton Parkway)♣P⌐

Holsworthy

Old Market Inn ♀ Ⓛ
Chapel Street, EX22 6AY (on A388 S of town square)

✪ 11-midnight (1am Fri & Sat); 12-11 Sun
☎ (01409) 253941 ⊕ oldmarketinn.co.uk
Bays Gold ⑤**; Clearwater Proper Ansome; Holsworthy Muck 'n' Straw** Ⓗ
Local CAMRA Pub of the Year 2012 situated in an historic market town. This family-run free house has stillage for six casks at the end of the single bar, plus four handpumps and autumn scrumpy cider from Winkleigh. Locally sourced food is served in the spacious rear restaurant. Local comedy club acts appear regularly, and during St Peter's Fair week in July a mini beer festival is held. Wednesdays are very busy thanks to a thriving local livestock and food market.
✿⊭◑ఉ🚃(X9)♣●P'—

Rydon Inn 🗓
Rydon Road, EX22 7HU (¾ mile W of Holsworthy on A3072 Bude road)
✪ closed Mon winter; 11.30-3, 6-11; 12-3, 6-10.30 (not winter) Sun ☎ (01409) 259444 ⊕ rydon-inn.com
Beer range varies Ⓗ
Free house and licensed wedding venue near both the market town of Holsworthy and the Cornish border. Extended from an original Devon longhouse, there is a thatched bar with a high vaulted ceiling and a cosy fire in winter, while the large conservatory restaurant serves high-quality locally sourced food. At least two local ales are kept and CAMRA members receive a discount. Outside, the spacious garden area has picturesque views over Holsworthy. Families with well-behaved children are welcome.
🏚Q⛱✿◑ఉ🅰🚃(X9,71,85)♣●P'—

Honiton

Holt 🗓
178 High Street, EX14 1LA
✪ closed Sun & Mon; 11-3, 5.30-11 (midnight Sat)
☎ (01404) 47707 ⊕ theholt-honiton.com
Otter Bitter, Amber, Bright, Ale, Head Ⓗ
The floor is slate, the walls are ochre, and the decor is smart with lots of exposed wood. The kitchen is fully open allowing you to watch the chefs preparing delicious main meals and tapas; it is a gastro-pub. However, as the pub is the first to be opened by the Otter brewery, you could simply call the place a brewery tap. Gastro-pub, or brewery tap? When food and drink are this good, who cares? ◑≢🚃(20,52b,367)

Horsebridge

Royal Inn
PL19 8PJ (off the A384 Tavistock-Launceston road) SX401748
✪ 12-3, 7-11 (10.30 Sun) ☎ (01822) 870214
⊕ royalinn.co.uk
Dartmoor Legend; St Austell Proper Job; Skinner's Betty Stogs Ⓗ**; guest beers** ⑤
Originally built as a nunnery in 1437 by French Benedictine monks and reported to have been visited by Charles I, the pub overlooks an old bridge on the River Tamar, connecting Devon to Cornwall. It now features half-panelling and stone floors in the bar and lounge, both traditional in style, with a further larger room off the lounge. There is a terraced garden with sheltered seating. The guest beers are usually served on gravity; the locally sourced food is recommended. 🏚Q✿◑P

Iddesleigh

Duke of York
EX19 8BG (off B3217 next to church) SS569082
✪ 11-11; 12-10.30 Sun ☎ (01837) 810253
Adnams Broadside; Cotleigh Tawny; guest beers ⑤
Fifteenth-century remote village pub ideally positioned near the Tarka Trail. The bar is simply furnished, with old beams, an inglenook log fire and a rocking chair. Faded currency notes are pinned to the beams and a collection of 1970s photos of locals adorn the walls. Well-behaved dogs are welcome. Three real ales are served from casks behind the bar, plus Sam's cider from Winkleigh. Food is served all day either in the bar or in one of the several dining areas. 🏚✿◑🅰♣●

Ide

Poachers Inn 🗓
55 High Street, EX2 9RW (3 miles from M5 jct 31, via A30) SX899903
✪ 12-midnight (1am Fri & Sat) ☎ (01392) 273847
⊕ poachersinn.co.uk
Bays Topsail; Branscombe Vale Branoc; Dartmoor Legend; guest beers Ⓗ
Typical busy village pub with a friendly atmosphere, serving a varied menu of home-made locally sourced produce, including excellent-value fish and chips to eat in or take away on Wednesday evenings. Dogs are welcome in the comfortably furnished bar, with old sofas, chairs and a big log fire in winter. There is also a large beer garden overlooking the glorious Devon countryside. Five ales are usually on handpump, with various guest beers from the West Country.
🏚✿⊭◑🅰🚃(360)♣P'—

Ideford

Royal Oak ✔
TQ13 0AY
✪ closed Mon; 12-2.30, 6-11.15; 12-3, 7-11 Sun
☎ (01626) 852274
Courage Directors; guest beers Ⓗ
A charming, traditional 17th-century inn with flagstone floor and beamed ceilings. The small, cosy single bar is festooned with historic memorabilia, mainly concerning Nelson and Trafalgar. At the rear is a small sheltered patio, with more tables across the road by the pub car park. Children and dogs are welcome. The hostelry is in the village centre and is popular with locals, hashers, cyclists, walkers and morris dancers.
🏚✿◑ఉ♣P'—

Ilfracombe

George & Dragon
4 Fore Street, EX34 9ED
✪ 10-midnight ☎ (01271) 863851
⊕ georganddragonilfracombe.co.uk
Exmoor Ale; Shepherd Neame Spitfire; Skinner's Betty Stogs Ⓗ
Dating from 1360, this is one of two remaining pubs in Fore Street where once there were many. Situated close to the pier and harbour, with out-front seating, there are three real ales on offer in an atmosphere of wooden beams and large fireplaces. A wide range of bar snacks and home-cooked meals is available every day using fresh local produce wherever possible, including

vegetables and herbs from the pub's garden. A quiz is held every Tuesday. Dogs are welcome. Q◑♣

Ship & Pilot L

10 Broad Street, EX34 9EE (opp bus station)
✪ 11 (12 Sun)-midnight ☎ (01271) 863562
Beer range varies Ⓗ
Close to the harbour and pier, this is a difficult place to miss, with its bright yellow painted front. The pub has been transformed recently into an atmospheric local, mainly due to the hard work of the young manager. The handpumps on the bar dispense six varying real ales, mainly from West Country brewers, plus a real cider and a perry. A refurbishment of the bar area is planned.
▲ᕫ(3,30,301)♣♨

Ivybridge

Bridge Inn

Harford Road, PL21 0AS (on B3213 on E side of town) SX637563
✪ 11.30 (11 Sun)-11 ☎ (01752) 897086
Greene King Abbot; St Austell Tribute; Sharp's Doom Bar Ⓗ
Since taking over the pub in 2010, Angie has transformed this town-centre Admiral Tavern into a lively, friendly community pub catering for young and old alike, with teams for pool, darts and euchre, twice-monthly live bands, live sports TV and also a quieter lounge with comfortable seating. The community noticeboard displays current local job vacancies. ▲◑ᕫᴥ♣

Kilmington

New Inn L ✔

The Hill, EX13 7SF (in village, S of A35)
✪ 11.30-2.30, 6-11; 12-3, 7-10.30 Sun ☎ (01297) 33376
Palmers Copper Ale, IPA, seasonal beers Ⓗ
Thatched Devon longhouse that became a pub in the early 1800s, and has appeared in every Guide, 21 of those years with the current landlord. It was rebuilt after a major fire in 2004, retaining a welcoming atmosphere and gaining excellent toilet facilities and disabled access. There is a large safe garden and a well-used skittle alley. A quiz on the first Sunday in the month and other events maintain this pub's position as an important part of village life. Q❀◑&ᕫ(380)♣P

Old Inn L ✔

EX13 7RB
✪ 11-3, 6-11; 12-3, 7-10.30 Sun ☎ (01297) 32096
⊕ oldinnkilmington.co.uk
Branscombe Vale Branoc, Best Bitter; Otter Bitter; guest beer Ⓗ
Thatched 16th-century inn on the A35. The Cricketers' bar, a lounge with a log fire, and a restaurant area are complemented by a suntrap patio and a raised lawn. Food, served lunchtimes and evenings (not Sun eve), is sourced locally, including good mussels, and the many specials are changed daily. See the website for more about beer fests held at the end of May and August and regular themed nights. A loyalty card system operates, earning points towards meal vouchers. ▲Q❀◑⊟▲ᕫ(380)P♪

Kings Nympton

Grove Inn L

EX37 9ST SS684195
✪ 12-3 (not Mon winter), 6-11; 12-4, 7-10.30 Sun
☎ (01769) 580406 ⊕ thegroveinn.co.uk
Beer range varies Ⓗ
A 17th-century, Grade II-listed thatched pub situated within this picturesque village. The single bar has low beams with bookmarks hanging from the ceiling and serves four real ales, plus Winkleigh Sam's Dry cider. Multi award-winning food is served, including the popular Tuesday fish and chip nights. A quiz night is held on the first Monday of each month, raising funds for local charities. Well-behaved children and dogs are welcome both in the pub and in the self-catering cottage nearby.
▲Q❀ᕫ◑&♣♨♪

Kingsbridge

King's Arms L

93 Fore Street, TQ7 1AB
✪ 12-11 ☎ (01548) 852071 ⊕ kingsarmskingsbridge.co.uk
Beer range varies Ⓗ
An 18th-century Grade II-listed coaching inn at the top of the main street. The beer range is varied, with an emphasis on the offerings of British microbreweries. Beer discovery and pie night takes place every Thursday. Old local pictures adorn the walls. The food is highly recommended, with both the dining and drinking areas having comfortable seating. There is an upstairs function room available for hire. B&B accommodation in modern bedrooms, some with four-poster beds, is offered.
▲ᕫ◑⊟P♪

Kingston

Dolphin Inn

TQ7 4QE (next to church) SX634478
✪ 12-3, 6-11; 12-3, 7-10.30 Sun ☎ (01548) 810314
⊕ dolphin-inn.co.uk
Courage Best Bitter; Sharp's Doom Bar; guest beers Ⓗ
The main building of the pub was originally three 16th-century cottages before being joined together and converted. A focal point for the local community, the Dolphin is also popular with tourists during the summer. The cosy interior features exposed stonework and pleasant low lighting. Home-cooked food from locally sourced ingredients is served on winter Sunday and Monday evenings. The family room, gents' toilets and large beer garden are across the road which, so to speak, runs through the pub.
▲Q☕❀ᕫ◑♣P♪

Kingswear

Ship Inn ✔

Higher Street, TQ6 0AG
✪ 12-midnight (closed 3.30-6 Mon-Thu winter)
☎ (01803) 752348 ⊕ theshipinnkingswear.co.uk
Adnams Southwold Bitter; Otter Bitter; Wadworth Henry's IPA; guest beers Ⓗ
Welcoming and busy 15th-century pub tucked away above the steam railway station and behind the church, comprising one horseshoe-shaped bar with log fires and a nautical theme, plus a restaurant area. The food comes highly recommended, especially the fish dishes. There are superb views from the front terrace over the river

towards Dartmouth. Four beers are available in the winter, with more offered in the summer.
ᴍQ☸⓪▥≑➥(22,24,120)'≞

Lutton

Mountain Inn ⓛ
Old Chapel Road, PL21 9SA SX595594
☻ 12 (4.30 Tue)-11 ☎ (01752) 837247
Dartmoor Jail Ale; guest beers Ⓗ
A traditional two-roomed pub with simple cob walls and real fires. The local favourite, Dartmoor Jail Ale, is accompanied by three wide-ranging guest ales, occasional draught ciders, and up to eight bottled ciders. Simple home-made pub food is served daily (no food Tue). Although situated in the foothills of Dartmoor, the pub's name is actually a corruption of Montain, the name of an old local landowner. An annual beer festival is held. ᴍQ☸⓪▥(58,59)➊P

Manaton

Kestor Inn ⓛ
TQ13 9UF (on main road through village)
☻ 11-11 ☎ (01647) 221626 ⊕ kestorinn.com
Dartmoor Legend; Otter Bitter, guest ales Ⓗ
Spacious local village inn on Dartmoor with a large open-plan L-shaped bar with plenty of seating, including alcoves. There is also a separate pool room and a long dining room, which can be used for functions. It has a friendly atmosphere, and a good selection of local real ales is on offer. The lobby area of the pub has been turned into a small shop selling basic items, and a book exchange scheme is in operation. Sam's Medium Cider is sold. ᴍQ☸⓪♣➊P

Meavy

Royal Oak ⓛ
The Village, PL20 6PJ (on the village green) SX541672
☻ 11-11; 12-10.30 Sun ☎ (01822) 852944
⊕ royaloakinn.org.uk
Dartmoor IPA, Jail Ale; guest beers Ⓗ
This popular gem of a pub can be found tucked away in an attractive valley – a must for fans of real ale, real cider and real conversation. It is a hostelry of two halves: the quiet, smart lounge provides good-quality locally-sourced food and relaxation, while the lively public bar provides a Devon welcome and a roaring fire. Check out the informative website for news of special offers, live music, morris dancing visits and beer and cider festivals. ᴍQ☸⓪▤▥(56)➊

Milton Combe

Who'd Have Thought It
The Village, PL20 6HP SX489661
☻ 12-3, 6-11; 12-11 Sat and summer; 12-3, 6-10.30 (12-10.30 summer) Sun ☎ (01822) 853313
⊕ whodhavethoughtitdevon.co.uk
Beer range varies Ⓗ
In a small village near Buckland Abbey, this quaint 16th-century free house is a must. The well-kept ale is usually sourced from the south west, with the emphasis on Sharp's, Skinner's and Teignworthy. The pub is popular for Sunday lunches, though drinkers are always welcome. The interior is divided into three sections, including the small characteristic main bar where board games are

available. To the rear, there is a small covered seating area overlooking the fast-moving stream.
ᴍQ☸▨⓪▥▲➥(55)P'≞

Moretonhampstead

Union Inn ⓛ
10 Ford Street, TQ13 8LN
☻ 11-11; 12-10.30 Sun ☎ (01647) 440199
⊕ theunioninn.co.uk
Fuller's London Pride; Red Rock Lighthouse, Red Rock, Breakwater Ⓗ
Sixteenth-century village-centre free house. The beamed bar and adjoining pool room display old photographs of the village. The function room – with its own bar and skittle alley – is reached via a corridor displaying many artefacts relating to the inn's history. Value-for-money Red Rock beers are given house names, and Gray's cider is available. The good home-cooked food is served all day on Sunday. There is an outside seating on a decking area next to the small rear car park.
ᴍ☸⓪ᵹ▥(173,359)♣➊P

Newton Abbot

Richard Hopkins ⊘
34-42 Queen Street, TQ12 2EW (400yds from railway station)
☻ 8-midnight ☎ (01626) 323930
Greene King Abbot; Ruddles Best Bitter; guest beers Ⓗ
A busy town-centre Wetherspoon's. Ten handpumps offer local and national beers including, usually, one from the nearby Hunter's Brewery. The spacious interior is divided into separate seating areas with illustrations depicting local people and historic events. Each year the pub holds three beer festivals – two national and one featuring Devon beers – plus a cider festival. Monday is quiz night. Outside, there is a covered seating area at the front of the pub.
☸⓪ᵹ≑▥➊'≞

Union Inn ⊘
6 East Street, TQ12 1AF (between magistrates' court and clock tower)
☻ 10-11 (midnight Fri & Sat); 12-11 Sun ☎ (01626) 354775
St Austell Tribute; Sharp's Doom Bar; guest beers Ⓗ
A traditional town-centre pub in a Grade II-listed building that stands on a site associated with the family of Sir Walter Raleigh. Three guest beers are usually selected from south-west breweries. The pub has a well-deserved reputation for locally sourced and reasonably priced food. Breakfasts are served from 8.30am. Local darts, football and euchre teams are supported and there is a Sunday night quiz. Tables are provided outside on the pedestrianised street. ☸▨⓪≑▥♣'≞

Newton St Cyres

Beer Engine ⓛ
EX5 5AX (N of A377 near station)
☻ 11-11; 12-10.30 Sun ☎ (01392) 851282
⊕ thebeerengine.co.uk
Beer Engine Rail Ale, 040 Shunter, Silver Bullet, Piston Bitter, Sleeper Heavy, seasonal beer Ⓗ
Georgian pub, built in 1850 on the Exeter to Barnstaple Tarka Line, two-thirds of a mile north of the A377. Popular with drinkers and diners alike, it is well frequented by locals, visitors and the cricket

team. The dining area adjoining the bar serves its own bread made with beer yeast, along with locally sourced wholesome food, available lunchtimes and evenings. The pub brews its own ales which, like the village pictures and old pub signs, reflect a railway theme.
ⓂQ☺◑&⇌�︎(50,51,315)♣P↳🖙

North Tawton

Railway Inn Ⓛ
Whiddon Down Road, EX20 2BE (1 mile S of town off A3124) SS665001
☼ 12-3 (Fri & Sat only), 6-11; 12-3, 7-11 Sun
☎ (01837) 82789
Teignworthy Reel Ale; guest beers Ⓗ
Traditional single-bar local that is part of a working farm. A warm welcome from the landlord is assured and there is a translation of his Devon dialect displayed in the bar area for the benefit of confused visitors. The guest ales are normally from the West Country and change regularly, with a real cider available in summer. The dining room is popular in the evening (no food Thu), with light meals served at lunchtime. No dogs allowed except guide dogs. ⓂQ◑♣P

Noss Mayo

Swan Inn
Pillory Hill, PL8 1EE
☼ 11-11 (10.30 Sun) ☎ (01752) 872392
⊕ swaninnnossmayo.co.uk
St Austell Tribute; Sharp's Doom Bar; guest beers Ⓗ
The pub is situated on the attractive River Yealm estuary, separated from its neighbouring village by a tidal creek, which can be crossed on foot at low tide. A bright and welcoming interior is complemented by an outside seating area down by the water's edge. There are regular community-oriented events such as live music and quiz nights. A full food menu is offered, with many dishes using local produce. The no. 94 bus to/from Plymouth stops by the pub (daytime only, not Sun).
ⓂQ☺◑🚎(94)

Okehampton

Plymouth Inn Ⓛ
26 West Street, EX20 1HH (W end of town near West Okement bridge)
☼ 11-midnight ☎ (01837) 53633
Beer range varies Ⓖ
Old coaching inn and friendly village-style local dating from the 17th century. The ales are mainly from West Country brewers, with a regularly changing cider from Devon. Two popular beer festivals take place in the function room, one coinciding with the Ten Tors Challenge in May, and the other with the Baring Gould Folk Festival in October. Reasonably priced, locally sourced food is served, with special theme nights held every six weeks or so. Children and dogs welcome.
♿☺◑🅰🚎(X9)♣🖙↳

Ottery St Mary

Lamb & Flag Ⓛ ✔
Batts Lane, EX11 1EY (off Yonder St)
☼ 10.30-11 (midnight Thu-Sat); 12-10.30 Sun
☎ (01404) 813704
Otter Bitter, Ale; guest beer Ⓗ

Old coaching inn with a strong local following. It has recently been renovated, with the main bar leading to a separate dining area that doubles up as a skittle alley, and another dining room/bar. It is renowned for its breakfasts and curry evenings. There are two pool tables and darts in the main bar area, and live music is performed on weekend evenings. One or two changing guest beers are on offer. Dogs (in the main bar) and families are welcome. The cider varies but is often Westons.
◑🅱&🚎(60A,380)♣🖙

Paignton

Isaac Merritt Ⓛ ✔
54-58 Torquay Road, TQ3 3AA
☼ 8-midnight ☎ (01803) 556066
Courage Directors; Greene King Abbot; Ruddles Best Bitter; guest beers Ⓗ
Busy town-centre Wetherspoon pub themed around the inventor of the Singer sewing machine. Its comfortable, friendly atmosphere with cosy seated alcoves makes it popular with all ages. This superb establishment has a deserved reputation for beer quality and choice. At the rear is a covered, heated seating area for smokers. There is a separate family dining area, with meals served all day. The pub is fully accessible to wheelchair users, with a designated ground floor toilet.
☺◑&⇌🚎(12)🖙↳

Waterside Inn ✔
128 Dartmouth Road, Goodrington, TQ4 6ND
☼ 11.30 (11 Sat)-11; 12-10.30 Sun ☎ (01803) 551113
Courage Best Bitter; guest beers Ⓗ
A 1930s pub with a single large open-plan bar featuring several TV screens and a dining area with carvery. Courage Best is usually available, together with two guest beers, often from south-west brewers. A small garden and patio is at the rear while there are more picnic tables around the building. It also has a covered smoking area. Books and videos are sold on behalf of a local hospice. Free Wi-Fi is available, and food is served all day.
☺◑&🅰🚎(12,120)♣P↳

Parkham

Bell Inn Ⓛ ✔
Rectory Lane, EX39 5PL (1 mile S of the A39 at Horns Cross) SS387212
☼ 12-2, 5.30-11; 5-11 Fri & Sat; 12-3, 6-10.30 Sun
☎ (01237) 451201 ⊕ thebellinnparkham.co.uk
Sharp's Doom Bar; guest beers Ⓗ
Historic 13th-century thatched inn with traditional oak beams, cob walls and open fires, originally a forge and two farmers' cottages. The single bar has up to four real ales available, one a local guest. A well-attended beer festival takes place in early June and summer spit roasts have become a popular feature. Locally produced food is available lunchtimes and evenings every day in the bar area or the raised dining room. Ⓜ☺◑♣P↳

Peter Tavy

Peter Tavy Inn Ⓛ
PL19 9NN SX512778
☼ 12-3, 6-11 (6.30-10.30 Sun) ☎ (01822) 810348
⊕ petertavyinn.com
Dartmoor Jail Ale; guest beers; Otter Bright Ⓗ

125

In a quiet village on the edge of Dartmoor, a good varying range of local beers can be found in the pub's small central bar. The pub is renowned for its food, but drinkers are made welcome. Traditionally attired throughout, there are two larger rooms, one for families. A patio and hidden garden are added attractions. The inn is situated on the No. 27 cycle route, and near a caravan and camping site.
▲Q🌣🕭🕪🅟AP

Plymouth

Artillery Arms 🅛
6 Pound Street, Stonehouse, PL1 3RH (behind Stonehouse Barracks and Millbay Docks)
🕓 11 (4 Mon & Tue)-midnight; 12-midnight Sun
☎ (01752) 262515
Dartmoor Jail Ale; Draught Bass; guest beers 🅗
Cracking back-street local tucked away in the old quarter of Stonehouse, close to the magnificent Grade I-listed Royal William Yard and maintaining the area's military connections. Good home-cooked food is served (no food Sun). Two south-west guest beers and Thatchers Heritage cider are normally available. An out-of-season beach party takes place on the last weekend in February, and charity monkey racing also features. This place is a real find and is popular with hockey teams, who use the nearby pitches. ▲Q🌣🕭🖭(34)🍴🛏

Britannia Inn 🅛 🅥
1 Wolseley Road, Milehouse, PL2 3BH
🕓 8am-midnight (1am Fri & Sat; 11 Sun) ☎ (01752) 607596
Greene King Abbot; Ruddles Best Bitter; Sharp's Doom Bar; guest beers 🅗
Large Edwardian Wetherspoon's that benefits from having always been a pub, situated opposite the Citybus depot and handy for Central Park and Plymouth Argyle FC's Home Park. It can be very busy on match days and in the evenings. Numerous buses from the city centre and railway station pass close by this multi award-winning gem. Draught Westons cider and perry are served. It is one of only a handful of pubs serving real ale in the western half of the city. ▲Q🌣🕭🖕🖭🍴🛏

Clovelly Bay Inn
11 Boringdon Road, Turnchapel, PL9 9TB
🕓 11-3, 6-11; 12-11 Sat; 12-4, 7-10.30 Sun
☎ (01752) 402765 ⊕ clovellybayinn.co.uk
Beer range varies 🅗/🅖
This family-run free house has an enthusiastic landlord with a passion for real ales and farm ciders. Up to 10 beers are available, mostly on gravity dispense. At least four significant beer and cider festivals are held during the year, with an emphasis on locally-sourced produce – check the website for details. There is a free jukebox available and the house is dog friendly. The pub is reachable by bus, or water taxi from the Barbican. Local CAMRA Pub of the Year 2011.
▲Q🌣🖐🕭🖕🖭(2)🍀🛏

Dolphin Hotel
14 The Barbican, PL1 2LS
🕓 10-11 (midnight Thu-Sat); 11-11 Sun ☎ (01752) 660876
Draught Bass; St Austell Tribute; guest beers 🅖
An unpretentious hostelry steeped in history, the Dolphin is a Plymouth institution. A recent makeunder has left the character thankfully untouched, with tiled floors, well-used wooden benches, together with a real open fire, all adding to the ambience. The walls are adorned with

paintings by local artist, the late Beryl Cook, who painted many of the characters she encountered at the Dolphin. Some of the best Bass in the West Country is served straight from casks behind the bar, with up to seven guest beers also available.
▲▱🖭(25)

Fortescue 🅛 🅥
37 Mutley Plain, Mutley, PL4 6JQ
🕓 11-11 (midnight Thu-Sat); 12-10.30 Sun
☎ (01752) 660673
Bays Devon Dumpling; St Austell Proper Job; Skinner's Cornish Knocker; South Hams XSB; guest beers 🅗
Winner of numerous local CAMRA awards, the Fortescue is a well-run bohemian pub with an eclectic mix of customers where conversation flourishes. Spingo Sunday is a local institution, with a home-cooked roast washed down with Spingo Special, and a quiz in the evening. A long through-bar leads to a popular beer garden, with heating in winter. Numerous evening events take place in the cellar bar, including open mic and acoustic nights. Up to eight real ales and one real cider are usually available. 🌣🚆🖭🍀🛏

Lounge
7 Stopford Place, Devonport, PL1 4QT
🕓 11.30-3 (not Mon), 6-11 (midnight Fri); 11.30-11 Sat; 12-11 Sun ☎ (01752) 561330
Draught Bass; guest beers 🅗
The Lounge is one of the few pubs to sell real ale in the western side of the city, and thus a haven for discerning drinkers. Nearby Stoke is crammed with pubs but do not be fooled; make sure you head straight here. One weaker, one stronger than the regular Bass is the rule for the guest beers, with lighter and darker brews also alternating. The wood-panelled bar is comfortable and relaxing, although may be busy if Plymouth Albion RFC are at home. Q🌣🕭🚆(Devonport)🖭🛏

Maritime Inn 🅛
19 Southside Street, PL1 2LD
🕓 12 (5 Mon & winter Tue)-11; 12-1am Fri & Sat; 12-10.30 Sun ☎ (01752) 664898 ⊕ themaritimeinn.co.uk
Summerskills MRB; guest beers 🅗
Spacious open-plan pub on Plymouth's historic Barbican and Sutton Harbour. The bar area opening onto the quay has slate floors and a large TV, attracting sports supporters and is often lively. There is also a more relaxed seating area opening onto Southside Street. No food is served but customers may bring in food from local traders. An exclusive beer from the local Summerskills Brewery is available at a competitive price, and seasonal strong beers feature alongside those from other local and national breweries. A meeting room and apartment can be hired. 🌣🖐🖭(25)🍀🛏

Prince Maurice 🅛 🅥
3 Church Hill, Eggbuckland, PL6 5RJ
🕓 11-3, 6-11; 11-11 Fri & Sat; 12-10.30 Sun
☎ (01752) 771515
Dartmoor Jail Ale; O'Hanlon's Stormstay; St Austell HSD; Sharp's Doom Bar; Summerskills Best Bitter; guest beer 🅗
There is very much a village feel to this four-times local CAMRA Pub of the Year, which is between the church and the green. It is named after the royalist general, the King's nephew, who had his headquarters nearby during the siege of Plymouth in the civil war. Up to eight beers are on offer. Log fires in winter keep you warm. Look out for the SS

Titanic memorabilia as you down your next pint. No food at weekends. Local CAMRA City Pub of the Year. ▲❀◑⊟📶(28A,28B)♣♨⅃

Swan Inn

15 St Andrews Street, PL1 2AX
🌣 12-midnight (1.30am Fri & Sat) ☎ (01752) 221094
Beer range varies Ⓗ
Reopened in early 2011 as a free house under its original name after a major refurbishment and modernisation, the Swan now has a more traditional pub feel than its recent bistro-bar incarnations. An interesting collection of unusual bottled beers is on display in cabinets. Up to three guest ales are available which are unusual to Plymouth, mainly sourced from Devon and Cornwall. The real cider varies. Free Wi-Fi is available. ➡🚃♣♨⅃

Thistle Park Tavern Ⓛ

32 Commercial Road, Coxside, PL4 0LE
🌣 12-1am (4am Fri & Sat) ☎ (01752) 204890
South Hams Devon Pride, XSB, Eddystone, seasonal beers Ⓗ
Brewery tap for the South Hams Brewery which, as Sutton, was formerly located next door. There is a roof garden and Thai restaurant upstairs. Biltong is available at the bar. Cheddar Valley cider is on offer, alongside four beers from the brewery's range. The pub can be accessed across the swing bridge from the Barbican (this shuts at 9.30pm), and from there is situated behind the National Marine Aquarium. Live music and extra-late opening feature at the weekend.
▲❀◑ᯤ🖥📶♣♨⅃

Plympton

George Inn

191 Ridgeway, PL7 2HJ SX545562
🌣 11-11; 11.30-midnight Fri & Sat; 12-11 Sun
☎ (01752) 342674 ⊕ thegeorgeplympton.co.uk
Courage Best Bitter; Dartmoor Jail Ale; guest beers Ⓗ
A 17th-century former coaching house on the old Plymouth to Exeter road. The flagstone bar is complemented by a spacious dining room, and the florally bedecked patio is especially popular during fine weather. There is a large function room available upstairs. A specials board supplements an extensive menu and booking is advisable at weekends. A popular quiz is held monthly on the second Sunday. Dogs on leads are welcome in the bar area. ▲Q🌣❀◑📶⊟(22)♣P⅃

Union Inn Ⓛ

17 Underwood Road, PL7 1SY
🌣 4-11 (11.30 Fri); 12-midnight Sat; 12-11 Sun
☎ (01752) 336756 ⊕ unioninnplympton.com
Beer range varies Ⓗ
Family-run community pub that offers a warm welcome to all those who enter this traditional, cosy, early 19th-century pub. The landlord's passion for ale is evident, as up to four guest beers vary to provide a year-round beer festival. There are also two real ciders served on gravity. All meals are freshly prepared using local produce, and booking is advisable, particularly on specially themed evenings. Lunchtime meals are only available at weekends. Dogs on leads are welcome. ▲Q❀◑♣♨P⅃

Plymtree

Blacksmith's Arms Ⓛ

EX15 2JU
🌣 6 (12 Sat)-midnight; 12-5 Sun ☎ (01884) 277474
⊕ blacksmithsplymtree.co.uk
Exe Valley Dob's Best Bitter; O'Hanlon's Yellowhammer; Otter Amber; St Austell Tribute; guest beers Ⓗ
Nestled in beautiful countryside in the attractive village of Plymtree and sought after by locals, ramblers and visitors, this traditional pub embraces the atmosphere of true village life. It features a range of 14 local ales, with three on tap at any one time. The wine cellar is extensive and this pub has a reputation for serving quality food with generous portions and punchy flavours. Full menu and bar snacks are served Tuesday-Saturday evenings, and weekend lunchtimes. Venton's real cider is served in summer. ▲🌣❀◑♣♨P⅃

Postbridge

East Dart Hotel Ⓛ

PL20 6TJ
🌣 11-11 (10 winter) ☎ (01822) 880213
⊕ theeastdarthotel.co.uk
Dartmoor IPA, Jail Ale; New East Dart Ale Ⓗ
On the B3212 at Postbridge, a stone's throw away from the famous clapper bridge, this 19th-century coaching inn offers a wide range of facilities. The interior of the pub has a traditional feel, with exposed beams and horse brasses. Outside there is an attractive beer garden and stables. The beers from the Dartmoor Brewery are complemented by locally sourced food, and the Sunday carvery is particularly popular. The pub is frequented by both locals and visitors to the National Park.
▲Q❀🚐◑ᯤ🅿⅃

Warren House Inn

PL20 6TA (on B3212, 2 miles NE of Postbridge) SX674809
🌣 11 (5 Mon & Tue winter)-11; 11-10.30 Sun
☎ (01822) 880208 ⊕ warrenhouseinn.co.uk
Otter Ale; guest beers Ⓗ
Isolated and exposed at 1425 feet above sea level, this is one of the highest pubs in England. The interior consists of several rooms and features exposed beams, wood panelling, rustic benches and tables, plus a famous fire. Daytime and evening menus offer home-cooked dishes using locally sourced ingredients. There is a large family room, and tables outside give breathtaking views over the moors. Countryman cider is available and guest beers vary with the seasons, with one strong ale usually featured. ▲Q🌣❀◑ᯤ⊟♨P⅃

Princetown

Plume of Feathers Ⓛ

The Square, PL20 6QQ SX591735
🌣 10.30-11 (midnight Fri & Sat) ☎ (01822) 890240
⊕ theplumeoffeathersdartmoor.co.uk
Dartmoor Dartmoor IPA, Jail Ale; St Austell Tribute; guest beers Ⓗ
Princetown's oldest building (dating from 1785) features granite walls, slate floors and slate-topped tables. A later addition is the large family/function room with its own bar. Food is served all day, with a carvery in the family room at weekend lunchtimes. There is ample outdoor seating on the spacious patio and a children's play area, plus a large car park, B&B accommodation and a campsite

and camping barn on site. An infrequent bus service is available from Tavistock and Yelverton. ▲Q➤✿⇔◀❶&▲⊒(98)P✒

Sampford Peverell

Globe Inn 𝕃
16 Lower Town, EX16 7BJ
✪ 8-midnight ☎ (01884) 821214 ⊕ the-globeinn.co.uk
Otter Bitter; St Austell Tribute; Sharp's Doom Bar; guest beers ℍ
Traditional Devon village inn backing onto the Grand Western Canal near Tiverton. Locally sourced food is available daily, with a carvery at weekends. An early breakfast can be booked 8-11am daily. A sheltered courtyard and large garden with children's play area are towards the rear. There are two function rooms and seven guest bedrooms available. Over Christmas, part of the car park is converted into a skating rink. Sheppy's Farmhouse Cider can be drunk here.
▲➤✿⇔◀❶&▲⇌(Tiverton Parkway)⊒(1)
♣●P✒

Sandford

Lamb Inn
The Square, EX17 4LW
✪ 9 (10.30 Sat)-midnight; 10.30-midnight Sun
☎ (01363) 773676 ⊕ lambinnsandford.co.uk
Otter Bitter; guest beers ℍ
A traditional 16th-century free house in the village centre, with a warm, welcoming atmosphere. It is well supported by locals and visitors alike, offering award-winning food, West Country ales and Sandford Orchards cider. Skittles is played four nights a week in the alley-cum-cinema-cum-conference venue. There are open mic music and comedy evenings. Six B&B rooms are available and children and dogs are welcome. It is frequented by the village football, squash and cricket teams.
▲Q➤✿⇔◀❶&⊒(369)♣●✒

Scorriton

Tradesman's Arms 𝕃
TQ11 0JB (near Buckfastleigh, about 3 miles from A38)
✪ 12-2.30, 6-11.30; 12-11 Sun ☎ (01364) 631206
⊕ thetradesmansarms.co.uk
Dartmoor IPA; guest beers ℍ
On the edge of Dartmoor, this pub reopened after it was bought by four locals who drank at the pub prior to its demise. It was renovated and updated, and has an L-shaped main bar with plenty of seating in a long alcove to one side, with a conservatory open to the pub at the other. There is a friendly atmosphere, and good local food is served together with a local real cider. One of the guest beers is from Hunter's. Accommodation is available. ▲Q➤✿⇔◀❶&▲♣●P

Shaldon

Clifford Arms 𝕃
34 Fore Street, TQ14 0DE
✪ 11-2.30, 5-11 (11.30 Fri & Sat); 11.30-3, 5.30-10.30 Sun
☎ (01626) 872311
Dartmoor IPA; Ringmore Oarsome Ale; guest beers ℍ
In the centre of a pretty coastal village, this pub has an attractive, modern interior, and a warming log fire in winter. The guest and seasonal beers are sourced mainly from West Country breweries. The

restaurant area at the rear serves good-quality food every day, and leads out onto a sunny, decked patio. Special menus are offered alongside modern jazz evenings on Monday and monthly Sunday lunchtime trad jazz sessions. The cider is Westons scrumpy. ▲✿◀❶⊒(11)●✒

Shaugh Prior

White Thorn Inn
PL7 5HA (on Cornwood to Bickleigh road S of Yelverton)
SX540632
✪ 12-3, 6-11; 12-10.30 Sun ☎ (01752) 839245
⊕ white-thorn-inn.co.uk
Beer range varies ℍ
Community village pub on the south-west side of Dartmoor, with three varying beers from Devon and Cornwall. It has a large open-plan bar with a central fireplace, and offers regular entertainment including pub quizzes and local events. A family-friendly venue, there is a children's play area and a large car park to the rear. Dogs are welcome. Situated one mile from the Plym Valley foot and cycle path. ▲✿◀❶&⊒(58,59)♣P✒

Shebbear

Devil's Stone Inn
Shebbear, EX21 5RU (in village square opp church)
SS438094
✪ 12-3, 6-11; 11-11 Fri-Sun ☎ (01409) 281210
⊕ devilsstoneinn.com
Beer range varies ℍ
This 17th-century former coaching inn at the heart of the village is a warm, cosy venue with wood beams, flagstone floors and several open fireplaces. The single bar has three handpumps serving a range of ales, and Sam's Cider from Winkleigh in summer. Apparently haunted, there is also a large garden, games room and separate dining room. In the church opposite you will find the Devil's Stone that is turned every year on 5 November to ward off evil spirits.
▲Q✿⇔◀❶&⊒(72)♣●P✒

Sidmouth

Swan Inn
37 York Street, EX10 8BY
✪ 11 (12 Sun)-11 ☎ (01395) 512849
Young's Bitter, Special; guest beer ℍ
A traditional and quiet back-street inn, established around 1770, that lies just off the centre of this quaint town, a short walk from the seafront and bus terminus. An old-style wood-panelled bar with an open fire attracts a strong local trade, and leads to a dedicated dining area serving good food. Three beers, all from the Wells & Young's range, are normally available. Dogs, but not children, are welcome indoors. Find out about the King of Chit – a traditional competition.
▲Q✿◀&⊒(52,157)♣✒

Silverton

Lamb Inn 𝕃 ✔
Fore Street, EX5 4HZ
✪ 11.30-2.30, 6-11 (1am Thu & Fri); 11.30-1am Sat; 12-11
Sun ☎ (01392) 860272 ⊕ thelambinnsilverton.co.uk
Exe Valley Dob's Best Bitter; Otter Ale; guest beer 𝔾
Popular family-run village pub with stone floors, stripped timber, old pine furniture and comfy bar

stools, as well as a good display of old pump clips to jog the memory of ales long gone. At least three ales are served by gravity from a temperature-controlled stillage behind the bar at very competitive prices. There is a well-used function room and skittles alley. Good-value home-cooked food is served lunchtimes and evenings, plus a popular Sunday roast. ⚼Q❀✿⑪🅖⛌🚃(55B)♣

Slapton

Queen's Arms 🅛
TQ7 2PN
❀ 12-3, 6-11 (7-10.30 Sun) ☎ (01548) 580800
🌐 queensarmsslapton.co.uk
Dartmoor Jail Ale; Otter Ale, Bright; guest beer 🅗
A warm welcome awaits at this 14th-century village centre pub. Numerous photographs depicting the wartime evacuation adorn the walls. A flower-filled garden with patios is at the rear. Children and dogs are welcome here. An extensive menu is available with daily specials; the chef's home-made pies are a local, noted speciality. During winter Sunday roasts are served (booking advisable). A takeaway food service is offered. ⚼❀⑪🅰🚃(93)♣P⅃

South Brent

Royal Oak 🅛
Station Road, TQ10 9BE (near old railway station)
❀ 12-2, 4-11; 12-11 Sat & Sun ☎ (01364) 72133
🌐 oakunline.net
Dartmoor IPA; Otter Ale; Teignworthy Gun Dog; guest beers 🅗
Village-centre pub on the edge of Dartmoor. The wood-panelled, L-shaped bar is surrounded by a large open-plan area with plenty of seating. An excellent range of real ales is available. At the rear a restaurant serves good-quality food, and a new function room can be found upstairs, which is available for meetings. There is a no-smoking courtyard outside and accommodation is offered. Occasional beer festivals are held, with a discount on real ales for CAMRA members. Q❀✿⑪🅖🅰

South Molton

Town Arms Hotel 🅛 ✅
124 East Street, EX36 3BU (100m E of town centre bus stop)
❀ 11 (12 Sun)-midnight ☎ (01769) 572531
Draught Bass; Exmoor Exmoor Ale; Sharp's Doom Bar 🅗
Main street local in this small, historic market town, ideally suited for exploring Exmoor and north Devon. There is one main bar with a pool table, open fire and interesting old photographs on the walls, and a quieter back room. The pub can get very lively on occasions, particularly Thursday market day. There is a strong commitment to real ale and CAMRA members receive a 10p per pint discount. Well-behaved dogs are welcome. ⚼🍺❀✿⑪🅖(X7,155,307)♣P⅃

Spreyton

Tom Cobley Tavern 🍺 🅛
EX17 5AL (off A3124 in village)
❀ 6.30-11 Mon; 12-3, 6-11 (1am Fri & Sat); 12-4, 7-11 Sun
☎ (01647) 231314 🌐 tomcobleytavern.co.uk

Clearwater Proper Ansome; Cotleigh Tawny; Dartmoor Jail Ale; Holsworthy Tamar Sauce; St Austell Proper Job; Skinner's Betty Stogs 🅗
Family-run 16th-century village local, which still maintains the standards that won it CAMRA's National Pub of the Year a few years ago. There is an open fire in the bar and in Jimmy's Snug children and dogs are welcome. On a warm day you can enjoy the surroundings of the large picturesque garden. Home-cooked food and daily specials are on the menu, plus traditional roasts on Sunday (booking advisable). Six comfortable guest rooms are available for night stops at this genuine gem. ⚼Q❀✿⑪♣🐾P

Sticklepath

Taw River Inn
EX20 2NW (on main road old A30 through village) SX642941
❀ 12-midnight (11 Sun) ☎ (01837) 840377
🌐 tawriver.co.uk
Greene King Abbot; St Austell Tribute; Sharp's Doom Bar; guest beers 🅗
This oak-beamed village local on the edge of Dartmoor can get lively. It is popular with walkers and ideal for visiting the Finch Foundry Museum (NT) opposite. The large single bar has a TV and hosts numerous sports and pub games played by locals. The varied real ales are sold at very attractive prices and good-value pub food is served. Well-behaved children and dogs are welcome and there is plenty of rear garden space. ⚼❀⑪🅖🚃(X9)♣P⅃

Teignmouth

Brass Monkey ✅
Hollands Road, TQ14 8SR
❀ 11 (12 Sun)-midnight ☎ (01626) 773961
St Austell Tribute, HSD 🅗
Town-centre community-oriented pub with a warm welcome from the long-serving and award-winning licensees. Ideally situated between the railway station and the town bus stops, it makes a perfect waiting room for travellers. It has regular sporting events on TV, with Tuesday quiz nights, weekend karaoke, free Wi-Fi and an early evening happy hour. It is a splendid retreat from the busy town centre, especially at the height of the holiday season. 🅖🚉🚃(2,11)♣

Throwleigh

Northmore Arms 🅛
Wonson, EX20 2JA (on A382 towards Chagford take signs to Wonford and Throwleigh) SX674897
❀ 11-4, 5-11; 11-11 Sun; 12-11 Sun ☎ (01647) 321428
🌐 thenorthmorearms.co.uk
Dartmoor IPA, Jail Ale 🅖
Unspoilt, traditional country pub on Dartmoor where patrons can take a step back in time. The cosy single bar has an open fire and serves at least two beers, plus cider from Sandford Orchards. Historic black and white photographs of locals adorn the walls. Good-value home-cooked food is served either in the bar, the adjacent side room or outside in summer. Sunday roasts are particularly popular. Not easy to find but well worth the effort. Dogs are welcome. ⚼Q❀⑪♣🐾P⅃

Tiverton

Rose & Crown Inn L
Calverleigh, EX16 8BA (on the old Rackenford Road)
✪ 11.45 (12 Sun)-midnight ☎ (01884) 256301
Butcombe Bitter; Otter Ale; guest beers Ⓗ
A traditional 17th-century country pub with
beamed ceilings and exposed stone walls, just a
mile from Tiverton town centre, with a restaurant,
beer garden and skittle alley that doubles as a
function room. Excellent home-cooked food made
with local produce where possible is available,
together with local cider from Palmershayes across
the road. Pub games include darts. Q❀◑ᏜᏔ♣☜P

Topsham

Bridge Inn ★ L
Bridge Hill, EX3 0QQ
✪ 12-2, 6-10.30 (11 Fri & Sat); 12-2, 7-10.30 Sun
☎ (01392) 873862 ⊕ cheffers.co.uk
Branscombe Vale Branoc; guest beers Ⓖ
Traditional, cosy 16th-century inn on the banks of
the River Clyst. Up to nine gravity-fed ales are
available. The inn has been run by six generations
of the same family since 1897, and was visited by
the Queen in 1998. Snacks and pies are available
lunchtimes, and till 8.30pm in the evenings. The
adjoining Malthouse is available for functions. The
new Exmouth to Exeter cycle track now runs past
the inn after crossing the Clyst.
♨Q❀◑⬗ᚑ❧(57)P

Exeter Inn L
68 High Street, EX3 0DY
✪ 11.30-11 (midnight Fri & Sat); 12-10.30 Sun
☎ (01392) 873131
Teignworthy Beachcomber; guest beers Ⓗ
Genuine community pub run by a welcoming and
enthusiastic couple. Originally a coaching house
dating from the 17th century, part of the building is
thatched. The pub has a choice of five ales, four of
which change regularly; these include both local
and national beers. Traditional pub games are
played, including euchre. There is a large-screen TV
for sporting events. The real ciders come from
Green Valley and Thatchers.
♨❀ᚑ❧(57,T)♣☜⸗

Torquay

Chelston Manor L ✔
Old Mill Road, Chelston, TQ2 6HW
✪ 12-2.30, 5-11; 12-10.30 Sun ☎ (01803) 605142
⊕ chelstonmanor.co.uk
Bays Topsail; Sharp's Doom Bar; guest beers Ⓗ
Set in a 17th-century former manor house in a
leafy suburb of Torquay, one mile from the town
centre and half a mile from the beach. Good home-
cooked food is served lunchtimes and evenings
(booking advisable for Sunday lunch). A large
south-facing garden hosts barbecues and music
events on Saturday evenings April-September. Up
to two guest beers are usually available. The cider
is Thatchers Heritage or Westons Katy.
♨❀ᚑ❧(32)☜⸗

Totnes

Bay Horse Inn
8 Cistern Street, TQ9 5SP
✪ 12-midnight ☎ (01803) 862088

Dartmoor Jail Ale; Otter Bitter; guest beers Ⓗ
A 15th-century coaching inn at the top of the
picturesque town of Totnes, serving a minimum of
four local real ales including one on gravity. A bar
menu is offered all day, with specials in the
evening. Live jazz features on Sunday night, with
folk and acoustic sessions on Monday and
Thursday. Beer festivals are held at Easter, during
the Totnes festival in September, and during the
winter months. At the rear is a large, attractive
garden with a heated patio and disabled access.
♨Q❀ᚑ◑ᏜᏔ⸗

Welcombe

Old Smithy Inn L
EX39 6HG (2 miles W of A39 at Welcombe Cross)
SS231179
✪ 12-midnight ☎ (01288) 331305 ⊕ theoldsmithyinn.co.uk
Sharp's Doom Bar; guest beers Ⓗ
Remote 17th-century country inn with an L-shaped
slate bar and a cosy dining area with open fire.
Three ales are available, including two different
guests. Ciders figure strongly here and include
Winkleigh Sam's Medium, Westons Traditional and
Thatchers Cheddar Valley. Regular folk, jam and
quiz evenings are held and a 16th-century function
room serves as an extra dining space. Wednesday
can be busy as it is a cheap food night. Well-
behaved children and dogs are welcome.
♨❀◑☜P

Whimple

New Fountain Inn L
Church Road, EX5 2TA
✪ 12-2 (not Mon, 3 Sat), 6.30-11; 12-3, 7-10.30 Sun
☎ (01404) 822350
Teignworthy Reel Ale; guest beer Ⓖ
A genuine free house. Converted from cottages in
around 1890, this pub has changed little over the
years, although modern toilets were added in a
tasteful extension to one of the bars in 2009. The
other has many original features including a real
fire in winter. The handpumps are not in use; ale is
fetched from the cellar. Good-value home-cooked
food is served. The village heritage centre in the
car park is worth visiting. Opening hours may
change; it is advisable to phone. ♨Q◑⬗ᚑ❧♣P

Widecombe in the Moor

Rugglestone Inn ♀
TQ13 7TF (¼ mile from village centre) SX721760
✪ 11.30-3, 6-midnight; 11.30-midnight Sat; 12-11 Sun
☎ (01364) 621327 ⊕ rugglestoneinn.co.uk
Dartmoor Legend; guest beer Ⓖ
Unspoilt pub in a splendid Dartmoor setting. This
Grade II-listed building was converted to an inn
back in 1832. The stone-flagged bar area has
seating, with beer also served through a hatch in
the passageway. An open fire warms the lounge. A
wide selection of home-cooked food is available.
Across the stream is a large grassed seating area
with a shelter. Local farm cider is sold, and the
house beer is brewed by Teignworthy. The pub's
car park is just down the road. Local CAMRA Pub of
the Year 2012. ♨Q➷❀◑⬗ᎪᏔ☜P⸗

Yarde Down

Poltimore Arms L

Brayford, EX36 3HA (2 miles E of Brayford jct on A399) SS725356

✪ closed Mon; 12-2.30, 6-11; 12-3 Sun ☎ (01598) 710381

Beer range varies G

Still powered by its faithful generator due to the lack of mains electricity, this old pub on the edge of Exmoor is believed to date back to the 13th century. Some modernisation has taken place but it is still warm, welcoming and comforting, with a roaring log fire and cozy atmosphere. The small bar serves up to three ales on gravity from local or West Country breweries, and there is a separate restaurant. Not easy to find, but the location only adds to its charm. Children and dogs are welcome.

🏚Q🌣🐕◑♣P🏵

Yealmpton

Volunteer Inn L

Fore Street, PL8 2JN SX578518

✪ 5-11; 12-11.30 Fri & Sat; 12-11 Sun ☎ (01752) 880463

Courage Best Bitter; Summerskills Hopscotch; guest beer H

Two-bar village pub recently tastefully refurbished inside. It attracts the locals and acts as a centre for the community. The public bar is lively, especially when rugby matches are screened, while the welcoming lounge is more relaxed, featuring a wood-burning stove and an area for dining. There is a small beer garden at the rear. Food, including tapas and light bites, is served until 9pm Tuesday to Saturday, with roasts on Sunday lunchtime. Regular daytime buses (not Sun) serve the village.

🏚🐕◑🍴🚌(93,94)♣🏵

Culm Valley Inn, Culmstock (Photo: Adrian Tierney-Jones)

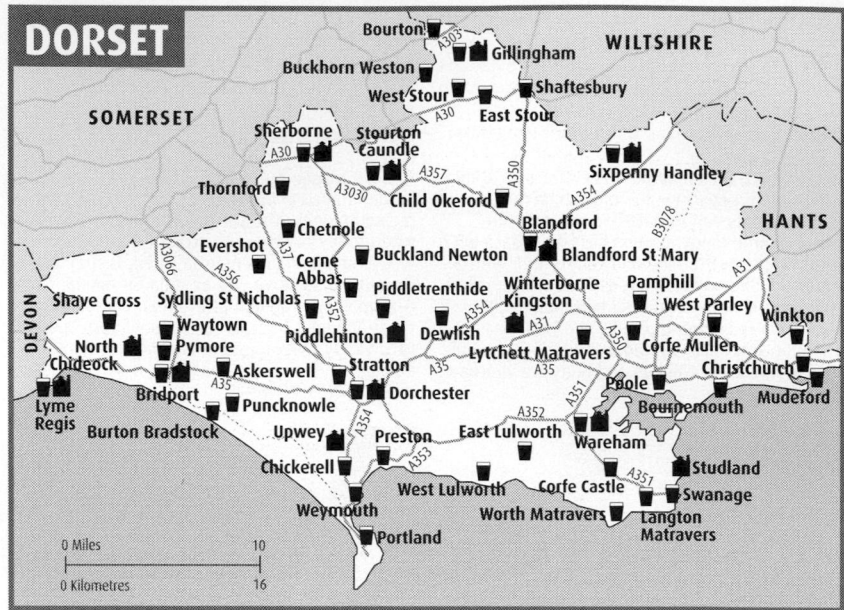

DORSET

Bourton
Gillingham
WILTSHIRE
Buckhorn Weston
West Stour
Shaftesbury
SOMERSET
East Stour
Sherborne
Stourton
Caundle
Sixpenny Handley
Thornford
Child Okeford
HANTS
Chetnole
Blandford
Evershot
Cerne
Abbas
Buckland Newton
Blandford St Mary
DEVON
Shaye Cross
Sydling St Nicholas
Piddletrenthide
Winterborne
Kingston
Pamphill
West Parley
Winkton
North
Chideock
Waytown
Pymore
Piddlehinton
Dewlish
Corfe Mullen
Askerswell
Stratton
Lytchett Matravers
Christchurch
Bridport
Punchnowle
Dorchester
Poole
Mudeford
Lyme
Regis
Burton Bradstock
Upwey
Preston
East Lulworth
Bournemouth
Wareham
Chickerell
Studland
West Lulworth
Corfe Castle
Swanage
Weymouth
Worth Matravers
Langton
Matravers
Portland

0 Miles 10
0 Kilometres 16

Askerswell

Spyway Inn
DT2 9EP SY528933
✪ 12-3, 6-11 ☎ (01308) 485250 ⊕ spyway-inn.co.uk
Otter Bitter, Ale; guest beer Ⓖ
Family-friendly 16th-century smugglers' inn
perched on a hill outside Askerswell on the road to
Eggardon hill fort. From March to October there is
usually a guest beer and a local cider on draught as
well as the Otter beers. The small lounge bar has
beams and a woodburner; a further bar has tables
for dining. The food menu features dishes made
with locally produced ingredients. Popular with
locals and walkers, the sunny garden enjoys a fine
view and the play area attracts families. Dogs are
welcome in the garden. ♨Q⚙✿➪⊕🐾P⁵⌐

Blandford

Dolphin ⃝ ✓
42 East Street, DT11 7DR
✪ 10-11 (midnight Fri & Sat) ☎ (01258) 456813
Dorset Piddle Piddle, Silent Slasher, seasonal beers;
guest beers Ⓗ
Friendly and often bustling pub in the centre of
town. It is owned by the Dorset Piddle Brewery and
features three or four of its beers on the seven
handpumps. The guest ales are from
microbreweries in the south-west and beyond. The
pub retains many original features including
wooden benches and oak panelling. Excellent food
is served daily at lunchtimes and evenings,
booking is recommended for Sunday lunch. Quiz
night is Sunday. ♨⊕➪(X8)🐾

Bournemouth

Brunswick
199 Malmesbury Park Road, Charminster, BH8 8PX
✪ 12-11 (midnight Fri); 10-midnight Sat ☎ (01202) 290197
Greene King IPA, Abbot; Ringwood Best Bitter; guest
beers Ⓗ

This Greene King pub is able to source a wide
variety of ales as a member of the select Head
Brewer's Club. An imposing street-corner
community local, it has two separate bar areas plus
an outside smoking room and a courtyard area. An
atrium has a welcoming log fire in winter. Children
are permitted in non-bar areas until 7pm. Food is
served Friday to Sunday until 8pm. The pub is a
short walk from the bus stops in Charminster.
♨⚙⊕ ➪&➪(M1,3,5a/b)🐾P⁵⌐

Cricketers Arms ✓
41 Windham Road, Springbourne, BH1 4RN
✪ 11-11 (10.30 Sun) ☎ (01202) 551589
Fuller's London Pride; guest beers Ⓗ
A splended Victorian gem dating back to 1847,
making it Bournemouth's oldest pub. Just a short
stroll from Bournemouth Travel Interchange, the
public bar hosts pool, darts and shove-ha'penny.
Mahogany and brass give the lounge a traditional
feel. A vaulted ceiling dominates the converted
stable room, once a boxing ring made famous by
Freddie Mills, former world champion. Posters
advertise forthcoming guest ales and regular folk
nights. Food is served Saturday (limited menu Sat)
and Sunday lunchtimes. ⚙➪&≈🐾P⁵⌐

Goat & Tricycle ✓
27-29 West Hill Road, BH2 5PF
✪ 12-11 (11.30 Fri & Sat) ☎ (01202) 314220
⊕ goatandtricycle.co.uk
Wadworth Henry's IPA, Horizon, 6X, seasonal beers;
guest beers Ⓗ
Formerly two adjoining pubs, the buildings have
been combined to form a popular and award-
winning split-level venue. The pleasant interior
offers space for diners and drinkers alike. Eleven
handpumps dispense Wadworth beers, one
draught cider, and constantly changing guest ales
mainly from small breweries. Good-value food is
served daily 12-9pm, with roasts on Sunday. A
partly covered courtyard caters for smokers and
alfresco drinking, and there is a separate meeting
room available to hire. ♨⚙⊕&➪🐾⁵⌐

Porterhouse ✅

113 Poole Road, Westbourne, BH4 9BG
⏰ 11-11 (midnight Fri & Sat); 12-11 Sun ☎ (01202) 768586
Marston's seasonal beers; Ringwood Best Bitter, Fortyniner, Old Thumper, seasonal beers Ⓗ
Previously known as the Old Thumper, this ever-popular Ringwood house offers the full range plus beers from other Marston's breweries. The cosy, welcoming, oak-panelled pub is popular with locals and visitors alike. Board games and cards are played and the sound of conversation dominates the friendly atmosphere. Sandwiches are served 12-2pm plus home-made roasts on Sunday. Haggis, neeps and tatties with interesting whiskies are served on Burns night.
Q◖�(Branksome)🚌(M1,M2,1b/1c)♣👍

Bourton

White Lion Inn ✅

High Street, SP8 5AT ST77863093
⏰ 12-3, 5-11; 12-11 Fri-Sun ☎ (01747) 840866
🌐 whitelionbourton.co.uk
Otter Amber; Sharp's Doom Bar; guest beer Ⓗ
The White Lion is a traditional inn dating from 1763. Originally separate rooms, the cosy flagstoned bar has been opened out but there is always a quiet corner to be found. The real cider is Thatchers. There is a comfortable, intimate restaurant and, to the rear, a large beer garden. The pub is set back from the B3081 with plenty of parking. ♨Q☀🛏🍴◖🚌(158)👍P

Bridport

Crown Inn ✅

59 West Bay Road, DT6 4AX (on roundabout on A35 between Bridport/West Bay)
⏰ 11.30-11 (1am Fri & Sat; 10.30 Sun) ☎ (01308) 422037
Palmers IPA, Copper, 200, Tally Ho! Ⓗ
A welcoming single-bar pub, much frequented by locals as well as beer and live music lovers from further afield. The full range of Palmers' beers is usually available and food is served throughout the day until 9pm. At weekends there is a great live music scene here, and a large TV screen, which can be viewed from around the bar, shows sports events. Outside is a beer garden and dogs are welcome. Popular with visitors in the summer months. ☀◖🍴♿🚌(X53)♣👍P🍴

George Hotel 🅛 ✅

4 South Street, DT6 3NQ
⏰ 10-11 (midnight Fri & Sat); 12-10.30 Sun
☎ (01308) 423187
Palmers Copper, IPA, 200, Tally Ho! Ⓗ
Fine, traditional and cheerful Palmers' pub at the centre of this busy market town. The long main bar has a warm, comfortable feel and there is a peaceful family room across the passageway with service through a hatch to the corridor. With the thatched Palmers Brewery less than a mile away, the real ales have few beer miles on the clock. There is no parking but several public car parks nearby. ♨Q♿◖🚌(X53)

Tiger Inn 🏆 🅛 ✅

14-16 Barrack Street, DT6 3LY
⏰ 12-11 (midnight Fri); 11-11 Sat ☎ (01308) 427543
🌐 tigerinnbridport.co.uk
Otter Bitter; Sharp's Doom Bar; guest beers Ⓗ

Bright and cheerful Victorian ale house offering a frequently changing beer list with two guests mainly from West Country breweries, plus Thatchers cider. The single split-level bar has TV for major sports events, plus pub games including a skittle alley. Children are allowed in the top bar. There is a pretty garden and a heated courtyard. Close to the town centre and shops, the Tiger is a well-hidden secret worth seeking out. Separate beer and cider festivals are held annually. A CAMRA discount scheme is offered. Local CAMRA Town Pub of the Year 2012. ♨Q☀🛏🚌(31)♣👍🍴

Buckhorn Weston

Stapleton Arms

Church Hill, SP8 5HS (between A303 and A30) ST757246
⏰ 11-3, 6-11; 11-11 Sat & Sun ☎ (01963) 370396
🌐 thestapletonarms.com
Butcombe Bitter; Moor Revival; guest beers Ⓗ
Imposing community inspired village pub with a large car park and secluded garden, with a relaxed and friendly bar and adjacent dining area. The two guest beers often reflect the seasons, including milds in May, robust winter brews and refreshing summer ales – frequently from local breweries. Real ciders and a wide selection of draught and bottled foreign beers are always available. Excellent food is served throughout as well as classic bar snacks such as hand-made pork pies, Scotch eggs and chutney. Children, dogs and muddy boots are welcome. Modern en-suite accommodation completes the Drink, Eat, Sleep motto. ♨Q☀🛏◖👍P

Buckland Newton

Gaggle of Geese

DT2 7BS SY050688
⏰ 11.30-3, 6-11.30; 12-10.30 Sun ☎ (01300) 345249
🌐 thegaggle.co.uk
Ringwood Best Bitter; St Austell Tribute; guest beers Ⓗ
Attractive pub down a back road in the village. The large garden accommodates two goose fairs in May and September, with beer festivals alongside. Chickens are kept in the pub orchard and goats and sheep in the paddock. Food is prepared with local ingredients such as pork, game and goats' cheese. Sunday lunches are served until 4pm and burgers and fish and chips are available to take away. Dorset cider and wines are stocked. Dogs welcome. ♨Q☀◖♣👍P🍴

INDEPENDENT BREWERIES

Art Brew/Chideock North Chideock
Blackmore Stourton Caundle (NEW)
Corfe Castle Wareham (NEW)
Dorset (DBC) Dorchester
Dorset Piddle Piddlehinton
DT Upwey
Hall & Woodhouse/Badger Blandford St Mary
Isle of Purbeck Studland
Mighty Hop Lyme Regis
Palmers Bridport
Sherborne Sherborne
Sixpenny (Wayland's Sixpenny) Sixpenny Handley
Small Paul's Gillingham
Sunny Republic Winterborne Kingston (NEW)
Town Mill Lyme Regis

Burton Bradstock

Three Horseshoes ✓
Mill Street, DT6 4QZ
☼ 11 (12 Sun)-11 ☎ (01308) 897259
⊕ three-horseshoes.com
Palmers Copper, IPA, Tally Ho! Ⓗ
Old thatched cottage-style stone pub in an
attractive village a mile from the sea, well used by
locals and visitors alike. The L-shaped beamed bar
has a large inglenook with a log fire in winter.
Good-value pub food is served in the bar, with a
more extensive menu specialising in local meat
and fish offered in the attractive restaurant.
Palmers Tally Ho! is available when brewed.
Outside is a small rear garden and dogs and
children are welcome. Very busy in summer.
曲❀①▶☷(X53)♣P

Cerne Abbas

Royal Oak
23 Long Street, DT2 7JG
☼ 11-3, 6-11 ☎ (01300) 341797
⊕ royaloakcerneabbas.co.uk
Badger First Gold, Tanglefoot, seasonal beer Ⓗ
A delightful thatched village pub built in 1540
using stone and other building materials from the
abbey, which was largely destroyed following the
Dissolution of the Monasteries. The present
landlord has returned after a long absence and he
and his staff are most welcoming. Good
wholesome food is served lunchtimes and
evenings with daily specials. 曲Q❀①▶♣⅃

Chetnole

Chetnole Inn
DT9 6NU
☼ 12-2.30, 6.30-11 (closed Mon winter); 12-2.30 Sun
☎ (01935) 872337 ⊕ thechetnoleinn.co.uk
Sharp's Doom Bar; guest beers Ⓗ
Traditional village pub with flagstone floors and
woodburners in both bars. Tables outside face the
church, and there is a pretty garden at the back
beyond the car park. Award-winning food ranges
from bar snacks such as big sandwiches with chips
to a full dining menu. Chetnole Halt, about 10
minutes' walk, is a request stop on the Yeovil-
Dorchester railway line. 曲Q❀☷①▶⑃⇌P

Chickerell

Lugger Inn Ⓛ
30 West Street, DT3 4DY
☼ 11-midnight (2am Fri & Sat) ☎ (01305) 766611
⊕ theluggerinn.co.uk
Dorset Jurassic; Palmers Copper, Dorset Gold; guest
beers Ⓗ
Large village pub with a split-level bar, a small
room suitable for families, a separate dining room
and 3-star English Tourist Board accommodation.
Breakfast is available from 8am; the bar opens at
11am. The carvery in the skittle alley is very
popular on Sundays. Authentic Mauritian curries
and local longhorn steaks feature on the extensive
menu. The local football team supports the pub and
a TV shows sports in the bar.
曲❄❀☷①▶&▲☷(X53)♣P⅃

Child Okeford

Saxon Inn
Gold Hill, DT11 8HD (along narrow lane N of village)
ST829135
☼ 12-3, 6-11 ☎ (01258) 860310 ⊕ saxoninn.co.uk
Butcombe Bitter; Gale's Seafarers Ale; guest beers Ⓗ
Situated at the north end of the village, close to the
iron age hill forts of Hambledon and Hod Hill near
the Stour Valley Way. This comfortable inn was
converted from three farm cottages in the 1950s.
Served by a corner bar, the main room has an open
fire and low beams, and an adjoining panelled
lounge with a wood-burning stove. A delicious
range of meals is offered including daily specials.
The large, quiet garden is at the rear.
曲Q❀☷①▶♣P

Christchurch

Olde George Inn ✓
2A Castle Street, BH23 1DT
☼ 10.30-11 (midnight Fri & Sat; 11.30 Sun)
☎ (01202) 479383
Dorset Piddle Jimmy Riddle, Piddle, Silent Slasher;
guest beers Ⓗ
A former coaching inn rebuilt after the civil war —
some of its stone foundations were looted from
the nearby castle. Today it is the original Piddle
Brewery tap and also serves locally sourced guest
beers. Excellent food is available all day plus a
Sunday carvery (booking recommended), which
makes it popular with locals and visitors alike.
Outside is a heated courtyard, a room available for
hire and a skittle alley. Seasonal beer festivals are
popular. ❀①▶&⇌☷(1b,1c)♣⅃

Corfe Castle

Greyhound Inn
The Square, BH20 5EZ
☼ 11-11 ☎ (01929) 480205 ⊕ greyhoundcorfe.co.uk
Ringwood Best Bitter; Sharp's Doom Bar; guest
beers Ⓗ
Claiming to be Britain's most photographed pub,
this Purbeck stone building is a former coaching inn
dating from 1580. The interior has a contemporary
feel, with flagstone floors and smaller rooms at the
back. The garden sits beneath Corfe Castle with
views of Swanage Steam Railway. Regular live
music, quality food, beer festivals and cider in
boxes ensure that most tastes are catered for.
Guest ales tend to be from south-west breweries,
with Bath Ales and Yeovil the regulars.
Accommodation is in the Banke's Arms over the
road.
❀☷①▶⇌(Swanage Steam Railway)☷(40)♣●

Royal British Legion Club
East Street, BH20 5EQ (on A351)
☼ 12-2.30, 6-11; 12-11 Sat & Sun ☎ (01929) 480591
Ringwood Best Bitter; Taylor Landlord; guest beer Ⓗ
Built in Purbeck stone, this friendly club has a bar
area with upholstered bench seating, wooden
tables and chairs. Major sporting events are shown
on TV; darts, shove-ha'penny and occasional live
music are played. Filled rolls are available at
lunchtime and an upstairs meeting room can be
hired. A lovely garden has a boules court and views
over the Purbecks. Show a CAMRA membership
card or a copy of this Guide for entry.
❀⇌(Swanage Steam Railway)☷(40)♣P⅃

Corfe Mullen

Lambs Green Inn ✪
Lambs Green Lane, BH21 3DN (500yds S of A31)
✪ 11-11 (10.30 Sun) ☎ (01202) 881974
Ringwood Best Bitter; St Austell Tribute; Sharp's Doom Bar; guest beers Ⓗ
Part-thatched former farmhouse with a lovely rustic atmosphere, retaining its original beamed ceilings and small rooms. At least one guest beer is always available and excellent food is served all day in the bar or a separate, pleasant dining area. The extensive rear garden is a gem with views over Wimborne Minster, and is home to a summer beer festival. Joint winner of local CAMRA Pub of the Year in 2011. ▲❀◑&▲묘(3)P⊑

Dewlish

Oak at Dewlish Ⓛ
DT2 7ND SY774981
✪ 11.30-2.30, 6-11; 12-2.30, 7-11 Sun ☎ (01258) 837352
⊕ oakpub.co.uk
Beer range varies Ⓗ
Unpretentious village inn with two or three ever-changing ales, mainly local. The horseshoe-shaped bar has a dining area and opens on to a patio and large garden. To the rear is a separate room with a pool table. A varied food menu offers good home-cooked dishes made using local produce. B&B and self-catering accommodation is available in a converted coach house next door. Dogs and children are welcome. ▲Q❧❀❀◑묘♣♠P⊑

Dorchester

Blue Raddle
9 Church Street, DT1 1JN
✪ 11.30-3 (not Mon), 6.30-11; 12-3, 7-10.30 Sun
☎ (01305) 267762
Butcombe Bitter; Otter Bitter; Sharp's Doom Bar; guest beers Ⓗ
Popular, genuine, town-centre free house with friendly staff and an enthusiastic landlord. In addition to the regular beers, two interesting guest ales and local ciders are also on offer. Good locally sourced food is served lunchtimes and Thursday, Friday and Saturday evenings. The pub takes part in local events and hosts regular folk music sessions. Piped comedy shows and Private Eye are available in the conveniences. No children, but dogs are welcome. Q◑&≠(South)묘♣♠

Colliton Club ✪
Colliton House, Colliton Park, DT1 1XJ (opp county hall and crown court)
✪ 9-3, 6-11.30; 10-3.30, 7-midnight Sat; closed Sun
☎ (01305) 224503 ⊕ collitonclub.co.uk
Greene King Abbot; Morland Old Speckled Hen; St Austell Dartmoor Best Bitter, Tribute; guest beers Ⓗ
Thriving club opposite County Council HQ with at least six real ales always available including guest beers from local brewers such as Flack Manor, Hop Back and Palmers. The club is housed in the mainly 17th-century Grade II-listed Colliton House and welcomes CAMRA members – just show your membership card. Busy in and out of office hours, this is a popular meeting place for a number of local associations. Evening snacks are served. Dogs and children are allowed. CAMRA Wessex Region Club of the Year 2007, 2008, 2010 and 2011.
Q❀◑≠(South/West)묘♣⊑

East Lulworth

Weld Arms Ⓛ
BH20 5QQ (off B3070)
✪ 12-3, 6-11.30 ☎ (01929) 400211 ⊕ weldarms.co.uk
Palmers Dorset Gold; Wells Bombardier; guest beer Ⓗ
Originally a row of cottages, this 17th-century thatched building was built by the Weld Family estate and is still owned by them. The attractive main bar leads to two other smaller rooms. The menu ranges from sandwiches to three-course meals, featuring locally sourced ingredients where possible. A family- and dog-friendly pub, it has a large garden boasting stunning views towards the neolithic hilltop Flowers Barrow. An ideal base for walks over the army firing ranges. ▲❀❀◑&P⊑

East Stour

King's Arms
East Stour Common, SP8 5NB (on A30, 3½ miles W of Shaftesbury) ST813231
✪ 12-3, 5.30-11; 12-midnight Sat; 12-10.30 Sun
☎ (01747) 838325 ⊕ kingsarmseaststour.com
St Austell Tribute; Sharp's Doom Bar; guest beer Ⓗ
This imposing roadside pub is a multi-roomed establishment served by a single bar, with many areas for diners. The bar is popular with locals, who have a say in the selection of the guest beers. The Scottish-influenced food is excellent, made with locally sourced ingredients where possible, and the all-day Sunday carvery can be very busy. The patio and enclosed garden are a welcome addition in summer, and there is accommodation year round. Dogs and muddy boots welcome. ▲❀❀◑&P⊑

Evershot

Acorn Inn ✪
28 Fore Street, DT2 0JW
✪ 11-11 (10.30 Sun) ☎ (01935) 83228 ⊕ acorn-inn.co.uk
Otter Ale; guest beers Ⓗ
Small, attractive 16th-century hotel with a fine pillared porch on the village main street. A large flagstoned room at the back is known as the village bar, adorned with local photographs and warmed by a wood-burning stove – a smaller bar and restaurant are at the front. There are always two ales available, often a third, plus local cider. Look out for the annual beer and cider festivals. The skittle alley can be hired for functions. This is the coaching inn that was mentioned in Thomas Hardy's Tess of the d'Urbervilles as the Sow & Acorn. ▲Q❧❀❀◑♣♠P⊑

Gillingham

Wine Bar
Queen Street, SP8 4DZ ST807268
✪ closed Mon; 12-2.30, 6.30-11 (midnight Fri & Sat); 12-midnight Sun ☎ (01747) 825825 ⊕ wineandgrill.co.uk
Fuller's London Pride; St Austell Tribute; guest beer Ⓗ
Once a confectionery shop, this stone-built town pub has been extensively modernised and is now a contemporary bar and grill. The regular beers are complemented by a guest ale, often from a Dorset micro. An annual beer festival is hosted in early August. The food is good value and there is a Sunday carvery. Music nights are held on the first and third Tuesdays, and the bar is extremely busy on Friday and Saturday nights. Outside is a large, secluded garden and decking area. ❀◑&▲≠⊑

Langton Matravers

Ship Inn ⃝
Coombe Hill, BH19 3EU
☼ 12-3, 5.30-11; 12-11 Fri-Sun and summer
☎ (01929) 426910 ⊕ shipinnlangton.co.uk
Isle of Purbeck Best Bitter, Fossil Fuel, Studland Bay Wrecked; guest beer Ⓗ
Founded in 1765 in the cottage next door, this attractive inn moved to the newly built premises in 1897. The landlord and landlady took over the pub in 2009, providing excellent local beers, food and accommodation. There is a small garden and covered smoking area near the car park, with step-free disabled access. A path beyond the car park connects to the Priests Way which leads from Worth Matravers to Swanage.
Q⊛✿✦⊙⅃&⊟(40)♣P⅃⚊

Lyme Regis

Harbour Inn
Marine Parade, DT7 3JF
☼ 11-11 (6 Sun winter) ☎ (01297) 441299
⊕ harbourinnlymeregis.co.uk
Otter Bitter, Ale; St Austell Tribute; Town Mill Lyme Gold Ⓗ
Beach-side inn in a row of three pubs overlooking the harbour and famous Cobb. The emphasis here is on home-made pub food made with local produce – there is no food-free bar space. A covered terrace faces the sea and there is a beach area with more tables. The pubs hosts music and other events. Note that plastic glasses are used in the beach area. ⊛⊙&▲⊟(31,X53,71)⅃⚊

Lytchett Matravers

Rose & Crown
178 Wareham Road, BH16 6DT
☼ 12-11 (2am Fri & Sat); 12-10.30 Sun ☎ (01202) 625325
Sharp's Doom Bar; guest beers Ⓗ
This welcoming, traditional pub has been a feature of the village since 1902, although recently refurbished and opened as a free house. The two changing guest beers often come from local breweries Yeovil, Butcombe and Palmers. There are two bars, one with a dartboard, a lawned garden area and a comfortable dining space to enjoy the excellent home-cooked food. The pub hosts regular comedy and live music events on-site and at the village hall, plus a village beer festival.
⊛⊙▲⊟(387,X8)⅃⚊

Mudeford

Nelson Tavern ✪
75 Mudeford, BH23 3NJ
☼ 10-12.30am ☎ (01202) 485105 ⊕ nelsontavern.com
Ringwood Best Bitter, Fortyniner; Taylor Landlord; guest beers Ⓗ
Situated a short walk from Avon Beach and Mudeford Quay, you are assured of a warm welcome at this traditional single-bar village pub. The three guest beers regularly come from Sixpenny, Andwell and Bowman breweries, and real ciders are also available. Bank holiday beer festivals prove popular in the garden. The pub holds a weekly quiz and frequent live music sessions, and screens Sky Sports. A spacious restaurant serves Thai and traditional English cuisine. ⋈⊛⊙&⅃⊟(X1,X2,111)♦P⅃⚊

Pamphill

Vine Inn ★
Vine Hill, BH21 4EE (off B3082) ST994003
☼ 11 (12 Sun)-3, 7-10.30 (11 Thu-Sat) ☎ (01202) 882259
Fuller's London Pride Ⓗ; guest beer Ⓖ
Identified by CAMRA as one of Britain's Real Heritage Pubs, this old bakehouse was converted by the landlady's grandfather. It comprises a tiny public bar, lounge and upstairs family/games room. The resplendent garden has heating and a climbing frame. Ciders include Westons plus local Cider by Rosie. Sandwiches and a hearty ploughman's lunch are served at lunchtimes only. Beers are generally sourced from small breweries. A conker and pumpkin festival is held in September. Winner of many local CAMRA awards.
Q⅄⊛✿⊟♣♦P⅃⚊

Piddletrenthide

Piddle Inn ⃝
DT2 7QF
☼ 11-2, 6-midnight; 11.30-midnight Fri & Sat; 12-11 Sun
☎ (01300) 348468 ⊕ piddleinn.co.uk
Dorset Piddle Piddle; St Austell Tribute; guest beer Ⓖ
Named after the river on whose banks it stands, this is the closest pub to the Dorset Piddle Brewery serving its ales. It has a spacious single bar and is brightly decorated throughout. A large restaurant seats 50, with dining also available in the bar. Popular locally, it hosts regular events including live music. There is a sunny garden and riverside patio. AA 4-star rooms are available. Children and dogs are welcome. All beers come from breweries in the south-west of England.
⋈⊛✿⊙&⊟(307)♣P⅃⚊

Poole

Bermuda Triangle
10 Parr Street, Lower Parkstone, BH14 0JY
☼ 12-2.30, 5-11 (midnight Fri); 12-midnight Sat; 12-11 Sun
☎ (01202) 748087
Beer range varies Ⓗ
As the name suggests, this bustling, multi-award-winning pub explores the mystery of the Triangle and carries a nautical theme. The single-room bar has a split-level interior and is bedecked with an intriguing range of curios, maps, newspaper cuttings and even part of an aircraft wing. Run by the same owner for 22 years, the bar has four handpumps offering an ever-changing range of ales sourced from far and wide alongside speciality German lagers and foreign beers.
⊛⇌(Parkstone)⊟(M1)

Blue Boar
29 Market Close, BH15 1NE
☼ 12-11 (midnight Fri & Sat) ☎ (01202) 682247
Fuller's London Pride, ESB; Gale's Seafarers Ale; guest beer Ⓗ
Formerly famous as the Cellar Club, this large, creeper-covered pub is at the junction of Market Close and Dear Hay Lane and is spread over three floors. The cellar hosts fortnightly jazz nights. At ground level is an L-shaped bar with a large fireplace as its centrepiece. The first floor has a function room with conference facilities and is available to hire. An extensive home-cooked food menu is offered. The pub is also home to a museum of military and diving artifacts. Weekly quiz nights are hosted. ⋈⊛⊙⇌⊟(9,152)

Branksome Railway Hotel Ⓛ

429 Poole Road, Branksome, BH12 1DQ (opp train station)
🕒 11-11; 12-10.30 Sun ☎ (01202) 769555
🌐 branksomerailwayhotel.co.uk
Hop Back Summer Lightning; Otter Ale; Sharp's Doom Bar; guest beer Ⓗ
This Victorian station hotel dating from 1894 still serves the main Weymouth to Waterloo rail link. The large, open-plan interior is divided into two areas, both served by one bar. The front space has a pool table and games machines with some seating. The rear has more comfortable seats with views of passing trains. A DJ and occasional live music play at weekends. En-suite accommodation is offered and a function room is available for hire. The bar may stay open later on Fridays and Saturdays. 🚪⬅️≈(Branksome)🚐(M1,M2)♣P

Brewhouse

68 High Street, BH15 1DA
🕒 11-11; 12-10.30 Sun ☎ (01202) 685288
Milk Street Mermaid, seasonal beers; guest beers Ⓗ
Popular local owned by the Milk Street Brewery of Frome, Somerset. The split-level interior has a bar at street level with two pool tables at the rear. Beers include Mermaid, which is almost exclusively brewed for the people of Poole, along with two other Milk Street beers and one well-chosen guest. You can sit outside and watch the world go by, or there is a patio at the back. 🏵️≈🚐♣⬅️

Bricklayers Arms Ⓛ

41 Parr Street, Lower Parkstone, BH14 0JX
🕒 12-2.30; 5-11 (midnight Fri); 12-midnight Sat; 12-11 Sun ☎ (01202) 740304
Hop Back Summer Lightning; Ringwood Best Bitter, Fortyniner; guest beers Ⓗ
Attractive pub with a clean, light and airy decor, fresh flowers and an open fire. Popular with locals, the L-shaped bar has plenty of seating at tables, both inside and out, creating a relaxed, friendly environment. There is decking to the front and a garden to the rear, with a modern rustic style. Children are permitted in outside areas but not after 9pm. Free Wi-Fi is available. 🏵️Q🏵️≈(Parkstone)🚐(M1,1b)⬅️

Portland

Clifton Hotel Ⓛ

50 Grove Road, DT5 1DA
🕒 12-11.30 (2am Fri & Sat) ☎ (01305) 820473
🌐 cliftonhotelportland.co.uk
Beer range varies Ⓗ
A friendly, family-oriented local, close to some spectacular cliff-top walks, serving three constantly changing ales. An extensive food menu ranging from bar snacks to full meals can be enjoyed in the bar, adjacent restaurant or on the deck overlooking the children's play area. Wide-screen TVs feature live football and other sporting events. Reasonably priced accommodation is available. 🏵️🚪◐P

Royal Portland Arms Ⓛ

40 Fortuneswell, DT5 1LZ
🕒 11-midnight (1.30am Fri & Sat); 12-midnight Sun ☎ (01305) 862255
Beer range varies Ⓗ/Ⓖ
Dating back 200 years, this Portland stone pub stands on the main road with public car parks nearby. George III is reputed to have stopped here

for a drink and some Portland mutton on a visit to the island. A basic one-bar pub with a friendly welcome, it offers a choice of local ales and ciders plus bar snacks. Live music plays on Fridays and Sunday afternoons in winter, and foodie events are popular. CAMRA members receive a discount on beer. Q🚐(1)♣♠🎱

Preston

Spiceship ✪

240 Preston Road, DT3 6BJ
🕒 11.30-midnight summer; 12-11 Sun & winter ☎ (01305) 834651 🌐 spiceship.co.uk
Ringwood Best Bitter; Sharp's Doom Bar; guest beers Ⓗ
Large, traditional coach house country pub with a friendly atmosphere and a well-regarded selection of ales. Guest beers are rotated on a regular basis, with Sharp's Doom Bar the most commonly available. There are a number of screens for televised sporting events which draw in the crowds, along with teams from the local darts leagues and live music events. Accommodation is available along with a good sized car park and grassy play area. Children and pets are welcome. 🏵️🚪◐🚐♣P⬅️

Puncknowle

Crown Inn ✪

DT2 9BN
🕒 12-3, 6-11; 12-11 (not eve winter) Sun ☎ (01308) 897711
Palmers Copper Ale, IPA, 200 Ⓗ
Lovely 16th-century thatched pub in the village – pronounced 'Punnel'. The bar has an open fire and books to read if you don't want to join in the conversation with the friendly staff and locals. Palmers Tally Ho! is served through the winter and Dorset Gold in the summer. Locally sourced home-cooked food is available in the bar and restaurant (no food Mon eve winter). There is a large garden at the back, and children and dogs are welcome. 🏵️Q🛏️🏵️🚪◐♿🚐(210)♠

Pymore

Pymore Inn

DT6 5PN
🕒 closed Mon; 12-3, 6-11; 12-4, 7-11 (closed eve winter) Sun ☎ (01308) 422625
Otter Ale; St Austell Dartmoor Best Ⓗ
Attractive Georgian ivy-clad free house about a mile north of Bridport. A cosy village local with a warm welcome, it offers a sensibly priced food menu and specials board featuring locally sourced ingredients. A third local beer is added in summer as well as real cider. Children and dogs are allowed in the large grassy garden. A function room is available for small parties. 🏵️Q🏵️◐♿P

Shaftesbury

Mitre

23 High Street, SP7 8JE ST863230
🕒 10.30-11 (1am Fri & Sat); 12-10.30 Sun ☎ (01747) 853002
Young's Bitter, Special, seasonal beers; guest beers Ⓗ
Historic pub close to the town hall at the top of famous Gold Hill, with grand views from the patio overlooking the beautiful Blackmore Vale. It attracts younger drinkers on Friday and Saturday evenings, but caters for all with an extensive food

menu ranging from morning coffee to cream teas to good pub food. Charity quizzes and live music nights are hosted regularly. There is always a seasonal beer from the Wells & Young's range as well as a regional guest beer. ⚠️♿🛏️🍴🍺🚲🚂♿

Shave Cross

Shave Cross Inn
DT6 6HW (W of B3162 Bridport-Broadwindsor road) SY415980
❀ closed Mon; 11-3, 6-1am; 12-3, 7-1am Sun
☎ (01308) 868358 ⊕ theshavecrossinn.co.uk
Dorset Weymouth Bitter; guest beers Ⓗ
Rural, stone-built, thatched 700-year-old inn that was historically a resting place for pilgrims for St White's shrine. It has a fine garden and impressive accommodation. Inside is a small stone-flagged bar and dining room. Award-winning food is often in Caribbean style (no food Sun eve). Three local beers and two ciders are usually served. Dogs are welcome. ⚠️Q❀🛏️🍴♿🐕P

Sherborne

Digby Tap ✪
Cooks Lane, DT9 3NS
❀ 11 (12 Sun)-11 ☎ (01935) 813148 ⊕ digbytap.co.uk
Beer range varies Ⓗ
Hidden away between the railway station and the abbey, Sherborne's only free house is worth seeking out for the building alone, which dates back to the 16th century. It was once the parish workhouse and many features of the original building remain. The interior feels like stepping back in time a generation, yet the pub remains popular with all ages. A supporter of West Country ales, beers come from small breweries all over the region. There are benches on a paved area outside for summer drinking. Excellent-value food is served at lunchtime. ⚠️Q❀🍴♿🚲🚂♿

Sixpenny Handley

Sixpenny Brewery Tap
Waylands Sixpenny Brewery, The Dairy Building, Manor Farm, SP5 5NU (turn off B3018 onto unclassified road ¼ mile S of village; signposted behind farm buildings) ST998166
❀ closed Sun-Tue; 4.30-6 (6.45 Fri); 11-1 Sat
☎ (01725) 762006 ⊕ sixpennybrewery.co.uk
Waylands Sixpenny 6d Original, 6d Best, 6d Gold, Special Ⓗ; **guest beer** Ⓖ
The bar, doubling up as the brewery shop, is attached to the brewhouse in the main farmyard. Usually, four regular real ales are served, but often an occasional or seasonal ale will be available on gravity. Due to complex leasing arrangements with the farm, opening hours are restricted, but when open the pub is extremely busy and popular. Although the actual bar is snug and welcoming, space is limited, but covered seating facilities are provided outside from which to take in the wonderful views. ❀🅰️🚲(184)🐕P♿

Stourton Caundle

Trooper Inn
Golden Hill, DT10 2JW (1½ miles E of A357) ST715149
❀ 12-2.30 (not Mon; 3.30 Sun), 6-midnight
☎ (01963) 362405
Beer range varies Ⓗ

Stone-built, single-room community pub with a separate function room/skittle alley. There is an attached camping and caravan site and a children's play area next to the beer garden. Good food is available lunchtimes and early evenings including a popular Friday fish and chips night. The pub now has its own microbrewery, brewing once a week. There are often two guest ales and a farmhouse cider. An annual beer festival is held in the spring. Dogs and walkers are welcome. Q❀🛏️♿🅰️♣🐕P

Stratton

Saxon Arms
20 The Square, DT2 9WG
❀ 11-3, 5.15-11; 11-11 Sat & Sun ☎ (01305) 260020
⊕ thesaxon-stratton.co.uk
Otter Ale; Purbeck Fossil Fuel; Ringwood Best Bitter; Taylor Landlord; guest beers Ⓗ
Celebrating its 10th anniversary in 2011, this flint and thatch pub has the feel of a country inn. Outside, a patio area overlooks the green and village hall. The bar divides into three areas including a dining space serving quality food from locally-sourced producers. This busy pub with helpful staff is an integral part of the local community. ⚠️Q❀🍴♿🚲P

Swanage

Red Lion
63 High Street, BH19 2LY
❀ 11-11.30; 12-11 Sun ☎ (01929) 423533
⊕ redlionswanage.co.uk
Palmers Copper Ale; Ringwood Best Bitter; Sharp's Doom Bar; Taylor Landlord Ⓗ; **guest beers** Ⓖ
A traditional ex-Strong's hostelry, centrally located and handy for the beach, steam railway and coastal path. Eighteen draught ciders are available and two guest beers in summer. The public bar has a real fire and dartboard, and the main bar includes a separate dining room and pool table area. Outside, there are covered and heated smoking areas in the large garden. Luxury accommodation is available in a separate coach house to the rear. ⚠️Q❀🛏️🍴🚲🚂(Swanage Steam Railway) ♣🐕P♿

Sydling St Nicholas

Greyhound Inn
26 High Street, DT2 9PD
❀ 11-3, 6-11; 12-3 Sun ☎ (01300) 341303
⊕ dorsetgreyhound.co.uk
Beer range varies Ⓗ
Sydling St Nicholas is hidden in a valley of chalk hills with a river running through it. This centuries-old coaching inn has a long bar, log fires, a restaurant and conservatory. Six bedrooms in a stable block have been recently refurbished. There are usually three guest ales to complement the award-winning food. ⚠️❀🛏️🍴P

Thornford

Lime Tree
Pound Road, DT9 6QD
❀ 12-2.30 (not Mon), 6-11 (not Mon summer); 12-2.30, 6-10.30 (closed eve winter) Sun ☎ (01935) 872294
⊕ thelimetreethornford.co.uk
Beer range varies Ⓗ

Formerly the King's Arms, this is a traditional free house in the centre of the village owned by the local Digby Estate, with four handpumps dispensing beers from Otter, Butcombe and another brewery. Offering a warm welcome to drinkers and diners alike, the bar area is simple in decor while the bright and airy new restaurant provides excellent food including a take-away service for villagers (but no food Mon). A coffee morning is hosted on Tuesday 10am-noon. Local CAMRA Rural Pub of the Year 2012.
🏚️✿◑≉🖵(74)♣P⅃

Wareham

King's Arms ✅
41 North Street, BH20 4AD
✪ 12-midnight (2am Fri & Sat; 11 Sun) ☎ (01929) 552503
Ringwood Best Bitter; guest beers Ⓗ
Joint local CAMRA Pub of the Year winner for 2011, this is a fine example of a traditional 16th-century public house. The frontage is unspoilt with a thatched roof and hanging baskets. The original flagstone floor and warming open fire add character to the cosy oak-beamed interior. Excellent home-cooked food is available at affordable prices lunchtimes and evenings. Traditional ciders and perries are always on offer, along with three guest beers. Dogs are welcome.
🏚️Q✿◑◱≉🖵(40,X53)♣🐾P⅃

Waytown

Hare & Hounds ✅
DT6 5LQ SY470978
✪ 11.30 (12 Sun)-3, 6.30 (6 summer)-11 ☎ (01308) 488203
Palmers Copper Ale, IPA, 200 Ⓗ
Hidden down winding lanes, this rural gem is an unspoilt village local and is well-worth seeking out. The garden, with stunning views across the Brit Valley, is a major attraction in summer with a play area and grassy expanse for children to let off steam. Bridge Farm cider is a regular and the attractive food menu features home-cooked meals and fresh local produce. A quiz replaces food on Sunday evenings in winter. Palmers Tally Ho! is available in winter months. The pub may close earlier on quiet nights or stay open later if busy.
🏚️Q✿◑♣🐾P

West Lulworth

Castle Inn 🏆 Ⓛ ✅
Main Road, BH20 5RN
✪ 12-2, 7-11; 12-3, 6-11 Sat; 12-3, 7-10.30 Sun
☎ (01929) 400311 ⊕ lulworthinn.com
Palmers Best Bitter Ⓖ**; guest beers** Ⓗ/Ⓖ
Winner of local CAMRA Rural Pub of the Year in 2011, this enchanting 16th-century thatched inn close to Lulworth Cove has two comfortable bars, one with a low ceiling, both beamed. Six mostly local ales and 13 traditional ciders are served alongside an extensive food menu offering good-value, home-made dishes in generous portions. At the rear is a tiered garden with a giant chess set. Board games are available inside. The inn has 15 bedrooms, 14 en suite, and is dog-friendly.
Q✿≉◑◱▲♣🐾P⅃

West Parley

Owl's Nest Ⓛ
196 Cristchurch Road, BH22 8SS
✪ 11.30-3, 5 (6 Sat)-11; 12-3, 6-10 Sun ☎ (01202) 572793
⊕ theowlsnest-westparley.com
Otter Ale; Ringwood Best Bitter, Fortyniner; guest beer Ⓗ
Tudor-style building with beamed ceilings and an open fire providing a welcoming and comfortable ambience. The pub is decorated with a number of collections – toby jugs hanging from the ceiling, military hats above the bar and many owls strategically positioned around the walls of the two rooms. Four handpumps serve Ringwood beers and a range of local guests. While the pub is geared towards dining, drinkers are welcome to enjoy a relaxing pint. 🏚️◑◱🖵(13,37)P⅃

West Stour

Ship Inn
SP8 5RP (on A30) ST78492257
✪ 12-3, 6-11; 12-11 (7 Nov-Feb) Sun ☎ (01747) 838640
⊕ shipinn-dorset.com
Beer range varies Ⓗ
Once a coaching inn, this popular roadside pub has fine views across the Blackmore Vale. The public bar features a flagstone floor and low ceiling; the separate restaurant area is light and airy with stripped oak floorboards and farmhouse furniture. There is a pretty patio and large garden to the rear. This friendly pub is renowned for superb home-cooked food (no meals Sun eve) and comfortable accommodation. Three changing beers are always available and a beer festival is held in July. Dogs are welcome in the bar. 🏚️Q✿≉◑♣🐾P⅃

Weymouth

Boot Inn ✅
High West Street, DT4 8JH
✪ 11-11; 12-10.30 Sun ☎ (01305) 770327
⊕ bootweymouth.co.uk
Marston's seasonal beers; Ringwood Best Bitter, Fortyniner, Old Thumper Ⓗ
Weymouth's oldest pub is hidden away by the inner harbour behind the former fire station. The single wood-floored bar area leads to small and intimate rooms at both ends. Three Ringwood beers are supplemented by two from the Marston's seasonal list plus Cheddar Valley cider. The pub's popularity leads to a spillage of customers onto the pavement. Entertainment includes live music on Tuesday, a quiz on Wednesday. A dog-friendly pub, where conversation rules. 🏚️Q✿◱≉♣🐾

Globe Inn ✅
24 East Street, DT4 8BN
✪ 11am-1am; 12-midnight Sun ☎ (01305) 786061
⊕ theglobeweymouth.co.uk
Dartmoor Jail Ale; Ringwood Old Thumper; St Austell Tribute; Sharp's Doom Bar; guest beers Ⓗ
Welcoming street-corner free house near Weymouth harbour and the town bridge, within walking distance of the town centre, main beach and esplanade. Up to six handpumps serve four regular beers plus two guests and a real cider. The separate games room has a pool table and pub games. Accommodation is available in four letting rooms. The local scooter club and local branch of the Royal Marine Association meet here every week. 🛏️◱♣🐾⅃

Ship Inn

Custom House Quay, DT4 8BE

✿ 11-11 (midnight Sat); 12-10.30 Sun ☎ (01305) 773879

⊕ shipweymouth.co.uk

Badger First Gold, Tanglefoot, seasonal beers ⊞

Spacious, open-plan Hall & Woodhouse-managed house situated on Weymouth harbourside, recently refurbished with a nautical theme. Food from an extensive, reasonably priced menu is served all day until 9pm (9.30pm Sat). Three handpumps serve two regular and one seasonal Badger beer. A large restaurant area and function room upstairs enjoy views of Weymouth Harbour. Outside is an enclosed rear garden area and seating on the harbourside. Occasional live music plays. Dog-friendly. ❀◑ઙ≉╚

Weatherbury

7 Carlton Road North, DT4 7PX

✿ 12-midnight ☎ (01305) 786040

Fuller's London Pride; guest beers ⊞

Down-to-earth free house in a residential part of the town. The single-bar interior is divided into different areas with a TV screen in each one. The London Pride is accompanied by three frequently changing guest beers. Outside there is a patio with a covered, heated area for smokers. Well-behaved children and dogs are welcome. Food may not be available on Sundays – phone to check. Q❀▱◑≉▤P╚

Wellington Arms

13 St Albans Street, DT4 8PY

✿ 10 (12 Sun)-11 ☎ (01305) 786963

Ringwood Best Bitter, Fortyniner; guest beer ⊞

You are assured of a warm welcome from the friendly landlord and his family at this peaceful and homely family-run oasis in the centre of Weymouth. A Grade II-listed green faience tile frontage dates from 1850 and the wood-panelled interior and mirrors are essential features of this former Eldridge Pope town pub. Good home-cooked food is served daily until 9pm (7pm Sun). In summer additional beers from the Marston's range are available. ⋈♘◑≉▤♣

William Henry ✔

1 Frederick Place, DT4 8HQ

✿ 7am-midnight ☎ (01305) 763730

Courage Directors; Greene King Abbot; Ringwood Old Thumper; Ruddles Best Bitter; guest beers ⊞

A popular Wetherspoon pub with friendly staff, conveniently located in the town centre with good transport links. Despite being a busy establishment, it retains a relaxed atmosphere, with sympathetic decor that celebrates the history of Weymouth. An excellent range of beers and ciders, both draught and bottled, is stocked, with frequently changing guests. Family-friendly and appealing to all ages, with plenty of seating, it is well worth a visit. Q◑▶≉▤♠╚

Winkton

Fisherman's Haunt ✔

Salisbury Road, BH23 7AS (on B3347)

✿ 11-11 (10.30 Sun) ☎ (01202) 477283

Fuller's London Pride, ESB; Gale's HSB ⊞

Built in the late 17th century, this imposing inn features a large patio at the rear and a drinking area at the front. Inside is a comfortable split-level bar with distinct drinking areas, one with a log fire, plus several areas mainly for dining, one dog friendly (dog biscuits supplied). An occasional guest beer accompanies the Fuller's range. The good, varied menu includes vegetarian options, and local produce is used where possible. There is a large car park including disabled spaces. Accommodation is next to the pub. ⋈❀▱◑ઙ▲▤(175)♣P

Worth Matravers

Square & Compass ★

BH19 3LF (off B3069) SY974777

✿ 12-3, 6-11; 12-11 Fri-Sun ☎ (01929) 439229

Palmers Copper Ale; guest beers Ⓖ

Iconic inn boasting both a museum and a book detailing its fascinating history. Featured in every edition of this Guide, its many awards are too numerous to list. The single serving hatch offers guest beers from near and far, plus a range of ciders including the landlord's own and Hecks. For the hungry there are pasties. The sea-facing beer garden features stone carvings from the annual Square Fair, and mutant pumpkins come autumn. In winter, real fires draw walkers from the coast path. Truly a pub for all seasons. ⋈Q❀▲▤(44)♠P

Castle Inn, West Lulworth

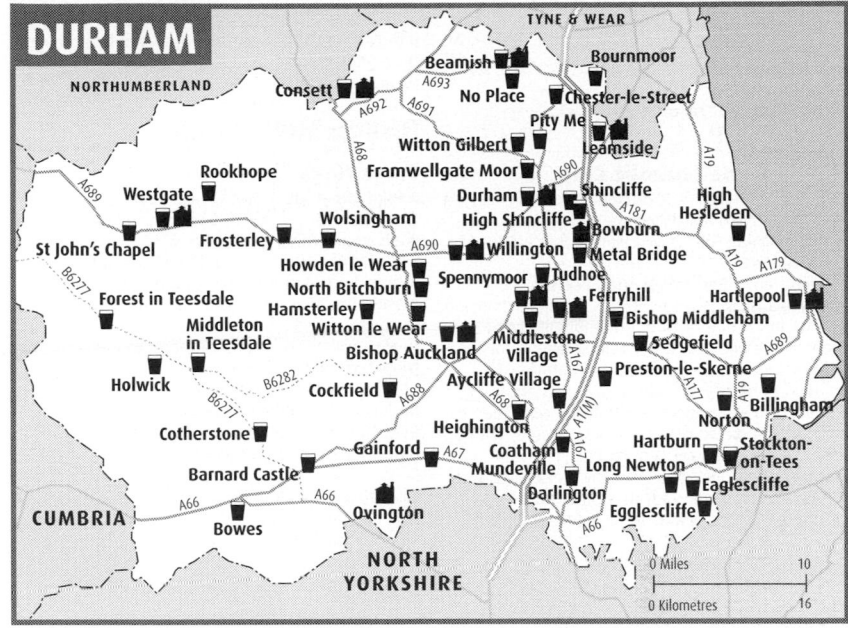

DURHAM

Co Durham incorporates part of the former county of Cleveland

Aycliffe Village

County ⅃

13 The Green, DL5 6LX
☼ 12-3, 6-11; 12-11 Sun ☎ (01325) 312273
⊕ thecountyaycliffevillage.com
Beer range varies Ⓗ
Overlooking the award-winning green in a
picturesque village, this attractive cream-coloured
country free house was originally three 17th-
century cottages. It is now open plan with the bar
and three dining areas unified by bright modern
decor, complemented by older beams and log
fireplaces. The current owners took over in 2008
and have a passion to marry good food with
excellent beers. Up to four guests come from
northern micros. Sunday is quiz night.
⌂Q❀☎◑⊟P♿▯

Barnard Castle

Old Well Inn ⅃

21 The Bank, DL12 8PH
☼ 12-11 ☎ (01833) 690130 ⊕ theoldwellinn.co.uk
Taylor Landlord; Courage Directors; guest beers Ⓗ
The boundary of this 17th-century town centre inn
incorporates part of the medieval castle wall. The
pub has a cosy front bar and a comfortable lounge,
a separate restaurant and an airy conservatory,
plus an enclosed beer garden. At least five well-
kept beers are available including three guests
from local micros. Excellent food is served every
day. A 10-day beer festival is held yearly. Thursday
is acoustic night, with guests from Barnard Castle
Folk Club on the last Thursday of the month.
Q❀☎◑⊞⊟(75,76)♿

Beamish

Black Horse ⅃

Red Row, DH9 0RW

☼ 11-11.30 (midnight Sat); 11-11 Sun ☎ (01207) 232569
⊕ blackhorsebeamish.co.uk
**Consett Ale Works White Hot, Red Dust; Wells
Bombardier** Ⓗ
A gem of a pub, the building was originally the first
and largest in a row of cottages and has been
beautifully restored, retaining all of its 300-year-
old charm and atmosphere, with the bar featuring
flagstone flooring and open fires. The spacious
restaurant offers a seasonal menu using fresh
ingredients sourced from over 10 acres of on-site
vegetable gardens and orchards. Outside there is
extensive seating with views over the Beamish
Valley. ⌂Q♿❀◑⊞♿P♿▯

Stables Bar & Restaurant ⅃

Beamish Hall Country House Hotel, DH9 0YB
☼ 11-11 (midnight Fri & Sat); 12-10.30 Sun
☎ (01207) 288750 ⊕ beamish-hall.co.uk/stables
Beer range varies Ⓗ
The Stables is attached to Beamish Hall Country
House Hotel, and has its own microbrewery. Stone
floors, old beams, solid furniture and crackling log
fires in winter help to create a relaxing
environment. Outside is a courtyard seating area
and, behind the pub, an excellent play area for

INDEPENDENT BREWERIES

Black Paw Bishop Auckland
Camerons Hartlepool
Consett Ale Works Consett
Durham Bowburn
Four Alls Ovington
Gambling Man Willington (NEW)
Hill Island Durham City
Just A Minute Spennymoor (NEW)
Leamside Leamside (NEW)
Stables Beamish
Weard'Ale Westgate
Yard of Ale Ferryhill

children. A beer festival is hosted in September, and the pub is also a popular live music venue. An extensive menu of locally produced food is served.
♨❀⇔◐◑♿●P⁵—

Billingham

Greenholme Catholic Club

37 Wolviston Road, TS23 2RU (on E side of old A19, just S of Roseberry Rd roundabout, next to bus stop)
⏲ 7-11 (midnight Fri); 12-midnight Sat; 12-10.30 Sun
☎ (01642) 551137
Copper Dragon Best Bitter; guest beers Ⓗ
Teesside's best-kept secret, this Victorian mansion and former school is now a friendly private members' club, with a genuine welcome for CAMRA members. Dedicated and enthusiastic volunteers ensure that the club's reputation for serving 150 different beers annually continues to grow. Three guest ales are usually offered, with up to 10 available during regular beer festivals, generally held over bank holiday weekends. The pub is also renowned for its vibrant R&B/rock scene, with guest bands most weekends.
❀♿▭(36)♣●P⁵—

Bishop Auckland

Grand Hotel

Holdforth Crest, DL14 6DU (on A6072, near Asda car park)
⏲ 5-11; 12-11.30 Fri-Mon ☎ 07746 360573
Beer range varies Ⓗ
The Grand is well regarded throughout the region for its live music on Saturday nights, and other social events. It hosts traditional pub games, a beer travel club, and is a meeting place for the local model railway club. There is a bar and music/function room across an open corridor. The smoking area in the yard is covered and heated. Usually four ales are on handpump, plus Old Rosie cider. Situated a five-minute walk from the railway station, past Asda and under the railway bridge.
❀♿≹♣●P⁵—

Pollards

104 Etherley Lane, DL14 6TW
⏲ 7-11 Mon; 12-2, 5-11.30; 12-2, 7-10.30 Sun
☎ (01388) 603539
Beer range varies Ⓗ
Smart local with a good atmosphere in four distinct drinking areas plus a large dining room. Two open fires, pub games and a renowned Sunday carvery help to create a welcoming feel. Food is available lunchtimes and evenings, and on Sunday night a free supper accompanies the popular quiz. There are picnic tables by the front door and a large heated patio to the rear, with views up the Wear Valley. Beers come from the Jennings/Marston's/Ringwood range. ♨Q❀◐◑⊟♿≹▭(94)♣P⁵—▯

Stanley Jefferson ✔

5 Market Place, DL14 7NJ
⏲ 9am-midnight (1am Fri & Sat) ☎ (01388) 452836
Greene King Abbot; Ruddles Best Bitter; guest beers Ⓗ
A former solicitors' office, the pub offers a typical range of Wetherspoon's facilities, with several comfortable drinking areas served from one long bar and an impressive glass roof. Stan Laurel, aka Mr Jefferson, lived in the town and went to school nearby. Ciders are Westons Old Rosie and Organic. Food is available all day and children are welcome, if dining, until 9pm. Outside is a large heated patio. Quiz night is Wednesday. The Bishop of Durham's palace and park are nearby. ❀◐◑♿≹▭●⁵—

Bishop Middleham

Cross Keys

9 High Street, DL17 9AR (1 mile from A177)
⏲ 12 (2.30 Mon)-11; 12-10.30 Sun ☎ (01740) 651231
Wells Bombardier; guest beer Ⓗ
Busy family-run village pub with a warm, friendly atmosphere and a good reputation for excellent meals. The spacious, open-plan lounge bar is complemented by a large restaurant/function room serving an extensive menu of freshly-prepared meals. Situated in excellent wildlife and walking country, a three-mile circular walk starts opposite. Quiz night is Tuesday, Teesside Tornadoes Bike Club meets on Wednesday and the pub has its own football team. ♨❀◐◑▭

Bournmoor

Dun Cow L

Primrose Hill, DH4 6DY
⏲ 12-midnight ☎ (0191) 385 2631
🌐 theduncowbournmoor.co.uk
Maxim Lambton's; guest beer Ⓗ
Welcoming 18th-century country pub with an often-sighted 'grey lady' ghost. Traditional English pub fare is served in the lounge and bar, and à la carte in the Lambton Conservatory restaurant. There is a function room for up to 100 people and a marquee for up to 400. Family-friendly with extensive gardens, it has beer festivals in March and October offering local ales, and live music festivals (first Saturday in June, last in September) featuring local folk and rock bands.
♨❀◐◑♿▭♣●P⁵—▯

Bowes

Bowes Club (CIU)

Arch House, The Street, DL12 9HR
⏲ 7 (3 Sat & Sun)-midnight ☎ (01833) 628431
Beer range varies Ⓗ
Previously the village lock-up, this 18th-century stone building is now a small, thriving club that hosts many community events, including quoits in the rear garden. There are two downstairs rooms – one with pool and darts, the other with a cosy fire in the fine old fireplace – and a meeting room upstairs. The single handpump features an ever-changing guest beer, often sourced locally. Guests including CAMRA members are welcome – if in the area you must experience this gem. Opening hours may vary. ♨❀⊟♣

Chester-le-Street

Butcher's Arms

Middle Chare, DH3 3QD (off Front Street on left from Market Place)
⏲ 11-11 ☎ (0191) 386 3605
Jennings Cumberland Ale; Marston's Pedigree; guest beers Ⓗ
A cosy pub in the centre of town acknowledged for the quality and quantity of its beers – and Joan Robinson, the landlady, is looking to increase the range of beers further. The pub is also noted for its food, with home cooking a speciality: Sunday

lunches are popular and good value for money. Teas and coffees are also served. Convenient for the railway station and all buses through the town. Q✿☗✍❶⇌❒♣⅄

Chester-le-Street Cricket Club 🅛 ✪
Ropery Lane, DH3 3PF
🕏 11-11 (midnight Fri-Sun) ☎ (0191) 388 3684
⊕ chesterlestreet-cc.com
Cumberland Corby Ale; guest beer Ⓗ
A splendid club house with two main rooms downstairs and an area outside for warm-weather drinking – all with fine views over the cricket ground. Sandwiches and pies are available from the bar on most days. Functions for up to 100 people (including wheelchair users) can be accommodated in the well-appointed function room on the first floor. Local CAMRA Club of the Year for the past five years. Shelter is provided outside for smokers. ✿⒟&⇌❒♣P⅄

Moorings Hotel 🅛
Hett Hills, DH2 3JU (off B6313) NZ240513
🕏 11-11 ☎ (0191) 370 1597 ⊕ themooringsdurham.co.uk
Beer range varies Ⓗ
Large, well-appointed, nautically-themed pub on two levels, extended by the addition of quality hotel accommodation – some rooms with hot tubs. The bar and bistro serve food all day, with a wide choice of traditional home-cooked English dishes. Upstairs, with splendid views, the Prime Rib restaurant offers quality food including seafood and fine cuts of local meats – ideal for special occasions. A smoking cabin is available outside. Wheelchair users can only access the ground floor. ✿✍❶&❒(28,28A)P⅄⚲

Pelaw Grange Greyhound Stadium
Drum Road, DH3 2AF (signed from Barley Mow roundabout on A167)
🕏 6.30-11 (closed Mon, Wed & Thu); 12-4 Sun
☎ (0191) 410 2141 ⊕ pelawgrange.co.uk
Beer range varies Ⓗ
Managed by a CAMRA member, this is the only greyhound stadium in Britain with real ales. The large open bar, Panorama restaurant and concert room all overlook the track. There is a lively atmosphere on race nights (Tue, Fri & Sat) – CAMRA members are admitted free. An annual beer festival is hosted on the Easter weekend and trips to local microbreweries are organised. The trackside terrace is available for smokers. Children are welcome. ✿❶&❒(21,22,50)P⅄

Smith's Arms 🅛
Castle Drive, Castle Dene, DH3 4HE NZ299507
🕏 4 (12 Sat)-11.30; 12-10.30 Sun ☎ (0191) 385 6915
Black Sheep Best Bitter; Jarrow Rivet Catcher, guest ale Ⓗ
A little off the beaten track, this traditional inn with well-kept beer has a small, cosy bar with a log-burning stove, a room with a pool table and a larger lounge with an open fire. The pub is reputed to be haunted. ♨Q⒝♣P⅄

Wicket Gate 🅛 ✪
Front Street, DH3 3AX
🕏 8-11 (midnight Thu; 2.30am Fri & Sat) ☎ (0191) 387 2964
Greene King Abbot; Ruddles Best Bitter Ⓗ
Large and well-appointed Wetherspoon Lloyds No. 1 Bar serving good food all day from breakfast onwards. Already established as a popular addition to the real ale venues in town, the Wicket Gate has

the added attraction of a DJ until the early hours on Friday and Saturday evenings each week and on bank holidays. ❶&♣♠

Coatham Mundeville

Foresters Arms
Brafferton Lane, DL1 3LU (on A167 ¼ mile S of A1M jct 59)
🕏 12 (4 Mon)-midnight; 12-10.30 Sun ☎ (01325) 320565
Black Sheep Best Bitter; Greene King IPA; Wells Bombardier Ⓗ
You can be sure of a warm welcome from the landlady at this Grade II-listed historic stone-built roadside inn close to the A1. The interior comprises a main bar with an adjoining restaurant/function room. The pub is a hub of the local community and many clubs use its facilities. A quiz is held every Thursday and live entertainment is hosted at weekends. To the rear is a large car park, garden and the Foresters Farm (chickens, ducks, sheep). Beware – the pub is reputedly haunted and mysterious happenings occur. ♨✿❶&▲❒♣P⅄

Cockfield

Queen's Head
106 Front Street, DL13 5AA
🕏 5 (11 Sat)-11; 12-11 Sun ☎ (01388) 710981
Beer range varies Ⓗ
Popular, community-focused local towards the north end of the village, with two constantly changing guest ales from the Jennings/Marston's range. The open-plan interior is divided into various sections for drinking and dining. A good-value set meal is served on Thursday from 1.30pm. The historic Cockfield Fell is just out the back, and visitors to this interesting area will find a warm welcome here. There is seating outside the front door and a bus stop nearby. ✿❶(6,8)♣P

Consett

Grey Horse 🅛 ✪
115 Sherburn Terrace, DH8 6NE (A692, then right along Sherburn Terrace)
🕏 12-12.30am (midnight Sun) ☎ (01207) 502585
⊕ thegreyhorse.co.uk
Consett Ale Works Steel Town Bitter, White Hot, Red Dust, Cast Iron, Black Bob, Men of Steel Ⓗ
Traditional pub dating back to 1848. The interior comprises a lounge and L-shaped bar, with a wood-beamed ceiling. Consett Ale Works Brewery is located at the rear. Beer festivals are held twice a year, live entertainment is hosted on Thursday and a quiz on Wednesday. The coast-to-coast cycle route is close by. ♨Q✿⒝&♣♠

Cotherstone

Red Lion
Main Street, DL12 9QE
🕏 12-3 (Sat only), 7-11; 12-4, 7-10.30 Sun
☎ (01833) 650236
Beer range varies Ⓗ
Nestling in a terrace of stone buildings dating from around 1738, this traditional local has changed little since the 1960s. The serving hatch bar supplies two rooms, each with its own fireplace, and there is a separate games room. There is no TV or jukebox, just good beer and conversation. Up to three guest ales are available. Local CAMRA

Community Pub of the Year, the venue is used by various local clubs. Children and dogs are welcome. There is a small beer garden and outside toilets. ♨Q🕭🌳🅰♣P

Darlington

Britannia

1 Archer Street, DL3 6LR (next to ring road W of town centre)
✪ 11.30-3, 5.30-11; 11.30-11 Thu-Sat; 12-10.30 Sun
☎ (01325) 463787
Camerons Strongarm; John Smith's Bitter; guest beers Ⓗ
Warm, friendly, popular local CAMRA award-winning inn – a bastion of cask beer for more than 150 years. The pub retains much of the appearance and layout of the private house it once was: a modestly enlarged bar and small parlour (used for meetings) sit either side of a central corridor. Prize-winning floral displays adorn the exterior in summer. Listed for its historic associations, it was the birthplace of teetotal 19th-century publisher JM Dent. Four countrywide guest beers are available. 🕭≒🖳♣P⅃🍴

Darlington Snooker Club Ⓛ

1 Corporation Road, DL3 6AE (corner of Northgate)
✪ 11-midnight (late Fri & Sat); 12-midnight Sun
☎ (01325) 241388
Beer range varies Ⓗ
First-floor, family-run and family-oriented private snooker club offering a warm, friendly welcome. Four guest beers from micros countrywide and a small range of real ales in bottles are stocked. A cosy, comfortable TV lounge is available for those not playing on one of the 10 top-quality snooker tables. Twice-yearly, the club plays host to a professional celebrity, and two beer festivals are held annually. Frequently voted CAMRA Regional Club of the Year, it welcomes CAMRA members on production of a membership card or copy of this Guide. Q🕭≒(North Rd)🖳♣

Number Twenty 2 Ⓛ ✪

22 Coniscliffe Road, DL3 7RG
✪ 12-11 (9 Mon); closed Sun ☎ (01325) 354590
⊕ villagebrewer.co.uk/our-pubs/number-twenty-2
Burton Bridge Bitter; Village Brewer White Boar, Bull Premium, Old Raby; guest beers Ⓗ
Town-centre ale house with a passion for cask beer and winner of many CAMRA awards. Ales are dispensed from up to 13 handpumps, including a stout or porter, along with nine draught European beers. Huge curved windows, stained glass panels and a high ceiling give the interior an airy, spacious feel. To the rear, The Canteen serves upmarket home-cooked lunches and early evening meals. This is the home of Village Brewer beers, commissioned from Hambleton by the licensee. Q🕽🕭≒🖳🍴

Old Yard Tapas Bar

98 Bondgate, DL3 7JY
✪ 11-11; 12-10.30 Sun ☎ (01325) 467385 ⊕ tapasbar.co.uk
Theakston Old Peculier; John Smith's Bitter; guest beers Ⓗ
Interesting mixture of a town-centre bar and Mediterranean-style taverna offering a range of real ales alongside a fascinating blend of international wines and spirits in a friendly setting. Five guest beers from micros local and countrywide are stocked. Although this is a thriving restaurant,

you are more than welcome to pop in for a pint, and maybe a tapa or two (Greek and Spanish). The excellent south-facing pavement café is popular in good weather. TV is for sport only. All Bar None 2011 winner for Darlington. 🕭🕽≒🖳⅃

Quakerhouse ♈ Ⓛ

2 Mechanics Yard, DL3 7QF (off High Row)
✪ 11 (12 Sun)-midnight ☎ 07783 960105
⊕ quakerhouse.net
Beer range varies Ⓗ
Nine times local CAMRA Town Pub of the Year, this bar is often the first point of call for CAMRA members visiting Darlington. The lively award-winning free house opened in 1998 in the former Quaker Coffee House in one of the old yards just off the pedestrianised town centre. The drinking establishment has the feel of a cellar bar, offering 10 guests from regional and microbreweries countrywide, and Old Rosie cider. A popular music venue, it caters for all tastes from acoustic to rock – on Wednesday there is a door charge after 7.30pm. 🕭🕭≒🖳♣🍴🍴

Tanners Hall ✪

63-64 Skinnergate, DL3 7LL
✪ 8-midnight (1am Sat) ☎ (01325) 369939
Greene King Abbot; Ruddles Best Bitter; guest beers Ⓗ
A popular Wetherspoon town pub with a varied clientele, named after the leather trade that dominated the town until the 18th century. Its 12 handpumps provide a good selection of real ales including up to seven guests, often from local micros. Converted from a furniture shop in 1998, its spacious interior makes it an ideal venue for holding its own beer festivals as well as the chain's national events. Reasonably priced food is served until 10pm. 🕭🕽🕭≒🖳🍴⅃

Durham

Bridge Hotel

40 North Road, DH1 4SE (200yds from Durham rail station)
✪ 11-11 (midnight Fri & Sat) ☎ (0191) 3868090
⊕ bridgehoteldurham.com
Caledonian Deuchars IPA; Theakston Black Bull Bitter; Wells Bombardier Ⓗ
Originally built in the 1850s as lodgings for the Irish navvies constructing the railway viaduct under which it sits, the building became a public house a few years after completion of the railway. Three immaculately kept ales are always available, one a weekly-changing guest. The comfortable dining area offers a diverse, high-quality menu of home-cooked food throughout the day at reasonable prices. It can get busy at the weekend. 🛏🕽🕭≒🖳

Colpitts Hotel

Colpitts Terrace, DH1 4EL
✪ 2 (12 Thu-Sat)-11; 12-10.30 Sun ☎ (0191) 386 9913
Samuel Smith OBB Ⓗ
An unspoilt gem, this late-Victorian pub has changed little since it was first built. Occupying a corner site, the building has an unusual A-shape with three rooms: a small lounge, a snug used as a pool room and the comfortable main bar partially divided by a fireplace. Like all Sam Smith's pubs, the noise comes from conversation not jukebox or games machines. A must-visit hostelry for anyone who appreciates pubs as they used to be. ♨Q🕭🕽≒🖳⅃

Court Inn
Court Lane, DH1 3AW
🕏 11-11 (11.30 Wed-Sat); 11-10.30 Sun ☎ (0191) 384 7350
🌐 courtinn.co.uk
Beer range varies Ⓗ
Large, popular urban oasis with a heavy focus on food (served 11am-10.20pm daily, with a 20 per cent discount Sun-Tue eves). The decor reflects the location of the pub near the Crown Court, with exposed brickwork and original artwork. The friendly pub is popular with students, and hosts a regular folk group. Accommodation is available in rooms above the premises. ⊛🛏◐≒

Dun Cow
37 Old Elvet, DH1 3HN (between Royal County Hotel & Durham Prison)
🕏 11-11.30; 12-10.30 Sun ☎ (0191) 386 9219
Black Sheep Best Bitter; Camerons Castle Eden Ale; Jennings Cumberland Ale Ⓗ
In 995AD Lindisfarne monks were searching for a resting place for the body of St Cuthbert when they came across a milkmaid looking for her lost cow. She directed them to Dun Holm (Durham). This Grade II-listed pub, part of which dates back to the 16th century, is named after the historic animal. At the front of the building is a friendly snug and a larger lounge to the rear. The story of the monks' legendary journey is told on the wall of the corridor alongside the two rooms. ♨Q⊛◐⊟♿≒🖾≒🖵

Half Moon Ⓛ ✅
86 New Elvet, DH1 3AQ (opp Royal County Hotel)
🕏 11-11 (midnight Fri & Sat); 12-11 Sun ☎ (0191) 383 6981
Draught Bass; Fuller's London Pride; Taylor Landlord; guest beer Ⓗ
A long-term regular in the Guide, this city-centre pub is named after the crescent-shaped bar that runs from the front room through to the lounge area. Run by the son of the landlord who ran it for 30 years, the interior is largely unchanged with traditional decor throughout and interesting photos of the pub at the beginning of the 20th century on the walls. Attracting a lively crowd on Friday and Saturday evenings, it has a large backyard next to the river which is popular in summer. The guest beer is from Durham Brewery. ⊛≒🖾(21)≒

Head of Steam Ⓛ
Reform Place, DH1 4RZ (through archway from North Road)
🕏 11-midnight (2am Fri & Sat); 11-11 Sun
🌐 theheadofsteam.co.uk
Beer range varies Ⓗ
Large, open-plan, modern pub over two floors. In addition to ale, the pub offers an extensive range of bottled European beers, alongside a range of real ciders. High-quality food is prepared on the premises, and the pub often holds special events, all featuring a wide choice of ales and ciders. During the day, the pub is family-friendly. One floor can be reserved for private functions. ⊛◐♿≒≒

Market Tavern
27 Market Place, DH1 3NJ
🕏 11-11 (midnight Thu; 1am Fri & Sat); 12-11 Sun
☎ (0191) 3862069
Beer range varies Ⓗ
Situated in Durham's historic market place, this single-roomed, L-shaped bar offers an array of six ales from all over Britain. The management makes full use of its guest list and has featured Mordue, Hydes, Beartown and Oakleaf breweries to name a few. One of the most improved venues in town, it serves good food up to 9pm. Although the interior is of basic wooden ale house appearance, friendly staff provide a warm welcome to both the regular and casual visitor. ◐♿≒

Olde Elm Tree Ⓛ ✅
12 Crossgate, DH1 4PS
🕏 12-11; 11-midnight Fri & Sat; 12-10.30 Sun
☎ (0191) 3864621
Wychwood Hobgoblin; guest beers Ⓗ
One of Durham's oldest pubs, dating back to at least 1600. As befits its age, it is reputed to have two ghosts. The interior comprises an L-shaped bar room and a top room linked by a set of stairs. A popular pub, it attracts a good mix including students, locals and bikers. Enjoy excellent home-cooked food, the Wednesday quiz (arrive early) and a folk group on Monday and Tuesday. Ask the landlord for details of the next Elm beer festival. ⊛◐♿≒♣♠◐P≒

Shakespeare Tavern
63 Saddler Street, DH1 3NU (100yds from Market Place)
🕏 11-11 (1am Fri & Sat) ☎ (0191) 3843261
Caledonian Deuchars IPA; Fuller's London Pride; guest beers Ⓗ
A CAMRA Real Heritage Pub in the city centre close to the Cathedral. The interior comprises a small bar with a recently spruced-up side snug and a back lounge that was enlarged in 2008. The pub was originally a haunt for 19th-century theatre actors and patrons, hence the name. Despite recent alterations and other ill-judged attempts at change over the years, it has largely maintained its character, except in the eyes of the purists. Popular with locals and students. Q⊟≒

Victoria Inn 🍸 ★
86 Hallgarth Street, DH1 3AS
🕏 11.45-3, 7-10.30 ☎ (0191) 386 5269
🌐 victoriainn-durhamcity.co.uk
Big Lamp Bitter; guest beers Ⓗ
This warm and welcoming Grade II-listed three-room Victorian pub remains almost unaltered since it was built in 1899. The quaint decor, coal fires, tiny snug and a genuine Victorian cash drawer help create an olde-worlde feel. Ales are mainly from local breweries and a wide selection of single malt whiskies is on display. No meals are served but toasties are available. Voted local CAMRA Pub of the Year for the seventh time in 2012. ♨Q♿⊟≒🖾(21)♣♠

Water House ✅
65 North Road, DH1 4SQ
🕏 8am-11.30 ☎ (0191) 370 6540
Greene King Abbot; Ruddles Best Bitter; guest beers Ⓗ
Situated in former water board offices and a short distance from the bus station, this pub is popular with young and old alike and extremely busy at weekends. A selection of beers from regional and microbrewers awaits, with single brewery weekends now a feature. The modern decor is complemented by coal-effect open fires. Good value food is served. An excellent Wetherspoon pub. ◐♿≒🖾

Eaglescliffe

Cleveland Bay
718 Yarm Road, TS16 0JE (jct of A67 and A135)

🕒 11-1am ☎ (01642) 780275
Beer range varies ⊞
A busy local's pub and previous local CAMRA award winner, under the stewardship of an enthusiastic licensee who has now established an enviable reputation for serving a fine range of traditional premium best bitters, as well as a free Sunday roast lunch buffet. The main bar, with four handpumps, has two sports TVs, while there is also a quieter lounge and a function room where live bands play on Friday evenings. Third-of-a-pint glasses are available. ❀✿🚌(7)P⚖-🏴

Egglescliffe

Pot & Glass ✪
Church Road, TS16 9DQ (300yds E of A135, opp church)
🕒 12-2 (not Mon), 6-11; 12-2, 5.30-midnight Fri; 12-2, 6-midnight Sat; 12-11 Sun ☎ (01642) 651009
Black Sheep Best Bitter; Caledonian Deuchars IPA; Draught Bass; guest beers ⊞
A previous local CAMRA award winner, this classic and ever-popular multi-roomed village local is situated in a quiet cul-de-sac opposite the parish church. Former licensee and cabinet maker Charlie Abbey, whose last resting place overlooks the pub, fashioned the ornate bar fronts from old country furniture. Tasting notes are available for the five handpumps, which include two guests. Outside is a large south-facing garden. Themed food evenings support the good value home-cooked menu.
Q✿👶🐶◑🚌(7)P⚖-🏴

Ferryhill

Surtees Arms ✪
Chilton Lane, DL17 0DH
🕒 4 (12 Sun)-11; 12-midnight Sat ☎ (01740) 655724
⊕ thesurteesarms.co.uk
Yard of Ale One Foot in the Yard, Surtees Gold; guest beers ⊞
Traditional multi-roomed pub that was a regional CAMRA Pub of the Year 2010 and local Pub of the Year 2011. Locally and nationally sourced ales and ciders are on offer here as well as beers from the on-site Yard of Ale Brewery (est 2008). Annual beer festivals are held in the summer and at Hallowe'en. Live music and charity nights are regular events. A large function room is available for private gatherings. Lunches are served on Sunday only. ♨Q✿👶✿◑🍴🚌♣🏴⚖

Forest in Teesdale

Langdon Beck Hotel ✪
DL12 0XP (on B6277, 8 miles NW of Middleton in Teesdale) NY853312
🕒 11-10.30 (closed Mon Nov-Easter); 12-10.30 Sun
☎ (01833) 622267 ⊕ langdonbeckhotel.com
Black Sheep Best Bitter; Jarrow Rivet Catcher ⊞
Known as the Sportsman's Rest in the early 1800s, this pub is situated in the North Pennines, three miles from the spectacular High Force and Cauldron Snout waterfalls and close to the Pennine Way. The welcoming inn has long been a destination for walkers, fishermen and those seeking hospitality in scenic and peaceful surroundings, whether staying overnight or just long enough to enjoy the excellent food and drink. A beer festival is held over the late May bank holiday weekend.
♨Q✿👶🛏◑◑👶🔑P

Framwellgate Moor

Tap & Spile ✪
Front Street, DH1 5EE (off A167 bypass)
🕒 12-3 (Fri & Sat only), 6 (5 Fri)-11; 12-3, 7-10.30 Sun
☎ (0191) 386 5451
Beer range varies ⊞
One of the last survivors of the old Cameron's chain, the inn has two front bars and a large back room which can be partitioned into two. Families are welcome in the back room until 9pm. A local CAMRA award winner, it has a varied selection of ales from near and far, with eight constantly changing handpumps. The pub has a very welcoming atmosphere, with friendly bar staff. Folk music nights are a weekly event.
Q✿👶🚌(21)🍴

Frosterley

Black Bull
Bridge End, DL13 2SL (100yds S of A689 at W end of village)
🕒 closed Mon & Tue; 10.30-11; 10.30-5.30 Sun
☎ (01388) 527784
Beer range varies ⊞
Local CAMRA Cider Pub of the Year 2012, this unique hostelry has four ales from local breweries, plus up to four ciders and perries. High-quality food is made from locally sourced ingredients, while the interior has a classic old-style feel, with stone and board floors. There are tables outside the front door and a covered yard to the side. Music, plays and story-telling feature regularly. It's the only pub in the country to have its own peal of bells. Winter hours may vary. ♨Q✿◑▶▲🚌(101)♣🍴P

Gainford

Cross Keys 🅛
High Row, DL2 3DN (on A67 between Darlington & Barnard Castle)
🕒 3-midnight Mon; 12-1am Sat; 12-midnight Sun
☎ (01325) 730237
Taylor Landlord; guest beer ⊞
Attractive pub built in 1759 overlooking the village green. The exterior has won Northumbria in bloom awards on several occasions. Inside, there is a split-level bar, pool room and lounge/restaurant – landlord Ian's curries on a Wednesday night are legendary. There is always a beer from local Mithril Ales on offer. Thursday is games night, Sunday is quiz night and there is monthly entertainment on a Saturday. The pictureque beer garden has a smoking shelter. Santa's sleigh sets off from here every Christmas Eve. ♨✿✿👶🚌(75,76)♣P⚖

Lord Nelson
40 Main Road, DL2 3DY (on A67)
🕒 12-midnight (1am Fri & Sat) ☎ (01325) 733233
⊕ lordnelsongainford.co.uk
Thwaites Wainwright; guest beers ⊞
Picturesque traditional family-run free house, built circa 1745, situated in this historic village on the road from Darlington to Barnard Castle. The interior comprises a dining room, bar and cosy snug. Hearty British food is served alongside a varied selection of guest ales, often from local micros. The pub has something for everyone – ramblers, fishermen and locals who enjoys a good pint – and dogs are welcome. Wednesday is curry night. The bus stops just outside. ♨Q✿◑👶🚌(75,76)

Hamsterley

Cross Keys ✓

DL13 3PX (2 miles S of A68) NZ115311
✪ 12-3, 5-11; 12-11 Sat & Sun ☎ (01388) 488457
⊕ thecrosskeyshamsterley.com
Beer range varies Ⓗ

A proper, popular village pub that also serves as restaurant, tourist meeting place and, most importantly, real local. Family run, it has a comfortable dining room, dog-friendly snug and a long bar/lounge across the front of the building with a huge open fire. Post can be collected here, and some groceries are available. Food is locally sourced, and a wine and cheese night is hosted on Tuesday. Central in the village, and close to Hamsterley forest. ⚲Q❀☎⊕◖Å♣P⌐

Hartburn

Parkwood Hotel ✓

64-66 Darlington Road, TS18 5ER (on Darlington Rd)
✪ 12-11 (midnight Fri & Sat) ☎ (01642) 587933
⊕ theparkwoodhotel.com
Adnams Broadside; Camerons Strongarm; Greene King Abbot; guest beers Ⓗ

A magnificent red-brick Victorian building with an imposing porch, tiled hallway, staircase and public rooms, this is the former home of the Ropner family – shipbuilders, ship owners and civic benefactors. A local CAMRA award winner, three regular ales are supplemented by two guests, usually rarities for the area, one sourced under the SIBA scheme. The ciders are Westons Old Rosie and Traditional Scrumpy. Accommodation is in six high quality en-suite bedrooms. Q❀☎⊕◖⌐♦P⌐

Hartlepool

Brewery Tap

Stockton Street, TS24 7QS (on A689 in front of Camerons Brewery)
✪ 11-4; closed Sun ☎ (01429) 868686
⊕ cameronsbrewery.com
Camerons Strongarm, seasonal beers Ⓗ

When Camerons discovered that it owned a somewhat derelict pub next to the brewery, the old Stranton's future was secured when it was converted into the brewery tap, museum and visitors' centre. Strongarm, Camerons' flagship brand, is always available, together with the brewery's monthly specials. The brewery tap also acts as the starting point for brewery tours, for which there is a small charge. Conferences, evening opening and social events can be arranged. Q♿⇌❀(36)P⌐

Causeway

Vicarage Gardens, Stranton, TS24 7QT (beside Camerons Brewery)
✪ 12-11 (11.30 Thu; midnight Fri & Sat) ☎ (01429) 273954
Banks's Bitter; Camerons Strongarm; guest beers Ⓗ

Marvellous multi-roomed, red-brick Victorian building and Camerons' unofficial brewery tap for more than a century, the Causeway is now owned by Marston's, though the sales of 'banked' Strongarm remain huge. A CAMRA multi award-winning pub, it even gets a mention in Hansard for the quality of its Strongarm. The licensee hosts an eclectic mix of live music most evenings, while Tuesday is quiz night. Three guest beers are sourced from the Marston's range. Good-value bar snacks are available. ⚲❀◖❀⇌❀(36)♣⌐

Fishermans Arms ✓

Southgate, Hartlepool, TS24 0JJ (on the headland close to the Fish Quay)
✪ 5-11.30; 3-midnight Fri & Sat; 3-11.30 Sun
☎ (01429) 266029 ⊕ thefishermans.co.uk
Black Sheep Best Bitter; Jennings Cumberland Ale; guest beer Ⓗ

The Fish is a friendly, family-run, one-room community pub close to the Fish Quay, the town wall and the site of the Anglo-Saxon monastery founded by St Aidan in 640AD. A choice of three handpumps includes a guest from Punch Taverns' list. There is no jukebox or TV. Quizzes are held twice weekly, while the pub supports darts teams, with the female team generally performing better. Details of the regular live bands and two annual beer festivals can be found on the pub's website. Q❀(7)♣⌐

Globe

26 Northgate, TS24 0LJ (on headland, towards Fish Quay)
✪ 11-11 ☎ (01429) 860097
Camerons Strongarm Ⓗ

Opposite the port that was once bustling with fishing boats, coal staithes and pit props, this friendly community establishment is under the stewardship of licensees celebrating 27 years of service to the trade. The pub comprises a main public bar and a smaller quieter lounge with a centrepiece Victorian fireplace and exposed brickwork. The price of the Strongarm (ask for a Hartlepool Head) reflects the pub's new-found freehold status where savings, negotiated with Camerons brewery, have been passed on to the customer. ⚲Q❀☎❀◖❀(7)♣⌐⊟

Jackson's Arms ✓

Tower Street, TS24 7HH (100yds S of railway/bus stations)
✪ 12-midnight (2am Fri & Sat) ☎ (01429) 862413
Beer range varies Ⓗ

Close to the Grand Central and Northern Rail railway station, the new bus station and Hartlepool United football ground, this warm, friendly, street-corner local was once offered as the prize in a raffle. However, at £100 a ticket there weren't many takers. There are two busy bars, one for convivial conversation and one for pool and darts. An upstairs function room is also available. Up to four premium beers are on offer, sourced from throughout the country. ◖⇌❀

Rat Race Ale House

Station Approach, TS24 7ED (on platform 1 of railway station)
✪ 12.02-2.15, 4.02-8.15; 12.02-9 Sat; closed Sun
☎ (07889) 828648 ⊕ ratracealehouse.co.uk
Beer range varies Ⓗ/Ⓖ

The station's former newsagent's is now an ale lovers' paradise, where approximately 200 different ales feature annually. A local CAMRA award winner, its opening/closing times coincide with the arrival/departure of the coast trains. No lager, no fizzy beer, no fizzy cider, no spirits, no alcopops, no food, no TV, no jukebox, no one-arm bandit, no quiz machine, no bar! Just four ever-changing real ales, real cider and real perry, all served in over-sized glasses at reasonable prices. Perfect. Q♿⇌❀♣♦⊟

Heighington

George & Dragon ✅
4 East Green, DL5 6PP
☼ 12-11 (midnight Fri & Sat); 12-10.30 Sun
☎ (01325) 313152
Black Sheep Best Bitter; guest beers H
A warm and welcoming pub in a picturesque village, situated in a fine position on the smaller green. An old coaching inn, it has been refurbished in a modern style. The main bar, with real log fire, serves a regular real ale, up to four guests and a real cider, ensuring its popularity with lovers of good beer. A separate bar has large-screen TV for sporting events. Excellent food is served daily in the lounge and conservatory-style restaurant area.
🛏Q🕏🐕🌓🍺♿🚲(1,16)♣

High Hesleden

Ship Inn
TS27 4QD (signed from the B1281, between A19 and Blackhall) NZ454382
☼ closed Mon; 12-3 (Sat only), 6-11; 12-9 Sun
☎ (01429) 836453 ⊕ theshipinn.net
Beer range varies H
Now in its 12th year of continual family ownership, complete satisfaction is guaranteed at this nautically-themed rural gem and 2011 local CAMRA award winner. The landlord serves seven ever-changing real beers, sourced mainly from microbreweries, and his wife runs the superb restaurant offering top-quality food at reasonable prices, including mid-week two-course specials. Six newly built chalets and the Crow's Nest self-contained flat provide good-value accommodation. There are stupendous coastal views from the well-kept gardens. 🛏Q🕏🛌🐕🌓🍺♿🚲(206)P🚫

High Shincliffe

Avenue Inn ✅
Avenue Street, DH1 2PT (150yds from A177)
☼ 12-11 ☎ (0191) 3865954 ⊕ theavenue.biz
Black Sheep Best Bitter; guest beers H
A friendly out-of-town pub offering decent B&B facilities, providing a handy base for walkers exploring the attractive countryside. The Monday night quiz and Thursday night dominoes knockout are popular with the regulars. The evening menu offers quality food at modest prices and the pub serves traditional Sunday lunches. Regular bus services stop just outside, providing easy access to historic Durham City nearby. 🕏🛌🌓♣P🚭

Holwick

Strathmore Arms Ⓛ
DL12 0NJ (just outside Middleton in Teesdale)
☼ 12-late ☎ (01833) 640362
Allendale Golden Plover, Adder Lager; guest beers H
Three miles off the B6277 at Middleton in Teesdale, this 17th-century stone and buttressed roadside pub has a welcoming bar with a stone flag floor, beams and real fire, and a separate lounge with tiled floor and pool table. Guest ales are usually from Allendale, and a cider is on handpull. Food is available during all sessions. Outside is a beer garden and camping field, and four en-suite letting rooms are available.
🛏Q🕏🛌🌓🅿P

Howden le Wear

Green Tree
Bridge Street, DL15 8EX
☼ 3 (12 Sat & Sun)-11 ☎ (01388) 762743
Beer range varies H
Lively village pub with a single open-plan room across the front of the building, with a partitioned dining area/pool room. Traditional pub pastimes such as darts, dominoes and pool are popular, and there is a quiz on Sunday, lively karaoke on Friday and live music on Saturday. Evening meals and Sunday lunches are available, and two of the guest ales are usually local. A big screen shows sporting events. Outside are a beer garden and smoking canopy. 🛏🕏🐕🌓(1)♣🚶P🚭

Leamside

Three Horseshoes Ⓛ
Pit House Lane, DH4 6QQ (½ mile N of A690 at West Rainton)
☼ 11-11 (midnight Fri & Sat) ☎ (0191) 584 2394
⊕ threehorseshoesleamside.co.uk
Jennings Cumberland Ale; Taylor Landlord H
A significant country pub, extended to provide a thriving restaurant, with a spacious garden area. The landlord is a past winner of local CAMRA and regional Pub of the Year competitions with previous pubs. The comfortable and well-maintained bar has an open fire in winter and offers a varied choice of real ales, a large range of whiskies and real cider from Westons. Food is served daily (booking advisable) including hot bar snacks. The pub is home to local cycle and clay pigeon clubs. Well worth a visit.
🛏🕏🌓🐕♣🚶P🚭

Long Newton

Vane Arms ✅
Darlington Road, TS21 1DB (W end of village, close to A66)
☼ 12-2 (not Mon), 5-11 (midnight Fri & Sat); 12-11 Sun
☎ (01642) 580401 ⊕ thevanearms.co.uk
Black Sheep Best Bitter, guests beers H
This lovely village pub had been left abandoned empty for 898 days when the pub management company eventually sold up. A local couple, new to the trade, bought the freehold, saved the pub from further dereliction and quickly established an enviable reputation for serving four real beers, often sourced from microbreweries, together with home-made and reasonably priced top-quality restaurant meals. A wonderful story, and the licensees have just celebrated the pub being open for another 898 days! 🛏Q🕏🌓🐕🚲(87A)♣P🚭

Metal Bridge

Old Mill Hotel
Thinford Road, DH6 5NX (off A1M jct 61, follow signs on A177 for 1¼ miles) NZ303351
☼ 12-11 (10.30 Sun) ☎ (01740) 652928
⊕ oldmilldurham.co.uk
Beer range varies H
Originally built as a paper mill in 1813, this spacious inn is now the venue of choice for discerning locals and visitors alike. Offering good-quality food and well-kept ales, three handpumps serve an ever-changing range, with the nearby Durham Brewery often supplying one of the beers.

The food menu is extensive with daily specials written up on a board above the bar. Larger groups are welcome in the conservatory. Accommodation is of a high standard, with all rooms en suite. ⏶⍟🅿🚭

Middlestone Village

Ship Inn ✪
Low Road, DL14 8AB (on B6287)
✪ 4 (12 Fri-Sun)-11 ☎ (01388) 810904
🌐 shipinnmiddlestone.co.uk
Beer range varies Ⓗ
There is always something going on at this bustling, popular local and, while very much at the heart of the community, regulars come from miles around to sample up to seven beers. Events include darts and dominoes on Monday, a quiz on Thursday, regular curry nights and twice-yearly beer festivals. The open-plan bar has three drinking areas providing spectacular views of the North Yorkshire Moors. Food is served lunchtimes and evenings Friday to Sunday, evenings only Monday to Thursday. ᛗ⍟🅭🚗(2,3)♣🅿

Middleton in Teesdale

Teesdale Hotel ✪
Market Place, DL12 0QG
✪ 11 (12 Sun)-11 ☎ (01833) 640264 🌐 teesdalehotel.co.uk
Black Sheep Best Bitter; guest beers Ⓗ
A former coaching inn with a fine stone-built exterior and archway, updated to provide excellent accommodation. This is a popular village local as well as a resting place for tourists and Pennine walkers – Middleton in Teesdale is often referred to as 'the capital of Upper Teesdale', with High Force and Cauldron Snout nearby. Up to two guest beers, often from local micros, may be found, especially in summer. Meals can be enjoyed in the main bar or the more comfortable restaurant. A farmers' market is held on the last Sunday of the month. ᛗQ⍟🅭🅿🚭

No Place

Beamish Mary Ⓛ
DH9 0QH (follow signs to No Place off A693 from Chester-le-Street to Stanley)
✪ 12-11.20 (10.50 Sun) ☎ (0191) 370 0237
Beer range varies Ⓗ
A former local CAMRA Pub of the Year that went into decline, the Beamish Mary has returned to something like its former glory under new ownership, now tenanted. This pub, full of character, is well respected for its warm welcome, generously portioned pub grub and ample choices of well-kept real ale and real cider. The location is handy for visitors to the nearby world-renowned Beamish Open Air Museum. ᛗ⍟🅭🚗(8,78)♣🍴🅿🚭

North Bitchburn

Red Lion
North Bitchburn Terrace, DL15 8AL (just off A689)
✪ 12-2 (not Mon; 3 Sun), 6.30-11 ☎ (01388) 763561
Black Sheep Best Bitter; Taylor Landlord; guest beers Ⓗ
Popular 250-year-old village pub with fine south-easterly views over the Wear Valley from the dining room. The bright, cheeerful interior is light and airy, with a comfortable bar, small pool room and larger restaurant with a second dining area down a couple of steps. The pub has a well-deserved reputation for good food, available lunchtimes and evenings, and excellent beer. Guest beers tend to come from smaller north-eastern breweries. Thursday is quiz night. Q⍟🅭🚗(1C)🅿

Norton

George & Dragon
109 High Street, TS20 1AA
✪ 12-11 (midnight Wed-Sun) ☎ (01642) 554150
Greene King Abbot; guest beer Ⓗ
Traditional community pub, described by one regular as 'how pubs used to be and how pubs ought to be'. The George comprises a bar, where drinkers sit on leather benches and photographs of yesteryear adorn the walls, a large lounge and a games room. The guest beer, always a premium bitter, is chosen by customers. Excellent-value home-made pub grub, including a whopping breakfast, is served. Going home thirsty or hungry is not an option. ⏶⍟🅭🚗(35,37,38)♣🚭

Pity Me

Lambton Hounds
Front Street, DH1 5DE (100yds from A167 bypass roundabout)
✪ 4-11; 11-midnight Fri & Sat; 12-11 Sun ☎ (0191) 3864742
🌐 lambtonhounds.com
Beer range varies Ⓗ
Situated on the Great North Road, this 250-year-old former coaching inn offers comfortable en-suite accommodation, a large restaurant, bar, lounge and snug. The bar has a pool table, TV, jukebox, and hosts live music. The lounge features the front of the bar from Titanic's sister ship, RMS Olympic, and is warmed by a welcoming fire in winter. The small snug has comfortable settees to relax in after a meal. Four handpumps dispense the beer range. The car park and garden are to the rear. ᛗQ⍟🅭🚗(21)🅿🚭

Preston-le-Skerne

Blacksmiths Arms Ⓛ
Ricknall Lane, DL5 6JH (1 mile E of A167 at Gretna Green)
✪ closed Mon; 11.30-2, 5.30 (6.30 winter)-11; 12-10.30 Sun ☎ (01325) 314873
Beer range varies Ⓗ
Welcoming free house known locally as the Hammers, situated in a rural location near Newton Aycliffe. A long corridor separates the bar, restaurant and a beamed lounge furnished in farmhouse style. The pub has an excellent reputation for home-cooked food, and up to three guest beers are available, sourced mainly from local micros. A former local CAMRA Rural Pub of the Year, it even has a helicopter landing pad. Q⏶⍟🅭🍴♣🅿🚭

Rookhope

Rookhope Inn
Rear Hogarth Terrace, DL13 2BG
✪ 12-midnight ☎ (01388) 517215
Beer range varies Ⓗ

Off the beaten track in the North Pennines, this Grade II-listed building dating from 1680 in a pretty former lead mining village retains the original open fires and wood beams. A welcome rest stop on the coast-to-coast cycle route, this friendly community inn also offers accommodation and a function room. The big fire in the bar is welcome in winter. Spectacular views of Upper Weardale can be enjoyed from the garden. The surrounding area provides ample opportunity for exploration. Thursday is cheese night. Opening hours are reduced in winter. ᐰQ✿✿⊯◑⊟⊟(101)♣P

St John's Chapel

Blue Bell ✅
12 Hood Street, DL13 1QJ
✪ 5 (12 Sat & Sun)-1am ☎ (01388) 537256
Beer range varies ⏄
Small, homely village local situated in beautiful Upper Weardale, very much at the heart of the community. The pub hosts ladies' and gents' darts and pool teams and runs a quiz on Sunday night. It has a leek club which holds an annual show, and there is a small library for customers' use. The local angling club is based here and fishing licences are on sale at the bar. The guest beers are usually from small local breweries. There is a covered and heated area outside. ᐰ✿✿⊟(101)♣♠P

Sedgefield

Nag's Head
8 West End, TS21 2BS
✪ 6 (5 Fri-Sat)-midnight; 12-3, 7-11 Sun ☎ (01740) 620234
Taylor Landlord; guest beers ⏄
Situated at the centre of the village, close to Sedgefield Racecourse, this free house is a classic local attracting all age groups – families with well-behaved children are welcome. There is a comfortable bar, a smaller lounge and a restaurant offering traditional Sunday lunch prepared with fresh local produce. Meals are also served in the bar (no food Sun and Mon eve). The landlord and landlady both come from the village. ᐰ✿◑⊟よ⊟♣

Shincliffe

Seven Stars Inn
High Street North, DH1 2NU (on A177, S of Durham)
✪ 11-11 (10.30 Sun) ☎ (0191) 384 8454
⊕ sevenstarsinn.co.uk
Black Sheep Best Bitter; Taylor Landlord; guest beers ⏄
Dating from 1724, this small, cosy, beamed pub is situated on the edge of a pleasant village. Local country walks and the long Weardale Way pass nearby. Walkers are welcome in the bar – just make sure your boots are clean – and well-behaved dogs are also permitted. Meals are served in the bar and traditional restaurant. Comfortable accommodation makes the pub a great base for visiting the city and other attractions in the area. ✿✿◑⊟⊟

Spennymoor

Frog & Ferret
Coulson Street, DL16 7RS
✪ 3 (12 Fri & Sat)-11; 12-10.30 Sun ☎ (01388) 818312
Beer range varies ⏄

Friendly, family-run free house offering four constantly changing real ales sourced from far and wide, with local and northern microbreweries well represented. A welcoming atmosphere greets you on arrival at the three-sided bar in the comfortably furnished lounge, with brick, stone and wood cladding. Darts and dominoes are played and bar snacks are available. Well-behaved children are permitted until 4pm. The pub hosts a quiz on Sunday evening, and a music quiz on the first Wednesday evening of the month. ᐰ✿よ♣P

Stockton-on-Tees

Sun Inn ✅
Knowles Street, TS18 1SU
✪ 11-11; 12-10.30 Sun ☎ (01642) 611461
Draught Bass ⏄
Popular town-centre drinkers' pub reputed to sell more Draught Bass than any other pub in the country. It was rescued from an uncertain future nine years ago by a regular at the pub who became the licensee and very quickly increased the sales of 'banked' Bass – his son-in-law is the current licensee. The pub supports darts and football teams and charitable causes. On Monday evening the function room is home to the famous Stockton Folk Club. ⇌(Stockton/Thornaby)⊟♣

Thomas Sheraton ✅
4 Bridge Road, TS18 1BH (at S end of High St)
✪ 9-midnight (11 Sun) ☎ (01642) 606134
Greene King Abbot; Ruddles Best Bitter; guest beers ⏄
This previous local CAMRA Pub of the Year winner is a fine Wetherspoon conversion of the Victorian law courts, and named after one of the country's great Georgian cabinet makers, born in the town in 1751. It comprises several distinct dining and drinking areas downstairs, and a balcony and patio upstairs. Eight guest beers are available, several sourced locally. Regular beer festivals, Meet the Brewer sessions and brewery trips are arranged. CAMRA members receive a 20 per cent discount on the food menu. ᐰ✿◑よ⇌(Stockton/Thornaby)⊟♠

Tudhoe

Black Horse Inn ⎣
4 Attwood Terrace, DL16 6TD (on B6288, 4 miles S of Durham)
✪ 11.30-11 ☎ (01388) 420662
Caledonian Deuchars IPA; Courage Directors; guest beers ⏄
Once closed down by a pubco as unviable, this is now a busy, atmospheric and friendly free house, reopened by the current owners in 2008. Two permanent and two regularly changing guest ales are always available. Excellent food is served lunchtimes and evenings in the restaurant and bar. Buses from Durham City pass the door. This family-friendly pub is well worth a visit. ✿◑よ⊟♣P

Westgate

Hare & Hounds
24 Front Street, DL13 1RX (on A689)
✪ 12-2.30 (Sat only), 6.30-11; 12-3, 6.30-9.30 Sun ☎ (01388) 517212
Black Sheep Best Bitter; Hare & Hounds Hare of the Dog ⏄

On the main road through the dale, on the banks of the Wear, this popular village pub has a large bar with two distinct areas and a separate dining room, as well as a brewery. Bench seats along one wall, three fires and stone floors add real character. There are tables to the front, and seats to the rear overlooking the river. Three pumps dispense the popular house beer and Black Sheep, while the Sunday carvery is justifiably renowned.
ᴁQ⊛❶⬥Å🚋(101)♣P

Willington

Black Horse

42 Low Willington, DL15 0BD (on A690 at N end of village) NZ205349

❸ 6 (12 Sat & Sun)-11 ☎ 07727 280196

Beer range varies Ⓗ

Superbly refurbished and modernised over the past two years, this is a bright and airy pub with a spacious open-plan arrangement. Up to four ales are available, often from local microbreweries. Sport, primarily football, is screened on TVs around the room. There are darts and dominoes teams and the pub is used by two local car clubs for their meetings. The pub is well positioned to serve as a stopping point between Durham City and Weardale. ᴁ⊛⬥P⅃

Witton Gilbert

Glendenning Arms ✅

Front Street, DH7 6SY (off A691 bypass)

❸ 4 (12 Sun)-11; 3-midnight Fri; 12-midnight Sat ☎ (0191) 371 0316

Black Sheep Best Bitter, Ale Ⓗ

Typical village community local and Guide regular with a small, comfortable lounge and a lively and welcoming bar with the original Vaux 1970s red and white handpulls. The bar is attractively decorated in a contemporary style while the lounge remains more traditional. The pub runs darts, dominoes and football teams. Situated on the village's main road, there is ample car parking. ᴁ⊛🚋(15)♣P⅃

Travellers Rest

Front Street, DH7 6TQ (off A691 bypass 3 miles from city centre)

❸ 11-11; 12-10.30 Sun ☎ (0191) 371 0458

Beer range varies Ⓗ

Open-plan country-style pub, popular with diners. The bar area is split into three sections with a conservatory off to the side where families are welcome. There is also a more private dining room. Now owned by TR Leisure Partnership, an extensive food menu suits all tastes, with dining throughout the pub. The restaurant was redesigned

two years ago and the kitchen upgraded to modern standards. Quiz nights are Tuesday and Sunday.
Q❧⊛❶⬥🚋(15)P⅃

Witton le Wear

Dun Cow

19 High Street, DL14 0AY

❸ 6 (1 Sat; 12 Sun)-11 ☎ (01388) 448294

Black Sheep Best Bitter; Jennings Cumberland Ale; Wells Bombardier Ⓗ

Genuine unspoilt stone pub dating from 1799, set back from the road in a quiet, pretty village, with a traditional single bar and seats outside the front of building. A large fireplace at one end of the room is topped by a set of impressive horns, another at the other end is guarded by a sleeping fox. Comfortable bench seats run along two walls to the left of the bar, and football memorabilia complete the decor. The view east over the Wear to Witton Castle is impressive. ᴁQ⊛♣P⅃

Wolsingham

Black Bull

27 Market Place, DL13 3AB

❸ 12-11 (11.30 Sun) ☎ (01388) 527332

Caledonian Deuchars IPA; guest beer Ⓗ

Proper Weardale hotel in the centre of the village, providing excellent food and accommodation. It has a bar, lounge, dining room and surprise suntrap garden, plus tables to the front. The pub runs various games nights and local Weight Watchers members enjoy the facilities after their meetings in the town hall opposite. It also serves as headquarters for the village cricket team in the summer and hosts social events. A good base for walkers and cyclists, near Weardale Way.
ᴁQ⊛❧❶⬥Å➔🚋(101)♣⅃

Black Lion

21 Meadhope Street, DL13 3EN (50yds N of market place)

❸ 6.30 (6 Fri; 12 Sat)-11; 12-10.30 Sun ☎ (01388) 527772

Beer range varies Ⓗ

On a pleasant residential street, just a few minutes' walk from the village centre, this establishment is well worth a visit. Comfortable surroundings and an open fire help to create a warm, friendly atmosphere. Sport is shown on TV and opening hours may be extended for big matches, particularly cricket. Local charities are supported in various events throughout the year, including a quiz on Sunday evening. Beer festivals are held two to three times a year. ᴁQ⊛🚋(101)♣

Choosing pubs

CAMRA members and branches choose the pubs listed in the Good Beer Guide. There is no payment for entry, and pubs are inspected on a regular basis by personal visits; publicans are not sent a questionnaire once a year, as is the case with some pub guides. CAMRA branches monitor all the pubs in their areas, and the choice of pubs for the guide is often the result of democratic vote at branch meetings. However, recommendations from readers are welcomed and will be passed on to the relevant branch: write to Good Beer Guide, CAMRA, 230 Hatfield Road, St Albans, Hertfordshire, AL1 4LW; or send an email to: **gbgeditor@camra.org.uk**

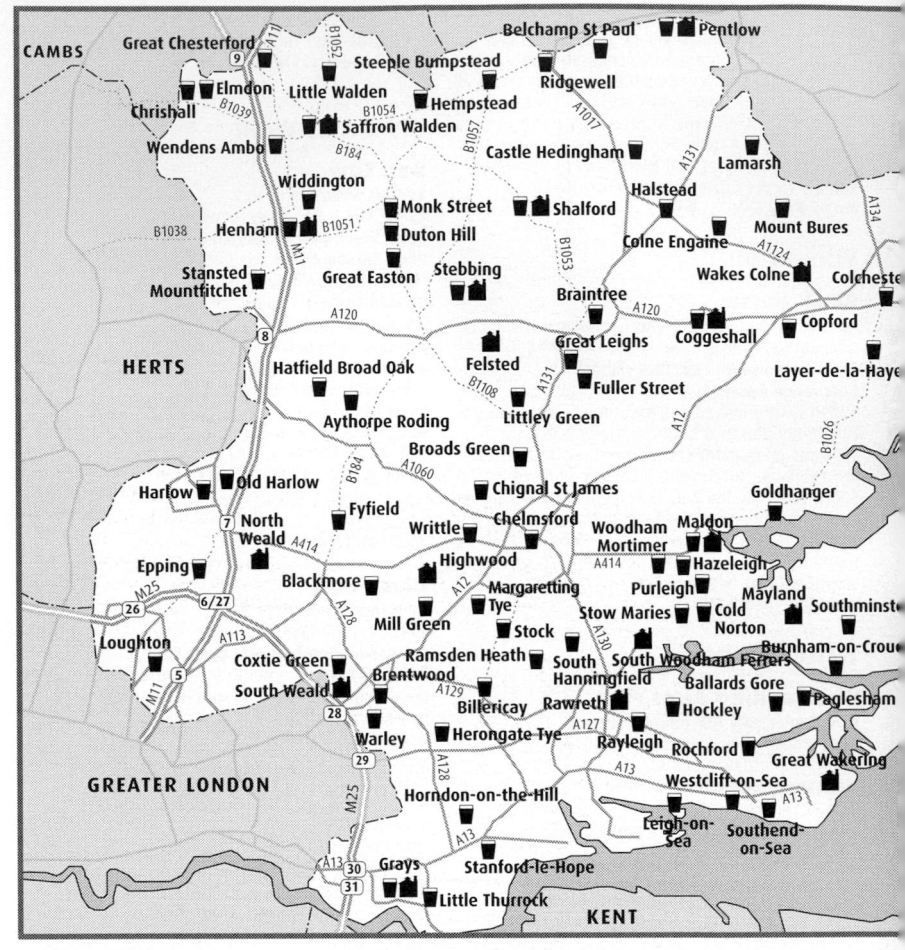

Aingers Green

Royal Fusilier 🄻
Aingers Green Road, CO7 8NH
☀ 6 (11 Sat)-11; 12-10.30 Sun ☎ (01206) 250001
Beer range varies Ⓗ
This friendly village pub is just under a mile's walk from Great Bentley station and is well established as part of the village community. The beer selection changes on a weekly basis. The landlord often keeps ales from local breweries but these are interspersed with beers not often seen in this part of Essex. Home to darts and pool teams, with satellite TV in the back bar. There are regular nights for quizzes, cribbage and dominoes. Well-behaved dogs welcome. ᛗQ⚘⊞ᕆ⚑(77)♣Pᒣ

Aythorpe Roding

Axe & Compasses 🄻 ✅
Dunmow Road, CM6 1PP (on B1845 5 miles SW of Dunmow) TL594154
☀ 12-11 (midnight Fri & Sat; 10.30 Sun) ☎ (01279) 876648
⊕ theaxeandcompasses.co.uk
Nethergate Axe Pale Ale Ⓗ; Sharp's Doom Bar Ⓖ; guest beers Ⓗ/Ⓖ
The Axe is an attractive thatched pub in open countryside south of Dunmow. The clientele is mixed – it is frequented by diners, drinkers, walkers and farming folk. Both good beer and good food are always available, with friendly and efficient service. Bar snacks are served and fine dining is in a separate restaurant. In winter there are log fires and in summer a pleasant garden, with views to the windmill. Winner of Best Pub Restaurant in the Essex Food and Drink Awards 2009 and 2011. ᛗQ⚘⊛⚑(7,18,346)Pᒣ

Ballards Gore (Stambridge)

Shepherd & Dog 🄻
Gore Road, SS4 2DA (between Rochford and Paglesham)
☀ 12-3, 6-11; 12-11 Sat; 12-10 Sun ☎ (01702) 258279
⊕ shepherddanddog.co.uk
Beer range varies Ⓗ
An excellent country pub with a warm welcome, and a previous winner of local CAMRA Pub of the Year and Country Pub of the Year awards. Three real ales generally come from local microbreweries such as Wibblers and Mighty Oak. There is also a real cider on handpump. The locally sourced, freshly prepared food is popular, so booking is advised for meals. Walkers, cyclists and coach groups are welcome. Open mic night is held fortnightly on Thursday evenings – check the website. ⚘⚑⊞(60)♣♠P

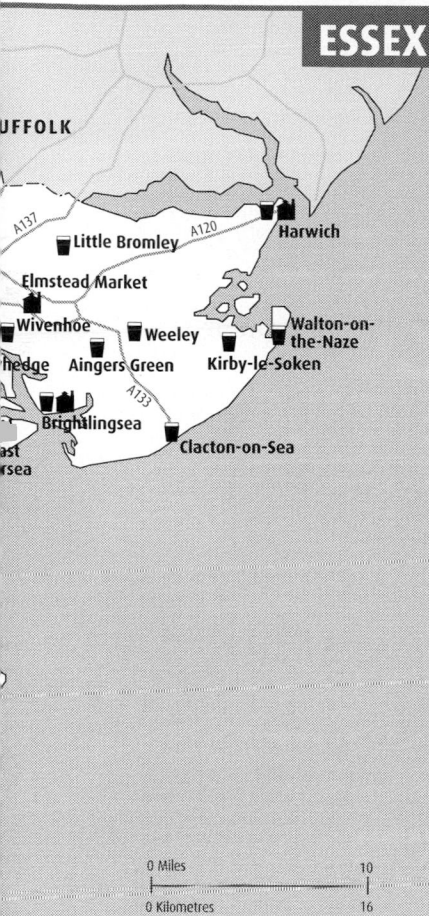

ESSEX

SUFFOLK

Little Bromley   Harwich
Elmstead Market
Wivenhoe   Weeley   Walton-on-the-Naze
hedge   Aingers Green   Kirby-le-Soken
Brightlingsea
ast   Clacton-on-Sea
rsea

| 0 Miles | 10 |
| 0 Kilometres | 16 |

Popular Wetherspoon venue, especially at weekends, with the usual suspects on handpump, plus guests from microbreweries, which are often local, such as Brentwood. The car park at the rear is Pay & Display but arriving here by public transport is easy, with the station and bus stops close by. Breakfast is available until noon, other meals until 10pm. There is no music, but there are fruit machines and muted TVs, and an outside area at the rear for drinking and smoking.
Q❀◑�&⇌☐(100)●┕

Coach & Horses 🅛
36 Chapel Street, CM12 9LU
🕑 10-11; 12-10.30 Sun ☎ (01277) 622873
⊕ thecoachandhorses.org
Adnams Southwold Bitter; Greene King Abbot; Sharp's Doom Bar; guest beer 🅗
Popular one-bar pub, situated off the High Street, with a cosy, welcoming ambience. Good-quality food is served Monday to Saturday lunchtimes and evenings, and all day Sunday, from an extensive menu featuring home-made pies and food made with locally sourced ingredients. The bar and food service is quick, efficient and friendly, enhancing the feel-good factor. The walls are adorned with prints and decorative plates, and there is a fine collection of ceramic and gleaming copper jugs.
♨Q❀◑⇌☐(100)P

Blackmore

Leather Bottle
Horsefayre Green, CM4 0RL
🕑 11-11 (midnight Fri & Sat); 12-11 Sun ☎ (01277) 821891
⊕ theleatherbottle.net
Adnams Southwold Bitter; Sharp's Doom Bar 🅗**; guest beers** 🅗/🅖
Large village pub with a small flagstone-floored bar area. Most of the interior is taken up by a good-quality restaurant. Two guest beers are generally available on handpump, with maybe a third on gravity at weekends in the summer, usually including a beer of around 5% ABV or higher. Westons Old Rosie cider is also sold. An annexe to the bar has a silent fruit machine.
♨❀◑🖥☐(32)●P

Braintree

King William IV 🅛
114 London Road, CM77 7PU (on B1053) TL749492
🕑 3-midnight; 12-1am Fri & Sat; 12-11 Sun
☎ (01376) 567755 ⊕ kingwilliamiv.co.uk
Beer range varies 🅖
Cosy 19th-century traditional free house with a main bar and a walk-through leading to a small back bar with a dartboard. The pub reopened in 2009, having been closed for two years. A range of three or four ales is served by gravity from a side cellar, usually featuring a Sharp's beer and Essex microbreweries. Cider from Westons and Cornish Orchards is sold. Beer festivals are held twice a year in a marquee in the large garden. Friendly dogs are welcome. ❀☐(70,352)♣●P

Belchamp St Paul

Half Moon
Cole Green, CO10 7DP TL792423
🕑 closed Mon; 12-3, 7-11 ☎ (01787) 277402
⊕ halfmoonbelchamp.co.uk
Greene King IPA; guest beers 🅗
Beautiful thatched rural pub dating from about 1685 opposite the village green, with a cosy interior and an attentive landlord and landlady. Three beers are on all year round, while guest beers change regularly. There is good local trade, and an excellent choice of bar and restaurant meals (no food Sun eve). A well-supported August bank holiday beer festival is held, with up to 35 beers, ciders and perries. In the past the pub provided one of the locations for the Lovejoy TV series. Outside there is a separate smoking area.
♨Q❀◑P┕

Billericay

Blue Boar ✅
39 High Street, CM12 9BA
🕑 8am-11.30 ☎ (01277) 655552
Courage Best Bitter, Directors; Greene King Abbot; Marston's Pedigree; Shepherd Neame Spitfire; guest beers 🅗

Wagon & Horses 🅛 ✅
53 South Street, CM7 3QD
🕑 12-11.30 (6 Sun) ☎ (01376) 552388
Beer range varies 🅗
The Wagon is the first of Greene King's Local Heroes pubs and the landlord is free to source

beers out of tie as well as from the brewery. Sixteen handpumps generally have eight beers on tap, four sourced from Greene King and then four others, often local. Occasionally mini beer festivals are held in which 16 different beers are offered. Food is hot pies and pasties available all day. Note the unusual glass-topped well inside. A beer garden can be enjoyed in the summer. Q❀≒P'⌐

Brentwood

Rising Sun ⓛ
144 Ongar Road, CM15 9DJ (on A128, at Western Rd jct)
✪ 3-11.30 (midnight Fri); 12-midnight Sat; 12-10.30 Sun
☎ (01277) 213749
Fuller's London Pride; Sharp's Cornish Coaster; Taylor Landlord; guest beers Ⓗ
Comfortable, friendly local with a good selection of real ales, in an area where beer choice can be fairly limited. This is very much a community pub: there is a charity quiz on Monday evening, Brentwood Chess Club plays here on Sunday evening, and there are frequent darts matches. Five handpumps are now used in the saloon bar, dispensing three regular ales plus a beer from Brentwood Brewery and a guest. Framed prints of the local area decorate the walls. Outside is a covered, heated smokers' area and patio. ⚏❀⪥🖰🖫♣P'⌐

Brightlingsea

Railway Tavern ⓛ
58 Station Road, CO7 0DT
✪ 5-10; 3-11 Fri; 12-11 Sat; 12-3, 7-10.30 Sun
Crouch Vale Best; guest beers Ⓗ
Making its 20th appearance in the Guide, this basic pub is a must for serious beer drinkers, almost always serving at least one real cider and three excellent real ales. One of these is usually dark, from its own brewery. The landlord may not always be in the best of spirits but his staff and locals more than make up for this with their friendly chat and banter, in which one can freely join. Animal tolerant. ⚏Q❀🖫(78)●

Broads Green

Walnut Tree ✪
CM3 1DT (¾ mile S of Great Waltham village) TL694125
✪ 12-midnight ☎ (01245) 360222
Greene King IPA; Morland Original Bitter; Ruddles Best Bitter; guest beer Ⓖ
Handsome Victorian brick-built pub overlooking a large green. The front door opens directly into a small snug. To the left is the wood-panelled public bar, little changed since it was built; to the right is the more modern lounge. Outside is a garden and seating in front of the pub. There is no food – the landlord prefers to concentrate on his beers (served on gravity from a half-cellar) and to maintain a traditional atmosphere. An outside Gents is still in use. ⚏Q❀⪥🖫(33,52)♣P

Burnham-on-Crouch

Queen's Head ⓛ
26 Providence, CM0 8JU (opp clock tower)
✪ 2 (5 Mon)-11; 12-11 Fri & Sat; 12-10.30 Sun
☎ (01621) 784825
Dark Star Hophead; Wibblers Providence IPA; guest beers Ⓗ

Traditional community local in this picturesque riverside town, recently benefiting from a sympathetic refurbishment that won the CAMRA/ English Heritage Joe Goodwin Award. It has a spacious single bar with simple furniture, a warm atmosphere and hops over the bar, which becomes a vibrant venue where the local RNLI and rugby team enjoy a pint. The two regularly changing guest beers are mostly from local micros, including Farmers and Red Fox. There is monthly live music and an August bank holiday beer festival. Walkers, cyclists and dogs welcome.
⚏❀⪥≒🖫(31X)♣●'⌐

Castle Hedingham

Bell ⓛ
10 St James Street, CO9 3EJ (signed off A1017)
✪ 12-3, 5.30-11; 12-midnight Fri & Sat; 12-11 Sun
☎ (01787) 460350 🌐 hedinghambell.co.uk
Adnams Southwold Bitter; Mighty Oak IPA, Maldon Gold; guest beers Ⓖ
A 15th-century coaching inn owned by Gray & Sons that is well-worth a visit. There are small rooms for drinking and dining alongside the two main bars. Beers come direct from the cask, and summer and winter beer festivals are held. Live jazz plays at lunchtime on the last Sunday of the month, the pub champions local musicians on Friday evening, and there is a regular quiz on Sunday night. Local Delvin End cider is usually available. Food includes Turkish specials prepared in a wood-fired stone oven. Local CAMRA Pub of the Year 2010 and 2011. ⚏Q🝙❀⪥⦿🖫♣●P'⌐

Chelmsford

Barista ⓛ
44-45 Duke Street, CM1 1JA
✪ 11.30-11 (midnight Wed & Thu; 2am Fri & Sat); closed Sun
☎ (01245) 493333 🌐 baristachelmsford.com
Beer range varies Ⓖ
New, modern bar with comfortable leather furniture and subdued lighting situated close to the railway and bus stations. Three varied, often local, gravity-fed beers change weekly and are dispensed from an upstairs cellar. Popular beer

festivals are held at least twice a year. Food is served weekday lunchtimes. Over-21s welcomed. 🐕👤♿≉🚊💪

Oddfellows Arms 🅛

195 Springfield Road, CM2 6JP
🕐 12-11 (midnight Fri & Sat) ☎ (01245) 490514
🌐 theoddfellowsarms.com

Adnams Broadside; Black Sheep Best Bitter; Mighty Oak Maldon Gold; Red Fox IPA; Sharp's Doom Bar Ⓗ
Newly refurbished, a pub with a modern wood interior but maintaining a local feel. There is a large U-shaped bar area with a back room containing a pool table leading out to the garden/smoking area. Beer festivals are hosted in mid February and late July. There is monthly live music and poker nights are held Tuesday and Thursday. Food is served lunchtimes and evenings weekdays, all day at weekends. 🐕◑🍴🚊(54,71,73)♣P💪

Orange Tree 🅛

6 Lower Anchor Street, CM2 0AS
🕐 12-11 (11.30 Fri & Sat) ☎ (01245) 262664 🌐 the-ot.com

Mighty Oak Oscar Wilde; Wibblers Apprentice Ⓗ; **guest beers** Ⓗ/Ⓖ
The Orange Tree is one of the best real ale pubs in Chelmsford and is runner-up local CAMRA Pub of the Year 2012. There are two permanent beers plus five guests on handpump and two from casks behind the bar (often including stouts or porters). Guests are from the Gray's listing and the cider is from the Westons range. There is a charity quiz every Tuesday, and rock/blues bands play one Saturday a month. Lunchtime food is served, including Sunday roasts, with a curry night Thursday evenings. Q🐕◑👤♿🍴🚊♣🚶P💪

Queen's Head 🅛

30 Lower Anchor Street, CM2 0AS
🕐 12-11 (11.30 Fri & Sat) ☎ (01245) 265181
🌐 queensheadchelmsford.co.uk

Crouch Vale Essex Boys Best Bitter, Brewer's Gold, Yakima Gold; guest beers Ⓗ
Crouch Vale Brewery's only pub, the Queen's Head sells three of its beers permanently, with a fourth Crouch Vale pump varying between a seasonal beer and Amarillo. The four guest ales from far and wide vary, but always include a dark beer. The cider, not always available in the winter, is from the Westons range. This popular local can be busy when there is a cricket match at the county ground, or when clubs and societies (such as the Essex Beard Club) meet. 🏰Q🐕◑👤♿🚊♣🚶P

Railway Tavern 🅛

63 Duke Street, CM1 1LW
🕐 11-11.30; 11.30-4.30 Sun ☎ (01245) 280679

Greene King Abbot; guest beers Ⓗ
A new landlord has rejuvenated this pub opposite the railway station. It now offers seven real ales from the large Gray's list, with six of them constantly changing. A Tardis-like corner pub, it has a central bar, seating towards the rear laid out like a railway carriage, and a garden where you can listen to the station announcements. Winner of local CAMRA Most Improved Pub Award for 2011. 🐕◑≉♣💪

Woolpack ✅

23 Mildmay Road, CM2 0DN (S of main road into town)
🕐 12-11 (midnight Fri & Sat) ☎ (01245) 259295
🌐 woolpack.net

H&H Kimberley Bitter; guest beers Ⓗ

Local CAMRA Pub of the Year 2010 and 2011, it offers six Greene King guest ales plus one guest free of tie. The small public bar has darts and a pool table. The large main lounge leads to an annexe with a large-screen TV. There is a quiz on Tuesday, monthly folk music, and beer festivals at Easter and in September. An ever-changing range of speciality sausages and spicy pickled eggs complements the food menu, which is available Monday to Friday and Sunday lunchtime. 🐕◑◗ 🍴🚊♣P💪

Chignal St James

Three Elms

Mashbury Road, CM1 4TZ
🕐 12-3, 6-11 Mon, Wed & Thu; 5-11 Tue; 12-11 Fri-Sun
☎ (01245) 443151 🌐 the-three-elms.com

Beer range varies Ⓗ
Friendly village local rejuvenated by new owners. Four constantly changing beers are served, usually including something local. The pub is particularly known for its range of real ciders, aiming to have at least 15 available all the time. In addition to lunchtime and evening meals, bar snacks include home-made pork pies and scotch eggs. 🏰🐕◑🍴♣🚶P💪

Chrishall

Red Cow

11 High Street, SG8 8RN (2 miles N of B1039) TL445394
🕐 closed Mon; 12-3, 6-11; 12-10.30 Sun ☎ (01763) 838792
🌐 theredcow.com

Adnams Southwold Bitter; guest beers Ⓗ
Thatched 14th-century pub close to an old barn in a small village near the Cambridge and Hertfordshire borders. Guest beers are usually from East Anglia. The owners welcome visitors and many local groups, including the cricket club (who run regular quizzes), the village book group, stallholders from the farmers' market, and the WI. Special occasions can be celebrated with meals from the extensive menu, either in the tiled bar or in the restaurant separated by original open timbering. A popular stop-off for ramblers, the pub is on the ancient Icknield Way. 🏰🐕◑P

Clacton-on-Sea

Old Lifeboat House 🏆

39 Marine Parade East, CO15 6AD
🕐 11-11; 12-10.30 Sun ☎ (01255) 476799

St Austell Proper Job; guest beers Ⓗ
Since the new landlords took over, this family-run pub has gone from strength to strength. They consistently obtain beers from all over the country, which means there are different ales to try weekly. A selection of real ciders is also available. On Wednesdays meals are served both lunchtime and evening and beers are offered at discounted prices. Beer festivals are held on the last weekends in April and October. 🐕◑♿≉🚶P💪

Coggeshall

Chapel Inn ✅

4 Market Hill, CO6 1TS
🕐 12-11 (1am Fri & Sat) ☎ (01376) 561655
🌐 thechapelinn.com

Fuller's London Pride; Red Fox Bitter; Wychwood Hobgoblin; guest beers Ⓗ

The pub is built on the site of a former chapel in the market square of Coggeshall. Up to four ales are offered, often including one from the local Red Fox Brewery in the town. A large seating area is sectioned off by beams. The pub prides itself on using mainly local produce for its varied menu, with food served every day except Tuesdays. A popular quiz is held every Sunday.
ᴹᴬ🏵🍴🍺(70)♣P²⌐

Colchester

Bricklayers
27 Bergholt Road, CO4 5AA (jct A134/B1508)
🏵 11-3, 5.30-11; 11-midnight Fri; 11-11 Sat; 12-7 Sun
☎ (01206) 852008
Adnams Southwold Bitter, Explorer, Broadside, seasonal beers; Fuller's London Pride; guest beers Ⓗ
An Adnams house offering up to nine ales with a good range of guests, as well as Crones Cider. The Brick is a lively, friendly pub and its close proximity to Colchester North station makes it popular with commuters and locals alike. There is a large lounge bar and a conservatory plus a busy public bar with dartboard and pool table. Run by a multi CAMRA award-winning family, it also offers good-value lunchtime food and an excellent Sunday roast.
🏵🍴🍺(North)🚌♣♠P²⌐

British Grenadier
67 Military Road, CO1 2AP (½ mile SE of Town station)
🏵 12-2.30 (not Tue or Wed), 5-11.30; 11-midnight Sat; 12-3, 7-11.30 Sun ☎ (07832) 215118
Adnams Southwold Bitter, seasonal beers; guest beers Ⓗ
A cosy and welcoming two-roomed, award-winning traditional corner pub. This Adnams tied house has a changing range of guest ales on its four handpumps – the array of pump clips adorning the walls is testament to this. An open brick fire warms the main bar during the winter, while a pool table dominates the small back bar. Darts is also regularly played and a fun quiz night is held every Sunday evening.
ᴹᴬ🏵🍴🚺🍺(Town)🚌(6,61,66)♣²⌐🚲

Fat Cat Ⓛ
65 Butt Road, CO3 3BZ (on B1026 near police station)
🏵 12-11 (midnight Fri & Sat) ☎ (01206) 577990
Crouch Vale Brewers Gold, Amarillo; Dark Star American Pale Ale; Fat Cat Honey; Woodforde's Wherry Ⓗ**; guest beers** Ⓖ
Well-established free house with guest ales mainly from East Anglia. Previous guests feature on the beer wall in the alcove. Pitfield bottled beers and a well-chosen selection of Belgian specialities provide plenty of choice. Regular events include a Sunday night quiz, live music on the last Saturday, and curries of the world on the last Thursday of the month. A real ale club is hosted on Sundays 3-7pm, and the popular West Country Beer Festival is held in May. 🏵🍴🍺(Town)🚌(1,63,64)♠²⌐

Hospital Arms
123-5 Crouch Street, CO3 3HA
🏵 12-11 (midnight Fri & Sat); 12-10.30 Sun
☎ (01206) 542398 🌐 colchester-hospitalarms.co.uk
Adnams Southwold Bitter, Explorer, Broadside, seasonal beers; guest beers Ⓗ
Busy Adnams pub on the outskirts of the town centre, opposite Essex County Hospital, and known locally as Ward Nine. Three separate bar areas serve up to seven ales, including guests on offer

from the Adnams range. Good home-cooked food is served lunchtimes, including a Sunday roast. There is no TV or loud music, and a pleasant suntrap courtyard is available to the rear for both smokers and alfresco drinkers. 🏵🍴🍺(Town)🚌(65,70,71)²⌐

Live & Let Live
12 Millers Lane, Stanway, CO3 0PS (off A1124)
🏵 12-11 (midnight Sat & Sun) ☎ (01206) 574071
Beer range varies Ⓗ
The venue comprises a public bar offering darts, pool and Sky Sports, plus a quiet homely saloon bar. Up to four ales are offered on handpump, with the pub keen to source the majority from LocAle. Good-value home-cooked food and bar snacks are available every day at lunchtime and in the evenings at weekends. A Beer & Sausage Festival is held summer and winter, and a local Classic Motorcycle Club holds regular meetings here.
ᴹᴬ🏵🍴🚺🚌(65)♣P²⌐

New Inn Ⓛ
36 Chapel Street South, CO2 7AX
🏵 12-11 (midnight Fri); 10.30-midnight Sat; 10.30-10.30 Sun
☎ (01206) 575277
Wells Eagle IPA; guest beers Ⓗ
Traditional two-bar back-street local that has been transformed into a free house, offering mainly ales from local micros and a fine selection of malt whiskies and wines at competitive prices. Live music is hosted in the public bar, where Sky Sports is screened, while the saloon bar boasts a welcoming open fire. There is free Wi-Fi throughout, along with a library. Breakfast is served at weekends. Dogs are welcome in the public bar, and a function room is available.
ᴹᴬ🏵🍺(Town)♣P²⌐

New Town Tavern Ⓛ
3 Kendall Road, CO1 2BN
🏵 4 (12 Sat & Sun)-11 ☎ (01206) 869490
Adnams Southwold Bitter; guest beers Ⓗ
Previously known as the Blue Boar, this is a proper free house in the New Town area of Colchester. The welcoming landlord offers up to five ales on handpump, mainly sourced from local breweries, often including a dark beer. Sky Sports is available along with traditional pub games including table football, and bar snacks are served. There is a large alfresco drinking area with a heated smoking shelter. 🏵🍺(Town)🚌(6,61,66)♣²⌐

Odd One Out Ⓛ
28 Mersea Road, CO2 7ET (on B1025)
🏵 4.30 (12 Fri & Sat)-11; 12-10.30 Sun ☎ (01206) 513958
Mauldons Silver Adder; guest beers Ⓗ
The Oddie is a multi CAMRA award-winning pub, including 2012 Pub of the Year and 2010/2011 East Anglian Cider Pub of the Year. Up to five ales are served, always including one dark and one strong. Four real ciders are also available plus a perry. A huge range of whiskies is stocked, along with the famous Nourishing Cheese Rolls. This local is dog-friendly but pay attention to the rules regarding mobile phones. The Oddie has one of the best open fires in town.
ᴹᴬQ🏵🍺(Town)🚌(8A,67,68)♠²⌐

Victoria Inn Ⓛ
10 North Station Road, CO1 1RB (opp Causton Road)
🏵 12-11 (midnight Fri & Sat); 2-11 Sun ☎ (01206) 514510
🌐 victoriainncolchester.co.uk
Crouch Vale Brewers Gold; guest beers Ⓗ

Recently transformed by real ale lovers from Yorkshire, this town pub serves up to four ales, primarily from micros, with many LocAle offerings. Up to four real ciders are also available. The pub is dog friendly, and has a real fire for a winter warmer, plus a sheltered courtyard for those lazy summer days. And with regular live music, quiz nights, traditional games and a monthly cheese club, the Vic is truly a proper pub.
㎡✿≈(North)🚆♣🐾'–

Cold Norton

Norton 🅛

54 Latchingdon Road, CM3 6JB
✪ 4.30 (11.30 Thu)-11; 12-midnight Fri & Sat; 12-11 Sun
☎ (01621) 826948 ⊕ savethenorton.org
Beer range varies Ⓗ
A community pub managed and staffed by 20-30 volunteers, this CAMRA LocAle-accredited free house offers a friendly welcome. At least one locally brewed beer is on handpump, with others sourced from all over the nation (see the website for what's on). CAMRA members benefit from a 10p discount on a pint of real ale. There is a two pint take-away service. Events include the annual beer festival, live music, open mic evenings, organised walks, and ladies' and gents' darts nights. Home-cooked food is available.
⤴✿⓿🗜P'–🍴

Colne Engaine

Five Bells 🅛 ✅

7 Mill Lane, CO6 2HY (2 miles E of Halstead) TL851303
✪ 12-3, 6-11 Mon-Wed; 12-11 Thu-Sun ☎ (01787) 224166
⊕ fivebells.net
Adnams Southwold Bitter; guest beers Ⓗ
A 16th-century free house set in the heart of the village on the Essex-Suffolk border offering a great range of ales from local breweries and micros, with Adnams a permanent feature. The pub has both dining and drinking areas plus a separate restaurant. Outside there is a terrace with a covered and heated space for smokers, which offers great views over the Colne Valley. The pub hosts an annual beer festival and has live music regularly. ㎡Q⤴✿⓿🗜👶♣P'–

Copford

Alma 🅛 ✅

Copford Green, CO6 1BZ
✪ 12-3, 5-11.30 (midnight Fri); 12-midnight Sat; 12-11 Sun
☎ (01206) 210607 ⊕ thealma.org.uk
Greene King IPA, Abbot; Red Fox Hunter's Gold Ⓗ
Picturesque 16th-century village pub offering LocAle Red Fox Hunter's Gold, plus the usual range of Greene King beers and its guests. The spring bank holiday beer festival is well-supported in the various drinking areas and rear garden where you can play garden chess. Lunchtime home-cooked meals are available including a popular Sunday roast, with evening meals served Thursday to Saturday. Free Wi-Fi and sports TV complement monthly quiz nights and local classic motorcycle and car club meetings. ㎡Q✿⓿👶♣P'–

Coxtie Green

White Horse 🅛

173 Coxtie Green Road, CM14 5PX (1 mile W of A128, at jct with Mores Lane) TQ564959
✪ 11.30-11 (midnight Fri & Sat); 12-11 Sun
☎ (01277) 372410
Fuller's London Pride; guest beers Ⓗ
Excellent country free house with a relaxed, friendly atmosphere. There is a comfortable saloon bar and a public bar with TV and dartboard. Seven beers are usually on handpump (soon to increase to 10), including at least one local guest from Brentwood Brewery. The pub has been extended, with larger bars, a new cellar, kitchen and ladies' toilet. There is a large garden at the rear, including a children's play area. A beer festival takes place in July, plus occasional small events. The bus service is limited but reliable. ✿⓿🗜👶🚆(71,72)♣🐾P'–

Duton Hill

Three Horseshoes 🅛

CM6 2DX (½ mile W of B184) TL606268
✪ 12-2.30 (not Mon-Wed; 3 Sat), 6-11; 12-3, 7-10.30 Sun
☎ (01371) 870681
Mighty Oak Captain Bob; guest beers Ⓗ
Cosy village local with a garden, wildlife pond and terrace overlooking the Chelmer Valley and farmland. The landlord hosts a weekend of open-air theatre in July. A millennium beacon in the garden, breweriana and a remarkable collection of Butlins memorabilia are features. Two guest beers are offered and a beer festival is held on the late spring bank holiday in the Duton Hill Den. Look for the pub sign depicting a famous painting, Our Blacksmith, by former local resident Sir George Clausen. ㎡✿👶🚆(313)♣P

Elmdon

Elmdon Dial 🅛

Heydon Lane, CB11 4NH TL461397
✪ closed Mon; 12-3, 6-11; 12-4, 6-10.30 Sun
☎ (01763) 837386 ⊕ theelmdondial.co.uk
Adnams Southwold Bitter; Mighty Oak Oscar Wilde; Taylor Landlord; guest beers Ⓗ
Friendly pub dating from 1450 owned by a real ale enthusiast. Previously called the King's Head, the pub was closed in 1998. After a seven-year planning battle and support from villagers and CAMRA, it was reopened with a new name and pub sign to commemorate a window sundial in the village church. The building was extended in 2006 to provide a modern kitchen and restaurant in addition to a tasteful bar. An à la carte menu is cooked fresh from local ingredients where possible, and changes with the seasons.
㎡Q✿⓿👶🚆♣P'–

Epping

Black Lion ✅

293 High Street, CM16 4DA (at N end of High Street)
✪ 10-11 Mon; 11-11 (midnight Fri & Sat); 12-10.30 Sun
☎ (01992) 578670 ⊕ theblacklionepping.co.uk
Greene King IPA; Young's Special; guest beers Ⓗ
There is a lively atmosphere here with a variety of sports shown live, including football, rugby and boxing. The pub has two bars with another room at the rear and a separate games room with a pool table. Guest beers and seasonal ales change

regularly. Outside there is a large heated smoking area. Bar snacks are available. Situated in the town centre about half a mile from Epping underground station, all buses through Epping stop outside.
୷Ⓐ⊛❻♣P╘

Forest Gate
111 Bell Common, CM16 4DZ (opp Bell Hotel) TL450011
✿ 10-2.30, 5-11; 12-3, 7-10.30 Sun ☎ (01992) 572312
Adnams Southwold Bitter, Broadside; Nethergate IPA
Ⓗ; guest beers Ⓗ/Ⓖ
Genuine free house set in a fine 17th-century building on the edge of Epping Forest and within walking distance from Epping. The pub is frequented by both locals and hikers. Basic food is usually available but the emphasis is very much on serving beer in a traditional atmosphere. There is no TV nor gaming machine. The peaceful setting within is mirrored on the outside as the pub is approached via a quiet lane. The extensive front lawn is popular with summer drinkers.
୷Q⊛❶🖾(213,214,575)♦P

Fuller Street
Square & Compasses Ⓛ
Fairstead, CM3 2BB (1½ miles E off the A131 at Gt Leighs, St Anne's Castle) TL748161
✿ 11.30-3, 5.30-11; 12-midnight Sat; 12-11 Sun
☎ (01245) 361477 ⊕ thesquareandcompasses.co.uk
Nethergate Stoker's IPA; guest beers Ⓖ
Known locally as the Stokehole, this is a 17th-century three-roomed free house with a first floor private dining room. There are exposed beams throughout and two inglenook fireplaces with woodburners. Old local woodworking tools adorn the Taproom Bar. Up to four beers and Westons cider and perry are sold. Food is prepared from locally sourced produce including game from the surrounding estates (not available Sun eve). A summer beer festival is hosted. Local CAMRA Food Pub of the Year 2010. ୷Ⓐ⊛❶🖾P╘

Fyfield
Queen's Head Ⓛ
Queen Street, CM5 0RY (off B184)
✿ 11-3.30 (not Mon), 6-11; 11-11 Sat; 12-10.30 Sun
☎ (01277) 899231 ⊕ thequeensheadfyfield.co.uk
Adnams Southwold Bitter, Broadside; guest beers Ⓗ
Although mainly geared for dining, customers popping in just for a beer are made welcome. An expansion to a new upstairs dining area has relieved previous overcrowding. A lovely garden leading to the River Roding is popular during summer months. Children and dogs are welcome in the garden but not in the pub. Up to three guest beers from independent breweries are normally on offer. No food Monday evenings. Note that this pub usually closes between Christmas and New Year.
୷Q⊛❶♦P

Goldhanger
Chequers ✔
The Square, CM9 8AS (500yds from B1026) TL904088
✿ 11-11; 12-10.30 Sun ☎ (01621) 788203
⊕ thechequersgoldhanger.co.uk
Crouch Vale Brewers Gold; St Austell Tribute; Woodforde's Nelson's Revenge; Young's Bitter; guest beers Ⓗ

Charming 15th-century inn with timbered rooms including a snug and games room with bar billiards. Changing guest ales are served, many locally sourced, and beer festivals are held in March and September. The large food menu offers excellent quality meals, with specials always available. A peaceful suntrap courtyard at the rear is popular in the summer. Local CAMRA Rural Pub of the Year 2011. ୷Q✪⊛❶🖳🖾(95)♣P╘

Grays
Theobald Arms
141 Argent Street, RM17 6HR
✿ 11-11 (midnight Fri & Sat); 12-11 Sun ☎ (01375) 372253
⊕ theobaldarms.com
Beer range varies Ⓗ
Genuine, traditional pub with a public bar that has an unusual hexagonal pool table. The changing selection of four guest beers features local independent breweries, and a range of British bottled beers is also stocked. Regular St George's and summer beer festivals are held in the old stables and on the rear enclosed patio. Lunchtime meals are served Monday to Friday. Darts and cards are played. A former local CAMRA Pub of the Year. ⊛❶❷🖳♣P╘

White Hart ✔
Kings Walk, Argent Street, RM17 6HR
✿ 12-11.30 (midnight Fri & Sat; 11 Sun) ☎ (01375) 373319
⊕ whitehartgrays.co.uk
Crouch Vale Brewers Gold; Sharp's White Hart Ale; guest beers Ⓗ
Traditional local just outside the town centre, rejuvenated since it was taken over in 2006. Two regular ales, including the house beer, White Hart, are supplemented by three guests and many bottled Belgian beers. There is a meeting/function room available and a beer garden. Darts and pool are played and sport is screened on TV. Live blues bands play on alternate Thursdays, and a beer festival is held in February/March. Local CAMRA Pub of the Year 2011. ୷Ⓐ⊛❶❷🖳🖾♣P╘

Great Chesterford
Crown & Thistle
High Street, CB10 1PL (near B1383)
✿ 12-3, 6-midnight; 12-3, 7-11 (not winter eve) Sun
☎ (01799) 530278
Adnams Southwold Bitter; Fuller's London Pride; guest beers Ⓗ
In an interesting village, this popular venue is frequented by locals, including the cricket team. The pub, built in 1528 and originally called the Chequers, was renamed and extended in 1603 to serve as a coaching inn. According to legend, James I stopped here on his way to London for his coronation. The magnificent inglenook fireplace in the bar is the earliest example of its type in Essex. A patio has seating for outdoor drinking and eating, with a heated smoking area. ୷Q⊛❶Å❄🖾P╘

Great Easton
Swan
The Endway, CM6 2HG (off B184) TL606255
✿ 12-3, 6-11; 12-3, 7-10.30 (not winter eve) Sun
☎ (01371) 870359 ⊕ swangreateaston.co.uk
Adnams Southwold Bitter; guest beers Ⓗ

A warm welcome is assured at this 15th-century free house in an attractive village. A log-burning stove, exposed beams and comfortable sofas feature in the lounge, while pool and darts are played in the public bar. Featured in CAMRA's Good Pub Food guide, all meals are prepared to order from fresh local produce, including the chips. The chef looks after the beers, chosen to complement the food. Accommodation is now available in four superb double rooms. ≜Q✿✲◐Φ✎♣P

Great Leighs

St Anne's Castle
Main Road, CM3 1NE
✪ 12-midnight (1am Fri & Sat) ☎ (01245) 361253
⊕ stannnescastle.co.uk
Beer range varies Ⓗ
A claimant to the title of oldest inn in England – the first to get a licence, in 1171 – and also reputedly haunted. The pub sign, depicting St Anne, won the Inn Sign Society's national award in 2011. There is a small public bar with darts and pool, and a larger bar where live music of all types takes place at least twice a week. Four changing beers are always available. ≜✿◐Φ✤▲🚲(70,352)♣P≟

Halstead

Dog Inn
37 Hedingham Road, CO9 2DB (on A1124)
✪ 4 (12 Sat)-11; 12-10.30 Sun ☎ (01787) 477774
⊕ innpubs.com/dog.php
Adnams Southwold Bitter; guest beers Ⓗ
Traditional local pub just two minutes' walk from the town centre. There are two separate drinking areas carpeted throughout and up to five ales are served, usually including a dark beer. Beer festivals are hosted at Easter and in October. Quizzes as part of the local league are held each Thursday and there is occasional live music. A large-screen TV shows primarily football and rugby. The large garden to the rear has a pétanque court and offers excellent rural views. ≜Q✿✲◐Φ🚲(88)♣●P≟

Harlow

Horns & Horseshoes Ⓛ
Foster Street, CM17 9HX
✪ 11.30-11 (1am Fri & Sat; 8 Sun) ☎ (01279) 422667
⊕ hornsandhorseshoes.co.uk
Courage Best Bitter; guest beers Ⓗ
A friendly family-run pub, still with original beams that are covered with a unique collection of brass containers of all sizes. It usually serves three or four guest beers sourced from local breweries. The spacious L-shaped bar has comfortable furniture for dining and drinking and a large open fireplace at one end. Fresh home-made food is prepared to order using local produce, including fresh fish on Friday. Outside there is an attractive garden, covered smoking area and a children's play space facing paddocks and stables. Entertainment is hosted on Saturdays. ✿◐P≟

Harwich

Alma Inn ✔
25 Kings Head Street, CO12 3EE
✪ 12-11 (midnight Fri & Sat) ☎ (01255) 318681
⊕ almaharwich.co.uk
Adnams Southwold Bitter, Broadside; guest beers Ⓗ

Enthusiastic new owners ensure a welcome return to the Guide for this historic pub. A tasteful refurbishment makes the most of the large main bar, which still manages to feel cosy. A corridor bar, back room and modest yard provide alternative places to sit and enjoy a quiet pint. Food, ranging from bar snacks to sumptuous meals, is served alongside a good selection of real ales, generally including offerings from Adnams and the Harwich Town Brewery.
≜✿◐≢(Town)🚲(103,104,102)♣

New Bell Inn
Outpart Eastward, CO12 3EN
✪ 11-3, 7-11 (midnight Fri & Sat); 12-4, 7-11 (12-11 summer) Sun ☎ (01255) 503545
Mighty Oak Oscar Wilde; guest beers Ⓗ
Home from home for a diverse and enthusiastic regular crowd as well as a welcoming haven for visitors to the old sea port, the New Bell is at the heart of its community. Beers from near and far are expertly cared for and served by knowledgeable staff, and the wholesome, hearty lunchtime food is popular. The front bar houses the pub's impressive collection of snow globes. A modest walled garden to the rear provides a tranquil space in the summer. Q✿◐Φ≢(Town)🚲(103,104,102)P

Hatfield Broad Oak

Cock Inn
High Street, CM22 7HF TL546164
✪ 12-11 (12.30am Fri & Sat); 12-10.30 Sun
☎ (01279) 718306
Adnams Southwold Bitter; Woodforde's Wherry; guest beers Ⓗ
Friendly village local that preserves a traditional atmosphere. Elegant but simple furniture and décor appropriately reflect the historic feel of the 16th-century Grade II-listed building. Sensibly priced meals using local produce are served in the main bar until 9pm daily (4pm Sun). A second bar accommodates the dartboard and satellite sports viewing; the third room is normally quiet. In the summer the pavement-side seating offers an opportunity to watch village life drift gently by.
≜Q✿✿◐Φ🚲(5,347)♣P

Hazeleigh

Royal Oak Ⓛ
Fambridge Road, Maldon, CM9 6PE
✪ 12-11 ☎ (01621) 853249 ⊕ the-royal-oak-maldon.co.uk
Adnams Southwold Bitter; Crouch Vale Brewers Gold; Dark Star Hophead; Farmer's Ales Dark Horse; Mighty Oak Oscar Wilde; Wibblers Apprentice Ⓗ
A friendly country pub, known as the Hazeleigh Oak, on the outskirts of Maldon, serving at least five ales from handpump and gravity. A selection of locally brewed ales is always on offer along with cider and perry. Food is available every lunchtime plus barbecues in the summer. The pub has a community feel about it: it hosts quiz nights, live folk music every third Friday in the month, and there are darts, shove-ha'penny, cards and dominoes available. The large garden overlooks farmland. A warm welcome awaits you.
≜Q✿◐Φ●P≟

Hempstead

Bluebell Inn
High Street, CB10 2PD (on B1054)
☼ 12-3, 6-11; 12-11 Fri & Sat; 12-8 (winter hours vary) Sun
☎ (01799) 599199
Adnams Southwold Bitter, Broadside; Woodforde's Wherry; guest beers H
Late 16th-century village pub with 18th-century additions, reputed to be the birthplace of Dick Turpin; the bar displays posters about his life. Six beers are usually available. The restaurant serves excellent meals from an extensive menu and the large bar has a log fire. Ample seating is provided outside, plus a children's play area. A folk evening is hosted on a Tuesday. ♨Q❀◑▭♣P⅃

Henham

Cock L
Church End, CM22 6AL (1 mile off B1051) TL546287
☼ 12-3, 5-11; 12-midnight Thu-Sun ☎ (01279) 850347
Greene King IPA; Sharp's Doom Bar; guest beers H
Traditional village pub in residential surroundings with outdoor seating at the front and a garden at the rear. The main and snug bars both have open fires. The snug has a large TV where major sporting events are screened. A large separate dining room is next to the bar. The Saffron Brewery is 100 yards away and one of its beers is always available here. There are regular quiz nights. No food on Sunday evening. ♨Q❀◑P

Herongate Tye

Olde Dog Inn L
129 Billericay Road, CM13 3SD (E of A128) TQ641909
☼ 11.30 (12 Sat)-11; 12-10.30 Sun ☎ (01277) 810337
⊕ theoldedoginn.co.uk
Crouch Vale Brewers Gold; Greene King Abbot H**; guest beers** G
This 17th-century weatherboarded free house is family owned and run, offering a variety of real ales. It has three regularly changing guest beers sourced from countrywide microbreweries, along with more established national brands and its own Olde Dog IPA brewed locally by Crouch Vale. Food is available at the bar, or in the separate restaurant area. The decor is traditional, with a variety of beer mats adorning the walls and ceilings. ♨❀◑&P⅃

Hockley

White Hart
274 Main Road, SS5 4NS
☼ 11-11; 12-10.30 Sun ☎ (01702) 203438
⊕ whiteharthockley.co.uk
Beer range varies H
A well-established friendly local, dating from the 18th century, facing the village green. The pub is community-oriented and supportive of local charities through its quiz nights and music events. Up to three changing guest ales are served. Lunchtime food is available all week, including roasts on Sunday, with evening meals served Tuesday-Saturday. Sporting events are shown in the separate function room. There is a large rear garden with seating and a patio area, plus picnic tables at the front. Q❀◑⇌▭(7,8)P

Horndon-on-the-Hill

Bell Inn
High Road, SS17 8LD (almost opp Woolmarket)
☼ 11-2.30 (3 Sat), 5.30-11; 12-4, 7-10.30 Sun
☎ (01375) 642463 ⊕ bell-inn.co.uk
Crouch Vale Brewers Gold H**; Draught Bass** G**; Greene King IPA; guest beers** H
Popular 15th-century coaching inn, where the beamed bars feature wood panelling and carvings. Note the unusual hot cross bun collection – a bun has been added every Good Friday for more than 100 years. Three regular beers are available, including ales from Essex breweries, plus up to four guests. The award-winning restaurant is open daily, lunchtimes and evenings, but it can get busy, so booking is advisable. Accommodation is available in 16 bedrooms.
♨Q❀⇌◑&▭(373)P⅃

Kirby-le-Soken

Red Lion
32 The Street, CO13 0EF
☼ 11 (12 winter)-11 ☎ (01255) 674832
Beer range varies H
Friendly village pub serving good home-cooked meals and fine ales. It is steeped in history and has a plethora of oak beams, a log fire in winter and, reputedly, a priest hole and a resident ghost. There is an excellent flower display in the summer and plenty of outdoor seating. The large garden has a dedicated children's play area and can cater for weddings. ♨Q❀◑●P

Lamarsh

Lamarsh Lion
Bures Road, CO8 5EP (1¼ miles NW of Bures) TL892355
☼ 12-11 (10.30 Sun) ☎ (01787) 227918
Adnams Southwold Bitter H**/**G**; Greene King IPA; guest beers** H
Rural 14th-century pub with fine views across the Stour Valley. The pub comprises a mixture of both stone flooring and carpeted areas, and comfortable seating is available throughout. A separate dining area offers a varied menu combined with regular specials. There is also a games room with a large-screen TV and sofa seating. Cyclists and ramblers are welcome and there is a large open fire to relax by. The large garden area includes a Wendy House to amuse the children. ♨⏴❀◑&♣P⅃

Layer-de-la-Haye

Layer Fox L
2 Malting Green Road, CO2 0JH (on B1026) TL968200
☼ 9am-11.30 (midnight Fri-Sun) ☎ (01206) 738723
⊕ thelayerfox.co.uk
Red Fox Bitter; guest beers H
Single-bar pub with various comfortable seating areas, plus a large child-friendly garden. Up to four beers are offered on handpump, mainly from local breweries. A varied and interesting menu is available, with Sunday roasts and a monthly curry night. A large fire and a pool table can be found in a separate room. Open daily from 9am with a delicatessen counter, PayPoint and cash machine. Accommodation is available in the Sleepy Fox B&B chalets. ♨Q⏴❀⇌◑▭(50)♣P⅃

Leigh-on-Sea

Crooked Billet 🍺 ✅
51 High Street, SS9 2EP (½ mile E of Leigh station)
⏰ 12-11 (10.30 Sun) ☎ (01702) 480289
Adnams Southwold Bitter; Sharp's Doom Bar; guest beers Ⓗ
This classic historic pub is at the heart of Old Leigh, a fishing village overlooking the Thames Estuary. Local CAMRA Pub of the Year 2012, it has two bars with bare floorboards and beamed ceilings. The walls are adorned with local fishing pictures. Beer tasting evenings are held occasionally. Traditional pub food is served daily. A small garden to the side is complemented by a large (but shared) waterside seating area. Popular in the summer, as is the Thornbridge Jaipur when available. Q❀⊄◗≠🚋

Elms Ⓛ ✅
1060 London Road, SS9 3ND (on A13)
⏰ 8am-midnight (1am Fri & Sat) ☎ (01702) 474687
Greene King Abbot; Ruddles Best Bitter; guest beers Ⓗ
Old coaching inn converted by Wetherspoon into a large, open pub decorated with old photos of the local area. Breakfast is available until noon, plus main meals and snacks until 10pm. Children are admitted until 9pm. Up to six changing guest ales including two LocAles and up to three Westons real ciders are served. There is no music but there are fruit machines and muted TVs. Outside is a paved, heated and covered area for smokers and a hedged front garden. ❀⊄◗&🚋🛒P≛

Little Bromley

Haywain Ⓛ
Bentley Road, CO11 2PL
⏰ closed Mon; 12-2.30 (not Tue), 6-10.30 (11 Fri & Sat); 12-5 Sun ☎ (01206) 390004 ⊕ thehaywain.co.uk
Adnams Southwold Bitter; guest beers Ⓗ
A traditional 18th-century free house, family-run by Dawn, Andy and Ernie, serving three to four real ales, with Nethergate and other Essex and Suffolk micros featuring regularly. The pub boasts two open fires in a comfortable beamed environment. Home-cooked food is served, including a number of vegetarian options. There is a large function room, with its own bar and toilets with wheelchair access. ♨❀⊄◗&🚋(2)P≛

Little Thurrock

Traitor's Gate
40-42 Broadway, RM17 6EW (on A126)
⏰ 3 (1 Fri)-11; 12-11 Sat; 12-10.30 Sun ☎ (01375) 372628
Beer range varies Ⓗ
Four guest beers are on offer, with forthcoming ales displayed on a blackboard above the bar, as well as two ciders on draught. This friendly hostelry has a wide and varied clientele, mostly local, showing how a good pub attracts a good trade. It boasts a bar billiards table. Sport is shown on large-screen TVs. Two beer festivals are held annually in April and August. The beer garden has won Thurrock in Bloom awards in recent years. It was voted local CAMRA Pub of the Year for 2010. ❀🚋(66)♣🌶≛

Little Walden

Crown
High Street, CB10 1XA (on B1052)
⏰ 11.30-2.30 (3 Sat), 6-11; 12-10.30 Sun ☎ (01799) 522475
⊕ thecrownlittlewalden.co.uk
Adnams Broadside; Greene King IPA, Abbot; Woodforde's Wherry; guest beers Ⓖ
Charming 18th-century beamed pub in a quiet hamlet. A feature is a large walk-through fireplace. The pub is popular with diners, especially at weekends, when booking is advisable. Evening meals are available Tuesday to Saturday. An excellent range of beers is dispensed direct from casks, which can be enjoyed on the covered patio area. The pub hosts traditional jazz on Wednesday evenings and has a function room for club meetings and private parties. ♨Q❀⊯◗🚋P

Littley Green

Compasses 🍺 Ⓛ ✅
CM3 1BU (turn off B1417 at former Ridley's Brewery, Hartford End) TL699172
⏰ 12-3, 5.30-midnight; 12-midnight Thu-Sun
☎ (01245) 362308 ⊕ compasseslittleygreen.co.uk
Adnams Southwold Bitter; guest beers Ⓖ
Local CAMRA Pub of the Year 2012, the former Ridley's Brewery tap is a picturesque Victorian country pub in a quiet hamlet. Beers are drawn direct from the cask in the half-cellar. The renowned filled huffers (giant baps) are available lunchtimes and evenings. There are seats and tables outside and in the large gardens. A folk evening is held monthly. Two or three guest beers are from local breweries, usually including one from Bishop Nick, and real ciders and perries are available. ♨Q❀⊯◗♣🌶P

Loughton

Victoria Tavern
165 Smarts Lane, IG10 4BP (off A121 at edge of forest)
⏰ 11-3, 5-11; 11-10.30 Sun ☎ (020) 8508 1779
Adnams Southwold Bitter; Greene King IPA; guest beers Ⓗ
Traditional pub on the edge of Epping Forest with one large and one small interconnected dark wood-panelled bar. It is decorated with old photos of West Ham United football teams and the local area, bottles and a small display of barrel bushes. Generous portions of well-cooked pub fare are served daily. There is occasionally a real fire in the bar. The pub is popular with locals, enjoys a lively atmosphere, and has occasional quizzes and charity events. Q❀⊯◗&⊖🚋(20,167)P≛

Maldon

Blue Boar Hotel Ⓛ
Silver Street, CM9 4QE (opp All Saints Church)
⏰ 11-11 ☎ (01621) 855888 ⊕ blueboarhotel.com
Adnams Southwold Bitter; Farmer's Ales Drop of Nelson's Blood, Pucks Folly, Golden Boar, seasonal beers Ⓖ
In this popular 14th-century coaching inn's two bars you will find original oak beams, a large brick fireplace, hunting trophies and maritime oil paintings. Farmer's Ales, brewed in the inn's stable block, are served by gravity in the rear bar. Further impressive oak beams may be found in the large function room over the bars, used by local folk and

jazz groups. Meals and bar snacks are available lunchtimes and evenings. Local CAMRA Pub of the Year for 2010 and 2011, it hosts two annual beer festivals. ▲Q🕮🍴◑ ⬕🖵(31,31X,75)P⁵🎁

Queen Victoria 🅛
Spital Road, CM9 6ED
✪ 11 (12 Sun)-11 ☎ (01621) 852923
Farmer's Ales Pucks Folly; Greene King IPA, Abbot; Wibblers Apprentice Ⓗ
A warm, friendly and comfortable Gray & Sons pub on the main road into Maldon, fronted by attractive hanging baskets. A single bar serves three linked rooms and offers four well-kept beers, including two from local breweries. A comprehensive menu of good home-cooked food, with many healthy eating options, is available lunchtimes and evenings. This is a popular community local, proud of its darts and dominoes teams. It is served by regular buses from Chelmsford.
🕮◑⬕க🖵(31,31X)♣P⁵

Queen's Head 🅛
The Hythe, CM9 5HN
✪ 11-11 (midnight Fri & Sat; 10.30 Sun) ☎ (01621) 854112
⊕ thequeensheadmaldon.co.uk
Adnams Southwold Bitter; Dark Star Hophead; Farmer's Ales Pucks Folly; Greene King IPA; Taylor Landlord; guest beers Ⓗ
A pleasant old coaching house on the river Blackwater at Maldon Quay, which is home to a fleet of Thames barges. It has a spacious riverside outdoor seating area with several large sun umbrellas. The front bar has a warming log fire and is a local meeting place. Fresh home-cooked food is served all day in the bars or the separate restaurant. Well-behaved children and dogs are welcome. Good disabled access and WC facilities.
▲Q🕮◑⬕க♣⁵

Margaretting Tye

White Hart Inn 🅛
Swan Lane, CM4 9JX TL684011
✪ 11.30-midnight (1am Fri-Sat); 12-midnight Sun
☎ (01277) 840478 ⊕ thewhitehart.uk.com
Adnams Southwold Bitter, Broadside; Mighty Oak IPA, Oscar Wilde; Red Fox Hunter's Gold; guest beers Ⓖ
Slightly off the beaten track, this fine pub has origins in the 17th century. Known for good food and ale, it generally offers two or three guest beers. Regular club meetings are held here for cyclists, car owners, ramblers and young farmers. Very much community-focused, a book stall raises money for charities, and beer festivals are held in July and November. ▲Q🚃🕮🍴◑க♣P⁵

Mill Green

Viper ★ 🅛
Mill Green Road, CM4 0PT TL641018
✪ 12-3, 6-11; 12-11 Sat; 12-10.30 Sun ☎ (01277) 352010
Mighty Oak Oscar Wilde; Viper Ales Jake the Snake, VIPA; guest beers Ⓗ
One of only a couple of pubs in the country with this name, the Viper is an isolated, unspoilt country pub with a lounge, public bar and wood-panelled snug. Jake the Snake is occasionally replaced by another Viper ale, commissioned from Mighty Oak and Nethergate, who also sometimes supply the two guest beers, although these may come from anywhere. Good home-cooked food is served at

lunchtime, and Westons cider is stocked. Beer festivals are held at Easter and over the August bank holiday. ▲Q🕮◑⬕♣ⓦP⁵

Monk Street

Farmhouse Inn 🅛
CM6 2NR (off B184, 2 miles S of Thaxted) TL612287
✪ 11-midnight (11 Sun) ☎ (01371) 830864
⊕ farmhouseinn.org
Greene King IPA; Mighty Oak Maldon Gold, seasonal beers Ⓗ
Built in the 16th century, this former Dunmow Brewery pub has been enlarged to incorporate a restaurant and accommodation; the bar is in the original part of the building. The quiet hamlet of Monk Street overlooks the Chelmer Valley, two miles from historic Thaxted. A disused well in the garden supplied the hamlet with water during World War II. The pub has a rear patio, front garden and a top field. Draught cider from Westons is usually sold in summer. Q🕮🍴◑க🖵(313)ⓦP⁵

Mount Bures

Thatchers Arms 🏆 🅛 ✅
Hall Road, CO8 5AT TL905319
✪ closed Mon; 12-3, 6-11; 12-11 Sat & Sun
☎ (01787) 227460 ⊕ thatchersarms.co.uk
Adnams Southwold Bitter; Crouch Vale Brewers Gold; guest beers Ⓗ
Family- and dog-friendly pub on the Essex/Suffolk border that offers exceptional views of the Stour Valley and in 2012 was local CAMRA Pub of the Year for the second year running. Up to five ales are offered, many LocAle, plus a good range of bottled British craft ales. The sumptuous menu is primarily sourced from local suppliers. Bar billiards is available and films are shown on Thursday nights in the cinema. There are beer festivals each spring and winter. Camping is available in the garden.
🕮◑♨♣P⁵

Old Harlow

Queen's Head 🅛
26 Churchgate Street, CM17 0JT TL483114
✪ 11.45-3, 5 (6 Sat)-11; 12-4, 7-10.30 (not winter) Sun
☎ (01279) 427266
Adnams Southwold Bitter; Crouch Vale Brewers Gold; Nethergate IPA Ⓗ
A traditional pub in a rural village setting. The building dates from the reign of Henry VIII when two adjoining cottages were constructed. It first started selling ale in 1750 when the two dwellings were merged to become the village inn. Wooden beams emphasise the historic feel in both the main bar and a smaller lounge that offers a welcoming open fire in winter. The beer range highlights East Anglian breweries. A full range of food is served.
▲Q🕮◑⬕🖵(7,59)P⁵

Paglesham

Punch Bowl
Church End, SS4 2DP (signed from Rochford)
✪ 11.30-3 (2.30 Mon), 6.30-11 (10 Mon); 12-10.30 Sun
☎ (01702) 258376
Adnams Southwold Bitter; Sharp's Doom Bar; guest beers Ⓗ
A 16th-century, south-facing building clad in white Essex board, formerly a bakers and sailmakers.

Situated in a quiet one-street village, it has been an ale house since the mid-1800s and was reputedly used by smugglers. The low-beamed single bar is adorned with a large collection of mugs, old local pictures and brassware. The small cosy restaurant next to the bar serves excellent reasonably priced food. Picnic tables are to the front of the pub. Q⚜🌢🌓♣P⅄

Pentlow

Pinkuah Arms

Pinkuah Lane, CO10 7JW (off B1064 in small lane, opp red phone box) TL816448
🌢 12-midnight (7 Mon & Sun) ☎ (01787) 280857
⊕ pinkuaharms.co.uk
Woodforde's Wherry; guest beers Ⓗ
Quite hard to find, this country pub is 350 years old, named after two spinsters who lived here. It has been tastefully refurbished, with beams, wooden floorboards, a low ceiling in part and a log fire. It has an interesting and varied menu with a good choice of Sunday roasts, and the credit crunch lunch is popular. There is outdoor seating. The pub offers many specials (quiz nights, steak nights) and themed menus. Westons Old Rosie is on handpump. Child- and dog-friendly. ♨Q⚜🌢🌓🐾P

Purleigh

Bell Ⓛ

The Street, CM3 6QJ
🌢 closed Mon; 11.30 (12 Sat)-3, 6-11; 12-4 Sun
☎ (01621) 828348 ⊕ purleighbell.co.uk
Adnams Southwold Bitter; Mighty Oak Captain Bob; guest beers Ⓗ
Traditional village pub dating back to the 14th century, standing on a hill with far-reaching views over the Blackwater Estuary. The interior includes an open fire in a large inglenook, three heavily beamed dining areas and a hop-decorated bar. Up to four ales are offered, with guests often from local microbreweries. The Bell has a reputation for good food, with a strong emphasis on seafood. It was once the home of George Washington's great-great-great grandfather, allegedly. ♨Q⚜🌢🌓♣P⅄

Ramsden Heath

Fox & Hounds Ⓛ

Church Road, CM11 1PW
🌢 12-midnight (11 Sun) ☎ (01268) 711625
⊕ foxandhoundsramsden.co.uk
Beer range varies Ⓗ
Friendly and welcoming village pub with three handpumps plus two real ales on stillage, and very supportive of local breweries such as Vens and Wibblers. It is community-focused, with quizzes, a golf society and many charity events, and puts on a popular summer beer festival. Good-value food, using fresh local produce, is served Tuesday to Saturday. Sunday lunches are a speciality (bookings preferred). Enjoy the huge beer garden in summer and the real fire in winter. ♨⚜🌓P⅄

Rayleigh

Roebuck ✓

138 High Street, SS6 7BU (close to library)
🌢 9am-midnight (1am Fri & Sat) ☎ (01268) 748430
Greene King Abbot; Ruddles Best Bitter; guest beers Ⓗ

Friendly Wetherspoon pub in the High Street located on the site of Reverend James Pilkington's Baptist School. It stocks an excellent range of guest beers. Children are welcome in a sectioned-off area for food. Meals are served all day until 11pm. Outdoor drinking and smoking is permitted in an area at the front and side. Wi-Fi is available. Rayleigh is served by many buses and a rail station. Q⚜🌢🌓♿⇌🚌(1,7,8)🐾⅄

Ridgewell

White Horse Inn Ⓛ

Mill Road, CO9 4SG (on A1017) TL736407
🌢 12 (6 Mon & Tue)-11 ☎ (01440) 785532
⊕ ridgewellwhitehorse.com
Beer range varies Ⓖ
CAMRA award-winning pub with a changing choice of beers, always including a dark mild, all gravity-dispensed, as are the two or three real ciders. The first week in March is the dark winter ale festival, and the first weekend in August the summer beer festival. This venue is famed locally for an excellent wine selection as well as for its home-made steak and ale pies and puddings, featuring local ingredients wherever possible. Luxury 4-star accommodation is available at reasonable prices and there are seasonal afternoon teas. ♨⚜🛏🌓♿♣🐾P⅄

Rochford

Golden Lion Ⓛ

35 North Street, SS4 1AB (200m N of town square)
🌢 11-midnight (1am Fri & Sat) ☎ (01702) 545487
⊕ goldenlionrochford.co.uk
Adnams Southwold Bitter; Greene King Abbot; Mighty Oak Maldon Gold; guest beers Ⓗ
Multi-award-winning pub situated within the town centre conservation area. A small 16th-century free house, it is covered in traditional Essex weatherboard, with stained glass windows and a pretty patio garden to the rear. The decor includes hops above the bar and a fireplace with a traditional logburner. Six ales are always available including three changing guests (one usually a dark beer) from local micros, and a real cider. This true community local has its own cricket team. ♨⚜🌓⇌🚌(7,8,60)🐾⅄

Horse & Groom Ⓛ

1 Southend Road, SS4 1HA
🌢 11.30 (12 Sun)-11 ☎ (01702) 544015
Mighty Oak Maldon Gold; guest beers Ⓗ
A fine locals' pub, a few minutes' walk from the town centre and station. Winner of local CAMRA Town Pub of the Year 2012, the guest ales include a selection from Essex breweries as well as from further afield. A real cider is always available. The separate restaurant provides good-value food, especially on Fridays when a varied fish menu is on offer. Evening meals are served most days, but it is best to check first. A function room is available for hire. ♨⚜🌓⇌🚌(7,8)🐾P⅄

Rowhedge

Olde Albion

High Street, CO5 7ES (3 miles SE of Colchester)
🌢 12-3 (not Mon), 5-11; 12-11 Thu-Sat; 12-10.30 Sun
☎ (01206) 728972 ⊕ yeoldealbion.co.uk
Beer range varies Ⓗ/Ⓖ

Friendly pub overlooking the River Colne with riverside seating available in summer. There is wooden flooring throughout the split-level pub, which has one bar and various seating areas. Beer festivals are held for St George's Day and the summer regatta, plus a mini festival each October. This free house offers a varied beer range from handpump and occasionally from gravity. There is live music on the last Saturday of each month. Biff, the friendliest pub dog, looks forward to welcoming you. ⚏⊛🚃(66)♣⌐

Saffron Walden

Old English Gentleman ▾
11 Gold Street, CB10 1EJ (E of B184/B1052 jct)
☼ 11-11 (midnight Tue-Thu; 1am Fri & Sat)
☎ (01799) 523595 ⊕ oldenglishgentleman.com
Adnams Southwold Bitter; Woodforde's Wherry; guest beers ⊞
An 18th-century town-centre pub with log fires and a welcoming atmosphere. It serves a selection of guest ales and an extensive menu of bar food and sandwiches that changes regularly. Traditional roasts and chef's specials are available on Sunday in the bar or the dining area, where a variety of works of art is displayed. Saffron Walden is busy on Tuesday and Saturday market days. There is a heated patio at the rear. Local CAMRA Pub of the Year 2012. ⚏⊛℄⌐

Railway
Station Road, CB11 3HQ (300yds SE of war memorial)
☼ 12-3, 6-11 (midnight Thu-Sat); 12-11 Sun
☎ (01799) 522208
Young's Bitter; guest beers ⊞
Typical 19th-century town-centre railway tavern, now opened out. Railway memorabilia, including a model train trundling back and forth above the bar, add a nice touch. Six handpumps feature Elgood's and Mighty Oak guest beers. Beer festivals are held at Easter (24 beers) and Whitsun (12 beers). The pub also has Erdinger Weissbier on draught, as well as an extensive food menu available lunchtimes and evenings. There are occasional live bands, with folk and blue grass prevailing. ⊛℄P⌐

Temeraire ✔
55 High Street, CB10 1AA
☼ 9am-midnight (1am Fri & Sat) ☎ (01799) 516975
Beer range varies ⊞
Fine Georgian building that was once a working men's club. At least one local beer from either Mighty Oak or Nethergate is always available. In addition to the regular Wetherspoon beer festivals, the pub hosts occasional Meet the Brewer sessions and beer tastings. It was the winner of a regional Wetherspoon food award, hosts a Monday quiz night, and always stocks draught ciders. Families are welcome, and there is a large garden and a covered smoking area. ⊛℄℉🚃(5,301,312)♠P⌐

Shalford

George ℓ ✔
The Street, CM7 5HH
☼ 12-3, 5-midnight; 12-midnight Sat & Sun
☎ (01371) 850207 ⊕ thegeorgeinnshalford.co.uk
Adnams Southwold Bitter; Greene King IPA; Woodforde's Wherry ⊞
Attractively beamed 15th-century inn, at the centre of village life. In summer it is pleasant to sit outside

on the patio, while in winter the roaring log fire draws you in. A true local, it attracts both drinkers and diners, and has a separate dining area. Various clubs and social events feature throughout the year including a summer beer festival. Shalford Brewery beers are always available. ⚏Q⊛℄℉㉄🚃♣P⌐

South Hanningfield

Old Windmill ℓ
South Hanningfield Road, CM3 8HT
☼ 12-11 (10.30 Sun) ☎ (01268) 712280
⊕ brunningandprice.co.uk/oldwindmill
Brunning & Price Original; guest beers ⊞
The Old Windmill was built in 1702 and has been a pub since 1799. It still retains much of the old architecture and all of the great atmosphere. The bar is the heart of the building, with dining areas and a restaurant surrounding it. Six real ales are on handpump, with five guests including at least two LocAles. An extensive food menu ranges from sandwiches to steaks. It is close to Hanningfield Reservoir, an Essex Wildlife Trust nature reserve. ⚏⊛℄℉🚃(15,15A)P⌐

Southend-on-Sea

Last Post ℓ ✔
Weston Road, SS1 1AS
☼ 9-midnight (1am Fri & Sat) ☎ (01702) 431682
Greene King Abbot; Ruddles Best Bitter; guest beers ⊞
The Last Post's décor reflects the building's former use as Southend's central post office. A well-managed and knowledgeable team has turned this into one of Wetherspoon's finest venues. The extensive beer range features Brentwood and Wibblers breweries (both LocAle) and Nethergate is also supported. Up to five ciders can be found. Situated just off the High Street, the pub is close to public transport and gets busy at weekends and for some live televised football matches. Q℄℉㉄(Central/Victoria)🚃♠⌐

Olde Trout Tavern ℓ
56 London Road, SS1 1NX (opp Sainsbury's)
☼ 11-11 (midnight Fri & Sat); 12-11 Sun ☎ (01702) 337000
⊕ theoldtrout.webs.com
George's Trout Ale; guest beers ⊞
Modern town-centre pub within walking distance of Southend High Street and both mainline railway stations. The house beer, George's Trout Ale, is from a local brewery in Great Wakering, with three other changing guests, often from other Essex breweries. Westons Traditional Scrumpy is served on handpump. Strong bottled beer is also available. Hot meals and snacks are served 12-7pm (4pm Sun). A quiz night is held fortnightly on Sundays. ℄㉄(Victoria/Central)♠⌐

Southminster

Station Arms ℓ
39 Station Road, CM0 7EW (near B1021)
☼ 12-2.30, 6 (5.30 Fri)-11; 2-11 Sat; 12-4, 7-10.30 Sun
☎ (01621) 772225 ⊕ thestationarms.co.uk
Adnams Southwold Bitter; Mighty Oak Oscar Wilde; guest beers ⊞
This is a classic among Essex weatherboarded pubs. Two beer festivals are held in January and May in an adjoining outbuilding to the rear, and a courtyard provides a pleasant place to enjoy the

excellent and varied range of ales throughout the seasons – weather permitting. Music nights showcase blues on the third Saturday and folk on the first Friday monthly. There is a darts team and weekly meat raffle. The pub has featured in the Guide for 22 consecutive years.
△Q✿≠➡(31X)♣♠⌐

Stanford-le-Hope

Rising Sun ♥ Ⓛ
Church Hill, SS17 0EU (opp church and near A1014)
✿ 3-10.30; 12-midnight Thu-Sun ☎ (01375) 671097
Beer range varies Ⓗ
Much-improved single-bar traditional town pub in the shadow of the church. The five guest beers are mainly from independent breweries, including LocAles, and up to three ciders or perries are stocked. Freshly prepared, locally sourced food is served Sunday lunchtime in a dining area at one end of the bar. Fortnightly cash quiz nights are held to raise money for a local charity. Beer festivals are hosted three times a year, in spring, summer and winter. Local CAMRA Pub of the Year 2012.
✿◑≠➡(11,100,200)♣♠P⌐

Stansted Mountfitchet

Rose & Crown
31 Bentfield Green, CM24 8HX (½ mile W of B1383)
✿ 12-3, 6-midnight; 12-10 Sun ☎ (01279) 812107
Adnams Southwold Bitter; guest beers Ⓗ
Typical family-run Victorian pub near a duckpond on the edge of a small hamlet. This free house has been modernised to provide one large bar but retains the atmosphere of a village inn and is well-used by locals. The front of the pub is brightened by floral displays. Food is traditional and good value, made from locally sourced produce (no meals Sun eve). Guest beers are from local breweries. The smoking area is covered and heated. Children and dogs are welcome.
△✿◑➡(7)♣P⌐

Stebbing

White Hart Ⓛ
High Street, CM6 3SQ
✿ 11-3, 5-11; 11-11 Sat; 12-10.30 Sun ☎ (01371) 856383
Hart of Stebbing IPA; Wells Eagle IPA Ⓗ
Friendly 15th-century timbered inn in a picturesque village. This comfortable pub features exposed beams, an open fire, eclectic collections from chamber pots to cigarette cards, an old red post box in an interior wall, and a section of exposed lath and plaster wall behind a glass screen. The Hart of Stebbing microbrewery opened in 2007 in the garage at the rear, producing one main beer and occasional specials, currently only available in the pub and at local beer festivals. Good-value food is served daily. There is a patio and a covered gazebo with heater. △Q✿◑➡♣P⌐

Steeple Bumpstead

Fox & Hounds ✔
3 Chapel Street, CB9 7DQ
✿ 12-3, 5-11; 12-11 Fri & Sat; 12-3, 7-11 Sun
☎ (01440) 731810 ⊕ foxinsteeple.co.uk
Beer range varies Ⓗ
A friendly welcome awaits at this cosy local in the centre of the village. It has a main bar with an

open fire and access to a rear courtyard area; two other rooms are mainly used for dining. The range of beers is sourced both locally and nationally, and the extensive restaurant-quality menu uses locally sourced produce (no food Mon). Occasional live music plays on Friday evenings, plus quiz nights. Reduced price beer and cheese are on offer on Wednesday evenings. △Q➔✿◑⌐➡♣P⌐

Stock

Hoop ✔
High Street, CM4 9BD (on B1007)
✿ 11-11 (midnight Fri & Sat); 12-10.30 Sun
☎ (01277) 841137 ⊕ thehoop.co.uk
Adnams Southwold Bitter Ⓗ; guest beers Ⓗ/Ⓖ
This traditional weatherboarded pub has been an ale house for about 450 years. The heavily beamed interior has lots of character and the pub welcomes drinkers and diners alike. A long-standing Guide entry, it has won a number of CAMRA awards. Four or five guest beers include some from local micros, and a cider or perry is usually available. Home-made food is served in the bar, or upstairs in the Oak Room, at lunchtimes, evenings and all day Saturday. Q✿◑⌐➡(100)♠⌐

Stow Maries

Prince of Wales ♥ Ⓛ
Woodham Road, CM3 6SA (near B1012) TL830993
✿ 11-11 (midnight Fri & Sat); 12-10.30 Sun
☎ (01621) 828971 ⊕ prince-stowmaries.net
Crouch Vale Brewers Gold; Elgood's Black Dog Ⓗ; guest beers Ⓗ/Ⓖ
This renowned ale house has had the same landlord since 1990 and always features an excellent range of beers. There are three cosy drinking areas, all with open fires, and an old baker's oven is used to cook legendary pizzas on Thursday evenings in winter. Regular events include a firework display on the last Saturday in October and a comedy festival on the third weekend in July. Guest ales are sourced from across Britain. △Q➔✿◑⌐➡♠P⌐

Walton-on-the-Naze

Victory ✔
Suffolk Street, CO14 8AR
✿ 11-11 (11.30 Fri & Sat); 12-10.30 Sun ☎ (01255) 677857
Greene King IPA, Abbot; guest beer Ⓗ
A traditional pub, run by father and son, well-supported by the local community and visitors to this seaside resort. It is in the town but close to the pier and beach. Always welcoming, the Victory has a characterful interior, with upper and lower bars and a separate dining area. The pub hosts regular varied live music evenings and is home to the world-famous Bah Humbug Club, whose members raise money for charity. A true guest ale is always available. △✿◑➔≠♣⌐

Warley

Brave Nelson
138 Woodman Road, CM14 5AL (½ mile E of B186)
✿ 12-3, 5.30-11; 12-11.30 Sat; 12-3.30, 7-10.30 Sun
☎ (01277) 211690
Brentwood Chestnut Stout; Nethergate Old Growler; guest beer Ⓗ

Cosy local featuring wood-panelled bars, with understated nautical memorabilia including pictures, drawings and plates. This is a rare, regular outlet in the area for Nethergate, while the guest beer is usually from either Brentwood or Caledonian. The weekly Sunday evening quiz is usually well attended. Darts, pool and crib are played, and wide-screen TVs often show sport. Live music features twice a month. Food is only served Thursdays-Saturdays. There is a sheltered smoking area in the garden. ⋈✿🜨◖⋐♣P⌐

Weeley

White Hart
Clacton Road, Weeley Heath, CO16 9ED (on B1441)
🕭 12-2.30, 4-11; 12-11 Fri-Sun ☎ (01255) 830384
Beer range varies Ⓗ
An oasis for real ale in the Clacton area. The friendly landlord serves consistently good-quality beer, which has resulted in the pub becoming a regular in the Guide. A hit with locals and CAMRA members, it offers at least two real ales and a cider, and has its own real ale club. Close to Weeley railway station and on the number 76 bus route from Clacton and Colchester. ✿▲🜨(76)♣ð P⌐

Wendens Ambo

Bell
Royston Road, CB11 4JY (on B1039)
🕭 11.30-3, 6-11; 11.30-12.30am Fri & Sat; 12-11.30 Sun
☎ (01799) 540382
Adnams Southwold Bitter; Woodforde's Wherry; guest beers Ⓗ/Ⓖ
Classic country pub at the centre of a picturesque village. A charity fundraising event is held in summer and there are small beer festivals throughout the year. Beers are straight from the cask. A chalkboard features beer tasting notes and forthcoming guest ales. Traditional pub food is served lunchtimes, main meals in the evenings, and roast lunches on Sundays, including a vegetarian option. There is a large garden with a play area and a pétanque pitch. A weekly quiz is held on Thursday. ⋈✿◖◗≢(Audley End)🜨P⌐

Westcliff-on-Sea

Cricketers Ⓛ
228 London Road, SS0 7JG (on A13)
🕭 11.30-midnight (2am Fri & Sat) ☎ (01702) 343168
Greene King Abbot; Sharp's Doom Bar; guest beers Ⓗ
A large street-corner Gray & Sons hostelry, close to Southend. Following a major refurbishment, it now houses a Thai restaurant, separate from the main bar. Up to eight ales can be found (including the two regulars); the guests are mainly from local breweries. There is also a real cider, a large selection of continental beers (mostly bottled, although some are available on draught) and a varied wine selection. Club Riga adjoins the premises, so the pub can get busy on music nights. ✿◖≢(Southend Victoria/Westcliff)🜨ð⌐

Widdington

Fleur de Lys
High Street, CB11 3SG
🕭 12-3 (not Mon), 6-11; 12-midnight Fri & Sat; 12-11 Sun
☎ (01799) 543280 🌐 thefleurdelys.co.uk
Beer range varies Ⓗ

There are rumours of a ghost at this welcoming 400-year-old village local, which boasts a large open fireplace and beams. The games room has a full-sized pool table, fuzzball table and dartboard. This was the first pub to be saved from closure by the north-west Essex branch of CAMRA after the branch's formation many years ago. Quality meals are offered, with fresh ingredients sourced locally (no food Mon). The venue is close to the source of the River Cam and Prior's Hall Barn, an English Heritage site. ⋈Q✿◖◗占🜨(322)♣P

Wivenhoe

Horse & Groom ✅
55 The Cross, CO7 9QL (on B1028)
🕭 10.30-3, 5.30-11 (midnight Fri); 12-4.30, 7-11 Sun
☎ (01206) 824928
Adnams Southwold Bitter, Broadside, seasonal beers; guest beers Ⓗ
Popular Adnams pub at the top end of this bustling village. Consisting of two traditional bars, the Public offers a dartboard and the Saloon a more relaxed and comfy seating area, plus a large garden to the rear. A range of well-kept Adnams beers and guests is served from handpump. Good-value home-cooked lunches are available every day except Sunday. Easily accessible from Colchester, and regular bus services pass by the front door. ✿◖🜨(61,62,78)♣P⌐

Woodham Mortimer

Hurdlemakers Arms Ⓛ
Post Office Road, CM9 6ST (off A414)
🕭 12-11 (9 Sun) ☎ (01245) 225169
🌐 hurdlemakersarms.co.uk
Farmer's Ales IPA; Greene King Abbot; Mighty Oak IPA; Wibblers IPA; guest beers Ⓗ
Popular with walkers, cyclists, locals and families, this 400-year-old Gray's country pub has a good beer range, including frequent specials from local breweries. Good-value home-cooked food is available daily. It has one of the largest beer gardens in the area, including a barbecue area along with a children's play space. A large marquee can be used for functions in season. An annual beer festival is held in June. ⋈Q✿◖◗占🜨(D2,31)♣ð P⌐

Writtle

Wheatsheaf Ⓛ
70 The Green, CM1 3DU (S of A1060)
🕭 11-2.30 (3 Fri), 5.30-11; 11-11 Sat; 12-10.30 Sun
☎ (01245) 420695 🌐 wheatsheafph-writtle.co.uk
Adnams Southwold Bitter; Farmer's Ales Drop of Nelson's Blood; Mighty Oak Oscar Wilde, Maldon Gold; Sharp's Doom Bar; Wibblers Apprentice Ⓗ
Traditional village pub with a small public bar, an equally compact lounge, and a covered patio for smokers by the road. It serves two guest beers from the wide Gray's list on gravity. The atmosphere is generally quiet, with Sky TV switched on only for occasional sporting events. A folk night is held on the third Friday of each month. Note the Gray's sign in the public bar. Q🜨(45)♣P⌐

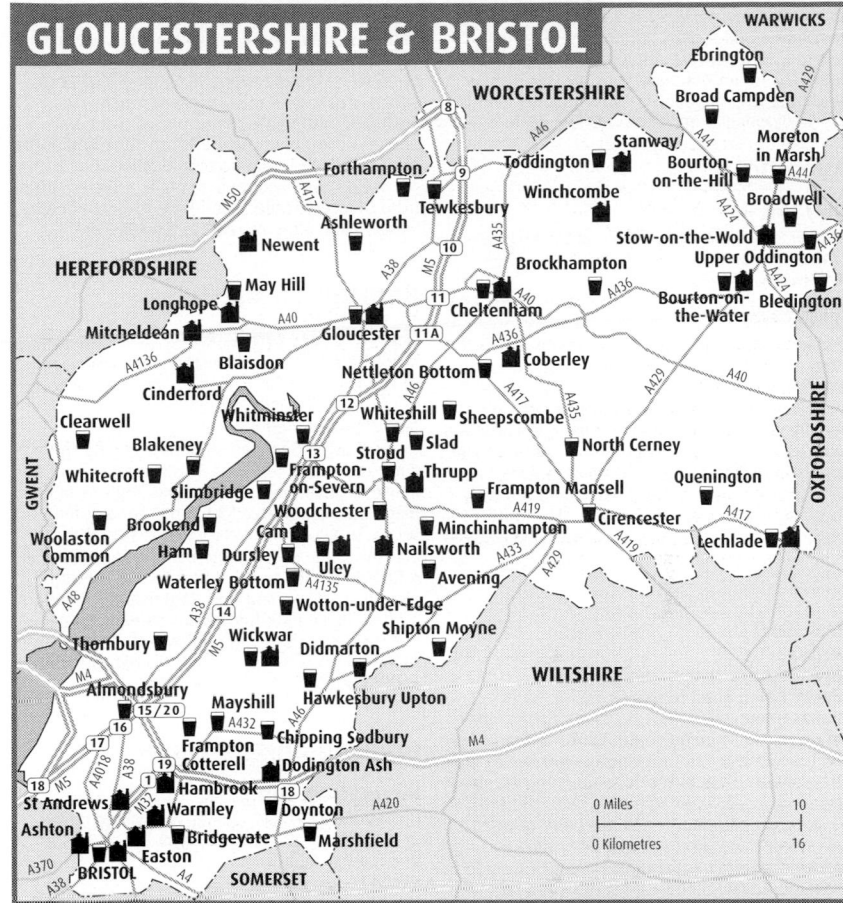

Almondsbury

Bowl Inn ✅
Church Road, BS32 4DT (next to church) ST604841
🕐 12-11 (10.30 Sun) ☎ (01454) 612757 🌐 thebowlinn.co.uk
Brains The Rev James; Butcombe Bitter; guest beers Ⓗ

Owned by Brains of Cardiff, the Bowl offers six beers including four changing guests, often from local breweries. The inn dates back to the 16th century and has a number of rooms, some used mainly for dining. Accommodation is available in the attached hotel. There is a long single bar with low beams and a good atmosphere for conversation. A function room is also available. The car park is Pay & Display, but with refunds at the bar. ᴹQ🕏🛏◐Pᴸ⸗

Ashleworth

Boat Inn Ⓛ
The Quay, GL19 4HZ (follow sign for quay from village) SO819251
🕐 closed Mon; 11-midnight (7-11 Wed); 11-11 Sun
☎ (01452) 700272 🌐 boat-inn.co.uk
Beer range varies Ⓖ

Owned by the same family for 450 years, this tranquil haven on the banks of the Severn is a real gem. The fireplace has a bread oven in it, and hops

INDEPENDENT BREWERIES

Arbor Bristol
Ashley Down Bristol: St Andrews
Bath Ales Bristol: Warmley
Battledown Cheltenham
Bespoke Mitcheldean (NEW)
Bristol Beer Factory Bristol: Ashton
Cotswold Bourton on the Water
Cotswold Lion Coberley (NEW)
Cotswold Spring Dodington Ash
Donnington Stow-on-the-Wold
Freeminer Cinderford
Gloucester Gloucester (NEW)
Goff's Winchcombe
Great Western Bristol: Hambrook
Halfpenny Lechlade
May Hill Longhope (NEW)
Nailsworth Nailsworth
Prescott Cheltenham
Severn Vale Cam
Stanway Stanway
Stroud Thrupp
Towles' Bristol: Easton (NEW)
Uley Uley
Whittington's Newent
Wickwar Wickwar
Zerodegrees Bristol

adorn most rooms. There is a covered courtyard with tables and a grass area on the river bank for relaxing. Six beers are offered from local micros and eight ciders. Soup and rolls are available at lunchtime. The pub has its own moorings and is especially popular in summer. Q❀♣♠P↳

Avening

Bell Inn L

29 High Street, GL8 8NF (on B4014 at bottom of village)
✪ 12-2.30, 5.30-11 (midnight Sat) ☎ (01453) 836422
⊕ thebellinnavening.co.uk
Brains The Rev James; Butcombe Gold; Wickwar BOB; guest beer Ⓗ
A friendly, confidently run old inn with exposed stone walls, two bay window seats and a roaring woodburner. This pleasant village local, where the jovial, amicable regulars are always chatty, now benefits from the addition of an upright piano. The attractive open bar offers up to four different ales, largely from local micros. The comfortable dining area serves a competitively priced and regularly changing menu. Catch this pub on the right evening and it can be difficult to leave. ♨Q❀❀◑♣

Blaisdon

Red Hart L

GL17 0AH
✪ 12-3, 6 (7 Sun)-11 ☎ (01452) 830477
Young's Bitter; guest beers Ⓗ
This charming old inn has flagstone floors, low beams and an open fire which, allied to chatty staff and friendly regulars, provides a warm, welcoming atmosphere. Three of the four beers are regularly changing, locally sourced guests, with the fifth handpump dedicated to either a perry or cider. A fine selection of good-value, quality food is available to enjoy in the dining areas or outside in the large, family friendly garden, where regular barbecues are hosted in summer. ♨❀◑♠P

Blakeney

Cock Inn L

Nibley Hill, GL15 4DB (bottom of Nibley Hill on main road S of Blakeney)
✪ 12-3 (not Tue & Wed), 6-11; 12-11.30 Fri & Sat; 12-8 Sun
☎ (01594) 510239 ⊕ thecockinnblakeney.com
Beer range varies Ⓗ
Over 200 years old, this attractive roadside pub retains many original features, including natural stone walling and old beams. A blazing log fire in winter adds to the welcoming atmosphere, which is enjoyed by locals and visitors alike (it has six letting rooms). The owner, who is a fine chef, serves some excellent food (no food Sun eves). Two varying real ales are available, plus a cider from McCrindles. The large garden offers both great views and children's play equipment. ♨❀🚪◑🛏(73)♠♠P

Bledington

King's Head L ✓

The Green, OX7 6XQ (on village green) SP243228
✪ 11.30-3, 6-11; 12-10.30 Sun ☎ (01608) 658365
⊕ kingsheadinn.net
Hook Norton Hooky Bitter; guest beers Ⓗ
Renowned, delightful, 16th-century inn, built in honey-coloured stone and overlooking the village

green, with its pretty brook, ducks and pet bantams. In the main bar, original old beams, an inglenook with kettle plus military brasses, an open wood fire, flagstone floors and high-back settles create a cosy atmosphere. Quality food is served in both public rooms and in a separate quieter dining room, while 12 en-suite bedrooms offer charming luxury accommodation. Guest ales are varied, well kept and carefully selected, often from Gloucestershire. Good local walks to nearby villages start close by. ♨Q🚲❀❀◑🚪♣P↳

Bourton-on-the-Hill

Horse & Groom L ✓

GL56 9AQ (at the top of the hill on the main road)
✪ 11-2.30 (3 Sat), 6-11; 12-3.30 Sun ☎ (01386) 700413
⊕ horseandgroom.info
Goff's Jouster; guest beers Ⓗ
Grade II-listed Georgian stone inn serving three good-value local real ales. This is a family-run free house in private ownership since 2005, winning many awards for excellent contemporary food served in two attractive dining areas and the bar. The light, airy separate bar has been tastefully refurbished with an open fire. Two miles from Moreton in Marsh and close to Batsford Arboretum, it offers five refurbished en-suite rooms for guests. The delightful sheltered garden has plenty of seating, with views over the Cotswold countryside. ♨Q❀🚪◑🚪P

Bourton-on-the-Water

Mousetrap Inn L

Lansdowne, GL54 2AR (300yds W of village centre)
✪ 11.30-3, 6-11; 12-3, 6-10.30 Sun ☎ (01451) 820579
⊕ mousetrap-inn.co.uk
Stroud Budding; guest beers Ⓗ
This attractive, traditional Cotswold-stone pub is a family-run free house, in the quieter Lansdowne part of Bourton. It is popular with the local community as well as offering 10 refurbished en-suite letting rooms. The pub is known for its friendly barman, keeping good-value real ales and serving excellent home-cooked meals. A welcoming, cosy atmosphere is created with a feature fireplace and coal-effect fire. The patio area in front with tables and hanging baskets provides a sheltered suntrap in summer. Q❀🚪◑🚪(801,855)♣P

Bridgeyate

White Harte

111 London Road, BS30 5NA (on A420 jct wth A4175 E of Bristol)
✪ 11-11; 12-10.30 Sun ☎ (0117) 967 3830
Bath Ales Gem; Butcombe Bitter; Courage Best Bitter; Marston's Pedigree; Wadworth 6X Ⓗ
A traditional pub dating from 1860, extended in 1987. It is often called the Inn on the Green because of the large village green at the front. An unusual bar counter incorporates old wooden spice drawers. Reasonably priced food attracts lunchtime diners, and the pub also gets busy in the evening. Pub games and sporting activities are likely conversation topics, and a quiz features on Monday evening. Black Rat cider is served. There is extra parking to the rear. ♨❀◑🚪(634,635)♣♠P↳

Bristol: Central

Bank

8 John Street, BS1 2HR (take lane by arcade in All Saints Lane)

☼ 12-midnight (1am Thu-Sat) ☎ (0117) 930 4691
⊕ banktavern.com
Beer range varies Ⓗ

Popular with a mixed crowd, this compact one-bar pub is right in the centre yet well hidden. A strong supporter of south-west microbrewers, the Bank offers three or four constantly varying ales, and is not afraid to sell dark or strong beers, plus varying guest ciders. Food is served 12-4pm daily, with popular roasts on Sunday. Many live events and party nights take place – including a summer fair and a Christmas party featuring live reindeer. Expect quirky humour, and ask about CAMRA discounts. Dogs allowed.

⚌❀◑≷(Temple Meads)🚍🖤‰

Barley Mow

39 Barton Road, The Dings, BS2 0LP (400yds from rear exit of Temple Meads station over footbridge)

☼ 12-3, 5-11; 12-11 Fri & Sat; 12-8 Sun ☎ (0117) 930 4709
⊕ barleymowbristol.com
Bristol Beer Factory No 7, seasonal beers; guest beer Ⓗ

A short walk from Temple Meads station brings you to this excellent pub, saved from closure by the Bristol Beer Factory in 2008. Located in the Dings renovation area, it is open plan, with a pleasant courtyard area outside. Local art and photos feature strongly, and there is occasional live music or a quiz. Good food is served lunchtimes and evenings Tuesday to Saturday, with roasts only 12-3pm on Sunday. It usually serves three beers from Bristol Beer Factory and a guest.

⚌❀◑≷(Temple Meads)🚍‰

Bell ✪

Hillgrove Street, Stokes Croft, BS2 8JT (off Jamaica St)

☼ 12-midnight (1am Fri); 5-1am Sat; 1-12am Sun
☎ (0117) 909 6612 ⊕ bell-butcombe.com
Bristol Beer Factory Sunrise; Butcombe Bitter, Gold, seasonal beer Ⓗ

Pleasant, eclectic, two-roomed pub where DJs often spin their discs from 10pm in the back room. Friday evenings attract drinkers on their way to nearby clubs, while local workers are regular customers for the lunchtime and early evening food. Sunday lunches are popular, too. A surprising feature is the pleasant rear garden with a patio, which is heated in colder weather. Local art on the wood-panelled walls adds a bohemian feel. There is a dartboard in the back room. ❀◑🚍‰

Bridge Inn

16 Passage Street, BS2 0JF

☼ 12-11.30 (11 Sun) ☎ (0117) 929 0942
Bath Ales SPA, Gem; guest beers Ⓗ

Tiny pub close to the station and surrounding hotels, yet only a short walk from the city centre. Music industry memorabilia features and a collection of vinyl records is available to play on a deck. A monthly quiz and other events are held, and there is free Wi-Fi. The pub is quite adventurous in its choice of real ales, with two from Bath Ales usually available plus two from high-quality microbreweries. All beer prices are reduced on Mondays. Lunch is served 12-3pm weekdays. Pavement tables increase capacity in good weather. ❀◑≷(Temple Meads)🚍

Colston Yard ✪

Colston Street, BS1 5BD

☼ 11 (12 Sun)-midnight ☎ (0117) 376 3232
⊕ colstonyard.butcombe.com
Butcombe Bitter, Gold, Rare Breed, seasonal beers; guest beers Ⓗ

Impressive renovation of the old defunct Smiles Brewery and tap site, reopened by Butcombe in late 2007. The pub has a pleasant contemporary and airy feel. In addition to the Butcombe range there are one or two guest ales and a number of interesting foreign draught and bottled beers, plus Ashton Still cider. An extensive bar and restaurant menu features local produce, served lunchtimes and evenings (lunch only Sun). Handy for the Colston Hall and Bristol Royal Infirmary. Outside tables are available in better weather.

❀◑点🚍(20)🖤

Commercial Rooms ✪

43-45 Corn Street, BS1 1HT

☼ 8am-midnight (1am Fri & Sat) ☎ (0117) 927 9681
Greene King Abbot; Ruddles Best Bitter; guest beers Ⓗ

Grade II-listed building dating from 1810 and impressively converted to Bristol's first Wetherspoon pub in 1995, offering up to ten guest beers. The interior features Greek revival-style décor, a stunning ceiling with dome, portraits and memorabilia from its days as a businessmen's club. There is a quieter galleried room, although the main bar can be busy at peak times. Disabled access is via the side entrance in Small Street. It always gets fully involved with Wetherspoon festivals and CAMRA events. CAMRA members receive a discount. Q◑点≷(Temple Meads)🚍🖤

Cornubia

142 Temple Street, BS1 6EN (opp fire station by former Courage Brewery)

☼ 12-11.30; closed Sun ☎ (0117) 925 4415
Beer range varies Ⓗ

Genuine free house now once again well established on the local scene. A great selection of guest beers of all styles, often local, is on offer across the 10 handpumps – plus a house beer brewed by Arbor and a changing real cider. The atmosphere is convivial with a real fire, subtle lighting, award-winning pictures, patriotic flags and numerous pump clips on the walls, and a turtle tank too. There is bench seating outside. This is a must-visit pub when in Bristol. Function rooms are available upstairs, and dogs are welcome. A CAMRA discount is offered.

⚌Q❀≷(Temple Meads)🚍🖤P‰

Eldon House

6 Lower Clifton Hill, BS8 1BT (off top of Jacobs Wells Rd)

☼ 12-3, 5-midnight; 12-1am Fri & Sat; 12-11 Sun
☎ (0117) 922 1271 ⊕ theeldonhouse.com
Bath Ales Spa, Gem; guest beers Ⓗ

A tasteful extension in 2009 has not detracted from the traditional look and feel of this cosy end-of-terrace pub, which lies close to the busy Clifton Triangle area. Get off a bus at the top of Park Street and head a short way down St Jacobs Well Rd. The three to five beers include guests from well-chosen independent brewers. Good-quality food is served daily and Sunday roasts are popular. There is free Wi-Fi and many events are hosted. Q◑🖤🚍

Grain Barge

Mardyke Wharf, Hotwells Road, Hotwells, BS8 4RU (moored on opp bank to SS Great Britain)
⚙ 12-11 (11.30 Fri & Sat) ☎ (0117) 929 9347
⊕ grainbarge.com
Bristol Beer Factory Acer, No 7, Sunrise, seasonal beers Ⓗ

Easily accessed on foot, by bus or ferry, this moored boat was built in 1936 and converted into a floating pub by Bristol Beer Factory in 2007, with great views of the SS Great Britain, the floating harbour, and passing boats from the two top decks. Popular themed food nights are held every Wednesday and Thursday. The kitchen is open lunchtimes and evenings. A downstairs bar and function room are available with live music on Fridays. ⚜⏺️⬛🚆⏴

Green Man

21 Alfred Place, Kingsdown, BS2 8HD
⚙ 4 (12 Fri & Sat)-11; 12-10.30 Sun ☎ (0117) 930 4824
Dawkins Green Barrel; guest beers Ⓗ

Small, dimly-lit Dawkins pub, formerly known as the Bell, offering a selection of four or five independent guest beers, some from the Dawkins range. Home-cooked food comes from a small but interesting changing menu, and is mainly organic or ethically produced (served all day Mon to Sat, 12-4pm Sun). Organic ciders are offered too. The pub hosts two beer festivals per year, and morris men appear sometimes. Q⏺️🚆(20)♣

Gryphon

41 Colston St, BS1 5AP
⚙ 1-11 (1.30am Fri & Sat); 6-11 Sun ☎ 07894 239567
⊕ gryphonbristol.co.uk
Beer range varies Ⓗ

Take a trip to the dark side! Totally transformed from its previous existence (as the Griffin), this is now a shrine to dark beer and great rock/heavy metal music. Triangular in shape due to its corner plot and just a few yards uphill from the Colston Hall, up to six handpumps dispense rapidly changing brews from all over – mostly dark and often strong. Food is served lunchtimes and all day Saturday. Live bands sometimes play upstairs and there are beer festivals in March and September. A CAMRA discount is offered. May open earlier than shown. ⏺️⬛🚆

Highbury Vaults

164 St Michaels Hill, Kingsdown, BS2 8DE (top of steep hill next to Bristol Royal Infirmary)
⚙ 12-midnight (11 Sun) ☎ (0117) 973 3203
⊕ highburyvaults.com
Brains SA; St Austell Tribute; Young's Bitter, Special; guest beers Ⓗ

In the same hands, and in this Guide, for many years, the pub is popular with students and hospital staff. Dating from the mid-19th century, its interior is dark and dimly lit, with a small front snug bar, main drinking area and a bar billiards table. Outside is a large heated patio and garden. Good-quality food is served every lunchtime and weekday evenings. Owned by Young's, the establishment is allowed some freedom with the beer range. Toilets are down steep stairs.
Q⚜⏺️⇌(Clifton Down)🚆(8,9)⏴

Hillgrove Porter Stores

53 Hillgrove Street North, Kingsdown, BS2 8LT
⚙ 4-midnight (1am Fri); 2-1am Sat; 2-midnight Sun
☎ (0117) 924 9818

Dawkins seasonal beers; guest beers Ⓗ

The first of the Dawkins Taverns, the brainchild of a local entrepreneur who also bought Matthews Brewery in 2009. An excellent community pub, it usually dispenses up to 10 guest ales, including two from Dawkins, dark beers and rare styles, plus guest ciders. The interior is horseshoe-shaped, with a wonderfully comfortable lounge area hidden behind the bar, and a pleasant patio. Sunday is quiz night. Mini beer festivals are held in conjunction with the other Dawkins pubs. Food is served 6-9pm, with – unusually – Sunday roasts 5-9pm. Q⚜⏺️🚆♣👜⏴

King's Head ★

60 Victoria Street, BS1 6DE
⚙ 11-11.30; 12-11 Sat; 12-2.30, 6.30-11.30 Sun
☎ (0117) 927 7860
Butcombe Gold; Hogs Back TEA; Sharp's Doom Bar; Skinner's Betty Stogs Ⓗ

Classic small pub, dating from at least 1660 and identified by CAMRA as one of Britain's Real Heritage Pubs. A narrow area around the bar leads to the tramcar snug at the rear. Pictures of old Bristol make fascinating viewing. An earlier landlady is reputed to haunt the pub. Popular food is served weekday lunchtimes only. It is a few minutes' walk from Temple Meads station on the way to town, and the pub is also well served by buses. There are tables for outside drinking in summer. Q⚜⏺️⇌(Temple Meads)🚆

Old Fish Market ✅

59-63 Baldwin Street, BS1 1QZ (200yds from city centre)
⚙ 12-11 (midnight Fri & Sat); 12-10 Sun ☎ (0117) 921 1515
Butcombe Bitter; Fuller's Discovery, London Pride, ESB, seasonal beers Ⓗ

Spacious Fuller's pub, once a fish market, that has become the main venue for those who enjoy a great pint with their TV sport – all big events are screened, when it can get extremely busy. It has a large front bar and an indoor patio to the side, as well as several discreet seating booths behind the bar for those wishing to avoid the sport. Thai and English meals are served lunchtimes and evenings Monday to Saturday and all day Sunday. ⏺️⬛♿⇌(Temple Meads)🚆

Orchard Inn

12 Hanover Place, Spike Island, BS1 6XT (off Cumberland Rd near SS Great Britain)
⚙ 12 (11 Sat & Sun)-11 ☎ (0117) 926 2678
Abbey Ales Bellringer; Bath Ales Gem; Fuller's London Pride; Otter Bitter Ⓗ**; guest beers** Ⓖ

Popular one-bar, street-corner local, 10-minutes' walk from the centre along the harbourside. The ferry service stops nearby. It serves two guest beers on gravity, and up to 24 different ciders at once. Good hearty food is served lunchtimes Wednesday to Friday only, with snacks at most other times. Popular with Bristol City fans before home games. Live music is played some Saturday evenings and there is a big screen for sport. ⚜⏺️🚆(500)♣👜⏴

Robin Hood

56 St Michaels Hill, BS2 8DX
⚙ 12-midnight (1am Fri & Sat) ☎ (0117) 929 4915
⊕ robinhoodfreehouse.com
Beer range varies Ⓗ

Pleasantly refurbished free house reopened in 2010, on a steep hill next to the maternity hospital.

A large plain front window looks in on light oak floors and pastel walls. Toilets and a function room are upstairs and there is a small rear outside patio. Four or five well-chosen changing beers often include one from Moor Brewery, and there is a good choice of continental beers. TVs show Sky Sports and good food is served all day until 9pm. Dogs welcome. ✿◑▶️🚃(8,9,20)

Seven Stars

1 Thomas Lane, Redcliffe, BS1 6JG (just off Victoria St)
✪ 12-11 (10.30 Sun) ☎ (0117) 927 2845
Beer range varies ℍ
This small free house was local CAMRA Pub of the Year 2010 and 2011. Generous discounts for CAMRA members apply at all times and for others in happy hour. Features are a pool table, a rock-oriented jukebox and outdoor seating. Eight changing pumps dispense a full range of styles and strengths, plus ciders and perries. Live acoustic music plays Thursday evening and weekend afternoons. Beeriodicals are held on the first Monday to Wednesday of every month, with 20 beers from a different county each time. Many who live miles away call this their local. Dogs welcome. ✿≠(Temple Meads)🚃(1,54,X39)♣♠⏱

Three Tuns 🍺

78 Georges Road, Hotwells, BS1 5UR (300yds from cathedral towards Hotwells)
✪ 12-2.30, 4-11.30; 12-11.30 Thu (midnight Fri & Sat); 4-10.30 Sun ☎ (0117) 907 0689
Beer range varies ℍ
Five minutes' walk from the city centre past the cathedral. Now run by Arbor Ales, this is independent beer nirvana. Seven pumps dispense the full range of beer styles, with two or three from Arbor and the rest mainly from top-rated British brewers. The L-shaped interior has scrubbed wooden tables and mixed seating. Food is limited to rolls and bar snacks. The covered, heated patio hosts unmissable beer festivals twice per year. A CAMRA discount applies. Free Wi-Fi is available and dogs are allowed. Local CAMRA Pub of the Year 2012. ♨✿🚃♠⏱

Bristol: East

Chelsea Inn

60-62 Chelsea Road, Easton, BS5 6AU
✪ 1-midnight ☎ (0117) 902 9186 ⊕ thechelseabs5.co.uk
Beer range varies ℍ
Street-corner community local with one large room and a collection of vintage sofas, armchairs and other furniture. Pictures from local artists are for sale or commission. In a cosmopolitan area, it attracts a varied crowd, many relatively young. Free Wi-Fi and a small exchange library are available. Up to four changing beers are served and two ciders. Live music plays on Tuesday (jazz), Wednesday and Saturday. Look for the interesting graffiti in the garden. Dog-friendly. ✿≠(Stapleton Rd)🚃(6,7)♣♠⏱

Old Stillage 🅛

145-147 Church Road, Redfield, BS5 9LA (on A420)
✪ 4-11; 12-midnight Fri & Sat; 12-10.30 Sun
☎ (0117) 939 4079
Arbor Ales Brigstowe, Hunny Beer, Single Hop; guest beers ℍ
Arbor's first pub acts as the brewery tap and testing ground for its many one-off brews. Low lighting and simple decor feature in this traditional town

venue. A pool table, dartboard and jukebox are all available, as is a large rear patio. Lunchtime food is served daily except Saturday. There is live music or a DJ at weekends, and Irish night on the last Thursday of the month. CAMRA members receive a discount on real ales. No dogs.
✿◑≠(Lawrence Hill)🚃♠⏱

Bristol: North

Annexe

Seymour Road, Bishopston, BS7 9EQ
✪ 11.30-3, 5-11.30; 11.30-11.30 Sat; 12-11 Sun
☎ (0117) 949 3931
Courage Best Bitter; Sharp's Doom Bar; St Austell Tribute; Taylor Landlord; Wye Valley HPA; guest beers ℍ
Community pub close to the county cricket ground behind the larger Sportsman pub and not far from the Memorial Stadium. Inside is a converted skittle alley and a large conservatory/family room to one side. Several TVs show live sport, including one out on the partially covered patio outside. Good wholesome food, including quality pizzas, is served, and a pool table is available. Monday is quiz night in this continuously improving pub, which is quite adventurous with guest beers too.
Q🛏✿◑&🚃♠⏱

Duke of York

2 Jubilee Road, St Werburghs, BS2 9RS
✪ 5-11; 4-midnight Fri; 3-midnight Sat; 3-11 Sun
☎ (0117) 941 3677
Beer range varies ℍ
This well-hidden free house serves an eclectic clientele. Visit in daylight for the enchanted forest mural exterior, then at night experience the warm glow of the grotto-like interior. The decor comprises fairy lights, odd memorabilia, wooden floors, a rare refurbished skittle alley, local art and more. There are two rooms, with an extra bar upstairs offering a quite different feel. Four handpumps serve unusual beers, plus real ciders from polypins and a good range of bottled ales.
✿≠(Montpelier)🚃(5,25)♣♠⏱

Miners Arms ✅

136 Mina Road, St Werburghs, BS2 9YQ (400yds from M32 jct 3)
✪ 4-midnight (1am Fri); 2-1am Sat; 12-midnight Sun
☎ (0117) 907 9874
Butcombe Gold; St Austell Tribute; guest beers ℍ
Located close to St Werburghs city farm and Bristol Climbing Centre, this is an excellent three-roomed street-corner local, part of the local Dawkins chain and free of previous beer ties. The split-level interior houses a hop-adorned bar where two guest beers and two from Dawkins join the regulars, along with Westons cider. Another small, quiet bar lies to the side, and a larger pool room to the rear. Children and dogs are welcome. The function room can be booked. Thursday is quiz night. ♨✿⊟≠(Montpelier)🚃(5,25)♣♠⏱

Wellington

Gloucester Road, Horfield, BS7 8UR (jct of Gloucester Rd and Wellington Hill)
✪ 12-11 (midnight Fri); 9-midnight Sat; 9-11 Sun
☎ (0117) 9513022
Bath Ales SPA, Gem, Barnsey, seasonal beers; guest beer ℍ
The largest in Bath Ales' pub portfolio, situated at a busy junction on the A38. This imposing hotel

offers B&B and weekend breakfast from 9am. It has a long, light and airy L-shaped bar, with various drinking areas arranged around it. The newer dining area leads to the extensive patio/garden. It is near the Memorial Stadium for rugby and football fans, but only home fans are admitted at policed football games. A good selection of bottled beers and traditional home-cooked food is served until 10pm. Q⊛🍽🕙👌👍🛏P⬥⬅

Bristol: South

Windmill

14 Windmill Hill, Bedminster, BS3 4LU (100yds from Bedminster station)

✪ 11-11 (midnight Fri); 12-midnight Sat; 12-10.30 Sun

☎ (0117) 963 5440 ⊕ thewindmillbristol.com

Bath Ales Gem; Bristol Beer Factory Sunrise; guest beers Ⓗ

With pastel colours and wooden flooring throughout, the pub is on two levels, with a family room on the lower area where children are welcome until 8pm. One beer from the nearby Bristol Beer Factory is always on offer plus one or two guests, as well as real cider and foreign bottled beers. Good food is served all day. Board games and kids' toys are available, and there is free Wi-Fi and an old 1970s jukebox. Outside is a small patio area to the front.

🏰🎄⊛🕽➔(Bedminster)🚍(75,76,77)⬥⬅

Bristol: West

Cambridge Arms ✔

Coldharbour Road, Redland, BS6 7JS

✪ 12-11 (11.30 Fri & Sat) ☎ (0117) 973 9786

Butcombe Bitter; Fuller's Discovery, London Pride, seasonal beers Ⓗ

Large, red-brick Edwardian Fuller's house, not far from the Downs, with an L-shaped bar, wooden floors and pastel walls. The pub can get busy with diners and those seeking refreshment after sporting exertions. There is a large south-facing garden at low level behind the pub. Fuller's seasonal beers and those from the former Gale's brewery are often available. Sunday roast is popular but no booking is allowed. Dogs are welcome. 🏰⊛🕽🚍(505)P⬅

Lansdown

8 Clifton Road, Clifton, BS8 1AF

✪ 4-11; 12-midnight Fri & Sat; 12-10.30 Sun

☎ (0117) 973 4949 ⊕ thelansdown.com

Severn Vale Session; St Austell Tribute; guest beers Ⓗ

Traditional pub that specialises in a great real ale offering. Four of the five beers come from within 20 miles and the range always features an excellent mix of styles, including a dark beer and a golden ale. Arbor ales alternate with Tribute. All beers are sold at similar upper-end prices irrespective of strength. There is an upstairs lounge/dining room available for functions. Good food is available weekend lunchtimes and Monday-Saturday evenings. The courtyard garden is heated and covered. ⊛🕽🚍(8,9)⬅

Portcullis

3 Wellington Terrace, Clifton, BS8 4LE (close to Clifton side of Suspension Bridge)

✪ 4.30 (12 Sat)-11; 12-10.30 Sun ☎ (0117) 908 5536

Dawkins Brassknocker, Green Barrel; guest beers Ⓗ

A pub since 1821, rescued by Dawkins in 2008, with a downstairs bar and a quieter upstairs lounge that can be used for functions and events and has a supply of board games. All pumps are occupied by small microbreweries, including at least five guest beers of all styles. Real ciders and American craft beers are also stocked. Frequent beer festivals and beer-themed events are held throughout the year. Free Wi-Fi is available, and dogs are welcome. Food may be reintroduced at some point. Find the secret garden if you can. Q⊛🍽(8,9)⬥

RAFA Club

Carlton Lodge, 38 Eastfield, Westbury on Trym, BS9 4BE (between Eastfield Rd and Grange Park)

✪ 12-2.30 (3 Fri & Sat), 7-11; 7.30-midnight Sat; 12-5 Sun

☎ (0117) 940 5300

Palmers Copper Ale Ⓖ**, Dorset Gold; Wadworth 6X; Wye Valley Butty Bach; guest beers** Ⓗ

Run entirely by unpaid volunteers, this was southwest regional CAMRA Club of the Year 2010. The ex-RAF social club, based in a Georgian country house, offers up to two guest ales plus the regulars. Show your CAMRA card to gain entry. The bar features RAF memorabilia, pictures and models. A pool table is downstairs, and a skittles alley in an outbuilding, plus darts. The club hosts themed evenings on saints' days, and an annual beer and cider festival. Live music plays on Saturday evening. Q⊛👌🚍(1,518)♣P⬅

Victoria

20 Chock Lane, Westbury on Trym, BS9 3EX (in small lane behind churchyard)

✪ 12-2.30, 6-11; 12-3, 7-10.30 Sun ☎ (0117) 950 0441

⊕ thevictoriapub.co.uk

Butcombe Bitter; Wadworth Henry's Original IPA, 6X, seasonal beer; guest beer Ⓗ

Once a courthouse, this traditional, relaxed and welcoming Wadworth-owned pub has been in this Guide for many years. A raised garden to the rear is a suntrap in summer. Pictures of Westbury as a village adorn the walls. Popular home-cooked food is available lunchtimes and evenings (no food Sun eve). Entertainment includes quizzes, themed meals and live blues on Sunday night. Various societies meet here. Bonus card offers are now available if you provide your email address. Q⊛🕽🚍(1,20)⬅

Victoria

2 Southleigh Road, Clifton, BS8 2BH (off St Pauls Rd)

✪ 4 (12 Sat)-11; 12-10.30 Sun ☎ (0117) 974 5675

Dawkins Brassknocker, Sixty Six; guest beers Ⓗ

Small 19th-century, Grade II-listed Dawkins' tavern, tucked away just off the bottom of Whiteladies Road and next to the Clifton Lido. Six pumps offer a changing selection of independent beers and ciders, always including two from Dawkins Brewery. The walls are adorned with pump clips and brewery mirrors, plus an amusing collection of obsolete keg fonts on a mantelpiece. Regular events, including beer festivals, are held. An ever-increasing stock of bottled Belgian beers is up to 25 and rising. Parking close by is difficult. 🏰Q➔(Clifton Down)🚍(1,40,54)⬥

Broad Campden

Bakers Arms Ⓛ

GL55 6UR (signed from B4081) SP158378

✪ 11.30-2.30, 5.30-11; 11.30-11 Fri, Sat & summer; 12-10.30 Sun ☎ (01386) 840515

Donnington BB; Stanway Stanney Bitter; guest beers Ⓗ
Genuine, excellent-value free house where the owners are celebrating their 15th year, characterised by Cotswold stone walls, exposed beams, an inglenook fireplace and an attractive oak bar counter where the local Stanney Bitter is a popular choice. Home-cooked meals, well prepared by the landlady, can be enjoyed in the bar or dining room. It is popular with locals and visitors, with a large car park and a variety of tremendous local walks. A traditional Cotswold pub at its best, close to Chipping Campden. ₳Q❀⒟♣♠P

Broadwell

Fox Inn Ⓛ
The Green, GL56 0UF (off A429 in village centre) SP202276
❀ 11-2.30, 6-11 (7-10.30 Sun) ☎ (01451) 870909
Donnington BB, SBA Ⓗ
This attractive stone-built hostelry overlooking the village green is one of the best Donnington pubs. The beers are good value, brewed only a few miles away, and popular with visitors. A friendly local, it offers good company and quality home-cooked food. Features include original flagstone flooring in the bar area, jugs hanging from beams and Aunt Sally played in the garden. At the back is a camping and caravan site with local walks. A special experience is assured at this family-run pub.
₳Q❀⒟Å⛝♣P╘

Brockhampton

Craven Arms ♥ Ⓛ
Kingsbury Street, GL54 5XQ (off A436 in centre of village) SP035224
❀ 12-3, 6-11; 12-11 Sat; 12-6 Sun ☎ (01242) 820410
Butcombe Bitter; Otter Bitter; guest beers Ⓗ
Spacious 17th-century pub, a proper free house, with carefully kept and selected beers. Set in an attractive hillside village with truly outstanding views and walks, it has a bar area with an open fire and an excellent dining room separated by church-style stone windows. A beer festival is held annually in summer in the sizeable garden. Handy for nearby Sudeley Castle, this is a well-managed gem, with a really enthusiastic friendly family who also organise functions for locals each month.
₳Q❀➧⒟⛝Å♣P

Brookend

Lammastide Inn Ⓛ
GL13 9SF
❀ 12-3, 7 (6 Fri)-midnight; 12-midnight Sat; 12-11 Sun
☎ (01453) 811337
Draught Bass; Wye Valley Bitter; guest beers Ⓗ
Single-bar pub built in 1932 which has six beer engines. Apart from a raised seating area in the bay window, the pub, garden and toilets are all accessible by wheelchair. The large dining area overlooks raised decking outside. The garden is equipped with children's play equipment and enjoys views of the Severn and Forest of Dean. The pub opens at 6.30pm on Monday and Tuesday to serve takeaway fish and chips, but there is no food on weekend evenings. ❀⒟⛝⛝♣P╘

Cheltenham

Adam & Eve Ⓛ
8 Townsend Street, GL51 9HD (near Tesco superstore)
❀ 10-2 (not Thu), 4-11; 10-11 Sat; 12-2, 4-10.30 Sun
☎ (01242) 690030
Arkell's 3B, Wiltshire Gold, seasonal beers Ⓗ
Run by the same landlady for more than 30 years, this friendly and unpretentious terraced local plays host to skittles, darts and quiz teams. A 15-minute walk from the town centre, it is readily accessible by public transport: buses stop at the end of the street. Seasonal beers are usually from Donnington Brewery. There is a separate lounge and the public bar provides a strong community focus. Street parking is limited and smoking is allowed in the narrow garden. Q➧⛝♣╘

Cheltenham Motor Club Ⓛ
Upper Park Street, GL52 6SA (access from A40 London Rd via Crown Passage)
❀ 6 (12 Sat; 7 Sun)-midnight ☎ (01242) 522590
⊕ cheltmc.com
Stroud Tom Long; guest beers Ⓗ
CAMRA members are more than welcome at this friendly club, which is just east of the town centre in the former Crown pub. Multiple winner of Gloucestershire and South-West CAMRA Regional Club of the Year, three regularly changing ales (four at weekends and busy times), from breweries throughout the country, feature alongside Stroud Tom Long and Thatchers cider. Parking is limited, but the club is served by Stagecoach service B. Local league quiz, darts and pool teams are based here. Q➧⛝(B)♣♠P╘

Jolly Brewmaster Ⓛ
39 Painswick Road, GL50 2EZ
❀ 12-11 (10.30 Sun) ☎ (01242) 772261
Beer range varies Ⓗ
Current local CAMRA Pub of the Year. Seven handpumps feature a regularly changing range of ales from Gloucestershire and beyond, alongside Black Rat cider and perry, plus a choice of Gwynt y Ddraig ciders. Booking is advised for the excellent-value Sunday lunch. Relaxed and friendly, featuring original etched windows and open fires, this busy pub appears in CAMRA's Good Cider Guide. The attractive beer garden is popular in the summer and offers some winter warmth for smokers.
₳Q❀⛝(10)♠╘

Kemble Brewery Inn Ⓛ ✔
27 Fairview Street, GL52 2JF (on one-way system off inner ring road at south-east corner)
❀ 11-11 (midnight Fri & Sat) ☎ (01242) 243446
Beer range varies Ⓗ
Small, popular, back-street local, hard to find but well worth the effort. It can get busy on race days, quiz nights (usually Tue) or if near-neighbours Cheltenham Town FC are at home. Six changing real ales from local breweries and further afield are usually available, alongside Westons Traditional scrumpy. Booking is necessary for the excellent Sunday lunch. Smoking is permitted in the attractive walled drinking area at the rear.
Q❀⒟♠╘

Royal Oak
43 The Burgage, Prestbury, GL52 3DL
❀ 11-3, 5.30-11; 11-11 Fri & Sat; 12-10.30 Sun
☎ (01242) 522344 ⊕ royal-oak-prestbury.co.uk
Taylor Landlord; guest beers Ⓗ

Cotswold stone local in Prestbury village with limited parking, the closest pub to Prestbury Park racecourse. The quiet public bar features oak beams, parquet flooring, equine prints and a logburner. Good-quality food is served in the lounge bar, with daily specials (booking advised). Two changing guest beers (see website for details) feature alongside Thatchers cider. A large garden hosts an annual beer festival in May and cider festival in August, and is home to the Pavilion skittle alley and function room.
ᴹᴬQ✿❄◑⌂(A)♠P⁵—

Royal Union Bar & Grill ᴸ
37 Hatherley Street, GL50 2TT
✪ 12-11 (midnight Fri & Sat) ☎ 07957 577450
Sharp's Doom Bar; guest beers Ⓗ
At least four changing guest ales from near and far supplement the two to three regulars (at least one being LocAle) in this locals' pub, which has been brought into the 21st century. A Belgian beer festival is hosted annually. Over 20 single malts are also stocked, as well as a great range of good-value wines. Steaks/burgers are available Wednesday-Friday evenings, Saturday lunch and evening, and Sunday lunchtime. Smoking is permitted in the courtyard at the rear of the pub.
ᴹᴬQ☎✿◑⌂(94)♣♠⁵—

Strand ᴸ
40-42 High Street, GL50 1EE
✪ 12-11; 10-midnight Sat; 12-10.30 Sun ☎ (01242) 511848
⊕ strandpub.co.uk
Beer range varies Ⓗ
Modern, comfortable town-centre pub offering five beers (one from the featured brewery of the month) and one cider. Good-value food is served daily (12-2.30, 6-9pm Mon-Fri; 12-8pm Sat; 12-4pm Sun), including a fish finger sandwich for lunch. An upstairs function room is available for hire, along with the cellar bar – home of live comedy on the first Thursday of the month, and live music every Friday. A large garden and patio provide a pleasant outdoor drinking venue.
✿◑⌂♠⁵—

Chipping Sodbury

Grapes
45 Rounceval Street, BS37 6AS
✪ 12-midnight (11 Sun) ☎ (01454) 310227
⊕ thegrapeschippingsodbury.co.uk
Courage Best Bitter; Sharp's Doom Bar; guest beers Ⓗ
After some years as part of the neighbouring Indian restaurant, the Grapes re-emerged as a community pub in its own right in 2009. It has since gone from strength to strength and now features four changing guest beers from all over the UK, including dark and/or strong brews. The interior features an open fireplace with a logburner and various bits of furniture and knick-knacks – some donated by locals. Darts and crib teams play here and board games are available. ᴹᴬ✿❄(342)♣⁵—

Cirencester

Corinium Hotel ᴸ
12 Gloucester Street, GL7 2DG (off A435 N of town centre)
✪ 11-11; 11-10.30 Sun ☎ (01285) 659711
⊕ coriniumhotel.co.uk
Beer range varies Ⓗ

An agreeable 2-star hotel with a discreet frontage entered via an attractive, narrow courtyard, leading into a stylish interior, with a comfortable lounge area complete with woodburner. The varying thicknesses of the walls hint at its heritage as an Elizabethan wool merchant's house. Three guest ales are usually offered including a LocAle. A smart dining area and a new vestibule lead into the pleasant suntrap of a garden at the rear of the premises. ᴹᴬ✿❄◑⌂&⌷P

Drillmans Arms
34 Gloucester Road, Stratton, GL7 2JY (on old A417 N of jct with A435)
✪ 11-2.30, 5.30-midnight; 11-midnight Sat; 12-4.30, 7-11 Sun ☎ (01285) 653892
Sharp's Doom Bar; guest beers Ⓗ
Current local CAMRA Pub of the Year, this busy roadside hostelry is a great community hub, its interior featuring low-beamed ceilings and a wood-burning stove to create a warm and welcoming atmosphere. Three of its ales change regularly, so there is always something different to sample. The lunchtime menu is popular with discerning drinkers. The smaller rear bar adjacent to the skittle alley/function room regularly fills with darts, pool and skittles teams. A popular beer festival is held in late August. ᴹᴬ✿◑⌂♣P⁵—

Clearwell

Lamb ᴸ
High Street, GL16 8JU SO570081
✪ 6-11 Wed & Thu; 12-3, 6-11 Fri & Sat; 12-4, 7-10.30 Sun ☎ (01594) 835441
Wye Valley Bitter; guest beers Ⓖ
A village local with two bars: a tidy snug with a woodburner, and a main bar with attractive settles flanking an open fire. The atmosphere is warm and inviting, with some interesting pictures adorning the walls. The beers are served from casks in the cellar directly behind the bar. This pub is a deserved favourite with local CAMRA members, and most of the guest ales are sourced from local brewers. No food is served here. ᴹᴬQ✿♠♣⁵—

Didmarton

King's Arms ᴸ
The Street, GL9 1DT (on A433)
✪ 11-11; 12-10.30 Sun ☎ (01454) 238245
⊕ kingsarmsdidmarton.co.uk
Taylor Landlord; Uley Bitter; guest beers Ⓗ
A previous local CAMRA Pub of the Year, the chatty locals and friendly staff can make this smartly attired village hostelry a hard place to leave at times. Its lively drinking area is adorned with copious amounts of reclaimed wood, giving warmth to the stylish interior, ably complemented by the smart furnishings of the popular restaurant. The low-key frontage only hints at the tasteful refurbishments contained inside this 17th-century coaching inn. The neat, private garden is popular in summer. ᴹᴬQ✿❄◑⌂♣P⁵—

Doynton

Cross House
High Street, BS30 5TF (2 miles from A420 at Wick)
✪ 11.30-3; 12-3, 6-11 Sat; 12-10.30 Sun ☎ (0117) 937 2261
Bath Ales Gem; Courage Best Bitter; Sharp's Doom Bar; Taylor Landlord; guest beer Ⓗ

Traditional country pub with a stone-walled exterior and a split-level interior. In a peaceful, pleasant and small village, it plays a pivotal role in local life. It is allegedly haunted by the ghost of Archie Carrow, who was landlord for 50 years. The garden is child-friendly and dogs are welcome. It is a rare outlet for Timothy Taylor Landlord in these parts. The TV is used sparingly for live sport, and darts is played. Superb-quality food cooked by the landlord is popular. ﾤQ☎◑◗⍰(635)♣P

Dursley

Old Spot Ⓛ
2 Hill Road, GL11 4JQ (next to bus station)
🕛 11 (12 Sun)-11 ☎ (01453) 542870 ⊕ oldspotinn.co.uk
Uley Old Ric; guest beers Ⓗ
Free house dating from 1776 and serving up to eight independent ales. Named after the Gloucestershire Old Spot pig, a porcine theme blends with the extensive brewery memorabilia, low ceilings and log fires to create a convivial atmosphere. The pretty garden has a heated, covered area. Wholesome, freshly prepared dishes complement the pub's enthusiasm for real ale. On the Cotswold Way, it holds regular beer festivals, and is adjacent to ample free parking.
ﾤQ☎◑&⍰♣●⍩

Ebrington

Ebrington Arms Ⓛ
GL55 6NH SP186399
🕛 12-11 (6 Sun) ☎ (01386) 593223
⊕ theebringtonarms.co.uk
Otter Bitter; Prescott Hill Climb; Stroud Budding; Uley Bitter; guest beers Ⓗ
Local CAMRA Pub of the Year 2009-11, this is an outstanding 17th-century Cotswold stone free house serving five selected beers, mainly from Gloucestershire. There is an attractive low-beamed bar with three cosy separate dining rooms, all with open fires. This young, enthusiastic, family-run inn serves home-cooked meals from a varied menu using local ingredients. Two miles from Chipping Campden and popular with the local community, it has three en-suite letting rooms. In summer you can picnic in a beautiful walled garden.
ﾤQ☎✉◑Å●P

Forthampton

Lower Lode Inn Ⓛ
GL19 4RE (follow sign to Forthampton from A438 Tewkesbury-Ledbury road) SO878317
🕛 12-midnight (2am Fri & Sat) ☎ (01684) 293224
⊕ lowerlodeinn.co.uk
Donnington BB; Malvern Hills Black Pear; Sharp's Doom Bar; guest beers Ⓗ
Brick-built 15th-century coaching inn, licensed in 1590, standing in three acres of lawned frontage looking across the River Severn to Tewkesbury Abbey. It has its own moorings and private slipway and is a licensed touring park site. En-suite accommodation, day fishing licences and a separate function room are also available. Regular ales are complemented by changing guests (two in winter, three in summer). The annual beer festival takes place in September. A ferry operates Easter to October. ﾤQ⍖☎✉◑&Å♣P⍩

Frampton Cotterell

Rising Sun
43 Ryecroft Road, BS36 2HN
🕛 11.30-11.30 (midnight Fri & Sat); 12-11 Sun
☎ (01454) 772330
Butcombe Bitter; Draught Bass; Great Western Maiden Voyage, Classic Gold, seasonal beers; guest beer Ⓗ
The brewery tap for the Great Western Brewery, owned by the same family that has run this excellent free house for many years. At least two Great Western beers and at least one guest are available. The three-roomed interior comprises the main bar, a small snug, and a conservatory/restaurant. Food is served all day (until 8pm Sun). There is also a skittle alley/function room, a covered smoking area, an enclosed child-safe beer garden and free Wi-Fi. Q☎◑⍰(581)♣P⍩

Frampton Mansell

Crown Inn Ⓛ
GL6 8JG (off A419 Cirencester to Stroud road opp petrol station)
🕛 12-11 ☎ (01285) 760601 ⊕ thecrowninn-cotswolds.co.uk
Stroud Organic Ale; Uley Laurie Lee's Bitter; guest beers Ⓗ
Attractive, thriving local dating from at least 1633, when it was known to be a cider house adjoining the village slaughterhouse. One of the first premises to be recorded under the 1737 Licensing Act, each of its three rooms is warmed by an open fire, with bare stone walls and wooden beams setting the tone. There is a modern 12-bedroom hotel annexe and function room, with ample car parking and some wonderful views over the Golden Valley. ﾤQ☎✉◑&P⍩

Frampton-on-Severn

Bell Inn
The Green, GL2 7EP
🕛 11-11 ☎ (01452) 740346 ⊕ thebellatframpton.co.uk
Butcombe Bitter; Fuller's London Pride; Moles Molecatcher; guest beer Ⓗ
Imposing three-storey Georgian inn, overlooking the longest village green in England where cricket is regularly played in summer. A former barn alongside is used for meetings and skittles; a second barn will delight children with its collection of farm animals. High-quality home-cooked food is served until 9pm daily, and there are themed evenings. Thatchers cider is available. Accommodation comprises two suites and two double rooms. On national cycle route 41, close to both the canal and M5. ﾤQ☎✉◑♣●P⍩

Gloucester

Cross Keys Inn Ⓛ
Cross Keys Lane, GL1 2HQ
🕛 11-11 (1am Fri & Sat); 7-1am Sun ☎ (01452) 523358
⊕ crosskeysinngloucester.co.uk
Beer range varies Ⓗ
Seventeenth-century timber-framed free house that has recently downsized. The large bar has become an antiques emporium, while the pub continues to function in the more intimate space of the former cocktail bar. Mature drinkers converse by day, and live and recorded music provide evening entertainment for all ages. Home-made

bistro-style food includes daily lunchtime specials. Both ales are usually local. A smart sun terrace is ideal for relaxation. Closed Sunday lunchtime.
🏠🌔🍴⇌🚬

Dick Whittington 🅛
100 Westgate Street, GL1 2PE
✪ 11-11; 12-10.30 Sun ☎ (01452) 502039
Butcombe Bitter; Wells Bombardier; guest beers 🅗
The imposing 18th-century brick frontage of this Grade I-listed building masks a 15th-century structure that was the Whittington family's town house until 1546. Offering up to six guest ales, including LocAles, a dark one and Thatchers Heritage cider, the Victorian-style bar blends with the spacious medieval interior. Home-cooked food is served 12-9pm (until 6pm Sun). There are occasional themed evenings, musical events and Meet the Brewer nights. A spacious cellar bar hosts private functions, with a patio/garden for smokers.
Q🏠🌔⇌🍴🚬

Fountain Inn
53 Westgate Street, GL1 2NW
✪ 11-11 (midnight Fri & Sat); 12-11 Sun ☎ (01452) 522562
⊕ fountaininngloucester.co.uk
Purity Gold, Mad Goose; St Austell Tribute; Taylor Landlord; guest beers 🅗
Seventeenth-century inn on a site where ale was almost certainly first served in 1216. The main entrance leads from Westgate Street into a courtyard ablaze with flowers in summer. The cathedral bar has a panelled ceiling, a carved stone fireplace and log fire. A modernised ground floor function room doubles as a bar overflow, while a second room upstairs hosts meetings and amateur dramatics. Excellent food is served lunchtimes and evenings. One Hook Norton beer always features.
🏠Q🏠🌔&⇌🍴🚬

Haywain
Bristol Road, Quedgeley, GL2 4PE
✪ 11.30-11; 12-10.30 Sun ☎ (01452) 720124
Banks's Bitter; Marston's Pedigree; Wychwood Hobgoblin; guest beer 🅗
Large pub built in 1985, but already with its third name. A reproduction of the Constable masterpiece greets customers, and a portrait of the artist complements framed pictures throughout. A horseshoe bar takes centre stage, and prominent pillars help to create discrete seating areas with table service for food. A quality two-for-one menu is available. Ideal for families, with internal and external children's play areas and a large outdoor seating area. 🏠🌔&P

Linden Tree ✔
73-75 Bristol Road, GL1 5SN (on A430 S of docks)
✪ 11.30-2.30, 6-11; 11.30-11.30 Sat; 12-11 Sun
☎ (01452) 527869
Wadworth Henry's IPA, Horizon, Boundary, 6X, Bishops Tipple 🅗**; guest beers** 🅖
This popular community pub is part of a Grade II-listed Georgian terrace. Its modest entrance masks an interior not untypical of a Cotswold pub. The open fire, warm colour scheme and somewhat eccentric decorative features contribute to a homely atmosphere. The skittle alley opens up to provide extra space when needed. Up to three guest beers are from family brewers. Substantial home-cooked meals are offered (no food Sat/Sun eves). Accommodation is reasonably priced.
🏠Q🏠🛏🌔🚃(12)🍴🚬

Ham

Salutation ▼ 🅛
Ham Green, Berkeley, GL13 9QH (from Berkeley take road signed Jenner Museum) ST681984
✪ 12-2.30 (not Mon), 5-11; 11-11 Sat; 12-10.30 Sun
☎ (01453) 810284 ⊕ salutationinn.biz
Cotswold Spring Stunner; Severn Vale Dursley Steam Bitter; guest beers 🅗
Finalist for CAMRA National Pub of the Year 2010 and current local CAMRA Pub of the Year, this attractive rural free house is situated in the Severn Valley within walking distance of the Jenner Museum, Berkeley Castle and Deer Park. A friendly, welcoming hostelry, it sources its beers and ciders from local producers and is popular with walkers and cyclists. There are two cosy bars with a log fire and a skittle alley/function room. Food is served lunchtimes and early evening. A pretty, child-friendly garden adorns the front. 🏠Q🏠🌔&♣🚬P

Hawkesbury Upton

Beaufort Arms 🅛
High Street, GL9 1AU (off A46, 6 miles N of M4 jct 18)
✪ 12-11 (10.30 Sun) ☎ (01454) 238217
⊕ beaufortarms.com
Bath Spa; Bristol Beer Factory No. 7; guest beers 🅗
Grade II-listed Cotswold stone free house built in 1602 and close to the historic Somerset Monument. With separate public and lounge bars, dining room and skittle alley/function room, this lovely, welcoming pub contains an ever-increasing wealth of ancient brewery memorabilia and has an attractive garden. It serves up to five ales and a traditional cider. As the fulcrum of most community activities, this is a fine example of the pub as the hub. 🏠Q🏠🌔&🚃♣🚬P

Lechlade

Crown Inn 🅛 ✔
High Street, GL7 3AE (opp traffic lights at A417/A361 jct)
✪ 12-midnight (11 Sun) ☎ (01367) 252198
⊕ crownlechlade.co.uk
Halfpenny Ha'penny Ale, Thames Tickler, Four Seasons, Old Lech, seasonal beers 🅗
Hub of the expanding Halfpenny Brewery empire, this twin-roomed, wooden-floored brewpub flourishes, with up to six Halfpenny ales available. Renowned locally for its parties, friendly clientele and unusual choice of games (including Aunt Sally), this enthusiastic establishment makes for a memorable drinking experience. Two fireplaces flank the front room, and an eclectic array of paraphernalia adorns the walls. Smokers can watch the brewing from a covered patio at the rear. Lunchtime bar snacks are now available (not Mon).
🏠🏠🛏🌔🚃♣🚬

Marshfield

Catherine Wheel
High Street, SN14 8LR (off A420 between Chippenham and Bristol)
✪ 12-11 ☎ (01225) 892220 ⊕ thecatherinewheel.co.uk
Courage Best Bitter; guest beers 🅗
Beautifully restored Georgian-fronted pub on the village high street, with a pretty dining room. An extensive main bar leads down from the original wood-panelled area, via stone-walled rooms, to

the patio area at the rear. A woodburner warms in winter. There are up to two local guest ales, usually from Cotswold Spring brewery, and imaginative and well-presented food is served in the bar or garden. Children are allowed and free Wi-Fi is available. Monthly acoustic music sessions are held. ≞Q✿⌂⊲◑◘➡(635)P⁵⌐

May Hill

Glasshouse
GL17 0NN (off A40 W of Huntley) SO710213
✿ 11.30-3, 6.30-11; 12-3 Sun ☎ (01452) 830529
Butcombe Bitter; Sharp's Doom Bar Ⓖ
Blessed with a handsome interior of flagstone floors, worn timber and reclaimed bricks, the various nooks and crannies of this sympathetically refurbished hostelry offer a plethora of drinking and dining areas. The conservatory is a taxidermist's delight, and is surrounded by the enclosed garden (popular with families on sunny days). There is a seat and canopy formed out of an old yew hedge in the car park. Good home-cooked food is offered, along with three new wooden cabins for letting. ≞Q✿⌂⊲◑◘➡P⁵⌐

Mayshill

New Inn ✪
Badminton Road, BS36 2NT (on A432 between Coalpit Heath and Nibley)
✿ 11.45-3, 5.30-11 (10 Mon; 10.30 Tue); 11.45-11 Fri & Sat; 12-10 Sun ☎ (01454) 773161
Beer range varies Ⓗ
A 17th-century inn hugely popular for its food, so book ahead. Expect three changing guest beers from far and wide – one of them likely to be dark – plus a changing cider. The main bar is warmed by a real fire in winter, and the rear area is more of a restaurant. Children are welcome until 8.45pm. The garden is pleasant in summer. Generous beer discounts are available to CAMRA members on Sunday and Monday evenings. The pub has free Wi-Fi. ≞Q✿◑◘➡(X42,342)◐P⁵⌐

Minchinhampton

Weighbridge Inn Ⓛ
Longfords, GL6 9AL (on road from Nailsworth to Avening near Longford Mill)
✿ 12-11 (10.30 Sun) ☎ (01453) 832520 ⊕ 2in1pub.co.uk
Uley Old Spot; Wadworth 6X; guest beer Ⓗ
Deceptively modern pub on the original packhorse trail to Bristol, which is now a footpath and bridleway. The road out front became a turnpike in 1822, when the weighbridge served the local mills. Today it is known for its popular 2in1 Pies. Inside, there are many exposed beams and open log fires to provide winter warmth. The bare stone walls display prints and memorabilia, and the guest beer is usually a LocAle. Children and dogs are welcome. ≞Q✿◑&P⁵⌐

Moreton in Marsh

Inn on the Marsh
Stow Road, GL56 0DW (on A429 at S end of town)
✿ 12-2.30 (3 Sun), 7-11; 11-3, 6-11 Thu-Sat & summer ☎ (01608) 650709
Banks's Mild; Marston's Burton Bitter, Pedigree; guest beer Ⓗ

A charming Marston's pub offering an interesting house guest ale, often from Ringwood. Next to a duck pond, this former bakery features woven hanging baskets on display. The bar area has a dedicated popular locals' section, and a welcoming lounge area with open fire and comfortable seating. The large conservatory serves good-value food with a Dutch East Indies influence, and is ideal for parties. Close to Moreton, it holds a beer festival each year. ≞Q✿◑&🗛⇌➡♣◐P⁵⌐

Nettleton Bottom

Golden Heart Ⓛ
GL4 8LA (on A417)
✿ 10.30-3, 5-11; 10.30-11 Fri & Sat; 12-10.30 Sun ☎ (01242) 870261 ⊕ thegoldenheart.co.uk
Brakspear Bitter; Festival Gold; Otter Bitter; guest beer Ⓗ
Three-hundred-year-old Cotswold free house, standing beside the short single carriageway section of the Swindon to Gloucester road. Little has changed here in a century, and the large log fire, bare stone walls, mixed furniture and assorted mementos ooze rustic charm. The finest locally sourced produce contributes to national award-winning food (served all day Sun), and children are catered for. To the rear, a large stone-paved patio and lawn abut a cow pasture. Two en-suite bedrooms are available. ≞Q✿⌂⊲◑P⁵⌐

North Cerney

Bathurst Arms Ⓛ
GL7 7BZ (on A435)
✿ 12-11 ☎ (01285) 831281 ⊕ bathurstarms.com
Box Steam Golden Bolt; Wickwar Cotswold Way; guest beers Ⓗ
Slaking thirsts since the Beer Act 1830, this old wheelwright's house (an original template still adorns part of the attractive garden) borders the River Churn. Built in 1699, the spacious hostelry has two main areas: the left hand side of the building for LocAle-seeking drinkers, featuring flagstone floors and an inglenook fireplace, the other half given over to the modern restaurant and dining areas. Several small beer festivals are hosted each year. ≞Q✿⌂⊲◑➡(151)P

Quenington

Keepers Arms
Church Road, GL7 5BL (from Fairford turn right at village green)
✿ 12-3 (not Mon & Tue), 7-11 ☎ (01285) 750349 ⊕ thekeepersarms.co.uk
Beer range varies Ⓗ
A previously dour village free house has been rejuvenated over the past six years by young, enthusiastic owners. As a proper community hub, dogs, children and cricketers are welcome in the refurbished oak bar with its three changing ales. With a good reputation for unpretentious food (no food Mon and Tue), there are food theme nights, quizzes and occasional live music. The petite front garden of this picturesque pub is popular with cyclists and ramblers in summer. Three en-suite rooms are now available. ≞✿⌂⊲◑♣P

Sheepscombe

Butchers Arms ✅

GL6 7RH (off A46 N of Painswick, or off B4070 N of Slad)
SO893105

✪ 11.30-3, 6.30 (6 Fri)-11; 11.30-11 Sat; 12-10.30 Sun
☎ (01452) 812113 ⊕ butchers-arms.co.uk

Butcombe Bitter; Moles Bitter; guest beer Ⓗ

Welcoming 17th-century Cotswold pub with a well-known sign, situated at the heart of the picturesque villages that lie in the famed combes (valleys) surrounding Stroud. It supports many local activities and offers three different regional beers. This inn is becoming renowned for its varied food menu, served in the bar and adjacent rooms, and in summer at the tables on the forecourt. The sloping garden above the building has fine views across the valley. ⚞Q✿◑▣♣P⁵⁻

Shipton Moyne

Cat & Custard Pot Ⓛ

The Street, GL8 8PN (on Tetbury road)

✪ 11-3, 6-11.30; 11.30-3, 6-11 Sun ☎ (01666) 880249

Bath Gem; Wadworth Henry's IPA, 6X; Wickwar BOB; guest beer Ⓗ

Blessed with an attractive, unique pub sign, this handsome village inn is largely open plan, the rooms opened out to cope with the demand for its popular menu. The busy main bar often appears to be the hub of the local dog-walking society, with the quiet (not always) snug behind it popular with families and social groups. There is an equestrian theme to the memorabilia adorning the walls; the origins of its unusual name is also displayed. ⚞Q✿◑♣P

Slad

Woolpack Ⓛ

GL6 7QA (on B4070)

✪ 12-midnight (1am Fri & Sat); 12-10.30 Sun
☎ (01452) 813429 ⊕ thewoolpackinn-slad.com

Butcombe Gold; Stroud Budding; Uley Bitter, Old Spot, Pig's Ear; guest beer Ⓗ

A popular village inn dating from the 16th century, offering superb views over the Slad valley. It is associated with the late Laurie Lee, author of Cider with Rosie, who was a regular customer and instrumental in the campaign that stopped Whitbread closing it. It has been thoughtfully restored, with a bar extending over the four rooms and wooden settles in the end room (where children are permitted). Real cider and perry are always available. Dogs and walkers welcome. ⚞Q✿◑▣♣◗P⁵⁻

Slimbridge

Tudor Arms Ⓛ

Shepherds Patch, GL2 7BP (from A38 1 mile beyond Slimbridge village)

✪ 11-11; 12-10.30 Sun ☎ (01453) 890306
⊕ thetudorarms.co.uk

Uley Bitter, Pig's Ear; Wadworth 6X; guest beers Ⓗ

Local CAMRA Country Pub of the Year 2007-12, this large family-owned and operated free house is near the Wildfowl and Wetlands Trust site. Two bars and five dining areas are constantly being improved, and excellent home-cooked food is available all day. Children are welcome. High-class accommodation is available in the modern lodge

alongside, and a separately owned caravan and camping park is immediately behind. Three guest ales from Palmers and local brewers complement up to eight ciders and perries. Q✿⇋◑▣&A♣◗P⁵⁻

Stroud

Crown & Sceptre Ⓛ

98 Horns Road, GL5 1EG (on B4070)

✪ 3 (12 Fri & Sat)-11; 12-10.30 Sun ☎ (01453) 762588
⊕ crownandsceptrestroud.com

Stroud Budding; Uley Bitter, Pigs Ear; guest beers Ⓗ

A fine example of a pub as the hub, regulars help select the guest beers at this community local. The comfortable front bar has a log fire, the rear features bar billiards, ringing the bull and televised sport. An eclectic selection of framed prints and posters graces most surfaces. A large oak table is popular, used by a knitting circle and the pub's own motorcycle society among others. Locally produced bar snacks are available. The terrace has panoramic views over Stroud. ⚞✿◑⇋♣P⁵⁻

Prince Albert Ⓛ ✅

Rodborough Hill, GL5 3SS

✪ 4.30-11.30 (12.30am Fri); 1-12.30am Sat; 12-10.30 Sun
☎ (01453) 755600 ⊕ theprincealbertstroud.co.uk

Otter Bitter; Stroud Budding; Taylor Landlord; guest beers Ⓗ

Lively, cosmopolitan, stone-built pub near Rodborough Common, managing to be simultaneously bohemian, homely and welcoming. It has an eclectic mix of furniture and fittings, and the walls are covered with many original film and music photos/posters. Three beer festivals are held each year as well as art exhibitions and themed nights – including backgammon, folk music and stand-up comedy. Some Tuesday events are ticketed (so check the pub website). Children, dogs and walkers are welcome. Local CAMRA Pub of the Year 2011. ⚞✿◑⇋♣⁵⁻

Tewkesbury

Nottingham Arms Ⓛ ✅

129 High Street, GL20 5JU

✪ 11-11 (midnight Thu-Sat); 12-midnight Sun
☎ (01684) 276346

Sharp's Doom Bar; St Austell Tribute; guest beers Ⓗ

Fourteenth-century town-centre pub with two welcoming rooms, both mostly timber: a bar at the front and a restaurant behind. Framed photographs of old Tewkesbury adorn the walls. Four real ales are usually offered, one from a local brewer, plus Westons Old Rosie cider. The pub is noted for its excellent, well-priced contemporary cuisine, served lunchtimes and evenings. Knowledgeable staff will happily tell you about the resident ghosts. Live music plays most Sunday evenings and Thursday is quiz night. ⚞◑🖵◗

Olde Black Bear

68 High Street, GL20 5BJ

✪ 11-11; 12-10.30 Sun ☎ (01684) 292202

Adnams Broadside; Wells Bombardier; guest beers Ⓗ

Built in 1308 and originally a coaching house, this is the oldest inn in Gloucestershire. As might be expected in such an historic building, the interior is rich in timber, both frames and beams. It is reputedly haunted by three ghosts, including a cavalier and an old lady, and was used as a hospital during the Wars of the Roses. Quiz nights are Sunday and Wednesday. Sky TV is screened inside and out. Private moorings and fishing are available. ⚒Q🚲🐕🍴◐🍽🏅🖼🚋

Royal Hop Pole 🅛 ✔

94 Church Street, GL20 5RS (between Abbey and Cross)
☀7am (8am Sun)-11 ☎ (01684) 274039
Greene King IPA, Abbot; guest beers 🅗
Large, town-centre landmark, an amalgamation of historic buildings dating from the 15th and 18th centuries. It has been known as the Royal Hop Pole since a visit from Princess Mary of Teck (Queen Mary, Royal Consort of George V) back in September 1891, and was mentioned in The Pickwick Papers. Current local CAMRA Pub of the Year (again), wood panelling graces the walls of this spacious, multi-roomed drinking establishment. There is an attractive patio and garden at the rear. Q🚲🐕🍴◐🍽🏅🖼P🏅

Theoc House 🅛

85 Barton Street, GL20 5PY (50yds from cross in town centre)
☀8.30am-11 ☎ (01684) 296562 ⊕ theochouse.co.uk
Bath Ales Gem; Severn Vale Severn Sins Stout 🅗
A fully refurbished town-centre hostelry that is a mixture of pub, café and coffee lounge. The owners aim for a relaxed atmosphere, and compete with a certain national pub chain by opening all day to serve good-value breakfast, brunch and evening meals. Only two real ales are regularly available, but there are plans to offer more. Quiz night is Sunday, jazz evenings are the second and fourth Wednesdays of the month. Q◐🖼

White Bear 🅛

Bredon Road, GL20 5BU
☀10.30-midnight ☎ (01684) 296614
Draught Bass; guest beers 🅗
On the north-western edge of the town centre, this good-value, family-run pub attracts a varied clientele. Situated close to the marina, it is popular with river users. The open-plan L-shaped bar offers room to play pool, cribbage and darts; there is also a skittle alley. Live music features every Sunday evening. The three guest beers change frequently and include many from smaller breweries. Three traditional ciders from Thatchers are served. 🖼♣🍺

Thornbury

Anchor 🅛 ✔

Gloucester Road, Lower Morton, BS35 1JY
☀11-11 ☎ (01454) 281375 ⊕ theanchorthornbury.co.uk
Draught Bass; guest beers 🅗
Licensed since 1695 and the second-oldest pub in Thornbury, this is a friendly, traditional inn serving good home-cooked food, five changing guest beers - often local - and a real cider. Dogs are welcome in the public bar, which was the original pub, and is home to darts, crib and dominoes teams. The pub also has its own cricket team and angling syndicate. The garden includes a boules piste and children's play area. The inn is the base for the local CAMRA branch; new members welcome – ask at the bar.
🐕◐🍴🖼(309,310)♣🍺🏅

Toddington

Pheasant Inn 🅛

The Roundabout, GL54 5DT (at jct of B4632 and B4077 between Winchcombe and Broadway)
☀11-11 ☎ (01242) 621271
Stanway Stanney Bitter, seasonal beer 🅗
A friendly, comfortable, independently owned pub serving several local villages, extensively refurbished in 1996. Parts of the large bar have hunting, racing and railway themes. The pub is handy for the Gloucestershire-Warwickshire railway, the Cotswold Way and Hailes Abbey, and is the brewery tap for Stanway Brewery located in the nearby Jacobean brewhouse of Stanway House. The quality of the beer is assured, often by the presence of the brewer. Thai food is available, and there's a shop. ⚒🐕🍴◐🍽🅿🚋♣P🏅

Uley

Old Crown 🅛

17 The Green, GL11 5SN (at top end of village)
☀12-11 ☎ (01453) 860502 ⊕ theoldcrownuley.co.uk
Uley Bitter, Pig's Ear; guest beers 🅗
Attractive 17th-century whitewashed coaching inn with a pleasant walled garden. A busy village local, it is also popular with walkers as it is close to the Cotswold Way footpath. The low-beamed bar has a welcoming fire, and serves food lunchtimes and evenings. This free house specialises in beers from local microbreweries. There is a covered smoking area and accommodation in four en-suite double bedrooms. ⚒Q🐕🍴◐♣P🏅

Upper Oddington

Horse & Groom 🅛

GL56 0XH (top of village signed off A436 E of Stow)
☀12-3, 5.30-11 (6-10.30 Sun) ☎ (01451) 830584
⊕ horseandgroom.uk.com
Wye Valley Bitter, Hereford Pale Ale 🅗
You are assured of a warm welcome at this attractive, privately-owned, 16th-century inn, run by friendly licensees, achieving many awards and now in its second year in the Guide. It has an extended bar area for locals, with a sitting room linked via a real open log fire in an inglenook setting. Good-value Wye Valley beers are always available, with guests changing weekly, usually from a Gloucestershire brewer. There is a large car park and an attractive garden and patio area. ⚒🚲🐕🍴◐🍽🖼P

Waterley Bottom

New Inn 🅛

Waterley Bottom, North Nibley, GL11 6EF (signed from North Nibley) ST758964
☀12 (7 Mon)-11; 12-10.30 Sun ☎ (01453) 543659
Beer range varies 🅗
Nestling in a scenic valley surrounded by steep hills, during the 19th century this was a cider house frequented by mill workers taking the footpath to Dursley. It has a cosy lounge/dining area with a pair of ancient unused beer engines and a small public bar. The child-friendly garden has a terraced decked area with a pool table. It offers an imaginative menu (no food Mon) and accommodation. The house beer is from Moles. Thatchers and Westons cider and perry are sold on gravity. ⚒Q🐕🍴◐🍽🏅♣🍺P🏅

Whitecroft

Miners Arms

The Bay, GL15 4PE (on B4234 near railway crossing)
SO619062
☼ 12-midnight (11 Sun) ☎ (01594) 562483
⊕ minersarmswhitecroft.com
Banks's Mild; Marston's Pedigree; guest beers Ⓗ
A village pub that for many years has offered a
wide range of ales and a fine selection of ciders.
There are two bars and a large skittle alley, which
doubles as a blues venue once a month. A boules
pitch is located in the front garden. Out back you
can hear the steam trains from the Dean Forest
Railway, and there is a solid structure for the
smoking fraternity. ⚞❀⌂⊄◑≈♣♠P╚

Whiteshill

Star Inn Ⓛ

Star Green, GL6 6AE
☼ 5-11; 12-midnight Fri-Sun ☎ (01453) 765321
⊕ stroud-starinn.co.uk
Bath Gem; Otter Amber; Purity UBU; guest beer Ⓗ
Local CAMRA Pub of the Year, this small stone
hostelry has been transformed into a comfortable
and welcoming village inn with B&B
accommodation in adjacent cottages. There is a
wood-burning stove in the main room, with a slate
floor and an intricate oak bar that dominates the
pub. Three ales are normally available direct from
racked casks. The TV prioritises rugby and there is
occasional live music, quizzes and an annual beer
festival. Food is available at weekends only
(Cornish pasties on Fridays). ⚞❀⌂⊄◑◫(93)♣P╚

Whitminster

Old Forge Inn ✪

GL2 7NP (on A38, close to M5 jct 13)
☼ 12-11 (midnight Thu-Sat); 12-10.30 Sun
☎ (01452) 741306 ⊕ theoldforgeinn.com
Butcombe Bitter; Greene King IPA; St Austell Tribute;
guest beer Ⓗ
Most of this listed wood-framed building with
mixed window styles dates from the 16th century.
Oak-beamed ceilings, carpeting and smart furniture
create a homely atmosphere, enhanced by the
landlady's personality, her aquariums, brasses and
collection of over 500 commemorative spoons.
Substantial meals are served lunchtimes and
evenings (not Mon eve winter), and all day at
weekends. Separate two-bedroom accommodation
is available. Q❀⌂⊄◑Å◫(12,91)♣P╚

Wickwar

Wickwar Social Club Ⓛ

35 High Street, GL12 8NP
☼ 12-1.30, 5-11; 12-2, 4-midnight Sat; 12-6 Sun
☎ (01454) 294221
Beer range varies Ⓗ

A comfortable two-bar social club where a friendly
atmosphere pervades and well-behaved children
are welcome. There is a walled drinking area as
part of the garden, including a covered designated
smoking area. The main bar has a pool table at one
end and a wide-screen TV for sport coverage. There
is a secluded quiet snug at the front of the club.
Show a CAMRA membership card or a current copy
of the Guide for entry on an occasional basis.
❀⌂◫♣╚

Woodchester

Ram Inn Ⓛ

Station Road, GL5 5EQ (signed from A46)
☼ 11-11 ☎ (01453) 873329 ⊕ raminn-woodchester.co.uk
Butcombe Bitter; Stroud Budding, Organic; Uley Old
Spot; guest beers Ⓗ
More than 400 years old, this much-altered and
expanded multi-roomed inn stands in superb
walking country south of Woodchester Mansion.
Lively banter fills the bar, with attractive wooden
furniture gracing the dining areas. Interesting guest
ales complement the LocAle offerings, and the
wheelchair access is good (drop off by the pub
before parking). A beautiful terrace has lovely
views over the valley. This is still a dog-friendly
village local, despite the numbers clamouring to try
the menu. ⚞Q❀◑⊄⌂♿(40,46)♣P╚

Woolaston Common

Rising Sun

GL15 6NU (1 mile off A48 at Woolaston) SO590009
☼ 12-2.30, 6.30-11.30; 12-3, 6.30-midnight Sat
☎ (01594) 529282
Butcombe Bitter; Wye Valley Bitter; guest beer Ⓗ
Off the beaten track but well worth finding. There
are spectacular views over the Forest of Dean, and
the hostelry features in circular walks of the area,
making it a popular stop-off for walkers. The cosy
snug just off the main bar is much sought after. The
food is home-cooked, using local produce where
possible (no food Mon eves). The guest ale is
usually a local brew. The cribbage league meet
here on Tuesdays. ⚞❀◑Å♣P╚

Wotton-under-Edge

Swan Hotel Ⓛ

16 Market Street, GL12 7AS (first left at top of Long St,
the main shopping area)
☼ 10-midnight (11 Sun) ☎ (01453) 843004 ⊕ swanhotel.biz
Fuller's London Pride; guest beers Ⓗ
Historic 16th-century coaching inn with an
imposing exterior at the top of the town, close to
the heritage centre. Open fires feature in one of
the two bars and the restaurant. A large function
room hosts live music every third Friday of the
month. This free house sources its beers from local
microbreweries and offers some unusual whiskies.
Its eight rooms are popular with tourists walking
the Cotswold Way. ⚞Q⏰⌂◑⊄♿♣╚

Your shout

If you think a pub not listed in the Guide is worthy of consideration, please let us know.
Send us the name, full address and phone number (if known). If a pub in the Guide has
given poor service, we would also like to know. Write to Good Beer Guide, CAMRA, 230
Hatfield Road, St Albans, Hertfordshire, AL1 4LW or email **gbgeditor@camra.org.uk**

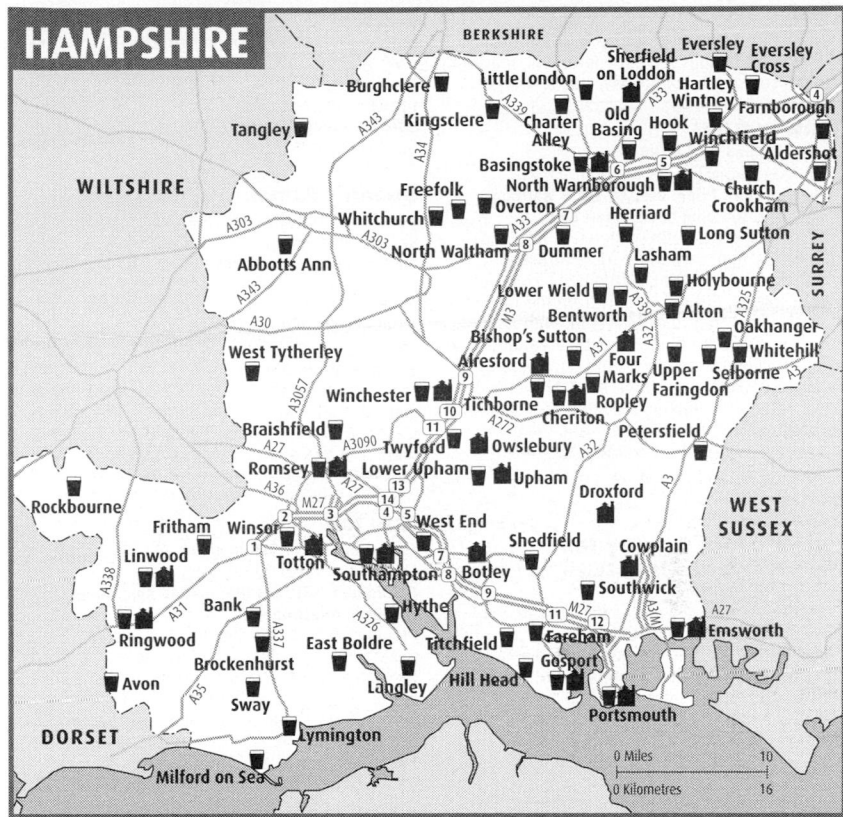

HAMPSHIRE

Abbotts Ann

Eagle Ⓛ
High Street, SP11 7BG SU328435
🕑 11.30-11; 12-10.30 Sun ☎ (01264) 710339
🌐 eagleabbottsann.co.uk
Skinner's Betty Stogs; guest beers Ⓗ
Located in a picturesque village just two miles south-west of Andover, this pub is at the heart of the community. Friendly conversation rules the house. The regular Betty Stogs is supplemented by three changing beers, often from local breweries, plus up to four real ciders. A beer festival with live music is held each summer. The public bar features pool and there is a skittle alley at the rear. Locally sourced food is available (no food Tue and Sun eves). ♨Q❀◖◗⌂⊞(77,87)♣♠P⅃

Aldershot

Garden Gate
Church Lane East, GU11 3BT
🕑 5-midnight; 4-1am Fri; 12.30-1am Sat; 12.30-10.30 Sun
☎ (01252) 321051
Greene King IPA; guest beers Ⓗ
Cosy town local that caters for many interests. There is a quiz night every Thursday, a poker night on Wednesday and a meat draw on Sunday. For music lovers, there is folk on the first Monday of the month, blue-grass on the third Wednesday, and traditional jazz on the last Sunday. There is also a dartboard and, for drinkers, a beer festival in November. Two guest beers feature, one of which is likely to be from Greene King. ❀⇌⊞♣P⅃

White Lion Ⓛ
20 Lower Farnham Road, GU12 4EA (200yds from A331/A323 jct)
🕑 1-11 (10.30 Mon; midnight Fri); 11-midnight Sat; 12-10.30 Sun ☎ (01252) 323832
Triple fff Alton's Pride, Pressed Rat & Warthog, Moondance, seasonal beers; guest beers Ⓗ
A genuine two-bar pub, in the eastern suburbs of the town, owned by Triple fff Brewery. It is popular with locals, visitors and vintage scooter enthusiasts, which is the landlord's passion. Three or four Triple fff beers are usually available, including the award-winning mild, supplemented by one or two guest beers from other microbreweries. It is only 15-minutes walk from the football ground, and visiting fans are always made welcome. Pizzas are available at all times. ♨❀⊞(3,20)♣⅃

Alton

Eight Bells
33 Church Street, GU34 2DA
🕑 11-11; 12-10.30 Sun ☎ (01420) 82417
Ballard's Best Bitter; Bowman Swift One; Sharp's Doom Bar Ⓗ
This popular free house, dating from circa 1640, is just outside the town centre on the Old Odiham Road turnpike. Opposite lies St Lawrence Church, site of the Civil War Battle of Alton. The pub has an original oak-beamed interior with a main bar and smaller drinking area, plus a restored listed smoking shelter incorporating a 17th-century well

in a secluded paved garden. Excellent filled rolls are available Monday-Saturday from noon. Look out for Phil's famous secret beer festival, following the late summer bank holiday. ♨Q❀⇌🚌⍭

Railway Arms 🏆 Ⓛ

26 Anstey Road, GU34 2RB

⌚ 12-11; 11-midnight Fri & Sat ☎ (01420) 82218

Triple fff Alton's Pride, Pressed Rat & Warthog, Moondance, seasonal beers; guest beers [H]

Friendly pub close to the Watercress Line and mainline station, owned by Triple fff Brewery, whose own beers are supplemented by ales from a host of micros. Bottled cider is from the local Mr Whitehead's. A rear function room, with its own bar, is available for hire. The patio area, designed with a traditional railway theme, incorporates a covered smoking area. There are tables outside at the front under a striking sculpture of a steam locomotive. Well-behaved dogs and CAMRA members are welcome. ❀⇌🚌(64,65)♣⍭

Avon

Tyrrell's Ford Country Inn

Ringwood Road, BH23 7BH (on B3347, Avon/Bisterne border) SZ148996

⌚ 10.30-11.30 ☎ (01425) 672646 🌐 tyrrellsford.co.uk

Ringwood Best Bitter; guest beers [H]

The 18th-century manor house residence of Lord and Lady Manners set in eight acres of grounds with a sweeping driveway, just 100 yards from the Avon Valley Path. Named after William Rufus's killer, this three-star inn has a comfortably furnished lounge bar overlooking the garden, a candlelit restaurant, open fires, a mural and a minstrels' gallery. Two local guest ales from Wadworth, Flack Manor, Goddards or others are always available. Family, dogs, horses and walkers are welcome, with many board games, bagatelle and bar billiards to keep the young and not so young amused. ♨Q♉❀⊟◐⛺♣P⍭

Bank

Oak ✔

Pinkney Lane, SO43 7FE (left fork on A35 1 mile W of Lyndhurst) SU286072

⌚ 11.30-3, 6-11; 11.30-11 Sat; 12-10.30 Sun

☎ (023) 8028 2350

Fuller's London Pride, seasonal beers; Gale's Seafarers Ale, HSB [P]

The Oak stands in a peaceful hamlet frequented by walkers, cyclists and ponies, a world apart from the nearby A35. Records of the white brick and slate building go back to the early 18th century. Its cosy interior is low-beamed and abounding in wood, including the barrel ends from which real ales are dispensed, propelled from the cellar by gas-driven pump. Food dominates (booking is recommended); specialities include game and seafood, with the addition of sandwiches at lunchtime. ♨❀◐♿P⍭

Basingstoke

Maidenhead Inn ✔

17 Winchester Street, RG21 7ED (at top of town)

⌚ 7-midnight (1am Fri & Sat) ☎ (01256) 316030

Greene King Abbot; Ruddles Best Bitter; guest beers [H]

Formerly home to a building society, this JD Wetherspoon pub is situated in the historic, and sometimes lively, Top of Town area, with 10 pumps dispensing local and guest ales. Local beers from Andwell, Loddon and Itchen Valley breweries regularly feature. A dining area at the front leads to the compact bar, with further seating to the rear over two levels, complemented by a courtyard beer garden to the rear. Q❀◐♿⇌🚌(1,2,3)⍭

Queen's Arms

Bunnian Place, RG21 7JE (100yds E of railway station)

⌚ 11-11 (midnight Fri & Sat) ☎ (01256) 465488

Courage Best Bitter; Sharp's Doom Bar; guest beers [H]

Just outside the main shopping area, this cosy pub is handy for all transport links. It attracts a wide-ranging clientele of all ages from all walks of life, and is a regular port of call for rail commuters. The choice of up to four guest beers is imaginative and the turnaround can be swift. Good-value home-cooked food is served lunchtimes and evenings. During warmer weather the shady courtyard garden at the rear is a popular attraction. ❀◐⇌🚌(1,2,3)⍭

Way Inn

Chapel Hill, RG21 5TB (opp Holy Ghost church)

⌚ 12-11 (10.30 Sun) ☎ (01256) 321520

Caledonian Deuchars IPA; Greene King Abbot; Taylor Landlord; guest beers [H]

Previously the Rising Sun, this pub, just north of the rail station, provides a comfortable environment for all age groups. It has a spacious, discreetly lit bar area at the front, with the rear bar area available for group reservations as well as occasional live music. There is a large car park, an outside patio and a south-facing garden. There are no TVs or bar games but there is an online jukebox. The menu offers home-cooked traditional food, available lunchtimes and evenings (no food Sun eve), with a good vegetarian range. ♨❀◐♿⇌🚌P⍭

Bentworth

Star Inn Ⓛ

Village Street, GU34 5RB (opp village crossroads)

⌚ 12-3, 5-11.30; 12-11 Fri-Sun ☎ (01420) 561224

🌐 star-inn.com

Fuller's London Pride; Palmers Copper Ale; Triple fff Moondance [H]

INDEPENDENT BREWERIES

Andwell North Warnborough
Botley Botley
Bowman Droxford
Dancing Man Southampton (NEW)
Emsworth Emsworth (NEW)
Flack Manor Romsey
Flowerpots Cheriton
Fulflood Arms Winchester (NEW)
Havant Cowplain
Hensting Owslebury (Brewing suspended)
Irving Portsmouth
Itchen Valley Alresford
Longdog Basingstoke (NEW)
Oakleaf Gosport
Red Shoot Linwood
Ringwood (Marston's) Ringwood
Sherfield Village Sherfield on Loddon
Triple fff Four Marks
Upham Upham
Vibrant Forest Totton (NEW)

Friendly Victorian free house with a bar warmed by open fires and an adjacent, quiet restaurant offering freshly cooked food. The pub is a social hub for the village community and equally welcoming to visitors. Its enthusiastic staff provide an active social calendar including steak nights, the Bentworth Cinema, quiz nights, live music on Friday evenings and a jam session on Sunday evenings. It hosts a popular annual blues festival with guest ales, but is free from intrusive music at other times. ⚒Q🍺🏵️🌓♿P♦

Bishop's Sutton

Ship Inn
Main Road, SO24 0AQ (on B3047)
☼ 12-2.30 (not Mon), 6-11; 12-3, 7-10.30 Sun
☎ (01962) 732863
Palmers Copper Ale; guest beers Ⓗ
Comfortable, genuine family-run free house with a split-level bar and a log fire providing a cosy, relaxing atmosphere. There are separate areas for pub games, families and dining, plus a restaurant. The food is home cooked, with daily specials on the board. Popular with walkers from the nearby St Swithun's Way, this pub is a key part of village life. The regular bus between Winchester and Alton stops outside, and the Watercress Line preserved steam railway is nearby. ⚒Q🍺🏵️🌓(64)♣P

Braishfield

Newport Inn
Newport Lane, SO51 0PL (signpost by red phonebox) SU373249
☼ 12-2.30 (not Mon), 6-11; 7-10.30 Sun ☎ (01794) 368225
Fuller's London Pride, seasonal beers; Gale's Seafarers Ale, HSB Ⓗ
Two-bar former Gale's pub, found down a narrow lane, run by the same family since 1941. Ham or cheese sandwiches or ploughman's are the only food available, but their quality and good value is legendary. The decor, inside and out, has changed little since the 1970s. Traditional singalongs round the piano are held on Saturday evenings and local folk musicians often play on Thursday evenings. Darts and other traditional pub games such as dominoes and cribbage are played in the public bar. ⚒Q🏵️🔄♣P

Brockenhurst

Rose & Crown
SO42 7RH (on A337)
☼ 11-11; 12-10.30 Sun ☎ (01590) 622225
⊕ rosecrownpubbrockenhurst.co.uk
Ringwood Best Bitter, Fortyniner; guest beers Ⓗ
Forest coaching inn dating from the 18th century, with extensions and the stable courtyard converted to accommodation. There is a beamed function and breakfast room, a skittle alley for hire and an extensive garden with illuminated sculptures. The separate public bar has TV for selective sport. Locally sourced and New Forest Marque food is all home cooked and available all day, with senior citizens lunchtime specials and a Sunday carvery. Quiz night is Sunday. Guest beers from the Marston's list may amount to six ales in peak season. Disabled access is to the restaurant only. ⚒Q🍺🏵️🔄🌓🏨♿🚶🚲🚊(6)♣P♦

Burghclere

Carpenters Arms
Harts Lane, RG20 9JY (off A34 at Tothill Services, follow signs to Sandham Memorial Chapel) SU463607
☼ 11 (12 Sun)-11 ☎ (01635) 278251
⊕ carpentersarms-burghclere.co.uk
Arkell's 3B, Kingsdown Ale Ⓗ
Small comfortable village pub with views over Watership Down from the patio and garden. Walkers, children and dogs are welcome. The food menu caters for all dietary requirements, with traditional roast meals on Sundays. Group bookings can be taken and food is served lunchtimes and evenings Monday to Saturday and lunchtimes on Sunday. Accommodation is in a separate cottage adjacent to the pub. ⚒Q🏵️🍽️🌓🏨(21,22)P♦

Charter Alley

White Hart
White Hart Lane, RG26 5QA (1 mile W of A340, opp turning for Little London) SU593577
☼ 12-2.30 (3 Sat), 7-11; 12-4, 7-10.30 Sun
☎ (01256) 850048 ⊕ whitehartcharteralley.com
Palmers Best Bitter; guest beers Ⓗ
Cosy coaching inn, built in 1819, the epicentre of this rural village, and all comers are assured of a friendly greeting. Welcoming features include log fires, oak beams and a capacious restaurant, serving a variety of quality food and home-made gourmet pies. The breweriana-decorated main bar has six pumps dispensing an array of ales that changes so frequently that an email notification service is available by subscription. It has been a stalwart Guide entry for the past 24 years. Sunday hours may change so check before visiting. ⚒Q🏵️🍽️🌓🏨♣P🏠

Cheriton

Flowerpots Ⓛ
SO24 0QQ (½ mile N of A272 between Winchester and Petersfield) SU581283
☼ 12-2.30 (3 Sat), 6-11; 12-3, 7-10.30 Sun
☎ (01962) 771318 ⊕ flowerpots-inn.co.uk
Flowerpots Perridge Pale, Bitter, Goodens Gold, seasonal beers Ⓖ
Four-square 1820s red-brick pub with two separate bars, popular with walkers and cyclists. A large rear marquee provides welcome overflow space on busy days. An outbuilding houses the pub's famous 10-barrel brewery and another has four comfortable B&B rooms. All the brewery's current beers (usually at least three) are served directly from casks. Good, home-cooked food is available daily (no food Sun eve). The publican also owns the Wheatsheaf at Shedfield, 10 miles south. Westons Old Rosie cider is available. ⚒Q🏵️🍽️🌓🏨🐶P♦

Church Crookham

Tweseldown Ⓛ
Beacon Hill Road, GU52 8DY SU819518
☼ 11-11.30 (midnight Fri & Sat); 12-11 Sun
☎ (01252) 613976 ⊕ thetweseldown.co.uk
Courage Best Bitter; Fuller's London Pride; Triple fff Alton's Pride; guest beer Ⓗ
Close to Tweseldown racecourse (which hosted the 1948 Olympics equestrian events), there has been a pub here since around 1840. This incarnation has a lively public bar with music, dartboard and pool

table, a quiet saloon bar, 60-seat barn function room and a garden. Friendly staff serve three permanent ales and a changing guest beer. Homemade food (main menu plus specials) is available. The decor is horse-racing themed. It has real log fires and dogs are welcome. Free Wi-Fi on request. ⚞Q🐾◐🍺👶♿🚆(70,71)♣P⃫

Dummer

Queen Inn
Down Street, RG25 2AD (in village close to M3, jct 7)
✪ 11-3, 6-11; 12-3.30, 7-10.30 Sun ☎ (01256) 397367
🌐 thequeeninndummer.com
Courage Best Bitter; Fuller's London Pride; guest beer Ⓗ
A fine 16th-century-style multi-roomed pub specialising in food, conveniently located close to the M3 in a quiet Hampshire village. A large open fireplace has a roaring fire in the winter. Ramblers and cyclists are welcome but no dogs. Meals are served all day. ⚞Q🐾◐P⃫

Sun Inn Ⓛ
Winchester Road, RG25 2DJ (on A30 1 mile S of jct 7 on M3) SU577465
✪ 12-11 (midnight Sat; 10.30 Sun) ☎ (01256) 397234
🌐 suninndummer.com
Triple fff Alton's Pride, Moondance Ⓗ
Formerly a coaching inn on the main London-Winchester road, the Sun has had a recent makeover and now provides a smart, clean and comfortable environment in which to enjoy the two local real ales and the locally sourced food from the stylish, well-presented menu. Big comfy sofas and tables grace the bar area, and there is a separate, more formal dining area. Conference facilities are available. Q🐾◐P⃫

East Boldre

Turfcutters Arms Ⓛ
Main Road, SO42 7WL SU374004
✪ 11-11 (10.30 Sun) ☎ (01590) 612331
🌐 the-turfcutters-new-forest.co.uk
Ringwood Best Bitter, Fortyniner; guest beers Ⓗ
Lovely brick-built, bay-windowed pub, standing on the edge of Bagshot Moor, and just a couple of miles from Beaulieu village. Its name derives from commoners' turbary rights; the old irons for this are displayed on the walls. The interior is cosy and rustic, with beams, stone floors, scrubbed tables and fireplaces; the bar, normally alive with conversation, dispenses four real ales. Two side rooms provide more seating for diners; food is served from midday till 9pm. Accommodation is three en-suite rooms in a former barn. ⚞Q🐾🍴◐♿🅰🚆(112)P⃫

Emsworth

Coal Exchange ✪
21 South Street, PO10 7EG
✪ 10.30-3, 5-11; 10.30-midnight Fri & Sat; 12-10.30 Sun
☎ (01243) 375866 🌐 thecoalexchange.co.uk
Fuller's London Pride, seasonal beers; Gale's Seafarers Ale, HSB; guest beers Ⓗ
A fairly small single-bar pub with a green tiled front (somewhat unusual for an ex-Gale's pub). Originally a pork butchery and ale house, the name derives from its time as a meeting place where local produce was traded for the coal delivered to the nearby harbour. In addition to the excellent quality beer, the pub serves award-winning food every lunchtime, as well as offering themed meals on Tuesday (curry) and Thursday (international) evenings. There is no entry after 10.30pm on Friday and Saturday evenings. ⚞🐾◐🚆(700)♣⃫

Eversley

Golden Pot Ⓛ
Reading Road, RG27 0NB (on B3272 W of cricket ground) SU788617
✪ 11.30-3, 5.30-11; 12-3.30 Sun ☎ (0118) 973 2104
🌐 golden-pot.co.uk
Beer range varies Ⓗ
A cosy red-brick cottage with creepers on the wall and attractive plants amid the front seating. The pub is supplied by nine breweries, six LocAle, with three ales on at any time. The bar has a striking stained glass feature and a prominent wood-burning stove. The focus is on food, with tables arranged for dining; quality ales complement the meals. A delightful feature is the garden at the rear. Opening hours may vary. Q🐾◐🚆(82)P

Eversley Cross

Frog & Wicket ✪
The Green, RG27 0NS SU796616
✪ 11-11 (midnight Fri & Sat); 12-10.30 Sun
☎ (0118) 9731126 🌐 thefrogandwicket.co.uk
Courage Best Bitter; Sharp's Doom Bar; Wadworth 6X; Young's Bitter; guest beer Ⓗ
A spacious double-fronted pub opposite the cricket green. In keeping with its name, the interior displays an array of both froggy and sporting memorabilia, and you can play Put the Ring on the Bull's Nose in the bar. A wood stove is in the separate dining room, adjacent to the main bar. There is also a skittle alley, and special food and music nights are held regularly. See the website for up-to-date information on regular live music. ⚞🐾◐♿🚆(82)♣P⃫

Fareham

Golden Lion
High Street, PO16 7AE
✪ 11.30-11 (9 Mon); 12-3.30 Sun ☎ (01329) 234061
🌐 thegoldenlionfareham.info
Fuller's London Pride; Gale's Seafarers Ale, HSB Ⓗ
Grade II-listed pub in the High Street conservation area, a short walk from the town centre. It has a traditional layout with a fresh and bright decor. The licensee holds the Fuller's Master Cellarman accolade. Children and dogs are welcome. Home-cooked traditional pub food (not Sun eve) is sourced through local suppliers. Book ahead for the weekly Sunday lunch and the first Saturday of the month steak night. A popular weekly charity quiz is held on Thursday and there is a folk band on the last Tuesday of the month. Q🐾◐🚆P⃫

Farnborough

Prince of Wales 🍺 Ⓛ ✪
184 Rectory Road, GU14 8AL
✪ 11.30-2.30, 5-11; 11.30-11 Fri & Sat; 12-10.30 Sun
☎ (01252) 545578 🌐 princeofwalesfarnborough.co.uk
Dark Star Hophead; Fuller's London Pride; Hop Back Summer Lightning; Ringwood Fortyniner; Young's Bitter; guest beers Ⓗ

Local CAMRA Pub of the Year since 2009 that simply exemplifies all a good pub should be. Welcoming to all comers, there is a single bar surrounded by separate drinking areas, with a covered, heated patio outside. Five well-known regular beers are on offer, supplemented by an eclectic range of five guest beers in the snug to your left, with local breweries and dark beers featuring strongly. Good quality lunches are served (no food Sun). ⊛◁⇌(North)🚆(73)P⊱

Freefolk

Watership Down Inn
Freefolk Priors, RG28 7NJ (just off B3400)
✪ 12-11 (10 Mon; midnight Fri & Sat); closed Tue; 12-10 Sun
☎ (01256) 892254 ⊕ watershipdowninn.info
Ringwood Best; Sharp's Doom Bar; guest beer H
Built in 1840, and still affectionately known locally as the Jerry, the pub has now been named in honour of local author Richard Adams' book Watership Down, set in the downland to the north of the pub. Local artwork and, notably, stained glass and jewellery, adorn the pub, while outside there is an extensive garden and family area. Local produce features strongly and sausages are made on site from the pub's own reared pork. An interesting menu includes dishes such as rabbit curry, and brie and beetroot tart. Takeaways are available. Real cider in summer months.
🏚⊛◁🚆(76,86)♣🍺P⊱

Fritham

Royal Oak L ✔
SO43 7HJ (1 mile S of B3078) SU232141
✪ 11.30-2.30 (3 summer), 6-11; 11-11 Sat; 12-10.30 Sun
☎ (023) 8081 2606
Bowman Wallops Wood; Flack Manor Double Drop; Hop Back Summer Lightning; Ringwood Best Bitter, Fortyniner; guest beers G
Thatched gem at the end of a New Forest track, with a main bar that leads to several interconnected areas featuring low beams and doors, colourwashed walls, log fires and wooden floors. Guest ales are from small local brewers – the house beer, Royal Oak, is Wallops Wood. Simple but excellent lunches include local cheeses. The vast garden has plenty of picnic tables and hosts barbecues and hog roasts. A warm welcome awaits walkers, cyclists and equestrians (facilities provided); dogs abound. 🏚Q⊛◁Å

Gosport

Junction Tavern L
Leesland Road, PO12 3ND
✪ 11-midnight (1am Fri & Sat); 10-midnight Sun
☎ (02392) 585140
Bowman Wallops Wood; guest beer H
Grade II-listed traditional community pub that was keg only until spring 2010. Then, taken over by the current management, real ale was reintroduced. It has been a free house from August 2011 and now has Wallops Wood as a LocAle regular, plus two guest ales from all over the country, mostly beers which will not be found elsewhere locally. It stocks real cider. An Easter weekend beer festival sees over a dozen ales. Usual weekly community pub activities include pool, darts and knitting. Live music features occasionally. ⊛🚆(E1,85)♣🍺⊱

Middlecroft L
Middlecroft Lane, PO12 3DH
✪ 11-midnight (1am Mon, Fri & Sat); 12-midnight Sun
☎ (023) 9258 2477
Oakleaf Some are Drinking H
Built in the 1930s, this pub is in the middle of a housing estate and still has two large bars, one of which is normally quiet. On the right of the entrance hall is the public bar with a games area (darts and pool). On the left is a lounge bar with a dance floor, which is sometimes used as a function room. An acoustic music session takes place on Wednesday evenings and there is occasional live music on Saturday evenings. 🏚Q⊛⊛♣P⊱

Queen's Hotel L
143 Queen's Road, PO12 1LG
✪ 11.30-2.30 (Fri only), 5-11; 11.30-11 Sat; 12-3, 7-10.30 Sun
☎ (023) 9258 2645
Oakleaf IPA; Palmers 200; Young's Bitter; guest beers H
Hidden away in the back streets, this beer drinkers' haven is a regular entry in this Guide, and a previous Wessex CAMRA Regional Pub of the Year. Two guest beers are normally available from Waverley. A regular beer festival takes place in October. Snacks are served Friday lunchtimes, and weekend opening hours are often extended by up to half an hour. A real cider is always available. 🏚⊛🚆♣🍺⊱

Hartley Wintney

Waggon & Horses 🍺
High Street, RG27 8NY
✪ 11-11 (midnight Fri & Sat); 12-11 Sun ☎ (01252) 842119
Courage Best Bitter H; **Gale's HSB; guest beers** G
A village pub whose landlord of 30 years has won several local CAMRA awards. HSB and Courage Best are regularly served alongside changing guest beers. The pub's lively public bar contrasts with a quieter lounge. Tables outside on the pavement enable guests to enjoy the atmosphere of the village, renowned for its antique shops. At the rear is a pleasant courtyard garden and a heated, covered smokers' area. Food is served lunchtimes only, not Sundays. 🏚Q⊛◁⊛🚆(100,72)🍺⊱

Herriard

Fur & Feathers L
Back Lane, RG25 2PN (on the old Basingstoke-Alton road, parallel to A339) SU671447
✪ closed Mon; 12-3, 5-11; 12-11 Fri & Sat; 12-6 Sun
☎ (01256) 384170 ⊕ franskitchen.co.uk
Sharp's Doom Bar; guest beers H
Victorian ale house built for local farmworkers in 1880, now open plan with a central bar area. The two guest beers are often from local breweries including Hogs Back, Flack Manor and Andwell. The two dining areas either side of the bar area provide a pleasant atmosphere in which to enjoy the mouthwatering menu that utilises the very best and most local ingredients available. A small, quality selection of whisky and brandy is available to complete your pub/dining experience, as is a selection of Havana cigars from the humidor. 🏚Q⊛◁⊛🚆(13)P⊱

Hill Head

Crofton 🍺 ✔
48 Crofton Lane, PO14 3QF
🕐 11-11; 12-10.30 Sun ☎ (01329) 314222
⊕ thecroftonpub.co.uk
Oakleaf Hole Hearted; Sharp's Doom Bar; guest beers ⓗ
Although seeming rather uninspiring from the outside, there is a good pub atmosphere inside, with locals exchanging conversation at both the main bars. Four guest beers are usually available, with beers from SIBA breweries in addition to those from the Punch Taverns portfolio. The function room has a skittle alley where special events are held, including a beer festival in the autumn. Home-cooked food is served all day at weekends. The real cider is from Westons.
🏚Q🐕🕐♿🅿🚼(33,35)♣🍴🅿⌐

Holybourne

Queen's Head
20 London Road, GU34 4EG
🕐 12-11 (11.30 Thu; 12.30am Fri & Sat); 12-10.30 Sun
☎ (01420) 86331
Greene King IPA; guest beers ⓗ
Traditional and friendly pub offering an interesting selection of local and guest ales. The Queen's comprises three recently refurbished rooms plus a covered and heated smoking area. Home-made hearty food is served daily featuring the pub's infamous pies. There is regular live music throughout the year, with 'Altonbury' the first Saturday in July. The popular extensive beer garden features a children's play area and dogs are permitted on a short lead. Happy hour is 4.30-6pm Monday-Friday. Q🐕🕐♿≠(Alton)🚌(X65)♣🅿⌐

Hook

White Hart 🍺 ✔
London Road, RG27 9DZ (5 mins fron M3 jct 5, next to Hook Texaco garage) SU732548
🕐 11-11; 12-10.30 Sun ☎ (01256) 762462
Sharp's Doom Bar; guest beers ⓗ
You will always get a warm welcome at the White Hart, a 16th-century coaching inn. Recently refurbished, it has a spacious bar area, oak beams and some nooks where you can sit. The bar area is busy and has softly piped music and TVs showing sport; the opposite end is much quieter and ideal for enjoying a meal. There is an extensive beer garden to the side and a large car park behind.
🏚🐕🍴🕐≠🚌(10,211)🅿⌐

Hythe

Ebenezer's 🍺
Pylewell Road, SO45 6AR
🕐 11-2.30, 5.30-11; 11-11.30 Fri & Sat; 12-11 Sun
☎ (023) 8020 7799
Flack Manor Double Drop; guest beers ⓗ
Delightful little pub, built in 1845 as a chapel. It has been a school and a store for flour and furniture, but now serves some of the best local ales in the area. The open-plan bar is modern, with a traditional feel that attracts seekers of conversation. Home-made pub food is available lunchtimes and evenings. Outside is a large covered smoking area. Nearby is the world's oldest pier railway. Q🐕🕐♿🚌(8,9)⌐

Kingsclere

Swan Hotel 🍺
Swan Street, RG20 5PP
🕐 11-3, 5.30 (6 Sat)-11 (11.30 Fri & Sat); 12-3.30, 7-10.30 Sun ☎ (01635) 298314 ⊕ swankingsclere.co.uk
Theakston XB; Young's Bitter; guest beers ⓗ
Traditional inn frequented by an eclectic mix of customers, serving five beers including three changing local guests. The pub is one of the county's oldest coaching inns, dating from 1449, and associated with the Bishop of Winchester for 300 years. A Grade II-listed building, close to the Watership Down beauty spot, it retains original oak beams and fireplaces, and offers nine en-suite bedrooms. Good food is served in both the dining room and the bar (no food Sun). 🏚Q🛏🕐🍴🚌♣🅿⌐

Langley

Langley Tavern 🍺
Lepe Road, SO45 1XR
🕐 11-11 (midnight Fri & Sat) ☎ (023) 8089 1402
Ringwood Best Bitter; guest beers ⓗ
A large, brick-built and crowstep-gabled pub erected in the 1930s for Brickwoods Brewery. It was refurbished in 2009, and the public bar is a venue for live music on most Friday and Saturday evenings. The lounge bar, furnished with tables, chairs and sofas, serves pub food. Outside is a large beer garden and children's play area. It is only 2½ miles from Exbury gardens and 1½ miles from Lepe beach and Country Park, with fine views across the Solent to the Isle of Wight. Q🐕🕐🍴🚌(9)♣🅿⌐

Lasham

Lasham Gliding Society Bar 🍺
Lasham Airfield, The Avenue, GU34 5SS (follow brown signs to Lasham Gliding. Bar in main club house) SU677438
🕐 12-2, 5.30-11; 12-11 Sat & Sun ☎ (01256) 384900
⊕ lashamgliding.com
Sharp's Doom Bar ⓗ
One of Europe's leading gliding centres, this club has a comfortable, recently refurbished lounge bar and an excellent restaurant, both free from recorded music. Open to the public at all times and welcoming children, it features a patio area with views of the flying operations and a children's playground. Check in advance for the evening opening hours, especially during the winter months. An annual beer festival is held over the Easter weekend. Q🐕🕐♿🅿⌐

Linwood

Red Shoot Inn ✔
Tom's Lane, BH24 3QT (4 miles NE of Ringwood) SU187094
🕐 11-3, 6-11; 11-11 Fri & Sat and summer; 11-10.30 Sun ☎ (01425) 475792 ⊕ redshoot.co.uk
Red Shoot New Forest Gold, Red White and Brew, Muddy Boot, Tom's Tipple; Wadworth Henry's IPA, 6X ⓗ
The pub, plus its caravan and campsite, provides an ideal base to explore this remote north-western part of the New Forest. Open all day in the summer, the Red Shoot welcomes families and dogs, and has its own brewery. Food is available every day from noon in the summer; in winter until 2.30pm weekdays, 9pm Saturday and 6pm Sunday.

Summer evening entertainment includes a Thursday quiz and live music on Sundays. There are beer festivals in April, July and October. ♨✿◑&Å♣P

Little London

Plough Inn ⃝
Silchester Road, RG26 5EP SU621596
✪ 12-3, 5.30 (6 Sat)-11; 12-3, 7-10.30 Sun
☎ (01256) 850628
Palmers Dorset Gold; Ringwood Best Bitter Ⓗ**; guest beers** ⒼWonderful village pub and recent CAMRA Regional Pub of the Year, where in winter you can enjoy a glass of beer in front of one of the log fires or play a game of bar billiards. A good range of baguettes is available (no food Sun eve). There is a secluded garden at the side of the pub. It is ideal for ramblers and cyclists visiting Pamber Wood or the extensive Roman ruins at nearby Silchester. CAMRA Branch Pub of the Year 2011. ♨Q☎✿吴(44)♣P⁵-

Long Sutton

Four Horseshoes
RG29 1TA (follow brown signs from B3349 Odiham to Alton road) SU748471
✪ 12-3 (not Mon & Tue), 6.30-11; 12-4 Sun
☎ (01256) 862488 ⊕ fourhorseshoes.com
Beer range varies Ⓗ
The veranda of this friendly pub provides splendid views over the countryside. The single-room bar, divided by the fireplace, is a comfortable place to enjoy reasonably priced, home-cooked meals washed down by well-kept beers, often from Palmers or the local Andwell brewery. Jazz lovers are catered for on the second and fourth Tuesdays of the month and the fourth Thursday is quiz night. Takeaway beer is keenly priced. Enquire in advance for accommodation and camping.
♨Q✿吴◑&ÅP

Lower Upham

Woodman
Winchester Road, SO32 1HA (on B2177, opp B3037 jct)
✪ 12-2.30, 7.15 (5.15 Fri)-11; 12-6.30, 7.30-11.30 Sat & Sun
☎ (01489) 860270
Beer range varies Ⓗ
The current landlord has lived in this 17th-century pub for over five decades. As it has been a freehouse for a few years, he has been able to offer a varied beer range. Sharp's and Palmers make regular appearances, with local beers also available. Two beers are usually served during the week, with an extra one at weekends. Over 150 whiskies are also available. There is live music on the first Wednesday of the month and a mini beer festival with a hog roast over the St George's Day weekend. ♨Q✿吴(69)P⁵-⊟

Lower Wield

Yew Tree ⃝
SO24 9RX SU636398
✪ closed Mon; 12-3, 6-11; 12-10.30 Sun ☎ (01256) 389224
⊕ the-yewtree.org.uk
Triple fff Alton's Pride; guest beer Ⓗ
Out-of-the-way rural local set in picturesque rolling Hampshire countryside, with an old yew tree growing outside (hence the name), situated on a quiet country lane opposite the local cricket pitch. The house beer is Triple fff Alton's Pride and the guest comes from a local brewery. All beers are sold at bargain-basement prices. The pub has a separate dining area where locally renowned and reasonably priced food is served. The nearest bus stop is Medstead, 1½ miles away. ♨Q✿◑P

Lymington

Borough Arms ✅
39 Avenue Road, SO41 9GP (off N end of New Street)
✪ 11-11 (midnight Fri & Sat); 12-10.30 Sun
☎ (01590) 672814
Ringwood Best Bitter, Fortyniner; guest beers Ⓗ
A lively, single-bar community pub with darts, pool, jukebox and selective TV sport. An adjoining, seated, carpeted lounge area is suitable for conversation. This is a former post house, built in 1855 and in the Jolliffe family for three generations. Guest ales are sought from both local and countrywide sources together with rapidly changing real ciders, including Black Rat and Moonshine. Bar snacks are generally available throughout the day. Handy for St Barbe Museum, library and town centre. ♨Q✿吴(X2)♣●P⁵-

Wheel Inn ⃝
Bowling Green, Sway Road, Pennington, SO41 8LJ (Ramiley Rd/Pitmore Lane jct, 2 miles W of Lymington) SZ297966
✪ 11 (12 winter)-midnight (1am Fri & Sat); 12-11 Sun
☎ (01590) 676122 ⊕ thewheelinnpub.co.uk
Ringwood Best Bitter; guest beers Ⓗ
Large, family-friendly bar in a Victorian building, formerly a pottery and then a blacksmith's. It specialises in sourcing unusual guest ales of differing styles. The separate Thai restaurant and takeaway occupies the lounge bar (no food Mon). There is stand-up comedy on the second Tuesday of each month, and acoustic music every Monday night. A pool table, jukebox and karaoke are on offer but this is mainly a pub for enlightened conversation. Camping (caravans only) is available. There is no weekend or evening bus service. Hours may be reduced in quiet periods.
♨✿◑&Å吴(X2)P⁵-

Milford on Sea

Red Lion
32 High Street, SO41 0QD (on B3058)
✪ 11.30-2.30, 6-11; 12-3 Sun ☎ (01590) 642236
Fuller's London Pride; Ringwood Best Bitter; guest beers Ⓗ
Imposing, extended 18th-century coaching inn with a notable fireplace. Run by Paul and June for 14 years, it has featured in the Guide for 12. Friendly, comfortable and relaxing, the single bar area is split up and arranged on several levels. One area is reserved for pool and darts with an unobtrusive gaming machine. Good-quality food is served and occasional live music events are staged. The cider is from Lilley's Cider Barn. No evening buses. ♨Q✿吴◑&Å吴(X2)♣●P⊟

North Waltham

Fox ⃝ ✅
Popham Lane, RG25 2BE (off Frog Lane, between village and A30, M3 jct 7) SU563458

❂ 11-11 (midnight Fri & Sat); 12-10.30 Sun
☎ (01256) 397288 ⊕ thefox.org
Brakspear Bitter; Sharp's Doom Bar; West Berkshire Good Old Boy; guest beer Ⓗ
Lovely country pub, overlooking farmland. The pub is divided into two – a popular restaurant and a public bar where food is also served (booking advisable). Outside there is an extensive beer garden and a children's adventure play area. Once a year the pub holds a charity oyster festival with a beer tent and many other stalls and attractions. The Ushers signage remains on the rear of the pub.
ᾼQ❂❂◖⊟ა⬛P♐

North Warnborough

Mill House
Hook Road, RG29 1ET (M3 jct 5; head towards Odiham) SU731521
❂ 11-11 ☎ (01256) 702953 ⊕ millhouse-hook.co.uk
Andwell King John; Brunning & Price Original; Three Castles Saxon Archer; guest beer Ⓗ
Listed as one of eight mills of Odiham in the Domesday Book, current sections are 17th-century additions, and it was last used as a corn mill in 1895. Most recently a restaurant, it is now under Brunning & Price ownership. It has a pleasant central bar area with eight handpumps, leading to separate tabled dining areas and a lower level view of the waterwheel and restaurant. The area surrounding the millpond fed from the Whitewater provides a pleasant outdoor seating area linking the function barn and parking. Disabled access is by request. ᾼQ◖⊟ა⬛(10)P♐

Oakhanger

Red Lion
GU35 9JQ SU770360
❂ 12-3, 6-11; 12-11 Sun ☎ (01420) 472232
Courage Best Bitter; Ringwood Fortyniner; Taylor Landlord; guest beer Ⓗ
Traditional unspoilt village pub catering for locals and visitors. There are views across the countryside from the front window seats. The restaurant has a good range of meals and in winter the pub is warmed by log fires – there is an inglenook fireplace. Dating from 1550, the pub was called the Rising Sun from 1700 until 1824. Acquired by Farnham United Breweries in 1927 and latterly Courage in 1951, the Red Lion is now an Enterprise Inn. ᾼQ❂❂◖⊟♣P♐

Old Basing

Bolton Arms
91 The Street, RG24 7DA SU667535
❂ 11-3, 5-11; 11-11 Fri & Sat; 12-6.30 Sun
☎ (01256) 819555 ⊕ thebolton.com
Andwell Ruddy Darter; guest beers Ⓗ/Ⓟ
Situated in quiet and picturesque Old Basing, the pub is less than two miles from Basingstoke centre. The building dates from 1490, and renovation in 2008 uncovered many period features including vaulted ceilings, oak beams and a central brick fireplace, all of which have added to its intimate ambience. There is an attractive landscaped beer garden at the rear of the property. The Inn Between bar was built from Basing House bricks and is renowned for sitings of The Cavalier ghost. The two guest beers may include another from Andwell and are often local. Q❂◖⊟ა⬛P♐

Millstone Ø
Bartons Lane, RG24 8AE (follow the signs from Bartons Lane to Basing House and car park) SU661531
❂ 11-11; 12-10.30 Sun ☎ (01256) 331153
⊕ millstoneoldbasing.co.uk
Wadworth Henry's IPA, Horizon, Boundary, 6X, seasonal beers; guest beer Ⓗ
An attractively situated Wadworth house, once part of a still-existing water mill that overlooks the River Loddon and a water meadow. The pub is a short walk from the historic and picturesque ruins of Basing House and a large medieval tithe barn. The Millstone features traditional pub food and six Wadworth cask ales, plus one rotating guest ale, served seven days a week by friendly staff. Children are welcome, as is the occasional duck from the river! ᾼ❂◖ა⬛P♐

Overton

Red Lion Ⓛ
37 High Street, RG25 3HQ SU514497
❂ 11.30-3, 6-11; 12-3 Sun ☎ (01256) 773363
⊕ redlion-overton.co.uk
Flowerpots Bitter; guest beer Ⓗ
Close to the village centre, this pub styles itself as a gastro-pub turned from boozie to foodie, with a good reputation for high-quality, freshly cooked food at reasonable prices. The main menu includes a vegetarian dish and there are daily specials with a contemporary flair – grilled Turkish figs and swordfish being examples. Three smartly decorated areas include a restaurant, main bar and snug with upholstered bench settees. Real ales are usually from a local Hampshire brewery. There is a car park at the rear and a partially covered patio area. A skittle alley/bar is available for private parties. ᾼQ❂◖⬛(76,86)P♐

Petersfield

George
28 The Square, GU32 3HH
❂ 9-11 (1am Fri & Sat); 9-10.30 Sun ☎ (01730) 233343
⊕ thegeorgepetersfield.co.uk
Beer range varies Ⓗ
One of the oldest buildings on the Square, this is a modern-looking bar and restaurant with a retro style. Two real ales and a real cider are available as well as an extensive range of locally sourced meals from breakfast to dinner. The bar area has comfortable settees while the larger restaurant is equipped with traditional wooden tables. There is a spacious courtyard garden to the rear and café seating is provided outside. ❂◖▶⇌⬛●

Good Intent Ø
40 College Street, GU31 4AF
❂ 11-3, 5.30-11 (11.30 Fri & Sat); 12-3, 7-11 Sun
☎ (01730) 263838 ⊕ goodintentpetersfield.co.uk
Fuller's London Pride, seasonal beer; Gale's Seafarers Ale, HSB; guest beers Ⓗ
A substantial 16th-century brick and timber coaching inn on the old road from London to Portsmouth, with a single bar and separate dining area. Some of the timbers used in building the pub came from the ship it is named after. An extensive menu of locally sourced food is available, as well as an all-you-can-eat curry night on Thursday. The inside is very traditional and there is a small paved outside drinking area to the front of the pub. ᾼ❂❄◖▶⇌P

Portsmouth

Artillery Arms L ✔
Hester Road, PO4 8HB
⏲ 12-11.30 (midnight Fri); 11-11.30 Sat ☎ (023) 9273 3611
Bowman Swift One; Fuller's ESB; Ringwood Fortyniner; guest beers Ⓗ
At the end of a cul-de-sac, this traditional two-bar back-street free house offers a selection of up to six ales from many southern breweries. Located just minutes from Fratton Park football ground, it can get lively on match days. The pub has a large walled garden with a children's play area. Food-wise, it offers good-value Sunday lunches, plus rolls and pies on match days. The pub also supports darts and pool teams and hosts a dominoes night.
Q❀🍴🚌(1c,6,17)♣P⁵–

Barley Mow L ✔
39 Castle Road, Southsea, PO5 3DE
⏲ 12 (11 Sat)-midnight; 12-11 Sun ☎ (023) 9282 3492
🌐 barleymowsouthsea.com
Fuller's London Pride; Gale's HSB; guest beers Ⓗ
This award-winning community pub hosts an amazing number of events including bands, quizzes, theme nights, a monthly moot for druids and of course egg yarping. It has pool and bar billiards tables, active darts, golf and cricket teams, plus a chess league. There are usually five beers on offer, including a mild, stout or porter. The garden is extremely well tended and is a must-see. Monday is quiz night, and there is a meat raffle on Sunday followed by good-natured competitions.
❀🍴♿⇌(Portsmouth & Southsea)🚌(1,1A,15)♣●

Bridge Tavern ✔
East Street, Old Portsmouth, PO1 2JJ
⏲ 11-11; 12-10.30 Sun ☎ (02392) 752992
Fuller's London Pride; Gale's Seafarers Ale, HSB Ⓗ
Situated right on Old Portsmouth's Camber Dock, this Grade II-listed building is decorated with a nautical theme throughout. It is popular with tourists and locals alike, especially when the weather is fine and customers can sit outside right on the jetty edge. Meals are served lunchtimes and evenings and fish is a speciality. Q❀◑🚌P⁵–

Eastfield Hotel ✔
124 Prince Albert Road, Southsea, PO4 9HT
⏲ 11-11 (12.30am Fri & Sat) ☎ (07894) 154488
Fuller's London Pride; Skinner's Cornish Knocker; guest beers Ⓗ
A large corner building in the residential area of Eastney, this two-bar pub has traditional tiling outside and wood panelling in the quieter lounge bar. The public bar is busier, with Sky Sports, darts and pool teams. The community aspect and local support continues with a Sunday quiz, barbecues and kids' events. Regular ale Cornish Knocker was originally picked as it shares the manager's name, but its popularity ensured its retention; guest ales are similarly chosen for quirky names.
🐴❀🍴🚌(1c,6,17)♣●

Eldon Arms L
11-17 Eldon Street, Southsea, PO5 4BS
⏲ 3 (12 Fri & Sat)-11; 12-10.30 Sun ☎ (023) 9229 7963
Fuller's London Pride; guest beers Ⓗ
A traditional tiled exterior belies an expansive interior, as the building encompasses the neighbouring cottage. This extension houses the games area with pool, darts and billiards; the other end of the bar has board games piled on a piano. Guest beers are both light and dark. There is a good community spirit, with a mixed clientele; although popular with students, this is not a student pub. Food is served lunchtimes, with a carvery on Sunday. The smoking shelter is heated.
❀◑⇌(Southsea)🚌(1,1A,15)♣●⁵–

Fifth Hants Volunteer Arms ✔
74 Albert Road, Southsea, PO5 2SL
⏲ 3-midnight; 12-1am Fri-Sun ☎ (023) 9282 7161
Fuller's London Pride; Gale's Seafarers Ale, HSB Ⓗ
A popular two-bar street-corner local that has been run by just two families since 1912. The public bar is simply decorated and lively, thanks to the enthusiastic management team, and has what is considered to be one of the best jukeboxes in town. It also displays the many certificates commemorating the pub's inclusion in this Guide. The smaller lounge bar is comfortable, decorated with memorabilia detailing the history of the pub's name and pictures of the pub's dogs past and present. 🍴🚌(17,18)♣

Florence Arms
18-20 Florence Road, Southsea, PO5 2NE
⏲ 12-midnight (11 Sun) ☎ (023) 9287 5700
Adnams Southwold Bitter, Broadside; Shepherd Neame Spitfire; guest beers Ⓗ
Surprisingly large back-street venue just two minutes' walk from the seafront. This well-run locals' pub is friendly to all visitors. A separate dining room serves good-value local food (no food Sat or Sun eves). Varied live entertainment includes blues, folk and poetry. A changing guest beer is sourced locally. It also has an excellent range of at least 30 ciders and perries.
Q◑🍴🚌(1,5A,6)♣●

Fountain Inn L
163 London Road, North End, PO2 9AA
⏲ 12 (11 Sat)-11.30; 12-11 Sun ☎ (023) 9266 1636
Gale's HSB; Irving Frigate Ⓗ
A large single-bar pub close to North End shops, this former Brickwoods house has retained its tiled frontage from 1898 when it was built by the Pike Spicer brewery. The landlady has collected a number of historic photographs of the surrounding area and these are displayed on the walls along with watercolour copies by local artists Tina Jones and Gary Knapp. The separate family/games room at the rear may be hired. A quiz is held on Thursdays. 🐴❀♿🚌(1,3,6)♣⁵–

Golden Eagle
1 Delamare Road, Southsea, PO4 0JA
⏲ 3-midnight (1am Fri); 12-1am Sat; 12-11 Sun
☎ (023) 9282 1658
Fuller's London Pride, seasonal beers; Gale's Seafarers Ale, HSB; guest beers Ⓗ
A substantial enthusiastically run street-corner pub, the Eagle, as it is known, is located in a residential part of Southsea between Fratton station and Albert Road. The larger front bar is comfortably decorated and hosts live music at weekends. The smaller back bar is wood panelled and has a pool table and access to a small patio garden. The pub publishes its own newsletter of forthcoming events and gigs. 🔥❀🚌(17,18,19)♣

Hole in the Wall 🍷 L
36 Great Southsea Street, Southsea, PO5 3BY
⏲ 2-11; 12-midnight Fri; 2-midnight Sat ☎ (023) 9229 8085
🌐 theholeinthewallpub.co.uk

Oakleaf Hole Hearted Ⓖ; guest beers Ⓗ/Ⓖ
A genuine free house, the Hole is probably the smallest pub in Portsmouth, but definitely has one of the best beer ranges. The current selection of beers is displayed on its website. Hole Hearted, originally brewed just for this pub, is on gravity. Real cider is always available. Weapons Grade ginger beer is stocked when available. Food is available 4-8pm apart from Mondays. Good quality sausages and suet puddings are the house speciality. No admittance after 11pm.
Q❶⇌(Southsea)🚋(1,1A,15)❀🖝🖓

Leopold Tavern Ⓛ ✅
154 Albert Road, Southsea, PO4 0JT
✿ 11-midnight; 12-11 Sun ☎ (023) 9282 9748
Beer range varies Ⓗ
A large street-corner pub with a green tiled exterior and bright, spacious interior with an island bar. The walls are decorated with local photographs and there are comfortable seats to the rear. The beer range is excellent, with up to 10 real ales from southern independent breweries, often including a stout or porter. The cider drinker is also well catered for, with up to three varieties available. A large sign outside proclaims its status as local CAMRA Pub of the Year for 2010 and 2011.
✿🚋(17,18,19)♣🖝🖢

Northcote Hotel Ⓛ
35 Francis Avenue, Southsea, PO4 0HL
✿ 11-midnight (1am Fri & Sat); 12-midnight Sun
☎ (023) 9278 9888 ⊕ northcotehotel.co.uk
Hop Back Summer Lightning; Irving Invincible; Taylor Landlord; Wadworth 6X Ⓗ
A traditional two-bar back-street local a few minutes' walk from Albert Road. The large public bar has a dartboard and pool table, and the smaller lounge is comfortably decorated with old cinema memorabilia, featuring comedy greats like Charlie Chaplin and the Marx Brothers, and the most famous of all fictional detectives, Sherlock Holmes. To the rear is a spacious patio garden equipped with heaters for the benefit of smokers in the colder months. ✿🖰🚋(17,18,19)♣🖢

Old Customs House ✅
Vernon Building, Gunwharf Quay, PO1 3TY
✿ 9-midnight (10.30 winter; 2am Fri & Sat); 9-11 Sun
☎ (023) 9283 2333
Fuller's London Pride, ESB, seasonal beers; Gale's Seafarers Ale, HSB Ⓗ
Set within the modern Gunwharf Quays retail and leisure complex, this pub is an award-winning conversion of the former Naval Pay Office in HMS Vernon. The layout of the Grade II-listed building comprises several rooms spread over the ground and first floors, many with period fittings. Complete redecoration in spring 2012 strengthened the nautical and naval theme throughout. It holds a popular Easter real ale festival.
Q✿🖰❶&⇌(Harbour)🚋🖢

Old House at Home ✅
104 Locksway Road, Milton, PO4 8RJ
✿ 12-midnight (1am Fri & Sat) ☎ (02392) 732606
Fuller's London Pride; Gale's HSB; Taylor Golden Best, Landlord Ⓗ
For the real ale enthusiast who enjoys live music, this is where to be at weekends. With four real ales on offer and 10 ciders plus guests, the variety is always interesting. The pub has a lovely warm atmosphere, especially in winter months, with

open fires in both bars; during the summer the large garden is the place to catch the rays. Traditional pub food is served, including the delicious Sunday roasts, but this is by no means a foodie pub. 🏚✿🖰❶&🖰&🚋(13,14)♣🖝P

Pembroke
20 Pembroke Road, Southsea, PO1 2NR
✿ 10-midnight (11 Mon); 12-4, 7-11 Sun ☎ (023) 9282 3961
Draught Bass; Fuller's London Pride; Greene King Abbot Ⓗ
Purpose built as a street-corner hostelry in 1711, this now single-room bar has a horseshoe-shaped interior and an L-shaped servery decorated with naval memorabilia. It is mentioned in the Captain Marryat novels under its original name of the Little Blue Line. It changed its name to the Pembroke in 1900. This pub is a rare haven for the discerning drinker, which explains its varied clientele, and it still serves probably the best pint of London Pride in Portsmouth. 🚋(6,6a)

Phoenix
13 Duncan Road, Southsea, PO5 2QU
✿ 10-midnight (1am Fri & Sat); 12-midnight Sun
☎ (023) 9278 1055
Beer range varies Ⓗ
A proper street-corner local that still retains its two bars. The public bar has a projector TV which is used to show various sporting events, and at weekends it has live music. The lounge is comfortable, with a piano and an antique telephone, and is adorned with memorabilia relating to the nearby Kings Theatre. Next to the lounge is a small walled patio garden and a separate games room, which was once part of the Dock End Brewery. A hidden gem well worth seeking out. ✿🖰🚋(17,18)♣🖢

Rose in June ✅
102 Milton Road, PO3 6AR
✿ 12-midnight (1am Fri & Sat) ☎ (023) 928 24191
⊕ theroseinjune.co.uk
Gale's HSB; Irving Invincible; Ringwood Best Bitter; Sharp's Doom Bar; guest beers Ⓗ
A substantial two-bar pub once owned by Allen's Buckland Brewery. Situated a 20-minute walk from Fratton Park, it is popular with football supporters. The first Wednesday of the month is curry night and there is a quiz every Tuesday evening. The pub has a spacious garden with a play area, barbecue and marquee (used for beer festivals in February and June). Ciders include Cheddar Valley, Old Rosie and Black Rat. ✿🖰&♣🖝🖢

Sir John Baker ✅
80 London Road, North End, PO2 0LN
✿ 7-11 (11.30 Thu; 12.30am Fri & Sat) ☎ (023) 9262 7960
Courage Directors; Greene King Abbot; Ruddles Best Bitter; guest beers Ⓗ
Named after a 19th-century MP and Lord Mayor and located in a busy main street, this Wetherspoon pub was converted from a former TSB bank and recently celebrated its 10th anniversary. The manager supports local microbreweries, and beers from Irving, Oakleaf, Triple fff, Itchen Valley and Goddards are often available. The cider and perry are from Thatchers and Broadoak. During the year two beer festivals and a cider festival are held. Food is available all day every day. Well served by buses.
❶&🚋(1,3,6)🖝🖢

HAMPSHIRE

Sir Loin of Beef 🅛
152 Highland Road, Southsea, PO4 9NH
�🕐 11 (12 Sun)-11.30 (midnight Fri & Sat) ☎ (023) 9282 0115
Plain Ales Sheep Dip; Titanic Plum Porter; guest beers Ⓗ
Unmissable from the outside and brightly decorated inside with painted vines and suspended umbrellas, this free house has a warm, almost Mediterranean feel. Eight beers with a mix of light and dark are sourced mainly from southern independent breweries, and a good range of bottle-conditioned beers is stocked. There is a Thursday quiz with hot dogs, Sunday lunchtime jazz once a month, and plenty of submarine paraphernalia. A jukebox, pinball machine, boxed cider and one value beer add to the appeal.
🅐🚃(1c,6,17)♣🍴

Still & West Country House ✅
Bath Square, Old Portsmouth, PO1 2LJ
🕐 10 (11 Sun)-11 ☎ (023) 92821567
Fuller's London Pride, ESB; Gale's HSB Ⓗ
Popular Grade II-listed building on the waterfront at the entrance to Portsmouth harbour, with fantastic views of the Gunwharf retail complex and Spinnaker Tower. Inside, the decor has a distinctly nautical theme and the ground floor bar includes a very impressive painted ceiling depicting Portsmouth's historical past. There is also a large photograph of HMS Vanguard, the Royal Navy's last battleship, which ran aground outside the pub in 1960 while being towed to the scrapyard.
🏰Q🕐🍴&

White Swan ✅
26 Guildhall Walk, PO1 2DD
🕐 9-11 (1am Fri & Sat) ☎ (023) 9289 1340
Beer range varies Ⓗ
An excellent recent renovation of a run-down city-centre pub. Although part of the Wetherspoon chain, this outlet has a more pubby feel. A varying range of up to six ales and three ciders is available, often featuring local breweries such as Hammerpot and Oakleaf. Food is served all day up to 10pm. There is a wide variety of board games and even a dartboard. Although the two televisions are always on they show news channels with subtitles and are kept silent. 🍴≈(Portsmouth & Southsea)♣🍴

Winchester Arms 🅛
99 Winchester Road, Buckland, PO2 7PS
🕐 3 (4 Mon)-11; 12-11 Sat & Sun ☎ (023) 9266 2443
🌐 thewinchpub.co.uk
Oakleaf Hole Hearted; Shepherd Neame Spitfire; guest beers Ⓗ
A proper back-street local, this friendly two-bar pub offers two regular beers and a varying guest. There is an annual spring bank holiday beer festival and live music every Sunday evening. The local science fiction group is hosted on the second Tuesday of the month and a darts team is fielded. There is a covered area in the garden for smokers. It may stay open beyond 11pm on Friday and Saturday if busy. Dogs welcome. 🏰Q🕐🍴🔧♣🍴

Ringwood

Inn on the Furlong ✅
12 Meeting House Lane, BH24 1EY (opp central car park and bus terminus)
🕐 9.30am-11 (midnight Fri & Sat); 10-11 Sun
☎ (01425) 475139

Jennings Cocker Hoop; Marston's seasonal beers; Ringwood Best Bitter, Fortyniner, Old Thumper, seasonal beers Ⓗ
This cream-painted Victorian house is a popular and convenient meeting place for mature customers, who benefit from the early opening times and breakfasts. Inside, a raised bar serves several interlinked rooms, including a family area and a conservatory. Outside are two small patios, one with a bar in fine weather and a weatherproofed TV. Masala, a nearby curry house, provides an Indian buffet on Wednesday night. The real cider is from Cheddar Valley. 🏰Q🎵🕐🍴🔧🅐🚃♣🍴🍴

Rockbourne

Rose & Thistle ✅
SP6 3NL SU113183
🕐 11-3, 6-11; 11-11 Sat; 12-10.30 (8 winter) Sun
☎ (01725) 518236 🌐 roseandthistle.co.uk
Fuller's London Pride; Palmers Copper Ale; Taylor Landlord; guest beer Ⓗ
Delightful 16th-century, thatched, chalk cob gem with beamed ceilings, two log fires and cottage garden frontage, in an attractive village close to a Roman villa. A locally sourced guest ale is added in summer and local game, fish and home-made sorbets and ice cream feature on an imaginative menu (no food Sun eve). The restaurant has a collection of Simon Drew animal caricatures. The pub is frequented by the local cricket team and set in good walking and cycling country. The car park entrance is narrow. A party is held on the second bank holiday Sunday in May. 🏰Q🕐🍴🍴P🍴

Romsey

Bishop Blaize 🅛 ✅
4 Winchester Road, SO51 8AA
🕐 12-11 (midnight Fri & Sat); 12-10.30 Sun
☎ (01794) 511777
Ringwood Best Bitter; guest beer Ⓗ
Named after the patron saint of woolcombers and built in the 1700s, this popular, welcoming local is a third of a mile from Romsey station and on a number of bus routes. Ringwood Best is served alongside a guest beer. Sports events are shown on the large screen at one end of the pub and in the paved garden in the heated smoking shelter. The pub hosts crib and darts teams and there is live music on Saturday nights. 🏰🎵≈🚃(4)♣P🍴

Cromwell Arms 🅛
Mainstone, SO51 8HG (on A3090 at W edge of town)
🕐 12-9.30 ☎ (01794) 519515 🌐 thecromwellarms.com
Flack Manor Double Drop; guest beers Ⓗ
Previously the Horse and Jockey and then a Spanish restaurant, this gastro-style pub, now with accommodation, is on the western edge of town across the street from the famous Broadlands estate. Good food, both full à la carte meals and bar snacks, is available at all times. The small but well-stocked bar has local ales on handpump and an extensive wine list. A covered patio looks onto woodland and the nearby River Test. There is no fruit machine or jukebox. Q🎵🍴🕐🚃(4)P🍴

Old House at Home
62 Love Lane, SO51 8DE (NE of town, next to Waitrose car park)
🕐 11-11 (11.30 Fri & Sat); 12-10.30 Sun ☎ (01794) 513175
🌐 theoldhouseathomeromsey.co.uk

Fuller's Discovery, London Pride, seasonal beers;
Gale's Seafarers Ale, HSB Ⓗ
Smart, white-painted pub, once two houses – one
of them thatched. This popular, efficiently run pub
was Fuller's Pub of the Year in 2010. Conveniently,
a gate leads into the sheltered patio garden from
the Waitrose car park. A good place to eat: at lunch
the menu is traditional, with wider choices in the
evening; roasts rule on Sunday lunch. The pub is
dog- and child-friendly too. Entertainments include
folk and blues on Mondays, and a quiz night every
other Sunday. Q❀◑≉🚃(4)P↖

Tudor Rose

3 Corn Market, SO51 8GB
✪ 11 (10 summer)-11; 10-midnight Sat; 12-11 Sun
☎ (01794) 512126
**Courage Best Bitter; Shepherd Neame Spitfire; guest
beer** Ⓗ
A small no-frills pub in a good central location on
the Corn Market and near the bus station. The
building's varied history includes time as a
workhouse, a brothel and a guildhall. The almost
square single bar has a fine timbered ceiling and
an ancient fireplace. Regulars choose the guest
beer in summer. A courtyard provides extra space
outside for drinkers and smokers. There is live
music every Saturday evening and Sunday
afternoon. 🏛❀≉🚃♣↖

Ropley

Anchor

The Dene, SO24 0BG (on A31 next to Shell Garage)
✪ 12-11 (midnight Fri; 1am Sat) ☎ 07973 178028
⊕ theanchorropley.com
**Stonehenge Danish Dynamite; Triple fff Alton's
Pride** Ⓗ
Small, friendly pub with large-screen TVs and a
wide range of music on computer, which can also
be used by customers. There is live music on
Saturday nights, and the venue is cyclist- and
motorcyclist-friendly. A tent site is available by
prior arrangement. There is also a skittle alley that
can be hired as a function house. January to March
opening is from 4pm. There are plans to have food
available – check the website. The Anchor is a 10-
minute walk from Watercress Steam Railway's
Ropley Station. 🏛❀▲🚃(64)P↖

Selborne

Selborne Arms ✪

High Street, GU34 3JR
✪ 11-3, 6-11; 11-11 Sat summer; 12-11 Sun
☎ (01420) 511247 ⊕ selbornearms.co.uk
**Courage Best Bitter; Oakleaf Old Dick; Ringwood
Fortyniner; guest beers** Ⓗ
A traditional award-winning village pub with real
fires and a friendly atmosphere, located at the foot
of the zig-zag path carved by famous naturalist
Gilbert White. Extensive menus showcase local and
home-made produce. Up to four guest beers come
from local microbreweries, and Mr Whitehead's
ciders are always available. A play area in the huge
garden is popular with children and parents, and
there are heaters and a woodburner to keep you
warm. 🏛Q❀◑💷🚃(72,X72)♣♦↖

Shedfield

Wheatsheaf Inn Ⓛ

Botley Road, SO32 2JG (on A334) SU558130
✪ 12-11 (10.30 Sun) ☎ (01329) 833024
⊕ thewheatsheafinnshedfield.co.uk
**Flowerpots Perridge Pale, Bitter, Gooden's Gold,
seasonal beer; guest beers** Ⓖ
This ever-popular country pub was local CAMRA
Pub of the Year 2011. It serves a selection of six
locally brewed real ales directly from casks behind
the bar. Two Thatchers real ciders are also
available. The home-cooked food is excellent (eve
meals Tue and Wed only). Live blues, jazz or folk
music features most Saturday evenings. A beer
festival is held over the late spring bank holiday
weekend. The garden's flowers are delightful in
summer. 🏛Q❀◑💷🚃(69)♣♦P↖

Southampton

Bitter Virtue Off Licence Ⓛ

70 Cambridge Road, SO14 6US
✪ closed Mon; 10.30-8.30 (2 Sun) ☎ (023) 8055 4881
⊕ bittervirtue.co.uk
Beer range varies Ⓖ
Speciality beer shop hidden in the back streets of
Portswood, selling nearly 500 different bottled
beers and ciders from around the world, including
Belgium, Germany, the US and Britain – many of
them local. At least one draught real ale and a cider
are available for takeaway. Polypins and firkins
from local breweries can be ordered upon request.
Badged glasses, brewery T-shirts and books can
also be purchased. ≉(St Denys)🚃

Cricketers

34 Carlton Place, SO15 2DX
✪ 12-12.30am (1am Thu-Sat); 12-11 Sun ☎ (023) 8022 6448
Keystone Bedrock Bitter; guest beers Ⓗ
Unpretentious busy city pub with a U-shaped
traditional bar and welcoming bar staff. Four locally
sourced ales (one is often from Bowman) and one
real cider are usually available. Home-cooked food
is served every day except Saturday, with burgers
and ribs the specialities. There are roasts on
Sundays in winter and barbecues in summer.
Outside is a courtyard beer garden, which hosts a
cider festival in May and a beer festival in July.
❀◑≉(Central)♦P

Guide Dog ♀ Ⓛ

38 Earl's Road, Bevois Valley, SO14 6SF (opp Aldi, off
Bevois Valley Rd)
✪ 12-11 (10.30 Sun) ☎ (023) 8022 5642
⊕ theguidedogsouthampton.co.uk
Flowerpots Goodens Gold; Fuller's ESB; guest beers Ⓗ
Single-roomed, back-street local that is a former
CAMRA Wessex Pub of the Year and Branch Pub of
the Year 2012. Up to six guest beers, mainly from
local breweries, are complemented by a range of
British and Belgian bottled beers and good-value
rolls. Within walking distance of St Mary's Stadium,
it is busy with home and visiting fans on match
days. Other attractions include the Friday meat
draw, October beer festival and charity events that
maintain the tradition that led to the pub's present
name. ≉(St Denys)🚃♣↖

Hop Inn Ⓛ

Woodmill Lane, SO18 2PH (corner of Oak Tree Rd)
✪ 11-11; 12.30-10.30 Sun ☎ (023) 8055 7723
Bowman Swift One; Gale's HSB; guest beers Ⓗ

By Riverside Park in Bitterne, the unassuming Hop Inn could be easily overlooked, but step inside the lounge bar and it instantly feels like home. A long L-shaped bar sits one side with seating on the other. The public bar is reached though a separate entrance and houses bar games and a jukebox. Up to six beers can be on offer. A quiz is held on the first Sunday of the month and competitors are treated to complimentary cheese and biscuits. ◑❦🖳♣●P⁝—

Key & Anchor 🅛
90 Millbrook Road East, Freemantle, SO15 1JQ
🌣 12-11 (midnight Fri & Sat); 12-10.30 Sun
☎ (023) 8090 0747
Itchen Valley Godfathers; Ringwood Fortyniner, Old Thumper; guest beer Ⓗ
Victorian street-corner local, opened on 12 September 1862. Four handpumps serve three regular and one guest beer. Full of characters, the pub has two real fires and prides itself on being dog friendly. A spacious garden features summer barbecues. There is karaoke and disco on Saturday evenings, an excellent jukebox and two darts teams. A covered area in the garden caters for smokers. 🚶❦≈(Central/Millbrook)🖳♣⁝—

Park Inn ✔
37 Carlisle Road, Shirley, SO16 4FN (jct of Carlisle Rd and Shirley Park Rd)
🌣 11.30 (12 Sat & Sun)-11.30 ☎ (023) 8078 7875
Wadworth Henry's IPA, 6X, Bishops Tipple, seasonal beers; guest beers Ⓗ
Early 1860s local that became a Wadworth house in the late 1980s. It is a single-bar pub but has two entrances and retains a two-bar feeling; many brewery-themed mirrors adorn the walls. Six handpumps serve the Wadworth range, plus seasonal and guest beers. The paved garden area has seating for alfresco drinking. Sundays are busy, with a lunchtime meat draw and a popular evening quiz. There are two annual beer festivals and free Wi-Fi. Q❦🖳♣●⁝—

Platform Tavern ✔
Town Quay, SO14 2NY (rear entrance in Winkle St)
🌣 12-11 (midnight Thu-Sat) ☎ (023) 8033 7232
🌐 platformtavern.com
Dancing Man seasonal beers; Fuller's London Pride; Gale's Seafarers Ale; guest beers Ⓗ
Named after the long-gone town quay gun platform, the decor of this attractive free house is a quirky mixture of Bohemian, African and original medieval town wall. The two-barrel Dancing Man Brewery, visible through an internal window in the bar, was installed in 2011, and its beers are proving popular. There is live music Thursday and Friday evenings and Sunday lunchtimes. Interesting menu choices are on offer lunchtime and evenings all week, and all day Thursday to Sunday. Ask at the bar for real cider from the back room. ◑🖳●

South Western Arms
38-40 Adelaide Road, St Denys, SO17 2HW (adjoins St Denys station down side)
🌣 12-11 (midnight Fri & Sat) ☎ (023) 8032 4542
🌐 southwesternarms.com
Bowman Swift One; guest beers Ⓗ
A traditional pub split over two floors with a large walled garden to the rear, with a heated smoking shelter. The bar always has a good variety of real ales, sometimes as many as 10, with beers sourced locally and from further afield. Westons Old Rosie

cider is always available. Beer festivals are held in May and November each year. The upper floor has a pool table and table football, while a dartboard is in a side room on the ground floor. ❦≈(St Denys)♣●P⁝—

Waterloo Arms 🅛
101 Waterloo Road, Freemantle, SO15 3BS (next door to the prominent Christ Church)
🌣 12-11 ☎ (023) 8022 0022
Hop Back GFB, Crop Circle, Entire Stout, Summer Lightning, seasonal beers; guest beers Ⓗ
There has been a pub here since the 1860s but the present pub was erected in the 1930s, becoming Hop Back's second house in 1991. It has a single L-shaped bar with a rear conservatory and paved garden with seating. Eight handpumps serve the Hop Back range, plus seasonal and guest beers. Families are welcome until 8pm in the conservatory. Lunchtime meals are served daily (except Wed), and Sunday roasts are always popular. Tuesday is quiz night and Sunday afternoon has a meat draw. Old Rosie cider is served. Regular beer festivals are held. 🚲❦◑≈(Millbrook)🖳●⁝—

Wellington Arms 🅛
56 Park Road, Freemantle, SO15 3DE (jct Mansion Rd and Park Rd)
🌣 12-midnight ☎ (023) 8022 0356
Fuller's London Pride, ESB; Ringwood Best Bitter, Old Thumper; guest beers Ⓗ
Dating from the 1860s, this pub was called the Swan until 1975. There are two distinct and dimly lit bars, with another room that leads to a paved garden area with a covered and heated smoking shelter. Eleven handpumps serve four regular beers and up to seven guests. Much Iron Duke memorabilia adorns the walls and there are many pre-decimal coins set into the bar counters. On Thursday evenings a popular quiz is held. The building has the rare distinction of being the Redondan consulate. ❦❦≈(Central)⁝—

Southwick

Golden Lion 🅛
High Street, PO17 6EB
🌣 12-3, 5.30-11 (midnight Fri); 12-midnight Sat; 12-10.30 (7 winter) Sun ☎ (023) 9221 0437
Oakleaf Old Dick, Skew Sunshine Ale; guest beer Ⓗ
Excellent, friendly, village free house steeped in history. Eisenhower and Montgomery drank together here to plan the D-Day landings. Although the brewhouse no longer brews (it is an excellent beer off-licence and museum), the regulars come from near and far to enjoy the award-winning food and excellent ales all sourced from local breweries. Occasionally folk or jazz music is played in the main bar. 🚶Q❦◑♣●P⁝—

Sway

Hare & Hounds ✔
SO41 6AL SZ283986
🌣 11-11 ☎ (01590) 682404
Ringwood Best Bitter; Taylor Landlord; guest beer Ⓗ
Long, narrow pub, built over 200 years ago as a coaching inn, on the edge of heathland. The beamed, farmhouse-style interior is divided into several separate seating areas. At the rear is a sheltered garden with a children's play area. Food

is served all day until 9.30pm. A Sunday quiz night and occasional Irish nights are held, and an annual beer and music festival over the last weekend in June. One and a quarter miles south is Sway Tower, 218 feet of unreinforced concrete, built around 1879 by a retired Indian judge. ⛺Q✿🕙 ♿️P🚲

Tangley

Cricketers Arms

SP11 0SH (towards Lower Chute) SU327528
☼ 11-3 (not Mon & Tue), 6-11; 12-3, 7-10.30 Sun
☎ (01264) 730283 ⏛ thecricketers.eu
Bowman Swift One, Wallops Wood Ⓖ
In attractive countryside, this 16th-century drovers' inn sits below the Berkshire Downs. The two Bowman ales, served from stillage behind the bar, may be supplemented by a local guest in summer months. The front bar, with its huge inglenook fireplace, is used mainly for drinking, while traditional home-cooked food is available in the flagstoned dining area at the rear.
⛺Q✿🍴🕙♿️🚃(C6)P🚲

Tichborne

Tichborne Arms

nr Alresford, SO24 0NA SU571304
☼ 11.45-3, 6-11 (midnight Fri); 12-11.30 Sat; 12-4 Sun
☎ (01962) 733760 ⏛ tichbornearms.co.uk
Palmers Copper Ale; guest beers Ⓖ
Thatched country pub comprising a compact public bar with traditional pub games and a larger rustic lounge with a woodburner, appreciated equally by customers and the four resident canines. At least two guests are served from breweries such as Bowman, Dark Star and Triple fff, and cider from Mr Whitehead's. The fine menu features home-cooked locally sourced food. The garden, which hosts a three-day beer festival every August, includes a well-appointed covered patio for smokers. Children and dogs welcome. ⛺Q✿🕙🍺♣🚲P🚲

Titchfield

Wheatsheaf Ⓛ

1 East Street, PO14 4AD (E end of East Street)
☼ 12-3, 6-11; 12-11 Wed & Thu; 12-midnight Fri & Sat; 12-11 Sun ☎ (01329) 842965
Flowerpots Bitter; Palmers Best Bitter; guest beers Ⓗ
Welcoming 17th-century free house and Guide regular, now with a new licensee who is a keen real ale fan. A cosy bar with a real fire leads into a separate snug and a newly refurbished restaurant. Food is served every day except Monday, with roasts on Sunday, and bar meals available at lunchtimes. At the rear, a covered smoking area and beer garden leads to a small private car park. Annual beer festivals are held during summer and winter. ⛺🐕✿🕙♿️🚃(57,72,80)P🚲

Twyford

Bugle Inn Ⓛ

Park Lane, SO21 1QT (jct of Park Lane and High St)
☼ 12-11 (10.30 Sun) ☎ (01962) 714888
⏛ bugleinntwyford.co.uk
Bowman Wallops Wood; Flowerpots Bitter; Lees Governor Ⓗ
Attractive, modernised pub, reopened in 2008 after several closed years and a campaign to save it from property developers. There is one long, open bar

with plush sofas at one end and a restaurant area at the other; the central bar has stools to accommodate casual drinkers. Good-quality food is a big feature, with the focus on local produce. The Bowman and Flowerpots ales may be differing brews, and sometimes an Upham beer is offered. Mr Whitehead's cider is available. Free Wi-Fi.
⛺✿🕙🚃(69)♦P🚲

Phoenix ✅

High Street, SO21 1RF
☼ 11.30-2.30, 6-11; 11.30-11 Fri & Sat; 12-7 Sun
☎ (01962) 713322 ⏛ thephoenixinn.co.uk
Greene King IPA, Abbot; guest beers Ⓗ
Village pub dating from the 17th century, when it was a coaching inn on the old Winchester to Portsmouth road. The single, long bar is multi-level and there is a popular skittle alley/private function room to the rear. Traditional pub food is served, with additional themed nights such as pizza on Wednesday, fish and chips Thursday and a curry evening every last Monday of the month. There is a large-screen TV for major sporting events. Occasional live music sessions and quiz nights are hosted. ⛺✿🕙🚃(69)♣P🚲

Upper Farringdon

Rose & Crown Ⓛ

Crows Lane, GU34 3ED (signed off A32) SU715351
☼ 12-3, 5.30-11; 12-11 Sat; 12-10.30 Sun ☎ (01420) 588231
⏛ roseandcrownfarringdon.co.uk
Triple fff Alton's Pride, Moondance Ⓗ
Built in 1810 by the Knight family of Chawton, the Rose & Crown is off the beaten track but worth seeking out. Enter this friendly pub to find a welcoming L-shaped bar with a seating area warmed by a log fire, and a dining area leading to a modern restaurant. An imaginative menu is supplemented by lunchtime bar snacks. Food is served lunchtimes and evenings, all day on Sunday. Families, walkers and dogs are welcome and there is a spacious garden. ⛺Q✿🕙P🚲

West End

Master Builder ✅

Swaythling Road, SO30 3AH
☼ 11 (12 Sun)-11 ☎ (023) 8047 2426
⏛ masterbuildersouthampton.co.uk
Wadworth Henry's IPA, 6X, Bishops Tipple; guest beers Ⓗ
Roadside inn on the A27 with an open-plan interior divided into three distinct areas: a raised space for dining, a bar area, and a games area with pool, darts and a real fire in winter. There is also a conservatory that can be used for private functions. A ramp outside gives access to the dining area, although the pub does not have full disabled facilities. Food is served all day at weekends. A quiz is held on Sunday evening and there are two beer festivals each year. ⛺✿🕙🚃(A,8A)♣P

West Tytherley

Black Horse Ⓛ

North Lane, SP5 1NF SU275301
☼ 7-10.30 Mon; 12-3 (not Tue), 6-11; 12-8 Sun
☎ (01794) 340308
Bowman Wallops Wood; Flowerpots Bitter; Hop Back GFB; Stonehenge Great Bustard Ⓗ

A gem of a free house, this convivial 17th-century coaching inn is the hub for local sports and social groups as well as thirsty cyclists and walkers from near and far – the pub is close to the Clarendon Way long distance walk. In addition to the two bars, there are side rooms and a skittle alley surrounding a sheltered courtyard. The locally sourced menu includes Pie of the Day. No food Monday evening. The beer and cider range may vary. ♨Q⛄☼◐⬗☐(37)♣●P⅄

Whitchurch

Bell Inn ⊘

Bell Street, RG28 7DD
⚙ 10-11; 12-10.30 Sun ☎ (01256) 893120
⊕ thebellwhitchurch.co.uk
Courage Best Bitter; Fuller's London Pride; Gale's Seafarers Ale Ⓗ
The 15th-century, half-timbered, family-run Bell just oozes the character of a traditional pub. Look carefully for the wooden nail in the timber work. Conversation and local gossip rule in both bars, while a separate area off the lounge with exposed beams provides space for enjoying a quiet pint or a meeting for a club or society. Acoustic music with local musicians features on alternate Sunday afternoons. There is a pool table and a small library that raises funds for charity. Outside is a small pleasant patio. The pub has an electric car charging point. Q☼⛄◐⬗☐(76,86)♣

Prince Regent Ⓛ

104 London Road, RG28 7LT SU469455
⚙ 12-11 (10.30 Sun) ☎ (01256) 892179
Hop Back Summer Lightning; Stonehenge Pigswill Ⓗ
The pub up the hill is a single-bar local free house on the edge of this country town, overlooking the higher reaches of the Test Valley. Local conversation takes pride of place among a mixed clientele who enjoy some of the best real ale prices in the area. There is an excellent jukebox, a pool table and sports TV, with an emphasis on football matches. ☐(76,86)♣P

Whitchurch Sports & Social Club

Longmeadow, Winchester Road, RG28 7RB (on S edge of town by football ground) SU471463
⚙ 7-11; 2-11.30 Sat; 12-3, 7.30-11 Sun ☎ 07963 159273
Bowman Swift One; guest beer Ⓗ
Next to the town football ground, the two-bar premises is home to the social, football, bowls and squash clubs. The large, comfortable lounge is adorned with historic pictures and overlooks an impressive indoor bowls green. The second bar can act as a function room for parties, dinners and music events, and has an impressive collection of football shirts as well as pool and darts. Check in advance if requiring food. Sunday roasts are available but need to be booked. The guest beer is often from another local brewery. ⛄☼◐☐(86)♣P⅄

White Hart Hotel ⊘

The Square, RG28 7DN
⚙ 11-11; 12-10.30 Sun ☎ (01256) 892900
⊕ whitehsarthotelwhitchurch.co.uk
Arkell's 3B, Moonlight Ale, Kingsdown Ale Ⓗ
This 15th-century coaching inn is a centre of community life, with a lively public bar, pleasant dining area and a quiet restaurant to the rear, also used for private functions and meetings. Local artists' work adorns the walls, and look out for

decorated bollards outside. One, facing the hotel, commemorates the author Charles Kingsley, who stayed here. Regular events are held, from discos and bands to charity challenges. In the square outside, the right to demonstrate was won for the country in the 19th century, and Lord Denning was born in the building across the road. Opens for breakfasts. ♨Q☼⛄◐⬗☐♿(76,86)P⅄

Whitehill

Woodlark

Petersfield Road, GU35 9AH
⚙ 11.30-11 ☎ (01420) 488367 ⊕ woodlarkpub.co.uk
Marston's Pedigree; Ringwood Best Bitter; Wychwood Hobgoblin Ⓗ
Only four years old, this single-bar Marston's pub offers a huge seating area divided into eight 'rooms', providing comfortable seating in pairs, fours or larger tables for drinkers and diners. There is an extensive food menu with various money-saving offers to tempt diners. Special menus are provided for Valentine's, Mother's Day and other occasions. The pub is close to Woolmer Forest, once army training land, now a Site of Special Scientific Interest – the only SSSI in Britain known to support all 12 species of reptiles and amphibians. ☼◐♿☐(13,18)P⅄

Winchester

Black Boy Ⓛ

1 Wharf Hill, SO23 9NQ (just off Chesil St, B3404)
⚙ 12-11 (midnight Fri & Sat); 12-10.30 Sun
☎ (01962) 861754 ⊕ theblackboypub.com
Flowerpots Bitter; Hop Back Summer Lightning; Itchen Valley Pure Gold; Ringwood Best Bitter; guest beers Ⓗ
Centuries-old rambling building comprising many interconnected rooms, resembling a well-stocked folk museum, serviced from a central bar. One room is themed as a country kitchen complete with working Aga, another a butcher's, with papier mâché joints, while other areas are tradesmen's workshops. Pub food is served Tuesday evening to Sunday lunchtime. Guest beers usually come from local breweries, often Bowman. A splendid medieval themed smoking shelter graces the patio/garden. The nearby Black Rat restaurant is in the same ownership. ♨Q☼◐☐⅄

Fulflood Arms Ⓛ

28 Cheriton Road, SO22 5EF (top of Western Rd, off Stockbridge Rd)
⚙ 4-11; 11-midnight Fri & Sat; 12-10.30 Sun
☎ (01962) 842996
Fulflood Arms Bitter; Greene King IPA; Itchen Valley Godfathers; guest beers Ⓗ
Now with its own integral one-barrel brewery, the original dark-green tiled façade and beautiful etched windows remain as evidence of this 19th-century pub's former Winchester Brewery ownership. Situated in a residential conservation area, a makeover has given the single bar a fresh look, with sofas, newspapers and flowers. The loyal, friendly locals, their banter, quizzes (Wed eves), live music and special events all make for a good atmosphere. Outside, drinkers and smokers have small patios front and rear. Available before 4pm for private functions. ☼◐⇌☐♣●⅄

Hyde Tavern L

57 Hyde Street, SO23 7DY (on B3047)
✪ 12.30-2.30 (Thu only), 5-11.30 (12.30am Fri); 12-midnight Sat; 12-11 Sun ☎ (01962) 862592
Flowerpots Bitter; Harveys Sussex Best Bitter H; **guest beers** H/G

An imposing double gable dominates the exterior of this small, medieval, timber-framed building. The three-roomed interior is below street level – beware of low ceilings and undulating floors. A cellar bar is used for literature evenings, a sewing circle, folk music and other functions. Up to seven beers from small local breweries feature, always including a mild, and real ciders are available. There is no regular food, but customers may order takeaways and a barbecue can be hired. Outside is a delightful, secluded garden. ▲Q☆≑🚃🚲●♪

Old Vine L ✓

8 Great Minster Street, SO23 9HA (2nd entrance in Little Minster Street)
✪ 11-11 (10.30 Sun) ☎ (01962) 854616
⊕ oldvinewinchester.com
Ringwood Best Bitter; guest beers H

In the heart of Winchester, with a vine growing over the front, the pub overlooks the cathedral green; it extends between Little and Great Minster Streets with entrances in both. The cosy bar features an oak-beamed ceiling, artwork from a local design house, leather sofas and an extensive selection of games. There are usually three guest beers, with local breweries featuring heavily, alongside the regular Ringwood. A curtain divides the pub from the award-winning restaurant, where home-cooked food made with local produce is served. ▲🛏🌰①≑🚃

St James Tavern ✓

3 Romsey Road, SO22 5BE
✪ 12-11 (midnight Fri & Sat); 12-10.30 Sun
☎ (01962) 861288
Wadworth Henry's IPA, Horizon, 6X, Bishops Tipple; guest beer H

This end-of-terrace pub on the steep Romsey Road hill has an L-shaped interior and a garden area. The split-level bar has a warm ambience enhanced by extensive wooden panelling and comfortable seating. The food menu features locally made sausages and has a good selection to suit all tastes. A quiz runs on Tuesdays, and the last Sunday of the month features live acoustic music. There are plans to extend into the adjoining house. Old Rosie cider is served. Q☆①≑🚃🚲●♪

Winchfield

Barley Mow ✓

The Hurst, RG27 8DE (from Winchfield Station car park turn right and follow Station Road for 1½ miles) SU787529
✪ 12-3, 5.30-11 (10 Mon); 12-3.30, 5.30-11.30 Fri & Sat; 12-10.30 Sun ☎ (01252) 617490 ⊕ barley-mow.com
Brakspear Bitter; Fuller's London Pride; Sharp's Doom Bar H

A cosy and spacious modernised pub in a pleasant rural location close to the Basingstoke Canal, so ideal for walkers. It has a real log fire, traditional wood flooring and comfortable seating. There are lots of nooks ideal for a quiet drink – three or four real ales are available – and it offers a good choice of pub food. A wide range of traditional pub and board games is available to borrow, including bar skittles, bagatelle and shove-ha'penny. There is a small step to negotiate to the toilets. ▲Q🛏☆①♣P♪

Winsor

Compass Inn

Winsor Road, SO40 2HE SU317143
✪ 12-11 ☎ (023) 8081 2237 ⊕ compassinn.co.uk
Flack Manor Double Drop; Fuller's London Pride; Gale's HSB; guest beers H

Walk into this cosy country pub and you discover a traditional bar with beamed ceilings, exposed brick walls and wooden floors. The pub is split into three sections, with a bar area in the centre, a cosy restaurant area on your right and a small area with a pool table on the left. There are real fires to warm you during winter months and a nice pub garden to enjoy the British summer. Dogs are welcome, with free doggy dinners offered. ▲☆①▲🚃(11)♣P♪

Good Intent, Petersfield (Photo: Geoff Marsh)

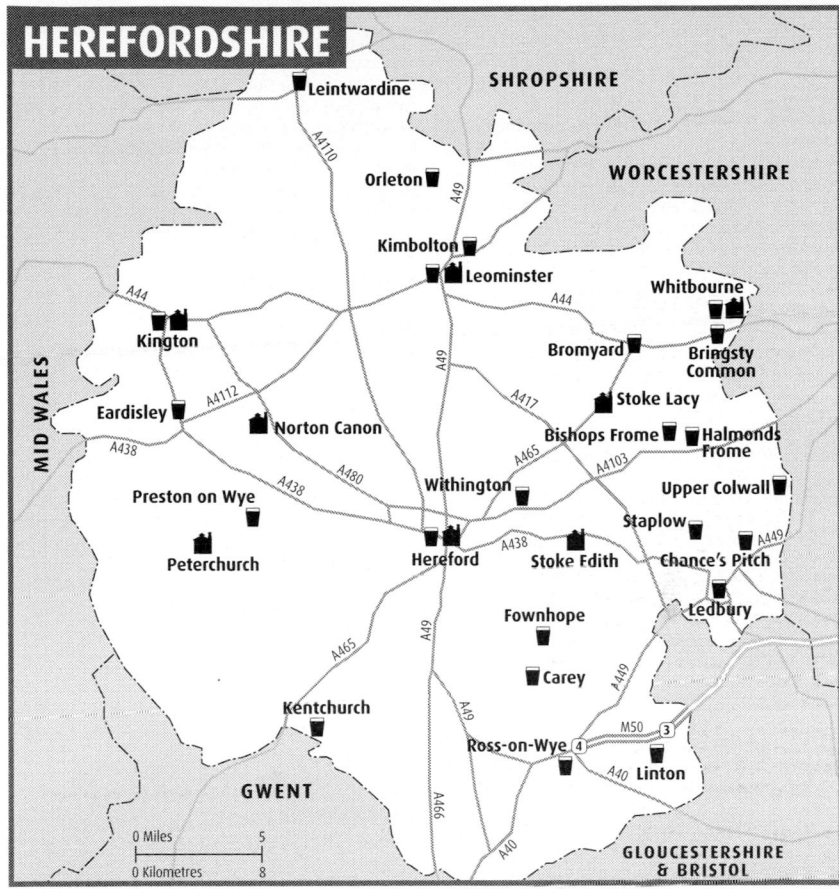

HEREFORDSHIRE

Leintwardine

SHROPSHIRE

Orleton

WORCESTERSHIRE

Kimbolton

Leominster

Whitbourne

Kington

Bromyard

Bringsty Common

Eardisley

Norton Canon

Stoke Lacy

Bishops Frome

Halmonds Frome

Preston on Wye

Withington

Upper Colwall

Peterchurch

Staplow

Chance's Pitch

Hereford

Stoke Edith

Ledbury

Fownhope

Kentchurch

Carey

Ross-on-Wye

Linton

GWENT

GLOUCESTERSHIRE & BRISTOL

0 Miles 5
0 Kilometres 8

Bishops Frome

Green Dragon L

WR6 5BP (just off B4214, in village)
🕙 5 (4 Fri, 12 Sat)-11.30; 12-4, 7-11 Sun ☎ (01885) 490607
Purple Moose Snowdonia Ale; Taylor Golden Best; Theakston Best Bitter; Wye Valley Butty Bach; guest beers Ⓗ
This 17th century inn has a warren of inviting rooms, complete with flagstone floors, low beams, a real fire in every room plus a paved garden to the rear. The inglenook in the main bar is particularly fine. Six handpumps dispense a range of local and regional beers, as well as real cider and perry. Bar meals are served in the evenings (until 8.15pm; not Sun) with steaks a speciality. Two beer festivals are held. ₳Q☽⌇✿◑ ⊟&♐(469,672)♣♠P⚊

Bringsty Common

Live & Let Live L

WR6 5UW (off A44, at Cat & Mouse sign follow right-hand track down onto common) SO699547
🕙 closed Mon; 12-11 (12-2.30, 6-11 Tue-Thu winter);
12-10.30 Sun ☎ (01886) 821462
🌐 liveandletlive-bringsty.co.uk
Malvern Hills Black Pear; Wye Valley Butty Bach; guest beer Ⓗ
Herefordshire's only thatched pub, this Grade II-listed ex-cider house was saved after CAMRA supported a locals' campaign to resist plans to convert it to a dwelling. Perched on the scenic Bringsty Common, it is accessed only via a gravel track (keep right as you go down). The owners have lovingly renovated the pub to a remarkable standard: downstairs is much exposed timber, flags, settles and a fine fireplace; upstairs is a restaurant. The garden affords fine views towards the Malvern Hills and hosts a beer festival each Easter. ₳Q☽✿◑▶♐⊟(420)P⚊

Bromyard

Queen's Arms L

30 High Street, HR7 4AE
🕙 11-11 (midnight Thu-Sat; 10.30 Sun) ☎ (01885) 483331
Hobsons Twisted Spire; Wye Valley Butty Bach; guest beer Ⓗ
A fine 400-year-old timber-framed building with a more modern frontage, recently rescued from decay and closure under pubco ownership. It has been renovated with a central bar, bare wood floor and light-painted beams. Furnishing is spartan at the front, but there are sofas to the rear.
Q✿⊟(420)♣♠P⚊

Rose & Lion L ✔

5 New Road, HR7 4AJ
🕙 11-11 (midnight Fri & Sat) ☎ (01885) 482381
Wye Valley Bitter, HPA, Butty Bach Ⓗ

One of the expanding Wye Valley estate, the Rosie has the atmosphere of a traditional village pub, but moved into town. It enjoys a loyal following by locals, and is never anything but friendly. The two small original rooms are complemented by a further bar to the rear plus an annexe with disabled toilets. Furnished in a modern but appropriate style, it acts as a venue for live folk music on Sunday nights. No food is served. The garden is to the side. Q❀✍️&🚪(420)♣P≛

Carey

Cottage of Content L ✅

HR2 6NG SO564310

🌫️ closed Mon; 12-2, 6.30 (6 Wed)-11; 12-2 Sun
☎ (01432) 840242 ⊕ cottageofcontent.co.uk

Hobsons Best Bitter; Wye Valley Butty Bach; guest beer H

A truly beautiful old, partly black and white building in delightful surroundings, some of it dating from 1485. It has two bars and a separate restaurant. Although food of high quality predominates, drinkers are welcome. Booking is advised at most times for the freshly prepared bar meals at lunchtime and à la carte in the evening. There is a large garden on the hillside to the rear. Dogs are allowed in the bar only. Winter opening times may vary. ✍️Q❀✍️🌔🍴P≛

Chance's Pitch

Wellington L

WR13 6HW (on A449, near B4218 junction)

🌫️ closed Mon; 12-3, 6.30-11; 12-4 Sun ☎ (01684) 540269
⊕ thewellingtoninnmalvern.co.uk

Goff's Tournament; guest beers H

On its own on the main Ledbury-Malvern road, this is a much-extended, multi-level building. The comfortable bar, with its drinkers-only area and reading material, has a traditional feel, while the lounge below has views across open country. There are two restaurant areas up to the rear. A wide range of locally sourced meals is on offer, from sandwiches through to full à la carte. Interesting guest beers are sourced as swaps from the local Goff's brewery. ✍️Q✍️❀🌔🚪(675)P≛

Eardisley

Tram Inn L

HR3 6PG (on A4111, in village)

🌫️ closed Mon; 12-3, 6-midnight (12.30am Fri & Sat); 12-3, 7-10.30 Sun ☎ (01544) 327251 ⊕ thetraminn.co.uk

Hobsons Best Bitter; Wye Valley Butty Bach; guest beer H

The name of this fine black and white inn refers to the Kington Railway, a horse-operated plateway that passed nearby until 1874. The much-altered 17th-century building has a public bar and a lounge with exposed beams and cosy corners, plus an informal dining room. Locally sourced, freshly-made pub meals and Sunday roasts are available (no food Sun eve). Bottled Orgasmic and Gwatkins ciders are stocked. ✍️Q❀🌔▲🚪(446,462)♣P≛

Fownhope

New Inn L

HR1 4PE (on B4224, in village)

🌫️ 12-2, 6 (5.30 Fri)-midnight; 11-midnight Sat; 12-midnight Sun ☎ (01432) 860350

Hobsons Best Bitter; Wye Valley Bitter, Butty Bach; guest beer H

This is first and foremost a locals' pub at the heart of a thriving two-pub village. A single bar serves two pleasant seating areas, one with large-screen TV. Fownhope football team uses the pub as a base. Typical pub food is served weekday lunchtimes, with a blackboard menu. Fish and chips, pie and curry evenings are held monthly, as well as jam sessions, singalongs plus a quiz evening. ✍️🐕❀✍️🌔▲🚪(453)♣P≛

Halmonds Frome

Majors Arms L

WR6 5AX (¾ mile N of A4103 at Bishops Frome)
SO675481

🌫️ 5 (4 Fri; 3 Sat; 12 Sun)-11 ☎ (01531) 641780
⊕ themajorsarms.co.uk

Ludlow Best; Thwaites Original; guest beer H

Small isolated pub that once achieved national fame when temporarily renamed the Miners Arms as the coalmines were being closed wholesale by John Major's government in 1991. Housed in what was once an old cider mill, it has a simple no-frills, high-ceilinged bar with bare stone walls and a large woodburner. From the patio are superb views over West Herefordshire and into Wales. Occasional live music is hosted. Home-produced Snails Bank cider is usually available. ✍️🐕❀✍️♣🍴P≛

Hereford

Barrels L ✅

69 St Owen Street, HR1 2JQ

🌫️ 11-11.30 (midnight Fri & Sat); 12-11.30 Sun
☎ (01432) 274968

Wye Valley Bitter, HPA, Dorothy Goodbody's Golden Ale, Butty Bach; guest beers H

Celebrating 25 consecutive years in this Guide, Barrels has been voted local CAMRA Pub of the Year on five occasions. Once home to Wye Valley Brewery, it enjoys a cult following in the city and beyond. Four distinct rooms cater for all age groups; a pool table occupies one, another has a large-screen TV (only for major sporting events), otherwise conversation rules. The cobbled and decked courtyard and adjacent brewery bar are home to a charity beer and music festival held each August bank holiday weekend. ❀✍️≈🚪♣🍴≛

Lichfield Vaults

11 Church Street, HR1 2LR

🌫️ 11-midnight (2am Fri & Sat) ☎ (01432) 266821

Adnams Broadside; Caledonian Deuchars IPA, Flying Scotsman; Draught Bass; Sharp's Doom Bar H

A well-run 18th-century city-centre venue tucked away in a charming cobbled alley leading to the Cathedral. Although opened out into a single bar area, the pleasant wood-panelled interior gives an intimate feel, while the secluded, decked beer garden extends some way back. Speciality Greek Cypriot dishes feature on the lunchtime menu, and there is a conventional roast on Sundays. The guest beer is often from a local brewery. Live blues plays on the last Sunday afternoon of the month. Quiz night is Sunday. ⏴️🏵️🍴♿🍺🚌♣️🚭

Kentchurch

Bridge Inn

HR2 0BY (on B4347)
☼ 12-2.30 (not Mon & Tue), 6-11; 12-11 Sat summer; 12-11 (12-5, 7-10.30 winter) Sun ☎ (01981) 240408
Otter Bitter; guest beers Ⓗ
Beautifully situated close to the Welsh border on the banks of the River Monnow, the building probably dates from the 14th century. It has a welcoming single front bar plus a restaurant with excellent views, and boasts riverside gardens and a pétanque piste for summer days. The freshly prepared food ranges from bar snacks to full à la carte (no food Sun eve). Guest beers are from regional and local breweries, usually including one from Wye Valley. A beer festival is held in May. ⏴️Q🏵️🍴♿🅰️♣️P🚭

Kimbolton

Stockton Cross Ⓛ

HR6 0HD (on A4112, W of village)
☼ closed Mon; 12-3, 7-11 (not Sun eve) ☎ (01568) 612509
Wye Valley HPA, Butty Bach; guest beer Ⓗ
Prominently situated on the edge of the village, this single-room black and white pub dates from the 16th century. The long narrow bar with its two cosy alcoves set either side of the large fireplace accommodates both drinkers and diners. The interesting menu, including a good vegetarian choice, is mainly sourced locally and freshly prepared. Regular events include an open mic night on the second Wednesday of the month and a curry and quiz night on the last Wednesday. ⏴️🚲🏵️🍴P🚭

Kington

Olde Tavern ★ Ⓛ

22 Victoria Road, HR5 3BX
☼ 6.30-10.30 (midnight Wed & Thu); 3.30-midnight Fri; 12-midnight Sat & Sun ☎ (01544) 239033
Hobsons Mild; Ludlow Best; Wye Valley Butty Bach; guest beer Ⓗ
Diminutive Grade II-listed two-room time warp. The entrance lobby, still with its off-sales hatch, leads to a main bar with many original features, and alcove seating. The old smoke room to the right has a flagstone floor and bench seating, plus a serving hatch to the bar. The Tavern offers a warm welcome from staff and locals alike. Regulars take pride in the pub-based activities, including the annual beer festival on the spring bank holiday. Q🏵️🚍♣️🚭

Ledbury

Prince of Wales Ⓛ ✅

Church Lane, HR8 1DL
☼ 11-11 (10.30 Sun) ☎ (01531) 632250 🌐 powledbury.com
Hobsons Best Bitter; Otter Bitter; Wye Valley HPA, Butty Bach; guest beers Ⓗ
Set in a delightful cobbled alley leading up to the imposing church, this 16th-century timber-framed

pub boasts two bars, one with a discrete alcove where a folk jam session is held on Wednesday evenings and alternate Sunday afternoons. This is a true community pub – bustling with locals and visitors. Draught cider from Westons is stocked, together with an extensive range of foreign beers, both draught and bottled. The bar meals are excellent value, including the Sunday roasts. 🚲🏵️🍴🚍≠🚌♣️🚭

Talbot Hotel Ⓛ

14 New Street, HR8 2DX
☼ 11-11 (midnight Fri & Sat) ☎ (01531) 632963
🌐 talbotledbury.co.uk
Wadworth Henry's IPA, 6X; Wye Valley Butty Bach; guest beer Ⓗ
An outstanding black and white half-timbered hotel and bar dating back to the 1590s, with direct links to the Civil War. Various comfortably furnished seating areas, with discreet nooks and corners, surround a central bar-servery facing a splendid fireplace. The restaurant, with its superb wood-panelling, offers affordable fine cuisine featuring locally sourced ingredients, while conventional bar snacks are also available. The guest beer is from Wadworth's seasonal range or Red Shoot subsidiary. ⏴️🏵️🏨🍴≠🚍♣️🚭

Leintwardine

Sun Inn 🏆 ★ Ⓛ

Rosemary Lane, SY7 0LP (off A4113, in village)
☼ 11 (5.30 Mon)-11; 11-10.30 Sun ☎ (01547) 540705
🌐 suninn-leintwardine.co.uk
Hobsons Mild, Twisted Spire, Best Bitter; guest beers Ⓗ
One of Britain's last remaining parlour pubs, the Grade II-listed marvel was saved after Herefordshire CAMRA led a successful 'Save the Sun' campaign in 2009. The red-brick public bar features bench furniture, a simple fireplace and gentle conversation, and the parlour is where ex-landlady of 74 years, Flossie, once held court. Recently added to the rear is a stylish new pavilion-style extension, overlooking the garden. A beer festival is held each August bank holiday Sunday. Some beer is served straight from a stillage – ask if you want your beer served by gravity. ⏴️Q🚲🏵️🍴🚍🅰️🚍(738,740)♣️♿

Leominster

Grape Vaults Ⓛ

2-4 Broad Street, HR6 8BS
☼ 11-11 ☎ (01568) 611404 🌐 thegrapevaults.co.uk
Ludlow Best, Gold; guest beers Ⓗ
One-room hard-core cider house whose plain façade conceals a real gem of a pub. The main bar area has a fireplace, bench seating and much original woodwork, plus a pull-down TV screen (used only for important sports fixtures). A small snug, tucked away to one side behind a part-glazed screen, is truly something to cherish. Pub food is served at affordable prices (no food Sun eve). Guest beers are from local breweries. The pub has the smallest Gents in the county. ⏴️Q🍴≠🚍

Linton

Alma Inn

HR9 7RY (off B4221, W of M50 jct 3) SO659255

✿ 12-3 (not Mon-Fri), 6-11 Sat; 12-3, 7-10.30 Sun
☎ (01989) 720355 ⊕ lintonfestival.org/pages/almainnlinton
Butcombe Bitter; guest beers Ⓗ
Two time local CAMRA Pub of the Year, the Alma is testament to the fact village pubs do not have to sell food to thrive. At the heart of its community and run with passion, there is always something happening here – events include a major music and beer festival in June held in the extensive grounds. A conventional front bar complete with real fire contrasts with a wood-panelled 'other' room, and a rear pool room. Up to three guest beers regularly come from Ludlow, Malvern Hills and Saxon City breweries. ▟Q☎☜✿⊟Å♣P╚

Orleton

Boot Inn Ⓛ

SY8 4HN (off B4361, in village)
✿ 12-3, 5.30-11; 12-11.30 Sat; 12-11 Sun ☎ (01568) 780228
⊕ thebootinnorleton.co.uk
Hobsons Best Bitter; Wye Valley HPA; guest beer Ⓗ
A comfortable and welcoming 16th-century black and white village pub with a large inglenook fireplace and original oak beams. The home-prepared food ranges from bar snacks to interesting gourmet meals. The Wye Valley HPA may alternate with Butty Bach. A charity quiz is held monthly on a Tuesday in winter and a beer festival in July in the beer garden, which includes a children's play area. ▟Q☜✿◑⊟(492)P╚

Preston on Wye

Yew Tree

HR2 9JT SO385414
✿ 7-midnight (1am Fri & Sat); 12-3, 7-11 Sun
☎ (01981) 500359
Beer range varies Ⓖ
A delightfully old-fashioned, welcoming village pub, popular with locals as well as canoeists and fishermen from the nearby River Wye. Simply furnished and warmed by a wood-burning stove in winter, boules, pool and quiz teams are based here. The single beer, from a local or regional brewery, is served direct from the cask behind the small central bar. Draught Thatchers cider is also on offer, with additional local ciders in summer. Evening meals are available in summer if ordered in advance. Live music plays monthly on Saturdays. ▟Q✿Å♣♦P╚

Ross-on-Wye

Mail Rooms ⊘

Gloucester Road, HR9 5BS
✿ 8-midnight (1am Fri & Sat) ☎ (01989) 760920
Greene King Abbot; Ruddles Best Bitter; guest beers Ⓗ
Behind the fine red-brick and stone façade of what was once the town's main post office is a single modern bar with vaulted ceiling, exposed air-conditioning ducts and a conservatory to the rear. At night the decor and subtle up-lighting create an intimate atmosphere. Good-value food is served all day, including a children's menu. The two regular beers are complemented by up to three guest beers from a diverse range of breweries, plus two Westons ciders. Local beer and cider festivals feature regularly. Alcohol is served from 9am. Q☜✿◑�⊟♦╚

Staplow

Oak Inn Ⓛ

HR8 1NP (on B4214)
✿ 12-11 (10.30 Sun) ☎ (01531) 640954
⊕ oakinnstaplow.co.uk
Bathams Best Bitter; Wye Valley Bitter; guest beers Ⓗ
The stylishly refurbished rural inn focuses primarily on food and enjoys a county-wide reputation for first class affordable dining, but drinkers are not ignored. The front bar divides into three areas: one with sofas and low tables, a snug and a dining room featuring an open kitchen. At the rear is a further room with scrubbed tables. Booking is essential for both food and the quality accommodation. The latter boasts bucolic views across nearby orchards.
▟Q☜✿➔◑ₕ⊟(417)P╚

Upper Colwall

Chase Inn Ⓛ

Chase Road, WR13 6DJ (off B4218, turning at upper hairpin bend signed British Camp) SO766431
✿ 12-3, 5-11; 12-11 Sat; 12-10.30 Sun ☎ (01684) 540276
Bathams Best Bitter; Hobsons Best Bitter; Sharp's Doom Bar; Wood's Shropshire Lad; guest beers Ⓗ
Conversation rules at this two-bar free house tucked away in a quiet wooded backwater on the western slopes of the Malvern Hills. It comprises a small lounge for informal dining and a narrow bar very much for drinkers and conversation. The suntrap rear garden commands views across Herefordshire to the Welsh Hills. One of the guest beers is always from St George's Brewery. A beer festival is held each August bank holiday weekend. ▟Q☜✿◑⊟(675)♣♦P╚☖

Whitbourne

Wheatsheaf Ⓛ

Bromyard Road, WR6 5SF (on A44)
✿ 12-11 (10.30 Sun) ☎ (01886) 822282
⊕ wheatsheaf-at-whitbourne.webs.com
Hobsons Mild; Wye Valley HPA; guest beers Ⓗ
A roadside pub that is really on the up. Bare wood, tiled floors and lighting create a modern yet intimate atmosphere, along with newly-established areas for pool, dining and relaxing. Traditional, good-quality pub meals are served all day plus snacks, and a traditional roast on Sunday. Up to six beers usually feature on the bar, sourced mainly from local microbreweries. The garden with its decking, pet menagerie and stream is a delight for children. ▟Q☜✿◑⊟(420)♣P╚

Withington

Cross Keys Ⓛ

HR1 3NN (on A465 in Withington Marsh)
✿ 5 (12 Sat)-11; 12-10.30 Sun ☎ (01432) 820616
Otter Ale; Wye Valley Bitter, Butty Bach; guest beer Ⓗ
Conversation rules in this traditional local, run by the same landlord for over 30 years. At the heart of the community, it is a CAMRA favourite for its atmosphere. A long and narrow single bar divides into two drinking areas, each with original beams, exposed stonework, a real fire and basic bench seating. A folk jam session is held on the last Thursday in the month. Filled rolls are available on Saturdays only. ▟Q☜✿Å⊟(420)♣P╚

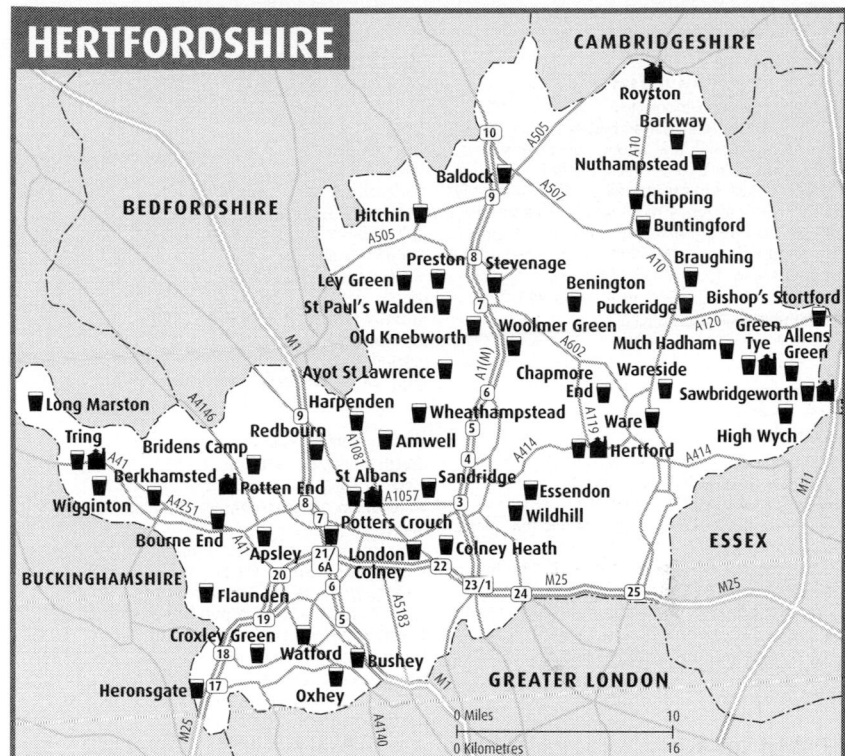

Allens Green

Queen's Head ♥ ℒ
CM21 0LS TL455170
🕓 12-2.30 (not Mon & Tue; 2 Wed), 5-11; 12-10.30 Sun
☎ (01279) 723393 ⊕ shirevillageinns.co.uk
Fuller's London Pride; Mighty Oak Maldon Gold ⊞;
guest beers Ⓖ
Popular with locals, cyclists, walkers and their dogs, this is a small traditional village inn with a large lawn for summer relaxation. Honest and simple food is served but the emphasis is on an interesting and varied beer range. Festivals are held every third weekend of the month and on bank holiday weekends, where beers are served by gravity from a temperature-controlled environment. A larger bar is planned, delivering all beers by gravity. Q✿♿♣P

Amwell

Elephant & Castle ✓
Amwell Lane, AL8 8EA TL167131
🕓 12-2.30, 5.30-11; 12-11 Sat; 12-10.30 Sun
☎ (01582) 832175
Greene King IPA, Abbot; H&H Bitter; guest beer ⊞
Hidden away in an attractive and peaceful setting, this deservedly popular, successful rural community pub dates from 1714 and has never forsaken real ale. Terracotta tiles in the front bar, a 200-foot well in the back, two real fires and two large gardens (one for adults only) complete the picture. Lunches are served daily and evening meals Tuesday to Saturday. The pub hosts Amwell Day, a local charity fundraising event in June each year. Dog-friendly. ▲✿♦P⅄

Apsley

Paper Mill ℒ ✓
Stationers Place, HP3 9RH (off London Road, A4251, opp station)
🕓 10.30-11 (midnight Fri & Sat); 11-10.30 Sun
☎ (01442) 288800
Fuller's London Pride, ESB; guest beer ⊞
Close to Apsley marina on the Grand Union Canal, this popular Fuller's pub is often busy but usually provides quick service. The large open-plan bar with a variety of tables, couches and stools attracts a mixed clientele. There is an extensive pub food menu with even more choice in the restaurant upstairs, which has additional tables on the balcony overlooking the canal. Free Wi-Fi inside and boat moorings adjacent. ▲✿♦♿≠⬛(500,501)P⅄

Ayot St Lawrence

Brocket Arms
Hill Farm Lane, AL6 9BT TL196168
🕓 11.30-11.30 (11 Sun) ☎ (01438) 820250
⊕ brocketarms.com
Greene King IPA, Abbot; Nethergate Brocket Bitter; Sharp's Doom Bar; guest beers ⊞
A classic country estate pub popular with ramblers, visitors to Shaw's Corner (NT) and country sports people. The setting is superb with a spacious garden surrounded by large trees and other listed buildings. There is a separate restaurant and bar snacks available in two bars, both with fires, one with a massive inglenook, the other with a large wood-burning stove. This building dates back to the 14th century and for 40 years was George Bernard Shaw's local. ▲Q❄✿♦♿♣P⅄

Baldock

Orange Tree Ⓛ ✅
Norton Road, SG7 5AW TL242339
✪ 12-2.30, 4.30-11; 12-midnight Fri & Sat; 12-10.30 Sun
☎ (01462) 892341 ⊕ theorangetreebaldock.com
Greene King XX Mild, IPA, Abbot; guest beers Ⓗ
Friendly, unspoilt two-bar local, dating back over 300 years, now run by Rob who has dramatically changed the pub since moving in. It features live folk, rock and pop music and hosts regular quiz nights and a quarterly mini beer festival. Outside is a large garden. The two free-of-tie handpumps serve Buntingford beers and a changing list of guests, plus locally produced Apple Cottage cider.
🏚🐧❄◑🍴♿🚇(94)♣👍P♨

Barkway

Tally Ho Ⓛ
London Road, SG8 8EX TL383350
✪ 11.30-11; 12-6 Sun ☎ (01763) 848389
⊕ tallyho-barkway.co.uk
Buntingford Highwayman IPA; Rebellion IPA; guest beer Ⓟ
Friendly rural free house offering two real ales, sometimes three when demand picks up. Bar snacks and home-made meals are available in the restaurant. The spirits menu features 58 whiskies, 12 gins and nine rums. Look out for the collection of cartoons, newspaper clippings and apocryphal stories. 🏚Q❄◑P

Benington

Lordship Arms
42 Whempstead Road, SG2 7BX TL307228
✪ 12-3, 6 (7 Sun)-11 ☎ (01438) 869665
⊕ lordshiparms.co.uk
Black Sheep Best Bitter; Crouch Vale Brewers Gold; Taylor Landlord; guest beers Ⓗ
Single-bar pub situated at the southern end of the village. A tidy bar is decorated with telephone memorabilia, even some of the handpumps are modelled on telephones. The well-maintained garden sports superb floral displays in summer. Good-quality sandwiches are available at lunchtime. Classic car club meetings are held here in summer. A repeat winner of local and county CAMRA Pub of the Year. 🏚Q❄◑🚇(384)👍P🏵

Berkhamsted

Rising Sun 🍷 Ⓛ ✅
1 Canal Side, George Street, HP4 2EG (at lock 55 on Grand Union Canal) SP997077
✪ 12 (3 winter)-11 (midnight Thu); 12-midnight Fri & Sat; 12-10.30 Sun ☎ (01442) 864913 ⊕ theriser.co.uk
Tring Riser; guest beers Ⓗ
Friendly pub in a wonderful setting, with canal lock-side seating and a sunken patio/smoking area that hosts beer festivals. Enter via steps up from the tow path into the bar, which has two conjoining rooms and an additional back room. Five real ales are available and 15 real ciders, alongside generous ploughman's. The innovative landlords offer plenty of diversions including pétanque, a charity book club, snuff to try/buy, cigars and plugged clay pipes, live music and quizzes. Dogs are welcome and a CAMRA discount offered. Local CAMRA Pub of the Year and Cider Pub of the Year 2012. ❄◑▶🚆🚇(500)♣👍♨

Bishop's Stortford

Bricklayers Arms Ⓛ
61 Hadham Road, CM23 2QY TL482214
✪ 12 (5 Mon)-midnight; 12-1.30am Fri & Sat; 12-11.30 Sun ☎ (01279) 657803
Beer range varies Ⓗ
Local beers are showcased here, usually including at least one each from Buntingford and Saffron breweries. Built on the site of a former brickworks, this popular pub has served the local community for 150 years. Once a Benskins house, it is now independent. There is a quiet, comfortable lounge and a lively sports-oriented public bar and pool room with several Sky HD screens. Outside there is a covered, heated smokers' patio and a large, secluded deck. Dogs are welcome throughout the pub. 🏚❄🍴🚆🚇P♨

Half Moon ✅
North Street, CM23 2LD TL486214
✪ 12-11 (midnight Wed-Sat) ☎ (01279) 834500
Caledonian Deuchars IPA; Wells Bombardier; guest beers Ⓗ
Five rotating guest beers, both light and dark, from near and far, make for an interesting, extensive range. Westons Old Rosie Cider is also available. This lively town centre pub has been thoroughly refurbished, yet the genuine character of the 16th-century building has been preserved throughout the three bars. Regular live acoustic, blues and jazz music is performed in the large separate function room. The heated patio outside is popular all year. ❄◑🚆🚇👍♨

Bourne End

White Horse Ⓛ
London Road, HP1 2RH (½ mile from A41 jct) TL023062
✪ 11-11; 12.30-10.30 Sun ☎ (01442) 863888
McMullen AK, Country Ⓗ
Large and comfortable McMullen pub with spacious areas inside and out. Two large but cosy open-plan sections has nooks and crannies for an intimate feel, with beams adding to its old world appearance. An ideal stop-off point between Hemel Hempstead and Berkhamsted, it is a short walk from the Grand Union Canal. The two beers showcase the brewery splendidly. Varied menus cover most tastes from snacks to full dinners all day, service is fast, and portions generous. 🏚Q❄◑♿🚇(500,501)P♨

Braughing

Golden Fleece ✅
20 Green End, SG11 2PG
✪ 11.30-3, 5.30-11; 11.30-midnight Sat; 12-10.30 Sun ☎ (01920) 823555 ⊕ goldenfleecebraughing.co.uk
Adnams Southwold Bitter; guest beers Ⓗ

INDEPENDENT BREWERIES
Buntingford Royston
Green Tye Green Tye
McMullen Hertford
Old Cross Hertford
Red Squirrel Potten End
Sawbridgeworth Sawbridgeworth
Tring Tring
Verulam St Albans

A large rural pub built in the early 1700s, with wooden floors, beams and a large fireplace. It was closed as a pub in 2003 but reopened in 2010 after extensive remodelling of the interior layout. Guest ales come from local breweries such as Buntingford, Tring and Red Squirrel. Food available is all gluten-free, and includes a changing range of daily specials, monthly tapas nights and themed food evenings. ⚑Q❧✿❁◗🖵(331,386)P

Bridens Camp

Crown & Sceptre ⅃

Red Lion Lane, HP2 6EY (from A4146 at Water End take Red Lion Lane up hill for ½ mile) TL044111
✪ 12-3, 5.30-11; 12-11 Sat & Sun ☎ (01442) 234660
⊕ crownandsceptrepub.co.uk
Greene King IPA, Abbot; guest beers Ⓗ
This friendly country pub goes from strength to strength. The U-shaped bar in the centre means you cannot see all the pump clips at the same time, and beware of the beams if you are taller than average. Beers from local breweries are regularly available. Outside is a patio and beer garden, plus a bar for beer festivals (also available for functions). The pub is popular with walkers and cyclists, and Gaddesden Cricket Club is opposite. No dogs are permitted inside.
⚑Q✿◗🖵(X31)♣●P⅃

Buntingford

Brambles ⅃

117 High Street, SG9 9AF TL360298
✪ 12-11 (10.30 Sun) ☎ (01763) 273158
Fuller's London Pride; Gale's HSB; guest beers Ⓗ
Brambles has two bars warmed by real fires and eight handpumps dispense the ales. Local beers from Buntingford and Red Squirrel breweries are usually available, and guests are often from Nethergate and Church End. The clientele is varied and can get exuberant at weekends. Unusually, Brambles has no pub sign outside.
⚑❧✿⊟🖵(331,700)♣❒

Bushey

Swan

25 Park Road, WD23 3EE TQ132954
✪ 11-11; 12-10.30 Sun ☎ (020) 8950 2256
Greene King Abbot; Young's Bitter; guest beers Ⓗ
Single bar in a residential street off Bushey High Street offering two regular and two guest ales. Two real fireplaces add to the homely and welcoming feel. Bar snacks are available all day including pies and toasties. Regular events are held to celebrate traditional dates such as Burns Night and Valentine's Day. There are three TV screens allowing for multiple sports to be shown simultaneously. The Ladies is in the back garden. Free Wi-Fi. ⚑✿🖵♣⅃

Chapmore End

Woodman ✪

30 Chapmore End, SG12 0HF (turn off B158 between Bengeo and A602 roundabout) TL328164
✪ 12-2.30 (not Mon), 5.30 (5 Fri)-11; 12-11 Sat & Sun
☎ (01920) 463143 ⊕ woodmanpub.com
Greene King IPA, Abbot; guest beer Ⓖ
Classic two-bar country pub in a quiet hamlet off the B158, popular with walkers. At this totally

unspoilt gem the beer is served straight from cooled casks. The large rear garden has chickens, rabbits and wild ducks, and a safe children's play area. Entertainment includes Sunday evening quiz nights, a pop quiz on the second Thursday of the month, and folk music sessions every second and fourth Monday. Beer and music festivals are held twice yearly. Outside is a bookable pétanque pitch.
⚑Q❧✿◗⊟♣▲P⅃

Chipping

Countryman

Ermine Street, SG9 0PG TL356319
✪ closed Mon-Thu; 12-11 Fri & Sat; 12-10.30 Sun
☎ (01763) 272721
Beer range varies Ⓗ
Built in 1663 and an inn since 1760, the Countryman is a single-bar, split-level pub. The interior boasts some well-executed carvings on the bar front, an impressive fireplace and some obscure agricultural implements. Two real ales are usually available from a varying range and tend to be around 4-4.5%. Note the restricted opening hours. ⚑Q❧✿🖵(331)P⅃

Colney Heath

Crooked Billet ⅃

88 High Street, AL4 0NP TL202060
✪ 11-2.30, 4.30-11; 11.30-11 Sat, 12-10.30 Sun
☎ (01727) 822128
Tring Side Pocket for a Toad; guest beers Ⓗ
Popular and friendly cottage-style village pub dating back over 200 years. A genuine free house, it stocks three to five guest beers from national, regional and microbreweries. A wide selection of good-value home-made food is served lunchtimes and Friday and Saturday evenings. Summer barbecues and Saturday events are held occasionally. This is a favourite stop-off for walkers on the many local footpaths. Families are welcome in the large garden (which has play equipment) and in the bar until 9pm.
⚑❧✿◗⊟🖵(304)♣●P⅃

Croxley Green

Sportsman ⅃

2 Scots Hill, WD3 3AD (at A412 jct with the Green) TQ069953
✪ 12-11 (10.30 Sun) ☎ (01923) 443360
⊕ croxleygreen.com/sportsman
Sharp's Doom Bar; Taylor Landlord; Tring Side Pocket for a Toad; guest beers Ⓗ
Comfortable community local with a warm welcome for all. Real ale is actively promoted with up to five guests, usually including a dark beer, and tasting trays are available. Beers by Buntingford, Dark Star and Salopian make regular appearances and Westons Bounds Brand cider is always available. Live music is staged every Saturday night and events include twice-yearly beer festivals, a book club and community activities. A 10-minute walk from Croxley station. Joint winner of local CAMRA Pub of the Year 2010.
✿🖵(320,321)♣●P⅃❒

Essendon

Candlestick ⅃

West End Lane, AL9 6BA TL262083

✪ 12-11 (10 Sun) ☎ (01707) 261322
⊕ thecandlestickpub.co.uk
Greene King IPA; guest beers Ⓗ
A remote country pub/restaurant where good food features strongly lunchtimes and evenings. It is popular with walkers and cyclists, who are rewarded with two guest ales from Hertfordshire brewers. Originally called the Chequers, the pub became known as the Candlestick because of the habit of a previous landlord who took the sole candle to the cellar when collecting the beer, leaving customers in the dark. Now a friendly, well-lit free house with a beer festival in June.
▟▷✿◑P⅃

Flaunden

Green Dragon ★
HP3 0PP (off Birch Lane towards Flaunden Hill) TL015008
✪ 12-11 (10.30 Sun) ☎ (01442) 832269
⊕ greendragon.org.uk
Fuller's London Pride, ESB; St Austell Tribute; Young's Bitter Ⓗ
Situated near the centre of a small village, this 17th-century free house has a superb tap room, decorated with old brewery posters, which is unchanged since 1868. The saloon was extended some years ago to form a comfortable, spacious bar. Among famous visitors are Charles I and the spy Guy Burgess, who was a regular before defecting to the Soviet Union. The restaurant, offering English & Thai menus, is open every day except Monday. Take-away meals are available.
▟Q✿◑▤♣P⅃

Green Tye

Prince of Wales Ⓛ
SG10 6JP TL444184
✪ 12-3 (3.15 Wed), 5.30-11 (1am Fri & Sat); 11.15-10.30 Sun
☎ (01279) 842517 ⊕ thepow.co.uk
Green Tye Union Jack, Hadham Gold; Wadworth Henry's Original IPA; guest beers Ⓗ
A traditional village local where Gary and Jenny extend a warm welcome to dog owners, cyclists and walkers. The beer range showcases smaller East Anglian breweries including Green Tye whose brewhouse is at one side of the pub. On the other side is a beer garden, which hosts major beer festivals in a marquee on the May Day weekend and in September. Home-cooked food and sandwiches are served. Live folk and other music features regularly. ▟Q✿◑♿♠P

Harpenden

Cross Keys Ⓛ ✪
39 High Street, AL5 2SD TL133144
✪ 11-11; 12-10.30 Sun ☎ (01582) 763989
⊕ cross-keys-harpenden.co.uk
Rebellion IPA; Taylor Landlord; Tring Jack O'Legs; guest beer Ⓗ
Tucked in among the shops in the town centre, this two-bar pub has retained its traditional charm with a fine pewter bar top and flagstoned floors. The original oak-beamed ceiling has tankards from past and present customers hanging from it. In spring and summer enjoy your pint in the secluded, attractive rear garden, and in autumn or winter relax in front of the saloon bar's real fire. Traditional home-cooked lunches are served Monday to Saturday. ▟Q▷✿◑≒▤♣⅃

Heronsgate

Land of Liberty, Peace & Plenty ♈ Ⓛ
Long Lane, WD3 5BS (exit jct 17 of M25, pub is ¾ mile on right) TQ023949
✪ 12-11 (midnight Fri & Sat); 12-10.30 Sun
☎ (01923) 282226 ⊕ landoflibertypub.com
Beer range varies Ⓗ
Welcoming country community pub with friendly locals, run by the same landlords for seven years. Six microbrewery beers of various styles are usually available along with ciders, perries and a growing range of single malt whiskies. Bar snacks are sold all day. Regular events are held throughout the year including beer festivals, club meetings and quizzes. Dogs are welcome and families are catered for in a large pavilion outside; no under-14s allowed in the bar. A previous CAMRA National Pub of the Year finalist. ▟✿♣♠P⅃☖

Hertford

Old Barge ✪
2 The Folly, SG14 1QD (ask for Folly Island and you'll find the Old Barge) TL326128
✪ 11-11 (midnight Fri & Sat); 12-11 Sun ☎ (01992) 581871
⊕ theoldbarge.co.uk
Dark Star Hophead; St Austell Tribute; Sharp's Doom Bar; guest beers Ⓗ
A free house hosting three beer festivals a year (one during St George's Day week), the pub is also rightly proud of its home-cooked food. Enjoy great beer while watching passing narrowboats. On August bank holiday children under 12 can take part in the Crayfish Festival. A quiz is held every Sunday and jazz nights on the second Thursday of the month. Look out for the 'Folly at the Folly' Sunday festival in August – music and fun supporting the National Deaf Children's Society.
▟▷✿◑≒(East)▤♣♠P⅃

Old Cross Tavern ♈ Ⓛ
8 St Andrew Street, SG14 1JA TL323126
✪ 12 (4 Mon)-11; 12-10.30 Sun ☎ (01992) 583133
Taylor Landlord; Old Cross Tavern Laugh 'n' Titter; guest beers Ⓗ
Superb town free house offering a friendly welcome. Up to eight real ales, usually including a dark beer of some distinction, come from brewers large and small, including the pub's own microbrewery, and there is a fine choice of Belgian bottle-conditioned beers. A popular beer festival is held over the spring bank holiday. No TV or music here, just good old-fashioned conversation. Home-made pies are available. ▟Q✿≒(North)▤♣

High Wych

Rising Sun
High Wych Road, CM21 0HZ TL463141
✪ 12-2.30 (not Tue; 2 Wed), 5.30-11; 12-3, 7-10.30 Sun
☎ (01279) 724099
Courage Best Bitter; Oakham JHB; guest beers Ⓖ
A regular in the Guide for many years, this small village pub has been recently refurbished with a stone floor in the original bar. Popular with walkers and friendly locals, it holds a monthly quiz and an annual vegetable competition. The pub has never used handpumps – all beers are served on gravity. Two or three guest ales usually come from small independent breweries. Parking is in the village hall car park opposite. Q✿▤(347)♣P

Hitchin

Half Moon ⓛ
57 Queen Street, SG4 9TZ TL186288
❂ 12-2.30 (2 Wed), 5-midnight; 12-1am Fri & Sat; 12-11 Sun
☎ (01462) 452448 ⊕ thehalfmoonhitchin.co.uk
Adnams Southwold Bitter; Young's Special; guest beers Ⓗ
Split-level single-bar pub dating back to 1748, once owned by Hitchin brewer W&S Lucas. Two regular beers are supplemented by guests, often from local micros. Five ciders and two perries are also available alongside a good choice of wines. Monthly quiz nights and themed food nights are popular in this friendly community pub, home to a successful cribbage team. Two beer festivals are held a year. Winner of local CAMRA Pub of the Year 2009 and 2010. ⓂⓈ⊛①♣◗P↲

Nightingale ⓛ
Nightingale Road, SG5 1RL TL192293
❂ 2.30 (3 Mon)-11; 12-midnight Thu-Sat; 12-10.30 Sun
☎ (01462) 457448 ⊕ nightingalehitchin.co.uk/pub
Tring Colley's Dog; guest beers Ⓗ
A local community pub where the evening's activities usually revolve around pub sport and lively discussions at the bar. Tring Brewery's Colley's Dog is a permanent fixture, alongside four ever-changing guest ales, and Westons Old Rosie for the cider drinkers. Behind the pub is a large semi-covered patio area complete with pond and goldfish. Those interested in local brewing history should note the Fordham's Ales & Stout sign on the front of the pub. ⊛⇌♣◗P↲

Radcliffe Arms ⓛ
31 Walsworth Road, SG4 9ST TL190295
❂ 8am (9am Sat & Sun)-11 ☎ (01462) 456111
⊕ radcliffearms.com
Buntingford Twitchell; guest beer Ⓗ
A gastro-pub with a clean, open, modern interior — the majority of the space is laid out for dining but there is a public bar area for drinkers. The bar is open all day every day and sports two handpumps, which will usually be found dispensing LocAle beers from North Hertfordshire's Buntingford Brewery. There are also several tables under umbrellas outside where occasional beer festivals are held during the summer months.
Ⓢ⊛①&⇌P↲₫

Ley Green

Plough
Plough Lane, SG4 8LA TL162243
❂ 12-11 ☎ (01438) 871394 ⊕ kingswalden.blogspot.com
Greene King IPA, Abbot; guest beers Ⓗ
An ale house as far back as 1846, this is a warm and friendly traditional pub in rolling farming country. A popular stop-off, it features in local guides for walks and cycle rides. The large patio enjoys idyllic views across the Bedfordshire/Hertfordshire countryside – look out for the red kites. There is an open invite to join in the acoustic music sessions on Tuesday evenings, and the snug bar is available for small functions. Hot and cold snacks are available throughout the week.
ⓂQⓈ⊛⑤⇌(88)♣P↲

London Colney

Bull ⊘
Barnet Road, AL2 1QU TL182037
❂ 12-11 (midnight Fri & Sat) ☎ (01727) 823160
⊕ thebullatlondoncolney.co.uk
Black Sheep Best Bitter; Greene King IPA Ⓗ**; guest beers** Ⓖ
Lovely old 17th-century timbered building near the River Colne with a cosy lounge and original fireplace. The large public bar features darts, pool and TV. Outside there is a children's play area. Evening events include a quiz on Sunday and live music on Saturday. Good-value home-made meals are served Monday to Saturday lunchtimes. Wednesday is food night and curry evenings are held monthly. ⊛①⇌♣◗P

Long Marston

Queen's Head ⊘
38 Tring Road, HP23 4QL SP899155
❂ 12-11 ☎ (01296) 668368 ⊕ qhlm.co.uk
Fuller's Chiswick, London Pride; Gale's HSB; guest beer Ⓗ
This delightful 16th-century village pub was once a coaching house and the stables next door have been converted into two B&B rooms. Inside there is a flagstone floor, open fire and exposed beams. The real ale on offer is a mix of Fuller's and Gale's with seasonal guests. The pub serves good-quality home-cooked food, locally sourced where possible, lunchtimes and evenings. Quiz night is Tuesday from 8pm. The chip van calls on Wednesdays around 10pm. Ⓜ⊛☒①&⇌(164)♣P↲

Much Hadham

Old Crown
Hadham Cross, SG10 6DF TL427196
❂ 12-3 (not Mon), 5.30-11 ☎ (01279) 842753
Adnams Southwold Bitter; Greene King IPA; Woodforde's Wherry; guest beer Ⓗ
Situated in the centre of the long, narrow village of Much Hadham, this former tied house once only offered large breweries' beers and eventually closed down. It reopened in 2009 as a free house and is now a shining example of what an independent landlord can achieve. Green Tye beers often feature, as the brewer lives almost next door and is a frequent visitor to the pub. Good traditional pub food is served. Q①⇌(351)

Nuthampstead

Woodman
Stocking Lane, SG8 8NB TL412344
❂ 4-8 Mon; 11-11 Tue-Sat; 12-7 Sun ☎ (01763) 848328
⊕ thewoodman-inn.co.uk
Adnams Southwold Bitter; Greene King IPA; guest beer Ⓖ
Family-run 17th-century free house with an L-shaped bar and wonderful open fires. Beer is dispensed by gravity from casks behind the bar. The restaurant offers à la carte meals as well as house specials and snacks (no food Sun eve). TV is restricted to major sports events. Functions are catered for in a marquee in the garden. During WWII the USAF 398th Bomber Group was based nearby and much memorabilia is displayed here. Ideally located for visiting local attractions such as Duxford Imperial War Museum. ⓂQ⊛☒①P

Old Knebworth

Lytton Arms ●
Park Lane, SG3 6QB TL230203
☼ 11-11; 12-10.30 Sun ☎ (01438) 812312
⊕ lyttonarms.co.uk
Adnams Southwold Bitter; Dark Star Hophead; Mighty Oak Maldon Gold; Sharp's Doom Bar; Tring Side Pocket for a Toad; guest beers Ⓗ
Nineteeth-century pub on the edge of the Knebworth House estate, built for Hawkes and Company of Bishop's Stortford whose original logo may still be seen in the wrought ironwork of the pub sign. Four house beers are supplemented by a changing mix from regional and microbrewers. Good home-made food is available every day. Outside is an attractive decked patio and garden. Live music features on Friday evenings.
♨⏰☆◑◐🍴(44,45)♣🖙P🕹

Oxhey

Villiers Arms
108 Villiers Road, WD19 4AJ TQ121950
☼ 4 (1 Sat)-midnight; 1-11 Sun ☎ (01923) 221556
⊕ thevilliersarms.co.uk
Beer range varies Ⓗ
This 19th-century free house provides a warm welcome with two real fires, while there is a garden for warmer weather. A rotating range of ales is available from three handpumps (often featuring Welsh or Hertfordshire beers) in comfortable surroundings. Suggestions for future guest beers are welcomed. The walls are covered by decorative plates, posters and other items. Food is available. Quiz night is the first Monday of the month. Dog-friendly. ♨Q⇌(Bushey)🖙♣

Potters Crouch

Holly Bush ●
Bedmond Lane, AL2 3NN TL116052
☼ 12-2.30 (3 Sat), 6-11; 12-3, 7-10 Sun ☎ (01727) 851792
⊕ thehollybushpub.co.uk
Fuller's Chiswick, ESB, London Pride; guest beer Ⓗ
An attractive early 17th-century pub in rural surroundings tastefully furnished throughout to a high standard and boasting large oak tables and period chairs. Spotless throughout, there are no jukeboxes, slot machines or TVs to disturb the drinker in any of the three separate drinking areas. The garden is ideal in summer. The food menu is not extensive but is of high quality. Children are welcome in the garden only. ♨Q☆◑◐&🖙P🕹

Preston

Red Lion 🏆 Ⓛ
The Green, SG4 7UD TL180247
☼ 12-2.30 (3.30 Sat), 6-11; 12-3.30, 7-10.30 Sun
☎ (01462) 459585 ⊕ theredlionpreston.co.uk
Fuller's London Pride; Young's Bitter; guest beers Ⓗ
This attractive Queen Anne free house on the village green was the first community-owned pub in Britain. It offers a changing list of beers, many from small breweries. Ray and Jo prepare home-made food using locally sourced ingredients where possible (no food Tue, and Sun eve). The pub hosts the village cricket teams and fundraises for charity. It holds a beer festival around November 5th. A regular CAMRA award winner and 2012 local Pub of the Year. ♨Q⏰☆◑◐🍴(88)♣🖙P🕹

Puckeridge

Crown & Falcon
33 High Street, SG11 1RN TL386233
☼ 12-3, 5.30-11 (midnight Fri); 12-4, 6.30-midnight Sat; 12-5, 7-11 Sun ☎ (01920) 821561
⊕ crown-falcon.demon.co.uk
Adnams Southwold Bitter; guest beers Ⓗ
A public house since 1530, mentioned in Pepys's diary for 1662. Changes to the interior layout can be traced on plans displayed in the bar. It is now one large open-plan room with a separate restaurant. A collection of Allied Breweries memorabilia is on display. The guest beers change weekly, and Westons cider is often available on handpump. Darts is popular, and there is a rare bar billiards table. A free computer is available in the bar for customers' use.
♨⏰☆◑◐🍴(700,331)♣🖙P🕹

Redbourn

Cricketers Ⓛ
East Common, AL3 7ND TL104119
☼ 12-11 (midnight Fri & Sat); 12-10.30 Sun
☎ (01582) 620612 ⊕ thecricketersofredbourn.com
Greene King IPA; guest beers Ⓗ
Redbourn's only free house dates back to 1725. Five real ales and a cider are always available and the food is excellent. The pub is opposite Redbourn's historic cricket pitch and common, making it a perfect setting for a summer's day drink. In winter a wood-burning stove makes for a cosy atmosphere. Summer beer festivals with local beers are held under marquees in the car park. Additional parking is available on the common.
♨Q⏰☆◑◐🍴(34,46,620)🖙P🕹

St Albans

Blacksmiths Arms ●
56 St Peter's Street, AL1 3HG TL150075
☼ 11 (10 Wed)-11; 11-12.30am Fri; 10-12.30am Sat; 12-10.30 Sun ☎ (01727) 868845
Wells Bombardier; guest beers Ⓗ
A large, welcoming high-street establishment with an open-plan bar and extensive beer garden at the rear. The pub is recovering well from its previous incarnation as a Hogshead bar. Two regular ales, along with up to seven guest beers and a handpumped cider, are offered. Good-quality reasonably priced pub grub is served and real ale festivals are a regular feature in the main and garden bars. A loyalty promotion is offered for real ale – buy seven, get one free. ♨⏰☆◑◐&🖙♣🖙🕹

Boot Inn ●
4 Market Place, AL3 5DG TL147072
☼ 12-midnight (12.45am Fri & Sat); 12-11.30 Sun
☎ (01727) 857533
Tring Side Pocket for a Toad; Adnams Southwold Bitter; Sharp's Doom Bar; guest beers Ⓗ
Dating back to the 1400s, this is a typical market-town-centre pub with low ceilings, exposed beams, log fire and wood flooring. On Wednesdays and Saturdays it is busy with bustling market traders and shoppers. The Clock Tower, Abbey and Verulamium Park are all nearby. Local bands play on Sunday afternoons and occasional midweek evenings. Cheese night is Wednesday 6-8pm, no food is available on Monday. Families are welcome until 6pm. The pub supports local breweries through SIBA. ♨⏰◑◐🖙🕹

Farmer's Boy L

134 London Road, AL1 1PQ TL152068
☼ 12-10.30 (midnight Wed & Thu; 1.30am Fri & Sat)
☎ (01727) 860535 ⊕ farmersboy.co.uk
Oakham Scarlet Macaw; Verulam Farmers Delight, Farmers Joy; guest beers H
The Farmer's Boy is St Albans' only brewpub, home of the Verulam Brewery. It supports CAMRA campaigns and always has a dark beer on offer. The three guest beers are sourced from small breweries nationwide and are often from other Hertfordshire breweries. Occasional beer festivals are held. There is also an interesting range of bottled beers. Live music plays on Thursday evenings and there are acoustic sessions on Sunday afternoons. No food Sunday evening. Local parking can be difficult.
⚞✵☎✖◑▶≷(City)⬚(724)♣♠!–

Farriers Arms L

32-34 Lower Dagnall Street, AL3 4PT (off A5183 Verulam Road) TL145073
☼ 12-2.30 (not Mon), 5.30-11; 12-11 Sat; 12-10.30 Sun
☎ (01727) 851025
McMullen AK, Cask Ale, Country; guest beer H
Originally a 19th-century grocer's and butcher's shop, the Farriers became a pub in the 1920s and is now a classic back-street local. The only pub in the city never to have forsaken real ale, a blue plaque on the wall outside marks the first meeting of the Hertfordshire branch of CAMRA The split-level interior has a small area fronting the bar for stand-up drinking, darts and cards. The back room has more comfortable seating and there is TV for sports. On-street parking can be difficult.
⚞✵◑◐♣♠!–

Garibaldi ✓

61 Albert Street, AL1 1RT (off Holywell Hill) TL149068
☼ 12-11.30 (midnight Fri & Sat), 12-11 Sun
☎ (01727) 855046
Fuller's ESB, London Pride; Gale's Seafarers Ale, HSB; guest beers H
Named after the Italian patriot who unified Italy in the 19th century, this is a welcoming, lively back-street local within walking distance of the Abbey. The central bar has plenty of standing and seating room – it is more spacious than the façade suggests. Good-value meals include popular Sunday roasts. CAMRA members are offered a discount on beer. There is a public car park nearby.
⚞✵☎◑▶≷(Abbey/City)♣!–

Six Bells L

16-18 St Michaels Street, AL3 4SH TL137074
☼ 12-11 (midnight Fri; 10.30 Sun) ☎ (01727) 856945
⊕ the-six-bells.com
Oakham JHB; Taylor Landlord; Tring Ridgeway; guest beers H
The owners of this 16th-century timbered free house are passionate about beer quality, offering three regular and two ever-changing guest ales, and a warm welcome to all. The only licensed premises within the walls of Roman Verulamium, it is also within walking distance of the city centre, Abbey, park and museum. Excellent food is served lunchtimes and evenings (no food Sun eve). The pub has a wood-burning fire in winter and a pleasant patio area for summer. Occasional quiz nights and live music are hosted.
⚞✵☎◑▶⬚(300,301)♣♠P!–

White Hart Tap ✓

4 Keyfield Terrace, AL1 1QJ TL150069
☼ 12-11 ☎ (01727) 860974 ⊕ whiteharttap.co.uk
Castle Rock Harvest Pale; Fuller's London Pride; Sharp's Doom Bar; Taylor Landlord; guest beers H
Welcoming, one bar, back-street local offering guest beers from the Punch Taverns range. Good-value home-cooked food, featuring fresh vegetables from the pub's own allotment, is served every lunchtime and Monday to Saturday evenings, with curries on Monday, fish and chips on Friday and roasts on Sunday. Quiz night is Wednesday and live music plays occasionally on Saturday. Barbecues are held in summer and several beer festivals, including one over the August bank holiday. There is a heated, covered smoking area outside and a public car park opposite.
⚞✵☎◑▶≷(Abbey/City)♠!–

White Lion L

91 Sopwell Lane, AL1 1RN TL149068
☼ 12-11 ☎ (01727) 850540 ⊕ thewhitelionph.co.uk
St Austell Tribute; Tring Side Pocket for a Toad; Young's Special; guest beers H
Two-bar 16th century timbered pub, full of conversation with a friendly welcome. There are plenty of guest beers and a beer festival is held in August. An interesting variety of quality home-made food is served daily. Live music features on Tuesday and Wednesday evenings. The large garden to the rear has a barbecue and pétanque piste and is popular with families in summer. The pub is handy for the famous St Albans Abbey.
⚞Q✵◑▶◁≷(Abbey/City)♣!–☐

St Paul's Walden

Strathmore Arms L

London Road, SG4 8BT TL193222
☼ 6-11 Mon; 12-2.30, 5-11 Tue-Thu; 12-11 Fri & Sat; 12-10.30 Sun ☎ (01438) 871654 ⊕ thestrathmorearms.co.uk
Buntingford Strathmore Bitter; guest beers H
The pub is on the Bowes-Lyon estate and caters for drinkers, diners and those wishing to play pub games. It hosts several beer festivals, obscure breweries are a speciality and 'tickers' will appreciate the ever-changing rota of guest beers. Bottled Belgian beers are also available along with a cider and a perry. The bar boasts a bar billiards table and the pub is well known for raising funds around the local area. A former Local CAMRA Pub of the Year and Community Pub of the Year.
Q✵☎◑▶◁▲⬚(304)♣♠P

Sandridge

Green Man

31 High Street, Sandridge, AL4 9DD TL169104
☼ 11-11 (midnight Fri & Sat); 12-11 Sun ☎ (01727) 854845
Black Sheep Best Bitter G; **Greene King IPA** H, **Abbot; guest beer** G
In the centre of Sandridge, this family-run locals' pub extends a warm welcome to all discerning ale and cider drinkers, with the current landlord now resident for 25 years. With up to three ales served straight from the cask, up to six ciders from Westons are available during the summer months. The pub is on the doorstep of the newly established 850-acre Heartswood forest, making it the ideal place for refreshment after a stroll in the woods. ⚞Q✵☎◑▶◁♣♠P

Queen's Head

7 Church End, AL4 9DL (just off B651 by church)
TL171104

☼ 11.30-2.30, 6-11 (midnight Fri); 11.30-midnight Sat; 12-11
Sun ☎ (01728) 855069

**Fuller's London Pride; Sharp's Doom Bar; Young's
Bitter; guest beer** Ⓗ

Friendly traditional local among old cottages. The
ancient heavily beamed front bar is complemented
by a more recent back bar where the handpumps
can be found; beyond is a covered patio
overlooking the graveyard. Dominoes and darts are
played and there are two football teams. Live
music takes place on alternate Sunday evenings.
Evening food is served (not Sun & Mon), mostly
home-made, and it is best to book meals on
Fridays and Saturdays. ♣◑⌂♿🚆♣╚

Sawbridgeworth

Gate Ⓛ

81 London Road, CM21 9JJ TL481150

☼ 11.30-2.30 (2 Wed), 5.30-11; 11.30-11 Fri & Sat; 12-11 Sun
☎ (01279) 722313 ⊕ thegatepub.com

Beer range varies Ⓗ

A lively pub particularly popular with sports fans as
there are satellite screens in all the bars. The small
Sawbridgeworth Brewery at the back provides
house beers. Large beer festivals are held over the
Easter and August bank holiday weekends. The pub
is home to several sports teams. No dogs are
allowed inside. ♣◑⌂♿🚆🚆(333,510,511)P╚

Stevenage

Our Mutual Friend Ⓛ

Broadwater Crescent, SG2 8EH TL249226

☼ 12-11 (11.30 Fri & Sat) ☎ (01438) 312282
⊕ omfpub.co.uk

Beer range varies Ⓗ

Thriving community pub on on the southern side of
Stevenage serving an ever-changing selection of
cask beers. Since being brought back from the cask
ale graveyard in 2002, it has appeared in every
issue of the Guide. At least eight real ciders and
perries are also on offer. Regular beer festivals are
held thoughout the year. Winner of many local
CAMRA awards including Pub of the Year. Can be
very busy on Stevenage FC match days.
Q☎♣◑⌂🚆(4,5)♣♣P╥

Standing Order ⊘

33 High Street, SG1 3AU TL233250

☼ 9-midnight (11 Sun) ☎ (01438) 316972

**Greene King Abbot; Ruddles Best Bitter; guest
beers** Ⓗ

There is a keen focus on cask ale here, with many
beers sourced from microbreweries far and wide.
Situated at the northern end of Stevenage Old
Town, the name reflects the pub's past history as a
bank from the early 1960s to the late 1990s. It was
converted to a Wetherspoon in 2000.
Q☎♣◑⌂🚆♣P

Tring

King's Arms

King Street, HP23 6BE (on corner of Queen St and King
St)

☼ 12-2.30 (3 Fri), 7-11; 11.30-3, 7-11 Sat; 12-4, 7-10.30 Sun
☎ (01442) 823318 ⊕ kingsarmstring.co.uk

Wadworth 6X; guest beers Ⓗ

Hugely popular 1830s free house serving five real
ales, mostly from microbreweries. It is painted pink
on the outside to distance itself from any brewery
livery. Inside it has wood-panelled and green-
painted walls festooned with beer paraphernalia,
and open fires in winter. The food is all home-
made and the menu is seasonal. Owned by the
same family for more than 30 years, it has been a
frequent winner of CAMRA Branch and Regional
Pub of the Year. ♨Q☼◑🚆(61,500,501)♣♣╚

Robin Hood Ⓛ ⊘

1 Brook Street, HP23 5ED SP925116

☼ 11.30-3, 5.30-11; 11.30-11.30 Fri; 12-11.30 Sat; 12-11 Sun
☎ (01442) 824912 ⊕ therobinhoodtring.co.uk

**Fuller's Chiswick, Discovery, London Pride, ESB; Gale's
Seafarers Ale; guest beer** Ⓗ

Welcoming 17th-century Fuller's pub situated on
the edge of Tring town centre. Two logburners,
beams and low ceilings give the pub a warm,
friendly feel. An interesting menu is served
lunchtimes and evenings, with fish a speciality – try
the beer sausages. Six real ales are on handpump.
There is a conservatory and covered courtyard at
the rear. Quiz night is Sunday and sometimes
Wednesday. The impressive toilets are well worth
a visit. ♨Q☼◑♿🚆(61,500)♣╚

Ware

Crooked Billet ⊘

140 Musley Hill, SG12 7NL (via New Rd from High St)
TL362150

☼ 12-2.30 (not Mon-Thu), 5.30-11.30 (midnight Fri);
12-midnight Sat; 12-11.30 Sun ☎ (01920) 462516

Beer range varies Ⓗ

Stuart and Sue have presided over the Billet for 18
years, with full use of the local SIBA delivery
scheme resulting in over 300 different ales being
sold – the pump clips adorn the walls. Three
handpumps offer the ales, always including a mild,
porter or stout. A fourth is sometimes available
from the cellar. The two small bars have real fires,
TV sports, pool and darts. Carlisle United and Ware
FC fans are always assured of a warm welcome.
♨☎♣♿🚆(395)♣╚

Worppell ⊘

35 Watton Road, SG12 0AD TL353147

☼ 12-2.30, 5-11; 12-11 Fri; 12-midnight Sat; 12-10 Sun
☎ (01920) 411666

Greene King Abbot, IPA; guest beer Ⓗ

George and Pat have run The Worppell for over 25
years, putting them among Hertfordshire's longest
serving landlords. The pub is small and cosy, with
food available Monday to Friday lunchtimes.
Greene King ales are always served to George's
high standard. The pub can be lively when football
is on TV (especially on Sundays), with the locals
often more entertaining than the match. ♣◑♣

Wareside

Chequers Ⓛ

Ware Road, SG12 7QY TL395156

☼ 12-3 (3.15 Wed), 6-11; 12-4, 6-10.30 Sun
☎ (01920) 467010

**Adnams Southwold Bitter; Buntingford Highwayman
IPA; guest beers** Ⓗ

A traditional free house run by the same family for
16 years. Dating from the 15th century, it was
originally a coaching inn and has three distinct bar

areas plus a restaurant. One guest beer is usually from a small brewery. All food is home-made, including vegetarian options. Walkers and cyclists are welcome, making this a good base for a country ramble. No machines or music, and there is a ban on swearing. ⚲Q⚙♿◐⬤&🖵(M3,M4)♣P

Watford

West Herts Sports & Social Club
8 Park Avenue, WD18 7HP (S of A412, near town hall) TQ103964
☼4 (12 Fri & Sat)-11; 12-10.30 Sun ☎ (01923) 229239
⊕ westhertssports.co.uk
Fuller's London Pride; Young's Bitter; guest beers Ⓗ
The clubhouse has a comfortable, modern bar decorated with a sporting theme. Major sporting events are screened and pub games are available. Up to three guest beers often come from small independent breweries such as Nethergate. Rolls are usually on offer. A function room, home of the CAMRA Watford Beer Festival, can be hired. CAMRA East Anglian Club of the Year for the past three years. Non-members can gain entry up to four times a year by showing a CAMRA membership card or this Guide. ⚙&⊖🖵♣P⌐🗓

Wheathampstead

Swan ✅
56 High Street, AL4 8AR TL177139
☼11-11 (midnight Fri & Sat); 12-11 Sun ☎ (01582) 833110
⊕ wheathampstead.net/swan/index.htm
Greene King IPA; guest beers Ⓗ
Dating from 1744, the inn retains many interesting features including exposed beams and an inglenook fireplace. A thriving village pub, it is popular with walkers and workers. Lunch, including excellent daily home-made specials, is served in the lower bar. The cellar has a 10-rack system and guest ales from local microbrewers are a regular attraction. There is a pool room to the rear plus darts and Sky TV. A beer and cider festival is held in September. Well-behaved and friendly dogs welcome. ⭢⚙◐⬤&🖵♣●P⌐

Wigginton

Greyhound Ⓛ ✅
Chesham Road, HP23 6EH SP938101

☼12-11.30 (midnight Fri & Sat); 12-11 Sun
☎ (01442) 824631 ⊕ greyhoundtring.co.uk
Tring Side Pocket for a Toad, Ridgeway; guest beers Ⓗ
A popular and friendly family-run village inn situated half a mile from the Ridgeway National Trail – an ideal stop-off for walkers and cyclists. Four beers, usually from local breweries, are available and excellent home-cooked, locally sourced food is served daily including the Ridgeway Sausage made using Tring's Ridgeway Bitter (no food Sun eve). There is a beer garden and childrens' play area to the rear, and three en-suite guest rooms are available. ⚲⚙♿◐⬤&🖵(387)♣P⌐

Wildhill

Woodman
45 Wildhill Road, AL9 6EA (between A1000 and B158) TL264068
☼11.30-2.30, 5.30-11; 12-2.30, 7-10.30 Sun
☎ (01707) 642618
Greene King IPA, Abbot; guest beers Ⓗ
Excellent, friendly village pub extending a warm welcome to a varied clientele of all ages. Voted local CAMRA Pub of the Year for a record seven times – and it shows. Six beers are available with four guests, usually at least one from a Hertfordshire brewery. Good pub grub is served at lunchtime (no food Sun). The large garden is ideal in summer. The annual Woodmanstick beer festival takes place in June. An all-round superb boozer! ⚲⭢⚙◐♣●P⌐

Woolmer Green

Chequers Ⓛ ✅
16 London Road, SG3 6JP (on B197) TL253185
☼12 (4 Mon)-11; 12-11.30 Fri & Sat; 12-8.30 Sun
☎ (01438) 813216 ⊕ benicksatthechequers.co.uk
Young's Bitter; guest beers Ⓗ
Large inn on the Great North Road at the southern end of the village. The interior is largely open plan with a central fireplace sporting a real fire during the cooler months. Cask ale is popular, with high quality compensating for a limited range. Good-quality, home-made food is made with fresh ingredients – the pies on Wednesday and Saturday are fantastic value. The garden features a collection of interesting birds and animals. ⚲⭢⚙♿◐🖵(300,301)●P⌐

The sign of the Bell

Mr Jones and Partridge travelled on to Gloucester. Being arrived here, they chose for their house of entertainment the sign of the Bell; an excellent house, and which I do most seriously recommend to every reader who shall visit this ancient city. The master of it is brother to the great preacher, Whitfield, but is absolutely untainted with the pernicious principles of Methodism, or of any other heretical sect. He is indeed a very honest, plain man, and in my opinion not likely to create any disturbance either in Church or State. His wife hath, I believe, had much pretension to beauty, and is still a very fine woman. Her person and deportment might have made a shining figure in the politest assemblies; but though she must be conscious of this and many other perfections, she seems perfectly contented with, and resigned to the state of life to which she is called – To be concise, she is a very friendly, good-natured woman; and so industrious to oblige that the guests must be of a very morose disposition who are not extremely well satisfied in her house.
Henry Fielding, The History of Tom Jones, 1749

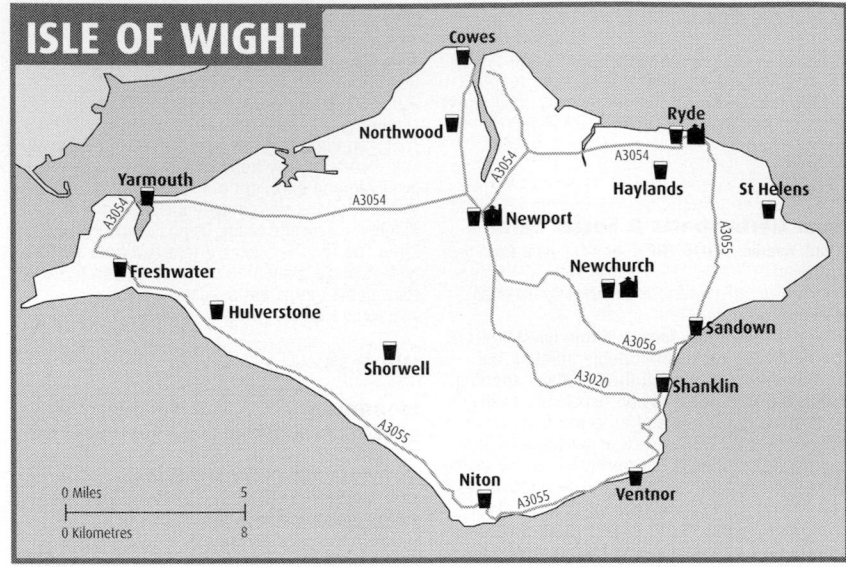

ISLE OF WIGHT

Cowes
Northwood
Ryde
A3054
Yarmouth
A3054
Haylands
St Helens
Newport
A3054
A3055
Freshwater
Newchurch
Hulverstone
Sandown
A3056
Shorwell
A3020
Shanklin
A3055
Niton
A3055
Ventnor

0 Miles 5
0 Kilometres 8

Cowes

Anchor Inn 🅛
1 High Street, PO31 7SA (opp Somerfields)
🕑 11-11 (midnight Fri & Sat); 12-10.30 Sun
☎ (01983) 292823 ⊕ theanchorcowes.com
Fuller's London Pride; Goddards Fuggle-Dee-Dum; Ringwood Best Bitter; guest beers 🅗
Originally the Trumpeters back in 1704, this high-street pub is next to the marina and ferry. Hugely popular during the summer, it has a covered area outside with tables for smokers. An extensive food menu is available all day, with families welcome. Live music plays outside in summer and in the stable bar in winter. One Island ale and two guests are always available. Accommodation is in seven comfortable rooms and there is a large public car park nearby. ⚐🛏🐾🍴🍽🚆(1)♣⚓

Union Inn
Watch House Lane, PO31 7QH (just off the Parade)
🕑 7.30-midnight (2am Fri & Sat); 12-10 Sun
☎ (01983) 293163 ⊕ unioninn.eu
Fuller's London Pride; Gale's Seafarers Ale, HSB; guest beer 🅗
A haven for yachting enthusiasts, locals and holidaymakers, one three-sided bar serves the lounge, snug, dining area and airy conservatory. A roaring fire in winter adds to the cosy atmosphere. It serves delicious family meals with portions for children and ingredients sourced from local suppliers. The pub may close at 11pm but frequently stays open later. There is pay parking on the Parade 25 yards away, free later in the day. ⚐Q🛏🐾🍴🍽🚆(1)♣

Freshwater

Prince of Wales 🅛
Princes Road, PO40 9ED SZ334874
🕑 3 (12 Sun)-11; 12-11.30 Fri & Sat ☎ (01983) 753535
Ballards Midhurst Mild; Yates' Mews; guest beers 🅗
Fine, unspoilt gem of a town pub run by possibly the longest-serving landlord on the Isle of Wight. Just off the main Freshwater shopping centre, it has

a large garden and pleasant public and lounge bars. It offers four frequently changing guest beers, usually including one from Andwell, so there is always something new to try. Q🛏🌞🍴🚆A🚆(12)♣P🖵

Haylands

Lake Huron
51 Upton Road, PO33 3HR (in Haylands Village)
🕑 12-11 ☎ (01983) 562653
Ringwood Fortyniner; Ruddles Best Bitter; guest beer 🅗
The only surviving pub from the Lake family's small Ryde pub empire, it was a wine and spirits shop called the Eclipse when it was taken over by the Lakes in 1878 and became a staging post for the Newport-Ryde coach. Unique with its many rooms, it remains a back-street local with a friendly and lively atmosphere. It keeps only a small range of beers, but they are always top quality. Live music is hosted on Friday and Saturday. ⚐Q🛏🌞🍴🚆

Hulverstone

Sun Inn
Main Road, PO30 4EH
🕑 11-11 (12-10.30 winter) ☎ (01983) 741124
⊕ sun-hulverstone.com
Beer range varies 🅗
Six hundred-year-old hostelry boasting uninterrupted views to the sea. It has a strong following for food with an extensive menu and daily specials served all day, plus a weekly curry night. There is a large restaurant and the pub caters for wedding parties in a stunning extension. Weekly music nights feature local musicians. Well-behaved children are welcome. The four ever-changing beers include at least one from the Island. ⚐🛏🌞🍴🍽🚆(77)♣P

Newchurch

Pointer Inn
High Street, PO36 0NN (next to church)
🌟 11-11; 12-10.30 Sun ☎ (01983) 865202
🌐 pointerinn.com
Fuller's London Pride, seasonal beers; Gale's HSB Ⓗ
Ancient village local where families are welcome. The home-cooked food is prepared by a chef with a vast experience of Island trade (booking is essential). Food is served until 9.30pm (9pm Sun). A highchair and toys are always available for children. Outside, the large garden has a pétanque terrain and there is a covered area for smokers.
Q✿ⓓP꤭

Newport

Newport Ale House Ⓛ
24A Holyrood Street, PO30 5AZ
🌟 12-11 (10.30 Sun); 11-midnight Fri & Sat ☎ 07515 493460
🌐 newportalehouse.co.uk
Beer range varies Ⓖ
This Grade II-listed building has previously traded as a hairdresser, coffin storage for an undertaker, posting house and stables for a coaching inn. It is the Island's newest pub and smallest ale house, no bigger than a front room. With no jukebox or TV, conversation comes easy, and regular local entertainment is hosted. Snacks include high-quality locally sourced pies, rolls and sandwiches. The owners have a passion for real ale – beers are served on gravity. Q🖳♣

Prince of Wales
36 South Street, PO30 1JE (opp bus station)
🌟 10.30-11; 12-10.30 Sun ☎ (01983) 525026
Beer range varies Ⓗ
Popular, unpretentious and historic town-centre locals' pub, well situated opposite the bus station, main car park and Morrisons. Bar snacks are served all day and three constantly changing beers are offered from the Punch portfolio. There is a thriving following for pub games. The Prince of Wales remains a street-corner hostelry in the traditional fashion. 🖳Q✿ⓓ🖳♣꤭

Niton

Buddle Ⓛ
St Catherines Road, Niton Undercliff, PO38 2NE (follow signs to St Catherine's Lighthouse) SZ507768
🌟 11-11 (midnight Fri & Sat); 12-10.30 Sun
☎ (01983) 730243 🌐 buddleinn.co.uk
Fuller's HSB, London Pride; Island Yachtsman's Ale; guest beers Ⓗ
Historic old smugglers' inn with flagstone floors, inglenook fireplace and black beamed ceilings. Extensive facilities include a separate bar, function room and garden with sea views. A popular destination dining pub, serving good locally sourced food, it also has a strong real ale following for the six ales served. 🖳Q🏃✿ⓓ🖳(6)♣P

White Lion Ⓛ
High Street, PO38 2AT SZ507768
🌟 11 (12 Sun)-11 ☎ (01983) 730293
Ringwood Fortyniner; Sharp's Doom Bar; Yates' Undercliff Experience; guest beer Ⓗ
Central to Niton, the pub sits opposite the village stores and bus stop, with recently extended car parking, children's area and garden. The interior includes a separate formal area/function room

with bar, as well as a popular public bar with room to enjoy the home-cooked fresh food and four excellent real ales. There is a covered, decked area outside for smokers. Live music plays occasionally. 🖳Q🏃✿ⓓ🖳🖳(66)♣P꤭

Northwood

Horseshoe Inn Ⓛ
353 Newport Road, PO31 8PL
🌟 12-5.30, 7-midnight (2am Fri & Sat); 12-midnight Sun
☎ (01983) 292349 🌐 thehorseshoe-iow.co.uk
Beer range varies Ⓗ
Pleasant 17th-century coaching inn, originally known as the Halfway Inn. There is a proper public bar with darts and pool, and a saloon that boasts a well. Sit in comfort and enjoy four excellent ales, chosen from a wide range, with a dark beer often available. Always expect to see the latest big game on two massive TV screens with HD and 3D. Well-behaved children are welcome. 🖳Q🏃✿🖳(1)♣P꤭

Travellers Joy Ⓛ
85 Pallance Road, PO31 8LS (on Northwood-Porchfield road) 480935
🌟 12-2.30, 5-11; 11-11 Thu-Sat; 12-11 Sun
☎ (01983) 298024 🌐 tjoy.co.uk
Island Wight Gold; guest beers Ⓗ
Offering one of the best choices of cask ale on the island, this long-standing old country inn was the Island's first beer exhibition house. Seven carefully chosen, varied and interesting ales rotate to supplement the Wight Gold, always including Island beers. A real cider is sometimes also available. A good range of home-cooked food is served lunchtimes and evenings. The pub is a popular venue for real ale followers, the local community and visitors seeking a friendly and amenable base. 🖳🏃✿ⓓ🖳(1)♣♣P꤭

Ryde

S Fowler & Co Ⓛ ✅
41-43 Union Street, PO33 2LF (top of Union St)
🌟 7am-midnight (1am Fri & Sat) ☎ (01983) 812112
Courage Directors; Greene King Abbot; Ruddles County; guest beers Ⓗ
Converted drapery store offering one of the most varied ranges of well-kept beers you will find anywhere. The pub's name was suggested by the local CAMRA branch – it was not just the name of the former drapery but also that of a founder member of CAMRA, whose life is commemorated in the pub. There is a selection of 12 ales, fewer during quieter periods. Food is served until 10pm. 🏃ⓓ🚉(Esplanade)🖳(4,9,3)♣

Simeon Arms Ⓛ
21 Simeon Street, PO33 1JG (opp Canoe Lake)
🌟 11-11 (11.30 Mon; 11.45 Thu-Sat); 12-11.30 Sun
☎ (01983) 614954
Courage Directors; Goddards Ale of Wight; guest beer Ⓗ
Thriving yet unlikely gem tucked away in a Ryde back street with a Tardis-like interior and annexed function hall. The pub is immensely popular with the local community who come to participate in various leagues including darts, crib and pool, and pétanque on the enormous floodlit terrain in summer. You can always expect to find a local ale, and food is available lunchtimes and weekend

evenings. Live music plays on Saturday and Sunday night. The smoking area outside is heated and covered. ゝ❀⯅⬛⇌(Esplanade)🚌♣�

Swans Nest
21 Player Street, PO33 2JB
✪ 11-3, 6-11 (midnight Fri & Sat); 12-6 Sun
☎ (01983) 565324
Draught Bass; Greene King IPA; guest beer H
Family-run, friendly local with a separate restaurant specialising in home-cooked Italian food. The interesting historic building with a distinctive frontage is said to have been an orphanage and monastic house in earlier times. Possibly one of the oldest buildings in Ryde, early photographic evidence shows it as an isolated building some distance from the shore line. A must for anyone interested in architectural curiosities. There is a small car park to the side.
🅰️❀⯅⇌(St Johns)🚌(2,3)P

St Helens

Vine Inn
Upper Green Road, PO33 1UJ
✪ 11-11 (12.20am Fri & Sat; 11.30 Sun) ☎ (01983) 872337
⊕ the-vine-inn.co.uk
Fuller's London Pride; guest beers H
The front of the pub overlooks what is possibly the biggest village green in the kingdom, known locally as Goose Island. An eclectic selection of memorabilia reflecting local history, from railways to hunting to breweries to maritime, decorates the walls. From Easter to late summer there is an additional tented area outside. Three guest beers include one from an Island brewery, with two extra on the bar during the summer. A public car park is nearby. ❀⯅♿⬅🚌(10,14,16)♣�

Sandown

Castle Inn
12-14 Fitzroy Street, PO36 8HY (off High Street)
✪ 11-11.30; 10.30-1am Fri & Sat; 12-10.30 Sun
☎ (01983) 403169 ⊕ sandowncastle.co.uk
Greene King Abbot; Young's Special; guest beers H
The Castle is an excellent town free house and locals' pub with four darts teams, crib and a pétanque terrain. Five real ales are always on offer including the best from local breweries. There is a children's room at the back and a patio for warm weather. The TV is not allowed to intrude, but is turned on for special occasions. Happy hour is popular, as is the Sunday quiz. Beer festivals are held several times a year, usually featuring local ales. ❀♿⇌🚌(10)♣�

Shanklin

Chine Inn L
Chine Hill, PO37 6BW
✪ 11-4, 7-11; 12-10.30 Sun ☎ (01983) 865880
Sharp's Doom Bar; guest beer H
This inn is a classic. The building, which has stood since 1621, must have some claim to being one of the oldest pubs with a licence on the Island. Completely refurbished, it has retained plenty of the original charm for which it was well known. Live music is hosted on Saturday night and Sunday afternoon. The Chine Inn ghosts – a girl in blue and an old man in the corner – have been seen by small children. The magnificent kitchens will be put to

good use during the summer months. There is frequently an Otter beer available.
🅰️Qゝ❀⯅⬛🚌(3,16)�

Shorwell

Crown Inn ♈ L ✅
Walkers Lane, PO30 3JZ SZ456830
✪ 10.30 (11.30 Sun)-11 ☎ (01983) 740293
⊕ crowninnshorwell.co.uk
Adnams Broadside; Goddards Fuggle de Dum; Sharp's Doom Bar; guest beers H
Expansive hostelry in the picturesque village of Shorwell with a central multi-sided bar and traditional bar areas offering a range of four to six beers and a good home-cooked pub menu all day produced by head chef Paul Hayward. The pub has a trout stream running through the garden, ducks in abundance to keep the children amused, and plenty of car parking. 🅰️Q❀⯅♿🚌(12)♣P

Ventnor

Crab & Lobster Tap L ✅
Grove Road, PO38 1TH (50yds from Central Car Park)
✪ 12-midnight (1am Fri & Sat; 10.30 Sun) ☎ (01983) 852311
⊕ crabandlobstertap.org.uk
Sharp's Doom Bar; guest beers H
Interesting town pub with a warm welcome. You may strike lucky and be there when one of the Rings league is taking place – Ventnor has one of the few leagues in Great Britain. Bar billiards is also played. The two guests beers come from the Punch portfolio and there is a small Beerex each year. From March, food is served Thursday to Sunday lunchtimes and evenings. A large public car park is nearby. Q❀⯅🚌(3,6)♣

Volunteer L
30 Victoria Street, PO38 1ES (50yds from bus terminal)
✪ 11-11 (midnight Fri & Sat); 12-10.30 Sun
☎ (01983) 852537 ⊕ volunteer-inn.co.uk
Courage Best Bitter; Greene King Abbot; guest beers H
Built in 1866, the Volunteer is one of the smallest pubs on the island. A past winner of local CAMRA Pub of the Year, between four and six guest beers are usually available including a local brew. No chips, no children, no fruit machines, no video games – just a pure adult drinking house and one of the few places where you can still play Rings and enjoy a traditional games night. Live music plays on Sunday afternoon. Westons Old Rosie cider is available. Q♿🚌(3,6)♣●☐

Yarmouth

King's Head ✅
Quay Street, PO41 0PB (opp ferry terminal)
✪ 11-11; 12-10.30 Sun ☎ (01983) 760351
Beer range varies H
Ancient 16th-century town pub with a big open fire and an interesting collection of old Island prints and local photographs. Stone floors, low ceilings and cosy corners in abundance help to create an intimate atmosphere. Home-cooked food includes fresh fish, with daily specials. Three changing ales are on offer, always including an Island beer. A handy place to wait for the Yarmouth-Lymington ferry. 🅰️❀⯅⬛🚌(7,11)�

South East Pub Walks

Bob Steel

South East Pub Walks is a pocket-sized, traveller's guide to some of the best walking and best pubs in South East England. It features 30 walks of varying lengths, all accessible by public transport and aimed at both the casual walker and more serious hiker. Each route has been selected for its unique and varied landscape, and its beer — with the walks taking you on a tour of the best real ale pubs the area has to offer. Full-colour Ordnance Survey maps and detailed route information, plus pub listings with opening hours, contact information and details of draught beers, make *South East Pub Walks* the essential guide for anyone wanting to see – and taste – the very best of South East England.

£9.99   ISBN 978-1-85249-287-8   CAMRA members' price £7.99   184 pages

For this and other books on beer and pubs visit the CAMRA bookshop at www.camra.org.uk/books

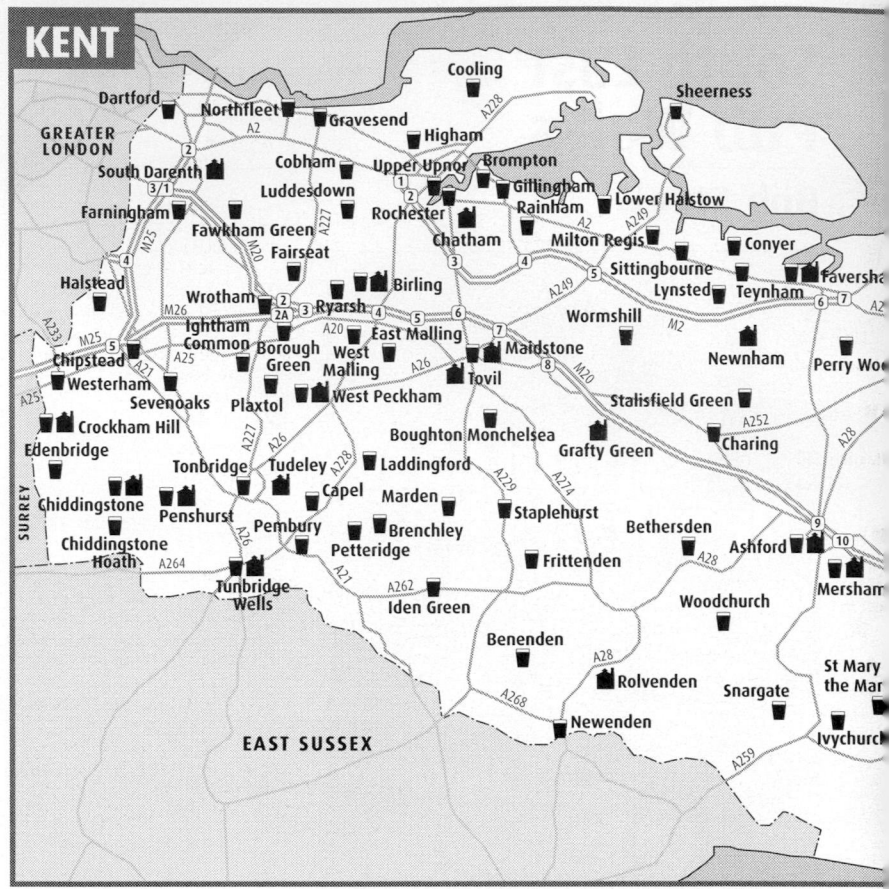

KENT

Ashford

County Hotel ✅
10 High Street, TN24 8TD
☼ 8-midnight (1am Fri & Sat) ☎ (01233) 646891
Greene King Abbot; Ruddles Best Bitter; guest beers Ⓗ
A welcome real ale oasis in the centre of Ashford, this building first became an inn around 1890. Now a spacious Wetherspoon pub, it has two bars with three distinct seating areas. Real cider is permanently on offer, dispensed from a polypin in the fridge. Food is available every day 8am-10pm. Children are allowed in the dining area.
ᗭ❀❶&♦P⅃

Benenden

Bull Ⓛ
The Street, TN17 4DE
☼ 12-midnight ☎ (01580) 240054
⊕ thebullatbenenden.co.uk
Dark Star Hophead; Harveys Sussex Best Bitter; Larkins Traditional; guest beer Ⓗ
Sizeable yet intimate free house in the village centre dating back to the early 17th century. The public bar features a large inglenook fireplace and there are wooden floors and exposed oak beams throughout. Food is prepared using locally grown produce and is available both in the bar area and separate restaurant (no food Sun eves). Booking is essential for the Friday fish and chips evening and Sunday lunchtime carvery. ᎯQ❀❶Ⓓ员(297)♣P⅃

Bethersden

George Inn
The Street, TN26 3AG (off A28, in centre of village)
☼ 11-11.30 (5 Sun) ☎ (01233) 820235
Brakspear Bitter; Harveys Sussex Best Bitter; Morland Old Speckled Hen; guest beers Ⓗ
Two-bar free house in a pretty Kentish village. Beer festivals are held on St George's Day and in July. Food is served lunchtimes (not Mon) and evenings (not Sun), the former saloon doubling as a restaurant. The public bar is a survivor of what village inns used to be like, with pub games, jukebox and good conversation. Buses from Ashford stop outside. Ꭿᗭ❀❶Ⓓ员(2)♦P⅃

Birling

Nevill Bull Ⓛ
1 Ryarsh Road, ME19 5JW
☼ 11-3, 6-11; 11-11 Fri & Sat; 12-5 Sun ☎ (01732) 843193
⊕ nevillbull.co.uk
Beer range varies Ⓗ

0 Miles 5

0 Kilometres 8

The pub sits at the heart of the village. It was renamed in 1953 in memory of local Lt Michael Nevill who was killed in World War II. Inside, the pub has an abundance of character, with bare brick walls and wooden beams. It is warmed in the winter months by a real log fire. Old table games are available for use. Blackboards list a popular locally sourced food menu. A stone's throw from the Kent Brewery, you will always find one of its beers available. ⚌Q☺◐▤(58)♣P⅄⊟

Bishopsbourne

Mermaid ⓛ
The Street, CT4 5HX
🕐 12-3.30, 6 (7 Sun)-11; 12-11 Sat ☎ (01227) 830581
Shepherd Neame Master Brew, seasonal beer Ⓗ
Built in 1865, this charming red-brick pub nestles in a pretty valley and is well worth the short detour from the A2. The two bars are a good place for a chat or a game of darts. Home-cooked meals are served at lunchtimes (no food Sun, and no payment by card). There is live music monthly, and occasional quizzes and summer barbecues. A heated and covered area is provided for smokers. Walkers and dogs are welcome, but children are allowed only in the attractive enclosed garden. A ramp is available for wheelchair users.
⚌☺◐☖♣⅄

Borough Green

Black Horse & Hoodens ⓛ ✅
76 Maidstone Road, TN15 8HF (on A25)
🕐 12-11.30 (midnight Fri & Sat) ☎ (01732) 885332
⊕ blackhorseandhoodens.com
Old Dairy Red Top; Westerham Hooden Brew; guest beers Ⓗ
Pleasantly refurbished main road community pub with a relaxed and friendly atmosphere. There is an emphasis on local produce including fresh eggs supplied by the pub chickens. Local ales are always on sale, including the house beer, a Westerham blend of Finchcocks and Freedom ales, along with a range of guests. The venue has one bar area with three sections and a large garden. Occasional live music and beer festivals are hosted, plus a regular comedy event on the first Monday of the month.
⚌☺◐⇌▤(70,222,308)♣P⅄

Boughton Monchelsea

Cock Inn ⓛ ✅
Heath Road, ME17 4JD
🕐 11-11; 12-10.30 Sun ☎ (01622) 743166
Shepherd Neame Master Brew, seasonal beers Ⓗ
A former coaching inn originally built to provide lodgings for Canterbury pilgrims, this 16th-century pub offers all the Shepherd Neame seasonal and pilot brewery beers. An excellent menu, specialising in seafood, is served in both the bar and good-sized restaurant (no food Sun eves). The oak beams in the drinking area are adorned with hops and there is a large inglenook fireplace with a log fire in the winter. Dog-friendly. Darts and board games are available. Outside is an extensive patio.
⚌☺◐🚻▤(59)♣P⅄

Bramling

Haywain ⓛ
Canterbury Road, CT3 1NB (on A257)

INDEPENDENT BREWERIES
Abigale Ashford
Canterbury Ales Canterbury
Canterbury Brewers Canterbury
Farriers Arms Mersham
Goacher's Tovil
Goody Herne (NEW)
Hop Fuzz West Hythe (NEW)
Hopdaemon Newnham
Kent Birling
Larkins Chiddingstone
Millis South Darenth
Moodley's Penshurst
Nelson Chatham
Old Dairy Rolvenden
Ramsgate (Gadds) Broadstairs
Ripple Steam Sutton (NEW)
Rockin Robin Maidstone (NEW)
Shepherd Neame Faversham
Swan West Peckham
Tír Dhá Ghlas Dover (NEW)
Tonbridge Tudeley
Tunbridge Wells Tunbridge Wells
Wantsum Hersden
Westerham Crockham Hill
Whitstable Grafty Green

7-11 Mon; 12-3, 6-11; 12-4 Sun ☎ (01227) 720676
🌐 thehaywainbramling.co.uk

Fuller's London Pride; Wells Bombardier; guest beers H

The welcoming main bar features hanging hop bines and assorted curios, while the cosy snug is mainly used for diners and meetings. Traditional games include darts and bat and trap. There is a Monday quiz night and a Wednesday crib night. One of the two guest beers is from a local brewery, and two annual beer festivals are hosted in marquees in the attractive garden. Excellent home-cooked food, using local produce, is served (no food Mon). In 2010 the pub was Taste of Kent Pub of the Year and local CAMRA Pub of the Year.
🏚️🏵️◑🔁🚃(13,14)♣P'—

Brenchley

Halfway House ❦ 🄻 ✅

Horsmonden Road, TN12 7AX (½ mile SE of village) TQ682413
12-11.30 ☎ (01892) 722526

Goacher's Fine Light Ale; Rother Valley Smild; guest beers G

Superb, atmospheric former coaching inn, where up to 10 beers, always including a mild, are served direct from the cask, in addition to real Kentish Chiddingstone cider. It is popular for food, especially weekends (no food Sun eve). The rambling wooden-floored rooms contain an abundance of old beams, agricultural tools and fascinating bric-a-brac. May and August bank holiday beer festivals with up to 50 ales are held in the extensive gardens. There are three charming B&B rooms. Conveniently, the bus from Tunbridge Wells will deliver you to the pub door.
🏚️Q🐕🏵️🛏️◑🔁🚃(297)♣◐P'—

Broadstairs

Brown Jug 🄻

204 Ramsgate Road, CT10 2EW
1-3, 6-11; 12.30-11.30 Sat; 12-11 Sun ☎ (01843) 862788

Ramsgate Gadds' No. 7; guest beers H

Tucked away in the Dumpton area, with a tiny public bar and a lounge that boasts a well-lit hearth, the Brown Jug is unique and has character in spades. It might have stepped straight from the '60s for so little has changed. Myriad jugs line the walls along with local pictures and other trinkets. Board games are littered among the tables and pétanque is played in the extensive garden, where you will also find the pub's outside toilets. On the Thanet Loop bus route.
🏚️Q🏵️🔁≠(Dumpton Park)🚃♣P'—

Brompton

King George V ✅

1 Prospect Row, ME7 5AL TQ761687
11.45-11; 12-10.30 Sun ☎ (01634) 842418
🌐 kgvpub.com

Adnams Southwold Bitter; guest beers H

Built in 1690 and known locally as the KG Five, patrons can choose from a wide range of guest beers including a dark mild and bottled Belgian beers, as well as malt whiskies, while admiring the naval and military memorabilia in all of the three inter-connecting rooms. Situated on

the Saxon Shore Way footpath and renowned for good food, the pub is near Fort Amherst, Chatham Historic Dockyard and the Royal Engineers Museum. Q🏵️🛏️◑🔁🚃(101,182)♣◐'—

Canterbury

Bottle Shop

The Goods Shed, Station Road West, CT2 8AN (adjacent to Canterbury West station)
closed Mon; 12-10.30 (4 Sun) ☎ (07515) 398685
🌐 bottle-shop.co.uk

Beer range varies G

The Bottle Shop is one of the market stands in the Goods Shed, a permanent farmers' market and food hall that has won acclaim in the national press. Customers can buy beers to take home throughout the day, or to enjoy on the premises in the historic surroundings of the Goods Shed. Over 250 beers, many unavailable anywhere else in the UK, are offered including seasonal British bottled real ales and ciders, international bottled beers, exclusive small batches and mini casks. See the website for details of special events and the monthly beer club. Q🏵️🖐≠(West)🚃(4,6)P'—

Dolphin ❦ 🄻

17 St Radigunds, CT1 2AA (off Northgate)
12-12.30am ☎ (01227) 455963
🌐 thedolphincanterbury.co.uk

Sharp's Doom Bar; Taylor Landlord; guest beers H

Friendly local decorated with 1950s-1970s memorabilia and free of TV screens. The Dolphin serves good pub food in generous portions daily, with roasts on Sunday. There is a comprehensive collection of board games, and free internet access. A pianist plays every Sunday from 8pm, and the infamous Dolphin Goat quiz rears its head on the first Monday of the month. The attractive enclosed veranda is popular with diners, and there is a large garden. Westons cider is served, and the guest beers are from Kent microbreweries. Next to St Radigunds car park. 🏚️🏵️◑≠(West)◐'—

Eight Bells

34 London Road, CT2 8LN
12-11 (midnight Thu-Sat); 12-10.30 Sun
☎ (01227) 454794

Wells Bombardier; Young's Bitter H

Small, traditional local dating from 1708 and rebuilt in 1902. It has original embossed windows and is decorated with memorabilia. There is live music fortnightly on Friday, and a monthly quiz, usually on the last Wednesday. Five darts teams play every week and their trophies are on display. Roast lunches are served on Sunday, and a simple menu at other times. There is an attractive, small walled garden. 🏵️◑≠(West)🚃(3,22)♣'—

Foundry Brew Pub 🄻

White Horse Lane, CT1 2RU (just off High Street)
12-midnight (3am Fri & Sat; 11 Sun) ☎ (01227) 455899
🌐 thefoundrycanterbury.co.uk

Canterbury Brewers Biggleston's Brown Ale, Foundryman's Gold, Helles, Torpedo, seasonal beers; guest beers H

A 19th-century building, the home of Canterbury Brewers, that was part of Drury and Biggleston's Foundry and is on two floors. There are usually seven ales, including one Kent guest beer, plus a local cider. The brewery's own bottled real ale can be bought to take away. Good-value pub food is available 12-6pm. A barbecue is held every Friday night on the small patio, and a DJ plays upstairs on Friday and Saturday nights. CAMRA members receive a 10 per cent discount on food and beer (also at the nearby sister pubs, the City Arms and Beercart Arms). ✿◖&⇌(East/West)▯●⌐

King's Head Ⓛ

204 Wincheap, CT1 3RY (on A28 S of city centre)
✪ 12-2.30, 4.45-midnight; 12-midnight Fri & Sat; 12-11.30 Sun ☎ (01227) 462885
Greene King IPA; Harveys Sussex Best Bitter; guest beers Ⓗ
Traditional and friendly Grade II-listed, 15th-century local, 15 minutes' walk from the city centre. Exposed beams, hanging hops and bric-a-brac add to its charm. Bar billiards and darts are played, while bat and trap league matches are held in the garden in summer. There is a monthly Sunday quiz from September to April, and a curry night every Thursday. One of the two guest beers is usually from a local microbrewery. Lunchtime food is Saturday and Sunday only, but evening food is every day. Three-star B&B is available, with parking for residents only. ✿⇐◖&▯⇌(East)▯(28,652)♣⌐

New Inn

19 Havelock Street, CT1 1NP (off ring road near St Augustine's Abbey)
✪ 12-3, 6-11 (11.30 Thu); 12-3, 5-midnight Fri & Sat; 12-3, 6-midnight Sun ☎ (01227) 464584
Greene King IPA; Harveys Sussex Best Bitter; guest beers Ⓗ
Victorian back-street terraced house close to St Augustine's Abbey, the cathedral and bus station. The main bar has red walls, a wooden floor and a jukebox. At the back is a long conservatory with two cosy alcoves, one known as the library. Biddenden cider is served and there are usually three guest beers. There are two beer festivals a year, on the Whitsun and August bank holiday weekends, held in the attractive garden as well as in the bar. Disabled access is through the garden and conservatory via Old Ruttington Lane. No food Mondays. ✿✪◖&▯♣●⌐

Unicorn Inn Ⓛ ✔

61 St Dunstan's Street, CT2 8BS
✪ 11.30-11 (midnight Fri & Sat) ☎ (01227) 463187
⊕ unicorninn.com
Sharp's Doom Bar; Shepherd Neame Master Brew; guest beers Ⓗ
Comfortable 1604 pub standing near the historic Westgate and boasting an attractive suntrap garden. Bar billiards is played, and a quiz, set by regular customers, is held weekly on Sunday evening. One of the guest beers is usually from a Kent microbrewery, and regular beer updates are posted on Twitter. The food ranges from pub favourites to imaginative specials, and is excellent value, with a 'two meals for £10' offer (no food Sun). Sporting events (not Sky) are televised unobtrusively. ✿✪◖⇌(West)▯(3,4,6)♣⌐

Capel

Dovecote Inn

Alders Road, TN12 6SU (½ mile W of A228 towards Tudeley) TQ643441
✪ 5.30-9.30 Mon; 12-3, 5.30-11; 12-9.30 Sun
☎ (01892) 835966
Gale's HSB; Harveys Sussex Best Bitter; guest beers Ⓖ

Tucked away in a hamlet surrounded by fruit and hop fields, the Dovecote is sought out by drivers, cyclists and walkers alike. Most enter from the rear door, adjacent to the car park and covered deck. The interior reveals exposed brickwork, beams decorated with hop garlands and real fires. Up to six ales, sometimes from the local Tonbridge microbrewery, are served by gravity. Westons real cider is also stocked. There is an interesting and popular menu (try the rosti). No food Monday or Sunday evenings. The large garden has a children's play area. ⋈Q✿◖♣●P⌐

Charing

Bowl Inn

Egg Hill Road, TN27 0HG TQ950514
✪ 4 (12 summer)-11.30; 12-midnight Fri & Sat; 12-11 Sun ☎ (01233) 712256 ⊕ bowl-inn.co.uk
Fuller's London Pride; guest beers Ⓗ
Remote 16th-century free house located high above Charing, on top of the North Downs, in an area of outstanding natural beauty, signed from the A20 and A251. It has been looked after by the present licensees since 1992. Guest beers are usually from regional brewers. A beer festival is held annually in mid July. The large garden is popular in summer and camping is available (booking essential). Hearty snacks are served, sandwiches are available all day and there are regular themed food evenings. Accommodation is in five en-suite bedrooms. ⋈✿⇐Å♣P

Chiddingstone

Castle Inn Ⓛ

TN8 7AH
✪ 10-11; 12-10.30 Sun ⊕ castleinn-kent.co.uk
Harveys Sussex Best Bitter; Larkins Traditional Ale, seasonal beer; guest beer Ⓗ
Long, rambling inn that dates from 1420 and sits in the middle of a picture-postcard village bequeathed to the National Trust. The public bar heaves with walkers and dogs at weekends, though at other times it is the ideal place for a quiet pint. Bar food is sold, but there is also a separate restaurant, and a function room for hire. The local Larkins Brewery beers are so popular they are sold from 18-gallon barrels. The dark winter warmer, Larkins Porter, is often mixed with the Traditional Ale to produce the less potent but tasty half-and-half. ⋈Q✿◖⇐♣

Chiddingstone Hoath

Rock Ⓛ

Hoath Corner, TN8 7BS TQ497431
✪ 12-11 (10.30 Sun) ☎ (01892) 870296
Larkins Traditional Ale, seasonal beers; guest beer Ⓗ
Remote rural inn west of Penshurst, named after characteristic outcrops nearby, where locals, visitors and dogs rub shoulders. This place is unspoilt and welcoming, with a well-worn brick floor and well-used woodburner in the main room and a small lounge to the right of the bar. A big draw is the tasty Larkins' beer from up the road, including summer and winter seasonals. Another draw for adults and children alike is the ring the bull bar game. The small front patio area is used to catch a few rays in sunny weather. ⋈Q✿◖♣P

Chipstead

Bricklayers Arms ✪
39 Chevening Road, TN13 2RZ
✪ 11.30-3.30, 5.30-11; 11.30-11 Fri-Sun ☎ (01732) 743424
⊕ the-bricklayers-arms.co.uk
Harveys Sussex Best Bitter Ⓖ, seasonal beer Ⓗ
Welcoming whitewashed village inn in an old row of cottages with a view across the sailing lake, rescued by Harveys Brewery after a fire under previous ownership. The pub is still popular for food, including curry and steak nights (not Sun eve). The cosy atmosphere is aided by a large open fire in the stone-flagged bar area, which is dominated by a row of beer casks nestling behind the bar. Other areas include an Indian restaurant and wooden-floored side rooms, with leather sofas and plenty of tables. Quiz night is Tuesday, and there is monthly live music. ⚏❀◑⅃&🚲(401)♣╚

Cobham

Darnley Arms
40 The Street, DA12 3BZ
✪ 12-3, 5-11; 12-10.30 Sun ☎ (01474) 814218
⊕ thedarnleyarms.co.uk
Dark Star Hophead; Greene King IPA; guest beers Ⓗ
Friendly local in the centre of a pleasant village. The decor features a wide range of local memorabilia including the coat of arms of the Darnley family, who lived at nearby Cobham Hall, and interesting artefacts including a time recording clock and apprentice indenture papers. A diverse menu of traditional English cooking is served, as well as a Thai menu on Wednesday evenings, and fish specialities (no food Sun eves).
⚏Q❀◐◑⅃&▲🚲(416)P

Coldred

Carpenter's Arms
The Green, CT15 5AJ
✪ 6 (7 Sun)-11 ☎ (01304) 830190
Beer range varies Ⓗ/Ⓖ
Overlooking the village green, this 18th-century two-roomed pub is one of CAMRA's Real Heritage Pubs. Its simple furniture and decor have remained largely unchanged for 50 years. It is a community pub for conversation, good fellowship and a place for local societies to meet. Two real ales are available from microbreweries including Hopdaemon and Ramsgate. Entertainment varies from darts, dominoes and skittles to auctions/competitions of local produce and an annual maggot race. Dog-friendly. May open in the afternoon for small groups. ⚏Q❀⊟♣P

Conyer

Ship Inn
The Quay, ME9 9HR TQ962648
✪ 12-3, 6-11 (midnight Fri); 11-11.30 Sat; 11-9.30 Sun
☎ (01795) 520881 ⊕ shipinnconyer.co.uk
Adnams Southwold Bitter; Shepherd Neame Master Brew; guest beers Ⓗ
Secluded pub, once the haunt of smugglers, on the quayside at Conyer Creek. Neglected by a pub company and sold on, the new owner has completely renovated and refurbished to a high standard. It is popular with sailors, walkers, cyclists and birdwatchers as well as locals. The food sets high standards (they make their own bread and sausages). Folk singing takes place on the first and third Tuesday of the month. Guest beers are sometimes from local micros such as Old Dairy. ⚏Q❀◑🚲(344,345,346)

Cooling

Horseshoe & Castle Ⓛ
Main Road, ME3 8DJ TQ759761
✪ 11.30 (5.45 Mon)-11 (midnight Fri & Sat); 12-11.30 Sun
☎ (01634) 221691 ⊕ horseshoeandcastle.co.uk
Shepherd Neame Master Brew; guest beer Ⓗ
Friendly local in the small and quiet village of Cooling, with a nearby RSPB reserve for birdwatchers. A ruined castle can be found nearby and the local graveyard was used in the film version of Great Expectations, where young Pip met the convict Magwitch. Snacks and bar food are available as well as an à la carte menu, served in the separate dining room (no food Mon). Draught Addlestones cider is stocked. Accommodation is of high quality. ⚏Q❀◐◑⅃&♣P╚

Crockham Hill

Royal Oak Ⓛ
Main Road, TN8 6RD (on B2026 opp Four Elms road jct)
✪ 12-3, 6-11 (midnight Fri); 12-9 Sun ☎ (01732) 866335
Westerham Finchcocks Original, British Bulldog, seasonal beers Ⓗ
Popular inn taken over a couple of years back by the local Westerham Brewery, restoring brewing links with the nearby town. Unsurprisingly, it serves a range of Westerham ales in top form. The refurbishment of the interior has given the place a more modern yet cosy feel, enhanced by subtle lighting and two real fires. Once separated, the public and lounge bars now merge into one long room (dogs welcome in the public area). Local societies including a ukulele club meet here. Food is available daily except Sunday and Monday evenings. ⚏Q❀◑⊟&🚲♣P╚

Dartford

Ivy Leaf Ⓛ ✪
72 Darenth Road, DA1 1LS
✪ 11-11; 12-10.30 Sun ☎ (01322) 220993
Sharp's Doom Bar; Wells Bombardier; guest beers Ⓗ
A medium-sized, single-bar pub situated midway between East Hill and Princes Road. Four guest ales are served, with one pump devoted to local microbrewery beers. Home-prepared snacks and sandwiches are sold at lunchtimes at reasonable prices. Tea and coffee are also available. It is the closest real ale outlet to Dartford FC ground, which is easily walkable from the pub.
⚏Q❀➔🚲(B)♣P╚

Malt Shovel
3 Darenth Road, DA1 1LP
✪ 12 (2 Mon)-11 ☎ (01322) 224381
St Austell Tribute; Young's Bitter; guest beers Ⓗ
Attractive two-bar pub just outside the town centre. The low-ceilinged tap room, featuring an original Dartford Brewery mirror, dates from 1673 and still exudes rural charm. The main bar retains

the large wooden malt shovel on display. The spacious modern conservatory leads to the garden that overlooks the parish church. Food is served lunchtimes and evenings. ♨Q🕭🍴❶🍺♿�MꝒ♬

Paper Moon L ✓
55 High Street, DA1 1DS
🕭 9-11 (midnight Sat) ☎ (01322) 281127
Greene King Abbot; Ruddles Best Bitter; Shepherd Neame Spitfire; guest beers ⊞
Town-centre corner pub, part of the Wetherspoon chain. Formerly Lloyds Bank, the name reflects the town's historic connection with the papermaking industry and is decorated with memorabilia recalling Dartford's past. The bar offers eight beers – three regular and five guests – plus a draught cider. This venue conducts regular brewery promotions and charity events. A community pub, it features regular darts competitions.
❶♿🚆🚍♣♨

Wat Tyler
80 High Street, DA1 1DE (next to parish church)
🕭 9-11 (midnight Fri & Sat); 10.30-10.30 Sun
☎ (01322) 272546
Courage Best Bitter; John Smith's Bitter; guest beers ⊞
Situated in the town centre and a five-minute walk from the train station, this early 15th-century pub is nevertheless a quiet local with a regular clientele. This is reflected in the range of three guest beers, which leans heavily towards milds, stouts and porters. It has a narrow bar with raised seating at the rear. 🍴🚆🚍

Deal

Dunkerley's
19 Beach Street, CT14 7AH
🕭 11-11 ☎ (01304) 375016 🌐 dunkerleys.co.uk
St Austell Tribute ⊞
Cheery seafront gastronomic venue, formerly the Pier Hotel, enjoying commanding views of Deal pier and seafront and the English Channel. The hotel has a cosy piano bar where you can enjoy your pint in a relaxing atmosphere. Unobtrusive live music plays occasionally. During the summer, while away the hours sitting on the terrace enjoying the sea views and watching life go by. A bar and restaurant menu is available that focuses on local produce and seafood. Q🕭🍴❶♿🚆🚍♬

Just Reproach
14 King Street, CT14 6HX
🕭 12-2, 5-9; 5-11 Fri & Sat; 12-2 Sun ☎ (07432) 413226
🌐 thejustreproach.co.uk
Beer range varies ⊞
This family-run, town centre micro-pub opened in December 2012. It has a welcoming, convivial atmosphere conducive to conversation. Three excellent real ales are on offer, usually from Kent, as is the real cider, along with wines and soft drinks. With its high benches and table service, the pub takes everything back to the absolute fundamentals: no keg, no spirits, no fruit machines, no music, and a fine is levied for using a mobile phone. Dogs and children welcome. Q🚆🚍♣

Prince Albert
187-189 Middle Street, CT14 6LW
🕭 6 (12 Sun)-11 ☎ (01304) 375425
Beer range varies ⊞

Situated just off the seafront, the unassuming Victorian exterior conceals a cheerful and welcoming local behind the unique curved doors. The cosy bar serves a varied range of three real ales from smaller, often local, breweries. Evening meals are available Wednesday to Saturday and roast lunches on Sunday. The small, sheltered courtyard garden is ideal in summer. This pub is a 10-minute walk north of the town centre and railway station. ♨Q🕭🍴❶🚆🚍(15A)♬

Ship
141 Middle Street, CT14 6JZ
🕭 11 (12 Sun)-11 ☎ (01304) 372222
Caledonian Deuchars IPA; Dark Star Hophead; Fuller's London Pride; Ramsgate Gadds' No. 7, Gadds' Seasider; guest beers ⊞
Unspoilt traditional pub in Deal's historic conservation area, just off the seafront. Dark wooden floors and subdued lighting give this pub a warm and comfortable atmosphere, complemented by a nautical theme. Five handpumps dispense a good range of beers including some from Ramsgate and Dark Star. The pub has a small cosy rear bar overlooking a large patio garden with a covered smoking area, accessed by a staircase. It is 10 minutes' walk from the town centre. ♨🕭🚆🚍(15A)♬

Dover

Eight Bells ✓
19 Cannon Street, CT16 1BZ
🕭 8-11 (midnight Fri & Sat) ☎ (01304) 205030
Greene King Abbot; Ruddles Best Bitter; Shepherd Neame Spitfire; guest beers ⊞
Popular Wetherspoon pub in the town's shopping precinct opposite the historic St Mary's Church. Inside, it has one large room with a long bar, sofas and a raised restaurant area. Twelve handpumps dispense a range of regular and guest ales, usually with at least one beer from a Kent microbrewery. There are real ale offers on Wednesdays and Sundays. Close to bus and railway stations.
❶♿🚆(Priory)🚍♣♬

Louis Armstrong
58 Maison Dieu Road, CT16 1RA
🕭 2 (7 Sun)-11 ☎ (01304) 204759
Hopdaemon Skrimshander; guest beers ⊞
Down-to-earth pub and renowned local music venue that has featured live music for 40 years, under the same landlady. The large L-shaped bar and stage are surrounded by music posters, a large mirror and long bench seating. Up to four real ales are on offer, principally from Kent microbreweries, with the occasional real cider. There is a beer garden at the rear. Two beer festivals are held each year and good-value food is served on Wednesday lunchtimes. Easily accessible by bus, with a public car park opposite. 🕭🚍♣♬

Red Lion
54 Charlton Green, CT16 2PS
🕭 11-11 ☎ (01304) 202899
Fuller's London Pride; Wells Bombardier ⊞
Friendly, welcoming two-bar pub with a traditional local feel to it. It has a good range of social activities, with darts, football and skittles teams. A big-screen TV shows sports and ESPN and there is also occasional live entertainment. The good-sized enclosed rear garden has a skittle alley and a

discrete smoking area. The pub is tucked just off Dover's one-way system and is a short bus ride from the town centre. ✿◗⊞🖾♣⌐

White Horse
St James Street, CT16 1QF
✪ 12-11 (10.30 Sun) ☎ (01304) 242974
Harveys Sussex Best Bitter; Loddon Ferryman's Gold; guest beers Ⓗ
The inn's history can be traced back to 1760, making this probably the oldest pub in Dover. The furniture is simple but comfortable and the walls are covered with the signatures of cross-Channel swimmers. Up to four real ales are served, with local microbreweries such as Ramsgate and Old Dairy regularly represented. Real cider is available in summer. The pub is convenient for cross-Channel visitors as there is public car parking nearby. A short walk from the bus station. ⊭➲✿⊞♣

East Brabourne

Five Bells Inn Ⓛ
The Street, TN25 5LP (in the lanes from A20 via Smeeth and Brabourne Lees or via Stowting from B2068)
✪ 11.30-11.30 ☎ (01303) 813334
⊕ fivebellsinnbrabourne.com
Beer range varies Ⓗ
Picturesque 16th-century inn extensively and thoughtfully refurbished, which now offers a warm and welcoming feel whether you wish to dine or indulge in a Kentish ale or cider. Nestling in the Kent countryside, it is well worth making the effort to visit, whether by car or on foot via the North Downs Way. A small shop selling local produce, as used in the restaurant, is at the side of the bar. ⊭Q➲✿⊨◗⛿⊞(10)♣P⌐

East Malling

Rising Sun Ⓛ
125 Mill Street, ME19 6BX
✪ 12-11 (10.30 Sun) ☎ (01732) 843284
Goacher's Fine Light; Theakston Best Bitter; guest beer Ⓗ
Community free house run by the same family for over 20 years. Its low prices and good quality are greatly appreciated. Guest beers may be local or national. Food is served weekday lunchtimes. There is a large patio garden to the rear for summer drinking. Sport is popular here and all major football matches and other sports events are shown on large TVs. The pub is home to several teams including darts, football and cricket. A lunchtime meat raffle is held on Sundays. ✿◗≈⊞(58)♣

Eastry

Five Bells ✔
The Cross, CT13 0HX
✪ 11-11.30 (1am Fri & Sat) ☎ (01304) 611188
⊕ thefivebellseastry.com
Greene King IPA; guest beer Ⓗ
Traditional two-bar community pub in the heart of the village. There is a comfortable lounge bar, and the public bar has pool, darts and TV. The old fire station, complete with historic memorabilia, is available as a function room. The events calendar includes a beer festival in April, live music, quiz

nights and poker evenings. Great home-made food, including a good value two-course table d'hote menu, is available all day. The suntrap patio has a children's play area and pétanque pitch. ✿⊭◗⊨⛿⊞(14,87,88)♣P⌐

Edenbridge

Old Eden Ⓛ
121 High Street, TN8 5AX
✪ 12-11 (midnight Fri & Sat); 11-11 Sun ☎ (01732) 862398
Taylor Landlord; Westerham 1965; guest beers Ⓗ
Originally a late 15th-century Kentish hall house, this inn is close to meadows by the River Eden. The impressive interior retains plenty of historic features, with heavy beams, cosy quiet corners and three open fires. Local Westerham beers are always among the five handpumps, including the house beer, along with two guests, often from Kent or Sussex. Westons Old Rosie real cider is often stocked. Bar food is supplemented by a full menu in the upstairs restaurant (no food Mon). It has a peaceful rear garden and boules is played in the car park. ⊭✿◗⛿⇌(Town)⊞(231,233,236)♣⊛P⌐

Elham

King's Arms Ⓛ
The Square, CT4 6TJ (in village square) TR176438
✪ 11-11.30; 12-10.30 Sun ☎ (01303) 840242
Harveys Sussex Best Bitter; Hopdaemon Golden Braid; Skrimshander IPA Ⓗ
Locals and visitors alike will find a friendly atmosphere here. In a building that originated in the early 17th century, the saloon bar/restaurant was originally used for brewing, and the public bar acts as the focal point for village activities. The pub is popular with walkers and has a spacious garden. Discounted meals are available Monday to Friday lunchtimes for senior citizens. Parking is in the square between the pub and a fine medieval church. ⊭➲✿◗⊨⊞(17)♣

Fairseat

Vigo Ⓛ
Gravesend Road, TN15 7JL (on A227)
✪ 6-11 (12.30am Fri); 12-12.30am Sat; 12-5, 7-11 Sun
☎ (01732) 822465 ⊕ vigoinn.co.uk
Beer range varies Ⓗ
A traditional ale drinkers' haven, this was a former drovers' inn on the north downs between Gravesend and Wrotham. It retains a traditional quiet bar with a large open fireplace at one end. Daddlums, a rare form of Kentish table skittles, is still played here. Beers from Goacher's and Old Dairy are regularly available, with occasional guests. Acoustic music sessions are held nightly Wednesday to Saturday evenings and Sunday lunchtime, with occasional poetry recitals on Sundays. ⊭Q⛿⊞(308)♣P

Farningham

Chequers
87 High Street, DA4 0DT (250yds from A20 jct 3 M25)
✪ 12-11 (10.30 Sun) ☎ (01322) 865222

Fuller's London Pride, ESB; Harveys Sussex Best Bitter; Taylor Landlord; guest beers Ⓗ
Popular, cosy, one-bar corner local in an attractive riverside village. The unusual decor includes murals depicting local scenes, two large decorative candelabra and a life-size model waiter. Ten handpumps dispense four regular beers and up to six guests. Food is served Monday to Saturday lunchtimes. Visitors can use community parking in the Lion Hotel car park. ◑🚋(412,427)

Faversham

Anchor
52 Abbey Street, ME13 7BP
✪ 12-11 (midnight Fri & Sat; 10 Sun) ☎ (01795) 536471
⊕ theanchorinnfaversham.com
Shepherd Neame Master Brew, Kent's Best, Spitfire, Late Red, Bishops Finger, seasonal beers Ⓗ
Traditional oak-beamed building over 300 years old and close to Faversham Creek quayside and boat moorings. The walls are adorned with a wealth of nautical memorabilia and there are many original features and an open fireplace. The pub proudly boasts a large range of Shepherd Neame ales, and has an impressive bar menu, as well as two restaurant areas and a large garden. Popular with locals, walkers and tourists. Live music plays most Sunday evenings. ₳Q◑Φ⊟⇌🚋'—

Bear Inn
3 Market Place, ME13 7AG
✪ 10.30-11; 12-10.30 Sun ☎ (01795) 532668
Shepherd Neame Master Brew, seasonal beers Ⓗ
Opposite the historic Guildhall in Market Place, this recently renovated 500-year-old building has three distinct wood-panelled bar areas off a long side corridor, and one room has an open fire. The pub has an unusual clock – instead of numbers it uses the pub's name spelled out around the dial. The landlord offers seasonal beers from Shepherd Neame's main and microbrewery. Guest beers from other breweries are featured when available. Home-cooked lunches are served every day. Regular quiz nights. ₳Q◑Φ⊟⇌🚋'—

Elephant ♈ Ⓛ ✪
31 The Mall, ME13 8JN
✪ closed Mon; 3 (12 Sat)-11; 12-7 Sun ☎ (01795) 590157
Beer range varies Ⓗ
Swale CAMRA Pub of the Year for the sixth consecutive year. This is a traditional ale house boasting five real ales, including a mild and now a real cider. The beers are mainly sourced from the south-east, including many from Kent microbreweries. An open log fire blazes in winter, and there is a walled garden for the summer. Live music from local bands/artists regularly features. Beer festivals are held throughout the year. ₳❀⇌🚋♣♦'—

Old Wine Vaults Ⓛ ✪
75 Preston Street, ME13 8PA
✪ 11-11 (10.30 Sun) ☎ (01795) 591817
⊕ theoldwinevaults.com
Beer range varies Ⓗ
A popular local dating back to the 17th century. The small street frontage opens to a deceptively large interior with ample seating. The traditional bar is set in the middle, with a mix of tables and chairs and many cosy corners. One ale from Hopdaemon is always available and there are three rotating

guest ales plus two ciders. There is an extensive menu and a pleasant beer garden. Local CAMRA Cider Pub of the Year in 2011. ☎❀◑⇌🚋♦'—

Phoenix Tavern ✪
98-99 Abbey Street, ME13 7BH
✪ 12-11 ☎ (01795) 591462
⊕ thephoenixtavernfaversham.co.uk
Harveys Sussex Best Bitter; guest beers Ⓗ
A 14th-century traditional English public house set in the heart of Faversham on one of England's longest medieval streets. It boasts two open fires and relaxing sofas. Real food is freshly prepared, such as local sausage and mash. A variety of real ales, often featuring guests from Otter, Timothy Taylor, Ringwood and occasionally Kent micros, is served; their real ale advisory board helps with the selection. It has an impressive and varied events calendar, including street plays, poetry, quizzes, and live jazz on Sunday afternoons. Outside is a secluded walled garden. ₳Q❀◑⇌🚋♣P'—

Shipwright's Arms Ⓛ
Ham Road, Hollowshore, ME13 7TU (1½ miles N of Faversham) TR017636
✪ closed Mon eve winter; 11-3, 6-10; 12-4, 6-11 Sat & summer; 12-4, 6-10.30 Sun ☎ (01795) 590088
⊕ theshipwrightsarmspub.co.uk
Goacher's Real Mild Ale, Shipwrecked; Whitstable EIPA; guest beer Ⓖ
Family-run traditional free house with beer straight from the cask; an extra beer in summer is normally Hopdaemon. This is a historic wood-clad pub behind the sea wall at the confluence of Faversham and Oare creeks, with many nooks and crannies, and decorated to reflect its maritime history. It is popular with walkers off the Saxon Shore Way and boat owners from the adjacent moorings, and is dog-friendly. Log fires blaze in winter and its large garden is popular. In deepest winter telephone to confirm opening. No food Sunday or Monday evenings. ₳Q❀◑P'—

Fawkham Green

Rising Sun Ⓛ
DA3 8NL (jct of Valley Rd and Brands Hatch Rd)
✪ 12-11 (10.30 Sun) ☎ (01474) 872291
⊕ risingsun-fawkham.co.uk
Courage Best Bitter, Directors; Fuller's London Pride; Harveys Sussex Best Bitter; guest beers Ⓗ
A 16th-century inn in a rural setting close to Brands Hatch motor racing circuit on the North Downs. The pub and associated restaurant is famed for its food, but also offers up to six draught ales at any one time – four regulars and two changing local beers. Quiz night is the first Monday of the month. The inn offers B&B accommodation including twin and four-poster beds. ₳Q☎❀🛏◑⊟♿P'—

Finglesham

Crown Inn
The Street, CT14 0NA
✪ 12-close ☎ (01304) 612555
⊕ thecrownatfinglesham.co.uk
Canterbury Wife of Bath; guest beers Ⓗ
A traditional village pub with wooden floors, real fires, a warm welcome and a friendly atmosphere. Three to four real ales, many from local microbreweries, and Biddenden cider on

handpump, are served. Good home-made food is available, served all day Friday to Sunday. Entertainment includes occasional quiz nights and live music. Bat and trap is played in summer. Families are welcome and there is a large children's play area in the garden. Dogs are permitted in the bar. It is a half mile from bus services. ᛗ☆✪❶Å⧐(13,14)♣♠P⌐

Folkestone

British Lion ✪

10 The Bayle, CT20 1SQ (close to church off pedestrian part of Sandgate Road)
✪ 11-4, 7-11; 12-4, 7-10.30 Sun ☎ (01303) 251478
Greene King Abbot; Young's Bitter; guest beers Ⓗ
A former Hanbury, Mackeson and Whitbread house dating from 1460 and now the oldest pub in Folkestone, visited by Charles Dickens when writing Little Dorrit. It has a relaxed and comfortable atmosphere in its drinking and dining areas. Two guest ales are normally stocked from the Punch Taverns Finest Cask selection, together with two real ciders. Good pub food, often local fish, is served in generous portions lunchtimes and evenings (no food Tue eve). ᛗQ⊱✿✪❶♣♠⌐

Chambers Ⓛ

Radnor Chambers, Cheriton Place, CT20 2BB
✪ 12-11 (1am Fri & Sat); closed Sun ☎ (01303) 223333
⏚ pubfolkestone.co.uk
Adnams Lighthouse; Gadds' Dogbolter; Hopdaemon Skrimshander IPA; Whitstable Kentish Reserve; guest beer Ⓗ
In this spacious cellar bar beneath a licensed coffee shop, guest beers, often from local breweries, and two real ciders are usually available. A beer festival is held over the Easter weekend. Food including Mexican and European dishes, and daily specials, is served (not Mon and Fri eves and Sun). Live music plays on Thursday, disco on Friday, and a quiz is held on the first Sunday of the month. Perry from local sources is served when available. No under-18s unless dining. ❶⇌(Central)⧐♣♠⌐

Guildhall

42 The Bayle, CT20 1SQ
✪ 12-11 (midnight Fri & Sat; 10.30 Sun) ☎ (01303) 251393
Greene King IPA; guest beers Ⓗ
A welcoming, traditional single-bar pub, close to the town centre. Large windows give the interior a light, airy feel. This is an ideal place to take a break from the hustle and bustle of the town centre and enjoy good ale. Three guest ales are normally stocked from the Punch Taverns Finest Cask selection. A real cider may be on offer in the summer. Good-value food is served at lunchtimes and occasionally evenings if pre-booked. ✿❶⧐♣♠P⌐

Pullman

7-9 Church Street, CT20 1SE (off Rendezous Street)
✪ 12-10 (11 Fri & Sat; 6 Sun) ☎ (01303) 240538
Beer range varies Ⓗ
A quiet haven next to the town-centre shopping area, with three distinct bar areas plus a suntrap garden. The inside is wood panelled, with prints of old Folkestone. Three or more beers from regional and local breweries, often including Hepworth's Pullman at 4.2% ABV, are usually available. Good-value food is served throughout the week until 8pm. ᛗQ⊱✿✪❶⧐♠⌐

Fordwich

Fordwich Arms Ⓛ

King Street, CT2 0DB
✪ 11-midnight (1am Fri & Sat); 12-11 Sun
☎ (01227) 710444 ⏚ fordwicharms.co.uk
Flowers Original; Sharp's Doom Bar; Shepherd Neame Master Brew; Wadworth 6X Ⓗ
Classic 1930s building opposite the ancient and tiny town hall in England's smallest town, by the River Stour. The large bar has a lovely fireplace and there is a separate dining room with wood panelling. Excellent meals are served in both areas (no food Sun eve). The pub hosts regular themed evenings including a popular pudding night on the second Wednesday of the month. Booking is essential. There is a folk club every second and fourth Sunday night and live jazz in the garden on summer Sunday afternoons once a month.
ᛗQ✿✪❶♿⇌(Sturry)⧐(4,6,7)P⌐

Frittenden

Bell & Jorrocks ✪

Biddenden Road, TN17 2EJ TQ815412
✪ 12 (11 Sat)-11; 12-10 Sun ☎ (01580) 852415
⏚ thebellandjorrocks.co.uk
Harveys Sussex Best Bitter; Woodforde's Wherry; guest beers Ⓗ
This village-centre pub, formerly known as the Bell, gained its present name when the other pub in the village, the John Jorrocks, closed some 40 years ago. A conversation piece par-excellence hangs over the fire – a propeller from a Heinkel 111 that was shot down locally during World War II. Although not on a main coaching route, there is an old stable block attached where a beer festival is held in mid April each year. No food Mondays.
ᛗ✿❶♿Å♣♠⌐

Gillingham

Frog & Toad ✪

38 Burnt Oak Terrace, ME7 1DR TQ774688
✪ 12-11 (10.30 Sun) ☎ (01634) 852231
⏚ thefrogandtoad.com
Fuller's London Pride; guest beers Ⓗ
Traditional back-street pub, 10 minutes' walk from Gillingham Station, three times past winner of local CAMRA Pub of the Year. London Pride, two rotating guest ales and Magic Bus cider are on handpump. It has a large patio garden area at the rear with tables and bench seating, and an outside bar for the popular beer festivals held three times a year. Traditional Sunday lunch is served (bookings only). The pub has a large screen for sports events, and hosts various sports teams including a golfing society. Q✿⇌⧐(176)♣♠⌐

Will Adams

73 Saxton Street, ME7 5EG TQ770683
✪ 7-11; 12.30-4 Sat; 12-3, 8-11 Sun ☎ (01634) 575902
⏚ thewilladams.co.uk
Beer range varies Ⓗ
A friendly single-bar local that was local CAMRA Pub of the Year in 2011, with a well-deserved reputation for well-kept beer. Three ales are usually on offer from breweries and micros across the country, plus draught ciders and perry – Old Rosie is the usual regular. The pub is named after a

local navigator adventurer, whose exploits are depicted on a mural. Opening times vary for Gillingham FC home games, when bar food is available. Away fans welcome. ⇌🖳♣👜

Gravesend

Crown & Thistle

44 The Terrace, DA12 2BJ
🌑 12-11 (10.30 Sun) ☎ (01474) 332387
Young's Bitter; guest beers Ⓗ
Small Georgian terraced pub, originally two fishermen's cottages. The name symbolises the union of England and Scotland, ratified on 1 May 1707, and the pub is believed to have opened in 1847. The convivial atmosphere is free from music and gaming machines. Four guest beers are on handpump. Double Vision and Westons cider are also available. Indian and Chinese takeaways can be ordered and eaten in the pub. Former CAMRA National Pub of the Year. Q🕸⇌👜🖳⚍

Jolly Drayman 🏆

1 Love Lane, Wellington Street, DA12 1JA
🌑 12-11.30 (10 Tue; midnight Fri & Sat; 11 Sun)
☎ (01474) 352355 ⊕ jollydrayman.com
Dark Star Hophead; St Austell Tribute; guest beers Ⓗ
Comfortable pub with original low ceilings just outside the town centre. The entrance is via what used to be the back of the pub, which looks out onto the alleyway opposite. It was once part of Walkers Brewery. It hosts men's and women's darts teams, and daddlums (Kentish skittles) is played on alternate Sundays. Four ales are available. Evening barbecues are held on some summer evenings, and beer festivals twice yearly. A bar billiards table has recently been installed. Q🕸🛋◖🍴&⇌🖳(490,499)♣P⚍

Rum Puncheon Ⓛ

87 West Street, DA11 0BL (on one-way system, next to Tilbury Ferry)
🌑 11 (12 Sat)-11; 12-10.30 Sun ☎ (01474) 353434
Beer range varies Ⓗ
Large riverside building between the ferry and town pier. The L-shaped bar has a log fire and chandeliers. Upstairs, a function room opens onto a balcony with river views. A rear terrace also enjoys these views. Eight ales rotate regularly, with beers from Adnams and Kent micros often appearing. There is a quiz night on the last Wednesday of each month. Home-cooked meals are available lunchtimes. Note the Russell's Brewery windows. 🕍🕸◖&⇌🖳(480,499)⚍

Great Mongeham

Leather Bottle

103 Mongeham Road, CT14 9PE
🌑 5 (12 Sat)-11; 12-9 Sun ☎ (01304) 375931
Theakston Lightfoot; guest beers Ⓗ
Street-corner free house on the outskirts of Deal. Recent renovations give the large bar room a relaxed, smart, modern feel. A locals' pub with no frills, but top ales and good company. Large-screen sports TVs and quality ale don't always agree, but they do here. There are darts and pool teams, and occasional live music, karaoke and quiz nights. Euchre night is Friday. Outside, there is a large garden and a small covered patio for smokers. Dog-friendly. 🕸🖳(14,82)♣P⚍

Halstead

Cock Inn ✅

Shoreham Lane, TN14 7DD
🌑 12-midnight (11.30 Sun) ☎ (01959) 533171
⊕ the-cock-inn.co.uk
Fuller's London Pride; Harveys Sussex Best Bitter; Wells Bombardier; guest beer Ⓗ
A multi-room pub sitting in the centre of a pretty village, built as a farmhouse in Elizabeth I's reign but licensed in 1718. Consequently beams abound inside, alongside the collection of water jugs and china cockerels. The licence was recently taken over by a local landlord with a reputation for keeping quality ale and providing good meals (available in the bar and side restaurant area). The busy bar room features a large fire. Charity quiz night is on the fourth Sunday each month, but cribbage boards are used for entertainment in between. 🕍Q🕸◖▶⚍🖳(R5,R10,402)♣P⚍

Hastingleigh

Bowl Inn 🏆 Ⓛ

The Street, TN25 5HU TR095449
🌑 closed Mon; 5 (12 Sat)-11.30; 12-10.30 Sun
☎ (01233) 750354 ⊕ thebowlonline.co.uk
Hopdaemon Incubus; guest beers Ⓗ
Lovingly restored village pub and local CAMRA Pub of the Year for 2012. This listed building retains many period features including a taproom, now used for playing pool, and is free from jukebox and games machines. Quiz night is Tuesday. The lovely garden has a tame European Eagle Owl and a cricket pitch to the rear, where matches are played most Sundays in the summer. A beer festival is held on August bank holiday Monday. Excellent sandwiches and baguettes are available weekends. 🕍Q🐾◖♣👜P⚍

Herne

Butcher's Arms Ⓛ

29A Herne Street, CT6 7HL (opp church)
🌑 closed Mon; 12-1.30, 6-9; 12.30-2.30 Sun
☎ (01227) 371000 ⊕ micropub.co.uk
Dark Star Hophead; Fuller's ESB; guest beers Ⓖ
The smallest pub in Kent, a real ale gem, and the inspiration for other micropubs. Once a butcher's shop, it still has the original chopping tables, with hooks and other implements. There is seating for 12 customers and standing room for about 20 – the compact drinking area ensuring lively banter. A variety of guest beers is offered, and customers can also buy beer to drink at home. The pub has won five CAMRA awards, and the landlord has been voted one of the top 40 CAMRA campaigners. Q🖳(4,6)

Herne Bay

Prince of Wales Ⓛ

173 Mortimer Street, CT6 5DS (at E end of town, between seafront and High St)
🌑 10am (12 Sun)-midnight ☎ (01227) 374205
⊕ princeofwaleshernebay.co.uk
Shepherd Neame Master Brew, Kent's Best, Spitfire, seasonal beers Ⓗ

Splendid refurbished Victorian pub full of memorabilia. The stylish woodwork, tiled fireplaces and etched glass are not overwhelmed by discreet TV screens for sporting events, and it has a unique collection of water jugs. Only a few yards from the seafront, the four bars include a large games room with pool and darts, and a small, beautifully decorated back bar. There is a patio with seating. Beers from Shepherd Neame's microbrewery, and guest ales, are occasionally available. ♨️🍽🏮♿🏠(4,6)♣️⁻

Higham

Stone Horse
Dillywood Lane, ME3 8EN (off B2000 Cliffe Road) TQ732713
😊 12-3, 6-11; 12-11 Fri & Sat; 12-3.30, 7-10.30 Sun
☎ (01634) 722046
Courage Best Bitter; guest beers Ⓗ
Two-bar country pub not far from Strood. It is surrounded by fields and is therefore handy for walkers. Good-value food with specials is served Monday to Friday lunchtime and also Tuesday and Wednesday evenings (no food Sun). The pub is dog-friendly, but no children are allowed in the bar. Up to three guest ales are usually served at this friendly local. ♨️Q🍽🌞🕐🍴♿🏠(133)♣️P⁻

Hythe

Three Mariners Ⓛ
37 Windmill Street, CT21 6BH
😊 4-10 Mon; 12-11 (midnight Fri & Sat) ☎ (01303) 260406
Young's Bitter; guest beers Ⓗ
Traditional two-bar local that is the jewel in the crown and a cask ale mecca in a town with several potential Guide candidates. Refurbished in 2009 from a run-down Shepherd Neame establishment, it was runner-up local CAMRA Pub of the Year in both 2010 and 2011. Well worth finding for the friendly and relaxed atmosphere as well as the range of guest ales, which features local microbrewers. A beer festival is usually held over the spring bank holiday. ♨️🍽🌞🍴♣️🐶⁻

Iden Green

Peacock
Goudhurst Road, TN17 2PB (1½ miles E of Goudhurst at A262/B2085 jct) TQ747374
😊 12-11 (6 Sun) ☎ (01580) 211233
⊕ peacockidengreen.co.uk
Shepherd Neame Master Brew, Late Red, Bishops Finger, seasonal beer Ⓗ
Peg-tiled and weatherboarded country pub dating back to 1397, with a large car park in front, named after the peacocks that strutted around the nearby Glassenbury Estate. The interior has exposed brickwork, beams, tiles and wooden floors. In winter, two fires welcome customers, one in the striking inglenook, while smokers can gather round the wood-burning stove overlooking the gardens. The pub hosts pheasant shoot breakfasts in season and is a regular venue for meetings of vintage car and motorbike clubs. ♨️Q🌞🕐🍴♿🏠(297)♣️P⁻

Ightham Common

Old House ★
Redwell, Redwell Lane, TN15 9EE (½ mile SW of Ightham village, between A25 and A227) TQ590558
😊 7-9 (11 Wed-Fri); 12-3, 7-11 Sat & Sun ☎ (01732) 886077
Beer range varies Ⓖ
Outstanding unspoilt pub in a secluded country lane, brick and tile hung and housing an entrance lobby and two separate bars. The public bar features a Victorian wood-panelled counter, parquet flooring and a large inglenook fireplace. The lounge bar has a chaise longue. Up to six beers are served by gravity from the cellar, always including at least one bitter, a golden ale and a dark beer (usually a mild or porter), selected by the landlord from a good range of breweries.
♨️Q🌞🍴♣️P⁻

Ivychurch

Bell Inn ✅
Ashford Road, TN29 0AL (signed from A2070 between Brenzett and Hamstreet) TR028275
😊 12-11 (10.30 Sun) ☎ (01797) 344355
⊕ thebellinnromneymarsh.co.uk
Black Sheep Best Bitter; Sharp's Doom Bar; Wadworth Henry's IPA; guest beers Ⓗ
Like many marsh pubs, this house is adjacent to the church; in fact it was carved off from the churchyard. Popular for its excellent ales and ciders as well as the selection of food, a warm welcome awaits. The current licensees have achieved an enviable reputation for the establishment, gaining the honour of local CAMRA Pub of the Year in 2010 and 2011. Well worth finding, it was once the centre of the Romney Marsh Owlers (smugglers).
♨️🍽🌞🕐🍴♣️🐶P⁻

Laddingford

Chequers ✅
The Street, ME18 6BP (1 mile SW of Yalding) TQ689481
😊 12-3, 5-11; 12-11 Sat; 12-10.30 Sun ☎ (01622) 871266
⊕ chequersladdingford.co.uk
Adnams Southwold Bitter; guest beers Ⓗ
Oak-beamed, 15th-century, community-focused pub with a frontage adorned with colourful window boxes and hanging baskets. The heavily beamed bar with split-level dining area has numerous artefacts throughout. The large garden, with children's play equipment, is popular during the April beer festival. Good-quality food is served (snacks only on Mon), with home-made sausages on Thursday, and regular themed food nights. One double bedroom is available for letting. A bus comes to the door, or there is a train to Beltring Halt, with a 20-minute walk.
♨️Q🌞🛏🕐🍴🏠(23,26)♣️P⁻

Lower Halstow

Three Tuns Ⓛ
The Street, ME9 7DY TQ859672
😊 12-11 (midnight Fri & Sat; 10.30 Sun) ☎ (01795) 842840
⊕ the-tuns.co.uk
Millis Kentish Best; guest beers Ⓗ
Spacious and charming listed building dating from 1468, in a quiet village on the Saxon Shore Way

coastal path. It has three separate rooms – a secluded dining area, a large lounge and main bar, and a games room/village bar. The pub is popular with locals, ale enthusiasts, ramblers, dog walkers and diners. There is a large, welcoming open fire in the main bar and a resident cat. The three beers are all from Kent micros and the real cider is also local; beer festivals are occasionally held.
🏠Q☺🐕☺◑🍴🍽🚃(327)♣♠P⚬�

Luddesdown

Cock Inn 🅛 ✅
Henley Street, DA13 0XB (1 mile SE of Sole Street station) TQ664672
☎ 12-11 (10.30 Sun) ☎ (01474) 814208
⊕ cockluddesdowne.com
Adnams Southwold Bitter, Lighthouse, Broadside; Goacher's Mild; Shepherd Neame Master Brew; guest beers Ⓗ
Superb rural traditional free house dating from 1713, under the same ownership since 1984. It has two bars and a large conservatory plus a very comfortable heated area at the side. Many local clubs and societies meet here and darts and pétanque are played. A selection of games is provided on the tables and there is also a bar billiards table. A devious free quiz is held on Tuesday evenings hosted by the landlord. Children are not permitted. 🏠Q☺◑🍴🍽♣♠P⚬⟵🛏

Lynsted

Black Lion
Lynsted Lane, ME9 0RJ (close to church) TQ943609
☎ 11-3, 6-11; 12-3, 7-10.30 Sun ☎ (01795) 521229
Goacher's Mild, Light, Dark, seasonal beers Ⓗ
With three or four beers from Goacher's on offer, this village local is sought out by discerning drinkers. The characterful landlord holds court with a cluster of regulars in the main bar, while the adjoining bar has a bar billiards table. Wooden floors throughout add to the character. Food is available daily and there is a large garden. The 345 bus runs every two hours or so past the pub (not eves or Sun). There are three letting rooms separate from the pub. Home-made political cartoons adorn the entrance hall.
🏠Q☺🚪◑🍴🚃(345)♣P⚬⟵

Maidstone

Dog & Gun 🅛
213 Boxley Road, ME14 2TL
☎ 12-midnight (1am Fri & Sat) ☎ (01622) 759046
⊕ dogandgunmaidstone.co.uk
Shepherd Neame Master Brew, Spitfire, seasonal beers Ⓗ
A community pub, it holds a music quiz on Tuesday and regular music evenings featuring groups and discos. Live bands play 5-7pm on Sundays, and there are both pool and darts teams. Many charities are supported including Help for Heroes and Air Ambulance, and Easter eggs have been distributed to retirement homes in the county. The garden has an outside bar and barbecues are held in the summer. Shepherd Neame microbrewery beers sometimes feature.
🏠☺◑🚉(East)🚃(79,130)♣⚬⟵

Flower Pot 🅛 ✅
96 Sandling Road, ME14 2RJ (off A229 N of town centre)
☎ 12 (11 Sat)-11; 12-10.30 Sun ☎ (01622) 757705
⊕ flowerpotpub.com
Goacher's Gold Star; Kent Brewery Pale; guest beers Ⓗ
A real ale lover's paradise, this split-level street-corner pub has nine handpumps adorning the bar, dispensing ales from the many Kent micros and the rest of Britain, including Thornbridge. TV screens display the beers on offer along with the strength and price, plus any forthcoming events such as music and jam nights. Occasional beer festivals are held and several ciders are sold. A must-visit when in the county town. CAMRA Kent regional Pub of the Year 2011/12. The landlord is planning to set up a microbrewery within the next year.
🏠Q☺◑🚉(East)🚃(101,155)♣⚬⟵

Pilot ✅
23-25 Upper Stone Street, ME15 6EU (on A229)
☎ 12-3 (not Mon), 6-11; 12-midnight Fri & Sat; 12-11 Sun
☎ (01622) 691167 ⊕ thepilotpub.net
Harveys Sussex XX Mild, Sussex Best Bitter, Armada Ale, seasonal beers Ⓗ
Maidstone's country pub in the town. A welcoming 16th-century, Grade II-listed pub with a beamed interior and inglenook fireplaces. Excellent Sunday roasts are served 12-3pm followed by live music and a fun quiz in the evening. Jam nights are held monthly on a Wednesday. No food Monday, Tuesday or Sunday evening. Darts is played and at the rear there is a pétanque piste and covered smoking area. Westons Old Rosie cider is sold.
🏠☺◑🚉(West)🚃♣⚬⟵

Rifle Volunteers 🅛
28 Wyatt Street, ME14 1EU
☎ 11-3, 6 (7 Sat)-11; 12-3, 7-10.30 Sun ☎ (01622) 758891
Goacher's Real Mild, Fine Light, Crown Imperial Stout Ⓗ
Quiet street-corner, single-bar pub owned by the local Goacher's Brewery. It retains most of its original features and has been a regular in this Guide for several years. The pub fields two quiz teams in the local league. Note the display of interesting old bottled beers and the unusual toy soldiers used to indicate a beer in the wood. A good old-fashioned pub free from music and fruit machines. Q☺🚉(East)♣⚬⟵

Swan 🅛 ✅
2 County Road, ME14 1UY (opp prison, near County Hall)
☎ 12-11 ☎ (01622) 751264 ⊕ theswaninnmaidstone.co.uk
Shepherd Neame Master Brew, Kent's Best, seasonal beers Ⓗ
Cosy end-of-terrace venue handy for local shops and workers. Dating back to 1840, the lower bar level area reflects expansion into adjoining property. The prison gates opposite featured in the movie Porridge and the TV sitcom Birds of a Feather. Shepherd Neame's seasonal and pilot microbrewery ales regularly feature, with mini festivals hosted. Swan-related memorabilia are to be found in all nooks and crannies, together with other historic and brewery-related pictures. Occasional live music plays at weekends, with quiz nights on alternate Wednesdays. 🏠☺🚉(East)♣⚬⟵

Marden

Stile Bridge ▼ Ⓛ ✔

Staplehurst Road, TN12 9BH (on A229 at foot of Linton Hill by jct with B2079)
✪ 11-11; 12-7 Sun ☎ (01622) 831236 ⊕ stile.co.uk
Adnams Southwold Bitter; Shepherd Neame Master Brew; guest beers Ⓗ
Large roadside pub and restaurant with separate drinking and dining areas. The rear snug bar features a large-screen TV for live sporting action. Pub and drink-related memorabilia festoon the walls. Five real ales and three ciders, including Double Vision, are always available, with local microbreweries supported. It also has an interesting selection of genuine continental beers and lagers. The popular Bridgestock beer and music festival is held over the spring and summer bank holidays, as well as regular quiz nights and live music evenings. ♨❀◑➡(5)♣P⁵⁻🍴

Margate

Lifeboat Ale & Cider House

1 Market Street, CT9 1EU
✪ 12-1am (2am Thu-Sat) ☎ (07837) 024259
⊕ thelifeboat-margate.com
Beer range varies Ⓗ
Excellent watering hole in the old town district, within walking distance of the Turner Contemporary art centre, which has been a welcome addition to the town's paltry ale scene since it opened in 2010. A wooden stillage divides the pleasant pub into a front and back room. Up to six real ales, mainly from Kent breweries, are offered, along with a wider selection of Kentish ciders and perries. All food is sourced from local suppliers. Live music plays most Thursdays. ♨◑➿➡(8,34)♣

Mechanical Elephant ✔

28-30 Marine Terrace, CT9 1XJ
✪ 9am-midnight (1am Fri & Sat) ☎ (01843) 234100
Greene King IPA, Abbot; Ruddles Best Bitter; guest beers Ⓗ
Lloyds No.1 bar ideally located opposite the main sands with a summer balcony offering the town's famous sunset views. A quiet daytime and evening pub during the week, it becomes busier on Friday and Saturday evenings. The name derives from a large roving mechanical elephant that gave rides along the seafront in the 1950s. A varied rota of ales, regularly including Kentish beers, as well as beer festivals, are offered in line with Wetherspoon's national promotions. Westons cider is available. ❀◑♿➿➡♣⁵⁻

Northern Belle

4 Mansion Street, CT9 1HE
✪ 11-11; 12-10.30 Sun ☎ (07810) 088347
Shepherd Neame Master Brew, seasonal beers Ⓗ
Margate's oldest standing pub is situated down a tiny road opposite the pier and a stone's throw from the Turner Contemporary art centre. In 1680 two fishermen's cottages were combined and a new pub was born, the Aurora Borealis. Its present name derives from a merchant ship that ran aground in 1857. Low ceilings and quirky nooks make this a rather cosy little pub. Music is regularly played on Sundays. A second Shepherd Neame beer is offered alongside Master Brew. ➿➡(8,34)

Mersham

Farriers Arms Ⓛ

The Forstal, TN25 6NU (through Mersham village turn right into Church Road; pub on left approx ½ mile)
✪ 11-11 (midnight Fri; 12.30am Sat; 11.30 Sun)
☎ (01233) 720444 ⊕ thefarriersarms.com
Old Forge Brewery Farriers 1606; guest beers Ⓗ
A friendly Grade II-listed pub dating back to 1606, with a large garden overlooking the River Stour. The pub and the adjacent Old Forge microbrewery, which brews Farriers 1606 and seasonal ales, is owned by local villagers. Food is available both in the Anvil restaurant and at the bar. Live music, classic car rallies, beer festivals and other organised events are regular features at the pub throughout the year. ♨Q❀❄◑♿➡(525,813)♣P⁵⁻

Milton Regis

Three Hats

93 High Street, ME10 2AR
✪ 11-11; 10-10 Sun ☎ (01795) 427645
Shepherd Neame Master Brew; guest beers Ⓗ
The oldest pub in Milton Regis, this popular and friendly local is to be found in the historic High Street. It has an open floor plan with two main areas. The front has low beams and a small dining section, providing good-value lunch and evening bar meals (no food Sat or Sun). The rear has a dartboard and bar billiards table. The landlord is a keen supporter of real ale and tries hard, despite guest beers and cider being restricted to the Enterprise and SIBA lists; he often features beers from the West Country when available. ♨❀◑➿(Sittingbourne)➡(347)♣♣⁵⁻

Newenden

White Hart Ⓛ

Rye Road, TN18 5PN (on A268) TQ834273
✪ 11-11; 12-10.30 Sun ☎ (01797) 252166
⊕ thewhitehartnewenden.co.uk
Harveys Sussex Best Bitter; Oakham Ales JHB; Rother Valley Level Best; guest beers Ⓗ
Reputedly haunted, this 16th-century free house stands on the Kent and East Sussex border. Regular customers mark the two guest ales for quality and make suggestions for future ales. Seasonal cider is sometimes available. The pub has six en-suite guest rooms and is a short walk from Northiam Station on the Kent & East Sussex Railway. Good-quality food is available and there is a large garden. ♨Q❄❀❄◑▲➡(340)♣P⁵⁻

Northfleet

Earl Grey

177 Vale Road, DA11 8BP
✪ 12-midnight ☎ (01474) 365240
Shepherd Neame Master Brew, Spitfire, seasonal beers Ⓗ
Distinctive late 18th-century cottage-style building with a Kentish brick and flint exterior that is rarely seen in this area. The interior consists of an L-shaped bar with a raised seating area at one end and exudes a homely convivial atmosphere. Darts and pool are played and the pub also hosts several football teams. ❀♿➡♣P⁵⁻

Pembury

King William

87 Hastings Road, TN2 4JS

✪ 12-11 (midnight Fri & Sat; 11.30 Sun) ☎ (01892) 825460
⊕ thekingwill.co.uk

Greene King IPA; Morland Old Speckled Hen; guest beers Ⓗ

A welcoming village pub, rejuvenated by the current licensees and winning the West Kent CAMRA Most Improved Pub award last year. Up to five cask beers are served. The Will is family- and dog-friendly, and all take advantage of the large front and rear gardens. There is plenty of entertainment on offer: darts, bar billiards, cribbage and occasional live music (including skiffle). Major calendar events including Burns Night, St George's Day and Bonfire Night are enthusiastically celebrated. Lunch is available Sundays only. ♨✿❂◑♿🚆(6,208,297)♣P⅃

Penshurst

Spotted Dog

Smart's Hill, TN11 8EE (turn off B2188 S of Penshurst) TQ523418

✪ 12-11 (3 Mon; 10.30 Sun) ☎ (01892) 870253
⊕ thespotteddogpub.co.uk

Harveys Sussex Best Bitter; Larkins Traditional Ale; guest beers Ⓗ

White weatherboard 15th-century inn clinging to the side of a hill, originally several cottages. There are spectacular views from the rear terrace, while inside the pub is divided into a number of small rooms with low-beamed ceilings. The emphasis is on home-cooked traditional English food, but casual drinkers, families, walkers and tourists are all given a warm welcome. Guest beers usually include one local brew (look out for Black Cat microbrewery beers from nearby Groombridge). Real local Chiddingstone cider is also served. A venue for regular classic car meetings. Beware of the step and door handle on entry. ♨✿❂◑🐾P⅃

Perry Wood

Rose & Crown

Crown Hill, ME13 9RY TR042552

✪ 11.30-3, 6.30-11 (not Mon eve); 12-10.30 Sun
☎ (01227) 752214 ⊕ roseandcrownperrywood.co.uk

Adnams Southwold Bitter; Harveys Sussex Best Bitter; guest beers Ⓗ

Historic 16th-century free house in the middle of Perry Wood, east Kent's highest point, set in outstanding countryside and popular with walkers, riders and cyclists. The attractive bar is adorned with old woodcutting tools and warmed in winter by a large inglenook fireplace. It has an extensive garden with a children's play area. The food menu is produced using locally sourced ingredients and served in the bar and separate restaurant (no food Mon eve). Winner of several green tourism and environmentally friendly awards. ♨Q✿❂◑♣P

Petham

Chequers Ⓛ

Stone Street, CT4 5PW (on B2068)

✪ 12-3 (not Mon), 6-11; 12-4, 7-10.30 Sun
☎ (01227) 700734

Dark Star Hophead Ⓗ**, Over the Moon; Harveys Sussex Best Bitter** Ⓖ**; Sharp's Doom Bar** Ⓗ**; Whitstable East India Pale Ale** Ⓖ**; Woodforde's Wherry** Ⓗ

On the Roman road from Canterbury to Hythe, the Chequers was built around 1830 and was local CAMRA Pub of the Year in 2011. The bar area has comfortable leather sofas, and there is a spacious dining area and restaurant at the back, with a tempting menu including a popular Sunday carvery (no food Sun and Mon eves). Darts and pool are played in the small side bar. Up to eight beers are available at busy times, and there are usually two beer festivals a year. It is close to a campsite. ♨✿❂◑Å🚆(620)♣P⅃

Petteridge

Hopbine

Petteridge Lane, TN12 7NE TQ668413

✪ 12-2.30, 6-11; 12-3, 7-10.30 Sun ☎ (01892) 722561

Hall & Woodhouse K&B Sussex Bitter, First Gold, seasonal beer Ⓗ

Cottage-style gem only half a mile from the bus route, an ideal refreshment stop for those walking the High Weald Landscape Trail or travelling National Cycle Route 18. There are two cosy rooms with a central log fire, and on balmy days picnic tables are put outside. Home-cooked food is served six days a week (not Wed). The Dorset Badger beers served are rare for Kent (it is the brewery's most eastern pub), and are in good condition, which is why the Hopbine has been in this Guide for a quarter of a century. ♨Q✿❂◑🚆(296,297)♣P

Plaxtol

Golding Hop

Sheet Hill, Topps Hill, TN15 0PT (¾ mile N of village) TQ600547

✪ 11-3 (2.30 Mon), 6-11 (5.30-11 Fri); 11-11 Sat; 12-3.30, 7-10.30 Sun ☎ (01732) 882150

Adnams Southwold Bitter; guest beers Ⓖ

Tucked away, the Golding Hop is nevertheless sought out by many, including ramblers and cyclists. The exterior is festooned with hanging baskets in the warmer months, while the interior is particularly cosy in winter with a wood-burning stove. Four ales, some from far afield, are served directly from the barrel. Unusually, there is list of real ciders on the chalkboard by the entrance, often including the home-made house rough. Traditional pub grub is cooked by the landlady (no food Sun-Tue eves). Dogs and children are welcome in the garden, which has a child's play area. ♨Q✿❂◑🚆(222,404)♣🐾P

Rainham

Three Sisters Ⓛ

Otterham Quay Lane, ME8 8QR (jct B2009, Lower Rainham Road and Otterham Quay Lane) TQ830667

✪ 12-midnight (2am Fri-Sat) ☎ (0634) 231991

Goacher's Goldstar, Fine Light Ⓗ

Friendly free house where the number of real ale handpumps has increased from two to five in the landlord's first two years. Selling ales from Kent breweries and Magic Bus cider, the pub has a full length front bar with open fire, a pool table to the

rear and a separate smaller bar. There is a large car park and an outside seating area at the rear, with a fenced-off children's play area. The separate function hall is used for beer festivals.
⚅🏮⬛⮃🏮(327)♣☀P⅃-🍺

Ramsgate

Artillery Arms 🅛
36 Westcliff Road, CT11 9JS
☼ 12-11 (midnight Fri-Sun) ☎ (01843) 853282
Beer range varies Ⓗ
Cosy corner pub with a warm welcome for locals and visitors alike, which focuses on its reputation as a traditional ale house. Allegedly built in 1812, it is said to have been used as an officers' billet, and stained glass windows depict battle scenes from the Napoleonic wars. You will normally find Ramsgate Gadds' beers along with guests, giving a good range of quality, well-served ales. 🏮(9,Loop)

Churchill Tavern
19-22 The Paragon, CT11 9JX
☼ 11.30-11 (1am Fri & Sat); 12-11 Sun ☎ (01843) 587862
⊕ churchilltavern.co.uk
Greene King IPA; guest beers Ⓗ
Built in 1816 as the Paragon Hotel, this is a spacious yet cosy pub overlooking Ramsgate's Royal Marina. It has six handpulls frequently offering ales from local craft breweries, plus a seventh offering Biddenden cider. A good selection of meals is available to eat in the bar or the separate dining area. The pub holds a quiz night on Mondays and live music on Saturdays and Sundays. It has a small outdoor roof terrace. Previous winner of Thanet CAMRA Pub of the Year.
⚅🏮⬤🏮(34,88)⅃-

Conqueror Alehouse 🍷 🅛
4C Grange Road, CT11 9LR
☼ closed Mon; 11.30-2.30, 5.30-9; 12-3 Sun
☎ (07890) 203282 ⊕ conqueror-alehouse.co.uk
Beer range varies Ⓗ
Superb micropub, probably the smallest free house in Thanet, offering a fine selection of mainly local ales straight from the cask, as well as local Broomfield cider. Opened in November 2010 by an ex-local CAMRA chairman, it has room for about 20 customers. Named after a two-funnelled paddle steamer that operated excursions from Ramsgate in the early 1900s, old photos of the ship and its crew adorn the walls. This cosy, friendly pub offers a pleasant music- and TV-free atmosphere.
Q⮃🏮☀

Great Tree
1 Margate Road, CT11 7SP
☼ 2 (6.30 Mon)-10.30; closed Tue ☎ (01843) 590708
⊕ thegreattreepub.co.uk
Beer range varies Ⓗ
Owned by opera singer Scheherazade Pesante and offering a great selection of real ales and real ciders in a relaxed and welcoming atmosphere, the Great Tree is a pub with a difference. A mouthwatering selection of Puerto Rican food and free bar snacks are always on offer. For the drivers, a selection of teas and coffees from China and Japan is also available. Opera nights, poetry readings and art and craft fairs feature alongside live music events. 🏮🍴⮃🏮(Loop)☀

Montefiore Arms 🅛
1 Trinity Place, CT11 7HJ
☼ 12-2.30 (not Wed; 4.30 Sat), 7-11; 12-3, 7-10.30 Sun
☎ (01843) 593265 ⊕ montefiorearms.co.uk
Ramsgate Gadds' No. 7; guest beers Ⓗ
Often voted Thanet CAMRA Pub of the Year, this charming back-street local offers a warm welcome to visitors and a home from home for locals. Named after local Jewish philanthropist Sir Moses Montefiore (1785-1885), the pub offers one handpull dispensing a regular local ale and two guest handpulls. Biddenden cider is also available on handpull. Behind the main bar there is a snug and a separate pool room. An absolute must for visitors who enjoy a warm and congenial atmosphere.
Q🏮🏮⮃(Dumpton Park)🏮(9,9X,Loop)♣☀⅃-

Sir Stanley Gray 🅛 ✅
Pegwell Bay Hotel, 81 Pegwell Road, CT11 0NJ
☼ 11-11 (midnight Fri & Sat); 11.30-10.30 Sun
☎ (01843) 599590 ⊕ pegwellbayhotel.co.uk
Ramsgate Gadds' No. 5; guest beers Ⓗ
Welcoming pub in the village of Pegwell with scenic views over Pegwell Bay and across the Channel. Connected to the Pegwell Hotel via a tunnel, the atmosphere is warm and friendly, with low beams and an intimate feel. There is a separate games room for pool, and a full pub food menu supplemented by home-cooked daily specials. Cask Marque-accredited, the pub offers four real ales including regionals and independents. ⚅🏮⬤🏮♣☀P⅃-

Ripple

Plough Inn
Church Lane, CT14 8JH TR348498
☼ 12 (3 Mon & Tue)-11; 12-10.30 Sun ☎ (01304) 360209
⊕ theploughripple.co.uk
Adnams Broadside; Sharp's Doom Bar; Shepherd Neame Master Brew Ⓗ
An attractive rural inn, just a couple of miles from Deal. This single-room, wood-beamed pub has a long bar with large tables and benches. National beers feature alongside ales from the local Ripple Steam Brewery. Popular with walkers, it is easily accessible by footpaths from the surrounding area. Food is served most days (but ring to check). Quiz night is Wednesday. It is about a mile's walk from regular bus number 14 at Great Mongeham. Families and dogs welcome. ⚅🏮🍴⬤🏮☀P⅃-

Rochester

Britannia Bar Café 🅛
376 High Street, ME1 1DJ
☼ 10-11 (2am Fri & Sat); 12-9 Sun ☎ (01634) 815204
⊕ britannia-bar-café.co.uk
Goacher's Fine Light; guest beers Ⓗ
Mid-way between Rochester and Chatham stations, this comfortable pub has been run by the present landlord for 11 years. Monthly themed dinner evenings are very popular. There is a well-planted garden area behind the pub. Q🏮⬤🏮⮃🏮⅃-

Coopers Arms
10 St Margaret Street, ME1 1TL
☼ 12-midnight (1am Fri & Sat) ☎ (01634) 404298
Courage Best Bitter; Young's Special; guest beers Ⓗ

A one-minute stroll past Rochester cathedral and castle, this charming old inn, originally dating from 1199, is one of the oldest in Kent. The front bar has beamed ceilings, exposed brickwork, a couple of impressive original fireplaces and items of historic interest. A passageway leads to a more modern rear bar and out to a large well-kept garden area, popular on sunny days. This venue features six real ales, Sunday roast and lunchtime specials. No children allowed in the bars.
🅼Q🅰🌳🅲🎏⌐

Eagle Tavern ✅

124 High Street, ME1 1JT
🌀 12-8 (11 Wed; midnight Thu & Fri); 11-midnight Sat; 12-10.30 Sun ☎ (01634) 409040 🌐 theeagletavern.org.uk
St Austell Tribute; Sharp's Doom Bar; Wells Bombardier; Wychwood Hobgoblin Ⓗ
Friendly, lively pub on the main high street which bills itself as Rochester's premier music venue, and gets very busy when live music plays (see the website for gig listings). It has a large garden area, and stands just outside the old city wall. Monday is curry night. No food is served on Sunday.
🌆🅰🌳⌐🈂🎏⌐

Good Intent

83 John Street, ME1 1YL
🌀 12-midnight; 12-11 Sun ☎ (01634) 843118
Beer range varies Ⓖ
Back-street local that was a recent Medway CAMRA Pub of the Year. Up to three beers and a cider are available, dispensed from casks racked behind the bar. Various events are held in the garden, when additional ales are on offer. The public bar has a large-screen TV for major sports events and a pool table. Live music gigs are hosted. There is a quieter back bar with posters reminding customers of past and upcoming events. Q🌆🌳🅰🎏🈂🎏🕯️P⌐

Man of Kent Ⓛ

6-8 John Street, ME1 1YN (200yds off A2 from bottom of Star Hill)
🌀 2-11; 12-midnight Fri & Sat; 12-11 Sun ☎ (07772) 214315
🌐 themanofkent.com
Goacher's Fine Light, Gold Star; guest beers Ⓗ
Medway CAMRA Pub of the Year 2010. Ales from 16 Kent brewers are served on 11 handpumps, plus seven ciders and various Kent wines. The friendly venue also has a large range of Belgian and German beers on tap and in bottles. Wednesday and Thursday nights are for live music. There is a pleasant enclosed garden. The pub offers a haven from Rochester High Street during the many festivals. 🅼🌳🈂🎏🕯️⌐🏳️

Two Brewers

113 Rochester High Street, ME1 1JS
🌀 11-11 (midnight Sat); 12-10.30 Sun ☎ (01634) 812448
🌐 twobrewersrochester.com
Shepherd Neame Master Brew, Spitfire, Bishops Finger, seasonal beers Ⓗ
Long and narrow traditional building reputed to be the smallest pub in Rochester. Built in 1683, the present façade was erected in 1775. The sign depicts two draymen carrying a barrel of beer on two poles (known as two brewers) between them. Photos of old Rochester adorn the walls. There is music Sundays from 4pm and a blues night on the first Thursday of the month. No food, except Sunday lunchtime roast. A large-screen TV shows major sports events. 🈂🎏

Who'd Ha' Thought It

9 Baker Street, ME1 3DN
🌀 12-11.30 (midnight Fri & Sat) ☎ (01634) 830144
🌐 whodha.co.uk
Beer range varies Ⓗ
Situated in a side street off Maidstone Road, this charming and welcoming pub has gained an increasing reputation among local real ale enthusiasts. It has a spacious main bar, wood-panelled with a variety of seating, and a TV and a log fire in winter. There is a recently decorated snug bar to the rear and a well-maintained garden. A selection of three real ales is served. It hosts a pub quiz once a month and live music. Bar snacks including rolls and pizzas are available. 🅼🌳🌆🏵️🎏⌐

Ryarsh

Duke of Wellington Ⓛ ✅

The Street, ME19 5LS
🌀 11-11; 12-10.30 Sun ☎ (01732) 842318
🌐 dukeofwellingtonryarsh.com
Harveys Sussex Best Bitter; Westerham Grasshopper; guest beers Ⓗ
A 16th-century pub in the village centre, dog-friendly and welcoming to ramblers. The central door opens to the main bar on the left and a popular restaurant to the right that has a varied main menu as well as Sunday roasts. There are large fireplaces in both areas for winter warmth. The large covered and heated patio opens onto the garden and pétanque piste. An enclosed area with tables at the front ensures safety for children. Live music is often played on Thursday evenings. 🅼🌳🅲🎏(58)🕯️P⌐

St Mary in the Marsh

Star Inn

TN29 0BX (opp church) TR065279
🌀 12-11 ☎ (01797) 362139 🌐 thestarinn-themarsh.co.uk
Young's Bitter; guest beers Ⓗ
The building, dating from 1476, is the hub of the village and offers a changing range of cask ales, draught cider and good-value food. Accommodation is available during the summer months in the pub, or in the adjacent self-catering cottage, which was once the home of Noel Coward and sits opposite the church where Edith Nesbit is buried. Frequent beer festivals are held in summer and a folk club meets on the second Tuesday of each month. 🅼🌳🌆🍴🅲🎏(11A)🕯️P⌐

Sandwich

Crispin Inn ✅

4 High Street, CT13 9EA
🌀 11-11 (midnight Fri & Sat; 10.30 Sun) ☎ (01304) 621967
🌐 sandwichpubs.co.uk
Adnams Broadside; Sharp's Doom Bar; guest beers Ⓗ
In the medieval town of Sandwich, this pub is by the Barbican and old toll bridge over the River Stour. Low ceilings, wooden beams and brick walls create an old world feel, providing a congenial ambience for locals and tourists alike. Relax by the windows and watch the world go by, or sit on the small patio at the back overlooking the river. Guest beers are usually from Kent microbreweries. There is occasional live music and the pub is only a short walk from local transport. 🅼🌳🌆🅲👤🈂🎏⌐

George & Dragon ✅

24 Fisher Street, CT13 9EJ
✪ 11-3, 6-11; 11-11 Sat; 11-4.30 Sun ☎ (01304) 613106
⊕ georgeanddragon-sandwich.co.uk
Shepherd Neame Master Brew; guest beers Ⓗ
A 15th-century pub and restaurant tucked away in the back streets of the Cinque Port. A wood-floored bar area, beamed ceilings and a real fire give the pub a welcoming and relaxed atmosphere. Superb home-cooked pies and Scotch eggs support the pub's standard menu. Guest ales vary, with occasional beers from Kent breweries including Wantsum and Hopdaemon. A small courtyard at the back provides a suntrap in the summer. Dogs are welcome. A short walk from bus and railway services. ▲❀◗➔ㅂ

Red Cow

12 Moat Sole, CT13 9AU
✪ 11-11 (midnight Fri & Sat) ☎ (01304) 613243
Fuller's London Pride; St Austell Tribute; Wells Bombardier; guest beers Ⓗ
You cannot miss the red cow on the front of this lively, timber-framed pub, with its tiled floors and exposed beams. Real ales from local breweries such as Old Dairy and Foundry feature alongside ciders from Broomfield and other producers. There is a large enclosed garden, which is used for occasional music events. The pub hosts its own mini beer festivals, and major football matches are shown on TV. Food is available all day, made from locally sourced ingredients. Close to the bus station. ▲❀◗&Å➔ㅂ◉P½

Sevenoaks

Anchor

32 London Road, TN13 1AS
✪ 11-3, 6-11; 10.30-11 Fri; 10.30-4.30, 7-11 Sat; 12-11 Sun
☎ (01732) 454898 ⊕ anchorsevenoaks.co.uk
Harveys Sussex Best Bitter; Sharp's Doom Bar; guest beer Ⓗ
A regular Guide entry, this lively pub is popular with all ages. It is one of the last traditional pubs in the town centre, with the longest-serving landlord in the area. The guest beer is usually sourced from a small independent brewery, often local. Good pub grub is served Monday-Friday lunchtimes. Live blues music plays twice a month, as well as open mic nights and poker evenings. Occasional Meet the Brewer events are hosted. ◗ㅂ♣½

Chequers ✅

73 High Street, TN13 1LD
✪ 12-10.30 (11 Tue-Thu); 12-midnight Fri & Sat
☎ (01732) 450144 ⊕ the-chequers-sevenoaks.co.uk
Black Sheep Best Bitter; Harveys Sussex Best Bitter; St Austell Tribute; guest beer Ⓗ
Lovely Grade II-listed 16th-century former staging post for coach routes. The town gallows and lime pit for disposing of the bodies were next to the pub. It has authentic timbers hung with hops, while the central bar sports a good array of handpumps. Westons Old Rosie cider is accompanied by a decent choice of ales. Lunchtimes are popular with local workers and good food is served. Quiz night is Wednesday, with live music once a month. ▲❀◗ㅂ◉½

White Hart Ⓛ

Tonbridge Road, TN13 1SG (on top of hill S of town centre on A225)

✪ 11-11; 12-10.30 Sun ☎ (01732) 452022
⊕ whitehart-sevenoaks.co.uk
Fuller's London Pride; Harveys Sussex Best Bitter; Old Dairy Blue Top IPA Ⓗ
Impressive, whitewashed 17th-century coaching inn on the site of the original Sevenoaks turnpike. Bought a few years ago by an independent pub chain from north-west England, the White Hart is now a firm favourite. The smart and sprawling interior bustles with friendly staff but maintains a relaxed atmosphere. In addition to the regular ales there is a house beer from the Phoenix Brewery in Manchester, several guest beers and real local Chiddingstone cider. Excellent food is served until 10pm and the garden and patio are a perfect suntrap for warm days. ▲Q❀◗&ㅂ(402)♣◉P½

Sheerness

Red Lion

61 High Street, Blue Town, ME12 1RW TQ911750
✪ 11-midnight (1am Thu-Sat); 12-midnight Sun
☎ (01795) 664354
Beer range varies Ⓗ
A pleasant and traditional locals' pub opposite the former naval dockyard wall, the only real ale outlet remaining in the old Blue Town district of Sheerness, with its cobbled High Street. Three beers are on handpump, mainly from microbreweries. The landlord takes pride in listening to customers' ale requests. No meals are served, but there is a free buffet on Sunday. Tables are available outside in the closed, heated courtyard. ▲❀ㅁ➔ㅂ♣½

Sittingbourne

Long Hop

80 Key Street, ME10 1YU (on A2)
✪ 12-11.30 (midnight Sat; 10.30 Sun) ☎ (01795) 425957
Shepherd Neame Master Brew; guest beer Ⓗ
Alongside the busy A2, almost two miles west of the town centre. This pleasant, welcoming pub is a sure favourite with the local community. The low ceilings, oak beams and wood flooring are enhanced by soft lighting and a homely open fire. Guest ales such as Sharp's Doom Bar or a Ringwood beer feature alongside the permanent Master Brew. The food is popular here both lunchtimes and evenings, especially the Sunday roast, so booking is advisable. The pub name refers to the Gore Court cricket ground opposite. ▲ㅎ❀◗ㅂ(333,334)♣P½

Snargate

Red Lion ★ Ⓛ

TN29 9UQ (on B2080, 1 mile NW of Brenzett) TQ990285
✪ 12-3, 7-11 (10.30 Sun) ☎ (01797) 344648
Beer range varies Ⓖ
Superb, unspoilt, three-room pub in a 16th-century building and in the same family for 100 years, universally known as Doris's. The interior is decorated with posters from World War II and the Women's Land Army. Identified by CAMRA as one of Britain's Real Heritage Pubs, it is on the road that separates Walland Marsh from Romney Marsh. Beers from small breweries are served, usually including Goacher's. ▲Q❀♣◉P½

Stalisfield Green

Plough Inn ⓁL

ME13 0HY TQ955529
✪ closed Mon; 12-3 (not Tue), 6-11; 12-11.30 Sat; 12-6 Sun
☎ (01795) 890256 ⊕ stalisfieldgreen.com
Beer range varies ⒽH

The country inn to search out, for the best in local microbrewery beer and locally sourced food. The pub makes its own bacon, sausages and even tomato sauce. An historic 600-year-old multi-roomed building in an attractive setting on the North Downs, its beers are almost always from a range of Kent's microbreweries. It has a large family-friendly garden. Live music plays on some Fridays (see website for details), and there is a beer festival over the August bank holiday weekend. The 660 bus from Faversham is infrequent, but may be of use.
🅐🅠❀◑ 🅐🚃(660)♣P

Staplehurst

Lord Raglan ⓁL

Chart Hill Road, TN12 0DE (½ mile N of A229) TQ786472
✪ 12-3, 6.30-11.30; closed Sun ☎ (01622) 843747
Goacher's Fine Light; Harveys Sussex Best Bitter; guest beer ⒽH

A hop-decorated bar runs across the front room of the pub, with a log fire at both ends. Excellent snacks and full meals are always available. It is a popular and unspoilt free house with no distractions, thereby restoring the art of conversation and giving the atmosphere of a country pub from days gone by. A side room gives access to the large garden, which is lovely on a summer day. The bus stops on the A229 at Cross-at-Hand. Double Vision cider and perry are on tap.
🅐Q❀◑🚃(5)♦P

Teynham

Swan ⓁL

78 London Road, ME9 9QH
✪ 12-midnight ☎ (01795) 521218
Wadworth 6X; guest beers ⒽH

A 1930s roadside inn with one large open bar. The pub is free from tie and offers a new and welcome addition to the drinker in Teynham; the enthusiastic landlord is keen on real ale and uses his freedom of choice to always offer a local beer from the wide selection of Kent microbreweries. The beer and real cider - Dudda's Tun from a local farm - are sold at competitive prices. Pub games include shut the box. Food is available lunchtimes and evenings (lunch only Sun).
🅐◑&🚃🚃(7,333,335)♣♦P⏪

Tonbridge

Humphrey Bean ✅

94 High Street, TN9 1AP (near castle and river)
✪ 9am-midnight (1am Fri & Sat) ☎ (01732) 773850
Greene King Abbot; Ruddles Best Bitter; guest beers ⒽH

The Bean goes from strength to strength, giving the best beer choice in town, combined with quality cellarmanship. This ex-post office is now basically one huge room, with areas of subdued

lighting and sofas, bright airy sections, a central fire and, lastly, surprisingly large gardens with views across the River Medway to the castle. Guest beers are often sourced from south-eastern breweries, expanding into top notch national independents (punters may be asked to vote on choices). Several real ciders, including Westons, complement the range of ales. The pub opens at 7am for breakfast.
❀◑&🚃🚃♦P⏪

Tunbridge Wells

Bedford ✅

21 High Street, TN1 1UX
✪ 11-11 (midnight Fri & Sat); closed Sun ☎ (01892) 544662
⊕ bedfordtw.co.uk
Greene King IPA, Abbot, seasonal beer; guest beers ⒽH

This pub just opposite the railway station has been given a new lease of life over the past year. It has eight handpumps dispensing beers from the owners Greene King, Royal Tunbridge Wells and guests – predominantly from Kent. The real cider is local, too. The pub is usually a quiet haven, but can reveal a hidden flat-screen TV for top sporting events. Popular at lunchtimes and with commuters in the evenings, good hearty snacks, locally sourced, are served. Regular music events, quizzes and beer festivals take place. A fabulous addition to the town's ale drinking scene. ◑🚃🚃♦

Bull

79 Frant Road, TN2 5LH
✪ 11-3, 5.30-11; 12-11 Sat; 12-10.30 Sun ☎ (01892) 536526
Shepherd Neame Master Brew, Spitfire ⒽH

A short walk from the Pantiles up Frant Hill brings you to the Bull. There is one large room with a central bar and open fire, accommodating drinkers and diners in their own space. A modern feel prevails, with expansive windows and light furnishings. Good locally sourced food, in generous helpings, ensures the pub is regularly busy. It also attracts a crowd when cricket is played at the nearby Neville ground. There is a courtyard garden for those wanting to take the air. The pool table, dartboard and wireless internet are free to customers. Dogs are welcome too.
🅐Q❀◑&🚃🚃(252,254,256)♣P

Grove Tavern ⓁL ✅

19 Berkeley Road, TN1 1YR
✪ 12-11 ☎ (01892) 526549 ⊕ grovetavern.co.uk
Harveys Sussex Best Bitter; Taylor Landlord; guest beers ⒽH

Reputedly the oldest and smallest pub in Tunbridge Wells, the Grove sits on a steep, narrow lane in the old village part of the town. It has a reputation for friendliness and inclusivity. Visitors can cosy up to the open fire in winter in the one-room bar, or just enjoy the warmth of conversation. The side alley is used for outside drinking in warmer weather. The beers are superbly kept and served with enthusiasm. Entertainment includes darts and lively quizzes. Dogs and children welcome.
🅐❀&🚃🚃♣

Ragged Trousers

44 The Pantiles, TN2 5TN
✪ 11 (10 Sat & Sun)-11 ☎ (01892) 542715
Larkins Traditional Ale; Taylor Landlord; guest beers ⒽH

Small, bustling pub right on the famous Pantiles area of the town. Seats are provided outside to observe the comings and goings and to listen to live jazz in July and August. It has a relaxing, intimate atmosphere inside aided by low lighting, candles and music. Good home-cooked lunches are served daily, and evening meals Wednesday and Thursday, by friendly young staff. Look out for the excellent beers from the town's own brewery, sometimes sold under the Spa Brewery name. ⊛◑⇌⊞

Royal Oak ⑤
92 Prospect Road, TN2 4SY
✪ 12-11 (10.30 Sun) ☎ (01892) 542546
⊕ theroyaloak.food.officelive.com
Harveys Sussex Best Bitter; Larkins Traditional Ale; guest beers Ⓗ
Just 10 minutes' walk from the railway station and well worth it. This popular corner local is remarkably spacious, with lots of quiet corners and a large central bar. With wood-panelled walls, leather sofas, plentiful table seats and bar stools, there is room for all. There is also a small patio to the front. Good home-made food is served in generous portions at good prices (no food Mon or Tue) to complement the four well-kept beers. Enthusiastic and friendly staff will happily give you a taster. Live jazz Sunday lunches are popular, as is the monthly quiz night. ⊱⊛◑⊞P↿

Upper Upnor

King's Arms ♚
2 High Street, ME2 4XG TQ757704
✪ 12-midnight (10.30 Sun) ☎ (01634) 717490
Adnams Southwold Bitter; guest beers Ⓗ
At the top of the cobbled high street lies this village local, offering traditional home-cooked food in the main bar and an à la carte menu in a separate restaurant. A choice of five well-kept ales always includes a mild. There is a range of European bottled beer as well as real cider and perry. The large garden gets very busy in summer, especially if a beer festival is on. At the other end of the street lies the historic Upnor Castle. Q⊛◑⊞⊞(197)⚫↿

Walmer

Berry ♚
23 Canada Road, CT14 7EQ
✪ 11 (5.30 Tue; 12 Thu)-11; 11.30-11 Sun
☎ (01304) 362411 ⊕ theberrywalmer.co.uk
Dark Star American Pale Ale; Harveys Sussex Best Bitter; guest beers Ⓗ
This unpretentious, traditional family-run ale house is far from ordinary. Serving eight real ales, two ciders and a perry (from large and small producers), there is always a great welcome and a good buzz, even at quieter times. Darts, pool and quiz teams keep the place busy, and there is a February beer festival, a May cider festival and occasional live music. Dogs are welcome. Local CAMRA Pub of the Year five years running and East Kent Pub of the Year 2011. The car park is over the road. ⋈⊛⊞(12,13,14)♣⚫↿

West Malling

Bull ⑤
1 High Street, ME19 6QH

✪ 12-2.30, 4-11; 12-11 Fri & Sat; 12-10.30 Sun
☎ (01732) 842753
Young's Bitter; guest beers Ⓗ
A convivial pub next to the railway line at the north end of this vibrant village. There are two wood-panelled bars, the smaller one available for meetings. Hop bines adorn the beams, and there is a splendid log fire. The keen landlord usually keeps five interesting beers, including one from each of local breweries Goacher's and Kent. ⋈⊛⇌⊞(72,151)♣↿

West Peckham

Swan on the Green
The Green, ME18 5JW (1 mile W of B2016 at Mereworth)
TQ644525
✪ 11-3.30 (4 Sat), 5.30-11 (11.30 Fri); 12-5 Sun
☎ (01622) 812271 ⊕ swan-on-the-green.co.uk
Swan Fuggles, Trumpeter, Cygnet, Bewick, seasonal beers Ⓗ
Situated overlooking the village cricket pitch, this pub brews all its cask ales, which mostly have swan-themed names. The light and airy L-shaped interior, featuring exposed brickwork and oak beams, has the bar and some tables along the front, while the left side is mainly used by diners sampling the award-winning food. No food is available Sunday evenings. On cooler days, two real fires ensure customers are kept warm and cosy. ⋈Q⊛◑P↿

Westerham

General Wolfe
High Street, TN16 1RQ (W of town on A25)
✪ 12-11 (midnight Fri & Sat; 10.30 Sun) ☎ (01959) 562104
Greene King IPA, Abbot; guest beer Ⓗ
Tucked away on the outskirts of town, this weatherboarded inn was named after General Wolfe of Quebec, once a Westerham resident. This is a long, thin building, the room divided into a number of areas, warmed by a real fire in the winter months. Keenly priced food is served (no food Mon), with a popular Sunday roast. A large range of malt whiskies is also on offer. Entertainment includes a quiz every Wednesday, live singalong on Saturday nights, and acoustic music on Sunday. There is limited parking adjacent to the pub, mainly on the road. ⋈Q⊛◑♿⊞(246,401,594)P

Westgate-on-Sea

Bake & Alehouse ⑤
21 St Mildred's Road, CT8 8RE (behind Carlton Cinema)
✪ closed Mon; 12-2, 5.30-9; 12-2 Sun ☎ (07581) 468797
⊕ bakeandalehouse.com
Beer range varies Ⓗ
Down an alleyway behind the Carlton Cinema, this welcoming new micropub is an oasis for the real ale drinker. It offers a selection of four varying beers, sourced mainly from Kentish breweries, served straight from the cask kept in a temperature controlled room. With seating for around 18 people, the well-considered layout makes the most of the small interior. Colanders are used as lampshades, with collages depicting baking and beer themes on the walls. Q⇌⊞(8,8A)⚫

Whitstable

Pearson's Arms L ✓
Horsebridge Road, Sea Wall, CT5 1BT (on seafront near Horsebridge Centre)
✪ 12-midnight (1am Fri & Sat; 11 Sun) ☎ (01227) 773133
⊕ pearsonsarmsbyrichardphillips.co.uk
Harveys Sussex Best Bitter; Whitstable East India Pale Ale; guest beer Ⓗ
Attractive wood-panelled pub, popular with visitors, just off the seafront. It is more than a gastro-pub; there is plenty of room for drinkers around the open fire and in the back bar. Dogs are welcome and there is live music every Tuesday. The upstairs restaurant, the brainchild of well-known chef Richard Phillips, has lovely views over the beach. Look out for the fixed price lunch menu. Imaginative bar snacks are available downstairs (no food Mon all day or Tue and Sun eves). Outside seating is limited but drinks can be taken onto the beach in plastic glasses. ﹏❀◑▲➡(4,6)

Ship Centurion L ✓
111 High Street, CT5 1AY
✪ 11-11; 12-7 Sun ☎ (01227) 264740
Adnams Southwold Bitter; Elgood's Black Dog; Fuller's London Pride; guest beer Ⓗ
A friendly and traditional town-centre pub, which is very busy at weekends. Colourful hanging baskets add to its charm in summer. There are pictures of old Whitstable in the main bar. A mild is always served, and regular guests usually include a beer from a local brewery. Home-cooked bar food (no food Sun) often features authentic German dishes, and there is always a schnitzel on the menu on Saturdays. Live music is played on Thursday evenings, except in January. A cider festival is held in the summer, and an October beer festival is being introduced from 2012. ◑➡⇌➡(4,5,6)⁵⁻

Wickhambreaux

Rose Inn ✓
The Green, CT3 1RQ
✪ 12-11 (10.30 Sun) ☎ (01227) 721763
⊕ theroseinnwickhambreaux.co.uk
Greene King IPA; guest beers Ⓗ
This 16th-century pub, beams festooned with hops, is just one of the beautiful buildings in this small village. There is a small snug behind the open fireplace. The wide range of pub grub includes ploughman's lunches and imaginative specials; food is served all day. The two guest beers change about twice a week, and four real ciders are served: Biddenden Dry, Westons Old Rosie, Gwynt y Ddraig Black Dragon and Two Trees Perry. There is a beer festival is in May and a quiz on the second Wednesday of each month. ﹏❀◑➡(11)👤P

Woodchurch

Six Bells ✓
Bethersden Road, TN26 3QQ (close to village green opp church) TQ942349
✪ 12-midnight ☎ (01233) 860246 ⊕ 6-bells.co.uk
Fuller's London Pride; Harveys Sussex Best Bitter; Hopdaemon Golden Braid; Taylor Landlord; guest beers Ⓗ
An unspoilt, popular and friendly village local where dogs are welcome. It has a separate public bar and a saloon bar with a dining area, but with plenty of bar space for drinkers. Beer festivals are held several times through the year. A good range of freshly prepared meals is available seven days a week – all day on Sunday. There are gardens to the front and rear; the large enclosed garden at the back is ideal for families.
﹏Q🐕❀◑➡❑♿➡(295)♣P⁵⁻

Wormshill

Blacksmiths Arms
The Street, ME9 0TU TQ 878571
✪ closed Mon & Tue; 7-11; 12-8 Sun ☎ (01622) 884386
⊕ blacksmiths-arms.com
Beer range varies Ⓗ
A Grade II-listed, timber-framed, 17th-century village pub, formerly three cottages, situated in rolling downland countryside near to the Pilgrims Way. It has a cosy bar with its original brick floor, and is warmed in winter by an inglenook log fire. Beers from Canterbury Ales appear on a regular basis, alongside ales from across the country. Food is served in the beamed and candlelit restaurant. Dogs are allowed in the bar, but not children under 14. ﹏Q❀❑P

Wrotham

Bull Hotel
Bull Lane, TN15 7RF
✪ 12-3, 6-11; 12-11 Sat & Sun ☎ (01732) 789800
⊕ thebullhotel.com
Dark Star Hophead, Partridge Best Bitter; guest beers Ⓗ
Well-appointed historic hotel, partly dating from the 14th century. The guest beer is often a Dark Star seasonal although other smaller breweries are represented. It has a good reputation for food, which is served lunchtimes and evenings, with curry on Thursday and fish on Friday. Regular theme nights take place, with jazz every last Wednesday evening of the month. The separate Buttery, formerly the village bakery, hosts corporate events, wedding receptions and birthday parties. ﹏Q❀🛏◑➡(306,308)P⁵⁻

Recipe for buttered beer

Take a quart of more of Double Beere and put to it a good piece of fresh butter, sugar candie an ounce, or liquerise in powder, or ginger grated, of each a dramme, and if you would have it strong, put in as much long pepper and Greynes, let it boyle in the quart in the maner as you burne wine, and who so will drink it, let him drinke it hot as he may suffer. Some put in the yolke of an egge or two towards the latter end, and so they make it more strength-full.
Thomas Cogan, The Haven of Health, 1584

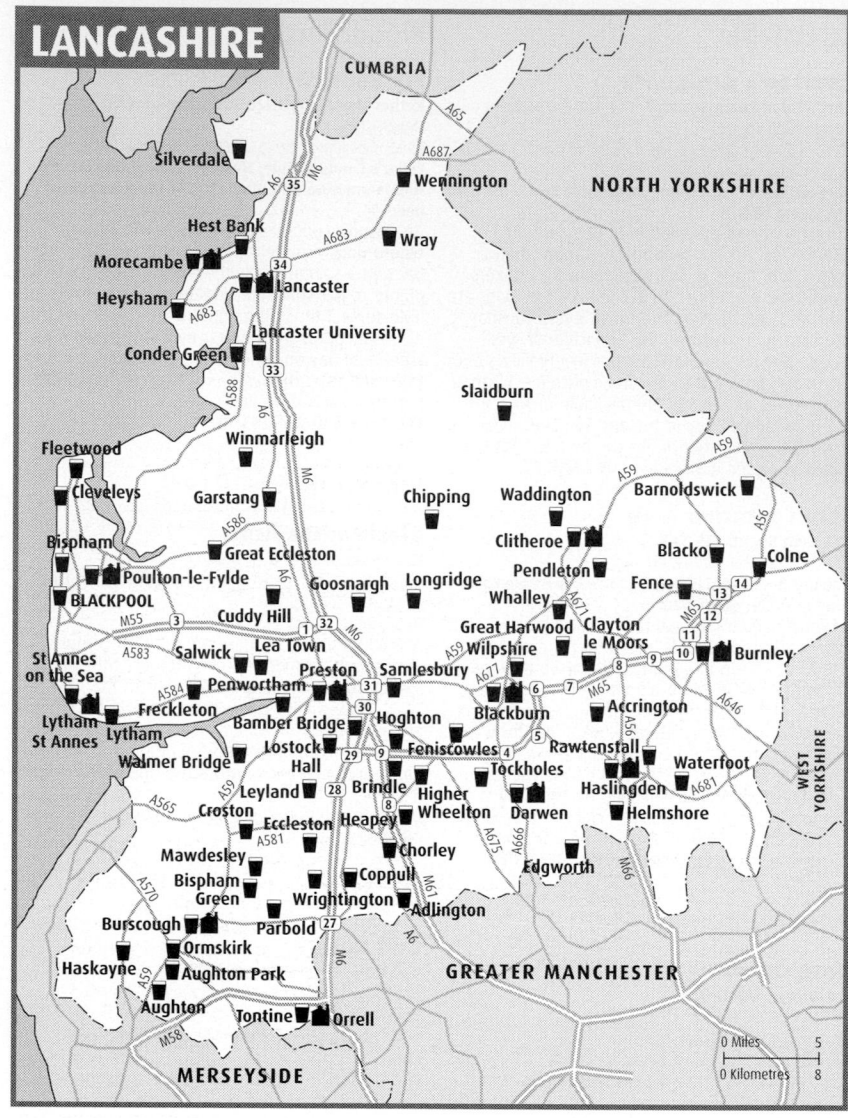

LANCASHIRE

CUMBRIA

NORTH YORKSHIRE

WEST YORKSHIRE

GREATER MANCHESTER

MERSEYSIDE

0 Miles 5
0 Kilometres 8

Silverdale
Wennington
Hest Bank
Wray
Morecambe
Heysham
Lancaster
Lancaster University
Conder Green
Slaidburn
Fleetwood
Winmarleigh
Cleveleys
Garstang
Chipping
Waddington
Barnoldswick
Bispham
Great Eccleston
Clitheroe
Blacko
Colne
Poulton-le-Fylde
Goosnargh
Longridge
Pendleton
Fence
BLACKPOOL
Whalley
Cuddy Hill
Great Harwood
Clayton
le Moors
St Annes
on the Sea
Salwick
Lea Town
Wilpshire
Burnley
Preston
Samlesbury
Penwortham
Freckleton
Hoghton
Blackburn
Accrington
Lytham
St Annes
Lytham
Bamber Bridge
Lostock
Hall
Feniscowles
Rawtenstall
Waterfoot
Walmer Bridge
Leyland
Brindle
Tockholes
Haslingden
Helmshore
Croston
Eccleston
Higher
Wheelton
Heapey
Darwen
Edgworth
Mawdesley
Chorley
Bispham
Green
Coppull
Wrightington
Adlington
Burscough
Parbold
Ormskirk
Haskayne
Aughton Park
Aughton
Tontine
Orrell

Accrington

Abbey
Bank Street, BB5 1HP
🕐 12-midnight (2am Fri & Sat; 1am Sun) ☎ (01254) 237043
John Smith's Bitter; guest beers Ⓗ
Just outside the town centre, this community local has a semi open-plan layout comprising a small front room with a dartboard, and a larger lounge at the rear. The pub is popular with the locals and can get busy at times. There are up to seven guest beers, generally from the major brewers, alongside the regular John Smith's. There is also usually at least one from a smaller brewery, which can include Bowland, Bank Top, Moorhouse's, Prospect and Timothy Taylor. ❀🕸🚌🚑(464,484,X41)♣🍴

Grants Ⓛ
1 Manchester Road, BB5 2BQ
🕐 12-11 (midnight Thu-Sat) ☎ (01254) 393938

Beer range varies Ⓗ
A large, imposing building on the edge of the town centre. Thoroughly modern on the inside, it is something of a place to be seen at weekends. A true free house, Grants supports local brewers, with up to seven beers generally from the north-west, including some from the Bowland, Prospect and Bank Top ranges. There is a separate function room upstairs for hire. ❀🕸🚌(464,484,X41)♣🍴

Peel Park Ⓛ ✅
Turkey Street, BB5 6EW (200yds from A679, adj to school)
🕐 12-11.30 ☎ (01254) 235830
Tetley Bitter; guest beers Ⓗ
Situated opposite the site of the old Accrington Stanley football ground, this is a true free house, with eight beers on offer, mainly from micros. The main bar is a large, open front room that is divided into two sections. There is a separate small pool

room, and a large room at the rear used as a restaurant or for meetings. Beer festivals are held twice a year, in May and November.
🏠⊛◑⇌🖳(23,263)♣P⚊

Adlington

Spinners Arms
23 Church Street, PR7 4EX
✪ 12-11 (midnight Fri & Sat) ☎ (01257) 483331
Rudgate Mild; Taylor Landlord; Thwaites Wainwright; guest beers Ⓗ
The pub is known as the Bottom Spinners to differentiate it from the other Spinners Arms in the village. Welcoming and friendly, a single bar serves three seating areas and there is a pleasant outdoor drinking area to the front. It has no pool table or gaming machine, just an open log fire. The bar menu offers home-cooked food with weekend specials. Four alternating guest beers, often sourced from local breweries, always include a mild. Small functions are catered for.
🏠Q⊛◑⇌🖳P⚊

Aughton

Stanley Arms ✅
St Michael Road, L39 6SA (off A59 at Aughton Springs)
SD391055
✪ 11-11 (12.30am Fri & Sat) ☎ (01695) 432241
Marston's Pedigree; Taylor Landlord; Tetley Dark Mild, Bitter; guest beers Ⓗ
Beside a historic Norman church, the Stanley Arms has distinctive 18th-century architecture and was originally a coaching stop for postal deliveries. Inside, the pub is decorated with Tudor-style woodwork and has several side rooms, one containing books on early brewing history. The centrally placed bar dispenses ales from six handpumps. The pub is a recent winner of the Lancashire Best Kept Pub award and is popular for its excellent home-cooked food. Regular beer festivals are held between spring and autumn.
🏠⊛◑🖳(311)P⚊

Aughton Park

Dog & Gun ✅
233 Long Lane, L39 5BU (near railway station)
SD413064
✪ 4 (12 Sat & Sun)-midnight ☎ (01695) 423303
Banks's Bitter; Marston's Pedigree; Ringwood Boondoggle; guest beers Ⓗ
A genuine community pub dating from 1891, the interior retains an intimacy unspoilt by the modern planner. Two rooms, one with a real fire, are set around the central bar, with ales served from six handpulls. The pub supports darts, quiz and bowling teams, and is also frequented by cycling and archery clubs. There are outside drinking areas to the front and rear, an award-winning floral display, and an impressive menagerie of animals including ducks, chickens, geese and pigs. Look out for Shirley the parrot. 🏠Q⏚⊛⇌♣P⚊

Bamber Bridge

Withy Arms ◖ ✅
122 Station Road, PR5 6QP
✪ 11-midnight (1am Fri & Sat) ☎ (01772) 697706
⊕ withyarms.com
Thwaites Wainwright; guest beers Ⓗ

On the main crossroads and 15 minutes' walk from the railway station, the pub was recently reopened after being bought by a local business for the office space. Being real ale enthusiasts, they decided to refurbish the pub and now it boasts four handpumps. Guest beers are usually from local micros, often Prospect or Moorhouse's. The house bitter is brewed by Thwaites. A Sunday roast has recently been introduced. Quiz night is Thursday. The bar manager is one of the youngest in the country, at barely 19 years of age.
🏠⏚⊛⇌🖳(125,113)P⚊

Barnoldswick

Greyhound
61 Manchester Road, BB18 5PW (short walk from town centre)
✪ 5 (2 Sat)-11; 2-10.30 Sun ☎ (01282) 850670
⊕ thegreyhoundbarlick.co.uk
Barlick Hare of the Dog; Moorhouse's Blond Witch, Pride of Pendle; guest beers Ⓗ
Traditional community local run by a syndicate, now also the home of Barlick microbrewery, the first brewery in Pendle for very many years. The historic three-storey stone building is set in the old part of town close to Bancroft Steam Mill. There is a separate games room for pool, darts and dominoes, with a real fire in the main room. A heated patio and beer garden can be found to the rear. Live music is played on Saturdays and a quiz on Sundays. 🏠⊛♿♣P

Bispham Green

Eagle & Child ◖
Malt Kiln Lane, L40 3SG (off B5246)
✪ 12-3, 5.30-11; 12-11 Sat; 12-10.30 Sun ☎ (01257) 462297
Beer range varies Ⓗ
An 18th-century pub with cheerful staff and eight handpumps with local ales showcased; Southport Carousel is always available and a variety of guest ales include Allgates, Prospect and Moorhouse's. This busy classic country pub is the Lancashire Dining Pub of the Year for the fifth time, so book early for a table. The beer garden, with its wildlife area and great views, hosts a beer festival on the May bank holiday. Quiz night is every Monday.
🏠Q⊛◑P⚊

Blackburn

Black Bull 🅛

Brokenstone Road, BB3 0LL (Heys Lane/Bog Height Road crossroads)
☼ 4-11 (midnight Fri); 12-midnight Sat; 12-10.30 Sun
☎ (01254) 581381 ⊕ threebsbrewery.co.uk
Three B's Stokers Slake, Bobbins Bitter, Tacklers Tipple, Pinch Noggin, Knocker Up 🅗
In the heart of rural Lancashire, this is an independent family-run pub with its relocated microbrewery attached. Serving from seven handpumps, there is a fine selection of Three B's real ales including the exclusive Black Bull Bitter, with a changing guest or cider; try the three beer wedges which are very popular. Built on a farmhouse in the 18th century, it was purchased by Robert Bell from Thwaites and transformed to a place for those who appreciate fine beer and friendly conversation. ₳Q❀&♣P⅃

Blacko

Rising Sun 🅛 ✔

330 Gisburn Road, BB9 6LS (on A682)
☼ 12-2, 5-11; 12-11 Thu; 12-midnight Fri & Sat; 12-11 Sun
☎ (01282) 612173
Moorhouse's Black Cat, Premier Bitter, Pride of Pendle, Blond Witch; guest beers 🅗
Enclosed in a row of cottages, the Rising Sun is the only tied Moorhouse's pub in Pendle, and the old hill with its witchcraft connections can be seen from the front patio. The traditional taproom is retained and the parlour has a collection of local breweriana. Dogs and walkers are made welcome. Bar snacks and meals are served daily (all day until 7pm at weekends). The local Pendleside delicacy of Stew an' Hard is popular. The licensee is a CAMRA member. ₳Q❀◗🖶(P70,P71)♣P

Blackpool: Bispham

Bispham Hotel

70 Red Bank Road, FY2 9HY (300yds from promenade)
☼ 12 (11 Sat)-11; 12-10.30 Sun ☎ (01253) 351752
Samuel Smith OBB 🅗
Well-maintained, mid-1930s Art Deco pub. A popular two-bar local, it is well-known for its low-priced ale drawn from oak casks. With no music, food, TV or children, it is a haven for a pint and a chat, and is only a four-minute walk from the promenade, sea front and the Blackpool-Fleetwood tramway. The pub sign features an old tram, a reminder that there used to be a tram depot behind the pub. Quizzes are on Thursday and Sunday. An upstairs meeting room is available. Q🗐&🖶🖵⅃

Blackpool: Town Centre

Blackpool Cricket Club 🅛 ✔

Barlow Crescent, West Park Drive, FY3 9EQ (follow brown signs to Stanley Park)
☼ 7 (12 Sat & Sun)-11 ☎ (01253) 393347
⊕ blackpoolcricket.co.uk
Thwaites Wainright; guest beers 🅗
The club is adjacent to Stanley Park and has numerous teams that play in the local leagues. County cricket matches are occasionally played here. The club has squash courts, and hockey teams from the Stanley Park pitches use the club's

facilities. Large-screen TVs show all sports events. A large function room is available upstairs for socials and meetings. Food is only available at weekends. ❀◗&P⅃

Gillespies ✔

87-89 Topping Street, FY1 3AA (off Church Street and close to Winter Gardens)
☼ 10-11 (midnight Fri & Sat) ☎ (01253) 627882
Beer range varies 🅗
Close to Church Street and the Winter Gardens, the pub sells four ales from the Greene King portfolio. This smart, popular town-centre establishment, with prominent TV screens and comfortable seating, has a café-bar ambience during the day and sports-bar atmosphere in the evenings. Food is available until 6pm. A discount on real ale is offered on production of a CAMRA membership card. ◗⇌(North)🖵⅃

No 4 & Freemasons 🅛 ✔

Layton Road, FY3 8ER (at jct with Newton Drive, B5266)
☼ 12-11 (midnight Sun) ☎ (01253) 398949
Thwaites Original, Wainright; guest beers 🅗
This smart suburban pub fronts on to Newton Drive and is located one mile inland from the seafront, with bus stops directly outside. The main lounge has both dining and drinking areas, with pool and darts in the rear games room. One or two guest beers feature from the Thwaites approved list. Meals are served lunchtimes and evenings Monday-Friday, and all day Saturday and Sunday. ❀◗🗐🖵(2,15)♣P⅃

Pump & Truncheon 🅛

13 Bonny Street, FY1 5AR (opp Bonny St police station)
☼ 11-11; 10-midnight Fri & Sat summer; 11-midnight summer Sun ☎ (01253) 624099
⊕ thepumpandtruncheon.co.uk
Beer range varies 🅗
Central Blackpool's cosy, hidden gem, close to the police station behind Madam Tussauds. The house beer is from Moorhouse's and guest beers are usually from a range of smaller, northern English breweries. A selection of bottled world beers, including Trappist and Belgian fruit beers, is a feature. Good-value meals are served until 6pm (later in summer). Show your CAMRA membership card for a discount on food and real ale. ₳◗&🖵(Central Pier)

Ramsden Arms 🅛

204 Talbot Road, FY1 3AZ (on A586 close to North railway station)
☼ 10.30-midnight (1am Sat); 12-midnight Sun
☎ (01253) 291713
Fuller's London Pride; guest beers 🅗
Serving four beers from the Punch range, this hostelry is on the edge of the town centre, close to Blackpool North station. The Rammy, with its black and white timbered appearance and real fires, offers a warm, friendly welcome, and has been part of Blackpool's real ale scene for many years. Beer tankards and sporting trophies adorn the walls. Bar snacks are available until 7pm every day. It has a smoking area to the rear, and limited parking at the side of the pub. Live sport is featured on large TV screens. ₳❀🗐⇌(North)🖵P⅃

Shovels 🅛 ✔

260 Common Edge Road, FY4 5DH (on B5261, ½ mile from A5230 jct)
☼ 12-11 (midnight Thu-Sat) ☎ (01253) 762702

Lytham Shovels Best; Wells Bombardier; guest beers Ⓗ
A large open-plan roadside venue that has won CAMRA Local Pub of the Year more than once. Six handpumps offer a range of guest beers, mainly from micros; Lytham Shovels Best is brewed exclusively for the pub. A beer festival is held every October. The pub is home to many sports clubs and has plasma screens for sporting events. Good food is popular and served all day. Steve, the manager, offers a warm and friendly welcome and is passionate about the selection of real ales. Buses are daytime only. ♨❀◑♿▲🚌(10,17)♣P⁵⌐

Brindle

Cavendish Arms ✔
Sandy Lane, PR6 8NG
❀ 12 (4 Mon & Tue, Jan & Feb)-11; 12-11.30 Wed-Sat; 12-11 Sun ☎ (01254) 852912 ⊕ cavendisharms.co.uk
Banks's Bitter; guest beers Ⓗ
At the heart of this attractive village, opposite the 13th-century church, the Cavendish was sadly boarded up for most of 2008. Now under new management, the pub and village have been revitalised. With a small room on the left as you enter and the large main bar area with rooms off, the pub has been tastefully restored and expanded inside. The three guest beers are from breweries on the Marston's group guest list. A beer festival is held in a marquee annually in June.
♨Q❀◑⊟🚌(118)P

Burnley

Boot Inn Ⓛ ✔
18 St James Street, BB11 1NG
❀ 8am-midnight ☎ (01282) 463720
Greene King Abbot; Moorhouse's Pendle Witches Brew; Ruddles Best Bitter; guest beers Ⓗ
A typical Wetherspoon's, this Grade II-listed building was designed by Blackpool architect H Thompson on the site of an earlier farmhouse-style inn; it celebrated its centenary in 2011. The former 19th-century Boot Inn had stables, used by the prize-winning colt Young Sampson, available to serve mares. It now offers a good choice of ales from many excellent East Lancashire local brewers. An extensive outdoor drinking area is popular in the summer months. Q❀◑≠🚌⁵⌐

Bridge Bier Huis ♀ Ⓛ
2 Bank Parade, BB11 1UH (behind shopping centre)
❀ closed Mon & Tue; 12-midnight (1am Fri & Sat); 12-11 Sun ☎ (01282) 411304 ⊕ thebridgebierhuis.co.uk
Moorhouse's Premier; guest beers Ⓗ
Free house with a large open-plan bar area and a small snug to one side. It offers two Moorhouse's beers and three changing guests, mainly from microbreweries, alongside a real cider. More than 60 foreign bottled beers are available as well as seven foreign beers on tap, usually including two rare German beers. Wednesday is quiz night and some weekends live music is hosted. This welcoming pub opens at 5pm on a Tuesday evening if Burnley FC are playing.
♨❀◑≠(Central)🚌♣●

Gannow Wharf Ⓛ
168 Gannow Lane, BB12 6QH (next to Leeds-Liverpool canal on Gannow bridge)
❀ 7 (5 Fri; 3 Sat & Sun)-11 ☎ (07855) 315498

Beer range varies Ⓗ
Popular canalside local offering a warm welcome to bikers and all lovers of real ale. A constantly changing array of up to six beers is sold, with an emphasis on local beers as part of the LocAle scheme. The pub hosts many activities such as pool, karaoke, charity nights and occasional live music. At the rear, overlooking the canal, is a heated, covered area for smoking.
❀≠(Rosegrove)🚌(4,5,65)⁵⌐

Ministry of Ale Ⓛ
9 Trafalgar Street, BB11 1TQ (100yds from Burnley Manchester Road station)
❀ closed Mon & Tue; 6-11 Wed & Thu; 4-midnight Fri; 12-midnight Sat; 1-11 Sun ☎ (01282) 830909
⊕ ministryofale.co.uk
Beer range varies Ⓗ
A friendly welcome is guaranteed at this small local, where the emphasis is on good beer and conversation. This is the home of the Moonstone Brewery, where the 2½-barrel plant can be viewed in the front room. Two Moonstone beers are usually available alongside two guests from other microbreweries. The pub has art exhibitions and there is a popular quiz on Thursday nights. This venue is situated at the junction of Trafalgar Street and Manchester Road.
Q≠(Manchester Road)🚌(X43,X44,1)⁵⌐

Talbot Hotel Ⓛ ✔
65 Church Street, BB11 2RS (on A56 close to town centre)
❀ 5-midnight; 4-1am Fri; 12-1am Sat; 12-midnight Sun ☎ (01282) 412074 ⊕ talbotburnley.co.uk
Copper Dragon Golden Pippin; Holt Bitter; Moorhouse's Premier; Taylor Landlord, Ram Tam; Thwaites Wainwright Ⓗ
You can be sure of a warm welcome at this free house which dates back to the 1800s. The licensee is a cask ale enthusiast and offers two guest beers in addition to the six regular ales. Live bands feature every weekend. There are two pool tables plus a large-screen TV for sports fans. The Talbot has its own Facebook page (search for talbotwednesdays). Four en-suite rooms are available for guests who also have use of the private car park.
♨❀✚≠(Central)🚌(X43,X44,4)♣P⁵⌐

Burscough

Hop Vine Ⓛ
Liverpool Road North, L40 4BY (on A59, near Burscough Bridge station)
❀ 10.30-midnight (12.30am Fri & Sat) ☎ (01704) 893799
⊕ thehopvine.co.uk
Burscough Priory Gold, Mere Blonde; guest beers Ⓗ
In the attractive village of Burscough, the Hop Vine brewpub dates from 1874 and was originally a coaching stop. Recently refurbished, the pub sports a classic country pub interior with wood panelling, mixed wood/tile flooring, and is decorated throughout with historic local maps, photographs and rare vintage bottled ales. Burscough Brewing Co operates from the charming cobbled flower garden at the rear. Large beer festivals are held over the May and August bank holiday weekends. Excellent home-cooked food is served throughout the day. ♨❀◑≠(Bridge)🚌(2A,2B)P⁵⌐

Ring o' Bells

Ring o' Bells Lane, Lathom, L40 5TF (take A5209 from Burscough, turn left at Ring o' Bells crossroads) SD459110
✿ 11-11 (10 Sun) ☎ (01704) 893157 ⊕ ainscoughs.co.uk/The-Ring-o-Bells
Thwaites Nutty Black, Wainwright; guest beers Ⓗ
Impressive country pub in large rural grounds and accessible by a 20-minute walk along the Leeds-to-Liverpool canal from Burscough village. Reopened in 2011 by a local pubco, the huge split-level interior boasts stone and wood floors and offers a separate locals' area and family area (with outdoor playpen). Six handpumps serve Thwaites beers and three or four local microbrewery ales. The outstanding food is well priced and locally sourced (beef is company farmed and slaughtered). An upstairs private function room is available. Dog-friendly, and 24-hour canal moorings are available.
🏚✿◑♿⚏≓(Hoscar)🚏(3A,337)P⚊

Ship Inn Ⓛ ✿

4 Wheat Lane, Lathom, L40 4BX (take School Lane from Burscough; turn left after hump-backed bridge) SD452116
✿ 12-midnight (1am Fri & Sat; 11.30 Sun) ☎ (01704) 893117
Moorhouse's Ship's Special; guest beers Ⓗ
A 10-minute walk from Burscough village, the Ship (or Blood Tub) consists of a series of 18th-century canalside cottages. The pub had a major refurbishment in 2011, retaining traditional stone floors, a real fire and original wood beams. Six handpumps serve Moorhouse's beers and four or five guest microbrewery ales. A separate dogs/walkers room boasts a welcoming wood-burning stove. Beer and food festivals are held in April and September. Excellent home-cooked food is served throughout the day (private dining is also available). 🏚✿◑♿≓(Bridge)P⚊

Chipping

Tillotsons Arms Ⓛ

18 Talbot Street, PR3 2QE
✿ 12-3 (not Mon), 5-midnight; 12-midnight Sat; 12-11 Sun ☎ (01995) 61568
Beer range varies Ⓗ
In a picturesque village in the Trough of Bowland, this two-roomed, beamed pub built in 1836 has four real ales from local micros, always including at least one from Bowland or Hawkshead, and often a Moorhouse's beer as well. Child- and dog-friendly, it has two real fires and a beer garden to the rear. Locally sourced home-cooked food is available lunchtimes and evenings, and all day Saturday and Sunday. The pub is on the SIBA direct delivery scheme. 🏚Q✿◑🚏(4)♣⚊

Chorley

Potters Arms Ⓛ

42 Brooke Street, PR7 3BY (next to Morrisons)
✿ 3-11 (midnight Fri); 12-4, 7-midnight Sat; 12-5, 7-11.30 Sun ☎ (01257) 267954
Black Sheep Best Bitter; Three B's Doff Cocker; guest beer Ⓗ
Small, friendly free house named after the owners, at the bottom of Brooke Street alongside the railway bridge. The central bar serves two games areas, while two comfortable lounges are popular with locals and visitors alike. The pub displays a fine selection of photographs from the world of music, as well as vintage local scenes. Regular

darts and dominoes nights are well attended and the chip butties go down a treat. The smoking area is covered. 🏚≓🚏(3,11)♣P⚊

Railway Inn ✿

20 Steeley Lane, PR6 0RD (under subway from train station)
✿ 12-midnight (1am Fri & Sat) ☎ (01257) 411449
⊕ therailwayhotelchorley.com
Beer range varies Ⓗ
Adjacent to the railway station and 100 yards from the bus station, this is a community local that offers a changing range of up to four real ales from the Marston's portfolio. Darts, dominoes, pool and pinball are popular with the locals, along with seasonal music festivals and Saturday night concerts. Open mic sessions on Sunday evening are successful, with the pub providing its own instruments and PA system to make participation easier. 🏚✿≓🚏♣⚊

Rose & Crown

15 St Thomas's Road, PR7 1HP
✿ 12-11 (midnight Fri & Sat) ☎ (01257) 368022
Deuchars IPA; Jennings Cumberland; Thwaites Wainwright; guest beer Ⓗ
Handy for Chorley town centre, this stone-built pub opposite the police station has a central bar covering two drinking areas. There is a mixed age range, with youth in the majority at weekends when it is busy and lively, but there are plenty of bar staff. All major sporting events are shown on the many wall-mounted TV screens and there are occasional live music nights. Good-value food is served at lunchtime Monday to Thursday. Dogs and children welcome. ✿◑≓🚏♣⚊

Swan with Two Necks Ⓛ

Hollinshead Street, Chorley Bottoms, PR7 1EP (at foot of steps off Park Road behind St Lawrence Church)
✿ 12-12.20am (1am Thu & Sun; 2.30am Fri & Sat) ☎ (01257) 266649
Beer range varies Ⓗ
A pub for all ages. Five handpumps serve beers from LocAle breweries including Bank Top, Bowland, Three B's, Hawkshead, Moorhouse's and Prospect. There are eight bar areas including a roof terrace and cocktail bar, so you can enjoy a peaceful pint or two in pleasant surroundings. It is a live music venue with open mic nights on Tuesday, live bands on Thursday, Friday and Saturday, and jazz on Sunday followed by a DJ and karaoke. There is a video jukebox at other times. Buffets, parties, weddings and christenings are catered for. 🏚✿≓🚏⚊

White Bull Ⓛ

135 Market Street, PR7 2SG (S end of Market St near Big Lamp)
✿ 12-11 (midnight Fri); 11-midnight Sat ☎ (01257) 232745
Bank Top Old Slapper; Courage Directors; Wells Bombardier; guest beers Ⓗ
Single-bar pub that is a beacon for real ale in an area where so many pubs around it are closing. The games room is partitioned to the right of the comfortable L-shaped lounge. The walls are adorned with memorabilia from the landlord's favourite football team, Preston North End. Pies are served all day. Children are permitted in the beer garden if supervised. ✿◑≓🚏♣⚊

Clayton le Moors

Forts Arms 🅛
1 Lower Barnes Street, BB5 5TA
✪ 4-midnight (1am Thu); 12-2am Fri & Sat; 12-midnight Sun
☎ (01254) 433713
Bowland Hen Harrier; guest beers 🅗
Partially opened out in a modern style, the pub also boasts a function suite. Guest beers often include ales from Prospect and Cross Bay. The Forts is one of four local pubs in the town that hold a twice-yearly beer festival, one over the spring bank holiday and the other, a winter ales festival, in November. A regular bus service stops at the end of Sparth Road, 300 yards from the pub.
✪🖾(6,7)♣🚲

Old England Forever 🅛
13-15 Church Street, BB5 5HT
✪ 12-11.30 (midnight Fri-Sun) ☎ (01254) 871506
Bank Top Port o' Call; guest beers 🅗
A mid-terrace pub that sits opposite the town square. The majority of the bar has been opened out, apart from the Smoke Room, which is quite compact. Beers from Prospect Brewery are often available. The Old England takes part in two beer festivals, one in May and the other in November (a winter ales festival), which are held jointly with three other local pubs. ✪🖾(6,7)♣🚲

Cleveleys

Jolly Tars 🅛 ✅
154-158 Victoria Road West, FY5 3NE
✪ 8-11 (11.30 Thu-Sat) ☎ (01253) 856042
Greene King Abbot; Ruddles Best Bitter; guest beers 🅗
A recently opened Wetherspoon pub with up to eight guest beers, usually including a selection of George Wright, Moorhouse's and Hawkshead brewery offerings. The pub theme is Cleveleys between the wars. The staff are friendly and efficient, and while the pub is open plan it includes several secluded booths. The venue is handy for the tram service and a number of bus routes.
🏺✪🕕♿🖾🚲

Victoria Hotel
183 Victoria Road West, FY5 3PZ (approx ½ mile from town centre, on B5412)
✪ 11-11; 12-10.30 Sun ☎ (01253) 853306
Samuel Smith OBB 🅗
Large main road 1930s pub in a residential area, a short walk to the shopping centre, the Blackpool-Fleetwood tramway and various bus routes. Wooden beams, leaded windows and two open fires feature in the comfortable, spacious lounge. The popular Vaults has a separate entrance. This local is well known for low-priced ale drawn from oak casks. There is no music, TV or food to distract from conversation in this relaxing pub. A separate meeting room is available.
🏺Q🕕♿🖾🖾(9,11,74)P

Clitheroe

New Inn 🅛
Parson Lane, BB7 2JN
✪ 11-11; 12-10.30 Sun ☎ (01200) 423653
Coach House Gunpowder Mild; guest beers 🅗
A beer drinker's paradise, with 11 real ales and a real cider in summer months. The beers do vary but always include a selection from local breweries

Moorhouse's and Bowland, as well as a variety of guest beers from across the country, including Goose Eye, Saltaire and Prospect. Close to Clitheroe Castle, this multi-room pub has an outside seating area at the front and a beer garden to the rear. There is an Irish music free-for-all every other Sunday afternoon. 🏺Q✪⚲Å🚲♣♣

Colne

Admiral Lord Rodney
Mill Green, BB8 0TA
✪ 4 (2 Fri; 12 Sat & Sun)-midnight ☎ (01282) 866206
⊕ theadmirallordrodney.co.uk
Beer range varies 🅗
Large multi-room pub, away from the town centre. It is a free house with five handpumps; one beer is normally from Ossett Brewery, the others come from micros from across the UK. Home-cooked bar meals are available. Live bands feature at weekends, with a folk night every other Tuesday. Worth the walk from the railway station. 🕕🚲P

Wallace Hartley ✅
35-37 Church Street, BB8 0EB
✪ 8am-11 (midnight Thu; 1am Fri & Sat) ☎ (01282) 857790
Greene King Abbot; Ruddles Best Bitter; guest beers 🅗
Formerly the King's Head, it became a Greek restaurant for a while, before reopening in 2008 as a popular Wetherspoon establishment. It is named after the bandmaster of the ill-fated Titanic, whose body was returned to Colne to be buried. Ten beers are usually available, including local ales. There is a friendly atmosphere, with a choice of seating areas, and the history of Wallace Hartley and old Colne decorate the walls. ✪🕕♿🖾🚲P🚲

Conder Green

Stork ✅
Corricks Lane, LA2 0AN
✪ 10-11 ☎ (01524) 751234 ⊕ thestorkinn.co.uk
Black Sheep Best Bitter; Taylor Landlord; guest beers 🅗
Delightful, hospitable country inn dating back to 1660, close to the estuaries of the Lune and Conder. There is a main bar, a restaurant and several small rooms including a pleasant snug and a playroom for children. The venue has a good-sized garden, with barbecues in summer.
✪⚲🕕Å🖾(89)P🚲

Coppull

Red Herring
Mill Lane, PR7 5AN (off B5251 next to Coppull Mill)
✪ 3-11; 12-11.30 Fri & Sat; 12-11 Sun ☎ (01257) 470130
Moorhouse's Pride of Pendle; guest beers 🅗
Real ale pub in the former offices of the next-door mill. It was converted to a pub some years ago; the bar area comprises a large single room plus an extension, with up to three microbrew beers usually available. TV sports fans are catered for, as are anglers, who use the pond opposite. The pub hosts regular music nights and barbecues, and has a large first-floor function room. Train spotters will enjoy close proximity to the West Coast main line.
✪🖾(1,362)♣P🚲

Croston

Lord Nelson

Out Lane, PR26 9HJ

✪ 3.30 (12 Fri & Sat)-midnight; 12-11 Sun

☎ (01772) 600387 ⊕ lordnelsoncroston.co.uk

Copper Dragon Golden Pippin; Jennings Cumberland Ale; guest beers Ⓗ

Former Higson's pub facing onto the village green. It claims to be the oldest pub in Croston, with some parts dating from 1640. There is a cosy central bar area and two separate rooms. Good-value food is served and the pub continues to be a welcoming venue for drinkers to congregate. The two guests are sourced from microbreweries and there is a changing guest cider (summer only). An annual beer festival is held in September. Food is available Friday-Sunday. ₩Q❀⏻♿↔🚃(7,112)♣👜P

Cuddy Hill

Plough at Eaves

Eaves Lane, PR4 0BJ (1 mile off B5269 from Broughton)

✪ closed Mon; 12-3, 5.30-11; 12-midnight Sat; 12-11 Sun

☎ (01772) 690233

Thwaites Original, Bomber; guest beer Ⓗ

A long, winding old drovers' road takes you to this stone and whitewashed country pub. It dates from 1645 and Cromwell fought a major battle nearby. It has a comfortable main bar with old beams and a roaring fire in winter. No children are allowed in the bar but there is a family room. There are separate dining and games rooms and a conservatory. The three beers (one rotating) come from Thwaites and the locally sourced food is excellent. ₩Q🐾❀⏻♿🅰♣P⁵⁻

Darwen

Number 39 Ⓛ

39 Bridge Street, BB3 2AA (in pedestrian street just off town centre)

✪ 12-11 ☎ (01254) 704305 ⊕ hopstarbrewery.co.uk

Hopstar Dizzy Danny, Lancashire Gold, JC; guest beers Ⓗ

Formerly a Thai restaurant, now the brewery tap for Hopstar Brewery, this is the newest place in town. New beers are tried out here first, with a changing guest beer. Real cider is also available plus a large variety of continental and world bottled beers, as well as draught Timmermans from Belgium. This is a good LocAle bar in the centre of town, with live music every Thursday night. Check out Facebook (Number 39 – Hopstar brewery tap) for weekly events and beers. ≈♣👜

Eccleston

Original Farmers Arms Ⓛ

Towngate, PR7 5QS (on B5250)

✪ 12-midnight (11.30 Sun) ☎ (01257) 451594

Black Sheep Best Bitter; Tetley Bitter; Wells Bombardier; guest beers Ⓗ

This white-painted village pub has expanded over the years into the cottage next door, adding a substantial dining area. However, the original part of the pub is still used mainly for drinking. The three rotating guest beers are predominantly sourced from local breweries large and small. Meals are available throughout the day seven days a week, and there is accommodation in four good-value guest rooms. ❀🛏⏻🚃(113,347)P⁵⁻

Edgworth

White Horse Ⓛ

2-4 Bury Road, BL7 0AY SD742168

✪ 5-11 Mon & Tue; 12-3, 5-midnight Wed & Thu; 12-midnight Fri & Sat; 12-11 Sun ☎ (01204) 852929

Bank Top Flat Cap; Black Sheep Best Bitter; Moorhouse's Pendle Witch's Brew; Taylor Landlord; Thwaites Wainwright; guest beers Ⓗ

Situated prominently at the Bolton-Bury road crossroads, this local is a large corner building. The impressively decorated interior has dining for locals and tourists, who come to enjoy exquisite cuisine. The range of real ales on five handpumps includes some from LocAle breweries. The pub name has heraldic origins, dating back to 1714-1800 – white being the colour of peace and the horse representing stead: readiness for all events in the name of the king. A wall plaque outside explains more. ₩❀⏻♿🚃(537)P⁵⁻

Fence

White Swan Ⓛ ✔

300 Wheatley Lane Road, BB12 9QA (off A6068)

✪ 5-10.30 Mon; 12-2.30, 5-11 Tue-Thu; 12-11.30 Fri; 10-11.30 Sat; 10-10.30 Sun ☎ (01282) 611773

⊕ whiteswanatfence.co.uk

Taylor Best Bitter, Golden Best, Landlord Ⓗ

A Timothy Taylor pub known locally as The Mucky Duck. Good, wholesome food made with fresh local ingredients is served throughout the day, including breakfasts at the weekend. Situated at the heart of the village community, a warm welcome awaits locals and visitors alike. Quiz night is on Wednesday and satellite TV shows football and six nations rugby in the bar area. Two open fires heat the small pub during the winter months. ₩Q⏻♿🚃(65)P⁵⁻

Feniscowles

Feildens Arms Ⓛ ✔

673 Preston Old Road, BB2 5ER (at jct of A674/A6062, 3 miles W of Blackburn)

✪ 12-12.30am (1am Fri & Sat; 10.30 Sun) ☎ (01254) 200988

Flowers IPA; guest beers Ⓗ

Stone-built pub on a busy road junction (A674/6062) three miles west of Blackburn. There are six handpumps on the bar, offering a range of beers including one or two from local breweries such as Moorhouse's and Bank Top. Guests have included Sharp's Doom Bar and Fuller's London Pride. Live football is screened and the pub hosts a poker league. ₩🛏♿≈(Pleasington)🚃(124,152)♣P⁵⁻

Fleetwood

Mount Hotel ✔

The Esplanade, FY7 6QE (on the seafront, close to Marine Hall)

✪ 12-midnight (11 Sun) ☎ (01253) 681501

Thwaites Wainwright; guest beers Ⓗ

Victorian building next to the local landmark from which it takes its name. The pub is close to the beach and provides great views across Morecambe Bay to the Lakeland Fells. Food is served until 9pm daily. Darts and pool can be played in a separate sports bar, with outside drinking on a terrace at the front of the pub. Regular live football matches are shown. 🐾❀⏻♿(London St)🚃♣

Strawberry Gardens ⓛ

Poulton Road, FY7 6TF

☺ 12-12.30am (1am Fri & Sat) ☎ (01253) 771991
🌐 strawberry-gardens.co.uk

Boggart Rum Porter; Fuzzy Duck Golden Cascade, Mucky Duck, Ruby Duck; guest beers ⓗ

Fuzzy Duck Inns recently reopened this pub. Up to 12 ales are on offer as well as Old Rosie and Cheddar Valley cider. Food is served until 8pm daily. The local folk club meets here Thursday evenings, and it is also home to the racing pigeon clubs and numerous crown green bowling teams. Pool, darts and dominoes can be played. A heated and covered smoking area is provided. See if you can make out the 1927 flood height marker at the front door.

Q❀⊕▶️⬛♿🚋(Fishermans Walk)🚋♣⬤P⁵⁻

Thomas Drummond ⊘

London Street, FY7 6JY (between Lord St and Dock St)

☺ 8am-11 (midnight Thu-Sat) ☎ (01253) 775020

Greene King Abbot; Ruddles Best Bitter; guest beers ⓗ

Wetherspoon pub in a former church hall and furniture warehouse, named after a builder who helped construct the town. A past winner of the local CAMRA Pub of the Season award, it has on display details of the founder of the town, Sir Peter Hesketh Fleetwood, and architect Decimus Burton. Food is served daily until 10pm, and children are welcome until 9pm. Cider is available. As an alternative to the pub's 50p vouchers, a discount is offered at the bar to CAMRA members.

❀⊕▶️🚋(London St)🚋(1,14)⬤⁵⁻

Freckleton

Coach & Horses ⊘

Preston Old Road, PR4 1PD

☺ 11-midnight ☎ (01772) 632284
🌐 coachandhorsesfreckleton.co.uk

Black Sheep Best Bitter; guest beers ⓗ

A pub with a warming atmosphere and home to the local brass band, whose awards can be seen in the cabinet. A place is reserved for mementos of the 8th Air Force, who served locally during World War II. The pub has a golf society and holds mini beer festivals and charity events in the car park. Up to three changing guest beers are available from the list supplied by the pubco. ❀⊕▶️♿🚋(68,78)P⁵⁻

Garstang

Wheatsheaf

Park Hill Road, PR3 1EL

☺ 10-midnight (1am Fri & Sat); 11.30-11.30 Sun
☎ (01995) 603398

Courage Directors; Theakston Best Bitter; guest beers ⓗ

Built as a farmhouse in the late 18th century, this is now a Grade II-listed building and was greatly extended in 2002. A disco is held every Friday. The pub serves breakfast, lunch and supper and there is a covered outdoor smoking area. A welcoming pub that attracts a varied clientele from all age groups. ❀⊕▶️🅰️🚋(40,42)♣P⁵⁻

Goosnargh

Horns Inn ★ ⓛ

Horns Lane, PR3 2FJ (corner of Inglewhite Rd, 2 miles NE of village) SD575391

☺ 11.30-3, 6-11; 12-9 Sun ☎ (01772) 865230
🌐 hornsinn.co.uk

Beer range varies ⓗ

Country pub dating from 1782 on the edge of the Forest of Bowland, with five small rooms including a very rare snug, one of only three in the country, where customers sit behind the bar counter while bar staff serve from the same area. Although marked private, it is open to all. This pub has at least one beer from Bowland and another from a local micro, and serves good food using locally sourced ingredients. Accommodation in a converted barn at the rear rewards the effort of finding it. 🛏️Q❀✎◀️⊕🅰️P

Great Eccleston

White Bull ⊘

The Square, PR3 0ZB (in village square)

☺ 11 (4 Tue; 12 Sun)-midnight ☎ (01995) 670203

Black Sheep Best Bitter; Everards Tiger; St Austell Tribute; guest beers ⓗ

Historic coaching inn in the heart of the village. A family-friendly, welcoming pub with flagged floors and an unspoilt atmosphere, it has a games room with pool, darts and the usual pub games. Three quieter rooms are for talking, drinking and dining. Locally sourced home-cooked food is good quality and excellent value. Interesting guest ales come from breweries on the SIBA list. For outdoor drinking there are seats at the front and rear. Accredited by Cask Marque in 2012.
🛏️Q🐾❀⊕🅰️🚋(82,42)♣⁵⁻

Great Harwood

Victoria ★ ⓛ ⊘

St John's Street, BB6 7EP

☺ 3-11 (midnight Fri & Sat); 12-10.30 Sun ☎ (01254) 885210

Black Sheep Best Bitter; Bowland Gold; Taylor Landlord; guest beers ⓗ

Art Nouveau interiors greet you in this comfortable, multi room local built in 1905. Note also the original internal etched glass including the rare sash shutters around the bar and the ornate staircase. The horseshoe-shaped bar with its eight handpumps serves a large corridor drinking area and a front vault. There is a heated smoking shelter to the rear of the pub and the old bowling green now serves as a beer garden. The pub sits alongside a well-used cycle path (off NR6 from Rishton). Q🐾❀🅰️♣⬤⁵⁻

Haskayne

King's Arms

Delph Lane, L39 7JJ SD361081

☺ 1 (12 Sat & Sun)-midnight ☎ (07712) 107088

Beer range varies ⓗ

Near the bridge where the A5147 crosses the Leeds-Liverpool canal, this pub is on the busy road from Southport to Maghull and Liverpool. It has two rooms with up to four real fires in winter, is home to two darts teams, and features bingo and a quiz on Thursday evenings. With many attractive original features, the pub has benefited from recent sympathetic refurbishment. The 300 Liverpool-Southport bus passes outside the door.
🛏️❀🚋🚋(300)♣P⁵⁻

Haslingden

Green Squirrel
148 Manchester Road, Rossendale, BB4 6NP
☼ 4 (2 Mon)-midnight; 4-1am Fri; 12-midnight Sat & Sun
Moorhouse's Premier, Blonde Witch, Pendle Witches Brew ⊞
Formerly the Crown Inn, this small pub has been renamed the Green Squirrel after the old cricket team the owners used to play in. It has a modern interior and a dedicated games room. The pub has strong roots in the local community and is quite friendly. There is a small sheltered area out the back for smokers and two wood-burning stoves for the winter. It is right on the main bus route between Rochdale and Accrington. Live music plays on Sunday evenings.
🏾🚃(464)♣ᐟᐟ

Heapey

Top Lock
Copthurst Lane, PR6 8LS (alongside canal at Johnson's Hillock)
☼ 11-11 ☎ (01257) 263376
Beer range varies ⊞
Excellent canalside pub where nine real ales are served in oversized lined glasses, mostly from micros, including a mild and either a porter or stout, together with a beer from Timothy Taylor and Coniston breweries, plus up to three real ciders. An annual beer festival is held in October, with around 100 ales to try in the pub and marquee. There is a covered smoking area. Live music plays on a Thursday. From Easter onwards there is an upstairs ice cream parlour. Locally produced food is available all day every day. A former local CAMRA Pub of the Year. Q❁◐●Pᐟᐟ⊟

Helmshore

Robin Hood ⃝
288 Holcombe Road, BB4 4NP (on B6235)
☼ 4-11; 12-midnight Sat & Sun ☎ (01706) 213180
Hydes Original, Jekyll's Gold, Finest; guest beers ⊞
Just down the road from Helmshore Textile Museum, the Robin Hood is a small heritage pub and a vital part of the community. With an original interior and windows, it has a good atmosphere that the locals add to. The pub has a range of Hydes beers and two locally sourced guests. The inside is divided into three rooms so it is easy to find a quiet corner near the pub's two open fires in the winter.
🏾🚃(11)♣

Hest Bank

Hest Bank ✅
2 Hest Bank Lane, LA2 6DN
☼ 11.30-11 (11.30 Fri); 11-11 Sat; 11-10.30 Sun
☎ (01524) 824339 ⊕ hestbankinn.com
Black Sheep Best Bitter; Lancaster Blonde; Thwaites Wainwright; guest beer ⊞
An historic pub dating from 1554 with canalside garden, it was formerly a coaching inn for travellers crossing Morecambe Bay to Grange-over-Sands. One of the older rooms in the pub functions as a locals' bar, while another smaller bar plus other rooms on differing levels are mostly used by diners. Wednesday is quiz night, Thursday steak night. 🏾Q❁◐⊞🚃(5,55)♣P

Heysham

Royal
7 Main Street, LA3 2RN (70yds towards St Patrick's Chapel from Heysham Village bus stop)
☼ 12-11.30 (12.30am Fri & Sat); 12-11 Sun
☎ (01524) 859298
Thwaites Lancaster Bomber; guest beers ⊞
A 15th-century inn in the heart of the village. As you enter the pub a tiny locals' bar is on the right and a restaurant is on the left; the main bar is accessed via a winding passage and opens onto a large landscaped garden (till 11pm). Six handpumps provide the beers, often including ales from York and Cross Bay. Forthcoming guest beers are usually listed on the website. Outside is a covered and heated smoking area.
🏾Q⌛❁◐▶⊞🚃(4,5)Pᐟᐟ

Higher Wheelton

Golden Lion ⃝ ✅
369 Blackburn Road, PR6 8HP (on A674)
☼ 12-midnight (1am Fri & Sat; 11.30 Sun) ☎ (01254) 830855
Thwaites Nutty Black, Original, Wainwright, Lancaster Bomber, seasonal beers; guest beers ⊞
In the centre of the village, this stone-built single-bar pub has a comfortable bar/lounge with a partitioned-off games area. The walls are adorned with old photographs of the area, and TV sports fans are well catered for. Outside drinking areas are to the front and rear, and good-value meals are served all day. Guest beers are from the Thwaites 1807 Cask Club range. 🏾❁◐🚃(124)♣Pᐟᐟ

Hoghton

Royal Oak ⃝ ✅
Blackburn Old Road, Riley Green, PR5 0SL (at A675/A674 jct)
☼ 11.30-11; 12-10.30 Sun ☎ (01254) 201445
Thwaites Nutty Black, Original, Wainwright, Lancaster Bomber, seasonal beers; guest beers ⊞
Stone-built pub on the old road between Preston and Blackburn, near Riley Green basin on the Leeds-Liverpool canal, popular with diners and drinkers. Rooms, including a dining room and alcoves, radiate from the central bar. Low-beamed ceilings and horse brasses give the pub a rustic feel. This Thwaites tied house is a regular award winner, and acts as an outlet for its seasonal beers and its guest range from the 1807 Cask Club. Hoghton Towers is nearby. 🏾Q❁◐🚃(152)P

Lancaster

Borough ✅
3 Dalton Square, LA1 1PP (near town hall)
☼ 9-11.30 ☎ (01524) 64170 ⊕ theboroughlancaster.co.uk
Lancaster Amber; guest beers ⊞
An upmarket town house built in 1824 but with a Victorian frontage, it is now a pub that succeeds in appealing both to food lovers and ale aficionados. The front area resembles a gentlemen's club, with deep-buttoned chairs and chandeliers, the large back room is a restaurant, and the bar is in a passage between them. Outside is a sheltered patio with covered smoking area. CAMRA members get a 30p discount. Poker night is Monday, comedy club Sunday evening. ❁◐&⇌🚃ᐟᐟ

Merchant's ✅

27 Castle Hill, LA1 1YN
✪ 11.30-11; 11-12.30 Fri & Sat; 12-11 Sun ☎ (01524) 66466
⊕ merchants1688.co.uk
Caledonian Deuchars IPA; Sharp's Doom Bar; guest beers ℍ
Converted wine merchants' cellars and an extensive outdoor drinking area create a peaceful haven from the hubbub of the city centre. The main drinking areas are in three separate tunnels, with a fourth forming the entrance and bar area. Quiz night is on Sunday. Look out for the stoneware bottles used in the construction of the cellar walls. ◑≒🖵

Penny Bank

51 Penny Street, LA1 1XF
✪ 11.30-11 (12.30am Fri & Sat); 12-11 Sun ☎ (01524) 61102
Caledonian Deuchars IPA; Tirril Old Faithful; guest beers ℍ
A former bank converted to a pub in the early 1990s, which has managed to create the feeling of a much older town-centre corner pub. Popular with shoppers during the day, it is part of the vibrant Lancastrian social scene during the evenings. Live music from local bands features every Wednesday. ≒🖵

Sun

63 Church Street, LA1 1ET (on B6480 S of Wennington)
✪ 10-midnight ☎ (01524) 66006
⊕ thesunhotelandbar.co.uk
Lancaster Amber, Black, Red, Blonde; guest beers ℍ
Quality is the name of the game here. The decor combines a mixture of exposed stonework, wood panelling and solid furniture, with ambient candlelight in the evenings. Some original features remain, including stone fireplaces and a well. The pub is the primary outlet for Lancaster Brewery in the city, as well as offering up to four guest beers. Wi-Fi internet access is available. Outside is a peaceful courtyard with a heated and covered smoking area. ⏱🏨◑≒🖵

Water Witch

Tow Path, Aldcliffe Road, LA1 1SU (on canal towpath near Penny Street bridge)
✪ 11-midnight; 12-11 Sun ☎ (01524) 63828
⊕ thewaterwitch.co.uk
Beer range varies ℍ
The Water Witch was a passenger packet boat that once plied the Lancaster canal. The building, originally a canal company stable block, assumed its present name and use in 1978, the first true canalside pub on this stretch of water. Wedged between the towpath and a retaining wall, it is long and narrow, with bare stone walls and floors. A mezzanine floor and the space underneath it are used mainly for dining. There are seats on the towpath. Quiz night is Thursday. 🏨🏨◑≒🖵

White Cross 🏆 ✅

Quarry Road, LA1 4XT (behind town hall, on canal towpath)
✪ 11.30-11; 11-12.30am Fri & Sat; 12-11 Sun
☎ (01524) 33999 ⊕ thewhitecross.co.uk
Caledonian Deuchars IPA; Sharp's Doom Bar; Theakston Old Peculier; Tirril Old Faithful; guest beers ℍ
Recently refurbished, this sympathetically converted canalside warehouse has a light, spacious feel. Outside seating on both the towpath and a secluded patio area is ideal for sunny days.

Up to 14 beers are on the menu on any one visit, many sourced from north-west brewers. There is a famous Tuesday night weekly quiz, and a beer and pie festival every April. 🏨◑&≒🖵♣●P🔚

Lancaster University

Graduate College Bar

Barker House Village, LA2 0PF
✪ 7-11; 5-11.30 Fri & Sat (term time); 8-11 Sun
☎ (01524) 592824
Beer range varies ℍ
The Graduate College can be found at Alexandra Park, south-west of the main campus, its bar attracting an age range higher than at the average student watering hole. The choice of beer is good, with eight handpumps often offering Barngates, Hawkshead or Goose Eye. Four ciders are also served, usually including Westons but with many unusual ones. There is a beer fest in June and a cider fest in October. Curry night is Friday, while open mic night alternates with live bands on a Thursday. 🏨&🖵(3,4)♣●P🔚

Lea Town

Smith's Arms 🅛

Lea Lane, PR4 0RP (rear of BNFL Salwick) SD476311
✪ 12-midnight ☎ (01772) 760555
Thwaites Original, Wainwright, Lancaster Bomber, seasonal beers; guest beers ℍ
Open-plan country pub near the Preston-Lancaster Canal on route 62 of the national cycle network, known as the Slip Inn from when farmers would slip in for a drink. This Thwaites pub offers guest beers alternating with the seasonal beers from the 1807 Cask Club range, and it regularly wins awards for its food, so it can get busy, particularly on Sundays when meals are served all day. Home to darts and dominoes teams, it has a covered smoking area with a real log fire and leather sofas. 🏨🏨◑&♣P🔚

Leyland

Barristers

Towngate, PR25 2LR
✪ 10-midnight (1am Thu & Sun; 2am Fri & Sat)
☎ (01772) 456585
Moorhouse's Blonde Witch; Tetley Bitter; Thwaites Wainwright; guest beers ℍ
After many years as a keg-only pub and enduring a period of closure, this venue, formerly known as the George IV, is now a lively addition to Leyland's growing cask ale scene. There are bare floorboards and a bustling atmosphere, with plenty of wide-screen TVs around the walls for showing sporting events. Up to three changing guest beers, often from local micros such as Prospect and Bank Top, are on offer, and good-value lunches are served (not Sun). No children allowed. 🏨◑🖵(109,111)

Railway at Leyland 🅛 ✅

1 Preston Road, PR25 4NT
✪ 12-11 (1am Fri & Sat) ☎ (01772) 458427
⊕ therailwayatleyland.co.uk
Black Sheep Best Bitter; Lancaster Blonde; guest beers ℍ
A pub that has gone from strength to strength since undergoing a complete refurbishment in 2007. The bright and airy interior makes it a

welcoming hostelry, with four cask ales including two rotating guests and an occasional cider. Although a large pub, it can get extremely busy on weekend evenings when there is live entertainment. A first floor function room was added in 2012, which can accommodate up to 100 people. An annual beer festival is held in the summer (see website for details).
🕸🕪&⇌🖾(111)♣P⅃

Longridge

Corporation Arms 🅛
Lower Road, PR3 2YJ (near B6243/B6245 jct)
🌣 11-11; 12-10.30 Sun ☎ (01772) 782644
🌐 corporationarms.com
Beer range varies 🅗
Eighteenth-century country inn close to the Longridge reservoirs on the road to Ribchester, and handy for local walks. This free house has a reputation for excellent ale, food, service and accommodation (booking advised). Four handpumps serve beers sourced from local breweries; Bowland, Copper Dragon and Phoenix are some of the favourites. Real cider is available during summer months. There is an annual beer festival on the spring bank holiday weekend. Note the old horse trough outside, reputedly used by Oliver Cromwell to water his horse on his way to the Battle of Preston. 🕮Q🕸🖼🕪&🖾(3,3A)♣P⅃

Lostock Hall

Anchor ✔
43 Croston Road, PR5 5LA (300yds from B5254)
🌣 4.30-11.30 (midnight Fri); 11-midnight Sat; 12-midnight Sun ☎ (01772) 335637
Beer range varies 🅗
Just a short distance from the Tardy Gate shopping area and alongside the Preston to Blackburn railway line, this friendly community pub offers five changing cask ales from the Heineken Cellarman's Reserve list. In May and September it holds a beer festival in marquees on a large grassy area adjacent to the pub. To the rear is a boules pitch used in summer. Meals are served Sunday only, 3-5pm. 🕸🕪⇌🖾♣P⅃

Lytham

Taps ✔
12 Henry Street, FY8 5LE (between West Beach and Market Square)
🌣 11-11 (midnight Fri & Sat); 12-11 Sun ☎ (01253) 736226
🌐 thetaps.net
Titanic Taps Bitter; Greene King IPA; guest beers 🅗
Multi award-winning, one-roomed pub in the final four of CAMRA's National Pub of the Year competition in 2010, and local Pub of the Year on several occasions. Six to eight varying guest beers, including a cask mild and a regularly changing cider, are served. The pub supports the local RNLI and Fyld RFC and hosts an annual charity bike ride. Good wholesome food is served lunchtimes. There is a heated outside area. A busy, vibrant pub.
🕮Q🕸🕪&⇌🖾(7,11,68)♣🌢⅃

Mawdesley

Black Bull ✔
Hall Lane, L40 2QY (off B5246)

🌣 12-11 (7 Mon winter); 12-midnight Fri & Sat
☎ (01704) 822202
Black Sheep Best Bitter; Moorhouse's Pride of Pendle; Robinsons Unicorn; guest beers 🅗
A pub since 1610, this low-ceilinged stone building boasts some magnificent oak beams. Older village residents know the pub as Ell 'Ob, a reference to a coal-fired cooking range. Certificates on display record the pub's success in Lancashire's Best Kept Village competition. It has also earned awards for its numerous hanging baskets. During summer months the well-kept beer garden is popular with both drinkers and diners. There are up to two guest beers, often from local breweries. No evening meals on Monday. 🕮🕸🕪&🖾(337,347)♣P

Morecambe

Eric Bartholomew ✔
10 Euston Road, LA4 5DD
🌣 8-11 (midnight Thu-Sat) ☎ (01524) 405860
Greene King Abbot; Ruddles Best Bitter; guest beers 🅗
Opened in April 2004, this Wetherspoon pub is dedicated to Eric Morecambe. Near the sea front, it functions on two levels with an upstairs lounge and diner area. The long bar services an open-plan interior with pictures of 19th-century Morecambe and some artwork with a Morecambe and Wise theme. Westons Vintage and Organic ciders are usually on offer. Close to the shops and a public car park. Q🕪&⇌🖾🌢

Palatine ✔
The Crescent, LA4 5BZ (overlooking prom opp clock tower)
🌣 10.30-midnight (1am Fri & Sat); 10.30-11.30 Sun
☎ (01524) 410503 🌐 thepalatine.co.uk
Lancaster Amber, Blonde, Black, Red; guest beers 🅗
An Edwardian mid-terrace pub, the ground floor was completely transformed in late 2008 with much bare stone and woodwork revealed. The bar room is quite small, with some intimate corners. An upstairs room is rather different. Cosy and carpeted, many of the fittings such as leaded lights, shelving, and the fireplace appear to be original. Enjoy the spectacular views across the bay, especially at sunset. There are seats on the pavement out front. 🕸🕪&⇌🖾🌢⅃

Smuggler's Den ✔
56 Poulton Road, LA4 5HB
🌣 3-11 (midnight Fri & Sat) ☎ (01524) 421684
Taylor Landlord; guest beers 🅗
The oldest pub in Morecambe, circa 1640, though remodelled, this is a welcoming hostelry with five handpumps. Regular live folk music features throughout the year. An impressive open fire warms the bar during the colder months. There are ladies' and gents' darts teams, and a pub quiz. Westons Traditional Scrumpy is served. A bike rack is available for customers.
🕮🕸⇌🖾(5,430)♣🌢P⅃

Ormskirk

Disraelis
26 Church Street, L39 3AN (between clock tower and church)
🌣 10-11 (midnight Fri & Sat) ☎ (01695) 570737
Marston's Pedigree; guest beers 🅗

Previously known as the Snig's Foot, Disraelis dates from 1872 and was formerly a brewery. This popular town-centre pub has a central bar with three handpumps, and numerous seating areas. It provides an extensive food menu, with special offers. Lunchtimes and early evenings are often quiet, but the pub comes alive later, with a weekly quiz, poker and DJ nights. An upstairs function room is available for hire. ◑➡️❄️🖨️

Eureka

78 Halsall Lane, L39 3AX (just off the Five Ways crossroads, 10 mins from Ormskirk town centre)
🏵 12-midnight ☎ (01695) 581824
Sharp's Doom Bar; Tetley Bitter; Triple fff Alton's Pride Ⓗ
The Eureka is a community pub situated in a residential area just under a mile from Ormskirk town centre, near the Fiveways crossroads. A selection of games is available in the main bar. The pub has an outside patio complete with children's play area. The 375/385 Southport-Wigan bus stops at the crossroads at the end of Halsall Lane.
🏵❄️♿🖨️(375,385)♣P⅃

Farmers Club ✅

65 Burscough Street, L39 2EL
🏵 12-11.30 ☎ (01695) 572172
Tetley Bitter; Black Sheep Best Bitter Ⓗ
The Farmers Club was the 2011 CAMRA Club of the Year for the West Pennines region. The venue has a grand portico frontage with an architecturally impressive interior. Inside there is a full-size snooker table and facilities for darts and skittles. As this is a members' club, visitors are asked to present either a CAMRA membership card or a current Guide to gain entry. The pub is near the library. ❄️➡️♣⅃

Parbold

Stocks Tavern Ⓛ

16 Alder Lane, WN8 7NN (on A5209)
🏵 12-11.30 ☎ (01257) 462874
Beer range varies Ⓗ
Charming local village pub close to an idyllic section of the Leeds-Liverpool canal. It has low-beamed ceilings, wood floor and panelling, and offers two real fires and a quirky public bar, with a small annexe containing leather sofas. The pub attracts canal enthusiasts, walkers, cyclists and locals. Excellent good-value food is served lunchtimes Monday to Friday, all day Saturday and Sunday. Five handpumps dispense mainly local beers. There is a 50p per pint discount for CAMRA members. ❄️◑❄️➡️🖨️P

Wayfarer Ⓛ

1-3 Alder Lane, WN8 7NL (on A5209)
🏵 12-3, 5-11; 12-midnight Fri & Sat; 12-11 Sun
☎ (01257) 464600 ⊕ wayfarerparbold.co.uk
Tetley Bitter; guest beer Ⓗ
With up to six guest beers, including at least one LocAle, and three food menus, there is something here that will tickle your tastebuds. Converted from cottages built in the 18th century, the Wayfarer has panoramic views outside and a variety of styles on the inside – including a thoroughly modern restaurant, a bar with nooks and crannies, and a sophisticated dining area. It is close to the Leeds-Liverpool canal, Parbold Hill, and welcomes walkers. ❄️❄️◑♿➡️🖨️P⅃

Pendleton

Swan with Two Necks Ⓛ

Main Street, BB7 1PT (½ mile E of A59 turn-off)
🏵 7-11 Mon; closed Tue; 12-2.30, 6-11; 12-10.30 Sun
☎ (01200) 423112 ⊕ swanwithtwonecks.co.uk
Copper Dragon Golden Pippin; guest beers Ⓗ
A well-deserved winner of the local CAMRA branch's Pub of the Year award 2011 and finalist in CAMRA's national competition. Home-made food cooked to order is popular and the portions are for hungry walkers. There is outdoor seating in the rear garden and in front of the pub, looking out on to a small stream running through the beautifully kept village, and cosy open fires in the winter months. Look for the eclectic collection of teapots and Rosie the 25-year-old cat. A pub well worth finding.
❄️Q❄️◑♣👜P⅃

Penwortham

Black Bull ✅

83 Pope Lane, PR1 9BA
🏵 11-11 (midnight Fri & Sat); 12-11 Sun ☎ (01772) 752953
⊕ blackbull-penwortham.co.uk
Greene King IPA; Ruddles Best Bitter; guest beers Ⓗ
Attractive cottage-style inn dating back to the 1800s, which has managed to retain a village pub atmosphere despite its location in a well-populated area. On entering, a narrow passageway leads through to a central bar serving a number of drinking areas including a separate public bar. A friendly community pub, the many social events include a popular Thursday quiz, while local charities are actively supported. Two guest beers are always available. A Beautiful Beer gold award winner. Q❄️❄️➡️🖨️(3,3A)♣P⅃

Fleece Inn ✅

39 Liverpool Road, PR1 9XD (next to old water tower)
🏵 11-11; 12-11.30 Sun ☎ (01772) 745561
Tetley Bitter; Wells Bombardier; guest beers Ⓗ
An ex-sheriff's house that from the front presents a cosy village inn appearance, but inside has been extensively modernised. The interior is mostly open plan with wall dividers, but retains separate seating areas including a quiet raised room. Guest beers are sourced from Northern Brewing with interesting microbreweries often represented. To the rear, a former bowling green is now a large outdoor drinking area and children's playground. The food is varied and popular, and the pub can get busy at times. ❄️❄️◑♿🖨️(2,3)P⅃

Poulton-le-Fylde

Castle Gardens ✅

Poulton Road, FY6 7NH
🏵 11.30-11 (midnight Fri & Sat) ☎ (01253) 890015
Black Sheep Best Bitter; Taylor Landlord; Thwaites Original; guest beers Ⓗ
Recently converted to the Ember pub and dining brand, the Castle Gardens proudly sports its Cask Marque and has between five and 10 cask ales on at any one time. It is a fantastic food pub with a variety of award-winning dishes and menus. Changing beer menus match the seasons and a warm, friendly welcome is given every time. The pub is perfect for drinking and family dining alike. A popular quiz is held on Tuesday.
❄️❄️❄️◑♿🖨️(14)P⅃

Old Town Hall ✅
5 Church Street, FY6 7AP
✪ 11-11 (11.30 Thu; 11.45 Fri & Sat); 12-11 Sun
☎ (01253) 892257
Copper Dragon Golden Pippin; Jennings Cumberland Ale; Moorhouse's Blonde Witch; Three B's Bee Blonde; guest beers ⊞
A venue that was converted from council offices in 1988 and originally called the Bay Horse. The first floor bar and lounge may open on busy weekend evenings. Live music is on Saturday evenings and occasonal Fridays, when it can get very busy. Large TVs show sports events. It has a range of up to five changing cask ales featuring Copper Dragon, Jennings, Moorhouse's and Three B's plus three other breweries. Handy for buses and trains. No car park but there is a large municipal one to the rear.
Q🕭🚲➡️(2,42,84)

Thatched House 🅛 ✅
30 Ball Street, FY6 7BQ
✪ 11.30-11 (11.30 Thu; midnight Fri & Sat); 12-11 Sun
☎ (01253) 891063
Lytham Thatched House Bitter; guest beers ⊞
A mock-Tudor building in the grounds of a Norman church. The present pub was built in 1910, replacing an ancient inn probably called the Green Man. Pictures of sporting heroes decorate the wooden panelled walls. There is occasional live music, and three coal fires blaze away in winter. Thatched House Bitter is brewed by Lytham brewery, served alongside five other ales. It hosts regular mini beer festivals from particular breweries or regions. It is handy for buses and trains and there is a large car park close by.
🏚🍺🕭➡️(2,42,84)♣︎⌐

Preston

Bitter Suite
53 Fylde Road, PR1 2XQ
✪ 12-3, 6-11 (not Mon eve); 12-midnight Fri & Sat; 7-11 Sun
☎ (01772) 827007 🌐 bittersuitepreston.co.uk
Beer range varies ⊞
A genuine free house, it serves six guest beers from microbreweries, with an emphasis on Yorkshire brewers. Guests change almost hourly and it hosts at least four mini festivals each year. It has a single-room bar set back from Fylde Road at the side of the unrelated Mad Ferret. Simple home-cooked lunches including pies and burgers are served weekdays. Although it is surrounded by university buildings, it is not primarily a student bar. Live music plays on Wednesday and Saturday, and an upstairs room is available for hire. Twice winner of local CAMRA Pub of the Year.
🎵🍺➡️(31,35,61)♣︎

Continental
South Meadow Lane, PR1 8JP (off Fishergate Hill)
✪ 12-midnight (1am Fri & Sat; 11.30 Sun) ☎ (01772) 499425
🌐 newcontinental.net
Beer range varies ⊞
Beside the River Ribble, the main railway line and Miller Park. A two-times winner of local CAMRA Pub of the Year, this place has a main bar area plus lounge with a real fire in winter and conservatories overlooking the garden. Live music and theatre feature regularly in a separate arts/events space that is also used for beer festivals – check the website or follow @newcontinenal on Twitter for details. Seven microbrewery beers are on offer

including the house ale from Marble, a beer from Pictish and a dark beer. Freshly cooked meals are served lunchtimes and evenings (no food Mon).
🏚Q🍺🕮🕭➡️(3A)👉P⌐

Grey Friar ✅
144 Friargate, PR1 2EJ (jct of Ringway)
✪ 9-midnight (1am Fri & Sat) ☎ (01772) 558542
Greene King Abbot; Ruddles Best Bitter; Theakston Old Peculier; guest beers ⊞
Modern open-plan Wetherspoon pub with raised areas to the side and rear, in a fine real-ale-drinking part of the city, formerly a carpet store. Preston's students and citizens, both young and old, appreciate the range of ales and food at good prices, with up to seven guests beers on sale. The social mix creates a bustling atmosphere and the bar can get extremely busy at weekends. The pub plays an active role in local CAMRA recruiting.
🕮🕭➡️

Market Tavern
33-35 Market Street, PR1 2ES
✪ 10.30-9 (11 Thu; midnight Fri & Sat); 12-9 Sun
☎ (01772) 254425
Beer range varies ⊞
Three handpumps serve a wide range of guest beers from all over the country, usually from micros with no particular emphasis. This is a small, popular, city-centre local in a pedestrianised area overlooking the historic Victorian outdoor market. A superb selection of imported bottled beers is also on offer, plus German Weisse on draught. Outside seating is available in summer. With two intimate seating booths, conversation rules in this former local CAMRA Pub of the Year. No food is served, but you are welcome to bring your own. Q🐾🚲

Old Black Bull ♟ ✅
35 Friargate, PR1 2AT
✪ 10.30-11 (midnight Fri & Sat); 12-10.30 Sun
☎ (01772) 823397
Beer range varies ⊞
Mock-Tudor city-centre pub now completely free of tie. A small front vault, a main bar with distinctive black and white floor tiles, two comfortable lounge areas and a pool table all combine to make this a popular venue. There is also a patio to the rear. Live music plays on Saturday evenings and all TV sport is shown. Nine guest beers come from micros or small independents sourced from all over Britain. Three times winner of local CAMRA Pub of the Year.
🐾🍺➡️➡️♣︎⌐

Old Vic 🅛
78 Fishergate, PR1 2UH
✪ 11.30-11 (midnight Fri; 1am Sat); 12-midnight Sun
☎ (01772) 254690
Courage Directors; guest beers ⊞
Opposite the railway station, and on bus routes into the city, the Old Vic is a popular pub that can get busy at weekends. Seven handpumps offer the widest range of LocAle beers in the area, with Moorhouse's and several smaller microbreweries usually represented. Big screens show sports events while the pub hosts thriving pool and darts teams. Meals are served 12-5pm (1-4pm Sun). To the rear is an outdoor decked smoking area and a car park that is only available Sunday and evenings.
🐾🕮🚲➡️♣︎⌐

Olde Dog & Partridge ✅
44 Friargate, PR1 2AT
🕐 11-3, 6-11.30; 11-1am Sat; 12-midnight Sun
☎ (01772) 252217
Holts Best Bitter; Taylor Landlord; Tetley Dark Mild; guest beers Ⓗ
Down-to-earth city-centre pub that specialises in rock music. Five real ales include two guest beers that come from the SIBA direct delivery scheme. The landlord has been at the pub for more than 30 years. There is a monthly live music night, a weekly quiz on Thursday and a rock DJ on Sunday evening. Excellent-value pub lunches are served (no food Sun) and a covered Smokey-O-Joes smoking area is provided at the rear.
❀⬭◖⇌🚌♣♠≜

Stanley Arms
24 Lancaster Road, PR1 1DA
🕐 12-9 (11 Thu & Sun; 2am Fri & Sat) ☎ (01772) 827957
Beer range varies Ⓗ
Adjacent to Preston's Guild Hall concert venue, and close to its iconic bus station, this wood-panelled and tiled pub has one room on the ground level, and an upstairs room for northern soul nights Friday and Saturday, which is also available to hire. Four handpumps dispense changing ales from the more interesting end of the Cellarman's Choice range. Full tasting notes are displayed behind the bar. Food is available lunchtimes Monday to Friday, 12-5pm Saturday. In summer there is outside seating in front of the pub. Q❀◖⇌🚌

Wheatsheaf Ⓛ
50 Water Lane, PR2 2NL (on A583)
🕐 11-11 (11.30 Fri & Sat); 12-10.30 Sun ☎ (01772) 725917
Courage Directors; guest beers Ⓗ
Victorian local on the way to Preston Marina, a mile from the city centre, owned by Amber Taverns, whose offices are upstairs. It normally has four guest beers, with at least one from Moorhouse's and others from small breweries from the north of England. Big on live sports (the heated outside courtyard has its own TV) and with beer prices among the lowest in the area, this is deservedly a popular venue. Live music plays Friday and Saturday nights. Daytime snacks are available. There is disabled access through the courtyard.
❀♿🚌(68,35)♣≜

Rawtenstall

Craven Heifer Ⓛ ✅
264-266 Burnley Road, BB4 8LA (on A682, N of Rawtenstall)
🕐 5 (11 Sat)-11, 12-11 Sun ☎ (01706) 214757
Moorhouse's Black Cat, Premier, Witch Hunt, Blond Witch, Pendle Witches Brew Ⓗ
A fantastic local pub with a comfortable interior that has a mixture of both modern and traditional styles. With all the Moorhouse's beers on handpump, including its seasonal specials, and a selection of spirits, the Craven Heifer is a quiet, friendly pub with lots of diversity and charm.
Q❀🚌(X43)♣≜

White Lion Ⓛ ✅
72 Burnley Road, BB4 8EW
🕐 4.30 (2 Fri; 12 Sat & Sun)-midnight ☎ (01706) 213117
Black Sheep Best Bitter; Copper Dragon Golden Pippin; guest beers Ⓗ
A large, friendly pub with enthusiastic and loyal locals. Changing guest beers, sourced both locally and from elsewhere around the country, help add to the classic atmosphere. A particular favourite for CAMRA meetings is the Black Coral Stout, from Hornbeam Brewery. Lively discussions about the beer or local politics are regularly heard around the bar. Situated on the main road from Manchester to Burnley, just out of Rawtenstall town centre.
❀🚌(X43)♣P≜

St Annes on the Sea

Fifteens of St Annes 🍴 Ⓛ ✅
42 St Annes Road West, FY8 1RF (in St Annes Square)
🕐 11-11 (midnight Fri & Sat); 12-11 Sun ☎ (01253) 725852
🌐 fifteensstannes.com
Hawkshead Stout; Moorhouse's Fifteens; guest beers Ⓗ
Converted from a former bank, Fifteens has one of the world's most luxurious snugs, which used to be the original bank vault. Five cask ales are always available, including a local brew as well as a traditional cider. The licensee is a true cask ale enthusiast. Afternoon tea with home-made cake is served. Once a month you can listen to a DJ playing Motown classics and northern soul favourites. Live sport is shown on three screens. There is a loyalty card scheme. ♿⇌🚌(11,68)♣♠≜

Trawl Boat Inn Ⓛ ✅
36-38 Wood Street, FY8 1QR (in side street off St Annes Square)
🕐 8am-midnight (1am Fri & Sat) ☎ (01253) 783080
Greene King Abbot; Moorhouse's Trawlboat; Ruddles Best Bitter; guest beers Ⓗ
A Wetherspoon's that used to be a solicitors' office, and is named after an old pub that closed many years ago. Spacious, warm and friendly, it caters for all tastes and runs a discount scheme for CAMRA members. Five different guest ales are always available. Situated just off the main square, it is handy for the shops, and a short walk from the promenade and beach. A credit to all.
🏛Q❀◖♿⇌🚌≜

Salwick

Windmill Tavern
Clifton Lane, PR4 0YE (off A583 via Clifton village, at BNFL Salwick works)
🕐 closed Mon; 12-11 (midnight Fri & Sat; 10.30 Sun)
☎ (01772) 687203 🌐 windmilltavern.com
York Yorkshire Terrier; guest beers Ⓗ
Built around 1778, Clifton windmill is the Fylde's oldest and tallest, constructed in stone. The tavern has only been a pub since 1974 and the restaurant was still a working mill until recently. Up to four beers are on sale, with ales from York and local breweries. There are plans to introduce real cider. Drink and relax beneath the main tower of the mill, or dine in the restaurant serving excellent locally sourced food. There is live music on Fridays. Trains stop four times a day (not Sun).
🏛❀◖⇌🚌(77,75)♣P≜

Samlesbury

New Hall Tavern Ⓛ
Cuerdale Lane, PR5 0XA (on B6230)
🕐 12-11 (midnight Thu-Sat) ☎ (01772) 877942
🌐 newhalltavern.com

Shepherd Neame Spitfire; guest beers Ⓗ
On a crossroads just off junction 31 of the M6, close to the InBev brewery, this pub has a large car park and a heated outdoor smoking area. Indoors it is divided up by wood and glass panels, providing separate areas for dining. Up to six real ales are served, with guests often from local micros. Home-cooked food is – where possible – sourced from local produce. Old photos and prints give an insight into the history of the area, which includes the nearby Samlesbury Hall. 﨡🏵️🅳🤝♣️P🗜️

Silverdale

Woodlands

Woodlands Drive, LA5 0RU
✪ 6-11; 12-midnight Sat; 12-11.30 Sun ☎ (01524) 701655
Beer range varies Ⓗ
Large country house dating from about 1878 on an elevated site, converted to a pub with only minimal alterations. Most of the trade is provided by locals. The bar has a large fireplace as big as the counter and enjoys great views across Morecambe Bay. Beer pumps are in another room with a list of the four ales on the wall. Home-made sandwiches are served at weekends. The smoking area is covered and sheltered. A beer festival takes place in October, and quiz night is the last Sunday of the month. 﨡Q🏵️🚲🍴🖼️(33)♣️👟P🗜️

Slaidburn

Hark to Bounty

BB7 3EP SD710524
✪ 9am-12.30am (1.30am Fri & Sat) ☎ (01200) 446246
⊕ harktobounty.co.uk
Theakston Best Bitter, Old Peculier; guest beers Ⓗ
Traditional country inn in the heart of the Forest of Bowland, serving up to four beers from a small central bar. Guests have included beers from Tirril, Caledonian and Brains. The pub prides itself on its home-cooked food, which includes breakfasts and afternoon teas, with a special fish night on Friday. Several real fires in the long, narrow interior welcome walkers on a wintry day. There is a large beer garden and nine en-suite rooms. A youth hostel is close by. 﨡Q🏵️🍴🅳🖼️(10,10a)P🗜️

Tockholes

Royal Arms 🄻

Tockholes Road, BB3 0PA (3 miles W of Darwen)
✪ 12-11 (6 Mon; 10.30 Sun) ☎ (01254) 705373
Beer range varies Ⓗ
Traditional free house, with many beers coming from local breweries. Formed from two cottages knocked together, the original stone walls have been retained, along with flagged and wooden floors within its four back-to-back rooms. It is on the edge of the west Pennine moors, close to Darwen Tower and overlooking Roddlesworth Woods. The pub welcomes walkers with a choice of three real fires in winter. There is an annual beer festival and good-value meals are offered Wednesday to Sunday. Note that it does not open on some Mondays during the year. 﨡Q🏵️🅳🖼️(223,535)P

Tontine

Delph 🄻

Sefton Road, WN5 8UJ (off B5206)

✪ 11.30-11.30 (12.30am Fri & Sat); 12-11.30 Sun
☎ (01695) 622239
Beer range varies Ⓗ
A warm welcome and a friendly atmosphere greet you here. The pub retains a separate vault with a pool table and TV. Good-value meals complement the various real ales served in a relaxed environment. Popular with all age groups, children are welcome. Darts, dominoes and pool are played in the local league and a quiz night is held on Wednesdays. 🏵️🅳🚉(Orrell)♣️P🗜️

Waddington

Waddington Arms

West View, BB7 3HP
✪ 11-11 ☎ (01200) 423262 ⊕ waddingtonarms.co.uk
Bowland Hen Harrier; Greys Best Bitter; Lancaster Blond; Tirril 1823; guest beers Ⓗ
In the middle of the pretty village from which it takes its name, this pub specialises in food, using local produce for bar meals and in its popular restaurant. There are fires in the winter and excellent outdoor areas for good weather. Public rooms are warm, clean and well-appointed. Moorhouse's brews The Waddy as a special for the pub and there is a good selection of bottled cider and wine. The pub has six bedrooms and is family friendly. 﨡Q🏵️🍴🅳🅖🖼️(C5,C15,10a)♣️P🗜️

Walmer Bridge

Walmer Bridge Inn ✪

65 Liverpool Old Road, PR4 5QE
✪ 4-midnight (1am Fri & Sat); 12-midnight Sun
☎ (01772) 612296
Robinson's Unicorn; guest beers Ⓗ
Village local comprising two rooms, a recently refurbished lounge and a vault popular with the sporting fraternity. Photographs of bygone Walmer Bridge and Longton adorn the walls. Outside there is a large garden with a children's play area. The keen landlord usually has two changing guest beers on offer, while he also supplies cask ales for functions at the nearby village hall. 🏵️🍴🖼️(2)♣️P🗜️

Waterfoot

Boot & Shoe

Millar Barn Lane, Rossendale, BB4 7AU (turn N up Townsend St and past Bacup and Rawtenstall Grammar School)
✪ 4 (12 Sun)-1am ☎ (01706) 213828
⊕ yeoldebootandshoe.co.uk
Banks's Mild; Moorhouse's Boot & Shoe, Pendle Witches Brew Ⓗ
Small, low-ceilinged pub that is one of those hidden gems you find tucked away, surprising you with its size and character. The pub has its own house beer brewed by Moorhouse's, and also serves from two other handpumps. A large-screen TV for big football matches is in a room off to one side, but there is almost always a quiet corner somewhere. A large selection of food is served in the restaurant at the back. B&B is offered. 🏵️🍴🅳🗜️

Wennington

Bridge

Tatham, LA2 8NL (on B6480 S of Wennington)

✪ 12-11 (closed 2.30-5 Wed & Thu); 12-10.30 Sun
☎ (01524) 221326 ⊕ gndlanc.webs.com
Black Sheep Best Bitter; Everards Beacon; York Guzzler; guest beer ⒣
Two linked buildings – one dating from 1642, the other from 1744 – make up a small, cosy, low-beamed bar and two dining rooms. The pub is set in an isolated spot south of Wennington, but attracts a surprisingly large number of locals, as well as walkers in the summer months. It has not succumbed to the gastro market, but offers good, well-priced food. The pub features in a Turner painting. Quiz night is Friday. There is an associated caravan park and helipad.
≜Q✿✿⊷⬤▲≈⊟(80,81b)♣P⸜

Whalley

Dog Inn
55 King Street, BB7 9SP
✪ 11-11; 12-10.30 Sun ☎ (01254) 823009
⊕ dog-innwhalley.co.uk
Beer range varies ⒣
One of four pubs at a crossroads in the village, the Dog is a real drinker's paradise. Offering up to six handpumps on the large bar, beers come from across the UK, including Oakham and BrewDog. Osset, Phoenix, Brightside and Moorhouse's are some of the Northern breweries that have featured. Cider is also on offer from Lancaster and the Ribble Valley. There are three distinct seating areas together with a separate space for the TV. Food is available lunchtimes only.
✿⬤≈⊟(26,27,225)●⸜

Wilpshire

Rising Sun
797 Whalley New Road, BB1 9BE (on A666)
✪ 12-11.30 ☎ (01254) 747379
Theakston Best Bitter; guest beers ⒣
Built around 1893, this former Matthew Brown house, whose name can still be seen on the windows, is about two miles from Blackburn town centre. In the lounge a coal fire is aglow on cold winter nights and a piano encourages a sing-along on Saturday evenings. There is a separate bar where you can play cards and dominoes, and displayed on the wall are photos of old Blackburn pubs. Guest ales here are often from the local Thwaites and Three B's breweries.
≜Q⊲⬐≈⊟(225)♣⸜

Winmarleigh

Patten Arms
Park Lane, PR3 0JU (on B5272 3 miles N of Garstang)
✪ 4-11 (midnight Sat); 12-10 Sun ☎ (01995) 791484
Jennings Cumberland Ale; Tetley Bitter; guest beers ⒣
Genuine, isolated free house situated away from villages on a B-road, yet enjoying regular local custom. This early 19th-century Grade II-listed building has a single bar with a country pub feel, high-backed bench seats, cream-painted walls and open fires. There is a separate restaurant, and terraced seating overlooking a bowling green. Food is served all day Saturday and Sunday, evening meals Wednesday to Friday only. ≜✿⬤▲♣P⸜

Wray

George & Dragon
Main Street, LA2 8QG (off B6480)
✪ 6-11 Mon; 12-2, 5-midnight; 12-midnight Sat; 12-11 Sun
☎ (01524) 221403
Everards Beacon; guest beers ⒣
A genuine village local that also has an excellent reputation for its food. Inside, there are two bar rooms, of quite different sizes, and a restaurant. Unusual pub games are available, as is Wi-Fi broadband. There is a Wednesday night quiz. The extensive beer garden has an aviary, as well as an unheated but covered smoking area. Wray hosts a popular scarecrow festival in May.
≜Q✿⬤⊟(80,81B)♣⸜

Wrightington

White Lion
117 Mossy Lea Road, WN6 9RE (on B5290)
✪ 10.30-10.30; 12-midnight Thu-Sat; 12-10.30 Sun
☎ (01257) 425977 ⊕ thewhitelionlancs.co.uk
Beer range varies ⒣
Extremely popular country pub, with a good mix of drinkers and diners. Eight handpumps are in constant use, serving beers from the Marston's range. There is a weekly quiz on Tuesday and a poker league on Thursday. Themed evenings are held in the restaurant. The pub is family friendly, with a large garden area. It is reputed to be haunted by the ghost of an old lady who used to inhabit one of the cottages now making up the restaurant. ✿⬤⊲⬐⊟P⸜

Beers suitable for vegetarians and vegans

A number of cask and bottle-fermented beers in the Good Beer Guide are listed as suitable for vegetarians and vegans. The main ingredients used in cask beer production are malted grain, hops, yeast and water, and these present no problems for drinkers who wish to avoid animal products. But most brewers of cask beer use isinglass as a clearing agent: isinglass is derived from the bladders of certain fish, including the sturgeon. Isinglass is added to a cask when it leaves the brewery and attracts yeast cells and protein, which fall to the bottom of the container. Other clearing agents – notably Irish moss, derived from seaweed – can be used in place of isinglass and the Guide feels that brewers should take a serious look at replacing isinglass with plant-derived finings, especially as the sturgeon is an endangered species.

Vegans avoid dairy products: lactose, a by-product of cheese making, is used in milk stout, of which Mackeson is the best-known example.

LEICESTERSHIRE & RUTLAND

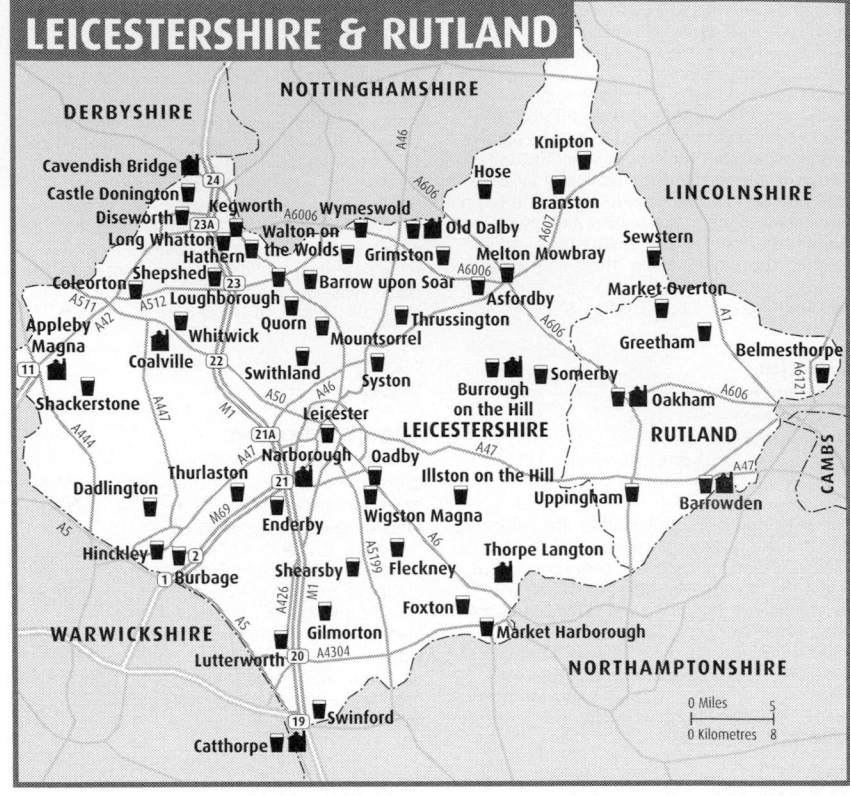

Asfordby

Horseshoes
128 Main Street, LE14 3SA
☼ 12-4, 7-11.30; 12-11.30 Fri ☎ (01664) 813392
Batemans XB, seasonal beers Ⓗ
At the heart of the village, this traditional community pub prides itself on providing a warm welcome to all. The pub is home to men's and ladies' darts teams as well as skittles and dominoes teams. Visitors to the Horseshoes will often see posters behind the bar advertising the landlord's annual trips to the Trooping the Colour event. At least two Batemans beers are always available and usually another from its seasonal range. ▲🚆(5,5A)⅃

Barrow upon Soar

Hunting Lodge
38 South Street, LE12 8LZ
☼ 11-midnight ☎ (01590) 412337
Adnams Broadside; Fuller's London Pride; guest beers Ⓗ
A comfortable bar, restaurant and inn with open fires and leather furniture. Good food from snacks to an à la carte menu can be enjoyed in the restaurant or alfresco in the large garden to the rear, with views towards Charnwood Forest. Accommodation is in six individually-styled bedrooms. ▲❀🚪◑&▲🚆(2)P⅃

Soar Bridge Inn
29 Bridge Street, LE12 8PN
☼ 12-11 (10.30 Sun) ☎ (01509) 412686

Everards Tiger, Original; guest beer Ⓗ
Situated next to the bridge that gave it its name, this pub is popular with walkers, boaters and drinkers. The large single-room interior divides into distinct areas, with a separate restaurant, function room and skittle alley. Outside there is a floodlit pétanque court, beer terrace and garden. Well-behaved dogs and children are welcome. Home-made food is available Tuesday to Sunday. The first Monday of the month is Grand Union Folk Club night and a weekly quiz is held on Thursday. The annual beer festival is a highlight.
▲❀◑▲🚆(K2,CB27)♣P⅃

Barrowden

Exeter Arms Ⓛ
28 Main Street, LE15 8EQ (1 mile S of A47)
☼ 12-2.30 (not Mon), 6-11; 12-3.30, 6-11 Sat; 12-5 Sun
☎ (01572) 747247

Barrowden Beech, Pilot, Hop Gear, Own Gear, seasonal ales Ⓗ
Collyweston slate-roofed pub with a fine view over the valley and village duck pond. It offers a warm welcome and serves highly regarded food. The patio area is the place to spend a sunny day. Pétanque is played here in the summer and dominoes in the winter. Folk music and quiz nights are hosted on alternate Mondays. Barrowden Brewery is situated in a barn to the rear. CAMRA award-winning ale Pilot won Beer of the Festival in Rugby. ▲Q✿⇆◑☙⌂(12)♣P⌐

Belmesthorpe

Blue Bell Ⓛ
Shepherds Walk, PE9 4JG TF042102
✪ 12-2 (not Mon), 6-11 (5-11.30 Fri); 12-11.30 Sat; 12-10.30 Sun ☎ (01780) 753081
Draught Bass; guest beers Ⓗ
Runner-up Rutland CAMRA Pub of the Year 2012, the Blue Bell is a historic village pub. Low ceilings, a roaring fire and stone walls are part of its charm. Six handpulls offer a wide range of well-kept guest beers, including at least one LocAle and real cider. Dogs on leads are welcome in the bar area. Good honest home-made pub food is available Tuesday to Sunday lunchtimes (booking advisable). ▲Q✿♣●P⌐

Branston

Wheel ☝ Ⓛ
Main Street, NG32 1RU
✪ closed Mon; 11-11; 12-10.30 Sun ☎ (01476) 870376
Batemans XB; guest beers Ⓗ
Like most of the buildings in the village, this attractive 18th-century pub is built using local stone. There is a small bar with some seating and a larger restaurant area, sympathetically renovated. The deceptively large outdoor area is quiet and relaxing in the summer months. The Wheel boasts an extensive lunch and evening food menu using locally sourced ingredients where possible, including produce from the nearby Belvoir Estate. There is regular live music and cask cider is often on the bar during the summer. Local CAMRA Pub of the Year 2012. ▲Q✿◑Ⅾ☙⌐P⌐

Burbage

Lime Kilns
Watling Street, LE10 3ED (on A5 between M69 jct and A47 Dodwells roundabout)
✪ 12-3, 5.30-11; 12-11 Sat; 12-10.30 Sun ☎ (01455) 631158
⊕ limekilnsinn.co.uk
Jennings Cocker Hoop; Marston's Burton Bitter, Pedigree; guest beers Ⓗ
Situated alongside the Ashby Canal, the pub was originally an 18th-century coaching inn. It offers customers free moorings, a large beer garden by the canal, a children's play area and free Wi-Fi. The first floor lounge has canal views and an open fire in winter. The guest beers change regularly and real ciders include Thatchers Traditional and Cheddar Valley. Traditional food is served, with special deals including Monday curry nights and pie and a pint on Wednesdays. ▲Q✿◑●P

Burrough on the Hill

Grant's Free House Ⓛ
Main Street, LE14 2JQ
✪ closed Mon; 6-11 Tue; 12-2, 5-11 (midnight Sat); 12-11 Sun
☎ (01664) 452141
Parish PSB, Farm Gold, Burrough Bitter, Poachers Ⓗ, Baz's Bonce Blower Ⓖ
Formerly a 16th-century inn known as the Stag & Hounds, Grant's Free House is a refurbished three-room, split-level pub, firmly established as the home of the Parish Brewery. A full range of Parish beers is always available from the adjacent brew house. A beer festival is held annually over the late May bank holiday weekend. ▲Q✿◑Ⅾ⌐P⌐

Castle Donington

Jolly Potters
36 Hillside, DE74 2NH
✪ 12 (11 Sat)-midnight; 12-10.30 Sun ☎ (01332) 811912
Draught Bass; Fuller's London Pride; Marston's Pedigree; Taylor Landlord Ⓗ
The landlord and locals are always happy to chat to visitors at this traditional, friendly pub, built at the turn of the 20th century. The open-plan front room divides into bar and lounge areas – the basic stone-floored bar has traditional wooden pews and there is a back room with jukebox, TV and dartboard. A collection of framed beer mats and cards decorates the walls, and cups, jugs and tankards hang from the ceiling. ▲✿♣⌐

Catthorpe

Cherry Tree
Main Street, LE17 6DB
✪ 12-2.30, 5-11 (12.30am Fri); 12-12.30am Sat; 12-11.30 Sun
☎ (01788) 860430 ⊕ cherrytree-pub.co.uk
Jennings Bitter; guest beers Ⓗ
Excellent free house at the heart of the community, welcoming to all. The range of three guest ales changes regularly, often including beers from Catthorpe's microbrewery, Dow Bridge. Locally sourced food is available, including a large selection of £5 specials. Railway and aviation memorabilia adorn the walls, including a jet fighter ejector seat. Outside, a south-facing decked area and small garden overlook the River Avon. The annual beer festival is on the last weekend in June. ▲Q✿◑Ⅾ▲⌐♣⌐

Coleorton

King's Arms
187 The Moor, LE67 8GD
✪ 12-11 ☎ (01530) 815435 ⊕ kingsarmscoleorton.co.uk
Draught Bass; guest beers Ⓗ
Lively yet cosy family-run free house set in the heart of the National Forest. The manager's father owns the Tap House Brewery and a range of Tap House beers is always available. Home-made, traditional food is served daily (no meals Sun eve and Mon). Outside there is a large car park, beer garden, secure children's play area and pétanque pitch. Regular events and beer festivals are publicised on the website. One of local CAMRA's Most Improved Pubs in 2011. ▲Q✿◑Ⅾ⌐P⌐

Dadlington

Dog & Hedgehog Ⓛ
2 The Green, CV13 6JB
🌣 12-11 (4 Sun) ☎ (01455) 213151
⊕ dogandhedgehog.com
Quartz Dadlington Hamlet; Tunnel Henry Tudor Red Ale; Wood Farm Best Bitter Ⓗ
A friendly free house saved from closure in 2011 by the present owners. Situated in a picturesque location, the terrace and beer garden overlook the Ashby Canal and famous site of the Battle of Bosworth (1485). The bar boasts three LocAles, two rebadged for the pub – Henry Tudor is Tunnel Nelson's Column and Dadlington Hamlet is Quartz Crystal. The restaurant serves the best in locally produced food. Whether dining or enjoying a pint, a warm welcome is assured. ♨Q✿◐🖶(86)P

Diseworth

Plough Inn ✅
33 Hall Gate, DE74 2QJ
🌣 11.30-3, 5-11; 11.30-11 Fri & Sat; 12-10.30 Sun
☎ (01332) 810333 ⊕ theploughdiseworth.com
Draught Bass; Greene King Abbot; Marston's Pedigree; guest beers Ⓗ
Situated in a village with many half-timbered buildings, this is a cosy, multi-roomed pub with parts dating back to the 13th century. Low-beamed ceilings and exposed brickwork are just some of the original features discovered during renovation work in the 1990s. There is an interesting display of old photographs of the area. Tasty home-made food is served. The spacious, well-presented beer garden is popular in summer. Joint local CAMRA Village Pub of the Year 2011. ♨✿◐🖤🖶♣♠P'—

Enderby

New Inn
51 High Street, LE19 4AG
🌣 12-2.30 (not Mon), 6-11; 12-3, 6 (5.30 Fri)-11.30 Thu-Sat; 12-3, 7-11 Sun ☎ (0116) 286 3126
Everards Beacon, Sunchaser, Tiger, Original, seasonal beers; guest beers Ⓗ
Friendly thatched village local dating from 1549 tucked away at the top of the High Street. Everards' first tied house, the pub is well known locally for the quality of its beer and is frequented by Everards' brewery staff. Three rooms are served by a central bar, with long alley skittles and a snooker room to the rear. Outside there is a patio area and garden. Lunches are served Tuesday to Saturday. Q✿◐🖶♣P'—

Fleckney

Golden Shield Ⓛ
46 Main Street, LE8 8AN
🌣 12-2.30 (not Mon & Tue), 4-11; 12-midnight Fri & Sat; 11.30-11 Sun ☎ (0116) 240 2366
Banks's Bitter; Greene King Abbot; John Smith's Bitter; Taylor Landlord; guest beers Ⓗ
Village pub in the heart of Leicestershire serving six real ales, including ever-changing LocAles and microbrewery beers. Regular beer festivals are also held. Home-cooked and à la carte meals are available lunchtimes Wednesday to Sunday and evenings Tuesday to Saturday – Sunday lunches are always popular. ✿◐🖼🖶(49B)♣P'—

Foxton

Bridge 61 Ⓛ ✅
Bottom Lock, LE16 7RA
🌣 10-11 ☎ (0116) 279 2285 ⊕ foxtonboats.co.uk
Adnams Southwold Bitter; guest beers Ⓗ
The smaller of the two pubs situated at the bottom of the famous flight of 10 Foxton locks, the two-roomed interior comprises a snug with a serving-hatch bar and a larger room with wide doors that open out onto the waterfront. The garden has barbecue facilities – an ideal spot for watching the boats pass by. At least one of the two guest beers is from the nearby Langton Brewery. ♨Q☾✿◐🖤🖶♠'—

Gilmorton

Red Lion ✅
Main Street, LE17 5LT
🌣 12-2.30 (not Mon), 5-11; 12-10.30 Sun ☎ (01455) 203564
⊕ theredliongilmorton.co.uk
Banks's Mild; Marston's Pedigree; guest beers Ⓗ
Village bistro pub, popular with locals and visiting diners, which can be busy at weekends. It is open plan, bright and spacious, with a friendly and modern feel. As well as the two regular beers, there are usually three guests from the Marston's list. Food is made with local produce where possible including eggs from the pub's chickens and herbs from the garden, all cooked on the premises. ♨✿◐🖤P'—

Greetham

Plough 🍷 Ⓛ ✅
23 Main Street, LE15 7NJ (1 mile off A1 towards Oakham on B668) SK925144
🌣 11-11 (11-3, 5-11 winter); 12-10.30 Sun
☎ (01572) 813613 ⊕ greethamplough.co.uk
Taylor Golden Best; guest beers Ⓗ
A true village pub with friendly staff and a warm atmosphere, serving excellent beer including a mild, and Westons Old Rosie real cider. Good food is available and a variety of pub games is on offer, plus a regular quiz. With the Viking Way close by, it is a popular spot for walkers, and Rutland Water is within easy reach by car or bicycle. Dogs are welcome. Local CAMRA Pub of the Year 2012. Q✿◐🖨🖤🖶(RF2)♣♠P'—

Grimston

Black Horse
Main Street, LE14 3BZ
🌣 12-3, 6-11; 12-6 Sun ☎ (01664) 812358
⊕ theblackhorsegrimston.co.uk
Adnams Southwold Bitter; Marston's Pedigree; Wychwood Hobgoblin; guest beer Ⓗ
Overlooking the village green, this pub is popular and busy lunchtimes and evenings. It has a large open-plan bar on two levels where a wide range of good food is available. A pétanque court hosts several local teams. A regular weekday daytime bus from Melton Mowbray stops outside the pub. Local CAMRA Pub of the Year 2010 and 2011. ♨✿◐🖤(23)♣'—

Hathern

Dew Drop ✅
49 Loughborough Road, LE12 5HY

❁ 12-3, 6-midnight (7-1am Fri-Sun) ☎ (01509) 842438
Greene King XX Mild, H&H Bitter; guest beers Ⓗ
Traditional two-roomed local with a large bar and
small, comfortable lounge with real fires. Do not
miss a visit to the totally unspoilt toilets with their
tiled walls and original features. A large range of
malt whiskies is stocked and cobs are available at
lunchtime. ♨Q🐕🍴🖳♣P🚭

Hinckley

Ashby Road Sports & Social Club Ⓛ
✔

Hangmans Lane, LE10 3DA (on N edge of town off
B4667 Ashby Rd) SP429959
❁ 7 (5 Fri; 12 Sat)-11.30; 12-11 Sun ☎ (01455) 615159
Sharp's Doom Bar; guest beers Ⓗ
CAMRA members are welcome at this Sports &
Social Club. The large bar has pool, darts, dominoes
and a monthly quiz. Major sports are televised on
Sky and ESPN. Large function rooms are for hire and
its six acres of grounds have facilities for team
events, campers and camper vans. Cask Marque
beers include Doom Bar all week and changing
micros and LocAles Wednesday to Sunday. Cobs are
served. Outside is a smoking shelter. The club has
ample car parking and is near bus routes.
🚌🐕♿▲🖳(48,81A,158)♣P🚭

New Plough Inn 🍷
Leicester Road, LE10 1LS (opp fire station) SP431942
❁ 4.45 (12 Fri-Sun)-midnight ☎ (01455) 615037
Marston's Burton Bitter, Pedigree; guest beers Ⓗ
Victorian building boasting original wood settles,
comfortable lounge areas and a traditional and
cosy ambience with rugby-themed memorabilia.
Darts, dominoes and skittles are played in the
games room. Dogs are welcome. Outside is a
sheltered beer garden and heated, covered
smokers area. The stables were recently converted
into a function room for corporate or party hire. The
landlady, a CAMRA member, runs a charity pub
quiz on the last Thursday of the month, chairs the
annual town carnival and sponsors Hinckley Rugby
Club. 🐕🖳(81,81A)♣P🚭

Queen's Head Inn ✔
40 Upper Bond Street, LE10 1RJ (just beyond police
station and courts)
❁ 5 (12 Fri & Sat)-11; 12-7 Sun ☎ (01455) 632018
Beer range varies Ⓗ
Rebuilt in Victorian times, this popular, friendly,
family-run free house originates from Queen
Anne's reign (1702-14). The cosy, relaxed
atmosphere and log fires add to a warm welcome.
Entertainment includes traditional live music every
Friday, darts, dominoes and cards during the week,
and charity quizzes on the second Monday of each
month. Regularly changing national guest beers
come from Timothy Taylor, Thornbridge, St Austell
and Bass as well as local micros. Real ale discounts
are available for CAMRA members.
♨🐕🖳(48,158)♣🚭

Hose

Rose & Crown Ⓛ
Bolton Lane, LE14 4JE
❁ 12-3 (not Tue), 6-10 (11 Wed & Thu; midnight Fri);
12-midnight Sat; 12-10 Sun ☎ (01949) 869458
🌐 theroseandcrownhose.co.uk
Adnams Southwold Bitter; Tetley Bitter Ⓗ

Set in the heart of the Vale of Belvoir, this
renowned 200-year-old country pub has
undergone a new lease of life over the past year.
Six cask ales are offered, with no smooth beer, and
a wide-ranging food menu using local produce (no
food Tue). The pub has a large, comfortable bar and
seating area, and a separate restaurant. Outside is
an attractive and spacious deck plus a paddock.
Regular live music events are held through the
year. ♨🐕◑♣P

Illston on the Hill

Fox & Goose
Main Street, LE7 9EG
❁ 6 (11 Sat & Sun)-midnight ☎ (0116) 259 6340
Everards Beacon, Tiger, seasonal beers; guest beers Ⓗ
Unique gem of a pub unscathed by the passing of
time, with many artefacts including pictures of
hunting scenes, McLachlan cartoons, animal traps,
farming implements and various taxidermy
exhibits. In 1997, when major structural work was
undertaken, photographs were taken before work
began to ensure that each item could be put back
in exactly the same place. A conkers contest and an
onion-growing competition are held annually to
raise funds for charities. Evening meals are served
Thursday to Saturday. Cider is available in summer.
♨Q🐕◑🍴♿♣🚭

Kegworth

Red Lion
24 High Street, DE74 2DA
❁ 11.30-11; 12-10.30 Sun ☎ (01509) 672466
🌐 redlionkegworth.com
**Adnams Southwold Bitter; Castle Rock Preservation;
Gale's HSB; Theakston Traditional Mild; guest beers** Ⓗ
Georgian building standing on the 19th-century
route of the A6, with four rooms served from one
bar. There are bench seats and original features
including coal fires. Eight cask ales and real cider
are available plus a good selection of malt
whiskies. Food is served every lunchtime and
weekday evenings. Outside is a large car park and
garden plus a pétanque court and children's play
area. En-suite accommodation is available. Local
CAMRA Pub of the Year 2010.
♨Q🚌🐕🛏◑🍴🖳♣♠P🚭

Knipton

Manners Arms Ⓛ
Croxton Road, NG32 1RH
❁ 11-11; 12-10.30 Sun ☎ (01476) 879222
🌐 mannersarms.com
**Batemans XB; Belvoir Dark Horse; Fuller's London
Pride; guest beer** Ⓗ
Impressive former Georgian hunting lodge set in
the heart of the Vale of Belvoir. The bar and
lounge, with its tall bookshelves and comfortable
seating, are warmed by an inviting open fireplace.
One long bar serves four cask ales, including a mild.
Light meals are available in the bar and a wide
range of interesting food made with local produce
is served in the restaurant. A wonderful patio and
garden area are ideal for lazing on a hot summer's
day. ♨Q🐕🛏◑♿P

Leicester

Ale Wagon

27 Rutland Street, LE1 1RE

☼ 11-11; 7-10.30 Sun ☎ (0116) 262 3330 ⊕ alewagon.co.uk

Hoskins Brothers HOB, IPA Ⓗ**, Old Navigation** ℗**, seasonal beers; guest beers** Ⓗ

Run by the Hoskins family, this city-centre pub with 1930s interior, including an original oak staircase, has two rooms with tiled and parquet floors and a central bar. There is always a selection of Hoskins Brothers ales and guests available. The pub is popular with visiting rugby fans and real ale drinkers. A function room is available to hire with catering. Handy for the nearby Curve Theatre. ﹰﹰﹰﹰ⇌🖫♣🌢

Black Horse Ⓛ

65 Narrow Lane, Aylestone, LE2 8NA (400yds from St Andrew's Church)

☼ 12-11 (midnight Fri & Sat) ☎ (0116) 283 7225

Everards Beacon, Tiger, Original; guest beers Ⓗ

A welcoming, traditional four-roomed Victorian pub with a distinctive bar servery in Aylestone Village Conservation Area. Eight real ales are always available and home-cooked food is served lunchtimes and evenings Monday to Friday, all day Saturday and Sunday. There is a large beer garden and children's play area. The skittle alley and function room are available for hire. Live music and a comedy club feature regularly plus a quiz every Sunday. Beer festivals are held and community events hosted. ﹰﹰﹰQ🕸⬤❶🖫🖫♣🌢⌐

Bridle Lane Tavern Ⓛ

2 Junction Road, LE1 2HS (under Belgrave flyover)

☼ 11-11 (midnight Thu-Sat) ☎ (0116) 251 0813

Belvoir Dark Horse; guest beers Ⓗ

A small wedge-shaped, single-roomed, cosy pub next to Belgrave flyover. To find it, look for Lower Willow Street, since Junction Road no longer runs this far. Despite its location just a few yards from the city centre ring road, it has the atmosphere and welcome of a country inn. New owners in 2011 introduced real ale for the first time since CAMRA was formed, and guest beers are constantly changing. Regular beer festivals are held and there is frequent live entertainment. 🕸🖫♣

Criterion

44 Millstone Lane, LE1 5JN

☼ 12-11 (10.30 Sun) ☎ (0116) 262 5418

Beer range varies Ⓗ

Two-roomed 1960s city-centre pub offering up to 10 guest ales from micros and regionals at weekends. Beer festivals are held regularly, with many beers on gravity from the cellar. More than 100 international bottled beers are stocked. Darts and dominoes are played in the bar. A pop quiz is hosted on Tuesday, general knowledge quiz on Wednesday and live music on Thursday and Saturday. Pub food is available Sunday and Monday, with Italian-style pizzas Tuesday to Saturday. 🕸⬤❶♣🌢⌐

Longstop Ⓛ

9 Churchgate, LE1 3AL (50yds from clock tower)

☼ 11-11 (midnight Fri & Sat); 12-10.30 Sun

☎ (0116) 262 1536 ⊕ longstoprealale.co.uk

Beer range varies Ⓗ

Leicester's most central hostelry, it is a family-run, traditional English pub, with a warm, welcoming atmosphere. There are six handpumps with regularly changing guest beers, usually LocAles. The pub has recently reopened following a three year period of closure. It hosts regular live music and DJ nights, and children are welcome until 9pm. Food is served from 12 to 5pm. ❶🖫

Old Horse

198 London Road, LE2 1NE (on A6 opp Victoria Park)

☼ 11-11.30 (midnight Fri & Sat; 11 Sun) ☎ (0116) 254 8384 ⊕ oldhorsepub.co.uk

Everards Beacon, Sunchaser, Tiger, Original, seasonal beers; guest beers Ⓗ

Nineteenth-century coaching inn immortalised by Michael Green in The Art of Coarse Rugby. It is popular with all sections of the community including students and the local church choir. Lots of interesting bric-a-brac hangs from ceilings. Weekly quiz nights and karaoke are held. The large garden features a children's play area, pétanque pitch, owls and a Tardis. CAMRA members receive a 10 per cent discount on beer. 🕸⬤❶&🖫(31,31A)♣🌢P⌐

Pub

12 New Walk, LE1 6TF (opp council offices)

☼ 12-11 (midnight Fri & Sat); 2-10 Sun

⊕ thepubleicester.co.uk

Beowulf Dragon Smoke Stout; Oakham Inferno; guest beers Ⓗ

Behind the small frontage lies a warm, welcoming interior with a modern bar offering a wide range of microbrewery ales and continental draught and bottled beers. The Pub is home to Leicester Morris Men and a firm favourite with rugby and football fans. LocAle breweries often feature among the 15 handpulls, supporting up to 12 changing guests. Food is served lunchtimes Monday to Saturday and evenings Tuesday to Saturday. ❶&⇌

Salmon ♉

19 Butt Close Lane, LE1 4QA

☼ 12-11 (8 Mon; midnight Fri & Sat; 6 Sun)

☎ (0116) 253 2301

Beer range varies Ⓗ

Victorian corner back-street free house, recently refurbished, with a friendly, welcoming atmosphere. It has a strong sports following, especially for rugby. The large, open U-shaped bar offers a selection of beers from six handpumps, mainly from microbreweries. Cellar runs are offered. One mild is always available along with a cider. St Margaret's bus station is nearby. Local CAMRA Pub of the Year 2012. 🕸⬤❶🖫🌢⌐

Shakespeare's Head

Southgates, LE1 5SH

☼ 12-midnight (8 Mon; 1am Fri & Sat; 11 Sun)

☎ (0116) 262 4378 ⊕ shakespeareshead.co.uk

Oakwell Dark Mild, Barnsley Bitter, Senior Ⓗ

This two-roomed local was built alongside the underpass in the 1960s and has changed little since then, retaining all the charm of a typical town pub of its era. Two large glass doors lead to an off-sales area with a bar to the left and lounge to the right. Formerly a Shipstones pub, it now sells Oakwell beers at reasonable prices. &🖫♣

Slug & Lettuce Ⓛ ✔

27 Market Street, LE1 6DP

☼ 10-11 (1am Fri & Sat) ☎ (0116) 255 5370 ⊕ slugandlettuce.co.uk/leicester

Oakham Inferno; Wells Bombardier; guest beers Ⓗ

A real ale establishment for everyone: young and old, families and football fans. The pub is passionate about promoting LocAle and offering an outlet for microbreweries, with three guest beers usually available. Regular beer festivals have seen the Slug cement its reputation in Leicester and beyond as a real ale pub for all who enjoy good honest beer. There is an extensive food menu with many special offers. ⚘🍴🕭🛇🚃

Swan & Rushes
19 Infirmary Square, LE1 5WR
🌣 12-11 (midnight Thu-Sat; 11.30 Sun) ☎ (0116) 233 9167
🌐 swanandrushes.co.uk
Batemans XB; Oakham JHB, Bishops Farewell, seasonal beers; guest beers Ⓗ
Comfortable, triangular, two-roomed pub in the city centre with a relaxed atmosphere, filled with breweriana and framed photos on the wall. Up to nine real ales (no nationals) are available or you can choose from the bottled beer menu featuring more than 100 international classics. Several food-linked beer festivals are held each year plus cider and cheese events. Thursday is quiz night and live gigs take place on some Saturdays. Home-made pizzas are available. ⚘🍴🕭🛇🚃♣●'—

Tom Hoskins ✔
131 Beaumanor Road, LE4 5QE
🌣 12-11 (midnight Fri); 10.30-midnight Sat; 10.30-11 Sun
☎ (0116) 266 9659
Banks's Mild; Black Sheep Best Bitter; Brains Bitter; Greene King IPA; guest beers Ⓗ
Hospitable, two-room, city-suburbs pub catering for the mature drinker. Between four and six ales are always available, including a mild and changing guest beers. If you are hungry there are freshly made cobs. Darts is played in the bar and the pub is popular with local football and rugby teams. Regular Sunday evening quiz nights are held. A barber is available 9am-2pm on Saturday and Sunday. ⚘🕭🛇♣P'—

Western
70 Western Road, LE3 0GA
🌣 12-midnight (1am Fri & Sat) ☎ (0116) 254 5287
Everards Tiger; Steamin' Billy Tipsy Fisherman, Bitter, Skydiver Ⓗ**; guest beers** Ⓗ/Ⓖ
Traditional two-roomed local in a residential location with a bar and lounge, popular with a good mixed clientele of all ages. Old pub signs decorate the walls. Food is served at lunchtime, with a carvery on Sunday. The pub gets busy on match days. 🏚⚘🍴🚃♣'—

Long Whatton

Royal Oak
26 The Green, LE12 5DB
🌣 12-11 (midnight Fri & Sat) ☎ (01509) 843694
🌐 theroyaloaklongwhatton.co.uk
Draught Bass; St Austell Tribute; guest beers Ⓗ
Tastefully modernised, award-winning gastro-pub welcoming real ale drinkers and diners alike. Regularly changing guest beers usually include one from Blue Monkey. The owners are passionate about their ale and hold two beer festivals a year. Local produce is used to create an interesting menu including 'nip & tuck' – four nips of beer and locally-produced nibbles on a platter. Convenient for East Midlands airport and Donington race circuit, accommodation is available in a separate building. Local CAMRA Village Pub 2011. ⚘🚃🍴🛇🚃P'—

Loughborough

Generous Briton 🏆
85 Ashby Road, LE11 3AB
🌣 12-11 (midnight Fri & Sat) ☎ (01509) 263565
🌐 bogiespubs.co.uk
Black Sheep Best Bitter; Castle Rock Harvest Pale; Oakham Citra; Taylor Landlord; guest beers Ⓗ
Reopened in 2011 as a genuine free house, the 'GB' is ideally situated between the town centre and university. The traditional bar has a dartboard and features old local photographs; the lounge has a pool table and jukebox. Satellite sport is shown throughout. A limited food menu is available but customers are welcome to bring their own food. There is an enclosed beer garden to the rear and families are welcome until 7.45pm. Joint local CAMRA Most Improved Pub 2011, Town Pub 2011 and Pub of the Year 2012. 🏚⚘🕭🚃(126)♣●'—

Moon & Bell Ⓛ ✔
6 Wards End, LE11 3HA
🌣 8-midnight ☎ (01509) 241504
Greene King Abbot; Marston's Pedigree; Nottingham Rock Mild; Ruddles Best Bitter; guest beers Ⓗ
Traditionally styled Wetherspoon venue set in the Grade II-listed Atherstone House, with a warm and welcoming atmosphere. It has a spacious beer garden to the rear, perfect for the summer months. An extensive food menu is available until 10pm every day. A fine selection of guest and house ales, always including a mild, is served, and frequent ale and cider festivals are hosted. Local CAMRA Pub of the Year 2011, Mild Pub 2009 and 2010. Q⚘🍴🛇🚃●'—

Swan in the Rushes
21 The Rushes, LE11 5BE
🌣 11-11 (midnight Fri & Sat) ☎ (01509) 217014
Adnams Southwold Bitter; Castle Rock Sheriff's Tipple, Harvest Pale, Elsie Mo; guest beers Ⓗ
Traditional three-room Castle Rock pub comprising two quiet, comfortable rooms and the Charnwood Vaults, a lively bar with a jukebox. A constantly changing range of up to six guest beers always includes a mild. Real cider, perry, a limited range of continental bottled and draught beers and a good choice of malt whiskies and country wines are also available. Upstairs is a skittle alley and function room that hosts comedy nights, live music and twice-yearly beer festivals. Local CAMRA Mild Pub for 2011. 🏚Q🛏⚘🍴🛇🚃≠🚃♣●P'—

Tap & Mallet
36 Nottingham Road, LE11 1EU
🌣 7 (5 Tue & Thu; 12 Sat; 3.30 Sun)-2am ☎ (01509) 210028
Abbeydale Deception; Batemans Dark Mild, XB; guest beers Ⓗ
Genuine free house specialising in beers from microbreweries not commonly found in the Loughborough area, plus seasonal brews from Abbeydale and Oakham. The interior has a large single room divided into two distinct drinking areas – a public bar with pool table, darts and boxed games, and a quieter lounge area that can be partitioned off for functions. Outside there is a large, secluded lawned garden and patio area with children's play equipment and pets' corner. Westons cider is available. 🏚⚘≠🚃♣●'—

Lutterworth

Fox

34 Rugby Road, LE17 4BN (400yds from Whittle Roundabout)

✪ closed Mon; 12-1am ☎ (01455) 552677

Courage Best Bitter; Draught Bass; Sharp's Doom Bar; Woodforde's Wherry; guest beer Ⓗ

A warm, friendly welcome awaits visitors, as does a range of top-quality real ales. Outside is a huge landscaped garden plus a function room catering for bands, private parties and dancing. The pub has a real community spirit, offering a quiz on Tuesday, Japanese food on Wednesday, jazz and swing on Sunday and a golf night once a month.
🏨✿◖🖢🖼♣Ｐ⅃

Greyhound

High Street, LE17 4EJ

✪ 6.30-11 ☎ (01455) 553307 ∰ greyhoundinn.co.uk

Ossett Excelsior; Salopian Shropshire Gold; Darwins Origin Ⓗ

A traditional coaching inn and hotel in the town centre with a large lounge and bar. The Grade II-listed Greyhound has a friendly, welcoming atmosphere. There is a paved courtyard outside with a covered smoking and drinking area with tables and chairs. The restaurant has a plush interior with olde worlde features and offers an excellent menu. A popular venue for private functions and weddings. Q✿🖤◖🖢�&🖼⅃

Unicorn ✪

29 Church Street, LE17 4AE (near church)

✪ 10.30-11 (midnight Fri & Sat) ☎ (01455) 552486

Adnams Broadside; Draught Bass; Greene King IPA; St Austell Tribute; guest beer Ⓗ

Friendly, traditional pub near the centre of town with a bar, lounge and restaurant area. Open fires welcome families in the lounge and there is live sports coverage in the bar. Darts, skittles and dominoes are popular with the locals – the Unicorn is well represented in local leagues. Lunchtime meals and bar snacks are available at reasonable prices. Well worth a visit when in Lutterworth.
🏨✿🖤◖ᴕ&🖼♣Ｐ⅃

Market Harborough

Admiral Nelson

49 Nelson Street, LE16 9AX

✪ 5 (3 Fri; 12 Sat)-midnight Sat; 12-11 Sun
☎ (01858) 433173

Wells Eagle IPA, Bombardier; guest beers Ⓗ

Welcoming, friendly locals' pub, built in 1900, a short stroll from the centre of the historic market town. Just off the beaten track, this pub is the town's best-kept secret, offering a lounge with TV (where they like their rugby) and bar with darts, pool, jukebox and another TV. A function room is available. Outside is a heated and covered smoking area with seating. Dogs are welcome. ✿🖲♣Ｐ⅃

Cherry Tree

Church Walk, Kettering Road, Little Bowden, LE16 8AE

✪ 12-2.30, 5-11; 12-11.30 Fri & Sat; 12-10.30 Sun
☎ (01858) 463525

Everards Beacon, Sunchaser, Tiger, Original; guest beers Ⓗ

Although this pub is situated in Little Bowden, it is very much part of the Market Harborough community. A spacious building with low beams and a thatched roof, there are many alcoves and seating areas for drinkers and diners to choose from. Outside is a large garden with children's play area. A beer festival is held over the August bank holiday. Guest beers are from the Everards' list. No food Sunday or Monday evenings. 🖢✿◖🖱⇌♣⅃

Market Overton

Black Bull Inn

2 Teigh Road, LE15 7PW (jct of Main St and Teigh Rd)

✪ 12-3, 6-11 (midnight Sat); 11.30-5, 7-11 Sun
☎ (01572) 767677 ∰ blackbullrutland.co.uk

Black Sheep Best Bitter; Theakston Black Bull Bitter; guest beers Ⓗ

Traditional village pub serving up to four real ales and good quality food, mainly cooked by the landlady. Close to the A1, the hostelry is more than 200 years old with cosy, comfortable rooms. The landlord is a real ale advocate and fan of old cars and bikes, occasionally hosting a vintage meet. For cider enthusiasts there are usually three on tap. A friendly, welcoming inn well worth a visit.
🖢✿🖾◖🖢🖢

Melton Mowbray

Anne of Cleves Ⓛ

12 Burton Street, LE13 1AE (just S of St Mary's Church)

✪ 11-11; 12-10.30 Sun ☎ (01664) 481336

Everards Beacon, Tiger, Original; guest beers Ⓗ

One of Everards' most historic pubs and an icon for the town. Part of the property dates back to 1327 when it was home to monks. The house was gifted to Anne of Cleves by Henry VIII as part of her divorce settlement. It is now a popular, busy hostelry following a sympathetic conversion and restoration of the building, with stone-flagged floors, exposed timber beams and wall tapestries. The building is said to be haunted and psychic research evenings have occasionally featured.
🏨Q✿◖⇌🖼(5,5A)Ｐ⅃

Boat ♟ ✪

57 Burton Street, LE13 1AF

✪ 12-3, 5-midnight; 11-midnight Fri & Sat; 12-4, 7-midnight Sun ☎ (01664) 560518

Caledonian Deuchars IPA; Theakston Best Bitter; Wells Bombardier; guest beer Ⓗ

A traditional single-roomed pub that takes its name from the long-vanished canal basin that was once adjacent. The walls are decorated with pictures of Melton Mowbray of yesteryear and a map of the course of the old Melton/Oakham canal whose workers used this establishment once served. The pub is usually busy with mature drinkers who enjoy a game of darts and good conversation with their pint. A warm welcome is always forthcoming from the licensees to old and new customers alike.
🏨⇌🖼(19)♣

Mountsorrel

Swan Inn

10 Loughborough Road, LE12 7AT

✪ 12-2.30, 5.30-11; 12-11 Sat; 12-3, 7-10.30 Sun
☎ (0116) 2302340 ∰ the-swan-inn.eu

Black Sheep Best Bitter; Ruddles County; Theakston XB, Old Peculier; guest beers Ⓗ

Traditional 17th-century, Grade II-listed coaching inn, under the present ownership since 1990. The split-level interior has open fires, stone floors and low ceilings, and includes a small dining area with a polished wood floor. Good quality, interesting food is cooked to order, with the menu changing weekly. Outside is a secluded riverside garden with moorings. Self-contained accommodation is available. ⚲❀☎◑🖼️P⬟⬩

Oadby

Lord Keeper of the Great Seal ✪

96-100 The Parade, LE2 5BF
❂ 8am-midnight ☎ (0116) 272 0957
Greene King Abbot; Ruddles Best Bitter; guest beers Ⓗ
Named after Sir Nathan Wright, a local landowner who held this position in the 17th century, this typical Wetherspoon conversion of a row of shops stands on the site of Sandhurst Infants School. It features pictures of old buildings and industries of Oadby and a varied library of books. Regular beer festivals and charity events are held.
⟝❀◑⛴🖼️(31,31A)⬩⬟⬩

Wheel Inn

99 London Road, LE2 5DP
❂ 12-midnight (10.30 Sun) ☎ (0116) 271 2231
Draught Bass; Marston's Pedigree; guest beers Ⓗ
Sports-oriented community pub where there is always something going on. As well as darts, dominoes and skittles teams, there are football, cricket, golf and fishing matches, casino nights, jazz evenings, train trips, cycle rides and anything else the landlord and customers can think of. Tasty home-cooked lunches are served from Sunday to Friday and an extensive selection of wines and spirits adds to the appeal. The Leicester bus stops outside. ❀◑⛴🖼️(31)⬦P⬟⬩

Oakham

Grainstore Ⓛ

Station Approach, LE15 6RE (next to Oakham station)
❂ 11-11 (midnight Fri & Sat) ☎ (01572) 770065
⬡ grainstorebrewery.com
Grainstore Rutland Panther, Cooking, Rutland Bitter, Triple B, 1050, seasonal beers Ⓗ
Pub and brewery in a cleverly converted small warehouse over four floors, retaining some original features. Brewery tours are available but must be booked in advance. The beer range always includes a mild, and a range of bottle-conditioned Belgian beers is also stocked. Home-made food is served at lunchtime. Live bands feature regularly during the month. An annual beer festival is held over the August bank holiday. Dog- and walker-friendly.
Q❀◑⛛🖼️⬦P⬟⬩

White Lion Hotel

30 Melton Road, LE15 6AY
❂ 12-3 (not Mon), 6-midnight ☎ (01572) 724844
Fuller's London Pride; Taylor Landlord; Wells Bombardier; guest beers Ⓗ
A repeat entry in the Guide confirms that standards, choice and hospitality have been maintained at the White Lion. A must-visit inn for home-made traditional food – make sure you are hungry as one size fits all. Beer is always of top quality and the guest changes regularly, often from Blue Monkey or Ossett breweries. Old-fashioned standards are upheld, with the landlord in collar and tie and Bruce, the peanut-eating pet, giving you a smile. ⚲❀☎◑⛛🖼️⬦P⬟⬩

Old Dalby

Sample Cellar Ⓛ

Belvoir Brewery, Station Road, LE14 3NQ
❂ 12-10 (8 Sun) ☎ (01664) 823455 ⬡ belvoirbrewery.co.uk
Belvoir Dark Horse, Beaver Bitter, seasonal beers Ⓗ
The brick-fronted Sample Cellar on the outskirts of the village incorporates a bar, visitors' centre and function room. The comfortable, spacious interior, filled with brewing artefacts, has a traditional bar area, and there is even room for long alley skittles and a bar billiards table. Two large internal windows provide views into the brewery. A full menu is served daily, with the focus on good wholesome food made with local produce. Local CAMRA Pub of the Year 2011. ❀◑⛛⬦P⬟⬩

Quorn

Manor House

Woodhouse Road, LE12 8AL
❂ 12-11 (midnight Sat; 10 Sun) ☎ (01509) 413416
⬡ themanorhouseatquorn.co.uk
Batemans XB; Draught Bass; Taylor Landlord; guest beers Ⓗ
Built in 1899 by the Great Central Railway, the Manor House was designed to serve passengers arriving at Quorn & Woodhouse Station, which it still does today – the preserved steam- and diesel-hauled trains pass by 200 yards from the door. The building was refurbished in 2005 and now has an open-plan bar and award-winning restaurant with a separate function/meeting room available to hire. A free house, two guest beers are available during the week and three at weekends. CAMRA members receive a discount. ❀◑⛛Å⛟🖼️P

Sewstern

Blue Dog

Main Street, NG33 5RQ
❂ 11-11; 12-10.30 Sun ☎ (01476) 860097
Greene King IPA; guest beers Ⓗ
Friendly and welcoming pub west of the village, handy for walkers at the southern end of the Viking Way. The unusual name reflects the tradition of local farm workers on the Tollemache estate being paid partly in blue tokens. The 300-year-old building was once a war hospital and has a ghost – a drummer boy called Albert. Guest ales often come from local breweries and a beer festival is held in May. A fish and chips menu is available on Wednesday evening. ⚲Q⟝❀◑⛛Å🖼️(55)⬦P⬟⬩

Shackerstone

Rising Sun Ⓛ

Church Road, CV13 6NN SK374066
❂ 10.30-2.30, 6-midnight; 11.30-midnight Sat & Sun
☎ (01827) 880215 ⬡ risingsunpub.com
Marston's Pedigree; Taylor Landlord; guest beers Ⓗ
A family-run free house since 1987 with a large, traditional wood-panelled bar area. The separate sports room has pool and Sky TV. Children are welcome in the conservatory and attractive beer garden. Two guest ales change regularly and Old Rosie real cider is sold. Meals are served in the bar and barn-conversion restaurant, with Sunday lunches always popular. The Battlefield Railway and Ashby Canal are nearby. Walkers are welcome, and regular charity fundraising walks support Guide Dogs. ⚲Q⟝❀◑⛛🖼️⬦⬟⬩

Shearsby

Chandlers Arms ⃝L
Fenny Lane, LE17 6PL (close to A5199)
⊕ 12-3 (not Mon), 7 (6 Fri)-11; 12-4, 6-11 Sat; 12-4, 7-10.30
Sun ☎ (0116) 2478384 ⊕ chandlersatshearsby.co.uk
Dow Bridge Acris; guest beers ⊞
Classic, quaint old country pub overlooking the
village green. Popular with walkers, cyclists, diners
and visitors from the city, it also has strong local
support. It was the first pub in CAMRA's Leicester
branch to be accredited to the LocAle scheme.
Microbrewery beers are always on the bar, often
locally sourced. Draught cider is available in
summer. No food is served Sunday evening or
Monday. Local CAMRA County Pub of the Year 2012
– for the fourth year in succession. ⊛⏴🍴♣🛏️

Shepshed

Black Swan
21 Loughborough Road, LE12 9DL
⊕ 6 (5.30 Tue-Thu; 4 Fri; 1.30 Sat; 12 Sun)-1.30am
☎ (01509) 502659
Draught Bass; Taylor Landlord; guest beers ⊞
Multi-roomed pub situated in a prominent position
close to the town centre, offering two guest beers
alongside the regulars. The main room has two
drinking areas, both with comfortable seating. A
further small room can be used by families. The
upstairs restaurant serves good quality food.
Shepshed Dynamo football ground is nearby.
⚑Q❀⏴🍴♣P⁼

Somerby

Stilton Cheese ⃝L
Main Street, LE14 2PZ
⊕ 12-3, 6 (7 Sun)-11 ☎ (01664) 454394
Grainstore Ten Fifty; Tetley Bitter; guest beers ⊞
Late 16th-century pub built in local ironstone, like
most of the buildings in the village. The interior
comprises two bars and a function room. Tall
customers will note the wide range of pump clips
on the low beams as they bang their heads on
them. A popular and lively village pub, booking is
advised for food. ⚑Q❀⏴🍴(113)♣P

Swinford

Chequers ✅
High Street, LE17 6BL (near church)
⊕ 7-11 Mon; 12-2.30, 6-11; 12-3, 7-11 Sun
☎ (01788) 860318 ⊕ chequersswinford.co.uk
Adnams Southwold Bitter; guest beers ⊞
Close to the M1, M6 and A14, the Chequers is a
welcome refreshment stop-off for travellers as well
as a popular local. The smart bars offer a regular
beer plus two guest ales and a good range of food
including vegetarian and children's dishes. The
large garden has children's play equipment. Three
beer festivals are held during the year. The 16th-
century Stanford Hall is nearby with a caravan park,
extensive gardens and motor museum.
⚑❀⏴🛏️♣P⁼

Swithland

Griffin Inn
174 Main Street, LE12 8TJ
⊕ 9-11 (10.30 Sun) ☎ (01509) 890535
⊕ griffininnswithland.co.uk

Everards Beacon, Tiger, Original; guest beers ⊞
Friendly and welcoming local with three
comfortable rooms. Set in the heart of Charnwood
Forest, there are many walking and cycling routes
nearby. Swithland Reservoir, Bradgate Park and the
preserved Great Central Railway are also close.
Alongside the regular food menu, light snacks are
available every afternoon including Melton
Mowbray pork pies. Guest ales are chosen from
Everards' Old English Ale Club, with three
frequently stocked in addition to the regulars.
⚑Q❀⏴🍴♿▲🛏️♣P⁼

Syston

Dog & Gun
Chapel Street, LE7 1GN
⊕ 12-midnight (11 Sun) ☎ (0116) 2609366
⊕ steamin-billy.co.uk
**Belvoir Dark Horse; Steamin' Billy Tipsy Fisherman,
Skydiver** ⊞**; guest beers** ⊞/Ⓖ
A recently refurbished traditional village drinking
pub with two rooms, a courtyard garden and a
function room available to hire. There are eight
handpulled ales alongside draught fruit beers and
scrumpy ciders. Bar snacks are served, but no hot
food; however buffets and barbecues are on offer
for parties. Q❀🍴⇄♣🍴⁼

Syston Social Club ⃝L
36 High Street, LE7 1GP
⊕ 7-11; 12-2.30, 5.30-midnight Fri; 12-midnight Sat; 12-4,
7-11 Sun ☎ (0116) 260 9086 ⊕ systonsocial.co.uk
Banks's Mild, Bitter; guest beers ⊞
Formerly the Bulls Head, this club is home to many
local societies and sports teams including darts,
crib, skittles and chess. It has a large function room,
available to hire. The range of six beers includes
four regularly changing guests, often from
microbreweries or from the Marston's list. An
annual beer festival is held in June. Show your
CAMRA membership card or a copy of this Guide for
entry. ❀♿⇄🛏️(5A)♣

Thrussington

Blue Lion
5 Rearsby Road, LE7 4UD
⊕ 12-2.30 (not Wed; 4 Sat), 5.30-11; 12-5, 7-10.30 Sun
☎ (01664) 424266
**Marston's Burton Bitter, Pedigree, seasonal beers;
guest beers** ⊞
This late 18th-century rural inn was once two
cottages. Good-value pub grub, featuring meat
supplied by the local butcher, is served in the
comfortable lounge. However, the bar is the heart
of the pub, where locals meet for high-pressure
darts and dominoes matches, kept under control by
licensees Mandy and Bob.
⚑Q❀⏴🛏️♿▲🛏️(128)♣P

Thurlaston

Elephant & Castle ⃝L
26 Main Street, LE9 7TP SP502990
⊕ 12-2.30 (not Mon & Tue), 6-11; 12-3, 7-10.30 Sun
☎ (01455) 888213
Everards Beacon, Tiger, Original; guest beers ⊞
A friendly local pub set in the heart of the village,
with a traditional bar area and two comfortable
rooms with beamed ceilings. The licensees are
award-winning real ale enthusiasts and CAMRA

members. Three Everards' beers, two changing guests and real cider are served. The landlady produces good-value home-cooked food – her speciality pies and Sunday lunches are a treat. Outside there is a patio, seating area and large car park. Walking and cycle routes pass through the village. Q☷❀❍❑❲❳▣(148)♣♠P♨

Uppingham

Crown Inn ℓ
19 High Street East, LE15 9PY
◷ 11-11; 12-10.30 Sun ☎ (01572) 822302
⊕ thecrownrutland.co.uk
Everards Beacon, Tiger, Original, seasonal beers; guest beers Ⓗ
A warm welcome is assured at this traditional market town pub dating from 1739. Recently refurbished to a high standard, it offers up to seven ales and good-quality, reasonably-priced, home-cooked food in the bar and restaurant. Live music plays monthly or more often and a beer festival is held every April over St George's Day. The pub is home to two local dominoes teams. En-suite accommodation is available. Rutland CAMRA Pub of the Year 2011. ❲❀❍❑▣(RF1,12,747)♣♠P♨

Walton on the Wolds

Anchor Inn
2 Loughborough Road, LE12 8HT
◷ 12-3 (not Mon), 7-11; 12-10.30 Sun ☎ (01509) 880018
Adnams Southwold Bitter; Black Sheep Best Bitter; Fuller's London Pride; Taylor Landlord; guest beer Ⓗ
The Anchor is situated in the centre of a small village within easy reach of Leicester and Nottingham via the A46. It is a popular venue for walkers who stop for a well-earned home-cooked lunch in front of the log fire. There is a menu to suit all tastes plus an extensive specials board. Outside is an elevated seating area to the front and a garden and large car park to the rear. En-suite B&B accommodation is available. ❲❀❍❑P

Whitwick

Three Horseshoes ★
11 Leicester Road, LE67 5GN
◷ 11-3, 6.30-11; 12-2, 7-10.30 Sun ☎ (01530) 837311
Draught Bass; Marston's Pedigree Ⓗ
Identified by CAMRA as one of Britain's Real Heritage Pubs, the Three Horseshoes is nicknamed 'Polly's' after a former landlady, Polly Burton. The pub was originally two separate buildings but now has two rooms. To the left is a long bar with a quarry-tiled floor and open fires, wooden bench seating and pre-war fittings; to the right is a similarly furnished small snug. ❲Q❑▣♣

Wigston Magna

William Wygston ✔
84 Leicester Road, LE18 1DR
◷ 9am-midnight ☎ (0116) 288 8397
Greene King Abbot; Ruddles Best Bitter; guest beers Ⓗ
Classic Wetherspoon establishment named after William Wygston (1456-1536), an extremely wealthy wool merchant, philanthropist, MP, and twice mayor of Leicester. Staffed by an efficient, friendly and helpful team of employees, it offers an ever-changing array of guest beers, often from local breweries Grainstore, Langton and Shardlow. Interesting pictures depicting bygone Wigston and Leicester adorn the walls. ☷❍❑▣♠

Wymeswold

Three Crowns ℓ ✔
45 Far Street, LE12 6TZ
◷ 12-11 ☎ (01509) 880153
Adnams Southwold Bitter; Marston's Pedigree; guest beers Ⓗ
Late 18th-century pub standing opposite the church. This friendly village local features a beamed ceiling in the bar and a split-level snug/lounge. Guest beers are usually from local breweries including Castle Rock, Belvoir or Nottingham. Evening meals are available Thursday to Saturday. There is a regular daytime bus service. ❲Q☷❍❑♣P♨

The language of beer

Nose: the aroma. Gently swirl the beer to release the aroma. You will detect malt: grainy and biscuity, often likened to crackers or Ovaltine. When darker malts are used, the nose will have powerful hints of chocolate, coffee, nuts, vanilla, liquorice, molasses and such dried fruits as raisins and sultanas. Hops add superb aromas of resins, herbs, spices, fresh-mown grass and tart citrus fruit – lemon and orange are typical, or grapefruit notes. Sulphur may also be present when waters are 'Burtonised'; i.e. gypsum and magnesium salts have been added to replicate the famous spring waters of Burton-on-Trent.

Palate: the appeal in the mouth. The tongue can detect sweetness, bitterness and saltiness as the beer passes over it. The rich flavours of malt will come to the fore but hop bitterness will also make a substantial impact. The tongue will also pick out the natural saltiness from the brewing water and fruit from darker malts, yeast and hops. Citrus notes often have a major impact on the palate.

Finish: the aftertaste, as the beer goes over the tongue and down the throat. The finish is often radically different to the nose. The aroma may be dominated by malt whereas hop flavours and bitterness can govern the finish. Darker malts will make their presence felt with chocolate or coffee notes; fruit character may linger. Strong beers may end on a sweet or biscuity note but in mainstream bitters, bitterness and dryness come to the fore.

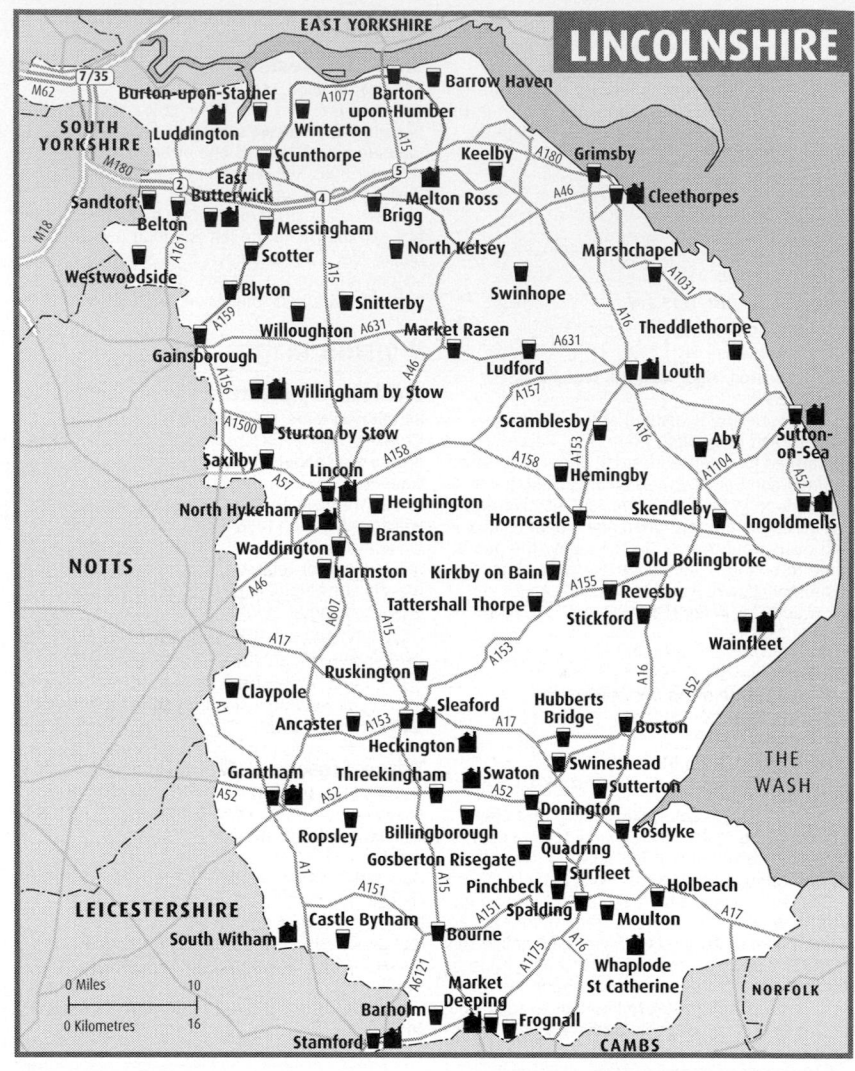

LINCOLNSHIRE

Aby

Railway Tavern

Main Road, LN13 0DR (off A16 via S Thoresby)
☼ 12-midnight (closed Tue winter) ☎ (01507) 480676
Beer range varies Ⓗ
Cosy village pub worth searching out for its varied
beer list and excellent food. A real community pub
(regional winner of the best community pub in the
2010 Great British Pub awards) with a warm
welcome for all, it has an open fire and a
Wednesday quiz night. Dogs are permitted and
there are plenty of good walks close by. Food is
home-made with locally sourced ingredients to the
Taste of Lincolnshire standard, and is usually
available until 8.30pm. ⚌Q♨❀◐&▲♣P⸺

Ancaster

Ancaster Sports & Social Club

Ermine Street, NG32 3PW
☼ 7 (12 Sat)-11; 12-10.30 Sun ☎ (01400) 230896
John Smith's Bitter; guest beer Ⓗ

Voted Local CAMRA Club of the Year 2012, this
village club is home to numerous sporting teams
and hosts local cup finals. The excellent well-kept
John Smith's is supplemented by different guest
beers. There is an airy conservatory and outside
seating area overlooking the sport pitches. ❀♣P⸺

Barholm

Five Horseshoes Ⓛ

Main Street, PE9 4RA
☼ 4 (1 Sat)-11; 12-10.30 Sun ☎ (01778) 560238
**Adnams Southwold Bitter; Oakham JHB; guest
beers** Ⓗ
A traditional 18th-century stone cottage-style pub
with flagstone floors and a Collyweston slate roof.
Inside there are two bars, two side rooms and a
room for pool and TV (no Sky). An open fire burns
throughout the winter. Outside there is a garden,
patio and a large car park. Barbecues are held in
the summer. The range of guest ales, on six
handpumps, is regularly updated by local and
regional microbreweries. ⚌Q❧❀P⸺

Barrow Haven

Haven Inn 🅛
Ferry Road, DN19 7EX (approx 1½ miles E of Barrow-upon-Humber) TA063230
☼ 11.30-11.30 ☎ (01469) 530247 ⊕ thehaveninn.co.uk
Black Sheep Best Bitter; Taylor Landlord; Tom Wood Best Bitter Ⓗ
The Haven Inn was built in 1730 as a coaching inn for travellers using the nearby ferry, and has remained a place renowned for hospitality, good food and comfortable lodgings ever since. Full of character, the bars have traditional, beamed ceilings, and a warm welcome awaits the weary traveller by the open fire in the lounge. Themed food events, such as pie night and stew/curry night, make this a great pub for both good food and good beer. ▥Q🟎⊛🖼◐🖿🕭🛌🗢♣🐾P⅃

Barton-upon-Humber

Wheatsheaf ✅
3 Holydyke, DN18 5PS
☼ 12-11.30 (12.30am Fri & Sat); 12-11 Sun
☎ (01652) 633292
Black Sheep Best Bitter; Theakston Best Bitter; Wells Bombardier; guest beers Ⓗ
Occupying a prominent position on the main road through Barton, this pub dates back to the 18th century, with a list of former licensees going back to 1791. It has an unspoilt, traditional atmosphere, with regulars enjoying classic bar games of dominoes and crib. The pub has a bar, snug and large drinking/dining area, plus a beer garden and a private car park. A range of excellent traditional pub food is served, and regular specials nights include steak and fish and chips.
▥Q⊛◐🖿🕭🛌(250,350)♣P⅃

Belton

Crown
Church Lane, Churchtown, DN9 1PA (off A161, behind church)
☼ 12-midnight (1.30am Fri & Sat) ☎ (01427) 872834
Batemans XB; Bradfield Farmer's Blonde; Copper Dragon Best; Jennings Cocker Hoop; Marston's EPA; guest beers Ⓗ
Difficult to find but well worth the effort, this hidden gem is a haven for the discerning drinker. Six cask ales are always on offer, including a rotating guest beer from the nearby Glentworth Brewery. Quizzes, live music and pub games are enjoyed at this friendly local, which also holds occasional beer festivals. Winner of Doncaster CAMRA District Pub of the Season award for Autumn 2010. ▥⊛🅰🛌(399)♣P⅃

Billingborough

Fortescue Arms ✅
27 High Street, NG34 0QB
☼ 12-3, 5.30-11; 12-11 Sat & Sun ☎ (01529) 240228
⊕ fortescuearms.co.uk
Adnams Broadside; Ringwood Fortyniner; guest beers Ⓗ
Fine, Grade II-listed inn with an interesting multi-roomed interior and a rustic feel. Popular with diners, it has a large patio to the rear. Nearby is the site of Sempringham Priory and its monument to Gwenllian, daughter of the Prince of Wales, who was confined to the priory in the 12th century.

Stone from the priory was used to build part of the inn. Guest beers are usually from micros.
▥Q🟎⊛◐🖿🛌🗢P⅃

Blyton

Black Horse
93 High Street, DN21 3JX
☼ 11.45-midnight ☎ (01427) 628277
⊕ blackhorseblyton.co.uk
Batemans XB; Marston's EPA Ⓗ
A 250-year-old establishment selling real ale and real food from a real pub, it is a very well-appointed and comfortable local but with a clean, new twist, serving good, home-made food using fresh local meat, fish and vegetables, prepared in a 5 star hygiene-rated kitchen. Pool and darts are played and a Friday quiz night is a regular event. The pub has a real community feel while remaining welcoming to visitors. B&B accommodation is now available on the premises.
▥⊛🖼◐🖿🛌🗢(100)♣🐾P⅃

Boston

Carpenters Arms
20 Witham Street, PE21 6PU (near marketplace)
☼ 12 (11 Sat)-midnight (1am Fri & Sat) ☎ (01205) 362840
Batemans Dark Mild, XB, XXXB; guest beer Ⓗ
Multi-roomed low-ceilinged traditional local hidden in a maze of side streets off the medieval Wormgate, and overlooked by the magnificent Boston Stump. Although a Batemans' house, the Carpenters always has a guest beer on handpump. There is a patio area outside for sunny days. The pub is close to the town centre but you may need to ask for directions more than once to find it. New this year is a lunchtime food menu.
▥⊛◐🖿🛌🗢♣⅃

Eagle
144 West Street, PE21 8RE
☼ 11 (11.30 Thu)-11 (midnight Fri & Sat) ☎ (01205) 361116
Banks's Bitter; Castle Rock Black Gold, Harvest Pale; Fuller's London Pride; guest beers Ⓗ
Part of the Castle Rock chain, the Eagle is known as the real ale pub of Boston. This two-roomed,

INDEPENDENT BREWERIES
8 Sail Heckington
Axholme Luddington (NEW)
Bacchus Sutton-on-Sea
Batemans Wainfleet
Blue Bell Whaplode St Catherine
Blue Cow South Witham
Brewsters Grantham
Cathedral Heights Lincoln (NEW)
DarkTribe East Butterwick
Fulstow Louth
Grafters Willingham by Stow
Hopshackle Market Deeping
Leila Cottage Ingoldmells
Melbourn Stamford
Newby Wyke Grantham
Oldershaw Grantham
Poachers North Hykeham
Riverside Wainfleet
Sleaford (Hop Me Up) Sleaford
Swaton Swaton
Tom Wood Melton Ross
Willy's Cleethorpes

friendly hostelry has an L-shaped bar with a large TV screen for major sporting events. The small cosy lounge has an open fire. The pub stocks a wide range of guest ales, usually including one or more Castle Rock beers, and at least one cider. A function room upstairs is home to Boston Folk Club. Thursday is quiz night – allegedly the hardest in town. ⚠Q🏠🍴🖕♿≠🚫♣🐾🏮

Moon Under Water ✅
6 High Street, PE21 8SH
🕓 9-midnight (1am Fri & Sat) ☎ (01205) 311911
Greene King Abbot; Ruddles Best Bitter; guest beers Ⓗ
Large, lively town-centre Wetherspoon pub near the tidal section of the River Witham. Formerly a government building, an imposing staircase leads from the lounge up to the toilets. A spacious conservatory-style dining area is supplemented by a second child-friendly dining room adjacent to the lounge. The pub offers a good number of guest ales and a large range of continental bottled beers. Local history photographs and information boards highlight important people associated with Boston. 🏠🍴♿≠🚫🐾🏮

Bourne

Smith's of Bourne Ⓛ
25 North Street, PE10 9AE
🕓 9am-11 (midnight Fri & Sat) ☎ (01778) 426819
🌐 smithsofbourne.co.uk
Beer range varies Ⓗ
Originally a family grocers' shop, this pub won a CAMRA/English Heritage award for the successful and imaginative conversion to a public house. Two bar areas serve a maze of interconnecting rooms over two floors. Each area has its own distinct theme, ranging from wooden pews and tables in the bar to high-backed curved leather sofas upstairs. Outside there is a well-equipped patio and large beer garden that hosts an annual beer festival in July. Guest beers are mainly from microbreweries. ⚠Q🏠🍴🖕♿≠🚫(101,102)🏮

Branston

Waggon & Horses
High Street, LN4 1NB
🕓 12-2 (Tue only), 5-midnight; 12-1am Sat; 12-midnight (6 winter) Sun ☎ (01522) 791356 🌐 branstonwaggon.co.uk
John Smith's Bitter; Sharp's Doom Bar; guest beers Ⓗ
A welcoming community pub in the heart of the village. The bar is home to pool, darts, TV and the moose head. Three rotating guests ales are included on the five handpumps. The lounge caters for diners up to 9pm (but Sunday roasts only) where good-value home-cooked food is served. Monday is quiz night, Tuesday jam night, while Saturday night features live entertainment. Regular fun and fund-raising events take place. Three rooms are available for B&B and bikers are welcome. 🏠≠🍴🖕≠🚫(2)♣P🏮

Brigg

Black Bull ✅
3 Wrawby Street, DN20 8JH
🕓 11-3, 7-11; 11-11 Wed-Sat; 12-11 Sun ☎ (01652) 652153
Everards Tiger Best Bitter; guest beer Ⓗ
Popular, cosy, town-centre public house, with a large open-plan seating/drinking area and a TV at

one end. Home-cooked pub meals can be eaten here or in the separate, raised dining area every lunchtime, and Wednesday to Sunday evenings until 7pm. Quiz night is Wednesday. Two changing guest beers supplement the single regular beer. A smoking area is provided at the rear of the building. The pub operates a no-swearing policy. 🏠🍴🚫(909)P🏮

Dying Gladiator
Bigby Street, DN20 8EF
🕓 11-11 (1 am Fri & Sat) ☎ (01652) 652110
Black Sheep Best Bitter; Everards Tiger Best Bitter; Tom Wood Dying Gladiator; guest beer Ⓗ
Uniquely named, traditionally styled town-centre local, with four discrete drinking areas. Two large rooms are simply but tastefully decorated and furnished, and there are sofas in one alcove and traditional pub seating in another. One room has pool, darts and a TV. Four real ales are served including Dying Gladiator, the house beer brewed by Tom Wood. Meals are served in the adjoining Stables, the pub's eatery, but are also available in the pub itself. A statue of the stricken gladiator overhangs the pub entrance. ⚠🏠≠🍴♿🚫(909)♣🏮

Burton-upon-Stather

Ferry House
Stather Road, DN15 9DJ (follow campsite signs through village)
🕓 6 (12 Sun)-11 ☎ (01724) 721783 🌐 theferryhouse.co.uk
Beer range varies Ⓗ
This friendly village local by the side of the River Trent has been in same family for over 52 years. The licensee is in the process of setting up a microbrewery at the pub. Local memorabilia are displayed in the large L-shaped bar, and the family room overlooks the river. A large outdoor seating area is available along with children's play facilities. The pub is a meeting place for local heritage groups. Guest beers mainly come from local breweries. Two beer festivals are held each year. 🐶🏠≠♣🐾P🏮

Castle Bytham

Castle Inn Ⓛ
High Street, NG33 4RZ
🕓 6-11; 10-2, 6-11 Sun ☎ (01780) 410504
Woodforde's Wherry; guest beers Ⓗ
A 17th-century village gem with Newby Wyke beers featuring permanently on the bar and regularly changing guest ales sourced both locally and nationally. A traditional cider and perry are also on offer. Folk nights are a regular feature. An excellent food menu is available every evening and Sunday lunchtime. ⚠Q🏠🍴🚫🐾🏮

Fox & Hounds Ⓛ ✅
6 High Street, NG33 4RZ
🕓 12.30-2.30 (not Mon-Wed), 6 (5 Sat)-11.30; 12.30-2.30, 6-10.30 Sun ☎ (01780) 410336
Marston's Pedigree; Oakham Bishops Farewell; guest beers Ⓗ
Village pub run by the same family for the past 15 years. Quiz night is the first Sunday of the month. Home-cooked food is always available. The first Thursday of the month is curry night – curries are supplied by the award-winning Bengal Clipper (Stamford). ⚠🏠🍴🐾🏮

Claypole

Five Bells 🍺
95 Main Street, NG23 5BJ
✪ 11 (4 Mon)-11; 12-10.30 Sun ☎ (01636) 626561
⊕ thefivebellsclaypole.co.uk
Greene King IPA; Tetley Bitter Ⓗ
Popular village hostelry and Grantham CAMRA Pub of the Year 2012, it features four beers and at least one real cider. The large public bar caters for all ages, and the small restaurant offers a range of home-cooked foods. Outside there is a children's play area and beer garden for the supervising adults. The pub has four well-appointed en-suite rooms. 🏨🍴◑🖵♣♠♦P≒

Cleethorpes

No. 2 Refreshment Room 🍺
Station Approach, DN35 8AX (on station)
✪ 7.30am-midnight ☎ (07905) 375587
Greene King XX Mild; H&H Olde Trip; Hancock's HB; Worthington's Bitter; guest beers Ⓗ
This is a little gem, a small and cosy pub with a reputation for good beer quality and serving four regular beers, plus two guests from both national and independent breweries. Its location on the station ensures a flow of customers enjoying a drink before or after their journeys. A free buffet is provided on Sunday evenings. Smokers may use a covered and heated area on the station concourse. Buses stop within 200 yards. 🏨⇌🖵≒

Nottingham House
5-7 Seaview Street, DN35 8EU
✪ 12-11 (midnight Sat & Sun) ☎ (01472) 505150
Tetley Mild, Bitter; Wychwood Hobgoblin; guest beers Ⓗ
Traditional local with three rooms, located at the highest point in town. The former snug is now a games room with a pool table and darts facilities, while upstairs there is a restaurant serving food lunchtimes Wednesday-Sunday and evenings Wednesday-Saturday. Meals may also be taken in any of the bars. Q🏨◑🖵⇌🖵(9,14)♣

Willy's
17 High Cliff Road, DN35 8RQ
✪ 11-11 (2am Fri & Sat) ☎ (01472) 602145
Draught Bass; Willy's Original; guest beers Ⓗ
Willy's overlooks the River Humber and beach through a glass frontage, giving spectacular views while enjoying the beers. Willy's Original is brewed on the premises and the brewery can be seen from the bar. Food is served lunchtimes as well as at the Tuesday and Thursday evening supper clubs. Extensive camping facilities are available at Meridian Park. Two real ciders are served and can include Moles Black Rat and Gwynt y Ddraig Black Dragon. There is a covered smoking area at the rear. 🏨◑▲⇌🖵(9,46)♦≒

Donington

Black Bull
7 Market Place, PE11 4ST
✪ 11 (12 Sun)-midnight ☎ (01775) 822228
⊕ blackbulldonington.co.uk
Batemans XB; John Smith's Bitter; guest beers Ⓗ
Busy local just off the A52. Four handpumps feature two regular beers and two varying guest beers from small brewers as well as large regionals; Westons cider is on handpump. The

comfortable bar has low, beamed ceilings, wooden settles and a cosy fire in winter. The restaurant offers a good choice of reasonably priced evening meals; lunches are served in the bar. Tables in the car park are used for outdoor drinking. Buses run from Boston and Spalding (not Sun). 🏨🌟◑🖵♦P≒

East Butterwick

Dog & Gun Ⓛ
High Street, DN17 3AJ (off A18 at Keadby Bridge E bank)
SE837058
✪ 5 (12 Sat & Sun)-11 ☎ (01724) 782324
DarkTribe Albacore, Spruce Goose; John Smith's Bitter; Ushers 1824 Ⓗ
Traditional village local alongside the River Trent, with three separate drinking areas linked around a polished wood bar. It is simply but tidily decorated and furnished, with a warming real fire in the bar, and is home to the on-site DarkTribe microbrewery, and two beers from its extensive range are always available. Darts is popular here, and the pub hosts monthly Wheels vehicle nights in summer. Spring and summer drinking can be enjoyed outdoors at riverbank tables, and a rear beer garden overlooks open fields. 🏨🌟🖵(12)♣P≒

Fosdyke

Ship Inn
Moulton Washway, PE12 6LH
✪ 12-3, 6-11 (10 Sun) ☎ (01205) 260764
⊕ maritimecruises.co.uk/ship inn.html
Adnams Southwold Bitter; Batemans XB; guest beer Ⓗ
Located just outside Fosdyke when travelling from Boston on the main A17. As its name suggests, this former Batemans' hostelry is dedicated to all things maritime; maps, photographs, charts and model ships of every description are in plentiful supply. The inn is located near to the busy Fosdyke Marina and boaters and landlubbers are well catered for, with excellent home-cooked food and a welcome cheer. 🏨Q🌟◑♿P

Frognall

Goat Ⓛ
155 Spalding Road, PE6 8SA
✪ 11-3, 6-11; 11.30-11 Sat; 12-10.30 Sun ☎ (01778) 347629
⊕ thegoatfrognall.com
Beer range varies Ⓖ
Friendly pub with a low-ceilinged bar, dining area and separate restaurant. The range of six cask ales, mostly from micros and independents, often includes local Hopshackle beers. Unusually, the pub normally offers two strong dark ales all year round. A large range of single malt whiskies is also on offer, as well as good quality food. The large garden has a play area for children and one for toddlers. A beer festival is held in June. 🏨Q🌟◑♿🖵(22,102)♦P🍴

Gainsborough

Blues Club
Northolme, North Street, DN21 2QW (adjacent to Gainsborough Trinity football ground)
✪ 7 (5 Fri; 12 Sat)-midnight (1am Fri & Sat); 12-midnight Sun
☎ (01427) 613688

Beer range varies Ⓗ
CAMRA members are always welcome at this club on production of a membership card or a copy of the Guide. There is a bar area with several TVs showing sport, a quieter lounge and a large function room that hosts regular live entertainment (admission charges may apply). Two changing real ales are always available, and details of forthcoming beers can be sent to customers by email on request. ⊞&♣

Canute Ⓛ

14-18 Silver Street, DN21 2DP (50yds S of marketplace)
⊙ 9am-midnight ☎ (01427) 678715
Wells Bombardier; guest beers Ⓗ
A typical, lively, town-centre pub where Charles Wells Bombardier is a permanent feature. Landlord Neil is keen to provide a varying range of other beers – there are usually at least five real ales available. Tasting notes are provided, which is a rarity for the area. Good-quality food is served and live sport is shown on many screens. The pub can be busy on Friday and Saturday nights.
☎❀◑&⊞P⁵⁻

Eight Jolly Brewers Ⓛ

Ship Court, Silver Street, DN21 2DW (behind the Canute, facing Riverside Gardens)
⊙ 11 (12 Sun)-midnight ☎ (07767) 638806
Glentworth Lightyear; guest beers Ⓗ
In the Guide for 18 years, this real ale haven based in a 300-year-old Grade II-listed building offers eight varying beers. Many are sourced from northern micros, but new breweries from all areas also feature. Real cider and a wide selection of continental bottled beers are also available. Quality live music can be heard on Thursday night. On Sunday lunchtimes customers bring in food to share. Near the bus station. Q&⊞♣P⁵⁻

R Bar

3 Lord Street, DN21 2DD (400yds W of market square)
⊙ 11-midnight (1am Fri & Sat); 12-midnight Sun
☎ (01427) 611265
Beer range varies Ⓗ
Records show this building was the Old Boar's Head in 1821, although it may have been a pub before then. It was the Hickman Arms until about 1930 and then a Rechabite hall until 2006. Three beers are available, with Ossett Brewery featuring regularly. Poker night is held on Monday, and sport is screened on satellite TV. The jukebox has a wide selection of music. Discounts on real ales are available to CAMRA members. ❀♣♣

Gosberton Risegate

Duke of York

105 Risegate Road, PE11 4EY
⊙ 12 (6.30 Mon)-11; 11-3, 7-10.30 Sun ☎ (01775) 840193
Batemans XB; Black Sheep Best Bitter; guest beers Ⓗ
A long-standing entry, this friendly pub has a deserved reputation for value-for-money beers and food. As well as regular beers, there are guests from a wide range of independent brewers. A good choice of cooked food is available, with portions to suit the largest appetite. Local community life is supported through charities, sports teams and other social events. ₪❀◑⊞&♣P⁵⁻

Grantham

Angel & Royal Ⓛ

High Street, NG31 6PN
⊙ 12-11 (Bistro Bar); 6-11 (Angel Bar, Fri & Sat only)
☎ (01476) 565814 ⊕ angelandroyal.co.uk
Oldershaw Mowbrays Mash Ⓗ
Dating back to the time of the Knights Templar, the Angel & Royal is arguably one of the oldest pubs in England. Both the Angel and Bistro bars feature impressive inglenook fireplaces. The historic Angel bar is only open Friday and Saturday evenings. Beer is supplied by LocAle brewer Oldershaw. Outside, there is a large well-appointed drinking area. ₪Q◑⊞P⁵⁻

Black Dog ✅

19 Watergate, NG31 6NS
⊙ 12-11 (midnight Sat) ☎ (01476) 978507
Mansfield Cask Ale; Marston's Pedigree; Wychwood Hobgoblin; guest beer Ⓗ
After a recent total refurbishment this much-improved quality Marston's pub is welcoming and friendly. The four handpumps serve three Marston's beers and a changing guest ale. With a large open-plan interior, the pub has a strong emphasis on good food every day at reasonable prices, including traditional Sunday lunch, Wednesday curry night and a Thursday grill night. Three screens show live Sky Sports and there is also a large screen in the beer garden. ❀◑⊞♣⁵⁻

Chequers Ⓛ

25 Market Place, NG31 6LR (on narrow paved side street between High St and Market Place Butchers Row)
⊙ 12-midnight (1am Fri & Sat) ☎ (01476) 570149
Beer range varies Ⓗ
This Victorian single-room pub has changed into a trendy public house. The separated drinking areas are furnished with leather sofas and comfortable chairs, making it a place to relax by day; popular with all ages, the pub comes alive at night. The three handpumps feature LocAles from Brewsters and Oldershaw plus guest ales. An outside seating area is available – British weather permitting. ♣

Lord Harrowby Ⓛ

65 Dudley Road, NG31 9AB
⊙ 3-11 (midnight Fri); 11-midnight Sat; 12-11 Sun
☎ (01476) 563515
Oldershaw Heavenly Blonde; Sharp's Doom Bar; guest beers Ⓗ
One of the last remaining back-street locals in Grantham. A traditional two-roomed pub with a log fire in winter, comfortable seating creates a cosy atmosphere. Five beers are available at all times, with guest ales sourced from far and wide. The pub hosts winter and summer beer festivals in a marquee in the garden. Sunday is quiz night. CAMRA members receive a discount on real ales.
₪❀⊞&♣⁵⁻

Nobody Inn Ⓛ

9 North Street, NG31 6NU
⊙ 12-11 (10.30 Sun) ☎ (01476) 565288 ⊕ nobodyinn.com
Marston's EPA, Pedigree; guest beers Ⓗ
The pub is a traditional local on the edge of town and is sport-oriented, with screens throughout, and has live music most weekends. The independently owned free house has six handpumps that support Grantham's three breweries, offering changing guest beers. Newby Wyke beers are always available, while Grantham Gold is brewed

exclusively for the pub. Please leave time to find the hidden entrance to the toilets and watch out for the spider. ✿👶🖪♣🏚

Grimsby

Barge
Riverhead, DN31 1NH
✿ 11-11 (2am Fri & Sat) ☎ (01472) 340911
Wells Bombardier; Wychwood Hobgoblin Ⓗ
The Barge is a converted grain barge moored on the River Freshney in the town centre. It has a slight list, which has been evident for over 20 years, but only adds to its character. It hosts a mix of shoppers by day, with some enjoying the home-cooked lunches. In the evening it caters more for the rock crowd, with a well-stocked jukebox. There is a quiet upstairs room and Monday is quiz night. It has a covered picnic area by the riverside. Cider is from Skidbrooke. ✿🐕🚲🖪♣🏚

Rose & Crown ✪
Louth Road, DN33 2HR (2 miles from town on A16)
✿ 11-11 (midnight Fri & Sat); 11.30-11 Sun
☎ (01472) 278517
Leeds Pale; Tetley Bitter; York Yorkshire Terrier; guest beers Ⓗ
Part of the Ember Inns chain, this popular and friendly pub typically has an emphasis on good, reasonably priced food but is rightly proud of its real ales. One large bar serves several seating areas. Quiz nights are Monday and Wednesday. Monday is pie night, Tuesday is grill night, Wednesday is fish night, while Thursday is curry night. There is a seated and heated patio out front. 🛏✿🕕👶🖪(8,51)**P**🏚

Spiders Web
180 Carr Lane, DN32 8LN
✿ 12-11 (midnight Fri & Sat) ☎ (01472) 692065
⊕ thespiderswebgy.co.uk
John Smith's Bitter; Taylor Landlord Ⓗ
Three-roomed and built in the '50s, this popular community pub holds regular music nights of various genres, with live music enjoyed most weekends. In the bar, games such as poker, darts and pool are played, and there is a weekly quiz night. Away from the bar, the lounge has plenty of seating, while the music room with a stage has a naval theme reflecting the ties with the Naval Association. ✿🕾🖪(14)♣**P**🏚

Walter's Cask Ale House
5-6 Old Market Place, DN31 1DT
✿ 11 (12 Sun)-11 ☎ (01472) 351710
Beer range varies Ⓗ
Formerly the Pestle & Mortar, this town-centre pub, with its mock-Jacobean exterior, is well served by buses and just a short walk from the railway station. It has a large main bar plus a spacious upstairs function room. A changing range of up to six guest beers is sourced from independent and national breweries. An uncovered courtyard at the rear is provided for smokers. The pub can be lively at weekends when local bands are hosted.
👶🚲(Town)🖪♣

Wheatsheaf ✪
47 Bargate, DN34 5AD
✿ 11.30 (12 Sun)-11 ☎ (01472) 246821
Everards Tiger Best Bitter; Leeds Pale; guest beers Ⓗ
A well-used Ember Inns pub, the Wheatsheaf provides its customers with a good, affordable

range of food, in addition to two regular beers and several guest ales. Two bars serve a split-level layout with various seating areas, and an outdoor space incorporates a heated patio for smokers. Quiz nights are Thursday and Sunday.
🛏🐕✿🕕👶👶🚲(Town)🖪**P**🏚

Yarborough Hotel ✪
29 Bethlehem Street, DN31 1JN
✿ 8-midnight (1am Fri & Sat) ☎ (01472) 268283
Greene King Abbot; Ruddles Best Bitter; guest beers Ⓗ
Three-times CAMRA local Pub of the Year, this spacious Wetherspoon establishment utilises the ground floor of what used to be an imposing Victorian railway hotel. Comprising two large bar areas, it also has a front and rear snug plus a seated patio area. It is always busy, particularly at weekends. Good-value meals are served from opening until late. Up to eight guest beers are available, together with cider. Located in the town centre, it is on most bus routes and adjacent to the railway station. **Q**🐕✿🕕👶🚲(Town)🖪♣🏚

Harmston

Thorold Arms
High Street, LN5 9SN
✿ 12-3 (not Mon & Tue), 6 (7 Sun)-11 ☎ (01522) 720358
⊕ thoroldarms.co.uk
Beer range varies Ⓗ
A 17th-century stone building housing a modern-style bar with an open fire, comfortable sofas and traditional tables and chairs. The four beers constantly change, often including something from Lincolnshire brewers. Another handpump offers a regularly changing cider. Community events feature charity evenings, acoustic jam nights, black tie dinners in the separate dining room, and the Harmstock music and beer festival on the August bank holiday. Local societies, such as the camera club, meet here. 🛏**Q**🐕✿🕕▶🖪(1)♣🚶**P**🏚

Heighington

Butcher & Beast
High Street, LN4 1JS
✿ 12-11 (10.30 Sun) ☎ (01522) 790386
⊕ butcherandbeast.co.uk
Batemans XB, XXXB; Castle Rock Harvest Pale; Everards Original; guest beers Ⓗ
With welcoming staff and award-winning publicans, this is an old stone Batemans' pub in the centre of the village on a regular bus route. The pub features distinct areas showing vintage photos and has pub games, charity quizzes and raffles. Westons and Thatchers cider, speciality bottled German and Belgian beers, plus a range of rare whiskies and gins, are available. Meals are served made with local produce, with weekly theme nights. Dogs are allowed in non-food areas. An award-winning floral display adorns the outside.
🛏**Q**🐕✿🕕▶🖪(2)♣🚶**P**🏚

Hemingby

Coach & Horses 🅛
Church Lane, LN9 5QF (1 mile from A158 at Baumber)
✿ 12-2 (not Mon & Tue), 7 (6 Wed-Fri)-11; 12-3, 7-10.30 Sun
☎ (01522) 578280
Riverside Dixon's Major; guest beers Ⓗ

Standing opposite the village church, this former coaching inn is one of the small community's few remaining facilities. The low beams are a hazard to taller customers. An impressive fireplace separates the main bar from the darts/pool area. Dominoes and quiz teams are hosted. Good home-cooked food regularly features in the Tastes of Lincolnshire awards. The camping field is busy when there is motor racing at nearby Cadwell Park. Two guest beers always include a mild. ஆQ♿❄◑▲₪(6)♣P⚊

Holbeach

Horse & Groom

65 High Street, PE12 7ED

✪ 12-3 (5 Fri & Sun), 7-12.30am (1.30am Fri); 12-1.30am Sat ☎ (01406) 422234 ⊕ horseandgroomholbeach.co.uk

Adnams Southwold Bitter; guest beer Ⓗ

Classic town-centre coaching inn dating from the 1800s, with low-beamed ceilings, feature fireplace and a log burner. Lively and welcoming, it offers good food and two well-kept ales, often from local independent breweries. There is a focus on traditional pub games, with many teams participating in local leagues. Live music is hosted occasionally. A winner of Holbeach in Bloom, it has an attractive family-friendly beer garden, and an excellent bus service stops at the door. Disabled access is through the rear car park and heated smoking area. ஆ❄⇔◑♿₪(505)♣P⚊

Horncastle

Red Lion

Bull Ring, LN9 5HT

✪ 11-11 (midnight Fri & Sat); 12-11 Sun ☎ (01507) 523338

Oakwell Barnsley Bitter, Senior Ⓗ

Typical market-town pub with a large bar/lounge with old bay windows overlooking the Bull Ring town centre. Above the bar a collection of 1,000 assorted key rings hangs on display, while framed photographs of Lion Theatre productions from 1988 adorn the walls. The theatre is part of the pub premises, located at the rear, and run by the Horncastle Theatre Company – productions sometimes star the landlord. A snug and a dining room also feature. No food Monday. ♿❄◑♿₪♣⚊

Hubberts Bridge

Wheatsheaf Inn

Station Road, PE20 3QR

✪ 12-2.30 (2 Mon), 5-11.30 ☎ (01205) 290347 ⊕ thewheatsheafinn.org

Batemans XB; Sharp's Doom Bar; guest beer Ⓗ

Pleasant rural free house that has been a pub for well over 100 years and is now run by a family partnership. It stands on the banks of the South Forty Foot Navigation, with moorings nearby. Eventually this waterway will link with the entire Midland canal system, with access currently available via the River Witham at Boston. The pub's first beer festival in 2009 was so successful that it has become an annual event. ஆQ❄◑▲⇆♣P⚊

Ingoldmells

Countryman

Chapel Road, PE25 1ND

✪ 12-midnight (winter times vary) ☎ (01754) 872268 ⊕ countryman-ingoldmells.co.uk

Leila Cottage Leila's Lazy Days, Ace Ale, Lincolnshire Life, Leila's One Off Ⓗ

The privately-owned Countryman appears to be a modern building but it incorporates the early 19th-century Leila Cottage, which gives its name to the brewery behind the pub. A notorious smuggler, James Waite, used to reside here when Ingoldmells was a wild and lonely place, but he certainly would not recognise the current holiday coast, with Skegness, Butlins and Fantasy Island all close at hand. The pub has its own touring caravan park. It is on northern bus routes from Skegness. ♿❄◑♿▲₪P⚊☗

Keelby

Nag's Head

8 Manor Street, DN41 8EF

✪ 12-midnight (10.30 Sun) ☎ (01469) 560660

Theakston Traditional Mild; guest beers Ⓗ

New visitors and locals will feel equally welcome in this two-roomed village pub. The bar features a regular mild and two guest beers often from northern English and Yorkshire breweries. A small garden includes a play area and a covered, lit and heated smoking area. Quiz night is on Tuesday, and there is Wednesday bingo and live music on some weekends. No food is available except for occasional summer weekend barbecues. Served by buses on the Cleethorpes-Hull route. ஆ❄▣₪(X1)♣P⚊

Kirkby on Bain

Ebrington Arms

Main Street, LN10 6YT

✪ 12-2 (not Mon), 6-11 ☎ (01526) 354560 ⊕ ebringtonarms.com

Batemans XB; Black Sheep Golden Sheep; Caledonian Deuchars IPA; Woodforde's Wherry; guest beers Ⓗ

Attractive country pub close to the River Bain and dating from 1610. World War II airmen used to slot coins into the ceiling beams to pay for beer when they returned from missions over Germany. Sadly, many of these coins are still in situ and make a unique memorial to the dead. The popular restaurant offers good food made with local produce (booking advised). There is a convenient caravan site within a mile of the pub. This year sees the introduction of a 42-whisky menu. ஆQ❄◑♿▲♣P⚊

Lincoln

Adam & Eve Tavern ✔

25 Lindum Road, LN2 1NT

✪ 12-11 (11.30 Thu; midnight Fri & Sat); 11-11 Sun ☎ (01522) 537108 ⊕ adamandevelincoln.co.uk

Caledonian Deuchars IPA; Greene King Abbot; guest beer Ⓗ

Standing on Lindum Hill, opposite the medieval Pottergate Arch and a stone's throw from the cathedral, the Adam & Eve claims to be one of the oldest taverns in Lincoln, dating back as far as 1701. It is a pub for all occasions, be it a meal with friends, the weekly quiz nights, live entertainment, or live sport on TV. Pool and darts are also popular with the locals. The bar has three handpumps, one with a regularly changing guest beer. ஆ❄◑▣₪♣P⚊

Dog & Bone

10 John Street, LN2 5BH

☼ 4.30 (12 Fri-Sun)-11 ☎ (01522) 522403

⊕ dogandbonelincoln.co.uk

Batemans XB; guest beers Ⓗ

Opposite the Arboretum is another Victorian oasis: a former local CAMRA Pub of the Year featuring a changing art exhibition and regular events including summer and winter beer festivals. The cosy lounge has a large book exchange library. Events include a folk jam session on the first Sunday of the month, Sunday lunch on the third (booking essential) and live music on the second Saturday. Occasional garden parties, cook-off competitions and gourmet nights also take place. A cider from the Westons range is sold.
🏚️⊛◐🖥️(4)♣♠🌡️

Golden Eagle

21 High Street, LN5 8BD

☼ 11-11 (11.30 Fri & Sat); 12-11 Sun ☎ (01522) 521058

Batemans XB; Castle Rock Harvest Pale; guest beers Ⓗ

Once a Georgian coaching inn, this traditional Castle Rock pub with 10 handpumps offers a good range of guest ales and a cider. Live sport is screened in the bar. The quiet lounge features a real fire and old Lincoln City football programmes (Sincil Bank Stadium is close by). Quiz night is Friday, with open mic on alternate Thursday evenings. A good-sized garden at the rear hosts a beer festival in the summer. Well-behaved dogs and children are welcome. A small function room is available. 🏚️➤⊛🖥️♣♠P🌡️

Jolly Brewer Ⓛ

27 Broadgate, LN2 5AQ

☼ 12-11 (midnight Wed, Fri & Sat) ☎ (01522) 567155

⊕ thejollybrewer.co.uk

Idle Black Abbot; Young's Bitter; guest beers Ⓗ

Regular Guide entry celebrating 30 years as a free house in 2012. The Art Deco interior comprises a long single bar and a separate corridor seating area. A large part-covered courtyard occasionally hosts community theatre productions and music. A good jukebox supports regular live music on Saturdays, while Wednesday is open mic night. Guest beers are often from local brewers. Westons perry and guest ciders from Broadoak and others are on gravity. 🏚️⊛➤(Central)🖥️♣♠P🌡️🍺

Morning Star

11 Greetwell Gate, LN2 4AW

☼ 11-midnight; 12-11 Sun ☎ (01522) 527079

Caledonian Deuchars IPA; Draught Bass; Greene King Abbot; Ruddles Best Bitter; Taylor Golden Best; Wells Bombardier Ⓗ

Dating back to the 18th century, this traditional pub is situated in the Uphill area close to the cathedral. Visitors can sit and relax in one of the two lounge areas, where conversation is the main activity, while sampling the fine cask ales on offer from the centrally located bar, complemented by its tiled floor and open fire. Locally sourced home-cooked food is available at lunchtimes except Sundays. Live music features weekly throughout the summer months. 🏚️Q⊛◐🖥️♣P🌡️

Ritz Ⓛ ✔

143-147 High Street, LN5 7PJ

☼ 8-midnight (1am Fri & Sat) ☎ (01522) 512103

Greene King Abbot; Ruddles Best Bitter; guest beers Ⓗ

A Wetherspoon pub, the Ritz is a prominent former cinema. The neon signlights have been a feature since the late '30s, illuminating the pub in the evening. The cinema closed in the 1990s but plans are in place to open a screen above the pub. Inside, framed displays of acts who graced the stage in years gone by can be seen. Guest beers from local and national breweries are showcased on the long bar. Westons Marcle Hill cider is ever-present.
Q➤⊛◐&⇌🖥️♿🌡️

Strugglers Inn Ⓨ Ⓛ ✔

83 Westgate, LN1 3BG

☼ 12-midnight (11 Sun & Mon; 1am Thu-Sat)

☎ (01522) 535023

Draught Bass; Taylor Landlord; guest beers Ⓗ

A small, welcoming community pub near the castle and cathedral. The main bar has photos and breweriana; the snug has pictures of old Lincoln and an open fire. The surprise garden, a suntrap, has TV for sport. The five guest beers are from the SIBA and Finest Cask lists, often from Lincolnshire, Nottinghamshire or Yorkshire – details are shown on a prominent price list. Simple pub snacks are always available. Sunday teatime live music is a regular feature. Local CAMRA Pub of the Year 2012.
🏚️Q⊛🖥️(7,8)🌡️

Treaty of Commerce

173 High Street, LN5 7AF

☼ 11-11 (1am Fri & Sat); 12-10.30 Sun ☎ (01522) 262940

⊕ treatyofcommerce.co.uk

Batemans XB, XXXB; guest beers Ⓗ

This old High Street pub, close to the railway station, was tastefully refurbished in 2011 with a new bar, including six handpumps and a seating area as you enter. Towards the rear is a new open fireplace and additional drinking and dining areas. Good-quality home-cooked food is served all week, with a special offer on match days of a pie and a free pint. The pub has a friendly, welcoming atmosphere and is a pleasant place to socialise.
🏚️⊛◐⇌(Central)🌡️

Victoria

6 Union Road, LN1 3BJ

☼ 11-midnight (1am Fri-Sat); 12-midnight Sun

☎ (01522) 541000

Batemans XB; Castle Rock Harvest Pale; Taylor Landlord; guest beers Ⓗ

A long-term Guide entry close to the castle's West Gate, the Vic is a small, traditional two-roomed pub with a long narrow bar that offers a range of five guest ales and regular beers plus a guest cider. The small lounge has pictures of Queen Victoria on the walls. Live music features once a month on a Saturday, and there are also monthly general knowledge and music quizzes. Outside is a patio and children's play area. CAMRA members receive a discount. Q⊛◐🖥️(7,8)♣

Wig & Mitre

30 Steep Hill, LN2 1LU

☼ 8.30am-11 (10.30 Sun) ☎ (01522) 535190

⊕ wigandmitre.com

Batemans XB; Everards Tiger Best Bitter; guest beer Ⓗ

Atop the famous cobbled Steep Hill, crowned the UK's best street in 2012, the Wig occupies buildings dating from the 14th century. The narrow frontage belies the extensive interior, with characterful rooms spread over two floors. A free house, it is renowned for the quality of its food but happily welcomes drinkers. Two guest pumps regularly feature beers from Black Sheep and Thwaites. The pub is family-friendly throughout and dogs are welcome downstairs. 🏚️Q🍽️

Louth

Boar's Head 🍺

12 Newmarket, LN11 9HH (next to cattle market)
🕐 closed Mon; 12 (9.30am Thu)-2.30, 6 (7 Wed & Thu)-11; 12-3, 6-11 Sun ☎ (01507) 603561
Batemans Dark Mild, XB, XXXB; guest beers 🅷
Batemans pub a short walk from the town centre, with a good guest beer list. The interior includes two main rooms plus the old snug, warmed by real fires in the winter, and always providing a friendly welcome. Pub games include darts, dominoes and a pool table. Thursday is cattle market day, which is why the pub opens earlier. Lunches are served daily except Monday, depending on the season; Sunday lunch is worth booking. 🏚️Q🍽️🍴♣️�)

Brown Cow

133 Newmarket, LN11 9EG
🕐 5-midnight; 12-3 Fri; 12-midnight Sat & Sun
☎ (01507) 605146
Adnams Southwold Bitter; Black Sheep Best Bitter; Castle Rock Harvest Pale; guest beer 🅷
Formerly the Newmarket Inn, this family-run, classically decorated free house is only five minutes' walk from the town centre. A free quiz is held every Sunday night and the local folk club meets here on a Tuesday evening. The popular bistro serves traditional home-cooked food made with locally sourced produce (booking is recommended). Food is available Wednesday to Saturday lunchtimes and evenings, 12-3pm only on Sunday. Q🟠🍽️P

Cobbles Bar

2 New Street, LN11 9PU (off Cornmarket)
🕐 10-midnight (2am Fri & Sat); 12-10 Sun ☎ (07736) 275262
Black Sheep Best Bitter; guest beer 🅷
Traditional pub-style bar based in the centre of town, with friendly staff at all times. This small but accommodating venue has multiple personalities, from bustling coffee shop serving light lunches to a busy pre-club local with DJs and live music at the weekend. It has a good beer trade, with two contrasting cask ales, as well as a huge selection of exotic spirits. Disabled access is right through the front doors. 🟠🍽️🍴🚇

Gas Lamp Lounge 🍷 🍺

13 Thames Street, LN11 7AD
🕐 5 (12 Sat & Sun)-11 ☎ (01507) 607661
Fulstow Marsh Mild, Fulstow Common, Northway IPA, Pride of Fulstow; guest beer 🅷
The tap for Fulstow Brewery, this is a warm and welcoming watering hole, with four regular beers from the upstairs brewery and a guest beer. Sample quality ales without the bother of noisy TVs and loud music in the bar of this recently converted building. Set along the canalside are benches for enjoying a drink in the summer, and inside is a roaring logburner to sit beside in the winter months. Dogs are welcome. 🏚️Q🍴♣️P

Joseph Morton 🍺 ✅

Pawnshop Passage, LN11 9EZ (small alleyway off Mercer Row)
🕐 9am-11 (midnight Fri & Sat) ☎ (01507) 353700
Greene King Abbot; Ruddles Best Bitter; guest beers 🅷

Wetherspoon pub opened in 2011 and comprising several combined properties, the tallest of which is a former warehouse built between 1808 and 1834, with cast-iron wall plates bearing the name of local ironmonger Joseph Morton. There is also a smaller warehouse facing Kidgate, rebuilt in 1818 along with two 19th-century houses in Pawnshop Passage. Some cast-iron gears were found in the renovation and are part of a ceiling decoration. 🟠🍽️🍴🍴🚇

Ludford

White Hart Inn

Magna Mile, LN8 6AD
🕐 closed Mon; 12-2 (not Tue-Thu), 6-11; 12-3.30, 7-11 Sun
☎ (01507) 313489
Beer range varies 🅷
Former 18th-century coaching house that is now a two-roomed rural village pub close to the Viking Way, popular with hikers and ramblers. It offers four different guest beers; the licensees pride themselves on serving real ale from microbreweries. All food is home made, using ingredients from local suppliers, and meals are available lunchtimes and evenings. There is guest accommodation separate from the pub.
🏚️Q🟠🛏️🍽️P

Market Deeping

Vine 🍺

19 Church Street, PE6 8AN
🕐 4-11 (midnight Fri); 12-midnight Sat; 12-11 Sun
☎ (01778) 218622
Sharp's Doom Bar; Wells Vine Ale; guest beers 🅷
Friendly two-bar pub, sympathetically refurbished a few years ago and a free house since 2011. The limestone building was formerly a Victorian prep school. The pub has a strong local following for the high-quality real ales on offer. Local Hopshackle beers often feature. Food is not available but free tiffin (bread and cheese) is provided Monday to Friday for early evening drinkers. The TV in the main bar is only used for major sporting events. 🟠🚇

Market Rasen

Aston Arms

18 Market Place, LN8 3HL
🕐 11-11 (11.30 Fri & Sat); 12-10.30 Sun ☎ (01637) 842313
John Smith's Bitter; Wells Bombardier; guest beer 🅷
Large pub sitting prominently at the head of the market square in the centre of the town. The single room is split into distinct areas, with beams and an inglenook as you enter, a games area towards the rear with TV screens for sport, plus a lounge area that is usually quieter. The pub is friendly and caters for all age groups. The food is good quality and value and this venue welcomes families.
🏚️🐕🟠🍽️🚆🚇(3,23)♣️P🚇

Marshchapel

White Horse

Sea Dyke Way, DN36 5SX
🕐 4 (12 Sun)-midnight; 12-1am Fri & Sat ☎ (01472) 388280
Beer range varies 🅷
Two-roomed coaching inn formerly part of Grimsby's Hewitts Brewery estate, now an Enterprise Inns pub. The landlord is the second

generation of the family to be the pub's licensee. Real ales outsell lager considerably and two well-rotated guest ales may come from Theakston, Black Sheep, Caledonian and St Austell. Food is locally sourced and served lunchtimes Friday-Sunday and evenings Wednesday-Saturday. There is bingo, a free quiz and a regular open night for musicians to bring in their instruments for a jam session. ▲❀◑ ⏛⛶(50)♣P⸜

Messingham

Horn Inn
61 High Street, DN17 3NU
❀ 11-11 (1.30am Wed; midnight Sat) ☎ (01724) 762426
Black Sheep Best Bitter; Taylor Landlord; guest beers Ⓗ
In the village centre, this venue is popular with locals and visitors for its regular, changing real ales and its excellent food. Quality home-made meals are available lunchtimes and evenings (no food Wed and Sat), and there is a raised dining area in the larger of the two rooms. Quiz night is Monday and live music is hosted on Wednesday and Saturday evenings. There are several distinct drinking areas, plus a sheltered patio at the rear for use in the warmer months. ▲Q❀◑ ⏛⛶♣P⸜

Pooleys
46 High Street, DN17 3NT
❀ closed Mon; 6 (7 Sun)-11 ☎ (01724) 762220
Batemans XB; guest beers Ⓗ
Pooleys is an attractive, well-appointed village tea room by day and a busy licensed bar in the evenings, increasingly popular with local drinkers and visitors alike. It has three separate drinking areas with rustic furniture and fittings, and a bar area serving Batemans XB as a stock beer plus three rotating guests, often from the likes of Batemans, Everards, Oakham, St Austell and Hook Norton. Unusual foreign keg beers and lagers are also available. Occasional mini beer festivals are planned. ▲Q◑⛶

Moulton

Swan ✔
13 High Street, PE12 6QB
❀ 11-11 ☎ (01406) 370349
Wells Bombardier; guest beers Ⓗ
A family-run pub in the centre of an attractive village that enjoys a good daytime bus service (Norfolk Green buses stop just across the road). One regular real ale and three changing guest ales are available as well as cider from Westons on handpump. The hostelry has an excellent reputation for food, with an interesting and varied menu, and serves credit crunch specials Mondays-Wednesdays. It is family- and dog-friendly, with a pleasant and popular garden. ▲❧❀◑ ⏛⛶♣●P⸜

North Hykeham

Centurion ✔
Newark Road, LN6 8LB
❀ 11.30-11 (midnight Thu-Sat) ☎ (01522) 509814
Leeds Pale; Tetley Bitter; York Yorkshire Bitter; guest beers Ⓗ
Part of the Ember Inns chain, this family-friendly pub is modern and fresh. There is a changing line-up of guest ales taken from Ember's Cask Club

selection. Food is reasonably priced and served until 10pm. Children are welcome when dining with the family. Regular quiz nights are held. The pub is a 20-minute bus ride from Lincoln city centre. ▲❀◑⛶⛶(27,46)P⸜

North Kelsey

Butchers Arms Ⓛ
Middle Street, LN7 6EH (off main road through village)
❀ 4-midnight (1.30am Fri); 12-1.30am Sat; 12-midnight Sun
☎ (01652) 678002
Tom Wood Best Bitter, Lincoln Gold, Bomber County Ⓗ
Traditional local in the centre of a quiet village, open plan in design, with a polished wood bar and overhanging hop bine. Simply but comfortably decorated in rustic style, it has a welcoming real fire. Three beers from the Tom Wood range are usually available, supplemented by an occasional guest beer. Weekly quiz nights are held, and a games area is used for darts. The pub has an attractive beer garden framed by mature trees, which is popular for alfresco drinking in spring and summer. ▲❀&♣P⸜

Old Bolingbroke

Black Horse Inn
Moat Lane, PE23 4HH
❀ closed Mon; 8.30-11 Tue; 12-3, 7-11 ☎ (01790) 763388
Milestone Black Pearl; Young's Bitter; guest beers Ⓗ
Situated in a splendid walking area, this fine old country inn has origins dating back to the 14th century but was largely rebuilt in 1930. Henry IV was born at nearby Bolingbroke Castle, which was also besieged during the Civil War. The battle of Winceby, which was fought a few miles from Bolingbroke in 1643, witnessed the first nationally important victory for Oliver Cromwell's cavalry. Still part of the Duchy of Lancaster, the Black Horse is a great place to visit when exploring the Lincolnshire Wolds. ▲Q❀◑&▲♣●P⸜

Pinchbeck

Bull Inn ✔
1 Knight Street, PE11 3RA
❀ 12 (11 Wed)-2.30, 5-11 (midnight Fri); 12-midnight Sat; 12-11 Sun ☎ (01775) 723022
John Smith's Bitter; guest beers Ⓗ
A welcoming, friendly village pub opposite the green, which still has the old stocks. The Bull has two comfortable bars: the public bar with a log fire, and the lounge, used mainly for dining. A carved bull's head features on the long bar front, with the bar rail representing its horns. The pub has a reputation for good food, from bar snacks to meals in the upstairs restaurant. Guest beers change regularly, often coming from local micros. ▲❀◑&⛶P⸜🍺

Quadring

White Hart
7 Town Drove, PE11 4PU
❀ 12-3 (not Mon-Wed), 6.30 (5 Fri)-11 ☎ (01775) 822178
Batemans XXXB Ⓗ
Friendly, small village pub, popular with locals. It serves only one, occasionally changing, real ale at a time, always in excellent condition. Kimes buses from Boston and Spalding stop at the nearby

crossroads (not eves or Sun). Pool and darts are offered in the bar – the landlord often joins in the pool. ⚐☺⛬♿🖵(59)♣P

Revesby

Red Lion
Main Road, PE22 7NU
☼ 12-11 (midnight Fri & Sat) ☎ (01507) 568665
⊕ redlion-revesby.co.uk
Batemans XB, XXXB; guest beer 🄷
In the heart of rural Lincolnshire, this newly refurbished Batemans' pub offers superb locally sourced foods in its separate restaurant. Game often features on the menu. Accommodation is available at sensible prices. Nearby attractions include the Lincolnshire Aviation Museum, Tattershall Castle and the Battle of Britain Memorial Flight. Well worth a visit. ⚐☺✉◑♿P⅃

Ropsley

Ropsley Fox
23-25 Grantham Road, NG33 4BX
☼ 12-3, 6-11; 12-midnight Fri & Sat; 12-11 Sun
☎ (01476) 585957 ⊕ ropsleyfox.co.uk
Adnams Southwold Bitter; Taylor Landlord; guest beers 🄷
Traditional village pub dating from 1657. With its low-beamed ceiling, the bar area is on the small side, but there is plenty of seating. A separate conservatory and dining area are available along with a games room and garden. A high standard of cuisine at pub prices is offered, supplemented with daily specials. ⚐☺◑♣P

Ruskington

Shoulder of Mutton
11 Church Street, NG34 9DU
☼ 12-11 ☎ (01526) 832220
John Smith's Bitter; Sharp's Doom Bar; Wells Bombardier; guest beer 🄷
A popular and thriving pub in the heart of the village that attracts a clientele of all ages. With its low wooden ceilings in its two main rooms it is probably one of the oldest buildings in the village and, reputedly, once housed a butcher's shop, hence the name. Although additions have been made in recent years they have not spoiled the essential character. There is a separate pool room. ☺⛬♿≈🖵♣P⅃

Sandtoft

Reindeer
Thorne Road, DN8 5SZ (follow signs for Sandtoft from A18)
☼ closed Mon; 12-midnight ☎ (01724) 710774
Black Sheep Best Bitter; Taylor Landlord; guest beers 🄷
Popular village pub with a reputation for good food as well as cask ale. Recently refurbished, the restaurant is notable for an impressive mural depicting the history of the Isle of Axholme by local artist Mary Daw. At least two ales are always available, with guest beers in the summer. Sandtoft Transport Museum is nearby. ⚐☺◑♿♣P⅃

Saxilby

Anglers
65 High Street, LN1 2HA
☼ 11.30-12.30am; 12-midnight Sun ☎ (01522) 702200
⊕ theanglerslincoln.co.uk
Caledonian Deuchars IPA; Greene King IPA; guest beers 🄷
A popular village local, home to crib, darts, dominoes, football and pool teams. This Victorian pub welcomes all. Old pictures of Saxilby are displayed around the lounge, where the village history group meets. The bar is popular with sporting locals, as can be seen from the memorabilia. Two guest beers are sourced from the Heineken UK list. ☺⛬≈🖵(100,105)♣P⅃

Scamblesby

Green Man
Old Main Road, LN11 9XG
☼ 12-2.30 (not Mon), 5-midnight; 12-midnight Thu-Sun
☎ (01507) 343282
Young's Bitter; guest beer 🄷
Welcoming village pub in picturesque wolds countryside, popular with walkers and visitors to Cadwell Park race circuit just a mile away. Accommodation is available, together with traditional good-value meals, served until 8.30pm. A spacious main bar and a quiet lounge are both patrolled by Alfie, the pub dog. Lots of motorcycle memorabilia is on display. The guest beer usually changes every month. ⚐Q☺⛬✉◑♿ΔP

Scotter

Sun & Anchor
54 High Street, DN21 3RX
☼ 12-midnight (1am Fri & Sat); 12-11 Sun ☎ (01724) 763444
Greene King IPA; guest beers 🄷
Village-centre pub near the A159, popular with locals both for the bar with traditional pub games and the spacious, comfortable lounge. There is a large outdoor seating area where visitors are free to use the pub barbecue. Several sports teams are based at the venue. One regular beer and two guests, often from Lincolnshire breweries, are served. TV features major rugby and football matches. ⚐☺⛬♿🖵(100,353)♣P⅃

Scunthorpe

Berkeley ★
Doncaster Road, DN15 7DS (½ mile from end of M181)
☼ 11.30-2.30, 5-11; 12-11 Fri & Sat; 12-10.30 Sun
☎ (01724) 842333
Samuel Smith Old Brewery Bitter 🄷
A 1930s Samuel Smith's hotel identified by CAMRA as one of Britain's Real Heritage Pubs. The landscaped front entrance leads to three rooms: the main lounge with a real fire and Art Deco interior, a restaurant area, and a ballroom with a staircase leading to seven hotel rooms. A side entrance provides access to the large public bar and beer garden. Lunchtime and evening meals are available, with a carvery on Sunday. The pub is five minutes' walk from Glanford Park football ground. ⚐Q☺✉◑⛬♿🖵P⅃

Blue Bell ✔
1-7 Oswald Road, DN15 7PU (at town-centre crossroads)

🌀 9am-11 (midnight Fri & Sat) ☎ (01724) 863921
Greene King IPA, Abbot; Ruddles Best Bitter; guest beers ⒣
Popular Wetherspoon pub with an open-plan layout on two levels, with tables for dining. Outside is a beer garden with a heated patio area for smokers. Beer festivals are held twice a year, as well as mini festivals with ales from regional breweries. Food is served lunchtimes and evenings. The pub celebrates special events such as Burns Night and Valentine's Day. Discounts apply for CAMRA members on real ales on Wednesdays, together with 10 per cent off food from the main menu all week. Q✿◗&⇌🖵🐾✆

Chancel
Cambridge Avenue, Bottesford, DN16 3LG
🌀 12-11 (midnight Thu-Sun) ☎ (01724) 840913
Beer range varies ⒣
Large community pub, recently refurbished, comprising two rooms – one is a public bar with pool and TV, the other an open-plan, spacious lounge that is attractively decorated and comfortably furnished. Meals are served in the lounge lunchtimes and evenings Wednesday to Saturday plus Sunday lunchtime (booking advisable). A grassed, outdoor patio area can be accessed from the lounge. Three rotating guest beers are available, and customers can request beers they would like to try. Quiz nights are held on Wednesday, Thursday and Sunday.
🛏✿◗🖵🖵(32A)♣✆

Malt Shovel Ⓛ
219 Ashby High Street, Ashby, DN16 2JP (in Ashby Broadway shopping area)
🌀 10-11 (midnight Fri & Sat); 12-11 Sun ☎ (01724) 843318
Exmoor Gold; Tom Wood Best Bitter; guest beers ⒣
Self-styled country pub in the town, with the widest choice of beer and cider in the area. Eight real ales include permanent, rotating Oakham beers and microbrewery guests. Twice-yearly week-long beer festivals are held in spring and autumn. The pub gets busy lunch and teatimes for good-value home-cooked food. Magazines, newspapers, book swap and members-only snooker facilities are available. Quizzes are on Tuesdays and Thursdays, with live music alternate Saturdays. Handy for the shops, but do your shopping first, otherwise you just might not bother.
✿◗&🖵🐾✆

Skendleby

Blacksmiths Arms
Main Road, PE23 4QE
🌀 12-3 (not Mon), 5.30-11 (not Sun eve winter)
☎ (01754) 890662
Batemans XB; guest beers ⒣
Dating back to the 18th century, this pub is set in an attractive Lincolnshire Wolds village. Ducking beneath the low door lintel, fortunately well-padded, you discover a cosy, friendly atmosphere in the small quarry-tiled snug bar, complete with range and settles. The cellar is visible through a glass panel behind the bar. The dining room at the rear incorporates the building's old well and there are fine views over the wolds. It is an ideal base for walking, with a cottage for overnight accommodation. 🚶Q✿🛏◗🖵♣✆

Sleaford

Packhorse Inn ✅
7 Northgate, NG34 7BH
🌀 8-midnight (1am Fri & Sat) ☎ (01529) 308730
Courage Directors; Greene King Abbot; Ruddles Best Bitter; guest beers ⒣
This 18th-century coaching inn on the London to Lincoln road has had several names during its lifetime, reverting to the original name when it was taken over by Wetherspoon a few years ago. Despite being remodelled as partly open plan, it retains an intimate atmosphere. As the Lion Hotel it hosted the opening dinner for the Sleaford Railway, an event that marked the start of the decline in coaching trade. The usual good-value Wetherspoon food menu is served.
Q🛏✿◗&⇌🖵✆

Snitterby

Royal Oak
High Street, DN21 4TP (½ mile off A15)
🌀 5 (12 Sat)-11; 12-10.30 Sun ☎ (01673) 818273
Greene King IPA; Rudgate Ruby Mild; Thwaites Original; guest beers ⒣
Good old-fashioned family-run community pub in a village setting, with a friendly welcome, going from strength to strength. It now has up to eight real ales on at any one time. In 2011, 116 guest ales were served from 62 breweries. The traditional interior is light and airy, with wooden floors and real fires. Outside, a seating area overlooks a stream. High-quality food made from carefully sourced local produce is served Thursday to Sunday. Mini beer festivals are held each bank holiday. Well-behaved dogs are welcome.
🚶Q✿◗🅰🐾P✆

Spalding

Ivy Wall ✅
18-19 New Road, PE11 1DQ
🌀 9am-midnight (1am Fri & Sat) ☎ (01775) 719770
Greene King Abbot; Ruddles Best Bitter; guest beers ⒣
The town-centre site on which this spacious, modern Wetherspoon pub now stands has had a variety of uses over the years, and was once on the bank of the former Westlode river. Excavations during the rebuild in 2005 discovered an undercroft and cellar from the late medieval period. Changing guest ales are normally sourced from local breweries, and there are Westons ciders dispensed by gravity. Food is available all day. Photographs and archaeological finds are displayed on the wall.
✿◗⇌🐾✆

Lincoln Arms
4 Bridge Street, PE11 1XA
🌀 11-12.30am; 11-4, 7-midnight Sun ☎ (01775) 710017
Mansfield Cask Ale; guest beer ⒣
Overlooking the picturesque River Welland and a stone's throw from Ayscoughfee Hall, this town local has the relaxed feel and atmosphere of a village pub, with a regular clientele, where lively conversation and pub games prevail. Regularly changing guest ales are from the Marston's stable. Every second Thursday of the month Spalding Folk Club holds a jam session. No meals are served, but a selection of rolls is available Monday to Saturday lunchtimes. 🚶⇌♣✆

Red Lion Hotel ✓

Market Place, PE11 1SU

🕙 10-midnight ☎ (01775) 722869

🌐 redlionhotel-spalding.co.uk

Draught Bass; Fuller's London Pride; Greene King Abbot; guest beer 🅷

A cosy and welcoming one-room traditional hotel bar popular with locals and visitors, overlooking the marketplace, with tables and chairs outside in the fine weather. The pub is a regular entry in the Guide and the staff take great pride in the quality of the cask ales. It is a rare outlet for Bass in the locality. The restaurant serves a selection of Indian cuisine. ❀🍴🖪🚶

Stamford

Green Man 🄻

29 Scotgate, PE9 2YQ

🕙 11 (12 Sun)-midnight ☎ (01780) 753598

Caledonian Deuchars IPA; guest beers 🅷

Stone-built former coaching inn dating from 1796 with an L-shaped split-level bar. There are always eight beers and up to seven ciders available, as well as a good range of European bottled beers. Two beer festivals are held each year on the secluded patio, which features one of only five stepping stones dating back to the inn's coaching days. Beer memorabilia adorn the walls.

🏚❀🍴◖🚶🖪(201)♣🐾💺⛴

Jolly Brewer 🄻

1 Foundry Road, PE9 2PP

🕙 11-midnight; 12-11.30 Sun ☎ (01780) 755141

🌐 jollybrewer.com

Oakham JHB; Sharp's Doom Bar; guest beers 🅷

Stone-built pub dating back to 1830. The interior comprises one L-shaped room around the bar and an adjoining small dining area. Locally sourced home-cooked food is served daily and Sunday lunches are always popular. A good community pub, it is home to pool, darts, crib and dominoes teams. It has six handpumps serving beers from far and wide as well as from several local breweries. Traditional cider is available as are around 30 whiskies. 🏚❀◖🚶🖪(9)♣🐾💺

Tobie Norris 🄻

12 St Paul's Street, PE9 2BE

🕙 11.30-11; 12-10.30 Sun ☎ (01780) 753800

🌐 tobienorris.com

Adnams Southwold Bitter; guest beers 🅷

Parts of this building date back to around 1280. In 1617 it was bought by Tobie Norris and used as a bell foundry. It was presented with CAMRA's Conversion to Pub Use Award when it was converted into a pub from a RAFA Club. Five handpumps serve many local beers and others from far and wide. Two beer festivals are held each year. The menu includes pizzas with unusual toppings. 🏚Q❀◖🚶🖪(202,203)♣💺

Stickford

Red Lion Inn

Church Road, PE22 8EP

🕙 closed Mon & Tue; 7 (6 Fri & Sat)-11; 12-2.30, 7-10.30 Sun ☎ (01205) 480395 🌐 redlionstickford.co.uk

Batemans XB; guest beer 🅷

The Red Lion is the most common pub name in England and is frequently found hereabouts thanks to the 14th century John of Gaunt, Earl of Lancaster,

whose heraldic emblem it was and who lived locally. This is a cosy, friendly pub with two bars and a small room used as a restaurant and for private functions. Food is served evenings and Sunday lunchtimes, using local produce such as rabbit pie. A beer festival is held, and camping and accommodation are projects for the near future. 🏚Q❀🖤🖪🛏♿P🚶

Sturton by Stow

Plough Inn

Till Bridge Lane, LN1 2BP

🕙 6.30-11 Mon & Tue; 12-2, 5-11 Wed-Fri; 12-midnight Sat; 12-11 Sun ☎ (01427) 788268

Batemans XB; Fuller's London Pride; guest beers 🅷

A small, comfortable, family-run pub at the centre of the village, close to stops for Lincoln-Gainsborough buses. Good value food is served (not Sun and Mon eves) – fish and chips are a speciality, and a carvery on Sunday. One of the two guest beers is often from a Lincolnshire brewery such as Grafters or Oldershaw. Westons Traditional cider is usually available. Q❀◖🖤🖪(100)♣P💺

Surfleet

Riverside Hotel

123 Station Road, Surfleet Seas End, PE11 4DG

🕙 12-2.30, 5.30-11; 12-midnight Fri-Sun ☎ (01775) 680675

🌐 theriversidesurfleet.com

Beer range varies 🅷

Pleasant riverside pub on the banks of the Glen on the edge of an attractive village. It has an L-shaped bar/lounge with offshoot dining rooms and a conservatory overlooking the river. Three guest beers, often from micros, change fairly regularly. Note the unusual marble table with supporting eagle near the entrance. Accommodation includes en-suite facilities. Riverside wildlife make this an attractive area for walks. ❀🍴◖🛏♿♣P💺

Sutterton

Thatched Cottage

Pools Lane, PE20 2EZ

🕙 11.30-11.30 ☎ (01205) 460870

🌐 thatchedcottagerestaurant.co.uk

John Smith's Bitter; guest beers 🅷

Picturesque thatched 17th-century listed building, a rarity in fen country, which was a private house until 1985. Although extended and modernised to the rear, the bar and separate dining room exhibit a wealth of ancient timbers and inglenook fireplaces – tall people beware. Behind the pub is a country farm store, and meat is butchered and cured on the premises. A country park and arboretum is being developed, with an area for pétanque and quoits. Q❀◖🖤♿🖪P💺

Sutton-on-Sea

Bacchus Hotel 🄻

17 High Street, LN12 2EY (on main A52 through town)

🕙 10-midnight (1am Fri & Sat) ☎ (01507) 441204

🌐 bacchushotel.co.uk

Bacchus Bittermans, Sutton Pride; Courage Directors; Ruddles County; Sharp's Doom Bar; guest beers 🅷

A long-established hotel selling a varied range of beers, including several from local breweries and the hotel's microbrewery. Well-attended beer festivals are held over the late spring and autumn

bank holiday weekends. The pub is used regularly by local clubs and societies and is also popular with tourists. A wide range of food is available, from bar snacks to restaurant dining. There is a large garden and patio area, and it is on the bus route between Skegness and Mablethorpe.
⚠Q⮧❀⛱◑⚅⛾🏠(9)♣P⏚

Swineshead

Pig & Whistle
Market Place, PE20 3LJ
✪ 5.30 (12 Sat)-11; 12-4, 7.30-11 Sun ☎ (01205) 821381
⊕ pig-and-whistle-real-ale.co.uk
Banks's Mild; Fuller's London Pride; guest beers Ⓗ
A great example of bringing a run-down and long-closed pub back to life as a vibrant and thriving village local. The owners have successfully blended old and new and recreated a genuine community pub with an emphasis on beer and traditional pub games. Guest beers come from a wide range of breweries and the food comprises home-made pizzas and bar snacks. ⚠❀♣●P⏚

Swinhope

Click 'em Inn
LN8 6BS (2 miles N of Binbrook on B1203) TF222973
✪ 12-3 (not Mon-Wed), 5-11; 12-11.30 Fri & Sat; 12-10.30 Sun ☎ (01472) 398253 ⊕ clickem-inn.co.uk
Batemans XXXB; Taylor Landlord; guest beers Ⓗ
Country pub set in the picturesque Lincolnshire Wolds, and a good stopping place for walkers and cyclists. The unusual name originates from the counting of sheep through a nearby clicking gate. Good home-cooked food is available in the bar and conservatory. A changing range of guest beers is offered alongside the house beer, Terry's Tipple (Hancock's HB). An outside covered but unheated area is available to smokers. Local CAMRA Country Pub of the Year 2012. Q❀◑♣P⏚

Tattershall Thorpe

Blue Bell Inn
Thorpe Road, LN4 4PE
✪ 12-3, 7-11 ☎ (01526) 342206 ⊕ bluebell-inn.com
Batemans XB; Shepherd Neame Spitfire; guest beers Ⓗ
An ancient building in a delightful location, this is one of Lincolnshire's oldest inns with 13th-century origins. It has a large open fire and beamed ceilings that are covered in signatures and photographs of airmen from World War II RAF squadrons who used the pub, including the 617 Dambusters and 627 Pathfinders. King Henry VIII reputedly visited the Blue Bell and there is a ghost in residence. ⚠Q❀◑⚅♣P⏚

Theddlethorpe

King's Head Inn
Mill Road, LN12 1PB (signed from A1031)
✪ closed Mon winter; 12-11; 12-10.30 (winter hours vary) Sun ☎ (01507) 339798 ⊕ kingsheadinn.com
Batemans XB; guest beers Ⓗ
Set on the edge of a picturesque village near the North Sea coast, this pub is the longest single-storey thatched public house in Britain, built in 1623. Entering it is like stepping back in time. Keep a lookout for two thrones in the restaurant. The bars are warmed by roaring open fires in the

winter months. Beware the low ceiling of the front bar. The restaurant has a good reputation and booking is recommended. There are picnic tables outside in the large garden. ⚠Q❀◑⚅♣P

Threekingham

Three Kings Inn
Saltersway, NG34 0AU
✪ closed Mon; 12-3, 6-11 (10.30 Sun) ☎ (01529) 240249
⊕ thethreekingsinn.com
Draught Bass; Taylor Landlord; guest beer Ⓗ
A fine country inn retaining charm and character. Its comfortable lounge and bar, with attractive and bright rural prints, and its panelled dining room serving locally sourced food, are deservedly popular with locals and visitors. Guest beers are usually from independent brewers. There is a pleasant terraced garden for the summer months, and a large function room. The pub name refers to the slaying of three Danish chieftains in 870 in a battle in nearby Stow; look for the effigies above the entrance. ⚠❀◑▶AP⏚

Waddington

Three Horseshoes
High Street, LN5 9RF
✪ 12 (3 Mon; 11 Sat)-midnight; 12-11 Sun ☎ (01522) 720448
John Smith's Bitter; guest beers Ⓗ
Tucked away in the centre of the village, this traditional pub provides visitors with a fine selection of up to four regularly changing cask ales sourced from microbreweries. The pub thrives on community spirit and is home to a number of local sports teams that add to the lively ambience. The main bar area is complemented by a smaller, quieter back room that benefits from a real fire. An annual beer festival is held in the summer months. ⚠⮧❀⚅🏠(1,13)♣⏚

Wainfleet

Batemans Brewery Visitors Centre
Salem Bridge Brewery, Mill Lane, PE24 4JE
✪ closed Mon, Tue & Jan; 11.30-4 (2.30 Feb-Mar, Oct-Dec) ☎ (01754) 882009 ⊕ bateman.co.uk
Batemans Dark Mild, XB, XXXB, seasonal beer; guest beer Ⓗ
A pilgrimage for many, Batemans draws real ale fans from far and wide, so the bar in the iconic windmill is the ideal place to sample those Good Honest Ales. A seasonal beer is also available, and a good selection of Tastes of Lincolnshire food is offered. Further entertainment is to be found in the Brewery Experience, brewery tours featuring the Theatre of Beers, traditional pub games, and the relaxing beer garden. Bar snacks are served 12-2pm and brewery tours are at noon and 2.30pm. ⚠❀◑⚅🚃🏠♣P⏚

Westwoodside

Carpenters Arms
Newbigg, DN9 2AT (on B1396 in centre of village)
✪ 4 (2 Sat; 12 Sun)-midnight ☎ (01427) 752416
Caledonian Deuchars IPA; Wells Bombardier; guest beers Ⓗ
This popular village local takes an active part in local community life and has raised significant sums of money each year for charities. Under the

present licensees, the beer range has increased – five are often on offer, including at least two sourced from microbreweries, and there are plans to add another handpump. Traditional games are a feature here, and the pub participates in the annual Haxey Hood contest. Winner of two local CAMRA Pub of the Season awards. ✿⬛🍴☖(391,399)♣P⅃

Willingham by Stow

Half Moon ♈ ⬛

23 High Street, DN21 5JZ (200yds from B1241 jct)
✪ 12-2 (Wed-Fri only), 6-11; 12-11 Sat; 12-10.30 Sun
☎ (01427) 788340
Grafters Traditional, Over the Moon, Brewers Troop, Moonlight; guest beers Ⓗ

Home to Grafters Brewery, this popular village pub goes from strength to strength. It offers four permanent Grafters ales, and four additional pumps serve a Batemans beer and three rotating guests, mostly from micros. Seasonal Grafters beers are also sold when brewed. The renowned home-cooked fish and chip meals are a must, available Thursday-Saturday evenings and Friday and Saturday lunchtimes (booking recommended). Sunday lunches are 12-3pm. Brewery tours can be arranged by appointment, which include food and a tasting session. ᴹQ◖⬛☖(100)♣⅃⊟

Willoughton

Stirrup Inn ⬛

1 Templefield Road, DN21 5RZ

✪ 5 (12 Sat)-midnight; 12-11.30 Sun ☎ (01427) 668270
Black Sheep Best Bitter; Grafters Traditional; guest beer Ⓗ

Built from local Lincolnshire limestone, this hidden gem in an out-of-the-way location is well worth seeking out. You are always assured of a warm welcome and in the colder months a roaring log fire burns. The pub just oozes character and is popular with locals and folk from further afield. It always has three real ales on sale, including the local award-winning Grafters Traditional, and the guest beer changes regularly. Pub quizzes are always popular and traditional pub games are played. ᴹQ✿♣P⅃

Winterton

George Hogg ⬛ ✅

Market Street, DN15 9PT
✪ 9.30am (1 Mon & Tue)-11 ☎ (01724) 732270
⊕ thegeorgehogg.co.uk
Tom Wood Best Bitter; York Guzzler; guest beer Ⓗ

Popular Grade II-listed marketplace pub and local CAMRA Pub of the Season award winner. It has a large lounge dining area and separate public bar, both with real fires. Good-value locally sourced food is served, plus home-made snacks, and it is open for Sunday breakfast at 9.30am. The guest beer is typically sourced from a local brewery. The pub has an annual beer festival, and is a popular meeting place for football teams and the local supporters club. An upstairs restaurant plus tea and coffee are also available. ᴹQ◖⬛☖(350)P⅃

Batemans Brewery Visitors Centre, Wainfleet

London index

*Shown on Inner London map

GREATER LONDON

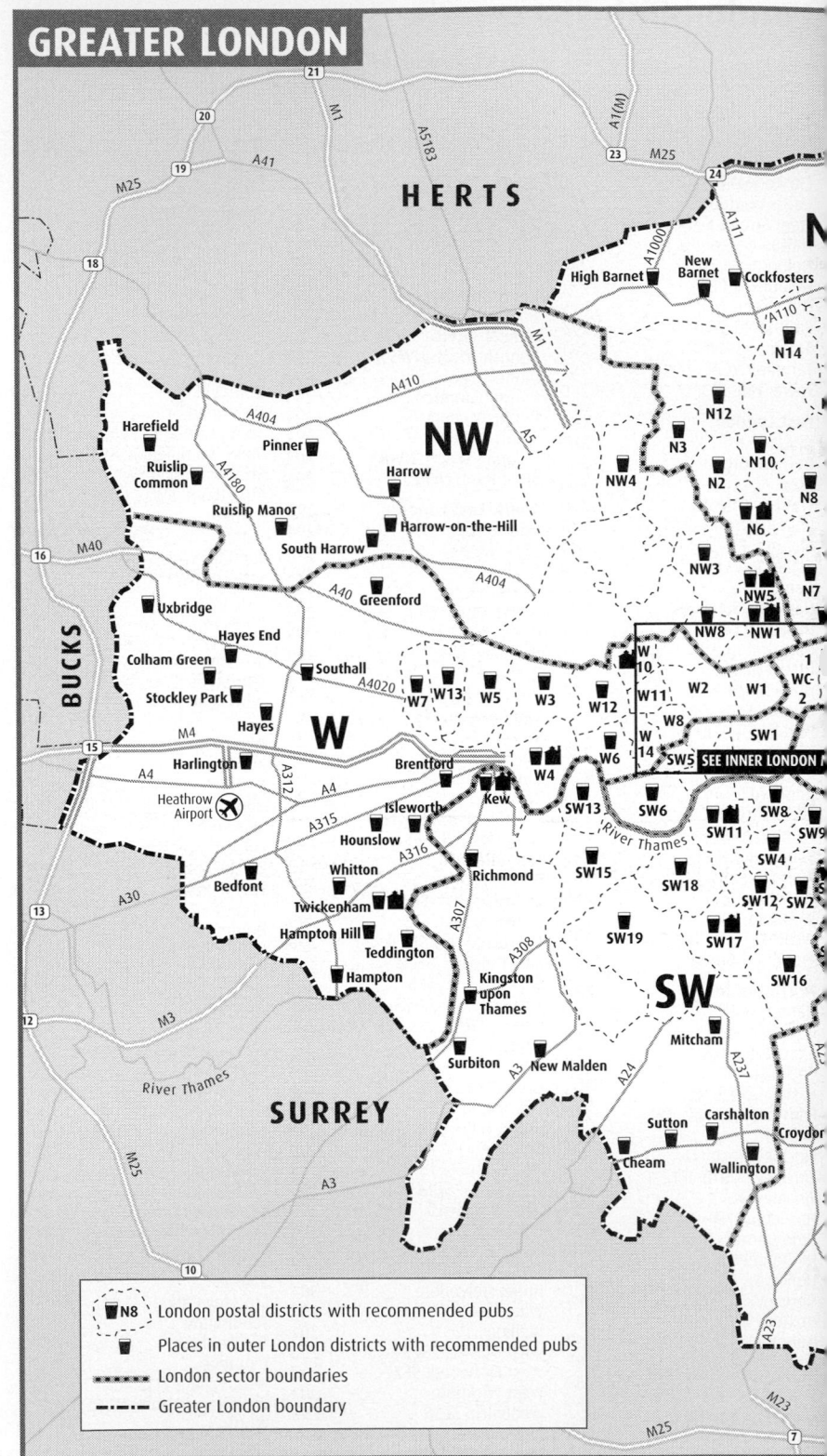

HERTS

BUCKS

SURREY

NW

W

SW

M

High Barnet
New Barnet
Cockfosters
N14
N12
N3
N10
NW4
N2
N8
N6
NW3
NW5
N7
NW8
NW1
W10
W11
W2
W1
WC
W7
W13
W5
W3
W12
W8
SW1
W6
W14
SW5
SW13
SW6
SW8
SW11
SW9
SW15
SW18
SW4
SW12
SW2
SW19
SW17
SW16
1
2

SEE INNER LONDON

Harefield
Pinner
Harrow
Ruislip Common
Ruislip Manor
Harrow-on-the-Hill
South Harrow
Uxbridge
Greenford
Hayes End
Colham Green
Southall
Stockley Park
Hayes
Harlington
Brentford
Heathrow Airport
Isleworth
Kew
Bedfont
Hounslow
Whitton
Richmond
Twickenham
Hampton Hill
Teddington
Hampton
Kingston upon Thames
Surbiton
New Malden
Mitcham
Sutton
Carshalton
Croydon
Cheam
Wallington

River Thames

Legend:
- N8 — London postal districts with recommended pubs
- Places in outer London districts with recommended pubs
- London sector boundaries
- Greater London boundary

ENGLAND

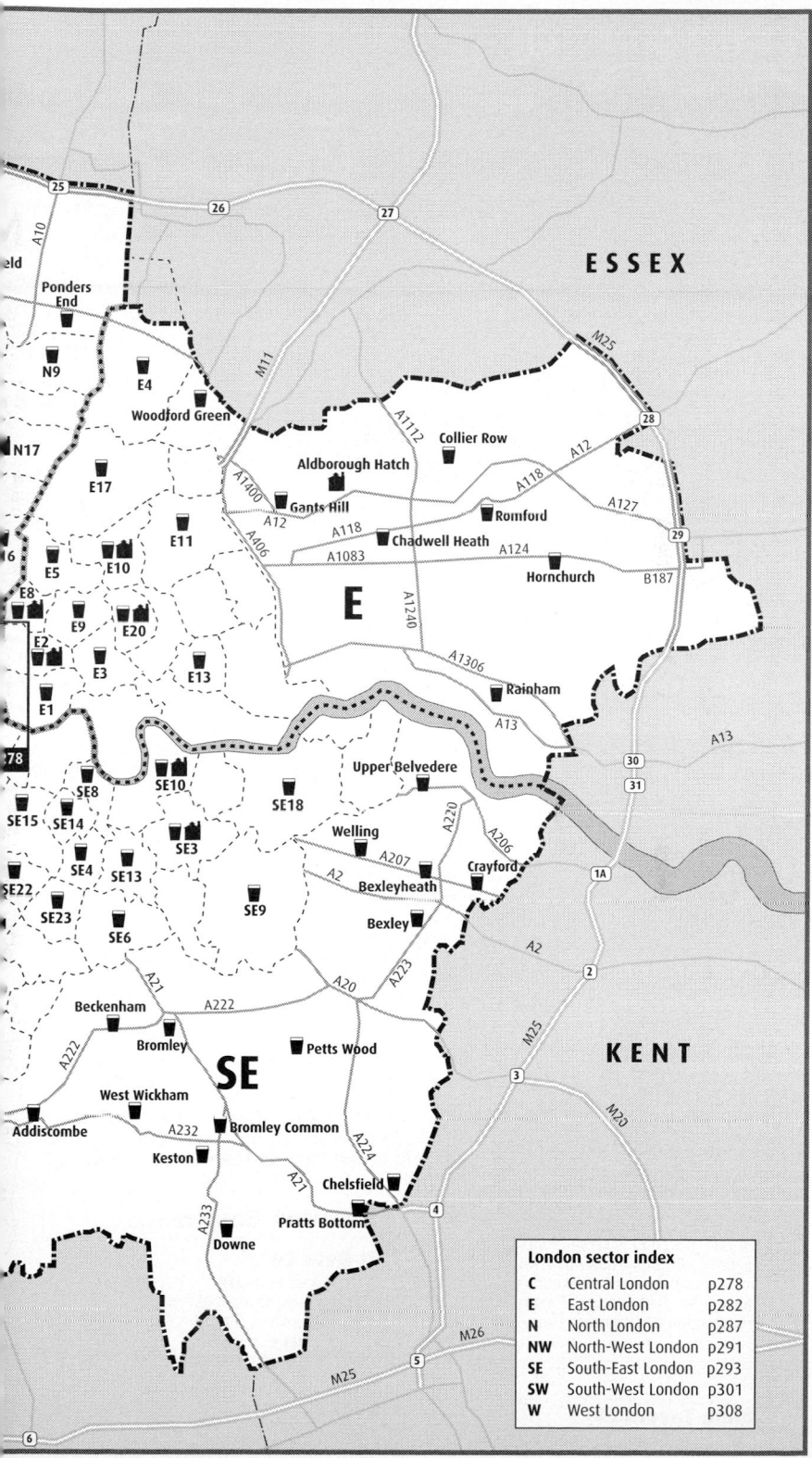

ESSEX

Ponders End

N9

E4

Woodford Green

N17

E17

Aldborough Hatch

Collier Row

Gants Hill

Romford

E11

Chadwell Heath

E5   E10

Hornchurch

E8

E9   E20

E

E2

E3

E13

E1

Rainham

78

Upper Belvedere

SE8   SE10

SE18

SE15   SE14

Welling

SE3

Crayford

SE4   SE13

SE22

Bexleyheath

SE23   SE9

Bexley

SE6

Beckenham

SE   Petts Wood

Bromley

West Wickham

KENT

Addiscombe

Bromley Common

Keston

Chelsfield

Pratts Bottom

Downe

London sector index

C	Central London	p278
E	East London	p282
N	North London	p287
NW	North-West London	p291
SE	South-East London	p293
SW	South-West London	p301
W	West London	p308

277

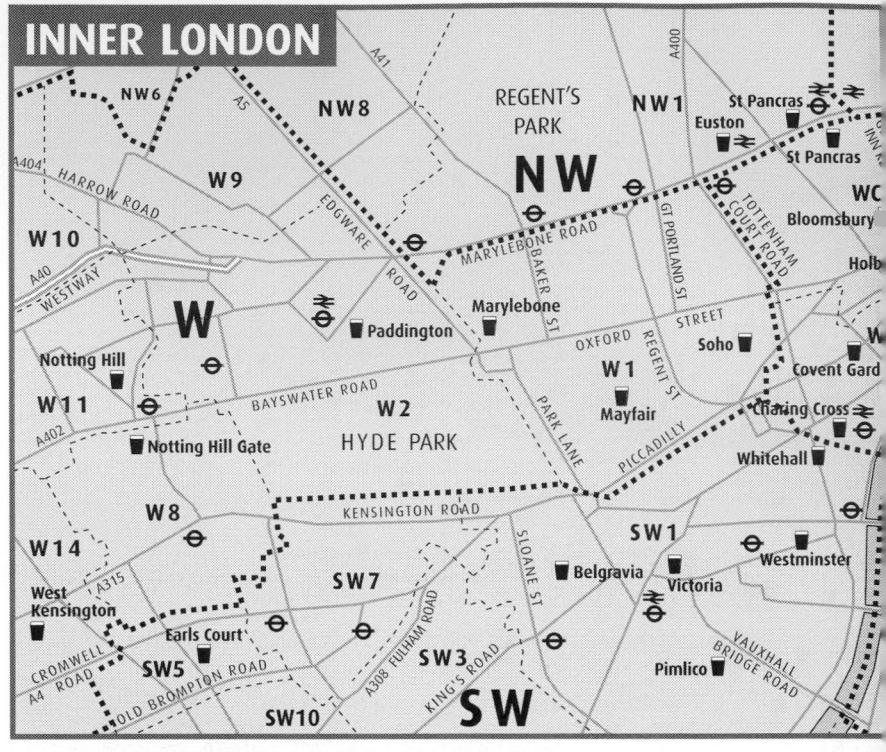

INNER LONDON

How to find London pubs

Greater London is divided into seven sectors: Central, East, North, North-West, South-East, South-West and West, reflecting postal boundaries. The Central sector includes the City (EC1 to EC4) and Holborn, Covent Garden and The Strand (WC1/2), where pubs are listed in postal district order. In each of the other six sectors the pubs with London postcodes are listed first in postal district order (E1, E2 etc), followed by those in outer London districts, which are listed in alphabetical order (Barking, Chadwell Heath etc) – see Greater London map. Postal district numbers can be found on every street name plate in the London postcode area.

CENTRAL LONDON
EC1: Clerkenwell

Gunmakers L ✪
13 Eyre Street Hill, EC1R 5ET
✪ 12-11; closed Sat & Sun ☎ (020) 7278 1022
🌐 thegunmakers.co.uk
Beer range varies Ⓗ
Just off Clerkenwell Road, this small pub is usually busy and drinkers often spill out on to the pavement. A Punch tenancy, it is free of tie for real ales and serves a range of five, mainly from microbreweries within 35 miles and mostly delivered directly. Food is served lunchtimes and evenings until 9.30pm. A quiet pub with no music, TV or machines, it closes at weekends except from 12 to 4pm on the first Sunday of every month.
Q ◖◗ ≠ (Farringdon) ⊖ (Chancery Lane/Farringdon) 🚌

Jerusalem Tavern ✪
55 Britton Street, EC1M 5UQ
✪ 11-11; closed Sat & Sun ☎ (020) 7490 4281

St Peter's Mild, Best Bitter, Golden Ale, seasonal beers Ⓐ
St Peter's Brewery's only pub, opened in 1996 as a re-creation of an 18th-century tavern – and it works. The interior has bare boards and wooden furniture. The bar area is small and can get crowded. Beers are served by air pressure from fake casks behind the bar. In one of the few pubs in London to sell mild regularly, up to six St Peter's cask beers are available along with a wide range of its bottled beers. ♨Q◖ ≠⊖(Farringdon)🚌

EC1: Hatton Garden

Craft Beer Co
82 Leather Lane, EC1N 7TR
✪ 12-11 (10.30 Sun) ☎ 07502 337339
🌐 thecraftbeerco.com
Beer range varies Ⓗ
Sixteen handpumps dispense a specially brewed house beer and 14 guests from independent microbreweries, plus a cider. Up to 20 keg and over 100 international bottled beers are also sold. The bar area is furnished with high tables and stools; further seating is available upstairs. Food is limited

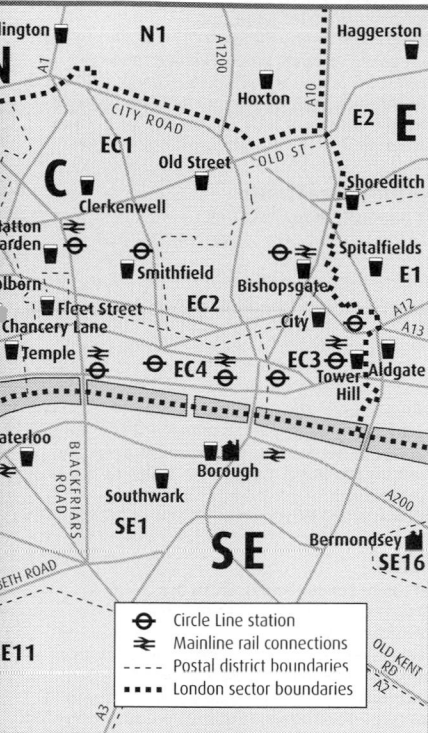

Legend

- ⊖ Circle Line station
- ⇌ Mainline rail connections
- - - - Postal district boundaries
- ■■■■ London sector boundaries

to good-quality Scotch eggs and pork pies. Note the mirrored ceiling downstairs, recalling its former Clock House name. Sunday closing time can depend upon custom; phone to check.
⊖(Chancery Lane)🚐♠🍺

Olde Mitre ★ ✓
1 Ely Court, Ely Place, EC1N 6SJ
🕐 11-11; closed Sat & Sun ☎ (020) 7405 4751
Fuller's London Pride, seasonal beer; guest beers Ⓗ
Hidden between Hatton Garden and Ely Place, this former local CAMRA Pub of the Year serves four guest ales selected from various regional breweries and holds regular beer festivals, including Mild Month. One of Britain's Real Heritage Pubs, it has extensive wood panelling in the two bars, the snug and a small function room upstairs. There has been a pub on this site since 1546; the current building is from the 18th century. Hanging jugs adorn the larger rear bar.
Q❄🍺⇌(Farringdon)⊖(Chancery Lane)🚐🍺

EC1: Old Street

Old Fountain Ⓛ
3 Baldwin Street, EC1V 9NU
🕐 11-11; closed Sat & Sun ☎ (020) 7253 2970
🌐 oldfountain.co.uk
Fuller's London Pride; guest beers Ⓗ
Privately owned free house split into two: one bar has a dartboard and the other a large fish tank. There is now a new roof garden, with two large tables covered by heated parasols. The comprehensive beer range comes mainly from local and microbreweries; the pub is noted for new brews and an extensive range of local bottled beers. The lunchtime menu is served 12-2.30pm;

evening menu 5-10pm. Check the website for beer festivals. Local CAMRA Pub of the Year 2011.
🏚❄🍺⇌⊖⊖🚐♠🍺

EC1: Smithfield

Old Red Cow Ⓛ
71-72 Long Lane, EC1A 9EJ
🕐 12-11 (midnight Fri & Sat) ☎ (020) 7726 2595
🌐 theoldredcow.com
Beer range varies Ⓗ
Reopened in 2010, this small, friendly, modern pub has five handpumps serving real ale from local brewers (Redemption and Windsor & Eton are regulars) and other larger micros, plus 12 craft keg and 60-70 bottled beers. With good food as well, this is a busy city pub. Look for special events such as beer and food pairings, beer tastings, brewery beer festivals and Meet the Brewer nights. An upstairs bar can be hired for functions.
🍺🍺⇌(Farringdon)⊖(Barbican)🚐(4,56,153)♠

EC2: Bishopsgate

Hamilton Hall ✓
Unit 32, The Concourse, Liverpool Street Station, EC2M 7PY
🕐 9am-11.30 ☎ (020) 7247 3579
Fuller's London Pride; Greene King IPA, Abbot; guest beers Ⓗ
A Wetherspoon pub in the opulent former ballroom of the Great Eastern Hotel by the eastern entrance to Liverpool Street Station. Ten handpumps dispense a varying range of ales at reasonable prices for the area. Bi-annual and brewery-themed festivals are held. It is always busy but the service is efficient. Both the upstairs and downstairs bars serve real ale and food is available all day. TV screens in the bar display train departure times.
Q🍺&⇌⊖(Liverpool St)🚐♠🍺

Magpie ✓
12 New Street, EC2M 4TP
🕐 11-11; closed Sat & Sun ☎ (020) 7929 3889
Fuller's London Pride; St Austell Tribute; Sharp's Doom Bar; guest beers Ⓗ
A typical M&B Nicholson's city-centre pub with dark wood, brass and glass screens predominating, on the site of one of London's first ambulance stations, down a pedestrianised street opposite the eastern entrance of Liverpool Street station. It has an L-shaped main bar with an upstairs bar and dining room. Six handpumps dispense three regulars and three changing guest ales. The pub can get busy at lunchtime and early evening, though efficient bar staff mean only a short wait for drinks. 🏚Q🍺&⇌⊖(Liverpool St)🚐🍺

EC3: City

Crosse Keys ✓
9 Gracechurch Street, EC3V 0DR
🕐 8am-11 (midnight Fri; 7 Sat); closed Sun
☎ (020) 7623 4824
Fuller's London Pride; Greene King IPA, Abbot; guest beers Ⓗ
Palatial pub in a magnificent former bank headquarters, complete with huge marble pillars and cupola. Twenty-four handpumps, with helpful overhead monitors showing 'Beers now being served', are all in use Thursday and Friday. Its own beer festival runs alongside the two main

Wetherspoon festivals, and separate brewery-themed festivals are held. There are quieter rooms for functions. Sporting events are shown on large TVs. Food is available until 10pm (6pm Sat). Disabled access is via the fire exit; ask staff to open.
⦅⦆≢(Cannon St/Liverpool St)⊖(Bank/Monument)🚇●ۥ

East India Arms ✪
67 Fenchurch Street, EC3M 4BR
✪ 11.30-8.30; closed Sat & Sun ☎ (020) 7265 5121
Shepherd Neame Master Brew, Kent's Best, Spitfire, seasonal beers Ⓗ
There has been a pub on this site since 1630. The current Grade II-listed red brick building dates from the 1820s, originally two bars but now one. One of only two London pubs recalling the East India Company, it was previously called the Magpie and the Station Tavern and had small booths by the windows. It features lots of wood panelling and old photographs.
⦅⦆≢(Fenchurch St)⊖(Aldgate/Tower Hill)🚇ۥ

EC3: Tower Hill

Peacock 🅛 ✪
41 Minories, EC3N 1DT
✪ 12-midnight; closed Sat & Sun ☎ (020) 7488 3630
Beer range varies Ⓗ
In the north-west corner of Ibex House, this pub was completed in 1937, is Grade II-listed, and is possibly the largest survivor of Streamline Moderne, a short-lived form of Art Deco. It is reputed to have been earmarked as Gestapo HQ had we lost World War II. The ground floor bar has a dartboard; two more and a pool table are upstairs. The landlord is passionate about ale: beers from East London and Redemption feature alongside brews from the likes of Hook Norton and Sharp's.
⦅≢(Fenchurch St)⊖(Aldgate/Tower Gateway/Tower Hill)🚇

EC4: Fleet Street

Castle
26 Furnival Street, EC4A 1JS
✪ 11-11; closed Sat & Sun ☎ (020) 7405 5470
Nethergate Red Car Best Bitter; guest beers Ⓗ
Small Red Car pub that enjoys a mixed clientele. Eight handpumps dispense beers mainly from new local and microbreweries. The dark wood panelling is offset by a selection of mirrors to brighten the atmosphere, and the long window shelf bar is divided by two small screens. The upstairs bar is mainly for lunchtime trade and private functions. Sourced fresh from Borough Market and Smithfield Market, the full menu is available 12-3pm, with snacks only in the evening.
🏛⦅⊖(Chancery Lane)🚇

WC1: Bloomsbury

Calthorpe Arms
252 Grays Inn Road, WC1X 8JR
✪ 11-11.30 (midnight Fri & Sat); 12-10.30 Sun
☎ (020) 7278 4732
Young's Bitter, Special, seasonal beer; guest beer Ⓗ
Unusual double doors lead into this single-bar corner local. With no music and an unobtrusive corner TV, it is easy either to strike up a conversation at a bar stool or take one of the tables

along the sides for more privacy. The upstairs dining room opens for lunch (12-2.30pm) but can be booked at other times. Evening meals are served 6-9.30pm. Young's bottle-conditioned beers are stocked. There is pavement seating outside. Multiple winner of local CAMRA Pub of the Year award. 🅿⦅⦆≢(King's Cross)⊖(Russell Sq)🚇ۥ

Jeremy Bentham
31 University Street, WC1E 6JL
✪ 11.30-11; closed Sat & Sun ☎ (020) 7387 3033
Beer range varies Ⓗ
Despite the appearance of a one-bar 1920s corner pub with original panelling, there are stairs leading up to a lounge providing welcome extra seating. Situated in the main University College London campus and attracting many academics from the university, it was renamed in 1982 to commemorate the 150th anniversary of the death of the recognised spiritual founder of UCL. This Punch pub serves four varying guest beers and Westons Old Rosie. Outside are tables on the pavement.
🅿⦅≢(Euston)⊖(Euston Sq/Warren St)🚇●ۥ

Lamb
94 Lambs Conduit Street, WC1N 3LZ
✪ 12-11 (midnight Thu-Sat); 12-10.30 Sun
☎ (020) 7405 0713
Courage Directors; Young's Bitter, Special, London Gold, seasonal beers; guest beers Ⓗ
Beautifully preserved, Grade II-listed and one of London's Real Heritage Pubs, with a small snug bar and etched glass snob screens in place above the bar. The glorious Victorian history of the pub and area is commemorated by a working polyphon (predecessor to the gramophone) which can be played in aid of charity. Three or four guest beers usually include one from Sambrook's. At the back is a small walled garden. Live music is hosted once a month. Q🅿⦅⦆⊖(Russell Sq)🚇

WC1: Holborn

Penderel's Oak ✪
286-288 High Holborn, WC1V 7HJ

INDEPENDENT BREWERIES

Beavertown N1: Islington (NEW)
Botanist Kew (NEW)
Brew Wharf SE1: Borough
Brodie's E10: Leyton
By the Horns SW17 (NEW)
Camden Town NW5: Kentish Town
East London E10: Leyton
Florence SE24: Herne Hill
Fuller's W4: Chiswick
Ha'penny Aldborough Hatch
Hackney E2: Hackney (NEW)
Kernel SE16: Bermondsey
Little Brew NW1: Camden (NEW)
London N6: Highgate (NEW)
London Fields E8: Hackney (NEW)
Meantime SE10: Greenwich
Moncada W10 (NEW)
Redchurch E2: Bethnal Green (NEW)
Redemption N17: Tottenham
Sambrook's SW11: Battersea
Tap East E20: Stratford (NEW)
Twickenham Twickenham
Zerodegrees SE3: Blackheath

✪ 9am-11 (midnight Thu; 1am Fri & Sat); 10-11 Sun
☎ (020) 7242 5669
Fuller's London Pride; Greene King Abbot; Ruddles Best Bitter; guest beers ⊞
Named after Richard Penderel, who helped Charles II hide in the oak tree, this large, busy Wetherspoon pub is on the site of Penderel House. The space is broken up by a raised seating area, settees, high stools and a back room. Lots of wood and subdued lighting add to the atmosphere. There is pavement seating on High Holborn and a cellar bar, which is available for hire. Food is served from 7am until 10pm and children are welcome during the day. Q✿✪◖&⊖(Chancery Lane/Holborn)🚌←

WC1: St Pancras

Mabel's Tavern ✪
9 Mabledon Place, WC1H 9AZ
✪ 11-11 (midnight Thu-Sat); 12-10.30 Sun
☎ (020) 7387 7739
Shepherd Neame Master Brew, Kent's Best, Spitfire, Bishops Finger, seasonal beers ⊞
Originally owned by Whitbread and called the Kentish Arms (note the plaque on the outside wall), the pub was renamed for landlady Mabel Macinelly, who is said to haunt these cosy premises. A snug is upstairs and a raised area at the back has a traditional fireplace with a large TV screen above it. Various prints and old photos adorn the walls. Food is served until 10pm (9pm Fri-Sun). Handy for the British Library.
✿◖≈⊖(King's Cross/St Pancras)🚌←

Queen's Head
66 Acton Street, WC1X 9NB
✪ 12 (4 Sat)-midnight; 12-11 Sun ☎ (020) 7713 5772
⊕ queensheadlondon.com
Dark Star Hophead; guest beers ⊞
Narrow, late Georgian side-street premises with a single bar, smoking patio at the rear and benches on the pavement. The piano is used for jazz and blues on Thursday evenings. Guest beers are from local breweries and one handpump serves cider, with three more real ciders and a range of foreign keg and bottled beers. Sharing platters of pub snacks are available at this comfortable locals' pub, with occasional tourists, off the Grays Inn Road. May close later weekdays.
✿◖≈⊖(Kings Cross/St Pancras)🚌●←

WC2: Chancery Lane

Knights Templar ✪
95 Chancery Lane, WC2A 1DT
✪ 9am-11.30 (midnight Thu & Fri); 11-5 Sat; closed Sun
☎ (020) 7831 2660
Courage Best Bitter; Greene King IPA, Abbot; guest beers ⊞
The Knights Templar owned land on which Chancery Lane was built and this imposing, listed, Wetherspoon's conversion of a former banking hall appeared in the film of The Da Vinci Code. Stairs at the rear lead to mezzanine level rooms, one reserved until 8pm for families. Twelve handpumps dispense up to six guest beers and two draught ciders. The venue can be hired for private functions on Saturday evening. TV screens show sport.
Q☙◖⊖🚌●

WC2: Charing Cross

Coal Hole
91-92 Strand, WC2R 0DW
✪ 10-11 (midnight Fri & Sat) ☎ (020) 7379 9883
Fuller's London Pride; Sharp's Doom Bar; guest beers ⊞
One of London's Real Heritage Pubs, built as part of the Savoy Court complex in 1903-4, then transformed into a pub named the Fountains Tavern. M&B Nicholson's has preserved the original decor, including friezes above the bar and original windows. The clientele consists largely of tourists, patrons of the Savoy Hotel and Charing Cross commuters. Guest beers are often from microbreweries such as Thornbridge. Attached is Edmunds wine bar, with separate street and internal entrances. ◖≈⊖🚌

Harp ▼ ⌊
47 Chandos Place, WC2N 4HS
✪ 10-11.30 (midnight Fri & Sat); 12-11 Sun
☎ (020) 7836 0291 ⊕ harpcoventgarden.com
Dark Star Hophead; Harveys Sussex Best Bitter; Sambrook's Wandle, Junction; guest beers ⊞
Small, friendly, independent free house that has become a haven for beer choice, generally including a mild or porter and London microbrewery seasonals. A fine range of real ciders is also offered. The narrow bar is adorned with mirrors and portraits. There is no intrusive music or TV and a cosy upstairs room provides a refuge from the busy throng. Numerous past awards culminated in 2010 in the ultimate accolade, CAMRA National Pub of the Year.
Q≈⊖(Charing Cross/Leicester Sq)🚌●

Ship & Shovell
2-3 Craven Passage, WC2N 5PH
✪ 11-11; closed Sun ☎ (020) 7839 1311
Badger First Gold, Tanglefoot, seasonal beers ⊞
Attractive, listed pub underneath the railway arches at Charing Cross main line station and uniquely divided into two halves on opposite sides of the passage. The pub is named after Admiral Sir Cloudesley Shovell whose portrait hangs in the main bar, along with a description of his fleet's grounding on the Scilly Isles in 1707. The venue has bevelled mirrors, engraved glass, nautical pictures, wood panelling and TV for sport. The smaller bar opposite has a dartboard and Crows Nest upstairs room. ◖≈⊖(Charing Cross/Embankment)🚌

WC2: Covent Garden

Cross Keys ⌊
31 Endell Street, WC2H 9BA
✪ 11-11; 12-10.30 Sun ☎ (020) 7836 5185
⊕ crosskeyscoventgarden.com
Brodie's Kiwi, London Fields, Bethnal Green, seasonal beer; Sambrook's Wandle; guest beer ⊞
The striking exterior, with its elaborate decoration obscured by extensive foliage, forms an immediate impression upon approaching this pub. Inside is a fascinating collection of bric-a-brac, ranging from copper kettles to musical instruments and even a diving helmet. There are also brewery mirrors, a large collection of portraits and pictures, including a good watercolour landscape, and two notable clocks. Leased by East London brewers Brodie's, this pub has a good range of its beers. ◖⊖🚌●

Freemasons Arms ✓

81-82 Long Acre, WC2E 9NG

✪ 12-11.30 (11 Fri & Sat); 12-10.30 Sun ☎ (020) 7836 3115
⊕ freemasonsarmscoventgarden.co.uk

Shepherd Neame Master Brew, Spitfire, seasonal
beers Ⓗ

Located near Freemasons Hall and convenient for
theatreland, this pub was first licensed in 1704 and
known as the Bull's Head until 1778. The
Geological Society was founded here in 1807 and
an extract from The Times shows that the Football
Association was created here in 1863. The interior
is comfortably furnished with leather banquettes
and wood panelling, but the background music can
be intrusive. There are four TV screens for sports
and two function rooms. ◑➍⊖⊞

Nell of Old Drury

29 Catherine Street, WC2B 5JS

✪ 12-2.30, 5-11.30 (midnight Fri); 12-midnight Sat; closed
Sun ☎ (020) 7836 5328 ⊕ nellofolddrury.com

Hook Norton Old Hooky; Sambrook's Wandle Ⓗ

Small and cosy pub opposite the Theatre Royal,
Drury Lane. A tunnel used by Charles II to visit Nell
Gwynne is reputed to link the two. The clientele is
a mix of locals, tourists, after-work drinkers and of
course theatregoers; there is an interval drinks
service available for the latter. The first floor offers
extra seating. If you are lucky you may be able to
bag the ground-floor bow window seats
overlooking Catherine Street. ⊖⊞

WC2: Holborn

Ship Tavern ✓

12 Gate Street, WC2A 3HP

✪ 11-11 (midnight Sat); 12-10.30 Sun ☎ (020) 7405 1992
⊕ theshiptavern.co.uk

Caledonian Deuchars IPA, 1549; St Austell Tribute;
Wells Bombardier; guest beers Ⓗ

Hidden in a passage behind Holborn Underground
station, a pub has been on this site since 1549. It
was one of the few Younger's pubs in London.
Decor is a mix of alcoves and stools, with
mahogany-coloured walls and prints of early 20th-
century ships. There are six handpumps for regional
beers, one guest and the aptly named house beer.
Food is available all day and regular pie promotions
are held. Upstairs is a restaurant also available to
hire for functions. ◑➍⊖⊞

WC2: Temple

Devereux ✓

20 Devereux Court, WC2R 3JJ

✪ 11-11; closed Sat & Sun ☎ (020) 7583 4562

Greene King Old Golden Hen; Young's London Gold;
guest beers Ⓗ

Attractive Grade II-listed pub built in 1844; part of
the site used to be the Grecian Coffee House. The
comfortable lounge with wood panelling has a bar
with five handpumps. There are prints on the walls
showing local places of interest and historic figures,
the judges and wigs reflecting proximity to the law
courts. Upstairs is a restaurant available for hire.
Ale drinkers can benefit from changing guest ales
from brewers such as Hop Back. ◑➍⊖⊞

Edgar Wallace

40 Essex Street, WC2R 3JF

✪ 11-11; closed Sat & Sun ☎ (020) 7353 3120

Crouch Vale Brewers Gold; Nethergate Edgar's Pale
Ale; guest beers Ⓗ

There has been a pub on this site since 1777. Now
leased from Enterprise, this one has so far collected
about 140 of the 170 or so books written by Edgar
Wallace. The comfortable downstairs room has a
fine wooden bar with seven handpumps and there
is also seating upstairs. The pub operates a try
before you buy policy but, to compensate for this,
half pints are charged at a premium rate. Look out
for beer festivals. Q◑➍⊖⊞

EAST LONDON

E1: Aldgate

Dispensary

19A Leman Street, E1 8EN

✪ 12-11; closed Sat & Sun ☎ (020) 7977 0486
⊕ thedispensarylondon.co.uk

Nethergate Florence NightingAle; guest beers Ⓗ

A recent local CAMRA Pub of the Year, this Grade II-
listed former hospital became a pub and dining
house in 2006. Alongside the house beer are up to
four interesting guests, normally including a dark
beer. A spacious bar with balcony seating, an
upstairs function room and smaller seating areas
make this an ideal place to eat and drink.
Q◑➍⊖(Aldgate East)⊞⚫♨

Goodman's Field ✓

87-91 Mansell Street, E1 8AN

✪ 9am-11 ☎ (020) 7680 2850

Fuller's London Pride; Greene King IPA, Abbot; guest
beers Ⓗ

A large, modern, well-appointed Wetherspoon pub
on the city fringe. Real ale has thrived under the
new manager, Kat, with three guest beers and
usually a real draught cider available. The value-
for-money food appeals greatly to residents, office
workers and visitors from nearby hotels. Breakfasts
are served from 7.30am on weekdays.
Q◑➍&≈(Fenchurch St)⊖(Tower Gateway/Tower
Hill)⊞⚫

White Swan ✓

21-23 Alie Street, E1 8DA

✪ 11-11; closed Sat & Sun ☎ (020) 7702 0448
⊕ whiteswanaldgate.co.uk

Shepherd Neame Master Brew, Spitfire, seasonal
beer Ⓗ

Comfortable pub built on the site of the Half Moon
Theatre on the fringe of the City, which can get
busy during lunchtimes and early evenings. One
bar serves two areas – the smaller area was the
original pub, which was extended into the next
door building in recent years. There is also a small
room upstairs used mainly for dining and functions.
Q◑≈(Fenchurch St)⊖(Aldgate/Aldgate East)⊞♨

E1: Shoreditch

Mason & Taylor

51-55 Bethnal Green Road, E1 6LA

✪ 5-midnight (2am Sat); 12-midnight Sun
☎ (020) 7749 9670 ⊕ masonandtaylor.co.uk

Dark Star Hophead; guest beers Ⓗ

Opened in 2010 and described as a craft beer bar,
offering a welcome choice in an area that has lost
many of its pubs. The decor is spartan with wooden
furniture. Three real ales from small breweries are
served alongside a variety of ciders and an
extensive menu of bottled beers, which changes

quarterly. The food could be described as British with a twist. Occasional beer festivals are held. The venue may close earlier on Sunday evenings. ❀◖♿❸(Shoreditch High St)🚃(8,388)●✿—

E1: Spitalfields

Pride of Spitalfields
3 Heneage Street, E1 5LJ
❂ 11-midnight (2am Fri & Sat) ☎ (020) 7247 8933
Crouch Vale Brewers Gold; Fuller's London Pride; Sharp's Doom Bar Ⓗ
A single bar pub just off Brick Lane, divided into two rooms by an arch. The bar back is full of spirit bottles and the stanchion is full of glasses and pump clips of previous guest ales. There is a working piano and a large comfortable sofa, and the walls are decorated with old photos of the local area, old bottles and earthenware jugs. Hot food and sandwiches are available at lunchtime. Children are allowed until early evening.
◖≈(Liverpool St)❸(Aldgate East/Shoreditch High St)🚃✿—

E1: Wapping

Town of Ramsgate
62 Wapping High Street, E1W 2PN
❂ 12-midnight (11 Sun) ☎ (020) 7481 8000
Fuller's London Pride; Sharp's Doom Bar; Young's Bitter Ⓗ
Historic pub in the old docklands among warehouses that have been converted into luxury flats. An Enterprise tenancy, it is popular with locals and with passing walkers and tour groups. The traditional bar is long and narrow, and there is a beer garden by the river. Home-cooked traditional English food is served all day. Children and dogs are welcome. A popular quiz is held on Monday nights.
Q❀◖❸🚃(100,D3)♣✿—

E2: Bethnal Green

Camel Ⓛ ✅
277 Globe Road, E2 0JD
❂ 4 (12 Fri-Sat)-11; 12-10.30 Sun ☎ (020) 8983 9888
Crouch Vale Brewers Gold; Sambrook's Wandle, Junction Ⓗ
Compact, one-bar pub behind the Bethnal Green Museum of Childhood, down an alley from the small park by the Underground station. The attractive brown-tiled exterior belies its plain wooden tables and bare floor. The beers may vary, but come mainly from local and smaller brewers. A range of pies and mash is served 12.30 9pm. There is a seated outdoor drinking area. Regular quiz nights are held and the pub has its own cricket team.
❀◖≈(Bethnal Green/Cambridge Heath)❸🚃●

Hare
505 Cambridge Heath Road, E2 9BU
❂ 12-midnight; closed Sat & Sun ☎ (020) 7613 0519
⊕ theharee2.co.uk
Fuller's London Pride; Greene King IPA; Taylor Landlord Ⓗ
Free house rebuilt in about 1860 with an attractive tiled exterior and notable sign. Quiz nights are held on Wednesdays and karaoke on Fridays. At the back of the single L-shaped area is a pool table, while football and rugby are shown on TV, with an outside screen for smokers. There is a small beer

garden. A resident cat is often on guard at one of the two doors, but is disdainful of customers.
❀≈(Cambridge Heath)❸🚃✿—

E2: Haggerston

Albion in Goldsmith's Row Ⓛ
94 Goldsmith's Row, E2 8QY
❂ 12-11 (1am Fri & Sat) ☎ (020) 7739 0185
Sharp's Doom Bar; Taylor Landlord; guest beers Ⓗ
Single-room free house named in honour of the guvnor's football team, West Bromwich. The pictures and memorabilia are similarly related and football is shown on match days. However, the pub attracts a wide, cosmopolitan clientele, being located between Broadway and Columbia Road markets. Every other Thursday offers an excellent quiz, and there is occasional live music. Families and dogs are welcome. Four beers on handpump include a guest from a local brewer such as Brodie's or East London.
❀≈(Cambridge Heath)🚃♣✿—

E3: Bow

Eleanor Arms
460 Old Ford Road, E3 5JP
❂ 12 (4 Mon)-11; 12-10.30 Sun ☎ (020) 8980 6992
⊕ eleanorarms.co.uk
Shepherd Neame Kent's Best, Spitfire, seasonal beers Ⓗ
Off the beaten track towards Old Ford but close to Victoria Park, and worth seeking out for the quality of its beer. The single room has a two-bar feel, the rear section containing a pool table and TV for major sporting events. A charity-themed quiz night on the first Thursday of the month is popular, as are the musical evenings: live jazz on the first Sunday and records from the landlord's extensive and eclectic collection on Friday and Saturday.
❀◖❸(Bow Church/Bow Rd)🚃(8)✿—

Palm Tree
127 Grove Road, E3 5RP (in Mile End Park; road access via Haverfield Rd)
❂ 12.30-midnight (2am Sat); 12-midnight Sun
☎ (020) 8980 2918
Beer range varies Ⓗ
Rebuilt by Truman's in the 1930s and marooned when most of the local terraces were demolished to create Mile End Park, this is one of London's Real Heritage Pubs. The curved main bar has a corner stage for live music and the impressive, smaller rear bar has fine panelling to the counter. There are always two changing real ales, and often jazz on CD. In fine weather the canalside and park are pleasant for a drink or a smoke.
❀◖♿❸(Mile End)🚃●P✿—

E4: Chingford

King's Head ✅
2b Kings Head Hill, E4 7EA
❂ 12-11 (midnight Fri & Sat) ☎ (020) 8529 6283
Fuller's London Pride; Sharp's Doom Bar; Taylor Landlord; guest beers Ⓗ
A large, double-fronted pub at the top of the hill, with one bar serving many different areas. This Stonegate house selects its guest ales mainly from regional breweries, but is starting to try smaller and local breweries. The decor is of modern design, described by some as John Lewis-style,

comfortable and welcoming, with lots of tables and different smaller areas for drinkers and diners. Quiz nights are Wednesday and Sunday. Food is served from opening until 9pm. ✿◖❺&≑⋤P⌐

Station House

134-138 Station Road, E4 6AN
✿ 12-11 (1am Fri & Sat) ☎ (020) 8529 8576
Banks's Bitter; Marston's Pedigree, seasonal beer; guest beer Ⓗ
Opposite Chingford bus and railway stations, this large open-plan pub was converted from a shop in 1999. Managed by Marston's until 2010, it is now a tenanted pub with four handpumps, and suggestions for the guest ale are welcome. Entertainment comprises quiz nights every Thursday, DJs Friday and Saturday and live music on Sunday night. There is a large-screen TV for most sporting events, plus a pool table and dartboard.
✿◖❺&Å≑⋤♣P⌐

E5: Clapton

Anchor & Hope ✅

15 High Hill Ferry, E5 9HG (800yds N of Lea Bridge Rd, along river path)
✿ 1-11 (midnight Fri & Sat); 12-11 Sun ☎ (020) 8806 1730
Fuller's London Pride, ESB; guest beer Ⓗ
Recent sympathetic refurbishment by Fuller's has restored this cosy riverside pub to its best, with new toilets. The small, single bar has four handpumps and a wall-mounted TV at the end of the main area, wood panelling and a dartboard in the rear room. Beside the River Lea, it provides good views and is busy in summer. Walkers, cyclists and rowers add to the local customers, creating a friendly mix for the pub.
✿≑⋤(393)♣⌐

E8: Hackney

Pembury Tavern

90 Amhurst Road, E8 1JH
✿ 12-11 ☎ (020) 8986 8597 ⊕ individualpubs.co.uk/pembury
Milton Minotaur, Sparta, Nero; guest beers Ⓗ
A real ale phoenix risen from the ashes of a serious fire. The Individual Pubs Company has, since 2006, transformed it into a vibrant Hackney social centre. Its appeal rests primarily on a core range of rotating Milton ales, with two dark beers usually available. Additionally, there is a selection from microbreweries such as Redemption. A varying draught cider is on handpump. Quality chef-prepared Mediterranean-influenced food is much appreciated. Check the website for beer festivals.
Q◖❺&≑(Hackney Downs)✪(Hackney Central) ⋤♣♦⌐⊟

E8: South Hackney

Dove

24-28 Broadway Market, E8 4QJ
✿ 12-11 (midnight Fri & Sat) ☎ (020) 7275 7617
Crouch Vale Brewers Gold; Flowers IPA; Taylor Landlord; guest beers Ⓗ
Located in the gentrified Broadway Market, this bustling free house is an iconic destination for lovers of Belgian beer, both draught and bottled. Six handpumps include three guest ales. The pub has one bar but lots of cosy nooks and crannies, with traditional wooden furniture. It also has tables

outside. There is an excellent food menu of Sunday roasts, Thai, Belgian and traditional pub food. Children are welcome.
Q✿❀&≑(London Fields)⋤(236,394)

E9: Homerton

Kenton Arms

38 Kenton Road, E9 7AB
✿ 4-11 (midnight Fri); 12-midnight Sat; 12-11 Sun
☎ (020) 8533 5041
Hop Back GFB; Taylor Landlord Ⓗ
Dog-friendly neighbourhood pub which, with its mixture of oddly matched furniture and bare wooden floors, invites you to come in and enjoy. The food is good basic pie and mash, and Sunday roasts. Entertainment is an eclectic mix: live music, world cinema screenings, DJs, quizzes, ladies' night (cocktails, cupcakes and jumble sale), rock-paper-scissors game, and the infamous rock 'n' roll bingo. There are also monthly arts exhibitions, comedy nights, free Wi-Fi and plenty of board games.
✿◖✪⋤

E10: Leyton

Drum Ⓛ ✅

557-559 Lea Bridge Road, E10 7EQ
✿ 9am-midnight (1am Fri & Sat) ☎ (020) 8539 9845
Greene King Abbot; Ruddles Best Bitter; guest beers Ⓗ
This, the 16th Wetherspoon pub, is smaller than most but has a larger choice of beer: up to 10 real ales from a list of 100 as well as up to three ciders. Direct deliveries include LocAle brews from East London and Redemption. There are two national beer festivals a year and brewery mini festivals including Meet the Brewer events. It can get busy at weekends. ✿◖✪(Midland Rd)⋤♦⌐

King William the Fourth Ⓛ

816 High Road Leyton, E10 6AE
✿ 11-midnight (1am Fri & Sat); 12-midnight Sun
☎ (020) 8556 2460 ⊕ williamthefourth.net
Beer range varies Ⓗ
Hotel rooms upstairs and Brodie's Brewery 12 feet away at the back make this large, ornately decorated two-bar pub all the more enjoyable to visit. Twenty handpumps snake along the front bar, with another five in the second bar. During special weekends, one in March/April and the Birthday Bash in September, all handpumps will be live with special or one-off ales. Food is served all day 1-9pm (8pm Sun). Book ahead for brewery tours and rooms. ✿✍◖✪❺✪(Midland Rd)⋤♣

Leyton Orient Supporters Club Ⓛ

Matchroom Stadium, Oliver Road, E10 5NF
✿ from 12.30 Sat match days; 5.30 weekdays (not during game) ☎ (020) 8988 8288 ⊕ orientsupporters.org
Mighty Oak Oscar Wilde; guest beers Ⓗ
Unlike their team, the O's supporters' bar regularly carries off the silverware, having been local CAMRA Club of the Year on several occasions and joint national winner once. Seven real ales and up to four ciders are served. Bi-annual beer festivals and brewery themed nights are held, with extended hours. A friendly atmosphere prevails at this volunteer-run club; show your CAMRA membership card to gain admission. Hours will be different for varying kick-off times (check website), and closing times vary. &✪⋤♦⌐

E11: Leytonstone

Birkbeck Tavern
45 Langthorne Road, E11 4HL
🌐 11-11 (midnight Fri & Sat); 12-11 Sun ☎ (020) 8539 2584
Rita's Special; guest beers Ⓗ
Traditional local, tucked away in the back streets near Leyton tube station, popular on Orient match days with both home and away fans. The excellent beer garden is recommended for summer. The pub is now managed by the What's Cookin' music promoters and there is live country or rock every Wednesday and Saturday or Sunday. As well as the house beer Rita's Special, the cask range includes two to four changing guests, often including a Mighty Oak beer. ✿Ⓠ&Ө(Leyton)🚇♣♪⁁

North Star
24 Browning Road, E11 3AR
🌐 12 (2 Mon)-11; 12-10.30 Sun ☎ (07961) 226197
Wells Bombardier; guest beers Ⓗ
Built in 1851 for Charrington's and now owned by Enterprise Inns, this pub is situated in a conservation area of Leytonstone. A friendly welcome awaits the visitor in a comfortable, traditional pub environment. There is live music on some Saturday and Sunday nights. Good-quality food is served every day (no food Mon) until 9pm (7pm Sun). Summer barbecues are held in the courtyard garden. ✿ⓆӨ🚇♣

Red Lion 🍺 Ⓛ
640 High Road Leytonstone, E11 3AA
🌐 12-11 (midnight Thu; 2am Fri & Sat) ☎ (020) 8988 2929
Beer range varies Ⓗ
A large corner house now transformed by Antic into a friendly and welcoming pub retaining some interesting architectural features. Ten handpumps on the single long bar offer a diverse selection of changing ales including local brews, alongside British and American craft keg and bottled British and European beers. Subdued lighting and candles provide a relaxing ambience. Food choice covers vegetarian, seafood, game and steak, and Sunday roasts. Local CAMRA Pub of the Year 2012. ✿ⒹӨ🚇♣🍴⁁

Walnut Tree ⊘
857-861 High Road Leytonstone, E11 1HH
🌐 9am-midnight (1am Fri & Sat) ☎ (020) 8539 2526
Courage Directors; Greene King Abbot; Ruddles Best Bitter; guest beers Ⓗ
Large, contemporary Wetherspoon pub, converted in 1997 from a gymnasium, carpet retailers and a co-operative store. On the long bar, 12 handpumps serve up to six guest ales and real cider. There are plenty of tables inside and out, and TV for major sporting events. Opposite the bar, a raised seating area is available free of charge for meetings or parties. There is an unusual sculpture at the beginning of the bar. ✿Ⓓ&Ө🚇♦⁁

E11: Wanstead

Nightingale ⊘
51 Nightingale Lane, E11 2EY
🌐 11-midnight (1am Fri & Sat); 12-midnight Sun
☎ (020) 8530 4540
Courage Best Bitter; guest beers Ⓗ
A country pub in the town beside the green, run by the same leaseholder for 25 years. The central bar separates the two main drinking areas; there is also a cosy snug with a fire and a small room for

meetings or functions. A small hatch is the servery in the rear room. This popular community pub has a quiz on Tuesdays and Irish folk music on Wednesdays. Home-made food includes hand-cut chips, a big breakfast, several fish options and roast dinners. ⚲ⒹӨ(Snaresbrook)🚇(W12)

E13: Plaistow

Black Lion ⊘
59-61 High Street, E13 0AD
🌐 11-11; 12-10.30 Sun ☎ (020) 8472 2351
Beer range varies Ⓗ
An early 16th-century coaching inn rebuilt about 280 years ago, retaining some original features including low ceilings, oak beams and a cobbled courtyard. This free house has two bars serving up to six different beers (check the chalkboard for those on and coming soon) selected from regional breweries – Mighty Oak features regularly. Excellent home-cooked food is available lunchtimes and early evenings. A function room is available for hire. The local West Ham boxing club uses the former stables. ✿ⒹӨ🚇P🍴⁁

E17: Walthamstow

Coppermill
205 Coppermill Lane, E17 7HF
🌐 11-11 (midnight Fri & Sat) ☎ (020) 8520 3709
Greene King IPA; Fuller's London Pride; Marston's Pedigree; guest beer Ⓗ
Small, friendly, back-street pub, close to Walthamstow Market. Originally an off-licence, it has been a pub since 1986, a free house offering a guest beer that changes twice a week. One bar is decorated with bric-a-brac. Major sporting events are shown on TV (the landlord is a fanatical Tottenham Hotspur supporter) and there are occasional live music nights and race nights. ✿⇌(St James St)🚇(W12)

Nag's Head Ⓛ
9 Orford Road, E17 9LP
🌐 4 (2 Fri; 12 Sat)-11; 12-10.30 Sun ☎ (020) 8520 9709
🌐 thenagshead17.com
Mighty Oak Oscar Wilde; St Austell Tribute; Taylor Landlord Ⓗ
In the Walthamstow Village conservation area, this single-room pub with attractive back patio is proudly cat-friendly; it hosts a cat-themed beer festival and challenged the royal wedding with its own famous cat wedding. A jazz band plays on Sunday afternoon, there is wine tasting once a month and pilates classes upstairs. This is a friendly, welcoming pub – when you sit on the comfortable sofa you just do not want to leave. The upstairs room is available for functions. Food is served 12-10pm.
✿ⒹⓍ Ө(Walthamstow Central)🚇(W12)⁁

Olde Rose & Crown Ⓛ
53-55 Hoe Street, E17 4SA
🌐 12-11 (midnight Fri & Sat) ☎ (020) 8509 3880
🌐 yeolderoseandcrowntheatrepub.co.uk
Beer range varies Ⓗ
Large Victorian family-friendly pub, open weekdays from 10am for coffee. Six handpumps dispense changing beers from independent breweries and there are two boxed ciders. Food is served 1-3pm daily, on Tuesday, Thursday and Friday evenings, and there is a traditional Sunday roast (1-4pm).

Events include regular live bands, open mic nights, shellac 78s nights, and art or craft exhibitions. The theatre upstairs has regular music and drama performances, comedy nights and a monthly quiz night. TV screens are absent.
✿◖≒⊖(Central)🍴🍽🚆

E20: Westfield Stratford City

Tap East 🄻
Great Eastern Market, Montfichet Road, E20 1ET (far end of lower ground mall near to Waitrose)
☼ 11-11; 12-10 Sun ☎ (020) 8555 4467
Tap East John Edwin Bitter, John Edwin Stout, guest beers Ⓗ
A cask brewpub in a shopping centre opposite the main entrance to Stratford International Station, operated by Utobeer of Borough Market, SE1, serving two or three of its own brews – not available elsewhere – alongside foreign beers and over 100 bottled beers. Furnished with high tables and a couple of sofas, this is a bar in a shop unit, not a cosy pub. Cold snacks are available and there are myriad places nearby whose food you can eat here.
✿🛇≒⊖(Stratford/Stratford International)🍴🚆

Chadwell Heath

Eva Hart ✪
1128 High Road, RM6 4AH (on A118)
☼ 9am-midnight ☎ (020) 8597 1069
Courage Directors; Greene King Abbot; Ruddles Best Bitter; guest beers Ⓗ
Large, comfortable Wetherspoon pub, previously the local police station, named after a local singer and music teacher who was one of the longest-living survivors of the Titanic disaster; photographs and memorabilia are on display. A splendid choice of four or more guest ales is normally available on handpump, usually including at least one stout or porter. Good-value food is served 9am-10pm.
✿◖🛇≒🍴🚆

Collier Row

Colley Rowe Inn ✪
54-56 Collier Row Road, RM5 3PA (on B174)
☼ 9am-11.30 ☎ (01708) 760633
Courage Directors; Greene King Abbot; Ruddles Best Bitter; guest beers Ⓗ
Pleasant Wetherspoon pub with some cosy alcoves, which provides some of the best real ale in the Romford area and is managed by a CAMRA member. Three or four guest beers are normally available, plus three real ciders from Westons, or sometimes a perry. Food is served all day, every day. The Colley is a 10-minute bus ride from Romford railway station (five routes). There is a segregated smoking area on the pavement.
Q◖🛇🍴🚆🍽

Gants Hill

Bar ♆
19 Sevenways Parade, Woodford Avenue, IG2 6JX (by A1400 at jct with A12 and A123)
☼ 12-11 (1am Fri & Sat); 12-10.30 Sun ☎ (020) 8551 7441
Beer range varies Ⓗ
Small, friendly free house by the Underground station (exit 2), with a pavement patio, offering a welcome choice and variety of beers (mainly from

Mighty Oak and Essex/London microbreweries) in an area with few mainstream real ales. It has seasonal beer festivals, light bar snacks, and shuffleboard is played. Karaoke/live music, jam'n and blues take place every Sunday. Several large-screen TVs show sports. Parking is at the rear (eves only). Local CAMRA Pub of the Year 2011 and 2012. ✿⊖🍴♣P🍽

Hornchurch

JJ Moons ✪
Unit 3, 46-62 High Street, RM12 4UN (on A124)
☼ 9am-midnight (12.30am Fri & Sat; 11.30 Sun)
☎ (01708) 478410
Greene King Abbot; guest beers Ⓗ
An impressive range of guest beers greets you at this busy Wetherspoon pub near the end of the High Street. The usual collection of local historic photographs and information includes a feature on John Cornwall, the boy hero of the Battle of Jutland. Breakfast is served until midday and food up to 11pm. A family area is available until 6pm. At the back is a covered smoking area.
Q◖🛇≒(Emerson Pk)🍴🍽

Rainham

Phoenix 🄻
Broadway, RM13 9YW (on B1335, near clock tower)
☼ 11-11; 12-3, 7-11 Sun ☎ (01708) 553700
Courage Directors; Fuller's London Pride; Greene King Abbot; John Smith's Bitter Ⓗ
Busy, spacious town pub close to Rainham station and convenient for the RSPB Rainham Marshes nature reserve. It has two bars: a public bar with dartboard, and a saloon for dining. Poker is played on Wednesday, quizzes and live entertainment/music alternate on Thursday and Saturday, and Sunday offers more entertainment. The large garden has five aviaries and a barbecue area. A family fun day is held every bank holiday Monday. Accommodation comprises seven twin rooms and one single. ✿🛏◖🍴≒🍴♣P🍽

Romford

Moon & Stars ✪
99-103 South Street, RM1 1NX
☼ 9am-midnight (1am Fri & Sat) ☎ (01708) 730117
Courage Directors; Greene King Abbot; Ruddles Best Bitter; guest beers Ⓗ
Popular Wetherspoon pub, handy for Romford railway station and buses. Five rotating guest beers range in strength from session bitters to strong ales, catering for all tastes. Friday and Saturday evenings are busy, which makes for an exciting atmosphere, although finding a table may be difficult. Breakfast is available from 7am to noon (beer from 9am), and good-value coffees are served. The full menu is available until 10pm. Real ciders come from the Westons range.
Q◖🛇≒🍴🍽

Woodford Green

Cricketers 🄻
299-301 High Road, IG8 9HQ (on A1099)
☼ 11.30-11 (midnight Fri & Sat) ☎ (020) 8504 2734
McMullen AK, Cask Ale, Country Bitter, seasonal beers Ⓗ

A pleasant, cosy two-bar local with a dartboard in the public bar and plaques in the saloon for all 18 first-class cricket counties, together with photographs of former local MP Sir Winston Churchill, whose statue stands on the green almost opposite. Good-value food is served Monday to Saturday lunchtimes. There are picnic tables on the front patio, and a covered smoking area with seating at the rear. Boules is played on a pitch behind the pub. Q☆❄◐♿➍☷(179,W13)♣P⁵⌐

Travellers Friend
496-498 High Road, IG8 0PN (on slip road off A104)
✪ 12-11; 12-4, 7-11 Sun ☎ (020) 8504 2435
Adnams Broadside; Courage Best Bitter; Wells Bombardier; guest beer Ⓗ
One of London's Real Heritage Pubs, this gem of a friendly, comfortable local features oak-panelled walls and rare original snob screens. There are normally two guest beers. Small beer festivals are held in April and September. As far as is known, the pub has never sold keg bitter. A pleasant heated patio/smoking area is at the rear, picnic tables are at the front and there is a small car park. Local CAMRA Pub of the Year 2010.
Q☆♿➍(20,179,W13)P⁵⌐

NORTH LONDON
N1: Hoxton
Baring
55 Baring Street, N1 3DS
✪ 12-11 (10.30 Sun) ☎ (020) 7359 5785
⊕ thebaringpub.co.uk
Shepherd Neame Spitfire; Taylor Landlord; guest beers Ⓗ
Guarding a corner of Baring Street facing towards Wilton Square, and close to the Regents Canal, this is very much a community pub, with its own cricket team. Featuring a long bar that wraps round at the right-hand end to give access to a garden area at the rear, it also has an upstairs function room that sees frequent use. Screens show major sporting events. One of the two guest ales comes from a local brewery. ♨☆◐➍⇌(Essex Rd)➍♣☝⁵⌐

Howl at the Moon Ⓛ
178 Hoxton Street, N1 5LH
✪ 12-11 (1am Fri & Sat) ☎ (020) 3341 2525
⊕ hoxtonhowl.com
Brodie's London Fields; Dark Star Partridge; Oakham JHB; guest beers Ⓗ
A pleasant conversion of a disused pub in a once run-down but now revived area. A range of five real ales is served with one real cider on tap plus two cider boxes behind the bar. A superb selection of music is played. Mixed seating consists of sofas and chairs around the bar and numerous interesting items adorn the walls. The pleasant staff offer tastings. Real English food is served lunchtimes and evenings at a reasonable price. Live blues features on Friday. ☆◐➋⊖➍♣☝⁵⌐

Prince Arthur
49 Brunswick Place, N1 6EB
✪ 11.30-midnight; 12-6 Sat & Sun ☎ (020) 7253 3187
Shepherd Neame Master Brew, Spitfire, seasonal beers Ⓗ
Friendly local tucked away near Old Street and Pitfield Street, always popular with local residents and office staff. There are two levels to the pub, with a dartboard much in demand on the lower

level. The decor reflects the long-standing landlord's boxing past, and horse racing pictures are also found. Snacks are available, and there is room to drink outside the front of the pub. It may close earlier on week nights. ☆⇌⊖(Old St)➍♣⁵⌐

N1: Islington
Barnsbury ✪
209-211 Liverpool Road, N1 1LX
✪ 12-11 (10.30 Sun) ☎ (020) 7607 5519
⊕ thebarnsbury.co.uk
Beer range varies Ⓗ
Large, traditional, friendly local with a separate dining area and rear garden terrace. A free house, it offers up to four changing real ales ranging from light to dark. There are regular pub favourites on the menu as well as more modern food. Recent refurbishment has subtly lifted the interior, which is comfortable and bright, with an interesting take on chandeliers. A relaxing oasis from the hubbub of nearby Angel. The various Sunday roasts are popular with locals. ☆◐➋⊖(Angel)➍⁵⌐

Charles Lamb
16 Elia Street, N1 8DE
✪ 12 (4 Mon & Tue)-11; 12-10.30 Sun ☎ (020) 7837 5040
⊕ thecharleslambpub.com
Dark Star Hophead; Triple fff Alton's Pride; guest beers Ⓗ
Charming, deservedly busy little pub serving four real ales, all from independent brewers and always in perfect condition. Service is fast, friendly and efficient. There is also a worthwhile range of bottle-conditioned ales. Food is a point of pride, but all seating is available to non-diners. Cask cider is on offer to warm you during the winter months. The decor is traditional with bare floorboards. There is some outside seating in a quiet street.
☆◐➋⊖(Angel)➍♣☝⁵⌐

New Rose ✪
84-86 Essex Road, N1 8LU
✪ 12 11 (midnight Thu; 2am Fri & Sat); 12-10.30 Sun ☎ (020) 7226 1082
Beer range varies Ⓗ
Two-room corner pub, with activities such as quizzes or DJs playing on one side. The quieter corner bar has a rose logo on the settle backs. Casual in style, with bare brickwork and distressed wood floors, it is popular with young people who demand a constantly rotating range of real ales from independent breweries. Pub grub and pizzas are available, and there is an annual beer festival in April. It has a flat floor but no disabled toilet, and benches on the pavement.
♨☆◐➋⇌(Essex Rd)⊖(Angel)➍⁵⌐

N1: Kingsland
Duke of Wellington Ⓛ ✪
119 Balls Pond Road, N1 4BL
✪ 3-midnight (1am Thu & Fri); 12-1am Sat; 12-11.30 Sun ☎ (020) 7275 7640 ⊕ thedukeofwellingtonN1.com
Sambrook's Wandle; guest beers Ⓗ
Pleasant Victorian two-room inn and former local CAMRA Pub of the Season. The front room has an island bar with many original features. The back room is more relaxed but can get busy for major sports events, comedy club, DJ and film nights. Three rotating guest ales are usually from small independents. Two ciders are served direct from

the cask. Bar snacks and pub grub are popular and beer festivals are held in January and July. There are benches at the side, and a garden in summer. ♨◑●(Dalston Jct/Dalston Kingsland)🚋🐾⁵⁻

N1: Newington Green

Clarendon 🅛 ✅
92 Mildmay Park, N1 4PR
✪ 12-11 (midnight Thu-Sat) ☎ (020) 7249 6430
Dark Star Hophead; Redemption Urban Dusk; Sharp's Doom Bar; guest beer Ⓗ
Spacious pub facing Newington Green, renamed from the Nobody Inn, with four handpumps for beer and three for cider (all Westons). Three areas, including one with large screens for TV sport, all have modern North London decor and are furnished with a mix of scrubbed tables, chairs and sofas. There are benches on the pavement, heated when necessary. Thai food is served lunchtimes and evenings. Board games are popular with the locals. ♨◑●(Canonbury)🚋🐾⁵⁻

N2: East Finchley

Bald Faced Stag 🅛
69 High Road, N2 8AB
✪ 12-11 (11.30 Thu; midnight Fri & Sat) ☎ (020) 8442 1201
⊕ thebaldfacedstagn2.co.uk
Beer range varies Ⓗ
An increasingly popular pub, this old-established corner local is now open plan around a three-sided bar, with a dining room at the rear. One of the Realpubs chain, owned by Greene King, but with complete autonomy on its choice of ales – the keen manager endeavours to stock local beers from brewers such as Camden and Redemption. The pub hosts its own beer festivals three times a year. Over 21s only. ❀◑&●🚋P⁵⁻

N3: Finchley

Dignity ✅
363 Regents Park Road, N3 1DH
✪ 12 (11 Sat & Sun)-midnight ☎ (020) 8349 1453
⊕ thedignityfinchley.co.uk
Sharp's Doom Bar; guest beers Ⓗ
A short walk from Finchley Central Station, located on the ground floor of Winston House. You will be greeted by friendly staff in this lively pub that has an L-shaped open-plan design with a raised section. The wide front patio has an area with partial cover and heaters. The two rotating guest beers are from the M&B portfolio. Wednesday is quiz night, Thursday open mic night, and Sunday evenings are dedicated to folk, blues or jazz. ❀◑●(Finchley Central)🚋⁵⁻

N4: Harringay

Old Ale Emporium ✅
405 Green Lanes, N4 1EU
✪ 11-midnight (1am Fri & Sat); 12-midnight Sun
☎ (020) 8348 6204
Fuller's London Pride; guest beers Ⓗ
Corner pub close to the Overground station. It has an outdoor smoking area with seating created by cutting back the front of the bar. Two or three varying guest beers are offered, and occasional beer festivals are held. It is popular for televised sporting events, but the back part of the bar, with a mini library, can offer some relief. Interesting old

prints of the locality adorn the walls, though a picture of the White Hart in Tottenham might suggest the pub's allegiance. ❀&●(Harringay Green Lanes)🚋♣⁵⁻

N5: Canonbury

Snooty Fox 🅛 ✅
75 Grosvenor Avenue, N5 2NN
✪ 4-11 (1am Fri); 12-10.30 Sat & Sun ☎ (020) 7354 9532
⊕ snootyfoxlondon.co.uk
St Austell Tribute; guest beers Ⓗ
Vibrant, spacious pub decorated with '60s icons and a 45rpm jukebox giving a retro feel. The light airy lounge leads to a small patio, a pleasant spot to enjoy one of its four real ales and watch the world go by. It has a regular DJ for music and several diverse beer festivals, always well attended. There is a revolving LocAle and two other changing guest beers. Good modern British food is cooked to order, and there are Sunday roasts. ❀◑●🚋⁵⁻

N6: Highgate

Gatehouse ✅
1 North Road, N6 4BD
✪ 9am-11.30 (midnight Fri & Sat); 9am-10.30 Sun
☎ (020) 8340 8054
Fuller's London Pride; Greene King Abbot; guest beers Ⓗ
Large, well-kept Tudor-style Wetherspoon on a busy corner in Highgate village that was once a toll house. With numerous booths and a separate 42-cover restaurant, it is panelled throughout and hung with photos depicting historic local views. It has a faux gas fire in an otherwise traditional fireplace, a fair-sized enclosed garden with heaters, and two screens for terrestrial TV sport. Upstairs, a variety theatre ranges from opera to modern drama and meal and ticket deals are sometimes available. Q❀◑&●🚋🐾⁵⁻

Prince of Wales ✅
53 Highgate High Street, N6 5JX
✪ 12-11 (midnight Fri & Sat) ☎ (020) 8340 0445
Butcombe Bitter; guest beers Ⓗ
Squeezed between the bustle of Highgate High Street and the calm of Pond Square, this pub offers up to three guest beers and an interior relatively unchanged over the years. It can get busy, particularly for the Tuesday quiz, reputedly one of the most testing in London. The pub sponsors a local cricket team. Thai food is served Monday-Friday lunchtimes and evenings and all day Saturday; Sunday roasts are available until 9pm. At the back is an outdoor drinking and smoking area. ♨Q❀◑●🚋♣⁵⁻

Red Lion & Sun ✅
25 North Road, N6 4BE
✪ 12-11 (midnight Fri & Sat); 12-10.30 Sun
☎ (020) 8340 1780 ⊕ theredlionandsun.com
Greene King Morland Bitter Ⓗ
Though rebuilt in 1926, there has been a pub on this site since the 1500s. The large front garden with heated smoking area leads to a single-roomed bar with simple and clean décor. A variety of pews, chairs and dining tables and two real fires provide an informal drinking and dining atmosphere. Hog roasts are a regular summer feature in the rear patio along with front garden

barbecues. Food is served all day every day, with highchairs for children. Dog- and walker-friendly. ♨♣♫◐♿⊖☒🐕⊏

N7: Holloway

Coronet ✓
338-346 Holloway Road, N7 6NJ
☼ 9am-11 (10.30 Sun) ☎ (020) 7609 5014
Greene King Abbot; Marston's Pedigree; Ruddles Best Bitter; guest beers Ⓗ
Impressive Wetherspoon conversion of an old cinema, adorned with large prints of movie stars and local entertainers of old, with an old projector the centrepiece of a raised dais towards the rear. A well-lit and heated area is provided at the back for smokers. Popular with all age groups, it frequently has up to six guest ales available, with single brewery festivals at times. Expect plastic glasses and higher prices when Arsenal are playing at home. Q♣◐♿⊖(Holloway Rd)☒🐕⊏

N8: Hornsey

Three Compasses Ⓛ ✓
62 High Street, N8 7NX
☼ 11-11 (midnight Fri & Sat); 12-11 Sun ☎ (020) 8340 2729
⊕ threecompasses.com
Fuller's London Pride; Redemption Pale Ale; Taylor Landlord; guest beers Ⓗ
Large front windows contribute to an airy, bright feel in the front bar of this award-winning community pub, a popular after-work venue for local young professionals and those heading for events at nearby Alexandra Palace. The rear bar is darker, with daylight from a large skylight roof, and has pool tables, a dartboard and a large-screen TV at the end. Three changing guest ales are served on the front bar. ◐♿≠☒(41,144,W3)♣Ⓣ

N9: Lower Edmonton

Beehive
24 Little Bury Street, N9 9JZ
☼ 12-midnight (1am Fri & Sat); 12-11 Sun
☎ (020) 8360 4358
Greene King IPA; Draught Bass; Greene King Old Speckled Hen; Sharp's Doom Bar; guest beer Ⓗ
Community one-bar pub with the four listed beers nearly always available, plus a guest from the Punch list. Fresh daily specials Tuesday-Saturday complement the regular pub food menu, plus Sunday roasts. There is a small garden area to the side and cover for smokers by the parking area to the front. Live bands play regularly but there is a quieter area to one side of the bar. No admittance or outside drinking after 11pm. ♣◐☒(329,W8)♣P⊏

N10: Muswell Hill

John Baird Ⓛ ✓
122 Fortis Green Road, N10 3HN
☼ 11-11 (midnight Fri & Sat); 12-10.30 Sun
☎ (020) 8444 8830 ⊕ thejohnbaird.co.uk
Purity Mad Goose; Redemption Trinity; Sharp's Doom Bar; guest beers Ⓗ
Large local pub named after the TV pioneer. Eight handpumps provide a changing selection of beers, with regular themed festivals. Dedicated cider and perry pumps ensure all are catered for. It incorporates the award-winning Black Orchid Thai

restaurant but food is served throughout the pub, and dining extends to the large rear patio where smokers are accommodated with a heated area. Traditional Sunday lunches are popular. TV screens show sport all around. ♨♣◐♿⊖☒🐕⊏

N12: North Finchley

Elephant Inn Ⓛ ✓
283 Ballards Lane, N12 8NR
☼ 11-11 (midnight Fri & Sat); 12-10.30 Sun
☎ (020) 8343 6110
Fuller's Discovery, London Pride, ESB; guest beer Ⓗ
A spacious U-shaped bar, divided into three drinking areas, serves a lively and mixed clientele. The landlady and bar staff enthusiastically promote real ale. There is a Thai restaurant upstairs open midday-10pm. Bar snacks are also available. At the front of the pub is a large patio. ♣◐⊖(West Finchley)☒♣⊏

N13: Palmers Green

Alfred Herring ✓
316-322 Green Lanes, N13 5TT
☼ 9am-11 (midnight Thu-Sat) ☎ (020) 3232 1083
Courage Directors; Greene King Abbot; Ruddles Best Bitter; guest beers Ⓗ
Named after a local World War I Victoria Cross holder, this pleasant, centrally located Wetherspoon shop conversion is popular with locals. The main dining area is conveniently divided off along one side of the pub. Families are welcome until 9.30pm. The pub was opened as a non-smoking pub before the ban; smoking is also not permitted along the front veranda. An extra bank of handpumps was recently installed. Sparklers may be used; if you are concerned, please ask for them to be removed. ◐♿≠☒(121,329,W6)

N14: Southgate

New Crown ✓
80-84 Chase Side, N14 5PH
☼ 9am-11.30 (12.30am Fri & Sat) ☎ (020) 8882 8758
Fuller's London Pride, ESB; Greene King Abbot; Ruddles Best Bitter; guest beers Ⓗ
Typical large Wetherspoon pub first opened in 1996 in a former high street Sainsbury's store. Staff are keen, efficient and knowledgeable when it comes to the ales. In addition to the regular national festivals, the pub hosts its own, often with a specific brewery theme and sometimes with a Meet the Brewer event. Sparklers may be used; if you are concerned, please ask for them to be removed. Ciders from Westons are available. ◐♿⊖☒♣

N16: Stoke Newington

Daniel Defoe ✓
102 Stoke Newington Church Street, N16 0LA
☼ 12-midnight (2am Fri & Sat) ☎ (020) 7254 2906
⊕ thedanieldefoe.com
Courage Best Bitter; St Austell Tribute; Wells Eagle, Bombardier; guest beers Ⓗ
A welcoming traditional local with authentic charm, newly decorated and light and spacious in the main bar. Outside is a large enclosed patio for enjoying a Sunday roast on balmy summer days. A tied Charles Wells' house with four regular ales, it

also offers a couple of changing guests like Barnsey from Bath Ales. There is a select menu of good pub grub at reasonable prices. ✿❶●❄₽🔥

Jolly Butchers 🅛
204 Stoke Newington High Street, N16 7HU
✪ 4-midnight (1am Fri); 12-1am Sat; 12-11 Sun
☎ (020) 7241 2185 ⊕ jollybutchers.co.uk
Beer range varies Ⓗ
Classic Art Deco bar boasting elaborate ironwork and glass with a lively modern feel and the enviable status of being a true free house. As such it offers a chameleon range of seven real ales from pale and hoppy through to sumptuous porters and stouts, some LocAle. There are also two ciders, a perry, numerous speciality lagers and extensive bottled beers from Europe and the US. The beer is complemented by great food, guaranteed to satisfy on quantity and quality. ✿❶●❄₽🔥

N21: Winchmore Hill
Dog & Duck
74 Hoppers Road, N21 3LH
✪ 12-11 (10.30 Sun) ☎ (020) 8886 1987
Fuller's London Pride; Greene King IPA; Taylor Landlord; Young's Bitter; guest beer Ⓗ
Small, friendly pub with one bar, popular with locals but welcoming to visitors. A large-screen TV shows sporting events. The walls are adorned with local history photographs and a Victorian map of the area. The patio-style walled garden at the rear welcomes dogs at quiet times and there is a covered and heated area for smokers. ✿❄₽(W9)🔥

Orange Tree
18 Highfield Road, N21 3HA
✪ 12-midnight (1am Fri & Sat); 12-11 Sun
☎ (020) 8360 4853 ⊕ orangetreepub.com
Greene King IPA, Old Speckled Hen; guest beer Ⓗ
In 2012 this popular community pub was 100 years old and the licensees celebrated 20 years here. Guest beers are not tied and local Redemption beers often feature. Home-cooked food is available at lunchtimes, including Sunday roasts. There is an area for pool and darts, and TV for main sporting events. A large attractive garden has a children's play area. Free Wi-Fi is available. No admittance after 11pm. ✿❶❄₽(329)♣P🔥

Cockfosters
Cock & Dragon ✪
14 Chalk Lane, EN4 9HU TQ277967
✪ 11-11 (11.30 Fri & Sat); 11-10.30 Sun ☎ (020) 8449 7160
⊕ cockanddragon-cockfosters.co.uk
Greene King IPA, seasonal beer; guest beer Ⓗ
A pub on the edge of countryside yet within 10 minutes' walk of the northern terminus of the Piccadilly Line. The London Loop footpath passes here. The large main bar has several alcoves. Bar meals at lunchtime are English and Thai; a separate restaurant is also available in the evenings until 10pm with Thai food only. The secluded rear garden has a large decked section and to the side is a covered, heated area. Disabled access is through a side entrance. ✿❶&⊖₽(298)P🔥

Enfield
Moon Under Water ✪
115-117 Chase Side, EN2 6NN
✪ 9am-11 (10.30 Sun) ☎ (020) 8366 9855
Courage Directors; Greene King Abbot; Ruddles Best Bitter; guest beers Ⓗ
Spacious Wetherspoon pub with two main seating areas around a U-shaped bar. It was a conversion from a dairy more than 20 years ago and has a refreshingly light and airy feel. Breakfasts are served until noon, meals until 10pm (families welcome until 8.30). Various brands of real cider are served on gravity. Sparklers may be used; if you are concerned, please ask for them to be removed. ✿❶&❄(Gordon Hill)₽(191,W9)♠P🔥

Wonder 🅛
1 Batley Road, EN2 0JG
✪ 11-11; 12-10.30 Sun ☎ (020) 8363 0202
McMullen AK, Cask Ale, Country Bitter, seasonal beer Ⓗ
The traditional feel of this popular, friendly local, cultivated by its previous hosts, has been retained by the new landlady. There are still two bars, neither with TV, one with a real fire and a dartboard, with cards and cribbage on request. Sessions on the piano take place on Saturday nights and Sundays. A selection of hot pies with mushy peas if you like is available all day. ▲Q✿✿❄(Gordon Hill)₽(191,W8)♣P🔥

High Barnet
Lord Nelson ✪
14 West End Lane, EN5 2SA
✪ 12-11 (midnight Fri & Sat); 12-10.30 Sun
☎ (020) 8449 7249 ⊕ thelordnelsonph.co.uk
Wells Bombardier; Young's Bitter, Special, seasonal beer; guest beer Ⓗ
Homely, dog-friendly pub on the outskirts of High Barnet, served by several bus routes. In keeping with its name, there are several marine artefacts, although a vast collection of cruet sets predominates. Good-value home-cooked food is served until 8.30pm. Cribbage, dominoes and scrabble sets are available. Look for the autographs of Richard Burton and Liz Taylor on the wall. There is one TV, used sparingly. ✿❶●₽♣🔥

Olde Mitre 🏆 ✪
58 High Street, EN5 5SJ
✪ 12-11 (1am Fri & Sat) ☎ (020) 8449 5701
Adnams Southwold Bitter; Taylor Landlord; guest beers Ⓗ
Extensive wood panels and wood flooring, basic seating and tables characterise this pub. The lower rear area leads out to a large garden with two further rooms known as Stable and Carriage from the pub's history as a coaching inn. The four frequently changing guest beers, together with its much improved ambience and facilities during the current licensees' tenure, have made it the local CAMRA Pub of the Year on several occasions. A real cider is always available. Q✿❶⊖₽♣🔥

New Barnet
Builders Arms
3 Albert Road, EN4 9SH
✪ 12-11 ☎ (020) 8216 5678
Greene King IPA, Abbot, seasonal beer; guest beer Ⓗ

In a side street off East Barnet Road just round the corner from the Railway Bell, this traditional two-bar pub has a quiet saloon to the front and a back bar with a pool table, jukebox and TV sport. There is an outside heated area for smokers. Q🌸🍴🏡⇌🖳♣🎵⌐

Ponders End

Picture Palace 🅛 ✔

Howard's Hall, Lincoln Road, EN3 4AQ (jct with High St)
🌣 9am-11 (midnight Fri & Sat) ☎ (020) 8344 9690
Greene King Abbot; Ruddles Best Bitter; guest beers Ⓗ

A superb Wetherspoon's conversion of a 1920s cinema – look up to appreciate the murals of the silent movie era. This oasis in a real ale desert has the bonus of LocAle guests from the Redemption Brewery only four miles away in Tottenham. Ciders are from Westons. There is a quieter family area as well as a patio to one side of the building. Sparklers may be used; if you are concerned, please ask for them to be removed. 🌸🍺👪⇌(Southbury)🖳🍴Pꝺⱶ

NORTH-WEST LONDON
NW1: Camden Town

Prince Albert 🅛 ✔

163 Royal College Street, NW1 0SG
🌣 12-11 (10.15 Sun) ☎ (020) 7485 0270
⊕ princealbertcamden.com
Young's Special; guest beers Ⓗ

A sensitive conversion of an old Charrington's pub by private owners. The leaded Toby windows and wooden floors have been tastefully restored. The outside tiling is striking but the main reason for visiting is the beer range. Guest beers include a LocAle from either Redemption or Sambrook's, and two others, often one from Otley. The garden is one of the most pleasant in Camden. There is a restaurant upstairs. 🌸🍺Ө(Camden Rd)🖳🍴ⱶ

NW1: Euston

Bree Louise 🅛

69 Cobourg Street, NW1 2HH
🌣 11.30-11; 12-10.30 Sun ☎ (020) 7681 4930
⊕ thebreelouise.com
Redemption Trinity; Windsor & Eton Conquerer, Knight of the Garter Ⓗ**; guest beers** Ⓗ/Ⓖ

One-bar corner pub, busy with locals and Euston commuters. A cooled gravity stillage, complemented by handpumps (beers change but usually feature LocAles), provides a large range, alongside up to eight ciders. Regular beer festivals are held. There is no music, just conversation, but occasional sport on TV (usually at the weekend). Outdoor seating is on the pavement. May close later on weekdays. 🌸🍺⇌Ө🖳🍴ⱶ

Doric Arch ✔

1 Eversholt Street, NW1 1DN
🌣 12-11 (10.30 Sun) ☎ (020) 7383 3359
Fuller's Discovery, London Pride, ESB, seasonal beer; guest beers Ⓗ

Go up the stairs to reach this single-bar pub where the raised seating area gives great views of the buses in front of Euston Station. Dark wood and subtle lighting create a convivial environment for the many commuters who call this a second home, if only to watch the sport on TV. Blackboards behind the bar list the beers. The cider, hidden under the bar, is from Westons. Toilets are downstairs; ask for the code. Food is served until 9pm daily. There is free Wi-Fi. 🍺⇌Ө🖳🍴

Euston Tap

West Lodge, 190 Euston Road, NW1 2EF
🌣 12-11.30 (10.30 Sun) ☎ (020) 3137 8837
⊕ eustontap.com
Beer range varies Ⓟ

Unusual pub in one of the old porters' lodges at the front of Euston station. It offers eight changing cask beers on tap. The dispense method is unusual: rather than using handpumps, the beers are pumped up to taps behind the bar. Space is rather limited although there is an outside drinking area as well as more seating upstairs. The opposite lodge, the Cider Tap, opening at 3pm, features six real ciders. 🌸⇌Ө🖳🍴ⱶ

NW1: St Pancras

Euston Flyer ✔

83-87 Euston Road, NW1 2RA
🌣 10-11 (11.30 Tue-Thu; midnight Fri & Sat)
☎ (020) 7383 0856
Fuller's Discovery, London Pride, ESB, seasonal beers; Gale's Seafarers Ale Ⓗ

Across the road from the British Library, this is a popular spot for office workers, commuters, sports fans and travellers using St Pancras International. A large open-plan pub divided into different sections and levels, it can be boisterous in the evenings and during major football matches. Two large-screen TVs plus a smaller one are always on for sporting events, often showing different matches. Meals are served all day, starting with breakfast. 🍺⇌Ө🖳

NW3: Hampstead

Duke of Hamilton 🅛 ✔

23-25 New End, NW3 1JD
🌣 11-11 (10.30 Sun) ☎ (020) 7794 0258
⊕ thedukeofhamilton.com
Fuller's London Pride; guest beers Ⓗ

Saved from conversion to flats by a vigorous local campaign and restored back to good health by sympathetic new owners, this free house offers up to five varying, rotating guest beers. Outside terraces at front and back and a cellar bar add to the attractions. An inn for nearly 300 years, it regularly shows televised sport, particularly rugby. A full menu is offered Thursday-Sunday and snacks (including a full breakfast) throughout the week. 🌸🍺Ө🖳(268,603)♣ⱶ

Holly Bush ✔

22 Holly Mount, NW3 6SG (up Holly Bush Steps from Heath St)
🌣 12-11 (10.30 Sun) ☎ (020) 7435 2892
Fuller's London Pride, ESB, seasonal beer; Gale's Seafarers Ale; Harveys Sussex Best Bitter Ⓗ

Handsome pub with a fine wood-panelled interior and several rooms of different sizes at different levels. A Grade II-listed building, originally the stables of artist George Romney's house, it retains many historic features and is one of London's Real Heritage Pubs. Food is good and unpretentious. At nearly the highest point in Hampstead (and one of the highest in London), this makes an excellent destination pub. 🏛Q🌸🍺Ө🖳(46,268,603)🍴ⱶ

NW4: Hendon

Greyhound
52 Church End, NW4 4JT
🌣 12-midnight (1am Fri; 11 Sun) ☎ (020) 8457 9730
Courage Best Bitter; St Austell Tribute; Wells Bombardier; Young's Bitter, Special; guest beers Ⓗ
Traditional cask ale house with three different drinking areas, one with wood-panelled walls and some comfortable seating. In a historic area beside St Mary's Church, it has a village feel about it. A large-screen TV shows sporting events, and there are quiz evenings on Monday and Wednesday and jazz every last Thursday of the month. Stone-baked pizza is a speciality. ⚒Q◕🌣🖵(143,183,326)♣🚴

NW5: Kentish Town

Junction Tavern Ⓛ
101 Fortess Road, NW5 1AG
🌣 5 (12 Fri; 11.30 Sat)-11; 12-10.30 Sun ☎ (020) 7485 9400
⊕ junctiontavern.co.uk
Sambrook's Wandle; guest beers Ⓗ
Busy, lively gastro-pub whose rear area extends through a conservatory into a large garden. As well as Wandle, there is usually a second LocAle and two more guest beers. The garden is hugely popular in the summer and children are welcome there until 7pm. Festivals are held at least twice a year. Q🌣◕🚆θ(Tufnell Pk)🖵(134)🚴

Pineapple 🍺 Ⓛ
51 Leverton Street, NW5 2NX
🌣 12-11 (10.30 Sun) ☎ (020) 7284 4631
Draught Bass; guest beers Ⓗ
A real community pub, saved from closure by the locals, Grade II-listed and one of London's Real Heritage Pubs, notable for its splendid bar-back. The comfortable seating around tables in the front bar leads through to an informal conservatory overlooking the patio garden. Two beer festivals a year include one at Easter with a popular bonnet parade. LocAles can include beers from Redemption and East London. Local CAMRA Pub of the Year 2012. Q🌣◕🚆θ🖵♣🚴

Southampton Arms
139 Highgate Road, NW5 1LE
🌣 12-11 (11.30 Fri & Sat) ☎ (020) 7485 1511
⊕ thesouthamptonarms.co.uk
Beer range varies Ⓗ
The 2011 CAMRA London Pub of the Year and 2010 London Cider Pub of the Year, this pub does what it says on the sign outside - Ale, Cider, Meat. Eighteen pumps on and behind the bar serve almost equal amounts of beer and cider from some of the best micros in the UK. Snacks include pork pies, cheese and meat baps. Only music on vinyl is played and the piano is in regular use. At the rear is a secluded patio. ⚒🌣🚆θ(Kentish Town)🖵(214,C2,C11)♣🚴

NW8: St John's Wood

Clifton Ⓛ ✔
96 Clifton Hill, NW8 0JT
🌣 12-11 (10.30 Sun) ☎ (020) 7372 3427
⊕ cliftonstjohnswood.com
Sambrook's Junction; guest beers Ⓗ
A hunting lodge 200 years ago before gaining a licence, this pub was given hotel status by King Edward VII so that he could visit Lily Langtry here, as royalty could not visit pubs. The front has a

decorative wooden island bar, with bronze inserts. To the rear are two rooms, one a restaurant. Many board games are available. One of two guest beers is usually from Adnams or Greene King. In summer one handpump is used for Westons cider. ⚒🌣◕θ(Kilburn High Rd/Kilburn Pk)🖵🚴

Harefield

Old Orchard
Park Lane, UB9 6HJ
🌣 11.30-11; 12-10.30 Sun ☎ (01895) 822631
⊕ oldorchard-harefield.co.uk
Brunning & Price Original; Fuller's London Pride; Tring Side Pocket for a Toad; guest beers Ⓗ
Brunning & Price establishment that was once a country house before becoming a restaurant. Refurbished in 2010, the pub is lined with bookcases and pictures and has an unfussy array of mismatched tables and chairs and several welcoming real fires. Three guest beers are usually available, mostly from local breweries. The Original is brewed by Phoenix. There are commanding views of the Colne Valley from the terrace and beer garden. ⚒Q🌣◕🚴🖵(U9)♣🅿🚴

Harrow

Moon on the Hill ✔
373-375 Station Road, HA1 2AW
🌣 8am-midnight (12.30am Fri & Sat) ☎ (020) 8863 3670
Greene King Abbot; Ruddles Best Bitter; guest beers Ⓗ
Small, busy Wetherspoon pub close to Harrow-on-the-Hill station and served by numerous bus routes. Serving food all day, it is popular with price-conscious regulars, office workers and students from the nearby University of Westminster. The pub gets extremely busy when there are sporting events on at nearby Wembley Stadium and plastic glasses may be used on these occasions. Q◕🚆θ🖵

Harrow-on-the-Hill

Castle ★ ✔
30 West Street, HA1 3EF
🌣 12-11 (midnight Fri & Sat) ☎ (020) 8422 3155
⊕ castleharrow.co.uk
Fuller's Discovery, London Pride, ESB, seasonal beers; Gale's HSB Ⓗ
Situated in the heart of historic Harrow-on-the-Hill, this is a popular and friendly Fuller's house. Built in 1901 and Grade II-listed, it is one of Britain's Real Heritage Pubs. Food is served until 9pm every day; reservations are recommended for Sunday lunchtime. Three real coal fires help to keep the pub warm and cosy in the colder months and a secluded beer garden is popular during the summer. ⚒Q🌣◕🖵(258,H17)🚴

Pinner

Queen's Head
31 High Street, HA5 5PJ
🌣 11-11 ☎ (020) 8868 4607
Adnams Southwold Bitter; Greene King Abbot; Wells Bombardier; Young's Special; guest beers Ⓗ
Historic pub in a conservation area, a Grade II-listed building dating back to 1540. Despite its suburban location, it has the appearance and feel of a traditional country inn, with its Tudor frontage, low

ceiling and exposed beams. It is closely involved in local activities and celebrates St George's Day with a hog roast. There is no music or TV but a quiz is held on Mondays. Local CAMRA Pub of the Year 2012. Q❀❶&⊖🚋P⅃

Ruislip Common

Woodman ✅
Breakspear Road, HA4 7SE
❂ 11 (12 Sun)-midnight ☎ (01895) 635763
⊕ thewoodmanruislip.co.uk
Courage Best Bitter; Otter Ale; guest beer Ⓗ
A cheerful and welcoming two-bar local in the northern area of Ruislip close to Ruislip Lido and woods, opposite Hillingdon Borough Football Club. The cosy lounge bar is traditional in atmosphere with no intrusive electronic machines, although the TV may be on for sport matches. Note the collection of bottled beers on display. There is also a good selection of single malt whiskies. The public bar is friendly and comfortable, with a dartboard and other pub games. ❀❶&🚋(331)♣P⅃

Ruislip Manor

JJ Moons Ⓛ ✅
12 Victoria Road, HA4 0AA
❂ 9am-midnight (1am Fri & Sat) ☎ (01895) 622373
Courage Directors; Fuller's London Pride; Greene King Abbot; Ruddles Best Bitter; guest beers Ⓗ
Large, busy Wetherspoon pub opened in 1990 in a former Woolworths and still with the same manager. There is a large raised area to the rear for diners. Accredited for LocAle in 2009, it offers guest ales from breweries such as Twickenham, Tring and Windsor & Eton. A real ale club every Wednesday helps the enthusiastic manager to decide which beers to order. Two Westons ciders are also regularly available on handpump. Local CAMRA Pub of the Year 2012. ≿❀❶&⊖🚋(114,398,H13)♣⅃

South Harrow

White Horse ✅
50 Middle Road, HA2 0HL
❂ 12-midnight (11 Mon & Tue; 10.30 Sun)
☎ (020) 8422 1215 ⊕ thewhitehorseharrow.co.uk
Fuller's London Pride, ESB; Gale's Seafarers Ale; guest beer Ⓗ
The landlord of this large pub takes pride in the good service that all his customers receive, the high standards he has set for his staff and for everything that is sold. There is a quiz every Thursday, and a dinner-dance on the last Saturday of the month. The home-cooked food, which is excellent, is available all day except Sunday, when last orders are taken at 6pm. ♒❀❶⊖🚋P⅃

SOUTH-EAST LONDON
SE1: Borough

Market Porter
9 Stoney Street, SE1 9AA
❂ 6-9am, 11-11; 12-11 Sat; 12-10.30 Sun
☎ (020) 7407 2495 ⊕ markettaverns.co.uk/
the_market_porter.html
Harveys Sussex Best Bitter; guest beers Ⓗ
A classic market pub serving up to 12 changing ales and ciders. Attached to the walls and ceiling is a vast range of pump clips of the ales that have

previously been on sale. It can get busy with drinkers spilling out on to the street, especially on market days. A small air-conditioned seating area is at the rear. Upstairs a restaurant serves lunches and is available for private hire in the evenings. ❶&⇌⊖(London Bridge)🚋♦

Old King's Head
King's Head Yard, 45-49 Borough High Street, SE1 1NA
❂ 11-midnight (1am Fri & Sat); 12-midnight Sun
☎ (020) 7407 1550 ⊕ theoldkingshead.uk.com
Harveys Sussex Best Bitter; St Austell Tribute, Proper Job; Sharp's Doom Bar; Wells Bombardier Ⓗ
Down a narrow, cobbled road off Borough High Street lies this traditional pub. The stained glass windows hint at a bygone era and the pictures adorning the walls tell the story of a pub, and an area, that has a rich history. The layout inside is simple: an L-shaped bar, with six pumps and three or four beers, serving the eclectic mix of tourists, office workers and marketgoers. ❶▶&⇌⊖(London Bridge)🚋

Rake
14 Winchester Walk, SE1 9AG
❂ 12 (10 Sat)-11; 12-8 Sun ☎ (020) 7407 0557
⊕ utobeer.co.uk/contactus_rake.html
Beer range varies Ⓗ
If you were to start a library of bottled beers, this pub, operated by Utobeer of Borough Market, would be about the best reference point. Alongside its vast range of bottles, it packs three handpumps and five taps into just four feet of bar. If you are looking for unusual guest ales, a world tour of beer and knowledgeable staff, this is an ideal place to visit. The heated patio doubles the area available, with overspill into the market when busy. ❀❶&⇌⊖(London Bridge)🚋

Royal Oak
44 Tabard Street, SE1 4JU
❂ 11 (12 Fri)-11.30; 12-9 Sun ☎ (020) 7357 7173
Harveys Sussex XX Mild, Pale, Sussex Best Bitter, Armada, seasonal beers Ⓗ
Victorian corner pub owned by Sussex brewers Harveys and stocking its full range of beers along with, usually, a Fuller's guest ale and real draught cider. Two bars are separated by an off sales area where you can also buy free range eggs and home-made preserves and chutneys. An interesting collection of prints and photographs adorns the traditional interior, including many theatre and music hall-related items. Look out also for the early 19th-century cartoon lampooning the temperance movement. Q❶▶&⇌(London Bridge)⊖🚋♦

Wheatsheaf
24 Southwark Street, SE1 1TY
❂ 11 (12 Sat)-11; 12-10 Sun ☎ (020) 7407 9934
Nethergate Redcar Best Bitter; Young's Bitter, Special; guest beers Ⓗ
Underneath the historic Hop Exchange, this Red Car pub is extremely popular with the work crowd on weekday evenings, and with good reason. A modern old-school feel sees the 10 handpumps rub shoulders with contemporary drinks dispensers, while the retro benches, stools and tables are complemented by modern partitioning and flat-screen TVs. Up to seven guest beers feature, including Mauldons and others from Nethergate. A must-visit on Saturdays to escape the bustle of the market. ❶▶⇌⊖(London Bridge)🚋♣♦

SE1: Southwark

Charles Dickens ✔

160 Union Street, SE1 0LH

12-11 (6 Sun) ☎ (020) 7401 3744

thecharlesdickens.co.uk

Beer range varies H

A back-street gem that demands a few minutes of extra walking, but you will be well rewarded with a superior, tranquil pub away from all hustle and bustle. Six varying guest beers from interesting microbreweries often include Mighty Oak's Oscar Wilde mild. Decor is largely traditional, with settles predominating. Food is served every day, with roasts on Sundays. A Victorian photo on one wall reveals that this was once the Red Lion, a Truman's pub. Q❀◑⇌(Waterloo East)⊖(Borough)🚌⚐

Doggett's Coat & Badge ✔

1 Blackfriars Bridge, SE1 9UD

10-11.30 (12.30am Thu-Sat); 10-11 Sun

☎ (020) 7633 9081 doggettscoatandbadge.co.uk

Brains SA Gold; Fuller's London Pride; St Austell Tribute; Sharp's Doom Bar; guest beer H

A large, multi-level M&B Nicholson pub at the south end of Blackfriars Bridge, situated on the South Bank halfway between Borough Market and the South Bank Centre. The ground floor bar has eight taps, serving a varied selection, and the terrace overlooking the river and covered beer garden at the back provide great outside drinking. The first floor is a restaurant, and the bars on the second and third floors are available for hire. ❀◑⇌(Blackfriars)⊖(Blackfriars)🚌⚐

SE1: Waterloo

Hole in the Wall

5 Mepham Street, SE1 8SQ

11-11 (11.30 Fri & Sat); 12-10.30 Sun ☎ (020) 7928 6196

Banks's Mild; Greene King IPA; Hogs Back TEA; Sharp's Doom Bar; Young's Bitter; guest beer H

A short hop across the road from Waterloo Station, this unusual free house enjoys the comforting rumble of trains overhead. It has a cosy, rugby-themed front bar, with a second bar in the large back room containing fruit machines and TVs. Alongside the impressive range of real ales, good food is served all day. The clientele is mixed and the pub gets busy when there is a game at Twickenham. Folk music plays on Sunday evenings. ❀◑⇌⊖🚌●⚐

King's Arms

25 Roupell Street, SE1 8TB

11-11; 12-10 Sun ☎ (020) 7207 0784

Adnams Southwold Bitter; Jennings Cumberland Ale; Ringwood Boondoggle; guest beers H

Tucked away in a historic street of 19th-century workers' cottages, this handsome free house, popular with office workers, locals, students and tourists, has a traditional horseshoe bar in the front saloon with an open fire. The rear large conservatory serves Thai food on a long central wooden table and counter with stool seating along one side. Packed with retro objets d'art, its rich history seeps through; it has been used as an undertakers and a magistrates court. ◑⇌⊖🚌●

SE3: Blackheath

Princess of Wales ✔

1a Montpelier Row, SE3 0RL

12-11 (10.30 Sun) ☎ (020) 8852 5784

princessofwalespub.co.uk

Fuller's London Pride; Sharp's Doom Bar; guest beers H

Long associated with Blackheath Rugby Club, this M&B pub sits on the edge of the heath. Summer drinkers spill out onto the vast green space and into the spacious walled garden. The L-shaped bar allows for large tables for groups as well as cosy sofas. The food is popular and the Sunday roasts are renowned. Guest beers come from micros and national breweries, with Purity and White Horse ales frequently featured. Real cider is often available in boxes. ❀◑♿⇌🚌●P

SE4: Brockley

Talbot

2 Tyrwhitt Road, SE4 1QG

12-11 (midnight Sat) ☎ (020) 8692 2665

Harveys Sussex Best Bitter; guest beers H

The sister pub of the Prince Regent in Herne Hill is building quite a reputation in the short space of time since it reopened in 2009. Serving a selection of ales and locally sourced, quality food, it strikes a nice balance between the old and the new, with modern decor and wooden furniture to give it a retro touch. Outside is a large seating area, perfect for enjoying the sunshine when the warmer weather is here. ❀◑♿⇌(St Johns)🚌⚐

SE5: Camberwell

Bear

296a Camberwell New Road, SE5 0RP

4-11 (midnight Fri & Sat); 12-11 Sun ☎ (020) 7274 7037

thebear-freehouse.co.uk

Beer range varies H

A true free house and a renovated Victorian pub, with tiled exterior, a lovely bar with cut glass mirrors, and stained glass toilet doors. Two real ales from different breweries are on tap. The menu emphasis is on traditional English and French food, with wine lists on chalkboards. It attracts a varied and discerning clientele. The front bar has piped music, with a quieter rear bar. Upstairs space is for hire, with swing dancing on Wednesday evenings. Sport is shown occasionally. ◑🚌()♣⚐

Hermit's Cave L

28 Camberwell Church Street, SE5 8QU

12-midnight (2am Fri & Sat) ☎ (020) 7703 3188

Caledonian Deuchars IPA; Loddon Gravesend Shrimpers; guest beers H

Just off Camberwell Green on a street corner, this family-run pub provides a haven from the bustle of the area. With a curved frontage, lovely Victorian windows and simple decor, it is popular with a lively, mixed clientele. There is no music, so conversation reigns. Sport is shown on muted TV in one corner or occasionally on a big screen. Real cider on handpump comes from a number of producers. Q⇌(Denmark Hill)🚌●

SE5: Denmark Hill

Fox on the Hill ✔

149 Denmark Hill, SE5 8EH

✪ 8am (9am Sun winter)-midnight (12.30am Fri & Sat)
☎ (020) 7738 4756
Fuller's London Pride; Greene King Abbot; Ruddles Best Bitter; guest beers Ⓗ
A former Charrington's pub, this large welcoming Wetherspoon is at the top of a steep hill. Its layout includes numerous cosy, low-screened booths. Outside is a spacious garden, smokers' terrace and front lawn with picnic tables. John Ruskin and other local notables are remembered in well-researched wall displays. Between four and six guest beers are served and, as well as national festivals, mini beer festivals featuring locally brewed beers are sometimes held. There are regular Meet the Brewer events. ⏰❀◑Ⓓ♿⇌🚇☕P🚭

SE5: East Dulwich

Hoopers ✪
28 Ivanhoe Road, SE5 8DH
✪ 5.30 (5 Fri)-11 (11.30 Wed; midnight Thu & Fri);
12.30-midnight Sat; 1-11 Sun ☎ (020) 7733 4797
🌐 hoopersbar.co.uk
Redemption Ivanhoe Ale; guest beers Ⓗ
A community pub on a wedge-shaped footprint, with two rooms served by an L-shaped bar. The main bar has breweriana displayed throughout and there is a snug to the rear. Three real ales are available most of the time, and beer festivals are held seasonally. Occasional Meet the Brewer events are hosted. A quiz is held on Thursdays and comedy on the first Sunday of the month. Eclectic live music features here every couple of weeks at the weekend. ⏰🚌⇌🚇(P13)♣☕🚭

SE6: Catford

London & Rye ✪
109 Rushey Green, SE6 4AF
✪ 9am-midnight ☎ (020) 8697 5028
Adnams Southwold Bitter; Fuller's London Pride; Greene King Abbot; Ruddles Best Bitter; guest beers Ⓗ
Formerly a DIY shop where you got your chisels sharpened, this is now a place to wet your whistle. Converted by Wetherspoon in 2000, it stocks a large selection of real ales, with microbreweries frequently represented among the choice of guests. Food is good value too, with further discounts for Lewisham employees with ID. Interesting local history displays on the walls inform us of a Catford of farmland and large country houses. How times change...
❀◑Ⓓ♿⇌(Bridge)☕

SE8: Deptford

Dog & Bell Ⓛ ✪
116 Prince Street, SE8 3JD
✪ 12-11.30 (midnight Sat); 12-11 Sun ☎ (020) 8692 5664
Fuller's London Pride, ESB; guest beers Ⓗ
An oasis in an area that has become something of a pub graveyard as the loss of local waterside industry killed off passing trade. A pub of this name has occupied this back street near the Thames for several hundred years, surviving now on its reputation for real ale, excellent food and events such as its celebrated annual Pickle Festival. Three interesting guest ales are always available. Parents with young children should beware of the steps where the floor is split level.
⏰Q❀◑Ⓓ⇌🚇(47,188,199)♣🚭

SE9: Eltham

Park Tavern
45 Passey Place, SE9 5DA
✪ 12-11 (midnight Fri & Sat); 12-10.30 Sun
☎ (020) 8850 8919
Fuller's London Pride; Harveys Sussex Best Bitter; St Austell Tribute; Taylor Landlord; guest beers Ⓗ
Attractive traditional Victorian pub with a tiled frontage and historic Truman's signage. The beautifully and warmly refurbished interior has elegant drapes, bar lamps and chandeliers, an impressive wood bar and a real log fire. Decorative plates and pictures line the walls. Vases of fresh flowers add to the relaxed atmosphere, with jazz and light classical background music, and an impressive selection of ales, whiskies and wines. A rear garden is available, plus seating to the front and side. ⏰Q❀◑⇌🚇♣🚭

SE10: East Greenwich

Pelton Arms ✪
23-25 Pelton Road, SE10 9PQ
✪ 12-midnight (1am Sat); 12-11 Sun ☎ (020) 8858 0572
🌐 peltonarmspub.com
Greene King IPA; Wells Bombardier; guest beers Ⓗ
This pub featured as the Nag's Head in an Only Fools and Horses prequel about the early life of Rodney Trotter. Tucked away down a quiet back street, it is delightfully cosy and friendly, with an L-shaped bar and decked out with comfy leather sofas, high stools and rustic wooden tables and chairs, made more inviting by soft lighting. The pub has many board games as well as darts, poker, quiz nights and even a knitters' club.
⏰❀🚌◑Ⓓ♿⇌(Maze Hill)🚇♣🚭

SE10: Greenwich

Plume of Feathers
19 Park Vista, SE10 9LZ
✪ 11-11 (midnight Fri & Sat); 12-11 Sun ☎ (020) 8858 1661
🌐 plumeoffeathers-greenwich.co.uk
Harveys Sussex Best Bitter; Sharp's Doom Bar; guest beers Ⓗ
With parts dating from 1691, this historic pub is opposite the northern end of Greenwich Park, close to the National Maritime Museum. It has a cosy atmosphere, especially in winter when the real fire is blazing. The maritime location is reflected inside the bar with much memorabilia on display. As well as bar meals, there is a separate restaurant to the rear, and also a pleasant garden area. Fortnightly quiz nights are held on Wednesdays.
⏰❀◑Ⓓ⇌(Maze Hill)⊖(Cutty Sark)🚇

SE13: Lewisham

Ravensbourne Arms
323 Lewisham High Street, SE13 6NR
✪ 4-11 (midnight Wed & Thu; 1am Fri); 12-midnight Sat;
12-11 Sun ☎ (020) 8613 7070
Adnams Lighthouse; guest beers Ⓗ
One of a number of recent adventurous pub renovations in the local area by Antic Ltd, this one (formerly the Coach & Horses) typifies shabby chic, with retro furniture, kitsch ornaments, a range of seating areas and a bar billiards table. A rotating range of guest beers, often from Thornbridge, Purity, Sharp's and Dark Star, complements a menu of foreign bottled beers. Cask cider is

often available, and good food is served from opening time until 10pm every day.
✪⦿❶⬧≢(Ladywell)🚊♣♥🏃

Watch House ✪

198-204 High Street, SE13 6JP
✪ 9am-midnight (1am Fri & Sat) ☎ (020) 8318 3136
Fuller's London Pride; Greene King Abbot; Ruddles Best Bitter; guest beers ⊞
On a busy high street by a market, this Wetherspoon establishment has plenty of capacity. Ceiling supports disguised as book shelves can make cross-pub views difficult, but they also create lots of different seating areas to choose from. Despite being well-lit, the interior can at times appear to be a little dark. The best place to enjoy breakfast is sitting in sunshine by the windows at the front. It is always a popular pub.
⦿❶⬧≢🅟🚊♥🏃

SE14: New Cross

Royal Albert ✪

460 New Cross Road, SE14 6TJ
✪ 4-midnight (1am Fri); 12-1am Sat; 12-midnight Sun
☎ (020) 8692 3737 ⊞ royalalbertpub.com
Beer range varies ⊞
An Antic pub with a moustache as its logo, and with a relaxed, homely ambience – almost romantic come evenings. Its L-shaped bar leads to a conservatory and an open-to-view kitchen. Guest beers come from microbreweries such as By the Horns, Dark Star, Kent, Purity and Thornbridge. The menu includes steaks, chops, pies and game. Two impressive stuffed birds are displayed. The clientele is a mixture of local academia, musicians and people out for an enjoyable time. A front patio offers outside drinking. Q✪✪⦿❶⬧≢🅟🚊♣♥🏃

SE15: Peckham

Gowlett ✪

62 Gowlett Road, SE15 4HY
✪ 12-midnight (1am Fri & Sat); 12-11.30 Sun
☎ (020) 7635 7048 ⊞ thegowlett.com
Fuller's London Pride; guest beers ⊞
Situated in a back street on the Peckham and Dulwich border, this is an oasis for real ale drinkers and is popular with people of all ages, and their dogs. It has a C-shaped bar with some attractive wood-panelled walls at one end. One regular beer, three changing guest beers and great pizzas are on offer. On Thursday nights you can play your own seven-inch records. On Sunday evening a DJ plays top choice music.
🚃✪⦿❶⬧≢(E Dulwich/Peckham Rye)🅟🚊🏃

Kentish Drovers ✪

71-79 Peckham High Street, SE15 5RS
✪ 9am-midnight ☎ (020) 7277 4283
Greene King Abbot; Ruddles Best Bitter; guest beers ⊞
Wetherspoon pub with a clientele reflecting the local, ethnically diverse area. A Jamaica stout has been instigated as a signature real ale which is available most of the time. The mosaic-tiled entrance floor used to form part of the public banking area when this was a bank. Its name today honours the long-time demise of nearby pubs of the same name, recalling livestock being driven to London from Kent. It has 53 tables accommodating up to 360 people. ✪⦿❶⬧≢(Peckham Rye)🚊🏃

SE18: Woolwich

Dial Arch

The Warren, Royal Arsenal, SE18 6GH (off No. 1 St)
✪ 9-11 (midnight Fri & Sat); 10-11 Sun ☎ (020) 3130 0700
⊕ dialarch.com
Meantime London Pale Ale; Wells Bombardier; Young's Bitter, Special, London Gold, seasonal beer ⊞
Situated in the former Royal Arsenal complex dating from 1720, this pub has a long bar with eight handpumps and a generous selection of bottles and casks behind it. The menu has an eclectic gastro vibe and bar snacks are available for a quick nibble. The large patio at the front is beautiful on a summer's evening, when there is little better than sitting with a pint and watching the sun set. ✪⦿❶⬧≢⊖(Woolwich Arsenal)🚊♥🏃

Prince Albert (Rose's)

49 Hare Street, SE18 6NE
✪ 11-11; 12-6 Sun ☎ (020) 8854 1538
Beer range varies ⊞
Behind a narrow, Victorian frontage lies a bright room, welcoming, homely and carpeted, with traditional dark wood tables, panelling and a pub dog. The long bar serves three or more microbrewery beers, often including Woolwich Ferry, a house beer brewed by Cottage. Towards the back is a mural of the Woolwich ferry, and two lizards, Ronnie and Reggie, live here in their vivarium. Darts and cribbage leagues play, and there are occasional beer festivals and live music.
Q🚃⦿≢⊖(Woolwich Arsenal)🚊♣

SE19: Crystal Palace

Grape & Grain ⦿

2 Anerley Hill, SE19 2AA
✪ 12-11 (midnight Fri & Sat); 12-10.30 Sun
☎ (020) 8778 4109 ⊕ thegrapeandgrainse19.co.uk
Purity Pure Gold; Westerham Finchcocks Original; guest beers ⊞
A warm welcome awaits you in this large, single-bar pub, whose future is now secured by a new 10-year lease. Rick and Angela supply fine beer and hearty food, including Sunday roasts. Twelve handpumps and two casks on gravity provide a varying selection of ales from brewers such as Westerham and Hogs Back, and ciders from Westons and Black Dragon. A recent local CAMRA Pub of the Year, it benefits from excellent transport links. ✪⦿❶⬧≢⊖🚊♣♥🏃🚩

SE19: Gypsy Hill

Railway Bell ✪

14 Cawnpore Street, SE19 1PF
✪ 12-midnight (1am Fri & Sat) ☎ (020) 8670 2844
Young's Bitter, Special, seasonal beer ⊞
A small and traditional Young's pub near to Crystal Palace Park and noted for its wall displays of railway memorabilia. There is satellite TV and a dartboard. To the rear of the pub is a function room and a large garden area which is covered in the winter, when there is also a cosy log fire inside. Quiz nights are held on Thursdays, and poker on Sundays, Mondays and Wednesdays. 🚃✪🚗🚊♣♥🏃

SE21: West Dulwich

Alleyns Head ✪

Park Hall Road, SE21 8BW

✪ 11.30-11 (midnight Fri & Sat) ☎ (020) 8670 6540
Fuller's London Pride; Taylor Landlord; Young's Bitter; guest beers Ⓗ
Situated a short walk from the centre of leafy Dulwich is this large, welcoming M&B Ember Inns pub. Unusually for the area, it offers a range of eight beers. Set on its own, the large bar has been effectively partitioned to provide an intimate and cosy environment, well served by the kitchen and its veritable smorgasbord of fish and meat dishes.
🏚️❀●ⅅ&≢🖳(3)♣P🍴

SE22: East Dulwich

Herne Tavern ★ ✪
2 Forest Hill Road, SE22 0RR
✪ 12-11 (1am Sat) ☎ (020) 8299 9521 ⊕ theherne.net
Greene King IPA; Sharp's Doom Bar; guest beers Ⓗ
Just off Peckham Rye Park, the Herne Tavern is one of Britain's Real Heritage Pubs for its original 1930s interior. There is a saloon bar and a dining room, and to the rear a conservatory leading to a landscaped garden with a separate function room, outside loo and children's climbing frame – ideal for families in summer. Westons cider or perry is served on handpump and occasional beer festivals are held. Popular sporting events are shown on TV; board games are on offer and sometimes live music. ❀●ⅅ🖳🍴

SE23: Forest Hill

All Inn One ✪
53 Perry Vale, SE23 2NE
✪ 12-midnight (1.30am Fri & Sat); 12-11.30 Sun
☎ (020) 8699 3311 ⊕ allinnone.org.uk
Brains SA; Caledonian Deuchars IPA; guest beers Ⓗ
Red brick free house, still known to locals as the Foresters, two minutes' walk behind Forest Hill railway station (use the subway next to WH Smith). The open-plan interior is surprisingly spacious. Outside, several garden areas variously cater for children, families, smokers and for those who require a little more tranquility. There is a quiz night on Sundays, and live acoustic music every Monday night, with the emphasis on blue grass. A separate restaurant serves evening meals and roast lunches on Sundays.
🏃❀●ⅅ&≢⊖🖳(122,185,356)🍴

Blythe Hill Tavern ♟
319 Stanstead Road, SE23 1JB
✪ 11-11.30 (midnight Thu-Sun) ☎ (020) 8690 5176
Courage Best Bitter; Dark Star Hophead; Fuller's London Pride; Harveys Sussex Best Bitter; guest beer Ⓗ
An imposing Victorian corner pub and one of London's Real Heritage Pubs for its interesting three-room interior and 1920s panelling. In this friendly local, the landlord and barmen uphold the tradition of serving customers in collar and tie. There is something here for everyone: sports screens (never too loud), quiz nights (Mondays, September to April), traditional Irish music on Thursday nights, and an attractive beer garden with children's play area.
🏚️Q❀☖≢(Catford/Catford Bridge)🖳(171,185)P🍴

Capitol ✪
11-21 London Road, SE23 3TW
✪ 9am-midnight (1am Fri & Sat) ☎ (020) 8291 8920

Fuller's London Pride; Greene King Abbot; Ruddles Best Bitter; guest beers Ⓗ
Close to the Horniman Museum, this spacious Wetherspoon pub occupies a converted 1929 Art Deco cinema, the only surviving complete cinema building by noted architect John Stanley Beard. An impressive frontage opens into a cavernous interior. Tours of the circle and other normally unseen areas are offered by arrangement; resident ghosts may be in attendance. There is assorted seating on three levels and a long bar across the former stage area. Community events are hosted. Book ahead for parties and groups. ❀●ⅅ&≢🖳🐾🍴

SE24: Herne Hill

Half Moon ★ ✪
10 Half Moon Lane, SE24 9HU
✪ 12-midnight (1am Fri & Sat); 12-10.30 Sun
☎ (020) 7274 2733
Adnams Southwold Bitter; Fuller's London Pride; Young's Bitter Ⓗ
One of Britain's Real Heritage Pubs, built in 1896. An L-shaped bar serves two main rooms. There is also a large function room and a beautiful snug with original etched glass, back-painted mirrors and an imposing chandelier. Renowned for eclectic live music three nights a week, including an open mic session, it also offers monthly comedy, occasional theatre and a weekly quiz. It has a TV for major sporting events, and board and card games. At the front is a spacious outdoor terrace.
❀●ⅅ≢🖳🐾🍴

Prince Regent ✪
69 Dulwich Road, SE24 0NJ
✪ 12-11.30 (12.30am Thu-Sat) ☎ (020) 7274 1567
⊕ theprinceregent.co.uk
Black Sheep Best Bitter; guest beers Ⓗ
Victorian corner pub opposite Brockwell Park with an elaborate exterior including a statue of the Prince Regent. The refurbished interior is just as impressive, with a wood and glass screen creating two separate rooms. A large brewery mirror indicates this was once a Truman's pub. Food, ranging from traditional to gastro, is served lunchtimes and evenings. Two upstairs rooms are available for hire. It does a meal deal on Mondays, a quiz Tuesdays, and has board games. Dog-friendly, with outdoor seating on a small covered front terrace. ❀●ⅅ&≢🖳🐾🍴

SE27: West Norwood

Hope ✪
49 Norwood High Street, SE27 9JS
✪ 11-11.30 (midnight Fri & Sat); 12-11 Sun
☎ (020) 8670 2035 ⊕ thehopepub.net
Wells Bombardier; Young's Bitter, Special, seasonal beer; guest beer Ⓗ
A comfortable, traditional, older-style Young's pub, dating from 1840, serving a diverse local and wider community around a central bar. Pleasant, relaxed and welcoming, it has a lovely walled, terraced beer garden with lighting and covered, heated bench seating around tables, a fish pond and an outside function room. Monthly live music, disco, karaoke and a quiz night take place, and it boasts a 3D sports TV, with screens in the garden in summer, when film nights also feature. Children and dogs are welcome. A beer festival is held in autumn. 🏚️❀●ⅅ≢🖳🍴

Addiscombe

Claret Free House
5A Bingham Corner, Lower Addiscombe Road, CR0 7AA
✪ 11.30-11 (11.30 Thu; midnight Fri & Sat); 12-11 Sun
☎ (020) 8656 7452
Palmers Best Bitter; guest beers Ⓗ
A small family-owned free house in a parade of shops close to the Tramlink stop. A rare outlet for Palmers' beers, it has been in this Guide continuously since 1989. The rather dimly lit interior has two TV sets and can be crowded during popular sporting events. There are five rapidly changing guest beers from the smaller breweries and micros, and at least two ciders. Current beers and those coming next are shown on a blackboard opposite the bar. ⬚(Tramlink)⬚(130,289,367)●

Cricketers
47 Shirley Road, CR0 7ER
✪ 12-midnight (11 Sun) ☎ (020) 8655 3507
Harveys Sussex Best Bitter; guest beers Ⓗ
Ray the publican is a real ale enthusiast and holds regular beer festivals, with up to 18 ales. This traditional community boozer has twice won local CAMRA Pub of the Year, most recently in 2010. Three real fires help provide a comfortable, lived-in atmosphere. Quiz nights and curry evenings feature regularly. Up to four guest beers are usually served, and real cider is occasionally available. The pub can be busy when Crystal Palace are playing. ⬚⬚◐⬚(Addiscombe/Blackhorse Lane) ⬚(130,367)♣●P⬚☗

Beckenham

Jolly Woodman
9 Chancery Lane, BR3 6NR
✪ 11 (4 Mon)-11 (midnight Fri & Sat) ☎ (020) 8663 1031
Adnams Southwold Bitter; Harveys Sussex Best Bitter; Skinner's Betty Stogs; Taylor Landlord; Young's Bitter; guest beers Ⓗ
This friendly local was originally an ale house. It benefits from a strong regular trade as well as discerning drinkers from further afield. The single L-shaped room has a small area in front of the bar and a larger seating area running to the rear. There are outdoor benches to the front and side of the pub and on the rear patio. Hot and cold food is served at lunchtimes. Special community occasions are celebrated with a hog roast. Q⬚◐⬚(Beckenham Jct)⬚(Beckenham Jct) ⬚(227,367)♣⬚

Bexley

Railway Tavern
38 Bexley High Street, DA5 1AH
✪ 11-11 (midnight Fri & Sat); 12-11 Sun ☎ (01322) 522779
Courage Best Bitter; guest beers Ⓗ
Characterful pub that is definitely one to get excited about. A policy of three changing guest beers from small breweries nationwide means you are always in for a surprise. The long bar is adorned with railway ephemera in keeping with its name and location. There are discounts for pensioners in the afternoon and commuters in the early evening, and many activities take place including poker on Thursdays and live music on Fridays and Sundays. ⬚⬚⬚♣●⬚

Bexleyheath

Earl Haig ✪
Little Heath Road, DA7 5HH
✪ 11.30-11 (midnight Fri & Sat) ☎ (01322) 449463
Fuller's London Pride; Harveys Sussex Best Bitter; Young's Bitter; guest beers Ⓗ
Large M&B Ember Inns pub situated away from Bexleyheath town centre but easily reached by bus. It has a steady trade and usually has guest beers from more unusual breweries for the area. The pub holds a quiz each Wednesday evening and is popular for its varied menu and specials evenings. ⬚⬚●◐⬚⬚(401,422,B12)P⬚

Furze Wren ✪
Broadway Square, 6 Market Place, DA6 7DY
✪ 8am-midnight ☎ (020) 8298 2590
Fuller's London Pride; Greene King Abbot; Ruddles Best Bitter; Shepherd Neame Spitfire; guest beers Ⓗ
Originally opened as a Lloyds No. 1 in 2002, it became the Furze Wren in 2006, named after a local bird, the Dartford Warbler. Situated around the shopping centre, it has a thorough mix of clientele throughout the day. Now sporting 10 handpumps, usually with a beer from Welton's (Sussex), this spacious Wetherspoon pub is all on one level, including the award-winning toilets. Relax and watch the innumerable buses and people as they pass by. Q◐⬚⬚●

Robin Hood & Little John ♈ ⅃
78 Lion Road, DA6 8PF
✪ 11-3, 5.30 (7 Sat)-11; 12-4, 7-10.30 Sun
☎ (020) 8303 1128
Adnams Southwold Bitter, Broadside; Brains The Rev James; Brakspear Bitter; Fuller's London Pride; Harveys Sussex Best Bitter; guest beer Ⓗ
Excellent back-street pub, dating from the 1830s, run by the Johnson family since 1980. As well as keeping eight real ales, it has a well-earned reputation for its food; it serves up home-cooked lunches (not Sun), with a reduced menu until 8.30pm Monday to Thursday. These can be enjoyed at tables made from old Singer sewing machines. CAMRA Greater London Pub of the Year three times and current local Pub of the Year. Over-21s only. Q⬚◐

Bromley

Partridge ✪
194 High Street, BR1 1HE
✪ 12-11.30 (12.30am Fri & Sat); 12-11 Sun
☎ (020) 8464 7656
Fuller's Discovery, London Pride, ESB, seasonal beers; Gale's Seafarers Ale, HSB Ⓗ
Opened in 1996, this Fuller's Ale & Pie house is a Grade II-listed former NatWest bank. It is popular with local shoppers and theatregoers and is often busy during major sporting events. There are two quieter rooms off the main bar room and a heated patio area that can be partially covered in bad weather. A recent introduction is a breakfast menu. This pub won third place in Fuller's 2010 Master Cellarman competition. ⬚◐⬚⬚(North)⬚

Red Lion ♈
10 North Road, BR1 3LG
✪ 11 (12 Sun)-11.30 ☎ (020) 8460 2691
Greene King IPA, Abbot; Harveys Sussex Best Bitter; guest beers Ⓗ

Managed by Chris and Siobhan, this is a traditional pub that, although small, has a big local reputation for its consistently well-kept real ales. Original features include wall tiles, and one wall is devoted to well-stocked book shelves. Good-value home-cooked food is served and five handpumps include two varying guest ales, as evidenced by the numerous pump clips displayed over the bar. 🏚Q🌡🕐≉(North)🚌(314)♣≟

Bromley Common

Two Doves
37 Oakley Road, BR2 8HD
🕐 12-3, 5-11; 12-11 Fri & Sat; 12-10.30 Sun
☎ (020) 8462 1627
Wells Bombardier; Young's Bitter, Special, London Gold Ⓗ
Friendly staff and locals inhabit this civilised pub, which has been tastefully decorated and restored to its former glory by its previous builder-owner. It looks especially inviting at night with light shining out through its stained glass windows. At the rear is a quiet and relaxing conservatory, opening on to a delightful garden full of flowers in summer. Watch out for the unusual mid-week, mid-afternoon closing times (for a couple of hours) to avoid disappointment. Q🌡🕐🚌(320)♣

Chelsfield

Five Bells ✓
Church Road, BR6 7RE
🕐 11.30-11; 12-10.30 Sun ☎ (01689) 821044
⊕ thefivebells-chelsfieldvillage.co.uk
Courage Best Bitter; Sharp's Doom Bar; guest beers Ⓗ
Well worth a detour from central Bromley, this semi-rural listed pub was built in 1664 and comprises two separate bars with original beams, a large garden, and a restaurant serving meals every day except Monday evenings. A popular stop for walkers and cyclists, it holds two beer festivals a year, Tuesday quiz nights, open mic nights on Wednesdays and regular live jazz. The bus service could not be more convenient, with a stop almost outside the door. Q🌡🕐🕐🗲🚌(R3)♣P≟

Crayford

Crayford Arms Ⓛ
37 Crayford High Street, DA1 4HH
🕐 2-11; 12-midnight Thu-Sat; 12-11 Sun
⊕ thecrayfordarms.com
Beer range varies Ⓗ
The pub sells up to five beers from Shepherd Neame. It has a traditional atmosphere and the saloon bar to the left retains many original features, with an attractive oak staircase leading to the function room and ladies' toilets. To the right is a standard public bar with pool table and dartboard. Live music is occasionally performed on a Saturday evening, there is a quiz on Sunday and a music quiz once a month. 🌡🗲≉🚌(96,428,492)♣P≟

Croydon

Builders Arms ✓
65 Leslie Park Road, CR0 6TP
🕐 12-11 (midnight Fri & Sat; 10.30 Sun) ☎ (020) 8654 1803
Fuller's Chiswick Bitter, London Pride, seasonal beers; Gale's HSB Ⓗ

An attractive, detached pub in a back street in the east of the town. The two bars differ in character: one has the feel of a public bar and the other has comfortable seating extending to a pleasant secluded garden at the rear. There are TVs for sport in both bars. Food is served until 9pm (8pm at weekends). Curry night is Monday. Children are welcome in the bars until 8pm. Occasional live music performances are held. 🏚🌡🕐≉(E Croydon)⊖(Lebanon Rd Tramlink) 🚌(197,312,410)♣≟

Dog & Bull
24 Surrey Street, CR0 1RG
🕐 11-11 (11.30 Fri & summer Sat); 12-10.30 Sun
☎ (020) 8667 9718
Young's Bitter, Special, seasonal beers Ⓗ
Recognised as Croydon's oldest pub, the building originated in the 16th century, was rebuilt in the 18th century, and is Grade II-listed. The interior features a main room with an island bar, and two adjoining rooms. The pub has a pleasant walled garden that hosts summer barbecues, weather permitting, and the landlord considers it one of Croydon's best-kept secrets. Quizzes are held every Tuesday and there is a small upstairs function room available for hire. 🌡🕐≉(East/West)🚌(W Croydon/Church St/George St)🚌≟

George ✓
17-21 George Street, CR0 1LA
🕐 8am-midnight (1am Fri & Sat) ☎ (020) 8649 9077
Dark Star Hophead; Fuller's London Pride; Oakham JHB; Surrey Hills Ranmore Ale; Thornbridge Jaipur IPA; guest beers Ⓗ
Through hard work and enthusiasm the manager and his team have pushed this bustling Wetherspoon pub into the company's top 10 best-performing pubs, with a growing reputation for a high quality and wide range of ales. Beers are served from bars at both ends of the pub, with locally sourced ales a regular feature. Local CAMRA Pub of the Year 2011, it is opening a large garden in 2012. Conveniently located in central Croydon for all transport links. 🌡🕐🕭≉(East/West)🚌(W Croydon/George St) 🚌🕭≟

Glamorgan
81 Cherry Orchard Road, CR0 6BE
🕐 12 (4 Sat)-midnight; closed Sun ☎ (020) 8688 6333
Harveys Sussex Best Bitter; Sharp's Doom Bar; guest beers Ⓗ
A welcoming corner pub, often busy at lunchtimes with trade from local offices. Its three rooms provide areas for drinking, dining and games, with a dartboard and pool table, and a TV (not used for live football). The pub serves good-quality food, and the menu has a distinct South African aspect. A pleasant patio garden also serves as a smoking area. Bookings are taken for private functions on Sundays, when the pub is otherwise closed. 🌡🕐≉(East)🚌(E Croydon)🚌≟

Green Dragon Ⓛ ✓
58-60 High Street, CR0 1NA
🕐 10-midnight (1am Fri & Sat); 12-10.30 Sun
☎ (020) 8667 0684 ⊕ greendragoncroydon.co.uk
Dark Star Hophead Ⓗ; **Hogs Back TEA** Ⓖ; **guest beers** Ⓗ/Ⓖ
A buzzing Stonegate pub near Croydon's historic market, popular with all ages and enthusiastically

run by young staff with a keen interest in ale. Six handpumps and two gravity casks dispense a variety of beers including some locally brewed. Real draught cider is usually available. Lunchtimes are quieter than evenings. A wide variety of music and other events takes place upstairs, including live jazz on Sunday afternoon.
⟨◑⟩&⇌(East/West)☒(W Croydon/George St)☒●

Half & Half 🅛
282 High Street, CR0 1NG
✪ 12 (3 Sat)-midnight; 3-11 Sun ☎ (020) 8726 0080
⊕ halfandhalf.uk.com
Dark Star Hophead; guest beer Ⓗ
A street-corner bar located between the town centre and the South End restaurant zone. The regular beer is complemented by a guest, usually sourced from a local microbrewery. A range of Czech, Belgian and German bottled beers is on offer. An interesting range of nuts, olives and other nibbles is available by the dish. There is also a downstairs room that can be booked for functions. The pub may close early on quiet evenings. Over-21s only. ☒(George St)☒

Royal Standard ✪
1 Sheldon Street, CR0 1SS
✪ 12-midnight (11 Sun) ☎ (020) 8688 9749
⊕ royalstandard-croydon.co.uk
Fuller's Chiswick Bitter, London Pride, ESB, Bengal Lancer, seasonal beers; Gale's HSB Ⓗ
A quiet street-corner local close to Croydon town centre, this is a regular entry in the Guide and a former local CAMRA Pub of the Year. Three drinking areas are available, each with its own character. Note the Victorian fireplace (occasionally lit) and misericord in the back bar. Beer festivals are held regularly, and the landlord has Fuller's Master Cellarman accreditation. The pub's quiet garden lies almost under the flyover opposite. Meals are available until 9pm. Q❀◑☒(George St)♣

Skylark ✪
34-36 South End, CR0 1DP
✪ 9am-midnight (1am Fri & Sat) ☎ (020) 8649 9909
Fuller's London Pride; Greene King Abbot; Ruddles Best Bitter; guest beers Ⓗ
Spacious Wetherspoon pub formerly a gym, with bars on two levels. A large garden caters for smokers as well as those choosing to drink outdoors. The range of guest beers includes local ales whenever possible as well as those from microbreweries, and the draught cider on offer can come from different parts of the country. The upstairs bar area can be booked for weddings and other celebrations. ❀◑&⇌(South)☒●⌐

Spreadeagle ✪
39-41 Katharine Street, CR0 1NX
✪ 11-11 (midnight Thu-Sat); 12-10.30 Sun
☎ (020) 8781 1134
Fuller's Chiswick Bitter, Discovery, London Pride, ESB, seasonal beers; Gale's HSB Ⓗ
A town-centre Fuller's Ale & Pie house next to Croydon Town Hall, in premises that were converted from a bank in 1996. The substantial building has rooms available for hire and a private cinema club. There are three TV screens downstairs showing sport, and a quiz is held every Sunday evening. The current manager holds Fuller's Master Cellarman accreditation and a good selection of Fuller's bottled ales is also available.
◑&⇌(East/West)☒(W Croydon/George St)☒⌐

Downe

Queen's Head
25 High Street, BR6 7US
✪ 12-11 (11.30 Fri & Sat; 10.30 Sun); 12-10.30 Sun
☎ (01689) 852145 ⊕ queensheaddowne.com
Harveys Sussex Best Bitter; Sharp's Doom Bar; guest beers Ⓗ
The pub was built in 1565 in the centre of this historic village, made famous by Charles Darwin, who lived in Downe House. Just 17 minutes by bus from Bromley South and Orpington, it is a traditional and comfortable pub with three fireplaces and several dining areas, and is popular with walkers all year round. Guest beers regularly include one from the nearby Westerham Brewery. The menu has daily specials and includes home-cooked vegetarian soups. 🏠❀◑☒(146,R8)P⌐

Keston

Greyhound
Commonside, BR2 6BP
✪ 11-11; 12-10.30 Sun ☎ (01689) 856338
Adnams Southwold Bitter; Greene King Old Speckled Hen; Ruddles Best Bitter; Taylor Landlord; guest beers Ⓗ
On the edge of Keston Common, this country-style pub is popular with walkers and village locals alike – and their dogs. Keston is fortunate in being able to enjoy two pubs, and this one is strongly engaged with the local community, with morris men dancing here regularly, beer festivals and fund-raising events. Other features are poker and quiz nights and monthly live music. An outside tea room is available for meetings and functions.
🏠❀◑☒(146,246,353)♣P⌐

Petts Wood

Sovereign of the Seas ✪
109-111 Queensway, BR5 1DG
✪ 9am-11.30 ☎ (01689) 891606
Adnams Broadside; Greene King Abbot; Ruddles Best Bitter; guest beers Ⓗ
Large Wetherspoon pub boasting 12 handpumps, six offering a changing range of guest beers, ciders and perries. The long, narrow layout gives the pub a cosier atmosphere than most 'Spoons, an impression enhanced by the varied seating styles, which include a couple of snug alcoves. There is also a community noticeboard. The pub's themes include reference to the ship after which it is named, and to a former resident, the daylight saving campaigner William Willett.
❀◑&⇌☒(208,R3)

Pratts Bottom

Bull's Head
Rushmore Hill, BR6 7NQ
✪ 11-11 (midnight Fri); 12-10.30 Sun ☎ (01689) 852553
⊕ thebullsheadpub.net
Courage Best Bitter; Young's Special; guest beers Ⓗ
All are welcome at this thriving S&N community pub, which started life as a coaching inn in 1575. Six handpumps dispense four beers from the Wells & Young's range plus changing guests. A quarterly guide lists regular events, with frequent theme nights often celebrating British historic occasions. The pub has a large enclosed garden where an occasional beer festival takes place. Good-value

home-cooked food is available, though the menu may change when an evening event is held. ᴁ☎⚶❍◗♿🚌(402,R5,R10)♣P⬅

Upper Belvedere

Prince of Wales 🅛
13a Woolwich Road, DA17 5EE
⊕ 12-11 (midnight Fri & Sat) ☎ (01322) 433737
Westerham British Bulldog; Young's Bitter; guest beers H
Built around 1863, this small cosy pub with a horseshoe-shaped bar stands on what was once Lesness Heath. Normally a Westerham beer is available and Dark Star beers, when stocked, are served in oversized, branded glasses. All beers are under 4.5% ABV. Sports fans can watch the large-screen TVs. Made-to-order snacks of the sandwich, baguette, toastie variety (with or without chips), plus a blackboarded dish of the day, are served 12-4pm. Free Wi-Fi is available. ⚶◗🚌(99,401)⬅

Welling

New Cross Turnpike 🅛 ✔
55 Bellegrove Road, DA16 3PB
⊕ 9am-midnight ☎ (020) 8304 1600
Adnams Broadside; Courage Best Bitter; Fuller's London Pride; Greene King Abbot; Ruddles Best Bitter; Shepherd Neame Spitfire; guest beers H
Wetherspoon pub, opened in 1998 and previously a NatWest bank, with an attractive layout on four levels, including a gallery, and two patios. Disabled access includes wheelchair lifts. Up to eight guest ales are dispensed by the helpful staff. Special offers include steak night on Tuesday and curry night on Thursday. ⚶◗♿🚌♦⬅

West Wickham

Railway Hotel ✔
Red Lodge Road, BR4 0EW
⊕ 11.30-11; 12-10.30 Sun ☎ (020) 8776 0043
Fuller's London Pride; Harveys Sussex Best Bitter; Young's Bitter; guest beers H
This is a good-sized M&B Ember Inns establishment, comfortably refurbished in recent years. Three bus routes and a railway station just across the road make it a convenient place to frequent for the attractions of its three regular ales, three guest ales and plentiful choice of food all day. The management has been responsive to beer requests from its discerning customers. Quiz nights are held on Tuesdays and Sundays. ᴁ⚶◗♿�₹🚌(119,194,352)

SOUTH-WEST LONDON
SW1: Belgravia

Antelope ✔
22-24 Eaton Terrace, SW1W 8EZ
⊕ 12-11 (11.30 Fri); 11-5 Sun ☎ (020) 7824 8512
Fuller's Discovery, London Pride, ESB, seasonal beers; guest beer H
Dating back to 1827, this pub is now operated by Fuller's after many years as a Nicholson's pub. Original features are preserved including etched glass windows, a side room used as a snug, and the central bar. This is very much an upmarket house and the clientele consists mainly of local professionals. The pub plays cricket matches

against the Churchill Arms (Notting Hill). The upstairs bar and side room can be hired for functions. ◗⊖(Sloane Sq)🚌

Grenadier ✔
18 Wilton Row, SW1X 7NR
⊕ 12-11.30 (10.30 Sun) ☎ (020) 7235 3074
Fuller's London Pride; Taylor Landlord; guest beers H
Originally built in 1720 as the Officers' Mess for the First Royal Regiment of Foot Guards, the Grenadier was licensed in 1818 as the Guardsman Public House. It was later renamed the Grenadier in honour of the Grenadier Guards' heroic deeds at Waterloo. The Duke of Wellington and King George IV frequented the pub. One of London's Real Heritage Pubs, with simple fittings indicating its origins, it has become an attractive and more upmarket destination for a drink and meal. Q◗◗⊖(Hyde Pk Corner)🚌

Horse & Groom
7 Groom Place, SW1X 7BA
⊕ 11.30-11 (midnight Thu & Fri); closed Sat & Sun ☎ (020) 7235 6980
Shepherd Neame Master Brew, Kent's Best, Spitfire H
You may have to search a little to find this traditional mews pub but it is well worth seeking out. The main wood-panelled downstairs room has etched glass front windows. There is also an upstairs room that is mainly used for dining. The pub is available for private hire at the weekend. A famous local resident could, theoretically, reach this pub by slipping over the back wall of Buckingham Palace. ⚶◗⊖(Hyde Pk Corner)🚌

Star Tavern 🅛 ✔
6 Belgrave Mews West, SW1X 8HT
⊕ 11 (12 Sat)-11; 12-10.30 Sun ☎ (020) 7235 3019
Fuller's Chiswick Bitter, Discovery, London Pride, ESB, seasonal beers H
In a cobbled mews near Belgrave Square, this Grade II-listed pub dates from 1848. It underwent a sensitive refurbishment in early 2008 and the ambience takes you back to when a pub looked like a pub. The landlord often organises the regulars to take part in charity fundraising events. A former local CAMRA Pub of the Year, the Star has featured in this Guide since its first edition. Q◗◗⊖(Hyde Pk Corner/Knightsbridge)🚌

SW1: Pimlico

Cask Pub & Kitchen 🅛
6 Charlwood Street, SW1V 2EE
⊕ 12-11 (10.30 Sun) ☎ (020) 7630 7225
⊕ caskpubandkitchen.com
Beer range varies H
Formerly a Lillington Gardens estate pub, this corner house has been transformed by the current operators into a destination real ale pub. Office workers and tourists from nearby hotels enjoy Dark Star, Arbor Ales and many other guest beers on 10 handpumps. There are also unusual German, Belgian and American keg beers and a vast range of bottled beers. Special events with visiting brewers are held here. A good range of food is available. Local CAMRA Pub of the Year in 2011. ◗⇌(Victoria)⊖(Pimlico/Victoria)🚌

Jugged Hare ✔
172 Vauxhall Bridge Road, SW1V 1DX
⊕ 11-11 (11.30 Fri & Sat); 12-10.30 Sun ☎ (020) 7828 1543

Fuller's Discovery, London Pride, ESB, seasonal beers Ⓗ
This Ale & Pie House is a 1996 conversion of a bank building, with an upstairs balcony that can be hired for functions. Its clientele is not only business people, but also a loyal base of locals, and tourists from nearby hotels. Sport is shown on TV with the volume turned down. Food is available all day; this includes jugged hare pie made with sustainable hare. ⑴⇌(Victoria)⊖(Pimlico/Victoria)🚋

SW1: Victoria

Cask & Glass ✪
39 Palace Street, SW1E 5HN
✪ 11-11; 12-8 Sat; closed Sun ☎ (020) 7834 7630
Shepherd Neame Master Brew, Kent's Best, Spitfire, seasonal beers Ⓗ
First licensed in 1862 as the Duke of Cambridge, this attractive one-room pub on the route between Buckingham Palace and Westminster Cathedral, adorned with flowers in summer, is a haven for tourists, office workers and local residents. The wood-panelled bar has pictures of local scenes and politicians. Look out for the bull's-eye windows and the two paintings of the pub on the way to the toilets. A cosy place for a pint after (or instead of) visiting the sights. ✿⇌⊖🚋↳

Wetherspoon's ✪
Unit 5, Main Concourse, Victoria Station, SW1V 1JT
✪ 8am-midnight (11 Sun) ☎ (020) 7931 0445
Fuller's London Pride; Greene King IPA, Abbot; guest beers Ⓗ
Attractive, comfortable, modern glass-fronted bar above WH Smith, between the two sides of the Victoria station concourse, accessed mainly by escalators. The clientele includes tourists, office workers and weekend football supporters enjoying a drink on arrival in London or before their train leaves. TV screens show times of train departures. A choice of guest beers and two Westons ciders are available. A good place perhaps for a Brief Encounter. Q⑴⇌⊖🚋

SW1: Westminster

Buckingham Arms
62 Petty France, SW1H 9EU
✪ 11-11; 12-6 Sat; closed Sun ☎ (020) 7222 3386
⊕ buckinghamarms.com
Wells Bombardier; Young's Bitter, Special, seasonal beer; guest beer Ⓗ
Originally a shop and then the Black Horse until 1901, this Young's pub has featured in every edition of this Guide. Recently refurbished, it retains many heritage features. The façade is elegant with its small window panes and the notable heraldic shield. The front bar and window are gracefully curved and behind the bar is an impressive set of decorated mirrors. A Sambrook's beer is now a regular guest. ⑴⊖(St James's Pk)🚋♣

Sanctuary House Hotel ✪
33 Tothill Street, SW1H 9LA
✪ 10-11 (10.30 Sun) ☎ (020) 7799 4044
Fuller's Chiswick Bitter, Discovery, London Pride, ESB, seasonal beers Ⓗ
A Fuller's Ale & Pie House plus 34-bedroom hotel in a building said to have formerly housed MI5. With plenty of wood panelling, bevelled mirrors, bright brass fittings at the bar, tall windows and generous, split-level hardwood or carpeted seating areas, it is comfortable and warm with a welcoming buzz, though the muzak may be irritating. A curious medieval style Book of Hours mural on the back wall is said to represent Sanctuary at nearby Westminster Abbey. 🛏⑴よ⊖(St James's Pk)🚋

Speaker 🅛 ✪
46 Great Peter Street, SW1P 2HA
✪ 12-11; closed Sat & Sun ☎ (020) 7222 1749
Taylor Landlord; Young's Bitter; guest beers Ⓗ
This friendly one-bar corner pub is a peaceful haven for locals, civil servants and MPs to enjoy conversation, unusual guest beers and home-made food without the intrusion of music, TV or children under 14. Like most bars in the area, it has its own division bell. Clay pipes and caricatures of MPs adorn the wood-panelled interior. Food is not available on busy Friday evenings. Themed beer weeks on the two guest handpumps are popular. Q⑴⊖(St James's Pk)🚋

SW1: Whitehall

Lord Moon of the Mall ✪
16-18 Whitehall, SW1A 2DY
✪ 9am-11.30 (midnight Fri & Sat; 11 Sun)
☎ (020) 7839 7701
Fuller's London Pride; Greene King IPA, Abbot; guest beers Ⓗ
Wetherspoon's 1995 conversion of a former bank building dating back to 1872. There is an open-plan seating area to the front; the rear of the pub is mainly reserved for dining, where tourists relax after taking in the nearby sites of Trafalgar Square and the Houses of Parliament. Local history is displayed on the walls. Food is available all day, but from a limited menu due to kitchen restrictions. ⑴⇌⊖(Charing Cross)🚋

SW2: Brixton

Elm Park Tavern 🅛
76 Elm Park, SW2 2UB
✪ 4 (12 Fri-Sun)-11 ☎ (07852) 345974
Purity Pure Gold, Pure UBU; Sambrook's Wandle, Junction Ⓗ
A much-improved, comfortable local, the last one left on the estate. This two-bar pub shows TV sport if requested, preferably in advance, and runs a Thursday quiz night. A unique portrait of 18th-century stage mimic Samuel Foote dominates the front bar and both rooms have some interesting stained glass. Beware the restricted weekday opening hours. ✿🖬🚋

SW2: Streatham Hill

Crown & Sceptre 🅛 ✪
2A Streatham Hill, SW2 4AH
✪ 9am-midnight (1am Fri & Sat) ☎ (020) 8671 0843
Greene King Abbot; Ruddles Best Bitter; Sambrook's Junction; guest beers Ⓗ
Set back from a busy junction on the South Circular road, the first Wetherspoon pub in south-west London retains an original Truman's façade and tiling. The interior is divided into several distinct areas, with some unusual framed floral artwork on the walls. The long-established manager serves extra Sambrook's and other local ales among his

guest beers, as well as a choice of Westons ciders. In an area with few surviving pubs, this one is a delight. 🌞🌓⬧⇌🖵🍴P⅃⚲

SW4: Clapham

Rose & Crown
2 The Polygon, SW4 0JG
☼ 4 (12 Sat)-midnight (1am Fri & Sat); 12-midnight Sun
☎ (020) 7627 5369
Greene King St Edmunds, Abbot; H&H Olde Trip; guest beers Ⓗ
Located in the heart of Clapham Common Old Town Conservation Area, this former Simonds pub is notable for its handsome tiled façade. Very much a drinkers' pub, it offers a varied range of guest ales from the Greene King list – Graham Greene himself once lived nearby. While enjoying the traditional pub atmosphere, complete with paintings and old photographs of local scenes, keep an eye out for Beyoncé and Betty, the resident cats. There is a heated pavement area for smokers. Over-21s only.
🌞⇌(Clapham High St)Θ(Clapham Common)🖵⅃⚲

SW5: Earls Court

Courtfield ✔
187 Earls Court Road, SW5 9AN
☼ 10-midnight, 12-11.30 Sun ☎ (020) 7370 2626
Wells Bombardier; Wychwood Hobgoblin; Young's London Gold; guest beers Ⓗ
Originally built in 1876 as the Courtfield Hotel, close to Earls Court Station, this pub has an impressive front bar with tall windows and a high ceiling. Chandeliers and lanterns suspended above the bar add to the period atmosphere. The rear area has attractive wood panelling and relaxing banquettes. Ale enthusiasts can sample guest beers from brewers such as St Austell. Sports matches are shown on screens situated around the pub. Friendly staff provide good service.
🌓⇌(W Brompton)Θ🖵

SW6: Parsons Green

White Horse 🄻 ✔
1-3 Parsons Green, SW6 4UL
☼ 9.30am-11.30 (midnight Thu-Sat) ☎ (020) 7736 2115
⊕ whitehorsesw6.com
Adnams Broadside; Harveys Sussex Best Bitter; guest beers Ⓗ
Large, light and airy M&B pub maintaining a long-standing reputation for quality beer and food. There are six guest ales from regional and microbreweries, a draught Severn cider or perry and unusual foreign beers. The former coach house at the rear is used as a restaurant or for stillage during four annual beer festivals. Upstairs a bar opens in the evening and at weekends. The covered patio area in front accommodates outdoor drinkers and smokers, with barbecues in summer.
🌞🌓⬧♿Θ🖵⅃⚲

SW8: South Lambeth

Priory Arms 🄻
83 Lansdowne Way, SW8 2PB
☼ 5 (3 Fri)-11; 12-11.30 Sat; 12-10.30 Sun
☎ (020) 7622 1884 ⊕ theprioryarms.co.uk
Beer range varies Ⓗ
Now in its 22nd consecutive year in the Guide, this celebrated free house offers five changing real ales and strongly supports London microbreweries. There is a good selection of bottled foreign beers and also wholesome food. The single corner bar with its big windows is supplemented by an upstairs function room. Various board games are available. 🌞🌓Θ(Stockwell)🖵♣⅃⚲

Surprise
16 Southville, SW8 2PP
☼ 11 (12 Sun)-midnight ☎ (020) 7622 4263
Young's Bitter, Special; guest beer Ⓗ
Small, characterful ale house at the end of a short cul-de-sac next to Larkhall Park. This is one of the few buildings in the vicinity to have survived World War II bombing. The pub is dog-friendly and there is a boules pitch outside. The back room is decorated with caricatures of the locals.
🚆🌞⇌(Wandsworth Rd)🖵♣⅃⚲

SW9: Brixton

Trinity Arms
45 Trinity Gardens, SW9 8DR
☼ 11-11 (12.30am Fri); 12-12.30am Sat, 12-11 Sun
☎ (020) 7274 4544 ⊕ trinityarmsbrixton.co.uk
Young's Bitter, Special, London Gold, seasonal beer Ⓗ
An oasis of peace and calm, this traditional pub is a cosy single-bar venue set in a quiet square off the busy Acre Lane and Brixton High Road. Named after an ancient asylum nearby, the pub is popular in the evening with office workers and locals, and is busy on Brixton Academy nights. The well-kept real ale is a big attraction. Families are welcome until 7.30pm and food is available until 10pm.
🌞🌓⇌Θ🖵⅃⚲

SW11: Battersea

Beehive ✔
197 St John's Hill, SW11 1TH
☼ 12-midnight ☎ (020) 7564 1897
Fuller's London Pride, ESB; guest beers Ⓗ
On the crest of St John's Hill, this cosy local is one of the few traditional pubs remaining in this thoroughfare. No gimmicks, just well-kept Fuller's ales, which are not common in this area. Classic pub decor includes old photographs and prints of Wandsworth as well as portraits of racehorses. On sunny days, watch the world and his dog go by from the pavement drinking area. Expect a friendly welcome from Snoopy, the female Doberman Pinscher as well. 🌞🌓⇌Θ(Clapham Jct)🖵⅃⚲

Eagle Ale House 🄻
104 Chatham Road, SW11 6HG
☼ 3 (12 Sat)-11; 12-10.30 Sun ☎ (020) 7228 2328
⊕ eaglealehouse.co.uk
Sharp's Doom Bar; Westerham Freedom Ale; guest beers Ⓗ
In a side street off the busy Northcote Road, this real ale haven with seven rapidly changing beers from Westerham and other microbreweries is an unspoilt, dog-friendly local with a somewhat chaotic interior: leather sofas, old bottles and dusty books. A loyal clientele is welcoming to all. The large-screen TV shows major sporting events. There is a heated marquee in the garden for special occasions, including beer festivals. Local CAMRA Pub of the Year runner up 2009-2011.
🚆🌞🖵(319,G1)♣⅃⚲

Falcon ★ 🏠 ✅

2 St John's Hill, SW11 1RU

🌑 10-11 (midnight Thu-Sat); 10-10.30 Sun

☎ (020) 7228 2076

Beer range varies 🅷

Close to Clapham Junction station, this flagship M&B Nicholson's pub is run by an enthusiastic young manager whose periodic beer festivals can double the 20 real ales available round the bar. Real cider is served in the summer. A late-Victorian gem among Britain's Real Heritage Pubs, it retains its partitions and etched and stained glass. The back half is in principle reserved for diners in the afternoons, but drinkers should not feel rejected.

⬤🔷&⇌⊖(Clapham Jct)�"

SW12: Balham

Nightingale 🏠

97 Nightingale Lane, SW12 8NX

🌑 11 (12 Sun)-midnight ☎ (020) 8673 1637

Sambrook's Wandle; Wells Bombardier; Young's Bitter, Special; guest beers 🅷

A Grade II-listed building, this multi award-winning community pub is a welcoming local for regulars and visitors alike and raises large sums for charities such as Help for Heroes. There is always something new happening at the Bird – be sure to read the newsletter. Food is served daily 12-10pm, and trays of third-of-a-pint glasses are available for sampling the good range of beers.

🏰Q🌲🐕🎦⬤&⇌(Wandsworth Common) ⊖(Clapham South)🚆(G1)♣ˈ⸝

SW13: Barnes

Red Lion ✅

2 Castelnau, SW13 9RU

🌑 11-11; 12-10.30 Sun ☎ (020) 8748 2961

Fuller's Chiswick Bitter, London Pride, ESB, seasonal beer; guest beer 🅷

Large Victorian landmark pub at the entrance to the Wetland Centre. It has been opened out in recent years, although the back room, with its ornate fireplace, chandelier, dark wood panelling and pillars, still has a more exclusive feel. Beyond is a decked patio and a spacious no-smoking garden. The landlord is a three times winner of the Fuller's Cellarman of the Year award. Excellent food is available from a varied, modern menu, and children are welcome during the day.

🏰🎦⬤&🚆Pˈ⸝

SW15: Putney

Bricklayer's Arms 🏠

32 Waterman Street, SW15 1DD

🌑 12-11 (10.30 Sun) ☎ (020) 8789 0222

🌐 bricklayers-arms.co.uk

Beer range varies 🅷

A regular local CAMRA Pub of the Year and twice regional winner, this small, welcoming, family-owned free house is a rolling festival of up to 12 microbrewery beers, typically including choices from Sambrook's and Dark Star and perhaps a Rudgate or Downton beer, complemented by a real cider or perry. Shove-ha'penny and bar skittles are played, and there is a pub cricket team. Regular beer festivals grace the patio outside. Its popularity with Fulham FC supporters tends to reduce the beer range after home matches.

🏰🎦⇌⊖(Putney Bridge)🚆♣"ˈ⸝

Green Man

Wildcroft Road, Putney Heath, SW15 3NG

🌑 11-11 (midnight Fri & Sat); 12-10.30 Sun

☎ (020) 8788 8096 🌐 greenmanputney.com

Young's Bitter, Special, seasonal beer; guest beer 🅷

On the edge of the heath opposite the bus terminus up Putney Hill, this charming, warm and welcoming Young's pub dates back to around 1700 and retains an intimate atmosphere. Outside are a sheltered front patio and a large, split-level back garden ideal for families in summer. Quiz night is Tuesday; poker night Wednesday. Board games are available. Meals are served lunchtimes and evenings Monday to Thursday and all day Friday to Sunday. 🏰🎦⬤&🚆♣ˈ⸝

SW16: Streatham

Earl Ferrers 🏠

22 Ellora Road, SW16 6JF

🌑 5 (12 Sat & summer)-midnight (11 Mon & Tue); 12-10.30 Sun ☎ (020) 8835 8333 🌐 earlferrers.co.uk

Sambrook's Wandle; guest beers 🅷

Home to various community activities, this Victorian back-street local, occupying a prominent corner site, is an oasis of calm in bustling Streatham. It serves up to five ales, mostly from London microbreweries, in a comfortable, tastefully decorated single bar with bare floorboards. An adventurous menu is available, plus a range of tempting bar snacks. The name commemorates the notorious fourth Earl, hanged for murder in 1760 – the last member of the House of Lords to die on the gallows.

🎦⬤⇌(Streatham/Streatham Common)🚆♣ˈ⸝

Pied Bull

498 Streatham High Road, SW16 3QB

🌑 12-11 (midnight Fri & Sat) ☎ (020) 8764 4003

🌐 thepiedbullstreatham.com

Young's Bitter, Special; guest beers 🅷

Landmark pub opposite the common. The public bar to the left features a skylight and attractive etched screens, while the open plan lounge bar welcomes children. There is a panelled games room to the rear with three pool tables. The paved garden is popular during warmer weather and smokers have a heated, covered area with a TV screen. Meals and bar snacks are available. The number of guest beers varies and may include Wells Bombardier or a Young's seasonal.

🏰🎦⬤&🔋⇌(Streatham/Streatham Common) 🚆♣ˈ⸝

SW17: Tooting

Antelope ✅

76 Mitcham Road, SW17 9NG

🌑 4 (12 Sat)-11 (midnight Fri; 1am Sat); 12-11 Sun

☎ (020) 8672 3888 🌐 theantelopepub.com

Adnams Lighthouse; Purity Pure UBU; guest beers 🅷

A cavernous Victorian Antic pub serving good food and a variety of ales; three or four guest beers change on a regular basis. It features an eclectic mix of retro furnishings and artefacts such as standard lamps and leather sofas. A real fire, lit candles and wood panelling give a cosy feel. The pub hosts a quiz night every Monday and occasional film and comedy nights. There is a large separate room at the back and a seating area outside. 🏰🌲🎦⬤&⊖(Tooting Broadway)🚆ˈ⸝

SW18: Wandsworth

Grapes ✔

39 Fairfield Street, SW18 1DX

⏲ 12-11 (midnight Fri & Sat); 12-10.30 Sun
☎ (020) 8874 3414

Young's Bitter, Special Ⓗ

A gem of a street-corner local providing an oasis of calm from the traffic on the Wandsworth one-way system and always friendly and welcoming. The well-decorated bar offers unobtrusive TV sport and there is a heated patio for smokers and a suntrap secret garden for everyone. A former local CAMRA Pub of the Year winner, this pub serves excellent beer as well as good-value lunches during the week. A seasonal ale is occasionally available.
❀◐⇌(Wandsworth Town)🚌⊷

Le Gothique

Royal Victoria Patriotic Building, John Archer Way, SW18 3SX

⏲ 12-midnight (weekend and winter hours vary)
☎ (020) 8870 6567 🌐 legothique.co.uk

Beer range varies Ⓗ

Well-established free house, French restaurant and wedding venue hidden within a vast, haunted, 1857 orphanage building, used by intelligence services in World War II and now housing apartments and studios. Wall panels illustrate its rich history. Three real ales are on offer, usually from Downton, Sambrook's and Shepherd Neame, although other small brewers may feature. Beer festivals are held the last weekends in March and October (Halloween). Phone first at weekends, as it is often closed for weddings. ❀◐◑♿🚌(77,219)P⊷

Old Sergeant 𝕃 ✔

104 Garratt Lane, SW18 4DJ

⏲ 12-11 (midnight Thu-Sat); 12-10.30 Sun
☎ (020) 8874 4099

Sambrook's Wandle; Wells Bombardier; Young's Bitter, Special; guest beers Ⓗ

A survivor among the industrial and council estates of Garratt Lane, the Old Sergeant has been owned by Young's since 1857. The upstairs John Young Room, named after the company's legendary chairman, is available for functions and contains something of a shrine to the erstwhile Wandsworth brewer. The modern decor of this friendly local includes a mural of the Ram Brewery in the covered and heated yard at the side. Guest beers often include others from Sambrook's.
❀◐◑♿🚌(44,270)⊷

SW19: South Wimbledon

Sultan

78 Norman Road, SW19 1BT

⏲ 12-11 (midnight Fri & Sat) ☎ (020) 8544 9323

Hop Back GFB, Entire Stout, Summer Lightning; guest beer Ⓗ

Traditional, well run and sometimes lively corner local that welcomes those seeking Hop Back beers in the brewery's only tied house in London. The smaller bar, usually open in the evenings, has a dartboard. A beer club with reduced prices operates Wednesday 6-9pm, and a weekend beer festival is held in the autumn. The guest beer is usually a Hop Back seasonal or from the Downton Brewery. The cat prefers to be left alone.
❀⊞♿⊖(Colliers Wood)🚌(200)♣⊷

Trafalgar 🏆 𝕃

23 High Path, SW19 2JY

⏲ 3 (12 Fri-Sun)-11 ☎ (020) 8542 5342 🌐 thetraf.com

Beer range varies Ⓗ

A small hidden gem with a strong local following – including darts and cricket teams – but also popular with visitors. The house beer, Market Ale, is from Ascot Brewery and there are up to five other beers, often including a dark one. Local beers from By the Horns are frequently available. Regular live music includes trad jazz on Sunday afternoons and Thursday is curry night. Local CAMRA Pub of the Year 2011. ♨⊖🚌♣●

SW19: Wimbledon

Hand in Hand 𝕃 ✔

6 Crooked Billet, SW19 4RQ

⏲ 11-11 (midnight Fri & Sat); 12-11 Sun ☎ (020) 8946 5720
🌐 thehandinhandwimbledon.co.uk

Courage Directors; Wells Bombardier; Young's Bitter, Special Ⓗ**; guest beers** Ⓗ/Ⓖ

A country house pub nestling on the outskirts of suburban London, with the feel of a genuine free house despite being part of the Young's estate. Eight real ales may include up to four guests. It has a wonderful grassy bank outside, a family room and interconnecting cosy bars within. Monthly cellar and tasting nights take place, two small beer and cider festivals a year, acoustic music on the last Sunday of the month plus a weekly quiz. No children are allowed in the main bar.
♨Q🐴❀◐◑🚌(200)♣⊷

Carshalton

Hope 🏆 𝕃

48 West Street, SM5 2PR

⏲ 12-11 (10.30 Sun) ☎ (020) 8240 1255
🌐 hopecarshalton.co.uk

W J King Horsham Best; Windsor & Eton Knight of the Garter; guest beers Ⓗ

A cosy, community-owned pub, free of tie, with a traditional, welcoming atmosphere and a large garden. Two regular and five guest beers, usually including a dark one and a strong one, are complemented by real ciders and a continental bottled beer selection. Regular ale festivals are held and bar billiards is available in the back room. Conversation is king, given that the venue is free of TV, muzak or machines. A full menu is served until 3pm, then bar meals until 10pm.
♨Q❀◐◑♿⇌🚌♣●P⊷🗑

Sun ✔

4 North Street, SM5 2HU

⏲ 12 (5 Mon)-11 (midnight Fri & Sat); 12-10.30 Sun
☎ (020) 8773 4549 🌐 thesuncarshalton.com

Sharp's Doom Bar; Taylor Landlord; guest beers Ⓗ

Refurbished by new owners in the past couple of years, this is a quality addition to the thriving local ale scene. Contemporary decor gives a café bar feel that fits well with the pub's older architecture. Four changing guests, with a local beer often represented, are supported by an extensive wine list. Board games are available, children are welcome until 7pm and the family room is well stocked with games, paper and crayons. There is also a beautiful walled garden with a sandpit for younger visitors. The menu is more gastro than grub. ♨🐴❀◐◑⇌🚌⊷

Windsor Castle ✅

378 Carshalton Road, SM5 3PT

🌣 11-11 (11.30 Fri & Sat); 12-10.30 Sun ☎ (020) 8669 1191
⊕ windsorcastlepub.com

Harveys Sussex Best Bitter; Shepherd Neame Kent's Best, seasonal beers; guest beers ℍ

Acquired by Shepherd Neame in 2009, this large corner pub is open plan but its distinct areas create a welcoming atmosphere. The restaurant serves lunch daily and dinner Tuesday-Saturday. Events includes a jam night and a jazz jam night on the first and third Mondays respectively, and a Thursday quiz – a lot goes on here. Outside, a covered courtyard leads to a garden and function room. Guest beers come from far and wide and there is an annual beer festival.
🏵️◖➤⇌(Carshalton Beeches)🚽♣P⌐

Cheam

Claret Wine Bar

33 The Broadway, SM3 8BL

🌣 11.30-11 (midnight Fri & Sat); 12-11 Sun
☎ (020) 8715 9002

Shepherd Neame Master Brew; guest beers ℍ

Small, friendly pub in a former shop, sister to the Claret in Addiscombe, which also appears in this Guide. The mock-Tudor interior is adorned with pump clips and other breweriana, and guest beers are often from small breweries such as Palmers and Sharp's. Food is served at lunchtimes, including Sunday roasts. The TV shows sporting events, and the pub has a function room available for hire.
◖&⇌🚽♣

Prince of Wales

28 Malden Road, SM3 8QF

🌣 11-11 (midnight Fri & Sat); 12-10.30 Sun
☎ (020) 8641 8106

Beer range varies ℍ

On the north side of Cheam village, this traditional pub has an L-shaped bar and a beer garden at the rear. The three guest ales usually available are likely to be session beers. The restaurant has special deals on Monday and Wednesday evenings and younger children eat free on Sundays. The pub hosts darts matches, and other events include charity auctions, a monthly quiz and an annual cricket match. Clubs include motor scooter and drama. Dogs welcome. 🏚Q🏵️◖&⇌🚽♣⌐

Kew

Botanist Brewery & Kitchen ✅

3-5 Kew Green, TW9 3AA

🌣 12-11 (midnight Fri & Sat); 12-10.30 Sun
☎ (020) 8948 4838 ⊕ thebotanistkew.com

Botanist Humulus Lupulus, 391, OK Bitter; guest beers ℍ

A lively pub-restaurant with its own microbrewery, the Botanist is favoured by local drinkers and diners alike. Originally a row of shops, its internal space divides into different areas, each with its own character. Pavement tables fronting Kew Green are popular in the summer, while a rear yard provides a refuge for smokers. As well as own-brewed ales, it offers a range of interesting British, American and continental bottled beers and a guest ale, often from near-neighbour Twickenham.
Q🏵️◖&⇌(Kew Bridge)⊖(Kew Gardens)
🚽(65,391)⌐

Kingston upon Thames

Boaters Inn 🅛 ✅

Canbury Gardens, Lower Ham Road, KT2 5AU (off A307 via Woodside Rd) TQ180699

🌣 11 (12 Sun)-11 ☎ (020) 8541 4672
⊕ boaterskingston.com

Beer range varies ℍ

The building is unusual, originally a council tea room in Canbury Gardens, beside the River Thames and with boat mooring (check in advance). It features five changing beers, many from local breweries. Inside there is one open area curving round the bar, with views of the river and gardens. The food is popular, especially on Sundays when jazz is played in the evening. The outside tables get filled up in good weather, when customers then spill out into the gardens. 🏵️◖&🚽(65)⌐

Druids Head ✅

2-3 Market Place, KT1 1JT

🌣 11 (12 Sun)-11 (midnight Thu-Sat) ☎ (020) 8546 0723

Greene King IPA, Ruddles Best Bitter, Abbot; guest beers ℍ

Kingston's oldest pub, originally a 17th-century coaching house, parts of which are Grade II-listed. The older public bar has a cosy feel while the split-level main bar tends to be busier. Two or three guest beers change on a regular basis. Food is available all day until 10pm and includes traditional Sunday roasts. Upstairs rooms are available to hire. The pub was once visited by the author Jerome K Jerome who left an inscription on an upstairs window. 🏚🏵️◖⇌🚽⌐

Willoughby Arms 🅛

47 Willoughby Road, KT2 6LN

🌣 10-midnight; 12-11 Sun ☎ (020) 8546 4236
⊕ thewilloughbyarms.com

Fuller's London Pride; guest beers ℍ

Friendly Victorian back-street local, divided into a sports bar with games and a big-screen TV, and a quieter lounge area. The pub belongs to the LocAle scheme and always features a Twickenham beer among others. An upstairs function room can be hired for events. Pizzas are available, cooked on the premises. Beer festivals are held around St George's Day and Halloween. The spacious garden includes a covered, heated and lit smoking area with another large TV screen.
Q🏵️🍴&🚽(371,K5)♣⌐

Wych Elm 🅛 ✅

93 Elm Road, KT2 6HT

🌣 11-3, 5-midnight; 11-midnight Sat; 12-11 Sun
☎ (020) 8546 3271 ⊕ thewychelm.co.uk

Fuller's Chiswick Bitter, London Pride, ESB, seasonal beer ℍ

Welcoming and friendly back-street local and a long-standing Guide entry where high beer quality has been maintained for more than 25 years. The comfortable saloon leads to an award-winning garden, and the basic but tidy public bar has a TV showing sport. Excellent home-cooked lunches are served daily (no food Mon). Live jazz features on the last Saturday of the month, and there are occasional barbecues. Q🏵️◖🍴⇌🚽(K5)♣⌐

Mitcham

Windmill

40 Commonside West, CR4 4HA

✪ 12-11 (1am Fri & Sat); 12-midnight Sun
☎ (020) 8685 0333
Young's Bitter; guest beer Ⓗ
Built in 1856, this homely, single-roomed free house, run by a landlady of almost 30 years standing, is close to the town centre, the Three Kings pond and its resident traffic-defying geese. Stained glass depicts windmills in the bow-fronted windows. There are live acoustic performances every other Friday, occasional themed music nights and a Christmas charity raffle. The TV is quiet except for sporting events. Families and dogs are welcome and the pub sponsors a Little League football team. ✿🚃⌐

New Malden

Woodies
Thetford Road, KT3 5DX TQ206673
✪ 11-11; 12-10.30 Sun ☎ (020) 8949 5824
⊕ woodiesfreehouse.co.uk
Adnams Broadside; Fuller's London Pride, ESB; Young's Bitter; guest beers Ⓗ
A former sports pavilion, this free house is festooned with sporting and theatrical memorabilia. Three changing guest ales mainly come directly from small breweries; forthcoming beers are listed on the website. Thatchers Traditional Dry cider, home-cooked lunches, a Sunday carvery and summer weekend barbecues are on offer, and a beer festival is held every August. The large patio outside has a covered and heated area for smokers. Local CAMRA Pub of the Year for 2011 and four of the previous five years. 🚶✿🕭&🚃(265)●P⌐

Richmond

Red Cow
59 Sheen Road, TW9 1YJ
✪ 11-11.30 (11 Sun & Mon; midnight Fri & Sat)
☎ (020) 8940 2511 ⊕ redcowpub.com
St Austell Tribute; Young's Bitter, Special; guest beers Ⓗ
Dating back at least 200 years, this popular community local maintains a traditional atmosphere despite extensive changes over the years. The Victorian painted glass panels can still be seen behind the bar. The first floor has four en-suite bedrooms providing B&B accommodation. A changing menu of home-cooked food is served until 10pm (not Sun eve). Tuesday is quiz night and live music is performed regularly. There is a front patio area and free Wi-Fi. Guest beers are often from Twickenham Fine Ales. ✿🍴◑≈♥🚃(33)⌐

White Cross
Riverside, off Water Lane, TW9 1TH
✪ 10-11 (10.30 Sun) ☎ (020) 8940 6844
⊕ thewhitecrossrichmond.com
Wells Bombardier; Young's Bitter, Special, London Gold, seasonal beer; guest beer Ⓗ
Prominent Young's pub on the waterfront built in 1748 and rebuilt 1838. A stained glass panel commemorates the site of a convent of the Franciscan Friary, whose insignia was a white cross. The entrance is reached by steps for good reason: the river often floods here. An island bar serves two side rooms (one a mezzanine); an unusual feature is a working fireplace beneath a window. The ground-level patio bar opens at busy times. Food is available every day. 🚶Q✿◑≈🚃⌐

Surbiton

Coronation Hall Ⓛ ✔
St Marks Hill, KT6 4LQ
✪ 9am-midnight ☎ (020) 8390 6164
Fuller's London Pride; Greene King IPA, Abbot; Shepherd Neame Spitfire; Wychwood Hobgoblin; guest beers Ⓗ
One of the better Wetherspoon conversions, this building has been a music hall, cinema, bingo hall and nudist health club. The decor is a mix of movie stars, film artefacts, the coronation of George V, and the planets. The pub has LocAle accreditation and beers from local micros always feature among the regularly changing guests. Local beer festivals are held as well as national events. Broad Oak perry, Gwynt y Ddraig and Mr Whitehead's cider are served. Q◑&≈🚃●

Lamb 🍷 Ⓛ
73 Brighton Road, KT6 5NF (on A243)
✪ 12-11 (midnight Thu-Sat) ☎ (020) 8390 9229
Sambrook's Junction; Surrey Hills Ranmore Ale; guest beer Ⓗ
Small, cosy, family-run pub that has evolved into a thriving community local under its current management. It is a free house and offers LocAles. Built in 1850 and formerly divided into four separate rooms, it retains its original horseshoe-shaped bar. Specialist cheeses are always available. The pub had a small brewery in Victorian times. Music and other events are regularly held. Local CAMRA Pub of the Year 2012. ✿≈🚃⌐

New Prince Ⓛ ✔
117 Ewell Road, KT6 6AL
✪ 11-11 (midnight Fri & Sat) ☎ (020) 8296 0265
Fuller's London Pride; Gale's Seafarers Ale, HSB; guest beer Ⓗ
Excellent example of a small, comfortable, welcoming community pub. It was built as a Charrington's house, the Prince of Wales, more than 150 years ago, and the beamed ceiling and photos of local bygone scenes give a traditional feel. The main bar is light and airy and a side room with dartboard leads off towards the surprisingly large garden, part-covered and with a pergola and outdoor heating. Disabled access is via the garden. ✿◑&≈🚃♣⌐

Sutton

Little Windsor ✔
13 Greyhound Road, SM1 4BY
✪ 12-11.30 (midnight Fri & Sat); 12-11 Sun
☎ (020) 8643 2574 ⊕ freewebs.com/little-windsor
Fuller's Chiswick Bitter, Discovery, London Pride, ESB, seasonal beers Ⓗ
A former CAMRA Sutton borough Pub of the Year, this small street-corner local in the heart of the New Town area, east of the town centre, is popular with locals, especially in the evenings and at weekends for football on TV. The L-shaped bar leads to a covered terrace, which is heated for smokers, and a garden. Quiz night is on Thursday and bridge night Monday. Food is served at lunchtimes and in the evenings, and children are welcome until 9pm. ✿◑≈🚃⌐

Wallington

Whispering Moon ✔
25 Ross Parade, SM6 8QF

❄ 9am-midnight (1am Fri & Sat) ☎ (020) 8647 7020
Courage Best Bitter; Greene King Abbot; Ruddles Best Bitter; guest beers Ⓗ
Here on the High Street close to the station, in a former Odeon cinema, you can be sure of a friendly welcome from the Wetherspoon staff. Opened in 1992, the pub is L-shaped, with a raised area for diners, and regular meal deals are offered. The decor includes historic photographs of the local area, and there is a good supply of tables and seating. Customers can use a book to express their preferences for guest ales. ⓓ♿⇌🚇💷

WEST LONDON
W1: Marylebone
Carpenters Arms
12 Seymour Place, W1H 7NE
❄ 11-11; 12-10.30 Sun ☎ (020) 7723 1050
Harveys Sussex Best Bitter; guest beers Ⓗ
A sister hostelry to the Market Porter in SE1, but with a smaller range of guest beers, this establishment is a haven from the bustle of Edgware Road. Many local people enjoy watching TV sport, and playing darts in the rear alcove. The pub has had a sensitive refurbishment, preserving the mosaics, and on the side wall is a display of facsimiles of woodworking tools. The upstairs function room is available for hire.
❀🚇(Marble Arch)🚇♣

W1: Mayfair
Coach & Horses ✓
5 Bruton Street, W1J 6PT
❄ 11.30-11; 12-8 Sat; closed Sun ☎ (020) 7629 4123
Fuller's London Pride; Greene King Old Golden Hen; Young's Gold; guest beer Ⓗ
An excellent refuge from the nearby Bond Street shopping area. First licensed in 1738, it was rebuilt in 1933 and has an imposing mock-Tudor exterior. Inside, the atmosphere is traditional, with wooden beams and panelling. Pictures on the walls feature caricatures of 19th-century politicians and clerics. Four handpumps include a changing series of guest ales. The small dining room with bar upstairs is available for private functions.
ⓓ🚇(Bond St/Green Pk/Oxford Circus)🚇

Windmill
6-8 Mill Street, W1S 2AZ
❄ 11-11; 12-4.30 Sat; closed Sun ☎ (020) 7491 8050
⊕ windmillmayfair.co.uk
Courage Best Bitter; Young's Bitter, Special; Wells Bombardier; guest beer Ⓗ
Licensed in 1988 in two adjoining buildings, one a former nightclub, the other an escort agency, this pub has a well-furnished lounge bar with wood panelling, decorative ceilings and frieze. The lower area at the rear is quieter and is available for private functions. There is a restaurant on the first floor. Pies are a speciality and the Pie Club claims 6,000 members. Qⓓ🚇(Oxford Circus)🚇

W1: Soho
Argyll Arms ★ ✓
18 Argyll Street, W1F 7TP
❄ 10-11 (11.30 Fri & Sat); 12-10.30 Sun ☎ (020) 7734 6117
Brains SA Gold; Fuller's London Pride; St Austell Tribute; Sharp's Doom Bar; guest beers Ⓗ
An 1860s pub, with current fittings dating from around 1895, this M&B Nicholson's house is one of Britain's Real Heritage Pubs and is Grade II*-listed. Inside are three snugs separated by etched glass partitions. Note the remarkable decorated Bass mirror. The bar back is impressive and adjacent is a rare survivor, a manager's office with etched glazing. The magnificent saloon is decorated with ornate mirrors. Drinkers can enjoy changing guest ales from brewers such as Green Jack and Leeds.
❀ⓓ🚇(Oxford Circus)🚇

Crown ✓
64 Brewer Street, W1F 9TP
❄ 10-11 (11.30 Fri & Sat); 12-10.30 Sun ☎ (020) 7287 8420
Fuller's London Pride; St Austell Tribute; Sharp's Doom Bar; guest beers Ⓗ
A popular M&B Nicholson's pub on the site of the Hickford Rooms, which were London's main concert rooms in the 1740s and '50s; there is an interesting notice showing the history of the pub. The main bar, with its banquettes, is a welcome retreat from the bustling street. Children are welcome, with parents, in the upstairs dining room. Food is served from 10am, including breakfast, up till 10pm every day. Three changing and often unusual guest beers are served.
ⓓ🚇(Piccadilly Circus)🚇

Dog & Duck ★ ✓
18 Bateman Street, W1D 3AJ
❄ 11-11 (11.30 Fri & Sat); 12-10.30 Sun ☎ (020) 7494 0697
Fuller's London Pride; St Austell Tribute; guest beers Ⓗ
In the bustling heart of Soho, this listed M&B Nicholson's outlet, built in 1897, is one of Britain's Real Heritage Pubs. An elaborate mosaic depicts dogs and ducks, and wonderful advertising mirrors adorn the walls. Changing guest beers include, for example, Fuller's Bengal Lancer, Caledonian Double Dark and Venus Black. The upstairs Orwell Bar can be hired for functions. The pub is small and so popular, especially with media people, that it is not just smokers who have to drink outside.
ⓓ🚇(Tottenham Ct Rd)🚇

Nellie Dean of Soho
89 Dean Street, W1D 3SU
❄ 11-11 (midnight Fri & Sat); 12-10.30 Sun
☎ (020) 7734 2572
Caledonian Deuchars IPA; Fuller's London Pride; Harveys Sussex Best Bitter; Meantime London Pale Ale; guest beer Ⓗ
Originally licensed in 1683 as the Dolphin, the current building dates from 1900 and is Grade II-listed. The pub now offers up to five real ales and reasonably priced food. The name was changed to Nellie Dean of Soho in 1967. The upstairs bar has a pool table and can be hired for functions.
ⓓ🚇(Tottenham Ct Rd)🚇

Three Greyhounds
25 Greek Street, W1D 5DD
❄ 10-11.30 (midnight Thu, 12.30am Fri & Sat); 10-11 Sun ☎ (020) 7494 0953
Fuller's London Pride; St Austell Tribute; Sharp's Doom Bar; guest beers Ⓗ
Popular M&B Nicholson's pub, just off Shaftesbury Avenue and full of tourists and wanderers through Soho, first licensed as a beer house in 1846, with weatherboarding added in 1925. It was refurbished in February 2012, and given a coat of paint, a new bar and handpumps. Recent guest beers have

included Cropton Elf Indulgence and Box Steam Tunnel Vision. It makes a comfortable break from the Soho streets, but does get rather crowded. ◑⊖(Leicester Sq/Tottenham Ct Rd)🖵🍺

W2: Paddington

Cleveland Arms
28 Chilworth Street, W2 6DT
🕐 11-11.30 (midnight Fri & Sat); 12-10.50 Sun
☎ (020) 7706 1759
Greene King IPA; Harveys Sussex Best Bitter; Taylor Landlord; guest beers ⓗ
A few minutes' walk from Paddington Station, this lovely 1852 Grade II-listed pub with its tiled ends is named after William Vane, first Duke of Cleveland. A friendly free house serving mainly locals, its guest beer often includes one seldom seen in London. The rear games room can be hired for functions. Quiz night is Tuesday, and there is a free bar buffet Sunday lunchtime. Children and dogs are welcome. Local CAMRA Pub of the Year runner-up in 2012. ◑⇌⊖🖵♣

Mad Bishop & Bear ✔
Upper Level, Paddington Station, W2 1HB
🕐 8am-11 (11.30 Fri); 10-10.30 Sun ☎ (020) 7402 2441
Fuller's Chiswick Bitter, Discovery, London Pride, ESB, seasonal beer; guest beer ⓗ
Above the shopping complex just behind the station concourse, the traditional pub interior features a long bar, mirrors, good prints and a rather grand chandelier, with train information screens and two TVs for sports. The raised area can be hired for events. It does not get too crowded, even in the rush hour. The bar may close early if there are football crowds passing through. 🏵◑♿⇌⊖🖵

Victoria ★ ✔
10A Strathearn Place, W2 2NH
🕐 11-11; 12-10.30 Sun ☎ (020) 7724 1191
Fuller's Chiswick Bitter, Discovery, London Pride, ESB, seasonal beers ⓗ
There is plenty to admire in this listed mid-Victorian inn, one of Britain's Real Heritage Pubs, including ornately gilded mirrors above a crescent-shaped bar, painted tiles in wall niches and numerous portraits of Queen Victoria. The walls display cartoons, paperweights and a Silver Jubilee plate. A recessed area at the back is furnished with a leather bench seat. Upstairs, via a spiral staircase, there is a library and theatre bar available for public use. Tuesday is quiz night.
Q🏵◑⇌⊖(Lancaster Gate/Paddington)🖵🍺

W3: Acton

Red Lion & Pineapple ✔
281 High Street, W3 9BP
🕐 9am-midnight ☎ (020) 8896 2248
Courage Directors; Greene King IPA, Abbot; guest beers ⓗ
A spacious two-room Wetherspoon pub featuring an oversized circular bar with large windows and two cast bronze lions. The smaller room is mainly for diners and families, and the walls are decorated with photographs of old Acton. Formerly owned by Fuller's, the site originally had two pubs, hence the unusual name. The cider can alternate between the handpumps and the fridge.
Q🚃🏵◑♿⊖(Acton Town)🖵🍺

West London Trades Union Club
33-35 High Street, W3 6ND
🕐 7pm-midnight ☎ (020) 8992 4557
Beer range varies ⓗ
Small and friendly club, run as a co-operative, which combines excellent real ale with a busy cultural and social life. One or two beers are normally served either from the Nelson Brewery range or from another small independent brewery. The Acton Community Theatre is upstairs, and the club hosts regular special events including summer barbecues in the courtyard. The local CAMRA branch is an associate member; show a CAMRA membership card or this Guide for entry.
🏵⊖(Acton Central)🖵🍺

W4: Chiswick

Fox & Hounds/Mawson Arms ✔
110 Chiswick Lane South, W4 2QA
🕐 11-8; closed Sat & Sun ☎ (020) 8994 2936
Fuller's Chiswick Bitter, Discovery, London Pride, ESB, seasonal beers ⓗ
On the corner of the Griffin Brewery, and its de facto brewery tap, this listed pub is the start of the Fuller's brewery tour. The unusual double naming is a historical relic of separate licences needed for beer and spirits. Hot food is available until 7pm and the pub is well known for its sausages and pies. Brewery memorabilia on the walls include ancestral portraits of the Fuller, Smith and Turner families. 🅿Q◑🖵(190)

George IV ✔
185 Chiswick High Road, W4 2DR
🕐 10.30-11 (midnight Fri & Sat); 12-11 Sun
☎ (020) 8994 4624
Fuller's Chiswick Bitter, London Pride, Bengal Lancer, ESB, seasonal beers ⓗ
In the heart of Chiswick, this is one of Fuller's Ale & Pie pubs and proud of its fresh food policy. There has been a pub here since 1777 and the present one is reputed to have its own ghost, George! The purpose-built Headliners Comedy Club within the pub plays host to a variety of events including top-class comedians, salsa dancing, jazz nights and silent movies. It is also available for private hire for parties and conferences.
🏵◑♿⊖(Turnham Green)🖵🍺

Old Pack Horse ✔
434 Chiswick High Road, W4 5TF
🕐 11-11 (midnight Thu-Sat); 12-10.30 Sun
☎ (020) 8994 2872
Fuller's Chiswick Bitter, London Pride, ESB, seasonal beers ⓗ
Well-preserved Edwardian corner pub with a frontage often featured in photographs of the area, and a view across Turnham Green. The interior retains ornate woodwork and glasswork including some stained glass panels; it is one of London's Real Heritage Pubs. Five drinking areas include a snug and a Thai restaurant at the back. A bar name refers to the long-gone nearby Chiswick Empire, and walls display theatre memorabilia.
🅿Q◑🍽⊖(Chiswick Pk/Gunnersbury)🖵🍺

Tabard 🄻 ✔
2 Bath Road, W4 1LW
🕐 12-11 (midnight Thu-Sat) ☎ (020) 8994 3492
Beer range varies ⓗ

A pub that dates back to 1880 and was built as part of the Bedford Park estate, the first London garden suburb. Notable features include the swing sign painted by TM Rooke, original tiling by William de Morgan and Walter Crane, and Arts & Crafts mirrors and pictures. Ten handpumps serve changing guest ales, including local beers. The first floor Tabard Theatre, an intimate 79-seat fringe theatre, has hosted the likes of Al Murray and Russell Brand. 　⊛ⅅ&⊖(Turnham Green)🚐⌐

W5: Ealing

Plough ✓

297 Northfield Avenue, W5 4XB
✪ 11-midnight (1am Thu-Sat) ☎ (020) 8567 1416
⊕ ploughnorthfields.co.uk
Fuller's Chiswick, Discovery, London Pride, ESB; guest beers Ⓗ
A large, mainly wood-panelled single-bar pub with several semi-private areas, a short walk south from Northfields Underground station on the Heathrow branch of the Piccadilly line. The enterprising management offers a wide range of events throughout the year, including regular Tuesday evening quiz and live jazz on Thursdays. There is a variety of interesting food throughout the day. The large garden with children's play facilities plays host to barbecues and hog roasts in the summer months. 　♨⊱⊛&ⅅ⊖(Northfields)🚐(E2,E3)P⌐

Questors (Grapevine Bar) Ⓛ ✓

12 Mattock Lane, W5 5BQ
✪ 7-11; 12-2.30, 7-10.30 Sun ☎ (020) 8567 0011
⊕ questors.org.uk/grapevine
Fuller's London Pride; guest beers Ⓗ
Friendly theatre bar opposite Walpole Park just south of the town centre. It regularly serves guest beers, usually including one from a local brewery, and also runs CAMRA-themed festivals twice a year. Books and board games are available, as are Belgian beers and obscure whiskies. The club is run by enthusiastic volunteers and is the 2012 national CAMRA Club of the Year.
Q⊛&⇌⊖(Ealing Broadway)🚐♣P⌐

Red Lion ✓

13 St Mary's Road, W5 5RA
✪ 12 (11 Sat)-11 (midnight Thu-Sat) ☎ (020) 8567 2541
⊕ redlionealing.co.uk
Fuller's Chiswick Bitter, London Pride, ESB, seasonal beer; guest beer Ⓗ
A popular local, affectionately known as Stage 6, opposite Ealing Studios. Photographs of TV and film stars who have been associated with the studios are on display alongside other memorabilia of the films that made them famous. The pub has gained its own reputation for home-made food in recent years and is unusual in the area for not having a TV or jukebox. The heated covered patio at the back now has braziers and hosts occasional beer festivals.
♨Q⊛ⅅ⇌(Ealing Broadway)⊖(Ealing Broadway/S Ealing)🚐(65)⌐

Sir Michael Balcon ✓

46-47 The Mall, W5 3TJ
✪ 9am-11.30 (midnight Fri & Sat) ☎ (020) 8799 2850
Adnams Broadside; Fuller's London Pride; Greene King IPA, Abbot; guest beers Ⓗ
On the busy Uxbridge Road just to the east of the main Ealing Broadway, this became a Wetherspoon pub in 2008, named after the legendary film

producer; the wall displays are devoted to him and films made at Ealing Studios. Eight real ales are usually available with guest beers often from Adnams, Hogs Back and Sambrook's. Westons cider is in the fridge. A glass-covered heated patio is available at the front for smokers.
♨Q⊛ⅅ&⇌⊖(Ealing Broadway)🚐●⌐

W6: Hammersmith

Andover Arms ✓

57 Aldensley Road, W6 0DL
✪ 12-midnight ☎ (020) 8748 2155 ⊕ theandoverarms.com
Fuller's Chiswick Bitter, London Pride; guest beers Ⓗ
A frequent entry in this Guide, tucked away in the side streets of Hammersmith, this popular local is an enduring real ale champion. The kitchen offers a wide range of meals lunchtime and evening. There is a TV for major sporting events, traditional pub games such as dominoes are available, and the pub holds regular quiz and live music nights. Two guest ales are a recent innovation and drinkers can sup beers from brewers such as Hook Norton.
♨ⅅ⊖(Ravenscourt Pk)🚐♣

Dove ✓

19 Upper Mall, W6 9TA
✪ 11-11; 12-10.30 Sun ☎ (020) 8748 9474
Fuller's London Pride, ESB, seasonal beers Ⓗ
Traditional Fuller's pub, a listed building overlooking the Thames and hence often crowded in summer. One of London's Real Heritage Pubs, it also holds the Guinness world record for the smallest bar area. Classic food with a twist is served every day; meals can take a little time to arrive at busy times but are worth the wait. The likes of Dylan Thomas, Ernest Hemingway and Alec Guinness have enjoyed a pint or two of excellent beer here. ♨Q⊛ⅅ⊖(Ravenscourt Pk)🚐♣⌐

Plough & Harrow ✓

120-124 King Street, W6 0QU
✪ 9am-11.30 ☎ (020) 8735 6020
Fuller's London Pride; Greene King IPA, Abbot; guest beers Ⓗ
A Plough & Harrow Inn stood here for centuries and at one stage had 'Established in 1419' painted above the entrance. The present cavernous Wetherspoon pub in a former car showroom dates from 2002 and has a mixture of stone floors and carpeted areas. Drinks and food – served from 8am to 10pm every day – are good value. Look out for the well-advertised beer festivals.
ⅅ&⊖(Hammersmith/Ravenscourt Pk)🚐

Swan ✓

46 Hammersmith Broadway, W6 0DZ
✪ 10-11 (midnight Fri & Sat; 10.30 Sun) ☎ (020) 8748 1043
Fuller's London Pride; St Austell Tribute; Sharp's Doom Bar; guest beers Ⓗ
Wood predominates in this bustling M&B Nicholson's pub, handily placed opposite Hammersmith Broadway. Ornate stairs lead to a first-floor restaurant and bar (and the toilets). It is well worth breaking your journey here to or from Heathrow Airport. Guest beers are from regional brewers such as Adnams, Elgood's and Thornbridge. Note the fine tessellated gables.
ⅅ⊖🚐

W7: Hanwell

Fox ⚑

Green Lane, W7 2PJ
❂ 11-11; 12-10.30 Sun ☎ (020) 8567 4021
⊕ thefoxpub.co.uk
Fuller's London Pride; Sharp's Doom Bar; Taylor Landlord; guest beers Ⓗ
Convivial back-street free house near Hanwell Locks, popular with walkers and canal users as well as locals. A traditional corner bar with plenty of seating, it offers a good range of beers and excellent food at reasonable prices. Booking is recommended for Sunday lunch. The pleasant garden has a games room. Local CAMRA Pub of the Year 2012. ⌂✿◐₪(195,E8)♣P⌐

W8: Notting Hill Gate

Churchill Arms ✅

119 Kensington Church Street, W8 7LN
❂ 11-11 (midnight Thu-Sat); 12-10.30 Sun
☎ (020) 7727 4242
Fuller's Chiswick Bitter, Discovery, London Pride, ESB, seasonal beers Ⓗ
The winner of awards ranging from Boozers in Bloom to the Griffin Award for Fuller's Pub of the Year, this is also one of London's Real Heritage Pubs. It is festooned with Churchillian and Irish memorabilia, and an antiques market hangs from the ceiling. There is even a signpost in the middle in case you get lost. Note the commemorative plaques to customers who are now spirits. The Thai food is recommended. This deservedly popular pub gets extremely busy. Q◐➲₪

Uxbridge Arms

13 Uxbridge Street, W8 7TQ
❂ 12-11 (10.30 Sun) ☎ (020) 7727 7326
Fuller's London Pride; Harveys Sussex Best Bitter; St Austell Tribute Ⓗ
A world away from nearby Portobello Road, this popular back-street local dates from 1836 as a beer house. Wood-panelled and carpeted throughout, the welcoming bar has a warm feel, with lots of photographs and plates as well as a lieutenant-colonel's dress tunic. The best seats are at the end of the bar by the Nicola Sunshine Fund charity collection bottle. Q✿➲₪⌐

W11: Notting Hill

Duke of Wellington

179 Portobello Road, W11 2ED
❂ 11-midnight (11 Sun) ☎ (020) 7727 6727
Wells Bombardier; Young's Bitter, Special, London Gold, seasonal beers Ⓗ
Dating from 1854, this Young's pub is an interesting combination of traditional and modern. Partitions with etched glass give an indication of an earlier layout. The impressive island bar with its tall bar-back is the most prominent feature, and the front bar retains a traditional ambience. The comfortable raised area at the rear has an attractive marble fireplace. Located close to the famous Portobello antiques market, the pub attracts many visitors.
◐➲(Ladbroke Grove/Notting Hill Gate)
₪(23,52,452)

W12: Shepherds Bush

Defectors Weld Ⓛ

170 Uxbridge Road, W12 8AA
❂ 12-midnight (2am Fri & Sat); 12-11 Sun
☎ (020) 8749 0008 ⊕ defectors-weld.com
Adnams Southwold Bitter; guest beers Ⓗ
On the corner of Wood Lane and Uxbridge Road. Downstairs is a large horseshoe-shaped main bar with five handpumps and a mix of sofas and table and chairs. Rotating every couple of days, guest beers come from Purity, Itchen Valley, Old Dairy, Cottage and Ringwood among others, with at least one LocAle from Moncada, Twickenham, Sambrook's or Redemption. An upstairs room with a bar is available for hire. DJs play music Thursday through to Sunday evenings. (Last entry Fri and Sat is midnight.)
⌂◐&➲(Shepherds Bush/Shepherds Bush Market)₪⌐

W13: West Ealing

Forester ★ Ⓛ ✅

2 Leighton Road, W13 9EP
❂ 10-11.30 (midnight Thu-Sat); 11-11 Sun
☎ (020) 8567 1654 ⊕ theforesterealing.com
Fuller's London Pride, ESB, seasonal beer; guest beers Ⓗ
One of Britain's Real Heritage Pubs, built in 1909 for the Royal Brewery of Brentford and designed by TH Nowell Parr, the Forester makes a welcome return to the Guide since its last appearance in 1994. Thai food is available daily except Sundays when the traditional carvery is served until 6pm. Wednesday is quiz night and on Thursday there are poker tournaments.
⌂✿⇦◐⭐&⇌➲(Northfields)₪(E2,E3)♣⌐

W14: West Kensington

Albion ✅

121 Hammersmith Road, W14 0QL
❂ 12-midnight ☎ (020) 7603 2826 ⊕ downthealbion.com
Courage Best Bitter; Caledonian Deuchars IPA, seasonal beer; Thwaites Wainwright; guest beers Ⓗ
Local CAMRA 2010 Pub of the Year runner-up, this corner pub halfway between Hammersmith Broadway and Olympia dates from 1925, but there have been licensed premises here since 1864. The walls display rock concert posters and photos. A good selection of food is available lunchtimes and excellent stone-baked pizzas in the evenings. Watch out for quiz nights and live music.
⌂◐⇌(Kensington Olympia)➲(Barons Ct/Hammersmith/Kensington Olympia)₪

Bedfont

Beehive

333 Staines Road, TW14 9HF
❂ 11-11 (midnight Fri & Sat); 12-11 Sun ☎ (020) 8890 8086
Fuller's Chiswick Bitter, London Pride, ESB, seasonal beer Ⓗ
Welcoming family-run pub, popular with the local community, a real ale oasis on the Staines to London Roman road. It has a public bar, main bar and an authentic Thai restaurant. English food is also served, including Sunday roasts. Darts and crib are played and major sporting events are shown on a wide-screen TV. The large garden at the back is popular in the summer. ✿◐⭐₪(116)♣P⌐

Brentford

Magpie & Crown ⃝L
128 High Street, TW8 8EW
✪ 12-midnight (1am Thu-Sat) ☎ (020) 8560 4570
⊕ magpieandcrown.co.uk
Twickenham Grandstand Bitter; guest beers Ⓗ
Mock-Tudor pub free of tie, a popular haunt for fans of Brentford Trilogy author Robert Rankin, as well as local ale drinkers. It usually has six real ales (always including one golden, one dark, one bitter), one cider and one perry on handpump, five Belgian draught beers such as Westmalle Dubbel, Fruli, Maredsous 6 and La Chouffe, plus British and continental bottled beers. There are tables and a cycle rack at the front, and a rear patio.
✪◑≠🖴♣🐾᠊

Colham Green

Hut
2 Old Orchard Close, UB8 3LH
✪ 12-midnight ☎ (01895) 437935 ⊕ thehutpub.com
Fuller's London Pride; St Austell Tribute Ⓗ
A friendly, family-run free house close to Stockley Country Park on the corner of two cul-de-sacs with additional pedestrian access from West Drayton Road and Stockley Road. It has been extended at one end with a games room and, at the other, a Thai restaurant serving Thai and English food (not Mon) and roasts on Sunday. Of particular note are old photographs of the area and a map locating pubs and breweries in Uxbridge 100 years ago. Over-21s only. ♒✪◑♿🖴(U5)♣P᠊

Greenford

Black Horse ✅
425 Oldfield Lane, UB6 0AS
✪ 11.30-11 (midnight Thu-Sat); 12-11 Sun
☎ (020) 8578 1384 ⊕ blackhorsegreenford.co.uk
Fuller's London Pride, ESB Ⓗ
Friendly canalside pub, on the Grand Union, with a committed local following. The large garden at the back is popular in the summer and the moorings nearby are regularly in use. The food is home-made, with a changing specials board. Poker night is Wednesday, a weekly quiz is held on Thursday and live music is offered once a month on a Saturday. Seasonal beers may also be available.
✪◑♿≠⊖🖴(92,395)♣P᠊

Hampton

Railway Bell
Station Road, TW12 2AP
✪ 11-11; 12-10.30 Sun ☎ (020) 8979 1897
⊕ therailwaybell.ph
Adnams Southwold Bitter; Courage Best Bitter; Skinner's Betty Stogs; guest beers Ⓗ
Down a driveway beside the Tudor Road bridge over the railway to the east of the station, this small cottage-style pub, known locally as the Dip, has a large, comfortable front terrace. Two separate bars are simply furnished, and one is decorated with old photographs of the locality. Guest beers are always available. Quiz night is the last Wednesday of every month. No evening meals are served on Saturday.
♒Q🐾✪◑≠🖴(111,216)♣᠊

Hampton Hill

Noble Green Wines
153-155 High Street, TW12 1NL
✪ 10-8; 11-6 Sun ☎ (020) 8979 1113
⊕ noblegreenwines.co.uk
Beer range varies Ⓖ
Innovative off-licence supplying not only a wide range of bottled beers from the UK and worldwide but also 16 changing cask ales from independent breweries (and cask cider and perry), available to take home in small containers as well as steel mini kegs or polypins. Well-informed and friendly staff offer good advice. It runs two popular beer festivals a year, introducing customers to a variety of interesting beers. The car park is off a side road.
≠(Fulwell)🖴🐾P

Roebuck
72 Hampton Road, TW12 1JN
✪ 11-11 (11.30 Fri & Sat); 12-4, 7-10.30 Sun
☎ (020) 8255 8133
St Austell Tribute; Sambrook's Junction; Young's Bitter; guest beers Ⓗ
There is almost always something new to see whenever you enter this Victorian corner local, but spotting it among such an extensive and eclectic collection is not easy; the wickerwork Harley Davidson is still the star of the show. Traffic lights in the bar and cosy award-winning garden (with octagonal gazebo for smokers) turn amber, then red as closing time approaches. There is also a summer house for cooler summer evenings. The two guest beers change regularly.
♒✪♨◑≠(Fulwell)🖴♣᠊

Harlington

White Hart ✅
158 High Street, UB3 5DP
✪ 11-11 (11.30 Thu; midnight Fri & Sat) ☎ (020) 8759 9608
⊕ whitehartharlington.co.uk
Fuller's London Pride, ESB, seasonal beer; guest beer Ⓗ
Large Grade II-listed Fuller's pub, refurbished in 2009, standing proud at the north end of the village. The single bar allows access to an open-plan area for sport on large TV screens and through to a seated area favoured by diners. Local history is the theme of the wall displays enjoyed by locals and visitors from nearby Heathrow Airport. Food is home cooked. ✪◑♿🖴(90,140,H98)P᠊

Hayes

Botwell Inn ✅
25-29 Coldharbour Lane, UB3 3EB
✪ 9am-midnight ☎ (020) 8848 3112
Courage Directors; Greene King Abbot; Ruddles Best Bitter; guest beers Ⓗ
A large Wetherspoon shop conversion with several areas for dining and drinking, with large settees in one part. There is a paved area to the front and a patio at the rear with large market-type parasols with heaters. Several beer festivals are held annually. At least one Westons cider is available.
Q✪◑♿≠(Hayes & Harlington)🖴🐾᠊

Hayes End

Angel ✅
697 Uxbridge Road, UB4 8HX

✪ 11-midnight (1am Fri & Sat) ☎ (020) 8848 8020
⊕ angelpub.net
Fuller's Chiswick, London Pride; Gale's HSB; guest beers Ⓗ
A real community local containing three bars, although the large back bar is mostly used for functions. The small saloon bar is quiet and the traditional atmosphere is maintained in the larger public bar, which has a pool table annexe. The pub is in both darts and pool leagues, has two six-a-side football teams and sponsors Hayes Alexander football team. Quiz and chips on Wednesdays and bingo on Sundays both support local charities.
Q✪◖⒠⊟(427,607,H98)♣P⅃

Hounslow

Moon Under Water ❷
84-88 Staines Road, TW3 3LF (W end of High St)
✪ 9am (12 Sun)-midnight ☎ (020) 8572 7506
Courage Directors; Greene King Abbot; Ruddles Best Bitter; guest beers Ⓗ
Early Wetherspoon shop conversion in original style and still displaying many local history panels and photos. Very popular, it has a diverse customer base. There are normally five guest ales, often locally sourced, but far more at festival times when all 12 handpumps offer different beers. The cider is usually Westons Old Rosie, supplemented by others for festivals. Children are welcome until 8.30pm; the rear is considered the family area and off that is an outside patio.
Q✪◖⒠⊖(Hounslow Central)⊟♦⅃

Isleworth

Red Lion Ⓛ ❷
92-94 Linkfield Road, TW7 6QJ
✪ 12-11.30 (11 Tue; midnight Fri & Sat); 12-11 Sun
☎ (020) 8560 1457 ⊕ red-lion.info
Greene King Morland Bitter; guest beers Ⓗ
Spacious two-bar free house with a strong community focus and often something going on: a performance by its own theatre group, live music (Mon, Wed and Sat eves, Sun afternoons), or the Thursday quiz. Up to eight guest beers complement the regular bitter, and up to five ciders or perries. Twice-yearly beer festivals feature champion beers; other weekend festivals have regional themes. Lunches are offered daily (except Mon) and evening meals Tuesday-Saturday. Local CAMRA Pub of the Year 2009 and 2010. ✪◖⒠⅋⇌⊟♦⅃

Southall

Conservative & Unionist Club Ⓛ
Fairlawn, High Street, UB1 3HB
✪ 11.30-2.30, 7-11; 11.30-3, 6-11 Fri & Sat; 12-3, 7-10.30 Sun
☎ (020) 8574 0261
Rebellion IPA, seasonal beers; guest beers Ⓗ
Virtually the last real ale outlet in this historic market town, situated behind the former town hall. A selection of beers from the Rebellion range is to be found inside. Meals are served some lunchtimes, there are four snooker tables and various events are held most evenings. This is an ideal meeting place before enjoying a curry in one of the many local restaurants. Show this Guide or a CAMRA membership card for entry. ✪◖⇌⊟♣P⅃

Stockley Park

White House ❷
The Arena, Bennetsfield Road, UB11 1AA
✪ 8am-10 (11 Thu-Sat) ☎ (020) 8589 7870
Fuller's London Pride; Ruddles Best Bitter; guest beer Ⓗ
A fairly modern Wetherspoon's Lloyds No.1 bar set in a small commercial complex servicing the Stockley Park business community and golf course. The long bar/restaurant, with a charming conservatory at the end, leads out on to a decked area overlooking a small lake, lovely on a summer's day. There is an outside patio with heaters and a large grassed area. A Westons cider is in the fridge. Q✪◖⒢⒠⊟(350,A10,U5)♦P⅃

Teddington

Clock House
69 High Street, TW11 8HA
✪ 11-11.30 (midnight Fri & Sat; 11 Sun) ☎ (020) 8977 3909
⊕ theclockhousepub.com
Fuller's London Pride; Sharp's Cornish Coaster; Taylor Landlord; Twickenham Naked Ladies Ⓗ
Popular former Isleworth Brewery pub that underwent a major makeover in 2008. The main bar area features a large traditional log fire. A comfortable seating area can be found to one side of the bar, and a small secluded dining room offers a good selection of food. There is access through the bar to an outside paved area with a covered section with TV. A function room is available and a small car park to the rear. Wi-Fi is free.
⌂✪◖⇌⊟P⅃

Masons Arms
41 Walpole Road, TW11 8PJ
✪ 12-11 (11.30 Fri & Sat); 12-10.30 Sun ☎ (020) 8977 6521
Downton Quadhop; Sambrook's Junction; guest beers Ⓗ
Small side-street community pub built in 1860, recently refurbished after becoming a free house in 2010. The four handpumps have bespoke wood handles with inlaid hardwoods, and the paraphernalia adorning the walls leaves you in no doubt that the publican is a beer enthusiast. Scrumpy cider is also served. The digital jukebox complements the convivial atmosphere on many evenings. Occasional quiz and themed nights take place. To the rear is a small patio.
⌂✪⒢⇌⊟♣♦⅃

Twickenham

Fox
39 Church Street, TW1 3NR
✪ 11-11.30 (midnight Thu; 12.30am Fri & Sat); 11-10.30 Sun
☎ (020) 8892 1535 ⊕ thefoxpubtwickenham.co.uk
Fuller's London Pride; Sharp's Doom Bar; Twickenham Naked Ladies; guest beers Ⓗ
A pub that has been at the heart of Twickenham for over 300 years. The street is now higher than when it was first built, so that visitors must step down into the small bar area. A much-needed restoration in 2011 has retained its character and original features. Live music with local bands is popular at weekends. It offers British-based food, a private, oak-panelled dining room and a superb beer garden with wheelchair access and facilities.
⌂Q☼✪◖⒢⇌⊟

Prince Blucher

124 The Green, TW2 5AG

✪ 11-11 (midnight Fri & Sat); 12-11 Sun ☎ (020) 8894 1824
Fuller's Chiswick Bitter, Discovery, London Pride, ESB,
seasonal beers Ⓗ

Historic 19th-century pub, the first built on the
newly enclosed Twickenham Green and reputedly
one of only two remaining in Britain still to pay
homage to the Duke of Wellington's left flanker at
Waterloo. Four separate bar areas will suit most
tastes. The landlord of 15 years' standing offers
home-cooked food all day, and in summer hosts
hog roasts and barbecues in the child-friendly
garden. Food and real ale festivals also feature.
▲Q✿❁◗⬤➤⇌(Strawberry Hill)🚌(110,490,H22)P⁼

Prince of Wales ☗

136 Hampton Road, TW2 5QR

✪ 12 (4 Mon)-11 (midnight Thu-Sat); 12-10.30 Sun
☎ (020) 8894 5054 ⊕ princeofwalestwickenham.co.uk
Marston's Pedigree; Ringwood Fortyniner;
Twickenham Naked Ladies; guest beers Ⓗ

An inn on this site was the final staging post on the
Windsor to London stagecoach route more than
150 years ago. The original stables survive and are
listed. Once an Isleworth Brewery pub and now run
by Lea Taverns, this is an unspoilt, two-room
community pub serving French-style cuisine.
Acoustic music plays on Tuesday and a quiz night is
hosted on Thursday. A comfortable child- and dog-
friendly hostelry, there is an attractive garden
outside. Local CAMRA Pub of the Year 2011.
▲Q✿❁◗⬤➤⇌(Fulwell/Strawberry Hill)🚌♣⁼

Sussex Arms ⓥ

15 Staines Road, TW2 5BG

✪ 12-11 (10.30 Sun) ☎ (020) 8894 7468
⊕ thesussexarmstwickenham.co.uk
Beer range varies Ⓗ

This restored community pub has become a firm
favourite with locals since reopening as an ale &
cider house. Eighteen handpumps dispense real
ales from independent breweries, usually including
Twickenham, plus ciders and perries. Acoustic blues
features on Tuesdays and Irish music fortnightly.
The kitchen serves Anthea's world-famous pies and
much more. A child- and dog-friendly pub, it has a
huge, well-equipped garden including a boules
pitch. Get your 10th pint free with the pub's loyalty
card. Wi-Fi is free too.
▲❁◗⬤➤⇌(Strawberry Hill)🚌(110,490,H22)⬤

William Webb Ellis ⓥ

24 London Road, TW1 3RR

✪ 9am-11.30 (midnight Thu; 1am Fri & Sat)
☎ (020) 8744 4300
Courage Directors; Fuller's London Pride, ESB; Greene
King IPA; Twickenham Naked Ladies; guest beers Ⓗ

Wetherspoon Lloyds No.1 bar in the centre of the
home town of English rugby named after the
alleged inventor of the game. It is large and
spacious, with live news and sports on silent
screens. Twelve handpumps are in constant use.
The rear patio is open to 9pm, food is served all day
and children are welcome until 8pm. A Monday Ale
Club offers reduced prices and third-of-a-pint
glasses. Free Wi-Fi. ✿❁◗⬤&⇌🚌⬤⁼

Uxbridge

Load of Hay

33 Villier Street, UB8 2PU

✪ 12-11.45 ☎ (01895) 234676
Sharp's Doom Bar; guest beers Ⓗ

Originally the officers' mess of the Elthorne Light
Militia, this became a pub in the 1870s. A genuine
free house, it usually sells two guest beers, mostly
from small and microbreweries, and at least two
real ciders. The pub hosts darts matches, an open
crib competition on Thursday and a quiz on
Tuesday. Live music on some weekend evenings
includes folk, and modern and traditional jazz. Car
parking is limited. ▲❁◗⬤&🚌(U3)♣⬤P⁼

Whitton

Admiral Nelson ⓥ

123 Nelson Road, TW2 7BB

✪ 11-11 (midnight Fri & Sat); 11-10.30 Sun
☎ (020) 8894 9998
Fuller's Chiswick Bitter, Discovery, London Pride, ESB,
seasonal beers Ⓗ

A former beer house, fully licensed in 1861 and
rebuilt in the 1930s, this large landmark pub with a
small patio area on the side stands in a prominent
position on the crossroads at the end of the high
street. The pub has both Nelsonian and rugby
themes. A 15-minute walk from Twickenham
Stadium and Twickenham Stoop, it is a haven for
rugby fans on match days. Sunday is quiz night.
Large TVs provide sports coverage.
▲❁◗⬤&⇌🚌(281,481,H22)⁼

Magpie & Stump

This favoured tavern, sacred to the evening orgies of Mr Lowten and his companions, was
what ordinary people would designate a public-house. That the landlord was a man of
money-making turn was sufficiently testified by the fact of a small bulkhead beneath the
tap-room window, in size and shape not unlike a sedan-chair, being underlet to a mender
of shoes; and that he was a being of philanthropic mind was evident from the protection
he afforded to a pieman, who vended his delicacies without fear of interruption on the
very door-step.

In the lower windows, which were decorated with curtains of a saffron hue, dangled two
or three printed cards bearing reference to Devonshire cider and Dantzig [sic] spruce,
while a large blackboard announcing in white letters to an enlightened public, that there
were 500,000 barrels of double stout in the cellars of the establishment, left the mind in a
not unpleasing state of doubt and uncertainty as to the precise direction in the bowels of
the earth, in which this mighty cavern might be supposed to extend.

Charles Dickens, The Pickwick Papers, 1837

London's Best Beer, Pubs & Bars

Des de Moor

London's Best Beer, Pubs & Bars is the essential guide to beer drinking in London. This practical book is packed with detailed maps and easy-to-use listings to help you find the best places to enjoy perfect pints in the capital. Laid out by area, find the best pubs serving the best British and international beers wherever you are. Features tell you more about London's rich history of brewing and the city's vibrant modern brewing scene, where well-known brands rub shoulders with tiny micro-breweries. The venue listings include a variety of real ale pubs, bars and other outlets with detailed information on opening hours, local landmarks, and public transport links to make planning any excursion quick and easy.

£12.99   ISBN 978-1-85249-285-4   CAMRA members' price £10.99   336 pages

For this and other books on beer and pubs visit the CAMRA bookshop at www.camra.org.uk/books

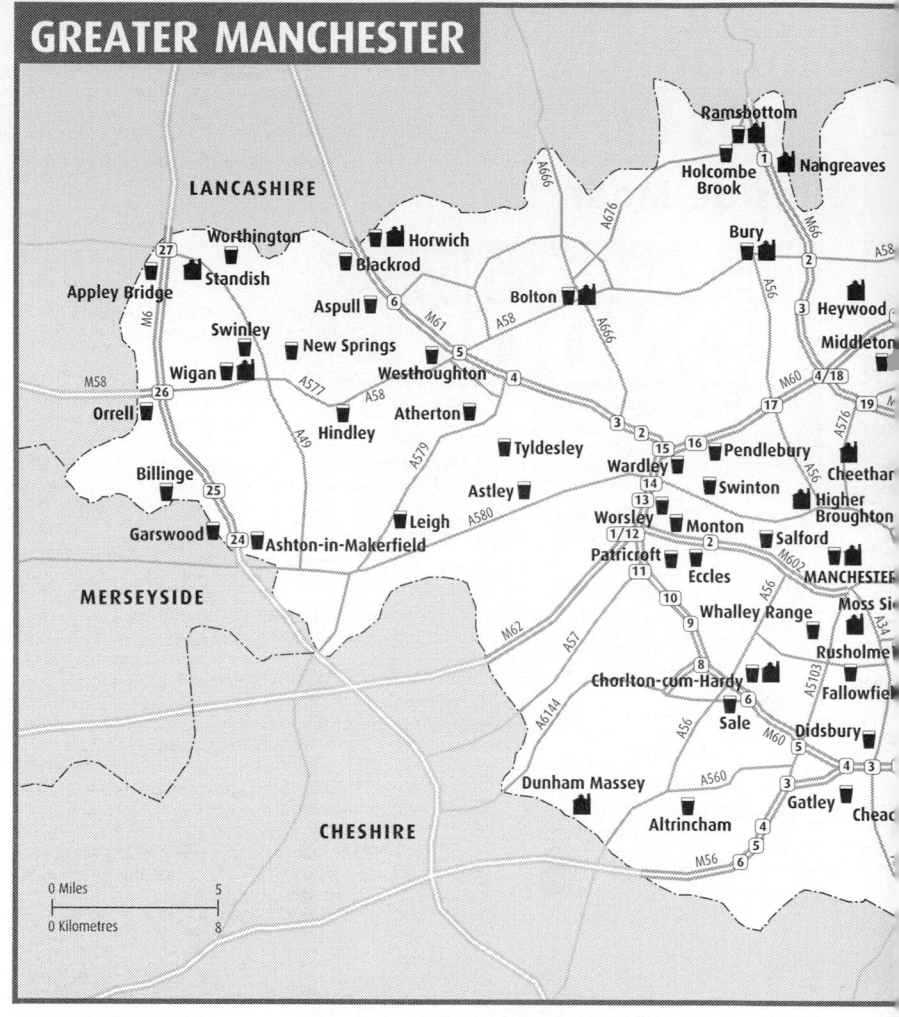

GREATER MANCHESTER

Altrincham

Costello's Bar ♥ 🛚

18 Goose Green, WA14 1DW

✪ 12-11 (midnight Fri & Sat); 12-10.30 Sun

☎ (0161) 929 0903 ⊕ costellosbar.co.uk

Dunham Massey Big Tree Bitter; guest beers ⊞

The Dunham Massey Brewing Company's only pub
and its brewery tap. The company brews over 25
different recipes and showcases them all in the
bar. Look out for the occasional guest from other
local breweries, too. Situated in Altrincham's
exclusive Goose Green, the pub opened in late
2010. It has a modern feel and is ever popular with
locals and visitors alike. ❀ 🖑 🗢 🖷 🖵 ♠

Old Market Tavern 🛚

Old Market Place, WA14 4DN (on A56)

✪ 12-11 (midnight Wed-Sat) ☎ (0161) 927 7062

**Caledonian Deuchars IPA; George Wright Drunken
Duck, Northern Lights; Phoenix Arizona; guest
beers** ⊞

Entertainment is always on offer here – Monday is
open mic jam night, Wednesday quiz night (with a
free buffet), Thursday open acoustic session and
rock bands play on Friday, Saturday and Sunday
evenings. Eleven handpumps are almost always in
use, with seven guests coming from local
microbreweries. A whiteboard opposite the bar
lists what is available including a real cider. Meals
are served until 4pm and children are welcome.
🏚 ❀ 🖑 🗢 🖷 🖵 ♠ 🖕 ⚓

Appley Bridge

Wheatsheaf ✔

287 Miles Lane, WN6 9DQ (on B5375 Shevington-
Appley Bridge road)

✪ 3 (12 Sun)-11; 2-midnight Fri, 12-midnight Sat

☎ (01257) 252299 ⊕ thewheatsheafatappleybridge.co.uk

Tetley Bitter; guest beers ⊞

Comfortable suburban pub within half a mile walk
of the Leeds & Liverpool Canal and railway station.
It has been revitalised by the current licensees
since taking over in 2009, and now has handpumps
dispensing Tetley Bitter, three rotating guests
always including a blonde beer, and a real cider.
The lounge bar area and homely quiet area are
divided by a fish tank, there is sport on TV in the
vault, and several areas outside, one also with a TV.

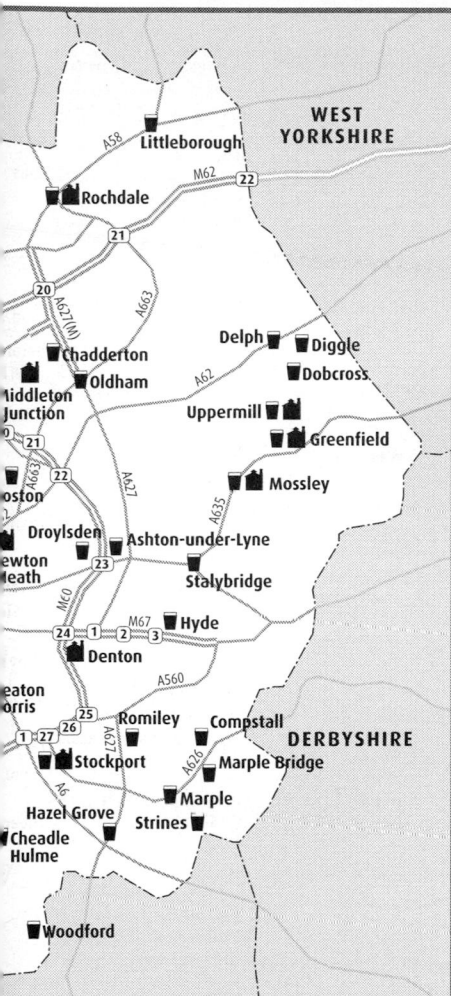

🕒 8am-midnight ☎ (0161) 339 9670
Greene King Abbot; Ruddles Best Bitter; Thwaites Wainwright; guest beers Ⓗ
Directly facing the fine Victorian Market Hall and square, this Wetherspoon pub has become one of the premier real ale destinations in the town centre. Families are welcome in the lower level; above are the bar and lounge/dining area which leads to the rear entrance and outdoor patio/smoking area. Wetherspoon's usual good value applies to the beers and food. 🏠◁️🚶⅙⩲🚃♿⌟—

Dog & Pheasant

528 Oldham Road, OL7 9PQ
🕒 12-11 (11.30 Fri & Sat; 10.30 Sun) ☎ (0161) 330 4894
Banks's Mild; Marston's Burton Bitter, Pedigree; guest beers Ⓗ
Nicknamed the Top Dog, this popular, friendly local near the Medlock Valley Country Park has been a regular Guide entry over the years. It has a large bar serving three areas, plus another room at the front. Up to three guest beers from the Marston's portfolio are available at all times, and the menu of good-value food includes vegetarian options. A quiz is held on Tuesday and Thursday evenings. Home to a local hiking group known as the Bog Trotters. 🚶🏠◁️🚃(409,419)P⌟—

Junction Inn Ⓛ

Mossley Road, Hazelhurst, OL6 9BX (on A670 2 miles N of town)
🕒 12-2.30 (not Mon & Tue), 5-11.30 (1am Fri); 12-1am Sat; 12-midnight Sun ☎ (0161) 343 1822
Robinson's 1892, Dizzy Blonde, Unicorn Ⓗ
A small pub of great character, the Junction remains little changed since the 19th century. Built of local stone, it is situated close to Ashton golf course and open country, and Hartshead Pike dominates the scene. The cosy, welcoming rooms include a front tap room served by the small bar through a hatch. The recently refurbished kitchen offers freshly prepared food to accompany the Robinson's beers. Q🏠🏠◁️🚃(350)♣

Home-made pizza and bar snacks are available evenings and weekends.
Q🏠🏠🚶⩲🚃(611,612,635)♣♦P⌟—

Ashton-in-Makerfield

Sir Thomas Gerard Ⓛ ✅

2 Gerard Street, WN4 9AN (on A58)
🕒 8am-midnight (1am Fri & Sat) ☎ (01942) 713519
Greene King Abbot; Ruddles County; guest beers Ⓗ
CAMRA award-winning Wetherspoon pub close to Haydock Park Racecourse. There are 12 handpumps with local ales often from Coach House, George Wright and Phoenix among others. As well as the national beer festivals, other themed festivals are held during the year. There is a beer garden for the hot summer months and during the winter the pub has a warm, cosy atmosphere.
🏠◁️⅙🚃(320,600,601)♦P⌟—

Ashton-under-Lyne

Ash Tree Ⓛ ✅

11-16 Wellington Road, OL6 6DA

INDEPENDENT BREWERIES

AllGates Wigan
Bank Top Bolton
Blackedge Horwich (NEW)
Boggart Hole Clough Manchester: Newton Heath
Bootleg Chorlton-cum-Hardy
Brightside Bury
Dunham Massey Dunham Massey
Dunscar Bridge Bolton
Green Mill Rochdale
Greenfield Greenfield
Holt Cheetham
Hornbeam Denton
Hydes Moss Side
Irwell Works Ramsbottom
Lees Middleton Junction
Leyden Nangreaves
Marble Manchester
Millstone Mossley
Outstanding Bury
Phoenix Heywood
Pictish Rochdale
Prospect Standish
Quantum Stockport
Robinson's Stockport
Saddleworth Uppermill
Star Inn Higher Broughton
Wilson Potter Middleton (NEW)

Aspull

Gerrard Arms Hotel 🅛
615 Bolton Road, WN2 1PZ (on B5239)
☼ 12 (4 Mon & Tue)-11; 12-midnight Fri & Sat
☎ (01942) 832346 ⊕ thegerrard.com
Bank Top Flat Cap; Prospect Silver Tally; Tetley Mild, Bitter; guest beer 🇭
A gem of a community pub, attracting visitors from far and wide for its excellent locally sourced food. Two TVs screen sport, usually with the volume off. A quiz night with supper is on Thursday. No under-16s allowed. Adjacent to Borsdane Wood, a local nature reserve. ⌖⊄🄿⊱

Astley

Boathouse Inn
Higher Green Lane, M29 7JB
☼ 12-midnight (11 Sun) ☎ (01942) 883300
Greene King Ruddles County; Taylor Landlord 🇭
Situated on the towpath of the Bridgewater Canal, the pub is located off Higher Green Lane. It was originally built with stabling for horses that pulled the barges. There is an old fashioned tap room with pictures of the area past and present, and a spacious lounge with wood decor, with big tables where you can spread out with the newspapers. Live music features most weekends. Good ales are served alongside excellent food. ⌖⊄🄿

Bull's Head ✅
504 Manchester Road, M29 7BP
☼ 11.30-11 (midnight Fri-Sun) ☎ (01942) 887109
Black Sheep Ale; Thwaites Original, Wainwright 🇭
A large, comfortable pub offering a good range of beers – you can even try before you buy. Outside, there are various seating areas, some with heaters for when it is chilly, plus lawns for sun worshippers. Quiz nights are held on Sunday, Monday and Wednesday. The pub welcomes children over 14 when dining with an adult in the evening. Occasional beer festivals are held. ⌖⌖⊄🄿

Atherton

Atherton Arms
6 Tyldesley Road, M46 9DD
☼ 11-11.30; 11.30-1am Fri & Sat; 12-12.30am Sun
☎ (01942) 01942 875996 ⊕ athertonarms.co.uk
Holts Mild, Bitter 🇭
Traditional public house with a great atmosphere and facilities, including a full-sized snooker table and function room. The pub is known for its superb beer garden, which has TV screens and heaters. The beer is competitively priced and promotions change on a monthly basis, with Happy Days Monday to Friday. Mid-week, the pub offers a wide range of entertainment. Friday and Saturday is Steve's karaoke and there is live entertainment every Sunday. ⌖⊄🄿⊱

Jolly Nailor 🅛
20-22 Market Street, M46 0DN
☼ 12-11 (midnight Sat & Sun) ☎ (01942) 792640
⊕ thejollynailor.com
AllGates California, seasonal beers 🇭
The Jolly Nailor is a revitalised local situated on the main Market Street in Atherton. The pub was purchased by AllGates in early 2010 and refurbished with the addition of six handpumps selling a range of cask beers plus draught cider. The interior is divided into three areas for live music, TV

sport and the weekly quiz. There is still space for the ladies' and men's darts teams. Meals are served every day except Wednesday. ⌖⊄🄿♣♠

Pendle Witch 🅛 ✅
2-4 Warburton Place, M46 0EQ
☼ 11 (12 Sun)-midnight ☎ (01942) 884537
Moorhouse's Black Cat, Premier Bitter, Pride of Pendle, Blonde Witch, Pendle Witches Brew, seasonal beers 🇭
A real gem hidden down a narrow alley. The entrance, part of a conservatory, leads to an open-plan bar that serves the full range of Moorhouse's beers plus up to two guests. The games area has a pool table and large-screen TV. Regular rock nights are hosted and occasional beer festivals are held. Food is served during the day, with a cheese night on Thursday. There is a well-kept garden for summer. Close to town-centre parking. ⌖⊄♣♠⊱

Billinge

Hare & Hounds 🅛
142 Upholland Road, WN5 7JH
☼ 4-11 (midnight Fri); 12-midnight Sat; 12-11 Sun
Thwaites Wainwright; guest beers 🇭
Friendly, welcoming, red-brick pub divided into a lounge and tap room (once the smoking room). Five handpumps dispense one regular beer and three guests. TVs in both rooms show live sport, especially rugby (ex Rugby League star Nick Du Toit is the licensee). Local league darts is played. Entertainment is provided on Saturday evenings and local pies are available. Wigan CAMRA Best New Cask Outlet 2011. ⌖⌖⊄(197,352)♣🄿⊱

Masons Arms 🅛
99 Carr Mill Road, WN5 7TY (off A571)
☼ 2-11 (midnight Thu & Fri); 12-midnight Sat; 12-10.30 Sun
☎ (01744) 603572 ⊕ masonsarmsbillinge.co.uk
Beer range varies 🇭
Built of local stone in 1779, the pub has been run by the same family for over 200 years. It is well placed for walking or cycling the local area. Five handpumps offer beers from George Wright and others. Mid-week sees regular folk and quiz nights. There is a luxurious smoking shelter with a bison's head and log burner, and the beer garden overlooks fields to the rear. The pub is just the place for a quiet chat as the Sky Sports TV is usually silent. Free Wi-Fi. ⌖⌖♠🄿⊱

Blackrod

Poacher ✅
Scot Lane, BL6 5SG
☼ 12-12.30am (1.30am Fri & Sat; midnight Sun)
☎ (01942) 832203
Jennings Dark Mild, Bitter, Cumberland Ale; Marston's Pedigree 🇭
Welcome new entry to the Guide, catering for the older, discerning drinker. A unique feature of this pub is that it has its own mini market with milk, bread and other groceries available. Up to five guest beers are served from the Marston's range, plus more than 60 single malts. Entertainment is hosted on the last Saturday of the month. Q⌖⊄≠(575)🄿⊱

Bolton

Alma ✓
152-154 Bradshawgate, BL2 1BA
✪ 12-1am; 4-midnight Sun & Mon ☎ (01204) 364113
Wychwood Hobgoblin Ⓗ
Small terraced public house on one of Bolton's busiest streets, just 300 yards from Trinity Street bus/rail interchange. Inside it has a wonderful cast-iron range and collages in the Gents and Ladies toilets. The guest beers come from the Marston's list, with up to three available. Popular with bikers and heavy rock/metal fans.
🏚️🏠🐕🚌♣🐾ⁱ🏚️

Bank Top Brewery Tap Ⓛ
68-70 Belmont Road, BL1 7AN (400yds from A666/A58 jct)
✪ 12-11 (11.30 Fri & Sat) ☎ (01204) 302837
Beer range varies Ⓗ
Bolton CAMRA Pub of the Year 2011, this is the brewery tap for Bank Top. It serves the complete range of Bank Top beers rotating on nine handpulls plus a guest. Beers are competitively priced and the brewery owner is often on site. A warm, comfortable pub on the edge of the West Pennine Moors, it is popular with walkers and their dogs. The large outdoor drinking area is busy in summer.
Q🏠🐕🚃👶🚌(537)♣ⁱ🏚️

Barristers
7 Bradshawgate, BL1 1HJ (on A575, near Market Cross)
✪ 12-1am (2am Fri & Sat) ☎ (01204) 365174
Black Sheep Best Bitter; Moorhouse's Blond Witch; Tetley Bitter Ⓗ
Barristers Bar is part of the Swan Hotel, a listed building dating from 1845. The wood-panelled interior has been retained and tastefully decorated to recreate a traditional pub atmosphere. The regular range of real ales is supplemented by six guests including some from local independent breweries. A heated courtyard with tables is used as a smoking area, and disabled toilet facilities are available. A pianist or guitarist plays live music most evenings. 🏠🐕🚌ⁱ🏚️

Bob's Smithy Inn Ⓛ
1448 Chorley Old Road, BL1 7PX (on B6226 uphill from A58 ring road) SD674111
✪ 4-11 (midnight Fri); 12-midnight Sat; 12-11 Sun
☎ (01204) 842622
Bank Top Flat Cap; Taylor Best Bitter; Tetley Bitter; guest beers Ⓗ
An intimate stone-built hostelry on the edge of the moors, now boasting its own restaurant, handy for walkers and visitors to the Reebok Stadium. The inn is some 200 years old and is named after a blacksmith who allegedly spent more time here than he did at his smithy across the road. This is a genuine free house, offering guest beers from small independent breweries. Dogs are welcome and there is a covered smoking area at the side of the pub. 🏚️Q🏠🐕🚌(125,126)Pⁱ🏚️

Brewhouse Ⓛ
987 Blackburn Road, Dunscar, BL1 7LG (on A666)
✪ 11-11 ☎ (01204) 301372
Dunscar Bridge Bombshell, Steeplejack, Wicketkeeper, Clocking Off Ⓗ
The Brewhouse is the tap for Dunscar Bridge Brewery, with the brewing plant viewable from the main bar area. Up to four guest beers are also available. The pub was formerly the Cheetham

Arms and is situated on the A666 two miles north of Bolton town centre. Quiz night is Wednesday. A friendly family establishment, it has four en-suite bedrooms and a new outdoor area for warmer weather. 🏠🛏️🐕🍴🚌(537)♠Pⁱ🏚️

Dog & Partridge Ⓛ
22 Manor Street, BL1 1TU
✪ 7-3am; 4-4am Sat ☎ (01204) 388596
Bank Top Flat Cap, Port O Call; Prospect Silver Tally; Thwaites Wainwright Ⓗ
Small free house just off Bolton town centre, popular with both young and old. Bands play every weekend, with an excellent outdoor staged area for summer gigs. Beers are competitively priced for a town-centre pub. A large selection of board games is available. 🏠🐕♣ⁱ🏚️

Finishers Arms ✓
487 Church Road, Heaton, BL1 5RE (opp Heaton Cricket Club)
✪ 12 (3 Mon)-11 (midnight Fri & Sat); 12-10.30 Sun
☎ (01204) 848244
Jennings Cumberland Ale; Thwaites Wainwright; Wells Bombardier Ⓗ
Situated opposite Heaton Cricket Club, this is one of the area's oldest public houses, dating from the mid-1700s. A friendly, homely drinkers pub, the guest beers are quite often Bank Top or Dunscar Bridge beers. It has a golf society, quiz nights and the occasional artiste, as well as competitively priced home-cooked food. A book library is available. Q🚌(501)♣ⁱ🏚️

King's Head
52 Junction Road, Deane, BL3 4NA (just off A676)
✪ 3.30 (12 Sat & Sun)-11 ☎ (01204) 62609
Bank Top Flat Cap; Wells Bombardier Ⓗ
Set back off the road in a lovely setting and close to Deane parish church, the oldest church in Bolton. The inn is a stone-built Grade II-listed building dating from the 17th century – it was named the King's Head in 1824 and was primarily used as a travellers' overnight stop. It has three rooms, two with low timber-framed ceilings, the other with a cast-iron range. At the rear is a bowling green, children's play area and outdoor seating. Local CAMRA Pub of the Year 2010. Q🏠🚌(540,715)Pⁱ🏚️

Spinning Mule ✓
Unit 2, Nelson Square, BL1 1JT (just off Bradshawgate)
✪ 9-midnight (1am Fri & Sat) ☎ (01204) 533339
Greene King Abbot; Ruddles Best Bitter; guest beers Ⓗ
Newly built in 1998, this town-centre pub is an open-plan split-level building with a comfortable dining area in a modern Wetherspoon style. It is named after Samuel Crompton's Mule, a revolutionary invention in cotton spinning that made Bolton famous throughout the world. The Mule supports Moorhouse's and other local breweries. Q🐕👶🚌

Bury

Art Picture House ✓
36 Haymarket Street, BL9 0AY (opp Metrolink station)
✪ 8am-midnight (2am Fri; 3am Sat) ☎ (0161) 705 4040
Greene King Abbot; Ruddles Best Bitter; guest beers Ⓗ
A beautifully restored former 1920s cinema featuring stills of black and white films and old historic photos of Bury's past times, this is a

Wetherspoon Lloyds No.1. With up to eight handpumps, it offers changing beers from around the country, regularly including Moorhouse's and Phoenix beers and others from local breweries. One handpump is reserved for real cider. Quiet during the day but music plays at night. ◑&◫◲◆

Automatic Café & Malt Real Ale Bar ℒ

Derby Hall, Market Street, BL9 0BW (500yds N from Interchange)
✪ 10am-11 (midnight Fri & Sat); 12-10.30 Sun
☎ (0161) 763 9399 ⊕ automaticcafé.com
Outstanding Silver Fox; guest beers ⊞
This welcoming independent café, restaurant and bar shares the Derby Hall with two theatres and an art gallery. The atmosphere is relaxed and comfortable, making it a popular choice with a discerning clientele. The smaller Malt Bar, with the cellar showing off an electric pulley system, provides an overspill for the busy daytime food trade, while at night it becomes a lovely, quiet, cosy space to enjoy a pint. Foreign bottled beers include Leffe, Duvel, Chimay and Budvar.
❀◑&≈(Bolton St)◫◲♣'–♬

Black Bull ✔

8 Lowercroft Road, BL8 2EY (on B6196)
✪ 12-midnight (1am Fri & Sat) ☎ (0161) 761 5961
⊕ theblackbullbury.co.uk
Thwaites Nutty Black, Original, Wainwright, Lancaster Bomber, seasonal beers; guest beers ⊞
Recently refurbished family-run local offering a warm and friendly atmosphere enjoyed by drinkers and diners alike. Guest beers are from Thwaites 1807 Cask Club range. Excellent meals, served daily, are prepared mainly from locally sourced top-quality produce. Diners are advised to book as the pub's reputation creates high demand for tables. A previous winner of the Thwaites Real Ale Pub of the Year. ❀◑&◫(486,510)P'–

Lamb Inn ℒ

533 Tottington Road, BL8 1UB (on B6123)
✪ 4.30-11 (midnight Fri); 1-midnight Sat & Sun
☎ (0161) 764 2714
Beer range varies ⊞
Built in 1831, the Lamb is a popular family-run pub. A stone fireplace with open fire and seating with plenty of scatter cushions helps to create a traditional and comfortable ambience. The landlord is enthusiastic about his real ales and regularly features beers from George Wright, Mallinsons, Phoenix, Brightside and Moorhouse's. The TVs are mute except for selected football matches and other major sporting events. Outside, the enclosed beer garden is busy during the summer months.
≛❀◑◫(468,469)P'–

Robert Peel ℒ ✔

5-10 Market Street, BL9 0LD (near parish church)
✪ 9am-midnight (1am Fri & Sat) ☎ (0161) 764 7287
Greene King Abbot; Ruddles Best Bitter; guest beers ⊞
Situated in Bury's cultural quarter, the Robert Peel is well established, popular and has the largest open public area in Bury, with a mixture of tables and booths. This Wetherspoon pub bears the name of the local mill owner and MP whose son became prime minister and founded the modern police force. The decor also celebrates other local worthies. Ciders are from Gwynt y Ddraig, Westons and Thatchers. ◑≈(Bolton St)◫◲◆

Trackside ℒ

East Lancashire Railway, Bolton Street Station, BL9 0EY (next to Bolton St station)
✪ 12 (9 Wed & Thu)-midnight; 9-12.30am Fri-Sun
☎ (0161) 764 6461 ⊕ eastlancsrailway.org.uk
Beer range varies ⊞
The Trackside has an enviable reputation for its ever-changing range of nine hand pulled cask ales from near and far, and boasts an appealing range of ciders, continental beers and malt whiskies. Set against the backdrop of the East Lancashire Railway, it is a true gem, providing a great venue for a quiet pint while reliving the days of steam. Hot food and snacks are available most days. The station platform provides an outdoor seating area. Ciders are from Thatchers, Broadoak and Westons.
❀◑&≈(Bolton St)◫◲◆'–

Chadderton

Rose of Lancaster ✔

7 Haigh Lane, OL1 2TQ
✪ 11.30-11 (11.30 Fri & Sat); 12-11 Sun ☎ (0161) 654 9245
Lees Brewer's Dark, Bitter, seasonal beers ⊞
Overlooking open countryside next to the Rochdale Canal, this large pub has a separate lounge and vault plus an extended area for dining. It attracts an eclectic mix of locals, walkers, canal boaters and diners. Food is popular and well priced. Quick and cheerful service adds to the experience, as well as a large range of Lees ales. There is a large outdoor drinking area for good weather. Buses and trains are a few strides away.
❀◑&≈(Mills Hill)◫(59,64)♣P'–

Cheadle

Cheshire Line Tavern

Manchester Road, SK8 2NZ (just N of M60 motorway bridge)
✪ 12-11 (10.30 Sun) ☎ (0161) 428 3352
Banks's Bitter; guest beers ⊞
A former railway station, this is a pleasant place to enjoy a drink or a meal. Situated below road level, it has an attractive twin-gabled frontage. Inside it feels very traditional with the central bar dividing several comfortable areas. At the rear, on the now enclosed former platform, you can see the occasional passing freight train. The Manchester Mini Car Club meets here every Wednesday. The guest beers tend to be from the extended Marston's stable.
≛Q☾❀◑&≈(East Didsbury)◫(X57,130)P'–

Crown ✔

81 High Street, SK8 1AA (on A560, opp church)
✪ 11-11 (midnight Fri; 12.30am Sat) ☎ (0161) 495 7247
Hydes Mild, Original Bitter, seasonal beers; guest beers ⊞
Some years ago Hydes converted this from a fish shop to a pub. It has a narrow interior that broadens out towards the rear, a bar accommodating seven handpumps and a raised seating area. A new seating arrangement has been added recently to give more space at the front. The pub attracts drinkers and weekly quiz-goers. Live artists at the weekend add a touch of pizazz. Hydes Best Tenanted pub for 2011 and runner-up Best-Kept Cellar. &≈(X57,371)'–

Cheadle Hulme

Cheadle Hulme

47 Station Road, SK8 7AA (on A5149 by railway station)
✪ 12-11 (midnight Fri & Sat); 12-10.30 Sun
☎ (0161) 485 4706
Holt Mild, Bitter, IPA, seasonal beers; guest beers Ⓗ
Formerly the Junction, this well-managed Holt house has an extensive bar serving four comfortably furnished spaces separated by half-glazed screens; one area has a dartboard. Staff are friendly and the service efficient. The pub maintains a traditional feel while serving excellent food, with meals from the carvery/hob available until 8.30pm daily. The regular Holt range is supplemented by up to four guest ales. Quiz night is Thursday, while one Saturday a month there is live entertainment in support of Christie Hospital.
🏠🕭◑🖳&🎿🖼(X57,313)♣P🚭

John Millington ✪

67 Station Road, SK8 7AA (on A5149)
✪ 11-11 (midnight Fri & Sat); 12-10.30 Sun
☎ (0161) 486 9226
Hydes Mild, Original Bitter, Manchester's Finest, seasonal beer; guest beers Ⓗ
Opened in 2004, this Hydes Heritage Pub is a successful conversion of Grade II-listed Millington Hall. It is now a busy multi-room establishment with well-regarded meals and snacks, yet the food does not dominate. It was one of the first Hydes outlets to feature guest beers and these are usually from local micros such as AllGates. Quiz night is Tuesday and a live band plays on Friday. A policy on under-21s restricts access at some times.
🏠🕭◑🖳&🎿🖼(X57,313)P🚭

Chorlton-cum-Hardy

Bar Ⓛ

533 Wilbraham Road, M21 0UE
✪ 12-11.30 (midnight Thu; 12.30am Fri); 11.30-12.30am Sat; 11.30-midnight Sun ☎ (0161) 861 7516
Marble Manchester, Ginger; guest beers Ⓗ
A good-sized venue, eight handpumps dispense a range of beers, with descriptions on the back wall. Regular beers are from Marble and a number of other local breweries are well represented. A good selection of bottled beers and lagers is also available. Children are welcome until 8pm.
🕭◑🖼🖼(16,85,276)🚭

Electrik Ⓛ

559 Wilbraham Road, M21 0AE
✪ 12 (3 Mon)-12.30am; 12-1.30am Fri; 11-1.30am Sat; 11-12.30am Sun ☎ (0161) 881 3315 🌐 electrikbar.co.uk
Thwaites Wainwright; guest beers Ⓗ
A modern, one-room bar, Electrik has become a firm favourite on the Chorlton pub scene. The four handpumps generally serve local ales plus a cider. Although quiet during the day, it can be extremely lively towards the weekend, assisted by a free jukebox and guest DJs. Quiz night is Tuesday. Recently awarded the coveted Bar of the Year 2011 by the Manchester Food and Drink Festival and a former CAMRA Trafford & Hulme Pub of the Season.
🕭◑&🖼🖼(16,85,276)🚭🚭

Horse & Jockey Ⓛ ✪

9 Chorlton Green, M21 9HS
✪ 12-11 (11.30 Thu; midnight Fri & Sat) ☎ (0161) 860 7794
🌐 horseandjockeychorlton.com
Bootleg Chorlton Pale Ale; guest beers Ⓗ

Large mock Tudor-fronted pub dating from the early 1800s. Extensively refurbished since 2009, it is now home to its own brewery, the Bootleg Brewing Co, and a separate restaurant on the upper levels. Food is also served in the bar until 10pm daily (6pm Sun). Up to six real ales are available including the house beers and an ever-changing range mainly from local microbreweries. Twice yearly beer festivals are held. Children and dogs are welcome. 🏠🕭◑&🖼🖼(276)♣🚭🚭

Oddest Ⓛ

414-416 Wilbraham Road, M21 0SD (over bridge across tram lines from Morrisons)
✪ 12 (10 Sat & Sun)-11.30 (1.30am Fri & Sat)
☎ (0161) 860 7515 🌐 oddbar.co.uk
Northern Oddest Ale; guest beers Ⓗ
Comfortable furniture, quirky decor and a spacious verandah make this an appealing venue. The six handpumps deliver an ever-changing mixture of six guest ales ranging from dark to light, with a focus on LocAle – featuring breweries such as Phoenix, Hornbeam, Northern and Bollington. Real cider and perry are also available. There is a free jukebox and food is served until 9pm (8pm Fri and Sat). 🕭◑&🖼🖼(16,85)🚭🚭

Pi Ⓛ

99 Manchester Road, M21 9GA (500yds from B5217/A6010 jct)
✪ 11-11 (midnight Wed & Thu; 12.30am Fri); 12-12.30am Sat; 12-11 Sun ☎ (0161) 882 0000 🌐 pi-chorlton.co.uk
Tatton Gold; guest beers Ⓗ
Popular café bar to the north of Chorlton's main street. Five handpumps serve four real ales and a guest cider or perry alongside a selection of 10 world beers on draught – no mainstream brands here. An impressive menu of 80 bottled beers from around the world is also offered. Gourmet Pieminister pies with trimmings are served until 11pm daily. The service is always friendly – it is the little touches like complimentary peanuts and blankets for those sitting outside that make Pi stand out from the crowd. ⛱🕭◑🖼🖼🚭🚭

Compstall

Andrew Arms

George Street, SK6 5JD
✪ 12-midnight ☎ (0161) 484 5392
Robinson's 1892, Dizzy Blonde, Unicorn Ⓗ
Traditional detached stone-built pub in a quiet former mill village, constructed in the 1820s by George Andrew for his workers. It lies close to Etherow Country Park, with its wildlife and river valley walks. The pub features a comfortable lounge, small, traditional games room and a separate dining room. This venue is the centre for many social activities. The kitchen serves good pub food and holds themed nights (no food Mon).
🏠Q🕭◑🖳🖼(383,384)♣P

Delph

Royal Oak (Th' Heights)

Broad Lane, Heights, OL3 5TX (via Tame Lane, off main Delph-Denshaw road) SD982090
✪ closed Mon; 7 (5 Thu & Fri)-11; 12-midnight Sun
☎ (01457) 874460
Black Sheep Best Bitter; Millstone Tiger Rut; guest beers Ⓗ

Isolated 250-year-old stone-built pub on a packhorse route overlooking the Tame Valley. In a popular walking area, this quintessential moorland inn benefits from outstanding views. The building comprises a cosy bar and three rooms, each with an open fire. The refurbished side room boasts a hand-carved fireplace, while the comfortable snug has exposed beams and old photos of the inn. Home-cooked food is served on Friday and Saturday evenings. The pub has featured in the Guide for 21 consecutive years. ♨Q❀◗♿P▯

Didsbury

Milson Rhodes ✔

1d School Lane, M20 6RD (off Wilmslow Rd, A5145)
⏲ 8-11.30 (12.30am Fri & Sat) ☎ (0161) 446 4100
Greene King Abbot; Ruddles Best Bitter; guest beers Ⓗ
Smart Wetherspoon pub near Didsbury metro station, named after Dr Milson Rhodes who treated local people suffering from learning difficulties and epilepsy. The pub has a main bar downstairs and a smaller room upstairs. There is space for outdoor drinking at the front and on the balconies. Two regular ales plus seven guests are stocked including a locally brewed house beer that changes every six months. Look out for regular beer and cider festivals. Q❀◖◗♿🚋(Village)🚌(42,142)P⁻

Royal Oak

729 Wilmslow Road, M20 6WF (on A5145, jct Old Oak St)
⏲ 11-11 (midnight Fri & Sat) ☎ (0161) 434 4788
Marston's Burton Bitter, Pedigree, seasonal beers; guest beers Ⓗ
Built around 1850, this multi-roomed venue is akin to the community centre of the village. The large central horseshoe-shaped bar displays an impressive collection of old porcelain spirit vats. The pub is famous for its award-winning cheese and pâté lunches (served Mon-Fri) which many have tried to copy but none has been able to surpass for choice or value. The pub can be particularly busy when live sport is screened on TV. Four guest beers are served each month.
❀◖🚋(Village)🚌(42,142)⁻

Diggle

Diggle Hotel 🄻 ✔

Station Houses, OL3 5JZ (½ mile off A670) SE007081
⏲ 12-3, 5-midnight (1am Fri); 12-1am Sat; 12-11 Sun
☎ (01457) 872741 🌐 digglehotel.co.uk
Black Sheep Best Bitter; Millstone Vale Mill; Taylor Landlord; Three B's Stoker's Slake; guest beers Ⓗ
Stone pub in a pleasant hamlet close to the Standedge Canal Tunnel. Built as a merchant's house in 1789, it became an ale house and general store on the construction of the nearby railway tunnel in 1834. Affording fine views of the Saddleworth countryside, the Diggle is a convenient base in a popular walking area. With a bar area and two rooms, the accent in on home-cooked food (served all day Sat and Sun). The pies and flans are popular. Q❀🛏◖◗🚌(184)P

Dobcross

Navigation Inn 🄻

21-23 Wool Road, OL3 5NS
⏲ 12-2.30, 5-11 (midnight Fri); 12-11 Sat; 12-10.30 Sun
☎ (01457) 872418
Millstone Tiger Rut; Moorhouse's Pendle Witches Brew; Thwaites Wainwright; Wells Bombardier; guest beers Ⓗ
A popular watering hole for Huddersfield Narrow Canal walkers and boaters, this is a family-run business. Dog- and family-friendly, it offers locally sourced, home-made and freshly prepared food every lunchtime and early evening, with special offers Monday to Saturday. Themed nights raise funds for local charities. The annual Rushcart Festival stops off at the pub in August.
Q❀◖◗🚌(184,353)P⁻

Droylsden

King's Head

169 Market Street, M43 7AY
⏲ 11.30-midnight; 12-11 Sun ☎ (0129) 827 7193
Holt Bitter, seasonal beers Ⓗ
Large, busy pub standing at the junction of Greenside Lane, a few minutes' walk from the crossroads in the centre of Droylsden and the new Metrolink line from Manchester to Ashton-under-Lyne. Droylsden FC football ground is close by. Attracting a mixed clientele, there is a choice of two lounges and a large public bar. This often unsung local is doing an excellent job – the use of 36-gallon barrels in the cellar is an indication of its popularity. ◖◗⊟♿🚌♣P⁻

Eccles

Eccles Cross ✔

13 Regent Street, M30 0BP (opp Metrolink terminus)
⏲ 8am-midnight (1am Fri & Sat) ☎ (0161) 788 0414
Greene King Abbot; Ruddles Best Bitter; guest beers Ⓗ
Named after a nearby stone cross, this Wetherspoon pub in the former New Regent cinema is smaller and has a more pub-like feel than most. A series of alcoves along one wall provides a degree of privacy for more intimate drinking, while the open areas are popular with older customers. Outside, the original brick and stone 1920s frontage is well maintained.
Q♨❀◖◗♿⇌🚋🚌●P⁻

Lamb Hotel ★

33 Regent Street, M30 0BP (opp Metrolink terminus)
⏲ 11.30-11 (midnight Fri & Sat); 12-11 Sun
☎ (07877) 850252
Holt Mild, Bitter; guest beer Ⓗ
One of the best of Holt's large Edwardian red-brick multi-roomed houses. Grade II-listed, it was completely restored a few years ago, including the stripping and French polishing of the fine mahogany woodwork and fireplaces. Original tiling and abundant etched glass add to the overall sumptuousness. The purpose-built billiards room has a full-sized table. There are two large lounges, a separate vault and a spacious floor-tiled corridor and lobby. Q⊟⇌🚋🚌♣P

Fallowfield

Friendship ✔

353 Wilmslow Road, M14 6XS (B5093, jct Egerton Rd)
⏲ 12-11 (midnight Fri & Sat) ☎ (0161) 224 5758
Hydes 1863, Original Bitter, Manchester's Finest, seasonal beers; guest beers Ⓗ

Impressive Victorian mansion in a busy student area. This is not purely the domain of the young, however, as it attracts a good mix of folk. A large horseshoe bar serves a variety of areas – some quiet, some raised. The rear extension completed a few of years ago created space for the provision of interesting and popular oriental food, including takeaways. Well-positioned TV screens provide for sports fans. Nine handpumps offer the Hydes range, as well as varying guest ales.
❀⟐&🚃(42,43)P↳

Garswood

Railway Hotel ✔
4 Station Road, WN4 0SA (opp station)
❀ 2-11 (11.30 Thu), 12-midnight Fri & Sat; 12-11 Sun
☎ (01942) 745187
Beer range varies Ⓗ
Family-friendly pub with a large beer garden and children's area. The central bar has three handpumps serving varying guest ales from the Punch Taverns range. Outside, there is a large heated smoking area and car park at the rear. A community pub, it regularly holds charity events, and is a previous winner of CAMRA Wigan Community Pub of the Year.
🏠❀⟐🚃🚃(156,157)P↳

Gatley

Horse & Farrier ✔
144 Gatley Road, SK8 4AB (jct of Church Road)
❀ 11-11 (midnight Fri & Sat); 12-10.30 Sun
☎ (0161) 428 2080
Hydes 1863, Original Bitter, Manchester's Finest, seasonal beers; guest beers Ⓗ
Hydes Heritage Inn formed from three cottages, with bay windows added and the elevations later rendered to look like stone, with a mock-Tudor upper floor. The central bar serves several spaces and a food bar to the rear. A carvery is offered on Sunday afternoon. A couple of seats are set cosily under the stairs that lead up to the Martingale function room and there is an outside smoking area. Occasional beer festivals are held throughout the year. Q❀⟐&🚃(44,371)🌼P↳

Greenfield

Railway Ⓛ
11 Shaw Hall Bank Road, OL3 7JZ (opp station)
❀ 12-midnight (1am Thu & Fri); 11.30-1am Sat
☎ (01457) 872307
Copper Dragon Golden Pippin; Millstone Tiger Rut; Moorhouse's Blonde Witch; Saltaire Blonde; Wells Bombardier; guest beers Ⓗ
Unspoilt pub comprising a central bar, games area and tap room decorated with old photos of Saddleworth. The Railway is a popular venue for live music on Thursday, Friday (unplugged night — all players welcome) and Sunday. It is also a stop-off on the Transpennine Real Ale Trail. A varying choice of ciders is served on gravity. In a picturesque area, the pub is a good base for outdoor pursuits and affords beautiful views across Chew Valley. Caravans are allowed.
❀🚃🚃🚃(180,184)🌼🌼P↳

Wellington Ⓛ
29 Chew Valley Road, OL3 7AF (100yds past Tesco)
❀ 12 (4 Mon-Thu)-11; 12-10.30 Sun ☎ (01457) 873450

Thwaites Nutty Black, Original, Wainwright; guest beers Ⓗ
Friendly village local, now a free house. On the end of a terrace, it comprises a small bar area, open-plan room for diners and a separate sports room with Sky TV, cribbage and a dartboard. Good home-made food includes pies, puddings and real chips, served Wednesday to Friday evenings and all day at the weekend. Up to five guest beers are available, and real cider in summer.
❀⟐🚃🚃(180,350,353)🌼🌼

Hazel Grove

Grapes
196 London Road, SK7 4DQ (on A6, jct with Hatherlow Lane)
❀ 11.30-11 (midnight Fri & Sat); 12-10.30 Sun
☎ (0161) 483 4479
Robinson's 1892, Unicorn, seasonal beer Ⓗ
A charming pub and one of the oldest in Hazel Grove. It retains a classic town-pub layout – the central bar separates the large vault on the left from the three-roomed lounge on the right, which still has some original-looking wooden beams. The back room displays images of old Hazel Grove, and to the rear is a small beer garden. Mild is offered at two different temperatures according to taste.
❀🍺🚃🚃(192,199)🌼P↳

Heaton Norris

Nursery ★ ✔
258 Green Lane, SK4 2NA (off A6, jct with Heaton Road)
❀ 11.30-11 (11.30 Fri; midnight Sat); 12-11.30 Sun
☎ (0161) 432 2044
Hydes 1863, Owd Oak, Original Bitter, Manchester's Finest, seasonal beers; guest beers Ⓗ
Now a Grade II-listed building, this former CAMRA National Pub of the Year is a classic, unspoilt 1930s pub with its own bowling green, hidden away in a pleasant suburb. The multi-roomed interior includes a traditional vault and a spacious, wood-panelled lounge where lunchtime diners enjoy home-cooked meals (no food Mon). Two changing guest beers are always available. Live singers and bands perform on weekend evenings, while jazz and folk often feature on Tuesdays and Thursdays. Several beer festivals are held each year.
Q❀⟐🍺🚃(22,364)🌼P↳

Hindley

Hare & Hounds Ⓛ
31 Ladies Lane, WN2 2QA (between railway station and town centre)
❀ 4 (12 Sat & Sun)-midnight
Beer range varies Ⓗ
A small, traditional pub that is thriving under the ownership of AllGates Brewery in Wigan. Alongside the AllGates beers there are usually a couple of guests from some of the best breweries in the UK. The pub has a cosy lounge featuring old photos of Hindley, which runs open plan into a bar/vault area. It is popular for TV sport, especially Premier League football. 🏮🍺🚃🌼↳

Holcombe Brook

Hare & Hounds ✔
400 Bolton Road West, BL0 9RY (on A676 at jct with Longsight Road)

🕒 12-11 (midnight Thu-Sat) ☎ (01706) 822107
🌐 hareandhoundsbury.com
Beer range varies H
Large rural community pub welcoming young, old and their dogs. Ten ever-changing countrywide cask ales are on handpump – the list can be seen on the website's ale cam. A small function room is available with a separate 40-handpump bar for beer festivals. Excellent food is served until 9pm. Free Wi-Fi available. Local CAMRA Pub of the Year 2011 and Area Pub of the Year 2012.
🏅⛲🌙🍴🛗🚃(472,474)♣P⚑

Horwich

Crown
1 Chorley New Road, BL6 7QJ (jct A673/B6226)
SD634118
🕒 11-11 (midnight Fri & Sat); 12-11.30 Sun
☎ (01204) 693109
Holt Mild, Bitter, seasonal beers H
A grand local landmark, handy for the Reebok Stadium, Rivington Pike and the West Pennine Moors. Lever Park across the road was a gift from Lord Leverhulme, the soap magnate and great benefactor to his home town. Darts and dominoes teams play on Tuesday and Thursday evenings and there is a vault and games room at the rear. Various artists provide entertainment on Sunday evening. Children are welcome at lunchtime when dining. 🌙🍴🛗🚃(125,575)♣P⚑

Original Bay Horse
206 Lee Lane, BL6 7JF (on B6226, 200yds from A673)
🕒 1-midnight; 12-12.30am Fri & Sat; 12-midnight Sun
☎ (01204) 696231
Bank Top Flat Cap; Coach House Gunpowder Mild; Lees Bitter; Moorhouse's Pride of Pendle; guest beers H
Dating from 1777, this stone-built pub with small windows and low ceilings has been run by the same family for many years and is locally known as the 'Long Pull'. In the lounge, pool and darts are played and live sports coverage on TV is popular, while on the left a cosy, traditional vault has some interesting football memorabilia. A Moorhouse's beer is usually available. 🌙🍴🚃(125,575)♣🍴⚑

Victoria & Albert ☆
114 Lee Lane, BL6 7AF (on B6226)
🕒 12-11 (midnight Fri & Sat) ☎ (01204) 770837
Holts Bitter H
Formally the Albert Arms, the pub is situated opposite Horwich Public Hall. Recently refurbished, it is now a modern and comfortable lounge-style pub with three separate seating areas. Two guest beers are offered, one usually from Moorhouse's. Outside is a beer garden and the toilets have disabled access. It is handy for the West Pennine Moors and walkers are always welcome. Over-21s only. Local CAMRA Pub of the Year 2012. 🚃(125)⚑

Hyde

Cheshire Ring
72 Manchester Road, SK14 2BJ
🕒 12 (4 Mon & Tue; 1 Wed; 3.30 Thu & Fri)-11; 12-10.30 Sun
☎ (07917) 055629
Beartown Kodiak Gold, Bearskinful, seasonal beers; guest beers H
One of the oldest pubs in Hyde and comprehensively overhauled by Beartown. Seven handpumps offer a range of Beartown ales and

guests from micros in addition to ciders, perries and continental beers. A selection of bottled beers is also stocked and occasional beer festivals offer additional drinking choice. Gentle background music plays and live bands perform. The opening hours vary with the season.
🌙⛲🚃(Central)🚃🍴⚑

Queen's Inn
23 Clarendon Place, SK14 2ND
🕒 11-11 ☎ (0161) 368 2230
Holt Mild, Bitter, seasonal beers H
A town-centre community pub with a warm welcome. Home to several sports teams, the interior is divided into four distinct areas to cater for all needs, including a large function room that is a favourite for wedding receptions. Close to Hyde bus station and the market, the Queen's is popular with shoppers during the day. A late licence is available for special events.
🌙⛲🚃(Central/Newton for Hyde)🚃♣⚑

Sportsman L
57 Mottram Road, SK14 2NN
🕒 11-11; 12-10.30 Sun ☎ (0161) 368 5000
Rossendale Floral Dance, Pitch Porter, Sunshine; guest beers H
Rossendale Brewery tied house offering the full range of its Pennine Ales plus up to three guests from micros. Bar snacks are served and there is a restaurant upstairs specialising in genuine home-cooked Cuban food and tapas. This former CAMRA Pub of the Region retains its character. The rear patio includes a covered and heated smoking area.
🏅Q⛲🌙🚃(Central/Newton for Hyde)🚃🍴P⚑

Leigh

Boar's Head L
2 Market Place, WN7 1EG
🕒 11-11 (1am Thu-Sat) ☎ (01942) 673036
Moorhouse's Premier Bitter, Pride of Pendle H
Opposite Leigh's parish church, the imposing red-brick exterior contains clues to the pub's history, from the Bedford Brewing Company to Walker's Warrington Ales, plus the odd Firkin brew-pub memento inside. A real free house, there are four pumps, two dispensing Moorhouse's beers and two ever-changing guests. The large pool room houses a collection of Rugby League team photographs from various eras, the dining area displays Lancashire colliery plates. A carvery is available on Sunday. Live music sessions are held most Saturdays, a quiz with hotpot on Sunday. 🌙🍴🚃♣⚑

Leigh Rugby Union Club
Round Ash Park, Hand Lane, WN7 3NA (off Beech Walk)
🕒 7 (12 Sat & Sun)-11 ☎ (01942) 673526
Coach House Round Ash Bitter, seasonal beers H
A true community club with men's and ladies' rugby teams plus crown green bowls, darts and dominoes. Put all that together with an enthusiastic, hard-working bar team and a friendly crowd of locals and you cannot go wrong. The Annual Scrumdown beer festival is held in May, with more than 30 real ales and ciders. Well worth the 10-minute walk from Leigh Bus Station. CAMRA Greater Manchester Club of the Year 2007-2011.
⛲P⚑

Thomas Burke L ✔

20A Leigh Road, WN7 1QR

🕃 9am-midnight (1am Fri & Sat) ☎ (01942) 685640

Greene King Abbot; Ruddles County Ⓗ

Popular with all ages, this Wetherspoon pub is named after a renowned Leigh tenor, known as the Lancashire Caruso. The pub divides into three areas: the main long bar, a raised dining area and, in what was once a cinema foyer, lounge-style seating. Ten handpumps offer a changing range of beers from local to distant breweries. ⬤🛒🏠⌐

White Lion ▼ L

6A Leigh Road, WN7 1QL

🕃 12-midnight (1am Fri) ☎ (07510) 905995

AllGates California, seasonal beers Ⓗ

Fully refurbished and reopened in 2011, the White Lion is situated opposite Leigh's historic parish church just a few minutes' walk from Leigh's centre. A friendly town-centre pub, you can choose whether to enjoy the comfort of the main bar, bar games in the vault, or the quiet of the snug. Six handpumps dispense a selection of AllGates real ales plus guests, and draught Gwynt Y Ddraig Cider. Local CAMRA Pub of the Year 2012. 🚃♣🏠⌐

Littleborough

Red Lion L

6 Halifax Road, OL15 0HB (on A58 adjacent to railway line)

🕃 2-midnight; 12.30-1am Fri & Sat; 1-midnight Sun
☎ (01706) 378195

Lees Bitter; Taylor Landlord; guest beers Ⓗ

Detached stone-built pub with four distinct rooms, each different in character. Beer and conversation dominate throughout the premises, with two rooms for games and TV sport. The main room is large and homely, the adjacent snug room has comfortable high-back chairs. Up to six guest beers supplement the two regulars and the house beer from Phoenix. Three German/Belgian beers are also on draught and one handpump supplies traditional cider from Thatchers and Westons. A proper community pub. Q🚃🚃(528,590)♣🏠P

White House

Blackstone Edge, Halifax Road, OL15 0LG (on A58 towards Halifax)

🕃 12-3, 6.30-midnight; 12.30-10.30 Sun ☎ (01706) 378456
🌐 thewhitehousepub.co.uk

Theakston Best Bitter; guest beers Ⓗ

High in the Pennines, a landmark on the Pennine Way, this 17th-century coaching house benefits from panoramic views. A family-owned and run free house for 28 years, it extends a warm and friendly welcome to all. There are two bars, both with log fires, and four handpumps serving one regular and three guests, often from local breweries. World bottled beers, cider and a good selection of wine complement the excellent menu and specials board. Open all day Sunday. 🚃Q🏠⬤▲🚃P⌐

Manchester: City Centre

Angel

6 Angel Street, M4 4BQ (off Rochdale Rd)

🕃 11am-midnight; 12-10.30 Sun ☎ (0161) 833 4786
🌐 theangelmanchester.com

Bob's White Lion; guest beers Ⓗ

Prominent in Manchester's real ale scene for 30 years, now in its smartest incarnation. Dedication to real ale is undiminished, with up to nine handpumps and two for cider. Bare floorboards remain in the L-shaped bar, warmed by one of the four real fires. To this, add a grand piano and restaurant on the first floor serving quality meals. Beers from microbreweries dominate here. 🚃🏠⬤⌐🚃(Victoria)🚃(Shudehill)🚃🏠P⌐

Bar Fringe

8 Swan Street, M4 5JN (30yds from A62/A665 jct)

🕃 12-midnight (12.30am Fri & Sat) ☎ (0161) 835 3815

Beer range varies Ⓗ

This Northern Quarter Guide regular is a compact continental bar with eccentric decor. Ornamental rats, Tin-Tin cartoons, continental beer posters and even a motorcycle adorn the walls. Up to five handpumps dispense ales from all over the country – Phoenix, Boggart and Cottage are often featured. There is also an extensive range of continental draught and bottled beers, mainly from Belgium. Thatchers Cheddar Valley Cider is a regular, with a guest often available. At the back is a good beer garden. 🏠⬤⌐🚃(Victoria)🚃(Shudehill)🚃🏠⌐

Cask

29 Liverpool Road, Castlefield, M3 4NQ

🕃 12-11 ☎ (0161) 819 2527 🌐 caskmanc.co.uk

Beer range varies Ⓗ

A converted shop with the bar on the left as you enter. At the rear is a large back room with comfortable seating. Although it sells four ever-changing cask ales, it specialises in continental beers with a number of unusual draught beers and a range of German and Belgian bottled beers. The staff are friendly and knowledgeable. No food is served but you can bring in your own food. 🏠⬤🚃(Deansgate)🚃(Deansgate/Castlefield)🚃⌐

Castle Hotel ✔

66 Oldham Street, M4 1LE (near Warwick St)

🕃 12-1am (2am Fri & Sat) ☎ (0161) 237 9485
🌐 thecastlehotel.info

Robinson's Unicorn, Cumbria Way, Dizzy Blonde, seasonal beers; guest beers Ⓗ

Robinson's flagship hostelry in the city, now serving guest beers in addition to several from its own range. The pub was refurbished in 2010 to a high standard and retains a small front vault, corridor and snug, complete with piano. A larger back room is used for music and arts events. Rather dimly lit, a daytime visit allows its many original features to be fully appreciated. 🏠⬤🚃(Victoria/Piccadilly)🚃(Market Street)🚃⬤⌐

City Arms L ✔

46-48 Kennedy Street, M2 4BQ

🕃 11.30-11 (midnight Fri); 12-midnight Sat; 12-8 Sun
☎ (0161) 236 4610

Moorhouse's Pride Of Pendle; Thwaites Original; guest beers Ⓗ

Relatively small two-room city-centre local tucked away on a back street close to Albert Square. It offers eight real ales including six ever-changing guests, with LocAle featuring via the SIBA Direct Delivery scheme, and real cider in a box on the bar. Meals are served lunchtimes only, but hot pies are available all day. Popular with office workers at lunchtimes and a regular evening crowd, it gets particularly busy on weekend evenings. 🏠⬤🚃(Oxford Rd)🚃(St Peter's Square)🚃(M3)♣⬤⌐

Jolly Angler ✔
47 Ducie Street, Ancoats, M1 2JW (behind Piccadilly rail station)
✪ 5.30 (12 Sat)-11; 1-6, 8-10.30 Sun ☎ (0161) 236 5307
Hydes Original Bitter Ⓗ
Pleasant, small, street-corner local, of a type that is slowly ebbing away. Welcoming and friendly, it is laid out with a single bar, overseeing what were two single rooms, with tasteful decor, and old photographs and prints depicting Manchester United legends and players (although it is frequented by City fans, as it is on the way to the stadium). Music sessions are played.
🏨≉(Piccadilly)🚋(Piccadilly)🚌

Knott Bar Ⓛ
374 Deansgate, M3 4LY
✪ 12-11.30 (midnight Thu; 12.30am Fri & Sat)
☎ (0161) 839 9229
Marble Ginger; guest beers Ⓗ
Long-established multi-award-winning specialist beer pub set in a converted railway arch adjacent to Deansgate station. Six cask ales selected from only the best microbreweries rotate on an almost daily basis. Marble and Pictish are near pemanent with others like RedWillow, Acorn and Summer Wine featuring alongside an impressive bottled range. Real cider is served from a tub on the back bar, but beware of non-real cider served by handpump. Meals are available until 8pm daily with all food cooked fresh.
🏵🍴🔥≉(Deansgate)🚋(Deansgate/Castlefield)🚌🚴🄿

Marble Arch ★
73 Rochdale Road, M4 4HY (on A664, 200m from A665 jct)
✪ 12-11 (midnight Fri & Sat; 10.30 Sun) ☎ (0161) 832 5914
Marble Draft, Pint, Best, Ginger, seasonal beers; guest beers Ⓗ
A showcase for the award-winning Marble Brewery's beers, this famous pub, just outside the city centre, is always busy. Two guest ales usually supplement the Marble range. The pub is listed and displays many interesting architectural features, from the imposing entrance to the sloping mosaic floor and the drinking frieze. A more modern back room is used primarily for dining. The food is justly popular and served until 8.45pm (7.45pm on weekends).
🏨🛏🏵🍴≉(Victoria)🚋(Shudehill)🚌🚴🄿

Micro Bar
Unit FC16, Manchester Arndale, 49 High Street, M4 3AH (inside Arndale Market, High St entrance)
✪ 11-6; 12-5 Sun ☎ (0161) 277 9666
Boggart Hole Clough Cascade, Rum Porter; guest beers Ⓗ
Offering a haven from the bustle of the Arndale Shopping Centre, this busy bar has up to five handpumps and a constantly changing, wide selection from both UK and foreign breweries. Run by Boggart Hole Clough Brewery, two of the brewery's award-winning ales are available, with the other three handpumps dispensing guest beers and a real cider/perry. There is also a good selection of bottles to buy.
≉(Victoria)🚋(Shudehill)🚌🚴🄳

Old Wellington Inn ✔
4 Cathedral Gates, M3 1SW (next to Cathedral)
✪ 10-11 (10.30 Sun) ☎ (0161) 839 5179

Jennings Cumberland Ale; Thwaites Original Bitter, Wainwright; guest beers Ⓗ
A large 16th-century timber-framed inn in the medieval quarter. The busy bar has three regular beers, plus up to five guests on handpump. The upper floors are used for more formal dining. A square outside provides an open drinking area, part covered by parasols. The inn was dismantled and rebuilt at its present location during redevelopment after the 1996 IRA bomb. A plaque gives a brief history and is worth a read. Food is served up to 10pm daily.
Q🛏🏵🍴🔥≉(Victoria)🚋(Victoria)🚌🄿

Paramount ✔
33-35 Oxford Street, M1 4BH (jct Portland St)
✪ 9-midnight (1am Fri & Sat) ☎ (0161) 233 1820
🌐 sandbaronline.net
Elland Paramount; Greene King Abbot; Phoenix Lancashire Pale Ale; Thwaites Wainwright; guest beers Ⓗ
While buzzing with life, this busy Wetherspoon pub has a more relaxed ambience than the frenetic atmosphere found in many other city pubs. However, what really gives it an edge is the passion the managers and staff have for cask beer. Around the walls are photos from Manchester's old theatreland in the vicinity of the pub (hence its name) and it is handy today for modern venues including the Palace Theatre, Bridgewater Hall and Manchester Central.
🍴≉(Oxford Rd)🚋(St Peter's Square)🚌(1,3)🚴🄿

Peveril of the Peak ★
127 Great Bridgewater Street, M1 5JQ
✪ 12-3 (not Sat), 5-11; 5-10.30 Sun ☎ (0161) 236 6364
Caledonian Deuchars IPA; Copper Dragon Golden Pippin; Everards Tiger; Jennings Cumberland Ale Ⓗ
Dating from around 1829, this classic pub boasts an array of original details and is one of Britain's Real Heritage Pubs. The venue is named after the stagecoach that ran from London to Manchester, and the landlady here celebrated 40 years as licensee in January 2011. The pub opens at noon on Saturday if Manchester United are playing at home. Look for the ancient table football.
🏨Q🏵🔥🍴≉(Oxford Rd)🚋(St Peter's Square)🚌(255,256)🚴🄿

Piccadilly ✔
71-73 Piccadilly, M1 2BS (near Piccadilly rail station approach)
✪ 8am-11 (midnight Thu; 1am Fri & Sat); 9am-11 Sun
☎ (0161) 236 9622
John Smith's Bitter; Marston's EPA; guest beers Ⓗ
Situated on a busy main thoroughfare, close to Piccadilly rail station, trams and bus station, this is a large split-level affair with the bar in the lower front section. Up to five real ales are available, with guest beers always an interesting selection. The pub caters for all tastes and the food menu vies with the nearby hostelries for special offers and meal deals. Due to its location, it gets a large crowd of people, especially on football match days.
🍴🔥≉(Piccadilly)🚋(Piccadilly)🚌

Port Street Beer House
39-41 Port Street, M1 2EQ (off Hilton St)
✪ closed Mon; 4 (2 Fri)-midnight; 12-1am Sat; 12-midnight Sun ☎ (0161) 237 9949 🌐 portstreetbeerhouse.co.uk
Beer range varies Ⓗ
Opened in 2011, this bar has become a mecca for beer lovers from far and wide. The knowledgeable

staff serve seven real ales plus an extensive selection of draught and bottled beers from the US, Belgium, Holland and beyond. Thornbridge, Dark Star and Prospect breweries usually feature. Beers here can be expensive, but customers pay for quality. Regular Meet the Brewer events are held. ☻&≠(Piccadilly)◼(Piccadilly Gardens)◼ᵗ—

Sandbar

120-122 Grosvenor Street, All Saints, M1 7HL (off Oxford Rd A34/B5117 jct)
✪ 12-midnight (1am Thu; 2am Fri-Sat) ☎ (0161) 273 1552
Bank Top Dark Mild; Holt IPA; Phoenix All Saints; guest beers Ⓗ
Excellent conversion of 18th-century town houses into a quirky and bohemian bar. In the heart of Manchester's student land, the bar is popular with students and university staff alike. Exhibitions of photographs and paintings adorn the walls and DJs do their thing at weekends. A good range of foreign beers complements the five handpulled cask ales and the changing guest cider, which often comes from smaller producers. Free Wi-fi available. ◐≠(Oxford Rd)◼(42,43)☻ᵗ—

Smithfield Hotel & Bar

37 Swan Street, M4 5JZ (on A665 between Rochdale Rd and Oldham Rd)
✪ 12-midnight ☎ (0161) 839 4424
⊕ the-smithfield-hotel.co.uk
Facer's Smithfield Bitter; Robinson's Dark 1892; guest beers Ⓗ
Situated in the Northern Quarter, this intimate bar has a local atmosphere. The front area includes a pool table and there is comfortable seating available near the bar. The house bitter is from Facer's and up to seven guests come from micros and family brewers from across the country. Beer festivals are held throughout the year. Reasonably priced accommodation is available.
☒≠(Victoria)◼(Shudehill)◼♣

Waterhouse Ⓛ ✔

67-71 Princess Street, M2 4EG
✪ 9am-midnight ☎ (0161) 200 5380
Buxton Moor Top; Phoenix Wobbly Bob; Thwaites Wainwright; guest beers Ⓗ
Standing in the shadow of Manchester Town Hall, this Wetherspoon differs from most in that it retains the many separate rooms of the civic palace it once was. It is named after the architect who designed it in 1877. Five frequently changing guest beers on the main bar, often from local micros, join the three regular beers hidden behind a pillar, and a good selection of real cider is also stocked. The Sunday evening CAMRA club offers a discount on real ale to CAMRA members.
Q☒☻◐&≠(Oxford Rd)◼(St Peter's Square)◼☻ᵗ—

Wheatsheaf

30 Oak Street, M4 5JE (off Oldham St)
✪ 12-11 (midnight Fri & Sat); 12-10.30 Sun
☎ (0161) 833 9445
Marston's Pedigree, seasonal beers; guest beers Ⓗ
A Marston's hostelry, the ales come from their range – Jennings, Ringwood and Brakspear breweries mainly – and change weekly. Darts is played and there is a pool table. Northern soul music features on Saturday night and karaoke on Sunday night. A pub not to be missed when in the Northern Quarter of the city centre.
☻≠(Victoria)◼(Shudehill)◼♣

Marple

Hare & Hounds

Dooley Lane, Otterspool, SK6 7EJ
✪ 11.30-11; 12-10.30 Sun ☎ (0161) 427 0293
Hydes 1863, Original Bitter; guest beers Ⓗ
Attractive pub by the River Goyt on the Marple-Romiley road. It is difficult to imagine that when this pub was built it was at the end of a row of terraced cottages, demolished long ago when the road was realigned. The pub's Hydes beers now provide some welcome variety in the area. The interior is open plan with a separate dining area and conservatory plus an improved and pleasant outdoor space. The pub offers something for everyone including good-value food. Q☻◐P ᵗ—

Railway

223 Stockport Road, SK6 6EN
✪ 12-11 (11.30 Fri & Sat; 10.30 Sun) ☎ (0161) 427 2146
Robinson's 1892, Unicorn, seasonal beers Ⓗ
This impressive pub first opened in 1878 alongside Rose Hill Station and many rail commuters still number among its customers. The pub has changed little externally, and is handy for walkers and cyclists on the nearby Middlewood Way. Two open-plan airy and relaxing rooms are complemented by an outside veranda and drinking area. A deservedly popular pub. ☻◐&≠(Rose Hill)◼P ᵗ—

Marple Bridge

Hare & Hounds ✔

19 Mill Brow, SK6 5LW (from A626 Lane Ends along Ley Lane for ¾ mile) SJ980896
✪ 12-3 (Fri only), 5-1am; 12-1am Sat; 12-midnight Sun
☎ (0161) 427 4042
Robinson's 1892, Dizzy Blonde, Unicorn, seasonal beers Ⓗ
Winner of the 2010 Robinson's Unicorn Shield for best-kept cellar, this is a hidden gem in the beautiful hamlet of Mill Brow. Extensively refurbished in 2008 to a high standard, this excellent country pub with a great atmosphere and a roaring fire in winter is the perfect place for both discerning drinkers and diners. Meals are freshly prepared and food is locally sourced. A genuine local that caters for everyone, including walkers, with some of the best views in the area.
Ａ☻◐&◼(394)♣P ᵗ—

Middleton

Olde Boar's Head ✔

111 Long Street, M24 6UE
✪ 12-11 (10.30 Sun) ☎ (0161) 643 3520
Lees Bitter, seasonal beers Ⓗ
Charming and ancient half-timbered pub near the parish church, dating back to at least 1632. Two bars serve a variety of rooms and alcoves. Features to note include stone flagged floors, a viewing panel for the wattle and daub walls and the large Sessions Room, once a local courthouse. Lees seasonal beers are sometimes sold. There is a covered and heated smoking shelter to the rear of pub. No food on Sunday. ☻◐◼(17)P ᵗ—

Ring o' Bells ✔

St Leonard's Square, M24 6DJ (up New Lane from Long St)
✪ 5 (12 Sun)-midnight; 12-1am Fri & Sat ☎ (0161) 654 9245
⊕ ringobellsmiddleton.co.uk
Lees Bitter, seasonal beers Ⓗ

Situated to the rear of Jubilee Park and opposite the historic parish church, this old pub has a strong place in the community. It hosts an annual maypole event on May bank holiday and a unique Pace Egg Play on Easter Monday. The pub features regular live music and popular quizzes. One main room is split by stairs to an upstairs function room featuring old collages made from butterflies. At the rear, there is a covered smoking area. ❀🚌(17)♣⚐

Monton

Park Hotel

142 Monton Road, M30 9QD (corner of Hawthorne Avenue)
⊙ 11-11 (11.30 Thu; midnight Fri & Sat); 12-10.30 Sun
☎ (0161) 834 3285
Holt Mild, IPA, Bitter, seasonal beers; guest beers Ⓗ
A busy, smart and well-run community local with a central bar serving three rooms. The main large lounge has TVs, the vault provides pool, darts and 3D TV, and the Bridgewater Room is quiet, with a fish tank and painted mural of the nearby canal system. Live entertainment is hosted on Saturday nights. Notice boards provide information on local activities. A freshwater angling club meets here with occasional sea fishing trips.
Q❀⊟🚌(33,68)♣P⚐

Mossley

Britannia Inn

217 Manchester Road, OL5 9AJ
⊙ 11.45 (2.45 Mon-Wed)-11 (midnight Fri & Sat); 12-midnight Sun ☎ (01457) 832799
🌐 britanniamossley.co.uk
Marston's Burton Bitter; guest beers Ⓗ
Imposing gritstone building yards from Mossley station. Marston's acquired it in 1961 when they bought Rothwell's, and the pub offers a range of beers that rivals many free houses, including ales from Millstone and other local breweries. Food is served from opening time until 7.30pm (5pm Sun). Smokers may use the seats and tables in the covered area in front of the pub.
❀◐◑⇌🚌(343,350)♣⚐

Dysarts Arms

Huddersfield Road, OL5 9BT (on B6175 ½ mile S of A635)
⊙ 12-midnight (1am Fri & Sat) ☎ (01457) 832103
🌐 dysartsarms.com
Robinson's 1892, Unicorn, seasonal beers Ⓗ
Located outside the town, bordering open farmland and close to the pre-1974 Lancashire/Yorkshire boundary, Robinson's acquired this pub when it took over Schofield's of Ashton-under-Lyne in 1926. The interior comprises a spacious, comfortable bar area and a cosy lounge with a real fire in winter. A partially covered patio to the side allows for outdoor drinking and smoking. The licensees organise the pub's walking and book clubs. No food is available on Monday.
♨❀◐⛺🚌(350)♣P⚐

Rising Sun

235 Stockport Road, OL5 0RQ
⊙ 12-midnight ☎ (01457) 238236 🌐 risingsunmossley.co.uk
Black Sheep Best Bitter; Millstone Tiger Rut; Taylor Landlord Ⓗ
From its bracing location nearly a mile from the station but a good deal higher, this pub offers good views eastwards over the Tame Valley towards Saddleworth Moor. The range of up to seven guest ales is complemented by a spendid variety of bottled beers from around the world. A pavement patio and covered area are available for smokers. Bluegrass music features on Tuesday evenings and bands perform on Mondays. ♨❀🚌(353)♣●P⚐

Moston

Blue Bell

493 Moston Lane, M40 9PY (opp St Joseph's cemetery)
⊙ 11-11 (midnight Fri & Sat); 12-11 Sun ☎ (0161) 834 3285
Holt Mild, Bitter Ⓗ
Imposing red-brick pub built in 1890 with a reputation for excellent ales. The interior comprises a lively vault to the right from the car park, two large rooms to the left and a smaller parlour beyond. All rooms are served from a central bar. Outside is a large patio area and a TV under a canopy for smokers. Quiz night is Wednesday and artists perform at weekends. The pub is home to the Salford Harriers Athletics Club.
❀⊟♿🚌(88,89)P⚐

New Springs

Crown Hotel 🄻

106 Wigan Road, WN2 1DP (on B5238 by canal bridge)
⊙ closed Mon; 5-11 (1am Fri); 12-1am Sat; 12-11 Sun
Prospect Gold Rush; guest beer Ⓗ
The licensee is renowned for his cellarmanship at this free house just two miles from Wigan centre, close to Haigh Country Park. Up to three handpumps serve a range of beers from local breweries, with Prospect featuring prominently. A real coal fire and woodburner add to the warm, welcoming ambience. High-quality food is a recent addition, and people travel from miles around for Dave's cabaret evenings on Friday and Saturday. Well worth a visit. ♨❀◑🚌P⚐

Oldham

Ashton Arms 🄻

28-30 Clegg Street, OL1 1PL (rear of Town Square shopping centre)
⊙ 11.30-11 (11.30 Fri & Sat; 7.30 Sun) ☎ (0161) 630 9709
Beer range varies Ⓗ
Once owned by Gartside Brewery, this free house is a permanent beer festival, offering seven different real ales from new and established brewers. Third-of-a-pint glasses are available to try something new. Continental beers, traditional ciders and perries (Valley Gold and guests) are stocked. Good-value food is served weekdays until 6pm (3pm Fri). The stone fireplace is more than 200 years old. Local CAMRA Cider Pub of the Year 2011 and Pub of Year 2010. ♨◐🚌♣●⚐🍺

Carrion Crow ✔

271 Huddersfield Road, OL4 2RJ (on A62 ¾ mile from town centre)
⊙ 12-midnight ☎ (0161) 633 4490
Marston's seasonal beers Ⓗ
Built in 1796, the Crow is a busy, thriving local on the A62. The landlord is an avid promoter of real ale, serving a wide selection from the Marston's range. Pub food is made with locally sourced produce, including the popular home-cooked Sunday roasts. The inn regularly hosts and supports charity events, plus football and quiz teams. Quiz

night is Thursday, and cask night is Monday, with the landlord's choice of discounted ales. Live entertainment features monthly.
❄️◗♿🍴(Mumps)🚇(81A,82,350)♣P⅃

Up Steps Inn L ✅
17-23 High Street, OL1 3AJ (between Town Square and Tommyfield Market)
🌐 8-midnight ☎ (0161) 6275001
Greene King Abbot; Ruddles Best Bitter; Theakston Best Bitter; guest beers Ⓗ
Traditional town-centre Wetherspoon on the main shopping street near the bus station and market. There are usually two regular beers and six rotating guests on offer, including some from local breweries under the LocAle scheme. The pub also hosts beer festivals featuring special beers and ciders. Food is available all day from 8am, and beer from 9am. The cider is usually from Westons, with others at festival time. ◗🍴(Mumps)🚇👤

Whittles L
27 King Street, OL8 1DP (near civic centre and police station)
🌐 12-8 (11 Wed & Thu; 1am Fri & Sat); 2-10 Sun
☎ (0161) 633 5468 ⊕ whittles-oldham.com
Beer range varies Ⓗ
The pub, formerly the Sergeant at Arms, dates from the early 1800s and served as the local militia HQ. Now Oldham's foremost live pub music venue, music features four nights a week (see website for details). Up to four real ales and one traditional cider are available including LocAles from Phoenix and other regional microbreweries. Ciders are usually from Westons. ❄️🍴🚇(180,409)👤⅃

Orrell

Running Horses
146 St James Road, WN5 7AA
🌐 4 (12 Fri & Sat)-midnight; 1-11.30 Sun ☎ (01942) 512604
Banks's Bitter; guest beers Ⓗ
Dating back to the 1800s, with a large extension added in 1920 and further modernisation in 2004, the pub offers a warm, cosy interior with sofas arranged around a fireplace. There is a separate pool and darts room. Sporting events are shown on a large pull-down screen and TV. Quality guest ales cover all tastes. Lunches are served on Sundays only (booking advisable). A regular Sunday night quiz and other charity events are held. There is a small covered smoking area outside.
❄️◗♿🚲🚇(197,362)♣P⅃

Patricroft

Bird in Hand
304 Liverpool Road, M30 0RY (by fire station)
🌐 11-midnight (1am Fri; 12.30am Sat) ☎ (0161) 211 6478
Holt Mild, Bitter, seasonal beer; guest beer Ⓗ
A red-brick Victorian pub with origins that seem earlier, located in a building that was formerly the Coroner's Court, with tunnels leading to the old police station. It still has separate rooms at the front, with some opening out to the rear. A pub with a great local atmosphere, friendly management and staff serve up to four real ales. It hosts fundraising events including a fancy dress dawdle to the brewery gates. There is a good beer garden outside with attractive floral displays.
❄️◗🚲(10,22,67)P⅃

Pendlebury

Lord Nelson
653 Bolton Road, M27 4EJ (A666 near B5231 jct)
🌐 11-11 (11.30 Fri); 12-11 Sun ☎ (07827) 850254
Holt Mild, IPA, Bitter Ⓗ
The Nelson, like his column, stands far above the other seven pubs on the road in terms of beer quality. The IPA is a recent addition. There are just two rooms – a vault and a lounge with a stage, reminiscent of a club room. A semi-secluded area, tucked away to the right of the lounge entrance, serves as a snug, albeit open to the main central bar. The pub is busy most times of the day.
◗🚉(Swinton)🚇(8,484)♣P⅃

Ramsbottom

First Chop L
43 Bolton Street, BL0 9HU
🌐 closed Mon; 4-midnight Tue; 12-midnight Wed & Sun; 12-1am Thu-Sat ☎ (01706) 827722 ⊕ thefirstchop.co.uk
Beer range varies Ⓗ
A friendly bar set over two floors, with a passion for beer, food and music. The landlord specialises in local ale and cider, with four of each always available. Live acoustic sessions feature on Thursday and a blues and soul jam on Sunday. CAMRA members receive every sixth pint in a week free, plus a 20 per cent discount on meals. The locally sourced home-cooked food, particularly the burgers, is excellent. Ciders are from Pure North, Dove Syke and guests. ◗♿🚇(472,474)👤

Irwell Works Brewery Tap
Irwell Works Brewery, BL0 9YQ (opp Morrisons)
🌐 11-11 (10.30 Sun) ☎ (01706) 825019
⊕ irwellworksbrewery.co.uk
Irwell Works Tin Plate Dark Mild, Copper Plate Bitter, Richard Mason's 1888, Steam Plate Best Bitter, Iron Plate Lancashire Stout Ⓗ
Irwell Works Brewery is situated in the former Irwell Steam, Tin, Copper and Iron Works. The building was used an engineering works until a few years ago. It now houses a six-barrel brewery above the entrance on Strag Street. Brewery tours are available by request. The bar sells a minimum of 10 beers including the brewery's own range plus guest beers and locally produced Ribble Valley Gold cider. Small plates of food are served at lunchtimes. Dogs are welcome. 🏃◗🚉👤🍴

Major Hotel L
158-160 Bolton Street, BL0 9JA
🌐 4-11 Mon; 12-midnight ☎ (01706) 826777
Bank Top Flat Cap; Copper Dragon Golden Pippin; St Austell Tribute; guest beers Ⓗ
The Major Hotel is a traditional stone-built property in keeping with its old mill town location. It benefits from having two separate areas, with a logburner in the lounge and many photographs of the local area. A dog- and family-friendly pub, it serves real home-cooked food with chips. A choice of four cask ales is always available, including local favourites and countrywide guests. Tuesday is quiz night, Thursday poker night. An easy stroll from East Lancashire Railway.
🏃❄️◗◗🚲🚉🚇(472,474)♣P⅃

Rochdale

Baum ▼ Ⓛ

33-37 Toad Lane, OL12 0NU (follow signs for Co-op Museum)
✪ 11.30-11 (midnight Fri & Sat; 10.30 Sun)
☎ (01706) 352186 ⊕ thebaum.co.uk
Beer range varies Ⓗ
A split-level hostelry with old world charm next door to the world's first co-operative store. The Baum has eight handpumps, one dedicated to cider, and a large variety of continental bottled beers. Excellent food includes vegetarian dishes, with a tapas menu available at weekends. There is an upstairs dining/function room. The large rear garden, overlooked by a conservatory, contains two full-size pétanque pistes. Local CAMRA Pub of the Year 2009 and 2012. Q❀◑⇥🖳♣🌳P⅃

Cask & Feather

1 Oldham Road, OL16 1UA
✪ 11-midnight (1am Fri & Sat); 12-midnight Sun
☎ (01706) 711476
Greenmill Gold; Phoenix Navvy; guest beers Ⓗ
Free house handily placed for the railway station. The interior is open plan with a long bar and pool area. Cask beer is keenly priced with the guests sourced from local micros. The rear of the pub is home to the Greenmill Brewery, which is a separate business. Good-value lunches are served daily. Outside is a beer garden and covered smoking area. Pool and poker are played on Monday and Tuesday, with a rock disco on Friday and live music on Sunday. ❀◑⇥🖳♣⅃

Cemetery Hotel ★ ✅

470 Bury Road, OL11 5EU (B6222 about 1 mile from town centre)
✪ 11.30-11 ☎ (07106) 645635
Beer range varies Ⓗ
This was Rochdale's original free house in the 1970s. Identified by CAMRA as one of Britain's Real Heritage Pubs, the building has a multi-roomed layout and retains impressive original features that make it well worth a visit. Upstairs is a restaurant noted for its traditional Lancashire fayre. The pub can get busy with Rochdale FC supporters on match days as it is handy for a pre- or post-match pint. Food is served 6-9.30pm Wednesday to Friday. Limited parking at the rear. ⋒❀◑🖳P

Flying Horse Hotel

37 Packer Street, OL16 1NJ
✪ 11-midnight (1am Fri & Sat); 12-midnight Sun
☎ (01706) 646412 ⊕ theflyinghorsehotel.co.uk
Lees Bitter; Taylor Best Bitter, Landlord; guest beers Ⓗ
Striking stone-built Edwardian free house in the Town Hall Square. Ten handpumps dispense a variety of beers including locals from Phoenix and Greenmill. Live sport is screened and live music plays on most Thursdays, Fridays and Saturdays. Reasonably priced food is served lunchtimes and evenings. There are 10 en-suite letting rooms and a large function room to hire. The main bus station is a three-minute walk. ⋓◑⇥🖳⅃

Healey Hotel

172 Shawclough Road, OL12 6LW
✪ 11.30-11.30 (midnight Fri & Sat); 12-11.30 Sun
☎ (01706) 645453
Robinson's Unicorn, seasonal beers Ⓗ
On the end of a row of stone terraced houses, this busy and friendly pub retains many original features. It serves excellent home-cooked food and hosts a pub quiz on Tuesday evening. Outside there is a beer garden to the side and a pétanque piste to the rear, along with a covered smoking area. Healey Dell Nature Reserve is nearby and there is a bridleway to the rear. Approximately two miles from Rochdale Centre, the 446 bus stops outside. Q❀◑🖳(446,466)🌳P⅃

Regal Moon Ⓛ ✅

The Butts, OL16 1HB (next to bus station)
✪ 9am-midnight (1am Fri & Sat) ☎ (01706) 657434
Greene King Ruddles Best Bitter; Thwaites Wainwright; guest beers Ⓗ
Large former cinema next to the main bus station retaining many original features including the imposing columns. Look above the bar and note the organ-playing mannequin. Boasting 18 handpumps, the pub was Wetherspoon Cask Pub of the Year in 2011, and quality beer from near and far is assured, with local beers featuring regularly. The cider is usually from Westons with an occasional guest. The standard range of meals and snacks is available. There is a patio to the rear for smokers. ❀◑&🖳🌳⅃

Star

691 Edenfield Road, Rochdale, OL12 7PP (on road to Norden)
✪ 12-11 ☎ (01706) 646479
Samuel Smith Old Brewery Bitter Ⓗ
A busy, family oriented local with friendly staff. The pub has been fully refurbished to a high standard with a traditional multi-roomed layout. An excellent and cheap pint of handpulled Sam Smith's is always available and a warm welcome is assured. The Star is handy for Rochdale AFC, with the ground less than a mile away. There is a large car park. ⋒Q❀◑&🖳♣P⅃

Romiley

Duke of York ✅

Stockport Road, SK6 3AN (on B6104, 100yds from bridge 14 on Peak Forest Canal)
✪ 12-midnight (12.30am Fri & Sat) ☎ (0161) 406 9988
Black Sheep Best Bitter; John Smith's Bitter; Thwaites Wainwright; Wells Bombardier; guest beer Ⓗ
Cosy, traditional village inn built in 1786 but tastefully and extensively refurbished in 2011, retaining its character and historic feel. A good range of cask-conditioned beers is always available and quality food is served six days a week (no food Mon) in the bar and first floor restaurant. A free-to-enter pub quiz is held every Wednesday evening, plus other weekly entertainment. A beer festival is held each autumn. ⋒Q❀◑🍴⇥🖳P⅃

Rusholme

Ford Madox Brown ✅

Unit 3 Wilmslow Park, Oxford Road, M13 9NG (opp Whitworth Park)
✪ 9-midnight ☎ (0161) 256 6660
Greene King Abbot; Ruddles Best Bitter; guest beers Ⓗ
Modern Wetherspoon pub named after the eminent Victorian Pre-Raphaelite painter (he lived nearby in Victoria Park) and built on the site of the old Rusholme Hall. Handy for the Curry Mile, MRI

Hospital, Whitworth Gallery and University, although many of its clientele are students it attracts a real cross-section of people. Although an open-plan pub, it has a warmer community feeling than you might expect, enhanced by charity and local events. Q✿❂◗⚅🖩(42,43)🍺⌐

Sale

J P Joule 🇱 ✅

2A Northenden Road, M33 3LF
❂ 9am-midnight (1am Fri & Sat) ☎ (0161) 928 9889
Greene King Abbot; Morland Old Speckled Hen; Phoenix Wobbly Bob; Ruddles Best Bitter; guest beers Ⓗ

Situated yards from Sale Metrolink station and on several major bus routes, this is an extremely popular Wetherspoon's named after the famous physicist, frequented by people of all ages from both near and far. The pub is spread over two floors connected by a stunning staircase, each floor having its own extensive bar hosting a total of 14 handpumps. Look for the CAMRA notice board on the ground floor at the far end of the bar.
✿◗⚅🖩🖩🍺⌐

Volunteer Hotel 🇱

81 Cross Street, M33 7HJ
❂ 12-midnight (11 Sun) ☎ (0161) 973 5503
Holt Mild, Bitter, seasonal beer Ⓗ

Dating back to the late 19th century, this once multi-roomed pub has been opened up into one large room served by a single bar. Major refurbishment in 2012 has highlighted the exterior's historic features. The interior is warm and welcoming, with friendly, helpful staff. Three darts teams are based here, which makes for some lively evenings, while a quiz night takes place on most Thursdays. There is a pool table and a fine oak-panelled room upstairs available for meetings.
✿⚅🖩P⌐

Salford

Crescent

18-21 The Crescent, M5 4PF (opp Salford University)
❂ 12-midnight (1am Fri & Sat); 12-11 Sun
☎ (0161) 736 5600 ⊕ thecrescentsalford.co.uk
Beer range varies Ⓗ

This Salford institution, housed in a Grade II-listed building, celebrated 25 consecutive years in the Guide in 2012. It has been revitalised by the enthusiastic new management. Up to 12 handpumps are available offering an ever-changing selection of beers sourced from far and wide, with up to four handpumps reserved for ciders. Entertainment includes a quiz night on Monday, open mic on Sunday, regular acoustic music sessions and curry night on Wednesday. Last entry 11pm Monday-Saturday.
🚅✿◗⇌(Crescent)🖩♣🍺P⌐

Mark Addy

Stanley Street, M3 5EJ (off New Bailey St)
❂ 11.30-11 (8 Sun) ☎ (0161) 832 4080 ⊕ markaddy.co.uk
Red Willow Mark Addy Fearless; guest beers Ⓗ

Named after a Victorian hero who saved many from drowning, this pub restaurant is situated wharfside on the River Irwell. Access is down steps from street level. Equal attention is focused on the award-winning food from renowned chef Robert Owen Brown and quality real ale. The house beer

Mark Addy Fearless is from Red Willow and up to five handpumps offer locally sourced ale. One handpump is for cider in summer. There is seating for drinkers by the bar. ✿◗⇌(Central)🖩🍺⌐

New Oxford 🏆

11 Bexley Square, M3 6DB (off Chapel St)
❂ 12-midnight ☎ (0161) 832 7082 ⊕ thenewoxford.com
Beer range varies Ⓗ

Situated just off the main A6, this regular local CAMRA Pub of the Year attracts locals as well as drinkers from further afield. A central bar serves two rooms. It offers up to 16 real ales at weekends, including a house beer from Moorhouse's, and has the widest range of bottled Belgian beers in the area. Occasional beer festivals are held. The pub was presented with a Community Pub Award by the local MP in 2011, a testament to its many charitable activities. ✿◗⚅⇌(Central)🖩🍺⌐

Racecourse Hotel

Littleton Road, Lower Kersal, M7 3SE (next to River Irwell)
❂ 12-11 (10.30 Sun) ☎ (0161) 792 1420
Oakwell Barnsley Bitter Ⓗ

Enter through revolving doors to be greeted by a massive rectangular bar, which served visitors to the Manchester Racecourse until its demise. Mementos of the racecourse abound, including a photograph of a young Lester Piggott winning the last race in 1963. The course fell victim to property developers, but fortunately this fine mock-Tudor community pub remains, playing host to a number of sports teams. Presented a 'fine example of an unspoilt pub' award by the local CAMRA Branch in 2012. Q🐕✿⚅🖩(93,95)♣P⌐

Star Inn

2 Back Hope Street, Higher Broughton, M7 2FR (off top of Great Clowes St)
❂ 1.30-11 (midnight Fri & Sat) ☎ (0161) 792 4184
⊕ staronthecliff.co.uk
Star Starry Night; guest beers Ⓗ

There used to be seven pubs in this area but now only this gem, run by a collective of locals, remains. With the look of a pebble-dashed 19th-century country inn and a welcoming interior with two attractive bay windows, it attracts a wide cross-section of customers. An occasional folk club night is held as well as the 'religious to quizzers' quiz on Sunday night. The Star houses its own brewery (formerly Bazens) in an outbuilding and holds a must-visit annual beer festival.
✿⚅◗(98)♣⌐

Stalybridge

Old Hunter's Tavern

51-53 Acres Lane, SK15 2JR
❂ 12-midnight ☎ (0161) 303 9477
Robinson's 1892, Unicorn, seasonal beers Ⓗ

Street-corner locals like this one, full of character, are becoming less common. This is a good pub that appeals to all. The brass poles with their circular shelves for holding pints are an unusual feature. The ladies' darts team meets every Tuesday evening (bringing their own Manchester log-end board). Quiz night is Thursday and the golf society meets monthly. There is a covered and heated area for smokers. No food at weekends. ✿◗⇌🖩♣P⌐

Stalybridge Station Refreshment Rooms (Buffet Bar)

Rassbottom Street, SK15 1RF (Platform 1)
✪ 10-11; 12-10.30 Sun ☎ (0161) 303 0007 ⊕ buffetbar.org
Flowers IPA; guest beers Ⓗ

Nobody minds delayed or missed trains at Stalybridge. This institution for educated drinkers serves a wide range of up to nine cask beers, usually from micros, often with rare brews as well. A good range of foreign and other bottled beers is also available, plus Broadoak Premium Perry. These can be enjoyed in convivial Victorian splendour by the roaring fire (but no drinking on the platform please). The conservatory adds to the charm and character of this gem. A folk club plays on Saturday, quiz night is Monday. Pies and peas and other light snacks are available. ⚃Q✿◑₫≢⊒◔P

White House Ⓛ ✅

1 Water Street, SK15 2AG
✪ 12-11 (midnight Sat) ☎ (0161) 303 2154
Hydes Original Bitter; guest beers Ⓗ

A light-touch refurbishment and an enthusiastic management have transformed this previously moribund town-centre pub close to the bus station. A well-balanced and intelligently chosen range of up to five guest beers complements those from Hydes. The pub is semi open plan, but the customer will appreciate the discreet and cosy individual areas. There is a quiz night on Wednesday, live entertainment on Friday and a folk night on alternate Thursdays. ◐≢⊒♣

Stockport

Arden Arms ★

23 Millgate, SK1 2LX (jct Corporation St)
✪ 12-11 ☎ (0161) 480 2185 ⊕ arden-arms.co.uk
Robinson's 1892, Unicorn, Double Hop Ⓗ**, Old Tom** Ⓖ**, seasonal beers** Ⓗ

Grade II-listed and and identified by CAMRA as one of Britain's Real Heritage Pubs, the Arden's distinctive curved, glazed bar, hidden snug, chandeliers and grandfather clock conjure up a Victorian ambience. Conveniently close to Stockport's historic market, the place is abuzz at lunchtimes, but more intimate in the evenings. The cellars, a former mortuary, retain body niches in their walls. A beautiful courtyard shows off the old stables and outbuildings. This is an unmissable gem. ⚃⛘✿◑₫⊒(300,384)♣ᵈ–

Armoury ✅

31 Shaw Heath, Edgeley, SK3 8BD (on B5465, jct Greek St)
✪ 11-midnight (1am Fri & Sat) ☎ (0161) 477 3711
Robinson's 1892, Unicorn, seasonal beers Ⓗ

Comfortable, recently refurbished multi-roomed local with a strong community involvement. It caters for a varied clientele from sport watchers to darts teams (with two leagues often playing on the same night) to quiet bookworms alike. Excellent well-priced food from a varied menu is now available (served until 5pm), with efficient, friendly service. Handy for the train station and football ground, outside is a pleasant suntrap of a beer garden. Q✿◑₫≢⊒(310,369)♣ᵈ–

Boar's Head

2 Vernon Street, Market Place, SK1 1TY
✪ 11-11; 12-6.30 Sun ☎ (0161) 4803978
Samuel Smith Old Brewery Bitter Ⓗ

A multi-roomed pub with a genuine cosy, town-centre feel. Owners Samuel Smith spent a fair sum some years back restoring this pub to what it may have once looked like. The front room is divided into a sparsely furnished public lounge and a more substantial, comfortably furnished main room. The latter is fitted out with cushioned pews, high-back chairs and stools. To the rear is a second lounge (once the music room) leading to a decked area outside. ⚃Q✿❀⊒(325,330)ᵈ–

Crown ✅

154 Heaton Lane, SK4 1AR (at jct with King Street West under viaduct)
✪ 12-11 (10.30 Sun) ☎ (0161) 480 5850
⊕ thecrowninn.uk.com
Beer range varies Ⓗ

A busy pub, especially in the evenings. It offers around 16 ever-changing beers, with helpful and knowledgeable staff to advise those confused by the choice. Pictish and Bollington beers are regulars, and there is usually a mild, stout/porter and a craft cider. Four rooms radiate from the busy bar: two compact snugs, a large lounge and a stand-up bar. Food is served until 3pm weekdays. Live music is a feature, with the rear yard often showcasing local bands at the weekend. A real gem. ⚃✿◑₫≢⊒(192)♣ᵈ–

Magnet

51 Wellington Road North, SK4 1HJ (A6 jct Duke St)
✪ 4 (12 Thu-Sun)-11 ☎ (0161) 429 6287
⊕ themagnetfreehouse.com
Beer range varies Ⓗ

Within less than two years of being rescued from failure, the rejuvenated Magnet won acclaim as both CAMRA Regional and local Pub of the Year 2011. It boasts 14 handpumps for beer and a draught cider, complemented by a large foreign bottled range. It has a bustling vault to the left, leading to a lower pool room, and a series of rooms separated by arched magnet doorways on the right. The upstairs beer terrace and function room are popular, as are the Monday cheese nights. The Cellar Rat Brewery is housed here. ⚃Q✿₫⊒(22,192)♣ᵈP–

Olde Vic

1 Chatham Street, Edgeley, SK3 9ED (jct of Shaw Heath)
✪ closed Mon; 5 (7 Sat)-late (last entry 10.15); 7-10.30 Sun ☎ (0161) 480 2410 ⊕ yeoldevic.com
Beer range varies Ⓗ

The first Stockport pub to offer changing guest beers, this quirky but extremely well-run free house continues to do the business to this day. Larger-than-life landlord Steve runs a tight ship (strictly no swearing) where conversation and banter are the order of the day. The beers come from north-west micros and also from farther afield, while the guest cider is often from a smaller maker. ⚃✿≢⊒(310,369)ᵈ–

Pineapple

159 Heaton Lane, SK4 1AQ (off A6, near viaduct)
✪ 12-11 (10.30 Sun) ☎ (0161) 480 3221
Robinson's 1892, Cumbria Way, Unicorn, seasonal beer Ⓗ

In 2013 the landlady will have been here for 25 years and her long-term commitment to quality shows throughout the pub. This longevity is also why this three-roomed pub in sight of Stockport's famous viaduct has remained a community local as well as a welcoming stop-off for shoppers and visitors to the nearby Hat Works and Plaza Theatre. The walls of the comfortable lounges are adorned with numerous plates brought back from foreign parts by customers over the years. ⍟◖⊞≠⊟(192)♣🍴

Railway

1 Avenue Street, Portwood, SK1 2BZ (jct Great Portwood St/A560)
✪ 12-11 (10.30 Sun) ☎ (0161) 429 6062
Pennine Floral Dance, Porter; Outstanding Sold Out, seasonal beers; guest beers Ⓗ
Bustling, street-corner house with 15 handpumps showcasing the ranges of Pennine, Outstanding and Pictish breweries, plus other guests. A changing mild and a real cider are also stocked, plus a wide selection of Belgian, German and other bottled beers. Occasional beer and cider festivals take place too. Note the model railway atop the bar canopy, and the amusing loco mural at the back. A bar billiards table is well used. A former local CAMRA Pub of the Year, its future may yet be threatened by a proposed supermarket development. Q⍟🐾⊟(325,330)♣🍴🍴

Railway

74-76 Wellington Road North, SK4 1HF (jct Georges Road)
✪ 12-midnight ☎ (0161) 477 3680
Holt Bitter; guest beers Ⓗ
Friendly pub with two front rooms, one with a feature fireplace and photos of old Stockport, the other more contemporary in decor with a raised stage area. A games room occupies the rear with a pool table and darts, and there is a function room upstairs. Live music includes open mic nights and jazz on a Sunday and the second Tuesday of the month. This 2010 local CAMRA Pub of the Year serves four guest ales (often from local microbreweries) alongside the permanent Holt Bitter. ⍟⊟⊟(22,192)♣🍴

Red Bull

14 Middle Hillgate, SK1 3AY (between Wellington and Edward streets)
✪ 12-11 (10.30 Sun) ☎ (0161) 480 1286
⊕ redbullstockport.co.uk
Robinson's 1892, Unicorn, Dizzy Blonde, seasonal beers Ⓗ
Refurbished and enlarged in 2008, the pub retains a homely, rustic atmosphere. Numerous dining and drinking areas radiate from a large central bar area, with a wooden and tiled floor. Outside are a cobbled courtyard and small car park. Full menus are provided plus daily meals at competitive prices. Situated 400 yards uphill from Robinson's Brewery, the Red Bull aims to maintain its flagship operation within the Robinson's estate. ㎖Q⍟◖◖≠⊟(313)P🍴

Swan with Two Necks ★

36 Princes Street, SK1 1RY
✪ 12-7 (11 Fri & Sat; 6 Sun) ☎ (0161) 480 2341
Robinson's Dark 1892, Unicorn, Old Tom, seasonal beers Ⓗ
Narrow-fronted with a mock-Tudor façade, the building was bought by Robinson's in 1924. Rejuvenated by a young couple with ideas and vigour, it is impressively panelled in light oak throughout in familiar Robinson's style, with labelled doors to match. The front door leads to a vault, then the bustling bar-corridor, beyond that a

cosy snug with an attractive skylight, and at the rear a small lounge and diner. Outside is a compact, walled drinking area. Quality lunchtime meals are served weekdays. The cider is Westons Scrumpy. ⍟◖⊞⊟(300,330)🍴

Strines

Sportsman 🏆

105 Strines Road, SK6 7GE (on B6101)
✪ 12-3, 5-11; 12-11 Sat & Sun ☎ (0161) 427 2888
⊕ the-sportsman-pub.co.uk
Beer range varies Ⓗ
Popular both with local drinkers and diners, this splendid white pub stands alone on the edge of the Goyt Valley. The comfortable lounge has large picture windows giving superb views over the wooded countryside; a monumental fireplace accommodates log fires in winter and there is a small separate tap room. Five guest beers, mainly from micros, are available and the landlord welcomes beer suggestions. Outside, a terrace and balcony are popular in summer and the pub is close to the Peak Forest Canal. ㎖Q⍟◖◖⊞Å≠⊟(62,358)♣P🍴

Swinley

Fifteens Swinley ✪

15 Upper Dicconson Street, WN1 2AD
✪ 12-11 (1am Fri & Sat) ☎ (01942) 820912
Beer range varies Ⓗ
Fifteens is a cosy pub spread over three levels with a pleasant drinking area outside at the front. It benefits from a homely environment and friendly, welcoming staff. The bar usually offers three real ales and a cider. Memorabilia adorn the walls. With five comfortable rooms on offer, the pub makes an ideal base for anyone wanting to explore the area. ⊟♣🍴

Swinton

White Horse ✪

384 Worsley Road, M27 0FH (on A572, near Moorside Rd)
✪ 12-11 ☎ (0161) 794 2404
Thwaites Wainwright; Wells Bombardier; guest beers Ⓗ
Dating back to the 17th century, this is Swinton's oldest pub. Although the exterior is listed, the interior has been much altered. As you enter from the front door the main lounge is to the left and the bar to the right. There are four quieter alcoves. At the rear is a large outdoor seating area which can be quite a suntrap on summer afternoons. A loyal following means the pub is usually busy. Food is served until 9pm daily. ⍟◖⊞⊟(12,26)♣P🍴

White Swan

186 Worsley Road, M27 5SN (jct A572/A580 north side)
✪ 12-11 (11.30 Fri; 10.30 Sun) ☎ (0161) 834 3285
Holt IPA, Bitter, seasonal beer Ⓗ
Built between the two world wars to replace a cottage pub, the Swan emulates much of the grandeur of the Edwardian estate. Originally five rooms, the two on the left had a dividing wall partly removed, but retain all the seating. The vault is front right and a large oak-panelled lounge is behind the bar. Far away to the rear is a separate room which serves for functions, football on TV, darts and a family room. ☸⍟⊞⊟(12,22,26)♣P🍴

Tyldesley

Mort Arms

235-237 Elliot Street, M29 8DG
☼ 12-midnight (1am Fri & Sat; 11 Sun) ☎ (01942) 883481
Holt Mild, Bitter Ⓗ
From the façade to the interior, this popular 1930s pub is recognisable as a Holt hostelry. The entrance has two etched doors directing you to the taproom or lounge, with a central bar serving both rooms. The taproom is a bright contrast and just how a taproom should be. A meeting place for the Tyldesley Brass Band, there is a secluded patio area at the rear. ⊞♣

Uppermill

Cross Keys

off Running Hill Gate, OL3 6LW (off A670, up Church Rd)
☼ 12-11.30 (midnight Fri & Sat) ☎ (01457) 874626
⊕ crosskeysuppermill.com
Lees Brewer's Dark, Bitter, Coronation Street, seasonal beers Ⓗ
Set in a conservation area, this attractive 18th-century stone building has exposed beams throughout. The public bar features a stone-flagged floor and Yorkshire range. The pub is the centre for activities including Mountain Rescue and the Saddleworth Runners. It is especially busy during annual events such as the Rushcart Festival and the Wartime Weekend. Folk nights take place on Wednesday and Sunday. Home-cooked food includes puddings and pies. Dogs are welcome and there is a covered and heated smoking area.
쌀Q⚙⏻⊞P≛

Hare & Hounds Ⓛ

68 High Street, OL3 6AW
☼ 12-midnight (12.30am Fri & Sat; 11.30 Sun)
☎ (01457) 873115
Lees Bitter; guest beers Ⓗ
Situated within close proximity to village amenities, this 18th-century inn welcomes dogs and walkers. Two guest beers are on handpump. Sky Sports is shown on a large screen and a pool table is available. The pub hosts a darts and crib team. Live entertainment features on Sunday evening and Monday is quiz night. Themed nights and charity events are held throughout the year. Uppermill football and cricket clubs are regularly supported, ensuring a strong local following.
≈(Greenfield)🚌(184,350)♣P

Waggon Inn

34 High Street, OL3 6HR
☼ 11.30-11 (midnight Fri & Sat); 12-11 Sun
☎ (01457) 872376 ⊕ thewaggoninn.co.uk
Robinson's Unicorn, Dizzy Blond Ⓗ**, Old Tom** Ⓖ**, seasonal beers** Ⓗ
Nineteenth-century stone-built inn providing Robinson's beers in picturesque Saddleworth. The building features a games room, lounge and snug serviced by a central bar. There is a separate restaurant and en-suite B&B is available. Monday is poker night, Sunday quiz night. Good home-cooked food includes senior specials and themed events (no eve meals Sun or Mon). Old Tom is available on gravity during the winter months.
Q⚙⏻⏻Å≈(Greenfield)🚌(184,350)♣P≛

Wardley

Morning Star

520 Manchester Road, M27 9QW (on A6 near motorway flyover)
☼ 12-11.30 (11 Sun) ☎ (0161) 794 4927
Holt Mild, IPA, Bitter, seasonal beers Ⓗ
Built in 1890, this fine red-brick building is a popular community pub on the outskirts of town – the vault to the left is the hub of social activities with men's and ladies' darts and dominoes teams. To the right is a small quiet lounge, which leads to a much larger lounge with larger TV screens showing sport – it can get busy here when football is on. There is regular live entertainment at weekends and quiz nights mid-week. The Holt seasonals alternate with a guest beer.
⚙⊞≈(Moorside)🚌(36,37)♣P≛

Westhoughton

Robert Shaw ⊘

34-40 Market Street, BL5 3AN (200yds from town hall)
☼ 8-midnight (1am Fri & Sat) ☎ (01942) 844110
Greene King Abbot; Ruddles Best Bitter Ⓗ
Large open-plan public house, formerly the Co-op. It is named after the actor who was born in Westhoughton. Wood panelling and bare brick dominate the decor in this modern Wetherspoon pub. Old photographs of the local Pretoria Pit Mine disaster that happened 100 years ago feature on the walls. The usual good-value Wetherspoon menu is served all day. The pub hosts four beer festivals a year. Q🛏⏻&🚌(540)♣P≛

Whalley Range

Hillary Step Ⓛ ⊘

199 Upper Chorlton Road, M16 0BH
☼ 4-11.30; 3-12.30am Fri; 12-12.30am Sat; 12-11.30 Sun
☎ (0161) 881 1978
Beer range varies Ⓗ
Recently extended modern bar in a small strip of shops and bars just north of Chorlton centre. A handpump is dedicated to each of Thwaites, Phoenix and Thornbridge breweries, with two further guest ales served alongside a good range of draught and bottled continental beers plus over 20 malt whiskies. Cheese boards, charcuterie and snacks are popular, plus a good range of other nibbles (olives, salami and nuts). Live jazz plays on Sunday evenings and quiz night is the first Tuesday of the month. No children.
⚙🚌(Firswood)🚌(86)♣≛

Wigan

Anvil Ⓛ ⊘

Dorning Street, WN1 1ND (next to bus station)
☼ 11-11 (10.30 Sun) ☎ (01942) 239444
AllGates Mild; Hydes Bitter; guest beers Ⓗ
Popular town-centre pub close to the bus station, winner of many local CAMRA awards (see the certificate wall). Seven handpumps dispense a selection of AllGates beers plus guests. A regular mild and a traditional cider as well as a range of continental draught and bottled beers are also available. Sport is shown on two TV screens. Outside is a covered smoking shelter and drinking area. ⚙≈(Wallgate/N Western)🚌♣≛

Berkeley L ✔

27-29 Wallgate, WN1 1LD
✪ 11.30am-11 (midnight Fri & Sat); 12-10.30 Sun
☎ (01942) 242041
Beer range varies Ⓗ

The Berkeley is a former coaching house opposite Wallgate rail station and three minutes from Wigan North Western. The pub has flexible seating including intimate booths that can be booked for celebrations. The large bar hosts a range of rotating guests and food is served daily until 7pm. Watch your favourite sporting event on one of the eight large flat-screen TVs and the massive projector screen. A first-floor function room is available for hire. ⓓ≒(Wallgate/N Western)🚃

Brocket Arms L ✔

Mesnes Road, Swinley, WN1 2DD
✪ 7am-midnight (1am Fri & Sat) ☎ (01942) 403500
Greene King Abbot; Marston's Pedigree; Ruddles County; guest beers Ⓗ

In a residential area a 15-minute walk from the town centre, the Brocket is also a Wetherlodge. The interior is large, open plan with two bars and intimate booths. Two conference rooms are available for private hire. Guest beers are always featured. In addition to the usual Wetherspoon menu, the Sunday carvery is popular here. There is a patio area to the front with benches and cover for smokers. Fundraising events are often held for various charities. ⓑ❀🍴ⓓ&🚃🐕P⅃

Royal Oak ♈ L

Standishgate, WN1 1XL (on A49 N of town centre)
✪ 4 (12 Sun)-midnight; 12-1am Fri & Sat ☎ (01942) 323137
Beer range varies Ⓗ

Built in the early 17th century and close to Wigan centre on the A49, the Grade II-listed Royal Oak has always been a landmark pub on the Wigan Lane crawl. It has recently undergone a major exterior restoration and refurbishment. The multi-room interior is served by a long bar stocking an excellent range of real ales, plus foreign draught and bottled beers. Live music and food festivals are hosted. The pleasant beer garden is ideal in summer. ❀&⅃

Standish Unity Club L

Cross Street, Standish, WN6 0HQ (opp library)
✪ 7.30-11 (midnight Fri & Sat) ☎ (01257) 424007
⊕ standishunityclub.com
Prospect Unity Gold; guest beers Ⓗ

Established for 11 years, this is an independent, non-profit-making club open to all. It has a comfortably furnished bar and function room with a separate pool/snooker room. It is also a music venue and available for private functions. There are quiz nights and the club has its own pool team. Prospect Unity Gold is a permanent beer with many local breweries also showcased. The club hosts its own beer festival annually and CAMRA members are welcome at all times. CAMRA Wigan Club of the Year 2011. Q♿&🚃(113,362)P

Tudor House

New Market Street, WN1 1SE
✪ 11-11 (1am Fri & Sat) ☎ (01942) 242190
Beer range varies Ⓗ

The Tudor is a town-centre pub yet slightly off the beaten track. It has genuine charm with a welcoming atmosphere, haphazard furniture and original decor. It is known for its music both live and on the jukebox, and has a large TV showing sporting events. There are two beer gardens with smoking areas. Reasonably priced food is served. ❀ⓓ≒(Wallgate)🚃🐕⅃

Woodford

Davenport Arms (Thief's Neck)

550 Chester Road, SK7 1PS (on A5102, jct Church Lane)
✪ 11-11; 12-10.30 Sun ☎ (0161) 439 2435
Robinson's 1892, Unicorn Ⓗ**, Old Tom** Ⓟ**, seasonal beers** Ⓗ

This is the 26th consecutive year in the Guide for this unspoilt farmhouse-style pub where the licence has now been in the same family for 80 years. The cosy rooms are warmed by real fires, and children are welcome at lunchtimes in the right-hand snug. Excellent food is mostly home made, with some adventurous specials. Outside, the spacious forecourt and attractive garden, set well away from the road, are popular in summer, when impressive floral displays are on show. 🏚ⓑ❀ⓓ♿🚃(157,X57)♣P⅃

Worsley

Bridgewater Hotel ✔

23 Barton Road, M28 2PD (on B5211, 200yds S of M60 jct 13)
✪ 10-11 ☎ (0161) 794 6206
Greene King IPA; guest beers Ⓗ

Built in 1903, this pub is set in a picturesque village. It is a large building overlooking the village green and the first canal in the UK. The interior is mostly separate rooms, with some parts open plan. The massive bar offers up to six handpumps dispensing a varied range of ales, often from Moorhouse's, Wychwood and St Austell breweries. A varied range of food is served, with breakfast from 10.30am. Well-behaved dogs are allowed in beer garden. 🏚ⓑ❀ⓓ♿🚃(33,68)P⅃

Worthington

Crown Hotel L

Platt Lane, WN1 2XF (off A5106 Chorley to Wigan)
✪ 12-11 (10.30 Sun) ☎ (08000) 686678
⊕ thecrownatworthington.co.uk
Facer's Northern Counties; guest beers Ⓗ

Privately owned free house in a country location with 10 en-suite bedrooms and function rooms. High-quality, home-cooked food is served in the bar and conservatory restaurant, and outside on the decked sun terrace at the rear. Up to 10 ales are offered and two or three ciders, with up to 16 different beers weekly. The pub hosts a cider festival in August and beer festivals throughout the year. An extensive selection of bottled beers is also stocked. Winner of six CAMRA awards. Qⓑ❀🍴ⓓ🚃(640,641)🐕P⅃

When you have lost your inns, drown your empty selves, for you will have lost the last of England. **Hilaire Belloc**, The Four Men, 1912

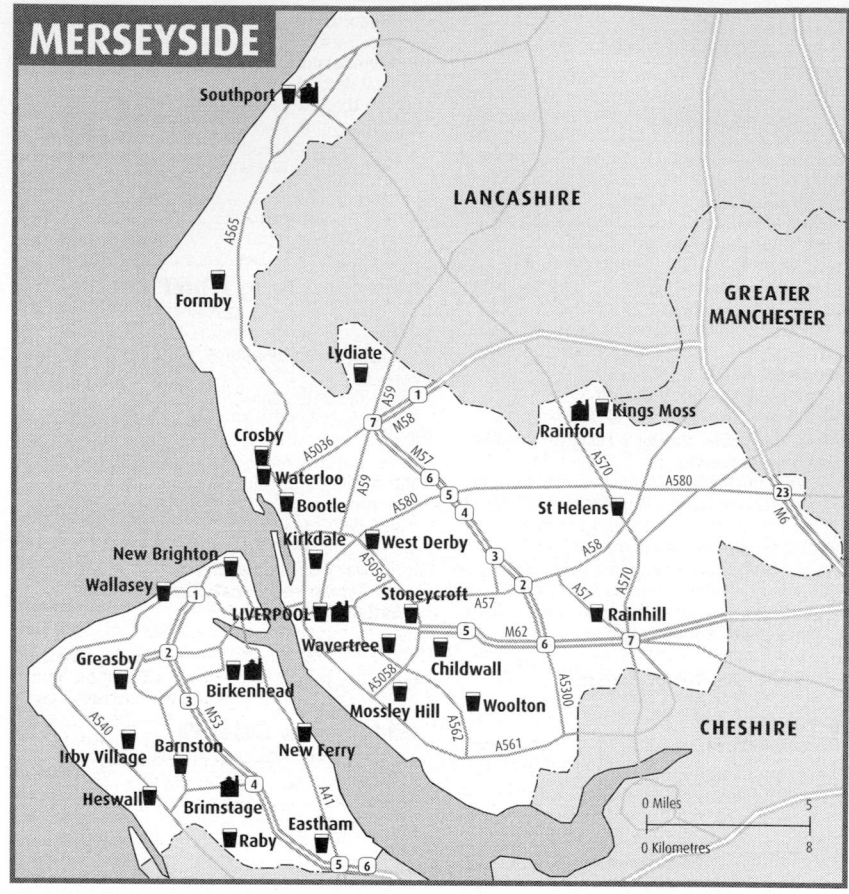

MERSEYSIDE

Southport

LANCASHIRE

Formby

GREATER
MANCHESTER

Lydiate

Kings Moss

Crosby
Rainford

Waterloo

Bootle

St Helens

New Brighton
Kirkdale
West Derby

Wallasey
Stoneycroft

LIVERPOOL
Rainhill

Greasby
Wavertree

Birkenhead
Childwall

Mossley Hill
Woolton

CHESHIRE

Irby Village
Barnston
New Ferry

Heswall
Brimstage
Eastham

Raby

0 Miles 5

0 Kilometres 8

Barnston

Fox & Hounds ✓
107 Barnston Road, CH61 1BW (on A551)
11-11; 12-10.30 Sun ☎ (0151) 648 7685
⏛ the-fox-hounds.co.uk
Brimstage Trappers Hat; Theakston Best Bitter, Old
Peculier; guest beers Ⓗ
Village pub with bar, lounge and snug full of bric-a-
brac, clocks, flying ducks, horse brasses, local
photos and other memorabilia. The lounge,
converted from tea rooms, is quiet with no music
or games machines. The pub retains its original
character including real fires in the bar and snug.
The stone courtyard is a profusion of colour in the
summer. Popular for its cask ales and real
lunchtime food, it offers a fish dish of the day, daily
specials and traditional Sunday roasts.
ⓂQ☺❄◑ⓈⓀ♿⇆☷♣Ⓟ↖

Birkenhead

Cock & Pullet Ⓛ
100 Woodchurch Road, CH42 9LP
12-midnight (1am Fri & Sat) ☎ (0151) 652 5437
Brimstage Trappers Hat; guest beers Ⓗ
Recently refurbished and transformed with many
photographs of old Wirral, the former Royal Hotel is
a welcome addition to the real ale scene in
Birkenhead and a strong supporter of local

breweries and traditional cider. Situated in a
residential area of the town, the locals are always
friendly and open to conversation. Quiz nights and
live music feature on Sunday evenings plus
televised live sport. ⛹♣

Gallaghers Pub & Barber's Shop �ⓎⓁ
20 Chester Street, CH41 5DQ
12-midnight (1am Fri & Sat) ☎ (0151) 649 9095
⏛ gallagherspubandbarbers.com
Brimstage Trappers Hat; guest beers Ⓗ
Genuine, welcoming free house close to the
famous Mersey ferries, resurrected after closure
and refurbished in 2010 by a former Irish
Guardsman as a unique pub with barber's shop.
One long bar sports six handpumps mainly serving
beers from local breweries plus real cider. A
fascinating range of memorabilia includes military

INDEPENDENT BREWERIES

Brimstage Brimstage
Cains Liverpool
George Wright Rainford
Liverpool Craft Liverpool
Liverpool One Liverpool
Liverpool Organic Liverpool
Peerless Birkenhead
Southport Southport
Wapping Liverpool

hats and photographs as well as a collection of Mersey shipping images. TV sport adds to a lively atmosphere. Local CAMRA Pub of the Year 2012. ❀◖►➔(Hamilton Sq)🖂●

Crosby

Stamps Bar 🅛
5 Crown Buildings, L23 5SR
❀ 12-11 (midnight Fri & Sat) ☎ (0151) 286 2662
⊕ stampsbar.co.uk
Beer range varies 🄷
'Real ale, real food, real music' is the Stamps motto and a visit will not disappoint. Five beers are available, with local brewers well represented and a regularly changing real cider. Home-produced food is served Thursday to Saturday until early evening. Local musicians play Friday to Sunday, with something to suit most tastes. There is a quieter upstairs lounge area away from the noise and bustle of the main bar. Free internet access and Wi-Fi is available.
◖►&➔(Blundellsands & Crosby)🖂●

Eastham

Tap
1a Ferry Road, CH62 0AU (1 mile from village)
❀ 12-11 (11.30 Thu; midnight Fri & Sat) ☎ (0151) 327 6810
⊕ thetap.net
Banks's Bitter; guest beers 🄷
Friendly and cosy country pub with fantastic views of the River Mersey, next to the site of the ferry pier and situated in Eastham Country Park. Known as a bikers' pub, it is popular with all. It has a quiz night on Thursday and live music on Saturday. Toasties are available at all times. The two guest beers are usually from the Marston's group.
🏚❀◖►🖂♣P

Formby

Freshfield Hotel 🅛
1a Massams Lane, Freshfield, L37 7BD (5 mins' walk from Freshfield train station)
❀ 11-11 (midnight Fri & Sat) ☎ (01704) 874871
Beer range varies 🄷
Up to 12 beers and three ciders are a feature of this community local. It is a Greene King pub with enlightened management that offers a broad range of beer and cider from across the country, with micros featuring strongly. Beers from Liverpool Organic provide the local element. A recent refurbishment has provided a more substantial food presence but the emphasis is decidedly on the beer. There is a heated smoking area outside.
🏚❀◖►&➔(Freshfield)🖂(162,165)●P'⸺

Greasby

Coach & Horses
Greasby Road, CH49 3NG
❀ 11.30-11 (midnight Fri & Sat); 12-11 Sun
☎ (0151) 677 1656
Taylor Landlord 🄷
Charming, whitewashed, traditional street-corner local dating back nearly 300 years. It became a pub in 1832 but was formerly a farmhouse where ale was brewed and sold from 1725. Time has changed little in this gem of a pub. Two main rooms with matching snugs lie either side of a compact bar. Ex-

Tranmere Rovers footballer Barrie Mitchell is an amiable licensee, and football memorabilia adorn the wall of one of the snugs. ❀&🖂(437)♣P

Irby Mill ✅
Mill Lane, CH49 3NT (on roundabout between Greasby and Irby)
❀ 12-11 (midnight Fri & Sat) ☎ (0151) 694 0194
⊕ irbymill.co.uk
Greene King Abbot; Jennings Cumberland Ale; Wells Bombardier; guest beers 🄷
Formerly Lumsdens Café and once frequented by touring motorcyclists, the pub sits on the site of a former mill. It comprises a small, L-shaped, stone-floored bar and a lounge used mainly by diners. The establishment has an excellent reputation for its home-made food. The nearby Royden Park and Thurstaston Common provide the pub with many passing hikers to supplement the strong local following. 🏚Q❀◖►🖂P

Heswall

Dee View Inn 🅛
Dee View Road, CH60 0DH
❀ 12-midnight (11 Sun) ☎ (0151) 342 2320
Black Sheep Best Bitter; Taylor Landlord; guest beers 🄷
Homely, traditional local built in the late 1800s offering a warm welcome. Redecorated in 2008, it has retained its character and friendly atmosphere. It sits on a hairpin bend by the war memorial and famous mirror, with views over the Dee Estuary and close to the Wirral Way path. A popular and entertaining quiz night is held on Tuesday and live music is a frequent attraction. Traditional home-cooked food is served and children are welcome if dining. ❀◖►🖂♣P'⸺

Irby Village

Shippons
8A Thingwall Road, CH61 3UA
❀ 12-midnight ☎ (0151) 648 0449 ⊕ shippons-irby.co.uk
Thwaites Nutty Black, Original, IPA, Wainwright, Lancaster Bomber; guest beers 🄷
A welcoming focal point for the community, this sandstone village pub was converted from old farm buildings. With up to seven quality real ales, including a mild and frequently a porter or stout, a range of beer styles is guaranteed. A good choice of interesting guests from the Thwaites' beer club is also on offer. The sheltered garden is a suntrap in summer, an ideal spot to relax and enjoy a few pints. Live music and sport on TV add to the enjoyment. ❀◖►&🖂(71)P'⸺

Kings Moss

Colliers Arms
Pimbo Road, WA11 8RD (follow signs for Houghwood Golf Club)
❀ 12-11 (10.30 Sun) ☎ (01744) 892284
⊕ colliersarms.org.uk
Black Sheep Best Bitter; guest beers 🄷
Situated in the rural hamlet of Kings Moss at the foot of Billinge Hill, the pub is part of a row of former miners' cottages near the site of the old Hillside Colliery. The interior comprises four distinct areas served from a central bar. Good quality home-cooked food is served. Books, mining memorabilia and photographs decorate the walls,

and there is a pleasant children's play area and beer garden to the rear, where they grow some of herbs and vegetables used in the meals.

⚲Q☗☺◑🖳(152,356)P

Liverpool: Bootle

Cat & Fiddle 🆕

St Martin's House, Stanley Street, L20 3LG

✪ 11.30-11 (1am Mon; 2am Fri & Sat; 10.30 Sun)

☎ (0151) 922 9561 ⊕ catandfiddlepub.co.uk

Beer range varies 🅷

Originally built as part of a '60s office block and owned by Tetley, the pub has been through a number of incarnations and, following a period of closure, reopened in 1999 as a real ale pub. Four handpumps offer a constantly changing range of guest beers including at least one Liverpool Organic ale. Good-value home-cooked food is served all day. Football is screened and there is a wide variety of entertainment in the evenings including quiz night every Wednesday.

☗◑≠(Bootle Oriel Rd/New Strand)⊖🖳'—

Liverpool: Childwall

Childwall Fiveways Hotel 🆕 ✅

179 Queens Drive, L15 6XS

✪ 9am-11.30 ☎ (0151) 738 2100

Greene King IPA, Abbot; guest beers 🅷

A former Higson's tied house, this large single-roomed pub opened as a Wetherspoon in 2010. Located in a leafy suburb, it has good motorway and public transport links. The refurbished interior is decorated with wood panelling, and outside there is a beer garden. A popular establishment, it can get busy, especially at weekends.

☗◑⬥≠(Broadgreen)🖳(61,79,81)P'—

Liverpool: City Centre

Augustus John 🆕

Peach Street, L3 5TX (off Brownlow Hill next to Blackwell's bookshop)

✪ 11.30 (12 Sat)-11; closed Sun ☎ (0151) 794 5507

Tetley Bitter; guest beers 🅷

Opened in 1901 and run by the University of Liverpool, the Augustus John is an open-plan pub popular with students, lecturers and locals. Up to four guest beers are available and a number of ciders – the pub was named Cider Pub of the Year 2011 by the local CAMRA branch. Pizza is served at all times, sport is screened and there is a jukebox. Closed over Christmas and the New Year.

☗⬥≠(Lime St)🖳(Central)🖳(79)♠'—

Baltic Fleet 🆕

33 Wapping, L1 8DQ

✪ 12 (10 Sat)-11; 10-10.30 Sun ☎ (0151) 709 3116

⊕ wappingbeers.co.uk

Wapping Bitter, Stout, Summer, seasonal beers; guest beers 🅷

Situated near the Albert Dock, Liverpool's only brewpub is in a Grade II-listed building based on the flat iron shape, with interior decoration on a nautical theme. Six handpumps serve beer from the Wapping Brewery located in the cellar plus occasional guests. Pies and home-cooked scouse are regularly available. Tunnels in the cellar have led to speculation of a dark period in the pub's history involving smuggling and press gangs.

⚲Q◑⬥🖳🖳(500)

Belvedere 🆕 ✅

8 Sugnall Street, L7 7EB (off Falkner St)

✪ 12-11 (10.30 Sun) ☎ (0151) 709 0303

Beer range varies 🅷

Tucked away in the Georgian area of the city, this small two-roomed community pub is a free house serving four rotating beers from mainly local microbreweries. Avoiding closure for housing redevelopment in 2006, this Grade II-listed building retains original fixtures and interesting etched glass features. It attracts a mixed local clientele including orchestra members from the famous Philharmonic Hall nearby. A pub where good conversation thrives, it was the local CAMRA branch's Pub of Culture in 2011.

⚲Q☗◑⬥≠(Lime St)🖳(Lime St)🖳'—♡

Caledonia 🆕 ✅

22 Caledonia Street, L7 7DX (on corner of Catherine St behind Philharmonic Hall)

✪ 12-11 (midnight Fri & Sat) ☎ (0151) 708 0235

Taylor Golden Best; guest beers 🅷

Situated in the Georgian quarter of the city, this single-room street-corner pub is on two levels with a small function room on the first floor. Named Live Music Pub of the Year 2011 by the local CAMRA branch, jazz plays on alternate Fridays and on alternate Sundays there is jazz in the early evening followed by a bluegrass band. Food is now served 12-3pm Tuesday to Friday, 5-8pm Wednesday evening and 12-6pm Saturday and Sunday.

🖳(Central)

Cracke 🆕

13 Rice Street, L1 9BB (off Hope St near Philharmonic Hall)

✪ 12-11.30 (midnight Fri & Sat) ☎ (0151) 709 4171

Thwaites Original; guest beers 🅷

Characterful multi-roomed back-street pub with two bars. In the public bar there are pictures of John Lennon outside the pub, from the time in the '50s when he attended the nearby art college. In the War Office a plaque states that this is where the locals discussed the Boer War. One room is used as a gallery by local artists. Ales come from a range of microbreweries, including LocAles, and farmhouse ciders.

☗◑⬥≠(Lime St)🖳(Central)🖳(86)♠

Crown ★ ✅

43 Lime Street, L1 1JQ

✪ 9am-11 (midnight Sat); 10am-midnight Sun

☎ (0151) 707 6027

Beer range varies 🅷

Grade II-listed Victorian pub built in 1905. Exterior stucco plasterwork, excellent plaster ceilings, dome and copperwork inside proclaim it as a Peter Walker house. But the original etched glass windows have been removed. Four beers are on handpump, often from Tetley, Cains or Greene King plus guests. The dining room upstairs and the back bar get fairly busy with shoppers and travellers using Lime Street Station next door.

◑≠(Lime St)⊖(Central)🖳

Dispensary 🆕

87 Renshaw Street, L1 2SP

✪ 12-11 (midnight Fri & Sat) ☎ (0151) 709 2180

Cains Bitter; George Wright Mild; guest beers 🅷

Local CAMRA Pub of the Year in 2010 and 2011, this lively local in the city is a haven for real ale drinkers of all ages. The licensee's impeccable attention to beer quality shines through, and the seven handpumps serve an ever-changing and imaginative choice of local and other interesting microbrewery beers, offering a good range in terms of both style and strength. The single-room interior has an attractive bar area with Victorian features, and a raised wood-panelled space to the rear. ❀≹(Lime St)🚊(Central)🚌

Excelsior ✅

121-123 Dale Street, L2 2JH (close to Birkenhead Tunnel entrance)
❀ 11 (12 Sun)-11 ☎ (0151) 236 0079
Caledonian Deuchars IPA; Taylor Landlord; guest beer Ⓗ
Large corner pub adjacent to what were the original Higsons Brewery offices. It reopened in 2010 after a comfortable refurbishment, attracting both business and leisure customers. The main room has a three-sided bar and an attractive area at the rear for meetings and functions. Six handpumps offer four changing beers from different regional breweries, including Adnams. Food includes award-winning pies, traditional dishes and tasty snacks. Local football is shown on three screens, and live music plays on Saturday night. ◑≹(Lime St)🚊(Moorfields)🚌

Fall Well Ⓛ ✅

St Johns Way, L1 1LS
❀ 8am-11.30 (midnight Fri & Sat) ☎ (0151) 705 2050
Greene King Abbot; Ruddles Best Bitter; guest beers Ⓗ
A former pet shop, this Wetherspoon pub is situated in a pedestrianised shopping area handy for the Playhouse, Royal Court and bus stops. The Fall Well was once an important source of water for the area and fed the fountain and garden of William Roe, a merchant who gave his name to Roe Street. The well stood on the site of the neighbouring Royal Court. Seasonal beer festivals are hosted. ❀◑&≹(Lime St)🚊(Lime St)🚌⏚

Fly in the Loaf ✅

13 Hardman Street, L1 9AS
❀ 12-11 (midnight Fri & Sat; 10.30 Sun) ☎ (0151) 708 0817
Okells Bitter, seasonal beers; guest beers Ⓗ
A Manx Cat Inn owned by Isle of Man brewer Okells. Originally the Kirklands bakery – whose slogan was: No flies in the loaf – it was refurbished with ecclesiastical fittings and opened in 2004. There are usually up to seven guest beers from microbreweries alongside the Okells beers, and a good selection of foreign bottled beers. The Fly attracts a wide cross-section of customers from students to theatregoers. The home-cooked meals are excellent, especially the Sunday roasts. There is also a function room with handpumps upstairs. An annual Oktoberfest is hosted.
◑&≹(Lime St)🚊(Central)🚌⏚

Globe ✅

17 Cases Street, L1 1HW (opp Liverpool Central Station)
❀ 11 (10 Sat)-11; 12-10.30 Sun ☎ (0151) 707 0067
Black Sheep Best Bitter; Cains Bitter; guest beers Ⓗ
Small, traditional two-roomed local in the city centre, close to railway stations and the main shopping area. A lively pub, it is popular with locals and visitors to the city. Drinkers need to be aware of the unique sloping floor that leads through to a quiet back room, which has a brass plaque commemorating the inaugural meeting of the Merseyside branch of CAMRA, held here in 1974.
≹(Lime St)🚊(Central)🚌

Grapes Ⓛ

60 Roscoe Street, L1 9DW
❀ 3.30-1am (2am Thu-Sat) ☎ (0151) 709 3977
🌐 thegrapesliverpool.co.uk
Beer range varies Ⓗ
Dating back to 1804, this traditional single-room hostelry originally stood on Roscoe Street but has expanded over the years to incorporate two adjoining houses on Knight Street. The exterior bears the sign: Mellors noted wines and spirits. A recent bar extension has made room for nine handpumps offering a wide variety of ales, some from local and microbreweries, as well as 13 different gins. Live jazz plays every Sunday night from 9pm. There is a cosy beer garden at the rear. ❀≹(Lime St)🚊(Central)🚌

Hole in Ye Wall Ⓛ ✅

4 Hackins Hey, L2 2AW
❀ 12-11 (11.30 Sat; 10.30 Sun) ☎ (0151) 227 3809
🌐 yeholeinyewall.co.uk
Tetley Bitter; guest beers Ⓗ
A traditional side-street pub rumoured to be the oldest hostelry in the city. Wood panelling and stained glass abound. Built on the site of an old Quaker graveyard, the beer cellar is unusually on the first floor above the bar. Another claim to fame is that in 1977 it became one of the last of the city's pubs to open its doors to women. Five guest beers are offered on rotation and may be from local and microbreweries. A great hidden gem. ≹(Lime St)🚊(Moorfields)🚌

Hub Ⓛ

12 Hanover Street, L1 4AA
❀ 10am-11 (midnight Thu); 9am-midnight Fri & Sat
☎ (0151) 709 2410 🌐 thehub-liverpool.com
Liverpool Organic 24 Carat; guest beers Ⓗ
A new pub in town but not a new building. The Grade II-listed ale house and kitchen occupy the Casartelli Building, built in 1760. Initially an Italian family-run scientific manufacturing business, it was latterly a wine warehouse. A period of decay led to dismantling in 2001. A campaign to 'Stop the Rot' led to reconstruction using as many original materials as possible. The house beer is Liverpool Organic 24 Carat and a rotating Lancaster Brewery beer is also offered. A good choice of lunchtime and evening meals is available.
◑≹(Lime St)🚊(Central)🚌(82,86)🚻

Lady of Mann

19 Dale Street, L2 2EZ
❀ 12-11 ☎ (0151) 236 5556
Okells Bitter; guest beers Ⓗ
Exposed beams and woodwork lend an almost rustic feel to this open-plan pub, owned by the Isle of Man brewery Okells. Three handpumps dispense the Okells Bitter and two guests. Sport is shown and the large rear room has a dartboard and can be booked for events. Cold food and snacks are available at all times. There is a courtyard for outside drinking shared with Thomas Rigby's, a fellow Okells pub. Q❀◑≹(Moorfields)🚌

Lion Tavern ★ Ⓛ ✅

67 Moorfields, L2 2BP
❀ 11-11; 12-11 Sun ☎ (0151) 236 1734 🌐 liontavern.com
Caledonian Deuchars IPA; Copper Dragon Golden Pippin; Moorhouse's Pride of Pendle; Young's Bitter; guest beers Ⓗ
The Lion is named after the locomotive that worked the Liverpool to Manchester Railway and is

now in the Museum of Liverpool. The Grade II-listed pub features exquisite artwork plus etched and stained glass and has been identified by CAMRA as one of Britain's Real Heritage Pubs. Regular society meetings are hosted plus occasional Meet the Brewer evenings. Westons cider is available. Lunchtime food is served with speciality pork pies available at all times. ◐♉🖳(Moorfields)🚈(26)

Liverpool One Bridewell L

1 Campbell Square, Argyle Street, L1 5FB
✿ 12-11 (midnight Fri & Sat) ☎ (0151) 709 7000
⊕ liverpoolonebridewell.com
Beer range varies Ⓗ
Grade II-listed building dating from around 1850, it was once used as a police station or bridewell. The cells provide an unusual focus for the downstairs bar area, where six handpumps dispense ales mainly from the Liverpool One Brewery. A good selection of continental bottled beers is also available. Traditional British food is served all day, with a full English breakfast at weekends. There is a large function room upstairs which can be booked for events. ✿◐●≈(Lime St)🖳(Central)

Peter Kavanagh's ★

2-6 Egerton Street, L8 7LY (off Catharine St)
✿ 12-midnight (1am Fri & Sat) ☎ (0151) 709 3443
Greene King Abbot; guest beers Ⓗ
A splendid back-street local, this gem is situated in the Georgian area of Liverpool and has been identified by CAMRA as one of Britain's Real Heritage Pubs. Murals by Eric Robinson adorn the walls, thought to have been commissioned to cover a debt. There are fine stained-glass windows with wooden shutters and two snugs with wooden benches – note the carved armrests, allegedly caricatures of the politically incorrect Peter Kavanagh. Up to four rotating guest beers are available alongside the Abbot. Q🖳(86)

Philharmonic ★ ✔

36 Hope Street, L1 9BX
✿ 10-midnight ☎ (0151) 707 2837
Beer range varies Ⓗ
A magnificent Grade II-listed building with stained-glass windows, a mosaic bar counter front, wood panelling and stucco ceilings, popular with locals, students and tourists alike. Divided into several ornate rooms, each with its own character, the pub retains a feeling of decadence, in the style of a private gentlemen's club. Famous for its marvellous marble-tiled gents' toilets, ladies are welcome to visit, but it is polite to ask first. Q◐●♉≈(Lime St)🖳(Central)🚈(86)

Richard John Blackler L ✔

Units 1 & 2 Charlotte Row, Great Charlotte Street, L1 1HU
✿ 7am-11.30 (midnight Wed-Fri); 8am-midnight Sat; 8am-11.30 Sun ☎ (0151) 709 4802
Greene King Abbot; Ruddles Best Bitter; guest beers Ⓗ
Close to Queen Square bus station, St John's shopping centre and Liverpool One, this Wetherspoon pub is always busy but is a good place to take a break before, during or after a shopping trip. It was originally the ground floor of the former Blacklers department store, where George Harrison of the Beatles served his electrician's apprenticeship. The rocking horse is a replica of one ridden by children who visited the

store – the original is at the city's children's hospital, Alder Hey.
♉◐●≈(Lime St)🖳(Central)🚈

Richmond Hotel L ✔

32 Williamson Street, L1 1EB (in pedestrian precinct, off Williamson Square)
✿ 10-11; 11-midnight Fri-Sun ☎ (0151) 709 2614
Beer range varies Ⓗ
Lively small single-room corner pub with large TV screens for sport. Formerly a Bass house, it retains the original Bass mirror, but the beers on the four handpumps are likely to come from Moorhouse's or Timothy Taylor. It is also a rare outlet for Southport Brewery's Golden Sands. The pub sign depicts Paddy Golden, a much-missed regular and one of the first to land on the Normandy beaches. The Victoria Cross and Lord Warden pubs, also in the city centre, are owned by the same family. ✿♉≈(Lime St)🖳(Central)🚈⌐

Roscoe Head 🏆 L

24 Roscoe Street, L1 2SX
✿ 11.30 (12 Sun)-midnight ☎ (0151) 709 4365
⊕ roscoehead.co.uk
Jennings Bitter; Tetley Cask Bitter; guest beers Ⓗ
One of the Magnificent Seven pubs that have been in every edition of the Guide, and 2012 local CAMRA Pub of the Year. This is a cosy four-roomed establishment where conversation and the appreciation of real ale rule. Run by members of the same family for more than 30 years, the name commemorates William Roscoe, a leading campaigner against the slave trade. Six handpumps feature two regular beers plus four changing guests mostly from microbreweries. Food is served Monday to Friday lunchtimes.
🛏Q♉◐♉≈(Central)🖳(Lime St)🚈(86)♣

Ship & Mitre

133 Dale Street, L2 2JH (by Birkenhead Tunnel entrance)
✿ 10-11 (midnight Thu-Sat) ☎ (0151) 236 0859
⊕ theshipandmitre.com
Beer range varies Ⓗ
The Ship & Mitre – whose name is a combination of two previous incarnations, the Flagship and the Mitre – is a 1930s Art Deco building partly hidden by the Queensway tunnel and the Churchill Way flyover. Thirteen handpulls serve an ever-changing array of beers from microbreweries, usually including Liverpool Organic, and ciders from a range of suppliers including Westons. There is also an impressive range of world beers. The pub also runs a bottle shop at 45a Whitechapel. Q◐●≈(Lime St)🖳(Moorfields)🚈🐾

Swan Inn

86 Wood Street, L1 4DQ
✿ 12-11 (2am Thu-Sat; 10.30 Sun) ☎ (0151) 709 5281
Hydes Original; Phoenix Wobbly Bob; guest beers Ⓗ
The Swan, with its distinctive blue-tiled façade and stained glass windows, has changed little over the years. The bar has eight handpumps and serves a selection of beers from national and microbreweries as well as Gwynt Y Ddraig Black Dragon cider. Seating is a combination of wooden pews and traditional bar stools, and the back room is lit with red light bulbs. The pub is renowned for its rock jukebox. Free Wi-Fi is available. A good selection of malt and blended whiskies is stocked. ♉≈(Lime St)🖳(Central)🚈🐾

Thomas Rigby's Ⓛ ✓
23-25 Dale Street, L2 2EZ
✪ 11.30-11 (10.30 Sun) ☎ (0151) 236 3269
Okells Bitter, Dr Okell's IPA, seasonal beers; guest beers Ⓗ
A large multi-roomed pub housed in a Grade II-listed building and boasting some fine wood panelling in the back room. Eight handpumps serve a mix of Okells' ales and guests, often from local breweries. A wide range of foreign beers and bottled lagers is also available as well as real cider from Cheddar Valley. Food is served daily until early evening. There is a courtyard at the back for outdoor drinking, shared with the Lady of Mann. ✪◑🖴✇(Moorfields)⚫

Vernon Arms Ⓛ
69 Dale Street, L2 2HJ
✪ 11.45-11.30 (12.30am Fri & Sat); 12-11 Sun
☎ (0151) 236 6132 🌐 vernonarms.co.uk
Boggart Rum Porter; Brains The Rev James; Wapping Johnnie Handsome; guest beers Ⓗ
Situated close to the business district, the Vernon retains the feel of a street-corner local. The single long-roomed bar serves three drinking areas including a back room with frosted glass windows advertising the Liverpool Brewing Company which used to serve the pub. The main bar has wood panelling, several large columns and a small snug area. Big-screen sport is shown. The exterior has recently been repainted due to the redevelopment of offices above. ◑🖴(Moorfields)

Victoria Cross ✓
1-3 Sir Thomas Street, L1 6BW
✪ 11am-11 (midnight Sat & Sun) ☎ (0151) 277 2265
Beer range varies Ⓗ
Recently taken over and renamed, this pub has gone through a variety of guises. The theme now is the Victoria Cross – many have been awarded to Liverpool regiments and there is a commemorative board celebrating their achievements. There is also a statue in Abercromby Square celebrating Noel Chavasse who lived there and is one of only three men to be awarded two VCs. Four ales are usually available from national and local breweries plus a range of foreign bottled beers.
⚆(Lime St)🖴(Central)🖴

White Star ✓
2-4 Rainford Gardens, L2 6PT
✪ 11.30-11; 12-10.30 Sun ☎ (0151) 231 6861
🌐 thewhitestar.co.uk
Caledonian Deuchars IPA; Draught Bass; guest beers Ⓗ
A true gem, this two-roomed public house is located among the glitzy and often noisy establishments of the world-famous Mathew Street area. Unsurprisingly, the walls are adorned with pictures of White Star liners as well as local memorabilia and an abundance of boxing photographs. Live football matches are shown. The pub is twinned with bars in both the Czech Republic and Norway.
✪◑🖴⚆(Lime St)🖴(Central/Moorfields)⚑

Liverpool: Kirkdale

Thomas Frost ✓
177-187 Walton Road, L4 4AJ
✪ 9-11.30 ☎ (0151) 207 8210

Greene King Abbot; Ruddles Best Bitter; guest beers Ⓗ
Wetherspoon pub occupying the ground floor of a Grade II-listed building, formerly the Thomas Frost Drapery Store (1885). The pub is near both Everton and Liverpool grounds and gets busy on match days. It has a spacious open-plan layout with a large family area. Food is served 9am to 10pm. To find out which beers are on, check out the Thomas Frost Facebook page. ✇◑🖴(20,21)

Liverpool: Mossley Hill

Pi
106 Rose Lane, L18 8AG
✪ 11-11 ☎ (0151) 222 - 0443 🌐 pi-roselane.co.uk
Tatton Tatton Blonde; guest beers Ⓗ
A large glass-fronted continental café-style bar, with wooden furniture and a stone tiled floor, situated in an affluent Liverpool suburb. Three real beers, often from regional breweries, are regularly served alongside eight foreign ales and 60 bottled beers. The cider is from Broadoak. Pieminister pies are available all day. There are plans for the single-room bar to extend into the shop next door.
◑⚆🖴⚫

Liverpool: Stoneycroft

Navigator Ⓛ ✓
694 Queens Drive, L13 5UH
✪ 9am-11.30 ☎ (0151) 220 2713
Greene King Abbot; Ruddles Best Bitter; guest beers Ⓗ
This branch of Wetherspoon, named after St Brendan the Navigator, the patron saint of sailors, occupies a former showroom. A welcome oasis on the edge of a busy shopping area, the open-plan layout is punctuated with alcoves along one side and there is a raised area set aside for families. The pub participates in Wetherspoon's national beer festivals. ✪◑🖴⚆(Broadgreen)🖴⚑

Liverpool: Wavertree

Edinburgh Ⓛ
4 Sandown Lane, L15 8HY
✪ 12-midnight ☎ (0151) 733 3533
Cains Bitter, FA, seasonal beers; guest beers Ⓗ
A small Victorian back-street hostelry housed in a Grade II-listed building and divided into two rooms. The bar offers Cains and guest beers, sometimes from local breweries. Popular with locals, the pub is a former winner of the local CAMRA Best Community Pub award. It hosts an Irish music night on Monday and a quiz on Tuesday, and sport is shown on TV screens. ✪🖴♣⚑

Liverpool: West Derby

Halton Castle ✓
86 Mill Lane, L12 7JD
✪ 11 (12 Sun)-midnight
Black Sheep Best Bitter; guest beer Ⓗ
Traditional Victorian multi-room pub with three real ales always on offer. All rooms have large flat-screen TVs featuring major football fixtures and other sporting events. During good weather drinkers can enjoy the decked area at the rear. There is also a covered, heated smoking shelter.
✪🖴(12,13,15)♣P⚑

Liverpool: Woolton

White Horse
2 Acrefield Road, L25 5JL
✪ 12-11 (midnight Sat & Sun) ☎ (0151) 428 1862
Cains Bitter; guest beers Ⓗ
Cosy local dating from the time when Woolton was a separate village, with a central bar and three drinking areas featuring wood panelling and brasswork. Run for many years by the same landlord, it has a warm, relaxing atmosphere. Good-value food is available until 8pm (5pm Sun) including a daily special. Sport is shown on TV. Two guest beers are available, usually from regional brewers. ⊛◑

Lydiate

Scotch Piper ★
Southport Road, L31 4HD (on A5147)
✪ 12-midnight ☎ (0151) 526 0503
Black Sheep Best Bitter; guest beers Ⓗ
A Grade II-listed building dating back to 1320, this three-roomed thatched inn takes its name from an incident in 1745 when a highland piper, injured in the Jacobite rebellion, took refuge here. The interior boasts traditional black wooden beams, low ceilings and whitewashed walls, and a roaring fire in winter. Three cask ales are always available from the small wooded bar. The toilets are in a small outhouse to the left of the entrance.
ᴪQ⊛☲(300)♣P

New Brighton

Magazine Hotel Ⓛ ❷
7 Magazine Brow, CH45 1HP (above Egremont Promenade)
✪ 12-11.30 (midnight Fri & Sat; 11 Sun) ☎ (0151) 639 3169
Draught Bass; guest beers Ⓗ
Dating from 1759, this multi-roomed, low-beamed pub suffered from a fire in 2010 but has been restored without losing its unique character. Overlooking Egremont Promenade, the pub affords fine views of the River Mersey. Three rooms lead off the main central bar area. Renowned over many years for its Draught Bass, it also offers guest ales including a local beer from Brimstage, Liverpool Organic or Peerless. Good-value lunchtime bar meals are served. A former local CAMRA award winner, it holds an annual beer festival. ᴪQ☎⊛◑♣P↲

Queen's Royal Ⓛ ❷
Marine Promenade, CH45 2JT
✪ 10.30-11 (10.30 Sun) ☎ (0151) 691 0101
⏛ thequeensroyal.com
Brimstage Trappers Hat; Hawkshead Windermere Pale; guest beers Ⓗ
An airy, modern bar in an imposing Victorian building, close to the Floral Hall Theatre and overlooking Marine Promenade, Marine Lake and Fort Perch Rock. A strong supporter of local ales, among the favourites are beers from Brimstage and Weetwood. The drinking area outside affords superb views over Liverpool Bay. Good-value, hearty meals are served in the bar; the adjoining restaurant offers excellent food including a popular Sunday carvery. ⊛☲◑⏦☲↲

Stanley's Cask
212 Rake Lane, CH45 1JP
✪ 11-11 (midnight Fri & Sat) ☎ (0151) 691 1093

Courage Best Bitter; guest beers Ⓗ
This ever-popular local returned to the Guide in 2010 after an absence of 14 years, and continues to thrive, due in no small part to the landlady who has a track record of serving good beer. Up to four guest ales are offered, mainly from national and regional breweries. A traditional, single-roomed community local, it hosts various sports teams, quiz nights and entertainment. ⊛☲(410)♣↲

Telegraph Inn ❷
25-27 Mount Pleasant Road, CH45 5EW
✪ 11.30-11; 12-10.30 Sun ☎ (0151) 639 1508
Wells Bombardier; guest beers Ⓗ
A traditional, friendly, multi-roomed local, the Telegraph is believed to be New Brighton's oldest as well as highest pub. It has a conservatory extension where good-value home-cooked food is served daily. The handpumps are in the main bar area, with four varying guest ales on offer from a mixture of national and microbreweries. Two popular beer festivals and a cider festival are held in the rear garden, and live folk music plays regularly. A former local CAMRA Pub of the Year. ⊛◑☲☲(410)♣P↲

New Ferry

Freddie's Club Ⓛ
36 Stanley Road, CH62 5AS
✪ 7 (5 Fri; 12 Sat & Sun)-11
Brimstage Trappers Hat Ⓗ
Popular social club converted from a former Conservative Club into a single-storey lounge bar and snooker room with two full-size tables. Situated in a residential street, a short walk from New Ferry centre, Freddie's is a former Wirral CAMRA Club of the Year. A LocAle outlet, there are two handpumps, one with a local ale. Freddie's features regular live entertainment. Guests are welcome – for entry show a CAMRA membership card or a copy of this Guide. ⇌(Bebington)☲♣P↲

John Masefield ❷
70-72 New Chester Road, CH62 5AD
✪ 9am-11 (11.30 Fri & Sat) ☎ (0151) 644 4250
Greene King Abbot; Ruddles Best Bitter Ⓗ
Comfortable open-plan Wetherspoon pub opened in 2007 in the town centre. Named after a former poet laureate with local links, controversy surrounded the opening when locals suggested that the portrait on the pub's sign looked more like Adolf Hitler – judge for yourself. Two banks of handpumps include beers from local microbreweries and further afield, and cask ales significantly outsell the other beers on the bar. The pub features Wetherspoon's meal deals, a Wednesday night quiz and regular vintage bus pub trips. ⊛◑♿⇌(Bebington)☲(41,401)◕↲

Raby

Wheatsheaf Inn Ⓛ
Raby Mere Road, CH63 4JH SJ311798
✪ 11.30-11 (midnight Fri & Sat); 12-10.30 Sun
☎ (0151) 336 3416 ⏛ wheatsheaf-cowshed.co.uk
Brimstage Trapper's Hat; Morland Old Speckled Hen; Taylor Landlord; Tetley Bitter; Thwaites Original; Wainwright Ⓗ
An inn for more than 350 years, this is Wirral's oldest pub. The thatched building was rebuilt following a fire in 1611 and is reputed to be

haunted by Charlotte, who died here. The bar has nine handpumps serving two rooms and a restaurant in a converted cowshed. Two guest beers are usually from local microbreweries, often Brimstage. No evening meals Sunday or Monday. ᴍQ⊛◑ℂ&🖳(85)P

Rainhill

Ship Inn ⓛ ✅

804 Warrington Road, L35 6PE (on A57, 400yds W of jct 7 M62)

☼ 12-11 (10.30 Sun) ☎ (0151) 426 4165

George Wright Ship to Shore; guest beers Ⓗ

Large 1930s roadhouse in a semi-rural location. There is a small, quiet front bar and a large rear lounge featuring live sport on TV and occasional live bands and charity nights. Four handpumps offer beers from microbreweries. A large restaurant serves both locals and the lodge behind the pub. There are outside drinking areas to the front and rear. The pub is dog-friendly away from dining areas. Free Wi-Fi is available.

ᴍ⊛🛏◑ ℂ&🖳(61,137,138)P⸗

St Helens

Duke of Cambridge ⍦

Duke Street, WA10 2JE

☼ 11-11 (1am Fri & Sat); 12-11 Sun ☎ (01744) 733340

Moorhouse's Blond Witch; guest beers Ⓗ

A small local pub on the edge of the town centre, the Duke of Cambridge is a welcome real ale outlet among the many keg-only bars on Duke Street. Two handpulls feature a Moorhouse's beer and guest ales often from local micros. Entertainment is high on the list of attractions, with live bands at the weekend and a jam night on Wednesday. 🖳

Glass House ⓛ ✅

5 Market Street, WA10 1NE

☼ 7am-midnight (1am Fri & Sat) ☎ (01744) 762310

Beer range varies Ⓗ

A former discount store, named to reflect the town's historic link with glass-making, situated a short distance from the award-winning World of Glass Visitor Centre and the main shopping centre in Church Street. The older and quieter of the two Wetherspoon outlets in the town, the pub is always busy. Large-screen TVs dominate the upper bar. Disabled access is via the rear patio area and children are allowed in the lower bar only if dining. ⊛◑&🖳●⸗

Olde England ⓛ ✅

113 Corporation Street, WA10 1SX

☼ 11-11 (1am Fri & Sat); 1.30-11 Sun ⊕ 1854pub.com

Beer range varies Ⓗ

Nineteenth-century town centre pub featuring a bar with pool and darts and a comfortable lounge decorated with pictures of old St Helens. Six beers are on offer from local microbreweries. The pub serves lunchtime food and crumpets toasted on a real fire on Tuesday afternoons in winter. Regular themed nights are held. ᴍ◑🖳♣●

Phoenix Hotel ⓛ

34 Canal Street, WA10 3LL

☼ 2-11; 12-1am Fri & Sat; 12-midnight Sun ☎ (01744) 751890

Beer range varies Ⓗ

Built in 1903, the pub has its name in mosaic tiles on an outer wall, and a mosaic tile floor. A community local, it offers up to six beers mostly from local microbreweries. The small bar is home to pool, darts and dominoes, and the spacious lounge is comfortable. Sky Sports is shown on numerous TVs. Music dominates, with karaoke on Friday nights and live Irish bands on Saturdays. A yard at the back has been converted into a heated smoking area. ⊛◑&♣●⸗

Running Horses ✅

Water Street, WA10 1BF

☼ 9-midnight (1am Fri & Sat; 11 Sun) ☎ (01744) 743400

Beer range varies Ⓗ

This Lloyds No.1 Bar is the larger and newer of the town's two Wetherspoon outlets. It is named after a long-demolished pub in a nearby location and offers everything you would expect from a Wetherspoon's. Lively on weekend nights but quieter during the week, it is a convenient starting point for a night out in town or a visit to the cinema next door. ◑&🖳

Turk's Head ⓛ ✅

49-51 Morley Street, WA10 2DQ

☼ 2-11.30 (12.30am Fri); 12-12.30am Sat; 12-11.30 Sun ☎ (01744) 751289

Beer range varies Ⓗ

A short distance from town, this popular pub was a previous CAMRA National Pub of the Year runner-up. Half-timbered, with etched glass windows, it was built in the 1870s by Ellis Warde Brewery, and features a distinctive turret inset with the brewery logo. It offers a constantly changing beer range, with 12 handpulls in use over the weekend, six at other times. Draught and bottled continental beers are also stocked. Thursday is curry and jazz night, and on Tuesday night there is a free quiz. Darts and dominoes are played. ᴍ⊛◑🖳♣●⸗☖

Southport

Barons Bar (Scarisbrick Hotel) ⓛ ✅

239 Lord Street, PR8 1NZ (on A565, opp A570 Eastbank St)

☼ 11-1am; 12-midnight Sun ☎ (01704) 543000

Moorhouse's Pride of Pendle; Tetley Bitter, Flag & Turret; guest beers Ⓗ

Set within the Scarisbrick Hotel, the Barons Bar is a single-room bar offering ales from seven handpumps. Traditionally Southport's premier real ale bar, there was some concern about its future in 2012 when Britannia Hotels acquired the Scarisbrick. No fear – purchases from local microbreweries recommenced in 2011 and the range is fast approaching its original quality. Britannia is to be congratulated for retaining the bar's CAMRA award-winning heritage. The best range of local microbrewery beers in Southport. Q🛏&≒🖳●P

Fishermen's Rest

2 Weld Road, Birkdale, PR8 2AZ

☼ 12-11 (midnight Fri & Sat) ☎ (01704) 569986

Caledonian Deuchars IPA; Theakston Best Bitter; Thwaites Wainwright; guest beers Ⓗ

The Fishermen's Rest is fast acquiring a reputation for its quality cask ales and good wholesome food. The pub was originally the coach house for the Birkdale Palace Hotel, which once welcomed stars such as Clark Gable and Frank Sinatra. It was also used as a temporary morgue for 14 sailors after the

Eliza Fernley lifeboat disaster of 1886. The brass mermaids that secure the bar's handrail commemorate them to this day along with photographs and illustrations around the walls. ⬤❙↧≷(Birkdale)🚇(15)P⬤←

Guest House ▼ Ⓛ

16 Union Street, PR9 0QE
⊘ 11.30-11 (11.30 Fri & Sat); 12-10.30 Sun
☎ (01704) 537660 ⊕ guesthouse-southport.blogspot.com/
Adnams Southwold Bitter; Caledonian Deuchars IPA; Jennings Cumberland Ale; Ruddles Best Bitter; Theakston Mild, Best Bitter ⓗ
Close to fashionable Lord Street, the pub boasts an impressive half-timbered Edwardian frontage and an unspoilt wood-panelled interior with three separate drinking areas. Southport Brewery beers are often sold, and a good range of malt whiskies is stocked. A Thursday quiz night and acoustic folk club on the first and third Monday evenings of the month attract a mixed clientele. Morris dancers perform on special occasions. There is outdoor seating to the front and a pleasant courtyard to the rear. Q⬤◐❙➞🚇⬤←

Inn Beer Shop Ⓛ

657 Lord Street, PR9 0AW (on A565, N end of Lord St)
⊘ 11-10 (10.30 Fri & Sat); 12-10 Sun ☎ (01704) 533054
Beer range varies ⓗ
Friendly café bar offering a huge selection of local, national and foreign bottled beers for takeaway or consumption on the premises. The long interior is lined with bottles and continental-style seating, leading to a comfy snug area complete with games. The bar serves foreign lagers, a Southport Brewery beer and two real ciders. Snacks and a tea/coffee china service with cakes is available throughout the day. Outside seating is on fashionable Lord Street. Dog-friendly, though the interior can get busy at weekends. ⬤➞🚇♣⬤←

Lakeside Inn

The Promenade, PR9 0EA (200yds from Lord St overlooking Marine Lake)
⊘ 11-11; 12-10.30 Sun ☎ (01704) 530173
Fuller's London Pride; guest beers ⓗ
Originally a sailing club store, this delightfully quirky little free house overlooking the Marine Lake retains a nautical theme. The tiny bar once featured in the Guinness Book of Records as Britain's smallest pub. Very friendly, the clientele includes performers from the nearby Southport Theatre. Monday is charity quiz night. Seating outside, some covered, offers fine views over the lake, especially at sunset. No children or dogs are permitted in the bar. Q⬤➞🚇⬤←

London Hotel

14 Windsor Road, PR9 0SR
⊘ 4-11 (10 Wed); 12-midnight Fri & Sat ☎ (01704) 542885
Oakwell Dark Mild, Barnsley Bitter ⓗ
Large Victorian community pub near railway sidings on the corner of Kensington Road in an area known as Little London. Handpumps on the bar dispense the reasonably priced Oakwell beers, unique in Southport. The large main room has a central bar, snug, function room and pool area. On display are many trophies won by the darts, quiz, pool and dominoes teams, all well-supported by the pub. Comfortable and friendly inside with a well-kept bowling green outside. ⟘⬤➞🚇(43,44)♣P⬤←

Park Hotel

36 Weld Road, Birkdale, PR8 2ED
⊘ 11-11 (midnight Fri & Sat); 12-11 Sun ☎ (01704) 569941
Marston's Pedigree; Thwaites Wainwright; Wells Bombardier ⓗ
Large comfortable pub situated in Birkdale village near to Birkdale Merseyrail station and the village shops. Recently refurbished, the pub is home to darts and football teams and offers Sky football coverage. Sunday is quiz night, Monday is poker night and Thursday features a sports quiz. Bus services 2X/X2 and 49/49A give regular links to Southport centre, Formby, Crosby, Liverpool and Preston. ⬤◐❙≷(Birkdale)🚇P⬤←

Sir Henry Segrave Ⓛ ✅

93-97 Lord Street, PR8 1RH (on A565, S end of Lord Street)
⊘ 8am-midnight (1am Fri & Sat) ☎ (01704) 530217
Greene King Abbot; Moorhouse's Pendle Witches Brew; Phoenix Wobbly Bob; Ruddles Best Bitter; Thwaites Wainwright ⓗ
Named after the former land speed world record holder who used to race on Southport flats, this is a spacious Wetherspoon pub with an attractive 19th-century exterior. The manager is a strong supporter of real ale and runs regular brewery and beer festival trips, and occasional Meet the Brewer evenings. The 12 handpumps offer the best all-round choice of microbrewery beers in Southport – regular orders are placed with Phoenix, Saltaire, Titanic and Hawkshead. There is outside seating on the famous Lord Street. ⬤◐❙➞🚇⬤←

Volunteer Arms Ⓛ

57-59 Eastbank Street, PR8 1DY
⊘ 11 (12 Sun)-midnight ☎ (01704) 543794
Thwaites Lancaster Bomber, Wainwright ⓗ
A newly refurbished Thwaites' pub, a short distance from the town centre, ably run by Alan and staff. The two Thwaites beers are always top-notch. Photographs of old Southport adorn the walls. The atmosphere is friendly, especially on sing-a-long Sunday. Lunches are served daily, from light snacks to hearty meals – the food is all good, making it a must for visitors. ◐➞🚇♣⬤←

Willow Grove ✅

387-389 Lord Street, PR9 0AG
⊘ 8am-midnight (1am Fri; 2am Sat) ☎ (01704) 517830
Greene King Abbot; Phoenix Wobbly Bob; Ruddles Best Bitter; guest beers ⓗ
Lloyds No.1 bar situated in the heart of town opposite the impressive 1920s War Memorial on Southport's famous mile-long Victorian Lord Street. The modern L-shaped interior leads to a brightly lit bar with nine handpumps and a good range of bottled beers and whiskies. There are flat-screen TVs, couches and alcoves, tall buffet chairs and a quieter bar upstairs serving only the two Greene King beers. The pub is often busy, particularly on Friday and Saturday evenings. ⬤◐❙➞🚇⬤←

Wallasey

Cheshire Cheese ✅

2 Wallasey Village, CH44 2DH
⊘ 12-11 (midnight Fri & Sat) ☎ (0151) 638 3641
⊕ thecheesewallasey.com
Theakston Best Bitter; guest beers ⓗ
Wallasey's oldest licensed premises, this is a friendly local with a separate bar, snug and lounge.

Outside is a walled garden where regular beer festivals are held. The handpumps are located in the lounge, with four guest beers on offer including a local ale, often from Liverpool Organic Brewery, plus real mild. Excellent home-cooked meals are served until early evening (no food Thu). Quiz nights are Monday and Wednesday, and the pub hosts a golf society and football, darts and bowls teams. Q❀◑♪⬚⇌(Village)🚲♣🌡

Waterloo

Old Bank 🄻 ✅

34 South Road, L22 5PE

⏣ 11-11.30; 12-12.30am Fri & Sat; 12-midnight Sun

☎ (0151) 928 7020 ⊕ theoldbankwaterloo.co.uk

Beer range varies ⊞

The addition of a fourth handpull and LocAle accreditation are cementing the Old Bank's quietly growing reputation for real ale. Beers are sourced largely from local brewers. The pub is a venue for live music and watching sport, and memorabilia adorn the walls. Although a quiet oasis on weekday afternoons, music nights and football on the big screen can lead to standing room only. A courtyard at the back provides space for outdoor drinking on warmer days. ❀⇌🚲(53)♣🌡

Stamps Too 🄻

99 South Road, L22 0LR (opp Waterloo Station)

⏣ 12-11 (11.45 Fri & Sat) ☎ (0151) 280 0035

Beer range varies ⊞

The first pub in the Liverpool CAMRA branch area to be LocAle accredited, it has six handpulls dispensing 90 per cent LocAle. Liverpool Organic, Southport, Brimstage and AllGates are the regulars, with a smattering of visitors from further afield for variety. Tranquil during the day, the long, narrow shop conversion opens its entire front to welcome in the sunshine, weather permitting. Live bands on Thursday to Sunday nights attract a good following. ♿⇌🚲(53)♣

Volunteer Canteen ★ ✅

45 East Street, L22 8QR

⏣ 2-11; 12-midnight Fri & Sat (10.30 Sun)

☎ (0151) 928 4676

Black Sheep Best Bitter; guest beers ⊞

A cosy, traditional pub housed in a Grade II-listed terraced building, the Volly, as it is known locally, still provides table service, plus a music- and sports-free environment in which to enjoy your pint. Nestling in the back streets of Waterloo, the pub dates back to 1871 and, until the 1980s, was owned by Higsons – the name remains, etched into the fine windows. Q❀⬚⇌🚲(53)♣

Roscoe Head, Liverpool: City Centre

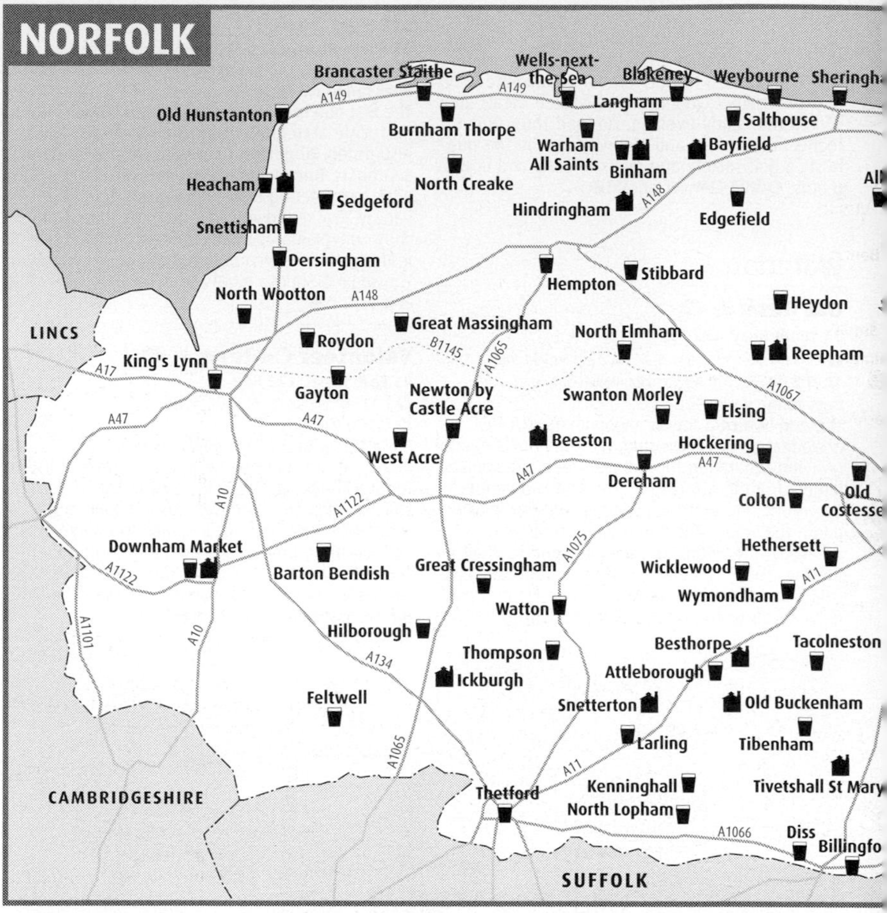

Alby

Horse Shoes Inn 𝕃

Cromer Road, NR11 7QE (on A140 halfway between Cromer and Aylsham, next to Alby Crafts) TG208324
✪ closed Mon; 12-2.30 (Fri & Sat), 6.30-11; 12-2.30 Sun
☎ (01263) 761378 🌐 albyhorseshoes.co.uk
Woodforde's Wherry; guest beers Ⓗ
A 19th-century inn on the main Norwich-Cromer road that offers four real ales, always from local breweries. There are two bars – one with an unusually low counter – a wood-burning stove, and a separate dining room. Traditional games of ring the bull and twister are located in the ceiling. Pictures of old cars adorn the walls, the landlord being a classic car enthusiast. Live music is '50s, '60s and traditional country, with a touch of local folk. Locally sourced home-cooked food is served. ⛰Q❀⇆◖◗♿🚌(44)♣P⚟

Attleborough

London Tavern 𝕃

Church Street, NR17 2AH
✪ 11-11 (1.30am Fri); 10-1.30am Sat; 10-11 Sun
☎ (01953) 457415
Wolf Werewolf; guest beers Ⓗ
Family-friendly pub in the town centre, opposite the main bus stops and 10 minutes' walk from the railway station. The range of four guest beers comes from all over the UK. The pub has a dining room and serves breakfast and lunch every day. Evening meals are by arrangement. Outside is a covered smoking area and garden. A beer festival takes place on the August bank holiday weekend. CAMRA members receive a discount. Free Wi-Fi is available. ⛰♉❀◖♿⇌🚌(6,6A,13)P⚟

Banningham

Crown Inn

Colby Road, NR11 7DY (adjacent to village green, just off B1145 or E of A140) TG217294
✪ 12-2.30, 6.30 (6 Sat)-11; 12-10.30 Sun ☎ (01263) 733534
🌐 banninghamcrown.co.uk
Greene King IPA, Abbot; guest beers Ⓗ
Traditional friendly free house in the heart of the village, opposite the parish church and village green, that has been run by the same family since 1991. Interior features include beams and a large working fireplace, in a building that has housed an inn since the 17th century. There is a patio with a covered smoking shelter, garden and barbecue area. Quality food, often made with locally sourced produce, is available lunchtimes and evenings. Monthly quiz nights and other special events are regularly held – see the website for details. ⛰❀◖◗♿▲🚌(18)P⚟

ever-present, with one or two guest beers depending on the season. Open long hours, with breakfast served 7-11am and meals from lunchtimes through to the evenings.
Q✿🍴◐🍽🕭🖾(580)♣P🚬🏠

Binham

Chequers Inn 🅛
Front Street, NR21 0AL (centre of village) TF983396
✪ 11.30-2.30, 6-11 (Fri & Sat 11.30); 12-2.30, 6-11 Sun
☎ (01328) 830297 ⊕ home.btconnect.com/
The-Chequers-Inn/index.html
Front Street Binham Cheer; guest beers 🅗
In the centre of the village and close to English Heritage's historic and picturesque Binham Priory, the Chequers is a single-room bar with welcoming roaring fires in winter. The pub is the home of the Front Street microbrewery, with three of its ales usually available, plus occasional guest beers from other breweries. There is also an extensive range of Belgian beers, bottled as well as on draught. Excellent meals are served at all sessions.
🏚✿◐🕭🖾(46)🍴P🚬

Blakeney

King's Arms
Westgate Street, NR25 7NQ (nr Blakeney harbour)
TG026440
✪ 9.30-11; 12-10.30 Sun ☎ (01263) 740341
Adnams Southwold Bitter; Greene King Old Speckled Hen; Marston's Pedigree 🅗; guest beers 🅗/🅖
Situated close to the harbour in one of Norfolk's most picturesque coastal villages, this old building was originally three fishermen's cottages. The interior comprises a series of interconnecting rooms, and there is a large garden to one side. Around five to six real ales are available, dispensed either by handpump or gravity, including

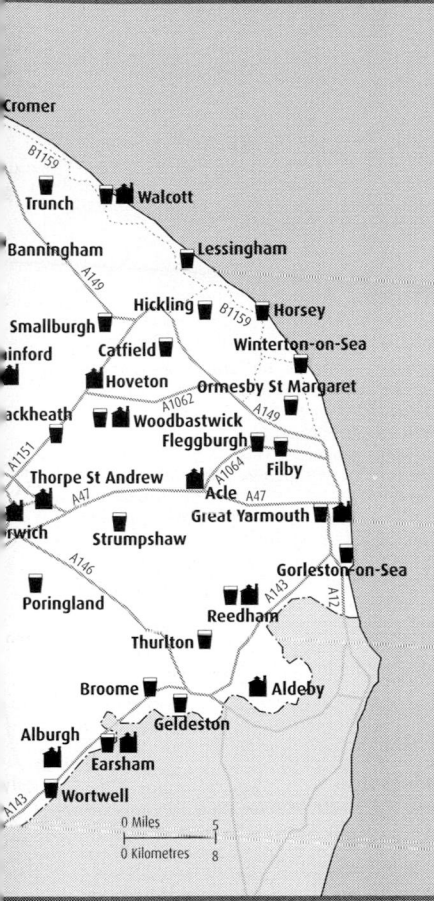

Barton Bendish

Berney Arms
Church Road, PE33 9GF
✪ 12-11 (10 Sun) ☎ (01366) 347995
⊕ theberneyarms.co.uk
Adnams Southwold Bitter, Broadside; guest beer 🅗
An old village local with a modern approach. There is a dining room that serves excellent food throughout the day, and luxury accommodation in the old stable block and blacksmith's forge. If all you want is a beer, the comfortable bar decorated with interesting pictures serves Adnams' ales, with the occasional guest. In the summer, an extensive beer garden offers an enticing alternative. Check out the afternoon teas. 🏚Q✿🍴◐P

Billingford

Horseshoes
Lower Street, IP21 4HL
✪ 11-11; 12-10 Sun ☎ (01379) 740414
⊕ horseshoesbillingford.co.uk
Adnams Southwold Bitter; guest beers 🅖
On the A143 Diss to Lowestoft road, this is an old hostelry that relies on passing trade but attracts locals for its beers. Handpumps advertise the ales on offer but all are dispensed straight from the casks in the taproom. Adnams Southwold Bitter is

INDEPENDENT BREWERIES

Bees Walcott
Beeston Beeston
Blackfriars Great Yarmouth
Buffy's Tivetshall St Mary
Chalk Hill Norwich
Elmtree Snetterton
Fat Cat Norwich
Fox Heacham
Front Street Binham
Golden Triangle Norwich
Grain Alburgh
Humpty Dumpty Reedham
Iceni Ickburgh
Norfolk Hindringham (NEW)
Norfolk Square Great Yarmouth
Norwich Bear Norwich
Ole Slewfoot Hainford
Opa Hay's Aldeby
Panther Reepham
Tipples Acle
Uncle Stuarts Hoveton
Wagtail Old Buckenham
Waveney Earsham
Why Not Thorpe St Andrew
Winter's Norwich
Wissey Valley Downham Market
Wolf Besthorpe
Woodforde's Woodbastwick
Yetman's Bayfield

at least one from Woodforde's. Morning cooked breakfasts are now available 9.30-11.30am, which is handy for campers and walkers. Children and dogs are welcome and en-suite accommodation is offered. ♨Q✿⌂✍◑▲⊟(Coasthopper)P

Brancaster Staithe

Jolly Sailors
Main Road, PE31 8BJ
✪ 11-11 (12-3, 6-11 winter); 12-10.30 (12-3, 6-10.30 winter) Sun ☎ (01485) 210314 ⊕ jollysailorsbrancaster.co.uk
Adnams Southwold Bitter; Woodforde's Wherry; guest beer Ⓗ
A cosy inn with several small drinking areas and two dining rooms. It has a garden and play area and is family- and dog-friendly. Four Brancaster beers are produced by a local brewery to the pub's recipes and these are rotated. There is regular live music in the winter and a beer festival in June. Food offerings include stone-baked pizza, with the oven visible from the bar. It is only a short walk to Brancaster harbour and the Norfolk coast path. Coasthopper buses stop outside.
♨Q✿◑▲⊟(Coasthopper)P⁵⁻

Broome

Artichoke Ⓛ
162 Yarmouth Road, NR35 2NZ (just off A143, on main road through village) TM352915
✪ closed Mon; 12-11 (midnight Fri & Sat) ☎ (01986) 893325 ⊕ theartichokeatbroome.co.uk
Adnams Southwold Bitter Ⓗ, **Broadside** Ⓖ; **Elgood's Black Dog** Ⓗ; **guest beers** Ⓗ/Ⓖ
Early 19th-century inn that was the home of the long-defunct Crowfoot Brewery. A large fireplace with a real fire, flagstones and wooden floors give a rural ambience to this friendly establishment. Delicious home-cooked food is available, served in the bar, dining room or garden. A range of up to eight beers is offered, always including an old, porter or stout, with an emphasis on local breweries – some served by gravity from the taproom. The pub also boasts a range of around 100 malt whiskies. ♨Q✿◑▲⊟(580,588)♣P⁵⁻

Burnham Thorpe

Lord Nelson
Walsingham Road, PE31 8HN (off B1355)
✪ 12-11 (12-3, 6-11 winter); 12-10.30 Sun
☎ (01328) 738241 ⊕ nelsonslocal.co.uk
Greene King Abbot; Woodforde's Wherry Ⓖ
Seventeenth-century pub about half a mile from the vicarage where Nelson was born, and which was his local when he had no ship between 1786 and 1793. He held a party here to celebrate his return to the sea. After Trafalgar it was the first pub renamed in his honour. The dispense is all by gravity from a traditional taproom, through a hatch to a cosy room with settles. The modern world is catered for by an extensive menu and occasional live bands. ♨Q✿◑ఉ♣P⁵⁻

Catfield

Crown Inn Ⓛ
The Street, NR29 5AA TG387218
✪ closed Mon; 12-2.30, 7-11; 12-3, 7-midnight Sat; 12-3, 7-10.30 Sun ☎ (01692) 580128 ⊕ catfieldcrown.co.uk
Greene King IPA; guest beer Ⓗ

Cosy, tastefully furnished, 300-year-old traditional village inn with a real fire in winter. The guest beer range changes regularly and often includes Green Jack beers. The landlord is also the chef, and excellent food, including Italian dishes, is a speciality. Fresh local ingredients are used where possible. There is a separate function/dining room and a secluded garden in summer. Accommodation is in a detached converted hall that was once the doctor's surgery. Close to the Broads and north Norfolk coast. ♨Q✿⌂✍◑⊟(12)P⁵⁻

Colton

Ugly Bug Inn Ⓛ
High House Farm Lane, NR9 5DG (2 miles S of A47. Turn off on roundabout on Honingham Rd) TG104908
✪ 12-2.30 (not Tue), 5-11; 12-3, 6-10 Sun
☎ (01603) 880794 ⊕ uglybuginn.co.uk
Beer range varies Ⓗ
Large remote rural pub with extensive gardens. Good-quality food is served in the spacious dining room. The single bar has exposed beams and comfortable seating. The two to three ales on offer are from the local Humpty Dumpty and Beeston microbreweries, and a guest beer, usually from East Anglia, is normally added in the summer months. Live jazz takes place monthly. The pub is closed on a Tuesday lunchtime. Eight en-suite bedrooms are available. ✿✍◑ఉAP

Cromer

Red Lion Ⓛ
Brook Street, NR27 9HD (on top of cliffs above pier and lifeboat station near parish church)
✪ 11-11 (10.30 Sun) ☎ (01263) 514964
⊕ redlion-cromer.co.uk
Adnams Southwold Bitter; Woodforde's Wherry; guest beers Ⓗ
Early 1800s pub and hotel at the top of the cliff, with commanding views of the promenade, sea and Cromer pier. The interior comprises two bars: one a traditional Edwardian bar with mahogany panels, the other with flint and brick walls adorned with photographs of Cromer's maritime past. There is a real fire in each bar. The guest beers usually come from local microbreweries. Regular beer festivals are held throughout the year. The award-winning Galleons restaurant offers an extensive menu. ♨✍◑ఉ⇌⊟(44)P

Dereham

Romany Rye ✪
Church Street, NR19 1DL
✪ 9-midnight (1am Fri & Sat); 12-midnight Sun
☎ (01362) 654160
Greene King Abbot; Ruddles Best Bitter Ⓗ
Situated in the mid-Norfolk market town of Dereham, the Romany Rye (formerly known as the Phoenix Hotel) is conveniently central, close to the marketplace and the 12th-century St Nicholas Parish Church. Typical of Wetherspoon, it has a large split-level bar with a range of rotating beers, including occasionals from local Norfolk micros such as Panther. There is a large beer terrace, and en-suite accommodation is available as well as a conference room. ♨⛌✿✍◑ఉ⊟♣⍟

Dersingham

Coach & Horses
77 Manor Road, PE31 6LN
✪ 12-midnight (11 Sun) ☎ (01485) 540391
⊕ norfolkinns.co.uk/coachhorse
Woodforde's Wherry; guest beers Ⓗ
Busy 19th-century carrstone pub close to
Sandringham House. Entertainment includes quiz
nights, bingo, poker games and live music on
Friday nights and some Sundays. It is a popular pub
for food, enjoyed by locals and tourists. There is a
large beer garden including a children's play area,
music stand, old red phone box and heated
smoking shelter. Three en-suite rooms are
available to let. A beer festival takes place in
September, with around 20 real ales and some
cider. ⚊Q⚒⛱🛏🌢🍽🚌(41A)P🚱

Diss

Cock Inn ✔
Lower Denmark Street, IP22 4BE
✪ 12-11 (midnight Fri & Sat) ☎ (01379) 643633
⊕ cockinndiss.co.uk
Adnams Southwold Bitter; guest beers Ⓗ
Popular edge-of-town pub in a pleasant location
opposite Fair Green. It has been sympathetically
restored and extended to provide four comfortable
seating/drinking areas grouped around a U-shaped
bar. It has a heavily beamed interior with a
logburner and lots of character. Three ales are
always on handpump, with Adnams Southwold
Bitter always available. Food is served 12-2pm and
6.30-9pm Wednesday-Sunday. Outside, there is
plenty of seating for those warmer days and for
watching the world go by. ⚊⚒🍽🚶🚌P🚱

Downham Market

Railway Arms Ⓛ
Downham Market Railway Station, PE38 9EN
✪ 10-5.30 (10.30 Thu & Fri); 10-12.10, 4-10.30 Sat; 12-2.30
Sun ☎ (01366) 386636 ⊕ railway-arms.co.uk
Beer range varies Ⓗ
A compact surprise, the Railway is contained in the
waiting rooms at Downham rail station. The
beer range majors in Elgood's ales but a good
variety is sourced from further afield, all on
gravity. Real cider from Cambridgeshire's Pickled
Pig features. The pub still acts as a waiting room
and has a small model railway running around at
ceiling height. Light snacks made from locally
sourced ingredients are available. A partition has
been removed recently, making the small bar feel
more spacious. Make sure you check out the
library. ⚊🚶🍴👜

White Hart Ⓛ
58 Bridge Street, PE38 9DH
✪ 12-midnight (1am Fri & Sat); 12-10.30 Sun
☎ (01366) 387720
Elgood's Blackdog Mild; guest beers Ⓗ
A typical basic 18th-century pub, the White Hart
has two large bars, one featuring a pool table.
Elgood's beers are always on, plus a widely
sourced range of guests. A no-nonsense drinkers'
pub, where a down-to-earth welcome awaits, this
venue is a short walk from the railway station, and
a great place for a mini pub crawl.
⚊⚒🛏🚶🚌🍴P🚱

Earsham

Queen's Head Ⓛ
Station Road, NR35 2TS (turn left off A143 signed to
Earsham) TM321891
✪ 12-11 (10.30 Sun) ☎ (01986) 892623
**Waveney East Coast Mild, Lightweight, seasonal beer;
guest beer** Ⓗ
Situated in the heart of the Waveney Valley on the
Norfolk-Suffolk border, this 17th-century pub has a
large front garden overlooking the village green.
The main bar has a flagstone floor, wooden beams
and a large fireplace with a roaring fire in winter. It
is home to the Waveney Brewing Co, with two
Waveney beers usually on offer, one a mild, plus at
least one guest from another brewer. There is a
separate dining area serving food at lunchtimes
(not Mon and Tue). ⚊⚒🍽🚌(580)🍴P🚱

Edgefield

Pigs
Norwich Road, NR24 2RL (on B1149) TG098343
✪ 11-3, 6-11; 12-10 Sun ☎ (01263) 587634
⊕ thepigs.org.uk
**Adnams Southwold Bitter, Broadside; Greene King
Abbot; Wolf Old Spot; Woodforde's Wherry; guest
beer** Ⓖ
Multi award-winning pub with its own local news
sheet, The Grunter, and famed for its barter system
where fresh produce can be exchanged for beer.
Enter through the foyer displaying fresh local
produce for sale. Beer is served by gravity from
casks behind the bar. There is a room to the left, a
restaurant area to the right, and outdoor seating
areas to the front and rear. The pub can become
busy during peak times. The mini bar on the
landing includes a handpump that dispenses the
house beer, Wolf Old Spot. Accommodation is
available. ⚊☕⚒🛏🌢🚌🍴P🚱

Elsing

Mermaid Inn Ⓛ
Church Street, NR20 3EA (opp church) TG053165
✪ 12-3, 7-11; 6-midnight Sat; 12-3, 6.30-11 Sun
☎ (01362) 637640 ⊕ elsingmermaidinn.co.uk
**Adnams Broadside; Woodforde's Wherry; guest
beers** Ⓖ
A 17th-century pub opposite the village church. The
large single room has a log-burning fire at one end
and a pool table at the other. There is also a
restaurant. Cask ales sold here are mainly, though
not exclusively, from local brewers, typically
Humpty Dumpty and Batemans, which are
dispensed by gravity. Food is served every
lunchtime and evening except Monday. The pub
menu features curries, steaks and pie specials. A
selection of books and pub games is available for
patrons' use. ⚊⚒🍽🌢🅰P🚱

Feltwell

West End ✔
43 Long Lane, IP26 4BJ
✪ 12-midnight ☎ (01842) 827711
Beer range varies Ⓗ
Lively pub that sits on the road to Southery and
backs on to RAF Feltwell, a mainly residential base
for American services. The real ales change all the
time, from a decent cask ale list that has
everything from Timothy Taylor to Marston's,

Sharp's and other independents, always in good condition. The West End does food, the Sunday carvery being particularly popular. Occasional live music and karaoke take place. Pub games include pool and darts. ⊛◖♣P

Filby

King's Head

Main Road, NR29 3HY (on main A1064 just E of village)
TG483133
✪ 12-11 ☎ (01493) 733948
Ruddles Best Bitter; guest beers Ⓗ
A traditional dog-friendly village local in an east Norfolk village, with one regular and two guest beers sourced from national and local breweries. The lounge/dining room has a log-burning fireplace and sofas. Traditional quality seasonal food is served. The pub is home to a number of sports teams. Families are welcome and there is outdoor seating. There is a separate covered and heated smoking area and Wi-Fi access is available.
🏛⊛◖⊟⚲▲🚃(730)♣P🏵💻

Fleggburgh

King's Arms

Main Road, NR29 3AG
✪ 12-11.30 (12.30am Fri & Sat; 11 Sun) ☎ (01493) 368463
Adnams Southwold Bitter; Fuller's London Pride; guest beers Ⓗ
Spacious one-room village pub, recently refurbished, offering two regular ales, up to six guests, and two to six ciders on gravity. It holds occasional mini beer festivals where the selection of guest ales is themed. Food is from local sources, served lunchtimes and evenings, 12-7pm Sundays. Fine dining is offered in the separate contemporary restaurant which permits a view of the professional kitchen during service. Booking is advised, particularly at weekends. Outside there are paved and grassed seating areas and a separate covered and heated smoking section.
🏛⊛◖⚲▲🚃(6,730)♣💧P🏵

Gayton

Crown Inn ✪

Lynn Road, PE32 1PA
✪ 12-11 ☎ (01553) 636252 ⊕ gaytoncrown.com
Greene King XX Mild, IPA, Abbot; guest beer Ⓗ
Originally built to house the stonemason and workers who built the local church in about 1240. The Crown has a charming atmosphere and has retained much of its 13th-century looks. It is a rare outlet for the XX dark mild as well as an occasional interesting guest beer. The large restaurant serves locally sourced food including game dishes. There are several drinking areas which include a very cosy snug bar and an outside patio area for the summer with attractive flower beds.
🏛Q🐕⊛🍴◖⚲🚃(48)

Geldeston

Locks Inn

Locks Lane, NR34 0HW (through village centre, turn left into Station Rd; after 300yds turn left onto track across marshes) TM390908
✪ 12-11; closed Mon-Wed winter; 12-11 (7 winter) Sun
☎ (01508) 518414 ⊕ geldestonlocks.co.uk

Green Jack Excelsior, Orange Wheat Beer, Trawler Boys, Gone Fishing, seasonal beers; guest beers Ⓗ
On the north bank of the River Waveney, the pub is accessed by a long, meandering track between dykes and marshes. The small main bar, with low ceiling beams and clay pamment floor, retains an authentic, welcoming feel, with candlelight adding to the atmosphere. It has live music on Thursday evenings and Sunday afternoons. Owned by the Green Jack Brewery, its range of beers is supplemented by guests and a selection of real ciders and perries. Excellent food is served lunchtimes and evenings, and in summer season weekends all day. 🏛Q🐕⊛◖♣💧P

Gorleston-on-Sea

Mariners Compass Ⓛ

21 Middleton Road, NR31 7AJ
✪ 10-12.30am (3 Sat); 10-11.30 Sun ☎ (01493) 659494
Ruddles Best Bitter; guest beers Ⓗ
Large two-bar pub opened in the 1930s and fitted out in brewers' Tudor style, retaining many of its original fittings inside. Saved from demolition in 2008, it is in the same hands as CAMRA Branch Pub of the Year winner Mariners Tavern in Yarmouth, and has become one of the major real ale venues for the area. The pub has two drinking areas, the real ale bar occupying the old saloon area. Beers change regularly and are invariably interesting. Good-value bar snacks are always available.
⊛◖⚲♿🚃♣💧P🏵🍴

New Entertainer

80 Pier Plain, NR31 6PG (off Englands Lane)
✪ 3-11 (midnight Sat); 12-11 Sun ☎ (01493) 441643
Greene King IPA; guest beers Ⓗ
Situated fairly close to the seafront, this traditional street-corner local with a curved frontage has an interesting design and layout. The interior includes a pool table and dartboard. There is always a fine choice of beers on offer, including at least six guests, many coming from local brewers, and a selection of bottled Belgian beers is also available. This dedicated free house is well worth seeking out, though the signposting is not always obvious. Q🚃♣💧

Great Cressingham

Windmill Inn

Water End, IP25 6NN (off A1065 S of Swaffham)
TF846019
✪ 11.30-11 ☎ (01760) 756232 ⊕ oldewindmillinn.co.uk
Adnams Southwold Bitter, Broadside; Greene King IPA; Hancock's Windy Miller Ⓗ; guest beers Ⓗ/Ⓖ
Family-run centuries-old rambling inn with a variety of bars and rooms offering real winter fire or conservatory sunshine. A good range of real ales includes the house beer, Windy Miller, plus two guest beers rotated weekly. One real cider is on the bar, often Westons Old Rosie. Thirty different malt whiskies are stocked. The pub offers live music nights, talent night and a games room. An extensive menu of home-cooked food is available daily lunch and dinner. Positioned for a stop-off from the Peddars Way.
🏛Q🐕⊛🍴◖⚲♿▲♣💧P🏵

Great Massingham

Dabbling Duck
11 Abbey Road, PE32 2HN
✪ 12-11 (10.30 Sun) ☎ (01485) 520827
⊕ thedabblingduck.co.uk
Adnams Broadside; Beeston Worth the Wait; Greene King IPA; Woodforde's Wherry; guest beers Ⓗ
Situated between two duck ponds in an attractive village, the pub features large bar areas with a roaring fire in winter. There is a separate restaurant for the many customers attracted by the food but also ample room for those who just wish to try one of the five or six beers on offer. An extensive garden hosts the occasional beer festival. See the wall map for details of local walks. Norfolk CAMRA Pub of the Year for 2011. ⚼⚘⛴⊄Ⓓ⊟⛁(48)♣P⅃

Great Yarmouth

Mariners Tavern Ⓛ
69 Howard Street South, NR30 1LN (between harbour and marketplace, 20yds from police station)
✪ 11 (12 Sun)-11 ☎ (01493) 332799
Beer range varies Ⓗ
Traditional two-bar pub in the town centre, winner of local CAMRA Pub of the Year 2010. With up to eight ales and real cider/perries on offer, visitors could be excused for thinking that a beer festival is always in progress, given the range and choice from all over the country. Regular beer festivals are held throughout the year, doubling the range available, the one at Easter a particular highlight, and the town's maritime festival is held in early September. ⚼⚲⚘⊞⚼⇌⊟(X1)♣⚫⅃⛉

Oliver Twist Ⓛ
62-63 North Market Road, NR30 2DX (to NE of Market Gates complex)
✪ 12-midnight (1am Fri & Sat summer) ☎ (07768) 120714
Blackfriars Bitter, Old Habit; guest beer Ⓗ
In a small back street conveniently near the Market Gates shopping complex, this cosy street-corner local always has a beer on from the local Blackfriars Brewery. Displays of scooters and rock 'n' roll highlight the landlord's twin passions. The main bar has a jukebox and there is a pool table in the adjoining bar. ⚘⊄Ⓓ⇌(Vauxhall)⊟♣⅃

St John's Head Ⓛ
58 North Quay, NR30 1JB
✪ 12-midnight (10.30 Sun) ☎ (01493) 843443
Elgood's Cambridge Bitter; guest beers Ⓗ
In one of the oldest areas of the town, this former Lacons Brewery pub is reputed to be built on land confiscated from monks of the Carmelite Order. A single bar houses a large TV screen for live sport, and the pub is busy on match days. There is a pool table in one area, plus a smoking shelter which is minimalist but heated on a pay-per-use basis. ⚘⚵⇌(Vauxhall)⊟♣⅃

Hainford

Chequers
10 Stratton Road, NR10 3AY (just off A140 on B1354, 5 mins from Norwich Airport, 8 miles from Norwich)
✪ 11-11 ☎ (01603) 891657 ⊕ hainford-chequers.co.uk
Hook Norton Old Hooky; Woodforde's Wherry Ⓗ
A lovely traditional country thatched pub just off the main A140 Norwich to Cromer road. The interior has a single bar with beamed ceilings and open fires. Four real ales are available. There is a

patio overlooking cottage gardens and a large garden with a children's play area. The emphasis is on food with locally sourced ingredients, and there are daily specials; it gets busy at weekends, so booking is advisable. A quiz night is held on Wednesday plus occasional live music. ⚘⚵Ⓓ P⅃⛉

Heacham

Fox & Hounds Ⓛ
22 Station Road, PE31 7EX
✪ 12-11 (10.30 Sun) ☎ (01485) 570345
Adnams Broadside; guest beers Ⓗ
Popular with locals and visitors, this is the home of the Fox Brewery. There are eight beers on offer including a selection from Fox, whose bottled beers are also sold, plus a range of imported beers. The restaurant offers beer recommendations to match the food. There is live music on Tuesday evening (mainly blues) and a quiz on Thursday. Beer festivals are hosted throughout the year. ⚼⚘Ⓓ⚵♣P⅃

Hempton

Bell
The Green, NR21 7LG (turn by the Fakenham Garden Centre off the A1065) TF913293
✪ 11-2.30 (not Tue), 5-midnight; 11-midnight Sat; 12-4, 7-midnight Sun ☎ (01328) 864579 ⊕ hemptonbell.co.uk
John Smith's Bitter; Woodforde's Wherry; guest beer Ⓗ
In a small village on the outskirts of Fakenham, this pub has been at the centre of the village community for around 400 years. A rare example of a rural pub that does not serve food, the Bell is friendly, traditional, and retains a two-bar layout little altered since the early 1970s. Pub games including dominoes, crib and darts are popular – you'll be welcome to get involved. The guest beer usually comes from a micro or independent brewery. P⅃

Hethersett

King's Head Ⓛ
36 Norwich Road, NR9 3DD (just off the B1172) TG154045
✪ 11-11 (midnight Fri & Sat) ☎ (01603) 810206
⊕ kingsheadhethersett.co.uk
Adnams Southwold Bitter; Fuller's London Pride; Taylor Golden Best; guest beer Ⓗ
In this 18th-century, two-roomed country pub the comfortable saloon bar boasts a large inglenook fireplace with a roaring fire in winter and a suit of armour. The public bar is a gem, unchanged for the past 50 years. Three regular real ales are always available plus a guest beer from the Woodforde's range, which changes on a regular basis. Food is served in a separate dining room lunchtimes and evenings (no food Sun eve). Outside there is a large grassed area and children's play equipment, with a large heated timber gazebo. ⚼⚘Ⓓ⚵⅃

Heydon

Earle Arms Ⓛ
The Green, NR11 6AD (just off the B1149, 5 miles from Aylsham and only 20 minutes from Norwich, opp village green) TG113273
✪ closed Mon; 12-3, 6-11; 12-10.30 Sun ☎ (01263) 587376
⊕ earlearms.vpweb.co.uk

Adnams Southwold Bitter; Panther Red; Woodforde's Wherry H
Lovely 16th-century former coaching inn situated opposite the green, in the centre of a privately owned picture-postcard village that has often been used as a film location. The bar is mainly candlelit, with a welcoming atmosphere and a log fire in winter; it also has an interesting collection of horse racing memorabilia. The food is seasonal and locally sourced, cooked to order and of the highest quality. The restaurant is separate, and booking is advisable. Superb pub, not to be missed.
🏚️❄️🍽️🚶P

Hickling

Pleasure Boat
Staithe Road, NR12 0YJ (from A149 take first right on entering village)
❀ 11.30-midnight; 12-11 Sun ☎ (01692) 598870
🌐 thepleasureboat.com
Adnams Southwold Bitter; Woodforde's Wherry, Nelson's Revenge H
An iconic Broadland pub with moorings 20 feet from its front door. There are always four real ales and two locally produced ciders (from award-winning East Norfolk Trading) available. Good home-cooked food is served using only fresh ingredients, locally produced whenever possible. Both child- and dog-friendly, enter to a welcoming real fire after exploring the nearby countryside and nature reserves. Well known both locally and by boating enthusiasts for a great atmosphere, music and quiz events are held on a regular basis. Real fire, real ale, real cider, real people!
🏚️Q🍽️❄️🍺🔓🏕️♣🚶P🚃

Hilborough

Swan Inn L
Brandon Road, IP26 5BW (on A1065)
❀ 11-11; 12-10.30 Sun ☎ (01760) 756380
🌐 hilboroughswan.com
Beer range varies H
The Swan is run by Claire and James, a husband and wife team. James is a chef and produces the home-made food, with steak and ale pie a speciality. A carvery is served on Sunday. Claire was born in Hilborough and comes from a family of gamekeepers; she has made the pub interior a comfortable space with a traditional local feel. The beers rotate regularly, with Elmtree, Humpty Dumpty and Beeston featuring. Accommodation is available. An ideal stop in lovely Breckland.
🏚️❄️🚪🍽️🏕️♣🚶P🚃

Hockering

Victoria
The Street, NR20 3HL (just off A47) TF863355
❀ 1 (12 Sat)-3, 6-11; 12-6 Sun ☎ (01603) 880507
Mighty Oak Oscar Wilde; Sharp's Doom Bar; guest beer H
Located just north of the A47 Norwich-Dereham road and conveniently opposite the X1 bus stop, this friendly pub offers a warm welcome – and a real fire in winter. The guest beer varies but is normally a golden ale. The large single bar has a dartboard and also offers shut-the-box and cribbage. Beer festivals are held in summer and at Christmas. Live music plays occasionally.
🏚️❄️🚶🚃(X1)♣🚶🚃

Horsey

Nelson Head
The Street, NR29 4AD (300yds E of B1159 coast road or 500yds from Horsey Staithe)
❀ 11-11; 12-10.30 Sun ☎ (01493) 393378
Woodforde's Wherry, Nelson's Revenge H
A rural pub close to the North Sea seals, Horsey Staithe, Horsey Mere nature reserve, the Broads and a famous mill. It is the ideal place for walkers, offering a good selection of hearty home-cooked meals made with locally sourced produce, available lunchtimes and evenings. Its beautiful views make it popular with boaters, artists and birdwatchers. Families and dogs are welcome, and there is a large garden area for children. Its warm friendly atmosphere, with local real ales and ciders, gives it the feel of a traditional pub. Well worth seeking out. 🏚️Q🍽️❄️🍽️🍺🏕️🚃♣🚶P🚃

Kenninghall

Red Lion ★
East Church Street, NR16 2EP (opp church) TM042859
❀ 12-3, 5.30-11; 12-11 Fri & Sat; 12-10 Sun
☎ (01953) 887849 🌐 redlionkenninghall.co.uk
Greene King IPA H**, Abbot** G**; Morland Old Golden Hen; Woodforde's Wherry; guest beers** H
Four-hundred-year-old pub situated opposite the parish church, comprising a bar with a real fire, a pine-panelled snug and a separate restaurant. The beer range comes mainly from Greene King and Woodforde's, with Abbot dispensed by gravity from a cask behind the bar. It serves good-quality, home-cooked food with themed food nights on some evenings. Live music is in the form of jam sessions on alternate Sunday afternoons. Accommodation is available, with four en-suite rooms. Directions for a short local walk can be obtained from the bar. 🏚️❄️🚪🍽️🚶P

King's Lynn

Crown & Mitre
Ferry Street, PE30 1LJ (off Tuesday Market Place)
❀ 12-2.30, 6-11 ☎ (01553) 774669
Beer range varies H
On entering it feels more like walking into a museum than a pub, with a huge collection of maritime and other objects. When you tire of these you can sit in the gallery overlooking the river. There are usually about five beers from small breweries on offer. Note that hours may vary, and the pub tends to close for the Mart (two weeks from February 14th). There are public car parks close by. 🏚️Q❄️🍽️

Lattice House ✅
Chapel Street, PE30 1EG
❀ 9-11 (1am Fri & Sat) ☎ (01553) 769585
Greene King Abbot; Ruddles Best Bitter; guest beers H
Unusually for a Wetherspoon pub there are no TV screens, and the interior is divided into a number of small areas. There are three bars, including one upstairs, which sometimes means that service can be a bit slow, but the choice of about 10 ales is worth the wait. Look out for the wall paintings and other features of this historic building. The usual food options are available and there is plenty of public car parking close by. 🏚️Q🍽️❄️🍽️🚶

Stuart House Hotel

35 Goodwins Road, PE30 5QX
6-11; 7-10.30 Sun ☎ (01553) 772169
stuart-house-hotel.co.uk
Beer range varies Ⓗ
There are usually two or three beers available in the bar of this independent hotel hidden down a gravel drive close to the Walks. Look out for live music, usually on the last Friday in the month, special themed evenings such as Murder Mystery dinners, and the annual beer festival in the last week in July, held in the large garden. Ask about special deals on accommodation for CAMRA members. Note that the bar is open in the evening only, unless by arrangement. ♨Q✿🛏◗⇌🚌P

Langham

Bluebell ✔

22-24 Holt Road, NR25 7BX (take B1156 S from Blakeney, then turn right into village) TG012411
11-3, 7-11; 11-11 Fri-Sun ☎ (01328) 830502
Adnams Southwold Bitter; guest beer Ⓗ
A traditional village local near the north Norfolk coast which has been run by same family for over 40 years. The red tiled main bar with traditional wooden furniture opens out to a spacious games room with darts and pool table. There is also a split-level dining room and a beer terrace to the rear. Up to two guest beers, one usually from Woodforde's, are on offer. Home-cooked food, made with locally sourced products where possible, is available every day lunchtime and evening (no food Wed). Families and dogs are welcome. ♨✿◖◗♿🚌(46)♣P⚟

Larling

Angel Inn

NR16 2QU (off A11 between Thetford and Norwich, signed by B1111 East Harling) TL983890
10-midnight; 11-11 Sun ☎ (01953) 717963
angel-larling.co.uk
Adnams Southwold Bitter; guest beers Ⓗ
A popular pub run by the same family since 1913, recognised as the local CAMRA Pub of the Year for 2010. Five real ales are always on handpump, including a mild. There is superb food, over 100 whiskies, and both the lounge and bar have open fires. The bar is enjoyed by friendly locals, passers-by and visitors who enjoy the Angel's campsite. A summer beer festival features more than 70 ales and the pub also hosts a whisky week.
♨Q✿🛏◖◗⊟♿⛺⇌(Harling Rd)P⚟

Lessingham

Star Inn Ⓛ

School Road, NR12 0DN (300yds off B1159 coast road) TG388283
12-3 (not Mon), 6-11 ☎ (01692) 580510
thestarlessingham.co.uk
Adnams Southwold Bitter; Buffy's Bitter; Greene King IPA; Woodforde's Wherry; guest beer Ⓗ
Excellent village local that offers well-kept beers to regulars from near and far, and has a relaxed welcoming atmosphere. Situated near the north-east Norfolk coast, it is convenient for those visiting nearby East Ruston Old Vicarage Garden. The large beer garden is perfect for summer drinking. The cider is Westons Old Rosie. Dogs are welcome in the bar. Bar snacks and freshly prepared high-quality lunches and dinners are available daily (no food Mon, and Sun eve).
♨Q✿🛏◖◗⛺🚌(34,36)♣●P

Newton by Castle Acre

George & Dragon Ⓛ ✔

Swaffham Road, PE32 2BX (on main road between Fakenham and Swaffham)
12-2.30, 6-11; 12-3 Sun ☎ (01760) 755046
Beer range varies Ⓗ
Three-roomed pub positioned on the A1065 opposite a turning into Castle Acre, with a large car park at the rear. The interior features wooden beams and a welcoming open fire. The venue supports LocAle, and two local beers are available at all times. A varying food menu is served in the restaurant, with some South African dishes from the landlady's homeland. There are popular gourmet meal nights three times a year, so book early. Entertainment includes regular music evenings and quiz nights. ♨Q🐴✿◖◗⊟🚌P

North Creake

Jolly Farmers

1 Burnham Road, NR21 9JW
closed Mon & Tue; 12-2.30, 7-11 (10.30 Sun)
☎ (01328) 738185 jollyfarmers-northcreake.co.uk
Adnams Southwold Bitter Ⓗ**; Woodforde's Wherry; guest beers** Ⓖ
Three small rooms with lots of wood and tile, leather chairs, classical music or jazz, and open fires all combine to create a wonderful atmosphere. Add the food, made from the finest local ingredients, and the beer, some of which comes straight from the cask, and we are coming close to describing the perfect village local – but note that it is closed Mondays and Tuesdays and in the afternoon. ♨🐴✿◖◗♿P⚟

North Elmham

Railway Ⓛ

Station Road, NR20 5HH TF995202
11-midnight ☎ (01362) 668300
Beer range varies Ⓗ/Ⓖ
A fine example of a rural community pub, situated in central Norfolk. A rotating choice of ales is available, with beers dispensed either by handpump or gravity. The range tends to favour local brewers such as Woodforde's and Elgood's, but beers from Somerset brewer Cottage also feature here regularly. There is an adjacent function room that hosts many music events. Home-cooked meals using mainly locally sourced ingredients are available. The pub now offers B&B and has a camping site at the rear. ♨✿🛏◖◗⛺P

North Lopham

King's Head ✔

The Street, IP22 2NE (2 miles N of A1066) TM037834
11.30-3 (not Mon), 5-11; 11.30-midnight Sat; 12-10.30 Sun
☎ (01379) 688007 lophamkingshead.co.uk
Adnams Southwold Bitter; Woodforde's Wherry; guest beer Ⓗ
Two-bar timber-framed pub dating from the 16th century and set back from the main road through the village. The public bar has an inglenook fireplace and a pool table, while the comfortable saloon and dining area have a wood-burner. The

guest beer varies but is normally over 4% ABV. Food is served lunchtimes and evenings Wednesday to Saturday and Sunday lunchtimes. The pub has its own crazy golf course; clubs and balls can be borrowed free of charge. Dog-friendly. ᨆ☀◑ᵫ♣P

North Wootton

Red Cat Hotel

Station Road, PE30 3QH (300yds from North Wootton church) TF640243
❀ 4.30-11; 12-2, 7-11 Sun ☎ (01553) 631244
⊕ redcathotel.com
Adnams Southwold Bitter; Woodforde's Wherry; guest beers Ⓗ
Informal yet friendly family-run country inn, built of local 'gingerbread' carrstone. Set in the picturesque village of North Wootton, it dates back to 1898. Recently refurbished to a high standard, it provides comfortable seating and a warm welcome from the staff. The three regular ales are of superb quality. The restaurant is available every evening and offers home-cooked food in a relaxing environment. A Wi-Fi hotspot zone is available for those who wish to surf the net. Q☀⇔◑ᵫ(3,7)P⁵⁻

Norwich

Beehive Ⓛ

30 Leopold Road, NR4 7PJ (between Newmarket and Unthank roads)
❀ 12 (5 Mon)-11; 12-midnight Fri & Sat ☎ (01603) 451628
⊕ beehivepubnorwich.co.uk
Fuller's London Pride; Wolf Golden Jackal; guest beers Ⓗ
Popular community pub that serves five guest ales mainly from East Anglia, with Green Jack being a regular. The pub is home to three darts teams, pool and korfball teams. A weekly quiz is held on Wednesday, a folk night is held monthly and free Wi-Fi and pub games round out the entertainment. It also hosts a popular beer festival in the first week of July along with regular charity barbecues during the summer months. Food is served lunchtimes only. ☀◑ᵫ(12,24)♣⁵⁻

Cottage Ⓛ

9 Silver Road, NR3 4TB (N of city within easy walking distance of rail station and city centre)
❀ 12-11 ☎ (01603) 665535 ⊕ thecottagenorwich.co.uk
Crouch Vale Brewers Gold; Mauldons Blackadder; guest beers Ⓗ
CAMRA Branch City Pub of the Year for 2011, this public house offers a warm and friendly welcome, with quality ales from the Mauldons range and up to 10 varied guests. Events include an annual St George's beer festival, monthly quiz nights, plus live music on Friday evening and Sunday afternoon. Excellent home-cooked food is served on a regular basis along with a monthly tapas evening. The pub has a pleasant beer garden to the rear which catches the sun in the summer. ☀⇌ᵫ(999)♣♠⁵⁻

Duke of Wellington

91-93 Waterloo Road, NR3 1EG
❀ 12-11.30 (10.30 Sun) ☎ (01603) 441182
⊕ dukeofwellingtonnorwich.co.uk
Elgood's Black Dog; Fuller's London Pride; Oakham JHB, Bishop's Farewell; Wolf Golden Jackal, Straw Dog; guest beers Ⓗ/Ⓖ

This regular Guide entry offers a range of ales from around the country, with many served from the small taproom, which can be seen from the bar area. The first Monday of the month is quiz night, while every Tuesday features folk music. The back patio/garden area holds the pub's annual beer festival during the late summer bank holiday and is picturesque in the sunshine. There is no food available but customers may bring their own. ᨆ☀ᵫ(9A,16)♣♠P⁵⁻

Fat Cat 🍺 Ⓛ

49 West End Street, NR2 4NA (just off Dereham Rd)
❀ 12-11 (midnight Thu-Sat) ☎ (01603) 624364
⊕ fatcatpub.co.uk
Adnams Southwold Bitter; Fat Cat Best Bitter Ⓗ, **Honey Cat, Wild Cat** Ⓗ/Ⓖ; **Fuller's ESB** Ⓖ; **guest beers** Ⓗ/Ⓖ
A beer lover's paradise that no visitor to Norwich should miss. This is an outstanding example of what a real ale pub should be – excellent service, quality ales from the Fat Cat Brewery, plus a selection of almost 30 guest ales from all over the UK. Brewery memorabilia is in abundance, reminding the customer of beer and breweries long gone. Draught and bottled continental beers from an extensive range are also available. Food is limited to good-value rolls and pies. Q☀ᵫ(16,19,20)♣♠⁵⁻

Fat Cat Brewery Tap

98-100 Lawson Road, NR3 4LF (along Sprowston Rd, about 15 mins walk from Anglia Sq)
❀ 12-11 (midnight Fri); 11-midnight Sat; 11-10.30 Sun
☎ (01603) 413153 ⊕ fatcattap.co.uk
Adnams Southwold Bitter; Crouch Vale Yakima Gold; Fat Cat Bitter, Marmalade; Harviestoun Bitter & Twisted; guest beers Ⓗ/Ⓖ
Sister pub to the award-winning Fat Cat, it is next door to the brewery, where pleasant smells often waft into the spacious but welcoming drinking area. A range of up to 10 varying guest ales from around the country is sold along with the Fat Cat range. There is even a beer post box for customers' own suggestions. Live music is provided Friday evening and Sunday afternoon, along with a fortnightly quiz night on a Thursday. Well worth seeking out. ☀ᵫᵫ(11)♣♠P⁵⁻

Gate House

391 Dereham Road, NR5 8QJ
❀ 12-11 (midnight Fri & Sat) ☎ (01603) 620340
Grain Oak Ⓖ; **Greene King IPA, Abbot** Ⓗ; **Woodforde's Wherry** Ⓖ
A quiet local two miles west of Norwich city centre. There is always a warm welcome in winter thanks to a log fire in the larger of the two oak-panelled bars. In the summer the garden area overlooking the Wensum is a delight. The pub is proud of its crib, ladies' darts and pool teams. Live music includes Irish folk on Wednesdays and folk nights on Sundays. Prices are very reasonable, making this lovely pub excellent value. ᨆQ☀⇌ᵫ(19,20)♣P⁵⁻

Ketts Tavern Ⓛ

29 Ketts Hill, NR1 4EX
❀ 3-11.30; 12-midnight Fri & Sat; 12-11 Sun
☎ (01603) 449654 ⊕ norwichbear.co.uk
Norwich Bear Classic, Legend, Pooh Bear, NPA; guest beer Ⓗ
Wood-beamed pub close to the railway station and a mile from the football ground, one of two taps

(with sister pub The Rose, Queen's Road) for the Norwich Bear brewery, owned by the proprietors. A full range of regular Norwich Bear beers is available, along with occasional specials and guest beers. Kitchen-cooked meals are served at lunchtimes Friday-Sunday and every evening, and in the evening the pub will also order and serve up meals from local takeaways. It offers a large child-friendly conservatory, pool table and outdoor smoking area. ⚫⚫⚫◐⇌⊟(19,20)P⬥⊷

King's Arms
22 Hall Road, NR1 3HQ
✪ 11-11 (11.30 Fri & Sat); 12-10.30 Sun ☎ (01603) 766361
⊕ kingsarmsnorwich.co.uk
Batemans XB, XXXB; Beeston Worth the Wait; Hop Back Summer Lightning; guest beers Ⓗ
A friendly Batemans public house serving an extensive range of guest ales to complement the Batemans beers, usually including a stout or porter. It is situated to the south of the city centre, about 10 minutes' walk from the bus station. The pub allows customers to bring their own food from various nearby takeaways (plates and condiments provided). Lunchtime food is now served, including the excellent Sunday roasts. The pub has regular monthly quiz nights, poker evenings and live music. Westons Old Rosie Cider is often available. ⚫◐&♣⬥⊷

King's Head Ⓛ
42 Magdalen Street, NR3 1JE (a few yards from Anglia Square shopping area)
✪ 12-midnight (11 Sun) ☎ (01603) 620468
⊕ kingsheadnorwich.com
Winter's King's Head Bitter; Woodforde's Nelson's Revenge; guest beers Ⓗ
A classic drinking establishment, where no keg beers of any sort are sold. This award-winning pub offers a friendly welcome to all, with many of the beers sourced from Norfolk breweries and the smaller East Anglian microbrewers. The extensive range also includes a local cider and a selection of continental bottled beers, all of which are well-priced. The pub plays host to the Norwich bar billiard league, with the table situated in the rear drinking area. Q⊟(9,10,11)♣⬥⊷⊟

Murderers/Gardeners Arms Ⓛ
2-8 Timberhill, NR1 3LB (close to Norwich Castle)
✪ 10-11.30 (1.30am Fri & Sat); 12-10.30 Sun
☎ (01603) 621447 ⊕ themurderers.co.uk
Fuller's London Pride; Woodforde's Wherry; guest beers Ⓗ
Popular city-centre free house in Norwich's main shopping area and close to the castle. There is always a large range of guest ales here, many from local micros. The interior contains a number of drinking areas on split levels and there are wide-screen TVs for live sports. The memorabilia has a macabre theme and the adjacent Murderers Café Bar is the location for popular beer festivals. There is a beer terrace outside by the front entrance. ⚫◐&⬥⊷

Plough ✪
58 St Benedicts, NR2 4AR
✪ 12-11 (midnight Fri & Sat; 10.30 Sun) ☎ (01603) 661384
⊕ theploughnorwich.co.uk
Grain Bitter, Oak, Blonde Ash Ⓗ
This popular pub is in one of the city's oldest areas near the Norwich Arts Centre. As the Grain Brewery tap, it offers the full range of ales together with

guests and cider. The interior is fairly small, with wooden chairs, tables and a roaring log fire in winter. At the back, the large Mediterranean-style courtyard has many different drinking areas, which makes it a fine place to while away a summer's evening. ⚫Q⚫⊟⊟(19,20,21)⬥⊷

Take 5 Ⓛ
17 Tombland, NR3 1HF TG233088
✪ 11-11 (midnight Fri & Sat); closed Sun ☎ (01603) 763099
Beer range varies Ⓗ
Take 5 opened under its present name in 2004 (previously the Louis Marchesi, home of the Round Table). It is a Grade II-listed building, dating in parts from the 15th century. A range of around four real ales is available, usually a Woodforde's plus three others sourced predominantly from Norfolk breweries. Real cider is served plus a selection of bottled beers, complementing the home-cooked food, which gives a slightly continental feel. A function room is upstairs. ⚫◐⇌⊟(9,10,11)⬥

Trafford Arms Ⓛ ✪
61 Grove Road, NR1 3RL
✪ 11-11 (11.30 Fri & Sat); 12-10.30 Sun ☎ (01603) 628466
⊕ traffordarms.co.uk
Adnams Southwold Bitter; Tetley Bitter; Woodforde's Wherry; guest beers Ⓗ
Close to the city centre, a warm welcome is assured at this public house run by the same licensees for over 20 years. It offers a wide range of beers, always including a mild. Kingfisher Farm Cider is available throughout the year. Excellent home-cooked food includes pie, curry and fish evenings each week. The annual Valentine's beer festival raises funds for charitable causes and 2013 will be the 20th festival. The monthly quiz nights are very popular and it is a former local CAMRA Pub of the Year. ⚫◐&⊟(9,18)♣⬥P⊷

Vine Ⓛ
7 Dove Street, NR2 1DE (close to Norwich Provision Market and Guildhall)
✪ 11-11; closed Sun ☎ (01603) 627362 ⊕ vinethai.co.uk
Brandon Gun Flint, Rusty Bucket; Oakham JHB Ⓗ
Norwich's smallest pub is a gem in the heart of the city, serving quality ales and traditional Thai cuisine in a winning combination that is hard to beat. Located just off the marketplace, the restaurant is upstairs, although some customers prefer to eat downstairs in the bar area. In summer, tables and chairs are set out in the pedestrianised street where customers can while away their time watching shoppers go by. Beer festivals are held in January and late spring. Q⚫◐⊟♣⊷

White Lion
73 Oak Street, NR3 3AQ (just within the inner link road, near Barn Road roundabout)
✪ 12-11 (10.30 Sun) ☎ (01603) 632333
⊕ individualpubs.co.uk/whitelion
Milton Dionysus, Nero, Pegasus, Sparta; guest beers Ⓗ
A comfortable and cosy pub, serving a range of beers from Milton Brewery's extensive portfolio, plus guests. In addition, many different ciders and perries can be sampled. There are a number of pub games on offer, including a bar billiards table. An outside smoking area adjoins the main building. Historic details of the surrounding area, and the many pubs that existed, adorn the walls. The pub hosts monthly quizzes, as well as local morris and molly dancers. ⚫⚫◐⊟(28)♣⬥⊷

Old Costessey

Bush 🄻
58 The Street, NR8 5DD TG174119
✪ 11 (12 Sun)-11 ☎ (01603) 747227
Fuller's London Pride; Theakston Traditional Mild; Woodforde's Wherry Ⓗ
Village pub dating back to the 19th century and once frequented by the artist Alfred Munnings. Inside, the pub has been modernised yet retains a beamed ceiling. The interior is divided into two bars, one with a dartboard – the pub has its own darts team – the other with a large open fire. Outside there is a large beer garden leading down to the river. Regular beers are from Woodforde's and Fuller's, with one guest ale. ﹩❀♣P🕮🕮

Old Hunstanton

Ancient Mariner ✪
Golf Course Road, PE36 6JJ
✪ 11 (12 Sun)-11 ☎ (01485) 534411
⊕ theancientmariner.co.uk
Adnams Southwold Bitter, Broadside; guest beers Ⓗ
A popular pub adjoining the Le Strange Arms Hotel, with a large beer garden that has access to the beach. The inn consists of old barns and stables and includes a family room and restaurants. At least four ales are available. Old Hunstanton is the only village on the east coast to face west and the pub offers superb views of spectacular sunsets over the sea from the decking at the rear.
﹩Q👁❀🚃🕮🕪♿⚓🚌(36)P

Ormesby St Margaret

Jolly Farmers
West Street, NR29 3RP
✪ 12-1am ☎ (01493) 730471
Fuller's London Pride; Woodforde's Wherry Ⓗ
Friendly single-roomed village local with a low beamed ceiling and screened seating lending it a cosy air. Two regular ales are offered plus two guests suggested by the locals. Good food, from local sources, is served lunchtimes and evenings (booking at weekends recommended). The pub is dog-friendly, provides Wi-Fi and has a covered and heated smoking area. ﹩❀🕪⚓🚌(1,6)♣P🕮

Poringland

Royal Oak ✪
44 The Street, NR14 7JT (on B1332) TG267023
✪ 11-11; 12-midnight Fri & Sat; 12-11 Sun
☎ (01508) 493734
Adnams Southwold Bitter; Fuller's London Pride; Woodforde's Wherry Ⓗ
This former local CAMRA Pub of the Year is an unashamedly beer-oriented pub that offers a large range of beers both from brewers locally and across the UK, together with up to three real ciders from Westons. It has an open-plan interior invitingly laid out, with numerous nooks and small seating areas, including a games area with a pool table and dartboard. No food is served but there is a fish and chip shop next door.
❀♿🚌(587,588)♣🕪P🕮🕮

Rackheath

Sole & Heel
2 Salhouse Road, NR13 6QH

✪ 12 (Mon 5)-11; 12-10.30 Sun ☎ (01603) 720146
⊕ soleandheel.co.uk
Coors Rackheath Liberator; guest beers Ⓖ
A warm and welcoming single-bar pub with a small separate restaurant area for about 25 diners. Rackheath Liberator, brewed in Burton, is the house ale, served on gravity from the cellar alongside four guest beers, split between local and national brews, and one or more real ciders. The restaurant has a large choice of fresh home-cooked and locally sourced food, including seasonal evening specials. There is a pleasant garden with decking, a children's play area, and regular live music and events. ❀🕪♿🚃♣P🕮🕮

Reedham

Ship 🄻
19 Riverside, NR13 3TQ TG422016
✪ 11-11 ☎ (01493) 700287
Adnams Southwold Bitter, Broadside; Woodforde's Wherry; guest beers Ⓗ
Located close by the famous railway swing bridge, rail enthusiasts and others can watch the backdrop of rail and river while enjoying a beer. There is a large riverside garden including a children's play area and a smoking shelter. The main bar is complemented by a separate public bar with pool table and two dining areas where families are welcome. The rear dining room is full of historic paraphernalia such as accordions, brass instruments, bedwarmers and chamber pots. Good food is a part of the pub's trade.
👁❀🕪🚃♿⚓🚌(730)P🕮

Reepham

King's Arms
Market Place, NR10 4JJ TG099231
✪ 11.30-3, 5.30-11; 11-11 Sat; 12-10.30 Sun
☎ (01603) 870345
Adnams Southwold Bitter; Greene King Abbot; Panther Pink; Woodforde's Wherry; guest beers Ⓗ
A former coaching inn dating back to 1667, situated in the picturesque square of this small market town. Extended sympathetically in the 1990s, original beams, Norfolk brickwork and open fires have been retained, providing several drinking and dining areas. At least one ale from the local Panther Brewery is always on handpump. The comprehensive menu includes food sourced from nearby butchers and bakers. Jazz bands play in the rear courtyard on summer Sunday afternoons, and a bar billiards table is available. Dogs are welcome. ﹩Q❀🕪♿🚌(25)♣🕮

Roydon

Union Jack ♈
30 Station Road, PE32 1AW
✪ 12 (4 Tue-Thu)-midnight ☎ (01485) 601347
Beer range varies Ⓗ
Voted local CAMRA Pub of the Year 2012, this is a traditional village drinking pub, dating back to 1884. Four handpumps dispense a variety of ales, mostly chosen from microbreweries. Beer festivals are held over the Easter and August bank holidays and usually feature local breweries. There is live music each month, regular bingo and quizzes, and weekly support for darts, crib and dominoes. Dogs are welcome. ﹩❀🚌(48)♣

Salthouse

Dun Cow

Coast Road, NR25 7XA (on A149) TG073439

🌑 11 (12 Sun)-11 ☎ (01263) 740467

⊕ salthouseduncow.com

Adnams Southwold Bitter; Greene King Abbot; Woodforde's Wherry ⊞

On the north Norfolk coast road, this venue welcomes walkers, families, dogs and birdwatchers alike. The entrance to the pub is via a courtyard surrounded by whitewashed flint buildings with a fountain in the centre. There is a large main bar, popular with diners, offering commanding views of Salthouse Marshes, plus a smaller, more intimate bar to one side. An extensive food menu is available all day featuring locally sourced food where possible. A guest beer is added in the summer. Coasthopper buses stop outside the pub. ᴪ❀⇆◖➟🖺(Coasthopper)P͏ؘ–

Sedgeford

King William IV

Heacham Road, PE36 5LU

🌑 11 (6 Mon)-11; 12-10.30 Sun ☎ (01485) 571765

⊕ thekingwilliamsedgeford.co.uk

Adnams Southwold Bitter, Broadside; Greene King Abbot; Woodforde's Wherry; guest beers ⊞

A large well-appointed village pub, popular for the locally produced food. Known by locals as the King Willie, it has an excellent reputation for quality food but still retains a pub atmosphere that attracts local drinkers. There are two bars and a restaurant divided into four areas. Six handpumps grace the bar, two of which are used for guest beers, usually from the same portfolio. A large garden at the rear has a superb outdoor covered drinking/dining area. Nine luxury rooms are available. ᴪⱲ❀⇆◖⊟&P͏ؘ–

Sheringham

Crown ✅

East Cliff, NR26 8BQ (on promenade)

🌑 10 (12 Sun)-11 ☎ (01263) 823213

⊕ crown-sheringham.co.uk

Fuller's London Pride; Greene King IPA, Abbot; Morland Old Speckled Hen; Woodforde's Wherry ⊞

Close to the promenade and next to Sheringham Lifeboat Museum, the Crown offers commanding views of Sheringham beach and the North Sea. It is a traditional-style pub, with an interior comprising three wood-panelled lounges and a central bar. A choice of five real ales is usually available throughout the year. Food is served ranging from bar snacks to Sunday roasts, and includes children's and vegetarian menus. The pub hosts regular pool and darts matches. ❀◖&▲➟🖺(Coasthopper)♣P͏ؘ–

Windham Arms �

15-17 Wyndham Street, NR26 8BA (just off High St)

🌑 12-11 (9 Sun) ☎ (01263) 822609

⊕ thewindhamarms.co.uk

Woodforde's Wherry; guest beers ⊞

CAMRA Branch Pub of the Year for 2011, this cosy two-bar local with Dutch-style gables is in a narrow back street just behind the High Street, comprising a main bar, restaurant and a separate function room. Outside is a small drinking area with views of the North Sea. Four regular Norfolk real ales are on offer. A range of bottled real ale from local brewers is also available. Greek food is the pub speciality, served lunchtimes and evenings. Q✖❀◖⊟▲➟🖺(Coasthopper)●P͏ؘ–

Smallburgh

Crown

North Walsham Road, NR12 9AD (on A149 NE of Wroxham) TG330245

🌑 12-3 (not Mon), 5.30 (7 Sat)-11; 12-4 Sun

☎ (01692) 536314

Adnams Southwold Bitter; Greene King IPA; Woodforde's Wherry; guest beers ⊞

A thatch-roofed former coaching inn in the village; original timbers and a log fire lend character to the cosy interior. Five ales, including two guests, give plenty of choice, and seasonal locally sourced produce is used in the home-cooked food. Meals may be enjoyed in the dining room, in the bar or, in summer, in the peaceful tree-fringed garden. Outside is a covered, heated smoking area. Close to the Broads and north Norfolk coast, a warm welcome awaits at this popular local pub. ᴪQ❀⇆◖🖺(6,34,36)♣P͏ؘ–

Snettisham

Rose & Crown

Old Church Road, PE31 7LX

🌑 11-11; 12-10.30 Sun ☎ (01485) 541382

⊕ roseandcrownsnettisham.co.uk

Adnams Southwold Bitter, Broadside; Woodforde's Wherry; guest beers ⊞

A busy village inn with small rooms at the front with exposed beams and a real fire. Head through the narrow passage to find a larger bar and dining areas with a contemporary feel. Well known for good food, it also remains popular with local drinkers, and the garden and play area make it appealing to families. Accommodation is available for those who wish to spend longer in this beautiful area. ᴪQ✖❀⇆◖⊟&🖺(10,11)P͏ؘ–

Stibbard

Ordnance Arms

Guist Bottom, NR20 5PF (on A1067) TF987267

🌑 12-2 (Sat only), 5.30-11; 12-11 Sun ☎ (01328) 829471

⊕ ordnancearms.co.uk

Adnams Southwold Bitter; Cottage Golden Arrow; guest beer ⊞

Situated in Guist Bottom on the A1067 Norwich-Fakenham road, this is a combination of traditional, welcoming pub and a Thai restaurant. There are three rooms: a cosy main bar with comfortable seating and a real fire, a second bar with hatch service, a real fire, stone flooring and simple wooden furniture, and a third room with a pool table. To the rear of the pub is the popular Thai restaurant offering excellent food five nights a week (closed Sun and Mon). ᴪQ◖🖺(X29)P͏ؘ–

Strumpshaw

Shoulder of Mutton

Norwich Road, NR13 4NT (on Brundall to Lingwood road S of A47) TG349078

🌑 10.30am-11 ☎ (01603) 712274

Adnams Southwold Bitter, Broadside; guest beers ⊞

Traditional hub of the community village local, deservedly popular. Most guest beers are from local Norfolk micros plus a few from further afield.

Quality wine is from a local importer. An extensive choice of freshly prepared meals using local produce is served in the separate restaurant – booking is advisable, particularly on themed evenings. The public bar has pool, darts, crib, Sky Sports and Wi-Fi, and pétanque is played. There is a covered, heated smoking area. Close to the RSPB reserve with nature walks, as well as the boating centre of Brundall. Ramblers welcome.
❀❍▸🍴&🖩(17A)♣P⌐

Swanton Morley

Angel

66 Greengate, NR20 4LX (on B1147 towards S edge of village) TG012162
✪ 12-11; 12-10 (6 winter) Sun ☎ (01362) 637407
⊕ theangelpub.co.uk
Hop Back Summer Lightning; Mighty Oak Oscar Wilde; Woodforde's Wherry; guest beer Ⓗ
At the south end of the village, this old inn dates back to 1610, and boasts a connection with Abraham Lincoln's family. The owners are keen CAMRA members. There is a spacious main bar with a real fire and hop-draped ceilings, and a dining room serving food lunchtimes and Monday to Saturday evenings. There are also themed food nights. A live folk group plays on the first Monday of each month. Four beers are usually available. The garden includes a bowling green. See website for details of the annual beer festival.
♨Q❀❍&🖩(4)♣🐾P

Tacolneston

Pelican Inn Ⓛ

136 Norwich Road, NR16 1PZ (on B1113)
✪ 5-11; 12-2, 6-11 (12-11 summer) Sat; 12-4 (11 summer) Sun ☎ (01508) 489521 ⊕ the-pelican-inn.co.uk
Beer range varies Ⓗ
Recently South Norfolk District Council Community Pub of the Year, this former coaching inn dating from the 17th century has an old rambling interior with lots of drinking areas, and a restaurant at the rear. A rotating range of four beers is usually available, mostly from local brewers such as Humpty Dumpty, Brandon and Elmtree. Live music on Sundays and various beer festivals take place during the year in the garden marquee (see website for details). The pub has a bottle shop selling more than 100 different beers, mostly from local micros. ♨Q🕿❀🚐❍&🖩(10A)♣P⌐

Thetford

Albion

93-95 Castle Street, IP24 2DN (opp Castle Hill)
✪ 12-11 (11.30 Thu; 12.30am Fri); 11-12.30am Sat
☎ (01842) 752796
Greene King IPA, Abbot Ⓗ
Recently refurbished with a longer bar and a change in decor, the Albion has changed markedly. The internal furnishings now include large, comfortable chairs surrounding low tables. The pub is still run by the same family and offers very reasonable beer prices indeed. The park opposite houses the Norman castle mound which is built on an Iceni hill fort 1,000 years older. Food is available by ordering out to surrounding restaurants.
♨❀≈♣⌐

Black Horse

64 Magdalen Street, IP24 2BP
✪ 12-11; 11-1am Fri; 11-midnight Sat ☎ (01842) 762717
Greene King IPA; Woodforde's Wherry; guest beers Ⓗ
A short distance from the town centre, this is a typical 19th-century town pub. The Black Horse continues to offer four real ales with interesting guests. Run by a husband and wife team, the interior is divided into three areas, with a nice garden for warm months. It features a menu of good pub food at very reasonable prices. Snacks are also available – try the nachos. The pub is home to several sports teams and features a darts playing area. ❀❍≈♣P⌐

Thompson

Chequers

Griston Road, IP24 1PX (signed in village)
✪ 11-3, 6.30-11; 12-3, 7-10.30 Sun ☎ (01953) 483360
⊕ thompsonchequers.co.uk
Beer range varies Ⓗ
Beautiful 16th-century building in the middle of Breckland with a steep thatch nearly touching the ground. It contains a very low beam in front of the bar – beware! Two to three guest ales, normally from Greene King, Adnams and Elgood's, are available. Food is served seven days a week, and booking is advisable for Sunday meals. The interior is mostly filled with food tables, with a small bar area, so in the summer chatting is best done at tables outside. ♨Q❀🚐❍♣P

Thurlton

Queen's Head Ⓛ

Beccles Road, NR14 6RJ (1 mile N of B1136 and 3 miles E of A146) TM414984
✪ 6-11; 5-midnight Fri; 12-midnight Sat; 12-10 Sun
☎ (01508) 548667 ⊕ thurlton-queenshead.co.uk
Beer range varies Ⓗ
In the centre of the village, this venue was saved from closure around six years ago by several local residents who joined together to purchase it, and it is now owned and run as a community pub by the local people. Four real ales are usually on offer, supplied mainly from local brewers such as Green Jack, Humpty Dumpty, Buffy's and Grain. The pub is family friendly, with children allowed in the bar, plus there is a good playing field adjacent.
♨❀&P⌐

Tibenham

Greyhound

The Street, NR16 1PZ (300yds from church) TM136895
✪ 12-3, 6-midnight; 12-11 Sun ☎ (01379) 677676
Adnams Southwold Bitter; Fuller's London Pride Ⓗ; **guest beers** Ⓗ/Ⓖ
In the heart of rural Norfolk countryside, this two-bar pub dates from 1710. Beers here come from Adnams and Fuller's, plus rotating guests (often including one from Shepherd Neame), with one usually served by gravity. There is a large car park, and a field at the rear that hosts regular events in summer, suitable for camping and caravanning, complete with electric hook-ups. Walkers may use the car park. ♨❀▸🍴▲♣P⌐

Trunch

Crown
Front Street, NR28 0AH (opp church) TG287348
⚙ 12-3 (not Mon), 5.30-11 (11.30 Fri & Sat); 12-7 Sun
☎ (01263) 722341 ⊕ trunchcrown.co.uk
Batemans XB, XXXB; Greene King IPA; guest beers Ⓗ
Set in the middle of a charming north Norfolk village with fine old flint cottages, close to the north Norfolk coast. The Crown, Batemans only pub in the area, offers an excellent choice of beers, and a friendly atmosphere. XXXB is often replaced by a Batemans seasonal beer, and the cider is from Westons. Bar snacks are available at all times. A quiz night is held on the second Wednesday in the month; the website lists beer festivals and other events. Dogs are welcome in the bar.
⌂Q✿🅷🚃(5,34,35)♠P≐

Walcott

Lighthouse Inn ✅
Coast Road, NR12 0PE (on B1159) TG359319
⚙ 11-11 ☎ (01692) 650371 ⊕ lighthouseinn.co.uk
Beer range varies Ⓗ
Spacious multi-roomed and family-friendly pub on the coast road between Cromer and Great Yarmouth, owned and run by the same landlord for over 20 years. It has been Cask Marque-accredited since 1999. A rotating range of up to four real ales is available in summer (fewer in winter), with beers usually supplied by Adnams, Woodforde's, Greene King and new local microbrewer Bees Brewery. Quality home-made food using locally sourced ingredients is available all day, including a children's menu and vegetarian options.
⌂✿🅷🅘Å♠P

Warham All Saints

Three Horseshoes
Bridge Street, NR23 1NL (2 miles SE of Wells) TF948417
⚙ 12-2.30, 6-11 ☎ (01328) 710547
Woodforde's Wherry; guest beers Ⓗ/Ⓖ
On entering the main bar of this pub in winter months customers are greeted by a roaring log fire. The interior comprises three connected rooms that are filled with a fascinating collection of antiques and pictures, including the traditional game of Norfolk Twister. Two to three beers are usually available, dispensed by handpump and gravity, one of which is normally Woodforde's Wherry. The real cider comes from Whin Hill. The pub is renowned for good plain cooking, featuring soups, pies and puddings. ⌂Q✿🅷🅘Å♠P≐

Watton

Willow House
2 High Street, IP25 6AE
⚙ 10.30-11 (midnight Thu; 12.30am Fri & Sat); 10.30-7 Sun
☎ (01953) 881181 ⊕ thewillowhouse.co.uk
Greene King IPA, St Edmunds; guest beers Ⓗ
The Willow House, now in its second year in the Guide, is a black and white thatched 16th-century inn. The interior features cosy low-ceilinged rooms with a separate restaurant. It offers four real ales with two changing guests from interesting sources. The menu is extensive and good value. Family run, this local has real heart, thanks to the team running it. Seven newly refurbished en-suite rooms are available. ✿🅷🅘P≐

Wells-next-the-Sea

Albatros
The Quay, NR23 1AT (moored on quayside)
⚙ 12-11 ☎ (07979) 087228 ⊕ albatros.eu.com
Woodforde's Wherry, Nelson's Revenge; guest beer Ⓖ
Possibly one of the Guide's most unusual entries – the Albatros is a Dutch North Sea clipper that is moored on the quayside of Wells harbour. The bar is in the hold of the ship and is adorned with much nautical memorabilia including many shipping maps. It sells two to three Woodforde's beers by gravity. Dutch pancakes, savoury and sweet, are a speciality here. Live bands perform regularly each Friday and Saturday night, as well as Sunday afternoons in high season. Being a 19th-century vessel, it is not wheelchair-friendly.
🅷🅘🚃(Coasthopper)

Crown Hotel ✅
The Buttlands, NR23 1EX
⚙ 8am-11 ☎ (01328) 710209 ⊕ thecrownhotelwells.co.uk
Beer range varies Ⓗ
This former coaching inn, whose interior has been much modernised, overlooks the picturesque Buttlands Green. Inside are a bar and two restaurants, one of which overlooks the rear garden. Despite the light, airy, modern feel, a sense of history remains about the place, and old photographs of the hotel are all around the bar. There are usually up to two beers from local East Barsham-based Kiwi brewery, plus up to two rotating guest ales.
⌂Q✿🅷🅘&🚃(Coasthopper)♠P⊟

West Acre

Stag Ⓛ
Low Road, PE32 1TR
⚙ closed Mon; 12-3, 6.30-11; 12-3, 5-11 Fri; 12-3, 6.30-11 Sat
☎ (01760) 755395 ⊕ westacrestag.co.uk
Beer range varies Ⓗ
The pub, popular with walkers and cyclists, can be found at the east end of picturesque West Acre, a village renowned for its historic ruins. There is a water trough for horses in the large car park. A supporter of LocAle, it maintains a high standard, with three varying beers. The popular restaurant offers a wide choice of food, and a monthly quiz on Sunday nights. ⌂Q✿🅘🅗&Å🚃♠P

Weybourne

Ship
The Street, NR25 7SZ (on A149 coast road) TG111430
⚙ 12-midnight summer; 12-3, 5-midnight winter;
12-midnight Sat & Sun ☎ (01263) 588721
⊕ shipinnweybourne.co.uk
Beer range varies Ⓗ
In the heart of an attractive north Norfolk coastal village, the pub's interior comprises three dining areas and a bar, all decorated with a seaside theme. Between six and 10 ales are on offer, coming largely from local brewers such as Grain, Humpty Dumpty and Winter's. One real cider is usually available. Home-cooked food is served lunchtimes and evenings. Close by are the Muckleburgh Military Vehicle Museum, and North Norfolk Railway's Weybourne Station. Three beer festivals are held in the New Year, April and summer. ⌂✿🅘🚃(Coasthopper)♠P≐

Wicklewood

Cherry Tree 🅛
116 High Street, NR18 9QA (1 mile E of B1108 Norwich-Watton road) TG075022
✪ 5 (3 Fri; 12 Sun)-11 ☎ (01953) 606962
Buffy's Bitter, Polly's Folly, Norwegian Blue 🅗/🅖
A Buffy's tied house with an L-shaped bar that boasts an unusual naturally curved top made from planks of solid oak. The pub hosts a number of evening entertainments including a monthly quiz night, jam session and folk night, and every Sunday lunchtime a chase the ace game. Home-cooked food is available evenings and all day Friday to Sunday. The Buffy's range varies, and occasionally beers from other breweries are available as guests.
🏵◑🖳(6)P

Winterton-on-Sea

Fisherman's Return
The Lane, NR29 4BN (off B1159) TG495194
✪ 11-2.30, 5-11; 11-11 Sat; 12-10.30 Sun ☎ (01493) 393305
🌐 fishermansreturn.com
Greene King H&H Olde Trip; Woodforde's Wherry 🅗,
Norfolk Nog 🅗/🅖
A large upmarket inn, over 300 years old, which retains many of its original features. There is a strong emphasis on food, and local ingredients are used where possible. In the 1920s the pub was a popular destination for day trippers from Great Yarmouth. The building to the rear, known as the Tinho, is a survivor of this period. The house ale is from Greene King. Three en-suite bedrooms are available all year round.
🏚🌄🏵🗐◑🖳🖏🖳(1a)🐾🌢P🕭

Woodbastwick

Fur & Feather Inn
Slad Lane, NR13 6HQ (just off B1140) TG328151
✪ 10-10 (11 Fri & Sat) ☎ (01603) 720003
🌐 thefurandfeatherinn.co.uk
Woodforde's Mardlers, Wherry, Sundew, Nelson's Revenge, Norfolk Nog, Admiral's Reserve, Headcracker 🅖
Converted from a row of three cottages, this large open-plan pub is largely food-oriented while offering customers the full range of beers from the adjoining Woodforde's Brewery. A tour of the brewery can be arranged in advance and combined with a meal. In summer the large garden provides an excellent area for a drink. The rare Norfolk Nip is occasionally available, usually as a bottle-conditioned strong ale, which is much prized locally. Q🌄🏵◑🖳🖏P🕭

Wortwell

Bell
52 High Street, IP20 0HH (off A143)
✪ 12-2.30 (not Mon), 5-11; 12-11 Fri & Sat; 12-10.30 Sun
☎ (01986) 788025 🌐 wortwellbell.co.uk
**Adnams Southwold Bitter; Woodforde's Wherry;
guest beers** 🅗
A charming village inn just off the A143, voted South Norfolk Community Pub of the Year 2010. Two regular ales are supplemented by up to three guests. There are separate dining areas where good home-cooked food is served. The pub is dog friendly, stages occasional quiz nights, and hosts live music once a month. A room at the rear is available for small private functions. Two campsites are within easy reach.
🏚Q🌄🏵◑🖏Å🖳(580)🐾P🕭

Wymondham

Green Dragon 🅛
6 Church Street, NR18 0PH (just off marketplace near Wymondham Abbey)
✪ 12-11 (midnight Fri & Sat; 10.30 Sun) ☎ (01953) 607907
🌐 wymondhamgreendragon.com
Beer range varies 🅗
A magnificent mid-15th century half-timbered inn, located between the marketplace and Wymondham Abbey. This building was one of the few to survive the great fire of 1615 – see the scorch marks on the external timbers. The interior has two bars and a snug that retain many of their original beamed timbers. The rotating beer range of four real ales includes brews from Green Jack, Nethergate, Wolf and Humpty Dumpty. Fifty malt whiskies are available. 🏚Q🏵◑🖏🍴🖳🐾🕭

Albatros, Wells-next-the-Sea (Photo: Kim Adams)

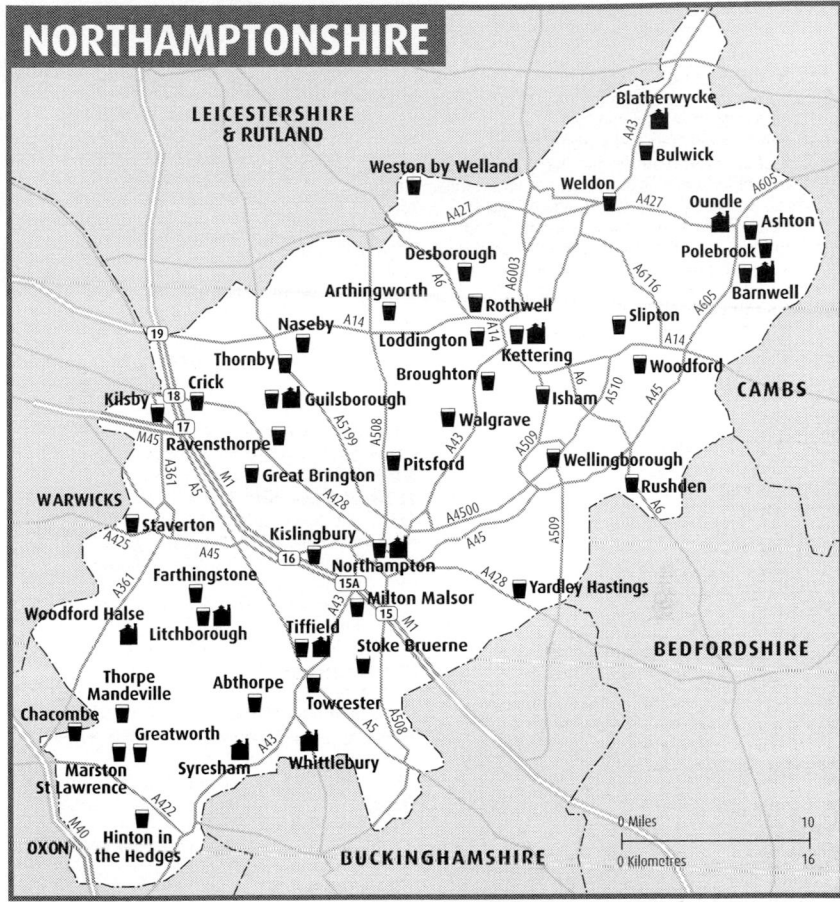

NORTHAMPTONSHIRE

Abthorpe

New Inn 🄻 ✅
Silver Street, NN12 8QR SP648465
⏱ 12-2.30 (not Mon & Tue), 6-11 (11.30 Sat); 12-10.30 Sun
☎ (01327) 857306 ⊕ slaptonmanor.plus.com/newinn.html
Hook Norton Hooky Bitter, Old Hooky; seasonal beers Ⓗ
A tranquil country hostelry, hidden up a cul-de-sac off the corner of the village green. This mellow sandstone local with its inglenook fireplace and low beamed ceilings is well worth searching out. Welcoming to visitors and locals alike, it offers high-quality meals cooked to order and served from the open kitchen, with much of the food locally sourced, including meat from the owners' farm. Hook Norton seasonal beers feature as guests. ⋈☎☀◗♣Ⓟ⅃⌐

Arthingworth

Bull's Head
Kelmarsh Road, LE16 8JZ (off A508)
⏱ 12-3, 6-11; 12-11 Sat & Sun ☎ (01858) 525637
⊕ thebullsheadonline.co.uk
Adnams Broadside; Thwaites Original; Wadworth 6X; guest beers Ⓗ
Nineteenth-century former farmhouse situated in rolling countryside. The pub has an opened-up bar with several cosy drinking areas and a restaurant to the front serving home-cooked fresh food from local producers. Ideal for ramblers and cyclists, this is an ideal place to finish a walk in the local area, or stay over in one of the annexe rooms. A beer festival is held over the August bank holiday on the suntrap patio. One regular guest ale is served; sparklers can be removed on request.
⋈Q☎⌂◗◖◗ᴗ♣Ⓟ⅃⌐

Ashton

Chequered Skipper 🄻
The Green, PE8 5LD

INDEPENDENT BREWERIES

Digfield Barnwell
Frog Island Northampton
Great Oakley Tiffield
Gun Dog Woodford Halse (NEW)
Hoggleys Litchborough
Hunsbury Craft Northampton (NEW)
Julian Church Kettering
Nene Valley Oundle (NEW)
Nobby's Guilsborough
Potbelly Kettering
Rockingham Blatherwycke
Silverstone Syresham
Whittlebury Whittlebury

✪ 11.30-3, 6-11; 11.30-11 Sat & Sun ☎ (01832) 273494
🌐 chequeredskipper.co.uk
Brewster's Hophead; guest beers Ⓗ
Rebuilt in 1997, this thatched stone-built pub
overlooks the green in the Rothschild's model
village of Ashton. The clean and bright main bar
area is now complemented by a small coffee bar
and a large function room to the rear. The bar
serves up to four real ales and is set out with table
and chairs for dining. Regularly changing guest
beers are often from local micros. Westons and
Thatchers ciders are regularly available. Two beer
festivals are held each year. Q✿❶&●P⁵⁻

Barnwell

Montagu Arms Ⓛ ✔
PE8 5PH
✪ 12-3 (not Mon), 6-11; 12-11 Sat; 12-10.30 Sun
☎ (01832) 273726
Adnams Southwold Bitter; guest beers Ⓗ
Inviting 16th-century inn with a public bar at the
front and a large restaurant to the rear. There is
disabled access to the dining room. The bar area is
busy and attractive with large original exposed
beams, an open fire and flagstone floors. This
LocAle pub frequently has four real ales on
handpump including one from the nearby Digfield
Brewery. Guest beers are mostly from
microbreweries. Most of the food in the restaurant
is locally sourced. ♨Q✿❶⊟&▲🚲(24)♣●P⁵⁻

Broughton

Red Lion Ⓛ ✔
7 High Street, NN14 1NF (off A43)
✪ 12-2, 5-11; 12-midnight Fri & Sat; 12-11 Sun
☎ (01536) 790239 🌐 redlionbroughton.co.uk
Beer range varies Ⓗ
Large 18th-century ironstone pub with three
rooms: a bar, lounge and semi open-plan dining
room. Very much a locals' pub, the regulars help
choose the beers. Six changing ales are served,
including one from local lad Julian Church and
another from a Northants brewery. Future beers
are listed on the bar and the website. The landlady
likes dark beers, so there is always a mild, stout, or
porter on offer. Good local food is available (not
Mon lunch or Sun eve). A recent CAMRA award
winner. Q✿❶⊟&🚲(39)P⁵⁻

Bulwick

Queen's Head Ⓛ
Main Street, NN17 3DY
✪ closed Mon; 12-3, 6-11; 12-10.30 (7 winter) Sun
☎ (01780) 450272 🌐 thequeensheadbulwick.co.uk
Shepherd Neame Spitfire; guest beers Ⓗ
Built in 1653, this pub has a central position in
Bulwick sited next to the village store and
overlooked by the church. Inside there is one bar
and three restaurant areas. New owners have
sympathetically refurbished the pub including
fitting the bar with five new handpumps, while
retaining the traditional low exposed beams and
stone floor. High-quality locally sourced food is
thoroughly recommended. Constantly changing
guest beers are mainly from microbreweries,
including Digfield and Oakham.
♨Q✿❶⊟♣●P⁵⁻

Chacombe

George & Dragon
1 Silver Street, OX17 2JR (between A361 and B4525
near Banbury)
✪ 11-midnight ☎ (01295) 711500 🌐 georgeanddragon.org
Everards Beacon, Tiger; guest beers Ⓗ
Welcoming, traditional, stone-built pub situated in
front of the small village green. Inside there is one
room for drinkers and three for diners, with three
impressive fireplaces. The bar area has a stone-
flagged floor and wooden beams, and the bar itself
features a glass top revealing a 26-foot well.
Outside is a pretty patio terrace. Aunt Sally is
played in the garden. This Everards' pub has two
regular beers and two changing guests. Cider is
stocked in summer only. ♨Q✿✿❶🚲(500)♣P⁵⁻

Crick

Royal Oak
22 Church Street, NN6 7TP
✪ 4-11; 3-10.30 Sun ☎ (01788) 822340
Oakham Bishops Farewell; guest beers Ⓗ
Wood-beamed, cottage-style free house, hidden
from the main A428 near the village church.
Friendly and welcoming, open fires warm the two
main drinking areas, giving the pub a cosy feel. A
separate function room can be booked, with
catering provided on request. The ever-changing
beer range features 10-12 guests available every
week. Northants skittles and darts matches are
played in the games room. ♨Q✿✿🚲♣P⁵⁻

Desborough

George Ⓛ
79 High Street, NN14 2NB
✪ 11-midnight (1am Fri & Sat); 12-midnight Sun
☎ (01536) 760271
Everards Beacon, Tiger; Fuller's London Pride Ⓗ
A 16th-century former coaching inn built from local
ironstone standing opposite the Desborough Cross.
The main bar is open plan with separate dining and
games areas and a lounge to the rear. The George
has been the current landlord's local for over 50
years and the pub is a supporter of local teams as
well as its own darts, pool, crib, Northants skittles,
football and tug-of-war pub teams. In summer the
part-covered suntrap yard comes into its own.
♨Q✿✿❶⊟&🚲(18,19)♣P⁵⁻

Farthingstone

King's Arms
Main Street, NN12 8EZ (opp church)
✪ closed Mon; 7-11 Tue-Thu; 6.30-midnight Fri; 12-4,
7-midnight Sat; 12-4, 9-11 Sun ☎ (01327) 361604
Beer range varies Ⓗ
A quintessentially English 18th-century free house
in delightful countryside in the heart of the county.
The listed building with its inglenook fireplace and
warming log fires has a unique and fascinating
secret garden. A separate games room has
Northants skittles. The pub is a retail outlet for fine
cheeses and Cornish fish. Lunchtime food is served
only at weekends, although speciality food
evenings with entertainment are held regularly.
♨Q✿❶♣●P

Great Brington

Althorp Coaching Inn (Fox & Hounds)
Main Street, NN7 4JA
✪ 11-11.45; 12-10.45 Sun ☎ (01604) 770651
⊕ althorp-coaching-inn.co.uk
Fuller's London Pride; Greene King IPA; guest beers Ⓗ
Thatched country pub dating back to 1765 close to Althorp House, home of the Spencer family. The interior features flagstone floors and a lounge with a large inglenook fireplace and oak beams, while outside there is a courtyard and an enclosed garden. Excellent food is served in the bar and separate restaurant. Monday is quiz night and a beer festival is held in August. Up to six guest ales are available. Well worth seeking out, the pub is often busy. ⚞Q✿✪❶❖P⅃

Greatworth

Inn Ⓛ
Capel Road, OX17 2DT
✪ 12-2.30, 6-11; 11-11 Sat; 12-11 Sun ☎ (01295) 710976
Hook Norton Hooky Bitter; guest beers Ⓗ
Stone-built village pub in the centre of the village. This enthusiastically run hostelry serves local real ales and good home-cooked food. The lovely cosy bar area has a large fireplace and low-beamed ceiling. To one side is a stepped restaurant and to the other a small snug with games. Outside is a patio, garden and family room, and the local game of Aunt Sally. Real cider is available in summer. ⚞❧✿✪❶❤(409,508)♣P⅃

Guilsborough

Ward Arms Ⓛ
High Street, NN6 8PY
✪ 12-2.30 (not Mon), 5.30-11; 12-midnight Fri & Sat; 12-10.30 Sun ☎ (01604) 740265 ⊕ thewardarms.webs.com
Nobby's Guilsborough Guzzler, Best, Guilsborough Gold; guest beers Ⓗ
Seventeenth-century pub situated in the heart of a historic rural village. Built from local ironstone with white rendering and a thatched roof, the old stables have been converted into Nobby's Brewery and visitor centre. Nobby's beers, including seasonals, feature heavily on the bar along with other guests. Traditional home-cooked, locally-sourced food is served. Live music features on the last Saturday of the month. Northants skittles and pool are played. ⚞❧✿❶❤♣P⅃☖

Hinton in the Hedges

Crewe Arms Ⓛ
Sparrow Corner, NN13 5NF (off A43/A422)
✪ 6-11 (midnight Thu & Fri); 12-11 Sat & Sun
☎ (01280) 705801 ⊕ thecrewearms.com
Hook Norton Hooky Bitter; guest beers Ⓗ
Tucked away in the village, this stone-built local is well worth seeking out. Inside there are four rooms – a traditional bar, lounge, relaxing snug and garden room. Smart and comfortable furnishings blend well with the original and newer parts of the building. Good-quality traditional home-cooked food is served (no food Mon). Guest beers are from national, regional and, more often, microbreweries. CAMRA members receive a 10 per cent discount on accommodation. ⚞Q✿❧❶P⅃

Isham

Lilacs ✅
39 Church Street, NN14 1HD (off A509 at church)
✪ 12-3, 5.30-midnight; 12-1am Fri & Sat; 12-midnight Sun
☎ (01536) 723948
Greene King IPA, Abbot; guest beers Ⓗ
Named after a breed of rabbit, this hard-to-find village pub is at the heart of the community – popular with locals, diners and drinkers enjoying a well-kept pint. The pub has a lounge and a cosy snug to the front, complemented by a large games room towards the rear with two pool tables, darts and Northants skittles. Quiz and live music nights are held regularly. The guest beers are from the Greene King guest list. ⚞Q✿✪❶❒(X4)♣P⅃

Kettering

Alexandra Arms ♈ Ⓛ
39 Victoria Street, NN16 0BU (400yds from bus station)
✪ 2 (12 Sun)-11; 12-midnight Fri & Sat ☎ (01536) 522730
Beer range varies Ⓗ
The Alex is a traditional back-street pub and home to the Julian Church Brewery. Two open rooms form the main bar, with walls and ceilings adorned with pump clips for 6,700 plus beers from more than 762 breweries served here over the past nine years. Two further rooms form the rear bar and games area, with darts and Northants skittles. Several times local CAMRA award winner, there is always a Julian Church, Nobby's and Marston's beer available, plus 10 interesting guests. Well worth the 15 minutes' walk from the railway station. Q✿❧❒≷♣⅃

Piper Ⓛ ✅
Windmill Avenue, NN15 6PS
✪ 11-3, 5-11; 11-4, 6-11 Sat; 12-10.30 Sun
☎ (01536) 513870
Hook Norton Hooky Bitter; Potbelly Best; guest beers Ⓗ
Popular 1950s two-roomed pub run by an enthusiastic CAMRA member. There is a quiet lounge to the left, and a more lively bar/games room to the right where a quiz is held on Sunday night. The four guests include two further Potbelly beers and often a Cottage beer. Traditional home-cooked food is available until 10pm, with a roast on Sunday (booking advisable). A beer festival is held on the third weekend in August. Close to Wicksteed Park, Britain's first theme park. The cider is Westons Old Rosie. Q✿❶❧❒⚲▲❒(B,X4)♣❖P⅃

Kilsby

George ✅
Watling Street, CV23 8YE (just off A361/A5 jct)
✪ 11.30-3, 5.30-11; 12-5, 6-10.30 Sun ☎ (01788) 822229
⊕ thegeorgeatkilsby.co.uk
Adnams Southwold Bitter; Fuller's London Pride; Taylor Landlord; guest beer Ⓗ
The George was rebuilt in the 1840s on the site of an old coaching inn using bricks from Kilsby railway tunnel. Ample car parking, a beer garden, dining room, lounge and public bar plus accommodation make this a popular venue for events and private functions. A quiz night on Sunday, themed food nights mid-week (see website), and biker Sundays (last of the month) all add to the community spirit. Celebrate St George's Day at the annual real ale and cider festival. Q✿❧❶❒▲❒♣P⅃

Kislingbury

Olde Red Lion

15 High Street, NN7 4AQ
✪ closed Mon; 12-2 (not Tue), 5-10.30 (11 Fri); 12-2.30, 5-11 Sat; 12-4 Sun ☎ (01604) 830219 ⊕ theolderedlion.co.uk
Black Sheep Best Bitter; Taylor Landlord Ⓗ
Traditional stone-built pub on the main route through the village. Formerly a farmhouse, dating from the late 1600s, it has been a public house since 1830. The present landlord is the third generation of the family to run the pub and is passionate about beer and food quality. A July beer festival features here, along with themed food evenings, live music events, Northants skittles and take-away fish and chips. A former winner of a Best Pub Restaurant Food award for the county.
🅐❀🖾🕪🍴🍺🔥🖥(D3)♣🐾P⌐

Litchborough

Old Red Lion Ⓛ

4 Banbury Road, NN12 8JF
✪ 2.30 (11 Sat)-11; 12-10.30 Sun ☎ (01327) 830064
Beer range varies Ⓗ
This compact, stone-built village pub is well worth seeking out. The bar area has flagstone flooring and a large inglenook with seats inside. A small passage leads to two further cosy rooms, one with a pool table. Near the Knightly Way footpath, the pub is popular with walkers and cyclists, and incorporates a mini shop selling local farm produce. A wide range of locally brewed bottled beers is stocked with Hoggleys Brewery a short distance away. Northants skittles is played in the new extension. 🅐Q❀🕭♣P⌐

Loddington

Hare Ⓛ

5 Main Street, NN14 1LA
✪ 12-3, 5.30-11; 12-11 Sat & Sun ☎ (01536) 710337
Greene King Abbot; guest beers Ⓗ
Set in a conservation area, this stone-built pub is listed, as is every other building on the main street. Formerly the Chequered Flag, the pub has recently been refurbished by the new owner. The single-room interior has four separate areas around a main bar, one set aside for diners. With a warm welcome guaranteed, the landlord promotes local ales and good traditional food. The three guest ales are often from Julian Church and well-established breweries. 🅐Q❀🕪🍴🕭P

Marston St Lawrence

Marston Inn Ⓛ ✔

The Green, OX17 2DB (off A422/B4525)
✪ 12-2 Tue-Fri summer only, 6-11; 12-4 Sun ☎ (01295) 711090
Hook Norton Hooky Bitter, seasonal beers Ⓗ
A traditional stone-built village pub converted from a row of cottages and set back from the road with a large, mainly lawned, front garden. The pub has three interconnecting rooms with the bar mainly in the middle. The smallest of the rooms is a cosy lounge and the second drinking area has a long wooden settle in front of an open fire. Outside is an Aunt Sally skittles alley. 🅐Q❀🕪♣P⌐

Milton Malsor

Compass Ⓛ

61 Green Street, NN7 3AT (follow signs for school)
✪ 5-11 (midnight Fri); 12-11 Sat & Sun ☎ 07956 135520
Beer range varies Ⓗ
The Compass is a drinkers' pub tucked away in the village. Two changing beers are available, usually local, often from Hoggleys Brewery. The long L-shaped interior has darts at one end and Northants skittles at the other, with four pub teams. Two beer festivals are held in outbuildings on the May and August bank holidays, and live music features occasionally. Well-behaved children are welcome until 8pm. 🅐Q❀👶🕭🅰🖾(8,89)♣P⌐

Naseby

Royal Oak ✔

Church Street, NN6 6DA (on B4036)
✪ 12-2, 5 (4.30 Fri & Sat)-11 (midnight Thu-Sat); 12-10.30 Sun ☎ (01604) 743310 ⊕ theroyaloaknaseby.com
Sharp's Doom Bar; Woodforde's Wherry; guest beers Ⓗ
A popular pub with walkers and Northants skittles players alike, the L-shaped single room is divided into three areas with a real fire in the wall between the main bar and games room. Three guest ales are served, always including one from Oakham Ales and usually another from a local brewery. An annual beer festival is held over the St George's weekend in an adjoining barn. Westons Stowford Press cider is available.
🅐❀🕪🕭♣P⌐

Northampton

Eastgate Ⓛ ✔

98-100 Abington Street, NN1 2BP (E end of pedestrianised zone)
✪ 9am-11 (midnight Thu & Fri; 1am Sat) ☎ (01604) 633535
Greene King Abbot; Ruddles Best Bitter; guest beers Ⓗ
Popular Wetherspoon pub now boasting two banks of four handpumps, with one pump dedicated to a dark beer. Local microbreweries are supported and beer festivals can feature international beers in racked casks served by gravity. Spread over two floors, there is a keg-only bar and smokers' balcony upstairs. The sound is usually muted on the TVs and there is no music. Q❀🕪🕭🍴♿⌐

Lamplighter Ⓛ

66 Overstone Road, NN1 3JS
✪ 12-midnight (1am Fri); 10-1am Sat; 10-11 Sun ☎ (01604) 631125
Grainstore Phipps IPA; guest beers Ⓗ
A delightful, traditional, street-corner pub just off the town centre attracting young and old alike. Three of the four handpumps offer ales from local breweries, with regular beer festivals and a selection of bottled beers. Home-cooked food is served until 8pm, and children are welcome during meal times. There is a roaring fire in the bar and a heated courtyard for the colder seasons. The pub hosts open mic and quiz nights, a disco on Friday and live music on Saturday, including touring bands. A recent CAMRA award winner. 🅐❀🕪🖥⌐

Malt Shovel Tavern Ⓛ

121 Bridge Street, NN1 1QF (opp Carlsberg brewery)
✪ 11.30-3, 5-11; 11.30-11 Fri & Sat; 12-10.30 Sun ☎ (01604) 234212 ⊕ maltsheveltavern.com

Frog Island Natterjack; Fuller's London Pride; Great Oakley Wot's Occurring, Harpers; Oakham Bishops Farewell; guest beers Ⓗ
Just off the town centre, this popular pub is a former local CAMRA Pub of the Year. The tap for the Great Oakley Brewery, its beers always feature among the 14 handpumps. A real cider and Belgian draught and bottled beers are also available. At least two beer festivals are held each year, usually over bank holidays. Blues bands play on Wednesday nights. The pub has a strong rugby following. Home-made lunches are served Monday to Saturday. Well worth visiting. Q❀⒤ᵹ⇋♿♣●🍴

Moon on the Square ✔

6 The Parade, NN1 2EA
❀ 9am-midnight (1am Thu-Sat; 11 Sun) ☎ (01604) 634062
Adnams Broadside; Batemans XXXB; Greene King Abbot; Ruddles Best Bitter; guest beers Ⓗ
Situated in the town centre opposite the historic market place, this large, open-plan pub is on two levels (lift provided), with a quiet conservatory to the rear. It offers a good selection of ales and cider, and holds beer festivals several times a year. Food is served all day, every day. There are TV screens with the volume turned down and free Wi-Fi is provided. ⊷⒤ᵹ⇋♿●🍴

Queen Adelaide 🄻

50 Manor Road, Kingsthorpe, NN2 6QJ (off A5199)
❀ 11.30-11.30; 12-10.30 Sun ☎ (01604) 714524
⊕ queenadelaide.com
Adnams Southwold Bitter, Broadside; Copper Dragon Golden Pippin; guest beers Ⓗ
This fine establishment has twice been local CAMRA Pub of the Year runner-up and is a regular Guide entry. An 18th-century listed stone-built friendly local, it has low beams and an uneven floor in the bar. Run by a real ale and cider enthusiast, it is known for high-quality beers and generous servings of good food. Up to four guest ales are often from local microbreweries. The Sunday roasts are exceptional (booking advised). A popular pub with rugby followers.
❀⒤ᵹ⇋(4,4A)♣●P🍴

Road to Morocco

Bridgewater Drive, Abington Vale, NN3 3AG (off A4500, near Abington Park)
❀ 12-11 (midnight Fri & Sat; 10.30 Sun) ☎ (01604) 632899
Greene King IPA, Abbot; Theakston Old Peculier; guest beers Ⓗ
A popular and welcoming two-roomed estate pub run by a landlord who enthusiastically promotes real ale, offering up to four guest beers as well as the regulars. Numerous themed events are held. Pool and darts are played in the lively public bar. Tuesday is quiz night and poker is played on Thursday in the quieter lounge. Live sport is shown on screens in both bars. Wi-Fi internet access is available. ❀ᵹ⇋(2,X46)♣🍴

Wig & Pen 🄻 ✔

19 St Giles Street, NN1 1JA
❀ 12-11 (10.30 Sun) ☎ (01604) 622178
⊕ wigandpennorthampton.co.uk
Fuller's London Pride; Greene King IPA; Morland Old Speckled Hen; guest beers Ⓗ
The frontage of this pub is over 300 years old, while the long L-shaped bar was added 150 years ago. Now in its second year under new ownership, this oak-beamed bar offers six frequently changing guest beers including a mild and a local microbrew.

A guest cider and a wide range of bottled beers are also available. Jazz bands play on Tuesday nights and live bands perform in the beer garden on summer evenings Friday to Sunday. Good home-cooked food features local ingredients. CAMRA members receive a 10 per cent discount on beer. ❀⒤ᵹ⇋♿♣●🍴

Pitsford

Griffin Inn 🄻

25 High Street, NN6 9AD (between A43 and A508)
❀ 6 (5 Fri)-11; 12-3, 7-11 Sun ☎ (01604) 880346
⊕ griffinpitsford.co.uk
Greene King Abbot; Potbelly Best; guest beers Ⓗ
Formerly cottages, this Grade II-listed 17th-century ironstone pub is family run and owned. It has retained most of its original character and is festooned with fascinating artefacts in both the cosy bar room and larger comfortable lounges to the rear. Reasonably priced good food is available in the restaurant. On Sunday there are quizzes at lunchtime and in the evening, while regular food-themed nights are held. The two guest beers are often from Potbelly too. Open all day on bank holidays. Q❀⒤ᵹ⇋(X7,62)P🍴

Polebrook

King's Arms 🄻

Kings Arms Lane, PE8 5LW
❀ 12-3, 6-11 (midnight Fri); 12-11.30 Sat; 12-11 Sun
☎ (01832) 272363 ⊕ thekingsarms-polebrook.co.uk
Beer range varies Ⓗ
Traditional stone-built thatched inn with a main bar and three areas for diners at the far end, including a glass-roofed function room. Five real ales are available, two from the nearby Digfield Brewery and another guaranteed to be from a local microbrewery. The food menu mixes traditional fare with Spanish tapas, plus a separate specials board. Outside is a small car park and enclosed garden. ⬰Q❀⒤ᵹ⇋(25)♣P🍴

Ravensthorpe

Chequers

Chequers Lane, NN6 8ER (between A428 and A5199)
❀ 12-3, 6-11; 12-11 Sat & Sun ☎ (01604) 770379
Fuller's London Pride; Greene King IPA; Oakham JHB; Thwaites Original; guest beer Ⓗ
The hosts have enjoyed more than 20 years at this friendly pub, which attracts locals, walkers and fishermen alike. The brick-built Grade II-listed free house has an L-shaped bar and a restaurant serving excellent home-cooked food. There is a collection of jugs on the beams, and bank notes on the half-panelled walls. Outside there is a children's adventure play area and a separate building for Northants skittles. Q❀⒤ᵹ⇋(96)♣●P🍴

Rothwell

Rowell Charter 🄻 ✔

Sun Hill, NN14 6AB (on old A6)
❀ 12-11 ☎ (01536) 710453
Fuller's London Pride; Gale's Seafarers Ale; guest beers Ⓗ
The Rowell Charter dates from 1642 and is built from Northamptonshire ironstone, with new rooms added to provide three split levels, with low door lintels and ceilings. Originally the Sun, the name

was changed 26 years ago to commemorate the signing of the Charter by King John in 1204 when the town was officially permitted to hold the annual fair and market. A proclamation is held every year on the first Monday after Trinity Sunday when the pub opens at 6am. Five guest ales are offered, two from local micros.
🏠🏮💳🔲�(19)🌺P🔄

Rushden

Rushden Historical Transport Society L

Station Approach, NN10 0AW (on ring road)
🕐 7.30 (6 Fri)-11, 12-11 Sat; 12-10.30 Sun
☎ (01933) 318988 ⊕ rhts.co.uk
Grainstore Phipps IPA; Oakham Bishops Farewell; guest beers H

This former Midland Railway station is now a mecca for real ale. A real gem, the bar occupies the former ladies' waiting room, with gas lighting and walls adorned with enamel advertising panels and railway photos plus many CAMRA awards including National Club of the Year 2010. On the platform, coaches including a Royal Mail postal van are used for meetings and skittles. Open weekends are held during the summer with steam- and diesel-hauled train rides. A beer festival is hosted in September. Day membership is £1 except on open days.
🏠Q🏮🚹🚪🚆(X46,M50)♣🌺🔄🍴

Slipton

Samuel Pepys L

Slipton Lane, NN14 3AR (off A6116)
🕐 12-3, 5-11; 12-11 Sat & Sun ☎ (01832) 731739
⊕ samuel-pepys.com
Digfield Fools Nook H; **guest beers** H/G

A lovely 16th-century ironstone village pub with a low-beamed and brick-floored traditional bar to the front where locals and visitors can chat or relax in cosy armchairs in front of a real fire. The stone-built dining/lounge bar and the conservatory restaurant are decorated and furnished in smart modern style. Five guest beers, some on gravity, often come from local micros, and in summer a real cider is also available. 🏠Q🏮🚹🚆(16)P🔄

Staverton

Countryman

Daventry Road, NN11 6JH (on A425)
🕐 12-3, 6-midnight (10.30 Sun) ☎ (01327) 311815
Fuller's London Pride; guest beers H

Formerly the New Inn, the Countryman is the last remaining of three pubs in this lovely village. The L-shaped bar, with wood beams throughout, serves four areas, some set aside for diners, and an open hearth fire between the spaces provides some seclusion. With a new enthusiastic landlord at the helm, a wide choice of reasonably priced food, sourced locally whenever possible, is served along with two changing guest beers, often from local breweries. 🏠🏮🚹🚹🍴▲🚆P

Stoke Bruerne

Boat Inn L

Bridge Road, NN12 7SB (opp canal museum)
🕐 11-11; 12-10.30 Sun ☎ (01604) 862428 ⊕ boatinn.co.uk

Banks's Bitter; Frog Island Best Bitter; Jennings Cumberland Ale; Marston's Old Empire; Wychwood Hobgoblin H

Situated on the banks of the Grand Union Canal, the Boat Inn has been run by the same family since 1877. The delightful Tap Bar's interconnecting rooms have canal views, open fires, original stone floors and window seats, while an adjoining room has Northants skittles. Popular with diners, a large extension houses the lounge, restaurant and bistro. Additional beers are sold in the summer. A canal boat is available to hire for parties. The cider is Thatchers Heritage. 🏠Q🚸🏮🚹🚹🚆(86)♣🌺P🔄

Thornby

Red Lion L

Welford Road, NN6 8SJ (on A5199)
🕐 12-2.30 (not Mon), 5-11; 12-11 Sat & Sun
☎ (01604) 740238 ⊕ redlionthornby.co.uk
Greene King IPA; Wadworth Henry's IPA; guest beers H

Situated on the old A50, this traditional village pub dates back more than 400 years. The compact bar has two drinking areas with a wood-burning open fire in the lounge. A motley collection of beer tankards, steins and framed photos is displayed throughout. To the rear is the restaurant, which occupies two linked rooms, one heavily beamed (no food Mon). Regular guest beers are from Church End, Elgood's and Grainstore, with five to choose from. During the summer, classic car meetings are held along with pig roasts.
🏠🏮🚹🚹P🔄

Thorpe Mandeville

Three Conies L ✓

Banbury Lane, OX17 2EX
🕐 11-midnight ☎ (01295) 711025 ⊕ threeconiesinn.co.uk
Hook Norton Hooky Bitter, Gold, Old Hooky, seasonal ales; guest beer H

Located in a picturesque untouched village, this popular pub dates from the 17th century when it was a drovers' inn. Inside are beamed bars with open fires at each end, along with a separate restaurant with a vaulted ceiling and welcoming woodburner stove. A Northants skittles team plays here; they are rewarded with an annual beer festival in the summer and a cider festival in April.
🏠🏮🚹🚹♣P🔄

Tiffield

George Inn L ✓

21 High Street, NN12 8AD (off A43)
🕐 12-3 (not Tue), 6-midnight (1am Fri); 12-1am Sat; 12-7 Sun
☎ (01327) 350587 ⊕ thegeorgeattiffield.co.uk
Vale VPA; guest beers H

Popular and welcoming village pub dating from the 16th-century with Victorian and more modern additions. It has three rooms: a cosy bar, games room with Northants skittles, and a back room that can be booked by clubs and groups. Two ever-changing guest beers and Old Rosie cider complement the Vale beer. Wednesday is live music night, with open mic sessions every other week. Two annual beer festivals are hosted.
🏠🚸🏮🚹🚆(8,89)♣🌺P🔄

Towcester

Plough
96 Watling Street, NN12 6BT
✪ 11-11 ☎ (01327) 350738 ⊕ theploughinn.biz
Wells Bombardier; Young's Bitter; guest beers Ⓗ
Situated in the centre of this Roman town, the Plough has two rooms: a cosy front bar with stone floors and a large bay window onto the main street, and a larger lounge bar/restaurant to the rear. A wide corridor runs from the front to back of the pub, where there is a small outdoor drinking area. Two constantly changing guest beers are available. No food Monday. Just behind the building stands Bury Mount, on which the town's fort once stood. ⊕▶ 🕭🚃(8,89)P⁵⌐

Walgrave

Royal Oak
Zion Hill, NN6 9PN (2 miles N of A43)
✪ 11.30-2.30, 5.30 (5 Fri & Sat)-11; 12-10.30 Sun
☎ (01604) 781248
Adnams Southwold Bitter; Greene King Abbot; guest beers Ⓗ
A mid-19th century ironstone-built pub set back from the main road. The front bar is semi open plan with a drinking area to the left of the bar and dining spaces on either side. The main feature is a stone inglenook fireplace and low beams. To the rear is a small bar, cosy lounge and a function area. Outside, there is a room for Northants skittles and children's play equipment in the garden. Three changing guest beers are available.
▲Q❀▶🚃(39)♣P⁵⌐

Weldon

Shoulder of Mutton Ⓛ
12 Chapel Road, NN17 3HP
✪ 5-10 Wed; 12-11 ☎ (01536) 266453
Beer range varies Ⓗ
Solid establishment comprising two large, brightly decorated rooms – the main bar to the front has been created by knocking through three smaller rooms, and the games room to the rear has a pool table, large-screen TV and bar football table. A set of patio doors leads outside to a separate enclosed area for smokers. There are six handpumps on the bar, four dispensing beers from local microbreweries. ▲❀▶🚃(X4)♣P⁵⌐

Wellingborough

Coach & Horses Ⓛ
17 Oxford Street, NN8 4HY
✪ 12-11 (9 Mon; 6 Sun) ☎ (01933) 441242
Beer range varies Ⓗ
Town-centre local with an enthusiastic landlord who is fully committed to offering a good choice of up to 14 beers and ciders, including two changing local microbrews, often from Great Oakley and Potbelly. A recent Local CAMRA Pub of the Year and a former East Midlands Regional Pub of the Year runner-up, the Victorian pub has a single L-shaped room with cosy corners. Lots of breweriana adorns the front bar area, which is warmed by a real fire. Traditional home-cooked food is served lunchtimes and evenings (no food Sun eve, Mon and Tue).
▲Q❀▶🕭🚃♣🍴⁵⌐

Locomotive Ⓛ
111 Finedon Road, NN8 4AL (on A510)
✪ 11-midnight; 12-11 Sun ☎ (01933) 276600
Grainstore Phipps IPA; Oakham JHB, Scarlet Macaw; guest beers Ⓗ
A popular locals' pub on the outskirts of the town, not too far from the railway station. A railway theme runs throughout, with a display of classic OO-gauge locomotives behind the bar and a railway running above the servery. There are three rooms, the front bar with armchairs and a piano for a relaxing ambience. Eight handpumps serve a wide range of microbrewery beers to suit all tastes. Bar billiards and skittles are played here. No food on Sunday. ▲Q❀❀▶🚃(45)♣🍴⁵⌐

Weston by Welland

Wheel & Compass
Valley Road, LE16 8HZ (off B664)
✪ 12-11 (10.30 Sun) ☎ (01858) 565864
⊕ thewheelandcompass.co.uk
Greene King Abbot; Marston's EPA, Burton Bitter, Pedigree; guest beers Ⓗ
The Wheel stands on the edge of the village surrounded by open countryside in the Welland Valley. Inside it has two open drinking areas and a large dining room to the side serving good-quality food at reasonable prices. The large family-friendly garden has swings and slides – a big attraction in the summer. Two guest beers come from all over the country. A luxury holiday apartment has recently been added at the back of the pub.
▲Q❀🛏️▶🕭🚃(167)🍴P⁵⌐

Woodford

Duke's Arms Ⓛ
83 High Street, NN14 4HE (off A14/A510)
✪ 12-11 ☎ (01832) 732224
Greene King IPA; guest beers Ⓗ
Popular village pub overlooking the village green and named after the Duke of Wellington who was a frequent visitor to Woodford. The interior comprises a bar, dining room, and games room to the rear featuring Northants skittles, darts and pool. Home-cooked meals using local produce are served daily (no food Sun eve). A beer festival is held on the Whit Sunday bank holiday weekend. Six guest beers include one from Oakham.
▲🍴❀▶🕭🚃(16)♣🍴P⁵⌐

Yardley Hastings

Rose & Crown Ⓛ
4 Northampton Road, NN7 1EX
✪ 5-11; 12-midnight Fri & Sat; 12-6 Sun ☎ (01604) 696276
⊕ roseandcrownbistro.co.uk
Grainstore Phipps IPA; Greene King IPA, Abbot; guest beers Ⓗ
A lovely ironstone pub extensively refurbished in the 1980s and now a single large room in olde-worlde style. It retains stone-flagged floors and beamed ceilings throughout, and has a small drinking area in the bay window. The emphasis is on traditional home cooking, with a menu that changes daily, some tempting dishes and good service. Regular live music events from jazz to rock to blues feature, along with a new boules court. The landscaped gardens are wonderful in summer. Northamptonshire Pub Restaurant of the Year 2011/12. ❀▶🚃(P1)P⁵⌐

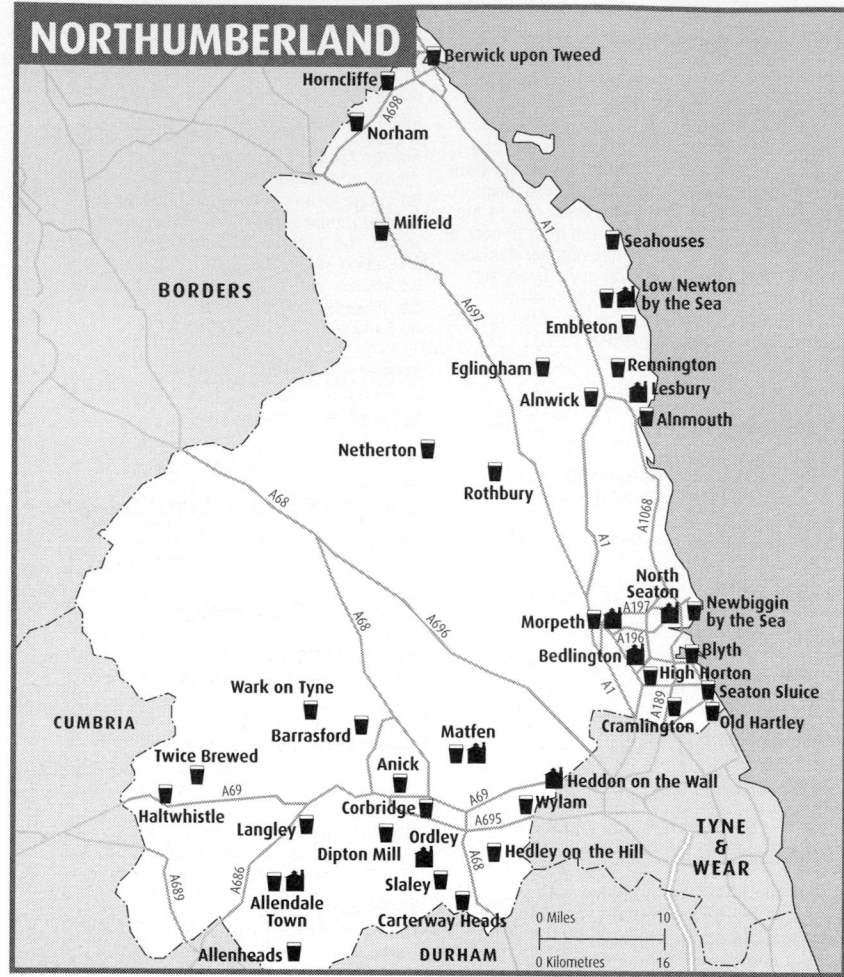

NORTHUMBERLAND

Berwick upon Tweed
Horncliffe
Norham
Milfield
BORDERS
Seahouses
Low Newton by the Sea
Embleton
Eglingham
Rennington
Lesbury
Alnwick
Alnmouth
Netherton
Rothbury
North Seaton
Newbiggin by the Sea
Morpeth
Bedlington
Blyth
High Horton
Wark on Tyne
Seaton Sluice
CUMBRIA
Barrasford
Matfen
Cramlington
Old Hartley
Twice Brewed
Anick
Heddon on the Wall
Haltwhistle
Corbridge
Wylam
Langley
Ordley
Dipton Mill
Hedley on the Hill
TYNE & WEAR
Slaley
Allendale Town
Carterway Heads
Allenheads
DURHAM

0 Miles 10
0 Kilometres 16

Allendale Town

Allendale Inn
Market Place, NE47 9BJ
☼ 12-midnight ☎ (01434) 683246
Taylor Landlord; guest beer Ⓗ
Pleasant pub nestling in the corner of Market Place with a friendly landlord. Popular with ramblers and locals, the pub is well supported and has darts, dominoes and pool teams. The nearby Allen Banks and superb countryside attract large numbers of ramblers who gladly quench their thirst here. Food is served lunchtimes and early evenings. Outside is a superb refurbished beer garden. Handy for the PlusBus via Hexham rail station.
🚶🐕✪◑🎁🍴♿🚃(688)♣🍴

Golden Lion Hotel Ⓛ
Market Place, NE47 9BD
☼ 12-1.30am (1am Wed; 2.30am Fri-Sun)
☎ (01434) 683225 ∰ goldenlionhotel.net
Taylor Landlord; Wylam Gold Tankard; guest beers Ⓗ
A friendly and hospitable pub in the market place, home to sociable locals and their dogs. The walls are adorned with photographs of the annual tar barrel procession, an experience in itself. The pub has a late licence at the weekend, and is an outlet

for Allendale Brewery's full range of bottled beers. The local choir practises here on Tuesday evening, and there is live Irish music on the last Wednesday of the month. 🚶🐕✪◑🎁🚃(688)

King's Head
Market Place, NE47 9BD (market place square, opp Co-op)
☼ 12-11 ☎ (01434) 683681
Jennings Cumberland Ale; guest beers Ⓗ
A welcoming, upmarket inn situated in the town square, next door to the Golden Lion. The refurbished bar retains original features such as an open log fire. Traditional pub food is served all day.

INDEPENDENT BREWERIES

Allendale Allendale Town
Brew Star Morpeth (NEW)
Gundog North Seaton (NEW)
Hexhamshire Ordley
High House Farm Matfen
Northumberland Bedlington
Ship Inn Low Newton by the Sea
VIP Lesbury (NEW)
Wylam Heddon on the Wall

The pub is popular with ramblers, cyclists and day trippers taking advantage of nearby countryside walks. Rail and bus links to Allendale are good, and it is handy for the PlusBus via Hexham rail station. Well worth seeking out in this small market town. ⚅Q☺🍴⚅⚅(688)

Allenheads

Allenheads Inn 🅛
Allenheads, NE47 9HJ
✪ 4 (12 Sat)-11; 12-10.30 Sun ☎ (01434) 685200
⊕ allenheadsinn.co.uk
Black Sheep Best Bitter; guest beers 🄷
Superb rural pub, popular with local ramblers and tourists. Originally the home of Sir Thomas Wentworth, the 18th-century multi-room building has a public bar with log fire, games room and dining room. The premises are bedecked with memorabilia and knick-knacks from a bygone age. Good bar meals are available at a decent price. Take care (and skis) in the winter. The pub will open early, if asked, for coach parties and groups. ⚅☺🍴⚅⚅(688)♣P

Alnmouth

Red Lion Inn ✅
22 Northumberland Street, NE66 2RJ
✪ 11-midnight ☎ (01665) 830584 ⊕ redlionalnmouth.com
Beer range varies 🄷
Charming 18th-century family-run coaching inn with a cosy lounge bar with attractive woodwork. Three guest beers often come from northern English or Scottish microbreweries, and a small range of continental bottled beers is available. Panoramic views across the Aln estuary can be enjoyed from the decked area at the bottom of the garden. Occasional live music plays – open air in summer. Well patronised by tourists and locals, dogs are welcome. An annual beer festival is held in October. Excellent en-suite B&B facilities. ⚅Q☺🍴⚅(518)♦P

Alnwick

John Bull Inn
12 Howick Street, NE66 1UY
✪ 12-3 (Sat & Sun only), 7-11 (10.30 Sun)
☎ (01665) 602055 ⊕ john-bull-inn.co.uk
Beer range varies 🄷
Many time CAMRA North Northumberland Pub of the Year winner, this 180-year-old inn thrives on its reputation as a 'back street boozer'. The passionate landlord offers a wide range of cask-conditioned ales at varying strengths, real cider, the widest choice of bottled Belgian beers in the county and over 120 single malt whiskies. The darts team competes in the local league, a cheese competition is held on Saturday night and the pub upholds the north-east tradition of an annual leek show. Q☺⚅(505)♣♦

Anick

Rat Inn
NE46 4LN (signed from Hexham A69 roundabout)
✪ 12-11 (3 Mon; 10.30 Sun) ☎ (01434) 602814
⊕ theratinn.com
Beer range varies 🄷
Superb 1750 country inn with spectacular views across Tyne Valley. The pub has a welcoming and

friendly feel to it and an excellent reputation for good food prepared with locally sourced ingredients, enhanced by inclusion in the prestigious Michelin Red Guide. Half portions are available for children. An open log fire is surrounded by several chamber pots hanging from the ceiling. Well worth the short taxi ride from Hexham Rail Station. ⚅Q☺🍴⚅⚅♣P⚑

Barrasford

Barrasford Arms
NE48 4AA
✪ 12-2 (not Mon), 6.30-11 (midnight Fri); 12-midnight Sat; 12-11 Sun ☎ (01434) 681237 ⊕ barrasfordarms.co.uk
Beer range varies 🄷
Splendid unspoilt 1870s country pub located in the heart of Barrasford village in the North Tyne Valley. The friendly bar is complemented by good ale and customer banter. It regularly hosts quoits tournaments, hunt meets, darts finals and vegetable competitions. Top chef Tony Binks has won several culinary awards. The nearby former railway station is used by the Scouts but the bar has several railway pictures from yesteryear that add to the pub's ambience. ⚅Q☺🍴⚅⚅♣P

Berwick upon Tweed

Barrels Ale House 🅛
59-61 Bridge Street, TD15 1ES (at town end of original Bridge)
✪ 12-midnight ☎ (01289) 308013
Stewart Pentland IPA; guest beers 🄷
There is an original Olde Curiosity Shop ambience to this pub, located in the old part of Berwick next to the original road bridge over the Tweed. The excellent real ale no doubt helps customers brave the 'dentist's chair' at the side of the bar. A downstairs bar is used by DJs and bands at weekends. Outside is a unique rear open drinking area surrounded by high walls. Winner of CAMRA Pub of the Year awards. ☺⚅⚅⚑

Pilot
31 Low Greens, TD15 1LZ
✪ 12 (11 Sat)-midnight ☎ (01289) 304214
Caledonian Deuchars IPA; guest beers 🄷
Well patronised by locals and sought out by train trippers who have heard about this gem. The stone-built end of terrace pub dates from the 19th century and and is a CAMRA Real Heritage Pub. It retains the original small room layout and boast several nautical artefacts over 100 years old. The pub runs darts and quoits teams and hosts music nights. The bar staff are welcoming and friendly. ⚅🍴⚅⚅♣

Blyth

Olivers 🅛
60 Bridge Street, NE24 2AP
✪ 12 (3 Mon-Fri)-11 (11.30 Sat); 12-10.30 Sun
☎ (01670) 368346
Caledonian Deuchars IPA; guest beers 🄷
A welcome real ale outlet within a beer desert, this warm and friendly one-roomed hostelry was converted from a newsagent's and is well supported by locals. It is close to the regenerated quayside of a port better known for the past (and recent) FA Cup exploits of its famous Spartans Football Club. Three real ales are available, one

usually locally sourced. Bus 308 passes outside and the bus station for services to Blyth is a five-minute walk. ◑🛏♣

Carterway Heads

Manor House Inn
DH8 9LX
✪ 11-11; 12-10.30 Sun ☎ (01207) 255268
⊕ themanorhouseinn.com
Beer range varies Ⓗ
Warm and hospitable country inn with three open fires and many rooms, situated just off the A68 10 miles south of Corbridge. A double-glazed window in the bar wall allows customers to view the well-maintained cellar. Proper home-cooked food is freshly prepared on the premises and popular with tourists and locals. Excellent accommodation is available. Derwent Reservoir is nearby.
♨⭐☺🛏◑🖤♣⮟P⭐

Corbridge

Angel Inn
Main Street, NE45 5LA
✪ 11 (12 Sun)-11 ☎ (01434) 632119
⊕ angelofcorbridge.co.uk
Hadrian Border Newburn No 1, Tyneside Blonde; guest beers Ⓗ
Superb former 1726 coaching inn located on the main road with good transport links. Seven handpulls offer a range of ales and it also keeps a wonderful selection of malt whiskies. Family-friendly with a reputation for good food, it is popular with tourists, ramblers and locals. A separate lounge area has comfy leather seating and outside is a relaxed seating area. The town has strong links with the Romans and Hadrian's Wall is nearby. ♨Q☺🛏◑⭐�🛏(10,685)P

Cramlington

Plough Ⓛ
Middle Farm Buildings, NE23 1DN
✪ 11-3 (3.15 Wed), 6-11; 11-11 Fri & Sat; 12-10.30 Sun ☎ (01670) 737633
Ruddles County; guest beers Ⓗ
Owned by the Fitzgerald pub chain and located within the old village centre of Cramlington, now surrounded by new town development, this is a sympathetic conversion of what used to be farm buildings into a traditional pub, including the time-honoured division between bar and lounge. Among the interesting architectural features is the former gin gan – a circular building in which a horse would be harnessed to a wheel to grind corn – in the lounge. The bar is smaller and busy with doors leading to a seating area outside. Children are welcome during the day. ⭐◑⭐P⭐

Dipton Mill

Dipton Mill Inn Ⓛ
Dipton Mill Road, NE46 1YA
✪ 12-2.30, 6-11; 12-3 Sun ☎ (01434) 606577
⊕ diptonmill.co.uk
Hexhamshire Devil's Elbow, Shire Bitter, Blackhall English Stout, Devil's Water, Whapweasel, Old Humbug Ⓗ
The tap for Hexhamshire Brewery, this small inn is run by a keen landlord who brews his own excellent beers – Blackhall English Stout has proved

so popular among drinkers that it has ousted the Guinness. To complement the ales there is great home-cooked food – Saturday is curry night. A cosy atmosphere and warm welcome make this pub well worth seeking out. The large garden has a stream running through it and there is plenty of countryside to explore. ♨Q⭐◑⮟P

Eglingham

Tankerville Arms Ⓛ
15 The Village, NE66 2TX
✪ 12-11 (12.30am Fri & Sat; 10.30 Sun) ☎ (01665) 578444
⊕ tankervillearms.com
Hadrian Border Tyneside Blonde; guest beers Ⓗ
Well-appointed, traditional country pub dating from 1851. The bar serves three locally sourced beers and has several framed pictures that enhance the surroundings. An excellent open-beam restaurant complements this establishment. The beer garden at the rear is very tranquil with superb rural views. The pub hosts meetings for the local golf and cricket clubs. Popular with tourists and ramblers, families and dogs are welcome. Accommodation is en suite. ♨Q☺⭐🛏◑⭐P

Embleton

Greys Inn ✪
Stanley Terrace, NE66 3UY
✪ 12-11 (10.30 Sun) ☎ (01665) 576983
Black Sheep Best Bitter; Hadrian Border Farne Island, Tyneside Blonde; guest beer Ⓗ
Pleasant traditional pub located at the rear of this lovely seaside hamlet, just a short walk to a wonderful beach. The pub has three open fires and a framed 1904 grocery list hangs on the wall. This is an excellent venue to enjoy a bite to eat washed down with a locally sourced real ale – hopefully relaxing outside on the superb patio. Home to a ladies' darts team, clay pigeon club and golf club. ♨☺⭐◑⭐🛏(501,518)♣⭐

Haltwhistle

Black Bull
Black Bull Lane, Market Square, NE49 0BL
✪ 12-11 (midnight Fri & Sat;10.30 Sun) ☎ (01434) 320463
Caledonian Deuchars IPA; guest beers Ⓗ
Warm, welcoming two-room pub with a genuine, friendly licensee, situated just off Market Place down a cobbled lane. Close to Hadrian's Wall, it is popular with locals and ramblers. The pub has a traditional ambience with a low beamed timber ceiling, open fire, horse brasses and six handpulls on the bar. Regular themed nights are held. Ring to check meal times and winter hours as they can vary. ♨Q☺◑🛏(685)⭐

Milecastle Inn Ⓛ
North Road, NE49 9NN (on B6318 Military Road)
✪ 12-11 ☎ (01434) 321372 ⊕ milecastle-inn.co.uk
Big Lamp Bitter, Prince Bishop, Sunny Daze Ⓗ
This 1600s inn adjacent to Hadrian's Wall only sells ale from Newburn-based Big Lamp Brewery. Located a mile and a half north of Haltwhistle, this rural pub has a homely feel. Food is locally sourced and diners come from as far away as Newcastle and Carlisle. Popular with ramblers and tourists, the Hadrian's Wall bus stops outside (April-Oct). There are also two holiday cottages. Check ahead for winter opening times. ♨Q☺⭐◑🛏(AD122)P

Hedley on the Hill

Feathers ✪

NE43 7SW (take Lead Road out of Greenside and follow signs)

☼ 12 (6 Mon)-11 ☎ (01661) 843607 ⊕ thefeathers.net
Beer range varies Ⓗ

Much acclaimed country pub set in a pleasant hamlet with superb views over three counties. The young and welcoming staff serve high-quality home-cooked food to complement the real ales. A beer festival is held at Easter with an uphill barrel race on Easter Monday. The pub has a comfortable feel with exposed stone walls and beams. The pub has won awards for food quality – book ahead for the popular Sunday lunch. ▲Q❤☀☺◑P⚲

High Horton

Three Horse Shoes Ⓛ

Hathery Lane, NE24 4HF (off A189 N of Cramlington, follow A192) N7276793

☼ 11-11 (midnight Fri & Sat); 12-11 Sun ☎ (01670) 822410
⊕ threehorseshoes-horton.co.uk

Greene King Abbot; Tetley Bitter; guest beers Ⓗ

Former coaching inn at the highest point in the Blyth Valley, with views of the Northumberland coast. The pub is open plan with distinct bar and dining areas plus a conservatory. Dedicated to real ale, there are regular beer festivals. Guest ales are sourced from all over the country but regularly come from local microbreweries. A house beer is brewed by Carlsberg and two pint carry-outs are available. An extensive range of meals and snacks is served lunchtimes and evenings, all day Friday to Sunday. Q☀◑🖫(X5)♣P⚲

Horncliffe

Fishers Arms

Main Street, TD15 2XW

☼ 12-3 (3.15 Tue; 2 Sun), 6-10.30 (11 Fri & Sat); closed Tue
☎ (01289) 386866
Beer range varies Ⓗ

Traditional pub at the heart of community life, offering a once-a-month buskers' session, food-themed nights, quiz nights, OAP lunch every Thursday, and the Hooky Mats club on Wednesday lunchtime. Part of a terrace in the village centre, the pub has separate dining and drinking areas. Reasonably priced home-cooked food is popular. The Tweed Cycle Way is nearby. B&B includes en-suite facilities. Q❤🛏◑🖫(67)♣

Langley

Carts Bog Inn Ⓛ

NE47 5NW (3 miles off A69 on A686 to Alston)

☼ 12-2.30 (not Mon; 2 Wed), 5-11; 12-11 Sat; 12-10.30 Sun
☎ (01434) 684338 ⊕ cartsbog.co.uk
Beer range varies Ⓗ

Excellent rural pub serving the local community and tourists. The building dates from 1730 and was built on the site of an ancient brewery (circa 1521). Carts really did get bogged down here. A large open fire divides the two-room interior and the walls proudly display pictures of bygone days. Good locally sourced food is served (booking essential for Sun lunch). Home to three quoits teams and a darts team. The pub hosts occasional live bands and an outdoor barbecue with marquees in the garden. ▲Q❤☀◑ 🍴👶🖫(688)♣P⚲

Low Newton by the Sea

Ship Inn

Newton Square, NE66 3EL (off B1340 between Seahouses and Craster)

☼ 11-11; 12-10.30 Sun ☎ (01665) 576262
⊕ shipinnnewton.co.uk

Ship Inn Sandcastles at Dawn, Sea Coal, Sea Wheat, Ship Hop Ale, Dolly Daydream Ⓗ

Pleasant pub nestling in the corner of a three-sides-of-a-square arrangement of former fishermen's cottages and graced by a small village green, this pub's location virtually on the beach is unique. Fine sea views can be enjoyed on the short walk from the car park. An excellent food menu features fresh locally-sourced ingredients. The pub serves its own beer from the brewery next door – please note that it is served colder than normal. A popular establishment that can get busy – opening times may vary in winter so phone first. ▲Q☀◑🍴⚲

Matfen

High House Farm Visitor Centre Ⓛ

NE20 0RG (turn right past Robin Hood on Military Road)

☼ 10.30-9 (5 Mon & Tue); closed Wed ☎ (01661) 886192
⊕ highhousefarmbrewery.co.uk

High House Farm Auld Hemp, Nel's Best, Matfen Magic, seasonal beers Ⓗ

Grade II-listed premises with a brewery and visitors centre on a 200-acre working farm. All real ales are sourced from the brewery, with brewery tours and tutored tastings available (book ahead). It has an award-winning restaurant and tea room, and a children's play area outside. Barbecues and hog roasts are hosted. Situated one and a half miles from the Military Road and not far from Roman Wall, touring caravans are welcome. Licensed for weddings and popular for wedding receptions. Q❤☀◑🍴♣P

Milfield

Red Lion

Main Road, NE71 6JD

☼ 11-2, 5-11 ☎ (01668) 216224 ⊕ redlioninn-milfield.co.uk
Black Sheep Best Bitter; guest beers Ⓗ

A true local pub at the heart of the village, just eight miles inside the border, dating back to the mid 1700s. Rescued by the current licensee from the tight grip of Heineken, the Red Lion is a proper free house, with many varied guest beers served from the third handpump. Freshly prepared food is available, with blackboards proudly displaying where the local produce is sourced. Home to the local leek-growing club. ▲☀🛏◑🍴P⚲

Morpeth

Tap & Spile Ⓛ

23 Manchester Street, NE61 1BH

☼ 12-2.30, 4.30-11; 12-11 Fri & Sat; 12-10.30 Sun
☎ (01670) 513894

Everards Tiger; Greene King Abbot; Hadrian Border Tyneside Blonde; Mordue Workie Ticket; Taylor Landlord; guest beers Ⓗ

Cosy, popular local, welcoming to all and handy for the nearby bus station. It has a busy, narrow bar to the front and a quieter lounge to the rear. A good choice of ales is on offer, often including local beers from Northumbrian breweries. Westons Old

Rosie real cider is stocked as well as a selection of fruit wines from Lindisfarne Winery. A traditional folk group plays on Sunday lunchtimes. Winner of local CAMRA awards. ₳Q✿✪◑❺♣♨╘

Netherton

Star Inn ★
NE65 7HD
✪ closed Sun, Mon & Thu; 7.30-10.30 (10 Wed)
☎ (01669) 630238
Beer range varies Ⓗ
Entering this gem, the only pub in Northumberland to appear in every edition of the Guide, is like entering the private living room of a big house. Beer is served on gravity from the cellar at a hatch in the panelled entrance hall. The bar area is basic with benches round the wall. On the walls are the pub's many awards. Children are not allowed in the bar. Please ring to check opening hours. **QP**

Newbiggin by the Sea

Queen's Head ✅
7 High Street, NE64 6AT
✪ 9.45am-midnight ☎ (01670) 817293
Beer range varies Ⓗ
A CAMRA Real Heritage Pub, the original Edwardian layout of the inn has been retained, with a public bar area, lounge area displaying many photographs of bygone Newbiggin, and snug to the rear. Outstanding features include the curved bar counter, bench seating, fireplace, etched windows and mosaic floors. The landlord sells competitively priced real ales and displays an ever-growing collection of guest-beer pump clips. Note the advantageous opening hours. All Newbiggin buses pass the door. ♣♨

Norham

Mason's Arms
17 West Street, TD15 2LB
✪ 12-3 (3.15 Wed), 7-11; 12-10.30 Sun ☎ (01289) 382326
⊕ tweed-sports.co.uk
Beer range varies Ⓗ
The cosy wood-panelled public bar, with a real fire at its heart, is the centre of this pub. The interior features an old Younger's brewery mirror, collections of fishing gear and joinery tools, plus photos of bygone Norham. Situated in an area popular with tourists, a ruined castle and former railway station museum are nearby. Cyclists on the Tweed Cycle Way stop here. ₳✿♠◑Ⓖ➡(67)♣

Old Hartley

Delaval Arms Ⓛ
NE26 4RL (by roundabout at jct of A193/B1325 S of Seaton Sluice)
✪ 12-11 (10.30 Sun) ☎ (0191) 237 0489
Beer range varies Ⓗ
Multi-roomed Grade II-listed building dating from 1748, with a listed World War I water storage tower behind the beer garden. Good-quality, affordable meals complement the beer, with guest ales coming from local micros. To the left as you enter there is a room served through a hatch from the bar and to the right a room where children are welcome. **Q**✿✪◑Ⓖ**P**╘

Rennington

Horse Shoes Inn
6 Rennington Village, NE66 3RS
✪ 12-3 (not Mon; 3.15 Wed), 7-11 ☎ (01665) 577665
⊕ thehorseshoesrennington.co.uk
Hadrian Border Farne Island; guest beer Ⓗ
Superb traditional family-run village pub dating from 1851. The bar is warm and friendly with hops hanging over the serving area. There is a large restaurant serving good food with locally sourced ingredients. The pub hosts a scarecrow competition every August bank holiday Saturday. Outside at the front is a pleasant beer garden. ♨✿✪◑♣**P**⊟

Rothbury

Queen's Head ✅
Townfoot, NE65 7SR
✪ 11-1am (midnight Sun) ☎ (01669) 620470
⊕ queensheadrothbury.com
Beer range varies Ⓗ
Friendly hotel dating from 1756 on the main street. Noted for its home-cooked meals made with local and seasonal produce, it is popular with locals, tourists and ramblers. Live folk music plays on the first Tuesday and last Thursday of the month (come early as it is often a sell out). The hotel has pool and darts teams who compete in local leagues. All bedrooms are en suite. There is an hourly bus service. ♨✿⇆◑Ⓖ₳➡(X14,144)♣**P**

Seahouses

Olde Ship Hotel
7-9 Main Street, NE68 7RD
✪ 11 (12 Sun)-11 ☎ (01665) 720200 ⊕ seahouses.co.uk
Black Sheep Best Bitter; Courage Directors; Hadrian Border Farne Island; Morland Old Speckled Hen; Ruddles County; Theakston Best Bitter; guest beers Ⓗ
A CAMRA Real Heritage Pub, this 1745 farmhouse was converted to the licensed trade in 1812 and has been family owned since 1910. It has three quality bars adorned with a veritable treasure trove of 19th and 20th century maritime memorabilia. Fully residential, the pub offers a unique menu of fish, fresh crab meals and snacks (no chips served). Seahouses harbour is nearby and handy for boat trips to the famous Farne Islands. ₳Q♨✿⇆◑Ⓖ₳➡(501)♣**P**╘

Seaton Sluice

Melton Constable
Beresford Road, NE26 4DA
✪ 12-11 (10.30 Sun) ☎ (0191) 237741
Beer range varies Ⓗ
Large roadside inn a few minutes' walk to the beach and local history sights. It overlooks a small harbour cut out of rock by the famous Delavals which is still in use today. The pub is named after the southern seat of Lord Hastings, a member of the Delaval family. A popular quiz is held on Wednesday evening. The ruins of Starlight Castle can be seen from the conservatory. Good wholesome food is served, making the pub a popular stop for walkers on the coastal route. Delaval Hall is close by. ♨✿◑Ⓖ➡(308,309)**P**

Slaley

Travellers Rest ⊘

NE46 1TT (on B6306 one mile N of village)
☼ 12-11 (10.30 Sun) ☎ (01434) 673231
⊕ travellersrestslaley.com
Black Sheep Best Bitter; Caledonian Deuchars IPA; guest beers ⊞
Former farmhouse from the 16th century, licensed for over 150 years. The pub has an excellent reputation for good food and accommodation. The bar has a large open fire, stone and flag floors, comfortable furniture and a beautiful wine rack carved from a large piece of wood. Children are welcome and there is a safe play area to the side.
ⱮQ⟓⊛⌂◖◗&♣P

Twice Brewed

Twice Brewed Inn

Military Road, Bardon Mill, NE47 7AN (on B6318)
☼ 11-11 (10.30 Sun) ☎ (01434) 344534
⊕ twicebrewedinn.co.uk
Yates Twice Brewed Bitter; guest beers ⊞
Superb remote inn, close to Hadrian's Wall and patronised by tourists and ramblers. It offers a range of bottled beers named Beers of the World. Outside, the pub has its own well for water, and excellent views from the rear garden, which hosts a marquee in summer and is home to two quoits teams. The inn acts as a rural transport interchange and has 16 bedrooms, seven en suite. It has full disabled access and an IT suite with internet connection. Q⟓⊛⌂◖◗⊟&ᵼP

Wark on Tyne

Battlesteads Hotel Ⅼ ⊘

Main Street, NE48 3LS
☼ 11-11; 12-10.30 Sun ☎ (01434) 230209
⊕ battlesteadshotel.com
Black Sheep Best Bitter; Durham Magus; guest beers ⊞
Well-appointed 1747 former farmhouse with a superb walled garden to the rear, restaurant and large conservatory. Five handpulls provide an excellent choice of beer with up to three guests. Ingredients for the excellent food menu are sourced within a 25 mile radius. With excellent accommodation including ground-floor rooms with disabled access, this family-friendly pub near Hadrian's Wall offers something for everyone. Future developments include a walking book based around the pub. Handy for the PlusBus via Hexham Rail Station. Ɱ⟓⊛⌂◖◗⊟&♣⊟(880)P⌐

Wylam

Black Bull

Main Street, NE41 8AB
☼ 4-11; 12-midnight Fri & Sat; 12-11 Sun ☎ (01661) 853112
⊕ blackbull-wylam.co.uk
Wylam Gold Tankard; guest beers ⊞
Run by a friendly landlord and staff, this cheerful pub on the main street in Wylam is popular with the locals. Regular themed nights are hosted, often in support of charities. Good food includes local home-cooked specialities, steak night on Wednesday, fish night on Friday and curry night on the last Thursday of the month. Nearby is Wylam Waggonway, a popular walk that passes George Stephenson's cottage. With six handpulls, real ale sales have increased – the beer is sourced mainly from the Wylam Brewery nearby. ⌂◖◗⊟≉♣⌐

Boathouse Inn Ⴤ Ⅼ

Station Road, NE41 8HR
☼ 11-11 (midnight Sat); 12-10.30 Sun ☎ (01661) 853431
⊕ theboathousewylam.co.uk
Beer range varies ⊞
Superb two-roomed pub with 15 handpulls, three dedicated to cider, with more ciders served from the cellar. Beers are sourced locally and nationwide, and on bank holidays themed beer festivals are held. Sunday lunches are popular, with good food available throughout the week. The pub is a popular stopping off point for 'Whistle Stops II' travellers. Fifteen CAMRA awards cover a wall, including North East Regional Pub of the Year 2011. Saturday afternoons and the first Wednesday evening in the month are for buskers.
ⱮQ⟓⊛◖◗≉●P

Olde Ship Hotel, Seahouses (Photo: Colin Anderson)

NOTTINGHAMSHIRE

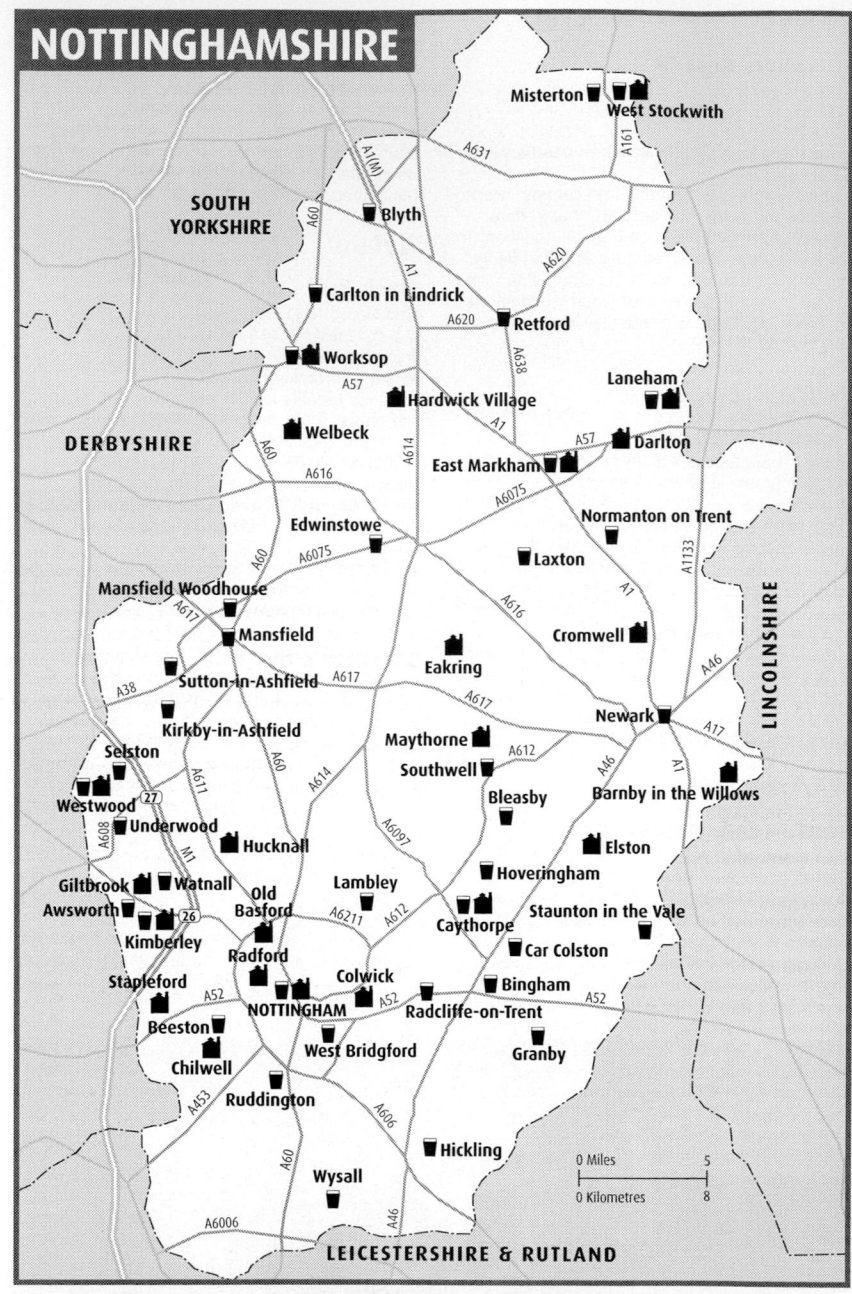

Misterton
West Stockwith
SOUTH YORKSHIRE
Blyth
Carlton in Lindrick
Retford
Worksop
Laneham
Hardwick Village
DERBYSHIRE
Welbeck
Darlton
East Markham
Normanton on Trent
Edwinstowe
Laxton
Mansfield Woodhouse
Cromwell
Mansfield
Eakring
Sutton-in-Ashfield
Kirkby-in-Ashfield
Newark
Maythorne
Selston
Southwell
Barnby in the Willows
Westwood
Bleasby
Underwood
Elston
Hucknall
Hoveringham
Giltbrook
Lambley
Watnall
Awsworth
Old Basford
Staunton in the Vale
Kimberley
Caythorpe
Radford
Car Colston
Stapleford
Colwick
Bingham
Beeston
NOTTINGHAM
Radcliffe-on-Trent
Granby
Chilwell
West Bridgford
Ruddington
Hickling
Wysall

LINCOLNSHIRE

LEICESTERSHIRE & RUTLAND

0 Miles 5
0 Kilometres 8

Awsworth

Gate Inn Ⓛ
Main Street, NG16 2RN
☼ 12-midnight (1am Fri & Sat) ☎ (0115) 932 9821
Burton Bridge XL; guest beers Ⓗ
Deemed to be unviable and sold at auction by the pub's former owners, the Gate Inn reopened in 2010 as a free house, and has quickly established itself as a quality real ale outlet, winning Nottingham CAMRA's Pub of Excellence award in 2011. A truly welcoming and friendly local, this late

19th-century pub has a bar, a lounge and a separate room housing a pool table. The current owners are gradually renovating the pub to realise its full potential. ᐸⓈ&✿⚅(R1)♣✿Pᐳ

Beeston

Crown Ⓛ
Church Street, NG9 1FY
☼ 12-11 ☎ (0115) 925 4738
Everards Sunchaser, Tiger; Fuller's London Pride; Leatherbritches Bounder, Cad, Scoundrel Ⓗ

A beer house since 1830 on a Grade II-listed site and fully restored by Everards. An outstanding cask ale emporium, it was East Midlands CAMRA Pub of the Year winner in 2010 and 2011. Five traditional rooms include the three-seat 'confessional' snug, reputedly once the vicar's hideaway, whisky bar and games room. The choice of 14 real ales include three from Leatherbritches, LocAles, dark beers, a range of guests plus six real ciders/perries. Rolls, pies and cheeseboard snacks are available.
Q ⚡🕎✿🕯🍴& ⇌🚃(36,Y36,R18)♠P↙—

Victoria Hotel L

85 Dovecote Lane, NG9 1JG (off A6005 by station)
🕗 10.30 (12 Sun)-11 ☎ (0115) 925 4049
🌐 victoriabeeston.co.uk
Blue Monkey Original; Castle Rock Harvest Pale; Everards Tiger; guest beers Ⓗ

Atmospheric Victorian architectural gem dating from 1899 – note the fine windows – with a dining area, public bar and covered, heated garden. This former Nottingham CAMRA Pub of the Year is a popular venue for drinkers and diners. The high-quality menu includes wide vegetarian and vegan options. Up to 16 beers are available including LocAles and always a mild and stout/porter, along with real ciders. Themed events are reflected in the beer range and beer festivals are held throughout the year. 🏚Q✿🕯🍴& ⇌🚃(13,14,R18)♠P

Bingham

Horse & Plough 🏆 ✅

25 Long Acre, NG13 8AF
🕗 11-11 (11.30 Fri & Sat); 12-11 Sun ☎ (01949) 839313
🌐 horseandploughbingham.com
Caledonian Deuchars IPA; Theakston XB; guest beers Ⓗ

Situated in the heart of a busy market town, this warm, friendly, one-room free house is a former Methodist chapel and has a cottage-style interior and flagstone floor. Six cask ales are served including four guests, with a 'try before you buy' policy, and a cider from Westons. Freshly prepared food is served weekday lunchtimes and evenings in the bar, and the first floor à la carte restaurant offers a varied seasonal menu. Local CAMRA Pub of the Year 2007, 2010 and 2012. 🍴& ⇌🚃♠

Bleasby

Waggon & Horses L

Gipsy Lane, NG14 7GE
🕗 12-2 (not Mon-Wed), 5-11 (4-midnight Fri), 12-midnight Sat; 12-11 Sun ☎ (01636) 830283
Batemans XB; Blue Monkey BG Sips; Nottingham Rock Mild; guest beers Ⓗ

Reversing the trend of village pub closures, the Waggon has been reborn. Now a free house, it offers six real ales including two from the award-winning Blue Monkey Brewery and a mild. This is a true village pub overlooking the church and green with no gimmicks or electronic gizmos, just conversation and banter. Well worth finding in a lovely Trent Valley village close to Southwell Minster and races – walkers with muddy boots and dogs with muddy paws all welcome.
🏚Q✿🕯🍴⇌🚃(3)♣♠P↙—

Blyth

Red Hart ✅

Bawtry Road, S81 8HG
🕗 12-11.30 ☎ (01909) 591221 🌐 redhart.co.uk
Beer range varies Ⓗ

An attractive village pub situated in the centre of Blyth – a previous winner of best-kept village. The pub has a separate lounge and bar areas with a reasonably sized dining room. The walls in the lounge are decorated with photographs and paintings of various locations around the village. Guest ales change regularly, with beers from microbreweries usually available. Restaurant-quality food at pub prices is served daily. The pub now hosts an annual beer festival on the late spring bank holiday. 🏚✿🕯🍴& 🚃P↙—

Car Colston

Royal Oak ✅

The Green, NG13 8JE
🕗 11.30-3 (not Mon), 5.30-midnight; 11.30-midnight Fri & Sat; 12-10.30 Sun ☎ (01949) 20247 🌐 brilliantpubs.co.uk/royaloaknotts
Ringwood Best Bitter; Marston's Burton Bitter; guest beers Ⓗ

Impressive country inn situated on one of England's largest village greens. The two-room interior includes a lounge and restaurant on one side and bar with comfortable seating on the other. Note the bar's vaulted brickwork ceiling – a legacy from the building's previous life as a hosiery factory. Good quality, traditional food is served lunchtimes and evenings. There is a skittle alley to the rear. The landlord maintains his 100 per cent record for entries in the Guide. 🏚✿🕯🍴& ▲♣P↙—

Carlton in Lindrick

Grey Horses

The Cross, S81 9EW

INDEPENDENT BREWERIES

Alcazar Nottingham: Old Basford
Blue Monkey Giltbrook
Castle Rock Nottingham
Caythorpe Caythorpe
Copthorne Darlton
Double Top Worksop
Flipside Colwick
Full Mash Stapleford
Funfair Elston
Grafton Worksop
Handley's Barnby in the Willows (NEW)
Holland Kimberley (brewing suspended)
Idle West Stockwith
Lincoln Green Hucknall (NEW)
Magpie Nottingham
Mallard Maythorne
Maypole Eakring
Medieval Nottingham (NEW)
Milestone Cromwell
Naked Westwood
Navigation Nottingham (NEW)
Nottingham Nottingham: Radford
Pheasantry East Markham (NEW)
Prior's Well Hardwick Village
Reality Nottingham: Chilwell
Springhead Laneham
Welbeck Abbey Welbeck

✪ 12-11.30 ☎ (01909) 730252
Beer range varies Ⓗ
The Grey Horses is situated in the heart of the village and serves at least three ever-changing guest beers. It has a front bar accessible from the street where locals gather to play cards and dominoes, and a large lounge bar area. Meals are served until 8pm Monday to Friday and until 4pm Saturday and Sunday. There is a separate function room upstairs. 🏚Q❀✿◑ 🖵🕭🖵(21,22)♣P'⎻

Caythorpe

Black Horse Ⓛ
29 Main Street, NG14 7ED
✪ closed Mon; 11.45-2.30, 6-11.30 (midnight Fri & Sat); 12-5, 8-11 Sun ☎ (0115) 966 3520
Caythorpe Dover Beck, One Swallow; Greene King Abbot; guest beer Ⓗ
The home of the Caythorpe Brewery, this classic unspoilt 18th-century country tavern has been run by the same family for 42 years and is reputedly a former haunt of Dick Turpin. Little has changed over the years – there is a comfortable lounge, a tiny snug bar with hatch servery, inglenook, bench seats, beams and wood panelling. A dining room is available for dinner parties. Bar food is popular, mostly cooked to order using fresh ingredients (booking essential). 🏚Q❀◑ 🖵🖵(103)♣P

East Markham

Queen's Hotel
High Street, NG22 0RE
✪ 12 (2 Mon)-11 ☎ (01777) 870288
⊕ queenshoteleastmarkham.co.uk
Adnams Southwold Bitter; Everards Beacon, Tiger; guest beers Ⓗ
Situated on the village main street, this cosy public house has a friendly atmosphere enhanced by an open fire in winter. A single bar serves the lounge, pool room and dining area. Food ranges from hot and cold snacks to full home-cooked meals. There is a large garden area at the rear where you can enjoy a drink on a warm summer's day. A previous winner of local CAMRA awards.
🏚Q❀◑🖵(36,37)♣P'⎻

Edwinstowe

Forest Lodge Hotel Ⓛ ✔
2-4 Church Street, NG21 9QA (by traffic lights on A6075 Mansfield-Ollerton road)
✪ 11.30-3, 5.30 (5 Fri)-11; 12-3, 6-10.30 Sun
☎ (01623) 824443 ⊕ forestlodgehotel.co.uk
Wells Bombardier; guest beers Ⓗ
A busy family-owned free house, this former coaching inn dating back to 1770 is located close to the 800-year-old Major Oak in Sherwood Forest. The central bar dispenses up to five real ales, often featuring paler beers, plus a LocAle. Refurbished to high standards, it retains a traditional feel and has a large impressive function room available for private hire. It offers 12 en-suite rooms. A former local CAMRA Branch Pub of the Year winner.
🏚Q❀✿◑🖵🖵(14,15)P'⎻

Granby

Marquis of Granby
Dragon Street, NG13 9PN

✪ 4-11 (midnight Fri); 12-midnight Sat; 12-11 Sun
☎ (01949) 859517
Brewster's Hophead, Marquis; guest beers Ⓗ
Believed to be the original Marquis of Granby, dating back to 1760 or earlier, this small two-roomed pub is now the brewery tap for Brewster's. York stone floors complement the yew bar tops and wood-beamed rooms, period wallpaper features throughout and the lounge has a welcoming open fire in winter months. Guest beers served alongside the Brewster's range usually come from micros, and include a mild, stout or porter. Fish and chips night is Friday. A former local CAMRA Pub of the Year. 🏚❀🖵🕭♣P

Hickling

Plough Inn Ⓛ
Main Street, LE14 3AH
✪ 12 – 12; 12 - 10.30 Sun ☎ (01664) 822225
⊕ theploughinnhickling.co.uk
Adnams Southwold Bitter; Belvoir Hickling Standard; Black Sheep Best Bitter; Castle Rock Harvest Pale; Draught Bass Ⓗ
Situated opposite the Hickling Basin, part of the Grantham Canal, this attractive traditional country pub is popular with walkers and cyclists using the towpath. The large main bar is upstairs while downstairs is a second bar with seating plus a smaller function room. Tuesday is quiz night and Wednesday pie night, with a full bar menu served seven days a week. Regular live music and open mic evenings are held throughout the year.
🏚❀◑🖵🕭♣❀P

Hoveringham

Reindeer Inn Ⓛ
Main Street, NG14 7JR SK699469
✪ 12-2 (not Mon & Tue), 5-11.30; 12-11.30 Sat & Sun
☎ (0115) 966 3629 ⊕ thereindeerinn.com
Black Sheep Best Bitter; Blue Monkey Original; Castle Rock Harvest Pale; guest beers Ⓗ
Genuine free house in a pleasant country village with traditional beams and a log fire for cold winter nights. A central servery divides the bar and restaurant areas of the pub. The well-kept ales are served alongside a good range of home-cooked food including vegetarian and vegan choices. The outside drinking area is served through the pub window and overlooks the village cricket pitch for those who like the sound of leather on willow as they drink. Dog-friendly.
🏚Q❀◑➿(Thurgaton)♣P'⎻

Kimberley

Nelson & Railway ✔
12 Station Road, NG16 2NR
✪ 11-midnight; 12-11.30 Sun ☎ (0115) 938 2177
⊕ nelsonandrailway.co.uk
H&H Bitter; guest beers Ⓗ
Run by the same family for more than 40 years, this popular Victorian pub lies in the shadow of the defunct Kimberley Brewery buildings. Beers are usually from the Greene King portfolio but guests also appear, including a local beer at weekends. This multi-roomed pub has plenty of seating throughout and is renowned for its quality food and accommodation, with 11 rooms available. There are attractive gardens at the front and rear plus ample car parking. ❀➿◑🖵🕭🖵(R1)♣P'⎻

Stag Inn L ✓
67 Nottingham Road, NG16 2NB
✪ 5 (1.30 Sat)-11; 12-10.30 Sun ☎ (0115) 938 3151
Adnams Southwold Bitter; Marston's Pedigree; Taylor Landlord; guest beers Ⓗ
Popular with all ages, this pub is located at the top of the hill, 200 yards from the town centre, and adjacent to Kimberley Town FC's ground. It dates from 1737, and has two rooms linked by a central bar. Pub games such as table skittles and dominoes are played, but at most times conversation reigns. The spacious rear garden includes a children's play area and ample seating. The annual beer festival, held in late May, raises money for charity. The guest beers always include a brew from a lesser-known local brewery. Q⊛&ⵗ무(R1)♣P¹⁻

Kirkby-in-Ashfield

Duke of Wellington
Church Street, NG17 8LA
✪ 12-11; 12-4, 7-11 Sun ☎ (01623) 753044
Marston's Pedigree; Wychwood Hobgoblin; guest beer Ⓗ
A friendly community pub in a 17th-century building with a separate bar and L-shaped lounge. There is a skittles alley, seats and children's play area outside. The popular meals, including vegetarian options, are available at lunchtimes and early evening. Quiz nights are Tuesday, Thursday and Saturday, and an open mic folk club meets on the last Wednesday of the month. CAMRA members receive a discount on beer.
ᴹQ⊛ⵗ⊕ⵗ&ⵗ무(9.3)♣P¹⁻

Lambley

Woodlark Inn L
Church Street, NG4 4QB
✪ 11-11; 12-5.30, 7-11 Sun ☎ (0115) 931 2535
Castle Rock Harvest Pale; Samuel Smith Old Brewery Bitter; Taylor Landlord; guest beer Ⓗ
Tucked away on the edge of the village just past the church, this delightful red-brick local is a quiet pub mercifully free of electronic machines, making the art of conversation a delight. A roaring coal fire greets you on cold winter nights. The bare brick and beamed bar is welcoming and dog-friendly while the comfortable lounge has a justifiable reputation for home cooking (booking recommended, even at lunchtime). The downstairs steak bar opens Friday and Saturday from 7pm.
ᴹQ⊛ⵗ⊕ⵗ무(7)♣♠P¹⁻

Laneham

Meg's Bar
Robin Hood Site, Main Street, DN22 0NA
✪ 4-11 Thu & Fri; 11-11 Sat; 11-8 Sun ☎ (01636) 821000
⊕ springhead.co.uk
Springhead Roaring Meg, The Leveller, Robin Hood Bitter, Maid Marian Blonde, seasonal beers Ⓗ
The brewery tap for Springhead Brewery following its move to Laneham in 2011. A small traditionally furnished single bar room on the brewery site, its windows overlook the plant. The start and finish for brewery tours, six Springhead beers are available at all times and popular brewery gift sets are sold. Events are held regularly throughout the year.
Q⊛무(89,90,736)♠P¹⁻

Laxton

Dovecote Inn
Cross Hill, NG22 0SX
✪ 11.30-3, 5 (6 Sat)-11; 12-10.30 Sun ☎ (01777) 871 586
⊕ dovecoteinnlaxton.co.uk
Beer range varies Ⓗ
Traditional inn situated in the centre of Laxton, a village known for having the last remaining working open field farming system in the country. The pub boasts three cosy wining and dining rooms, a locals' drinking room and a welcoming foyer. Three real ales are available and the pub holds an annual beer festival. Food is served daily lunchtimes and evenings, 12.30-6.30pm on Sunday. The large beer garden has access to Laxton's Visitor Centre. ᴹ⊛ⵗ⊲◖ⵗ&ⵗ무(33,36)P¹⁻

Mansfield

Bold Forester L ✓
Botany Avenue, NG18 5NF
✪ 11-11 (midnight Fri & Sat); 12-11.30 Sun
☎ (01623) 623970
Greene King IPA, Abbot; Morland Old Speckled Hen; Nottingham EPA; Ruddles County; guest beers Ⓗ
Hungry Horse pub and restaurant run by the same landlord for 14 years. Twelve real ales plus Westons Old Rosie cider are available. Food is served all day until 9pm. The spacious interior is open plan, with a raised dining area. Large-screen TVs show live sport. The pub hosts four beer festivals every year, offering up to 30 real ales. A regular winner of local branch CAMRA awards and a regular in the Guide. ⊛◖ⵗ&ⵗ무♠P¹⁻

Court House ✓
Market Place, NG18 1HX (next to town hall)
✪ 9am-11 (midnight Fri & Sat) ☎ (01623) 412720
Greene King Abbot; Ruddles Best Bitter; Marston's Mansfield Cask; guest beers Ⓗ
This friendly community pub in the town centre gets busy, especially at weekends. It offers a comprehensive range of at least five beers, often from local breweries including Springhead and Milestone, plus two regular ciders. Food is served until 10pm every day, offering the typical excellent value and quality associated with Wetherspoon's. Families are welcome. A local CAMRA award winner. Q🌣◖ⵗ&ⵗ무♠¹⁻

Nell Gwyn L
117 Sutton Road, NG18 5EX
✪ 2-midnight (2am Fri & Sat); 12-midnight Sun
☎ (01623) 659850 ⊕ nell-gwyn.com
Copthorne Nell Gwyn; guest beers Ⓗ
One of the first dwellings on Sutton Road, originally a farmhouse, the building became a gentlemen's club in 1927 and now claims to be Mansfield's best-kept secret. The community establishment is home to darts, dominoes and football teams, stages regular charity events and has a loyalty card scheme. The real ale named after the pub is usually on offer, or another local ale. Customers mainly prefer darker bitters. ᴹ무♣¹⁻

Railway Inn L
9 Station Street, NG18 1EF
✪ 11-11 ☎ (01623) 623086
Beer range varies Ⓗ
A true real ale gem with a strong community focus. Two small front rooms lead into the main bar serving three constantly changing, mainly lighter

coloured beers – at least one a LocAle. Westons Old Rosie and another real cider are available, plus a selection of bottled ales. Excellent reasonably priced home-cooked meals are served lunchtimes and evenings. There is a small walled garden and heated smoking area. Dogs are welcome.
Q❀◐◑⊟⇌🚌●⅟–

Redgate 🄻
189 Westfield Lane, NG19 6EH
✪ 12-11 ☎ (01623) 624406 🌐 redgateinn.co.uk
Beer range varies 🄷
A thriving community-focused pub with a friendly and welcoming atmosphere. It has a large public bar with a separate pool and darts area, a skittles alley to the rear and an enclosed illuminated garden. Up to five real ales are available, many from independent micros, including at least one LocAle. Good-quality food is served in the new comfortable restaurant, and also in the bar on request. Sporting photographs and colliery plates are displayed on the bar walls. Dogs are welcome in the bar. ♛❀◐◑⊟🚌(6,23B)♣P⅟–

Stag & Pheasant ✔
Unit 4 Clumber Street, NG18 1NU
✪ 8am-midnight (1am Thu; 2am Fri; 3am Sat)
☎ (01623) 412890
Greene King Abbot; Ruddles Best Bitter; Thornbridge Jaipur IPA; guest beers 🄷
Spacious Lloyds No.1 bar not far from the town centre. It gets busy at weekends, with music after 6pm and a DJ after 9pm on Friday and Saturday, when an entry charge applies. Three regular beers and three guests are usually on offer, plus two regular ciders. The pub serves Wetherspoon's excellent-value meals until 10pm every day.
◐◑♿⇌🚌(1,11,14)●⅟–

Widow Frost ✔
41 Leeming Street, NG18 1NB
✪ 8am-midnight (1am Fri & Sat) ☎ (01623) 666790
Greene King Abbot; Ruddles Best Bitter; guest beers 🄷
Spacious pub situated not far from the town centre. It gets busy, especially at weekends, but it is still possible to find a quiet corner. The full range of excellent value Wetherspoon meals is served until 10pm every day, with a separate family dining area. Up to six beers are available, plus two real ciders, served by friendly staff from a large bar. Regular Meet the Brewer events are held. A local CAMRA award winner numerous times.
Q⛐◐◑♿⇌🚌(1,10,16)●⅟–

Mansfield Woodhouse

Greyhound
82 High Street, NG19 8BD
✪ 12-11 (midnight Fri & Sat); 12-10.30 Sun
☎ (01623) 464403
Adnams Broadside; Caledonian Deuchars IPA; guest beers 🄷
A regular entry in the Guide for the past 19 years. This stone-built pub on the site of a 400-year-old coaching inn is now a thriving community establishment with a comfortable lounge and separate tap room where pool, darts and dominoes are played. The pub holds two mini beer festivals each year. Up to five real ales are available, plus Westons Old Rosie. Quiz nights are Monday and Wednesday. Dogs are welcome in the tap room.
Q❀⊟⇌🚌(1,10)♣●P⅟–

Misterton

Haxey Gate Inn
Haxey Road, DN10 4BA
✪ 12-11 ☎ (01427) 890746 🌐 haxeygate.co.uk
Batemans XB; guest beers 🄷
Occupying an idyllic position beside an ancient bridge over the River Idle, the Haxey Gate Inn is a friendly local specialising in good, wholesome, reasonably priced food and well-kept beer. Diners can enjoy their refreshments throughout the inn, but the front-facing conservatory is popular, with plenty of seating. A choice of four real ales is available including Batemans XB. ♛❀◐◑⊟P⅟–

Newark

Castle 🄻
5 Castlegate, NG24 1AZ
✪ 11-midnight (1am Thu-Sat); 12-midnight Sun
☎ (01636) 640733
Everards Sunchaser; Oldershaws Castle Ale; Sharp's Doom Bar; guest beers 🄷
A lively pub situated opposite the famous Newark Castle. Over the years it has become a popular music venue with open mic sessions on a Sunday afternoon. There are also quieter times when you can enjoy a pint served by friendly, helpful staff. CAMRA members receive a discount. Beer festivals are hosted occasionally. ⇌(Castle)🚌

Just Beer Micropub 🏆 🄻
Swan & Salmon Yard, 32A Castlegate, NG24 1BG
✪ 1-11; 11-midnight Fri & Sat; 12-10 Sun ☎ (07983) 993747
🌐 justbeermicropub.biz
Beer range varies 🄷
Situated just off the historic Castlegate and near Newark Castle, Just Beer opened in 2010 and is Newark CAMRA's Pub of the Year 2012. The single small room has minimalist decor, helpful bar staff and a varied clientele. At least four ever-changing beers are sourced from small or microbreweries and rare beers are often available. Cider and perry are also served. No spirits, keg, lager, smooth or bottles, and no pool or TV.
Q♿Å⇌(Castle)🚌♣●P🗑

Prince Rupert 🄻
46 Stodman Street, NG24 1AW (between Castlegate and market place)
✪ 11-midnight (1am Fri & Sat); 12-midnight Sun
☎ (01636) 918121 🌐 theprincerupert.co.uk
Beer range varies 🄷
Historic building dating back to around 1452, lovingly restored after years of closure. It retains several rooms with original features; there is also an outside drinking area in the courtyard. Beers are sourced from breweries the length and breadth of the UK, and beer festivals are held on a regular basis. High-quality pub food includes speciality pizzas and toppings. A recent addition is a separate room called the Venue, with a separate bar for regular live music events. ♛Q❀◐◑⇌(Castle)🚌●

Vine 🄻
117 Barnbygate, NG24 1QZ
✪ 4 (3 Sat)-11; 12-11 Sun ☎ (07855) 530 5009
Springhead Leveller, Roaring Meg, seasonal beers; guest beers 🄷
Victorian street-corner pub owned by the Springhead Brewery, comprising two main rooms, an L-shaped bar with a pool table and gaming machines, and a lounge with a dartboard. A typical

offering is at least two Springhead beers and one or two guests. The landlord is an enthusiastic CAMRA member and always happy to discuss his beers. 🏠🍴♿🚭(Northgate)♣♪⌐

Normanton on Trent

Crown 🅛
South Street, NG23 6RQ (exit A1 at B1164, follow signs to Normanton) SK792688
🕐 12-11 ☎ (01636) 821973 ⊕ milestonebrewery.co.uk
Beer range varies ⓗ
The only pub owned by the Milestone Brewery, the Crown was sympathetically extended and refurbished several years ago. Although very much a community pub, it is friendly and welcoming to all. The food has a good reputation and the Sunday lunches are popular. There is a safe play area at the back and the car park is a good size. Two to three Milestone beers are always available and the guest is often from another small local brewery.
🏨🏠🕐♿🚪(39)♣P♪⌐

Nottingham: Central

Canalhouse 🅛
48-52 Canal Street, NG1 7EH
🕐 11-11 (midnight Thu; 1am Fri & Sat); 11-10.30 Sun
☎ (0115) 955 5060 ⊕ thecanalhouse.co.uk
Castle Rock Harvest Pale, Preservation; guest beers ⓗ
Listed three-storey Castle Rock pub with a canal inlet on the inside, traversed by wooden walkways. It used to house a canal museum before it was converted to an open-plan pub that retains a certain quiet cosiness. One floor doubles as a function room where many beer festivals have been hosted. The canal-side decked patio is popular in summer, half-covered and heated for overcast evenings. Food, available daily, is varied in choice. 🏠🕐♿🚪(Station St)🚪⌐

Cross Keys 🅛
15 Byard Lane, NG1 2GJ (opp Fletcher Gate car park)
🕐 8am-1am; 9am-1am Sun ☎ (0115) 941 7898
⊕ crosskeysnottingham.co.uk
Batemans XB; Fuller's London Pride; guest beers ⓗ
Reopened in 2010 following a sympathetic refurbishment, the Cross Keys is adjacent to the Lace Market area and tram stop. The interior is welcoming, with high ceilings, wood floorboards and panelling, a mixture of seating and tables, and artwork provided by local artists. A lower level to the rear offers a more comfortable and quiet area to relax in. It usually offers Navigation beers brewed at the sister pub, the Trent Navigation on Meadow Lane, which is also recommended.
🏠🕐♿🚪(Lace Market)🚪(50)

Dragon 🅛 ✔
67 Long Row, NG1 6JE (opp Central Library)
🕐 12-11 (midnight Thu; 1am Fri & Sat); 11-11 Sun
☎ (0115) 941 7080 ⊕ the-dragon.co.uk
Adnams Southwold Bitter, Broadside; Castle Rock Harvest Pale ⓗ
Small and welcoming unspoilt pub with a long, split-level, fairly narrow interior and laid-back ambience. Seating is a combination of bar stools and comfortable benches. There is a delightful enclosed beer garden at the back with seating. An extensive menu of fresh home-cooked food is available until 9pm weekdays and 5pm weekends. 🏠🕐🚪(Market Sq)🚪⌐

Hand & Heart 🍷 🅛
65 Derby Road, NG1 5BA
🕐 12-midnight (11 Mon; 2am Fri & Sat); 12-10.30 Sun
☎ (0115) 958 2456 ⊕ thehandandheart.co.uk
Dancing Duck Round Heart; guest beers ⓗ
Although not apparent from the outside, the pub is built into hollowed-out sandstone rock. The dining area to the rear extends deep into the 'cave', where a large choice of high-quality food is on offer until 9.30pm. Up to eight beers are served from the dual bars, as well as real cider and/or perry. Local ales feature heavily, including at least one beer from a LocAle brewery. Nottingham Pub of the Year 2012. Music nights are generally Tuesday and Thursday. Q🕐♿🚪♣

Kean's Head 🅛
46 St Mary's Gate, NG1 1QA (opp St Mary's Church)
🕐 11.30-11 (12.30am Fri & Sat); 12-10.30 Sun
☎ (0115) 947 4052
Castle Rock Harvest Pale, Preservation, Screech Owl; guest beers ⓗ
Cosy one-room pub opposite the imposing St Mary's Church in the historic Lace Market district – the building was once a lace factory. Named in honour of the 19th-century actor Edmund Kean, it is busy at weekends and attracts a diverse and varied clientele. Owned by the Castle Rock group, it serves inventive, freshly-prepared traditional English and European food from an ever-changing menu. Three guest beers are usually available, often including a dark beer.
🕐♿🚪(Lace Market)🚪

King William IV
6 Eyre Street, Sneinton, NG2 4PB
🕐 12 (11 Sat)-11 ☎ (0115) 958 9864
Oakham JHB, Bishops Farewell; guest beers ⓗ
Nicknamed the King Billy, this cosy Victorian gem nestling on the edge of town is just a stone's throw from the Capital FM Arena. A family-run free house that oozes charm and character, it is a haven for real ale drinkers, with a choice of seven microbrewery ales from near and far, as well as a cider. Occasional live music and televised sports feature. A fine selection of rolls is available. Not to be missed on a visit to Nottingham.
🏠♿🚪(43)♣♪⌐

Lincolnshire Poacher 🅛
161-163 Mansfield Road, NG1 3FR
🕐 11-11 (midnight Thu-Sat); 12-11 Sun ☎ (0115) 941 1584
Castle Rock Harvest Pale, Screech Owl; guest beers ⓗ
Friendly pub with a large bar area on two levels, a snug, conservatory and covered patio area. Thirteen handpumps offer a wide selection of guest beers, mainly from microbreweries, including a mild, stout or porter. Real cider, continental bottled beers and a large selection of malt whiskies are also available. A popular choice of food uses locally sourced ingredients. Live music features on Sundays and Wednesdays. Twinned with the In de Wildeman bar in Amsterdam, this pub is a former local CAMRA Pub of the Year. Q🏠🕐♿🚪♣♪⌐

Malt Cross 🅛
16 St James Street, NG1 6FG (off Market Square)
🕐 11-11 (1am Fri-Sat; 6 Sun) ☎ (0115) 9411048
⊕ maltcross.com
Brewster's Music Hall; guest beers ⓗ
A recent addition to the local real ale scene, this Grade II-listed former Victorian music hall was built by Edwin Hill in 1877 and is now owned by a

charitable trust. Arts projects are hosted in the on-site gallery. The first floor is a gallery of a different kind, viewing the ground floor from all sides. The five handpumps host an ever-changing selection of beers, mainly from local microbreweries. Meals are served until 8pm (5pm Sun). Monday is quiz night and live music plays every Tuesday.
⊄╿☰(Old Market Sq)🚋♣

Organ Grinder ℝ

21 Alfreton Road, Canning Circus, NG7 3JE
✪ 12-11 (11.30 Thu; midnight Fri-Sat) ☎ (0115) 9700630
Batemans XB; Blue Monkey BG Sips, Guerilla, seasonal beers; guest beers Ⓗ
Previously the Red Lion, this pub was bought and refurbished by Blue Monkey Brewery, and is now its brewery tap, hence the name. The single-roomed pub boasts a wood-burning fire, and outside is a decked garden leading to a small first-floor function room, available for hire. The guest beers are usually from other microbreweries, and two real ciders and a perry are always available. No meals, but bar snacks such as pork pies are sold. A welcome addition to the Canning Circus area known for its real ale pubs. ⋈☸╿♣🍺⌐

Round House ℝ

Standard Court, NG1 6FS
✪ 11-11; 12-10.30 Sun ☎ (0115) 924 0120
⊕ theroundhousenottingham.co.uk
Dancing Duck Roundheart; Theakston Black Bull; guest beers Ⓗ
Formerly part of the General Hospital, the building is perfectly circular, hence the name. Main access is via a curved staircase, with disabled access to the side. Polished wood furnishings, comfortable seating areas, low mood lighting and a painted mural ceiling adorn the interior, giving a cosy yet spacious feel. Six beers are available, including house beer Roundheart, with guests from local microbreweries and the East Midlands area, and an occasional real cider. Well known for a quality food menu and bar snacks.
☸╿♿⇌☰(Old Market Sq)🚋♣⌐

Salutation Inn ℝ

Hounds Gate, Maid Marian Way, NG1 7AA
✪ 12-midnight (2am Fri & Sat) ☎ (0115) 947 6580
⊕ salutationpub.com
Beer range varies Ⓗ
Steeped in history, this lively 17th-century inn with oak beams and stone floor is a favourite venue with young and old. Regular live rock music plays upstairs while downstairs there are quieter snugs for drinking and conversation. The pub sells a range of ciders and perries and promotes local beers. A Halloween beer festival is an annual highlight. Good food is based on local produce and cooked on the premises. The labyrinth of caves under the pub is reputed to be haunted.
⋈☸╿♿⇌☰(Market Sq)🚋🍺⌐

VAT & Fiddle ℝ

12-14 Queen's Bridge Road, NG2 1NB
✪ 11-11 (midnight Fri & Sat); 12-11 Sun ☎ (0115) 985 0611
Castle Rock Sheriff's Tipple, Harvest Pale, Preservation, Screech Owl; guest beers Ⓗ
Adjacent to the Castle Rock Brewery and a minute's walk from the railway station, an extension in 2011 added an extra room and a brewery visitors' centre. With 12 handpumps, the full range is offered, including the monthly Wildlife Trust beers, and a guest mild. To the front is a seating area

where patrons can admire the building's Art Deco frontage, the floral displays in summer, or simply watch the traffic go by. Hot food is served weekdays, plus Sunday lunch.
Q☸⊄╿♿⇌☰(Station St)🚋♣🍺⌐

Nottingham: East

Bread & Bitter ℝ

153-155 Woodthorpe Drive, Mapperley, NG3 5JL
✪ 10-11 (midnight Thu-Sat); 11-11 Sun ☎ (0115) 960 7541
Castle Rock Black Gold, Harvest Pale, Preservation, Screech Owl; guest beers Ⓗ
Castle Rock pub built in 2007 on the premises of the old Judge's Bakery on Mapperley Top. The original baker's oven fronts are still embedded in an inside wall, giving the place a warm and welcoming feel. The pub started a revival of real ale outlets in Mapperley. Up to 12 beers, including LocAles, a mild and rotating guests, are available, along with an extensive foreign bottled beer list. Food is all home cooked and varies frequently – look for the specials board. Q☸⊄╿♿☰(25,45)⌐

Nottingham: North

Gladstone ℝ ✅

45 Loscoe Road, Carrington, NG5 2AW (off A60)
✪ 5 (3 Fri; 12 Sat)-11 (11.30 Thu-Sat); 12-11 Sun
☎ (0115) 912 9994
Castle Rock Harvest Pale; Fuller's London Pride; Nottingham EPA; Taylor Landlord; guest beers Ⓗ
In the middle of a Victorian terrace, this two-roomed back-street local has a narrow public bar with memorabilia on display and a TV showing sporting events. A similarly shaped lounge is pleasantly decorated with old bottles, brass ornaments and pictures. Customers may browse the shelf of old books, if so inclined. The Carrington Folk Club has been meeting in the upstairs function room on a Wednesday night for more than 25 years. Beer festivals are held in May and September. ☸╿☰♣⌐

Horse & Groom ℝ ✅

462 Radford Road, Basford, NG7 7EA
✪ 12 (4 Mon & Tue)-11 (midnight Fri; 11.30 Sat)
☎ (0115) 970 3777 ⊕ horseandgroombasford.com
Caledonian Deuchars IPA; Shepherd Neame Spitfire; guest beers Ⓗ
Popular corner pub situated a few yards away from the defunct Shipstones Brewery. The main entrance is via steps to the front door, but there is disabled access towards the rear on request. Although small, the pub has several distinct areas on two levels, including a function room, each with its own character. The bar accommodates nine handpumps serving mainly microbrewery beers, including a mild, and at least one local guest. There is a quiz on Monday night.
⋈Q╿☰(Shipstone St)🚋(L12-14)♣🍺

Hotel Deux ℝ

Clumber Avenue, Sherwood Rise, NG5 1AP
✪ 5-11 (11.30 Fri & Sat) ☎ (0115) 985 6724
⊕ theguitarbar.co.uk
Blue Monkey BG Sips; guest beers Ⓗ
Formerly a hotel, now a pub with a friendly, comfortably furnished main bar overlooking the front garden. The range of four beers varies, but usually includes a beer each from Whim and Blue Monkey. Off the main bar is the Guitar Bar,

featuring live entertainment at weekends from local, national and sometimes international artists (see website for details). A separate function room is much used by the local community. Board games are available. ✿🖳P🏃‍♂️

Nottingham: West

Johnson Arms 🅛 ✅
59 Abbey Street, Lenton, NG7 2NZ
✿ 12 (4 Sat)-11 ☎ (0115) 978 6355 ⊕ johnsonarms.co.uk
Adnams Southwold Bitter; guest beers 🖽
Popular with students and hospital workers due to the proximity of the University of Nottingham and QMC hospital, this former Shipstones house retains the original etched windows, complemented by a green-tiled frontage. The pub prides itself in its guest ales including LocAles, as well as real cider, quarterly beer festivals and traditional home-cooked food. An open-plan split-level bar area leads out to the magnificent beer garden with a pétanque court, where the annual Johnsonbury Music Festival is held. ✿🌓🚌(13,14)♣👣🏃‍♂️

Plough 🅛 ✅
17 St Peters Street, Radford, NG7 3EN
✿ 12-midnight ☎ (0115) 970 2615
Nottingham Rock Mild, Rock Bitter, Legend, EPA 🖽
Linked with the old Nottingham Brewery since 1887, the Plough is now the brewery tap for the revived company. A full range of Nottingham beers is served, four regular and four rotating. The present building, a 1932 two-room house with a central servery, is largely unchanged. Attracting regulars from a wide area, this 'village pub in the city' has retained its local feel in a period of rapid change, offering real fires, an outside skittle alley and a popular quiz night. 🏘️Q✿🌓🍴♿🖳♣👣P🏃‍♂️

Radcliffe-on-Trent

Horse Chestnut 🅛 ✅
49 Main Road, NG12 2BE
✿ 12-3, 5-11 Mon, 12-11 (11.30 Fri & Sat)
☎ (0115) 933 1994 ⊕ horsechestnutradcliffe.com
Batemans XB; Castle Rock Harvest Pale; Sharp's Doom Bar; guest beers 🖽
Previously known as the Cliffe Inn, this LocAle-accredited pub was totally refurbished in 2006 with a smart 1920s-style decor. Six reasonably priced real ales are served including ever-changing guests. Very much a smart local pub that sells food, rather than a restaurant that sells beer, the high quality meals are made with local ingredients. Thursday is quiz night, on Wednesday there is a themed food night, Saturday is steak night and Friday features fish and chips. ✿🌓♿🚅🖳👣P🏃‍♂️

Retford

Brick & Tile Inn
81 Moorgate, DN22 6RS
✿ 12-3 (5 Sat; 4 Sun), 7-11 ☎ (01777) 703681
Beer range varies 🖽
A quiet pub situated on the main road between Retford and Gainsborough. There is always a choice of two real ales available here – one a light beer and the other dark, usually from local breweries Idle, Springhead and Milestone. Two twin rooms and two single rooms are available. Q✿🛏🖳P🏃‍♂️

Rum Runner
Wharf Road, DN22 6EN (by fire station)
✿ 12-midnight (1am Fri & Sat) ☎ (01777) 860788
Batemans XB, XXB; guest beers 🖽
Formerly home to the now-closed Broadstone Brewery, the interior includes a long room warmed by a real fire and a second room, with its own serving hatch through to the bar, which can be used for meetings. A quiz night is held on Wednesday and frequent music nights are hosted. Mini beer festivals are a regular feature. Outside is a large enclosed beer garden. 🏘️Q✿🌓🖳♣👣🏃‍♂️

Turk's Head ✅
Grove Street, DN22 6LE
✿ 11-2.30, 5-11; 11-11 Sat; 12-11 Sun ☎ (01777) 702742
Beer range varies 🖽
Situated close to the main Market Square, entry to this pub is via two large oak doors, which both lead into an open-plan area served by an L-shaped bar. The room features plenty of oak panelling and has a large warming open fire. At the far end is a pool table. Four real ales are served. 🏘️🖳♣🏃‍♂️

Ruddington

Three Crowns 🅛
23 Easthorpe Street, NG11 6LB
✿ 12-3 (not Mon & Tue), 5-11; 12-11 Sat; 12-10.30 Sun
☎ (0115) 921 3226 ⊕ ruddingtonbeer.co.uk
Fuller's London Pride; Nottingham Rock Mild, EPA; guest beers 🖽
Modern, friendly local pub serving great real ale. One of the most popular pubs in the village, it is known as the Top House because of its position at the top end of Easthope, a street of three pubs. It is properly named the Three Crowns due to its roof-top chimneys. Excellent Indian food is available in the Dine India restaurant, which is open in the evenings at the rear of the building. The pub participates in the annual village beer festival. CAMRA discounts are offered. 🏘️🌓🚌

White Horse 🅛
60 Church Street, NG11 6HD
✿ 12-11 (11.30 Thu-Sat); 12-10.30 Sun ☎ (0115) 984 4550
⊕ whitehorseruddington.co.uk
Belvoir Beaver Best Bitter; Wells Bombardier; guest beers 🖽
Traditional community local with two light and airy rooms and a central bar where the emphasis is on quality beer and good conversation. The pub hosts the annual village beer festival, held for the past 10 years. There is a spacious, attractive courtyard complete with sunny aspect and barbecue on occasion. Food is served lunchtimes Tuesday to Sunday, evenings Tuesday to Thursday. Quiz night is Thursday. Situated on the south side of the village, with regular bus services to Nottingham. Q✿🌓🍴🖳♣👣P🏃‍♂️

Selston

Horse & Jockey 🍷 🅛
Church Lane, NG16 6FB SK459535
✿ 12-3.30, 5-1am; 12-4, 7-1am Sun ☎ (01773) 781012
Adnams Broadside 🖽**; Greene King Abbot; Taylor Landlord** 🅖**; guest beers** 🖽
A drinking man's pub dating back to 1664 with large open fires and old flagstone floors. Up to six real ales are available, two served from the jug plus four changing guests including a LocAle. Two

real ciders are always available. A quiz is held on Sunday evening and a folk night every Wednesday. No hot food is served. A winner of many CAMRA awards including local Pub of the Year 2012.
🅜Q🐾🕪🕭🖫(90,331)🍀🍺P⬗

Southwell

Final Whistle 🅛
Station Street, NG25 0ET
✪ 12-11.30 (midnight Fri & Sat; 11 Sun) ☎ (01636) 814953
Everards Tiger; Leatherbritches Cad, Bounder; guest beers 🅗
Brilliant Everards renovation of a previous pub at the terminus of the Southwell Trail, formerly the Beeching-cut rail line. A superb reconstruction of a 1920s railway station, it is full of railway memorabilia with booking offices, fireplaces and an open waiting room. The beer garden is styled as the platform, with seating and the old railway track alongside. Ten real ales plus six real ciders are always available in tip-top condition. Filled rolls, pies and cheeseboard snacks are served. Occasional live music plays.
🅜Q🐾🕪🖫(100)🍀🍺P⬗

Hearty Goodfellow 🅛
81 Church Street, NG25 0HQ
✪ 12-3 (not Mon), 5-midnight; 12-1am Fri & Sat; 12-midnight Sun ☎ (01636) 812365 ⊕ heartygoodfellowpub.co.uk
Everards Tiger; guest beers 🅗
A friendly pub dating from the 18th century with a warm welcome for all. Good food, served lunchtimes only, is sourced from local ingredients. The large attractive garden is particularly family friendly with a play area for children. A recent addition is the barn, a separate room available for hire. Eight handpulls offer at least one beer from the Mallard Brewery, brewed by landlord Steve in a nearby village. 🐾🕪🖫(90,100)🍀P⬗

Staunton in the Vale

Staunton Arms 🅛
NG13 9PE
✪ 12-11 (midnight Fri & Sat); 11-10 Sun ☎ (01400) 281218 ⊕ stauntonarms.co.uk
Castle Rock Harvest Pale; Draught Bass; guest beer 🅗
Two hundred-year-old listed pub in the far north of the Vale of Belvoir, carefully restored to retain its original character. The large bar offers comfortable seating for drinkers and diners, with a further separate raised restaurant area. The pub serves freshly prepared meals lunchtimes and evenings, and three cask beers, one always a LocAle. Mini-festivals are held occasionally, with upcoming events publicised on the website. 🅜Q🐾🚗🕪⬗🅟

Sutton-in-Ashfield

Masons Arms 🅛
Unwin Road, NG17 4NB (on corner of Eastfield Side and Unwin Rd)
✪ 12-11 ☎ (01623) 472704 ⊕ themasonsarmspub.co.uk
Beer range varies 🅗
Easily recognisable with its solar panels on the roof, the pub has become a thriving community hostelry with a friendly atmosphere. The comfortable lounge and large public bar are served from a central bar dispensing two ever-changing real ales and one real cider. Blue Monkey, Welbeck Abbey and Abbeydale often feature. Dominoes is played

and darts is popular, with the pub boasting four teams. A new conservatory has been added to the rear. Dogs welcome. Q🐾🕪🖫(17)🍀🍺P⬗

Underwood

Red Lion
Church Lane, NG16 5HD (off B600)
✪ 12-11 (midnight Fri & Sat) ☎ (01773) 810482
Jennings Cumberland Ale; Marston's Pedigree; guest beers 🅗
Parts of this friendly local are over 300 years old, with more recent extensions. Four real ales are available, including two ever-changing guests. The beamed ceiling displays pump clips from the many different guest beers served. The pub gets busy lunchtimes and evenings for food, offering an extensive menu featuring specials, all cooked to order. Children are welcome in the restaurant and there is a large play area outside. Q🐾🕪🖫P⬗

Watnall

Queen's Head
40 Main Road, NG16 1HT
✪ 12 (11.30 Thu & Fri)-midnight ☎ (0115) 938 6774
⊕ thequeensheadwatnall.co.uk
Adnams Broadside; Everards Tiger, Original; Morland Old Speckled Hen; Wells Bombardier; guest beer 🅗
A 17th-century rural gem with a lounge/dining space, a small snug hidden behind the bar and an unusual locals' area with a grandfather clock. The extensive garden has children's play equipment, making the pub popular all year. The internal fittings around the bar are original, and old photos adorn the walls adding to the pub's ambience. Home-cooked English food is served lunchtimes and weekday evenings. The pub is reputedly haunted. Occasional beer festivals and live music feature. 🅜Q🐾🕪🕭🗗(331)P⬗

West Bridgford

Poppy & Pint 🅛
Pierrepont Road, NG2 5DX
✪ 9.30am (10am Sun)-11 ☎ (0115) 981 9995
Castle Rock Black Gold, Harvest Pale, Preservation, Screech Owl; Fuller's London Pride; guest beers 🅗
Former British Legion Club converted in 2011 to become Castle Rock's largest pub. It has separate rooms, a large main bar with a raised area and a family area (children welcome until 9pm), and a café bar, all with a homely, welcoming feel. Look for the old snooker table ends on one wall. A large function room is upstairs. The beer garden overlooks a bowling green and is adjacent to tennis courts. Eleven handpumps dispense the Castle Rock beers plus ales from new breweries. Excellent food is served. Q🐾🕪🕭🖫🍺P⬗

Stratford Haven 🅛
2 Stratford Road, NG2 6BA
✪ 10.30-11 (midnight Thu-Sat); 12-11 Sun
☎ (0115) 982 5981
Batemans XB; Castle Rock Sheriff's Tipple, Harvest Pale, Elsie Mo; Everards Tiger; Hop Back Summer Lightning 🅗
A former pet shop, the pub has a single narrow bar with a larger seating area at the back and a secluded snug to one side. Up to 13 cask ales are available at any one time, including LocAles from owner Castle Rock's portfolio. A wide range of food

includes curry night on Monday and pie night on Tuesday. Sunday is quiz night and a brewery evening is held on the second Tuesday of the month. Q❀◑▧⌨⏚

West Stockwith

White Hart
Main Street, DN10 4ET
❀ 12-11 ☎ (01427) 890176
Idle Idle Landlord; guest beers Ⓗ
Small country pub with a little garden overlooking the River Trent, Chesterfield Canal and West Stockwith Marina. One bar serves the through bar, lounge and dining area. The Idle Brewery is situated in outbuildings at the side of the pub and the range of five real ales usually includes three from Idle. The area is especially busy during the summer, due to the canal and river traffic.
Q◑▧Å⌨(97)♣P

Westwood

Corner Pin Ⓛ
75 Palmerston Street, NG16 5HY (off B6016)
❀ 1-11 (midnight Fri); 12-midnight Sat & Sun
☎ (07908) 531901
Naked Hopsession, Kiss M'Willie, Oracle, Palindrome; guest beer Ⓗ
A free house with its own on-site Naked brewery, the licensee is the head brewster. It has separate lounge and public bars with open fires, plus a function room and games room for pool and skittles. Six handpumps dispense the house beers and guests from local micros. An annual beer festival is held and dogs are welcome. Poker is played. Winner of numerous local CAMRA branch awards. ⋈Q❧❀⌨(R1,90)♣♠P⏚

Worksop

Grafton Hotel
157-161 Gateford Road, S80 1UJ
❀ 3 (12 Sat & Sun)-11.30 ☎ (01909) 768089
Grafton Dark Lady; guest beers Ⓗ
The brewery tap for the Grafton Brewing Company, at least three of its beers are always available at reasonable prices as well as guests from other local breweries. A lively community pub, it has a spacious bar area and restaurant serving good-value food. It is situated close to the railway station and Worksop Town Football Club, and offers good accommodation. ⋈⌂◑▧⇌⌨♣⏚

Mallard ⏨
Station Approach, S81 7AG (on railway platform)
❀ 12 (5 Mon; 11 Fri & Sat)-11; 12-10.30
Sun ☎ 07973 521824

Beer range varies Ⓗ
Formerly the Worksop station buffet, the Mallard is situated within the railway station buildings, with access from the car park. The pub offers a warm welcome as well as four real ales usually including one from the Double Top Brewery, a selection of foreign bottled beers and country fruit wines. A further room is available downstairs for special occasions – such as the three beer festivals the pub holds each year. Q⇌⌨P

Shireoaks Inn
Westgate, S80 1LT
❀ 11.30-4, 6-11; 11.30-11 Sat; 12-10.30 Sun
☎ (01909) 472118 ⊕ shireoaksinn.co.uk
Beer range varies Ⓗ
Warm, friendly pub converted from cottages. The public bar houses a pool table and large-screen TV, and the comfortable lounge bar has a separate dining area. Tasty home-cooked food is good value for money. The two handpulls dispense regularly changing guest ales. A small outside area with tables is available in the summer.
Q❀◑▧Å⌨♣⏚

Station Hotel
Carlton Road, S81 7AG (opp railway station)
❀ 11 (12 Sun)-11 ☎ (01909) 474108
⊕ thestationhotelworksop.co.uk
Acorn Barnsley Bitter; guest beers Ⓗ
Situated opposite Worksop railway station on the edge of the town centre. Four regularly changing real ales are available alongside the Barnsley Bitter. One long bar serves a large bar area with a separate dining room, and there is a further small room suitable for functions and meetings. Food is served lunchtimes and evenings and accommodation is offered. ❀⌂◑Å⇌⌨P⏚

Wysall

Plough Inn Ⓛ ✅
Main Street, Keyworth Road, NG12 5QQ
❀ 12-midnight ☎ (01509) 880339 ⊕ ploughatwysall.co.uk
Draught Bass; Greene King Abbot; Taylor Landlord; guest beers Ⓗ
A busy country pub in existence for more than 150 years, and for the last 14 years owned by the same family. This pleasantly updated village free house retains many period features and much original character, with an attractive beer garden at the front. A sensibly priced menu of traditional home-cooked pub favourites is available at lunchtime. Dogs are welcome after 3pm when food is finished. There is a separate area for pool, and a quiz is hosted on Tuesday. ⋈Q❀◑⌨(63)♣P⏚

The discreet barman

Over the mahogany, jar followed jorum, gargle, tincture and medium, tailor, scoop, snifter and ball of malt, in a breathless pint-to-pint. Discreet barman, Mr Sugrue thought, turning outside the door and walking in the direction of Stephen's Green. Never give anything away – part of the training. Is Mr so-and-so there, I'll go and see, strict instructions never to say yes in case it might be the wife. Curious now the way the tinge of wickedness hung around the pub, a relic of course of Victorianism, nothing to worry about as long as a man kept himself in hand.
Jack White, The Devil You Know, 1962

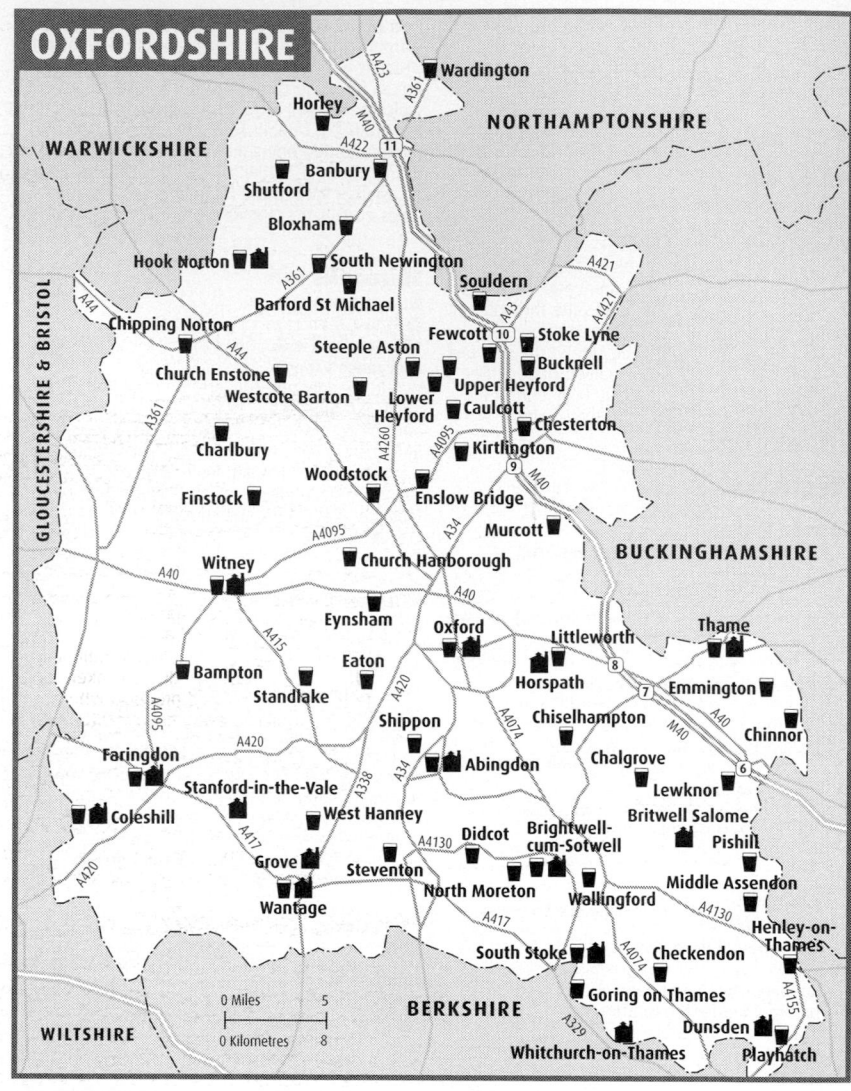

OXFORDSHIRE

Wardington
Horley
WARWICKSHIRE
NORTHAMPTONSHIRE
Banbury
Shutford
Bloxham
Hook Norton
South Newington
Souldern
Barford St Michael
GLOUCESTERSHIRE & BRISTOL
Chipping Norton
Fewcott
Stoke Lyne
Steeple Aston
Bucknell
Church Enstone
Upper Heyford
Westcote Barton
Lower
Caulcott
Heyford
Chesterton
Charlbury
Kirtlington
Woodstock
Finstock
Enslow Bridge
Murcott
BUCKINGHAMSHIRE
Witney
Church Hanborough
Eynsham
Oxford
Littleworth
Thame
Bampton
Eaton
Horspath
Emmington
Standlake
Shippon
Chiselhampton
Chinnor
Faringdon
Abingdon
Chalgrove
Stanford-in-the-Vale
Lewknor
Coleshill
West Hanney
Britwell Salome
Pishill
Grove
Didcot
Brightwell-
Middle Assendon
Steventon
cum-Sotwell
Wantage
North Moreton
Wallingford
Henley-on-
Thames
South Stoke
Checkendon
0 Miles   5
Goring on Thames
0 Kilometres   8
Dunsden
WILTSHIRE
BERKSHIRE
Whitchurch-on-Thames
Playhatch

Abingdon

Brewery Tap 🅻 ✅
40-42 Ock Street, OX14 5BZ
🕑 11-11.30 (1am Fri & Sat); 12-11 Sun ☎ (01235) 521655
🌐 thebrewerytap.net
**Loose Cannon Abingdon Bridge; Morland Original;
guest beers** Ⓗ
Morland created a tap for its brewery in 1993 by
converting three Grade II-listed town houses. The
brewery closed and its site was redeveloped in
2000, following a takeover by Greene King, but the
pub, run by the same family since it opened, has
thrived. There are usually four regularly changing
guest beers, including local ales not from the
Greene King list. The pub holds three beer festivals
a year. ♨Q🐕🛏◄🕮🖶(X3)♣P🚫

Bampton

Morris Clown
High Street, OX18 2JW

🕑 5 (1 Sat)-11; 12-10.30 Sun ☎ (01993) 850217
Brakspear Bitter; guest beers Ⓗ
A regular in the Guide and run by the same family
for two generations, the walls of this popular pub
are decorated with murals featuring past
customers. The single-bar inn is heated in the
winter by a huge log fire. Bar billiards is played,
while Aunt Sally features in the sprawling rear
garden. Real cider is available in the summer
months. The local community and morris dancers
are much in evidence at this true free house.
♨Q🐕🖶(18)♣♠P🚫

Banbury

Bell Inn ✅
12 Middleton Road, OX16 4QJ
🕑 1-3 (not Mon & Tue), 7-11; 1-11 Fri & Sat; 12-5.30, 8-10.30
Sun ☎ (01295) 253169
Adnams Southwold Bitter; guest beers Ⓗ
A regular Guide entry, the Bell is a comfortable,
unpretentious two-bar local, offering consistently

good beer. Run by the same family for decades, it hosts quiz nights, darts, dominoes, pool and Aunt Sally. Adnams Southwold Bitter is the regular on handpump supplemented by two other beers such as Cairngorm Trade Winds and Tring Side Pocket. The pub holds a beer festival in late March and is a venue for Banbury Folk Festival in October. Handy for bus and railway stations. ♨❀◐⊟≈⊟♣P⁻

Barford St Michael

George Inn

Lower Street, OX15 0RH (off B4031)

12-3 (Sat only), 7-11; 12-4 Sun ☎ (01869) 338226

Beer range varies H

At the heart of the village, this charming thatched free house dates from 1672. Landlord Martin provides a friendly welcome and a changing range of beers plus cider and perry from Westons and others. Labrador Dillon assists, but has been known to purloin items from low-lying handbags! A beer festival is held in summer. No food is served but weddings and functions can be catered for with a marquee in the garden. Opening hours can be varied to suit groups on request. Q❀⊟Å♣●P⁻

Bloxham

Elephant & Castle ✔

Humber Street, OX15 4LZ (off A361 4 miles W of Banbury)

10-3, 6-11; 10-11 Sat; 12-11 Sun ☎ (01295) 720383

bloxhampub.co.uk

Hook Norton Hooky Bitter, seasonal beers; guest beer H

Warm, welcoming 16th-century pub, in the hands of the same family for 40 years. The arched carriageway entrance once straddled the turnpike from Banbury to Chipping Norton. The old bread oven can still be seen in the dining area. Good food is served at lunchtimes (no food Sun). Dogs on leads are welcome. Current CAMRA Branch Cider Pub of the Year, with five or six ciders and perries from Westons. ♨❀⊟◐⊟♿⊟(488)♣●P⁻

Brightwell-cum-Sotwell

Red Lion 🏆 L

Brightwell Street, OX10 0RT

12-3, 6-11 (7-10.30 Sun) ☎ (01491) 837373 redlion.biz

Loddon Hoppit; West Berkshire Good Old Boy; guest beers H

A fine 16th-century village pub, popular with both locals and visitors. Excellent ales come from nearby breweries such as Loddon, Appleford and West Berkshire, as well as from further afield. Quality, locally sourced food is served including beef and lamb from Little Wittenham and vegetarian choices. Pub and community events are well supported, with pudding nights, pub quizzes, music festivals, art classes and French conversation lessons. Firmly established as one of South Oxfordshire's outstanding pubs, it was local CAMRA Pub of the Year 2012. ♨Q❀◐◑⊟(131)P⁻

Bucknell

Trigger Pond ✔

Bicester Road, OX27 7NE

12-11 ☎ (01869) 252817 triggerpond.co.uk

Wadworth IPA, 6X, Malt 'n' Hops; guest beer H

Three miles from jct 10 of the M40, this is a delightful country inn on the outskirts of Bicester, with two log fires, big comfy armchairs and a lovely conservatory dining room. At least four Wadworth ales are usually on handpump at any one time. Great food is served every day, made with locally sourced produce. Highlights include an outstanding Sunday roast, curry night on Thursday and fish on Friday. The large beer garden is ideal for summer evening relaxation. ♨Q❀◐◑♣P⁻▯

Caulcott

Horse & Groom L

Lower Heyford Road, OX25 4ND (on B4030 between Middleton Stoney and Lower Heyford)

12-3, 6-11; 12-3, 7-10.30 Sun ☎ (01869) 343257

horseandgroomcaulcott.co.uk

White Horse Bitter; guest beers H

A small pub with a big welcome —the French landlord/chef offers excellent food and the Bastille Day beer festival is not to be missed. A genuine free house, three guest ales often come from local micros and Cornish brewers. Real cider is sold in summer. Booking is advised for meals, especially Sunday lunch. No dogs or under-sevens permitted inside. The garden is popular in summer; car parking is available nearby. Local CAMRA Pub of the Year 2010. ♨Q❀◐◑♿●⁻

Chalgrove

Red Lion

115 High Street, OX44 7SS SU635970

11.30-3, 6-midnight (all day Sat summer); 12-11.30 Sun

☎ (01865) 890625 redlionchalgrove.co.uk

Butcombe Bitter; Fuller's London Pride; guest beers H

Church-owned village local run by a friendly husband and wife team, both trained chefs. Good food is a speciality at this picturesque 16th-century pub. The interior is divided into several distinct areas and the pub is used by a wide cross-section of the village community. Outside drinking is available in both front and rear gardens. ♨Q❀◐◑♿⊟(101,106)♣⁻

Charlbury

Rose & Crown ✔

Market Street, OX7 3PL

INDEPENDENT BREWERIES

- **Adkin** Wantage
- **Appleford** Brightwell-cum-Sotwell
- **Bellingers** Grove
- **Betjeman** Wantage
- **Brakspear (Marston's)** Witney
- **Complete Pig** Britwell Salome
- **Faringdon** Faringdon (NEW)
- **Hen House** Whitchurch-on-Thames (NEW)
- **Hook Norton** Hook Norton
- **Loddon** Dunsden
- **Loose Cannon** Abingdon
- **Old Bog** Oxford
- **Old Forge** Coleshill
- **Ridgeway** South Stoke
- **Shotover** Horspath
- **Thame** Thame
- **White Horse** Stanford-in-the-Vale
- **Wychwood (Marston's)** Witney

🕐 12-11 (1am Fri); 11-1am Sat ☎ (01608) 810103
🌐 roseandcrown.charlbury.com
Ramsbury Bitter; guest beers Ⓗ
Accomplished town-centre free house featuring in 26 consecutive editions of the Guide. It offers one of the best beer selections in the area, with one regular ale and six guests from micros across the UK (often Wye Valley and Loddon, and golden ales from Abbeydale, Kelham Island and Salopian). The simply furnished bar hosts fortnightly Saturday live music, and there is a comfortable rear lounge with a pool table. Outside is a small patio. A popular annual beer festival is held at the end of January.
🏚🛏🏮♿🚲🚃(X9,S3)♣🐾⌐

Checkendon

Black Horse
Burncote Lane, RG8 0TE (500yds along narrow lane NE from Checkendon-Stoke Row road) SU666841
🕐 12-2 (3 Sun), 7-11 ☎ (01491) 680418
West Berkshire Old Father Thames, Good Old Boy; White Horse Bitter Ⓖ
Buried in the Chilterns woods, the effort of finding this old-fashioned, 300-year-old Guide regular, which has been run by the same family for 107 years, is rewarded by three excellent gravity-dispensed beers. The two-roomed pub welcomes an eclectic mix of locals, walkers, horse riders and cyclists. The outside toilets are not to be missed. Unusually for the area, filled rolls at lunchtime are the only food that is available. During the winter months opening times may vary.
🏚Q🛏🏮♿🚃(142,145)P⌐

Chesterton

Red Cow
The Green, OX26 1UU
🕐 12-3, 6-11; 12-12.30am Fri & Sat; 12-10.30 Sun
☎ (01869) 241337
Greene King IPA, seasonal beer; guest beer Ⓗ
A welcoming community pub on the outskirts of the village on the back road from Bicester Avenue and the A41. The landlady makes imaginative use of the guest beer list and a non-Greene King beer is regularly found alongside the seasonal ale. The single-room bar has a separate dining area where good home-cooked food is made to order. A coffee morning is held every Tuesday. The garden is popular in summer. 🏚🏮🍴🚃(25,25A)♣P⌐

Chinnor

Red Lion
3 High Street, OX39 4DL (on B4009)
🕐 12-2, 5-11; 12-10.30 Sun ☎ (01844) 353468
🌐 redlionchinnor.co.uk
Beer range varies Ⓗ
Situated near the centre of the village, this 300-year-old local was originally three cottages. Set in the heart of the fine Chiltern countryside, it is also close to the local steam railway station. Guest ales often come from local breweries, including seasonal beers, and usually change twice weekly. Quiz nights are held monthly. Wooden decking with lighting and heating provides an outside drinking area. Families and well-behaved dogs are welcome. No meals Sunday evening.
🏚Q🏮🍴🚲🚃(40)♣P⌐

Chipping Norton

Chequers ✓
Goddards Lane, OX7 5NP (next to theatre, on corner of Spring Street)
🕐 11-11 (midnight Fri & Sat) ☎ (01608) 644717
🌐 chequers-pub.com
Fuller's Chiswick Bitter, Discovery, London Pride, ESB; Gale's HSB; guest beers Ⓗ
Traditional English pub with an emphasis on real ale and home-cooked food. Up to eight ales from the Fuller's range are available plus guests, as well as a range of bottled ales. The pub is a popular meeting place for discerning drinkers and also convenient for theatregoers. The bar has four separate areas and there is an airy restaurant and function room to the rear. Look out for the annual beer festival in September and tasting evenings. CAMRA members receive a five per cent discount Monday to Wednesday. 🏚Q🍴🚃

Fox Hotel ✓
Market Place, OX7 5DD
🕐 10-11.30; 12-4 Sun ☎ (01608) 642658
🌐 thefoxatchippy.co.uk
Hook Norton Hooky Bitter, Old Hooky; guest beer Ⓗ
Located in the centre of Chipping Norton, this is one of only two Hook Norton Brewery hotels, with a committed local clientele. A popular venue for local interest groups, it hosts monthly folk evenings, the annual Boxing Day meet, a carol service with the town's Silver Band and other seasonal events. Good food includes daily changing specials and an à la carte menu with traditional Sunday roasts. All ages are welcome, and dogs too. Adjacent to bus stops for all routes, the town's only taxi rank is outside. 🏚Q🛏🏮🍴🛌🚃♣🐾⌐

Red Lion
Albion Street, OX7 5BJ
🕐 9.30-11 ☎ (01608) 644641
Hook Norton Hooky Bitter; guest beer Ⓗ
The smallest pub in Chipping Norton, dating back to 1684, this is an ideal place to visit for a pint of Hook Norton beer and some good conversation. There are no jukeboxes or machines. The pub has a roaring fire in winter and a beer garden for the summer, and a giant vegetable competition is held each year. Pub lunches are served. A real community pub, much fundraising for charities is carried out. Wi-Fi available. 🏚Q🏮🚃♣

Chiselhampton

Coach & Horses Ⓛ
Watlington Road, OX44 7UX (on B480)
🕐 11-11; 11-3.30, 7-10.30 Sun ☎ (01865) 890255
🌐 coachhorsesinn.co.uk
Hook Norton Old Hooky; guest beers Ⓗ
This 16th-century hotel and restaurant provides visitors with good-quality ales and an à la carte menu. There are several dining areas and a dedicated bar. The large patio area has ample room for those who like their alfresco summer drinking. The River Thame is only 200 yards away, providing excellent local fishing and walking. For those looking to stay, there are nine en-suite bedrooms and free Wi-Fi. 🏚🏮🛌🍴♿🚃(101,106)P

Church Enstone

Crown
Mill Lane, OX7 4NN (off A44, on B4030)

✪ 12-3, 6-11; 12-4 Sun ☎ (01608) 677262
Hook Norton Hooky Bitter; guest beers Ⓗ
Enchanting 17th-century Cotswold stone village inn – a wonderful place to visit after a walk in the countryside. A popular pub for locals and tourists alike, features include an inglenook fireplace and wood beams. Local photographs of days gone by adorn the exposed stone walls. The absence of a jukebox or games machines encourages polite conversation. An award-winning menu features locally sourced produce. Well-behaved dogs are welcome, as are children. ♨Q✿❀◑🛏(S3)P

Church Hanborough

Hand & Shears

Church Road, OX29 8AB
✪ 12-3, 6-11; 12-4, 6-10.30 Sun ☎ (01993) 881392
⊕ handandshearswitney.co.uk
Wells Eagle IPA, Bombardier Ⓗ
'When you are in here we are in good company' is the motto over the fireplace of this family-run pub. The traditional village inn, situated opposite the Church with its famous steeple, dates back to the 17th century. The spacious interior has well-furnished bars and dining areas, providing ample room for drinkers and diners alike. Two draught ales are always available. Quality home-cooked, locally sourced food is served seven days a week. Walkers and dogs are welcome. ♨◑▣🛏♣

Coleshill

Radnor Arms Ⓛ

32 Coleshill, SN6 7PR (on B4019)
✪ 12-11; 12-10.30 Sun ☎ (01793) 861575
⊕ radnorarmscoleshill.co.uk
Old Forge Anvil Ale, Blacksmiths Gold, Hammer & Tongs, Sledgehammer Ⓗ/Ⓖ
Set in a beautiful National Trust village, the 18th-century building was the former smithy to the Coleshill estate. Old blacksmith's tools are displayed in the split-level two-room interior; one room has its own snug. This is the brewery tap for the on-site Old Forge Brewery. The beers are dispensed by gravity and handpump to be enjoyed with the traditional home-cooked pub fare. Walkers, children and well-behaved dogs are welcome. Local, county and regional CAMRA Pub of the Year 2011. ♨Q✿❀◑♿🛏(64)♣♠P⌐

Didcot

Wheatsheaf ✪

Wantage Road, OX11 0BS (on B4493)
✪ 11-midnight (12.30am Thu; 1am Fri & Sat); 12-11 Sun ☎ (01235) 519114
Beer range varies Ⓗ
There has been a Wheatsheaf on this site since the 17th century – the present pub was built in 1909. This tie-free town hostelry has recently gained a well-deserved reputation for the quality and variety of its beers, with up to seven ales and two real ciders at any time. The main bar features darts and a pool table, with a quieter room off to the side. There is a large garden and children's play area, and Aunt Sally is played in the summer. Live music features most Saturdays and two beer festivals are held each year. ♨✿▣♿⇌(Parkway)🛏(32,X32)♣♠P⌐

Eaton

Eight Bells Ⓛ

High Street, OX13 5PR (off B4017 between Cumnor and Appleton)
✪ closed Mon; 12-3, 7-11; 12-11 Fri-Sun ☎ (01865) 862261
⊕ eightbellseaton.co.uk
Loose Cannon Abingdon Bridge; guest beers Ⓗ
The pub is located in the centre of the hamlet and reopened as a free house in 2009. Once a simple cottage, extensions and projections have been added over the years that have lent a certain charm. Inside, the basic, no-frills public bar with wooden benches and tables retains the pub's original character, and there is a larger, simply furnished lounge bar where traditional home-made food is served. ♨Q✿❀◑▣🛏(66)♣♠P

Emmington

Inn at Emmington

Sydenham Road, OX39 4LD
✪ 12 (4 Mon & Tue)-11; 12-10 Sun ☎ (01844) 351367
⊕ theinnatemmington.co.uk
Brakspear Bitter; Fuller's London Pride; guest beers Ⓗ
Situated in view of the Chiltern Hills, the Inn is popular with locals, walkers, cyclists and many visitors who come to enjoy the cask ales, convivial atmosphere and excellent food. There are seven bedrooms providing guests with a comfortable base to enjoy the inn and its rural surroundings. The pub has a bar and small restaurant area, split by an open gas-burning fireplace, plus a large well-kept garden featuring a 150-year-old walnut tree. ✿🛏◑🛏(40)⌐

Enslow Bridge

Rock of Gibraltar

OX5 3AY
✪ 11 (4 Tue)-midnight; 12-10.30 Sun ☎ (01869) 331373
⊕ therockofgibraltar.co.uk
Beer range varies Ⓗ
Large canalside free house dating to the 1780s. The spacious garden attracts visitors in good weather and narrowboaters make use of the moorings to enjoy this popular pub. It offers up to three beers mainly from local brewers, with Wye Valley Butty Bach a regular visitor. Good home-cooked food is served in the restaurant with Greek nights a speciality. Thursday is folk music night. No food is served Sunday evenings or Tuesdays. ♨✿◑▲🛏(25,25a)♣P

Eynsham

Queen's Head

17 Queen Street, OX29 4HH
✪ 12-2.30, 5-11; 12-3, 7-10.30 Sun ☎ (01865) 881229
⊕ thequeenshead.net
Sharp's Doom Bar; guest beers Ⓗ
Eighteenth-century inn tucked away in the back streets of Eynsham. Popular with locals and visitors alike, it has two bars – one decorated with railway memorabilia and featuring a wood-burning stove, the other more spacious with a seating area, TV and pool table. Outside is a large garden. The landlord, with 28 years at the helm, has long been a keen supporter of small breweries and offers a wide range of guest beers. ♨Q✿◑▣♿🛏(S1)♣⌐

Faringdon

Swan [L]
1 Park Road, SN7 7BP
✪ 12-midnight (2am Fri & Sat) ☎ (01367) 241480
⊕ faringdonbrewerytap.co.uk
Faringdon Folly; guest beers [H]
Home to the Faringdon Brewery, the pub was completely renovated in 2010. With up to six real ales available from the local Old Forge and Halfpenny breweries and the on-site Faringdon brewery, there is always a wide choice available. Live music and folk jamming sessions keep the ever-increasing regular clientele entertained. Pub games include bar billiards, table skittles, bagatelle and many more. Q✿◑❶▤(66)♣♠⁵⁻

Fewcott

White Lion
Fritwell Road, OX27 7NZ (1 mile from jct 10 M40)
✪ 7 (5.30 Fri; 12 Sat)-11; 12-6.30 Sun ☎ (01869) 346639
Beer range varies [H]
Popular and friendly, this free house at the hub of the local community offers a constantly changing selection of four ales, mainly from microbreweries. A stout, porter or mild is always available. The pub is ideal for conversation and watching sport on TV, though it can be busy on darts nights. There is a large garden for use in summer and accommodation is available (just one single en-suite room, so book early). Local CAMRA Pub of the Year 2011. ⌂Q✿◑&♣P⁵⁻

Finstock

Plough Inn
The Bottom, High Street, OX7 3BY (off B4022)
✪ closed Mon; 12-2.30, 6-11; 12-11 Sat; 12-3 Sun
☎ (01993) 868333 ⊕ theplough-inn.co.uk
Adnams Broadside; St Austell Trelawny; guest beer [H]
A traditional thatched pub dating to 1777. The atmosphere is convivial, with three real ales and scrumpy cider always on handpump. The interior comprises a front bar/dining room, inglenook fireplace, back bar and billiards room. Outside is a rear patio and garden. Popular with locals and walkers, this is also a cosy dining venue and well-behaved children are welcome. Bella the mellow golden lab is unobtrusive but happy to receive a pat on the head (and handouts!). Midweek meal deals include special offer fish and chips on 'Tuppence Tuesdays'. ⌂Q✿◑❶▤(X9,53,69)♣♠P

Goring on Thames

Goring Social Club
High Street, RG8 9BA
✪ 6.30-11; 4.30-11 Fri; 12-11 Sat; 12-10.30 Sun
☎ (01491) 873105 ⊕ goringsocialclub.co.uk
Butcombe Bitter; West Berkshire Old Father Thames; guest beer [H]
Established in 1888 as a Working Men's Club, this venue is truly at the heart of Goring. Dropping the 'Working Men's' in the 1960s, it has become a wonderful community-based establishment. Offering all you could possibly ask for from a club, a warm and friendly welcome is assured. The ales are excellent and it was recognised in 2010 as Central Southern CAMRA Club of the Year. Traditional pub games, TV and a function room are available. CAMRA members will need to show their membership card and non members a copy of this Guide (paper or electronic) for entry. ✿&₰▤(Goring & Streatley)▤(133,134,135)♣P⁵⁻

John Barleycorn ✪
Manor Road, RG8 9DP
✪ 11-11; 12-10.30 Sun ☎ (01491) 872509
⊕ thejohnbarleycornpub.co.uk
Brakspear Bitter, seasonal beers; Ringwood Fortyniner [H]
Located in the centre of the village and within 100 yards of the River Thames, this popular local haunt is on both the Ridgeway and Thames Path. The building, formerly three cottages, dates from the 17th century. It has four rooms on the ground floor and a small function room upstairs accessible only by a winding staircase. The landlord, formerly the village butcher, and his wife run a friendly pub serving good traditional food. ⌂Q✿₰◑❶▤₰(Goring & Streatley)▤(134,135)♣⁵⁻

Henley-on-Thames

Bird in Hand
61 Greys Road, RG9 1SB SU760824
✪ 11.30-2, 5-11; 11.30-11 Sat; 12-10.30 Sun
☎ (01491) 575775 ⊕ henleybirdinhand.co.uk
Fuller's London Pride; Hook Norton Hooky Dark; guest beers [H]
A Guide regular, the 'Bird' is a deservedly frequent winner of local CAMRA Pub of the Year (2006, 2008 and 2010) and always popular. The two regular beers are complemented by three ever-changing guests, often supplied by local micros. The pub hosts darts and cribbage teams. The family room leads onto a delightful rear garden, with an aviary and a pond. Various events are held here, including mini beer festivals in May and September. TVs (including 3D) show sporting events. Dogs on leads are welcome. ⍩✿◑Å₰▤(151,152)♣⁵⁻

Hook Norton

Pear Tree ✪
Scotland End, OX15 5NU (off A361, follow signs to brewery)
✪ 12-11.30 (midnight Fri & Sat) ☎ (01608) 737482
Hook Norton Hooky Dark, Hooky Bitter, Hooky Gold, Old Hooky; guest beers [H]
The brewery tap for the Victorian tower brewery at Hook Norton, the Pear Tree has undergone a tasteful refurbishment while retaining the character of a popular village local. The full range of Hooky ales is on offer. A large beer garden features a play area. Accommodation is available, making it an ideal base for a brewery tour or exploring the Cotswolds. The pub was a local CAMRA Pub of the Year finalist in 2011 and 2012. ⌂✿₰◑&▤(488)♣P

Horley

Red Lion
Hornton Lane, OX15 6BQ SP418438
✪ closed Mon; 6-11; 12-6 Sun ☎ (01295) 730427
Hook Norton Hooky Bitter; St Austell Tribute; guest beer [H]
At the heart of the local community, this popular locals' pub offers a friendly welcome to visitors. Little changed over the years, it is a traditional

beer-only hostelry. Poker, darts and dominoes are played during the week, and sport is shown on TV. The pub hosts occasional beer and music festivals. Aunt Sally is played during the summer. ♨❀♣♦�⊷

Kirtlington

Oxford Arms
Troy Lane, OX5 3HA (next to Post Office)
✪ 12-3, 6-11 (10.30 Mon; closed Sun eve)
☎ (01869) 350208 ⏅ oxford-arms.co.uk
Brakspear Bitter; Hook Norton Hooky Bitter; guest beers Ⓗ
From the large wood-burning stove to the church candles on pine tables, this stripped stone 19th-century inn has it all. The beer quality is matched by the quality of the food; locally sourced or grown in the pub's own kitchen garden (the triple-cooked hand-cut chips are a must!). This is a popular venue during the Kirtlington Lamb Ale festival, held every year over the weekend of Trinity Sunday, 56 days after Easter Sunday, with 'dancing, mirth and merry glee'. ♨Q❀☀❶Å�(25/25A)♦P⏌⊷

Lewknor

Leathern Bottle
1 High Street, OX49 5TW (off B4009 nr M40 jct 6) SU716976
✪ 11-2.30 (3.30 Sat), 6-11; 12-3.30, 7-10.30 Sun
☎ (01844) 351482 ⏅ theleathernbottle.co.uk
Brakspear Bitter; guest beer Ⓗ
A classic 17th-century pub that has featured in all but one edition of the Guide. The pub has built up a strong reputation for great ale, home-cooked pub food featuring locally sourced meats, roaring log fires, a warm welcome and a garden that is child- and pet-friendly. Walkers and cyclists are welcome, but do take off your muddy boots before entering. Easily reached by car or the Oxford Tube coach. A guest beer, occasionally two, is from the Brakspear Pub Co approved list. ♨⏍❀☀❶&🚌(121,124,W1)P

Littleworth

Cricketer's Arms Ⅼ
38 Littleworth, OX33 1TR
✪ 12-3 (not Wed & Thu), 6-11; 12-11 Fri; 12-3, 7-10.30 Sun
☎ (01865) 872738 ⏅ cricketers-arms.co.uk
Hook Norton Hooky Bitter; Shotover Prospect; guest beers Ⓗ
A friendly, family-run free house, the pub was the first in the Oxford branch area to gain LocAle accreditation, and was CAMRA Branch Town and Village Pub of the Year in 2011. All four cask ales are from local breweries, and one is always a dark ale. There is also a huge range of local bottled beers available. Great-value home-cooked food is served. Popular with walkers, dogs and children are welcome. Beer and sausage festivals are held in February and September.
Q❀❶🚌(104,280)♣♦P⏌⊷

Lower Heyford

Bell
21 Market Square, OX25 5NY
✪ 12-3; 5-11; 12-11 Fri & Sat; 12-10.30 Sun
☎ (01869) 347176
Beer range varies Ⓗ
Large multi-roomed pub in the centre of the village close to the railway and canal. Up to three guest

ales change regularly, often from micros near and far, with a real cider or perry always available. A beer festival is held in early September. Regular live music nights promote local bands. A large garden has a covered smoking area and Aunt Sally is played in summer. CAMRA Branch Cider Pub of the Year 2010.
♨❀❶&⇌(Heyford)🚌(25A)♣♦P⏌⊷

Middle Assendon

Rainbow
Stonor Road, RG9 6AU (on B480) SU738858
✪ 12-3, 6-11 (not Mon eve winter); 12-3, 7-10.30 Sun
☎ (01491) 574879 ⏅ rainbowinnhenley.co.uk
Brakspear Bitter Ⓗ
An exceptional 17th-century public house situated within the Stonor Valley. A warm and friendly welcome is always waiting, along with a wet nose (Brian the pub dog). The pub has a cosy bar (mind your head) and a large lounge area serving traditional home-cooked fresh food. Ideally situated for walking and cycling around the Chilterns, it is also only a short drive from the Regatta town of Henley-on-Thames. A lively local and the hub of the village, it hosts special events throughout the year (details on the pub website).
Q❀❶🚌♣P

Murcott

Nut Tree
Main Street, OX5 2RE
✪ closed Mon; 12-11; 12-6 Sun ☎ (01865) 331253
⏅ nuttreeinn.co.uk
Vale Best Bitter; guest beers Ⓗ
Idyllic village hostelry complete with a pond in the front garden and spacious suntrap patio to the rear. Although one of the only Michelin-starred pubs in Oxfordshire, beer drinkers are warmly welcomed and bar snacks are available. Beer is mostly from local breweries, and the food is also sourced locally whenever possible, with pigs reared in the back garden. A fine example of a local pub that serves stunning food while still attracting discerning drinkers. ♨Q❀❶P

North Moreton

Bear at Home Ⅼ
High Street, OX11 9AT (S off A4130) SU561894
✪ 12-3, 6-11; 12-11 Sat & summer Sun; closed evenings Jan-March Sun ☎ (01235) 811311 ⏅ bear-at-home.co.uk
Taylor Landlord; West Berkshire Bear Beer; guest beers Ⓗ
Friendly village local dating back to the 15th century. The main bar features sofas, an open fire and plenty of tables for diners to enjoy the excellent pub food. The four handpumps deliver a range of mostly local ales, including Bear Beer, brewed exclusively for the pub by West Berkshire. During the summer one handpump is converted to real cider. The Bear adjoins the village cricket ground and cricket matches are played on most summer weekends – a four-day beer and cricket festival is held at the end of July. Local CAMRA Pub of the Year 2011. ♨❀❶🚌(95,130,131)♣P

Oxford

Bear Inn ✅
6 Alfred Street, OX1 4EH

✪ 11-11; 11.30-10.30 Sun ☎ (01865) 728164
Fuller's London Pride, ESB; Gale's HSB; Shotover Prospect ⒣
One of Oxford's oldest and most atmospheric pubs, the Bear is tucked away behind the Town Hall, close to Christ Church and Corpus Christi Colleges. Popular with students and visitors, it is renowned for its collection of thousands of ties displayed on the walls and ceiling. A small pub, it can be crowded at busy times, but there is ample outside seating in a paved public square to the rear.
🏬Q🕮🅳🍴🚆🚧

Chequers ✔

131 High Street, OX1 4DH
✪ 11 (12 Sun)-11 ☎ (01865) 727463
Brakspear Bitter, Oxford Gold; guest beers ⒣
Down a narrow medieval passageway off the High Street, the Chequers is a fine old inn, much of it dating back to 1500 when it was converted from a house into a tavern. The pub has built a reputation for its fine selection of real ales as well as its food. There are five frequently changing guest beers, and tasting notes are provided for all real ales. A cobblestoned courtyard provides alfresco drinking, dining and smoking facilities. 🕮🅳🚆🚧🍴

Far from the Madding Crowd 🍽 🅛 ✔

10-12 Friars Entry, OX1 2BY (alley off Magdalen St)
✪ 11.30-11 (midnight Thu-Sat); 12-10.30 Sun
☎ (01865) 240900 ⊕ maddingcrowd.co.uk
Brakspear Bitter; guest beers ⒣
An award-winning free house, with six handpumps and a beer choice that changes daily. One ale is always sold at a discounted price. Four beer and two cider festivals are held annually, and real cider is always available. A quiz and curry night is hosted on Sunday, Monday is open mic (no food), and pizza night on Thursday is popular. The pub is located close to Gloucester Green and handy for the city's theatres. Local CAMRA City Pub of the Year 2011. 🅳🚆🚧🅿🚆🍴

Lamb & Flag

12 St Giles, OX1 3JS
✪ 12-11 (10.30 Sun) ☎ (01865) 515787
Palmers IPA; Shepherd Neame Spitfire; Skinner's Betty Stogs; Theakston Old Peculier; guest beers ⒣
Grade II-listed building run by St John's College as a free house. The profits from the pub support student scholarships. Guest beers often come from the West Country – the house beer Lamb & Flag Gold is brewed by Palmers of Bridport, and beer festivals feature occasionally. The inn was used by Thomas Hardy as a setting in his novel Jude the Obscure. Q🅳🚆🚆🍴

Masons Arms 🅛 ✔

2 Quarry School Place, Headington Quarry, OX3 8LH
✪ 7-11 Mon, 5 (11 Sat)-11; 12-4, 7-10.30 Sun
☎ (01865) 764579 ⊕ themasonsarmshq.co.uk
Harviestoun Bitter & Twisted; Rebellion Mutiny; West Berkshire Good Old Boy; guest beers ⒣
Family-run community pub full of character, hosting many pub game leagues, including bar billiards and Aunt Sally. Old Bog Brewery's beers feature regularly among the guest ales. A range of local and foreign bottled beers is stocked, with Old Bog brews also available in mini-cask. It is home to the Headington beer festival in September. A heated decking area and garden lead to the function room. Events include twice-monthly music nights. 🕮♣🍴P🚧

Rose & Crown

14 North Parade Avenue, OX2 6LX (½ mile N of city centre, off Banbury Road)
✪ 10-midnight (1am Fri & Sat); 12-11 Sun
☎ (01865) 510551 ⊕ rose-n-crown.com
Adnams Southwold Bitter; Hook Norton Hooky Bitter; Shotover Prospect; guest beer ⒣
Now a free house, this popular Victorian local on a vibrant north Oxford street attracts a good mix of academics, students and passers-by. This pub is a gem for the warm welcome, lively conversation and superb beer. It has three small rooms, a cottage used as a function room to the rear, and a covered courtyard. No intrusive music, mobile phones or children permitted. Opening hours may vary. Q🕮🅳🚆(2)🍴

Royal Blenheim 🅛

13 St Ebbe's Street, OX1 1PT
✪ 11-11 (11.30 Wed, Thu & Sun; midnight Fri & Sat)
☎ (01865) 242355 ⊕ royalblenheim.co.uk
White Horse Bitter, Village Idiot, Wayland Smithy, seasonal beers; guest beers ⒣
Street-corner Victorian pub with a bright, airy interior, next to the Museum of Modern Art. The pub is owned by Everards but leased to the White Horse Brewery. Ten handpumps dispense a range of White Horse beers, plus guests (including one from Everards) and a real cider. TVs show rugby and various American sports, usually with the sound turned down. The single room has raised seating around the perimeter, and can get very busy, especially for the Wednesday quiz.
🅳🚆🚧🅿🍴

White Hart

12 St Andrew's Street, OX3 9DL
✪ 12-11.30 (12.30am Fri & Sat) ☎ (01865) 761737
Everards Sunchaser, Tiger; guest beers ⒣
This 17th-century establishment, located in the picturesque Cotswold stone area of Old Headington, opposite a 12th-century church, was once an alehouse/brothel run by the notorious Joan of Headington. The decor includes wooden flooring and furniture. To the rear is one of the loveliest walled gardens in the Oxfordshire area. A good selection of guest beers changes weekly and the food is traditional and home-made, with pies a speciality. An annual beer festival is held in spring. 🕮🅳🅲🚆🍴

White Horse 🅛 ✔

52 Broad Street, OX1 3BB
✪ 11-midnight ☎ (01865) 204801
⊕ whitehorseoxford.co.uk
Hook Norton Hooky Bitter; St Austell Tribute; Shotover Prospect; Taylor Landlord; guest beers ⒣
Claiming to be the smallest pub in Oxford and sandwiched between the two entrances to Blackwell's famous bookshop, this classic Grade II-listed 16th-century city centre inn has a long and narrow bar and a small snug at the rear. Popular with students and tourists, the pub featured regularly in Inspector Morse and more recently Lewis. Both Winston Churchill and Bill Clinton are reputed to have frequented the White Horse in their student days. Q🅳🚆🚧🍴

Pishill

Crown Inn

Stonor Road, RG9 6HH (on B480) SU718902

12-2.30, 6-11; 12-10 Sun ☎ (01491) 638364
⊕ thecrowninnpishill.co.uk
Brakspear Bitter; guest beers Ⓗ
A beautiful, picturesque 15th-century pub in the
Stonor Valley, boasting magnificent scenery, walks
and cycling. Smuggling, murder, religious conflict,
suicide, seductive wenches and a ghost all feature
in its long local history. Diners and drinkers come
for the freshly cooked food, made to order, and
great beer. The garden is popular during the warm
months of the year, with the log fire the attraction
during the winter. The 400-year-old converted barn
is available for weddings and other functions and
holds a licence for civil services. ⚏Q❀☎⏿◑ ⊟P

Playhatch

Flowing Spring
Henley Road, RG4 9RB (on A4155) SU745766
closed Mon; 12-midnight (11.30 Sun) ☎ (0118) 969 9878
⊕ theflowingspringpub.co.uk
Fuller's Chiswick Bitter, London Pride, ESB Ⓗ
The oldest part of the building dates from the
1700s and the spring under the pub (hailed as a
cure for eyesight problems) supplied its water until
1981. Much improved by enthusiastic new
management, the pub now features events such as
the annual ferret show and astronomy nights. The
menu specialises in vegetarian, gluten-free and
dairy-free food. Check out 'Quirky Corner', where a
slant of almost a foot difference across the pub
starts and continues to the balcony overlooking the
large stream-side garden. ⚏❀◑⏰(800)P↻

Shippon

Prince of Wales Ⓛ
60 Barrow Road, OX13 6JQ (off A415, NW of Abingdon)
12-3, 5-midnight; 12-midnight Fri-Sun ☎ (01235) 538546
**Black Sheep Best Bitter; Loose Cannon Abingdon
Bridge; Shotover Prospect; Taylor Landlord; guest
beers** Ⓗ
At the centre of the village, this traditional country
pub is rumoured to be haunted. There are two
large log fires, one dominating the lounge. An
ever-changing menu of English food is available
alongside a large selection of malt whiskies. The
pub hosts regular beer and cider festivals and live
traditional jazz and folk music evenings. It caters
for all types of visitors including walkers, cyclists
and dogs. ⚏Q❀◑ ⊟占⏰(4)♣♠P↻

Shutford

George & Dragon ✅
Church Lane, OX15 6PG (3 miles off A422, next to
church)
12-2.30 (not Mon-Thu), 6-11, 12-11 Sat; 12-10.30 Sun
☎ (01295) 780320 ⊕ thegeorgeanddragon.com
Hook Norton Hooky Bitter; guest beers Ⓗ
Traditional 13th-century listed building in the heart
of the village nestling in the hillside beside the
church. The lively bar room has an inglenook
fireplace, tiled floor and a well-stocked bar with
Hooky Bitter and four guests usually available, plus
a restaurant serving good food. The pub hosts
traditional games including darts and Aunt Sally.
There is a separate TV room with Sky and ESPN for
sport. ⚏Q❀◑ ⊟♣⏰

Souldern

Fox Inn Ⓛ
Fox Lane, OX27 7JW (off B4100)
12-3, 5-11; 12-11 Sat; 12-4, 6-10.30 Sun
☎ (01869) 345284 ⊕ thefoxatsouldern.co.uk
Hook Norton Hooky Bitter; guest beers Ⓗ
Free house situated at the centre of the village just
off the B4100. Two guest beers come from local
micros and a good mix of brewers; though expect
to see something from Yorkshire. A beer festival is
held on the fourth weekend of July when northern
micros feature strongly. Aunt Sally is played in the
large garden, which is busy in good weather. The
car park is small, but on-road parking is available
nearby. Accommodation is in four en-suite rooms.
⚏❀☎◑♣P↻

South Newington

Duck on the Pond
Main Street, OX15 4JE (on A361)
11-3, 5-11; 11-11 Sat; 11-10.30 Sun ☎ (01295) 721166
⊕ duckonthepond.co.uk
Hook Norton Hooky Bitter; guest beer Ⓗ
Parts of this attractive village pub date back to the
16th century. Built of local stone, it has been
lovingly restored, retaining many of the original
features such as oak beams and a bread oven
hidden behind the large open fire. A spacious patio
area overlooks the pond where ducks and fish co-
exist. Picturesque views are a treat from the
garden. The menu features locally sourced produce
served to a high standard. ❀⏰(488)♣P↻

South Stoke

Perch & Pike
The Street, RG8 0JS (off B4009)
11.30-3, 5.30-11; 11.30-11 Sat; 12-10.30 Sun
☎ (01491) 872415 ⊕ perchandpike.co.uk
Brakspear Bitter, Oxford Gold Ⓗ
This 17th-century brick and flint pub of traditional
build has an adjoining barn that houses four
comfortable en-suite bedrooms and a restaurant.
The pub is on the Ridgeway and is a good stop for
walkers, with three separate areas for drinking, in
addition to a well-kept garden. The pub is at the
heart of the small village and has a real fire and
daily papers, and home-cooked food served
lunchtimes and evenings.
⚏Q❀☎◑占⏰(134,135)♣P↻

Standlake

Black Horse
81 High Street, OX29 7RH
11-3, 5-11; 11-11 Sat & Sun ☎ (01865) 300307
⊕ blackhorsestandlake.co.uk
Hook Norton Hooky Bitter; guest beers Ⓗ
The Black Horse has been here since 1672, and the
building, once owned by Lincoln College, is a low-
beamed stone inn typical of the period. There is a
small bar with dining room adjoining, and a
separate back room. In summer a marquee in the
garden gives more covered space. The pub has
built a reputation for good beer and good food – a
mix of pub classics with a specials board and fresh
fish daily from the Really Interesting Crab
Company. ⚏Q❀◑▲⏰(18,X15)♣

Steeple Aston

Red Lion 🄻 ✆
South Side, OX25 4RY
✪ 12-11 summer (12-3, 5.30-11 winter); 12-10.30 (5 winter)
Sun ☎ (01869) 340225 ⊕ redlionsteepleaston.co.uk
Hook Norton Hooky Dark, Hooky Bitter; guest beer ⊞
Set back off the road, the pub is situated about a mile from Heyford station and the Oxford Canal. In summer it boasts an impressive display of hanging baskets on the front patio. Hook Norton Double Stout is a regular guest beer. The TV shows rugby and major sporting events, although this is in no way a sports bar. Regular beer and food matching is popular. Wheelchair access is from the car park to the rear of pub. ♨⊛◑♿⛴(S5)P🚲

Steventon

North Star ★ 🄻
2 Stocks Lane, OX13 6SG (end of the Causeway off B4017)
✪ 5 (3 Fri)-11; 12-11.30 Sat; 12-11 Sun
Loose Cannon Abingdon Bridge; Morland Original; guest beers �servG
Identified by CAMRA as one of Britain's Real Heritage Pubs and situated next to the Causeway, a listed ancient monument. This wonderful unspoilt village inn has been run by the same family for 160 years. Popular with locals and visitors, it hosts many village clubs and social events. Inside it has two rooms, one with a snug space with three settles around an open fireplace. There is no bar counter – beers are served through a stable door or hatch. An ideal stop-off for walkers and their dogs. ♨Q⊛Å⛴(32C,X2)♣P🚲

Stoke Lyne

Peyton Arms
Main Street, OX27 8SD (¾ mile off B4100) SP567284
✪ closed Mon; 12-2, 5-close; 12-7 Sat & Sun
☎ (01869) 345285
Hook Norton Hooky Bitter, Old Hooky ⒼG
Entering this classic old-fashioned pub is like visiting another world, yet it is situated just two miles from junction 10 of the M40. One simply appointed bar serves two Hooky ales straight from casks in the cellar behind the bar, with home-made rolls often available. The legendary host and regulars from the local community provide much character, as does the interesting memorabilia around the walls. No dogs allowed, and children are welcome in the garden only. ♨Q⊛🚲

Thame

Cross Keys ♟
East Street, OX9 3JS
✪ 12-2, 5-11; 12-11 Sat; 12-10.30 Sun ☎ (01844) 218202
Vale Best Bitter; guest beers ⊞
Local CAMRA Pub of the Year 2012, a surprisingly large number of handpumps feature guest beers from microbreweries, with milds and porters usually on show. No food is available although there is no objection to bringing in a takeaway from one of the local fish & chip shops. Lots of games are available and an upstairs room is handy for private meetings. The pub is also home to Thame Brewery which opened in 2009. Beers are brewed about twice a week and don't tend to last long. ♨Q⊛Å⛴(280)♣🚲

Upper Heyford

Barley Mow
Somerton Road, OX25 5LB
✪ 12-2.30, 5-11; 12-11 Sat; 12-4, 7-10.30 Sun
☎ (01869) 232300
Fuller's Chiswick Bitter, London Pride; guest beers ⊞
A warm welcome is assured at this community-focused local, situated not far from the end of the runway of a disused US Airforce base. The landlord is a Fuller's Master Cellarman and the guest beer could be a Fuller's seasonal or come from a regional brewer. There is a large open bar area and a separate dining space, with food home-cooked to order. Aunt Sally is played in a garden area to the rear. ♨⊛◑⛴(25)♣P🚲

Wallingford

Coachmakers Arms
37 St Marys Street, OX10 0EU SU606891
✪ 12-3, 5-11; 12-11 Fri; 12-10.30 Sun ☎ (01491) 832231
⊕ thecoachmakersarmswallingford.co.uk
Brakspear Bitter; guest beers ⊞
Known locally as the Cat, this lively and friendly drinkers' pub offers a warm welcome to all. The interior is divided into two rooms – the Ramping Cat bar and a second room that hosts music sessions and themed nights. Good-value food is served at lunchtimes and the pub is renowned for excellent Sunday lunches. It is also popular for darts and home to a cycling club that meets each Thursday in summer. Wallingford can be reached by heritage train or riverboat on selected weekends. ⊛⌂◑♿Å⇌⛴(X39,X40)♣🚲

Wantage

Royal Oak Inn 🄻
Newbury Street, OX12 8DF (S of Market Square)
✪ 5.30-11; 12-2.30, 7-11 Sat; 12-2, 7-10.30 Sun
☎ (01235) 763129 ⊕ royaloakwantage.co.uk
Wadworth 6X; West Berkshire Maggs Mild, Old Father Thames, Dr Hexter's Wedding Ale, Dr Hexter's Healer; guest beers ⒼG
This multi-award-winning street-corner pub is a mecca for the discerning drinker and is a meeting place for many local clubs. Photographs of pubs bearing the pub's name adorn the walls. The lounge bar features wrought-iron trelliswork covered in pump clips. The pub is the primary outlet for West Berkshire ales in the area – two beers carry the landlord's name – and also offers an extensive changing range of ciders and perries. Local, county, regional and national finalist CAMRA Pub of the Year 2010. 🍽⛴♣👜

Shoulder of Mutton ♟ 🄻
38 Wallingford Street, OX12 8AX (E of market square)
✪ 10.30-midnight ☎ (07870) 577742 ⊕ themutton.co.uk
Beer range varies ⊞
Corner pub recently renovated by an enthusiastic landlord, renowned for its friendly atmosphere. The 10 beers are constantly changing, with a strong emphasis on LocAle – it is the main outlet for Betjeman beers. The interior comprises public and lounge bars with traditional decor and furnishings, a small, cosy snug and a 'lay-by' – the corridor leading to the outdoor patio and function room. It also has a vegetarian restaurant. Regular folk music evenings are hosted and there is a weekly raffle. Local CAMRA Pub of the Year 2012. ♨Q🍽⊛◑🍽⛴👜🚲

Wardington

Hare & Hounds 🅛 ✅

Edgecote Lane, OX17 1SH (just off A361)
✪ 12-3, 5-11; 12-11 Fri & Sat; 12-8 Sun ☎ (01295) 750645
Hook Norton Hooky Gold; guest beers 🅗
Serving good beer and hearty pub food, this community oriented establishment run by Carol and Jamie is the hub of village life. Two handpumps dispense Hook Norton and Cask Marque-accredited ales. Numerous charity fundraising events are organised throughout the year including real ale festivals, and regular themed evenings such as Burns night are held in a separate restaurant area. The pub supports teams in local darts, quiz, Northants skittles and dominoes leagues. ᗰQ🕭🅓&♣P⅃

West Hanney

Plough 🅛

Church Street, OX12 0LN
✪ closde Mon; 12-3, 6-11; 12-10.30 Sun ☎ (01235) 868674
⊕ plough-westhanney.co.uk
Beer range varies 🅗
Welcoming, atmospheric, 16th-century thatched free house. The Grade II-listed building has a cosy beamed and alcoved split-level bar with an open fire and separate dining room serving locally renowned, traditional British food. A large garden plays host to Aunt Sally and outdoor skittles in summer Two beer festivals are held annually. The late May bank holiday features Oxfordshire ales, while the August festival is a real village and family occasion full of live music and a variety of entertainments. ᗰQ🕭🅓♣P⅃

Westcote Barton

Fox Inn 🍸

27 Enstone Road, OX7 7BL (on B4030 Enstone-Bicester road)
✪ 12-3, 5-11 (1am Fri); 11-1am Sat; 12-3, 6-11 Sun
☎ (01869) 340338 ⊕ the-fox.net
Hook Norton Hooky Bitter; guest beer 🅗
Seventeenth-century roadside pub offering a hearty welcome and up to four guest beers from micros as well as regionals – SIBA list is well used. A music and beer festival over the August bank holiday is always a crowd puller. Good home-cooked food is available in the restaurant Tuesday to Sunday lunchtimes, with Sunday roasts proving popular as well as Jacqui's curries. The spacious garden has distractions for the kids as well as an Aunt Sally pitch. ᗰ🕭🅓🚍(S4)♣P

Witney

Eagle Tavern ✅

22 Corn Street, OX28 6BL
✪ 11-3, 5-midnight (2am Fri); 11-2am Sat; 12-midnight Sun
☎ (01993) 700121
Hook Norton Hooky Bitter, Hooky Gold, Old Hooky, seasonal beers; Wychwood Hobgoblin 🅗
Following acquisition and an excellent refurbishment by Hook Norton Brewery, this wood-panelled and stone-floored building has become a gem of a locals' establishment. The landlord has been running pubs in Corn Street for 20-odd years and is proud of his award-winning cellar. An unobtrusive jukebox, friendly locals, welcoming staff and quality beer all add up to a 'must visit' pub. ᗰ🕭🚍(S1,S2)♣⅃

New Inn 🅛 ✅

111 Corn Street, OX28 6AU
✪ 5 (12 Sun)-midnight; 12-1am Sat ☎ (01993) 703807
Black Sheep Best Bitter; Sharp's Doom Bar; Theakston Old Peculier; Tring Side Pocket for a Toad; guest beers 🅗
Slightly away from the town centre, the New Inn is a relaxing place to enjoy a quiet pint during the week. With six real ales, there is something for everyone. Friday and Saturday nights are busy, as are televised rugby match nights, when the atmosphere is lively. The pub itself dates back to 1805, though the cellar is older. A separate building at the rear is used for occasional beer festivals. Live music plays every Saturday and some Fridays. ᗰ🕭&🚍(S1,S2)♣P

Woodstock

Black Prince

2 Manor Road, OX20 1XJ (on A44 just N of town centre)
✪ 12-11 ☎ (01993) 811530
Vale Best Bitter; guest beer 🅗
Delightful 16th-century riverside pub sitting opposite Blenheim Palace. Inside you will find stone walls, ancient fireplaces, old beams and even a suit of armour. There is a choice of four real ales and home-cooked food is available at reasonable prices. A room at the side of the pub is available for meetings. Each August a Mock Mayor ceremony is carried out and there is a duck race in June. Families, walkers and dogs are all welcome. ᗰQ🕭🅓P⅃

Ale conner

The official ale-tester wore leather breeches. He would enter an inn without warning, draw a glass of ale, pour it on a wooden bench, and then sit down in the puddle he had made. He would sit for half an hour and would not change his position. At the end of the half hour, he would make as if to rise, and this was the test of the ale; for if the ale was impure, if it had sugar in it, the tester's leather breeches would stick fast to the bench, but if there was no sugar in the liquor, no impression would be present – in other words, the tester would not stick to the seat.

17th-century description of the work of the ale conner, a public official who inspected inns, taverns and ale houses to test the quality of the beer. William Shakespeare's father was an ale conner.

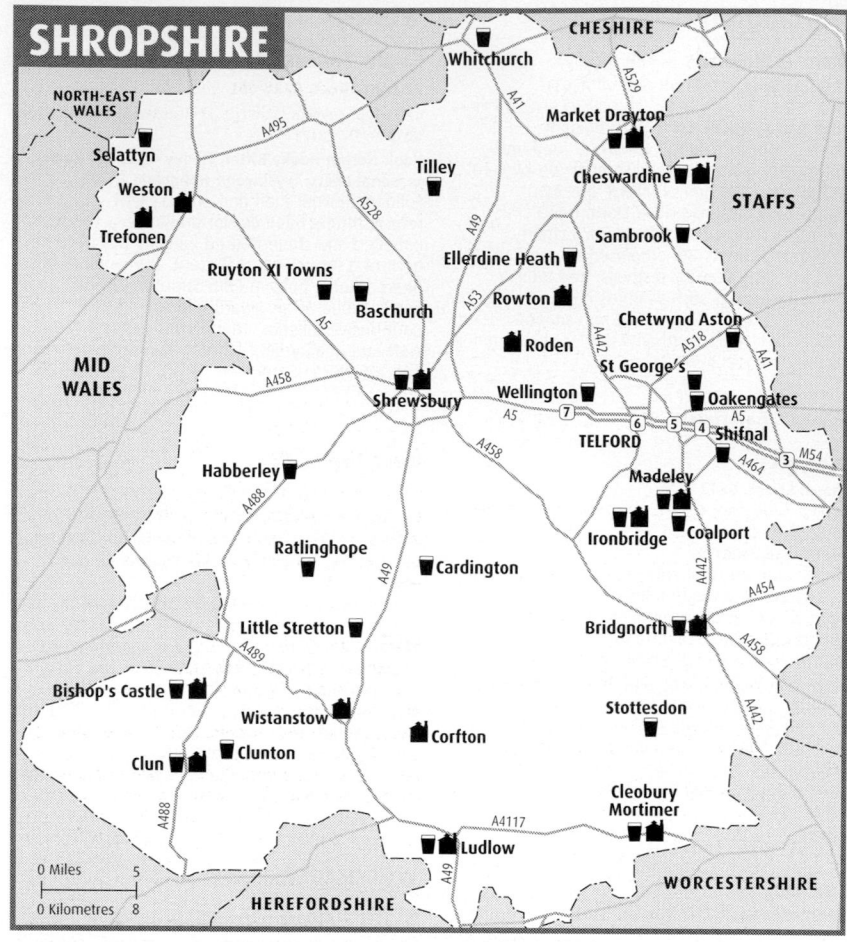

SHROPSHIRE

CHESHIRE

Whitchurch

NORTH-EAST WALES

Market Drayton

Selattyn

Tilley

Cheswardine

STAFFS

Weston

Trefonen

Sambrook

Ruyton XI Towns

Ellerdine Heath

Baschurch

Rowton

Chetwynd Aston

MID WALES

Roden

St George's

Shrewsbury

Wellington

Oakengates

TELFORD

Shifnal

Habberley

Madeley

Ironbridge

Coalport

Ratlinghope

Cardington

Bridgnorth

Little Stretton

Bishop's Castle

Stottesdon

Wistanstow

Corfton

Clun

Clunton

Cleobury Mortimer

Ludlow

0 Miles   5

0 Kilometres   8

HEREFORDSHIRE

WORCESTERSHIRE

Baschurch

New Inn Ⓛ
Church Road, SY4 2EF (off B5067 opp church)
✪ closed Mon; 11-3, 6-11; 11-11 Sat; 12-10.30 Sun
☎ (01939) 260335 ⊕ thenewinnbaschurch.co.uk
Banks's Bitter; Hobsons Best Bitter; Stonehouse Station Bitter; guest beer Ⓗ
Sixteenth-century former post office and inn, first granted a licence by Wrexham Brewery in 1850. Refurbished in 2005, the family-run pub has an open-plan layout with three distinct areas – the modern bar area has wood and tile flooring and comfortable seating, with exposed beams and an inglenook fireplace adding character. Food and drink are sourced as locally as possible. Dogs, walkers and cyclists are all welcome. Real cider is stocked in summer. Bus 576 stops in the village.
⌂Q✿ⓓ❂&🚌(576)Pᐦ╴

Bishops Castle

Crown & Anchor Vaults Ⓛ
High Street, SY9 5BQ
✪ 4 (2 Sun)-11 ☎ 07971 213728
Ludlow Gold; Monty's Sunshine; Wye Valley HPA; guest beer Ⓗ

Known locally as the Vaults, this no-frills boozer has been purchased by the current landlady. Extensive alterations to the interior have created an open space around the central bar so that customers can appreciate the pub's regular music sessions. It relies entirely on ale sales to survive so that while customers bringing in their own food are not frowned upon, it's always best to ask first. Dogs are most welcome. ✿Åᚋ❂ᐦ╴

Six Bells Ⓛ
Church Street, SY9 5AA
✪ 12-2.30 (not Mon), 5-11; 12-11 Sat & Sun
☎ (01588) 638930 ⊕ sixbellsbrewery.co.uk
Six Bells Big Nev's, Ow Do, Cloud Nine; guest beers Ⓗ
The Six Bells Brewery tap – the adjoining Six Bells Brewery was re-established on the site of the original one, which closed in the early 1900s. You can be sure of a friendly greeting in the wood-beamed bar where three ales are on handpump, plus monthly specials and real cider in summer. Excellent fresh food is served in the dining/lounge bar (no food Sun, Mon and Tue eves). The town beer festival in July offers around 90 ales (20 at the Six Bells) and real ciders plus live music in the courtyard. Opening hours may vary on Sunday.
⌂Q✿ⓓ❂Åᚋ(553)♣❀ᐦ╴

Three Tuns ⓛ
Salop Street, SY9 5BW
☼ 12-11 (10.30 Sun) ☎ (01588) 638797
⊕ thethreetunsinn.co.uk
Three Tuns 1642 Bitter, XXX, Cleric's Cure, seasonal beers Ⓗ

One of the truly historic pubs in the country, this is one of the Famous Four who were still brewing in the early 1970s. Together with the adjoining, but separately owned, Three Tuns Brewery, from where it gets all its beers, it has been on this site since 1640. It has now been extended into four rooms – on one side is the dining lounge, on the other the ever-popular front bar leading to the central characterful snug and the extended timber-framed glass-sided dining room. As well as good food, the pub offers music sessions, including jazz, in the upper floor function room. Dogs are welcome. 🏠Q🕭🐕❶🍴❸🗻🅿(443,745)♣🐾🚶

Bridgnorth

Hare & Hounds ⓛ
8 Bernards Hill, Low Town, WV15 5AX (200yds up Bernards Hill off A442 by Fox)
☼ 5 (3 Sun)-midnight; 3-1am Sat ☎ (01746) 768819
⊕ hareandhounds.biz/index.php
Hobsons Mild, Town Crier; guest beers Ⓗ

Community family pub with wonderful views of the Severn Valley Railway and Bridgnorth. A free house, the two guest beers often come from local brewers, served in two drinking areas, both with real fires. Ideal for quiet conversation mid-week, the pub comes alive at weekends with live entertainment. Fresh crusty cobs with chips and salad are served daily. An annual beer festival is held in the large beer garden at the rear on the last weekend in July. Visitors from Stanmore and Riverside Caravan Parks are welcome including families and well-behaved dogs.
🏠🕭🐕🗻🅿(101,114)♣🐾🚶

King's Head ⓛ
3 Whitburn Street, High Town, WV16 4QN
☼ 11-11 (midnight Fri & Sat); 12-10.30 Sun
☎ (01746) 762141 ⊕ kingsheadbridgnorth.co.uk
Hobsons Twisted Spire, Best Bitter, Town Crier; Holden's Golden Glow; Wye Valley HPA, Butty Bach; guest beers Ⓗ

Sympathetically renovated Grade II-listed 16th-century coaching inn complete with timber beams, flagstone floor, leaded windows and roaring log fires in winter. The King's Head bar has two regular and three guest beers. The extensive menu includes a pub grub section and daily blackboard specials made with locally sourced produce. The Stable Bar to the rear has several handpulls and an impressive display of wine bins (open evenings and daytimes if busy). The courtyard has a pleasant seated area. 🏠Q🕭❶🐾🗻🚶

Old Castle ⓛ ✔
10/11 West Castle Street, WV16 4AB (end of High Street)
☼ 11.30-11 ☎ (01746) 711420 ⊕ oldcastlebridgnorth.co.uk
Greene King IPA; Hobsons Town Crier; Sharp's Doom Bar; guest beer Ⓗ

Low-beamed pub dating from the 1600s, divided by a central chimney breast. The front is for diners where good, home-made hearty meals are served lunchtimes and evenings. The bar has a wood-burning stove, the rear is a conservatory/games room with darts and pool table, and a small function room. Dogs are welcome. Outside is a beer garden with flower borders, a children's play area and raised decking. There are four handpulls serving a LocAle, two nationals and a guest.
🏠🛏🕭🐕❶🐾🗻🚶

Railwayman's Arms ⓛ
Bridgnorth Station, Hollybush Road, WV16 5DT (follow signs for SVR)
☼ 11.30-4, 6-11; 11.30-11 Fri; 11-11 Sat; 12-10.30 Sun
☎ (01746) 764361 ⊕ svr.co.uk
Bathams Best Bitter; Hobsons Mild, Best Bitter, Town Crier; guest beers Ⓗ

A licensed refreshment room since 1861, owned by SVR, this is a busy drinking spot attracting steam enthusiasts as well as a popular pub for locals. The landlord is proud of his cellarmanship and serves an excellent pint of real ale. A free house with 10 handpulls, it offers five LocAle beers (with a special from Bewdley), three guests, one cider and a perry in summer. The platform drinking area is perfect for soaking up the atmosphere of the steam era, with plenty of railwayana on display in the bar. A CAMRA beer festival is held here every September.
🏠Q🕭🗻🚶🐾🅿🚶

White Lion ⓛ
3 West Castle Street, WV16 4AB
☼ 11-11; 10.30-midnight Fri & Sat ☎ (01746) 763962
⊕ whitelionbridgnorth.co.uk
Banks's Bitter; Ludlow Gold; Olde Swan Original; St Austell Tribute; guest beers Ⓗ

This 18th-century inn offers a warm welcome. Murals depicting regulars and Shropshire views adorn the interior and exterior walls. Freshly made bar food is available all day, including the famous White Lion Scotch Egg. Seven handpulls offer a range of LocAles, national ales, ales from its own 2½-barrel Hop & Stagger Brewery, and traditional cider. Outside are a terraced heated area, lawned garden and children's play area. The pub is dog-friendly. Entertainment includes a monthly folk club and Tales from the Edge storytellers.
🏠Q🛏🕭🐕❶🐾🗻♣🚶

Cardington

Royal Oak
SY6 7JZ

INDEPENDENT BREWERIES
Clun Clun
Corvedale Corfton
Dickensian Roden
Hobsons Cleobury Mortimer
Hop & Stagger Bridgnorth (NEW)
Ironbridge Ironbridge
Joules Market Drayton
Lion's Tale Cheswardine
Ludlow Ludlow
Offa's Dyke Trefonen
Rowton Rowton
Salopian Shrewsbury
Shires Madeley
Six Bells Bishop's Castle
Stonehouse Weston
Three Tuns Bishop's Castle
Wood Wistanstow

✪ closed Mon; 12-2.30, 6.30-midnight (11 Tue & Wed); 12-3.30, 7-midnight Sun ☎ (01694) 771266
🌐 at-the-oak.com

Hobsons Best Bitter; Marston's Pedigree; guest beers Ⓗ

Reputedly the oldest continuously licensed pub in Shropshire. This ancient 15th-century free house in a conservation village retains the character of a country pub. The low-beamed bar has a roaring fire in winter in a vast inglenook fireplace. The dining room has exposed old beams and studwork. Guest beers come mainly from local breweries. The menu includes Fidget Pie made to a Shropshire recipe that has been handed down from landlord to landlord. Dog-friendly, and free Wi-Fi is available.
🏚Q✿◑▶♿♣P⌐

Cheswardine

Fox & Hounds

High Street, TF9 2RS

✪ 5-11 (10 Mon); 12-2, 5-midnight Fri; 12-midnight Sat; 12-10.30 Sun ☎ (01630) 661244

Joule's Blonde, Original Pale Ale, Slumbering Monk Ⓗ

Joule's tied house in the high street oppposite the historic village church. Very much a traditional pub, it offers well-kept cask ales plus a Westons cider. In addition, there is a great selection of popular pub fare ranging from sandwiches and baguettes to full, hearty meals. The decor is tasteful and the lobby door incorporates an original Joule's etched window. Outside, the pub garden is a suntrap for when it shines. 🏚☎✿◑♿♣♠P⌐

Red Lion

High Street, TF9 2RS

✪ 7-10.30 Mon; 4 (5 Thu & Fri)-11; 12-3, 7-10.30 Sun ☎ (01630) 662234

Lion's Tale Blooming Blonde, Lionbru, Chesbrewnette; Marston's Burton Bitter Ⓗ

Home of the Lion's Tale Brewery, with three of its beers always on sale. This quiet pub also boasts over 130 whiskies, which the landlord will be happy to advise on. A music session night is held on the second Tuesday of every month, showcasing local talent. With its quieter corners and old time charms, the Red Lion is ideal whatever mood you are in. 🏚Q⊟♿P⌐

Chetwynd Aston

Fox

Pave Lane, TF10 9LQ (½ mile W of A41)

✪ 12-11 (10.30 Sun) ☎ (01952) 815940
🌐 fox-newport.co.uk

Three Tuns XXX; Wood Shropshire Lad; guest beers Ⓗ

An open-plan pub retaining the original fireplace for winter warmth. Good food and a range of beers attract an appreciative clientele from near and far. There is often a mild or stout available as well as the house Brunning & Price Original brewed by Phoenix. At least one mini beer festival is held each year. It's also a popular dining establishment, with food served until 10pm (9.30pm Sun). Note the interesting old maps, pictures, bills of sale and other artefacts that adorn the walls. There is an extensive garden for summer visitors.
🏚Q✿◑♿P⌐

Cleobury Mortimer

Kings Arms Ⓛ

6 Church Street, DY14 8BS

✪ 10-11 (midnight Thu-Sat; 10.30 Sun) ☎ (01299) 271954
🌐 kingsarms-cleobury.co.uk

Hobsons Mild, Twisted Spire, Best Bitter, Town Crier; guest beer Ⓗ

Opposite the church, this welcoming 15th-century pub has original beams, a log-burning fire and sofas to sink into with the daily newspapers, helping to create the perfect ambience in which to enjoy Hobsons' local award-winning ales, plus a frequent guest beer. Hobsons in bottles is also available to take away. The excellent lunchtime menu features locally sourced ingredients and generous portions – try the ham, egg and chips. Breakfast is available from 10am. Dogs welcome. The town is known as the Gateway to the Shropshire Hills. 🏚☎✿🛏◑♿🚌(292)⌐

Clun

White Horse Inn Ⓛ ✔

The Square, SY7 8JA

✪ 12-midnight ☎ (01588) 640305 🌐 whi-clun.co.uk

Clun Clun Pale; Hobsons Mild, Best Bitter; Salopian Shropshire Gold; Stonehouse Station Bitter; Wye Valley Butty Bach; guest beers Ⓗ

Comfortable 16th-century coaching inn and post house that stands in the old market square at the centre of a wonderfully timeless town, described by AE Housman as 'one of the quietest places under the sun'. It now boasts its own 'nano' brewery, Clun Brewery. A friendly local, it has an L-shaped bar with low beams and an adjoining dining room serving excellent, reasonably priced food. Westons 1st Quality cider and a perry are stocked. Outside is a secluded garden. Jam nights are held once a month. Dogs welcome.
🏚Q☎✿🛏◑▶♿🚌(773,860)♣♠⌐🚬

Clunton

Crown Inn Ⓛ

SY7 0HU (on B4368)

✪ 3 (4 Tue; 12 Fri-Sun)-11 ☎ (01588) 660265
🌐 crowninnclunton.co.uk

Hobsons Best Bitter; Stonehouse Station Bitter; guest beer Ⓗ

Community-owned inn now run by a local family. It is set in the Clun Valley in a designated area of outstanding natural beauty. A genuine pub, it has three rooms, one a smart restaurant. The pub hosts a popular fish and chips night every Wednesday (including takeaway) and an acoustic folk night on the third Wednesday of the month. It is part of the annual Clun Valley Beer Festival.
🏚Q✿◑⊟♿🚌♣♠P⌐

Ellerdine Heath

Royal Oak Ⓛ ✔

Hazles Road, TF6 6RL (2 miles off A442 towards A53) SJ604225

✪ 12-11 ☎ (01939) 250300

Hobsons Best Bitter; Rowton Bitter; Salopian Shropshire Gold; guest beers Ⓗ

Known locally as the Tiddly, this friendly rural pub serves locally sourced food and quality ales throughout the year. Six handpulls dispense three house ales complemented by three changing guests. Dining facilities cater for up to 30 people, plus buffets and parties. Entertainment is occasionally hosted over weekends as well as a folk night every third Tuesday. Families and dogs are welcome. A real cider is usually available and a cider festival takes place on the last weekend in July. ♨⊛◑🕭&♣♠P'⌐

Habberley

Mytton Arms Ⓛ
SY5 0TP (S of Pontesbury off A488) SH398035
✪ 4 (12 Fri-Sun)-11 ☎ (01743) 792490
Hobsons Best Bitter; Three Tuns XXX; guest beers Ⓗ
This quintessential country pub continues to survive and is now at the heart of this small village. Off the entrance lobby are a separate lounge and bar. It supports various pub teams from its extended open-plan, part-tiled, part-carpeted, U-shaped bar, which is divided into various nooks and crannies. The exterior has seats to the front and a paved area with a pagoda. Guest beers come from local and national breweries and tend to be around the 4-4.5% mark. Accessible in summer by the Long Mynd & Stiperstones Shuttle bus. ♨Q⊛🖰♣P'⌐

Little Stretton

Ragleth Inn Ⓛ
Ludlow Road, SY6 6RB
✪ 12-3, 6-midnight; 12-11 Sun ☎ (01694) 722711
⊕ theragletinn.co.uk
Hobsons Best Bitter; guest beers Ⓗ
Dating from 1663, this friendly, welcoming pub overlooks half an acre of well-maintained shrubs and trees between the gentle slopes of the Long Mynd and Ragleth Hill. The dining room and the two lounges with red-bricked walls, wooden beams, an inglenook fireplace with a woodburner, have ample room for drinkers and diners, attracting locals, walkers, visitors and their dogs. Reasonably priced, home-prepared meals are available. The garden has plenty of seating and spectacular views. ♨Q⊛◑A🖰♣P'⌐

Ludlow

Charlton Arms Ⓛ
Ludford Bridge, SY8 1PJ (by Ludford Bridge)
✪ 11 (12 Sun)-11 (midnight Fri & Sat) ☎ (01584) 872813
⊕ thecharltonarms.co.uk
Hobsons Best Bitter; Ludlow Gold, Stairway; Wye Valley Butty Bach; guest beers Ⓗ
Now extensively refurbished, this fine building is situated to the south, overlooking the River Teme and across the historic Ludford Bridge up towards Ludlow's last remaining fortified gate and the town centre. It has an attractive bar and spacious lounge leading to a separate dining room with a terrace. The impressive function suite and roof bar offer fine views across the river towards the town. Accommodation is in 10 en-suite rooms. Dogs are allowed in the bar. ♨Q♜⊛🖰◑⊜&A⇌🖰♣P'⌐

Queens
113 Lower Galdeford, SY8 1RU
✪ 12-11 (midnight Fri & Sat; 10.30 Sun) ☎ (01584) 879177
⊕ thequeensludlow.com
Hobsons Best Bitter; Ludlow Gold; Three Tuns 1642 Bitter; Wye Valley Butty Bach; guest beer Ⓗ
Popular pub/café bar with a decent range of local ales. The light and airy L-shaped bar has two

distinct areas, with dining down a short flight of steps. Good-value quality meals are freshly cooked from locally sourced food, and booking is advised at weekends. Live music features regularly. It has a large enclosed patio-style garden with views over Ludford. The pub is the home of the Ludlow venison pie and is a regular award winner at the Ludlow Festival. A family-run, friendly local. Dogs allowed. ⊛◑A⇌🖰(192)♣'⌐

Market Drayton

Red Lion
Great Hales Street, TF9 1JP
✪ 11-11 (midnight Fri & Sat) ☎ (01630) 652602
⊕ joulesbrewery.co.uk
Joule's Blonde, Original Pale Ale, Slumbering Monk Ⓗ
Home to the Joule's Brewery, this former coaching house originally built in 1623 is warmed by a log fire and has a traditional snug atmosphere. The long bar has its own well – once the source for the on-site brewery. The adjacent mouse room features unique wood panelling carved by Robert Thompson – his trademark was to carve a mouse into each of his works and there are seven to find here. The pub offers locally produced food that rounds a visit off nicely. ♨Q♜⊛◑&🖰♣P'⌐

Ratlinghope

Bridges Ⓛ
SY5 0ST
✪ 11-11 ☎ (01588) 650260 ⊕ thebridgespub.co.uk
Three Tuns seasonal beers Ⓗ/Ⓐ, 1642 Bitter, XXX, Cleric's Cure Ⓗ
Formerly called the Horseshoe, the pub reopened in 2011, after several months of restoration, as the only tied house for the Three Tuns Brewery, Bishops Castle. A long, low building of some age, it is situated in the picturesque setting of the South Shropshire Hills west of the Long Mynd, on the banks of the River East Onny. Inside there is a large drinking and dining area on the left and a cosy bar to the right. The pub is popular with walkers. Live music features from time to time. ♨Q♜⊛🖰◑AP'⌐

Ruyton XI Towns

Talbot Country Inn Ⓛ
Church Street, SY4 1LA
✪ 11.30-3, 6-11; 11.30-midnight Sat; 12-10.30 Sun ☎ (01939) 262882 ⊕ thetalbotcountryinn.co.uk
Hobsons Best Bitter; Salopian Shropshire Gold; Stonehouse Station Bitter; guest beers Ⓗ
Opened in 2010 after a full refurbishment, this Grade II-listed former coaching inn caters for a quick drink or more leisurely dining, whether a light bite lunch or a full meal. There are three distinct areas including the bar with an open real fire, and dogs are welcome. All food is sourced locally wherever possible. Monday is supper and real ale night and Tuesday is a themed food night. The 576 bus stops outside during the day (not Sun). ♨Q⊛🖰◑⊜&🖰(576)P'⌐

Sambrook

Three Horseshoes
TF10 8AP (½ mile E of A41)
✪ 12-2 (not Mon), 5 (4 summer)-11; 11-10.30 (11 summer) Sun ☎ (01952) 551133

Banks's Mild; St Austell Tribute; Salopian Shropshire Gold; guest beers ℍ
A cosy village pub unspoilt by time, with a welcoming woodburner in the quarry-tiled bar for winter and a patio garden area for summer. A popular watering hole for visitors from far and wide, it is a favourite for country music groups and the young farmers. Dominoes and darts add to the traditional ambience. To complement the beer there is good locally sourced food served in the restaurant. ♨Q❀①❶⚌♣P⌐

Selattyn

Cross Keys ★ 🄻
Glyn Road, SY10 7DH (on B4579 Oswestry-Glyn Ceiriog road)
❀ closed Mon & Tue; 7 (6 Fri)-11; 12-5, 7-11 Sun
☎ (01691) 650247
Stonehouse Station Bitter; guest beers ℍ
Dating from the 17th century, this building has been an inn since 1840 and identified by CAMRA as one of Britain's Real Heritage Pubs. It is situated next to the church in a small village close to the Welsh border and Offa's Dyke. The small cosy bar with a quarry-tiled floor has a large topical cartoon redrawn each December above the fireplace. There are two further rooms and a function room. The pub opens at lunchtimes during the week by prior arrangement. Accommodation is available in a self-catering cottage. The landlord is a keen campanologist. Local CAMRA Pub of the Year 2012. ♨Q❀✉❶🅰♣P

Shifnal

Odfellows Wine Bar ✅
Market Place, TF11 9AU
❀ 12-midnight (1am Fri & Sat; 11.30 Sun) ☎ (01952) 461517
🌐 odleyinns.co.uk/odfellows
Salopian Shropshire Gold, Oracle; guest beers ℍ
Great wine bar in the centre of Shifnal serving up to four cask ales including guests from the local area. The emphasis here is on food with an extensive well-priced menu. Live music nights are hosted on a regular basis. Comfortable B&B accommodation is available. Although open late on Friday and Saturday, entry must be before 11pm.
♨❀✉①⚌⇌P⌐

White Hart 🄻 ✅
4 High Street, TF11 8BH
❀ 12-11 ☎ (01952) 461161
Holden's Black Country Mild, Black Country Bitter; Salopian Shropshire Gold; Wye Valley HPA, Butty Bach; guest beers ℍ
A regular in the Guide for 20 years, this popular pub has two rooms and a large patio area. Many times local CAMRA Pub of the Year, it regularly achieves maximum Cask Marque accreditation. With seven handpulls dispensing the regular range plus two guests, it has established itself as the premier pub in the area. It is Grade II-listed, circa 1600, and community aware, home to dominoes, darts, quizzes and charity auctions, and runs a spectacular hanging basket competition in summer. Home-cooked food is served lunchtimes except Sunday.
Q🅂❀①⚌⇌♣P⌐

Shrewsbury

Admiral Benbow 🄻
24 Swan Hill, SY1 1NF (just off main square)
❀ 5 (12 Sat)-11; 7-10.30 Sun ☎ (01743) 244423
Ironbridge Foundry Gold; Ludlow Gold; Monty's Sunshine; Six Bells Cloud Nine; Titanic Iceberg; Wye Valley HPA; guest beers ℍ
Spacious free house offering a range of eight Shropshire and Herefordshire ales, six ciders from Gwatkin (including Foxwhelp and Yarlington Mill) and Rosie's Perfect Pear perry. A good range of Belgian beers is also available. A small room off the bar can be used for private functions. Children are not permitted and under 30s are served at the management's discretion. Outside seating and a smoking area are available. ♨Q❀⚌⇌♣●⌐

Coach & Horses 🄻 ✅
Swan Hill, SY1 1NF
❀ 11.30-midnight (12.30am Fri & Sat); 12-11.30 Sun
☎ (01743) 365661 🌐 odleyinns.co.uk/coach-horses/
Salopian Shropshire Gold, Oracle; Stonehouse Station Bitter; guest beers ℍ
Set in a quiet street off the main shopping area, the Coach & Horses provides a quiet haven, with magnificent floral displays in summer. Victorian in style, the pub has a wood-panelled bar, a small side snug area and a lounge for dining. It is recognised as having an interior of regional historical interest. Cheddar Valley cider is sold alongside the ales. Live music, electro-acoustic in the main, plays most Sunday evenings in the lounge/restaurant. Q①⚌❶⇌⊞●⌐

Nag's Head
Wyle Cop, SY1 1XB (on RH side of Wyle Cop)
❀ 11.30 (12 Sun)-midnight (1am Fri & Sat)
☎ (01743) 362455
Caledonian Deuchars IPA; Hobsons Best Bitter, Town Crier; Sharp's Doom Bar; Three Tuns XXX; Taylor Landlord; guest beer ℍ
Situated on the historic Wyle Cop, the main features of this timber-framed building are best appreciated externally, in particular the upper storey jettying and to the rear the timber remnants of a 14th-century hall house including a screened passage that provided protection from draughts (and now provides shelter for smokers). The old-style interior has remained unaltered for many years. The pub can be very busy at times, attracting a mixed clientele. The building is reputed to be haunted and features on the Shrewsbury Ghost Trail. ❀❶⇌⊞♣⌐

Prince of Wales 🄻
Bynner Street, Belle Vue, SY3 7NZ
❀ 5-midnight; 12-1am Fri-Sun ☎ (01743) 343301
🌐 princeofwaleshotel.co.uk
Greene King IPA; Hobsons Mild; St Austell Tribute; Salopian Golden Thread; guest beers ℍ
Welcoming two-roomed community pub with a large decked suntrap garden and heated smoking shelter with bowling green. The green is overlooked by a 19th-century maltings. Darts, dominoes and bowls teams abound. Two beer festivals are held each year – a winter ales festival in February and another in May. Shrewsbury Town FC memorabilia adorn the building inside and out, with some of the seating from the old Gay Meadow ground skirting the bowling green. Meals served Friday-Sunday lunchtimes only.
♨🅂❀①⚌❶⇌⊞♣P⌐🍷

Salopian Bar 🏆 🗒 ✅

Smithfield Road, SY1 1PW

✪ 11-11 (midnight Wed, Fri & Sat) ☎ (01743) 351505
⊕ thesalopianbar.co.uk

Salopian Oracle; Stonehouse Station Bitter; guest beers Ⓗ

This pub has a modern, comfortable atmosphere with tasteful, non-invasive decor. The dedicated management continually strives to increase the beer, cider and perry range to satisfy public demand. Regular cider and perry are provided by Westons and Thatchers. An ever-increasing range of bottled beer (Belgian and American) is also available. Major sports events are shown on large-screen TV. Local artists' paintings on display are for sale. Frequently voted local CAMRA Pub of the Year including 2011 and 2012. ♿🎗🛏🐕🕯🎵

Three Fishes 🗒 ✅

Fish Street, SY1 1UR

✪ 11.30-3, 5-11; 11.30-11.30 Fri & Sat; 12-4, 7-10.30 Sun
☎ (01743) 344793 ⊕ realaleshrewsbury.com

Sharp's Doom Bar; Stonehouse Station Bitter; Taylor Landlord; guest beers Ⓗ

Fifteenth-century building standing in the shadow of two churches, St Alkmund's and St Julian's, within the maze of streets and passageways in the medieval quarter of the town. Freshly prepared food is available at lunchtime and early evening Monday to Saturday. The pub offers a range of up to six local and national ales, with some dark beers featuring regularly although not guaranteed, plus a varied range of real ciders and perries. Local CAMRA Pub of the Year 2010. Q🎗🛏🎵

Woodman Inn

Coton Hill, SY1 2DZ (750yds from train station on Ellesmere Rd A528)

✪ 4 (12 Sat & Sun)-midnight ☎ (01743) 351007

Greene King Abbot; Salopian Shropshire Gold; Wye Valley Butty Bach; guest beers Ⓗ

Half-brick and half-timbered black and white corner pub originally built in the 1800s but destroyed by fire in 1923 and rebuilt in 1925. The pub is reputedly haunted by an ex-landlady who died when the pub burnt down. With an interior of historic interest, it has a wonderful oak-panelled lounge with two real log fires and traditional settles. The bar has the original stone-tiled flooring, wooden seating, log fire and leaded windows. The courtyard seating area doubles as a heated smoking area. Real cider is usually available in summer. ⌂Q🎗🛏🎵🕯

Stottesdon

Fighting Cocks 🏆 🗒

1 High Street, DY14 8TZ

✪ 6 (12 Sat)-midnight; 5-1am Fri; 12-10.30 Sun
☎ (01746) 718270

Hobsons Mild, Twisted Spire, Best Bitter; guest beer Ⓗ

Set in the heart of rural south Shropshire, this local CAMRA award-winning pub (Pub of the Year 2012) is well worth visiting. A thriving community pub with its own shop, it serves local Hobsons beers and a guest. The traditional bar with log fire leads up to one of two dining rooms where locally sourced food is served (Sat and Sun lunch only, not Sun and Mon eves). Live music plays most Saturday nights. A function room is available. Apple Day is celebrated every October and a beer festival hosted in November. ⌂🎗🐾🕯

Telford: Coalport

Shakespeare 🗒

High Street, TF8 7HT (near Tar Tunnel and China Museum)

✪ 5-11; 12-midnight Sat & Sun ☎ (01952) 580675
⊕ shakespeare-inn.co.uk

Everards Tiger; Hobsons Twisted Spire; Ludlow Gold; guest beers Ⓗ

Cosy but spacious village pub within the Ironbridge Gorge area with views of the river and close to local museums. A good selection of real ales includes many locally brewed favourites such as the award-winning Hobsons Twisted Spire and Ludlow Gold. Good food is always popular so book ahead. Friendly and welcoming staff create a pleasant and warm atmosphere. ⌂Q🎗🛏🕯

Telford: Ironbridge

Golden Ball

Newbridge Road, TF8 7BA (off B4373 – Madeley Road Hill)

✪ 11.30-11 (midnight Sat & Sun) ☎ (01952) 432179
⊕ goldenballinn.com

Everards Tiger; guest beers Ⓗ

A hidden gem situated off the Madeley to Ironbridge road, this historic inn is well worth finding. Warm and welcoming with a vibrant atmosphere in the bar, it has three main areas set around the central bar. Regular ales vie with an ever-changing list of guest beers. Delicious home-cooked food is served in the bar or separate dining areas. Handy for the local museums around the Ironbridge Gorge and a must if visiting the Severn Gorge. ⌂Q🎗🛏P

Robin Hood Inn

33 Waterloo Street, TF8 7HQ

✪ 11-midnight; 12-11.30 Sun ☎ (01952) 434089

Holden's Black Country Bitter, Golden Glow, Special; guest beers Ⓗ

Across the road from the River Severn, this lovely looking pub is close to the modern Jackfield Bridge on the outskirts of historic Ironbridge. Two bars serve five rooms where good-value food, often locally sourced, is served along with three regular and three guest ales. Quality Sunday lunches are popular. Family friendly, with full disabled access, outdoor patio areas and a large car park, the pub is rarely without the hum of voices and smiling faces. ⌂Q🎗🛏(88,89)🕯P

Telford: Madeley

All Nations 🗒

20 Coalport Road, TF7 5DP (off Legges Way opposite Blists Hill Museum)

✪ 12-midnight ☎ (01952) 585747

Shires Best Bitter, Dabley Gold; guest beers Ⓗ

A local institution, this is a multi-award-winning pub loved by everyone. Stuck in a time-warp, it refuses to change. Out the back you will find the Shires Brewery and the toilets along with various drinking areas; inside you'll find a warm welcome, a single-roomed bar, four real ales and a cider or perry from Westons. Made-to-order rolls complement the drinks. A TV that uses a 36-gallon barrel as a stand is set up for international Rugby Union matches. ⌂Q🎗🕯P

Telford: Oakengates

Crown Inn 🅛 ✅
Market Street, TF2 6EA
✪ 12-11 ☎ (01952) 610888 ⊕ crown@oakengates.net
Hobsons Best Bitter; guest beers Ⓗ
A warm welcome is guaranteed at this convivial hostelry. The licensees were pioneers when they introduced a diverse range of cask ales to Oakengates way back in the '90s, a theme that continues to the present day. Thursday night is given over to entertainment which is popular with folk from near and far. The Telford Beer Festival is held twice a year in May and October, offering rare brews alongside favourites, all dispensed via a bank of handpumps. ⚒Q♿🍴🅓♿➝🖨♣♠🐾

Old Fighting Cocks
48 Market Street, TF2 6DU
✪ 3 (11 Fri-Sun)-11 ☎ (01952) 615607
Everards Tiger; Ironbridge Foundry Gold, Wenlock Stout; guest beers Ⓗ
Reopened in 2010, Ironbridge Brewery has restored this pub to its former glory. Off the two-room bar there is a separate snug and a dining area where you are encouraged to bring your own food or order from nearby – cutlery and plates provided. Four of the handpulls are dedicated to Ironbridge beers including Ironbridge Blonde, giving plenty of scope for guest beers, with seven available, and a rotating cider. Guaranteed no karaoke or open mic nights! ⚒Q♿🍴🅓♿➝🖨♣♠🐾

Station Hotel
42 Market Street, TF2 6DU
✪ 10-11; 10.30-3.30, 7-11 Sun ☎ (01952) 612949
Salopian Shropshire Gold; guest beers Ⓗ
Multi-roomed genuine free house serving a splendid selection of ever-changing beers sourced from both near and far as well as a traditional cider. Food is generally baps only, however Wednesday is home-made curry night. A warm welcome is always assured. ⚒Q🅓♿➝🖨♣♠🐾

Telford: St George's

St George's Sports & Social Club
Church Road, TF2 9LU
✪ 7-11; 6-midnight Fri; 12-12.15am Sat; 12-10.30 Sun
☎ (01952) 612911
Banks's Mild, Bitter; Jennings Bitter; guest beers Ⓗ
At the heart of the community, this club has much to offer including a superb range of quality cask ales and excellent outdoor sports facilities. The establishment is CAMRA local Branch 2012 Club of the Year, and was a 2011 West Midlands regional finalist. Good-value food is on sale at most times. CAMRA members are always welcome in the club, which has a friendly and relaxed atmosphere. There is a separate hall available to hire for functions. 🚆♿🍴🖨♣♠P

Telford: Wellington

Cock Hotel
148 Hollyhead Road, TF1 2DL
✪ 4 (12 Thu)-11.30; 12-midnight Fri & Sat; 12-4, 7-11 Sun
☎ (01952) 244954 ⊕ cockhotel.co.uk
Hobsons Mild, Best Bitter; guest beers Ⓗ
The Old Wrekin Tap is the main bar of this frequent winner of CAMRA Branch and Regional Pub of the Year awards. Eight handpulls serve the regular Hobsons beers and Black Rat cider, with five other changing beers including a stout or porter. The stable yard of this 18th-century coaching inn has picnic benches and a covered smoking area. A quiet drink can be enjoyed in the wood-panelled dining room; or connoisseurs can sample quality beers from across Europe in the Brasserie de Haan. Accommodation has been recently refurbished and upgraded. ⚒Q♿🍴🅓♿➝🖨♣♠P🐾

William Withering ✅
43-45 High Street, TF1 1LU
✪ 8am-midnight ☎ (01952) 642800
Greene King Abbot; Ruddles Best Bitter; Salopian Shropshire Gold; guest beers Ⓗ
Previously a shopping complex, this is one of the newest pubs Wetherspoon has opened, named after a local physician and geologist. The Withering's decor mixes period 1700s features with a typical modern bar area. The 10 handpulls provide three regular ales and seven constantly changing guests from up and down the country. A real cider is sometimes also available. Good-value food is served until 10pm in a relaxed atmosphere. 🅓♿➝🖨🐾

Wrekin Inn
26 Wrekin Road, TF1 1RH (near police station and leisure centre)
✪ 4-11; 2-midnight Fri; 12-midnight Sat; 12-10.30 Sun
☎ (01952) 244865
Beer range varies Ⓗ
Modern corner pub with distinct areas in an open plan layout. One regular beer from Titanic and five changing guest beers are on handpump as well as two ciders. Darts and dominoes are played and there is a weekly poker night and monthly quiz. Live music features on Friday evening and late Sunday afternoon, with an occasional open mic night during the week. Freshly made bar snacks are available to order plus an interesting nuts menu. Outside is a decked seating area. Beer or cider festivals are held four times a year. ⚒♿➝🖨♣♠P🐾

Tilley

Tilley Raven 🅛 ✅
SY4 5HE (signed off A49 just S of Wem by railway bridge)
✪ 12-11 (1am Fri; midnight Sat) ☎ (01939) 234419
⊕ tilleyraven.com
Hobsons Best Bitter; Three Tuns 1642 Bitter; guest beers Ⓗ
An 18th-century pub in the hamlet of Tilley on the edge of Wem. The inside has been modernised but retains character with an oak floor, an inglenook fireplace that once held an Aga oven and old exposed brickwork. Four cask beers are stocked, one either a mild, stout or porter from a local brewery. Excellent home-cooked food is prepared by the chef/owner made with locally produced ingredients. Live music plays on Friday nights. ⚒Q♿🅓♿➝(Wem)🖨🐾P🐾

Whitchurch

Anchor 🅛
7 Pepper Street, SY13 1BG (off High Street)
✪ 11 (10 Fri)-11; 12-10.30 Sun ☎ (01948) 663806
⊕ theanchorbarandrestaurant.co.uk
Titanic Anchor Bitter; guest beers Ⓗ
Located just off the High Street, this tastefully restored Victorian former hotel is divided into four

areas and still retains the original floorboards in the public bar. Comfortable chairs are provided in the lounge area around the island bar, which has six handpulls serving a varying range of mainly local beers. The pub has a separate dining room where a range of locally sourced home-cooked food is served with a daily specials board. Q◑▷🍴&⇌🚲P🚳⌐

Black Bear 🄻

49 High Street, SY13 1AZ

🕔 12-3, 6-11; 12-11 Sat & Sun ☎ (01948) 663800 ⊕ theblackbearpub.co.uk

Phoenix Monkeytown Mild; guest beers Ⓗ

Attractively renovated black and white corner pub situated opposite the historic St Alkmund's church. The ornate bar has six handpulls, one dedicated to cider, and the remainder serving an ever-changing range of guest beers from both local and lesser-known national microbreweries, with pump clips adorning the walls, ceiling and bar area. The pub

has two separate dining areas serving locally sourced home-cooked food from an ever-changing menu. Q🕸◑▷⇌🚲

Whitchurch Cricket Club 🄻

SY13 3JG (via Greenfoot Lane off Tilstock Road or Cycle Route 45)

🕔 6 (10 Sat; 6.30 Sun)-11 summer; 6.30-11 (closed Wed) winter ☎ (01948) 663923 ⊕ whitchurchcc.play-cricket.com

Thwaites Nutty Black; Woodlands Midnight Stout; guest beers Ⓗ

This four-times local CAMRA Club of the Year goes from strength to strength. The bar has nine handpulls serving a range of beers from Shropshire and Cheshire microbreweries. Two ticker-friendly festivals are held in February and June making use of 26 handpulls. The club offers discounts to CAMRA members. This dog-friendly venue is sometimes hired out for private functions so ring ahead prior to travelling. 🕸&▲⇌🚲(511)♣🐾P🚳⌐

Three Fishes, Shrewsbury (Photo: sisaphus)

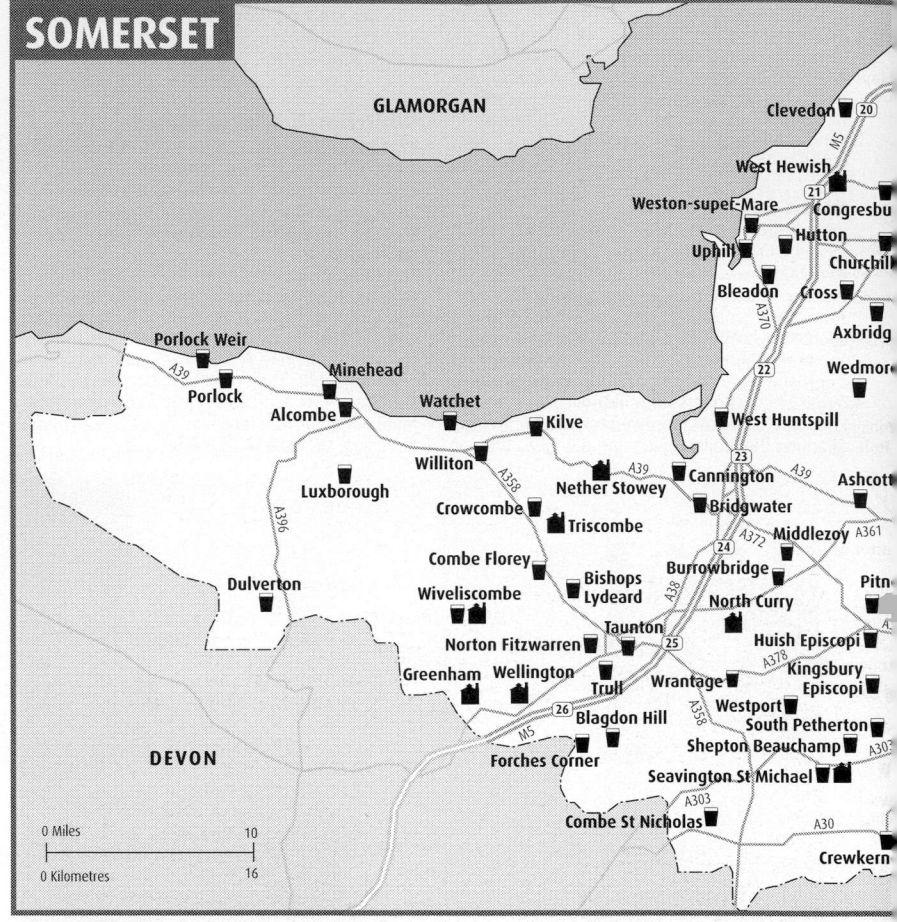

SOMERSET

GLAMORGAN

Clevedon 20

West Hewish

21

Weston-super-Mare Congresbu

Uphill Hutton

Bleadon Churchill

Cross

Axbridg

22 Wedmor

Porlock Weir

Minehead

Porlock

Alcombe Watchet West Huntspill

Kilve

23

Williton Cannington Ashcott

Luxborough Nether Stowey Bridgwater

Crowcombe Triscombe

24

Combe Florey Burrowbridge Pitn

Dulverton Bishops Middlezoy

Wiveliscombe Lydeard North Curry

Norton Fitzwarren Taunton Huish Episcopi

25 Kingsbury

Greenham Wellington Wrantage Episcopi

Trull Westport

DEVON 26 Blagdon Hill South Petherton

Forches Corner Shepton Beauchamp

Seavington St Michael

0 Miles 10

0 Kilometres 16 Combe St Nicholas

A30

Crewkern

Alcombe

Britannia Inn ✓

1 Manor Road, TA24 6EH

✪ 10.30-11 (midnight Fri & Sat); 12-11 Sun

☎ (01643) 702384 ⊕ britanniaalcombe.co.uk

Brains SA; Courage Best Bitter; guest beers Ⓗ

One of the oldest free houses in the Minehead area, the Britannia offers a comfortable public bar and saloon plus a safe and secluded walled garden. There is also a skittle alley and private function room with cocktail bar. The traditional bar food menu is extensive, with daily home-cooked specials, and the function room caters for either a set menu or à la carte lunches and dinners. The medieval village of Dunster, the Quantock Hills and Exmoor National Park are close by. Accommodation is en-suite. ⊕⇌◗Ⅾ⊟ᵹⅆ▲⊟(18,28)♣⊱

Ash

Bell Inn Ⓛ

3 Main Street, TA12 6NS

✪ 12-midnight ☎ (01935) 822727 ⊕ thebellinnash.co.uk

Beer range varies Ⓗ

The Bell has been recently refurbished, enhancing its rustic charm and fine, welcoming atmosphere. At the bar you will find up to four real ales, mainly from Somerset breweries. Good-quality home-

cooked seasonal food is available six days a week (no food Mon). The Sunday lunchtime carvery is exceptional, as are the daily specials. Live music is well supported and also the Sunday evening quiz. A warm open fire ensures cosy sessions. Look out for the belfry antiquities adorning the walls. ⊭Q⊛◗Ⅾᵹ⊟(N9A,52)♣P⊱

Ashcott

Ring O' Bells

High Street, TA7 9PZ

✪ 12-2.30, 7-11 (10.30 Sun) ☎ (01458) 210232

⊕ ringobells.com

Beer range varies Ⓗ

An 18th-century family-run free house in the village, divided into three traditional areas on split levels with a separate restaurant; old fireplaces and beams help enhance a warm ambience. There is a contrasting modern skittle alley/function room and an enclosed garden. Families are welcome. Three ales on handpump support mainly local microbreweries but also more distant ones. Wilkins cider is served. Good home-cooked food is available; takeaway meals and ales can be arranged. Close to Ham Wall and Shapwick Heath nature reserves. ⊛◗Ⅾ⊟(19,29,375)♣●P⊱

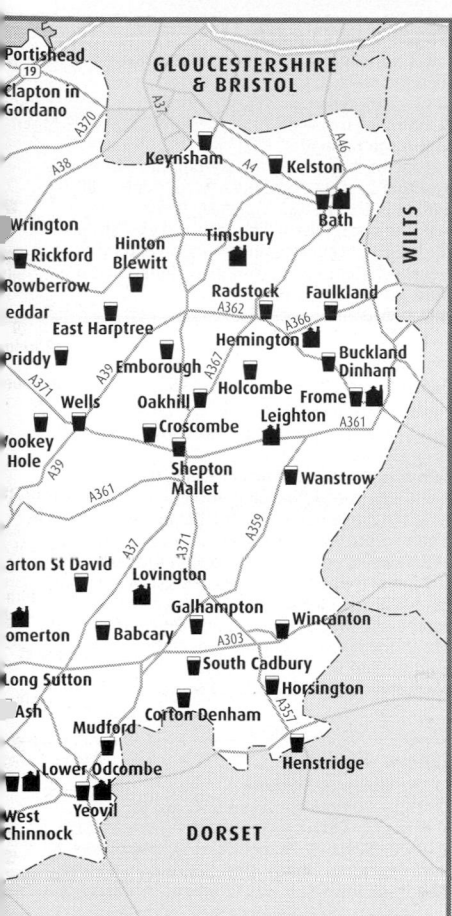

restaurant have flagged floors and beams. The back bar features ancient furniture and plenty of traditional bar games. The menu has dishes to suit all tastes and local produce is used whenever possible. Guest chef nights are popular. Families are welcome and dogs too. Teignworthy ales are usually on handpulls, as are many other locally sourced beers. ⌂Q🕾🕭🕨🕭🖎♣🐾P

Barton St David

Barton Inn
Main Street, TA11 6BZ
🕛 12-2.30 (not Mon), 4.30-11 (midnight Sat & Sun)
☎ (01458) 850451 🌐 barton-inn.co.uk
Beer range varies Ⓖ
Park the muddy dog next to the fire to dry before sampling some of the local ales racked behind the counter, or real cider if you prefer. A proper country pub full of both character and characters, eccentricity appears to be the norm here. The single bar manages to retain the appearance of the original two rooms and maintains a cosy feeling. While this pub is somewhat off the beaten track, those making the effort to find it will be rewarded. ⌂🕭🕭🕭🖎(667)♣🐾P🍴

Bath

Bell
103 Walcot Street, BA1 5BW
🕛 11.30-11; 12-10.30 Sun ☎ (01225) 460426
🌐 thebellinnbath.co.uk
Abbey Bellringer; Bath Ales Gem; Butcombe Bitter; Hop Back Summer Lightning; Otter Ale; RCH Pitchfork; Stonehenge Danish Dynamite Ⓗ
The Bell features bands on Monday and Wednesday evenings and Sunday lunchtimes. There is a long main bar and a number of seating areas. The wall space inside is taken up with posters for local events. A computer is available for free internet access and Wi-Fi. At the back of the pub is a garden with covered seating, behind which is the Love Lounge (open mic on Thursday nights) and a launderettette (sic). 🕭🕭🗲(Spa)🖎♣🍴

Garrick's Head
7-8 St John's Place, Sawclose, BA1 1ET (next to Theatre Royal)
🕛 12-11.30 (midnight Sat); 12-10.30 Sun ☎ (01225) 318368
🌐 garricksheadpub.com
Beer range varies Ⓗ
A theatre pub for over 200 years, but originally the town house of Beau Nash, Bath's 18th-century Master of Ceremonies, this local is reputedly the most haunted pub in the city. Three or four real ales, mostly from local microbreweries, include some rarities, while local ciders are often complemented by a perry. Traditional food sourced from local ingredients is served lunchtimes and evenings. Tables in the pedestrianised area outside are an ideal place to watch the world go by. 🕭🕭🗲(Spa)🖎🐾🍴

Hop Pole
7 Albion Buildings, Upper Bristol Road, BA1 3AR
🕛 12-11 (midnight Fri & Sat) ☎ (01225) 446327
Bath Ales SPA, Gem, Barnsey; guest beers Ⓗ
Bath Ales pub half a mile west of the city centre, close to Royal Victoria Park and the River Avon. Five or six real ales are available, including four from

Axbridge

Lamb ✓
The Square, BS26 2AP
🕛 11.30-3, 6-11 Mon-Wed; 11.30-11 (11.30 Fri & Sat); 12-10.30 Sun ☎ (01934) 732253 🌐 lamb.butcombe.com
Butcombe Bitter, Gold, seasonal beer; Fuller's London Pride Ⓗ
Butcombe-owned Grade II-listed coaching house in the village square. The National Trust's medieval King John's Hunting Lodge lies directly opposite. There is a large low-beamed bar area and several smaller, quieter areas leading off from it. Outside drinking areas are to the front and rear via the courtyard. Lunchtime and evening meals (not Sun) are served. London Pride is occasionally replaced by guest beers. The cider is Thatchers. The Weston to Wells 126 bus stops in the main square during the day. ⌂Q🕭🕭🖎(126)♣🍴

Babcary

Red Lion
TA11 7ED (off A37 N of Podimore jct with A303)
🕛 12-3, 6-midnight; 12-midnight Sun ☎ (01458) 223230
🌐 redlionbabcary.co.uk
Beer range varies Ⓗ
A 14th-century pub that is well worth a visit for good food and excellent beers. The lounge bar and

Bath Ales, plus a range of bottled foreign beers. The enclosed and spacious beer garden is popular with families. Food is served lunchtimes and evenings Monday to Friday, all day on Saturday and till 4pm on Sunday. Home-made bar snacks – nuts, pork scratchings and Scotch eggs – are also on offer. ♨⌂☺◑▣⌐

King William

36 Thomas Street, London Road, BA1 5NN (on A4 London Road around ½ mile NE of city centre)
☼ 12-3 (not Mon & Tue), 5-11 (midnight Fri); 12-midnight Sat; 12-11 Sun ☎ (01225) 428096 ⊕ kingwilliampub.com
Palmers Dorset Gold; guest beers Ⓗ
Tiny, two-bar Victorian pub that has kept the look and feel of a bustling street-corner local, while garnering awards for the quality of its home-cooked, locally sourced food. The varying range of local beers generally includes one from Palmers and three from local microbreweries. Local cider is also available. A monthly book club meets in the restaurant upstairs and the quiz on the first Monday of each month is gaining in popularity. ◑▣●

Old Green Tree ★

12 Green Street, BA1 2JZ
☼ 11-11; 12-10.30 Sun ☎ (01225) 448259
Blindmans Green Tree Bitter; Butcombe Bitter; RCH Pitchfork; guest beers Ⓗ
Classic, unspoilt pub in a 300-year-old building. The three oak-panelled rooms include a superb northern-style drinking lobby, where it is nigh impossible not to strike up a conversation. Although it can get crowded, there is often space in the comfortable back bar. Beers are generally sourced from local microbreweries, with a stout or porter usually on offer in the winter months. A local farmhouse cider is also available, along with a range of fine wines and malt whiskies.
Q◑⌐♿(Spa)▣●

Pig & Fiddle

2 Saracen Street, BA1 5BR
☼ 11-11.30; 12-10.30 Sun ☎ (01225) 460868
Butcombe Bitter; Fuller's London Pride; Wadworth Henrys IPA; guest beers Ⓗ
A large and busy town-centre pub with a varied clientele and a friendly atmosphere. One end is an old shop front, the other a courtyard with drinking benches and covered heaters. The decor is an esoteric collection of art displays and sports memorabilia. Up to three guest beers come from local breweries. Table football is available, and there are regular live music and open mic nights. The pub is popular with rugby fans and there are several large TV screens. ☺◑♿(Spa)▣♣●⌐

Raven

6-7 Queen Street, BA1 1HE
☼ 11.30-11 (midnight Fri & Sat); 12-10.30 Sun
☎ (01225) 425045 ⊕ theravenofbath.co.uk
Blindmans Raven, Ravens Gold; guest beers Ⓗ
Busy 18th-century free house in the heart of Bath that was CAMRA local City Pub of the Year 2010. The six ales include two brewed exclusively by Blindmans. Guest ales come from far and wide, with several mini beer festivals a year. The main bar and the quieter first-floor bar serve the same range of ales. Famous for its sausages and Pieminister pies, the Raven is one of the few pubs in Bath serving food on Sunday evening.
◑♿(Spa)●☐

Royal Oak (Twerton)

Lower Bristol Road, Twerton, BA2 3BW (on A36 at intersection with road to Windsor Bridge)
☼ 4 (12 Fri-Sun)-midnight ☎ (01225) 481409
⊕ theroyaloak-bath.co.uk
Beer range varies Ⓗ
A range of up to seven beers from microbreweries near and far are served here. Local ciders and bottled beers are also available. There are folk music sessions (alternating Irish and English) on Wednesday evenings and live music plays most weekends. Outside is a secluded garden and a small on-site car park.
♨Q☺♿(Oldfield Park)▣●P⌐

Salamander

3 John Street, BA1 2JL
☼ 10 (9am Sat)-11 (midnight Fri & Sat); 10-10.30 Sun
☎ (01225) 428889
Bath Ales SPA, Gem, Barnsey, Golden Hare Ⓗ
Eighteenth-century building, tucked away in a side street, that opened as a coffee bar in 1957 and got a pub licence five years later. Taken over by Bath Ales 12 years ago and revamped in the company's inimitable style, it looks and feels like a pub that has been there for a century or more. Wooden floorboards, wood panelling and subdued lighting add to the ambience of the ground-floor bar, created from several small rooms. There is a popular restaurant upstairs. ◑♿(Spa)▣

Star ★ ✅

23 The Vineyards, BA1 5NA
☼ 12-2.30, 5.30-midnight (1am Fri); 12-1am Sat; 12-midnight Sun ☎ (01225) 425072 ⊕ star-inn-bath.co.uk
Abbey Bellringer Ⓗ**; Draught Bass** Ⓖ**; guest beers** Ⓗ
Now the tap for Abbey Ales, Bath's only brewery, this classic town pub was fitted out by Gaskell & Chambers in 1928. Its four small rooms have benches around the walls, wood panelling and roaring fires. The smallest room has just a single bench, called Death Row, while the pub, which dates from around 1760, is coffin-shaped. Bass is served from the cask and complimentary snuff is available. There is a Friday night folk session and a monthly quiz. ♨Q♿♿(Spa)▣♣●

INDEPENDENT BREWERIES

Abbey Ales Bath
Blindmans Leighton
Butcombe Wrington
Cheddar Ales Cheddar
Cotleigh Wiveliscombe
Cottage Lovington
Dawkins Timsbury
Devilfish Hemington
Exmoor Wiveliscombe
Glastonbury Somerton
Masters/Blackdown Greenham (NEW)
Milk Street Frome
Moor Pitney
North Curry North Curry
Odcombe Lower Odcombe
Quantock Wellington
RCH West Hewish
Six Trees Triscombe (NEW)
Stowey Nether Stowey
Windy Seavington St Michael (NEW)
Yeovil Yeovil

White Horse

Shophouse Road, Twerton, BA2 1EF (off A36 Lower Bristol Rd, at top of Jews Lane) ST730643
🌞 3-11 (midnight Thu); 2-midnight Fri; 12-midnight Sat; 12-11 Sun ☎ (01225) 340668 🌐 thewhitehorsebath.com
Otter Ale; Moorhouse's Blonde Witch; guest beers Ⓗ
Local CAMRA Branch Pub of the Year in 2011 and Bath City Pub of the Year 2012, this friendly community pub, perched high on a hill overlooking the city, is celebrating its sixth year under the current landlord. Up to five beers are available, with Otter and Moorhouse's beers the semi-regulars, and guests generally sourced from local microbreweries. There are four beer festivals a year, a regular open mic night, and a charity event in aid of the local church. Children are welcome.
Q ⛲😊🍴 ♿ ▲ 🚲 (Oldfield Park) 🚃 ♣ ♠ P 𝄢 ⊟

Bishops Lydeard

Bird in Hand ⅃ ✅

34 Mount Street, TA4 3LH
🌞 12-11 (10 Sun) ☎ (01823) 432090
🌐 thebirdinhand34.com
Cotleigh Tawny; Exmoor Gold; guest beers Ⓗ
Very much a community pub, this free house is at the centre of the village and only 10 minutes' walk from West Somerset Railway. Four ales are served, mainly from local and south-west breweries. The bar and dining area are slate floored and warmed by an open fire in winter. Good food is locally produced and home cooked. The skittle alley also accommodates functions, and there is a large garden where families and dogs are welcome. Look out for mini beer festivals.
🏨😊🍴 ▲ 🚲 🚃 (18,28) ♣ P 𝄢

Blagdon Hill

Lamb & Flag ⅃

TA3 7SL (4 miles S of Taunton)
🌞 11-2.30, 5-11; 11-midnight Fri; 11-11 Sat; 12-10.30 (12-6 winter) Sun ☎ (01823) 421736 🌐 lambandflag.co.uk
Beer range varies Ⓗ
Privately owned 16th-century free house with frequently changing ales on the northern slopes of the Blackdown Hills and popular with locals and visitors. The main bar has the original flagstone floor and there is a candle-lit dining area. Good food is locally sourced and home made. There is also a skittle alley and function room. The large garden has panoramic views across the Brendon, Quantock and Mendip Hills. Folk music and quiz nights are held fortnightly. 🏨Q😊🍴 ♣ P 𝄢

Bleadon

Queen's Arms ✅

Celtic Way, BS24 0NF (off A370)
🌞 11.30-11; 12-10.30 Sun ☎ (01934) 812080
🌐 queensarms.butcombe.com
Butcombe Bitter, Gold, Rare Breed, seasonal beer Ⓗ
Seventeenth-century stone-built pub in the centre of the village. Three rooms converge on the bar; the largest is the main dining area. Food sales are strong, but not at the expense of ale drinkers - the pub is owned by the local Butcombe Brewery. Thatchers cider is also sold. Two real fires and exposed beams add to the cosy atmosphere. There is also a garden/patio with a sales hatch and families are welcome. Regular buses serve the village from Weston. 🏨Q😊🍴🚃(83)♠ P 𝄢

Bridgwater

Carnival Inn ✅

37 St Mary Street, TA6 3LX
🌞 8am-midnight (1am Fri & Sat) ☎ (01278) 726180
Greene King Abbot; Ruddles Best Bitter; guest beers Ⓗ
Town-centre Wetherspoon that takes its name from Bridgwater's famous carnival. It serves a consistently good range of real ales, often featuring beers from Somerset breweries. There is a large bar area with another large room off to one side. At the back up two steps is a family area and there is space in the garden at the rear for those who wish to smoke. Every Wednesday is ale night with reduced prices on beer. Q😊🍴♿➕🚃🚌♠ 𝄢

Buckland Dinham

Bell

High Street, BA11 2QT (on A362 Frome-Radstock road) ST752512
🌞 12-3 (not Mon & Tue), 6-midnight; 12-2.30, 7-11.30 Sun ☎ (01373) 462956 🌐 bellatbuckland.co.uk
Butcombe Bitter; Wychwood Hobgoblin; guest beers Ⓗ
A warm and cosy local pub that takes part in community activities - it has produced a village recipe book and holds film nights. It also offers a facility to order and pay for beer online. A three-day summer beer festival with live music is run in August and a cider festival in October. Local beers feature in home-prepared dishes. The pub is convenient for the campsite (featuring a collection of bikes), attracting CAMRA members from all over the UK. 🏨⛲😊🍴 ♿▲🚃♣♠ P 𝄢

Burrowbridge

King Alfred Inn ⅃

TA7 0RB (on A361)
🌞 12-2.30, 5.30-11 (8.30 Mon); 12-3, 6-midnight Sat; 12-9.30 Sun ☎ (01823) 698379 🌐 kingalfredinn.com
Butcombe Bitter; Milk Street Funky Monkey; guest beers Ⓗ
Traditional unspoilt Grade II-listed country pub full of warmth and character, at the foot of Burrow Mump, reputed to be the vantage point chosen by King Alfred when he withdrew his army in 878. There is live music every Sunday afternoon and some evenings. One of the guest beers is usually from Otter. Most menu items are sourced locally, many from the landlord's family farm (no food Sun eve or Mon). A beer festival takes place over the August bank holiday weekend. Self-catering cottages are available. CAMRA members receive a discount on beer. 🏨⛲😊🍴▲🚃(29)♣♠ P 𝄢

Cannington

Rose & Crown

30 High Street, TA5 2HF
🌞 12-11 (10.30 Sun) ☎ (01278) 653190
Greene King IPA, Abbot; guest beers Ⓗ
Atmospheric, friendly 17th-century pub with a loyal local following. Original beams are covered with interesting objects donated by locals and there is a large collection of clocks. The single L-shaped bar has a pool table and a collection of games hand made by locals. The Outside Inn is a comfortable covered smoking area in the large award-winning garden. 🏨😊🚃(14)♣ P 𝄢

Churchill

Crown Inn

The Batch, Skinners Lane, BS25 5PP (off A38, ¼ mile S of A368 jct)
🌣 11.30-11 (midnight Fri & Sat); 12-10.30 Sun
☎ (01934) 852995
Cotleigh Batch; Draught Bass; Palmers IPA; RCH Hewish IPA, PG Steam; St Austell Tribute; guest beers Ⓖ

Long-time Guide regular and winner of many CAMRA awards, the Crown has been in the same hands for over 25 years. It is tucked away down a small lane yet close to the village centre. Several small rooms with stone-flagged floors are warmed by two log fires and offer an assortment of seating. Excellent food is provided (lunchtimes only) using local ingredients. Up to nine beers are served on gravity, usually from local breweries. Outside drinking is to the front and rear. Dog-friendly.
🏚Q🕸🏵◖▲�︎(121)P♿︎—

Clapton in Gordano

Black Horse

Clevedon Lane, BS20 7RH (2 miles from M5 jct 19) ST473739
🌣 11-11; 12-10 Sun ☎ (01275) 842105 ⊕ thekicker.co.uk
Butcombe Bitter; Courage Best Bitter; Exmoor Gold Ⓖ**; Otter Bitter; Wadworth 6X** Ⓗ

Excellent 14th-century pub hidden away down a small lane. The snug was once the village lock-up. A large fireplace with a display of old rifles dominates the main bar. Beers are served from a small serving hatch – some but not all on gravity. The games room doubles as a family room, with a children's play area in the pleasant garden. The Gordano Valley cycle route is nearby. Dogs are welcome. Thatchers Dry and Heritage ciders are sold. Bar meals are served 12-2pm Monday to Saturday. 🏚Q🌂🕸🏵◖▲♣♠P♿︎—

Clevedon

Royal Oak ✓

35 Copse Road, BS21 7QN (behind ice cream parlour near pier) ST402717
🌣 12-11 (midnight Fri & Sat) ☎ (01275) 547416
⊕ royaloakclevedon.com
Butcombe Bitter; Fuller's London Pride; Sharp's Doom Bar; guest beer Ⓗ

Lively, friendly, mid-terrace pub close to the sea front and connected to it via an alley. It has a large front window and a Tardis-like interior of many rooms. This epitome of a community pub is home to darts, cribbage and cricket teams. The winner of various awards, it hosts many events, including cooking competitions and dancing ranging from morris men through belly dance to real Zulus. There is a quiz on Monday and folk music on Wednesday. It has its own taxi too. 🏚Q🏵🚫🚏♣♠

Combe Florey

Farmers Arms Ⓛ

TA4 3HZ (on A358 between Bishops Lydeard and Williton)
🌣 12-11 (10.30 Sun) ☎ (01823) 432267
⊕ farmersarmsatcombeflorey.co.uk
Cotleigh Tawny Owl; Exmoor Ale, Gold; St Austell HSD Ⓗ

Family-run 19th-century thatched country pub that boasts Innserve's Regional Best Kept Cellar award for the past two years. Four regular ales are available and the bar area has a cosy and friendly atmosphere with a log fire. The restaurant serves excellent home-cooked food and there is also a large beer garden to enjoy, where you can listen to the nostalgic sounds of steam trains on the nearby West Somerset Railway. 🏚Q🕸🏵◖🚏(18,28)P♿︎—

Combe St Nicholas

Green Dragon Ⓛ

TA20 3NG
🌣 12-2.30 (not Mon), 6-midnight; 12-midnight Sat; 12-4, 7-11 Sun ☎ (01460) 63311
Otter Bitter; guest beer Ⓗ

A large green dragon carved by the landlord greets visitors to this friendly free house, which has origins in the 17th century. More woodcarvings can be found in both bars. The guest beer usually comes from a West Country brewery. A varied menu of good-value, home-cooked food is served at lunchtimes (no food Mon) and Tuesday to Saturday evenings. Local ingredients are used where possible and there is a popular pie and a pint night on Wednesday. Live music features on alternate Fridays. Q◖🏵⬗▲🚏(99)♣P♿︎—

Congresbury

Plough

High Street, BS49 5JA (off A370 at B3133 jct)
🌣 11.30-2.30, 4.30-11; 11.30-midnight Fri; 12-3, 7-11 Sun
☎ (01934) 877402 ⊕ the-plough-inn.net
Butcombe Bitter; St Austell Tribute; guest beers Ⓗ

Characterful village pub with flagstone floors and many original features, decorated with interesting local artefacts. Three or four guest beers are served from a row of old cask heads behind the bar, sourced mainly from local breweries. Thatchers cider is also stocked. Food is served daily lunchtimes and evenings, except Sunday evening, which is quiz night. The pub has real fires, no TV, and children and dogs are welcome. Mendip morris men meet here. 🏚Q🕸🏵◖🚏(X1,353)♣♠P♿︎—

Corton Denham

Queen's Arms Ⓛ ✓

DT9 4LR (3 miles S of A303)
🌣 10-11; 12-10.30 Sun ☎ (01963) 220317
⊕ thequeensarms.com
Moor Queen's Revival; guest beers Ⓗ

Cosy, friendly 18th-century pub in a secluded village well worth seeking out. It is a regular outlet for Moor Brewery, some of whose beers are pioneered here, and Queen's Revival is the house beer. There is also local cider available. Food ranges from local pork pies with mustard and pickles to a selection of main meals made using local ingredients whenever possible. The accommodation is highly rated and the garden has lovely views. Dogs and muddy boots are welcome in the bar. 🏚Q🕸🏵🛏◖♿︎♠P♿︎—

Crewkerne

Old Stagecoach Inn

Station Road, TA18 8AL (next to station)
🌣 12-2, 7-11 (closed Tue & Sun eves) ☎ (01460) 72972
⊕ stagecoach-inn.co.uk

Beer range varies Ⓗ

Pleasant, comfortable pub, once called the Queen's Hotel, close to the railway station. There is a good selection of local real ales, supplemented by a range of Belgian beers. At the rear is a large garden. A varied menu of good-value meals to suit all tastes is served. Accommodation is in 13 en-suite rooms at the rear of the main building. ⚌✿⊜◫ₐ♿☆ₑ(47,99)P╘

Croscombe

Bull Terrier

Long Street, BA5 3QJ (on A371 between Wells and Shepton Mallet) ST590443

✪ 12-3, 7-midnight (closed Mon winter); 12-3, 7-11 Sun ☎ (01749) 343658 ⊕ bullterrierpub.co.uk

Cheddar Ales Gorge Best; Greene King Abbot; guest beers Ⓗ

Originally a 15th-century priory, this cosy village-centre free house was first granted a licence in 1612. The name changed from Rose & Crown to Bull Terrier in 1976. A single bar serves three areas: the inglenook room with flagstone floor, the cosy snug and, to the rear, the common bar. There is also a pretty walled garden. The two guest beers are normally sourced from local micros. Thatchers Cheddar Valley cider is served, and there is an extensive food menu. The kitchen is closed on Sunday evenings in winter. ⚌Q✿⊜◫ₐ◫Å♿(371)♣♠P

George Inn

Long Street, BA5 3QH (on A371 between Wells and Shepton Mallet) ST589443

✪ 12-2.30, 6-11; 2-3, 6-11 Sun ☎ (01749) 342306 ⊕ thegeorgeinn.co.uk

Blindmans King George the Thirst Ⓖ**; Butcombe Bitter; guest beers** Ⓗ

A 17th-century inn, refurbished by the landlord, serving at least two guest ales and hosting two beer festivals a year, at Whitsun and in late October. There is a large main bar, a snug with a fireplace, a family room and a separate dining room. Food is home-cooked using locally sourced ingredients. To the rear is a skittle alley and a garden with a covered terrace. Guests are from West Country independents. The Blindmans King George is exclusively brewed for the pub. ⚌Q✿⊜◫ₐ◫Å♿(371)♣♠P╘

Cross

New Inn ✓

Old Coach Road, BS26 2EE (on A38/A361 jct)

✪ 12-11 (midnight Fri & Sat) ☎ (01934) 732455

Otter Ale; guest beers Ⓗ

Roadside inn on the A38, close to the historic medieval town of Axbridge. Popular for its extensive food menu served all day until 9pm (8pm Sun) and twice-yearly beer festivals, it usually has three guest beers that can often be adventurous. There is a function room on the first floor. A large hillside garden with children's play facilities offers a fine view of the Mendip Hills and Somerset Levels. Families are welcome – dogs too. There is a small car park opposite. Ale is discounted on Thursdays. ✿◫☆(126)♣P╘

Crowcombe

Carew Arms Ⓛ

TA4 4AD (village signed off A358)

✪ 12-11 (closed 3-6 Jan-Mar) ☎ (01984) 618631 ⊕ thecarewarms.co.uk

Exmoor Ale; Otter Bright; guest beers Ⓗ

A classic rural pub in the village at the foot of the beautiful Quantock Hills. The flagstone public bar has a historic inglenook, and the large garden looking towards the Brendon Hills makes this popular with locals, walkers and dogs. Three to four guest ales come from local microbreweries, the real cider from Thatchers. A local ales festival is held in August. The larger bar/restaurant serves excellent locally sourced food. Accommodation consists of six rooms, ideal for walkers and bikers. ⚌Q✿⊜⊜◫ₐ◫◫♿☆(18,28)♣♠P╘

Dulverton

Bridge Inn Ⓛ ✓

20 Bridge Street, TA22 9HJ

✪ 12-3, 6-11 (not Mon winter); 12-11 Fri-Sun ☎ (01398) 324130 ⊕ thebridgeinndulverton.com

Exmoor Ale; guest beers Ⓗ

Close to the River Barle, this warm, welcoming pub dating from 1845 has a cosy single-room bar featuring a wood-burning stove and Exmoor memorabilia. Good food is available lunchtimes and evenings. At the southern gateway to Exmoor, good walking and country pursuits are nearby. The Bridge holds a Green Tourism Award in recognition of the environmentally friendly way it is run. A beer festival is held each year to coincide with the local folk festival that takes place over the Whitsun holiday. ⚌Q✿◫ₐÅ☆(25,398)♣P╘

Rock House Inn Ⓛ

1 Jury Road, TA22 9DU

✪ 12-11 ☎ (01398) 323131 ⊕ rockhouseinndulverton.com

Sharp's Doom Bar; guest beers Ⓗ

Lively free house at the top of this bustling Exmoor town. Built on the side of a rock face, it was first licensed in 1837, although part of the property, which once comprised a saddlery and a hayloft, is said to be much older. The single bar is where the locals congregate and there is an adjoining dining room. Food is served at all times except Sunday evening and Monday lunchtime. ⚌✿◫ₐÅ☆(25,398)♣♠╘

East Harptree

Castle of Comfort

BS40 6DD (on B3134 just N of jct with B3135)

✪ 12-3, 6-11; 12-11 Sun ☎ (01761) 221321 ⊕ castlecomfort.com

Butcombe Bitter; Sharp's Doom Bar; guest beers Ⓗ

Splendid sprawling isolated inn on the Mendip Hills, within reach by car of both Cheddar Gorge and Wookey Hole caves. The name is believed to derive from the time when the pub housed condemned criminals on their last night. A hostelry since 1684, it is popular for locally-sourced generously portioned food. Two guest beers feature regularly from the south west and sometimes further afield. The child-friendly garden is busy in summer. Dogs are allowed in the lower bar. Moles Black Rat is the cider. ⚌Q✿◫ₐ♣♠P╘

Emborough

Old Down Inn 🅛

BA3 4SA ST628513
✪ 12-2, 6.30-11.30; 12-10.30 Sun ☎ (01761) 232398
Butcombe Bitter; Draught Bass Ⓖ
A free house first licensed in 1640, this establishment was once an important coaching inn. The spirit of the past lives on in the main bar, where beer is served straight from the cask. Guests from local breweries are generally available. The bar snacks are excellent value, and likewise the main meals. This friendly and popular hostelry is a classic example of a traditional Somerset inn and is the centre of many local community activities.
Q🌣🕏🍴🕪🕀🕹🏃🛏🏆🅿🌡

Faulkland

Tucker's Grave ★

BA3 5XF (on A366 1 mile E of village) ST751551
✪ 11.30-3, 6-11; 12-3, 7-10.30 Sun ☎ (01373) 834230
Butcombe Bitter; Fuller's London Pride Ⓖ
One of CAMRA's Real Heritage Pubs, this place was built in the mid-17th century and has changed very little since then. It was named after Tucker, who hanged himself and was buried at the crossroads outside, and featured in a song by the 1970s punk band The Stranglers. Beers and Thatchers cider are served from an alcove rather than a bar. Shove-ha'penny is played and there is a skittle alley. Camping is available in the grounds. A warm welcome is guaranteed. 🏚Q🕏🅰🍀🏆🅿🌡

Forches Corner

Merry Harriers

EX15 3TR (3 miles SE of Wellington)
✪ 12-3 (not Mon), 6.30-11; 12-3 Sun ☎ (01823) 421270
⊕ merryharriers.co.uk
Otter Head; guest beers Ⓗ
Friendly, family-owned free house on the Blackdown Hills bordering Somerset and Devon. The bar separates the lounge from the dining area, where excellent meals using fresh fish, meat and game are served. Two changing guest beers are offered from local microbreweries, with Exmoor beers featuring regularly, as well as Bollhayes cider. Despite a somewhat remote location, the pub has a thriving trade attracted by its reputation for quality food. The large, pleasant garden is ideal for families in summer. 🏚Q🌣🕏🕪🕀🕹🍀🏆🌡

Frome

Griffin Inn

Milk Street, BA11 3DB
✪ 5-11; 4-1am Fri & Sat; 1-9 Sun ☎ (01373) 467766
Milk Street Usual, Funky Monkey, Beer Ⓗ
Situated in the older part of Frome, known as Trinity or Chinatown, the Griffin is owned by Milk Street Brewery, with the small brewhouse at the back. It produces a wide range of ales served alongside seasonal beers. The single bar retains original features including open fires, etched windows and wooden floors, and a stained glass griffin is behind the bar. Monday is pub quiz night and live music plays regularly. A small garden opens all year. Food is limited to summer barbecues and Sunday lunches. 🕏🚞🛏🍀🌡

Galhampton

Old Pub 🅛

High Road, BA22 7BA (on A359 between Sparkford and Castle Cary)
✪ closed Mon; 12-2.30, 6-10 (11 Fri & Sat); 12-4 Sun
☎ (01935) 440395 ⊕ theoldpub.com
Bath Ales Gem; guest beers Ⓗ
Recently refurbished, with a good reputation for fine ales and food, the friendly licensees always make visitors and locals most welcome. Regular ales are usually from Bath and St Austell breweries, with guest beers from around the country. The pub is comfortable, with log-burning stoves and traditional oak tables. It supports many local groups who often book most of the rear dining area, but there is always room for visitors and the service is prompt. 🏚Q🕀🕹🕀🛏(1)🅿🌡

Henstridge

Bird in Hand

2 Ash Walk, BA8 0RA (100yds S of A30/A357 jct) ST723199
✪ 11-2.30, 5.30-11; 11-11 Sat; 12-3, 7.30-10.30 Sun
☎ (01963) 362255
Beer range varies Ⓗ
Old stone village pub with low ceilings, beams, a fireplace at each end of an attractive long bar, and a games room housing a TV. There is an adjoining skittle alley. Excellent quality rotating guest ales and good-value snacks makes a visit to this friendly pub well worthwhile. 🏚Q🕀🕹🕀🛏🍀🏆🅿

Hinton Blewitt

Ring o' Bells ✅

Upper Road, BS39 5AN (2 miles W of Temple Cloud from A37) ST594569
✪ 12-3, 5-11 (midnight Fri); 12-midnight Sat; 12-11 Sun
☎ (01761) 452239
Butcombe Bitter, seasonal beer; Fuller's London Pride Ⓗ
Butcombe pub dating from the 19th century. A dining/function room with its own garden was more recently added, and blends nicely with the cosy bar and snug. Quality food is served, using local produce when possible. Local sports clubs meet here and much memorabilia is on show, particularly cricket-related. Cyclists, walkers, children and dogs are all most welcome. Thatchers Cheddar Valley cider is available. 🏚Q🕀🕹🕀🍀🏆🌡

Holcombe

Duke of Cumberland 🅛 ✅

Edford Hill, BA3 5HQ
✪ 9am-midnight ☎ (01761) 233731
⊕ thedukeholcombe.co.uk
Blindmans Edford Gold; Butcombe Bitter Ⓗ
The landlord here has a good knowledge of and interest in real ale, and local activities are supported. Refurbished to a high standard prior to reopening, the pub is on the edge of the Mendip Hills in a fine walking area, with a beer garden on the banks of the river. Excellent bar and restaurant food are available at all times. There is a skittle alley and the cider is Thatchers Cheddar Valley. 🏚🕀🕹🕀🛏🍀🏆🅿🌡

Horsington

Half Moon Inn ✔

Duck Lane, BA8 0EF (200yds NE of A357) ST701239
✪ 12-2.30 (closed Mon lunch winter), 6-11; 12-4 Sun
☎ (01963) 370140 ⊕ horsington.co.uk

Fuller's London Pride; Wadworth 6X; guest beers Ⓗ

Owned and run by the same couple for over 20 years, this pub is the focal point of a lovely village. Up to three guest beers are available, and over 1,000 different beers have been served so far. There are gardens to the front and rear, a separate skittle alley, a large function room, an ample car park and 10 letting rooms. Reasonably priced food is available at all sessions. The annual beer festival is well worth a visit.
🏨Q🌞🚭🛏&≠(Templecombe)🚌(58)♣P

Huish Episcopi

Rose & Crown (Eli's) ★

Wincanton Road, TA10 9QT (on A372)
✪ 11.30-2.30, 5.30-11; 11.30-11 Fri & Sat; 12-10.30 Sun
☎ (01458) 250494

Teignworthy Reel Ale; guest beers Ⓗ

A 17th-century thatched inn, known locally as Eli's, that has been in the same family for generations. Although severely flooded three years ago, it has managed to retain its original character and unusual features, giving visitors the feeling they have stepped back in time. A now rare, counterless, flagstoned tap room adjoins several small cosy rooms where locals and visitors chat over a drink. Good wholesome food is available at lunchtime and in the early evening (no food Mon and Sun eves). 🏃🌞🍴🚌♣♠P½

Hutton

Old Inn

Main Road, BS24 9QQ
✪ 11.30-11 (midnight Fri & Sat); 12-11 Sun
☎ (01934) 812336

Butcombe Gold; Fuller's London Pride; RCH Hewish IPA; guest beers Ⓗ

A genuine free house owned by a long-standing Guide landlord and now a thriving local, the Old Inn offers a varied range of guest ales, often from nearby brewers, especially RCH. The pub is extremely popular for its excellent food, particularly the Sunday carvery. Dogs are welcome. The car park behind the pub is accessed by narrow one-way lanes either side. The Old Inn is a perfect example of how a struggling pub can succeed in the right hands. 🏨🏃🌞🍴&(5,5A)P½

Kelston

Old Crown ✔

Bath Road, BA1 9AQ (3 miles from Bath on A431)
✪ 11.30-11; 12-10.30 Sun ☎ (01225) 423032
⊕ oldcrown.butcombe.com

Butcombe Bitter, Gold, seasonal beer; Draught Bass; Fuller's London Pride Ⓗ

Attractive multi-roomed 18th-century coaching inn owned by Butcombe Brewery. The rare cash register handpumps, flagstone floors, open fires and settles all help create a friendly atmosphere. No restaurant food is served Sunday or Monday evenings, but from 6pm on Monday the landlord and regular customers contribute tapas dishes. In summertime, barbecues and live musical events

are occasionally held in the large, attractive garden. Sunday is quiz night. Butcombe's own Ashton Still cider is sold. Take care crossing the busy road. 🏨Q🌞🚭🍴🚌(319,332)●P

Keynsham

Lock Keeper

Keynsham Road, BS31 2DD (on A4175)
✪ 11 (12 Sun)-11 ☎ (0117) 986 2383
⊕ lockkeeperbristol.com

Bath Ales Gem; Young's Bitter, Special, seasonal beers Ⓗ

Multi-roomed Young's pub, noted for its food, by Keynsham lock on the River Avon. The original 17th-century cottage once brewed its own beer and was named the White Hart. It divides into two parts, with the older bar facing the canal, while the large conservatory and heated veranda overlook the river, pétanque pitches and the popular garden. Families are welcome and dogs allowed in the bar area. Occasional live music features in summer. The pub may stay open later when busy.
Q🌞🍴≠🚌(318)P½

Old Bank

20 High Street, BS31 1DG
✪ 10-11 (midnight Fri & Sat); 11.30-10 Sun
☎ (0117) 904 6356

Sharp's Doom Bar; guest beers Ⓗ

Located at one end of the High Street, this is a basic and welcoming pub. The single bar is decorated with pictures of bygone Keynsham. There are two or three guest beers, often unusual and interesting, as well as a small selection of foreign beers. Quiz night is Monday. The car park is to the rear.
🏨🌞≠🚌(318,339,649)♣P½

Kilve

Hood Arms Ⓛ

TA5 1EA (on A39)
✪ 11-11 ☎ (01278) 741210 ⊕ thehoodarms.com

Exmoor Ale; Otter Head; guest beers Ⓗ

Former 17th-century coaching inn set beside the main road. It has oak beams, an open fireplace, a comfortable bar and a separate restaurant. There is also a landscaped walled garden where boules is played in summer. A bar billiards knockout takes place every Sunday night. Special events for charities are held regularly. There are 12 en-suite rooms and a lodge available to rent. It is an ideal base for walkers and fossil hunters at the nearby beach. Well-behaved dogs are welcome.
🏨🌞🚭🛏&🍴🚌(14)♣●P½

Kingsbury Episcopi

Wyndham Arms Ⓛ ✔

TA12 6AT
✪ 12-1am ☎ (01935) 823239 ⊕ wyndhamarms.com

Butcombe Bitter; Otter Ale; guest beers Ⓗ

Fine old pub around 400 years old with log fires in the dining area and bar, where antique settles enhance a relaxed atmosphere. Outside is the skittle alley that doubles as a function room and a heated smoking area, and also has a pool table. Another function room upstairs is used for meetings and occasional live music. Burrow Hill is the pub's cider, and good-quality home-cooked food is served. Local charities are actively supported. Well worth a visit. 🏨Q🌞🍴♣●P½

Long Sutton

Devonshire Arms
TA10 9LP
🔆 12-3, 6-11 (10.30 Sun) ☎ (01458) 241271
⊕ thedevonshirearms.com
Beer range varies Ⓗ
Grade II-listed former hunting lodge facing an idyllic village green. A combined bar and restaurant area in a contemporary style is furnished with comfortable chairs around the log fire. Real ales always include a beer from Moor Brewing Company and guests are often from Somerset breweries. A blackboard gives tasting notes for beers on handpump. Locally made cider is served. Alfresco areas include a courtyard, a large walled garden and a terrace overlooking the village green. En-suite accommodation is available.
🏚Q🅿🖧🌀🔌&💀P🏷

Lower Odcombe

Masons Arms
41 Lower Odcombe, BA22 8TX (off Yeovil to Montacute road)
🔆 12-2.30, 6-midnight ☎ (01935) 862591
⊕ masonsarmsodcombe.co.uk
Odcombe No. 1, Spring, seasonal beers Ⓗ
A picturesque thatched free house in the main street of an attractive village. A small brewery to the rear of the pub brews for the pub only. Good food is served using local produce and booking is advisable for the restaurant. The monthly curry night is especially popular. Well-behaved children and dogs are welcome. Local events are held on the pub field. B&B accommodation is offered and there is also a caravan site at the rear with hook-ups, showers and a laundry room.
🅿🖧🔌🗼🖳(81)💀P🏷

Luxborough

Royal Oak Inn
TA23 0SH (about 2½ miles from B3224 between Wheddon Cross and Raleghs Cross)
🔆 12-2.30, 6-11; 12-11 Sat & Sun ☎ (01984) 640319
⊕ theroyaloakinnluxborough.co.uk
Exmoor Ale, Gold; St Austell Tribute; guest beers Ⓗ
Ancient village pub with an original stone-flagged public bar, serving hatches, large inglenook fireplace and a further bar/children's room to the rear. In the old dining room you can sample meals freshly cooked to order using fresh seasonal produce. The pub is popular in season with shooting parties and walkers as well as locals. Quiz evenings are held. As well as locally produced ales, Thatchers Cheddar Valley cider is sold. Situated in an Exmoor valley, it is an ideal base for walking. 🏚Q🅿🖧🔌🖧🌀💀P🏷

Middlezoy

George Inn Ⓛ
42 Main Street, TA7 0NN (off A372, 1 mile NW of Othery)
🔆 closed Mon; 12-3, 7 (6.30 Fri & Sat)-midnight; 12-4, 7-11 Sun ☎ (01823) 698215 ⊕ thegeorgeinnmiddlezoy.co.uk
Butcombe Bitter; guest beers Ⓗ
Friendly 17th-century free house with stone flag floors and exposed beams. The two guest beers are mainly from south-west England. Excellent locally sourced food is available Wednesday to Saturday.

The South African landlord keeps his beers in top condition and runs a beer festival each year at Easter. Westcroft traditional cider is served. This pub may be a little remote but is well worth seeking out. 🏚Q🅿🖧🔌🗼🖳(16)🌀💀P🏷

Minehead

Kildare Lodge Hotel
Townsend Road, TA24 5RQ
🔆 11-3, 6.30-11; 12-5, 7-10.30 Sun ☎ (01643) 702009
⊕ kildarelodge.co.uk
St Austell Trelawney, Dartmoor Best, Tribute; guest beers Ⓗ
Situated just two minutes from Minehead town centre, this Grade II-listed building in the Arts and Crafts style retains many interesting features. It is an ideal base for exploring the Exmoor countryside, and medieval Dunster is also nearby. Accommodation includes 12 en-suite rooms and a bridal suite with four-poster bed. There is a small bar, two separate lounges and a dining room. The beers are reasonably priced for the area.
🏚Q🖧🔌🖧&🖳(18,28,398)💀P🏷

Queen's Head Ⓛ
Holloway Street, TA24 5NR (off the Parade)
🔆 11-11 (midnight Wed-Sat) ☎ (01643) 702940
Draught Bass; Exmoor Gold; St Austell Tribute; Sharp's Doom Bar; guest beers Ⓗ
In a side street just off the Parade, this popular town pub sells up to eight ales. The spacious single bar has a raised seating area for dining and families. There is a games room at the rear and a skittle alley. Good-value food is served daily lunchtimes and evenings – try the home-made pies. A carvery is offered on Tuesday, Thursday and Sunday lunchtimes, and there are twice-yearly beer festivals. 🔌🗼🚆🖳(18,28,398)🌀🏷

Mudford

Half Moon
Main Street, BA21 5TF (on A359 between Yeovil and Sparkford)
🔆 12-11 (10.30 Sun) ☎ (01935) 850289
⊕ thehalfmooninn.co.uk
Beer range varies Ⓖ
Welcoming 17th-century village roadside inn with a good trade in food and drink. The bar is divided into several cosy areas. An extensive menu is displayed on blackboards, and daily specials are offered. Two regular West Country ales, usually from RCH, are on stillage behind the bar, together with two Westons ciders. Reduced-price takeaways are also available. There is a courtyard for warmer days. Accommodation is in the pub and the converted skittle alley. Guide dogs only are allowed. Q🖧🔌🖧&🖳(1)💀P🏷

Norton Fitzwarren

Cross Keys Ⓛ ✅
TA2 6NR (at A358/B3227 jct W of Taunton)
🔆 11-11; 12-10.30 Sun ☎ (01823) 333062
Beer range varies Ⓗ
Busy 19th-century former coaching inn and stables now converted into a pub and restaurant, comprising several separate seating areas with open fires, exposed beams and timber floors. There is a large garden to the rear and a car park to the side. Four constantly changing real ales from local,

regional and national breweries are usually available. There is a large menu offering traditional pub food, which is served all day, a skittle alley and regular live music. ⚏✿❸❶❺➤🚆(18,25,28)P¹⏚

Oakhill

Oakhill Inn ✓

Fosse Road, BA3 5HU (on A367 between Radstock and Shepton Mallet) ST635472

❂ 12-3, 5-11 (midnight Fri); 12-midnight Sat; 12-11 Sun
☎ (01749) 840442 ⊕ theoakhillinn.com

Butcombe Bitter; guest beers Ⓗ

Large village-centre pub that is both a popular local and a family-friendly gastro-pub, with a strong emphasis on organic and locally sourced food. The bar serves two areas with an open feel. Regular quiz nights are held. Up to two changing guest ales, normally sourced from local micros, are on offer along with a range of mainly bottled ciders. There is a garden at the rear and the car park is 20 yards up the road in the Shepton Mallet direction. Accommodation is in five 4-star rooms.
⚏✿❇❶❶🚆❤P

Pitney

Halfway House Ⓛ

Pitney Hill, TA10 9AB (on B3153)

❂ 11.30-3, 5.30-11 (midnight Fri & Sat); 12-11 Sun
☎ (01458) 252513 ⊕ thehalfwayhouse.co.uk

Butcombe Bitter; Hop Back Summer Lightning; Otter Bright; Teignworthy Reel Ale; guest beers Ⓖ

Serving at least nine local ales on gravity alongside many international bottled beers, this basic but buzzing pub deserves its many accolades, most recently Somerset CAMRA Pub of the Year 2011. No music or fruit machines disturb the hum of conversation here. Superb home-cooked food is based on local produce, including the popular Sunday roast lunch (no food Sun eve). Local ciders from Wilkins and Hecks are served, and the pub puts on a beer festival in March.
⚏Q✿❶❶🚆(54)❤❤P¹⏚

Porlock

Ship Inn Ⓛ ✓

High Street, TA24 8QD

❂ 11-midnight ☎ (01643) 862507 ⊕ shipinnporlock.co.uk

Cotleigh Tawny Owl; Exmoor Ale; Otter Bitter; St Austell Tribute, Proper Job; guest beers Ⓗ

Known locally as the Top Ship, this 13th-century inn was in RD Blackmore's Lorna Doone. The bar appears not to have changed much since then, with flagstoned floors, inglenook fireplaces, a good selection of real ales and Cheddar Valley cider. Located at the bottom of the notorious Porlock Hill, it offers home-cooked food, a three-tiered patio garden, a skittle alley and four en-suite bedrooms. The dog-friendly hostelry also welcomes well-behaved children. A joint beer festival with the Ship at Porlock Weir is held annually.
⚏Q❂✿❇❶❶🚆❺🚆(39)❤❤P¹⏚

Porlock Weir

Ship Inn Ⓛ

TA24 8PB (take B3225 from Porlock)

❂ 11-11 (10.30 Sun) ☎ (01643) 863288
⊕ thebottomship.co.uk

Exmoor Ale, Stag; St Austell Tribute, Proper Job; guest beers Ⓗ

With possibly the best view from any pub in Somerset, the Ship overlooks the harbour and Bristol Channel towards South Wales. In the Exmoor National Park, this place is more than 400 years old. Good-value food is served by friendly staff. Friday night in winter is fish, chips and a pint night. Ideal for walkers, it is close to Porlock village and the famous hill. The large nearby Pay & Display car park can be busy during holiday periods. A joint beer festival with the Ship at Porlock is held annually. ⚏Q❇❶❶❺▲🚆(39)❤❤¹⏚

Portishead

Windmill Inn

58 Nore Road, BS20 6JZ (next to municipal golf course above coastal path)

❂ 11-11; 12-10.30 Sun ☎ (01275) 843677
⊕ thewindmillinn.org

Butcombe Bitter, Gold; Courage Best Bitter; Draught Bass; guest beers Ⓗ

Large split-level free house with a spacious patio to the rear, plus a recent extension enjoying panoramic views. Above the coastal path on the edge of town, the Severn Estuary and both Severn bridges can be seen on clear days. A varied menu is served all day and is enormously popular. One large area is set aside for families. The two guest ales are often locally sourced and there is an Easter beer festival. Thatchers cider is stocked.
Q❄❇❶❺➤🚆(359)❤P¹⏚

Priddy

Hunters Lodge

BA5 3AR (isolated crossroads 1 mile from A39 close to TV mast) ST549500

❂ 11.30-2.30, 6.30-11; 12-2, 7-11 Sun ☎ (01749) 672275

Butcombe Bitter; Cheddar Potholer Ⓖ**; guest beers** Ⓗ

Timeless, classic roadside inn near Priddy, the highest village in Somerset, popular with cavers and walkers. The landlord has been in charge for well over 40 years. Three rooms include one with a flagged floor, and there are beer casks behind the bar. Wilkin's cider is served. The simple home-cooked food is excellent and exceptional value. A folk musicians' drop-in session is held on Tuesday evening in the back room. The garden is pleasant and secluded. Mobile phones are not welcome but dogs are. ⚏Q❄✿❶❶❹❤❤P

Queen Victoria Inn ✓

Pelting Drove, BA5 3BA

❂ 12-11 ☎ (01749) 676385 ⊕ queenvictoria.butcombe.com

Butcombe Bitter, seasonal beer; Fuller's London Pride Ⓗ

Creeper-clad inn, a pub since 1851, with four rooms that feature low ceilings, flagged floors and three log fires. A wonderfully warm and relaxing haven on cold winter nights, it is popular during the Priddy Folk Festival in July and the annual fair in August. Reasonably priced, home-cooked food is a speciality. Children and dogs are allowed and there is a play area by the car park. Cheddar Valley cider is sold. May close briefly on some afternoons.
⚏Q❇❶❶▲❤❤P¹⏚

Radstock

Fromeway
Frome Road, BA3 3LG (¾ mile from Radstock centre on A362 Frome Road) ST697547
✪ closed Mon; 12-3, 6-11; 12-11 Sun ☎ (01761) 432116
⊕ fromeway.co.uk
Butcombe Bitter; Plain Indulgence; Wadworth 6X Ⓗ
This friendly free house has been in the same family for five generations. The present landlord has been in charge for more than 36 years and produces his own sausages, faggots and home-cured hams for the excellent bar and restaurant meals. Popular with locals, the Fromeway has a warm and relaxing atmosphere. A single bar serves three regular ales, and there are weekly guest beers. The pub organises many functions, quizzes and walks for charity. Three charming bedrooms are available. Q❀❁✍❍◑♿⬛P⬥

Rickford

Plume of Feathers ✪
Leg Lane, BS40 7AH (off A368 2 miles from A38 jct)
✪ 12-11 ☎ (01761) 462682 ⊕ theplumeoffeathers.com
Butcombe Bitter, seasonal beer; guest beers Ⓗ
A 15th-century, Grade II-listed building that has been a pub since the 1800s. If approaching from Churchill, the left U-turn into Leg Lane is extremely tricky. The interior is divided into a bar, restaurant and family room. The pub provides a pleasant and convenient base from which to walk, fish or explore the Mendips. It has a garden at the rear and a stream running along the front, leading to a ford. Parking is limited. There are plans to extend the beer range. Dogs welcome. ❀Q❁❀✍❍♣P

Rowberrow

Swan Inn ✪
Rowberrow Lane, BS25 1QL
✪ 12-3, 6-11; 12-11 Sat; 12-10.30 Sun ☎ (01934) 852371
Butcombe Bitter, Rare Breed, seasonal beer; guest beer Ⓗ
Believed to date from around the late 17th century, this Butcombe Brewery-owned country pub enjoys an attractive setting, nestling beneath the Dolebury Iron Age hill fort. A convenient stop for walkers on the Mendip Hills, the emphasis is on home-cooked food with unusual specials, but customers who just want a drink are welcome. There is a collection of artefacts around the walls and a grandfather clock. Thatchers cider is available. The large, attractive beer garden and car park are opposite. ❀Q❁❍♣P⬥

Seavington St Michael

Volunteer
New Road, TA19 0QE
✪ 12-2.30, 6.30-11; 12-3, 7-11 Sun ☎ (01460) 240126
⊕ thevolly.co.uk
Beer range varies Ⓗ
Fine old village pub on the old A303 between South Petherton and Ilminster. Five ales are usually on the menu, with beers from St Austell and other West Country breweries also available to take away. There is a recently built microbrewery at the rear of the pub. Good food is on offer and walkers and their dogs are made welcome. Wednesday pie night is well worth trying. En-suite accommodation is available. ❀Q❁✍❍⬛♿⬛(N10,91)♣P⬥

Shepton Beauchamp

Duke of York Ⓛ
North Street, TA19 0LW
✪ 12 (5.30 Mon; 4 Tue & Wed winter)-midnight; 12-10.30 Sun ☎ (01460) 240314 ⊕ thedukeshepton.co.uk
Otter Ale; Teignworthy Reel Ale; guest beers Ⓗ
Friendly village pub that hosts several local darts and skittles teams. On pleasant days, the tables on the raised pavement outside enable patrons to enjoy a voyeuristic view of rural Somerset life: the butcher's, post office, school, church and village hall all panoramically displayed. Dogs and walking boots are welcomed. The pool room is separate from the bar area. Recently built accommodation is popular with visitors. No food Sunday evening or Monday. ❀❁❀✍❍♣P⬥

Shepton Mallet

Swan Inn
27 Town Street, BA4 5BE (N of town centre) ST618437
✪ 11-midnight ☎ (01749) 344995 ⊕ swanatshepton.co.uk
Dawkins Bob Wall; guest beer Ⓗ
Situated in a terrace of small shops. Inside, the front area is arranged mainly for diners (no meals Mon afternoon or Sun and Mon evenings), with chairs and tables extending out onto the pavement. The bar area at the rear offers darts and shove-ha'penny. Live music features once or twice a month. Guest ales are chosen from local small brewers, and cider is from Hecks and Thatchers. The car park is at the rear. ❀✍❍♿▲⬛♣●P⬥

South Cadbury

Camelot Ⓛ
Chapel Road, BA22 7EX (just off A303 between Sparkford and Wincanton)
✪ 11-midnight (closed 3-5 winter); 11.30-11 Sun
☎ (01963) 440448 ⊕ thecamelotpub.com
Beer range varies Ⓗ
A large attractive pub in the centre of this pleasant village. The floor is flagstoned throughout, with a logburner at each end. A display case contains information about the nearby Cadbury Castle (reputed to be King Arthur's Camelot) and artefacts found in various excavations. Beers from local breweries such as Yeovil Ales are always available, and the cider is from the next village. Excellent home-cooked food is served at all sessions. Well worth the short detour off the busy A303. ❀Q❁❍♿♣●P⬥

South Petherton

Brewers Arms Ⓛ ✪
18 St James Street, TA13 5BW (½ mile off A303)
✪ 11.30-2.30, 6-11; 11.30-midnight Fri & Sat; 12-11 Sun
☎ (01460) 241887
Otter Bitter; guest beers Ⓗ
Consistently among the finalists for local CAMRA Pub of the Year, the venue has offered more than 1,700 ales in 17 years. Village events and organisations are enthusiastically supported, especially the Carnival Club. Trips to sporting events still leave time for an in-house alphabet trail and two beer festivals on the late May and August holidays. There is a good adjoining restaurant. Dogs on leads and children are welcome. Just two minutes from the A303. ❀❁❍▲⬛(81,91)♣●⬥

Taunton

Castle Green Inn 🍷 🗓

Castle Green, TA1 4AE (by Castle Hotel)
🕒 9am-11 (midnight Fri & Sat); 10-9 Sun ☎ (01823) 257688
⊕ castlegreeninn.co.uk
Bays Topsail; guest beers 🅷

In the town centre near the bus station, this open-plan pub has a stone-floored bar at the centre with seating/dining areas to each side. Four to five ales come mainly from local and south west breweries, and the real cider is Thatchers Heritage. Good-value food is served. Join the Beer Society for discounted beers on Wednesday evenings, and check the website for beer festival and Meet the Brewer sessions. Jazz and other bands appear regularly. Local CAMRA Pub of the Year 2012. ⌂🏠🕒◑⅄🖩🌳●ᐟᤢ

Racehorse 🗸

157 East Reach, TA1 3HT
🕒 12-4, 6-11 (midnight Thu); 12-12.30am Fri & Sat; 12-11 Sun ☎ (01823) 327513
St Austell Trelawney, Tribute, Proper Job 🅷

Friendly, popular pub just off the town centre at the top of East Reach, multi-roomed with front and rear bars, a small lounge with comfortable armchairs, and two further drinking areas as well as a large walled beer garden. This traditional town hostelry is the place to go for good conversation and a great atmosphere. On display are various pieces of memorabilia such as old tin signs and musical instruments. No food is served, but regular live music is featured. 🏠🖽🖩♣ᐟᤢ

Wyvern Club 🗓

Mountfields Road, TA1 3BJ
🕒 7-11; 12-3, 7-10.30 Sun ☎ (01823) 284591
⊕ wyvernclub.co.uk
Exmoor Ale; guest beers 🅷

Large, busy sports and social club, home to cricket, rugby and squash teams. It offers a variety of West Country beers, with guest ales changing frequently – beers from three different breweries are usually on offer, at club prices. Meals are served each evening until 9pm, plus Sunday lunchtime. The club premises are available for daytime meetings and evening functions. Show this Guide or your CAMRA membership card to be signed in as a guest. A real ale festival is held in October. Children are welcome. ⅄🏠◑⅄🖩(1A,99)♣P

Trull

Winchester Arms

Church Road, TA3 7LG
🕒 12-3, 6.30-11 ☎ (01823) 284723
⊕ winchesterarmstrull.co.uk
St Austell Tribute; guest beers 🅷

Thriving family-run community pub on the outskirts of Taunton near the Blackdown Hills. The comfortable bar area is separated from the long dining area by an impressive coal-effect fireplace. Three ales are mainly from local breweries. Real cider is served in summer only. The locally sourced home-cooked food is excellent (booking ahead at popular times). The streamside gardens, perfect for family and dogs, are the venue for entertainment and barbecues. Accommodation is good value. ⌂Q🖾◑⅄🖩(97)♣Pᐟᤢ

Uphill

Ship Inn

56 Uphill Way, BS23 4TN
🕒 11.30 (12 Sat & Sun)-11 ☎ (01934) 621470
⊕ theshipinn-uphill.co.uk
Hook Norton Old Hooky; guest beer 🅷

Spacious family-oriented pub, where customers of all ages mix harmoniously. A real hub of the community, it has its own skittles teams and a pool table. Food is served lunchtimes and evenings, both in the main pub and upstairs restaurant area. Most of the pub is easily accessible and there is a covered and heated smoking area in the rear garden. Disabled groups meet here weekly. Dogs are welcome. There is a quiz on Thursdays and occasional live music. ⌂Q⅄🏠◑⅄🖩(5,5A,5B)♣Pᐟᤢ

Wanstrow

Pub

Station Road, BA4 4SZ ST711416
🕒 6.30-11 Mon; 12-2.30 (3 Fri & Sat), 6-11; 12-3, 7-11 Sun ☎ (01749) 850455
Blindmans Golden Spring; Draught Bass; guest beers 🅷

An absolute gem, this friendly village local has a lounge bar with open fire and flagstone floors that leads to a small restaurant. The pub serves two regular and two guest beers, sourced from almost anywhere, along with Thatchers Traditional and Cheddar Valley ciders. Games include skittles, bar billiards and ring the bull. A small but imaginative menu is offered and all food is home cooked. ⌂Q🏠◑🖾♣●P

Watchet

Esplanade Club 🗓 🗸

The Esplanade, TA23 0AJ (opp marina)
🕒 12-3 (Sun only), 7-midnight ☎ (01984) 634518
Beer range varies 🅷

Somerset CAMRA Club of the Year 2010, 2011 and 2012, with splendid views over the marina and Bristol Channel. Decked out with old photographs and memorabilia, it was built in the 1860s as a sail-making factory, but has been a club since the 1930s. Live entertainment features every weekend, with folk and open mic nights during the week. A short walk from the West Somerset Railway, visitors showing this Guide or a CAMRA membership card are welcome. Also home to the boat owners' club. ⅄🅰�🖩(14,18,28)♣●

Star Inn 🗓

Mill Lane, TA23 0BZ
🕒 12-3.30, 6.30-midnight; 12-4, 7-midnight Sun ☎ (01984) 631367
Beer range varies 🅷

Local CAMRA Pub of the Year again in 2010, the Star offers four different beers from local and regional breweries. It has a cosy main bar with small side rooms and a large garden. Mouthwatering food, including seafood, is locally sourced where possible. There are quiz and dart teams and the infamous Sunday Bad Boys Club. Port and cheese nights and beer trips are run. The pub is near the marina and West Somerset Railway, and handy for walks on the Quantock Hills. Dogs welcome. ⌂🏠◑🅰�🖩(14,18,28)♣●ᐟᤢ

Wedmore

New Inn L
Combe Batch, BS28 4DU
🟢 12-2.30 (not Mon), 5-midnight; 12-2am Fri; 12-1am Sat; 12-10.30 Sun ☎ (01934) 712099
Butcombe Bitter; guest beers H
This traditional village inn holds many events including the annual turnip prize, conkers, spoof, penny chuffin' and apple bobbin'. There is a public bar, lounge and dining areas, with beer gardens to the front and rear. A chalkboard lists forthcoming guest ales, with the three handpumps dispensing ales mainly from local breweries. Traditional, good-value pub food is served. There is also a skittle alley/function room. Q❀◐▶Å🖪(668,670)♣🐾P🍴

Wells

City Arms
69 High Street, BA5 2AG ST547456
🟢 10-11 (10.30 Sun); 9am-midnight Fri & Sat
☎ (01749) 673916 ⊕ thecityarmsatwells.com
Glastonbury Hedgemonkey, Golden Chalice, Penny's Pride H
In 1810 the City of Wells jail closed and later became the City Arms. The main bar retains the small barred windows and low-vaulted ceilings of its former existence. The building encloses a courtyard on three sides, with outdoor seating. There is extensive food service in the bar, bistro and restaurant, made to order using fresh local produce. Between five and seven beers are normally available, mainly from local brewers, with a Molson Coors rebadged beer, Cathedral City. ⏂❀◐🖪♣🐾🍴

West Chinnock

Muddled Man L ✅
Lower Street, TA18 7PT
🟢 11-2.30, 7-midnight; 11-midnight Fri & Sat; 12-11 Sun
☎ (01935) 881235
Beer range varies H
Excellent cosy free house run by the same friendly family for over 12 years serving a good range of West Country ales from three handpumps, with some additional guest beers served straight from the cask. Superb, reasonably priced food is available and the Sunday lunch needs to be booked in advance due to demand. Many visitors have been converted to real ale and become regulars at this fine pub. Burrow Hill cider is served. The skittle alley is available for hire. ♨Q❀🛏◐👤🐾🍴

West Huntspill

Crossways Inn L
Withy Road, TA9 3RA (on A38)
🟢 12-midnight (11.30 Sun) ☎ (01278) 783756
⊕ crosswaysinn.com
Butcombe Bitter; Sharp's Doom Bar; guest beers H
Seventeenth-century inn with six handpumps offering a wide range of guest beers. There are several bar areas, and two fireplaces with roaring fires during the winter. It also has an outside fireplace to keep the smokers warm. There is a dining room and skittle alley that can be used as a function room, and outside areas to the front and back. An extensive menu of good-value food is complemented by a specials board. ♨Q❀🛏◐👤Å🖪(15,21,21A)♣🐾🍴

Weston-super-Mare

Criterion
45 Upper Church Road, BS23 2DY
🟢 12-11 (10.30 Sun) ⊕ criterioninns.co.uk/the-criterion.html
Courage Directors G; guest beers H
Genuine free house and traditional community pub, just off the sea front in the Knightstone area. Believed to be one of the oldest pubs in town, it has interesting local photos on the walls. Pub games feature strongly, with darts, bar billiards and table skittles, plus a quiz on Tuesday. Bar snacks are available, with filled rolls at lunchtime. Two or three guest beers are offered, with all beer styles and local breweries well supported. The Directors is served by gravity. Thatchers cider is served. ♨🖪(1)♣🐾

Dragon Inn ✅
15 Meadow Street, BS23 1QG
🟢 8am-midnight (1am Fri & Sat) ☎ (01934) 621304
Greene King Abbot; Ruddles Best Bitter; guest beers H
Relatively small Wetherspoon situated in the town centre, serving an interesting variety of local and regional beers and often featuring RCH, Box Steam or Cottage breweries, with at least one cider too. It is family-friendly, with the usual JDW fare served all day. Smokers have the benefit of a heated rear courtyard, and free Wi-Fi is available. There is good disabled access, but it can get busy, especially at weekends and lunchtimes in school holidays. A CAMRA discount is given. Q❀◐👤🛏🐾🍴

Regency
22-24 Lower Church Road, BS23 2AG
🟢 9.45am-11.30 (midnight Fri & Sat); 10.45-11.30 Sun
☎ (01934) 633406
Butcombe Bitter; Draught Bass; Flowers IPA; guest beers H
Comfortable and friendly town-centre local, attracting a mixed clientele and popular with students at lunchtime. The pub has pool, skittles and crib teams, but also offers a quiet refuge for conversation. The pool room with TV and jukebox is separate from the main bar area, and children are welcome here. Home-cooked food at keen prices is served (lunchtimes plus Wed and Thu eves). There are patios to the front and rear. Monthly mini beer festivals and pub outings feature, plus occasional live bands. ⏂❀◐🛏🖪(4,5,7)♣🐾

Waverley
69 Severn Road, BS23 1DR
🟢 12-11 ☎ (07810) 198332
Greene King Abbot; St Austell Tribute; guest beers H
Genuine old-fashioned community free house in an area with few pubs, to the south of the town centre but walkable from the station. Two guest beers are usually on, including some of the more unusual ales. Thatchers ciders are served. A weekly quiz features, as does live music at weekends in what is known as the air raid shelter to the rear. It also stages a regular farmers' market. Food is limited to basic snacks. ❀🛏🖪(7)🐾🍴

Westport

Old Barn Owl Inn
TA10 0BH (between Ilminster and Curry Rivel on B3168)
🟢 12-3, 6-11; 11-11 Sat; 12-10 Sun ☎ (01460) 281391
⊕ oldbarnowlatwestport.co.uk

Beer range varies Ⓗ
Large, welcoming roadside pub with three separate dining areas, but also plenty of space for those just wanting a drink. Beers from Cotleigh, Cottage and Otter breweries feature regularly. An extensive range of home-cooked food is available, including a mid-week menu of good-value meals. A range of exotic meats usually features for those wishing to try something a little different. Tribute acts are hosted in the function room and jazz plays monthly on Sunday. ᗰ❀◐▣♣Pᐟ⌐

Williton

Masons Arms
2 North Road, TA4 4SN
❂ 11-2.30, 6-11; 12-3, 7-10.30 Sun ☎ (01984) 639200
⊕ themasonsarms.com
Sharp's Doom Bar; Skinner's Betty Stogs; guest beers Ⓗ
Thatched 16th-century pub with oak beams throughout, with a reputation for good real ales, cider and locally sourced food. The pub hosts quiz teams, is in the local boules league, and has a pleasant beer garden where locals and visitors alike sit and relax. Rich's draught cider is always available and the beers tend to be from Devon or Cornwall breweries. Accommodation is in an outside annexe with five en-suite rooms.
❀🛏◐�රⴳ▣(14,18,28)♠Pᐟ⌐

Wincanton

Nog Inn ♟ 🅛
South Street, BA9 9DL (50yds from market sq)
ST71312856
❂ 10.30-11 (midnight Fri & Sat); 12-11 Sun
☎ (01963) 32998 ⊕ thenoginn.com
Otter Bitter; Sharp's Own; guest beers Ⓗ
Tucked away a short distance from the market square, this attractive listed pub fronts a long, narrow building with parts dating back to the 16th century. A secluded sunny garden with covered seating can be found at the far end of the property. The guest ales are often seasonal and an extensive range of continental draught beers is always available, as are real ciders. CAMRA members receive a 10 per cent discount on real ale. CAMRA Regional Pub of the Year 2011. ᗰQ❀◐රⴳ▣(58)♣♠Pᐟ⌐

Unicorn Inn
Bayford, BA9 9NL (on old A303) ST72692914
❂ closed Mon; 12-11; 11-11 Sat; 12-6 Sun ☎ (01963) 34941
Butts Jester; guest beers Ⓗ
Former 17th-century coaching inn with a comfortable bar, wood-burning stove and flagstone floor. The landlord is a real ale and cider enthusiast who regularly holds cider festivals and prides himself on sourcing unusual guest beers. Muddy boots and dogs are welcome. The ciders come from Thatchers and Burrow Hill. Good-value Sunday lunches are served and evening specials Wednesday to Friday. A decked seating area is at the rear and the car park is through the arch.
ᗰQ❀▣(158,667)♣♠P

Wiveliscombe

Bear Inn 🅛
10 North Street, TA4 2JY

❂ 11-11 (midnight Thu-Sat); 12-11 Sun ☎ (01984) 623537
⊕ thebearwiveliscombe.co.uk
Otter Amber; Sharp's Doom Bar; guest beers Ⓗ
Family-run, lively community pub in the centre of this traditional brewing town. Two rooms share a single bar, and there is a children's play area and garden at the rear and also a skittle alley. Cotleigh and Exmoor breweries are a short walk away and their brews regularly feature among the guests. An extensive menu offers good-value meals using local produce where possible. The pub forms an ideal base for exploring Exmoor and the Brendon Hills. Local heritage trail leaflets are available.
ᗰ⌂❀🛏◐▣(25)♠Pᐟ⌐

Wookey Hole

Wookey Hole Inn
High Street, BA5 1BP (opp Wookey Hole caves)
❂ 12-11 (6 Sun) ☎ (01749) 676677 ⊕ wookeyholeinn.com
Beer range varies Ⓗ
Charismatic, picturesque gastro-pub with a unique contemporary style, situated opposite the famous caves. Usually two, but up to four, changing guest beers from small, often local or unusual brewers, are served, plus Wilkins cider and a wide choice of draught continental beers and lagers. Top-quality food is available at restaurant prices, ideal for special occasions (book ahead at weekends). The huge sculpted rear garden is impressive. A lurid pink function room and five highly individual bedrooms complete the picture. The bus service is limited. ᗰ❀🛏◐▲▣♠Pᐟ⌐

Wrantage

Canal Inn 🅛
TA3 6DF (on A378 towards Langport, SE of Taunton)
❂ 12-3, 5-11 (midnight Thu & Fri); 12-11 Sat; 12-10.30 Sun
☎ (01823) 480210 ⊕ the-canal-inn.com
Beer range varies Ⓗ
Recently renovated 200-year-old roadside pub about five miles south-east of Taunton. There is a constantly changing range of ales available, often featuring beers from Cottage and Exmoor breweries, as well as guests from around the region. Good home-cooked food is served in the restaurant (no food Sun eve). The pleasant enclosed beer garden is available for private functions. Q❀◐රⴳ▣(54)Pᐟ⌐

Yeovil

Quicksilver Mail ✔
168 Hendford Hill, BA20 2RG (at jct of A30 and A37)
❂ 11-midnight; 12-11 Sun ☎ (01935) 424721
⊕ quicksilvermail.com
Adnams Broadside; Butcombe Bitter; St Austell Tribute Ⓗ
A friendly and comfortable roadside pub beside a roundabout. The pub's name is unique in Britain and commemorates a high-speed mail coach. The large single bar is separate from a lower-level dining area. A former pub sign features in the bar together with sporting and musical memorabilia. Excellent food is served – Sunday lunch, curry and steak nights are popular. The large function room hosts regular live music. ❀🛏◐▣(47,99)♣♠Pᐟ⌐

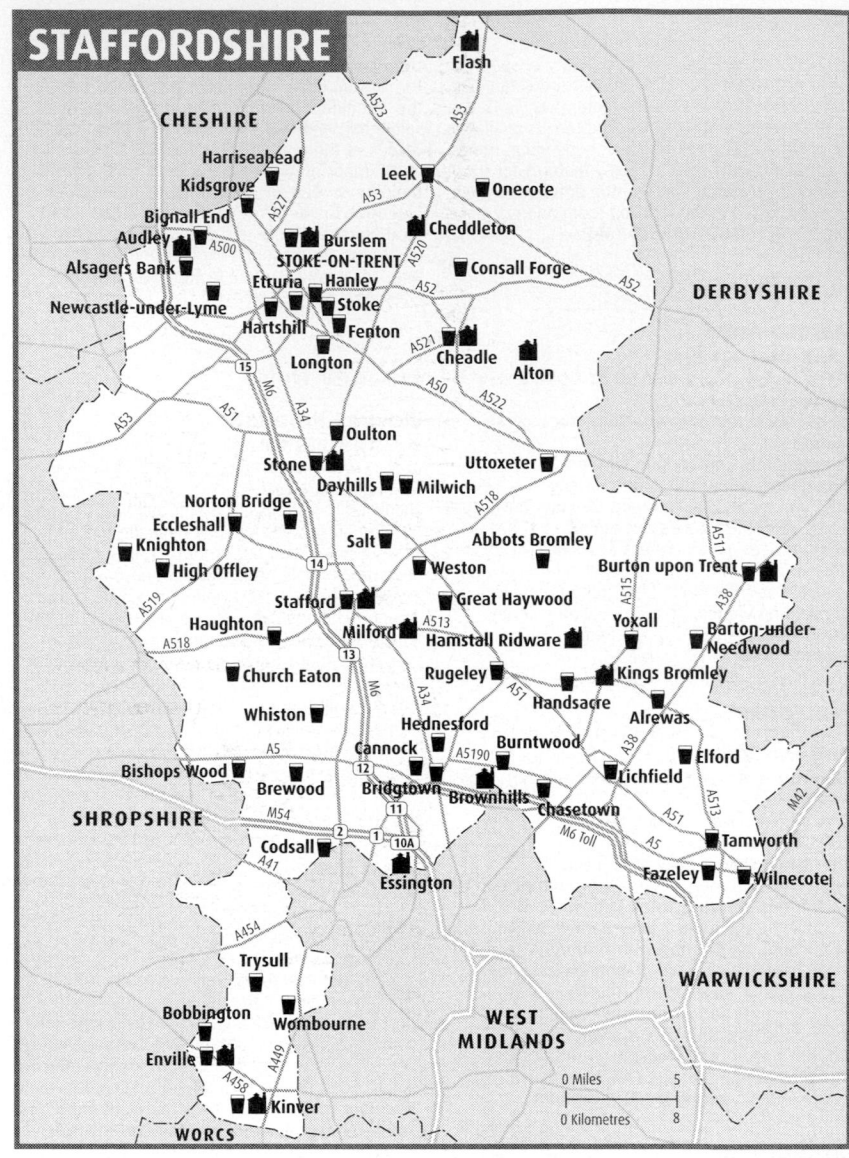

STAFFORDSHIRE

Flash

CHESHIRE

Harriseahead
Kidsgrove
Leek
Onecote
Bignall End
Audley
Burslem
Cheddleton
Alsagers Bank
STOKE-ON-TRENT
Consall Forge
Newcastle-under-Lyme
Etruria
Hanley
Stoke
Hartshill
Fenton
Longton
Cheadle
Alton

DERBYSHIRE

Oulton
Stone
Dayhills
Milwich
Uttoxeter
Norton Bridge
Eccleshall
Salt
Abbots Bromley
Knighton
Weston
Burton upon Trent
High Offley
Stafford
Great Haywood
Yoxall
Barton-under-Needwood
Haughton
Milford
Hamstall Ridware
Church Eaton
Rugeley
Kings Bromley
Whiston
Handsacre
Alrewas
Hednesford
Cannock
Burntwood
Elford
Bishops Wood
Brewood
Bridgtown
Brownhills
Lichfield
Codsall
Chasetown
Tamworth
Essington
Fazeley
Wilnecote

SHROPSHIRE

WEST
MIDLANDS

WARWICKSHIRE

Trysull
Bobbington
Wombourne
Enville
Kinver

WORCS

0 Miles 5
0 Kilometres 8

Abbots Bromley

Coach & Horses

High Street, WS15 3BN (on B5014, at E end of village)
☼ 5.30-midnight Mon; 12-2.30, 5.30-midnight; 12-midnight
Sun ☎ (01283) 840256
⊕ coachandhorsesabbotsbromley.co.uk
**Black Sheep Best Bitter; Marston's Pedigree; guest
beer** ⊞

Grade II-listed coaching inn dating back to 1745,
although the building is even older, with links to
Burton Abbey. Inside, the long narrow lounge bar
features a beamed ceiling and an assortment of
memorabilia and bric-a-brac, such as brasses and
old photographs. There are several dining areas,
and a dining/function room to the rear. Occasional
live entertainment and other events take place.
Abbots Bromley is famous for its annual Horn
Dance. ♨❀◑▷🚆(403,428)♣P╚

Alrewas

George & Dragon

120 Main Street, DE13 7AE
☼ 11 (12 Sun)-11 ☎ (01283) 791476
⊕ georgeanddragonalrewas.co.uk
**Banks's Bitter; Marston's Burton Bitter, Pedigree;
guest beers** ⊞

Imposing three-storey village local with a
welcoming feel, thought to be a former coaching
inn and dating back to the early 1700s. The
comfortable main bar area is split into three
distinct cosy sections and there is a separate
lounge/dining room to one side. It was Marston's
Community Pub of the Year 2010. The Trent &
Mersey Canal runs along the edge of the village,
about 300 yards distant, and the National Memorial
Arboretum is a mile to the east. No meals served
Sunday evening. ♨❀◑◑₺▲🚆(7,7A,7E)♣P╚

Alsagers Bank

Gresley Arms 🏳

High Street, ST7 8BQ (on B5367 3 miles N of Newcastle-under-Lyme)
🌣 12 (3 Mon-Wed)-11 ☎ (01782) 722469
⊕ gresleyarms.co.uk
Beer range varies Ⓗ
Sat at the top of Alsagers Bank with breathtaking views from the beer garden and dining rooms, the pub is perfect for enjoying a well-earned pint after a walk in nearby Bateswood or Apedale country parks. The Gresley offers four rooms including a newly refurbished bar with slate floors, 200-year-old oak beams, a real fire and a warm and friendly lounge. The bottom room is home to monthly folk nights and the dining room serves hearty meals.
🏚Q🕿☎🍴 ⬤▲🖼(94,94A)🐾P🚭

Barton-under-Needwood

Royal Oak 🍷 ✅

74 The Green, DE13 8JD (½ mile from B5016 via Wales Lane)
🌣 12-midnight (1am Fri & Sun; 11 Sun) ☎ (01283) 713852
Marston's Pedigree; guest beers Ⓗ/Ⓖ
Bustling community local on the southern edge of the village, home to many traditional pub games teams and an over-40s football team. While parts of the building date back to the 16th century, the pub has only existed since the mid-1800s. Public bar and lounge customers are served from a central sunken bar, the floor being below the level of the rest of the ground floor. Beers are available on handpump or by gravity, direct from the cask, on request. 🏚Q🕿☎⬤🖼(7,7A,7E)🐾P🚭

Shoulder of Mutton ✅

16 Main Street, DE13 8AA (on B5016)
🌣 12-midnight (1am Fri & Sat) ☎ (01283) 712568
⊕ shoulderofmutton.com
Draught Bass; Marston's Pedigree; guest beer Ⓗ
A 17th-century former coaching inn with some 19th-century additions, located at the centre of this historic village, opposite the church. Two rather smart Bass lanterns illuminate the front entrances, which directly access the simple public bar and comfortable lounge, the latter featuring a low-beamed ceiling, wood panelling and inglenook, plus dining areas to the side and rear. There is a small landscaped patio garden at the back, adjoining the car park. See the website for details of live music nights. Breakfast is available from 7am. 🏚☎🍴⬤ ⬤▲🖼(7,7A,7E)🐾P🚭

Bignall End

Bignall End Cricket Club

Boon Hill, ST7 8LA (400yds from B5500)
🌣 7 (12 Fri-Sun)-midnight ☎ (01782) 720514
Wells Bombardier; guest beers Ⓗ
Welcoming village cricket club in a semi-rural location not far from a main road, with splendid views of Cheshire from the clubhouse. Established for over 100 years, the club hosts two annual beer festivals, one in summer and one in winter, plus other events, in the upstairs function room. A public bar and snooker room are downstairs. A varied range of cask beers is available from an independent wholesaler. CAMRA members always welcome. ☎♿🖼(34)P🚭

Swan

Chapel Street, ST7 8QD (just off B5500 ½ mile E of Audley)
🌣 12-11 (midnight Fri & Sat; 10.30 Sun) ☎ (01782) 720622
Dartmoor Legend; Draught Bass; Oakham Citra; guest beers Ⓗ
Popular street-corner pub, known to the locals as The Duck, just off the main road through the village. It comprises a large traditional public bar and a smaller comfortable lounge, plus a pleasant beer garden and smoking area at the rear. The pub serves an excellent and varied selection of beers, plus four traditional ciders and a perry on handpull. The new licensees have worked hard to maintain the reputation for real ale that the Swan has acquired. 🏚☎☎⬤🖼(34)🐾⬤🚭

Bishops Wood

Royal Oak 🏳

Ivetsey Bank Road, ST19 9AE
🌣 12 (4 Mon)-midnight (1am Fri-Sun) ☎ (01785) 841802
⊕ royaloak-bishopswood.co.uk
Enville Ginger Beer; Holden's Golden Glow; Salopian Shropshire Gold; Sarah Hughes Dark Ruby Mild; Wye Valley Butty Bach; guest beers Ⓗ
Situated only half a mile from Boscobel House where King Charles II reputedly hid from parliamentary forces, this original Royal Oak comprises a small bar and a larger lounge/restaurant. However, the new owners intend to reverse the rooms to create a larger traditional bar, with further alterations for the lounge/restaurant. By early 2013 it is hoped a microbrewery will have been installed behind the pub. Traditional cider is available during summer. No meals on Monday or on Sunday evening. 🏚Q☎⬤ ⬤♿🖼(88,88A)🐾⬤P🚭

Bobbington

Red Lion

Six Ashes Road, DY7 5DU
🌣 12-3, 5-11; 12-11 Sat; 12-10.30 Sun ☎ (01384) 221237
⊕ redlioninn.co.uk
Morland Old Speckled Hen; Wye Valley HPA Ⓗ
First recorded as an alehouse brewing its own ale, cider and porter in 1820, this pub has been family

INDEPENDENT BREWERIES

Beowulf Brownhills
Black Hole Burton upon Trent
Blythe Hamstall Ridware
Burton Bridge Burton upon Trent
Burton Old Cottage Burton upon Trent
Enville Enville
Flash Flash (NEW)
Gates Burton Burton upon Trent (NEW)
Kinver Kinver
Leek Cheddleton
Lymestone Stone
Marston's Burton upon Trent
Morton Essington
Peakstones Rock Alton
Quartz Kings Bromley
Shugborough Milford
Slater's Stafford
Titanic Burslem
Toft Cheadle
Tower Burton upon Trent
Town House Audley

run for over 20 years. The bar leads to a room housing traditional and modern games. Do not be alarmed by the pouncing lion and tiger as you enter the large restaurant. An expansive garden has a children's play area and provides a pleasant place to enjoy a beer on a summer's afternoon. The house beer is from Enville and happy hour is Monday to Friday 5-7pm, with a 50p reduction on real ales. Seventeen modern en-suite rooms, including two suites, provide excellent accommodation (CAMRA members receive a discount). ♿⊛✍⬤❶ 🍴♿♿▲P'—

Brewood

Swan Hotel 🍷 Ⓛ ✅
15 Market Place, ST19 9BS
⊛ 11.45-midnight ☎ (01902) 850330
⊕ swanbrewood.co.uk
Caledonian Deuchars IPA; Courage Directors; Theakston Black Bull Bitter; guest beers Ⓗ
This comfortable central-village pub is at the heart of the community. The former 15th-century coaching inn, with low wood-beamed ceilings and seasonal log fires, is only five minutes' walk from the Shropshire Union Canal and the Staffordshire Way. Cosy snugs displaying early prints of the area flank the central bar and there is a traditional skittle alley upstairs available for hire. Three handpulls feature LocAle beers and, unusually, there is a selection of over 50 malt whiskies. Cheese and ham baguettes are available at lunchtimes. ⬛Q⊛♿🖥(76,88A)♣P'—

Bridgtown

Stumble Inn
264 Walsall Road, WS11 0JL (200yds from A34/A5/M6 toll jct)
⊛ 12-2, 6-11 (5-midnight Fri); 7-midnight Sat; 12-10.30 Sun
☎ (01543) 502077 ⊕ thestumble.net
Beer range varies Ⓗ
Comfortable split-level one-room pub with a darts and pool area as well as a small function room. It is a popular, fun place, with a Friday night disco, live bands on Saturday and karaoke on Sunday. Various charity events take place plus an annual beer festival in September. The pub has showcase nights on the second and fourth Tuesdays of the month for local bands and wannabes. Good-value weekday lunches are served and a choice of guest beers. ⊛◗♿⭠(Cannock)🖥(1,2)♣P'—

Burntwood

Drill Inn ✅
33 Springlestyche Lane, WS7 9HD (left off the northbound Rugeley Road out of Burntwood) SK061102
⊛ 12-midnight (10.30 Sun) ☎ (01543) 675799
Beer range varies Ⓗ
Tucked away down a country lane, you would hardly know that the Drill is less than a mile from Burntwood. Despite the relative isolation, the pub ensures a healthy footfall by the quality of its ales, the good food, and the cheery welcome. The airy main room is partnered with a small snug, a large elevated beer garden to the rear, plus a children's play area. Three changing ales are served, plus occasional beer festivals. No food available on Monday. ⬛Q⊛◗▲♣P'—

White Swan
2 Cannock Road, WS7 0BJ
⊛ 4.30 (12 Sun)-11; 4-11.30 Fri; 12-11.30 Sat
☎ (01543) 670555
Adnams Southwold Bitter; Greene King Abbot; Purity Mad Goose; guest beers Ⓗ
An ale-led community pub with a mainly local trade, although visitors and passing trade are made very welcome. The main room is a comfortable lounge, with the counter featuring a rustic lapped-wood roof which probably seemed a good idea at the time! There is a smaller separate room for games and meetings. Two changing guest beers are usually available, mostly through the SIBA list. A regular bus service from Lichfield stops a few yards from the pub. ♿⊛🖥(60)♣♥P'—

Burton upon Trent

Alfred
51 Derby Street, DE14 2LD (on A5121)
⊛ 11-2.30 (not Tue), 5-11; 11-midnight Fri & Sat; 12-10 Sun
☎ (01283) 562178
Burton Bridge Golden Delicious, Bridge Bitter, Burton Porter, Stairway to Heaven, Festival Ale; guest beer Ⓗ
Double-fronted terrace pub, now part of the Burton Bridge estate, that was once the long-gone Truman's Brewery tap. A central bar counter serves two rooms, each featuring wood partitions topped with leaded stained glass. The raised area in the left-hand room is generally used for dining. There is also a small snug/family room to the rear. It is known locally for its range of English fruit wines, Monday poker nights, and Wednesday quiz nights. Meals are available Thursday-Saturday evenings and Sunday lunchtimes (to 5pm). Cider is usually from Thatchers. ⬛♿⊛◗⭠(Burton)🖥♣♥P'—

Burton Bridge Inn
24 Bridge Street, DE14 1SY (on A511, at town end of Trent Bridge)
⊛ 11.30-2.30, 5-11; 11.30-11.30 Fri & Sat; 12-3, 7-11 Sun
☎ (01283) 536596 ⊕ burtonbridgeinn.co.uk
Burton Bridge Golden Delicious, Sovereign Gold, Bridge Bitter, Burton Porter, Festival Ale, seasonal beers; guest beer Ⓗ
This 17th-century pub is the flagship of the Burton Bridge Brewery estate and fronts the brewery itself. Sensitively refurbished in 2000, it has two rooms served from a central bar: a smaller front room, with wooden pews and displaying many awards and brewery memorabilia, and a back room featuring oak beams and panels. The beer range is supplemented by a selection of malt whiskies and fruit wines. A small dining/function room and a skittle alley are upstairs and available for hire. No lunches Sunday. ⬛Q⊛◗⭠🖥♣'—

Coopers Tavern ★
43 Cross Street, DE14 1EG (off Station St)
⊛ 6 (12 Sun)-11; 12-2.30, 5-11 Wed & Thu; 12-11.30 Fri & Sat
☎ (01283) 532551 ⊕ cooperstavern.co.uk
Draught Bass Ⓖ; Joule's Blonde, Original Pale Ale, Slumbering Monk Ⓗ; guest beers Ⓗ/Ⓖ
A classic, unspoilt 19th-century ale house, once the Bass Brewery tap and now part of the Joule's estate. The intimate inner taproom has barrel tables and bench seating where the beer is served from a small counter, next to the cask stillage, using a mixture of gravity and handpumps. The more comfortable lounge leads to a third small room. Awarded CAMRA Regional Cider Pub of the

Year 2008-11, it offers a choice of up to four ciders/perries plus fruit wines. Local folk musicians meet here on Tuesday evenings for impromptu sessions. Well-behaved dogs welcome. 血Q❀❅╆⇆❊●⅃

Devonshire Arms
86 Station Street, DE14 1BT
✪ 5-11 Mon; 12-3, 5 (7 Sun)-11; 12-11 Fri & Sat
☎ (01283) 562392
Burton Bridge Golden Delicious, Bridge Bitter, Damson Porter, Stairway to Heaven, seasonal beers; guest beer ⒣
One of six Burton Bridge Brewery hostelries in the area, this popular old pub dates from the 19th century and is Grade II-listed. It comprises a public bar at the front and a larger, more comfortable, split-level lounge to the rear. Note the 1853 map of Burton, old photographs and unusual arched wooden ceilings. An enclosed rear patio features flower borders and hanging baskets. A number of continental bottled beers and English fruit wines are also stocked. 血❀❅⇆❊♣P⅃

National Brewery Centre (Brewery Tap) ✪
Horninglow Street, DE14 1NG (on A511, at Guild St jct)
✪ 11-11 (6 Mon & Tue); 12-6 Sun ☎ (01283) 532880
⊕ nationalbrewerycentre.co.uk
Worthington's Red Shield, Brewery Tap, Worthington E, White Shield, seasonal beers; guest beer ⒣
Formerly the Bass Museum/Coors Visitor Centre, the site has been operating under new management since 2010. The associated Brewery Tap showcases beers from the new William Worthington's Brewery, including the seasonal Shield beers. While the comfortable single-room bar still features an illuminated ice block-look bar counter with chrome fonts and handpumps, the decor has been toned down since a 2007 refurbishment. Food is served in the bar and the adjacent restaurant, while an L-shaped conservatory overlooks the garden and enclosed children's play area. ⚓❀❅◖❺❒P⅃

Old Cottage Tavern
36 Byrkley Street, DE14 2EG (off Derby St A5121, behind town hall)
✪ 12-11 (10.30 Sun) ☎ (01283) 511615
Burton Old Cottage Oak Ale, Stout, Halcyon Daze; guest beers ⒣
While leased from the Tadcaster Pub Company and no longer owned by the brewery, this welcoming community local continues to operate as the Burton Old Cottage Brewery tap. The main public bar at the front and the wood-panelled lounge to the rear are served from a central bar. There is also a cosy snug to one side of the public bar, and a games/function room (with demountable skittle alley) upstairs. Guest beers are usually sourced from other SIBA members. 血❀❅❅⇆❊●⅃

Cannock

Linford Arms ✪
79 High Green, WS11 1BN
✪ 8-midnight (1am Fri & Sat) ☎ (01543) 469360
Greene King Abbot; Ruddles Best Bitter; guest beers ⒣
A local Wetherspoon pub that prides itself on serving good beers at the right price. Situated in a busy town centre and near the bus station, the pub

is a listed building dating back to at least the 17th century. It has lots of charming areas to sit in and a vibrant social area for weekends. ⚓◖❅♿⇆❒●⅃

Chasetown

Uxbridge Arms
2 Church Street, WS7 3QL
✪ 12-midnight ☎ (01543) 677852
Beer range varies ⒣
Renowned both for the quality and choice of the five changing ales, this welcoming local is just 10 minutes' walk from Chasewater Country Park. A wide range of country wines and malt whiskies is available. Sport is popular here, with bowls, darts and football teams. The bar features bar billiards as well as sport on a large screen. Good food is available in the lounge and upstairs restaurant (no food Sun eve). Dogs are welcome in the bar. ❀◖❅❒♣●P

Cheadle

Huntsman ⌦
The Green, ST10 1XS
✪ 12-midnight ☎ (01538) 750502
⊕ thehuntsmancheadle.com
Joule's Slumbering Monk; Marston's Pedigree; Titanic Iceberg; guest beers ⒣
A family-friendly pub, close to Alton Towers and the Peak District. A must for real ale enthusiasts, it offers changing guest beers, with one from local micro Peakstones Rock always available. Good food is reasonably priced; meat comes from the farm across the road. This local has a good-sized car park, three separate rooms and a central bar with TVs in two showing sport. A beer festival is held at the end of May. Look out for the pub cat. 血❀❅◖♿⇆❒●P⅃

Church Eaton

Royal Oak ⌦
High Street, ST20 0AJ (village signed from A518 at Haughton) SJ932019
✪ 5-11; 12-9 Sun ☎ (01785) 823078
⊕ theroyaloakchurcheaton.co.uk
Banks's Bitter; guest beers ⒣
Once threatened with closure but saved by a local consortium, the Royal Oak is now a thriving pub at the centre of the community. The interior is split into a lounge area, a restaurant and an area with a dartboard, pool table and TV. Many of the guest beers are sourced from local breweries and the restaurant is noted for its good food. The pub is about a mile north-east of the Shropshire Union Canal at High Onn Bridge. 血Q⚓❀◖♿▲❒(482)♣P⅃

Codsall

Codsall Station ⌦
Chapel Lane, WV8 2EJ
✪ 11.30-2.30, 5-11; 11.30-11.30 Fri & Sat; 12-10.30 Sun ☎ (01902) 847061
Holden's Black Country Mild, Black Country Bitter, Golden Glow, Special; guest beers ⒣
Sensitively converted from the waiting room, offices and stationmaster's house, the Grade II-listed building now comprises a bar, lounge, snug and conservatory and displays worldwide railway memorabilia. A raised terrace overlooks the

working platforms and the occasional steam train may be spotted. Bar meals are served all week except Sunday, when sandwiches are on offer until 5pm. Two guest beers are regularly available. A popular beer festival is held on the weekend after the August bank holiday.
🏚Q🏠🍴🐕🕭♿☕➴🚃(5,88)Pᐟᵔ

Firs Club 🅛 ✅

Station Road, WV8 1BX (entrance along drive from shared Co-op car park)
✪ 7.30-11 (midnight Fri); 12-5, 7.30-midnight Sat; 12-5, 7.30-11 Sun ☎ (01902) 844674 ⊕ firsatcodsall.co.uk
Banks's Mild, Bitter ℗; guest beers Ⓗ
Formerly the Conservative Club, this venue has a bar area, two lounges and an upstairs games room with snooker and darts. Interesting photos of old Codsall and surrounding areas are on display. Up to three guest ales are served, often from local breweries, and a beer festival is held in November. A large function room is available for hire. Show this Guide or a CAMRA membership card to be signed in. Q🏠♿➴🚃(5,88)♣Pᐟᵔ

Consall Forge

Black Lion

ST9 0AJ (off A522 follow signs to Consall Gardens then Consall Forge. At bottom of hill turn left along track to car park)
✪ 12-11 (10.30 Sun) ☎ (01782) 550294
⊕ blacklionpub.co.uk
Peakstones Rock Black Hole; guest beers Ⓗ
The Churnet Valley Heritage Railway, Cauldon Canal and the River Churnet all have to be crossed from a large car park to reach this destination pub. The range of beers and ciders is extensive, sourced mainly from microbreweries. Two beer and cider festivals are held each year. Food is served daily; portions are large and reasonably priced – there is also a regular hog roast. A rural gem in the Churnet Valley, well worth the search.
🏚Q🐕🏠🍴Å➴🚃♣Pᐟᵔ

Dayhills

Red Lion

Uttoxeter Road, ST15 8RU (3 miles E of Stone on the B5027)
✪ 5 (4 Fri & Sat)-11; 12-10.30 Sun ☎ (01889) 505474
Draught Bass; guest beer Ⓗ
Welcoming country pub known locally as the Romping Cat, unspoilt and full of character. Along with the adjoining farm, it has been in the same family since 1920. The main room has a timeless feel with its quarry tile floor, meat hooks in the ceiling and inglenook fireplace. The atmosphere is undisturbed by music, gaming machines or TV.
🏚Q🏠🍴♿Å♣Pᐟᵔ⚑

Eccleshall

Bell Inn 🅛 ✅

16 High Street, ST21 6BZ
✪ 11-12.30am; 12-midnight Sun ☎ (01785) 850378
⊕ thebelleccleshall.com
Holden's Black Country Bitter, Golden Glow; Titanic Anchor Bitter, Captain Smiths; guest beers Ⓗ
A busy pub in the centre of this small market town, now a firm favourite with regulars from far and wide. This former coaching inn has a multi-room layout. The sympathetic restoration has continued

with the completion of the garden. The number of handpulls has increased with the recent addition of Joule's. The pub also hosts regular beer festivals together with Thursday night quizzes and a range of live music events (check website for details).
🏚🐕🏠🍴🔔◖🍴♿Å🚃(350,432)♣🚶Pᐟᵔ⚑

George Hotel 🅛

Castle Street, ST21 6DF (at main crossroads)
✪ 11-midnight (11 Sun) ☎ (01785) 850300
⊕ thegeorgeeccleshall.com
Slater's Original, Top Totty, Premium; guest beers Ⓗ
Slater's Brewery has moved to Stafford, but the six handpulls serving nearly the full range of Slater's award-winning ales are still the main attraction at the George; the pub has LocAle accreditation. Originally a 17th-century coaching inn, this venue has thrived under the Slater family's ownership. It now boasts an attractive bar and lounge area with food available all day every day. There are evenings of live music on a regular basis.
🏚Q🐕🏠🍴◖🍴♿Å🚃(350,432)♣🚶Pᐟᵔ⚑

Royal Oak

25 High Street, ST21 6BW
✪ 11-11 (midnight Fri & Sat) ☎ (01785) 859988
⊕ royaloakeccleshall.co.uk
Joule's Blonde, Pale Ale, Slumbering Monk Ⓗ
Recently refurbished to a high standard by Joule's of Market Drayton, featuring lots of light oak and specially commissioned stained glass. Portraits of the Joule's family of past times together with advertisements from the post-war period adorn the walls. Further investments for the disused upper floors and ballroom are planned. A welcome addition to the Eccleshall real ale scene.
🏚Q🐕◖🍴♿🚃(350,432)🚶Pᐟᵔ⚑

Star Inn 🅛 ✅

Copmere End, ST21 6EW (leave Eccleshall on the B5026 and turn left at the sign for Copmere End. The pub is at the crossroads) SJ803294
✪ 12-3 (not Mon), 6-11; 12-6 Sun ☎ (01785) 850279
⊕ thestarinn-eccleshall.co.uk
Draught Bass; Titanic Anchor Bitter; Wells Bombardier; guest beer Ⓗ
A thriving 100-year-old pub in the heart of the beautiful Staffordshire countryside, adjacent to the Cop Mere Lake and central to numerous walks. The next door post office has been closed for a number of years but a Victorian post box is retained. An excellent selection of bar meals and an à la carte menu are offered lunchtimes and evenings. The pub has won awards for its locally sourced food and is Taste of Staffordshire accredited.
🏚Q🐕🏠🍴♿Å♣Pᐟᵔ⚑

Elford

Crown Inn

The Square, B79 9DB (600m E of A513)
✪ 6 (12 Sat & Sun)-midnight ☎ (01827) 383602
Draught Bass; guest beers Ⓗ
Welcoming, cosy, 18th-century village pub with a bar, lounge and dining room. Beamed ceilings feature throughout and there are real fires in the bar and lounge. Two changing guest beers are offered, one usually from Burton Bridge. Food is served evenings Wednesday to Friday, 12-10pm Saturday, 12-5pm Sunday. Bar snacks are available at all times. In the 18th century the upstairs rooms were used as a courthouse, and today's dining room once served as the cells. 🏚◖🚃♣Pᐟᵔ

Enville

Cat ⃝L
Bridgnorth Road, DY7 5HA (on A458)
✪ 12-3 (not Mon), 5-11; 12-11 Sat; 12-6 Sun
☎ (01384) 872209
Enville Ale, Ginger Beer; guest beers Ⓗ
Parts of this traditional country pub date back to the 16th century. It has three oak-beamed rooms, two with real fires. There is also a family/function room. Hanging baskets adorn the beer garden and courtyard during summer months. Up to four guest ales are served including beers from local breweries. Home-made dishes and daily specials, using local produce whenever possible, are served. A separate menu is offered in the restaurant.
🅜Q🛏🐕🌣◐⌂&P

Fazeley

Three Horseshoes
New Street, B78 3RD (nr A4091/B5404 jct)
✪ 12-3, 6.30-11; 12-11 Fri-Sun ☎ (01827) 289754
Adnams Southwold Bitter; Draught Bass; Marston's Pedigree Ⓗ
Welcoming back-street local, a three-storey red brick building that looks rather more ancient on the outside than within. The single main room features a central bar of wood and tilework, with a quarry tiled floor. A side area is cosier, with carpeting and various knick-knacks around the walls. The pub is close to Drayton Manor Park, and sits near the junction of the Coventry and Birmingham & Fazeley canals. Car parking is possible on surrounding streets. 🌣🚌(110,780)♣⬛

Great Haywood

Clifford Arms ✅
Main Road, ST18 0SR (off A51 4 miles NW of Rugeley, 200yds from canal junction) SJ997227
✪ 12-11.30 (midnight Fri & Sat; 11 Sun) ☎ (01889) 881321
🌐 thecliffordarms.co.uk
Adnams Broadside; Morland Old Speckled Hen; guest beers Ⓗ
Village-centre inn with a large bar providing plenty of seating and a restaurant adorned with past photos of the pub. A busy local, it is home to cribbage, dominoes and quiz teams as well as a tug o' war team. It is also popular with walkers, cyclists, boaters and visitors to the nearby Shugborough Estate (National Trust). The Staffordshire Way and bridge 73 of the Trent & Mersey Canal are 200 yards along Trent Lane. Dog-friendly. 🅜Q🛏🐕🌣◐&▲🚌(841)♣🐾P⬛

Handsacre

Olde Peculiar ✅
The Green, WS15 4DP
✪ 12-2.30 (not Mon & Tue), 5.30-midnight; 12-3, 6-11 Sun
☎ (01543) 491891 🌐 theoldepeculiar.co.uk
Marston's Pedigree; Theakston Black Bull Bitter, Old Peculier; guest beer Ⓗ
A pleasantly decorated free house that is popular with locals and visitors alike. The single-room interior is divided into three distinct drinking areas. Food is served daily lunchtimes and evenings (not Mon and Tue). A changing guest beer comes from across the Midlands accompanies the regular ales. Accommodation is available at reasonable prices, and the pub is dog-friendly. 🌣🚪◐🚌(825)P⬛

Harriseahead

Royal Oak
42 High Street, ST7 4JT
✪ 7 (5 Fri & Sat; 12 Sun)-11 ☎ (01782) 513362
🌐 royaloak-harriseahead.com
Courage Directors; Fuller's London Pride; Joule's Original Pale Ale; Samuel Smith OBB; guest beers Ⓗ
A warm welcome awaits at this excellent, two-roomed free house, popular with locals and walkers. The guest beers come from microbreweries, and an upstairs function room provides extra space for meetings and the annual beer festival in December. A good selection of Belgian bottled beers is available, and monthly quizzes are held for local charities. There are also pork pies and filled baps for the hungry. An excellent place to stop off after a walk round Mow Cop folly. 🅜Q🌣🚪🚌♣P⬛

Haughton

Bell Inn ✅
Newport Road, ST18 9EX (on A518)
✪ 12-3, 5-midnight; 12-midnight Fri-Sun ☎ (01785) 780301
🌐 thebellhaughton.co.uk
Banks's Mild; Marston's EPA, Pedigree; Taylor Landlord; guest beer Ⓗ
This friendly village pub is the hub of the community. The building was a farm about 200 years ago. The L-shaped interior has the restaurant at the rear and the bar at the front. A large TV in the bar is used for screening major sporting events. The guest beer regularly changes. Booking is recommended for dining.
🅜Q🛏🌣◐🚪&▲🚌(481)♣🐾P⬛

Hednesford

Cross Keys Hotel ▼ ⃝L
42 Hill Street, WS12 2DN
✪ 12-midnight ☎ (01543) 879534
Brains The Rev James; Draught Bass; Greene King Abbot; Holden's Golden Glow; Ruddles County; Skinner's Betty Stogs; guest beers Ⓗ
Former coaching inn dating back to 1746, serving up to eight real ales including several guests. Hednesford Town Football Club was originally based behind the pub and links are still strong as the licensee is an ex-player and manager. Sky and ESPN sports are available to view on TV. The pub is home to several dominoes teams and hosts a monthly quiz night. It is rumoured that the infamous highwayman Dick Turpin stopped here on his ride to York. Local CAMRA Pub of the Year 2010 and 2011. 🌣🚪🚌(33A,60,23)♣P📺

High Offley

Anchor Inn ★
Peggs Lane, Old Lea, ST20 0NB (by bridge 42 of the Shropshire Union Canal) SJ775256
✪ 12-3, 7-11; winter hours vary ☎ (01785) 284569
Wadworth 6X Ⓗ
A Victorian canalside inn that has changed little, run by generations of the same family since 1870. It remains a rare example of an unspoilt country pub and has two small bars where cask ale and Westons cider are often served from jugs. Freshly made sandwiches are always available. There is a large award-winning garden. Difficult to reach by road, it is well worth finding. 🅜Q🛏🌣🚪▲🐾P⬛

Kidsgrove

Blue Bell
25 Hardingswood, ST7 1EG (off A50 near Tesco)
✪ closed Mon; 7.30-11; 1-4, 7.30-11 Sat; 12-10.30 Sun
☎ (01782) 774052 ● bluebellkidsgrove.co.uk
Beer range varies Ⓗ
Genuine free house that benefits from the absence of TV and games machines. It has a lively conversational atmosphere that draws everyone in. Informal live music is played on Sunday evenings and the pub attracts customers from a wide area, together with visitors from the Trent & Mersey and Macclesfield canals, which meet a few yards away. Six handpumps deliver a changing range of beers from microbrewers. Belgian and German ales, plus real cider and perry, are available.
Q✿≈☐(20,20A,34A)●P⑤⌐

Kinver

Kinver Constitutional Club Ⓛ
119 High Street, DY7 6HL
✪ 5-11; 4-midnight Fri; 11.30-midnight Sat; 12-10.30 Sun
☎ (01384) 872044
Enville Ale; Hobsons Best Bitter, Town Crier; Kinver Brewery Edge; Olde Swan Bumble Hole Bitter; Wye Valley HPA; guest beers Ⓗ
Built in 1902 on the site of an old pub, this converted hotel has a smart restaurant, a large snooker room and a bar always dispensing eight real ales and as many as 18 for special events, at reasonable prices. The club enjoys an enviable sporting reputation and hosts regular quiz and music nights. Meals are served Sunday lunchtime and Thursday to Saturday evenings – booking advised. CAMRA members are welcome but must be signed in; groups should book ahead. The bus from Stourbridge stops nearby. Winner of local CAMRA awards 2007-2012 and National Club of the Year 2011. ㊉✿◑🚼☐(227,228)♣P⑤⌐

Knighton

Haberdasher's Arms
Knighton, ST20 0QH (between Adbaston and Knighton)
SJ753275
✪ 12.30 (7 Wed & Thu)-midnight (1am Fri & Sat)
☎ (01785) 280650
Banks's Mild; guest beers Ⓗ
Traditional country pub, built about 1840, offering a warm, friendly welcome. This former local CAMRA Pub of the Year has four compact rooms all served from a small central bar. It hosts a range of events such as the annual Potato Club Show and occasional music festivals. It is also available for private hire. Well worth the drive through leafy country lanes to get here. ㊉Q✿🚼Å♣●P⑤⌐

Leek

Cock Inn Ⓛ
19 Derby Street, ST13 6HN
✪ 10-11 (midnight Fri & Sat; 10.30 Sun) ☎ (01538) 387467
Joule's Blonde, Original Pale Ale, Slumbering Monk; guest beer Ⓗ
One of the Joule's chain, the Cock is on the main street in Leek. The usual three Joule's beers are available and one rotating guest ale. The pub is split level: the bar area has a real log fire and comfortable leather armchairs, while the upper area is suitable for dining. Good food is served here

and locally sourced, with menus reflecting the occasion. A different menu is offered at weekends. The pub is pleasantly decorated throughout. ㊉✿◑🚼♣⌐

Den Engel
11 Stanley Street, ST13 5HG (off Market Square)
✪ 4 (11 Sat; 12 Sun)-11 ☎ (01538) 373751
Beer range varies Ⓗ
If you want to experience a taste of Belgium in Staffordshire then this is the place – a contemporary Belgian bar where you can sample 10 draught foreign beers or, if none takes your fancy, choose from over 100 bottled beers. Four handpumps offer real ale; a permanent Titanic and three guest beers are available. Café-style seating is at the front of the bar and a larger seating area is to the rear. Q✿◑🚼⌐

Wilkes Head Ⓛ
15 St Edward Street, ST13 5DS
✪ 12 (3 Mon)-midnight (11 Sun) ☎ 07976 592787
Whim Arbor Light, Hartington Bitter, Flower Power; guest beers Ⓗ
One of Leek's oldest pubs, dating back to the 1700s, with the oldest cellar in the town. A rustic-style interior adds to the atmosphere of the place. The pub is a regular in the Guide and a friendly place to visit. There are seven real ales, four brewed by Whim, with three guest beers from microbreweries. At least two real ciders are also on at any time. The licensee is a professional musician. Q✿☐(18)♣●⌐

Lichfield

Duke of Wellington
Birmingham Road, WS14 9BJ
✪ 4 (12 Fri & Sat)-midnight; 12-11 Sun ☎ (01543) 256584
Fuller's London Pride; Holden's Golden Glow; Marston's Pedigree; Wye Valley HPA Ⓗ
A traditional local, highly popular for the ale quality, well worth the 15-minute walk from the city centre. The interior is essentially open plan with three distinct drinking areas. Crusty cobs, locally produced sausage rolls and pork pies are available from the snack menu. The pub is home to darts and dominoes teams, and live sports are shown on three large screens. During the summer months the spacious back garden is popular. Dogs are welcome. ㊉✿🚼☐(112)♣●P⑤⌐

Duke of York
23-25 Greenhill, WS13 6DY
✪ 12-11 (midnight Fri & Sat) ☎ (01543) 300386
Joule's Blonde, Original Pale Ale, Slumbering Monk; guest beers Ⓗ
Deservedly popular Grade II-listed pub tastefully restored just over two years ago by Joule's Brewery. Both the bar and lounge boast oak-panelled walls and woodburners. A third room is available for meetings, events, or for more space during busy times. Food is served lunchtimes Monday-Saturday. Two changing guest beers are available alongside the Joule's range. There is a paved garden and car park to the rear. Dogs are welcome if accompanied by well-behaved owners. ㊉Q✿◑🚼≈(City)☐♣●P⑤⌐

George & Dragon ♈ ✅
28 Beacon Street, WS13 7AJ
✪ 11-midnight (1am Fri & Sat); 12-11.30 Sun
☎ (01543) 254854

Banks's Mild, Bitter; Marston's Pedigree; guest beers Ⓗ

A warm welcome is assured at this traditional two-roomed local near the cathedral. Up to four guest ales are served from the Marston's portfolio, and snacks are available. In the large rear garden a plaque marks the position of an artillery battery used during the 1643 siege of Lichfield. Darts, dominoes and board games are played and a charity quiz is held on a Thursday night. The pub is dog-friendly. ⚘⌂⌖≷(City)⊟♣P'⌐

Horse & Jockey
8-10 Sandford Street, WS13 6QA

☼ 11.30-11 (11.30 Fri & Sat) ☎ (01543) 410033

Fuller's London Pride; Holden's Golden Glow; Marston's Pedigree; guest beers Ⓗ

Genuine free house with a large U-shaped bar serving up to five guest ales, mainly from local micros, alongside the regular beers. The pub is host to darts and dominoes teams and a small separate games room is located at the rear of the bar. Good-value food is served lunchtimes Monday to Saturday, and pork pies are available during all sessions. The pub is dog-friendly. Note that there is an over-21 entry policy. ⚘⌖◖≷(City)⊟♣P'⌐

Queen's Head
4 Queen Street, WS13 6QD

☼ 12-11.30 (12.30am Fri & Sat) ☎ (01543) 410932

Banks's Mild; Brakspear Oxford Gold; Marston's Pedigree; Taylor Best Bitter; guest beers Ⓗ

In this highly popular, single-roomed pub, the friendly, welcoming atmosphere is enhanced by the art of conversation among locals, staff and visitors alike. Two guests from the Marston's portfolio are on handpump alongside the regular ales. Good-value, home-cooked food is served Wednesday to Sunday lunchtimes and weekday evenings. Thursday is curry night and a cheese and pâté selection is available during all sessions. Well-behaved dogs are welcome. Q⚘◖≷(City)⊟♣'⌐

Milwich

Green Man ⓛ
Milwich, ST18 0EG (on B5027 in centre of village)

☼ 12 (5 Mon-Wed)-11 ☎ (01889) 505310

⊕ greenmanmilwich.com

Holden's Black Country Bitter; guest beers Ⓗ

A pub since 1775, this free house offers guest beers from regionals and microbreweries nationwide, and holds regular beer festivals (see website for forthcoming guests). The long-serving licensee has been there for over 20 years, and the venue displays a list of his predecessors dating back to 1792. A popular hostelry with walkers and cyclists, there is a small restaurant area off the bar. Westons or Thatchers cider is stocked. ⚘Q⛄⚘◖⊟⌖Å♣⚘P'⌐

Newcastle-under-Lyme

Castle Mona ✅
4 Victoria Street, ST5 1NT

☼ 4 (12 Sat)-midnight; 12-11.30 Sun ☎ (01782) 244142

Taylor Landlord; Wells Bombardier; Young's Special; guest beer Ⓗ

A gem of a corner pub in a residential area close to the A34, a five-minute walk from Newcastle bus station and on the 101 bus route. It has a splendid cosy panelled lounge and a traditional bar where

pool and table skittles are played. There is a large, pleasant beer garden and a notable beer festival is held annually. The venue has a genuine community spirit and a warm welcome is guaranteed. Major sports fixtures are screened. ⚘⚘⊟⊟(101)♣'⌐

Freebird ⓛ
96 Liverpool Road, ST5 2AX

☼ 5-11 (midnight Fri); 12-midnight Sat; 12-11 Sun

Beer range varies Ⓗ

Named after a Lynyrd Skynyrd song, the Freebird is a real ale and music pub, welcoming to bikers. The bar sports a friendly atmosphere with a pool table and plenty of conversation. A second bar is in the Gig Room. This local has a total of nine handpumps. Lymestone ales are regularly available, with guest beers from local and nationwide microbreweries. Real cider is also on offer, while the bars are well stocked with wines, spirits and other beverages. ⊟♣⚘P

Norton Bridge

Railway Inn
Station Road, ST15 0NT

☼ 5 (12 Sat)-11; 12-10.30 Sun ☎ (01785) 760289

Thwaites Original; guest beer Ⓗ

Saved from closure, this venue is now a thriving and popular community village hostelry. It plays host to traditional pub games and also the bi-monthly meetings of the North Staffordshire BSA Motorcycle Owners Club. A good range of home-cooked meals is served (Mon-Sat eves) and is not to be missed. The food can be savoured with a traditional pint in a cosy atmosphere. Draught cider appears regularly during the summer and soon, with luck, all year round. ⚘Q⛄⚘◖⊟⌖Å≷⊟(490)♣⚘P'⌐

Onecote

Jervis Arms ⓛ
ST13 7RU (nn B5053 N of A53 Leek-Ashbourne road)

☼ 12-3, 7 (6 Sat)-midnight winter; 12-midnight Sun & summer ☎ (01538) 304206

Titanic Steerage, Iceberg; Wadworth 6X; guest beers Ⓗ

A regular in this Guide, the pub has shown a long-term commitment to the real ale scene. Situated in the Peak District National Park, it is close to Alton Towers. Family friendly, the beer garden has a river running through it and a good children's playground. There is a large car park just beyond. The landlord is fanatical about real ale, sourcing his guest beers from breweries near and far. Dogs are permitted in the bar. ⚘⛄⚘◖◖⌖Å♣⚘P'⌐

Oulton

Brushmakers Arms
8 Kibblestone Road, ST15 8UW (500yds W of A520, 1 mile NE of Stone)

☼ 12-midnight (1am Fri & Sat) ☎ (01785) 812062

Thwaites Original; guest beer Ⓗ

Named after a local cottage industry, the Brush is a pub where time stands still. It has a traditional quarry-tiled bar and a small ornate lounge. Pictures and postcards adorn the walls, reflecting a bygone era. The small rear patio garden is a real suntrap and doubles as a smoking area. With no games machines or jukebox, conversation flows in this excellent village local. Well-behaved dogs are welcome. The guest ale can be from a local micro. ⋈Q🐾🗟🕭▲⇌(Stone)🚋(250)♣P'⌐

Rugeley

Plaza ✅
Horsefair, WS15 2EJ
🕒 9-11.30 (12.30am Fri & Sat) ☎ (01889) 586831
Greene King Abbot; Ruddles Best Bitter; guest beers 🅗
A spacious Wetherspoon pub that has retained a great deal of the former cinema building's atmosphere. The airy interior allows for three widely separated levels, and the outside drinking areas are similar, with balcony, terrace and beer garden. A good selection of guest ales is offered; the focus is usually on Staffordshire micros, with an ever-present ale from Blythe Brewery. There are occasional Meet the Brewer evenings. Note the car park is Pay & Display. Q🏵🌑🗟⇌(Town)🚋🐾P'⌐

Yorkshireman
Colton Road, WS15 3HB (at jct of Colton Rd B5013 with Blithbury Rd)
🕒 12-2.30, 5.30-11; 12-11 Sat; 12-6 Sun ☎ (01889) 583977
⊕ wine-dine.co.uk
Blythe Bagot's Bitter, Palmers Poison 🅗
Close to Rugeley Trent Valley railway station, just north of the River Trent, this classic pub reopened as a free house in 2007 after a short period of closure and has flourished ever since. While a large part of the pub is set aside for dining, it is known as much for fine ale as fine cuisine, with casual drinkers welcome in the elegant Oak Room bar. The well-regarded local Blythe Brewery ales have featured for some years. Occasional themed food nights are held. ⋈🏵🌑🗟▲⇌(Trent Valley)P'⌐

Salt

Holly Bush Inn ✅
ST18 0BX (turn left off A518 opp Weston Hall) SJ959277
🕒 12-11 (10.30 Sun) ☎ (01889) 508234
⊕ hollybushinn.co.uk
Adnams Southwold Bitter; Marston's Pedigree; guest beers 🅗
The pub claims to have origins as far back as 1190 and is believed to be the second oldest inn to be granted a licence. The oldest part of the building retains a thatched roof. With extensions and alterations over the centuries, there are now three distinct areas: a bar area, dining room and snug. Many awards have been won for the superb-quality meals. ⋈Q🐾🏵🌑🗟🚋P'⌐

Stafford

Greyhound 🅛
12 County Road, ST16 2PU (off A34, opp jail)
🕒 4-11.30; 3-midnight Fri & Sat; 12-11 Sun
☎ (01785) 222432
Wells Bombardier; guest beers 🅗
A short walk from the town centre and opposite Stafford's jail, this site has housed a pub since the 1830s. Eight different beers are on offer at all times, mostly from microbreweries: just look at the beer menu on the wall. A range of Meet the Brewer sessions takes place throughout the year. The Greyhound has lost none of its vitality and energy. Cold snacks are available. ⋈Q🏵🗟⇌🚋♣🐾P'⌐

Joxer Bradys
4 St Martin's Place, ST16 2LA (in the corner of market square)
🕒 11.30-11 Mon & Tue; 11-11 Wed; 11.30-midnight Thu-Sat; 12-11 Sun ☎ (01785) 228183
Banks's Bitter; Jennings Cocker Hoop; Wychwood Hobgoblin; guest beers 🅗
A welcoming multi-roomed pub in the corner of Stafford's market square. It hosts a broad range of five varying well-kept ales as well as Thatchers Heritage traditional cider. The pub was formerly known as the Chains and is reputed to have an underground tunnel leading to the dungeons of the once-nearby crown court. Regular live music and comedy events are hosted. The bar also offers Stafford's best whisky menu. 🗟🕭⇌🚋♣🐾'⌐🍴

Lamb Inn
Broad Eye, ST16 2QB (opp Sainsbury's on Chell Road)
🕒 12-11 (midnight Fri & Sat); 12-10.30 Sun
☎ (01785) 603902
Fuller's London Pride; Wells Bombardier; guest beers 🅗
A traditional street-corner local that is just outside the town centre, with a warm and welcoming atmosphere and community spirit. The railway station is within walking distance and there are several bus stops close by, giving easy access to the public transport system. Although the pub car park is small there is a large local authority car park opposite. The regular beers, Bombardier and London Pride, are Cask Marque-accredited. The two guest beers change weekly. Q🐾🏵🗟🕭⇌🚋(1,2,3)♣P'⌐

Sun 🍷 🅛
7 Lichfield Road, ST17 4JX (close to town centre, opp the pictures)
🕒 11.30-11 (midnight Fri & Sat); 12-11 Sun
☎ (01785) 248310 ⊕ thesunstafford.co.uk
Everards Tiger Best Bitter; Titanic Steerage, Anchor Bitter, Iceberg, White Star, Captain Smiths; guest beers 🅗
One of six pubs in the Titanic Brewery fleet, this venue has been extensively renovated. Six regulars from the Titanic range along with four changing guest beers and three guest ciders will leave you spoilt for choice. A good-value food menu is served throughout the day using ingredients sourced as locally to the pub as possible. The original pub sign has been replaced by a replica that now hangs at the front; the original can be seen inside. ⋈🐾🏵🌑🗟🕭⇌🚋(1,2,3)♣🐾P'⌐

Vine Hotel
Salter Street, ST16 2JU
🕒 11-11; 12-10.30 Sun ☎ (01785) 244112
Banks's Bitter; guest beers 🅗
In the town centre, this Grade II-listed building started life as a 15th-century coaching inn called the Saracens Head. The current name derives from the grape vines growing outside. Reputed to be the oldest licensed building in Stafford, it is haunted by a young girl who has been seen in the mirror above the fireplace. There are many stories of local interest attached to the building, some displayed outside. Banks's Bitter is supported by two changing guest beers from the Marston's range. Q🐾🏵🍴🌑🗟🕭⇌🚋♣P'⌐

Stoke-on-Trent: Burslem

Bull's Head ⓛ

14 St John's Square, ST6 3AJ

☼ 3-11 (11.30 Wed & Thu); 12-midnight Fri & Sat; 12-11 Sun

☎ (01782) 834153

Titanic Steerage, Anchor Bitter, Iceberg, White Star; guest beers ⓗ

The Bull's Head is Titanic's brewery tap and flagship pub. Situated in the centre of Burslem, a short walk from Port Vale's ground, the pub welcomes all football fans, both home and away. The range of nine excellent real ales is complemented by a selection of up to 10 real ciders, a wide choice of single malt whiskies, fruit wines, and draught and bottled Belgian beers. Bar billiards and table skittles are played in the public bar.
ᴁ✿⊞◨♣☙🚆

Duke William ⓛ

2 St Johns Square, ST6 3AJ

☼ 11.30-11 (midnight Fri & Sat); 12-10.30 Sun

☎ (01782) 814809 ⊕ dukewilliamburslem.com

Joule's Slumbering Monk; Oakham Citra; Sharp's Doom Bar; guest beers ⓗ

Imposing pub that has undergone a sympathetic restoration, with most of the original features still in place, including the horseshoe-shaped bar and its heated foot rail, bell pushes in the lounge, serving hatch and leaded windows. Eight handpumps dispense a range of beers, including five guest ales. There is a smoking area to the rear and an restaurant upstairs with an English menu and its own bar. One beer festival is usually held each year; phone for details. ᴁ◖⊟᪥⊞(98)♣☙🚆

Post Office Vaults ⓛ

3 Market Place, ST6 3AA

☼ 10-10.45 (12.45am Fri & Sat); 10-10.30 Sun

☎ (01782) 811027

Fuller's London Pride; Greene King Abbot; Oakham Inferno; Thornbridge Jaipur IPA; guest beers ⓗ

Small, one-roomed pub in the centre of Burslem, popular with the local football club and community. The guest beers can hail from a wide variety of microbreweries. Real cider is also available. Sport and live music feature on the array of TV screens, and there is a heated and lit smoking area to the rear with its own TV. Post office memorabilia adorn the walls, including a factory clocking-in machine. The pub is dog-friendly.
≋(Longport)⊞(20,21,98)☙🚆

Stoke-on-Trent: Etruria

Holy Inadequate ⓛ

67 Etruria Old Road, ST1 5PE

☼ 4-11; 12-midnight Fri-Sun ☎ (01782) 915170

Joule's Original Pale Ale; guest beers ⓗ

A new and welcome entry to the Guide, this recently opened and refurbished pub is a shining light in the search for quality ales, a free house that already has a growing reputation among locals and visitors alike. With Joule's Pale the house beer, the other four pumps vary, with a strong preference given to microbrewers. The local delicacy, oatcakes, are made and sold on the premises. Plans are underway to expand the beer range. ᴁQ✿⊟⊞(34,34A)☙🚆

Stoke-on-Trent: Fenton

Malt 'n' Hops

295 King Street, ST4 3EJ

☼ 12-4 (not Tue), 7-11; 12-11 Fri; 12-midnight Sat; 12-11 Sun

☎ (01782) 313406 ⊕ maltnhops.com

Greene King Abbot; Tower Bursley Bitter; guest beers ⓗ

A traditional free house run by the Turner family since 1986. A favourite with many CAMRA members, it is regularly among the top 10 for the Potteries Pub of the Year. The open-plan, split-level layout gives the impression of separate bar and lounge areas. There are six rotating guest beers available; many are from local microbreweries. These are accompanied by the two permanent ales, a draught Belgian beer and bottled beers. Beer festivals are staged. ⊞(26,6)♣☙🚆

Stoke-on-Trent: Hanley

Coachmakers Arms ★

Lichfield Street, ST1 3EA (off A5008 Potteries Way ring road)

☼ 12-11.30 (midnight Fri & Sat; 10.30 Sun)

☎ (01782) 262158

Draught Bass; guest beers ⓗ

A warm atmosphere and friendly character welcome you to the Coachmakers Arms, situated near to Hanley bus station. This pub, recently refurbished and redecorated, provides five varying guest beers including a mild and stout, along with cider from a cask box. The pub is popular with local drinkers as well as having many fans from outside Stoke-on-Trent. Possible redevelopment of the area has put this building in jeopardy, so do not miss the opportunity to visit a gem.
ᴁQ🐾⊟⊞♣☙🚆

Unicorn Inn ✓

40 Piccadilly, ST1 1EG

☼ 12-1am (midnight Sun) ☎ (01782) 281809

Fuller's London Pride; guest beers ⓗ

One-room city centre pub opposite the Regent Theatre, consisting of a comfortably furnished lounge and a popular snug at the rear. A favourite with theatregoers both before and after the show, interval drinks can be pre-ordered. Acoustic nights are held on the last Sunday in the month and the local poker league meets here on the same night. In the alley alongside is a narrow gauge tram track, along which draymen used to deliver barrels. All this, plus the resident ghost. ◖☙🚆

Stoke-on-Trent: Hartshill

Greyhound ⓛ

67 George Street, ST5 1JT

☼ 12-11.30 (midnight Wed & Thu; 12.30am Fri & Sat)

☎ (01782) 635814

Everards Tiger Best Bitter; Titanic Steerage, Iceberg, White Star, Captain Smiths; guest beers ⓗ

On the edge of Newcastle town centre, this roadside pub is a joint venture between Titanic and Everards. There are nine handpumps on the bar, dispensing a range of Titanic, Everards and guest beers. Hot and cold snacks are served all day, with local oatcakes a speciality. A monthly sausage and mash evening is also organised. The interior has an L-shaped, open-plan layout, with a separate room to the right-hand side. The pub is dog-friendly.
ᴁQ◖▶⊞(25,26,101)♣☙🚆

Stoke-on-Trent: Longton

Congress ▼ L
14 Sutherland Road, ST3 1HJ (opp police station)
✪ 12-11 (midnight Fri-Sun) ☎ (01782) 763667
Holden's Black Country Mild; Wadworth Henry's IPA,
6X ⊞; guest beers ⊞/Ⓖ
Spacious two-roomed pub, comprising a large bar
area and meeting room. The landlord won first
place in the 2011 local CAMRA Pub of the Year
competition. A beer festival is held every May,
when two bars are added, both serving beer from
the cask, to supplement the regular range. The pub
also hosts various events and societies. How can
you fit so much in one pub? It's like Doctor Who's
Tardis... bigger on the inside! A pleasure to drink in.
⇌➡♣●'–

Stoke-on-Trent: Stoke

Glebe
35 Glebe Street, ST4 1HG
✪ 12-11 (11.30 Fri & Sat; 10.30 Sun) ☎ (01782) 844600
Joule's Blonde, Original Pale Ale, Slumbering Monk ⊞
Situated an equally short walk from both the rail
station and Stoke town centre, this new entrant to
the Guide is a recently reopened and beautifully
restored corner tavern, and is the flagship pub for
the reinvigorated Joule's Brewery. Amazing stained
glass windows, wooden panelling and an open fire
all add to the welcoming feel on entering. Home-
made food is available lunchtimes and evenings,
with Staffs organic cheeses and pork pies on all
day. ◖⇌➡(21,21A,F10)●

Wheatsheaf L ✔
84-92 Church Street, ST4 1BU
✪ 9-midnight (1am Fri & Sat) ☎ (01782) 747462
Courage Directors; Greene King Abbot; Ruddles Best
Bitter; guest beers ⊞
Situated in Stoke town, this regular entry in the
Guide has a well-earned reputation as one of the
best real ale outlets in the Wetherspoon chain. It is
a cosy pub that actively supports the LocAle
scheme, so much so that Lymestone has a
permanent ale featured in the range of up to five
guest beers. Breakfast and beer are served from
9am. Meet the Brewer nights are held, and the
Tuesday steak night and Thursday curry night are
always popular. Q☽◖&⇌➡'–

White Star
63 Kingsway, ST4 1JB (off Church Street)
✪ 11-11 (midnight Fri-Sun) ☎ (01782) 848732
Everards Tiger Best Bitter; Titanic Steerage, Anchor
Bitter, Iceberg, White Star; guest beers ⊞
One of the Titanic Brewery fleet, this award-
winning pub has a convenient town-centre
location and is a popular local. With its 10
handpumps offering five from Titanic's superb
range, plus Everards Tiger and four well-sourced
guest ales, it is easy to see why. In the comfortable
split-level bar festooned with remembrances of the
ill-fated Titanic, delicious home-made food is
served lunchtimes and evenings. An upstairs
function room is available.
Q◖&⇌➡(23,25,26)♣●'–

Stone

Royal Exchange L
Radford Street, ST15 8DA
✪ 12-11 (midnight Fri & Sat) ☎ (01785) 812685

Everards Tiger Best Bitter; Titanic Mild, Steerage,
Iceberg, White Star ⊞, Captain Smiths ⊞/Ⓖ; guest
beers ⊞
Although one room, there are four distinct drinking
areas in this 2008 refurbishment by Everards and
Titanic. It is a welcome addition to the town's real
ale scene. Up to six guest ales, many from micros,
and a real cider, complement ales from the Titanic
and Everards ranges. Acoustic music nights
occasionally feature on Tuesdays. Lunchtime food,
locally sourced, is good value. There is a good
selection of single malts. Well-behaved dogs are
welcome, and children are allowed until 9pm.
Town car parks are nearby.
🏠Q☽&❄◖&⇌➡(250,101,400)♣●'–🍴

Swan Inn L
18 Stafford Street, ST15 8QW (on A520)
✪ 12-11 (12.30am Tue; midnight Wed); 11-1am Thu & Fri
☎ (01785) 815570 ⊕ swaninnstone.co.uk
Beer range varies ⊞
Grade II-listed and carefully renovated in 1999, this
thriving free house has served beers from over 450
breweries so far on its seven handpulls. A range of
guest ales from Thornbridge, Abbeydale,
Townhouse, Sharp's, Blythe and Dark Star is on
offer alongside an increasing selection of real
ciders. Tuesday and Friday are quiz nights, with
Thursday and Saturday live music, and there is a
free Sunday buffet. An annual beer festival is held
the second week of July. Over-18s only.
🏠❄◖&⇌➡(101,250,490)♣●'–🍴

Tamworth

Globe Inn
Lower Gungate, B79 7AT
✪ 11-11; 12-3, 7-10.30 Sun ☎ (01827) 60455
⊕ theglobetamworth.com
Draught Bass; Holden's Black Country Mild;
Worthington's Bitter; guest beer ⊞
Comfortable town-centre hotel bar attracting a
clientele of all ages. The single changing guest
beer sometimes comes from a local microbrewery.
The mild, hard to find in the area, is keenly priced
and has a strong following. Three public areas
include a raised dining space where Sunday
lunches are popular. A separate function room is
available for hire. The pub can get busy when live
sporting events are shown on the two large-screen
TVs. 🛏◖⇌➡♣

Sir Robert Peel
13-15 Lower Gungate, B79 7BA
✪ 2-11 (midnight Fri); 12-midnight Sat; 12-11.30 Sun
☎ (01827) 300910
Sharp's Doom Bar; guest beers ⊞
Popular ale house named after the local MP who
served two terms as Prime Minister and laid the
foundations for the modern police force. Up to five
ales are on offer, with regularly changing guests.
Ale choice is never predictable but often includes
Oakham beers and selections from the many
excellent local micros. A real cider is always
available, usually Westons. Weekends can be busy,
with Monday and Wednesday ideal for a quiet pint.
⇌➡●

Trysull

Bell L
Bell Road, WV5 7JB SO852940

❄ 11.30-3, 5-11.30; 11.30-midnight Sat; 12-11.30 Sun
☎ (01902) 892871
Bathams Best Bitter; Holden's Black Country Mild, Black Country Bitter, Golden Glow, Special; guest beer Ⓗ
A fine 18th-century building next to the village church, comprising a smallish but cosy bar, pleasant lounge and a large restaurant/dining room. Food is served lunchtimes and evenings, and 12-4pm Sunday. As well as the Holden's range, Bathams Best Bitter is a regular together with a changing guest, often sourced from a microbrewery. A patio area is to the front of the pub. Popular with walkers – the Staffordshire & Worcestershire canal is a 15-minute walk away.
Q❧☺❀◐Ⓓ♿➾(584,585)P

Uttoxeter

Old Swan Ⓛ ✅
Market Place, ST14 8AN
❄ 7-midnight (1am Fri & Sat) ☎ (01889) 598654
Greene King Abbot; Ruddles County; guest beers Ⓗ
Opened by Wetherspoon in December 2006, this is an excellent example of a one-room pub, and has rapidly become a favourite among Uttoxeter drinkers. There is a strong emphasis on real ales served through the eight handpulls, with beers coming from local breweries such as Lymestone and Slater's as well as the regulars from national brewers. The pub has recently become more active in its promotion of beers and hosts Meet the Brewer evenings. ⋈Q❧☺❀◐Ⓓ♿➾(841)♣♠⅃

Weston

Woolpack Inn
The Green, ST18 0JH (off A518) SJ977268
❄ 11-11 ☎ (01889) 270218 ⊕ woolpackpubweston.co.uk
Banks's Bitter; Marston's Pedigree; guest beers Ⓗ
Known locally as the Inn on the Green, the Woolpack is a welcoming village local with an extensive dining area, while another area hosts dominoes and darts. Over the years the low-ceilinged pub has been thoughtfully extended while retaining the original bar area. Four bays inside reflect the pub's origins as a row of cottages and a blacksmith's workshop. The property is recorded as being owned by the Bagot family in the 1730s. ⋈Q❧☺❀◐Ⓓ♿Å➾(X1)♣♠P⅃

Whiston

Swan Inn Ⓛ
ST19 5QH (in Penkridge turn W off A449 at roundabout near Texaco garage onto Rungham Lane, cross Cuttlestone Bridge and follow signs to Whiston) SJ895144
❄ 12-3 (not Mon), 5-11; 12-11 Sun ☎ (01785) 716200
⊕ swanwhiston.co.uk
Holden's Black Country Mild, Black Country Bitter; guest beers Ⓗ
Although remotely situated, high-quality, well-kept ales and superb food make this a thriving pub. Built in 1593, burned down and rebuilt in 1711, the oldest part today is the small bar housing an inglenook fireplace. The lounge features an intriguing central double-sided log fire. Six acres of grounds include a children's obstacle course, aviary and rabbits. Discount on ales are available to CAMRA members. Branch Pub of the Year 2011 and Cider Pub of the Year 2011.
⋈Q❧☺❀◐Ⓓ♿Å➾(88,88A)♣♠P⅃

Wilnecote

Globe Inn
91 Watling Street, B77 5BA (on B5404 opp church)
❄ 12-11 ☎ (01827) 280885
Marston's Pedigree; guest beer Ⓗ
A regular Guide entry, the pub is renowned for the quality of its Pedigree, which sells in good volumes. A guest beer from the Marston's portfolio is also usually available. This is very much a locals' pub, but visitors can be assured of a friendly welcome from bar staff and customers alike. Games are popular, with darts, dominoes and football teams featuring. The pub is close to the M42 motorway, and a 15-minute walk from Wilnecote rail station. Q❀❅➾(8,9)♣⅃

Wombourne

New Inn ☗ Ⓛ
1 Station Road, WV5 9EY
❄ 12-11 (11.30 Thu; midnight Fri & Sat) ☎ (01902) 892037
Banks's Mild, Bitter Ⓗ/Ⓟ**; Jennings Cocker Hoop; guest beers** Ⓗ
Large open-plan pub with a strong emphasis on good-quality food at reasonable prices. Dining is mainly in the lounge area, while drinkers have their own space at the far end of the pub. Banks's beers are on offer plus three or four other changing guests from the Marston's stable. The large garden at the rear and the patio at the front can get busy in summer. Regular karaoke and quiz nights are held. There is a discount of 20 per cent for CAMRA members from 6pm on Mondays. Local CAMRA Pub of the Year 2012. ❧❀◐♿➾(255,256)P⅃

Yoxall

Golden Cup
Main Street, DE13 8NQ (on A515)
❄ 12-3, 5-midnight; 12-1am Fri & Sat; 12-midnight Sun
☎ (01543) 472295 ⊕ goldencupyoxall.co.uk
Marston's Pedigree; guest beer Ⓗ
Impressive family-run 300-year-old inn at the centre of the village, opposite St Peter's Church, bedecked with attractive floral displays for much of the year. The pub features a smart L-shaped lounge with beamed ceiling, primarily catering for diners, and a plainer public bar with Sky Sports TV. Colourful murals with a classical theme enhance both the ladies' and men's toilets. The award-winning pub gardens stretch down to the River Swarbourn and include a camping area (caravans and motor homes only). ⋈Q❀❅◐Ⓓ♿Å➾(7,7E)♣P⅃

By George!

It was my Uncle George who discovered that alcohol was a food well in advance of modern medical thought.
P G Wodehouse, The Inimitable Jeeves, 1923

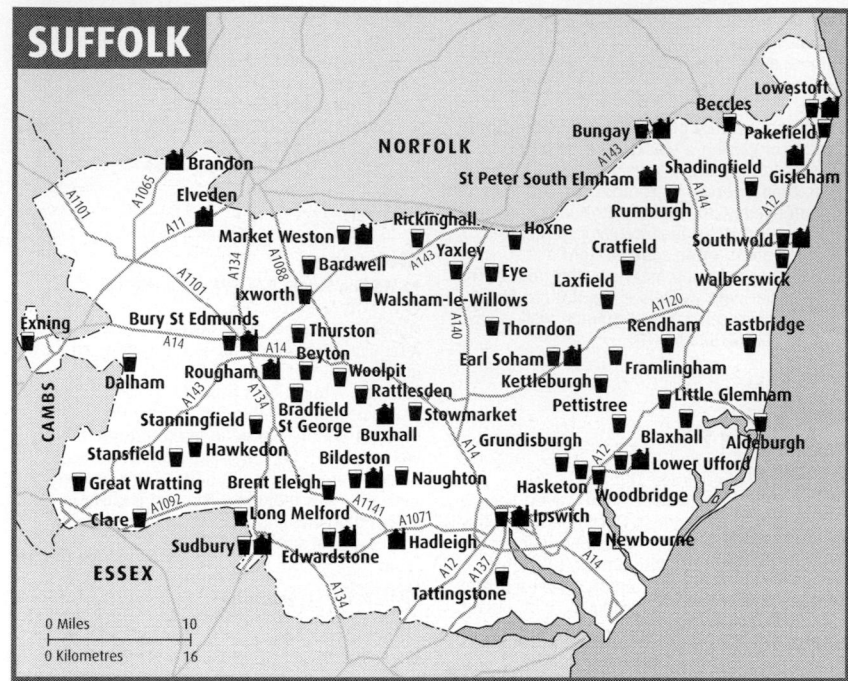

SUFFOLK

NORFOLK

Lowestoft
Beccles
Bungay
Pakefield
Brandon
Shadingfield
Gisleham
Elveden
St Peter South Elmham
Rumburgh
Rickinghall
Hoxne
Cratfield
Southwold
Market Weston
Yaxley
Bardwell
Eye
Laxfield
Walberswick
Ixworth
Walsham-le-Willows
Bury St Edmunds
Exning
Thurston
Thorndon
Rendham
Eastbridge
Beyton
Earl Soham
Framlingham
Woolpit
Kettleburgh
Dalham
Rougham
Rattlesden
Pettistree
Little Glemham
Stanningfield
Bradfield
Stowmarket
St George
Blaxhall
Aldeburgh
Stansfield
Hawkedon
Buxhall
Grundisburgh
Bildeston
Lower Ufford
Great Wratting
Brent Eleigh
Naughton
Hasketon
Woodbridge
Clare
Long Melford
Ipswich
Sudbury
Hadleigh
Newbourne
Edwardstone
ESSEX
Tattingstone

0 Miles 10
0 Kilometres 16

Aldeburgh

Mill Inn 🅛
Market Cross Place, IP15 5BJ (opp Moot Hall)
❂ 11-11; 12-10.30 Sun ☎ (01728) 452563
🌐 themillinnaldeburgh.com
Adnams Southwold Bitter, Broadside, seasonal beers Ⓗ
Recently refurbished throughout, the pub has new seating and stripped-back wooden flooring and tiling in the main bar areas plus a new servery. The food menu specialises in local produce, particularly fish that comes directly from nearby beach fishermen. A popular stop-off for walkers on the Suffolk coastal path, the Mill also welcomes bikers, bird spotters and dogs and their owners. CAMRA members receive a 10 per cent discount. Recently highly commended for its best-kept cellar. ⛲◑&

Bardwell

Dun Cow ✔
Up Street, IP31 1AA (approx 1 mile off A143 at Stanton)
❂ 11.30-2, 5-midnight; 12-midnight Sat; 12-10.30 Sun
☎ (01359) 250806
Greene King IPA, seasonal ales; Morland Old Golden Hen Ⓗ
A traditional pub in a pleasant village set in the Suffolk countryside. The pub has two bars and offers speciality food nights. Party bookings are taken and coaches are welcome if booked in advance. ᴁQ⛲◑🖶♣P⅃

Beccles

Caxton Club 🅛
Gaol Lane, NR34 9SJ (next to supermarket car park)
❂ 12-1.30 (not Tue), 7-11; 12-2, 6.30-11 Fri; 12-11 Sat;
12-10.30 Sun ☎ (01502) 712829
Theakston Black Bull; guest beers Ⓗ

Spacious club conveniently situated a short walk from train and bus stations and close to the town centre. All members and guests are warmly welcomed (just show this Guide or CAMRA membership card to be signed in as a guest). It has a central bar, TV and darts room, and snooker room. There is also a large function room where music events are held on Friday and Saturday evenings. Some guest beers are locally sourced. ᴁ⛲&≒🖶♣⅃

Beyton

Bear Inn
Tostock Road, IP30 9AG
❂ 12-2, 5-11; 12-4, 7-10.30 Sun ☎ (01359) 270249

Adnams Broadside; Woodforde's Wherry; guest beer H

Rebuilt in 1900 after the original thatched Bear burnt down in a July thunderstorm – you can read a full account of this event in the bar. The pub has been run by the same family since 1922. The current landlord has updated the building without spoiling a traditional inn, with a public bar, and a separate bar with restaurant serving excellent food (Fri-Sun lunchtimes, Fri & Sat eves). There is easy access from the A14 as the building was originally on the main Ipswich to Cambridge road. ⋈Q✿⊞▲⊟♣P⌐

Bildeston

King's Head L

132 High Street, IP7 7ED (on B1115)

✿ closed Mon & Tue; 6 (4 Fri; 12 Sat)-midnight; 12-10.30 Sun

☎ (01449) 741434 ⊕ bildestonkingshead.co.uk

Bildeston Best; Brandon Rusty Bucket; Earl Soham Victoria; King's Head Landlady; Mauldons Silver Adder H

The home of the King's Head Brewery since 1996, this former coaching inn, dating from around 1530, has a single bar and retains exposed carved timbers and an inglenook fireplace. A friendly drinking house atmosphere has evolved, with food available at the weekend only. There is a fully enclosed rear garden with covered patio area, lawns and play equipment. The May bank holiday beer festival is well established. ⋈✿◑♠

Blaxhall

Ship L

School Road, IP12 2DY

✿ 12-3, 6-midnight; 12-midnight Sat & Sun

☎ (01728) 688316 ⊕ blaxhallshipinn.co.uk

Adnams Southwold Bitter; Woodforde's Wherry; guest beers H

Traditional two-roomed 16th-century pub on the edge of Suffolk Sandlings with a long-established reputation for singing in the bar. It is also renowned for good food, the menu offering a wide choice using locally sourced ingredients, including home-made pies and puddings. Live music features at least once a week with regular folk music sessions. Eight chalets to the side of the pub provide B&B accommodation, and dogs are welcome. The bus service is hourly during the day. ⋈Q❧✿⊯◑⊟P

Bradfield St George

Fox & Hounds

Felsham Road, IP30 0AB

✿ closed Mon; 12-11 (midnight Fri & Sat; 10.30 Sun)

☎ (01284) 386379

Adnams Southwold Bitter, Lighthouse H

On the village outskirts, close to the historic coppiced woodland of the Suffolk Wildlife Trust, this beautifully restored Victorian building is a free house and country restaurant. Now refurbished to appeal to drinkers and diners, it also offers B&B accommodation, all with excellent service. The cosy public bar, with a woodblock floor and logburner, is served by two main bars. The camping and caravan site in an adjoining meadow has space for 10 tents and five caravans. ⋈Q✿⊯◑⊞♣P

Brent Eleigh

Cock Inn ★

Lavenham Road, CO10 9PB

✿ 12-4, 6-11; 12-11 Fri & Sat; 12-10.30 Sun

☎ (01787) 247371

Adnams Southwold Bitter; Greene King Abbot; guest beer H

Unspoilt gem, identified by CAMRA as one of Britain's Real Heritage Pubs. In winter both bars are snug and warm; in summer with the doors open, the bar is at one with its surroundings. The Bitch and Stitch knitting club meets here every Wednesday evening. Walkers and cyclists exploring the area will be pleased to hear that Deborah is a great cook and that food service, available at all times, is not intrusive. ⋈Q✿⊯◑⊞♣♦P

Bungay

Green Dragon L

29 Broad Street, NR35 1EE

✿ 11-3, 5-11; 11-midnight Fri; 12-midnight Sat; 12-3, 7-11 Sun ☎ (01986) 892681

Green Dragon Chaucer Ale, Gold, Bridge Street, seasonal beers H

Bungay's only brewpub, on the edge of town, the Green Dragon is a regular entry in this Guide. Ales are brewed in outbuildings next to the car park at the rear of the building (brewery tours are available by appointment). This town pub has a separate public bar and a spacious lounge with a small side garden. Bottle conditioned and seasonal ales are often available including a strong dark mild in the winter. ⋈❧✿⊞▲⊟P

Bury St Edmunds

Beerhouse L

1 Tayfen Road, IP32 6BH

✿ 5 (12 Sat)-11; 12-10 Sun ☎ (01284) 766415

⊕ burybeerhouse.co.uk

Brewshed Pale Ale, Best Bitter, American Blonde, seasonal beers; guest beers H

Unusual semi-circular, brick-built Victorian building (previously called the Ipswich Arms) quite close to the railway station. The building was refurbished in 2010 prior to reopening in 2011 as an ale-focused traditional pub with a new microbrewery in the yard behind, now trading as the Brewshed Brewery and currently supplying two local pubs. Eight handpumps provide a varied selection of well-kept real ales and four ciders. Q✿⇌⊟♣♦⌐

Dove L

68 Hospital Road, IP33 3JU

✿ 5-11; 12-3, 6-11 Sat; 12-3, 6-10.30 Sun ☎ (01284) 702787

⊕ thedovepub.co.uk

Mauldons Gold; Woodforde's Wherry, seasonal beers; guest beers H

A traditional Victorian ale house that won CAMRA Regional Pub of the Year in 2010/11. Situated just five minutes' walk from the historic town centre, the Dove has six handpumps and real ciders but no TV, music, gaming machines or lager. The no-frills main bar has scrubbed floorboards alongside a carpeted parlour. The staff offer a warm, friendly welcome and are knowledgeable about the ever-changing beers, which come mainly from East Anglia together with ales from established regional brewers. Q✿⊟♣♦P⌐

Old Cannon 🅛
86 Cannon Street, IP33 1JR
❂ 12-11 ☎ (01284) 768769 ⊕ oldcannonbrewery.co.uk
Adnams Southwold Bitter; Old Cannon Best Bitter, Brass Monkey, Gunner's Daughter Ⓗ
Formerly the St Edmund's Head, this brewpub is on the site of the original Cannon Brewery. The interesting, upwardly extended bar area is also home to the brewing vessels. As well as its own real ales and guests, a wide range of foreign beers is offered. Good food, locally sourced, is served (no food Sun). Accommodation is available with limited parking. ⌂Q✿✿🛏◑⇄🖳P🅿🚆

Rose & Crown ✪
48 Whiting Street, IP33 1NP
❂ 11.30-11.30; 11.30-3, 7-11.30 Sat; 12-2.30, 7.30-11.30 Sun ☎ (01284) 755934
Greene King XX Mild, IPA, Abbot, seasonal beers Ⓗ
In sight of Greene King's Westgate Brewery, this is a traditional pub with two bars and a separate off-sales area. The present tenants have run this house for 25 years, and it was previously run by the landlady's father. Wholesome and good-value lunches are served Monday to Saturday. The public house itself is a listed building close to a conservation area with many fine buildings. Children are not allowed in the bars but are welcome in the garden. Q✿◑🖳♣🚆

Clare

Cock
3 Callis Street, CO10 8PX
❂ 12-3 (not Mon), 5-11; 12-midnight Sat & Sun ☎ (01787) 277391
Adnams Southwold Bitter, Broadside Ⓗ
A popular 16th-century Adnams' inn set back from the highway on the Stradishall Road close to Clare's magnificent church. Run by Clare's longest-serving landlords, the bar is welcoming with much of its history on display. A separate lower dining room and large enclosed rear garden provide plenty of space. An interesting menu at a fair price uses organic local produce where possible, with the pub's own allotments growing salads in summer. No food on Monday. Q✿◑P

Cratfield

Poacher 🅛
Bell Green, IP19 0BL TM312751
❂ closed Mon; 12-2.30 (Wed-Fri summer only), 6-11; 12-midnight Sat & Sun ☎ (01986) 798206
Adnams Southwold Bitter Ⓗ**; guest beers** Ⓗ/🅖
A large, rustic, split-level rural pub that can be difficult to find in this rather dispersed village. But it is well worth the effort seeking out this friendly, comfortable establishment, with a good selection of locally produced real ales including six to eight guest beers. Live music features on occasion including the Trembling Wheelbarrows who play here in their own unique style. A pool table and other pub games are available. Food is served until about 8.30pm. ⌂Q❧✿◑♣P

Dalham

Affleck Arms 🅛 ✪
Brookside, CB8 8TG
❂ 12-2.30 (not Mon), 5-11; 12-11 Sun ☎ (01638) 500306
Black Sheep Best Bitter; guest beers Ⓗ

Situated in the thatched village of Dalham, dating back to the 16th century, this friendly pub has a cosy restaurant and a sleepy bar with original beams and a prominent inglenook fireplace. It offers two cask ales from local microbreweries and hosts an annual beer fest every June. The home-cooked food is exceptional and well priced, attracting families and walking parties. Outside is a rear patio and a garden for diners and drinkers overlooking the river. ⌂Q✿◑♿🖳♣P🚆

Earl Soham

Victoria 🅛
The Street, IP13 7RL (on A1120)
❂ 11.30-3, 6-11; 12-3, 7-11 Sun ☎ (01728) 685758
Earl Soham Victoria, Albert, Sir Rogers Porter, Brandeston Gold, seasonal beers Ⓗ
Traditional Victorian pub with two small bars and a large fire in winter months, which has changed little over the years. The Earl Soham Brewery is just 150 yards from the pub. An interesting, ever-changing food menu is offered. It gets busy at weekends and especially on sunny days when even a seat in the garden can be difficult to find. A must-visit for anyone who appreciates a great pub – it still has the outside loo, too. ⌂Q✿◑🖳P

Eastbridge

Eels Foot 🅛
Leiston Road, IP16 4SN (close to entrance to Minsmere nature reserve) TM452661
❂ 11.30-3, 6-11; 11.30-11 Sat & Sun ☎ (01728) 830154 ⊕ theeelsfootinn.co.uk
Adnams Southwold Bitter, Broadside, seasonal beers Ⓗ
Located adjacent to the famous nature reserve where avocets and otters are local success stories, the pub is popular with ramblers and bird watchers. It also has a good reputation for locally sourced home-cooked food and has a separate restaurant area and a new kitchen. Live traditional music sessions feature on Thursday evenings and folk music plays monthly. En-suite accommodation is available for visitors exploring the heritage coastline and there is cycle hire behind the pub. ⌂Q❧✿🛏◑P

Edwardstone

White Horse 🅛
Mill Green, CO10 5PX TL951426
❂ 12-3, 5-11; 12-midnight Fri & Sat; 12-11 Sun ☎ (01787) 211211 ⊕ edwardstonewhitehorse.co.uk
Adnams Southwold Bitter; Mill Green Mawkin Mild, White Horse, Loveleys Fair, seasonal beers Ⓗ
Well off the beaten track, this lovely rural free house has been recently extended and refurbished. An ideal holiday base, alongside the pub and its own Mill Green Eco Brewery there is a campsite and two self-catering chalets, all supplied with power from the site's own wind generator. Delicious home-made food uses locally sourced organic ingredients where available. Beer and music festivals are held and the pub has a late licence when trade demands. Castings Heath Cottage ciders are stocked. ⌂Q✿🛏◑🖳🅰♣🍺P🖵

Exning

White Horse
Church Street, CB8 7EH
☼ 12-11 ☎ (01638) 577323
Taylor Landlord; Woodforde's Wherry; Young's Special Ⓗ
The Exning White Horse has been run by the same family since 1923 and is mentioned in the Domesday Book. It is a real village pub with a thriving restaurant and public bar. An excellent menu of home-cooked food specialises in seafood, steaks and classic British dishes (booking advisable). Happy hour is 5.30-6.30pm, extended to 7pm on Friday. A private room is available to hire. ▲❀♿☕♣P⅃

Eye

Queen's Head Ⓛ ✅
Cross Street, IP23 7AB
☼ 12-3, 5-10.30; 12-11 Fri-Sat; 12-5 Sun ☎ (01379) 870153
⊕ queensheadeye.co.uk
Adnams Southwold bitter; guest beers Ⓖ
Dating from 1590, now the only pub in town, and incorporating the former butcher's shop (the Cross Street bar). It has recently been sympathetically restored. A minimum of two guest beers are on tap, and at least one of these is local. Beers are dispensed direct from the cask in the bar with a water-cooling system. Full of character, both bars have log fires in winter. There is extensive outside seating, and a good selection of pub food, with tapas a speciality, is served. Dogs on leads welcomed. ▲Q❀❶♿P⅃

Framlingham

Station Ⓛ
Station Road, IP13 9EE (on B1116) TM284630
☼ 12-3, 5-11; 12-4, 7-10.30 Sun ☎ (01728) 723455
⊕ thestationhotel.net
Earl Soham Gannet Mild, Victoria, Brandeston Gold, seasonal beers Ⓗ
Small, cosy, two-bar pub set in a former station buffet that was built in 1859 (the branch line closed in 1963). It enjoys a good reputation for food, which is all locally sourced and prepared on the premises – the ever-changing menu is displayed on chalkboards. Beers are dispensed from a set of Edwardian German silver handpumps and a guest cider is also available. The small snug bar leads to an enclosed patio and can be booked for private parties. A beer festival is held at the end of July. ▲Q☺❀❶☕P⅃

Great Wratting

Red Lion
School Road, CB9 7HA (on B1061 2 miles N of Haverhill)
☼ 11-2.30, 5-11; 11-1am Sat; 12-3, 7-10 Sun
☎ (01440) 783237
Adnams Southwold Bitter, Broadside, seasonal beers Ⓗ
Traditional local pub with a well-stocked log fire. A separate restaurant serves good food lunchtimes and evenings, which is popular with families. The landlord and local residents are most welcoming. Over the porch are two whale rib bones which have stood there for more than 400 years. ▲❀❶♣P

Grundisburgh

Dog Ⓛ
The Green, IP13 6TA TM224509
☼ closed Mon; 12-2.30, 5.30-11; 12-11 Fri-Sun
☎ (01473) 735267 ⊕ grundisburghdog.co.uk
Adnams Southwold Bitter; guest beers Ⓗ
Centrally placed in the village, set back from the road, this traditional pub has a separate public bar with timber-beamed ceiling, flagstone flooring and comfortable seating. A selection of pub games can be played including darts and dominoes. The lounge bar is set for dining, with a good selection of home-cooked meals and snacks. Outside there are seating areas to the front and rear of the building, and a children's play area. The house beer is supplied by a Suffolk brewer.
Q❀❶☕♿☕(70,70a,936)♣P⅃

Hasketon

Turk's Head Ⓛ
Low Road, IP13 6JG TM247506
☼ 12-11 (midnight Fri & Sat; 10.30 Sun) ☎ (01473) 610907
⊕ hasketonturkshead.co.uk
Adnams Southwold Bitter; Woodforde's Wherry; guest beers Ⓗ
A community-run pub with a timber-beamed ceiling and quarry-tiled floor around the bar. The building is set off the road with a large garden to one side with raised seating. Indoors, a cosy area near the inglenook fireplace includes a high-back settle. To the side of the main bar is a dining area where meals and snacks are served (lunchtimes and evenings weekdays, all day Sat and Sun). There is also a large camp site and a barn used for live music and private functions. ▲Q❀❶♿▲☕♣P⅃

Hawkedon

Queen's Head
Rede Road, IP29 4NN
☼ 12 (4 Mon-Thu)-11 ☎ (01284) 789218
⊕ hawkedonqueen.co.uk
Adnams Southwold Bitter; Woodforde's Wherry; guest beers Ⓗ/Ⓖ
Fifteenth-century free house with an unspoilt interior and an enormous open fire in the main bar. As well as good beers, it also serves traditional cider and perry. The food is home cooked and of excellent quality; a butcher's shop was recently opened on the premises. Various events are held including an excellent beer festival in July, and it is a meeting place for classic car clubs (see website for details). A friendly welcome is assured. ▲Q❀❶▲♣☕P⅃

Hoxne

Swan ✅
Low Street, IP21 5AS TM179771
☼ 12-3, 6-11; 12-10.30 Sun ☎ (01379) 668275
⊕ hoxneswan.co.uk
Adnams Southwold Bitter, Broadside Ⓖ; Woodforde's Wherry; guest beers Ⓗ
Good food made with fresh, seasonal, locally-sourced ingredients is served alongside a selection of fine real ales. The timber-framed Grade II country pub was built in 1480 by the Bishop of Norwich and is full of history. It has three main rooms including a front bar with a large fireplace

and high beamed ceiling. The spacious garden backs onto the river and is close to where King Edmund, last Saxon king of East Anglia, was killed by the invading Danes. A beer festival is held in summer. ⚏🏠🌣🕪🍴🍺❧

Ipswich

Arboretum 🛈
43 High Street, IP1 3QL
🕐 11-2.30, 6-11; 11-11 Fri & Sat; 12-11 Sun
☎ (01473) 222177 ⊕ the-arboretum.net
Beer range varies ℍ
Small single-bar pub offering beers from local small brewers including Green Jack and St Peter's, complemented by a selection of local bottled beers and wines. It has a separate restaurant/function room upstairs, specialising in contemporary British food including light lunches available daily (booking not essential but recommended). There is 20 per cent off all drinks 5-6.30pm weekdays. Outside is a patio garden. 🌣🕪➡🚆❧

Brewery Tap 🛈
Cliff Quay, IP3 0AT
🕐 11-3, 6-11; 11-11 Sat; 11-10.30 Sun ☎ (01473) 225501
⊕ thebrewerytap.org
Cliff Quay Bitter, Tolly Roger, seasonal beers; Earl Soham Victoria; guest beers ℍ
Old brewer's house located close to the former historic brewery with a large main bar area and various more intimate spaces. Alongside beers that are mainly brewed locally is an extensive food menu with home-produced fare. Themed food nights, home-made pickled eggs and bar snacks are offered. There are great views of the River Orwell through a bay window in the bar, despite new sea defences being added. Regular live music plays. Two private function rooms are available and there is a secluded garden.
⚏🏠🌣🕪🚆(1,6)♣❧

Dove Street Inn 🛈
76 St Helens Street, IP4 2LA TM170445
🕐 12-midnight (10.30 Sun) ☎ (01473) 211270
⊕ dovestreetinn.co.uk
Adnams Broadside; Crouch Vale Brewers Gold; Fuller's London Pride ℍ**; Elgoods Black Dog Mild** ℂ**; guest beers** ℍ/ℂ
A popular multi-roomed pub serving a large selection of real ales in oversized glasses – including various milds and traditional ciders – plus a choice of continental beers. Beers from the new house brewery are also offered on handpump and there is a new brew shop next door. Home-cooked food and bar snacks are available at all times. Well-behaved dogs and children are welcome during the day. Last entry is 10.45pm. Three beer festivals are held annually, each with more than 60 cask ales.
Q🏠🌣🚃🕪🚆(66)♣❧🍴

Fat Cat 🍸 🛈
288 Spring Road, IP4 5NL TM181448
🕐 12-11 (midnight Fri & Sat) ☎ (01473) 726524
⊕ fatcatipswich.co.uk
Crouch Vale Brewers Gold; Fuller's London Pride; Woodforde's Wherry; guest beers ℂ
With no background music or games machines, this cosy drinking pub is a joy to visit. Walls display a selection of original enamel signs, posters and other artefacts. Up to 16 beers are dispensed from a taproom behind the bar. A secluded garden and patio provide extra space for occasional barbecues

on summer afternoons. Snacks are available and plates provided for customers to order in takeaways (not Fri or Sat eve). No children or dogs. Local CAMRA Branch Pub of the Year 2012.
Q🌣⇌(Derby Rd)🚆(2,75)♣❧

Greyhound 🛈
9 Henley Road, IP3 3SE
🕐 11-2.30, 5-11; 11-midnight Fri & Sat; 10-10.30 Sun
☎ (01473) 252862 ⊕ thegreyhoundipswich.co.uk
Adnams Southwold Bitter, Explorer, Broadside, seasonal beers; guest beers ℍ
The pub has been refurbished but retains a timeless quality. It has a cosy, small public bar at the front and a larger drinking and dining area to the side and rear. The outside drinking space can be busy in the summer months. Fresh home-made food from a blackboard menu is served daily. Occasional live music and arts events are hosted and TVs screen sporting events. Cooked breakfasts are now available on Sunday 10-11.30am.
🌣🕪🕻🚆♣❧

Lord Nelson 🛈
81 Fore Street, IP4 1JZ
🕐 12-11.30 (12.30am Fri & Sat); 12-11 Sun
☎ (01473) 407510 ⊕ lord-nelson.co.uk
Adnams Southwold Bitter, Explorer, Broadside, seasonal beers ℂ
Nautically-themed pub steeped in history. Dating back to the 17th century, it has a half-timbered frontage and dormer windows and is close to the historic waterfront. An unusual gravity dispense system is used that incorporates a row of wooden casks to good effect and also guarantees temperature-controlled real ales. Families are welcome and there is an enclosed patio area outside. The public car park to the rear (off Star Lane) is free after 8pm. Q🏠🌣🕪⇌❧

Robert Ransome ✔
Trafalgar House, Tower Street, IP1 3BE
🕐 9am-midnight (2am Fri & Sat); 11-11 Sun
☎ (01473) 341920
Beer range varies ℍ
A spacious two-storey pub adjacent to Tower Ramparts bus station that opened in 2009 to replace a former nightclub. It is close to the Cricketers pub – another large, popular Wetherspoon venture in town. With two large bar serveries and up to seven draught beers alongside Wetherspoon's standard value-for-money food fare, the ground-floor bar is popular all day. The upstairs bar is open 11-8 (and until late Fri & Sat), when loud music and dancing feature. 🕪🕻⇌🚆🌢

Ixworth

Greyhound ✔
High Street, IP31 2HJ
🕐 11-2.30, 6-11; 11.30-2.30, 5-11 Fri & Sat; 12-3, 7-11 Sun
☎ (01359) 230887
Greene King XX Mild, IPA, Abbot; Ruddles Best Bitter ℍ
Situated on the town's pretty High Street, this traditional inn has three bars including a lovely central snug. The heart of the building dates back to Tudor times. The pub is a rare outlet for XX Mild. Good-value lunches and early evening meals are served in the restaurant. Dominoes, crib, darts and pool are played in leagues and for charity fundraising. There is an area outside for camping and caravanning. 🌣🕪🚃🍴🚆♣P

Kettleburgh

Chequers 🅛 ✅
The Street, IP13 7JT TM263600
☼ 12-2.30, 6-11; 12-2.30, 7-10.30 Sun ☎ (01728) 724369
⊕ thechequers.net
Elgoods Black Dog Mild; Greene King IPA; guest beers 🅗
Large single-bar pub built to replace an earlier building destroyed by fire just 100 years ago. The massive rear garden eventually leads down to the River Deben and provides an excellent location for a relaxing afternoon on sunny days. An unusual arrangement of branches, lights and other ornaments adorns the bar ceiling and gives the room much character. Food includes various à la carte options and specials that change regularly. There are three letting rooms including a self-catering family apartment. ▨☎❀◐P

Laxfield

King's Head (Low House) ★ 🅛
Gorams Mill Lane, IP13 8DW (behind churchyard)
TM296724
☼ 12-3, 6-midnight; 11-midnight Fri & Sat summer; 12-4, 7-11 Sun ☎ (01986) 798395 ⊕ laxfieldkingshead.co.uk
Adnams Southwold Bitter, Broadside, Ghost Ship, Sole Star, seasonal beers; guest beer 🅖
Gem of a pub dating from about 1560 which has changed little over the years. With a warren of rooms, low ceilings and high-back settles, beers are served straight from their casks in a taproom with no bar counter. Traditional home-cooked food using seasonal local ingredients is available – look out for special meal deals. Outside, there is a large garden where croquet and pétanque are played. An annual beer festival is hosted. B&B and self-catering accommodation are offered. ▨Q❀⊠◐⊞♣P⌐

Little Glemham

Lion Inn 🅛 ✅
Main Road, IP13 0BA
☼ closed Mon; 12-2.30, 6-11; 12-3, 7-10.30 Sun
☎ (01728) 746505 ⊕ lioninnlittleglemham.co.uk
Adnams Southwold Bitter; Woodforde's Wherry; guest beers 🅗
Friendly pub on the main road, popular with locals and visitors, providing an ideal stopping-off point close to the Suffolk heritage coast. Food is traditional, home cooked and locally sourced, with vegetarian options, meal deals and a children's menu available (no food Sun & Mon). Themed food evenings are always popular (especially the 'starters & puddings' and curry nights). Monthly bingo sessions and quiz nights are also hosted. The car park and garden are to the rear of the building. ▨☎❀◐🚌(63,64)P

Long Melford

Crown
Hall Street, CO10 1JL
☼ 11.30-11; 12-10.30 Sun ☎ (01787) 377666
⊕ thecrownhotelmelford.co.uk
Adnams Southwold Bitter; Greene King IPA; guest beers 🅗
In the antiques centre of Suffolk, this 17th-century inn is a traditional family-run free house in the centre of the village. A central servery provides

access to the bar, lounge and restaurant. There is a large patio/garden area for summer drinking and dining. As well as two regular beers there are two ever-changing guests, all well kept, and an excellent bar and restaurant food menu. Accommodation is in 12 guest bedrooms.
Q❀⊠◐⊞⛽&🚪P⌐

Lower Ufford

White Lion 🅛
Lower Street, IP13 6DW
☼ 11.30-2 (not Mon), 6-11; 12-3 Sun ☎ (01394) 460770
⊕ uffordwhitelion.co.uk
Adnams Southwold Bitter, Broadside; guest beers 🅖
Cosy, small, single-bar pub with a quarry-tiled bar close to the historic church on the edge of a tiny settlement. Many special events are held in the evening including highly popular bingo sessions and themed food events such as hog roasts. Food is available lunchtimes and evenings (not Mon). The large garden leading to the River Deben is the perfect place to relax and enjoy the gravity beers. A large marquee hosts parties and entertainment on summer days. Since summer 2011 the range usually features one or two house beers brewed on the premises under the name of Uffa's brewery. ▨Q❀❀◐♣P

Lowestoft

Mariner's Rest
60-62 Rotterdam Road, NR32 2HA
☼ 11-midnight (2am Fri & Sat); 12-11.30 Sun
☎ (01502) 218077
Beer range varies 🅗/🅖
This welcoming community local is part of the Mariners pub chain. The comfortable open-plan interior has a central bar with a TV screen used mainly for sporting events and hosts live music some weekends. It has a good-sized garden with a covered, heated, smoking area. A vast range of real ales and ciders is available on handpump or gravity dispense (CAMRA members receive a discount). The pub has raised a considerable amount for local charities. ❀⇄🚪♣♠⌐

Norman Warrior 🅛 ✅
Fir Lane, NR32 2RB
☼ 11-midnight (12.30am Fri & Sat); 12-10.30 Sun
☎ (01502) 561982 ⊕ thenormanwarrior.co.uk
Greene King IPA; guest beers 🅗
Popular twin-bar local within a 20-minute walk of Oulton Broad North railway station. It comprises a public bar with pool table and dartboard, a comfortable lounge and a spacious restaurant serving home-cooked food daily. Outside is a large beer garden and terrace where a well-attended beer and cider festival is held over the August bank holiday weekend. Guest beers are usually supplied by local brewers and CAMRA members receive a discount. ❀◐⊞⇄(Oulton Broad North)🚪♣♠P⌐

Oak Tavern 🅛
Crown Street West, NR32 1SQ
☼ 10.30-11; 12-10.30 Sun ☎ (01502) 537246
Adnams Southwold Bitter; Greene King Abbot; guest beers 🅗
Well-run, lively community pub situated on the northern side of town. It has an open-plan bar divided into two areas. Four real ales are usually available, often including a dark beer during the

winter months. Belgian brewery memorabilia adorn the walls, reflecting a range of Belgian bottled beers also on offer. The pub raises money for charities. Outside is a patio and car park. ⊛≒⊟♣P꜀⊾

Stanford Arms 🅛

94 Stanford Street, NR32 2DD
🌐 12-midnight (1am Fri & Sat; 11 Sun) ☎ (01502) 587444
⊕ stanfordarms.co.uk

Green Jack Excelsior, Orange Wheat, Trawlerboys, Lurcher Stout, Gone Fishing, seasonal beers 🇭
The Green Jack Brewery tap, five minutes' walk from the brewery. It has six hundpumps dispensing ales from its own range plus real cider. The single-room bar has been modernised in the style of a Belgian brown bar and features church pew seating throughout. A fine collection of beer trays and other breweriana decorates the walls. There is a large courtyard garden to the rear. A few minutes from Lowestoft FC and a short walk from Lowestoft train station. ⊛≒♣🐕꜀⊾

Triangle Tavern 🅛

29 St Peters Street, NR32 1QA
🌐 11-11 (midnight Thu; 1am Fri & Sat); 12-10.30 Sun
☎ (01502) 582711 ⊕ thetriangletavern.co.uk

Green Jack Excelsior, Orange Wheat, Trawlerboys, Lurcher Stout, seasonal beers; guest beers 🇭/🇬
The flagship for local brewery Green Jack, this popular community town hostelry was originally two pubs, now they are one. The cosy front bar has wood panelling surrounds and benches giving the feel of a front parlour, and hosts live music on Friday nights. A corridor leads to an open-plan back bar. Both bars are decorated with brewery awards and memorabilia and are dog-friendly. Westons and Burnard's cider are available. Local CAMRA Pub of the Year in 2011. ⊛⊕≒⊟🐕꜀⊾

Market Weston

Mill Inn 🅛

Bury Road, IP22 2PD TL979776
🌐 11-3 (not Mon), 5-11; 12-3, 7-11 Sun ☎ (01359) 221018
Old Chimneys Military Mild, Scarlet Tiger; guest beers 🇭
Striking white brick and flint-faced inn standing at a crossroads. It is the closest outlet to the Old Chimneys Brewery, located on the other side of the village. Run by the same landlady for more than 16 years, it offers an excellent choice of beers complemented by a good menu of home-cooked meals (no food Mon eve). ᎙Q🌑♣P

Naughton

Wheelhouse

Whatfield Road, IP7 7BS (450yds off B1078)
🌐 5-11 (9 Mon; 8 Tue); 6-11 Sat; 12-10.30 Sun
☎ (01449) 740496
Beer range varies 🇭
Splendid rural pub well worth seeking out, with an interesting selection of beers always available. A thatched, timber-framed building, look out for the low ceiling in the main bar that remains a hazard, despite the tiled floor now being much lower than it once was. The bar is warmed by a welcoming fire on cold nights. The more spacious public bar is brighter and more modern, and leads to a games room with pool table and darts. Opening times vary to suit local demand. Dog-friendly. ᎙Q⊛♿⊟♣P

Newbourne

Fox 🅛 ✅

The Street, IP12 4NY (close to village church) TM273431
🌐 12-11 (10.30 Sun) ☎ (01473) 736307
⊕ debeninns.co.uk/fox

Adnams Southwold Bitter, seasonal ales; guest beers 🇭
Nestling in the centre of the village and overlooked by the parish church, this 13th-century timber-framed building has quaint old-world charm. Reputedly some of the timber used in its construction came from sailing ships. Good food includes a full à la carte menu, gluten-free options and daily specials. The garden has a pond with fish and wildfowl. Popular with families, ramblers and locals, there is camping close by. George Page, the Suffolk giant who stood 7ft 7in tall and died in 1870 is burried nearby. ᎙Q⊗⊛🌑♿⊾Å⊟P꜀⊾

Pakefield

Oddfellows 🅛

6 Nightingale Road, NR33 7AU
🌐 11-11; 12-10.30 Sun ☎ (01502) 538415
Adnams Southwold Bitter; guest beers 🇭
Small, cosy pub close to the cliff top, popular with local drinkers, holiday makers and those walking the heritage coastal path. The interior comprises three open-plan areas, with wooden flooring and panelling throughout. One side of the main drinking area has space reserved for diners, and two TV screens show sport. Up to four ales are available, usually including one from Green Jack Brewery. The pub hosts a popular beer festival in summer on the green opposite. ⊛🌑⊟

Pettistree

Greyhound 🅛

The Street, IP13 0HP
🌐 12-3 (not Mon), 6-11 ☎ (01728) 746451
⊕ pettistreepub.co.uk
Earl Soham Victoria; Woodforde's Wherry; guest beers 🇭
Dating from 1349, this two-roomed historic village inn retains several interesting features including traditional outdoor toilets. Food is all locally sourced and prepared on the premises. The garden is popular on summer evenings and hosts pétanque games, morris men visits, car rallies and other locally advertised events. An annual beer festival is also held. Folk music plays on the second Monday evening of the month and the pub hosts book club meetings, local church bell ringer socials and monthly quiz nights. ⊗⊛🌑♣P

Rattlesden

Five Bells 🅛

High Street, IP30 0RA
🌐 12-12.30am (11.30 Sun) ☎ (01449) 737373
Beer range varies 🇭
Set on the high road through a picturesque village, this is a good old Suffolk drinking house – few of its kind still survive. Three well-chosen ales on the bar are usually sourced direct from the breweries. The cosy single-room interior has a games room on a lower level and occasional live music plays. Pub games include shut the box and shove-ha'penny, and pétanque and croquet in summer. This is a dog-friendly pub. ᎙Q⊛♣꜀⊾

Rendham

White Horse L
Bruisyard Road, IP17 2AF
☼ 12-2.30 (not Mon-Fri), 6-11; 12-3, 7-10.30 Sun
☎ (01728) 663497 ⊕ whitehorserendham.co.uk
Earl Soham Victoria; guest beers G
Cosy, old-fashioned inn with two comfortable seating areas divided by a central fireplace and a large single bar. Good home-made food includes traditional English dishes, freshly prepared and made with locally sourced produce. The pub hosts regular quiz nights on the first Monday of the month plus other themed evenings. Pétanque is played on summer evenings. A beer festival is held over the August bank holiday. Camping is available about a mile away in Sweffling. ▨⊠☼❍♠♣P

Rickinghall

Bell Inn L ✔
The Street, IP22 1BN (adjacent to Botesdale)
☼ 11-11 (midnight Fri & Sat) ☎ (01379) 898445
⊕ thebellrickinghall.co.uk
Adnams Southwold Bitter, Broadside H
This pub dates back to the 17th century when it was an inn used by travellers going from Great Yarmouth to Bury St Edmunds and London. It was a popular stop-off because of its extensive stabling, accommodation and lively bar. More recently, it has become the focal point of the village, popular with locals as well as visitors. The lounge has a log fire and beamed ceilings. Food is available seven days a week. Children and dogs are welcome. ▨☼⊠❍➡♣P½⊟

Rumburgh

Buck ♥ L
Mill Road, IP19 0NS
☼ 11.45-3, 6.30 11; 12-3, 7-10.30 Sun ☎ (01986) 785257
Adnams Southwold Bitter, seasonal beers; guest beers H
Popular local at the heart of village life, full of character and charm. Interlinked rooms have been added to the original historic core, which retains its timber frame and flagstone floor. There are now two dining rooms where you can enjoy good food, a bar and a games room. Outside there is a small garden. Guest beers and ciders are often locally sourced. Mini beer festivals feature occasionally alongside folk music and local craft events. Local CAMRA Pub of the Year. ☼❍⊟♠♣♥P

Shadingfield

Fox L
London Road, NR34 8DD (on A145)
☼ 12-3, 6-11.30; 12-5 Sun ☎ (01502) 575100
⊕ shadingfieldfox.co.uk
Fuller's London Pride H; guest beers H/G
A charming and cosy rural inn just a short drive from busy Beccles. The Fox straddles the boundary of two parishes – Shadingfield and Willingham St Mary. The original inn dates back to the 16th century, and the arched doors and carved fox heads on beams have been retained. The interior comprises a bar with comfortable seating and conservatory plus a restaurant. Two beer festivals are held each year – one over the Father's Day weekend and the other close to Guy Fawkes Night. ▨Q⊠☼❍P½

Southwold

Lord Nelson L ✔
42 East Street, IP18 6EJ
☼ 10.30-11; 12-10.30 Sun ☎ (01502) 722079
Adnams Southwold Bitter, Explorer, Broadside, seasonal beers H
There is no shortage of pubs selling Adnams in Southwold, and they all have their own merits, but the Lord Nelson is a special place to drink Adnams' ales. Situated between the town centre and the nearby cliff top, with coastal views, it is cosy and homely, with a flagstone floor and a roaring fire in the winter. A busy and lively hostelry where locals and visitors mix and mingle, the pub is timeless in an ever-changing world. ▨⊠☼❍♠➡½

Stanningfield

Red House
Bury Road, IP29 4RR
☼ 12-3, 5-11.30; closed Wed; 12-11 Sat & Sun
☎ (01284) 828330
Greene King IPA; guest beers H
Built in 1866 in Victorian red brick, the building was originally a cobbler's workshop but licensed in 1900. Now a free house, it has recently been sympathetically extended to incorporate two extra bar rooms and three en-suite B&B breakfast rooms. Well supported, the pub fields teams in local leagues for cribbage, darts and bar billiards. Between Bury St Edmunds and Sudbury, close to Lavenham, and surrounded by beautiful countryside, it is handy for places of interest. ▨Q☼➡❍⊠➡♣P½

Stansfield

Compasses
High Street, CO10 8LN
☼ closed Mon; 12-2, 5-11; 12-11 Sat & Sun
☎ (01284) 789486 ⊕ compasses.uk.com
Adnams Southwold Bitter; Woodforde's Wherry H
A pleasant, friendly 200-year old village pub, the age of the building limits development and thus it retains much of its original charm. The wooden-floored bar area is bright and welcoming. Behind the brick chimney breast is a smaller tiled dining area, and another small room is home to a bar billiards table. The friendly Dutch landlord will set up the shuffleboard on request. A selection of locally sourced food is available. Well-behaved dogs are welcome. ▨Q☼❍♠➡(343)♣P½⊟

Stowmarket

King's Arms
Station Road, IP14 1RQ
☼ 11 (10.30 Sun)-11.30 ☎ (01449) 675232
Woodforde's Wherry; guest beers H
Built about 1850, closed in 1958 and reopened again in 2009, this friendly three-roomed pub is just a short walk from the railway station and town centre. Games are regularly played, and occasional live music, seasonal beer festivals and barbecues hosted. Food is available all day including stews, hotpots, chillis and omelettes. The patio to the rear leads to outside rooms that are used for live music and private parties. Two or three ciders are usually available including Westons. Dogs are welcome when the pub is not busy. Q⊠☼❍➡➡(87B,88)♣♥P½

Royal William

53 Union Street, IP14 1HP (off Stowupland St)
⏲ 11-11; 12-10.30 Sun ☎ (01449) 674553
Beer range varies Ⓖ
Tucked away down a side street and just a short walk from the town centre, this is a gem of a pub. An end-of-terrace back-street boozer, it is well supported by locals and visitors alike. Regular darts and crib matches are played and sport is shown on TV. Ales are all served from a cellar behind the bar by gravity dispense. ❀≢▣♣⁻

Sudbury

Brewery Tap 🏆 Ⓛ

21 East Street, CO10 2TP (200yds from Market Place)
⏲ 11-11 (midnight Fri & Sat); 12-10 Sun ☎ (01787) 370876
🌐 blackaddertap.co.uk
Mauldons Mole Trap, Silver Adder, Suffolk Pride; guest beers Ⓗ
An oasis in a desert of national brewers' beer, this is the first of Mauldons' two tied pubs. All the brewery's beers are on offer together with seasonal specials and up to five guests, all superbly kept. Sandwiches, pies and soup are available and takeaways can be ordered in. Beer festivals are held in April and October together with regular jazz/music sessions and a breakfast club on the last Sunday of the month. A traditional pub where conversation dominates – not to be missed. Local CAMRA Pub of the Year 2012. Q❀♿≢▣♣⁻🗑

Tattingstone

White Horse Ⓛ

White Horse Hill, IP9 2NU TM136382
⏲ 12-3, 6-11; 12-11 Fri & Sat; 12-10 Sun ☎ (01473) 328060
🌐 whitehorsetattingstone.co.uk
Adnams Southwold Bitter; Cliff Quay Tumble Home; Crouch Vale Blackwater Mild, Brewers Gold; guest beer Ⓗ
Grade II-listed, 17th-century inn with a heavily beamed main bar and log-burning stove. Excellent home-cooked food is available including gluten-free options, and a curry night on the last Thursday of the month is popular. Beers include a changing mild, and the cider is from Westons. Dog- and biker-friendly, it hosts folk nights, barbecues and other events. There are excellent outside toilets and a caravan and campsite to the rear. The statue at the front of pub is said to have come from the famous Great White Horse in Ipswich.
♨Q♘❀◐◑⊟▲▣♣●P⁻

Thorndon

Black Horse

The Street, IP23 7JR
⏲ 12-3, 5 (6 Sat)-11; 12-10.30 Sun ☎ (01379) 678523
🌐 theblackhorsethorndon.co.uk
Adnams Southwold Bitter; Greene King IPA; guest beers Ⓗ
Traditional country pub in the heart of this pretty village. Dating back to the 1600s and full of character, there are many historic photos of the village on display. The central bar has a log fire and two adjoining restaurant areas. Two guest ales are usually on offer, typically local and often from Brandon, Grain or Woodforde's breweries. At lunchtime there is a carvery and evening meals are served seven days a week. Dogs are welcome on a lead in the main bar. ♨Q❀◐◑P⁻

Thurston

Fox & Hounds Ⓛ ✔

Barton Road, IP31 3QT
⏲ 12-2.30, 5-11; 12-midnight Fri & Sat; 12-10.30 Sun
☎ (01359) 232228 🌐 thurstonfoxandhounds.co.uk
Adnams Southwold Bitter; Greene King IPA; guest beers Ⓗ
A listed building, this busy local pub sits in the middle of the village and is at the centre of local life. The restaurant, serving good home-cooked food, is within the public bar area but separated by uprights from an original wall. There is a separate bar for pool, darts and Sky TV. On bank holidays and special occasions live music is performed. Conker competitions are a feature in season. B&B accommodation is provided.
❀🛏◐◑⊟▲≢▣♣P⁻

Walberswick

Anchor Ⓛ ✔

Main Street, IP18 6UA
⏲ 11-4, 6-11; 11-11 Sat; 12-11 Sun ☎ (01502) 722112
🌐 anchoratwalberswick.com
Adnams Southwold Bitter, Broadside, seasonal beers Ⓗ
Rebuilt in the 1920s, this hotel is a classic example of brewer's Tudor. Situated in a picturesque coastal village, the Anchor caters for holidaymakers and locals alike. The open front bar is bright and comfortable, with oak flooring, wood panels and a smattering of local scenes on the walls. A large restaurant to the rear serves high quality local produce. Apart from the perfect Adnams' ales, there is a generous selection of global craft and bottled beers. Accomodation is available in the shape of four bedrooms in the main building and six additional garden chalet rooms.
♨Q♘❀🛏◐◑⊟♿▲P⁻

Walsham-le-Willows

Six Bells

Summer Road, IP31 3AA (opp church)
⏲ 11.30-2.30, 5.30 (6.30 Sat)-11; 12-2.30, 7-11 Sun
☎ (01359) 259726
Greene King XX Mild, IPA; Ruddles Best Bitter Ⓗ
A former wool merchant's house in the centre of a pretty village, this thatched building partly dates from the 16th-century. A huge fireplace and dark timbers create a cosy atmosphere, together with exposed, heavily carved timbers in the main bar. This traditional community pub, home to darts and crib teams, is run by a local couple who were regulars before taking it on 19 years ago. The emphasis here is firmly on beer. ♨Q❀⊟▣♣P⁻

Woodbridge

Angel

2 Theatre Street, IP12 4NE TM270491
⏲ 12-3, 5-11 (midnight Fri & Sat); 12-10.30 Sun
☎ (01394) 383808 🌐 theangelwoodbridge.co.uk
Adnams Southwold Bitter; Sharp's Doom Bar; Woodforde's Wherry; guest beers Ⓗ
A popular and lively 16th-century inn just off the market square with a quarry-tiled entrance and wooden floors in three separate bar areas. One bar is used for dining or private hire (by arrangement), with a good menu of home-made food on offer, including meal deals Monday to Wednesday. The

bar areas are furnished in a homely style with settles, armchairs and tables, warmed by open fires. Three guest beers complement the regulars. Families welcome. ♨♣☺◐●🖤🍴♿🅿♣

Old Bell & Steelyard ✅
103 New Street, IP12 1DZ
☼ 12-3, 6-11.30 (12.30am Fri & Sat); 12-3, 7-11 Sun ☎ (01394) 382933 ⊕ yeoldebellandsteelyard.co.uk
Greene King IPA; guest beers Ⓗ
Large multi-roomed pub with oak beams in two bars and a separate function room. The steelyard – a former cart weighbridge that still works – dates from 1650 and was on show at the Great Exhibition in 1851. Traditional games include bar billiards, chess and bar skittles. A good range of home-cooked food includes occasional Hungarian dishes. To the rear of the building is a large heated and covered patio area. An annual beer and cheese festival is held in July. Dog- and family-friendly. ♨☺☺◐●🖤🍴♿🅿♣🐾

Old Mariner
26 New Street, IP12 1DX TM273491
☼ 11-3.30, 5 (6 Sat)-11; 12-10.30 Sun ☎ (01394) 382679
Adnams Southwold Bitter; Fuller's London Pride; Woodforde's Nelson's Revenge; Young's Bitter Ⓗ
Intimate, two-bar pub with a small restaurant to the rear. The decor is simple and traditional throughout, with quarry-tiled floors and scrubbed wooden tables. A large TV is particularly well used on international rugby days, when the locals gather in force to watch matches in the lively front bar. Food is popular, with casseroles, stews and roasts all freshly prepared on the premises (booking recommended for Sun lunch). Outside is a smoking area and garden. ♨Q☺◐●🍴♿🅿♣

Woolpit

Bull ✅
The Street, IP30 9SA
☼ 11-3, 6-11 (midnight Fri); 12-4, 6-midnight Sat; 12-4, 7-10.30 Sun ☎ (01359) 240393 ⊕ bullinnwoolpit.co.uk
Adnams Southwold Bitter; guest beers Ⓗ
Large family-run inn on the old Ipswich to Cambridge road through the village. Visitors can choose between the community-minded front bar, hosting various charity events throughout the year, games room, comfortable conservatory and a spacious restaurant to the rear. Wholesome, home-cooked food is served – lunch only on Sundays. A garden with children's play area leads off the car park beside the pub. B&B is available. ☺☺🛏◐●🍴♿🅿♣

Yaxley

Cherry Tree
Old Norwich Road, IP23 8BH TM121743
☼ 12-3 (not Tue), 6-midnight; 12-7 Sun ☎ (01379) 788050
Adnams Southwold Bitter; Brandon Rusty Bucket; Woodforde's Wherry; guest beers Ⓗ
Pleasant village local incorporating a post office and local store. Outside, there is an enclosed garden to one side and seating to the front. Over 300 East Anglian ales have been served since the landlord took over nine years ago. New for 2013 is a 'foreign beer' handpump for ales from outside East Anglia. Beer festivals are held twice a year and barbecues on every bank holiday Monday. The pub dates back to the mid-1800s and displays numerous historic photos of the village in the front bar. Dogs on leads welcome. ♨☺☺◐●♿🍴🅿♣

Lord Nelson, Southwold

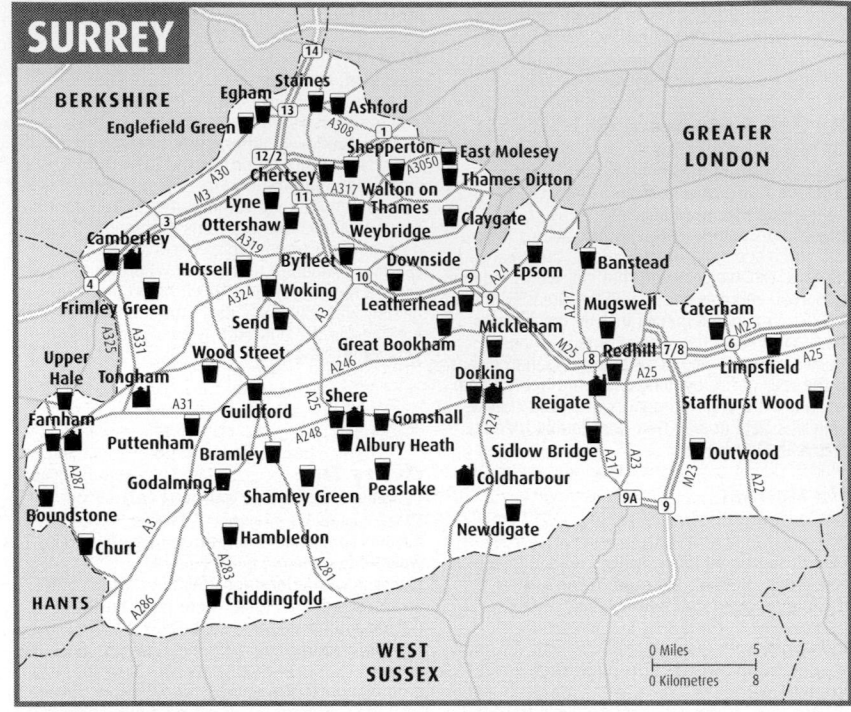

SURREY

BERKSHIRE
Egham
Staines
Englefield Green
Ashford
Shepperton
East Molesey
Chertsey
Walton on Thames
Thames Ditton
Lyne
Ottershaw
Weybridge
Claygate
Camberley
Horsell
Byfleet
Downside
Epsom
Banstead
Frimley Green
Woking
Leatherhead
Mugswell
Caterham
Send
Mickleham
Wood Street
Great Bookham
Redhill
Limpsfield
Upper Hale
Tongham
Dorking
Farnham
Guildford
Shere
Reigate
Staffhurst Wood
Puttenham
Bramley
Gomshall
Sidlow Bridge
Outwood
Godalming
Albury Heath
Coldharbour
Boundstone
Shamley Green
Peaslake
Newdigate
Churt
Hambledon
Chiddingfold
HANTS

GREATER LONDON

WEST SUSSEX

0 Miles 5
0 Kilometres 8

Albury Heath

William IV ⓛ
Dark Lane, Little London, GU5 9DG TQ066467
✪ 11-3, 5.30-11; 11-11 Sat; 12-10.30 Sun ☎ (01483) 202685
⊕ williamivalbury.com
Hogs Back TEA; Surrey Hills Ranmore Ale, Shere Drop;
Young's Bitter ⓗ
The building has its origins in the 16th century and
boasts beams, flagstones and a large fireplace
where a welcoming wood fire burns brightly in
winter. Set on a quiet lane adjoining extensive
woodland, the area is popular with walkers. There
are two traditional bars with a dining room up a
few steps. Excellent home-made meals are served
(no food Sun eve). Dishes includes Gloucester Old
Spot pork from the pigs kept in the field behind the
pub. Shove-ha'penny can be played.
ᛘQ❀◑♣●P⅃

Ashford

King's Fairway ⓛ ✿
91 Fordbridge Road, TW15 2SS (on B377)
✪ 11.30-11 (midnight Fri & Sat) ☎ (01784) 423575
Fuller's London Pride; Sharp's Doom Bar; guest
beers ⓗ
Popular rambling modern pub in a cosy, traditional
style. Six handpumps dispense two regular real
ales and four frequently changing guests from the
Ember Inn seasonal selection, all good value for
money. Food is also reasonably priced (families
allowed in dining area). Two gas fires provide
comfort in the winter months. Quiz nights are
Wednesday and Sunday and curry night is
Thursday, with additional themed food evenings.
There is a small TV area for sport and a heated and
covered smokers' refuge alongside the patio.
Q❀◑&🚇(290)P⅃

Banstead

Woolpack ✿
186 High Street, SM7 2NZ (on B2217)
✪ 11-11; 12-10.30 Sun ☎ (01737) 354560
⊕ thewoolpackbanstead.co.uk
Shepherd Neame Master Brew, Spitfire, Bishops
Finger; guest beers ⓗ
Bright and friendly pub at one end of the High
Street, the Woolpack is a real ale oasis in the area,
offering excellent beer with two ever-changing
guests, usually from local breweries. Good-value
home-made food of high quality is also available.
The single bar is divided into a number of areas,
with plenty of room for all. A beer festival is held
over the August bank holiday. Live jazz plays on
the first Tuesday afternoon of the month.
ᛘ❀◑&🚇P⅃

Boundstone

Bat & Ball
Bat and Ball Lane, GU10 4SA (off Sandrock Hill Road via
Upper Bourne Lane) SU833444
✪ 11-11; 12-10.30 Sun ☎ (01252) 792108
⊕ thebatandball.co.uk
Hogs Back TEA; Young's Bitter; guest beers ⓗ

INDEPENDENT BREWERIES

Ascot Camberley
Dorking Dorking
Farnham Farnham
Hogs Back Tongham
Leith Hill Coldharbour
Pilgrim Reigate
Surrey Hills Dorking
Tillingbourne Shere (NEW)

Dating back to the 17th century, this popular pub offers a range of beers from four guest pumps, often including ales from local breweries, as well as serving excellent food. The pub is family-friendly with a front room for dining and a children's play area in the garden. The bar, with beams, wood panelling and an open fire, is a cosy haven for adults. The well-kept garden plays host to an annual beer festival. ▲Q☼❄✪◖Ġ☟(16)P⁻⌐

Bramley

Jolly Farmer 🄻
High Street, GU5 0HB (on A281)
✪ 11-3, 6-11 Mon; 11-11; 12-11 Sun ☎ (01483) 893355
⊕ jollyfarmer.co.uk
King Horsham Best Bitter; Sharp's Doom Bar; guest beers Ⓗ
The Jolly Farmer has a welcoming atmosphere and is full of character. A real fire, beer mats, bank notes and other memorabilia decorating the low ceilings and oak beams all add to the ambience. Up to eight real ales are available from different parts of the country, often selected from smaller and family brewers. There is a large dining area and good food is available every day, from a wide and frequently changing menu. A wonderful village pub. ▲☼✎◖Ġ☟(53,63)♣P⁻⌐

Byfleet

Plough ✪
104 High Road, KT14 7QT (off A245)
✪ 11-3, 5-11; 12-11 Sat; 12-10.30 Sun ☎ (01932) 354895
Beer range varies Ⓗ
A cosy village local with plenty of character, the Plough has nine handpumps delivering ever-changing guests (reduced to six in quiet times to ensure beer quality). There is an L-shaped bar with two roaring fires in winter, and exposed beams and brickwork. The emphasis here is on conversation – mobile phones are banned. Children are allowed in the conservatory, which has a TV for occasional terrestrial sport. ▲Q☼◖☐P⁻⌐

Camberley

Claude du Vall 🄻 ✪
77-81 High Street, GU15 3RB
✪ 8-midnight (12.30am Wed; 1am Fri & Sat)
☎ (01276) 672910
Greene King Abbot; Ruddles Best Bitter; guest beers Ⓗ
Since opening in 2002, this Wetherspoon pub has gone from strength to strength, and this is its third consecutive year in the Guide. Five cask ales are on offer, usually including at least one LocAle. Westons cider is also on draught, and a wide range of foreign beers is available in bottles. Quiz night is Monday and Sunday is poker night. Conveniently located near the station and bus stops. ☼◖Ġ☐♣⁻

Caterham

King & Queen ✪
34 High Street, CR3 5UA (on B2030)
✪ 11-11 (midnight Fri); 12-10.30 Sun ☎ (01883) 345438
Fuller's Chiswick Bitter, London Pride, ESB, seasonal beers Ⓗ
Originally three 17th-century cottages, this friendly pub has been serving the local community for

around 170 years. It retains three distinct areas – the front part has the feel of a public bar, the back room is used for darts and the central area is warmed by a log fire. Good food and snacks are available (not Fri eve). The landlady is rightly proud of her cask beer, which is just one of the reasons the pub has featured in the past 19 editions of the Guide. ▲Q☼✪◖Ġ☐(400,409)♣P⁻⌐

Chertsey

Coach & Horses ✪
14 St Ann's Road, KT16 9DG (on B375)
✪ 12-11 (8 Sun) ☎ 01932 583085
⊕ coachandhorseschertsey.co.uk
Fuller's London Pride, ESB; Gale's Seafarers Ale Ⓗ
Attractive, tile-hung, busy community local close to the town's cricket and football grounds, dedicated exclusively to three of Fuller's cask ales. This frequent Guide entry is recognised as providing the best London Pride in the area. Good-value English food is available on weekdays (not Mon eve) but the landlady likes to keep a 'proper pub' for beer and conversation at weekends. League darts is played. There is an awning for smokers at the front. Frequent buses to Staines and Woking stop nearby. Free Wi-Fi. ▲☼✪◖☐(446)♣P⁻⌐

Thyme at the Tavern ♟ 🄻
20 London Street, KT16 8AA (jct of London St and Heriot Rd)
✪ 12-2.30, 5 (4 Sat)-midnight; 12-midnight Sun
☎ (01932) 429667 ⊕ thymeatthetavern.co.uk
Courage Best Bitter; Fuller's London Pride; guest beers Ⓗ
Previously the Town Hall Tavern, this lively free house received a welcome boost under its enthusiastic new owner and is local CAMRA Pub of the Year in the year it makes its debut in the Guide. Alongside the two regular cask beers, two guests from local breweries are provided. Bottle-conditioned ales and continental bottled beers are also stocked. Beer festivals on a LocAle theme are held several times a year. The pub is heavily involved in local charity fundraising. Dog-friendly, with free Wi-Fi and regular live music. ▲☼✎≈☐♣⁻

Chiddingfold

Swan Inn ✪
Petworth Road, GU8 4TY SU960353
✪ 11-11 ☎ (01428) 684688 ⊕ theswaninnchiddingfold.com
Beer range varies Ⓗ
Traditional meets modern in this welcoming hotel bar. Inside it is relaxed and cosy with a feature fireplace and a logburner, wood beams wrapped with hops and pictures around the walls. There is also a separate bistro-style dining area. Outside there is a terraced garden for warmer days and plenty of parking across the road. A varying range of beers is served, usually including Adnams and Langham ales. ▲☼✎◖Ġ P⁻⌐

Churt

Crossways
Churt Road, GU10 2JE (on A287)
✪ 11-3, 5-11; 11-11 Fri & Sat; 12-4, 7-10.30 Sun
☎ (01428) 714323
Bowman Warbler; Courage Best Bitter; Hop Back Crop Circle Ⓗ; guest beers Ⓖ

Travellers and locals mingle happily in the comfortable saloon and small public bar, reminiscent of a 17th-century Dutch painting. The five changing guest beers, served directly from the cellar, are mainly from microbreweries. Four ciders sit on stillage behind the bar. Food is served lunchtimes only except for fish and chips on Wednesday evenings. The garden is popular in summer. A festival of over 40 beers is held in July and a cider festival in September. CAMRA Regional Cider Pub of the Year. Q❀✪⊈▲�'(19)♣🐕P'⌐

Situated just a short distance from the High Street, this food-oriented pub is a welcome respite for shoppers. Inside there is rather minimalist decor with bare boards and comfortable seating; outside is a covered decking area and pleasant patio garden with tables and umbrellas for smokers. Wi-Fi and newspapers are available and dogs are allowed. Weekly poker and monthly comedy and music nights are hosted. A blackboard lists freshly prepared home-made specials (no food Sun eve). ❀⊈�'P'⌐

Claygate

Griffin
50 Common Road, KT10 0HW TQ160635
✪ 11-11 (midnight Thu-Sat); 12-11 Sun ☎ (01372) 463799
Fuller's London Pride; Young's Bitter; guest beers Ⓗ
Friendly family-run two-bar pub over 100 years old in a residential area. The lively sports bar with TV and darts is separated from a quieter lounge by a leaded glass partition. Up to two guest beers often include a local Surrey brew. Sandwiches, tapas and traditional pub fare is available lunchtimes and evenings (not Sun eve). There is a small rear garden and heated patio at the front. Children and well-behaved dogs are welcome. Note the original Mann, Crossman & Paulin windows.
🏰Q❀✪⊈�'(K3)♣P'⌐

Dorking

Cobbett's Ⓛ
23 West Street, RH4 1BY (on A25 eastbound)
✪ closed Mon; 12 (10am Fri & Sat)-8; 12-6 Sun
☎ (01306) 879877 ⊕ cobbettsrealales.co.uk
Beer range varies Ⓖ
Excellent off-licence offering cask beer and cider at very fair prices. The number of beers varies from two at the beginning of the week to four or five at the end. LocAle breweries are always represented, often including Dark Star, along with some from further away. There is usually a 'hop monster' on tap towards the weekend, and perry is available in summer. Many bottled beers from the UK and overseas are also sold (mail order available). CAMRA members receive a five per cent discount.
Q⇌(West)�'🐕

Cricketers Ⓛ ✔
81 South Street, RH4 2JU (on A25 westbound)
✪ 12-11 (midnight Thu & Sat; 1am Fri) ☎ (01306) 889938
⊕ thecricketersdorking.co.uk
Fuller's Chiswick Bitter, London Pride, ESB; guest beer Ⓗ
Small family-run pub with bare brick walls decorated with old photographs and Fuller's beer adverts. A large-screen TV is used for major sporting events on terrestrial TV, especially rugby. A dartboard is at one end of the bar, and past this is one of the pub's best features – a walled split-level Georgian garden, where the pub's beer festivals are held. There is also a TV in the garden. Monthly live music plays. Children are welcome until early evening. ❀✪⊈♣♣'⌐

Red Bar & Lounge Ⓛ
45 Dene Street, RH4 2DW (off A25 High Street)
✪ 12-11 (midnight Fri & Sat; 10 Sun) ☎ (01306) 882222
Dark Star Hophead; Harveys Sussex Best Bitter; guest beer Ⓗ

Downside

Plough Ⓛ
Plough Lane, KT11 3LT TQ107582
✪ 11-11; 12-10.30 Sun ☎ (01932) 589790
⊕ theploughcobham.co.uk
Courage Best Bitter; Hogs Back TEA; Sharp's Doom Bar; guest beer Ⓗ
Catering for both drinkers and diners, the Plough overlooks meadows close to the River Mole. The interior retains original features including a large fireplace with real fire. There are two separate drinking areas and a restaurant. The pub is popular with both regulars and visiting diners. Dogs and children are welcome. The guest beer changes regularly and is usually sourced from a small local independent brewer. Live music plays occasionally – check the website for details.
🏰❀✪⊈&�'(513)P'⌐

East Molesey

Albion ✔
34 Bridge Road, KT8 9HA (off B3379)
✪ 11-11 (10.30 Sun) ☎ (020) 8783 9342
Fuller's London Pride; Young's Bitter; guest beers Ⓗ
Open-plan locals' pub, part of the Ember Inns estate. The central bar serves separate drinking/dining areas with comfortable seating. Reasonably priced food is available from opening time until 9pm each day; several vegetarian options are included on the menu. The pub is a short walk from Hampton Court Palace and the River Thames. The guest beers come from regional and larger microbreweries. ✪⊈&⇌(Hampton Court)�'

Egham

United Services Club Ⓛ
111 Spring Rise, TW20 9PE (close to A30 Egham Hill)
✪ 12-11 (midnight Fri & Sat) ☎ (01784) 435120
⊕ eusc.co.uk
Rebellion IPA; guest beers Ⓗ
CAMRA National Club of the Year finalist in 2010, and a mecca for the discerning real ale or cider drinker. Eight handpumps offer an ever-changing range of ales and ciders, with bottle-conditioned beers also available. Three beer festivals per year attract visitors from across the UK to enjoy the eclectic range of ales, mostly from newer microbreweries, and ciders. Live music plays most Saturdays, with satellite TV and free Wi-Fi available. A copy of this Guide or CAMRA membership card secures entry. ❀⇌🚑♣🐕P'⌐🍺

Englefield Green

Happy Man
12 Harvest Road, TW20 0QS (off A30)

✪ 12-11.30 (midnight Fri & Sat; 10.30 Sun)
☎ (01784) 433265
Beer range varies Ⓗ
Originally two Victorian cottages, the building was converted to a pub to serve the workers building Royal Holloway College. Recently refurbished but virtually unchanged, it is now a popular student haunt. Four handpumps dispense a constantly changing range of guest ales from microbreweries around the country and the landlord, passionate about real ale, sometimes has additional beers on gravity from the cellar. Darts is played and food is available all day. The attractive rear garden has a heated smokers' refuge. ✿◑🏠🚃🚶♿♨—

Epsom

Barley Mow Ⓛ ✓
12 Pikes Hill, KT17 4EA (off A2022)
✪ 12-11 (midnight Fri & Sat; 10.30 Sun) ☎ (01372) 721044
Fuller's London Pride, ESB; guest beer Ⓗ
Well-run pub, originally three cottages, tucked away down a narrow side road. Smart in a traditional, rustic way, it has various alcoves and seating areas around a central bar. Old-style wooden furnishings and ornate leaded windows add to the ambience. An alleyway from the pub's garden leads to the Upper High Street public car park. Food is served all day at weekends. A beer festival is held in July. The guest beer is supplied by Fuller's and may be from another family brewer. 🏠✿◑♿🚃🚶♣♨—

Jolly Coopers 🍴 Ⓛ ✓
84 Wheelers Lane, KT18 7SD TQ197605
✪ 12-11.30 (12.30am Thu-Sat; 10.30 Sun)
☎ (01372) 723222 ⊕ jollycoopers.co.uk
Beer range varies Ⓗ
More than 200 years old, this traditional pub is situated in the middle of a residential area just over half a mile west of the town centre. It has a quiet lounge bar, a sports bar where darts is played, and a snug area. Beers are generally from micros in Surrey and Sussex. Roasts are served on Sundays. Live music and quiz nights are held. Local CAMRA Pub of the Year 2011 and 2012. 🏠Q✿◑Ⓒ🏠🚃(E9)♣P♨—

Rising Sun
14 Heathcote Road, KT18 5DX (off B290) TQ211605
✪ 11-11 (midnight Fri & Sat); 12-10.30 Sun
☎ (01372) 740809 ⊕ therisingsunepsom.com
St Austell Tribute; Young's Bitter, Special; guest beer Ⓗ
Back-street pub which is food-led but retains a traditional bar area at the front. It has a covered patio and large garden to the rear, which hosts summer barbecues. The guest beer is from the Wells & Young's portfolio. Excellent English and continental cuisine is available, made on the premises with locally sourced ingredients – the pub has its own curing and smoking room. The Rising Sun was the birthplace of the Society for Preservation of Beers from the Wood in the 1960s. 🏠Q✿◑▶🚃—

Farnham

Hop Blossom ✓
50 Long Garden Walk, GU9 7HX
✪ 12-3, 5-11; 12-midnight Fri & Sat; 12-10.30 Sun
☎ (01252) 710770

Fuller's Chiswick Bitter, Discovery, London Pride, ESB; guest beer Ⓗ
Fuller's pub situated in a quiet back street close to the town centre. It has a friendly atmosphere and is a cosy retreat in winter with its open fire (chestnuts and crumpets provided). The interior comprises three main areas, including a large area for bigger groups. Take a moment to look around the walls and see the eclectic mix of memorabilia while enjoying a pint. The guest beer may be a seasonal Fuller's ale, but is often from another brewery. 🏠Q✿◑Ⓒ🚃🚶

Lamb
43 Abbey Street, GU9 7RJ
✪ 11-2.30, 5-11; 11-midnight Fri & Sat; 12-10.30 Sun
☎ (01252) 714133
Shepherd Neame Kent's Best, Spitfire Ⓗ, **seasonal beers** Ⓗ/Ⓖ
Situated between the town centre and the railway station, this friendly pub is a great place to enjoy a pint or two. Quiet and relaxed in the day, it draws a crowd in the evenings, particularly when sport is screened. Most Fridays there is live music, so bring your dancing shoes. Traditional pub food is available at lunchtimes and most evenings. Outside there is an elevated garden, accessed via a metal staircase. 🏠✿◑♿🚃🚶—

Queen's Head ✓
9 The Borough, GU9 7NA
✪ 10-11 (midnight Fri & Sat); 11-11 Sun ☎ (01252) 726524
Fuller's London Pride, seasonal beers; Gale's HSB; guest beer Ⓗ
Warm, friendly pub in the heart of the town with cosy wood-panelled drinking areas. Quiet during the day, it can get lively in the evening when candles adorn the pub, adding to the atmosphere. Entertainment includes quiz and open mic nights on alternate Thursdays and live acoustic music on Sunday evenings. Locally sourced food is served until 4pm daily; Wednesday is steak night. A small rear courtyard garden is used by smokers. Fuller's Pub of the Year and local CAMRA Town Pub of the Year 2011. 🏠✿◑Ⓒ🚃🚶♣♨

William Cobbett
4 Bridge Square, GU9 7QR
✪ 11-11.30 (12.30am Fri); 11.30-12.30am Sat; 11.30-10.30 Sun ☎ (01252) 726281
Fuller's London Pride; guest beers Ⓗ
A wonderfully dark interior full of eclectic memorabilia plus Sophie the pet tarantula, table football and an upstairs pool area. The cottage-style exterior has a number of drinking areas, including a covered smokers' space with the luxury of sofas. There is a good '60s/'70s jukebox and an open mic night/band night on Wednesday evenings. Four guest beers are often from local microbreweries. Burgers are served Friday and Saturday evenings. A busy favourite with younger drinkers during UCA term times. ✿◑🚃🚶P♨—

Frimley Green

Rose & Thistle ✓
1 Sturt Road, GU16 6HT (on B3411)
✪ 12-midnight (1am Fri & Sat) ☎ (01252) 834942
⊕ theroseandthistlefrimleygreen.co.uk
Fuller's London Pride; Sharp's Doom Bar; guest beers Ⓗ
A relatively large pub, divided into different areas, including a conservatory for dining (and available

for private functions). Well used by the local community, it is often lively in the evenings. Three or four cask ales are available as well as draught Westons cider. A good, varied menu of pub food and more substantial dishes is offered. Nice to see a pub with a dartboard. Occasional live music plays. ✇❶♿➍(3,11)♣➎P⅃

Godalming

Jack Phillips 🗓️ ✅
48-56 High Street, GU7 1DY
✇ 7am-11 (midnight Thu; 1am Fri & Sat) ☎ (01483) 521750
Greene King Abbot; Ruddles Best Bitter; guest beers Ⓗ
The bar has a pleasant, airy feeling enhanced, on fine days when the French windows are opened at both ends of the pub. A room at the rear, where families are welcome until 9.30pm, overlooks the Wey Valley. Alternatively, sit outside on the patio at the front and enjoy Godalming's historic High Street. Four ciders and six guest ales are available, with a few local beers to complement the Wetherspoon list. Q🌥❶♿≠➍➎

Gomshall

Compasses 🗓️
50 Station Road, GU5 9LA (on A25)
✇ 11-11; 12-10.30 Sun ☎ (01483) 202506
∰ thecompassesinn.co.uk
Surrey Hills Ranmore Ale, Shere Drop, seasonal beers Ⓗ
Standing between the A25 and the River Tillingbourne, this 19th-century roadside pub offers a traditional bar with three handpumps and a dining room where home-made meals are served (no food Sun eve). Old farming and other tools decorate the wooden pillars and beams in the bar. There is a garden and outdoor seating beside the stream. Live music plays every Friday and a music festival is held in August – see the website for details. There are two en-suite rooms for B&B. ✇🛏️❶≠➍(32)P⅃

Gomshall Mill 🗓️
52 Station Road, GU5 9LB (on A25)
✇ 12-11 (10.30 Sun) ☎ (01483) 203060
∰ gomshallmill.hcpr.co.uk
Beer range varies Ⓗ
The pub is located in a 17th-century timber-framed and clad watermill, astride the River Tillingbourne. The two water wheels, formerly used to produce flour, are open to view from the centre of the pub, with the mill-race running beneath your feet. While the emphasis is on excellent dining, the bar, with real fire, features four handpumps serving constantly changing brews, usually including two LocAles such as Tillingbourne. Dining areas are set on several different levels and outside is a pleasant garden. ⛪🌥✇❶♿≠➍(32)♣➎P

Great Bookham

Anchor ✅
161 Lower Road, KT23 4AH (off A246)
✇ 11.30-11 (12.30am Fri); 12-10.30 Sun ☎ (01372) 452429
∰ theanchorbookham.co.uk
Brakspear Bitter; Courage Best Bitter; Fuller's London Pride; Skinner's Cornish Knocker; Wells Bombardier Ⓗ
Grade II-listed inn dating from the 15th century. Low beamed ceilings, wooden floors, exposed

brickwork and an inglenook with a real fire burning in the winter give the pub a traditional and homely feel. Lunchtime snacks and meals are served daily. A charity quiz night is held every Tuesday. Darts, dominoes, cribbage and other card games are played. There is a garden and a heated smoking area. Children under 14 are not allowed in the bar. ⛪Q✇❶➍(479)♣➎⅃

Guildford

Keystone
3 Portsmouth Road, GU2 4BL (on A3100)
✇ 12-11 (midnight Fri & Sat; 5 Sun) ☎ (01483) 575089
∰ thekeystone.co.uk
Triple fff Alton's Pride; Wadworth 6X; guest beers Ⓗ
A well-kept, modern, town-centre pub with a slight rustic feel thanks to the wooden floors and decor. You can enjoy art with your beer at the Keystone and many of the paintings on the walls are by local artists. Four real ales are complemented by good food and themed evenings include the popular Thursday pie night. See the website for forthcoming events, including occasional live music and an annual cider festival in July. Darts, bar billiards and various board games are played here. ✇❶≠➍♣⅃

King's Head ✅
27 King's Road, GU1 4JW (on A320 Stoke Road)
✇ 11-11 (11.30 Thu; 12.30am Fri & Sat); 12-11 Sun
☎ (01483) 568957
Fuller's Chiswick Bitter, London Pride, ESB, seasonal beers; guest beers Ⓗ
Built in 1860 as two small houses, this attractive pub has a deceptively large interior after many extensions. Extensively refurbished, there are various separate seating areas around the island bar and a heated, covered courtyard for smokers. The circular floor hatch at the rear covers a well. The pub serves traditional British food all day and offers a large selection of Belgian bottled beers. A recent winner of the Guildford in Bloom competition. Quiz night is Thursday. Free Wi-Fi. ⛪✇❶♿≠(London Road)➍(3,34)➎P⅃

Row Barge 🏆 🗓️ ✅
7 Riverside, GU1 1LW
✇ 12-11 (midnight Fri & Sat) ☎ (01483) 573358
∰ rowbargeguildford.com
Andwell King John; Ascot On The Rails, Posh Pooch, Compass Point; guest beer Ⓗ
Built in 1856 and extended for the post-war Bellfields Estate, this two-bar pub with pool room is 1½ miles along the River Wey towpath from the town centre. Overnight moorings are available for customers. The exclusive house ale is Compass Point from Ascot and the guest is from a local micro. A beer festival is held at the end of May. Live music features on Wednesday, Friday and Saturday, and alternate Sundays. Cyclists get a rack for their bikes and there is free Wi-Fi. ⛪✇❶➍(3,34)♣➎⅃

Royal Oak
Trinity Churchyard, GU1 3RR
✇ 12-11 (11.30 Thu; 1am Fri); 11-1am Sat; 12-10.30 Sun
☎ (01483) 459023
Fuller's London Pride, seasonal beers; Gale's HSB; guest beers Ⓗ
Part of an early 17th-century terrace of houses converted to a pub about 1870. It is tucked away on the hillside between the High Street and

Sydenham Road overlooking the graveyard of Holy Trinity. The single bar has the atmosphere of an old house. The new landlord continues to extend the beer range, aided by a cellar that is larger than the pub. There is live music on alternate Mondays and Thursdays together with three beer festivals per year. ✿◑❂♠♣✦💺

Hambledon

Merry Harriers ☐
Hambledon Road, GU8 4DR SU967391
✪ 11-2.30, 5.30-11; 11-11 Sat; 11-8 Sun ☎ (01428) 682883
⊕ merryharriers.com
Langham Hip Hop; Surrey Hills Shere Drop; guest beers Ⓗ
Old-fashioned 16th-century inn down small country lanes with basic wooden furniture and flooring. There is a separate dining area with an interesting menu using local produce. The three guest ales are selected from the local area. The pub serves the community in many ways and hosts local events including a pantomine. The landlord is proud of the llama trekking days. Pub games are available as well as a boules pitch. There is a sizeable car park opposite. ♨Q♞❂♠❄◑♣✦●P💺⛭

Horsell

Crown
104 High Street, GU21 4ST
✪ 12-11 (midnight Fri & Sat) ☎ (01483) 771719
⊕ thecrownhorsell.co.uk
Beer range varies Ⓗ
A classic community local, the Crown is one of just a few pubs in this area to retain two bars. Two handpumps dispense beers from a short list of regulars, while the third features plenty of local ales as well as visitors from anywhere in the country. Pizzas are available at any time to eat in or take away. The garden has a climbing frame for younger customers and a pétanque piste. ❂◑♠♣(28)♣P💺

Leatherhead

Running Horse ✅
38 Bridge Street, KT22 8BZ (Off B2122)
✪ 11-11.30; 12-10.30 Sun ☎ (01372) 372081
⊕ therunninghorse.biz
Shepherd Neame Master Brew, Kent's Best, Spitfire, Bishops Finger, seasonal beers; guest beer Ⓗ
Grade II-listed pub dating back to 1403. It has a cosy lounge bar with a real fire, low ceilings and exposed beams, and a public bar with TV, pool and a dartboard. Outside is a patio and garden with a tuck shop and play area for children. Traditional pub games include bar skittles and shove-ha'penny, and quiz nights and live music nights are hosted. The guest beer is from Surrey Hills. On take-away evenings home-prepared food like pie and mash or fish and chips are offered to eat in or take home. Dog friendly. ♨Q❂◑♠♣♦♠♣P💺

Limpsfield

Bull ☐
High Street, RH8 0DR (off A25)
✪ 12-3, 6-11 (11.30 Fri); 12-11.30 Sat; 12-7 Sun
☎ (01883) 713402 ⊕ thebulllimpsfield.com
Beer range varies Ⓗ

Grade II-listed former coaching inn dating from the 16th century and situated in the middle of an attractive village. It continues to thrive by offering good quality food, wine and beer. Inside are three separate drinking areas and a restaurant, all decorated to a high standard. At least one ale is from Westerham Brewery. The nearby churchyard is the resting place of conductor Sir Thomas Beecham and composer Frederick Delius. ♨Q❂◑♠(236,594)♣P💺

Lyne

Royal Marine
Lyne Lane, KT16 0AN (off B386) TQ013663
✪ 12-2.30, 5.30-11 (6.30-11.30 Sat); 12-3 Sun
☎ (01932) 873900 ⊕ royalmarinelyne.co.uk
Sharp's Doom Bar; guest beers Ⓗ
This country community local celebrates its 10th year in the Guide. The name of the beer house commemorates Queen Victoria's review of her troops nearby on Chobham Common in 1853. Marine memorabilila, a large collection of drinking jugs and other bric-a-brac are on display although there is still space for a dartboard. The guest beers come from far and wide. Generous portions of home-cooked food are served lunchtimes and Tuesday to Friday evenings. The pub closes on some winter Saturday evenings – ring to check. ♨Q❂◑♣P💺

Mickleham

King William IV ☐
Byttom Hill, RH5 6EL (off A24 southbound) TQ174538
✪ 11-3, 6-11; 12-5 (10.30 spring & summer) Sun
☎ (01372) 372590 ⊕ king-williamiv.com
Hogs Back TEA; Surrey Hills Shere Drop; Triple fff Alton's Pride; guest beer Ⓗ
Friendly 18th-century free house clinging to the hillside overlooking Mole Valley and Norbury Park. It has two separate rooms, both with real fires. An extensive home-cooked menu offers traditional pub food plus more exotic dishes and vegetarian options. The patio and terraced garden are popular on sunny days, and barbecues are hosted. Opening hours are extended in spring and summer. Steep steps can make access difficult. The shared car park is on the A24 southbound at the foot of Byttom Hill. ♨Q❂◑♠(465)P💺

Mugswell

Well House Inn ☐ ✅
Chipstead Lane, CR5 3SQ (off A217) TQ259552
✪ 12-11 (10.30 Sun) ☎ (01737) 830640
⊕ wellhouseinn.co.uk
Adnams Southwold Bitter; Fuller's London Pride; Surrey Hills Shere Drop; guest beers Ⓗ
The ghost of Harry the Monk is said to be a regular visitor at this Grade II-listed 16th-century pub. There are three bars, each with a log fire, and a conservatory. The two guest beers change frequently and are usually from local microbreweries; the cider is from Millwhites. The Domesday Book mentions the well outside – known as Mag's Well, hence the area's name. There is no evening food on Sunday or Monday. Families are welcome until 9pm. ♨❂◑♠♣●P

Newdigate

Surrey Oaks ♥ 🄻
Parkgate Road, Parkgate, RH5 5DZ TQ205436
🌂 11.30-2.30 (3 Sat), 5.30 (6 Sat)-11; 12-10 (9 Jan-Feb) Sun
☎ (01306) 631200 ⊕ surreyoaks.co.uk
Harveys Sussex Best Bitter; Surrey Hills Ranmore Ale; guest beers 🄷
Great 16th-century pub offering a selection of ales from microbreweries (hoppy beers and dark ales always popular) plus cider and perry. Third of a pint glasses are available. Good home-made food is served in the bar and restaurant (no food Sun or Mon eves). Low beams, flagstones and an inglenook feature; outside are two boules pitches and a skittle alley in the barn. Beer festivals are held on the late spring and August bank holidays. Local CAMRA Pub of the Year 2003 to 2012 and Surrey Pub of the Year 2005 to 2011.
🅰Q⌛🅳♣🚻P

Ottershaw

Castle ❷
220 Brox Road, KT16 0LW (signed off A320) TQ 022631
🌂 11-11 (midnight Fri); 12-10.30 Sun ☎ (01932) 872373
⊕ the-castle-ottershaw.co.uk
Greene King Abbot; Harveys Sussex Best Bitter; Sharp's Doom Bar; Taylor Landlord 🄷
Attractive tile-hung pub that has retained its two-bar layout. Built as a beer house in 1840, the pub was extended in 1905 and a conservatory added to the side more recently. The emphasis is on lively conversation in a music-free environment. The rustic feel is enhanced with agricultural (and some more sinister looking) implements around the walls inside and out, and each bar has an open fire. Well prepared home-cooked food is available. Outside is a heated wooden gazebo for smokers.
🅰Q⌛🅳🚲🚭(557)P🚲

Outwood

Castle 🄻
Millers Lane, RH1 5QB TQ 317453
🌂 12-3, 5.30-11; 12-11 Sat; 12-8 Sun ☎ (01342) 842754
⊕ castleoutwood.co.uk
Harveys Sussex Best Bitter; Pilgrim Surrey Bitter, Progress; guests beers 🄷
Friendly and comfortable village pub, popular with locals and visitors alike. Three separate drinking areas and good dining facilities make this a well-balanced pub, enhanced by log fires in winter and a garden for summer. Seasonal locally sourced food is served alongside local ales. The pub is dog-friendly and is an ideal stop for walkers and cyclists. Occasional beer festivals and other events are held. 🅰Q⌛🅳🚭P🚲

Peaslake

Hurtwood Inn 🄻
Walking Bottom, GU5 9RR TQ086446
🌂 12-11 (midnight Fri; 10.30 Sun) ☎ (01306) 730851
⊕ hurtwoodinnhotel.com
Fuller's London Pride; Hogs Back TEA; Surrey Hills Shere Drop; guest beer 🄷
Dating from 1920, this three-star privately-owned hotel has a bright and contemporary bar offering a wide range of bar snacks and meals as well as mostly LocAle beers. Furnishings include easy chairs and sofas, and there is a modern open

fireplace and artwork featuring classic cars. The hotel's location at the heart of the beautiful Surrey Hills makes it a welcome stop-off for weary ramblers and cyclists. There is a separate restaurant and 21 en-suite rooms. 🅰⛵🚲🅳🚭(25)P

Puttenham

Good Intent ❷
60-62 The Street, GU3 1AR (off B3000) SU931478
🌂 12-3, 6-11.30 (11 Mon); 12-11.30 Sat; 12-10.30 Sun
☎ (01483) 810387 ⊕ thegoodintentpub.co.uk
Otter Bitter; Sharp's Doom Bar; Taylor Landlord; guest beers 🄷
Puttenham is a small Surrey village sitting below the ridge of the Hogs Back and has the last hop-growing field in the county. The Good Intent is a welcoming 16th-century inn popular with villagers, cyclists and walkers, with real fires lit in winter. Three guest beers are served and a beer festival is held over the late May bank holiday weekend. Good home-cooked food is available lunchtimes and evenings (no food Sun and Mon), with fish and chips every Wednesday. 🅰Q⌛🅳🅰♣P🚲

Redhill

Garland ❷
5 Brighton Road, RH1 6PP (on A23)
🌂 11.30-11.30 (12.30am Fri; midnight Sat); 12-11.30 Sun
☎ (01737) 760377
Harveys Sussex XX Mild, Hadlow Bitter, Sussex Best Bitter, Armada Ale, seasonal beers 🄷
Classic Victorian street-corner local dating from 1865. Although close to the town centre, it has the atmosphere of a country pub, and is home to a number of darts, bar billiards and quiz teams. Eight handpumps supply the full range of Harveys beers (including all seasonals and specials), helping to attract visitors from near and far. A side room is available for private use. Lunchtime meals offer good value (no food Sat). The pub is on the London-Brighton Vintage Vehicle runs.
⌛🅳🚲🚭♣P🚲

Hatch ❷
44 Hatchlands Road, Shaws Corner, RH1 6AT (on A25)
🌂 11-midnight (12.30am Fri & Sat); 12-midnight Sun
☎ (01737) 765104 ⊕ thehatchpub.co.uk
Shepherd Neame Master Brew, Spitfire, Bishops Finger, seasonal beer 🄷
The Hatch dates from the 17th century, and is a former workhouse with a hayloft for horses. There is a single L-shaped bar, home to a bank of eight handpumps. To the left is a small room with more seating. Beyond this, up a few steps and quite hidden away, is a pool room. Good home-made food is available and there is an extensive wine range. Beers from the Shepherd Neame micro-plant are often sold. 🅰⌛🅳🚲🚭(420,460)♣🚻🚲

Home Cottage
3 Redstone Hill, RH1 4AW (on A25)
🌂 11-11 (midnight Fri & Sat); 12-11 Sun ☎ (01737) 762771
⊕ homecottageredhill.com
Wells Bombardier; Young's Bitter, Special, seasonal beers 🄷
Just off the town centre and behind the station, this large mid-19th-century inn was extensively refurbished in 2011. It still retains distinct drinking areas and original features such as an interesting old bank of five handpumps in what used to be the

front bar, drawing in loyal Young's drinkers. Good food is served all day in the bars, on the patio outside and in the dining room until 10pm (9pm Sun). ♨🛏🕮🌣◑⊃⇌🍺⌐—

Jolly Brickmakers ✓
58-60 Frenches Road, RH1 2HP
🕓 12-11 (midnight Fri & Sat) ☎ (01737) 789388
🌐 jollybrickmakers.co.uk
Brakspear Bitter; Ringwood Fortyniner; guest beer Ⓗ
To the north of town, this basic but friendly pub is very much part of the local community. The wood-panelled interior is effectively two bars with a public section containing some unusual moulded heraldic wall badges. The saloon area is distinguished by a Bass mirror, bar billiards table and a library of paperback books. Occasional beer festivals are held in the small garden. The guest beer comes from the Marston's list. No meals, but cutlery and plates are provided for takeaways.
🌣🍺(430,435)♣—

Send

New Inn
Send Road, GU23 7EN
🕓 11-11; 12-10.30 Sun ☎ (01483) 762736
Adnams Southwold Bitter; Fuller's London Pride; Greene King Abbot; Ringwood Best Bitter; guest beer Ⓗ
Located by the Cart Bridge on the Wey Navigation which provides over 20 miles of pleasant walking and boating from the Thames at Weybridge to Godalming via Guildford, the New Inn is popular with boaters, walkers and families. It has a long single room divided into a number of areas by exposed brick partitions, and offers good home-cooked meals plus occasional barbecues in summer. A guest beer is available in addition to the four regulars. ♨🌣◑⊃🍺(462,463)P—

Shamley Green

Bricklayers Arms
The Green, GU5 0UA TQ033437
🕓 11-11 ☎ (01483) 898377 🌐 bricklayersarmspub.co.uk
Exmoor Ale; Fuller's London Pride; Sharp's Doom Bar; guest beers Ⓗ
This Georgian pub is an ideal place to stop off while exploring the Surrey Hills Area of Natural Beauty. The bar has been opened out, leaving exposed brickwork and space for different seating areas including a couple of large sofas around an open fire. There are usually two guest ales available, one from the local area. The food is all home made and occasional themed menus are offered including curry night and fresh fish specials.
♨🌣◑⊃♿🍺(53,63)♣P—

Shepperton

Barley Mow 🅛
67 Watersplash Road, TW17 0EE (off B376 in Shepperton Green)
🕓 12-11 (10.30 Sun) ☎ (01932) 225326 🌐 themow.co.uk
Hogs Back TEA; Hop Back Summer Lightning; guest beers Ⓗ
Beer, live music and conversation rule in this friendly Shepperton Green local where the wall space is gradually being obscured by past pump clips and CAMRA awards. The landlord is a keen supporter of local breweries and the pub was one of the first North Surrey pubs to receive LocAle accreditation. Entertainment includes live rock or blues bands on Friday and Saturday nights, jazz on Wednesday, a quiz night on Thursday and a charity meat raffle on Sunday afternoon. Bar billiards is played. The smoking refuge is an ornate metal gazebo. ♨🌣🍺(438,458)♣♠P—

Shere

William Bray 🅛
Shere Lane, GU5 9HS
🕓 11-11; 12-10.30 Sun ☎ (01483) 202044
🌐 thewilliambray.co.uk
Sharp's Doom Bar; Surrey Hills Ranmore Ale, Shere Drop Ⓗ
Set in a prominent position just above the centre of the village, this gastro-pub is named after the 18th-century Lord of the Manor. Formerly the Prince of Wales, it was renamed in 2009, when it was bought by former F1 driver Julian Bailey. It has a bar with a wood-burning stove and a popular restaurant. Hay, tethering rings and mounting blocks are provided for those who arrive on horseback, and there are cycle racks for cyclists. ♨🌣◑⊃🍺(32)P

Sidlow Bridge

Three Horseshoes 🅛
Ironsbottom, RH2 8PT (off A217) TQ252461
🕓 12-11 (9.30 Sun) ☎ (01293) 862315 🌐 sidlow.com
Dark Star Hophead; Fuller's London Pride, ESB; Surrey Hills Shere Drop; Young's Bitter; guest beers Ⓗ
The Shoes is a fine old-fashioned country pub, with parts of the building dating back 300 years. It was once home to a forge, hence the name, and was a coaching inn on the London to Brighton route. A beer festival is held on the first May bank holiday. Good food, including daily specials, is available lunchtimes and evenings, with barbecues held in the large garden. Two guest beers are sold with another pump reserved for a varying cider.
Q🌣◑⊃♠P—

Staffhurst Wood

Royal Oak 🅛 ✓
Caterfield Lane, RH8 0RR TQ407485
🕓 11-3, 5-11; 11-11 Thu-Sat; 12-10.30 Sun
☎ (01883) 722207 🌐 theroyaloakinn.net
Adnams Southwold Bitter; Harveys Sussex Best Bitter; Larkins Traditional Ⓗ**; guest beers** Ⓗ/Ⓖ
A rural free house well worth seeking out for local beer, real cider and perry, and excellent locally sourced food. An interesting selection of bottled beer is also sold. Staffhurst Wood is a nature reserve and the pub welcomes walkers and their dogs. A log fire is cosy in winter and a large garden with extensive views is popular in summer. CAMRA members receive a discount on beer. Branch Cider Pub of the Year 2011 and 2012.
♨Q🌣◑⊃♿♣♠P—

Staines

Bells
124 Church Street, TW18 4ZB (off B376)
🕓 12-3, 5-11; 12-midnight Fri & Sat; 12-11 Sun
☎ (01784) 454240
Courage Best Bitter; Young's Bitter, Special, seasonal beers; guest beer Ⓗ

Friendly, comfortable, 18th-century pub opposite St Mary's Church close to the Thames Path and within easy walking distance of the town centre. Regular beers and seasonals from Wells and Young's are available plus a guest. Noted locally for the quality of its food, it is often busy in the evenings. The pleasant rear patio garden, with a large heated smokers' canopy, is especially popular in summer, attracting local workers and shoppers.
Q❀❀◐◖&☷(305)↰

George ✅

2-8 High Street, TW18 4EE (on A308, opp town hall)
❀ 9am-midnight (1am Fri & Sat) ☎ (01784) 462181
Courage Best Bitter; Greene King Abbot; Ruddles Best Bitter; guest beers Ⓗ
Ever-popular, two-storey, town-centre Wetherspoon pub built in the 1990s. The spacious downstairs bar with its mixture of tables and intimate booths is always busy but a quieter bar can be reached via a spiral staircase. Up to six guest ales are dispensed from one bank of handpumps, with the national brands and two real ciders from Westons on the rear bank. A varied selection of foreign bottled beers and ciders is also stocked. Value-for-money pub food is served all day.
◐◖&≢☷♠

Wheatsheaf & Pigeon Ⓛ ✅

Penton Road, TW18 2LL (off B376, corner of Wheatsheaf Lane and Penton Road) TQ 038701
❀ 12-11; 12-10.30 Sun ☎ (01784) 452922
⊕ thewheatsheafandpigeon.co.uk
Courage Best Bitter; Fuller's London Pride; St Austell Tribute; Sharp's Doom Bar Ⓗ
Welcoming and friendly community local between Staines and Laleham, a short walking distance from the Thames Path and Staines Town FC, now training ground for the Chelsea ladies' team. Well-kept ales and good-value food is served every day (no food Sun eve); there is also a small dining area. Outside there is seating for the summer months plus a covered smoking area. Quiz night is Sunday. Child- and dog-friendly. Beer festivals are held and the pub is particularly busy on football match days.
❀◐☷(218)P↰

Thames Ditton

George & Dragon ✅

High Street, KT7 0RY (on B364)
❀ 11 (12 Sun)-11 ☎ (020) 8398 2206
⊕ georgeanddragonthamesditton.co.uk
Shepherd Neame Master Brew, Spitfire, seasonal beers Ⓗ
Run by the same popular landlord for 10 years, the pub has won a number of plaudits, most recently Sheps' best community pub. It has an open-plan layout around a central bar, with plenty of dark wood and comfortable leather seating. Various items of sports memorabilia decorate the walls. The menu, including sandwiches and a couple of veggie options, is reasonably priced for the area. Jazz club night is Tuesday. Outside is a patio along with two outdoor smoking areas, one heated with a TV. ❀◐&≢☷(514,515)P↰

Upper Hale

Alfred Free House

9 Bishops Road, GU9 0JA SU837490

❀ 5-11; 12-11 Sat; 12-10.30 Sun ☎ (01252) 820385
⊕ thealfredfreehouse.co.uk
Brakspear Bitter; Ringwood Best Bitter; guest beers Ⓗ
A great little find in a residential area of Hale, this classic family-run pub serves a range of traditional ales as well as home-cooked food – look out for the occasional themed evening. The cosy main bar is welcoming, as is the slightly larger smart dining area next to it. Outside there is a well-maintained seating space for warmer evenings. The Alfred aims to be a community pub and runs regular beer festivals – check the website for details.
⚑Q❀◐☷P↰

Walton on Thames

Old Manor

113 Manor Road, KT12 2NZ (off A3050) TQ098667
❀ 11-11 (midnight Fri & Sat); 12-10.30 Sun
☎ (01932) 221359
Courage Best Bitter; Sharp's Doom Bar; Young's Bitter, Special Ⓗ
Down the back roads of Walton, towards the river, this small, cosy locals' pub has one central bar with seating in front of it and to one side. A long bench faces the bar next to the brick fireplace and various brass implements hang from the cross beam, with wrought ironwork above the bar. The pub backs onto a small park and the manor house where a previous occupant signed the death warrant for King Charles I. An occasional guest beer complements the range. ⚑❀☷♣↰

Regent ✅

19 Church Street, KT12 2QP (on A3050)
❀ 9-midnight (1am Fri & Sat) ☎ (01932) 243980
Ruddles Best Bitter; Greene King Abbot; guest beers Ⓗ
A pleasantly furnished town-centre Wetherspoon pub in what was previously a cinema dating from the 1920s. Art Deco in style, it has reflecting lights hanging from the long curved ceiling and high wood panels around the walls. A long bar runs along the right-hand side, with wooden cubicles on the other side. Steps at the far end lead to a raised seating area. Westons and Gwynt y Ddraig cider are sold. Q❀◐◖&☷♠↰

Weybridge

Old Crown

83 Thames Street, KT13 8LP (off A317)
❀ 10-11; 12-10.30 Sun ☎ (01932) 842844
⊕ theoldcrownweybridge.co.uk
Courage Best Bitter, Directors; Young's; guest beer Ⓗ
Weatherboarded, Grade II-listed building dating back to at least 1729, alongside the River Thames where it meets the Wey. It has been run by the same family for over 50 years, now in their third generation. Wood-panelled drinking areas include a snug, public bar and dining room, with a conservatory to the rear. It has two gardens, one running to the waterside where there is access for small boats. Food is available lunchtimes and Wednesday to Saturday evenings. Q❀◐◖☷♣P

Woking

Herbert Wells Ⓛ ✅

51-57 Chertsey Road, GU21 5AJ
❀ 8am-midnight (1am Fri & Sat) ☎ (01483) 722818

Courage Best Bitter, Directors; Greene King Abbot; Hogs Back TEA; guest beers Ⓗ

Long-established Wetherspoon pub with an invisible man in the window and a time machine in the ceiling in honour of local author HG Wells. Four guest ales are usually available including beers from many local breweries as well as the current Wetherspoon list. Beer festivals feature many extra beers on top of the published list. Four ciders include two from Mr Whiteheads. Local CAMRA Pub of the Year in 2010 and 2011. Q⊕▸ᕊ⇌🖳☙🕯⌐

Sovereigns ⊘

Guildford Road, GU22 7QQ (on A320)
✪ 11.30-11 (midnight Fri & Sat) ☎ (01483) 751426
Adnams Broadside; Ringwood Best Bitter; Sharp's Doom Bar; guest beers Ⓗ

Eight handpumps greet visitors to this large and comfortable Ember Inns pub, situated just off the town centre. The guest beers change every couple of weeks and food is served until 10pm. There is a large heated area at the front of the pub and a patio to the rear. Quiz nights are Monday and Wednesday. There is a charge for the car park, which is refundable in the pub. ♨🌣⊕ᕊ⇌🖳P🕯⌐

Woking Railway & Athletic Club

Goldsworth Road, GU21 6JT
✪ 10.30-11 (11.30 Fri & Sat); 11.30-10.30 Sun
☎ (01483) 598499
Beer range varies Ⓗ

A warm welcome awaits at this lively social club tucked away near Victoria Arch. Two ever-changing ales are available, often from local breweries. One side of the bar is sport oriented, hosting thriving darts and pool teams plus Sky Sports, the other is quieter, allowing conversation to flow. Children are welcome and there is wheelchair access. Filled rolls are available on Saturday afternoon. For entry show a CAMRA membership card or copy of this Guide. Local CAMRA Club of the Year 2010 and 2011. ⇌🖳♣🕯⌐

Wood Street

Royal Oak Ⓛ

89 Oak Hill, GU3 3DA
✪ 11-3, 5-11; 12-3, 7-10 Sun ☎ (01483) 235137
Courage Best Bitter; Surrey Hills Shere Drop; guest beers Ⓗ

This fine country local has been a regular in the Guide for many years and winner of numerous CAMRA awards. The warmly upholstered drinking area looks on to a bar offering four changing guest ales including a mild, and two real ciders. From Monday to Saturday there is a range of good wholesome home-made food on offer involving a large range of vegetables but no chips. In summer the large garden is an ideal place for families. Q🌣⊕🖳(17)♣🕯P

Running Horse, Leatherhead (Photo: Bob Steel)

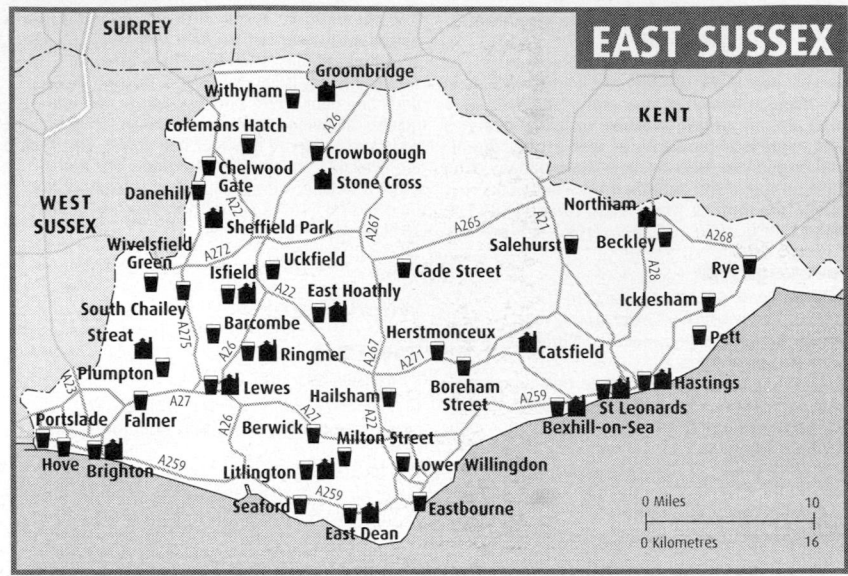

SUSSEX (EAST)

Barcombe

Royal Oak ✔
High Street, BN8 5BA
🌐 10 (12 Sun)-11 ☎ (01273) 400418
🌐 royaloakbarcombe.co.uk
Harveys Sussex XX Mild, Hadlow Bitter, Sussex Best Bitter, seasonal beers Ⓗ
Situated in the heart of this quiet Sussex village near Lewes, easily accessed from the A26 or A275. Parking is available outside and in the village car park 50 yards away. The pub has a Victorian front bar and a large quiet bar to one side. Attached to the building is a separate skittle alley which can be hired for functions. This family-run pub has three Harveys beers permanently on and a friendly clientele. Good food is served.
🏚Q🐕❀🕽🕭🚆(125)♣🗝

Beckley

Rose & Crown
Northiam Road, TN31 6SE (N end of village)
🌐 11.30-midnight; 12-11.30 Sun ☎ (01797) 252161
Fuller's ESB; Harveys Sussex Best Bitter; Taylor Landlord; guest beers Ⓗ
Spacious free house with a warm ambience and up to five cask beers on offer, including some from local breweries. The pub is popular with walkers, is dog-friendly and families are welcome. The main bar area has two real fires, wooden floors and decorative hops around the bar. There is a separate dining area next to it and good-value home-cooked food is available (no food Sun eves). The garden enjoys fine views.
🏚Q🐕❀🕽🕭🚆(344)♣P🗝

Berwick

Cricketers' Arms Ⓛ ✔
Berwick Village, BN26 6SP (S of A27)

🌐 11-3, 6-11; 11-11 Sat & summer; 12-10.30 Sun
☎ (01323) 870469 🌐 cricketersberwick.co.uk
Harveys Sussex Best Bitter, Armada Ale, seasonal beers Ⓖ
Close to the South Downs Way and popular with walkers, this tied house serves Harveys ales on gravity from the cellar room behind the bar. Rustic in appearance, it was originally two cottages that were converted into a pub during the 18th century. Peaceful cottage gardens make this an ideal place to idle away the hours on a hot summer's day, with real fires keeping it cosy in the winter. Good-quality food is served all day. 🏚Q❀🕽♣P

Bexhill-on-Sea

Albatross Club
15 Marine Parade, TN40 1JS
🌐 11.30-2.30, 7-11 (closed Thu eve); 12-2.30 Sun
☎ (01424) 212916 🌐 bexhillrafa.co.uk
Beer range varies Ⓗ
On Bexhill seafront near the De la Warr Pavilion, close to the town centre. A friendly club, which welcomes CAMRA members, it has three handpumps dispensing beers from all over the country, mostly from microbreweries. Good food is served lunchtimes and live jazz bands perform on the last Tuesday of each month. Voted CAMRA Regional Club of the Year 2011. Q🕽🕭🚄🚆

Boreham Street

Bull's Head Ⓛ ✔
BN27 4SG
🌐 12-3, 6-11; 12-11 Fri & Sat; 12-10.30 (6 winter) Sun
☎ (01323) 831981 🌐 bullsheadborehamstreet.co.uk
Harveys Sussex Best Bitter, seasonal beers Ⓗ
The first tied house in the Harveys estate has been popular with locals and visitors alike, since reopening a few years ago. A traditional village pub with wooden floors and panelling, it has a main bar area with a real fire plus two smaller rooms. Three beers are served, Old throughout the winter and Olympia in the summer, plus seasonal ales. Quiz night is Monday. Good-quality, locally

sourced food is served lunchtimes except Monday and evenings except Sunday.
🏨Q🕮🌓▲🚃(98)♣P🚃

Brighton

Basketmakers Arms ✓
12 Gloucester Road, BN1 4AD
🕒 11-11 (midnight Fri & Sat); 12-11 Sun ☎ (01273) 689006
🌐 thebasketmakersarms.co.uk
Fuller's Discovery, London Pride, ESB, seasonal beers; Gale's Seafarers Ale; guest beers Ⓗ
Popular two-room Victorian street-corner pub on the outer edge of the North Laine area of the city. Eight handpumps serve the Fuller's range plus guests. Reasonably priced, locally sourced home-made food is available, from snacks to full mains, including traditional roast on Sundays. An array of metal boxes and signs covers the walls. Real ale in a bottle is available to take away. Also stocks around 100 whiskies. 🕮🌓🚃🚃

Evening Star Ⓛ
55-56 Surrey Street, BN1 3PB (150yds S of station)
🕒 12-11; 11.30-midnight Fri & Sat ☎ (01273) 328931
🌐 eveningstarbrighton.co.uk
Dark Star Hophead, seasonal beers; guest beers Ⓗ
A flagship Dark Star pub with four of its beers always available, plus three from other microbreweries. Real cider and sometimes a perry are available on handpump. A varied selection of bottled beers and worldwide beers on draught is also available. A Guide regular, the pub is popular with a varied clientele of all ages and from all over the country. Occasional beer festivals and live music are also staged. There is a patio seating at the front. 🕮🚃🚃🚃

Greys Ⓛ
105 Southover Street, BN2 9UA (500yds E of A270 opp the Level)
🕒 4-11 (11.30 Thu; 12.30am Fri); 12-12.30am Sat; 12-11 Sun ☎ (01273) 680734 🌐 greyspub.com
Harveys Sussex Best Bitter; Taylor Landlord Ⓗ
A friendly pub in the Hanover district reminiscent of a Belgian brown bar offering a wide selection of Belgian beers. Excellent food from an à la carte menu is served Tuesday-Thursday and Saturday evenings as well as a popular Sunday lunchtime roast. A quiz is held every Sunday evening and a music quiz on the third Monday of the month. Regular live music events take place, including international artists. Posters of past acts adorn the walls of the stairs. 🕮🌓🚃(37,37B)🚃

Hampton
57 Upper North Street, BN1 3FH (behind Argos)
🕒 12-midnight (11 Sun) ☎ (01273) 731347
WJ King Brighton Best; guest beers Ⓗ
Lively single-bar pub close to the main shopping area with plenty of tables inside and a south-facing patio outside. A popular choice for the younger (or young at heart) beer lovers, there are generally four or five well-kept ales, mostly from Sussex breweries. Music is played at a reasonable volume, with occasional live music or a DJ. Quiz night is Monday. Food is served lunchtimes and evenings, all day at the weekend. 🏨🕮🌓🚃🚃

Lord Nelson Inn ✓
36 Trafalgar Street, BN1 4ED
🕒 11.30-11; 12-10.30 Sun ☎ (01273) 695872
🌐 thelordnelsoninn.co.uk

Harveys Sussex XX Mild, Hadlow Bitter, Sussex Best Bitter, Armada Ale, seasonal beers Ⓗ
Popular back-street pub close to Brighton Station. The full range of Harveys regular and seasonal beers is stocked. There is a folk club on the first Monday of the month, quiz night on Tuesday, and occasional live music. Home-cooked food is served lunchtimes, and in the evening pizzas may be ordered from a nearby restaurant and eaten in the pub. Occasional live televised sport is shown. Children and well-behaved dogs are welcome. Free Wi-Fi. 🌓🕮🚃🚃

Mitre Tavern ✓
13 Baker Street, BN1 4JN
🕒 10.30-11.30 (midnight Fri & Sat); 12-10.30 Sun
☎ (01273) 683173 🌐 mitretavern.co.uk
Harveys Sussex XX Mild, Sussex Best Bitter, Armada Ale, seasonal beers Ⓗ
Within walking distance of Brighton main and London Road stations, this street corner local is close to the Open Market, London Road shops and many bus routes. The main bar is long and narrow, with seating around the edge and at the bar. There is also a cosy snug off the main bar. A Harveys tied house, the five handpumps serve two seasonal beers alongside the regulars. The pub is a key stop on the local Ale Trail. 🌓🕮🚃🚃🚃

Prestonville Arms ✓
64 Hamilton Road, BN1 5DN (between Preston Circus and Seven Dials)
🕒 5-11; 12-midnight Fri & Sat; 12-11 Sun ☎ (01273) 701007
🌐 theprestonvillearms.co.uk
Fuller's London Pride, seasonal beers; Gale's Seafarers Ale, HSB; guest beers Ⓗ
Popular Fuller's street-corner local in a residential area. The half-panelled interior has a variety of seating round a horseshoe-shaped bar. Entertainment includes live music on some weekends, an entertainment quiz on Tuesdays, a general knowledge quiz on Sundays and a Wednesday curry night. There is often a guest beer to complement the Fuller's/Gale's range. 🌓🕮🚃🚃

Pump House Ⓛ ✓
46 Market Street, BN1 1HH (in the Lanes)
🕒 10-11 (midnight Fri & Sat) ☎ (01273) 827421
Fuller's London Pride; Harveys Sussex Best Bitter; guest beers Ⓗ
Part of the Nicholson's chain located in the famous Brighton Lanes shopping area. Four or five

changing real ales are generally available, at reasonable prices for central Brighton. One of the oldest buildings in the town, the bar has wood-panelled walls and the cellar is reputed to date from medieval times. The interior is welcoming, with plenty of seating and tables. Food is served all day until 10pm. ᴁ⓪≠⊒●⌐

Royal Oak Ⓛ
46 St James Street, BN2 1RG
✪ 11-11 (midnight Fri & Sat); 12-11 Sun ☎ (01273) 621093
⊕ theroyaloakbrighton.co.uk
Fuller's London Pride; Gale's HSB; Harveys Sussex Best Bitter; Otter Ale; Taylor Landlord, guest ales Ⓗ
A traditional pub in the heart of Kemptown with two large bars and a courtyard. It serves five regular beers including Harveys Best, London Pride and Gale's HSB. Guest ales include Harvest Pale, Fuller's ESB and Hepworth Old. Live jazz plays every Wednesday and usually another live music session features one day a week. Home-made food is served 12-8.30pm (8pm Sun). ᴁ✿⓪⊒

Sir Charles Napier ●
50 Southover Street, BN2 9UE
✪ 4-11.30; 3-12.30am Fri; 12-12.30am Sat; 12-11 Sun ☎ (01273) 601413
Fuller's London Pride, seasonal beers; Gale's Seafarers Ale, HSB; guest beers Ⓗ
A splendid Victorian corner local where little has changed over past decades. Although a single-bar pub, it naturally divides into two areas to suit most tastes. A good mixed clientele comes here for food (a good range is served), beer, a game of cribbage or just a chat. The regular Sunday night quiz is well supported and various other events take place. The landlord is a winner of Fuller's Master Cellarman award. ᴁQ✿⓪⊒(37,81)♣⌐

Cade Street

Half Moon Ⓛ
TN21 9BS
✪ 12-11 (10.30 Sun) ☎ (01435) 868646
⊕ halfmoon-inn.co.uk
Harveys Sussex Best Bitter; 1648 Triple Champion; guest beers Ⓗ
A Victorian village local, biker- and child-friendly, with one large bar subdivided into distinct areas, including one set for diners. Quiz night is the second Sunday of the month. The menu features tapas and pizza. There is a large garden with panoramic views of the South Downs 15 miles distant. The two guest ales change regularly and Biddenden cider is sometimes available. Bar billiards can be played. Live music features on special occasions. ᴁ✿⓪♣P⌐

Chelwood Gate

Red Lion
Lewes Road, RH17 7DE (on the A275) TQ415302
✪ closed Mon; 12-3, 5-11; 12-6 Sun ☎ (01825) 740265
⊕ raffansredlion.co.uk
Harveys Sussex Best Bitter; Shepherd Neame Spitfire, seasonal beers Ⓗ
In the heart of Ashdown Forest, the Red Lion has been a pub since 1874. In 1963 President Kennedy and Harold Macmillan enjoyed a pint here, and it was filmed as Arthur Dent's local in The Hitchhiker's Guide to the Galaxy. There is a welcoming bar with log fire and a dining area with

garden views, plus a large garden to the rear. Children and dogs are welcome but not on Friday and Saturday evenings. ᴁQ✿⓪⅊⊒(270)P⌐

Colemans Hatch

Hatch Inn Ⓛ
TN7 4EJ (400yds S of B2110) TQ452334
✪ 11.30-3, 5.30-11; 11.30-11 Sat & Sun ☎ (01342) 822363
⊕ hatchinn.co.uk
Harveys Sussex Best Bitter; Larkins Traditional; Sharp's Doom Bar Ⓗ
Based on three 15th-century cottages, this has been an inn for over 200 years. The attractive low-beamed building is ideally situated for visiting Ashdown Forest and has two gardens for summer drinking and dining. A daily menu uses locally produced food and regular beers are local. An annual beer festival is held in May. The picturesque pub has featured in TV programmes. Pooh Bridge and a llama farm are nearby. ᴁQ✿⓪⊒(291)P

Crowborough

Coopers Arms Ⓛ
Coopers Lane, TN6 1SN
✪ 12-2.30 (not Mon), 5-11; 12-11 Sat & Sun ☎ (01892) 654796
Black Cat Original; Dark Star Hophead, Partridge Best Bitter; guest beers Ⓗ
A friendly pub run by a knowledgeable landlord. There are at least two beer festivals a year as well as other themed events. A selection of bottled beers is also stocked and draught cider is available in the summer. This simply furnished pub consists of a classic long bar with a logburner forming the main drinking area, with a separate restaurant and side bar with open fire. The garden has views over the Sussex Weald to Kent. ᴁQ✿⓪⊒♣P

Wheatsheaf Ⓛ ●
Mount Pleasant, Jarvis Brook, TN6 2NF
✪ 12-11 (10.30 Sun) ☎ (01892) 663756
⊕ wheatsheafcrowborough.co.uk
Harveys Sussex XX Mild, Hadlow Bitter, Sussex Best Bitter, Armada Ale, seasonal beers Ⓗ
Unspoilt 18th-century pub tucked away down an old back road, giving the feeling of a country pub. Inside, an unusual three-sided bar provides three cosy drinking areas on two levels. Each area has an open fire, and the lower bar has an unusual copper fireplace. This tied house always has a good range of Harveys beers, and runs two beer festivals, usually in May and October. ᴁ✿⓪≠⊒♣●P⌐

Danehill

Coach & Horses Ⓛ
School Lane, RH17 7JF (off A275) TQ412286
✪ 11-3, 6-11; 12-11 Sat; 12-10.30 Sun ☎ (01825) 740369
⊕ coachandhorses.danehill.biz
Harveys Sussex Best Bitter; guest beers Ⓗ
A traditional country pub built in 1847 and retaining many original features. The former adjoining stables has been converted to a restaurant serving high-quality locally sourced food. There are separate public and saloon bars with real fires and simple farmhouse-style furniture. It has a large garden to the front with a children's play area and a rear patio with extensive farmland views. The cider is seasonal. Dogs are welcome. ᴁQ✿⓪⅊⊒(270)♣●P⌐

East Dean

Tiger Inn L ✓
The Green, BN20 0DA TV557978
☼ 11-11 ☎ (01323) 423209
Beachy Head Original, Legless Rambler, seasonal beer; Harveys Sussex Best Bitter Ⓗ
Fifteenth-century smugglers' and wreckers' inn with plenty of outdoor seating on the traffic-free village green. It is near the South Downs Way, making it popular with walkers and cyclists. The main bar has beams, an inglenook and woodburner. There is a smaller bar and a recently extended dining area, tastefully decorated combining old and new. Freshly cooked meals are served and the pub is the brewery tap for nearby Beachy Head Brewery. Luxury B&B accommodation is offered. ᴁQ♿⛵☕🍴♿♨️🍺(12)♣Pᵇ⊸

East Hoathly

King's Head L
1 High Street, BN8 6DR
☼ 11-11 (midnight Fri & Sat); 12-11 Sun ☎ (01825) 840238
⊕ 1648brewing.co.uk
Harveys Sussex Best Bitter; 1648 Triple Champion, Signature, seasonal beers; guest beer Ⓗ
Traditional friendly 17th-century local in the village centre, decorated with posters, old prints of the pub and photographs of local events and sports clubs. Five handpumps serve beers from the 1648 Brewery next door, along with regular guests. The U-shaped main bar includes a family area and a dining area serving excellent locally sourced home-cooked food, with takeouts available. Function rooms are to the side. There is a rear walled beer garden and further seating at the front. ᴁQ⛵☕🍴♨️(54)♣Pᵇ⊸

Eastbourne

Counting House L ✓
Star Road, BN21 1NB
☼ 12-11 (midnight Fri & Sat); 12-10.30 Sun ☎ (01323) 731158
1648 Triple Champion; guest beers Ⓗ
Attractive 16th-century Grade II-listed building, with the feel of a country pub in town. Its large garden makes it popular in summer. The part-panelled main bar has beams, inglenook and a woodburner. There are two smaller rooms, one set for diners during service times when good, freshly cooked food is served. Popular with all ages, entertainment includes jam nights, film nights and a pool table. Seasonal beer festivals are held. The two guests are usually from local microbreweries. ᴁ⛵☕🍴♨️🚊Pᵇ⊸

Dew Drop Inn
37-39 South Street, BN21 4UP
☼ 12-midnight (1.30am Fri & Sat) ☎ (01323) 723313
Greene King Dew Drop Inn Ale; H&H Olde Trip; guest beers Ⓗ
A friendly inn, located in the Little Chelsea area, popular with drinkers of all ages. Evenings attract a mainly younger crowd. The horseshoe-shaped bar area is divided in two, with ample comfortable seating. Up to eight handpumps serve regularly changing guest beers, and beer and cider festivals are held. A range of pub food, including speciality burgers, is served until 9pm. For warmer weather there is a small pleasant garden at the rear. CAMRA members are offered a discount. ᴁ☕🍴♿🚊🚊Pᵇ⊸

Eagle L
57 South Street, BN21 4UT
☼ 11-11 (midnight Fri & Sat) ☎ (01323) 417799
⊕ theeagleeastbourne.co.uk
Harveys Sussex Best Bitter; guest beers Ⓗ
Former Kemptown Brewery pub featuring some fine restored internal decoration, including a large illuminated stained glass arch window as a bar-back. It has a small roof terrace. Several TVs, including a 100-inch HD projection screen, show popular sports. A pool table and dartboard are available. Five changing beers from local breweries and a real cider are offered alongside an excellent range of pub food, served until 9pm. Regular beer festivals are held. CAMRA members receive a discount. ᴁ☕🍴🚊🚊♣🚊ᵇ⊸

Ship Inn L
33-35 Meads Street, BN20 7RH
☼ 10-11 (midnight Fri; 10.30 Sun) ☎ (01323) 733815
Beachy Head Original, Legless Rambler; Harveys Sussex Best Bitter; guest beer Ⓗ
A large comfortable roadside establishment, with a decked area and an impressive garden to the rear. The two bar areas have easy chairs and low coffee tables that enable the visitor to relax and savour the delights of local beers and good food. Two separate areas are designated for dining. Located in the Meads area, it is a short walk to the beach by St Bede's School and access to the Downs. ᴁQ☕🍴🚊(3)

Star Inn
Star Road, BN21 1PD
☼ 12-11 (midnight Fri & Sat; 10.30 Sun) ☎ (01323) 403168
Courage Best Bitter; Harveys Sussex Best Bitter; Young's Special; guest beer Ⓗ
This traditional local boozer is a double-fronted Grade II-listed building in Eastbourne's old town and is all that remains of the Star Brewery, which brewed from 1777 to 1967. A two-sided bar serves two separate rooms, one with fascinating murals and a small stage where jam nights are hosted, the other with bar billiards and darts where pub teams play. Quiz night is Wednesday. 🚊♿🚊🚊♣ᵇ⊸

Victoria Hotel L ✓
27 Latimer Road, BN22 7BU (behind TAVR Centre)
☼ 11-11 (midnight Fri & Sat); 12-10.30 Sun ☎ (01323) 722673 ⊕ victoriaeastbourne.co.uk
Harveys Sussex Best Bitter, Armada Ale, seasonal beers Ⓗ
Friendly family-run local, serving all Harveys seasonal ales. TVs show major sporting events. A large floor bar features brewery memorabilia and prints of Victorian portraits, a smaller back bar has pool and toad in the hole tables, and there is a rear garden for barbecues and summer functions. A beer festival is held over the Easter weekend. Good-value home-made food is available Thursday to Sunday lunchtimes and Thursday to Saturday evenings. The cider is Westons Old Rosie. ☕🍴🍴🚊♣🚊ᵇ⊸

Falmer

Swan Inn
Middle Street, BN1 9PD (just off A27 in N of village)
☼ 12-11 (4 Mon); 12-10.30 Sun ☎ (01273) 681842
Palmers Best, seasonal beers; guest beers Ⓗ
This three-bar pub has a central snug and two larger bars either side. A German model railway

sits above the bar. Music plays on the last Tuesday of the month. It is close to the Amex Stadium and very popular on match days, when a bar tent, marquee and seats are provided in the car park. Dependent upon the fixture, entry for football fans may be restricted to Brighton & Hove Albion followers only. Food is available lunchtimes, with a barbecue on Saturday match days.
🏛Q🏠🌑🏮🍴🔥🚻🚆🚃(28,29)♣P¾🚬

Hailsham

King's Head 🅻 ✓
146 South Road, BN27 3NJ
✪ 5-11; 12.30-3, 4.30-11 Fri; 12-3, 6-11 Sat; 12-3, 7-10.30 Sun ☎ (01323) 440447
Harveys Sussex Best Bitter, seasonal beers 🅗
Branch CAMRA Pub of the Year 2011 and a tied Harveys house since 1841, the pub dates from 1700. There are two separate bars, exposed beams, open fireplaces and a quiet snug, while outside is a large beer garden. A friendly welcome awaits from the staff, locals and Benson the dog. This community local has several darts teams, a pool team, knitting club, a weekly Sunday quiz and an annual summer beer festival. Traditional pub games include toad in the hole and shove-ha'penny. 🏛Q🏠🌑🚆🚃(51,54,98)♣P¾🚬

Hastings

Dolphin ✓
11-12 Rock-a-Nore Road, TN34 3DW
✪ 11-11 (midnight Sat) ☎ (01424) 431197
Courage Directors; Dark Star Hophead; Harveys Sussex Best Bitter; guest beers 🅗
Pub in the old town that is at the heart of the fishing community, overlooking the unique Hastings fishermen's huts at Rock-a-Nore. It is decorated with fishing memorabilia and is particularly busy at weekends and holidays. Good food includes the speciality fish platter (no eve meals at weekends). Live music takes place on occasional weekdays, quiz night is Thursday and sport TV is available. 🏛Q🏠🌑🌑🚃(20,100)¾🚬

First In Last Out 🅻
14-15 High Street, TN34 3EY (in old town, near Stables Theatre)
✪ 12-11 (midnight Fri); 11-midnight Sat ☎ (01424) 425079
🌐 thefilo.co.uk
FILO Mike's Mild, Crofters, Old Town Tom, Cardinal, Churches Pale Ale; guest beers 🅗
Located in the picturesque Old Town, this building has been an inn since 1896, but dates back to the 1500s. Formerly home to the FILO Brewery (now 300 yards away), the popular pub has a large bar warmed by a central open fire. Five beers are usually available, including guests. Fresh home-cooked food is served Monday to Saturday lunchtimes and some evenings – Monday is tapas night. Beer festivals are held in the rear function room/restaurant over most bank holiday weekends, with real cider also available. 🏛Q🌑🌑🚃(20,100)♣🐾🚬

Stag Inn
14 All Saints Street, TN34 3BJ
✪ 12-midnight (11 Sun) ☎ (01424) 425734
Shepherd Neame Kent's Best, Spitfire, Bishops Finger, seasonal beers 🅗

Probably the oldest surviving pub in Hastings, in its present form it dates from 1547 and has many interesting and quirky features, including mummified cats on display. As a tied house, it is one of a few pubs to take beers from Shepherd Neame's microbrewery, and these are often available to complement the regular ales. Food is usually on offer (check first in winter months). Monday is quiz night, Tuesday folk night, Wednesday blue grass and Thursday singers. 🏛Q🏠🌑🌑🚃(20,100)♣¾

White Rock Hotel 🅻
1-10 White Rock, TN34 1JU (opp pier)
✪ 10 (12 Sun)-11 ☎ (01424) 422240
🌐 thewhiterockhotel.com
Beer range varies 🅗
Large hotel next door to the theatre of the same name, featuring a stylish, contemporary bar with ample seating and an extensive terrace overlooking the seafront. The four beers on offer are always from independent Sussex breweries, and a good range of freshly prepared food is available all day. Many of the en-suite guest rooms have fantastic sea views; try and book one on the first floor with a balcony. Q🏠🛏🌑🌑🚆🚃🐾

Herstmonceux

Brewers Arms 🅻
Gardner Street, BN27 4LB
✪ 12-11 (midnight Fri & Sat) ☎ (01323) 832226
Greene King IPA, seasonal beers; guest beers 🅗
Originally two 15th-century cottages, this beamed, wood panelled and floored building has been a pub since the 1830s. Recently it has been sympathetically refurbished, and decorated with old prints of the village. Under the Greene King Local Heroes scheme, three of its beers are stocked and three guests, usually from Dark Star, FILO, 1648, or Old Dairy and Royal Tunbridge Wells from Kent. Freshly cooked food (with meat from a local butcher) is on offer including Sunday roasts and reduced weekday lunchtime prices for seniors. 🏛🏠🌑🌑🚃(98)♣P¾

Hove

Cliftonville Inn ✓
98-101 George Street, BN3 3YE
✪ 8-11 (midnight Fri & Sat) ☎ (01273) 726969
Courage Directors; Greene King Abbot; Ruddles Best Bitter; guest beers 🅗
Single-storey pub, formerly a furniture store, left open plan with a single bar. This Wetherspoon pub is not to be confused with the one next to Hove station, which was the original Cliftonville before being renamed twice. The name derives from a local area of Hove. Apart from the regular beers, the range varies from nationals to local breweries. Food is available from 8am every day. Q🌑🚆🚃🐾

Downsman
189 Hangleton Way, BN3 8ES (N of Hangleton)
✪ 11.30-4.30, 6 (7 Sun)-11 ☎ (01273) 711301
Harveys Sussex Best Bitter; guest beers 🅗
Cordial and inviting two-room pub just off the A27 providing great access to Devils Dyke and the South Downs. Bring your dog along and relax in front of the fire or, in the summer months, chill out and enjoy the views from the beer garden. In addition to Harveys Best one or two well-kept guest ales

are served by the friendly and knowledgeable bar staff, and would go well with the traditional pub food on offer. ♨☼◑⎕🍴(5,5A,5B)P♿—

Neptune Inn
10 Victoria Terrace, Kingsway, BN3 2WB
🕐 12-1am (2am Fri & Sat; midnight Sun) ☎ (01273) 736390
⊕ theneptunelivemusicbar.co.uk
Greene King Abbot; Harveys Sussex Best Bitter; guest beers Ⓗ
Traditional single-bar free house on the Brighton to Shoreham coast road close to central Hove. The front door opens on to a long oak-panelled bar area displaying pictures of musicians and posters for current and historic gigs. Five handpumps dispense regular favourites plus frequently changing guest ales, always in peak condition. Live music is strongly supported with blues and rock every Friday and jazz on Sunday, together with occasional open mic and poetry evenings. 🚌(700)♿—

Icklesham

Queens Head
Parsonage Lane, TN36 4BL (opp village hall)
🕐 11-11; 12-10.30 Sun ☎ (01424) 814552
⊕ queenshead.com
Harveys Sussex Best Bitter; guest beers Ⓗ
Award-winning Guide regular, this early 17th-century inn, once comprising two dwellings, always stocks five beers, up to eight at weekends. Local beers and cider are prominent. The interior has five areas warmed by log fires in winter and adorned with an eclectic mix of decorations and memorabilia. With an interesting, affordable menu, live music most Sunday afternoons and an annual autumn mini beer festival, a visit is always worthwhile. A spacious garden offers fine views towards Winchelsea and Rye. ♨☼◑🚌(100)♣♠P♿—🍺

Robin Hood ♈ Ⓛ
Main Road, TN36 4BD
🕐 11-3, 6-11; 11-11 Fri & Sat; 12-4, 7-10.30 Sun
☎ (01424) 814277
Beer range varies Ⓗ
This family-run roadside 17th-century pub, with some parts rebuilt in 1812 following fire damage, serves up to five beers, often from local breweries. It comprises two bars – one with a pool table and open fire, the other leading to a dining area where good home-cooked food is served (no food Tue eve). To the rear is a large garden and a spacious car park. The successful village beer festival is held in an adjacent field each July. Local CAMRA Branch Pub of the Year 2012. ♨☼◑⎕🍴(100)♣♠P♿—

Isfield

Laughing Fish ✅
Station Road, TN22 5XB (off A26 between Lewes and Uckfield) TQ452172
🕐 11.30-11 ☎ (01825) 750349 ⊕ laughingfishonline.co.uk
Greene King IPA, seasonal beers; H&H Kimberley, Olde Trip; guest beers Ⓗ
The pub abuts the preserved Lavender Line and was formerly the Station Hotel. It had an eventful World War II (see website). Tenants Andy and Linda have now expanded the beer range to include local brews, and good-quality pub food is served. Morris dancers occasionally perform and

annual events include an Easter beer race. The pub hosts bar billiards, darts and toad in the hole teams. There is a large outdoor play area for children. ♨☼◑⎕👶Ⓐ🚌(29)♣P♿—

Lewes

Brewers Arms ♈ Ⓛ
91 High Street, BN7 1XN (near Lewes Castle)
🕐 10-11; 12-10.30 Sun ☎ (01273) 475524
⊕ brewersarmslewes.co.uk
Harveys Sussex Best Bitter; guest beers Ⓗ
Genuine family-run free house catering for most tastes in its two bars. At the front, the comfortable saloon offers a range of seating with books and games available. The rear bar has a pool table and two TVs show sporting events. It is popular on match days with Lewes FC, Brighton & Hove Albion and away fans. Food, including traditional breakfasts, is served until 6.30pm. The exterior proclaims the former owners, Page & Overtons, Brewers of Croydon. Q☼◑⎕🚋🚌(28,29)♣♠—

Elephant & Castle Ⓛ
White Hill, BN7 2DJ (off Fisher St, near old police station)
🕐 11.30-11 (midnight Fri & Sat); 12-11 Sun
☎ (01273) 473797 ⊕ elephantandcastlelewes.co.uk
Harveys Sussex Best Bitter; Taylor Landlord; guest beers Ⓗ
Dating from 1838, nowadays the pub attracts a varied but mainly younger crowd, and gets busy on match days when multiple games can be shown on the TVs. The sports theme continues with various rugby, stoolball, toad in the hole and other teams based here. Societies including a folk club, CAMRA, and the Commercial Square Bonfire Society use the upstairs function room. Some of the regalia of the Bonfire Society decorates the pub. Look for the skunk! The real cider is Westons Old Rosie. ♨☼◑🚋🚌(127)♣♠—

Gardener's Arms Ⓛ
46 Cliffe High Street, BN7 2AN
🕐 11-11; 12-10.30 Sun ☎ (01273) 474808
Harveys Sussex Best Bitter; guest beers Ⓗ
Genuine free house in the historic Cliffe area of Lewes and close to Harveys Brewery. The five guest beers change regularly and are usually from small breweries from all over the country, often including a dark beer. Harveys seasonal ales often feature. Bottled and draught real cider is available. Food consists of basic pub grub (pies, pasties). A Guide and Ale Trail regular, the pub was voted most popular on the 2011 Trail. No children allowed. 🚋🚌(28,29)♣♠

John Harvey Tavern Ⓛ ✅
Bear Yard, Cliffe High Street, BN7 2AN (opp Harveys Brewery)
🕐 11-11; 12-10.30 Sun ☎ (01273) 479880
⊕ johnharveytavern.co.uk
Harveys Hadlow Bitter Ⓗ**, Sussex Best Bitter** Ⓖ**, Armada Ale, seasonal beers** Ⓗ
In the lane opposite Harveys brewery shop, the pub occupies what was once the stables of the Bear Hotel, where John Harvey first brewed. Despite its modernity, the main bar has character – some of the seats are made from wooden fermenting vessels. There is a second quiet room and another room upstairs which can be used for functions. In winter Old Ale is available on gravity. Live music is performed at the weekend. ♨Q☼◑🚋🚌(28,29)♿—

Lewes Arms ✓

1 Mount Place, BN7 1YH
✪ 11-11 (midnight Fri & Sat); 12-11 Sun ☎ (01273) 473152
⊕ thelewesarms.co.uk
Fuller's London Pride, seasonal beers; Gale's HSB; Harveys Sussex Best Bitter; guest beers Ⓗ
In the heart of the county town, the pub is a traditional alehouse popular with visitors and locals alike. Fuller's beers are served plus Harveys Best and a guest. It is home to the world pea-throwing championship, dwyle flunking, spaniel racing and other unusual events. A three-day music festival is hosted in August and an annual pantomime in March in the upstairs function room in aid of a local charity. Home-made food is available every day until 8.30pm. ♨Q❀☎☀❀❶❷⬅➡(28,29)♣♥⅃

Snowdrop Inn ✓

119 South Street, BN7 2BU
✪ 12-midnight (11 Sun) ☎ (01273) 471018
⊕ thesnowdropinn.com
Dark Star Hophead, seasonal beers; Harveys Sussex Best Bitter, seasonal beers; guest beers Ⓗ
Six real ales and fantastic food greet visitors to this pub, which has two Harveys beers and at least two from Dark Star on handpump. Guest ales tend to be either local or those that are hard to find. There is always a real cider on, usually from Gwynt y Ddraig. All meat and poultry on the menu is free range and vegetarians are well catered for. The pub is child- and dog-friendly, and hosts live music in the upstairs room. ❀❶⬅➡(28,29)♣♥⅃

Litlington

Plough & Harrow Ⓛ ✓

The Street, BN26 5RE
✪ 11 (12 Sun)-11 ☎ (01323) 870632 ⊕ thepandh.co.uk
Longman Sussex Pride; Dark Star Hophead; Harveys Sussex Best Bitter; Longman Long Blonde, Best Bitter Ⓗ
With parts dating from the 16th century, this pretty village free house is situated in the South Downs National Park. The interior offers a variety of comfortable seating, including cut-down beer casks. As well as the main bar area, there is a separate dining area and an unusual snug with an inglenook fireplace. To the rear is an attractive garden with seating and barbecue. Food is served with an emphasis on home-cooked local produce and home-made desserts. The pub is now the tap for the local Longman Brewery. ♨Q❀☎❶♣P⅃☖

Lower Willingdon

British Queen

The Triangle, BN20 9PG
✪ 11-11 (11.30 Thu; midnight Fri & Sat); 12-10.30 Sun
☎ (01323) 484166
Dark Star Hophead; Fuller's London Pride; Harveys Sussex Best Bitter; guest beers Ⓗ
Originally two cottages, the pub was part of the old Star Brewery estate and was rebuilt in mock-Tudor style in the 1930s. It is a large two-bar establishment with darts, pool and sports TV in the public bar, which is also used for regular live music. A meat raffle and quiz night are weekly features. Good food is available. Harveys Old Ale is served in the winter, otherwise a varying guest is on offer. Q❀❶❷⬅➡(32,51,54)♣P⅃

Milton Street

Sussex Ox Ⓛ ✓

BN26 5RL (signed off A27) TV533040
✪ 11.30-3, 6-11; 12-3, 6-10.30 (12-5 winter) Sun
☎ (01323) 870840 ⊕ thesussexox.co.uk
Dark Star Oxhead; Harveys Sussex Best Bitter; guest beers Ⓗ
Set overlooking the Cuckmere valley, this popular free house has stunning views from the large garden area to the rear of the pub. The beer range includes Dark Star Oxhead, which is brewed for the pub, and a changing guest ale, often from a Sussex microbrewery. The separate internal dining areas are fairly large, with the stone-floored small bar area adjacent to them. Sat Nav users take care: some devices have difficulty finding this pub! ♨☎❀❶♣P

Pett

Two Sawyers ✓

TN35 4HB
✪ 12-11 (10.30 Sun) ☎ (01424) 812255
⊕ twosawyers.co.uk
Harveys Sussex Best Bitter; Ringwood Fortyniner; guest beers Ⓗ
In the village centre, this welcoming pub serves at least three, often five, real ales, some from local breweries, and a real cider. It comprises two main bars, one with an open fire, a separate restaurant also with an open fire, and a number of smaller dining areas. Popular with locals, walkers and campers, it has an excellent menu, large beer garden, pétanque piste and three B&B rooms. Reflecting the pub's name, many areas are decorated with antique saws. ♨Q❀❦❶❷❸⬅➡(347)♣♥P⅃

Plumpton

Half Moon Inn

Ditchling Road, BN7 3AF
✪ 12-11 (10.30 Sun) ☎ (01273) 890253
⊕ halfmoonplumpton.com
Harveys Sussex Best Bitter; guest beers Ⓗ
Situated about two miles south of Plumpton railway station, this pub lies at the foot of the South Downs, close to Plumpton Agricultural College. High-quality locally produced food is served from the gastro-style menu lunchtimes and evenings, with sandwiches available during the afternoon. Drinkers are just as welcome as diners; the guest beers all come from Sussex breweries, including nearby Rectory Ales. Real cider and perry are available all year round. There is camping nearby at Blackberry Farm and Hatton Farm. ♨☎❀❶❸⬅➡(166,824)♥P⅃

Portslade

Stanley Arms

47 Wolseley Road, BN41 1SS
✪ 4 (3 Wed-Fri)-11; 12-11 Sat; 12-10.30 Sun
☎ (01273) 430234 ⊕ thestanley.com
Beer range varies Ⓗ
Genuine free house that has been in the same ownership for the past 10 years. It is a street-corner local just five minutes' walk from Fishersgate station. The seven handpumps offer a changing range of beers. This eight-times winner of local CAMRA Branch Pub of the Year hosts three beer

festivals a year on the second weekends of February, June and September. Quiz night is Wednesday, football is often on TV, and live music features some weekends.
⚐Q✿≈✿⊟(2,2A,46)♣●⚑–⊟

Ringmer

Anchor Inn
Lewes Road, BN8 5QE
✪ 11-11 (midnight Fri & Sat); 11.30-10.30 Sun
☎ (01273) 812370 ⊕ anchorinnringmer.co.uk
Harveys Sussex Best Bitter; guest beers Ⓗ
Family-run village pub dating back to 1742 opposite the village green in the centre of Ringmer, with two large beer gardens and a Mediterranean-style patio. The interior is divided into three distinct areas, with a raised seating space opposite the bar servery. The timber-panelled walls are decorated with pictures of local scenes. Food is served all day every day except Sunday evening. Real cider is available on handpump during the summer. Live entertainment and quizzes are posted on the events board.
⚐✿✪◑⊟(28,29B,143)●P⚑–

Cock Inn ✪
Uckfield Road, BN8 5RX (1 mile from village on slip road off A26)
✪ 11-3, 6-11; 11-11 Sun ☎ (01273) 812040
⊕ cockpub.co.uk
Harveys Sussex Best Bitter, seasonal beers; guest beers Ⓗ
Traditional family-run pub with an extensive menu of quality food. Vegetarian, vegan and gluten-free dishes are available. Guest beers rotate and often include Harveys Old, as well as beers from Adnams, Dark Star and Hogs Back. Harveys bottled beers feature all year round and include Bonfire Boy and Christmas Ale. The bar has a huge inglenook fireplace, exposed beams and a flagstone floor. There is a large dining area, beer garden and car park. ⚐Q✿◑▲⊟(29)P⚑–

Rye

Queen's Head Inn Ⓛ
Landgate, TN31 7LH
✪ 12-11 (midnight Sat) ☎ (01797) 222181
⊕ queensheadrye.com
Dark Star Hophead; Old Dairy Copper Top; guest beers Ⓗ
This spacious 17th-century free house offers two changing guest beers, often from local breweries, alongside its regulars and draught ciders. The pub is well known for live music every Saturday evening as well as assorted musical events on Fridays. It is large enough to accommodate the music and leave quiet drinkers undisturbed. There are three B&B rooms. The pub offers a good menu of home-made food, real fires, bar billiards and pool tables, a library and function room.
⚐Q✿◠◑≈⊟♣●⚑–

St Leonards

Horse & Groom
4 Mercatoria, TN38 0EB
✪ 11-11; 12-10.30 Sun ☎ (01424) 420612
Adnams Broadside; Fuller's London Pride; Harveys Sussex Best Bitter; guest beer Ⓗ

Free house at the heart of old St Leonards. The outside gives no clue to the unusual horseshoe-shaped bar, with a separate, narrow, quieter room at the rear. Food is not served in the pub, but there is an adjoining restaurant open Tuesday to Saturday evenings and Sunday lunchtimes. The pub is a short walk from the seafront and Warrior Square. ⚐Q✿⇔≈(Warrior Sq)♣⚑–

North Star Inn ✪
Clarence Road, TN37 6SD
✪ 11-midnight (1am Fri); 12-midnight Sun
☎ (01424) 436576
Harveys Sussex Best Bitter; Taylor Landlord; guest beers Ⓗ
Decorated with railway memorabilia and recently refurbished, this friendly local is hidden away in a back street in the Bohemia area. The large U-shaped bar room with an open fire offers a good range of up to three changing guest beers, often from local microbreweries. There is a popular curry evening on Wednesdays.
⚐Q✿≈(Warrior Sq)⊟(99,100)♣●⚑–⊟

Salehurst

Halt
Church Lane, TN32 5PH (by church)
✪ closed Mon; 12-3, 6-11 Tue & Wed; 12-11 Thu-Sun
☎ (01580) 880620 ⊕ salehursthalt.co.uk
Harveys Sussex Best Bitter; guest beers Ⓗ
Visitors will find a warm welcome at this dog-friendly, traditional family-run pub which was originally a railway stop on a hop-picking line. The two guest beers are often from local microbreweries. In the summer three ciders are served, one in the winter. Good food is on the menu, locally sourced. From the garden, which has a pizza oven, there is a view over the beautiful Rother Valley. Inside there is a selection of board games and, on every second Sunday of the month, live music. ⚐Q✿◑⇔♣●⚑–

Seaford

Cinque Ports ✪
49 High Street, BN25 1PP (bottom of Broad St)
✪ 11-midnight; 12-11.30 Sun ☎ (01323) 892391
Black Sheep Best Bitter; Harveys Sussex Best Bitter; Wychwood Hobgoblin; guest beers Ⓗ
A central bar and three pillars greet you through the porch of this friendly locals' town pub. It curves round to a darts room past the fire; in fact three dartboards are used on busy tournament nights. To the right a side yard offers either fresh air or a smokers' area, depending. The furniture is eclectic and you will note the generous opening hours. The pub opens an hour earlier on Sunday for breakfast.
⚐Q◑⇔≈⊟(12,12A)♣–

South Chailey

Horns Lodge Ⓛ
South Street, BN8 4BD (on A275)
✪ 11.30-2.30 (not Tue), 5.30-11; 11.30-11 Sat; 12-10.30 Sun
☎ (01273) 400422 ⊕ hornslodge.com
Harveys Sussex Best Bitter, seasonal beers; guest beers Ⓗ
Roadside pub that was originally a coaching inn on the London to Brighton postal service route. The bar has a games area for bar billiards, darts and toad in the hole. Home-cooked food is available

lunchtimes and evenings (no food Tue). The pub has a beautiful, recently renovated, garden with a covered and heated smoking area. There are annual beer, cider and sausage festivals and a Mr & Mrs contest. A charity quiz is held on the last Tuesday of each month. ⚧✿☙⊀❶▣(121)♣🍴Pᵇ⸗

Uckfield

Alma ✅
65 Framfield Road, TN22 5AJ (on B2102)
✪ 11-11; 12-10.30 Sun ☎ (01825) 762232
⊕ alma-arms.co.uk
Harveys Sussex XX Mild, Sussex Best Bitter, seasonal beers Ⓗ
About five minutes' walk from the town centre, bus and railway stations, this Harveys pub is among the few to offer XX Mild. Most seasonal ales are served when in brew; Thatchers Heritage is the chosen cider offering. Food is available lunchtimes and evenings (not Mon & Tue), with a carvery on Sunday lunchtimes. Bar billiards, shove-ha'penny, crib, toad in the hole and darts are played. The pub offers separate meeting and function rooms.
✿❶◗⛢❺⇌▣(318)♣🍴Pᵇ⸗

Withyham

Dorset Arms Ⓛ ✅
TN7 4BD
✪ 12-midnight ☎ (01892) 770278 ⊕ dorset-arms.co.uk
Harveys Hadlow Bitter, Sussex Best Bitter, seasonal beers Ⓗ
Originally a 16th-century farmhouse, in the 18th century it became an inn – the Ale House. The pub sign depicts the arms of the Sackvilles, Earls of Dorset. There is an upright desk with an etched glass screen, as well as many Tudor and Elizabethan features, massive beams and wood floors. It is local to Ashdown Forest, of Winnie the Pooh fame. A varied menu of traditional pub food and continental themed fare is offered, prepared mainly with local ingredients. A beautiful historic pub. ⚧Q✿❶◗⛢▣(273,291)♣Pᵇ⸗

Wivelsfield Green

Cock Inn Ⓛ
North Common Road, RH17 7RH (900yds E of B2112)
✪ 12-11 (10.30 Sun) ☎ (01444) 471668
⊕ cockinn-wivelsfield.co.uk
Harveys Sussex Best Bitter, seasonal beers; guest beers Ⓗ
The pub is on the eastern edge of the village and is popular with walkers, cyclists and locals alike. A more frequent bus service is available at the other end of the village on routes 40/40X. Two guest beers supplement the Harveys Best; in winter one of these is always Harveys Old Ale. In summer real cider is available. Darts, pool and bar billiards are played in the public bar and a portable skittle alley is available for hire. ⚧Q✿❶◗⛢▣(166,824)♣Pᵇ⸗

SUSSEX (WEST)

Alfold Bars

Sir Roger Tichborne
Loxwood Road, RH14 0QS
✪ 11-11 ☎ (01403) 751873 ⊕ thetichborne.co.uk
Beer range varies Ⓗ

Familiar to all those who once completed the King & Barnes Ale Trail, this small country pub, whose origins date back to medieval times, reopened in 2009 after a period of closure followed by complete refurbishment. The restaurant enjoys extensive views of the surrounding countryside. It is now an attractive free house selling a variety of mostly local guest ales. Happily much of its original rustic rural charm remains. ⚧Q✿❶◗Pᵇ⸗

Amberley

Sportsman 🍷 Ⓛ
Rackham Road, Cross Gates, BN18 9NR (½ mile E of village off B2139) TQ039135
✪ 11 (12 Sun)-11 ☎ (01798) 831787
⊕ thesportsmaninn.org.uk
Harveys Sussex Best Bitter; Langham Hip Hop; guest beer Ⓗ
A warm welcome, tasty home-cooked food using locally sourced produce, and well-kept ales await you at this 17th-century hostelry. A central bar dispensing only local brews, including guests from Hammerpot and King, serves three separate rooms. In addition, a conservatory restaurant and outdoor terrace offer excellent views over the Wild Brooks – a birdwatchers' paradise, particularly in the winter when the area floods. This place is popular with walkers, cyclists, drinkers and diners. Sussex CAMRA Pub of the Year runner-up 2011 and local Pub of the Year 2010-2012. ⚧Q✿☙⊀❶◗⛢♣P

Barns Green

Queen's Head Ⓛ ✅
Chapel Road, RH13 0PS
✪ 11.30-2.30, 6 (5 Fri)-11; 11.30-11 Sat; 12-10.30 Sun
☎ (01403) 730436 ⊕ thequeensheadbarnsgreen.co.uk
Fuller's London Pride; WJ King Horsham Best Bitter; Sharp's Doom Bar; guest beers Ⓗ
Cosy 17th-century village pub, with old timber beams and a large inglenook, and a log fire in winter. It is mainly open plan, with three seating areas and a small separate room. During the summer holiday season the pub may open all day. Some guest beers are dispensed by gravity from pins owned by the landlord and filled by local breweries. The pins are jacket-cooled, so may not be on in hot weather. There are two real ciders on draught. Good home-made food from locally sourced produce is on the menu.
⚧Q✿❶◗▲▣(74)🍴Pᵇ⸗

Bolney

Eight Bells Ⓛ
The Street, RH17 5QW
✪ 11-11 (1am Fri & Sat) ☎ (01444) 881396
⊕ theeightbellsbolney.co.uk
Harveys Sussex Best Bitter; guest beers Ⓗ
Attractive village pub in the main Bolney street, close to the A23 London to Brighton road. Dating from 1753, original fireplaces are retained in two separate bars and are in use during the winter. There is a separate restaurant. Four-star rated B&B accommodation is provided in a cottage opposite the pub. A beer festival is held annually in August. Other events celebrated here include Burns Night, St George's Day, a summer party and Halloween.
⚧Q✿☙⊀❶◗⛢♿▣(273,89)♣Pᵇ⸗

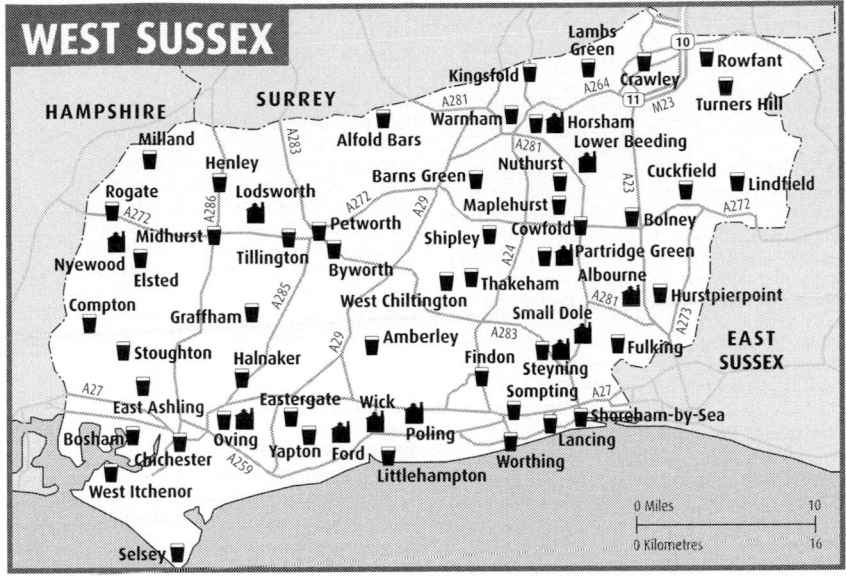

Bosham

White Swan ⓛ
Station Road, PO18 8NG (beside A259 roundabout)
☼ 12-11; 11.30-11.15 Fri & Sat; 11.30-10 Sun
☎ (01243) 578917 ⊕ thewhiteswanbosham.com
Dark Star Hophead; Sharp's Doom Bar Ⓗ; **guest beers** Ⓗ/Ⓖ
Cosy Grade II-listed free house that reopened in 2011 after extensive refurbishment, with tasteful use of stone flags on the bar floor and much reclaimed timber. The restaurant area serves reasonably priced home-cooked food and has the old bread oven in the wall from its days as the village bakery. Up to two guest beers are usually available, as well as locally-sourced wines. In fine weather outside seating to the front can be used. Opens 10-11.30am Friday and Saturday for breakfast, but there is no food Sunday evenings.
Q✿◑❤▭(700,56)♣P⅃

Byworth

Black Horse ⓛ
GU28 0HL (just off A283, 1 mile SE of Petworth)
☼ 12-11 ☎ (01798) 342424 ⊕ theblackhorsebyworth.com
Flowerpots Bitter; Young's Bitter; guest beers Ⓗ
Delightful, unspoilt 16th-century village inn with a vast log fire to welcome you in winter. The dining areas are full of character, including some secluded nooks with views of the countryside and the steeply terraced garden. Guest beers are often from local breweries such as Langham. The Worthing to Midhurst bus stop is just a short distance away. Evening meals are served every day, except Sundays in winter.
♨Q✿◑❤▭(1)♣P

Chichester

Bell Inn
3 Broyle Road, PO19 6AT (on A286 just N of Northgate)
☼ 11.30-2.30, 5-midnight; 12-3, 7-11 Sun ☎ (01243) 783388
Beer range varies Ⓗ

Cosy and comfortable city local with a traditional ambience enhanced by exposed brickwork, wood panelling and beams. A rear suntrap garden has a covered smoking area heated by a coal stove in winter. The pub tends to become busiest after 10pm, when the nearby Festival Theatre empties out. The beer selection usually comprises two from the Enterprise range and one from a local micro, complemented by an extensive food menu chalked up on the blackboard (no food Sun eve).
Q✿◑❤▭(60)♣P⅃

Bull Inn ⓛ
4-5 Market Road, PO19 1JW (at Eastgate opp market)
☼ 12-11; 11-midnight Fri & Sat ☎ (01243) 792432
Beer range varies Ⓗ
Situated opposite the market car park at Eastgate, this airy and friendly city local sells up to eight beers, mostly from local microbreweries. The famous O'Hagan's sausages are always available either in bar meals or to take away from the butcher's counter. The landlord's sense of humour is evident in the forever growing display of potato mashers on one of the high beams. A meeting room is available and there is a covered garden and smoking area behind the pub.
♨Q✿◑❤▭(51,700)⅃

INDEPENDENT BREWERIES

Adur Steyning
Anchor Springs Wick
Arundel Ford
Ballard's Nyewood
Baseline Small Dole (NEW)
Bedlam Albourne (NEW)
Dark Star Partridge Green
Gribble Oving
Hammerpot Poling
Hepworth Horsham
King Horsham
Kissingate Lower Beeding
Langham Lodsworth
Welton's Horsham

Chichester Inn ⃤
38 West Street, PO19 1RP (at Westgate roundabout)
☼ 12-11.30 (midnight Fri & Sat); closed 2.30-5.30 Mon-Thu Jan-Apr; 12-10.30 Sun ☎ (01243) 783185
⊕ chichesterinn.co.uk
Dark Star Hophead; Langham Hip Hop; guest beers Ⓗ
New to the Guide, this pleasant two-bar pub has a high-ceilinged front lounge with a log fire and comfy chairs around it, as well as a mixture of wooden chairs and tables. A larger public bar to the rear doubles as a live music venue on Friday, Saturday and Wednesday evenings (see website). Behind the pub your beer can be enjoyed in the pleasant walled garden or in the heated and covered smoking area. Guest beers from local micros are stocked, especially at weekends. Food includes Sunday lunches. Two B&B rooms are available. ⁜⊛⊠⊪⊕⊟⇌⊟♣P⅃

Eastgate ✅
4 The Hornet, PO19 7JG (500yds E of Market Cross)
☼ 12 (11 Wed)-11; 10-12.30am Sat; 12-11.30 Sun
☎ (01243) 774877 ⊕ theeastgatepub.org.uk
Fuller's London Pride, ESB; Gale's Seafarers Ale, HSB; guest beer Ⓗ
Welcoming town pub with an attractive open-plan bar, a wood-burning stove and an area for diners. Good-value traditional pub meals are home-cooked and served daily, with organic roasts offered on Sunday. There is a heated patio garden to the rear, which is the venue for a beer festival in July. The pub attracts locals, holidaymakers and shoppers from the nearby market with its warm welcome and traditional pub games such as darts, cribbage and pool. ⁜⊛⊪⇌⊟(51,700)♣⅃

Four Chesnuts ⃤
234 Oving Road, PO19 7EJ (900yds E of Market Cross)
☼ 12 (4 Mon)-11; 12-midnight Fri & Sat; 12-10.30 Sun
☎ (01243) 779974 ⊕ the4chesnuts.co.uk
Ballard's Midhurst Mild; Taylor Landlord; guest beers Ⓗ
A traditional town hostelry, the Chesnuts has been converted to a single bar but retains distinct drinking areas. The skittle alley doubles as a dining room at busy times and occasionally as a venue for beer festivals. Two guest beers come from a variety of independent brewers. The menu features hearty meals at reasonable prices. There is a Saturday music night, local folk club on Tuesday, quiz night on Wednesday and regular poker night. Sport is shown on TV. ⁜⊛⊪⇌⊟(51,700)♣P⅃

Compton

Coach & Horses ⃤
The Square, PO18 9HA (on B2146)
☼ 12-3, 6-11; 12-4, 7-10.30 Sun ☎ (023) 9263 1228
Dark Star Hophead; guest beers Ⓗ
Sixteenth-century pub in a remote but charming village, popular with walkers and cyclists. The front bar is warm and welcoming, with an open fire and a wood-burning stove. Internal window shutters and wooden floors give the bar a traditional feel. This bar connects to the oldest part of the pub, now the restaurant, featuring a small bar, exposed beams and another wood-burning stove. An adventurous menu of high-quality food is served every day, all sourced locally. Up to five beers are on offer from independent breweries. There is a bar billiards table, and seats outside in the village square. ⁜Q⊛⊪⊟(54)♣⌂

Cowfold

Hare & Hounds ⃤
Henfield Road, RH13 8DR
☼ 11-3, 5-11; 11-11 Sat; 12-11 Sun ☎ (01403) 865354
Harveys Sussex Best Bitter; guest beers Ⓗ
Convivial village local where you can be sure of a warm welcome. It has a large stone-flagged bar area, a separate carpeted dining space, and an adjacent area for drinking. The log fire creates a cosy feel on chilly days. This free house frequently offers Dark Star beers along with other local ales; often a mild or dark beer is available. An annual beer festival is held in July, and food is served at all sessions. A pub that welcomes diners and drinkers alike. ⁜Q⊛⊪⊟(17,86,100)P

Crawley

Brewery Shades ⃤
85 High Street, RH10 1BA
☼ 10-11.30 (1am Sat; 10.30 Sun) ☎ (01293) 514105
Dark Star Original; Greene King Abbot; Morland Old Speckled Hen; guest beers Ⓗ
Arguably the oldest building in Crawley High Street, dating back to 1400 and complete with two active ghosts. As befits such a building, the pub is unashamedly wet-sales led. The licensee has a true passion for the trade, demonstrated by the positively inspired range of guest ales available, always in excellent condition. The haunted upstairs room is now available for meetings. Good food is served during the day and evening – try the mixed grill. ⊛⊪⇌⊟●

Swan ⦅Ⓨ⦆ ⃤ ✅
1 Horsham Road, West Green, RH11 7AY
☼ 12-11 (1am Fri & Sat) ☎ (01293) 527447
⊕ theswanpubcrawley.co.uk
Dark Star Hophead; Fuller's London Pride; guest beers Ⓗ
The Swan is a gem, located five minutes' walk from the busy town centre. There are two bars and an outside patio area. The pub hosts live rock music evenings and has a pool table. The landlord promotes local breweries as well as those from further afield and includes strong beers on handpump. Themed beer festivals are held in spring and Halloween and the pub supports CAMRA's Mild Campaign in May.
⁜⊛⊞&⇌⊟(23,24)♣●⅃

Cuckfield

Ship Inn ⃤
Whitemans Green, RH17 5BY (at B2115/B2036 jct)
☼ 12-2.30 (not Wed), 5.30-11; 12-11 Sat; 12-4 Sun
☎ (01444) 413219
Harveys Sussex Best Bitter; guest beers Ⓖ
The landlocked Ship is a traditional family-run free house at the northern end of Cuckfield village. The four handpumps are for decoration – the beer comes direct from casks in a cool room behind the bar. There is a lounge area with comfortable sofas, and a pleasant garden at the rear. In winter a central real fire makes for a cosy atmosphere. Food is available at all sessions. No children allowed. Two twin-bedded letting rooms are available.
⁜Q⊛⊪⊪⊟(271,272)P⅃

East Ashling

Horse & Groom ⓛ

PO18 9AX (on B2178)

✪ 12-3, 6-11; 12-11 Sat; 12-6 Sun ☎ (01243) 575339

⊕ thehorseandgroomchichester.co.uk

Dark Star Hophead; Hop Back Summer Lightning; Sharp's Doom Bar; Young's Bitter; guest beer Ⓗ

An inn for over 200 years, this fine country free house has a compact bar featuring flagstones, settles, half-panelled walls and a fine old range. Sympathetically extended, it remains unspoilt. The beers are meticulously presented and are sold at consistently good-value prices. A blackboard reveals the diverse, high-quality menu of home-made dishes, all sourced locally (no food Sun eve). En-suite accommodation is dog-friendly, some in a converted 17th-century oak-beamed flint barn.

🗮Q🏠🍴◑♿Å⇄(Bosham)🚃(54)♣Pⁱ-ö

Eastergate

Wilkes Head ⓨ ⓞ

Church Lane, PO20 3UT (off A29 in old village)

✪ 12-3, 5-11; 12-11 Fri-Sun ☎ (01243) 543380

⊕ wilkesheadeastergate.co.uk

Adnams Southwold Bitter; guest beers Ⓗ

Named after 18th-century radical John Wilkes, this small Grade II-listed red-brick pub dates from 1803. There is a cosy lounge to the left of the central bar and a larger main bar with inglenook, flagstones and low beams, plus a separate restaurant. The large garden houses a comfortable heated smokers' shelter. Four guest beers come from Punch's Finest Cask range or SIBA local direct delivery. A beer festival is staged in September. Local CAMRA Pub of the Year 2012.

🗮Q🏠◑🚃🚃(66,66A,84)♣●Pⁱ-

Elsted

Three Horseshoes

GU29 0JY (E end of village)

✪ 11-2.30, 6-11; 12-3, 7-10.30 Sun ☎ (01730) 825746

Flowerpots Bitter; Langham Hip Hop; Young's Bitter; guest beers Ⓖ

Low-beamed cosy rural inn with small rooms including a back room for dining only, and a room with a blazing log fire in winter. Outside, the large, pleasant garden enjoys superb views over the Downs. In summer there are five beers (mainly from local micros), and three in winter, all served by gravity dispense from a stillage alongside the bar. Meals are substantial and of high quality. This is an old, comfortable and homely pub that you will be reluctant to leave. 🗮Q🏠◑🚃(91)P

Findon

Snooty Fox ⓛ

High Street, BN14 0TA

✪ 12-2.30, 6-11; 12-10.30 Sun ☎ (01903) 872733

⊕ findonmanor.com

Harveys Sussex Best Bitter; Sharp's Doom Bar; Taylor Landlord; guest beers Ⓗ

Part of the 16th-century Findon Manor Hotel set in the picturesque village of Findon, this quiet, cosy and friendly bar has recently been refurbished. The bar has kept some of its original features, including oak beams and a brick fireplace incorporating a cheery woodburner. Good-quality food, a good range of beers, and a large garden for summer

visits add to the appeal. The pub is on a half-hourly bus route to and from Worthing. Children welcome.

🗮Q🏠🍴◑♿🚃(1)P

Fulking

Shepherd & Dog ⓛ ⓞ

The Street, BN5 9LU

✪ 11-10.30; 12-8 Sun ☎ (01273) 857382

⊕ shepherdanddogpub.co.uk

Harveys Sussex Best Bitter; SouthDowns Ruskin's Ram, Devils Dyke Porter; guest beers Ⓗ

At the foot of the South Downs and popular with walkers in summer, this pub is now the brewery tap for the SouthDowns Brewery, which uses water from the local spring. The building dates from the 17th century, with knurled oak beams, wobbly walls, an inglenook fireplace and low ceilings. Up to six local ales are served, as well as local cider. Food, sourced locally where possible, is served daily. 🗮Q🏠◑♿Å●Pⁱ-

Graffham

Foresters Arms

The Street, GU28 0QA (3 miles W of A285) SU930177

✪ 12-3, 6-11 (closed Mon winter); 12-3, 6-10.30 (not eve winter) Sun ☎ (01798) 867202 ⊕ forestersgraffham.co.uk

Dark Star Hophead; Harveys Sussex Best Bitter; guest beers Ⓗ

Fine Grade II-listed traditional country pub built in 1609 and extended in Victorian times. An attractive garden and an impressive inglenook with blazing logs in winter make this a popular venue, as does its proximity to the South Downs Way and other fine walking country. The guest beers are sourced from local independent breweries. There are three cosy en-suite rooms in the adjoining converted stables. The 99 bus runs 2½ miles away, but will divert if booked ahead. An extensive food menu is available in the restaurant; booking recommended.

🗮Q🏠🍴◑Å🚃(99)♣Pⁱ-

Halnaker

Anglesey Arms ⓛ

Stane Street, PO18 0NQ (on A285)

✪ 11-3, 5.30-11.30; 11-11 Fri & Sat; 12-10.30 Sun ☎ (01243) 773474 ⊕ angleseyarms.co.uk

Black Sheep Best Bitter; Young's Bitter; guest beers Ⓗ

Close to the Goodwood Estate, which owns the freehold, this family-run, listed, Georgian pub and dining room features a wood and flagstone-floored public bar with a log fire, plus a comfortable restaurant renowned for good food made with local produce (reservation essential). Two local SIBA guest beers are usually available. Cribbage and cricket are played by pub teams. There is a two-acre rear garden with a pétanque court, and dogs are welcome in the bar.

🗮Q🏠◑Å🚃(55,99)♣P

Henley

Duke of Cumberland Arms ⓛ

Henley Village, GU27 3HQ (off A286, 3 miles N of Midhurst) SU894258

✪ 11-11; 12-10.30 Sun ☎ (01428) 652280

⊕ dukeofcumberland.com

Harveys Sussex Best Bitter; Langham Hip Hop, Sundowner, Best Bitter Ⓖ

Stunning 15th-century inn nestling against the hillside and set in 3½ acres of terraced gardens with extensive views. The rustic front bar has scrubbed-top tables and benches, plus a log fire at both ends, while to the rear is a new extension that blends in perfectly with the original pub and offers much-needed additional space, particularly for diners. Outside is a smokers' shelter with its own woodburner. A former local CAMRA Pub of the Year, this is a rural gem. ▲Q❀◑🖰(70)♣♠P⁵⁻

Horsham

Black Jug

31 North Street, RH12 1RJ
❂ 11.30-11; 12-10.30 Sun ☎ (01403) 253526
⊕ blackjug-horsham.co.uk
Caledonian Deuchars IPA; Harveys Sussex Best Bitter; guest beers Ⓗ
Large bustling town-centre pub, the Jug is something of a Horsham institution. It has a welcoming interior with bookshelves, pictures and a fire, and friendly and efficient staff. Two regular ales are available with rotating guests and cider. Excellent food is served all day and the pub is equally popular as a venue to meet and chat, with no intrusive music. Close to the railway station and opposite the Arts Complex. ▲Q❀◑Ⴑ⇌🖰♠⁵⁻

Piries Bar Ⓛ

Piries Alley, The Carfax, RH12 1NY
❂ 11 (12 Sun)-midnight ☎ (01403) 267846
⊕ piriesbar.co.uk
Dark Star Hophead; Taylor Landlord Ⓗ
In a building dating from the 15th century with exposed timber beams, the pub is tucked away down a narrow alley adjoining Horsham's Carfax. It comprises a small downstairs room, an upstairs lounge bar and a small modern extension in character with the building. Regular charity events are organised. Evenings here can be lively, with karaoke on Sundays, occasional live music and late opening until midnight. With two cask ales always available, this bar is well worth a visit. ◑⇌🖰

Hurstpierpoint

Poacher

139 High Street, BN6 9PU
❂ 12-11.30 ☎ (07799) 085053
Dark Star Hophead; Harveys Sussex Best Bitter; guest beers Ⓗ
On the eastern side of the village in an area formerly known as Lower Trumpkins, this single-bar community pub was originally a cottage belonging to the nearby Danny estate; following a single-storey extension to the front of the building in Victorian times it became a pub under the name Queen's Head Inn. The guest beers are generally from family brewers such as Brains or Hook Norton. The real cider is Westons Old Rosie. ▲❀◑🖰(33,273)♠⁵⁻

Kingsfold

Owl Ⓛ

Dorking Road, RH12 3SA
❂ 10.30-11; 11.30-9.30 Sun ☎ (01306) 628499
⊕ theowl-kingsfold.co.uk
Hogs Back TEA; Otter Bitter; guest beers Ⓗ
Large friendly pub set back from the road with a large car park. It features a long bar with Horsham

Stone flagstones in front and red tiles. The restaurant area is carpeted. The pub has an open aspect but some areas do give some privacy. Old wood beams indicate the age of parts of the pub. In the past, when it was known as the Wheatsheaf, it served the smugglers who came up from the coast with their contraband. ▲Q❀◑Ⴑ🖰(52,93)♣♠P⁵⁻

Lambs Green

Lamb Inn Ⓛ

RH12 4RG (2 miles N of A264) TQ220368
❂ 11.30-3, 5.30-11; 11.30-11 Fri & Sat; 12-10.30 Sun
☎ (01293) 871336 ⊕ thelambinn.org
Dark Star Hophead; guest beers Ⓗ
Lovely old pub with a mixture of flagstones and wood floors interspersed with wrought-iron work, low-beamed ceilings and exposed brick walls. Furnishings include high-backed settles and soft sofas, and a real fire adds warmth in winter. This welcoming pub with a friendly landlord and staff is committed to LocAle – all beers come from within 25 miles. The cider is from Biddenden. Both landlords are chefs, serving quality home-made, locally sourced food. The conservatory can be hired for functions and the pub can also provide outside catering. ▲Q❀❀◑🖰(52)♣♠P⁵⁻

Lancing

Crabtree Inn

140 Crabtree Lane, BN15 9NQ
❂ 12-11 (11.30 Thu; 12.30am Fri & Sat); 12-11.30 Sun
☎ (01903) 755514
Beer range varies Ⓗ
Traditional Kemptown house that offers a wide-ranging selection of real ale. The large public bar has pool, darts and table football and the Spitfire lounge bar offers quieter, more relaxed drinking. This room can also be booked for functions free of charge. Live bands are featured monthly. There is a spacious child- and dog-friendly garden and covered smoking area. The Crabtree is also known for its home-made steak pies and the popular Sunday lunch carvery. ❀◑⬚⇌🖰(7,16)♣P⁵⁻

Lindfield

Stand Up Inn

47 High Street, RH16 2HN
❂ 11.30-11.30; 11-midnight Fri & Sat; 12-11.30 Sun
☎ (01444) 482995 ⊕ standupinn.co.uk
Dark Star Hophead, Partridge Best, seasonal beers; guest beers Ⓗ
Two-roomed pub on the village high street, one of four Dark Star pubs. The bar areas feature timber-beamed ceilings, a mural of the Lindfield Pond adjacent to the entrance door, myriad pump clips adorning the walls and many certificates from the local CAMRA Branch. There is a garden to the rear of the premises where the remains of the old Durrants Brewery may be seen. Real cider and/or perry is available. Look out for the bat! ▲Q❀🖰(30,270)♣♠⁵⁻

Littlehampton

Crown Ⓛ ✅

29 High Street, BN17 5EG
❂ 9am-midnight (2am Thu-Sat) ☎ (01903) 719842
⊕ thecrownlittlehampton.co.uk

Anchor Springs LA Gold, seasonal beers; Sharp's Doom Bar; guest beers Ⓗ
The Anchor Springs Brewery tap, with three of its beers always available. The pub is decorated with a big collection of nautical bric-a-brac large and small, and attracts a cosmopolitan mix of customers. There are regular live music nights. Drinkers are welcome to bring in a Cornish pasty from the shop opposite to accompany their pints.
🏛️🌂🕭🚊🖂(9,700)♣🐾♪'─

New Inn Ⓛ
5 Norfolk Street, BN17 5PL (E end of seafront)
🌂 11-11 (midnight Fri & Sat); 12-11 Sun ☎ (01903) 713112
🌐 newinnla.co.uk
Arundel Gold, seasonal beers; Courage Best Bitter; guest beer Ⓗ
By day this street-corner local, only a short walk from the beach, comprising an L-shaped front bar, a smaller rear bar and a games room, provides a pleasant, relaxed atmosphere in which to enjoy the beers. In the evening there are traditional pub games and regular music, theme and quiz nights. Good home-cooked food is available until 6pm, and until 9pm on Thursday steak night (vegetarian option available). 🏛️🌂🕭🚊🖂(9,700)♣♪'─

Maplehurst

White Horse Ⓛ
Park Lane, RH13 6LL
🌂 12-2.30, 6-11 (11.30 Fri & Sat); 12-3, 7.30-11 Sun
☎ (01403) 891208
Harveys Sussex Bitter; Welton's Pride & Joy; guest beers Ⓗ
Simon and Beth celebrated their 30th year at the pub in January 2012. The White Horse has featured in the Guide continuously for the past 27 years and is as popular as ever with locals, walkers, cyclists and members of clubs and societies. Among clubs meeting here are Harley-Davidson, Horsham Historic and Morris Register. A French folk night is held on the last Monday of the month. The extensive garden is popular with families.
🏛️Q🌂🕭🚊♣🐾♪P'─

Midhurst

Swan Inn Ⓛ ✅
1 Red Lion Street, GU29 9PB (opp church)
🌂 11-11 (midnight Fri); 12-midnight Sat; 12-11 Sun
☎ (01730) 812853 🌐 theswaninnmidhurst.co.uk
Harveys Sussex Best Bitter, seasonal beers Ⓗ
Old split-level town pub with a boisterous lower section with a dartboard and various TVs showing sport, particularly football. The upper section is quieter and cosier with sofas for relaxing in front of the fire, wooden beams and more TVs in silent mode. Old Ale or Olympia is available according to season, plus other Harveys seasonal beers. To the right of the side door is a small area used mainly for dining, offering a good menu of seasonal and local dishes, and roast lunches on Sundays. Accommodation is in three en-suite rooms. Limited public parking nearby. 🏛️🌂🕭🚊(1,60)'─

Milland

Black Fox Inn Ⓛ
Portsmouth Road, GU30 7JJ (on B2070) SU829291
🌂 12-2 (not Mon), 6-11 (midnight Fri & Sat); 12-4 Sun
☎ (01428) 723218 🌐 theblackfoxinn.co.uk

Bowman Swift One; Young's Special; guest beers Ⓗ
Situated on the B2070 and the West Sussex Border Path, this remote and comfortable free house has an air of spaciousness about its L-shaped bar, high ceilings and brick arches. Food from an extensive menu can be enjoyed in the restaurant, which overlooks the patio and the enclosed garden with a playhouse for children. There is also a skittle alley for hire, four B&B rooms and a covered smoking area to the rear. Up to two guest beers usually come from Hants and Sussex micros. Q🌂🚊🕭P'─

Nuthurst

Black Horse Ⓛ
Nuthurst Street, RH13 6LH (off A281 at Monks Gate)
🌂 12-3, 6-11; 12-11 Sat; 12-10.30 Sun ☎ (01403) 891272
🌐 theblackhorseinn.com
Dark Star Hophead; Harveys Sussex Best Bitter, seasonal beers; guest beers Ⓗ
Multi-roomed village pub on various levels following the contours of the site. Timber beams abound, unusually painted the same colours as the walls. The main bar is dominated by an inglenook fireplace with flagstone floors, with access to a lower room for general bar use. Upper rooms are used mainly for dining. To the rear of the pub is an outside terraced area alongside a running stream. CAMRA members receive a discount. 🏛️🌂🕭 🐾P'─

Oving

Gribble Inn Ⓛ
Gribble Lane, PO20 2BP (W end of village) SU900050
🌂 11 (12 Sun)-11 ☎ (01243) 786893 🌐 gribbleinn.co.uk
Gribble Ale, Fuzzy Duck, Reg's Tipple, Plucking Pheasant, Pig's Ear, Mokka Mild Ⓗ
Once home to a Miss Gribble, this attractive thatched cottage has been a traditional village pub for 30 years and is also home to the Gribble Brewery. A wide range of Gribble draught beers is always on offer, complemented by seasonal brews throughout the year. Always cosy, with open log fires in winter, home-made food is served in the bar/restaurant. In summer a large attractive garden offers occasional weekend barbecues and the skittle alley is also available for functions.
🏛️Q🚌🌂🕭🖐🚊(84,85)♣P'─

Partridge Green

Partridge Ⓛ
Church Road, RH13 8JS
🌂 12-11 ☎ (01403) 710391
Dark Star Hophead, Partridge Best, seasonal beers; guest beers Ⓗ
The Dark Star Brewery tap is near the brewery, and large photographs of the plant decorate the wall behind the bar. An interesting guest beer is always available. The spacious lounge has wooden panels, an unusual blue glass ceiling and a collection of old local photographs; it leads to a patio and a garden with a children's playground. There are no evening meals Sunday or Monday. 🏛️🌂🕭🚊(17)🐾P🖥️

Petworth

Angel Inn Ⓛ ✅
Angel Street, GU28 0BG
🌂 11-11; 12-10.30 Sun ☎ (01798) 344445
🌐 angelinnpetworth.co.uk
Arundel Castle; Langham Best Bitter; guest beer Ⓗ

A welcome return to the Guide for this fine part timber framed inn, first licensed in 1740 but possibly built in the 14th century, which has recently reopened after a tasteful refurbishment. With well-kept LocAles, good-quality food from a varied menu, several separate cosy areas with open fires and en-suite accommodation, it has quickly established a reputation for excellence that attracts both locals and visitors to this fascinating, compact, historic market town. A large sunny rear patio garden is popular for alfresco drinking and dining. ♨Q❀✿◑◻🚃(1,99)♣P╘

Rogate

White Horse Inn ⅃ ✪

East Street, GU31 5EA (on A272)
❄ 11-midnight (1am Fri & Sat); 12-midnight Sun
☎ (01730) 821333
Harveys Hadlow Bitter, Sussex Best Bitter, Armada Ale, seasonal beers Ⓗ
Dating from the 16th century, this old coaching inn has oak beams, flagstone floors and a huge log fire. A Harveys tied house, you can expect up to five of its draught beers, including Olympia or Old depending on season, plus other seasonal brews. Half the pub is used for dining – a large range of meals using local ingredients includes vegetarian choices (no food Sun eve). The car park overlooks the village sports field behind the pub, where camping can be arranged.
♨❀◑ ▲🚃(92,54)♣P╘

Rowfant

Rowfant House ⅃

Wallage Lane, RH10 4NG TQ325373
❄ 11.30-midnight; 12-10.30 Sun ☎ (01342) 714823
⊕ rowfanthouse.co.uk
Harveys Sussex Best Bitter, seasonal beers; Welton's Rowfant Best Ⓗ
Set in 22 acres of parkland including a lake, Rowfant House is a 16th-century Grade II-listed manor house, owned by the Latvian Church since 1962 and set up as a registered charity. Rowfant House offers a unique setting for enjoying a range of cask ales. There are two comfortable rooms with a bar and further rooms available for dining and social functions. The bars are open until midnight Monday to Saturday. Families are welcome.
♨Q🐕❀✿◑&P╘

Selsey

Seal Hotel ⅃ ✪

6 Hillfield Road, PO20 0JX (on B2145, 600yds from sea)
❄ 10.30-midnight; 12-11 Sun ☎ (01243) 602461
⊕ the-seal.com
Dark Star Hophead; Greene King Abbot; Young's Bitter; guest beers Ⓗ
Popular free house, family-run for 41 years. A focal point for the local community, visitors also converge here to partake of the quality home-cooked food including locally caught fish (booking advised), and the many guest beers, mostly from local micros. Acoustic live music often features on Sunday. The patio has seating and umbrellas to cater for smokers. Camping is available nearby at West Sands Caravan Park. The 12 en-suite B&B rooms are popular. Q❀✿◑▶&▲🚃(51)♣P╘

Shipley

Countryman ⅃

Countryman Lane, RH13 8PZ
❄ 10-4, 6-11; 10-11 Sat; 11-9.30 Sun ☎ (01403) 741383
Harveys Sussex Best Bitter; Fuller's London Pride; guest beer Ⓗ
Previously a blacksmith's cottage, the Countryman has been a pub since the early 18th century. Popular with many local groups, it has two bars, a separate restaurant and an attractive south-facing garden. This is a quintessential Sussex country pub, set in idyllic surroundings; Hilaire Belloc lived locally. Home-grown produce is available in the restaurant and is also sold in the pub. The guest ale is sourced from local breweries. Dog-friendly.
♨❀◑ ⊖P╘

Shoreham-by-Sea

Buckingham Arms

35 Brunswick Road, BN43 5WA (opp railway station)
❄ 11-11; 12-10.30 Sun ☎ (01273) 453660
Greene King Abbot; Harveys Sussex XX Mild, Sussex Best Bitter; Hogs Back TEA; Hop Back Summer Lightning; Ringwood Best Bitter Ⓗ
The first thing to catch the eye on entering the Buck is the seemingly endless row of pumps. Six sell the regular beers, including a mild, with the rest dispensing a changing selection. If that is not enough, there are regular beer festivals held throughout the year. A large covered and heated patio caters for smokers or those just wishing to sit and watch the world go by. Occasional live music plays at weekends. ❀◑⇌🚃(2,2A)👤╘

Duke of Wellington ⅃

368 Brighton Road, BN43 6RE (on A259)
❄ 12-midnight (1.30am Fri & Sat; 11 Sun) ☎ (01273) 389818
Dark Star Hophead, seasonal beers; guest beers Ⓗ
The Duke of Boots, as it is known to some, is an old Kemptown Brewery pub. A small raised area serves as a platform for live bands, with music most weekends. The pub serves mainly Dark Star ales, usually three or four plus a guest or two. The large garden to the rear contains a roofed-over smoking area with a wood stove for cold winter days. One real cider is always on handpump. Look for the giant boot sign. ♨❀⇌🚃(2,2A,700)♣👤╘

Red Lion

Old Shoreham Road, BN43 5TE
❄ 11.30-11; 12-10.30 Sun ☎ (01273) 453171
⊕ redlionshoreham.co.uk
Harveys Sussex Best Bitter; guest beer Ⓗ
In Shoreham's old village, north of the main town, close to the Amsterdam, the 10th-century church and the old river crossing, now a footbridge. Converted from three low cottages knocked together, it is quite small and cosy. Nevertheless, a huge beer festival is held each Easter weekend, accommodated by covering the garden with a marquee. The September airshow at the nearby airport draws large crowds. Harveys is a regular, plus four guests from interesting breweries. Real cider is available in summer.
♨Q❀◑▶🚃(2A,9)♣👤P╘

Sompting

Gardeners Arms ⅃

West Street, BN15 0AR (on S side of West Street)

✪ 11-11; 12-midnight Fri & Sat; 12-11 Sun
☎ (01903) 233666
Draught Bass; Harveys Sussex Best Bitter; Sharp's Doom Bar; guest beers 🅷
A friendly 19th-century free house located roadside in the original village main street. A unique feature is the 1962 BR passenger carriage built on to the side of the pub, which houses toilets and storage space. Prints of old Sompting adorn the walls. A cribbage team is based here. Tuesday is quiz night. One of the guest beers is usually a Harveys dark ale. There is a south-facing decked area with covered smoking space. Home-cooked food is served daily. ➡🏠🐕🌙🍴🛏🚃(7)♣P⚑—

Steyning

Chequer Inn 🅻 ✅
41 High Street, BN44 3RE
✪ 10-11 (midnight Fri & Sat) ☎ (01903) 814437
⊕ chequerinnsteyning.co.uk
Gale's HSB; Harveys Sussex Best Bitter; Taylor Landlord; guest beers 🅷
Deservedly popular 15th-century coaching house in a pretty village. Guest beers often come from Sussex breweries. The large public bar has TVs and a 100-year-old snooker table, while the historic saloon bar is a more cosy affair, and a small room has an interesting painting of local residents. Outside is a covered courtyard. Home-cooked traditional food using locally sourced ingredients is available, with breakfasts ever popular.
➡Q🏠🍴🌙🚃(2A,100)♣P⚑—

Stoughton

Hare & Hounds
PO18 9JQ (off B2146, through Walderton) SU803116
✪ 11-3, 6-11; 11-11 Fri & Sat; 12-10.30 Sun
☎ (02392) 631433 ⊕ hareandhoundspub.co.uk
Harveys Sussex Best Bitter; Taylor Landlord; guest beer 🅷
An ideal base for walking, this is a traditional country pub in a beautiful downland valley. A large dining room serves fresh local produce while the public bar, with pictures of vintage racing cars and its own open fire, is the locals' choice. There are three open fires which, along with stone-flagged floors, beams and simple furniture, create a wonderful atmosphere. Outside is a paved drinking area at the front and a garden at the back. The bus stops on the B2146, a mile away. The cider is Westons. ➡Q🏠🐕🍴🛏🚶(54)♣🐕P

Thakeham

White Lion Inn 🅻
The Street, RH20 3EP (just off B2139) TQ108174
✪ 11-11; 12-10.30 Sun ☎ (01798) 813141
Fuller's London Pride; Harveys Sussex Best Bitter; Sharp's Doom Bar; guest beers 🅷
Stone steps lead up from the street to this charming 15th-century inn set in a picturesque village to the north of the downs. The interior features three separate bar areas and a restaurant adorned with local photographs from earlier times. The menu is locally sourced wherever possible, and a speciality is the Kobe steakburger. A wood-burning fire warms the pub in winter, and in the summer a terrace and small garden are popular. Dogs are welcome (the pub has three of its own). ➡Q🏠🍴🌙♣P⚑—

Tillington

Horseguards Inn
Upperton Road, GU28 9AF (100yds N of A272)
✪ 12-11.30 (11 Sun) ☎ (01798) 342332
⊕ thehorseguardsinn.co.uk
Harveys Sussex Best Bitter; guest beers 🅷
Originally three cottages, this charming 350-year-old pub, sitting high above the village street opposite the church, is named after a regiment that was stabled in Petworth Park during the Napoleonic Wars. The welcoming, rustically furnished main bar, plus three other rooms at different levels, all have open fires. Outside is a small front terrace plus an award-winning rear garden where chickens and cats roam freely. Top quality food is served seven days a week, and three B&B rooms are available. Two local guest beers come from the SIBA Direct Delivery scheme.
➡🏠🐕🍴🌙🚃(1)♣🐕

Turners Hill

Crown ✅
East Street, RH10 4PT
✪ 9am-3, 6-11 (midnight Fri & Sat) ☎ (01342) 715218
⊕ thecrownturnershill.co.uk
Harveys Sussex Best Bitter; Morlands Old Speckled Hen; St Austell Tribute 🅷
A 16th-century farmhouse and 17th-century barn with Jacobean oak beams go to make up this pub, which converted to an inn in 1706. It holds a St George's Day celebration, a beer festival to coincide with the London to Brighton cycle ride, and a 30-ale festival in October. Leather settees surround a large open fire in the bar area, with another open fire in the restaurant serving traditional English dishes. There is an enclosed garden to the rear and patio area to the front.
➡🏠🍴🌙🚃(82,84,291)P⚑—

Warnham

Sussex Oak 🅻 ✅
2 Church Street, RH12 3QW
✪ 11-11 (10.30 Sun) ☎ (01403) 265028
⊕ thesussexoak.co.uk
Fuller's London Pride; Harveys Sussex Best Bitter; Taylor Landlord 🅷
Large, popular village pub, open plan but with a separate dining area and four other seating areas. Eight handpumps dispense three regular beers and two or three guests, usually local. LocAle is actively supported. An extensive menu of high-quality, reasonably priced food, mainly local, is available. It has a large garden with plenty of seating and is dog friendly. There is also a heated and covered smokers' area. Jazz nights are on the second and last Thursday of the month, and beer festivals are held on bank holidays. The pub has featured in the Guide for the past 10 years.
➡Q🏠🍴🌙🚃(93)🐕P⚑—

West Chiltington

Five Bells 🅻
Smock Alley, RH20 2QX (1 mile SE of village) TQ091170
✪ 12-3, 6-11 (7-10.30 Sun) ☎ (01798) 812143
⊕ fivebellsinn.co.uk
Harveys Sussex Best Bitter; Palmers Copper Ale; guest beers 🅷

One long bar featuring an unusual copper fireplace runs across this inter-war former King & Barnes pub, now a free house. The three guest pumps feature a beer range that always includes a mild and a local ale. With a heated conservatory and a large garden, this is a popular venue at any time of the year. Mine hosts, Bill and Joan, recently celebrated 25 years at the pub. Excellent home-cooked food includes locally sourced produce (no food Sun eve). ₪Q✿❀☕◐Ⓟ(1)♣♠P

West Itchenor

Ship Inn

The Street, PO20 7AH (on main street, 100yds from waterfront) SU799014
🌣 11-11; 12-10.30 Sun ☎ (01243) 512284
🌐 theshipinnitchenor.co.uk
Arundel Castle; Ballard's Best Bitter; WJ King Horsham Best Bitter; guest beer Ⓗ
Popular pub in the main street of an attractive village on the shore of picturesque Chichester harbour. Cosy bars decorated with yachting memorabilia add to the pub's character and are complemented by a pleasant patio, a suntrap in summer. The two bars have dining facilities, offering a wide range of traditional meals, often including locally landed fish. Three West Sussex ales are normally available, with one guest usually from a local brewery. Accommodation includes a four-bed family apartment. Buses stop on the B2179, 1⅓ miles away.
₪Q✿❀☕◐ ⬦&Ⓟ(52,53)♣P⅄

Worthing

George & Dragon ✅

1 High Street, Tarring, BN14 7NN (S end of High St)
🌣 11-11 (midnight Fri & Sat); 12-10.30 Sun
☎ (01903) 202497 🌐 ganddtarring.co.uk
Courage Directors; Greene King Abbot; Harveys Sussex Best Bitter; Hop Back Summer Lightning; Sharp's Doom Bar; Young's Bitter Ⓗ
Seventeenth-century coaching inn in the unspoilt part of Tarring village. A welcoming, traditional locals' pub, it has oak beams throughout and a choice of several split-level seating areas, including a cosy lounge with a coal-effect fire and a good-sized enclosed rear garden with a suntrap patio. Excellent home-cooked food is available lunchtimes and Monday to Thursday evenings. A poker league and darts team play here every Monday, and there is a pub quiz on Wednesdays. Dog friendly. ❀◐≷(West)Ⓟ(6,16)♣P⅄

North Star ✅

Littlehampton Road, Durrington, BN13 1QY (on A2032, ½ mile N of Durrington station) TQ126046
🌣 11.30-11 (midnight Fri & Sat) ☎ (01903) 526110
🌐 emberinns.co.uk/thenorthstarworthing/
Fuller's London Pride; Ringwood Best Bitter; St Austell Tribute; guest beers Ⓗ
Spacious 1930s road house with decor updated by current owner Ember Inns. It offers one rambling bar with many nooks and crannies, and a garden for alfresco drinking. Aiming, to quote, at a grown-up crowd that really enjoy drinking and eating out, it has achieved a well-mixed clientele. Guest beers are from the Ember Inns seasonal selection, and are always interesting and frequently inspired.
₪≥❀◐&≷(Durrington)Ⓟ(5,6)P⅄

Richard Cobden ✅

2 Cobden Road, BN11 4BD
🌣 11-11 (11.30 Fri & Sat); 12-10.30 Sun ☎ (01903) 236856
🌐 therichardcobden.co.uk
Hop Back Summer Lightning; Ringwood Best Bitter; guest beers Ⓗ
A traditional street-corner pub featuring an L-shaped bar with a real fire at one end and a dartboard at the other, and an attractive enclosed courtyard garden outside. The two guest ales often include a mild. On Sunday there is a meat raffle, in the evening shuffleboard is played. Slate shove-ha'penny and cribbage are among the other pub games available. A local morris side performs a traditional mummers' play on New Year's Day featuring the pub Father Christmas.
₪❀&≷Ⓟ♣⅄

Selden Arms Ⓛ

41 Lyndhurst Road, BN11 2DB (near Worthing hospital)
🌣 11-11 (11.30 Fri); 12-11.30 Sat; 12-10.30 Sun
Dark Star Hophead; guest beers Ⓗ
Nestling in the lee of the now disused gasometer, between Lidl and the hospital, this classic one-bar pub continues its 15-year run of Guide listings. There are always six beers from micro and craft breweries, plus a selection of draught and bottled Belgian and German beers, adding to the growing list of over 1,600 ales served from the polished copper-topped bar. The interior walls are adorned with a photographic archive of Worthing's pubs. Proper pub food is served. ₪◐≷Ⓟ(9,16)♠

Swan Inn Ⓛ

79 High Street, BN11 1DN
🌣 11-11 (midnight Fri & Sat); 12-11 Sun ☎ (01903) 232923
Harveys Sussex Best Bitter; Sharp's Doom Bar; Shepherd Neame Spitfire; guest beers Ⓗ
Traditional 19th-century inn that was refronted in 1938. It has an open-plan U-shaped bar with agricultural implements and brass and copper artefacts hanging from the beamed ceiling. Swan ornaments adorn the pub. Two white swan stained-glass windows give a historic feel, showing evidence of the Kemptown Brewery. Four bar billiards teams are based here. Discos and open mic sessions are held at the weekend, with a quiz on Wednesday night. The cider is Westons Old Rosie. ₪❀◐≷Ⓟ(9,16)♣♠⅄

Yapton

Maypole Inn Ⓛ

Maypole Lane, BN18 0DP (off B2132 1 mile N of village; pedestrian access across railway from Lake Lane) SU978042
🌣 11.30-11 (midnight Fri & Sat); 12-11 Sun
☎ (01243) 551417
Dark Star Hophead; guest beers Ⓗ
Small flint-built free house hidden away from the village centre, down a narrow lane ending in a pedestrian crossing over the railway (1¼ miles east of Barnham and 1¾ miles west of Ford stations). The cosy lounge boasts two open fires and a row of eight handpumps, dispensing up to four guest beers including a mild. There is a traditional public bar and a skittle alley/function room with a bar billiards table. Bar meals are served lunchtimes Monday-Saturday. Dogs are welcome. Local CAMRA Pub of the Year 2011.
₪Q❀◐&≷(Barnham/Ford)Ⓟ(66,66A,700)♣♠P⅄

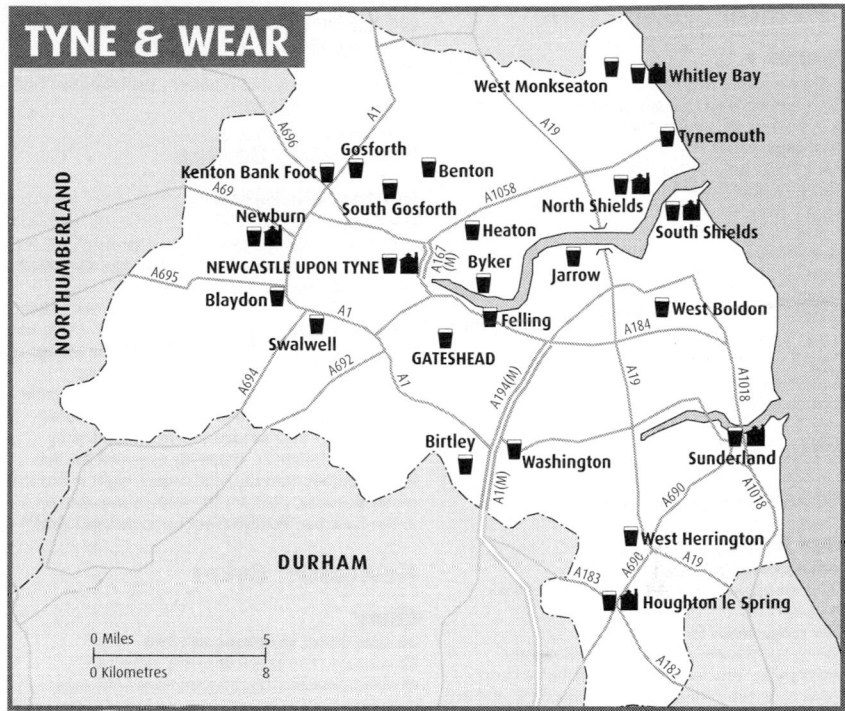

Birtley

Barley Mow
Durham Road, DH3 2AG (at jct of Durham Rd and Vigo Lane)
☼ 11-midnight; 10-11.30 Sun ☎ (0191) 410 4504
⊕ thebarleymowinn.co.uk
Harviestoun Bitter & Twisted; Rudgate Viking; guest beers Ⓗ
A 1930s roadhouse-style pub on the southern edge of the town, with up to seven guest beers (often from northern microbreweries) alongside two regulars. There is a public bar, split-level lounge and separate dining area. The seasoned tenants run a weekly quiz alongside darts and dominoes teams. Dogs are welcome in the bar. Regular and varied live music takes place plus two music- and beer-themed festivals each year, in February and August. ⌂⌖⌂⌂⌂♣P⌐

Blaydon

Black Bull ✓
Bridge Street, NE21 4JJ
☼ 2 (12 Sun)-11; 12-midnight Fri & Sat ☎ (0191) 414 2846
⊕ blackbull-blaydon.co.uk
Black Sheep Best Bitter; Caledonian Deuchars IPA; Wychwood Hobgoblin Ⓗ
Two-roomed pub with traditional values —'No pool table, no jukebox, no bandit' boasts the proud landlord. There has been a pub on this site since the 1800s; the bar has over 40 framed photographs of old Blaydon. Two folk nights feature weekly, plus a buskers' night, quiz night and live bands once a month. Barbecues are held in the superb beer garden during the summer months. There are excellent views of the River Tyne and Tyne Valley. The premises are patronised by the local blind club. Dog-friendly. ⌂Q⌂⌂⌂⌂(10,602)♣♦P

Gateshead: Felling

Old Fox
10-14 Carlisle Street, NE10 0HQ
☼ 2-11; 1-midnight Fri & Sat; 12-11 Sun ☎ (0191) 440 4815
⊕ theoldfoxpub.co.uk
Camerons Old Fox Ale; Castle Rock Harvest Pale Ale; guest beers Ⓗ
Superb traditional/community street pub restored to its former glory by the previous landlord now back in charge. It is a short walk from Felling Metro. The open fire gives the bar a homely feel. Monday is local buskers' night, Tuesday ladies' darts, Wednesday poker 'n' pool, Thursday quiz, Friday men's darts, and Saturday live bands or disco/karaoke. You are assured of a friendly welcome by a landlord who knows how to treat customers as people as opposed to a source of income.
⌂⌂⌂⌂⌂⌂(27,93,94)♣P⌐

Wheat Sheaf Ⓛ
26 Carlisle Road, NE10 0HQ
☼ 5 (12 Fri & Sat)-11; 12-10.30 Sun ☎ (0191) 420 0659
⊕ wheatsheaf-felling.co.uk
Big Lamp Sunny Daze, Bitter, Prince Bishop Ale, seasonal beers Ⓗ
Welcoming street-corner pub owned by the Big Lamp Brewery, popular with a loyal band of regulars who often travel quite a distance to drink here. The pub features some original details, mismatched furniture and, when needed, real coal fires, and the outdoor toilets have original Victorian urinals. There is a fortnightly Monday night quiz, traditional folk music featuring keen local musicians on Tuesday and dominoes night on Wednesday. An original CAMRA clock keeps time behind the bar. ⌂⌂⌂⌂⌂(27,93,94)♣♦

Gateshead: Town Centre

Central ★ L
Half Moon Lane, NE8 2AN
☺ 12-midnight (1am Fri & Sat) ☎ (0191) 478 2543
🌐 theheadofsteam.co.uk/gateshead
Beer range varies Ⓗ
Marvellous mid 19th-century Grade II-listed four-storey wedge-shaped building recently impressively revived by the Head of Steam group. It now has a revamped public bar, two function rooms for regular live music, and a rooftop terrace. However, the main attraction is the quite magnificently restored buffet, designated by CAMRA as a historic interior of national importance. It was fitted out circa 1900 with a great carved U-shaped counter and bar-back, plasterwork frieze and panelling. There is also a triangular snug with dartboard. The 14 handpulls dispense a range of beer from many local microbreweries.
❀◑⊟♿⇋⊟♣●⚡

Houghton le Spring

Copt Hill L
Seaham Road, DH5 8LU (on B1404)
☺ 11-midnight; 11.30-11.30 Sun ☎ (0191) 584 4485
🌐 copthill.co.uk
Beer range varies Ⓗ
With a spectacular vista over the Houghton countryside, this former Vaux pub has a close connection with the local Maxim Brewery and acts as its unofficial tap, so at least one of its beers is always available, complemented by four guest ales, usually sourced locally. Excellent food including breakfast is served all day from an extensive menu – booking for the recently refurbished restaurant is advisable as it can get busy at evenings and weekends. Live music plays every Sunday night. ♨❀◑⊟♿⊟(20)P⚡

Jarrow

Robin Hood L
Primrose Hill, NE32 5UB (on old road parallel to A194)
☺ 12-11 (11.30 Fri & Sat) ☎ (0191) 428 5454
🌐 jarrowbrewery.co.uk
Jarrow Bitter, Rivet Catcher, Westoe IPA, McConnells Irish Stout Ⓗ
Originally a coaching inn dating back to 1824, the Robin Hood is tastefully decorated and retains its old charm. A previous CAMRA local Pub of the Year, and the original home of the Jarrow Brewery, it is adorned with awards for both the brewery and the pub. It has three function rooms, live entertainment every Friday and Sunday, and a good range of award-winning Jarrow ales constantly on offer plus one guest.
Q❀◑⊟♿⇋(Fellgate)⊟●P⚡

Newburn

Keelman L
Grange Road, NE15 8NL
☺ 11-11; 12-10.30 Sun ☎ (0191) 267 1689
🌐 keelmanslodge.co.uk
Big Lamp Sunny Daze, Bitter, Summerhill Stout, Prince Bishop, seasonal beers Ⓗ
A tastefully converted Grade II-listed former pumping station, this is now home to the Big Lamp Brewery and the Keelman is the brewery tap. A conservatory restaurant serves excellent food and quality accommodation is provided in the adjacent Keelman's Lodge and Salmon Cottage. Attractively situated by Tyne Riverside Country Park, the Coast-to-Coast cycleway and Hadrian's Wall National Trail.
❀⊟◑⊟♿⊟(22)P⚡

Newcastle: Benton

Benton Ale House
Front Street, NE7 7XE
☺ 11-11 (midnight Fri & Sat); 12-11 Sun ☎ (0191) 266 1512
Banks's Bitter; Jennings Cumberland Ale; Ringwood Boondoggle, Fortyniner; guest beers Ⓗ
Well-appointed, traditional pub with a horseshoe bar, run by a friendly manager and staff. Large bay windows give a light and airy feel to the lounge at the front, and the public bar is to the rear. Reasonably priced, good-quality food is available – the menu proudly boasts 'fresh meat in home-made dishes and Sunday lunches supplied by Lemington butchers' (booking essential for Sun lunch). Family friendly, and a quiz night is hosted on Wednesday. Look for the interesting abstract art in the back bar. ◑♿⇋(Four Lane Ends)⊟(1)♣P⚡

Newcastle: Byker

Cluny
36 Lime Street, Ouseburn, NE1 2PQ
☺ 11.30-11; 12-10.30 Sun ☎ (0191) 230 4474
🌐 theheadofsteam.co.uk/newcastle-outlets-the-cluny/
Beer range varies Ⓗ
Large former industrial building converted into a pub, art gallery and live music venue. The pub runs frequent themed beer festivals and always has a good selection of British and foreign draught and bottled products available. The art gallery shows work of all kinds ranging from final degree shows to local independent established artists in all media, with the displays changing monthly. Live music sessions are held most evenings and include a wide range of British, European and American musicians. ◑♿●

Cumberland Arms L
James Place Street (off Byker Bank), Ouseburn, NE6 1LD
☺ 4.30 (12.30 Sat)-11; 12.30-10.30 Sun ☎ (0191) 265 6151
🌐 thecumberlandarms.co.uk
Wylam Rapper; guest beers Ⓗ
Three-storey pub rebuilt more than 100 years ago and relatively little changed since. It stands in a prominent position looking down and across the lower Ouseburn Valley. Home to traditional dance and music groups, the house beer Rapper from Wylam Brewery is named after a traditional dance. A multiple winner of CAMRA's regional Cider Pub of

INDEPENDENT BREWERIES

Big Lamp Newburn
Bull Lane Sunderland
Cullercoats North Shields (NEW)
Darwin Sunderland
Delavals Whitley Bay
Hadrian Border Newburn
Jarrow South Shields
Maxim Houghton le Spring
Mordue North Shields
Ouseburn Valley Newcastle upon Tyne
Three Kings North Shields (NEW)
Tyne Bank Newcastle upon Tyne

the Year award, it generally offers up to six ciders and perries. Winter and summer beer festivals are held each year. ▲Q❀✿✢⬛♣✿P

Free Trade Inn L

St Lawrence Road, Ouseburn, NE6 1AP
✪ 11-11 (midnight Fri & Sat); 12-10.30 Sun
☎ (0191) 265 5764
Mordue IPA; guest beers Ⓗ
Often described as 'basic', this pub, full of character and characters, looks upstream with wonderful views of the bridges over the Tyne, and the Newcastle and Gateshead quaysides. Service is smiling, friendly and knowledgeable. Up to nine beers and two ciders are available on the bar, with cellar runs willingly offered. Interesting beers come from far and wide, and tasty sandwiches from a long-established local delicatessen are available. The jukebox is classic and free. ▲❀☷☷(Q2,106)✿

Newcastle: City Centre

Bacchus ♥ L

42-48 High Bridge, NE1 6BX
✪ 11.30-midnight; 12-10.30 Sun ☎ (0191) 261 1008
Jarrow Rivet Catcher; guest beers Ⓗ
CAMRA Tyneside Pub of the Year four years running, this smart, comfortable city-centre establishment boasts nine handpumps offering a wide range of rapidly changing guest beers, with one pump dedicated to cider and another to beer from Orkney's Highland Brewing Company. A seasonal house beer is brewed by Yorkshire Dales, and a large range of draught and bottled foreign beers is available. Regular beer and food matching events are held. Photographs and posters showing the industries in which this region used to lead the world cover the walls. ◀&☷(Monument)✿

Bodega L

125 Westgate Road, NE1 6BX
✪ 11-11 (midnight Fri & Sat); 12-10.30 Sun
☎ (0191) 221 1552
Big Lamp Prince Bishop; Durham Magus; guest beers Ⓗ
Two fine stained-glass domes are the architectural highlights of the pub, which stands next to the Tyne Theatre and is popular with football and music fans. TVs show sporting events and the pub can be busy on match days. The interior offers a number of standing and seating areas, with separate booths for more intimate drinking. A number of old brewery mirrors adorn the walls. A good selection of foreign bottled and draught beers is available. ◀⇌(Central)☷(Central)✿

Bridge Hotel L

Castle Garth, NE1 1RQ
✪ 11.30-11 (midnight Fri & Sat); 11.30-10.30 Sun
☎ (0191) 232 6400
Caledonian Deuchars IPA; Black Sheep Best Bitter; guest beers Ⓗ
Large Fitzgerald pub situated next to Stephenson's spectacular High Level Bridge – the rear windows and the patio have views of the city walls, River Tyne and Gateshead Quays. The main bar area, adorned with many stained-glass windows, is divided into a number of seating areas with a raised section at the rear. Several guest beers come from far and wide. Among the live music events held in the upstairs function room is what is claimed to be the oldest folk club in the country. ❀◀⇌(Central)☷(Central)✿⌐

Broad Chare L

25 Broad Chare, Quayside, NE1 3DQ
✪ 11-11 (10 Mon) ☎ (0191) 211 2144
⊕ thebroadchare.co.uk
Wylam The Writer's Block; guest beers Ⓗ
A warm welcome awaits in this cosy bar just off Newcastle's historic, bustling Quayside. Stripped floors and exposed brickwork make this a comfortable, quiet bar to relax in and enjoy a pint. Bar food is served all day and there is a restaurant upstairs if you wish to dine in style. ◀▶☷(Monument)☷(Q2)

Centurion L ✅

Central Station, Neville Street, NE1 5DG
✪ 10-11 (midnight Fri & Sat) ☎ (0191) 261 6611
⊕ centurion-newcastle.co.uk/bar.asp
Black Sheep Best Bitter; Caledonian Deuchars IPA; Jarrow Rivet Catcher; guest beers Ⓗ
This beautiful bar, recently enhanced with improved lighting, was built in 1893 as a sumptuous waiting lounge for first class passengers – a major feature is the exquisite tiling which is today worth £3.8 million. It was closed in the 1960s, when the Transport Police used it as cells. Since its restoration, the grandeur of the John Dobson-designed interior is now enjoyed by thousands of locals and visitors to Newcastle. A popular starting point for Whistle Stops II real ale outings. ☎❀◀▶&⇌(Central)☷(Central)☷♣✿

Crown Posada ★ L

33 Side, NE1 3JE
✪ 12-11; 11-1am Fri; 7-10.30 Sun ☎ (0191) 232 1269
Beer range varies Ⓗ
An architecturally fine establishment, identified by CAMRA as one of Britain's Real Heritage Pubs. Behind the narrow street frontage with two impressive stained-glass windows lie a small snug, bar counter and a longer seating area. There is an interesting coffered ceiling, local photographs and cartoons of long-gone customers and staff on the walls. Small brewers are enthusiastically supported, with three regular local ales. The pub has been sympathetically refurbished over the years and is an oasis of calm near the busy Quayside drinking, dining and clubbing circuit. Q☷(Q1,Q2)⌐

Five Swans ✅

14 St Mary's Place, NE1 7PG
✪ 8am-midnight (1am Fri & Sat) ☎ (0191) 232 3893
Beer range varies Ⓗ
Multi-roomed Wetherspoon venue opposite Newcastle Civic Centre and close to the main shopping areas. The beer range includes guests from all the local brewers as well as from further afield. Food is served all day. There is an outside drinking area to the front of the pub and a 'secret' courtyard through the maze of rooms. ☎❀◀▶&☷(Haymarket)⌐

King's Manor L

132 New Bridge Street, Manors, NE1 2SZ
✪ 11-11; 12-10.30 Sun ☎ (0191) 232 1618
Hadrian Border Tyneside Blonde; guest beers Ⓗ
The brewery tap for Hadrian Border Brewery, this updated pub is next door to Manors Metro. It is well patronised by locals and also the student community including Northumbria Real Ale Society. English, German and Spanish football is shown on several TVs. Sandwiches and toasties are always available. A recently installed wood-burning stove

adds to the pleasant ambience. Framed pictures of several former English monarchs adorn the walls. Bands play in the downstairs room most Saturdays. ᴹᴬ⊞⊞(Manors)⊟♣♠

Lady Grey's 🛋 ⊘
20 Shakespeare Street, NE1 6AQ
✪ 12-11 ☎ (0191) 232 3606 ⊕ ladygreys.co.uk
Mordue Northumbrian Blonde; guest beers Ⓗ
Close to the historic Theatre Royal and busy shopping areas, this pub, formerly the Adelphi, is a welcome addition to the city-centre real ale scene. Beers are mainly from local brewers Mordue, Hadrian Border, Allendale and Wylam, with guests from all over the country. Food is served all day.
◑▶⊟(Monument)♠

Mile Castle ⊘
Westgate Road, NE1 5XU (corner of Grainger St and Westgate Rd)
✪ 7-midnight (1am Thu-Sat) ☎ (0191) 211 1160
Greene King Abbot; Ruddles Best Bitter; guest beers Ⓗ
Opened in 2009, this Lloyds No.1 bar boasts 20 handpulls across three floors. Impressively redecorated, it has a boothed area for diners on the second floor although meals are served throughout the day and evening to all areas. The name refers to the Roman forts that were built a mile apart and there is one reputed to be situated nearby. Transport links are excellent, with rail and Metro stations nearby and a bus stop outside the front door. ⊶◑▶&⇌(Central)⊟(Central/Monument)⊟♠

New Bridge 🛋
2 Argyle Street, NE1 6PF
✪ 11-11 (11.30 Thu & Fri); 12-10.30 Sun ☎ (0191) 232 1020
Tyne Bank Monument Bitter; guest beers Ⓗ
Just east of Newcastle city centre, well served by buses and the Metro, this pub has no regular beers but offers an ever-changing choice from independent brewers. Although very much a locals' pub, all are warmly welcomed. The pub is next to a business park and faces a large new extension to Northumbria University, so attracts a mixed lunchtime and early evening crowd enjoying the beer and home-made food. ⊛◑⊞⊟(Manors)⊟♠

Newcastle Arms 🛋
57 St Andrew's Street, NE1 5SE (20yds from Chinese Arch at Gallowgate end of Stowell St)
✪ 11-11; 12-10.30 Sun ☎ (0191) 260 2490
⊕ newcastlearms.co.uk
Beer range varies Ⓗ
Hosted by a great licensee, this multi award-winning back-street boozer known locally as the 'Top Arms' boasts more than 160 years of tradition. It holds frequent beer festivals highlighting new, original and innovative microbreweries – a house beer is from Big Lamp, the North East's oldest micro. The single-room pub is next to St James' Park and Chinatown, and gets busy on match days and beer festival opening nights.
Q⊞&⊟(Monument/St James)⊟♠

Town Wall ⊘
Pink Lane, NE1 5HX
✪ 12-midnight (1am Fri & Sat; 11 Sun) ☎ (0191) 232 3000
⊕ thetownwall.com
Beer range varies Ⓗ
The Town Wall is housed within the elegant Bewick House, a Grade II-listed building that was once the home and workplace of the Northumberland artist, naturalist and engraver Thomas Bewick. It is named the Town Wall in recognition of the historic importance of the site, which formed part of the original 24 wards that fortified the old boundaries of the City of Newcastle upon Tyne. Regular ales are from Wylam, Mordue and Allendale, complemented by an excellent range of guest beers. Food is served all day. ◑▶&⇌(Central)⊖♠

Newcastle: Gosforth

County ⊘
High Street, NE3 1HB
✪ 12-11 (10.30 Sun) ☎ (0191) 285 6919
Black Sheep Best Bitter; Caledonian Deuchars IPA; Daleside Blonde; Fuller's London Pride; Wells Bombardier; guest beers Ⓗ
Standing at the southern edge of Gosforth High Street – one of the main roads into the city centre – the County is one of the best-known real ale outlets in Newcastle. Several guest beers are available. The large L-shaped bar attracts a variety of visitors, from office workers to students, and can get very busy, especially at weekends. A separate quiet room at the back offers respite from the hustle and bustle of the main bar, and also doubles as a small function room. ⊛⊟(Regent Centre)P

Job Bulman 🛋 ⊘
St Nicholas Avenue, NE3 1AA
✪ 9am-11.30 ☎ (0191) 223 6230
Greene King Abbot; Ruddles Best Bitter; guest beers Ⓗ
Impressive Wetherspoon conversion of the old post office building just off busy Gosforth High Street. The unusual horseshoe-shaped interior houses a large bar area in the centre, complemented by more discrete dining areas to each side. Up to eight ales are on offer at any one time, including six guest beers, at least two from local microbreweries. A church group and war widows group meet monthly. Food is available from 8am, alcohol from 9am. An outside courtyard caters for smokers. ⊶⊛◑▶⊟(Regent Centre)⊟♠⬏

Queen Victoria 🛋 ⊘
206 High Street, NE3 1HD
✪ 12-11 (midnight Fri); 11-midnight Sat ☎ (0191) 285 8060
⊕ leopardleisure.com/queen_victoria
Mordue Workie Ticket; guest beers Ⓗ
Big pub on the corner of the High Street with a large upper-storey bay window, recently acquired by Leopard Leisure and refurbished to a high standard after a long period of closure. Previously called the Northern Lights and also Ye Olde Jockey, it has now reverted to its original name. Six handpumps serve beers from the Punch list. ◑&⊟(Regent Centre)♠

Newcastle: Heaton

Chillingham 🛋
Chillingham Road, NE6 5XN
✪ 11-11 (midnight Fri & Sat); 12-11 Sun ☎ (0191) 265 5915
Black Sheep Best Bitter; Jarrow Rivet Catcher; Mordue Workie Ticket; guest beers Ⓗ
A large two-roomed pub with contrasting styles – the public bar in traditional dark wood with panelling and a historic mirror recalling the past glories of nearby Wallsend, and the lounge with a contemporary feel, flat-screen sports TVs and

excellent artwork depicting the sights of Newcastle. The upstairs function room hosts live music and comedy nights. Appealing to the widest possible customer base, it offers an excellent choice of local microbrewery beers, as well as a bottled beer, whisky and wine of the month. ⊛⊄⊟⊠(Chillingham Rd)⊟(62, 63)♣♠P

Newcastle: Kenton Bank Foot

Twin Farms
22 Main Road, NE13 8AB
✪ 11-11 (11.30 Fri); 12-10.30 Sun ☎ (0191) 286 1263
Black Sheep Best Bitter; Caledonian Deuchars IPA; guest beers ⊞
Large stone-built former farmhouse standing in its own grounds. Comfortably furnished, it has various areas inside and out to sit and enjoy the extensive selection of beers on offer. The management runs various events for regulars, including brewery visits and Meet the Brewer sessions. The pub aims to reduce food miles and the ingredients used in meals are locally sourced from named suppliers.
⋒Q⤫⊛⊄⊕⊠⊟(Bank Foot)⊟(X77,X78)P

Newcastle: South Gosforth

Brandling Villa
Haddricks Mill Road, NE3 1QL
✪ 12-midnight (10.30 Sun) ☎ (0191) 284 0490
⊕ brandlingvilla.co.uk
Jarrow Rivet Catcher; Wylam Gold Tankard; guest beers ⊞
Now run by an enthusiastic real ale licensee, this established public house has two pleasantly furnished and decorated rooms. Regular beer festivals are held, alongside sausages and pies specially provided by a local butcher. The basement is home to the Ouseburn Valley Brewery.
⋒⊛⊕⊠⊟♠P

Millstone ◉
Haddricks Mill Road, NE3 1QL
✪ 11-11; 12-10.30 Sun ☎ (0191) 285 3429
Draught Bass; guest beers ⊞
Recently refurbished by a new entrepreneurial pub group, this is now a modern, stylish two-roomed pub, with the lounge to the front and a small public bar to the rear. The enthusiastic CAMRA licensee sources beers from local microbreweries as well as national favourites. Bass has been the regulars' top choice for many years. The function room upstairs, also recently renovated, hosts CAMRA events.
⤫⊛⊕⊠P⅃

North Shields

Oddfellows Ⓛ
7 Albion Road, NE30 2RJ
✪ 11 (12 Sun)-11 ☎ (0191) 257 4288
⊕ oddfellowspub.co.uk
Greene King Abbot; Jarrow Bitter; guest beer ⊞
The walls of this small, friendly, single-room lounge bar are covered with historic maps and photographs of pre-war North Shields, which are also shown on a large flat-screen TV and relayed to the outside smoking area. The pub has strong sporting links with past boxing champions and current national darts players, and is home to football and darts teams. It fundraises for charity and holds a beer festival annually in May.
⊛⊕⊠(306)♠⅃

South Shields

Alum Ale House ◉
Ferry Street, NE33 1JR (next to Ferry Landing)
✪ 11-11 (midnight Fri & Sat); 12-11.30 Sun
Banks's Bitter ⊞/℗, **Original; Jennings Cumberland Ale, Cocker Hoop; Marston's Pedigree; Wychwood Hobgoblin** ⊞
The Alum Ale House is situated on the south bank of the River Tyne, adjacent to the Ferry Landing and close to the Market Place. The open-plan bar, with its eight handpumps, is the venue for a fortnightly buskers' night on alternate Thursdays and a lively Irish music session on the first Sunday of the month. In addition to traditional bar games such as dominoes, the pub also hosts a chess club and organises quiz nights. Beers are all from the Marston's stable. ⋒Q⊛⊕⊟♣P⅃

Maltings Ⓛ
Claypath Lane, NE33 4PG (off Westoe Rd)
✪ 12-11.30 (10.30 Sun) ☎ (0191) 427 7147
⊕ jarrowbrewery.co.uk
Jarrow Jarrow Bitter, Isis; guest beers ⊞
The Maltings is located on the first floor of the building, above the Jarrow Brewery. Take the staircase or lift to a partitioned room with a large central bar and plenty of seating. At least two Jarrow beers are always available on handpull, complemented by a selection of guest beers and an excellent range of imported ales. Food is available daily. Q⊕⊠⊟⅃

Steamboat ◉
Coronation Street, Mill Dam, NE33 1EQ (follow signs for Customs House)
✪ 12-11 (midnight Thu-Sat; 11.30 Sun) ☎ (0191) 454 0134
Beer range varies ⊞
Offering an impressive range of beers from independent and microbrewers on eight handpumps plus a real cider, the Steamboat has won CAMRA Pub of the Year for the past three years. A pub full of character and atmosphere, run by friendly staff, it has a large bar with a raised seating area and a small lounge. The South Shields ferry and Custom House theatre are nearby. Beer festivals, cheese and ale and Meet the Brewer nights are arranged on a regular basis. ⊠⊟♣♠

Trimmers Arms Ⓛ
34 Commercial Road, NE33 1RW
✪ 12-11.30 (1am Fri-Sun) ☎ (0191) 597 9023
Beer range varies ⊞
In 2004, rising from the ashes of the West End Vaults and the earlier Trimmers Arms, came the new and partly rebuilt pub of the same name. It has a large bar and a raised lounge with an area for live music at the weekend. Five handpulls provide a constantly changing range of guest beers, plus a real cider. A separate restaurant room opens on Sunday afternoon with a carvery.
⊕⊠(Chichester)⊟♠

Wouldhave Ⓛ ◉
16 Mile End Road, NE33 1TA
✪ 9am-midnight ☎ (0191) 427 6014
Greene King Abbot; Ruddles Best Bitter; guest beers ⊞
Wetherspoon pub named after the 18th-century boat builder William Wouldhave, who was co-inventor of the self-righting lifeboat. Set on two floors, the ground floor has a long bar featuring six handpulls for four guests and two regular ales.

Cider is also available. More seating can be found upstairs. Old photographs of South Shields decorate the walls. Occasional beer festivals are held during the year and CAMRA members receive a discount.
◑⑆🅿🚌🚏🖐

Sunderland

Avenue 🅛
26 Zetland Street, Roker, SR6 0EQ (just off Roker Avenue)
🕒 12 (11 Sun)-11; 11-midnight Fri & Sat ☎ (0191) 567 7412
Beer range varies 🅗
Just a short walk from the Stadium of Light, this local pub hosts various themed nights throughout the week including music, bingo, football and a popular Thursday night quiz, often followed by a live band. The bar area has a pool table and there is a full-size snooker table and two dartboards in the upstairs games room. A function room provides extra space during busier periods and is available to hire.
🏮🚋(St Peters/Stadium of Light)🚌(E1,E6)♣🅿⤙

Fitzgerald's 🏆 🅛
10-12 Green Terrace, SR1 3PZ
🕒 11-11 (midnight Fri & Sat); 12-10.30 Sun
☎ (0191) 567 0852
Fyne Jarl; Jarrow Rivet Catcher 🅗
One of Sunderland's largest range of cask beers can be found at this busy city-centre pub run by the real-ale-friendly Sir John Fitzgerald group. There are two separate rooms, with the smaller Chart Room quieter than the main bar. The pub is an enthusiastic supporter of North-East microbreweries, with eight guest beers usually on offer. CAMRA members receive a discount on ale. Quizzes are held on Tuesday and Thursday.
🏮◑🚉🚋(University)🚌🖐⤙

Harbour View 🅛
Benedict Road, Roker, SR6 0NU
🕒 10.30-11.30 (midnight Fri & Sat) ☎ (0191) 567 1402
Caledonian Deuchars IPA; Taylor Landlord 🅗
A modern, open plan bar with good views of the River Wear and the sea. It offers two regular ales as well as a good choice of four guests. Quiet during the week, the pub is livelier at weekends – match days are best avoided if you like a peaceful pint as it can get hectic. 🏮⑆🚌(E1,18,19)⤙

Isis 🅛
26 Silksworth Row, SR1 3QJ
🕒 12-11.30 ☎ (0191) 514 7684 🌐 jarrowbrewery.co.uk
Beer range varies 🅗
Closed for two years, Jarrow Brewery has reopened and refurbished this pub, revealing the long-lost Victorian interior. A long and narrow wood, chrome and glass bar holds 12 handpulls serving three changing Jarrow beers and six guests, plus two ciders and a perry. The lounge is off to the side of the bar. The interior features wood panels and old black and white photographs on the walls. Candles on the tables help to create an atmospheric mood.
🛏⑆🚉🚋(University)🚌(10,11)🖐

King's Arms 🅛
Beach Street, Deptford, SR4 6BU
🕒 12-11 (midnight Fri & Sat; 10.30 Sun) ☎ (0191) 567 9804
🌐 threehorseshoesleamside.co.uk/kings_arms
Taylor Landlord; guest beers 🅗
A traditional wood-panel and bare-boards pub with a large main room and a small snug. One of

Sunderland's oldest establishments, dating from 1834, it is adjacent to the industrial area of Deptford, nestling next to the River Wear. Seven guest beers from microbreweries are usually available. There are regular small beer festivals and live music/barbecues held in the marquee. Light snacks are available all day. A former CAMRA Local Pub of the Year and North East award winner.
🏕🏮🚋(Millfield)🚌(10,11)🖐⤙

Museum Vaults 🅛
33 Silksworth Row, Millfield, SR1 3QJ
🕒 12-11 (3 Tue; midnight Thu-Sat; 10.30 Sun)
☎ (0191) 565 9443
Beer range varies 🅗
Two blazing open fires welcome you to this small, friendly hostelry, managed by the same family for more than 30 years. This former Vaux pub has a long connection to both the brewery and the local football team, with numerous pieces of memorabilia adorning the walls. Three handpulled beers are available, one always from Maxim Brewery, the others alternating between local and national microbrews. A selection of bottle-conditioned beers is also stocked, often from Durham Brewery.
🏕🏮🚋(University)🚌(10,11)🖐🅿⤙

Railway Tavern 🅛
1 Westbury Street, Millfield, SR4 6EF (corner with Hylton Rd)
🕒 10 (11 Sun)-midnight ☎ (0191) 565 1411
Beer range varies 🅗
Traditional street-corner local with a compact public bar at the front and a larger games room to the rear. One handpump dispenses beer from either Bull Lane Brewery or, occasionally, Maxim Brewery. Railway-themed artefacts decorate the walls and windows. 🚋(Millfield)🚌(10,20)

TJ Doyles 🅛
Hanover Place, Deptford, SR4 6BY
🕒 4-11; 12-midnight Sat & Sun ☎ (0191) 510 1554
🌐 tjdoyles.com
Beer range varies 🅗
A friendly welcome awaits you in this authentic Irish pub. Six handpulls offer a range of local beers from Bull Lane, Maxim and Jarrow, as well as national ales. Memorabilia celebrating Gaelic and local sports and Irish culture adorn the walls. Live music features throughout the week, and if any Irish national team is playing you can be sure the game will be showing here. There is a smoking area and decked beer garden to the rear of the pub. 🏮🍴🚉🚋(11,36A/C)🖐🅿⤙

William Jameson 🅛 ✅
30-32 Fawcett Street, SR1 1RH
🕒 8am-midnight ☎ (0191) 514 5016
Greene King Abbot; Ruddles Best Bitter 🅗
Sunderland's first JD Wetherspoon is in a former department store under the City Library and Arts Centre and opposite the Winter Gardens. All the usual features associated with the chain can be found is this busy pub at the heart of the city centre. Twelve handpumps offer up to four guest beers to complement the regular range. The pub is a keen supporter of local brewers. ◑⑆🚉🚌🚏

Wolsey
40 Millum Terrace, Roker, SR6 0ES
🕒 12-11 (midnight Fri & Sat) ☎ (0191) 514 0389
🌐 thewolsey.co.uk

Beer range varies Ⓗ
The exterior of this traditional pub has been recently redecorated and given a modern sign. Inside there is a log-burning fire, pool table, big screen and TVs. A free quiz is hosted on Thursday night, karaoke on Friday and live music on Saturday. Food is served until 7pm (4pm Sun). The atmosphere is friendly and welcoming, and the regulars are happy to recommend a beer.
Q(E1)P

Swalwell

Sun Inn ✔

Market Lane, NE16 3AL (just off roundabout at end of Front St)
11-midnight; 12-11 Sun
Brakspear Oxford Gold; Jennings Cocker Hoop; Ringwood Boondoggle Ⓗ
No-nonsense, welcoming, community pub situated in the heart of the historic village that spawned many internationally renowned engineers and industrialists, and of course the famous Swalwell cabbage. It has been providing good company for locals and strangers alike for more than 100 years. Sword dancers, darts, dominoes, a monthly pie competition and buskers' nights all feature. The enthusiastic licensees have increased the handpulls from one to four, and real cider is also on draught. Bar food and snacks are available, free on Sundays.

Tynemouth

Cumberland Arms ✔

17 Front Street, NE30 4DX
12-11 (10.30 Sun) ☎ (0191) 257 1820
cumberlandarms.co.uk
Courage Directors; Jennings Cumberland Ale; Tetley Bitter; guest beers Ⓗ
Cosy, split-level pub with friendly bar staff. Families are welcome in the dining area at the rear which serves good-value meals. Disabled access is via the front to the lower bar; a side alley gives access to the upper bar. Beer is dispensed in both rooms from a cabinet with six handpulls. Attractive stained-glass windows and historic artefacts feature throughout. Wednesday is grill night and Thursday curry night. With three guest ales complementing the regular beers, the pub is popular with CAMRA members.
(Tynemouth)(306)

Turk's Head ✔

41 Front Street, NE30 4DZ
11-11 (11.30 Thu-Sat); 12-11.30 Sun ☎ (0191) 257 6547
Caledonian Deuchars IPA; Courage Directors; Wells Bombardier; guest beers Ⓗ
Popular main-street pub with two linked rooms – the front bar tends to be more lively and the rear room much quieter, welcoming families up to 7pm. TVs throughout screen live sport. An interesting pub architecturally, it has a white tiled exterior and stained-glass windows; the interior contains Willie, the famous stuffed dog. A wide range of seating and wooden floors add character.
(306)

Tynemouth Lodge Hotel

Tynemouth Road, NE30 4AA
11-11; 12-10.30 Sun ☎ (0191) 257 7565
tynemouthlodgehotel.co.uk
Caledonian Deuchars IPA; Draught Bass; Sharp's Doom Bar; guest beer Ⓗ
This attractive externally tiled free house was built in 1799 and has featured in every issue of the Guide since 1983 when the current owner took over – he is now approaching his 30th anniversary. The comfortable U-shaped lounge with the bar on one side and hatch on the other is noted in the area for reputedly selling the highest volume of Draught Bass on Tyneside. Three regular ales and one guest are usually available. The pub is next to Northumberland Park and near the Coast-to-Coast cycle route. Q(1)P

Washington

Courtyard Ⓛ

Arts Centre, Biddick Lane, Fatfield, NE38 8AB
11-11 (midnight Fri & Sat); 12-11 Sun ☎ (0191) 417 0445
artscentrewashington.co.uk/courtyard.aspx
Taylor Landlord; guest beers Ⓗ
Located within the lively arts centre, this light and airy café/bar offers a warm welcome to drinkers and food lovers alike. Eight handpumped beers, one real cider, one perry and a range of bottled Belgian beers are available. An extensive range of food is served throughout the day, with early evening specials. The pub hosts a weekly quiz and buskers' nights. Outdoor seating is within the spacious courtyard. Two popular beer festivals are held annually, on the Easter and August bank holidays. Q(M1)P

Sir William de Wessyngton Ⓛ ✔

2-3 Victoria Road, Concord, NE37 2SY (opp bus station)
8am-11 ☎ (0191) 418 0100
Greene King Abbot; Ruddles Best Bitter; guest beers Ⓗ
Large open-plan Wetherspoon pub housed in a former snooker hall and ice cream parlour. It is named after a Norman knight and lord of the manor whose descendants later emigrated to the United States. A real ale oasis, it is the only cask beer outlet in Concord and offers value-for-money beer and the usual well-priced Wetherspoon menu. The regular ales are complemented by up to four guests, and occasional beer festivals are held.
Q

West Boldon

Black Horse

Rectory Bank, NE36 0QQ (off A184)
11-11; 12-11.30 Sun ☎ (0191) 536 1814
blackhorsewestboldon.co.uk
Jennings Cumberland Ale; guest beer Ⓗ
An old-fashioned pub with unusual bric-a-brac adorning the walls and candles on the tables. The photographs on display are by the talented chef, and prints are available for sale. It has one small L-shaped bar and, with a popular restaurant serving high-quality food, can get busy evenings and weekends. Live music features on Sunday night.
P

West Herrington

Stables

McLaren Way, DH4 4ND (off B1286)
12-11 (midnight Fri & Sat) ☎ (0191) 584 9226
Black Sheep Best Bitter; Taylor Landlord; guest beer Ⓗ

Located just off the main road, at first sight this pub looks like a private dwelling, as there is no pub sign. The small beer garden leads to a converted stable block, with low ceilings, flagstone floor and welcoming peat fire in winter. The main area is open plan, with a cosy snug behind the bar. Three ales are offered, including one changing guest. Quality food is served until 3pm and dogs are welcome. ⚛Q✿◐♿⏍(35)P

West Monkseaton

Beacon Hotel ✅
Earsdon Road, NE25 9PT
✪ 11.30-11 (midnight Fri & Sat) ☎ (0191) 253 6911
Caledonian Deuchars IPA; guest beers Ⓗ
Superb modern pub set back from the main road, popular with locals. The cellar has been updated to dispense beer at the correct temperature. Try the rack of ale – a wooden rack that holds three third-of-a-pint glasses of the customer's choice. Excellent food is available at reasonable prices, with themed nights Monday to Thursday and chef's specials on Friday and Saturday. Quiz nights are Sunday and Wednesday. Children over 14 are welcome with an adult. Cask ale prices are reduced on Monday nights. ⚛Q✿◐♿⏍P

Whitley Bay

Briar Dene
71 The Links, NE26 1UE
✪ 11-11; 12-10.30 Sun ☎ (0191) 252 0926
Black Sheep Best Bitter; guest beers Ⓗ
Fitzgerald's pub with a large, attractive lounge with sea views to the links and St Mary's Lighthouse, and a more compact rear bar with wide-screen TV, pool and darts. The pub is well known for its food, with local fish and chips a speciality. Guest beers change regularly. Children are welcome in a family area in the lounge, and there is seating outside at the front of the pub. The Tuesday quiz is especially popular. Q✿✿◐♿⏍(308,309)♣🐾P

Rockcliffe Arms
Algernon Place, NE26 2DT
✪ 11-11 (11.15 Fri & Sat); 12-11 Sun ☎ (0191) 253 1299
Beer range varies Ⓗ
Outstanding back-street Fitzgerald's pub, a few minutes' walk from the Metro station. This one-room establishment has distinct bar and lounge areas with a snug in between. There are four constantly changing guest beers, with details written on notices above the dividing arch. Regular darts and dominoes matches are held in the snug. ✿⏍♣🍺

Bodega, Newcastle: City Centre (Photo: Cat Button)

WARWICKSHIRE

STAFFORDSHIRE

Polesworth
10
Grendon
Atherstone
A5

LEICESTERSHIRE & RUTLAND

Nether Whitacre
9
Ridge Lane
Hartshill
Shustoke
8
Ansley
Nuneaton

WEST MIDLANDS

M6
4
Corley Moor
2
Monks Kirby
Willey

A444
A5
M1
M6
1

Rugby

M42
3
3A
16
Rowington
Kenilworth
Bubbenhall
A452
A46
A45

A4177
M40
Warwick
Cubbington
Long Itchington

Henley-in-Arden
Studley
Great Alne
Alcester
A4189
A3400
A46
15
14
13
Leamington Spa
12
Harbury

Hampton Lucy
Wellesbourne

Stratford-upon-Avon
A429
A422
M40

NORTHANTS

WORCS

A44
A422

Stretton-on-Fosse
GLOUCS & BRISTOL
Whichford
OXFORDSHIRE

0 Miles 5
0 Kilometres 8

Alcester

Holly Bush

37 Henley Street, B49 5QX (behind church and town hall)

☼ 12-11 ☎ (01789) 762482 ⊕ thehollybushalcester.co.uk

Black Sheep Best Bitter; Hobsons Town Crier; Purity Pure Gold; Sharp's Doom Bar; guest beers ⑭

A frequent CAMRA Branch Pub of the Year, this is a traditional 17th-century local in a historic market town. Restoration has preserved its five rooms and many original features within the pub. There is also a function room and a pretty walled garden at the rear. Four regular ales and up to four guests are available and beer festivals are held in June and October. It has both traditional English and à la carte menus (no food Sun eve). Regular folk sessions are held monthly and spontaneous music may strike up at any time. White Hart Morris Men practise here on Monday evenings.

ⓜ✿⓪⑤❺⊜⊟(26,246,247)♣⌐

Three Tuns

34 High Street, B49 5AB (next to post office)

☼ 12-2, 5.30 (6 Mon & Tue)-11; 12-11 Sat & Sun

☎ (01789) 762626

Hobsons Best Bitter; guest beers ⑭

A must visit, this local CAMRA award-winning pub has no music, no pool and no food – just how a real pub should be. Inside there is a single room with low beams, stone-flagged floor and an exposed area of wattle and daub. Up to seven ales from micros and independents provide a permanent yet ever-changing mini beer festival.

Q⊟(26,246,247)♣

Turk's Head

4 High Street, B49 5AD (near church)

☼ 12-11 ☎ (01789) 765948 ⊕ theturkshead.net

Wye Valley Bitter, HPA; guest beers ⑭

A central location makes this a popular place. The publican is a cask enthusiast and sources beers as

473

locally as possible. There are four regular handpulls plus a good range of changing bottled beers – the most requested making it to draught on occasion. Beer festivals are staged during the summer months. The interior is divided into two rooms with real fires, and good traditional pub food is available (booking advised). A regular quiz and open mic night are hosted. ⚠️🅿️🍴◑🚭🚪🚌(26,246,247)⌐

Ansley

Lord Nelson Inn
Birmingham Road, CV10 9PQ
🕐 12-11 (10.30 Sun) ☎ (024) 7639 2305
⊕ thelordnelsoninnansley.co.uk
Beer range varies Ⓗ

Warwickshire CAMRA Pub of the Year 2011, this is a family-friendly establishment with plenty to offer. Nautically themed throughout, the restaurant serves a wide range of food with week-night promotions. Four ales are usually on tap including two sourced from local breweries, especially Church End and Tunnel, with beer from the Sperring brewery behind the pub regularly available. Outside is a pleasant enclosed paved area that hosts real ale and cider festivals accompanied by a barbecue. 🅿️◑🚭🚌🅿️⌐

Atherstone

New Dolphin Inn ♈
162 Long Street, CV9 1AE
🕐 6 (12 Fri-Sun)-midnight ☎ (01827) 713167
Beer range varies Ⓗ

Comfortable, friendly town pub that excels itself with its choice of interesting ales. Free of tie, at least two keenly priced beers are the norm, usually from favourite micros of the West Midlands. Blythe and Beowulf ales feature frequently. The pub is host to a darts and dominoes team, and also features a pool table. Dogs are welcome. A part-grassed suntrap beer garden offers a quiet summer retreat. Closed Monday-Thursday lunchtimes, but will open for booked groups. 🅿️🚭🚌(48,765)♣⌐

Bubbenhall

Malt Shovel Ⓛ
Lower End, CV8 3BW SP362725
🕐 12-11 ☎ (024) 7630 1141
⊕ themaltshovelbubbenhall.co.uk
Hook Norton Hooky Bitter; Wells Bombardier; guest beers Ⓗ

Friendly village free house in a 17th-century Grade II-listed building comprising a large L-shaped lounge bar at the front and a small public bar to the rear. Outside is a small front patio and behind the spacious car park lies a large walled garden and adjacent bowling green, with woods available in the summer. Home-cooked food is served including daily specials. At least one of the two guest beers is usually local, frequently from Church End. Convenient for Ryton Pools Country Park. Q🅿️◑🚭🚶🚌(539)♣🅿️⌐

Corley Moor

Bull & Butcher ♈ ✅
Common Lane, CV7 8AQ SP279850
🕐 10-midnight (1am Fri & Sat; 11 Sun) ☎ (01676) 540241
Draught Bass; Greene King Abbot; M&B Brew XI; guest beer Ⓗ

This pub successfully manages to retain a traditional village public bar while running a busy restaurant at the rear. The front entrance leads to an old-fashioned wood-beamed flagstone bar with a couple of completely unspoilt cosy snugs. A separate restaurant entrance leads to a comfortable dining area serving good-value locally sourced food. Outside is a wonderful display of hanging baskets. The large garden is filled with play equipment. ⚠️Q🅿️◑🚭🚶🅿️⌐

Cubbington

King's Head
2 Church Hill, CV32 7JY (E end of village next to church)
🕐 12-midnight ☎ (01926) 887142
Flowers IPA; Greene King Abbot; Hobsons Mild; Wells Bombardier; Wye Valley HPA Ⓗ

Attractive village pub dating to the 1890s in the shadow of the church. It comprises two old cottages with varying roof lines, now knocked together and painted white. Inside, a number of distinct drinking areas reflect the original old rooms. The large games area was once the garage. The pub is popular with ramblers and sports teams who raise funds for deserving causes. A mixed clientele gives a nice feel to this hostelry. A few tables are on the pavement outside. 🅿️◑🚌(68)♣

Hampton Lucy

Boar's Head Ⓛ
Church Street, CV35 8BE
🕐 12-10; 11.30-11.30 Fri & Sat summer; 11.30-3, 5-10.30 (11.30 Fri); 11.30-11.30 Sat; 12-7 Sun winter
☎ (01789) 840533
Greene King IPA; guest beers Ⓗ

Friendly, comfortable village pub dating back to the 17th century, with five to seven real ales on offer, always at least one LocAle. The menu offers fresh, home-made food with daily specials, including locally sourced rare meats such as pheasant and squirrel (no food Sun eve). Tapas and afternoon teas are also available. Outside is a walled garden. An annual themed beer festival is held at Easter. Shakespeare CAMRA Pub of the Year 2009/ 10 and Warwickshire County Champion Pub of the Year 2010. ⚠️Q🅿️◑🚭🚌🅿️⌐

Harbury

Old New Inn
Farm Sreet, CV33 9LS (SW of village)
🕐 3.30 (12 Fri & Sat)-midnight; 12-11 Sun ☎ (01926) 614023

Beer range varies Ⓗ
Fine stone-built pub on the edge of the village with a splendid family-friendly garden at the rear. Inside, the two rooms have low ceilings reflecting the age of the building. The beer range changes regularly, with a county brewery usually represented. Sport is popular here and the TV shows major fixtures. Pub teams are well supported – darts, dominoes and pool are all played. ⛽🚌🏵️🅿️Ⓗ🅗♿🅐🚌(64A,65,66)♣🅿️⬥

Hartshill

Malt Shovel
39 Grange Road, CV10 0SS
✪ 12-11.30 ☎ (024) 7639 2501
Banks's Mild, Bitter; Marston's Pedigree; guest beer Ⓗ
Ideally situated for country walks, both in Hartshill Hayes Country Park and along the Coventry Canal, this pub is well known for its value-for-money meals, both in the day and evening. The main bar shows sporting fixtures on screen and there is a separate restaurant. The garden has seating and a play area for children. ⛽🏵️🅒🅓🅗🚌(48,765)🅿️⬥

Henley-in-Arden

Black Swan ✅
23 High Street, B95 5AA SP15106640
✪ 12-11 (midnight Fri & Sat) ☎ (01564) 795338
Batemans XB; Sharp's Doom Bar; guest beer Ⓗ
Friendly pub on a classic high street in a lovely old market town. Children and dogs are welcome. Traditional pub games include dominoes, crib and darts. Karaoke features every Friday and a quiz every Thursday. An open mic night is hosted on the first Wednesday of the month and occasional live music. No food is available on Sunday and Monday evenings. ⛽🏵️🅒🅗🅓♿🚌(X20)♣♣🅿️⬥

Kenilworth

Clarendon Arms 🄻
44 Castle Hill, CV8 1NB
✪ 11.30-3, 5.30-11.30; 11.30-12.30am Fri & Sat; 12-11.30 Sun ☎ (01926) 852017 ⊕ clarendonarmspub.co.uk
Wye Valley Butty Bach; guest beers Ⓗ
Multi-roomed restaurant and bar opposite Kenilworth Castle warmed by a log-burning stove in winter. In addition to the regular beer there is a frequently changing selection of guests from Church End, Purity, Slaughterhouse, Hook Norton and Warwickshire. An excellent range of food is available all day. TV screens show Six Nations and World Cup games. There is a function room upstairs and a paved patio outside with tables and umbrellas. On-street parking is limited but there is an adjacent Pay & Display car park. ⛽🏵️🅒🅓⬥

Old Bakery
12 High Street, CV8 1LZ (near A429/A452 jct)
✪ 5.30 (5 Fri & Sat)-11; 5-10.30 Sun ☎ (01926) 864111
⊕ theoldbakery.eu
St Austell Trelawny; Wye Valley Bitter, HPA; guest beer Ⓗ
Open evenings only, this pleasant two-roomed bar is in an old town hotel near Abbey Fields. It offers a convivial atmosphere and mainly mature clientele. One guest handpump often features Midlands independents such as Hobsons, Purity or Church End. The Wye Valley Bitter is sold as Old Bakery

Bitter. Monday is fish and chips night (until 7.30pm). Disabled access is via the rear car park and small patio area. Roadside parking is limited. Four en-suite bedrooms are available.
Q🏵️🅔🅓♿🅗🚌(12)🅿️

Royal Oak ✅
New Street, CV8 2EZ (250yds from A429/A452 jct)
✪ 4 (12 Sat)-11; 12-10.30 Sun ☎ (01926) 856906
Adnams Southwold Bitter; Black Sheep Ale; Castle Rock Harvest Pale; guest beer Ⓗ
Situated close to the crossroads at the heart of old Kenilworth, the Grade II-listed Royal Oak is one of the town's few remaining traditional pubs. The atmosphere is convivial and welcoming and the clientele diverse. This community-spirited pub is home to two darts teams, pool and poker leagues and a chess club. Twice-monthly live acoustic music is hosted on Sundays. There is a patio and garden to the rear. The number 12 bus between Coventry and Leamington stops right outside the door.
🏵️🚌(12)♣⬥

Wyandotte Inn
Park Road, CV8 2GF (jct of Park Rd and Stoneleigh Rd)
✪ 11.30-midnight ☎ (07827) 017470
Jennings Cocker Hoop; guest beer Ⓗ
The pub is named after a tribe of Native Americans. It was originally a home-brew pub built in 1868, and remained in the same family for many years, but it is now a Marston's tied house and the guest beers come from the Marston's stable. Thatchers cider is also available. A community pub, it screens sporting events on TV, and live music and DJs often feature. A well-known landmark for many bus routes. ⛽🏵️🚌(16,X17)♣🅿️⬥

Leamington Spa

Benjamin Satchwell ✅
112/114 The Parade, CV32 4AQ (opp town hall)
SP318658
✪ 7-midnight (1am Fri & Sat) ☎ (01926) 883733
Greene King Abbot; Ruddles Best Bitter; guest beers Ⓗ
The Benjamin Satchwell, named after a former Leamington benefactor, bears all the hallmarks of typical Wetherspoon style. (The real Benjamin Satchwell discovered Leamington's second spring in 1784.) Converted from two shops, the pub is large, stretching back to Bedford Street, with an impressively long bar on the upper level and comfortable seating areas. On the walls are panels depicting the history of Leamington and its benefactors. It's a rare real cider outlet for town. Q🅓♿🅗🚌♣

Jug & Jester ✅
11/13 Bath Street, CV31 3AF
✪ 8am-midnight (1am Fri & Sat) ☎ (01926) 331820
Greene King Abbot; Ruddles Best Bitter; guest beers Ⓗ
Converted by Wetherspoon in late 2009 from a pub of the same name, this building was originally Leamington's Theatre Royal. It is situated in Old Town only a short distance from the railway station and the Grand Union Canal. The pub comprises four areas, with the serving bar split between two rooms. Guest ales are varied but expect offerings from Sadler's and Warwickshire. The real cider alternates between Westons Marcle Hill and Gwynt Y Ddraig Black Dragon. ⛽Q🚌🏵️🅒🅓♿🅗🚌♣

Somerville Arms 🍺 ✅
4 Campion Terrace, CV32 4SX
🕐 12-2, 5.30-11; 12-11 Sat & Sun ☎ (01926) 426746
🌐 somervillearms.co.uk
Adnams Southwold Bitter, Broadside; Everards Beacon Bitter, Sunchaser Blonde, Tiger, Original; guest beer Ⓗ

An excellent Victorian local situated on a street corner in a pleasant suburb of north-east Leamington. The 'Ville' has benefited from a subtle and sympathetic refurbishment by Everards, retaining a simple bar room and a small comfortable snug. The wooden bar sports a fine set of seven matching handpumps. A popular community venue, regular open music nights are well supported. The courtyard has won awards for its flowers. Local CAMRA Pub of the Year 2011. 🏚Q❀🖰🖵(67)♣🐾⌐

Talbot Inn
34 Rushmore Street, CV31 1JA
🕐 12-11 (midnight Fri & Sat) ☎ (01926) 428883
Oakham Citra; Wye Valley HPA, Butty Bach; guest beers Ⓗ

Friendly free house standing at the end of a Victorian terrace between St Mary's and Clapham Terrace canal bridges. The converted Victorian building is notable for the large mural painted on the side near the Grand Union canal. The pub is popular with locals, canal users and walkers. Changing guest ales augment the three regular beers, and a draught cider is always available. The pub is still referred to as Hector's House after a previous landlord. Q❀🐱🖰⇋🖵♣🐾⌐

Woodland Tavern Ⓛ
3 Regent Street, CV32 5HW
🕐 12-midnight (1am Fri & Sat; 11.30 Sun) ☎ (01926) 425868
Slaughterhouse Saddleback Best Bitter; Wychwood Hobgoblin; guest beer Ⓗ

A traditional Victorian street-corner drinkers' pub, handy for the town centre, with a separate lounge and public bar. The friendly mixed clientele and the cosy rooms produce a lively atmosphere. Murals featuring local events and jokes decorate the walls. There is a small walled beer garden, partly sheltered in the old covered entrance. The only regular outlet for Slaughterhouse beer in Leamington Spa. ❀🐱🖰⇋🖵♣⌐

Long Itchington

Green Man ✅
Church Road, CV47 9PW
🕐 5-11 (midnight Fri); 12-midnight Sat; 12-10.30 Sun
☎ (01926) 812208 🌐 greenmanlongitchington.co.uk
Black Sheep Best Bitter; Fuller's London Pride; St Austell Tribute; guest beer Ⓗ

Parts of this fine country inn date back to the early 1700s, notably the original beams and low ceilings. The building has a number of linked drinking areas and a function room. It is home to several pub teams and hosts an annual beer festival in May. There are benches on the front courtyard and a good-sized garden. The landlord is rumoured to be so passionate about real ale that he sings to his beer each morning to help it condition. 🏚Q🐂🐱🖰🖰🐾🅰🖵(64)♣🐾P

Harvester Ⓛ
6 Church Road, CV47 9PE (off A423 at village pond, then first left)

🕐 12-2.30, 6-11; 12-3, 7-10.30 Sun ☎ (01926) 812698
🌐 theharvesterinn.co.uk
Hook Norton Hooky Bitter; guest beers Ⓗ

Friendly village local situated on the corner of a small village square. The unassuming building has two drinking areas and a separate restaurant serving good-value and popular food, with steaks a speciality. The pub participates in the annual village May bank holiday beer festival and sold 50 different beers last year alone. Look out for the rare Budvar Dark, and often a hard-to-find Belgian beer on draught. Local pickles are on sale. Free Wi-Fi available. Q🍷🖰🅰🖵(64)P

Monks Kirby

Denbigh Arms
Main Street, CV23 0QX
🕐 5.30-11.30; 11.30-midnight Fri & Sat; 12-11 Sun
☎ (01788) 832303
Brains SA, The Rev James; Copper Dragon Best Bitter; Sharp's Doom Bar; Taylor Landlord; Wood Farm Victorious; guest beers Ⓗ

The landlord is a cask ale enthusiast and tries to include one local ale among the range on offer. This welcoming multi-roomed village pub is renowned for its home-cooked food – Sunday lunch is a must. Traditional pub games include table skittles and darts. Summer beer festivals with live music are held in the outbuildings. Alfresco drinking and a small garden for summer days make this a shining example of how a village pub should be run. 🏚Q❀🐱🖰🖵♣🐾P⌐

Nether Whitacre

Dog Inn ✅
Dog Lane, B46 2DU SP232930
🕐 12-3, 6-11; 12-11 Sat & Sun ☎ (01675) 481318
Marston's Pedigree; guest beers Ⓗ

Well-hidden black and white rural pub with a peaceful beer garden. The marvellously elaborate carved frontage to the bar, including two pairs of stuffed jays, came from the local Whitacre Hall. Brass knick-knacks abound, and the bar features a church pew for seating and two overly snug sofas. There are two cosy, intimate dining rooms to the side. Between two and four rotating guest beers are served, some sourced from local breweries. Complimentary bar nibbles are available on Sunday lunchtimes. 🏚❀🖰P

Gate Inn
Gate Lane, B46 2DS
🕐 12-11 (10.30 Sun) ☎ (01675) 481292 🌐 thegateinn.com
Banks's Mild, Bitter; Jennings Cumberland Ale; Marston's Pedigree; Ringwood Fortyniner; guest beer Ⓗ

Convivial community local with a variety of rooms, ales and food, topped off with a warm welcome. Diners tend to favour the conservatory and large lounge while drinkers gravitate to the quarry-tiled bar. Both main rooms feature wood-burning stoves. The pool table is in a small separate room. The guest ale is from the Marston's portfolio. To the rear is a large, child-friendly garden, plus a separate beer garden for adults. Local eggs are sold at the bar. ❀🖰🖵♣🐾P⌐

Nuneaton

Crown

10 Bond Street, CV11 4BX (between rail and bus stations)

🌑 12-11 (midnight Fri & Sat) ☎ (024) 7637 3343

Oakham Bishops Farewell; guest beers Ⓗ

This Guide regular boasts 10 handpulls for eight real ales and two ciders. It also offers a large selection of malt whiskies and a variety of foreign bottled beers. Live bands play on Saturday nights. A function room is available for hire, and there is a large garden at the rear. Beer festivals are held in June and December. Food is only available 4-9pm Friday, 12-6pm Saturday and a popular Sunday lunch 12-4pm. ♨🏠🅮🍴≉🚃🅿🏃

Felix Holt ⊘

3 Stratford Street, CV11 5BS

🌑 8am-midnight (1am Fri & Sat) ☎ (024) 7634 7785

Greene King Abbot; Ruddles Best Bitter; Thornbridge Jaipur IPA; guest beers Ⓗ

Large Wetherspoon outlet in the town centre. The pub takes its name from the novel by local author George Eliot, and its decor continues in a literary theme with two walls covered in old books and pictures of local history. An interesting range of six guest ales is offered alongside the regular beers. The pub is family friendly with children allowed until 8pm and food service 8am to 10pm. There is a heated area for smokers. Q🅮👶≉🏃

Horseshoes Ⓛ

2 Heath End Road, CV10 7JQ

🌑 12-11 (1am Fri & Sat) ☎ (024) 7767 5066

⊕ thehorseshoesbrewerytap.co.uk

Everards Tiger; Tunnel Late Ott, Trade Winds, Nelson's Column; guest beers Ⓗ

Refurbished traditional Edwardian-style English pub with two coal fires and a welcoming ambience. Ten handpulled ales and a varied selection of bottled beer are on offer here as well as regular beer festivals held in the garden. Live music and weekly quiz nights also feature. Excellent home-cooked food includes speciality cuisine evenings and a popular Sunday carvery. The snug is available for private functions. This is a family-friendly pub close to the Coventry Canal and a welcome addition to the local real ale scene. ♨Q🅮🍴👶🚃🐕🅿🏃

Royal Oak ⊘

The Square, CV11 4JY

🌑 12 (4.30 Mon-Thu winter)-midnight; 12-11 Sun

☎ (024) 7638 3613

Draught Bass; Morland Old Speckled Hen; guest beers Ⓗ

The Royal Oak continues to retain a village inn feel due to the main road bypassing the old village, leaving it unchanged. Popular with locals, the red-tiled public bar area is usually lively with conversation. The lounge is accessed by a passage and steps and is the venue for social events and quiz nights. Lounge service is via a hatch to the bar where there are six handpulls. Seasonal beer festivals are held in the garden, which has a pleasant seating area. ♨🏠🚃🏃

Polesworth

Bull's Head

Tamworth Road, B78 1JH (by canal bridge on westbound B5000)

🌑 11-midnight (11 Sun) ☎ 07796 538415

Marston's Pedigree; guest beer Ⓗ

Unpretentious canalside boozer with a feel of the 1960s. The L-shaped bar is usually busy, with conversation drowning out the camel music. Football on the TV sometimes dominates. A pair of arches segregates the quieter lounge. The guest ale is generally from an interesting micro. The pub is home to many games teams including cribbage and bowls. Feeling peckish? Eat in the independent Indian restaurant upstairs and they will fetch ale for you from downstairs. 🚆🚃(765,785)🐕🅿

Ridge Lane

Church End Brewery Tap

CV10 0RD (2 miles SW of Atherstone) SP295947

🌑 closed Mon-Wed; 12 (6 Thu)-11; 12-10.30 Sun

☎ (01827) 713080 ⊕ churchendbrewery.co.uk

Beer range varies Ⓗ/Ⓖ

Long-standing brewery tap, offering at least eight beers from the adjoining Church End Brewery, visible through a large glass panel. First time visitors may wish to try a 'coffin' of third-of-a-pint tasters. A range of Belgian bottled beers is also available plus a mild and at least one real cider. Dogs are welcome inside but children and smokers are relegated to the extensive rural beer garden. Customers are welcome to bring their own food. Q🅮👶⛺🐕🅿

Rowington

Rowington Club Ⓛ

Rowington Green, CV35 7DB (just E of B4439, opp village hall) SP1998070150

🌑 2 (12 Sat & Sun)-11 ☎ (01564) 782087 ⊕ rowington.org/Rowington/rowington_club

Wye Valley HPA; guest beers Ⓗ

Busy and thriving community club, popular with locals, also open to non-members (free entry for CAMRA members). Frequent entertainment is hosted plus seasonal events such as ladies' day, August beer festival, marrow Sunday and game fair. Three real ales are on offer at all times plus traditional ciders. Bar snacks are available but no meals. The large beer garden overlooks the village cricket ground. The club is handy for local walking and cycling. Always friendly, it's well worth seeking out. ♨🐕👶≉(Lapworth)🐕🅿🏃

Rugby

Alexandra Arms Ⓛ

72 James Street, CV21 2SL (next to John Barford car park)

🌑 11.30-11.30 (midnight Fri & Sat); 12-11.30 Sun

☎ (01788) 578660 ⊕ alexandraarms.co.uk

Atomic Fission; Fuller's London Pride; Hook Norton Hooky Gold, Old Hooky; guest beers Ⓗ

Bought in 2011 by Atomic Brewery, this town-centre pub has a comfortable lounge bar where good-value pub food is served lunchtimes only. The back bar has the best rock jukebox in the county. Outside, the large garden hosts beer fests and local bands, especially jazz and rock, and the Atomic Brewery building is to the rear. Seven times local CAMRA Pub of the Year. Q🅮🍴🐕≉🐕🏃

Lawrence Sheriff ⊘

28-29 High Street, CV21 3BW

🌑 8am-midnight (3am Thu-Sat) ☎ (01788) 517640

Greene King Abbot; Ruddles Best Bitter; Shepherd Neame Spitfire; guest beers H
Built in Art Deco style during the '30s for Boots the Chemist, this is now a Wetherspoon Lloyds No.1 Bar named after the founder of Rugby School. Ten handpumps offer guest ales alongside the regular Wetherspoon's range. Breakfast is served from 8am, with food available all day until 9pm. Frequented by all age groups, the weekends are especially popular with the younger set – the music gets loud after 9pm. ♻🍺🕭🍴🚉🅿️🚏

Merchants Inn ✓

5-6 Little Church Street, CV21 3AW (behind Marks & Spencer)
✪ 12-midnight (1am Fri & Sat; 11 Sun) ☎ (01788) 571119
⊕ merchantsinn.co.uk
Batemans XB; Oakham Bishops Farewell; Purity Mad Goose; guest beers H
This must-visit real ale emporium surrounds the visitor with an abundance of brewery memorabilia in an atmospheric setting. The interior features wooden seating, comfortable sofas, flagstone floors and an open fireplace. On the bar there are nine real ales, traditional cider and perry plus bottled European beers. Live music is hosted on Tuesdays. Beer festivals are held in spring and autumn plus themed events such as cider, Belgian and German evenings, all with appropriate food and music. ♨🍺🛏🅿️🍴🚏

Raglan Arms

50 Dunchurch Road, CV22 6AD (opp Rugby School)
✪ 4-midnight (1am Fri); 12-1am Sat & Sun
☎ (01788) 544441 ⊕ raglanarmsinn.co.uk
Fuller's London Pride, ESB; Greene King Abbot; guest beers H
Situated opposite Rugby School playing fields, the Raglan Arms was awarded local CAMRA Pub of the Year in 2010, for the third consecutive year. The interior has a comfortable feel and friendly atmosphere. A large choice of real ales is kept in the pub's two cellars. The cosy snug bar with a coal-effect fire is for general use and meetings. Snacks are served all day. Major sporting events are screened on Sky TV. Q♻🍺🕭🚉🅿️🚏

Squirrel Inn

33 Church Street, CV21 3PU
✪ 12-11; 4-10.30 Sun ☎ (01788) 544154
Marston's Pedigree; guest beers H
A real fire adds to the warm and friendly atmosphere at this traditional free trade Guide regular. Visitors are welcome to join the regulars in topical discussions at the bar while enjoying the changing guest ales, always including a LocAle, often from Dow Bridge. Live acoustic music is a major part of the weekly calendar of events. A wide selection of tabletop games is available. ♨🚉🅿️🚏

Victoria Inn 🏆

1 Lower Hillmorton Road, CV21 3ST
✪ 12 (4 Mon-Wed)-midnight ☎ (01788) 544374
⊕ downthevic.com
Atomic Strike, Fission, Fusion, Half Life, Bomb, Power; guest beers H
Local CAMRA Pub Of The Year 2011, the Vic is the Atomic Brewery tap and also offers guest ales and micro beers on 14 handpumps. Regular beer fests and events are held throughout the year. This Victorian hostelry has a traditional bar with a comfortable lounge, two snugs and an enclosed

courtyard. A wide variety of sport is shown on TV and it is home to many teams including vets football. Quiz night is Sunday. Often the first/last pub visitors encounter on the way to/from the station. Q🍺🕭🚉🅿️🚏

Shustoke

Griffin Inn

Church Road, B46 2LB (on B4116 on sharp bend)
✪ 12-2.30, 7-11; 12-10.30 Sun ☎ (01675) 481205
Hook Norton Old Hooky; Jennings Dark Mild; Marston's Pedigree; RCH Pitchfork; Theakston Old Peculier; guest beers H
Thriving family-run Guide regular with its own brewery next door. A Griffin beer usually features alongside the regular ales and four guests. Occasional beer festivals are overwhelmingly popular. The low-beamed interior is blessedly music and TV-free. In winter it is superbly cosy with the log-burning stoves roaring away. Summer is the time for the patio seating and large grassy play area. Children are welcome in the conservatory. No food served Sunday. Local eggs are sold at the bar. ♨Q♻🍺🅿️🚏

Stratford-upon-Avon

Bear at the Swan's Nest Hotel 🅻 ✓

Swan's Nest Lane, CV37 7LT (S end of Clopton Bridge)
SP20545480
✪ 12-11 (midnight Fri & Sat) ☎ (01789) 265540
⊕ thebearfreehouse.co.uk
Hook Norton Hooky Bitter, Old Hooky; Wye Valley Butty Bach; guest beers H
Historic pub with a waterside location, five minutes' walk from the town centre, serving eight real ales. The focus tends to be on local and regional brewers such as Wye Valley, Hook Norton, Hobsons and Warwickshire Brewing Co, with seasonal beers available. The Bear is decked out with wood panelling, a pewter bar and picnic tables for riverside drinking. Excellent, home-made bar meals are served in a warm, friendly, welcoming atmosphere. Board games and newspapers are always available. ♻🍺🕭🚉(23)🅿️

West End 🅻

9 Bull Street, CV37 6DT (400yds SW from council offices)
✪ 11.30-11; 12-10.30 Sun ☎ (01789) 268832
⊕ thewestendstratford.co.uk
Cannon Royal Millwards Muket Ale; Sharp's Doom Bar; Taylor Landlord; guest beers H
Stratford's hidden gem. Although situated just a short walk from the centre, the pub has the feel of a village local. The landlord aims to offer cask ales that cannot normally be found in the town. In-house cask ale weeks feature regularly, and an annual beer festival has been recently introduced. Darts, pool, dominoes and quiz events are also held. Freshly prepared food, using locally sourced produce, is available daily, plus regular food themed nights. The pub is dog-friendly. Q🍺🕭🚉🚏

Stretton-on-Fosse

Plough Inn

GL56 9QX
✪ 12-2.30 (not Mon), 6-11; 12-3, 6-11 (closed eves winter) Sun ☎ (01608) 661053

Sharp's Doom Bar; Wickwar Brand Oak Bitter; Wye Valley Bitter; guest beer Ⓗ
A superb 17th-century stone-built village pub with oak beams and flagstoned bar. Four real ales and a cider are available and delicious food is home-cooked by the owner, French chef Jean Pierre. The large inglenook fireplace is used to slow roast a joint of meat on winter Sundays. Traditional pub games and quizzes are played in the bar. A former local CAMRA Pub of the Year. ⚞Q✿◑♣➍P'⌐

Studley

Little Lark
108 Alcester Road, B80 7NP (Tom's Town Lane jct with A435) SP075632
☼ 12-3, 6-11; 12-midnight Fri & Sat; 12-10.30 Sun
☎ (01527) 853105
Adnams Broadside; Taylor Landlord; guest beer Ⓗ
Popular village local serving a great selection of traditional fruit wines and single malt whiskies as well as real ale. A former Mad O'Rourke pub, it used to publish its own newspaper, and framed front pages decorate the walls. Food is served lunchtimes and evenings, all day on Sunday – the Desperate Dan Cow Pie is a speciality. The pub runs an annual cheese festival and regular beer festivals as well as monthly Wednesday evening themed food events. ⚞Q✿◑Ⓖ♿➍(26,143,247)♣➍'⌐

Warwick

Wild Boar
27 Lakin Road, CV34 5BU
☼ 12-11 (midnight Fri & Sat; 10 Sun) ☎ (01926) 491663
⊕ thewildboarwarwick.co.uk
Everards Sunchaser Blonde; Slaughterhouse Saddleback Best Bitter; guest beers Ⓗ
Traditional two-roomed community pub and Slaughterhouse brewery tap close to Warwick station. A two-barrel brewery supplying special beers for the pub can be viewed from the wood-panelled tasting room. Nine handpumps dispense the regular Slaughterhouse and Everards beers plus a changing selection of guest ales and a draught cider. Special events and festivals are held in the separate beer hall and hop garden. Limited home-made food and beer bites are sometimes available. ⚞✿�Ⓡ(X17)➍'⌐

Wellesbourne

Stag's Head
Chestnut Square, CV35 9QS

☼ 11.30-3, 6-11; 11-11 Fri & Sat; 12-10.30 Sun
☎ (01789) 840266
Dow Bridge Morgan's Chedham Ale; Fuller's London Pride; Shepherd Neame Spitfire; Taylor Landlord; guest beers Ⓗ
Grade II-listed black and white timber-framed thatched pub dating back to the 17th century. The family-friendly village local is near to Chedham's Yard. Comfortable and welcoming, it has seven pumps for the regular beers plus ever-changing guests. Good, reasonably priced home-made food is available and there are five B&B rooms. The pub has two darts teams and a dominoes team, and holds regular quiz nights. Q✿⟰◑Ⓖ♿Ⓡ➍'⌐

Whichford

Norman Knight ♟ Ⓛ
CV36 5PE
☼ 11-11 summer; 12-3 (not Mon), 6 (7 Mon)-11 winter; 12-3, 6-11 Sun ☎ (01608) 684621 ⊕ thenormanknight.co.uk
Hook Norton Hooky Bitter; Patriot Morris, Kiwi; guest beers Ⓗ
A traditional country pub in the centre of Whichford overlooking the green. Very much a community pub at the heart of village life, it has won many local and regional awards for the quality of its beers, food and facilities. Music nights are held frequently and every third Thursday owners of classic cars and bikes meet here. It is also a popular pub for walkers who enjoy the delicious home-cooked meals. The Patriot Brewery is to the rear of the bar. ⚞Q✿✿◑♿⟰Ⓡ♣➍P'⌐

Willey

Wood Farm Brewery Tap Ⓛ
Coalpit Lane, CV23 0SL
☼ 12-10 (8 Sun) ☎ (01788) 833469
⊕ woodfarmbrewery.co.uk
Wood Farm 1823 Dark Mild, Webb Ellis, Best Bitter, Victorious, Union, No 8; guest beers Ⓗ
The Wood Farm brewery tap is situated just outside the village of Willey. Set in 35 acres of farmland, it is a barn conversion over two floors with the brewery viewed through windows from the ground floor bar. Woodburners keep it warm in winter. The full range of beers, plus seasonals and guests, is available, and good home-made food is served – try the pork and Webb Ellis sausages. Book ahead for a guided tour of the brewplant. ⚞✿◑♿P'⌐

The Maypole

All bars are snug place, but the Maypole's was the very snuggest, cosiest and completest bar, that ever the wit of man devised. Such amazing bottles in old oaken pigeon-holes; such gleaming tankards dangling from pegs at about the same inclination as thirsty men would hold them to their lips; such sturdy little Dutch kegs ranged in rows on shelves...such closets, such presses, such drawers full of pipes, such places for putting away in hollow window-seats, all crammed to the throat with eatables, drinkables, or savoury condiments; lastly, and to crown all, as typical of the immense resources of the establishment, and its defiance to all visitors to cut and come again, such a stupendous cheese.

Charles Dickens, Barnaby Rudge, 1841. The model for the Maypole is the King's Head, Chigwell, Essex

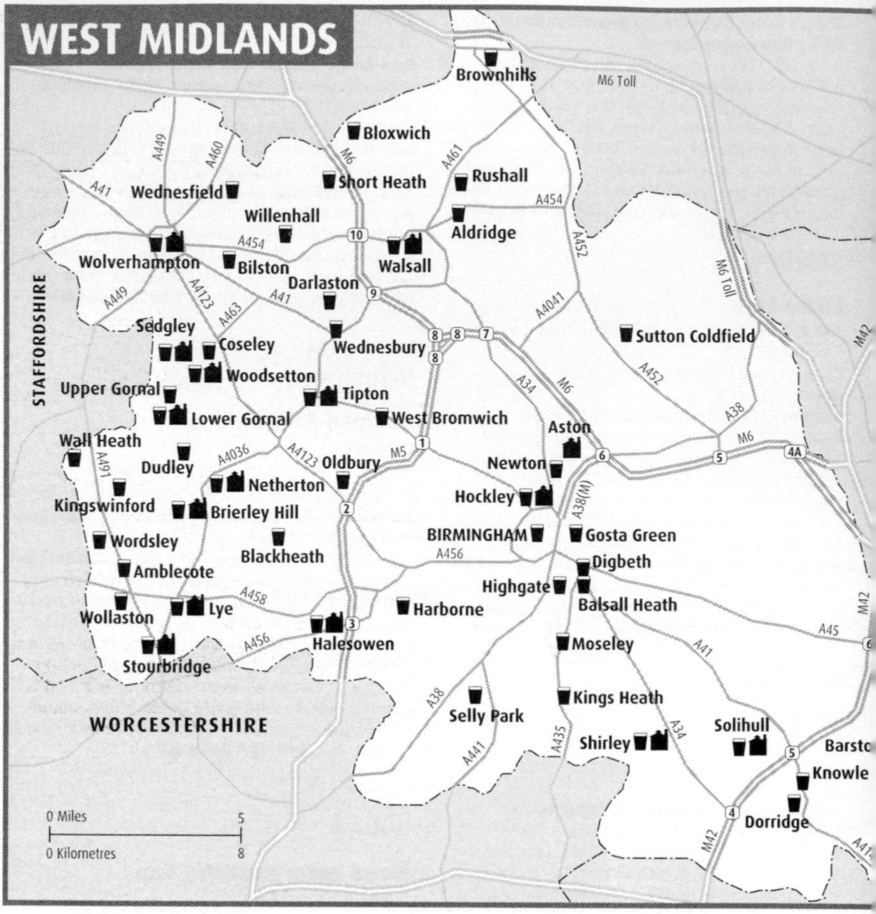
WEST MIDLANDS
Brownhills
M6 Toll
Bloxwich
M6
A461
A449
A460
A41
Wednesfield
Short Heath
Rushall
A454
Willenhall
Aldridge
A452
A454
10
Walsall
Wolverhampton
Bilston
M6 Toll
Darlaston
A449
A4123
A41
9
A4041
STAFFORDSHIRE
A463
Sedgley
8
7
Coseley
Wednesbury
Sutton Coldfield
M42
Woodsetton
A452
A34
M6
Upper Gornal
Tipton
Lower Gornal
West Bromwich
Aston
A38
Wall Heath
M6
A4036
A4123
Oldbury
M5
1
6
5
4A
A491
Dudley
Newton
Netherton
Hockley
A38(M)
Kingswinford
Brierley Hill
2
BIRMINGHAM
Gosta Green
Wordsley
Blackheath
A456
Digbeth
Amblecote
Highgate
A458
Lye
Harborne
Balsall Heath
M42
Wollaston
3
A45
A456
Halesowen
Moseley
A41
Stourbridge
A38
Kings Heath
Selly Park
WORCESTERSHIRE
A34
Solihull
A435
Shirley
A441
5
Barston
Knowle
0 Miles
5
0 Kilometres
8
4
M42
Dorridge
A41

Aldridge

Lazy Hill Tavern 🄻

196 Walsall Wood Road, WS9 8HB

⏲ 6-11; 12-2.30, 7-10.30 Sun ☎ (01922) 452040

Greene King IPA, Abbot; guest beers 🄷

Family-run free house with the same licensee for 30 years. Originally a farmhouse, it became a country club, then a pub in 1986. Four separate rooms are all similarly and comfortably furnished, with original beams exposed in the middle two. The large 160-seater function room is used mid-week by local sports/community organisations and can be booked for weddings and the like. Live entertainment is provided every other Tuesday. A new deal means that the licensee is able to have better control over the beers sold and more LocAle breweries are being supported. ♨**Q**🚌(367,56)**P**

Amblecote

Maverick 🄻 ✔

Brettell Lane, DY8 4BA (on jct of A491 and A461)

⏲ 12-midnight (1am Wed, Fri & Sat); 12-11 Sun

☎ (01384) 824099

Jennings Cumberland Ale; guest beers 🄷

Large corner pub, a former local CAMRA Pub of the Year. The Maverick has a Wild West theme and is a live music venue for blues, folk, rock and more. Four beers are permanently available, with three guests – two from local breweries. Sky Sports can be watched in a separate area when no music is on. There is a covered, heated, smoking area and a small garden. An occasional beer festival, locally advertised, is held. **Q**❀🚌(256,257,246)♣⁻

Robin Hood 🄻

196 Collis Street, DY8 4EQ (on A4102 one-way street off Brettell Lane A461)

⏲ 12-3 (not Mon & Tue), 5-11; 12-midnight Fri & Sat; 12-11 Sun ☎ (01384) 821120

Bathams Best Bitter; Enville Ale, Ginger Beer; Salopian Oracle; guest beers 🄷

Fine ales, high quality food and a warm welcome – what more could you ask from a Black Country local? A recent extension to the dining area and an innovative sign featuring the tree opposite demonstrate the Robin's forward-looking approach, while managing to retain traditional values. The pub houses an interesting collection of beer bottles and hosts an annual beer festival in October. ♨❀🛏◑♿🚌(246)●**P**⁻🛡

Starving Rascal ✔

1 Brettell Lane, DY8 4BN

⏲ 4 (12 Sat & Sun)-11 ☎ 07843 670163

Holden's Golden Glow; guest beers 🄷

Three linked rooms surround a central bar which forms the hub of this pub. There is a pool room, a

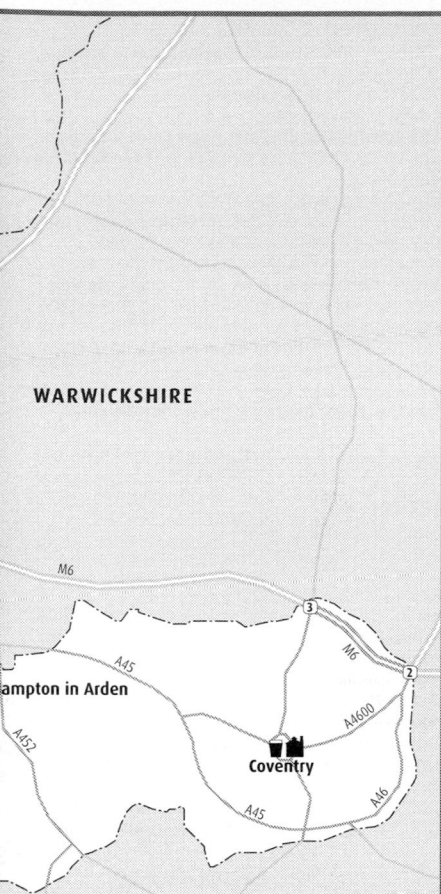

WARWICKSHIRE

M6

M6

A45

lampton in Arden

A452

A4600

3

2

Coventry

A45

A46

---

bar area with TV showing sport, and a quiet lounge. The usual pub games plus some board and other games are on offer. It is a warm, friendly hostelry generally serving local guest beers from the SIBA direct delivery scheme, and occasionally from further afield. A large range of single malt whiskies is also available. ♨️🚌(246)♣️P

Barston

Bull's Head ♈ Ⓛ ✅
Barston Lane, B92 0JU (in village opp church)
SP2073378090
✪ 11-2.30, 5-11; 11-11 Fri & Sat; 12-10.30 Sun
☎ (01675) 442830 🌐 thebullsheadbarston.co.uk
Adnams Southwold Bitter; Hook Norton Old Hooky;
Purity Mad Goose; guest beer Ⓗ
A true countryside local, with its history as a coaching inn dating back to 1490 reflected in its three beamed rooms. It has two comfortable bars with real fires and racing memorabilia, plus an intimate restaurant. Seasonal home-cooked food is available plus the standard menu (no food Sun eve). Cask Marque and LocAle accredited, it offers three regular ales and a changing guest. The pub has featured in the Guide for over 20 years and has won local Pub of the Year on five occasions. With a secluded beer garden and a warm welcome, it is definitely worth a visit. ♨️Q🌳🐾🌸◑🍴⬆️

Bilston

Olde White Rose Ⓛ
20 Lichfield Street, WV14 0AG
✪ 12 (11 Sat)-midnight (11.30 Mon); 12-11.30 Sun
☎ (01902) 498339
Castle Rock Harvest Pale; Greene King Abbot; Hop Back Summer Lightning; Kelham Island Pale Rider; Sarah Hughes Dark Ruby Mild; Thornbridge Jaipur IPA; guest beers Ⓗ
Revamped listed pub with 12 handpumps offering a wide range of real ales including six regulars. At least one cider is also available plus a large selection of food. There is a discount on pints for CAMRA members. The location close to the metro and bus stations makes it convenient for public transport. It offers quiz nights on Tuesday and Wednesday and is close to the Robin 2 music venue. The pub has its own hotel with 13 en-suite rooms. 🛏️◑♿🚆(Central)🚌🐾

Birmingham: Balsall Heath

Old Moseley Arms Ⓛ
53 Tindal Street, B12 9QU
✪ 12-11 (midnight Fri & Sat) ☎ (0121) 440 1954
Bathams Best Bitter; Enville Ale; Purity Mad Goose; Wye Valley HPA; guest beers Ⓗ
Former Ansells back-street local that is a welcoming establishment. The two-door entrance leads to two drinking areas – the left bar has a large TV screen showing sporting events and the right bar is a large seating area with a jukebox featuring classic rock among the playlist. Beer festivals are held at regular intervals. There is a large outdoor area at the rear. Tandoori dishes have been introduced to the food menu which is available from lunchtime. ♨️🐾◑🚌(50)♣️⬆️

Birmingham: City Centre

Old Fox Ⓛ ✅
54-56 Hurst Street, B5 4TD (opp Hippodrome Theatre)
✪ 11.30-midnight (2am Fri & Sat); 12-midnight Sun
☎ (0121) 622 5080
Morland Old Speckled Hen; St Austell Tribute; guest beers Ⓗ
Victorian two-roomed pub with stained glass windows, located between Chinatown and the gay village. A central bar serves both a public room with wood and brass decor and a carpeted lounge with comfortable seating. The venue is theatre themed, with many framed posters adorning the walls. It can get busy with a mixed clientele when performances are on at the Hippodrome Theatre opposite, or the nearby Glee Club. Guest beers are often from Backyard, Milestone and Slater's. ◑♿⬆️🚆(New St/Moor St)🚌(45,47)

Old Joint Stock Ⓛ ✅
4 Temple Row, B2 5NY (opp St Philip's cathedral)
✪ 11-11; 12-5 Sun ☎ (0121) 200 1892
🌐 oldjointstocktheatre.co.uk
Fuller's Chiswick Bitter, Discovery, London Pride, ESB; Gale's HSB; guest beers Ⓗ
Formerly the Old Joint Stock Bank, this imposing Victorian Grade II-listed building boasts elaborate features both externally and internally. There is a large island bar with a club room at the rear and a separate balcony for drinking/dining. The theatre hosts plays throughout the year and also showcases local comedians and live jazz. Good-quality food is served, with many pies on the

menu. There is a stairlift by the paved area at the back down Wellington Passage.
♿⚙🍴♿⚡(New Street/Snow Hill)🚇(Snow Hill)🚃

Old Royal ✅

53 Church Street, B3 2DP (off Colmore Row)
✪ 9-11 ☎ (0121) 200 3841
Brakspear Oxford Gold; Marston's EPA, Pedigree; guest beer 🅷
Elaborately designed Victorian pub, with the national emblems of England, Scotland, Ireland and Wales incorporated into the leaded windows, on the edge of Birmingham's business district, with a large upstairs function room. This pub is often quite busy, with a mainly middle-aged clientele. Two TVs are present, showing major sporting events. Food is traditional and good-value pub grub.
⚡♿⚡(Snow Hill/New St)🚇(Snow Hill)🚃

Post Office Vaults 🅛

84 New Street, B2 4BA (entrances are on both New St and Pinfold St)
✪ 11-11 (midnight Fri & Sat); 12-11 Sun ☎ (0121) 643 7354
⊕ postofficevaults.co.uk
Hobsons Mild; Salopian Oracle; guest beers 🅷
Just one minute's walk from the Navigation Street entrance to New Street Station, with an excellent range of eight real ales, this subterranean pub is a great place for lovers of traditional ale. There is so much more on offer too: over 200 bottled beers from all over the world, more than 10 real ciders and perries, and staff who really know how to advise you on your drink choice. Free bar billiards and quirky humour complete the experience.
Q♿(Moor St/New St/Snow Hill)🚇(Snow Hill)🚃♣🍴

Pub du Vin 🅛

25 Church Street, B3 2NR
✪ 12 (1 Sat)-11; closed Sun ☎ (0121) 200 0600
Kinver Light Railway; Purity Mad Goose; guest beer 🅷
The downstairs bar of the Hotel du Vin, in a central square format with lounge-style seating surrounding. It has a comfortable, calming ambience. The large-screen TV and piped music are never obtrusive. A separate lounge is available for hire. The bar is popular with all types but specifically office workers. The guest beer, like the two regulars, is locally sourced, and it stocks a vast range of wines and whiskies, with bookable tastings. Closed some days of the week for functions, so check ahead.
🛏⚡♿(Snow Hill/New St)🚇(Snow Hill)🚃

Shakespeare 🅛 ✅

31 Lower Temple Street, B2 4JD
✪ 10-11 (midnight Fri & Sat); 10-10.30 Sun
☎ (0121) 616 2196
Brains The Rev James; Purity Mad Goose; Sharp's Doom Bar; guest beers 🅷
Part of the M&B Nicholson's chain, a stone's throw from the rear entrance of New Street station. Reopened in December 2010 after a lengthy refurbishment, it now resembles a smart Victorian pub, with traditional decor and discreet lighting. There is strong emphasis on food and the back is given over to diners. Outside at the front is a fenced-off alfresco seating area. The pub attracts a wide range of drinkers, but be aware that it may close before the stated times if not busy.
⚡♿⚡(New Street/Moor Street/Snow Hill)
🚇(Snow Hill)🚃🍴

Wellington 🍷 🅛 ✅

37 Bennetts Hill, B2 5SN (5 mins from New St and Snow Hill stations)
✪ 10-midnight ☎ (0121) 200 3115
⊕ thewellingtonrealale.co.uk
Black Country Ales Bradley's Finest Golden; Oakham Citra; Purity Mad Goose; Wye Valley HPA; guest beers 🅷
With 17 handpumps, the Welly is a mini beer festival for 14 hours a day. A constant stream of seasonal beer festivals, cheese nights, darts competitions and quiz nights ensure there is always something on offer for its varied clientele. Three real ciders and an extensive range of bottled beers complement the unrivalled selection of cask ales. The bar has lots of local information, CAMRA publications and knowledgeable staff. You are able to bring your own food.
Q♿(Snow Hill/New St)🚇(Snow Hill)🚃♣🍴

Birmingham: Digbeth

Anchor ★ 🅛

308 Bradford Street, B5 6ET
✪ 11-11.30 (midnight Fri & Sat); 12-11 Sun
☎ (0121) 622 4516
Hobsons Mild; guest beers 🅷
Run by the Keane family for 39 years, this multiple winner of CAMRA Branch Pub of the Year is an ale enthusiast's destination, with up to a dozen different guests plus real cider. Ales are predominantly from newer micros, and there are regular beer festivals and themed weekends. Sport is shown on large-screen TVs, usually football, and the pub will be busy when Birmingham City play at home. Grade II-listed building and identified by CAMRA as one of Britain's Real Heritage Pubs.
⚙⚡⬛(Moor St/New St)🚇(37,50)🍴

Birmingham: Gosta Green

Sacks of Potatoes 🅛 ✅

10 Gosta Green, B4 7ER
✪ 10 (12 Sun)-11 ☎ (0121) 503 5811
⊕ sackofpotatoes-birmingham.co.uk
Marston's EPA; guest beers 🅷
A lively pub run by an enthusiastic landlady on Aston University campus, popular with students and local office staff. The U-shaped bar is

INDEPENDENT BREWERIES

ABC Birmingham: Aston
Angel Halesowen
Backyard Walsall
Bank's & Hanson's (Marston's) Wolverhampton
Bank's (Marston's) Wolverhampton
Batham Brierley Hill
Beer Geek Birmingham: Aston (NEW)
Black Country Lower Gornal
Broughs Wolverhampton
Byatt's Coventry
Craddock's Stourbridge
Highgate Walsall
Holden's Woodsetton
Olde Swan Netherton
Sadler's Lye
Sarah Hughes Sedgley
Silhill Solihull
Toll End Tipton
Two Towers Birmingham: Hockley
Whitworth Shirley (NEW)

surrounded by seating areas, with ample room and stools at the bar itself, while outside tables offer views overlooking the campus. Silent TVs screen sport coverage. This hostelry has good-value food and reasonable ale prices, and holds beer festivals throughout the year.
🏮🌑🕭✦≋(Snow Hill)🚆(Snow Hill)🚍(66)♣P🏷←

Birmingham: Harborne

Green Man 🅛 ✅
2 High Street, B17 9NE
🌑 11.30-11 (1am Fri & Sat) ☎ (0121) 428 3581
Purity Pure UBU; guest beers 🅷
A busy M&B community pub furnished like other Ember Inns, with an open fire. It offers reasonably priced food until 10pm. Beer from the Ember portfolio is priced competitively. There is outside seating at the front and a covered area to the rear. Regular quizzes are held on Wednesdays and Sundays, and other community charity fundraising activities take place. It is considered by some to be ideally placed for the start of a pub crawl at the beginning of the High Street.
🚶🏮🌑🕭🚍(22,24,29)P🏷←

Harborne Club 🅛
39 Albany Road, B17 9JX (200yds down road, last house on left)
🌑 12.30-3.30 (not Mon-Fri), 5.30-midnight; 12.30-3.30 Sun
☎ (0121) 427 1638 ⊕ theharborneclub.co.uk
Holden's Black Country Bitter; guest beer 🅷
The Harborne Club, a private members' establishment, welcomes CAMRA members by signing the attendance book. A snooker room is upstairs and a comfortable and friendly bar downstairs. The club was originally founded by local businessmen returning from work in the city. In keeping with the residential character of the area, there is little indication it exists apart from cellar doors and a small brass sign on the door.
🚍(22,24,29)♣

Plough 🅛 ✅
21 High Street, B17 9NT
🌑 11-11 (midnight Thu & Fri); 10-midnight Sat; 10-10.30 Sun
☎ (0121) 427 3678 ⊕ theploughharborne.co.uk
Purity Mad Goose; Wye Valley Butty Bach; guest beers 🅷
An attractive, popular pub that appeals to many and can get very busy. It serves a good selection of beers, presently two regular ales and two predominantly local guests. The food menu features extensive home-cooked food, with a good pizza selection, a brunch menu and afternoon tea. A quiz takes place on Tuesday and live music on Thursday. It has a large, quirkily designed pub garden, with a covered area for smokers. Cakes and traditional sweets, along with more usual bar snacks, are also available. 🏮🌑🕭🚍(22,23,24)🏷←

Birmingham: Highgate

Lamp 🅛
157 Barford Street, B5 6AH (500yds from A441 Pershore Road near bottom of Hurst Street)
🌑 12-11 ☎ (0121) 688 1220
Everards Tiger Best Bitter; Stanway Stanney Bitter; guest beers 🅷
Popular and intimate one-room back-street boozer and regular Guide entry run by long-standing landlord Eddie for 20 years. The pub is close to the

lively Hurst Street gay district and the Chinese quarter. The only outlet in the West Midlands for Stanway beers, there is a changing range of four or five guests, including a local mild. The large function room at the rear is used by a variety of local groups including CAMRA. Occasional late licence. ≋(New St)🚍(35,45,47)

Birmingham: Hockley

Black Eagle 🅛
16 Factory Road, B18 5JU (turn right out of Soho Benson Road metro station, cross road and walk 200yds)
🌑 11.30-3, 5.30-11; 11.30-11 Fri; 12-3, 7-11 Sat; 12-3 Sun
☎ (0121) 523 4008 ⊕ blackeaglepub.co.uk
Bathams Best Bitter; Marston's Burton Bitter; Taylor Best Bitter; guest beers 🅷
A gem of a pub in a real ale desert; six times Birmingham CAMRA Pub of the Year and run by former thespian Tony Lewis for more than 20 years. This Victorian pub retains many original features, including Minton tiles on the bar. The pub consists of two small bars that can get crowded, and a larger restaurant specialising in traditional home-cooked meals with daily specials. The beer festival held in the beer garden every July attracts a large following.
🚶Q🏮🌑🕭🚍(Soho Benson Rd)🚍(101)🏷←

Brown Lion 🅛
18 Hall Street, B18 6BS
🌑 11-11 ☎ (0121) 233 2285 ⊕ brownlion.co.uk
Two Towers Mott Street Mild, Baskerville Bitter, Hockley Gold, Complete Muppetry, Chamberlain Pale Ale, Birmingham Special Ale; guest beer 🅷
The brewery tap of Two Towers Brewery, this friendly traditional pub is located in Birmingham's Jewellery Quarter, a short walk from the city centre. The attentive staff take pride in serving a range of Two Towers beers. A changing guest beer and real ciders are available along with freshly cooked meals. Popular live music sessions held on Saturdays and Sundays add to the relaxed atmosphere enjoyed by a mixed clientele. CAMRA members get a discount on Two Towers ales.
🚶🌑≋(Jewellery Quarter)🚆(Jewellery Quarter)♣🏷←

Drop Forge 🅛
6-10 Hockley Street, B18 6BL
🌑 11-11 (midnight Fri & Sat); 12-7 Sun ☎ (0121) 448 4578
⊕ thedropforge.com
Purity Pure Gold; guest beers 🅷
The former industrial manufacturing building has been transformed into a contemporary bar and restaurant, yet respecting its history and heritage. A selection of original drop forge machinery has been retained behind a screen. An unusual patio and smoking area is on the first floor and a meeting room is available for hire. The beer range varies, with four always available. Good food is served every day. Directly opposite the Jewellery Quarter station.
🏮🌑🕭≋(Jewellery Quarter)🚆(Jewellery Quarter)🚍🏷←

Lord Clifden
34 Great Hampton Street, B18 6AA
🌑 10-midnight ☎ (0121) 523 7515
Wye Valley HPA; guest beers 🅷
The simple exterior belies what this pub has to offer. The interior is eclectic but comfortable. The walls are adorned with urban art by Banksy, the

large suntrap garden has table football and table tennis, and a beer festival is held in the garden in July. Sport is shown on a number of screens in the front bar and garden. Good-quality food, especially an interesting selection of burgers, is served all day.
❀❶🏠♿🚆(Jewellery Quarter)🚇(Jewellery Quarter)🚃♣💷⅃

Red Lion Ⓛ
94/95 Warstone Lane, B18 6NG
🕓 10-midnight (2am Fri & Sat) ☎ (0121) 233 9144
⊕ theredlionbirmingham.com
Bathams Best Bitter; guest beers Ⓗ
Traditional two-roomed pub with a smart quirky feel; there is a lively front bar and a cosy, secluded back lounge. Excellent food is served all day, in particular for the Cow Club on Mondays. There are three changing guest beers and two regularly changing ciders. A good-sized function room is available and there is a well-appointed patio and smoking area to the rear. Regular quiz nights are held. Situated close to the heart of the Jewellery Quarter.
❀❶🏠♿🚆(Jewellery Quarter)🚇(Jewellery Quarter)🚃(8,101)💷⅃

Birmingham: Kings Heath

Kings Heath Cricket & Sports Club Ⓥ
Charlton House, 247 Alcester Road South, B14 6DT
🕓 12-midnight ☎ (0121) 444 1913
⊕ kingsheathsportsclub.co.uk/
Wye Valley Bitter, HPA; guest beers Ⓗ
Welcoming sports club with two rooms, the comfortable lounge for relaxed drinking and the large room for watching sporting events on large screens and also housing two full-size snooker tables. Beer festivals are held in April and November as well as other social events, including live music. CAMRA members are welcome on production of a membership card (maximum 10 visits per year). The beer range always includes a rotating guest ale, with a minimum of five real ales available. Q❀❀❶🏠♿🚃(50)♣P⅃

Pear Tree Ⓛ Ⓥ
25-27 Alcester Road South, B14 7JQ
🕓 9-11.30 (midnight Thu; 1am Fri & Sat) ☎ (0121) 441 6710
Greene King Abbot; Ruddles County; guest beers Ⓗ
An excellent Wetherspoon outlet run by an enthusiastic manager who is a keen CAMRA member. The guest beers are highly driven by the LocAle policy where many local beers feature; at least four guest ales are available. The building is a former bank and is easily accessible by local transport. In winter months a large gas fire in the middle of the pub gives an open-fire impression. Food is the standard Wetherspoon fare.
🍴❶♿🚃♣💷

Birmingham: Moseley

Elizabeth of York Ⓛ Ⓥ
12A St Marys Row, B13 8JG
🕓 8-11 (11.30 Thu; 12.30am Fri & Sat) ☎ (0121) 442 5250
Greene King Abbot; Ruddles Best Bitter; guest beers Ⓗ
A Wetherspoon shop conversion with two entrances, one from St Mary's Row and the other from the car park at the rear. It is a spacious and welcoming establishment in the centre of Moseley.

Breakfast is available from 8am, and the typical Wetherspoon menu till 10pm. There is a regular LocAle rotation of its beer, alongside the usual Wetherspoon's ales. Fridays and Saturdays are popular, with a vibrant atmosphere.
❶♿🚃(1,35,50)💷P

Prince of Wales Ⓛ Ⓥ
118 Alcester Road, B13 8EE
🕓 12-11 (12.30am Fri & Sat) ☎ (0121) 449 4198
⊕ theprincemoseley.co.uk
Holden's Golden Glow; Oakham Bishops Farewell; St Austell Tribute; Taylor Landlord; Thornbridge Jaipur IPA; guest beers Ⓗ
Traditional Victorian pub that is a lively place in the heart of Moseley village. At the front of the pub is a bar area with 10 handpumps, a real fire and a TV showing sports. At the rear is a snug area and cigar emporium. There is a heated, partially tented area, ideal to use any time of the year. There is also a cocktail bar outside selling numerous foreign beers and various wines. ♨Q❀🏠♿🚃(50)⅃

Birmingham: Newtown

Bartons Arms ★
144 High Street, B6 4UP (at A34/B4144 jct, opp Newtown Baths)
🕓 12-11 (10.30 Sun) ☎ (0121) 333 5988
⊕ bartons-arms.co.uk
Oakham Inferno, Citra, Bishops Farewell; guest beers Ⓗ
Grade II-listed building that is a classic example of late Victorian splendour. From the main bar the superb original stained-glass windows can be viewed with the M&B logo as it was in 1901. There are ornate Minton tiles and a fancy tiled staircase. The restaurant is well known for its excellent selection of Thai cuisine. As well as the regular Oakham beers and seasonals, at least one guest ale is usually available.
♨Q🍴❶🏠♿🚃(33,34,51)💷P

Birmingham: Selly Park

Selly Park Tavern Ⓥ
592 Pershore Road, B29 7HQ
🕓 11.30 (12 Sun)-11 (midnight Fri & Sat) ☎ (0121) 472 4392
M&B Brew XI; Marston's Pedigree; guest beers Ⓗ
An Ember Inns red-brick pub dating back to 1901, run by the same manager for over 10 years, with a varied clientele. The interior is one large room but there are smaller areas so you can still get privacy. Two regular and four guest ales are served by friendly staff. There is an active bowling club and a skittle alley at the rear. Less than a mile from Edgbaston Cricket Ground, it is handy for visiting fans. ❀❶♿🚃(45,47)♣P⅃

Blackheath

Britannia Ⓥ
124 Halesowen Street, B65 0ES
🕓 7-11 (midnight Mon; 1am Fri); 9-1am Sat; 9-midnight Sun ☎ (0121) 559 0010
Greene King Abbot; Ruddles Best Bitter; guest beers Ⓗ
Formerly known as the Traveller's Rest, this friendly, open-plan community pub is popular with a wide variety of customers, and serves up typical Wetherspoon's fare from 7am until 10pm. The walls are adorned with pictures of local historic

figures detailing the area's industrial legacy. Up to seven guest beers are available at any given time. The pub gets busy at weekends and is readily accessible by buses from Birmingham, Dudley and West Bromwich, which stop nearby. A garden area at the back makes for a pleasant, peaceful drinking area.

🏰🏠🅾️◗&♿≠(Rowley Regis)🚍(128,140,241)♦P⏴

Bloxwich

Turf Tavern ★
13 Wolverhampton Road, WS3 2EZ (opp Bloxwich Park)
🌑 1-2.30, 7-11; 12-3, 7-11 Sat; 12-2.30, 7-10.30 Sun
☎ (01922) 407745
Oakham Bishops Farewell; Otter Bright; RCH Pitchfork; guest beer Ⓗ
Known locally as Tinky's, after a former licensee, this pub has been in the same family since around 1875. The three rooms are dominated by the bar with its splendid tiled floor and twin fireplaces. The building is steeped in nostalgia and is a haven for quiet conversation, which adds to its traditional charm. Outside is a rustic courtyard that serves as a pleasant spot for smokers and summer drinkers alike. Not to be missed. 🏰Q🏠🏵️🅾️🍴&♿🚍(301)⏴

Brierley Hill

Vine (Bull & Bladder)
10 Delph Road, DY5 2TN
🌑 12-11 (10.30 Sun) ☎ (01384) 78293
Bathams Mild Ale, Best Bitter Ⓗ
Classic, unspoilt brewery tap with an ornately decorated façade proclaiming the Shakespearian quotation: 'Blessing of your heart, you brew good ale.' Step inside and you enter an elongated pub with a labyrinthine feel. The rooms have contrasting characters. The front bar is small and staunchly traditional while the larger rear bar, with its own servery and leather seating, houses the dartboard at the far end. On the other side of the central passageway is a homely lounge partly converted from former brewery offices. Good-value Black Country lunches are served weekdays. A car park is across the road.
🏰Q🏠🏵️◗🍴🚍(X96)♦P⏴

Brownhills

Royal Oak Ⓛ
68 Chester Road, WS8 6DU (on A452, approx 500yds from Anchor Bridge towards Shire Oak)
🌑 12-11 (midnight Thu-Sat) ☎ (01543) 452089
🌐 theroyaloakpub.co.uk
Greene King Abbot; Hobsons Best Bitter; Purity Mad Goose; St Austell Tribute; Taylor Landlord; guest beer Ⓗ
More commonly referred to as the Middle Oak, this Art Deco-style pub is set back from the main road. The traditional bar plays host to darts and dominoes teams and there is poker on Sunday night, while the comfortable lounge provides a more relaxed atmosphere. The pub also boasts its own skittle alley, a separate dining room and a patio drinking area that leads to a large garden at the rear. Good-value food is served lunchtimes and evenings (no food Sun eve).
🏠🏵️◗🍴🚍(10,33,56)♣⏴

Coseley

New Inn Ⓛ
35 Ward Street, WV14 9LQ (backs onto A4123)
🌑 4-11 (10.30 Mon; 11.30 Fri); 12-11.30 Sat; 12-10.30 Sun ☎ 07927 459470 🌐 thenewinncoseley.co.uk
Holden's Black Country Mild, Black Country Bitter; guest beer Ⓗ
Popular suburban local just off the Birmingham New Road (the 126 bus passes the rear car park). The lounge is housed in a late 20th-century extension and the bar in the older 19th-century part of the building, separated by the modern bar counter that is the hub of the establishment. The regular beers are supplemented by Holden's Golden Glow or seasonal special. Pub food, particularly home-made specials, is served Tuesday-Friday evenings.
🏰Q🏠◗&♿🚍(126)♣P⏴

Coventry

Biggin Hall ✅
214 Binley Road, CV3 1HG
🌑 12-midnight (1am Fri & Sat) ☎ (024) 7644 3196
🌐 thebigginhall.com
Marston's Burton Bitter, Pedigree; guest beers Ⓗ
Built in 1923, this pub has barely changed. In the lounge the fireplace with inglenook, centre table and chairs are all original; the public bar is similar though the smoke room and accommodation have gone. The two guest beers are carefully chosen from the Marston's stable to ensure a good range is available, with an emphasis on stronger ales. The upstairs function room holds up to 120 people and is available for hire. Live music is played most Friday evenings. No food on Mondays.
🏰🏠🏵️◗🍴&🚍(13,86)♣P⏴

Boat Ⓛ ✅
31 Shilton Lane, Walsgrave, CV2 2AB
🌑 11 (12 Sun)-midnight ☎ (024) 7661 2191
Draught Bass; Thwaites Original; guest beers Ⓗ
Charming Victorian pub sympathetically refurbished seven years ago. Two regular and up to five guest ales are available in the public bar and lounge. There are two additional rooms: one was used for smoking meat (the meat hooks are still visible), the other a quiet snug. Pictures adorn the walls, which add to the Victorian character. The pub hosts darts and domino teams in local leagues. Children are welcome when dining until 9.30pm; no food Sunday evenings. 🏵️◗🍴&🚍(30)♣P⏴

Broomfield Tavern
14-16 Broomfield Place, Spon End, CV5 6GY
🌑 12-11 (1am Fri & Sat; 10.30 Sun) ☎ (024) 7663 0969
Draught Bass; guest beers Ⓗ
Five handpumps feature two or more beers from small breweries and one draught cider. There is no TV, no fruit machine, although live music is played some weekends. This local is in a quiet street, with parking space usually available, just behind a main bus route. Benches at the front of the pub form a smoking area overlooking the park. A garden at the back is only opened for special events. Occasional beer festivals, with more than 12 handpumps, are hosted. Lunches only available Sundays. 🏵️🍴♣♦⏴

City Arms Ⓛ ✅
1 Earlsdon Street, Earlsdon, CV5 6EP (on roundabout at centre of Earlsdon)
🌑 8-midnight (1am Fri & Sat) ☎ (024) 7671 8170

Greene King Abbot; Ruddles Best Bitter; guest beers H

Built in 1930 on the site of the original Victorian pub of the same name, and an example of the mock-Tudor style. Part of the Wetherspoon chain, this local is an enthusiastic supporter of real ale and the largest Wetherspoon outlet for ale in the city. It is largely open plan with plenty of seating, attracting a mix of clientele, particularly at weekends. The community notice board is well-used by local groups. ✿ℂ▷&ℝ(5,12)●P↑—

Craven Arms

58 Craven Street, Chapelfields, CV5 8DW (1 mile W of city centre, off Allesley Old Road)
✪ 12 (4 Tue)-11.30 (midnight Fri & Sat) ☎ (024) 7671 5308
Flowers Original; Holden's Golden Glow; Oakham Bishops Farewell; guest beer H

Busy street-corner pub in a popular drinking area. The long one-roomed bar has a pool table and darts in a raised area off the bar. Up to three guest beers are available alongside the other regulars. There is a weekly quiz, karaoke and a disco with live music on Sunday evenings. Scooter memorabilia is on display, and occasional mod-themed weekend events are held. Outside is a pleasant patio with a heated and covered area for smokers. Dogs welcome. ⚐✿ℝ(10,18)♣↑—

Gatehouse Tavern L

46 Hill Street, CV1 4AN (city centre, near jct 8 of ring road)
✪ 11-11 Mon (11.30 Thu; midnight Fri & Sat); 11-3, 5-11; 12-11 Sun ☎ (024) 7663 0140
Beer range varies H

A pub rebuilt by the landlord from the shell of the former Leigh Mills gatehouse. The garden is the largest within the city centre. Stained-glass windows depicting the rugby Six Nations give a clue to the sporting preference of the pub. A free house, there are normally seven handpulls, two offering LocAles. Lunchtime meals are served Monday-Saturday, evening meals Tuesday-Friday. ✿ℂ▷ℝ↑—

Greyhound Inn ♥

Sutton Stop, Hawkesbury Junction, CV6 6DF (off Grange Rd at jct of Coventry and Oxford canals)
✪ 11-11; 12-10.30 Sun ☎ (024) 7636 3046
⊕ greyhoundinn.org
Draught Bass; Marston's Pedigree; guest beers H

Voted best pub in Coventry by CAMRA in 2010 and 2011, this popular free house is also four-times winner of the Godiva Award for best pub in Coventry & Warwickshire. A canalside inn with a terrace overlooking the junction of two canals, it dates from circa 1830. An extensive menu of freshly cooked food is available. Two major beer festivals take place annually. A separate beer garden bar serves an additional two real ales. It is a pleasant 25-minute canalside walk from Ricoh Arena. ⚐Q✿ℂ▷ℝ♣●P↑—

Hearsall Inn L

45 Craven Street, Chapelfields, CV5 8DS (1 mile W of city centre, off Allesley Old Road)
✪ 12 (11 Sat)-midnight ☎ (024) 7671 5729
⊕ hearsallinn.com
Beer range varies H

Busy community pub in the historic watchmaking area, one of the few free houses in Coventry and now a regular outlet for Byatt's, the first commercial Coventry brewery for nearly 90 years.

The four handpumps include Bass, one from Byatt's and one from Church End, with the fourth beer usually another local - the landlord is a strong supporter Of LocAle. His Irish roots are evident throughout the pub. ⚐⛵✿ℂℝ(10)♣↑—

Nursery Tavern

38-39 Lord Street, Chapelfields, CV5 8DA (1 mile W of city centre, off Allesley Old Road)
✪ 12-11.30; 11-midnight Fri & Sat; 12-11 Sun
☎ (024) 7667 4530
Courage Best Bitter; Fuller's London Pride; guest beers H

Community pub in a Victorian terraced street in the old watchmaking quarter. Comprising three rooms, the front two are served by a central bar. The rear room hosts monthly quizzes, local society and club meetings, a music night promoting local talent, and serves as a restaurant providing excellent-value traditional roast meals at Sunday lunchtimes. The pub has a collection of Rugby Union and Formula I paraphernalia. Beer festivals are held in the rear garden every June and December. Dogs are welcome. Q⛵✿ℂℝ(6,10)♣●↑—

Old Windmill

22-23 Spon Street, CV1 3BA (behind IKEA)
✪ 11 (3 Mon)-11 (1am Fri & Sat); 12-11 Sun
☎ (024) 7625 1717
Morland Old Speckled Hen; Sharp's Doom Bar; Taylor Landlord; Theakston Old Peculier; Wychwood Hobgoblin; guest beer H

Friendly and popular pub reputedly the oldest in Coventry, situated in medieval Spon Street. It is colloquially known as Ma Brown's, after a long-standing landlady.The multi-roomed, half-timbered building retains many original features. An old brewhouse can be seen in one of the many small rooms. A discount is offered for CAMRA members. Regular beer festivals are held. Meals are served until 9pm, 7pm on Friday and Saturday (but no food Sun & Mon). An eclectic mix of shoppers, cinemagoers, bikers and ice hockey fans frequent this pub. ℂℝ

Town Wall Tavern ✪

Bond Street, CV1 4AH (behind Belgrade Theatre)
✪ 12-11 (midnight Fri); 11.30-midnight Sat; 12-6 Sun
☎ (024) 7622 0963 ⊕ townwalltavern.co.uk
Adnams Southwold Bitter, Broadside; Caledonian Deuchars IPA; Draught Bass; Marston's Pedigree; guest beer H

One of the few traditional two-bar locals left in the city centre. As well as the lively bar and relaxing lounge, look out for the Donkey Box, a small snug at the front that is just big enough to hold a donkey. Popular with actors and journalists, it is gaining a good reputation for its imaginative food offering. The pub is built on the line of the ancient city wall, hence the name. ⚐✿ℂℝ●↑—

Whitefriars Olde Ale House

114-115 Gosford Street, CV1 5DL
✪ 12-midnight (1am Fri & Sat; 11 Sun) ☎ (024) 7625 1655
⊕ whitefriarscov.com
Sharp's Doom Bar; guest beers H

A 14th-century building once part of the Whitefriars monastery, subsequently made into a butcher's shop before being renovated and made into a pub. The small front room was a kitchen used by the friars, now with a welcoming fire in the winter months. The upstairs room is worth viewing for the mural on the wall and uneven floors. Eight changing guest ales are available. Beer festivals offering cider and perry and featuring live music are held regularly. No food on Sundays. ᵐ⊛ℂ&᠗(8,9)♣ᵗ╌

Darlaston

Spring Head Tavern
83 Walsall Road, WS10 9JU
✪ 12-midnight ☎ (0121) 526 6636
Black Country Ales Bradley's Finest Golden, Pig on the Wall, Fireside; guest beers Ⓗ
Darts is played in the small front bar, decorated with advertisements of sports equipment from yesteryear. The large lounge has soft bench seats and old world prints on the walls, with a big-screen TV at one end, mainly for sports events. There is a benched yard with a sheltered smokers' area. Poker night is Tuesday, Free and Easy guitar Thursday, and karaoke every Friday. A singer features once a month on Saturday. Regular brewery trips are organised, and an annual beer festival is held. Various cobs are available daily. ⊛᠗᠗(34,39)♣ϕPᵗ╌

Dorridge

Railway ✪
Grange Road, B93 8QA (½ mile SW from station)
SP16455743
✪ 11-3, 4.30-11; 11-11 Sat; 12-10.30 Sun ☎ (01564) 773531
Draught Bass; Hook Norton Hooky Bitter; Purity Mad Goose; guest beers Ⓗ
A popular pub that has been run by the same family for almost a century. Up to three guest beers are available as well as a real cider. Good-value food is served (all day Sun and bank holidays) and game is on the menu when in season. The large garden, with a children's play area and heated outdoor patio, is busy on summer days and evenings, while the real fire in the public bar provides a warm welcome in winter. ᵐQ⅀⊛ℂ᠗&᠗(S3)♣ϕPᵗ╌

Dudley

Court House ⓛ
30 New Street, DY1 1LP (a short walk from bus station towards police station)
✪ 12-11 (10.30 Sun) ☎ (01384) 240062
Black Country Ales Bradley's Finest Golden, Pig on the Wall, Fireside; guest beers Ⓗ
Acquired by Black Country Traditional Inns in early 2009 and extensively refurbished to create a specialist real ale pub. The regular beers come from the company's own brewery alongside a large selection of guest ales from across the country. The pub has developed a reputation for regularly offering a dark beer. Cider drinkers are well catered for with a choice of four from Thatchers and Gwynt y Ddraig. The small snug and the upstairs function room complement the facilities. Snacks are available lunchtimes. CAMRA Cider Pub of the Year. Q᠗&᠗(1)♣ϕ

Lamp Tavern ⓛ
116 High Street, DY1 1QT
✪ 12-11 (10.30 Sun) ☎ (01384) 254129
Bathams Mild Ale, Best Bitter Ⓗ
Classic Bathams' pub with a large front bar with traditional games and a cosy back room with a more relaxed feel. The old Queens Cross brewery has been converted into a large function room

available for hire and staging music nights. An outside area for drinking overlooks the southern area of the Black Country to the Clent Hills beyond. B&B accommodation is in the adjacent Lamp Cottage (discount for CAMRA members, ring for details). Q⅀⊛⊠᠗&᠗♣Pᵗ╌

Halesowen

Somers Sports & Social Club ✪
2 Grange Hill, B62 0JH (at A456/B4551 jct)
✪ 12-2.30, 6-11; 12-11 Sat & Sun ☎ (0121) 550 1645
⊕ somersclub.co.uk
Bathams Mild Ale, Best Bitter; Holden's Black Country Bitter; Olde Swan Original; Wye Valley HPA; guest beers Ⓗ
Grade II-listed building set in acres of landscaped grounds. The long bar features eleven beers including six guests, many local, usually including an Oakham ale. The lounge overlooks the large garden, which has a children's play area and a crown bowling green. Pub food is served at lunchtimes (not Sun) and regular evening entertainment is hosted. CAMRA members are welcome; large groups should phone ahead. Three times winner of CAMRA National Club of the Year and current local Club of the Year. ᵐQ⅀⊛ℂ᠗(9,241)♣Pᵗ╌

Waggon & Horses ⓛ
21 Stourbridge Road, B63 3TU (on main A458, ½ mile from bus station)
✪ 12-11.30 (12.30am Fri & Sat) ☎ (0121) 550 4989
⊕ waggonales.co.uk
Bathams Best Bitter; Bob's White Lion; Holden's Golden Glow; Nottingham Extra Pale Ale; Oakham Inferno; guest beers Ⓗ
Thoroughly welcoming pub with an enviable reputation for its wide selection of expertly kept beers. Fourteen ales are always available, usually including a stout or mild, plus real cider and draught Belgian beers. The traditional interior has a long bar flanked by quieter seating areas at both ends. Top-quality home-made hot and cold food is now served Monday to Saturday until early evening, with a regular steak and curry night on Monday. Qℂ᠗(9)ϕᵀ

Hampton in Arden

White Lion ✪
10 High Street, B92 0AA (opposite the church)
SP2025080900
✪ 12-midnight (10.30 Sun) ☎ (01675) 442833
⊕ thewhitelioninn.com
Hobsons Best Bitter; M&B Brew XI; Purity Mad Goose; St Austell Tribute; Sharp's Doom Bar Ⓗ
Charming 17th century timber framed building with Grade II listed status, the White Lion has been licensed since 1838. It has an L-shaped lounge, a light, airy and open plan dining area, and a separate public bar with lovely real fires. Quality British pub food with a French accent is served lunchtime & evenings only. Since the current proprietor took over in 2010 he has increased the quantity and quality of the real ales on offer, to such an extent it won a local CAMRA Most Improved Pub award. ᵐQ⊛⊠ℂ᠗&⇌᠗(82)Pᵗ╌

Kingswinford

Park Tavern ⓛ
182 Cot Lane, DY6 9QG (corner of Cot Lane and Broad St)
SO884884
🌣 11-11 (1am Fri & Sat) ☎ (01384) 287178
Bathams Best Bitter; Enville Ale; Purity Mad Goose; guest beers ⓗ
Popular, lively old pub in the back streets of Kingswinford. The separate bar and lounge each have their own feel, but TV does dominate when there are sporting events on. The landlord has worked hard to raise the quality and quantity of real ales, currently serving five or six. For the peckish, there is a selection of cobs, including Tiger cobs, which are especially popular. There is a large marquee attached to the rear for smokers and sports enthusiasts alike. Show your CAMRA membership card for a discount on real ales.
🍺🚽(256,257)♣P⌐

Knowle

Vaults
St John's Close, B93 0JU (off High St A4141) SP181767
🌣 12-2.30, 5-11; 12-11.30 Fri & Sat; 12-11 Sun
☎ (01564) 773656
Adnams Lighthouse; Sharp's Doom Bar; St Austell Tribute; Tetley Bitter; guest beers ⓗ
Traditional pub that can be relied on for a wide range of quality real ales, as well as real cider from the Westons range. In recent years it has been a regular winner of local CAMRA Branch Pub of the Year, and is a popular meeting place for those visiting the many local restaurants. Wi-Fi is available and major sporting events are shown on ESPN Sports TV. Light meals are served 12-2pm (not Sun). 🍺(S2,S3)♥⌐

Lower Gornal

Black Bear
86 Deepdale Lane, DY3 2AE
🌣 5 (4 Fri; 12 Sat)-11; 12-10.30 Sun ☎ (01384) 253333
Beer range varies ⓗ
Once a farmhouse and now a traditional Black Country pub, serving four or more guest beers. Subsidence has taken its toll and there is a distinct slope to the split-level interior, and large buttresses support the downhill exterior walls. The views are stunning, the natives friendly, the ambience warm, and dogs are welcome here. There are bus stops close by; alternatively, you could choose to walk (uphill) from the bus station at Gornal Wood. Kinver Black Bear is the house beer. 🏚🍺🚽(27,257)♣

Five Ways
375 Himley Road, DY3 2PZ (jct of B4176/4175, 3 mins from Gornal Wood bus station)
🌣 9-midnight (1am Fri & Sat) ☎ (01384) 252968
Bathams Best Bitter ⓗ
Family-friendly Gornal Wood corner house, its one J-shaped room dividing the bar into two distinct areas. There is a raised decking area overlooking the car park at the back of the pub. Buses 257 and 297 pass close by and it is only a short walk from Gornal Wood bus station. Opens early at 9am for home-cooked breakfasts seven days a week. 🏚🚽(257,297)♣P

Fountain
8 Temple Street, DY3 2PE (on B4157 5 mins from Gornal Wood bus station)
🌣 12-11 (10.30 Sun) ☎ (01384) 242777
🌐 fountainrealales.com
Greene King Abbot; Hobsons Town Crier; Morland Old Speckled Hen; RCH Pitchfork; guest beers ⓗ
Regular finalist and twice winner of Dudley CAMRA Pub of the Year, this excellent free house offers nine real ales accompanied by draught Belgian beers, real cider and 12 fruit wines. The busy, vibrant bar is complemented by an elevated dining area serving excellent food all week. During the summer months the rear garden is a suntrap and a pleasant area to while away an hour or two. You may need to ask about traditional cider, which is kept in the cellar. 🍺🏚🍴🚽(27)♣♦

Red Cow ⓛ
84 Grosvenor Road, DY3 2PR
🌣 4 (12 Sat & Sun)-midnight ☎ 07943 189351
Beer range varies ⓗ
Early 19th-century hostelry in a cul de sac off Grosvenor Road. A convivial public bar to the left is complemented by a cosy lounge to the right. This is divided into two by a large chimney breast supporting an abundance of oak beams overhead and housing a double-sided wood-burning stove. A large garden at the rear hosts barbecues in summer. The six beers on offer can be from far and wide, though local beers such as Enville, Pardoe's and Holden's are popular regulars. Five minutes' walk from the bus stop in Corncrake Road. 🏚🍺🚽(257)♣P⌐

Lye

Shovel ⓛ
81 Pedmore Road, DY9 7DZ (on A4036, just S of Lye Cross)
🌣 5.30-11 (midnight Thu); 5-midnight Fri; 2.30-midnight Sat; 12-11 Sun ☎ (01384) 423998 🌐 theshovelinn.co.uk
Enville Ale, Ginger Beer; Holden's Golden Glow; Ludlow Gold; Morland Old Speckled Hen; Purity Mad Goose; guest beers ⓗ
Extensive refurbishment by the owner has given this pub a smart feel. A central bar full of handpumps serves three separate areas: a bar area with TV showing sport, a plush lounge, and a rear seating area. The outside Mediterranean smoking area is covered and heated by a real fire and also has a real ale wall featuring over 1,000 pump clips. Good-value evening meals include regular Mexican and Balti nights. Traditional Sunday lunches are served. 🏚🍴🚽(9,276)♣⌐

Windsor Castle Inn ⓛ
7 Stourbridge Road, DY9 7DG (at Lye Cross)
🌣 12-11 ☎ (01384) 897809
Sadler's Mellow Yellow, Worcester Sorcerer, Thin Ice, Hop Bomb, Red IPA, Mud City Stout, seasonal beers ⓗ
Tap house for the family-owned Sadler's Ales since 2004, showcasing its full range of regular beers along with seasonal specials. The modern yet cosy interior creates an atmosphere that is relaxed and laid back during the week, livening up at weekends. Tasty home-made food is served daily from a varied award-winning menu, including gourmet burger night on Tuesday. Brewery tours are Mondays at 7pm - booking essential. There is live music Sundays from 7pm.
Q🏚🍴🚽(9,276)P⌐

Netherton

Olde Swan ★ 🄻

89 Halesowen Road, DY2 9PY (in Netherton centre on A459 Dudley-Old Hill road)

🕘 11-11; 12-4, 7-11 Sun ☎ (01384) 253075

Olde Swan Original, Dark Swan, Entire, Bumble Hole Bitter 🄷

One of the last four remaining English home-brew pubs from 1974, deservedly identified by CAMRA as one of Britain's Real Heritage Pubs and home to the Olde Swan Brewery, resurrected in 2000. The front bar is an unspoilt treasure and there is a cosy rear snug. Food is available in the lounge weekday lunchtimes and Monday evening.The upstairs restaurant is highly regarded for its à la carte menu (open Tue-Sat). Sunday lunches are popular, with booking essential. ♨Q❀⊕❿◗♿🖷(243,244,81)P

Oldbury

Jolly Collier 🄻

43 Junction Street, B69 3HD (off A457)

🕘 12-2.30, 5-11; 12-11 Fri & Sat; 12-10.30 Sun ☎ 07817 286827

Beer range varies 🄷

Friendly locals' pub popular with a wide clientele. Traditional pub games and comprehensive TV coverage of live sporting events are available here. There is a heated, covered smoking patio and a large elevated decked area overlooking the garden, which is ideal for supervising children as they play on the grassed games area. The beers, which change regularly, are nearly always LocAles. Three beer festivals are organised each year, usually one coinciding with Cask Ale week. Sandwiches are available at the bar.

🏃❀♿⇒(Sandwell & Dudley)🖷(87)♣●⬩

Rushall

Manor Arms ★ 🄻

Park Road, off Daw End Lane, WS4 1LG (off B4154 at Canal Bridge)

🕘 12-midnight (11 Sun) ☎ (01922) 642333

Banks's Mild, Bitter; Jennings Cocker Hoop; Wychwood Hobgoblin; guest beers 🄷

With a reputation for being haunted, this pub is thought to have been built around 1105 and to have held a licence to serve ale since 1248. It still retains exposed beams and there is an open fire in both bars. The beer pulls come straight out of the wall, resulting in the pub being known locally as 'the pub with no bar'. Previously voted Best Canalside Pub in the Country, its large beer garden is near the canal and a local county park. Good food is served Saturday and Sunday from April through to September only. Dog friendly.

♨Q🏃❀❿🖷(355,356)P⬩

Sedgley

Beacon Hotel 🏆 ★ 🄻

129 Bilston Street, DY3 1JE (A463)

🕘 12-2.30 (3 Fri), 5.30-11; 12-3, 6-11 Sat; 12-3, 7-10.30 Sun ☎ (01902) 883380

Sarah Hughes Pale Amber, Sedgley Surprise, Dark Ruby Mild; guest beers 🄷

In the shadow of the ancient Sedgley Beacon atop the hill, this old hotel has sat virtually unchanged for decades. Identified by CAMRA as one of Britain's Real Heritage Pubs, time seems to have stood still, but make no mistake, it is vibrant. At its heart is a central servery with hatches. Then there is a lounge, a tap room, a further lounge, and a family room. The Sarah Hughes Brewery lives in a tower out the back and supplies the pub. CAMRA Branch Pub of the Year 2012. The Beacon lives up to its name: it shines. Q❀🏃❀🖷(545)P⬩

Bull's Head

27 Bilston Street, DY3 1JA (A463)

🕘 9-11 ☎ (01902) 661676

Holden's Black Country Mild 🄷, **Black Country Bitter** 🄷/Ⓟ, **Golden Glow, Special** 🄷

Not far from the centre of Sedgley village sits this listed building. The bar area extends across the front of the pub and into the two bay windows. A bit more drinking space is available further back in the raised area to the side. Beyond that is now housed a Thai restaurant that also provides some basic English dishes, open lunchtimes and evenings. Breakfasts are served 9-2.30pm and the pub is licensed from 9am. ♨❀❿◗🖷(1,27)♣⬩🛏

Mount Pleasant (Stump)

144 High Street, DY3 1RH (A459)

🕘 6.30 (7 Mon & Tue)-11; 12-3, 7-10.30 Sun ☎ 07950 195652

Beer range varies 🄷

Known locally as the Stump by its many regulars, this friendly, popular free house serves an interesting selection of eight beers. It possesses a Tardis-like interior and a mock-Tudor frontage. The front bar has a convivially warm atmosphere while the lounge has an intimate feel, with two rooms on different levels and two real coal stoves. Food is limited to ham or cheese cobs. Dog-friendly, it is on the Dudley/Wolverhampton bus route, or five minutes' walk from Sedgley centre.

♨Q❀❹🖷(1)♣P⬩

Shirley

Bernie's Real Ale Off-Licence 🄻

266 Cranmore Boulevard, B90 4PX (off A34, opp TRW research site) SP1287077635

🕘 11.30-2, 4-10; 11.30-10 Fri & Sat; closed Sun ☎ (0121) 744 2827

Taylor Landlord; guest beers 🄷

This long-standing Guide entry proudly displays a wide choice of real ale pumps as though it were a pub. The guest beers offer a range of styles, mainly from small or microbreweries from the north of England; some newer local breweries are proving popular too. Traditional Rich's cider is always available. Various takeaway containers are supplied for draught ale and complement the wide range of bottled ales, ciders and continental beers (260 at the last count). ♿🖷(76,6,5)●

Short Heath

Duke of Cambridge

82 Coltham Road, WV12 5QD

🕘 12-11 ☎ (01922) 712038

Black Country Ales Bradley's Finest Golden, Pig on the Wall, Fireside; guest beers 🄷

A traditional welcoming pub converted from 17th-century cottages about 200 years ago. There are three comfortable rooms including a tastefully refurbished family lounge/family room, with a pool table. The public bar has a solid fuel burner, and original beams feature in the other room. A

quiz is held every other Wednesday. The pub is on the Facebook social networking site.
🏚Q❧✿❄⬛🖼(341,369)♣⚹

Whimsey ⬛
13 High Road, WV12 4JR
❂ 1-midnight (1am Sun); 12-1am Fri & Sat
☎ (01902) 630634
Enville Ale; Hop Back Summer Lightning; Taylor Landlord; guest beer ℍ
A popular street-corner local with two rooms and a beer garden. The staff and regulars are friendly and welcoming, creating a comfortable atmosphere. The guest beer is normally Wye Valley HPA but does vary occasionally. Bar snacks are available.
🏚❧✿⬛(326)♣P⚹

Solihull

White Swan ✅
32-34 Station Road, B91 3SB (by main bus stops opp Touchwood shopping centre)
❂ 8-midnight (1am Fri & Sat) ☎ (0121) 711 5180
Greene King Abbot; Ruddles Best Bitter; guest beers ℍ
Large, modern, open-plan pub serving two regular ales and a varying range of up to five guest beers, often from local brewers such as Purity and Silhill. Decorations include a number of prints showing aspects of the town centre's history and some original works by local artists. Food is the standard Wetherspoon's fare. The pub can get very busy on Friday and Saturday nights. ❧◑♿⇌⬛⚹

Stourbridge

Duke William ♟ ⬛ ✅
25 Coventry Street, DY8 1EP (corner of Coventry St and Duke St)
❂ 12-11 ☎ (01384) 440202
Craddock's Low Gravity, Saxon Gold, Crest, Capra, Troll; Wye Valley Butty Bach; guest beers ℍ
Beautifully restored Edwardian pub with high ceilings, lovely exposed brickwork chimneys – with real wood fires – and oak floors. To complement the home-brewed ales, real cider, perry and an impressive range of bottled Belgian beers are served. Live music is in the front bar on Thursdays. The rear room at the back of the pub is quiet. CAMRA Branch Pub of the Year for the second year running. Craddock's Bewery, with large viewing windows, is at the rear. Cobs available.
🏚Q✿⬛♿⇌(Town)⬛♥⚹🚪

Plough & Harrow ⬛
107 Worcester Street, DY8 1AX (on A451 at jct of B4186 Heath Lane)
❂ 12-11 (11.30 Fri & Sat) ☎ (01384) 397218
Craddock's Crest; Hobsons Best Bitter; Taylor Landlord; Wye Valley HPA; guest beers ℍ
Friendly former Pub and Cider Pub of the Year where the main priority is to serve well-kept real ale and cider. The U-shaped bar serves three separate areas and conversation is not interrupted by TV or loud music. Three real fires create a cosy atmosphere inside, where dogs on leads are welcome. Outside there is a garden with covered smoking area and a log-burning stove. Car park (daytime) at Mary Stevens park opposite.
🏚Q✿⇌(Town)⬛♥⚹

490

Sutton Coldfield

Bishop Vesey ♟ ✅
63 Boldmere Road, B73 5UY
❂ 8-11 (midnight Fri & Sat) ☎ (0121) 355 5077
Courage Directors; Greene King Abbot; Ruddles Best Bitter; guest beers ℍ
Boasting 12 consecutive years in the Guide and local CAMRA Pub of the Year 2012, this busy Wetherspoon has a loyal local clientele and thriving darts team. It comprises an open-plan layout with upstairs seating and outside patio/smokers area. Children are welcome in the family area until 9pm. Three regular beers and up to six guests feature, many from local micros, together with regular beer festivals and Meet the Brewer evenings. ✿◑♿⬛⚹

Butlers Arms ✅
444 Lichfield Road, B74 4BL (near corner with Butlers Lane)
❂ 12-11 (midnight Fri & Sat); 12-10.30 Sun
☎ (0121) 308 0765 ⊕ butlersarms.co.uk
Beer range varies ℍ
Fronted by a spacious car park and close to the nearby station at Butler's Lane. Peruse the interior, an eclectic mix of styles; enjoy the leather sofas, Shaker chairs, modern lamps and mirrors dotted round the tall bar, reflecting the landlord's inimitable taste. Four guest beers often include Caledonian and Greene King Abbot. The fabulous food boasts a chalkboard full of fish specials and a menu with meat and vegetarian alternatives, all with good prices. This is a family-run pub with great staff and a comfortable feel.
Q❧✿◑♿⇌(Butlers Lane)⬛(112,966,905)P⚹

Duke Inn ✅
12 Duke Street, B72 1RJ
❂ 12-11; 11-midnight Fri & Sat ☎ (0121) 355 1767
Caledonian Deuchars IPA, Flying Scotsman; Greene King Abbot; Wells Bombardier; Young's Bitter ℍ
Old-fashioned side-street boozer, a welcome break from chain pubs. The main bar features a pale wood gantry complete with mirrors and clock; note also the etched glass in the doors. A small lounge to the rear is more cosy, but the best drinking area is the short corridor abutting the bar, featuring elaborate floor tiles and decorated mirrors, and even a short panel of snob screens. It has a large grassy beer garden. Beers can be pricey. Parking is Pay & Display. ✿❄⇌⬛♣⚹

Horse & Jockey ✅
90 Birmingham Road, B72 1LU
❂ 11.30-11 (midnight Fri & Sat) ☎ (0121) 321 2412
M&B Brew XI; Marston's Pedigree; Purity Pure UBU; guest beers ℍ
Prominent multi-gabled street-corner Ember Inn. The mock-Tudor exterior features deep bay windows and elaborate hanging lamps. The well-decorated cosy interior is warmed by three flaming gas fires and displays pictures of old Sutton. Two interesting guest beers feature, changing about once a week, and ale prices are keen for the area. Good pub grub is offered, with a dining area where children are permitted until 9pm. Car parking is Pay & Display. ✿◑♿⬛P⚹

Mare Pool ✅
297 Lichfield Road, B74 2UG (behind shops on E side of Lichfield Rd)
❂ 8am-midnight (1am Fri & Sat) ☎ (0121) 323 1070

Greene King Abbot; Ruddles Best Bitter; Wychwood Hobgoblin; guest beers Ⓗ
Opened in 2011, this pub has the usual Wetherspoon food offerings and child-friendly policy. The name refers to one of the many pools that used to surround Sutton, and the watery theme includes hundreds of hanging glass droplets. The interior features a canopied gas fire, while the suntrap beer terrace has an unusually shaped chimenea. There is occasional showing of big-screen sport. Up to five guest ales, often featuring Backyard and Purity beers, are on handpump. Ale discount for CAMRA members.
Q⊛❶ᵫ⇌(Four Oaks)🚆(6,112,902)P⌐

Three Tuns ✅
19 High Street, B72 1XS (uphill N from town centre)
✪ 11.30-midnight (11 Sun & Mon; 11.30 Tue; 1am Fri & Sat)
☎ (0121) 355 2996 ⊕ threetuns.net
Thwaites Original, Wainwright, Lancaster Bomber; guest beer Ⓗ
Grade II-listed, 16th-century coaching inn boasting a quality refurbishment. This has provided a glazed canopy to envelop both sides of the pub and shield the courtyard from the weather. The interior has four rooms: one for quiet contemplation, a bar for chat, a lounge for food and regular live music and a Sky Sports and games room. The beer range includes a special from Thwaites. Food is served all day and children are welcome until 9pm.
Q❶ᵫ⇌🚆♣P

Tipton

Tamebridge
45 Tame Road, DY4 7JA (off A461) SO975921
✪ 12-11 ☎ (0121) 557 2496
RCH Double Header; Wye Valley HPA; guest beers Ⓗ
Situated alongside the Oldbury arm of the River Tame, the Tamebridge stands out with its bright red painted brickwork. The bar, which has a large coal fire, leads onto a small cosy snug area, and there is also a family room, all rooms having large-screen TV. There is a patio outside with a covered heated smoking area. Currently serving four real ales including two changing guests.
🏚🏠⊛❶ᵫ⇌(Dudley Port)🚆(74)P⌐

Upper Gornal

Britannia (Sally's) ★ Ⓛ
109 Kent Street, DY3 1UX (on A459)
✪ 12-11 (10.30 Sun) ☎ (01902) 883253
Bathams Mild Ale, Best Bitter Ⓗ
Identified by CAMRA as one of Britain's Real Heritage Pubs thanks to the tap room at the rear named after legendary former landlady Sally Perry, with its wall-mounted handpumps. Service can be obtained from the main front bar, itself a comfortable place to be, with both areas warmed with roaring open fires. There is also a family/games room with TV. Behind the pub is the former brewhouse, and a delightful garden with a smoking shelter. A good selection of bar snacks is available. 🏚Q🏠⊛❶ᵫ🚆(1)♣⌐

Jolly Crispin
25 Clarence Street, DY3 1UL (A459)
✪ 4 (12 Fri & Sat)-11; 12-10.30 Sun ☎ (01902) 672220
Beer range varies Ⓗ
Lively pub on the main route from Dudley to Sedgley. This 18th-century former shoemaker's

house has a beer festival every day. The locals are friendly, and the fires glow. The beer, a regular Titanic house beer (Crispy Nail) and eight guest pulls are complemented by a real cider. A twice-yearly cider festival is held in the garden and the number 1 bus from Dudley to Wolverhampton stops outside. 🏚⊛❶🚆(1)♣🐷P⌐

Wall Heath

Wall Heath Tavern Ⓛ
14 High street, DY6 0HA (on A449)
✪ 12-midnight ☎ (01384) 287319
Enville White, Ale, Old Porter, Ginger Beer; Holden's Golden Glow; guest beers Ⓗ
After a long period under different names, this former Ansells pub has been reinstated as the Wall Heath Tavern. Serving up to 10 real ales, with a major emphasis on Enville Ales, it can get busy, particularly at weekends. The lounge is predominantly a dining area, especially in the evenings, when good-value food is served. There is a large patio area at the rear, which is busy in the summer months. A CAMRA discount applies on all real ales. 🏚🏠⊛❶ᵫ🚆P⌐

Walsall

Butts Tavern
44 Butts Street, WS4 2BJ (200yds from Arboretum's Lichfield St entrance)
✪ 12-midnight (2am Fri & Sat); 12-11 Sun
☎ (01922) 629332 ⊕ buttstavern.co.uk
Bathams Best Bitter; Burton Bridge Bramble Stout; Greene King Abbot; Olde Swan Bumble Hole Bitter; Slater's Original; Wye Valley Bitter; guest beers Ⓗ
The Butts Tavern is a welcoming, friendly and lively free house recently refurbished by Richard and Lydia. Tuesday is quiz night, Friday is karaoke with Mark James, Saturday is a live band (advertised in the monthly programme), and the last Sunday of every month is acoustic night. Two large screens show Sky and ESPN sports. Six real ales are available in the two lounges, with many favourites to suit all real ale connoisseurs. Bathams is a Sunday speciality. The hosts pride themselves on providing quality ales at competitive prices.
🏠⊛ᵫ🚆(22,394,977)♣⌐

King Arthur
59 Liskeard Road, Park Hall, WS5 3EY (off A34 next to Gillity shopping centre)
✪ 12-11 (midnight Fri & Sat) ☎ (01922) 631400
⊕ thekingarthurpub.co.uk
Greene King IPA, Abbot; Sharp's Doom Bar; St Austell Tribute; Taylor Golden Best; Wye Valley HPA Ⓗ
An urban gem located in Park Hall estate, which is hard to find but definitely worth the effort. A two-roomed community pub, it has a bar area with a big screen and five TVs boasting comprehensive sports viewing. The front lounge is popular with diners and is famous for its steaks (large parties should book ahead for food). The pub is decorated with sporting memorabilia. There is a heated smoking area outside next to the large car park, also front and rear beer gardens.
⊛❶ᵫ🚆(274.)P⌐

Lyndon House Hotel Ⓛ
9-10 Upper Rushall Street, WS1 2HA (between the market and St Matthew's church)

✪ 11.30-11 (midnight Fri & Sat); 12-11 Sun
☎ (01922) 612511 ⊕ lyndonhousehotel.co.uk
**Bathams Best Bitter; Burton Bridge XL Bitter;
Caledonian Deuchars IPA; Greene King Abbot;
Theakston Best Bitter; guest beer** Ⓗ
Part of a complex also containing a hotel, the bar
(formerly the Royal Exchange) was converted in
the '80s. It incorporates old brick and many old
timbers to warm and cosy effect. The luxurious
hotel was once a Salvation Army hostel. Popular
with business people, the clientele is drawn from
all over the town to give a slice of Walsall life.
There is occasional live entertainment. Lunchtime
meals are served all week (with a carvery on
Sunday), and evening meals Monday-Thursday
only. ᴪQ❀✍❶❺占🖵(51,377)P⬩⬟

Rose & Crown 🄻
55 Old Birchills, WS2 8QH (off A34)
✪ 12-midnight (1am Fri & Sat) ☎ (01922) 720533
**Black Country Ales Bradley's Finest Golden; guest
beers** Ⓗ
Grade II-listed, this three-roomed corner pub dates
from 1901, when it was owned by Lord's Brewery,
noted for the quality of its buildings. You enter into
a central corridor that also serves as a drinking
area. The long bar has a fine bar back and the room
contains glazed tiling. It hosts live entertainment
on the last Saturday evening of the month. A pool
table, function room and Sky Sports are also
available. Up to 10 guest ales are served and beer
festivals are held in June and December.
ᴪQ❧占🖵♣⬩⬟

Walsall Cricket Club
Gorway Road, WS1 3BE (off A34, by University campus)
✪ 8-10.30; 12-11 (4-10.30 winter) Sat;12-11 (12-8 winter)
Sun ☎ (01922) 622094 ⊕ walsallcricketclub.com
Wye Valley HPA; guest beers Ⓗ
Established in 1830, Walsall Cricket Club has
occupied this site since 1907. It has a comfortable
single-roomed lounge displaying cricket
memorabilia, and two large screens for sporting
events. The bar is staffed by members. On match
days the cricket can be viewed through panoramic
windows, and in good weather the lounge is
opened onto the patio area. On summer evenings
it is a rural retreat in the heart of town. Beer
festivals are held. Entry to the club for non-
members is by CAMRA membership card.
❀占🖵(51)♣P

Wheatsheaf
4 Birmingham Road, WS1 2NA
✪ 12 (5 Mon)-midnight ☎ (01922) 628992
**Black Sheep Best Bitter; St Austell Tribute; guest
beers** Ⓗ
Originally a small multi-roomed local, in the mania
for destroying pubs it was all knocked into a large
one-roomed layout incorporating the adjoining
house. There is a bar area and the present tenants
have created a cosy snug area around an open fire.
A delight here is to occupy a tub armchair and put
your feet up on a pouffe, gentlemen's club-style. It
is family- and dog-friendly. It has live bands on
Friday and Saturday evenings, and a monthly quiz.
Lunchtime meals served Tuesday-Friday and
evening meals Wednesday-Friday only.
ᴪ❀❶占⇌🖵(51)♣⬩⬟

White Lion ✪
150 Sandwell Street, WS1 3EQ (at jct of Sandwell St and
Little London)

✪ 12-11 (midnight Thu & Fri); 11-midnight Sat
☎ (01922) 628542
Greene King IPA; Taylor Landlord; guest beers Ⓗ
This imposing late-Victorian back-street local is a
great community melting pot. The classic sloping
bar, with its deep and shallow ends, is the best in
town. There is a plush, comfortable lounge for the
drinker who wants to languish, and it has a small
walled garden. Steak night is Tuesday, live bands
play every Friday, jazz night is the first Monday of
the month, open mic night is Thursday, darts team
plays on Wednesday and dominoes on Thursday.
Children are welcome until 8.30pm.
ᴪ❧❀占🖵(404)♣⬩⬟

Wednesbury

Bellwether ✪
3-4 Walsall Street, WS10 9BZ
✪ 8-midnight (1am Fri & Sat) ☎ (0121) 502 6404
**Greene King Abbot; Ruddles Best Bitter; guest
beers** Ⓗ
Typical lively Wetherspoon outlet in the town
centre, close to the bus station. Popular with
shoppers, it can get exceptionally busy on Fridays
and Saturdays. Up to 10 ales are available, with
Springhead Roaring Meg and Holden's beers often
featured. As well as the usual Wetherspoon
festivals, the Bellwether frequently showcases a
particular brewery's beers throughout a week. A
beer garden is at the rear. ❧❀❶占🖵♣⬩⬟

Old Blue Ball 🄻
19 Hall End, WS10 9ED (just off B4200 Whitley St; buses
311A and 313 pass by)
✪ 12-3, 5-11; 12-11 Fri-Sun ☎ (0121) 556 0197
**Everards Original; Olde Swan Original; Wells
Bombardier; Wye Valley Butty Bach; guest beers** Ⓗ
A traditional back-street local with six handpulls.
There are three rooms, a small bar through a
sliding door on the right, a family room with a
dartboard on the left and a quieter back room snug
opposite. Drinking is acceptable in the corridor
which, like the snug, has a serving hatch. The large
garden with seating and a children's play area is
especially popular in summer. Chips and hot pork
and stuffing sandwiches are served on Fridays and
Saturdays. Q❧❀❶占🖵(311A,313)♣⬟

Olde Leathern Bottel ✪
40 Vicarage Road, WS10 9DW (just off A461; bus 311
from Walsall is a 5 min walk)
✪ 12-2.30 (not Mon), 6-11; 12-3, 6-11.30 Fri; 12-11.30 Sat;
12-4, 7-11 Sun ☎ (0121) 505 0230
Beer range varies Ⓗ
The Bottel is set in cottages dating from 1510. It
has four rooms adorned with old photos, including
a snug that is also used as a function room. Two
beers are available (three at weekends), with Wye
Valley HPA often making an appearance. There is a
quiz on Sunday evenings, and occasional beer
festivals have proved to be popular. Closed Monday
lunchtimes. Q❀❶ 🖵(311)♣P⬟

Wednesfield

Vine 🍷 ★ 🄻
35 Lichfield Road, WV11 1TN
✪ 12-11 ☎ (01902) 733529
**Black Country Ales Bradley's Finest Golden, Pig on the
Wall, Fireside; guest beers** Ⓗ

A rare intact example of a simple inter-war working class pub built in 1938. Identified by CAMRA as one of Britain's Real Heritage Pubs and Grade II-listed, it retains the original bar, lounge and snug. Six changing guest beers, often including other LocAles, complement the three regular beers. A covered smokers' shelter and a beer garden provide outdoor drinking areas. This true community pub was winner of local CAMRA Pub of the Year 2012. ⛃Q✿❀◖⊟(59,89)♣P⌐⌐

West Bromwich

Old Hop Pole
474 High Street, B70 9LD
☼ 12-2 (3 Mon & Tue), 5-11; 12-1am Sat & Sun ☎ 07946 579957
Wye Valley HPA; guest beers Ⓗ
Popular community pub, a short distance from West Bromwich town centre, where a warm welcome is always guaranteed. The central bar is surrounded by a busy, traditional, bustling front bar, with two conversely quieter, homelier drinking areas. The pub gets extremely busy at weekends when West Bromwich Albion play at home (opens at 11am) as it is a mecca for fans, as testified by the club memorabilia decorating the walls. Live bands play on Saturday evenings. Up to three guest beers are served from regional breweries or larger micros. ⛃➳◖⊟(Dartmouth St)⊟(74,79)♣⌐

Wheatsheaf Ⓛ
379 High Street, B70 9QW
☼ 11 (12 Mon)-11 (1am Sat); 12-1am Fri; 12-11 Sun
☎ (0121) 553 4221
Holden's Black Country Mild Ⓐ, Black Country Bitter, Golden Glow, Special; guest beers Ⓗ
Popular, community-centred Holden's gem easily identifiable by its conspicuously designed and colourful mock-Tudor exterior. The elongated central servery is surrounded by a bustling, friendly front bar contrasting with a more secluded, peaceful lounge. The generously portioned and keenly priced food is popular with office workers at lunchtimes and also served in the evenings. Like the Old Hop Pole opposite, the pub is jam-packed when West Bromwich Albion play at home. Quizzes are held every Wednesday and live bands play fortnightly at weekends.
Q➳✿◖⊟(Guns Village)⊟(74,79)♣⌐⊟

Willenhall

Falcon Ⓛ
77 Gomer Street West, WV13 2NR (off B4464, behind flats)
☼ 12-11 (10.30 Sun) ☎ (01902) 633378
Exmoor Gold; Olde Swan Dark Swan, Bumble Hole Bitter; Salopian Oracle; Thornbridge Jaipur IPA; guest beers Ⓗ
The Falcon has long been the flagship real ale pub in Willenhall. Boasting seven keenly priced beers, this venue has been run by the same family for the past 28 years and has established a strong local following. Built in 1936, it has two rooms, a lively bar and a quieter lounge, with friendly staff.
Q✿❀⊟(525,529)♣⌐⊟

Malthouse Ⓛ ✓
The Dale, New Road, WV13 2BG
☼ 9-midnight (1am Fri & Sat) ☎ (01902) 635273

Greene King Abbot; Ruddles Best Bitter; Springhead Roaring Meg Ⓗ; guest beers Ⓗ/Ⓖ
Centrally located Wetherspoon that started life as a malthouse, becoming the Dale Cinema, then a bingo hall. It consists of an L-shaped single room with a rear patio area. The accent here is on the quality of the food and real ales on offer, rather than the amount of choice. Two traditional ciders are also usually available. As well as the usual bi-annual beer festival, this pub offers occasional mini beer festivals and often has CAMRA promotion nights on Wednesdays. ✿◖&⌐⌐

Robin Hood Ⓛ
54 The Crescent, WV13 2QR (200yds from A462/B4464 jct)
☼ 12-11 ☎ (01902) 635070
Black Country Ales Bradley's Finest Golden, Pig on the Wall Ⓗ, Fireside Ⓗ/Ⓖ; guest beers Ⓗ
A small, warm and friendly pub with a single comfortable U-shaped room. The mainly local trade supports the many charity events held throughout the year. This venue is frequented by the local archery club, who practise in the adjacent field. There are usually nine real ales on and one real cider. Bar snacks are available all day. No TV.
⛃✿⊟(529)♣⌐P⌐⌐

Wollaston

Graham's Place Ⓛ
73 Bridgnorth Road, DY8 3PZ (on A458 towards Bridgnorth, just before Wollaston)
☼ 11-midnight (1am Fri & Sat; 11.30 Sun) ☎ (01384) 440315
⊕ grahams-place.co.uk
Enville Ginger Beer; Salopian Oracle; guest beers Ⓗ
Long, single-room pub with a modern, clean decor and a variety of different feels within the bar area. Freshly prepared meals made from locally sourced ingredients are served in the conservatory to the rear (Mon-Fri eves only), with a more intimate, cosy drinking area to the front and a long narrow bar separating the two. Up to seven real ales are on handpull. Outside is a small covered smoking area and a large garden – pleasant in summer.
✿◖⊟(227,228,X96)P⌐⌐

Unicorn Ⓛ
145 Bridgnorth Road, DY8 3NX (on A458 towards Bridgnorth)
☼ 12-11; 12-4, 7-11 Sun ☎ (01384) 394823
Bathams Mild Ale, Best Bitter Ⓗ
Former brewhouse purchased by Bathams in the early 1990s following the death of the last member of the Billingham family. The brewhouse is still there, but not in use. Since joining the Bathams' estate this venue is widely recognised as serving one of the best pints of both of the brewery's beers. The pub is still a traditional two-bar drinking house popular with all age groups in the local community. Cobs can be freshly made on request. Bathams XXX is available at Christmas.
⛃Q✿◖&⊟(227,228,X96)P⌐⌐

Wolverhampton

Chindit Ⓛ ✓
113 Merridale Road, WV3 9SE
☼ 4 (12 Sat & Sun)-11 ☎ (01902) 425582 ⊕ thechindit.co.uk
Enville Ale; Wye Valley HPA; guest beers Ⓗ
Street-corner local, built in the 1950s originally as an off-licence. It is thought to be the only pub in

the country named after the Chindits, a special force who fought in Burma in World War II – their history is displayed on the wall of the lounge. The bar is decorated with music memorabilia and hosts live music every Friday evening. Cobs are usually on offer behind the bar. ✿⊄🚃(3,4)P↻

Combermere Arms Ⓛ

90 Chapel Ash, WV3 0TY (on A41 Tettenhall Rd)
🕭 11-3, 5.30-11; 12-midnight Fri & Sat; 12-10.30 Sun
☎ (01902) 421880
Banks's Mild, Bitter; guest beers Ⓗ
Famous for having a tree growing in the gents' toilet, this quaint little terrace pub lies just a short distance from the city centre. Although small, it still has three separate rooms, plus a covered backyard where live music is often played at the weekend. The small car park at the rear is accessed via Bath Road around the corner. There are always two or three guest beers available. Good-value weekday lunches are popular with the business folk.
🗠✿⊄🚃P↻

Dog & Gun Ⓛ ✅

1 Wrottesley Road, Tettenhall, WV6 8SB (off A41 Wergs Rd)
🕭 12-11 (midnight Thu-Sat) ☎ (01902) 747943
Banks's Bitter; Marston's Pedigree; Purity Pure UBU; guest beers Ⓗ
Comfortable and welcoming Ember Inns pub with individual seating areas around a large U-shaped bar. It attracts a wide age range, including a local writers' group and a rambling club who meet here regularly. Food quality, a varied range of LocAle beers and an imaginative choice of guest beers, often dark, ensure a busy and friendly atmosphere, particularly on weekend evenings. There is a patio for outside drinking and a covered, heated area for smokers. ✿⊄🚃(1,891)P↻

Great Western Ⓛ

Sun Street, WV10 0DJ (via subway from high level station and city centre)
🕭 11-11 (10.30 Sun) ☎ (01902) 351090
Bathams Best Bitter; Holden's Black Country Mild, Black Country Bitter, Golden Glow, Special; guest beers Ⓗ
Former CAMRA National Pub of the Year with four distinct drinking areas. This listed pub gets its name from its proximity to the city's disused GWR station. Plenty of Wolves and old railway memorabilia is on display. The pub is just a short walk from Wolverhampton's bus and railway stations and is popular on Wolves match days. Good-value traditional pub grub is on the menu. Monthly charity quiz nights are well attended.
🗠✿⊄≢🚃(St George's)🚃P↻

Hog's Head Ⓛ ✅

186 Stafford Street, WV1 1NA
🕭 10-midnight (1am Fri & Sat); 12-midnight Sun
☎ (01902) 717955
Wells Bombardier; guest beers Ⓗ
Deserved winner of CAMRA Local Pub of the Year competition in 2011 for its commitment to real ale. A varying range of up to nine ales is available, always including beers from local microbreweries, plus Thatchers cider. This large one-roomed city-centre pub is split into many areas, featuring large-screen TVs showing sport and music videos. It can get busy at weekends and when Wolves are playing at home. CAMRA members get a discount on real ales. ✿⊄≢🚃(St George's)🚃🍺↻

Horse & Jockey Ⓛ ✅

64 Robert Wynd, Woodcross, WV14 9SB
🕭 12-11 (11.30 Fri & Sat) ☎ (01902) 662268
Banks's Mild; Greene King Abbot; Hobsons Town Crier; St Austell Tribute; Young's Bitter; guest beers Ⓗ
Friendly and welcoming, this is a thriving community local with a bar, lounge and a large beer garden at the rear. The bar features horse racing pictures, and the contemporary lounge has an open fire and an old Black Country canal map. Quiz nights raise money for local charities and a chalkboard announces forthcoming guest ales. Good-value food, with vegetarian options, is served every day (no food Sun eve).
🗠🍴✿⊄🚃(81)♣P↻

Moon Under Water Ⓛ

53-55 Lichfield Street, WV1 1EQ (opp Grand Theatre)
🕭 7-midnight (1am Fri & Sat) ☎ (01902) 422447
Banks's Mild; Greene King Abbot; Ruddles Best Bitter; guest beers Ⓗ
Wetherspoon pub opened in 1995 on the ground floor of the former Co-op building and featuring a display of Old Wolverhampton photographs. Opposite the Grand Theatre, it attracts pre-show drinkers and diners as well as students and real ale enthusiasts. The pub gets very busy on weekend evenings and when Wolves are playing at home. It is close to the rail and the new bus station, making it easy to reach by public transport.
⊄🚃≢🚃(St George's)🚃🍺

Newhampton Ⓛ ✅

19 Riches Street, Whitmore Reans, WV6 0DW
🕭 11-11 (midnight Fri & Sat); 12-11 Sun ☎ (01902) 746747
Caledonian Deuchars IPA; Courage Best Bitter; Enville Ale; Fuller's London Pride; Taylor Landlord; Wye Valley HPA Ⓗ
Locals of all descriptions are catered for, with three main bars supplemented by a bowls pavilion bar, function room and an award-winning garden around the bowling green. Its street-corner location disguises an extensive range of drinking areas, with eight handpumps offering seven real ales and a real cider. Hot food from the pot is almost always available. A discount is offered on beer to CAMRA members. 🗠✿⊄🚃🍺↻

Penn Bowling & Social Club Ⓛ

10 Manor Road, Penn, WV4 5PY
🕭 12-midnight (1am Fri & Sat; 11 Sun) ☎ (01902) 342516
⊕ pennbowlingclub.com
Banks's Mild, Bitter Ⓟ**; guest beers** Ⓗ
The hub of this well-used community club is a large bar overlooking the floodlit crown bowling green. It has a pool table and dartboard, and is surrounded by TV screens which show the major sport and music channels. A small quiet lounge, the Red Room, is accessed from the main bar. There is a further large function room where the club holds a Classic Northern Soul and Motown evening on the last Saturday of each month.
✿⊄🚃(255,256)♣P↻

Posada Ⓛ

48 Lichfield Street, WV1 1DG (opp art gallery)
🕭 12-11 (1am Fri & Sat); closed Sun
Beer range varies Ⓗ
A splendid Victorian listed city-centre pub that has retained some of its original features, although it has been converted to one room. It attracts a varied customer base – quiet during the day and with recorded music on weekend evenings. There

is a courtyard to the rear for summer drinking, and a smoking area. CAMRA members receive a discount on real ales. The pub is usually closed on Sundays but opens when Wolves are playing at home. ✿≠ℜ(St George's)🚾⍭

Royal Oak Ⓛ

70 Compton Road, WV3 9PH (on A454 300yds from Chapel Ash jct)
✿ 11.30-11 (midnight Fri & Sat) ☎ (01902) 422845
Banks's Mild, Bitter; guest beers Ⓗ
Historic local pub, less than 10 minutes' walk from the city centre, with a lively and friendly atmosphere in its single-bar room. The two changing guest beers are from a Marston's-owned brewery. Traditional pub food is served at lunchtimes. There is an open mic night every Tuesday and DJs play in the bar on Saturday evenings. The large covered patio provides shelter for smokers, and also stages live music in the summer months. ✿◖&🚾(10,890)🐾P⍭

Stile Inn Ⓛ

3 Harrow Street, Whitmore Reans, WV1 4PB (off Newhampton Rd East)
✿ 11.30-11 (midnight Fri; 1am Sat) ☎ (01902) 425336
Banks's Mild, Bitter; guest beers Ⓗ
Late-Victorian street-corner pub built in 1900 replacing a former pub on the site. It is a true community local with a sporting prominence: darts and dominoes feature inside and bowling on the unusual L-shaped bowling green outside. The public bar, smoke room and snug are popular with Wolves fans on match days – the football ground is a short distance away. Guest ales are from the Marston's range, and excellent-value food, including Polish dishes, is served all day, every day. ☞✿◖🚾🍴(5,6)♣⍭🖥

Swan (at Compton) Ⓛ

Bridgnorth Road, Compton, WV6 8AE (at Compton Island, A454)
✿ 12-11 (11.30 Thu; midnight Fri & Sat) ☎ (01902) 754736
Banks's Mild, Bitter; guest beers Ⓗ
A Grade II-listed inn, this unspoilt gem has a convivial atmosphere, with guest ales from the

Marston's range. The traditional bar features exposed beams, wooden settles and a faded painting of a swan dated 1777. The bar and L-shaped snug are supplied from a central servery, and a separate lounge doubles as a games room. Local angling, cycling and pigeon clubs meet here regularly. The heated patio is partially covered for smokers. Dogs are welcome in the bar.
Q✿🍴🚾(10,890)♣P⍭

Woodsetton

Park Inn Ⓛ

George Street, DY1 4LW (on A457, 200yds from A4123) SO939926
✿ 12-11 (10.30 Sun) ☎ (01902) 661279
Holden's Black Country Mild, Black Country Bitter, Golden Glow, Special; guest beers Ⓗ
Vibrant suburban brewery tap, held by the Holden family since 1915. Radiating out from the spacious main bar are a small games room, a raised dining area and a separate conservatory. Functions are catered for and reasonably priced food is served 12-8pm (4.30pm Sun). There is a 10p discount on pints for CAMRA members. Note that the new brewery centre is on the right of the car park.
🏠☞✿◖🚾(126)♣P⍭

Wordsley

New Inn Ⓛ

117 High Street Wordsley, DY8 5QR (A491)
✿ 12-11 (10.30 Sun) ☎ (01384) 295614
Bathams Mild Ale, Best Bitter Ⓗ
On the main Wolverhampton to Stourbridge road, the building has an imposing three-storey Victorian façade. One of the Bathams 11, it has become popular and can be extremely busy. An L-shaped bar serves a single room with a small annexe at one end, and a patio area outside. Car parking is at the rear. Children are not allowed but an outside play area is available in the summer. Bar snacks are on offer. The pub largely caters for the surrounding community and has the feel of a proper local. Live music features occasionally. ✿&🚾(256,257)♣P⍭

LocAle

A growing number of entries in the guide refer to pubs supporting the LocAle system. This was devised by CAMRA members in Nottingham and is now in widespread use in England, Wales, Scotland and Northern Ireland.

The aim is to encourage publicans to stock at least one cask beer that comes from a local brewery – the distance between pub and brewery varies but is now generally accepted to be not more than 30 miles. The scheme also encourages publicans to use the Direct Delivery Scheme run by SIBA, the Society of Independent Brewers. SIBA members deliver direct to pubs in their localities rather than going through central warehouses. The overall aim of LocAle is to cut down on 'beer miles'. Research by CAMRA shows that food and drink transport accounts for 25 per cent of all HGV vehicle miles in Britain. Taking into account the miles that ingredients have travelled on top of distribution journeys, an imported lager produced by a multi-national brewery could have notched up more than 24,000 'beer miles' by the time it reaches a pub.

£10 spent on locally-supplied goods generates £25 for local economies. Keeping trade local helps enterprises, creates more economic activity and jobs, and makes other services more viable. The scheme also generates consumer support for local breweries. Pubs that support the LocAle scheme receive a special window sticker. For more information, see the CAMRA website: **www.camra.org.uk**

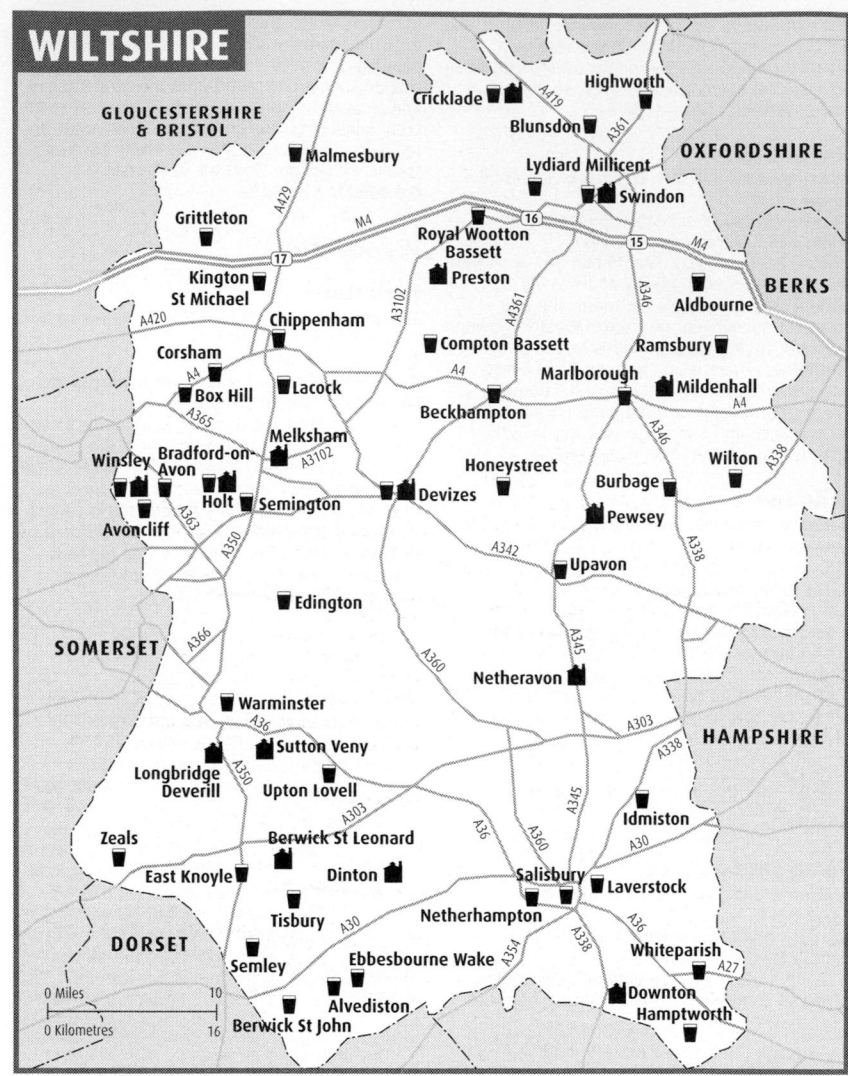

WILTSHIRE

Aldbourne

Blue Boar ⌷

20 The Green, SN8 2EN
✪ 11.30-3, 5.30-11.30; 11.30-midnight Fri & Sat; 12-10.30
Sun ☎ (01672) 540237 ⊕ thepubonthegreen.com
Wadworth Henry's IPA, 6X; guest beer Ⓗ
Friendly, comfortable and traditonal pub in a
wonderful location by the village green. Food is
home-cooked, and there are dining areas inside
and out. Beer festivals are held annually in April
and October. A large collection of bottled beers
from around the country adorns the walls. The pub
featured in a 1971 episode of Dr Who.
⋈Q✿◑♿Å⛢(46,48)

Alvediston

Crown Inn ⌷

The Street, SP5 5JY (off A30 near Donhead) ST977234
✪ 12-3, 5.30-11; 12-11 Sat & Sun ☎ (01722) 780335
⊕ thecrown-inn-alvediston.co.uk

**Hop Back Summer Lightning; Ringwood Best Bitter;
Wadworth Henry's IPA; Wayland's Sixpenny
Alvediston Ale** Ⓗ
Picturesque 15th-century thatched free house in
the heart of the Chalke Valley. The huge garden
offers outstanding views in summer and real log
fires make the pub cosy in winter. A good selection
of local ales and West Country ciders complements
a sumptuous food menu, with locally sourced
produce cooked to order. A beer festival is held in
May. There is en-suite accommodation and a large
car park. ⋈Q✿◒◑♿⛢(29)⏹P⁼⊟

Avoncliff

Cross Guns

BA15 2HB ST805599
✪ 10-midnight (1am Sat) ☎ (01225) 862335
⊕ crossguns.net
**Box Steam Golden Bolt, Tunnel Vision, seasonal
beers; guest beer** Ⓗ

Sixteenth-century canalside inn with sloping terraces down to the River Avon, popular with walkers and cyclists. Features include an inglenook fireplace, priest's hole, garden bar, weekend barbecues and a resident ghost. Live music plays every Tuesday and third Thursday in the month. Five beers from Box Steam are complemented by a guest sourced from far and wide, with a dark and a blonde always in the mix. Up to seven real ciders are also available. Just 100 yards from Avoncliff station, there are car parks nearby. Children and dogs are welcome. ♨Q☺🍴⌖◑⬥🅰🚲♣🐾🚪

Beckhampton

Waggon & Horses Ⓛ ✅
SN8 1QJ
🕒 11-11; 12-10.30 Sun ☎ (01672) 539418
🌐 waggonandhorsesbeckhampton.co.uk
Wadworth Henry's IPA Ⓗ, 6X Ⓖ, seasonal beers Ⓗ
Built originally in 1669 as the Black Bear, this pretty and historic thatched inn was an overnight stop on the journey from London to Bristol. Its most famous guest was reputedly Charles Dickens who used it as his model for an inn in The Pickwick Papers. The pub no longer provides accommodation but there is excellent food. Check the website for winter opening hours. Three seasonal Wadworth ales are served alongside the regulars. ♨☺◑🚪(49)P

Berwick St John

Talbot
The Cross, SP7 0HA (S of A30, 5 miles E of Shaftesbury)
🕒 12-2.30, 6-11; 12-4 Sun ☎ (01747) 828222
Draught Bass; Ringwood Best Bitter; Wadworth 6X; guest beers Ⓗ
Set in a small, rural, peaceful village, the Talbot opened as a beer house circa 1832 despite vehement opposition from the local parson's wife. The building is predominantly stone built, with a long, low bar with beams and an inglenook fireplace. As well as offering three regular beers, the landlord is keen to promote local microbreweries with a choice of guest ales. The more inquisitive visitor may find the cosy dining room behind the inglenook. The pub is popular with walkers from the local downs and cyclists on the 160-mile Wiltshire Cycleway.
♨Q☺◑🚪(29)♣P🚪

Blunsdon

Heart in Hand
43 High Street, SN26 7AG
🕒 12-3.30, 5.30-11; 12-10.30 Sun ☎ (01793) 721314
🌐 heartinhand.co.uk
Beer range varies Ⓗ
This is a friendly, family-run, local pub with good-value home-cooked food. There are two guest beers in the winter, three in the summer; one is usually a local one. Outside there is a large garden and children's play area at the back. Meals are served Sunday lunchtimes, and lunchtimes and evenings the rest of the week. It also has darts and crib teams. Dogs are allowed in the bar, and the pub has four en-suite rooms. ☺🍴◑🚪(24)♣P

Box Hill

Quarryman's Arms
SN13 8HN (S of A4 between Corsham and Box) ST834693

🕒 11-11.30 ☎ (01225) 743569 🌐 quarrymans-arms.co.uk
Butcombe Bitter; Moles Best Bitter; Wadworth 6X; guest beer Ⓗ
Tucked away off the main routes, it is a steep uphill walk from the nearest bus stop, but this 300-year-old miners' inn is well worth the effort. Offering a friendly welcome, the pub is renowned for high-quality food and ales, served in the bar, restaurant or garden. Quiz night is every second Wednesday, and county-themed beer festivals are held regularly (check website for details). Black Rat cider is on offer. Accommodation is available.
Q🛏☺🍴◑🍴⬥🚪(X31,231,232)♣🐾P🚪

Bradford-on-Avon

Castle Inn
10 Mount Pleasant, BA15 1SJ ST827612
🕒 9-11; 10-10.30 Sun ☎ (01225) 865657
🌐 flatcappers.co.uk
Three Castles Barbury Castle, Vale Ale; guest beers Ⓗ
Acquired by pubco Flatcappers in 2006 and transformed by wholesale refurbishment, this quiet, cosy, relaxing pub caters for a wide clientele. The interior comprises a large bar with flagstone floor, lime-washed walls, open fireplace and magnificent reclaimed mahogany bar, and three smaller rooms with elm floorboards, exposed walls and worn club chairs. Food is served throughout the premises. The garden and terrace enjoy commanding views towards Salisbury Plain. The Vale Ale is badged as Flatcapper while the four guests are sourced from local micros. Real cider is available in summer. ♨Q☺🍴⬥🚲P🚪

Rising Sun
231 Winsley Road, BA15 1QS ST824613
🕒 12 (4 Tue)-11; 12-10.30 Sun ☎ (01225) 862354
🌐 therisingsunatbradfordonavon.co.uk
Beer range varies Ⓗ
Popular local at the top of a hill with two bars: a small, quiet lounge and a more spacious, livelier saloon with TV screens. At the back is a walled beer garden with patio. The pub is home to darts, quiz, crib, pool and football teams, and hosts regular live music including a Rhythm & Booze beer festival over the August bank holiday. The three beers change week by week and the cider is Cheddar Valley. The pub's ancient spaniel is still there, ready to welcome you. ♨☺🍴🚲♣🐾🚪

Burbage

Three Horseshoes ⓛ

1 Stibb Green, SN8 3AE
☼ 12-2 (not Mon), 6-11; 12-2, 7-10.30 Sun
☎ (01672) 810324
Wadworth Henry's IPA, 6X, seasonal beer Ⓗ
A traditional thatched pub standing next to the village green. Constructed during the railway boom in the 19th century, it features railway memorabilia from the three railways that operated in the area. The same landlord has been behind the bar for more than 20 years and he knows how to serve an excellent pint of Wadworth's beers and the occasional guest. With good quality food (no meals Mon eve) and Budweiser Budvar on tap, this pub has something for everyone.
🅼Q🌣🕊🍽🚫(X5,80)♣P⏴⏵

Chippenham

Gladstone Arms

34 Gladstone Road, SN15 3BW
☼ 11-3, 5.30-11; 11-midnight Fri & Sat; 12-11 Sun
☎ (01249) 660535 ⊕ thegladstonearms.co.uk
Bath Ales Gem; Butcombe Bitter; St Austell Tribute Ⓗ
Friendly and welcoming town-centre pub near the bus station catering for a broad age range of customers. Lively at weekends, the lounge is mainly used for bistro-style dining, where a tempting menu is served, but there is also a comfortable separate public bar if you just want a drink. A TV shows news, with the volume only turned up for major sporting events. Occasional guest beers supplement the standard range. The large garden adjoins an innovative eco-friendly house, designed and occupied by a local architect.
🌣🕊🚫🍽P⏴⏵

New Inn

New Road, SN15 1HS
☼ 12 (4 Tue; 11 Sat)-midnight ☎ 07764 820587
Courage Best Bitter; guest beers Ⓗ
This two-roomed terraced pub is a typical friendly back-street boozer. Opened in 1815, its frontage is on New Road, which was built in 1792. The landlord is renowned for the best-kept Courage Best in the area and his cellarmanship is second to none. Two guest beers selected from the Punch Taverns ale list are also available. Crib, dominoes and darts are regularly played by a clientele of all ages. The winter fire enhances the warm welcome offered all year round. 🅼🚫🍽🚫♣⏴⏵

Old Road Tavern

Old Road, SN15 1JA (200yds N of railway station over footbridge)
☼ 11-11.30 (12.30am Fri & Sat); 12-11.30 Sun
☎ (01249) 652094
Bath Ales Gem; Hop Back Summer Lightning; Otter Bitter; guest beers Ⓗ
Grade II-listed, 140-year-old traditional community local with a large garden that is popular in summer. A diverse mix of regulars ensures lively and friendly conversation. Two frequently changing guest beers come from local and distant breweries. The home of folk music in Chippenham, the pub is a venue for the annual folk festival held over the end of May bank holiday weekend. Folk also features informally on the first and third Sundays of the month in the lounge bar. 🌣🕊🚫🍽♣⏴⏵

Three Crowns ⓛ

18 Causeway, SN15 3DB
☼ 12-2.30, 4.30-11 (midnight Fri); 12-midnight Sat; 12-11 Sun ☎ (01249) 449029 ⊕ threecrownschippenham.co.uk
Beer range varies Ⓗ
A pub since the 18th century with 19th-century additions, the Three Crowns closed in 2009, crippled by pubco rents and prices, but has revived under new family owners to become a beer and cider exhibition establishment. The beer range includes at least two dark beers and four other varying ales, with LocAle breweries well represented. To that add three ciders and a perry, all from small local producers. Entertainment includes comedy nights hosted by a local stand-up, film and poetry nights, plus other special events and occasional beer festivals. 🅼Q🚫🚫🍽♣⏴⏵P🍴

Compton Bassett

White Horse Inn ⓛ

SN11 8RG (2 miles off A4 Calne to Marlborough road)
☼ closed Mon, 12-3, 6-11; 12-4 Sun ☎ (01249) 813118
⊕ whitehorse-comptonbassett.co.uk
Bath Ales Gem; Box Steam Tunnel Vision; Wadworth 6X; guest beers Ⓗ
An award-winning family-run rural gem that always offers a friendly welcome. This traditional country inn is situated in an area of outstanding natural beauty with the Marlborough Downs and Avebury nearby. All food is freshly prepared from locally sourced meat and vegetables, and the fish is from a fresh Cornish catch. The real cider is Old Rosie. There is a large beer garden and function room, and the pub holds a monthly quiz night. Accommodation is available in eight en-suite rooms. 🅼🌣🛏🕊🚫♣🍴P⏴⏵

Corsham

Hare & Hounds ✅

48 Pickwick, SN13 0HY
☼ 11-11 ☎ (01249) 701106
Bath Ales Gem; Caledonian Deuchars IPA; Gale's HSB; guest beers Ⓗ
A large, busy 17th-century coaching inn on the A4. Five ales are usually available including two ever-changing guest beers from local breweries. The occasional beer festival and a Tuesday evening quiz are held. A variety of good food is always on the menu. The pub has three drinking areas – the large lounge can be reserved for private functions. There is outside seating in the garden, which includes cider apple trees and a covered, heated smoking area. Dogs are welcome.
🅼Q🐕🌣🕊🚫(231,233)P⏴⏵

Two Pigs

38 Pickwick, SN13 0HY
☼ 7-11; 12-2.30, 7-10.30 Sun ☎ (01249) 712515
⊕ the2pigs.info
Stonehenge Pigswill, Danish Dynamite; guest beers Ⓗ
This classic free house is a gem of a pub. Several times local CAMRA Pub of the Year, it has featured in the Guide continuously for 23 years. With flagstone floors and wood-panelled walls, the pub dates back to the 18th century. Four ales are usually available, including two alternating guests. Live music plays on Monday evening, usually local blues bands. The covered outdoor drinking area is known as The Sty. 🌣🚫(231,232)

Cricklade

Red Lion ⒧
74 High Street, SN6 6DD
☼ 12-11 (10.30 Sun) ☎ (01793) 750776
⊕ theredlioncricklade.co.uk
**Butcombe Bitter; Moles Best Bitter; Wadworth 6X;
guest beers** Ⓗ
Friendly and comfortable pub, parts of which are
quite ancient – the old town wall passes through
the building. Ten real ales plus cider are on
handpumps. Food is served in what used to be the
back bar, now the restaurant (no food Sun eve).
There is a large garden at the back. Five rooms are
available for B&B. A past winner of CAMRA South
West Regional Pub of the Year. Well worth a visit.
ᄤQ❀⇔◑�døᰁ(51,53)P

Devizes

British Lion ✅
9 Estcourt Street, SN10 1LQ (on A361 London road)
☼ 11-11 (midnight Fri & Sat); 12-11 Sun ☎ (01380) 720665
⊕ britishliondevizes.co.uk
Beer range varies Ⓗ
The Lion is a real ale lover's dream come true, with
an ever-changing range of beers from mainly West
Country breweries, from session ales through to
5% ABV and above, plus porters and stouts. Time it
right and you can sample eight beers on a busy
evening. The landlord has been here for 20 years
and is an authority on the brewing industry. With a
three-sided bar, wooden floors, lively conversation
and interesting locals, this is a genuine 'must visit'
pub. ❀ᰁ(49)♣●P⁵⚊ō

Hare & Hounds ✅
Hare & Hounds Street, SN10 1LZ
☼ 11-3, 7-midnight; 11-midnight Thu-Sat; 12-midnight Sun
☎ (01380) 723231
Wadworth Henry's IPA, 6X, seasonal beers Ⓗ
Consistently the best Wadworth's cellar in town,
the pub has one long bar, comfortable seating, bar
stools, friendly locals and a warm, relaxed
atmosphere. Wadworth's seasonals include Horizon
and Swordfish. The pub is carpeted throughout,
with pristine toilets and a good line in local banter.
Dogs and children are allowed, as long as their
owners and parents behave. Well worth the five-
minute stroll from the town centre.
Q❀◑ᰁ(49)♣P⁵⚊

Silk Mercer ✅
38 St John's Street, SN10 1BL
☼ 7-11 (midnight Fri & Sat) ☎ (01380) 736760
Beer range varies Ⓗ
The Mercer occupies a Grade II-listed building;
refurbishment has made it the smartest pub in
Devizes, with carpets throughout, luxurious
seating, spotless toilets and a good atmosphere. At
least five ales are available at all times from all
areas of the UK. CAMRA Devizes branch is well
supported by the pub, with tasting evenings and
good liaison with the management. Regular beer
festivals are held, with up to 50 ales available over
the festival period. Food is served all day.
❀◑ㅿᰁ(49)⚊

Southgate Inn
Potterne Road, SN10 5BY
☼ 4 (12 Sun)-11; 12-midnight Fri & Sat ☎ (01380) 722872
Beer range varies Ⓗ

Once a regular in the Guide, the Southgate has
been brought back to life by the landlord who took
over the pub two years ago. Dimmed lighting, lots
of nooks and crannies, relaxed background music
and a warm welcome combine to make it a great
stop for a couple of beers. A Hop Back pub, its three
handpumps generally have two Hop Back beers,
sometimes a Downton ale and occasional guests.
There are three small bar areas and a large
courtyard with benches outside. ❀●P⁵⚊

East Knoyle

Fox & Hounds
The Green, SP3 6BN (signed from B3089 close to jct
A303) ST871314
☼ 11.30-3, 5.30-11 ☎ (01747) 830573
⊕ foxandhounds-eastknoyle.co.uk
Beer range varies Ⓗ
Attractive old thatched black and white pub
situated high on a hillside with extensive
panoramic rural views. Comfortable and cosy
inside, the warm welcome is enhanced in winter
by a blazing log fire in a huge inglenook fireplace.
Three ales are always available, encompassing a
wide range of strengths and varying continuously,
with local beers given prominence. The real cider is
Thatchers Cheddar Valley. Food is served at all
sessions. An adjacent skittle alley doubles as a
function room. ᄤQ❀◑♣●P

Ebbesbourne Wake

Horseshoe Inn
The Cross, SP5 5JF (just off A30) ST993239
☼ 12-3 (not Mon), 6.30-11; 12-4 Sun ☎ (01722) 780474
**Bowman Swift One; Otter Bitter; Palmers Copper Ale;
guest beer** Ⓖ
Unspoilt 18th-century pub in a remote rural setting
at the foot of an old ox drove. This friendly pub has
two small bars that display an impressive collection
of old farm implements, tools and lamps, a
restaurant, conservatory and a pleasant garden.
Good local food is served Tuesday to Sunday and
the five beers are served direct from casks stillaged
behind the bar. The original serving hatch just
inside the front door is still in use. Cider is often
available. Q❀⇔◑ ᰁᰁ(29)●P

Edington

Three Daggers
Westbury Road, BA13 4PG
☼ 11-11 Sat & summer (11-3, 5-11 winter); 11-10 (9 winter)
Sun ☎ (01380) 830940 ⊕ threedaggers.co.uk
Wadworth Henry's IPA; guest beer Ⓗ
Once called the Lamb, this pub was renamed the
Paulet Arms but has now reverted to its original
name. It was extensively refurbished in 2010 and
offers good locally sourced food and an interesting
range of bar snacks (no food Sun eve). The main
bar has three drinking areas, sofas and a small
alcove. There is a dining area and stairs leading
upstairs to the accommodation and a small
function room. The restaurant is off to the side and
leads out to the garden. TV screens are hidden
behind two mirrors. Regular events are hosted
each month. Dog-friendly. ᄤ❀⇔◑ㅿᰁ♣P

Grittleton

Neeld Arms 🄻
The Street, SN14 6AP
🌣 12-3, 5.30-11; 12-4, 7-11 Sun ☎ (01249) 782470
⊕ neeldarms.co.uk
Wadworth Henry's IPA, 6X; guest beers 🄷
Cosy, comfortable stone-built 17th-century inn set in a beautiful and unspoilt south Cotswold village with old prints and photographs adorning the walls and a welcoming log fire in winter. A good selection of home-made food is offered with theme nights a highlight. An ever-changing choice of guest beers means there is always something different to try. Popular with locals and visitors, the pub is central to the community. Tourist attractions including Castle Combe, Malmesbury and Bath are close by. 🏚Q🏵🚪🌢◐🅳🚃(35)Pゝ

Hamptworth

Cuckoo Inn 🄻
Hamptworth Road, SP5 2DU (follow signs from A36 for Hamptworth Golf Club) SU244197
🌣 12-3, 5.30-11; 12-11 Fri & Sat; 12-10.30 Sun
☎ (01794) 390302
Bowman Elderado; Hop Back GFB, Summer Lightning; Ringwood Best Bitter; guest beers 🄶
Characterful thatched country pub on the edge of the New Forest. Three small rooms are served by one bar with a fourth room to the rear. All beer is dispensed direct from the cask. GFB and Elderado are sold as Old School and Cuckoorado. Frams scrumpy is sold in the summer. A beer festival is held in late summer. Food is available lunchtimes, snacks Monday and Tuesday, meals Wednesday to Sunday. 🏚Q🌣🏵◐♣ 🍴Pゝ

Highworth

Rose & Crown ✅
19 The Green, SN6 7DB
🌣 12-midnight Mon; 12-3, 5-midnight Tue-Thu; 12-2am Fri; 12-1am Sat; 12-11.30 Sun ☎ (01793) 766287
Courage Best Bitter; Wadworth 6X; Wells Bombardier; guest beers 🄷
This is one of the oldest pubs in Highworth. As well as five real ales, the landlord also keeps a collection of around 70 malt whiskies and hosts tasting sessions on the last Sunday of the month. Good home-cooked food is available from Wednesday evening to Sunday lunchtime. Special nights and parties can be catered for. Games including darts, cards and chess are played and the back garden boasts a boule piste.
🏚🏵◐🚻🚃(7,64,74)♣P

Holt

Tollgate Inn
Ham Green, BA14 6PX (on B3105 between Bradford-on-Avon and Melksham) ST858616
🌣 10-2.30, 5.30 (6 Mon)-11; 11-3 Sun ☎ (01225) 782326
⊕ tollgateholt.co.uk
Beer range varies 🄷
A real gem, this old village pub has an upmarket atmosphere with a wood-burning stove, oak floors, and comfy sofas to relax in. The range of four or five beers, which changes daily, is imaginative, with a good selection of local beers alongside many from smaller breweries further afield. The food in both the upstairs restaurant and the bar is

excellent. The garden at the rear has a small petting zoo/farm for children, complete with miniature goat. 🏚🌣🚪◐🚃(237)🍴Pゝ

Honeystreet

Barge Inn 🍺 🄻
SN9 5PS
🌣 11.30-3 (not Tue), 6-11 (5-midnight Fri); 11.30-midnight Sat; 12-10.30 Sun ☎ (01672) 851705 ⊕ the-barge-inn.com
Fuller's London Pride 🄷
Sitting next to the Kennet & Avon Canal, this is a popular stop for thirsty boaters, but the pub's main appeal is to crop circle enthusiasts, for which the area is renowned. Now run as a community pub, it featured in the BBC series Village SOS and underwent refurbishment in 2011. There is a large caravan and camping field next to the pub. The three house beers are brewed by Stonehenge Brewery and the traditional pub food is of high quality. 🏚🏵◐⊟Å🍴Pゝ

Idmiston

Earl of Normanton 🄻
Tidworth Road, SP4 0AG (on A338) SU195382
🌣 12-2.30, 6-11; 12-3, 7.45-10.30 Sun ☎ (01980) 610251
⊕ earlofnormanton.co.uk
Flowerpots Bitter; Hop Back Summer Lightning; guest beers 🄷
Popular roadside pub with a loyal village clientele and a welcoming atmosphere enhanced by two real fires in winter months. LocAle accredited, it offers two guest ales mostly from local breweries. Good value home-cooked food is served (not Sun eve). There is a small, pleasant garden on the steep hill behind the pub and a heated, covered smoking area. B&B is available. A former Salisbury CAMRA Pub of the Year. 🏚Q🌣🚪◐🚃(66)Pゝ

Kington St Michael

Jolly Huntsman 🄻
80 Kington St Michael, SN14 6JB (signed from A350, between Chippenham and M4 jct 17)
🌣 11.30-3, 6-11 (midnight Fri & Sat); 12-3, 7-10.30 Sun ☎ (01249) 750305 ⊕ jollyhuntsman.com
Moles Tap Bitter; Wadworth 6X; guest beers 🄷
Situated on the high street, at the heart of the village, there is always a friendly welcome at this free house, with an open log fire in winter. A varying range of real ales and ciders is always on offer. The excellent food menu features regularly changing chef's specials and themed evenings. Quiz night is usually the first Monday of the month (check website) and other entertainment includes live jazz and blues. Accommodation is all en-suite with free Wi-Fi. 🏚Q🌣🚪◐🚻Å🚃(99)♣🍴Pゝ

Lacock

Bell Inn 🍺
The Wharf, Bowden Hill, SN15 2PJ (½ mile E of Lacock)
🌣 11.30-2.30, 5-11; 11.30-11 Sat; 12-10.30 Sun
☎ (01249) 730308
Bath Ales Gem; Palmers Best Bitter; guest beers 🄷
On the edge of the National Trust village of Lacock, this free house has been run by the same family for more than 10 years. Local CAMRA Pub of the Year on many occasions, it has an excellent reputation for quality food and ever-changing guest ales. An annual winter beer festival is held in late January/

early February. Originally canal cottages, the pub lies beside the National Cycle Route, with excellent cycle tracks and walks between Chippenham and Melksham. Q✪❀⊙♣♠P⅃⌐

Laverstock

Duck Inn 🅛

Duck Lane, SP1 1PU (signed from village centre)
SU160303
✪ 12-midnight (10.30 Sun) ☎ (01722) 327678
Downton seasonal beer; Hop Back GFB, Crop Circle, Summer Lightning, seasonal beer 🅗
Large open-plan pub with ample car parking. A full menu is available lunchtimes and evenings, with a popular Sunday roast and a regular barbecue. There is satellite TV, live music at weekends and a quiz on Wednesdays. Pool is played in a side room. Music festivals and other events such as themed dinner nights are held. Well situated for walkers on the Clarendon Way. ✪⊙&🅟(R2,R6)♣P⅃⌐

Lydiard Millicent

Sun

The Street, SN5 3LU
✪ 12-2, 5.15-10.30; 10.30-2.30, 5-midnight Fri; 12-2.30, 5-midnight Sat; 12-2.30, 5.30-10.30 Sun ☎ (01793) 770886
⊕ thesunatlydiard.com
Sharp's Doom Bar; Wadworth 6X; guest beers 🅗
A traditional village pub near the grounds of picturesque Lydiard Park. The large garden and tented area hosts various functions throughout the year including an annual beer festival held on the first weekend of May. The interior has low-beamed ceilings and there is comfortable seating around an open fireplace. The chef's attractive dishes can be enjoyed in two separate dining areas. The pub is open all day on weekends throughout the summer. Wi-Fi available. ♨✪⊙🅟(53)P⅃⌐

Malmesbury

Whole Hog 🅛

8 Market Cross, SN16 9AS
✪ 11-11.30 (midnight Fri & Sat); 12-10.30 Sun
☎ (01666) 825845
Stonehenge Pigswill; Young's Bitter; Wadworth 6X 🅗
Located between the 15th-century Market Cross and Abbey, the building has at various times served as a cottage hospital, gas showroom and café/restaurant before becoming licensed premises. This pub is a popular local serving five real ales including two guests, frequently from nearby breweries. Food is served in the bar at lunchtime and in a separate dining room. A warm and friendly atmosphere is guaranteed. Traditional cider alternates between Westons and the local Sherston Village Brew. Q🝮⊙🅟(91,92)♠

Marlborough

Green Dragon

12-13 High Street, SN8 1AA
✪ 11-11 (1am Fri); 10-1am Sat; 10-10.30 Sun
☎ (01672) 514847
Wadworth Henry's IPA, 6X; guest beers 🅗
This large, multi level pub is one of the oldest in Marlborough. It has a bar and front room at street level and a smaller room, pool room and dining area at a lower level at the back. Outside is a large garden, very pleasant for alfresco drinking in the summer. There are two guest beers, one often also from Wadworth and one from another brewery. The pub is one of the venues for the Marlborough Jazz Festival in July. Free Wi-Fi available.
🝮✪⊙🍴🅟(X5,70)

Netherhampton

Victoria & Albert 🍷 🅛

SP2 8PU (opp church) SU108298
✪ 11-3.30, 5.30-11; 12-3, 7-10.30 Sun ☎ (01722) 743174
Beer range varies 🅗
This welcoming classic thatched inn dates from 1540. Inside, a log fire greets customers in the winter while outside a large garden and patio await. Three handpulls dispense an ever-changing range of real ales from far and wide. Food is prepared in the pub, ranging from light snacks to full meals. Local CAMRA Pub of the Year 2012. Quintessential England – a gem.
♨Q✪⊙▲♣♠P⅃⌐

Ramsbury

Crown & Anchor 🅛

1 Crowood Lane, SN8 2PT
✪ closed Mon; 12-3, 6.30 (6 Sun)-11 ☎ (01672) 520335
⊕ crownramsbury.co.uk
Ramsbury Kennet Valley, Gold; Wadworth Henry's IPA; guest beers 🅗
A quiet and welcoming 19th-century country pub with a small bar and three rooms, two with fireplaces. Interesting bric-a-brac adorns the low ceiling beams including 200-year-old blacksmith's fixings and a Victorian beer engine that was used behind the bar and is now on display. Thursday is acoustic music night and a quiz is held every Sunday evening. There is a garden area behind the pub. ♨Q🝮✪❀🍴⊙🅟(46,48)P⅃⌐

Royal Wootton Bassett

Five Bells 🅛 ✔

Wood Street, SN4 7BD
✪ 12-3, 5-11.30; 12-midnight Fri-Sun ☎ (01793) 849422
Black Sheep Best Bitter; Fuller's London Pride; guest beers 🅗
This cosy thatched local with a beamed ceiling opened before 1841. The bar dispenses ales from six handpumps, usually including a guest from Braydon Ales just down the road. Westons Old Rosie is on another pump. Special events are held throughout the year including a quiz night on the last Sunday of the month, a Tuesday book club and a summer beer festival. The pub also has darts and crib teams. ♨✪⊙🍴🅟(55)♣♠⅃⌐

Salisbury

Anchor & Hope

59 Winchester Street, SP1 1HL
✪ 10 (11 Sun)-11 ☎ (01722) 501660
Beer range varies 🅗
Friendly, traditional pub, close to the town centre. The landlord is a keen diver and the pub hosts the Hidden Depths Dive Club. It is also home to pool, darts and cribbage teams. Three draught beers, varying seasonally, and a traditional cider are served on handpump. There is a courtyard garden with a covered, heated area for smokers.
✪⊙≠🍴♣♠⅃⌐

Deacons 𝕃
118 Fisherton Street, SP2 7QT
✪ 5 (4 Fri; 12 Sat)-11; 12-10 Sun ☎ (01722) 504723
Hop Back GFB, Summer Lightning; Sharp's Doom Bar ⊞
A welcoming no frills town-centre locals' pub with a basic wooden-floored front bar and a larger back room with sofas and tables. Unusual artefacts abound on the walls and ceilings. A smoking area is available outside at the rear. This conveniently located pub is between the town centre and the railway station. Last entrance is 10.40pm Monday to Saturday. ≹🚌♣⚐

King's Head ✔
Bridge Street, SP1 2ND
✪ 7am-midnight (1am Thu-Sat) ☎ (01722) 342050
Greene King Abbot; Ruddles Best Bitter; guest beer ⊞
Wetherspoon Lloyds No.1 bar arranged over two floors of what was once the County Hotel. There has been a pub on this site since 1470 when it was known as Bores Place. It became the King's Head around 1520 and the County Hotel in the 1880s. Four ever-changing guest ales include many from local breweries, and there is a large selection of bottled beers and ciders. The food is Wetherspoon's standard fare, and beer festivals are held twice a year. ♘❀⇌◐◑♿≹🚌●⚐

Rai d'Or 𝕃
69 Brown Street, SP1 2AS
✪ 5-11; closed Sun ☎ (01722) 327137
Beer range varies ⊞
Thirteenth-century characterful pub with a fascinating history. An inglenook fireplace and low ceilings make for an appealing ambience. Excellent, reasonably priced Thai food is complemented by two ever-changing, usually local, beers. It can be busy at food times, but drinkers are always welcome. There is a discount on food before 6.30pm and on beer for CAMRA members. Former local CAMRA Pub of the Year. ◑🚌♣

Village Freehouse 𝕃
33 Wilton Road, SP2 7EF (on A36 near St Paul's roundabout)
✪ 11 (3 Mon-Thu)-11; 12-11 Sun ☎ (01722) 329707
Downton Quadhop; Taylor Landlord; guest beers ⊞
Friendly city local close to the railway station with three changing guest beers. The focus is on local microbreweries and beers unusual for the area, with requests welcome. The only regular outlet in the city for dark beers, a dark ale, mild, porter or stout is always available. Major sports are screened and there is free Wi-Fi. Popular with rail users, it features rail memorabilia and books. Recent renovations have not altered the intrinsic character of this former Salisbury CAMRA Pub of the Year. ≹🚌

Winchester Gate 𝕃
113-117 Rampart Road, SP1 1JA
✪ 12 (2 Mon-Wed)-11 ☎ (01722) 322834
🌐 winchestergate.co.uk
Hop Back Crop Circle; guest beers ⊞
An inn since at least the 17th century, this free house once provided for travellers arriving at the city's east tollgate. Three handpumps offer ales from across the UK and a real cider is often available. Beer festivals are held in the garden at least twice a year. There is a pétanque terrain and boules available for anyone to have a go. Live music is hosted every weekend, and an open mic night is held on the third Wednesday of each month. Filled rolls are available. Salisbury CAMRA Pub of the Year 2010. ❀●P⚐

Wyndham Arms 𝕃
27 Estcourt Road, SP1 3AS
✪ 4.30 (12 Thu)-11.30; 12-midnight Fri & Sat; 12-11.30 Sun ☎ (01722) 331026
Hop Back Heracles, GFB, Crop Circle, Taiphoon, Summer Lightning; guest beer ⊞
The birthplace of Hop Back Brewery, the Wyndham celebrated 25 consecutive years in the Guide in 2012 and was local CAMRA Pub of the Year in 2011. A traditional ale house, it has a single bar with six handpumps serving a selection of Hop Back ales plus a guest pump featuring Hop Back or Downton seasonal beers or an ale from further afield. There is also a fine selection of bottled beers and wines. This is a pub for conversation, good-natured banter and fine ale. ♘🚌(R2,R6,11)♣

Semington

Somerset Arms
High Street, BA14 6JR (N from roundabout on A361) ST898607
✪ 10-11 (10.30 Sun) ☎ (01380) 870067
🌐 somersetarmssemington.co.uk
Bath Ales Gem; guest beers ⊞
A coaching inn dating back to perhaps the 16th century, this village-centre pub was acquired by a local family in 2009 and turned into a smart, cosy, welcoming free house. Awarded Community Pub of the Year by the local CAMRA branch in 2010, the regular beer and three guests come from micros within 50 miles, while the highly regarded food is made from local ingredients. Close to the Kennet & Avon Canal, it is popular with boaters. Accommodation is in three luxury en-suite bedrooms. ♨❀⇌◐◑♿🚌(234)●P⚐

Semley

Benett Arms
SP7 9AS (off A350, 4 miles N of Shaftesbury) ST891270
✪ 12-3, 5-11 ☎ (01747) 830221 🌐 benettarms.co.uk
Beer range varies ⊞
A former Gibbs Mew country pub, this is now a genuine free house sitting by the village green and pond in a quiet village, with a single small bar and separate dining areas. The beer choice varies but there are usually three to choose from, either on handpump or direct from the cellar. Excellent home-cooked food is available at all sessions. A warm welcome is extended to all, including families and dogs, in an area popular with walkers. ♨Q❀⇌◐◑♿🚌(84,247)♣P⚐

Swindon

Beehive
55 Prospect Hill, SN1 3JS
✪ 12-midnight (1am Thu-Sat) ☎ (01793) 523187
🌐 bee-hive.co.uk
Greene King IPA; H&H Olde Trip; Morland Old Speckled Hen; guest beers ⊞
The multi-levelled, bare-boarded pub is divided into four areas in this wedge-shaped building and populated by an eclectic mix of people of all ages. A venue for non-mainstream live music on Thursdays, Fridays and Sundays, it even hosts

occasional poetry readings. The walls are covered in works of art and announcements about cultural events. The beer range is interesting, but with the exception of IPA rather expensive. Monday is poker night. Wi-Fi available. ⚑🖿(11,22)♣

Blunsdon Arms ✆
Lady Lane, SN25 2NA
🕐 11-11 (midnight Thu-Sat) ☎ (01793) 729801
Beer range varies 🅷
Opened in 2006 in a forever expanding part of north Swindon, this Ember Inns house with friendly staff can get quite busy. The large open-plan interior has plenty of comfortable seating. A range of more than 18 beers is served on six handpumps throughout the month, as well as real cider. Wednesday and Sunday are quiz nights, grill night is Tuesday and curry night is Thursday. Food is served every day until 10pm. ✿◑🖿(11,13)♠P

Dockle Farmhouse ✆
2 Bridge End Road, Stratton St Margaret, SN3 4PD
🕐 8am-midnight (1am Fri & Sat) ☎ (01793) 838910
Greene King Abbot; Ruddles Best Bitter; guest beers 🅷
Formerly the Greenbridge, this pub is now a Wetherspoon Lloyds No.1 Bar. It is a very extended pub, spread over several buildings, with various bars and seating areas, including an outdoor patio. One bar is primarily for food service, the other has all the guest beers. A quiz is held every Monday night, and a beer festival is hosted annually. Children are permitted during the day, with a play area outside. ✿◑♿🖿(7)P

Glue Pot 🅻
5 Emlyn Square, SN1 5BP
🕐 12 (4.30 Mon; 11.30 Fri & Sat)-11; 12-10.30 Sun
☎ (01793) 325993
Hop Back Odyssey, Crop Circle, Summer Lightning; White Horse Bitter; guest beers 🅷
The Glue Pot is part of the historic sandstone Swindon Railway Village built in the 1840s. It offers six Hop Back or Downton ales, two guest beers and five real ciders. Food is served Wednesday to Friday lunchtimes. Although usually a quiet pub, it can get busy on weekend evenings. A pub quiz is held on Thursday night. Well worth a visit. ✿◑≒🖿(8,14)♠

Tisbury

Boot Inn 🅻
High Street, SP3 6PS
🕐 12-2.30, 7 (5 Fri)-11; 12-4 Sun ☎ (01747) 870363
Beer range varies 🅶
Fine village pub built of Chilmark stone, licensed since 1768, with a relaxed, friendly atmosphere appealing to locals and visitors alike. Run by the same landlord since 1976, it became a free house in 2009. It offers three or four ales sourced from local breweries, as well as from further afield, with a Sixpenny beer often available. Excellent food is served (pizza only on Tue) and there is a spacious garden. A former local CAMRA Pub of the Year. ⚑✿◑≒🖿(25,26)♠P

Upavon

Ship 🅻
10 High Street, SN9 6EA
🕐 11-12.30am (1am Thu-Sat); 12-12.30am Sun
☎ (01980) 630313 ⊕ upavonpc.co.uk/ship

Butcombe Bitter; Wadworth 6X; guest beers 🅷
Parts of the Ship Inn date from the 15th century. Completely refurbished in recent years, it now combines traditional wooden beams with a light, open appearance, and has a wood-burning pizza oven at the back. The decorations, including a huge model of the Cutty Sark in the dining room, are of nautical or local interest. The four guest ales are usually local and three ciders from Westons are stocked. Tuesday is fish and chip night. There is limited parking outside. Dog-friendly. ⚑✿◑♿🖿(X5)♠P

Upton Lovell

Prince Leopold
Up Street, BA12 0JP (off A36 between Warminster and Salisbury) ST943411
🕐 12-3, 6-midnight; 12-4, 7-10 Sun ☎ (01985) 850460
⊕ princeleopoldinn.co.uk
Beer range varies 🅷
Recently celebrating a year under new ownership, this lovely riverside pub goes from strength to strength. The beer range includes regular ales from Butcombe and Wadworth, plus a guest, often Keystone, together with an interesting selection of bottled ales. Good food is served in the bar and restaurant, which overlooks the pretty beer garden and the River Wylye. There is a cosy snug area with log fire, books – some on the pub's links with Prince Leopold, Queen Victoria's youngest son – and board and card games. ⚑➹✿⚑◑♿🖿♣P⅃

Warminster

Fox & Hounds 🍷
6 Deverill Road, BA12 9QP ST870445
🕐 11-11 ☎ (01985) 216711 ⊕ pitcherpubs.co.uk
Wessex Foxy's Best, Warminster Warrior; guest beer 🅷
This friendly two-bar pub is local CAMRA Pub of the Year 2012 and was Community Pub of the Year in 2011. One of the bars is a cosy snug, the other has a pool table and TV at the back. A large skittle alley and function room opened in 2009. Three real ciders from Rich's and Thatchers are a mainstay of the pub. A regular outlet for the Wessex Brewery, the guest beer is usually sourced from another local micro. Closing time may be later than 11pm. ⚑Q✿⚑♿≒🖿(24,264,265)♣♠P⅃

Organ Inn ✆
49 High Street, BA12 9AQ ST872451
🕐 4 (12 Sat)-midnight; 4-11 Sun ☎ (01985) 211777
⊕ theorganinn.co.uk
Beer range varies 🅷
An inn from 1770 to 1913, the building was converted back to a drinking establishment from shop premises in 2006. The welcoming interior comprises three rooms with a traditional feel, along with a snug, games room and skittle alley. Up to five ciders or perries are served from a separate bar – three from Westons and two guests. The beer range includes Organ Bitter (a closely guarded secret recipe) plus two guests, usually sourced from local breweries. A beer festival is also held. There is an art gallery upstairs. ⚑Q✿✿♿≒🖿(24,264,265)♣♠⅃

Whiteparish

Parish Lantern 🗈
Romsey Road, SP5 2SA (on A27)
🌣 11-3, 5-11; 11.30-11 Fri-Sun ☎ (01794) 884392
⊕ theparishlantern.co.uk
Flack Manor Flack's Double Drop; guest beers 🖽
A welcoming pub run by the same couple since 1991, serving a range of changing guest beers from local breweries. The single bar has a central fireplace and areas for dining, pool and darts. The pub organises family events on bank holidays and occasional beer festivals. Food is served lunchtimes and evenings, including regular themed nights. A spacious garden with play equipment for children and a chicken coop leads to a camping area with space for five caravans.
🏚️⊛🕽🕭🛠️🚃(34,X7/X71)♣P⸦

Wilton

Swan 🗈
SN8 3SS
🌣 12-3, 6-11; 12-11 Sat; 12-10.30 Sun ☎ (01672) 870274
⊕ theswanwilton.co.uk
Ramsbury Gold 🖽**; guest beers** 🖽/🖪
This is a pretty red brick village pub near the Kennet & Avon canal with an attractive interior. There is an emphasis on good local beer and food, which ranges from traditional pub meals to haute cuisine. Some of the beers are on stillage and gravity fed. There are four varying guest beers plus traditional draught ciders. The pub lends itself for inclusion in a circular walk starting at Great Bedwyn along the canal to the beam engines and the windmill at Wilton. No evening meals on Sunday.
🏚️⊛🕽🚃(X5,22)♣P⸦

Winsley

Seven Stars ✅
BA15 2LQ ST799608
🌣 12-2, 6.30-11; 12-2.30, 6-11 Fri & Sat; 12-4 Sun
☎ (01225) 722204 ⊕ sevenstarswinsley.co.uk
Devilfish Devil Best, Bomb Shell; Wadworth 6X; guest beer 🖽
Lovely old village pub dating in parts back to the early 1700s. It is the brewery tap for the Devilfish Brewery, situated a few miles away over the Somerset border on a farm near Norton St Philip. As well as the Devilfish beers there are usually one or two guests available. The home-made food uses locally sourced ingredients from the West Country and comes highly recommended. There is a peaceful garden with plenty of seating, and a large car park. Dogs are welcome in the bar. The 264 bus stops right outside.
🏚️Q⊛🕽🕭🛱(Avoncliff)🚃(264)♣P

Zeals

Bell & Crown
New Road, BA12 6NJ ST782318
🌣 11-3, 5-11; 11-11 Fri & Sat; 11-4 Sun ☎ (01747) 840404
Wadworth Henry's IPA; guest beers 🖽
Refurbished in the last few years, with an open fire and flagstone floors, this is now a fine dining pub with a traditional bar and real ales. The layout allows for almost complete separation of the bar and dining areas. The owner has run several highly regarded pubs in the past and ensures that the beer choice changes regularly, with West Country breweries well represented. The pub attracts locals as well as visitors to the nearby National Trust property of Stourhead. 🏚️Q🕽🛠️🚃(158)P⸦

Tollgate Inn, Holt

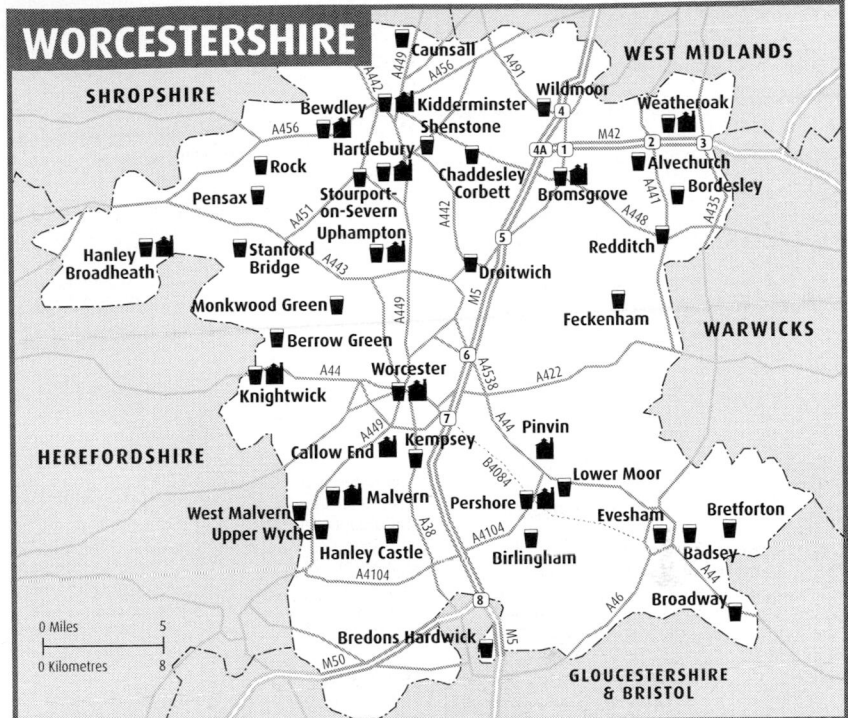

Alvechurch

Weighbridge ♥ 🄻

Scarfield Wharf, Scarfield Hill, B48 7SQ (follow signs to marina from village) SP022721

🕘 12-3 (4 Sat & Sun summer), 7-11; 12-3, 7-10.30 Sun

☎ (0121) 445 5111 ⊕ the-weighbridge.co.uk

Beer range varies 🄷

Alongside the canal next to Alvechurch marina, this cosy pub has two lounges and a public bar. It has won many CAMRA awards and runs popular spring and autumn beer festivals. Good-value home-cooked food is served lunchtimes and evenings (but no food Tue and Wed) with excellent Sunday lunches. Ample outdoor seating includes a heated marquee that can be used for functions. Two house beers, Kinver Bargees and Weatheroak Tillerman's Tipple, are available and three changing guest beers, including a mild, plus a real cider/perry.

🏚Q🕱🌣🅿◑🖳🖳🖵(146)🌢🅿⌐

Badsey

Round of Gras

47 Bretforton Road, WR11 7XQ (B4035/B4085 jct)

🕘 11-11 ☎ (01386) 830206 ⊕ roundofgras.co.uk

Flowers IPA; Uley Pigs Ear; guest beer 🄷

Open-plan roadside inn with a restaurant area, games area with a pool table, comfortable bar and seating, and an attractive beer garden. The pub was named to celebrate the world-famous local asparagus, which features on the menu from March to July. The interior is decorated with photographs and old farming implements. Food is served all day, with a good-value carvery Tuesday to Thursday lunchtimes. Ciders include Westons Old Rosie and a changing guest cider or perry, usually from Thatchers. 🛏🌣◑🖳🖵(247,554)🌢🅿⌐

Berrow Green

Admiral Rodney 🄻

WR6 6PL SO748584

🕘 12-3 (not Mon), 5-11; 12-11 Sat; 12-10.30 Sun

☎ (01886) 821375 ⊕ admiral-rodney.co.uk

Wye Valley Bitter, HPA; guest beers 🄷

A light, airy country pub with three main bar areas and a restaurant serving locally produced food including excellent fish and chips and the pub's own award-winning sausages. Guest ales are often from local microbreweries along with real cider and perry. The pub has a skittle alley, covered and heated patio, floodlit garden with views of the Malvern Hills, and disabled toilet. Folk music features on the third Wednesday of the month. The accommodation is popular with walkers on the Worcestershire Way. 🏚Q🕱🛏🖳◑🖵🛇♣♠🌢🅿⌐

Bewdley

Little Pack Horse 🄻 ✅

31 High Street, DY12 2DH (near Lax Lane 300yds from St Anne's Church)

🕘 12-3, 6-11 (midnight Fri); 12-midnight Sat; 12-10.30 Sun

☎ (01299) 403762 ⊕ littlepackhorse.co.uk

Bewdley Worcestershire Way; St Austell Tribute; guest beer 🄷

Dating from the 15th century, this welcoming inn has a great reputation. Three ales are always available including one from the nearby Bewdley Brewery. The food menu specialises in pies from around the world such as Moroccan Chicken, Bombay Potato and Veg and the famous Desperate Dan. Daily specials are on the chalkboard. Live blues/folk plays on the last Saturday of the month. The pub has a red light shining over the entrance when it is open. 🏚🛏🌣◑🖳🖵(SVR)🖵⌐

Mug House 🏠 ✅

12 Severnside North, DY12 2EE (150yds from bridge)
🟢 12-11 (11.30 Fri & Sat) ☎ (01299) 402543
🌐 mughousebewdley.co.uk
Bewdley Worcestershire Way; Taylor Landlord; Wye Valley HPA; guest beers 🅷
Situated on the side of the River Severn, the Mug House is not to be missed. A dog-friendly pub, it welcomes locals and visitors alike. Current beers and one or two guests can be viewed on yourround.co.uk. There is a real fire and to the rear a glass-covered patio and sun terrace in lovely surroundings with grape vines and wisteria. Fine food is available in the evenings in the restaurant and lunches are served daily throughout the pub.
🏠Q❄🍴🍺🔊♿❤≈(SVR)�🅿↙

Old Waggon & Horses

91 Kidderminster Road, DY12 1DG (on Bewdley-Kidderminster road, Catchem's End)
🟢 12-11; 11.30-1am Fri & Sat ☎ (01299) 403170
🌐 waggonbewdley.co.uk
Banks's Mild, Bitter; Bathams Best Bitter; guest beer 🅷
Popular locals' pub with a single bar serving three distinct areas. The small wooden-floored snug has settles, tables and a dartboard; the larger room has a roll-down screen for major sporting events, bench seating and a TV. An old kitchen range in the dining area adds to the cottagey feel. Food is available lunchtimes and evenings, with a carvery on Sundays. The attractive terraced garden is on many levels. Guest ales come from local independents. ❄🍴♿≈(SVR)🚃♣❤🅿↙

Woodcolliers Arms 🏠 ✅

76 Welch Gate, DY12 2AU (200yds from St Anne's Church up Welch Gate)
🟢 5-midnight (11 Mon & Wed); 12.30-midnight Sat; 12.30-11 Sun ☎ (01299) 400589 🌐 woodcolliers.co.uk
Kinver Edge; Ludlow Gold; St George's Friar Tuck; Three Tuns 1642 Bitter; guest beer 🅷
A short walk from Bewdley centre, this friendly pub keeps a constantly changing range of local guest beers. The Cordon Bleu chef offers a Russian and English menu freshly prepared seven days a week – no microwave used. The Grade II-listed dog-friendly pub has beams and open fires, and no piped music. It stores bikes and fishing tackle for guests and provides a luggage service for Severn, Geopark and Worcestershire Way walkers. Quiz night is Tuesday. 🏠Q❄🍴🍺≈(SVR)🚃♣❤🅿↙

Birlingham

Swan 🏠

Church Street, WR10 3AQ
🟢 12-3, 6.30-11 (10.30 Sun) ☎ (01386) 750485
🌐 theswaninn.co.uk
Wye Valley Bitter; guest beers 🅷
Black and white thatched free house dating back over 500 years in a quiet village. The open bar/lounge boasts exposed beams and a wood-burning stove. Over 300 guest beers are served over the course of a year alongside two real ciders (one from Thatchers, the other Moles Black Rat). Two beer festivals are hosted in May and September. Traditional home-cooked food is served in the conservatory (no food Sun eve). Crib, darts and dominoes are played in the bar. Dogs are welcome. There is a pleasant garden and a large car park opposite. 🏠❄🍴🚃(382)♣❤🅿↙

Bordesley

Meadow Farm

Dagnall End Lane, B98 9BJ SP042693
🟢 11.30-11 (11.30 Tue & Thu); 11-11.30 Fri & Sat; 12-11 Sun
☎ (01527) 585639 🌐 meadowfarmpubredditch.co.uk
Banks's Mild, Bitter; Brakspear Bitter; Marston's Pedigree, Old Empire; Ringwood Best Bitter; guest beers 🅷
This is a large, modern and friendly barn conversion pub that serves good food all day but also has dedicated drinking-only tables. Six regular real ales are offered and three guests. An exceptional smoking area is provided which is heated and well lit. There is a Travelodge next door. ♿❄🍴♿🚃🅿↙

Bredons Hardwick

Cross Keys Inn 🏠

GL20 7EE
🟢 12-3 (not Mon-Thu), 6-11 ☎ (01684) 772626
Beer range varies 🅷
Traditional pub with two rooms: one with the bar and a parakeet, the other with a bar billiards table and dartboard. There is always one local real ale among the range. An extensive range of pies is available. Quiz night is Tuesday and live bands play on Friday evening, March to January.
🏠Q❄❄🍴🚃♣♣🅿↙

Bretforton

Fleece Inn ★ 🏠 ✅

The Cross, WR11 7JE (near church)
🟢 11-11.30 (10.30 Sun) summer; 11-3, 6-11; 11-11.30 Wed-Sat; 12-10.30 Sun winter ☎ (01386) 831173
🌐 thefleeceinn.co.uk
Uley Pigs Ear; Wye Valley Bitter; guest beers 🅷
Famous old National Trust-owned village pub, sympathetically restored after a fire in 2005 and recognised by CAMRA as one of Britain's Real Heritage Pubs. It houses a world-famous collection of 17th-century pewter. Up to four ciders are available, including one produced at the Fleece itself using apples from various NT premises. The pub has its own orchard garden with play equipment. Folk sessions feature every Thursday. Great British food is served and there is a medieval barn for functions and weddings. Pebworth Morris Men meet here. 🏠Q❄🍴🍺♿❤🚃(554)♣❤↙

Broadway

Crown & Trumpet 🍷 🏠 ✅

14 Church Street, WR12 7AE (just off Cotswolds Way)
🟢 11-2.30, 5-11; 11-11 Fri-Sun ☎ (01386) 853202

Cotswold Spring Codrington Codger; **Stanway** Cotteswold Gold; **Stroud** Tom Long; guest beer ⊞
Picturesque 17th-century Cotswold stone inn on the road to Snowshill, complete with oak beams and log fires along with plenty of Flowers Brewery memorabilia. The menu offers specials featuring locally grown produce, enjoyed by locals, tourists and walkers. The hostelry has an unusual range of pub games and entertainment including live music. The Stanway beers alternate throughout the seasons, and other guest beers are sourced from Gloucestershire microbreweries. A regular mini beer festival is held over the Christmas period and Gwatkins cider is sold. ♨☀♇⌑⬧⬧🖴(559)♣🕯P⌐

Bromsgrove

Golden Cross Hotel ⓛ ✅
20 High Street, B61 8HH (S end of High Street)
☼ 8am-midnight (1am Fri & Sat) ☎ (01527) 870005
Greene King Abbot; **Ruddles** Best Bitter; guest beers ⊞
The Golden Cross Hotel was rebuilt in 1932 on the site of one of Bromsgrove's oldest coaching inns of the same name. This Wetherspoon venue offers a changing selection of up to 12 beers, many LocAles, often from Sadler's, Wood and Titanic. There are also monthly beer festival events. Good-value food is available from early morning breakfast to supper, with special deals available. CAMRA members receive a discount. The rear car park is Pay & Display. Q☀☀⬧⬧⬧🖴🕯P⌐

Caunsall

Anchor Inn ♀
DY11 5YL (off A449 Kidderminster-Wolverhampton road)
☼ 12-11, 4-7-11; 11-3, 7-10.30 Sun ☎ (01562) 850254
⊕ theanchorinncaunsall.co.uk
Hobsons Best Bitter, Town Crier; **Ludlow** Gold; **Wye Valley** HPA, Butty Bach; guest beer ⊞
Popular village pub run by the same family since 1927. This friendly traditional local is renowned for its six real ales, ciders and well-filled cobs. A central doorway leads into the little-changed bar with its original 1920s furniture and horse racing memorabilia. The friendly staff welcome an impressive mix of customers, as well as their dogs, and the pub gets especially busy at lunchtimes. Easily reached from the nearby canal, this gem is well worth a visit. Q☀⬧⬧⬧♣🕯P⌐

Chaddesley Corbett

Swan
The Village, DY10 4SD SO892737
☼ 11 (12 Sun)-11 ☎ (01562) 777302
Bathams Mild Ale, Best Bitter; guest beer ⊞
Village pub dating from 1606 with a large lounge, snug, comfy public bar and restaurant. Evening meals are served Thursday to Saturday; rolls, pork pies and snacks are available at lunchtime daily. Jazz nights are held in the lounge every Thursday. There is a large garden and children's play area overlooking the beautiful local countryside and the pub is well used by walkers. Dogs are welcome in the bar. Bathams XXX is served during the winter months and Westons Old Rosie cider is kept. ♨Q☀⬧⬧⬧♣🕯P⌐

Droitwich

Hop Pole ⓛ
40 Friar Street, WR9 8ED SO898634
☼ 12-11 (10.30 Sun) ☎ (01905) 770155 ⊕ thehoppole.com
Enville Ale; **Malvern Hills** Black Pear; **Wye Valley** HPA, Butty Bach; guest beer ⊞
A popular and friendly 18th-century pub with black and white timbers. It has a raised alcove for those who like to enjoy quiet conversation as well as bar-side seating for the locals. A separate pool room adjoins the bar and there is a heated patio area outside for smokers. Guest beers are mostly from local breweries. Good-value home-cooked food is served at lunchtime. Close by is the newly restored Droitwich barge canal that offers secure moorings. ➶☀⬧⬧🖴♣⌐

Ring o' Bells ⓛ
The Holloway, WR9 8HD (off Hanbury Rd) SO903633
☼ 1.30 (12 Sun)-11.30; 12-midnight Sat ☎ (01905) 770083
⊕ ringobells.webs.com/
Wye Valley HPA; guest beers ⊞
Small pub just off the town centre and close to the restored Junction Canal. The modern, single bar has an area to the side with a TV. There is also a function room and a games bar to the rear with a pool table, darts and fruit machine. Live music features occasionally. Horse racing is keenly followed by the locals on Saturdays. Bar snacks are available lunchtimes. Up to three guest ales come from local breweries such as Bathams, Hobsons and Three Tuns. ➶☀🖴🖴♣🕯P⌐

Evesham

Old Swanne Inne ✅
66 High Street, WR11 4HG (by bus station)
☼ 8-midnight (1am Fri & Sat) ☎ (01386) 442650
Greene King Abbot; **Ruddles** County; guest beers ⊞
Modern, family-friendly town centre Wetherspoon, on the High Street by the bus station, offering the widest range of beers in Evesham and an extensive food menu. The comfortable, open-plan bar area displays items of historic interest and many photographs of old Evesham. Six guest ales usually include at least one local, with beers from Purity and Sadler's appearing regularly. Westons Old Rosie and Broadoak Perry are always available, and beer and cider festivals are hosted throughout the year. ➶☀⬧⬧⬧🖴🕯⌐

Feckenham

Rose & Crown
High Street, Feckenham, B96 6HS SP009615
☼ 11-3, 6-11; 12-11 Sat & Sun ☎ (01527) 892188
⊕ roseandcrownfeckenham.co.uk
Brakspear Oxford Gold; guest beers ⊞
Welcoming 19th-century Grade II-listed village pub serving up to three real ales. The guest beer range varies, and the pub hosts an annual beer festival during the August bank holiday, as well as occasional music sessions. There is a separate lounge and restaurant, with a large beer garden. A pre-theatre menu is available for cinemagoers. The pub has limited parking but there is a free car park 200 yards away. ♨Q☀⬧⬧🖴🕯⌐

Hanley Broadheath

Fox Inn L

WR15 8QS (on B4204) SO671652

✪ 5-midnight; 12-12.30am Fri & Sat; 12-10.30 Sun
☎ (01886) 853189 ⊕ jhstraditionalbrewery.com

Bathams Best Bitter; Holden's Golden Glow; JHS Foxy Lady; guest beer ⊞

Black and white, timbered, 16th-century, rural free house. Three local real ales are available including at least two from the pub's own JHS on-site brewery, plus occasional real cider in summer. The friendly, family-owned inn is warmed by a welcoming wood-burning stove throughout the winter. Meals are served Tuesday, Friday and Saturday evenings and Sunday lunchtime, but lunches can be ordered ahead on other days. Live music plays occasionally and brewery trips are arranged. Annual lawnmower racing is held in the adjoining field in August. ∰Q❤☺⊕◑⑤▲♣P⇌

Hanley Castle

Three Kings ★ L

Church End, WR8 0BL (signed off B4211) SO838420

✪ 12-3, 7-11 (10.30 Sun) ☎ (01684) 592686

Butcombe Bitter; Hobsons Best Bitter; guest beers ⊞

Recognised by CAMRA as one of Britain's Real Heritage Pubs, this unspoilt 15th-century country inn on the village green near the church has been run by the Roberts family since 1911. The three-room interior comprises a small snug with large inglenook, serving hatch and settle wall; a small side room; and Nell's Lounge with another inglenook, beams and its own entrance. Three interesting guest ales are on offer, often from local breweries, plus cider from Westons. Regular live music sessions are hosted, and a popular beer festival in November. Events to support Acorns Children's Hospice have raised over £33,000 in recent years. ∰Q❤☺⊛◑⑤(363)♣⬤P

Hartlebury

Hartlebury Club L

Millridge Way, Waresley, DY11 7TJ (off A449, down track on Waresley Court Rd)

✪ 6-11 (11.30 Fri); 12-11.30 Sat; 12-10 Sun
☎ (01299) 250252

Cannon Royall Honey Bear, Arrowhead Bitter, Grapeshot, Ombersley Pale Ale; guest beer ⊞

Although off the beaten track, this friendly, welcoming club on the edge of Hartlebury is well worth seeking out. It offers four local ales from Cannon Royall Brewery plus a guest beer. The large bar area has plenty of seating and welcomes families and dogs. Food is served in the bar or, if you wish, in a separate dining area on Wednesday and Saturday evenings. There is seating outside for warmer days. Non-members are welcome. Q❤☺◑⑤⑤(303)♣P⇌☗

Kempsey

Walter de Cantelupe L ✓

34 Main Road, WR5 3NA (on A38 next to post office) SO852489

✪ closed Mon; 12-2, 6-11; 12-3, 7-10.30 Sun
☎ (01905) 820572 ⊕ walterdecantelupe.co.uk

Cannon Royall Arrowhead Bitter; Mayfields Copper Fox; Taylor Landlord; guest beer ⊞

Named after a 13th-century bishop of Worcester, the pub features a cosy drinking area, a large settle from the 1700s and an imposing inglenook fireplace. High-quality food is home made using local ingredients wherever possible. Regular events throughout the year include a paella party in the attractive walled garden in June. Local beers are served in lined glasses and third-of-a-pint glasses are available. CAMRA members receive a 10 per cent discount. Occasional real cider is kept in summer. The pub may stay open all day on summer weekends. ∰Q❤☺⊛◑⑤⑤▲⑤(32,362)P⇌☗

Kidderminster

King & Castle

Comberton Hill, DY10 1QX

✪ 11-11; 12-10.30 Sun ☎ (01562) 747505

Bathams Best Bitter; Hobsons Mild; guest beers ⊞

Atmospheric recreation of a refreshment room in a GWR terminus station that is the gateway to the Severn Valley Railway. Real ale pubs along the line and at Bridgnorth attract locals and visitors. Six handpumps dispense three regular beers and three constantly changing guests from breweries as far flung as Cornwall and Scotland. Royal Piddle is brewed especially for the pub. Bottled beers are served on the trains. Good-value lunchtime meals are served daily in the adjacent refreshment room. ∰Q❤◑⑤⑤⬤⇌⬤P

Olde Seven Stars L

13-14 Coventry Street, DY10 2BG

✪ 11-11 (11.30 Fri & Sat); 12-11 Sun ☎ (01562) 755777
⊕ yeoldesevenstars.co.uk

Beer range varies ⊞

With six ever-changing real ales and one draught cider, this traditional family-friendly pub is well worth visiting. Cobs and pork pies are available but no hot food, however you are more than welcome to bring your own (with plenty of takeaways nearby): plates, crockery and condiments provided. Live bands perform monthly and a quiz is held fortnightly. The large rear garden is popular and well-behaved dogs are always welcome. Worcestershire CAMRA Pub of the Year 2011. ❤☺⑤⇌⬤⇌

Station Inn

7 Farfield, DY10 1UG

✪ 1-11; 12.30-10.30 Sun ☎ (01562) 822764

Beer range varies ⊞

Popular community pub just a short walk from both the main line and Severn Valley Railway stations. Two rooms are served from a central bar and there is a large beer garden at the rear. Up to three ever-changing guest ales may come from local breweries such as Enville or Sadler's. Regular live music events are held, with proceeds donated to charity. The pub is home to a golf society and darts team. ∰Q⊛⇌P

Swan

Vicar Street, DY10 1DE

✪ 10-11.30 (1am Fri & Sat); 12-5 Sun ☎ (01562) 823008

Brains The Rev James; St Austell Tribute; guest beers ⊞

A family-run town-centre pub opposite the town hall, dating back to 1865. Five real ales are on offer, usually including one from Brains and a couple from local breweries. Bar food is served Monday to Saturday, with breakfast until 11.45am.

This one-room pub attracts a mixture of locals, shoppers, and office workers. It has a small raised stage for live music on Thursday evenings and hosts discos on Friday and Saturday evenings. A mini beer festival is held in early September. ⊛◑⌐

Knightwick

Talbot 🅛

WR6 5PH (on B4197, 400yds from A44 jct) SO733560
🕓 11-midnight; 12-10.30 Sun ☎ (01886) 821235
🌐 the-talbot.co.uk
Hobsons Best Bitter; Teme Valley t'Other, This, That Ⓗ
Originally a 14th-century coaching inn, the pub has been recently refurbished and extended. Food is local and imaginative with a separate restaurant area as well as bar tables. Filled rolls are also sold. Three or four beers from the Teme Valley Brewery behind the pub are usually on offer. There is a farmers' market on the second Sunday of the month and the Green Hop Beer Festival in early October is popular. Dog- and walker-friendly.
🏚Q🐾⊛✍◑ ⊕⅊Åᕁ(420)♣🕭P

Lower Moor

Old Chestnut Tree 🅛

Manor Road, WR10 2NZ
🕓 12-3, 5-midnight; 12-1am Fri & Sat; 12-midnight Sun
☎ (01386) 860380 🌐 theoldchestnuttreeinn.webeden.co.uk
Malvern Hills Black Pear; guest beers Ⓗ
Sixteenth-century black and white farmhouse featuring an inglenook fireplace with stones scavenged from Pershore Abbey after the Dissolution. It has an open bar and snug with exposed beams, a separate games room and a back room that serves as a post office and shop. Two or three guest beers are on offer, often from local breweries, and the cider is ever changing. Beer festivals are held at Easter, August bank holiday and Christmas, and a music festival in mid-July. 🏚Q🐾◑♿ᕁ(551)♣🕭P⌐

Malvern

Great Malvern Hotel 🅛

Graham Road, WR14 2HN (by crossroads with Church St)
🕓 10-11; 11-10.30 Sun ☎ (01684) 563411
🌐 great-malvern-hotel.co.uk
Draught Bass; guest beers Ⓗ
Popular hotel public bar just a short walk from the Malvern Theatres complex, ideal for pre- and post-performance refreshment. At least one beer comes from a local brewery – often Malvern Hills. Meals are served in the bar and the adjoining brasserie, and there is a separate comfortable lounge with sofas. Fresh coffee, daily newspapers and free Wi-Fi are on offer. Live music sessions feature during the week – check the website for details. Parking on-site is limited but there is plentiful public parking nearby. 🐾✍◑➟� P

Morgan 🅛 ✔

52 Clarence Road, WR14 3EQ
🕓 12-3.30, 5-11; 12-3, 6.30-10.30 Sun ☎ (01684) 578575
Wye Valley Bitter, HPA, Butty Bach; guest beer Ⓗ
The Wye Valley Brewery has transformed a previously unloved side-street pub into a real ale magnet, named after the town's Morgan car factory. The open-plan interior is divided into a games area with bar billiards and darts, a general drinking area and a slightly raised seating area

with comfortable settees to relax in. Outside, the welcoming garden has seating with landscaping, a fish pond and 'Them Organ' gates. Varied activities throughout the week include a book club, quizzes and live music. Q🐾⊛◑♿➟�⌐

Nag's Head ✔

21 Bank Street, WR14 2JG
🕓 11-11.15 (11.30 Fri & Sat); 12-11 Sun ☎ (01684) 574373
Banks's Bitter; Bathams Best Bitter; St George's Friar Tuck, Charger, Dragons Blood; Sharp's Doom Bar; guest beers Ⓗ
Free house offering eight permanent beers, including several from the owner's brewery St George's, and up to six guests plus two ciders. Random knick-knacks and furniture, nooks and crannies provide a homely environment, although the pub does get busy most evenings and every weekend. It offers a high-class food menu. There is a large, covered, heated outdoor area to the front and a garden to the rear. A no swearing rule is enforced. The car park is small but there is ample on-street parking. 🏚⊛◑�(44,44A)♣🕭P⌐

Star 🅛

59 Cowleigh Road, WR14 1QE
🕓 closed Mon; 4.30-10.30 (11.30 Fri & Sat); 12-10.30 Sun
☎ (01684) 891918 🌐 star-malvern.co.uk
Beer range varies Ⓗ
A fusion of Chinese restaurant and English pub, drinks and simple meals are served in the bar (note the ornate bar-back) and there is a separate restaurant for more formal dining (evening food from 5pm, Sunday lunch 12-3pm). A take-away service is also available – enjoy a pint while you wait. The patio includes a sheltered smoking area. Wye Valley HPA and Fuller's London Pride make regular appearances. ◑�(44,44A,675)P⌐

Monkwood Green

Fox

WR2 6NX (S edge of Monkwood Nature Reserve)
SO803601
🕓 5 (12 Sat) 11; 12-10.30 Sun ☎ (01886) 889123
Malvern Hills Feelgood; Wye Valley HPA, Butty Bach Ⓗ
Single-bar, dog-friendly village local set on the common near the nature reserve renowned for butterflies and moths. There is seating around the fireplace and hearth at one end, games at the other. The pub is home to events including skittles and indoor air rifle shooting, and music nights feature on the last Friday of the month. Food can be provided by arrangement for groups and parties. A rare outlet for Barkers cider and perry. Note that the bus service is limited.
🏚Q🐾⊛Åᕁ(308)♣🕭⌐

Pensax

Bell 🅛

WR6 6AE (on B4202 Clows Top-Great Whitley road)
🕓 closed Mon; 12-2.30, 5-11; 12-10.30 Sun
☎ (01299) 896677
Bewdley Worcestershire Way; Exmoor Gold; Hobsons Best Bitter; Wye Valley HPA; guest beers Ⓗ
Local CAMRA Pub of the Decade and previous West Midlands Pub of the Year, this family- and dog-friendly pub is well worth making a detour to visit. At least five constantly changing real ales are on offer, plus local cider and perry. There is a separate

dining room with fine views and a snug where families are welcome. Local seasonal ingredients are used in the range of pub food. Wooden floors, hanging hops, open fires and pew seating give a true country feel. A beer festival is held at the end of June. ⚒Q🎱❀🕽❶🐾P↕─🍴

Pershore

Brandy Cask ℒ
25 Bridge Street, WR10 1AJ
✪ 11.30-2.30, 7-11 (11.30 Thu); 11.30-3, 7-11.30 Fri & Sat; 12-3, 7-11 Sun ☎ (01386) 552602
Brandy Cask Whistling Joe, Brandy Snapper, John Baker's Original; guest beers Ⓗ
At least three house ales are always available as well as a wide range of guest beers from around the country. Cheddar Valley cider is also usually stocked. Food is good and reasonably priced (no food Tue winter). The beautifully kept rear garden runs down to the River Avon where mooring for boats is available. This is a classic brewpub well worth a visit. ⚒Q🎱❀🕽❶🐾(382,550,551)❀

Redditch

Gate Hangs Well ✔
98 Evesham Road, B97 5ES (on main Evesham to Redditch Road) SP037659
✪ 11-2.30, 6-11; 11-2.30, 5.30-11.30 Fri; 6-11.30 Sat; 12-3, 7-11 Sun ☎ (01527) 401293 🌐 gatehangswell.com
Greene King Abbot; Hook Norton Hooky Bitter; Purity Mad Goose; St Austell Tribute; Wadworth 6X; guest beer Ⓗ
A cosy open-lounge pub with a real fire, offering up to six real ales. Popular quiz nights run on Sundays and Mondays from 9pm, and a cheese night runs monthly. A lunchtime menu is served weekdays. The pub produces a monthly newsletter that includes details of future guest ales. Dominoes and darts are also popular here. Note that it is closed Saturday lunchtime. ⚒Q❀🕽❶🐾(70,247)♣↕

Royal Enfield ✔
Unicorn Hill, B97 4QR
✪ 9-midnight (2am Fri-Sun) ☎ (01527) 590970
Greene King IPA, Abbot; guest beers Ⓗ
Previously a cinema, this Lloyds No.1 bar is named after a local motorcycle manufacturer, and memorabilia including a full-size bike adorn the walls of this large open-plan town-centre pub. The circular bar offers up to eight real ales including a LocAle and a guest cider. Balcony-style seating at the front allows smokers to watch the world go by. A DJ attracts the crowds on Friday and Saturday evenings. 🎱❀🕽❶🐾≠🐾P↕

Woodland Cottage
102 Mount Pleasant, Southcrest, B97 4JH (10 mins walk from bus station) SP038668
✪ 12 (5 Tue)-midnight ☎ (01527) 402299
Sharp's Doom Bar; Taylor Landlord; guest beers Ⓗ
Four beers are usually available at this friendly open-lounge locals' pub, two of which are changing guests. Photographs of old Redditch pubs adorn the walls alongside pictures painted by a local artist, while a rear balcony with smoking shelter overlooks the beer garden. The pub is host to a local darts team and live music is played most Saturday evenings. Closed Tuesday lunchtimes. ⚒❀≠🐾(55,56,143)P↕

Rock

Rock Cross Inn
Rock Cross, DY14 9SD (signed from A456)
✪ 5 (4 Fri; 12 Sat)-midnight; 12-11 Sun ☎ (01299) 832533
🌐 therockcrossinn.co.uk
Beer range varies Ⓗ
A traditional free house, situated on the crossroads in the heart of the village, offering a public bar, lounge bar, restaurant and a small beer garden for lazy days. The beamed interior has a central serving area and log fires in winter. The public bar has a pool table, dartboard and TV. The lounge bar is quieter with a raised dining area where a range of local produce is served – specials include curry night on Wednesday and steak night on Friday. Walkers, children and dogs are all welcome. ⚒Q❀🕽❶🍴🐾(291)♣🐾P↕

Shenstone

Plough
DY10 4DL (off A450/A448) SO865735
✪ 12-3, 6 (7 Sun)-11 ☎ (01562) 777340
Bathams Mild Ale, Best Bitter Ⓗ
Traditional rural community pub at the heart of the village since 1840. A long single bar serves both the lounge and public room areas, each with its own real fire. Pork pies are worthy of mention, as is the friendly welcome from the locals and staff. A large enclosed courtyard serves as an overflow area where children are permitted. The pub hosts local morris dancing teams in the summer. Bathams XXX is also on handpump during the winter months. ⚒Q🎱❀🕽❶⅃♣🐾P↕

Stanford Bridge

Bridge Hotel ℒ
WR6 6RU (signed 100yds off B4203) SO716658
✪ 12-11.30 Mon-Wed; 11-1am ☎ (01886) 812771
🌐 stanfordbridgepub.co.uk
Hobsons Twisted Spire; Wye Valley HPA; guest beers Ⓗ
A former hotel near the River Teme, popular with local residents. The lively, friendly atmosphere is considerably heightened during the Wednesday-night quiz. Traditional pub pastimes are played in the separate games room. Four real ales are offered plus Thatchers Heritage cider and, in summer, Westons perry. Bar meals are served alongside an à la carte menu in the restaurant (no food Mon). There is a heated seating area outside and a large car park. 🎱❀🕽❶♣🐾P↕

Stourport-on-Severn

Angel ✔
14 Severn Side, DY13 9EW
✪ 11-11 ☎ (01299) 822661 🌐 theangel-stourport.co.uk
Banks's Mild, Bitter; Marston's Old Empire; guest beer Ⓗ
Old-fashioned single-bar pub situated on the bank of the River Severn, close to the barge lock of the canal basin, with public moorings nearby. As well as providing bitter and mild from Banks's, guest beers are also regularly offered. Traditional pub games such as crib, darts and dominoes are actively supported, and a pool table is available in a separate room. Home-made food is a summer speciality. ⚒❀🕽❶🍴⅃♣🐾P↕

Hollybush

Mitton Street, DY13 9AA
☼ 12-11 (midnight Fri & Sat; 10.30 Sun) ☎ (01299) 827435
⊕ hollybushrealalespub.co.uk
Black Country Bradley's Finest Golden, Pig on the Wall, Fireside; guest beers Ⓗ
This traditional pub specialising in real ales and good food was recently presented with a Most Improved Pub award by the local CAMRA branch. Three regular ales from Black Country are served in a friendly atmosphere along with three ever-changing guests from independent breweries. A single bar serves a split-level bar area, a newly refurbished upper function room and a beer garden. Regular events include live music, quizzes, TV coverage of sport and beer festivals.
ﾑQ👜🐕❄️◑◪&♣️🐾🅿️⁵⁻

Uphampton

Fruiterer's Arms Ⓛ

Uphampton Lane, WR9 0JW (off A449 at Reindeer pub) SO838648
☼ 12.30-3.30, 5-11.30; 12.30-midnight Fri; 12-midnight Sat; 12-11.30 Sun ☎ (01905) 620305
Cannon Royall Fruiterer's Mild, Kings Shilling, Arrowhead Bitter, Ombersley Pale Ale; guest beer Ⓗ
Located down a lane off the A449, the pub has been in the same family for 162 years, with Ted working here since 1951. The ales from the independent Cannon Royall Brewery at the rear of the pub are reasonably priced in both the bar and comfortable beamed lounge. Guest beers are Cannon Royall seasonals. Local perry and cider are stocked. Filled rolls are available Friday to Sunday and a range of home-made pickles is sold at the bar. Children under 14 are welcome until 9pm.
ﾑQ◑◪♣️🐾🅿️⁵⁻

Upper Wyche

Wyche Inn Ⓛ

Wyche Road, WR14 4EQ SO769437
☼ 12 (11 Sat)-11; 11-10.30 Sun ☎ (01684) 575396
⊕ thewycheinn.co.uk
Hobsons Best Bitter; Wye Valley HPA; guest beers Ⓗ
Set on the side of the Malvern Hills adjacent to the Wyche Cutting, this free house has panoramic views towards the Cotswolds. Ideally situated for hill walkers, it offers two bars, one with traditional games, a dining area and a patio. Tony and Stephanie offer an ever-changing ale list (check the website for current and upcoming beers). Good home-cooked food is served, with special themed nights. The accommodation is AA 4-star rated, with fantastic views over the Severn Vale.
❄️🛏️◑◪🐾(362,363,675)♣️P

Weatheroak

Coach & Horses Ⓛ

Weatheroak Hill, B48 7EA (Alvechurch-Wythall road) SP057740
☼ 11.30-11; 12-10.30 Sun ☎ (01564) 823386
⊕ coachandhorsesinn.co.uk
Hobsons Mild, Best Bitter; Holden's Special; Weatheroak Hill Icknield Pale Ale, WHB; Wood's Shropshire Lad; guest beers Ⓗ
On the corner of Icknield Street and Weatheroak Hill, this is the home of the Weatheroak Hill Brewery. It has a public bar with quarry-tiled floor and real fire, a split-level lounge/bar and a modern restaurant with disabled access and toilets. Restaurant/bar meals are available daily. Summer beer festivals, barbecues and morris dancing take place in the large family-friendly garden. Children under 14 are not allowed in the bars. A recipient of numerous local CAMRA awards.
ﾑQ👜❄️◑◪&♣️🐾⁵⁻

West Malvern

Brewers Arms Ⓛ

Lower Dingle, WR14 4BQ (down track by pub sign on B4232) SO76404565
☼ 12-3, 6-midnight; 12-midnight Fri-Sun ☎ (01684) 568147
Malvern Hills Black Pear; Marston's Burton Bitter, Pedigree; Wye Valley HPA; guest beers Ⓗ
A comfortable, traditional pub that is both the centre of the village community and an ideal refreshment stop for visitors to the Malvern Hills. Up to eight real ales are available and a beer festival is held in early October. Home-cooked food is served lunchtimes and evenings. The cosy bar can get busy at times, but extra dining space is available in the function room or in the garden with the 'best pub view in Britain' to the Black Mountains beyond. Cider is from Westons.
ﾑQ❄️◑◪🐾(675)🐾⁵⁻

Wildmoor

Wildmoor Oak Ⓛ ✅

Top Road, B61 0RB SO963756
☼ 5-10.30 Mon; 12-11 (midnight Fri & Sat; 10.30 Sun)
☎ (0121) 453 2696 ⊕ wildmooroak.com
Beer range varies Ⓗ
Rural country inn with patio and gardens, serving an interesting beer range and one or two local real ciders and perries. An award-winning chef specialises in both British and Caribbean food, and Caribbean nights are held on the last Thursday of the month (booking essential). Special themed nights, quizzes, and an annual beer and cider festival attract a varied clientele. A 10 per cent reduction for those dining is available to CAMRA card-holders. ﾑ👜❄️◑◪♣️🐾🅿️⁵⁻

Worcester

Bell

35 St Johns, WR2 5AG (W side of the Severn off A44)
☼ 10 (11 Sun)-11.30 ☎ (01905) 424570
Fuller's London Pride; Thwaites Wainwright; guest beers Ⓗ
A community pub dating from the 17th century with two small rooms on one side and the main bar on the other, divided by a central corridor. At the rear is a second bar used at busy times and available for functions. There is also a popular skittle alley. One guest beer is from Hobsons and two more are often from local independent brewers. Live music frequently features at weekends. ﾑ❄️◪♣️⁵⁻

Berkeley Arms

School Road, WR2 4HF
☼ 12-2, 5-midnight; 12-12.30am Fri & Sat; 12-3.30, 8-11.30 Sun ☎ (01905) 421427
Banks's Mild, Bitter Ⓟ**; Jennings Dark Mild; guest beers** Ⓗ
Family-run local with two main drinking areas served by a single bar. There is also a small adjacent room used as a family room or for

functions, and an outside patio at the rear partially covered and heated for the benefit of smokers. Traditional pub games are popular. The draught cider is Thatchers Heritage.
Q❂❀❀🖵(44,44A)♣🍺P🛈

Dragon Inn
51 The Tything, WR1 1JT (on A449, 300yds N of Foregate St Station)
❂ 4.30 (12 Fri & Sat)-11; 12-3, 4.30-11 Wed & Thu; 1-4.30, 7-10.30 Sun ☎ (01905) 25845
Beer range varies Ⓗ
The owner of this ale-centric pub is passionate about beer quality. Six ever-changing beers from smaller independent brewers are on offer, usually including at least one from the co-owned Little Ale Cart brewery in Sheffield. Bottle-conditioned Belgian beers and Thatchers cider are also stocked. The walls feature mementos of life in the pub – note the list of banned conversation topics. Good-value lunches are served on Friday and Saturday only. There is a partially covered rear patio for outdoor drinking in warmer weather, and well-behaved dogs are welcome.
❀◖≢(Foregate St)🖵♣🍺🛈

Firefly ♥ �🅛
54 Lowesmoor, WR1 2SE
❂ 4-midnight (1am Thu); 3-1am Fri; 1-2am Sat; 1-11 Sun
☎ (01905) 616996
Beer range varies Ⓗ
Offering period comfort in a regenerated part of the industrial city, the old vinegar works' manager's Georgian residence is now a delightful drinking establishment featuring its own brewery, with soft furnishing and subtle lighting, warmed by an open fire. Downstairs is a cosy snug with bench sofas. The upstairs bar opens at weekends and occasionally during the week for live music. There is a paved partially covered beer garden. Pie and a pint night is Wednesday. A member of the Oakademy of Excellence, beer festivals are held throughout the year. Westons or Devon cider is sold. ❀❀◖≢(Foregate St)🖵🍺🛈

Plough �🅛
23 Fish Street, WR1 2HN (next to fire station)
❂ 12 (4.30 Thu)-11 (11.30 Fri & Sat; 10.30 Sun)
☎ (01905) 21381
Hobsons Best Bitter; Malvern Hills Black Pear; guest beers Ⓗ
A must for any visitor to Worcester, this friendly Grade II-listed pub offers four ever-changing guest ales from breweries in Worcestershire and surrounding counties, as well as draught cider and perry from local producer Barbourne. A short flight of stairs leads to a bar flanked by two rooms, each with a fire and many original features. A small patio area provides views towards the Cathedral.
❀❂❀❀◖≢(Foregate St)♣🍺🛈

Postal Order ✅
18 Foregate Street, WR1 1DN
❂ 8-midnight (1am Fri & Sat) ☎ (01905) 22373
Greene King Abbot; Ruddles Best Bitter; guest beers Ⓗ
This classic Wetherspoon pub was originally the Worcester telephone exchange. The Postal Order has one of the largest real ale sales in Wetherspoon's West Midlands region and offers a wide range of beers. It holds regular mini festivals featuring local breweries' beers. Traditional cider and Broadoak Perry are also available. Good-value food is served daily until 10pm.
Q❂◖🅍≢(Foregate St)🖵🍺🛈

Wheatsheaf Inn �🅛
192 Henwick Road, WR2 5PF
❂ 12-11 ☎ 07891 668030
Banks's Mild; Marston's Burton Bitter, Pedigree; guest beers Ⓗ
A small Grade II-listed 18th-century terraced local attracting both young and old. A varied selection of guest ales includes at least one from St George's. The rear balcony gives views of the River Severn down to the Cathedral and a footpath up from the riverside also leads to the pub. Dogs are welcome and there is a separate family-friendly pool room. Televised sport creates a lively atmosphere. Hot and cold pies and snacks are served all day and newspapers and Wi-Fi are available. ❀❂❀❀❀🖵♣🍺

Walter de Cantelupe, Kempsey

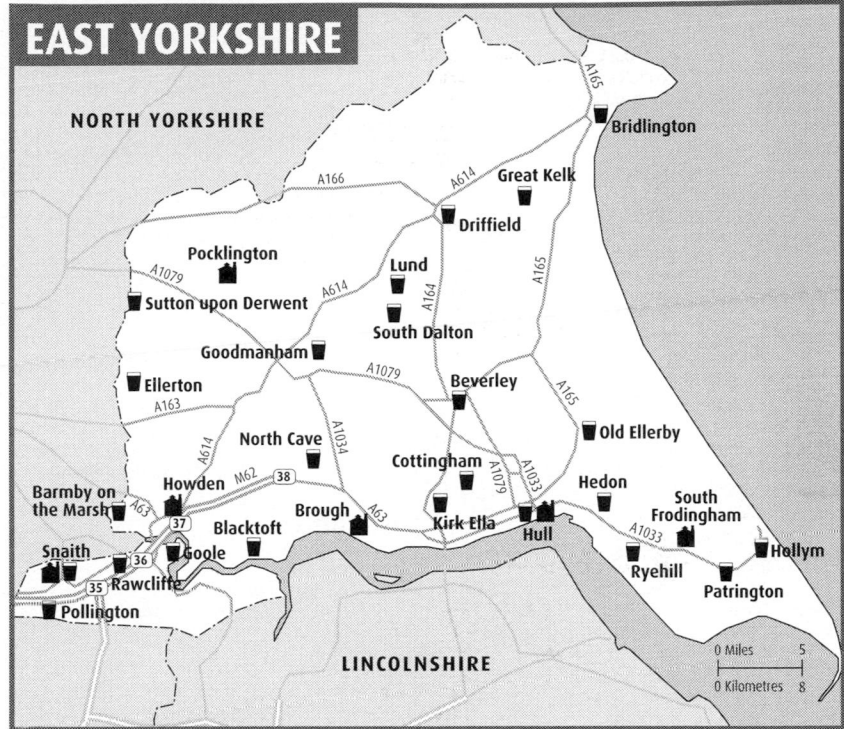

EAST YORKSHIRE

NORTH YORKSHIRE

A165 — Bridlington

A166 — A614 — Great Kelk

Driffield

Pocklington — A1079 — Lund — A164

Sutton upon Derwent — A614

South Dalton — A165

Goodmanham — A1079 — Beverley — A165

Ellerton — A163

North Cave — A1034 — Cottingham — Old Ellerby

Howden — M62 — 38 — A1079 — A1033 — Hedon

Barmby on the Marsh — A63 — 37 — Brough — A63 — South Frodingham

Blacktoft — Kirk Ella — Hull — A1033 — Hollym

Snaith — 36 — Goole — Ryehill — Patrington

35 — Rawcliffe

Pollington

LINCOLNSHIRE

0 Miles 5
0 Kilometres 8

YORKSHIRE (EAST)

Barmby on the Marsh

King's Head 🄻 ✅
High Street, DN14 7HT (3 miles from Knedlington on B1228 near Howden on no through road) SE688286
🕙 12-2, 5-11 (not Mon & Tue eve); 12-midnight Sat; 12-11 Sun ☎ (01757) 630705 ⊕ thekingsheadbarmby.co.uk
Black Sheep Best Bitter; guest beers Ⓗ
Busy village pub that is well worth finding. Refurbished and extended in 2008, but dating back to the early 1800s, the pub is now a spacious and welcoming watering place and eatery. There is a bar with a stone-flagged floor for drinkers, a comfortable lounge and a restaurant renowned for its quality food using locally sourced ingredients. Four handpumps are in constant use, with three guests often from local breweries. ⌂❀◖&♣P♿

Beverley

Cornerhouse
2-4 Norwood, HU17 9EY
🕙 closed Mon; 5-midnight (1am Fri); 10-1am Sat; 10-11 Sun ☎ (01482) 882652
Abbeydale Deception; Black Sheep Best Bitter; Taylor Landlord; Tetley Bitter; guest beers Ⓗ
The Cornerhouse looks like a gastro-pub, but the customers are mainly here for the real ale on 12 handpumps, and the real cider on two handpumps. Yorkshire brewers feature prominently and there is usually a mild available. A coal fire warms the far end of the bar and there is unusual gallery seating off the bar. Curry night is Tuesday and quiz night Wednesday. Food is served weekday evenings and all day weekends, plus breakfasts. ⌂❀◖🍴♿☕

Dog & Duck
33 Ladygate, HU17 8BH
🕙 11-4, 7-midnight; 11-midnight Fri & Sat; 11.30-3, 7-11 Sun ☎ (01482) 862419
Batemans XB; Black Sheep Best Bitter; Copper Dragon Golden Pippin; John Smith's Bitter; Ringwood Boondoggle; guest beers Ⓗ
Just off the main Saturday Market, next to the historic Picture Playhouse building (now Browns), the Dog & Duck was built in the 1930s and has been run by the same family for 40 years. It comprises three areas: a bar with a period brick fireplace and bentwood seating, a front lounge and a rear snug. The good-value, home-cooked lunches are popular. Guest accommodation is in six purpose-built self-contained rooms to the rear. Close to Beverley bus station. ⌂🛏◖🍴♣

Durham Ox
48 Norwood, HU17 9HJ
🕙 10.30 (12 Sun)-11 ☎ (01482) 679444
John Smith's Bitter; guest beer Ⓗ
Victorian local on the A1035, 200 yards east of the bus station. This two-roomed pub has been refurbished after consultation with CAMRA's local pub preservation officer. The lounge was extended

to include a games area but retains its original etched windows; the public bar has the old wooden floor, with an off-sales hatch in the entrance lobby. The pub fields five darts and two dominoes teams. Off-street parking is possible directly opposite. Meals are served daily, and a quiz is held on Wednesday night. ❀◖▶ ⊕☷(121,246)⚊

Green Dragon ✪
51 Saturday Market, HU17 8AA
✪ 11-11 (midnight Thu-Sat); 12-11 Sun ☎ (01482) 889801
Beer range varies ⒣
Historic Tudor-fronted inn renamed the Green Dragon in 1765. Up to seven beers from breweries throughout Yorkshire and the UK are featured. Beer festivals are held in the spring and at Halloween. The pub was extensively refurbished and extended several years ago; most internal fittings of note were lost, although some wood panelling remains. Meals are served daily until 10pm; Tuesday and Wednesday are quiz nights. Friday and Saturday nights are busy, and the pub opens at 10am on race days. Outdoor seating is provided in a patio area. ❀◖▶ ♿☷♣⚊

Blacktoft

Hope & Anchor
Main Street, DN14 7YW (3½ miles S of Gilberdyke railway station, following signs to Blacktoft)
✪ 12 (4 Mon)-11; 12-10.30 Sun ☎ (01430) 440441
Greene King Abbot; Marston's Pedigree; Old Mill Mild; guest beers ⒣
Thriving village local in a superb location on the bank of the River Ouse. The RSPB's Blacktoft Sands bird sanctuary is visible on the far bank. Humour, past and present, is a feature of the old pub – look out for the Laurel and Hardy memorabilia. The conservatory offers fine river views and popular home-cooked meals – serving times are lunchtimes and evenings during the week, all day at weekends. Two guest beers change regularly. Runner-up Hull & East Yorks CAMRA Branch Village Pub of the Year. ➤❀◖▶ ♿♠♣P⚊

Bridlington

Marine Bar
North Marine Drive, YO15 2LS (1 mile NE of centre)
✪ 11-11 (11.30 Sat) ☎ (01262) 675347 ⊕ marine-bar.co.uk
John Smith's Bitter; Taylor Landlord; Wold Top Bitter; guest beers ⒣
Large, triangular, open-plan bar, part of the Expanse Hotel, on the seafront to the north-east of the town. The bar attracts a good mix of regulars throughout the year and is welcoming to the influx of summer visitors. A good menu of home-cooked food, including vegetarian options, is available daily. There is ample car parking on the promenade at the front. Guest beers are normally sourced from a local brewery. An outdoor seating area with spectacluar sea views is one of the attractions. ❀⇄◖♿☷⚊

Prior John ✪
34-36 The Promenade, YO15 2QD (near bus station)
✪ 9am-midnight ☎ (01262) 674256
Greene King Abbot; Ruddles Best Bitter; guest beers ⒣
Large, busy Wetherspoon, close to the bus station. Modern in appearance, the interior is basically one large half-moon-shaped room. To the right of the

serving area is a first-floor gallery, reached by a sweeping metal staircase. The downstairs room is a clever mix of metal and wood, with a segmented ceiling supported by steel pillars. The decor is plain and bright, using mainly pastel colours. Six guest beers are usually available, including a dark brew. Food is served all day. Q❀◖▶ ♿☷♣⚊

Telegraph Inn
110 Quay Road, YO16 4JB
✪ 12-midnight (1am Fri & Sat) ☎ (01262) 674592
Beer range varies ⒣
Free house saved and lovingly refurbished by its current owners, who have dedicated themselves to creating a pub that appeals to local residents and seasonal visitors. A wide range of real ales is served, usually from local breweries. An extensive outdoor area creates a tranquil environment in which to enjoy an alfresco pint. Sunday lunches are served and there are plans to provide accommodation in due course. The pub is within a 10-minute walk of the railway station. ❀⇄☷

Cottingham

Blue Bell ✪
West Green, HU16 4BH
✪ closed Mon; 11-11 (midnight Fri & Sat); 12-10.30 Sun
☎ (01482) 847113 ⊕ bluebellinn-cottingham.co.uk
Brakspear Bitter; Ringwood Boondoggle; guest beers ⒣
In a picturesque setting overlooking the green near the village centre, this attractive building is split into a bar and restaurant. The restaurant has a log fire and enjoys a high reputation. The modern bar has deep armchairs and low-level music. To the rear there is a secluded beer garden with a covered smoking area and heaters. Open mic music night is Wednesday and live jazz plays on Sunday evening. Dogs are welcome in the bar. ㊙❀♿☷P⚊

Duke of Cumberland ✪
10 Market Green, HU16 5QG
✪ 11 (12 Sun)-midnight ☎ (01482) 847199
Jennings Cocker Hoop, Cumberland Ale; Marston's Pedigree; guest beers ⒣
Thought to be the oldest pub in the village, dating from the 18th century, it has an L-shaped lounge offering a warm, friendly atmosphere. There is a downstairs function room in which several local clubs meet, and another upstairs for wedding and birthday parties. Live music features every Wednesday and a talent night is held on the first Thursday of the month. The beer garden has a covered area and faces the former stables. Food is served daily 12-8pm. ❀◖⇄☷(105,115)⚊

King William IV ✪
152 Hallgate, HU16 4DB
✪ 11-11 (midnight Fri & Sat); 12-11 Sun ☎ (01482) 875996
Jennings Cumberland Ale; Marston's Pedigree; guest beers ⒣
Village-centre pub with a traditional bar and lounge, both free of music. At the rear a former brewery has been converted into a function room offering live music and special events. The pub also hosts weekly quiz nights and an annual music festival. The rear beer garden and side courtyard have covered smoking areas. Excellent-value meals are served in large and small portions. Up to six guest beers are on handpump.
Q❀◖▶ ⊕⇄☷♣⚊

Driffield

Bell Hotel ✅
46 Market Place, YO25 6AN
❁ 9.30am-11; 12-10.30 Sun ☎ (01377) 256661
Beer range varies Ⓗ
With a feeling of elegance, this inn features a long, wood-panelled bar and red leather seating, substantial fireplaces, antiques and prints. Two or three real ales are available, usually from local breweries, and more than 300 malt whiskies are stocked. A covered courtyard functions as a bistro, and there is a splendid lunchtime carvery buffet Monday to Saturday; Sunday lunch must be booked. Children are welcome until 7.30pm.
Q☕🛏️🌙&≏🚆(121)P

Mariners Arms
47 Eastgate South, YO25 6LR
❁ 3 (12 Sat & Sun)-midnight ☎ (01377) 253708
Brakspear Bitter; Jennings Bitter; seasonal beers Ⓗ
A street-corner local that is well worth seeking out. The beer range is from Marston's portfolio, as an alternative to the John Smith's outlets that dominate the capital of the Wolds. Formerly part of the Hull Brewery estate, its four small rooms have now become two: a basic bar and a more comfortable lounge. Live sport is shown and the pub fields various sports teams. The long-standing licensees enjoy a loyal following among locals and offer a friendly welcome to all visitors.
🐾🍴≏♣P🔒

Rose & Crown 🏆
North Street, YO25 6AS (400yds N of centre)
❁ 3 (12 Fri-Sun)-midnight ☎ 07525 817175
John Smith's Bitter; guest beers Ⓗ
A welcoming locals' pub opposite Driffield's park, comprising a main bar/lounge and a pool room. Between three and four guest ales are usually available; the local Wold Top brewery is well represented as the landlord is often able to offer its commemorative brews. The pub serves as a hub for people to meet and is very much a part of the community. Benches are provided outside for summer drinking, and live sport is shown on TV. The railway station is a 20-minute walk. CAMRA East Yorkshire Town Pub of the Year 2011. 🐾♣P🔒

Ellerton

Boot & Shoe
Main Street, YO42 4PB (just off B1228 road to Howden)
❁ 5.30 (12 Sat & Sun)-midnight ☎ (01757) 288346
Dark Horse Old Boot; Tetley Bitter; Warwickshire Darling Buds Ⓗ
A welcoming country village inn of character dating from the 17th century. The building wraps around a large tree and features low-beamed ceilings. There is a cosy bar area with exposed brick and an open fire, plus two intimate separate dining rooms. Three real ales are on offer in this free house, including Old Boot brewed by the Dark Horse brewery. Food is served Friday and Saturday evenings and Sunday lunchtime (booking advisable). 🏚️Q♣P

Goodmanham

Goodmanham Arms 🏆
Main Street, YO43 3JA
❁ 11-midnight ☎ (01430) 873849
⊕ goodmanhamarms.co.uk

Black Sheep Best Bitter; Taylor Landlord; Theakston Old Peculier; guest beers Ⓗ
Close to the Wolds Way footpath and an ideal resting place for walkers. There is a small beer garden at the front and a small car park to the side. This traditional village pub serves up to seven real ales, usually including a mild – Old Peculier is from the wood. A microbrewery on the site commenced brewing in 2012, producing All Hallows beers. Food is available lunchtimes and Friday evening. Local CAMRA Pub of the Year. 🏚️Q🐾🌙&🛏️🐕P🔒

Great Kelk

Chestnut Horse
Main Street, YO25 8HN
❁ closed Mon & Tue; 6 (5.30 Fri & Sat)-11; 12-10.30 Sun
☎ (01262) 488263
Wold Top Bitter; guest beers Ⓗ
Built in 1793, this delightful Grade II-listed rural community pub is situated between the Wolds and Holderness. It has a cosy bar with a real fire and a comfortable games room that doubles as a daytime family room. Darts, dominoes and chess are played. Two guest beers are available alongside Belgian bottled beers delivered in authentic glasses. The pub is well regarded for its wide variety of home cooked pies, from conventional to exotic, served until 8.30pm.
🏚️Q🐾🌙♣P🔒

Hedon

Haven Arms
Havenside, Sheriff's Highway, HU12 8HH (½ mile S of A1033 crossroads)
❁ 11-11 (midnight Fri & Sat); 12-10.30 Sun
☎ (01482) 897695 ⊕ havenarms.co.uk
Black Sheep Best Bitter; Camerons Strongarm; Taylor Landlord; guest beers Ⓗ
Situated in the historic Haven area of town, once the largest port on the Humber. The bar is divided into different areas, and the concert and cabaret room serves as the focal point for the activities of a number of community clubs and teams. Reasonably priced pub food, freshly prepared from local ingredients, is served all day. Three guest beers are available, one usually from a local microbrewery. One real cider increases to two or three from April to September.
🏚️🐾🌙&🚶🚆(75,76,77)♣🐕P🔒

Hollym

Plough Inn
Northside Road, HU19 2RS
❁ 12 (5 Mon)-midnight summer; closed Mon, 12 (2 Tue-Thu)-midnight winter; 12-midnight (11 winter) Sun
☎ (01964) 612049 ⊕ theploughinnhollym.co.uk
Tetley Bitter; guest beers Ⓗ
Family-run, 200-year-old free house of wattle and daub construction offering five real ales, with Bradfield and Great Newsome beers regularly available. Primarily a locals' pub, a base for Withernsea rugby club and the local running club, it is a haven for discerning holidaymakers in summer, and dogs are permitted. Photographs in the bar depict its role as a World War II ARP station, and the right-hand side room doubles as a dining room (booking essential on Sun). Accommodation comprises three en-suite letting rooms.
🏚️🐾🛏️🌙🚶🚆(75,76,77)♣P🔒🍴

Hull

Admiral of the Humber ✔

1 Anlaby Road, HU1 2NT

⊗ 8am-midnight ☎ (01482) 381850

Greene King Abbot; Ruddles Best Bitter; guest beers Ⓗ

Wetherspoon pub that was formerly a home decorating shop, yet the site has connections to Hull's seafaring history, which is reflected in its name. It is a spacious single room largely on one level, an ideal destination for those who find steps and stairs a problem. A designated area is set aside for diners during the day, and meals are served 8am-10pm; families are welcome until 6pm. The beer range varies. Sports are shown on TV.
⊛◑☵⇌☕🚲♿

Hop & Vine

24 Albion Street, HU1 3TG (near Hull New Theatre)

⊗ closed Sun & Mon; 11 (4 Tue)-11 ☎ 07500 543199

Beer range varies Ⓗ

Atmospheric basement bar free house close to Hull New Theatre, serving three changing guest beers from independent breweries, plus rare farmhouse ciders and a perry. Oversized lined glasses are used, and a good range of Belgian bottled beers plus Budweiser Budvar and Pilsner Urquell are stocked. An interesting selection of freshly made snacks and hot drinks is served until 9pm. Joint winner of CAMRA National Cider Pub of the Year 2010 and Yorkshire Regional Cider Pub of the Year 2010, 2011 and 2012. Closed between Christmas and New Year. ◑⇌☕♣🚲♿🅟

Lion & Key ☗

48 High Street, HU1 1QE

⊗ 12-11 ☎ (01482) 225212

Beer range varies Ⓗ

There is always a particularly friendly welcome for all customers here. There has been a pub at this address for many years and it has recently returned to its original name. Up to seven real ales and three ciders are available at any time; the beer range is largely sourced from microbreweries in Yorkshire, complemented by bottled beers from around the world. Delicious freshly cooked food is served at lunchtime throughout the week and on some week nights. Local CAMRA Pub of the Year. ◑♿

Olde Black Boy ★

150 High Street, HU1 1PS

⊗ 12.30 (5.30 Mon & Tue)-11.30

⊕ yeoldeblackboy.weebly.com

Wychwood Hobgoblin; guest beers Ⓗ

Historic pub, licensed since 1729 but which has also been, variously, a wine merchant and a tobacco dealer – traditionally represented by an Indian chief or black boy. It was refitted in 1926 when the office became the panelled front smoke room – note the carved boy's head above the fireplace – and the warehouse became the back bar. First Mondays of the month are for folk music and Wednesday nights are for open mic sessions. Guest beers vary widely and Westons Old Rosie cider is also available. A modern rarity – bring your own vinyl LPs to play. ⏧☕♣♿

Olde White Harte ★

25 Silver Street, HU1 1JG

⊗ 11 (12 Sun)-midnight ☎ (01482) 326363

⊕ yeoldewhiteharte.co.uk

Caledonian Deuchars IPA, Flying Scotsman; Theakston Best Bitter, Lightfoot, Old Peculier; guest beers Ⓗ

Historic pub in a 17th-century merchant's house. The existing ground floor interior dates back to a major refurbishment in 1881, which was an idealised re-creation of an old English inn, complete with massive inglenook fireplaces and stained glass windows. The first floor has restaurant facilities and the Plotting Parlour is available for meetings and functions. There is also a courtyard with heating providing an all-weather outdoor drinking area. Hull & East Yorkshire CAMRA Branch's most recent recipient of Committed to Cask award. Q⊛◑⇌☕♿

Pave ✔

16-20 Prince's Avenue, HU5 3QA

⊗ 11-11.30 (midnight-Fri & Sat) ☎ (01482) 333181

⊕ pavebar.co.uk

Caledonian Deuchars IPA; Theakston Best Bitter, XB; guest beer Ⓗ

A continental-style café bar that attracts a diverse range of customers. As well as the regular real ales, there will be a guest ale which is usually sourced locally, and a varied range of European draught and bottled beers. Food including vegetarian options is served every day. Complimentary live entertainment is provided on Tuesday evenings and Sunday afternoons, but the bar closes to the general public when comedy nights and world music nights are held - further details on the bar's website. ⊛◑☕🚲♣♿

Three John Scotts ✔

Lowgate, HU1 1XW

⊗ 9am-midnight (1am Fri & Sat) ☎ (01482) 381910

Greene King Abbot; Ruddles Best Bitter; guest beers Ⓗ

Originally an Edwardian post office, this open-plan Wetherspoon features modern decor and works of art. It is named after three past incumbents of the church opposite. The pub has established a broad customer base appealing to all types of clientele. Wetherspoon's club meal offers are available Tuesday, Thursday and Sunday throughout the year. Up to 10 real ales and additional real ciders are available, and bi-annual Wetherspoon beer festivals are held. Children are welcomed up to 7pm. ⊛◑☵⇌☕♿

Walters

21 Scale Lane, HU1 1LF

⊗ 12-11 ☎ (01482) 224004 ⊕ waltersbar.co.uk

Beer range varies Ⓗ

The pub's name recalls an 1820s barber shop on the same premises. It is now a modern café bar in style, attracting a broad cross-section of drinkers, offering up to 16 real ales and five real ciders. Many new microbreweries are given their Hull debut here, and established local breweries are also supported. Continental draught and bottled beers are also available. An over-21s door policy operates on Friday and Saturday evenings. Runner-up local CAMRA Pub of the Year 2011. ☵♿

Wellington Inn

55 Russell Street, HU2 9AB

⊗ 4-11; 12-midnight Fri & Sat; 12-11 Sun ☎ (01482) 329486

Wellington 1st Duke; guest beers Ⓗ

Hidden free house gem and past local CAMRA Pub of the Year, just off Freetown Way. It began brewing in 2011 and serves up to seven real ales, with three from the brewery. Around 100 imported bottled beers are stored in a glass-fronted walk-in cooler. Real ciders and perry are also on sale, plus draught specialist European beers. No food is served, but you can bring your own sandwiches. Quiz night is Wednesday, jazz plays on the last Thursday of the month and folk on the first and third Sunday afternoons. ⊛≷⊟♣♠P¼

Whalebone
165 Wincolmlee, HU2 0PA (500yds N of North Bridge on W side of River Hull)
☼ 12-midnight ☎ (01482) 226648
Copper Dragon Best Bitter; Taylor Landlord; Tetley Bitter; Whalebone Neckoil Bitter; guest beer Ⓗ
Built in 1796, the pub is situated in a former industrial area – look for the illuminated M&R Ales sign. The comfortable saloon bar is adorned with photos of bygone Hull pubs, CAMRA awards and the city's sporting heritage. The adjacent Whalebone Brewery opened in 2003. Whalebone Diana Mild is available in spring/summer. Broad Oak Kingston Black and Westons Old Rosie ciders are sold, together with European draught and bottled beers. Hot snacks are available. ₩♣♠

Kirk Ella

Beech Tree ✔
Southella Way, HU10 7LY
☼ 11.30-11 (midnight Thu-Sat) ☎ (01482) 654350
Caledonian Deuchars IPA; Taylor Golden Best; Tetley Bitter; guest beers Ⓗ
Open-plan pub on the western outskirts of Hull, owned by a pub company committed to cask ale. Up to eight real ales are available, and try before you buy is encouraged. Food is available 12-10pm every day. Tuesday is curry night and Thursday is grill night – both from 5pm. Monday and Wednesday are quiz nights. Families with children are served in the restaurant area. Buses stop close to the pub until early evening and later stop 10 minutes' walk away. ⊛◖&⊟(154,180)P¼

Lund

Wellington Inn
19 The Green, YO25 9TE
☼ 12-3 (not Mon), 6.30-11 (11.30 Fri & Sat); 12-11 Sun
☎ (01377) 217294 ⊕ thewellingtoninn.co.uk
Theakston Best Bitter; guest beers Ⓗ
Enjoying a prime location on the green in this award-winning Wolds village, most of the pub's trade comes from the local farming community. Renovated by the present licensee, it features stone-flagged floors, beamed ceilings and three real fires. The multi-roomed interior includes a games room and candle-lit restaurant serving evening meals Tuesday-Saturday. Good food can also be enjoyed at lunchtime from the bar menu and specials board. ₩⊛◖⊟&♣P¼

North Cave

White Hart ✔
20 Westgate, HU15 2NJ
☼ 12-11 (midnight Fri & Sat) ☎ (01430) 470940
⊕ whitehartnorthcave.co.uk
Beer range varies Ⓗ
This welcoming, traditional village pub is a credit to the community it serves. It has three rooms, one now only used for Sunday lunches. The long bar to the side and rear is where the three real ales are

dispensed, and the front room is used by real ale drinkers. Real fires are lit during the winter months, providing further home from home comfort. The owners welcome walkers and customers with dogs. ₩⊛⊟(155)P¼

Old Ellerby

Blue Bell
Crabtree Lane, HU11 5AJ
☼ closed Mon; 7-11.30; 12-4.30, 7-midnight Sat; 12-6, 8-11 Sun ☎ (01964) 562364
Tetley Bitter; guest beers Ⓗ
A 16th-century inn with an L-shaped bar and a single room divided into distinct areas, including a snug to the right and a rear pool area where children are welcome until 8.30pm. The pub has a strong community feel and is home to several darts and dominoes teams. Two guest beers in winter increase to three in summer. Outside is a fish pond and bowling green. Popular with walkers (wipe your boots please). ₩Q⊛&▲♣P¼

Patrington

Holderness Inn
9 High Street, HU12 0RE
☼ 12-11 ☎ (01964) 630335
Tetley Bitter; Wye Valley HPA; York Guzzler; guest beer Ⓗ
The original entrance porch and two rooms to the left have now become one large L-shaped room. To the right, a door takes you into the comfortable front lounge, which retains some of its original features and extends into a more basic room behind it. St Austell Tribute, or a guest beer, is usually available as well as the regular range of ales. Dogs are welcome.
₩Q⊛◖⊟&▲⊟(75,76,77)♣P¼

Station Hotel ✔
Station Road, HU12 0NE
☼ 12-11 (midnight Sat) ☎ (01964) 630262
Black Sheep Best Bitter; guest beers Ⓗ
A family-owned free house on the western edge of the village, this hotel used to service passengers on the Hull-Withernsea railway, which closed in the 1960s. The Anglo-German owners have completely refurbished the old building in a welcoming modern-rustic style, and have added a snug and family room. The hotel is renowned locally for the quality of its food, served 12-9pm every day. Two guest beers are sourced from far and wide.
⊛◖&▲⊟(75,76,77)P¼

Pollington

King's Head Ⓛ ✔
Main Street, DN14 0DN
☼ 5.30-11.30; 12.30-12.30am Sat & Sun ☎ (01405) 861507
Tetley Bitter; guest beers Ⓗ
Excellent village pub situated conveniently for the Aire and Calder canal and Transpennine Trail. Popular with regulars, walkers and visitors, the pub offers B&B accommodation and ample parking. The interior is open plan, comprising a comfortable lounge area and another area with pool table, darts and TV sport. Quiz night is every Friday. Guest ales are sourced from small, independent breweries, with at least one locally brewed beer always available. ⊟&♣P¼

Rawcliffe

Jemmy Hirst at the Rose & Crown 🍷 Ⓛ

26 Riverside, DN14 8RN (from village green turn N on Chapel Lane) SE683231
✿ 6 (5 Fri)-11; 12-11 Sat & Sun ☎ (01405) 831038
Taylor Landlord; guest beers Ⓗ
Outstanding village pub, well known in the region and winner of numerous local CAMRA Branch awards, including seven times Pub of the Year and Yorkshire Winner 2011. A warm welcome awaits you from the owners, locals and Bruno the dog. Book-lined walls and an open fire provide a haven on a cold winter's day. It is the perfect place to sample the four guest ales; a traditional cider can also be enjoyed. The patio or river bank beckon in warmer weather. ⚞Q❀☆ዪ(88,400)●P²⌐

Ryehill

Crooked Billet ✔

Pitt Lane, HU12 9NN (off A1033 E of Thorngumbald)
✿ 4-midnight (1am Fri); 12-1am Sat & Sun
☎ (01964) 622303
Jennings Cumberland Ale; Marston's Burton Bitter; Wychwood Hobgoblin; guest beers Ⓗ
Sixteenth-century coaching inn with stone floors, upholstered bench seating and a rear dining area. Customers can expect a warm welcome – and that is guaranteed in the colder months, with a real fire next to the entrance door. Five handpumps offer four Jennings or Marston's beers, plus an occasional guest. Home-cooked food is served Thursday to Saturday evenings and Sunday lunchtimes. ⚞❀◑ዪ(75,76)♣P²⌐

Snaith

Brewer's Arms Ⓛ

10 Pontefract Road, DN14 9JS (on A645)
✿ 11.30-11.30; 12-11 Sun ☎ (01405) 862404
Old Mill Bitter, Blonde Bombshell, Red Goose, seasonal beer Ⓗ
This impressive former town house is the flagship pub and brewery tap for the Old Mill estate. Converted in 1986, it is of split-level design, with four distinct drinking/dining areas, and includes a well, complete with a fake but realistic skeleton at the bottom. Four Old Mill ales are on offer, plus Old Rosie cider. Fresh seafood complements a high-quality food menu on most Fridays and Saturdays, with seafood festivals throughout the year. Q❀❀✍◑占❧ዪ(401)♣●P²⌐

South Dalton

Pipe & Glass

West End, HU17 7PN (follow signs from B1248)
✿ closed Mon; 12-11 (10.30 Sun) ☎ (01430) 810246
⊕ pipeandglass.co.uk
Black Sheep Best Bitter; guest beers Ⓗ
Delightful hostelry that stands at the site of the original gatehouse to Dalton Hall. It features exposed beams and custom-made furniture. The pub holds a Michelin star for the second year running; meals are served lunchtimes and evenings. Three guest beers come from Yorkshire breweries and the real cider from Moorlands Cyder. Two double rooms are available to let, and walkers are made welcome. The pub closes for two weeks in January. ⚞❀◑占●P²⌐

Sutton upon Derwent

St Vincent Arms Ⓛ

Main Street, YO41 4BN (on B1228 S of Elvington)
✿ 11.30-3, 6-11; 12-3, 6.30-10.30 Sun ☎ (01904) 608349
⊕ stvincentarms.co.uk
Fuller's London Pride Ⓗ, **ESB** Ⓖ; **Old Mill Bitter; Taylor Golden Best, Landlord; Wells Bombardier; York Yorkshire Terrier; guest beer** Ⓗ
Winner of many York CAMRA awards over the years, this pretty white-painted village free house on a bend in the road has been family-owned and well run for many years. It has a consistent but varied beer range, and serves excellent food in the restaurant every day, including many fish dishes. The bar, featuring a large Fuller, Smith & Turner mirror, is popular with locals. Another small bar with a serving hatch leads to the dining rooms. Q❀◑❧P

YORKSHIRE (NORTH)

Aldbrough St John

Stanwick Ⓛ ✔

High Green, DL11 7SZ (1 mile from B6275)
✿ 12-3, 5.30 (6.30 Sat)-11; closed Mon Jan & Feb; 12-10.30 Sun ☎ (01325) 374258 ⊕ thestanwickinn.co.uk
Daleside Bitter; Jarrow Rivet Catcher; guest beers Ⓗ
In a picturesque North Yorkshire village on one of the country's largest village greens, this welcoming 19th-century inn overlooks the meandering beck. It has two bars: one for drinkers and one for the two excellent restaurants, where locally sourced food is served seven days a week. The Stanwick offers two guest ales, always including one from Mithril Ales in the village. You can stay at the pub and explore the Yorkshire Dales and Teesdale. ⚞Q❀✍◑ ዪ(29)♣P²⌐—⎕

Appletreewick

Craven Arms Inn Ⓛ

BD23 6DA
✿ 11-11 (10.30 Sun) ☎ (01756) 720270
⊕ craven-cruckbarn.co.uk
Dark Horse Hetton Pale Ale; Thwaites Nutty Black, Original; guest beers Ⓗ
Dating from 1548, this multi-roomed Dales free house has stone-flagged floors, oak beams and gas lighting. The main bar features an original Yorkshire range while the cosy taproom has ring the bull. A snug behind the bar leads to the cruck barn, added in 2006 and built using traditional techniques. The four to six guest beers come from Lancashire and Yorkshire breweries and the house beer, Cruck Barn Bitter, is brewed by Dark Horse. Guest beers are served in summer. ⚞Q❀◑ Æ(74)♣●P

New Inn Ⓛ

BD23 6DA (W end of village)
✿ 12-11 ☎ (01756) 720252
⊕ the-new-inn-appletreewick.com
Black Sheep Best Bitter; Daleside Bitter, Blonde; Tetley Bitter; Theakston Old Peculier; guest beer Ⓗ
Friendly village local with good views of the Wharfe Valley from the outside seating area. All welcome including walkers, horse riders, well-behaved dogs and cyclists (there is a nearby cycle livery). The main bar and separate newly refurbished dining room are both warmed by real

fires. Black and white photographs of bygone Appletreewick adorn the walls. A fine range of bottled beers from around the world is always available. Ilkley-Grassington bus no 74 passes Monday-Saturday. 🏠⛲🍴◑Å🚌(74)♣P

Aysgarth

George & Dragon L

DL8 3AD (on main A684 between Hawes and Leyburn)
❁ 8am-midnight ☎ (01969) 663358
⊕ georgeanddragonaysgarth.co.uk
Black Sheep Best Bitter; John Smith's Bitter; Yorkshire Dales George & Dragon; guest beers Ⓗ
Located in this beautiful village in the heart of the Yorkshire Dales near the famous Aysgarth falls, the George & Dragon is a 17th-century coaching inn that offers both en-suite accommodation and a restaurant with good food. The bar is cosy with dark wooden panelling, and the five real ales usually include two from the local Yorkshire Dales brewery. Dogs are welcome. The outside drinking area has thatched umbrellas and great views.
🏠Q⛲🍴◑Å🚌(156)♣P

Barkston Ash

Boot & Shoe L ✔

Main Street, LS24 9PR (100yds off A162 in village)
❁ 5-11 (midnight Fri & Sat); 12-10.30 Sun
☎ (01937) 557374 ⊕ bootandshoe.info
Brown Cow Boot & Shoe IPA; Leeds Pale; Tetley Bitter; Theakston Black Bull Bitter; guest beers Ⓗ
A classic two-roomed village free house dating back to the 18th century, with a friendly welcome. Four regular cask beers and one guest are on handpump, usually from local breweries. Traditional good-value food is served daily (no food Mon) as well as Sunday lunch, and there are pizzas to eat in or take out. Take-away beer cartons are also available. An annual beer festival in the decked beer garden takes place on the second full weekend in July.
🏠Q⛲◑&⇆(Church Fenton)🚌(492,493)♣P⅃—

Beck Hole

Birch Hall Inn ★

YO22 5LE (1 mile N of Goathland)
❁ 11-11 summer; 11-3, 7.30-11 (closed Mon eve & Tue) winter ☎ (01947) 896245
Birch Hall Beckwater; Black Sheep Best Bitter; guest beers Ⓗ
An unspoilt, family-run rural gem, resting in the middle of a hamlet of nine cottages, run by the same licensee for 32 years. A CAMRA multi-award winner, it comprises the big bar and the small bar that, uniquely, sandwich a traditional sweet shop. Local rural scenes, painted by the licensee herself, adorn the walls. The house ale, Beckwater, is organically brewed by North Yorkshire Brewing. Guest beers are sourced locally. Sandwiches, pies, beer cake and traditional sweets are always available. 🏠Q⛄⛲⛐♣

Bishop Monkton

Masons Arms ✔

St Johns Road, HG3 3QU (1 mile S of A61)
❁ 11.30-3, 6.30-11; 12-11 Sat & Sun ☎ (01765) 676631
⊕ masonsarmsbishopmonkton.org.uk
Tetley Bitter; guest beers Ⓗ

A friendly pub at the heart of village life, it hosts frequent events including quizzes, bingo, steak nights, poker and a pub cinema that also screens sport. The varied guest beers come from all over, as the collection of pump clips testifies. There is a formal dining room to the back, with bar meals served in the open-plan bar at the front. The pub is hiker- and child-friendly. 🏠⛲◑🚌(56)P

Boroughbridge

Black Bull Inn

6 St James Square, YO51 9AR
❁ 11-midnight; 12-11 Sun ☎ (01423) 322413
John Smith's Bitter; Taylor Best Bitter; guest beer Ⓗ
Nestling in a corner of the market square, the inn has been serving ale since it was first built in 1278. The bar is situated in a small, cosy snug, and a separate hatch serves the lounge, with its wooden settles and open fire. The guest beer is locally sourced. An unusual attraction – although not guaranteed – is that ghostly figures have been seen within the pub by both the landlord and customers on a number of occasions. The ancient Roman site of Aldborough (Isurium) is nearby.
🏠Q🍴◑⅊Å🚌(142)♣P

Borrowby

Wheatsheaf

Main Street, YO7 4QP (1 mile from A19 in village centre)
❁ 5.30 (12 Sun)-11 ☎ (01845) 537274

INDEPENDENT BREWERIES

Barkston Barkston Ash (NEW)
Black Sheep Masham
Brown Cow Barlow
Captain Cook Stokesley
Conquest Whitby (NEW)
Copper Dragon Skipton
Daleside Harrogate
Dark Horse Hetton
East Coast Filey
Great Heck Great Heck
Great Yorkshire Cropton
Hambleton Melmerby
Hop Studio Elvington (NEW)
Litton Litton
Marston Moor Tockwith
Mithril Aldbrough St John
Naylor's Cross Hills
North Riding Scarborough
North Yorkshire Pinchinthorpe
Redscar Redcar
Richmond Richmond
Rooster's Knaresborough
Rudgate Tockwith
Samuel Smith Tadcaster
Scarborough Scarborough (NEW)
Theakston Masham
Three Peaks Settle
Treboom Shipton-by-Beningbrough (NEW)
Truefitt Middlesbrough (NEW)
Urban York
Wainstones Stokesley
Wall's Northallerton
Wensleydale Bellerby
Wold Top Wold Newton
York York
Yorkshire Dales Askrigg
Yorkshire Heart Nun Monkton

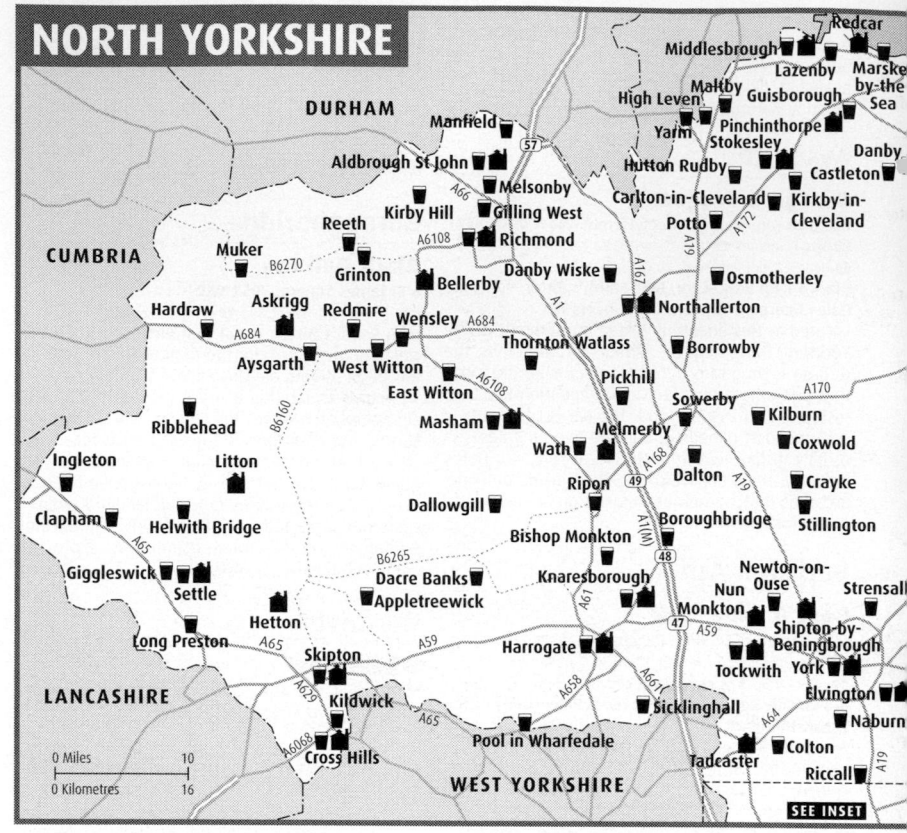

NORTH YORKSHIRE

Redcar
Middlesbrough
Lazenby
Marske-by-the-Sea
DURHAM
Manfield
High Leven
Maltby
Guisborough
Danby
Aldbrough St John
Yarm
Pinchinthorpe
Stokesley
Castleton
Hutton Rudby
Melsonby
Carlton-in-Cleveland
Kirkby-in-Cleveland
Kirby Hill
Gilling West
Potto
Reeth
CUMBRIA
Muker
Grinton
Richmond
Danby Wiske
Osmotherley
Hardraw
Askrigg
Redmire
Wensley
Bellerby
Northallerton
Aysgarth
West Witton
Thornton Watlass
Borrowby
Ribblehead
East Witton
Pickhill
Kilburn
Masham
Melmerby
Sowerby
Coxwold
Ingleton
Litton
Wath
Dalton
Crayke
Clapham
Helwith Bridge
Dallowgill
Ripon
Boroughbridge
Stillington
Giggleswick
Dacre Banks
Bishop Monkton
Newton-on-Ouse
Strensall
Settle
Appletreewick
Knaresborough
Nun Monkton
Shipton-by-Beningbrough
Hetton
Harrogate
Tockwith
York
Elvington
Long Preston
Skipton
Naburn
LANCASHIRE
Kildwick
Sicklinghall
Colton
Cross Hills
Pool in Wharfedale
Tadcaster
Riccall
WEST YORKSHIRE
SEE INSET
0 Miles 10
0 Kilometres 16

Daleside Bitter; guest beers Ⓗ
Attractive 17th-century free house near the North York Moors and close to the A19 trunk route. A huge stone fireplace dominates the low-beamed public bar, with another drinking area to the rear and a small dining room with convertible pool table across the passage. Home-cooked food is served on Wednesdays and themed food nights are common on Fridays and Saturdays. However, this is predominantly a thriving and welcoming locals' pub, which is also very dog- and child-friendly. ⌂Q❄☆♿⇦♣P⌐

Burn

Wheatsheaf Ⓛ
Main Road, YO8 8LJ (on A19 3 miles S of Selby)
SE594286
☼ 12-11 ☎ (01757) 270614 ⊕ wheatsheafburn.co.uk
John Smith's Bitter; Taylor Best Bitter; guest beers Ⓗ
A Guide pub for more than 12 years, renowned for its reasonably priced beers, always including one dark and often from local breweries such as Brown Cow. A narrow entrance leads to the bar and spacious lounge with its huge open fire. A collection of bottled beers, artefacts from bygone days and memorabilia of 578 Squadron stationed at Burn in World War II adorn the walls. Food is served every lunchtime and Wednesday to Saturday evenings. Frequent beer festivals and monthly jazz nights are held.
⌂Q❄◑⇦(150,405,407)♣P⌐

Carlton-in-Cleveland

Blackwell Ox Inn
Main Street, TS9 7DJ (400yds E of A172)
☼ 11.30-11 ☎ (01642) 712287 ⊕ theblackwellox.co.uk
Beer range varies Ⓗ
In a beautiful area on the edge of the National Park, this impressive, multi-roomed village inn is renowned for its good-value cuisine as well as its fine ales. Winter Monday evening Thai buffets can easily become habit forming. Look out also for early evening year-round specials. But you do not have to eat, as drinkers are made most welcome. Four handpumps provide an eclectic range of varying beer styles. The garden has an extensive children's play area. ⌂Q❄☆⇦◑♿▲⇦(80)P

Castleton

Eskdale Inn
Station Road, YO21 2EU (next to railway station, 400yds N of village centre)
☼ 12-midnight (11 Sun) ☎ (01287) 660333
⊕ eskdaleinn.co.uk
Black Sheep Best Bitter; Tetley Bitter; guest beer Ⓗ
Between the Esk Valley railway station and the River Esk, this former station hotel offers a friendly welcome. The casks sit in a cool cellar directly beneath the handpumps and well away from the warming fire. The guest beer is often chosen by the locals themselves and is usually something interesting. A good-value menu, served all day every day, includes a specials board and a

includes oak panelling, the other has walls with photos and cartoons depicting caving and is home to pub games. Children are welcome in the restaurant. The railway station is a mile away. ⚏✿🏠◖◗⇌🚻(581)♣P

Old Manor House

Church Avenue, LA2 8EQ
🕐 12-6 (7 Fri & Sat) ☎ (01524) 251144 🌐 claphambunk.com
Beer range varies Ⓗ
The old manor house, dating back to circa 1620, is home to a bunkhouse, a café and a bar called the Reading Room. A huge fireplace (dated 1701) holds a wood-burning stove, the floor is flagged, and art for sale hangs on the walls. Snacks such as soup, paninis and baked potatoes are available 4-7pm. Giant Jenga is played. Do not overlook the bottled beers and ciders; the draught cider is Westons Scrumpy. The station is a mile away. ⚏Q✿🏠◖△⇌🚻(581)♣

Cloughton

Bryherstones Inn

Newlands Road, YO13 0AR (1000yds up Newlands Rd off A171 at Cloughton)
🕐 closed Mon & Tue; 12-3, 6-midnight (11 Sun)
☎ (01723) 870744 🌐 bryherstones.info
Taylor Landlord; Wold Top Bryherstones Ale Ⓗ
Nestling between the North York moors and the coast, just outside the village of Cloughton. The pub is now back in the hands of the Shipley family and has been restored to its former glory. Its many rooms are full of features, and there is a separate games room. An extensive locally sourced menu is offered – booking is advised on an evening. The spacious beer garden has a children's play area, the pub is child- and dog-friendly and there is a large car park. ⚏✿◖◗🍴♣P

Hayburn Wyke Inn

Newlands Road, YO13 0AU (off Ravenscar Rd, 1½ miles N of jct with A171) TA007968
🕐 11-midnight; 11-3, 6-midnight Mon Fri winter
☎ (01723) 870202 🌐 hayburnwykeinn.co.uk
Black Sheep Ale; Daleside Bitter; Theakston Old Peculier Ⓗ
Eighteenth-century coaching inn located in woodland adjacent to the disused Scarborough to Whitby railway line. Home-made food is served every lunchtime and evening, with the Sunday carvery a local favourite. En-suite accommodation is available. Outside is a well provisioned children's play area and a sizeable heated and covered smoking area. Situated only minutes away from the Cleveland Way coastal path and rocky beach, it is popular with cyclists and walkers. ⚏✿🏠◖◗△🚻P⌐

Colton

Old Sun Inn Ⓛ ✔

Main Street, LS24 8EP (left into village, along Colton Lane, 1 mile S of Bilbrough Services on A64) SE544448
🕐 12-2, 6-11; 12-11 Sun ☎ (01904) 744261
🌐 yeoldsuninn.co.uk
Black Sheep Ale, Best Bitter; York Guzzler; guest beer Ⓗ
A 17th-century village pub with an award-winning restaurant and deli. It has four cosy dining areas, together with a newly developed drinkers-only bar. The interior features traditional low-beamed

children's menu. The pub supports two darts and one pool team. Two letting bedrooms are available. ⚏Q✿🏠◖◗&⇌🚻♣P⌐🍴

Cawood

Ferry Inn

2 King Street, YO8 3TL (over the bridge, first right)
🕐 12 (3 Mon)-midnight (1am Fri); 12-11 Sun
☎ (01757) 268515
Caledonian Deuchars IPA; Taylor Landlord; guest beers Ⓗ
Wooden-beamed, 16th-century inn, with a homely ambience and three open fires to welcome visitors on winter days. Summer months showcase a picturesque backdrop of river views, open countryside and the adjacent swing bridge from the vantage point of the popular outside terrace. Regular quizzes, pub games, live music and extended opening hours ensure this establishment keeps both visitors and the local community well satisfied. ⚏Q🐕✿🏠◖◗&🚻(415)♣P⌐

Clapham

New Inn

LA2 8HH
🕐 11-midnight; 9-11 Sun ☎ (01524) 51203
🌐 newinn-clapham.co.uk
Black Sheep Best Bitter; Copper Dragon Best Bitter, Golden Pippin; Taylor Landlord Ⓗ
In a major tourist village, this spacious 18th-century coaching inn features two lounge bars. One

ceilings and in winter there are two real fires. For the summer there is a patio and a large picnic area. Next door is a B&B owned by the publican.
🏚️🏵️🛏️◑♿🚌(21)P

Coxwold

Fauconberg Arms 🅛
YO61 4AD
✪ 11-3, 6-midnight; 11-midnight Sat & Sun
☎ (01347) 868214 ⊕ fauconbergarms.com
Hambleton Bitter; Theakston Best Bitter; guest beers 🅗
Seventeenth-century country inn, close to Shandy Hall and Newburgh Priory, with a cosy, beamed front bar, a rear bar with dartboard and piano, and a separate dining room. Guest ales come from local microbreweries, and there is also local Galtres Gold real cider. In spite of its excellent reputation for food and accommodation, the pub is still the village local. It holds regular quizzes, food events, music nights on Sundays and even an annual pantomime. A village shop is incorporated at the rear. No food Sunday evenings.
🏚️🏵️🛏️◑🚌(31X)♣🐕P⁵⁄

Crayke

Durham Ox
Westway, YO61 4TE SE562704
✪ 12-11.30 (10.30 Sun) ☎ (01347) 821506
⊕ thedurhamox.com
Black Sheep Best Bitter; Taylor Landlord; Theakston Best Bitter 🅗
Unashamedly food-oriented and with a good selection of local beers, this renowned pub lies in a beautiful village within the Howardian Hills, 30 minutes' drive north of York. Also conveniently located on the Easingwold-York bus route, there are numerous interesting villages nearby. Incorporating characterful cottage-style accommodation, a marquee and barbecue area, it offers formal dining, a bar/restaurant and a cosy public bar. It holds weekly music, themed dining, cooking, and beer and wine nights. There are great views of the Vale of York from the car park.
🏚️Q🏵️🛏️◑🍴♿🚌P⁵⁄

Cropton

New Inn 🅛 ✪
Woolcroft, YO18 8HH (5 miles off the A170 Pickering-Kirkbymoorside road) SE755888
✪ 11-11 (midnight Fri & Sun) ☎ (01751) 417330
⊕ newinncropton.co.uk
Beer range varies 🅗
The Cropton Brewery tap, this is a family-run pub on the edge of the North Yorkshire Moors National Park. In an attractive stone building, it is a perfect base for walking and cycling, offering good food in the bars, conservatory or restaurant, and B&B or camping accommodation. With up to half a dozen of the well-regarded Cropton ales, it doesn't get more LocAle than this. A legendary beer festival is held every November, plus a music festival in summer. Dogs welcome. Q🎪🏵️🛏️◑▲♣P

Cross Hills

Old White Bear 🅛
6 Keighley Road, BD20 7RN (on A6068, close to jct with A629)

✪ 11-11 ☎ (01535) 632115 ⊕ oldwhitebear.co.uk
Naylor's Pinnacle Mild, Bitter, Blonde, seasonal beers 🅗
Popular four-room village pub with exposed timbers said to have come from a ship of the same name. Built in 1735, it had a chequered history as a hotel, brothel, council meeting room and dance hall before becoming a pub. The top room, with stone-flagged floor, is used mainly as an eatery, with good-value meals available. Children and dogs are welcome. The back room has darts and ring the bull. A regular outlet for Naylor's Brewery.
🏚️🏵️◑🚌(66,66A)♣P⁵⁄

Dacre Banks

Royal Oak Inn
Oak Lane, HG3 4EN
✪ 11.30-11; 12-10.30 Sun ☎ (01423) 780200
⊕ the-royaloak-dacre.co.uk
Rudgate Viking; guest beers 🅗
A family-run, Grade II-listed pub dating from 1752, in the heart of Nidderdale. At the rear are views of the dale, while a cosy seating area at the front is complete with a real fire. Outside is an attractive garden and boules is played beside the car park. Up to four real ales from Rudgate and Marston Moor are available. Food majors on local produce and is served in the bar and a separate restaurant.
🏚️Q🏵️🛏️◑🚌(24)♣P

Dallowgill

Drovers Inn
HG4 3RH (2 miles W of Laverton on road to Pateley Bridge) SE210720
✪ closed Mon; 6.30 (7 winter)-11; 12-3, 6.30-11 Sat & Sun
☎ (01765) 658510
Black Sheep Best Bitter; Hambleton Bitter; guest beers 🅗
The inn, as the name implies, was built in 1860 on the site of an old hut to provide food, drink and shelter for passing herdsmen on the adjacent drove road. Nowadays it serves the local farming community as well as walkers and tourists exploring this beautiful part of the Yorkshire Dales. The small one-roomed interior has a tiny bar and in winter a roaring fire. Excellent-value home-cooked meals are available daily until 8.30pm.
🏚️Q🏵️◑▲♣P

Dalton

Jolly Farmer 🅛
Brookside, YO7 3HY (off A19 or A168)
✪ 7 (6 Thu)-11; 12-2.30, 6-11 Fri; 12-11 Sat & Sun
☎ (01845) 577359
Theakston Best Bitter; guest beers 🅗
Popular with locals, this family-run pub dating from the mid-1800s is at the heart of the village. Its four handpumps feature beer from local micros chosen by the regulars. Freshly prepared home-made dishes using local produce are served from the kitchen (booking advisable for Sunday lunch). Three en-suite rooms provide an ideal base for exploring the Dales and North Yorkshire Moors.
🏵️🛏️◑♿▲♣P⁵⁄

Danby

Duke of Wellington 🍷
2 West Lane, YO21 2LY (200yds N of railway station)

⚙ 12-3 (not Mon), 7-11; 12-11 Fri & Sat; 12-3, 7-10.30 Sun
☎ (01287) 660351 ⊕ dukeofwellingtondanby.co.uk
Copper Dragon Scotts 1816; Daleside Bitter; guest beer Ⓗ

An 18th-century inn, and 2012 CAMRA Pub of the Year, set in idyllic National Park countryside, close to the Moors Visitor Centre and Esk Valley railway station. It was used as a recruiting post during the Napoleonic Wars. A cast-iron plaque of the first Duke of Wellington, unearthed during restorations, hangs above the fireplace. All the beers come from local breweries, while the menu offers traditional British home-cooked meals, using locally sourced meat, fish and game. Cider and perry are served Easter-October. ᗅQ❁✉🌙≥🚫♣👍

Danby Wiske

White Swan 🏆 Ⓛ

DL7 0NQ (approx 3 miles N of Northallerton off A167) 336986
⚙ 12-11 Easter-October; closed Tue; 7 (6 Fri)-11; 12-3, 6-11 Sat winter; 12-3, 7-10.30 Sun ☎ (01609) 775131
⊕ thewhiteswandanbywiske.co.uk
Beer range varies Ⓗ

Renovated a couple of years ago after a long closure, this lovely pub has a welcome for Coast-to-Coast route walkers, and B&B and camping facilities for them to rest. The open bar area has a splendid stone floor and wood-burning stoves. Locally sourced food features meat from just a mile away (ring first for winter availability). The landlord fiercely champions real ale, especially local breweries like Wall's of Northallerton, with up to five changing beers depending on the time of year. ᗅQ❁✉🌙⛺♣P

East Witton

Cover Bridge Inn Ⓛ

DL8 4SQ (½ mile N of village on A6108) SE144871
⚙ 11-midnight; 12-11.30 Sun ☎ (01969) 623250
⊕ thecoverbridgeinn.co.uk
Black Sheep Best Bitter; John Smith's Bitter; Taylor Landlord; Theakston Best Bitter, Old Peculier; guest beers Ⓗ

An ancient inn in beautiful countryside on a sharp bend on the Masham to Middleham road, this true country pub has won countless CAMRA awards. A warm welcome awaits in the unspoilt public bar, dominated by its splendid hearth and open fire. A tiny lounge leads to an attractive garden with a play area backing on to the River Cover. The pub has an enviable reputation for food, serving lunchtime and evening meals daily. The car park is across the road. Two real ciders and a perry are on offer. ᗅQ⛄❁✉🌙🚌(159)♣👍P🚬

Egton

Wheatsheaf Inn

High Street, YO21 1TZ
⚙ closed Mon; 11.30-2.30, 5.30-11; 11.30-11 Sat & Sun
☎ (01947) 895271 ⊕ wheatsheafegton.com
Black Sheep Best Bitter; Taylor Landlord; guest beer Ⓗ

Winner of many CAMRA awards, this Grade I-listed 19th-century pub is now in its 13th year in the Guide, and remains under the stewardship of a licensee who has had 26 years of continuous Guide recognition. Church pews, collectables from auctions and a roaring range add to the character.

The upmarket menu features local meat, fish and game. The grassy area to the front and boules to the rear are ideal for summer. Six bedrooms and a holiday cottage are available. ᗅ❁✉🌙🍴🚌≥🚫(99)♣P🚬

Egton Bridge

Horseshoe Hotel

YO21 1XE (down hill from Egton station)
⚙ 11.30-3, 6-11; 11.30-11 Sat; 12-11 Sun ☎ (01947) 895245
⊕ egtonbridgehotel.co.uk
Black Sheep Best Bitter; John Smith's Bitter; Theakston Best Bitter; guest beers Ⓗ

Secluded 18th-century gem in a horseshoe-shaped hollow and easily accessed either by road, from the railway station, or from across the stepping stones of the River Esk. Old-fashioned settles, a large fire and angling memorabilia adorn the bar, while a large raised grassy bank makes outdoor drinking a pleasure. Five handpumps provide a wide selection of differing beers. The menu and specials board are locally sourced and represent good value. Accommodation is in six letting bedrooms. ᗅQ⛄❁✉🌙🍴≥(Fgton)🚫(99)P🚬

Elvington

Grey Horse

Main Street, YO41 4AG (on B1228 6 miles SE of York)
⚙ 5 (3 Fri)-midnight; 12-midnight Sat & Sun
☎ (01904) 608335 ⊕ thegreyhorse.com
Copper Dragon Golden Pippin; Taylor Landlord; guest beers Ⓗ

Welcoming Punch-owned beamed country local opposite the village green, dating from the 17th century. The comfortable lounge area has a glass wall of bottled beers, a wooden propeller, an odd wooden hand seat and a collection of vintage radios. The lively bar has a dartboard. The central bar serves two regular and two to three guest beers from a countrywide selection, and is warmed by wood-burning stoves. Sunday lunch is a carvery only. There is a pleasant front garden with picnic tables and a covered, heated smoking area to the rear. ᗅ⛄❁✉🍴🚫(36)♣P🚬

Filey

Bonhomme's Bar

Royal Crescent Court, The Crescent, YO14 9JH
⚙ 11 (12 winter)-midnight; 11-1am Fri & Sat; 12-midnight Sun ☎ (01723) 515325
East Coast Bonhomme Richard; guest beers Ⓗ

Just off the fine Victorian Royal Crescent Hotel complex, the bar's name celebrates John Paul Jones, father of the American Navy. His ship, the Bonhomme Richard, was involved in a battle off nearby Flamborough Head during the War of Independence. Five handpumps serve one East Coast beer plus four rotating guests. A fun quiz is held on Saturday, and the main quiz is on Sunday. Voted local CAMRA Rural Pub of the Year 2010. ≥🚫👍

Giggleswick

Hart's Head Hotel Ⓛ

Belle Hill, BD24 0BA (on B6480 ½ mile N of Settle)
⚙ 12-2.30 (not Wed & Thu), 5.30-11; 12-11.30 Fri & Sat; 12-11 Sun ☎ (01729) 822086 ⊕ hartsheadinn.co.uk

Copper Dragon Golden Pippin; Tetley Bitter; guest beers H

Open-plan 18th-century coaching inn. The bar separates the comfortable lounge from the bar area where pub games are played and sport is shown on TV. Freshly prepared meals from a varied menu are served in the adjacent dining room. The pleasant sloping beer garden at the rear is a great place to soak up the summer sun. Four changing guest beers are available from smaller Yorkshire, Lancashire and Cumbrian breweries such as Dent, Kirkby Lonsdale and Lancaster.

ᴍᴍ✿⌑◖◗&▲➔(580,581)♣P⌐

Gilling West

White Swan Inn L

51 High Street, DL10 5JG (2 miles W of Scotch Corner, off A66)
✪ 12-11 (3am Mon); 10.30-11 Sun ☎ (01748) 821123
Beer range varies H
Friendly 17th-century country inn with an open-plan bar with a real fire and a dining room offering an extensive menu. This free house sources its four guest beers from local and national microbreweries, and as it is the brewery tap for the local Mithril Ales, one of its beers is always featured. A real cider is stocked, and there is a yearly beer festival. The hostelry has a beer garden. Live acoustic music plays on alternate Wednesdays – avoid the Grumpy Seat.

ᴍᴍQ✿◖◗▲➔(29)♣♠⌐

Great Heck

Bay Horse

Main Street, DN14 0BQ (follow signs to village from A19) SE594210
✪ 12-11 (midnight Fri & Sat) ☎ (01977) 661121
Old Mill Bitter, Blonde Bombshell, seasonal beer H
Traditional, open-plan village pub with exposed beams and a real fire, subdivided into three separate areas for drinking and eating. Part of the Old Mill Brewery group, there are three of its beers on handpump, including one seasonal. Food is served daily and is all freshly prepared by the award-winning chef. There is no TV or bandit, just unobtrusive background music and a friendly atmosphere. Quiz night is Thursday. Outside is a heated smoking area and a walled patio seating area. ᴍᴍ✿◖◗P⌐

Grinton

Bridge Inn

DL11 6HH (on B6270, 1 mile E of Reeth) SE046984
✪ 12-midnight (11 Sun) ☎ (01748) 884224
⊕ bridgeinngrinton.co.uk
Jennings Cumberland Ale; guest beers H
A friendly, family-run country hostelry in the heart of Swaledale and on the Coast-to-Coast and Inn Way walks, as well as the Dales Cycle Way. It serves fresh, home-made food all day in the wood-panelled bar, lounge or two restaurant rooms. Close to the River Swale and the towering hills of Fremington Edge and Harkerside, the premises have the added quirk of Grinton Beck running through them, as well as clear warnings about the use of mobile phones.

ᴍᴍQ⛟✿⌑◖◗⊟▲➔(30,36,831)♣P

Grosmont

Crossing Club

Co-operative Building, Front Street, YO22 5QE (opp NYMR car park)
✪ 8-11 ☎ 07766 197744
Beer range varies H
Situated opposite the NYMR and Esk Valley railway stations, what was once the village Co-operative store's upstairs delivery bay has been converted by dedicated volunteers into a railway-themed private members' club. Four handpumps, one usually dedicated to Wold Top, have served more than 700 different beers during the club's 13-year existence. A warm welcome is always extended to CAMRA members. Access is gained by ringing the door bell.

Q⇌➔♣⌐

Guisborough

Globe

81 Northgate, TS14 6JP (at jct with Church Lane)
✪ 5 (3 Thu & Fri)-11.30; 12-midnight Sat; 12-10.30 Sun
☎ (01287) 639465
Camerons Strongarm; Jennings Cumberland Ale; Wychwood Hobgoblin; guest beer H
A welcome return to the Guide for this two-roomed, street-corner community pub, nicely situated just off the main road, and certainly well worth the 200-yard walk up Northgate. Three regular beers and a guest from the Marston's range are served. With its three sports TVs, the pub gets hectic on big match days. The licensee supports quiz nights and live music, together with football, pool and both male and female darts teams. Outside is a smokers' paradise. ⛟✿⊟&♣P⌐

Hardraw

Green Dragon L

DL8 3LZ (about 1 mile N of Hawes, just off Buttertubs road) 868913
✪ 10-2am (1am Sun) ☎ (01969) 667392
⊕ greendragonhardraw.com
Taylor Landlord; Theakston Best Bitter H, Old Peculier G; guest beers H
Old pub of character with origins dating back to the 13th century and specialising in locally brewed ales. In the grounds is Hardraw Force, England's highest single-drop waterfall, a noted beauty spot (pay at the bar for admission). Regular live music events include a folk weekend in July and a brass band competition in September. The bar has flagged floors, low beams and two impressive ranges. Meals are served all day. Real cider is stocked in summer only. Accommodation, from suites to a bunkhouse, is available.

ᴍᴍ⛟✿⌑◖◗⊟▲➔♣♠P⌐

Harrogate

Blues Bar

4 Montpellier Parade, HG1 2TJ (down the hill 50yds from Betty's Tea Room)
✪ 10-1am; 12-12.30am Sun ☎ (01423) 566881
⊕ bluesbar.org.uk
Beer range varies H
Small single-room bar in the town centre overlooking the lovely Montpellier Gardens, with four rotating guest beers. Noted for live music seven days a week, with two sessions on a Sunday, it is popular with music lovers and can get busy.

Modelled on an Amsterdam café bar, it has been going for more than 20 years. Food is served lunchtimes (except Sun) and upstairs there is an Egyptian restaurant open Tuesday to Saturday. ◑⇌�(24,36)

Coach & Horses 🅛
16 West Park, HG1 1BJ (opposite West Park Stray)
🕓 11-11; 12-10.30 Sun ☎ (01423) 561802
🌐 thecoachandhorses.net
Copper Dragon Golden Pippin; Daleside Bitter; Ilkley Gold; Taylor Landlord; Tetley Bitter; guest beer 🅗
A central bar is surrounded by snugs and alcoves, creating a cosy atmosphere. Excellent meals are served at lunchtime, with frequent themed food evenings. Many of these, together with a Sunday night quiz, have raised over £200,000 so far for a local children's hospice. Six real ales, usually sourced from local breweries, including one from Rooster's, are always available. A few tables and chairs are placed outside for smokers in summer. Window boxes provide year-round colour, with a quite spectacular display in summer. Q◑⇌�(24,36)

Fat Badger 🆗
2 Cold Bath Road, HG2 0NF
🕓 11-midnight (10.30 Sun) ☎ (01423) 505681
🌐 thefatbadger.co.uk
Black Sheep Best Bitter; Copper Dragon Golden Pippin; Tetley Bitter; Theakston Best Bitter; guest beers 🅗
New single-room pub created in part of the historic White Hart Hotel. It has a large bar area with high-quality ornate finishings throughout. Raised floor levels around the edges interspaced with part-glazed screens along one wall lend an intimate atmosphere. Outside is a large partly-covered patio area for year-round drinking and dining. A beer club is held once a month where quality food and real ales are paired. Bar meals are available until early evening, or you can choose the separate adjoining restaurant. ⊛🅟◑⇌🅟⅃

Hales Bar 🅛 🆗
1-3 Crescent Road, HG1 2RS
🕓 12-midnight (1am Thu-Sat; 11.30 Sun) ☎ (01423) 725570
🌐 halesbar.co.uk
Copper Dragon Golden Pippin; Daleside Old Legover; Draught Bass; Taylor Landlord; guest beers 🅗
Harrogate's oldest pub, and a CAMRA Real Heritage Pub. Featured in the film Chariots of Fire, the lounge has a Victorian-style interior with original gas lighting over the bar, and there is a separate snug. There are six handpumps, two serving a changing range of guest beers. Karaoke features on a Thursday night, Wednesday is quiz night, and occasional party nights are hosted. The venue prides itself on its floral displays in season. Food is available lunchtimes and evenings. Q◑◲⇌�(24,36)⅃

Old Bell Tavern 🆗
6 Royal Parade, HG1 2SZ (500yds W of A61)
🕓 12-11 (10.30 Sun) ☎ (01423) 507930
Black Sheep Best Bitter; guest beers 🅗
Part of the Market Town Taverns chain, the Old Bell opened in 1999 on the site of the Blue Bell Inn, which closed in 1815 and was later demolished. In 2001 it expanded into the former Farrah's toffee shop – plenty of Farrah's memorabilia is still on show. Eight real ales are available – many are local and one is always a mild – complemented by a

good range of bottled beers. Excellent-quality bar food is served every day and a separate upstairs restaurant offers a tranquil haven and opens evenings (except Sun). Q◑⇌🚶

Swan on the Stray 🆗
17 Devonshire Place, HG1 4AA (just off Skipton Rd)
🕓 11-11; 12-10.30 Sun ☎ (01423) 524587
Black Sheep Ale; Daleside Bitter; Ilkley Mary Jane; Taylor Landlord; guest beers 🅗
Formerly known as the Black Swan, this pub was extensively and tastefully refurbished in a modern style and reopened in early 2010. Eight real ales are available with four changing regularly, many from Yorkshire micros, though not exclusively so. A range of foreign beer is available on draught plus a real cider and an added selection in bottles. Allied to a good wine choice and excellent bar meals, the pub appeals to all age groups. Well-behaved children are welcome in the beer garden at the rear. Q⊛◑å🚶(1)♣🅟⅃

Helwith Bridge

Helwith Bridge 🅛 🆗
BD24 0EH (turn off B6479 at Helwith Bridge and cross river) SD810695
🕓 2.30 (12 Fri-Sun)-11 ☎ (01729) 860220
🌐 helwithbridge.com
John Smith's Bitter; Three Peaks Pen-y-ghent Bitter, Ingleborough Gold; Wells Bombardier; guest beers 🅗
Despite its relative isolation in the tiny hamlet of Helwith Bridge, this is a thriving, no-frills community local, run by the genial host with warmth and a sense of humour. His interests are reflected in the numerous paintings, photos and railway memorabilia on display. The three guest beers are usually sourced from the Heineken UK list, and the house beer is from Three Peaks Brewery. See the beer list fastened to the ceiling. ⛺⊛◑å▲å🚶(B1)♣🅟

High Leven

Fox Covert
Low Lane, TS15 9JW (on A1044, 1½ miles E of Yarm)
🕓 11.30-11 (midnight Fri & Sat); 12-11 Sun
☎ (01642) 760033 🌐 thefoxcovert.com
Caledonian Deuchars IPA; Theakston Old Peculier 🅗
A previous local CAMRA award winner, this popular, long-established and uniquely named inn has been in the same family for more than 25 years. Originally a farmhouse, it was built in the traditional longhouse style, with whitewashed walls and a pantiled roof. Inside it is warm and cosy, with two open fires and two drinking areas offering superbly kept beers. The pub is noted for its food, served all day every day. Conference facilities are available. ⛺⊛◑å🚶(507)🅟

Hinderwell

Brown Cow
55 High Street, TS13 5ET (on A174)
🕓 11 (12 Sun)-1am ☎ (01947) 840694
Beer range varies 🅗
Between the moors and the coast, this family-run pub has a strong local following as well as attracting visitors. Two busy handpumps serve weaker beers mid-week and stronger beers at weekends. The pub supports darts teams, charity nights, dominoes and whist drives, and has a

separate pool room. Children and dogs are welcome, and smokers are also well provided for. There are snacks in addition to lunchtime and evening meals. Accommodation is in three bedrooms. A previous local CAMRA award winner. ▲▷❀🛏️◑🍴🛇🪑♿(4,5)♣P⚊

Hutton Rudby

King's Head

36 North Side, TS15 0DA (W end of village)
❂ 12-11 (10.30 Sun) ☎ (01642) 700342
Camerons Strongarm; Jennings Cockerhoop, Cumberland Ale; guest beer Ⓗ
Set in a beautiful village, this previous local CAMRA award winner is a superb traditional locals' pub where a friendly welcome is assured. It comprises a main bar that is always busy, and a snug where children are welcome. Four ales on handpump include a guest from the Marston's range. Real fires, a popular quiz night on Tuesday, steak nights on Wednesday and Friday and live music on Saturday all add to the experience. Outside is a smokers' paradise, complete with TV.
▲▷❀🍴(82)⚊

Ingleton

Wheatsheaf ✅

22 High Street, LA6 3AD
❂ 12-11 (10 Sun) ☎ (01524) 241275
⊕ thewheatsheaf-ingleton.co.uk
Black Sheep Best Bitter; guest beer Ⓗ
Handy for the finish of the Waterfalls Walk, the Wheatsheaf has a good reputation for food and accommodation, as well as beer. The long, narrow bar is divided into different areas: one end has a pool table, the other leads into the restaurant, which is as large as the bar. A wood-burning stove is a focal point. ▲❀🛏️◑🍴(80)♣P

Kilburn

Forresters Ⓛ ✅

YO61 4AH (centre of village)
❂ 11-11 ☎ (01347) 868386 ⊕ forrestersarms.com
Hambleton Best Bitter; John Smith's Bitter; guest beer Ⓗ
A country pub in the centre of Kilburn. The bar, lounge and dining room are mainly furnished with items from the nearby workshops of Mousey Thompson. Traditional pub food is available and there is a specials board offering restaurant food. Outside at the front is a seating area that faces a cobbled square, and there is a covered smoking area at the rear. The White Horse at Sutton Bank is nearby. ▲Q❀🛏️◑🍴(59)P⚊

Kildwick

White Lion Ⓛ ✅

Priest Bank Road, BD20 9BH
❂ 12-11 (midnight Fri & Sat; 10.30 Sun) ☎ (01535) 632265
⊕ thewhitelionkildwick.co.uk
Copper Dragon Best Bitter; Ilkley Brewery Black; Taylor Landlord; Tetley Bitter Ⓗ
Centuries-old, two-roomed pub in a quiet village that has recently undergone refurbishment. It is opposite the medieval church and near the Leeds-Liverpool Canal. The pleasant lawned beer garden is south-facing, affording views across the Aire Valley. The venue hosts the Keighley and Craven Athletic Club and makes a good base for walks over Kildwick Moor or along the canal. Traditional pub food is served daily, and families are welcome. ❀🛏️◑🍴(66)♣P⚊

Kirby Hill

Shoulder of Mutton

DL11 7JH (2½ miles from A66, 4 miles NW of Richmond)
❂ 12-3 (not Mon-Fri), 6-11.30; 12-3, 6-11 Sun
☎ (01748) 822772 ⊕ shoulderofmutton.net
Daleside Bitter; guest beers Ⓗ
Ivy-fronted country inn in a beautiful hillside setting overlooking Lower Teesdale and the ruins of Ravensworth Castle. The pub has an open front bar that links the lounge with a cosy restaurant to the rear. Three guest beers (four in summer) are chosen by the pub's regulars. On the edge of the Yorkshire Dales, this is a popular venue for walkers. There are five en-suite guest bedrooms. Excellent food is available Wednesday to Sunday, although the bar area remains for drinkers.
▲Q❀🛏️◑🍴♣P⚊

Kirk Smeaton

Shoulder of Mutton

Main Street, WF8 3JY (follow signs from A1)
❂ 5-midnight (1am Fri & Sat); 11.30-midnight Sun
☎ (01977) 620348
Black Sheep Best Bitter; guest beer Ⓗ
Award-winning traditional village inn situated conveniently for the Went Valley and Brockadale Nature Reserve, popular with walkers and the local community. This attractive pub comprises a large lounge with open fires and a cosy, dark-panelled snug. Outside there is ample parking and a spacious beer garden with a covered and heated shelter for smokers. The superb beers are sourced directly from independent breweries – the guest is usually from Dark Horse. Quiz night is Tuesday. ▲❀🍴(409)P⚊

Kirkby-in-Cleveland

Black Swan

Busby Lane, TS9 7AW (½ mile W of B1257)
❂ 12-midnight ☎ (01642) 712512
Black Sheep Best Bitter; Copper Dragon Golden Pippin; Taylor Landlord; guest beer Ⓗ
Nestling at the foot of the North York Moors, and at the crossroads of this ancient village, this warm and cosy free house, comprising a bar, lounge/restaurant and conservatory, affords a friendly and genuine welcome. Three regular beers and a guest beer, all usually sourced from Yorkshire, are served 364 days of the year – the pub shuts at 3pm on Christmas Day. Bar snacks and a full menu including daily specials represent good value. There is a pool table. ▲Q❀◑🍴🪑♿(89)♣P⚊

Knaresborough

Blind Jack's Ⓛ

19 Market Place, HG5 8AL
❂ 4 (12 Fri & Sat)-11; 12-10.30 Sun ☎ (01423) 869148
Black Sheep Best Bitter; Harviestoun Bitter & Twisted; Marble Blind Jack's Bitter; Taylor Landlord Ⓗ
Multi-roomed pub with bare brick walls, wooden floorboards and panelling. An award-winning ale house, it provides a focal point for both locals and the many visitors who appreciate the excellent

selection of ales, cosy ambience and lively banter. The beer range usually includes the house beer brewed by Marble and one Village Brewer beer. Cheese and pâté platters complement the beers. The pub has its own small brewery producing exciting, radical beers. Of particular interest is the trompe-l'oeil painting to the exterior, which features the pub's namesake, Blind Jack Metcalfe. Q★⚭🖵(1)

Cross Keys ✅

Cheapside, HG5 8AX (near town centre)
✪ 12-11 (midnight Fri & Sat; 10.30 Sun) ☎ (01423) 863562
Fuller's London Pride; Ossett Yorkshire Blonde, Silver King, Excelsior Ⓗ
Refurbished as a traditional pub by Ossett Brewery, the Cross Keys is close to the marketplace, with a stone-flagged floor in front of the single bar and wood floors to the sides. Eight handpumps dispense four regular beers and four changing guests, usually from microbreweries or those within the Ossett Brewery group. Monday is pie night and Thursday quiz night. Good food is available daily with a special menu on Sunday. ◑★🖵(1)

Mitre ✅

4 Station Road, HG5 9AA (opp railway station)
✪ 12-11 ☎ (01423) 868948 ⊕ mitre.squarespace.com
Black Sheep Ale; Copper Dragon Golden Pippin; Thwaites Wainwright; guest beers Ⓗ
The Mitre offers a modern split-level bar, a side function room, a brasserie/restaurant and an outside drinking area. As with other Market Town Taverns, there are eight handpumps, usually serving Yorkshire beers. Look out for the speciality bottled beer menu; some foreign beers are also available on draught. There is live acoustic music on Sunday evenings, and dogs are welcome. No evening meals on Sundays. Q⚭❀⚭◑★🖵(1)

Union ✅

Calcutt, HG5 8JL (½ mile from Knaresborough centre in Calcutt village)
✪ 12-2 (not Mon & Tue), 5-11; 12-11 Fri & Sat; 12-10.30 Sun ☎ (01423) 862084 ⊕ theunionknaresborough.co.uk
Jennings Cumberland Ale; Mansfield Cask Ale; guest beer Ⓗ
A warm, welcoming, traditional two-roomed pub with modern decor. The front room is a public bar while the lounge is more suitable for dining. Each has its own bar selling between three and five ales from the Marston's stable. A good menu of pub food is available (no food Sun eve). Summer visitors will enjoy the outside drinking area looking down over the local cricket ground. Situated half a mile from Knaresborough town centre, across the river Nidd via Low Bridge, the pub is well worth a visit. ⌂Q❀◑⚭🖵(56,57)♣P

Lazenby

Lazenby Social Club

High Street, TS6 8DX (in centre of village, off A174)
✪ 11.30-11; 12-10.30 Sun ☎ (01642) 453905
Brains The Rev James; guest beer Ⓗ
In a pleasant village, wedged between the remnants of Teesside's heavy industries and the Cleveland Hills, this private members' club extends a warm welcome to CAMRA members. A free house, it comprises a lounge, a large bar/games room, a concert room and a conservatory that houses a full-size snooker table. It was dry for years

during Teesside's industrial heyday, but the club has now gained a deserved reputation for selling fine real ales. ❀⚭⚭🖵(70,71)♣P⅃

Lealholm

Board Inn

Village Green, YO21 2AJ (by River Esk)
✪ 9am-midnight (2am Fri & Sat) ☎ (01947) 897279
Black Sheep Best Bitter; Camerons Strongarm; guest beers Ⓗ
Family-run 17th-century free house, alongside the River Esk, serving four beers, four real ciders and a huge selection of whiskies. It has a busy main bar, lounge and restaurant, and a riverside patio where a beer festival is held each Easter. The menu, which reflects the seasons, is virtually all sourced and traceable to within 500 yards of the pub. The licensees air-cure their hams, keep hens, own a herd of prime beef, and also have local fishing rights. There are five letting bedrooms. ⌂Q❀⚭◑⚭⚭Å★🖵(99)♣●P⅃

Leavening

Jolly Farmers

Main Street, YO17 9SA SE785631
✪ 7 (6 Fri)-midnight; 12-midnight Sat & Sun ☎ (01653) 658276
Taylor Landlord; York Guzzler; guest beers Ⓗ
Seventeenth-century pub on the edge of the Yorkshire Wolds between York and Malton. The multi-room interior has been extended but still retains a cosiness in two small bars, a family room and dining rooms. Former local CAMRA Pub of the Year, its varied guest beers from independent breweries and two beer festivals a year make this an essential visit. The extensive menu includes locally caught game dishes in season. ⌂Q⚭❀◑♣P⅃⊟

Loftus

Station

Station Road, TS13 4QB (100yds S of A174)
✪ 3-midnight; 12-1.30am Sat & Sun ☎ (01287) 640373
Beer range varies Ⓗ
The Station Hotel is now a free house, with the last passenger train having left in the 1960s – though the platform is still there. The licensee, a keen musician and local independent councillor, has worked here for 21 years, and only serves best/premium bitters – anything under 4% ABV generally meets with disapproval. The venue comprises a separate bar, a lounge and a function room where regular live music plays. Fans of eccentric railway memorabilia are particularly well catered for. ⌂❀❀⚭⚭🖵(4,5)♣P⅃

Long Preston

Maypole Inn Ⓛ ✅

Main Street, BD23 4PH
✪ 11 (12 Sun)-11 ☎ (01729) 840219 ⊕ maypole.co.uk
Moorhouse's Premier Bitter; Taylor Landlord; guest beers Ⓗ
On the village green complete with maypole, this friendly, welcoming pub has been in the same capable hands for 27 years. Dogs are welcome in the taproom, which has carved Victorian bench seating. Good-quality home-cooked food is available all day in the dining room and in either

bar. Two guest beers are usually available, often from Bowland, Moorhouse's or other local breweries, and two Westons ciders are served. ⚒Q✿🏠🍴◑🅱🄰⇌🚻(580)♣👜P⚓

Maltby

Manor House
High Lane, TS8 0BN (at jct of A1044 and A1045, 2½ miles E of Yarm and just W of A19)
✪ 11-11; 12-10.30 Sun ☎ (01642) 764153
Black Sheep Best Bitter; guest beers 🅷
Situated on the western outskirts of this pretty village, the hostelry is also adjacent to one of Europe's largest private housing estates. Now in its fourth year of operation following extensive renovations, this large, busy establishment has a welcoming cosiness and warmth to it. Food is served all day every day, and enthusiastic staff ensure that two, usually three, guest beers provide an interesting mix of different styles. Quiz night is Monday. ✿◑🛁🚻(507)P⚓

Malton

Crown Hotel (Suddaby's)
12 Wheelgate, YO17 7HP
✪ 11-11 (11.30 Fri & Sat); 12-11 Sun ☎ (01653) 692038
691812 ⊕ suddabys.co.uk
Suddaby's Double Chance, seasonal beers; Thwaites Original; guest beers 🅷
Grade II-listed market-town pub that has been in the same family for 139 years and in the Guide for over 25. Double Chance is brewed by Leeds Brewery, other Suddaby's beers by Brown Cow. Beer festivals are held at Easter, in summer and at Christmas. The on-site shop stocks more than 200 different beers, specialising in Belgian and local British microbreweries, plus wine and breweriana. A covered smoking patio is at the rear. Accommodation is available, with a discount for CAMRA members staying two nights or more. ⚒Q✿🏠⇌🚻♣P⚓

Manfield

Crown Inn 🄻
Vicars Lane, DL2 2RF (500yds from B6275)
✪ 5 (12 Sat)-11.30; 12-11 Sun ☎ (01325) 374243
Village White Boar; guest beers 🅷
A regular local CAMRA award winner, this attractive 18th-century inn sits in a quiet village. Recently refurbished, it has two bars, a games room, a large beer garden and a trellised heated smoking area. A mix of locals and visitors creates a friendly atmosphere. Seven guest beers come from microbreweries countrywide, along with up to two ciders or perries. Two beer festivals and a cider festival are held, and there is a monthly quiz on a Tuesday night. ⚒Q✿◑🚻(29)♣👜P⚓🍴

Marske-by-the-Sea

Clarendon
88-90 High Street, TS11 7BA
✪ 11-11 (11.30 Fri-Sun) ☎ (01642) 490005
Black Sheep Best Bitter; Camerons Strongarm; Copper Dragon Golden Pippin; Theakston Best Bitter, Old Peculier; guest beer 🅷
The middle house, as it is known, is a family-run, one-room locals' pub. It serves five regular beers plus a guest from an island bar, which is a rarity in

this area. There is no TV, no jukebox, no pool table, no one-armed bandits, no children/teenagers – just the locals indulging in convivial conversation. There is no catering either as such, but tea and coffee are available, together with excellent home-made scones at lunchtimes, while a substantial finger buffet is provided on Tuesday evenings. It has a pleasant south-facing outdoor drinking area. ✿♿⇌🚻(4,81)P⚓

Frigate
49 Hummershill Lane, TS11 7DH (300yds E of A1085, next to cricket club)
✪ 3-11 (11.30 Wed & Thu); 12-12.30am Fri; 12-1am Sat; 12-midnight Sun ☎ (01642) 483270
Beer range varies 🅷
What still remains a community pub, in the middle of a housing estate, has now been transformed by an enthusiastic licensee into a venue that also provides an eclectic mix of both beer and R&B/rock music. Up to five guest beers are served at this free house. The atmosphere then heats up at 9pm on Thursday, Saturday and Sunday evenings when live bands perform. There is no food, just beer and music. An ideal party venue. ✿⇌🚻(4,81)♣P⚓🍴

Masham

Bay Horse 🄻
Silver Street, HG4 4DX
✪ 11-midnight (1am Fri & Sat) ☎ (01765) 689236
⊕ bayhorsemasham.co.uk
Black Sheep Best Bitter; Greene King H&H Olde Trip; Morland Old Speckled Hen; Theakston Best Bitter 🅷
Friendly pub welcoming tourists and locals alike with a range of ales unusual to Masham. As well as the front bar there is a cosy snug up a short flight of steps. The roaring winter-time fire comes with an invitation to stoke up as needed. A wide variety of home-cooked food is served, with ingredients coming mainly from local suppliers. There are six letting rooms and a holiday cottage sleeping six close by. Dogs are welcome throughout. ⚒Q✿🏠◑🄰🚻(159)♣⚓

White Bear 🄻 ✅
Wellgarth, HG4 4EN (follow brown tourist signs on A6108)
✪ 11-midnight ☎ (01765) 689319
⊕ thewhitebearhotel.co.uk
Caledonian Deuchars IPA; Theakston Best Bitter, Black Bull Bitter, Lightfoot, XB, Old Peculier 🅷
Theakston Brewery's tap, an award-winning hostelry, and a great favourite with the locals, as well as directors and staff from the brewery. One area is set aside mainly for dining, while the cosy taproom offers the full range of Theakston's beers including the seasonal specials. There are 14 bedrooms and conference facilities. Oddly for the Yorkshire Dales, the pub was a victim of wartime bombing and derelict for many years. ⚒✿🏠◑🅱🚻(159)♣P⚓

Melsonby

Black Bull
19 West Road, DL10 5ND (1 mile N of A66 and 1 mile from A1)
✪ 5.30-11 (midnight Fri); 4-midnight Sat; 4-11 Sun ☎ (01325) 718811
Beer range varies 🅷

Late 18th-century community pub with a warm and friendly welcome. This long single-roomed pub has seating either end of the central bar. Upstairs there is a function/games room available for parties. It has unusual pub games, including ring the bull. Up to three beers from national and local micros are on handpump, including a weekly beer from local Mithril Ales. Quizzes take place on alternate Tuesdays, and it has an internet café. It runs men's and women's darts teams, dominoes on Mondays, and various clubs hold meetings here. 🏚️🏵️🚃(29)♣️⁵⁻

Middlesbrough

Star

14 Southfield Road, TS1 3BX (opp university)
🌼 11-11 (1am Fri & Sat); 12-11 Sun ☎ (01642) 245307
Beer range varies Ⓗ
Large and popular pub opposite the university campus that attracts a wide-ranging clientele. The licensee is dedicated to promoting a wide variety of real beers from four handpumps. Friendly staff help promote a contemporary, relaxed atmosphere, with sofas and easy chairs adding to the ambience. The pub can get extremely busy at weekends. Good-value pub food is on offer. The outdoor areas are heated and covered.
🏵️🅞🕙&⇌🚃⁵⁻

Muker

Farmers Arms Ⓛ

DL11 6QG
🌼 11-11 ☎ (01748) 886297 ⊕ farmersarmsmuker.co.uk
Black Sheep Best Bitter; Theakston Best Bitter, Old Peculier; Yorkshire Dales Muker Silver Ⓗ
A traditional Dales inn offering local ales, good food and a warm welcome in the heart of the spectacular Swaledale walking country. Walkers, cyclists and dogs are welcome and the stone-flagged floor can cope with boots and paws, whether you are tackling the nearby Coast-to-Coast and Pennine Way routes or just a local stroll. On a fine day, the view from the terrace outside is splendid. 🏚️Q🏵️🖂🕙Å♣P

Naburn

Blacksmiths Arms

Main Street, YO19 4PN (take B1222 from A19, heading SW of York) SE598455
🌼 11.30-11.30 (12.30am Fri & Sat); 12-11.30 Sun
☎ (01904) 623464 ⊕ blacksmithsarmsnaburn.co.uk
Marston's EPA, seasonal beers; guest beers Ⓗ
A fantastic riverside village pub, with a selection of real ales, excellent food and a great community ethos. The pub is the hub for much local life, often coordinating village events. There is a pleasant, fairly new outdoor area, and the pub is easily accessible by road, river or the York-Selby cycle path. There are camping facilities nearby and a holiday cottage in the grounds. Children are welcome in the pub – there is even a large pick 'n' mix sweet stand. 🏚️🚲🏵️🅞🕙🍴&Å🚃(42)♣P⁵⁻

Newton-on-Ouse

Dawnay Arms

YO30 2BR (on main street of village) SE510601
🌼 closed Mon; 12-2.30, 6-11; 12-9.30 Sun
☎ (01347) 848345 ⊕ thedawnayatnewton.co.uk

Taylor Golden Best; guest beers Ⓗ
Country pub with an emphasis on locally sourced food and Yorkshire beer. The modern British menu often includes local game. It is on the Top Gastro Pubs list and booking is advisable. The interior is a mix of rustic wooden tables and comfortable upholstered chairs. There are two open fires in winter, and a pleasant garden that leads down to the River Ouse. Riverside mooring is available. The pub is handily placed for the bus to and from York. 🏚️Q🏵️🅞🕙&🚃(29)P⁵⁻

Northallerton

Standard

24 High Street, DL7 8EE (on A167, 400yds N of town centre opp Sainsbury's)
🌼 12-2.30, 5-11.30; 12-11.30 Fri-Sun ☎ (01609) 772719
⊕ thestandard-pub.co.uk
Copper Dragon Golden Pippin; Hambleton Stallion; Taylor Landlord; guest beer Ⓗ
The pub takes its name from the Battle of the Standard, a famous English defeat of the Scots which took place just outside Northallerton in 1138. It is now home to a more recent military memorial, a genuine ex-RAF Jet Provost aircraft in the beer garden to the rear. It has the atmosphere of a real community local and is well known for its good value, wholesome meals (no food Sun-Tue eves) in the stone-flagged bar. Spring bank holiday sees an annual beer festival. Q🏵️🅞🍴🚃♣⁵⁻

Tickle Toby Ⓛ

180 High Street, DL7 8JZ
🌼 11-11 (midnight Thu-Sat); 12-11 Sun ☎ (01609) 778760
Black Sheep Best Bitter; guest beers Ⓗ
Long, narrow market-town pub with a single bar, popular with all age groups and named after a notorious highwayman and pickpocket who once frequented the area. At the heart of the High Street, it is busy at weekends and features an open-plan layout at the front, narrowing towards the rear where separate booths give a train-like feel. Guest beers are mainly from Yorkshire and the North East. Evening meals are available weekdays throughout the year and Wednesdays to Fridays in winter. Q🅞🍴⇌🚃♣

Tithe Bar & Brasserie Ⓛ ✅

2 Friarage Street, DL6 1DP (just off High St near hospital)
🌼 12-11 (midnight Fri & Sat) ☎ (01609) 778482
Beer range varies Ⓗ
Just off the busy High Street, this bar offers the town's best selection of cask ales and has the feel of a continental beer café. Ales are usually from smaller brewers, supplemented by a wide array of foreign beers. Part of the small Market Town Taverns chain, renowned for its strong commitment to cask beer, it offers good-value meals, with a brasserie upstairs open Tuesday-Saturday evenings. It also features occasional music and quiz nights. Q🅞🕙&⇌🚃♣

Old Malton

Royal Oak

47 Town Street, YO17 7HB (400yds off A64 Malton bypass)
🌼 closed Mon; 12-midnight (1am Fri & Sat); 12-midnight Sun
☎ (01653) 699334

Copper Dragon Golden Pippin; Tetley Bitter; York Guzzler; guest beers Ⓗ
Popular historic old inn in a picturesque village off the A64 close to the Eden Camp military museum. At the front of the pub is a cosy snug, to the rear is a larger room with original beams and a log fire, leading to an extensive beer garden with a large covered smoking area. Four handpumps serve beers mainly from Yorkshire. Traditional home-cooked meals are available Thursday to Saturday evenings and Saturday and Sunday lunchtimes. Children are welcome but guide dogs only. The bus stops outside. ⚒☀️◑ⴾ⊟(843,840)♣P⁵-

Osgodby

Wadkin Arms Ⓛ ✅

Cliffe Road, YO8 5HU (just off A63 in village) SE641335
✪ 12-11 (midnight Fri & Sat) ☎ (01757) 702391
⊕ wadkinarms.co.uk
Brown Cow White Dragon; John Smith's Bitter; guest beers Ⓗ
Cosy old pub in the centre of the village, featuring real fires and wholesome food served at limited times – teatimes can be busy. Guest beers regularly come from nearby breweries such as Great Heck and Brown Cow, and a dark mild and a pale beer are usually available. An annual beer festival is now established. The pub has a good local atmosphere and is frequented both by Osgodby residents and nearby villagers alike. ⚒🦮☀️♣P⁵-

Osmotherley

Golden Lion

6 West End, DL6 3AA (in village centre, 1 mile E of A19)
✪ 12-2.30 (not Mon & Tue), 6-11; 12-midnight Sat; 12-10.30 Sun ☎ (01609) 883526 ⊕ goldenlionosmotherley.co.uk
Beer range varies Ⓗ
Set in prime walking country on the edge of the North York Moors National Park, the bar is imaginatively decorated with whitewashed walls and mirrors. The emphasis is on food but there is a warm welcome given to drinkers. The food is made from locally sourced produce and has an excellent reputation. An annual beer festival is held in November and many of the frequently changing beers come from Yorkshire breweries such as Timothy Taylor. Dogs are welcome with well-behaved owners. ⚒Q🛏️◑Å⊟(80,89)

Pickering

Sun Inn

136 Westgate, YO18 8BB (on A170 400yds W of traffic lights in town centre)
✪ 4-11; 2.30-midnight Fri; 12-midnight Sat; 12-11 Sun
☎ (01751) 473661 ⊕ thesuninn-pickering.co.uk
Leeds Best Bitter; Tetley Bitter; guest beers Ⓗ
Friendly local CAMRA Rural Pub of the Year a short walk from the busy town centre and NYMR steam railway, with three guest beers from Yorkshire. Well-behaved children, walkers and dogs (on leads) are welcome. There is just one room, recently extended to form an L-shaped bar, cosy in winter with real fires, where pub games and newspapers are provided. The large beer garden is popular in summer. An acoustic open session features in the bar on the third Sunday of the month and a vinyl night every third Wednesday. ⚒Q☀️🚆⊟(128)♣👍⁵-

Pickhill

Nag's Head Ⓛ ✅

YO7 4JG (1 mile off A1 just N of jct with B6261 Masham-Thirsk road) SE345833
✪ 11 (12 Sun)-11 ☎ (01845) 567391
⊕ nagsheadpickhill.co.uk
Black Sheep Best Bitter; Theakston Best Bitter; guest beers Ⓗ
Although focusing principally on food, this village inn handy for the A1 strikes a good balance between a local pub and a fine place to eat in a relaxed atmosphere. Food is served in the restaurant, lounge and bar and there is also high-class accommodation, making this an ideal base to explore the Yorkshire Moors, Dales and Vale of York or take in the local race meetings. Guest beers are generally Yorkshire brewed. ⚒Q☀️🛏️◑⊞Å♣P⁵-

Pool in Wharfedale

Hunters Inn Ⓛ

Harrogate Road, LS21 2PS (on A658 between Otley and Harrogate)
✪ 11-11; 12-10.30 Sun ☎ (0113) 2841090
Theakston Best Bitter; Thwaites Nutty Black; guest beers Ⓗ
When you enter this welcoming roadside pub, do not forget to check out the impressive range of up to nine cask ales on the board on the right. A separate board gives tasting notes. The large single-room interior incorporates a raised area with a warming real fire during the colder months. Well-behaved children are allowed in the pub until 9pm accompanied by an adult. ⚒☀️⊟(737,X52,X53)♣👍P⁵-

Potto

Dog & Gun ✅

2 Cooper Lane, DL6 3HQ
✪ 12-2.30 (not Mon), 5.30-midnight; 12-midnight Sat; 12-11 Sun ☎ (01642) 700232 ⊕ thedogandgunpotto.com
Beer range varies Ⓗ
Country inn under the stewardship of an enthusiastic licensee who also runs the Captain Cook Brewery. Friendly staff ensure that a laid-back ambience prevails in this contemporary setting, which comprises a comfortable main bar, classy restaurant, private dining areas, five luxury bedrooms and conference facilities. Alongside a selection of the various beers brewed by Captain Cook, a guest beer is sourced from a local microbrewery. Outside, open terraces are ideal for summer drinking. Live acoustic music plays on Friday. ⚒☀️🛏️◑♿⊟(89)P

Redmire

Bolton Arms Ⓛ ✅

DL8 4EA
✪ 11-midnight ☎ (01969) 624336
⊕ boltonarmsredmire.co.uk
Black Sheep Best Bitter; John Smiths Bitter; Theakston Best Bitter; guest beer Ⓗ
At the eastern edge of the Yorkshire Dales National Park, this warm and friendly pub has a separate dining area and outside patio. There are many walks in the area and snacks are available all day, as well as lunchtime and evening meals. Parking is limited, but the western terminus of the Wensleydale Railway is a few minutes' walk away

and a bus stop is in the centre of the village. Accommodation is available and the ground floor rooms are easily accessible. The guest beer may be from either a local or national brewer.
🏨❀🛏◑🅰🚆🚲(157)P

Reeth

Buck Hotel ✔
DL11 6SW
🕑 12-midnight ☎ (01748) 884210 ⊕ buckhotel.co.uk
Black Sheep Best Bitter; Caledonian Deuchars IPA; Copper Dragon Best Bitter; Taylor Landlord; guest beer Ⓗ
In the centre of Reeth, the capital of Swaledale, the Buck was originally a coaching inn and retains many original features, with beamed ceilings, an open fire and an ice house. It now offers five cask ales and three real ciders along with good food. There are regular music events with occasional visits from some surprisingly well-known bands. A little quieter, quoits is popular in the summer and there is free Wi-Fi. 🏨🍴❀🛏◑👟🅰🚆♣🚲

Ribblehead

Station
LA6 3AS (on B6255 nr B6479 jct)
🕑 11-11; 12-10.30 Sun ☎ (01524) 241274
⊕ thestationinn.net
Black Sheep Best Bitter; guest beers Ⓗ
A welcome refuge in a bleak spot in the midst of superb walking country and close to the famous viaduct. A surprisingly large number of locals frequent the plainly furnished bar. There is a good train service – times are above the bar counter – but buses are rare. It has a bunk barn next door, with wild camping behind. Station Ale, one of the guest beers, is brewed by Dent.
🏨❀🛏◑🅰🚆🚲(831)♣P🚲

Riccall

Greyhound Inn Ⓛ ✔
Main Street, YO19 6TE (on A19 10 miles S of York)
SE620380
🕑 12 (3 Mon-Wed Nov-Feb)-midnight; 12-11.30 Sun
☎ (01757) 249101 ⊕ thegreyhoundriccall.co.uk
Tetley Mild, Bitter; Theakston Best Bitter; guest beer Ⓗ
In a quiet village between Selby and York, this pub offers a friendly welcome and an enthusiastic guest beer policy. Home-made food is available daily (no food Mon; Sat and Sun lunchtime only), plus take-away fish and chips. Home to keen darts and dominoes teams, the pub is also popular with cyclists and walkers using the York-Selby cycle path (note the old Cyclists Touring Club emblem). There is a large garden to the rear for summer meals and drinks. 🏨Q❀🛏◑🚆(415)♣P🚲

Richmond

Bishop Blaize
40 Market Place, DL10 4QL
🕑 10-midnight (1am Fri & Sat) ☎ (01748) 823065
Taylor Landlord; guest beers Ⓗ
Town-centre pub and CAMRA commendation winner on the historic cobbled marketplace, run by committed cask ale enthusiasts, with good-value meals and accommodation. All buses to Richmond stop outside the pub, where thirsty travellers can find refreshment. Pool and live sports and music TV set the scene but there are also occasional folk nights. 🛏❀🛏◑🚲🚆🚲

Ralph Fitz Randal Ⓛ ✔
6 Queens Road, DL10 4AE (edge of town centre on main Scotch Corner road)
🕑 9am-midnight (1am Fri & Sat) ☎ (01748) 828080
Greene King Abbot; Ruddles Best Bitter; guest beers Ⓗ
Once the town's post office and telephone exchange, this Wetherspoon house has a single bar set on three levels, decorated in simple and contemporary style and including a large family dining area. Low-volume TVs cater for sports fans but the main focus is on the beer, with up to eight guest ales and themed monthly beer festivals, usually featuring a particular brewery or beer style, and earning several well-deserved CAMRA awards. Opens at 8am for breakfast. ❀◑👟🚆🐶🚲

Ripon

Magdalens Ⓛ
26 Princess Road, HG4 1HW (5-minute walk from city centre past fire station)
🕑 12 (4 Mon; 1 Tue & Wed)-midnight; 12-midnight Sun
☎ (01765) 604276
John Smith's Bitter; Theakston Best Bitter; guest beers Ⓗ
A real community pub with darts, dominoes, pool and football teams. The guest beers change on a regular basis. The landlord, who is a keen gardener, has created an award-winning beer garden. A grassed play area for children is provided at the rear of the pub. Inside, the walls are covered with old photographs, and a large cabinet filled with trophies is witness to the prowess of customers over the years. ❀🚆♣P🚲

One-Eyed Rat Ⓛ ✔
51 Allhallowgate, HG4 1LQ (near bus station)
🕑 5 (12 Fri & Sat)-11; 12-10.30 Sun ☎ (01765) 607704
⊕ oneeyedrat.com
Black Sheep Best Bitter; guest beers Ⓗ
A regular entry in the Guide, the pub is set within a terrace of 200-year-old houses, with a narrow frontage that leads to a warm and welcoming family-run hostelry. One regular beer is served along with seven changing guests. There is always a pump dedicated to a mild or stout/porter, and another for a stronger beer at around 5%, plus a real cider. The pub hosts regular live music and holds two beer festivals a year. 🏨Q❀🚆♣🐶🚲

Royal Oak ✔
36 Kirkgate, HG4 1PB (just off Market Square)
🕑 11-11 (midnight Fri & Sat); 12-10.30 Sun
☎ (01765) 602284 ⊕ royaloakripon.co.uk
Taylor Dark Mild, Golden Best, Best Bitter, Landlord Ⓗ
This old coaching inn between the cathedral and Market Square has a modern airy feel to its interior while retaining period features. The full range of Timothy Taylor's beers is stocked and there is also an emphasis on locally sourced food. At the Obelisk in the nearby Market Square at 9pm every night the Ripon Hornblower sets the night watch – which has happened for 1,000 years. The pub has six en-suite bedrooms. 🏨❀🛏◑🚆🚲

Saltburn-by-the-Sea

Saltburn Cricket, Bowls & Tennis Club

Marske Mill Lane, TS12 1HJ (next to leisure centre)
✪ 8-midnight (1am Fri & Sat); 2-midnight Sat match days; 11.30-3, 8-midnight Sun ☎ (01287) 622761
Beer range varies H

Casual visitors are made welcome at this 2011 local CAMRA award winner. A private sports club, well-supported by the local community, it fields cricket, tennis and bowls teams, and is also the watering hole for the local diving club. The bar sits in a spacious, comfortable lounge, which can be divided for different functions and social events. The balcony, ideal for those lazy summer afternoons, overlooks the cricket field. Two changing beers are served. 🏵️&≒⊟(X4,48)♣P⁵⌐

Sawdon

Anvil Inn

Main Street, YO13 9DY (2 miles off A170)
✪ closed Mon & Tue; 12-2.30, 6-11; 12-3, 6-10.30 Sun
☎ (01723) 859896 ⊕ theanvilinnsawdon.co.uk
Daleside Bitter; guest beers H

A heart-of-the-village pub, on the edge of the North York Moors National Park, Dalby Forest and close to the coast, in excellent walking, cycling and mountain biking country. Formerly the village blacksmith's, it still retains the forge and, of course, the anvil. It has a cosy bar, with a separate lounge and dining area, and three handpumps serving beers from local independents. Food of the highest standard is served so booking is recommended. There are two well-appointed letting cottages.
🏠🏵️❶♣P

Scarborough

Angel

46 North Street, YO11 1DF
✪ 11 (12 Sun)-midnight ☎ (01723) 365504
Copper Dragon Golden Pippin; Tetley Bitter; Wells Bombardier; York Yorkshire Terrier H

Friendly town-centre local close to the main shopping area, with a single-room horseshoe bar displaying an excellent collection of saucy seaside postcards. An interest in sport and games is reflected in the impressive array of trophies won by various pub teams and the large-screen TVs for viewing sporting events. Occasional guest beers are added in summer. It has a surprisingly spacious and well-appointed patio garden at the rear.
🏵️≒⊟♣⁵⌐

Cellars

35-37 Valley Road, YO11 2LX
✪ 12-midnight; 4-11 winter; 12-10.30 Sun
☎ (01723) 367158
Jennings Snecklifter; Camerons Strongarm H

A family-run pub converted from the cellars of a Victorian house. Six handpumps dispense guest beers from micros around the country. Excellent locally sourced, home-cooked food is available lunchtimes and evenings, with Sunday lunches particularly popular. Quiz night is Tuesday, open mic night is Wednesday, local acoustic acts appear on Thursday, and Saturday is live music night. The patio fronting the pub is popular in summer. Children and dogs are welcome and accommodation is available. 🏵️🏠❶≒⊟(4)♣P

Indigo Alley

4 North Marine Road, YO12 7PD
✪ 4 (12 Fri-Sun)-11 ☎ (01723) 350599
Wychwood Hobgoblin; guest beers H

Recently upgraded into a welcoming open-plan pub retaining a rustic feel and sporting a logburner, this venue has come back on the real ale and traditional cider trail after a few years in the wilderness. It is a true free house, with bare floorboards and the advantage of pool, darts, dominoes and chess. Locally brewed Indigo Ale and draught Thatchers cider complement specialist lagers. It is dog- and child-friendly, with live entertainment every Friday and Saturday.
🏠🏵️≒⊟♣🐕

North Riding Brew Pub 🏆

161-163 North Marine Road, YO12 7HU
✪ 12-midnight (1am Fri & Sat) ☎ (01723) 370004
⊕ northridingbrewpub.com
Taylor Landlord; York Guzzler; guest beers H

Scarborough's only brewpub and current Local CAMRA Town Pub of the Year, it is on the North Bay, just down from the cricket ground. It has now served nearly 2,000 guest beers in addition to its own North Riding beers. Two or more guests come from microbreweries from far and wide and it is a regular outlet for Elland, Thornbridge and Yorkshire Dales. The pub has a public bar, a quiet lounge and an upstairs dining room serving home-cooked food, all with real fires. Quiz night is Thursday.
🏠Q🏠❶🍴⊟(3A)♣⁵⌐

Old Scalby Mills

Scalby Mills Road, YO12 6RP
✪ 11 (12 winter)-11 ☎ (01723) 500449
Wold Top North Bay; guest beers H

This popular seafront local was originally a watermill but has seen many uses over the years – old photographs and prints chart its history. Admire the superb views of the North Bay from the sheltered patio, conservatory or lounge. The Cleveland Way reaches the seafront here and there is a Sealife Centre nearby. Children are welcome in the lounge. North Bay ale from the local Wold Top Brewery is only available here; guest beers invariably include a stout, porter or mild.
Q🐕🏵️❶🍴▲⊟(3A)♣⁵⌐

Scholars

Somerset Terrace, YO11 2PW
✪ 4.30 (12 Fri-Sun)-midnight ☎ (01723) 360084
Copper Dragon Golden Pippin; Hambleton Nightmare; Theakston Lightfoot; York Yorkshire Terrier; guest beers H

A warm, friendly atmosphere prevails at this town-centre pub at the rear of the main shopping centre. It has a large front bar and a games room. Seven handpumps serve a rotating range of beers from Ossett, Fernandes, Rat and other breweries throughout the Yorkshire region. Numerous screens show major sporting events. Twenty-eight pints are the prize at the Thursday quiz, and more free beer can be won rolling dice on Monday, Tuesday, Wednesday and Sunday nights. &≒⊟♣

Valley

51 Valley Road, YO11 2LX
✪ 12-midnight (1am Thu-Sat) ☎ (01723) 372593
⊕ valleybar.co.uk
Theakston Best Bitter; guest beers H

A cellar bar with seven handpumps offering mainly microbrewery beers, usually including one or more

from Scarborough Brewery. Up to eight real ciders and perries are also available, together with over 100 bottles of Belgian beers including Cantillon. Further rooms offer additional seating upstairs, which can be used for meetings. There is also a pool table. Sandwiches are available all day.
爵幽≠♣♠●'☐

Settle

Thirteen 🄻
13 Duke Street, BD24 9DU (between Market Place and railway station)
✪ 4-8 Mon; 11-9 Tue; 11-10 Wed-Thu; 11-11 Fri-Sat; closed Sun ☎ (01729) 824356 ⊕ thirteencafébar.co.uk
Dark Horse Best Bitter; Goose Eye Chinook Blonde; Three Peaks Ingleborough Gold 🄷
The owners are hands-on at Thirteen, offering a friendly welcome to locals and tourists. The venue has a smart wine bar ambience, but walking boots are also welcome. Created in 2005 from a small hardware store on the main street near a pedestrian crossing, real ale was added in 2009. The beers are all from local micros and a range of bottled Belgian beer is also stocked. Themed dining evenings include steak night and tapas.
🄳&≠🚐(580,581)

Sicklinghall

Scotts Arms 🄻
Main Street, LS22 4BD (3 miles W of Wetherby) SE361485
✪ 11-11 (10 Sun) ☎ (01937) 582100 ⊕ scottsarms.com
Black Sheep Best Bitter; Theakston Old Peculier; guest beers 🄷
Welcoming village inn with an excellent reputation for food, available in two large but intimate lounges. The L-shaped bar serves a new seating area which has been built for drinkers. This is great walking territory. Guest beers tend to be from northern breweries. The garden area is popular with families in summer, and the pub also houses the village shop, with a visiting post office one day a week. 幽▲爵🄳&🄿'

Skipton

Bistro des Amis
1 Jerry Croft, BD23 1DT
✪ 10-11 (10.30 Sun) ☎ (01756) 797919
⊕ lebistrodesamis.co.uk
Ilkley Mary Jane; Taylor Landlord 🄷
As the name suggests, this is a French-style bistro focusing on quality food and comfortable relaxed dining. There are two handpumps and also some less common foreign beer selections served from fonts. While the emphasis is on food, the drinker is made welcome, and once ensconced in a comfortable chair with beer served at the table it can be difficult to leave. Lunchtime and evening meals are available all week. 🄳&≠🚐

Narrow Boat 🄻 ✔
38 Victoria Street, BD23 1JE (alleyway off Coach St near canal bridge)
✪ 12-11 ☎ (01756) 797922
Black Sheep Best Bitter; Copper Dragon Ilkley Best; Ilkley Mary Jane; Taylor Landlord; guest beers 🄷
Just off the main street, there is no piped music, jukebox or gaming machines to disturb the conversation. Guest ales, always including a dark

beer, are mainly from northern independents and there is a good selection of continental bottled and draught beers, plus up to four ciders or perries. Folk club is on Monday evenings and quiz night Wednesday. Well-behaved dogs are welcome. Children under 14 are only admitted when dining.
Q爵🄳&≠🚐●'—

Woolly Sheep Inn 🄻 ✔
38 Sheep Street, BD23 1HY
✪ 10-11 (midnight Thu; 1am Fri & Sat); 12-11 Sun
☎ (01756) 700966 ⊕ woollysheepinn.co.uk
Taylor Dark Mild, Golden Best, Best Bitter, Landlord, Ram Tam; guest beer 🄷
Deceptively large 18th-century pub in the town centre. There is a lounge at the front, a flagged area around the bar and a large back room on two levels, mainly used for dining. The sheltered decked beer garden at the rear has heating and comfortable seating, making it popular almost all year round. Traditional pub food is served throughout the day, and until 4pm on Sundays. It is the only Timothy Taylor's pub in Skipton.
幽爵幽🄳≠🚐♣'—

Sowerby

Crown & Anchor 🄻
138 Front Street, YO7 1JN (in village ½ mile from Thirsk town centre)
✪ 12-midnight (1am Thu-Sat; 11 Sun) ☎ (01845) 522448
⊕ crownandanchorsowerby.co.uk
Black Sheep Best Bitter; John Smith's Bitter; guest beers 🄷
A community pub with several distinct drinking areas at the heart of the village on the edge of Thirsk; it is easy to see why it has won several CAMRA awards. There are usually four guest ales on handpump, and regular beer festivals take place, plus a cider festival in May, making good use of the outside bar at the rear. Occasional live music is hosted. Good, no-nonsense food ranges from bar snacks to Sunday lunches (booking advised).
爵🄳&▲🚐(146,148,149)♣🄿'—

Staithes

Captain Cook Inn
60 Staithes Lane, TS13 5AD (off A174, by village car park)
✪ 11-midnight ☎ (01947) 840200
Beer range varies 🄷
Local CAMRA multi award-winning pub sitting high above this pretty coastal village and close to Boulby Cliffs, the highest in England. Six handpumps provide an eclectic mix of beer styles, now including its own in-house brews. The pub hosts five annual beer and pork pie/sausage festivals, held to celebrate St Patrick's Day, St George's Day, Lifeboat Week, Halloween/Guy Fawkes and, finally, there is Winter Warmers week, held between Christmas and New Year. Accommodation is in four bedrooms and a holiday cottage. 幽Q爵幽🄳🚐(5)♣🄿

Stillington

White Bear Inn 🄻
Main Street, YO61 1JU
✪ 12-2.30 (not Mon), 5.30-11; 12-midnight Sat & Sun
☎ (01347) 810338

Black Sheep Best Bitter; Marston's Burton Bitter; Samuel Smith's Old Brewery Bitter; guest beers ⊞
An unpretentious village pub that punches well above its weight. It serves excellent food but is not foody, it provides a wide choice of ale at affordable prices, and plays an important role in local sporting and social life. Guest beers regularly rotate, often featuring some rarer local offerings; a pub well worth seeking out. ⓓ⏚🖵(40)♣P'⌐

Stokesley

Spread Eagle
39 High Street, TS9 5AD
✪ 11-1am; 12-12.30am Sun ☎ (01642) 710278
Camerons Strongarm; Marston's Pedigree; guest beers ⊞
A fine welcome is assured at this small, unspoilt market-town pub. Friendly regulars drink at one end and an open fire welcomes diners at the other. Excellent, good-value home-cooked food, complete with details of where the produce has been sourced, is served all day. Two interesting and stronger guest beers are always available. Children are welcome. A rear garden leads down to the tranquil River Leven, where over-fed ducks amuse children and adults alike. Tuesday is live music night. ♨Q✿ⓓ▸Å🖵(80,81)'⌐

White Swan ✅
1 West End, TS9 5BL (at W end of town)
✪ 11.30 (12 Sun)-11 ☎ (01642) 710263
⊕ thewhiteswanstokesley.co.uk
Captain Cook Sunset, Slipway, Endeavour, Discovery, Black Porter; guest beer ⊞
A local CAMRA award winner, this traditional one-room 18th-century local also acts as the brewery tap for the Captain Cook Brewery, sited within the pub's outdoor drinking area. Seven handpumps serve the brewery's range of beers, together with a guest sourced from a local microbrewery. The pub holds a quiz night on Wednesday and music nights are held monthly. Beer festivals take place at Easter and in October. Ploughman's lunches are served Wednesday-Saturday. Children are not allowed in the pub. ♨Q✿ⓓ⏚(29,81)

Strensall

Ship Inn
23 The Village, YO32 5XS
✪ 12-11 (11.30 Fri & Sat; 10.30 Sun) ☎ (01904) 490302
John Smith's Bitter; Taylor Landlord; guest beers ⊞
Approximately five miles north-east of York, this quiet village local has built on its reputation, with dedicated bar and lounge areas and a separate restaurant room. Outside seating is provided and there is a children's play area. The bar now has two permanent cask beers and two handpumps for guest beers, one mainly dedicated to microbreweries. The pub holds regular quiz and music nights as well as supporting local charities, and is popular with cyclists, ramblers and caravanners in summer. The bus stop is virtually outside the front door. Q✿ⓓ♿🖵(5)P'⌐

Thixendale

Cross Keys
YO17 9TG SE845611
✪ 12-3 (not Mon, or Tue-Thu winter), 6-11; 12-3, 7-10.30 Sun
☎ (01377) 288272

Tetley Bitter; guest beers ⊞
Evidence of activity in Thixendale has existed for 10,000 years, and this single-room hostelry appears on a map dated 1851. At the heart of 16 dry valleys, it is popular with walkers, including those on the Wolds Way and, though remote, is well worth seeking out. Guest beers come from independent breweries and are usually not more than 4% ABV. Children are welcome in the beer garden. Good-value, traditional food is served. Accommodation is in the adjoining converted stable. ♨Q✿🛏ⓓ♣

Thorganby

Ferry Boat Inn Ⓛ
Ferry Lane, YO19 6DD (1 mile NE of village, signed from main road, by the River Derwent) SE697427
✪ closed Mon; 12-4, 7-11; 12-midnight Sat
☎ (01904) 448224
Beer range varies ⊞
Yorkshire CAMRA Pub of the Year 2010, this is a warm, welcoming local in a beautiful and secluded rural setting, run by the same family for over 60 years. Free of tie, the landlord favours beers from local micros and Yorkshire breweries, served in oversized glasses. It has a cosy bar with a real fire, a lounge with pub games, and a large riverside garden where dogs are welcome. Caravan hook-ups and fishing permits are available. Folk night is on the third Sunday of the month.
♨Q🛏✿♿Å🖵(35)♣P⊟

Thornton Watlass

Buck Inn Ⓛ ✅
The Village Green, HG4 4AH (off B6268 between Bedale and Masham)
✪ 11-11 ☎ (01677) 422461 ⊕ thebuckinn.net
Black Sheep Best Bitter; Theakston Best Bitter; guest beers ⊞
Overlooking the village green, this traditional country inn features a cosy bar room with a real fire, a lounge/function room – The Long Room – and a separate dining area. Regular beers are from Black Sheep and Theakston breweries just down the road in Masham, with up to three rotating guests usually from northern micros. The pub hosts regular jazz sessions. Food is sourced locally and served lunchtimes and evenings. Outside is an attractive tree-lined beer garden. ♨Q✿🛏ⓓ⏚P

Thornton-le-Dale

Buck Hotel ✅
Chestnut Avenue, YO18 7RW
✪ 12-midnight; 12-10 Mon summer, 4-10.30 Mon winter
☎ (01751) 474212
Tetley Bitter; guest beers ⊞
A welcoming small hotel with a traditional pub atmosphere. Two guest beers (one in winter) come from Yorkshire independents such as Copper Dragon and Ossett. Home-made pub food is served daily until 8.30pm (3pm Sun). Pool, darts and quizzes including a Sunday music quiz are held weekly. The beer garden is a suntrap in summer, where you can relax after a day in Dalby Forest or on the moors, or just sit soaking up the beautiful village atmosphere.
♨🛏✿🛏ⓓ⏚🖵(128,840)♣P'⌐

Tockwith

Spotted Ox Inn L ✓
Westfield Road, YO26 7PY
✪ 12.30-2, 5-11; 12-11 Sat; 12-10.30 Sun ☎ (01423) 358387
⊕ thespottedox.co.uk
Taylor Landlord; Tetley Bitter; guest beers H
Traditional village pub situated midway between the city of York and the town of Wetherby, from where the historic village is well-served by buses. It has separate dining and public bar areas and offers four quality ales, one usually from the nearby Rudgate Brewery, alongside hearty dishes made using locally sourced ingredients. Dominoes, darts, cricket and football teams are based here and skittles and shove-ha'penny are played too. Regular entertainment and quizzes feature.
🏚🕭◐⊟🖼(412)♣P🏷

Wath

George at Wath ✓
Main Street, HG4 5EN (3 miles N of Ripon; village signed from the A61 Melmerby crossroads)
✪ 5 (12 Sat & Sun)-11 ☎ (01765) 641324
⊕ thegeorgeatwath.co.uk
Rudgate George Blonde; Theakston Best Bitter; guest beers H
Country inn lying off the beaten track some three miles north of Ripon. It has acquired a deserved reputation for the quality and provenance of its food, all sourced locally, and this commitment is also reflected in the choice of beers, all from Yorkshire breweries, with the house beer, George Blonde, from Rudgate Brewery. Sympathetically refurbished in 2009, the stylish interior utilises a mix of traditional materials including oak and stone to create an inviting atmosphere. 🏚🕭🛏◐�&♣P

Wensley

Three Horseshoes L
DL8 4HJ (on A684)
✪ 11-3 (not Mon), 5.30-11; 11-11 Sat; 12-10.30 Sun
☎ (01969) 622327
John Smith's Bitter; Theakston Best Bitter; Yorkshire Dales Three Horseshoes; Wall's Gun Dog Bitter; guest beers H
A cosy and atmospheric traditional country pub of character in a small village on the A684. The bar and adjoining dining room both feature low beams and real fires. Wholesome, reasonably priced lunchtime and evening meals are served daily. Outside, the terraced beer garden to the rear offers glorious views across Wensleydale.
🏚Q🌣🕭◐⊟&🖼(156,157)♣P

West Haddlesey

George & Dragon L
Main Street, YO8 8QA (1 mile W of A19, 5 miles S of Selby) SE565266
✪ 5-midnight (1am Fri); 2-1am Sat; 12-10.30 Sun
☎ (01757) 228198
Brown Cow White Dragon; guest beers H
Privately owned traditional free house supporting local microbreweries. It has low ceilings and a cosy bar with a real fire, an area with large-screen TV showing sporting events, a separate room for diners and an attractive outside decked area for summer days. Food is served evenings (not Sun and Mon) as well as Saturday and Sunday lunch. A

weekly quiz night and frequent jazz music nights take place. Occasional beer festivals are held, including an annual April festival on the weekend closest to St George's Day.
🏚Q🕭🛏◐⊟&🖼(405)♣P🏷

West Witton

Fox & Hounds L
Main Street, DL8 4LP (on A684)
✪ 12-3, 6-midnight; 12-midnight Sat & Sun
☎ (01969) 623650 ⊕ foxwitton.com
Black Sheep Best Bitter; John Smith's Bitter; guest beer H
Friendly, family-run free house full of character, with a down-to-earth bar and games room popular with locals and visitors alike. Good-value meals are served all week, with a roast on Sunday. Parts of the pub date from the 1400s, when it was a rest house for monks from Jervaulx Abbey, and the dining room boasts an inglenook fireplace, complete with beehive oven. A pleasant patio to the rear leads onto the quoits pitch; beware the tight entry to the car park. Real cider is often available. 🏚🕭◐⊟(156)♣🍴P🏷

Whitby

Black Horse ✓
91 Church Street, YO22 4BH (E side of bridge on approach to abbey steps)
✪ 11-11; 12-10.30 Sun ☎ (01947) 602906
⊕ the-black-horse.com
Adnams Southwold Bitter; Black Dog Rhatas; Black Sheep Ale; guest beers H
Dating from the 1600s, this previous local CAMRA award winner offers a warm welcome. The frontage, with its frosted glass windows, together with one of Europe's oldest public serving bars, was built in the 1880s and remains largely unchanged. Beer is dispensed from five handpumps along with hot meals during the winter months. Snuff, tapas, olives, Yorkshire cheeses and hot drinks are always on offer. The cider is Westons Traditional scrumpy. Accommodation is in four bedrooms.
Q🛏◐⊟&🏃🚶⇌🖼(93)♣🍴

Endeavour
66 Church Street, YO22 4AS (on E side of river, 100yds from swing bridge)
✪ 12-1am (11.30 Sun) ☎ (01947) 603557
John Smith's Bitter; guest beers H
Named in celebration of James Cook's three-year voyage to the South Seas, this cosy one-room town pub has an open fire that adds to the warm welcome from an enthusiastic licensee. Alongside the John Smith's, five handpumps serve approximately 140 different guest beers annually, sourced from throughout the country. A tremendous atmosphere prevails, enhanced during Whitby's various folk and Gothic celebrations. Regular folk/Irish music sessions are held on Friday/Saturday evenings and Sunday afternoons. Two bedrooms are available. 🏚🛏🚶⇌🖼(93)

Station Inn ✓
New Quay Road, YO21 1DH (opp bus station)
✪ 10-midnight (11.30 Sun) ☎ (01947) 603937
Black Dog Whitby Abbey Ale; Camerons Strongarm; Copper Dragon Challenger IPA; Taylor Golden Best; guest beers H

Next to the harbour and marina, a warm welcome awaits you at this popular multi-roomed pub and 2011 local CAMRA Pub of the Year. The enthusiastic licensees ensure that the eight beers always represent a superb range of varying styles, while Westons cider and a dozen fruit wines mean there is something for everyone. Opposite the bus station and the NYMR/Esk Valley railway terminus, the pub has become the discerning traveller's waiting room. Live entertainment features on Wednesday, Friday and Saturday evenings. ⟲🖂(93)🌣

Yarm

Black Bull
42 High Street, TS15 9BH (by town hall)
✪ 11-midnight (1am Fri & Sat) ☎ (01642) 791251
Draught Bass; York Terrier; guest beers Ⓗ
With by far the best beer garden in the area, this popular pub has been the favourite haunt of Teesside's 30-somethings, and older, for decades. A dedicated licensee has now increased the number of handpumps to five, which are busy during the day, and even busier each evening and at weekends. There are two separate bars inside, and a third outside on the heated patio. Good-value pub food is served all day.
🏠🌣🌓⚓🖂(7,82)⌐

York

Blue Bell ★ Ⓛ
53 Fossgate, YO1 9TF
✪ 11-11; 12-10.30 Sun ☎ (01904) 654904
Black Sheep Best Bitter; Bradfield Farmers Blonde; Rudgate Ruby Mild; Taylor Landlord; guest beers Ⓗ
A wonderful city-centre pub, one of only a few left on a street that once boasted dozens. The interior is unchanged since 1903 and the Blue Bell is identified by CAMRA as one of Britain's Real Heritage Pubs. It is wood panelled throughout, with two small rooms and a corridor with a serving hatch. Sandwiches are served at lunchtimes but big groups are discouraged due to the lack of space. A great real ale pub and reputed to be the birthplace of York City FC. Q🌓⚓🖂

Brigantes Bar & Brasserie Ⓛ ✅
114 Micklegate, YO1 6JX (100yds from Micklegate Bar)
✪ 12-11 ☎ (01904) 675355
Beer range varies Ⓗ
A real ale haven, with 10 handpumps featuring Yorkshire beers, including one from Leeds, York, Black Sheep, Great Heck and Timothy Taylor alongside five other guests. It is located just inside the city walls. Part of the Market Town Taverns chain, the pub also stocks a selection of continental beers and a draught cider. The ground floor bar area leads to a lounge area, while upstairs is a period Georgian function/dining room. The menu features daily specials and a pie of the day.
Q🌓&⟲🖂🌣

Golden Ball ★
2 Cromwell Road, YO1 6DU
✪ 5-11 (11.30 Thu); 4.30-11.30 Fri; 12-11.30 Sat; 12-11 Sun
☎ (01904) 652211 ⊕ goldenball-york.co.uk
Caledonian Deuchars IPA; Everards Tiger Best Bitter; John Smith's Bitter; Wells Bombardier; guest beer Ⓗ
In the residential Bishophill district, this is a fine, welcoming Victorian street-corner local. It has an

impressive glazed brick exterior and was extensively refurbished by John Smith's in 1929. Identified by CAMRA as one of Britain's Real Heritage Pubs, it has four very different rooms – a main bar, back room, comfortable lounge and snug. Outside is a large south-facing beer garden. This is a true community pub where several local societies hold their meetings. Q🌣&⟲⚓⌐

Guy Fawkes Inn
25 High Petergate, YO1 7HP (next to St Michael le Belfry church)
✪ 11-11; 12-10.30 Sun ☎ (01904) 623716 ⊕ gfyork.com
Guy Fawkes Dark Force Treason; guest beers Ⓗ
Hugely atmospheric inn with up-market chic accommodation in the shadow of York Minster. Purported to be the birthplace of Guy Fawkes, it has retained many of the features from this period. Timber floors and plentiful oak furniture are lit by candles and gas lamps to complete the old world experience with a flourish. Six handpumps dispense Dark Force Treason brewed especially by Great Heck, plus rotating local ales. Gastro-type pub grub is served in the rooms adjoining the bar.
🏠🌣⚓🌓⚑⌐

Maltings Ⓛ
Tanners Moat, YO1 6HU (below Lendal Bridge)
✪ 11-11; 12-10.30 Sun ☎ (01904) 655387 ⊕ maltings.co.uk
Black Sheep Best Bitter; York Guzzler; guest beers Ⓗ
The pub that all real ale enthusiasts should visit on a trip to York. Situated halfway between the railway station and York Minster, this iconic ale house has been quenching the thirst of locals and visitors alike since 1993. Three popular Yorkshire beers are always available, but the four guests can hail from any part of the country. The lunchtime menu is legendary, but do be prepared for a spot of overcrowding at peak times. 🏠🌓⟲🖂🌣

Minster Inn
24 Marygate, YO30 7BH
✪ 2-11; 11-midnight Fri & Sat; 12-10.30 Sun
☎ (01904) 624499
Jennings Snecklifter; Marston's Burton Bitter; guest beers Ⓗ
A traditional, unspoilt local pub that retains its multi-roomed layout. You can always find someone to talk to in the friendly bar, meet with friends in one of the three other rooms, or seek out a quiet spot. There are table-top games to keep everyone busy (or frustrated) for hours. Although tied to Marston's, it makes the best of the range of beers available, always selecting the seasonal ones. Dogs are welcome. 🏠Q🐾🌣⚑⟲🖂♣⌐

Phoenix
75 George Street, YO1 9PT
✪ 6 (4.30 Fri)-11; 12.30-11.30 Sat; 2.30-11.30 Sun
☎ (01904) 656401 ⊕ thephoenixinnyork.co.uk
Copper Dragon Golden Pippin; Timothy Taylor Landlord; Wold Top Bitter; guest beer Ⓗ
Unspoilt traditional and independently run pub. A major refurbishment took place a few years back that preserved the historic features of the pub. It is adjacent to the city walls and close to tourist attractions such as Jorvik Viking Centre and Castle Museum. The pub has five real ales mainly from northern breweries and hosts small beer festivals. Live jazz can be heard two nights a week, and a quiz night and traditional pub games (bar billiards and shove-ha'penny) help create a convivial atmosphere. 🏠Q🌣🌓⚑🖂♣

Rook & Gaskill ⓛ

12 Lawrence Street, YO10 3WP (near Walmgate Bar)
✪ 4-11; 12-midnight Fri & Sat; 12-11 Sun ☎ (01904) 674067
**Castle Rock Black Gold, Harvest Pale, Screech Owl;
guest beers** Ⓗ

The most northerly Castle Rock outlet, offering one of the widest ranges of beers in York. Just outside the ancient city walls, this popular and simply furnished local, with a single split-level bar, keeps a varied clientele happy with nine constantly rotating guest beers to supplement three Castle Rock regulars. Two more handpumps serve traditional cider. There are quarterly beer festivals and open mic nights every Thursday.
🖵(8,10)♣●'–

Slip Inn ⓛ

20 Clementhorpe, YO23 1AN
✪ 5-11.30 (midnight Fri); 12-midnight Sat; 12-11 Sun
☎ (01904) 621793 ⊕ theslipinnyork.co.uk
**Ilkley Best; Leeds Pale; Rudgate Ruby Mild; Wold Top
Wold Gold; guest beer** Ⓗ

An independent free house since 2010, this traditional community pub is situated just outside the city walls. There are two bars and a snug, plus a paved outdoor area often covered for events such as the annual beer festival (run jointly with the Swan just up the road), other beer festivals and featured brewery days. The regular beers are sometimes replaced by others from the same brewery. Live music features at many of the events. ❀≠🖵♣'–

Swan Inn ★ ⓛ ✓

16 Bishopgate Street, YO23 1JH
✪ 4-11 (11.30 Thu; midnight Fri); 12-midnight Sat; 12-10.30
Sun ☎ (01904) 634968
**Saltaire Blonde; Taylor Landlord; Tetley Bitter; guest
beers** Ⓗ

This popular Tetley Heritage Inn has a West Riding layout and features on the cover of Yorkshire's Real Heritage Pubs. Three regular and three rapidly changing guest beers, plus two real ciders, are served from a central bar to the drinking lobby, lounge and public bar. To the rear is a paved and walled garden, with a covered and heated smoking area. It holds an annual beer festival with the nearby Slip Inn. ㎡❀⊕≠🖵♣'–

Three-Legged Mare ⓛ

15 High Petergate, YO1 7EN
✪ 11-midnight (11 Sun) ☎ (01904) 638246
**York Guzzler, Terrier, Wonkey Donkey, Centurion's
Ghost; guest beers** Ⓗ

A modest frontage gives way to a roomy pub with plenty of seating. Enjoy the view of the Minster from the settee by the door, spot the red piano occasionally used by buskers around town or navigate the spiral staircase in search of the loos. The York Brewery range (including the unique Wonkey Donkey brew) is supplemented by an interesting choice of guests – something for everyone at any time of day. Q❀♿≠🖵'–

Waggon & Horses ♟ ⓛ

19 Lawrence Street, YO10 3BP
✪ 5-11.30; 12-2am Fri & Sat; 6.30-11.30 Sun
☎ (01904) 637478 ⊕ waggonandhorsesyork.co.uk
Batemans XB, seasonal beers; guest beers Ⓗ

The only Batemans'-owned pub in York, refurbished to a high standard with a multi-room layout, situated just outside the city walls (Walmgate Bar). It is now free of tie for guest beers

and features a constantly rotating range from near and far. The pub is a supporter of LocAle and offers a varied selection of beers from local microbreweries including Rooster's and Great Heck. Popular for live entertainment and quiz nights. Good-value accommodation is offered.
㎡❀🛏♿🖵(8,10)♣●P'–

YORKSHIRE (SOUTH)

Aughton

Robin Hood Inn ⓛ ✓

64 Main Street, S26 3XJ (2 miles from jcts 31 & 33 of
M1)
✪ 12-11.30 (11 Sun) ☎ (01142) 871010
Beer range varies Ⓗ

Built in the 1600s as a farmhouse, this traditional pub has been known as the Robin Hood since 1865. Original features include low-beamed ceilings, an open fire and different seating areas. An attractive conservatory has proved popular with diners enjoying home-cooked food and excellent fish and chips. An outbuilding used in World War II by the Home Guard has been converted into accommodation. Five guest beers are always on offer, with at least three from local breweries.
㎡❀🛏◑♿🖵(25,49)♣P'–

Barnsley

Commercial ⓛ

Summer Lane, S70 2NN
✪ 4.30 (4 Fri)-11; 12-11 Sat & Sun ☎ (01226) 215277
Oakwell Barnsley Bitter; guest beers Ⓗ

Popular, lively, community local on the edge of town, a great example of a pub for everyone. This free house offers three real ales, with most of them coming from local breweries. No messing around with top-ups here, the landlord insists that drinks are served in a lined glass. The pale décor gives the pub a fresh feel while the garden out the back is not just for the smokers. Football or other sport is on large screens.
❀≠(Interchange)🖵(14,43)♣'–☐

Conservative Club ⓛ

36 Pitt Street, S70 1AW (200yds out of town centre)
✪ 11.30-3.30 (Fri & Sat only), 6.30-midnight; closed Sun
☎ (01226) 282571
Phoenix Wobbly Bob; guest beer Ⓗ

Stone-fronted club just a short walk from the town centre. There is plenty of comfortable seating in the lounge, bar or snooker rooms, and a large-screen TV shows sports or popular programmes. The two full-sized snooker tables are for the members. Darts, cards and dominoes are played most evenings. The bar offers two real ales; one is always changing and is usually from a local brewery. Show this Guide or a CAMRA membership card and you will be made most welcome.
≠(Interchange)♣

Courthouse ⓛ

Regent Street, S70 2HG
✪ 9am-11 (midnight Fri & Sat) ☎ (01226) 779056
Beer range varies Ⓗ

Something is always happening at this lively town-centre pub, from Sky Sports to live music on Friday evenings. The long bar offers up to two changing real ales from the local brewery Acorn. Real cider is also available. The split-level seating areas and

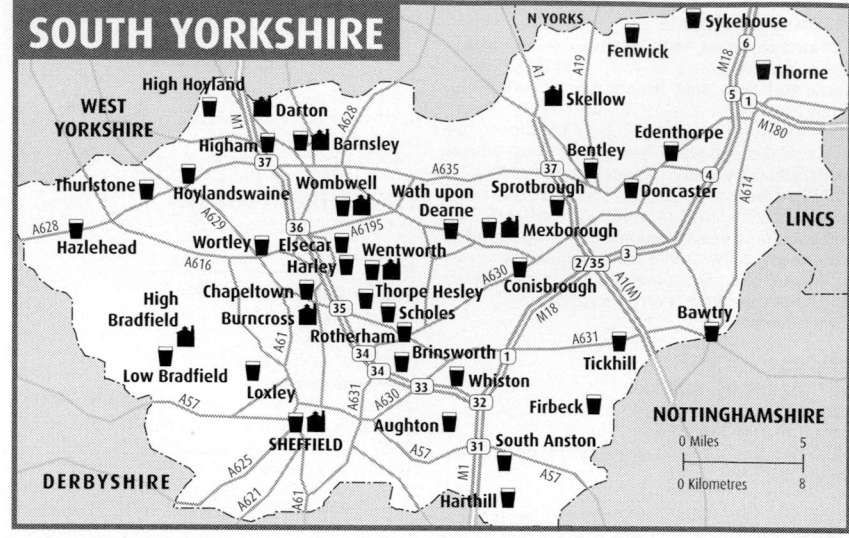

SOUTH YORKSHIRE

snug make this pub popular for groups of drinkers, couples and the lone drinker; however, the pub is seldom quiet. It is convenient for the train and bus station. Food is served till 6pm.
❀◐♿⇄(Interchange)♣●⅃

Joseph Bramah 🄻 ✓
15 Market Hill, S70 2PX
❀ 9am-midnight (1am Fri & Sat) ☎ (01226) 320890
Greene King Abbot; Ruddles Best Bitter; guest beers Ⓗ
Up to four additional microbrewery guest beers, plus one real cider, add to the permanent Wetherspoon beer offerings. This Lloyds No.1 offers value-for-money meals that keep it a busy town-centre pub. Set over two floors (there is good disabled access, including a lift), the T-shaped layout allows for some quieter areas, especially in the smaller upstairs bar. Outside is a sheltered and heated smoking courtyard. This popular watering hole caters for all. ❀◐♿⇄(Interchange)●⅃

Old No. 7 🍺 🄻
7 Market Hill, S70 2PX
❀ closed Mon; 12-midnight ☎ (01226) 244735
⊕ oldno7barnsley.co.uk
Acorn Barnsley Bitter, Yorkshire Pride, Barnsley Gold; guest beers Ⓗ
Acorn Brewery's first public house, it has quickly become popular with real ale drinkers in the area. An ale house in the heart of Barnsley, it offers at least eight real ales and a range of continental beers, British lagers and real ciders. The pub has regular beer festivals and other beer-related entertainment, including occasional beer tasting sessions. The main bar is open at all times, while the cellar bar is open weekend evenings and match days. ●⒟

Silkstone Inn 🄻 ✓
64 Market Street, S70 1SN (160yds from Peel Square up Market St)
❀ 9am-midnight (1am Fri & Sat) ☎ (01226) 320860
Greene King Abbot; Ruddles Best Bitter; guest beers Ⓗ
In the centre of the town, this Wetherspoon's pub is deservedly popular. A modern fireplace gives a

warm feel and wooden bookcases fill up the open-plan space. A coal-themed interior (the Silkstone coal seam stretched under Barnsley) keeps everything dark, even down to the black pendants in the lights. The long black bar is well lit and offers two permanent beers and up to four guest ales, plus a real cider, to satisfy the client mix.
Q❀◐♿⇄(Interchange)●⅃

Bawtry

Ship ✓
Gainsborough Road, DN10 6HT (on A631 near traffic lights)
❀ 12-11 (10.30 Sun) ☎ (01302) 710275
Beer range varies Ⓗ
One of the Doncaster and District CAMRA's success stories. The current licensees took over this once run-down roadside pub in 2007 and transformed it. Refurbished inside and out, the Ship offers good-quality meals at reasonable prices. Four cask ales from the Marston's range are always available and the pub holds beer festivals twice a year. Quizzes and theme nights are popular. Local CAMRA District Pub of the Year in 2011. ❀◐🄺🚗♣P⅃

Turnpike

28-30 High Street, DN10 6JE (on A638 opp marketplace)
☼ 11-11; 12-10.30 Sun ☎ (01302) 711960
Caledonian Deuchars IPA; John Smith's Bitter; Ruddles Best Bitter; guest beers ⊞
Opened in 1986 and still with the original licensee, the Turnpike celebrates 25 years in this Guide. Situated opposite the old marketplace, it is arranged over three levels and features glass and wood panelling together with flagstone floors. The decor includes a county cricket tie collection and photographs of the former RAF Finningley, now Robin Hood Airport. The venue has received several local CAMRA awards over the years. ☼⊲🖳(21,25)⌐

Bentley

Three Horse Shoes Ⓛ

St Mary's Bridge, Town End, DN5 9AG (on roundabout where A638 meets new bridge on route N from Doncaster)
☼ 12-11 (midnight Sat); 12-10.30 Sun ☎ 07878757474
Acorn Barnsley Bitter; guest beers ⊞
Friendly, traditional multi-roomed pub, which recently featured in CAMRA's Yorkshire Real Heritage Pubs guide, only a five-minute walk from Doncaster centre over the old North Bridge. A beer garden overlooks the River Don, one of many improvements made by the owner of this free house, while still keeping its character. Note the unchanged pub frontage with leaded glass. ⋈Q☼⊲🖳≠🖳♣♠

Brinsworth

Sidings

Whitehill Lane, S60 5HE
☼ 12-11 (11.30 Fri & Sat) ☎ (01709) 296024
⊕ thesidingspub.co.uk
Marston's Pedigree, seasonal beers ⊞
A red brick pub that has a friendly taproom with cosy alcoves, and a large carpeted lounge, exposed roof beams and a real fire. Food here is as highly rated as the beer. The classic British menu, locally sourced and all freshly cooked from scratch, even down to the home-made sauces, is excellent value. Hand-made pies are a speciality as is game when available, or try the hand-cut fish finger sandwich with real tartare sauce and mushy peas. ⋈☼⊲🖳(31,87)♣P

Chapeltown

Commercial Ⓛ

107 Station Road, S35 2XF
☼ 12-3, 5.30-11; 12-midnight Fri & Sat; 12-11 Sun ☎ (0114) 2469066
Wentworth Imperial, WPA, Bumble Beer; guest beers ⊞
Built in 1890, this well-established free house is a regular outlet for Wentworth beers, as well as five guest ales including a stout or porter, and there is also a rotating cider. An island bar serves the lounge, games room and snug. Popular beer festivals are held at the end of May and November. Outdoor drinking facilities are to the side and rear, and there is an upstairs function room, which is home to regular live folk sessions. Children are welcome. No meals Sunday evening. ⋈Q☼⊲🖳(265)♣♠P⌐

Conisbrough

Hilltop Hotel Ⓛ

Sheffield Road, DN12 2AY (on A630 at jct of Sheffield Rd and Old Rd)
☼ closed Mon; 4 (3 Fri)-midnight; 12-midnight Sat & Sun ☎ (01709) 868811 ⊕ thehilltophotel.co.uk
Black Sheep Best Bitter; guest beers ⊞
A traditional free house serving up to four ales. On the outskirts of Conisbrough, it offers a relaxed and friendly atmosphere. It is split into a public bar and lounge/dining area, the latter incorporating Bully's Steakhouse and serving locally sourced produce. The owner strives to provide a range of ales, including local beers from Wentworth, Wellbeck and Acorn, alongside its regular Black Sheep. Quiz night is Wednesday. A former local CAMRA Pub of the Season. ⋈☼⊲🖳(X78)♣P⌐

Doncaster

Cask Corner 🏆 Ⓛ

3 Cleveland Street, DN1 3EH
☼ 12-midnight (1am Fri & Sat) ☎ (01302) 366277
⊕ caskcornerdoncaster.co.uk
Theakston Old Peculier; Thwaites Original; guest beers ⊞
Centrally located bar featuring 12 handpumps, including two real ciders. Also available are draught fruit beers and 100 bottled beers from around the world. Unusual, quirky decor includes pump clips, old records and a cornucopia of useless bric-a-brac, some even suspended from the ceiling. Upstairs is a rear heated seating area. A classic jukebox provides unobtrusive background music. Live music takes place on Fridays and Saturdays. Customers are allowed to bring food or takeaways. Local CAMRA Pub of the Year 2012. ☼&≠🖳♠⌐

Corner Pin 🍺

145 St Sepulchre Gate West, DN1 3AH (on W side of dual carriageway)
☼ 12-11.30 ☎ (01302) 340670
York Guzzler; guest beers ⊞
Award-winning, traditional street-corner hostelry offering a variety of guest beers sourced from small, independent, often local, breweries, and Westons Old Rosie cider. Convenient for the town centre and the Travel Interchange, this popular pub comprises a smart lounge area and public bar, with an outside decked drinking area to the rear. Pub food is served from lunchtime onwards, and the Sunday lunches are excellent. Local CAMRA Pub of the Year 2011. ☼⊲≠🖳♣♠⌐🖵

Plough ★ Ⓛ

8 West Laith Gate, DN1 1SF (close to Frenchgate shopping centre)
☼ 11-11 (midnight Fri & Sat); 11.15-4, 7-11 Sun ☎ (01302) 738310
Acorn Barnsley Bitter; guest beers ⊞
The Little Plough, as the locals know it, is a welcoming haven for those wishing to escape the town-centre bustle. CAMRA-friendly, the pub offers local guest ales and twice-yearly beer festivals. The interior dates from 1934 and the Plough has been identified by CAMRA as one of Britain's Real Heritage Pubs. There is a public bar at the front and a comfortable lounge at the rear, with pictures of old agricultural scenes. A winner of several CAMRA awards, and well worth a visit. Q⊲≠🖳⌐

Red Lion ✅

37-38 Market Place, DN1 1NH (S corner of Market Place)

☼ 9-11 (midnight Fri & Sat) ☎ (01302) 732120
Greene King Abbot; Ruddles Best Bitter; guest beers ⓗ

The Red Lion has stood on this site for over 260 years and has many associations with Doncaster's most famous horse race, the St Leger – a list of post-war winners and jockeys is maintained on one wall. Converted to a Wetherspoon's about nine years ago, the pub has seven handpumps serving up to five guest ales, including a range of dark, light and local beers. Its lively atmosphere is popular with local characters, especially on market days. Q⑾⅙➔🖫♣⅃

Salutation Hotel ⓛ ✅

14 South Parade, DN1 2DR (off South Parade, opp Regent Square)

☼ 12-midnight (1am Fri & Sat; 11 Sun) ☎ (01302) 340705
⊕ thesalutationdoncaster.co.uk
Black Sheep Best Bitter; guest beers ⓗ

A winner of many CAMRA awards, this 18th-century coaching inn is a favourite with local members. It is just a 10-minute walk from the town centre. The open-plan lounge features a magnificent bar, boasting seven handpulls. The licensee, Sue, is a self-confessed real ale fanatic, and keeps an eclectic range of beers from national and local breweries. There is a large function room upstairs and a patio area behind the pub. ⚌Q❀⑾🖫♣⅃

Tut 'n' Shive ✅

6 West Laith Gate, DN1 1SF (next to Frenchgate shopping centre)

☼ 11-11 (1am Fri & Sat); 12-midnight Sun ☎ (01302) 360300
Abbeydale Moonshine; Black Sheep Best Bitter; Greene King IPA, Abbot; guest beers ⓗ

Six real ales are available at this busy town-centre pub, featuring a stone floor and walls decorated with pump clips from past guest beers. Quiz nights are on Wednesday and Sunday. Classic rock is well represented on the jukebox, and is featured with a DJ on Sunday nights. A large-screen TV shows major sporting events. Trains and buses and town-centre shopping are only yards away. A lively atmosphere ensures that all over-18s feel welcome. ⑾⅙➔🖫⅃

Edenthorpe

Beverley Inn

117 Thorne Road, DN3 2JE (on A18)

☼ 12-3, 5-11 (8-10.30 Sun) ☎ (01302) 882724
⊕ beverleyinnandhotel.co.uk
Beer range varies ⓗ

An excellent establishment, with friendly and efficient staff serving at least three changing guest beers. The pub is in the east of the town, with many buses serving the route, and it is close to the bus stop on the main Thorne Road. Quality food is served in either the restaurant or bar, depending on what you eat, with a carvery to die for at Sunday lunchtime. TV and accommodation are also available. Highly recommended. ❀🚄⑾🖫⅙♣P⅃

Elsecar

Milton Arms ⓛ

Armroyd Lane, S74 8ES (2 mins' walk from Elsecar Heritage Centre)

☼ 12-3, 7 (6 Fri)-midnight; closed Wed; 12-5, 7-midnight Sun ☎ (01226) 742240
Black Sheep Best Bitter; guest beers ⓗ

Outstanding friendly pub in a village with several good real ale outlets. With three rooms, a conservatory and an award-winning beer garden, the Milton is a great place to relax and enjoy a pint. Alongside the ales the landlord/chef provides great food Thursday to Sunday. Among other activities, the pub hosts the annual Milton 6 Road Race with entries from all over Yorkshire. ⚌❀⑾➔🖫(66,227)♣P⅃🛏

Fenwick

Baxter Arms

Fenwick Lane, DN6 0HA

☼ 5.30 (11.30 Sat & Sun)-midnight ☎ (01302) 702671
Theakston Best Bitter; guest beers ⓗ

A gem of a pub, a little off the beaten track but well worth seeking out. A farmhouse until 1973, it has a lounge and another smaller bar with a snooker table, both with real fires. Evening bar food is available and cooked to order with daily themed specials. The guest beer is mainly sourced from a local, independent brewery. Wednesday is quiz night. Outside is a large, sheltered garden with a small play area. ⚌Q❀⑾⅙Å♣P⅃

Firbeck

Black Lion 🍷 ⓛ

9 New Road, S81 8JY (opp village hall) SK5688

☼ closed Mon; 12-3, 5.30-11; 12-5 Sun ☎ (01709) 812575
John Smith's Bitter; guest beers ⓗ

Traditional village pub and restaurant, now a free house. Excellent home-cooked food attracts diners, walkers and the local community. Four guest beers are offered, usually including one from a local microbrewer. Pictures of old Firbeck adorn the walls of the snug area. A quiz is held every Tuesday, with folk music every third Monday. There are two letting rooms. The famous St Leger horse race was first held in fields near the pub in 1776. Local CAMRA Pub of the Year 2012. ⚌Q❀🚄⑾⅙♣P⅃

Harley

Horseshoe Inn ⓛ

9 Harley Road, S62 7UD (off A6135 on B6090 1 mile from Wentworth)

☼ 4 (1 Sat)-11; 12-10.30 Sun ☎ (01226) 742204
Beer range varies ⓗ

Street-corner local hosting regular events and home to football and pool teams. Guest beers change regularly, ensuring their quality, with ales often coming from Wentworth and other local breweries. Sunday lunchtime is a carvery; book to avoid disappointment. The Horseshoe has been the hub of the local community for well over a century, and is handy for walking around the Wentworth estate as well as for the Needles Eye and Elsecar Heritage Centre. ❀⑾🖫(44)♣

Harthill

Beehive Inn L ✔

16 Union Street, S26 7YH (opp church 1½ miles from Kiveton Park rail station)

☼ 11.30-3 (not Mon), 6-11; 11-11 Sat & Sun

☎ (01909) 770205

Kelham Island Easy Rider; Taylor Landlord; Tetley Bitter H

Welcoming and award-winning village inn on the Five Churches walk and close to Rother Valley Country Park. It caters for drinkers and diners and is home to a number of local clubs, including a Friday folk club and the Harthill morris men. The rear room houses a full-sized snooker table, and the upstairs function room has stairlift access. The Beehive has been a pub since at least 1833 – its name is believed to be a reference to the lime kilns once prevalent in the area.

Q❀❂🍴🐕🛇♿🚃(25,49)♣P½⊟

Blue Bell

4 Woodall Lane, S26 7YQ

☼ 5-11; 2-11.30 Sat; 12-11 Sun ☎ (01909) 770391

Bradfield Farmers Blonde; guest beer H

A welcoming, friendly mock-Tudor pub comprising a public bar with TV for sport and pool table and a large comfortable lounge with a real fire. Behind the car park there is a sheltered garden for when it is warmer. This lively village community local is ideal for those who want an excellently kept pint without being surrounded by diners.

🏰❀🐕♿🚃(25,49)♣P½⊟

Hazlehead

Dog & Partridge L

Bord Hill, S36 4HH (1¼ miles westbound on A628 Flouch roundabout) SE179011

☼ 12-11 ☎ (01226) 763173 🌐 dogandpartridgeinn.co.uk

Acorn Barnsley Bitter; guest beers H

Surrounded by stunning scenery winter and summer alike, the Dog & Partridge is a 4-star Yorkshire Tourist Board Country Inn. The bar serves four quality locally sourced real ales, and close by is a large roaring open log fire to take away the chills of the winter months. The Transpennine Way and Saltersbrook packhorse trails are nearby. Traditional country cooking uses local produce when possible and pork dishes come from the pub's own rare breed pigs. 🏰🛏️❀🍴♿P½⊟

High Hoyland

Cherry Tree L ✔

Bank End Lane, S75 4BE

☼ 12-3, 5.30-midnight; 12-midnight Sun ☎ (01226) 382541

Acorn Barnsley Bitter; Black Sheep Best Bitter; Taylor Landlord; guest beers H

Busy rural pub with spectacular open views across the valley, overlooking Cannon Hall Country Park. Popular with locals and visitors, the pub is used as a starting and finishing point for walkers. The interior is long and narrow with a central bar, two dining areas, trendy armchairs and plenty of drinking space in front of the bar. Five cask ales are on handpump with two changing guest beers. Good-quality food means it is advisable to book a table. Q❀🍴♿P½⊟

Higham

Engineers Arms

Higham Common Road, S75 1PF

☼ 12-3, 7-11; 12-3.30, 7-10.30 Sun ☎ (01226) 384204

Samuel Smith Old Brewery Bitter H

Lively community Grade II-listed pub built in 1849 and owned by Samuel Smith's. The pub offers a warm welcome to locals and visitors alike. There is no TV or music here – conversation is king. One remarkable feature is the split-level bar with the public bar on the upper level. The public bar has a Yorkshire doubles dartboard. The lower level bar serves the lounge, has original still photographs from the TV show Last of the Summer Wine, and a pool table. Q❀🍴♿🚃(92A)♣P

Hoylandswaine

Hoylandswaine Sports & Athletic Club L

Haigh Lane, S36 7JJ

☼ closed Mon; 8 (2 Sat)-midnight; 12-6 Sun

☎ (01226) 765726

Beer range varies H

With panoramic views over the borough, this is the ideal place to watch the world go by – or a game of cricket. The club is located in the heart of the village and is popular with locals. The changing guest ales are sourced from local breweries. Outside is a lovely terrace area to enjoy the views. A warm welcome is guaranteed, and club non-members just need to show a copy of this Guide or a CAMRA membership card on entry. ❀♿🚃(92)P

Low Bradfield

Plough Inn L ✔

New Road, S6 6HW SK263916

☼ 12-11 ☎ (0114) 285 1280

Bradfield Farmers Blonde, Plough; guest beers H

Lying in the heart of the Loxley Valley, this former 18th-century farm celebrated 200 years as a pub in 2009. This free house, it provides two guest ales as well as stocking seasonal beers from the nearby Bradfield Brewery. Good home-cooked food is available lunchtimes all week, evenings Wednesday to Saturday, and all day Sunday, made from locally sourced produce, with pies a speciality. Thursday is curry night. A music evening is held on the first Tuesday of every month.

🏰❀🍴🐕♿🚃(61,62)♣🐾P½⊟

Loxley

Nag's Head L ✔

Stacey Bank, S6 6SJ SK906289

☼ 12-midnight ☎ (0114) 285 1202

Bradfield Farmers Blonde, Farmers Brown Cow, Yorkshire Farmers, seasonal beers H

A two-roomed country pub on the main road out of Loxley, birthplace of Robin Hood, towards High Bradfield. This is the nearby Bradfield Brewery's recently acquired tap, with up to five from the range, including seasonal beers and specials. Good home-cooked food is available lunchtimes (no food Mon) and evenings Tuesday to Friday. A three-quarter-size snooker table fills the room to the left of the entrance. Excellent views overlooking the Loxley Valley can be enjoyed from the outside patio. 🏰❀🍴🐕🚃(61,62)♣P½⊟

Mexborough

Concertina Band Club ⓛ

9A Dolcliffe Road, S64 9AZ (off Bank St, on left halfway up hill)
✪ 2-4; 12-5 Fri; 12-4 Sat; 12-3, 7.45-10.30 Sun
☎ (01709) 580841
Concertina Club Bitter, Bengal Tiger, Dark Attic; John Smith's Bitter Ⓗ

Long-established and now unique club and brewery with an interesting history. Pictures and memorabilia of the Concertina Band who began in 1887 decorate the main room. The Tina provides three regular ales, including the award-winning Bengal Tiger. An array of CAMRA and beer awards around the bar cover many years of dedicated achievements. CAMRA members are welcome on production of a copy of the Guide or a CAMRA membership card. ✿⇌🚋(220,221,222)♣⌐🕁

Imperial Club & Brewery ⓛ

Arcadia Hall, Cliff Street, S64 9HU (opp bus station off dual carriageway)
✪ 4 (12 Sat & Sun)-midnight ☎ 07712200382
Imperial Bitter, Blonde, Stout; guest beer Ⓗ

A friendly club and brewery opposite the bus station; the railway station is close by. The club regularly provides five real ales – award-winning Blonde and Stout often feature – as well as a guest beer or an Imperial seasonal beer; a real cider is also served. There is regular entertainment, with a buskers' night on Wednesday, Friday night prize bingo and a Saturday live singer, while Sundays offer a carvery at lunch and brass band concerts in the evening. It has a separate pool/games area. Families are welcome. ✿◑&⇌🚋♣👕⌐

Rotherham

Bluecoat ⓛ ✔

The Crofts, S60 2JD (behind town hall, off A618 Moorgate Rd)
✪ 7am-midnight (1am Fri & Sat) ☎ (01709) 580841
Greene King Abbot; Ruddles Best Bitter; guest beers Ⓗ

Originally a charity school opened in 1776, it became a pub called Ffeoffes in 1981 and then a Wetherspoon in 2001. The wide selection of beers on offer is listed on a screen at the end of the bar. Westons Old Rosie or Organic cider is served from a cask behind the bar. The pub frequently holds Meet the Brewer events, and has special curry and steak nights. Winner of local CAMRA Pub of the Year five times. ✿◑&⇌🚋👕P⌐

Bridge Inn ⓛ

1 Greasbrough Road, S60 1RB (alongside Chantry Bridge, between bus and rail stations)
✪ 12-11; 3-1am Sat; closed Sun ☎ (01709) 836818
Old Mill Bitter, Blonde Bombshell, Yorkshire Porter, seasonal beer; guest beers Ⓗ

The spiritual home of Rotherham CAMRA, this is an Old Mill tied house, built in 1930 using stone from the original Bridge Inn, which dated back to the 1700s. Two guest beers are usually sourced from microbreweries, and the real cider changes. There is live music every Saturday evening, with folk and jazz once a month, and two function rooms upstairs. Close to the medieval chapel on the bridge and a short walk to the Minster. &⇌🚋♣👕

Colin

1 Old Wortley Road, Kimberworth, S61 1NQ (opp school, 2 miles from M1 jct 34)
✪ 12-midnight; 11-11 Sun ☎ (01709) 554585
Greene King IPA, Abbot, seasonal beer Ⓗ

Recently refurbished Greene King pub where the Abbot and seasonal beers alternate. Dating from at least 1858 and named Sir Colin Campbell after the Field Marshall's part in the relief of Lucknow in 1837, it now officially bears its former local nickname. This thriving local is home to sports clubs and quiz nights. There is an outside area at the rear of the pub, which is handy for Keppel's Column, Kimberworth Manor and Grange Golf Course. The curry night on Thursdays is highly recommended. ✿◑🖳&🚋(6,7,8)♣P⌐

Scholes

Bay Horse ⓛ ✔

Scholes Lane, S61 2RQ (off A629, 1 mile from M1 jct 35)
✪ 5 (12 Sat & Sun)-11 ☎ (0114) 246 8085
Bradfield Farmers Blonde; Kelham Island Pale Rider; Taylor Landlord; guest beers Ⓗ

Traditional village pub by the cricket ground, on the Rotherham Round Walk and the Transpennine Trail. It serves home-cooked food including Dan's Cow Pie (certificate presented if you finish everything on the plate), curries and Sunday lunches. Pork pie competitions are held and hog roasts feature up to four times a year. A choir performs on Thursday and two quizzes are hosted. Handy for visiting Keppel's Column and walks to Thorpe Hesley and Wentworth. A regular local CAMRA award winner. ⌂Q✿◑&🚋(44)P⌐

Sheffield: Central

Bath Hotel ★

66 Victoria Street, S3 7QL
✪ 12-11; 7-10.30 Sun ☎ (0114) 249 5151
Thornbridge Lord Marples; guest beers Ⓗ

A careful restoration of the 1930s interior gave this two-roomed pub a conservation award and acknowledgment by CAMRA as one of Britain's Real Heritage Pubs. The bar lies between the tiled lounge, a small corridor drinking area, and the cosy well-upholstered snug. There are usually three Thornbridge beers and three guests, plus a good choice of malt whiskies and continental beers. Live jazz/blues plays Sunday, Irish music Monday, a blues session on the first Wednesday of the month and jazz on the second Wednesday.
Q🖳(West St/University)🚋🕁

Devonshire Cat ✔

49 Wellington Street, S1 4HG
✪ 11.30-11 (1am Fri & Sat); 12-10.30 Sun
☎ (0114) 279 6700
Abbeydale Deception; Kelham Island Pale Rider; Oakwell Barnsley Bitter; Thornbridge Jaipur IPA; guest beers Ⓗ

With 12 handpumps adorning the bar (the house beer is brewed by the local Bradfield Brewery) and over 100 beers from around the world, the Dev Cat is a great place for the discerning drinker. The menu features light snacks through to hearty meals. The clientele is a mix of beer enthusiasts, students and anyone else in search of an excellent range of the best beers. An essential calling point if you are on a short visit to the city.
◑&🚋(West St)🕁

Fat Cat ⅃

23 Alma Street, S3 8SA
✪ 12-11 (midnight Fri & Sat) ☎ (0114) 249 4801
Kelham Island Best Bitter, Pale Rider; Taylor Landlord; guest beers Ⓗ

Opened in 1981 and still ferociously independent, this is the pub that started the real ale revolution in the area. Beers from around the country are served alongside those from the adjacent Kelham Island brewery. Vegetarian and gluten-free dishes feature heavily on the menu (evening food to 8pm, not Sun). The walls are covered with the many awards presented to the pub and brewery. Beer festivals are held every August and at various other times. Monday is curry and quiz night.
₳Q✿❶&☖(Shalesmoor)☖➌P⟜

Harlequin ⅃

108 Nursery Street, S3 8GG
✪ 11.30-11 (11.30 Thu & Fri; midnight Sat)
☎ (0114) 275 8195 ⊕ theharlequinpub.co.uk
Brew Company Best Bitter, Blonde; guest beers Ⓗ

Operated by the Brew Company, the Harlequin (formerly the Manchester) takes its name from another former Wards pub around the corner, now demolished. The large open-plan interior features a central bar, with seating on two levels. As well as local brews, the nine handpumps serve beers from far and wide, with an emphasis on microbreweries, and there are regular beer festivals. A range of boutique bottled beers, many from Flying Dog, is also available. Wednesday is quiz night and there is live music at weekends.
Q✿❶☖(Castle Square)☖(47,48,53)♣➌⟜

Henry's ⅃

38 Cambridge Street, S1 4HP
✪ 11-11 (1am Fri & Sat) ☎ (0114) 273 8742
Clarks Henry's Long Blonde; guest beers Ⓗ

Former café/bar reopened as a free house in 2010 after being derelict for a couple of years. Now thriving again, it offers one of the largest selections of cask ales in the city centre, with up to 11 guest beers. The ground floor is open plan, with seating at various levels around the long bar counter. Meals prepared from good locally sourced food are served daily from 11-7pm in the main bar area. The in-house Aardvark Brewery is being established on site. ✿❶⇌☖(City Hall)☖➌⟜

Kelham Island Tavern 🏆 ⅃ ✓

62 Russell Street, S3 8RW
✪ 12-midnight ☎ (0114) 272 2482
⊕ kelhamislandtavern.co.uk
Abbeydale Deception; Acorn Barnsley Bitter; Bradfield Farmers Blonde; Pictish Brewers Gold; Thwaites Nutty Black; guest beers Ⓗ

Former CAMRA National Pub of the Year, this small gem was rescued from dereliction in 2002. Twelve handpumps dispense an impressive range of beers, always including a mild, a stout and a porter, so you are sure to find something to suit your palate. In the warmer months you can relax in the pub's multi award-winning beer garden. Regular folk music features on Sunday and quiz night is Monday; no meals Sunday.
Q✿❶&☖(Shalesmoor)☖➌⟜🖫

Old House

113-117 Devonshire Street, S3 7SB
✪ 12-1am (2am Fri & Sat) ☎ (0114) 272 0569
⊕ theoldhousesheffield.com
Abbeydale Moonshine; guest beers Ⓗ

Unlike many of the trendy strip of bars that form Division Street/Devonshire Street, the Old House provides a homely atmosphere. There are seating areas either side of the entrance corridor leading into the main bar area, which is decorated with classic album covers and old photos, while the shelves are stacked with retro artefacts. Food ranging from snacks to hearty mains is home-cooked and available throughout the day. Guest beers are mostly local. ₳❶☖(West St)☖

Red Deer ⅃ ✓

18 Pitt Street, S1 4DD
✪ 12-midnight (11 Sun & Mon; 1am Fri & Sat)
☎ (0114) 2722890 ⊕ red-deer-sheffield.co.uk
Black Sheep Best Bitter; Kelham Island Easy Rider; Moorhouse's Pride of Pendle; Taylor Landlord; guest beers Ⓗ

A genuine, traditional local in the heart of the city. The small frontage of the original three-roomed pub hides an open-plan interior extended to the rear with a gallery seating area. As well as the impressive range of cask ales, including up to four guest beers, there is also a selection of continental bottled beers. Meals are served 12-9pm (until 3pm Sun). There is a function room upstairs which can be booked, and a pub quiz every Tuesday.
Q✿❶☖(West St)☖➌⟜

Riverside

1 Mowbray Street, S3 8EN
✪ 12-11 (midnight Fri & Sat) ☎ (0114) 281 3621
⊕ riversidesheffield.co.uk
Brew Company Kraken, Riverside Pale; guest beers Ⓗ

On the banks of the River Don, with a pleasant terrace that overlooks the river. The interior is largely open plan but with a separate room to the right of the main entrance. Furnishings comprise a mix of comfortable sofas and armchairs together with more spartan former school desks. The two house beers are complemented by a changing selection of guest ales, mostly from local breweries. Live music is featured at weekends.
✿❶&☖(47,48,53)➌⟜

Rutland Arms ⅃

86 Brown Street, S1 2BS
✪ 12-11 (midnight Thu-Sat) ☎ (0114) 272 9003
⊕ rutlandarmspeople.co.uk
Blue Bee Nectar Pale Ale, Bees Knees; guest beers Ⓗ

Occupying a corner spot in the Cultural Industries Quarter and near Sheffield's main railway station, this pub reopened as a free house in 2009. The comfortable interior provides ample seating either side of the central entrance, and the walls are decorated with changing displays of work from local artists, as well as photos of old Sheffield pubs. Most of the guest beers are sourced from local breweries, and both beer and cider festivals are held annually. Food is served throughout the day.
✿❶⇌☖☖➌⟜🖫

Shakespeare's ⅃

146-148 Gibraltar Street, S3 8UB
✪ 12-11.30 (1am Fri & Sat) ☎ (0114) 275 5959
⊕ shakespeares-sheffield.co.uk
Abbeydale Deception; guest beers Ⓗ

Originally built as a coaching inn in 1821, the pub reopened as a free house in the summer of 2011. The central bar serves two small rooms and the corridor, and there are two further rooms together with a recent extension. Up to eight changing guest beers are available, together with real cider and a selection of some 80 whiskies. There is regular live music in the upstairs function room and a quiz is held on Thursday. Several beer festivals are held each year. Q⚜♿🖼(Shalesmoor)🚌♣🍴–🚻

Sheffield Tap L

Platform 1b, Sheffield Station, Sheaf Street, S1 2BP

🕐 11-11; 10-midnight Fri & Sat ☎ (0114) 273 7558

🌐 sheffieldtap.com

Thornbridge Brother Rabbit, Kipling; guest beers H

Opened in 2009, this was originally the first-class refreshment room for Sheffield Midland station, built in 1904. After years of neglect the main bar area has been the subject of an award-winning restoration and retains many original features, including the ornamental bar fittings and tiled walls. Further seating has been provided in the corridor leading from the Sheaf Street entrance, and two more rooms have been opened up to the right of the bar. There are usually four beers from the Thornbridge range and up to six guest beers. Q⚜♿🚆🖼🚌🍴

Ship Inn L ✅

312 Shalesmoor, S3 8UL

🕐 12-3.30, 5.30-11.30 ☎ (0114) 281 2204

Abbeydale Moonshine; guest beers H

Behind the impressive Tomlinson's frontage lies a friendly community local, with two lounge areas around the central L-shaped bar, and a small pool room to the rear. Although the pub is tied to Greene King, the three handpumps dispense beers from local breweries. Good quality lunchtime meals are available. The pictures and ornaments mostly have a nautical theme in keeping with the pub's name. ◖🖼(Shalesmoor)🚌(11,12,14)♣P🍴–🚻

Sheffield: East

Carlton

563 Attercliffe Road, S9 3RA

🕐 11-11; 12-9 Sun ☎ (0114) 244 3287

Beer range varies H

Built in 1862, this former Gilmour's house lies behind a deceptively small frontage, but offers the most impressive range of real ales in the area. The main room around the bar is comfortably furnished in traditional style. To the rear is the refurbished games room leading on to a newly established snug and a recently created garden. A strict no-swearing policy enhances the friendly atmosphere. Beers are mainly from small breweries, with some local but mostly from further afield. ⚜🖼(Woodbourn Rd)🚌(52,69)♣🍴

Sheffield: North

Blake Hotel

53 Blake Street, S6 3JQ

🕐 12-11.30 ☎ (0114) 233 9336

Bradfield Farmers Blonde; guest beers H

At the top of a steep hill, this community pub reopened as a free house in 2010 after seven years of closure. Extensively restored, it has many traditional Victorian features, original etched windows and mirrors from bygone breweries. A large decked garden has been developed to the rear. There are five guest beers, usually including a stout or porter, mostly from small independent breweries. Q⚜🖼(31,95)🍴–

Gardeners Rest L

105 Neepsend Lane, S3 8AT

🕐 3-11 (midnight Fri & Sat); 12-11 Sun ☎ (0114) 272 4978

Sheffield Crucible Best, Five Rivers, Porter, Seven Hills, seasonal beers; guest beers H

The tap of the Sheffield Brewery reopened in 2009 after refurbishment following severe flooding in 2007. The clean, bright interior has retained the cosy lounge. The main bar features art exhibitions, live music Friday and Saturday, and the restored bar billiards table. To the rear is a conservatory leading to the beer garden overlooking the River Don. There are usually at least four Sheffield beers, together with six guests from other local and regional breweries. The popular quiz night is on a Sunday. Q⚜♿🖼(Infirmary Rd)🚌(53)♣🍴–🚻

Hillsborough Hotel L

54-58 Langsett Road, S6 2UB

🕐 12-11 (midnight Fri & Sat) ☎ (0114) 232 2100

Wood Street Pale Ale, Traditional Bitter, Stannington Stout, seasonal beers; guest beers H

Privately owned hotel serving home-cooked food. The guest ales are supplemented by beers from the house brewery in the cellar, which brews under the Wood Street name, with at least four of its range always available. Brewery tours can be booked. The conservatory and raised terrace at the rear feature panoramic views along the upper Don Valley. Attractions include seasonal beer festivals, regular themed events, folk music on Sunday and a popular quiz night on Tuesday. Q⚜🛏🍽♿🖼(Langsett Primrose View)🚌♣🍴

New Barrack Tavern L

601 Penistone Road, S6 2GA

🕐 11-11 (midnight Fri & Sat); 12-11 Sun ☎ (0114) 234 9148

Acorn Barnsley Bitter; Bradfield Farmers Bitter; Castle Rock Harvest Pale, Screech Owl; guest beers H

Multi-roomed pub offering up to five guest beers including seasonal ales from Castle Rock. The home-cooked food is available daily, with a carvery on Sunday. The front bar has bar billiards, the main room features live music Friday and Saturday, there is a comedy club on the first Sunday of the month, and Monday is folk night. A wide choice of continental beers, single malts and a real cider is served. Outside is an award-winning heated, covered patio garden. 🏚Q⚜🍽♿🖼(Bamforth St)🚌(53)♣🍴

Wellington L

1 Henry Street, S3 7EQ

🕐 12-11; 12-3.30, 7-10.30 Sun ☎ (0114) 249 2295

Beer range varies H

Popular street-corner pub, also known as the Bottom Wellie, that champions a varying range of beers from small independent brewers, with 10 handpumps always offering a stout or porter and a real cider, plus a range of continental bottled beers. The house brewery, which adjoins the secluded garden at the rear, recommenced brewing late in 2009. It now produces a wide range of brews, usually pale and hoppy, under the Little Ale Cart name, normally with three on sale. 🏚Q⚜🖼(Shalesmoor)🚌(11,12,14)🍴–🚻

Sheffield: South

Archer Road Beer Stop L

57 Archer Road, S8 0JT

✪ 11 (10.30 Sat; 5 Sun)-10 ☎ (0114) 255 1356
⊕ archerroadbeerstop.com
Beer range varies H
Small corner shop real ale off-licence. Up to four handpulled ales are available at a time, in addition to an extensive range of bottle-conditioned beers, Belgian beers and other world favourites. The shop has received the local CAMRA branch award for its outstanding contribution to real ale, and has appeared in this Guide every year since 1997.
🖳(97,98)

Sheaf View

25 Gleadless Road, Heeley, S2 3AA
✪ 11.30-11.30 ☎ (0114) 249 6455
Kelham Island Easy Rider; Wentworth Sheaf Pale Ale; guest beers H
Former John Smith's and Marston's pub superbly restored in 2000 after a period of dereliction. It reopened as a genuine free house and since then has become an integral part of the Heeley drinking scene, offering a wide range of real ales, Belgian beers and whiskies, all at realistic prices. A winner of many CAMRA branch awards, it is busy at most times, especially on Wednesday quiz nights and Sheffield United match days.
Q✿✿&🖳(20,20A,53)♣🍺P🏷–

White Lion L ✓

615 London Road, S2 4HT
✪ 3-11 (11.30 Wed; midnight Thu; 1am Fri); 12-1am Sat; 12-11.30 Sun ☎ (0114) 255 1500 ⊕ whitelionsheffield.co.uk
Abbeydale Moonshine; Tetley Bitter; Thornbridge Jaipur IPA; Wells Bombardier; Wychwood Hobgoblin; guest beers H
Lovingly maintained pub dating from 1781. A tiled corridor links a number of small distinct rooms, including a delightful snug. The larger concert room at the rear caters for live bands on Thursdays and Saturdays, and folk and jazz sessions on alternate Tuesdays. Wednesday is quiz night. The separate rooms create an intimate and pleasant drinking environment. Visitors should note the interesting spelling of Windsor on the original Gilmour's windows. ✿🖳(20,20A,53)♣🏷–

Sheffield: West

Cobden View L

40 Cobden View Road, Crookes, S10 1HQ
✪ 1-midnight; 12-1am Fri & Sat; 12-midnight Sun ☎ (0114) 266 1273 ⊕ thecobdenview.co.uk
Bradfield Farmers Blonde; Caledonian Deuchars IPA; Copper Dragon Best Bitter; Greene King IPA; Wychwood Hobgoblin H
Off the main Crookes thoroughfare, this busy community pub caters for a varied clientele, ranging from students to retired folk. The original room layout is still apparent, with the bar serving a snug at the front, a games area with pool and darts to the rear, and a lounge to the right of the front entrance. A quiz is held on Sunday evenings and there is live music most Thursdays and Saturdays. The well-kept rear garden hosts summer barbecues. ✿&🖳(52,95)♣🍺🏷–

Ranmoor Inn L ✓

330 Fulwood Road, S10 3GD
✪ 11.30-11; 12-10.30 Sun ☎ (0114) 230 1325
Abbeydale Deception; Bradfield Farmers Bitter, Farmers Blonde; Taylor Landlord; guest beers H
Renovated Victorian local with original etched windows lying in the shadow of Ranmoor Church.

Now open plan, the seating areas reflect the old room layout. A friendly, old-fashioned pub, it has a diverse clientele that includes choirs and rugby and cricket teams. The piano by the bar is often played by regulars. Outside, there is a small front garden plus the former stable yard, which has been opened as a partly covered and heated drinking area. Lunches are available Tuesday to Saturday.
Q✿◖🖳(120)🏷–

Rising Sun L ✓

471 Fulwood Road, S10 3QA
✪ 12-11 ☎ (0114) 230 3855 ⊕ risingsunsheffield.co.uk
Abbeydale Daily Bread, Brimstone, Moonshine, Absolution, seasonal beers; guest beers H
Operated by local brewer Abbeydale, this is a large suburban roadhouse in the leafy western side of the city. The two rooms are comfortably furnished, with a main bar and raised area to the rear. A range of Abbeydale beers is always available, with up to six guests, mainly from micros, dispensed from the impressive bank of 13 handpumps. Entertainment includes live music on Monday and quizzes on Sunday and Wednesday. An annual beer festival, Sunfest, is held in July.
Q✿◖&🖳(120)♣P🏷–

University Arms L

197 Brook Hill, S3 7HG
✪ 12-11 (midnight Fri & Sat); closed Sun ☎ (0114) 222 8969
Acorn Thirst Degree; guest beers H
Owned by the University of Sheffield, this former staff club became a pub in 2007. There is a bar in a small alcove seating area adjoining, and a main lounge area. A conservatory at the rear leads to the extensive beer garden. Up to six guest beers are available, many sourced locally. Entertainment includes a quiz on Tuesday night, live jazz or blues at weekends and regular beer festivals. No food on Saturday evening.
Q✿◖🖳(University)🖳(51,52)♣🏷–

York L

243-247 Fulwood Road, S10 3BA
✪ 11.30-11 (midnight Fri & Sat) ☎ (0114) 266 4624
⊕ theyorksheffield.co.uk
True North Blonde, Porter; guest beers H
Occupying a prominent site in the centre of Broomhill, the York reopened as a free house in 2010 after a period of closure following its disposal by a pubco. Extensively refurbished, with parquet flooring and wood-panelled walls, it now offers high quality dining complemented by a range of up to five mainly local guest ales and two real ciders, and has introduced an annual beer festival in the autumn. Q✿◖&🖳(52,120)🍺🏷–

South Anston

Loyal Trooper L ✓

34 Sheffield Road, S25 5DT (off A57, 3 miles from M1 jct 31 heading for Worksop)
✪ 12-11 (midnight Fri & Sat) ☎ (01909) 562203
Adnams Southwold Bitter; Taylor Landlord; Tetley Bitter; guest beers H
Friendly oak-beamed village local selling a range of real ales and good wholesome food at reasonable prices. Guest beers often come from local breweries. Largely unchanged since the 1960s, parts of the building date back to 1690. The interior comprises a public bar, snug, lounge and a function room upstairs used by many local groups, including a thriving folk club. Close to St James's Church, it is

on the Five Churches walk and handy for Anston Stones Wood and the nearby Butterfly Farm.
Q✿❶❷🖶(19,19B,29)♣P♿

Sprotbrough

Boat Inn ✪
Nursery Lane, DN5 7NB (down hill from village; walk along canalside)
✪ 12-11 (10.30 Sun) ☎ (01302) 858500
Black Sheep Best Bitter; York Yorkshire Terrier; guest beer Ⓗ
An attractive, multi-roomed pub situated conveniently for the canal, Don Gorge, Sprotbrough Flash and the Transpennine Trail, and popular with walkers, drinkers and diners. Good food from an extensive menu is served throughout the day and the real ales are sourced from independent breweries. The guest beer is chosen from a new batch of specials which Vintage Inns regularly makes available. Outside is a large courtyard drinking area, ideal for warm summer evenings, and ample parking. ♨✿❶&P♿

Sykehouse

Old George ✪
Broad Lane, DN14 9AU
✪ 12-midnight ☎ (01405) 785635
Tetley Bitter; guest beers Ⓗ
A 200-year-old building in this linear village, the Old George is well worth seeking out. The pub features an open fire in winter and a warm welcome from staff all year round. A free house, two guest ales are sourced from countrywide breweries are always available. Excellent meals are served, including OAP specials and a Sunday carvery. Outside is a patio area and garden where barbecues are held in summer, and a large playground including a children's bathing pool. ♨✿❶&▲🖶(69)♣P♿

Thorne

Windmill Ⓛ
19 Queen Street, DN8 5AA (close to Sainsbury's in town centre)
✪ 2-11 (midnight Fri & Sat); 12-midnight Sun
☎ (01405) 812866
Black Sheep Best Bitter; Thorne Pale Ale; guest beers Ⓗ
A friendly community pub in the middle of a residential area close to the heart of Thorne. The compact and cosy lounge bar has many historic photographs of Thorne and is linked to the public bar by an archway. The public bar has a large-screen TV often showing live football or rugby; the pub is used as a base by several local sports clubs. The regular beer is Black Sheep, with guests from the Thorne Brewery. ✿⇌(North)P♿

Thorpe Hesley

Masons
106 Thorpe Street, S61 2RP
✪ 12-3, 5.30-11; 12-3.30, 7-10.30 Sun ☎ 0845 2915467
⊕ masonsarmsthorpehesley.co.uk
Beer range varies Ⓗ
Friendly local where various musical artists perform once a week. Note the collection of jugs above the bar and around the beamed ceilings, and the early local photographs. Good-value, home-cooked food

is served from a varied menu. Handy for the Transpennine Trail, the pub is home to many local groups. Up to three different guest beers are on handpump at any one time. ✿❶🖶(6,44,66)♣P

Thurlstone

Huntsman Ⓛ
136 Manchester Road, S36 9QW (on A628)
✪ 6 (5 Sat)-11; 12-10.30 Sun ☎ (01226) 764892
⊕ thehuntsmanthurlstone.co.uk
Black Sheep Best Bitter; Taylor Landlord; Tetley Bitter; guest beers Ⓗ
An untypical roadside pub with its oak beams and two real fires that welcomes travellers and locals with both arms. Come one, come all and bring your dogs! Enjoy the beer, enjoy the chat, revel in good old-fashioned Yorkshire bonhomie. The hub of its community, the pub satisfies all tastes, from footpath runners to dominoes players. A real precious gem. ♨Q🖶(23,25)♣

Tickhill

Scarbrough Arms
Sunderland Street, DN11 9QJ (on A631 near Buttercross)
✪ 12-11 (10.30 Sun) ☎ (01302) 742977
Greene King Abbot; John Smith's Bitter; Morland Old Speckled Hen; Shepherd Neame Spitfire; guest beers Ⓗ
A deserving entry since 1990, this three-roomed stone-built pub has won several local CAMRA awards over the years. Originally a farmhouse, the building dates back to the 16th century. Although structural changes have taken place, the snug is a delight, with its barrel-shaped furniture and real fire, while bar billiards can be played in the bar. An outbuilding doubles as a covered smoking area and an extension for beer festivals – held in spring and autumn. Real cider is available in summer. ♨Q✿⇌🖶(22,205)♣●P♿

Wath upon Dearne

Church House Ⓛ ✪
Montgomery Square, S63 7RZ
✪ 9am-midnight ☎ (01709) 879518
Marston's Pedigree; Ruddles Best Bitter; guest beers Ⓗ
Large pub with an impressive frontage set in a pedestrian square in the town centre, with excellent access to local bus services. It was built in 1810, consecrated by the nearby church in 1912, became a pub in the 1980s, and then a Wetherspoon in 2000. Handy for exploring the RSPB Old Moor Wetlands Centre and for Manvers, it serves a wide variety of beers from both national and local brewers, including the nearby Acorn and Wentworth breweries. Westons ciders are on handpull. ♨✿❶&🖶(22,220,229)●P♿

Wentworth

George & Dragon Ⓛ
85 Main Street, S62 7TN (stands back from road on B6090)
✪ 10-11 (10.30 Sun) ☎ (01226) 742440
⊕ georgeanddragonwentworth.co.uk
Taylor Landlord; guest beers Ⓗ
In a picturesque village, just 500 yards from Rotherham's only brewery, this free house offers

up to four ales from the brewery along with beers from local and national brewers. The pub has a car park and patio, and a grassed area at the rear with a children's adventure playground and a craft shop. Home-cooked food is popular here. This local is near to historic Wentworth Woodhouse and Hoober Stand, and has been licensed since 1804.
🏚Q🌣🌓🗑(44,227)P‧

Whiston

Chequers Inn
Pleasley Road, S60 4HB (on A618, 1½ miles from M1 jct 33)
🌣 12 (4 Mon & Tue)-11; 12-11.30 Fri & Sat
☎ (01709) 829168 ⊕ thechequers.whiston.co.uk
Jennings Cumberland Ale; Tetley Bitter; guest beers Ⓗ
Next to a 13th-century thatched barn, this friendly local replaced the original inn when the road was widened in 1933. One side of the bar acts as a taproom, with a split-level lounge to the right. The large garden features a barbecue area. In the heart of Whiston, the pub is a regular local CAMRA award winner. The food is home-cooked by chefs. Features include quiz nights, discos, occasional live music and scooter club meets. Close to Whiston Meadows and Ulley Country Park.
🌣🌓🗑(21,25,25A)♣P‧

Hind ✓
285 East Bawtry Road, S60 4ET (on A631 link road between M1 and M18)
🌣 12-11 (midnight Thu-Sat) ☎ (01709) 704351
Taylor Landlord; Tetley Bitter; guest beers Ⓗ
Large pub, built for Mappins Brewery of Rotherham in 1936, on the border of Whiston and Rotherham and serving the extensive estates in the area. Originally known as King Edward VIII, it was renamed when the king abdicated. Since refurbishment the interior has been opened out, creating good disabled access. There are extensive gardens and a patio to the rear, with a snooker table upstairs (membership required to play). Daytime and evening food is popular, and third-of-a-pint tasting racks are available. Historic Canklow Woods are a short walk away.
🏚Q🌣🌓🗑(10,10A,19B)P‧

Wombwell

Anglers Rest Ⓛ
66 Park Street, S73 0HS (on Park St 5 mins' walk from town centre)
🌣 5-midnight; 12-1am Sat; 12-midnight Sun
☎ (01226) 751031
Black Sheep Best Bitter; guest beers Ⓗ
Small three-room roadside locals' pub. The enthusiastic activist landlady leads locals into traditional games, fundraising events, books, chess and anything else she can think of. Top-quality real cider or perry is always available alongside a varying range of guest beers, all from small or microbreweries. One beer is always from local Wombwell brewery Acorn. The outside drinking area has a wood-burning stove for those cold nights. Q🌣🌓🗑(22,222,226)♣P‧

Wortley

Wortley Arms Ⓛ
Halifax Road, S35 7DB

🌣 12-11.30 (midnight Sat; 9 Sun) ☎ (01142) 885218
⊕ wortley-arms.co.uk
Taylor Landlord; guest beers Ⓗ
If you are after quality ale and excellent food then the Wortley Arms is certainly worth a visit. Upstairs is Montagu's fine dining restaurant run by chef Andy Gabbitas; early booking is advised. The main traditional bar offers a superb range of ales from local breweries. Accessed through a revolving door, the building dates back to 1753 with lots of exposed stone, timber beams and an inglenook fireplace. 🏚Q🌓🗑(23,29)P

Wortley Mens Club & Institute Ⓛ
Reading Room Lane, S35 7DB (directly behind the Wortley Arms on A629)
🌣 2 (11.30 Sat)-11; 11.30-10.30 Sun ☎ (0114) 2882066
Taylor Landlord; guest beer Ⓗ
In the heart of a pretty village and surrounded by open countryside, this local with an opulent interior and ornate ceilings has a small bar area, a plush lounge and a large games room. The outside of the club is equally impressive, with traditional timber framing and a small beer garden. The guest ale is from a local brewery and a changing guest draught cider is always available. Show your CAMRA membership card or a copy of this Guide for entry.
🏚Q🌣🗑(23,29)♣P

YORKSHIRE (WEST)

Ackworth

Angel
Wakefield Road, WF7 7AB (on A638 ½ mile W of A628/A638 roundabout)
🌣 12-3, 5-11 (11.30 Fri & Sat); 12-11 Sun ☎ (01977) 611276
Black Sheep Best Bitter; guest beers Ⓗ
One of five real ale pubs and clubs in Ackworth, the Angel has a thoughtful and well-designed open-plan layout centred around a large arched wooden bar. High-quality home-made bar meals using local produce are served during the week, plus a Sunday lunchtime carvery. There is a popular quiz on Wednesday evening. The adjacent Dando Way provides a good start and finish point for walking/cycling in the nearby country park and surrounding area. The Ackworth Road Runners set out from here on Tuesday and Thursday evenings.
🏚🌣🌓🗑(35,245,485)P‧

Addingham

Swan Inn Ⓛ ✓
106 Main Street, LS29 0NS
🌣 5.30-11; 12-2, 5-11 Fri; 12-midnight Sat; 12-10.30 Sun
☎ (01943) 831999 ⊕ swan-addingham.co.uk
Beer range varies Ⓗ
Friendly village local retaining a four-room layout arranged around a central bar. The stone-flagged bar, snug and taproom are all warmed by real fires in winter. Live bands perform on Saturday evenings, Monday is folk night and Wednesday is quiz night – see the website for additional events. Food is served Wednesday, Friday and Saturday evenings and Friday, Saturday and Sunday lunchtimes. At least four beers are available, sourced from the SIBA and Enterprise lists. Well-behaved dogs are welcome.
🏚🌣🌓🗑(X84,762,765)♣P

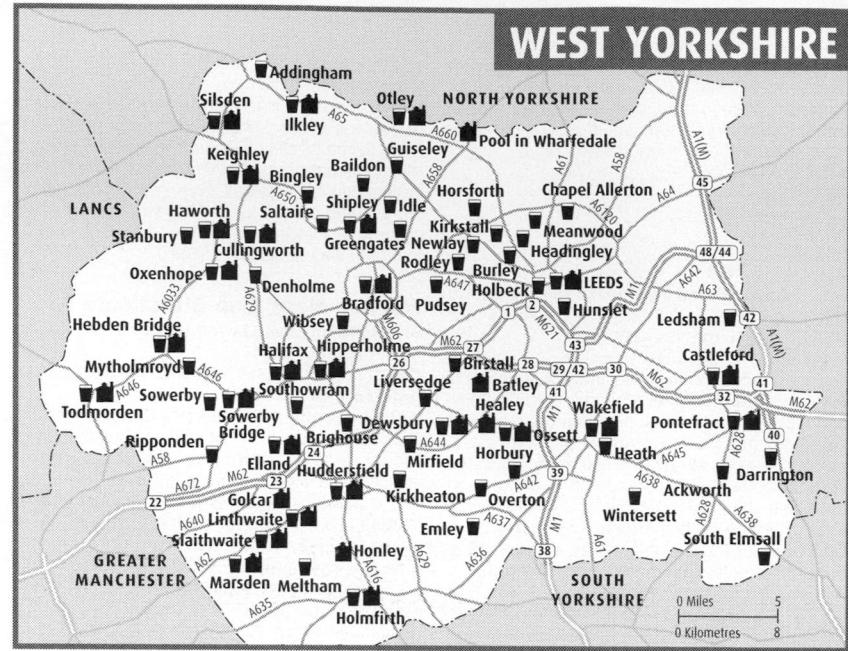

WEST YORKSHIRE

Baildon

Junction 🅛

1 Baildon Road, BD17 6AB (on Otley road)
🌣 12-midnight (1am Fri & Sat) ☎ (01274) 582009
Fuller's ESB; Oakham JHB; Saltaire Blonde; Tetley Bitter; guest beers 🅗
On a busy road junction, this award-winning friendly local has three rooms – bar, games and lounge. Three guest beers complement the four regulars. Home-made food is available weekday lunchtimes, and at other times by arrangement. A quiz night is held Thursday and a jam session Sunday. An annual beer festival takes place in late July. Sporting events are popular on TV. A microbrewery has been installed and is due to start operating soon. Plans for another room are ongoing. ❀✪◖≑(Shipley)🚋(656,658,737)♣♠⚑⚑

Bingley

Brown Cow 🅛 ✅

Ireland Bridge, BD16 2QX
🌣 12-3, 5-11 (midnight Fri); 12-midnight Sat; 12-10.30 Sun
☎ (01274) 564345
Taylor Dark Mild, Golden Best, Best Bitter, Landlord, Ram Tam 🅗
On the riverside next to a 13th-century bridge, a warm welcome awaits both drinkers and diners at this comfortable hostelry. Not all tables are set for dining, and settees, armchairs and bar stools are provided. An upstairs function room plays host to a variety of local groups. A small range of Belgian bottled beers is stocked. Live music features on Saturday, quiz night is Tuesday. Book ahead for meals, especially at weekends. Free Wi-Fi provided. ♨✿✪◖≑🚋(662,760)P⚑

Myrtle Grove 🅛 ✅

141 Main Street, BD16 1AJ
🌣 8am-midnight ☎ (01274) 568637

Greene King Abbot; Ruddles Best Bitter; guest beers 🅗
Town-centre Wetherspoon outlet that is in its 13th year. Originally a cinema, the large single room retains the high ceiling, and cosy alcoves with comfortable high-backed settles occupy the back wall. The pub is popular with all age groups and has a well-established clientele of regulars. Five guest beers are always available, with local breweries represented, such as Saltaire, Naylor's, Elland, Ossett, Moorhouse's and Daleside. Regular Meet the Brewer evenings are hosted. The train station is close by. Q◖♿≑🚋(662,760)♠

Birstall

Horse & Jockey ✅

97 Low Lane, WF17 9HB (200yds W of marketplace)
🌣 12-midnight ☎ (01924) 472559
Black Sheep Golden Sheep; Copper Dragon Golden Pippin; guest beers 🅗
The former Horse & Groom, a country-style pub first licensed in the 1750s, lies west of the village centre. The open-plan bar divides into four alcoves and has half-panelled walls and beamed ceilings. Photos show it as having been a Kirkstall Brewery house. Darts, dominoes and pool are played. Outside is a paved patio drinking and smoking area. Good-value pub food is served weekday lunchtimes (no food Wed), with plans to expand. Pub policy is that hats must be removed. ❀◖🚋♣P⚑

Bradford

Castle Hotel 🅛

20 Grattan Road, BD1 2LU
🌣 12-11; 1-9 Sun ☎ 07967 144474
Jennings Cumberland Ale; guest beers 🅗
An established real ale pub in the city centre within easy reach of the transport network, this former

Webster's house now stocks a changing range of beers, supporting local breweries, including an ale from Old Spot Brewery. A real cider is often available. The 19th-century building features a semicircular wraparound bar, forming two almost separate areas, with a dartboard and TV at one end. Live folk music is on Friday.
&≡(Forster Square/Interchange)🚌(662)●

City Vaults 🅛 ✅
33 Hustlergate, BD1 1NS
✪ 10.30-11 (midnight Fri & Sat) ☎ (01274) 739697
Black Sheep Best Bitter; Salamander Golden Salamander; Saltaire Blonde; Tetley Bitter 🅗
Bustling city-centre pub in former bank premises opposite the famous Wool Exchange. There are five ales on handpump, with local breweries strongly supported, and sometimes a seasonal beer from Salamander. Home-cooked food is served all day (until 6pm Sat and Sun). The pub retains a traditional feel, with fine stained glass and a wrought-iron spiral staircase to the upper drinking area. There is live music Saturday, jazz every Sunday, and a popular quiz on Wednesday.
❀◑&≡(Forster Square/Interchange)🚌●⌐

Corn Dolly 🅛
110 Bolton Road, BD1 4DE
✪ 11.30-11; 12-10.30 Sun ☎ (01274) 720219
Black Sheep Best Bitter; Everards Tiger Best Bitter; guest beers 🅗
Award-winning pub that has been a Guide entry for many years, only a 10-minute walk from the city centre. It used to be called the Wharf as it was near the former Bradford canal, and it opened its doors for the first time in 1834. An open-plan layout incorporates a separate games area. Good-value food is served weekday lunchtimes. It is popular for a pint before Bradford City matches. A collection of over 1000 pump clips adorn the beams.
🏨❀◑&≡(Forster Square/Interchange) 🚌(611,640)●P⌐

Fighting Cock 🅛
21-23 Preston Street, BD7 1JE
✪ 11.30-11; 12-10.30 Sun ☎ (01274) 726907
Copper Dragon Golden Pippin; Greene King Abbot; Taylor Best Bitter, Landlord; Theakston Old Peculier; guest beers 🅗
Popular, unassuming pub, just a short walk or bus ride from the city centre. Twelve real ales are usually on sale, including at least one dark beer. Additionally ciders, foreign bottled beers and fruit wines are stocked. The pub attracts a wide variety of customers, from loyal locals to well-travelled real ale enthusiasts. Lunches are served Monday to Saturday. A regular award winner and local CAMRA Pub of the Year 2011. 🏨◑&🚌(607,615,636)●

Ginger Goose 🅛 ✅
Market Street, BD1 1LH
✪ 10-11 ☎ (01274) 390584
Ilkley Mary Jane; Saltaire Blonde; guest beers 🅗
Large open-plan pub just a few minutes' walk from the bus and train interchange. It is friendly and welcoming, serving up six real ales, many supporting local microbreweries. There is a first-floor function room but the only bar is on the ground floor, with easy access throughout for all visitors. The impressive City Hall is visible from the front of the pub.
◑&≡(Forster Square/Interchange)🚌

Haigy's 🅛 ✅
31 Lumb Lane, Manningham, BD8 7QU
✪ 5 (12 Sat)-2am; 2-11 Sun ☎ (01274) 731644
Tetley Mild, Bitter; guest beers 🅗
Friendly locals' pub, a former Bradford CAMRA Pub of the Year, on the edge of the city centre. It offers up to four guest ales, mainly from local micros, and Westons Old Rosie cider. The comfortable lounge sports a fine collection of porcelain teapots and an extensive range of pictures. It has a heated smoking area and a large-screen TV, and is popular with Bradford City and away fans on match days.
❀≡(Forster Square/Interchange)🚌(620,621)●P⌐

New Beehive Inn ★ 🅛
171 Westgate, BD1 3AA
✪ 12-11 (1am Fri & Sat); 6-11 Sun ☎ (01274) 721784
⊕ newbeehive.co.uk

INDEPENDENT BREWERIES

Barearts Todmorden
Barley Bottom Silsden (NEW)
Bob's Healcy
Brass Monkey Sowerby Bridge
Brewery Tap Leeds
Bridestones Hebden Bridge
Bridgehouse Oxenhope
Briscoe's Otley
Burley Street Leeds
Cap House Batley (NEW)
Clark's Wakefield
Eastwood Elland
Elland Elland
Empire Slaithwaite
Fernandes Wakefield
Five Towns Wakefield
Golcar Golcar
Goose Eye Keighley
Halifax Steam Hipperholme
Haworth Steam Haworth
Ilkley Ilkley
James & Kirkman Pontefract (NEW)
Kirkstall Leeds
Landlord's Friend Halifax
Leeds Leeds
Linfit Linthwaite
Little Valley Hebden Bridge
Magic Rock Huddersfield
Mallinsons Huddersfield
Milltown Huddersfield (NEW)
Nook Holmfirth
Oates Halifax (NEW)
Old Bear Keighley
Old Spot Cullingworth
Ossett Ossett
Owenshaw Mill Sowerby Bridge
Partners Dewsbury
Pennine Batley (NEW)
Rat Huddersfield (NEW)
Revolutions Castleford
Ridgeside Leeds
Riverhead Marsden
Rodham's Otley
Salamander Bradford
Saltaire Shipley
Sportsman Huddersfield
Summer Wine Honley
Tigertops Wakefield
Timothy Taylor Keighley
WharfeBank Pool in Wharfedale

Beer range varies ⊞
Gas-lit pub on the fringe of the city centre. Built in 1901, this imposing building deserves to be identified by CAMRA as one of Britain's Real Heritage Pubs for its multi-roomed interior. Note its external features, too. Beers are almost exclusively from local micros. A separate cellar bar offers weekend music, and folk and jazz can sometimes be experienced in the pub itself. See the splendid paintings in the back bar. No food is sold on Sunday. Three-star en-suite accommodation is available.
꧁꧂⚐⊙▣⇌(Forster Square)🚐(617,618)
♣♠P⌂⌐

Sir Titus Salt ⏛ ✅
Unit B, Windsor Baths, Morley Street, BD7 1AQ (behind Alhambra Theatre)
☼ 9am-midnight (1am Fri & Sat) ☎ (01274) 732853
Greene King Abbot; Ruddles Best Bitter; guest beers ⊞
An excellent conversion of former public baths by Wetherspoon. Named in honour of a local industrialist, the interior decoration includes photographs and other artefacts relating to his life and times. Close to the National Media Museum and the city's famous curry houses.
Q⊙&⇌(Forster Square/Interchange)🚐♠

Sparrow Bier Café ⏚ ⏛
32 North Parade, BD1 3HZ
☼ 11-8 (11 Wed & Thu; midnight Fri & Sat)
⊕ thesparrowbradford.co.uk
Beer range varies ⊞
Welcome addition to the city-centre beer scene opened in 2011 by local enthusiasts. On two floors, it is simply furnished and features local art on the walls. Four rotating cask ales are from quality breweries such as Salamander, Kirkstall, Saltaire, Thornbridge and Magic Rock. There are always two real ciders on sale, together with an extensive range of international beers. No meals are provided but deli sandwiches and platters are available.
⇌(Forster Square/Interchange)🚐(622,662,680)♠

Brighouse

Red Rooster ⏛
123 Elland Road, Brookfoot, HD6 2QR (on A6025)
☼ 3 (12 Fri & Sat)-11; 12-10.30 Sun ☎ (01484) 713737
Abbeydale Deception; Marble Pint; Moorhouse's Blond Witch; Taylor Landlord; guest beers ⊞
Small stone pub that lies on the inside of a sharp bend approximately half a mile out of town. Its former four-roomed layout is still apparent, with a stone-flagged floor throughout. A charity week is held in mid-August and a beer festival in September. Part of the decking area to the front is covered to provide a smoking shelter. Live music features on the last Sunday afternoon of the month. Guest ales always include a dark beer.
☼🚐(571,E8)♣⌐

Richard Oastler ⏛ ✅
Bethell Street, HD6 1JN SE145227
☼ 9am-11 (1am Fri & Sat) ☎ (01484) 401756
Greene King Abbot; Ruddles Best Bitter; guest beers ⊞
A Grade II-listed former Methodist chapel converted to a successful Wetherspoon pub. It has a magnificent but inaccessible upper floor with original chapel pews, and the impressive ceiling is

retained. Eight guest ales are served, always including a dark beer, and local microbreweries are regularly featured. Two traditional ciders from the Westons range are also available. The usual good-value Wetherspoon food menu is served all day.
☼⊙&⇌🚐♠⌐

Castleford

Glass Blower ⏛ ✅
15 Bank Street, WF10 1JD (just off town centre)
☼ 8am-midnight (1am Fri & Sat) ☎ (01977) 520390
Greene King Abbot; Ruddles Best Bitter; guest beers ⊞
Characterful former post office converted by Wetherspoon. The name refers to the town's history of glass bottle manufacture, with some examples on display. Locally born sculptor Henry Moore is represented via reproductions adorning the walls. It is a popular venue for families and rugby supporters on match days, and Meet the Brewer events and brewery visits are held. Excellent-value food is served all day and children are welcome in the family area. Q☼⊙&⇌🚐♠⌐

Junction ⏛
Carlton Street, WF10 1EE (in town centre)
☼ 12-11 (midnight Fri & Sun) ☎ (01977) 278867
Beer range varies ⊞
Town-centre community pub just two minutes' walk from bus and train stations. Open fires and lively banter keep the large horseshoe-shaped bar warm and friendly. There is a separate stove-heated snug, which is also available for functions and meetings. Up to six guest ales, mainly from Yorkshire micros, including Ridgeside beers from the wood, are served, as well as a good selection of Sam Smith's bottled beers. Quiz night is Wednesday. Rare for the area is a bar billiards table. Dog- and child-friendly. ꧁⇌🚐♣

Shoulder of Mutton ⏛
18 Methley Road, WF10 1LX (on A6032 500yds from town centre)
☼ 12-3, 7-midnight; 12-4, 7-1am Sat; 12-4, 7-midnight Sun ☎ (01977) 736039
Tetley Dark Mild, Bitter; guest beers ⊞
A traditional free house that started life as a farmhouse in 1632, now packed with breweriana by the landlord, known as Tetley Dave Parker, a great supporter of micros and a fount of knowledge on pub-keeping. He is justifiably proud of his many cellarmanship awards. There is no pool table or jukebox, just lively conversation. Motorcycle meets and poetry readings feature, as does live music on the last Sunday, and the George Formby Society on the last Wednesday, of each month.
꧁Q☼&▣⇌🚐(153,189)♣P⌐

Cullingworth

George Hotel ⏛
Station Road, BD13 5HN
☼ 4 (12 Wed & Thu)-11; 12-midnight Fri & Sat; 12-11 Sun ☎ (01535) 275566 ⊕ thegeorgecullingworth.co.uk
Old Spot Light But Dark, Spot Light, OSB, Spot o' Bother; guest beers ⊞
A lovely old-fashioned village pub rescued from oblivion by local brewery owners, in a pleasant setting by the church. Four distinct drinking areas, one primarily for dining, welcome the visitor. The customer will find good news at the bar, as a fine

range of the local beer is always available; Old Spot Brewery is nearby. Children are welcome until 9pm. An extensive and imaginative food menu will impress. The pub dog is ever curious but lovable. ♨Q☆◑▶️☒(697)♣P

Darrington

Spread Eagle 🅛
Estcourt Road, WF8 3AP (W of A1 on main road through village)
☼ 12-3 (not Mon), 5-11; 12-10.30 Sun ☎ (01977) 699698
Beer range varies Ⓗ
A friendly and welcoming community pub in the heart of the village. The landlady is particularly adventurous in her choice of three guest ales. Good-quality food is served both in the bar and a small dining area (no food Sun eve or all day Mon). Monday is quiz night. There is a pleasant function room for hire. It is said there have been sightings here of the ghost of a boy who was shot for horse rustling in 1685. Q☆◑▶️🅖☒(408)P⬳

Denholme

New Inn 🅛
Keighley Road, BD13 4JT
☼ 4-11; 2-midnight Sat; 2-11 Sun ☎ (01274) 833871
Old Spot Light But Dark; Tetley Bitter; guest beers Ⓗ
A warm welcome is assured at this lovely pub that supports local microbreweries and often offers guest ales from further away. Local beers from Salamander and Goose Eye are often found here, and all beers are keenly priced. Tuesday night hosts a jam session while on Thursday free snacks are available from 6pm. The pub sits high on the hillside with stunning views. For the energetic the Great Northern walking/cycling trail is nearby. ♨Q☆☒(696,697)♣P⬳

Dewsbury

Huntsman 🅛
Chidswell Lane, Shaw Cross, WF12 7SW (400yds from A653/B6128 jct)
☼ 12-3 (not Mon), 7 (5 Thu & Fri)-11 ☎ (01924) 275700
Taylor Landlord; guest beers Ⓗ
Under half a mile from Leeds Road, this is a homely country pub with a warm atmosphere and a choice of four ales, including two interesting guests. It has excellent views to the front and rear. With one large room and two smaller rooms, the converted farm cottages are made cosy with horse brasses, a Yorkshire range and other period features. Lunches are served Tuesday to Saturday, evening meals Thursday and Friday. The house beer, Chidswell Bitter by Highwood, may be available. ♨☆◑▲☒(205,119)P

Leggers Inn
Calder Valley Marina, Mill Street East, WF12 9BD (off B6409; follow brown signs to Canal Basin)
☼ 10.30-11 (midnight Fri & Sat); 11-10.30 Sun ☎ (01924) 502846
Abbeydale Moonshine; Everards Tiger Best Bitter; guest beers Ⓗ
Once the hayloft above stables by the canal basin, the building's low beams, powerful stove, deep seating and quirky items on display make for a unique atmosphere. Six beers listed on the school blackboard include ale from Rooster's, plus one rotating cider. Outside, a large decked area is

excellent in summer. Light meals are served all day until 8pm and there is a pool table and a function room. Bus and rail stations are just within a mile. ♨☆◑♣☒P⬳

Shepherds Boy 🅛 ✅
157 Huddersfield Road, WF13 2RP (on A644 ½ mile from town centre)
☼ 4-11; 3-midnight Fri; 12-midnight Sat; 12-11 Sun ☎ (01924) 454116
Ossett Pale Gold; guest beers Ⓗ
Ten minutes' walk from the railway station, this Ossett Brewery pub, with its nicely reconstructed interior, has many retained or reinstated original features and four separate, comfortable drinking areas. A trademark brick arch separates the front and rear of the pub. A well-balanced range of beers includes several from the Ossett group, varying local guest beers and one from Fuller's. At least three choices of real cider and perry are always available. The pub hosts two well-supported annual beer festivals. ☆🅖⇌☒♣●P⬳

West Riding Licensed Refreshment Rooms ♛ 🅛 ✅
Railway Station, Wellington Road, WF13 1HF (platform 2 Dewsbury Station)
☼ 12-11 Mon; 11-11 Tue, Wed & Sun; 11-midnight Thu & Fri; 10-midnight Sat ☎ (01924) 459193 ⊕ imissedthetrain.com
Black Sheep Best Bitter; Taylor Dark Mild, Landlord; guest beers Ⓗ
Multi award-winning pub in a Grade II-listed Victorian building. A Transpennine Rail Ale Trail mainstay, it serves a broad range of rotating beers as well as two real ciders or perries, often from West Yorkshire producer Pure North. The pub is famed for good-value, quality food. An annual beer festival is held in June, with live music every weekend in summer. A large, decked, partially covered patio serves as a beer garden. Lunches are available daily, evening meals Tuesday to Thursday. ♨☆◑🅖⇌☒●⬳

Elland

Drop Inn 🅛 ✅
12 Elland Lane, HX5 9DU (off the link road from the A629 to the town centre)
☼ 4-11; 12-midnight Fri & Sat; 12-11 Sun ☎ (01422) 387484
Ossett Pale Gold, Yorkshire Blonde, Silver King; guest beer Ⓗ
Stone flags and floorboards, and a brick arch between rooms, exhibit the Ossett Brewery pub style. French Renaissance pictures add to the decor along with cigar containers, stone jars and tankards. A stove occupies a large cottage fireplace in the side room. Food is served Friday lunch only. Beer festivals take place in March and September and a quiz is held every Thursday. Guest beers are from Fuller's, other Ossett group breweries and microbreweries. Outside is a heated smoking shelter. Q☆◑☒(278,503)♣⬳

Emley

White Horse 🅛 ✅
2 Chapel Lane, HD8 9SP (on main road through village)
☼ 12 (4 Mon)-11 ☎ (01924) 849823
⊕ white-horse-emley.co.uk
Ossett Pale Gold, Emley Cross, Excelsior; guest beers Ⓗ

Friendly local that is Ossett Brewery's only tenanted pub, traditional in style with a stone floor and range. A small flight of steps leads up to another room with a stove, which is used as a family room. The regular Ossett beers are complemented by five guests from small local and further afield breweries; there is always a mild, stout or porter on handpump as well as a real cider. Bar meals are served, as is Sunday lunch. ▲⌂✿◑➾(232)♣♠P¹⌐

Greengates

Albion Inn

25 New Line, BD10 9AS (on main Keighley-Leeds road)
✪ 12-11 (midnight Fri & Sat) ☎ (01274) 613211
Acorn Barnsley Bitter; Tetley Bitter; guest beers Ⓗ
Busy roadside local on a regular bus route. It has an L-shaped lounge and a separate taproom where pub games are played. The pub is home to a thriving social club and strangers are made welcome. Traditional values are maintained in this friendly neighbourhood pub, where consistent beer quality is due to dedicated staff. Look out for the Grafters Tea on Fridays, after work. ◲➾(760)♣P

Guiseley

Coopers Ⓛ ✔

4-6 Otley Road, LS20 8AH (opp Morrisons on A65)
✪ 12-11 (midnight Fri & Sat) ☎ (01943) 878835
Black Sheep Best Bitter; Copper Dragon Golden Pippin; Taylor Golden Best; guest beers Ⓗ
A light, modern, airy bar/diner converted from a former Co-operative store, and now a Market Town Tavern. Eight ales are served, generally from Yorkshire and northern independents and micros, with a dedicated dark beer pump and a large selection of continental bottled beers. A diverse range of meals is available until 9pm. The large upstairs function room has regular music events and a comedy club, and this area also serves as extra dining space. Q✿◑♿⇌➾(33,33A,97)♠¹⌐

Guiseley Factory Workers Club Ⓛ

6 Town Street, LS20 9DT (in Towngate near to St Oswald's church)
✪ 1-11 (midnight Fri); 11.30-midnight Sat; 11-11 Sun
☎ (01943) 874793 ⊕ guiseleyfactoryworkersclub.co.uk
Tetley Bitter; guest beers Ⓗ
Founded over 100 years ago by the Yeadon and Guiseley Factory Workers Union, this is a friendly club serving three changing guest ales; normally one of these will be a dark beer. There is a small lounge bar, a larger concert room and a snooker room with two tables. The club holds an annual beer festival in April. Show your CAMRA membership card or a copy of this Guide for entry. Former National CAMRA Club of the Year. ✿⇌➾(33A,97,737)♣P¹⌐

Halifax

Big Six

10 Horsfall Street, Saville Park, HX1 3HG (off A646 Skircoat Moor road at King Cross) SE081241
✪ 4 (3.30 Fri)-11; 11-11 Sat & Sun ☎ (01422) 350169
Courage Best Bitter; guest beers Ⓗ
An unusual pub in the middle of a terrace of houses adjacent to the Free School Lane recreation ground. Dogs are always welcome at this busy and friendly venue. A through corridor separates the bar and

games room from the two lounges. Memorabilia from the Big Six mineral water company, which operated from the premises a century ago, adorn the walls. Three changing guest beers from regional or microbreweries are sold. A quiz features every Monday. ▲Q✿➾(577,832)♣

Dirty Dick's Food & Ale Emporium Ⓛ

1 Clare Road, HX1 2HZ
✪ 12-11 ☎ 07887 510354
Empire Dirty Dicks Ale; guest beers Ⓗ
Impressive Grade II-listed building built in 1931 from timbers from HMS Newcastle, an 1860 gunship. Many of its original features remain, including the oak panelling. The pub's new owner has brought back this traditional local, also reinstating the popular beer triangle. You will not find loud music or entertainment here; with up to eight rotating guest beers enticing customers it is the place to be for drinking and socialising. ▲◑⇌➾

New Prospect Ⓛ

1 Crowroyd Place, Range Bank, HX3 6JR (best reached from New Bank A58 via Prospect St)
✪ closed Mon winter; 4 (12 Fri-Sun)-midnight
☎ (01422) 367232 ⊕ thenewprospectinn.co.uk
Beer range varies Ⓗ
This white-painted local is prominent on the hillside overlooking the end of the Burdock Way viaduct. The interior has been partially opened out while retaining distinct spaces. The beer garden with views over Halifax is popular with families in summer and has a play area. The pub has gained a reputation for its restaurant facilities, and guest beers are usually from LocAle microbreweries. The Canopy adjoining the entrance provides a covered smoking area. ▲✿◑➾P¹⌐

Sportsman Inn Ⓛ

Bradford Old Road, Swalesmoor, HX3 6UG (off A647, 1 mile N of centre)
✪ 12-2.30 (not Mon), 6-11 (midnight Fri); 12-midnight Sat; 12-11 Sun ☎ (01422) 367000
Tetley Bitter; guest beer Ⓗ
Set on a hilltop, next to a popular leisure complex that includes a dry ski slope, from where you get good views of Halifax and the surrounding countryside. It is a family-friendly traditional pub, with exposed stone walls, old beams and a fireplace, popular for both traditional ales and food. It specialises in beer from local microbreweries, serving up to seven rotating guests. Food is available both lunchtime and evening, making this place a popular venue for all. ▲⌂✿◑➾(576)P¹⌐

Three Pigeons ★ Ⓛ ✔

1 Sun Fold, South Parade, HX1 2LX
✪ 4 (12 Fri-Sun)-11.30 ☎ (01422) 347001
Ossett Pale Gold, Big Red, Excelsior; guest beers Ⓗ
Built by Websters in 1932, the Three Pigeons retains many of the original Art Deco fixtures and fittings. Its three main rooms are connected by an octagonal drinking lobby where drinks are served. Owned by Ossett Brewery, the pub serves beers from its own range and up to four guests. A range of Belgian bottled beers is also available. Popular with drinkers, the pub has a lively atmosphere while retaining its traditional appeal. ▲✿⇌➾♠¹⌐

Haworth

Fleece Inn L ✓

67 Main Street, BD22 8DA
☼ 12-11 (11.30 Fri); 10-11.30 Sat; 10-10.30 Sun
☎ (01535) 642172 ⊕ fleece-inn.co.uk
Taylor Golden Best, Best Bitter, Landlord, Ram Tam Ⓗ
A three-storey former coaching inn halfway up the historic steep cobbled Haworth main street. The Haworth brass band can be heard outside on some evenings rehearsing in their band room above the pub, which offers good beer, food and accommodation to visitors and is popular with locals. The beer garden is three storeys up from the bar. A range of foreign bottled beers is available.
🏨🏕️⇦🕭🖧🛱🛆🚶🚲(KWVR)🚌(663,664,665)♣♦🍴

Heath

King's Arms ★ L ✓

Heath Common, WF1 5SL (off A655 Wakefield-Normanton Rd)
☼ 12-11 (midnight Fri & Sat) ☎ (01924) 377527
Ossett Silver King, Yorkshire Blonde, seasonal beer; Tetley Bitter Ⓗ
Stone terrace from the 1700s converted to a pub in 1841, the King's Arms has stone-flagged floors, gas lighting, oak settles and blazing fires in winter. At the rear is a conservatory overlooking a large beer garden. There is wheelchair access. A weekly quiz is held every Tuesday at 9.30pm.
🏨Q🏕️🕭🖧🛆🚌(188)🍴

Hebden Bridge

Moyles L

4-10 New Road, HX7 8AD (on A646 opp canal marina)
☼ 12-midnight ☎ (01427) 845272 ⊕ moyles.com
Pictish Brewers Gold; guest beers Ⓗ
A modern and upmarket bar with a restaurant on the right of the entrance; the bar has tables, chairs and sofas over to the left. Five beers are served in these comfortable surroundings, which attract local drinkers as well as diners. Bar snacks are available lunchtimes and Monday-Thursday evenings. Tasting notes for the beer range are displayed on the bar counter. Discounts are offered to CAMRA members. Q🏕️⇦🕭🛆🚶🚲🚌(590,591,592)🍴

Stubbing Wharf L

King Street, HX7 6LU (on A646 ½ mile W of Hebden Bridge)
☼ 12-11 (midnight Fri & Sat); 12-10.30 Sun
☎ (01422) 844107 ⊕ stubbingwharf.com
Black Sheep Best Bitter; Copper Dragon Golden Pippin; Taylor Landlord; guest beers Ⓗ
A popular local with an increasing reputation for food, so tables can be limited during dining times. Three guest beers and two ciders are always available here, Calderdale's 2012 Cider Pub of the Year. Apple days and cider festivals are notable attractions. Situated next to the canal, there is outdoor seating beside the towpath, and walking groups and others can take advantage of the function room. Events include open mic every Wednesday, a quiz every Thursday and monthly storytelling. 🏨🏕️🕭🛆🚌(590,592)♦🍴

Hipperholme

Cock o' the North L

The Conclave, South Edge Works, Brighouse Road, HX3 8EF (on A644)
☼ 5 (4 Fri)-11; 12-11 Sat & Sun ☎ 07974 544980
⊕ halifax-steam.co.uk
Halifax Steam Lily Fogg, Jamaican Ginger, Uncle Jon, Child Catcher, seasonal beers Ⓗ
The sectional building shared with the brewery, next to the imposing red-brick Vulcan works, belies a well-fitted-out single-roomed bar with polished floors and fittings, inspired by 1930s Art Deco ocean liners. The atmosphere is relaxed, with a friendly, varied clientele. The bar is a showcase for the extensive range of Halifax Steam beers, with at least 10 on sale. It has two or three beer festivals a year. Wednesday is quiz night and the second Sunday of every other month features Beer and Hymns. Q🏕️🚌(548,549)P

Travellers Inn L ✓

53 Tanhouse Hill, HX3 8HN
☼ 12-midnight (11 Sun & Mon; 11.30 Tue & Wed); 12-11 Sun
☎ (01422) 202494
Fuller's London Pride; Ossett Pale Gold, Yorkshire Blonde, Excelsior; guest beers Ⓗ
Opposite the former railway station, this traditional 18th-century, stone-built local has taken in adjoining cottages to create a series of distinct spaces. The floor is stone-flagged in the lower area, with plain floorboards in the upper part. Children and dogs are welcome until 7pm when quiet. There is a small south-facing roadside seating area. A covered yard with heating is provided for smokers. Guest beers include two from Ossett, Riverhead or Fernandes, and a dark beer.
🏨🏕️🚌(255,548,549)♦🍴

Holmfirth

Rose & Crown (Nook) L ✓

7 Victoria Square, HD9 2DN (down alley off Hollowgate)
☼ 11.30 (12 Sun)-midnight ☎ (01484) 682373
⊕ thenookbrewhouse.co.uk
Nook Yorks, Best, Blond, Red, Oat Stout; guest beers Ⓗ
Holmfirth is notable for being the location for the filming of Last of the Summer Wine, and the Rose & Crown is a favourite of locals and tourists alike. The pub dates from 1754, and has appeared more than 30 times in this Guide. Known as the Nook, it serves home-cooked food all day and has been dispensing beers from its own Nook Brewhouse since 2009. There is a popular folk club every Sunday evening, and real ale festivals throughout the year, with the main one over the August bank holiday. 🏨🏕️🕭🛆🚌(308,312,313)♣♦🍴

Horbury

Cricketers Arms ♟ L ✓

22 Cluntergate, WF4 5AG (on eastern edge of town)
☼ 12-11; 11-midnight Fri & Sat ☎ 07788 506797
Black Sheep Best Bitter; Taylor Dark Mild, Landlord; guest beers Ⓗ
A former Tetley's house that has now reopened as a genuine free house. The pub has had a tasteful refurbishment that has extended the length of the bar. There is a bus stop close by with a frequent service to Wakefield and Dewsbury. Local CAMRA Pub of the Year 2011.
🏨Q🐕🏕️🚌(126,127,231)♣♦P🍴

Huddersfield

Grove ⎣

2 Spring Grove Street, HD1 4BP

☼ 12-11 (midnight Thu-Sat) ☎ (01484) 430113

Magic Rock Curious; Taylor Landlord; Thornbridge Jaipur IPA; guest beers ⊞

The Grove has an almost unrivalled choice of beer, with three permanent ales, eight handpumps dedicated to rotating beers from Thornbridge, Fuller's, Gadds', Dark Star, Marble, Durham, Buxton and Magic Rock breweries, and at least a further seven guest ales, many rare for the region. Mild, stout and strong ale are regularly available. In addition there are over 250 foreign bottled beers from Europe, the US and the rest of the world. This pub is an absolute gem and a connoisseur's delight. Q✿❀⊞⇌⊟●'─🍴

King's Head

St George's Square, HD1 1JF (in station buildings, on left when exiting station)

☼ 11.30-11; 12-10.30 Sun ☎ (01484) 511058

⊕ the-kings-head-huddersfield.co.uk

Bradfield Farmers Blonde; Taylor Landlord; guest beers ⊞

A popular Guide entry, this pub's distinctive character gives it an unmistakable individuality. Its sound management ensures that the 10 beers available are all top quality and sold at competitive prices. There are always two dark ales, and real cider on handpull is also available. A mosaic-tiled floor dominates the main room, which hosts live bands on Sunday afternoons, piano singalongs on Tuesday evenings, and monthly folk and blues sessions. It can get busy at weekends, but is well worth discovering. 🚋&⇌⊟●'─

Rat & Ratchet ⎣ ✓

40 Chapel Hill, HD1 3EB (on A616 below ring road)

☼ 3-midnight; 12-12.30am Fri & Sat; 12-11 Sun

☎ (01484) 542400

Ossett Silver King, Excelsior; guest beers ⊞

A perennial entry in the Guide, this multi award-winning pub returned to brewing with the establishment of the Rat Brewery in 2011. Alongside three of its own rotating Rat beers, Fuller's, Mallinsons, Pictish and Ossett feature regularly among its 13 handpumps. Beers always include a mild and a stout/porter. The pub was runner-up Yorkshire CAMRA Cider Pub of the Year 2010, and offers six ciders and two perries. Pub games are available and a quiz is held every Wednesday. ✿⇌⊟♣●P'─

Slubbers Arms ⎣

1 Halifax Old Road, Hillhouse, HD1 6HW (off A641)

☼ 12-11 ☎ (01484) 429032

Taylor Best Bitter, Landlord; guest beers ⊞

Friendly and inviting free house where the focus is firmly on quality ale and good conversation; it is a former Timothy Taylor pub, with a heritage of over 150 years. An assortment of memorabilia from Huddersfield's textile past, militaria and breweriana adorn the walls of this wedge-shaped, multi-room corner-terrace pub. Good-value pub fare is available at all times, and is particularly popular on match days, when the pub is busy. It has a large suntrap beer terrace/smoking area. A cider and a perry are always available. 🚋✿◖&⊟(363)●'─

Sportsman ♈ ⎣

1 St John's Road, HD1 5AY

☼ 12-11; 11-midnight Fri & Sat ☎ 07766 131123

⊕ undertheviaduct.com

Black Sheep Golden Ale; Taylor Landlord; guest beers ⊞

Restored 1930s pub that has won a CAMRA English Heritage Conservation Pub Design award. It has recently established its own on-site brewery, the Sportsman Brewing Company, and regularly features at least three of its own beers among its eight handpumps; these include dedicated handpumps for mild and stout/porter. Three ciders and a perry are also available. This pub has established itself as a firm favourite of the Huddersfield drinking scene, and was local CAMRA Pub of the Year in 2012. 🚋✿◖⇌⊟●'─

Star Inn ⎣

7 Albert Street, Folly Hall, HD1 3PJ (off A616)

☼ closed Mon; 5 (12 Sat)-11; 12-10.30 Sun

☎ (01484) 545443 ⊕ thestarinn.info

Pictish Brewers Gold; Taylor Best Bitter, Landlord; guest beers ⊞

Multi award-winning pub with a warm welcome for locals and visitors alike. There is a changing range of guest ales to suit all tastes, sourced nationally and locally, including a dedicated Mallinsons pump. With no jukebox, pool table or games machine, there is always a great atmosphere, with lively conversation around the bar and a real fire during winter months. The pub holds three beer festivals annually in its marquee, which are recognised as being among the best in the country. 🚋Q✿&⊟●'─

Vulcan

32 St Peter's Street, HD1 1RA

☼ 9am-2am ☎ (01484) 302040

Copper Dragon Golden Pippin; guest beers ⊞

A traditional town-centre pub with a long-standing licensee. It has five handpumps usually offering competitively priced beers from Yorkshire and Lancashire breweries – often Mallinsons and Moorhouse's. Bargain-priced lunches are available every day, and free food is served for regulars Friday teatime. There is a daily happy hour extended on Wednesday evenings. The pub attracts all age groups, catering for enthusiasts of pool, karaoke and televised horse racing on Racing UK. Live music is featured on Sunday evenings. ✿◖&⇌⊟♣●'─🍴

White Cross Inn

2 Bradley Road, Bradley, HD2 1XD (on A62, 3 miles from town centre, at Leeds Rd/Bradley Rd crossroads)

☼ 11.45-11 (midnight Fri & Sat); 12-10.30 Sun

☎ (01484) 425728

Copper Dragon Golden Pippin; John Smith's Bitter; guest beers ⊞

A cheerful pub serving a wide range of the community. The pub dates from 1806 and has a large lounge extending across both sides of the central bar, where the two regular beers are supplemented by three or four varied guests. Home-cooked food is served lunchtimes (no food Sat). The games area offers pool, darts and dominoes. A popular beer festival is held in February in the upstairs meeting room. ✿◖&⊟(202,203,229)♣P'─

Idle

Brewery Tap L
51 Albion Road, BD10 9QE
🕔 4-11 (midnight Thu-Sat); 2-11 Sun ☎ 07515 469441
Saltaire Blonde; Tetley Bitter; Wells Bombardier; guest beers Ⓗ
Single-roomed pub with an island bar, behind which is the cellar trap door and its vertiginous steps. This pub was part of the Trough Brewery estate until its demise. Locally famous for its regular live rock bands, it attracts talent and customers from afar. The garden area is well sheltered. Look around you for pithy mottoes as well as evidence of the Trough era, and ask about the ashes in the niche. Two different ciders are always on sale. The beer festival is in August.
🏵🖼(640,641,760)♣🍺

Symposium Ale & Wine Bar L ✅
7 Albion Road, BD10 9PY
🕔 12-2.30 (not Mon-Wed), 5.30-11; 12-11 Fri & Sat; 12-10.30 Sun ☎ (01274) 616587
Copper Dragon Golden Pippin; Thwaites Wainwright; guest beers Ⓗ
A Market Town Taverns pub that always has six real ales on. It is a popular bar/restaurant with a rolling beer festival, predominantly featuring northern breweries. Beers from many parts of the world are also on sale, draught and bottled, and the wine list is impressive. Excellent meals are available from an inventive menu with regular themes. The rear snug leads to an elevated terrace, popular in summer. This is a warm and quiet pub in an old suburban village, and easy to find.
🏵◑🖼(610,611,612)🏵

Ilkley

Bar T'at L ✅
7 Cuncliffe Road, LS29 9DZ
🕔 12-11 ☎ (01943) 608888
Black Sheep Best Bitter; Copper Dragon Golden Pippin; Ilkley Mary Jane; Taylor Landlord; guest beers Ⓗ
Popular side-street pub in the Market Town Taverns group, renowned for the quality of its beer and food. The four regular beers are supplemented by four guest ales, usually including a mild, stout or porter, plus brews from Yorkshire micros. A wide range of good foreign beers is available, bottled and draught. Home-cooked food is on the menu every day. This three-storey building has a music-free bar area and stands next to the main town centre car park. Q🏵◑🚲🖼🍺

Keighley

Boltmakers Arms 🍷 L ✅
117 East Parade, BD21 5HX
🕔 11-midnight (11 Mon); 12-11 Sun ☎ (01535) 661936
Taylor Dark Mild, Golden Best, Best Bitter, Landlord, Ram Tam; guest beers Ⓗ
Local CAMRA Pub of the Year 2012, this is a classic Keighley town centre pub – the de facto Taylor brewery tap. It has a tiny split-level layout, but this adds to the character of the place. Brewery, whisky and music memorabilia adorn the walls. The guest beer and handpulled cider are from various sources at the licensee's whim, and there is a fine selection of single malts. Quiz night is every Tuesday and occasional live music plays. 🏵🚲🖼♣🍺

Brown Cow L
5 Cross Leeds Street, BD21 2LQ (bottom of West Lane, corner of Oakworth Rd)
🕔 4-11; 12-10.30 Sun 🌐 browncowkeighley.co.uk
Taylor Dark Mild, Golden Best, Best Bitter, Landlord, Ram Tam; guest beers Ⓗ
Warm, friendly local, with a comfortably furnished lounge and a small separate meeting room. The pub features local breweriana including the original sign from Bradford's Trough Brewery. The licensees are keen local historians and the landlord is the official town mace bearer and steward. Guest beers are sourced mainly from local micros. The pub has a no bad language policy favoured by its customers. 🏵🖼♣P

Cricketers Arms
Coney Lane, BD21 5JE
🕔 11.30-11 (midnight Fri & Sat); 12-11 Sun
☎ (01535) 669912 🌐 cricketersarmskeighley.co.uk
Yates Bitter; guest beers Ⓗ
Welcoming pub on the quieter side of town, only seven minutes' walk from the railway station and five minutes from the bus station. Alongside the regular Yates Bitter, the guest beer range features ales from regional and microbreweries that are rare for the area. A selection of bottled beers is also offered. Occasional beer festivals take place, and the pub is a regular live music venue. 🏵🚲🖼🏵

Kirkheaton

Yeaton Cask L
4 Town Road, HD5 0HW (at crossroads in centre of village)
🕔 4-9 Mon; 4-11 Tue; 12-11 (11.30 Fri & Sat); 12-10.30 Sun ☎ 07796 641003 🌐 yeatoncask.co.uk
Hawkshead Red; Thwaites Wainwright; guest beers Ⓗ
A true community local that reopened in 2010 after an extensive renovation, where modern sits happily alongside traditional. This genuine free house is a real ale oasis, with seven handpumps serving four guests ales, a real cider and a selection of bottle-conditioned beers. The house beer is from a West Yorkshire microbrewery. The pub is a past CAMRA Pub of the Season. Live music features with a band on the first Sunday of the month (check the website for events). 🏵🏵◑🖼(262)🍺P🏵

Ledsham

Chequers Inn
Claypit Lane, LS25 5LP (near A1M jct 42)
🕔 11-11; closed Sun ☎ (01977) 683135
Brown Cow Ledsham Sessions; John Smith's Bitter; Taylor Landlord; Theakston Best Bitter Ⓗ
A respected pub with a restaurant and garden, across the road from what is possibly Yorkshire's oldest church, All Saints. It has two rooms each side of the bar plus two small rooms with oak beams, log fires, jugs, brasses, sporting memorabilia and beer mats from previous guest ales to complement the old photos on the walls. A range of meals and sandwiches is served. There is an outside area for alfresco dining or just for drinking.
🏵🏵◑🖼(175,405)P🏵

Leeds: Burley

Fox & Newt L
9 Burley Street, LS3 1LD
🕔 12-11 (1am Fri; midnight Sat) ☎ (0113) 245 4527

Burley Street Laguna Sec, Bricklayer; guest beers ⊞
Just a short walk from the city centre, this is the home of Burley Street Brewhouse. The single room is wood-floored with a raised section at one end, and is frequented by a good mix of clientele from the city and the university. The centrally placed bar has eight handpumps, three dispensing the house regulars and seasonal beers. Guest beers are mainly sourced from local microbreweries. A regular pub quiz is held on Sunday night.
🏠⊕🏃♿�(49,50,50A)

Leeds: Chapel Allerton

Regent ℒ ✅
15-17 Regent Street, off Harrogate Road, LS7 4PE
✪ 12-11 (midnight Fri & Sat); 12-10.30 Sun
☎ (0113) 293 9395
Caledonian Deuchars IPA; Leeds Pale; Taylor Landlord; Tetley Bitter; guest beers ⊞
Dating from 1827, this stone-built two-roomed pub retains an old-fashioned feel despite sympathetic modernisation. A welcoming venue, it attracts a growing clientele of all ages, both male and female, drawn by the selection of guest ales. Quiz nights are Mondays, Tuesdays and Thursdays, a jukebox is available in one room and food is served lunchtimes and evenings. Occasional charity nights are held and TVs show current sporting events.
🏠⊕🚃♣P⌐

Three Hulats ℒ ✅
13 Harrogate Road, LS7 3NB
✪ 8am-midnight (1am Fri & Sat) ☎ (0113) 262 0524
Greene King Abbot; Ruddles Best Bitter; guest beers ⊞
Eight changing beers give a superb choice to the most discerning drinker in this local community pub located 200 yards downhill from the centre of Chapel Allerton. It holds regular beer festivals, has a Wednesday ale club with discounts for CAMRA members, and food until 10pm. Guest beers are from near and far, both micros and regionals. There is an outside drinking area and families are welcome until 9pm. A farmers' market is held on the last Sunday of the month. Q🏠⊕♿🚃P

Leeds: City Centre

Hop ℒ ✅
The Dark Arches, Granary Wharfe, Neville Street, LS1 4BR
✪ 12-midnight ☎ (0113) 243 9854 ⊕ the-hop.co.uk
Ossett Pale Gold, Yorkshire Blonde, Big Red, Silver King, Excelsior; guest beer ⊞
Directly under platform 17 of Leeds railway station in the Dark Arches, this venue offers a varied programme of weekly events ranging from a pub quiz to Sunday gatherings of live bands. Ten handpumps dispense the Ossett range along with ales from Riverhead, Fernandes, Rat and Fuller's as guests. It is a rare outlet in Leeds for perry. Food offerings include award-winning pies from AJ Pies of Huddersfield. Disabled access to the ground floor with a stage area is situated on the first floor gallery. 🏠🚃♥⌐

Mr Foley's Cask Ale House ℒ
159 The Headrow, LS1 5RG
✪ 11-11 (1am Fri & Sat) ☎ (0113) 242 9674
York Guzzler; Yorkshire Terrier; guest beers ⊞
In the impressive Pearl Chambers building, Mr Foley's is named after Patrick James Foley, founder of Pearl Life Assurance, whose statue is at the top of the premises. In the multi-level interior there is a range of seating from comfortable armchairs to high stools near the bar. With 10 handpumps on the bar, a good range of both local beers and ales from smaller breweries countrywide is offered. An extensive choice of beers from the rest of the world is also available. ⊕♿🚃🚃

North ℒ
24 New Briggate, LS1 6NU
✪ 12-2am (1am Mon & Tue); 12-midnight Sun
☎ (0113) 242 4540 ⊕ northbar.com
Beer range varies ⊞
One of the most enduring and popular bars in Leeds, where real ale drinkers mingle happily with world beer lovers and whisky aficionados. Its winning formula is simple: minimalist decor with interesting local art shows, friendly staff, unfussy food, regular beer festivals and a long bar packed with bottles, fonts and pumps. Striking a balance between local beers and those from further afield, the five handpumps dispense one house ale and a good range of light and dark beers. ⊕🚃🚃♥

Palace ℒ ✅
Kirkgate, LS2 7DJ
✪ 10-11.30 (midnight Fri & Sat); 10-11 Sun
☎ (0113) 244 5882
Draught Bass; Fuller's London Pride; guest beers ⊞
On the eastern edge of the city centre in the shadow of Leeds Parish Church, this former Melbourne Brewery house still retains its bowing courtiers on several windows. A time module, which would be more at home in a railway station, dominates a single-roomed drinking area opened out from what was once a three-roomed hostelry. This place is an avid supporter of local ales, with usually one or two beers from Leeds Brewery.
🏠⊕♿🚃♥

Scarbrough Hotel ℒ
Bishopgate Street, LS1 5DY
✪ 11-midnight; 10-10.30 Sun ☎ (0113) 243 4590
Fuller's London Pride; Tetley Bitter; guest beers ⊞
Busy city-centre pub conveniently close to the main train station. It is named after an early owner, Henry Scarbrough, although in his time the venue was known as the King's Arms; the name was changed in the 1890s. At either end of the long bar are comfortable seating areas. Alongside the regular beers a selection of guests is served, mostly from local breweries. Normally both real cider and perry are available. The menu includes an extensive range of pies. 🏠⊕♿🚃(City)🚃(1)♥⌐

Veritas Ale & Wine Bar ℒ ✅
43 Great George Street, LS1 3BB
✪ 11-11; 12-10.30 Sun ☎ (0113) 242 8094
Ilkley Mary Jane; Thwaites Wainwright; guest beers ⊞
A modern but relaxed bar hosting one large L-shaped wood-floored room divided into four areas. Guest beers concentrate on local microbreweries and a cider or perry is usually available. Good food is served all day and occasional ale and food themed evenings are held. Local produce is available from the deli counter to eat in or take away. As its name suggests, a good range of wines is present, along with draught and bottled foreign beers. Q⊕♿🚃🚃♥

Victoria Family & Commercial 🅛 ✔
28 Great George Street, LS1 3DL (behind town hall)
🌣 11-11 (midnight Fri); 10-midnight Sat; 12-8 Sun
☎ (0113) 245 1386
Acorn Barnsley Bitter; Leeds Pale; guest beers 🅗
The pub retains the original Victorian frontage and signs, although the hotel function has now ceased. The interior displays Victorian grandeur but is, however, mostly quality reproduction. The central hallway leads to a main long bar, with its cosy booths, and two smaller lounges, which can be hired. Up to six guest beers are usually available from smaller breweries across the UK. Food is served up to 10pm. ◖▮≒⊟

Whitelocks First City Luncheon Bar ★ 🅛 ✔
Turks Head Yard, off Briggate, LS1 6HB (near Marks & Spencer)
🌣 11-11 (midnight Fri & Sat); 12-6 Sun ☎ (0113) 245 3950
Caledonian Deuchars IPA; Leeds Pale; Theakston Best Bitter; guest beers 🅗
The Turk's Head, as it was originally called, has been licensed since 1715. A walk up the yard to the top bar reveals how Whitelocks has absorbed what were once cottages dating from around 1790. Inside the pub there has been little change since it was laid out by the Whitelock family in 1886. The sumptuous display of faience tiling is just one of the many items of historic interest at this must-visit hostelry. ﷯Q❀◖▮≒⊟

Leeds: Headingley

Arcadia Ale & Wine Bar 🅛 ✔
34 Arndale Centre, Otley Road, LS6 2UE (corner of Alma Road)
🌣 12-11 ☎ (0113) 274 5599
Black Sheep Best Bitter; Taylor Landlord; guest beers 🅗
Cleverly converted former bank that is a well-established and multi award-winning pub. The bar has ground floor rooms plus an upstairs mezzanine level, and is a dog-friendly environment. Eight beers are offered from Copper Dragon, Elland, Ilkley and other breweries locally and from around the region. Draught and bottled foreign beers plus a range of wines also feature. Food is served Thursday to Sunday, and a waiter service is sometimes offered on busy nights. Children are not permitted. Q◖▮⅋⊟

Leeds: Holbeck

Grove Inn 🅛
Back Row, LS11 5PL
🌣 12-11 (midnight Fri & Sat) ☎ (0113) 243 9254
🌐 thegroveinn.com
Daleside Blonde; Moorhouse's Black Cat, Pride of Pendle; guest beers 🅗
Surrounded by office blocks, the Grove is a survivor and typifies a traditional pub although it attracts a varied clientele. Its four rooms host a wide range of live music, singers and more. The five guest beers are always from local breweries such as Ridgeside, Wharfebank, Leeds, Kirkstall, Salamander and Elland. Old Rosie cider is served. This place is winner of many Leeds CAMRA awards in recent years. If he likes you, Donut (the resident dog) may grace you with his presence. ﷯Q❀◖▯≒⊟♣●⅃

Midnight Bell 🅛
101 Water Lane, LS11 5QN
🌣 11.30-11 (midnight Fri & Sat); 12-11 Sun
☎ (0113) 244 5044 🌐 midnightbell.co.uk
Leeds Pale, Best, Midnight Bell; guest beers 🅗
In Holbeck Urban Village, this contemporary Leeds Brewery pub is popular with local office workers. The downstairs is aimed primarily at drinkers, but with an intimate corner tailored towards dining. Upstairs, the restaurant doubles as a function room. The menu includes a number of dishes containing the brewery's own beer. A Leeds seasonal brew and two guests from microbreweries complement the core range, and a real cider is usually available in warmer months. To the rear is a pleasant open courtyard for alfresco drinking. ﷯❀◖⅃▮≒⊟●⅃

Leeds: Horsforth

Town Street Tavern 🅛 ✔
16-18 Town Street, LS18 4RJ
🌣 12-11 (10.30 Sun) ☎ (0113) 281 9996
Black Sheep Best Bitter; Copper Dragon Golden Pippin; Leeds Pale; Taylor Golden Best; guest beers 🅗
Part of the Market Town Taverns chain, with eight handpumps serving ales from northern microbreweries, and a selection of continental beers on draught and in bottle. The upstairs brasserie serves meals from 6pm, while a bar menu is offered at lunchtimes and until 6pm at weekends. A small patio provides an area for outdoor drinking, which also doubles as a smoking area. Accompanied children are allowed in the main bar until 6pm. Dogs welcome. Q❀◖⊟(50,50A)⅃

Leeds: Hunslet

Garden Gate ★ 🅛
3 Whitfield Place, LS10 2QB (off Church St, to right of Penny Hill Centre)
🌣 12-3, 5-11; 12-midnight Fri & Sat; 12-9 Sun
☎ (0113) 277 7705 🌐 gardengateleeds.co.uk
Leeds Pale, Best, Midnight Bell; guest beer 🅗
The Garden Gate is Leeds' most beautiful pub. Designed by local architect W Mason Coggill of Stourton, it was built in 1903, with almost all the work carried out by local firms. The pub was purchased by Leeds Brewery in 2010 and at the same time was awarded a Grade II* listing by English Heritage, making it one of only a handful of pubs in the country to hold this accolade. ﷯Q⅃❀◖▯⅃♣

Leeds: Kirkstall

West End House 🅛 ✔
26 Abbey Road, LS5 3HS
🌣 11.30-11; 12-midnight Sat; 12-11 Sun ☎ (0113) 228 9108
🌐 westendleeds.co.uk
Beer range varies 🅗
Traditional, welcoming pub close to Kirkstall Abbey, with a central bar surrounded by comfortable seating and a dining area serving high-quality food. The main area provides a convivial atmosphere for visitors and locals alike. Popular quiz nights are Tuesday and Thursday. Constant rotation on four handpumps supplies beers from local breweries and further afield. There are also handpumps for Old Rosie cider and Westons County perry. ❀◖▯⅃≒(Headingley)⊟(33,33A,757)●⅃

Leeds: Meanwood

East of Arcadia ☐ ✅
607 Meanwood Road, LS6 4HQ
✪ 11-11 (11.30 Fri & Sat); 12-11 Sun ☎ (0113) 2755 488
Black Sheep Best Bitter; Ilkley Mary Jane; Leeds Pale; Taylor Landlord; guest beers Ⓗ
Newly built pub with one large curved room lit by huge windows, which is divided into two areas. The wood-floored drinking space features tables made from large wooden casks. The carpeted area provides seating for drinkers and diners who can enjoy the excellent food. Guest beers concentrate mainly on northern microbreweries and there is one handpump dedicated to Ridgeside. A range of wines plus draught and bottled foreign beers also feature. Wednesday is quiz night. Q◑&

Leeds: Newlay

Abbey ☐
99 Pollard Lane, LS13 1EQ (vehicle access from B6157 only) SE239367
✪ 12-11 (10.30 Sun) ☎ (0113) 258 1248
⊕ theabbey-inn.co.uk
Kirkstall Pale; guest beers Ⓗ
Popular pub between the River Aire and the Leeds-Liverpool canal, close to Newlay Locks, with moorings nearby. The building is Grade II-listed, with low ceilings, and is named after the nearby 12th-century Kirkstall Abbey. There is live music most weekends, a music quiz on Thursdays and a general knowledge quiz on Sundays. Various beer festivals are held throughout the year. It is handy for walkers, cyclists and narrowboat users exploring the valley. ⚹≿◑♣●P⅄

Leeds: Rodley

Owl ☐
1 Rodley Lane, LS13 1LB (on corner of Bagley Lane)
✪ 12-11.30 (midnight Fri & Sat) ☎ (0113) 256 5242
⊕ theowlatrodley.co.uk
Black Sheep Best Bitter; Taylor Landlord; guest beers Ⓗ
Occupying a prominent position on the corner of Rodley Lane and Bagley Lane, up to eight real ales are served here. The traditional taproom at the front has a dartboard and pool table. The open-plan lounge/restaurant to the rear has many ornamental owls on display. Entertainment throughout the week includes live music on Fridays and Saturdays, and a quiz night on Thursdays. There is 10 per cent off all cask ales on production of a CAMRA membership card. ≿❁◑☐Ɽ♣P⅄

Rodley Barge ☐ ✅
182-184 Town Street, LS13 1HP (by Leeds-Liverpool canal)
✪ 12-3, 5-11; 12-11 Fri-Sun ☎ (0113) 257 4606
Clark's Rodley Barge Bitter; Leeds Pale; Tetley Bitter; guest beers Ⓗ
Comfortable street-corner local that serves up to five real ales, with guest ales mostly from local microbreweries. There are outside drinking areas to both front and rear, with the rear outdoor terrace right next to the canal. The smaller back bar serves as a family room. Various quizzes are held throughout the week, including a music quiz on Sundays. A popular beer festival takes place over the August bank holiday weekend.
⚹≿❁◑Ɽ(8,9,16A)♣P⅄

Linthwaite

Sair Inn ☐ ✅
139 Lane Top, HD7 5SG (top of Hoyle Ing, off A62)
✪ 5 (12 Fri & Sat)-11; 12-10.30 Sun ☎ (01484) 842370
Linfit Bitter, Gold Medal, Swift, Special, Autumn Gold, Old Eli Ⓗ
Iconic brewpub high on a hillside above the Colne Valley, where the same landlord will soon have been in charge for 30 years. The reasonably priced Linfit beers are available only in the pub itself, brewed in the new bespoke brew plant. The laid-back feel of the place is accentuated by its cluster of small rooms radiating from the central bar, and also by the real fires in winter. Westons 1st Quality cider is available. ⚹Q❁Ɽ(181,182,183)♣●

Liversedge

Black Bull ☐ ✅
37 Halifax Road, WF15 6JR (on A649, near A62)
✪ 12-midnight (1.30am Fri & Sat) ☎ (01924) 403779
Fuller's London Pride; Ossett Pale Gold, Yorkshire Blonde, Silver King, Excelsior; guest beers Ⓗ
A regular Guide entry, this pub is an excellent, sociable community local with a warm welcome. The drinking area is a blend of cosy corners and open spaces where groups can mix. A highlight is the so-called chapel with its stained glass and woodwork. Nine handpumps dispense a range of beer styles including a mild or dark ale. Quiz night Tuesday is always popular. Last admission is 30-60 minutes before closing. ⚹≿❁❀(254)♣P⅄

New Inn ☐ ✅
139 Roberttown Lane, Roberttown, WF15 7NP (near Roberttown village centre)
✪ 3-10.30 Mon; 12-11.30; 12-10.30 Sun ☎ (01924) 402069
Abbeydale Moonshine; Leeds Best; Mallinsons Bobtown Blonde; guest beers Ⓗ
Given a new lease of life under private ownership, this true free house is the social centre of the village. There are six ales, three rotating and usually including a dark beer. Bobtown Blonde is brewed specially by local brewery Mallinsons. The pub has a pool room, a traditional taproom, a popular, sociable lounge and a function room used for occasional live music and events including themed food evenings. The Wednesday quiz is recommended. ⚹❁Ɽ(229,253)♣P⅄

Marsden

Riverhead Brewery Tap ☐ ✅
Argyle Street, HD7 6BR (overlooking River Colne in the centre of Marsden)
✪ 12-midnight (1am Fri); 11-1am Sat ☎ (01484) 841270
Ossett Pale Gold, Silver King; Riverhead Sparth Mild, Butterley Bitter, March Haigh; guest beers Ⓗ
A friendly and welcoming pub at the centre of village life. Formerly a Co-op store, it is now part of the growing chain of Ossett Brewery pubs. Great pictures of Marsden adorn the walls. Fantastic food is served in the restaurant and there is a riverside terrace for alfresco drinking. The microbrewery is visible from the bar – LocAle does not get any more local than this. Up to 10 beers are available: usually six from Riverhead, two from Ossett, London Pride and a guest. Dogs are welcome.
Q❁◑&≈Ɽ(185)●

Meltham

Wills o' Nats ✪
Blackmoorfoot Road, HD9 5PS SE091121
✪ 11.45-3, 5-midnight; 11.45-midnight Sat & Sun
☎ (01484) 850078
Black Sheep Best Bitter; Greene King IPA; Taylor Landlord; Tetley Bitter; guest beers Ⓗ
In 1890, William, son of Nathaniel, became landlord of the Spotted Cow. Soon it became known as the Wills, and eventually the name was changed to Wills o' Nats. Today it is renowned for its locally sourced home-cooked food and five ales. Live music events are held on the last Saturday of each month in the summer. It is in Last of the Summer Wine country, close to the Peak District, with stunning views, and is a welcome stop for families, walkers and their dogs.
🏰❀◑ᕁᗎ(388)Ｐ⚊

Mirfield

Navigation Tavern
6 Station Road, WF14 8NL (between rail station and canal)
✪ 11.30-11; 12-10.30 Sun ☎ (01924) 492476
John Smith's Bitter; Theakston Best Bitter, Black Bull Bitter, XB, Old Peculier; guest beers Ⓗ
Popular canalside free house serving up to five rotating guest and Caledonian ales plus regulars, and a registered ambassador for Theakston beers at competitive prices. Close to Mirfield railway station, it features on the Transpennine Rail Ale Trail. It has Saturday night entertainment, regular beer festivals, active sports and pool teams, a large function room and en-suite B&B. At least two real cider/perry choices are offered. Open for tea and coffee from 7.30am Monday to Saturday.
❀ᕮᕁᗎ♣◗Ｐ⚊

Old Colonial Ⓛ
Dunbottle Lane, WF14 9JJ (off A644 up Church Lane, 1 mile NNE of station)
✪ 4.30 (3 Sat)-12.30am; 12-11 Sun ☎ (01924) 496920
⊕ theoldcolonial.co.uk
Copper Dragon Best Bitter; guest beers Ⓗ
Formerly a private members' club, it is run by an enthusiastic real ale supporter. Six real ales are from Thwaites, Lees and a wide range of small brewers, and often include one-off or commemorative brews. The excellent-value Sunday lunch is popular. There is a Royal British Legion memorial in the garden and local charities are well supported. The spacious conservatory is popular for meetings and functions. Evening meals are available Thursday, Friday and Saturday.
🏰⛵❀◑ᕁᗎ(202,205)♣Ｐ

Pear Tree Ⓛ
259 Huddersfield Road, WF14 9DL
✪ 11-midnight (1am Fri & Sat) ☎ (01924) 491360
Copper Dragon Golden Pippin; Wells Bombardier; guest beers Ⓗ
A popular, warm and inviting pub boasting an excellent riverside beer garden, on the main road a mile from Mirfield centre and the railway station. The relaxed and cosy atmosphere combined with home-cooked food served lunchtimes and evenings is appealing to locals and visitors alike. On the bar rotating guest ales and traditional handpulled cider feature. Thursday is quiz night from 9pm and on Sunday evenings an acoustic jam session is held. ❀◑ᕁᗎ(278)◗Ｐ⚊

Mytholmroyd

Shoulder of Mutton Ⓛ
38 New Road, HX7 5DZ (on B6138, near station)
✪ 11.30-3 (not Tue), 7-11; 11.30-11 Sun; 12-10.30 Sun
☎ (01422) 883165
Black Sheep Best Bitter; Taylor Golden Best, Landlord; guest beers Ⓗ
Village inn with a strong community feel and a warm welcome for walkers and other visitors. Excellent-value, home-cooked food is available lunchtimes and evenings (no food Mon and Tue). Two guest beers are from the Enterprise list. Major sporting events are shown on a large-screen TV, but there is normally a quiet corner to be found. The bar displays memorabilia relating to the Cragg Vale Coiners, a gang of 18th-century forgers. There is a heated smoking shelter. ❀◑ᕮᕁᗎ♣Ｐ⚊

Ossett

Brewers Pride Ⓛ
Low Mill Road, WF5 8ND (at bottom of Healey Road, 1½ miles from town centre)
✪ 12-11 (10.30 Sun) ☎ (01924) 273865
⊕ brewers-pride.co.uk
Bob's Brewing Co White Lion; Rudgate Ruby Mild; guest beers Ⓗ
A genuine free house on the outskirts of Ossett, five minutes' walk from the Calder & Hebble Canal. Two resident beers plus seven guest ales from a wide range of microbreweries are served. The excellent-value menu (often themed) is available lunchtimes and evenings. Monday is quiz night, and live music is on the first Sunday of each month. Dogs and well-behaved children are welcome until 7pm. This venue puts on an annual August bank holiday beer festival. 🏰Q❀◑ᗎ(102)⚊

Tap Ⓛ
2 The Green, WF5 8JS (from town centre turn left onto Queen St, which becomes The Green)
✪ 3 (12 Thu & Sun)-1am; 12-2am Fri & Sat
☎ (01924) 272215
Ossett Excelsior, Pale Gold, Silver King; guest beers Ⓗ
On the edge of the town centre and formerly known as the Mason's Arms, the pub was bought by the Ossett Brewery and is now its brewery tap. Alongside the three regular Ossett beers there is usually a special or seasonal beer from Ossett and five guest ales – one from Fuller's and two each from Rat and Riverhead. A real wood fire and stone-flagged floors give the pub an old-fashioned feel. Disabled access is to the bar only.
🏰Q❀ᕁᗎ(117)Ｐ⚊

Otley

Bowling Green Ⓛ ✪
18 Bondgate, LS21 3AB
✪ 8am-midnight (1am Fri & Sat; 11 Sun) ☎ (01943) 858980
Greene King Abbot; Ruddles Best Bitter; guest beers Ⓗ
A JD Wetherspoon free house representing an excellent conversion of the previous Bowling Green pub, which has stood on this site since 1825. The Grade II-listed building has previously been a court, assembly rooms and a place of worship, and was originally built in 1757. The traditional lounge is at the front, while the atrium by the bar retains the original cobbles. Some of the guest ales are from local microbreweries, including Wharfebank, which is less than two miles away. 🏰Q❀◑ᕁᗎ◗

Fleece L ✓

Westgate, LS21 3DT

✪ 11.30-11.30; 12-11.30 Sun ☎ (01943) 465034

⊕ fleece-otley.co.uk

Wharfebank Camfell Flame, Slingers Gold, Tether Blond, Verbeia Pale Ale, seasonal beer; guest beers ℍ

A tastefully refurbished Grade II-listed building retaining many original features such as the moulded plaster panelling. The main room is divided into three separate drinking areas; to the left of the entrance is a snug with its own real fire where dogs are welcome. A unique feature is the slate tile wall, which carries the food menu. An attractive garden with a terrace containing plentiful picnic tables stretches down to the River Wharfe. ▲⊛◑&🖵(X84,33A)♣🌰P⌐

Horse & Farrier L

7 Bridge Street, LS21 1BQ

✪ 11-11 ☎ (01943) 468400

Black Sheep Best Bitter; Ilkley Mary Jane; guest beers ℍ

A modern open-plan pub with one large room divided into three wood-floored drinking areas and a carpeted area for diners. The rectangular bar has eight handpumps dispensing a variety of styles of ale. A Copper Dragon beer is always available as well as one from Timothy Taylor. Guest beers concentrate mainly on northern microbreweries. Real cider is stocked in summer. A good selection of bottled foreign beers and a choice of wines is stocked. Dogs are welcome and children may accompany diners until 8pm. ▲⊛🛏◑&🖵(33A,X84)🌰P⌐

Junction L

44 Bondgate, LS21 1AD (corner of Bondgate and Charles Street)

✪ 11-11 (11.30 Thu; midnight Fri & Sat); 12-10.30 Sun ☎ (01943) 463233

St Austell Tribute; Taylor Best Bitter, Landlord; Theakston Best Bitter, Old Peculier; guest beers ℍ

An ale mecca that occupies a prominent street-corner site on the approach from Leeds. Up to 11 ales from around the country are served, along with a real cider. There is a central fireplace, and a collection of leather harnesses and saddles hangs from the ceiling. Pictures of old Otley and some interesting metal beer advertisements and mirrors complete the decor. There is live music on Tuesdays, and a DJ Sundays. Roadside tables allow for outdoor drinking. Dog-friendly. ▲⊛🖵♣🌰⌐

Old Cock 🍺 L

11-13 Crossgate, LS21 1AA (opp bus station)

✪ 11-11 ☎ (01943) 464424 ⊕ theoldcockotley.co.uk

Ilkley Mary Jane; Theakston Best Bitter; guest beers ℍ

A genuine free house opened in 2012, this compact, three-roomed stone inn was converted from a former café. The six guest ales are mostly from local breweries, usually including Otley-based breweries Wharfebank, Rodham's and Briscoe's. There are two rotating real ciders plus a wide range of global beers. Sandwiches are available from the bar. No admittance to under-18s. ▲Q&🖵🌰

Overton

Reindeer L

204 Old Road, WF4 4RL (turn left off A642 in Middlestown, continue for 1 mile, pub on right after village)

✪ 12 (4 Mon)-midnight; 12-11 Sun ☎ (01924) 848374

John Smith's Bitter; guest beers ℍ

A traditional free house, this pub is the tap for Cap House Brewery. Guest beers are mainly from local breweries and there is also real cider on handpull. Home-cooked food, including real chips, is served in the separate restaurant or conservatory, which leads to the beer garden overlooking the National Coal Mining Museum. A free quiz and supper are hosted on Wednesday night. The games room has a pool table, dartboard, dominoes and games machines. Outside is a covered smoking area. ▲Q☔⊛◑🖵(128,232)♣🌰P⌐

Oxenhope

Waggon & Horses Inn

Dyke Nook, Hebden Bridge Road, BD22 9QE (on A6033 Keighley to Hebden Bridge road, 1 mile up the hill from village) SE020338

✪ 12-3, 5-11 Mon-Thu winter; 12-11 ☎ (01535) 643302

⊕ waggonandhorsesoxenhope.co.uk

Beer range varies ℍ

Up on the moors overlooking the Worth Valley, West Yorkshire's highest free house enjoys magnificent views on sunny days, and is a warm, welcome haven with real fires when the weather turns. This well-appointed open-plan roadside hostelry, with a single bar, offers a range of guest beers mainly from microbreweries. Home-cooked food is served daily, with good-value weekday special lunches for senior citizens. The bus between Keighley and Hebden Bridge stops outside. ▲⊛🛏◑🖵(500)P

Pontefract

Broken Bridge L ✓

5 Horsefair, WF8 1PD (close to bus station)

✪ 8-midnight (1am Sat) ☎ (01997) 781640

Greene King Abbot; Moorhouse's Pontus Fractus; Ruddles Best Bitter; guest beers ℍ

Close to the bus station, this Wetherspoon's outlet is a former charity shop and is named after the Latin name for Pontefract. There are numerous pictures depicting the history of the town adorning the walls. Popular at weekends, the small entrance belies the large one-room interior, which features two open fires in winter. Food is served daily and the guest beers come from Moorhouse's, Saltaire, Wentworth and Clark's. There are regular monthly events such as Meet the Brewer evenings. A rear courtyard can be used by smokers. ▲⊛◑&≒(Monkhill/Baghill/Tanshelf)🖵🌰⌐🍴

Robin Hood

4 Wakefield Road, WF8 4HN (on jct of A639 and A645 at edge of town)

✪ 5-midnight; 12-1.30am Fri & Sat; 12-midnight Sun ☎ (01977) 702231

Draught Bass; East Coast Little John, Tuck's Tipple ℍ

Busy pub near the notorious Town End traffic lights, known as Jenkins' Folly. There are four separate drinking areas including a public bar. Quizzes are held on Sunday and Tuesday evenings and darts and dominoes teams play in the local charity leagues. The on-site brewery opened in summer 2012. ▲⊛&≒(Tanshelf/Monkhill/Baghill)🖵♣🌰⌐

Pudsey

Fleece 🅛 ✅
100 Fartown, LS28 8LU
🍺 12-11 (10.30 Sun) ☎ (0113) 236 2748
🌐 fleecefartown.co.uk
Taylor Landlord; Tetley Bitter; guest beers 🅷
A beacon of what a community hostelry stands for, and a deserved winner of Leeds CAMRA awards. This stone-built inn is a comfortable two-roomed local – the snug is a small taproom where you can catch up on the latest sporting action or admire sporting memorabilia, and the larger lounge is quaintly adorned with pot pigs. The outdoor area features more pigs. 🚶🏵🍴&🚌(40,40A,205)♣P

Ripponden

Old Bridge Inn 🅛
Priest Lane, HX6 4DF
🍺 12-3, 5.30-11; 12-11 Fri & Sat; 12-10.30 Sun
☎ (01422) 822595 🌐 theoldbridgeinn.co.uk
Taylor Dark Mild, Golden Best, Best Bitter, Landlord; guest beers 🅷
Old riverside pub overlooked by a packhorse bridge, popular with both drinkers and diners. The Pork Pie Club meets on Saturday and holds an annual championship for charity. There are three rooms: one has panelling, the centre room - open to the roof - contains the bar, and a lower room displays a fine cruck beam. Imaginative menus are displayed on blackboards including buffet lunches on weekdays (no eve meals Sun). It is on the Calderdale Way footpath, but no dogs please. 🚶Q🏵◖🚌(528,560)P

Saltaire

Fanny's Ale & Cider House 🅛 ✅
63 Saltaire Road, BD18 3JN (on A657 opp fire station)
🍺 12 (5 Mon)-11; 12-midnight Fri & Sat ☎ (01274) 591419
🌐 fannysalehouse.com
Taylor Golden Best, Landlord; Theakston Old Peculier; guest beers 🅷
Near the historic Salts Mill and world heritage site of Saltaire Village, this cosy pub was originally a beer shop. It is now a fully licensed free house stocking an excellent range of beers and serving a number of draught ciders. A recent extension increased the seating capacity downstairs and added disabled access, while an upstairs room has comfortable seating. The gas-lit lounge is adorned with breweriana; real fires add nicely to the warm welcome. Bradford CAMRA Pub of the Year 2010. 🚶&🚆🚌(662,760)♣🍴

Victoria 🅛
192 Saltaire Road, BD18 3JF (5 mins' walk from railway station)
🍺 12-11.30 (12.30am Fri & Sat) ☎ (01274) 593725
Copper Dragon Golden Pippin; guest beers 🅷
Traditional community pub close to Saltaire Village world heritage site, with a friendly atmosphere where children and dogs are welcome. There is a lounge with real fires, and a separate public bar with a pool table, jukebox and pinball machine. A quiz is held on Wednesday nights and live music plays each Saturday, with an acoustic jam session on Thursday. See the Facebook group Vic Saltaire for information. Six regularly changing ales including beers from local breweries are on sale. 🚶🏵🍴🚆🚌(662,760)♣P🍴

Shipley

Ring O' Bells 🅛 ✅
3 Bradford Road, BD18 3PR (on A650)
🍺 11-midnight; 12-11 Sun ☎ (01274) 584386
Copper Dragon Golden Pippin; Ilkley Mary Jane; Saltaire Blonde; Tetley Bitter; guest beers 🅷
Traditional broad-based local with a warm, homely feel showing all the up-to-date sports matches on several TV screens. Occasional bands perform and the pub takes part in popular poker games and weekly quizzes. Small functions can be catered for and there are facilities for activity groups, which currently include writers and anglers. 🏵◖🍴&🚆(Saltaire)🚌(662)♣P🍴

Sir Norman Rae 🅛 ✅
Victoria House, Market Place, BD18 3QB (50yds from clock tower)
🍺 8-11 (midnight Fri & Sat) ☎ (01274) 535290
Greene King Abbot; Ruddles Best; guest beers 🅷
The typical conversion by Wetherspoon from a previous use. Formerly a Co-op department store, this example opened originally as a Lloyds No.1, but was converted to the standard format nearly two years ago. Real ale usually centres on local breweries, with Greene King products also on the bar. Regular Meet the Brewer nights are held. Situated at the edge of the bus interchange and close to the railway. Q◖&🚆🚌🍴

Silsden

King's Arms 🅛
9 Bolton Road, BD20 0JY
🍺 12-midnight ☎ (01535) 653216
Saltaire Blonde; Theakston Best Bitter; guest beers 🅷
There is always something going on at the King's of an evening: Tuesday folk, Thursday open mic, Wednesday quiz, and other events such as themed food nights wedged in where there is time. The effort put in made the pub a deserved winner of local CAMRA Branch Pub of the Year in 2011. Guest beers are from the Punch Finest Cask list, and the pub is a regular outlet for Westons cider. The bus between Keighley and Addingham stops outside. Dogs and well-behaved children are allowed. 🚶🏵◖🚌(70,712,762)♣🍴P🍴

Slaithwaite

Commercial 🅛
1 Carr Lane, HD7 5AN (village centre, off A62)
🍺 12-midnight (1am Fri & Sat) ☎ (01484) 846258
🌐 commercial-slaithwaite.co.uk
Empire Moonraker Mild, Commerciale; guest beers 🅷
Since reopening in 2009, this village-centre free house has enjoyed enviable success. Nine handpumps provide ample variety, with the keenly priced house beer, Commerciale, and mild supplied by Empire Brewery. A rotating real cider/perry is available, often from Westons. Very community-focused, it nonetheless has a varied clientele including locals, enthusiasts tackling the Transpennine Rail Ale Trail, ramblers and their dogs – the pub is dog-friendly. Light snacks and beverages are served Friday-Sunday. An upstairs function room is available free of charge. Q🏵🚆🚌(181,335,339)♣🍴🍴

South Elmsall

Barnsley Oak ✅

Mill Lane, WF9 2DT (on B6474, off A638 Wakefield-Doncaster road)

🕓 12 (11.30 Sun)-11.30 ☎ (01977) 643427

John Smith's Bitter; guest beer Ⓗ

This former mining area is fortunate to be served by such a fine community pub. It has built up a loyal following for cask ale and often features a guest ale brewed in Yorkshire. Excellent-value food is served every day, and there is also a popular lunchtime carvery. Children are welcome and meals can be taken in the conservatory, which affords panoramic views. Outside seating is popular on sunny days. Quiz nights are Tuesday and Sunday. ⊛◑≢(Moorthorpe)🚆(46,496)P⟵

Southowram

Shoulder of Mutton Ⓛ

14 Cain Lane, HX3 9SB

🕓 2-11; 12-midnight Fri & Sat; 12-10.30 Sun ☎ 07707 358697

Saltaire Blonde; guest beers Ⓗ

A popular village local that has won awards for the floral display on its frontage, and for its strong community spirit. The L-shaped lounge includes exposed stonework behind the bar, and a separate room has a pool table. Timber lintels over some windows suggest the pub is quite old. One or two guest beers are from small breweries. Activities include a Thursday evening quiz. Dogs are welcome. 🚆(571,572)♣⟵

Sowerby

Church Stile

Sowerby New Road, HX6 1JZ (opp St Peter's Church)

🕓 1-11 (midnight Fri); 12-midnight Sat; 12-11 Sun ☎ (01422) 836696

Taylor Golden Best; guest beers Ⓗ

A friendly semi-rural pub high above Sowerby Bridge with superb views across the Calder Valley. It comprises a welcoming and convivial bar room with an open fire, and a separate games room where families with children are welcome until 9pm. The pub hosts young farmers' meetings and has a football team. One of the guest beers is from the Timothy Taylor range. No hot meals are served, but delicious pork pies are always available. Dogs welcome. ⚶⏾⊛🚆(577,579)♣⟵

Sowerby Bridge

Jubilee Refreshment Rooms 🏆 Ⓛ

Station Road, HX6 3AB (at railway station)

🕓 12-10 ☎ (01422) 648285

⊕ jubileerefreshmentrooms.co.uk

Beer range varies Ⓗ

Recently converted railway station building, dating from 1876, which has been impressively renovated as a café bar. The room is lit with Art Deco lamps hanging from the ceiling, and railway memorabilia decorate the walls. It is run by real ale enthusiasts, and interesting beers from up to 17 local microbreweries are served from up to six handpumps. Ideally situated for commuters on the Calder Valley rail ale trip and walkers on the Calderdale Way. ⚶Q⏾≢P⟵

Puzzle Hall

21 Hollins Mill Lane, HX6 2RF (400yds from A58)

🕓 3-midnight; 1-1am Sat; 1-midnight Sun ☎ (01422) 835547 ⊕ puzzlehall.com

Beer range varies Ⓗ

The Puzzle Hall has a welcoming atmosphere and great beer quality. It can be found nestling between the canal and the river. Opened in the 1700s, this former brewpub is dominated by the tower of the old brewery. It has six handpumps serving a variety of beers from microbreweries, and also offers an extensive range of continental and UK bottled beers. Live music features every Thursday and Saturday night. ⚶⊛≢🚆🐾⟵

Shepherd's Rest Ⓛ ✅

125 Bolton Brow, HX6 2BD (on A58 towards Halifax)

🕓 3 (12 Fri-Sun)-11.30 ☎ (01422) 831937

Ossett Pale Gold, Shepherd's Rest, Excelsior; Taylor Landlord; guest beers Ⓗ

This pub was built in 1877, using the name of an old inn that stood on the other side of Bolton Brow. It was purchased by Ossett Brewery in 2005, and the available space has been used to good effect. From the entrance steps a triangular drinking area leads to the bar, which faces the cosy lounge with its large brick-arched fireplace and stone-flagged floor. Quiz night is Monday. ⚶Q⊛≢🚆🐾⟵

White Horse Ⓛ

Burnley Road, Friendly, HX6 2UG

🕓 12-11 (10.30 Sun) ☎ (01422) 831173

Tetley Bitter; guest beer Ⓗ

Served by regular bus services, the White Horse stands back from the busy A646 Burnley Road at Friendly. The small seating area to the front is an ideal spot to enjoy the impressive floral window boxes that are a feature each summer and have earned prizes for the pub. The cosy and compact two-roomed interior has a semi-divided lounge bar and an adjacent taproom that are listed in CAMRA's Yorkshire's Real Heritage Pubs guide. The pub is also noted for its fundraising efforts for the local hospice. ⊛🍴🚆(590,591,592)♣P⟵

Works Ⓛ

12 Hollins Mill Lane, HX6 2QG

🕓 12-11 (10.30 Sun) ☎ (01422) 834821

⊕ theworkssowerbybridge.co.uk

Taylor Golden Best, Best Bitter, Landlord; guest beers Ⓗ

Converted from a former joinery, the pub won Best Conversion to Pub Use in 2007. This large open-plan local features exposed beams and floorboards, and is beside the Rochdale Canal on the western side of the town centre. Nine real ales are served, including three from Timothy Taylor and six rotating guests. Food, made with love, is served both lunchtimes and teatime. Entertainment includes jazz, folk or comedy. ⚶⊛◑≢🚆🐾P⟵

Stanbury

Friendly Ⓛ

54 Main Street, BD22 0HB (on Colne Road between Haworth and Colne)

🕓 12-11 (10.30 Sun) ☎ (01535) 645528

Goose Eye Bronte Bitter; guest beers Ⓗ

Popular village local that also attracts those walking the Pennine Way or visiting the ruined farmhouse that claims to be Wuthering Heights. This is a three-room pub with two lounges either side of a central bar plus a separate games room. Stanbury is only two miles from Haworth but a million miles from its tourist hustle and bustle. ✿&▲🖾(664,916,917)♣P

Old Silent Inn 🅛

Hob Lane, BD22 0HW SE002371
🕓 12-11 (midnight Sat; 10.30 Sun) ☎ (01535) 647437
⊕ old-silent-inn.co.uk
Theakston Old Peculier; Taylor Landlord; guest beers Ⓗ
A 400-year-old roadside inn at the west edge of the village, only five minutes' walk from the bus stop. With oak beams, flagged floors and open fires, it is a building with considerable charm. Drinkers are welcome and award-winning food is served. Walkers will find it close to the Pennine Way, Bronte Way and Millennium Way. Rotating guest beers are usually from local breweries. ▲🖾✿🛏🚲◑▷🖾(664,916,917)P

Todmorden

Polished Knob 🅛 ✓

31 Burnley Road, OL14 7BU SD936242
🕓 10-1am (2am Fri & Sat) ☎ (01706) 810480
Bridestones Pennine Gold; Thwaites Wainwright, Nutty Black; guest beers Ⓗ
Popular pub that once contained the lock-up for the villains of Todmorden and Walsden. It is positioned opposite the local open-air market. The pub has a bright feel about it and is furnished with a mix of comfortable chairs and traditional seating. To the rear is a patio garden with covered seating, and outside at the front there are tables and chairs for alfresco drinking. Quality food is served into the early evening, and local bands play here at the weekend. ▲✿◑▷⇌🖾P⸗

Staff of Life 🅛

550 Burnley Road, Lydgate, OL14 8JF SD916257
🕓 12-2 (not Mon & Tue), 5.30-11; 12-11 Fri-Sun
☎ (01706) 819033 ⊕ staffoflifeinn.org.uk
Moorhouse's Blond Witch; Taylor Golden Best, Landlord; guest beers Ⓗ
Set in a dramatic valley landscape beneath Eagles Crag, this welcoming free house was built in 1838. The layout is semi-open, with seating around the cosy bar area. There are two further rooms, one of which contains a vaulted stone chamber originally used as the cellar. Quality home-cooked food with continually changing specials is served, and a regular quiz night is hosted. Parking for the pub is on Knotts Road, 70 yards to the east. B&B is available. ▲Q✿🛏◑▷🖾(589,592)●P

Wakefield

Alverthorpe WMC 🅛 ✓

111 Flanshaw Lane, Alverthorpe, WF2 9JG (between Dewsbury and Batley Roads, 2 miles from city centre)
🕓 2 (11.30 Fri & Sat)-11; 12-3.30, 7-11 Sun
☎ (01924) 374179
Bob's Brewing Co White Lion; Tetley Mild, Bitter; guest beers Ⓗ
Multi-roomed CIU-affiliated club with a cosy interior with unusual stained glass features and an extensive collection of pot horses. A wide selection of guest ales is featured, mainly from local micros. The club holds an annual beer festival in November and is a regular winner of local CAMRA awards. Live entertainment takes place on Saturday and Sunday.

Snooker and darts are among the traditional games, with a wide-screen TV for the armchair enthusiasts. It has sporting teams and also a floodlit bowling green. ✿🅟&🖾(114,115)♣P⸗

Black Rock ✓

19 Cross Square, WF1 1PQ (at top of Westgate, near Bull Ring)
🕓 11-11 (midnight Sat); 12-10.30 Sun ☎ (01924) 375550
Tetley Bitter; guest beers Ⓗ
An arched, tiled façade leads into this compact city-centre local, with a warm welcome and comfortable interior including photographs of old Wakefield. The Rock stands as one of the few proper pubs left in the middle of the clubs and bars of Westgate, and is popular with drinkers of all ages looking for a real pint. Customers are encouraged to suggest beers to try, with three different ales on offer. There is a free function room available. ⇌(Westgate/Kirkgate)🖾⸗

Bull & Fairhouse 🅛

60 George Street, WF1 1DL (left out of Westgate station, right at the lights, left at the bottom of the hill and the pub is 200yds on the left)
🕓 4-11; 12-midnight Fri & Sat; 12-11 Sun ☎ (01924) 362930
Bob's Brewing Co White Lion; Great Heck Golden Bull; guest beers Ⓗ
The tap for the Great Heck Brewery, the pub has reverted to an earlier name alluding to the cattle market and fairground in the area. The comfortable multi-roomed premises now enjoys a lighter feel, with a new lounge at the front and the toilets relocated to the rear, with limited disabled access via a passageway. A lively bingo quiz with meat raffle and hot supper is held on Thursdays, with live music at weekends. A changing real cider or perry is served on gravity. ▲✿&⇌(Westgate/Kirkgate)🖾(443,444)⸗

Fernandes Brewery Tap & Bier Keller 🅛 ✓

5 Avison Yard, Kirkgate, WF1 1UA (turn right 100yds S of George St/Kirkgate jct)
🕓 Pub: 4-11 (11.30 Thu); 12 midnight Fri & Sat; 12-11 Sun; Bier Keller: 4-midnight Fri & Sat ☎ (01924) 386348
Beer range varies Ⓗ
Owned by Ossett Brewery, although Fernandes Brewery still brews in the cellar, with a beer range that includes Ossett, Fernandes and Fuller's beers. The pub has 10 handpulls, one dedicated to a mild, stout or porter, and also a draught cider. The Bier Keller has several premier foreign beers on draught, plus Ossett Pale Gold and a cider on handpump. There is live music on Sunday afternoon. Pets are welcome. Q⇌(Westgate/Kirkgate)🖾●⸗

Harry's Bar 🅛 ✓

107B Westgate, WF1 1EL (out of Westgate Station, turn left and cross the road, then take 2nd alley on right)
🕓 5 (4 Sat)-1am; 12-midnight Sun ☎ (01924) 373773
Bob's Brewing Co White Lion; Leeds Pale; Ossett Silver King; guest beers Ⓗ
Small, one-roomed pub with an exposed brick and wood interior complemented by a sun deck and a shady yard. Hidden away down an alley off Westgate, it is secluded from the fizz and music youth zone of the city centre. Harry's is a thriving community local with many new friends to meet. Live music features on Wednesday. There is a Pay & Display car park adjacent. ▲✿⇌(Westgate/Kirkgate)🖾●⸗

Hop Ⓛ ✓

19 Bank Street, WF1 1EH (down Bank St off Westgate, opp Opera House)

✪ 4-midnight (2am Fri); 12-2am Sat; 4-11 Sun

☎ (01924) 367111 ⊕ the-hop-wakefield.co.uk

Fuller's London Pride; Ossett Yorkshire Blonde, Silver King, Excelsior; guest beers Ⓗ

Converted into a venue for music, comedy and conversation, this Georgian building retains bare brick walls, fireplaces and other original features, along with new additions including a VW camper van converted into a bar. The main bar has nine handpumps, one reserved for a dark beer and one for a Fernandes or Riverhead Beer; there is also a selection of bottled Belgian beers. Open mic night is on Mondays, quiz on Tuesdays, and live music Thursdays, Fridays and Saturdays. Rooms are available for private hire.

ᐱQ✿&≷(Westgate/Kirkgate)🚋╘

Wakefield Labour Club (The Red Shed)

18 Vicarage Street, WF1 1QX (at the top of Kirkgate turn right, then first left onto Vicarage St)

✪ 12-4 (Fri only), 7-11; 11-4, 7-11 Sat ☎ (01924) 215626 ⊕ theredshed.org.uk

Beer range varies Ⓗ

The Red Shed is an old army hut that has survived the redevelopment of the area. Home to many trade union, community and charity groups, quiz night is on Wednesdays and live music plays on the second and last Saturdays of the month. There are three rooms; two can be hired for functions. An extensive collection of union plates and badges is displayed over the bar, and numerous CAMRA awards adorn the walls. The beers are usually from micros nationwide.

Q≷(Westgate/Kirkgate)🚋♣♠P╘

Wibsey

Dog & Gun

St Enoch's Road, BD6 3BU

✪ 2-11; 12-midnight Fri & Sat; 12-11 Sun ☎ (01274) 677727

Caledonian Deuchars IPA; Tetley Bitter; guest beers Ⓗ

Warm and welcoming traditional local on the outskirts of Bradford, set back from the road, with a large car park. Inside it has three distinct areas with very different feels. The bar serves the smart front lounge, which has a small games room at the side. A further lounge at the rear often shows live sport. Two guest beers are always available from the Cellarman's Reserve list. Monday is poker night and a weekly quiz is held on Wednesday. The pub may open earlier Monday-Thursday during the summer.

✿🚋(570,571,640)♣P

Wintersett

Angler's Retreat Ⓛ

Ferry Top Lane, WF4 2EB (between Crofton and Ryhill) SE382157

✪ closed Tue; 12-3, 7-11; 12-11 Sat; 12-3.30, 7-10.30 Sun ☎ (01924) 862370

Acorn Barnsley Bitter; Samuel Smith Old Brewery Bitter; guest beers Ⓗ

Rural ale house that is an increasingly rare example of an old-fashioned, no frills community pub. There is a loyal local clientele with many old pitmen and many old tales to be told. Close to the Anglers Country Park, Haw Wood and the Transpennine Trail, it is also frequented by birdwatchers, walkers, cyclists and bikers. There are benches and a garden for fine-weather drinking, with a large car park opposite. Due to its isolated location it may close early if trade is slow.

ᐱQ✿🚋(194,195,196)♣P╘

Ship Inn, Sheffield: Central (Photo: Tom Stainer)

SHETLAND

NORTHERN ISLES

HIGHLANDS
&
WESTERN ISLES

ABERDEEN
& GRAMPIAN

TAYSIDE

ARGYLL &
THE ISLES

FIFE

LOCH LOMOND
STIRLING
& THE
TROSSACHS

EDINBURGH & LOTHIANS

GREATER
GLASGOW &
CLYDE VALLEY

BORDERS

AYRSHIRE
& ARRAN

DUMFRIES &
GALLOWAY

NORTHERN
IRELAND

NORTHUMBER-
LAND

TYNE &
WEAR

CUMBRIA

DURHAM

ISLE OF
MAN

NORTH
YORKSHIRE

LANCASHIRE

EAST
YORKS

MERSEYSIDE

WEST
YORKS

GREATER
MANCHESTER

SOUTH
YORKS

LINCOLN-
SHIRE

NW
WALES

NE
WALES

CHESHIRE

DERBYSHIRE

NOTTINGHAM-
SHIRE

SHROPSHIRE

STAFFORD-
SHIRE

NORFOLK

CAMBRIDGE-
SHIRE

LEICESTERSHIRE
& RUTLAND

MID
WALES

WEST
MIDLANDS

NORTHAMPTON-
SHIRE

SUFFOLK

WORCESTER-
SHIRE

WARWICK-
SHIRE

HEREFORD-
SHIRE

BEDFORD-
SHIRE

WEST
WALES

GWENT

GLOUCS &
BRISTOL

OXFORD-
SHIRE

HERTFORD-
SHIRE

ESSEX

BUCKINGHAMSHIRE

GLAMORGAN

GREATER
LONDON

WILTSHIRE

BERKSHIRE

SURREY

KENT

SOMERSET

HAMPSHIRE

WEST
SUSSEX

EAST
SUSSEX

DEVON

DORSET

CHANNEL
ISLANDS

CORNWALL

ISLE OF
WIGHT

Wales

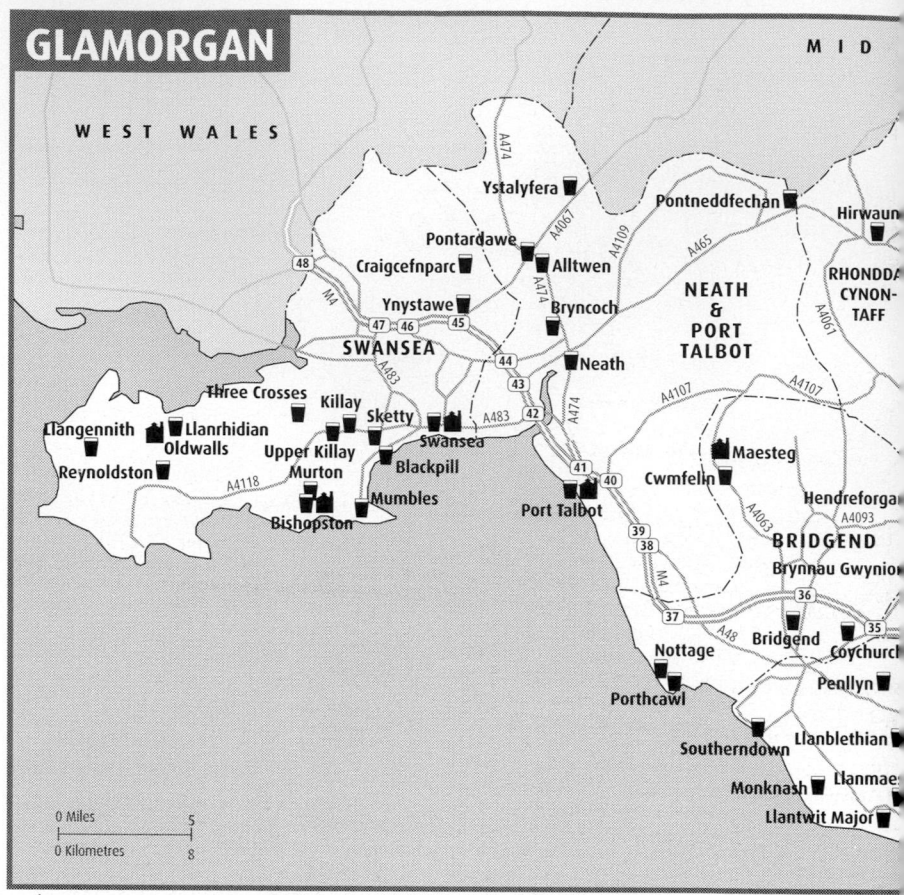

GLAMORGAN

Authority areas covered: Bridgend UA, Caerphilly UA, Cardiff UA, Merthyr Tydfil UA, Neath & Port Talbot UA, Rhondda, Cynon & Taff UA, Swansea UA, Vale of Glamorgan UA

Aberdare

Red Cow ♥ 🄻
6 Merthyr Road, Llwydcoed, CF44 0YE (on B4276)
☼ 12 (6 Mon & Tue)-midnight ☎ (01685) 873924
⊕ theredcowpub.com
Beer range varies Ⓗ
Local CAMRA Pub of the Year 2011 and 2012, the Red Cow is now home to Grey Trees Brewery. Up to six good-value guest beers are available, including beers brewed on site – check the website for what's on. Two ciders are also stocked. Excellent food is on offer at affordable prices. The rear conservatory opens out into an enclosed garden. The pub sponsors local sport and children's events, and holds two beer festivals each year.
🛏Q🍴🕭❀🄳🍴🍽(6)♦P🍽

Alltwen

Butchers at Alltwen
Alltwen Hill, SA8 3BP (off A474)
☼ 12-4, 6-11; 12-midnight Fri & Sat; 12-11 Sun
☎ (01792) 863100 ⊕ thebutchersarmsalltwen.co.uk
Beer range varies Ⓗ
This recently refurbished public house retains an easy atmosphere for a quiet drink, although the main focus is on serving quality food in the bar and restaurant. Two guest ales are available, predominantly from Marston's and Wye Valley breweries. Live music features on alternate Sunday afternoons. The decking outside the pub makes the most of the location, giving a panoramic view of the Lower Swansea Valley. 🛏❀🕭❀🄳🍽(122)P🍽

Barry

Sir Samuel Romilly ⊘
Romilly Buildings, Broad Street, CF62 7AU
☼ 7-midnight (1am Fri & Sat) ☎ (01446) 724900
Greene King Abbot; Ruddles Best Bitter; guest beers Ⓗ
Spacious Wetherspoon pub named after a legal reformer of the 1800s. It opened in 2009 in a building that was previously a market hall, theatre and a bank – the vault is used as a seating area. A large mural above the side entrance depicts life in old Barry, with many more pictures of the town inside. A typical range of guest ales includes regular appearances from Bullmastiff and Vale of Glamorgan breweries. Q❀🕭🄳🍴🚆🐾🍽

Bishopston

Joiners Arms 🄻
50 Bishopston Road, SA3 3EJ

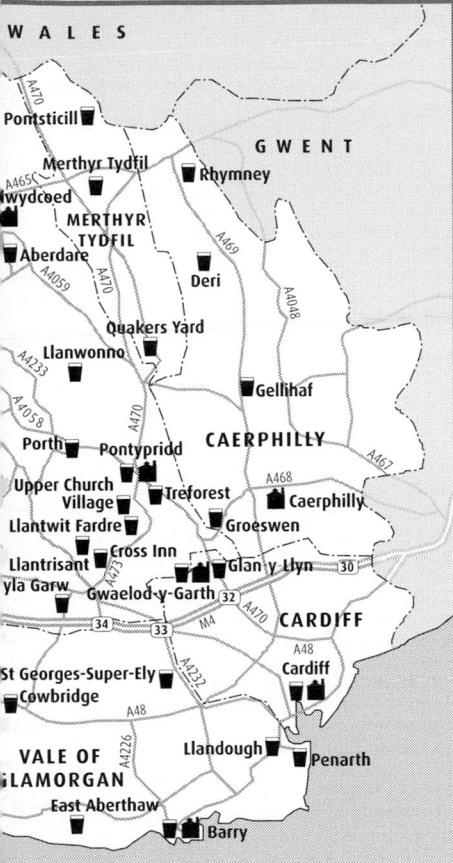

WALES

Bridgend

Coach
37 Cowbridge Road, CF31 3DH
⏱ 11.30-11; 12-10.30 Sun ☎ (01656) 649231
Beer range varies Ⓗ
With good-quality real ale hard to find in this town, it is good to see a new outlet making a go of it and entering the Guide for the first time. This up-and-coming single-bar pub is situated on the edge of the town centre near Bridgend College. Three real ales are available on the bar, along with a real cider and a selection of bottled beers from around the world. ⥱🚇♣💀🍽

Wyndham Arms ✪
Dunraven Place, CF31 1JE
⏱ 7am-midnight (1am Fri & Sat) ☎ (01656) 673500
Greene King Abbot; Ruddles Best Bitter; guest beers Ⓗ
Dating back to 1792 and named after an old local family, this establishment was reopened as a Wetherspoon pub and 25 bedroom hotel in 1999. Situated in the pedestrianised area in the centre of Bridgend, next to the post office and war memorial, it has one bar serving three areas, one used for family dining. 🛏🌀◐👤⥱🚇

Bryncoch

Dyffryn Arms
Neath Road, SA10 7YF (on A474)
⏱ 12-midnight ☎ (01639) 636184
Beer range varies Ⓗ
A cosy and comfortable family-friendly country pub north-west of Neath with two changing guest ales available at all times. Excellent home-cooked meals are reasonably priced and served all day, including a carvery on Wednesday and Sunday (booking essential). An outside play area provides activity for children. Q🌀◐👤🚇(122,132)P💀

Brynnau Gwynion

Mountain Hare
Brynna Road, Pencoed, CF35 6PG (off A473 between Pencoed and Llanharan)
⏱ 5-11.30; 2-midnight Fri & Sat; 12-11 Sun
☎ (01656) 860458 🌐 mountainhare.co.uk
Bullmastiff Welsh Gold; Wickwar BOB; guest beers Ⓗ
Traditional roadside family-owned pub comprising a bar and lounge with log fires and a games room. Sporting memorabilia, particularly rugby, adorn the walls of the bar, along with a 1905 picture of the Worthington Brewery of Burton upon Trent.

⏱ 3-10.30 Mon & winter Tue; 11.30-11; 12-10.30 Sun
☎ (01792) 232658
Courage Best Bitter; Swansea Bishopswood, Three Cliffs Gold, Original Wood; guest beers Ⓗ
Situated in the heart of the village, this 1860s free house is popular with locals and busy in both bars. Home of the Swansea Brewing Company, beer festivals and music events are held occasionally. Good-value food is served lunchtimes and evenings (not Mon and eve Sun). The pub has won several local CAMRA awards. There is a small car park. 🛏🌀◐👤🚇(14,114)P💀

Blackpill

Woodman ✪
120 Mumbles Road, SA3 5AS (near turn off for B4436)
⏱ 12-11 (10.30 Sun) ☎ (01792) 402700
Beer range varies Ⓗ
Local scenes of yesteryear decorate the various rooms and nooks of this spacious, recently refurbished establishment situated between the seafront and the entrance to the beautiful Clyne Gardens. Popular with both families and diners, the pub is also welcoming to those wishing to forego the ubiquitous electronic sounds and screens. A constantly changing range of guest ales is offered. There are three outside seating areas including a small beer garden. Meals are served until 10pm (9.30pm Sun). 🛏Q🌀◐👤🚇(2,3,14)P💀

INDEPENDENT BREWERIES

Artisan Cardiff
Brains Cardiff
Bullmastiff Cardiff
Celt Experience Caerphilly
Cerddin Maesteg
Gower Oldwalls (NEW)
Grey Trees Llwydcoed (NEW)
Neath Port Talbot
Otley Pontypridd
Swansea Bishopston
Tomos Watkin (Hurns) Swansea
Vale of Glamorgan Barry
Violet Cottage Gwaelod-y-Garth (NEW)
Zerodegrees Cardiff

Outside, a lawned beer garden lies beyond a covered smoking area. An on-site brewery is nearing completion. Q☆✲੪ᵭ🖵(44,244)♣P

Cardiff

Albany
105 Donald Street, CF24 4TL
✪ 12-11 (11.30 Fri & 10.30 Sun) ☎ (029) 2031 1075
Brains Dark, Bitter, SA, SA Gold; guest beers Ⓗ
A locals' pub in an area with a large student population, the Albany continues to attract a varied clientele through its beer quality, ambience and range of activities. The public bar is lively, with TVs showing sport, while the lounge bar offers the chance for quiet conversation. The pub holds a twice-weekly poker league night, weekly quiz and karaoke on Saturday nights. It has a covered and heated smoking area, skittle alley and beer garden. Q☆✲੪🖵(57,58)♣🍴⊵

Birchgrove Ⓛ ✔
Caerphilly Road, CF14 4AE
✪ 12-11 (midnight Thu-Sat) ☎ (029) 2031 1319
Brains Dark, Bitter, SA, The Rev James; Sharp's Doom Bar; guest beer Ⓗ
Busy suburban community pub in a prominent position at a major crossroads. Built in Arts & Crafts style but modernised in recent years, it has retained original features including wood panelling in the public bar and two red-brick fireplaces. The full range of Brains is served together with seasonals and guest ales from family and microbreweries. A changing guest cider is also on handpump. The pub has a traditional skittle alley.
✲✪੪ᵭ≢(Heath High/Low Level/Birchgrove)🖵🍴⊵

Chapter Arts Centre
Market Road, Canton, CF5 1QE
✪ 12-11 (12.30am Fri; midnight Sat; 10.30 Sun)
☎ (029) 2030 4400 🌐 chapter.org
Ringwood Best Bitter; guest beers Ⓗ
Former school, now a bright, attractive Arts Centre with a fantastic bar. One section of the long bar counter is dedicated to fine, good-value food. Beyond that, the real business begins with a handpumped cider and six real ales, half from the Marston's stable and the others from interesting independents. There is also a lip-smacking range of continental beers including many from smaller German breweries. Contemporary art adorns the walls. ⚲✲✪ᵭ⚥≢(Ninian Park)🖵(17,18)🍴P⊵

City Arms 🏆 ✔
Quay Street, CF10 1EA
✪ 11-11 (midnight Fri & Sat); 12-10.30 Sun
☎ (029) 2064 1913
Brains Dark, SA, Bitter, The Rev James Ⓗ; **guest beers** Ⓗ/Ⓖ
A must-visit city-centre pub in the shadow of the Millennium Stadium. This is a Brains house with a marked departure from the usual guest beer policy. The keen licensee is free to order guest beers as he sees fit and what is on offer reflects his knowledge of good real ales, mainly from microbreweries from across the UK, some dispensed via gravity from cooled casks. Festivals and other events are held regularly. Frequent visitors should obtain a loyalty card. Local CAMRA Pub of the Year 2012. Q੪ᵭ≢(Central)♣🍴🍴

Cottage Ⓛ ✔
25 St Mary Street, CF10 1AA
✪ 11-11 (midnight Fri & Sat) ☎ (029) 2033 7195
Brains Dark, Bitter, SA, The Rev James, SA Gold; guest beer Ⓗ
Behind an ornate wood and glass frontage, the Cottage has a long, narrow interior. Built around 1750, it is one of the oldest inns in Cardiff. A classic Brains pub, it serves a full range of the brewery's ales and a guest beer, along with home-cooked food until mid-evening. Decorated with old photographs of the city, this is a convivial retreat on a main street where the nightlife can be hectic – it is usually busy on international rugby match days. ⊄▶≢(Central)🖵

Deri ✔
Heol y Deri, Rhiwbina, CF14 6UH
✪ 12-midnight ☎ (029) 2062 6237
Brains Bitter; Hancock's HB; Sharp's Doom Bar; guest beers Ⓗ
A large suburban pub on the northern outskirts of Cardiff that has been much altered, extended and modernised over the years. Popular and busy, it has a large lounge bar, stylishly furnished and divided into several distinct areas. The regular beers are supported by a changing range of four guest ales from regional and microbreweries from all over the UK. Two quiz evenings are hosted each week. There is a large car park, outside seating space and covered smoking area.
Q✲✪ᵭ≢(Rhiwbina)🖵(21,23)P⊵

Discovery
Celyn Avenue, Lakeside, CF23 6EH
✪ 12-11 (midnight Fri & Sat; 10.30 Sun) ☎ (029) 2075 5015
🌐 thediscoverypubcardiff.co.uk
Butcombe Bitter; Greene King Abbot; Sharp's Doom Bar; guest beer Ⓗ
Spacious community pub situated close to the north end of Roath Park Lane. The bar has a big screen for sports enthusiasts and caters for the usual pub activities including darts and quizzes. The large quieter lounge has two impressive Tiffany ceiling lights. There is also a large function room which can cater for parties. Food is served until 9pm (4pm Sun). The pub holds occasional mini beer festivals and hosts charity events.
✲✪ᵭ≢(Heath High/Low Level)🖵(52A)♣P⊵

Goat Major Ⓛ ✔
33 High Street, CF10 1PU
✪ 12-midnight (6 Sun) ☎ (029) 2033 7161
Brains Dark, Bitter Ⓗ, **SA** Ⓖ; **guest beer** Ⓗ
Popular city-centre Brains pub with a traditional appearance and friendly bar staff, attracting a brisk trade from both locals and visitors. It is named after the mascot of the Royal Welsh Regiment, a fact that is proudly illustrated in the many photographs adorning the cosy interior. Traditional Welsh food is served into the early evening. A handy watering hole if visiting Cardiff Castle and other local attractions. ⊄▶≢(Central)🖵

Half Way Ⓛ ✔
247 Cathedral Road, Pontcanna, CF11 9PP
✪ 12-11.30 (midnight Fri); 10-midnight Sat; 12-11 Sun
☎ (029) 2066 7135
Brains Dark, Bitter, SA, SA Gold, The Rev James; guest beers Ⓗ
Managed by an enthusiastic licensee, this busy open-plan establishment has a large central bar and three drinking and dining areas to choose

from. Real fires add warmth and character, and the pub has a genuine, comfortable feel to it. Popular with a mixed clientele, it has the added attraction of a full range of Brains beers and guest ales, with a beer festival hosted in late summer. There is a traditional skittle alley. ⛰❀◐♿⛺🚌♣⚡

Mochyn Du

Sophia Close, CF11 9HW

⏲ 12-11 (midnight Fri & Sat; 10.30 Sun) ☎ (029) 2037 1599 🌐 ymochyndu.com

Vale of Glamorgan Cwrw'r Mochyn Du, Cwrw Cymru; guest beers Ⓗ

Located near Glamorgan County Cricket ground, this large free house is known for the quality and variety of its beer, as well as for its Welsh pride. At least four real ales are always available, more during the rugby season – often from local microbreweries. The conservatory provides a smart and comfortable place to enjoy the menu of freshly cooked Welsh food, while large decked areas outside offer pleasant surroundings in fair weather. Sport is screened on TV. ❀◐⛺🚌P⚡

New Conway 𝕃

58 Conway Road, Pontcanna, CF11 9NW

⏲ 12-11 (midnight Fri & Sat; 10.30 Sun) ☎ (029) 2022 4373 🌐 theconway.co.uk

Greene King IPA; guest beers Ⓗ

In a quiet side street in the residential district of Pontcanna, the pub has an L-shaped drinking area divided into spaces devoted to drinking and dining. Good-quality food, with an emphasis on local ingredients, is available from a frequently changing menu. At least three guest beers are kept, generally sourced from recently established Welsh brewers. There is an outdoor drinking area to the front of the pub. ❀◐🚌♣🍎⚡

Rummer Tavern ✔

14 Duke Street, CF10 1AY

⏲ 11.30-11 (midnight Fri & Sat); 12-11 Sun ☎ (029) 2023 5091 🌐 therummertaverncardiff.co.uk

Hancock's HB; Wye Valley HPA; guest beers Ⓗ

Traditional wood panelling features heavily throughout this pub, which is divided into various seating areas, with a function room upstairs available to hire. The bar is to the rear and stocks a good selection of ales, including three guests. Food is served all day from a traditional menu, with specials on a chalkboard. The central location of this pub makes it a must-visit when in the city. ◐⇌(Central)🚌

Zerodegrees 𝕃

27 Westgate Street, CF10 1DD

⏲ 12-midnight (11 Sun) ☎ (029) 2022 9494

Zero Degrees Pilsner, Black Lager, Pale Ale, Wheat Ale, Mango; seasonal beers Ⓗ

Situated across the street from the Millennium Stadium, the brewery can be seen from the street as well as from inside the bar. The beers are slightly cooler than cask beers are normally served. A wide variety of pizzas is available, as well as mussels, pasta, risotto, salads and sausage and mash. The upper floors are reserved for diners. A welcoming pub with friendly staff. ◐♿⛺⇌(Central)🚌

Cowbridge

Bear Hotel

63 High Street, CF71 7AF

⏲ 11-11 (midnight Fri & Sat); 12-10.30 Sun ☎ (01446) 774814 🌐 bearhotel.com

Brains SA; Hancock's HB; Sharp's Doom Bar; guest beers Ⓗ

Smart hotel, part of a small chain, in the centre of this attractive market town. Steeped in history, it was a coaching inn in the 18th century, but some features of its town house origins going back to the 16th century remain. Two bars either side of the entrance corridor both serve real ale, and up to three guest beers are generally available. There is a rear courtyard for outdoor drinking and a heated and covered smoking area. Food is served every day until 9pm from an extensive menu of main meals and snacks. ⛰Q❀🛏◐🚌P⚡

Vale of Glamorgan Inn 🏆

53 High Street, CF71 7AE

⏲ 11.30-11 (midnight Fri & Sat); 12-11 Sun ☎ (01446) 772252

Hancock's HB; Shepherd Neame Bishops Finger; Wye Valley HPA, Butty Bach; guest beer Ⓗ

Popular single-roomed pub in the centre of town. The wooden-floored bar area has a warming fire; go down a step to the carpeted lounge section where you will find more seating. Outside there is an attractive beer garden with a separate covered and heated smoking area. Good-value food is served at lunchtime (no food Sun). The autumn beer festival coincides with the town's Food & Drink Festival. Accommodation is basic. Local CAMRA Pub of the Year 2012. ⛰Q❀🛏◐🚌🍎⚡

Coychurch

White Horse ✔

Church Terrace, CF35 5HD

⏲ 12-11 (midnight Fri & Sat; 10.30 Sun) ☎ (01656) 652583

Brains Bitter, SA, The Rev James; Greene King Old Speckled Hen; guest beers Ⓗ

Situated opposite the village church, the pub serves five real ales alongside its popular all-day food menu, with a range of offers throughout the week. Cask cider is also on offer during the summer months. The single-room L-shaped interior maintains a homely feel – the bar area is clearly defined and comfortably set out. Outside there is a large car park, beer garden and smoking areas. Well worth a visit. ❀◐♿🚌♣🍎P⚡

Craigcefnparc

Rock & Fountain 𝕃

Rhyddwen Road, SA6 5RA

⏲ 5 (4 Fri; 3 Sat)-11; 12-10.30 Sun ☎ (01792) 843347

Felinfoel Celtic Pride, Stout; guest beer Ⓗ

Friendly local situated on the side of a steep hill close to the RSPB Cwm Clydach bird sanctuary. There is an outside patio area with seating where you can enjoy the view across the valley. The pub has a comfortable lounge featuring pictures of local interest and pub memorabilia, with a separate games bar for pool, darts, dominoes and sport on TV. ❀🀄🚌(121)♣P⚡

Cross Inn

Cross Inn Hotel

Main Road, CF72 8AZ

⏲ 12-11 ☎ (01443) 223431

Hancock's HB; Sharp's Doom Bar; Shepherd Neame Spitfire; guest beer Ⓗ

WALES

A warm, welcoming, lively single-roomed pub, popular with locals and visitors. Poker is played on Monday and Thursday nights, and Wednesday is curry night. Sunday lunches are popular – booking is advised. ❀❶ⅅ✿⊠♣P⌐

Cwmfelin

Cross Inn

Maesteg Road, CF34 9LB (on A4063)
🌣 11.45-midnight (1am Fri & Sat) ☎ (01656) 732476
⊕ cerddinbrewery.co.uk
Cerddin Solar, Cascade; Wye Valley Butty Bach ⊞
In an area where good real ales are hard to find, this friendly multi-roomed pub with its own green-energy-run Cerddin Brewery is a breath of fresh air. Cerddin is Welsh for rowan tree which, in mythology, has magical properties. The pub is situated between Maesteg and Bridgend, with buses stopping at the front door and the railway station within walking distance. A recent runner up in the Vale of Glamorgan CAMRA Pub of the Year competition. Q❀❀⊟⇌(Garth)⊠(32)♣⌐

Deri

Old Club ✓

93 Bailey Street, CF81 9HX
🌣 5 (12 Sat & Sun)-midnight ☎ (01443) 830278
Beer range varies ⊞
A proudly independent establishment that makes a virtue of its freedom from tie. Two guest beers are always available, three at weekends. The vast collection of pump clips on display records an eclectic beer range, with ales mainly from small independent brewers. Rail passengers can take the short undulating bus ride from Bargoed Station, or a gentle 45-minute stroll or cycle ride along the ex-railway Cwm Darran path. Nearby is Cwm Darran country park and hilltops popular with ramblers and paragliders. ▲⊠(1)♣

East Aberthaw

Blue Anchor

CF62 3DD
🌣 11-11; 12-10.30 Sun ☎ (01446) 750329
⊕ blueanchoraberthaw.com
Brains SA; Theakston Old Peculier; Wadworth 6X; Wye Valley HPA; guest beer ⊞
Reputedly dating from 1380, this pub has been in the same family for over 70 years. Its thick stone walls and attractive thatched roof house a labyrinth of rooms, with stone floors, wooden beams and open fires adding to the character. Award-winning food is served in the bar and the upstairs restaurant (no food Sun). The guest beer is usually from a microbrewery, frequently local, and the cider is normally from Gwynt-y-Ddraig. ♨Q☎❀❶ⅅ⊠♣P⌐

Gellihaf

Coal Hole

Bryn Road, NP12 2QE (on A4049 S of Fleur-de-Lys)
🌣 12-3, 6.30-11; 11-11 Fri & Sat; 12-10.30 Sun
☎ (01443) 830280
Greene King Old Speckled Hen, Abbot ⊞
Pleasant one-bar pub converted from farm buildings during the 19th century. Food is served in the bar and a separate dining room, with popular traditional roast dinner served on Sundays. B&B is

available in two single and one double room. The pub takes its name from the former mine shaft (now safely capped) in the car park. From here there are commanding views of the iconic Hengoed Viaduct spanning the Rhymney Valley. ♨❶ⅅP⌐

Glan-y-Llŷn

Fagin's Ale & Chop House ⬡

9 Cardiff Road, CF15 7QD
🌣 11-11 (midnight Thu & Fri); 12-midnight Sat; 12-10.30 Sun
☎ (029) 2081 1800 ⊕ faginsalehouse.co.uk
Otley O4 Columbo ⊞; **guest beers** ⊞/ⓖ
Top-quality free house set in a classic Valleys terrace at the northern end of Taffs Well. Three gravity-dispensed guest ales change daily, with big hop flavours favoured. Handpulls offer Otley Brewery beers and Gwynt y Ddraig ciders. The traditional flagstone floor and log fire are a delight on winter days. Good-value meals are served (no foof Sun eve or Mon). Streetside tables form an outside drinking area. Situated near the M4, the pub is well served by buses and trains. A recent CAMRA Mid-Glamorgan Pub of the Year winner. ♨❀❶ⅅ⊠(26,132)♣

Groeswen

White Cross Inn

CF15 7UT
🌣 4 (12 Fri-Sun)-11 ☎ (029) 20851332
⊕ thewhitecrossinn.co.uk
Beer range varies ⊞
With commanding views over Caerphilly, this delightful rural stone-built pub shares its origins with the adjacent Groeswen Chapel of 1742. The beer range comprises three local or regional guest ales, including a dark, plus a local cider. Road access is easiest via Nantgarw or Hendredenny, though all routes are unsuitable for large vehicles. Rhymney Valley Ridgeway Walk passes close by. ♨Q❀♣♠P

Gwaelod-y-Garth

Gwaelod-y-Garth Inn

Main Road, CF15 9HH
🌣 10-11; 12-10.30 Sun ☎ (029) 2081 0408
⊕ gwaelodinn.co.uk
Wye Valley Bitter; guest beers ⊞
Award-winning pub in the heart of the village with superb views across the valley. Expect to find five real ales, invariably from small breweries, and a cider. The characterful interior with a number of interesting features has recently been expanded to utilise a room beneath the car park. There is a dining room upstairs but diners are equally welcome to eat in the bars. The keen publican has plans for an on-site brewery. ♨Q❀♨❶ⅅ⊠(26B)♣♠P⌐

Hendreforgan

Griffin Inn

Gilfach Goch, CF39 8YL (From Tonyrefail on A4093, turn S after Gilfach Goch village sign) OS988875
🌣 7 (6 Fri)-11, 12-11 Sat & Sun ☎ (01443) 670379
Brains SA ⊞
Although just one cask ale is served, this pub situated at the end of a country lane is well worth seeking out. Listed in CAMRA's Real Heritage Pubs

of Wales, the Griffin has been in the same family for over 50 years. Period features in the back bar include a splendid Victorian counter with an 1870 till, plus oak furniture and gleaming brasses.
♨Q☎☀♿⊕▤(150,172)P⚲—

Hirwaun

Glancynon Inn
Swansea Road, CF44 9PH
☼ 11-11 ☎ (01685) 811043 ⊕ glancynoninn.co.uk
Greene King Abbot; guest beers Ⓗ
This large country pub with oak beams and a friendly atmosphere is the main real ale outlet for the area. A little off the beaten track, it is nevertheless easy to find. The pub features a pleasant lounge and public bar leading to a well-kept beer garden. Guest beers are often from Welsh breweries and the popular restaurant uses local organic produce whenever possible. Lunches are served daily, evening meals Monday to Saturday. Demand is high at weekends (booking advisable). ☀◑⊕♿▤(9)♣P⚲—

Killay

Village Inn ♻ Ⓛ
5-6 Swan Court, The Precinct, Gower Road, SA2 7BA
☼ 10.30-11.30; 12-11 Sun ☎ (01792) 203311
Evan Evans Warrior; Fuller's London Pride; Taylor Landlord; guest beer Ⓗ
Cosy pub with an L-shaped bar and wood panelling, situated in a small shopping precinct. Home-made food is served until 8pm daily from a wide-ranging, daily-changing menu, both in the bar and separate restaurant (booking essential). The pub offers Sky Sports, holds a quiz on Sunday and Tuesday evenings and hosts monthly gatherings of a Song Writers Guild. An annual beer festival is held in April. Local CAMRA Pub of the Year 2012. ◑♿▤(20,21)♣P⚲—

Llanblethian

Cross Inn
Church Road, CF71 7JF (on B4270)
☼ 11-11 (9 Sun) ☎ (01446) 772995
⊕ crossinncowbridge.co.uk
Hancock's HB; Wye Valley Butty Bach; guest beer Ⓗ
Sixteenth-century inn, popular with locals, passing trade and walkers, with a friendly public bar, warmed by a log stove, and a separate room for diners. The pub prides itself on serving locally sourced food where possible and caters for vegetarians and children. Two small beer festivals in spring and autumn stimulate interest in more unusual beers, but locally brewed ales are also popular. Real cider is available occasionally. ♨Q☀◑⊕▤(V1)♣👍P⚲—

Llandough

Merrie Harrier
117 Penlan Road, CF64 2NY (on jct of A4055 and B4267)
☼ 12-11; 11.30-11.30 Fri & Sat ☎ (029) 2030 3994
Brains Dark, Bitter, SA; guest beer Ⓗ
A large Brains pub on a busy road junction close to Llandough Hospital. This traditionally styled road house has a tiled floor in the front bar giving way to wooden floorboards, and a raised seating area where you can relax in a leather sofa and

armchairs. A good range of food is available all day, and in warm weather meals can be enjoyed outside on the patio area. There is live music on Saturday evenings, and sport is screened on TV.
♨☀◑♿⇄(Cogan)▤(X45,95)P⚲—

Llangennith

King's Head Ⓛ
SA3 1HX
☼ 11-11; 12-10.30 Sun ☎ (01792) 386212
⊕ kingsheadgower.co.uk
Gower Brew One, Sampson Jack, Best Bitter, Gold, seasonal beers; guest beers Ⓗ
A row of three 16th-century stone-built cottages, the pub has been owned and run by the same family for many years. The full range of ales from nearby Gower Brewery is available plus a cask cider. An impressive variety of home-made food is served all day with dishes inspired by fresh, local produce. Situated a short distance from the sandy stretches of Llangennith Beach, the pub offers quality 4-star accommodation. A gem of a hostelry.
♨Q☀▣◑♿▲▤(116)♣👍P⚲—

Llanmaes

Blacksmiths Arms Ⓛ ✅
CF61 2XR
☼ 12-11.30 (10.30 Sun) ☎ (01446) 795996
⊕ blacksmithsarmsllanmaes.co.uk
Brains The Rev James; Hancock's HB; guest beers Ⓗ
A pub for everyone and their dog. Diners and drinkers, locals and strangers, families and pets are equally welcome at this village inn. The sizeable patio is popular in summer, and in winter two open fires warm the bar. Meals are served in the bar as well as the separate restaurant. Quiz nights are Wednesday and Sunday, there is occasional live music, and a beer festival is held in summer. Two guest beers are available at all times.
♨Q☎☀◑♿▲▤(V1)P⚲—

Llanrhidian

Dolphin Inn
SA3 1EH (just off B4295 N Gower Road)
☼ 1 (6 Mon)-11 summer; 6 (1 Fri & Sat)-11 winter; 12-10.30 Sun ☎ (01792) 391069
Brains The Rev James; Fuller's London Pride; guest beers Ⓗ
Cosy village pub on the north side of Gower next to a 13th-century church, with stunning views of the estuary from the lovely beer gardens. A characterful single room, it has a central bar and a dartboard. Friendly and knowledgeable staff help to create a welcoming atmosphere. There is a children's play area at the rear with a fenced area for rabbits and poultry to roam. Cold snacks are available until 8pm. ☀▤(116)♣P⚲—

Greyhound Inn Ⓛ
Oldwalls, SA3 1HA (1 mile W of Llanrhidian on B4295)
☼ 11-11 ☎ (01792) 391027
⊕ thegreyhoundinnoldwalls.co.uk
Gower Brew One, Sampson Jack, Best Bitter, Gold, seasonal beers; guest beers Ⓗ
Traditional 19th-century inn with a welcoming atmosphere, offering the full range of ales from the pub's on-site microbrewery. An extensive home-cooked bar menu is served until 9pm every day. There is a dartboard and pool table. Outside at

the rear is a large beer garden with a children's play area and wonderful views over the Gower countryside. Home of the Halfpenny Folk Club every Sunday evening. ⋈✿☺◑⬚♿🛆🅰(116)♣P⌐

Llantrisant

Wheatsheaf
High Street, CF72 8BQ
🌣 5 (3 Sat)-1am; 12-midnight Sun ☎ (01443) 226841
⊕ wheatsheafllantrisant.com
Beer range varies ⊞
Traditional pub with a central bar serving four rooms, one a family room. The landlord, a Cornishman, is extremely knowledgeable about real ales and passionate about how they are kept. A Cornish brew often features among the five ever-changing handpulled beers, and ales brewed on the premises make occasional appearances. CAMRA members receive a discount. Monday is a popular cheese night, with generous platters provided for customers. Two beer festivals are held each year. ⋈Q☺✿♣🌣⌐

Llantwit Fardre

Bush Inn
Main Road, CF38 2EP
🌣 4-midnight (1am Thu); 3-1am Fri; 12-1am Sat; 12-midnight Sun ☎ (01443) 203958
Hancock's HB; guest beers ⊞
Busy village local offering up to three guest beers, which can be from any brewer, large or small, with up-and-coming ales noted at the bar. Entertainment includes popular quizzes on Tuesday and Wednesday, open mic on Thursday and a live band on Saturday – all nights can be busy. Pool and darts are played in a separate area. ✿♿🛆(100,400)♣P⌐

Crown Inn
Main Road, CF38 2HL
🌣 12-midnight ☎ (01443) 218277 ⊕ freewebs.com/crowninn
Wickwar Coopers WPA; guest beers ⊞
Bright, friendly pub with a single large bar and dining area. One or two guest beers are available – they may be from local brewers or from further afield. Good food includes traditional and international choices. Live music plays on Saturday, a quiz is hosted on Sunday. A popular beer and cider festival is held in late August. ✿◑🛆(100,400)P⌐

Llantwit Major

King's Head
East Street, CF61 1XY
🌣 11.30-11; 12-10.30 Sun ☎ (01446) 792697
Brains IPA, Bitter, SA; guest beers ⊞
Family-run town-centre local making its 14th consecutive appearance in the Guide. A traditional two-room pub, the public bar is flagstoned and well used by darts and pool teams. The comfortable lounge features wood panelling, a fish tank and an entrance to the beer garden. Good-value lunches are served and there is a large-screen TV for sport in both bars. Occasional mini beer festivals are held with beer stillaged in the bar. Parking space is limited to two cars. ⋈Q☺✿◑🅰🛱🛆P⌐

Old Swan Inn
Church Street, CF61 1SB
🌣 12-11 (10.30 Sun) ☎ (01446) 792230 ⊕ oldswaninn.co.uk
Beer range varies ⊞
The oldest pub in town overlooks St Illtyd's Church to the side and the town hall at the front in this historic old part of Llantwit. Two ever-changing beers are offered during the week and up to four at weekends, with south Wales breweries strongly supported. The front bar is popular with diners and drinkers, the busy back bar is a bit livelier. A beer festival is held in late summer. Free public parking is available behind the town hall. ⋈✿◑🛆🅰🛱♣🌣⌐

Llanwonno

Brynffynon Hotel
CF37 3PH ST030955
🌣 12-11 (10.30 Sun) ☎ (01443) 790272
⊕ brynffynonhotel.com
Beer range varies ⊞
Remote country inn resting high in the middle of the forest between the Cynon and Rhondda Fach valleys. The lounge has a comfortable, relaxed feel with leather couches and a wood-burning stove, and the dining room offers food of an excellent standard (booking recommended). Two guest ales are available at the bar, and regular beer festivals are held throughout the year. A new patio offers views of the forest and churchyard. ⋈✿🛱◑🅰P⌐

Merthyr Tydfil

Rose & Crown
20 Morgan Street, The Quar, CF47 8TP (off A4102 Brecon Rd S of Cyfarthfa Park)
🌣 12 (11.30 Sat & Sun)-midnight ☎ (01695) 722726
Rhymney Best Bitter; guest beers ⊞
A welcome return to the Guide for this comfortable back-street local, just off the Brecon Road. Well worth a visit for the warm welcome, it offers a range of beers complemented by good home-cooked meals (try the Irish Chicken Curry) served until 7pm. Historic maps and photographs proudly display how industry shaped Merthyr Tydfil. ◑♿🛆(26)♣⌐

Monknash

Plough & Harrow
CF71 7QQ (off B4265 between Wick and Marcross) SS918705
🌣 12-11 ☎ (01656) 890209 ⊕ ploughandharrow.org
Beer range varies ⊞/Ⓖ
Renowned 14th-century pub, originally a monastic farmhouse for Neath Abbey, with many original features remaining. Up to eight real ales are offered, four on handpump and the others direct from casks behind the bar, with local breweries well supported, along with real cider and perry. Good home-cooked food is served, and the large log fires add warmth in winter. The spacious garden is popular, and hosts beer festivals in summer. Vale of Glamorgan CAMRA Cider Pub of the Year 2012. ⋈Q✿◑🛆(145)♣⌐

Mumbles

Newton Inn

New Well Lane, Newton, SA3 4SR (1 mile N of Mumbles on Newton Rd)

☼ 12 (3 Mon)-midnight (1am Fri & Sat) ☎ (01792) 363226

Worthington Bitter; guest beers Ⓗ

Comfortable, spacious pub with a separate lounge and bar. Five handpumps serve the regular Worthington's cask and three or four guest ales. Home-made food includes pub classics and more upmarket dishes, plus daily fish specials (no food Sun eve or Mon). Quiz night is Wednesday and dogs are allowed in the bar. ♨⤳✿❀⟨⟩🍴♿⏚

Park Inn Ⓛ

23 Park Street, SA3 4AD

☼ 4 (12 Fri-Sun)-midnight ☎ (01792) 366738

Felinfoel Stout; guest beers Ⓗ

A regular Swansea CAMRA Pub of the Year award winner, with five handpumps dispensing an ever-changing range of beers, with particular emphasis on independent breweries from Wales and the west of England. The convivial atmosphere in this small establishment attracts discerning drinkers of all ages, though the games room is particularly popular with younger people. Alongside a fine display of pump clips are pictures of old Mumbles and its pioneering railway. ♨Q🚐(2,3)♣⏚

Murton

Plough & Harrow

88 Oldway, SA3 3DJ

☼ 12-3, 5-11; 12-11 Sat; 12-10.30 Sun ☎ (01792) 234459

Brains Bitter, IPA, SA; guest beers Ⓗ

One of Gower's oldest pubs, the Plough & Harrow has been enlarged and renovated in recent times, but retains its character and popularity. The pub combines a busy food trade with the traditions of a local. The bar area has TV and pool, and there is a quieter space for conversation or a meal. Tuesday is quiz night. Heaters are used to warm the large, covered and decked outdoor area, which unusually also has a pool table. ♨✿⟨⟩♿🚐(14,114)P⏚

Neath

Borough Arms

2 New Henry Street, SA11 1PH (off Briton Ferry road)

☼ 4-11 (9 Mon); 12-11 Sat; 12-8 Sun ☎ (01639) 644902

Draught Bass; guest beers Ⓗ

Welcoming traditional pub with a reputation for quality ales and a strong local following. A central bar serves two distinct areas, offering a constantly changing range of up to five beers with an emphasis on local ales. An annual beer festival is held every autumn. The pub is three quarters of a mile from the town centre but well worth the walk. Local CAMRA Pub of the Year for three consecutive years, and runner up in 2012. Q✿♿≒🚐♣⏚

Smiths Arms Ⓛ

New Road, Neath Abbey, SA10 7DG (off A465 on A4320 to Skewen)

☼ 2-11; 12-midnight Sat & Sun ☎ (01639) 641770

Neath Firebrick, Witch Hunter Ⓗ

A Grade II-listed building, this traditional pub is close to the ruins of Neath Abbey, a former Cistercian monastery. The interior is attractively decorated and comprises a bar, lounge and function room. The lounge features an open hearth fire. Pool and darts are available in the bar and

sport is screened on TV. Live music plays occasionally. A local outlet for the Neath Brewery. ♨✿⟨🚐♣⏚

Nottage

Rose & Crown Hotel

Heol y Capel, CF36 3ST

☼ 11-11 (midnight Fri & Sat); 12-10.30 Sun

☎ (01656) 784850 ⊕ roseandcrownporthcawl.com

Brains Bitter, SA, The Rev James; guest beers Ⓗ

Part of a hotel group run by Brains in a little village on the northern outskirts of Porthcawl. This cosy pub, which is made up of two old cottages, one having been an ale house in the past, has plenty of little bar areas, as well as a dining section offering a good range of food all day throughout the week. ♨✿🛏⟨⟩♿🅿🚆●P⏚

Penarth

Bear's Head ✪

37-39 Windsor Road, CF64 1JD

☼ 8am 11.30 ☎ (029) 2070 6424

Bullmastiff Son of a Bitch; Greene King Abbot; Ruddles Best Bitter; guest beers Ⓗ

A typical Wetherspoon outlet in the town centre with an extensive open-plan interior, and a smaller area upstairs comfortable for families. A clientele of all ages enjoys a variety of up to eight ales, with locally brewed Vale of Glamorgan, Bullmastiff, Newmans and other Welsh beers making regular appearances. There is a steady trade most of the week, but it can get busy Friday and Saturday evenings. The pub's name is a rough English translation of Penarth – pen meaning head and arth meaning bear. Q⟨⟩♿≒🚐●⏚

Golden Lion

69 Glebe Street, CF64 1EF

☼ 11-11 (midnight Fri & Sat) ☎ (029) 2070 1574

Beer range varies Ⓗ

A lively JW Bassett pub situated a short walk from the town centre. Recently refurbished and modernised to a high standard, the pub offers good-value food and two real ales from Welsh breweries. 3D HD Sky Sports is offered throughout, even in the small beer garden, and the jukebox has an impressive 20,000 tracks. Regular events include a quiz night on Monday and poker on Tuesday. The pub has a darts team. ✿⟨⟩♿≒●⏚

Windsor

93 Windsor Road, CF64 1JF

☼ 9am-11.30 (11 Sun) ☎ (029) 2070 2821

Greene King Abbot; St Austell Tribute; Taylor Landlord; guest beers Ⓗ

A large collection of pump clips on the wall, along with a good range of up to five beers on handpump, are tribute to the landlord's commitment to real ale. The open-plan interior features Welsh rugby and nautical themes, and with background music kept low, the pub is comfortable for conversation. Regular activities include live jazz on Wednesday, unplugged music on Sunday, and bingo on Monday in the adjoining function room, which also hosts live music and community events. ✿⟨⟩≒(Dingle Rd)🚐⏚

Penllyn

Red Fox

CF71 7RQ (half mile off A48) SS973763

✪ 12-11 (10.30 Sun) ☎ (01446) 772352 ⊕ redfoxinn.co.uk

Hancock's HB; Tomos Watkins OSB; guest beers Ⓗ

A genuine welcome is guaranteed at this friendly village local. The main bar area with traditional stone walls and floors is warmed by a log fire, and a separate restaurant serves good British pub food. Outside, there is an attractive patio to the front and a large enclosed garden to the rear – the perfect place to while away the time with a good pint and a quality meal in warmer weather. Activities including a mussels and ales festival take place throughout the year. ⌂Q✿◑❒♣P▞

Pontardawe

Dillwyn Arms Hotel

The Cross, SA8 4EB

✪ 12-midnight ☎ (01792) 863310 ⊕ dillwynshotel.com

Young's Special; guest beer Ⓗ

Free house on Pontardawe Cross with a comfortable bar and a large dining area. One regular beer and one guest are supplied by local and national brewers. The good-value home-made food menu (try the real chips) has meal deals for adults and children. A large function room and accommodation are available. The outdoor seating overlooks the river. ✿⇔◑❒৬❒(120,125)♣P▞

Pontneddfechan

Angel Inn Ⓛ

Pontneathvaughan Road, SA11 5NR (just off A465 on B4242 1 mile from Glynneath)

✪ 11.30 (12 Sun)-11 ☎ (01639) 722013

Neath Firebrick; guest beer Ⓗ

Traditional country pub convenient for the famous Waterfall Walks and opposite the Waterfalls Centre. It has a large area catering mainly for diners with quality home-cooked food, and a separate bar for use by hikers and for screening live rugby matches on TV. The outside tables are popular with walkers and diners in fine weather. The pub may close in the afternoon in winter if quiet.
Q✿◑❒৬❒(X5)P▞

Pontsticill

Red Cow ⊘

CF48 2UN (follow signs for Brecon Mountain Railway)

✪ 10.30-midnight ☎ (01685) 384828

Wye Valley Bitter; guest beers Ⓗ

Set within the Brecon Beacons National Park, this traditional inn has flagstone floors and an enthusiastic landlord. A popular locals' pub, it also attracts walkers and visitors to the beautiful Pontsticill reservoirs. The Brecon Mountain Railway is a modest but steep walk away. A few pints here may tempt you to join the unusual Snipers Club – ask at the bar for details. Lunches served 12-4pm.
⌂✿◑❒(24)♣P▞

Pontypridd

Bunch of Grapes Ⓛ

Ynysangharad Road, CF37 4DA (off A4054)

✪ 11-1am (midnight Sun) ☎ (01443) 402934

⊕ bunchofgrapes.org.uk

Otley 01 Ⓗ**; guest beers** Ⓗ/Ⓖ

A must-visit for quality food and drink. The short walk from the town centre is amply rewarded by up to eight ales, often eclectic and innovative. An impressive range of foreign beers also features, plus real cider and perry, and some unusual soft drinks. The pub has an esteemed restaurant where quality is the watchword, offering locally sourced foods and friendly service (booking advisable). Allow time to experience the fabulous atmosphere here – this is a hostelry that is hard to leave.
⌂✿◑❒♣⬥P▞

Llanover Arms

Bridge Street, CF37 4PE (opp N entrance to Ynysangharad Park, off A470)

✪ 12-midnight (11 Sun) ☎ (01443) 403215

Brains Bitter; guest beer Ⓗ

The history of this free house can be traced back to the late 18th century. It is just a short stroll from the bus station, close to the museum and historic old bridge. The three rooms and passageway each have their own distinct atmosphere and attract a loyal clientele. The walls are festooned with a variety of artefacts including old mirrors, paintings and clocks. ⌂Q✿◑❒⇌❒♣P

Patriot Bar ⊘

25B Taff Street, CF37 4UA (at N end of main street opposite Iceland)

✪ 10 (12 Sun)-midnight ☎ (01443) 407915

Rhymney Hobby Horse, Dark, Bevans Bitter, Bitter, Export Ⓗ

Previously a shop, this new Rhymney Brewery pub (known locally as the Wonky Bar) is close to the Muni entertainment venue, the historic centre, and the famous town bridge. Simply and functionally furnished, with a popular jukebox, the Patriot offers keenly priced ales to an appreciative and varied clientele. Real cider from Gwynt y Ddraig is sometimes on sale. ৬⇌❒▞

Port Talbot

Lord Caradoc ⊘

69-73 Station Road, SA13 1NW

✪ 9am-midnight (1.30am Fri & Sat) ☎ (01639) 896007

Brains SA; Rhymney Export; Ruddles Best Bitter; guest beers Ⓗ

Popular Wetherspoon pub in the centre of town a short distance from the railway station and bus terminus. The bar has an L-shaped layout with a raised drinking area. Children are welcome in the family area towards the rear and the patio area outside. The usual value-for-money fare is served, with steak and curry nights always popular. At least one cider is available. A public car park is situated at the rear of the pub. ✿◑৬⇌❒⬥▞

Porth

Rheola

Rheola Road, CF39 0LF

✪ 2-midnight; 1-1am Fri; 12-1am Sat; 12-midnight Sun ☎ (01443) 682633

Draught Bass; Theakston XB; guest beer Ⓗ

Large detached free house situated at the point where the Rhondda Valley divides, and easily accessible by bus or train. Loud music can sometimes dominate, but the lounge tends to be a little quieter. One guest beer is added every Friday. The outdoor smoking area is sheltered. Last admission is strictly 10.30pm. ✿❒⇌❒♣P

Porthcawl

Lorelei Hotel

36-38 Esplanade Avenue, CF36 3YU
✪ 5 (11 Fri & Sat)-11; 12-10.30 Sun ☎ (01656) 788342
Draught Bass Ⓖ; **Rhymney Export** Ⓗ; **guest beers** Ⓗ/Ⓖ

Flowerpot men guard the entrance to this small friendly hotel in a terraced street just off the seafront near the Grand Pavilion Theatre. An oasis for real ale in the area, the front bar features an old central fireplace and the smaller bar at the back leads to the garden. Alongside the real ales, the pub offers European beers including Czech Budvar. Real cider is available in summer.
🏚Q☞🕸🍴🍽🚽🏮🛡

Quakers Yard

Glantaff Inn

Cardiff Road, CF46 5AH
✪ 11-4, 6-1am; 11-1am Fri & Sat; 11-midnight Sun
☎ (01443) 410822
Beer range varies Ⓗ

Pleasant riverside pub popular with locals as well as walkers and cyclists from the nearby Taff Trail. The interior is adorned with a large collection of water jugs, many interesting early photographs of the locality, plus boxing memorabilia. Meals are both generous and good value, and local Welsh ales are often available. The pub hosts meetings of the local mountaineering club. ◑🍽(7,78)🛡

Reynoldston

King Arthur Hotel Ⓛ

Higher Green, SA3 1AD (on village green)
✪ 11-11 ☎ (01792) 390775 ⊕ kingarthurhotel.co.uk
Felinfoel Double Dragon; Tomos Watkin OSB; guest beers Ⓗ

Traditional family-owned hotel with efficient and friendly staff. Situated at the foot of Cefn Bryn in beautiful Gower, overlooking the village green, outdoor seating is available. The cosy, atmospheric main bar is open to drinkers and diners, serving home-cooked food with a difference made with local produce. Main meals are served lunchtimes and evenings, snacks are available all day. Beer can be bought to take out.
🏚☞🕸🍴◑🍴🚽🍽(118)🍀P🛡

Rhymney

Farmers Arms

Old Brewery Lane, NP22 5EZ
✪ 12-11; 12-3.30, 7-11 Sun ☎ (01685) 840257
Beer range varies Ⓗ

Large, traditional pub and restaurant near the site of the original Rhymney Brewery, recalled in photographs and breweriana. Three rooms, full of individual character, surround a central serving area. Two guest beers from regional and national brewers are usually on offer. The bar is delightfully restful, with a flagstone floor and real fire. A large function room is available. The pub hosts the local Silurian Choir and a popular Thursday quiz night. Rhymney railway station is a modest walk. No evening food Sunday and Monday. 🏚Q🕸◑🍀🍀P

St Georges-Super-Ely

Greendown Inn

Drope Road, CF5 6EP (off A48 Culverhouse Cross then Michaelston Road) 104765
✪ 12-2 (not Mon & Tue), 6-11; 12-11 Sat; 12-10.30 Sun
☎ (01446) 760310 ⊕ greendownhotel.com
guest beer Ⓗ

Just outside the Cardiff city boundary, this 15th century pub has an L-shaped bar with low beams and two log stoves. It offers a single regularly changing ale, often from a local Welsh brewery, plus real cider and perry. The seperate restaurant is used for Sunday lunches and functions, and accommodation is available. The pub is an active supporter of charities. It may close early in the evening if quiet. 🏚Q🕸🍴◑🍽(320,322)🍀🍀P

Sketty

Vivian Arms ✪

104 Gower Road, SA2 9BZ
✪ 12-11 (midnight Fri & Sat) ☎ (01792) 516194
Brains Bitter, SA, The Rev James; guest beers Ⓗ

Situated on the main crossroads in Sketty, this spacious pub attracts a wide range of customers young and old. It offers a mixture of seating areas with comfortable sofas, a real fire and plenty of TV screens throughout showing live sport. Two frequently changing guest beers are available alongside the Brains standards. The pub has a small meeting room and is suitable for family dining. Meals are served until 9pm (6pm Sun).
🏚🕸◑🍴🍽(20,21)🛡

Southerndown

Three Golden Cups

CF32 0RW
✪ 12-11 (midnight Fri & Sat; 10 Sun) ☎ (01656) 880432
⊕ thethreegoldencups.co.uk
Sharp's Doom Bar; guest beers Ⓗ

One of the few pubs on the Glamorgan Heritage Coast with a view to the sea. The public bar has pool and darts, and the restaurant/lounge has a stone and wooden decor and is named after the Maria Jose, a ship wrecked nearby in 1914 – some crew members were cared for here. Guest beers tend to be well-known national brands. Regular music evenings are held and summer barbecues are popular. There is a heated, covered shelter for smokers. Well-behaved dogs welcome.
🏚🕸◑🍴🍽(145)🍀P🛡

Swansea

Bank Statement ✪

57/58 Wind Street, SA1 1EP
✪ 9-midnight (1am Wed, Thu & Sun; 1.30am Fri; 2am Sat)
☎ (01792) 455477
Greene King Abbot; Ruddles Best Bitter; guest beers Ⓗ

A former Midland Bank, sympathetically transformed by Wetherspoon and retaining its original ornate interior. Trading as a Lloyds No.1 Bar, the pub is at the heart of the city's popular bar quarter and has a large ground floor with plenty of seating. Popular with all ages, it is busy throughout the week as well as at the weekend. An increased commitment to real ale has resulted in the availability of four guest beers and a cask cider.
◑🍴🚉(High St)🍀🛡

Brunswick Arms

3 Duke Street, SA1 4HS (between St Helens Rd and Walter Rd)

✪ 11.30-11; 12-10.30 Sun ☎ (01792) 465676

🌐 brunswickswansea.co.uk

Courage Best Bitter; Greene King Old Speckled Hen, Abbot ⊞; guest beer ⑤

Well-run side-street pub with the air of a country inn in the city. Wooden beams and comfortable seating create a traditional, relaxing atmosphere. The walls are adorned with interesting, ever-changing displays of artwork, with pictures for sale. Food is available until 7.45pm during the week, 2.45pm at the weekend. A quiz is held on Monday evening and live music plays on Sunday, Tuesday and Thursday. The guest beer is gravity dispensed, often from a local microbrewery. Cask cider also available. ♨️◐♿♣🐕

No Sign Bar

56 Wind Street, SA1 1EG

✪ 11-11 (1am Fri & Sat); 12-10.30 Sun ☎ (01792) 456300

🌐 nosignbar.co.uk

Brains The Rev James; guest beers ⊞

Historic narrow bar established in 1690, formerly known as Mundays Wine Bar and reputedly a regular haunt of Dylan Thomas. The premises has recently been extended, but fortunately the pub's charm has been retained and it continues to offer a wonderful drinking experience. Quality food and wine are available and there are usually three cask ales on sale. Live acoustic music features on Sunday and local bands play in the extensive Vault basement on Friday and Saturday evenings. ♨️🕸️◐♿🚄(High St)💷

Potters Wheel Ⓛ ✓

85 The Kingsway, SA1 5JE

✪ 8am-midnight (1am Thu-Sat) ☎ (01792) 465113

Brains SA; Greene King Abbot; Marston's Pedigree; Ruddles Best Bitter ⊞; guest beers ⊞/⑤

A city-centre Wetherspoon outlet named after the old pottery industry. The long sprawling bar area has various seating layouts and attracts customers of all ages and backgrounds. A strong connection to the local CAMRA branch is evident from the real ale information board. An interesting selection of guest beers and a commitment to local microbreweries, enhanced by the introduction of casks on back bar stillage, has boosted the pub's sale of real ales. Cask cider is always available. ◐♿🚄(High St)🐕💷

Queen's Hotel

Gloucester Place, SA1 1TY (near Waterfront Museum)

✪ 11-11 (11.30 Sat); 12-10.30 Sun ☎ (01792) 521531

Brains Buckley's Best Bitter; Theakston Best Bitter, Old Peculier; guest beer ⊞

This vibrant free house is near the Dylan Thomas Arts Centre, City Museum, National Waterfront Museum and marina. The walls display photographs depicting Swansea's rich maritime heritage. The pub enjoys strong local support and home-cooked lunches are popular. Evening entertainment includes a Sunday quiz and live music on Saturday. This is a rare local outlet for Theakston Old Peculier in addition to a seasonal guest beer from a local microbrewery. Beware the bear. 🕸️◐♿💷

Uplands Tavern ✓

42 Uplands Crescent, Uplands, SA2 0PG

✪ 11-11 (midnight Fri & Sat) ☎ (01792) 458242

Greene King IPA, Abbot; guest beer ⊞

In the heart of Swansea's student quarter, this large, single-room pub is currently enjoying something of a renaissance under its present management, attracting regulars from all walks of life. Another former haunt of Dylan Thomas, commemorated in a separate snug area, it now has a deserved reputation for the quality and variety of its live music. There is a large outdoor drinking area at the front. Quiz night is Wednesday, and major sporting events are screened on TV. 🕸️♿🚆(20,21)♣💷

Westbourne

1 Brynymor Road, SA1 4JQ

✪ 11-11.30 (11 Mon; 12.30am Fri & Sat); 12-11 Sun

☎ (01792) 476637 🌐 westbourneswansea.com

Greene King Abbot; guest beers ⊞

Located on the western fringe of the city centre, this street-corner single-bar pub has a refurbished interior. Renowned in the area, it is now the place to go to for young and old alike. Four ales are always available – customers are able to request a particular beer on the pub's website. Food is served until 6pm (4pm Sun). A quiz is held on Tuesday evening. 🕸️◐♿🚆(2,3)💷

Three Crosses

Poundffald ✓

Tir Mynydd Road, SA4 3PB

✪ 11-midnight ☎ (01792) 873428 🌐 poundffald.com

Greene King Abbot; Sharp's Doom Bar; guest beer ⊞

Community village pub in north Gower with equestrian hardware on display on the wooden beams. It has a separate bar and lounge/dining room with real fires. Home-cooked, locally produced food ranges from snacks to main meals, served daily. A discount on beer is available to CAMRA members. An annual beer festival is held during the spring/summer months. ♨️🕸️◐🍴♿🚆(21)℗💷

Treforest

Otley Arms

Forest Road, CF37 1SY (on gyratory system)

✪ 11-midnight (1am Sat); 12-midnight Sun

☎ (01443) 402033 🌐 otleyltd.co.uk

Otley O1, O5 Gold; guest beers ⊞

The original Otley family pub, this end-of-terrace local has spread into adjacent houses. The beer range gives equal prominence to the Otley beers alongside two or three guests from micros and occasionally regionals. A bustling beer festival is held annually in October. Popular with university students and locals, this establishment is well served by train and bus, and easily accessible from Cardiff and many valley towns. Inside, it has a number of drinking areas, and outside is a heated and covered smoking area. ◐🚄🚆(100,244)♣💷

Rickards Arms

61 Park Street, CF37 1SN (100yds N of railway station)

✪ 10-midnight (1am Fri & Sat); 11-11 Sun ☎ (01443) 402305

Otley O1; guest beer ⊞

Popular with students and locals alike, the pub is a one-bar conversion of an old local, and retains a cosy atmosphere. It divides into four separate areas including the old vaulted cellar and an upstairs dining room. Good-value bar food includes ample breakfasts. Outside is a small beer garden. Quizzes and music nights feature regularly. The Otley O1 is increasingly substituted for another from the Otley range. ❀◗➽🖾(100,244)⌐

Tyla Garw

Boar's Head

Coedcae Lane, CF72 9EZ (600yds from A473 over level crossing) ST029815

🌼 4-10 Mon; 12-11; 12-10 Sun ☎ (01443) 225400

Beer range varies ⒣

This pub has several rooms, each with a cosy character of its own, including three mainly used for dining. One bar serves the whole pub, with up to eight handpumps offering an ever-changing range of beer. Knowledgeable staff are able to advise on suitable choices. Sunday lunches are busy (booking advised), and Tuesday steak and Wednesday curry nights are also popular. A direct path to/from Pontyclun station cuts through a small industrial area. **Q**❀◗➽(Pontyclun)**P**⌐

Upper Church Village

Farmers Arms

St Illtyd Road, CF38 1EB

🌼 3-11; 12-midnight Thu-Sat; 12-10.30 Sun
☎ (01443) 205766

Brains The Rev James; guest beer ⒣

One-room village local with pleasant areas outside. The guest beer is usually a bitter from a larger independent brewer. A popular quiz is held on Tuesdays, and curry and music night on Thursdays. At other times, beer and conversation are the main attractions unless there is a rugby match showing on TV, or a visiting choir (possibly two or three at Christmas). No food Monday evening. ⚏❀◗🖾(11,100)**P**

Upper Killay

Railway Inn Ⓛ

553 Gower Road, SA2 7DS

🌼 12-11 (10.30 Sun) ☎ (01792) 203946

Swansea Deep Slade Dark, Bishopswood, Three Cliffs Gold, Original Wood; guest beers ⒣

A classic locals' pub set in woodlands at the top end of Clyne Valley. The adjacent former railway line now forms part of route 4 of the National Cycle Network. In the winter the real fire in the lounge provides welcome warmth and cheer. Traditional cider and at least one guest beer are kept alongside the Swansea Brewing Company beers. Hot pies are available daily. A large area outside hosts occasional barbecues and the annual Steam-Up. Local CAMRA Pub of The Year 2011. ⚏❀⬗🖾(20,21)♣♠**P**⌐

Ynystawe

Millers Arms

634 Clydach Road, SA6 5AX (on B4603, ½ mile N of M4 jct 45)

🌼 11.30-3, 6 (5 Sat)-11; 12-3, 7-10.30 Sun
☎ (01792) 842614 ⊕ millers-arms.co.uk

Greene King Abbot; guest beers ⒣

Friendly community pub with a highly decorative interior including an extensive teapot collection, celebrity photo of the landlord with Tom Jones, and artwork by Katherine Jenkins. Busy periods require booking for meals, which are good value and home-cooked, served in the pub and separate restaurant. In the spring a garden nesting box is on CCTV for the twitchers. Occasional brewery trips are run for locals. The pub is on the main bus routes to/from Swansea Valley and on cycle path 43. ❀◗⬥**P**⌐

Ystalyfera

Wern Fawr Ⓛ

47 Wern Road, SA9 2LX

🌼 7 (6.30 Fri; 12 Sun)-11 ☎ (01639) 843625

Bryncelyn Buddy Marvellous, Holly Hop, Oh Boy, seasonal beers ⒣

This iconic pub is listed in CAMRA's Real Heritage Pubs of Wales publication and is also the Bryncelyn Brewery tap. The bar has a traditional Welsh theme filled with local ephemera, while the lounge has a nice '60s feel. A central bar serves both rooms with three regular Bryncelyn beers including a mild and a seasonal beer. ⚏**Q**❀⬗🖾(X25,125)♣⌐

City Arms, Cardiff

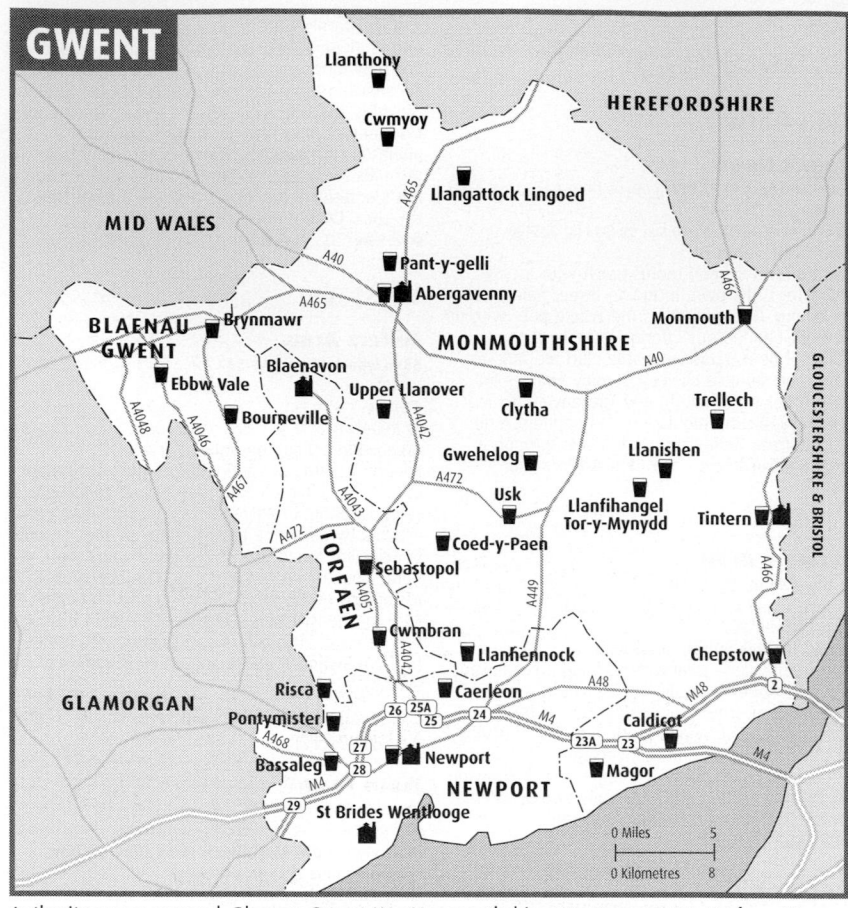

GWENT

Llanthony

Cwmyoy

HEREFORDSHIRE

Llangattock Lingoed

MID WALES

Pant-y-gelli

Abergavenny

BLAENAU
GWENT

Brynmawr

Monmouth

MONMOUTHSHIRE

Blaenavon

Ebbw Vale

Upper Llanover

Clytha

Trellech

Bourneville

Gwehelog

Llanishen

Usk

Llanfihangel
Tor-y-Mynydd

Tintern

Coed-y-Paen

Sebastopol

TORFAEN

Cwmbran

Llanhennock

Chepstow

GLAMORGAN

Risca

Caerleon

Pontymister

26 25A
25

24

Caldicot

Bassaleg

27

Newport

23A   23

Magor

28

NEWPORT

29 St Brides Wentlooge

0 Miles   5

0 Kilometres   8

Authority areas covered: Blaenau Gwent UA, Monmouthshire UA, Newport UA, Torfaen UA

Abergavenny

Angel Hotel

15 Cross Street, NP7 5EW
✪ 10-2.30, 6-11 (11.30 Fri & Sat; 10.30 Sun)
☎ (01873) 857121 ⊕ angelhotelabergavenny.com
Sharp's Doom Bar; Wye Valley HPA; guest beer Ⓗ
A meeting place where people have come to eat
and drink for generations – the wood panelling in
the Foxhunter Bar is over a century old. Contrast
this with the latest addition – a funky little room
that leads off the bar next to the imposing
fireplace. There are several such discrete drinking
areas, each with its own distinctive character and
decoration, which in part explains the hotel's
enormous appeal and growing popularity.
🏚Q🛏🍽🕑◑🕭♿P

Grofield Ⓛ

Baker Street, NP7 5BB
✪ 11 (5 Mon)-11; 11-11.30 Thu-Sat ☎ (01873) 858939
Rhymney Bitter; Sharp's Doom Bar; guest beers Ⓗ
Friendly, modern lounge bar, with comfortable
seating and decor, serving lunchtime meals only.
Just off the main thoroughfare, and close to the
cinema and library, this is the ideal place for a pre-
film drink – you won't find a rowdy crowd here. The
two regular ales, and guest, are always top quality,
and are occasionally supplemented by another

guest from a microbrewery. An enclosed garden at
the rear is a welcome refuge in summer.
Q🛏🍽🕑🍴♣🚲

Station

37 Brecon Road, NP7 5UH
✪ 5 (2 Wed; 1 Thu & Fri; 12 Sat; 11.30 Sun)-11; 11-11.30
Thu-Sat ☎ (01875) 854759
**Draught Bass; Fuller's London Pride; Wye Valley HPA;
guest beers** Ⓗ
Featuring in CAMRA's Real Heritage Pubs of Wales,
this is a classic town pub with a large public bar
and much smaller and quieter lounge. Railway
memorabilia reflects the fact that the pub once
served the long-gone Brecon Road station. Pictures
of jazz greats adorn the bar walls – the landlord is a
well-known jazz drummer on the south Wales
music circuit. Three guest beers often include
choices that are unusual for the area.
🕑🚌(X4,X43)♣P🚲

WALES

Bassaleg

Tredegar Arms ✔

Caerphilly Road, NP10 8LE
☼ 12-11 (midnight Fri); 11-midnight Sat; 12-11.30 Sun
☎ (01633) 893247
Greene King IPA, St Edmunds Ⓗ, **Abbot** Ⓖ, **Old Speckled Hen; Ruddles County** Ⓗ; **guest beers** Ⓖ
Less than a mile from junction 28 on the M4, the 'TA' is an imposing 200-year-old coaching inn at the top of Forge Lane. The pub sells a good selection of Greene King ales plus one or two guests and the occasional cider. A recent refurbishment has improved the ambience of the place, which is proving popular with diners and drinkers. A beer and cider festival is held annually.
Q✿☻◑ ⊟☖ (37,50) ♣P⅃

Bourneville

Tilers Arms Ⓛ

Abertillery Road, NP13 3EB
☼ closed Mon; 12-2, 6-11; 12-4 Sun ☎ (01495) 292000
⊕ tilersarms.com
Beer range varies Ⓗ
A fine pub with a good reputation for food and local real ale – the owner is a strong supporter of local breweries. While food led, with a cosy restaurant and a lunchtime carvery in the main bar, there is room for drinkers in the bar outside dining times, and a small snug centred around a real fire on cold days. Interesting local paintings are on display and some are available to buy.
🏛Q✿☻◑ (X15,X16) ♣P

Brynmawr

Hobby Horse

30 Greenland Road, NP23 4DT
☼ 12-3, 7-11; 11.30-midnight Sat; 11.30-10.30 Sun
☎ (01495) 310996 ⊕ freewebs.com/hobbyhorseinn/home.htm
Beer range varies Ⓗ
This charming community hub is home to several local clubs and societies. Two ever-changing guest beers often include one from a Welsh brewery. The food is popular and can be enjoyed in the restaurant or main bar. Next to the bar counter is an intimate snug with pump clips and various sporting memorabilia colourfully displayed on the ceiling, while on the wall are autographed football shirts and a signed football commemorating a famous Welsh win over Italy in 2002.
✿☻🚃◑ ⊟☖♣P⅃

Caerleon

Bell Inn ✔

Bulmore Road, NP18 1QQ
☼ 12 (11 Sat)-11; 11-10.30 Sun ☎ (01633) 420613
⊕ thebellatcaerleon.co.uk
Beer range varies Ⓗ
An impressive stone exterior fronts a cosy low-beamed restaurant, fireside bar and snug, with a pleasant, secluded garden to the rear. Customers are drawn from near and far to sample fine food and select from an impressive drinks range which, as well as real ales, includes an extensive choice of ciders and perries – as you would expect from the regional CAMRA Cider Pub of the Year. Real ale and cider festivals are hosted twice a year in the Cwtch.
✿☻◑ ⊟☖ (27/28,60) ♣🍴P⅃

Caldicot

Castle Inn

64 Church Road, NP26 4HW
☼ 12-11 (midnight Fri & Sat) ☎ (01291) 420509
Beer range varies Ⓗ
Miniature cannons at the front are a reminder that this attractive pub lies close to Caldicot Castle & Country Park. The pleasant low-beamed interior has a lounge/dining room on one side of the servery, with a cosy bar with a large fireplace as its focal point on the other. Two changing guest ales are sourced from national, regional and family brewers. Food is popular, with a good choice from an extensive menu. The garden includes a large play fort for children. 🏛☻✿◑ ⊟🚃 (14,74)P⅃

Chepstow

Chepstow Athletic Club Ⓛ

Mathern Road, Bulwark, NP16 5JJ (off Bulwark Rd)
☼ 7-11 (11.30 Fri); 12.30-11.30 Sat; 12-3.30, 7-11 Sun
☎ (01291) 622126
Brains SA; Flowers IPA; Rhymney Bitter; guest beers Ⓗ
Hospitable, thriving and well-run club that is highly regarded by locals and visitors. You do not need a sporting disposition to enjoy its friendliness, conversation and good-value ales. CAMRA members are warmly received, as are families, clubs, organisations and societies who meet here. Sports-wise, rugby reigns supreme, but the club's footballers, archers, bowlers, tennis players, cricketers and their friends and followers are all equally welcome at the bar. A large function room upstairs also serves real ale. ☻✿☖⊟🚃♣P⅃

Chepstow Castle Inn Ⓛ

12 Bridge Street, NP16 5EZ
☼ 12-11 ☎ (01291) 630956 ⊕ chepstowcastleinn.co.uk
Bath Gem; Otter Ale; guest beer Ⓗ
Real ale and real music blend happily at this pub, across the road from reputedly the earliest stone-built castle in Europe. Besides slaking thirsts of customers (including the town's Widders morris dancers) the pub serves traditional hearty meals – try the renowned home-cooked fish pie. The three-level bar provides a good variety of seating and, towards the rear, a regular venue for acoustic singers, musicians and their audiences. A surprise delight is an enormous well-sheltered back garden.
✿◑🍴⊟♣

Coach & Horses 🍺 Ⓛ

Welsh Street, NP16 5LN
☼ 12-11 (10.30 Sun) ☎ (01291) 622626 ⊕ sabrain.com/coach-and-horses
Brains Bitter, SA, The Rev James; guest beers Ⓗ
Welcoming family-run inn featuring a single split-level bar with a comfortable range of seating. Six letting rooms are popular with visitors to this ancient market town and the pub attracts regulars from near and far. The range of ales often includes rare and distinctive light-coloured brews alongside the regular Brains ales, plus summertime Westons cider. Four ale-based festivals each year (including one to delight fans of real sausages) reinforce the pub's strong community commitment. Local CAMRA Pub of the Year 2012. ☻✿◑🍴⊟⅃

Clytha

Clytha Arms 🄻

Groesonen Road, NP7 9BW (on B4598 between
Abergavenny and Raglan) SO366088
🕒 12-3 (not Mon), 6-11; 12-11 Sat (10.30 Sun)
☎ (01873) 840206 ⊕ clytha-arms.com
Rhymney Bitter; Wye Valley Bitter; guest beers 🄷

A pub that is rapidly acquiring legendary status for
the range and quality of the beers it serves over
the course of a year. Set in extensive grounds with
fine views, inside you can sit in front of a real fire
and play traditional pub games. The famous Welsh
cider festival and the Welsh beer and cheese
festivals held in the gardens have recently been
supplemented by a German beer and dumplings
weekend. ♨Q🌣🏵🏩◑🖰🖵(83)♣🐾P🛂

Coed-y-Paen

Carpenters Arms

NP4 0TH (turn off A4042 S of Pontypool and aim for
Llandegfedd Reservoir, cross the reservoir dam, pub is
about ½ mile on the left) SO986334
🕒 closed Mon; 12-3, 6-11; 12-midnight Sat; 12-5 Sun
☎ (01291) 672621 ⊕ thecarpenterscoedypaen.co.uk
**Sharp's Doom Bar; Wye Valley Butty Bach; guest
beer** 🄷

Significant investment that almost doubled the size
of the pub has paid handsome dividends for the
chef/owner. On entering you find yourself in a
flagstoned bar, with a cosy restaurant with a log
fire down to the right, and new smart function
rooms and a large restaurant to the left. Booking is
recommended for meals at all times. Three
handpumps dispense the two regular ales with
either Draught Bass, Hancock's HB or an occasional
guest taking up the third handpump.
♨Q🌣🏵◑🖰🕭♿P🛂

Cwmbran

Mount Pleasant 🄻

Wesley Street, NP44 3LX
🕒 12 (4 Mon)-11; 12-midnight Fri & Sat ☎ (01633) 712176
⊕ mountpleasantcwmbran.co.uk
Beer range varies 🄷

A homely establishment at the end of a terrace set
off the road in the middle of old Cwmbran village.
A genuine community pub, a good clientele mix
helps foster a friendly and welcoming atmosphere.
One half of the management team is a culinary
master who produces popular quality food, from
traditional pub meals to à la carte dishes (booking
advisable). An adventurous guest beer policy has
seen a wide range of ales pass this way, many
from local breweries. 🌣🏵◑🖵(6)♣P🛂

Queen Inn

Upper Cwmbran Road, Upper Cwmbran, NP44 5AX
🕒 12-11.30 (11 Sun) ☎ (01633) 484252
Beer range varies 🄷

Attractive hillside pub set beside a mountain
stream with ducks living on its banks. Photographs
at the entrance dating from 1963 provide a
historical snapshot of the pub. The interior
comprises a public bar, lounge/diner and dining
room, and there is a good outdoor play area for
children to enjoy. The licensees and customers
work hard to raise funds for local charities in a pub
that has grown in popularity in recent years.
Cottage and Wye Valley ales are regular visitors.
♨🌣🏵◑🖰🖵(1,8)♣🐾P🛂

Cwmyoy

Queen's Head

NP7 7NY (leave A465 at Llanfihangel Crucorney and take
lane signed to Llanthony) SO311221
🕒 11-2.30 (not Tue; 3 Sat), 6-11; 12-3, 7-10.30 Sun
☎ (01873) 890241
Beer range varies 🄷

A pub that has guarded the lane to the remote
Llanthony valley for generations, presided over by
possibly Gwent's longest-serving landlord. The
simple stone building has low ceilings and a wood-
burning stove for cold days. Outside, the grounds
slope away to the river and then up to the hills
beyond in a quiet, yet reasonably accessible part of
the national park. At weekends the regulars are
joined by walkers and trekkers. Food is available at
lunchtimes only. ♨Q◑P

Ebbw Vale

King's Arms 🄻

Newchurch Road, Newtown, NP23 5BD
🕒 7 (5 Sat)-midnight; 12-11 Sun ☎ (01495) 352822
Brains The Rev James; guest beer 🄷

A short stroll from the town centre and bus station,
this welcoming pub has a traditional interior with a
bar and lounge, and an additional bar/function
room. Comfortably furnished throughout, the public
bar displays Rugby Union memorabilia and is the
haunt of Ebbw Vale rugby fans. Close to the Eugene
Cross Park ground, Saturday opening at 1pm on
match days makes this a popular pre-game and
half-time venue. B&B accommodation is available.
♨Q🌣🏵🏩🖰🖵(X4,22)♣P

Gwehelog

Hall Inn 🄻

Old Raglan Road, NP15 1RB
🕒 12-3 (not Mon), 5.30-11; 12-11 Sat & Sun
☎ (01291) 672381
**Brains The Rev James; Rhymney Hobby Horse; Wye
Valley Butty Bach** 🄷

Attractive roadside inn with an outside space
alongside a paddock with livestock. Inside, the
stone-flagged Country Bar is very much in a rural
style with much stonework centred around a
fireplace. Pictures of country scenes are dotted
around while two deer heads peer down on
proceedings. The restaurant with low beams and
thick stone walls has an intimate feel, making it a
popular venue for diners to enjoy good home-
cooked food. The beer range reflects the locals'
choice here. ♨🌣🏵🏩◑🖰🖵(60)♣P

Llanfihangel Tor-y-Mynydd

Star Inn 🍸 ✅

Llansoy, NP15 1DT
🕒 12-11 summer; 12-3 (not Mon), 6 (5 Sat)-11 winter; 12-4
Sun ☎ (01291) 650256 ⊕ thestarinn.org.uk
Butcombe Bitter; guest beers 🄷

Popular country pub with a public bar displaying
patriotic Union Jack memorabilia, and a cosy snug
with a great fireplace. The restaurant is stylish and
extends into a conservatory, which gives access to
the spacious garden and play area at the rear. A
beer and cider festival is held in the summer. Local
CAMRA Pub of the Year 2012. ♨🌣🏵◑🖰🕭♣P🛂

Llangattock Lingoed

Hunters Moon Inn

NP7 8RR (by village church) SO363201

✪ closed Mon; 12-2.30 (Sat only), 6.30-midnight (1am Fri);
12-3, 7-11 Sun ☎ (01873) 821499

⊕ hunters-moon-inn.co.uk

Otter Bitter; Wye Valley HPA; guest beer ⊞

Attractive 13th-century country inn set in a tiny
hamlet near Offa's Dyke and alongside the equally
ancient St Cadoc's Church. The old stone-flagged
bar is full of character while the adjoining
reasonably priced restaurant – a recent winner of
Matt Dawson's Golden Spoon Award – with its thick
stone walls forms part of the original building. The
attractive waterfall garden and decked patio offer
excellent outdoor facilities.
🏨Q✿⍾❀🛏⌒◑🖪🕭♣🐾P

Llanhennock

Wheatsheaf

Caerleon, NP18 1LT ST353927

✪ 11-11; 12-3, 7-10.30 Sun ☎ (01633) 420468

⊕ thewheatsheafatllanhennock.webs.com

Fuller's London Pride; guest beers ⊞

Over 25 consecutive years in this Guide is
testament to the beer quality at this unspoilt
country pub, formed by merging two cottages in
the 19th century. The main bar is to the right and a
snug to the left. It has fine views from front and
back and a pleasant secluded outside drinking area.
One of the two guest beers is usually from a local
brewery. The pub is a mecca for local boules
players. Closing time may be earlier on Monday if
quiet. 🏨✿◑🖪🕭♣P

Llanishen

Carpenters Arms

NP16 6QH

✪ closed Mon; 12-3 (not Tue), 6 (6.30 Thu, 5.30 Fri & Sat; 7
Sun)-11 ☎ (01600) 860812

Wadworth 6X; guest beer ⊞

Sixteenth-century coaching house, pleasantly
furnished with a traditional country inn layout. The
licensees have established a fine track record for
well-kept cask ale and good-value home-cooked
food. The curries are highly rated, as are the fish
dishes; vegetarian meals are appropriately listed
on a green board. The landlord often sources the
guest beer from a local brewery such as Kingstone.
Two self-catering flats make this a handy base
from which to explore the beautiful surrounding
countryside. ✿❀🛏◑🖪🕭(65)♣P

Llanthony

Half Moon

NP7 7NN (leave A465 Hereford Road at Llanfihangel
Crucorney, take lane signposted Llanthony. The pub is a
few hundred yards beyond the Priory) SO286279

✪ 12-3, (not winter), 7-11; closed Tue; 11-11 Sat; 12-4,
7-10.30 Sun ☎ (01873) 890611

Bullmastiff Son of a Bitch; guest beers ⊞

At times the silence is broken only by the sheep on
the mountains rising steeply on either side of this
remote pub situated a short distance along the
lane from the romantic ruins of Llanthony Priory.
But more often the background noise is of locals
enjoying themselves, frequently joined by the
many walkers and pony trekkers who flock to this

idyllic spot, especially on hot summer days. Best
ring ahead to check opening times, but visit you
should. Q✿🛏⌒🕭P

Magor

Wheatsheaf ⌷

The Square, NP26 3HN

✪ 11-11 (midnight Fri & Sat); 12-11 Sun ☎ (01633) 880608

Beer range varies ⊞

Large village pub that offers something for
everyone. Food may be enjoyed in the spacious
restaurant while there is plenty of room for those
just wishing to enjoy a drink, either in the cosy
lounge or traditional Tap Room public bar. The
interior is characterful with exposed stonework and
low beams. Expect to see a Rhymney ale alongside
guest beers from national and local breweries.
Open mic sessions add to the entertainment along
with weekly quiz and poker nights.
✿❀◑🖪⌒🖪(14,74)♣🐾P⌷

Monmouth

King's Head Hotel ✪

8 Agincourt Square, NP25 3DY

✪ 7am-midnight ☎ (01600) 713417

**Greene King Abbot; Ruddles Best Bitter; guest
beers** ⊞

Wetherspoon hotel adjacent to the historic Shire
Hall offering a choice of comfortable drinking and
dining areas, many retaining original features. A
family room on the ground floor has a fine old
fireplace above which is an impressive Stuart
plaster cast, believed to have been salvaged from
the nearby castle, along with some Stuart portraits.
Pictures and pictorial histories of famous people
and organisations associated with Monmouth are
displayed. There is a garden at the rear for warmer
weather. Q✿❀🛏◑⌒🛏🖪🕭⌷

Newport

Pen & Wig ⌷

22-24 Stow Hill, NP20 1JD

✪ 11-11 (midnight Fri & Sat); 12-10.30 Sun
☎ (01633) 666818

Draught Bass; Kite Cwrw Gorslas; guest beers ⊞

A pub formed from former business premises, the
interior is essentially open plan but is skilfully
divided into a number of different sections. The
decor is dominated by wood panelling – note the
patterned bar panels. The pub attracts a good
cross-section of customers and showcases beers
from small Welsh breweries among its guest ales.
An extensive upstairs function room is home to
occasional beer festivals. Lunchtime food is
popular, especially the traditional British Sunday
roast. ❀◑⇌🖪♣P

St Julian Inn ✪

Caerleon Road, NP18 1QA

✪ 11.30-11.30 (midnight Fri & Sat); 12-11 Sun
☎ (01633) 243548 ⊕ stjulian.co.uk

**John Smith's Bitter; Wells Bombardier; Young's Bitter;
guest beer** ⊞

Situated in the most glorious of settings, with a
riverside balcony giving views across the
countryside and towards ancient Caerleon, this
pub's great popularity is no surprise. The
comfortable interior offers a choice of public bar,
sports room and lounge positioned around a

central bar counter as well as a downstairs skittles alley and function room. Twenty one consecutive years in this Guide says much about how well kept the ales have been under the watchful eye of the management team. ⬡⬡⬡⬡⬡(27/28,60)♣P⅃

Pant-y-gelli

Crown Inn 🅛
Old Hereford Road, NP7 7HR
✪ 12-2.30 (not Mon; 3 Sat), 6-11; 12-3, 6-10.30 Sun
☎ (01873) 853314 ⊕ thecrownatpantygelli.com
Draught Bass; Rhymney Best Bitter; Wye Valley HPA; guest beers Ⓗ
Still going from strength to strength, the Crown's inclusion in CAMRA's book Great British Pubs is among its many accolades. Run by a great family team, one half tends to the consistently excellent beers, the other half is in charge of the high-quality food, creating a gastro-pub of the highest order. Set in beautiful countryside but close to Abergavenny, it is popular with walkers. On hot days many enjoy the well-maintained patio with its views towards Skirrid Mountain.
⌂Q⬡⬡⬡♣P⅃

Pontymister

Commercial ✅
Commercial Street, NP11 6BA
✪ 11 (12 Sun)-11.30 ☎ (01633) 612608
⊕ thecommercialpontymister.com
Beer range varies Ⓗ
Comfortably furnished pub with an adjoining lounge and bar/games areas. A spacious front patio with tables can be covered by a retractable awning when required. The menu offers a good range of popular main meals plus lighter bites including baguettes and sandwiches. A good selection of frequently changing ales is available, which may include a beer from the local Tiny Rebel Brewery, plus an occasional cider or perry. Three-time local CAMRA Pub of the Year winner.
⬡⬡⬡⬡⬡(Risca & Pontymister)⬡♣⅃

Risca

Fox & Hounds
Park Road, NP11 6PW
✪ 12-midnight (10.30 Sun) ☎ (01633) 612937
Beer range varies Ⓗ
Friendly, old-fashioned venue overlooking the local park, shops and bus stops. The interior is divided into several areas, with a good-sized garden as well as a smaller, somewhat secluded, outdoor area accessed via the pool room. Sport and music are popular here with live music on Friday evening. Games include 'corks' on a Sunday, very much a local game, and a quiz night on Thursday. The single guest ale changes regularly, and cider is also a mainstay here.
⬡⬡(Risca & Pontymister)⬡♣⬡P

Sebastopol

Open Hearth
Wern Road, NP4 5DR
✪ 11.30-12.30am (1.30am Fri & Sat); 12-11.30 Sun
☎ (01495) 763752 ⊕ theopenhearth.co.uk
St Austell Tribute; Wye Valley HPA; guest beers Ⓗ
Charming family-run canalside pub with a spacious garden, play area and tow path that are popular in

good weather. It has served as a cowman's cottage, a wash house, and a hotel when owned by the Great Western Railway, before eventually becoming the welcoming pub it is today. The cosy multi-roomed layout is appealing to drinkers and diners. A rotation of well-known nationally listed ales accompanies tasty food selected from a well-balanced menu. Last admittance is 11pm.
⬡⬡⬡⬡⬡♣P⅃

Sebastopol Social Club 🅛
Wern Road, NP4 5DU
✪ 12-11 (midnight Fri & Sat; 10.30 Sun) ☎ (01495) 763808
⊕ sebastopolsocial.org.uk
Beer range varies Ⓗ
A regular CAMRA Club of the Year winner at regional and national levels, the club attracts a clientele from well outside its locality. This friendly, well-run venue offers live entertainment, bingo and various games, while major sporting events are screened in both downstairs rooms. One of the attractions is the keenly priced beer range, with ales sourced from local breweries as well as other UK independent brewers. A popular beer and cider festival is held in June. Visitors are welcome subject to entry rules. ⬡⬡⬡♣⬡P⅃

Tintern

Anchor Inn
Chapel Hill, NP16 6TE (off A466 at Tintern Abbey)
✪ 11-11; 12-10.30 Sun ☎ (01291) 689582
⊕ theanchortintern.com
Otter Ale; Wye Valley Bitter; guest beers Ⓗ
On a fine day, sit and sup in the expansive garden and drink in one of Wales' grandest structures – Tintern Abbey, towering above. The Anchor itself also bustles with history, not least as a former cider mill once run by Cistercian brothers. The massive mill takes centre stage in a comfortable main bar complemented by a separate restaurant and several seating areas, including a summertime garden café. This welcoming family-run free house is in high repute for its ales and meals.
⌂⬡⬡⬡⬡(69)⬡P

Wye Valley Hotel
NP16 6SQ
✪ 11-3, 6-11; 12-3, 6-10.30 Sun ☎ (01291) 689441
⊕ thewyevalleyhotel.co.uk
Wye Valley Bitter; guest beers Ⓗ
Distinctive multi-angled 1930s pub and hotel on the main road, a popular calling point for locals and visitors in an impressively scenic location. The bottle collection of special and commemorative brews around the walls impresses, too. Rich seasonal floral displays form the backdrop for the outside seating at the front. A long-term purveyor of Wye Valley ales, the pub also offers a broad range of food in the main bar and adjoining restaurant. ⌂⬡⬡⬡⬡(69)P

Trellech

Lion Inn
NP25 4PA
✪ 12-3, 6 (7 Mon)-11 (midnight Thu); 12-midnight Fri & Sat; 12-4.30 Sun ☎ (01600) 860322 ⊕ lioninn.co.uk
Beer range varies Ⓗ
Pub at the heart of the village with a split-level interior, with the bar ahead and to the right on entering, and a slightly larger dining room to the

left. The owner is a chef and there are usually some interesting meals chalked up on the board. Three beers are on offer, plus polypins of cooled cider and perry from local producers. The June beer festival has long been a local fixture while the November beer festival and August cider festival are becoming so, too. ⚌⚘◑⊟⟐(65)●P'

Upper Llanover

Goose & Cuckoo ⓛ

NP7 9ER (turn off A4042 at the sign to Upper Llanover then follow the hand-written signs) SO292073
✪ closed Mon; 11.30-3, 7-11; 11.30-11 Fri & Sat; 12-10.30 Sun ☎ (01873) 880277 ⊕ gooseandcuckoo.com
Beer range varies ⒣
Serving drinkers for the past two centuries, there is a time-warp feel here as little seems to have changed over the years. Just as you think the twisting, narrow lane up from the main road is about to give up, you arrive at this wonderful, remote pub. From the garden the views go on for miles, while inside the low ceilings and wood stove keep the place warm on cold days. Beer and music festivals each Whitsun and August bank holiday draw a lively crowd. ⚌Q⥂⚘⊟◑♣P'

Usk

King's Head Hotel

18 Old Market Street, NP15 1AL
✪ 11-11 (10.30 Sun) ☎ (01291) 672963
Fuller's London Pride; Greene King Abbot; Taylor Landlord ⒣
Entrance is through a short corridor into a cosy bar on two levels, with much hunting and fishing memorabilia scattered about. A number of books adorn the walls. The interior has plenty of old

world charm with its low-beamed ceilings. A good selection of food is available both in the bar and the adjoining Lionel Sweet room. A mix of en-suite and budget accommodation makes this a useful base for exploration of the area. ⚌Q⥂◑Ġ⊟(60,63)P

Nag's Head ⓛ

Twyn Square, NP15 1BH
✪ 9.30am-2.30, 5-11 (10.30 Sun) ☎ (01291) 672820
Brains The Rev James; Sharp's Doom Bar; guest beer ⒣
A fascinating old multi-roomed pub, dating back to 1641, which has been in the same family for over 40 years. Situated in the main town square, almost in the shadow of Usk Castle, this regular Guide entry is well known for a good range of locally sourced produce. Note the unusual brass taps on the front panel of the bar (not in use). A fine collection of plaques from businesses, numerous old photos and adverts adorn the walls. Q⥂◑Ġ⊟(60,63)'

Usk Conservative Club ⓛ

16 Maryport Street, NP15 1AB
✪ 12-3, 7-11 (10.30 Sun) ☎ (01291) 672634
Marston's Pedigree; guest beer ⒣
Established in an elegant former town house set in its own grounds, this private members' club provides offices for local Conservative politicians. A smart well-appointed bar services a comfortably furnished lounge with a games area on one side and a dining room on the other. Three handpumps dispense a choice of beers from a variety of local and UK brewers from further afield. A friendly club, non-members are welcome but club entry rules may be applied. Q⥂⚘◑⊟(60,63)♣P'

Crown Inn, Pant-y-gelli (Photo: Adrian Tierney-Jones)

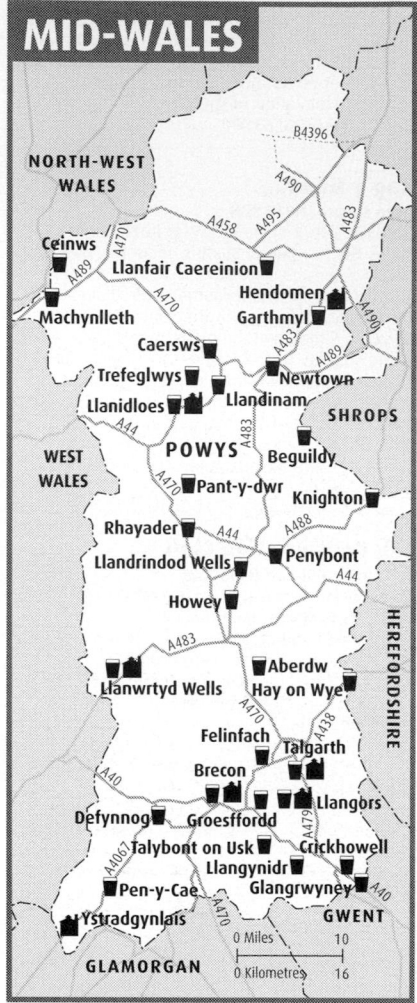

MID-WALES

NORTH-WEST WALES

Ceinws
Llanfair Caereinion
Machynlleth
Hendomen
Garthmyl
Caersws
Trefeglwys
Newtown
Llanidloes
Llandinam
SHROPS
POWYS
Beguildy
WEST WALES
Pant-y-dwr
Knighton
Rhayader
Llandrindod Wells
Penybont
Howey
Aberdw
Llanwrtyd Wells
Hay on Wye
Felinfach
Talgarth
Brecon
Llangors
Defynnog
Groesffordd
Talybont on Usk
Crickhowell
Llangynidr
Pen-y-Cae
Glangrwyney
Ystradgynlais
GWENT
GLAMORGAN

HEREFORDSHIRE

0 Miles 10
0 Kilometres 16

Authority area covered: Powys UA

Aberedw

Seven Stars
LD2 3UW (off B4567)
✪ 12-3, 6.30 (6 Fri & Sat)-11; 12-3.30, 6.30-10.30 Sun
☎ (01982) 560494 ⊕ 7-stars.co.uk
Beer range varies Ⓗ
A village local that claims links back to the 13th century and the legend of the fall of Llywelyn ap Gruffydd, the last native Prince of Wales. The main bar is friendly, with rugged, exposed stone walls and a real fire. The restaurant is comfortable, and popular with residents and visitors. The B4567 road runs along the opposite bank of the River Wye from the main A470 and the Seven Stars makes an excellent pit stop for motorists using this alternative route. ♨Q╬◑♿♣🏠P

Beguildy

Radnorshire Arms ✪
LD7 1YE (on B4355)
✪ closed Mon; 7-midnight (1am Fri & Sat); 12-3, 7-midnight Sun ☎ (01547) 510634

Fuller's London Pride; Stonehouse Station Bitter; guest beer Ⓗ
Impeccable pub high up in the Teme Valley. It has a snug, low-ceilinged bar leading to a larger seating area and games room, and a cosy restaurant to the left as you enter. Guest beers are sourced from local breweries including Breconshire, Hobsons, Ludlow and Six Bells. No meals are available on Sunday evenings, booking is recommended at other times. A pleasant garden lies to the side. ♨Q❀◑♿♣P╙

Brecon

Brecon RFC
63 The Watton, LD3 7EL
✪ 5 (11 Fri & Sat)-midnight; 12-11 Sun ☎ (01874) 624848
⊕ breconrfc.co.uk
Beer range varies Ⓗ
Friendly and welcoming club, open to all, with a large main bar, separate lounge and large function room with a projector screen for important rugby matches. There is also a large patio garden complete with the 16 pistes of the Brecon Pétanque Club. Three handpumps adorn the bar, with beers from Brecon Brewing and Wye Valley frequently available. Bottled ciders from Gwynt y Ddraig are also on offer. The club gets busy during the rugby season, particularly when Wales are playing. Local CAMRA Club of the Year 2012. ❀◑♿♣🚃P╙

Caersws

Red Lion
Main Street, SY17 5EL (on B4569)
✪ 3-11 (midnight Fri, Sat & summer) ☎ (01686) 688023
Beer range varies Ⓗ
Wood-beamed village locals' pub with two bars, attracting a varied clientele of all ages. Early evenings can be busy and boisterous as many villagers call in on their way home from work. The four changing ales usually include two locally produced beers, and a local cider is also sold. A summer beer festival is held in the large car park and there are drinking areas outside to the front and rear. ♨❀╬◑♿➡🚃(X75,X85)♣🏠P

Ceinws

Tafarn Dwynant
SY20 9HA (off A487 3 miles N of Machynlleth) SH759059
✪ 5.30 (3 Sat & Sun)-11; closed Mon & winter Sun
☎ (01654) 761660 ⊕ tafarndwynant.co.uk
Purple Moose Snowdonia Ale; guest beer Ⓗ
Situated in a quiet village, this friendly community free house is three miles from Machynlleth. The landlord's own artwork is on display. Home-prepared food uses locally and ethically sourced ingredients (evening meals served Tue-Sun in summer, Wed-Sat in winter). Occasional mini beer

festivals are held and the front patio is used for alfresco drinking. The local 34 bus stops near the pub; longer-distance buses stop on the main road, just across the river from the village.
🏠🕸🌑🅰️🚆(34)🌡️

Crickhowell

Bear Hotel
High Street, NP8 1BW
☀️ 11-3, 6-11 (7-10.30 Sun) ☎ (01873) 810408
🌐 bearhotel.co.uk
Brains The Rev James; Draught Bass; guest beer Ⓗ
Formerly a 15th-century coaching inn, the Bear is now an award-winning hotel. The multi-roomed bar enjoys grand surroundings with exposed beams, wood panelling and fine settles, and an eclectic selection of furnishings and decorations. There are open fireplaces in both bar rooms and a side room. An excellent and varied food menu is offered, featuring much local produce. The hotel is an ideal base for exploring the surrounding Black Mountains and Brecon Beacons National Park.
🏠Q🕸♿🛏️🌑🚃♿🚆(X43)P🌡️

Defynnog

Tanners Arms
LD3 8SF
☀️ 5 (12 Sat & Sun)-midnight ☎ (01874) 638032
🌐 tannersarmspub.com
Beer range varies Ⓗ
Originally three separate workers' cottages for the nearby tannery, this is now a fabulous village-centre community pub. An ideal base for exploring the Brecon Beacons, it now offers B&B accommodation. The main bar boasts six handpumps, four given over to an ever-changing range of beers (some local, some from further afield), with Gwynt y Ddraig ciders on the other two. Excellent food is available to eat in or take away. The large suntrap garden is popular in summer. 🏠🕸♿🌑🅰️🚆(X63)♣🐾P

Felinfach

Griffin Ⓛ
LD3 0UB (just off A470 3 miles NE of Brecon)
☀️ 12-11.30 ☎ (01874) 620111 🌐 eatdrinksleep.ltd.uk
Brecon Wandering Beacons; Monty's Sunshine; Tomos Watkins OSB; Waen Festival Gold Ⓗ
The pub's ethos – the simple things in life done well – says it all. A welcoming country pub, restaurant and hotel, the emphasis is on good beer and excellent food. The multi-roomed layout allows for discrete areas for drinking and dining. A huge fireplace between the bar and main dining area dominates during winter, while a full-sized Aga lurks in a side room, providing warmth throughout. The large garden affords superb views of the Brecon Beacons and Black Mountains. Regular beer-themed events are growing in popularity. 🏠Q🕸♿🌑♿🚆🌡️

Garthmyl

Nag's Head Inn
SY15 6RS (on A483)
☀️ 12-midnight ☎ (01686) 207207 🌐 thenagsinn.co.uk
Monty's Mischief, Sunshine; guest beer Ⓗ
Plush canal/roadside hotel with a slate-floored central bar, three wood-floored drinking spaces

and a restaurant area. There are plenty of wood beams and comfortable seating throughout. A wood-buring stove separates the central and right-hand areas while another stove warms the third section, giving a cosy and comfortable feel to the hotel. There is a rear patio for outdoor drinking.
🏠Q🕸♿🌑🚆(X75)

Glangrwyney

Bell
NP8 1EH (on A40)
☀️ 12-midnight (10.30 Sun) ☎ (01873) 811115
🌐 thebellcountrypub.co.uk
Brains Bitter, SA; guest beers Ⓗ
A large multi-roomed and well-appointed stone-built pub situated on the A40. The beamed interior has undergone recent restoration to a high standard and has a welcoming atmosphere. The Bell prides itself on the quality of its meals and is a winner of the Brains Food Pub of the Year award. The main bar is child-friendly. Guest beers are usually available and beer festivals are held throughout the year.
🏠🕸♿🌑🚃🅰️🚆(X43)♣🐾P🌡️

Groesffordd

Three Horseshoes
LD3 7SN
☀️ 12-3 (not Mon), 5-11; 12-11 Fri-Sun ☎ (01874) 665672
🌐 threehorseshoesgroesffordd.co.uk
Beer range varies Ⓗ
Busy village pub in the heart of the Brecon Beacons, boasting superb views from both the front and rear outdoor seating areas. The pub is just a 10-minute walk from the Brynich Lock on the Monmouthshire & Brecon Canal, and is a popular stopping off point for boaters and other visitors to the area. Excellent food, sourced locally, is on offer, and quizzes and other events take place regularly. Brynich Caravan Site and the Brecon YHA are also close by. 🏠🕸🌑♿🅰️♣🐾P🌡️

Hay on Wye

Kilverts Ⓛ ✅
The Bull Ring, HR3 5AG
☀️ 11-11 (midnight Fri & Sat) ☎ (01497) 821042
🌐 kilverts.co.uk
Brecon Wandering Beacons; Wye Valley Butty Bach; guest beers Ⓗ
Popular with locals and visitors alike, this award-winning inn has a large beer garden and en-suite accommodation. The focus is on quality beer, with tutored tastings, food pairings, regular Meet the Brewer events and an August bank holiday beer festival. Five handpumps boast ales from near and far, alongside three pumps for ciders from Gwynt y Ddraig and a selection of world beers. Fresh home-made food includes local organic specialities. Tuesday is open mic night and jazz plays on the lawn throughout the summer.
🏠🕸♿🌑♿🅰️🚆♣🐾P🌡️

Howey

Laughing Dog
LD1 5PT (100yds off A470)
☀️ 6 (5.30 Fri)-11; 11-11 Sat; 11-10.30 Sun
☎ (01597) 822406 🌐 thelaughingdog.co.uk
Wye Valley Bitter; guest beer Ⓗ

Located on an old drovers' road, now a loop off the main A470, this 18th-century building has been a pub since the 19th century. The interior is rustic and friendly with solid timber furniture. There is a separate, large games room and restaurant, with food served on Friday and Saturday evenings plus Sunday lunchtime. As the name says, friendly dogs are always welcome. ⚌🏵🅭🌢▲🚃(T4,44)♣

Knighton

Horse & Jockey
Wylcwm Place, LD7 1AE
✪ 11-11.30 (11 Sun) ☎ (01547) 520062
⊕ thehorseandjockeyinn.co.uk
Greene King Old Speckled Hen; Hobson's Best Bitter; Three Tuns XXX Ⓗ
Attractive pub sprawling around a courtyard in the town centre. First on the left is a cosy lounge bar. Next is a larger public bar, which leads to a pool room. At the end of the courtyard lies a restaurant, with letting bedrooms above. There is seating in the courtyard for fine weather. A coaching inn since the 14th century, the pub is ideally situated for exploring Offa's Dyke. The regular beers may be replaced by alternative ales from the same breweries. Book ahead for meals at weekends. ⚌Q🍴🏵🅭🌢🅴🌢▲🚃(41,740)♣🛏

Llandinam

Lion
SY17 5BY (on A470)
✪ closed Mon; 12-midnight (12-3, 6-midnight winter)
☎ (01686) 688233
Hancock's HB; Sharp's Doom Bar Ⓗ
Comfortable, relaxing village hotel with a bar dominated by a large wooden beam and an open stone fire. The hotel is now owned by an award-winning chef and has a large restaurant. The venue is popular and a large selection of bar meals is available (booking advised). There are wooden benches at the rear for outside drinking. The hotel aims to be the hub of the village and families are welcome. ⚌🏵🅭🅭🚃(X75)P

Llandrindod Wells

Conservative Club
South Crescent, LD1 5DH
✪ 11-2, 5.30-11; 11-11.30 Fri & Sat; 11.30-10.30 Sun
☎ (01597) 822126
Hancock's HB; Marston's Pedigree; guest beer Ⓗ
Located in the centre of Victorian Llandrindod Wells, the Conservative Club is a smart and friendly destination for those wishing to enjoy a quiet drink. Visitors will find a large lounge, TV room, games bar, snooker and pool tables, and a small front patio. Lunches are available Thursday, Friday and Sunday. Live entertainment is hosted occasionally in the evening. CAMRA members are welcome but non-members must be signed in. Q🏵🅭🌢🚃🛏

Llanfair Caereinion

Goat Hotel
High Street, SY21 0QS (off A458)
✪ 11-11 (midnight Fri & Sat) ☎ (01938) 810428
Beer range varies Ⓗ
This excellent inn has a welcoming atmosphere and attracts both locals and tourists. The plush lounge, dominated by a large inglenook with an open fire, has comfortable leather armchairs and sofas, complemented by a dining room serving home-cooked food and a games room at the rear. The choice of three real ales always includes one from the Wood Brewery. ⚌🏵🅭🅭♣P

Llangors

Castle Inn
LD3 7UB
✪ 5-11; 12-midnight Fri-Sun ☎ (01874) 658819
Beer range varies Ⓗ
Hospitable and traditional village local with stone walls, wood bar, large fireplace and great service. Popular with locals and visitors, the pub provides a hub for ramblers, boaters, horse riders and explorers. Excellent beers are brought in from near and far, and locally sourced food is served in the evenings and at weekends. ⚌🏵🅭♿▲🚃🚃♣🛏P

Llangynidr

Red Lion
Duffryn Road, NP8 1NT (off B4558)
✪ 11-11; 12-10.30 Sun ☎ (01874) 730223
⊕ theredlion1.vpweb.co.uk
Beer range varies Ⓗ
Popular village local with a warm welcome for walkers, boaters, families and dogs. The beer range changes regularly, sourced from local brewers, as well as from further afield. Good-value home-cooked food is served in the bar. A separate games area, outside seating and children's play area make this a pub with something for everyone. Regular quiz nights are hosted as well as live music and food themed events. ⚌🍴🏵🅭🅭🅭♣P

Llanidloes

Angel Hotel
High Street, SY18 6BY (off A470)
✪ 11.30-2.30 (not Wed), 5-1am; 12-3, 7-midnight Sun
☎ (01686) 412381
Everards Tiger; Greene King Abbot; guest beer Ⓗ
Friendly edge-of-town pub with two comfortable bars. The larger of the two rooms has a big stone fireplace and old photographs on the wall. The smaller room has an interesting bar inlaid with old pennies. There is a restaurant at the rear that can seat 40 people (booking recommended). The building was built in 1748 and Chartists held meetings here between 1838 and 1839. Outside seating is available at the front of the pub. 🏵🅭🚃(X75,525)♣

Crown & Anchor Inn ★
41 Long Bridge Street, SY18 6EF (off A470)
✪ 11-11; 12-10.30 Sun ☎ (01686) 412398
Brains The Rev James; Worthington Bitter Ⓗ
Wonderful, unspoilt town-centre gem with a relaxed and friendly atmosphere, identified by CAMRA as one of Britain's Real Heritage Pubs. The landlady has been in charge since 1965 and throughout that time the pub has remained unchanged, retaining its public bar, lounge, snug and two further rooms, one with a pool table and games machine. Serving hatches connect the small end rooms to the bar and there is another hatch to pass drinks into the games room. 🚃🚃(X75,525)♣

Red Lion Hotel

Long Bridge Street, SY18 6EE (off A470)
🕐 11-midnight (1am Fri & Sat) ☎ (01686) 412270
Brains The Rev James; Taylor Landlord; guest beers Ⓗ
Wood-beamed town-centre hotel with a plush lounge and red leather sofas in the lounge bar. The public bar is divided into two areas – the front area has an interesting wood-panelled fireplace, the rear space has a pool table and games machines. Up to four real ales are usually available with the guests usually coming from local breweries. There is a patio to the rear for alfresco drinking in warmer weather. ⚶✿✐⬤⬤⎗(X75,525)♣P

Stag

15 Great Oak Street, SY18 6BU (off A470)
🕐 12 (11 Sat)-12.30am ☎ (01686) 414824
Shepherd Neame Bishops Finger; Snowdonia Purple Moose; guest beer Ⓗ
Dog- (and people-) friendly town-centre pub offering three ales. The long premises are divided in two – the wooden-floored front space has wall seating and a wood-burning stove, the rear area through an archway has comfortable sofas, a pool table and a piano. There is an outside drinking area to the rear. The pub hosts live music on Fridays and Sundays and take-away tea and coffee are available. ⚶✿⎗(X75,525)♣

Llanwrtyd Wells

Neuadd Arms Hotel Ⓛ

The Square, LD5 4RB
🕐 9.30am-midnight (1am Fri & Sat) ☎ (01591) 610236
⬤ neuaddarmshotel.co.uk
Heart of Wales Aur Cymreig, Bitter, Noble Eden, Welsh Black, Innstable, seasonal beers Ⓗ
Large Victorian hotel serving as the Heart of Wales Brewery tap. The Bells Bar features a large fireplace and an eclectic mix of furniture. The bells that once summoned servants remain on one wall, along with winners' boards from some of the town's more unusual competitions, such as bog-snorkelling or man v horse. The lounge bar has deep carpets and sofas. The hotel takes part in the town's annual events, including food festivals, and holds a beer festival in November. Gwynt y Ddraig ciders are served. ⚶Q✿✐⬤⬤Å⬤♣⬤P

Stonecroft Inn

Dolecoed Road, LD5 4RA
🕐 5-midnight; 12-1am Fri-Sun ☎ (01591) 610332
⬤ stonecroft.co.uk
Brains The Rev James; guest beers Ⓗ
Warm and friendly community pub that participates in the town's many and varied festivities – bog-snorkelling, beer and food festivals, real ale rambles and much more. The hostelry has three main areas for drinking, dining and games, plus a large riverside garden. Excellent food complements the fine range of beers. Lodge accommodation is popular with walkers and mountain bikers. ⚶✿✐⬤Å⬤♣⬤P

Machynlleth

White Horse

42 Maengwyn Street, SY20 8DT
🕐 12-3 Wed-Fri, 7 (6 Fri)-11.30; 12-11.30 Sat & Sun
Beer range varies Ⓗ
Friendly locals' pub on the main street of this bustling market town, once the capital of Wales –

just across the street, the site of Owain Glyndwr's Parliament House of 1404 now houses a visitor centre. Both bars have open log fires in winter, and there is a pool table. Two real ales are usually on offer, drawn from a wide range of family and microbrewers. The beer garden at the rear affords access for disabled customers. ⚶✿⬤⬤⬤⎗P⬤

Newtown

Elephant & Castle

Broad Street, SY16 2BQ (off A483)
🕐 11-11 ☎ (01686) 626271 ⬤ elephantandcastlehotel.co.uk
Six Bells Big Nev's; guest beers Ⓗ
Open-plan town-centre hotel next to the River Severn with a number of drinking areas off the main bar. Old photographs and prints adorn the walls, and several TVs show sporting events. There are three beers on offer, two local, usually from Monty's or Six Bells breweries. To the rear is a separate building used for functions. Outside, there is bench seating by the river wall. ✿✐⬤⬤♣P

Railway Tavern

Old Kerry Road, SY16 1BH (off A483)
🕐 12-2.30, 6-midnight Mon, Wed & Thu; 11-1am Tue, Fri & Sat; 12-11 Sun ☎ (01686) 626156
Draught Bass; Worthington Bitter; guest beer Ⓗ
Traditional locals' pub on the edge of the town centre and handy for the railway station. The friendly, welcoming atmosphere and devoted clientele are down to the long-serving landlord and landlady who have been in charge for more than 27 years. The pub is home to a successful darts team and match nights can get busy. Guest beers come from a wide range of independent breweries. Beware the cellar hatch which is right in front of the dartboard. ✿⬤⎗(X75)♣

Sportsman Ⓛ ✅

Severn Street, SY16 2BQ (off A483)
🕐 closed Mon; 12-11 (10.30 Sun) ☎ (01686) 623978
Monty's Manjana, Midnight, Sunshine, Mischief; guest beers Ⓗ
Monty's Brewery flagship pub. Five Monty's beers are usually available alongside two guest ales and a cider. There are three areas to drink in – the main bar with a brick fireplace and wood-burning stove, a quiet area with comfortable leather seating, and a rear space with slate-tiled floor, pool table and TV. The muted TV in the main bar shows classic children's cartoons and silent comedies. The walls of the bar display Monty's brewing awards. ⚶✿⬤⬤♣⬤

Pant-y-dwr

Mid Wales Inn

LD6 5LL (on B4518 5 miles N of Rhayader)
🕐 5-midnight; 12-2am Sat (1am Sun) ☎ (01597) 870076
Monty's Sunshine; guest beers Ⓗ
At the geographical centre of Wales, and on a popular north-south route for motorists, this is worth a stop-off. The half-timbered pub is formed from three old buildings in a short terrace. Attractive and well-maintained inside, the carved wooden bar fronts are outstanding. Despite its remote location, the pub hosts eight sports teams including five pool teams. Two guest beers are usually available from Monty's. Note that the pub closes on Tuesday in lambing season. ⚶Q✿✐⬤⬤⬤⎗(47)♣P⬤

Pen-y-Cae

Ancient Briton ▼

Brecon Road, SA9 1YY (on A4067 between Ystradgynlais and Dan-yr-Ogof caves)
◎ 12-midnight ☎ (01639) 730273 ⊕ ancientbriton.co.uk
Wye Valley Ancient Briton, Butty Bach; guest beers Ⓗ
Local CAMRA Pub of the Year for the past four years and Regional Pub of the Year 2012, this establishment is ideally situated in the Brecon Beacons National Park with many local attractions within easy reach. The pub offers hotel accommodation and is introducing full camping and caravan facilities. However, it is the magnificent array of 13 handpumps that sets the pub apart. The landlord and staff take great pride and care in the constantly changing selection of ales, ciders and perry.
🏛Q✿⇔◁◑▲🚐(X63)♣♚P⅃

Penybont

Severn Arms

LD1 5UA
◎ 11-2.30 (3 Sat), 5.30-11; 12-3, 7-9.30 Sun
☎ (01597) 851224 ⊕ severn-arms.co.uk
Beer range varies Ⓗ
An 18th-century coaching inn on the main Aberystwyth road. The walls of the large main bar are hung with pictures of sports teams and other items of local interest. Beyond lies a pool room and a smokers' courtyard, leading to a large garden that slopes down to the River Ithon. To the left of the entrance is an attractive, comfortable lounge/restaurant. Four handpumps dispense beers from microbreweries near and far, with a fifth reserved for more mainstream beers.
🏛Q✿⇔◁◑⬚▲🚐(461)♣P⅃

Rhayader

Crown Inn

North Street, LD6 5BT
◎ 11-11 (midnight Fri & Sat, closed Mon Jan & Feb); 12-10.30 Sun ☎ (01597) 811099 ⊕ thecrownrhayader.co.uk
Brains Dark, Bitter, The Rev James; guest beer Ⓗ
A 16th-century beamed pub with an open-plan bar plus a restaurant. The bar is decorated with photographs of local residents and scenes. Look for the item describing the eccentric Major Stanscombe, a former owner. The guest beer will either be Brains IPA, sold at a bargain price, or a Brains seasonal beer. This is a rare outlet locally for real mild. An area at the rear serves as a car park in the winter and a beer garden in the summer.
✿⇔◁◑⬚▲🚐(47)♣P⅃

Talgarth

Tower Hotel ⓛ

The Square, LD3 0BW
◎ 4-11; 12-midnight Fri-Sun ☎ (01874) 711 253
⊕ towerhoteltalgarth.co.uk
Rotters Utter Rotter, Grounds for Divorce, seasonal beer Ⓗ
Recently refurbished, bright yet cosy modern pub with two bars and a pool room area leading out to the garden. The on-site Rotters microbrewery provides most of the beers and a spring beer festival is hosted alongside a bike festival. The large screen shows Sky Sports and is popular for major rugby and football matches. Real ciders are available in bottles.
✿⇔◁◑⬚&▲🚐(39,39A)♣♚P⅃

Talybont on Usk

Star Inn ▼ ⓛ

LD3 7YX (on B4558 between Brecon and Crickhowell)
SO114226
◎ 11-3, 5-11; 12-11 Sun ☎ (01874) 676635
⊕ starinntalybont.co.uk
Beer range varies Ⓗ
Large and lively pub alongside the Monmouthshire & Brecon Canal with a spacious garden that is extremely popular in summer. The beer range varies, with five handpumps offering ales from local brewers and those from further afield. Real cider is also available. Live music evenings are held regularly, and quiz nights are popular. The excellent food makes good use of local produce. Popular beer festivals feature throughout the year. A multiple winner of Local CAMRA Pub of the Year, including 2012. 🏛✿⇔◁◑⬚&▲🚐(X43)♣♚

Trefeglwys

Red Lion

SY17 5PH (on B4569)
◎ 5 (2 Fri)-11; 12-midnight Sat; 12-11 Sun
☎ (01686) 430934 ⊕ redliontrefeglwys.co.uk
Celt Experience Celt Golden; Greene King Old Speckled Hen; Sharp's Doom Bar; guest beer Ⓗ
Beamed village pub with a pleasant view across the valley. The public bar is wood panelled and has an impressive stone inglenook and wood-burning stove. A pool room is situated off the bar down a couple of steps, and a restaurant area is to the right as you enter. The pub attracts a mixed clientele from the village and has a relaxed feel to it. There are outside drinking areas at the front and rear.
🏛✿◑

The soul of beer

Brewers call barley malt the 'soul of beer'. While a great deal of attention has been rightly paid to hops in recent years, the role of malt in brewing must not be ignored. Malt contains starch that is converted to a special form of sugar known as maltose during the brewing process. It is maltose that is attacked by yeast during fermentation and turned into alcohol and carbon dioxide. Other grains can be used in brewing, notably wheat, but barley malt is the preferred grain as it gives a delightful biscuity / cracker / Ovaltine note to beer. Unlike wheat, barley has a husk that works as a natural filter during the first stage of brewing, known as the mash. Cereals such as rice and corn / maize are widely used by global producers of mass-market lagers, but craft brewers avoid them.

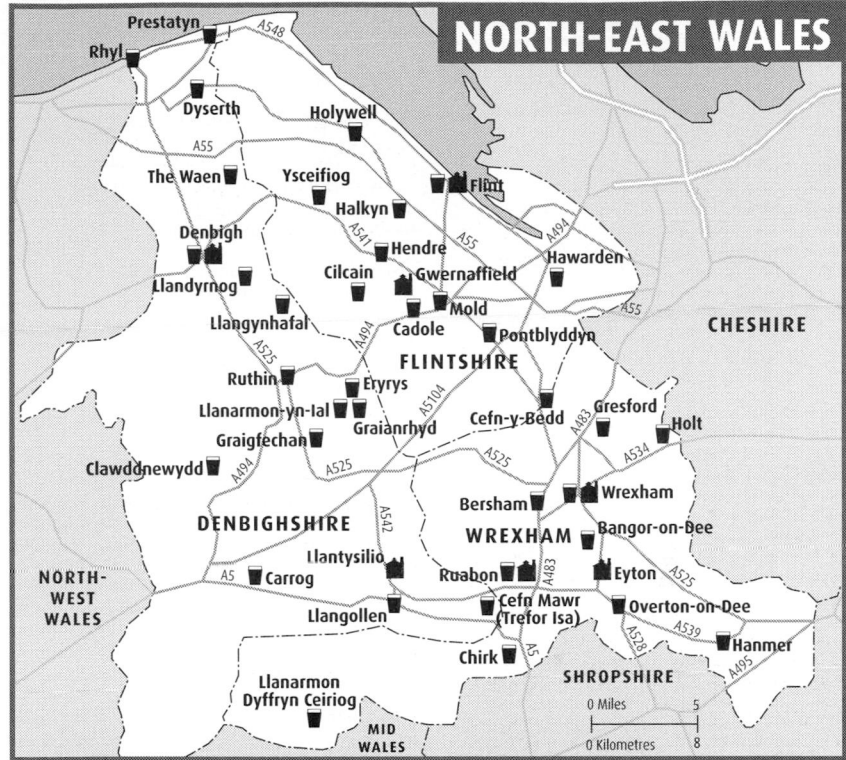

NORTH-EAST WALES

WALES

Authority areas covered: Denbighshire UA, Flintshire UA, Wrexham UA

Bangor-on-Dee

Buck House Hotel ⃝L

High Street, LL13 0BU (opp church)
⊕ 11-midnight; 12-11.30 Sun ☎ (01978) 780336
⊕ buckhousehotel.co.uk
Tetley Bitter; guest beers ⊞
Traditional family-run village inn with a warm, friendly atmosphere. The main bar has pub games and Sky TV and there is a red telephone box and an old well in the lobby. There are two quiet lounges, both with an amazing collection of teapots. The separate restaurant can be extended with a marquee for private functions. On race days a minibus shuttles punters to and from the course. The pub has two beer festivals a year – check the website for details. ⌂◗⊕&⊟(146)♣P⌐

Bersham

Black Lion ✔

LL14 4HN (off B5099 near Bersham Heritage Centre)
⊕ 11.30-12.30am (1am Fri & Sat); 11.30-1am Sun
☎ (01978) 365588
Hydes Original Bitter, seasonal beers ⊞
Also known as the Hole in the Wall, this is a pub with a real local feel. Popular with walkers and visitors to the Heritage Centre, it overlooks the River Clwyedog. The wood-panelled bar serves two rooms, heated by coal fires in winter. There is a games room and an outside play area in the garden. Locally sourced food is available all day. Beer and music festivals feature in July and October. ⌂⊕⊟&⊟♣P⌐

Cadole

Colomendy Arms

Village Road, CH7 5LL (off A494 Mold-Ruthin road)
⊕ 7 (6 Thu; 4 Fri)-11; 2-11 Sat & Sun ☎ (01352) 810217
Beer range varies ⊞
Friendly, traditional village local on the edge of Loggerheads Country Park, popular with park visitors, walkers, runners and cyclists as well as locals. There is a single bar, heated by coal fires in winter, serving two rooms, both with a distinctive '60s feel. An ever-changing selection of ales on five handpumps comes from both local and more distant breweries. ⌂Q⅍⊕⊟⊟♣P

Carrog

Grouse Inn

LL21 9AT (on B5437) SJ113437
⊕ 12-11.30 (12.30am Sat & Sun) ☎ (01490) 430272
⊕ thegrouseinncarrog.co.uk
Lees Bitter, John Willie's ⊞
Alongside the River Dee, with spectacular views of the valley and the Berwyn Mountains, the Grouse was originally a farm and brewhouse. Today, this

INDEPENDENT BREWERIES

Denbigh Denbigh (NEW)
Facer's Flint
Hafod Gwernaffield (NEW)
Llangollen (Abbey Grange) Llantysilio
McGivern Ruabon
New Plassey Eyton
Sandstone Wrexham

long-standing Guide entry has a single bar serving two agreeable and separate dining rooms, a games room and a covered patio area. The western terminus of the Llangollen Railway is a short walk away. Lees seasonal beers are available occasionally. ᛗ✿◑ ➤ ➤➚ (5,X94)P⁵⛎

Cefn Mawr (Trefor Isa)

Mill

Mill Lane, LL14 3NL SJ275424
✿ 12-midnight (1am Fri & Sat) ☎ (01978) 821799
Beer range varies Ⓗ
Small basic locals' pub hidden down a narrow one-way lane in the lower part of an old industrial village. A games room and small snug with upholstered benches lead off the central bar. The smoking area backs on to the gurgling mill stream. Beers are usually sourced from local micros. Nearby are the famous Pontcysyllte Aqueduct on the Llangollen Canal and Cefn Druids FC. Parking can be difficult but buses pass nearby. ✿➚➚(2,5)♣⁵

Cefn-y-Bedd

Ffrwd

Ffrwd Road, LL12 9TS (1 mile along B5102 from A541)
✿ closed Mon; 6.30-midnight; 12.30-10 Sun
☎ (01978) 757951
Beer range varies Ⓗ
The Ffrwd (Fast Flowing Stream) is a typical roadside pub situated on the edge of a small wood and stream. Inside, a single bar serves the cosy main bar with a real fire, and a large dining area, both with timber-beamed ceilings. Good home-cooked meals are available throughout the day but lunchtime only on Sundays. A TV shows most sporting events. ᛗ✿◑ ➚➚➚●P⁵⛎

Chirk

Hand Hotel Ⓛ

Church Street, LL14 5EY
✿ 10.30-11 (midnight Thu-Sat); 12-10.30 Sun
☎ (01691) 773472 ∰ thehandhotelchirk.co.uk
Stonehouse Station Bitter, Cambrian Gold Ⓗ
Delightful inn in the centre of Chirk on the old coaching road from Holyhead to London. Built in 1610, it is one of the oldest in north-east Wales. Bar snacks are available in the cosy front lounge bar. The hotel restaurant is decorated in period 1800s style. Three handpumps serve Stonehouse beers with an occasional guest.
ᛗ✿➚◑➚➚➚P⁵⛎

Cilcain

White Horse

The Square, CH7 5NN (signed from A451 Mold-Denbigh road) SJ177651
✿ 12-3, 6-11; 12-11 Sat; 12-10.30 Sun ☎ (01352) 740142
Banks's Bitter; guest beer Ⓗ
Picturesque, whitewashed pub in an attractive village beside the Clwydian range, popular with walkers exploring the nearby Offa's Dyke and Moel Famau. It has a separate, quarry-tiled public bar where prices are lower and both walkers and dogs are welcome. The beers are from the Marston's list, with a regularly changing guest. Four log fires keep the pub warm in winter. Food is served lunchtimes and evenings throughout the week.
ᛗQ✿◑➚➚➚(14C)♣P⁵⛎

Clawddnewydd

Glan Llŷn Ⓛ

LL15 2NA (on B5105) SJ083524
✿ 5-midnight (1am Sat); 12-11 Sun ☎ (01824) 750754
Facer's Flintshire Bitter; guest beers Ⓗ
In the centre of the village, this 16th-century multi-roomed pub acts as a hub for the local community, and is a meeting place for local football, pool, darts and dominoes teams. The house beer is brewed by Facer's, with a varying range of guest beers. Exposed beams and stonework lend a traditional feel while a central stove adds to the cosy atmosphere. ᛗ➚✿◑➚♣●P⁵⛎

Denbigh

Brookhouse Mill Ⓛ

Ruthin Road, LL16 4RD (off A525 south of Denbigh)
SJ072658
✿ 12-3, 6-11.30; 12-11 Sun ☎ (01745) 813377
∰ brookhousemill.co.uk
Conwy Welsh Pride; guest beers Ⓗ
Situated by the River Ystrad, this former water mill has been converted into a smart restaurant, with a central bar serving a number of satellite dining areas. Upstairs is a conservatory and separate function area. The old mill cogs and wheels can still be seen in the low-beamed interior. Two cask beers are available from local north Wales microbreweries. Q✿◑➚➚➚P

Guildhall Ⓛ

Hall Square, LL16 3NU (in town square, behind library)
✿ 12-11 ☎ (01745) 816533 ∰ guildhalltavernhotel.co.uk
Brains The Rev James; Facer's Flintshire Bitter; guest beers Ⓗ
The Grade II-listed Guildhall Tavern, formerly known as the Bull, a 17th-century coaching hotel tucked away just off the town square, has been refurbished with 11 plush bedrooms. There are three main public areas including a conservatory with an ancient covered well and the hotel restaurant. Three real ales are served, including one brewed locally by Facer's, supplemented by Happy Daze, a real cider. Denbigh Castle, built by Edward I, is 200 yards up the hill behind the hotel. Hotel parking is reserved for residents.
ᛗ➚➚➚➚➚●P⁵⛎

Railway

2 Ruthin Road, LL16 3EL SJ059664
✿ 12-midnight ☎ (01745) 812376
Beer range varies Ⓗ
Situated in the lower part of Denbigh, about half a mile from the historic castle, this traditional, many-roomed local takes its name from its proximity to the now-demolished Vale of Clwyd railway line to Rhyl and Ruthin. Its heritage is reflected throughout the interior decorations, although sports screens and a pool table cater for modern tastes. Two ales are available, with Purple Moose beers a regular favourite. Q➚➚➚♣P⁵⛎

Dyserth

New Inn

Waterfall Road, LL18 6ET (on B5119 close to Dyserth Waterfall) SJ054794
✿ 12-11 ☎ (01745) 570482 ∰ thenewinndyserth.co.uk
Banks's Mild; Marston's Burton Bitter, Pedigree; guest beer Ⓗ

Close to the foot of Dyserth Waterfall, this 400-year-old pub, now greatly modernised and extended, focuses on food. Nevertheless, five real ales – including hard-to-find cask-conditioned mild – are a good reason to call in for a drink at this TV-free zone. There is also a pleasant outdoor drinking area. Q🌜🕭⌚◑🚻♿🚍(19,35,36)P🏃

Eryrys

Sun Inn
Village Road, CH7 4BX
☼ 3.30-11; 1-10.30 Sun ☎ (01824) 780402
Theakston Best Bitter; guest beers Ⓗ
Welcoming village inn built from local stone and set in an attractive countryside location close to the Flintshire/Denbighshire border. Popular with locals, walkers and cyclists, the small bar serves a low-beamed lounge with a wood-burning stove and TV. A separate quiet room at the back is mostly used for dining. One or two guest ales are available, often sourced from local micros. Good-quality home-produced food is served lunchtimes and evenings (no food Mon or Sun eve). 🏚🌜◑🕭🚍P🏃

Flint

Royal Oak
6 Church Street, CH6 5AE (at traffic lights on A548 jct with A5119)
☼ 9.30am-midnight (1am Fri & Sat); 11-12.30am Sun
☎ (01352) 732239
Oakwell Old Tom Mild, Barnsley Bitter, Senior Ⓗ
An oasis in the beer desert of Flint, the Royal Oak serves three Oakwell beers, including the only real mild for miles. This friendly town-centre local has two bars with many photos of Flint's past plus a separate games room with darts and a pool table. Tuesday is quiz night and weekends can be busy with karaoke. There is a free car park adjacent. Flint Castle, where Richard II was imprisoned, is close. No food on Monday. 🏚◑🕭🚆🚍♣🏃

Graianrhyd

Rose & Crown
Llanarmon Road, CH7 4QW (on B5430, off A5104)
SJ218560
☼ 4 (12 Fri & Sat)-11; 12-10.30 Sun ☎ (01824) 780727
⊕ theroseandcrownpub.co.uk
Flowers IPA; guest beers Ⓗ
Welcoming 200-year-old village pub, appealing to the local community and walkers alike. The main bar area has an open fire and traditional copper-topped tables, and the smaller side bar has a log-burning stove and satellite TV. Two ever-changing guest ales feature, mainly sourced from local microbreweries, and real cider is also on offer from time to time. Excellent-value hearty food is popular, with lunchtime bar snacks and full evening meals available (no eve meals Mon). 🏚Q◑🕭🚍P🏃

Graigfechan

Three Pigeons Inn
LL15 2EU (on B5429 about 3 miles S of Ruthin) SJ145545
☼ 12-3 (not Mon), 5-11; 12-11 Sat; 12-10.30 Sun
☎ (01824) 703178 ⊕ threepigeonsinn.co.uk
Sharp's Doom Bar; guest beers Ⓗ

Multi-roomed pub with a spacious dining room and a games room with pool table and darts. The bar offers three changing guest beers, which can be served in earthenware tankards on request. A central lounge area features a well-stocked bookcase, interesting old pictures, posters, brasses, pottery and real fires. Rustic decoration, with oak beams and pew-style seating, adds to the relaxed atmosphere. There are stunning views of the Clwydian range from the garden. The pub participates in the Route 76 beer festival each July. 🏚🌜🕭🚐◑🚪♿🚍(76)♣👟P🏃

Gresford

Griffin
Church Green, LL12 8RG
☼ 4-11.30 (11 Sun) ☎ (01978) 852231
Adnams Southwold Bitter; Courage Best Bitter; guest beers Ⓗ
Presided over by Jean, the landlady since 1973, this friendly community pub has some equally long-standing regulars. The irregular open-plan single-room interior is adorned with a variety of interesting pictures. A lawned area to the side has seating. Children are welcome in some areas until 8pm. The 15th-century All Saints Church is adjacent – its bells are one of the Seven Wonders of Wales. Q🕭♿🚍(1)P🏃

Pant-yr-Ochain
Old Wrexham Road, LL12 8TY (off A5156, E from A483, follow signs to The Flash) SJ347534
☼ 12-11 (10.30 Sun) ☎ (01978) 853525
⊕ pantyrochain-gresford.co.uk
Brunning & Price Original; Flowers Original; Purple Moose Snowdonia Ale; guest beers Ⓗ
Extensively converted 16th-century manor house, set in award-winning landscaped gardens with a view over a small lake. It is renowned for high-quality food, especially the excellent Sunday roasts. A variety of light and airy rooms, adorned with interesting prints and bric-a-brac, are served by a single bar. The irregular, open-plan layout includes a large conservatory and smaller areas adjacent to the 16th-century inglenook fireplace. In summer the lawn is ideal for relaxing or dining. 🏚Q🕭◑♿P🏃

Halkyn

Blue Bell Inn Ⓛ ✓
Rhosesmor Road, CH8 8DL (on B5123) SJ209703
☼ 5-11 (midnight Fri); 12-midnight Sat; 12-11 Sun
☎ (01352) 780309 ⊕ bluebell.uk.eu.org
Beer range varies Ⓗ
Situated on Halkyn Mountain with spectacular views across the Dee Estuary and local countryside. Winner of many awards, including CAMRA Regional Pub of the Year, the landlords are enthusiastic supporters of real ale and cider. Four beers, two ciders and a perry are available including two house regulars from local brewery Facer's plus ever-changing guests from Welsh micros. The pub is a focal point for the local community, with regular walks, music including Sunday jazz, and a class in conversational Welsh. CAMRA members receive a discount. 🏚Q🕭🚪♿🚪🚍(126)♣👟P🏃

Hanmer

Hanmer Arms Hotel ⓛ

SY13 3DE (just off A495 1 mile from jct with A525)
✪ 11-11 (12.30am Fri & Sat) ☎ (01948) 830532
⊕ hanmerarms.co.uk
Stonehouse Station Bitter; guest beers Ⓗ
Attractive hotel-restaurant situated in a bucolic corner of the North Wales Borderlands between Wrexham and Whitchurch. Meals are served from an extensive menu throughout the day and high-quality accommodation is available in 11 en-suite bedrooms. Drinkers are welcome and up to three cask beers are on offer including at least one from a local micro such as Salopian.
🏨Q✿✿⬅◑⊟♿☒(146)♠P⭑

Hawarden

Crown & Liver ✔

The Highway, Ewloe, CH5 3DN (on B5125, ½ mile from A494)
✪ 12-midnight (2am Fri & Sat) ☎ (01244) 531182
⊕ crownandliverhawarden.co.uk
Jennings Bitter Ⓗ
Drinkers are welcomed in this Marston's local with a well-kept range from the owner's list. The main T-shaped bar has an unusual decor of musical and 1950s Hollywood emblems and leads to an extensively furnished outside area with a large water feature, smokers' patio and a small summer bar. An additional bar has a dartboard, jukebox and TV. On Saturday there is piano music followed by a live band. ✿◑♿➡☒(X44)P⭑

Hendre

Y Dderwen (The Oak) ♟ ⓛ

Denbigh Road, CH7 5QE (on A541) SJ191677
✪ 7-midnight ☎ (01352) 741466 ⊕ ydderwen-theoak.com
Beer range varies Ⓗ
Roadside pub with a strong community focus. The central bar serves two rooms, each with an impressive pottery collection. Two cask ales are usually available, at least one from a local microbrewery, often a house beer from Hafod. The pub is a popular meeting point for ramblers and visitors to the surrounding countryside, and it hosts a range of social activities. Local CAMRA Pub of the Year 2012. 🏨Q✿✿♿▲☒(14)P⭑–🍺

Holt

Peal o' Bells

12 Church Street, LL13 9JP (400yds S of Holt-Farndon bridge)
✪ 4 (6 Mon)-11; 4-12.30am Fri; 12-12.30am Sat; 12-10.30 Sun ☎ (01829) 270411 ⊕ pealobells.co.uk
Beer range varies Ⓗ
Family-friendly village pub situated next to St Chad's Church on the road to the River Dee. The bar serves two front rooms and a back room with a dartboard and pool table. The large fully enclosed garden has a small play area and excellent views of the Dee Valley and Peckforton Hills. Perry is available and guest ales come from the SIBA list. The pub usually stages a beer festival on one of the May bank holidays. 🏨Q✿✿♿☒(C56)♠P⭑

Holywell

Old Wine Vaults ⓛ

Cross Street, CH8 7LP (at jct of High St & Cross St)
✪ 10-midnight (2am Fri & Sat) ☎ (01352) 714801
Theakston Best Bitter; guest beers Ⓗ
The open-plan bar has three handpumps, two serving Welsh national and micro beers. Home to a Sunday League football team, there are many TV screens showing all types of sport; an enclosed drinking and smoking area also has its own TV. At one time the pub was used as the pay office for local lead miners – the safes can still be seen. The landlord's family has run pubs in the area for 40 years and a customer loyalty scheme is offered.
🏨☒(X11,11A)⭑–

Llanarmon Dyffryn Ceiriog

Hand at Llanarmon

LL20 7LD (end of B4500 from Chirk) SJ157328
✪ 11-11 (12.30am Fri & Sat); 12-11 Sun ☎ (01691) 600666
⊕ thehandhotel.co.uk
Beer range varies Ⓗ
Centrally situated village inn at the head of the Ceiriog Valley, surrounded by the Berwyn Mountains. The cosy and atmospheric bar is hard to leave once you have settled by the log fire. There is always a cask beer on offer from an independent, such as Weetwood, and two at busier times. The imaginative and interesting menu and the accommodation are both of a high standard. This popular base for walkers and cyclists welcomes well-behaved dogs. 🏨✿✿⬅◑⊟♿☒♣P⭑

Llanarmon-yn-Ial

Raven Inn ⓛ

Ffordd-Rhew-Ial, CH7 4QE (signed 500yds west of B5430) SJ191562
✪ closed Mon; 5-10.30 (11 Fri); 12-11 Sat; 12-9 Sun
☎ (01824) 780833 ⊕ raveninn.co.uk
Beer range varies Ⓗ
The Raven has been a pub since 1772. It was rescued from housing developers by the village locals and is run almost entirely by them. Within, it has four drinking areas, one with a tiled floor where walkers and their dogs are welcome. The house beer is brewed by Purple Moose, with two local beers changing constantly; real local cider is also stocked. Local CAMRA Pub of the Year 2011.
🏨Q✿✿✿◑♿▲♣P⭑

Llandyrnog

Golden Lion ⓛ ✔

LL16 4HG (on B5429, opp village stores) SJ108650
✪ 4-11 (12.30am Thu); 2-1am Fri & Sat; 2-11 Sun
☎ (01824) 790373
Facer's DHB; Greene King Old Speckled Hen; guest beer Ⓗ
Situated at the heart of the village, this welcoming drinkers' establishment has strong links with the local football team; players and supporters like to drink here after matches. Live music and ESPN TV feature at weekends. The pub has two main areas – a public bar and a room with wooden floor and fixtures, and a pool table. It participates in the July Route 76 inter-pub beer festival, and real cider is usually available in the summer.
🏨✿✿✿♿▲☒(76)♣♠P⭑

Llangollen

Abbey Grange Hotel L

Horseshoe Pass Road, Llantisylio, LL20 8DD (on A542, 1½ miles NW of Llangollen)
🕒 12-11 (may close in the afternoon on weekdays in winter)
☎ (01978) 860753 ⊕ abbey-grange-hotel.co.uk
Llangollen Bitter; guest beer ⊞
Former slate quarry owner's residence boasting an enviable location in eight acres of countryside at the foot of the Horseshoe Pass. Close by are the evocative ruins of the Cistercian Valle Crucis Abbey that dates from the 13th century. Up to four cask ales are available, mainly from the hotel's own brewery, which began operations in 2010. Good-value meals are served throughout the day. The pub may close on weekday afternoons in winter.
🏨❀🖂🕽🍽占♣♠P꓿

Sun Inn

49 Regent Street, LL20 8HN (½ mile E of town centre on A5)
🕒 12 (5 winter)-1am; 12 (3 winter)-2am Fri & Sat; 12 (3 winter)-1am Sun ☎ (01978) 860079
Purple Moose Snowdonia; Salopian Shropshire Gold; guest beers ⊞
A superb free house serving at least two changing ales from microbreweries. The large room at the front, with two real fires and a games area, hosts live music Wednesday to Saturday evenings, featuring folk, jazz and rock bands. A small snug at the rear of the bar leads to a covered seating area outside with a large-screen TV. Winter hours may vary – phone ahead to check. 🏨❀🖂🍽🖂♣꓿

Llangynhafal

Golden Lion Inn

LL16 4LN (at village crossroads) SJ131634
🕒 closed Mon; 6-11; 4-midnight Fri; 12-midnight Sat; 12-11 Sun ☎ (01824) 790451 ⊕ thegoldenlioninn.com
Holt Bitter; guest beer ⊞
Welcoming inn at a village crossroads with an L-shaped counter serving a public bar with a pool table, lounge and dining area. A regularly changing guest beer, often from Facer's or Purple Moose, supplements the Holt Bitter. The licensees are enthusiastic supporters of the inter-pub Route 76 beer festival each July; their outlet was also twice voted as local CAMRA Pub of the Year.
🏨Q🚲❀🖂🕽🍽Å🖂(76)♣♠P꓿

Mold

Glasfryn

Raikes Lane, CH7 6LR (off A5119 ½ mile N of Mold) SJ240649
🕒 11.30-11; 12-10.30 Sun ☎ (01352) 750500
⊕ glasfryn-mold.co.uk
Flowers Original; guest beers ⊞
The Glasfryn stands in its own grounds near to Theatre Clwyd and was originally a residence for circuit judges attending the nearby court; it was more recently converted into the large upmarket pub and restaurant that it is today. The house beer is brewed by Phoenix Brewery and many national and local north Wales beers are dispensed from 12 handpumps. Food is served all day.
🏨Q❀🕽占🖂(28,X44)P꓿

Gold Cape ✅

8-8A Wrexham Road, CH7 1ES (next to Market Square crossroads)
🕒 8am-midnight (1am Fri & Sat); 9am-midnight Sun
☎ (01352) 705920
Greene King Abbot; Ruddles Best Bitter; guest beers ⊞
This Wetherspoon establishment is an enthusiastic supporter of cask beer - it offers five beers and four ciders, with Welsh micros often represented. The pub is named after a 4,000-year-old gold peytrel found nearby (a replica of this cape-like relic can be seen in Mold Heritage Centre and Museum). Handily situated in the market town centre, it offers a discount to CAMRA members and is a popular venue for local real ale fans.
Q🚲❀🕽占🖂♠꓿

Overton-on-Dee

White Horse Inn

21 High Street, LL13 0DT (on A528)
🕒 closed Mon; 12-2.30 (not Tue), 5.30-midnight (10.30 Tue); 12-midnight Sat; 12-11 Sun ☎ (01978) 710111
⊕ thewhitehorseoverton.co.uk
Joule's Pale Ale ⊞
Attractive red-brick, mock Tudor building situated in the heart of the village and part of the small but impressive Joule's estate. A CAMRA pub design winner, it features frosted and latticed windows, pristine wooden partitioning and restored fireplaces. A former pantry, coal shed and wash house for the rear have been converted into dining spaces, decorated with Joule's breweriana. Excellent food is served lunchtimes and evenings, including a Sunday lunchtime carvery and weekly curry nights. A weekly quiz is held. Dogs are welcome. 🏨❀🕽占🖂(146)♣꓿

Pontblyddyn

Bridge Inn

Wrexham Road, CH7 4HN (on A541 3 miles S of Mold)
🕒 12-11 ☎ (01352) 770087
Deer range varies ⊞
Set in a 16th-century building that has been a hostelry since 1803, this community village inn offers two changing beers usually from independent breweries. Good-value food is served both in the bar area and the separate restaurant, with themed evenings a speciality (no food Mon). On Sunday there is a carvery until 7.30pm. Outside, the riverside beer garden has a children's play area. 🏨❀🕽占🖂(26,27)P꓿

Prestatyn

Halcyon Quest L

17 Gronant Road, LL19 9DT (on A547 just E of town centre) SJ069826
🕒 3-11.30 (12.30am Fri & Sat); 12-11.30 Sun
☎ (01745) 852442 ⊕ halcyonquest-hotel.com
Facer's Flintshire Bitter; guest beers ⊞
The Halcyon Quest is a pleasant one-roomed bar with much sporting memorabilia, including cricket, golf and baseball equipment – there is even a rowing boat suspended from the ceiling. The outside covered drinking area has been renewed recently. Accommodation is available in nine bedrooms. The northern end of Offa's Dyke is close by. ❀🖂Å⇌🖂(35,36)♣P꓿

Rhyl

Sussex ✅

26 Sussex Street, LL18 1SG

⚙ 8am-midnight (1am Fri & Sat; 10.30 Sun)

☎ (01745) 362910

Greene King Abbot; Marston's Pedigree; Ruddles Best Bitter; guest beers Ⓗ

Wetherspoon pub situated in a pedestrianised part of the town centre with a drinking area at the front. In the past the building has been used as a Welsh Wesleyan Chapel and The Old Comrades Club before becoming a pub in 1992; it was taken over by Wetherspoon in 2001. Inside are three areas, with pictures of Rhyl's history alongside modern art. The Sussex is popular with locals and holidaymakers alike. The guest beer sometimes comes from Conwy Brewery while Westons supplies real cider. Q ⇆ ◑ ᴅ & ≠ 🖛 ●

Swan ✅

13 Russell Road, LL18 3BS

⚙ 11-11 (midnight Fri & Sat); 12-11 Sun ☎ (01745) 336694

Thwaites Nutty Black, Original, Lancaster Bomber; guest beer Ⓗ

One of Rhyl's oldest pubs, this popular local is situated just off the town centre. The lounge is wood panelled and used for both drinking and dining; background music is maintained at a pleasant volume and pictures on the wall show something of Rhyl's history. The public bar is equipped for darts and pool, and TVs show a variety of sports. Outside is a covered smoking and seating area. In 1951 the Swan was among the first pubs in Britain to hold a TV licence. Nowadays it is one of the few pubs in the area to serve cask-conditioned mild. ⊛◑ᴅ≠🖛♣⌐

Ruabon

Bridge End Inn ♈ Ⓛ

5 Bridge Street, LL14 6DA (on B5605)

⚙ 5 (4 Fri)-11; 12-11 Sat & Sun ☎ (01978) 810881

⊕ mcgivernales.co.uk

Beer range varies Ⓗ

This former coaching inn near the station, owned by the McGivern Brewery with brewing on the premises, was voted CAMRA National Pub of the Year 2012. The welcoming three-roomed local has a whitewashed exterior and cosy public bar, reputed to be 300 years old, with a beamed ceiling and walls adorned with old breweriana. Children are welcome in the lounge until 7pm and there is a quiet room. Six changing guest ales include a stout and McGivern ale, plus a real cider. Groups can be catered for by arrangement. Live music features on Wednesday. ♨Q⇆⊛⊕≠🖛♣●P⌐🖥

Ruthin

Morning Star Ⓛ

55 Clwyd Street, LL15 1HH (just off town centre)

⚙ closed Mon; 11-3, 5-midnight; 11-1am Sat & Sun

☎ (01832) 703017 ⊕ themorningstarinn.com

Beer range varies Ⓖ

One of the oldest inns in Ruthin, formerly called the Star, situated a short walk from the town centre. The pub has a cosy interior with a large fireplace and a bistro-style dining area. Three beers from Welsh micros are served straight for the cask on a stillage behind the bar. Ruthin Gaol, situated across the road, was originally a house of correction, built in 1654 and closed in 1916. On-site parking is reserved for B&B guests; however, municipal parking is available nearby. ♨☀⊠◑ᴅ ⅄₪ (X50,51,76) ●P⌐

The Waen

Farmers Arms Ⓛ

LL17 0DY (1 mile S of A55 jct 28, signed for Trefnant) SJ061731

⚙ closed Mon & Tue; 5.30-11 Wed-Sat; 12-3, 5.30-10 Sun

☎ (01745) 582190 ⊕ the-farmers-arms.co.uk

Beer range varies Ⓗ

The Farmers Arms has public and lounge bars with two dining areas. There are also two rooms used for functions. The inn is particularly popular for evening meals and Sunday lunches. Several societies meet here, including Rhyl Motor Club. Usually, there are two house beers on handpump, sourced from local brewer Facer's. There may not always be the full range of real ales in winter. ♨Q⇆⊛◑ᴅ ⅄P⌐

Wrexham

Elihu Yale Ⓛ ✅

44-46 Regent Street, LL11 1RR

⚙ 7am-midnight (1am Fri & Sat) ☎ (01978) 366646

Beer range varies Ⓗ

A large, popular Wetherspoon pub, the Elihu Yale owes its name to one of the founders of Yale University, New Haven, Connecticut, who is buried in nearby St Mary's Church. The large single-room interior has various seating areas. Beers are the standard Wetherspoon selection plus some locally sourced brews, and are enthusiastically looked after and presented by the staff. Located in the town centre, close to bus and train stations, the pub has a lively atmosphere, and is often busy. ♨Q⇆◑ᴅ&≠●⌐🖥

Royal Oak

35 High Street, LL13 8HY

⚙ 12-11 (midnight Fri & Sat) ☎ (01978) 358547

Joule's Pale Ale, Slumbering Monk; guest beers Ⓗ

The Royal Oak has proved a popular addition to Wrexham's drinking scene. The Grade II-listed building is known locally as the Polish Embassy after its most recent use, before major refurbishment by the Joule's Pub Company. The interior is long and narrow, with wood panelling and etched brewery mirrors around the bar creating a comfortable ambience. No food is available but crockery and cutlery can be provided if you want to bring your own. ♨☀&≠🖛⌐

Ysceifiog

Fox ★

Village Road, CH8 8NJ (signed from B5121) SJ153714

⚙ 4 (3 Fri; 1 Sat & Sun)-11 ☎ (01352) 720241

Thwaites Original, Lancaster Bomber; guest beers Ⓗ

Identified by CAMRA as one of Britain's Heritage Pubs, this classic village inn's four-roomed interior has remained intact since the 1930s. The tiny front bar, accessed via a sliding door, has bench seating attached to the front counter, which may be unique to the Fox. The guest beers usually come from Welsh breweries. No food on Wednesdays. ♨Q⊛◑ᴅ ₪

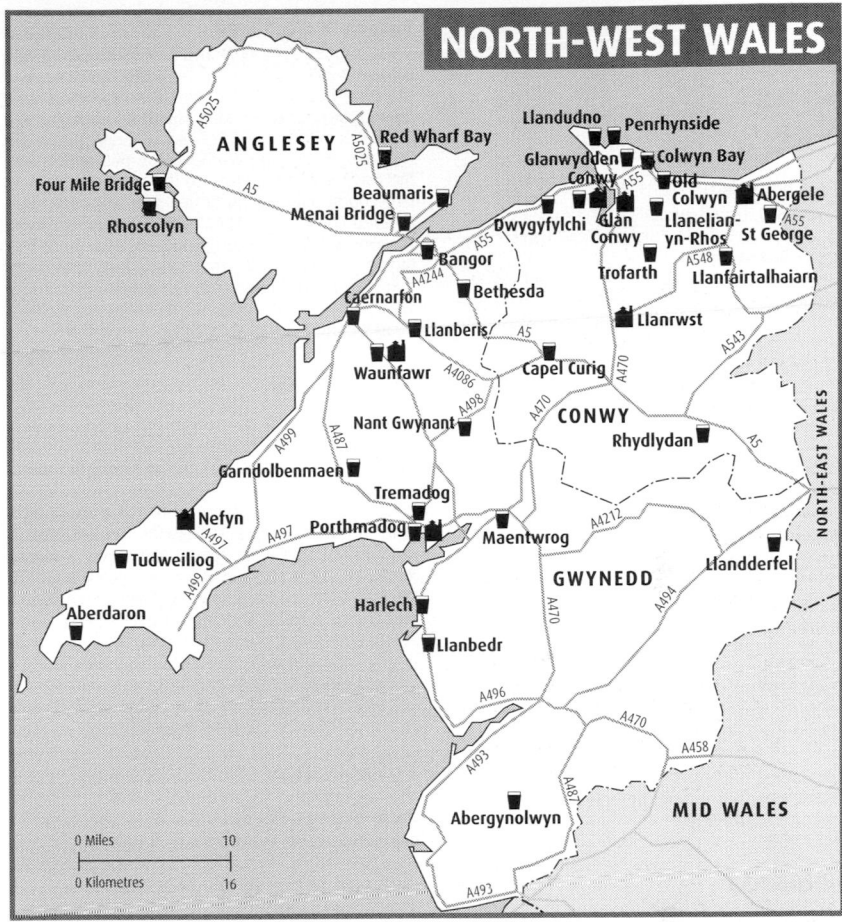

NORTH-WEST WALES

WALES

NORTH-EAST WALES

ANGLESEY

Red Wharf Bay
Llandudno   Penrhynside
Glanwyddan   Colwyn Bay
Four Mile Bridge   Conwy   Old
Rhoscolyn   Beaumaris   Colwyn   Abergele
Menai Bridge   Dwygyfylchi   Llanelian-   St George
Glan   yn-Rhos
Conwy
Bangor   Trofarth   Llanfairtalhaiarn
Caernarfon   Bethesda
Llanberis   Llanrwst
Waunfawr   Capel Curig
CONWY
Nant Gwynant   Rhydlydan
Garndolbenmaen   Tremadog
Nefyn   Porthmadog   Maentwrog
Tudweiliog   Llandderfel
GWYNEDD
Aberdaron   Harlech
Llanbedr

MID WALES
Abergynolwyn

0 Miles   10
0 Kilometres   16

Authority areas covered: Anglesey UA, Conwy UA, Gwynedd UA

Aberdaron

Ship Hotel
LL53 8BE
⊕ 11-11 ☎ (01758) 760204 ⊕ theshiphotelaberdaron.co.uk
Beer range varies Ⓗ
In the centre of the village, the Ship Hotel has two bars, one with a games area. Excellent food made with fresh locally sourced ingredients is highly recommended. Two handpumps in summer and one in winter dispense local Welsh beer. The village has a bus service but check times first.
🏠🐾🛏️🍽️🌏🍺👜🚶‍♂️🅿️♣

Abergynolwyn

Railway Inn
LL36 9YN (on B4405)
⊕ 12-midnight (11 Sun) ☎ (01654) 782279
Beer range varies Ⓗ
Hospitable community local in the centre of the village not far from the Talyllyn Railway. You can still see the remains of the old incline that brought goods traffic down from the railway to the village. Excellent food is served and, following a refit, the range of beers is set to increase. The pub has stunning views of the nearby hills and there is wonderful walking nearby. 🏠Q🌏🍽️🍺👜🚶

Bangor

Boatyard
Garth Road, LL57 2SF (off old A5, follow pier signs)
⊕ 11 (12 Sun)-11 ☎ (01248) 362462
Marston's Burton Bitter, Pedigree; guest beers Ⓗ
Formerly the Union Garth, this large multi-roomed pub is in lower Bangor. It has been refurbished and now has a well-appointed restaurant and pleasant seating areas. The garden area overlooks the sea and Penrhyn Harbour. Guest beers are usually from the Marston's range. The Boatyard is popular with clubs, students and locals. 🏠Q🌏🍽️🍺👜🅿️🚭

Mostyn Arms
27 Ambrose Street, LL57 1BH (off Beach Road)
⊕ 3 (1 Sat & Sun)-midnight ☎ (01248) 364752
Beer range varies Ⓗ

This small, friendly back-street pub has been completely refurbished with a pool area, lounge space with Sky Sports and a small bar. Beers are sourced locally, usually from Purple Moose and Great Orme breweries. No food is served. Note the selective opening hours.

Tap & Spile

Garth Road, LL57 2SW (off old A5, follow pier signs)
🕛 12-11 (11.30 Tue, Fri & Sat) ☎ (01248) 370835
Beer range varies Ⓗ
Busy pub attracting locals, students and visitors to Bangor, with a changing range of up to six real ales from different breweries. It enjoys excellent views of the magnificent pier, Menai Straits and over to Beaumaris. Good wholesome food including vegetarian options is served at sensible prices, and seven letting rooms are available. CAMRA Local Branch Pub of the Year for 2010. ⓓ♣

Beaumaris

Olde Bull's Head Inn

Castle Street, LL58 8AA
🕛 11-11; 12-10.30 Sun ☎ (01248) 810329
⊕ bullsheadinn.co.uk
Draught Bass; Hancock's HB; guest beer Ⓗ
Grade II-listed building that was the original posting house of the borough. In 1645 General Mytton, a parliamentarian, commandeered the inn while his forces laid siege to the nearby castle. The Royalists surrendered on 25 June 1646. Dr Johnson and Charles Dickens were famous guests and each bedroom is named after a Dickens character. The beamed bar has a large open fire. Parking is limited. ⚏Q✍ⓓ☒P

Bethesda

Douglas Arms Hotel ★

London Road, LL57 3AY
🕛 6-11; 3.30-midnight Sat; 1-3, 7-11 Sun ☎ (01248) 600219
Marston's Burton Bitter, Pedigree; guest beer Ⓗ
Built in 1820, this was an important coaching inn on the historic Telford post route from London to Holyhead. The Grade II-listed building is recognised by CAMRA as one of Britain's Real Heritage Pubs. The four-room interior has not changed since the 1930s and includes a snug, lounges and a large tap room with a full-size snooker table. Bethesda is convenient for buses to the Ogwen Valley and the surrounding mountains. Q⚏Å☒♣

Caernarfon

Black Boy Inn ✔

Northgate Street, LL55 1RW (near marina)
🕛 11-11 (11.30 Fri & Sat); 12-10.30 Sun ☎ (01286) 673604
Brains The Rev James; Draught Bass; Hancock's HB; guest beer Ⓗ
The pub is set within the town walls between the marina and castle. This historic town, a World Heritage Site, is well worth a visit, ending with a welcome pint at the Black Boy. The public bar and small lounge are warmed by roaring fires. Good-value food is served and the guest beer usually comes from Purple Moose. There is a drinking area outside on the traffic-free street. A previous local CAMRA award winner. ⚏✿✍ⓓ⚏Å⇄P

Tafarn Y Porth ✔

5-9 Eastgate Street, LL55 1AG (just off Bangor Rd near Barclays Bank)
🕛 9-midnight ☎ (01268) 662920
Big Bog Bitter; Greene King Abbot; Ruddles Best Bitter Ⓗ
Friendly, welcoming Wetherspoon pub opposite the town walls and close to the castle. It has a large open-plan interior and a spacious partly covered courtyard outside with plenty of seating. The real ale range often includes a beer from the Big Bog Brewing Company in Waunfawr, just a few miles away. The pub's location is handy for the Welsh Highland Railway, which takes you to the heart of Snowdonia. Q♿✿ⓓ♿Å⇄☒♣♦P⁻

Capel Curig

Plas y Brenin ᴸ

LL24 0ET
🕛 12-2, 6-11 (10.30 Sun); 11-11 Sat ☎ (01690) 720214
Beer ranges varies Ⓗ
Plas y Brenin is an outdoor centre in a lovely rural area. The raised bar overlooks the two lakes of Llŷnnau Mymbyr, with spectacular views of Mount Snowdon in the distance. The furnishing is basic but modern with wooden floors and wooden tables and chairs. A good selection of hearty and reasonably prices meals is served. There is a large dining area and a TV. The three handpumps dispense local beers from Nant, Purple Moose and Conwy breweries. An alfresco pint is the best way to enjoy the view. Q♿✍ⓓ♿Å☒P⁻

Colwyn Bay

Pen-y-Bryn ♀ ᴸ

Pen-y-Bryn Road, LL29 6DD (top of King's Road)
SH842782
🕛 11.30-11; 12-10.30 Sun ☎ (01492) 533360
⊕ penybryn-colwynbay.co.uk
Brunning & Price Original; Purple Moose Snowdonia Ale; guest beers Ⓗ
Open-plan pub popular with all ages, with large bookcases and old furniture, and real fires in the winter months. The walls are decorated with old photographs and memorabilia from the local area. Panoramic views of Colwyn Bay and the Great Orme can be admired from the terrace and garden. Imaginative bar food is served – the menu is updated daily. Four guest beers are mainly sourced from local and independent breweries. Local CAMRA Pub of the Year 2012. ⚏Q✿ⓓ♿☒♣P

Conwy

Albion Ale House ★ ᴸ

Uppergate Street, LL32 8RF
🕛 12 (5 winter)-11; 12-midnight Fri & Sat; 12-11 Sun
☎ (01492) 582484
Beer range varies Ⓗ
Multi-room heritage pub superbly refurbished by the current owners. Each room retains original 1920s features and several have amazing fireplaces. There is no music, TV or slot machines. The pub is managed by four local brewers – Conwy, Great Orme, Nant and Purple Moose – and showcases their beers as well as guest ales. There are two guest Welsh ciders. The licensee is a former CAMRA award winner. An excellent wine list and a good selection of malt whiskies are also offered. ⚏Q✿⚏☒♣♦🍴

Castle Hotel Ⓛ

High Street, LL32 8DB

✪ 10.30-11.30 (11 Sun) ☎ (01492) 582800

⊕ castlewales.co.uk

Beer range varies Ⓗ

An old coaching inn dating back to the 15th century, standing on the site of a Cistercian abbey. This privately owned hotel had a major refurbishment a few years ago and the public bar is now an upmarket meeting place. One of the partners is also head of the Welsh National Culinary Team, so it's no surprise that the excellent food menu, available in the bar and restaurant, features the finest local produce. The beer is also local, coming from the nearby Conwy Brewery, and the cider is supplied by Gwynt-y-Ddraig.

Q❀✿⊕❀⇆🖳❀P⅄

Old White House

Bangor Road, LL32 8DP (½ mile W of Conwy on old A55) SH770780

✪ 4 (12 summer)-11; 12-midnight Thu-Sun

☎ (01492) 573133 ⊕ oldwhitehouseconwy.com

Taylor Landlord; Tetley Bitter; guest beer Ⓗ

This 17th-century building was once the coach house stable for a now-demolished hotel. The long central bar, featuring a large log-burning stove and a high-beamed roof space, serves the open-plan front lounge and a small rear dining area. The pub hosts a general knowledge quiz on Tuesday, a music quiz on Friday night and live entertainment on Saturday night. Food is available Tuesday to Sunday evening and all day every day in the summer. ⚟Q❀⊕Å⇆🖳(5,X5)❀P⅄

Dwygyfylchi

Gladstone Ⓛ ✔

Ysgubor Wen Road, LL34 6PS (off jct 16 A55) SH730772

✪ 12-11 (midnight Fri & Sat); closed Mon & Tue winter

☎ (01492) 623231 ⊕ thegladstone.co.uk

Beer range varies Ⓗ

Renowned for its magnificent sea views, this recently refurbished pub retains many original features including the alcoves and traditional decor with wood panelling and old photographs. Comfortable sofas surround a wood-burning stove and a galleried balcony with tables and booths overlooks the bar. The restaurant offers imaginative food sourced locally. There is a function room, accommodation in six luxury rooms and the pub has a wedding licence. Live music plays on Saturday nights. ⚟❀✿⊕Å🖳P⅄

Four Mile Bridge

Anchorage Hotel

LL65 2EZ (on B4545, just past bridge to Holy Island)

✪ 11 (12 Sun)-11 ☎ (01407) 740168

Draught Bass; Taylor Landlord; Theakston XB; guest beer Ⓗ

Family-run hotel situated on Holy Island close to Trearddur Bay. It has a large, comfortable lounge bar and a dining area serving a wide selection of meals. The hotel is near some fine sandy beaches and coastal walks. Its proximity to the A55 makes it a useful stopping-off point for Holyhead Port.

Q❀✿⊕Å🖳P⅄

Garndolbenmaen

Cross Foxes

LL51 9TX (between Caernarfon and Porthmadog off A487)

✪ 6-11; closed Mon & Tue winter; 12.30-2.30, 6.30-11 Sun

☎ (01766) 530246 ⊕ crossfoxesinn.co.uk

Beer range varies Ⓗ

Two-roomed village inn dating from the 19th century with a central bar. The pub is popular with locals and visitors for an ever-changing range of beer and good home-cooked food. Meals are served Sunday lunchtime and every evening. The dining area converts into a popular skittle alley in winter. The local bus stops close by, with regular services Monday to Saturday to Porthmadog and Caernarfon. ⚟❀⊕🖳❀P

Glanwydden

Queen's Head Ⓛ

LL31 9JP SH817804

✪ 11.30-3, 6 (5.30 Fri)-10.30; 11.30-10.30 Sat & Sun

☎ (01492) 546570 ⊕ queensheadglanwydden.co.uk

Adnams Southwold Bitter; Great Orme Orme; guest beer Ⓗ

Former wheelwright's cottage in the centre of the village, welcoming locals and holidaymakers alike. Run by the same owner for more than 20 years, the olde-worlde pub has a traditional front bar with a cosy atmosphere and a rear bar with a dining area. Excellent quality, locally sourced food includes fish and chips in Great Orme beer batter and steak and ale pie with Great Orme ale. There is a heated seating area outside. ⚟Q❀✿⊕☖Å🖳P⅄

Harlech

Branwen Hotel

Ffordd Newydd, LL46 2UB (on A462 below Harlech Castle) SH583312

✪ 11-11 ☎ (01766) 780477 ⊕ branwenhotel.co.uk

Beer range varies Ⓗ

Warm and welcoming family-run hotel and bar overlooked by Harlech Castle. The hotel is named after a princess whose tales are found in a collection of Welsh myths known as Y Mabinogion. The popular and stylish bar offers a wide range of cask ales as well as foreign beers. A large selection of wines and malt whiskies is also stocked. Ask for your favourite malt – they are sure to have it. A former local CAMRA award winner. ❀✿⊕☖Å⇆🖳❀P⅄

Llanbedr

Ty Mawr Hotel

LL45 2HH

✪ 11-11 ☎ (01341) 241440 ⊕ tymawrhotel.com

Beer range varies Ⓗ

Small country hotel set in its own grounds. The modern lounge bar has a slate-flagged floor and cosy wood-burning stove. Unusual flying memorabilia reflect connections with the local airfield. French windows open out on a veranda and landscaped terrace with seating. A beer festival is held in a marquee on the lawn each year. Popular with locals and walkers, dogs and children are welcome. Meals are served all day. ⚟❀✿⊕☖Å⇆P

Llanberis

Heights
74 High Street, LL55 4DT
🌣 12 (4 Mon-Fri winter)-midnight ☎ (01286) 871179
⊕ heightshotelsnowdon.com
Beer range varies Ⓗ
The Heights has been completely refurbished downstairs with bistro-style decor. There are several dining areas away from the main bar and a larger conservatory room to the rear. In the centre of Llanberis, the pub is well situated for walking, the Snowdon Railway, visiting the slate museum and the Dinorwic Power Station. One of the beers is usually a local ale. 🌣🏠🌣🕪🚻⇌🚃Pᐟ

Llandderfel

Bryntirion Inn Ⓛ
LL23 7RA (on B4401 4 miles E of Bala) SJ986364
🌣 11 (12 Sun)-11 ☎ (01678) 530205 ⊕ bryntirioninn.co.uk
Beer range varies Ⓗ
This old coaching inn, situated in a rural setting with views of the River Dee, is a recent CAMRA Vale of Clwyd Branch Pub of the Year. One beer from Purple Moose is always on offer plus one guest on handpump. Meals are served in a separate, quieter lounge and bar snacks are also available. The pleasant public bar leads to a room where families are welcome. There is outdoor seating in the front car park and at the rear is a larger parking area and courtyard. Three bedrooms offer good-value accommodation.
🏰Q🌣🏠🌣🕪🛏🚃(X94)♣Pᐟ

Llandudno

Cottage Loaf Ⓛ ✔
Market Street, LL30 2SR SH781824
🌣 11-11 (11.30 Fri & Sat) ☎ (01492) 870762
⊕ the-cottageloaf.co.uk
Conwy Welsh Pride; Courage Directors; guest beers Ⓗ
The building was previously a bakery, hence the name. The interior features stone-flagged floors, an impressive fireplace and a raised timber-floored area – much of the wood came from the Flying Foam, a schooner shipwrecked at Llandudno's West Shore. With great home-cooked food served daily, the Loaf is a popular meeting place for people of all ages. Live bands play on Saturday and Sunday evenings, and there is an annual beer and music festival in the summer. 🏰🌣🕪⇌🚃ᐟ

Llanelian-yn-Rhos

White Lion
LL29 8YA (off B583) SH863764
🌣 closed Mon; 11.30-3, 6-midnight; 12-11 Sun
☎ (01492) 515807 ⊕ whitelioninn.co.uk
Marston's Burton Bitter, Pedigree; guest beer Ⓗ
A regular in the Guide for more than 20 years, this 16th-century inn situated in the hills above Old Colwyn, next to St Elian's Church, offers a warm welcome. Gracing the entrance are two stone white lions, leading into the bar area with its slate-flagged flooring and large comfortable chairs around the log fires. Decorative stained glass is mounted above the bar in the tiny snug. A spacious restaurant serves delicious home-cooked food, with a wide menu choice. Jazz night is Tuesday, quiz night Thursday. 🏰Q🌣🏠🕪🛏♣Pᐟ

Llanfairtalhaiarn

Black Lion Hotel
Swan Square, LL22 8RY SH 927703
🌣 3-10 Mon; 12-11 ☎ (01745) 720205
⊕ theblacklionnorthwales.co.uk
Robinson's 1892, Unicorn, Double Hop Ⓗ
Idyllically situated beside the Afon Elwy, the Black has recently undergone major refurbishment, with the emphasis now on quality dining and accommodation. Here you will find a warm and welcoming place to drink, dine and stay. A great range of Robinson's real ales is complemented by fine food, locally sourced wherever possible, and accommodation that exudes comfort and luxury. The open-plan layout divides into three distinctive areas: a dining space, public bar and games room.
🏰Q🌣🏠🕪🛏♣Pᐟ

Maentwrog

Grapes Hotel
LL41 4HN (on A496 near A487 jct)
🌣 12-late ☎ (01766) 590365 ⊕ grapes-hotel.co.uk
Evans Evans Cwrw, Best, Warrior, seasonal beers Ⓗ
A former coaching inn, this hotel dates back to the 17th century and overlooks the Vale of Ffestiniog. The interior comprises a lounge, public bar, veranda and large dining room. All the beers are from the local Evan Evans Brewery in Llandeilo, including the full seasonal range. Good-value food is popular, especially the ribs. The railway station nearby is on the Ffestiniog line.
🏰Q🌣🏠🕪🛏⇌🚃Pᐟ

Menai Bridge

Anglesey Arms ✔
Mona Road, LL59 5EA (by Menai Suspension Bridge)
🌣 11-11 (midnight Thu-Sat); 12-11 Sun ☎ (01248) 712305
⊕ anglesey-arms.co.uk
Lees Bitter, Governor Ⓗ
Dating back more than 200 years, this old coaching house has recently been completely refurbished. Just over Telford's famous suspension bridge, it is on the main route to Holyhead and ideally situated for Snowdonia, the Llŷn Peninsula, the resorts of Anglesey and the Irish Ferries. Guest beers and seasonal ales are from the JW Lees list and local produce is used in most meals. The large rear rooms are available for functions.
🌣🏠🕪🛏🚃Pᐟ

Tafarn y Bont (Bridge Inn)
Telford Road, LL59 5DT
🌣 11-midnight; 12-10.30 Sun ☎ (01248) 716888
Banks's Bitter; Marston's Pedigree; guest beers Ⓗ
Mid 19th-century former shop and tea rooms, close to the famous bridge, now a brasserie-style pub with an excellent restaurant. A beamed interior, log fires and numerous hideaway rooms give the pub an old-fashioned feel. Snowdonia is a short drive away and the Anglesey Coastal Path is close. A former local CAMRA award winner.
🏰🌣🕪🛏ᐟ

Nant Gwynant

Pen-y-Gwryd Ⓛ
LL55 4NT (at jct of A486 and A4086)
🌣 11-11 (winter hours limited) ☎ (01286) 870211
⊕ pyg.co.uk

Purple Moose Madog's Ale, Glaslyn Ale H
Built in 1810 and Grade II-listed, this famous hotel is situated in the heart of Snowdonia. It was used by the team who made the first ascent of Everest. The Everest room has famous signatures on the ceiling and there are two other small rooms plus a dining room. The hotel is featured in CAMRA's Real Heritage Pubs of Wales and Great British Pubs. Please note that winter opening is restricted but the bar does open for festivities over the New Year. ⚶Q✿≉🍴◑⊟▲⊠♣P⚑

Old Colwyn

Red Lion
385 Abergele Road, LL29 9PL (on main Colwyn Bay to Abergele road) SH868783
✪ 5 (12 Sun)-11; 4-midnight Fri; 12-midnight Sat
☎ (01492) 515042
Brains Dark; Marston's Burton Bitter; guest beers H
Free house serving up to five guest ales from independent and local brewers. A winner of many awards, the popular local is a former CAMRA Branch Pub of the Year. It has a cosy L-shaped lounge featuring a real coal fire, antique brewery mirrors and other memorabilia, and a traditional public bar with a pool table, darts and TVs. To the rear is a superb Victorian-style covered and heated smoking conservatory. The Real Ale Club every Thursday offers nine beers at reduced prices. Guest ciders are also available. ⚶Q✿⊟♣♦⚑

Penrhynside

Cross Keys Inn Ⓛ ✓
Pendre Road, LL30 3DD (off B5115) SH814815
✪ 5-midnight (11 Mon); 3-midnight Fri; 12-midnight Sat & Sun ☎ (01492) 547070 ⊕ crosskeys-inn.co.uk
Facer's Flintshire Bitter; guest beers H
A former local CAMRA award winner, this family-owned and run 19th-century free house offers a warm and friendly welcome. It has a cosy front room with a central bar, rear pool room and side lounge boasting unrivalled views of the surrounding area towards Penrhyn Bay and Rhos-on-Sea. Occasional karaoke and live music nights are hosted. ⚶✿⊟▲⊠♣

Penrhyn Arms Ⓛ
Pendre Road, LL30 3BY (off B5115) SH814816
✪ 5.30 (4.30 Thu; 4 Fri)-midnight; 12-1am Sat; 12-11 Sun
☎ (07780) 678927 ⊕ penrhynarms.com
Banks's Bitter; Marston's Pedigree; guest beers H
A winner of many awards including local CAMRA Pub of the Year, plus regional, Welsh and national cider awards including National Cider Pub of the Year finalist 2012. The welcoming local has up to four guest beers including local ales, Belgian beers and a winter ale on gravity at Christmas. The spacious L-shaped bar has pool, darts and a wide-screen TV. Thursday is cheese night. Accommodation is available in a self-contained flatlet for up to eight people. ⚶✿≉▲⊠♣♦⚑

Porthmadog

Ship Inn ✓
14 Lombard Street, LL49 9AP
✪ 12-2.30, 5.30-11 (11.30 Thu-Sat) ☎ (01766) 512990
Beer range varies H
Traditional pub set in a picturesque location behind the park in the centre of this harbour town. Friendly

and efficient staff dispense frequently changing ales and serve quality food, including pub favourites steak and ale pie, lasagne and barbecue ribs. The pub has a separate bar and lounge, and a room available for private events, and is popular with locals and tourists. A quiz is hosted on Thursday night. Local CAMRA Pub of the Year 2011. ⚶Q✿◑≉⊟(1,3,X32)P

Spooner's Bar
Harbour Station, LL49 9NF
✪ 10-11; 12-10.30 Sun ☎ (01766) 516032 ⊕ festrail.co.uk
Beer range varies H
An all-year-round mini beer festival – Spooner's has built its reputation on an ever-changing range from small breweries, including the local Purple Moose. Situated in the terminus of the world-famous Ffestiniog Railway, steam trains are outside the door most of the year. Food is served every lunchtime, evening meals Tuesday to Saturday, but check first out of season. A former local CAMRA Pub of the Year award winner. Q✿◑⚅≉⊟P

Station Inn
LL49 9HT (on mainline station platform)
✪ 11-11 (midnight Thu-Sat); 12-11 Sun ☎ (01766) 512629
Brains The Rev James; Purple Moose Snowdonia; guest beer H
Situated on the Cambrian Coast railway platform, this pub is popular with locals and visitors alike. It has a large lounge and a smaller public bar, and can get busy at the weekend and on nights when live football is shown on TV. A range of pies and sandwiches is available all day. ✿⊟▲≉⊠♣P

Red Wharf Bay

Ship Inn ✓
LL75 8RJ (on A5025 between Pentraeth and Benllech)
✪ 11-11 (10.30 Sun) ☎ (01248) 852568
⊕ shipinnredwharfbay.co.uk
Adnams Southwold Bitter; Brains SA; guest beers H
Red Wharf Bay was once a busy port exporting coal and fertilisers in the 18th and 19th centuries. Previously known as the Quay, the Ship enjoys an excellent reputation for its bar and restaurant, with meals served lunchtimes and evenings. It gets busy with locals and visitors in the summer. The garden has panoramic views across the bay to south-east Anglesey. The resort town of Benllech is two miles away and the coastal path passes the front door. Beers can be expensive. ⚶Q✿✿◑⊟P⚑

Rhoscolyn

White Eagle
LL65 2NJ (off B4545 signed Traeth Beach) SH271755
✪ 12-3, 6-11; 12-11 Sat; 12-10.30 Sun ☎ (01407) 860267
⊕ white-eagle.co.uk
Marston's Burton Bitter, Pedigree; Weetwood Eastgate Ale; guest beers H
Saved from closure by new owners, this pub has been renovated and rebuilt with an airy, brasserie-style ambience. It has a fine patio enjoying superb views over Caernarfon Bay and the Lleyn Peninsula to Bardsey Island. The nearby beach offers safe swimming with a warden on duty in the summer months. The pub is also close to the coastal footpath. Excellent food is available lunchtimes and evenings, all day during the school holidays. ⚶Q✿◑⊟⚅▲P

Rhydlydan

Giler Arms

LL24 0LL SH892508

✪ 12-3 (not Mon-Thu), 6 (7 winter)-11

☎ (01690) 770612 01690 ⊕ giler.co.uk

Bathams Mild Ale, Best Bitter, XXX H

Friendly country hotel set in six acres of grounds with a one-acre lake, camping and caravan site with recently refurbished facilities, and picturesque gardens beside the small River Merddwr. It offers a welcoming, comfortable lounge, a separate public bar popular with locals, and a small pool room. The restaurant has lovely views over the lake. Quiz night is the middle Wednesday of the month. B&B accommodation is in seven bedrooms and children and dogs are welcome. ♨Q♙☺✿⌂◑ ⊟Å⊟♣P⌐

St George

Kinmel Arms

LL22 9BP SH974758

✪ closed Sun & Mon; 12-3, 6-11 (11.30 Fri & Sat)

☎ (01745) 832207 ⊕ thekinmelarms.co.uk

Thwaites Original; guest beers H

A local CAMRA Pub of the Year winner, this former 17th-century coaching inn is set on a hillside overlooking the sea. A central bar serves a large combined dining and drinking area with a real log fire in one corner and a spacious conservatory at the rear. Two guest beers come from independent breweries, plus a Welsh cider or perry and a selection of Belgian and continental beers. The pub has a reputation for good food. Luxury accommodation is available in four comfortable suites. ♨Q♙✿⌂◑ ⊟Å⊟♠P⌐

Tremadog

Golden Fleece ✔

Market Square, LL49 9RB (on A487)

✪ 11.30-3, 6-11; 12.30-3, 6-10.30 Sun ☎ (01766) 512421

⊕ goldenfleeceinn.com

Draught Bass; Purple Moose Glaslyn Ale; guest beer H

Situated in the old market square, this former coaching inn is now a friendly local. The pub has a lounge bar, snug and a covered area outside with decking and bench seats. Bar meals are good value and there is a bistro upstairs (booking advisable). Guest beers come from small breweries. Live acoustic music plays on Tuesday night. ♨Q♙✿⌂◑Å⊟

Union Inn ✔

7 Market Square, LL49 9RB

✪ 12-2, 5.30-12.30am (11 Sun) ☎ (01766) 512748

⊕ union-inn.com

Big Bog Bog Standard Bitter; Great Orme Great Welsh Bitter; Purple Moose Snowdonia Ale H

Friendly village local situated in the village square, with two separate cosy bars and a restaurant at the rear. The pub has a policy of using locally sourced produce, and the ale range features mainly local beers. Children are welcome and there are board games available. Excellent food is served in the bar and restaurant. Tremadog was the birthplace of Lawrence of Arabia. Frequent bus services pass the building.

♨Q♙◑⊟✿⇄(Porthmadog)⊟(1A,X32)♣⌐

Trofarth

Holland Arms L

Llanrwst Road, LL22 8BG SH840708

✪ 12-3 (not Thu), 7 (6 Fri & Sat)-11; closed Wed; 12-10.30 Sun ☎ (01492) 650777 ⊕ thehollandarms.co.uk

Beer range varies H

Eighteenth-century coaching house set in a country landscape within sight of Snowdonia. Family-run with a warm welcome for locals and visitors alike, it has a pleasantly furnished bar, lounge and restaurant areas. Excellent, value-for-money meals are available daily, with a special themed menu on Mondays. Beers are all local from Conwy, Great Orme, Purple Moose and Nant. Live music features occasionally. The pub has picked up many local CAMRA awards in recent years. ♨Q♙◑♣P

Tudweiliog

Lion Hotel

LL53 8ND (on B4417)

✪ 11-11 (12-2, 6-11 winter); 11.30-11 Sat; 11-10.30 (12-3 winter) Sun ☎ (01758) 770244

Beer range varies H

The origins of this free house go back more than 300 years. A village inn set on the glorious, quiet north coast of the Lleyn Peninsula, cliffs and beaches are a mile away by footpath, a little further by road. Up to three beers are served depending on the season, with Purple Moose a firm favourite. The pub is accessible by number 8 bus from Pwllheli during the day only. Closed Monday lunchtimes in winter. Former local CAMRA Pub of the Year. Q♙✿⌂◑Å⊟P

Waunfawr

Snowdonia Park ♥ L ✔

Beddgelert Road, LL55 4AQ

✪ 11-11 (10.30 Sun) ☎ (01286) 650409

⊕ snowdonia-park.co.uk

Beer range varies H

Home of the Snowdonia and Big Bog Breweries, this is a popular pub for walkers, climbers and families, with children's play areas inside and out. Meals are served all day. The pub adjoins Waunfawr station on the Welsh Highland Railway – stop off here before continuing on one of the most scenic sections of narrow gauge railway in Britain. There is a large campsite adjacent on the riverside. Local CAMRA Pub of the Year 2012.

Q♙✿◑⊟Å⇄⊟♣P

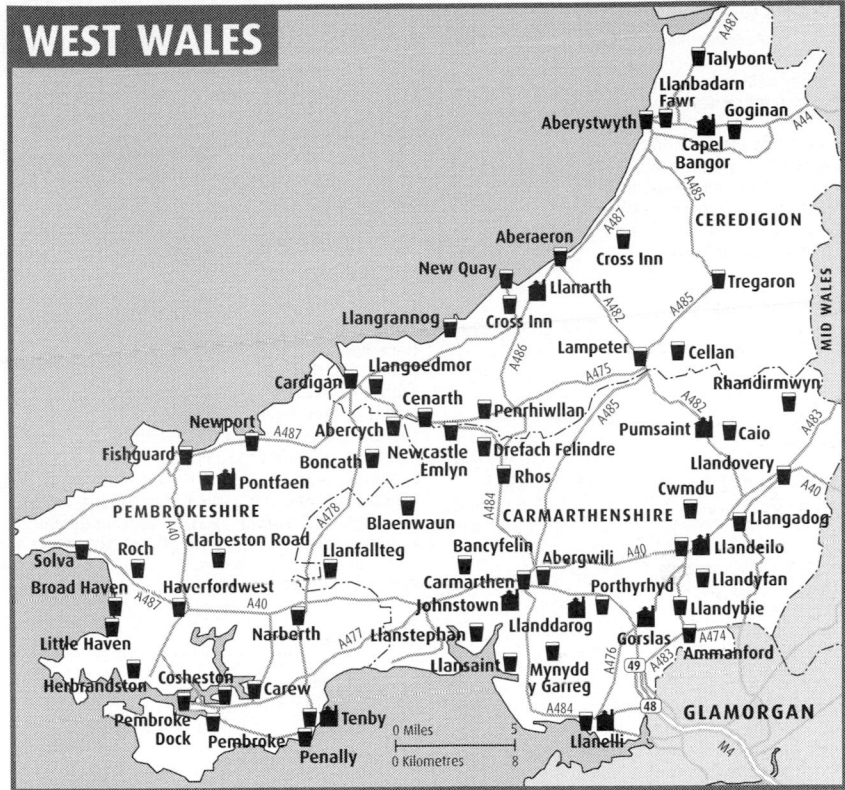

WEST WALES

Talybont
Llanbadarn Fawr
Goginan
Aberystwyth
Capel Bangor
CEREDIGION
Aberaeron
Cross Inn
New Quay
Llanarth
Tregaron
Llangrannog
Cross Inn
Lampeter
Cellan
Llangoedmor
Rhandirmwyn
Cardigan
Cenarth
Penrhiwllan
Newport
Abercych
Pumsaint
Caio
Fishguard
Boncath
Newcastle Emlyn
Drefach Felindre
Llandovery
Pontfaen
Rhos
Cwmdu
PEMBROKESHIRE
Blaenwaun
CARMARTHENSHIRE
Llangadog
Solva
Roch
Clarbeston Road
Llanfallteg
Bancyfelin
Abergwili
Llandeilo
Broad Haven
Haverfordwest
Carmarthen
Porthyrhyd
Llandyfan
Little Haven
Johnstown
Llanddarog
Llandybie
Narberth
Llanstephan
Gorslas
Ammanford
Herbrandston
Cosheston
Carew
Llansaint
Mynydd y Garreg
GLAMORGAN
Pembroke Dock
Pembroke
Tenby
Penally
Llanelli

0 Miles 5
0 Kilometres 8

Authority areas covered: Carmarthenshire UA, Ceredigion UA, Pembrokeshire UA

Aberaeron

Cadwgan
10 Market Street, SA46 0AU
☼ 12-11 (midnight Fri & Sat; 5 Sun) ☎ (01545) 570149
Hancocks HB; guest beer Ⓗ
Taking its name from the last ship to be built in Aberaeron harbour, the Cadwgan is a small traditional pub overlooking the inner harbour. Visitors receive a warm welcome from the locals and the single bar is a cosy spot to enjoy an ever-changing guest beer, conversation, and televised rugby. The small pavement drinking area is a suntrap and there is a free car park opposite. Dogs welcome. ⚏❀▲♿(40,50,550)⟵

Harbourmaster
2 Quay Parade, SA46 0BT (off A487, overlooking harbour)
☼ 8am-11.30 ☎ (01545) 570755 ⊕ harbour-master.com
Purple Moose HM Best, Cwrw Glaslyn; guest beer Ⓗ
Light, modern bar and restaurant occupying a former grain warehouse overlooking Aberaeron harbour. Welsh culture is celebrated, staff are bilingual, paintings by Welsh artists adorn the walls and award-winning food is locally sourced. The guest beer, available Easter to October, comes from a Welsh brewery. While the bar is usually free of electronic entertainment, an exception is made for rugby internationals on TV. In the summer, pints can be enjoyed outside overlooking the water. The boutique-style hotel accommodation has been widely praised – parking is for residents only. Q❀⟷◑♿▲⟵(40,50,550)P

Abercych

Nag's Head
SA37 0HJ (on B4332 between Cenarth and Eglwyswrw)
☼ 11-3 (not Mon), 6-11; 12-10.30 Sun ☎ (01239) 841200
Beer range varies Ⓗ
Well restored old smithy boasting a beamed bar and riverside garden. The bar area is furnished with collections of old medical instruments, railway memorabilia, beer bottles and timepieces showing the time in various parts of the world. The pub's own brewery, unused since 2001, is due to start brewing once more. Abercych is a hamlet in the beautiful Cych valley, which features in the Welsh tales of the Mabinogion. ⚏⟱❀◑♿P⟵

Abergwili

Black Ox
High Street, SA31 2JB

✪ 12-midnight ☎ (01267) 231257
Marston's Pedigree; Ringwood Fortyniner; guest beers Ⓗ
Friendly village local a couple of miles from the county town of Carmarthen. It has an open-plan bar, a separate dining room serving good-value food, and a small covered beer garden to the rear. Live music plays on alternate Saturdays and occasional quiz and bingo evenings are hosted. The Carmarthenshire County Museum in the former Bishops Palace is close by.
✪◖⟶&🖵(280,281)♣P⟵

Aberystwyth

Glengower Hotel ✪
3 Victoria Terrace, SY23 2DH (N end of promenade)
✪ 12-11 ☎ (01970) 626191 ⊕ glengower.co.uk
Wye Valley Butty Bach; guest beers Ⓗ
Traditionally a student haunt but welcoming to all, this seafront hotel enjoys excellent coastal views. Outside seating is on the front terrace, which catches the sun but can be bracing in winter. Butty Bach (or a Wye Valley seasonal beer) is joined by one or two guest beers, usually from microbreweries in Wales or the borders. Well-behaved accompanied children are welcome until 9pm. Buses call nearby en route from university campus to town. Meals finish at 6pm Sundays, 8pm weekdays. The pub also closes for a fortnight over the Christmas-New Year period.
✪⟶◖ Å⟷🖵(2)♣⟵

Mill Inn
Mill Street, SY23 1HZ
✪ 4-midnight (1am Fri); 12-1am Sat; 1-midnight Sun
Purple Moose Cwrw Glaslyn Ⓗ
Under the same ownership as the Ship & Castle, this one-bar pub offers a single real ale and Westons Old Rosie cider to its largely student and sports-oriented clientele. The main drinking space, housing both a pool table and a chessboard table, is flanked by a smaller carpeted area adjacent to the bar counter. The pub supports a number of university sports clubs. Å⟷🖵♣👄

Ship & Castle
1 High Street, SY23 1JG
✪ 2-midnight (1am Fri & Sat) ☎ (07773) 778785
⊕ shipandcastle.co.uk
Wye Valley HPA; guest beers Ⓗ
Its 2009 refurbishment wearing well, this street-corner pub in the old town remains the area's real ale mecca. HPA is a constant, flanked by four ever-changing guests, often from Welsh or borders micros; Gwynt y Ddraig supply the cider and perry. The spring and autumn beer festivals are eagerly awaited highlights. While the interior is essentially one room, the pool area is well segregated and there is a more secluded area at the rear. Decor features an old OS map, a mural illustrating the pub's name, and a variety of nautical photographs. Televised rugby is passionately and knowledgeably followed. Å⟷🖵♣👄

Ammanford

Ammanford Hotel
Wernolau House, 31 Pontamman Road, SA18 2HX
✪ 5.30-11 (10 Mon); 3-11 Sat; 12-10 Sun ☎ (01269) 592598
Beer range varies Ⓗ

Originally a colliery manager's house, this pleasant hotel stands on the outskirts of the town, set in five acres of landscaped grounds and woodland. It is renowned not only for the choice and quality of its beer but also for the warm welcome. Log fires burn in winter and there is a large function room catering for weddings and private events.
⟜Q✪⟜◖⟶Å🖵(124,125)P

Bancyfelin

Fox & Hounds
SA33 5ND (just off A40)
✪ 11.30-2.30, 5.30-9 (closed Mon winter); 12-midnight Fri-Sun ☎ (01267) 211341 ⊕ foxandhounds-bancyfelin.co.uk
Beer range varies Ⓗ
Situated in the heart of the village, this is a pub with a real Welsh welcome. Lunches and evening meals are served in the lounge/dining area and there is a separate locals' bar with a pool table, jukebox and games machines for those who prefer a more traditional bar atmosphere. The pub is located near the West Wales showground with a good bus service. Two guest beers in winter and up to four in summer are usually offered from a mix of small and larger breweries.
Q⟊✪◖⟜&🖵(222)♣P

Blaenwaun

Lamb Inn
SA34 0JD SN236271
✪ 4.30-midnight (2am Fri & Sat) ☎ (01994) 448899
Beer range varies Ⓗ
The Lamb is set in an idyllic area and has an original old local ambience with a relaxing atmosphere and welcoming and friendly staff. It offers a range of three to four real ales alongside one or two ciders. A small, quaint pub, darts and pool are played here. There is plenty of parking available and a camp site half a mile away.
⟜✪◖Å👄⟵

Boncath

Boncath Inn
SA37 0JN (on B4332 between Cenarth and Eglwyswrw)
✪ 11-11; 12-8.30 Sun ☎ (01239) 841241
Worthington Bitter; guest beers Ⓗ
This pub dates back to the 18th century and is the centre of life in this attractive village, which developed as a result of the opening of the now long-closed Whitland-Cardigan railway. The interior is divided into several seating areas creating an intimate atmosphere, and the walls display items of local historic interest. The home-cooked meals are recommended. A beer festival is held each August bank holiday weekend.
⟜✪◖⟶&Å🖵(430)♣P⟵

Broad Haven

Galleon
35A Enfield Road, SA62 3JW (on seafront)
✪ 10-midnight (1am Fri & Sat) ☎ (01437) 781152
Brains Bitter, SA, The Rev James; guest beer Ⓗ
The Galleon's hospitable and welcoming landlady helps to bring a cosy atmosphere to this friendly pub with splendid views over St Brides Bay. Converted from a tea room in the 1980s, the pub has now become a widely appreciated feature of the Havens community. With a delightful sandy

beach, Broad Haven remains popular as a holiday resort for day trips and longer stays.
ᐱQ🕭🍽️➔❖◑ᵭ▲🗐(311)♣🐾⚊🗓️

Caio

Brunant Arms

SA19 8RD (off A482 near Pumsaint)
🌣 11-11 (1am Fri & Sat) ☎ (01558) 650483
Beer range varies Ⓗ
Family-run pub in the centre of the village near the Dolaucothi Gold Mines. Good food is served until 9pm every day. There are plenty of outdoor pursuits nearby including pony trekking, and a horse tethering rail is provided at the pub. A legendary Welsh wizard is buried in the church opposite. One real ale is offered in winter, two in summer. ᐱ❀🍽️◑ ▲♣⚊

Cardigan

Grosvenor

Bridge Street, SA43 1HY
🌣 11 (12 Sun)-11 ☎ (01239) 613792
Greene King Abbot; Worthington Bitter; guest beer Ⓗ
Situated on the edge of the town centre next to Cardigan Castle and the River Teifi, this large pub offers a good choice of ales, including a selection of bottled beers. The large open-plan bar/lounge provides various areas to relax, eat and drink, and there is an extra room upstairs for dining or functions. Good-value food is served lunchtimes and evenings every day. ❀◑ᵭ🗐⚊

Carew

Carew Inn

SA70 8SL (off A477 before Pembroke Dock)
🌣 11-11 (11.30 Sun) ☎ (01646) 651267 🌐 carewinn.co.uk
Brains The Rev James; Evan Evans Cwrw Ⓗ
Situated close to Carew's historic Celtic Cross, castle and tidal mill, this former estate pub of the Trollope-Bellew family makes an ideal stop-off with its village location and many local attractions. A pine-boarded bar features photographs of the local area from the past. Outside there is a marquee and a large grassed garden with a children's play area. ᐱ❀◑ ▲🗐(361)P⚊

Carmarthen

Friends Arms

Old St Clears Road, Johnstown, SA31 3HH
🌣 12-11 (midnight Fri); 11-midnight Sat; 11-11 Sun
☎ (01267) 234073
Evan Evans Cwrw; guest beers Ⓗ
Excellent local hostelry half a mile from Carmarthen town centre, with a cosy and friendly atmosphere and a warm welcome, enhanced by two open fires. Popular with sports fans, it has Sky Sports and ESPN, plus pool and darts. A quiz and bingo are held on alternate Wednesdays. Three real ales are usually offered, with a 10 per cent discount for CAMRA members. Local CAMRA Pub of the Year 2011, with its own microbrewery producing a selection of ales. ᐱQ❀🗐(222,322)⚊

Hen Dderwen ✅

47-48 King Street, SA31 1BH
🌣 9-midnight (11 Sun) ☎ (01267) 242050
Greene King Abbot; Ruddles Best Bitter; guest beers Ⓗ

This Wetherspoon pub opened in 2000 and is named after the Carmarthen legend of Merlin and the Old Oak – the story is told in pictures and plaques on the walls. The interior is divided into two distinct spaces – the principal drinking area is at the front while the area to the rear tends to be mainly used by diners. A good selection of real ales is offered. Food is served all day including the chain's standard meal deals. ◑➔🗐🐾⚊

Queen's Hotel

Queen Street, SA31 1JR
🌣 11-11 ☎ (01267) 231800
Beer range varies Ⓗ
Town-centre pub near Carmarthenshire county hall with a bar, lounge and small function room. The public bar is used by locals and has TV for sporting events. Local beers are usually on sale. The patio nestles beneath the castle walls and is a suntrap during the summer months. Upstairs function rooms are available, and the local CAMRA branch meets here. ❀➔🗐⚊

Stag & Pheasant

34 Spilman Street, SA31 1LQ
🌣 12-midnight (11 Sun) ☎ (01267) 232040
Ringwood Fortyniner Ⓗ
A busy and friendly locals' pub close to the centre of town, it also attracts a strong tourist trade. Two large screens show Sky TV, making it a popular venue for viewing live sport. The pub boasts an excellent beer garden with outdoor heaters at the rear. Historically it was a stable block serving the hotel opposite. ❀ᵭ➔🗐♣⚊

Cellan

Fishers Arms

SA48 8HU (on B4343)
🌣 4.30 (12 Sat & Sun)-11 ☎ (01570) 422895
Beer range varies Ⓗ
Situated close to the River Teifi, one of Wales' premier trout and salmon rivers, the pub dates from 1580 and was first licensed in 1891. The main bar has a logburner and flagstone floor. The guest beer changes weekly and is usually from a Welsh microbrewery. Meals are available 6.30-8.45pm on Thursday, Friday and Saturday. Live music plays every Sunday afternoon. The pub is served by buses from Lampeter and Aberystwyth until early evening (not Sun). ᐱQ❀◑ᵭ▲🗐(585)♣P

Cenarth

Three Horse Shoes

SA38 9JL
🌣 11 (12 winter)-11 ☎ (01239) 710119
Evan Evans Best Bitter Ⓗ
A gem of an inn in a popular tourist village in west Wales. The interior has been modified in recent years but retains an abundance of original features including an inglenook fireplace that is big enough to sit in and huge, exposed beams. The pub can be touristy in high season but retains a local atmosphere. Good food is available lunchtimes and evenings. ᐱ❀◑ ▲🗐(460)P⚊

Clarbeston Road

Cross Inn ✅

SA63 4UL (N of railway station) SN019211
🌣 12-midnight (1am Fri & Sat) ☎ (01437) 731506

Courage Directors; Greene King Abbot; guest beer Ⓗ
Multi-roomed village inn, well worth seeking out, with stone and wood floors and original oak beams in abundance. The large bar area housing pool, TV for sport and jukebox is complemented by two small snugs and a dining room where reasonably priced home-cooked food from a largely grill-based menu is served Thursday to Saturday evenings and Sunday lunchtime. Outside there are more spacious drinking areas. A beer festival is held in summer.
ꔫ❀◗ᕼ➔ᕱ(313)♣P'⌐

Cosheston

Brewery Inn
SA72 4UD
❀ closed Mon; 12-3, 6-11; 12-4, 7-11 Sun ☎ (01646) 686678
Courage Best Bitter; guest beers Ⓗ
Set between Cosheston Pill and the Carew Estuary just north east of Pembroke, this light and airy stone-built inn boasts a traditional slate floor and bar, roof beams and comfortable seating with old tables. Paintings and drawings by local artists adorn the walls. The outdoor smoking area is heated in winter. Despite the name, there has been no brewery here since 1889. Q➥❀◗ᕼ&P'⌐

Cross Inn (Llanon)

Rhos yr Hafod Inn
SY23 5NB (at B4337/B4577 crossroads)
❀ closed Mon; 5-11; 12-3 Sun ☎ (01974) 272644
⊕ rhos-yr-hafod-inn.co.uk
Young's Bitter; guest beer Ⓗ
Quiet, friendly pub in a small village offering a regularly changing guest beer, often from a Welsh brewery, alongside Young's Bitter. Cosy drinking areas cluster around a small central bar; the back room has old photographs of local scenes. The roadside drinking area at the front captures the evening sun and there is a large, attractive garden at the rear. Easy to find at a prominent country crossroads, this pub is a haven for local real ale fans and visitors alike. Ample parking, dogs welcome.
ꔫQ➥❀ᕼᕱÅ♣P'⌐

Cross Inn (New Quay)

Penrhiwgaled Arms
SA44 6LN (2 miles S of New Quay on A486)
❀ 12-late ☎ (01545) 560238
⊕ penrhiwgaled.moonfruit.co.uk
Beer range varies Ⓗ
Close to the popular coastal resort of New Quay, this village pub has a surprisingly urban and often bustling atmosphere, its bare-boards main bar flanked at opposite ends by a pool area and dining room. Just one real ale is served from November to March, two or three at other times – frequently from larger microbreweries, though regional brewers sometimes feature. Hearty portions of food are served from an extensive menu all day until 9pm. The pub has its own shooting club. There is a TV, mainly for sport, but no jukebox.
ꔫ❀◗ Åᕱ(50,550)♣P'⌐

Cwmdu

Tafarn Cwmdu
SA19 7DY (off B4302 at Halfway)
❀ 7-11; closed Sun-Tue ☎ (01558) 685088 ⊕ cwmdu.com
Beer range varies Ⓖ

Owned by the National Trust and run by the local community, this is one of CAMRA's Real Heritage Pubs of Wales. The pub is the centre of activities for the village alongside the local shop and post office, also run by the community. A folk night features on the first Friday of the month. The pub will open at the request of visitors for a special occasion and can also be hired for private parties. There is a sitting room upstairs with free access to a computer. ꔫQ❀➔P

Drefach Felindre

Tafarn John Y Gwas
SA44 5XG (over stone bridge, near school and church)
SN354383
❀ 5-11, 4-midnight Fri; 12-midnight Sat & Sun
☎ (01559) 370469
Beer range varies Ⓗ
Early 19th-century village tavern offering a warm welcome to locals and tourists alike. There is an emphasis on small breweries and local produce at the bar. A wide variety of bottled beers and ciders is always available to complement the guest ales. There are plenty of local walks and places of interest to help you work up a thirst before stopping off for a drink. ꔫ❀ᕼᕱ(460)♣●P'⌐

Fishguard

Pendre Inn
High Street, SA65 9AT (on A487 300yds SW of market square)
❀ 11 (4 Mon)-midnight; 12-11.30 Sun ☎ (01348) 874128
Worthington Bitter; guest beers Ⓗ
Friendly, traditional pub on the main road south out of town with a good local following and a growing reputation for its beer. Two guest beers change regularly and may come from anywhere in the UK – sometimes from the Gwaun Valley Brewery, a few miles away up the valley. Pool and darts are played in the big back bar. ꔫ❀ᕼᕱ(412,413)P'⌐

Goginan

Druid Inn
High Street, SY23 3NT (on A44 6 miles E of Aberystwyth)
❀ 12-midnight (1am Fri & Sat) ☎ (01970) 880650
Wye Valley Bitter, Butty Bach; guest beer Ⓗ
Thriving community local with an L-shaped main bar flanked by a side dining room and separate pool room. It continues to serve friendly regulars and many visitors with quality ales and excellent home-cooked food (no meals Tue lunch). The guest beer, available at most busy times, is typically from a micro in Wales or the Marches, often a Wye Valley monthly special. A second guest is occasionally also on offer. Real cider sometimes appears in summer. Live bands play at least monthly. ➥❀ᕼᕱ(525, X47)♣P'⌐

Haverfordwest

Bristol Trader ✅
Quay Street, SA61 1BE
❀ 11-11 (1am Sat); 12-10.30 Sun ☎ (01437) 762122
Worthington Bitter; guest beers Ⓗ
Dating back to Haverfordwest's days as a port, this pub retains some character despite modernisation. A quiet venue in the daytime, popular for dining, food is served in a large dining area or at outside

tables overlooking the river. It gets lively in the evening. In the late '50s this was the first pub in town to have carpet on the floor. Two guest ales are served – beers can be dispensed without tight sparkler on request. ◑&≉⊞P

Pembroke Yeoman
11 Hill Street, SA61 1QQ
✪ 11-11 ☎ (01437) 762500
Draught Bass; Flowers IPA; guest beers Ⓗ
A little off the beaten track, conversation rules at this local pub, though there is a well-stocked jukebox should it flag. Two guest ales come from small breweries and change often. Food is served in generous portions. Known as the Upper Three Crowns until the 1960s, the pub's name was changed to reflect the presence nearby of the local yeomanry headquarters. ⋒Q◑⊟♣

William Owen ✔
Quay Street, SA61 1BG
✪ 9-midnight (1am Fri & Sat) ☎ (01437) 771900
Greene King Abbot; Ruddles Best Bitter; guest beers Ⓗ
Pembrokeshire's first and so far only Wetherspoon pub occupies a handsome 19th-century building, formerly a shop, hotel and restaurant, now with a spacious extension to the rear. Beer from one of the county's two breweries is often available. The pub offers the chain's customary menus, promotional deals and policies (with 7am opening for hot drinks and breakfast). ❀◑&≉⊟'–

Herbrandston

Taberna Inn ♟
SA73 3TD (3 miles W of Milford Haven)
✪ 12-11 ☎ (01646) 693498
Hop Back Summer Lightning; guest beers Ⓗ
Designed and built in 1963 by a local carpenter and builder with an eye to the area's then rapidly developing oil and petrochemical industry, this pub has a pleasant atmosphere and welcoming locals. Two guest beers are served alongside Westons and Moles Black Rat cider, and the pub issues a list of all the guest beers sold throughout the year. Local CAMRA Pub of the Year 2012.
⋒Q❀≉◑⊟&♥P'–

Lampeter

King's Head
14 Bridge Street, SA48 7HG
✪ 5-12.30am (1.30am Fri-Sun) ☎ (01570) 421498
Marston's Old Empire; Ringwood Old Thumper; guest beer Ⓗ
Town-centre pub with two bars and a large function room, popular with a good mix of customers – locals, students and tourists – in this university town. It can get lively. Good food is served, with hot dogs offered late into the evening. The pub is tied to Marston's and the guest ale, usually from the Marston's group, changes frequently. Open mic night is Tuesday, and there is a large-screen TV. ⋒❀◑⊟Å⊟(40)♣P'–

Little Haven

Castle
1 Grove Place, SA62 3UG (opp beach)
✪ 10-11 (1am Fri) ☎ (01437) 781445

Banks's Mansfield Cask Ale; Jennings Cocker Hoop; Marston's Pedigree; guest beer Ⓗ
The main bar of this tastefully modernised pub is split into separate areas by pillars and low dividers. A separate games area has darts and pool. Steeped in local history, the Castle opened in 1871 and is reputedly haunted – a phenomenon attributed by some to its use in former times as a place to lay out the bodies of drowned sailors, washed ashore on the beach, to await burial. ⋒❀◑⊟&Å'–

Saint Bride's Inn
St Brides Road, SA62 3UN
✪ 10.30-midnight (11-3 winter) ☎ (01437) 781266
⊕ saintbridesinn.co.uk
Banks's Bitter; Marston's Pedigree; guest beer Ⓗ
Formerly known as the New Inn, the pub acquired its present name, taken from the bay in which the village is set, in 1904, and is noted for the ancient well in the cellar. The attractive interior includes a separate dining area, and there are heaters on the patio in the pretty suntrap garden for outdoor drinking. Live music is performed occasionally. ⋒Q❀≉◑'–

Llanbadarn Fawr

Black Lion ✔
SY23 3RA
✪ 12-midnight (11.30 Sun) ☎ (01970) 623448
Banks's Bitter; guest beers Ⓗ
Set in the village centre, a mile from the university town of Aberystwyth, this modernised pub is popular with locals and students alike. The spacious main bar has seating at one end, darts and pool at the other, while the rear function room can also be used to enjoy home-cooked, locally sourced food (lunches Tue-Sun, evening meals Thu-Sat). The large rear beer garden, next to the village's ancient church, has a delightful air of rural seclusion. Two guest beers are from the Marston's list – customers are consulted on the selection. ❀◑Å⊟(1,2)♣P'–

Llandeilo

White Horse
Rhosmaen Street, SA19 6EN
✪ 11-11; 12-10.30 Sun ☎ (01558) 822424
Evan Evans Cwrw, seasonal beers; guest beers Ⓗ
Grade II-listed coaching inn dating from the 16th century. The tap for the local Evan Evans Brewery, this multi-roomed pub is popular with all ages. There is a small outdoor drinking area to the front and a large council car park to the rear with access to the pub down a short flight of steps. The covered area for smokers has its own TV showing sport. ❀≉⊟(103,X13)♣'–

Llandovery

King's Head
1 Market Square, SA20 0AB
✪ 10am-11 ☎ (01550) 720393
⊕ kingsheadcoachinginn.co.uk
Evan Evans Cwrw; guest beer Ⓗ
Former coaching inn dating from the 1700s in a historic town on the edge of the Brecon Beacons. Newly refurbished yet still traditional, it is a popular base for many organisations including the Rotary Club and cattle breeders. Good food ranges from bar meals to à la carte. Guest beers usually include local Welsh ales. Across the courtyard is the

Red Lion, a CAMRA Real Heritage Pub whose limited opening hours depend on whether the local rugby team is playing. Q✸⏰◑⟍🛆⇌🖵(280,281)P

Llandybie

Ivy Bush

Church Road, SA18 3HZ (100yds from church)
✪ 12-midnight (11 Mon); 11-midnight Sat & Sun
☎ (01269) 850272
Taylor Landlord; guest beer Ⓗ
The oldest pub in the village, this friendly local dates back nearly 300 years. The single-bar room has two comfortable seating areas. Pub games and quizzes are run weekly and a large-screen TV shows sport. The guest beer changes regularly. The railway station nearby is on the Heart of Wales line.
✸⇌🖵(103,X13)♣♠P¹⌐

Llandyfan

Square & Compass

SA18 2UD (between Ammanford and Trapp)
✪ 12 (1 Sat)-11 summer; 5-11 winter; 12-6 Sun
☎ (01269) 850402
Beer range varies Ⓗ
Originally the village blacksmith's, this 18th-century building was converted into a pub in the 1960s. Nestling on the western edge of the Brecon Beacons National Park, it offers magnificent local views and plenty of walking opportunities. A traditional family pub, it has a wonderful rustic charm and a warm, friendly welcome. Usually two, occasionally three, guest beers are kept, at least one from a local brewery. Opening hours vary in winter – ring first to check. Q◑⟍🛆P¹⌐

Llanelli

Harry Watkins

2 Millfield Road, SA14 8HY (on A476)
✪ closed Mon; 12-11 ☎ (01554) 776644
Banks's Bitter; Ringwood Fortyniner Ⓗ
Renamed after a local rugby hero of yesteryear who features on the pub walls, the pub was originally called the Bear. The open-plan, split-level, family-friendly hostelry has defined dining spaces and a function room. There are covered and open drinking areas outside. There is no car park but there is usually ample room on the road. National cycle and walking paths to the Swiss Valley and beyond are nearby.
🕏✸◑🖵(128,196)¹⌐

York Palace ✓

51 Stepney Street, SA15 3YA (opp Town Hall Square Gardens)
✪ 9am-11 (midnight Thu; 1am Fri & Sat) ☎ (01554) 758609
Greene King Abbot; Ruddles Best Bitter; guest beers Ⓗ
This former cinema in the town centre is a typical Wetherspoon conversion. The walls are adorned with photographs of local industrial history including Llanelli's famous tin plate industry. Guest beers are discounted on Wednesday and Sunday (CAMRA members receive a discount at all times). There is easy access to the bus station and the train station is a 10-minute walk. ◑⟍⇌🖵♠¹⌐

Llanfallteg

Plash ♟

SA34 0HN (off A40 at Llanddewi Velfrey)
✪ 5-11; 12-midnight Wed-Sun ☎ (01437) 563472
Greene King IPA; Wye Valley Butty Bach; guest beer Ⓗ
Terrace-style cottage pub with a garden. An inn for more than 180 years, it has had four different names in that time. The Plash is the centre of village life, with welcoming locals. The guest beer is usually from a small, independent brewery. Home-made pizzas are a speciality, and a small selection of bar snacks is also available. The disabled entrance is to the rear. A small cottage is available to let. Local CAMRA Pub of the Year 2012.
🏠Q✸✸◑⟍♣P

Llangadog

Red Lion

Church Street, SA19 9AA
✪ 12-midnight ☎ (01550) 777357
⊕ redlioncoachinginn.co.uk
Evan Evans Cwrw; guest beers Ⓗ
Refurbishment of this Grade II-listed 16th-century coaching inn has taken it back to its origins. It was reputed to be a safe house for Royalist soldiers during the Civil War. Family-friendly, it is full of character and atmosphere. Its excellent, fresh, locally sourced food attracts locals and tourists alike. Guest beers include Welsh ales as well as those from across the border. Car parking is through the arch. 🏠✸✸◑⟍🛆⇌🖵(280,281)P

Llangoedmor

Penllwyndu

SA43 2LY (on B4570, 4 miles E of Cardigan) SN241458
✪ 12-11 (midnight Sun) ☎ (01239) 682533
Brains Buckleys Best Bitter; guest beers Ⓗ
Old-fashioned ale house standing at an isolated crossroads where Cardigan's evil-doers were once hanged – the pub sign is worthy of close inspection. The cheerful and welcoming public bar retains its quaintness with a slate floor and inglenook with wood-burning stove. Good home-cooked food including traditional favourites is available all day in the bar and separate restaurant. Free live music plays on the third Thursday evening of the month. 🏠✸◑♣P¹⌐

Llangrannog

Pentre Arms

SA44 6SP (at seaward end of B4321/B4334)
✪ 12-midnight ☎ (01239) 654345 ⊕ pentrearms.co.uk
Gale's Seafarers Ale; St Austell Tribute; guest beer Ⓗ
Right on the shore in a former seafaring village, this welcoming pub enjoys stunning sea views. The main bar is complemented by a games room offering darts and pool. A guest beer, usually from a Welsh brewer, is available at busy times. Live music plays on alternate Monday evenings, and quiz nights and Welsh language classes are offered. The Cardi Bach coastal tourist bus runs in summer, when the village's narrow lanes can get busy. The village firework display draws crowds in November. ✸◑🛆♣

Llansaint

King's Arms
13 Maes yr Eglwys, SA17 5JE
✪ 12-2.30 (not Mon-Fri), 6-11; closed Tue; 12-2.30,
6.30-10.30 Sun ☎ (01267) 267487
Beer range varies ⒣
A former local CAMRA Pub of the Year, this friendly
village local has been a pub for more than 200
years. Situated near an 11th-century church, it is
reputedly built from stone recovered from the lost
village of St Ishmaels. Music and poetry nights are
held on the third Friday of the month. Two guest
beers from smaller breweries are usually offered.
Good-value home-cooked food is served.
Carmarthen Bay Holiday Park is a few miles away.
⋈Q✿✿⇘◖)▲⊟(198)♣P

Llanstephan

Castle Inn ⌊
The Square, SA33 5JG
✪ 11.30am-11 (midnight Fri & Sat); 12-10.30 Sun
☎ (01267) 241225
Felinfoel Cambrian Bitter; guest beer ⒣
Guest beers are usually from local breweries
including Evan Evans at this welcoming pub in the
centre of a popular seaside village. The south-
facing patio is favoured by visitors and villages
alike. Inside, there is a separate area for TV and a
space away from the bar for families. The pub hosts
the local cricket and football clubs and many
village functions. The menu offers wholesome pub
grub with some unusual twists – curries are a
speciality with takeaways available. ✿◖⊟(227)

Mynydd y Garreg

Prince of Wales
SA17 4RP
✪ 5-11; closed Sun ☎ (01554) 890522
Bullmastiff Welsh Black, Son of a Bitch; guest beers ⒣
Well worth seeking out for both its beer range and
its ambience, this little gem of a pub was local
CAMRA Pub of the Year in 2010. As well as the two
regular Bullmastiff beers there are up to four
rotating guest ales, usually from smaller breweries.
A real cider is also often available in the summer.
The cosy single-room bar is packed with a treasure
trove of miscellaneous bric-a-brac. Q✿●P

Narberth

Angel Inn
43 High Street, SA67 7AS
✪ 11-3, 5.30-11; 7-10.30 Sun ☎ (01834) 860215
Brains The Rev James; guest beers ⒣
Long-established but modernised and extended
former coaching inn in the town centre with a
small public bar and larger lounge/dining area. It
offers two guest beers and popular food. With a
warm and friendly welcome, it can be busy at
times. Outside is a good-sized beer garden for the
summer months. Note that Narberth Railway
Station is a mile from the town.
Q◖)⇘▲⊟(322,381,430)'–

New Quay

Queens
2 Church Street, SA45 9NZ
✪ 6-11; closed Sun ☎ (01545) 560650

Beer range varies ⒢
Self-described as 'the quirky pub', the Queens
offers a distinctive pub-going experience. A side
room serves as a dining area and secondhand
bookshop, and the books spill out into the main bar
and back room. Beers are stillaged on the bar
counter and come from brewers such as Evan
Evans, Golden Valley and Heart of Wales – one or
two in winter, three or four in summer. Cider is
from Gethin's of Pembrokeshire. Events include
snail racing and an October beer festival; games
include Jenga and shove-ha'penny. There is a patio
for alfresco drinking. ⋈✿●▲⊟(50,550)♣P'–

Newcastle Emlyn

Ivy Bush ✪
Emlyn Square, SA38 9BG
✪ 10-11; 12-6 Sun ☎ (01239) 710542
Draught Bass; guest beer ⒣
Very much a local pub with a traditional separate
bar area and plenty of small, intimate nooks.
Located at the top end of the market town of
Newcastle Emlyn, it has lots of local parking,
shopping and public transport links. Pool and darts
are available in an area to the rear of the pub. No
food is served but there is a chip shop/café next
door. ⋈⊟&⊟(460)♣

Newport

Castle Hotel
Bridge Street, SA42 0TB
✪ 11-11; 12-10.30 Sun ☎ (01239) 820742
Greene King Old Speckled Hen; Theakston Best Bitter,
XB; guest beer ⒣
Friendly, popular local in a characterful small town
halfway between Cardigan and Fishguard, with an
attractive bar featuring some impressive wood
panelling. Food is served at lunchtimes and in the
evening in the extensive dining area. An off-street
car park is situated behind the hotel. A wealth of
prehistoric remains adds interest to the many local
walks. ⋈⏴✿✿⇘◖)▲⊟(412)P'–

Golden Lion
East Street, SA42 0SY (on A487)
✪ 12-midnight (11 Sun) ☎ (01239) 820321
Brains The Rev James, Draught Bass; guest beers ⒣
Another of the town's sociable locals, this one is
reputed to have its own resident ghost. A number
of internal walls have been removed to form a
spacious open-plan bar area, with distinct sections
helping to retain a cosy atmosphere. Car parking
space is available on the opposite side of the road.
⋈Q◖)▲⊟(412)P'–

Pembroke

Royal Oak
138-140 Main Street, SA71 4HN
✪ 2 (12 Sat & Sun)-midnight ☎ (01646) 682537
Hancock's HB; guest beers ⒣
Situated at the east end of the town, this well-
established pub with coach arch and stable yard –
now used as beer garden – offers a warm and
friendly welcome from an enthusiastic licensee.
The traditional interior features exposed oak beams
in the bar. Pub games include shove-ha'penny.
Two guest beers are usually offered, one is either
Sharp's Doom Bar or Brains Rev James.
⋈⊟&≠⊟(349,356)♣'–

Pembroke Dock

First & Last
London Road, Waterloo, SA72 6TX (on A477)
✪ 10-1am (1.30am Thu-Sat) ☎ (01646) 682687
Brains The Rev James; Worthington Bitter; guest
beer Ⓗ
Small, friendly, single-bar local in the same family
for the last 50 years. The walls display an eclectic
mix of photos and prints. Food is standard pub fare.
Formerly the Commercial, the pub acquired its
current more distinctive name in 1991 to reflect its
edge-of-town location. It is handy for the Cleddau
Bridge giving easy access to Haverfordwest and the
beaches and other attractions of west and north
Pembrokeshire. ✪◗≠⊞(349,356)♣P

Station Inn
Hawkestone Road, SA72 6HN (in station building)
✪ 7-11 Mon; 11-3, 6-midnight (12.30am Fri & Sat); 12-3,
7-10.30 Sun ☎ (01646) 621255
Beer range varies Ⓗ
Housed in the town's railway station where trains
still depart for Carmarthen and Swansea (and, on
summer Saturdays, far-off Paddington), this town-
centre pub is close to both the Irish Ferries terminal
and popular Pembrokeshire Coast Path. Meals are
excellent value (no lunches Mon, evening meals
Wed-Sat only). Three real ales are generally on
sale, with Young's Bitter a frequent visitor and a
new beer coming on every Tuesday. The June beer
festival offers around 20 beers. Live music is
performed on Saturday evenings.
🏠Q✿☆◗🛏�590P≠⊞P'←

Penally

Cross Inn
SA70 7PU
✪ 12-11 (12.30am Fri & Sat); 12-midnight Sun
☎ (01834) 844665
Hancock's HB; guest beers Ⓗ
Situated in a picturesque village with some well-
preserved Georgian and Victorian houses, the pub
has a wood and brick bar leading to the restaurant.
Local pictures and shields of regiments stationed in
a nearby barracks adorn the walls. The sporting
prowess of the locals is evident from the cups and
shields on the trophy shelf. A signed photo and a
set of darts used by Phil 'The Power' Taylor is
framed in an alcove. Food is sometimes available –
ring to check first. ✿A≠⊞(349)'←

Penrhiwllan

Daffodil
SA44 5NG
✪ 11.30-3, 5.30-11 ☎ (01559) 370343 ⊕ daffodilinn.co.uk
Beer range varies Ⓗ
Formerly the Penrhiwllan Inn, the Daffodil is a
family-run pub and restaurant dating from 1750, in
a country village 20 minutes from the popular
coastal resort of New Quay. It has been
modernised in an elegant style to provide
separate, intimate dining areas and cosy drinking
spaces catering for all, and has excellent disabled
facilities. Two handpumps, three in the summer,
dispense beers mostly from nationals, with guest
ales from Welsh breweries. 🏠Q⏳✿◗🛏&P'←

Pontfaen

Dyffryn Arms ★
SA65 9SE (off B4313)
✪ opening hours vary ☎ (01348) 881305
Draught Bass Ⓖ
This much-loved pub, a reminder of how many
country pubs must once have looked, is the hub of
life in a secluded valley whose distinctive cultural
traditions include a long history of farmhouse
brewing. There is no bar counter – beer is still
served by the jug through a sliding serving hatch.
Conversation is the main form of entertainment,
and the pub's relaxed atmosphere is captivating.
The well-regarded Gwaun Valley Brewery is close,
but the regulars are loyal to their Bass. A timeless
gem to be treated with respect. 🏠Q✿&A♣

Porthyrhyd

Mansel Arms
Banc y Mansel, SA32 8BS (on B4310 between
Porthyrhyd and Drefach)
✪ 5-11; 3-midnight Sat; 12-6 Sun ☎ (01267) 275305
Beer range varies Ⓗ
Friendly 18th-century former coaching inn with
wood fires in each room. The original limestone
flags have been broken up and used in the
fireplace, and low beams have been added to
create atmosphere, with numerous jugs hanging
from them in the bar. Pool and darts are played in
a room to the rear, which was originally used for
slaughtering pigs. Beers are varied with the
Young's range always popular as well as local ales.
Food is served Friday and Saturday evenings and
Sunday lunchtime. 🏠Q◗A⊞(129)♣♠

Rhandirmwyn

Royal Oak
SA20 0NY
✪ 12-2, 6-11 (7-10.30 Sun) ☎ (01550) 760201
⊕ theroyaloakinn.co.uk
Beer range varies Ⓗ
Remote, stone-flagged inn with excellent views of
the Tywi Valley and close to an RSPB bird
sanctuary. Originally built as a hunting lodge for
the local landowner, it is now a focal point for
community activities and popular with fans of
outdoor pursuits. Two or three guest beers are
offered, a range of interesting bottled beers and
whiskies is stocked, and the good wholesome food
is recommended. There are panoramic views from
the beer garden at the side of the pub. Four-time
local CAMRA Pub of the Year. 🏠Q✿☆◗A♣P

Rhos

Lamb of Rhos
SA44 5EE (on A484)
✪ 4-midnight Mon; 12 (4 Tue-Thu winter)-close
☎ (01559) 370055 ⊕ thelambofrhos.co.uk
St Austell Tribute; guest beer Ⓗ
Taken over in 2010 and family-run, this large
country establishment with a quirky interior has
seen a revival in its fortunes. The pub is rapidly
becoming a hub for the community, its function
room used for a range of daytime events. The
owners believe in a correlation between quality
beer and good food, which equates to a great all-
round pub. Two ales are offered during busier
periods, one in winter. 🏠✿🛏◗&⊞(460)♣P

WALES

Roch

Victoria Inn
SA62 6AW (on A487)
✪ 12-2.30am (10.30 Sun) ☎ (01437) 710426
Beer range varies ⊞
A little gem with views across St Brides Bay, this locals' pub offers a warm welcome. The inn was established in 1851 although parts are older, and it has retained much of its olde-worlde charm, with beamed ceilings and low doorways. The menu features home-made Welsh dishes made with local produce where possible. Curry and a pint night is Friday. For those in a hurry there is a beer carry-out service. Live music plays occasionally.
🏰Q🏵🚳🍴⑩🍺🛏🚃(411)♣P

Solva

Harbour Inn ✪
SA62 6UU (on A487 next to harbour)
✪ 11-11 ☎ (01437) 720013
Brains Dark, SA; guest beers ⊞
Delightful seaside inn next to the tiny harbour, now the haunt of leisure sailors but once a port of embarkation for North America. It continues to showcase Brains beers including seasonals and sometimes guests from other breweries. A community pub with a traditional atmosphere, it serves as a base for many village activities and is popular with locals who come to enjoy a quiet, relaxing pint. The nearby camping facilities cater for both caravans and tents.
🏰Q🏵🚳⑩🛏🚃(411)P🚆

Talybont

White Lion (Llew Gwyn) ✪
SY24 5ER (7 miles N of Aberystwyth on A487)
✪ 11 (12 Sun)-late ☎ (01970) 832245
Banks's Mild, Bitter; guest beer ⊞
Friendly, family-run community pub facing the village green. The main bar features a slate floor, settles, ceiling hooks once used for hanging meat, and a local history display. There is also a games room, rear lounge and large garden. Home-cooked food is good value – Thursday curry nights are particularly popular. The guest beer usually comes from the Marston's group. Folk sessions are held monthly on a Sunday afternoon.
🏰🏵🚳⑩🍺🚃(X28,X32)♣P🚆

Tenby

Crown Inn
Lower Frog Street, SA70 7HU
✪ 12-11 (11.30 Sun) ☎ (01834) 842796
Brains The Rev James; guest beers ⊞
Close to the town's famous beaches and within the old town wall, the pub is convenient for Tenby's many attractions and is on the coastal footpath. A poker night is held each week and numerous charity events are hosted throughout the year. In 1891 the licensee denied a charge of serving after hours, claiming that the Coast Brigade gunners found in the pub at midnight were only waiting for the tide to go out so that they could walk back to their fort on an offshore island. 🏵🚳Å🚆🚃♣🚆

Hope & Anchor
St Julian Street, SA70 7AS
✪ 11-11; 12-10.30 Sun ☎ (01834) 842131
Brains The Rev James; guest beer ⊞
Once the haunt of Tenby fishermen – 'we were drunk for a week' read one Victorian account following a bumper haul of bream – this extended pub, handy for the harbour and North Beach, now caters for locals and tourists alike. Bar snacks and full meals are available. The medieval town walls, one of this historic town's chief glories, can be seen nearby. 🏰🏵⑩Å🚆🚃♣🚆

Tregaron

Y Talbot 🍷
The Square, SY25 6JL
✪ 11-11 (1am Fri & Sat) ☎ (01974) 298208 ⊕ ytalbot.com
Felinfoel Double Dragon; guest beers ⊞
Former drovers' inn at the heart of the town oozing character and heritage with its old beams, flagstone floors and inglenook fireplace. The front snug is one of the cosiest in Wales, the perfect place to enjoy well-chosen guest beers from Wales and the borders. Ciders come from Gwynt y Ddraig. Excellent, good-value food – pie of the day is recommended – is served lunchtimes and evenings. The back bar has a TV, elsewhere conversation rules. This much-improved pub is well worth seeking out. Dogs and muddy-booted walkers are welcome. Local CAMRA Pub of the Year 2012. 🏰Q🏵🚳⑩🍺🛏Å🚃(585,588)♣🖤P🚆

The beauty of hops

There are many varieties of hops: global brewers use 'high alpha' varieties (high in alpha acids) purely for bitterness. Craft brewers prefer to use varieties that deliver aroma and flavour as well as bitterness. The two most widely used English hops are Fuggles and Goldings, often blended together in the same beer, the Fuggle primarily for bitterness but with earthy and smoky notes, the Golding for its superb resiny, spicy and peppery character. Bramling Cross delivers rich fruity (blackcurrant) notes, Challenger has a citrus/lime edge while the workhorse of the hop fraternity, Target, offers citrus and pepper. First Gold is the most successful of the new 'hedgerow' varieties that grow to only half the height of conventional hops and are therefore easier to pick. It offers piny and apricot notes. American varieties used in Britain include Willamette (an offshoot of the Fuggle) and Cascade, both of which give rich citrus/grapefruit aromas and flavours. The Styrian Golding, renamed Bobek, (actually a type of Fuggle) from Slovenia is widely used as an aroma hop in Britain for its luscious floral and citrus character.

101 Beer Days Out

Tim Hampson

101 Beer Days Out is the perfect handbook for the beer tourist wanting to explore beer and brewing culture in their local area and around the UK. From historic city pubs to beer festivals; idyllic country pub walks to rail ale trails; tourist brewery tours to serious brewing courses – Britain has beer and brewing experiences to rival any in the world. *101 Beer Days Out* brings together for the first time the best of these experiences, ordered geographically and with full visitor information, maps and colour photography – the perfect way to celebrate Britain's national drink.

£12.99   ISBN 978-1-85249-288-5   CAMRA members' price £10.99   224 pages

For this and other books on beer and pubs visit the CAMRA bookshop at www.camra.org.uk/books

NORTHERN ISLES

SHETLAND

HIGHLANDS & WESTERN ISLES

ABERDEEN & GRAMPIAN

TAYSIDE

LOCH LOMOND, STIRLING & THE TROSSACHS

FIFE

ARGYLL & THE ISLES

EDINBURGH & LOTHIANS

GREATER GLASGOW & CLYDE VALLEY

AYRSHIRE & ARRAN

BORDERS

DUMFRIES & GALLOWAY

NORTHERN IRELAND

NORTHUMBER-LAND

TYNE & WEAR

CUMBRIA

DURHAM

ISLE OF MAN

NORTH YORKSHIRE

LANCASHIRE

WEST YORKS

EAST YORKS

MERSEYSIDE

GREATER MANCHESTER

SOUTH YORKS

CHESHIRE

DERBYSHIRE

NOTTINGHAM-SHIRE

LINCOLN-SHIRE

NW WALES

NE WALES

SHROPSHIRE

STAFFORD-SHIRE

LEICESTERSHIRE & RUTLAND

NORFOLK

MID WALES

WEST MIDLANDS

WORCESTER-SHIRE

WARWICK-SHIRE

NORTHAMPTON-SHIRE

CAMBRIDGE-SHIRE

SUFFOLK

WEST WALES

HERTFORD-SHIRE

GWENT

GLOUCS & BRISTOL

OXFORD-SHIRE

BUCKINGHAM-SHIRE

BEDFORD-SHIRE

HERTFORD-SHIRE

ESSEX

GLAMORGAN

BERKSHIRE

GREATER LONDON

WILTSHIRE

SURREY

KENT

SOMERSET

HAMPSHIRE

WEST SUSSEX

EAST SUSSEX

CHANNEL ISLANDS

DEVON

DORSET

ISLE OF WIGHT

CORNWALL

Scotland

ABERDEEN & GRAMPIAN

Authority areas covered: Aberdeenshire UA, City of Aberdeen UA, Moray UA

Aberdeen

Aitchies Ale House

10 Trinity Street, AB11 5LY
✪ 8am-10 (11 Fri & Sat); closed Sun ☎ (01224) 581459
Orkney Dark Island; guest beer Ⓗ
This small corner bar is the closest real ale outlet to the city rail/bus stations and the Union Square shopping complex. Renovated in 1994, it retains the flavour of an old-fashioned Scottish pub. Bar food is best described as traditional Scottish pub grub, including roast beef stovies. A good selection of whiskies includes Bell's special edition decanters. The guest beer is frequently Caledonian Deuchars IPA. The friendly service here is second to none. ♿≉🚃♣

Archibald Simpson ⊘

5 Castle Street, AB11 5BQ (corner of Union St & King St)
✪ 8am-midnight (1am Fri & Sat); 9am-11 Sun
☎ (01224) 621365
Greene King Abbot; Ruddles Best Bitter; guest beers Ⓗ
One of many monumental granite buildings in central Aberdeen designed by local architect Archibald Simpson. The former local headquarters of Clydesdale Bank, this Wetherspoon pub retains many original architectural features. The main room is the high-ceilinged central hall, and there are additional seating areas to the side. The long bar features 12 handpumps offering a variety of beers, frequently from Scottish breweries, plus house ales Aberdeen Granite and Archibald

Simpson from Houston and Castlegate from Isle of Skye. Local CAMRA Pub of the Year 2009. Free Wi-Fi is available. ❄️◑♿≉🚃♣

Brentwood Hotel

101 Crown Street, AB11 6HH
✪ 11-2.30 (not Sat), 4.30-midnight; 6-11 Sun
☎ (01224) 595440 ⊕ brentwood-hotel.co.uk
Beer range varies Ⓗ
Mirrored downstairs bar, formerly known as Carriages, in the basement of a modernised hotel, with lots of comfortable couches and seating areas. A winner of numerous local CAMRA awards, it offers 10 changing beers, usually a mix of national brands and Scottish micros typically from Black Sheep, Houston, Highland and Orkney breweries. Lunches are available in the bar, and the adjoining restaurant serves good food in the evening. Railway and bus stations are easily reached by descending the stairs from nearby Crown Terrace to Bridge Street. Free Wi-Fi is available. 🛏️◑≉🚃P↳

Grill 🍽 ★

213 Union Street, AB11 6BA
✪ 10-midnight (1am Fri & Sat); 12.30-midnight Sun
☎ (01224) 573530 ⊕ thegrillaberdeen.co.uk

Caledonian 80; Harviestoun Bitter & Twisted; guest beers Ⓗ
With an exquisite interior redesigned in 1926 and remaining largely unchanged since, this has been identified by CAMRA as one of Britain's Real Heritage Pubs. For men only until 1975, ladies' toilets were not provided until 1998. Situated across from the Music Hall, musicians often visit during concert breaks. The pub has a large selection of whiskies and has won numerous awards from lovers of the malt. Guest ales are frequently from Fyne Ales or Orkney breweries. Bar snacks are served and free Wi-Fi is available. CAMRA Branch Pub of the Year 2012. ⚅⇌🖼

Moorings
2 Trinity Quay, AB11 5AA (opp quayside near Market St)
⚙ 12 (1 Sun)-midnight; 1-3am Fri & Sat ☎ (01224) 587602
Inveralmond Moorings Ale; guest beers Ⓗ
Historic harbourside bar combining pirate and hard rock decors. It changes character from friendly laid-back local to raucous music bar on weekend evenings, when there may be a cover charge. The eclectic jukebox is in regular use by the varied clientele. Sword dancers and a classical quartet have both been spotted. Movies are shown on Sunday afternoons. A wide selection of guest beers comes mainly from Scottish micros, with a discount for CAMRA members. Local CAMRA City Pub of the Year 2010 and 2011. ⇌🖼♣🏵

Old Blackfriars ✅
52 Castle Street, AB11 5BB
⚙ 12-midnight (1am Fri & Sat; 11 Sun) ☎ (01224) 581922
⊕ old-blackfriars.co.uk
Belhaven IPA; Inveralmond Ossian Ale; guest beers Ⓗ
On the Castlegate in the historic centre of the city, this Belhaven pub is on two levels, with bars on both, and offers at least three guest beers, many from Scottish micros plus the obligatory ones from the Greene King range. Unobtrusive background music plays and there is no TV. The pub has a reputation for good pub food, served daily until 9pm. Quiz night is every Tuesday and traditional music plays on Thursday. Occasional themed beer festivals are hosted. Free Wi-Fi is available.
🌓⚅⇌🖼

Prince of Wales ✅
7 St Nicholas Lane, AB10 1HF (opp Marks & Spencer)
⚙ 10-midnight (1am Fri & Sat); 11-midnight Sun
☎ (01224) 640597
Caledonian 80; guest beers Ⓗ
One of the oldest bars in Aberdeen, the Prince of Wales has possibly the longest bar counter in the city, a friendly atmosphere and a large following of regulars. One of CAMRA's Real Heritage Pubs, it offers up to eight ales including a varied selection of Scottish ales, typically from Fyne Ales, Stewart, Houston or Kelburn, plus various English ales, often Pale Rider or Summer Lightning, and the usual Greene King/Belhaven suspects. The house beer, Prince of Wales, is brewed by Inveralmond. Folk music plays on Sunday evening and a quiz is hosted on Monday. Good value food is served daily until 9pm (5pm Sun). Q🌓⇌🖼

St Machar Bar
97 High Street, Old Aberdeen, AB24 3EN
⚙ 12-11 (6 Sun) ☎ (01224) 483079 ⊕ themachar.com
Caledonian Deuchars IPA; guest beers Ⓗ
Located in the photogenic and historic Old Aberdeen conservation area amid the university

buildings and close to Kings College, the pub is frequented by academia and locals alike. Up to three guest beers are normally from Scottish microbreweries, including at least one from Inveralmond. The bar also has a great selection of malt whiskies. A splendid mirror from the long-gone Thomson Marshall Aulton Brewery down the street adorns the wall just inside the front door, and one from the Devanha Brewery is outside the toilets. CAMRA members receive a discount. Open until midnight during university term.
🌓⚅⚅🖼(20)♣🏵

Under the Hammer
11 North Silver Street, AB10 1RJ (off Golden Square)
⚙ 5 (4 Fri)-midnight (1am Thu & Fri); 2-1am Sat; 6-11 Sun
☎ (01224) 640253
Caledonian Deuchars IPA; Inveralmond Ossian Ale; guest beer Ⓗ
Located in a quiet side street near Golden Square just minutes off Union Street, this regular Guide entry is located in a basement next to an auction house – hence the name. Works by local artists displayed on the walls are for sale if they take your fancy. Convenient for the Music Hall and His Majesty's Theatre, the large noticeboard has posters advertising forthcoming events in town. Guest beers tend to contrast in style from the two regulars, with local Burnside beers frequent favourites plus Taylor Landlord. Unobtrusive background music plays. ⇌

Auchleven

Hunter's Moon
3 The Belts, AB52 6QB
⚙ closed Mon & Tue; 5-11; 4-1am Fri (12.30am Sat); 11-11 Sun ☎ (01464) 820380
Beer range varies Ⓗ
A friendly welcome is assured at this recently refurbished village local, with green wood panelling all around. An interesting, seasonal menu of freshly cooked, locally sourced food is available in both the restaurant and spacious bar (Wed-Sun eves plus Sun brunch). Children are permitted until 8pm. Pool and darts are played. Quiz night is the first Thursday of the month, folk night on the fourth Thursday. Ever-changing beers often come from Scottish microbreweries, with ales from the Cellarman's Reserve list selected by the regulars.
🏨🌓⚅♣🏵

Ballater

Alexandra Hotel 🄻
12 Bridge Square, AB35 5QJ (E of village on A93, adjacent to Dee bridge)
⚙ 11-2.30, 5-midnight; 11-midnight Fri-Sun
☎ (01339) 755376 ⊕ alexandrahotelballater.co.uk
Beer range varies Ⓗ
Originally built as a private home in 1800 and becoming the Alexandra Hotel in 1915, this smart and recently refurbished lounge bar is popular with locals for bar suppers and regular drinkers too. Ales come from Cairngorm, Inveralmond and Orkney breweries. The house beer is Chiel's Ale, with 10p per pint donated to a local charity of the same name. Handy for a stop-off on your way to Braemar for the Highland Games or for a visit with the royals at Balmoral. 🏵🛏🌓⚅▲🖼(201,202)♣🏵

Balmoral Bar Ⓛ

1 Netherley Place, AB35 5QE
✪ 11-midnight (1am Thu-Sat); 12.30-midnight Sun
☎ (01339) 755462
Caledonian Deuchars IPA; Inveralmond
Thrappledouser Ⓗ
Smart and recently refurbished public bar, situated on a corner opposite the square, with two large plasma screen TVs. The adjacent pool room also has two screens usually featuring sport. Evening meals are served only in summer. The St Machar Bar in Aberdeen is owned by the same people.
◖❙▲🚃(201,202)♣

Banchory

Douglas Arms Hotel

22 High Street, AB31 5SR
✪ 11-midnight (1am Fri & Sat); 11-11 Sun
☎ (01330) 822547 ⊕ douglasarms.co.uk
Caledonian Deuchars IPA; guest beers Ⓗ
Small hotel offering relatively inexpensive accommodation. It has three bars and rooms with plasma TVs where different sports are screened. The public bar is a classic Scottish long bar with etched windows, vintage mirrors and is identified by CAMRA as one of Britain's Real Heritage Pubs. The lounge is in three parts, divided by former exterior and internal walls and fireplace, and is primarily used for bar suppers. To the rear is a large, south-facing decking area, ideal for fair-weather drinking. There is also a separate function room. The guest beer range usually features one from the local Deeside Brewery. The public bar is usually not open till 3pm.
🏚🕭🍴◖❙🌳❳▲🚃(201,202)♣

Ravenswood Club (Royal British Legion)

25 Ramsay Road, AB31 5TS (parallel to, and north of, the main A93)
✪ 11-11 (midnight Fri & Sat) ☎ (01330) 822347
⊕ banchorylegion.com
Beer range varies Ⓗ
Large British Legion Club with a comfortable lounge adjoining a pool and TV room, and a spacious function room used by local clubs and societies as well as members. Darts and snooker are popular and played most evenings. The two handpumps offer excellent value and the beer choice is constantly changing, with ales consistently the best quality in the village. An elevated terrace has fine views of the Deeside hills. Show a copy of this Guide or your CAMRA membership card for entry.
🕭🍴◖❳▲♣P

Banff

Ship Inn

8 Deveronside, AB45 1HP (at mouth of Deveron, close to harbour)
✪ 12-midnight (1am Fri & Sat) ☎ (01261) 812620
⊕ theshipbanff.co.uk
Fuller's London Pride; guest beer Ⓗ
The interior of this historic nautical-themed inn featured in the film Local Hero. It has a wood-panelled bar and lounge with sea views through the small windows. A blocked carriage arch hints at the earlier history of the building. Banff Marina, Duff House Gallery (National Gallery of Scotland) and Macduff Aquarium are close by, as are several golf courses. The pub has a fine view across the mouth of the Deveron to Macduff. Bar snacks are served all day. Karaoke and live music feature at weekends. Wi-Fi is available. One guest ale is selected by the regulars. 🏚🚲▲🚃(305)♣

Brodie

Old Mill Inn

IV36 2TD (on main A96 between Forres and Nairn)
✪ 11.30-11 ☎ (01309) 641605 ⊕ oldmillinnbrodie.com
Beer range varies Ⓗ
This gem is a spacious, family-friendly pub-restaurant with a cosy fireside area, smart restaurant, function room and a charming conservatory with views of the old watermill and garden. Up to five ales are on handpump, mainly from Scottish micros. Light lunches, cream teas and traditional Scottish high teas are served, plus a full restaurant menu with steak on Monday, fish on Friday and roasts on Sunday. Live Scottish/Irish instrumental music plays on Sunday evening. A beer festival is held in June. Local CAMRA Country Pub of the Year 2012.
🏚Q🕭🍴◖❙🌳▲🚃(10,11,305)P⅃

Catterline

Creel Inn

AB39 2UL (on coast off A92, 5 miles S of Stonehaven)
NO868782
✪ 12-2, 5-midnight (1am Fri & Sat); closed Mon & Tue;
12-midnight Sun ☎ (01569) 750254 ⊕ thecreelinn.co.uk
Beer range varies Ⓗ
Predominantly a restaurant, but the cosy bar area around the fireplace is well frequented by local villagers. The restaurant has been extended into an adjoining row of fishermen's cottages. A walk round the back to enjoy the view from the cliff top will be well rewarded. Three varying cask ales are on offer, with at least two from Scottish microbreweries. The house beer, Creal Ale, is from the Houston Brewery. Crawton Bird Sanctuary and Todhead Lighthouse are close by and Kinneff Old Church lies to the south. 🏚Q🕭◖♣P

Craigellachie

Highlander Inn

10 Victoria Street, AB38 9SR (on A95)
✪ 12-11 (12.30am Fri & Sat) ☎ (01340) 881446
⊕ whiskyinn.com
Cairngorm Trade Winds; guest beers Ⓗ
Picturesque whisky and cask ale bar on Speyside's Whisky Trail, close to the Speyside Way. It offers a fine selection of malt whiskies and good-value tasting sessions, alongside a selection of ales from three handpumps (two in winter). CRAC (Craigellachie Real Ale Club) meets on the first Wednesday of the month, and its members, whose etched glass tankards hang above the bar, help to choose the pub's guest ales with the support of the owners and staff. The area is good for fishing and walking. Free Wi-Fi. Q🕭🍴◖🚃(336)♣P⅃

Cullen

Three Kings

17-21 North Castle Street, AB56 4SA
✪ 12-2, 5-11 (12.30am Thu-Sat) ☎ (01542) 840031
Beer range varies Ⓗ
Situated close to impressive but now defunct railway viaducts, this small, family-run pub was

converted 40 years ago from 150-year-old railway workers' cottages. A low-beamed roof and real fire help to create a cosy atmosphere on colder days. There is a separate restaurant to the rear and a large outdoor drinking area complete with pétanque courts. Three beers are served, mainly from Scottish micros including Deeside, Cairngorm and Orkney. ▲⊛≠◖◗⊒(305)P¹⊷

Dyce

Granite City ✅
Main Terminal, Aberdeen Airport, AB21 7DU
✪ 6am-10; 8am-6 Sat; 8am-8 Sun ☎ (01224) 725711
Greene King Abbot Ⓗ
In the main terminal of Aberdeen Airport, the pub was taken over by Wetherspoon in 2010 and fully refurbished. It is popular with airport staff, travellers and offshore workers. The walls feature informative framed photographs of local personalities including Thomas Blake Glover, 'The Scottish Samurai' – one of the prime movers of Japan's industrialisation in the late 19th century. An extensive outdoor area features The Baby Boar – a sculpture carved from a one-tonne boulder of local Kemnay granite. ⊛◖◗ら⊒(27,727)¹⊷

Elgin

Muckle Cross ✅
34 High Street, IV30 1BU
✪ 11-midnight (1am Fri & Sat); 12.30-11.45 Sun
☎ (01343) 559030
Greene King Abbot; guest beers Ⓗ
Typical small Wetherspoon converted from what was once a bicycle repair shop, then a Halfords branch. The long pleasant room has ample seating, a family area and a long bar. It can get busy, particularly at weekends. Eight handpumps offer a wide range of beers from national and Scottish microbreweries, including one beer from Isle of Skye, as well as a cider. The pub also stocks a wide range of malt whiskies from more than 20 local distilleries. Open from 8am for coffee and breakfast (9am Sun). ◖◗らき⊒⊒⊛

Ellon

Tolbooth
21-23 Station Road, AB41 9AE
✪ 12-11 (midnight Thu; 12.30am Fri & Sat); 12.30-11.30 Sun
☎ (01358) 721308
Greene King Abbot; guest beers Ⓗ
A large pub, popular with all ages, close to the centre of the town and recently refurbished. There are separate seating areas on split levels as well as an airy conservatory. The range of ales depends on availability, but tends to focus on national brands, but not to the exclusion of Scottish micros such as Fyne and Orkney. Several National Trust Scotland properties are nearby. No food is served. ⊛ら⊒(260,267,268)¹⊷

Findhorn

Kimberley Inn
94 Findhorn, IV36 3YG
✪ 12-midnight ☎ (01309) 690492 ⊕ kimberleyinn.com
Beer range varies Ⓗ
Styling itself as Moray's seafood pub, it is situated right on the shore of Findhorn Bay, with superb views from the tables on the patio outside. The bar

is wood panelled with snugs at either end. Two handpumps dispense a wide variety of beers, mainly from Scottish micros. The menu of home-cooked food features local fish and even local ice cream. Findhorn is a breezy village with views over the sands to the Moray Firth, framed by distant hills. ▲Q⊱⊛◖◗ら▲⊒(332)♣P¹⊷

Fraserburgh

Elizabethan Lounge
36 Union Grove, AB43 9PH (jct Union Grove and Dennyduff Rd)
✪ 9.30am (11 Sun)-1am ☎ (01346) 515148
Beer range varies Ⓗ
Set in the middle of a housing estate and near to the local Academy, with a mock-Tudor exterior, the pub has a large bar and lounges in three distinct sections, with TV sport usually featuring in two of them. The Elizabethan has a formidable reputation for its variety of quality ales from throughout the country. Local CAMRA membership has increased as a direct result of the landlord's avid promotion of real ale, and a CAMRA discount applies. The bar also features well-over 150 malts – the largest collection in the area. CAMRA Pub of the Year 2011. ⊱⊟▲⊒(267,268,269)¹⊷

Garlogie

Garlogie Inn
AB32 6RX (on B9119)
✪ 11-2.30, 5-10.30 (11.30 Fri & Sat); 12.30-9 Sun
☎ (01224) 743212 ⊕ garlogieinn.com
Beer range varies Ⓗ
Roadside inn dating from the early 19th century run by the Quinn family for more than 25 years. Numerous extensions have been added to the original building, forming a large restaurant area, and the pub has a reputation for excellent food (booking advised). Drinkers are welcome in the small bar area, with beers from Scottish breweries including Harviestoun Bitter & Twisted and Deuchars IPA, and English ales Black Sheep Bitter and Shepherd Neame Spitfire. A house beer will feature during the summer, replaced by a variety of guests in winter. Drum Castle and Cullerlie Stone Circle are close by. ▲Q⊛◖◗ら⊒(210)P

Inverurie

Black Bull
50 North Street, AB51 4RS
✪ 12-3, 5-midnight; 11-12.30am Sat; 11-11 Sun
☎ (01467) 621242 ⊕ blackbullinn.moonfruit.co.uk
Beer range varies Ⓗ/Ⓖ
Formerly a staging inn, this is now a small family-run hotel and friendly local pub. There is live music each Saturday and a quiz night on Thursday. The pub is home to four darts teams. One Inveralmond beer is served on handpump, and a guest beer, normally from a Scottish microbrewery, is served on gravity. The pub also stages a yearly real ale and cider festival. Free Wi-Fi is available. ▲⊛≠らき⊒(10,307,737)♣P¹⊷

Edwards
2 West High Street, AB51 3SA
✪ 10-midnight (2am Fri & Sat) ☎ (01467) 629788
⊕ edwardsinverurie.co.uk
Beer range varies Ⓗ

Tastefully converted from a town-centre hotel into a bar diner a few years ago, the decor is modern with just a hint of Art Deco. Situated in the heart of a thriving town and close to the railway station, the upstairs function room doubles as a disco at weekends. Three beers are always available, usually two from Scottish breweries and one from further afield. Free Wi-Fi is available.
①❶♿⇄➡(10,307,737)'–

Gordon Highlander ✓
West High Street, AB51 3QQ
✪ 9am-11.30 (1am Fri; 12.30am Sat) ☎ (01467) 626780
Caledonian Deuchars IPA; Greene King Abbot; guest beers Ⓗ

A new Wetherspoon outlet in a splendid Art Deco building that used to be the Victoria Cinema. The name refers to the famous local regiment, and also to a preserved steam engine named after the regiment, which was based at the now defunct Inverurie Locomotive Works nearby. Both historic references are documented in various displays. The books on the shelves are free to read and take home (and donations are welcome). There are at least three guest ales. ▲☎❶♿⇄➡(10,307,737)

Methlick

Ythanview Hotel
Main Street, AB41 7DT
✪ 11-2.30, 5-11 (1am Fri); 11-12.30am Sat; 12-11 Sun
☎ (01651) 806235 ⊕ ythanviewhotel.co.uk
Beer range varies Ⓗ

Traditional inn in the village centre, close to the Laird's Cricket Ground, home to the Methlick Cricket Club. The small public bar at the rear is heavily sports themed. Log fires warm both the lounge and public bar. The pub is renowned for Jay's special curry with whole chillies – a challenge worth taking. Thursday is steak night. Bands play on some Saturdays and quiz nights are also hosted. Beers are mainly from Scottish micros and the Waverley guest list. Haddo House, Tolquhon Castle and Pitmedden Garden are nearby.
▲①🍴❶➡(290,291)♣P'–

Milltown of Rothiemay

Forbes Arms Hotel
AB54 7LT
✪ 12-2.30 (not Mon & Tue), 5-11 ☎ (01466) 711248
⊕ forbesarms.co.uk
Beer range varies Ⓗ

Small family-run hotel in a pleasant country location near the River Deveron. It has public and lounge bars and a separate dining area. Fishing and shooting activities are nearby. The local folk club hosts a live session on the second Thursday of the month. Two beers are usually available, sourced from Scottish micros and from Welsh breweries, including Brains. More than 60 malt whiskies are stocked. Accommodation is in six en-suite rooms.
①🍴❶♿P'–

Monymusk

Grant Arms Hotel
The Square, AB51 7HJ (on village green)
✪ 11-11 (11.30 Fri & Sat) ☎ (01467) 651226
⊕ monymusk.com
Taylor Landlord; guest beer Ⓗ

Former coaching inn dating from the 18th century with later additions, now a small hotel with lounge and public bars. Food is served in the lounge and a separate restaurant area. Situated at the centre of a conservation area, this is a popular haunt for walkers as well as salmon and trout fishermen on the River Don (the hotel owns the fishing rights to more than 10 miles of the river). The Pitfichie and Cairn William mountain bike trails are close by. A guest beer is added occasionally in summer. A premium is paid for half-pint drinking.
▲Q①🍴❶♿➡(X20,220,421)♣

Netherley

Lairhillock Inn
AB39 3QS (¼ mile E of B979, signed from B979 and A90)
✪ 11-11 (midnight Fri & Sat) ☎ (01569) 730001
⊕ lairhillock.co.uk
Caledonian Deuchars IPA; Taylor Landlord; guest beer Ⓗ

The 'INN' sign on the roof of this rambling building in attractive open countryside makes it easy to spot from the road. It has a traditional, wood-panelled bar warmed by a large log fire in winter, and a lounge with a large conservatory area, popular for dining. A separate restaurant, the Crynoch, is available for finer dining. The guest beer is usually from Cairngorm Brewery. Convenient for the attractions of Stonehaven and Royal Deeside.
▲Q🌳①🍴❶♿♣P

Oldmeldrum

Redgarth Hotel
Kirk Brae, AB51 0DJ (off A947 towards golf course)
✪ 11-3, 5-11 (11.45 Fri & Sat); 12-3, 5-11 Sun
☎ (01651) 872353 ⊕ redgarth.com
Beer range varies Ⓗ/Ⓖ

Renowned local hotel and pub with imposing views over the eastern Grampian mountains. A winner of many local CAMRA awards, it retains a strong reputation for its imaginative choice of beers, sourced from, among others, Timothy Taylor, Highland and Inveralmond breweries. A successful blend of popular family restaurant and marvellous real ale pub, it is appreciated by a dedicated core of regulars. During occasional Brewers in Residence evenings, three handpumped ales may be supplemented by many more on gravity.
🌳①🍴❶▲➡(305,325)♣P'–

Peterhead

Cross Keys ✓
23-27 Chapel Street, AB42 1TH
✪ 8am-11 (1am Fri & Sat); 9am-11 Sun ☎ (01779) 483500
Caledonian Deuchars IPA; Greene King Abbot; Isle of Skye Cross Keys; guest beers Ⓗ

A typical Wetherspoon outlet located in the centre of a bustling port, close to the local museum, where you can learn about the town's maritime history. The pub is named after the chapel dedicated to St Peter that previously stood on the site. The long single-room interior has the bar towards the front and a large seating area to the rear. A sheltered and heated area outside caters for hardy souls and smokers. At least one guest ale is available, often from a Scottish micro. Children are welcome until 8pm if dining.
①❶♿➡(260,263)●'–

Stonehaven

Marine Hotel

9-10 Shorehead, AB39 2JY (on harbour front)
☼ 11-midnight (1am Fri & Sat; 11 winter Sun)
☎ (01569) 762155 ⊕ marinehotelstonehaven.co.uk
Caledonian Deuchars IPA; Taylor Landlord; guest beers Ⓗ

Small harbourside hotel featuring simple wood panelling in the bar and a rustic lounge with an open fireplace. The upstairs restaurant has its own handpumps. Outside seating enjoys a splendid view of the harbour. Guest ales are mostly sourced from local and regional breweries. Several Belgian beers are also on draught and there is a massive choice of bottled Belgian beers – ask for the beer menu. Historic Dunnottar Castle is one mile south. The pub has plans to start its own brewery. Local CAMRA Pub of the Year 2010. ⋈✿☛❹◗◻⌐☐

Ship Inn

5 Shorehead, AB39 2JY (on harbour front)
☼ 11-midnight (1am Fri & Sat) ☎ (01569) 762617
⊕ shipinnstonehaven.com
Beer range varies Ⓗ

Traditional harbour-front hotel, with a maritime themed, wood-panelled bar and an outdoor seating area overlooking the water. In the bar, a mirror from the defunct Devanha Brewery is a prominent feature. Two beers are offered, one from the Inveralmond Brewery. An extensive range of malt whiskies is stocked. A modern restaurant, with panoramic harbour views, is adjacent to the bar, with food available all day at the weekend. Accommodation is in 11 guest rooms. ⋈✿☛❹◗◻⌐

Tarland

Aberdeen Arms

The Square, AB34 4TX
☼ 12-2.30, 5-11 (1am Tue & Fri); 12-1am Sat; 12-11 Sun
☎ (01339) 881225 ⊕ aberdeenarmshotel.co.uk
Inveralmond Minstrel Ale; guest beer Ⓗ

Part of a 300-year-old listed building in the village centre. This traditional inn has a wood-lined bar area, stripped wooden floors, low ceilings and a real fire. Live music features on Tuesday nights and the Cromar Folk Club meets on the last Friday of the month. Craigievar Castle, the Grampian Transport Museum at Alford and the Queen's View beauty spot are close by. Closed winter Mondays. ⋈✿◗♿♣P

Douglas Arms Hotel, Banchory

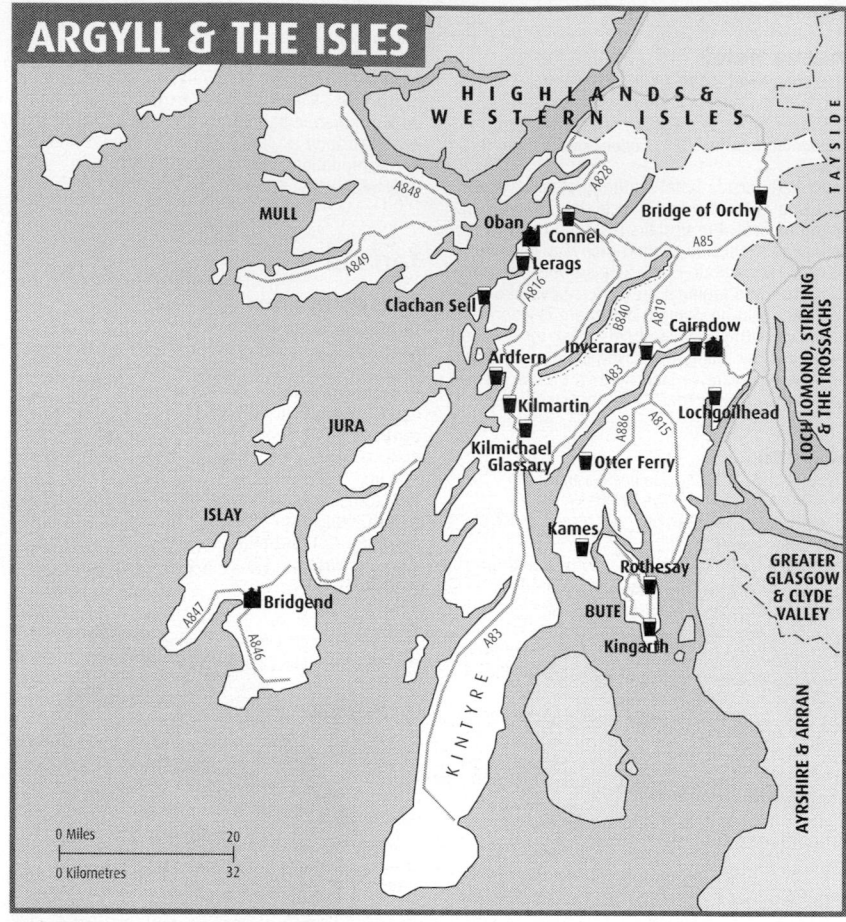

ARGYLL & THE ISLES

Authority area covered: Argyll & Bute UA

Ardfern

Galley of Lorne Inn

PA31 8QN (near marina) NM805043
☼ 12-1am (5-midnight Mon-Fri winter); 12-1am (midnight winter) Sun ☎ (01852) 500284 ⊕ galleyoflorne.co.uk
Beer range varies Ⓗ
An old drovers' inn, dating from 1680, now catering for different travellers due to its location at a popular yachting marina and chandlery. Up to four widely sourced beers are available from handpumps in the bar, which has wooden beams and pillars, rustic seating and two fireplaces. The lounge has dining tables and there is also a spacious restaurant with large picture windows offering attractive views over the loch. The sizeable beer garden is a delight on sunny days.
曲స⊛⊯◑ ⊟&▲P

Bridge of Orchy

Bridge of Orchy Hotel ✔

PA36 4AD (on A82 at N end of Glen Orchy between Tyndrum & Glencoe) NN296396
☼ 11-11 (midnight Fri & Sat); 12.30-11 Sun
☎ (01838) 400208 ⊕ bridgeoforchy.co.uk
Caledonian Deuchars IPA; guest beers Ⓗ

Set amid mountain and forest scenery, this hotel is surprisingly accessible. Located on the main A82 to Glencoe and near the West Highland Way and the rail station, it provides an ideal point to take a break from travelling. In the bar, the two guest beers come from a wide range of breweries. Hearty meals are served both in the bar and the restaurant, which offers scenic views. The bunkhouse rooms are popular with climbers and walkers. 曲స⊛⊯◑≠⊟(914)♠P

Cairndow

Stagecoach Inn

PA26 8BN (near head of Loch Fyne) NN181109
☼ 11-11 (1am Fri & Sat); 11-midnight Sun
☎ (01499) 600286 ⊕ cairndowinn.com
Beer range varies Ⓗ
Situated at the foot of Glenkinglas on the shores of Loch Fyne, this inn provides a resting point before the long ascent over the Rest and Be Thankful, and makes a handy base for enjoying the local scenery. The old stables have been converted into an old-world restaurant with views over the loch, and the friendly public bar beside it serves beers from the nearby Fyne Ales brewery – two in summer and one at quieter times.
曲స⊛⊯◑&▲⊟(926,976)♣P⊱⊟

Clachan Seil

Tigh an Truish 🄻

PA34 4QZ (on B844 5 miles W of A816 jct, by Clachan Bridge) NM784197
❄ 11-11; 11-2.30, 5-8 winter; 12-1am (8 winter) Sun
☎ (01852) 300242 ⊕ tighantruish.co.uk
Beer range varies 🄷

Fancy a day trip across the Atlantic? Traverse the Clachan Bridge to visit this delightful, traditional family-run inn and and you have done just that! Historically important, it is where kilts were exchanged for trousers after Culloden. Today there is no such restriction, just a cosy, welcoming interior with beers from Fyne Ales and other Scottish micros. The beer garden and front patio are wonderful and the pub is set in fantastic scenery, ideal for a short walk and photography.
🏚Q🌤☀🏘◑⅃🕭⅊(418)♣P⅃—

Connel

Glue Pot Bunkhouse & Bar

at The Oyster Inn, PA37 1PJ (on A85 near Connel Bridge) NM910343
❄ 11-midnight (1am Fri-Sun) ☎ (01631) 710666
⊕ oysterinn.co.uk
Caledonian Deuchars IPA 🄷

Once the site of glue making, the Glue Pot is otherwise known as Ferryman's from times before the Connel Bridge. A small wooden horseshoe bar projects into a cosy room with stone walls incorporating a log-burning fireplace. Local maps cover the ceiling and the windows give views of Loch Etive. A TV to the rear shows news and sport at appropriate times. Food is available 12-9pm (check times in winter) or, for a more diverse menu, try the attached Oyster Inn restaurant.
🏚☀🏘◑⅃🕭⅊(405,408)P⅃—

Inveraray

George Hotel

Main Street East, PA32 8TT
❄ 11 (12 Sun)-12.45am ☎ (01499) 302111
⊕ thegeorgehotel.co.uk
Beer range varies 🄷

Two private homes, dating from 1770, were joined 90 years later to form this town-centre hotel by the Clark family who still own and manage it. The original flagstone floors, stone walls and peat/log fires help retain much of the original ambience. Beers, mostly sourced from Fyne Ales, are available both in the lively public bar and the cocktail bar to the rear, generally two in summer and one in winter. Food in the restaurant and bar has an emphasis on local produce.
🏚Q☀🏘◑⅃🕭⅊(926,976)P⅃—

Kames

Kames Hotel 🄻

PA21 2AF (down small road off B8000 above the shore) NR974712
❄ 12 (4 Mon-Thu winter)-midnight (1am Fri & Sat); closed Jan
☎ (01700) 811489 ⊕ kames-hotel.com
Fyne Highlander; guest beer 🄷

Perched on a hillside above a rocky beach, this impressive hotel provides stunning views of its attractive 15-mooring marina, the Kyles of Bute, the Bute hills and Argyll mountains. Two handpumps in the central bar serve Highlander and other Fyne Ales. The bar counter extends into the lounge, with comfortable chairs, and a pool room with darts, TV showing sports and wood-burning stove. Nautical pictures of old sailing ships and historic characters adorn the walls.
🏚☀🏘◑⅃ Δ🕭(478)P⅃—

Kilmartin

Kilmartin Hotel 🄻

PA31 8RQ (on A816 10 miles N of Lochgilphead) NR835989
❄ 12-midnight (1am Sat) summer; 5-11 (1am Sat) winter; 12-midnight (11 winter) Sun ☎ (01546) 510250
⊕ kilmartin-hotel.com
Beer range varies 🄷

It is impossible to miss this tall white family-run hotel by the A816, perched on a hill overlooking scenic Kilmartin Glen. The two beers offered include one from Fyne Ales, with the other usually from another Scottish micro. Tasty home-made meals can be enjoyed inside or in the beer garden, which has a covered, heated smoking area. The local museum has details of the historic 5,000-year old glen and Neolithic sites to visit.
🌤☀🏘◑⅃ Δ🕭(423)P⅃—

Kilmichael Glassary

Horseshoe Inn

Bridgend, PA31 8QA (off A816 3 miles N of Lochgilphead) NR852928
❄ 5-11; 12-midnight Sat; 12-11 Sun ☎ (01546) 606369
⊕ horseshoeinn.biz
Beer range varies 🄷

Four-roomed hotel just off the A816 near the Crinan Canal and ancient hill fort of Dunadd set in historic Kilmartin Glen. Up to two ales are available in summer, mainly local from Fyne Ales. Food in the bar, lounge and dining room is excellent and there is a games room. A convenient place for a stopover en-route to Oban and the isles, or a stay while exploring the cairns, standing stones and stone circles of the scenic glen.
🏚☀🏘◑⅃ 🔌🕭(423)P⅃—

Kingarth: Isle of Bute

Kingarth Hotel

PA20 9LU (jct with road to Kilchattan Bay) NS094563
❄ 12-midnight ☎ (01700) 831662 ⊕ kingarthhotel.co.uk
Beer range varies 🄷

A pleasant coastal bus ride from Rothesay delivers you to this secluded country inn amid a verdant agricultural landscape. It affords fine views of the countryside and Kilchattan Bay – reached by the bus or a healthy walk. Dining, drinking and pool are easily accommodated in the welcoming interior, while the beer garden catches the afternoon sun. Two handpumps offer a truly eclectic beer range. Enjoy a meal, a game of bowls or simply sit and relax with a pint. 🏚☀🏘◑⅃🕭(490)P⅃—

INDEPENDENT BREWERIES

Argyll Oban
Fyne Cairndow
Islay Bridgend

SCOTLAND

Lerags

Barn

Cologin, Lerags Glen, PA34 4SE (down minor road off A816) NM853260

☼ 12-11; 11-11 Sun summer; closed Mon-Thu, 5-11 Fri; 11-11 Sat & Sun winter ☎ (01631) 564618 ⊕ cologin.co.uk

Fyne Highlander; guest beer Ⓗ

Cologin farmhouse forms the centre of a range of holiday chalets and lodges in a secluded glen three miles by road south of Oban. The Barn was originally the cattle byre and some of the slate stalls have been retained as backrests, contributing to the cosy ambience. Regulars come from local villages and enjoy a folk session on Sunday afternoons. The guest beer comes from Fyne Ales. In winter ring ahead to confirm opening hours. Wi-Fi is available. ⋈Q❀◑☾♠P≒

Lochgoilhead

Shore House Inn Ⓛ

PA24 8AD (at head of Loch Goil) NN197014

☼ 12-11; closed Tue ☎ (01301) 703340 ⊕ theshorehouse.net

Beer range varies Ⓗ

Accessed from the B839 along a driveway or gate next to a chapel by the loch. The rectangular bar room has a wooden roof with skylights. One beer (two in summer) from Fyne Ales is offered. A speciality of the varied menu are pizzas cooked in a wood-fired pizza oven. Those seated at the restaurant windows or in the delightful beer garden can enjoy stupendous views down Loch Goil. Note, the pub closes January to mid-February. ❀≒◑☾▲🚍(484)♣P≒

Otter Ferry

Oystercatcher Ⓛ

PA21 2DH (on B8000 on E coast of Loch Fyne) NR930844

☼ summer 11-11 (5-11 Fri; 11-11 Sat; closed Mon-Thu winter); 12.30-11 (5 winter) Sun ☎ (01700) 821229 ⊕ theoystercatcher.co.uk

Fyne Highlander; guest beers Ⓗ

It is well worth making the scenic journey along Loch Fyne to this oasis catering for locals, holidaymakers and yachtsmen. The Oystercatcher offers majestic views over the loch to Kintyre, a large lawn and beach. It has 15 moorings and a pontoon, and caters for various shoreline activities. Pine wood features in the bar with a divider to the snug, with iron stove and fireplace respectively, and a restaurant/function room. Home-made dishes, especially seafood, feature on a diverse menu. ⋈❀◑☾♣P≒

Rothesay: Isle of Bute

Black Bull Inn

3 West Princess Street, PA20 9AF (opp harbour)

☼ 11-11 (midnight Fri & Sat); 12.30-11 Sun ☎ (01700) 502366

Belhaven St Andrews Ale; Caledonian Deuchars IPA Ⓗ

After a pleasant train ride along the Clyde from Glasgow, take the ferry from the splendour of Wemyss Bay station, perhaps visit the Victorian toilets on Rothesay Pier and look at the rare Victorian postbox by the Discovery Centre before enjoying a beer in this two-bar pub, which offers good food in a separate dining area. A visit to Mount Stuart House may be taken before a final beer and the ferry home. ◑🍴🚍

Shore House Inn, Lochgoilhead

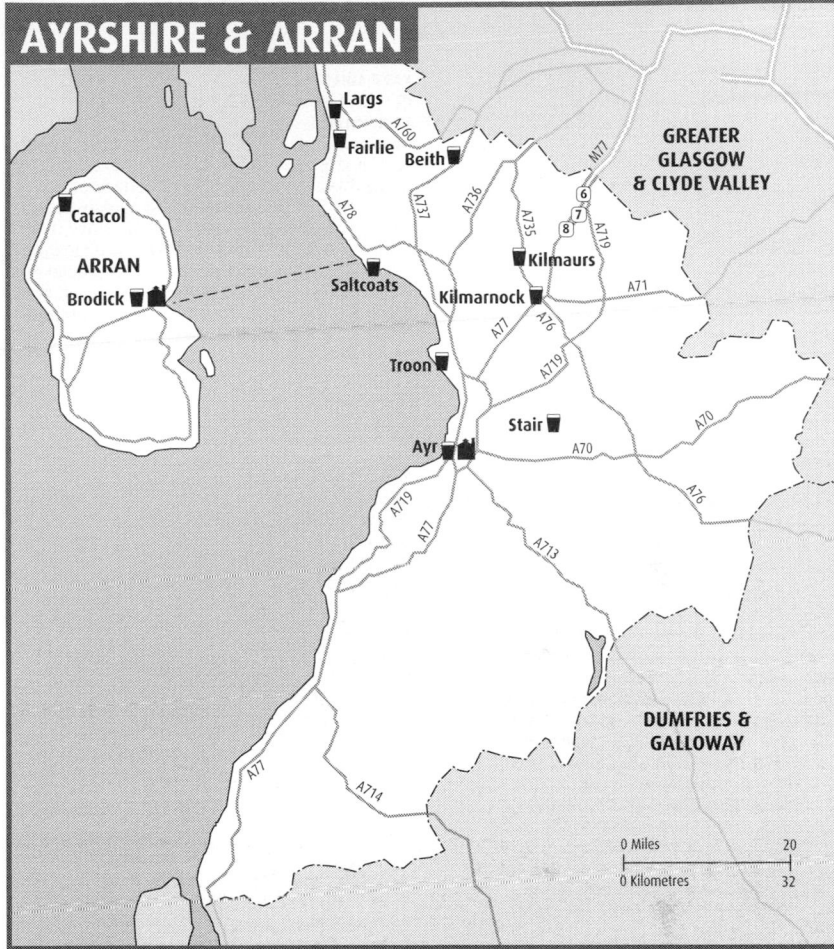

Authority areas covered: East Ayrshire UA, North Ayrshire UA, South Ayrshire UA

Ayr

Abbotsford Hotel
14 Corsehill Road, KA7 2ST
✪ 10-12.30am (midnight Sun) ☎ (01292) 261506
⊕ abbotsfordhotel.co.uk
Caledonian Deuchars IPA; guest beer Ⓗ
Family-run hotel situated in a residential area south of the town centre, convenient for the seafront, local golf courses, Burns-related attractions and other delights of the area. Two real ales are offered in the Copper Bar – its name accurately describes its decor. Meals are served in both the bar and a separate restaurant area. There is also a pool/TV room and a function room/conservatory. The guest beer tends to be from a larger brewery – often a darker English beer. ⬗✿🛏◑🚪(57,361)P↝

Chestnuts Hotel
52 Racecourse Road, KA7 2UZ (A719, 1 mile S of centre)
✪ 10-midnight (12.30am Sat) ☎ (01292) 264393
⊕ chestnutshotel.com
Beer range varies Ⓗ
Three changing real ales, from both local and larger regional breweries, are offered in The 19th Hole – the bar at this well appointed, family-run hotel.

The bar is a focal point for locals and tourists and features golfing prints and memorabilia, discreet seating around a cosy log fire and a vaulted ceiling that displays a record-breaking collection of whisky water jugs. High-quality meals are served in the bar and separate restaurant. ⬖✿🛏◑♿🚪(9)P

Geordie's Byre
103 Main Street, KA8 8BU (N of centre, over river towards Prestwick)
✪ 11-11 (midnight Thu-Sat); 12.30-11 Sun
☎ (01292) 264925
Beer range varies Ⓐ
CAMRA award-winning 18th-century pub, located in the Newton area of Ayr, serving up to four guest ales sourced from far and wide. It is one of the few Scottish pubs using traditional Scottish tall founts. Both the public bar and the lounge feature a wealth of memorabilia. A wide selection of malt whiskies and rums is also available. Handy for several local bus routes. 🚪⇌(Newton-on-Ayr)🚌

INDEPENDENT BREWERIES
Arran Brodick: Isle of Arran
Ayr Ayr

Glen Park Hotel ⓛ

5 Racecourse Road, KA7 2DG
✪ 10-12.30am (midnight Sun) ☎ (01292) 263891
⊕ glenparkhotel.com
Ayr Leezie Lundie, Jolly Beggars; guest beer Ⓗ
A short walk from the town centre, this attractive
1860s B-Listed Victorian building is a splendid
modern hotel offering guests and non-residents
alike the warmest of welcomes. Home to Ayr
Brewing Company, the guest beer is its seasonal
brew, and the restaurant features fresh local
produce. The front patio has fine views in the
summer months. 🚲🏩♿⬤🍴♿⇌🚌(9,57,444)P⅄

Wellingtons Bar

17 Wellington Square, KA7 1EZ
✪ 11-12.30am; 12.30-midnight Sun ☎ (01292) 262794
⊕ welliesbar.weebly.com
Beer range varies Ⓗ
A large Wellington boot advertises the location of
this basement bar. Close to the seafront, bus
station and local government offices, it attracts
tourists and office workers alike. The Wednesday
evening quiz is popular and weekend music
features live bands or a DJ on Saturday and an
acoustic session on Sunday. Two changing ales
usually include at least one from either Kelburn or
Fyne Ales. Good-value food is served lunchtimes
and Thursday to Sunday evenings. ⬤🍴⇌🚌

West Kirk ⓛ ✓

58A Sandgate, KA7 1BX (close to bus station)
✪ 10-12.30am (midnight Sun) ☎ (01292) 880416
Greene King Ruddles Best Bitter; guest beers Ⓗ
Wetherspoon conversion of a former church
retaining many original features – access to the
toilets is via the pulpit. Up to six changing guest
ales are offered and local micros are usually well
represented. Meals are available all day, with
breakfast from 8am. Outside, the front drinking
area has a shelter for smokers. ♿⬤♿⇌🚌⅄

Beith

Masonic Arms ⓛ

21 Main Street, KA15 2AD
✪ 11-midnight ☎ (01505) 502786
Beer range varies Ⓗ
Small, traditional pub where well-behaved dogs
are welcome, situated on a narrow main street
close to bus routes heading north, south and west.
A friendly, sports-oriented pub, pool, darts and
dominoes are played here. Beers are normally
from Houston and a large selection of malt
whiskies is also available. Children are not
permitted. 🚌(X34,X36)♣

Brodick: Isle of Arran

Ormidale Hotel

Knowe Road, KA27 8BY (off A841 at W end of village)
✪ 12.30-2.30 (summer only), 4.30 (12 Sat & Sun)-midnight
☎ (01770) 302293 ⊕ ormidale-hotel.co.uk
Arran Ale, Blonde; guest beers Ⓐ
Large red sandstone hotel with a small bar and
spacious conservatory set in seven acres of
grounds. Beers are served from traditional Scottish
tall founts on the boat-shaped bar. Home-cooked
meals are recommended. Discos and folk nights
are held, and the attractive beer garden has views
across Brodick Bay. Accommodation is only
available in the summer. 🚲🏩♿⬤🍴🚌(324)♣P⅄

Catacol: Isle of Arran

Catacol Bay Hotel

KA27 8HN
✪ 11-midnight (1am Thu-Sat) ☎ (01770) 830231
⊕ catacol.co.uk
Houston Peter's Well; Taylor Landlord Ⓗ
Former manse sitting in its own grounds adjacent
to the Twelve Apostles, a listed terrace of former
estate workers' houses. Both the garden and the
bar, which now has a wood-burning stove, offer
superb views over Kilbrannan Sound to Kintyre.
Run by the same family since 1979, this hotel is an
ideal base for exploring the north and west of
Arran. Bar meals are served all day, every day.
🚲🏨♿🏩⬤🍴🚌(324)♣P⅄

Fairlie

Village Inn

46 Bay Street, KA29 0AL
✪ 11-midnight (1am Fri & Sat); 12.30-midnight Sun
☎ (01475) 568432 ⊕ villageinnfairlie.co.uk
Beer range varies Ⓗ
Opposite the site of the Fife boatyard, the walls of
this village local are covered with spectacular
pictures by local photographer Marc Turner. The inn
reopened in 2010 after two years of closure and
the locals, determined not to lose it again, support
the Tuesday night quiz and occasional live music
nights. Two regularly changing real ales are served,
usually Scottish. The pub has quickly gained a
reputation for excellent food and friendly staff.
Children are welcome until 10pm, although the
public bar is a child-free oasis.
🚲Q♿⬤🍴🚌(585)P⅄

Kilmarnock

Brass & Granite

53 Grange Street, KA1 2DD
✪ 11-midnight (12.30am Thu-Sat); 12.30-midnight Sun
☎ (01563) 523431
Beer range varies Ⓗ
Open-plan pub in Kilmarnock town centre, close to
Rugby Park Football Ground. Guest beers are
usually sourced from local or Cumbrian brewers
and there is also a wide range of draught and
bottled Belgian beers on sale. Food is available all
day and there are several TVs in the pub showing
live sport. Quizzes are held every Sunday, Monday
and Wednesday. ⬤🍴♿⇌🚌♣⅄

Wheatsheaf Inn ✓

70 Portland Street, KA1 1JG (near bus and rail stations)
✪ 10-11 (midnight Thu; 1am Fri & Sat) ☎ (01563) 572483
**Greene King Abbot; Ruddles Best Bitter; guest
beers** Ⓗ
Sizeable town-centre Lloyds No.1 bar, originally the
historic Wheatsheaf Hotel, famous for its links to
Robert Burns, who was first published in
Kilmarnock. The bar is divided into various seating
areas, with booths, sofas and a raised dining space.
DJs entertain on a Friday and Saturday, with
karaoke early Friday evening, but otherwise
conversation holds sway. Food is standard
Wetherspoon fare and nine handpumps dispense a
range of ales plus real cider. Open from 9am for
breakfast. 🚲♿⬤🍴♿⇌🚌♣⅄

SCOTLAND

Kilmaurs

Weston Tavern

27 Main Street, KA3 2RQ
☼ 11-midnight (1am Fri & Sat); 12.30-midnight Sun
☎ (01563) 538805 ⊕ westontavern.co.uk
Beer range varies Ⓗ
Housed in the former manse of reformist minister David Smeaton, a contemporary of Robert Burns, this is a classic country pub and restaurant with a tiled floor, stone walls and a wood-burning fire. It sits beside the Jougs, a former jailhouse and tollbooth (jougs were iron collars used to restrain miscreants and a set still hangs from the walls today). A single pump dispenses ale from a rotating list of local breweries. The pub holds regular live music and quiz nights.
🏠⊛❍♿⇌🚌(1,13,337)

Largs

Charlie Smith's

14 Gallowgate Street, KA30 8LX (on A78, opp pier)
☼ 10-midnight (1am Fri & Sat) ☎ (01475) 672250
Beer range varies Ⓗ
Friendly, one-roomed pub situated on the seafront near the pier and Cumbrae ferry terminal, close to the railway station. A child-free establishment with a modern feel to it, good-quality pub food is served daily. There is one ever-changing ale, sometimes from a local brewer, but frequently from further afield. Handy for the Waverley paddle steamer in summer. ❍♿⇌🚌(585,906)♣

JG Sharps Bar

34-36 Nelson Street, KA30 8LW
☼ 11-midnight (1am Fri & Sat); 12.30-midnight Sun
☎ (01475) 675515 ⊕ jgsharps.co.uk
Caledonian Deuchars IPA Ⓗ
Set back from the seafront and Main Street on the corner of Nelson Street and Boyd Street, this is a large traditional pub with many different drinking areas. An open fire warms the bar area and there is space for smokers in the beer garden outside. Good quality pub meals are served at lunchtime and Friday to Sunday evenings. Games and TV both feature and there is occasional live music.
🏠🐕⊛❍♿⇌🚌♣⌐

Waterside

14 Bath Street, KA30 8BL (on side street behind seafront)
☼ 12-11 (1am Fri & Sat; midnight Sun) ☎ (01475) 672224
Beer range varies Ⓗ
Formerly the Clachan, this pub has been tastefully refurbished throughout. Approximately 100 yards from the ferry terminal, it is accessible from the promenade or Bath Street. There is one ever-changing real ale, with a second from Easter to October. Evening entertainment includes live music, quiz nights, karaoke and poker. A small snug off the main bar offers privacy for families and private meetings. Quality pub food is available lunchtimes and until 7pm at the weekend.
🐕❍♿⇌🚌♣⌐(585,906)♣⌐

Saltcoats

Salt Cot Ⓛ ✔

7 Hamilton Street, KA21 5DS
☼ 10-11 (midnight Thu; 1am Fri & Sat) ☎ (01294) 465924
Greene King Abbot; Ruddles Best Bitter; guest beers Ⓗ
A good Wetherspoon conversion of a former cinema, the pub gets its name from the original cottages at the salt pans. One of the guest beers usually comes from Strathaven Ales. Although there are TVs in the bar area, the sound is only turned on a few times a year for rugby internationals. It has an area where children are permitted and there is a family menu. Opens at 9am for breakfast. Local CAMRA Pub of the Year 2010. Q❍♿♿⇌🚌

Stair

Stair Inn

KA5 5HW (on B730 7 miles E of Ayr)
☼ 12-11 (1am Fri & Sat) ☎ (01292) 591650 ⊕ stairinn.co.uk
Beer range varies Ⓗ
Well worth seeking out, although this family run hotel on the banks of the River Ayr is not accessible by public transport. The comfortable bar and adjacent restaurant feature bespoke hand-made furniture and the bedrooms are furnished in a similar style. A single real ale is available, usually from Houston Brewery. The food menu relies heavily on local produce and fish from the inn's own smokehouse is a speciality. Booking for meals at weekends is strongly recommended.
🏠Q⊛♣❍♿P⌐

Troon

Bruce's Well

91 Portland Street, KA10 6QN
☼ 12-12.30am (midnight Sun) ☎ (01292) 311429
Caledonian Deuchars IPA; guest beer Ⓗ
A friendly, spacious and comfortable lounge bar, close to Troon town centre and a short walk from Troon Station. There are a number of TVs around the bar area that show football and other sporting events but the volume is usually low or off. The bar may open earlier if there is a big sporting event on TV. The guest ale comes from the Belhaven list and changes regularly. Unusually, the cellar is situated in a temperature-controlled room off the main bar area. The pub was awarded Cask Marque accreditation in 2011. ⇌🚌(10,14,110)⌐

Fullartons ✔

10 Portland Street, KA10 6EA
☼ 10-11.30 (12.30am Fri & Sat) ☎ (01292) 311212
⊕ fullartons.co.uk
Cairngorm Wildcat; guest beers Ⓗ
Smart, comfortable lounge bar decorated to a high standard and situated close to Troon cross. One or two guest ales are sourced from the Belhaven guest list. The gantry also features speciality malt whiskies, vodkas and rums. Locally sourced food, prepared daily in the bar's kitchen, is popular. Live music sessions are held on Saturday nights.
❍♿⇌🚌(10,14,110)⌐

A glass of bitter beer or pale ale, taken with the principal meal of the day, does more good and less harm than any medicine the physician can prescribe. **Dr Carpenter**, 1750

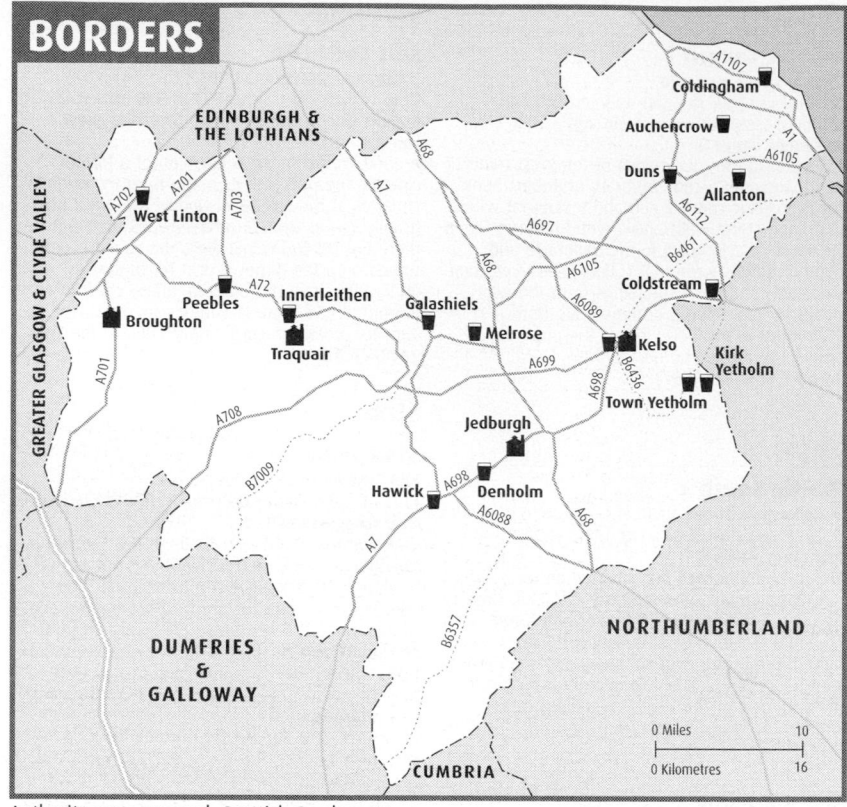

BORDERS

EDINBURGH &
THE LOTHIANS

GREATER GLASGOW & CLYDE VALLEY

Coldingham

Auchencrow

Duns

Allanton

West Linton

Peebles
Innerleithen
Galashiels
Coldstream

Broughton

Melrose
Kelso

Traquair

Kirk
Yetholm

Town Yetholm

Jedburgh

Hawick
Denholm

DUMFRIES
&
GALLOWAY

NORTHUMBERLAND

0 Miles   10
0 Kilometres   16

CUMBRIA

Authority area covered: Scottish Borders UA

Allanton

Allanton Inn

TD11 3JZ
☼ 12-11 ☎ (01890) 818260 ⊕ allantoninn.co.uk
Beer range varies Ⓗ
Dating back to the 18th century, this old coaching
inn still has hitching rings for those arriving by
horse. Inside, the inn has been refurbished in a
bright, airy style. The front dining rooms focus on
quality food, while the rear bar looks out over the
beer garden to the countryside beyond. Beers are
often from Scottish Borders Brewery and other
Scottish micros. For those visiting on their own
there is plenty to read. Families are welcome and
there is free Wi-Fi access. ⚊Q✿≠⊲◗⊟♣P

Auchencrow

Craw Inn

TD14 5LS (signed from A1)
☼ 12-2.30, 6-11 (midnight Fri); 12-midnight Sat; 12.30-11
Sun ☎ (01890) 761253 ⊕ thecrawinn.co.uk
Beer range varies Ⓗ
This friendly 18th-century village inn is the hub of
the community. The traditional single bar features
beams festooned with pump clips, a wood-burning
stove and ample seating. Excellent home-cooked
food is served in both the bar and the well-
appointed restaurant, and families are welcome. In
summer, drinking and dining can be enjoyed on
the outdoor decking. A beer festival is held in
November. Free Wi-Fi access. ⚊Q✿≠⊲◗&⊟♣P

Coldingham

New Inn

1 Bridge Street, TD14 5NG
☼ 11-midnight ☎ (01890) 771315
⊕ thenewinncoldingham.co.uk
Beer range varies Ⓗ
The focus is on dining at this village pub, with local
fish and seafood featuring regularly. Families are
made welcome and food is served all day Saturday
and Sunday. The small wooden-floored bar has a
cosy atmosphere and a roaring fire when the
weather dictates. The two real ales change very
regularly and are often from smaller breweries.
Check opening times ahead during winter months.
Free Wi-Fi is available. ⚊Q✿◗Å⊟

Coldstream

Besom ✓

75-77 High Street, TD12 4AE
☼ 11-midnight (1am Fri & Sat); 12.30-midnight Sun
☎ (01890) 882391
Caledonian Deuchars IPA; guest beer Ⓗ
One of the first and last pubs in Scotland, this
three-roomed gem has remained relatively

unchanged since it was built in the 1890s and revamped circa 1910. The cosy bar retains its original counter and gantry, while the diverse range of memorabilia, bookshelves and comfortable seating gives the feel of a living room more than a pub. Leading through from the lounge is a room dedicated entirely to the memory of the Coldstream Guards. Families are welcome in the lounge and dogs are permitted in the bar. ⚌Q🌣◑⊟⊟♣╚

Denholm

Auld Cross Keys Hotel
Main Street, TD9 8NU
🕓 12-11 (midnight Thu; 1am Fri & Sat); 12.30-midnight Sun
☎ (01450) 870305 ⊕ crosskeysdenholm.co.uk
Scottish Borders Game Bird; guest beer 🅗
Overlooking the village green, this small hotel retains the character of an inn. The plain public bar may be favoured by drinkers, however there is also a more comfortable lounge bar. The guest beer is often from Northumberland Brewery. Renowned for good honest home-cooked food, meals are served all day on Sunday. The bedrooms are of a good standard. Folk music sessions and concerts are regular events. Families are welcome until 9pm, but dogs are only allowed in the bar. Free Wi-Fi access. ⚌Q🌣✍◑⊟⊟♣P╚

Fox & Hounds Inn
Main Street, TD9 8NU
🕓 11.30-3, 5-midnight Mon & Wed; 11.30-midnight (1am Fri & Sat); 12.30-midnight Sun ☎ (01450) 870247
Scottish Borders Game Bird; guest beer 🅗
A village local, built in 1728, overlooking the green. The small bar is half wood-panelled with pictures and memorabilia decorating the walls, and a real fire creates a cosy feel in winter. The rear lounge has a coffee-house feel and there is an upstairs dining room used in the evening. A courtyard provides space for smokers and a sheltered outdoor drinking area in warmer weather. The guest beer is often from Wylam Brewery. Dogs are welcome and families until 8pm. Free Wi-Fi access. ⚌🌣✍◑⊟⊟(20)♣╚

Duns

Black Bull Hotel
15 Black Bull Street, TD11 3AR
🕓 11-midnight (1am Fri & Sat); 12-midnight Sun
☎ (01361) 883379
Beer range varies 🅗
Family-run 200-year-old hotel just off the town square. The cosy wood-panelled front bar is popular with locals, and the lounge area with bench seating is more suited to families. There is also a restaurant specialising in fresh fish, which has an intimate, relaxed and candlelit atmosphere. The secluded beer garden can be enjoyed during the summer. Dogs are welcome in the bar. The letting rooms are all named after local historic figures. Free Wi-Fi access. 🌣✍◑⊟&⊟♣P╚

Galashiels

Ladhope Inn
33 High Buckholmside, TD1 2HR (A7, ⅓ mile N of centre)
🕓 4-11 (midnight Thu); 3-midnight Fri; 11-midnight Sat; 12-midnight Sun ☎ (01896) 752446

Caledonian Deuchars IPA; guest beer 🅗
Comfortable, friendly local with a vibrant Borders atmosphere. Originating circa 1792, it has been altered considerably inside. Now a single room, it is decorated with a large inked map of the Galashiels area and a wee alcove has a golfing theme. Three flat-screen TVs ensure the pub is busy during sporting events. The guest beer is often from Scottish Border Brewery but changes regularly. Frequent live music is hosted. Excellent home-made soup is served on Sundays. Dogs are welcome, but no children. 🌣▲⊟(95)♣

Hawick

Bourtree 🅥
22 Bourtree Place, TD9 9HL
🕓 9-midnight (1am Fri & Sat) ☎ (01450) 360450
Beer range varies 🅗
Overlooking the small village square, this well-appointed coaching inn enjoys a good reputation for its food. The small wood-panelled bar is adorned with sporting artefacts and leads through to two comfortable lounge areas. The real ales are frequently from little-known English breweries. Families are welcome, but dogs may only be taken in to the bar. Free Wi-Fi access. ⚌Q🌣◑&⊟(20,95)P╚

Exchange Bar (Dalton's)
1 Silver Street, TD9 0AD (off W end of High St)
🕓 11-11 (1am Fri & Sat); 12.30-11 Sun ☎ (01450) 376067
Beer range varies 🅗
Hidden away in Silver Street behind High Street, this pub was once Hawick Corn Exchange. Nestled between the imposing St Mary's Parish Kirk with its winkie bells and the Hawick Heritage Hub, it is a Victorian gem with dark wood panelling and ornate cornice work. A previous owner was named Dalton and the name has stuck ever since. The bar is popular with locals and there is a comfortable lounge for families, parties and Friday karaoke. ⊟⊟(20,95)

Innerleithen

Traquair Arms Hotel
Traquair Road, EH44 6PD (B709, off A72)
🕓 11-11 (midnight Fri & Sat); 12-11.30 Sun
☎ (01896) 830229 ⊕ traquairarmshotel.co.uk
Caledonian Deuchars IPA; Taylor Landlord; Traquair Stuart Ale 🅗
Elegant 18th-century hotel in the scenic Tweed Valley. The comfortable lounge bar features a welcoming real fire in winter and a relaxing tropical fish tank. An Italian bistro area and separate restaurant provide plenty of room for diners. Food is served all day at weekends. One of the few outlets for draught ales from Traquair House. Families are welcome, as are dogs. There is free Wi-Fi access. ⚌🌣✍◑&▲⊟(62)P╚

Kelso

Cobbles Inn 🏆
7 Bowmont Street, TD5 7JH (off NE side of town square)
🕓 11-11 (1am Fri); closed Mon winter; 12-11 Sun
☎ (01573) 223548 ⊕ thecobblesinn.co.uk
Beer range varies 🅗
An award-winning gastro pub offering an eclectic mix of British classics, Pacific Rim and modern European cuisine using the finest locally sourced

SCOTLAND

and seasonal ingredients. Though the focus is on food, drinkers are welcome here. To the right of the main dining area is a lounge bar where beers from Tempest, the pub's own microbrewery, are featured. Families are welcome and private functions are catered for upstairs. Free Wi-Fi available. Local CAMRA Pub of the Year 2012.
🏚️❄️◑⬤👜⛽

Kirk Yetholm

Border Hotel
The Green, TD5 8PQ
❂ 11-midnight (1am Fri & Sat); 12-11 winter; 12-midnight Sun ☎ (01573) 420237 ⊕ theborderhotel.com
Beer range varies Ⓗ
A mecca for walkers, this 260-year-old coaching inn is situated at the official end of the Pennine Way and on the ancient St Cuthbert's Way. Those completing the Pennine Way are entitled to a free half pint, a tradition from Wainwright's time. The hotel is noted for its hearty food served in the bar and conservatory. Families are welcome and dogs in the bar only. Free Wi-Fi available.
🏚️❄️🍴◑🅰️👜🐾P

Melrose

George & Abbotsford Hotel
High Street, TD6 9PD
❂ 11-11 (midnight Fri & Sat); 12-11 Sun ☎ (01896) 822308 ⊕ georgeandabbotsford.co.uk
Beer range varies Ⓗ
A spacious hotel overlooking the main street with a comfortable bar and lounges offering real ales from both sides of the border. There is also a small shop selling an interesting selection of bottled beers. Look out for the hotel's beer festivals. Meals are served all day until 8.30pm and families are welcome. Dogs are permitted and there is free Wi-Fi access. Q❄️🍴◑🅰️👜(62)🐾P⅃

King's Arms Hotel ✓
High Street, TD6 9PB
❂ 11-11 (midnight Fri & Sat); 12-11 Sun ☎ (01896) 822143
Caledonian Deuchars IPA; guest beers Ⓗ
Old coaching inn dating from 1793. The bar has a wooden floor and church pew seating, and is decorated with rugby memorabilia and old local photographs. A large-screen TV shows sports events. The quieter lounge is comfortably furnished and has a lovely old carved door set into the ceiling. There are dining rooms upstairs. Families are welcome in the lounge until 8pm. Dogs are also permitted and Wi-Fi access is free. National Cycle Route 1 passes the door.
🏚️Q🍴◑🍽️🅰️👜🐾P⅃

Peebles

Bridge Inn
Portbrae, EH45 8AW
❂ 11-midnight (1am Fri & Sat); 12-midnight Sun
☎ (01721) 720589
Caledonian Deuchars IPA; guest beers Ⓗ
Cheerful single-roomed town-centre local, also known as 'the Trust'. The mosaic entrance floor shows it was once the Tweedside Inn. The bright, comfortable bar is decorated with jugs, bottles, memorabilia of outdoor pursuits and photos of old Peebles. An outdoor heated patio area overlooks the river. The gents is superb, with well-maintained original Twyford Adamant urinals. No children admitted, but dogs are welcome.
❄️🅰️👜🐾⅃

Town Yetholm

Plough Hotel
High Street, TD5 8RF
❂ 11-midnight (1am Fri & Sat) ☎ (01573) 420215
⊕ ploughhotelyetholm.co.uk
Beer range varies Ⓗ
A friendly village inn dating from 1710 set in a rural village near the end of the Pennine Way. A large wood-burning stove sitting beneath two stags heads dominates the bar where the locals are happy to chat with visitors. A separate functional games room has a pool table and video machine. Hearty home-cooked meals are served in the bar and the attractive little dining room. Dogs are permitted in the bar and families are welcome until 8pm. Free Wi-Fi available.
🏚️❄️🍴◑🍽️👜🅰️👜🐾P

West Linton

Gordon Arms Hotel
Dolphinton Road, EH46 7DR (on A702)
❂ 11-11 (midnight Tue; 1am Fri & Sat); 12-11 Sun
☎ (01968) 660208 ⊕ thegordon.co.uk
Caledonian Deuchars IPA; guest beer Ⓗ
The hotel is situated in a picturesque village on the main road from Edinburgh to Biggar. It has a large L-shaped airy bar with stone walls and cornicing more reminiscent of an Edinburgh tenement pub than a village local. There is a roaring log fire in winter and you can relax in one of the comfortable sofas or chairs. Meals are available lunchtimes and evenings during the week and all day Saturday and Sunday in the bar, restaurant or covered outdoor area. Families and dogs are welcome. Free Wi-Fi access. 🏚️❄️🍴◑🍽️🅰️👜🐾P⅃

Learned drinker

He was a learned man, of immense reading, but is much blamed for his unfaithfull quotations. His manner of studie was thus, he wore a long quilt cap, which came two or rather three inches at least over his eies, which served him as an umbrella to defend his eies from the light. About every three houres his man was to bring him a roll and a pot of ale to refocillate (refresh) his wasted spirits so he studied, and dranke, and munched some bread and this maintained him till night, and then he made a good supper.
An Oxford man, William Prynne (1600-69), as described by **John Aubrey** in Brief Lives, ed. John Buchanan-Brown, 2000

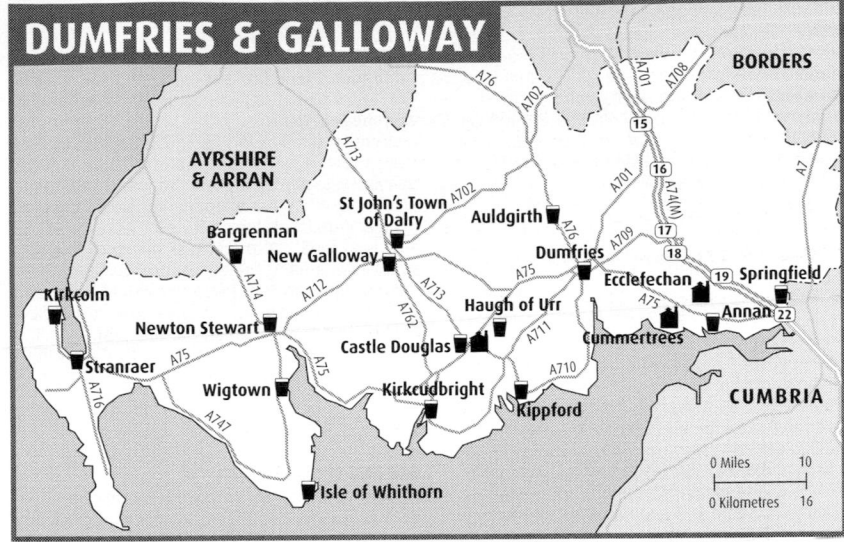

Authority area covered: Dumfries & Galloway UA

Annan

Blue Bell Inn
10 High Street, DG12 6AG
🕓 11-11 (midnight Thu-Sat); 12.30-11 Sun
☎ (01461) 202385
Caledonian Deuchars IPA; guest beers Ⓗ
A focus for cask ale enthusiasts in the Annan area for many years, this pub has won local CAMRA Branch's Pub of the Year title on several occasions. A former coaching inn, the busy, friendly hostelry offers three or four ales from anywhere in the UK. The outside courtyard at the rear provides a pleasant seated area in summer. The pub retains traditional features from its time within the Gretna & District State Management Scheme, notably the wood-lined interior. ⛺≠🚇P⅃

Auldgirth

Auldgirth Inn
DG2 0XJ (next to the A76 Dumfries-Kilmarnock road)
🕓 12-midnight (1am Sat) ☎ (01387) 740250
🌐 theauldgirthinn.co.uk
Beer range varies Ⓗ
Built in the 1500s as a sanctuary for monks travelling from Melrose to Galloway, the building has been a blacksmith's and a fishing bar before becoming a pub/hotel. It offers an impressive range of freshly prepared food using local produce, available Wednesday to Sunday lunchtimes and every evening. Two cask ales are usually on offer from a range of UK breweries. The bar is popular with locals and outdoor enthusiasts, including cyclists, anglers and shooters. ⛺❄🚇◑▶ⒶҨP

Bargrennan

House o' Hill Hotel
DG8 6RN (just off A714 on Glentrool road) NX350769
🕓 12-11 (closed Mon Nov & Feb) ☎ (01671) 840243
🌐 houseohill.co.uk
Beer range varies Ⓗ
Close to the Southern Upland Way and situated within the Galloway Forest Park, this small hotel is popular with walkers, climbers, anglers and cyclists. Fully refurbished, it has an attractive interior including a small function room. Two beers are offered, mainly from Scottish microbreweries, and occasional three-day beer festivals with food and live music are held. The hotel specialises in good-value home cooking featuring locally sourced ingredients as well as home-grown produce. Wood-burning open fires add to the warm and relaxed ambience. Regular music events featuring local artists are held throughout the year.
⛺Q🕏❄🚇◑🕏Ⓐ🚌(359)♣P⅃

Castle Douglas

Sulwath Brewery Tap Room Ⓛ
The Sulwath Brewery, 209 King Street, DG7 1DT
🕓 10am-6; closed Sun ☎ (01556) 504525
🌐 sulwathbrewers.co.uk
Beer range varies Ⓗ
The taproom and visitor centre for Dumfries & Galloway's principal brewery, the bar is popular with real ale lovers in Castle Douglas and surrounds. Six of the brewery's award-winning ales are offered, although not all are in cask-conditioned form, along with two draught ciders. Guest ales from other breweries are available on occasion. Mini festivals are held in May and June, the latter in conjunction with the Food Town celebrations. Q🕏Ⓐ🚌♦⅃

Dumfries

Cavens Arms 🏆
20 Buccleuch Street, DG1 2AH (next to Barbours department store)
🕓 11-11 (midnight Thu-Sat); 12.30-11 Sun
☎ (01387) 252896
Beer range varies Ⓗ

INDEPENDENT BREWERIES

Andrews Cummertrees (NEW)
Madcap Ecclefechan
Sulwath Castle Douglas

Recently renovated and extended, this busy town-centre pub offers three house ales and four guest beers drawn from breweries north and south of the border. Great-value meals are served until 9pm daily except Monday, and occasional themed nights are hosted. Local CAMRA Pub of the Year 2006-2011 and joint winner in 2012. Runner-up Scotland and Northern Ireland Pub of the Year in 2009 and 2010. ◑◮&≈⊟⌐

New Bazaar

39 Whitesands, DG1 2RS (on Whitesands opposite River Nith)

☼ 11-11 (midnight Thu-Sat); 12.30-11 Sun
☎ (01387) 268776

Greene King Abbot; Theakston XB; guest beers ⊞

Former coaching inn beside the River Nith with a pleasant airy bar featuring an impressive Victorian gantry and a warming coal fire in winter. It usually serves four cask ales – two regulars and two varying guests. A favourite with football supporters before and after matches at nearby Palmerston Park, it is also ideally situated for local tourist attractions. There is a good area outside for smokers. The pub may close early if quiet.
⌂※&≈⊟♣P⌐

Robert the Bruce ⌶ ✪

81-83 Buccleuch Street, DG1 1DJ

☼ 11-midnight (1am Fri & Sat); 12.30-midnight Sun
☎ (01387) 270320

Caledonian Deuchars IPA; Greene King Abbot; guest beers ⊞

A former Methodist church, sensitively converted by Wetherspoon. A popular meeting place in the town centre, it has a relaxed atmosphere. Seven cask ales are usually available, including beers from local breweries. Real ale festivals are a regular feature, with up to 40 ales on offer. The food menu is varied, with a range of good-value meals served all day, every day. There is a pleasant seating area outside. Q☎※◑&≈⊟P⌐

Ship Inn

97-99 St Michael Street, DG1 2PY (opp St Michael's churchyard)

☼ 11 (12.30 Sun)-11 ☎ (01387) 255189

Caledonian Deuchars IPA; Greene King Old Speckled Hen; guest beers ⊞

A long-time favourite with real ale enthusiasts in the Dumfries area, this small, traditional pub has up to six beers on handpump. Welcoming to locals and visitors, it has a front bar and small back lounge. No meals are served but toasties are available. The pub is opposite St Michael's churchyard where Robert Burns is buried and 200 yards from Burns House where he spent his final years. Q≈⊟♣P⌐

Tam o' Shanter ⌶

114-117 Queensberry Street, DG1 1BH (off High Street near Burns statue)

☼ 11-11 (midnight Wed-Sat); 12.30-7.30 Sun ☎ 07855 473 933

Broughton Clipper, Exciseman; guest beers ⊞

Well positioned just off the High Street, this 17th-century coaching inn has featured highly in the Dumfries beer scene for many years. The cosy traditional pub has a comfortable public bar and a couple of small quiet rooms. A rotating range of five ales includes three from Broughton Brewery. Dogs are welcome. Q≈⊟♣

Haugh of Urr

Laurie Arms Hotel

11-13 Main Street, DG7 3YA (on B794, 1 mile S of A75)

☼ 12 (12.30 Sun)-3, 5.30-midnight ☎ (01556) 660246

Beer range varies ⊞

Welcoming family-run pub and restaurant on the main street in a charming, quiet location. It has a genuine village pub atmosphere, enhanced on cold winter nights by the warming log fire in the bar. Popular with locals and visitors for its range of ales and good food, up to four cask beers, mainly from small independent breweries, are available depending on the season. The toilets feature an interesting selection of saucy seaside postcards. Former CAMRA Scottish Pub of the Year and joint winner Dumfries & Stewartry CAMRA Pub of the Year 2012. ⌂Q※◑⊟♣P

Isle of Whithorn

Steam Packet Inn ✪

Harbour Row, DG8 8LL (B7004 from Whithorn)

☼ 11-11 (1am Fri; 12.30am Sat) summer; 11-midnight (11 Mon); 11-3, 6-11 Tue-Thu winter; 12-11 Sun
☎ (01988) 500334 ⊕ steampacketinn.biz

Taylor Landlord; guest beers ⊞

Traditional and historic family-run hotel overlooking the harbour and surrounding area, welcoming to locals and visitors alike, including families and pets. The public bar has stone walls and a multi-fuel stove, and there are pictures of the village and maritime events throughout. Four guest ales from a wide variety of breweries are available in both bars. The extensive food menu features local produce – the Sunday hot buffet is a speciality and there are various themed food nights. CAMRA members receive a discount on B&B. ⌂Q☎※⊯◑⊟&⊟(415)♣⌐

Kippford

Anchor Hotel

DG5 4LN

☼ 11-3, 6-11 (midnight summer); 12.30-11 (midnight summer) Sun ☎ (01556) 620205 ⊕ anchorkippford.co.uk

Beer range varies ⊞

Popular sailing centre with fine views over the Urr estuary. Two cask ales are always available, with another added during the summer season, usually from the local Sulwath Brewery. This busy establishment has a dining area serving excellent food from a varied menu using local produce, with good vegetarian options (book ahead for the restaurant). Outside seating overlooking the Solway estuary is pleasant in summer.
⌂Q※⊯◑&▲⊟P

Kirkcolm

Blue Peter Hotel ⚐

23 Main Street, DG9 0NL (A718 5 miles N of Stranraer)

☼ 6 (4 Fri)-11.30; 12-midnight Sat; 12.30-11.30 Sun
☎ (01776) 853221 ⊕ thebluepeterhotel.co.uk

Beer range varies ⊞

A small family-run hotel with two bars packed with memorabilia and, outside, a decked patio for viewing the abundant wildlife – including red squirrels. Two handpumps in each bar dispense a constantly changing range of ales, and occasional mini beer festivals are hosted. Home-cooked food is served at weekends, using fresh and local

produce. The bar is popular with walkers, bird and wildlife watchers and real ale enthusiasts. Good-value B&B is available, with a discount for CAMRA members. Local CAMRA Pub of the Year.
🏠Q🍴🅿️🛏️◑🖤🛜👤🚃(408)♣🍺

Kirkcudbright

Selkirk Arms 🅛 ✅
High Street, DG6 4JQ
◐ 11-11; 12.30-11 Sun ☎ (01557) 330402
⊕ selkirkarmshotel.co.uk
Sulwath The Grace; guest beer 🅗
Traditional hotel with an excellent reputation for meals and accommodation. Two cask ales are available in the lounge and public bars. Outside is a large garden area with tables for the summer months. Kirkcudbright is notable for its artistic heritage and houses a number of interesting galleries and museums. Robert Burns is reputed to have written his famous Selkirk Grace while visiting the hotel, hence the name of the hotel's house ale.
Q🍴🅿️🛏️◑🖤🛜👤🚃🅿️🍺

New Galloway

Ken Bridge Hotel 🅛
DG7 3PR (next to river bridge at head of Loch Ken on A713)
◐ 11 (12 Sun)-11 ☎ (01644) 420211
⊕ kenbridgehotel.co.uk
Beer range varies 🅗
The hotel sits on the banks of the River Ken at the head of Loch Ken, both renowned for good fishing and picturesque views. The owners of this family-run establishment have local connections reaching back through generations. Good freshly-cooked meals are served in the restaurant and bar with two or more cask ales available, usually at least one from the local Sulwath Brewery. A superb centre for water sports and outdoor pursuits or for simply relaxing and taking in the spectacular scenery. 🏠Q🍴🅿️🛏️◑🖤🛜👤🚃🅿️🍺

Newton Stewart

Creebridge House Hotel
Minigaff, DG8 6NP (on B7079, E of river)
◐ 12-2.30, 6-midnight ☎ (01671) 402121
⊕ creebridge.co.uk
Houston Creebridge Gold; guest beers 🅗
Traditional country house hotel set in three acres of gardens and woodland next to the River Cree and close to the town centre. It features two handpumps dispensing a Houston house brew and guest ale or, occasionally, Caledonian Deuchars IPA. Food choices are excellent and locally sourced meat, game and fish are served in the top-class restaurant and adjacent informal brasserie. The bar and lounge areas have real fires. Regular games and quiz nights and open music sessions are hosted. 🏠Q🍴🍴🅿️🛏️◑🖤🛜👤🚃(X75,430)♣🍺

St John's Town of Dalry

Clachan Inn
8-10 Main Street, DG7 3UW
◐ 11-11; 12-11 Sun ☎ (01644) 430241
⊕ theclachaninn.co.uk

Beer range varies 🅗
In a picturesque village, this hotel has an established reputation for excellent food, cosy, well-appointed bedrooms and a welcoming atmosphere. It features an attractive, traditional main bar with a separate restaurant. Two cask ales, usually from Scottish breweries, are always available. A varied menu, featuring local produce including organic lamb and venison, offers excellent daily specials. The Clachan suits the needs of hunters, fishermen, cyclists and all visitors enjoying country life, and is a handy stop for those walking the Southern Upland Way.
🏠Q🍴🅿️🛏️◑🖤🛜👤🚃🅿️🍺

Springfield

Queen's Head
Main Street, DG16 5EH
◐ 5-11 (midnight Thu & Fri); 12-11 Sat; 12.30-11 Sun
☎ (01461) 337173
Caledonian Deuchars IPA 🅗
Although slightly off the beaten track, this single-room village pub is actually little more than a stone's throw from Gretna, wedding capital of the country. It is close to the A74(M) and about a mile from Gretna Green railway station. Just one real ale is served in this friendly, unpretentious local. Note there is no lunchtime opening on weekdays.
Q🍴🛜🚃(Gretna)🚃♣P

Stranraer

Grapes
4-6 Bridge Street, DG9 7HY
◐ 11-11.30 (midnight Thu-Sat); 12.30-11.30 Sun
☎ (01776) 703386
Beer range varies 🅗
Popular, historic public bar with an impressive mirror and gantry, which has altered little in over 50 years. There is also a separate refurbished snug bar, an upstairs function room with 1930s Art Deco gantry and counter, and a small courtyard with tables and chairs. Regular live music is hosted in the public bar on Friday evenings and occasional music nights in the function room. There are two handpumps, although only one ale, usually from the Belhaven guest list, is served in winter. Occasional beer festivals are held. 🍴🖤🚃♣🍺

Wigtown

Wigtown Ploughman Hotel
30 South Main Street, DG8 9HG
◐ 11-midnight summer; 2 (12 Thu-Sat)-midnight winter; 11 (12 winter)-11 Sun ☎ (01988) 403236
⊕ wigtownploughman.co.uk
Caledonian Deuchars IPA; guest beer 🅗
Situated in the centre of Wigtown, Scotland's National Book Town, this is a traditional coaching inn with an authentic cast-iron pub sign outside. It is well placed to explore local attractions including Bladnoch Distillery and the Cradle of Christianity in Whithorn. The comfortable bar with wood-burning stove and games area offers one beer in winter plus a Houston or other Scottish guest in summer. Fine locally sourced food is served in the bar area and adjoining restaurant.
🏠Q🍴🅿️🛏️◑🖤🛜🚃(415,416)♣🍺

I never drink water. I'm afraid it will become habit-forming. **W C Fields**

EDINBURGH & THE LOTHIANS

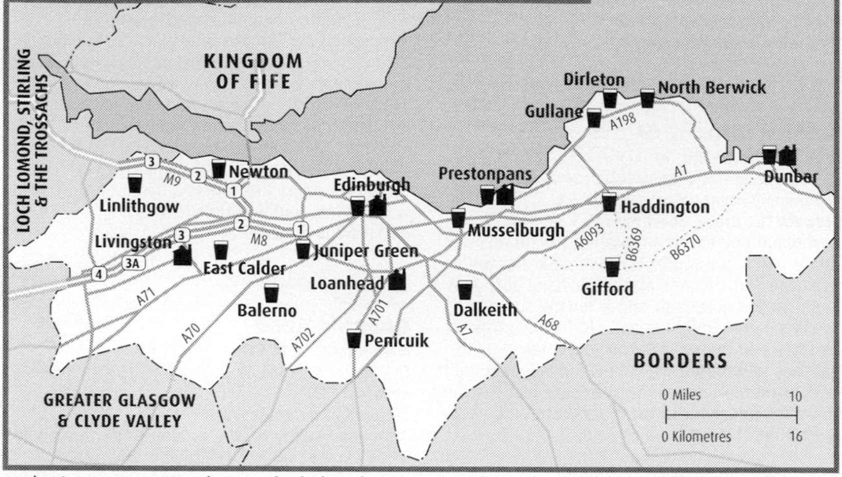
KINGDOM
OF FIFE
LOCH LOMOND, STIRLING
& THE TROSSACHS
Dirleton
North Berwick
Gullane
A198
Newton
Edinburgh
Prestonpans
A1
Dunbar
Linlithgow
M9
Haddington
Musselburgh
Livingston
M8
A6093
B6369
B6370
East Calder
Juniper Green
Loanhead
Gifford
Balerno
Dalkeith
A71
A70
A702
A701
A7
A68
Penicuik
BORDERS
GREATER GLASGOW
& CLYDE VALLEY
0 Miles
10
0 Kilometres
16

Authority areas covered: City of Edinburgh UA, East Lothian UA, Midlothian UA, West Lothian UA

Balerno

Grey Horse

20 Main Street, EH14 7EH (off A70, in pedestrian area)
☼ 10 (12.30 Sun)-1am ☎ (0131) 449 2888
🌐 greyhorsebalerno.com
Caledonian Deuchars IPA; Greene King Old Speckled Hen; guest beers Ⓗ
Traditional stone-built village-centre pub, dating from 200 years ago. The public bar retains some original features with wood panelling and a fine Bernard's mirror. The pleasant lounge has green banquette seating. The restaurant next door is part of the pub so you can have a drink with your meal in the evening. Families are welcome in the lounge until 9pm, and dogs are offered water and biscuits. Free Wi-Fi available. ♨Q❀◑◐⊞☐♣⁻

Dalkeith

Blacksmith's Forge ✔

Newmills Road, EH22 1DU
☼ 9am-11 (1am Fri & Sat) ☎ (0131) 561 5100
Caledonian Deuchars IPA; Greene King Abbot; guest beers Ⓗ
A Wetherspoon establishment with a mixture of differently styled seating areas, including a family area. Although the pub tends to be busy at weekends, it has a reasonably quiet atmosphere. Dimmed lighting helps to produce a soothing ambience, despite the two small TVs and a gaming machine. Meals are served all day. An outdoor drinking area can be used until 10pm. Free Wi-Fi available. ❀◑◐♿☐⁻

Dirleton

Castle Inn

Manse Road, EH39 5EP (off A198)
☼ 11-11 (1am Fri & Sat) ☎ (01620) 850221
🌐 castleinndirleton.com
Belhaven IPA; Caledonian Flying Scotsman, 80 Ⓗ
Attractive 19th-century inn overlooking the village green and opposite the castle ruins. Sympathetically refurbished throughout in 2009, to the right when you enter is a bar area with a small dining space to the rear and to the left is a comfortable bistro area, with meals available all day. A separate spacious restaurant completes the layout. Families are welcome at any time and dogs are permitted in the bar. Free Wi-Fi available. ♨❀⊟◑◐♿Å☐♣P

Dunbar

Volunteer Arms

17 Victoria Street, EH42 1HP
☼ 12-11 (midnight Thu; 1am Fri & Sat); 12.30-midnight Sun
☎ (01368) 862278
Beer range varies Ⓗ
Close to Dunbar harbour, this is a friendly traditional locals' pub. The cosy panelled bar is decorated with fishing and lifeboat-oriented memorabilia. Two real ales are available, usually from smaller breweries, and local real cider. Upstairs is a restaurant serving an excellent good-value menu with an emphasis on seafood. In summer, meals are served all day until 9.30pm. Families are welcome until 8pm and dogs after 9pm. ❀◑◐Å≠☐♣●⁻

East Calder

Grapes

130 Main Street, EH53 0HD
☼ 12-11 (midnight Thu; 1am Fri); 11-1am Sat; 12.30-11 Sun
☎ (01506) 881896 🌐 thegrapeseastcalder.co.uk
Beer range varies Ⓗ
Dating from the 19th century, this traditional stone-built small village local is located on the outskirts of Livingston New Town. The modern

INDEPENDENT BREWERIES

Alechemy Livingston (NEW)
Barney's Edinburgh (NEW)
Belhaven (Greene King) Dunbar
Caledonian Edinburgh
DemonBrew Prestonpans
Stewart Loanhead

interior comprises two rooms served from a central horseshoe bar, and a separate pool room. Popular with the local villagers, the pub serves reasonably priced meals all day, and hosts live music at the weekend once or twice a month. Free Wi-Fi available. ✿◖❾❺◗♣⎔(27,28)♣P⅃⌐

Edinburgh

Abbotsford Bar & Restaurant ★

3 Rose Street, EH2 2PR (city centre)
✪ 11-11 (midnight Fri & Sat); 12.30-11 Sun
☎ (0131) 225 5276 ⊕ theabbotsford.com
Beer range varies Ⓗ/Ⓐ

This traditional Scottish bar is one of CAMRA's Real Heritage Pubs. The magnificent island bar and gantry in dark mahogany have been a fixture since 1902. The ornate plasterwork and corniced ceiling are outstanding and highlighted by concealed lighting. Beers are usually from Scottish microbreweries and there is an extensive menu, with food served all day in the bar. There is also an upstairs restaurant (children over five permitted) where real ale from downstairs can be enjoyed.
Q✿◖◗⇌(Waverley)⎔

Athletic Arms (Diggers) ✔

1-3 Angle Park Terrace, EH11 2JX (1 mile SW of centre)
✪ 11 (12.30 Sun)-1am ☎ (0131) 337 3822
Caledonian Deuchars IPA, Flying Scotsman; Stewart Diggers 80/- Ⓐ; **guest beers** Ⓗ

Situated between two graveyards, the name 'Diggers' became synonymous with this Edinburgh pub legend, which opened in 1897. Banquette seating lines the walls, and a compass drawing in the floor aids the geographically challenged. A smaller back room has a dartboard and further seating. Quieter now than in its heyday, though packed when Hearts are at home, it continues to extend a warm welcome to local characters and visitors alike (but children not usually admitted). Dogs are welcome. Free Wi-Fi available. ⎔♣

Auld Hoose ✔

23/25 St Leonards Street, EH8 9QN (¾ mile S of centre)
✪ 12 (12.30 Sun)-12.45am ☎ (0131) 668 2934
⊕ theauldhoose.co.uk
Caledonian Deuchars IPA; Wychwood Hobgoblin; guest beer Ⓗ

Traditional pub dating back to the 1860s with a large central U-shaped bar and lots of pictures of old Edinburgh. The friendly pub has a wide clientele including students and hosts a pub quiz every Tuesday. The jukebox features metal and punk. Good food is served all day including vegetarian and vegan options, with a 10 per cent discount for students. The guest beer is usually from a Scottish micro. Dogs are welcome on a lead, children are not normally admitted. Free Wi-Fi access available. ◖◗⎔♣

Beehive Inn ✔

18-20 Grassmarket, EH1 2JU (Old Town)
✪ 11-midnight (1am Fri & Sat); 12.30-midnight Sun
☎ (0131) 225 7171
Beer range varies Ⓗ

On the site of a 16th-century inn, the Beehive is a large, multi-roomed pub and restaurant. An upstairs room features the condemned cell door from the old tollbooth. The beer garden is one of the best kept secrets in the city and has great views up to the castle. Meals are served all day. Music and a DJ on Friday and Saturday evenings

caters for hen and stag parties and ensures a lively but rather noisy atmosphere. Comedy club evenings are also popular. Free Wi-Fi is provided. Children not normally admitted.
✿◖◗❺⇌(Waverley)⎔⅃⌐

Bennets of Morningside

1 Maxwell Street, Morningside, EH10 5HT (1½ miles S of centre)
✪ 11-12.30am (1am Wed-Sat); 12.30-12.30am Sun
☎ (0131) 447 1903 ⊕ bennetsofmorningside.co.uk
Caledonian Deuchars IPA; Taylor Landlord; guest beers Ⓐ

In the Morningside area of the City, this cosy tenement boozer has recently been tastefully refurbished. Photographs of old Edinburgh adorn the walls. One of the beers is always on sale at a competitive price. Pub grub is available at lunchtime with an extended menu at weekends. There is a paved outdoor drinking area to the front. Dogs on leads are welcome, but children are not admitted. ✿⎔⅃⌐

Blue Blazer

2 Spittal Street, EH3 9DX (SW side of centre)
✪ 11 (12.30 Sun)-1am ☎ (0131) 229 5030
Cairngorm Trade Winds Ⓐ; **Orkney Dark Island** Ⓗ; **Stewart Pentland IPA** Ⓐ, **80/-; guest beers** Ⓗ

Wooden floors, high ceilings and old brewery window panels give this two-roomed pub a traditional feel, complemented by candles in front of the handpumps in the evening. Named after a local school uniform, there is a blue blazer inlaid on the floor. Close to theatres and cinemas, it stays open later during August and December. The pub specialises in beers from Scottish micros. Dogs are welcome but do not bring the kids. Free Wi-Fi is available. ⇌(Haymarket)⎔♣

Bow Bar

80 West Bow, EH1 2HH (Old Town, off Grassmarket)
✪ 12-midnight; 12.30-11.30 Sun ☎ (0131) 226 7667
Broughton Coulsons EPA; Fyne Avalanche; Stewart Edinburgh No.3; guest beers Ⓐ

One of the first re-creations of a classic Scottish one-roomed ale house dedicated to traditional Scottish air pressure dispense and upright drinking. The five guest beers can be from anywhere in the UK. The walls are festooned with original brewery mirrors and the superb gantry does justice to an award-winning selection of around 200 single malt whiskies. Bar snacks are available at lunchtime. Dogs are welcome but children are not admitted. Free Wi-Fi is available. Q⇌(Waverley)⎔

Café Royal ★ ✔

19 West Register Street, EH2 2AA (E end of Princes St)
✪ 11-11 (midnight Thu; 1am Fri & Sat); 12.30-11 Sun
☎ (0131) 556 1884 ⊕ caféroyal.org.uk
Caledonian Deuchars IPA; guest beers Ⓗ

Identified by CAMRA as one of Britain's Real Heritage Pubs, with one of the finest Victorian pub interiors in Scotland, the room is dominated by an impressive oval island bar with ornate brass light fittings and magnificent ceramic tiled murals of innovators made by Doulton from pictures by John Eyre. The superb sporting windows of the Oyster Bar were made by the same firm that supplied windows for the House of Lords. Guest beers are usually from Harviestoun and Kelburn. Meals are served all day and children are welcome in the restaurant. Free Wi-Fi is available.
◖◗⇌(Waverley)⎔

Caley Sample Room

56 Angle Park Terrace, EH11 2JR (1 mile W of city centre)
🌢 12-midnight (1am Fri); 11-1am Sat; 11-midnight Sun
☎ (0131) 337 7204 ⊕ thecaleysampleroom.co.uk
Caledonian Deuchars IPA; guest beers Ⓗ
Large one-roomed bar with iron pillars and brick walls, resembling the sample cellar at the nearby Caledonian brewery. The real ales are generally from Scottish micros, and there is an interesting range of bottled beers. Food is popular and served all day. The atmosphere is usually relaxed but hots up when Hearts are at home. Families are welcome until 8pm and dogs permitted away from the food area. Free Wi-Fi access. Ⓦⓑ🖪🕂

Canon's Gait

232 Canongate, EH8 8DQ (lower half of Royal Mile)
🌢 12-11 (midnight Fri; 1am Sat); 12.30-11 (closed Oct-Apr) Sun ☎ (0131) 556 4481
Hadrian Border Tyneside Blonde; guest beers Ⓗ
Situated on the historic Royal Mile, this bar is on two levels. At street level there is a comfortable lounge bar with walls adorned with interesting drink-related quotations and observations. A good range of beers is available, many from smaller Scottish breweries, with one always offered at a competitive price. Good food is served all day every day. Downstairs is a stone-floored bar used for functions. Ⓦ⇌(Waverley)♣🕩

Cask & Barrel

115 Broughton Street, EH1 3RZ (E edge of New Town)
🌢 11-12.30am (1am Thu-Sat); 12.30-12.30am Sun
☎ (0131) 556 3132 ⊕ caskandbarrel.co.uk
Caledonian Deuchars IPA, Draught Bass; Hadrian & Border Broughton St Domestic Ale; Highland Orkney Best; Young's Special; guest beers Ⓗ
Spacious and busy ale house drawing a varied clientele of all ages, ranging from business folk to football fans. The interior features an imposing horseshoe bar, bare floorboards, a splendid cornice and a collection of brewery mirrors. Old barrels act as tables for those who wish to stand up, or cannot find a seat. The guest beers, often from smaller Scottish breweries, come in a range of strengths and styles. Sparklers can be removed on request. ✿Ⓦ⑁⇌(Waverley)🖪🕩

Cask & Barrel (Southside)

24-26 West Preston Street, EH8 9PZ (1 mile S of centre)
🌢 12-midnight (1am Fri); 11-1am Sat; 12.30-midnight Sun
☎ (0131) 667 0856
Caledonian Deuchars IPA; Highland Orkney Best; Stewart 80/-; guest beers Ⓗ
Modern re-creation of a Scottish city or tenement boozer. A room with windows front and back is divided by a horseshoe bar with a dark wood gantry, adorned with decorative wooden casks. The walls support a fine range of old photos, framed advertisements and historic brewery and distillery mirrors. A good place to try beers from Scottish breweries, along with some from 'down south'. Children are not admitted. Free Wi-Fi is available. CAMRA Edinburgh Pub of the Year 2012. 🖪

Cloisters Bar

26 Brougham Street, EH3 9JH (SW edge of centre)
🌢 12-midnight (1am Fri & Sat); 12.30-midnight Sun
☎ (0131) 221 9997
Cairngorm Trade Winds; Highland Scapa Special; Stewart Pentland IPA, Holy Grale; guest beers Ⓗ

A former parsonage, this bare-boarded ale house is popular with a broad cross-section of drinkers. Old pews give the pub a friendly feel and a fine selection of brewery mirrors adorns the walls. The wide range of single malt whiskies does justice to the outstanding gantry. Bar meals are freshly prepared from local ingredients (no food Mon or Fri and Sat eves). Dogs are welcome, but no children admitted. Wi-Fi access is free. ⓆⓌⓑ🖪♣🕩

Dagda Bar

93-95 Buccleuch Street, EH8 9NG (¾ mile S of centre)
🌢 12 (1 Sun)-1am ☎ (0131) 667 9773
Beer range varies Ⓗ
Convivial, cosy bar in the university area attracting a wide-ranging clientele. The single room has banquette seating on three sides and the bar counter on the other. The stone-flagged floor is a little uneven in places. The staff are happy to let you try the four ales before you buy, which are usually from smaller breweries. There is also a good range of Belgian bottled beers and whiskies. Fresh ground coffee and quality tea are available. Dogs are admitted, but not children. 🖪♣

Guildford Arms

1 West Register Street, EH2 2AA (off E end of Princes St)
🌢 11-11 (midnight Fri & Sat); 12.30-11 Sun
☎ (0131) 556 4312 ⊕ guildfordarms.com
Caledonian Deuchars IPA; Harviestoun Bitter & Twisted; Orkney Dark Island; guest beers Ⓗ
Large city-centre pub built in the golden age of Victorian pub design. The high ceiling, cornices and friezes are spectacular, as are the window arches and screens. An unusual gallery above the main bar, where the restaurant is located, is also noteworthy. There is a large standing space around the canopied bar plus seating areas to the rear. The diverse beer range includes various Scottish microbrews, with specific breweries regularly showcased. Ⓦ⇌(Waverley)🖪♣

Halfway House

24 Fleshmarket Close, EH1 1BX (up steps opp station's Market St entrance)
🌢 11-midnight (1am Fri & Sat); 12.30-midnight Sun
☎ (0131) 225 7101 ⊕ halfwayhouse-edinburgh.com
Beer range varies Ⓗ
Cosy bar hidden halfway down an old town 'close'. Railway memorabilia and current timetables adorn the interior of this small, often busy, bar. Four interesting beers are usually available from smaller Scottish breweries. Good-quality, reasonably priced food is served all day. The bar may stay open until 1am at busy times of the year. Dogs are welcome. CAMRA members receive a discount of 20p per pint. ✿Ⓦ⇌(Waverley)🖪♣🕂

Malt & Hops

45 The Shore, Leith, EH6 6QU (1½ miles S of centre)
🌢 12-11 (midnight Wed & Thu; 1am Fri & Sat); 12.30-11 Sun
☎ (0131) 555 0083
Caledonian Deuchars IPA; guest beers Ⓗ
One-roomed public bar dating from 1749 and in the heart of 'new' Leith's riverside restaurant district. Wood panelling gives an intimate feel, with numerous mirrors, artefacts and a large oil painting adding interest. The superb collection of pump clips, many from now defunct breweries, reflects the ever-changing and interesting range of guest beers, often from Scottish breweries. Meals are served on Friday only. Families and dogs are welcome. 🏛✿Ⓦ🖪♣

Oxford Bar ★

8 Young Street, EH2 4JB (New Town, off Charlotte Sq)
✪ 11-midnight; 12.30-11 Sun ☎ (0131) 539 7119
⊕ oxfordbar.co.uk
Caledonian Deuchars IPA; guest beers Ⓗ
Small, basic, vibrant New Town drinking shop unaltered since the late 19th century. It is renowned as one of the favourite pubs of Rebus and his creator Ian Rankin, and a haunt of many other famous and infamous characters over the years, so you never know who you might bump into. Guest beers are normally from Scottish microbreweries. A real taste of New Town past, and recognised by CAMRA as one of Britain's Real Heritage Pubs. Bar snacks are available. Dogs are welcome, but children are not admitted. 🖨♣💷

Queen's Arms

49 Frederick Street, EH2 1EP (new town)
✪ 11 (12.30 Sun)-1am ☎ (0131) 225 1045
⊕ queensarmsedinburgh.com
Caledonian Deuchars IPA; guest beers Ⓗ
Basement bar, named after Mary Queen of Scots, divided into two rooms by an impressive copper-topped semi-circular bar. The main area is traditional in style, with a proper bookcase, bare stone walls and an attractive fireplace. The secondary room has unusual booth seating with doors, comfortable leather seats and access to a private dining room. Real ales are always Scottish. Locally sourced award-winning food is served all day. Children are not admitted. ❀ⅅ≉(Waverley)

Sandy Bell's

25 Forrest Road, EH1 2QH (½ mile S of centre)
✪ 12-1am; 12.30-midnight Sun ☎ (0131) 225 2751
Caledonian Deuchars IPA, 80; Harviestoun Bitter & Twisted; Inveralmond Ossian; guest beer Ⓗ
Very much a part of Edinburgh folklore, the pub has been central to the traditional music scene for many years. An arch, the gantry bar counter and wall panelling are all in dark wood, in marked contrast to the atmosphere which is far from gloomy. Folk music plays every night and on Saturday and Sunday afternoons. Bring along an instrument and join in! Dogs are well catered for but no children. ≉(Waverley)🖨♣

Stable Bar

Mortonhall Park, 30 Frogston Road East, EH16 6TJ (S edge of City by camp/caravan site)
✪ 11-11 (midnight summer); 12.30-11 Sun
☎ (0131) 664 0773
Belhaven IPA; Stewart Edinburgh Gold, 80/- Ⓗ
A country pub in the city accessed by a cobbled courtyard. The main bar is dominated by a large fireplace and the walls are adorned with horse brasses and photographs of old Edinburgh. Food is served all day in both the main bar and the dining room to the rear. Do not forget to ask for the Little Miss Muffet seat. The pub has a charity book exchange and a quiz is held every second Friday in winter. Families and dogs are very welcome. ﹢❀ⅅ▲🖨♣P💷

Stockbridge Tap

2-4 Raeburn Place, Stockbridge, EH4 1HN (¾ mile S of centre)
✪ 12-midnight (1am Fri & Sat); 12.30-midnight Sun
☎ (0131) 343 3000
Cairngorm Trade Winds; Stewart Pentland IPA, 80/-; guest beers Ⓗ

A specialist real ale house, this establishment offers unusual and interesting beers from all over the UK and holds occasional beer festivals. The L-shaped room, with a bright bar area, boasts mirrors from lost breweries including Murray's and Campbell's. Plenty of seating is available as well as ample space for vertical drinking. The food menu is excellent (no food Mon or Fri-Sun eves). Children are not admitted but dogs are welcome. Free Wi-Fi. ⓘ♿🖨♣💷

Teuchters Landing

1c Dock Place, Leith, EH6 6LU (1½ miles N of centre)
✪ 11 (12.30 Sun)-1am ☎ (0131) 554 7427
Caledonian Deuchars IPA; Fyne Jarl; Highland Dark Munro; Inveralmond Ossian; guest beer Ⓗ
Converted from the former waiting room for the Leith to Aberdeen ferry, to the front is a comfortable bar with a series of interesting Scottish place names listed around the top. The wood-panelled ceiling is in the shape of an upturned boat. To the rear is a larger restaurant and bistro, with a conservatory extension that opens out onto a pontoon floating on the Water of Leith. Good-quality food is served all day. Free Wi-Fi is provided. Dogs welcome in the bar until 6pm. Q❀ⅅ♿🖨💷

Windsor Buffet

45 Elm Row, EH7 4AH (¾ mile N of centre)
✪ 11 (12 winter; 12.30 Sun)-1am ☎ (0131) 556 4558
Caledonian Deuchars IPA; guest beers Ⓗ
Late-Victorian establishment on busy Leith Walk, significantly altered in recent years. Still very much a locals' bar, it retains a traditional look, but is now brighter and more open plan. The beer selection has recently been expanded, with three guests coming from a range of Scottish breweries. Comfortable green leather armchairs and bench seating throughout complement the extensive wood panelling. Dogs are welcome but children are not admitted. ❀≉(Waverley)🖨♣

Winstons ✔

20 Kirk Loan, Corstorphine, EH12 7HD (3 miles W of centre, off St Johns Road)
✪ 11-11.30 (midnight Thu-Sat); 12.30-11 Sun
☎ (0131) 539 7077 ⊕ winstonslounge.co.uk
Caledonian Deuchars IPA; guest beers Ⓗ
A comfortable lounge bar situated in Corstorphine, just over a mile from Murrayfield Stadium and half a mile from the zoo. The small, modern building houses a warm and welcoming active community pub. The single room is used by old and young alike. The decor features golfing and rugby themes along with historic photos of Corstorphine. Lunchtime meals feature wonderful home-made pies (no food Sun). Dogs are welcome, but children are not admitted. Free Wi-Fi access. ❀ⅅ🖨💷

Gifford

Goblin Ha' Hotel ✔

Main Street, EH41 4QH
✪ 11-11 (1am Fri & Sat) ☎ (01620) 810244 ⊕ goblinha.com
Caledonian Deuchars IPA; Hop Back Summer Lightning; Taylor Landlord; guest beer Ⓗ
A long-established inn near the village green. The focus is on food (served 11-9.30pm) in the smart contemporary lounge bar and conservatories, with light-stained wood and colourful decor, though an area is available for drinking. Gluten-free meals are available. Non diners may prefer the more rustic

633

public bar, with its half-wood, half-stone walls. A games room leads off the bar. Families are welcome in the lounge areas until 8pm. Dogs are permitted in the bar. Live music features occasionally. Free Wi-Fi. ♨☣☎◑◐♿⚏➗♣

Gullane

Old Clubhouse

East Links Road, EH31 2AF (W end of village, off A198)
☼ 10.30-11 (midnight Thu-Sat); 11-11 Sun
☎ (01620) 842008 ⊕ oldclubhouse.com
Caledonian Deuchars IPA; Taylor Landlord; guest beer ℗
There is a colonial touch to this pub, with views over the golf links to the Lammermuir Hills. The half-panelled walls are adorned with historic memorabilia and stuffed animals. Caricature statuettes of the Marx Brothers and Laurel and Hardy look down from the gantry. Food features highly and is served all day – the extensive menu includes seafood, pasta, barbecue, curries, salads and burgers. Families are welcome until 8pm and dogs are permitted. ♨☼◐➗♣⅃

Haddington

Tyneside Tavern ✓

10 Poldrate, EH41 4DA (B6368, ⅓ mile S of centre)
☼ 11-11 (midnight Thu & Sun; 1am Fri & Sat); 12.30-11 Sun
☎ (01620) 822221 ⊕ tynesidetavern.co.uk
Caledonian Deuchars IPA, 80; guest beers ℍ
Dating from the 18th century, this community pub lies next to an old water mill by the River Tyne. On the left on entering is the long narrow main bar, popular for TV sport and boasting a real fire in winter. On the right is the more spacious lounge bar. The pub is known for its excellent selection of guest ales. Hearty, good-value meals are served in both bars and are available all day at weekends. Families and dogs are welcome. Wi-Fi is free. ♨☼◑⚏♿➗

Victoria Inn & Avenue Restaurant

9 Court Street, EH41 3JD
☼ 11-11 (midnight Fri & Sat); 12.30-11 Sun
☎ (01620) 823332 ⊕ theavenuerestaurant.co.uk
Belhaven IPA; guest beer ℍ
A stylish inn overlooking the town square. The focus is on quality food, served all day on Sunday, however drinkers are made most welcome. The cosy bar with its horseshoe counter has bar chairs and two tall tables backing the ground-floor dining area. In summer an outside area in front of the inn is a popular suntrap where you can sit and watch the world go by. Families are welcome until 10pm if dining. Free Wi-Fi available. ♨Q☼☣◑♿➗

Waterloo Bistro ✓

Poldrate, EH41 4DA (B6368, ⅓ mile S of centre)
☼ 12-11 ☎ (01620) 822100 ⊕ waterloobistro.co.uk
Caledonian Deuchars IPA, Flying Scotsman; guest beer ℍ
Lying on the banks of the River Tyne beside an old mill stream, this bistro takes its name from the nearby bridge. An inviting courtyard leads to the bar on the left and bistro on the right. Meals are served all day on Sunday. In summer the courtyard gives a continental feel and is a popular place to sit. Families are welcome, Wi-Fi access is free and dogs are permitted in the bar. Q☼◑♿➗℗

Juniper Green

Juniper Green Inn

542 Lanark Road, EH14 5EL
☼ 11-11 (midnight Thu-Sat); 12.30-11 Sun
☎ (0131) 458 5395
Caledonian Deuchars IPA; Taylor Landlord; guest beers ℍ
Well-appointed, single-roomed lounge bar in a late 1800s building. The decor is clean and attractive throughout, and a strong community spirit exists within the pub. The bar counter is mahogany and a more modern gantry is designed to match. Pictures of the old Balerno branch line provide interest. The food is freshly cooked to a high standard. A secluded patio and garden are popular in summer. Children are not admitted in the bar. Free Wi-Fi. Q☼☣➗⅃

Linlithgow

Four Marys ☐ ✓

65-67 High Street, EH49 7ED
☼ 11-11 (midnight Wed & Thu; 12.30am Fri & Sat); 12.30-11 Sun ☎ (01506) 842171 ⊕ thefourmarys.co.uk
Belhaven 80/-, St Andrews Ale; Caledonian Deuchars IPA; guest beers ℍ
Much commended pub in the main street opposite Linlithgow Palace, the birthplace of Mary Queen of Scots, and named after her ladies-in-waiting. The pub walls are decked with mementos of Mary. The building has seen many uses in its 500-year history, from dwelling house to shop. It holds popular beer festivals in May and October when 20 or more beers from around the UK are available in two bars. Local CAMRA Pub of the Year 2011. ☼◑⚏⇌➗⅃

Platform 3 ☐ ✓

1A High Street, EH49 7AB (just below railway station)
☼ 10.30-midnight (1am Fri & Sat); 12.30-midnight Sun
☎ (01506) 847405 ⊕ platform3.co.uk
Caledonian Deuchars IPA; guest beers ℍ
Small, friendly hostelry on the railway station approach, originally the public bar of the hotel next door. It was purchased and renovated in 1998 as a pub in its own right, and is now closely involved with the local community. Look out for the train that journeys above the bar. One of the guest beers always comes from Stewart Brewing and the other from another Scottish brewery. Live music includes regular folk sessions. Dogs are welcome, with biscuits 'on tap'. ⇌➗♣

Musselburgh

Levenhall Arms

10 Ravensheugh Road, EH21 7PP (B1348, 1 mile E of centre)
☼ 12-11 (midnight Thu & Sun; 1am Fri & Sat); 12.30-11 Sun
☎ (0131) 665 3220
Inveralmond Ossian ℗; guest beers ℍ
Three-roomed hostelry dating from 1830, popular with locals and racegoers. The lively, cheerfully decorated public bar is half timber-panelled and carpeted. A smaller area leads off, with a dartboard and pictures of old local industries. The quieter lounge, where families are welcome, has a hardwood floor and comfortable seating, and is used for dining, with food served all day until 8pm. Dogs are welcome in the bar. Opening times and the menu may vary in winter. Free Wi-Fi. Q☼◑⚏▲⇌(Wallyford)➗♣⅃

Volunteer Arms (Staggs)

81 North High Street, EH21 6JE (behind Brunton Hall)
✪ 12-11 (11.30 Thu; midnight Fri); 11-midnight Sat; 12.30-11 Sun ☎ (0131) 665 9654 ⊕ staggsbar.com
Caledonian Deuchars IPA; guest beers H
Superb pub run by the same family since 1858. The bar and snug are traditional with a wooden floor, wood panelling and mirrors from defunct local breweries. The attractive gantry is topped with old casks. The more modern lounge opens at the weekend. Up to six guest beers, mostly pale and hoppy but always including a darker brew, change regularly. Dogs are welcome in the bar. Local CAMRA Pub of the Year 2012 and winner of many previous awards – proudly displayed on a wall in the bar. ✪❄️🍴🖨️♣️≈

Newton

Duddingston Arms L

13-15 Main Street, EH52 6QE (1 mile W of South Queensferry on A904 Boness/Linlithgow road)
✪ 12-2.30, 4.30-10; 12-11 Fri & Sat; 12.30-10 Sun
☎ (0131) 331 1948 ⊕ duddingstonarms.com
Beer range varies H
Decked out with hanging baskets, this building is easy to spot on the main road through the village – close to a viewpoint over the River Forth and the Bridges. A family-owned business since 1832, the pub has three handpulls serving beers from Tryst, Stewart and Kelburn, with ales from further afield making regular appearances. The pub acts as a gallery for local artists, with pictures for sale. Very much a community establishment, ramblers, cyclists, fishermen and dogs are all welcome. 🚍❄️🍴♿🖨️(474)≈

North Berwick

Nether Abbey Hotel

20 Dirleton Avenue, EH39 4BQ (A198, ¾ mile W of centre)
✪ 11-11 (midnight Thu; 1am Fri & Sat) ☎ (01620) 892802 ⊕ netherabbey.co.uk
Belhaven IPA; Taylor Landlord; guest beers P
Busy family-run hotel in a stone-built villa offering a bright, contemporary interior comprising open-plan, split-level rooms. The lower area is the Fly Half bar and the upper a restaurant. The marble-topped bar counter has a row of modern chrome founts. The middle ones, with horizontally moving levers, dispense the real ales. Food is served all day Friday to Sunday. Families are welcome until 9pm and dogs are permitted. Free Wi-Fi available. ✪🚍🍴♿🅿🖨️♣️P≈

Ship

7-9 Quality Street, EH39 4HJ
✪ 11-11 (1am Thu-Sat) ☎ (01620) 890676
Caledonian Deuchars IPA H; **guest beers** H
Spacious, atmospheric open-plan bar located beneath a tenement block at the leafy east end of town. It is divided into two areas by a twice pierced wall, with pine floor boards, a mahogany counter and dark-wood gantry. The various guest beers tend to be higher ABVs. The pub is popular for food, served all day until 8pm, and the menu recommends a beer to complement each dish. Family-friendly until 9pm and dogs are also welcome. Live music features regularly on weekend evenings. Free Wi-Fi available. ✪🍴🅰≈🖨️♣️≈

Penicuik

Navaar

23 Bog Road, EH26 9BY (just W of centre)
✪ 12-1am (midnight Sun) ☎ (01968) 672683
Beer range varies H
A lively pub with a strong community spirit, situated in an old private house, built circa 1870. The large bar is open plan with a log and coal fire and TV screens for sport. The real ale is usually from Stewart or Fyne Ales. The restaurant, with an extensive à la carte menu, serves meals all day. Snacks are available in the bar. A large patio and decked area is popular in summer. Dogs are welcome. 🚍❄️🚪🍴🖨️♣️P≈

Prestonpans

Prestoungrange Gothenburg ★

227 High Street, EH32 9BE (W edge of town)
✪ closed Mon; 12-3, 5-11; 12-midnight Fri & Sat; 12.30-11 Sun ☎ (01875) 819922 ⊕ thegoth.co.uk
Demon Brew Demon Pale, Fowler's Gothenburg Porter; guest beers A
Superb Gothenburg pub identified by CAMRA as one of Britain's Real Heritage Pubs, with a magnificent painted ceiling in the bar that has to be seen to be appreciated. The pub's microbrewery can be viewed from the bar as you sample the beers. There is also a bistro and, upstairs, a lounge and function room with superb views over the Forth. The walls throughout are covered in murals and paintings depicting past local life. Meals, including gluten-free options, are served all day Friday to Sunday. Families are welcome. 🚍🍴♿🚪🅰🖨️P

Johnnie Dowie's tavern

Johnnie Dowie was the sleekest and kindest of landlords. Nothing could equal the benignity of his smile when he bought in a bottle of ale to a company of well-known and friendly customers. It was perfect treat to see his formality in drawing the cork, his precision in filling the glasses, his regularity in drinking the health of all present in the first glass (which he always did, and at every successive bottle) and then his douce civility in withdrawing. Johnnie lived till within the last few years and with laudable attachment to the old costume, always wore a cocked hat, buckles at knee and shoes, as well as a cane with a cross top, somewhat like an implement called by Scottish gardeners 'a dibble'. **William Home**, The Year Book, 1839. Dowie died in 1817. His Edinburgh tavern was frequented by Robert Burns and Adam Smith.

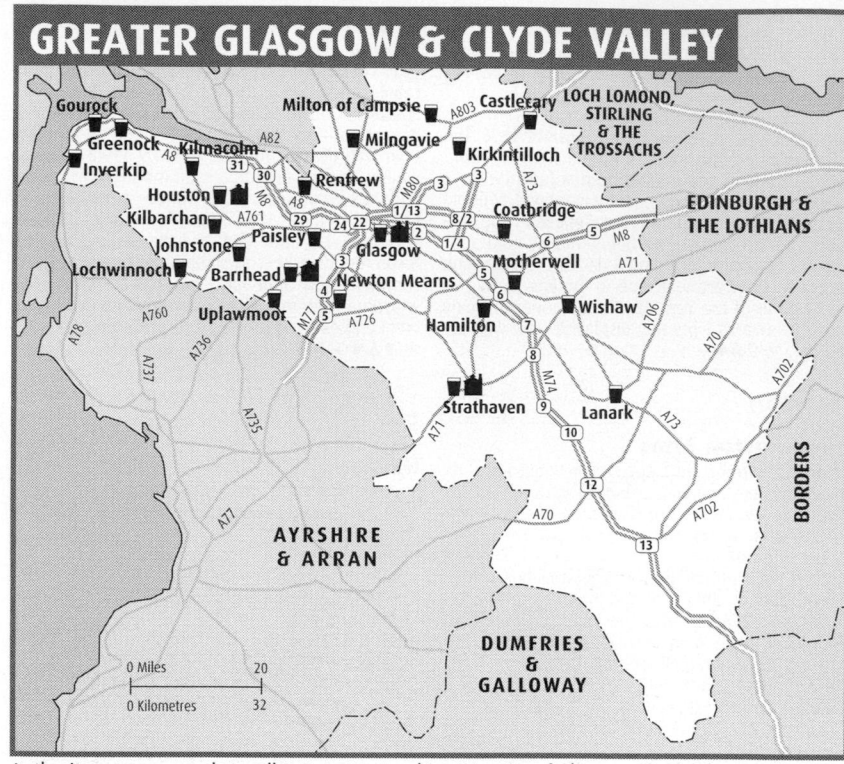

GREATER GLASGOW & CLYDE VALLEY

Authority areas covered: Argyll & Bute UA, Ayrshire UAs, City of Glasgow UA, Dunbartonshire UAs, Inverclyde UA, Lanarkshire UAs, Renfrewshire UAs

Barrhead

Cross Stobs Inn 🅛
2-6 Grahamston Road, G78 1NS (on B7712)
❂ 11-11 (midnight Thu & Sat; 1am Fri); 12.30-11 Sun
☎ (0141) 881 1581
Kelburn Misty Law; guest beer 🆶
Eighteenth-century coaching inn on the road to Paisley. The restaurant leads out to an enclosed rear garden. There is also an outside drinking area at the front of the pub. The bar leads to a pool room and a function suite that can be hired privately. The guest beer is always from the nearby Kelburn Brewery. ♨Q❀◑₲&≠🚆(51,101)◄–🗗

Waterside Inn 🅛
The Hurlet, Glasgow Road, G53 7TH (A736 near Hurlet, on edge of Barrhead)
❂ 11-11 (midnight Fri & Sat); 12.30-11 Sun
☎ (0141) 881 2822 ⊕ thewatersideinn.net
Beer range varies 🆶
Comfortable, friendly bar and restaurant near Levern Water. Food is the main focus here but there is a cosy area with a real log fire for those just wanting to enjoy a relaxing drink. The decor includes old local photographs on the walls. One or two beers are offered from the local Kelburn Brewery range. ♨Q◑₲🚆(103,X44B)P🗗

Castlecary

Castlecary House Hotel
Castlecary Road, G68 0HD (just off A80 near M80 jct 7)

❂ 11-11 (11.30 Fri & Sat); 12.30-11 Sun ☎ (01324) 840 233
⊕ castlecaryhotel.com
Belhaven IPA; Tryst Bottleneck; guest beers 🆶
A large hotel in a small village within two miles of Cumbernauld and near a famous rail viaduct, this establishment has long been a favourite among CAMRA members. A central bar serves three different rooms so look for the blackboard if you cannot see the handpumps. The largest room, the Poachers Bar, is divided into separate alcoves to suit groups of different sizes. Tryst Bottleneck is unique to the hotel – other beers are sourced from English and Scottish micros.
Q❀🛏◑₲&🚆(X37,X39)P◄–

Coatbridge

Vulcan ✔
181 Main Street, ML5 3HH (jct with Dunbeth Rd)
❂ 11-midnight (1am Fri & Sat) ☎ (01236) 437 972
Beer range varies 🆶
Possibly the smallest Wetherspoon in the west of Scotland, and a welcome real ale outlet for north Lanarkshire. It was named after the world's first iron-hulled boat that sailed on the nearby Monkland Canal. Greene King Abbot, Ruddles Best Bitter and Caledonian Deuchars IPA are frequently

INDEPENDENT BREWERIES
Clockwork Glasgow
Houston Houston
Kelburn Barrhead
Strathaven Strathaven

on offer, supported by up to three guests, often from Scottish breweries. Local CAMRA Pub of the Year 2010. ❶❸&≹(Sunnyside)❒(62)❦

Glasgow

Babbity Bowster

16-18 Blackfriars Street, Merchant City, G1 1PE
❸ 11 (12.30 Sun)-midnight ☎ (0141) 552 5055
Caledonian Deuchars IPA; Kelburn Misty Law; guest beer Ⓐ

The bar of this hotel/restaurant offers a welcome retreat from Glasgow's increasingly busy Merchant City. Paintings and photographs are illuminated by large windows overlooking the pedestrianised street. Scottish traditional tall founts dispense a guest ale plus two regulars. Quality bar and restaurant meals feature local produce including game, fish and seafood. Patrons are warmed by a peat-burning fire in winter and can enjoy a game of boules in the garden in summer.
ᐰQ❀❬❶❸≹(High St/Argyle St/Queen St) ❒(Buchanan St)❒P❜

Blackfriars Ⓛ

36 Bell Street, Merchant City, G1 1LG
❸ 11 (12.30 Sun)-midnight ☎ (0141) 552 5924
⊕ blackfriarsglasgow.com
Beer range varies Ⓗ

Traditional corner local in Glasgow's modern Merchant City. Locals, students, city workers, theatre- and concert-goers all keep the friendly staff busy manning five handpumps dispensing Kelburn and other local/Scottish ales and guests from afar. Rare foreign bottled beers and occasional real ciders are also available. Meals are served until 9pm. Events including quizzes, live music, dancing and a comedy club are held in the bar and basement.
❀❶❸&≹(High St/Argyll St/Queen St)❒(Buchanan St)❒(18,62)❦❜

Bon Accord Ⓛ ✔

153 North Street, G3 7DA
❸ 11 (12.30 Sun)-midnight ☎ (0141) 248 4427
⊕ thebonaccord.com
Caledonian Deuchars IPA; Marston's Pedigree; guest beers Ⓗ

The Bon Accord opened in the same year that CAMRA was founded and has promoted real ale ever since. Ten handpumps serve eight guest beers from all over Britain, with regular themed beer festivals. The friendly staff are knowledgeable about both beer and malt – the pub has a large and growing collection of whiskies. Food is available until 8pm, there is music on Saturday nights and a quiz on Wednesdays. But mostly it's about the beer, as numerous Glasgow CAMRA Pub of the Year awards testify.
❀❶❸&≹(Charing Cross/Anderston)❒(62)❦❜

Camperdown Place Ⓛ ✔

4-5 West George Street, G2 1DR
❸ 11 (12.30 Sun)-midnight ☎ (0141) 331 6600
Cairngorm Wildcat; Caledonian Deuchars IPA; Greene King Abbot; Ruddles Best Bitter; guest beers Ⓗ

Comfortable bar situated below street level. This Wetherspoon establishment has a more local feel than many due to its modest size, low ceiling, comfortable upholstered furniture and attractive Tiffany lampshades. Eight handpumps dispense four regular and four guest ales. Wherever possible local beers are sourced directly from the breweries.

Stairs, with wheelchair lift, lead up to the outside area with views of George Square.
Q❀❶&≹(Queen St)❒(Buchanan St)❒❦❜

Drum & Monkey ♟ ✔

91 St Vincent Street, G2 5TF (corner with Renfield St)
❸ 11-11 (midnight Fri & Sat); 12.30-11 Sun
☎ (0141) 221 6636
Beer range varies Ⓗ

Local CAMRA Pub of the Year 2011, this Nicholson corner bar was formerly a bank as the decor indicates. Convenient for both main rail stations and bus routes, it is usually busy. Several diverse areas are created by the long U-shaped counter and split levels within the main room. Diners may prefer to use the quieter rear dining room. From local and national favourites to innovative microbrews, the choice of ales should satisfy even the most eclectic of tastes.
❶❸&≹(Central/Queen St)⊖❒(Buchanan St)❒

Esquire House ✔

1487 Great Western Road, Anniesland, G12 0AU (opp Anniesland rail station)
❸ 11-11 (midnight Fri & Sat); 12.30-11 Sun
☎ (0141) 341 1130
Caledonian Deuchars IPA; Greene King Abbot; guest beers Ⓗ

Newly built smaller-than-average Wetherspoon establishment with the friendly feel of a community pub. It is near a good shopping area and lies on a major bus route to the city centre. The clientele is a mix of locals from the residential area and students from the nearby college. Ten handpumps serve a wide variety of British beers.
❀❶&≹(Anniesland)❒(20,66,118)❦P❜

Granary ✔

10 Kilmarnock Road, G41 3NH
❸ 12-11 (midnight Fri & Sat); 12.30 11 Sun
☎ (0141) 649 0594
Caledonian Deuchars IPA; guest beer Ⓗ

This Nicholson pub is shaped like the prow of a ship. The front room is only open at weekends. Caledonian Deuchars IPA and one guest beer are on handpump at the front of the rear bar, the remaining area is exclusively for dining. A fine selection of foreign beers and whiskies is also stocked. Served by regular buses from the city.
❶&≹(Crossmyloof)❒

Hengler's Circus ✔

351-363 Sauchiehall Street, G2 3HU
❸ 11 (12.30 Sun)-midnight ☎ (0141) 331 9810
Greene King Abbot; guest beers Ⓗ

Sited on a corner near King's Theatre and the School of Arts, this Wetherspoon is patronised by theatregoers, office workers, students, locals and an ever-growing number of real ale drinkers. Friendly staff man the eight handpumps, offering a wide beer range – during the last week of each month a different local brewery is featured. There is a family room to one side and windows view busy Sauchiehall Street and Holland Street.
Q❧❶&≹(Charing Cross)❒(9,44,62)❦

Horse Shoe Bar ★ ✔

17-19 Drury Street, G2 5AE
❸ 11 (12.30 Sun)-midnight ☎ (0141) 248 6368
⊕ horseshoebar.co.uk
Caledonian Deuchars IPA Ⓗ**; Harviestoun Bitter & Twisted; guest beer** Ⓐ

Sited in a narrow street near Central Station and dating from 1884, the Horse Shoe is a Glasgow institution and identified by CAMRA as one of Britain's Real Heritage Pubs, famously claiming the longest continuous bar in Britain with a superb gantry and a mosaic floor. Basic food is available until 8pm. Famous past customers include Keith Floyd and Billy Joel. Frankie Miller and Atomic Kitten have performed numbers in the upstairs karaoke bar, which Travis used as a rehearsal room.
◑ ≹(Central/Queen St) ⍾(St Enoch/Buchanan St) 🚌

Mulberry St

778 Pollokshaws Road, G41 2AE
⏲ 11-11 (midnight Fri & Sat); 12.30-11 Sun
☎ (0141) 424 0858 🌐 mulberrystbarbistro.com
Harviestoun Bitter & Twisted; guest beer 🄷
Friendly contemporary-style family-run bar and bistro in a conservation area, with large windows helping to give a spacious feel even on busy weekends. Outside, the patio is popular on sunny days. Up to two real ales, including a guest from Fyne Ales, are available, supplemented by a small selection of foreign bottled beers. An international menu including Scots specialities is served in both bar and bistro until late. Monday is quiz night. Frequent buses to the city centre stop outside.
❀ ◑ ♿ ≹(Queen's Park/Pollokshields West) 🚌 ⚟

Pot Still 🄻

154 Hope Street, G2 2TH
⏲ 11 (12.30 Sun)-midnight ☎ (0141) 333 0980
🌐 thepotstill.co.uk
Beer range varies 🄷
A cosy city gem, also popular with whisky aficionados who come to sample the world-famous collection of 300 malts. An ideal place for a chaser, with up to four ales on offer from mainly local breweries. A recently expanded range of basic bar food is available. Note the mezzanine corner, iron circular columns, roof beams with ornate cornicing and coloured glass panels, and etched windows.
◑ ≹(Central/Queen St) ⍾(Buchanan St) 🚌

Sir John Moore ✔

260-292 Argyle Street, G2 8QW
⏲ 11 (12.30 Sun)-midnight ☎ (0141) 222 1780
Caledonian Deuchars IPA; Greene King Abbot; Ruddles Best Bitter; guest beers 🄷
This Wetherspoon has a more local feel than is usual for the chain. The wide pavement and patio area outside looks on to busy Argyle Street and catches the sun in summer. An overhead cover is appreciated by smokers. The pub's location close to Central Station makes it popular with travellers as well as city workers, locals and clubbers.
Q ❀ ◑ ♿ ≹(Central) ⍾(St Enoch) 🚌 🍎 ⚟

Sir John Stirling Maxwell ✔

Unit 13B, 140 Kilmarnock Road, Shawlands, G41 3NN
⏲ 11-11 (midnight Fri & Sat); 12.30-11 Sun
☎ (0141) 636 9024
Greene King Abbot; guest beers 🄷
Situated at the southern end of Shawlands Shopping Centre, 'Maxi' is popular with shoppers and local drinkers who keep the 10 handpumps serving up to nine guest ales, mostly from local breweries, continually busy. Cairngorm Wildcat and beers from Kelburn Brewery are especially appreciated. The raised area to the rear is used by families, while outside an awing provides shelter for smokers. ◑ ♿ ≹(Pollokshaws East) 🚌 🍎

Society Room

151 West George Street, G2 2JJ
⏲ 11 (12.30 Sun)-midnight ☎ (0141) 229 7560
Caledonian Deuchars IPA; guest beers 🄷
Modern Lloyds No.1 bar popular with a wide range of pubgoers. In the day, families enjoy meals and silver suppers drain the casks, to be joined later by the post-5pm crowd. Soon, young pre-clubbers add a dash of glamour, before departing to their chosen late night venues. Attentive staff note drinkers' beer requests and try to get favourite ales. A board shows ales on, conditioning and in cellar to inform customers of the beer situation. Weekend evening music can be loud.
◑ ♿ ≹(Queen St/Central) ⍾(Buchanan St) 🚌 🍎

State Bar 🄻

148 Holland Street, G2 4NG
⏲ 11 (12.30 Sun)-midnight ☎ (0141) 332 2159
Caledonian Deuchars IPA, 80; Houston Killellan; Stewart Edinburgh No.3; guest beers 🄷
An island bar blends well with the older dark wood walls and stained-glass panels, providing a timeless feel that belies its relatively recent heritage. Photographs reflect the proximity of the Kings Theatre. Three guest beers are often from Scottish breweries but also from further afield. The lunches are popular and a blues band plays on Saturdays. Downstairs, one handpump lubricates a Saturday comedy club.
◑ ⊟ ≹(Charing Cross) ⍾(Cowcaddens) 🚌

Tennents ✔

191 Byres Road, G12 8TN
⏲ 11-11 (midnight Thu-Sat); 12.30-11 Sun
☎ (0141) 339 7203
Brains The Rev James; Caledonian Deuchars IPA; Harviestoun Natural Blonde; Jennings Cumberland Ale; Marston's EPA; guest beers 🄷
Opened late in the 19th century, many of Tennents' regulars recently campaigned to ensure that the iconic character of the large U-shaped bar was retained in development plans. The bar is adorned with 12 handpumps, four used for guest beers. Good-value food is served all day and TV screens show the big games.
◑ ♿ ⍾(Hillhead) 🚌(44)

Three Judges ✔

141 Dumbarton Road, G11 6PR
⏲ 11-11 (midnight Thu-Sat); 12.30-11 Sun
☎ (0141) 337 3055 🌐 threejudges.co.uk
Caledonian Deuchars IPA; guest beers 🄷
Originally taken from boxing, 'Judges' now refers to the legal fraternity. There is no doubting the appeal of this traditional corner tenement pub at Partick Cross. Customers come to enjoy the eight guest ales from breweries both local and further afield. Several thousand different beers have been served over the past 20 years. A guest cider is available on handpump and an annual cider festival is held. On Sunday afternoons a jazz band entertains customers. ≹(Partick) ⍾(Kelvinhall) 🚌(9,16,62) 🍎

Gourock

Spinnaker Hotel

121 Albert Road, PA19 1BU
⏲ 11-midnight (12.30am Thu; 1am Fri & Sat); 12.30-midnight Sun ☎ (01475) 633107 🌐 spinnakerhotel.co.uk
Belhaven 80/-; guest beer 🄷

Seafront hotel with splendid views over the Firth of Clyde towards Dunoon and the Holy Loch in one direction and Killcreggan in the other. Sit in the beer garden and see the ferries travel from Gourock to Dunoon and back, as well as watching all kinds of sailing boats go by. If the weather is poor, the bay window in the bar enjoys the same glorious view. The Spinnaker has been selling real ale since the 1970s. Q❀✿◑◗≓🚲(901,907,908)

Greenock

James Watt ✅
80-92 Cathcart Street, PA15 1DD
❀ 8-11 (midnight Thu; 1am Fri & Sat) ☎ (01475) 722640
Greene King Abbot; Ruddles Best Bitter; Marston's Pedigree; guest beers Ⓗ
Situated across the road from Greenock Central Station and 200 yards from the bus station, this large open-plan Wetherspoon, in a former post office, is named after one of Greenock's famous sons who improved steam engine technology and has the SI unit of power named after him. The chain's standard value-for-money food is available all day and beer festivals are hosted at various times throughout the year. This pub is an oasis in a beer desert. ❀◑♿≓(Central)🚲(X7,X7A)⌐

Hamilton

George Bar
18 Campbell Street, ML3 6AS (off Cadzow St)
❀ 12-11.45 (1am Fri); 12.30-11.45 Sun ☎ (01698) 424 225
Beer range varies Ⓗ
Traditional, family-run pub in a pedestrianised section with café seating outside, just off a main street. Food is served Monday to Saturday 12-6pm and there is ample seating. On the bar, the three handpumps offer a changing ale range with one frequently from local Strathaven Ales. The railway and bus interchange are a short walk away. A winner of CAMRA Glasgow Branch awards for many years and Lanarkshire Pub of the Year in 2011. ❀◑♿≓(Central)🚲⌐

Houston

Fox & Hounds 🏆 Ⓛ ✅
South Street, PA6 7EN
❀ 11-midnight (12.30am Fri & Sat); 12.30-midnight Sun ☎ (01505) 612448 ⊕ houston-brewing.co.uk
Houston Killellan, Peter's Well, APA, Slainte, Warlock Stout; guest beer Ⓗ
Established in 1779 and home to the Houston Brewing Company. The Fox & Vixen lounge offers the full range of Houston beers including Peter's Well, CAMRA Champion Best Bitter 2011, along with a seasonal beer and a guest, often from an English brewery. A viewing window allows customers to see into the brewery. The Stables bar serves three Houston beers and has multiple TV screens for all sporting occasions. Beer festivals are held every May and August. CAMRA Scotland & NI Pub of the Year 2011. ♨Q◑♿≓🚲(X7,8)P⌐

Inverkip

Inverkip Hotel
Main Street, PA16 0AS
❀ 11 (12.30 Sun)-11.30 ☎ (01475) 521478 ⊕ inverkip.co.uk
Beer range varies Ⓗ

Small, family-run hotel just a short walk from the large Inverkip Marina, making it an ideal staging post for those just messing about on the river or passing through on the way to Largs and the Ayrshire coast. This is the only outlet in the area that regularly sells beer from the Isle of Arran Brewery, with a second beer usually from another local brewery. ❀✿◑◗♿≓🚲(578,580)P⌐

Johnstone

Callum's Ⓛ
26 High Street, PA5 8AH
❀ 11-11.30 (1am Fri & Sat); 12.30-11.30 Sun
☎ (01505) 322925 ⊕ callums-bar.com
Caledonian Deuchars IPA; guest beers Ⓗ
Popular town-centre pub offering a friendly welcome and a comfortable atmosphere. A large but unobtrusive TV screen features major sporting events. The lounge has an area set out for formal meals with themed nights including Thursday curry and Friday steak. There is a function room for private parties. Quiz night is Thursday, live music plays on Saturday and open mic night is Sunday. Six real ales are available mainly from local breweries Kelburn and Houston. ◑♿≓🚲(36,38)

Rennies
8 Collier Street, PA5 8AR
❀ 11-midnight (1am Fri & Sat); 12.30-midnight Sun
☎ (01505) 326486
Beer range varies Ⓗ
Upmarket bar/café decorated in the style of Charles Rennie Mackintosh, famous Glasgow architect and designer. The front lounge is comfortably furnished with low tables and armchairs. The bar leads to a dining area where imaginative food is served. Live music features at the weekend. One of the two regularly changing beers comes from the local Kelburn brewery, complemented by a large bottled beer menu from around the world. ◑♿≓🚲(36,38)⌐

Kilbarchan

Glen Leven Inn ✅
25 New Street, PA10 2LN
❀ 11.45-11 (midnight Thu; 1am Fri & Sat); 12.30-midnight Sun ☎ (01505) 702481
Beer range varies Ⓗ
Ales are from the Punch Taverns list and two-pint containers are popular with locals to take home their favourite brew. The busy local has an open fire with comfortable seating – look out for 'Piper Habbie' above the fireplace. Live music features every Saturday and most Sunday nights plus a quiz on Tuesday evenings. The beer garden is popular in summer for alfresco drinking, with a children's play area available until 8pm. In August a music weekend festival is held with a different theme each year. ♨❀◑♿🚲(36)P

Trust Inn ✅
8 Low Barholm, PA10 2ET
❀ 11.45-midnight (1am Fri & Sat); 12.30-midnight Sun
☎ (01505) 702401
Greene King Old Speckled Hen; guest beers Ⓗ
Popular local pub in the centre of a conservation village. Live music can be enjoyed most Friday evenings and a quiz night is held every Tuesday. Old village photographs adorn the walls. Both guest beers are from the Punch Taverns range.

SCOTLAND

Lunchtime and evening meals are available and children are welcome until 8pm if dining. Locals say fajitas is a favourite dish. A short walk away is the famous Weaver's Cottage owned by the National Trust. ◑&≠(Milliken Park)♍(36)

Kilmacolm

Pullman Tavern

Elthinstone Court, Lochwinnoch Road, PA13 4LG
✪ 11-11 (midnight Wed; 1am Fri & Sat); 12.30-11 Sun
☎ (01505) 874501
Beer range varies ℍ

The only pub in this small conservation village, the building was originally a railway station and is on the Sustrans cycle path between Paisley and Gourock. Seating outside is south facing and a suntrap in summer months, attracting walkers, cyclists and families. The pub is popular with village residents and various local organisations including the drama club. Beers are rotated from the Mitchells & Butlers range and Caledonian Deuchars IPA is often available.
❀◑ ⭙&♍(1,X7)P↩

Kirkintilloch

Kirky Puffer ✔

1-11 Townhead, G66 1NG (next to canal)
✪ 11 (12.30 Sun)-midnight ☎ (0141) 775 4140
Caledonian Deuchars IPA; Greene King Abbot; guest beers ℍ

Near the town centre, the Forth & Clyde Canal and the ancient Roman Antonine Way, this is a large and busy Wetherspoon. Split-level and alcove areas provide space for drinkers and families, with settees in quieter spots to relax in. Pictures of boats including puffers from yesteryear adorn the walls. The four guest ales may be local or from further afield. Food is served until 10pm. There are regular bus services to Glasgow. Q⭧◑&♍

Lanark

Clydesdale Inn ✔

15 Bloomgate, ML11 9ET
✪ 11-11 (1am Fri; midnight Sat); 12.30-11 Sun
☎ (01555) 678 740
Caledonian Deuchars IPA; Greene King Abbot; guest beers ℍ

In the centre of town, this former hotel became a Wetherspoon pub about a decade ago. Since then it has become increasingly popular with locals and is a handy stop-off for visitors to the nearby New Lanark World Heritage Site. Eight handpumps in the bar serve three separate rooms, one primarily for diners and one a family room which is often used for functions or entertainment in the evenings. Beers from Scotland's microbreweries frequently feature. Q⭧◑&▲≠♍♣♠P↩

Lochwinnoch

Brown Bull

32 Main Street, PA12 4AH
✪ 12-11 (midnight Fri; 11.45 Sat); 12.30-11 Sun
☎ (01505) 843250
Caledonian Deuchars IPA; guest beers ℍ

This village pub, a family-run free house, is more than 200 years old and popular with locals and visitors alike. Quiz night is Tuesday and live music features every second Sunday. An ever-changing

choice of three guest ales is offered. The restaurant, situated upstairs, uses local produce and bar meals are also available.
❀✪◑&≠♍♠↩

Milngavie

Talbot Arms

30 Main Street, G62 6BU
✪ 11-midnight; 12.30-11 Sun ☎ (0141) 955 0981
Caledonian Deuchars IPA; guest beers ℍ

Traditional corner bar with modern furniture, popular with locals and also convenient for walkers as Milngavie is at the start/end of the West Highland Way. The staff welcome guest ale suggestions from their regular drinkers. Evening entertainment includes live bands, an open mic night and a quiz at weekends. Three screens show big football matches and other sporting events. Customers regularly play traditional board and card games and local clubs are encouraged.
◑&▲≠♍(8,10)♣

Milton of Campsie

Kincaid House Hotel

Birdston Road, G66 8BZ (signed on B757, just S of village) NS650760
✪ 12-11.30 (1am Fri; midnight Sat); 12.30-midnight Sun
☎ (0141) 776 2226 ⊕ kincaidhouse.com
Beer range varies ℍ

A long wooded driveway eventually leads to an imposing country house hotel. However, the real ales are to be found in an unassuming building to the rear. The central counter serves up to two beers, usually from Caledonian and Houston breweries. To one side lies a pool table and to the other a dining area and fireplace. A large and pleasant conservatory looks out to a child-safe, sheltered garden, a treat in summer. The good food is popular with locals and guests.
❀❀♐◑&♍(X85)P↩

Motherwell

Brandon Works ✔

54-60 Merry Street, ML1 1LZ
✪ 11-midnight (1am Fri & Sat) ☎ (01698) 210280
Greene King Abbot; Ruddles Best Bitter; guest beers ℍ

Busy town-centre Wetherspoon located at the edge of the shopping centre five minutes from the station. The name reflects Motherwell's industrial heritage and a collection of prints in the elevated section to the left recalls the early days of the coal and steel industries and the co-operative and labour movements. A long bar on the right serves up to five real ales and a draught cider. Breakfast and coffee are available from 9am each day.
◑&≠♍♠

Newton Mearns

Osprey ✔

Stewarton Road, G77 6NP
✪ 12-11 (10.30 Sun) ☎ (0141) 639 7453
Caledonian Deuchars IPA; guest beer ℍ

Recently refurbished but retaining its original ambience, this country pub in the heart of the city, overlooking Balgray Reservoir, is a retreat from city life. The interior is open plan, with two large dining areas both enjoying the full effect of a real wood-burning fire. Oak beams and stone floor retain a rustic charm reminiscent of a converted stable block. All areas are served from the central bar area with its expansive seating. The location is ideal for visitors to the nearby Pollok House and Burrell Collection. ≜⊛◑⅏⚷≠(Patterton)➡(44A)P≒

Paisley

Bull Inn ★ L ✔

7 New Street, PA1 1XU

✪ 11-midnight (1am Fri & Sat); 12.30-midnight Sun
☎ (0141) 849 0472 ⊕ bullinnpaisley.co.uk
Caledonian Deuchars IPA; guest beers H

Established in 1901 and identified by CAMRA as one of Britain's Real Heritage Pubs, this is the oldest inn in Paisley. The building retains many original features including stained-glass windows, three small snugs and a spirit cask gantry, and boasts the only original set of spirit cocks left in Scotland. Guest ales are usually Scottish with an emphasis on the local Houston and Kelburn breweries. ≜◑≠(Gilmour St)➡(9,36)

Harvies Bar L

86 Glasgow Road, PA1 3NU

✪ 11-midnight (1am Fri & Sat); 12.30-midnight Sun
☎ (0141) 889 0911
Kelburn Goldihops; Theakston XB H

Popular tenement-style local situated on the main Paisley to Glasgow road. The spacious open-plan bar, with raised seating, has three large TV screens showing sport and music videos with the volume turned down low. The pub can get busy during major football matches. Sunday features a quiz night and Monday is poker night. Live music or a DJ play occasionally. ◑⚷≠(Hawkhead)➡(9,36)

Last Post ✔

2 County Square, PA1 1BN

✪ 8-midnight (1am Fri & Sat) ☎ (0141) 849 6911
Greene King Abbot; Ruddles Best Bitter; guest beers H

Large Wetherspoon converted from the town's main post office. Open plan in design, there is plenty of seating. The standard food menu is available. Next to Gilmour Street railway station and close to the bus station, it is handy for a pint between trains or buses. It was the first Wetherspoon pub to hold a Battle of the Brewers competition and continues to run them regularly throughout the year. Six guest ales are usually available. ◑⚷≠(Gilmour St)➡(9,36)

Wee Howff

53 High Street, PA1 2AN

✪ 11-midnight (1am Fri & Sat); 12.30-midnight Sun
☎ (0141) 889 2095
Beer range varies H

The Wee Howff has appeared in the last 23 editions of the Guide and is a little piece of heaven in an otherwise crowded area of cheap drinking establishments. A small, traditional pub with a loyal regular clientele, the Howff offers up to three guest ales from all four corners of Britain. It has an open mic night on the first Monday of each month and a pub quiz every Thursday. The jukebox caters for even the most eclectic of tastes. ≠(Gilmour St)➡(9,36)

Renfrew

Lord of the Isles

Unit 21 Xscape, Kings Inch Road, PA4 8XQ

✪ 8-midnight (1am Fri & Sat) ☎ (0141) 886 8930
Greene King Abbot; guest beers H

Large, purpose-built Wetherspoon establishment attached to the Xscape Leisure Complex with its cinema, ski slope, rock climbing and more at the Braehead Retail Park. Throughout the pub the walls display photographs depicting the history of industry on the River Clyde. A short stroll allows you to watch the ships docked at Yarrows Shipyard. The outside seating area is south facing and a real sunspot during warm summer days. Food is available all day and three ever-changing guest ales are on handpump. ⊛◑⚷➡P≒

Strathaven

Weavers L

1-3 Green Street, ML10 6LT

✪ 11 (4.30 Tue-Thu)-midnight (1am Thu-Sat); 2-1am Sun ☎ 07749 332914
Beer range varies H

This single-roomed local takes its name from the town's principal trade of years gone by. The interior of the family-run pub has a bright, modern feel, featuring a collection of music and movie star photos on the walls. While most customers come for a drink with friends, the pub is also a meeting place for a wide variety of groups and clubs. It has four handpumps, one exclusively dispensing ale from the nearby Strathaven Brewery. ⚷➡(13)

Uplawmoor

Uplawmoor Hotel L

66 Neilston Road, G78 4AF (off A736)

✪ 11-11 (midnight Sat); 12.30-11 Sun ☎ (01505) 850565
⊕ uplawmoor.co.uk
Houston Killellan; Kelburn Red Smiddy H

Situated in a tranquil village setting about 10 miles from Glasgow, the building dates back to the 18th century. It was originally a coaching inn used by travellers and customs officers chasing smugglers en-route between Glasgow and the south-west coast of Scotland. Today the hotel continues to offer travellers the opportunity to relax and explore. The interior is rustic and cosy, with a separate pool room. Bar meals are served until 9.30pm. ≜Q⊛≜◑⚷⅏➡(395,X44B)P≒

Wishaw

Wishaw Malt ✔

62-66 Kirk Road, ML2 7BL

✪ 11-midnight (1am Fri & Sat) ☎ (01698) 358806
Greene King Abbot; Ruddles Best Bitter; guest beers H

Housed in a former furniture store in the centre of town, this large pub is a welcome watering hole in what is otherwise a real ale desert. The guest beers come from local breweries as well as further afield, and the pub enthusiastically supports Wetherspoon's twice-yearly beer festivals. Named after a 19th-century distillery that fell victim to the local temperance movement, no such impediments limit the enthusiasm of today's customers. ⊛◑⚷≠➡(240,267)◖≒

HIGHLANDS & WESTERN ISLES

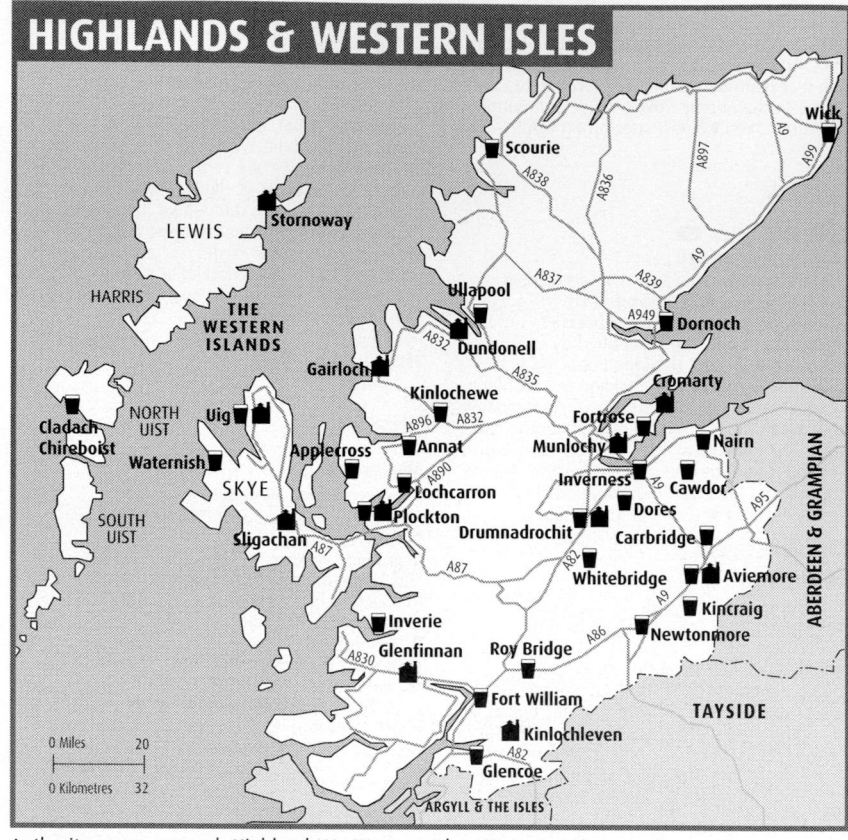

Authority areas covered: Highland UA, Western Isles UA

Annat

Torridon Inn ⃞ ✓

IV22 2EY (close to Loch Torridon)

☼ 8am-11 (Thu-Sat only Nov-Mar); 8am-11 (5 Nov-Mar) Sun

☎ (01445) 791242 ⊕ thetorridon.com

Beer range varies ⒣

One ale from An Teallach is served in the winter and up to six in summer, often from local Isle of Skye and Cairngorm breweries. Real cider is also sometimes available in the summer months. An excellent base for outdoor activity enthusiasts and families alike, it opens early for breakfast and serves good food all day in generous portions, made with locally sourced ingredients. Traditional music features weekly in the summer and there is a beer festival in October. ⌂🛏☼🍴🕙🚻🅿

Applecross

Applecross Inn

Shore Street, IV54 8LR NG710444

☼ 11-11.30 (midnight Fri); 12.30-11.30 Sun

☎ (01520) 744262 ⊕ applecross.uk.com/inn

Isle of Skye Red Cuillin, Young Pretender ⒣

On the shore of the Applecross Peninsula, enjoying views of the Isles of Skye and Raasay, the inn is reached by a single track road over the highest vehicular ascent in Britain, or by a longer scenic coastal route, but is well worth finding. Two Isle of Skye beers are served alongside a large malt whisky selection. Accommodation is available and

local seafood is a speciality. Dogs are welcome and there is a handy 24-hour petrol pump close by. ⌂🛏🍴🕙🚻🅿🚲

Aviemore

Cairngorm Hotel ⃞

Grampian Road, PH22 1PE (opp train station)

☼ 11-midnight (1am Fri & Sat); 11.30-midnight Sun

☎ (01479) 810233 ⊕ cairngorm.com

Cairngorm Gold, Stag ⒣

The lounge bar of this privately owned hotel, though large, has a cosy feel. Though the trade is mainly holidaymakers, the bar is popular with locals, with a large-screen TV showing sport. Decorated with tartan wall coverings, there is a Scottish theme throughout the hotel, and Scottish entertainment features on many afternoons and evenings. ☼🛏🕙🚻🅿🚲

Old Bridge Inn ⃞

Dalfaber Road, PH22 1PU NH894117

☼ 11-midnight (1am Fri & Sat); 12.30-midnight Sun

☎ (01479) 811137 ⊕ oldbridgeinn.co.uk

Caledonian Deuchars IPA; Cairngorm Tradewinds; guest beers ⒣

Busy pub, popular with outdoor enthusiasts, serving good-quality food. Originally a cottage and now greatly enlarged, it lies on the road to the Strathspey Steam Railway overlooking the River Spey. The two guest handpumps dispense the seasonal offering from the local Cairngorm Brewery plus another Scottish ale. Live music features regularly including traditional Scottish music and bands. Children are welcome and there is a bunkhouse attached. ♨✿✍◀❶◐&▲⇌☷(15,15X)P⤙

Carrbridge

Cairn Hotel Ⓛ
PH23 3AS (on B9153)
✪ 11-midnight (1am Fri & Sat); 12.30-11 Sun
☎ (01479) 841212 ⊕ cairnhotel.co.uk
Beer range varies Ⓗ
Traditional Highland inn with seven guest rooms. It is in the Cairngorm National Park and is popular with both locals and visitors. Freshly cooked, seasonal bar meals are available alongside three real ales. Local beers from the Black Isle and Cairngorm breweries are favourites, and the third pump features a different Scottish guest ale with every cask. ♨✿✍◀❶⇌☷♣P⤙

Cawdor

Cawdor Tavern ✅
The Lane, IV12 5XP
✪ 11-11 (midnight Fri & Sat); 11-3, 5-11 (midnight Fri) Oct-Apr; 12.30-11 Sun ☎ (01667) 404777
⊕ cawdortavern.com
Beer range varies Ⓗ
At the heart of this conservation village, the family-run pub is a short walk from the famous castle and within easy reach of local historic attractions. It has a spacious lounge and cosy public bar, both wood panelled with log fires, and a large restaurant. Up to four handpumps offer Orkney and Atlas ales as the family also owns the Orkney Brewery at Quoyloo. ♨Q✿◐◀Ⓖ&♣P

Cladach Chirebost: North Uist

Westford Inn
HS6 5EP (4 miles NW of A867/865 jct) NF781655
✪ 12-11; winter hours vary ☎ (01876) 580653
⊕ westfordinn.co.uk
Beer range varies Ⓗ
A Georgian listed building, set in a remote area of the Outer Hebrides on the edge of the Atlantic. Popular with walkers, shooting parties and tourists, this friendly pub has a traditional atmosphere – no pool table, fruit machines, jukebox or deep fat frier. Home-cooked pub food is available lunch and evenings in summer and there are real peat-fuelled fires. Dogs are welcome. Winter times depend on custom. Ales are from the Isle of Skye Brewery on up to three handpumps, and a good range of bottled beers is stocked. ♨Q✿✍◀❶Ⓖ▲☷♣P

Dores

Dores Inn
IV2 6TR (on B862 from Inverness at jct with B852)
✪ 11-11 (midnight Fri & Sat); 12.30-11 Sun
☎ (01463) 751203 ⊕ thedoresinn.co.uk
Beer range varies Ⓗ
Situated on the south side of Loch Ness just eight miles from Inverness, this inn enjoys spectacular views and is ideal for Nessie spotting. The cosy wood-finished bar serves up to four ales, nearly always from Scottish independent breweries such as Cairngorm, Highland and Fyne Ales, with an

occasional English ale featured. The welcoming, extended dining room serves good food made with locally sourced ingredients and can get busy at times. Home baking is available and the inn opens at 10am for coffee. ♨Q✿◐◀☷(302,303)P

Dornoch

Dornoch Castle Hotel
Castle Street, IV25 3SD
✪ 11-11 (1am Fri; 11.45 Sat); 12.30-11 Sun
☎ (01862) 810216 ⊕ dornochcastlehotel.com
Beer range varies Ⓗ
Upmarket 500-year-old converted Scottish castle situated in the centre of town, famous for its golf course, and opposite a 13th-century cathedral, which makes it a popular venue for weddings. Three handpumps are enthusiastically employed although during the winter season this can be reduced to one. Ales are sourced from Orkney, Cairngorm and the new Cromarty Brewery on the Black Isle. ♨Q⤸✿✍◀❶&▲☷(X99,25X)P⤙

Drumnadrochit

Benleva Hotel ♉ Ⓛ
Kilmore Road, IV63 6UH (signed, 800yds from A82)
✪ 12-midnight (1am Fri); 12.30-11 Sun ☎ (01456) 450080
⊕ benleva.co.uk
Loch Ness Dark Ness, Hoppy Ness; guest beers Ⓗ
Popular, friendly village inn near Loch Ness, catering for locals and visitors. A 400-year-old former manse, the sweet chestnut outside was once a hanging tree. Six handpumps dispense the hotel's own Loch Ness Brewery ales accompanied by other Scottish offerings and two real ciders. Lunches, evening meals and Sunday roasts are available. Entertainment includes occasional quiz nights and traditional music. Home of the famous Loch Ness Beer Festival in September, this is the 2012 local CAMRA Pub of the Year. ♨Q✿✍◀❶Ⓖ▲☷♣♥P⤙

Fort William

Ben Nevis Inn
Claggan, Achintee, PH33 6TE (at start of Ben Nevis footpath) NN125729
✪ 12-11 (closed Mon-Wed Nov-Mar); 12.30-11 Sun
☎ (01397) 701227 ⊕ ben-nevis-inn.co.uk
Beer range varies Ⓗ
Popular with walkers, mountaineers and locals alike, this friendly bar and restaurant is in a unique location, housed in a traditional 200-year-old stone-built barn and warmed by a log-burning stove. There is usually a choice of three ales, mainly from Cairngorm, An Teallach and Isle of

INDEPENDENT BREWERIES

An Teallach Dundonell
Black Isle Munlochy
Cairngorm Aviemore
Cromarty Cromarty (NEW)
Cuillin Sligachan: Isle of Skye
Glenfinnan Glenfinnan
Hebridean Stornoway: Isle of Lewis
Isle of Skye Uig: Isle of Skye
Loch Ness Drumnadrochit
Old Inn Gairloch
Plockton Plockton
River Leven Kinlochleven (NEW)

Skye breweries. The daily-changing food menu is a mix of fresh local produce and innovative international dishes. Live music is a regular feature. Bunkhouse accommodation sleeps up to 20 people. ♨Q☺☕◑&▲P⌐

Cobbs at Nevisport

Airds Crossing, High Street, PH33 6EU (beneath Nevisport shop) NN110742
🌑 11-11 (1am Fri & Sat); 12.30-11 Sun ☎ (01397) 704790
⊕ cobbs-at-nevisport.co.uk
Beer range varies Ⓗ
Convenient for Glen Nevis and at the end of the West Highland Way, this large but cosy bar is a favourite meeting place for walkers, climbers and skiers. Traditional Scottish breakfasts, bar meals and home-baked cakes are served in the bar and the upstairs restaurant where children are welcome. Beers are mainly Scottish, often from Orkney and Isle of Skye breweries.
♨☺◑&▲⇌🚊⌐

Grog & Gruel 🄻 ✔

66 High Street, PH33 6AE
🌑 12-11.30 (12.30am Thu-Sat); 12.30 (5 winter)-11.30 Sun
☎ (01397) 705078 ⊕ grogandgruel.co.uk
Beer range varies Ⓗ
This traditional ale house has featured in the Guide since 1994. It keeps up to six beers in summer, fewer in winter, usually Scottish, often including something from Glenfinnan and River Leven breweries. The bar is busy with locals, tourists and outdoor enthusiasts. Light meals and snacks are available all day in the bar, and evening meals in the upstairs restaurant. Events includes regular live music, open mic nights and beer festivals. ☺◑▲⇌🚊⌐

Fortrose

Anderson

Union Street, IV10 8TD
🌑 4 (12.30 Sun)-11.30 ☎ (01381) 620236
⊕ theanderson.co.uk
Beer range varies Ⓗ
The owners are an international beer writer and self-confessed beer geek, and his wife, a New Orleans-trained chef. Serving ale and cider from more than 250 breweries since 2003, this beer drinkers' mecca also offers more than 240 malts and 100 Belgian beers. Entertainment includes winter beer festivals, regular quizzes, music sessions and knitting nights. Food is reasonably priced, high-quality international cuisine. CAMRA members are offered a discount on accommodation in winter.
♨☺☕◑🍴▲🚊(26)♣♦P⌐

Glencoe

Clachaig Inn 🄻 ✔

PH49 4HX (on slip road ½ mile off A82) NN128567
🌑 11-11 (11.30 Fri; midnight Sat); 12.30-11 Sun
☎ (01855) 811 252 ⊕ clachaig.com
Beer range varies Ⓗ
Serving mainly local ale from 16 handpumps plus occasional real cider in the large, rustic Boots Bar, this is a popular destination for climbers and outdoor enthusiasts. Ales are also available in the comfortable Bidean Lounge, with good pub grub on offer throughout, as well as regular beer festivals and live music. There are 23 well-

appointed en-suite bedrooms for overnight stays to enjoy the peaceful location and dramatic scenery. ♨Q☺☕◑ 🍴&▲🚊(916)♦P⌐

Inverie

Old Forge

PH41 4PL (100yds from ferry terminal)
🌑 11am (3 winter)-11 Mon & Wed; 3-11 Tue & Thu; 12-midnight Fri & Sat; 1-11 Sun ☎ (01678) 462267
⊕ theoldforge.co.uk
Beer range varies Ⓗ
The most remote pub in mainland Britain can be reached only by a seven-mile ferry crossing from Mallaig or a 16-mile hilly walk. In a spectacular setting on the shore of Loch Nevis, it provides an ideal location for walking the rough bounds of Knoydart. Moorings welcome waterborne visitors. Two handpumps usually include a beer from Isle of Skye or Glenfinnan breweries. Excellent food is served all day featuring locally caught seafood and game, with roasts on Sunday. ♨Q☺◑▲⌐

Inverness

Blackfriars 🄻 ✔

93-95 Academy Street, IV1 1LU
🌑 11-midnight (1am Fri; 12.30am Sat); 1-9 (closed Nov-Feb) Sun ☎ (01463) 233881 ⊕ blackfriarshighlandpub.co.uk
Beer range varies Ⓗ
This popular traditional pub has a spacious single-room interior with a large standing area by the bar and ample seating in comfortable alcoves. The five handpumps celebrate Scottish beers, often from Inveralmond, Orkney and Highland. Local ales are from Loch Ness, Cairngorm and An Teallach. Good-value home-cooked Scottish fare is served with daily specials. A welcoming music-oriented venue, with bands performing at weekends. ◑&⇌🚊

Castle Tavern 🄻

1 View Place, IV2 4SA (top of Castle Street) NH666449
🌑 11-1am (12.30am Sat); 12.30-midnight Sun
☎ (01463) 718178 ⊕ castletavern.net
Cairngorm Trade Winds; guest beers Ⓗ
A warm welcome is assured at this cosy city-centre pub that has all the friendliness of a village local. A Victorian-style canopy covers the large beer patio that overlooks the end of the Great Glen Way and has impressive views over the River Ness. Bar meals are served all day, and there is a restaurant on the first floor. Six handpumps dispense a changing selection of mostly Scottish beers, often including a house ale from the Isle of Skye Brewery. ☺◑▲⇌🚊(6,7,14)⌐

Clachnaharry Inn

17-19 High Street, Clachnaharry, IV3 8RB (on A862 Beauly Road) NH648466
🌑 11-1am; 12-11.45 Sun ☎ (01463) 239806
⊕ clachnaharryinn.co.uk
Beer range varies Ⓗ
Popular with locals and visitors, this friendly 17th-century coaching inn offers high-quality food made with locally sourced ingredients lunchtimes and evenings, and families are welcome. Five handpumps dispense Scottish beers from Inveralmond, Orkney/Atlas and Cairngorm as well as some from Greene King breweries. The large patio area affords fine views over the Caledonian Canal sea lock and Beauly Firth toward the Munro Ben Wyvis. ♨Q☺◑ 🍴&▲🚊(28A)♣P

King's Highway ✅
72-74 Church Street, IV1 1EN
✪ 11-midnight (1am Thu & Fri); 12.30-11 Sun
☎ (01463) 251830
Caledonian Deuchars IPA; Greene King Abbot; guest beers Ⓗ
This former hotel is now a Wetherspoon pub with a 27-room lodge attached. The vast single-roomed bar is broken up by several pillars and plenty of comfortable seating in alcoves. Up to 10 handpumps serve the regular ales alongside a good mix of guests, including beers from Houston, Cairngorm and An Teallach. Real cider is also available. Food is standard Wetherspoon, with breakfasts served from 7am. Customers are the typical eclectic mix and the pub gets busy at weekends. ♨◑&⚡☒♦

Snowgoose ✅
Stoneyfield, IV2 7PA (on A96)
✪ 12-11 (10.30 Sun-Thu Jan-Mar) ☎ (01463) 701921
Caledonian Deuchars IPA; guest beers Ⓗ
This traditional inn supports a popular, mostly local, bar trade, with an area reserved for drinkers. A converted 1788 coach house, the single large L-shaped room has alcoves and log fires to give it a more cosy and intimate feel. A wide variety of food is offered all day at reasonable prices. The two guest handpumps feature ever-changing ales from the Mitchells & Butlers Vintage Inn list.
♨Q❄◑&⚡(1,10)Pᐧ

Kincraig

Suie Hotel Ⓛ
PH21 1NA
✪ 5-11 (1am Fri & Sat) ☎ (01540) 651344 ⊕ suiehotel.com
Cairngorm Trade Winds; guest beers Ⓗ
Victorian character hotel located at the south end of the village, run by only the second owner in 108 years. The wooden-floored bar features a large wood-burning stove plus a pool table and jukebox. Up to two guest pumps dispense a selection from the local Cairngorm Brewery. Close to the River Spey and Loch Insh, the bar is popular with locals, hillwalkers, skiers and cyclists. Traditional Scottish music features occasionally. Good food is served.
♨❄⚡◑⚡(209)♣Pᐧ

Kinlochewe

Kinlochewe Hotel Ⓛ
IV22 2PA NH028619
✪ 11-11 ☎ (01445) 760253 ⊕ kinlochewehotel.co.uk
Beer range varies Ⓗ
The ambience in this refurbished bar is friendly and welcoming. Freshly cooked food uses the best of seasonal high-quality local produce, including seafood, game and beef, with an emphasis on simplicity and flavour. Set in the heart of the magnificent Torridon Mountains at the foot of Beinn Eighe, this is an ideal base for exploring the wild scenery of the North Western Highlands. Up to five handpumps serve ales from An Teallach and Orkney. ♨Q♨◑▲⚡♦P

Lochcarron

Lochcarron Hotel
Main Street, IV54 8YS
✪ 11 (12.30 Sun)-1am ☎ (01520) 722226
⊕ lochcarronhotel.com

Beer range varies Ⓗ
With magnificent views across upper Loch Carron, this family-run hotel offers a pleasant, comfortable bar opening on to a spacious dining area. One English and two Scottish ales, usually from Isle of Skye and Cairngorm, plus a varied food menu featuring local ingredients, make a visit well worth while. The hotel is an ideal base for exploring the beautiful west coast of Scotland as well as walking and climbing numerous hills and Munros. Breakfast is served from 7am.
♨Q♨☒◑&⚡(164,702,704)Pᐧ

Nairn

Braeval Hotel Ⓛ ✅
Crescent Road, IV12 4NB
✪ 12-midnight (12.30am Thu-Sat); 5-midnight Mon & Tue Jan-Mar; 12.30-midnight Sun ☎ (01667) 452341
⊕ braevalhotel.co.uk
Beer range varies Ⓗ /Ⓖ
The award-winning Bandstand Bar is part of the Braeval Hotel, close to Nairn beach. It has up to nine handpumps offering a wide selection of Scottish ales, often from Cairngorm and Highland, as well as a range of English ales and a Westons cider. The restaurant in this family-run hotel enjoys spectacular sea views overlooking the Moray Firth. The bar hosts a beer festival every spring featuring at least 60 ales. CAMRA Highlands & Western Isles Pub of the Year 2009 and 2011.
Q♨❄⚡◑&▲⚡☒♦Pᐧ⚁

Newtonmore

Glen Hotel Ⓛ ✅
Main Street, PH20 1DD
✪ 11 (12.30 Sun)-midnight ☎ (01540) 673203
⊕ theglenhotel.co.uk
Beer range varies Ⓗ
Small, welcoming, family-run Edwardian hotel with the Monadhliath and Cairngorm mountain ranges on its doorstep. It has a good local trade and is also popular with outdoor enthusiasts and tourists. There is a large bar room and separate games and dining rooms, and regular quiz and games nights are held. Up to four handpumps dispense mainly Scottish beers, usually including one from Cairngorm and Caledonian breweries, plus a Westons cider or perry. An extensive menu includes a good selection of vegetarian dishes.
♨❄⚡◑&▲☒♦Pᐧ

Plockton

Plockton Inn Ⓛ ✅
Innes Street, IV52 8TW NG803333
✪ 11-1am (12.30am Sat; 11 Sun) ☎ (01599) 544222
⊕ plocktoninn.co.uk
Plockton Plockton Bay; guest beers Ⓗ
Located in a picture postcard Highland village, this popular inn has been owned and run by a local family for many years. Locally caught fish and shellfish take pride of place on the menu – the seafood platter includes fish smoked on the premises. Every Tuesday and Thursday there are live music sessions in the public bar and all are welcome to join in. A regularly changing selection of real ales includes locally brewed Plockton Brewery beers. ♨Q♨❄⚡◑&≷♣Pᐧ

Roy Bridge

Stronlossit Inn ✓

PH31 4AG

☼ 11-11.45 (1am Thu-Sat); 12.30-11.45 Sun
☎ (01397) 712253 ⊕ stronlossit.co.uk
Beer range varies Ⓗ

An ideal base for outdoor activities or touring the Highlands. Bar meals featuring local seasonal produce are available all day. The three handpumps dispense a selection of Scottish beers, often from Highlands and Islands breweries, and an occasional cider. Opening times vary in December and January. Budget accommodation is available alongside standard rooms.
🏨🌠🛏️🕪🍴🚃🚐🐾Pⁿ⇐

Scourie

Scourie Hotel Ⅼ

IV27 4SX (on A894 between Laxford Bridge and Kylesku)

☼ 11-2.30, 5-11; 12-2.30 Sat summer; 5-9.30 (10.30 Fri; 11 Sat) winter; 12-2.30, 6-10.30 Sun ☎ (01971) 502396
⊕ scourie-hotel.co.uk
Beer range varies Ⓗ

Fabulously remote hotel in the picturesque village of Scourie, 25 miles south of Cape Wrath. It lies close to the bird reserve of Handa Island and the peaks of Arkle and Foinavon, and has numerous fishing beats held exclusively for guests. The dining room serves high quality four-course meals featuring seafood, and lunchtime meals are available in the bars. Four handpumps in summer, fewer in winter, serve Scottish beers and one cider.
Q🌠🛏️🕪🍴🐾Pⁿ⇐

Uig: Isle of Skye

Bakur Bar Ⅼ

The Pier, IV51 9XX

☼ 11.30-11 (midnight Thu; 1am Fri; 12.30am Sat); 12.30-11.30 Sun ☎ (01470) 542212
Isle of Skye Red Cuillin, Black Cuillin; guest beers Ⓗ

Traditional West Coast bar conveniently located on the pier at Uig adjacent to the Western Isles ferry terminal and a stone's throw from the Isle of Skye Brewery, which supplies all the pub's ales. During the summer months up to four beers are available, with a more limited range in the quieter winter season. The Bakur also has a pool table and is popular with the locals. 🌠🕪🍴🚐Pⁿ⇐

Ullapool

Argyll Hotel Ⅼ ✓

18 Argyll Street, IV26 2UB

☼ 11-1am (midnight Sat); 12.30-11.30 Sun
☎ (01854) 612422 ⊕ theargyllullapool.com
Beer range varies Ⓗ

Busy, small hotel offering breakfast, lunch and dinner all made with locally sourced produce wherever possible. The beer range includes a changing English guest plus another from An Teallach. Live music features on Monday, and regular live bands play on Tuesday and Saturday. Weekly quiz and poker nights keep the lounge bar busy. A pool table is available through the back, and a dartboard in the public bar. Dogs are welcome. Hours can vary out of season.
🏨🌠🛏️🕪🍴🚐🐾Pⁿ⇐

Morefield Motel Ⅼ

North Road, IV26 2TQ (off A835) NH125947

☼ 12 (12.30 Sun)-11 ☎ (01854) 612161
⊕ morefieldmotel.co.uk
Beer range varies Ⓗ

Locally-caught seafood is the speciality on the menu and the three ales are predominantly from local Highland breweries at this friendly and welcoming hostelry. The annual Ullapool Beer Festival is held here in October. The Western Isles ferry terminal in the centre of Ullapool is a short distance away. Afternoon opening can be subject to seasonal variation. Q🌠🛏️🕪🍴🐾🚃🐾Pⁿ⇐

Waternish: Isle of Skye

Stein Inn ✓

Waternish, IV55 8GA (N of Dunvegan, on B886) NG263564

☼ 11-midnight (1am Fri; 12.30am Sat) summer; 12-11 (midnight Fri & Sat) winter; 11.30 (12.30 winter)-11 Sun
☎ (01470) 592362 ⊕ steininn.co.uk
Beer range varies Ⓗ

Traditional family-run pub, the oldest on the Isle of Skye, in a beautiful setting among a smattering of whitewashed cottages strung along the shores of Loch Bay. Locally caught seafood, landed at the nearby jetty, is served in the bar and restaurant. Facilities for seafarers include council moorings, showers, food supplies (by arrangement) and message relay services. 🏨Q🛥️🌠🛏️🕪🍴🐾Pⁿ⇐

Whitebridge

Whitebridge Hotel Ⅼ

IV2 6UN

☼ 11-11 (11-2.30, 5-11 Nov-Mar); 12.30-11 Sun
☎ (01456) 486226 ⊕ whitebridgehotel.co.uk
Beer range varies Ⓗ

Built in 1899, this hotel has fishing rights on two local lochs. Inside, the attractive pitch pine panelled bar, with a welcoming wood-burning stove, has an alcove with a pool table and a separate area used for dining. Most of the traditional pub food is home cooked. One or two ales are stocked, usually from Cairngorm and Isle of Skye. The hotel has a green tourism policy.
🏨Q🌠🛏️🕪🍴🚐🐾P

Wick

Alexander Bain ✓

Market Place, KW1 4LP

☼ 11-midnight (1am Fri & Sat); 12.30-11.45 Sun
☎ (01955) 609920
Caledonian Deuchars IPA; Greene King Abbot; guest beers Ⓗ

A former post office, this is the most northerly Wetherspoon, named after a local man who invented the electric clock in 1841. Bright and welcoming, the pub has comfortable alcoves, seating in the spacious bar area and a licensed outdoor space. The majority of guest ales are shipped across from the nearby Orkney Isles. Food is from the standard Wetherspoon menu and breakfast is available from 7am.
🏨🛥️🌠🕪🍴(X97,81,82)🐾⇐

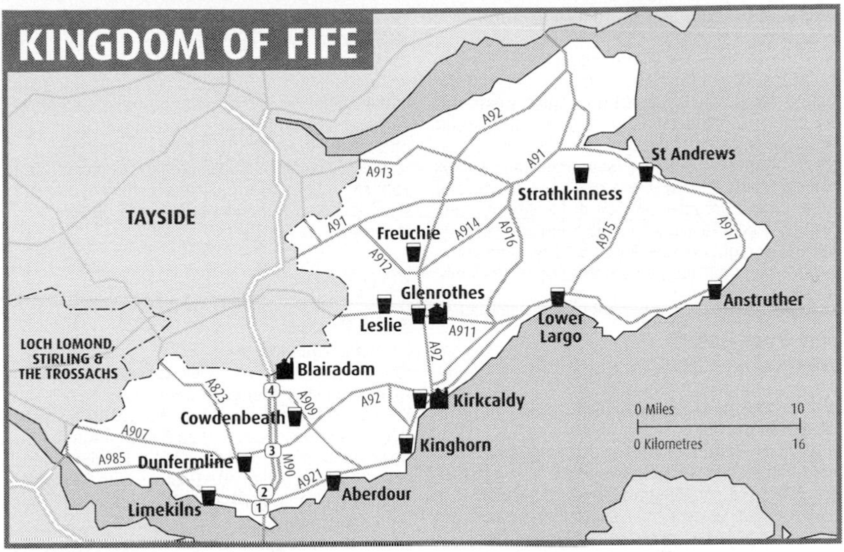
KINGDOM OF FIFE
TAYSIDE
LOCH LOMOND, STIRLING & THE TROSSACHS
St Andrews
Strathkinness
Freuchie
Glenrothes
Leslie
Lower Largo
Anstruther
Blairadam
Kirkcaldy
Cowdenbeath
Kinghorn
Dunfermline
Aberdour
Limekilns
A92
A91
A913
A914
A916
A912
A915
A917
A911
A823
A909
A907
A985
A921
M90
0 Miles 10
0 Kilometres 16

Authority area covered: Fife UA

Aberdour

Cedar Inn ✔

20 Shore Road, KY3 0TR

⌚ 11 (12.30 Sun)-11.45 ☎ (01383) 860310

🌐 thecedarinn.co.uk

Caledonian Deuchars IPA; guest beers Ⓗ

To the right through the front door is a quiet bar where you will find the real ale handpumps and a range of whiskies. Carry on and you will come to another bar with a band area where live music plays every other Friday. On the wall is a lovely Alloa Brewery mirror as well as two TVs. To the left as you enter is a comfortable lounge bar with a centrally situated Cotswold-stone fireplace. Meals are served in the lounge and a separate restaurant, and bar snacks are available.

⛰❀⛟◑⊟≹⊟(7,7A)P⁵–

Anstruther

Dreel Tavern

16 High Street, KY10 3DL

⌚ 11 (12.30 Sun)-midnight ☎ (01333) 310727

Caledonian Deuchars IPA; guest beers Ⓗ

A former Fife CAMRA Pub of the Year, situated in an old fishing village with links to James IV, the Dreel is an old stone building with traditional crow-step gables and a pantile roof. Wood panelling and stone walls with an ornamental stove at one end of the bar all add to a cosy atmosphere. The games room has a pool table and the conservatory to the rear provides home-cooked meals. The pub has now inherited a piano and hosts music nights on the second Friday of the month.

⛰Q❀◑⊟⊟(X60,95)♣⁵–

Ship Tavern

49 Shore Street, KY10 3AQ (next to Scottish Fisheries Museum)

⌚ 11-midnight (1am Fri & Sat); 12.30-midnight Sun

☎ (01333) 310347

Beer range varies Ⓗ

This old, traditional pub on the harbour front is a popular meeting place for fishermen, locals and visitors to the museum next door. The main bar has a flagstone floor and a picture window overlooking the busy harbour, next door to the famous Anstruther Fish & Chip Restaurant. Above the mirror behind the bar, covering two walls, is a mural of the harbour. A back room has a pool table. Ales from microbreweries often feature, including the pub's own house beer, The Reaper Ale from Harviestoun, named after the Fifie herring drifter.

⊟⊟(X60,95)♣

Cowdenbeath

Woodside Hotel

109 Broad Street, KY4 8JR

⌚ 11 (12.30 Sun)-midnight ☎ (01383) 511598

🌐 woodsidehotelcowdenbeath.co.uk

Beer range varies Ⓗ

Large single-roomed bar with two handpumps serving ales from local and north of England microbreweries in lined glasses. On one side of the room are a pool table and dartboard, and four plasma screens show sport. A warm, friendly atmosphere prevails, with poker played on Thursday night and live entertainment at the weekend. A separate lounge is available for small functions, and bar lunches are served Thursday to Saturday. There is a covered, decked area with seating outside, which is a lovely suntrap in summer. ❀⛟◐⊟♿≹⊟(19,17,X54)♣P⁵–⊟

Dunfermline

Commercial Inn

13 Douglas Street, KY12 7EB

⌚ 11-11 (midnight Fri & Sat); 12.30-11 Sun

☎ (01383) 733876

INDEPENDENT BREWERIES

Fyfe Kirkcaldy
Loch Leven Blairadam
St Andrews Glenrothes (NEW)

Caledonian Deuchars IPA, 80; Courage Directors; guest beers H
Well-known ale house in a building dating back to the 1820s, situated opposite the post office off the High Street. A cosy town-centre establishment, this is a place for conversation, with quiet background music. Good-quality food and friendly service attract an eclectic clientele. Seven ales are always available, plus a cider at times. An extensive food menu includes regular specials at lunchtime, and evening meals Tuesday-Thursday and Saturday, with steak night on Tuesday and curry night on Wednesday. A former Fife CAMRA Pub of the Year. ⊕♨♠

East Port Bar ✅
7 East Port, KY12 7JG
☼ 11.30-11 (midnight Fri & Sat); 11-11 Sun
☎ (01383) 736678 ⊕ eastportbar.co.uk
Caledonian Deuchars IPA H
Busy town-centre pub with welcoming staff who pride themselves on friendly service. The interior features wood panelling and a wood bar and gantry, alcove seating and comfortable sofas at the rear. An old Maclay mirror decorates the stairs leading to the beer garden. Two plasma screens show sport, from football to golf, and soft background music usually plays. Value-for-money bar food is served 12-3pm. The pub received a Best Bar None award every year 2008-2011 from Fife Constabulary. ❀⊕♿♠♨'-

Freuchie
Albert Tavern
2 High Street, KY15 7EX
☼ 5 (12 Fri & Sat; 12.30 Sun)-midnight ☎ 07876 178863
Beer range varies H
Friendly village local, reputedly a coaching inn when nearby Falkland Palace was a royal residence. Wainscot panelling and two old brewery mirrors adorn the walls of the bar. Both bar and lounge feature beamed ceilings and new carpets. A TV in the lounge screens sport. Four handpumps offer weekly changing beers from the Flying Firkin range, usually including a dark mild. A multi-award winner, including Scottish CAMRA Pub of the Year, National Pub of the Year runner-up, local CAMRA Pub of the Year for the past three years and runner up 2012. ♨Q❀⊕♨(36,X54,64)P'-

Lomond Hills Hotel
High Street, KY15 7EY
☼ 11-2, 5-midnight; 11-midnight Fri & Sat; 12.30-midnight Sun ☎ (01337) 857329 ⊕ lomondhillshotel.com
Beer range varies H
Comfortable country hotel, originally a coaching inn established in 1733, with a marvellous view of the Lomond Hills. The small, welcoming public bar sports a carved bar top and wood panelling on the walls. A plasma screen shows sport. Two beers are always available. Meals are served in the family lounge and a separate dining room. Outside there is a smoking area and beer garden. The hotel has a leisure area with heated pool and sauna available to guests and a conservatory available for functions. ♨♥❀⊕⊕♿♨(36,X54,64)P'-

Glenrothes
Golden Acorn ✅
1 North Street, KY7 5NA (next to bus station)

☼ 11-midnight; 12.30-11 Sun ☎ (01592) 755252
Greene King Abbot; guest beers H
Large Wetherspoon venue with its own accommodation. In the bar, scenes of the local area in days gone by decorate various pillars. Real ale on four handpumps and an occasional cider are on offer, as well as the usual Wetherspoon beer festivals and special deals. Breakfast is served from 7am (8am Sun). Plasma screens show sport, and there is a smoking and seating area outside. ♥❀♨⊕♿♠♨♠P'-

Kinghorn
Auld Hoose
6-8 Nethergate, KY3 9SY
☼ 12 (11 Sat; 12.30 Sun)-midnight ☎ (01592) 891074
Fuller's London Pride; guest beers H
Busy village family-run local situated on a steep side street leading off the east end of Kinghorn main street, handy for the station, Kinghorn beach and the Fife Coastal Path. Popular with locals and visitors, the main bar has a TV and pool table to keep sports fans happy and features dominoes competitions at the weekend. Hot snacks, pies and sausage rolls are served and also tea and coffee. The lounge is quieter and more comfortable, with a relaxed atmosphere. ⊕♠♨(7,7A)♣

Crown Tavern
55-57 High Street, KY3 9UW
☼ 11 (12.30 Sun)-11.45 ☎ (01592) 890430
Beer range varies H
Bustling two-roomed local, also called The Middle Bar, situated to the west end of the High Street. Two ever-changing ales are dispensed by cheery bar staff. Attractive stained-glass panels adorn the windows and door, and the high ceilings feature ornate plaster work. Mainly a sports bar, two TVs and a large projector screen show games, and there is a pool table in a side room. Live bands play monthly. A collection of footballs autographed by Scottish Premier League players is displayed at the end of bar. ♠♨(7,7A)♣

Kirkcaldy
Harbour Bar
471-475 High Street, KY1 2SN (opp harbour)
☼ 11-3, 5-midnight; 11-midnight Thu-Sat; 12.30-midnight Sun ☎ (01592) 264270
Beer range varies H
Situated on the ground floor of a tenement building, this old pub has been described by regulars as a village local in the middle of town. It has a light and airy lounge with ornate cornices. Six handpumps sell up to 20 different beers each week from micros all over Britain. Fife CAMRA Pub of the Year on numerous occasions and a Scottish Pub of the Year runner-up. Q⊕'-

Robert Nairn ✅
2-6 Kirk Wynd, KY1 1EH
☼ 11 (12.30 Sun)-midnight ☎ (01592) 205049
Caledonian Deuchars IPA; Greene King Abbot; guest beer H
A Wetherspoon Lloyds No.1 with a split-level lounge and pictures of old Kirkcaldy on the walls. Six handpumps dispense a variety of beers – check the noticeboard to see which beers are on and what to look forward to. There is also a good selection of bottled ciders. Beer festivals are held

throughout the year. The lively pub attracts a mixed clientele, young and old, who all enjoy the real ales. Breakfast is available from 9am and meals are served until 10pm. ⅋◑&♿🖵🕯🍴

Leslie

Burns Tavern
184 High Street, KY6 3DB
❖ 12 (11 Fri & Sat; 12.30 Sun)-midnight ☎ (01592) 741345
Taylor Landlord; guest beers Ⓗ
Typical Scottish two-room main-street local in a town once famous for papermaking. The public bar is on two levels, the lower lively and friendly with an open fire, the upper with a large-screen TV, pool table and football memorabilia on the walls. The lounge bar is quieter and more spacious. Competitions and quizzes are held weekly, with karaoke on Saturday. Leslie Folk Club meets and plays here on a Sunday. Two beers are usually available in this good, honest, friendly local.
🏰♿▲🖵(X1,201)♣P🍴

Fettykil Fox ✅
Leslie Roundabout, KY6 3EP (next to Holiday Inn Express)
❖ 12-11 (10.30 Sun) ☎ (01592) 749613
Caledonian Deuchars; guest beer Ⓗ
A traditional olde worlde-style building with coal fires at both ends. The decor is a mix of stone, wood panelling and rough plaster on the walls, with oak-beamed ceilings throughout. The bar is furnished with comfortable couches and wooden tables, and decorated with pictures of the local village. Food is served all day in two dining areas. The soft background music is a joy. There is also an enclosed beer garden and large car park.
🏰Q❄◑♿▲🖵(X1,201)P🍴

Limekilns

Ship Inn
Halkett's Hall, KY11 3HJ (on promenade)
❖ 11-11 (midnight Fri & Sat); 12.30-11 Sun
☎ (01383) 872247
Black Sheep Best Bitter Ⓗ
Traditional white coastal building on the waterfront with seating outside providing superb views of the River Forth to watch the ships go by. There is always a friendly welcome here, with fresh flowers, cosy alcoves and a maritime theme throughout. Three guest ales from local micros are on handpump. Meals are served lunchtimes, with fish and seafood the speciality. Runner-up Kingdom of Fife Pub of the Year 2011 and 2012.
Q❄◑🖵(76)P🍴

Lower Largo

Railway Inn
1 Station Wynd, KY8 6BU
❖ 11 (12.30 Sun)-midnight ☎ (01333) 320239
Beer range varies Ⓗ
Small two-room pub with a cosy real fire close to the picturesque forgotten harbour of Largo. The bar has a railway theme and displays photographs of the last trains to pass on the viaduct overhead before the Beeching measures of the 1960s. TV screens in each room show sport. Bar snacks are available. The four handpumps serve various beers from all over Britain. 🏰Q♿🖵(95)🍴

St Andrews

Central Bar 🍷 ✅
77-79 Market Street, KY16 9NU
❖ 11-11.45 (midnight Fri & Sat); 12.30-11.45 Sun
☎ (01334) 897684
Courage Directors; Fuller's London Pride; Inveralmond Lia Fail; Theakston Old Peculier Ⓗ
A good mix of students, locals, business folk and tourists makes this an interesting, bustling hostelry. It has a Victorian-style island bar, large windows and ornate mirrors creating a late 19th-century feel. There are tables outside on the pavement, weather permitting. Food is available until 9pm. The bar manager is dedicated to his ales and the staff are friendly. CAMRA members receive a discount on real ale. Local Pub of the Year runner up in 2010 and 2011, and winner in 2012.
❄◑🖵🍴

Criterion ✅
99 South Street, KY16 9QW
❖ 11-midnight (1am Fri & Sat); 12.30-midnight Sun
☎ (01334) 474543
Caledonian Deuchars IPA; guest beers Ⓗ
Lovely pub with a big picture window and oak-panelled walls adorned with photographs of St Andrews in days gone by. The hostelry is famous for its home-made pies including steak and ale, chicken and ham, and lamb and rosemary, served until 5pm. Background music plays and a plasma screen shows sport. Open music night on Monday is popular with local artists, and a regular quiz night is hosted during the week. ◑🖵

Whey Pat Tavern ✅
1 Bridge Street, KY16 9EX
❖ 11-11.30 (11.45 Fri & Sat; midnight Sun)
☎ (01334) 477740
Caledonian Deuchars IPA; Greene King IPA; guest beers Ⓗ
Town-centre pub on a busy road junction just outside the old West Port Gate. There has been a hostelry on this site for several centuries. The front bar is L-shaped with a dartboard and TV, and there is an airy lounge and meeting room to the rear. Seven beers are on handpump. Delicious bar snacks are served all day. A mixed clientele of all ages frequents this usually busy venue.
🏰◑♿🖵♣🍴

Strathkinness

Tavern
4 High Road, KY16 9RS (just off A91)
❖ 5-11; 12-midnight Sat & Sun ☎ (01334) 850085
⊕ strathkinnesstavern.co.uk
Beer range varies Ⓗ
Public bar with seating and a comfortable lounge at one end, with two handpulls offering a choice of changing guest ales. There is a separate room with a dartboard, pool table and Sky TV. Quiz nights are the first and third Mondays of month, ceilidh evenings the second and fourth Mondays. Lunches and evening meals are served in the bar and a separate restaurant. There is a beer garden to the rear and the front of the pub affords lovely views over the river estuary – a good location for plane spotting. Q❄◑♿▲🖵(64,96,91)♣P🍴

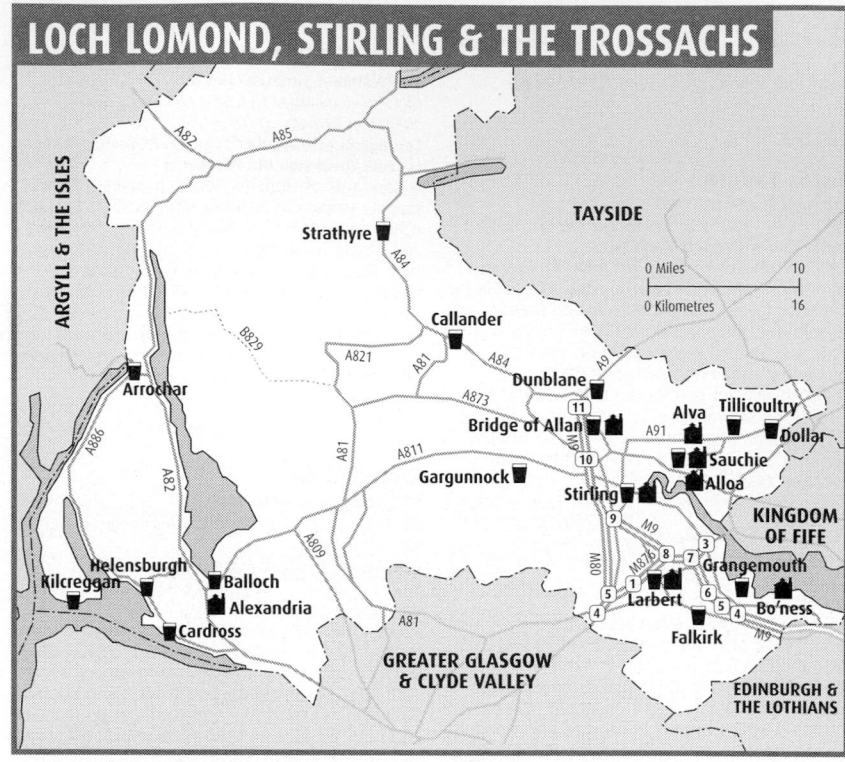

LOCH LOMOND, STIRLING & THE TROSSACHS

Authority areas covered: Argyll & Bute UA (part), Clackmannanshire UA, Falkirk UA, Stirling UA, West Dumbartonshire UA

Arrochar

Village Inn ✪

Shore Road, G83 7AX (on A814) NN293034
🕒 11-midnight (1am Fri & Sat); 12-midnight Sun
☎ (01301) 702279 ⊕ villageinnarrochar.co.uk
Beer range varies Ⓗ
Welcoming inn with impressive views over Loch Long and the Arrochar Alps. Up to three guest ales come from Fyne Ales and other Scottish breweries, and occasionally others from further afield. The varied food menu in the bar and restaurant offers the perfect way to recharge after walking or climbing the mountains. An easy walk from Arrochar rail station or bus stop.
🏨Q❀🍴🌢🕭&♿🚆(926,976)P♩

Balloch

Tullie Inn Ⓛ ✪

Balloch Road, G83 8SW (next to rail station)
🕒 11-midnight (1am Fri & Sat) ☎ (01389) 752052
Caledonian Deuchars IPA; Greene King Abbot; Morland Old Speckled Hen; guest beers Ⓗ
An older building houses the hotel and dining room, and modern pub food is served in both areas. Guest beers usually come from Fyne Ales and sometimes other Scottish or English breweries. The large and well-furnished beer garden includes a covered and heated smoking area. There is a quiz and music at weekends. Conveniently situated next to Balloch rail station, with frequent trains from Glasgow. ❀🍴🕭&♿🚆🚆P♩

Bridge of Allan

Allanwater Brewhouse Ⓛ

Queens Lane, FK9 4NU (behind Adamo Hotel)
🕒 12-5 ☎ (01786) 834555
Tinpot 70/-, 80/-; guest beer Ⓗ
The brewery tap for Tinpot is a working brewery and pub in one. It is furnished with historic pieces of brewery equipment and offers free tasters and brewery tours. Children and well-behaved dogs are welcome. Tinpot's beers include the unusual and interesting Marmalade Pot, Thai Pot and Chilli Pot, and a range of gluten-free beers. Q🚆🚆P

Callander

Waverley Hotel ✪

88-92 Main Street, FK17 8BD
🕒 11-midnight (1am Fri & Sat) ☎ (01877) 330245
⊕ thewaverley.co.uk
Beer range varies Ⓗ
Popular bar that offers an excellent base for visitors wishing to explore this scenic area. Usually offering

INDEPENDENT BREWERIES

Devon Sauchie
Harviestoun Alva
Kinneil Bo'ness (NEW)
Loch Lomond Alexandria (NEW)
Tinpot Bridge of Allan
Traditional Scottish Ales Stirling
Tryst Larbert
Williams Alloa

a choice of at least four ales, the hotel also runs beer festivals in September and December. Children are allowed in the seated area until 10pm and dogs on a lead are welcome. Belhaven and Greene King beers often feature. Q☺☞❀✦➊❶ ▲🚌(59,C59/60)⏏

Cardross

Coach House Inn
Main Road, G82 5JX (opp golf club) NS347775
☺ 11-midnight (1am Thu-Sat) ☎ (01389) 841358
🌐 coachhouseinn-cardross.com
Caledonian Deuchars IPA; guest beer Ⓗ
A spacious yet cosy inn with well-defined dining, drinking and games areas and a pool table. It is a valuable hub for the community in the village and locality as well as a good base to start or finish a walk from Loch Lomond or along the Firth of Clyde coast. Easily reached by train from Glasgow, you can be sure of a warm welcome. Caledonian Deuchars is supported by an ever-changing second guest ale. Regular live music enhances the ambience. 🏚❀☞❶⛓♿➊🚌(216)♣P⏏

Dollar

King's Seat ✓
19-23 Bridge Street, FK14 7DE
☺ 12-midnight (1am Fri & Sat) ☎ (01259) 742515
🌐 kingsseat.com
Harviestoun Bitter & Twisted; guest beers Ⓗ
Cosy, welcoming bar and restaurant situated in the quaint village of Dollar. It offers up to six ales and ciders along with menus for bar snacks and restaurant food. Dogs and children are welcome and there are tables and chairs outside for warmer weather. Occasional barbecues and live folk music are hosted. There are many great walks and attractions nearby. Q❀☞❶♿▲🚌(23,65)♣⏏

Dunblane

Dunblane Hotel ✓
10 Stirling Road, FK15 9EP (opp station)
☺ 11-midnight (1am Fri & Sat) ☎ (01786) 823178
Greene King Abbot; Taylor Landlord; guest beers Ⓗ
The bar is decorated with brewery mirrors, and real ale ordered here will be brought through from the lounge. Four cask ales are available in the comfortable lounge, which is adorned with pictures with angling and golf themes. A good view of the Allan River is afforded through the rear window. Last orders for food is 8pm. Quiz night is every other Thursday. ❀☞❶⛓♿➊🚌♣P⏏

Tappit Hen ✓
Kirk Street, FK15 0AL (opp cathedral)
☺ 11-midnight (1am Fri & Sat) ☎ (01786) 825226
Belhaven IPA; guest beers Ⓗ
A varied range of five real ales is on offer at this friendly and welcoming pub. The staff are knowledgable and welcome locals and tourists alike. At least one beer festival is held, usually in October or May. Tuesday is folk night – all are encouraged to bring along an instrument and join in the fun. Local CAMRA Pub of the Year 2012 finalist. ➊🚌♣

Falkirk

Behind the Wall ✓
14 Melville Street, FK1 1HZ
☺ 5-9 (11 summer; 1am Fri & Sat); 12.30-midnight Sun
☎ (01324) 633338 🌐 behindthewall.co.uk
Caledonian Deuchars IPA; guest beers Ⓗ
This spacious venue for drinking, dining and entertainment was once a bra factory. Popular for watching live sports events, it has plenty of seating and several wide screens in a large room that doubles as a live music and comedy venue with bands both local and from many parts of the UK. Eglesbrech is the real ale and whisky bar upstairs, divided into two rooms with timber furnishings and a wood-burning stove. 🏚❀❶⛓➊➡(Grahamston)🚌

Carron Works Ⓛ ✓
Bank Street, FK1 1NB (near rail and bus stations)
☺ 9.30am-11 (midnight Thu; 1am Fri & Sat); 11-11 Sun
☎ (01324) 673020
Caledonian Deuchars IPA; Greene King Abbot; guest beers Ⓗ
In a converted cinema, this is an excellent Wetherspoon venue with helpful staff dispensing the chain's guest beers. It is centrally situated, with a spacious interior. It has frequent festivals and is keen to promote real ale. The standard Wetherspoon menu is available all day. ❀❶➡(Grahamston)🚌♣⏏

Wheatsheaf Inn ✓
16 Baxters Wynd, FK1 1PF
☺ 11-midnight (1am Fri & Sat); 12.30-midnight Sun
☎ (01324) 638282
Caledonian Deuchars IPA; guest beers Ⓗ
Dating from the late 18th century, this public house can be found off the High Street via one of the vennels. The wood-panelled bar is furnished in traditional style and retains much of its original character. Guest beers come from microbreweries in Scotland and England, with two on offer midweek and three at the weekend. A must-visit venue, it is CAMRA Forth Valley South Pub of the Year for 2012. ❀➡(Grahamston)🚌⏏

Gargunnock

Gargunnock Inn
Main Street, FK8 3BW
☺ closed Mon; 5-11 (11 Fri); 12-1am Sat; 12-11 Sun
☎ (01786) 860333 🌐 caféalbert.co.uk
Beer range varies Ⓗ
Originally an 18th-century staging inn, it has been extended over the years to provide a restaurant and function room. The pub sponsors local football and cricket teams and holds charity events. The bar offers a rotating range of local and regional ales. Regular entertainment is hosted and a beer festival is held on the second Sunday in August. CAMRA Forth Valley Rural Stirlingshire Pub of the Year 2012. ❀❶♿🚌(12)♣P

Grangemouth

Earl of Zetland ✓
Bo'ness Road, FK3 8AN
☺ 9-11 (1am Fri & Sat) ☎ (01324) 499940
Caledonian Deuchars IPA; Greene King Abbot; guest beers Ⓗ
Excellent Wetherspoon conversion of an old church in the town centre. Ample seating, either at tables or in pew booths, is provided, allowing the

SCOTLAND

ecclesistical features such as the organ pipes above the bar and stained glass windows to be enjoyed while savouring your pint. Two permanent beers are supplemented by two guests midweek and up to four at the weekend. TVs screen major sporting events with news channels on silent at other times. ◑♿🍴◉

Helensburgh

Commodore Hotel ✅
112-117 West Clyde Street, G84 8ER (on seafront)
✪ 11-11; 12.30-10.30 Sun ☎ (01436) 676924
⊕ innkeeperslodge.com
Caledonian Deuchars IPA; guest beer Ⓗ
Take a pleasant walk from the station along the seafront and it is impossible to miss this large, modern hotel overlooking the Gareloch. Sit in the sunny beer garden and watch the sailing boats, or relax in a comfortable chair in the sizeable lounge and enjoy a drink and perhaps a meal from the diverse menu. The bar offers an ever-changing guest ale from anywhere in Britain to complement the Deuchars IPA.
🏨🏵️🍴◑♿≠(Central)🚌(216)P⌐

Kilcreggan

Kilcreggan Hotel Ⓛ
Argyll Road, G84 0JP (tip of Rosneath Peninsula)
NS238805
✪ 11.30-midnight (1am Fri & Sat); 12-midnight Sun
☎ (01436) 842243 ⊕ kilcregganhotel.com
Beer range varies Ⓗ
Built on a commanding position with great views over the Firth of Clyde, the hotel can reached by ferry from Gourock or bus from Helensburgh. The large lounge bar serves up to four ales, always including a Scottish microbrew and often Draught Bass. You can enjoy good food in the dining area. In summer the outside patio and garden, with a large covered area, is a floral treat.
♿🏵️🍴◑🚌(316)P⌐

Larbert

Station Hotel
2 Foundry Loan, FK5 4AW (near station)
✪ 12-11 (midnight Thu; 1am Fri & Sat); 12.30-11 Sun
☎ (01324) 557186
Caledonian Deuchars IPA; guest beers Ⓗ
This hotel has been a focal point for the town for several years. It has a large traditional public bar and a smaller lounge area and games room. Three cask ales, including Caledonian's monthly guest, are offered and the hotel is popular with locals and passing visitors. There are 11 bedrooms and conference facilities are available. Four large TVs show major sporting events.
🏵️🍴♿≠🚌(10,11)P⌐

Sauchie

Mansfield Arms ✅
7 Main Street, FK10 3JR
✪ 11-11.30 (12.30am Fri & Sat); 12.30-11.30 Sun
☎ (01259) 722020 ⊕ devonales.com
Devon Original, Thick Black, Pride Ⓟ
The oldest operating microbrewery in the county, this pub brews three Devon ales which are dispensed via Scottish tall founts. Family owned and run, situated within an ex-mining community,

the bar is popular with the locals, and families come to enjoy good-value meals served in the lounge. The pub is on the Stirling via Alloa circular bus route. ◑♿🍴🚌(60,62)P🖥

Stirling

No. 2 Baker Street ✅
2 Baker Street, FK8 1BJ
✪ 11-midnight (1am Fri & Sat); 12.30-midnight Sun
☎ (01786) 448722
Greene King Abbot; guest beers Ⓗ
In the city centre, this busy pub is part of the Belhaven/Greene King chain. The interior is open plan with bare floorboards and local paintings helping to create a traditional atmosphere. Popular with locals, students and tourists, it holds a weekly quiz night on Tuesday, open-mic night on Thursday, live music monthly on a Saturday and occasional ceilidh. The beer range is mainly Scottish with regular guests such as Taylor Landlord and London Pride. 🏵️◑≠🚌

Portcullis Hotel
Castle Wynd, FK8 1EG
✪ 11.30-midnight (11 Mon & Tue); 11.30-11 Sun
☎ (01786) 472290 ⊕ theportcullishotel.com
Beer range varies Ⓗ
Popular pub at the top of the town featuring exposed stone walls and an open fireplace with ornate surround, creating a traditional ambience in the heart of old Stirling. Frequented by locals and tourists alike, the pub is renowned for its food and regularly changing selection of Scottish real ales, mainly from the far north and west. Always busy, diners are advised to reserve a table.
🏨Q🏵️🍴◑≠🚌P

Strathyre

Inn & Bistro
Main Street, FK18 8NA (on A84)
✪ 12 (12.30 Sun)-11 ☎ (01877) 384224
⊕ innatstrathyre.com
Beer range varies Ⓗ
Cosy, popular pub, serving meals in the bar or bistro, all made with local produce. Hill walking, fishing, golf and watersports are all close at hand, and Stirling, Callander and the Trossachs are within easy travelling distance. Accommodation is available and dogs and children are permitted in the bar. The beers are mainly Scottish during the summer tourist season and from below the border off season. 🏨Q🏵️🍴◑♿▲🚌🐾P⌐

Tillicoultry

Woolpack Inn ♈
1 Glassford Square, FK13 6AU
✪ 11-midnight (1am Sat) ☎ (07976) 988909
Beer range varies Ⓗ
Originally a drovers' inn on the Southern foothills of the Ochil Hills, this is a genuine pub, well used by locals, with a comfortable feel, log fire and low ceilings, and no intrusive TV or music. Ales on three handpumps change regularly and there is a good selection of malt whiskies. Meals are available at weekends only. CAMRA Branch Pub of the Year 2012. 🏨Q🏵️🍴🚌(62,63)🐾⌐

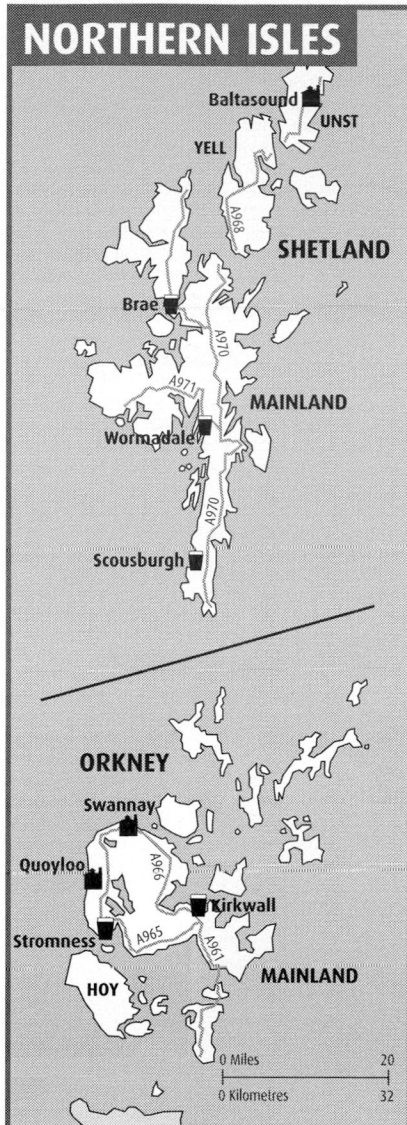

NORTHERN ISLES

Baltasound
UNST
YELL
A968
SHETLAND
Brae
A970
MAINLAND
Wormadale
A970
A971
Scousburgh

ORKNEY
Swannay
Quoyloo
A966
Kirkwall
Stromness
A965
A961
MAINLAND
HOY

0 Miles   20
0 Kilometres   32

Authority area covered: Highland UA

Brae: Shetland

Busta House Hotel
ZE2 9QN HU345669

☼ 12-midnight ☎ (01806) 522506 ⊕ bustahouse.com

Beer range varies Ⓗ

Rambling mansion house on many different levels converted to a friendly country house hotel. Dating from 1588 with numerous later additions, it is set in extensive grounds running down to the seashore. The beamed main bar area is lined with ship drawings. One beer, usually from Valhalla, is supplemented by an extensive range of over 150 malt whiskies. The hotel is near the centre of the Shetland mainland and Mavis Grind, where the Atlantic and the North Sea are separated only by the width of the road. Allegedly haunted by the ghost of Barbara Pitcairn. ⚠Q✿⇦◖P

Kirkwall: Orkney

Bothy Bar (Albert Hotel)
Mounthoolie Lane, KW15 1HW

☼ 11-11.30 (1am Thu-Sat); 12-11.30 Sun ☎ (01856) 876000
⊕ alberthotel.co.uk

Highland Scapa Special; Orkney Red MacGregor; guest beers Ⓗ

Risen from the ashes of a fire several years ago, the bar was rebuilt using much of the original timber and is now more spacious than the previous building. Ideally located in the centre of town, it is handy for shops, buses and ferries to the outer isles. Busy in the early evening after work, it is also a lively part of the night scene at weekends. A range of Orkney and Highland brewery beers is available in high season but the beer range is restricted in winter. Wi-Fi available. ⚠⇦◖▲

Helgi's Bar
14 Harbour Street, KW15 1LE

☼ 11-11 (1am Thu-Sat); 12.30-11 Sun ☎ (01856) 879273
⊕ helgis.co.uk

Highland Scapa Special; Orkney IPA; guest beer Ⓗ

Converted from a former shipping office, this small, smart bar has the look of a modern café. Take your drinks to the cosy upstairs room overlooking the harbour while filling in time before island-hopping on the many ferries to the outlying parts. Coffee, home-bakes and sandwiches are available all day. The guest pump rotates the Highland Brewing Company's range of beers. CAMRA Northern Isles Pub of the Year. ◖

Shore
6 Shore Street, KW15 1LG

☼ 11 (9 Sat & Sun)-midnight (1am Fri & Sat)
☎ (01856) 872200 ⊕ theshore.co.uk

Highland Scapa Special Ⓗ

Smart, modern bar in a refurbished hotel overlooking the harbour. An ideal base for island-hopping, using the many ferries available to Westray, Sanday and most of the other Orkney Islands. A darts player's haven, it has dartboards at both ends of the bar room. TVs screen all serious sporting fixtures and background music plays at a level that allows easy chat. Complimentary newspapers are available. ⇦◖

Scousburgh: Shetland

Spiggie Hotel
Dunrossness, ZE2 9JE (signed from A970 off B9122)
HU379174

☼ 12-2 (not Mon & Tue), 5.30-11; 12-11 Sat & Sun
☎ (01950) 460409 ⊕ thespiggiehotel.co.uk

Beer range varies Ⓗ

Family-run hotel with a small stone-floored bar and adjacent restaurant built as the original terminus of the Northern Isles ferries. On an elevated site, it enjoys views of St Ninians Isle, Fitful Head and the Loch of Spiggie. The gleaming white Scousburgh Sands are a five-minute walk and Sumburgh Head, Jarlshof and Old Scatness are a short drive away. Birdwatching and trout fishing on the loch can be arranged. One beer from the local Valhalla brewery

INDEPENDENT BREWERIES

Highland Swannay: Orkney
Orkney/Atlas Quoyloo: Orkney
Valhalla Baltasound: Unst

SCOTLAND

plus guests are on tap in summer. In winter a single ale is served, usually from the Waverley portfolio. The hotel has six bedrooms and various self-catering lodge options. Phone to check food availability and opening hours in winter.
Q✿≠◑P

Stromness: Orkney

Ferry Inn

John Street, KW16 3AA (100yds from ferry terminal)
✪ 10-11 (midnight Fri-Sun) ☎ (01856) 850280
⊕ ferryinn.com
Highland IPA, Scapa Special, seasonal beers; Orkney Red MacGregor, seasonal beers; guest beer Ⓗ
A former temperance hotel, this inn is a welcome sight after the ferry crossing from Scrabster. Refurbished by new owners at the end of 2011 giving a much-improved interior, the hostelry is popular with locals and visitors alike, particularly the divers who come to Orkney to explore the wrecks of Scapa Flow. Local folk musicians meet here regularly, and the pub hosts annual blues and folk festivals in conjunction with the Stromness Hotel. A swearing ban is in force. ✿≠◑Ⓐ⊟

Stromness Hotel

15 Victoria Street, KW16 3AA (opp pier head)
✪ 12-midnight (1am Fri-Sun) ☎ (01856) 850298
⊕ stromnesshotel.com

Highland Scapa Special; Orkney Red MacGregor; guest beers Ⓗ
On the first floor of this hotel is a large bar, the Hamnavoe Lounge (not normally open till 5pm Mon-Thu), with views overlooking the harbour and a fire in winter. Used as an army HQ during World War II, the hotel is well placed for visiting attractions such as Scara Brae and the Ring of Brodgar. Annual music and beer festivals are held. The hotel itself closes during January and February, but the Flattie Bar downstairs, with one handpump serving Scapa, remains open. In high season various other Orkney and Highland beers are added to the range. ⋈✿≠◑Ⓐ⊟P

Wormadale: Shetland

Westings Inn

ZE2 9LJ (8 miles N of Lerwick on A971) HU403465
✪ 12.30-2.30, 5.30-10.30; 6.30-9 Sun ☎ (01595) 840242
⊕ westings.shetland.co.uk
Beer range varies Ⓗ
Isolated white-painted inn on the side of Wormadale Hill with extensive sea views from the comfortable lounge and adjacent games area. One ale is usually available from the local Valhalla Brewery and up to two guests in summer. The bar may stay open until 1am if busy. Phone to check food availability/hours before travelling. Tents and caravans are welcome on the campsite.
✿≠◑&Ⓐ♣P

Stromness Hotel, Stromness: Orkney (Photo: rockmasterp)

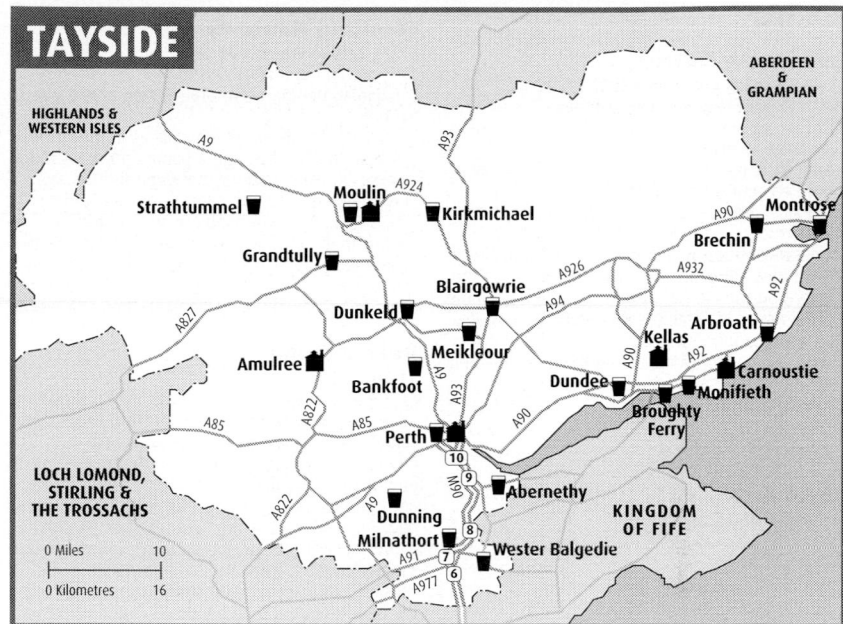

Authority areas covered: Angus UA, City of Dundee UA, Perth & Kinross UA

Abernethy

Crees Inn

Main Street, PH2 9LA

☼ 11-2, 5-11; 11-11 Sat & Sun ☎ (01738) 850714
⊕ creesinn.co.uk

Beer range varies Ⓗ

Comfortable former farmhouse in a quiet village, lying in the shadow of the imposing Abernethy Tower, one of only two Pictish watchtowers in Scotland. A free house, it has timber panels and beams that display an impressive collection of pump clips reflecting the varied beer range. Up to six ales are available, mostly from English breweries. A good varied selection of meals is served lunchtimes and evenings made with fresh local produce. Abernethy village was once the southern Pictish capital of Scotland.
Q❀🚱🌓🕭⅏🚆(36)P

Arbroath

Corn Exchange ✅

Market Place, DD11 1HR

☼ 11-midnight (1am Fri & Sat); 12.30-midnight Sun
☎ (01241) 432430

Greene King Abbot; Ruddles Best Bitter; guest beers Ⓗ

Located just off the High Street, this well-managed Wetherspoon pub occupies a 19th-century former corn exchange. Two guest beers are usually available in addition to the two regular offerings. Although largely open plan there are a number of booths offering some privacy. Food is served daily from 8am or you could try the famous Arbroath smokies from one of the local producers. Boat trips offering fishing or a visit to the 200-year-old Bell Rock lighthouse can be found at the nearby harbour. ⅏🕭⅏🚆🍴🚬

Bankfoot

Bankfoot Inn

Main Street, PH1 4AB (just off A9)

☼ 5.30-11 (11.45 Thu; 12.30am Fri); 12-12.30am Sat;
12.30-11.30 Sun ☎ (01738) 787243 ⊕ bankfootinn.co.uk

Beer range varies Ⓗ

Traditional 18th-century coaching inn situated on the main street in the village, the 'old road to the Highlands'. Extensively refurbished over the past few years, it has a small public bar, a lounge with a fine oak bar and an adjoining restaurant. Two real fires in winter make it a cosy howff. The owners are real ale enthusiasts and strongly committed to local breweries. Live music nights are held regularly. Catering for all interests – golf, fishing, shooting, hiking and cycling – dogs are also welcome with their owners. ⨇❀🚱⅏🕭⅏🚆(22)

Blairgowrie

Ericht Alehouse ▿ Ⓛ

13 Wellmeadow, PH10 6ND (on N side of park in town centre) NO180452

☼ 1-11 (11.45 Thu; 12.30am Fri & Sat); 1-11.30 Sun
☎ (01250) 872469

Beer range varies Ⓗ

Classic town-centre pub with a friendly atmosphere. There are two seated areas separated by a well-stocked bar, and an open log fire in the lounge adds to the warm welcome. Up to six handpumps serve a wide range of ever-changing ales and a cider. A range of bottled continental beers is also available. No food is served but customers are welcome to bring their own. Occasional live music plays on Friday evenings. A winner of Local CAMRA Pub of the Year several times during the last decade.
⨇Q🍺⅙🕭🚆(57,58)🚬⅏

Brechin

Caledonian Hotel
43-47 South Esk Street, DD9 6DZ
✪ 5-11 (midnight Fri); 3-1am Sat; 3-11 Sun
☎ (01356) 624345
Beer range varies ℍ
Taking its name from the privately run railway whose terminus is opposite, the Caledonian features a large bar and dining area. The extensive use of wood creates a warm and inviting appearance. Houston and Inveralmond provide the regular ales although guest beers sourced by the landlord on trips to Hampshire are often available. A wide range of continental bottled beers is also stocked. Live folk music on the last Friday of the month is popular. Phone ahead to check opening hours as these may vary in summer.
🏚Q🌞🍴🌙◑🚽(30)♣�"

Broughty Ferry

Royal Arch 🅛 ✔
285 Brook Street, DD5 2DS
✪ 11 (12.30 Sun)-midnight ☎ (01382) 779741
⊕ royal-arch.co.uk
Caledonian Deuchars IPA; guest beers ℍ
A busy, popular local in the centre of 'the Ferry', near the rail station (improved but still limited service). There are three TVs in the public bar for the many sports fans and meals are served in the Art Deco lounge. Pavement tables are popular in clement weather and with smokers. Ales from all over Britain are served and local beers from Angus Ales and Inveralmond are regularly available. The gantry in the public bar was rescued from the demolished Craigour Bar in Dens Road as part of the pub's refurbishment. 🌞◑🍴🌆🚽(5,73)�"

Ship Inn
121 Fisher Street, DD5 2BR
✪ 11 (12.30 Sun)-midnight ☎ (01382) 779176
⊕ theshipinn-broughtyferry.co.uk
Caledonian Deuchars IPA; Taylor Landlord; guest beers ℍ
The Ship Inn is a traditional free house situated on the waterfront at Broughty Ferry, with amazing views over the Tay towards Fife. Dating back to 1847, this cosy retreat is atmospheric and interesting. The staff are friendly, hospitable and consistently provide a good choice of well-kept real ales. A range of tasty bar meals is on offer and there is also an excellent restaurant upstairs.
🌞◑🍴🚽

Dundee

Bank Bar
7-9 Union Street, DD1 4BN
✪ 11 (12.30 Sun)-midnight ☎ (01382) 205037
Beer range varies ℍ
Former bank with a collection of pictures celebrating the old local banking industry decorating the walls. Now a no-nonsense ale house, it has a bare-boards floor, wood furniture and a series of alcoves with tables in the tradition of older Scottish city pubs. The management is enthusiastic about supporting small brewers and, while beers from many parts are available, Angus Ales and Inveralmond feature regularly among the two or three ales on handpump. Food is served until 7pm. Live music plays on Friday and Saturday nights. ◑🍴🚽

Counting House ✔
67-71 Reform Street, DD1 1SP
✪ 11-midnight ☎ (01382) 225251
Caledonian Deuchars IPA; Greene King Abbot; guest beers ℍ
A converted bank with high ceilings in the heart of Dundee, this has become a popular local for many city ale drinkers. Halfway between the Overgate and Wellgate shopping centres, on the corner of Albert Square, it is a handy watering hole for visitors to the McManus Galleries. Thatchers cider is on regularly, with additions during beer festivals. Guest beers frequently include seasonal ales from Caledonian. Food is available 8am-10pm. ◑🍴🚽🍴

Duke's Corner
13 Brown Street, DD1 5EG
✪ 12-2.30am (midnight Mon & Tue) ☎ (01382) 205052
BrewDog Trashy Blonde; Williams Fraoch Heather Ale, Ceilidh Lager, Seven Giraffes; guest beer 🅖
Revived in late 2009 by Fuller & Thompson, this is now a smart establishment geared to live music and comedy as well as food service throughout the day. The unusual bar arrangement has 30 taps along the wall behind the staff, with no fonts on the bar counter. Real ale traditionalists may be surprised to see the good stuff dispensed by turn-top handles rather than handpulls. The outside area is also much improved with tables, umbrellas and lights. 🌞◑🍴"

Phoenix
103 Nethergate, DD1 4DH
✪ 11-midnight ☎ (01382) 200014
Caledonian Deuchars IPA; Taylor Landlord; guest beers ℍ
Splendidly re-created traditional local (only the ceiling and pillars are original) which has proved to be one of the city's most popular real ale outlets down the years both as the Phoenix and, previously, the Town & Gown. Eccentric in decor, it has sturdy wooden seats and tables and green leather benches, plus intimate nooks for a quiet drink. Look out for the Ballingall's Brewery mirror, a rarity. The atmosphere is always friendly and busy – it is handy for the Rep Theatre, Dundee Contemporary Arts and Bonar Hall. Free Wi-Fi available. ◑🍴🚽

Dunkeld

Royal Dunkeld Hotel
Atholl Street, PH8 0AR
✪ 11-11 (12.15am Fri & Sat); 12-11 Sun ☎ (01350) 727322
⊕ royaldunkeld.co.uk
Cairngorm Trade Winds; Stewart Pentland IPA; guest beer ℍ
Located on the main street of the cathedral town of Dunkeld, this former coaching inn is now a comfortable hotel. It has a restaurant, lounge bar and public bar with an open fire. Three handpulls serve real ale. A pool room with dartboard is adjacent. Outside, the large beer garden is a suntrap in summer. Good food is served in the bar

INDEPENDENT BREWERIES

Angus Carnoustie
Inveralmond Perth
MôR Kellas (NEW)
Moulin Moulin
Strathbraan Amulree (NEW)

and restaurant. An ideal base for a variety of outdoor activities including walking, fishing and golf. ᴍ❀✍◑❨❓❤(23)Pᵇ┖

Dunning

Kirkstyle Inn ✔
Kirkstyle Square, PH2 0RR NO019144
✪ 11-2.30 (not Mon winter), 5-11 (midnight Fri); 11-midnight Sat; 12.30-11 Sun ☎ (01764) 684248
⊕ kirkstyle-dunning.co.uk
Beer range varies Ⓗ
Traditional village inn dating from 1760 overshadowed by the impressive Norman steeple of St Serf's Church, which contains the ancient Dupplin Cross and other Pictish relics. Up to three ales in the small public bar come from a variety of Scottish independents, as well as English and Welsh regional breweries. A small snug area is next to the bar and there is a separate restaurant. Around a mile west of Dunning village stands a 20ft high stone cross, a memorial to Maggie Wall who was burned here as a witch in 1657.
ᴍQ❀◑❨❓(17)

Grandtully

Grandtully
PH9 0PL
✪ 12-11 (12.30am Fri-Sun); 5 (12 Sat & Sun)-11 winter
☎ (01997) 840357 ⊕ thegrandtully.com
Beer range varies Ⓗ
This budget-priced hostel was formerly a fishing and shooting lodge. It has a good-sized bar area, with real fire and comfortable sofas adjacent. Four handpulls were introduced in 2011, dispensing ales from different Scottish micros. A good whisky selection is also stocked and rums are a house speciality. The hostel attracts outdoor sporty types, especially canoeists on the challenging River Tay, just across the road. Live bands are a regular feature. ❀✍◑❓(23)

Kirkmichael

Strathardle Inn ⌱
PH10 7NS (on A924) NO082599
✪ 12-2, 6-11 (11.30 Fri & Sat) ☎ (01250) 881224
⊕ strathardleinn.co.uk
Beer range varies Ⓗ
Small, friendly hotel set in a peaceful environment, with a bar room with a coal fire and horse brasses around the mantelpiece. Up to three ales are available from Scottish micros, and good lunches and evening meals are served. This historic coaching inn, dating back to the late 1700s, has a 700-yard fishing beat on the River Ardle, which passes in front of the inn. The Cateran Trail also passed by on its way from Bridge of Cally to Enochdhu. The Southern Highlands, Glenshee ski slopes, Deeside and Angus glens are all within reach. ᴍQ❧❀✍◑♿P

Meikleour

Meikleour Hotel ⌱
PH2 6EB
✪ 11-3, 6-11; 11-11.45 Fri & Sat; 12-11 Sun
☎ (01250) 883206 ⊕ meikleourhotel.co.uk
Beer range varies Ⓗ
Originally a coaching inn and posting house dating back to 1820, this welcoming family-owned

country inn has an informal stone-flagged bar and comfortable lounge/dining room with a log fire in an Adam-style fireplace. Up to three ales are available including the house beer The Lure of Meikleour, brewed by Inveralmond. The excellent food is made with locally sourced ingredients. Outside is an ample-sized car park and beer garden. Nearby is the famous beech hedge planted in 1745 that now stands 100ft high and is a third of a mile long. ᴍQ❀✍◑❨♿❓(58)P

Milnathort

Village Inn
36 Westerloan, KY13 9YH
✪ 2-11 (midnight Fri); 12-midnight Sat; 12.30-11 Sun
☎ (01577) 863293
Caledonian Deuchars IPA; Inveralmond Thrappledouser; guest beer Ⓗ
Located in the heart of the village, this friendly local has a semi open-plan interior featuring classic brewery mirrors and local historic photographs. A comfortable lounge area is at one end with low ceilings, exposed joists and stone walls, and at the other end is the bar area with log fire. The games room at the rear has a pool table. This pub has been family-owned since 1985. Milnathort links some great cycling routes through the Ochils, via Burleigh Castle, to the more leisurely Loch Leven Heritage Trail. ᴍ❀♿❓(23,56)♣

Monifieth

Milton Inn
Grange Road, DD5 4LU NO484327
✪ closed Mon; 12-2.30, 5-11; 12-midnight Fri & Sat; 12-11 Sun ☎ (01382) 532620 ⊕ themiltoninn.co.uk
Beer range varies Ⓗ
Set back from the road with large gardens and a sunny deck area to the rear, this family-run inn offers a genuinely warm and friendly welcome. The interior is bright but cosy, and the decor is a refreshing combination of traditional and modern styles. The well-kept ales change frequently and two interesting session beers can usually be found alongside a seasonal one from Caledonian. These are complemented by excellent food and an impressive selection of single malt whiskies, all served by pleasant, enthusiastic and knowledgeable staff. Q❀✍◑❓(73,39A)Pᵇ┖

Montrose

Market Arms
95 High Street, DD10 8QY
✪ 11-midnight (1am Thu-Sat) ☎ (01674) 673384
Beer range varies Ⓗ
Stylishly renovated a few years ago, this town-centre pub provides a comfortable retreat for a wide mix of customers. Two handpulls are conveniently sited on a long bar near the entrance in the main open area. Several satellite TVs show live sporting events but there is a small snug at the front for those wishing to enjoy a quiet pint. The beers are usually sourced from Scottish brewers. Visitors to Montrose may admire the town's many statues and beautiful church with a tall spire and resident peregrine falcon. ♿Å⇄❓(X7)

Moulin

Moulin Inn

11-13 Kirkmichael Road, PH16 5EH NN991642
☼ 11 (12 Nov-Apr)-11 (11.45 Fri & Sat); 12-11 Sun
☎ (01796) 472196 ⊕ moulininn.co.uk
Moulin Light, Braveheart, Ale of Atholl, Old Remedial Ⓗ
Situated in the shadow of Ben Vrackie, this delightful haven of highland hospitality in picturesque Moulin village was founded in 1695. The interior of the cosy hostelry is divided into small alcoves warmed by two log fires. Its four ales are produced in the hotel's own brewery in the former coach house and stable behind the hotel. A good choice of home-cooked fare is served all day. A popular destination for hill walkers and tourists visiting Pitlochry and the surrounding area.
🏨Q🐕☆🍴◑♣P

Perth

Capital Asset Ⓛ ✔

26 Tay Street, PH1 5LQ
☼ 11-11.30 (12.30am Thu-Sat); 12-midnight Sun
☎ (01738) 580457
Caledonian Deuchars IPA; Greene King Abbot; guest beers Ⓗ
The name of this Wetherspoon pub recalls the building's original purpose as a savings bank and Perth's status in medieval times as capital of Scotland, with Scottish kings crowned at nearby Scone Palace. The high ceilings and ornate cornices have been retained and pictures of old Perth adorn the walls of the open-plan lounge, which overlooks the River Tay. The large safe from its banking days can be found in the children's area. A variety of five ales is dispensed and food is available all day. Beer festivals twice a year are popular with local ale drinkers. Q🐕☆◑&≒🚊⌐

Cherrybank Inn Ⓛ

210 Glasgow Road, PH2 0NA
☼ 11-11 (midnight Fri & Sat) ☎ (01738) 624349
⊕ cherrybankinn.co.uk
Inveralmond Ossian; guest beers Ⓗ
Tayside CAMRA Pub of the Year for 2011, this 250-year-old former drovers' inn is a popular watering hole and stop-over for travellers. Five ales from Inveralmond and other Scottish independents are available from the multi-roomed public bar or in the larger L-shaped lounge with views up to a woodland walk. Good bar lunches and evening meals are served. The inn has seven well-appointed en-suite rooms and golf can be arranged for residents. Q🍴◑🛏🅿🚐(7)P⌐

Greyfriars

15 South Street, PH2 8PG
☼ 11-11 (11.45 Fri & Sat); 3-11 Sun ☎ (01738) 633036
⊕ greyfriarsbar.com
Beer range varies Ⓗ
City-centre lounge bar serving up to four ales often including an Inveralmond beer. Good-value lunches are available in the bar or in a small upstairs seating area. The pub takes its name from the former Greyfriars monastery, which was gutted by followers of John Knox in 1559 and subsequently demolished. Ideally located on the edge of the shopping area, nearby attractions include a Victorian theatre, art gallery, museum and concert hall. This may well be the smallest lounge bar in Perth but it has an enviable reputation among locals and visitors as one of the friendliest pubs in the Fair City. ◑≒🚊

Strathtummel

Loch Tummel Inn Ⓛ

PH16 5RP (9 miles W of Pitlochry on B8019) NN819602
☼ 11-11 (closed Mon & Tue winter) ☎ (01882) 634272
⊕ lochtummelinn.co.uk
Beer range varies Ⓗ
Located on a hillside with spectacular views across Loch Tummel, this 200-year-old former coaching inn is an ideal place to stop off and enjoy warm and friendly highland hospitality. The bar area comprises the former coach house and stables, with pews and a wood-burning stove adding to the traditional ambience. The outside drinking area overlooking the loch is a superb spot to linger on a summer's day. Two ales are usually available, often from Inveralmond, and good food is served daily.
🏨Q☆🍴◑&P⌐

Wester Balgedie

Balgedie Toll Tavern

KY13 9HE (2 miles E of M90 at jct of A911 and B919) NO164039
☼ 11-11 (11.30 Thu; 12.30am Fri & Sat); 12.30-11.30 Sun
☎ (01592) 840212
Harviestoun Bitter & Twisted; guest beer Ⓗ
Welcoming and comfortable rural tavern dating from 1534 where travellers had to break their journey to pay tolls. Now much extended, the oldest part of the building (the toll house) is at the southern end. It has three seating areas plus a small bar with low ceilings, oak beams, horse brasses, wooden settles and works of art by a local painter. A good selection of meals and bar snacks is available. Guest beers are rotated, mainly from Scottish independent breweries.
☆◑🚐(201,205)P⌐

Cask breather

Where an entry states that some beers in a pub are served with the aid of cask breathers, this means that demand valves are connected to both casks and cylinders of gas; as beer is drawn off, it is replaced by applied gas (either carbon dioxide, nitrogen or both) to prevent oxidation. The method is not acceptable to CAMRA as it does not allow beer to condition and mature naturally. The Campaign believes brewers and publicans should use the size of casks best suited to the turnover of beer in order to avoid oxidation. If a pub in the Good Beer Guide uses cask breathers, we list only those beers that are free of the device.

SHETLAND

NORTHERN ISLES

HIGHLANDS & WESTERN ISLES

ABERDEEN & GRAMPIAN

TAYSIDE

LOCH LOMOND STIRLING & THE TROSSACHS

FIFE

ARGYLL & THE ISLES

GREATER GLASGOW & CLYDE VALLEY

EDINBURGH & LOTHIANS

BORDERS

AYRSHIRE & ARRAN

DUMFRIES & GALLOWAY

NORTHUMBER-LAND

TYNE & WEAR

NORTHERN IRELAND

CUMBRIA

DURHAM

ISLE OF MAN

NORTH YORKSHIRE

LANCASHIRE

WEST YORKS

EAST YORKS

MERSEYSIDE

GREATER MANCHESTER

SOUTH YORKS

LINCOLN-SHIRE

NW WALES

NE WALES

CHESHIRE

DERBYSHIRE

NOTTINGHAM-SHIRE

NORFOLK

SHROPSHIRE

STAFFORD-SHIRE

LEICESTERSHIRE & RUTLAND

CAMBRIDGE-SHIRE

SUFFOLK

MID WALES

WEST MIDLANDS

WORCESTER-SHIRE

WARWICK-SHIRE

NORTHAMPTON-SHIRE

BEDFORD-SHIRE

HERTFORD-SHIRE

ESSEX

WEST WALES

HERTFORD-SHIRE

GWENT

GLOUCS & BRISTOL

OXFORD-SHIRE

BUCKINGHAM-SHIRE

GREATER LONDON

GLAMORGAN

BERKSHIRE

SURREY

KENT

WILTSHIRE

HAMPSHIRE

WEST SUSSEX

EAST SUSSEX

SOMERSET

DEVON

DORSET

ISLE OF WIGHT

CHANNEL ISLANDS

CORNWALL

Northern Ireland
Channel Islands
Isle of Man

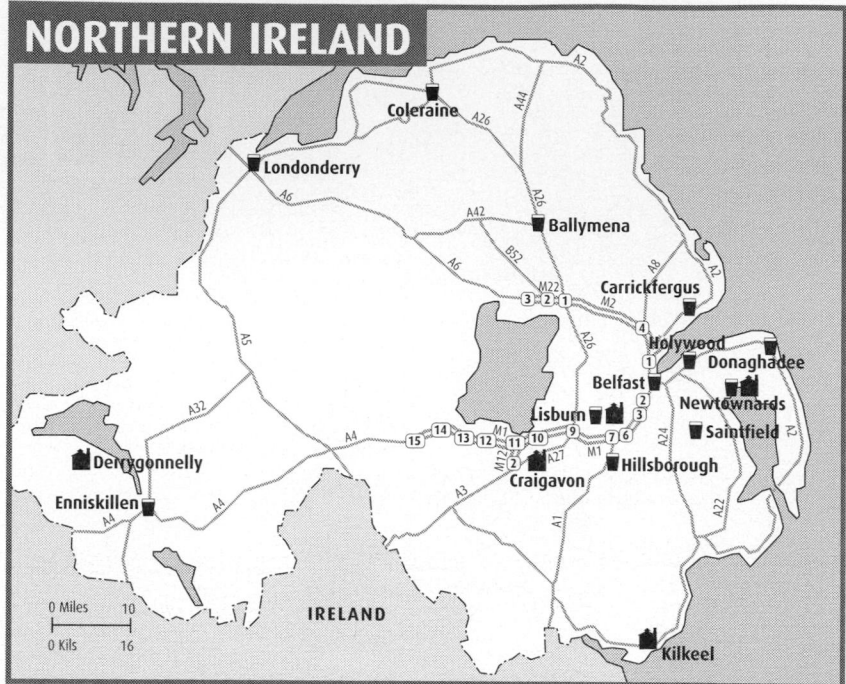

NORTHERN IRELAND

Ballymena

Spinning Mill 🍷 ✅
17-21 Broughshane Street, BT43 6EB
☼ 8-11 (midnight Fri & Sat) ☎ (028) 2563 8985
Greene King Abbot; guest beers Ⓗ
Town-centre Wetherspoon in a busy part of
Ballymena. Converted from a keg-only pub, it has
two bars – the upstairs area has a cosy fireplace
while downstairs there is some interesting church-
sourced woodwork. Up to eight real ales are
offered with the maximum at beer festival times.
The pub opens for breakfast from 8am but in
common with other Wetherspoon pubs in the
province alcohol is not served until 11.30am
(12.30pm Sun). Local CAMRA Pub of the Year 2012.
🏭🛏️🌗️🍽️🚻

Belfast

Botanic Inn
23-27 Malone Road, BT9 6RU
☼ 11.30-1am; 12-midnight Sun ☎ (028) 9050 9740
⊕ thebotanicinn.com
Whitewater Belfast Ale Ⓗ
'The Bot' is a long-established pub near Queen's
University. It claims to be the largest pub in
Northern Ireland and has three busy bars.
Downstairs is the main bar where you will find the
handpump serving real ale. Beside it is the public
bar where ale is a little cheaper. Both are
decorated with sporting memorabilia and have
numerous screens for sports events. Upstairs is a
nightclub open Wednesday to Saturday.
🍷🚭♿️🚍(8B)🚻

Bridge House ✅
37-43 Bedford Street, BT2 7EJ
☼ 8-midnight (1am Fri & Sat); 12-midnight Sun
☎ (028) 9072 7890

Greene King IPA, Abbot; guest beers Ⓗ
Wetherspoon pub close to the railway station and
City Hall. Set on two floors, the main bar is
downstairs and the family area and toilets upstairs.
Eight handpumps dispense two regular beers and
up to six constantly changing guests from quarterly
lists. Two annual beer festivals are held and
occasional festivals featuring Hilden beer. The
usual good-value Wetherspooon food menu is
available. A busy pub, especially at weekends, with
friendly, helpful, knowledgable staff. Local CAMRA
Pub of the Year 2010 and 2011.
🚭🍷♿️🚉(Gt Victoria St)🚍🍽️🚻

Crown ★ ✅
46 Great Victoria Street, BT2 7BA (opp Europa Hotel and
Great Victoria St station)
☼ 11.30-midnight; 12.30-11 Sun ☎ (028) 9024 3187
⊕ crownbar.com
Whitewater Belfast Ale, Copperhead Ⓗ
Corner bar, dating from 1840, transformed in the
1880s into a fine example of Victorian pub design.
Five years ago the mosaic-tiled floor, yellow, red
and gold painted ceiling, brocaded walls, granite-
topped bar, snugs and woodwork were all restored
to their former beauty. Pictures of the restoration
can be seen on the pub's website. A masterpiece in
pub architecture and a real ale delight – a must-
visit venue for visitors to Belfast.
🍷♿️🚉(Gt Victoria St)🚍

INDEPENDENT BREWERIES

Ards Newtownards (NEW)
Clanconnel Craigavon
Hilden Lisburn
Inishmacsaint Derrygonnelly
Whitewater Kilkeel

Horatio Todd's Bar & Restaurant

406 Upper Newtownards Road, BT4 3EZ
⊕ 11.30-1am (11 Mon-Wed); 12-midnight Sun
☎ (028) 9065 3090 ⊕ horatiotodds.com
Whitewater Belfast Ale H

Part of the Botanic Inns group, Horatio Todd's is the only real ale outlet in the east of the city. The spacious interior includes a large L-shaped bar, a snug and comfortable sofas. Whitewater Copperhead ale is often offered as an alternative to the Belfast. Along with the King's Head, this is one of the classier establishments selling real ale in the city. The crowd tends to be well dressed and it can be busy. ⊕&₩⅄

John Hewitt

51 Donegal Street, BT1 2FH (100yds from St Anne's Cathedral)
⊕ 11.30 (12 Sat)-1am; 7-midnight Sun ☎ (028) 9023 3768
⊕ thejohnhewitt.com
Hilden Ale, Twisted Hop H

This popular bar, near St Anne's Cathedral, does not have TV or piped music but concentrates on live music and events including quizzes and art exhibitions. It is owned and run by the Belfast Unemployed Resource Centre and helps to fund the organisation's work. High-quality food is served at lunchtime with specials on the blackboard. Q⊕&₩

King's Head

829 Lisburn Road, BT9 7GY (opp Kings Hall at Balmoral)
⊕ 12-1am (midnight Mon); 12-midnight Sun
☎ (028) 9050 9950
Whitewater Belfast Ale H

Formerly a mansion house, the King's Head is now a bar, restaurant and music complex. The real ale is available in the public bar – to one side is an open-plan drinking area while on the other is a comfortable lounge. The restaurant is upstairs, serving quality food with excellent service. Note the glass case displaying beer and wine bottles by the staircase. Well worth a visit, with bus and rail stops nearby. Q⊛⊕&≠(Balmoral)P⅄

Carrickfergus

Central Bar ✓

13-15 High Street, BT38 7AN (opp Castle)
⊕ 8-11 (1am Fri & Sat); 9-11 Sun ☎ (028) 9335 7840
Greene King IPA, Abbot; guest beers H

Town-centre Wetherspoon convenient for the railway station. This is a community pub with many devoted regulars and a family dining area upstairs offering the standard good-value menu. The first floor enjoys fantastic views from many windows over Belfast Lough and Carrick Castle. Handpumps on both levels dispense the two house beers plus up to three guests, usually from Scottish and English micros. Alcohol is served from 11.30am (12.30pm Sun). Q⅄⊕&≠₩(563)

Coleraine

Old Courthouse ✓

Castlerock Road, BT51 3HP
⊕ 9-11 (1am Fri & Sat) ☎ (028) 7032 5820
Greene King IPA, Abbot; guest beers H

A remarkable Wetherspoon conversion, it has kept the look of the old courthouse it once was. The pillars and black and white tiled flooring help retain something of the building's original courtly ambience. Food and drink can be enjoyed in the main bar area, on the balcony upstairs, or at outside tables. There are five handpumps dispensing a changing range of guests in addition to the two regular beers. Alcohol is served from 11.30am (12.30pm Sun). ⋈⅄⊛⊕&₺

Donaghadee

Moat Inn

102 Moat Street, BT21 0ED
⊕ 11.30-11.30; 12.30-10 Sun ☎ (028) 9188 3297
⊕ moatinn.co.uk
Beer range varies H

On the main road into Donaghadee, the Moat has a public bar, lounge, upstairs restaurant and garden area for summer days. There are two handpumps in the public bar supplying beers mainly from the Whitewater Brewery, often Belfast Ale and Copperhead, with occasional guests. The seaside town is well known for the lighthouse and the picturesque harbour just a few hundred yards away. The pub and locality are well worth a visit. ⊛⊕&₩(7)P⅄

Enniskillen

Linen Hall ✓

11-13 Townhall Street, BT74 7BD
⊕ 8-midnight (11 Mon & Tue; 1am Sat); 8-11 Sun
☎ (028) 6634 0910
Greene King Abbot; guest beers H

The Linen Hall is centred on Enniskillen's busy main street. On three levels, it is long and narrow, and tends to be busy despite being surrounded by many competing bars. It has five handpumps serving a variety of ales and occasionally a real cider. In common with other Wetherspoons in the province, alcohol is served from 11.30am (12.30pm Sun). ⅄⊛⊕&⚘⅄

Hillsborough

Hillside

21 Main Street, BT26 6AE
⊕ 12-11.30 (1am Fri & Sat); 12-11 Sun ☎ (028) 9268 9233
⊕ hillsidehillsborough.co.uk
Hilden Hilden Ale, Twisted Hop; guest beer H

An outlet for the Hilden Brewery from the neighbouring city of Lisburn, three handpumps serve Hilden products with an occasional guest. The rustic interior has two drinking areas with a restaurant at the back. The walls are adorned with pictures of hunting and old Hillsborough. Live music acts play at the weekend and there is a summer beer festival. Outside is a pretty cobblestone beer garden. ⋈Q⊛⊕&₩(38,238)⅄

Parson's Nose Ⓛ

48 Lisburn Street, BT26 6AB
⊕ 12-11 (1am Fri & Sat) ☎ (028) 9268 3009
⊕ theparsonsnose.co.uk
Whitewater Copperhead H

This pub has been transformed from a keg-only bar to a more upmarket establishment selling real ale. You can drink in the bar without dining but it is mostly frequented by diners before or after eating. The restaurant is upstairs and offers excellent cuisine made by an award-winning chef. The bar area is on two levels and has some interesting woodwork to admire. Closing times vary depending on how busy it is. ⋈⊛⊕&₩(38,238)⅄

Plough Inn

The Square, BT26 6AG
🕐 11.30-11 (12.30am Thu-Sat) ☎ (028) 9268 2985
Whitewater Copperhead Ⓗ
One of three real ale outlets in the village of
Hillsborough. The Plough, a former CAMRA
Northern Ireland Pub of the Year, now sells
Whitewater ales, usually Copperhead but
sometimes Belfast Ale. The interior has a central
bar surrounded by drinking areas on different
levels. The walls are decorated with wood
panelling and a variety of memorabilia. Two
screens show football matches and the bar can be
congested when a big game is on. Friendly and
helpful staff add to a welcoming atmosphere.
🏨🕸🌓🕭☶☵(38,238)🗙

Holywood

Dirty Duck Ale House

3 Kinnegar Road, BT18 9JN (300yds from railway
station)
🕐 11.30-11.30 (1am Thu-Sat); 12.30-11 Sun
☎ (028) 9059 6666 🌐 thedirtyduckalehouse.co.uk
Beer range varies Ⓗ
On the County Down side of Belfast Lough, this
welcoming inn is a previous CAMRA Northern
Ireland Pub of the Year and has won various
awards for its food. The four handpumps often
feature ales from Hilden, Tom Wood and
Inveralmond breweries. The picture windows, both
upstairs and downstairs, offer superb views of
shipping in the lough and the county Antrim coast.
The pub has a golf society, a quiz on Tuesday, a real
ale club on Wednesday and live music Thursday to
Sunday evenings. 🏨🕸🌓☵☶🗙

Lisburn

Tap Room

Hilden Brewery, Hilden, BT27 4TY (5 mins walk from
Hilden railway halt)
🕐 closed Mon; 12-2.30, 5.30-9; 12-3 Sun ☎ (028) 9266 3863
🌐 taproomhilden.com
Hilden Hilden Ale, Twisted Hop Ⓗ
The Tap Room nestles beside Hilden Brewery in the
courtyard of the Scullion's Georgian mansion. It is a
long building with restaurant, bar and seating
areas. As a licensed restaurant, alcohol is only
available with a meal. High-quality seasonal,
locally sourced food is served alongside two ales
from the brewery next door. The Tap Room often
hosts functions, including an annual beer festival,
and brewery tours can be arranged.
🏨Q🕸🌓☵☶(Hilden)☶(325H)P🗙

Tuesday Bell ✅

4 Lisburn Square, BT28 1TS
🕐 8-11 ☎ (028) 9262 7390
Greene King IPA, Abbot; guest beers Ⓗ
Now in its 10th year, the Tuesday Bell is still the
only pub in Lisburn City that sells real ale. It has
both upstairs and downstairs bars with a total of

eight handpumps. These dispense a variety of
beers from the Wetherspoon's list and the local
brewery at Hilden. The bars have different
characters with the younger crowd preferring to go
upstairs. Alcohol is served from 11.30am (12.30pm
Sun). 🌓☵☶☶☵🗙

Londonderry

Diamond ✅

23-24 The Diamond, BT48 6HP (centre of walled city)
🕐 8-1am (11 Mon & Tue; midnight Wed & Thu; midnight Sun)
☎ (028) 7127 2880
Greene King IPA, Abbot; guest beers Ⓗ
In the heart of the main shopping district is the
Diamond, one of the city's two Wetherspoon
establishments. In an elevated location inside the
city walls, this two-storey pub has good views from
the upper floor. There are large bars on both floors
with a total of 10 handpumps. A varied range of
guest ales is usually available alongside the
regulars. Alcohol is served from 11.30am (12.30pm
Sun). ☴🌓☵☶☶🗙

Newtownards

Spirit Merchant ✅

54-56 Regent Street, BT23 4LP (next to bus station)
🕐 9am-11 (midnight Fri & Sat) ☎ (028) 9182 4270
**Greene King IPA, Abbot; Ruddles Best Bitter; guest
beers** Ⓗ
Wetherspoon pub adjacent to the bus station and
near the town centre. Warm and welcoming, it has
the feel of a local with knowledgable, friendly and
helpful staff. In addition to the three regular beers,
up to two changing guests are offered. It features
two annual beer festivals, three TV screens, a
smoking area at the front and a heated courtyard
to the side. The usual good-value Wetherspoon's
menu is served, with breakfast from 9am. Alcohol
is available from 11.30am (12.30pm Sun).
🕸🌓☵☶(5,7,9)☶P🗙

Saintfield

White Horse

49-53 Main Street, BT24 7AB
🕐 11.30-11.30; 12-10.30 Sun ☎ (028) 9751 1143
🌐 whitehorsesaintfield.com
**Whitewater Copperhead Ale, Belfast Ale, Crown
Glory; guest beers** Ⓗ
Situated in the historic town of Saintfield some 10
miles from Belfast. Formerly a coaching inn, it is
now a modern pub with bar, lounge and bistro
areas. Effectively the brewery tap for Whitewater,
three or more of its ales are always on offer. A
previous winner of CAMRA Northern Ireland Pub of
the Year, the annual beer festival is a 'must do' in
the local branch's social diary.
🏨🕸🌓☵☶(15,215)🗙

George and the dragon

Belated traveller arrives at an inn, the George & Dragon. He bangs on the door for a long
time. Eventually an upstairs window opens and a furious female head is thrust out. 'What
the hell d'you want at this time o'night?' 'Can I speak to George, please?'
Yorkshire story

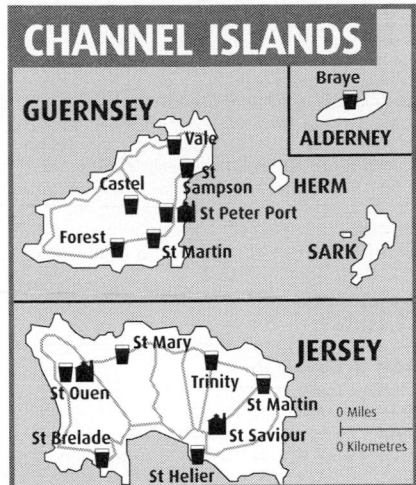

CHANNEL ISLANDS

GUERNSEY
Vale
St Sampson
Castel
St Peter Port
Forest
St Martin
Braye
ALDERNEY
HERM
SARK

St Mary
St Ouen
Trinity
St Martin
St Brelade
St Saviour
St Helier
JERSEY
0 Miles
0 Kilometres

ALDERNEY
Braye

Coxswain Bar
Braye Street, GY9 3XT
🌀 9am-11 ☎ (01481) 822421
Randalls Patois 🖻
The small Coxswain Bar and Boathouse Bistro together form The Moorings, a venue that is popular with locals as well as visitors. The bar's welcoming landlords are enthusiastic about quality real ale, and guest beers may be on sale during the summer. Another attraction is the lovely location just 100 yards from the harbour. Good-value food is served from April to October. 🕮🕪

GUERNSEY
Castel

Fleur du Jardin ✪
Kings Mills, GY5 7JT
🌀 10.30-11.45 ☎ (01481) 257996 ⊕ fleurdujardin.com
Greene King Old Speckled Hen; Sharp's Doom Bar 🖻
A building of unique charm with two bars – one traditional, small and cosy, attached to the restaurant, the other recently renovated in a more contemporary style to create a comfortable, relaxing area to enjoy a beer. A door from this area leads to a large covered patio and out to the garden. Menus in both the bar and restaurant feature fresh local produce. 🕮Q🌸🕪👌P🕯

Rockmount Hotel
Cobo, GY5 7HB
🌀 10.30-midnight (12.45am Fri & Sat) ☎ (01481) 256757
Black Sheep Best Bitter; Randalls Patois 🖻
A pub for all seasons with a choice of bars – a public to the rear, and a large front bar with a comfortable seating area, a main area for dining and a sports-oriented space. In winter a warming fire makes it a cosy retreat from the gales. A good range of tasty food is served and the pub is just across the road from a sandy beach. The perfect place to relax and enjoy one of Guernsey's legendary sunsets. 🕮🕪🖨🚽P🕯

Forest

Deerhound ✪
Le Bourg, GY8 0AN
🌀 11-11 ☎ (01481) 238585
Liberation Ale 🖻
Modern pub on the main road to the airport. The emphasis is on food, and a popular choice of meals is served. Tables cannot be booked ahead and the bar can get busy in the evenings. Outside, there is a large, decked patio perfect for summer dining, as well as benches dotted about on the grass. The car park fills up quickly at peak times. 🌸🕪▶🚽P

St Martin

Captain's Hotel ✪
La Fosse, GY4 6EF
🌀 11-11 (midnight Fri & Sat); 12-4 Sun ☎ (01481) 238990
Fuller's London Pride; Greene King Old Speckled Hen 🖻
In a secluded location down a country lane, this is a popular locals' pub with a lively, friendly atmosphere. It has a small, raised area in front of the bar furnished with a sofa to make a comfy zone. Meals can be eaten in the bar or bistro area, or you can take away a pizza. A meat draw is held on Friday. The car park to the rear fills up quickly. 🚽🕪P🕯

St Peter Port

Cock & Bull
Lower Hauteville, GY1 1LL
🌀 11-2.30, 4-12.45am; 11-12.45am Fri & Sat; closed Sun
☎ (01481) 722660
Beer range varies 🖻
Popular pub, just up the hill from the town church, with five handpumps providing a changing range of beer and cider. Live music takes place throughout the week, with salsa, baroque or jazz on Monday, open mic on Tuesday, jazz on Wednesday, Irish on Thursday and on Saturday a silent set – gentle music that won't hinder good conversation. A meat draw is held on Friday. Seating is on three levels. The pub only opens on Sunday when there is rugby on. 🍺🕯

Cornerstone Café Bar ♈
La Tour Beauregard, GY1 1LQ (top of Cornet Street)
🌀 10 (8am Thu & Fri)-midnight; 12-6 Sun ☎ (01481) 713832
⊕ cornerstoneguernsey.co.uk
Beer range varies 🖻
Situated across the road from the States Archives, this café has a small bar area to the front and further seating to the rear. Regular quiz evenings are held. The menu offers a wide range of good-quality hot and cold meals, plus a daily specials board (no food Sun). There is a large screen for sporting events. Ales from Randalls or Liberation Brewery are usually on handpump – check the website for what's on now and what's up and coming. 🕪

Drunken Duck
La Charroterie, GY1 1EL (opp Charles Frossard House)
🌀 11 (12 Sun)-12.45am ☎ (01481) 726170
Beer range varies 🖻
After a return to its distinctive name, this is once again a welcoming locals' hostelry. The bar is divided into two areas. At the front, the comfortable zone with a couple of sofas has been

ISLANDS

retained, alongside plenty of traditional pub seating. To the rear, the original bench seats around the walls have returned and there is now a dartboard. Light bites such as baguettes and toasties are available. ⭲

Ship & Crown ✓

North Esplanade, GY1 2NB (opp Crown Pier car park)
✪ 10-12.45am; 12-10 Sun ☎ (01481) 721368
⊕ crowsnestguernsey.com
Beer range varies Ⓗ
Situated in the heart of St Peter Port, opposite the Victoria Pier, with superb panoramic views of the marina and neighbouring islands. Excellent bar meals are served in generous portions throughout the day until 9pm, with a daily changing range of specials. The Crows Nest above the pub serves meals lunchtimes and evenings but there is no handpump – only bottles. However, if they are not too busy the staff will bring beer up from the bar for you. Real cider is also on handpump. ◖❿

St Sampson

La Fontaine

Vale Rord, GY2 4DS
✪ 11 (10 Sat)-midnight,; 12-6 Sun ☎ (01481) 247644
Randalls Patois Ⓗ
The pub is situated on the main road leading from the Halfway towards L'Ancresse Common and Pembroke Bay. Inside, there is a public bar at the front and a large back bar with a serving hatch into the lounge. The beer is served from a bar in the middle. A popular locals' pub, shove ha'penny is played in the public bar. There is a car park to the rear and buses stop nearby. ❀◖❒♣P⭲

Pony Inn ✓

Les Capelles, GY2 4GX
✪ 11-10.30 ☎ (01481) 244374
Fuller's London Pride Ⓗ
The pub was heavily modernised some years ago and the emphasis is now on good-quality food, with families welcome. The handpumps are on the bar in the dining area. To the side there is a public bar with its own entrance – although there is no handpump here the staff will happily bring you a pint from the main bar. To the front is a large car park with an outside seating area. ❀◖◖⊟P⭲

Vale

Houmet Tavern ✓

Rousse, GY6 8AR (between Vale Church and Rousse Tower)
✪ 10-12.45am (6 Sun) ☎ (01481) 242214
Liberation Ale Ⓗ
A popular locals' pub, the Houmet has two bars – the Anchor Bar, which is the public bar at the rear with pool and darts available, and the recently renovated Front Bar, with a more contemporary feel and picturesque views of the north of the island. Guest beers may be on sale during the summer. A good-quality food menu offers a mix of old favourites and new ideas. ◖⊟❒P⭲

JERSEY
St Brelade

Old Smugglers Inn ✓

Le Mont du Ouaisne, JE3 8AW

✪ 11-11 (winter hours vary) ☎ (01534) 741510
⊕ oldsmugglersinn.com
Draught Bass Ⓗ; **Greene King Abbot** Ⓖ; **Wells Bombardier; guest beers** Ⓗ
Perched on the edge of Ouaisne Bay, the Smugglers has been the jewel in the crown of the Jersey real ale scene for many years. It is set on several levels within granite-built fishermen's cottages dating back hundreds of years. Up to four real ales are usually available including one from Skinner's, and mini beer festivals are regularly held. The pub is well known for its good food and fresh daily specials. ᗶQ◖◗

St Helier

Dog & Sausage

9 Halkett Street, JE2 4WJ
✪ 10-11 ☎ (01534) 730982
Skinner's Ginger Tosser, Betty Stogs Ⓗ
Down a back lane near the central market, with a corner entrance and a small alfresco area, the Dog has a character all of its own. A local pub for local people, but welcoming to all, there is usually a choice of two well-looked-after Skinner's ales on offer. Lunchtime snacks are served and there is a jukebox but no TV. Probably the coldest toilet on the Island... ◖

Forum ❢ Ⓛ ✓

13 Grenville Street, JE2 4UF
✪ 11-11.30 ☎ (01534) 768105
Liberation Ale, seasonal beers; guest beers Ⓗ
Situated just on the outskirts of the town centre, the pub is named after the cinema that once occupied the site opposite. It has a modern interior but with a classic feel and includes a number of brass plaques that were taken from the old Royal Court building. This is not a quiet pub – live sport and background music often feature. Three real ales are always available, and a large range of real ciders. Food is served in the bar from the Indian restaurant directly above. Local CAMRA Pub of the Year 2010 and 2011. ◖⅋❿⭲

Lamplighter Ⓛ

9 Mulcaster Street, JE2 3NJ
✪ 11-11 ☎ (01534) 723119
Ringwood Best Bitter, Fortyniner; Wells Eagle IPA, Bombardier Ⓗ; **guest beers** Ⓖ
A traditional pub with a modern feel. The gas lamps that gave the pub its name remain, as does the original antique pewter bar top. An excellent range of up to eight real ales is available including one from Skinner's – four are served direct from the cask. A real cider is sometimes also on offer. Previous local CAMRA Pub of the Year. ◖❒(5)❿

Peirson Ⓛ ✓

17 Royal Square, JE2 4WA
✪ 10 (11 Sun)-11 ☎ (01534) 722726
Draught Bass; Liberation Ale Ⓗ; **guest beer** Ⓖ
Recently redecorated, the pub is nestled in the corner of the Royal Square in the centre of St Helier. Named after Major Francis Peirson, it contains historical reminders of the Battle of Jersey

in 1781. Two ales are always on handpump plus an occasional additional ale on gravity. Excellent food is served at lunchtime throughout the year, with evening meals also offered during the summer. The pub has a good reputation with locals and visitors alike. Outside seating is extremely popular in the summer months. Q❀①❶♿➍

Post Horn 🅛
Hue Street, JE2 3RE
✪ 10 (11 Sun)-11 ☎ (01534) 872853
Liberation Ale, seasonal beer; guest beer Ⓗ
Busy, friendly pub adjacent to the precinct and five minutes' walk from the Royal Square. Popular at lunchtimes with its own nucleus of regulars, it offers three draught ales plus a guest. The large L-shaped public bar extends into the lounge area where there is an open fire and TV showing sport. A good selection of freshly cooked food is served. There is a large function room on the first floor, a drinking area outside and a public car park nearby. ♨❀①♿➍

St Martin

Royal
La Grande Route de Faldouet, JE3 6UG
✪ 9.30am (11 Sun)-11 ☎ (01534) 856289
Ringwood Best Bitter; Draught Bass Ⓗ**; guest beer** Ⓖ
Large, traditional, country-style inn at the centre of St Martin with sizeable public and lounge bars and a restaurant area. Owned by Randalls, it has been under the same management team for 25 years. The interior features traditional furnishings, cosy corners and a real fire in the colder months. Guest ales are from the Marston's, Sharp's and Skinner's stables. Quality food is popular with locals and visitors alike, with a good menu served lunchtimes and evenings until 8.30pm (no food Sun eves). ♨Q❀①❶♿▲➍(3)P➍

Rozel Bar & Restaurant ✔
La Valle de Rozel, JE3 6AJ
✪ 10-11 ☎ (01534) 863478 ⊕ rozelbarandrestaurant.co.uk
Draught Bass; Liberation Ale Ⓗ
A charming hostelry tucked away in the north-west corner of the Island, under new management as a Liberation Group partner pub. It has a delightful beer garden and an excellent restaurant upstairs. Bar meals are served in the public bar and snug, where there is a real fire in the winter. Guest beers from Skinner's and Ringwood are often available. Locals are friendly if sometimes a little rumbustious. ♨➤❀①❶♿➍(3)P➍

St Mary

St Mary's Country Inn 🅛 ✔
La Rue des Buttes, JE3 3DS
✪ 10 (11 Sun)-11 ☎ (01534) 482897
Liberation Ale; guest beers Ⓗ
An archetypal country inn from the outside, this 17th-century farmhouse is sited opposite the parish church that has a history dating back to Norman times. Following refurbishment in 2009, the interior is contemporary with a main bar and an extensive dining area. The four handpumps serve Liberation and three guest beers, and reasonably priced good food is available daily from an extensive menu. The inn has a comfortable and relaxed atmosphere with seating outside front and rear for when the sunshine prevails. A reasonable walk from the north coast. ♨➤❀①❶♿➍P➍

St Ouen

Moulin de Lecq ✔
Le Mont de la Greve de Lecq, JE3 2DT
✪ 11-11 (winter hours vary) ☎ (01534) 482818
⊕ moulindelecq.com
Greene King Abbot Ⓖ**, Old Speckled Hen, seasonal beers; Wells Bombardier; guest beers** Ⓗ
Another free house on the island offering a range of real ales, the Moulin is a converted 12th-century watermill situated in the valley above the beach at Greve de Lecq. The waterwheel is still in place and the turning mechanism can be seen behind the bar. A restaurant adjoins the mill. There is a children's play space and a barbecue area used extensively in the summer. ♨Q❀①❶➍(9)➍P➍

Trinity

Trinity Arms 🅛 ✔
La Rue es Picots, JE3 5JX
✪ 11-11 ☎ (01534) 864691
Liberation Mary Ann Best Ⓐ**, Ale** Ⓗ
Sporting the parish's ancient symbol of the Trinity, this 1976-built pub is modern by Jersey country pub standards but has plenty of character. Owned by the Liberation Group, the pub is central to and popular within village community life. It has a public bar and restaurant where food is served lunchtimes and evenings. There is seating outside, a children's play area and car parking. ❀①♿➍(4)♣P➍

The ale diet

Boniface: Sir, I have now in my cellar ten tun of the best ale in Staffordshire; 'tis smooth as oil, sweet as milk, clear as amber, and strong as brandy; and will be just 14 years old the fifth day of next March, old style.

Aimwell: You're very exact, I find, in the age of your ale.

Boniface: As punctual, sir, as I am in the age of my children. I'll show you such ale: I have lived in Lichfield, man and boy, about eight-and-fifty years, and, I believe, have not consumed eight-and-fifty ounces of meat.

Aimwell: At a meal, you mean, if one may guess your sense by your bulk.

Boniface: Not in my life, sir, I have fed purely upon ale; I have eat my ale, drank my ale, and I always sleep upon ale.

George Farquhar, The Beaux-Stratagem, 1701

ISLANDS

Good Bottled Beer Guide

Jeff Evans

A pocket-sized guide for discerning drinkers looking to buy bottled real ales and enjoy a fresh glass of their favourite beers at home. The 7th edition of the **Good Bottled Beer Guide** is completely revised, updated and redesigned to showcase the very best bottled British real ales now being produced, and detail where they can be bought. Everything you need to know about bottled beers; tasting notes, ingredients, brewery details, and a glossary to help the reader understand more about them.

£12.99   ISBN 978-1-85249-262-5   CAMRA members' price £10.99   384 pages

For this and other books on beer and pubs visit the CAMRA bookshop at **www.camra.org.uk/books**

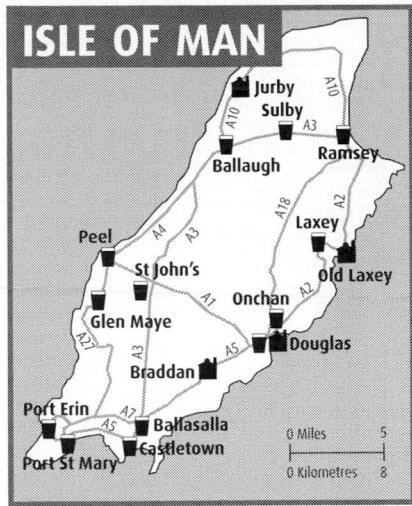

Ballasalla

Whitestone 🅻 ✅
Station Road, IM9 2DD
🕐 12-11 (midnight Fri & Sat) ☎ (01624) 822334
Okells Bitter; guest beers Ⓗ
Large multi-roomed village pub, a short walk from the steam railway station. There is a small separate public bar with a pool table and TV. Additionally there is plenty of space in two comfortable lounge areas, with an area for diners. A varied food menu is offered and live entertainment most weekends. The Okells bitter is usually complemented by one or two guest ales. Q❀ᗕ◖₠Ģᖘ⪪(IMR)▱(1,2)♣Pˡ⸺

Ballaugh

Raven 🅻 ✅
The Main Road, IM7 5EG
🕐 12-midnight ☎ (01624) 896128
Okells Bitter, Raven's Claw; guest beers Ⓗ
Established in 1740, the Raven is situated on the famous TT course near Ballaugh Bridge. Pictures of the TT are displayed throughout the inn. The house brew, Raven's Claw, is especially made by Okells, served alongside regularly changing guests. This family-friendly country inn has a separate dining area with food served all day. A popular quiz is held on Tuesday evening and theme nights monthly. There is a separate pool room and log fire in the bar. ≜❀ᗕ&ᗕⓅᖘ(5,6)♣Pˡ⸺

Castletown

Castle Arms (Glue Pot) 🅻 ✅
The Quay, IM9 1LD
🕐 12-11 (midnight Fri & Sat) ☎ (01624) 824673
Draught Bass; Okells Bitter; guest beers Ⓗ
Established around 1750, the Castle is known locally as the Glue Pot because once inside you are stuck there like glue. The pub overlooks the picturesque quayside and is adjacent to the historic Castle Rushen. The interior has a nautical feel, with pictures of the island's seafaring and TT tradition decorating the walls. It is the only pub to appear on a banknote (the Manx pound). Two guest beers are on offer plus a real cider.
Q❀⪪(IMR)▱(1,2)♣🐾ˡ⸺

Sidings 🍷 🅻
Victoria Road, IM9 1EF (next to railway station)
🕐 11.30-11.30 (12.30am Fri & Sat) ☎ (01624) 823282
🌐 thesidings.im
Bushy's Ruby Mild, Bitter, Castletown Bitter; Okells Bitter; guest beers Ⓗ
The Sidings stands next to the Victorian steam railway station. Locals call it by its former name, The Duck's Nest, after the original licensee, Mr Duck. Freshly cooked good-value food is served daily. Four local ales and eight changing guests are on offer. A beer festival with up to 50 real ales and ciders is held during the first fortnight in July. There is a log fire for cold days, separate pool room, darts and regular live entertainment. A winner of local CAMRA Branch Pub of the Year several times.
≜Q❀ᗕ◖⪪(IMR)▱♣Pˡ⸺

Douglas

Albert Hotel 🅻 ✅
3 Chapel Row, IM1 2BJ (next to bus station)
🕐 10-11 (11.45 Fri & Sat); 12-11 Sun ☎ (01624) 673632
Bushy's Castletown Bitter; Okells Mild, Bitter; guest beers Ⓗ
The nearest Guide pub to the sea terminal and ferries, the Albert is an unspoilt backstreet local with many regulars. It has a traditional central bar, dark wood panelling, a pool table in one room and interesting pictures of Steam Packet boats in the other. Sport on TV is a frequent feature but never loud enough to spoil conversation. The house beer, Jough (Manx for drink), brewed by Okells, is often available, though sometimes it is replaced by a guest. A rare outlet for Okells Mild.
₠⪪(IMR)▱♣ˡ⸺

Horse & Plough 🅻 ✅
Isle of Man Business Park, Cooil Road, Braddan, IM2 2QZ
🕐 12-3, 5-11; 12-midnight Fri & Sat; 12-11 Sun
☎ (01624) 626060
Okells Bitter; guest beers Ⓗ
A large, modern pub serving the Isle of Man business park and adjacent housing estate. With a choice of rooms, there is ample space for customers to relax in an informal atmosphere. The large conservatory leads to a seating area outside at the rear. There is a pool table and TV for sporting events, complemented by old photographs on the walls. Good-value pub food as well as an excellent Thai menu are offered to accompany the four real ales. ❀◖&▱(4)♣Pˡ⸺

Old Market Inn 🅻
Chapel Row, IM1 2BJ (near bus station)
🕐 9-midnight (11 Sun) ☎ 07624 381076
Bushy's Old Bushy Tail; guest beer Ⓗ
The Old Market Inn appeared in the Guide in 2007, but stopped selling real ale for a while. Now that the beer is back – with Bushy's and a changing guest – you can once again use this small (probably the smallest on the Island), friendly pub as a waiting room for bus, boat and horse trams during the summer. Keep an eye on the time though, or

continued below / independent breweries

INDEPENDENT BREWERIES

Bushy's Braddan
Doghouse Jurby (NEW)
Okells Douglas
Old Laxey Old Laxey

ISLANDS

you're bound to get caught up in conversation with fellow imbibers and miss your transport. The steam railway is also not far away. 🏚🚋≈(IMR)🚆♣♿

Prospect Hotel Ⓛ
Prospect Hill, IM1 1ET
✪ 12-11 (midnight Fri); 6-midnight Sat; closed Sun
☎ (01624) 616773
Okells Bitter; guest beers Ⓗ
Opened in 1857, the pub is situated in the finance sector of the island's capital, opposite the Tynwald Parliament building. It is busy and popular, especially among office workers. A library area is for visitors wanting a quiet drink. Close to the law courts, the walls feature many pictures relating to the law profession. Up to six changing guest beers are available. Ⓓ≈(IMR)🚆

Queen's Hotel Ⓛ
Queen's Promenade, IM2 4NL (on seafront, N end of promenade)
✪ 12-11 (midnight Fri & Sat) ☎ (01624) 674438
Okells Bitter; guest beers Ⓗ
One of a few remaining pubs on Douglas promenade, refurbished and popular with visitors and locals alike. Outside, there is plenty of seating under heated awnings, and great views of Douglas bay, ferries and trams. The interior has three distinct areas, one with a pool table and the others with low-volume TVs screening sport. Up to two guest beers are available alongside the Okells. Pub grub is served seven days a week and there is live music at the weekend. 🏵Ⓓ≈🚆♣♿

Rovers Return Ⓛ
11 Church Street, IM1 2AG (behind town hall)
✪ 12-11 (midnight Fri & Sat) ☎ (01624) 676459
Bushy's Bitter, Ruby Mild, seasonal beers; guest beers Ⓗ
This wonderfully atmospheric town-centre pub comprises a labyrinth of rooms, including the Inner Sanctum – a shrine to Blackburn Rovers FC, served by a single bar featuring handpumps fashioned from polished brass firehose branches. The Rovers showcases Bushy's range of beers plus three guests and Westons real cider (rare on the Island), and serves wholesome pub lunches in Desperate Dan-sized portions. One of its greatest assets is a truly eclectic mix of loyal and enthusiastic regulars. 🏚🏵Ⓓ≈(IMR)🚆♣👕♿

Terminus Tavern Ⓛ ✔
Strathallan Crescent, IM2 4NR
✪ 12-11 (midnight Fri & Sat) ☎ (01624) 624312
Okells Bitter; guest beers Ⓗ
Refurbished a few years ago, the Terminus offers guest beers alongside Okells Bitter. The spacious front bar is comfortable, with alcoves around the large front windows. There is also a back bar/games room. Popular for dining, the pub can get busy during peak times. The large seating area outside is next to the starting point for the seasonal horse trams and Manx Electric Railway, with views across Douglas Bay. 🏚Q🏵Ⓓ🍴♿≈(MER)🚆(25,26,27)♣♿

Woodbourne Hotel Ⓛ ✔
Alexander Drive, IM2 3QF
✪ 3 (12 Fri-Sun)-midnight ☎ (01624) 676754
Okells Bitter, seasonal beers; guest beers Ⓗ
Imposing Victorian red-brick pub retaining its three-bar layout, although sadly few original fittings remain. The cosy central bar features a splendid series of watercolour caricatures of regulars from the not-so-long-ago days when this was the Gents Only bar. A games room features pool, darts and occasional live music. Under the stewardship of the current manager, the Woody has become a showcase for Okells fine beers in addition to an ever-changing selection of guests. Q🍴🚆♣♿

Glen Maye

Waterfall Ⓛ
Shore Road, IM5 3BG
✪ 12-11 ☎ (01624) 840626 🌐 thewaterfall.im
Okells Bitter; guest beers Ⓗ
Situated at the head of the beautiful Glen Maye, this attractive traditional country pub has an open terrace at the front. Popular with walkers and families on summer weekends, the pub also enjoys a local following in the evenings. Good hearty food is available alongside between two and four varied real ales on handpump. Three linked areas around the bars cater for diners, drinkers and pool players. 🏚Q🏵Ⓓ🚆P♿

Laxey

Bridge Inn Ⓛ
6 New Road, IM4 7BE
✪ 12-11 (midnight Fri & Sat) ☎ (01624) 862414
🌐 bridgeinn.im
Bushy's Mild, Bitter; guest beers Ⓗ
Traditional historic local in the heart of the village, divided into two rooms. The lively saloon bar to the right features pool, darts and a large TV screen, with more comfortable seating and a piano in the lounge bar to the left. The pub cellar area was used as a temporary morgue after the nearby Snaefell mining disaster in 1897 in which 20 men perished. 🏚Q🏵🛏Ⓓ≈(MER)🚆(3,3a)♣P♿

Shore Hotel Ⓛ
Old Laxey Hill, Old Laxey, IM4 7DA (signed from main road)
✪ 12-midnight ☎ (01624) 861509 🌐 theshorehotel.im
Old Laxey Bosun Bitter Ⓗ
The Island's only brewpub, this comfortable village inn nestles beside the river in the quaint setting of Old Laxey, close to the picturesque harbour. The well-appointed single bar has a nautical theme but also features two framed cycling shirts worn by international cyclist and local sporting hero Mark Cavendish. The pub participates in the annual Laxey Big Wheel Blues Festival and other live music events. 🏚🏵Ⓓ♿🅰♣P♿

Onchan

Manx Arms Ⓛ
Main Road, IM3 1BE
✪ 12-11 (midnight Fri-Sun) ☎ (01624) 675484
Okells Bitter; guest beers Ⓗ
Sometimes lively, always friendly, this traditional village pub is situated on the main road, with a lounge and bar with pool, darts and dominoes, and large-screen TVs for sport. Live music features on most Saturday evenings and occasional karaoke nights are hosted. A heated patio at the front provides shelter for smokers and there is another at the rear next to the large car park. A seasonal or guest beer is usually offered alongside the Okells. 🏵🚆♿(3,23)♣P♿

Peel

Creek Inn L ✓

Station Place, IM5 1AT (overlooking Peel Marina)
✪ 10-midnight (12.30am Fri & Sat); 12-midnight Sun
☎ (01624) 842216 ⊕ thecreekinn.co.uk
Okells Bitter; guest beers Ⓗ
Traditional friendly, welcoming, marina-side pub, popular with locals and tourists. The lounge bar has separate seating areas and a nautical theme, with etched glass screens featuring sailing ships, and mirrors rescued from bygone Manx pubs. A good selection of ales, with up to 15 available at busy times, is on offer to complement the comprehensive food menu. Locally caught Manx queenies (queen scallops) and lobster are specialities. A sausage festival is held in January. Live music features every weekend.
🅗⬤🚆♿🅰🚃(5,6)🌸⚓

Marine Hotel L

Shore Road, IM5 1AH
✪ 12-midnight ☎ (01624) 842337 ⊕ marinehotelpeel.co.uk
Bushy's Bitter; Okells Bitter; guest beers Ⓗ
The Marine Hotel first opened in 1890 and overlooks the beautiful sandy beach and historic Peel Castle. It has two bar areas and a large refurbished restaurant serving a wide variety of food including excellent children's meals every day. Pictures of Peel and maritime images adorn the walls. With a much-improved real ale selection in recent years, it usually offers locally brewed Bushy's and Okells beers plus two guests.
🅜🅗⬤🚆♿🅰🚃(5)♣

White House Hotel L ✓

Tynwald Road, IM5 1LA (150yds from bus station)
✪ 11-midnight ☎ (01624) 842252
⊕ thewhitehousepeel.com
Bushy's Ruby Mild, Bitter; Moorhouse's Pride of Pendle; Okells Bitter; guest beers Ⓗ
A truly traditional pub – cosy, friendly and welcoming – with snugs and a large room for TV sport and live Manx music on Saturdays. The Whitey is one of just a few Manx pubs that sell real cider, and the only Manx pub to have won CAMRA Branch Pub of the Year three years in a row, 2008 to 2010. The regulars are complememted by up to four guest beers. The landlords source their ales from microbreweries all over the British Isles and are not afraid to experiment with new styles.
🅜Q🅗⬤🚆🅰🚃(5,6)♣🌸P

Port Erin

Bay Hotel L

Shore Road, IM9 6HL (far end of lower promenade)
✪ 12-midnight (1am Fri & Sat) ☎ (01624) 832084
Bushy's Ruby Mild, Bitter, Castletown Bitter, Old Bushy Tail, seasonal beers; guest beers Ⓗ
Bushy's flagship pub is on one of the best beaches on the island. Beach concerts and a promenade patio make The Bay a great summertime venue, with local bands playing in the winter. The full range of Bushy's brews is available, and can be sampled with a special taster tray. The interior comprises four traditional rooms – public bar, quiet room, dining room and band area. Wi-Fi access,

---

Beer makes you feel the way you ought to feel without beer. **Henry Lawson**

---

newspapers and good food help make this a popular pub for local ale fans and bikers during TT week. 🅜Q🚆🅗⬤🚃♿🚆≈(IMR)♣🌸⚓

Falcon's Nest Hotel L

Station Road, IM9 6AF (200yds from railway station)
✪ 11-midnight (1am Fri & Sat) ☎ (01624) 834077
Bushy's Bitter; Okells Dr Okells IPA; guest beers Ⓗ
The Falcon's Nest hotel enjoys panoramic views over a picturesque crescent-shaped bay. A free house, the bar is open to the public and hotel guests, offering a range of local ales as well as the warmth of a real fire. With a nearby sandy beach, this is a child-friendly hotel and pets are welcome too, but not in dining areas. Food is served until 9pm in the restaurant, conservatory and bars, with a popular Sunday carvery 12-2pm. There is a smoking area with TV.
🅜Q🚆🏠⬤🚃🚆≈(IMR)🚃♣⚓

Station Hotel L ✓

Station Road, IM9 6AE (opp railway station)
✪ 10.30-11 (midnight Fri & Sat); 12-11 Sun
☎ (01624) 838991
Okells Bitter, seasonal beers; guest beers Ⓗ
Large Heron & Brearley pub situated opposite the steam railway station and close to the bus station. Refurbished in recent years with wood-panelled bar areas and surround, there are comfortable tables and seating areas for diners, with raised alcove spaces and large bay windows. For those not dining, to the right of the bar area lies a separate well-furnished side room, ideal for a relaxed pint during peak periods.
⬤♿≈(IMR)🚃P⚓

Port St Mary

Albert Hotel L

Athol Street, IM9 5DS (next to bus terminal)
✪ 11-midnight; 12-1am Fri & Sat; 12-midnight Sun
☎ (01624) 832118
Bushy's Bitter, Old Bushy Tail; Okells Bitter; guest beer Ⓗ
The last pub in the village, with a bus stop right outside the door. Situated next to the quaint old harbour, this traditional inn has a nautical theme and is decorated with original artwork and fishing tackle. The interior features Manx Gaelic language quotations on the walls. Note the handsome sailing ship pub sign and the 'very low bend or bump' doorway to the Gents. It has three rooms, including spaces for TV and games, dining and a quiet lounge. 🅜Q🚆🏠⬤🚃🚆♣P⚓🍴

Ramsey

Plough L

40 Parliament Street, IM8 1AN
✪ 4-11.30 (12.30am Fri); 12-12.30am Sat; 12-11.30 Sun
☎ (01624) 813323
Okells Bitter; guest beer Ⓗ
Busy pub on Ramsey's main street. Shoppers taking a break mingle with football fans during the day and in the evening a mixed clientele vies for space in the two small bars. This free house has sold Okells Bitter for several years and has recently added an ever-changing guest. The Plough is a proud sponsor of Shennaghys Jiu – a Manx music festival held in Ramsey at the end of March/ beginning of April. 🅜⬤♣⚓

Trafalgar Hotel L ✓
West Quay, IM8 1DW (on quayside)
☼ 11-11 (12.15am Fri & Sat); 11.30-11 Sun
☎ (01624) 814601
Moorhouse's Black Cat; Okells Bitter; guest beers Ⓗ
Established in 1870, this cosy, friendly and popular pub is a traditional quayside free house, overlooking the Sulby river and a short walk from the shopping area. Close to the course, it is popular with bikers in TT week. A good and varied selection of local, seasonal, and guest ales is always available. Beers are listed on a chalkboard for convenience. Q✤⚲≠(MER)🚍(3,5,6)♣

St John's

Glen Helen Inn L
Glen Helen, IM4 3NP (continue round TT course from St Johns for 1 mile)
☼ 11-11 (11.45 Fri & Sat) ☎ (01624) 801294
🌐 glenheleninn.com
Bushy's Bitter; Okells Bitter; guest beers Ⓗ
Completely refurbished in recent years, the inn nestles among trees in the heart of the Glen Helen on the famous TT motorcycle course. With a contemporary decor and a relaxed and informal atmosphere, the main bar comprises a mixture of tables and lounge-style seating areas. There are further offshoot dining areas, and seating outside overlooking the river. Popular for weddings and functions, the Glen Helen carries a surprisingly large cask ale range for its idyllic rural location.
❀⛲◑&♣P⚊

Sulby

Ginger Hall Hotel L
Ballamanagh Road, IM7 2HB
☼ 12 (4 Mon)-midnight ☎ (01624) 897231
🌐 gingerhallhotel.com
Bushy's Castletown Bitter; Moorhouse's Black Cat; guest beers Ⓗ
The original licensee brewed ginger ale on this site, hence the name Ginger Hall. Situated on the TT course, the pub is a shrine to the races, with a TT map filling the ceiling of the main bar and pictures and memorabilia covering the walls. There is a separate dining area, pool room, dartboard and a log fire in the bar. Guest ales change regularly and a food take-away service is available. Nine en-suite B&B rooms are available. ≒⛲◑&✤🚍(5,6)♣P⚊

Sulby Glen Hotel L ✓
Main Road, IM7 2HR
☼ 12-midnight (1am Fri & Sat); 12-11 Sun
☎ (01624) 897240 🌐 sulbyglen.net
Bushy's Bitter; Okells Bitter; guest beers Ⓗ
A friendly welcome from staff is guaranteed at this country inn with 11 en-suite rooms, situated on the TT course on the Sulby Straight. The large rural pub has two lounges, a separate dining area and a real fire in winter. The motorcycle engine on the bar is a talking point; it is used to dispense keg beers and lagers. Home-cooked food is first class and the pub hosts beer and cider festivals. CAMRA members receive a discount. The bus stop is right outside.
≒Q⛄❀⛲◑⚲&✤🚍(5,6)♣P⚊

All hands to the pumps

British beer is unique and so are the methods used for serving it. The best-known English system, the beer engine operated by a handpump on the pub bar, arrived early in the 19th century. It coincided with and was prompted by the decline of the publican brewer and the rise of commercial companies that began to dominate the supply of beer to public houses. In order to sell more beer, commercial brewers and publicans looked for faster and less labour-intensive methods of serving beer.

In The Brewing Industry in England, 1700-1830, Peter Mathias records that 'most beer had to be stored in butts in the publicans' cellars for the technical reason that it needed an even and fairly low temperature, even where convenience and restricted space behind the bar did not enforce it. This meant, equally inevitably, continuous journeying to and from the cellars by the potboys to fill up jugs from the spigots: a waste of time for the customer and of labour and trade for the publican. Drawing up beer from the cellar at the pull of a handle at the bar at once increased the speed of sale and cut the wage bill.'

The first attempt at a system for raising beer from cellar to bar was patented by Joseph Bramah in 1797. But his system – using heavy boxes of sand that pressed down on storage vessels holding the beer – was so elaborate that it was never used. But his idea encouraged others to develop simpler systems. Mathias writes: 'One of the few technical devices of importance to come into the public house since the publican stopped brewing his own beer was the beer engine. It was, from the first, a simple manually operated pump, incorporating no advances in hydraulic knowledge or engineering skill, similar in design to many pumps used at sea, yet perfectly adapted to its function in the public house.'

By 1801, John Chadwell of Blackfriars, London, was registered as a 'beer-engine maker' and soon afterwards Thomas Rowntree in the same area described himself as a 'maker of a double-acting beer-machine'. By the 1820s, beer engine services had become standard throughout most of urban England and Gaskell & Chambers in the Midlands had become the leading manufacturer, employing more than 700 people in their Birmingham works alone.

White Horse, Parsons Green, London (p303).

St Austell brewery, St Austell, Cornwall (p829

The
Breweries

Holding on to Hard-Won Victory

Since its embryonic first edition in 1974, the *Good Beer Guide* has extolled the virtues of great British beer in great British pubs, to become established as an annual progress report, chronicling an age of brewing revolution and 'revitalisation' far beyond the wildest imaginings of CAMRA's founding fathers.

Celebrate by all means...

A glance back through the early Guides serves as a reminder of just how much has been achieved. In 1976 the presentational format of the breweries section took shape, much as it is today: an alphabetical gazetteer of breweries listing all their regular real ales. Then, however, there were only 154 breweries, operated by fewer than 100 independent companies; and no more than about 300 brands, categorised by simple symbols into just three styles (mild, bitter and old/special ale). Compare that with this year's brewery entries, the number of permanent brands and variety of beer styles – not forgetting to factor in all the seasonals and specials that are far too numerous to collate and mention – and the urge to grin like a Cheshire Cat and punch the air in jubilation is almost impossible to resist!

There is indeed much cause for celebration. Britain has a youthful, vibrant and invigorated brewing industry, which the Society of Independent Brewers – itself an evolving product of the last thirty-plus years – is immensely proud to represent. Brewing businesses proliferate and prosper, and bring innovation and imagination to a time-honoured and traditional craft; and evered survivors that pre-date CAMRA have re-invented themselves and their beer portfolios so as to retain their rightful place in the modern era.

The upshot for consumers is unprecedented choice and endless opportunity to try something new. The beer drinker really has never had it so good, and the *Good Beer Guide* is a testament to that – a fact we should all be delighted to celebrate.

...but don't forget to campaign

'The purpose of pub conversation is to find areas of agreement and common ground.' Wise words from the late Richard Boston, pioneering beer journalist and true champion of good ale and pubs, in his groundbreaking *Beer and Skittles* (also 1976). He goes on to write that, 'Confrontation and controversy are usually avoided', which is no doubt why the rules of pub etiquette traditionally impose a ban on certain contentious and potentially divisive subjects. Foremost among these, of course, is politics – even though in its long history the pub has served as a meeting place and breeding ground for fledgling movements of political thought and activism.

The convention is that politics should be kept out of pub chat, as Richard writes, so a visit to your local provides the satisfying and relaxing

The SIBA bar at the 2011 Great British Beer Festival – an event which celebrates the variety of cask beer

SIBA brewers supporting the campaign to axe the beer-tax escalator

CAMRA's membership stands at an all-time high of more than 140,000 – a force to be reckoned with only if every one of that number counts him or herself as a campaigner, rather than just belonging to a cosy club dedicated to enjoying the malt and hops (and sometimes fruits) of victory.

The pub is the new battleground, where the fight against duty escalation, cheap supermarket booze and anti-beer and anti-pub misinformation from health lobbyists, and the campaign for meaningful government support for a responsible pub culture that can help restore our community cohesion, will define our future and the future of the British local itself. It behoves us all to enlist for this struggle – and the rule about talking politics in pubs is hereby duly waived!

leisure time it's supposed to, without punters squaring up to each other about the relative lack of merit of Maggie, Tony, David, Nick or Ed or whoever's currently at the forefront of the Westminster scene.

But if ever politics had a role to play in the pub it's now. It's all very well congratulating ourselves and singing the praises of the brilliant British beer world we've helped to create; but it hasn't happened by accident and it isn't automatically here to stay. The real ale campaign may appear to be won, but the Campaign for Real Ale – together with SIBA and other industry bodies – still faces many political challenges.

SIBA's sponsorship of the *Good Beer Guide* unites brewers and beer drinkers in appreciation of this golden age of real ale. We should by all means celebrate great local beer and great local pubs, but to be a truly meaningful and effective partnership between industry and customer we must use them as our campaigning tools to ensure their survival and prosperity for generations to enjoy.

SIBA Locals: Great local pubs... great local beer!

Pubs that are proud to serve local beers forge a natural link between brewers and drinkers and give focus to our united campaign.

The **SIBA Locals** scheme is seeking to build a national network of on-trade local beer champions within the broader membership of SIBA, which encompasses not just brewers but their many and various supplier associates, representing the total supply-chain infrastructure of a vital British manufacturing industry.

Working alongside CAMRA's own excellent **'LocAle'** initiative, **SIBA Locals** strive to embody the ideals and ethics of local brewers, the dedication and enterprise of community publicans, and the commitment and campaigning zeal of discerning beer drinkers.

Could you be the next SIBA Local?

If you are in the pub trade and would like to know more, please go to **http://siba.co.uk/** and click on the **SIBA Locals** link.

How to use the Breweries section

Breweries are listed in alphabetical order. The independents (regional, smaller craft brewers and brew-pubs) are listed first, followed by the nationals and the globals. Within each brewery entry, beers are listed in increasing order of strength. Beers that are available for less than three months are described as 'occasional' or 'seasonal' brews. If a brewery also produces bottle-conditioned beers, this will be mentioned in the main description: these are beers that have not been pasteurised and contain live yeast, allowing them to continue to ferment and mature in the bottle as a draught real ale does in its cask.

KEY TO SYMBOLS

≣   A brew-pub: a pub that brews beer on the premises.

◉   The brewery is affiliated with the Cyclops system for describing beers to consumers.

◆   CAMRA tasting notes, supplied by a trained CAMRA tasting panel. Beer descriptions that do not carry this symbol are based on more limited tastings or have been obtained from other sources. Tasting notes are not provided for brew-pub beers that are available in fewer than five outlets.

🏆   A CAMRA Beer of the Year in 2011.

🏆   One of the 2012 CAMRA Beers of the Year: a finalist in the Champion Beer of Britain competition held during the Great British Beer Festival in London in August 2012, or the Champion Winter Beer of Britain competition held earlier in the year.

☺   The brewery's beers can be acceptably served through a 'tight sparkler' attached to the nozzle of the beer pump, designed to give a thick collar of foam on the beer.

⊗   The brewery's beers should NOT be served through a tight sparkler. CAMRA is opposed to the growing tendency to serve southern-brewed beers with the aid of sparklers, which aerate the beer and tend to drive hop aroma and flavour into the head, altering the balance of the beer achieved in the brewery. When neither symbol is used it means the brewery in question has not stated a preference.

ABBREVIATIONS

OG   Stands for Original Gravity, the measure taken before fermentation of the level of 'fermentable material' (malt sugars and added sugars) in the brew. It is only a rough indication of strength and is no longer used for duty purposes.

ABV   Stands for Alcohol by Volume, which is a more reliable measure of the percentage of alcohol in finished beer. Many breweries now only disclose ABVs but the Guide lists OGs where available. Often the OG and the ABV of a beer are identical, i.e. 1035 and 3.5 per cent. If the ABV is higher than the OG, i.e. OG 1035, ABV 3.8, this indicates that the beer has been 'well attenuated' with most of the malt sugars turned into alcohol. If the ABV is lower than the OG, this means residual sugars have been left in the beer for fullness of body and flavour: this is rare but can apply to some milds or strong old ales, barley wines and winter beers.

SIBA   Indicates a member of the Society of Independent Brewers.

IFBB   Indicates a member of the Independent Family Brewers of Britain.

EAB   Indicates a member of East Anglian Brewers Co-operative.

NOTE: The Breweries section was correct at the time of going to press and every effort has been made to ensure that all cask-conditioned beers are included.

The independents

The breweries listed in this section include micro, small, family and regional companies. Some sell their beers widely, others are restricted to their home areas, and a few are brew-pubs. Listings for new national brewers and global brewers operating in Britain follow this section.

1648 SIBA 👁

❚ 1648 Brewing Co Ltd, Old Stables Brewery, Mill Lane, East Hoathly, East Sussex, BN8 6QB
☎ (01825) 840830
✉ brewmaster@1648brewing.co.uk
🌐 1648brewing.co.uk
Tours by arrangement

⊗ The 1648 brewery, set up in the old stable block at the King's Head pub in 2003, derives its name from the year of the deposition of King Charles I. One pub is owned and more than 40 outlets are supplied. Seasonal beers: see website. Bottle-conditioned beers are also available.

Brew Master (OG 1040, ABV 3.9%)
A chestnut/brown-coloured bitter with a long aftertaste.

Triple Champion (OG 1041, ABV 4%)
A chestnut-coloured traditional English ale, deeply flavoured and full-bodied.

Signature (OG 1044, ABV 4.4%)
Very pale, light, crisply refreshing ale with a bitter aftertaste.

4Ts

4Ts Brewery Ltd, Rydal Avenue, Warrington, Cheshire, WA4 6AT
☎ 07917 730184 ✉ johnwilkinson530@yahoo.co.uk

4Ts (The Tavern Tasty Tipples) began brewing in 2010. The 0.5-barrel plant is located in a private garage and a further five-barrel plant is also used at a location in Runcorn. Beer are usually available in the Tavern, Warrington.

Old School Dark Mild (ABV 4%)

Bitter (ABV 4.2%)

Coff-Stout-ee (ABV 6%)

8 Sail SIBA

8 Sail Brewery, Heckington Windmill, Hale Road, Heckington, Lincolnshire, NG34 9JW
☎ (01529) 469308 ☎ 07866 183479
✉ a.pygott@btinternet.com ✉ 8sailbrewery.co.uk
Shop Thu-Sun 12-5pm

8 Sail Brewery was established in 2010 and operates on a six-barrel brew plant. The brewery nestles in the shadow of Heckington Windmill, Britain's only eight sailed windmill, from where the brewery takes its name. The brewery shop stocks Lincolnshire bottle-conditioned beers alongside local ciders. Plans are ongoing to develop a display telling the history of pub drinking vessels. All beers are also available bottle conditioned.

Millwright Mild (OG 1035, ABV 3.5%)
Rich dark flavours balanced with Fuggles and Goldings hops.

Ale (OG 1038, ABV 3.8%)

Windmill Bitter (OG 1038, ABV 3.8%)

Dark and fruity session beer. Pleasant and easy-drinking.

Hops 4 Heroes (OG 1040, ABV 4%)
Pale blonde beer, well-hopped. Mainly produced as a bottled beer with a donation going towards the Bridge for Heroes charity but a few casks available from each brew.

Merry Miller (OG 1041, ABV 4.1%)
A traditional bitter. Mid-brown in colour with a nutty, malty flavour.

Flour Power (OG 1042, ABV 4.2%)
Light, floral and hoppy.

Golden Ale (OG 1044, ABV 4.4%)
Pale beer with a good balance of hop flavour, aroma and bitterness.

Damson Porter (OG 1050, ABV 5%)
Fruit flavoured version of the Victorian Porter.

Victorian Porter (OG 1050, ABV 5%)
Brewed to a classic Victorian porter recipe. Slight bitterness at the end. Only lightly hopped. Full-bodied, dark and dominated by dark malt flavours.

John Barleycorn IPA (OG 1055, ABV 5.5%)
Traditional English IPA. Light copper-coloured.

Abbey Grange

See Llangollen

Abbey Ales SIBA 👁

Abbey Ales Ltd, Abbey Brewery, Camden Row, Bath, Somerset, BA1 5LB
☎ (01225) 444437 ✉ enquiries@abbeyales.co.uk
🌐 abbeyales.co.uk
Tours by arrangement

Founded in 1997, Abbey Ales was the first brewery in Bath for over fifty years. It supplies more than 80 regular outlets within a 20-mile radius of Bath, while selected wholesalers deliver beer nationally. It has four tied houses one of which, the Star Inn in Bath, is one of CAMRA's Real Heritage Pubs. Seasonal beers: see website.

Bellringer (OG 1042, ABV 4.2%) 🍺
A notably hoppy ale, light to medium-bodied, clean-tasting, refreshingly dry with a balancing sweetness. Citrus, pale malt aroma and dry, bitter finish.

Abbeydale SIBA 👁

Abbeydale Brewery Ltd, Unit 8, Aizlewood Road, Sheffield, South Yorkshire, S8 0YX
☎ (0114) 281 2712
✉ info@abbeydalebrewery.co.uk
🌐 abbeydalebrewery.co.uk

Since starting in 1996, Abbeydale Brewery has grown steadily; it now produces upwards of 130 barrels a week, and recent investment has enabled further growth. The regular range is complemented by ever-changing seasonals – see website.

THE BREWERIES

Daily Bread (OG 1037, ABV 3.8%)

Brimstone (OG 1039, ABV 3.9%)
A russet-coloured bitter beer with a distinctive hop aroma.

Deception (OG 1040.3, ABV 4.1%)

Moonshine (OG 1041.2, ABV 4.3%)
A well-balanced pale ale with a full hop aroma. Pleasant grapefruit traces may be detected.

Absolution (OG 1050, ABV 5.3%)
A fruity pale ale, deceptively drinkable for its strength. Sweetish but not cloying.

Black Mass (OG 1065, ABV 6.7%)
A strong black stout with complex roast flavours and a lasting bitter finish.

ABC SIBA

ABC Brewery Ltd, Unit 21, Birch Road, Witton, Aston, Birmingham, B6 7DD
☎ (0121) 328 2655 ✉ paul@abcbrewery.co.uk
⊕ abcbrewery.co.uk

⊗ ABC started brewing in 2008 and is situated near Villa Park football ground. 2010 saw the opening of its first pub, Malt in Lichfield. Around 40 other outlets are supplied regularly.

Aston Dark (OG 1033, ABV 3.6%)

Aston Mild (OG 1033, ABV 3.6%)

Hoppy Gold (OG 1036, ABV 3.8%)

Dizzy Blonde (OG 1040, ABV 4.4%)

Sporting Gold (OG 1040, ABV 4.4%)

Rotunda Red (OG 1045, ABV 4.8%)

Power Cut (OG 1048, ABV 5%)

Aston Distressway (OG 1058, ABV 6%)

Abigale

Abigale Brewing Co Ltd, Unit 4, Javelin Enterprise Park, Javelin Way, Ashford, Kent, TN24 8DE
☎ (01233) 661310 ☎ 07734 342278
✉ enquiries@abigalebrewing.co.uk
⊕ abigalebrewing.co.uk
Tours by arrangement

⊗ Abigale began brewing in 2010 using a 10-barrel plant. Outlets are supplied in the East Kent area. 10-litre in a box and five-litre mini kegs are available for home use.

Ridgeway (OG 1037, ABV 3.8%)
A blonde pale ale with a fruity blackcurrant hop aroma giving way to well-balanced malt characteristics and a soft hop bitterness on the palate.

Samphire (OG 1039.5, ABV 4.1%)
A light, copper-coloured bitter. A hoppy aroma gives way to well-balanced malt characteristics and hop bitterness on the palate. A refreshing ale, clean and dry to taste.

Nailbourne (OG 1042, ABV 4.5%)
A copper-coloured bitter with a fresh, hoppy aroma giving way to well-balanced caramel and biscuit malt characteristics with hop bitterness on the palate. A full-flavoured, robust ale.

Hoyman's Porter (OG 1045, ABV 4.7%)
A dark, complex ale with rich roast coffee and chocolate flavours.

Acorn SIBA ◉

Acorn Brewery of Barnsley Ltd, Unit 3, Aldham Industrial Estate, Mitchell Road, Wombwell, Barnsley, South Yorkshire, S73 8HA
☎ (01226) 270734 ✉ sales@acorn-brewery.co.uk
⊕ acorn-brewery.co.uk
Shop Mon-Fri 9am-5pm
Tours by arrangement

☺Acorn was set up in 2003 with a 10-barrel ex-Firkin plant. Expansion to a 20-barrel plant was completed when the brewery moved to larger premises. All beers are produced using the original Barnsley Bitter yeast strain, dating back to the 1850s. The brewery currently has a 160-barrel a week capacity, and recently purchased its first pub, the Old No. 7 in Barnsley. Seasonal beers: see website. Bottle-conditioned beers are available.

Yorkshire Pride (OG 1037, ABV 3.7%) ◆
A golden-coloured bitter with a hint of wheat and a clean, bitter finish. A very drinkable session beer.

Barnsley Bitter (OG 1038, ABV 3.8%) 🍴 ◆
A smooth, malty bitter with notes of chocolate and caramel. Fruity, bitter finish.

Barnsley Gold (OG 1041.5, ABV 4%) ◆
Fruit in the aroma and taste. There is also a hoppy flavour throughout. A well-hopped, clean, dry finish.

Blonde (OG 1040.5, ABV 4%) ◆
A clean-tasting, hoppy beer with a refreshing bitter and fruity aftertaste.

Old Moor Porter (OG 1045, ABV 4.4%) 🍴 ◆
A rich tasting porter, smooth throughout with a hint of chocolate.

Sovereign (OG 1044, ABV 4.4%) ◆
Malt and hop aroma, a roast nut and burnt bitterness and a hint of sulphur throughout.

Gorlovka Imperial Stout (OG 1058, ABV 6%) 🍴 ◆
Full of chocolate and liquorish flavours. Rich and smooth with a fruity creamy finish.

Adkin

Adkin Brewery, correspondence only: c/o 52 Adkin Way, Wantage, Oxfordshire, OX12 9HW
☎ 07709 086149 ✉ adkinbrewery@googlemail.com
⊕ adkinbrewery.co.uk
Tours by arrangement (limited to 4 persons)

Adkin was established on a 0.5-barrel plant in 2007 after producing charity beers in 2005 and 2006 at the Oxford Beer Festival. Eleven brews are rotated and are produced when required (prior orders only). The beers are most easily found at regional beer festivals but are starting to make their way into the local free trade. No beer is kept at the correspondence address. Bottle-conditioned beers are available.

Adnams SIBA ◉

Adnams plc, Sole Bay Brewery, East Green, Southwold, Suffolk, IP18 6JW
☎ (01502) 727200 ✉ info@adnams.co.uk
⊕ adnams.co.uk
Shop 10am-6pm daily
Tours by arrangement

⊗ The company was founded by George and Ernest Adnams in 1872, who were joined by the Loftus family in 1902; a member of each family is still a director of the company. Real ale is available in all 70 pubs and there is national distribution. All beers are now from a new energy-efficient 300-barrel brewery, built within the confines of the present site. Seasonal beers: see website. Bottle-conditioned beers are also available.

Lighthouse (OG 1037, ABV 3.4%) ◆
A quaffable beer with bitterness predominating.

Southwold Bitter (OG 1037, ABV 3.7%) 🍴 ◆
Aromas of toffee apple, caramel and sulphur. Taste is a complex mix of malt toffee and roast bitterness with hops. Malty bitter and apple flavours linger into the aftertaste.

Gunhill (OG 1045, ABV 4%)

Explorer (OG 1042, ABV 4.3%) 🍴 ◆
Fruity bitter taste with very delicate sweet aftertaste.

Ghost Ship (OG 1046, ABV 4.5%)
American-style pale ale.

Broadside (OG 1049, ABV 4.7%) 🍴 ◆
Rich, malty aroma with blackberries and dried fruit. Rich and full flavours of malt and fruit, with roast and caramel notes and subtle hops. Well-balanced, long-lasting aftertaste.

Adur

Adur Brewery Ltd, Brick Barn, Charlton Court, Mouse Lane, Steyning, West Sussex, BN44 3DG
☎ (01903) 867614 ✉ info@adurvalleycoop.com
⊕ adurvalleycoop.com
Tours by arrangement

⊠ Adur Brewery was launched in 2008 on a 5.5-barrel plant, marking the return of brewing to the Adur Valley after an interval of nearly 100 years. A large part of the output is sold as bottle-conditioned beer. At the time of going to print the brewery was in the course of a transition to a co-op. See the website for the latest information.

Ropetackle Golden Ale (OG 1036, ABV 3.4%)
A light, golden ale with an initial sweetness and delicate aroma balanced by a dry finish.

Hop Token: Amarillo (OG 1040, ABV 4%)
An amber bitter with notes of peach and grapefruit, a good bitterness and a long, dry finish.

Hop Token: Summit (OG 1040, ABV 4%)

Velocity (OG 1044, ABV 4.4%)
Traditional best bitter with a hoppy aroma and a hint of marmalade in the taste.

Black William (OG 1055, ABV 5%)
A rich, black stout with dark chocolate aromas and roasted flavours.

Robbie's Red (OG 1050, ABV 5.2%)
A strong red-brown ale with an aroma of malt and hops. Slight initial sweetness leads into complex flavours including orange peel and a satisfying bitterness which persists into the long finish.

Alcazar SIBA

☰ Alcazar Brewing Co Ltd, Alcazar Brewery, Rear of Fox & Crown, 33 Church Street, Old Basford, Nottingham, NG6 0GA
☎ (0115) 978 2282

Office: Turnstone Taverns, c/o The Railway Tavern, 188 Station Road, Langley Mill, Nottinghamshire, NG16 4AE ☎ (01773) 510863

✉ alcazarbrewery@ntlworld.com
⊕ turnstonetaverns.co.uk
Tours by arrangement

Alcazar was established in 1999 and is located behind its brewery tap, the Fox & Crown. The brewery is full mash with a 10-barrel brew length. Seasonal beers are available.

Sheriffs Gold (OG 1036, ABV 3.6%) ◆
Slightly sweet yellow session bitter made with First Gold and Goldings hops.

Alcazar Ale (OG 1040, ABV 4%) ◆
Flagship golden ale, full of citrus hops with a dry, bitter aftertaste.

New Dawn (OG 1045, ABV 4.5%) ◆
Full-bodied golden ale, brewed with Cascade hops.

Foxtale Ale (OG 1049, ABV 4.9%) ◆
A strong malty and bitter brown ale. Named 'Brush Bitter' in the brewery tap.

Vixen's Vice (OG 1052, ABV 5.2%) ◆
A premium strength hoppy pale ale.

Alechemy (NEW)

Alechemy Brewing Ltd, Unit 2C, Young Square, Brucefield Industry Park, Livingston, West Lothian, EH54 9BX
☎ 07748 156973
✉ james.davies@alechemybrewing.com
⊕ alechemybrewing.com
Tours by arrangement

☺Alechemy began brewing in 2012. Seasonal beers are available and new beers are being produced regularly: see website.

Cairnpapple IPA (OG 1042, ABV 4.1%)
A light IPA with a lingering citrus taste.

Five Sisters (OG 1045, ABV 4.3%)
A rich, dark amber beer with a hint of citrus.

Cockleroy (OG 1049, ABV 4.8%)
An intriguing juxtaposition of dark malt colours and the full citrus and floral aromas of a traditional IPA.

Alehouse

See Verulam

Ales of Scilly SIBA

Ales of Scilly Brewery, 2b Porthmellon Industrial Estate, St Mary's, Isles of Scilly, Cornwall, TR21 0JY
☎ (01720) 423233 ☎ 07810 816681
✉ mark@alesofscilly.co.uk
Shop – please ring first
Tours by arrangement

⊠ Opened in 2001 as a two-barrel plant and expanded in 2004 to five barrels, Ales of Scilly is the most south-westerly brewery in Britain. Nine local pubs are supplied, with regular exports to mainland pubs and beer festivals. The brewery moved to new premises in 2007. Seasonal beers are available.

Scuppered (OG 1043, ABV 4.6%) ◆
Faint aroma of malt and fruit in this tawny ale leads to a rich and creamy sweet maltiness on the tongue, balanced by bitterness and fruit esters. Long bittersweet finish.

Allendale SIBA ⊙

Allendale Brew Co Ltd, Allen Mills, Allendale Town, Northumberland, NE47 9EQ
☎ **(01434) 618686** ✉ **tom@allendalebrewery.com**
⊕ **allendalebrewery.com**
Shop Mon-Fri 9am-5pm
Tours by arrangement

⊛Brewing returned to Allendale in 2006 – the original brewery having closed in 1887 – when Tom Hick and his father Jim opened the site. Tom now runs the brewery with his wife using a 10-barrel plant. More than 300 outlets are supplied across the north of England. The brewery tap is the Crown in Catton, which was saved in 2008 after nine years of closure. Seasonal beers: see website.

Wagtail Best Bitter (OG 1037, ABV 3.8%) ◈
Amber bitter with spicy aromas and a long, bitter finish.

Golden Plover (OG 1039, ABV 4%) ◈
Light, refreshing, easy-drinking blonde beer with a clean finish.

Adder Lager (OG 1050, ABV 5%)
A traditional cold-fermented Pilsner-style lager.

Wolf (OG 1053, ABV 5.5%) ◈
Full-bodied red ale with bitterness in the taste giving way to a fruity finish.

AllGates SIBA ⊙

AllGates Brewery Ltd, The Old Brewery, Brewery Yard, off Wallgate, Wigan, WN1 1JU
☎ **(01942) 234976**
✉ **information@allgatesbrewery.com**
⊕ **allgatesbrewery.com**
Tours by arrangement (max. of 36)

⊛AllGates commenced brewing in 2006 in a Grade II-listed building at the rear of Wigan Main Post Office. The building is an old tower brewery that has been lovingly restored, but with a modern five-barrel plant. With the brewery now at full capacity, expansion plans are under consideration. Beers are distributed through its own estate of seven pubs, regionally and through wholesalers. Seasonal beers and monthly specials: see website.

All Black (OG 1039, ABV 3.6%) ◈
Dark brown beer with a malty, fruity aroma. Creamy and malty in taste, with blackberry fruits and a satisfying aftertaste.

California (OG 1037, ABV 3.8%) ◈
A pale yellow beer with a restrained hoppy and fruity aroma. Clean and fresh tasting, with hops and fruit in the mouth and a bitter, hoppy finish.

Napoleon's Retreat (OG 1038, ABV 3.9%)
A deep golden/copper-coloured session bitter.

Pretoria (OG 1039, ABV 3.9%)

Deux Citra (OG 1042, ABV 4.2%)

All Nations

See Shires

Allsaints

Allsaints Brewery Co, c/o Coastal Brewery, Unit 10B, Cardrew Industrial Estate, Redruth, Cornwall, TR15 1SS
☎ **07790 274112**

Formerly known as Doghouse Brewery, which closed in 2007, Allsaints recommenced production in 2008 using spare capacity at Keltek Brewery. In 2009 the brewery began using spare capacity at Coastal Brewery in Redruth. Four regular beers are produced (see Coastal for beer list) and changing seasonal beers.

Alnwick

See Hadrian Border

Amber SIBA

Amber Ales Ltd, Unit A, Asher Lane Business Park, Pentrich, Ripley, Derbyshire, DE5 3SW
☎ **(01773) 512864** ✉ **info@amberales.co.uk**
⊕ **amberales.co.uk**
Shop: Off sales from brewery tap
Tours by arrangement

Amber Ales began production in 2006 on a five-barrel plant. Amber produces five core beers and a range of experimental and seasonal ales all available at its brewery tap, the Talbot Taphouse in Ripley. Around 50 outlets are supplied direct. Bottle-conditioned beers are available and are suitable for vegetarians and vegans.

Chocolate Orange Stout (OG 1040, ABV 4%) ⊟

Original Black Stout (OG 1040, ABV 4%)

Barnes Wallis (OG 1040, ABV 4.1%)

Dambuster (OG 1051, ABV 5.5%)

Imperial IPA (OG 1058, ABV 6.5%)

Anchor Springs SIBA

Anchor Springs Brewery Co Ltd, Lineside Way, Wick, West Sussex, BN17 7EH
☎ **(01903) 719842/715111**
✉ **debbie@jenkinslittlehampton.co.uk**

Kevin Jenkins, owner of the Crown in Littlehampton, established the brewery in 2010 using the five-barrel plant previously used at the Dark Star Brewery. The beer is sold in the Crown (brewery tap), the Spy Glass in Worthing and at beer festivals and via wholesalers. Seasonal beers are also available.

LA Gold (OG 1039.5, ABV 3.7%)
A golden session ale. An initial sweetness leads to a citrus kick and a lingering crisp, clean finish.

IPA (OG 1042.5, ABV 4%)
A full-bodied, complex beer with a good mouthfeel and lingering hop finish. Light gold in colour, the initial sweetness gives way to malt then a dry aftertaste.

Rip Tide (OG 1045, ABV 4.1%)
Copper-coloured ale. Malted caramel nose and initial sweetness of milk chocolate leads to a complex palate and lingering bitter finish.

Undercurrent (OG 1045, ABV 4.2%)
A light, copper-coloured traditional English bitter with a modern twist. Hoppy aroma and initial taste leads to nutty, chocolate palate and finish.

Andrews (NEW)

Andrews Ales, 1 Railway Cottage, Cummertrees, Dumfriesshire, DG12 5QG

☎ (01461) 700387
✉ aemmerson999@googlemail.com

Andrews Ales began brewing in 2011 using a one-barrel plant but soon expanded to three-barrels. 15 outlets are supplied direct.

Supus Lupus (OG 1036, ABV 3.6%)
A light session ale with a citrus sweet finish.

Cummertrees Pale Ale (OG 1040, ABV 4%)
An IPA-style beer.

Tinfast (OG 1044, ABV 4.3%)
A traditional Scottish ale.

Andwell SIBA ◉

Andwell Brewing Co LLP, Andwell Lane, North Warnborough, Hampshire, RG27 1HA
☎ (01256) 761044 ✉ beer@andwells.com
⊕ andwells.com
Shop Mon-Fri 10am-6pm; Sat 10.30am-1pm
Tours by arrangement

⊗ Brewing commenced in 2008 on a 10-barrel plant. The brewery relocated and expanded in 2011 to an idyllic riverside location with a new bespoke 20-barrel plant. Beer is distributed within a 40-mile radius of the brewery. More than 200 outlets are supplied. Seasonal beers are also available.

Resolute Bitter (OG 1038, ABV 3.8%) ◄
A well-balanced session bitter. A malty aroma leads into an initially malty flavour with some bitterness and a sweetish finish.

Gold Muddler (OG 1039, ABV 3.9%) ◄
Although light golden in colour, this is a standard bitter, with an aroma of hops and malt. These characteristics are carried into the flavour with a solid bitterness and a dry, biscuity finish.

King John (OG 1042, ABV 4.2%) ◄
Malty best bitter, low in hops with a short initial bitterness and a underlying sweetness, leading to some dryness in the finish.

Ruddy Darter (OG 1047, ABV 4.6%)
A ruby chestnut ale with a hoppy, spicy aroma and a full-bodied and fruity taste with a dry finish.

Angel SIBA

Angel Ales Ltd, 62a Furlong Lane, Halesowen, West Midlands, B63 2TA
☎ 07847 300350 ✉ angelales@hotmail.co.uk
⊕ angelales.co.uk

Angel Ales is the brainchild of Nick Pritchard and Andy Kirk. The brewery building has been a Chapel of Rest, a coffin makers' workshop and a pattern makers before becoming a brewhouse. All beers are produced using organic materials and there are plans to use spring water below the brewery. Commercial brewing began in 2011. Occasional ales are available: see website.

Ale (OG 1042, ABV 4.1%)
A very pale beer with citrus nose and a lingering bitter finish.

Anglo Dutch

See Partners

Angus SIBA

Angus Ales, 14b Panmure Industrial Estate, Carnoustie, DD7 7NP
☎ 07708 011649 ✉ info@angus-ales.co.uk
⊕ angus-ales.co.uk
Tours by arrangement

⊗ Angus Ales was established in 2009 using a four-barrel plant. Situated in the golf town of Carnoustie, the regular brews have golf-related names.

Gowfers' Gold (OG 1038, ABV 3.8%)
A pale, refreshing golden ale.

Mashie Niblick (OG 1042, ABV 4.2%)
A full-flavoured malty ale.

Ann Street

See Liberation

An Teallach

An Teallach Ale Co Ltd, Camusnagaul, Dundonnell, Garve, Ross-shire, IV23 2QT
☎ (01854) 633306 ✉ ataleco1@yahoo.co.uk
Tours by arrangement

An Teallach was formed in 2001 by husband and wife team David and Wilma Orr on Wilma's family croft on the shores of Little Loch Broom, Wester Ross. The business has grown steadily each year. 60 pubs are supplied. All beers are also available bottled.

Beinn Dearg Ale (OG 1038, ABV 3.8%) ◄
A well-balanced malty, sweetish beer with a long, malty aftertaste.

Ale (OG 1042, ABV 4.2%) ◄
A classic beer in the Scottish 80/- tradition. Plenty of malt in the nicely-balanced, bittersweet taste.

Crofters Pale Ale (OG 1042, ABV 4.2%) ◄
A good quaffing, lightly-flavoured golden ale. Hops in the taste and with a slight astringency in the finish.

Suilven (OG 1043, ABV 4.3%) ◄
A refreshing golden ale with a creamy sweetish taste and a pleasant sulphurous nose.

Kildonan (OG 1044, ABV 4.4%) ◄
Plenty of fruit and a good smack of bitterness in this golden ale.

Appleford SIBA

Appleford Brewery Co Ltd, Unit 14, Highlands Farm, High Road, Brightwell-cum-Sotwell, Wallingford, Oxfordshire, OX10 0QX
☎ (01235) 848055
✉ sales@applefordbrewery.co.uk
⊕ applefordbrewery.co.uk

⊗ Appleford Brewery opened in 2006 when two farm units were converted to house an eight-barrel plant. Deliveries are made to a number of local outlets as well as nationally, via the brewery or wholesalers. Occasional and bottle-conditioned beers are available.

Brightwell Gold (OG 1041, ABV 4%)

Power Station (OG 1043, ABV 4.2%)
A copper-coloured, slightly malty bitter.

THE BREWERIES

Arbor SIBA ⟨◎⟩

Arbor Ales Ltd, Unit 4, Lawrence Hill Industrial Estate, Croydon Street, Bristol, BS5 0EB
☎ (0117) 329 2711 ✉ beer@arborales.co.uk
⊕ arborales.co.uk

⊠ Arbor Ales opened in 2007 in the back of the Old Tavern pub. In 2008 it moved to Kingswood and expanded to a 5.5-barrel plant. Further expansion took place in 2009. In 2012 it moved and expanded to a new 12-barrel plant. Arbor Ales also bought its first pub, the Old Stillage, in 2009, and took on a second, the Three Tuns, in 2010. A wide range of beers are brewed with particular pride taken in the darker ales due to the brewer's involvement with the Bristol & District Rare Ales Group (www.badrag.co.uk). Seasonal beers are available: see website. Around 200 outlets are supplied direct.

Single Hop (OG 1037, ABV 4%) ◣
Very pale, well-hopped ale. While hops lead, sweet malt and fruit balance the palate while a powerful hop bitterness marks the aftertaste.

Hunny Beer (OG 1041, ABV 4.2%) ◣
Speciality bitter, pale amber in colour. Honey is discernible in the malty-fruity aroma and taste. The aftertaste is bittersweet and short.

Brigstow (OG 1042, ABV 4.3%) ◣
Fairly bitter version of the typical Bristol Best. Mid-brown with plenty of hop flavour and a hint of roasted barley.

Oyster Stout (OG 1046.5, ABV 4.6%) ◣
A smoky stout with real oysters added in the copper – a hint of the sea in the dry aftertaste. Fruity, roast and burnt flavours, liquorice notes and a creamy mouthfeel.

Archers

See Evan Evans

Ards (NEW)

Ards Brewing Co, 34B Carrowdore Road, Newtownards, Co Down, BT22 2LX
☎ 07515 558406

Ards began brewing in 2011 using a 100 litre plant. No beer list was available at the time of going to press.

Argyll SIBA

⧉ Argyll Breweries Ltd, Oban Bay Brewery, Back building, 60 George Street, Oban, Argyll, PA34 5DS
☎ (01631) 564492 ✉ info@obanbaybrewery.co.uk
⊕ obanbaybrewery.co.uk

⊠ Argyll Breweries Ltd was formed in 2010 following the merger of Oban Bay and Isle of Mull breweries. Cask production is currently only at the Oban site. Bottle-conditioned beers are available.

Island Pale Ale (OG 1038, ABV 3.9%)

Kilt Lifter (OG 1038, ABV 3.9%)

Galleon Gold (OG 1041, ABV 4.1%)

Skinny Blonde (OG 1042, ABV 4.1%)

Ginger Jakey (OG 1041, ABV 4.2%)

Red Monk of Iona (OG 1042, ABV 4.2%)

Skelpt Lug (OG 1042, ABV 4.2%)

Terror of Tobermory (OG 1045, ABV 4.6%)

Arkell's SIBA IFBB ⟨◎⟩

Arkell's Brewery Ltd, Kingsdown, Swindon, Wiltshire, SN2 7RU
☎ (01793) 823026 ✉ arkells@arkells.com
⊕ arkells.com
Brewery merchandise can be purchased at reception
Tours by arrangement

⊠ Arkells Brewery was established in 1843 and is still run by the family. The brewery owns 99 pubs in Berkshire, Gloucestershire, Oxfordshire and Wiltshire. Seasonal beers: see website.

2B (OG 1032, ABV 3.2%) ◣
Light brown in colour, malty but with a smack of hops and an astringent aftertaste. It has good body for its strength.

3B (OG 1040, ABV 4%) ◣
A medium brown beer with a strong, sweetish malt/caramel flavour. The hops come through strongly in the aftertaste, which is lingering and dry.

Wiltshire Gold (OG 1040, ABV 4%)
A golden ale. Satisfyingly sweet flavour with a distinctive hop aroma.

Moonlight (OG 1045, ABV 4.5%)
A golden beer with a lingering taste, toasty aroma and citrus hoppiness.

Kingsdown Special Ale (OG 1050, ABV 5%) ◣
A rich, deep russet-coloured beer, a stronger version of 3B. The malty/fruity aroma continues in the taste, which has a hint of pears. Hops come through in the aftertaste.

Arkwright's SIBA

Arkwright's Brewery, c/o The Real Ale Shop, 47 Lovat Road, Preston, Lancashire, PR1 6DQ
☎ 07944 912326 ✉ info@realaleshop.net
⊕ realaleshop.net

Arkwright's began brewing at the rear of the Real Ale Shop in 2010 using a 2.5-barrel plant.

Trouble at Mill (ABV 4%)

Run of the Mill (ABV 4.1%)

Arran SIBA ⟨◎⟩

Arran Brew Ltd t/a Arran Brewery, Cladach, Brodick, Isle of Arran, North Ayrshire, KA27 8DE
☎ (01770) 302353 ✉ info@arranbrewery.co.uk
⊕ arranbrewery.com
Shop Mon-Sat 10am-5pm, Sun 12.30-4.30pm summer; Mon-Sat 10.30am-4.30pm, Sun closed winter
Tours by arrangement

⊠ The brewery opened in 2000 using a 20-barrel plant. Production is up to 100 barrels a week with additional bottling capability. 300 outlets are supplied direct. Seasonal beers are brewed and bottle-conditioned beer is also available.

Ale (OG 1038, ABV 3.8%) ⊟ ◣
An amber ale where the predominance of the hop produces a bitter beer with a subtle balancing sweetness of malt and an occasional hint of roast.

Red Squirrel (OG 1038, ABV 3.9%)
A session beer with a balanced malty, hop blend containing hints of liquorice and burnt toffee with a characteristic nutty aroma.

Dark (OG 1042, ABV 4.3%) ◆
A well-balanced malty beer with plenty of roast and hop in the taste and a dry, bitter finish.

Sunset (OG 1042, ABV 4.4%)
A mid-amber ale with a lightly perfumed aroma, good balance of malt, fruit and hops with a pleasant, dry finish.

Clyde Puffer (OG 1045, ABV 4.9%)
A stout with a deep, dark colour. Sweet and mellow.

Blonde (OG 1048, ABV 5%) ◆
A hoppy beer with substantial fruit balance. The taste is balanced and the finish increasingly bitter. An aromatic strong bitter that drinks below its weight.

Arrow

Arrow Brewery, c/o Wine Vaults, 37 High Street, Kington, Herefordshire, HR5 3BJ
☎ (01544) 230685 ✉ deanewright@yahoo.co.uk

Brewer Deane Wright built this five-barrel brewery at the rear of the Wine Vaults and started brewing in 2005. The Wine Vaults is the only pub outlet for Arrow Bitter.

Bitter (OG 1042, ABV 4%)

Art Brew SIBA

Art Brew, The Art Brew Barn, Northend Farm, off Venn Lane, North Chideock, Dorset, DT6 6JY
☎ 07881 783626 ✉ artbrewdorset@googlemail.com
⊕ artbrew.co.uk

Brewing started in 2008 on a five-barrel plant with its own water source near the Jurassic Coast. Around 60 outlets are supplied from Dorset towards Berkshire and London. Seasonal beers: see website. Beers are also available under the Chideock Brewery name.

Art Nouveau (OG 1039, ABV 3.9%)
Golden and hoppy.

iBeer (OG 1039, ABV 4%)
Speciality vanilla beer.

Hip Hop Green Bullet (OG 1040, ABV 4.3%)

Tempest Stout (OG 1046, ABV 4.6%)

Monkey IPA (OG 1058, ABV 6.4%)
Massively hopped proper IPA.

Spanked Monkey IPA (OG 1058, ABV 6.4%)
As above but with root ginger and chilli added to the cask.

Brewed under Chideock Brewery name:

Marshwood Pale (ABV 3.9%)

Marshwood Gold (ABV 4.3%)

Martyr's Bitter (ABV 4.5%)

Artisan

Artisan Brewing Co Ltd, 183a Kings Road, Cardiff, Glamorgan, CF11 9DF
☎ 07505 401939 ✉ info@artisanbeer.co.uk
⊕ artisanbeer.co.uk

Tours by arrangement (small groups only)

⊠ Artisan was established in 2008. All beers are unfiltered, without additives or preservatives and suitable for vegans. Bottle-conditioned beers are available.

ALT Beer (ABV 5%)

Bohemian Style Pils (ABV 5%)

Chocolate Wheat (ABV 5%)

Helles Style Lager (ABV 5%)

Vienna Lager (ABV 5.2%)

Bavarian Style Wheat Beer (ABV 5.3%)

Smoked Lager (ABV 5.4%)

The 'Real' IPA (ABV 5.6%)

Baltic Porter (Espresso) (ABV 6%)
Infused with coffee beans.

Arundel SIBA ◉

Arundel Brewery Ltd, Unit C7, Ford Airfield Industrial Estate, Ford, Arundel, West Sussex, BN18 0HY
☎ (01903) 733111
✉ arundelbrewery@dsl.pipex.com
⊕ arundelbrewery.co.uk
Off-sales available Mon-Fri 9am-4pm at brewery

⊠ Founded in 1992, Arundel Brewery is the historic town's first brewery in more than 70 years. A range of occasional brands is available in selected months. Seasonal beers: see website.

Castle (OG 1038, ABV 3.8%) ◆
A pale tawny beer with fruit and malt noticeable in the aroma. The flavour has a good balance of malt, fruit and hops, with a dry, hoppy finish.

Sussex Gold (OG 1042, ABV 4.2%) ◆
A golden-coloured best bitter with a strong floral hop aroma. The ale is clean-tasting and bitter for its strength, with a tangy citrus flavour. The initial hop and fruit die to a dry and bitter finish.

ASB (OG 1045, ABV 4.5%)
A special bitter with a complex roast malt flavour leading to a fruity, hoppy, bittersweet finish.

Stronghold (OG 1047, ABV 4.7%) ◆
A smooth, full-flavoured premium bitter. A good balance of malt, fruit and hops comes through in this rich, chestnut-coloured beer.

Trident (OG 1050, ABV 5%)
An amber-coloured strong beer with a citrus, fruity aroma. The taste is clean and refreshing with a hoppy, fruity flavour and a pleasant dry, bitter finish.

Ascot SIBA ◉

Ascot Ales Ltd, Unit 5, Compton Place, Surrey Avenue, Camberley, Surrey, GU15 3DX
☎ (01276) 686696 ✉ info@ascot-ales.co.uk
⊕ ascot-ales.co.uk
Shop Mon-Fri 10am-3pm
Tours by arrangement

⊠ Ascot Ales began production in 2007 on a four-barrel plant. Current owner and head brewer Chris Gill took over the brewery in late 2007. Since adding a third fermenter the extra capacity has given scope for more seasonal/one off brews. Seasonal beers: see website. Bottle-conditioned beers are also available and are suitable for vegetarians and vegans.

Alley Cat Ale (OG 1038, ABV 3.8%) ◆
A pale brown session bitter with citrus hop present throughout, but balanced by malt. Dry with a lasting bitter finish.

On the Rails (OG 1039, ABV 3.8%) ◆
Dark, fruity and roasty mild with a notable hop character throughout, bittersweet in the taste and aftertaste.

Posh Pooch (OG 1042, ABV 4.2%) ◆
A hoppy best bitter with balancing biscuity malt sweetness. The citrus fruitiness lasts throughout. Clean hoppy aftertaste.

Alligator Ale (OG 1047, ABV 4.6%) ◆
American hops provide grapefruit notes in this golden ale. Hop and bitterness dominate, but there is some balancing biscuit in the aroma and taste. A residual sweetness remains even in the sharp, dry finish.

Anastasia's Exile Stout (OG 1049, ABV 5%) 🍷 ◆
Burnt coffee aromas lead to a roast malt flavour in this black beer. Notably fruity throughout. The presence of some hop feeds into the bittersweet aftertaste.

Ashley Down

Ashley Down Brewery Ltd, 15 Wathen Road, St Andrews, Bristol, BS6 5BY
☎ (0117) 983 6567

Ashley Down began brewing in 2011 using a 3.5-barrel plant in the owner's garage.

Vanguard (OG 1042, ABV 3.9%)
A dark ale brewed with stacks of roast malt, complemented with residual sweetness.

Best (OG 1040, ABV 4.2%)
A well-balanced best bitter.

Pale Ale (OG 1040, ABV 4.3%)
A good balance between malt and hoppy bitterness.

Ashover SIBA

🏠 Ashover Brewery, 1 Butts Road, Ashover, Chesterfield, Derbyshire, S45 0EW
☎ 07803 708526
✉ ashoverbrewery@googlemail.com
⊕ ashoverbrewery.com
Tours by arrangement

⊗ Ashover Brewery first brewed in early 2007 on a 3.5-barrel plant in the garage of the cottage next to the Old Poet's Corner pub. The brewery caters mainly for this and its sister pub, the Poet & Castle in Codnor and the Princess Victoria in Matlock Bath, but other local free houses and festivals are also supplied. Seasonal beers are available.

Light Rale (OG 1037, ABV 3.7%) ◆
Light in colour and taste, with initial sweet and malt flavours, leading to a bitter finish and aftertaste.

Poets Tipple (OG 1040, ABV 4%) ◆
Complex, tawny-coloured beer that drinks above its strength. Predominantly malty in flavour, with increasing bitterness towards the end.

Hydro (OG 1043, ABV 4.3%) 🍷 ◆

Easy to drink golden beer with a predominantly hoppy aroma. Hop and fruit flavours and an initial sweetness lead to a dry, clean finish and aftertaste.

Rainbows End (OG 1045, ABV 4.5%) ◆
Slightly smooth, bitter beer with an initial sweetness. Grapefruit and lemon hop flavours come through strongly as the beer gets increasingly dry towards the finish, ending with a bitter, dry aftertaste.

Coffin Lane Stout (OG 1050, ABV 5%) ◆
Excellent example of the style, with a chocolate and coffee flavour, balanced by a little sweetness. Finish is long and quite dry.

Butts Pale Ale (OG 1055, ABV 5.5%) ◆
Pale and strong yet easy to drink. A combination of bitter and sweet flavours mingle with an alcoholic kick, leading to a warming yet bitter finish and aftertaste.

Aston Manor

Aston Manor Brewery Co Ltd, 173 Thimble Mill Lane, Aston, Birmingham, West Midlands, B7 5HS
☎ (0121) 328 4336 ✉ sales@astonmanor.co.uk
⊕ astonmanor.co.uk

Aston Manor is the former owner of the Highgate Brewery in Walsall (qv). Its own plant concentrates on cider. Beer is bottled at Highgate but is not bottle conditioned.

Atlantic

Atlantic Brewery, Treisaac Farm, Treisaac, Newquay, Cornwall, TR8 4DX
☎ (0870) 042 1714 ✉ stuart@atlanticbrewery.com
⊕ atlanticbrewery.com

Atlantic started brewing in 2005. All beers are organic, Soil Association certified and suitable for vegetarians and vegans. It concentrates on bottle-conditioned beers with occasional casks, mainly Blue: Gold (ABV 4.6%, summer), Blue (ABV 4.8%), Red (ABV 5%), Fistral (ABV 5.2%).

Atlas

See Orkney

Atomic

Atomic Brewery, Alexandra Arms, 72-73 St James Street, Rugby, Warwickshire, CV21 2SL
☎ 07986 983984 ✉ sales@atomicbrewery.co.uk
⊕ atomicbrewery.com
Tours by arrangement

⊗ Atomic Brewery started production in 2006 and is run by CAMRA members Keith Abbis and Nick Pugh. Two pubs are owned, the Victoria Inn and the Alexandra Arms in Rugby, the latter being where the brew plant resides.

Strike (OG 1039, ABV 3.7%)

Fission (OG 1040, ABV 3.9%)

Half-Life (OG 1051, ABV 5%)

Bomb (OG 1054, ABV 5.2%)

Attwood (NEW) SIBA 👁

Attwood Ales Ltd, Hartlebury Brewery, Station Road, Hartlebury, Worcestershire, DY11 7YJ
☎ (01384) 220046 ✉ enquiries@attwoodales.com
⊕ attwoodales.com

Attwood was established in late 2011 using a 10-barrel plant. The brewery is housed in railway buildings at the rear of the Old Ticket Office pub and restaurant, a conversion of Hartlebury railway station.

Driver's Bitter (OG 1031.8, ABV 2.6%)

Farmers Dark Ale (OG 1038.8, ABV 3.7%)
A smooth, dark session ale; slightly smoky with a caramel finish.

Nectar Bitter (OG 1043.8, ABV 4.2%)
A light golden bitter, well-balanced with a gentle sweetness throughout.

O'Ryan's (OG 1049.8, ABV 5%)
A dark premium bitter, full-flavoured with both malt and hops evident in equal measure.

AVS

See Loddon

Axholme (NEW)

Axholme Brewing Co, 2 Garthorpe Road, Luddington, Lincolnshire, DN17 4QT
☎ 07551 910040 ✉ info@axholmebrewing.co.uk
⊕ axholmebrewing.co.uk

Former Thorne brewer Mike Richards commissioned Scunthorpe's first ever microbrewery in 2012 using a 2.5-barrel plant from Brupaks. Seasonal and one-off brews are also available.

Best Bitter (ABV 3.8%)
A traditional English bitter packed full of both bittering and aroma hops for maximum flavour while remaining an easy-drinking session beer. Malty fruitcake flavours dominate with a peppery hop finish.

IPA (Isle Pale Ale) (ABV 4.1%)
A pale and refreshing beer; powerfully hopped. A fresh and spicy take on the pale ale style with grassy and herbal flavours dominating with a rounded, bitter finish.

Aylesbury (NEW)

Aylesbury Brewhouse, Hop Pole, 83 Bicester Road, Aylesbury, Buckinghamshire, HP19 9AZ
☎ (01844) 239237
✉ info@aylesburybrewhouse.co.uk
⊕ aylesburybrewhouse.co.uk
Shop at rear of pub Wed-Sat 12-6pm

Established in 2011 as a sister brewery to Vale in Brill and operated by the same team using the eight-barrel plant previously used by Vale. Limited edition, one-off beers are brewed on a weekly basis.

Ayr SIBA

Ayr Brewing Co Ltd, 5 Racecourse Road, Ayr, KA7 2DG
☎ (01292) 263891
✉ anthony.valenti@btinternet.com
Tours by arrangement

Ayr began brewing in 2009 on a five-barrel plant and is located in the Glen Park Hotel. As well as the hotel, around 25 other outlets are supplied in central and southern Scotland and the north of England. Seasonal beers are available.

Leezie Lundie (OG 1037.5, ABV 3.8%)
A pale golden session ale with hints of grapefruit and a dry, lingering finish.

Jolly Beggars (OG 1041, ABV 4.2%)
A complex best bitter with plenty of character and lingering malty aftertaste.

Rabbie's Porter (OG 1042.5, ABV 4.3%)
A robust, full-bodied porter with well-balanced toffee, fruity malt and a slightly smoky finish.

Towzie Tyke (OG 1044.5, ABV 4.6%)
An amber ale with a dry, long, bitter finish.

B&T SIBA EAB 👁

B&T Brewery Ltd, The Brewery, Shefford, Bedfordshire, SG17 5DZ
☎ (01462) 815080 ✉ brewery@banksandtaylor.com
⊕ banksandtaylor.com
Tours by arrangement (CAMRA branches only)

Banks & Taylor – now just B&T – was founded in 1982. It produces an extensive range of beers, including monthly special brews together with occasional beers: see website for details. There are six tied houses, all operated with guest beers as well as B&T beers.

Two Brewers Bitter (OG 1036, ABV 3.6%)
Bronze-coloured bitter with citrus hop aroma and taste and a dry finish.

Shefford Bitter (OG 1038, ABV 3.8%)
A pale brown beer with a light hop aroma and a hoppy taste leading to a bitter finish.

Shefford Dark Mild (OG 1038, ABV 3.8%)
A dark beer with a well-balanced taste. Sweetish, roast malt aftertaste.

Golden Fox (OG 1041, ABV 4.1%)
A golden, hoppy ale, dry tasting with a fruity aroma and citrus finish.

Fruit Bat (OG 1045, ABV 4.2%)
A warming straw-coloured beer with a generous taste of raspberries and a bitter finish.

Black Dragon Mild (OG 1043, ABV 4.3%)
Black in colour with a toffee and roast malt flavour and a smoky finish.

Dunstable Giant (OG 1044, ABV 4.4%)
Dark tawny bitter with a subtle blend of malt and hops.

Dragon Slayer (OG 1045, ABV 4.5%)
A golden beer with a malt and hop flavour and a bitter finish. More malty and less hoppy than is usual for a beer of this style.

Edwin Taylor's Extra Stout (OG 1045, ABV 4.5%)
A complex black beer with a bitter coffee and roast malt flavour and a dry bitter finish.

Shefford Pale Ale (SPA) (OG 1045, ABV 4.5%)
A well-balanced beer with hop, fruit and malt flavours. Dry, bitter aftertaste.

SOD (OG 1050, ABV 5%)

SOS (OG 1050, ABV 5%) ◆
A rich mixture of fruit, hops and malt is present in the taste and aftertaste of this beer. Predominantly hoppy aroma. SOD is the same beer with caramel added.

Bacchus

Bacchus Brewing Co, Bacchus Hotel, 17 High Street, Sutton-on-Sea, Lincolnshire, LN12 2EY
☎ (01507) 441204 ✉ info@bacchushotel.co.uk
⊕ bacchushotel.co.uk
Tours by arrangement

⊗ Bacchus began brewing in 2010 on a one-barrel plant supplying the Bacchus Hotel.

Best Bitter (OG 1039, ABV 3.9%)

Bittermans (OG 1043, ABV 4.3%)

Sutton Pride (OG 1045, ABV 4.5%)

Backyard SIBA ◉

Backyard Brewhouse, Unit 8a, Gatehouse Trading Estate, Lichfield Road, Brownhills, Walsall, West Midlands, WS8 6JZ
☎ 07591 923370
✉ enquiries@thebackyardbrewhouse.com
⊕ thebackyardbrewhouse.com
Tours by arrangement

⊕ Backyard began brewing in 2008 on a five-barrel plant, expanding to 12 barrels in 2012. Four core beers are produced plus seasonal and monthly specials – see website for further details. Around 100 outlets are supplied direct.

Bitter (OG 1040, ABV 3.8%)

The Hoard (OG 1040, ABV 3.9%)

Blonde (OG 1041, ABV 4.1%)

Premium (OG 1046, ABV 4.5%)

Badger

See Hall & Woodhouse

Ballard's SIBA ◉

Ballard's Brewery Ltd, The Old Sawmill, Nyewood, Petersfield, GU31 5HA
☎ (01730) 821362 ✉ service@ballards-brewery.co.uk ⊕ ballards-brewery.co.uk
Shop Mon-Fri 8am-4pm
Tours by arrangement

⊗ Launched in 1980 by Mike and Carola Brown at Cumbers Farm, Trotton, Ballard's has been trading at Nyewood since 1988 and now supplies 70-80 outlets. Seasonal beers: see website. Bottle-conditioned beers are also available.

Midhurst Mild (OG 1034, ABV 3.4%)
Traditional dark mild, well-balanced, refreshing, with a biscuity flavour.

Golden Bine (OG 1038, ABV 3.8%) ◆
Amber, clean-tasting bitter. A roast malt aroma leads to a fruity, slightly sweet taste and a dry finish.

Best Bitter (OG 1042, ABV 4.2%) ◆
A copper-coloured beer with a malty aroma. A good balance of fruit and malt in the flavour gives way to a dry, hoppy aftertaste.

Wild (ABV 4.7%)
A blend of Mild and Wassail.

Nyewood Gold (OG 1050, ABV 5%) ◆
Robust golden brown strong bitter, hoppy and fruity throughout, with a balanced finish.

Wassail (OG 1060, ABV 6%) ◆
A strong, full-bodied, tawny-red, fruity beer with a predominance of malt throughout, but also an underlying hoppiness.

Bank Top SIBA ◉

Bank Top Brewery Ltd, The Pavilion, Ashworth Lane, Bolton, Lancashire, BL1 8RA
☎ (01204) 595800 ✉ dave@banktopbrewery.com
⊕ banktopbrewery.com
Tours by arrangement

⊕ Bank Top was established in 1995. Since 2002 the brewery has occupied a Grade II-listed tennis pavilion. In 2007 the brewing capacity was doubled with the installation of a new 10-barrel plant and in 2008 David Sweeney became the sole proprietor.

Barley to Beer (OG 1036, ABV 3.6%)
A pale bitter with a citrus lemon and herbal finish.

Sweeney's (OG 1038, ABV 3.8%)
An amber bitter with a bold, crisp flavour and a delicate, slightly spicy aroma.

Bad to the Bone (OG 1040, ABV 4%)
A tan-coloured beer with floral qualities and delicate citrus notes.

Dark Mild (OG 1040, ABV 4%) ☐ ◆
Dark brown beer with a malt and roast aroma. Smooth mouthfeel, with malt, roast malt and hops prominent throughout.

Flat Cap (OG 1040, ABV 4%) ▮ ◆
Amber ale with a modest fruit aroma leading to a beer with citrus fruit, malt and hops. Good finish of fruit, malt and bitterness.

Gold Digger (OG 1040, ABV 4%) ◆
Golden coloured, with a citrus aroma, grapefruit and a touch of spiciness on the palate; a fresh, hoppy citrus finish.

Old Slapper (OG 1042, ABV 4%)
A blonde bitter with an initial fruitiness complemented by a pronounced hoppiness in the finish.

Pavilion Pale Ale (OG 1045, ABV 4.5%) ◆
A yellow beer with a citrus and hop aroma. Big fruity flavour with a peppery hoppiness; dry, bitter yet fruity finish.

Blonde (OG 1050, ABV 5%)
An extremely pale ale made with New Zealand hops resulting in a pleasant woody flavour and distinct berry aroma.

Port O Call (OG 1050, ABV 5%) ◆
Dark brown beer with a malty, fruity aroma. Malt, roast and dark fruits in the bittersweet taste and finish.

Leprechaun Stout (OG 1060, ABV 6%)
A pitch black stout with hints of blackcurrant and spicy fruit.

Banks's

See Marston's in New Nationals section

Barearts

Barearts Ltd t/a Barearts Brewery, 290-292 Rochdale Road, Todmorden, West Yorkshire, OL14 7PD
☎ (01706) 839305 ✉ info@barearts.com
⊕ barearts.com
Shop Wed-Fri 4-9.45pm, Sat 12-9.45pm, Sun 12-9.45pm

A four-barrel craft brewery that began production in 2005 and is named after an art gallery dedicated to nude artwork. Beer is available only from the beer shop and studio bar or by mail order. All beers are sold in bottles or 5-litre mini casks and are all conditioned by secondary fermentation.

Barge & Barrel

See Eastwood

Barkston (NEW)

Barkston Brewery, Orchard House, Saw Wells Court, Barkston Ash, North Yorkshire, LS24 9JU
☎ 01764 750959 ✉ info@barkstonbrewery.com
⊕ barkstonbrewery.com

Barkston was established in 2011 in the picturesque village of Barkston Ash.

3b (OG 1040, ABV 4%)
A session bitter with a creamy head and smooth taste.

Blonde (OG 1040, ABV 4%)
A light golden beer with an intense, hoppy flavour.

Belle (OG 1046, ABV 4.7%)
A dark ruby beer with a biscuit flavour.

Barley Bottom (NEW)

Barley Bottom Brewery, Unit 1a, Howden Hall Industrial Estate, Howden Road, Silsden, West Yorkshire, BD20 0HJ
☎ (01535) 656797 ☎ 07954 173473
⊕ barleytrading.co.uk

Barley Bottom began brewing in 2012 using a one-barrel plant.

Cobbydale Bitter (ABV 4%)

Cobbydale Blonde (ABV 4%)

Cobbydale Gold (ABV 4%)

Barlow SIBA

Barlow Brewery Ltd, Units 5 & 6, Shippen Rural Business Centre, Church Farm, Barlow, Derbyshire, S18 7TR
☎ (0114) 289 1767
✉ enquiries@barlowbrewery.co.uk
⊕ barlowbrewery.com
Ring for shop opening times

Barlow began brewing in 2009 using a self-built 2.5-barrel plant located in renovated farm buildings. The Hare & Hounds in Barlow is supplied on a permanent basis as well as several other outlets in Derbyshire and South Yorkshire.

Heath Robinson (OG 1039, ABV 3.8%)
A traditional dark bitter with a malty background and a balanced, bitter finish.

Carnival Ale (OG 1042, ABV 4%)
A light, golden pale ale with a citrus finish.

Dark Horse (OG 1043, ABV 4.2%)
A dark bitter with a coffee aroma and well-balanced finish.

Black (OG 1051, ABV 5%)
A dark ale with strong roast and malty flavours and a well-balanced, bitter finish.

Three Valleys IPA (OG 1052, ABV 5%)
An American-style IPA bursting with tropical fruit and citrus flavours with a clean, bitter finish.

Full Monty (OG 1067, ABV 6.5%)
A strong, full-flavoured IPA. Golden in colour with complex passion fruit, citrus and mandarin orange flavours with a warming finish.

Anastasia (OG 1080, ABV 8%)
Strong, dark and smooth with complex malt flavours, chocolate coffee and a hint of fruit.

Barney's (NEW) SIBA

Barney's Beer Ltd, Summerhall Brewery, 1 Summerhall, Edinburgh, EH9 1PL
☎ 07512 253660 ✉ barneysbeer@gmail.com
⊕ barneysbeer.com

Barney's began brewing in 2011 at the Behind the Wall pub in Falkirk. In 2012 the brewery expanded and moved to new premises in Edinburgh using a six-barrel plant. Seasonal and bottle-conditioned beers are available.

Good Ordinary Pale Ale (ABV 3.8%)

Red Rye (ABV 4.5%)

Volcano IPA (ABV 5%)

Barngates SIBA ◉

Barngates Brewery Ltd, Barngates, Ambleside, Cumbria, LA22 0NG
☎ (01539) 436575 ✉ info@barngatesbrewery.co.uk
⊕ barngatesbrewery.co.uk
Tours by arrangement

⊚Barngates Brewery started brewing in 1997 and initially provided only the Drunken Duck Inn. The brewery became a limited company in 1999 upon expansion to a five-barrel plant. Further expansion in 2008 included a brand new, purpose-built 10-barrel plant. Around 150 outlets are supplied direct throughout Cumbria, Lancashire, Yorkshire and Northumberland. Occasional beers are produced.

Cat Nap (OG 1037, ABV 3.6%) 🍺 🍂
Pale beer unapologetically bitter with a dry astringent finish.

Cracker Ale (OG 1038, ABV 3.9%) 🍂
A flavoursome malty bitter, fruity but not sweet. Dry in taste rather than finish.

Westmorland Gold (OG 1043, ABV 4.2%) 🍂
A golden ale with a good balance of malt and hops, perhaps not as intense as previously.

Tag Lag (OG 1044, ABV 4.4%) 🍂
A pale amber beer, smooth and sweetly malty to begin but a lasting, bitter finish.

Barnsley

See Wentworth

THE BREWERIES

Barrowden

⊟ Barrowden Brewing Co, c/o Exeter Arms, 28 Main Street, Barrowden, Rutland, LE15 8EQ
☎ (01572) 747247
✉ enquiries@exeterarmsrutland.co.uk
⊕ exeterarmsrutland.co.uk

⊗ The brewery was established in 1998. Martin Allsopp bought the pub and brewery in 2005, which is situated in a barn at the back of the Exeter Arms. Seasonal beers: see website.

Pilot (OG 1028, ABV 2.6%)

Beech (OG 1040, ABV 3.8%)

Own Gear (OG 1040, ABV 4%)

Hop Gear (OG 1046, ABV 4.4%)

Bartrams EAB

Bartrams Brewery, Rougham Estate, Ipswich Road (A14), Rougham, Suffolk, IP30 9LZ
☎ (01449) 737655 ☎ 07768 062581
✉ marc@bartramsbrewery.co.uk
⊕ bartramsbrewery.co.uk
Shop Tue & Sat 12-6pm
Tours by arrangement

The brewery was set up in 1999. In 2005 the plant was moved to a building on Rougham Airfield, the site of Bartram's Brewery between 1894 and 1902 run by Captain Bill Bartram. His image graces the pump clips. Beers are available in a selection of local pubs and there is a large amount of trade through local farmers' markets. Marld, Beltane Braces and all porters and stouts are suitable for vegetarians and vegans, as are all bottled beers. Seasonal beers: see website.

Marld (OG 1033, ABV 3.4%)
A traditional mild. Spicy hops and malt with a hint of chocolate, slightly smoky with a light, roasted finish.

Premier Bitter (OG 1038, ABV 3.7%)
A traditional quaffing ale, full-flavoured but light, dry and hoppy.

Rougham Ready (OG 1038, ABV 3.8%)
A light, crisp bitter, surprisingly full bodied for its strength.

Red Queen (OG 1039, ABV 3.9%)
Typical IPA style, chocolate malt in the foreground while the resiny hop flavour lingers.

Cat's Whiskers (OG 1040, ABV 4%)
A straw-coloured beer with ginger and lemons added; a unique flavour experience.

Grozet (OG 1040, ABV 4%)
Gooseberries are added to give an appealing extra dimension.

Bee's Knees (OG 1042, ABV 4.2%)
An amber beer with a floral aroma; honey softness on the palate leads to a crisp, bitter finish.

Catherine Bartram's IPA (OG 1043, ABV 4.3%)
A full-bodied malty IPA style; tangy hops lead the malt throughout and dominate the dry, hoppy aftertaste.

Jester Quick One (OG 1044, ABV 4.4%)
A sweet reddish bitter using fruity American Ahtanum hops.

Beltane Braces (OG 1046, ABV 4.5%)
Smooth and dark.

Stingo (OG 1045, ABV 4.5%)
A sweetish, fruity bitter with a hoppy nose. Light honey softens the bitter finish.

Beer Elsie Bub (OG 1048, ABV 4.8%)
Originally brewed for a Pagan wedding, this strong honey ale is now brewed all year round.

Captain Bill Bartram's Best Bitter
(OG 1048, ABV 4.8%)
Modified from a 100-year old recipe, using full malt and traditional Kentish hops.

Captain's Stout (OG 1049, ABV 4.8%)
Biscuity dark malt leads to a lightly smoked aroma, plenty of roasted malt character, coffee notes and a whiff of smoke.

Cherry Stout (OG 1048, ABV 4.8%)
Sensuous hints of chocolate lead to a subtle suggestion of cherries.

Suffolk 'n' Strong (OG 1050, ABV 5%)
A light, smooth and dangerously potable strong bitter, well-balanced malt and hops with an easy finish.

Comrade Bill Bartram's Egalitarian Anti-Imperialist Soviet Stout (OG 1070, ABV 6.9%)
A Russian stout by any other name, a luscious easy-drinking example of the style.

Barum SIBA

⊟ Barum Brewery Ltd, c/o Reform Inn, Pilton, Barnstaple, Devon, EX31 1PD
☎ (01271) 329994 ✉ info@barumbrewery.co.uk
⊕ barumbrewery.co.uk
Tours by arrangement

Barum was formed in 1996 by Tim Webster and is housed in a conversion attached to the Reform Inn that acts as the brewery tap and main outlet. Distribution is exclusively within Devon. Seasonal beers are brewed.

Original (OG 1044, ABV 4.4%)

EPA (OG 1046, ABV 4.6%)

Breakfast (OG 1048, ABV 5%)

Baseline (NEW)

Baseline Brewing Ltd, Golding Barn Industrial Estate, Henfield Road, Small Dole, West Sussex, BN5 9XH
☎ (01903) 879111 ✉ info@baselinebrewing.co.uk
⊕ baselinebrewing.co.uk

Baseline began brewing in 2012 using a five-barrel plant.

Thunderbolt Bitter (ABV 4%)
A full-flavoured, copper-coloured session bitter.

Dark Matter (ABV 5.5%)
A dark, full-bodied ale with roasted malt and spicy hop flavours and a fruity but dry bitter finish.

English Electric Lightning (ABV 6%)

Batch Brew (NEW)

Batch Brew, c/o 17 Sussex Street, Winchester, Hampshire, SO23 8TG
☎ 07917 035625 ✉ phil.whitwell@batchbrew.com
⊕ batchbrew.com

Established in 2012, Batch Brew's bottle-conditioned beer is contract brewed by Oakleaf Brewery at present: Batch 9 (ABV 5%).

Batemans SIBA IFBB ⊙

George Bateman & Son Ltd, Salem Bridge Brewery, Mill Lane, Wainfleet, Lincolnshire, PE24 4JE
☎ (01754) 880317 ✉ enquiries@bateman.co.uk
⊕ bateman.co.uk
Visitor Centre & Shop: ring or see website for opening times
Tours by arrangement

⊙Bateman's Brewery is one of the few remaining independent family-owned and managed brewers. Established in 1874 it has been brewing award-winning beers for four generations of the family. All but one of the 66 tied houses serve cask-conditioned beer. See website for seasonal and speciality beers.

Dark Mild (OG 1030, ABV 3%) ⬚ ▨ ◆
Gentle roast fruity airs preface this red-brown, caramel-infused brew. Malt and a stewed plummy sweetness initially give depth. Caramel dominates the short simple finish.

XB (OG 1037, ABV 3.7%) ◆
A well-rounded, smooth malty beer with a blackcurrant fruity background. Hops flourish initially before giving way to a bittersweet dryness that enhances the mellow malty ending.

All Seasons (OG 1042, ABV 4.2%)

XXXB (OG 1048, ABV 4.5%)
A blend of malt, hops and fruit on the nose with a bitter bite over the top of faintly banana maltiness that stays the course.

Salem Porter (OG 1048, ABV 4.7%) ▨ ◆
A black and complex mix of chocolate, liquorice and cough elixir.

Bath Ales SIBA ⊙

Bath Ales Ltd, Units 3-7, Caxton Business Park, Crown Way, Warmley, Bristol, BS30 5LW
☎ (0117) 947 4797 ✉ hare@bathales.co.uk
⊕ bathales.com
Shop Mon-Fri 9am-5pm; Sat 9am-12pm
Tours by arrangement

Bath Ales started brewing in 1995. Around 400 outlets are supplied direct. It owns its own bottling plant and also bottles for more than 25 other breweries. 10 pubs are owned, all serving cask ale. Seasonal beers: see website.

SPA (OG 1039, ABV 3.7%) ◆
Nicely-balanced pale session bitter. A citrus hop aroma, fruity taste and long bitter aftertaste.

Gem (OG 1042, ABV 4.1%) ◆
Well-balanced pale brown best bitter. Ripe fruits with a hint of caramel. Hops come through on the aftertaste, which can also be astringent.

Barnsey (OG 1045, ABV 4.5%) ◆
A honey/caramel nose to this dark roast, smooth, strong bitter, almost an Old Ale but with more hops. A sweetish taste of caramel and fruit develops into a lingering roast aftertaste with a suggestion of hops.

Batham IFBB

⧮ **Daniel Batham & Son Ltd, Delph Brewery, Delph Road, Brierley Hill, West Midlands, DY5 2TN**
☎ (01384) 77229 ✉ info@bathams.com
⊕ bathams.com

⊙A classic Black Country small brewery established in 1877. Tim and Matthew Batham represent the fifth generation to run the company. The Vine, one of the Black Country's most famous pubs, is also the site of the brewery. The company has 11 tied houses and supplies around 30 other outlets. Batham's Bitter is delivered in 54-gallon hogsheads to meet demand. Seasonal beer: see website.

Mild Ale (OG 1036.5, ABV 3.5%) ◆
A fruity, dark brown mild with malty sweetness and a roast malt finish.

Best Bitter (OG 1043.5, ABV 4.3%) ▨ ◆
A pale yellow, fruity, sweetish bitter, with a dry, hoppy finish. A good, light, refreshing beer.

Battledown SIBA ⊙

Battledown Brewery LLP, Keynsham Works, Keynsham Street, Cheltenham, Gloucestershire, GL52 6EJ
☎ (01242) 693409 ☎ 07734 834104
✉ info@battledownbrewery.com
⊕ battledownbrewery.com
Shop open Wed/Thu/Sat am – see website for times
Tours by arrangement

⊠ Established in 2005 by Roland and Stephanie Elliott-Berry, and joined in 2006 by Ben Jennison-Phillips (ex-Whittingtons), Battledown operates an eight-barrel plant from an old engineering works and supplies more than 250 outlets. Visitors are always welcome. There is an online shop for mail order purposes. Seasonal beers are also brewed.

Sunbeam (OG 1037, ABV 3.8%)
A golden pale ale with a refreshing aroma and sharp but smooth taste leaving a dry, hoppy aftertaste which lingers on the palate.

Natural Selection (OG 1041, ABV 4.2%)
A deep golden beer, the malts evident but giving way to the triple hop addition that leaves a spicy and slightly citrus finish.

Premium (OG 1046, ABV 4.6%)
A rich amber ale. A malty aroma and taste with a deep satisfying, full-bodied fruit and malt texture leaving a well-rounded mellow aftertaste.

Special (OG 1050, ABV 5.2%)
A well-balanced and crisp pale ale.

Battlefield

See Tunnel

Bays SIBA ⊙

Bays Brewery Ltd, Aspen Way, Paignton, Devon, TQ4 7QR
☎ (01803) 555004 ✉ info@baysbrewery.co.uk
⊕ baysbrewery.co.uk
Shop Mon-Fri 8am-5pm
Tours by arrangement

⊠ Bays Brewery opened in early 2007 in an old steel fabrication unit in Paignton on a 20-barrel plant. Seasonal and bottle-conditioned beers are also available.

Best (OG 1037, ABV 3.7%)

Topsail (ABV 4%)

Gold (OG 1042, ABV 4.3%)

Devon Dumpling (OG 1048, ABV 5.1%)

Bazens'

See Star Inn

Beachy Head SIBA

**Beachy Head Brewing Co Ltd, Seven Sisters Sheep
Centre, Birling Manor Farm, Gilberts Drive, East Dean,
East Sussex, BN20 0AA**
☎ (01323) 423313 ✉ charlie@beachyhead.org.uk
⊕ beachyhead.org.uk
Tours by arrangement

⊗ The 2.5-barrel brew plant was installed at the
rear of the sheep centre in late 2006. Beachy Head
Brewery produces both cask and bottle-
conditioned ales, supplied regularly to around 15
outlets, three of which are local pubs. The full
range of ales (including seasonals) can be sampled
at the Tiger Inn in East Dean village, which is the
brewery tap.

Southdowns Ale (ABV 4.4%)

Beachy Original (ABV 4.5%)

Legless Rambler (ABV 5%)

Beartown SIBA ◉

**Beartown Brewery Ltd, Bromley House, Spindle
Street, Congleton, Cheshire, CW12 1QN**
☎ (01260) 299964
✉ headbrewer@beartownbrewery.co.uk
⊕ beartownbrewery.co.uk
Shop Mon-Fri 9am-5pm; Sat 9am-4pm
Tours by arrangement

⊕Congleton's links with brewing can be traced
back to 1272. Two of its most senior officers at the
time were Ale Taster and Bear Warden, hence the
name of the brewery. Both the brewery's
Navigation in Stockport and the Beartown Tap have
been named CAMRA regional pubs of the year.
Beartown supplies 250 outlets and owns five pubs.
Seasonal beers: see website.

Best Bitter (OG 1037, ABV 3.7%)
A copper-coloured session beer with a full palate of
malt and crisp hops.

Bear Ass (OG 1040, ABV 4%) ✦
Dark ruby-red, malty bitter with good hop nose and
fruity flavour with dry, bitter, astringent aftertaste.

Ginger Bear (OG 1040, ABV 4%)
The flavours from the malt and hops blend with the
added bite from the root ginger to produce a
quenching finish.

Kodiak Gold (OG 1040, ABV 4%) ✦
Hops and fruit dominate the taste of this crisp
yellow bitter and these follow through to the
dryish aftertaste. Biscuity malt also comes through
on the aroma and taste.

Bearskinful (OG 1042, ABV 4.2%) ✦
Biscuity malt dominates the flavour of this amber
best bitter. There are hops and a hint of sulphur on
the aroma. A balance of malt and bitterness follow
through to the aftertaste.

Bearly Literate (OG 1045, ABV 4.5%)
A golden pale ale. Floral scented with summer fruit
and lemon flavours ending with a smooth dryness.

Polar Eclipse (OG 1048, ABV 4.8%) 🖩 ✦
Classic black, dry and bitter stout, with roast
flavours to the fore. Good hop on the nose follow
through the taste into a long dry finish.

Blackbear (OG 1050, ABV 5%) ✦
Advertised as a strong mild, this beer is rather
bitter for the style. Bitter and malt flavours are
balanced and there is also a good roast character
along with a hint of liquorice. Aftertaste is short
and reasonably dry.

Bruins Ruin (OG 1050, ABV 5%)
A deep copper-coloured premium ale. Full of malty
character and a palate of sweet, smooth, fruity
flavours.

Beavertown (NEW) SIBA

**目 Beavertown Brewery, Duke's Brew & Que, 33
Downham Road, De Beauvoir Town, London, N1 5AA**
☎ (020) 3006 0794
✉ info@beavertownbrewery.com
⊕ beavertownbrewery.com

Brewing began in 2012 using a five-barrel plant.

Neck Oil (ABV 4.3%)

Smog Rocket (ABV 5.4%)

8 Ball (ABV 6.2%)

Beckstones

**Beckstones Brewery, Upper Beckstones Mill, The
Green, Millom, Cumbria, LA18 5HL**
☎ (01229) 775294
✉ david@beckstonesbrewery.com
⊕ beckstonesbrewery.co.uk

⊗ Beckstones started brewing in 2003 on the site
of an 18th-century mill with its own water supply.
It's a five-barrel, one-man operation. The beer
names often have a connection to the long-closed
Millom Iron Works or local characters. The brewer
also designs the distinctive pump clips. Occasional
and seasonal beers are also brewed.

Barley Juice (OG 1033, ABV 3.4%) ✦
Full-flavoured, beautifully balanced, emphatically
fruity, hoppy beer.

Beer O'Clock (OG 1036, ABV 3.5%) ✦
A fascinating blend of flavours delivering ever-
changing mouthfuls of sweet fruity and hoppy
bitterness.

Black Gun Dog Freddy Mild
(OG 1038, ABV 3.8%) ✦
A full-bodied, beautifully balanced ruby dark mild,
replete with fruit and roast malt.

Iron Town (OG 1038, ABV 3.8%) ✦
Creamy sweet brown ale full of well-balanced fruit
and hop.

Border Steeans (OG 1040, ABV 4.1%) ✦
An old-fashioned tawny bitter with a sweet start,
some bitter notes and plenty of aftertaste.

Rev Rob (OG 1044, ABV 4.6%) ✦
A golden beer with a pronounced grapefruit aroma
and taste. The hoppy bitterness lasts through to the
aftertaste.

Bedlam (NEW)

**Bedlam Brewery, Albourne Farm, Shaves Wood Lane,
Albourne, West Sussex, BN6 9DX**

✉ bedlambrewery@gmail.com
⊕ bedlambrewery.co.uk

Bedlam began brewing in 2012. No beer list was available at the time of going to press.

Beer Engine SIBA

⧪ Tuttles Unique Co Ltd t/a The Beer Engine, Newton St Cyres, Devon, EX5 5AX
☎ (01392) 851282 ✉ info@thebeerengine.co.uk
⊕ thebeerengine.co.uk
Tours by arrangement

⊠ Beer Engine was developed in 1983 and is the oldest continuously-working micro-brewery in Devon, still employing the original brewer, Ian Sharp. The brewery is visible behind glass downstairs in the pub. A few outlets are supplied as well as all local beer festivals. Seasonal beers are also available.

Rail Ale (OG 1037, ABV 3.8%) ⬥
A straw-coloured beer with a fruity aroma and a sweet, fruity finish.

Piston Bitter (OG 1043, ABV 4.3%) ⬥
A mid-brown, sweet-tasting beer with a pleasant, bittersweet aftertaste.

Sleeper Heavy (OG 1052, ABV 5.4%) ⬥
A red-coloured beer with a fruity, sweet taste and a bitter finish.

Beer Geek (NEW)

Beer Geek Brewery Ltd, Unit D3, Aston Seedbed Centre, Aston, Birmingham, B7 4NT
☎ 0844 272 7207 ✉ sales@beergeekbrewery.com
⊕ beergeekbrewery.com

Beer Geek began brewing in 2012 using 15-barrel brewery.

Geek Unique (ABV 4.3%)
A dark bitter with sweet, malty flavours and a bold, fruity aftertaste.

Great White Geek (ABV 4.5%)
A full-flavoured ale with floral aromas and a lingering, hoppy finish.

Legend of the Golden Geek (ABV 4.5%)
A well-hopped golden beer with citrus notes leading to a crisp, refreshing aftertaste.

Dark Side of the Geek (ABV 5.5%)
A malty, dark ale with soft, fruity aromas.

Beer Works

See Abbeydale

Bees

Bees Brewery, Plot 2, Coast Road, Walcott, Norwich, NR12 0LS
☎ 07971 577526 ✉ bees-brewery@hotmail.co.uk

Bees first brewed in 2008 and was initially based at Queniborough near Leicester. It relocated to Norfolk towards the end of 2009 and the five-barrel plant is now located in a static caravan overlooking the sea. Brewer Alec Brackenbury operates the brewery on a part-time basis and mainly supplies pubs within a 10-mile radius of Walcott.

Amber (OG 1038, ABV 3.8%)

Navigator (OG 1045, ABV 4.5%)

Stripey Jack (OG 1046, ABV 4.6%)

Wobble (OG 1050, ABV 5%)

Honey (OG 1052, ABV 5.2%)

Beeston SIBA EAB

Beeston Brewery Ltd, Fransham Road Farm, Beeston, Norfolk, PE32 2LZ
☎ (01328) 700844 ☎ 07768 742763
✉ mark@beestonbrewery.co.uk
⊕ beestonbrewery.co.uk
Tours by arrangement

⊠ The brewery was established in 2006 in an old farm building using a five-barrel plant. Brewing water comes from a dedicated borehole and raw ingredients are sourced locally whenever possible. All beers are also available bottle conditioned and in 5-litre mini casks.

The Squirrels Nuts (OG 1035, ABV 3.5%)

Afternoon Delight (OG 1036, ABV 3.7%)
An easy-drinking blonde ale.

Worth the Wait (OG 1041, ABV 4.2%) ⬥
Well-balanced and complex with a soft hoppy nose. An initial burst of passion fruit mingles with malt and hops in a delightful first taste. A long-lasting finish develops a bittersweet dryness.

Stirling (OG 1045, ABV 4.5%)
A rich, malty red bitter with toffee notes.

Village Life (OG 1047, ABV 4.8%)
An amber bitter with an abundance of interesting hop character.

On the Huh (OG 1048, ABV 5%) ⬥
Deceptively smooth bitter with a fruity raisin aroma. A bittersweet maltiness jousts with caramel and roast. A dry hoppiness gives depth to a strong finale.

Norfolk Black (OG 1060, ABV 6%)
A warming, full-bodied, strong stout.

Old Stoatwobbler (OG 1065, ABV 6%)

For Brancaster Brewery:

Best (OG 1038, ABV 3.8%)

Malthouse Bitter (OG 1042, ABV 4.2%)

Oyster Catcher (ABV 4.4%)

The Wreck (ABV 4.8%)

Belhaven

See Greene King in New Nationals section

Bellingers SIBA

Bellingers Brewery, Station Road, Grove, Oxfordshire, OX12 0DH
☎ (01235) 772255 ✉ info@bellingersbrewery.co.uk
⊕ bellingersbrewery.co.uk
Shop Mon-Sat 6am-9pm; Sun 7am-8pm
Tours by arrangement

⊠ The late Mike Bellinger established Bellinger's Brewery as a family partnership in 2011. The five-barrel plant produces three core beers plus seasonals: see website.

Blenheim (OG 1037, ABV 3.9%)

Original Bitter (OG 1040, ABV 4.1%)
A light and refreshing easy-drinking beer.

Best Bitter (OG 1046, ABV 4.9%)

Belvoir SIBA

Belvoir Brewery Ltd, Crown Park, Station Road, Old Dalby, Leicestershire, LE14 3NQ
☎ (01664) 822015 ✉ colin@belvoirbrewery.co.uk
⊕ belvoirbrewery.co.uk
Shop open from 12pm daily (until evening)
Tours by arrangement

⊗ Belvoir (pronounced 'beaver') Brewery was set up in 1995 by former Shipstone's and Theakston's brewer Colin Brown. Long-term expansion has seen the introduction of a 20-barrel plant that can produce 50 barrels a week. There is also a visitor centre incorporating brewery memorabilia, a bar, restaurant and shop (open seven days a week). Around 150 outlets are supplied direct. Seasonal and bottle-conditioned beers are also available.

Dark Horse (OG 1035, ABV 3.4%)

Whippling (OG 1037, ABV 3.6%)
A golden, light, crisp and refreshing beer.

Star Bitter (OG 1039, ABV 3.9%) ◈
Reminiscent of the long-extinct Shipstone's Bitter, this mid-brown bitter lives up to its name as it is bitter in taste but not unpleasantly so.

Gordon Bennett (OG 1041, ABV 4.1%)
Light chestnut beer with a biscuity character and a pleasant hop finish.

Beaver Bitter (OG 1043, ABV 4.3%) ◈
A light brown bitter that starts malty in both aroma and taste, but soon develops a hoppy bitterness. Appreciably fruity.

Oatmeal Stout (OG 1044, ABV 4.3%)
A full-bodied creamy dark stout.

Old Dalby (OG 1050, ABV 5.1%)
A rich, smooth ruby red strong ale with a pleasant hop character.

For Hoskins Brothers, Leicester:

Hobs Best Mild (OG 1035, ABV 3.5%)

Brigadier Bitter (OG 1036, ABV 3.6%)

Hobs Bitter (OG 1040, ABV 4%)

White Dolphin (OG 1040, ABV 4%)

Tom Kelly's Stout (OG 1042, ABV 4.2%)

Ginger Tom (OG 1052, ABV 5.2%)

Beowulf SIBA ◉

Beowulf Brewing Co, Chasewater Country Park, Pool Road, Brownhills, Staffordshire, WS8 7NL
☎ (01543) 454067 ✉ beowulfbrewing@yahoo.co.uk
⊕ beowulfbrewery.co.uk
Tours by arrangement

Beowulf Brewing Company beers appear as guest ales predominantly in the central region but also across the country. The brewery's dark beers have a particular reputation for excellence. Seasonal beers: see website. Bottle-conditioned beer is also available.

Beorma (OG 1038, ABV 3.9%) ◈
A perfectly balanced session ale with a malty hint of fruit giving way to a lingering bitterness. Background spice excites the palate.

Chasewater Bitter (OG 1043, ABV 4.4%) ◈
Golden bitter, hoppy throughout with citrus and hints of malt. Long mouth-watering, bitter finish.

Dark Raven (OG 1048, ABV 4.5%) 🍴 🍺 ◈
So dark with apple and bonfire in the aroma, so sweet and smooth like liquid toffee apples with a sudden bitter finish.

Swordsman (OG 1045, ABV 4.5%) ◈
Pale gold, light fruity aroma, tangy hoppy flavour. Faintly hoppy finish.

Folden Cross (ABV 4.6%)

Dragon Smoke Stout (OG 1048, ABV 4.7%) ◈
Black with a light brown creamy head. Tobacco, chocolate, liquorice and mixed fruity hints on the aroma. Bitterness fights through the sweet and roast flavours and eventually dominates. Hints of a good port emerge.

Finn's Hall Porter (OG 1049, ABV 4.7%) 🍴 ◈
Dark chocolate aroma, after dinner mints, coffee and fresh tobacco. Good bitterness with woodland hints of autumn. Long late bitterness with lip drying moreishness.

Mercian Shine (OG 1048, ABV 5%) ◈
Amber to pale gold with a good bitter and hoppy start. Plenty of caramel and hops with background malt leading to a good bitter finish with caramel and hops lingering in the aftertaste.

Berrow

See Towles'

Bespoke (NEW) SIBA

Bespoke Brewing Co, Unit 5, The Mews, Mitcheldean, Gloucestershire, GL17 0DD
☎ (01594) 546557 ✉ mike@bespokebrewery.co.uk
⊕ bespokebrewery.co.uk
Tours by arrangement

Brewing commenced in 2012 on a 5.5-barrel plant located on the site of the old Wintles Brewery in Mitcheldean. The brewery includes a tap which opens on Friday evenings (4-8pm).

Saved By The Bell (OG 1038, ABV 3.8%)
A light, refreshing session bitter with a spicy hop bite and a light, floral aroma from the late hop addition.

Running the Gauntlet (OG 1046, ABV 4.4%)
A full, malty-flavoured bitter with rich roasted undertones balanced with good hop bitterness with spicy blackcurrant aromas from late hopping.

Money for Old Rope (OG 1049, ABV 4.8%)
A classic stout with rich, dry flavours of malt and grain with deep hop bitterness.

Over a Barrel (OG 1052, ABV 5%)
Richly-coloured fruity strong ale with a generous peppery finish.

Betjeman

🍴 Betjeman Brewery, Shoulder of Mutton, 38 Wallingford Street, Wantage, Oxfordshire, OX12 8AX
☎ 07870 577742 ✉ peter@themutton.co.uk
⊕ themutton.co.uk

⊗ Established in 2011, the brewery is situated at the rear of the Shoulder of Mutton in Wantage. The brewer is award-winning Peter Fowler, previously of Pitstop Brewery. Brewing currently takes place at a separate site due to expansion plans.

Wantage Bells (OG 1054, ABV 5%)

Slough Bomb (OG 1066, ABV 6%)

Sebastopol (OG 1076, ABV 7%)

Bewdley SIBA

Bewdley Brewery Ltd, Unit 7, Bewdley Craft Centre, Lax Lane, Bewdley, Worcestershire, DY12 2DZ
☎ (01299) 405148 ✉ sales@bewdleybrewery.co.uk
⊕ bewdleybrewery.co.uk
Tours by arrangement

⊗ Bewdley began brewing in 2008 on a six-barrel plant in an old school. Brewing experience days are offered; ring for details. Beers are brewed with a railway theme for the nearby Severn Valley Railway. Seasonal beers: see website. Bottle-conditioned beers are also available.

Worcestershire Way (OG 1036, ABV 3.6%)
A light beer with citrus notes.

Old School Bitter (OG 1038, ABV 3.8%)
Session bitter with a hoppy finish.

Senior School Bitter (OG 1041, ABV 4.1%)
A premium bitter, amber-coloured with malty taste and hoppy finish.

Worcestershire Sway (OG 1049, ABV 5%)
A stronger version of Worcestershire Way, slightly sweeter with more body.

Big Bog (NEW)

▤ Big Bog Brewing Co, c/o Tafarn Snowdonia Parc, Waunfawr, Gwynedd, LL55 4AQ
☎ 07769 110791 ✉ big.bog@btinternet.com
⊕ bigbog.co.uk
Tours by arrangement

Big Bog was established in 2011 by Paul Jefferies of Hydes Brewery. 40 outlets are supplied direct. Seasonal beers are available.

Bog Standard Bitter (OG 1034.9, ABV 3.6%)

WPA (Welsh Pale Ale) (OG 1039.5, ABV 4.2%)

Swampy (OG 1045.9, ABV 4.7%)

Quagmire (OG 1058.4, ABV 6%)

Bog Super (OG 1066.2, ABV 7%)

Big Lamp

Big Lamp Brewers, Grange Road, Newburn, Newcastle upon Tyne, Tyne & Wear, NE15 8NL
☎ (0191) 267 1689
✉ admin@biglampbrewers.co.uk
⊕ biglampbrewers.co.uk
Tours by arrangement

⊙Big Lamp started in 1982 and relocated in 1997 to a 55-barrel plant in a former water pumping station. It is the oldest micro-brewery in the north-east of England. Around 160 outlets are supplied and two pubs are owned. Seasonal and bottle-conditioned beers are available.

Sunny Daze (OG 1036, ABV 3.6%) ◆
Golden, hoppy session bitter with a clean taste and finish.

Bitter (OG 1039, ABV 3.9%) ◆

A clean-tasting bitter, full of hops and malt. A hint of fruit with a good, hoppy finish.

One Hop (OG 1040, ABV 4%)
Dark amber beer with a smooth finish and a hint of hazelnut.

Lamp Light (OG 1042, ABV 4.2%)

Summerhill Stout (OG 1044, ABV 4.4%) ◆
A rich, tasty stout, dark in colour with a lasting rich roast character. Malty mouthfeel with a lingering finish.

Prince Bishop Ale (OG 1048, ABV 4.8%) ◆
A refreshing, easy-drinking bitter. Golden in colour, full of fruit and hops. Strong bitterness with a spicy, dry finish.

Premium (OG 1052, ABV 5.2%) ◆
Hoppy ale with a good bitter finish.

Keelman Brown (OG 1057, ABV 5.7%)
A full-bodied ale with a hint of toffee.

Big River (NEW)

Big River Brewery Ltd, 48 Grange Park, Brough, East Yorkshire, HU15 1AA
☎ 07737 820922
✉ contactus@bigriverbrewery.co.uk
⊕ bigriverbrewery.co.uk

Big River was established by Mark Storey and began brewing commercially in 2011 on a 0.5-barrel plant in his garage. This has since been upgraded to a 2.5-barrel plant. Local freehouses in Hull and East Yorkshire are supplied as well as CAMRA beer festivals. Bottle-conditioned beers are available. The Big River is the Humber.

Halcyon Daze (ABV 3.4%)
A golden ale with a citrus overtone and bright hop aroma.

Ropewalk (ABV 3.5%)
An amber session ale with a mellow and rounded aroma.

Big Red (ABV 3.9%)
A rich ruby red ale with a complex taste including malt and autumn berries.

Windjammer (ABV 4.7%)
A strong, hoppy golden ale.

Sailmakers Porter (ABV 5.2%)
A dark beer with roast coffee and liquorice flavours.

Binghams SIBA

Binghams Brewery Ltd, Unit 10, Tavistock Industrial Estate, Ruscombe Business Park, Ruscombe Lane, Ruscombe, Berkshire, RG10 9NJ
☎ (0118) 934 4376 ✉ info@binghams.co.uk
⊕ binghams.co.uk
Shop Mon-Thu 2-6pm; Fri 2-7pm; Sat 12-6pm; closed Sun & bank hols
Tours by arrangement

⊗ Binghams started brewing in 2010 using a 10-barrel plant and produces 40 firkins in each batch.

Twyford Tipple (OG 1040, ABV 3.7%)
Tawny-coloured beer with a citrus hop finish.

Brickworks Bitter (OG 1045, ABV 4.2%)
Chestnut-coloured best bitter with a slightly nutty hint. The hops balance the maltiness to provide a well-rounded ale.

Coffee Stout (OG 1052, ABV 5%)

A mellow stout with dark malts that complement the coffee flavour.

Doodle Stout (OG 1052, ABV 5%)
A blend of dark malts provide a complex character. Named after the brewery dog (a Labradoodle called Stout).

Ginger Doodle Stout (OG 1056, ABV 5%)
Stout infused with root ginger to produce a refreshing zing that's not overpowering.

Hot Dog Chilli Stout (OG 1056, ABV 5%)
A stout with a warm chilli afterglow.

Space Hoppy IPA (OG 1050, ABV 5%)
A pale golden ale with a citrus flavour.

Vanilla Stout (OG 1052, ABV 5%)
Infused with vanilla pods for a smooth-drinking, dark stout.

Bird Brain

Bird Brain Brewery Ltd, 30 Hailgate, Howden, East Yorkshire, DN14 7SL
☎ (01430) 432166 ☎ 07790 615915
✉ birdbrainbrewery@tiscali.co.uk

⊛Bird Brain began brewing in 2009 using a two-barrel brew plant expanded to a four-barrel in 2012. Local pubs and beer festivals are supplied. Seasonal beers are available.

Puffin Pale Ale (OG 1038, ABV 3.8%)

Howden Bittern (OG 1038, ABV 3.9%)

Jemmy Wren (OG 1038, ABV 3.9%)

Capercaillie (OG 1042, ABV 4.1%)

For the Victoria Hotel, Goole:

Shiny (OG 1038, ABV 3.9%)

Birds SIBA ◉

Birds Brewery, Ladybird Barn, Old Burcot Lane, Bromsgrove, Worcestershire, B60 1PH
☎ (01527) 889870
✉ brewmaster@birdsbrewery.co.uk
⊕ birdsbrewery.co.uk
Tours by arrangement

⊛Birds began brewing in 2009, supplying their beers to pubs across the West Midlands. The number of beers available has been gradually increasing since then as brewer Ian Hughes experiments with different malts and hops to create a balanced range of beers. One-off brews are created for special events and bottle-conditioned, vegan versions of the range are also available.

Thunderbird (OG 1038, ABV 3.8%)
A malty beer with a hint of sweetness and a distinctive nutty finish.

Natural Blonde (OG 1040, ABV 4%)
A pale blonde beer; floral on the nose, plenty of fruit and hops in the mouth with balanced malt. A pleasantly hoppy aftertaste with a gently crisp, bitter finish.

Amnesia (OG 1045, ABV 4.5%)
A pale ale with a fruity zest and a slight orange citrus undertone combining with a mixture of hops to provide a dry, hoppy finish.

Black Widow Stout (OG 1045, ABV 4.5%)

A traditional smooth stout with a roasted malt flavour, a bitter edge and overtones of blackcurrant, raisins and liquorice.

Bishop Nick (NEW) SIBA

Bishop Nick Ltd, c/o The Chestnuts, Chelmsford Road, Felsted, Essex, CM6 3ET
☎ (01371) 822814 ✉ info@bishopnick.com
⊕ bishopnick.com

Bishop Nick was launched in 2011 by Neilion Ridley, a member of the family that ran Ridley's Brewery near Chelmsford. Three beers are brewed by Felstar while Neilion finds premises for his own brewery.

Ridley's Rite (ABV 3.6%)

1555 (ABV 4%)

Heresy (ABV 4%)

Blackawton

Blackawton Brewery, Barnlee Lodge, Ilsington, Devon, TQ13 9RG
☎ (01364) 661524 ☎ 07971 871546
✉ enquiries@blackawtonbrewery.co.uk
⊕ blackawtonbrewery.com

Blackawton was once Devon's oldest operating brewery, but relocated to Cornwall in 2000 with ownership changing in 2004 and again in 2010. In 2011 it returned to Devon. Brewing is currently suspended.

BlackBar (NEW)

BlackBar Brewery, Unit B3, Button End Industrial Estate, Harston, Cambridgeshire, CB22 7GX
☎ (01223) 872131 ✉ info@BlackBar.co.uk
⊕ blackbar.co.uk

BlackBar Brewery was established in 2011. 10 outlets are supplied direct.

Bitter (OG 1036, ABV 3.4%)

Black Economy (OG 1046, ABV 4.6%)

Blackbeck

⬟ Blackbeck Brewery, Blackbeck Inn, Egremont, Cumbria, CA22 2NY
☎ (01946) 841661
✉ drink@blackbeckbrewery.co.uk
⊕ blackbeckbrewery.co.uk

⊛Blackbeck was established in 2009 using a five-barrel plant and was extended a year later. Owned by a father and daughter team, it uses a purpose-built steam system. Beers are available in bottled form and mini casks.

Belle (OG 1038, ABV 3.8%) ❦
Sweet, tasty, dark mild.

Trial Run (OG 1037, ABV 3.8%) ❦
A fresh and fruity yellow beer with a lasting hoppy finish.

Black Cat SIBA

Black Cat Brewery, Eridge Road, Groombridge, Kent, TN3 9NJ
☎ 07948 387718 ✉ info@blackcat-brewery.com
⊕ blackcat-brewery.com

Tours by arrangement

⊗ Black Cat began brewing in 2011 on a 2.5-barrel brew plant. The brewery is owned and run by airline pilot Marcus Howes. Bottle-conditioned and seasonal beers are also available.

Original (OG 1042, ABV 4.2%)
A hoppy, bitter amber beer balanced with malt.

Black Country SIBA ⟨⊙⟩

▤ Black Country Ales, Rear of Old Bulls Head, 1 Redhall Road, Lower Gornal, Dudley, West Midlands, DY3 2NU
☎ (01384) 480156

Office & Beer Deliveries: Unit 4, Tansey Green Road, Pensnett, Dudley, West Midlands, DY5 4TL
✉ info@blackcountryales.co.uk
⊕ blackcountryinns.co.uk
Tours by arrangement

Brewing started on the site in the 1830s and continued until 1934. Brewing recommenced in 2004. In 2012 much of the equipment was replaced or refurbished. Seasonal beers: see website. Beers are also brewed under the Thomas Guest Brewing Company name.

Bradley's Finest Golden (BFG) (OG 1040, ABV 4.2%)
A straw-coloured quaffing beer with a bold citrus hop aroma, fruity balanced sweetness and a lingering, refreshing aftertaste.

Pig on the Wall (OG 1042, ABV 4.3%)
A refreshing chestnut brown beer with a complex flavour of light hops giving way to a bittersweet blend of roasted malt. Suggestions of chocolate and coffee undertones.

Fireside (OG 1047, ABV 5%)
A well-rounded premium bitter, amber in colour, clean in taste leading to a pleasant, dry finish.

Brewed under Thomas Guest Brewing Co name:

Puddlers (ABV 4.1%)
A light, creamy bitter. Initial malt and fruit notes and a mellow, dry bitterness to finish.

Cobblers (ABV 4.4%)
A pale bitter, finely balanced with a malty start leading to a long, dry finish.

Black Dog

Black Dog Brewery, The Grange, High Street, Thornton le Dale, North Yorkshire, YO18 7QW
☎ (01751) 474423 ✉ tony.bryars@btinternet.com

☺Black Dog started brewing in 1997 in the centre of Whitby, but closed in 2000. In 2006 Tony Bryars purchased the original Black Dog recipes, and re-established the brewery. The beers are currently contract brewed by Hambleton Ales (qv) in Melmerby, North Yorkshire.

Blackdown

See Masters

Blackedge (NEW) SIBA

Blackedge Brewing Co Ltd, Engine House No. 2, Hampson Street, Horwich, BL6 7JH

☎ 07719 438587
✉ enquiries@blackedgebrewery.co.uk
⊕ blackedgebrewery.co.uk

Blackedge began brewing in 2011 and uses a five-barrel brew plant.

Hop (OG 1039, ABV 3.8%)

Blonde Ale (OG 1046, ABV 4.5%)

Blackfriars SIBA

Blackfriars Brewery Ltd, The Courtyard, Main Cross Road, Great Yarmouth, Norfolk, NR30 3NZ
☎ (01493) 850578 ✉ info@blackfriars-brewery.co.uk ⊕ blackfriars-brewery.co.uk
Shop: Mon-Fri 12-2pm; closed Sat & Sun
Tours by arrangement

⊗ The brewery was established in 2004 using a purpose-built five-barrel plant and was extended in 2007. In 2008 the brewery relocated and now has a shop, visitor centre and fully-licensed bar. More than 50 outlets are supplied. Following a recent takeover by JV Trading, the brewery have acquired various recipes from the famous old Lacons Brewery, which closed in 1968, and have started trial brews using the original yeast with the intention of reviving the name and expanding production. Some beers are also available in bottle-conditioned form. Specials and seasonal beers: see website.

Abbey (ABV 3.5%)
A traditional copper-coloured bitter, with warm malt and caramel flavours throughout.

Yarmouth Bitter (OG 1038, ABV 3.8%) ◆
Lots of blackberry and malt on the nose. A complex beer, copper coloured with a grainy mouthfeel. The initial malty fruitiness fades to a long, vinous, hoppy ending.

Whyte Angel (OG 1045, ABV 4.5%) ◆
Fragrant hoppy aroma leads to a strong bitter first taste. Golden hued with honey notes softening the dryness of the bitter hops. Gentle malt background throughout.

Black Hole SIBA

Black Hole Brewery Ltd, Unit 63, Ground Floor, Imex Business Park, Shobnall Road, Burton upon Trent, Staffordshire, DE14 2AU
☎ (01283) 534060 (Office) ☎ (01283) 619943 (Brewery) ✉ beer@blackholebrewery.co.uk
⊕ blackholebrewery.co.uk
Tours by arrangement

⊗ The brewery was established in 2007 with a purpose-built 10-barrel plant in the former Ind Coope bottling stores. Fermenting capacity now enables the production of up to four brews per week. Over 400 outlets are supplied direct and many more via wholesalers. Seasonal beers are available throughout the year and occasional beers are produced to mark special anniversaries and events.

Bitter (OG 1040, ABV 3.8%) ◆
Amber glow and malt and spicy hop aroma. Fresh lively session beer with a clean, crisp finish of hoppy dryness and touch of astringency.

Cosmic (OG 1044, ABV 4.2%) ◆
Almost golden with an initial malt aroma. The complex balance of malt and English hops give

THE BREWERIES

lingering tastes of nuts, fruit and dry hoppy
bitterness.

Red Dwarf (OG 1045, ABV 4.4%) ◣
Red as named with a sugary sweet fruits start with
citrus notes. Malt is elbowed aside by the hops that
dominate the tongue-tickling, bitter end.

Supernova (OG 1048, ABV 4.8%) ◣
Pure gold. Like marmalade made from Seville
oranges and grapefruit, the aroma mimics the
sweet start but gives way to the hops that deliver a
dry, lingering, bitter finish.

Milky Way (OG 1059, ABV 6%) ◣
Honey and banana nose announces the sweet
taste but not the sweet, dry spicy finish from this
wheat beer.

Black Iris (NEW) SIBA

▤ Black Iris Brewery, Flowerpot, 23-25 King Street,
Derby, DE1 3DZ ✉ blackirisbrewery@gmail.com
⊕ blackirisbrewery.co.uk
Tours by arrangement

Black Iris began brewing in 2011 using a six-barrel
plant behind the Flowerpot pub in Derby.
Occasional and seasonal beers are brewed: see
website.

White Fang (OG 1042, ABV 4.2%)

Bitter (OG 1045, ABV 4.3%)

**Great Eastern Transatlantic Porter
(OG 1048, ABV 4.6%)**

Peregrine Pale (OG 1045, ABV 4.6%)

Iron Gate Stout (OG 1055, ABV 5.5%)

West Coast IPA (OG 1060, ABV 6.2%)

Black Isle SIBA

Black Isle Brewing Co Ltd, Old Allengrange, Munlochy,
Ross-shire, IV8 8NZ
☎ (01463) 811871
✉ greatbeers@blackislebrewery.com
⊕ blackislebrewery.co.uk
Shop Mon-Sat 10am-6pm; Sun 11am-5pm (Apr-
Sep)
Tours by arrangement

⊠ Black Isle Brewery was set up in 1998 in the
heart of the Scottish Highlands. The five-barrel
plant was upgraded to a 30-barrel plant in 2010. All
beers are organic and have Soil Association
certification. Bottled (including bottle-conditioned)
beers are suitable for vegetarians and vegans and
are available by mail order to anywhere in
mainland Britain. Seasonal beer: see website.

Yellowhammer (OG 1038, ABV 3.9%) ◣
A refreshing, hoppy golden ale with light hop and
passion fruit throughout. A short, bitter finish.

Red Kite (OG 1042, ABV 4.2%) ◣
Tawny ale with light malt on the nose and some
fruit on the palate. Slight sweetness in the taste
and a short bitter finish.

Porter (OG 1046, ABV 4.6%) ◣
A hint of liquorice and burnt chocolate on the nose
and a creamy mix of malt and fruit in the taste.

Blackmore (NEW)

Blackmore Ales, Golden Hill, Stourton Caundle,
Dorset, DT10 2JW
☎ (01963) 362405 ✉ kevinstaunton@aol.com

Blackmore Ales is a small 0.5-barrel brewery
established in 2011. It currently produces one brew
a week with a range of three beers.

Ale (OG 1038, ABV 3.8%)

Bitter (OG 1038, ABV 3.8%)

Pale (OG 1040, ABV 4%)

Black Paw SIBA

Black Paw Brewery, Unit 4, Westgate Road, Bishop
Auckland, County Durham, DL14 7AX
☎ (01388) 602144 ☎ 07557 020664
✉ paw@blackpawbrewery.co.uk
⊕ blackpawbrewery.co.uk

Black Paw began brewing in 2011 using a 12-barrel
plant. Pubs are supplied across the North East.
Seasonal beers are available.

Paragon Ale (ABV 2.8%)

Bishop's Best (ABV 3.8%)

Paw's Gold (ABV 4%)

Black Paw IPA (ABV 5%)

Dark Seam (ABV 5%)

Black Sheep SIBA ◉

Black Sheep Brewery plc, Wellgarth, Masham, Ripon,
North Yorkshire, HG4 4EN
☎ (01765) 689227 ⊕ blacksheepbrewery.co.uk
Visitor Centre Bistro, bar and shop 10.30am-5pm
daily
Tours by arrangement

☺Black Sheep was established 1992 by Paul
Theakston, a member of Masham's famous
brewing family, in the former Wellgarth Maltings.
The traditional Yorkshire Square fermenting system
is used. The company has enjoyed continued
growth and now supplies a free trade of around
600 outlets, has national exposure through pubcos
and wholesale channels, but owns no pubs. The
brewery specialises in cask ales (75% of
production) and bottled ales.

Best Bitter (OG 1038, ABV 3.8%) ◣
A hoppy and fruity beer with strong bitter
overtones, leading to a long, dry, bitter finish.

Ale (OG 1044, ABV 4.4%) ◣
A premium bitter with rich fruit aromas and hints of
orange and roast coffee maltiness. Bittersweet in
the mouth with a dry finish with deep fruit notes.

Riggwelter (OG 1059, ABV 5.9%) 🍾 ◣
A fruity bitter, with complex underlying tastes and
hints of liquorice and pear drops leading to a long,
dry, bitter finish.

Blakemere

See Northern

Blencowe

See Barrowden

Blindmans SIBA

Blindmans Brewery Ltd, Talbot Farm, Leighton, Frome, Somerset, BA11 4PN
☎ (01749) 880038 ✉ info@blindmansbrewery.co.uk
⊕ blindmansbrewery.co.uk
Tours by arrangement

Blindmans Brewery was established in 2002 in a converted milking parlour and purchased by its current owners, Paul Edney and Lloyd Chamberlain, in 2004. The five-barrel brewery has its own water spring. The range of ales is regularly on tap at the Lamb Inn in Frome, which was recently renamed the Cornerhouse. Seasonal beers: see website.

Buff (OG 1036, ABV 3.6%)
Amber-coloured, smooth session beer.

Golden Spring (OG 1040, ABV 4%)
Fresh and aromatic straw-coloured beer, brewed using selected lager malt.

Icarus (OG 1045, ABV 4.5%)
Fruity, rich, mid-dark ruby ale.

Blue Anchor SIBA

⊟ Blue Anchor Inn Brewery, 50 Coinagehall Street, Helston, Cornwall, TR13 8EL
☎ (01326) 562821
✉ theblueanchor@btconnect.com ⊕ spingoales.com
Tours by arrangement

⊗ Dating back to the 15th century, this is the oldest brewery in Cornwall and was originally a monks' hospice. After the dissolution of the monasteries it became a tavern brewing its own uniquely flavoured beer called Spingo at the rear of the premises. Brewing has continued to this day. Spingo is available across the country, supplied by an independent distributor for whom Blue Anchor also brew unique beers. Other outlets in Cornwall are also supplied direct. All draught beers are available in bottle-conditioned form and seasonal beers are brewed.

Flora Daze/Spingo Original (ABV 4%)
A well-hopped, light tan bitter with a strong floral/citrus aroma from the late addition of hops. A good hop character flavour with a smooth, delicate, dry finish.

Jubilee IPA (ABV 4.5%)
A clean-tasting, hoppy beer.

Ben's Stout (ABV 4.8%)
A lightly-hopped classic stout with a bittersweet taste and a roasted barley and coffee aroma.

Spingo Middle (OG 1050, ABV 5.1%) ◆
Tawny in appearance, aromatic malt and esters lead into a sweet, malty and bitter taste with hints of green apple and grapefruit. The finish has lingering malt and dry bitterness.

Spingo Special (ABV 6.6%)
A dark-coloured, sweet beer.

Blue Ball

Blue Ball Brewery Ltd, Units 11-12 EBL Centre, Picow Farm Road, Runcorn, Cheshire, WA7 4UA
☎ (01928) 238442 ✉ info@beerrepublic.com
⊕ blueballbrewery.com
Shop Mon-Fri 9am-5.30pm; Sat 9am-5pm

Blue Ball originally started brewing as Bridgewater Brewery in 2010 behind a homebrew shop in Frodsham. The business relocated and expanded later the same year using a five-barrel plant. A bar and restaurant, Kash, opened in Chester in 2011.

Mild Mannered Mae (OG 1033, ABV 3.5%)
A black/brown mild with a sweet, malty aroma. A sweet taste is kept in check by a light bitterness from the hops and a subtle coffee note from the roasted malt.

Indie Girl (OG 1036, ABV 3.8%)
A pale gold beer with an aroma of citrus and tropical fruits. The finish is clean and dry with a long, hoppy aftertaste.

Laid Back Lucille (OG 1036, ABV 3.8%)
An auburn bitter with a light malt profile showing some caramel notes with a floral and citrus fruit aroma. The finish is bitter and full but not overpowering.

Gold Digger (OG 1038, ABV 4%)
A subtle malt profile makes way for a tropical fruit explosion from the Citra hops. The nose is sweet and fruity giving hints of passion fruit. The taste is crisp and bitter with a refreshing dry finish.

Zeppelin (OG 1053, ABV 5.5%)
German style unfiltered wheat beer.

Spank (Industrial IPA) (OG 1059, ABV 6%)
A sweetish, strong ale.

Blue Bee SIBA

Blue Bee Brewery Ltd, Unit 29-30, Hoyland Road Industrial Estate, Sheffield, S3 8AB
☎ 07791 662484 ✉ bluebeebrewery@hotmail.co.uk
⊕ bluebeebrewery.co.uk
Tours by arrangement

Blue Bee Brewery was set up in 2010 by award-winning brewer Richard Hough. The core range is complemented by an eclectic mix of seasonal beers – see website. The beers are available to the free trade across Yorkshire, the Midlands and north west England.

Bees Knees Bitter (ABV 4%)
A russet-brown bitter with lots of hop character.

Nectar Pale (ABV 4%)
A pale, well-balanced ale with a quenching bitter finish.

Lustin' For Stout (ABV 4.8%)
A rich, complex stout. Full-bodied and black in colour with roast malt flavours continuing to a satisfying bitter finish.

Tangled Up IPA (ABV 6%)
A hoppy, floral aroma with citrus flavours and a hoppy, bitter finish.

Emergency! (ABV 9.99%)
A powerful barley wine, pale in colour with hop flavours, rich fruit on the palate and a vinous alcoholic kick.

Blue Bell

Blue Bell Brewery, Cranesgate South, Whaplode St Catherine, Lincolnshire, PE12 6SN
☎ (01406) 701000 ☎ 07813 819746
✉ beer@bluebellbrewery.co.uk
⊕ bluebellbrewery.co.uk
Tours by arrangement

⊚ The Blue Bell Brewery was founded in 1998 in a former potato shed located behind the Blue Bell pub, Whaplode St Catherine. The brewery operates as a separate business from the Blue Bell pub but the pub does act as the brewery tap. Around 30 outlets are supplied. Bottle-conditioned beers are available.

Frightened Pheasant (OG 1037, ABV 3.7%)

Old Honesty (OG 1040, ABV 4.1%)

Old Resurgence (OG 1043, ABV 4.3%)

For Blue Bell Inn, Whaplode St Catherine:

Ingle Dingle (OG 1054, ABV 5.1%)

Blue Buzzard

Blue Buzzard Brewery, 17 Joseph Street, Darwen, Lancashire, BB3 3HT
☎ 07578 278013 ✉ brewery@bluebuzzards.com

Blue Buzzard is a small craft brewery run by an enthusiastic home brewer, licensed in 2010. Local festivals and the occasional pub and bar are supplied.

Dark Matter (ABV 3.8%)

Supernova (ABV 4%)

Nebula (ABV 4.3%)

Eclipse (ABV 4.5%)

White Dwarf (ABV 4.8%)

Solar Winds (ABV 5%)

Blue Cow

⊟ Blue Cow Inn & Brewery, High Street, South Witham, Lincolnshire, NG33 5QB
☎ (01572) 768432 ✉ enquiries@bluecowinn.co.uk
⊕ bluecowinn.co.uk
Tours by arrangement

☺Owned by Simon Crathorn since 2005, Blue Cow is a traditional 13th-century pub with a brewery. The beer is only available in the pub or at CAMRA beer festivals.

Best Bitter (OG 1038, ABV 3.8%)

Witham Wobbler (OG 1046, ABV 4.5%)

Blue Monkey SIBA

Blue Monkey Brewing Ltd, 10 Pentrich Road, Giltbrook Industrial Park, Giltbrook, Nottinghamshire, NG16 2UZ
☎ 0800 028 0329
✉ sales@bluemonkeybrewery.com
⊕ bluemonkeybrewery.com
Shop Mon-Sat 9.30am-4.30pm

☺Blue Monkey was established in 2008 as a 10-barrel plant but moved in 2010 to a bigger site to meet increasing demand. It now brews around 15,000 pints a week to supply over 200 local outlets and selected national distributors. The name stems from a nickname for the blue flames that used to rise from the chimneys of Stanton Ironworks, a prominent local foundry.

Original (OG 1039, ABV 3.6%) ◀
Full-bodied pale brown session bitter. Slightly sweet but predominantly malty.

BG Sips (OG 1040, ABV 4%) ◀
Pale golden hoppy beer, brewed mainly with Brewers Gold hops. Very fruity and bitter.

99 Red Baboons (OG 1042, ABV 4.2%) ◀
Red in colour with a malty fruitiness. Not overly hoppy.

Evolution (OG 1043, ABV 4.3%) ◀
Amber-coloured ale with a floral hop aroma. Bitter and hoppy with a dry aftertaste.

Guerrilla (OG 1053, ABV 4.9%) ◀
A creamy stout, full of roast malt flavour and a slightly sweet finish.

Ape Ale (OG 1053, ABV 5.4%)
A pale, strong ale with aromas of resinous pine and orange. A dry finish and moderate bitterness make this deceptively quaffable.

Blythe SIBA

Blythe Brewery, Blythe House Farm, Lichfield Road, Hamstall Ridware, Rugeley, Staffordshire, WS15 3QQ
☎ 07773 747724 ✉ info@blythebrewery.plus.com
⊕ blythebrewery.co.uk
Tours by arrangement

⊗Robert Greenway started brewing in 2003 using a 2.5-barrel plant in a converted barn on a farm. As well as specials, seasonal beers are produced on a quarterly basis. Fifteen outlets are supplied. Seasonal and bottle-conditioned beers are also available.

Ridware Pale (OG 1042, ABV 4.3%) ◀
Bright and golden with a bitter floral hop aroma and citrus taste. Good and hop-sharp, bitter and refreshing. Long, lingering bite with ripples of citrus across the tongue.

Chase Bitter (OG 1044, ABV 4.4%) ◀
Fresh fruity aroma touched by malt from this amber beer. Sweet biscuity start with caramel support and fruit hints. Hops emerge and intensify to give a satisfyingly bitter finish.

Staffie (OG 1044, ABV 4.4%) 🗂 ◀
Hoppy and grassy aroma with hints of sweetness from this amber beer. A touch of malt at the start is soon overwhelmed by hops. A full hoppy, mouth-watering finish.

Palmer's Poison (OG 1045, ABV 4.5%) ◀
Refreshing darkish beer. Tawny but light headed. Coffee truffle aroma, pleasingly sweet to start but with a good hop mouthfeel.

Johnson's (OG 1056, ABV 5.2%) 🍾 ◀
Black with a thick head. Refreshingly hoppy and full bodied with lingering bitterness of chocolate, dates, coal smoke and liquorice.

Bob's SIBA

Bob's Brewing Co Ltd, Healey Brewery, The Brewers Pride, Low Mill Road, Healey, West Yorkshire, WF5 8ND
☎ 07789 693597
Tours by arrangement

☺The brewery was founded in 2002 by Bob Hunter, a former partner in Ossett Brewery, in outbuildings behind the Red Lion pub. In 2009 brewing relocated to an eight-barrel plant in part of the original Ossett brewhouse behind the Brewers Pride in Healey. The beers appear regularly in more than 25 free houses across West Yorkshire and in the West Midlands via wholesalers. Other beers are brewed on an occasional basis.

White Lion (OG 1043, ABV 4.3%)
Pale, flowery, lager-style beer.

Chardonnayle (OG 1051.5, ABV 5.1%)
Complex, stylish strong pale ale with hints of lemongrass and fruits.

Boggart Hole Clough SIBA

Boggart Hole Clough Brewing Co, Building 7, Wilsons Park, Monsall Road, Newton Heath, Manchester, M40 8WN
☎ (0161) 277 9666 ✉ boggartoffice@btconnect.com
⊕ boggart-brewery.co.uk

☺The brewery was set up by Mark Dade in 2001 next to Boggart Hole Clough Park in former engineering works. In 2009 the brewery moved to the former Wilson's Brewery site. The site also houses Boggart Beer/Cider Distribution, launched in 2003 delivering to more than 250 outlets throughout the country. A large number of monthly specials are produced as are bottle-conditioned beers from the regular beer list. In 2009 the brewery opened its first outlet, the Micro Bar and Shop, in the food hall of Manchester's Arndale Centre.

Boggart's Dark Mild (ABV 4%)
A classic dark mild.

Cascade (ABV 4%)
A bitter, hoppy session ale.

I Am Beer (ABV 4.2%)
A light-coloured beer with a distinctive fresh fruit flavour.

Rum Porter (ABV 4.6%)
A classic porter with a smooth roast finish, enhanced by a sweet spicy hop taste, complemented with a hint of dark rum.

Bollington SIBA

Bollington Brewing Co Ltd, Adlington Road, Bollington, Cheshire, SK10 5JT
☎ (01625) 575380 ✉ lee@valeinn.co.uk
⊕ bollingtonbrewing.co.uk
Tours by arrangement

⊗ Lee Wainwright bought the Vale Inn, a closed freehouse in Bollington in 2005 and started brewing in 2008. The brewery is situated just 50 metres from the pub. Around 40 outlets are supplied direct. All cask ales are also available bottle conditioned. A second pub, the Park Tavern in Macclesfield, opened in 2011.

Light Nancy (OG 1035, ABV 3.4%)
A light, pale beer with good body and grapefruit and lemon hop flavours.

Bollington Nights (OG 1038, ABV 3.9%)
A smooth, traditional dark ale with a light flavour and aroma but a definite bitterness.

Long Hop (OG 1039, ABV 3.9%)
A pale, lager-style bitter with fruity, refreshing hops.

Park Life (OG 1041, ABV 4.1%)
A light golden bitter with a slightly spicy aroma and hoppy aftertaste.

White Nancy (OG 1040, ABV 4.1%)
Very pale, light bitter with a good hoppiness and light body.

Best (OG 1041, ABV 4.2%) 🗊

A golden hoppy bitter. Clean and crisp with a refreshing bitter aftertaste.

Dinner Ale (OG 1042, ABV 4.3%)
A deep copper-coloured beer with a fresh, slightly fruity nose and a dry, hoppy finish.

Oat Mill Stout (OG 1049, ABV 5%)
An oatmeal stout with a twist. A hoppy, bitter taste keeps the sweetness in check.

Bootleg

≣ Hoi Polloi Pub Co Ltd t/a Bootleg Brewing Co, Horse & Jockey, 9 Chorlton Green, Chorlton-cum-Hardy, Manchester, M21 9HS
☎ (0161) 860 7794
✉ info@horseandjockeychorlton.com
⊕ horseandjockeychorlton.com
Tours by arrangement

⊗ Brewing began in 2010 using a four-barrel brew plant at the Horse & Jockey (also known as the Inn on the Green). Seasonal beers are also available.

Chorlton Pale Ale (OG 1040, ABV 4%)
A refreshing blonde beer with a hint of citrus and a long, dry finish.

Lawless (OG 1047, ABV 4.7%)
A dry, copper-coloured ale with a hint of spice in the nose and slight presence of caramel in the aftertaste.

Borough Arms

≣ Borough Arms, 33 Earle Street, Crewe, Cheshire, CW1 2BG
☎ (01270) 254999
✉ info@borougharmscrewe.co.uk
⊕ borougharmscrewe.co.uk
Tours by arrangement

☺A two-barrel brewery opened in 2005 to supply the pub. The beers are available at the pub and local beer festivals. Regular seasonal ales are brewed.

Blonde Temptation (ABV 3.8%)
A light session ale.

Borough Gold (ABV 4.2%)
A hoppy, golden ale.

Botanist (NEW)

≣ Botanist Brewery, Botanist, 3-5 Kew Green, Kew, TW9 3AA
☎ (020) 8948 4838
✉ enquiries@thebotanistkew.com
⊕ thebotanistkew.com
Tours by arrangement

The Botanist Brewery brews for both the Botanist pub, which is its home and main outlet, and other pubs within the Convivial Group. Seasonal and one-off beers are also produced.

Humulus Lupulus (ABV 3.8%)

Three Nine One (ABV 4%)

OK (ABV 4.2%)

Kew Green (ABV 4.8%)

Queen Charlotte (ABV 5.2%)

Botley SIBA

Botley Brewery, Botley Mills, Mill Hill, Botley,
Hampshire, SO30 2GB
☎ (01489) 784867 ☎ 07830 369573
✉ botleybrewery@hotmail.co.uk
Tours by arrangement

⊗ Botley Brewery was established in 2010 by
experienced brewer Andy Ingram using a five-
barrel plant. Seasonal and bottle-conditioned beers
are also available.

Mill (OG 1038, ABV 3.8%)
A well-balanced light copper bitter.

Pale Rider (OG 1040, ABV 3.9%)
A crisp and hoppy session beer.

Best Bitter (OG 1044, ABV 4.2%)
A traditional amber ale.

Gringo's Gold (OG 1047, ABV 4.5%)
A light golden ale with a fresh, clean finish.

Old Cooperage (OG 1053, ABV 5%)
A strong, full-flavoured ale with a powerful hop
aroma.

Bottle Brook

Bottle Brook Brewery, Church Street, Kilburn, Belper,
Derbyshire, DE56 0LU
☎ (01332) 880051 ☎ 07971 189915

⊗ Bottle Brook was established in 2005 using a
2.5-barrel plant on a tower gravity system. New
World hops are predominantly used. The core
range of beers is supplemented by one-off brews.

Columbus (OG 1040, ABV 4%)

Heanor Pale Ale (OG 1041, ABV 4.2%)

Roadrunner (OG 1047, ABV 4.8%)

Mellow Yellow (OG 1054, ABV 5.7%)

Rapture (OG 1058, ABV 5.9%)

Sand in the Wind (OG 1060, ABV 6.1%)

Bowland SIBA

Bowland Beer Co Ltd, Bashall Town, Clitheroe,
Lancashire, BB7 3LQ
☎ (01200) 443592 ☎ 07952 639465
✉ richardbakerbb@btconnect.com
⊕ bowlandbrewery.com
Shop Mon-Sun 10.30am-5pm
Tours by arrangement

☺Bowland started brewing in 2003 and has
steadily expanded capacity to 50 barrels per week,
supplying more than 100 outlets in the north west.
Further expansion is planned. Five litre mini-casks
and bottles are sold through the on-site shop and
visitor centre. Artisan Gold, a premium bottle-
conditioned beer, sold in 750ml champagne
bottles, was launched in 2010. Seasonal beers: see
website.

Pheasant Plucker (OG 1036, ABV 3.6%)

Sawley Tempted (OG 1038, ABV 3.7%)
A copper-coloured fruity session bitter with toffee
in the mouth and a spicy finish.

Gold (OG 1039, ABV 3.8%)
A hoppy golden bitter with intense grapefruit
flavours.

Hen Harrier (OG 1040, ABV 4%)

A pale gold bitter with soft citrus, peach and apricot
flavours throughout.

Dragon (OG 1043, ABV 4.2%)
A golden bitter with rounded fruit in the mouth and
a refreshing finish.

Admiral of the Blues (OG 1046, ABV 4.4%)

Bowman SIBA ◉

Bowman Ales Ltd, Wallops Wood, Sheardley Lane,
Droxford, Hampshire, SO32 3QY
☎ (01489) 878110 ✉ info@bowman-ales.com
⊕ bowman-ales.com
Tours by arrangement

⊗ Brewing started in 2006 on a 20-barrel brew
plant housed in converted farm buildings. The
brewery supplies more than 100 outlets. In
addition to the standard beers a range of
celebratory and seasonal brews are produced.
Bottle-conditioned beers are also available.

Elderado (OG 1036, ABV 3.5%) ◖
Straw-coloured beer flavoured with elderflower. A
citrus aroma with a fruity, bitter taste. Good
hoppiness and a background sweetness. A dry,
bitter finish.

Swift One (OG 1038, ABV 3.8%) ◖
A golden ale characterised by strong hoppiness
throughout. Aroma of grapefruit leads to a pleasing
bitterness and a background sweetness. A long, dry
finish.

Wallops Wood (OG 1040, ABV 4%) ◖
Well-balanced bitter, with no particular flavour
dominating this well-crafted beer. Malt flavours
throughout are balanced by toffee notes and
sweetness in the flavour and a slightly dry finish.

Quiver Bitter (OG 1045, ABV 4.5%) 🍺 ◖
A fruity best bitter, golden in colour with a hoppy
aroma leading to a balanced, bittersweet taste and
a refreshing hoppy finish.

Warbler (OG 1046, ABV 4.8%)
A premium bitter with an initial sweetness giving
way to a dry chestnut finish. Smooth, full-bodied
and fragrant. Brewed for the Hampshire & Isle of
Wight Wildlife Trust.

Bowness Bay (NEW)

Bowness Bay Brewing, Green Lane, Winster, Cumbria,
LA23 3NL
☎ 07768 116794
✉ mashtun@bownessbaybrewing.co.uk
⊕ bownessbaybrewing.co.uk

Bowness Bay began brewing in 2012 using a four-
barrel plant from the closed Northcote Brewery in
Norwich.

Swan Blonde (OG 1039, ABV 4%)

Swift Bitter (OG 1044, ABV 4.5%)

Box Steam SIBA ◉

Box Steam Brewery, The Midlands, Holt, Wiltshire,
BA14 6RU
☎ (01225) 782700 ✉ info@boxsteambrewery.com
⊕ boxsteambrewery.com
Tours by arrangement

⊗ The brewery was founded in 2004 and boasts a
Fulton steam-fired copper, hence the name. Under

present ownership since 2006, the brewery has undergone a series of expansion work to increase production capacity and moved to larger premises in 2011. Two pubs are owned and more than 100 outlets supplied. Seasonal beers are brewed.

Golden Bolt (OG 1037.5, ABV 3.8%)
A straw-coloured bitter with a slightly dry, hoppy aftertaste.

Chuffin Ale (OG 1040, ABV 4%)
A full-flavoured bitter, chestnut brown in colour with a fruity aroma and smooth, rich taste.

Tunnel Vision (OG 1040.5, ABV 4.2%)
A well-rounded light amber bitter. Clean-tasting with a slight bitterness in the finish.

Steam Porter (OG 1045, ABV 4.4%)
A smooth-drinking, well-rounded porter with a slightly smoky aroma. Roasted malts give way to chocolate undertones on the palate.

Funnel Blower (OG 1045, ABV 4.5%)
Dark brown in colour with a subtle vanilla aroma. Vanilla sweetness contrasts nicely with the slight bitterness from roasted barley and chocolate malts.

Piston Broke (OG 1045, ABV 4.5%)
A fine, full-bodied deep golden ale with a refreshing hoppy, citrus palate and a subtle fruit hop aroma.

Derail Ale (OG 1049, ABV 5.2%)
A hoppy, traditional IPA. Full-flavoured with an intense floral aroma finished with well-balanced bitterness.

Bradfield SIBA ◉

Bradfield Brewery, Watt House Farm, High Bradfield, Sheffield, South Yorkshire, S6 6LG
☎ (0114) 285 1118 ✉ info@bradfieldbrewery.com
🌐 bradfieldbrewery.co.uk
Shop Mon-Sat 10am-4pm

◉Bradfield Brewery, established in 2005, is a family-run business, based on a working farm in the Peak District. Only the finest ingredients are used, along with pure Millstone Grit spring water from a borehole on the farm. In 2009 the brewery bought its first brewery tap, the Nags Head, Loxley. Seasonal beer: see website. Bottle-conditioned beers are also available along with five-litre mini kegs.

Farmers Bitter (OG 1039, ABV 3.9%)
A traditional copper-coloured malty ale with a floral aroma.

Farmers Blonde (OG 1041, ABV 4%)
Pale, blonde beer with citrus and summer fruits aromas.

Farmers Brown Cow (OG 1042.5, ABV 4.2%)
Deep chestnut-coloured ale with a smooth, creamy head. A citrus taste gives way to a long, dry finish.

Farmers Stout (OG 1045, ABV 4.5%)
A dark stout with roasted malts and flaked oats and a subtle, bitter hop character.

Farmers Pale Ale (OG 1049, ABV 5%)
A full-bodied pale ale with a powerful floral bouquet leaving a predominantly dry aftertaste.

Farmers Sixer (OG 1056, ABV 6%)
A strong, lager-type ale with a fruity, pleasant finish.

Brains IFBB ◉

S A Brain & Co Ltd, Crawshay Street, Cardiff, CF10 1SP
☎ (029) 2040 2060 ✉ enquiries@sabrain.com
🌐 sabrain.com

◉Brains began trading at the Old Brewery in Cardiff in 1882 when Samuel Arthur Brain and his uncle Joseph Benjamin Brain purchased a site founded in 1713. The company has remained in family ownership ever since. The full range of Brains ales is now produced at the company's Cardiff Brewery (formerly Hancock's), bought from Bass in 1999. The company owns more than 270 pubs, spread throughout Wales, the West Country and the Midlands. Brains is the official sponsor of the Wales Rugby Union team, the Football Association of Wales and Glamorgan County Cricket Club. Seasonal beers: see website.

Dark (OG 1035.5, ABV 3.5%) ◀
A tasty, classic dark brown mild, a mix of malt, roast, caramel with a background of hops. Bittersweet, mellow and with a lasting finish of malt and roast.

Bitter (OG 1036, ABV 3.7%) ◀
Amber coloured with a gentle aroma of malt and hops. Malt, hops and bitterness combine in an easy-drinking beer with a bitter finish.

SA (OG 1042, ABV 4.2%) ◀
A mellow, full-bodied beer. Gentle malt and hop aroma leads to a malty, hop and fruit mix with a balancing bitterness.

Rev James (OG 1045.5, ABV 4.5%) ◀
A faint malt and fruit aroma with malt and fruit flavours in the taste, initially bittersweet. Bitterness balances the flavour and makes this an easy-drinking beer.

SA Gold (OG 1047, ABV 4.7%) ◀
A golden beer with a hoppy aroma. Well balanced with a zesty hop, malt, fruit and balancing bitterness; a similar satisfying finish.

Brakspear

See Marston's in New Nationals section

Brampton SIBA

Brampton Brewery Ltd, Unit 5, Chatsworth Business Park, Chatsworth Road, Chesterfield, S40 2AR
☎ (01246) 221680 ✉ info@bramptonbrewery.co.uk
🌐 bramptonbrewery.co.uk
Tours by arrangement

◉The old Brampton Brewery closed in 1955. After a lapse of 52 years the Brampton name was re-registered for a new brewery a stone's throw away from the original. The first commercial brew took place in 2007 on the eight-barrel plant. Around 35 outlets are supplied. Two tied houses are within a mile of the brewery. Seasonal beers and bottle-conditioned beers are available. For off sales please contact the brewery.

Best (OG 1041, ABV 3.8%) ◀
Classic, drinkable bitter with a predominantly malty taste, balanced by caramel sweetness and a developing bitterness in the aftertaste.

Golden Bud (OG 1037, ABV 3.8%) ◀
Crisp and refreshing golden bitter with a pleasant balance of citrus, sweetness and bitter flavours. Light and easy to drink.

1302 (OG 1040, ABV 4%)

Griffin (OG 1041, ABV 4.1%)

Jerusalem (OG 1046, ABV 4.6%)

Wasp Nest (OG 1049, ABV 5%) ◆
Strong and complex with malt and hop flavours and a caramel sweetness.

Brancaster EAB

Brancaster Brewery, c/o Jolly Sailors, Brancaster Staithe, Norfolk, PE31 8BJ
☎ (01485) 210314 ✉ info@brancasterbrewery.co.uk
⊕ brancasterbrewery.co.uk

Brancaster opened in 2003 using a five-barrel plant squeezed into a converted ocean-going steel container adjacent to its own pub/restaurant. The brewery closed in 2008 but was resurrected by the current licensee, James Nye, in 2010. Beers are brewed to the Brancaster recipes by Mark Riches of Beeston Brewery (see Beeston listing for regular beers). Seasonal beers are also brewed.

Brandon

Brandon Brewery, 76 High Street, Brandon, Suffolk, IP27 0AU
☎ (01842) 878496 ☎ 07876 234689
✉ enquiries@brandonbrewery.co.uk
⊕ brandonbrewery.co.uk
Shop Mon-Sat 9am-5pm (please ring before visiting); closed Thu
Tours by arrangement

Brandon started brewing in 2005 on the site of an old dairy. Beers are based on traditional styles which include unique recipes and incorporate locally-sourced ingredients. All beers are also available bottle conditioned.

Breckland Gold (OG 1038, ABV 3.8%)
A combination of Goldings and Fuggles hops give a delicate, smooth, slightly spicy taste and a dry, lingering, malty finish.

Old Rodney (OG 1040, ABV 4%)
Spicy and aromatic with a satisfying finish.

Paddys Pride (OG 1040, ABV 4%)
A dark ruby mild with smooth malt flavours ending with a little roast bitterness.

Saxon Gold (OG 1040, ABV 4%)
A pale, golden beer with a subtle aroma of hops. The taste is a clean, crisp mix of spice and bitter fruits with a dry, hoppy finish.

Strawberry Wheat (OG 1040, ABV 4%)
A pale ale, includes torrefied wheat and pulped strawberries.

Waxies Dargle (OG 1040, ABV 4%)
A copper-coloured brew with rich malt flavours and hoppiness.

Molly's Secret (OG 1041, ABV 4.1%)
A pale ale based on an old recipe.

Norfolk Poacher (OG 1041, ABV 4.1%) ◆
A rich malty roast aroma that follows through to flavours of malt, hops, fruit and sweetness. Sweetness dominates the long complex finish.

Royal Ginger (OG 1041, ABV 4.1%)
A refreshing summer ale with a distinctive mix of malt and hoppy spice, balanced with a gentle ginger flavour and finish.

Gun Flint (OG 1042, ABV 4.2%)
Roasted malts are used to produce a malty, chocolate flavour. This combines well with spicy, citrus hops to give a dry, bittersweet, roasted malt finish.

Wee Drop of Mischief (OG 1042, ABV 4.2%)
An amber-coloured premium bitter. Gentle malt flavours give way to a delightful hop character and a dry, increasingly bitter aftertaste.

Rusty Bucket (OG 1044, ABV 4.4%) ◆
Aromas of figs and malt with dried fruit, and flavours of malt and hops, lead to a bitter, biscuity aftertaste. A well-balanced traditional brown best bitter.

Grumpy Bastard (OG 1045, ABV 4.5%)

Slippery Jack (OG 1045, ABV 4.5%)
A dark brown stout. Complex but well-balanced flavours of roasted grain and hop bitterness. Dry with a lingering, pleasantly bitter finish.

'Old On To Your 'At (OG 1047, ABV 4.7%)
Dark amber in colour with big malt flavours overlaid with a tangy fruit bitterness.

Nappertandy (OG 1050, ABV 5%)
A reddish amber beer, full-bodied with a malty aroma. Crisp and spicy with an underlying citrus flavour and a dry, malty, bitter fruit finish.

Brandy Cask

▤ Brandy Cask Pub & Brewery, 25 Bridge Street, Pershore, Worcestershire, WR10 1AJ
☎ (01386) 552602
Tours by arrangement

⊕Brewing started in 1995 in a refurbished bottle store in the garden of the pub. Brewery and pub now operate under one umbrella, with brewing carried out by the owner/landlord.

Whistling Joe (ABV 3.6%) ◆
A sweet, fruity, copper-coloured beer that has plenty of contrast in the aroma. A malty balance lingers but the aftertaste is not dry.

Brandy Snapper (ABV 4%) ◆
Golden brew with low alpha hops. Plenty of fruit and hop aroma leads to a rich taste in the mouth and a lingering aftertaste.

John Baker's Original (ABV 4.8%) ◆
A superb blend of flavours with roasted malt to the fore. The rich hoppy aroma is complemented by a complex aftertaste.

Branscombe Vale SIBA ⊚

Branscombe Vale Brewery Ltd, Branscombe, Devon, EX12 3DP
☎ (01297) 680511
✉ branscombebrewery@yahoo.co.uk
⊕ branscombebrewery.com

⊠ The brewery was set up in 1992 by former dairy workers Paul Dimond and Graham Luxton in cowsheds owned by the National Trust. Paul and Graham converted the sheds and dug their own well. The NT has twice built extensions for the brewery for more space and new fermenters. In 2008 a new 25-barrel plant was added to the brewhouse. Around 80 outlets are supplied. Seasonal and bottle-conditioned beers are also available.

Mild (OG 1036, ABV 3.7%)

Branoc (OG 1038, ABV 3.8%) 🍺 ◆
Pale brown brew with a malt and fruit aroma and a
hint of caramel. Malt and bitter taste with a dry,
hoppy finish.

Draymans Best Bitter (OG 1042, ABV 4.2%)

BVB Best Bitter (OG 1045, ABV 4.6%) ◆
Reddy/brown-coloured beer with a fruity aroma
and taste, and bitter/astringent finish.

Summa That (OG 1049, ABV 5%)
Light golden beer with a clean and refreshing taste
and a long hoppy finish.

Brass Castle (NEW)

**Brass Castle Brewery, 92 Market Street, Brass Castle
Hill, Pocklington, North Yorkshire, YO42 2AB**
☎ 07563 579723 ✉ info@brasscastlebrewery.co.uk
⊕ brasscastlebrewery.co.uk
Tours by arrangement

Brass Castle is a one-barrel brewery within a
townhouse in the centre of Pocklington with plans
to expand to a larger dedicated brewhouse with
visitor facilities. Production is boosted by using
spare capacity at Lord Halifax's Garrowby Estate
four-barrel brewhouse.

#1 (OG 1038, ABV 3.6%)

Cliffhanger (OG 1040, ABV 3.8%)

Best Bitter (OG 1046, ABV 4.5%)

Bad Kitty (OG 1060, ABV 5.5%)

Sunshine (OG 1061, ABV 5.7%)

Brass Monkey SIBA

**Brass Monkey Brewery Co Ltd, Unit 25, Asquith
Bottom Mill, Sowerby Bridge, West Yorkshire,
HX6 3BS**
☎ (01484) 660790
✉ richard@thebrassmonkeybrewery.co.uk
⊕ thebrassmonkeybrewery.co.uk

Brass Monkey was established in 2008 on a
seven-barrel brew plant. Capacity was doubled in
2009 with the addition of two fermenters. Around
150 outlets are supplied. Seasonal beers: see
website.

Son of Silverback (ABV 3.6%) ◆
Straw-coloured grainy bitter with a light hoppiness
in the aroma. Fruity and hoppy in the mouth with
bitterness developing in the aftertaste.

Bitter (ABV 3.8%) ◆
Pale brown, grainy bitter with a pronounced hoppy
aroma and flavour. It has a long-lasting satisfying
bitter finish.

Golden Monkey (ABV 4.1%) ◆
Smooth, tawny-coloured best bitter. It has a full,
hoppy flavour and citrus/spicy aroma, finishing
with a bitter finish.

Mandrill (ABV 4.2%) ◆
This grainy golden ale has a floral hop nose. Hops
fill the mouth balanced by tangy fruit. The finish is
deep and long.

Silverback (ABV 5%) ◆
Grainy yellow pale ale. A hoppy aroma is followed
by a mellow fruity flavour. There is a lingering
bitter aftertaste.

Braydon SIBA

**Braydon Ales Ltd, The Brewhouse, Preston West Farm,
Preston, Chippenham, Wiltshire, SN15 4DX**
☎ (01249) 892900 ✉ info@braydonales.co.uk
⊕ braydonales.co.uk
Tours by arrangement

⊠ In 2009 three business partners bought the
former Burford Brewery and relocated to a former
farm building in Wiltshire, close to the area once
covered by Braydon Forest. Brewing takes place on
a five-barrel plant and pubs and clubs are supplied
in the area. Seasonal beers are also available.

RWB (Royal Wootton Bassett) (OG 1040, ABV 4%)
A light copper-coloured ale with a gentle bitter
taste.

Yertiz (OG 1042, ABV 4.1%)
Triple-hopped but well-balanced standard bitter.

Potwalloper (OG 1043, ABV 4.4%)
A malty, ruby-coloured ale.

Brecon SIBA

**Brecon Brewing, 8a Brecon Enterprise Park, Brecon,
Powys, LD3 8BT**
☎ (01874) 620800 ✉ beer@breconbrewing.co.uk
⊕ breconbrewing.co.uk
Tours by arrangement

Brecon was established in 2011 by Buster Grant.
Seasonal and special beers are also available
including beers from the Genesis Project: see
website.

Bronze Beacons (ABV 3.9%)
A full-bodied bronze ale with plenty of hop flavours
and a refreshing finish.

Twilight Beacons (ABV 4%)
A full-bodied session ale with a distinctive hoppy
finish.

Gold Beacons (OG 1042, ABV 4.2%)
A deep golden ale with a soft yet well-defined
bitterness which balances the blend of malts.

Bright Beacons (OG 1045, ABV 4.5%)
A very pale straw-coloured best bitter.

Wandering Beacons (OG 1050, ABV 5%)
A chestnut-coloured, full-bodied strong premium
bitter.

Breconshire SIBA

**Breconshire Brewery Ltd, Ffrwdgrech Industrial
Estate, Brecon, Powys, LD3 8LA**
☎ (01874) 623731
✉ sales@breconshirebrewery.com
⊕ breconshirebrewery.com
Shop Mon-Fri 8.30am-4.30pm

⊠ Breconshire Brewery was founded in 2002 as
part of C H Marlow, a wholesaler and distributor of
ales, beers, wines and spirits in the south Wales
area for more than 30 years. The 10-barrel plant
uses British malts blended with a range of British
whole hops. The beers are distributed throughout
Wales and the west of England to around 200
outlets. Seasonal beers: see website. Bottle-
conditioned beers are also available.

Brecon County Ale (OG 1037, ABV 3.7%) ◆
A traditional amber-coloured bitter. A clean hoppy
flavour, background malt and fruit, with a good
thirst-quenching bitterness.

Welsh Pale Ale (OG 1037, ABV 3.7%)
Pale golden, mildly hopped session ale. Brewed to
an old Welsh style of pale ale.

Golden Valley (OG 1042, ABV 4.2%) ◆
Golden in colour with a welcoming aroma of hops,
malt and fruit. A balanced mix of these flavours
and moderate, building bitterness lead to a
satisfying, rounded finish.

Cribyn (OG 1045, ABV 4.5%)
A pale, straw-coloured aromatic best bitter.
Brewed with Northdown, Challenger and Bramling
Cross hops.

Red Dragon (OG 1047, ABV 4.7%)
A red-hued premium ale brewed with a complex
grist and a blend of hops for extra bite.

Ramblers Ruin (OG 1050, ABV 5%) ◆
Dark amber, full-bodied with rich biscuity malt and
fruit flavours; background hops and bitterness
round off the beer.

Brentwood SIBA 👁

**Brentwood Brewing Co Ltd, Frieze Hall Farm, Coxtie
Green Road, South Weald, Essex, CM14 5RE**
☎ (01277) 375577
✉ enquiries@brentwoodbrewing.co.uk
🌐 brentwoodbrewing.co.uk
Shop Mon-Fri 9am-5pm
Tours by arrangement (for groups of 10+)

⊠ Since its launch in 2006 Brentwood has steadily
increased its capacity and distribution. A major
expansion and relocation in 2008 included a new
18-barrel plant. More than 70 outlets are supplied
direct as well as national pub chains. Seasonal/
occasional beers: see website. Bottle-conditioned
beers are also available.

IPA (OG 1039, ABV 3.7%)
A lightly hopped, pale session beer.

Marvellous Maple Mild (OG 1038, ABV 3.7%)
Dark brown mild with a hint of maple syrup.

Spooky Moon (OG 1040, ABV 3.8%) ◆
Well-balanced session bitter. The sweet
marmalade aroma hints at the citrus bitterness to
be found in the finish.

Best (OG 1042, ABV 4.2%)
A traditional, straw-coloured best bitter with a
well-rounded flavour and aroma.

Gold (OG 1043, ABV 4.3%)
A heavily hopped golden beer with a fruity taste
and bitter finish.

Hope & Glory (OG 1046, ABV 4.5%)
A dark, full-bodied bitter.

Lumberjack (OG 1052, ABV 5.2%)
A strong bitter with a rounded, hoppy finish.

Brew Company

**Brew Company Ltd, Unit C, G4 Business Centre,
Carlisle Street East, Sheffield, South Yorkshire, S4 7QN**
☎ (0114) 270 9991 ✉ thebrewcompany@gmail.com
🌐 thebrewcompany.co.uk
Tours by arrangement

Brewer Pete Roberts set up this eight-barrel plant
in part of a former factory in Sheffield's industrial
east end in 2008. House beers are brewed for the
nearby Harlequin pub, the Riverside and the
Devonshire Cat. Seasonal beers: see website.

Brewers Gold (OG 1038.8, ABV 4%)

Slaker Pale Ale (OG 1038.8, ABV 4%)
Pale, crisp and fruity.

Hop Ripper IPA (OG 1041.7, ABV 4.3%)
A pale IPA, bitter and hoppy.

Hop Monster (OG 1043.6, ABV 4.5%)

St Petrus (OG 1048.4, ABV 5%)

For Devonshire Cat, Sheffield:

Devonshire Cat Pale Ale (ABV 3.8%)

For Harlequin, Sheffield:

Harlequin Blonde (ABV 4%)

Harlequin Best Bitter (ABV 4.2%)

For Riverside, Sheffield:

Riverside Pale Ale (ABV 4.2%)

BrewDog SIBA

**BrewDog Ltd, Unit 1, Kessock Workshops, Kessock
Road, Fraserburgh, AB43 8UE**
☎ (01346) 519009 ✉ info@brewdog.com
🌐 brewdog.com
Tours by arrangement

BrewDog was established in 2007 by James Watt
and Martin Dickie. Seven bars are owned and a
new brewery is being built. Most of the production
goes into bottles with some keg production. No
cask beers are produced at the moment.

Brewery Tap

🍺 Brewery Tap Brewhouse, 18 New Station Street,
Leeds, West Yorkshire, LS1 5DL
☎ (0113) 243 4414 ✉ info@brewerytapleeds.co.uk
🌐 brewerytapleeds.co.uk

Owned by the Leeds Brewery, the Brewery Tap has
its own 2.5-barrel plant and brews beer under the
Leeds name for use in the pub.

Brewhouse

See Dunscar Bridge

Brewmeister (NEW)

**Brewmeister, Westhall, Kincardine Estate, Kincardine
O'Neil, Aberdeenshire, AB34 5AE**
☎ 07917 633263 ✉ production@brewmeister.co.uk
🌐 brewmeister.co.uk
Shop Sat 10am-4pm
Tours by arrangement

☺Brewmeister began brewing in 2012. 10 outlets
are supplied direct.

Deeside Pale Ale (OG 1040, ABV 4%)

Lochnagar Spray (OG 1042, ABV 4%)

Brew On

**Brew On CIC, Brockhampton Brewery, Oast House
Barn, Whitbourne, Herefordshire, WR6 5SH**
☎ (01584) 711031 ☎ 07974 685388
✉ nick.comley@brew-on.co.uk 🌐 brew-on.co.uk

Brew On is a six-barrel brewery located on the
National Trust Brockhampton Estate. It's a social
enterprise providing employment for

disadvantaged adults. All beers are bottle-conditioned and produced under the brand name 'Trusted' for sale in National Trust properties and local shops and restaurants. Ciders and soft drinks are also available.

Brewshed (NEW) SIBA

Brewshed Brewery, 1 Tayfen Road, Bury St Edmunds, Suffolk, IP32 6BH
☎ (01284) 848066 ✉ info@brewshedbrewery.co.uk
⊕ brewshedbrewery.co.uk
Tours by arrangement

⊠ Brewshed began brewing in 2011 using a five-barrel brew plant. Beer is available in its three pubs as well as a few other local outlets.

Pale Ale (OG 1040, ABV 3.9%)

Best Bitter (OG 1044, ABV 4.3%)

American Blonde (OG 1051, ABV 5.5%)

Brew Star (NEW) SIBA

Brew Star Brewery, Unit 5, The Whitehouse Farm Centre, Morpeth, Northumberland, NE61 6AW
☎ (01670) 789755 ✉ sales@brew-star.co.uk
⊕ brew-star.co.uk
Shop 11am-5.30pm daily
Tours by arrangement

Brew Star began brewing in 2012 using a 10-barrel plant. An on-site bar/lounge sells all beers and is available for small functions. Bottle-conditioned beers are planned.

Blonde St*r (ABV 4.1%)
A lightly-hopped pale session ale.

Sinist*r (ABV 4.3%)
A dark, sweet ale with a big molasses finish.

Brewster's SIBA ◉

Brewster's Brewing Co Ltd, Unit 5, Burnside, Turnpike Close, Grantham, Lincolnshire, NG31 7XU
☎ (01476) 566000 ✉ sara@brewsters.co.uk
⊕ brewsters.co.uk
Tours by arrangement

⊠ Brewster is the old English term for a female brewer and Sara Barton is a modern example. Brewster's Brewery was set up in the heart of the Vale of Belvoir in 1998 and moved in 2006 to its current premises. Beer is supplied to around 250 outlets throughout central England and further afield via wholesalers. Seasonal beers: see website.

Hophead (OG 1036, ABV 3.6%) ◆
This blonde beer has a floral/hoppy character; hops predominate throughout before finally yielding to grapefruit in the lasting finish.

Marquis (OG 1038, ABV 3.8%) ◆
A well-balanced and refreshing session bitter with maltiness and a dry, hoppy finish.

Hop A Doodle Doo (OG 1043, ABV 4.3%)
A copper-coloured ale with a rich, full-bodied feel and fruity hop character.

Decadence (OG 1044, ABV 4.4%)
Well-balanced, full-flavoured golden ale with pronounced hop notes.

Rutterkin (OG 1046, ABV 4.6%) ◆

A premium bitter with a golden appearance. A zesty hop flavour from American Mount Hood hops combines with a touch of malt sweetness to give a rich, full-bodied beer.

Brew Wharf

▤ Brew Wharf Co Ltd, Brew Wharf Yard, Stoney Street, London, SE1 9AD
☎ (020) 7378 6601 ✉ brewwharf@vinopolis.co.uk
⊕ brewwharf.com

Brew Wharf opened in 2005 and has a bar plus a restaurant where dishes are matched with beer. Two changing special beers are brewed each month.

Bridestones SIBA

Bridestones Brewing, Smithy Farm, Long Causeway, Blackshaw Head, Hebden Bridge, West Yorkshire, HX7 7JB
☎ (01422) 847104 ✉ bridestones@hotmail.co.uk
⊕ bridestonesbrewery.co.uk

☺Bridestones started brewing in 2006 and supplies over 60 outlets. Its brewery tap is the New Delight Inn, Blackshaw. Seasonal and bottle-conditioned beers are available.

Indians Head (ABV 3.7%)
A light amber session bitter with a citrus hop finish.

Sandstone (ABV 3.9%)
A pale session ale with a smooth, clean taste.

Pennine Gold (OG 1043, ABV 4.3%) ◆
Good hop aroma and flavour without being over bitter. Fruity, refreshing and easy-to-drink golden ale.

Dark Mild (ABV 4.5%) ◆
Dark brown strong mild with a complex nose of caramel and roasted malt. Good balance of sweetness and bitterness on the palate. Upfront bitterness in the finish.

American Pale Ale (ABV 5%)
A premium golden bitter.

Bridgehouse SIBA

Bridgehouse Brewery Ltd, Hawkcliffe Works, Hebden Road, Oxenhope, West Yorkshire, BD22 9SY
☎ (01535) 642893
✉ mark@bridgehousebrewery.co.uk
⊕ bridgehousebrewery.co.uk
Tours by arrangement

Bridgehouse began brewing in 2010 using a 10-barrel plant. The brewery moved to its present site in 2011 to take advantage of the spring water available.

Blonde (OG 1040, ABV 4%)

Porter (OG 1045, ABV 4.5%)

Moorland Bitter (OG 1052, ABV 5.2%)

Bridgetown

▤ Bridgetown Brewery, Albert Inn, Bridgetown Close, Totnes, Devon, TQ9 5AD
☎ (01803) 863214
Tours by arrangement

⊠ Bridgetown started brewing in 2008 on a 2.5-barrel plant. Seasonal beers are available.

Albert Ale (OG 1038, ABV 3.8%)

Joyces Choice (OG 1040, ABV 4%)

Whaler (OG 1043, ABV 4.3%)

Realaleativity (OG 1046, ABV 4.8%)

Brightside

Brightside Brewing Co Ltd, 1 New George Street,
Bury, Lancashire, BL8 1NW
☎ (0161) 705 2625 ☎ 07870 207442
✉ carley@brightsidebrewing.co.uk
⊕ brightsidebrewing.co.uk

Brightside is a family business established in 2010,
which began commercial production in 2011. It is a
2.5-barrel plant currently housed in the back room
of the family's bakery with plans to move into
industrial premises during 2012. 40 regular outlets
are supplied.

Odin (OG 1041, ABV 3.8%)

The Beast (OG 1042, ABV 3.8%)

Best Bitter (OG 1044, ABV 4.3%)

Solstice Golden Ale (OG 1043, ABV 4.5%)

Darkside Stout (OG 1053, ABV 4.6%)

Maverick IPA (OG 1047, ABV 4.8%)

Brimstage SIBA

Brimstage Brewing Co Ltd, Home Farm, Brimstage,
Wirral, CH63 6HY
☎ (0151) 342 1181 ☎ 07870 968323
✉ info@brimstagebrewery.com
⊕ brimstagebrewery.com

⊗ Brewing started in 2006 on a 10-barrel plant in a
redundant farm dairy in the heart of the Wirral
countryside. This is Wirral's first brewery since the
closure of the Birkenhead Brewery in the late
1960s. Around 60 outlets are supplied. Seasonal
beers are brewed.

Sandpiper Light Ale (OG 1036.5, ABV 3.6%)
A light and refreshing session beer with tropical
fruit flavours.

Trappers Hat Bitter (OG 1037.5, ABV 3.8%)
Gold-coloured with a complex bouquet, it provides
a mouthful of fruit zest, with hints of orange and
grapefruit. A refreshingly hoppy session beer.

Rhode Island Red Bitter (OG 1039, ABV 4%) ◆
Red, smooth and well-balanced malty beer with a
good dry aftertaste. Some fruitiness in the taste.

Scarecrow Bitter (OG 1041, ABV 4.2%)
Orange marmalade in colour, this well-balanced
session brew has a distinct citrus fruit bouquet and
a bitter finish.

Oystercatcher Stout (OG 1043, ABV 4.4%)
A smooth, easy-drinking stout with rich chocolate
aromas leading to a mellow roasted coffee flavour
and lingering bitter finish.

Briscoe's

Briscoe's Brewery, 16 Ash Grove, Otley, West
Yorkshire, LS21 3EL
☎ (01943) 466515 ✉ briscoe.brewery@virgin.net

The brewery was launched in 1998 by
microbiologist/chemist Dr Paul Briscoe in the cellar
of his house with a one-barrel brew length.

Following a spell brewing on a larger scale at the
back of a local pub, Dr Briscoe is currently
producing one brew per week on his original plant.
Several beers are produced on an irregular basis,
those listed below are most likely to be available.

Chevin Light (OG 1039, ABV 3.8%)
A golden, hoppy bitter.

Lighter Shade of Pale (OG 1039, ABV 4%)

Bristol Beer Factory SIBA

Bristol Brewing Co Ltd, t/a Bristol Beer Factory, Unit
A, The Old Brewery, Durnford Street, Ashton, Bristol,
BS3 2AW
☎ (0117) 902 6317
✉ enquiries@bristolbeerfactory.co.uk
⊕ bristolbeerfactory.co.uk
Shop Mon-Fri 9am-5pm
Tours by arrangement

⊗ The Beer Factory is a 10-barrel micro-brewery in
a part of the former Ashton Gate Brewing Co,
which closed in 1933. 50 outlets are supplied and
output and brewing capacity are steadily
increasing. Seasonal beers are also available.

Acer (OG 1040, ABV 3.8%) ◆
Pale session bitter than punches above its weight.
A powerful aroma of citrus/floral hop precedes a
slightly sweet and fruity taste and bitter aftertaste.

Bristol Stout (OG 1040, ABV 4%) ◆
Plenty of roast malt with vinous notes on the nose
then a creamy, full-bodied stout whose ripe dark
fruits fade into roast bitterness.

Seven (OG 1042, ABV 4.2%) ◆
Mid-brown best bitter with grainy mouthfeel. A
malty taste finishes dry and astringent with a little
hint of roast.

Sunrise (OG 1044, ABV 4.4%) ◆
Golden best bitter, malt and fruit (orange
marmalade notes) in the mouth and a bitter
aftertaste.

Britannia (NEW) SIBA

⊟ Britannia Brewery, Royal Standard of England,
Forty Green, Buckinghamshire, HP9 1XS
☎ (01494) 673382 ✉ theoldestpub@btconnect.com
⊕ rsoe.co.uk

Britannia began brewing in 2012 at the Royal
Standard of England pub.

Pale (ABV 4%)

Gold (ABV 4.2%)

Brodie's SIBA

Brodie's Brewery, 816a High Road, Leyton, London,
E10 6AE
☎ 07828 498733 ✉ james@brodiesbeers.com
⊕ brodiesbeers.com
Tours by arrangement

Siblings James and Lizzie began commercial
brewing in 2008 on a five-barrel plant at the back
of the William IV pub in East London. Beers are
available at the William IV and their small chain of
family-owned pubs as well as other local outlets.
All cask ales are available bottle conditioned.
Seasonal ales and festival specials are also brewed
regularly – see website for more information.

Citra (OG 1031, ABV 3.1%) ◆
Refreshing light golden ale. Citrus and tropical fruit in the aroma and flavour, which is dry and bitter but with a faint malty sweetness. The bitterness grows on drinking.

Amarilla (OG 1042, ABV 4.2%)
Golden ale with strong grapefruit on the nose with a little passion fruit. Grapefruit dominates the flavour, fading to a dry bitter finish, which is softened slightly by the smooth mouthfeel.

California (OG 1053, ABV 5.3%) ◆
A smooth, yellow-coloured beer with citrus fruit on the nose. Sweet citrus fruit with a hint of honey is balanced with bitterness on the palate and aftertaste.

Broughs

Broughs Ltd, Springfield Brewery, Grimstone Street, Wolverhampton, West Midlands, WV10 0JP
☎ 07814 158292 ✉ broughsltd@yahoo.co.uk
Tours by arrangement

☺Broughs is a small family-run company. After using spare capacity at several breweries in the West Midlands region it now has its own premises on the site of the Old Springfield Brewery in Wolverhampton.

Bitter (OG 1043, ABV 4.3%)

Pale Ale (OG 1048, ABV 4.8%)

Broughton SIBA

Broughton Ales Ltd, Broughton, ML12 6HQ
☎ (01899) 830345 ✉ beer@broughtonales.co.uk
⊕ broughtonales.co.uk
Shop Mon-Fri 8am-4pm
Tours by arrangement

☺Founded in 1979, Broughton Ales was then one of the first microbreweries. Broughton has developed since then and though more than 60% of production is bottled for sale in Britain and abroad, it retains a sizeable range of cask ales. Seasonal beers: see website. All beers are suitable for vegetarians.

Coulsons EPA (OG 1034, ABV 3.5%)
A light, yellow-coloured ale with a mellow lingering flavour and tangy aftertaste.

The Reiver (OG 1038, ABV 3.6%)
A light-coloured session ale with a predominantly hoppy flavour and aroma on a background of fruity malt. The aftertaste is crisp and clean.

Bramling Cross (OG 1041, ABV 4.2%)
A golden ale with a blend of malt and hop flavours followed by a hoppy aftertaste.

Clipper IPA (OG 1042, ABV 4.2%)
A light-coloured, crisp, hoppy beer with a clean aftertaste.

Merlin's Ale (OG 1042, ABV 4.2%) ◆
A well-hopped, fruity flavour is balanced by malt in the taste. The finish is bittersweet, light but dry.

Exciseman's 80/- (OG 1046, ABV 4.6%)
A traditional 80/- cask ale. A dark, malty brew. Full drinking with a good hop aftertaste.

Old Jock (OG 1070, ABV 6.7%)
Strong, sweetish and fruity in the finish.

Brown Cow

Brown Cow Brewery, Brown Cow Road, Barlow, Selby, North Yorkshire, YO8 8EH
☎ (01757) 618947
✉ susansimpson@browncowbrewery.co.uk
⊕ browncowbrewery.co.uk

☺Established in 1997 by brewster Susan Simpson and joined by husband Keith in 2004, the brewery has steadily expanded, the six-barrel plant now brewing at its capacity of 17 barrels per week. In addition to the five regular beers a range of seasonal, occasional and one-off brews is crafted using an extensive stock of different hop varieties and a wide range of coloured malts. Beers are supplied direct throughout Yorkshire and to outlets in southern counties. Bottle-conditioned beers are also available.

Sessions (OG 1033, ABV 3.6%)
A pale, hoppy session beer with a refreshing finish and citrus notes in the aftertaste.

Bitter (OG 1038, ABV 3.8%)
Copper-coloured classic bitter brewed with English hops. Round and full in flavour with a smooth finish.

White Dragon (OG 1039, ABV 4%)
A pale, aromatic beer with a good level of bitterness, citrus undertones and a clean finish.

Captain Oates Mild (OG 1044, ABV 4.5%)
A dark mild with complex mix of malts and oats. Well-balanced with undertones of coffee and chocolate.

Mrs Simpson's Thriller in Vanilla Porter (OG 1049, ABV 5.1%)
A rich porter brewed with fresh vanilla pods complementing the dark malts.

Brunswick 👁

Brunswick Brewery Ltd, 1 Railway Terrace, Derby, DE1 2RU
☎ (01332) 290677
✉ thebrunswickinn@btconnect.com
Tours by arrangement

The Brunswick is a purpose-built tower brewery that started brewing in 1991. A viewing area allows pub users to watch production. Bought by Everards in 2002, it is now a tenancy supplying beers to local outlets and the Everard's estate. Seasonal beers are also brewed.

White Feather (OG 1038, ABV 3.6%)
Very pale citrus/floral session beer. Full-bodied with a grassy finish.

Triple Hop (OG 1038, ABV 4%) ◆
A pale gold colour and citrus hop bouquet promise sweetness but the hops deliver a firm, dry, lasting bitterness.

The Usual (OG 1042, ABV 4.2%) ◆
This tawny best bitter, also known as The Usual, presents an aroma of sulphur and hops that continue throughout, accompanied by a striking bitterness and astringency.

Porter (OG 1045, ABV 4.3%)
Typical English porter – dark black chocolate and caramel with deep bitter undertones.

Station Approach (OG 1048, ABV 4.7%)
Straw-coloured bitter with lingering hints of citrus, with a hoppy aftertaste.

THE BREWERIES

Old Accidental (OG 1050, ABV 5%)
A well-balanced, malty beer leading to a bitter finish with warming aftertaste. A light, vinous floral hop has underlying malt notes.

Father Mike's Dark Rich Ruby (OG 1055, ABV 5.8%) 🍺 🍺 ◆
A smooth, near black mild with a hint of red. Well-balanced and filled with sweet roast flavours that conceal its strength.

Black Sabbath (OG 1058, ABV 6%) 🍺
A genuine mild with a voluptuous feast of coffee, chocolate and caramel flavours. High alcohol balanced with fine body.

Bryncelyn

Bryncelyn Brewery, Unit 303, Ystradgynlais Workshops, Trawsffordd Road, Ystradgynlais, SA9 1BS
☎ (01639) 841900
✉ bryncelynbrewery@hotmail.co.uk
⊕ bryncelynbrewery.org.uk
Tours by arrangement

☺A one-quarter barrel brewery was opened in 1999 by William Hopton (owner) and Robert Scott (brewer) and capacity was increased to a three-quarter barrel plant in the same year. The brewery relocated to its present premises in 2008 with a six-barrel plant acquired from the old Webb's Brewery of Ebbw Vale. As the beer names imply, the owner is fond of Buddy Holly: Feb 59 (seasonal) commemorates the singer's death. Seasonal beers: see website.

Everyday Ale (OG 1038, ABV 3.8%)

Holly Hop (OG 1039, ABV 3.9%) 🍺 🍺 ◆
Pale amber with a hoppy aroma. A refreshing hoppy, fruity flavour with balancing bitterness; a similar lasting finish. A beer full of flavour for its gravity.

Buddy Marvellous (OG 1040, ABV 4%) ◆
Dark brown with an inviting aroma of malt, roast and fruit. A gentle bitterness mixes roast with malt, hops and fruit, giving a complex, satisfying and lasting finish.

Buddy's Delight (OG 1042, ABV 4.2%)

Not Fade Away (OG 1042, ABV 4.2%)

Cwrw Celyn (OG 1044, ABV 4.4%)

CHH (OG 1045, ABV 4.5%) ◆
A pale brown beer with hints of red malt and an inviting hop aroma, with fruit and bitterness adding to the flavour. The finish is clean and hoppy-bitter.

Maybe Baby (OG 1045, ABV 4.5%)
A dark-coloured ale with a balance of malt and hops, finishing with a hint of caramel.

Oh Boy (OG 1045, ABV 4.5%) ◆
An inviting aroma of hops, fruit and malt, and a golden colour. The tasty mix of hops, fruit, bitterness and background malt ends with a long, hoppy, bitter aftertaste. Full-bodied and drinkable.

Buddy Confusing (OG 1050, ABV 5%)

Rave On (OG 1050, ABV 5%)

Buckingham (NEW) ⓈⒾⒷⒶ

Buckingham Brewery Ltd, 57 Waine Close, Buckingham, MK18 1FF

☎ (01280) 422830 ✉ info@buckingham-brewery.co.uk ⊕ buckingham-brewery.co.uk

⊗ Buckingham began brewing in 2011 using a 2.5-barrel plant and is the only microbrewery in Buckingham; the first to brew in the historic market town since 1897.

Golden (ABV 3.8%)

Bitter (ABV 4%)

Mild (ABV 4%)

Buffy's ⓈⒾⒷⒶ EAB 👁

Buffy's Brewery Ltd, Rectory Road, Tivetshall St Mary, Norfolk, NR15 2DD
☎ (01379) 676523 ✉ buffysbrewery@gmail.com
⊕ buffys.co.uk
Tours by arrangement

⊗ Buffy's was established in 1993. The brewery owns two pubs, the Cherry Tree at Wicklewood and the White Hart at Foulden. Barley for all brewing is grown in Norfolk. Around 150 outlets are supplied. Seasonal and bottle-conditioned beers are available.

Norwich Terrier (OG 1036, ABV 3.6%) ◆
A fragrant peachy aroma introduces this refreshing, gold-coloured bitter. Strong bitter notes dominate throughout as hops mingle with grapefruit to produce a long, increasingly dry finish.

Bitter (OG 1039, ABV 4%) ◆
The strong malty aroma contrasts with the dry bitterness of the taste. A pale brown beer with an increasingly hoppy finish that grows and grows.

Mild (OG 1042, ABV 4.2%) ◆
A complex brew, deep red with a smooth but grainy feel. Caramel and blackcurrant bolster the heavy malt influence that is the main characteristic of this understated, deceptively strong mild.

Polly's Folly (OG 1043, ABV 4.3%) ◆
Complex and well-balanced with a definitive malty spine. An elderberry sweetness complements the malty character throughout as a bittersweet dryness defines the long finale.

Hopleaf (OG 1044.5, ABV 4.5%) ◆
Pale brown beer with a gentle hop nose. Strawberries mingle with the hops and malt, remaining as the malt gently subsides to leave a bittersweet, dry finish.

Mucky Duck (OG 1044, ABV 4.5%) ◆
Roasted malt with sweet fruitiness giving depth without becoming dominant. Chewy mouthfeel and lingering finish.

Norwegian Blue (OG 1049, ABV 4.9%) ◆
A nutty aroma with caramel and malt. A well-balanced mix of malt and bitterness floats above a background of caramel, hops, and sweetness. A strong, increasingly bitter finish.

Ale (OG 1055, ABV 5.5%)

Festival 9X (OG 1089, ABV 9%)

Bull Lane

⧌ Bull Lane Brewing Co, Clarendon Hotel, 143 High Street East, Sunderland, Tyne & Wear, SR1 2BL
☎ (0191) 510 3200
✉ bulllanebrewingco@hotmail.co.uk
⊕ bull-lane-brewing.co.uk
Tours by arrangement

☺Sunderland's first brew-pub started production in 2005 in the cellar of the Clarendon pub. A new head brewer in 2011 saw the introduction of new beers. The beers are supplied to pubs within a 30-mile radius of Sunderland and are regularly available in Sir John Fitzgerald's pubs.

Nowtsa Matta BB (OG 1037, ABV 3.7%)

Ryhope Tug (OG 1039, ABV 3.9%)

TJ Doyles Neck Oil (OG 1042, ABV 4.3%)

Bullmastiff SIBA

Bullmastiff Brewery, Unit 14, Bessemer Close, Leckwith, Cardiff, CF11 8DL
☎ (029) 2066 5292 ✉ bob.bullmastiff@live.co.uk

⊗ An award-winning small craft brewery run by brothers Bob and Paul Jenkins since 1987. The name stems from their love of the bullmastiff breed. They have no ambitions for expansion or owning any pubs, preferring to concentrate on quality control. 50 outlets are supplied. Seasonal beers are also brewed.

Welsh Gold (OG 1039, ABV 3.8%) ◄
A hoppy and fruity aroma leads into the same juicy blend of flavours. Bittersweet initially, an easy-drinking and refreshing beer.

Jack the Lad (OG 1041, ABV 4.1%)
A copper-coloured best bitter.

Thoroughbred (OG 1046, ABV 4.5%) ◄
A good hop aroma leads to a hoppy flavour with accompanying fruit, malt and balancing bitterness. There is a quenching hoppy bitterness in the finish.

Welsh Black (OG 1050, ABV 4.8%)
Easy-drinking porter with a finish of wild berries.

Welsh Red (OG 1048, ABV 4.8%)
A premium ale.

Olde Snarler (OG 1053, ABV 5.1%)
A strong bitter.

Son of a Bitch (SOB) (OG 1062, ABV 6%) ◄
A complex, warming amber ale with a blend of hops, malt and fruit flavours, with increasing bitterness.

Special Reserve (OG 1068, ABV 6.5%)
A tawny, reddish ale bursting with flavours leading to a delicate butterscotch finish.

Buntingford SIBA

Buntingford Brewery Co Ltd, Greys Brewhouse, Therfield Road, Royston, Hertfordshire, SG8 9NW
☎ (01763) 250749 ☎ 07879 698541
✉ contact@buntingford-brewery.co.uk
⊕ buntingford-brewery.co.uk
Tours by arrangement

⊗ Brewing commenced on the current site in 2005 and has expanded to a capacity of around 60 barrels per week. Two regular beers are brewed year round alongside seasonal/occasional brews and various themed specials. The beers are brewed using water from an on-site well and all liquid waste is treated in a reed bed. The brewery is located on a conservation farm and there is a wide variety of bird life visible from the doors of the brewhouse, often including endangered species.

Highwayman (OG 1036, ABV 3.6%)

Twitchell (OG 1038, ABV 3.8%)

Burley Street SIBA ◉

☰ Burley Street Brewhouse Ltd, Fox & Newt, 9 Burley Street, Leeds, West Yorkshire, LS3 1LD
☎ 07506 741039 ✉ dawn@zigzaglighting.co.uk
Tours by arrangement

☺Burley Street Brewhouse is in the cellar of the Fox & Newt pub, where the first brewery was installed by Whitbread in the 1980s. The freehold was purchased by the current owners and brewing recommenced in 2010. 12 outlets are supplied direct.

The Brickyard (OG 1038.5, ABV 3.7%) ◄
A drinkable bitter beer with a good mix of malt and hops. Although light on aroma, this is a pale brown, proper session bitter with a refreshing, clean finish.

SPA Francorchamps (OG 1039.5, ABV 3.8%)
A pale, crisp session bitter with a refreshing lemon aroma and flavour.

Laguna Seca (OG 1041, ABV 4%) ◄
A hoppy bitter beer with citrus fruit flavours, balanced with some sweetness. This golden amber bitter beer has a lingering though not particularly strong bitter finish.

Burnside SIBA

Burnside Brewery, Unit 3, Laurencekirk Business Park, Laurencekirk, Aberdeenshire, AB30 1EY
☎ (01561) 377316 ✉ gary@brewmet.com
⊕ burnsidebrewery.co.uk
Tours by arrangement

Burnside began brewing in 2010 using a 2.5-barrel plant, upgraded in 2012 to 10-barrels. Beer festivals and local outlets are supplied. Bottle-conditioned beers are available.

Black Katz (OG 1036, ABV 3.6%)

3 Bullz (OG 1038, ABV 3.8%)

Mad Dogz (OG 1038, ABV 3.8%)

Golden X (OG 1041, ABV 4.1%)

Wild Rhino (OG 1043, ABV 4.5%)

M-Pire (OG 1048, ABV 5.2%)

Burscough SIBA

Burscough Brewing Co Ltd, c/o Hop Vine, Liverpool Road North, Burscough, Lancashire, L40 4BY
☎ 07831 225656
✉ enquiry@burscoughbrewery.co.uk
⊕ burscoughbrewery.co.uk
Tours by arrangement

Burscough began brewing in 2010 in renovated outbuildings in the cobbled courtyard behind the Hop Vine in Burscough. The four-barrel plant was purchased from Oban Ales. Exclusive beers are brewed for the Hop Vine with all regular beers available to the wider trade. Seasonal beers are available.

Flat Rib Mild (OG 1036, ABV 3.6%)

Priory Gold (OG 1038, ABV 3.8%)
A golden session ale with light body and moderate bitterness.

Mere Blonde (OG 1040, ABV 4%)

Black Canon Stout (OG 1045, ABV 4.5%)

Mug Billy (OG 1045, ABV 4.5%)

Thorougood (OG 1051, ABV 5.1%)

Sutlers IPA (OG 1055, ABV 5.4%)

Burton Bridge SIBA ⊚

Burton Bridge Brewery Ltd, 24 Bridge Street, Burton upon Trent, Staffordshire, DE14 1SY
☎ (01283) 510573
✉ bbb@burtonbridgebrewery.fsnet.co.uk
⊕ burtonbridgebrewery.co.uk
Shop at Bridge Inn 11.30am-2.15pm, 5-11pm
Tours by arrangement (Wed evenings)

⊚The brewery was established in 1982 by Bruce Wilkinson and Geoff Mumford and owns six pubs in the local area, including its CAMRA award-winning brewery tap. More than 300 outlets are supplied direct. An ever-changing range of seasonal/monthly beers and bottle-conditioned beers are available.

Golden Delicious (OG 1037, ABV 3.8%) ◀
A Burton classic with sulphurous aroma and well-balanced hops and fruit. An apple fruitiness, sharp and refreshing start leads to a lingering mouth-watering bitter finish with a hint of astringency. Light, crisp and refreshing.

Sovereign Gold (OG 1040, ABV 4%) ◀
Sweet caramel aroma with a grassy hop start with malt overtones. Fresh and fruity with a bitterness that emerges and continues to develop.

XL Bitter (OG 1039, ABV 4%) ◀
Another Burton classic with sulphurous aroma. Golden with fruit and hops and a characteristic lingering aftertaste hinting of toffee apple sweetness.

Bridge Bitter (OG 1041, ABV 4.2%) ◀
Gentle aroma of malt and fruit. Good balanced start finishing with a robust hop mouthfeel.

Burton Porter (OG 1044, ABV 4.5%) ◀
Chocolate aromas and smooth taste of smoky roasted grain and coffee.

Damson Porter (OG 1044, ABV 4.5%)
A fruity beer with a bittersweet aftertaste.

Bramble Stout (OG 1049, ABV 5%) ▣

Stairway to Heaven (OG 1049, ABV 5%) ◀
Golden bitter. A perfectly balanced beer. The malty and hoppy start leads to a hoppy body with a mouth-watering finish.

Top Dog Stout (OG 1049, ABV 5%) ◀
Black and rich with a roast and malty start. Fruity and abundant hops give a fruity, bitter finish with a mouth-watering edge. Also available as Bramble Stout.

Festival Ale (OG 1054, ABV 5.5%) ◀
Caramel aroma with plenty of hop taste balanced by malty sweetness.

Thomas Sykes (OG 1095, ABV 10%) ◀
Kid in a sweetshop aroma. Rich fruity spirited tastes – warming and dangerously drinkable.

Burton Old Cottage SIBA

Burton Old Cottage Beer Co Ltd, Unit 10, Eccleshall Business Park, Hawkins Lane, Burton upon Trent, Staffordshire, DE14 1PT
☎ 07909 931250 ✉ jwsaville@tiscali.co.uk
⊕ oldcottagebeer.co.uk
Tours by arrangement

⊚Old Cottage was originally installed in the old Heritage Brewery, once Everard's production plant in Burton. When the site was taken over, the brewery moved to a modern industrial unit. The brewery was sold in 2005 and 2006 saw heavy investment in new production and storage facilities by the new owners. Around 10 outlets are supplied. Seasonal beers are brewed.

Oak Ale (OG 1044, ABV 4%) ◀
Tawny, full-bodied bitter. A sweet start with balanced fruit gives way to a slight roast taste with some caramel for interest. A dry, hoppy finish satisfies the palate.

Chestnut (OG 1042, ABV 4.2%)
A dark session ale with a touch of bitterness and a pleasant, full aftertaste.

Stout (OG 1047, ABV 4.7%) ◀
Roast aroma with background fruit; roast tastes with gentle sweetness. Bitterness develops from the sweet start to leave a sharp-edged mouthfeel. Roast throughout, with a malt background.

Pastiche (OG 1050, ABV 5.2%) ◀
A smooth, balanced ale with a complex taste and aroma.

Halcyon Daze (OG 1050, ABV 5.3%) ◀
Tawny and creamy with touches of hop, fruit and malt aroma. Fruity taste and finish.

Burtonwood

Thomas Hardy Burtonwood Ltd, Bold Lane, Burtonwood, Warrington, Cheshire, WA5 4TH
☎ (01925) 220022 ⊕ thomashardybrewery.co.uk

Burtonwood is now Thomas Hardy's only brewery, run by Peter Ward as a contract operation. Most cask beer production has stopped with the demise of Webster's Green Label and Yorkshire Bitter.

Bushy's SIBA

Mount Murray Brewing Co Ltd, Mount Murray Brewery, Mount Murray, Braddan, Isle of Man, IM4 1JE
☎ (01624) 661244 ✉ info@bushys.com
⊕ bushys.com
Tours by arrangement

⊚Set up in 1986 as a brew-pub, Bushy's moved to its present site in 1990 when demand outgrew capacity. It owns three tied houses and the beers are also supplied to 25 other outlets. Bushy's goes one step further than the Manx Pure Beer Law, which permits only malt, hops, sugar and yeast, preferring the German Reinheitsgebot (Pure Beer Law) that excludes sugar. Seasonal beers are numerous and include Oyster Stout (ABV 4.2%) – see website.

Castletown Bitter (OG 1035, ABV 3.5%)
A light, golden beer full of floral and citrus hints. A refreshing session beer.

Ruby (1874) Mild (OG 1035, ABV 3.5%) ▣ ◀
Classic full-bodied malty, ruby mild with sweet caramel flavours throughout, and well-balanced hops.

Bitter (OG 1038, ABV 3.8%) ◀
A traditional malty and hoppy beer with good balance. The fruit lasts through to the bitter finish.

Old Bushy Tail (OG 1045, ABV 4.5%)

A reddish-brown beer with a pronounced hop and malt aroma, the malt tending towards treacle. Slightly sweet and malty on the palate with distinct orangy tones. The full finish is malty and hoppy with a hint of toffee.

Butcombe SIBA 👁

Butcombe Brewery Ltd, Cox's Green, Wrington, Bristol, BS40 5PA
☎ **(01934) 863963** ✉ **info@butcombe.com**
⊕ **butcombe.com**
Shop Mon-Fri 9am-5pm; Sat 9am-12pm
Tours by arrangement

⊗ Established in 1978 by Simon Whitmore and sold to Guy Newell and friends in 2003, Butcombe moved to a new purpose-built brewery with a 150-barrel plant in 2005. It supplies around 500 outlets directly and similar numbers via wholesalers and pub companies. The brewery has an estate of 21 free houses. Seasonal beers: see website.

Bitter (OG 1039, ABV 4%) ◆
Pale brown bitter with satisfying, slightly astringent bitter aftertaste. Malt, fruit and hints of hop, caramel and sulphur in the aroma and taste.

Adam Henson's Rare Breed (OG 1044, ABV 4.2%)

Gold (OG 1045, ABV 4.4%) ◆
Very well-balanced, strongish golden bitter. Aroma of hop and sulphur; bitter taste with malt, fruit and caramel. The bitterness lingers and becomes astringent as the other flavours fade.

Butts SIBA

Butts Brewery Ltd, Northfield Farm, Wantage Road, Great Shefford, Berkshire, RG17 7BY
☎ **(01488) 648133** ✉ **sales@buttsbrewery.com**
⊕ **buttsbrewery.com**

⊗ The brewery was set up in a converted Dutch barn in 1994. In 2002, the brewery took the decision to become dedicated to organic production: all the beers brewed use organic malted barley and organic hops when suitable varieties are available. All beers are certified by the Soil Association. Around 60 outlets are supplied. Seasonal, occasional and bottle-conditioned beers are also available.

Jester (OG 1036, ABV 3.5%) ◆
A pale brown session bitter with a hoppy aroma and a hint of fruit. The taste balances malt, hops, fruit and bitterness with a hoppy aftertaste.

Traditional (OG 1040, ABV 4%) ◆
A pale brown bitter that is quite soft on the tongue with hoppy citrus flavours accompanying a gentle bittersweetness. A long, dry aftertaste is dominated by fruity hops.

Barbus Barbus (OG 1046, ABV 4.6%) ◆
Golden ale with a fruity hoppy aroma and a hint of malt. Hops dominate taste and aftertaste, accompanied by fruitiness and bitterness, with a hint of balancing sweetness.

Buxton SIBA

Buxton Brewery, Unit 7D & E, Staden Business Park, Staden Lane, Buxton, Derbyshire, SK17 9RZ
☎ **(01298) 244200** ✉ **geoff@buxtonrealale.co.uk**
⊕ **buxtonrealale.co.uk**
Shop Thu & Fri 4-6pm; Sat 10am-1pm

Tours by arrangement

Buxton Brewery was set up in 2009 after acquiring the former Wild Walker plant and began brewing at the current site in 2010. Bottle-conditioned beers are available.

Moor Top (OG 1037, ABV 3.6%)
A dry-hopped blonde ale with a citrus flavour and aroma. It has a sweetness balanced with a lingering bitter finish backed up with a late grapefruit hit.

Bitter (OG 1040, ABV 3.8%)
A classic English bitter, copper-coloured with light malty and caramel flavours complemented with a gentle, fruity hop character.

Kinder Stout (OG 1044, ABV 4.1%)
A black stout with a creamy head. Aromas of burnt roast coffee, malty molasses, prunes and a hint of smoke. Gently sweet and sour with a moderate bitterness.

Old Big 'Ead (OG 1042, ABV 4.1%)

SPA (Special Pale Ale) (OG 1041, ABV 4.1%)
Light and refreshing, delicately hopped ale with a clean taste, a creamy mouthfeel and nutty notes.

Best Bitter (OG 1045, ABV 4.3%)
A hoppy, amber, rye best bitter.

Kinder Downfall (OG 1043, ABV 4.3%)
A refreshing, full-flavoured, hoppy golden ale.

Blonde (OG 1046, ABV 4.6%)
Clear, crisp and malty, mashed with a blend of barley and wheat for a zesty, fruity character.

English Pale Ale (OG 1049, ABV 4.9%)
A celebration of English hops.

Kinder Sunset (OG 1050, ABV 5%)
A ruby red bitter with a complex taste profile and malty richness, tempered by a bitter, citrus finish.

Gold (OG 1052, ABV 5.2%)

Black Rocks (OG 1055, ABV 5.5%)
A black IPA.

Wild Boar (OG 1057, ABV 5.7%)

High Tor (OG 1062, ABV 6.3%)

Byatt's SIBA

Byatt's Brewery Ltd, Unit 10, Lythalls Lane Industrial Estate, Lythalls Lane, Coventry, West Midlands, CV6 6FL
☎ **(02476) 637996** ☎ **07850 236882**
✉ **info@byattsbrewery.co.uk** ⊕ **byattsbrewery.co.uk**

Lee Byatt established this six-barrel plant in 2011 in an industrial estate on the north side of Coventry. At first supplying the Coventry and Warwickshire area the brewery has taken on more staff and expanded into the West and East Midlands regions. Bottle-conditioned beers are also available.

XK Dark (OG 1038, ABV 3.5%)

Coventry Bitter (OG 1038, ABV 3.8%)

Phoenix Gold (OG 1042, ABV 4.2%)

Urban Red (OG 1047, ABV 4.5%)

Regal Blond (OG 1053, ABV 5.2%)

THE BREWERIES

By the Horns (NEW) SIBA

By the Horns Brewing Co Ltd, Unit 25, Summerstown, London, SW17 0BQ
☎ (020) 3417 7338 ✉ info@bythehorns.co.uk
⊕ bythehorns.co.uk
Shop – please ring for hours
Tours by arrangement

⊗ By the Horns began brewing in 2012 using a 5.5-barrel plant. It was set up by two friends combining a love of great beer with London life. Seasonal beers are available.

Stiff Upper Lip (OG 1040, ABV 3.8%) ◀
A classic amber-coloured bitter, well-balanced with hops to the fore and a hint of citrus. Dry, bitter finish.

Bobby on the Wheat (OG 1045, ABV 4.7%) ◀
Citrus fruit is present throughout this wheat beer, which has some spice on the nose and a little banana on the palate. The finish is bitter with a slight dryness.

Diamond Geezer (OG 1050, ABV 4.9%)

Lambeth Walk (OG 1057, ABV 5.1%)

Robert Cain ◉

Robert Cain Brewery, Stanhope Street, Liverpool, Merseyside, L8 5XJ
☎ (0151) 709 8734 ✉ info@cains.co.uk
⊕ cains.co.uk
Shop 12-10pm daily
Tours by arrangement

☺The Dusanj brothers, Ajmail and Sudarghara, bought the brewery in 2002, but after investing heavily and following a reverse takeover of the Honeycombe leased pubs estate, Cains Beer Co went into administration in 2008. The brewing operation was then sold back to the Dusanj family. Nine pubs are owned all serving cask beer and around 300 outlets are supplied. Seasonal beers include Dark Mild; see website.

IPA (OG 1036, ABV 3.5%)
A light, full-flavoured session beer with a subtle hop aroma.

Finest Bitter (OG 1041, ABV 4%) ◀
Blackcurrant fruit and malt dominate the aroma. A sweetish malty bitter with hints of roast and caramel. Hops come through in the dry, bitter aftertaste.

Formidable Ale/FA (OG 1049, ABV 5%) ◀
A bitter and hoppy beer with a good dry aftertaste. Sharp, clean and dry.

Cairngorm SIBA ◉

Cairngorm Brewery Co Ltd, Unit 12, Dalfaber Industrial Estate, Aviemore, Highlands, PH22 1ST
☎ (01479) 812222 ✉ info@cairngormbrewery.com
⊕ cairngormbrewery.com
Shop Mon-Sat 10am-5.30pm (online shop also available)
Tours by arrangement

☺The brewery produces seven regular cask beers along with a rolling programme of seasonal ales. Expansion has taken the weekly capacity to 140 barrels. The free trade is supplied as far as the central belt with national delivery via wholesalers. Seasonal beers: see website.

Caillie (OG 1039.5, ABV 3.8%)
Refreshing amber bitter. Light, sweet malt flavour balanced with a bitter hop tang. The aftertaste is dry and spicy with a hint of orange.

Nessies Monster Mash (OG 1040, ABV 4.1%)
A predominantly malty, lightly hopped beer giving a satisfying fullness of flavour with a warming finish.

Stag (OG 1040, ABV 4.1%) ▣ ◀
A fine best bitter with plenty of roast and hop bitterness throughout. This tawny brew also has plenty of malt in the lingering bitter aftertaste.

Trade Winds (OG 1043, ABV 4.3%) ◀
A multi-award winning beer. A massive citrus fruit, hop and elderflower nose leads to hints of grapefruit in the mouth. The exceptional bittersweetness in the taste lasts through the long, lingering aftertaste.

Black Gold (OG 1044, ABV 4.4%) ▢ ▣ ◀
With a hint of smoked sausage, roast malt dominates throughout, but the liquorice and blackcurrant in the taste and nose give it a background sweetness. Very long, dry bitter finish.

Gold (OG 1044, ABV 4.5%) ◀
Fruit and hops to the fore with a hint of caramel in this sweetish brew. Also known as Sheepshaggers Gold.

Wildcat (OG 1049.5, ABV 5.1%) ◀
A full-bodied strong bitter. Malt predominates but there is an underlying hop character through to the well-balanced aftertaste. Drinks less than its 5.1%.

Caledonian

See Heineken in Global Giants section

Callow Top

See Haywood Bad Ram

Calvors

Calvors Brewery Ltd, Home Farm, Coddenham Green, Ipswich, Suffolk, IP6 9UN
☎ (01449) 711055 ✉ info@calvors.co.uk
⊕ calvors.co.uk

No real ale. Calvors Brewery was established in 2008 and brews real lagers without any additives or adjuncts: Calvors Suffolk Lager (ABV 3.8%), Calvors Premium (ABV 5%) and Calvors Dark (ABV 4.7%), which are available bottled and on draught.

Cambridge Moonshine

Cambridge Moonshine Brewery, Hill Farm, Shelford Road, Fulbourn, Cambridgeshire, CB21 5EQ
☎ (01223) 514366 ☎ 07906 066794
✉ mark@moonshinebrewery.co.uk
⊕ moonshinebrewery.co.uk

⊗ Established in 2004, the brewery moved in 2010 to larger premises incorporating a five-barrel plant. Locally produced ingredients are used including water from the brewery's own well. It mainly concentrates on supplying CAMRA beer festivals, with two outlets supplied direct. Bottle-conditioned beers are available.

Sparkling Moon (OG 1036, ABV 3.7%)

A light blond lager beer with a delicate hop aroma and a crisp, clean taste with hints of vanilla.

Spiritual Matter (OG 1036, ABV 3.7%)

Shelford Crier (OG 1038, ABV 3.8%)
An amber-coloured session beer.

Harvest Moon Mild (OG 1040, ABV 3.9%)
Smooth fruit notes combine with coffee and chocolate flavours, lightly hopped. A well-balanced beer, slightly sweet with plenty of character.

Barton Bitter (OG 1040, ABV 4%) ◀
Pale brown with red and amber highlights, balanced malt and hops and a fruity backdrop on both nose and palate. A bittersweet flavour dries as fruit and sweetness diminish.

CB1 Best Bitter (OG 1041, ABV 4.2%)
Amber-coloured traditional best bitter with a good blend of malt and hops with a rounded, hoppy finish.

Red Watch Blueberry Ale (OG 1040, ABV 4.2%)
A red-coloured beer brewed with fresh blueberries. A refreshing, fruity ale.

Reel Ale (OG 1041, ABV 4.2%)
Straw-coloured beer with an initial malt sweetness giving way to a long and lasting hoppy finish.

Budding Moon (OG 1043, ABV 4.5%)
A smooth, refreshing golden wheat beer, with a citrus hop bouquet and a rich, malty fruit flavour.

Nightwatch Porter (OG 1043, ABV 4.5%)
Five types of malts, four varieties of hops plus locally-produced honey from the Cambridge Beekeepers Association are blended together to create a unique and rounded flavour.

Minion of the Moon (OG 1044, ABV 4.6%)
A premium, light-coloured, full-flavoured fruity beer. Rich malt, fruit and hops dominate the taste. The fullness of flavour is sustained throughout leading to a bittersweet finish.

Black Hole Stout (OG 1048, ABV 5%) 🍺
Full-bodied stout with a complex malt and caramel profile and a dry-roasted, bitter flavour that is rich, smooth and long-lasting.

Chocolate Orange Stout (OG 1068, ABV 6.7%)
Full-bodied, rounded soft stout. Loaded with chocolate and coffee flavours with a good hop balance that has a hint of orange on the nose.

Cambrinus

See Liverpool Organic

Camden Town

Camden Town Brewery, 55-59 Wilkin Street Mews, Kentish Town, London, NW5 3NN
☎ (020) 7485 1671
✉ brewingbeer@camdentownbrewery.com
⊕ camdentownbrewery.com

⊠ A modern, automated brewhouse housed in five railway arches underneath Kentish Town West railway station. A brewery tap is also on site.

Bitter (OG 1038, ABV 3.8%) ◀
The aroma is predominantly malty in this pale brown beer. The flavour has a touch of hops and peach fruit with a bittersweet finish.

Pale Ale (OG 1045, ABV 4.5%)

A golden ale with grapefruit on the nose with a sweet fudge character and a bitterness that lingers into the aftertaste.

Wheat Beer (OG 1045, ABV 4.5%)

Hells Lager (OG 1048, ABV 4.8%)

Camerons 👁

Camerons Brewery Ltd, Lion Brewery, Stranton, Hartlepool, Co Durham, TS24 7QS
☎ (01429) 852000
✉ martindutoy@cameronsbrewery.com
⊕ cameronsbrewery.com
Shop Mon-Sat 12-4pm
Tours by arrangement

☺Founded in 1865, Camerons was bought in 2002 by Castle Eden brewery, which moved production to Hartlepool. In 2003 a 10-barrel micro-brewery, the Lions Den, opened to produce and bottle small brews of guest ales and to undertake contract brewing and bottling. 75 pubs are owned, with five selling real ale. Seasonal beers have been dropped in favour of monthly guest beer production.

Best Bitter (OG 1036, ABV 3.6%) ◀
A light bitter, but well-balanced, with hops and malt.

Strongarm (OG 1041, ABV 4%) ◀
A well-rounded, ruby-red ale with a distinctive, tight creamy head; initially fruity, but with a good balance of malt, hops and moderate bitterness.

Trophy Special (ABV 4%)
An amber ale, slightly sweet and malty, fruity and hoppy from the addition of Styrian Golding hops in the cask.

Cannon Royall ⟨SIBA⟩

🏳 Cannon Royall Brewery Ltd, Fruiterer's Arms, Uphampton Lane, Uphampton, Worcestershire, WR9 0JW
☎ (01905) 621161 ✉ info@cannonroyall.co.uk
⊕ cannonroyall.co.uk
Tours by arrangement (CAMRA only)

Cannon Royall's first brew was in 1993 in a converted cider house behind the Fruiterer's Arms. It has increased capacity from five barrels to more than 16 a week. The brewery supplies a number of outlets in Worcestershire and the West Midlands. Seasonal beers are regularly produced. Bottle-conditioned beers are also available.

Fruiterer's Mild (OG 1037, ABV 3.7%) ◀
This black-hued brew has rich malty aromas that lead to a fruity mix of bitter hops and sweetness, and a short balanced aftertaste.

Honey Bear (OG 1038, ABV 3.8%)

King's Shilling (OG 1038, ABV 3.8%) ◀
A golden bitter that packs a citrus hoppy punch throughout.

Arrowhead Bitter (OG 1039, ABV 3.9%) ◀
A powerful punch of hops attacks the nose before the feast of bitterness. The memory of this golden brew fades too soon.

Arrowhead Extra (OG 1045, ABV 4.3%)

Fistful of Hops (OG 1043, ABV 4.3%)

For A Few Hops More (OG 1043, ABV 4.3%)

Grapeshot (OG 1044, ABV 4.3%)

Hartlebury Tipple (OG 1043, ABV 4.3%)

Hood (OG 1043, ABV 4.3%)

Ombersley Pale Ale (OG 1045, ABV 4.5%)
A slight initial sweetness leads to a dry, bitter finish.

Canterbury Ales SIBA

Canterbury Ales, Unit 7, Stour Valley Business Park, Ashford Road, Canterbury, Kent, CT4 7HF
☎ (01227) 732541 ☎ 07944 657978
✉ canterbrew@gmail.com ⊕ canterbury-ales.co.uk
Tours by arrangement

Brewing commenced in 2010 using an eight-barrel plant. Over 25 outlets are supplied direct.

The Wife of Bath's Ale (OG 1038, ABV 3.9%) ◆
A golden beer with strong bitterness and grapefruit hop character, leading to a long, dry finish.

The Reeve's Ale (OG 1040, ABV 4.1%)

The Miller's Ale (OG 1044, ABV 4.5%)

Canterbury Brewers SIBA

▤ Canterbury Brewers, The Foundry Brew Pub, Whitehorse Lane, Canterbury, Kent, CT1 2RU
☎ (01227) 455899 ✉ manager@stonesetinns.com
⊕ thefoundrycanterbury.co.uk

The Foundry is a craft brewery, restaurant and bar occupying an industrial two storey building, originally a Victorian foundry, tucked away in the heart of Canterbury.

Foundryman's Gold (OG 1042, ABV 4%)

Haka (OG 1043, ABV 4.1%)

Helles (OG 1039, ABV 4.1%)

Torpedo (OG 1046, ABV 4.5%)

Red Rye (OG 1056, ABV 5.6%)

Streetlight Porter (OG 1060, ABV 5.8%)

Cap House (NEW)

Cap House Brewery, 444-446 Bradford Road, Batley, West Yorkshire, WF17 5LW
☎ (01924) 479909 ☎ 07981 858270
✉ sales@caphousebrewery.co.uk
⊕ caphousebrewery.co.uk

Cap House began brewing in 2011 using a 2.5-barrel brew plant. It is a joint venture between Peter Lister, who has a plastics business at the address where the brewery is located, and Gary Wardman of the Reindeer Inn in Overton, which serves as the brewery tap and distribution depot. There were plans to increase capacity in 2012. Seasonal and special beers are planned.

Miners A Pint (OG 1038, ABV 3.8%)

Gold (OG 1040, ABV 4%)

Love At First Brew (OG 1040, ABV 4%)

Ruby (OG 1054, ABV 5.6%)

Captain Cook SIBA ◉

▤ Captain Cook Brewery Ltd, White Swan, 1 West End, Stokesley, North Yorkshire, TS9 5BL
☎ (01642) 710263
✉ mail@captaincookbrewery.com
⊕ captaincookbrewery.com

Tours by arrangement

◉The Captain Cook Brewery is located within the 18th-century White Swan pub. The brewery, which started in 1999, has a six-barrel plant brewing up to 26 barrels a week supplying local and regional outlets. Seasonal beers are available.

Resolution (OG 1037, ABV 3.7%)
A pale golden beer brewed with New Zealand hops.

Red Bay (OG 1040, ABV 4%)
An Irish-style hoppy ale.

Sunset (OG 1040, ABV 4%)
An extremely smooth, light ale with a hint of citrus flavours.

Slipway (OG 1042, ABV 4.2%)
A light-coloured hoppy ale with bitterness coming through from Challenger hops. A full-flavoured ale with a smooth malt aftertaste.

Endeavour (OG 1043, ABV 4.3%)
A brown ale with a bitter finish.

Black Porter (OG 1044, ABV 4.4%)
Chocolate notes and dominant roast flavours lead to a dry, bitter finish.

Discovery (OG 1044, ABV 4.4%)
A malty ale with a bitter finish.

Schooner Granville (OG 1047, ABV 4.7%)
A classic dry stout.

Castle Rock SIBA ◉

Tynemill Ltd t/a Castle Rock Brewery, Queens Bridge Road, Nottingham, NG2 1NB
☎ (0115) 985 1615
✉ admin@castlerockbrewery.co.uk
⊕ castlerockbrewery.co.uk
Shop Mon-Thu 10.30am-6pm, Fri 10.30am-4pm; Sat 10.30am-2pm
Tours by arrangement

◉Castle Rock was established in 1998. Since then capacity has steadily increased with the largest expansion taking place in 2010 when additional brewing equipment was installed in the neighbouring building giving a total capacity of 340 barrels a week. Beers are distributed through its own estate of 21 pubs and further afield through wholesalers. A different beer is brewed monthly to support the Nottinghamshire Wildlife Trust and a unique Nottinghamian Celebration beer is brewed quarterly. A visitor centre opened in 2011. Seasonal beers: see website. Bottle-conditioned beers are also available.

Sheriff's Tipple (OG 1035, ABV 3.4%)
A tawny brown session bitter with a malty, bitter taste.

Black Gold (OG 1037, ABV 3.8%) ◆
A dark ruby mild. Full-bodied and fairly bitter.

Harvest Pale (OG 1037, ABV 3.8%) ⬡ ◆
Pale yellow beer, full of hop aroma and flavour. Refreshing with a mellowing aftertaste. Champion Beer of Britain 2010.

Preservation Fine Ale (OG 1044, ABV 4.4%) ⬡ ◆
A traditional copper-coloured English best bitter with malt predominant. Fairly bitter with a residual sweetness.

Elsie Mo (OG 1045, ABV 4.7%) ⬡ ◆

A strong golden ale with floral hops evident in the aroma. Citrus hops are mellowed by a slight sweetness.

Midnight Owl (OG 1055, ABV 5.5%)

Screech Owl (OG 1055, ABV 5.5%) ◆
A classic golden IPA with an intensely hoppy aroma and bitter taste with a little balancing sweetness.

Castle SIBA

Castle Brewery, Unit 9a-7, Restormel Industrial Estate, Liddicoat Road, Lostwithiel, Cornwall, PL22 0HG
☎ (01726) 871133 ☎ 07800 635831
✉ castlebrewery@aol.com

Castle started brewing in early 2008 on a two-barrel plant. Only bottle-conditioned ales are produced: Cornish Best Bitter (ABV 4.2%), Moat Mild (ABV 4.4%), Battle Stout (ABV 4.6%), Once A Knight (ABV 5%), Lostwithiale (ABV 7%), Kernow Kurb Kisser (ABV 7.4%), Hung, Drawn & Slaughtered (ABV 10%).

Castor SIBA

Castor Ales, 30 Peterborough Road, Castor, Peterborough, Cambridgeshire, PE5 7AX
☎ (01733) 380337 ✉ duncan@castorales.co.uk
⊕ castorales.co.uk
Tours by arrangement

This three-barrel brewery, established in 2009, is located in a specially converted outhouse in the garden of the founder brewer. The Prince of Wales Feathers in Castor village features the beers as well as the Beehive in Peterborough.

Roman Gold (OG 1037, ABV 3.7%)
Golden-coloured session bitter.

Edmund Tyrell Artis (OG 1039, ABV 4%)
Low-hopped, copper-coloured traditional bitter.

Imperial Palace Ale (OG 1045, ABV 4.6%)

Old Scarlet (OG 1045, ABV 4.6%)

Falcon Stout (OG 1050, ABV 5.3%)

Cathedral Heights (NEW) SIBA

Cathedral Heights Brewery, 54 Hadrians Road, Bracebridge Heath, Lincoln, LN4 2UO
☎ 07545 090318 ✉ marsie@ntlworld.com
⊕ chbrewery.co.uk

Cathedral Heights began brewing in 2011 and was established by Steve Marston after previous experience of brewing at Milestone and Cathedral Ales. Named after the small housing estate in which the brewery is located, there are plans for relocation and expansion.

Just Married (OG 1035, ABV 3.7%)

Steep Hill (OG 1038, ABV 4%)

Devil's Nightmare (ABV 4.2%)

Caythorpe SIBA

Caythorpe Brewery Ltd, c/o Black Horse, 29 Main Street, Caythorpe, Nottinghamshire, NG14 7ED
☎ (0115) 966 4933
✉ caythorpebrewery@btinternet.com
⊕ caythorpebrewery.co.uk
Tours by arrangement

Caythorpe was established in 1997 and was one of the first microbreweries in the county. In 2010 the brewery was upgraded with the installation of a six-barrel plant.

Dark Gem (OG 1033.3, ABV 3.5%)
A subtly hopped dark mild with a hint of chocolate.

One Swallow (OG 1034, ABV 3.6%)
A golden bitter, crisp and well-hopped.

Bitter (OG 1034.7, ABV 3.7%)
Copper-coloured, light flavoured bitter.

Dover Beck (OG 1037, ABV 4%) ◆
Pale brown, well-balanced session bitter. Initial malt is offset by a slight hoppy bitterness.

Classic (ABV 4.6%)
A traditional copper-coloured premium bitter, malty and well-hopped.

Celt Experience SIBA

Celt Experience Ltd, Unit 2E, Pontygwindy Industrial Estate, Pontygwindy Road, Caerphilly, CF83 3HU
☎ (02920) 867707 ☎ 07855 221453
✉ celt@theceltexperience.co.uk
⊕ theceltexperience.co.uk
Shop Mon-Fri 10am-4.30pm
Tours by arrangement

⊗ Celt Experience was established in 2007 by Tom Newman. In 2012 selected beers from its sister brewery, Newmans, were integrated to form one brand. Beers are distributed widely. A small cellar brewery (Y Bragdy Fach) is also situated at its tied house, the Wheatsheaf in Llantrisant.

Celt Iron Age (OG 1039, ABV 3.6%)

Celt Dark Age (OG 1042, ABV 4%)

Celt Golden (OG 1043, ABV 4.2%)

Celt Native Storm (OG 1045, ABV 4.4%)

Celt Bronze (OG 1046, ABV 4.5%)

Celt Red Castle Cream (OG 1047, ABV 4.7%)

Celt Cryf (OG 1053, ABV 5.2%)

Celt Bleddyn (OG 1058, ABV 5.6%)

Cerddin SIBA

Cerddin Brewery, c/o Cross Inn, Maesteg Road, Maesteg, Mid Glamorgan, CF34 9LB
☎ (01656) 732476
✉ enquiries@cerddinbrewery.co.uk
⊕ cerddinbrewery.co.uk

Cerddin was established in 2010 by husband and wife team David Morgan and Gillian Scott-Morgan using a 2.5-barrel brewery. Beer is available in the owner's pub, the Cross Inn, as well as several other local outlets. Bottle-conditioned beers are planned and seasonal beers are available.

Solar (ABV 4%)
A reddish beer with good bittering and a blackberry aftertaste.

Cascade (ABV 4.8%)
A straw-coloured beer with a citrus flavour.

Chalk Hill

▤ Chalk Hill Brewery, Rosary Road, Norwich, Norfolk, NR1 4DA
☎ (01603) 477078 ✉ chalkhillinns@ntlworld.com

Tours by arrangement

Chalk Hill began production in 1993 on a 15-barrel plant. It supplies local pubs and festivals.

Tap Bitter (OG 1036, ABV 3.6%) ◆
Easy-drinking, well-balanced bitter with a light, hoppy character in both aroma and taste. Initially malt provides some contrast but fades rapidly in a quick, increasingly dry and bitter finish.

CHB (OG 1042, ABV 4.2%) ◆
Malt comes to the fore as a fruity cooking apple beginning melds into the hoppy bittersweet background. A gentle malt aroma and sticky mouthfeel. Long finish.

Gold (OG 1043, ABV 4.3%) ◆
Light hoppy airs introduce this yellow-gold ale. Grapefruit, banana and hops mingle in a well-balanced beginning. The finish develops a growing bitterness as it slowly subsides.

Dreadnought (OG 1049, ABV 4.9%) ◆
A rich, resinous aroma fittingly introduces a heavily malt-influenced brew. Raisin and plum vie with each other to match the sweet malty backbone. Malt remains in a decidedly singular and abrupt ending.

Flintknapper's Mild (OG 1052, ABV 5%) 🍷 ◆
Red hued with a creamy mouthfeel. Malt emerges from a well-balanced mix of flavours including roast, sweetness and dates. Eventually only a malty sweetness remains.

Old Tackle (OG 1056, ABV 5.6%) ◆
A strong banana aroma overshadows a somewhat understated malty body. Banana notes swirl in the background to give depth and sweetness. A smooth, undemanding brew.

Cheddar Ales SIBA ◉

Cheddar Ales Ltd, Winchester Farm, Draycott Road, Cheddar, Somerset, BS27 3RP
☎ (01934) 744193 ✉ brewery@cheddarales.co.uk
⊕ cheddarales.co.uk
Shop Mon-Fri 8am-4pm; Sat-Sun by appointment
Tours by arrangement (15+ people)

⊗ Cheddar Ales is a 20-barrel brewery established in 2006 with a capacity of 25,000 pints per week. Around 200 outlets are supplied direct. Bottle-conditioned and seasonal beers are also available.

Bitter Bully (OG 1038, ABV 3.8%) ◆
Pale yellow/straw coloured bitter. Citrus hops on aroma and palate with hints of gooseberries and quince. Fine tasting and refreshing.

Gorge Best (OG 1039.5, ABV 4%) ◆
Amber best bitter with pleasant mouthfeel, balanced aroma and taste – malt, hops and pale fruit with hints of roast and caramel. Fairly bitter aftertaste.

Potholer (OG 1043.5, ABV 4.3%) 🍷 ◆
Pale best bitter with slight floral spicy hop and pale malt aromas, hints of toffee in the balanced taste of malt and hops. Short, bitter finish.

Totty Pot Porter (OG 1044.5, ABV 4.5%)

Goat's Leap IPA (OG 1054.5, ABV 5.5%) ◆
A pale amber-coloured IPA with good hop character. Full-bodied with pale fruit flavours, apricot notes and a bittersweet finish.

Chiltern SIBA ◉

Chiltern Brewery, Nash Lee Road, Terrick, Aylesbury, Buckinghamshire, HP17 0TQ
☎ (01296) 613647 ✉ info@chilternbrewery.co.uk
⊕ chilternbrewery.co.uk
Shop Mon-Thu & Sat 9am-5pm; Fri 9am-7pm
Tours by arrangement

⊗ Founded by the Jenkinson family in 1980, Chiltern is one of the first micro-breweries in the country and is the oldest independent brewery in Buckinghamshire and the Chiltern Hills. Now run by the second generation of the family it supplies more than 80 pubs and independent outlets including its own brewery tap, the Farmers' Bar at the King's Head in Aylesbury. Seasonal beers: see website. Bottle-conditioned beers are also available.

Chiltern Ale (OG 1037, ABV 3.7%) ◆
An amber, refreshing beer with a slight fruit aroma, leading to a good malt/bitter balance in the mouth. The aftertaste is bitter and dry.

Beechwood Bitter (OG 1043, ABV 4.3%) ◆
This pale brown beer has a balanced butterscotch/toffee aroma, with a slight hop note. The taste balances bitterness and sweetness, leading to a long bitter finish.

Chough

See Cornish Chough

Julian Church

Julian Church Brewing Company, c/o Alexandra Arms, 39 Victoria Street, Kettering, Northamptonshire, NN16 0BU
☎ 07794 289559

Office: 79 Edmund Street, Kettering, Northamptonshire, NN16 0HS
✉ julianchurch@ymail.com ⊕ jchurchbrewery.co.uk
Tours by arrangement

Julian Church started brewing in early 2009 on Nobby's Brewery's old five-barrel plant. The brewery is based beneath the Alexandra Arms in Kettering, where at least one of the beers is always available. Parson's Nose is rebadged as Father Nip for the Alexandra Arms. Seasonal and one-off beers are produced.

More Tea Vicar (OG 1035, ABV 3.7%)

Parson's Nose (OG 1037, ABV 3.9%)
Mahogany-coloured with a nutty taste and a warm, spicy finish.

Lion's Den (OG 1040, ABV 4%)

Martyr (OG 1040, ABV 4.1%)
An amber-coloured beer with a caramel flavour and a light, bitter finish.

Midnight Mass (OG 1040, ABV 4.2%)
A dark, rich, malty stout.

Ale Mary (ABV 4.3%)

Wonky Spire (OG 1045, ABV 4.7%)
A fruity light ale.

Church End SIBA ◉

Church End Brewery Ltd, Ridge Lane, Nuneaton, Warwickshire, CV10 0RD

☎ (01827) 713080
✉ stewart@churchendbrewery.co.uk
⊕ churchendbrewery.co.uk
Shop during tap opening hours
Tours by arrangement

⊗ Stewart Elliot started brewing in 1994 and moved to the present site and upgraded to a 10-barrel plant in 2001 with further expansion to a 20-barrel plant in 2008. The brewery tap opened in 2002 and a further pub, the George & Dragon in Stoke Golding, was purchased in 2011. A portfolio of around 60 non-regular beers is produced as well as many one-off specials. 500 outlets are supplied. Seasonal and bottle-conditioned beers are also available.

Poachers Pocket (OG 1036, ABV 3.5%)

Cuthberts (OG 1038, ABV 3.8%) ◆
A refreshing, hoppy beer, with hints of malt, fruit and caramel taste. Lingering bitter aftertaste.

Goat's Milk (OG 1038, ABV 3.8%) 🛈

Gravediggers Ale (OG 1038, ABV 3.8%) ◆
A premium mild. Black and red in colour, with a complex mix of chocolate and roast flavours, it is almost a light porter.

What the Fox's Hat (OG 1044, ABV 4.2%) ◆
A beer with a malty aroma, and a hoppy and malty taste with some caramel flavour.

Vicar's Ruin (OG 1044, ABV 4.4%) ◆
A straw-coloured best bitter with an initially hoppy, bitter flavour, softening to a delicate malt finish.

Stout Coffin (OG 1046, ABV 4.6%)

Fallen Angel (OG 1050, ABV 5%)

For Cape of Good Hope, Warwick:

Two Llocks (ABV 4%)

City of Cambridge EAB

City of Cambridge Brewery Co Ltd, Ely Road, Chittering, Cambridge, CB5 9PH
☎ (01223) 864864 ✉ sales@cambridge-brewery.co.uk ⊕ cambridge-brewery.co.uk

City of Cambridge opened in 1997 and moved to its present site in 2002. The brewery site is in the process of being redeveloped. At present all brewing is being done under contract by Wolf Brewery (qv). In addition to prizes for its cask beers, the brewery holds a conservation award for the introduction of native reed beds at its site to treat brewery water. Seasonal beers are also available.

City of Stirling

See Traditional Scottish Ales

Clanconnel

Clanconnel Brewing Co Ltd, PO Box 316, Craigavon, Co Armagh, BT65 9AZ
☎ 07711 626770 ✉ info@clanconnelbrewing.com ⊕ clanconnelbrewing.com
Tours by arrangement

Clanconnel started producing bottled beer in late 2008: McGrath's Irish Black (ABV 4.3%), McGrath's Irish Red (ABV 4.3%), Weaver's Gold (ABV 4.5%). Cask ale is seen occasionally.

Clark's SIBA 👁

HB Clark & Co (Successors) Ltd, Westgate Brewery, Wakefield, West Yorkshire, WF2 9SW
☎ (01924) 373328 ☎ 07801 922473
✉ brewery@hbclark.co.uk ⊕ hbclark.co.uk
Tours by arrangement

☺Founded in 1906, Clark's ceased brewing during the 1960s/70s but resumed cask ale production in 1982 and now delivers to around 220 outlets. Three pubs are owned, all serving cask ale, though one is leased to Ossett Brewery. Seasonal beers are also produced.

Traditional Bitter (OG 1038, ABV 3.8%)
A copper/brown bitter with a hoppy aroma and a lasting, refreshing bitter aftertaste.

Classic Blonde (ABV 3.9%)
A pale, straw-coloured beer with a fruity aroma and a light, citrus taste.

Westgate Gold (ABV 4.2%)
A golden, creamy ale with a malty aroma and a sharp, dry finish.

Clearwater SIBA

Clearwater Brewery Ltd, 2 Devon Units, Hatchmoor Industrial Estate, Great Torrington, Devon, EX38 7HP
☎ (01805) 625242
✉ sales@clearwaterbrewery.co.uk
⊕ clearwaterbrewery.co.uk
Tours by arrangement

⊗ Clearwater began brewing in 1999 but a change of ownership saw a re-branding in 2010. Four regular beers are brewed under its 'Devon's Own' labelling plus seasonal ales. Around 200 outlets are supplied direct and via Waverley TBS. All beers are also available bottle conditioned.

Real Smiler (OG 1036, ABV 3.7%)
A nose of crisp, fresh-cut apples and melon accompanies a honeyed tone. A light biscuit taste with the most delicate of tannins.

Devon Dympsy (OG 1041, ABV 4%) ◆
Mid-brown, full-bodied best bitter with a burnt, rich malt aroma and taste, leading to a bitter, well-rounded finish.

Proper Ansome (OG 1043, ABV 4.2%)
Hoppy aromas and caramel colour. Honeyed sweetness and a herbal edge.

Devon Darter (OG 1046, ABV 4.5%)

Cliff Quay

Cliff Quay Brewery, c/o Earl Soham Brewery, The Street, Earl Soham, Suffolk, IP13 7RT
☎ (01728) 684097
✉ cliffquaybrewery@btconnect.com
⊕ cliffquay.co.uk

Cliff Quay was established in 2008 by former Wychwood brewer Jeremy Moss and John Bjornson on part of the historic Tolly Cobbold riverside site. In 2012 the site was vacated due to redevelopment by its new owners and beers are brewed under contract by the Earl Soham Brewery (qv) until a new site is found.

Clockwork

⬛ The Clockwork Beer Co, Maclay Inns PLC, 1153-1155 Cathcart Road, Glasgow, G42 9HB
☎ (0141) 649 0184 ✉ clockwork@maclay.co.uk
⊕ maclay.com
Tours by arrangement

☺Established in 1997, Clockwork has been taken over by Maclay Inns. The beers are stored in cellar tanks where fermentation gases from the conditioning vessel blanket the beers (but not under pressure). A wide range of ales, lagers and specials are produced. Most beers are naturally gassed while the Original Lager and Hazy Daze Ginger are pressurised. Some updated Maclay's recipes have been introduced as guest ales.

Amber IPA (ABV 3.8%)

Red Alt (ABV 4.4%)

Lager (ABV 4.8%)

Hazy Daze Ginger (ABV 5%)

Oregon IPA (ABV 5.5%)

Thunder & Lightning (ABV 6%)

Clun SIBA

⬛ Clun Brewery, White Horse Inn, The Square, Clun, Shropshire, SY7 8JA
☎ (01588) 640305 ✉ pub@whi-clun.co.uk
⊕ whi-clun.co.uk
Tours by arrangement

Clun was previously a 9 gallon nano-brewery but this was replaced with a 2.5-barrel plant in 2012 to produce beers for the pub.

Pale Ale (OG 1040, ABV 4.1%)
A pale, clean-tasting bitter beer.

Citadel (OG 1054, ABV 5.4%)

Coach House SIBA 👁

Coach House Brewing Co Ltd, Wharf Street, Howley, Warrington, Cheshire, WA1 2DQ
☎ (01925) 232800 ✉ djbcoachhouse@hotmail.com
⊕ coach-house-brewing.co.uk

☺Coach House was founded in 1991 following the closure of Greenall Whitley Brewery, which had a presence in Warrington since 1762. With a fermentation capacity of 240 barrels, the brewery produces permanent beers, seasonal and occasional brews and a range of fruit and spiced beers.

Coachman's Best Bitter (OG 1037, ABV 3.7%) ◄
A well-hopped, malty bitter, moderately fruity with a hint of sweetness and a peppery nose.

Gunpowder Mild (OG 1037, ABV 3.8%) ◄
Biscuity dark mild with a blackcurrant sweetness. Bitterness and fruit dominate with some hints of caramel and a slightly stronger roast flavour.

Honeypot Bitter (OG 1037, ABV 3.8%)

Farrier's Best Bitter (OG 1038, ABV 3.9%)

Cheshire Gold (OG 1042, ABV 4.1%)

Dick Turpin (OG 1042, ABV 4.2%) ◄
Malty, hoppy pale brown beer with some initial sweetish flavours leading to a short, bitter aftertaste. Sold under other names as a pub house beer.

Flintlock Pale Ale (OG 1044, ABV 4.4%)

**Innkeeper's Special Reserve
(OG 1045, ABV 4.5%)** ◄
A darkish, full-flavoured bitter. Quite fruity, with a strong, bitter aftertaste.

Postlethwaite (OG 1045, ABV 4.6%) ◄
Thin bitter with a short, dry aftertaste. Biscuity malt dominates.

Gingernut Premium (OG 1050, ABV 5%)

Posthorn Premium (OG 1050, ABV 5%) ◄
Dry golden bitter with a blackcurrant fruitiness and good hop flavours leading to a strong, dry finish. Well-balanced but slightly thin for its gravity.

Coastal SIBA

Coastal Brewery, Unit 10B, Cardrew Industrial Estate, Redruth, Cornwall, TR15 1SS
☎ (01209) 212613 ☎ 07875 405407
✉ coastalbrewery@btconnect.com
⊕ coastalbrewery.co.uk

Coastal was set up in 2006 on a five-barrel plant by Alan Hinde, former brewer and owner of the Borough Arms in Crewe, Cheshire. It moved to larger premises in 2009. Seasonal beers and two monthly specials are produced as well as bottle-conditioned beers.

Hop Monster (OG 1038, ABV 3.7%)

Pale Sunlight (OG 1038, ABV 3.8%)

Handliner (OG 1040, ABV 4%)

Merry Maidens Mild (OG 1040, ABV 4%) 🏳

Poseidon (OG 1040, ABV 4%)

Angelina (OG 1042, ABV 4.1%)

Golden Hinde (OG 1044, ABV 4.3%)

Winnies Honey Heaven (OG 1044, ABV 4.4%)

Cornish Riviera (OG 1050, ABV 5%)

Sea King (OG 1056, ABV 5.5%)

Golden Sands (OG 1058, ABV 5.8%)

St Pirans Porter (OG 1060, ABV 6%)

Sunseeker (OG 1060, ABV 6%)

Kernow Imperial Stout (OG 1090, ABV 9%)

For Allsaints Brewery:

St Moses the Black (OG 1040, ABV 4%)

St Piran Cornish Best Bitter (OG 1040, ABV 4%)

St Ambrose (OG 1046, ABV 4.6%)

St Arnold (OG 1046, ABV 4.6%)

Colchester (NEW) SIBA

Colchester Brewery Ltd, Viaduct Brewhouse, Unit 16, Wakes Hall Business Centre, Wakes Colne, Essex, CO6 2DY
☎ (01787) 829422 ✉ sales@colchesterbrewery.com
⊕ colchesterbrewery.com
Shop Mon-Fri 9am-5pm
Tours by arrangement (via email tom@colchesterbrewery.com). CAMRA members only Apr-Sep

Colchester was set up in 2012 up by three friends, Tom Knox, Roger Clark and Andy Bone, using the 'double drop' process. Popular during the early 20th century this process requires additional brewing vessels in a two-tier system resulting in clean beer with pronounced flavours. Special beers are also brewed.

Diesel (ABV 3.6%)
A session bitter, rich amber in colour.

Metropolis (ABV 3.9%)
A golden, hoppy beer with enormous depth of flavour and a long, spicy finish.

No. 1 (ABV 4.1%)
A classic English best bitter, copper in colour.

Red Diesel (ABV 4.2%)
A red best bitter, well-balanced with a long, rich finish.

Coles

▤ Coles Family Brewery, White Hart Thatched Inn & Brewery, Llanddarog, Carmarthen, SA32 8NT
☎ (01267) 275395 ✉ bestpubinwales@aol.com
⊕ colesfamilybrewery.co.uk
Shop 12-3pm, 7-10pm daily (not Wed)
Tours by arrangement

The brewery is based at the ancient White Hart Inn, built in 1371. Centuries ago beer was brewed on site, but brewing only started again in 1999 on a nine-gallon plant. A one-barrel plant was fitted in 2000. Coles produces many unique ales throughout the year, the style depending on the season. In 2012 the brewery was opened to the public. Cider is also produced.

Bramling Cross (ABV 4%)

Merlins Brew (ABV 4%)

Nettle Ale (ABV 4%)

Beetroot Ale (ABV 4.2%)

Llanddarog Ale (ABV 4.2%)

Swn Y Dail (ABV 4.2%)

Cwrw Blasus (ABV 4.4%)

College Green

College Green Brewery, 1 College Green Mews, Botanic Avenue, Belfast, BT7 1LW
☎ (02892) 660800 / (02890) 322600
✉ irishbeers@hildenbrewery.co.uk
⊕ hildenbrewery.co.uk

☺College Green was set up in 2005 by Owen Scullion as a sister brewery to Hilden Brewery. All beers are brewed at Hilden.

Colonsay SIBA

Colonsay Brewery, The Brewery, Isle of Colonsay, PA61 7YT
☎ (01951) 200190 ✉ info@colonsaybrewery.co.uk
⊕ colonsaybrewery.co.uk

Colonsay began brewing in 2007 on a five-barrel plant. Beer is mainly bottled or brewery conditioned for the local trade: Lager (ABV 4.4%), 80/- Ale (ABV 4.2%), IPA (ABV 3.9%).

Compass SIBA

Compass Brewery, Office: 6 Compass Close, Oxford, OX4 3SX
☎ 07988 928724 ✉ info@compassbrewery.com
⊕ compassbrewery.com

Compass started brewing in 2009. It is run by Mattias Sjoberg who previously worked for Scottish & Newcastle at the Reading brewery. It uses other brewery's facilities to produce its beers. Small batch bespoke beers are also brewed for customers.

Isis Pale Ale (ABV 4.1%)
Malty aromas on a backdrop of distinct Cascade hops. Sweet malt with some fruity esters and a gentle bitterness that lingers.

Baltic Night Stout (ABV 4.8%)
Well-balanced roasted bitterness as well as a hoppy aroma with floral notes. A high percentage of roasted barley gives it a hint of coffee and a long, dry cocoa finish.

King's Shipment IPA (ABV 6%)
A strong IPA with hoppy bitterness balanced with malty sweetness. Dry hopped with oak chips. Based on East London Bow Brewery's IPA brewed in the 1790s for shipment to India.

Complete Pig

The Complete Pig, Red Lion Farm, Britwell Salome, Oxfordshire, OX49 5LG
☎ 07742 861882 ✉ henry@thecompletepig.co.uk
⊕ thecompletepig.co.uk

⊠ Based on an Oxfordshire pig farm, The Complete Pig's main business is making free-range pork products. The brewery was started in 2010 to provide another product for the farmer's markets and so the livestock could be fed on the spent grain and yeast. Originally only bottle-conditioned beers were produced but proved popular so are now also supplied in casks to an ever-increasing number of local pubs.

Perfecta Porcus (OG 1035, ABV 3.6%)

Oxfordshire Black Porter (OG 1037, ABV 3.8%)

Hallacre Gold (OG 1040, ABV 4.2%)

Red Lion Best (OG 1043, ABV 4.5%)

Concertina SIBA

▤ Concertina Brewery, 9a Dolcliffe Road, Mexborough, South Yorkshire, S64 9AZ
☎ (01709) 580841 ✉ concertina@btconnect.com
Tours by arrangement

The brewery started in 1992 in the cellar of a club once famous as the home of a long-gone concertina band. The plant produces up to eight barrels a week for the club, other occasional direct outlets and the wider trade as beer wholesalers. Other beers are increasingly brewed on a seasonal basis and as specials.

Club Bitter (ABV 3.9%) ◆
A fruity session bitter with a good bitter flavour.

Old Dark Attic (OG 1038, ABV 3.9%)
A dark brown beer with a fairly sweet, fruity taste.

One Eyed Jack (OG 1039, ABV 4%)
Fairly pale in colour with plenty of hop bitterness. Brewed with the same malt and hop combination as Bengal Tiger, but more of a session beer. Also badged as Mexborough Bitter.

Bengal Tiger (OG 1043, ABV 4.6%) ◆
Light amber ale with an aromatic hoppy nose followed by a combination of fruit and bitterness.

Dictators (OG 1044, ABV 4.7%)

Extreme (OG 1047, ABV 5.1%)

Ariel Square Four (OG 1046, ABV 5.2%)

Concrete Cow SIBA

Concrete Cow Brewery, 59 Alston Drive, Bradwell
Abbey, Milton Keynes, Buckinghamshire, MK13 9HB
☎ (01908) 316794 ☎ 07889 665745
✉ dan@concretecowbrewery.co.uk
⊕ concretecowbrewery.co.uk
Tours by arrangement

⊗ Concrete Cow opened in 2007 on a 5.5-barrel
plant. The beers are named after aspects of local
history and all are available bottle conditioned as
well as in casks. The brewery supplies pubs,
farmers markets, local shops and restaurants.
Seasonal beers: see website. Bottle-conditioned
beers are also available.

Pail Ale (OG 1036, ABV 3.7%)
A light-coloured ale brewed using Lager malt.

Fenny Popper (OG 1039, ABV 4%)
A light-coloured, zesty ale.

Cock 'n' Bull Story (OG 1041, ABV 4.1%)
A dark amber malty beer.

Cloven Hoof (OG 1045, ABV 4.5%)
A dark vanilla stout flavoured with natural vanilla
pods.

Old Bloomer (OG 1045, ABV 4.7%)
A dark ruby best bitter.

Coniston SIBA ◉

Coniston Brewing Co Ltd, Coppermines Road,
Coniston, Cumbria, LA21 8HL
☎ (01539) 441133 ✉ beer@conistonbrewery.com
⊕ conistonbrewery.com
Shop (in Black Bull Inn) 11am-11pm
Tours by arrangement

☺ A 10-barrel brewery set up in 1995 behind the
Black Bull inn, Coniston, it now brews 40 barrels a
week and supplies 70 local outlets while the beers
are distributed nationally by wholesalers. One pub
is owned. Some bottle-conditioned Coniston beers
are brewed using Hepworth's Horsham plant:
Bluebird (ABV 4.2%), Bluebird XB (ABV 4.4%),
Oldman Ale (ABV 4.8%). Others are bottled on site.

Oliver's Light Ale (OG 1035, ABV 3.4%) ◄
A fruity, hoppy, straw-coloured bitter with plenty of
flavour for its strength.

Bluebird Bitter (OG 1036, ABV 3.6%) ◄
A yellow-gold, predominantly hoppy and fruity
beer, well-balanced with some sweetness and a
rising bitter finish.

Bluebird Premium XB (OG 1040.5, ABV 4.2%) ◄
Well-balanced, hoppy and fruity golden bitter.
Bittersweet in the mouth with dryness building.

Old Man Ale (OG 1040.5, ABV 4.2%) ◄
Delicious fruity, vinous beer with a complex, well-
balanced richness.

Special Oatmeal Stout (OG 1045, ABV 4.5%) ◄
A well-balanced, easy-drinking stout, fruity with a
balanced ratio of malt to hop bitterness. A good
starting point for novice stout drinkers.

Thurstein Pilsner (OG 1044.5, ABV 4.8%)

Blacksmiths Ale (OG 1047.5, ABV 5%)

A well-balanced strong bitter with hints of Xmas
pudding.

Infinity IPA (OG 1055, ABV 6%)
A highly-hopped India Pale Ale.

No 9 Barley Wine (OG 1087.5, ABV 8.5%) 🍺

Conquest (NEW) SIBA

Conquest Brewery, Unit 2B, Larpool Lane Industrial
Estate, Larpool Lane, Whitby, North Yorkshire,
YO22 4LX

Conquest was established in 2012. The brew plant
was built from scratch by a keen home brewer and
supplies pubs in the local area.

Broadsword (ABV 4.2%)

Consett Ale Works SIBA ◉

▤ Consett Ale Works Ltd, Grey Horse, 115 Sherburn
Terrace, Consett, Co Durham, DH8 6NE
☎ (01207) 591540 ✉ jeffhind@aol.com
⊕ consettaleworks.co.uk
Tours by arrangement

☺ The brewery opened in 2006 in the stables of a
former coaching inn, the Grey Horse, Consett's
oldest pub. The name commemorates the historic
Consett Steel Works that closed in 1980. The
brewery expanded in 2007 to cope with demand.
Around 100 outlets are supplied direct.

Steel Town Bitter (OG 1039, ABV 3.8%)
A dark, rich, full-flavoured bitter.

White Hot (OG 1040, ABV 4%)
A refreshing, light, straw-coloured ale.

Cast Iron (OG 1040, ABV 4.1%)
A deep aromatic bitter.

Men of Steel (OG 1045, ABV 4.3%)

Stout (OG 1045, ABV 4.3%)
A rich, malty stout.

Red Dust (OG 1045, ABV 4.5%)
A rich ruby ale.

Conwy SIBA

Conwy Brewery Ltd, Unit 3, Morfa Conwy Enterprise
Park, Parc Caer Selon, Conwy, LL32 8FA
☎ (01492) 585287
✉ enquiries@conwybrewery.co.uk
⊕ conwybrewery.co.uk
Shop Mon-Fri 9am-5pm (please ring if making
special trip)
Tours by arrangement

☺ Conwy started brewing in 2003 and was the first
brewery in Conwy for at least 100 years. Around 50
outlets are supplied. Seasonal beers: see website.
Bottle-conditioned beers are also available.

Welsh Pride/Balchder Cymru
(OG 1040, ABV 4%) ◄
A clean-tasting, malty bitter. Fruit in aroma and
taste with a crisp, grainy mouthfeel and a lingering
hoppy bitter aftertaste.

Celebration Ale (OG 1041, ABV 4.2%) ◄
Sweetish best bitter with a fruity nose and palate,
and a good hoppy finish.

Honey Fayre/Cwrw Mel (OG 1044, ABV 4.5%) ◄
Amber best bitter with hints of honey sweetness in
the taste balanced by an increasingly hoppy, bitter

finish. Slightly watery mouthfeel for a beer of this strength.

Rampart (ABV 4.5%)

Telford Porter (ABV 5.6%) 🍺 🏆

For Cobdens Hotel, Capel Curig:

Cobdens Hotel Bitter/Cwrw Gwesty Cobdens (OG 1042, ABV 4.1%)

Copper Dragon SIBA 👁

Copper Dragon Brewery, Snaygill Industrial Estate, Keighley Road, Skipton, North Yorkshire, BD23 2QR
☎ (01756) 702130 ✉ post@copperdragon.uk.com
🌐 copperdragon.uk.com
Bistro/Bar/Shop: see website for opening times
Tours by arrangement (see website for details)

☺Copper Dragon began brewing in 2003. Commissioned during October 2008, the purpose-built 'double 60' brewhouse is the centrepiece of an impressive and technologically advanced operation. The site also boasts a visitor centre, shop, conference facilities and a bar/bistro. Beer distribution is widespread across northern England. The main beers are supplemented by limited edition ales throughout the year.

Black Gold (OG 1036, ABV 3.7%) ◀
This creamy dark ale has a malty, roast character throughout with coffee notes and a bitter roast finish.

Best Bitter (OG 1036, ABV 3.8%) ◀
A traditional Yorkshire bitter with a gentle, hoppy, fruity aroma. A hoppy bitterness in the taste is balanced by nutty malt and hints of fruit and followed by a bitter finish.

Golden Pippin (OG 1037, ABV 3.9%) ◀
This golden ale has a citrus aroma and flavour, characteristic of American Cascade hops. The dry, bitter astringency increases in the aftertaste.

Challenger (OG 1040, ABV 4%) ◀
Amber-coloured, this is a best bitter in the traditional style. Initial malt and hops give way to fruit and a growing bitter, dry finish.

Scotts 1816 (OG 1041, ABV 4.1%) ◀
This best bitter is fruity and malty with a bitter finish. Look for hints of nuts, tropical fruits and vanilla in the aroma and taste.

Coppice Side

Coppice Side Brewery Ltd, Unit 3, Small Business Centre, Adams Close, Heanor Gate Industrial Estate, Heanor, Derbyshire, DE75 7SW
☎ 07790 305682 ✉ chris_coppice@yahoo.co.uk

Brewing began in 2012 using a five-barrel plant in a tower set-up. The site is shared with Leadmill Brewery (qv) although the two breweries are separate enterprises. Traditional English hops are used wherever possible and the range of beers brewed is dependent on hop availability. The brewery tap is the Butchers Arms in Langley, jointly leased with Leadmill.

Nottingham Blonde (OG 1040, ABV 4%)
Crisp and hoppy with a fruity aroma.

Owd Miner (OG 1040, ABV 4%)
A traditional copper ale with good hop characteristics.

Unit 3 IPA (OG 1041, ABV 4.2%)

XOB (OG 1043, ABV 4.4%)

Coppice Light (OG 1044, ABV 4.5%)

Ninkasi (OG 1045, ABV 4.6%)

Scary Crow (OG 1052, ABV 5%)
Flagship premium pale ale. Full mellow flavour with citrus and floral notes.

Copthorne

Copthorne Brewery, Majors Farm, Woodcotes Lane, Darlton, Nottinghamshire, NG22 0TL
☎ 07523 340989 ✉ copthornebrewery@gmail.com

☺Former Milestones head brewer Dean Penney started production in 2010 in converted outbuildings at the Nags Head in Sutton-on-Trent. The brewery relocated to larger premises in 2011. Small scale bottling is planned.

Gold (ABV 3.6%)
A straw-coloured hoppy ale.

Diamond Nine (ABV 3.7%)

Classic (ABV 3.8%)
A crisp, golden ale with a hint of honey.

Finest Hour (ABV 3.8%)
A chestnut ale with a creamy head.

Trafalgar (ABV 3.9%)
A golden, hoppy ale.

Comanche (ABV 4%)
A copper-coloured ale with caramel overtones.

Darlton Pale Ale (ABV 4.2%)
A single-hopped pale golden ale.

Cherry Porter (ABV 4.3%)

Cossack (ABV 4.3%)
A well-balanced, full-bodied bronze ale with hints of toffee and fruit.

Black Beauty (ABV 4.8%)
A full-bodied traditional porter.

Corfe Castle (NEW)

Corfe Castle Brewery Ltd, PO Box 7597, Wareham, Dorset, BH20 9BP
☎ (01929) 480730
✉ info@corfecastlebrewery.co.uk

Corfe Castle is a family-owned brewery established in 2012 brewing in the beautiful Corfe Valley in Dorset.

Raven (ABV 3.9%)
A smooth porter with a rich blend of roasted malts and traditional English hops.

Castle Ale (ABV 4.3%)
A refreshing, golden, light ale. Well-balanced with a light malt taste and crisp, dry hop finish.

Gloriette (ABV 4.7%)
A traditional English best bitter with a fine balance of malt and hops.

Sovereign (ABV 4.9%)
A complex, full-flavoured golden ale with a dry finish.

Cornish Chough

Cornish Chough Brewery, Trethvas Farm, Lizard, Cornwall, TR12 7AR
☎ (01326) 290908

Tours by arrangement

Formerly known as Chough, the brewery was sold in 2011 and relocated as Cornish Chough to a farm complex on the Lizard. The farmer has planted hops for the brewery. The beers can be found in several local outlets and further afield through wholesalers. Bottle-conditioned beers are available.

Serpentine (OG 1037, ABV 4%) ◆
Light-bodied tawny best bitter with a gentle malt and ripe fruit aroma. Strongly malty in taste with sweetness and a delicious bitterness plus a hint of grapefruit that lingers into a dry finish.

Kynance Blonde (OG 1039, ABV 4.2%) ◆
Refreshing gold bitter with soft malt and fruit aroma. Bitterness strikes the tongue balanced by malt and citrus fruit. Finish is sharp and clean, becoming dry.

Cornish Crown (NEW) SIBA

Cornish Crown Brewery, End Unit, Badger's Cross Farm, Badger's Cross, Penzance, Cornwall, TR20 8XE
☎ (01736) 449029 ☎ 07870 998986
✉ cornishcrown@gmail.com ⊕ cornishcrown.co.uk

Cornish Crown began brewing in 2012 on a six-barrel plant. Head brewer is Josh Dunkley, the landlord of the Crown Inn in Penzance, which acts as the brewery tap.

Bitter (OG 1036, ABV 3.6%)

Ale (OG 1039, ABV 3.9%)
A session beer, light brown in colour with medium bitterness and a citrus finish.

SPA (Strong Pale Ale) (OG 1048, ABV 4.8%)
An easy-drinking but strong pale golden ale with medium bitterness, a strong hop aroma and a citrus finish.

Corvedale SIBA ⊚

⊟ **Corvedale Brewery, Sun Inn, Corfton, Craven Arms, Shropshire, SY7 9DF**
☎ (01584) 861239 ✉ normanspride@btconnect.com
⊕ corvedalebrewery.co.uk
Tours by arrangement

☺Brewing started in 1999 in a building behind the pub. Landlord Norman Pearce is also the brewer and he uses only British malt and hops, with water from a local borehole. Seasonal beers are also brewed. All beers are on sale in the pub in bottle-conditioned form and are suitable for vegetarians and vegans.

Dale Ale (OG 1040, ABV 4%)

Katie's Pride (OG 1040, ABV 4.3%)

Norman's Pride (OG 1043, ABV 4.3%)
A golden amber beer with a refreshing, slightly hoppy taste and a bitter finish.

Farmer Rays Ale (OG 1045, ABV 4.5%)
A clear, ruby bitter with a smooth, malty taste.

St George's Stout (OG 1045, ABV 4.5%)

Dark & Delicious (OG 1045, ABV 4.6%)
A dark ruby beer with hops on the aroma and palate and a sweet aftertaste.

Cotleigh SIBA

Cotleigh Brewery Ltd, Ford Road, Wiveliscombe, Somerset, TA4 2RE
☎ (01984) 624086 ✉ sales@cotleighbrewery.com
⊕ cotleighbrewery.co.uk
Shop Mon-Fri 9am-4pm
Tours by arrangement for select CAMRA groups

Situated in the historic brewing town of Wiveliscombe, Cotleigh has become one of the most successful independent breweries in the West Country. The brewery, which started trading in 1979, is housed in specially converted premises with a modern plant capable of producing 165 barrels a week. 300 pubs and 250 retail outlets are supplied; the beers are also widely available through select wholesalers. Cotleigh's charitable partner is The Hawk and Owl Trust. Seasonal beers: see website. Bottle-conditioned beers are also available.

Harrier (OG 1035, ABV 3.5%)
A golden beer with a delicate floral and fruity aroma and a refreshing, sweet and lightly hopped finish.

Tawny Owl (OG 1038, ABV 3.8%) ◆
Well-balanced, tawny-coloured bitter with plenty of malt and fruitiness on the nose, and malt to the fore in the taste, followed by hop fruit, developing to a satisfying bitter finish.

25 (OG 1040, ABV 4%)
A golden beer with a fresh aroma and fruit-filled finish.

Commando Hoofing (OG 1040, ABV 4%)
A pale golden beer with an explosion of fruit-filled flavours.

**Golden Seahawk Premium Beer
(OG 1042, ABV 4.2%)** ◆
A gold, well-hopped premium bitter with a flowery hop aroma and fruity hop flavour, clean mouthfeel, leading to a dry, hoppy finish.

Barn Owl Premium Ale (OG 1045, ABV 4.5%) ◆
A pale to mid-brown beer with a good balance of malt and hops on the nose; a smooth, full-bodied taste where hops dominate, but balanced by malt, following through to the finish.

Honey Buzzard (OG 1045, ABV 4.5%)
Copper-coloured ale infused with local Wiveliscombe honey. A smooth, creamy and chocolate palate giving a subtle bittersweet finish.

Buzzard Dark Ale (OG 1048, ABV 4.8%)
A traditional dark ale, deep copper red in colour. The chocolate malt gives a dry, nutty flavour with hints of amarone biscuit. The finish in the mouth is dry with a smoky but smooth finish.

Cotswold SIBA

Cotswold Brewing Co Ltd, College Farm, Stow Road, Bourton on the Water, Gloucestershire, GL54 2HN
☎ (01451) 824488 ✉ lager@cotswoldlager.com
⊕ cotswoldlager.com
Shop Mon-Fri 9am-5pm
Tours by arrangement

Cotswold Brewing Co is an independent producer of lager and speciality beers. The brewery was established in 2005 in rented accommodation on part of a working farm in Foscot, Oxfordshire. It moved to its current location in 2010. More than 60 outlets are supplied. Seasonal and bottle-conditioned beers are also available.

3.8 Lager (OG 1035, ABV 3.8%)
A well-hopped lager; full-flavoured and well-rounded.

Lager (ABV 4%)
An easy-drinking lager with hints of tropical fruits and elderflower.

Wheat Beer (OG 1040, ABV 4.2%)
An aromatic wheat beer with pronounced banana and tropical fruit notes.

Stout (ABV 4.3%)

Premium Lager (OG 1044, ABV 5%)
A smooth, subtle lager with a soft, fruity flavour.

Dark Lager (ABV 5.5%)
A dark lager with a smooth, rich taste of chocolate malt.

Cotswold Lion (NEW)

Cotswold Lion Brewery Ltd, Grain Store 5, Downmans Farm, Coberley, Gloucestershire, GL53 9QY
☎ (01242) 870164
✉ drinkbeer@cotswoldlionbrewery.co.uk
⏺ cotswoldlionbrewery.co.uk

Brewing began in 2012 using the 10-barrel plant from the closed Festival Brewery. A five-barrel plant is also used. Seasonal beers are available.

Shepherd's Delight (ABV 3.6%)
A crisp, tart, light ale full of citrus flavours.

Best in Show (ABV 4.2%)
A well-balanced best bitter, malty and hoppy.

Golden Fleece (ABV 4.4%)
An IPA filled with Jamaican fruit flavours.

Under Festival Brewery name:

Gold (OG 1042.6, ABV 4.4%)
Refreshing golden ale with sweet floral aroma and a dry finish.

Ruby (OG 1045.5, ABV 4.7%)
A strong bitter, ruby-coloured with a rich and warming character.

Cotswold Spring SIBA ◉

Cotswold Spring Brewery Ltd, Dodington Ash, Chipping Sodbury, Gloucestershire, BS37 6RX
☎ (01454) 323088 ✉ info@springbrewery.co.uk
⏺ springbrewery.co.uk
Shop Mon-Fri 9am-5pm; Sat 10am-1pm
Tours by arrangement

⊗ Cotswold Spring opened in 2005 with a 10-barrel plant. All the beers are produced using spring water sourced from a borehole on site. Seasonal beers: see website. Bottle-conditioned beers are also available.

Ambler (OG 1040, ABV 3.8%) ◕
Amber session bitter with pronounced hop finish. Plenty of malt and fruit on the nose; at first a sweet taste that soon fades into spicy bitterness. There are hints of red apples and passion fruit.

Stunner (OG 1041, ABV 4%)
Straw-coloured ale with an initial dryness on the palate, mouth-filling malt and fruit and a long, sweet finish.

Codger (OG 1042, ABV 4.2%) ◕

Pale and crystal malt on the nose preludes a big malty taste to the pale brown best bitter. Hints of dates as the taste develops an increasingly hoppy bitter finish.

Cottage SIBA ◉

Cottage Brewing Co Ltd, The Old Cheese Dairy, Hornblotton Road, Lovington, Somerset, BA7 7PS
☎ (01963) 240551 ✉ sales@cottagebrewing.co.uk
⏺ cottagebrewing.co.uk
Tours by arrangement

⊗ The brewery was established in 1993 in West Lydford and moved to larger premises in 1996, doubling brewing capacity at the same time. In 2001, Cottage installed a 30-barrel plant. 1,500 outlets are supplied. The names of beers mostly follow a railway theme. Seasonal beers are also brewed.

Southern Bitter (OG 1039, ABV 3.7%) ◕
Gold-coloured beer with malt and fruity hops on the nose. Malt and hops in the mouth with a long fruity, bitter finish.

Broadgauge Bitter (OG 1040, ABV 3.9%)
A light tawny-coloured session bitter with a floral aroma and a balanced bitter finish.

Golden Arrow (OG 1043, ABV 4.5%) ◕
A hoppy golden bitter with a powerful floral bouquet, a fruity, full-bodied taste and a lingering dry, bitter finish.

Goldrush (OG 1051, ABV 5%)
A deep golden strong ale brewed with Cascade hops.

Country Life SIBA

Country Life Brewery, The Big Sheep, Abbotsham, Bideford, Devon, EX39 5AP
☎ (01237) 420808 ☎ 07971 267790
✉ simon@countrylifebrewery.co.uk
⏺ countrylifebrewery.co.uk
Shop 1-4pm daily (Apr-Oct)
Tours by arrangement

⊗ The brewery is based at the Big Sheep tourist attraction that welcomes more than 100,000 visitors in the summer. The brewery offers a beer show and free samples in the shop during the peak season (Apr-Oct). A 15.5-barrel plant was installed in 2005, making Country Life the biggest brewery in north Devon. Around 100 outlets are supplied. All cask ales are also available in bottle-conditioned form plus Devonshire Ten-der. Seasonal beer is also brewed. All beers are also available in the brewery's managed pub, Lacey's in Bideford.

Old Appledore (OG 1037, ABV 3.7%)

Lacey's Ale (OG 1042, ABV 4.2%)

Golden Pig (OG 1046, ABV 4.7%) ⏺

Country Bumpkin (OG 1058, ABV 6%)

Cox & Holbrook EAB

Cox & Holbrook, Manor Farm, Brettenham Road, Buxhall, Suffolk, IP14 3DY
☎ (01449) 736323
Tours by arrangement

⊗ First opened in 1997, the brewery concentrates on producing a range of bitters, four of which are available at any one time, along with more specialised medium strength beers and milds. There is also a strong emphasis on the preservation and resurrection of rare and traditional styles. Bottle-conditioned versions of draught beers are available at varying times of the year.

Crown Dark Mild (OG 1037, ABV 3.6%) ◆
Thin tasting at first but plenty of malt, caramel and roast flavours burst through to give a thoroughly satisfying beer.

Shelley Dark (OG 1036, ABV 3.6%)
Full-flavoured and satisfying.

Beyton Bitter (OG 1038, ABV 3.8%)
A traditional bitter, pale tawny in colour, malty with Fuggles and Goldings hops.

Old Mill Bitter (OG 1038, ABV 3.8%)
Pale, hoppy and thirst quenching.

Rattlesden Best Bitter (OG 1043, ABV 4%)
A full-bodied and malty best bitter.

Albion Pale Ale (OG 1042, ABV 4.2%)
Refreshingly clean, hoppy ale.

Remus (OG 1045, ABV 4.5%)
An amber ale, soft on the palate with full hop flavours but subdued bitterness.

Goodcock's Winner (OG 1050, ABV 5%)
An amber ale, rather malty yet not too heavy, with a sharp hop finish.

Ironoak Single Stout (OG 1051, ABV 5%)
Full-bodied with strong roast grain flavours and plenty of hop bitterness plus a distinct hint of oak.

Stormwatch (OG 1052, ABV 5%)
An unusual premium pale ale with a full, slightly fruity flavour.

Stowmarket Porter (OG 1056, ABV 5%) ◆
Strong caramel flavour and lingering caramel aftertaste, balanced by full malt and roast flavours. The overall impression is of a very sweet beer.

Uncle Stan Single Brown Stout (OG 1053, ABV 5%)
Unusual soft malt and fruit flavours in a full and satisfying bit of history.

Prentice Strong Dark Ale (OG 1053, ABV 5.3%)
A strong porter.

East Anglian Pale Ale (OG 1059, ABV 6%)
Well-matured pale beer with a strong Goldings hop character.

Craddock's

▤ Craddock's Brewery, Duke William, 25 Coventry Street, Stourbridge, West Midlands, DY8 1EP
☎ (01384) 440202 ✉ thedukewilliam@gmail.com
⊕ thedukewilliam.com

Craddock's began production in 2011 at the back of the Duke William pub in Stourbridge using a four-barrel plant. Bottle-conditioned beer is also available at the local farmers' market.

Saxon Gold (OG 1038, ABV 4%)

Crest (OG 1042, ABV 4.4%)
A classic, copper-coloured premium ale. Well-balanced and full-bodied. A smooth, easy-drinking beer.

Stout (OG 1043, ABV 4.5%)
An easy-drinking stout with coffee, burnt toast and bitter fruits, edging towards a dry finish.

Troll (OG 1052, ABV 5.4%)

A deceptively strong golden ale with a bittersweet taste and dry hop finish.

Croglin

See Nine Standards

Cromarty (NEW)

Cromarty Brewing Co, Davidston, Cromarty, Ross-shire, IV11 8XD
☎ (01381) 600440
✉ enquiries@cromartybrewing.co.uk
⊕ cromartybrewing.co.uk
Shop Mon-Sat 10am-4pm
Tours by arrangement

Cromarty began brewing in 2011 using a new Bavarian brewhouse.

Happy Chappy (OG 1040, ABV 4.1%)

Brewed Awakening (OG 1048, ABV 4.7%)

Red Rocker (OG 1049, ABV 5%)

Cropton

See Great Yorkshire

Cross Bay SIBA ◉

Cross Bay Brewery, Newgate Brewery, White Lund Industrial Estate, Morecambe, Lancashire, LA3 3PT
☎ (01524) 39481 ✉ info@crossbaybrewery.co.uk
⊕ crossbaybrewery.co.uk
Shop Mon-Fri 9am-4pm; Sat 9.30am-11.30am; Sun 10-11am
Tours by arrangement

☺The brewery, occupying the old premises of Bryson's, opened in 2011 using a 30-barrel plant. Seasonal beers: see website. A brewery tap is planned.

Nightfall Pale Bitter (OG 1038, ABV 3.8%)
A finely balanced session ale with a robust body, following through with a moderate bitterness that boasts a huge spicy fruit finish.

Dusk Ruby Bitter (OG 1040, ABV 4%)
A ruby ale kicking in with a strong, fruity nose bursting on to the palate with a roasted but fruity bitter body with hints of cocoa, following through with a floral/blackcurrant aroma.

Sunset Blonde Bitter (OG 1043, ABV 4.2%)
A light, refreshing ale with a sharp start moving on to leave a smooth orange and lemon rind aftertaste.

Zenith (OG 1050, ABV 5%)
A light-coloured, refreshing IPA with a distinct tropical aroma. Zesty fruit flavours give way to a long, bitter finish.

Crouch Vale SIBA

Crouch Vale Brewery Ltd, 23 Haltwhistle Road, South Woodham Ferrers, Essex, CM3 5ZA
☎ (01245) 322744 ✉ info@crouchvale.co.uk
⊕ crouchvale.co.uk
Shop Mon-Fri 8.30am-5pm
Tours by arrangement

⊠ Founded in 1981 by two CAMRA enthusiasts, Crouch Vale is now well established as a major craft brewer in Essex, having moved to larger premises in 2006. The company is also a major wholesaler of cask ale from other independent breweries, which it supplies to more than 100 outlets as well as beer festivals throughout the region. One tied house, the Queen's Head in Chelmsford, is owned. Seasonal beers: one beer available each month, details on website.

Blackwater Mild (OG 1037, ABV 3.7%) ◀
A dark bitter rather than a true mild. Roasty and very bitter towards the end.

Essex Boys Best Bitter (ABV 3.8%)

Brewers Gold (OG 1040, ABV 4%) ◀
Pale golden ale with a striking citrus nose. Sweet fruit and bitter hops are well matched throughout.

Yakima Gold (ABV 4.2%)

Amarillo (OG 1050, ABV 5%)
A strong golden ale with a spicy aroma, juicy malt mouthfeel and an extremely long and bitter hop finish.

Crown

See Wood Street

Cuerden

Cuerden Brewing, Smithy Farm, Blackshaw Head, West Yorkshire, HX7 7JB
☎ 07938 000530 ✉ cuerdenbrewing@gmail.com

☻Cuerden was established in 2010 using spare capacity at Bridestones Brewery. Specially designed beers for individual groups and outlets are also brewed.

Munich (ABV 3.7%)
A golden-coloured, well-balanced, clean beer.

Mild (ABV 3.9%)
A session beer, deep ruby in colour with plenty of body.

Gold (ABV 4%)
A pale, sunny beer. Clean, dry and hoppy with a smooth aftertaste.

Pale (ABV 4.2%)
A traditionally brewed bitter, not too dry and refreshingly sharp.

For the Fountaine Inn, Linton and Spread Eagle, Sawley:

Individual Pale (ABV 4.2%)

Cuillin

▤ **Cuillin Brewery Ltd, Sligachan Hotel, Sligachan, Carbost, Isle of Skye, IV47 8SW**
☎ (01478) 650204 ☎ 07795 250808
✉ steve@cuillinbrewery.co.uk
⊕ cuillinbrewery.co.uk
Tours by arrangement

☻The five-barrel brewery opened in 2004 and is situated in central Skye, close to the famous Cuillin mountain. The water provides a distinctive colour and taste to the ales. Specials and seasonal ales are available throughout the year. The brewery is closed in winter.

Skye Ale (OG 1041, ABV 4.1%)

Black Face (OG 1043, ABV 4.3%)

A good balance of blackcurrant fruit and malts highlight this dark ruby red strong mild. Liquorice and roast also evident in the creamy mouthfeel.

Glamaig (OG 1045, ABV 4.5%)

Pinnacle (OG 1047, ABV 4.7%) ◀
The hoppy and fruity nose leads to more hop and plenty of pale malt flavour in this drinkable golden amber bitter.

Cullercoats (NEW) SIBA ◉

Cullercoats Brewery Ltd, 17 St Oswins Avenue, Cullercoats, North Shields, Tyne & Wear, NE30 4PH
☎ (0191) 252 8765
✉ cullercoatsbrewery@gmail.com
⊕ cullercoatsbrewery.co.uk

⊠ Cullercoats was established in 2011.

Lovely Nelly (OG 1040, ABV 3.9%)
A premium pale ale, full-bodied with a malty flavour and smooth bitterness.

Jack the Devil (OG 1045, ABV 4.5%)
A rich, dark bitter with a balance of malty nuttiness and a fresh, hoppy aroma.

Cumberland

Cumberland Breweries Ltd, The Green, Great Corby, Carlisle, Cumbria, CA4 8LR
☎ (01228) 560899
✉ enquiries@cumberlandbreweries.co.uk

☻Cumberland was established in 2009 using a bespoke 10-barrel plant in what was once the village blacksmiths.

Corby Ale (ABV 3.8%) ◀
A fruity session beer with sweetness leading to gentle bitterness in the aftertaste.

Corby Blonde (ABV 4.2%) ◀
Melon fruity hoppiness gives a light refreshing drink.

Cumbrian Legendary SIBA ◉

Cumbrian Legendary Ales Ltd, Old Hall Brewery, Esthwaite Water, Hawkshead, Cumbria, LA22 0QF
☎ (01539) 436436
✉ info@cumbrianlegendaryales.com
⊕ cumbrianlegendaryales.com
Tours by arrangement

☻The Old Hall Brewery was established in 2006 in a renovated barn on the shores of Esthwaite Water. It was taken over in 2009 by Loweswater Brewery with Hayley Barton as head brewer. 100 outlets are supplied direct. The success of Loweswater Gold has meant the brewery is thriving and extra fermenting and conditioning tanks have been installed.

Esthwaite Bitter (OG 1038.5, ABV 3.8%) ◀
Amber session ale with sweetness, fruit and hoppiness in fine balance.

Langdale (OG 1040, ABV 4%) ▤ ◀
Golden ale with fresh grapefruit aromas, hoppy fruity flavours and crisp long hop finish making for a well-balanced beer.

Grasmoor Dark Ale (OG 1044.5, ABV 4.3%) ◀
Dark fruity beer with complex character and roast nutty tones leading to a short, refreshing finish.

Loweswater Gold (OG 1041, ABV 4.3%) ▱ ◀

A dominant fruity body develops into a light bitter finish. A beer that belies its strength.

Daleside SIBA ⟨◉⟩

Daleside Brewery Ltd, Camwal Road, Starbeck, Harrogate, North Yorkshire, HG1 4PT
☎ (01423) 880022
✉ enquiries@dalesidebrewery.com
⊕ dalesidebrewery.com
Shop Mon-Fri 9am-4pm (Off sales only)

☺Opened in 1991 in Harrogate with a 20-barrel plant, the brewery delivers direct to a range of outlets including pubs, restaurants and farm shops from Newcastle to Chesterfield as well as nationally via wholesalers. Seasonal beers: see website.

Bitter (OG 1039, ABV 3.7%) ◆
Pale brown in colour, this well-balanced, hoppy beer is complemented by fruity bitterness and a hint of sweetness, leading to a long, bitter finish.

Blonde (OG 1040, ABV 3.9%) ◆
A pale golden beer with a predominantly hoppy aroma and taste, leading to a refreshing hoppy, bitter but short finish.

Old Legover (OG 1043, ABV 4.1%)
Well-balanced mid-brown refreshing beer that leads to an equally well-balanced fruity bitter aftertaste.

Special Bitter (OG 1043, ABV 4.1%)
A mid-amber beer with a malty nose and a hint of fruitiness. Hops and malt carry over to leave a clean, hoppy aftertaste.

Monkey Wrench (ABV 5.3%)
Powerful, strong mid-brown ale. Aromas of fruit, hops, malt and roast malt give way to well-balanced fruit hoppiness and some sweetness.

Morocco Ale (ABV 5.5%)
A rich, dark, spiced ale.

Dancing Duck SIBA

Dancing Duck Brewery, 1 John Cooper Buildings, Payne Street, Derby, DE22 3AZ
☎ 07581 122122
✉ rachel@dancingduckbrewery.com
⊕ dancingduckbrewery.com

Dancing Duck was established in 2010 in a former motor engineering unit using a 10-barrel plant. Head brewer is Rachel Matthews who designed the brewery together with her husband, Ian Murfin. An increasing number of local outlets are supplied. In 2011 the brewery became partners in the operation of the Exeter Arms in Derby where the beers can always be found.

Ay Up (OG 1041, ABV 3.9%)
A pale session ale with subtle malt and floral notes matched with citrus hop and rounded off with a slightly dry finish.

Nice Weather (OG 1042, ABV 4.1%)
A copper-coloured fruity beer packed with blackberry, strawberry and floral rose notes in balance with a malt character.

22 (OG 1044.1, ABV 4.3%)
A well-balanced best bitter with malty flavour and dark fruit notes offset by a strong hop and clean finish.

Dark Drake (OG 1051, ABV 4.5%)

Malty caramel and liquorice flavours combine in a smooth-drinking oatmeal stout with freshly roasted coffee and tea finish.

Gold (OG 1046.5, ABV 4.7%)
A modern IPA with powerful hoppy bitterness and aroma balanced with strong malt notes. English First Gold hops give peppery, plum-like and orange zest flavours.

Abduction (OG 1053, ABV 5.5%)
Myriad tropical flavours in balance with a hoppy bitterness, a good malt character and clean finish.

Dancing Man (NEW)

☰ Dancing Man Brewery, Platform Tavern, Town Quay, Southampton, SO14 2NY
☎ (023) 8033 7232 ✉ stewart@platformtavern.com
⊕ dancingmanbrewery.com

Dancing Man began brewing in 2011 using a one-barrel plant. Seasonal beers are available.

Pilgrim's Pale Ale (ABV 3.9%)

Troubadour (ABV 4.1%)

DNA (Dark Nomadic Ale) (ABV 4.7%)

Fiddler's Jig (ABV 4.8%)

Big Casino (ABV 5%)

Last Waltz (ABV 5.3%)

Dark Horse SIBA

Dark Horse Brewery, Coonlands Laithe, Hetton, Nr Skipton, North Yorkshire, BD23 6LY
☎ (01756) 730555
Tours by arrangement

☺Formerly the Wharfedale Brewery, Dark Horse opened in 2008 with new owners. The brewery is based in an old hay barn within the Yorkshire Dales National Park. More than 15 outlets are supplied direct.

Best Bitter (OG 1038, ABV 3.8%) ◆
This well-balanced tawny bitter has biscuity malt and fruit on the nose, which continue into the taste. Bitterness increases in the finish.

Hetton Pale Ale (OG 1041, ABV 4.2%) ◆
A well-balanced and full-bodied golden pale ale with hoppy bitterness on the palate overlaying a malty base and a strong citrus fruit character.

Dark Star SIBA

Dark Star Brewing Co Ltd, 22 Star Road, Partridge Green, Horsham, West Sussex, RH13 8RA
☎ (01403) 713085 ✉ info@darkstarbrewing.co.uk
⊕ darkstarbrewing.co.uk
Shop Mon-Fri 9am-5pm; Sat 9am-1pm
Tours by arrangement

⊗ Dark Star started in the cellar of the Evening Star in Brighton, moved to a 15-barrel brewery near Haywards Heath in 2001 and in 2010 moved to its current premises using a 45-barrel plant. Copies of classic European, American or old English beer styles are regularly produced and the brewery increasingly undertakes collaboration brews with other breweries. Three local pubs are owned. Beers are distributed directly, through wholesalers and via brewery swaps with other small craft brewers. The range of beer is divided between permanent, seasonal and monthly specials: see website. Bottle-conditioned beer is also available.

Hophead (OG 1040, ABV 3.8%) 🍶 🔷
A golden-coloured bitter with a fruity/hoppy aroma and citrus/bitter taste and aftertaste. Flavours remain strong to the end.

Partridge Best Bitter (OG 1041, ABV 4%)
A traditional Sussex-style best bitter.

Espresso (OG 1043, ABV 4.2%)
A black beer brewed with freshly ground coffee.

American Pale Ale (OG 1048, ABV 4.7%) 🍶
Light gold in colour with a clean, malty body balanced by crisp bitterness and a full citrus hop aroma.

Festival (OG 1051, ABV 5%) 🍶
A chestnut, bronze-coloured bitter with a smooth mouthfeel and fruit aroma.

Original (OG 1051, ABV 5%) 🔷
Dark, full-bodied ale with a roast malt aroma and a dry, bitter, stout-like finish.

Winter Meltdown (OG 1051, ABV 5%)
A deep bronze-coloured beer with Chinese stem ginger and other spices to produce an aromatic warmth.

Revelation (OG 1056, ABV 5.7%)
Big juicy pale malt flavours with layers of bitterness and pronounced hop aromas of tangerine and tropical fruit.

DarkTribe

🍺 DarkTribe Brewery, Dog & Gun, High Street, East Butterwick, Lincolnshire, DN17 3AJ
☎ (01724) 782324 ✉ dixie@darktribe.co.uk
🌐 darktribe.co.uk
Tours by arrangement

☺A small brewery was built during the summer of 1996 in a workshop at the bottom of his garden by Dave 'Dixie' Dean. In 2005 Dixie bought the Dog & Gun pub and moved the 2.5-barrel brewing equipment there. The beers generally follow a marine theme, recalling Dixie's days as an engineer in the Merchant Navy and his enthusiasm for sailing. Local outlets are supplied. Seasonal beers are also produced.

Dixie's Mild (OG 1034, ABV 3.6%)

Honey Mild (OG 1032, ABV 3.6%)

Admiral Sidney Smith (OG 1034, ABV 3.8%)

Full Ahead (OG 1034, ABV 3.8%) 🔷
A malty smoothness is backed by a slightly fruity hop that gives a good bitterness to this amber-brown bitter.

Captain Floyd (OG 1035, ABV 3.9%)

Albacore (OG 1036, ABV 4%)

Red Duster (OG 1036, ABV 4%)

Red Rock (OG 1037, ABV 4.2%)

Sternwheeler (OG 1037, ABV 4.2%) 🍶

Intelligent Whale (OG 1038, ABV 4.3%)

RAMP (Richard's Amazing Magical Potion) (OG 1038, ABV 4.3%)

Bucket Hitch (OG 1040, ABV 4.4%)

Dixie's Bollards (OG 1040, ABV 4.5%)

Old Gaffer (OG 1038, ABV 4.5%)

Twin Screw (OG 1044, ABV 5.1%) 🔷
A fruity, rose-hip tasting beer, red in colour. Good malt presence with a dry, hoppy bitterness coming through in the finish.

Dartmoor SIBA

Dartmoor Brewery Ltd, The Brewery, Station Road, Princetown, Devon, PL20 6QX
☎ (01822) 890789 ✉ ale@dartmoorbrewery.co.uk
🌐 dartmoorbrewery.co.uk
Tours by arrangement

⊗ Established in 1994, it is the highest brewery in England at 1,400 feet above sea level. It moved into a new purpose-built building in 2005. In early 2010 the capacity was increased to 300 barrels per week by the addition of two 60-barrel fermenters with a further one added in 2012. The brewery changed name from Princetown to Dartmoor in 2008 with no change to the structure or ownership of the company. It is the first brewery to market its own brand of crisps, Jail Ale Crisps. Bottle-conditioned beers are available.

Dartmoor IPA (OG 1039.5, ABV 4%) 🔷
There is a flowery hop aroma and taste with a bitter aftertaste to this full-bodied, amber-coloured beer.

Legend (OG 1043.5, ABV 4.4%)
Golden brown in colour, smooth, full-flavoured and balanced with a crispy malt fruit finish.

Jail Ale (OG 1047.5, ABV 4.8%) 🔷
Hops and fruit predominate in the flavour of this mid-brown beer, which has a slightly sweet aftertaste.

Darwin SIBA

Darwin Brewery Ltd, 1 West Quay Court, Sunderland Enterprise Park, Sunderland, Tyne & Wear, SR5 2TE
☎ (0191) 549 9450 ✉ info@darwinbrewery.com
🌐 darwinbrewery.com
Tours by arrangement

☺Established in 1994, the Darwin Brewery is now based in purpose-built premises in Sunderland with a 3.5-barrel brew plant. The brewery supports students on Brewlab brewing courses who produce many unique specialist and international beers, often available locally. A range of established Darwin beers are also produced, some based on historical analysis or student initiatives.

Evolution Ale (OG 1040, ABV 4%)

Beagle Blond (OG 1040, ABV 4.1%)

Richmond Ale (OG 1045, ABV 4.5%)

Rolling Hitch (OG 1053, ABV 5.2%)

Galapagos Stout (OG 1056, ABV 5.8%)

Killer Bee (OG 1060, ABV 6%)
A strong but light ale matured with honey.

Extinction Ale (OG 1075, ABV 8.3%) 🍶

Davenports

See Highgate

Dawkins SIBA

Dawkins Ales Ltd, The Now Thus Brewery, Unit 7, Timsbury Workshop Estate, Hayeswood Road, Timsbury, Bath, BA2 0HQ
☎ (01761) 472242 ✉ sales@dawkins-ales.co.uk
⊕ dawkins-ales.co.uk
Tours by arrangement

The established Dawkins Taverns group of independent Bristol pubs bought the former Matthews Brewery in 2009. The regular Matthews' recipes continue unchanged under the Dawkins' banner. Five pubs are owned and around 80 outlets are supplied direct. Seasonal beers: see website. Bottle-conditioned beers are planned.

Brassknocker (OG 1037, ABV 3.8%) ◆
A pale gold beer with a full, hoppy, citrus flavour and a satisfying dry finish.

Bristol Best (OG 1039, ABV 4%) ◆
Accent on fruit on both aroma and taste of this brown, well-hopped bitter. An initial sweetness fades in the bitter aftertaste.

Green Barrel Bitter (OG 1039, ABV 4%) ◆
Amber-coloured best bitter; well-balanced taste and clean bittersweet aftertaste. No longer brewed with organic ingredients.

Bob Wall (OG 1041, ABV 4.2%) ◆
Fruity best bitter; roasty hint with intense forest fruit and rich malt flavour continuing to a well-balanced finish.

DB SIBA

DB Brewery, Clifton Road, Runcorn, Cheshire, WA7 3EH
☎ 07739 325742 ✉ tony@dbbrew.com
⊕ dbbrew.com
Tours by arrangement

DB started brewing in 2011 on a small industrial site in the Clifton area of Runcorn. As well as brewing they also develop brewing technology: see website.

Tankslapper (ABV 4%)

Transporter (ABV 4.1%)

Mersey Porter (ABV 4.2%)

Traitor (ABV 4.2%)

Ugly Australian (ABV 4.2%)

Blonde (ABV 4.3%)

Laycock (ABV 6.5%)

Deeside

Deeside Brewery Ltd, c/o Aulton Farm, Auchattie, AB31 6PT
☎ (01339) 883777 ☎ 07765 124162

Office: Escape Business Technologies, 5 Carden Place, Aberdeen, AB10 1UT ✉ tim@deesidebrewery.co.uk
⊕ deesidebrewery.co.uk

⊠ Originally established as Home Brewery (Hillside Brewery) in 2005. The brewery relocated to the Deeside Activity Park in 2008 with a new 10-barrel plant. This was subsequently moved to a small farm owned by the majority shareholder of the new company that bought the business in 2012. Seasonal beers: see website. Bottle-conditioned beers are also available.

Abhainn (OG 1037, ABV 4.1%)
A fruity pale ale.

Laf (OG 1037, ABV 4.1%)
A California steam beer.

Macbeth (OG 1037, ABV 4.1%)
A robustly hopped bitter.

Nechtan (OG 1037, ABV 4.1%) 🍺

Talorcan (OG 1051, ABV 4.5%)
A smooth, creamy stout.

Delavals SIBA

Delavals (Brewers) Ltd, 26 Windsor Gardens, Whitley Bay, NE26 3BG
☎ 0844 504 2214 ✉ info@delavals.com
⊕ delavals.com

Delavals began brewing in 2010 reviving an 18th century ale for Seaton Delaval Hall in partnership with the National Trust. They continue to work closely to create a range of ales that help to promote and preserve regional landmarks. Currently brewing on a two-barrel plant and directly supplying 50 outlets.

Souter Lighthouse Best Bitter (OG 1037.5, ABV 3.8%)
Well-rounded, bittersweet with a little malt and rich fruity aromas.

Lindisfarne Castle Dark Ale (OG 1039, ABV 4%)
A sweet, malty ale made with hyssop to give a subtle minty chocolate taste and a silky finish.

Seaton Delaval Hall Pale Ale (OG 1040.6, ABV 4.2%)
Crisp and refreshing with a hoppy aroma and dry finish.

Washington Old Hall Honey Beer (OG 1045.4, ABV 4.6%)
A light, sweet, golden ale made with honey. A blend of biscuity malt, light floral aromas and warming honey.

DemonBrew

⊟ DemonBrew, 227-229 High Street, Prestonpans, East Lothian, EH32 9BE
☎ (01875) 819922 ☎ 07974 107453
✉ dave@demonbrew.com ⊕ demonbrew.com
Tours by arrangement

⊚DemonBrew uses the microbrewery in the award-winning pub, the Prestoungrange Gothenburg. Originally installed in 2004 and trading as Fowler's Ales then Prestopans, brewer Dave Whyte commenced DemonBrew in 2011. Beer is available in the pub and distributed to other outlets in Edinburgh and the Lothians and throughout Britain. Further beers are planned.

Firehead (ABV 3.9%)
A golden session ale. Citrus hops and slightly bitter.

Demon Black (ABV 4.4%)
Jet black with hints of roasted coffee and chocolate.

Denbigh (NEW)

⊟ Denbigh Brewery (Bragdy Dinbych), c/o Hope & Anchor Inn, 94 Vale Street, Denbigh, LL16 3BW
☎ (01745) 817021 ✉ bragdy@shworth.com

Brewing commenced in 2012 at the rear of the Hope & Anchor pub. Beers are mainly supplied to the pub although the brewery is run as a separate operation.

Cockpit (Cadlas Ceiliog) (ABV 4%)

Dent SIBA ◉

Dent Brewery Ltd, Hollins, Cowgill, Dent, Cumbria, LA10 5TQ
☎ (01539) 625326 ✉ laptop@dentbrewery.co.uk
⊕ dentbrewery.co.uk
Merchandise available from George & Dragon, Dent
Tours by arrangement

Dent was set up in 1990 in a converted barn next to a former farmhouse in the Yorkshire Dales National Park. In 2005 the brewery was completely refurbished and capacity expanded. One pub is owned. Over 150 outlets are supplied direct.

Bitter (OG 1036, ABV 3.7%)

Golden Fleece (OG 1035, ABV 3.7%) ◄
Light, hoppy, fruity, easy-drinking summer bitter with a lingering bitter aftertaste.

Aviator (OG 1039, ABV 4%) ◄
This medium-bodied amber ale is characterised by strong citrus and hoppy flavours that develop into a long bitter finish.

Ramsbottom Strong Ale (OG 1042, ABV 4.5%) ◄
This complex, mid-brown beer has a warming, dry, bitter finish to follow its unusual combination of roast, bitter, fruity and sweet flavours.

Kamikaze (OG 1047, ABV 5%) ◄
Hops and fruit dominate this full-bodied, golden, strong bitter, with a dry bitterness growing in the aftertaste.

T'owd Tup (OG 1056, ABV 6%) ◄
A rich, full-flavoured, strong stout with a coffee aroma. The dominant roast character is balanced by a warming sweetness and a raisiny, fruitcake taste that linger on into the finish.

Derby SIBA ◉

Derby Brewing Co Ltd, Masons Place Business Park, Nottingham Road, Derby, Derbyshire, DE21 6AQ
☎ (01332) 242888 ☎ 07887 556788
✉ sales@derbybrewing.co.uk ⊕ derbybrewing.co.uk
Tours by arrangement

A family-run, craft microbrewery, established in 2004 in the old Masons Paintworks Varnish Shed by head brewer Trevor Harris, founder and former brewer at the Brunswick Inn, Derby. The business has grown massively over the years and three pubs are now owned around Derby. More than 400 outlets are supplied including major retailers. In addition to the core range there are at least four new beers each month.

Hop Till You Drop (OG 1039, ABV 3.9%)
A blonde brew with fruity overtones and a dry finish.

Triple Hop (OG 1041, ABV 4.1%)
A well-balanced classic pale ale.

Business As Usual (OG 1044, ABV 4.4%)
An easy-drinking, flavoursome copper-coloured beer. Perfectly balanced, smooth and malty with a satisfying finish.

Dashingly Dark (OG 1045, ABV 4.5%)
A smooth, dark brew with complex flavours and a chocolate roasted finish.

Double Mash (OG 1046, ABV 4.6%)
A balanced ruby brew.

Penny's Porter (OG 1046, ABV 4.6%)
A rich, very dark, robust brew with a fine hop balance.

Old Friend (OG 1047, ABV 4.7%)
A classic, well-rounded brew. Balanced and full-bodied.

Old Intentional (OG 1050, ABV 5%)
A full-bodied, malty premium beer. Rich chestnut in colour and well-balanced with a delicate sweet aroma and smooth finish.

Derventio SIBA

Derventio Brewery Ltd, Long Mill, Darley Abbey Mills, Darley Abbey, Derbyshire, DE22 1DZ
☎ (01332) 380199 ☎ 07525 689095
✉ enquiries@derventiobrewery.co.uk
⊕ derventiobrewery.co.uk
Tours by arrangement

Derventio Brewery was established in 2005 and first brewed in 2006 at Trusley Brook Farm in Trusley. In 2011 the six-barrel brewery relocated to the Grade-I listed Long Mill, which is part of the Derwent Valley Mills World Heritage Site. The brewery tap can be hired for private parties. A popular 'Day with the Brewer' is available, by prior arrangement, for up to three people on Saturday mornings. The brewery is involved in sponsorship of local cricket teams as well as numerous outside events and is one of the founding members of the Derbyshire Brewers Collective. Seasonal beers and monthly specials are also brewed.

Cleopatra (OG 1048.4, ABV 5%)
A complex beer with a hint of apricot.

Derwent Rose

See Consett Ale Works

Derwent SIBA

Derwent Brewery, Units 2a-2c, Station Road Industrial Estate, Silloth, Cumbria, CA7 4AG
☎ (01697) 331522/331523
✉ sales@derwentbrewery.co.uk
⊕ derwentbrewery.co.uk

Derwent was set up in 1996 in Cockermouth and moved to Silloth in 1998. It is involved with the Silloth Beer Festival every September and has supplied Carlisle State Bitter to the House of Commons, a beer that recreates one produced by the former state-owned Carlisle Brewery. More than 300 outlets are supplied in the north of England. Seasonal beers: see website.

Carlisle State Bitter (OG 1036, ABV 3.7%) ◄
Malty, biscuity, hoppy beer with a gold colour.

W&M Dark Mild (OG 1036, ABV 3.7%)

Parsons Pledge (OG 1039, ABV 4%) ◄
Amber ale with a biscuity tang and a slightly fruity finish.

Derwent Blonde (ABV 4.2%)

Mutineer (ABV 4.4%)

W&M Pale Ale (ABV 4.4%)

THE BREWERIES

Deverells (NEW)

Deverells Brewery, Unit 16, Globe Industrial Estate, Grays, Essex, RM17 6ST
☎ 07843 627791

Brewing began in 2012 on a 2.5-barrel plant. Seasonal beers are available.

Tall Hot Blonde (ABV 4%)

Redemption (ABV 4.5%)

Devil's Dyke

⊟ Devil's Dyke Brewery, Dyke's End, 8 Fair Green, Reach, Cambridgeshire, CB25 0JD
☎ (01638) 743816
Tours by arrangement

⊠ Devil's Dyke came on stream in 2007 using a plant bought from the Red Rose Brewery. It is situated in outbuildings to the rear of the Dyke's End pub, the freehold of which was bought by the village in the late 1990s to save it from being turned back into a private house. Several outlets are supplied in the area. Seasonal beer is also brewed.

No. 7 Pale Ale (OG 1039.8, ABV 4.1%)

Bitter (ABV 5%)

London Porter (OG 1052, ABV 5.5%)

Devilfish SIBA

Devilfish Brewery Ltd, Highchurch Farm, Chickwell Lane, Hemington, Somerset, BA3 5XT
☎ 07725 983004 ⊠ info@devilfishbrewery.com
⊕ devilfishbrewery.com

Devilfish began brewing in 2011 using a 4.5-barrel plant. Seasonal and bottle-conditioned beers are also available.

Devil Best (ABV 4.2%)
A medium-bodied beer with a malty character and hoppy edge.

Bomb Shell (ABV 4.5%)
Silky with a slight lemony backdrop and zingy aftertaste. Light and refreshing.

Stingray (ABV 5.5%)
Full-flavoured, malty and fruity with strong aromas and a deep finish.

Devon Ales

⊟ Devon Ales Ltd, Mansfield Arms, 7 Main Street, Sauchie, Clackmannanshire, FK10 3JR
☎ (01259) 722020 ⊠ martingibson66@gmail.com
⊕ devonales.com
Tours by arrangement

☺Established in 1992 to produce high quality cask ales for the Mansfield Arms, Sauchie, Devon is the oldest operating brewery in the county. A second pub, The Inn at Muckhart, was purchased in 1994. The brewery also now sells beer to the open market.

Original (70/-) (OG 1038, ABV 3.8%)
A full-bodied session ale with a prominent malty flavour and distinct hoppiness.

Thick Black (OG 1042, ABV 4.2%)
A traditional Scottish stout.

Pride (OG 1046, ABV 4.8%)

A flavourful, full-bodied beer.

Devon Brewing (NEW)

Devon Brewing Co, Lower Yelland Farm, Yelland, Devon, EX31 3EN
☎ 07976 724243 ⊠ matt@devonbeer.co.uk
⊕ devonbeer.co.uk

Devon Brewing was established in 2011 supplying local pubs and beer festivals.

Pale Ale (ABV 4.2%)

Devon Earth SIBA

Devon Earth Brewery, Office: 7 Fernham Terrace, Torquay Road, Paignton, Devon, TQ3 2AQ
☎ 07927 397871 ⊠ info@devonearthbrewery.co.uk
⊕ devonearthbrewery.co.uk

⊠ Devon Earth was launched in 2008 on a 2.5-barrel plant located on the edge of Dartmoor (Buckfastleigh) and is run on a part-time basis. It supplies beer festivals and pubs, mainly in the Torbay area. As well as three regular ales, seasonal specials are also produced.

Devon Earth (ABV 4.2%)

Grounded (ABV 4.7%)

Lost in the Woods (ABV 5.2%)

Dickensian

Dickensian Brewery, Roden Lane, Roden, Shropshire, TF6 6BP ⊠ sales@dickensianbrewery.co.uk
⊕ dickensianbrewery.co.uk

Dickensian took on the brewery plant at the Dolphin Inn on a rental basis in 2011. In 2012 a new purpose-built brewhouse in Roden began brewing. No beer list was available at the time of going to print.

Digfield SIBA

Digfield Ales, Lilford Lodge Farm, Barnwell, PE8 5SA
☎ (01832) 273954 ⊠ brewery@digfield-ales.co.uk
⊕ digfield-ales.co.uk

Digfield Ales started brewing in 2005 on a five-barrel plant, which was later expanded to seven barrels. Increased demand led to a move to larger premises in 2012, still in the Barnwell area. A reed bed effluent system has been installed and brewing capacity increased to 15 barrels with new equipment. More than 40 free houses are supplied. Seasonal beers: see website.

Fool's Nook (OG 1037, ABV 3.8%) ◆
The floral aroma, dominated by lavender and honey, belies the hoppy bitterness that comes through in the taste of this golden ale. A fruity balance lasts.

Barnwell Bitter (OG 1039, ABV 4%) ◆
A fruity, sulphurous aroma introduces a beer in which sharp bitterness is balanced by dry, biscuity malt.

Shacklebush (OG 1044, ABV 4.5%) ◆
This amber brew begins with a balance of malt and sulphury hop on the nose that develops on the palate, complemented by a mounting bitterness. Good dry finish with lingering malt notes.

IPA (OG 1046, ABV 4.7%)

A strong flavoured pale ale with a hoppy aroma and a dry, lingering finish.

Mad Monk (OG 1047, ABV 4.8%) ◆
Fruity beer with bitter, earthy hops in evidence.

Doghouse (NEW)

Doghouse Brewery Ltd, Unit 7, The Paddocks, Jurby Industrial Estate, Jurby, Isle of Man, IM7 3BD
☎ (01624) 890039 ✉ doghousebrewery@manx.net

Brewing began in 2012 using a six-barrel plant originally owned by Freedom Brewery.

Bitter (OG 1036, ABV 3.7%)

IPA (OG 1039, ABV 4%)

Gold (OG 1042, ABV 4.3%)

Donnington IFBB

Donnington Brewery, Upper Swell, Stow-on-the-Wold, Gloucestershire, GL54 1EP
☎ (01451) 830603 ✉ info@donningtonales.com
⊕ donningtonales.com
Shop Mon-Fri 8am-3pm

Thomas Arkell bought a 13th-century watermill in 1827 and began brewing on the site in 1865; the waterwheel is still in use. Thomas' decendant Claude owned and ran the brewery until his death in 2007, supplying 20 outlets direct. It has now passed to Claude's cousin, James Arkell, also of Arkells Brewery, Swindon (qv). Bottle-conditioned beer is available.

BB (OG 1035, ABV 3.6%) ◆
A pleasant amber bitter with a slight hop aroma, a good balance of malt and hops in the mouth and a bitter aftertaste.

SBA (OG 1045, ABV 4.4%) ◆
Malt dominates over bitterness in the subtle flavour of this premium bitter, which has a hint of fruit and a dry malty finish.

Dorking SIBA

Brewery at Dorking Ltd, Engine Shed, Dorking West Station Yard, Station Road, Dorking, Surrey, RH4 1HF
☎ (01306) 877988 ✉ info@dorkingbrewery.com
⊕ dorkingbrewery.com
Tours by arrangement

Dorking started brewing in 2008 and supplies an increasing number of local pubs and clubs. Seasonal beers are available.

DB Gold (OG 1042, ABV 3.8%) ◆
A hoppy bitterness dominates this golden-coloured ale but balancing malt is also present. New Zealand hops result in a green hop character. Dry bitter finish.

DB Number One (OG 1045, ABV 4.2%) ◆
Hoppy best bitter with underlying orange fruit notes. Some balancing malt sweetness in the taste leads to a dry bitter finish.

Red India Ale (OG 1051, ABV 5%)
A strong, hoppy beer similar to an IPA. The colour of dark cherries, this beer has a fruity sweetness with a smooth, full-bodied taste.

Dorset SIBA 👁

Dorset Brewing Co Ltd (DBC), Unit 7, Hybris Business Park, Warmwell Road, Crossways, Dorchester, Dorset, DT2 8BF
☎ (01305) 777515 ✉ info@dbcales.com
⊕ dbcales.com
Tours by arrangement

The Dorset Brewing Company was founded in Hope Square, Weymouth, famous as the home of the Devenish and Groves breweries, where brewing has taken place since 1256. Originally called the Quay Brewery, it was situated in part of the old brewery buildings. In 2008 Dorset took over the running of Dorchester's brewpub, Tom Brown's (Goldfinch Brewery). In 2010 the brewery moved to purpose-built premises near Dorchester with new state of the art brewing equipment. Beers are available in local pubs and selected outlets in the south-west. Seasonal beers: see website.

Weymouth Harbour Master (OG 1036, ABV 3.6%) ◆
Light, easy-drinking session beer. Well-balanced, with a long, bittersweet, citrus finish.

Goldfinch Tom Brown's (OG 1039, ABV 4%)
A pale-coloured bitter with a fruity nose. The taste is bittersweet with malt, fruit and some hop. Complex aftertaste.

Weymouth Best Bitter (OG 1038, ABV 4%) ◆
Complex bitter ale with strong malt and fruit flavours despite its light gravity.

Jurassic (OG 1040, ABV 4.2%) ◆
Clean-tasting, easy-drinking bitter. Well balanced with lingering bitterness after moderate sweetness.

Ammonite (OG 1043, ABV 4.5%)
A fruity, copper-coloured beer with a long, fruity finish.

Yachtsman (OG 1048, ABV 4.7%)
A pale golden bitter beer with hints of vanilla and honey in the aroma and aftertaste.

Durdle Door (OG 1046, ABV 5%) ◆
A tawny hue and fruity aroma with a hint of pear drops and good malty undertone, joined by hops and a little roast malt in the taste. Lingering bittersweet finish.

Dorset Piddle SIBA 👁

Dorset Piddle Brewery Ltd, 24 Enterprise Park, Piddlehinton, Dorset, DT2 7UA
☎ (01305) 849336
✉ vic@dorsetpiddlebrewery.co.uk
⊕ dorsetpiddlebrewery.co.uk
Tours by arrangement

Dorset Piddle began brewing in late 2007 on an eight-barrel plant. In 2011 the brewery moved to larger adjacent premises. It currently brews on an eight-barrel plant with plans to expand further. Seasonal beers are also available.

Jimmy Riddle (OG 1040, ABV 3.7%) ◆
Pale brown session beer with a good depth of malty flavours for its strength.

Piddle (OG 1041, ABV 4.1%) ◆
An enjoyable, well-balanced bitter with a lingering bitter finish.

Yogi (OG 1051, ABV 4.9%)

Smooth with a hint of red, an easy-drinking beer with a rounded fruitiness giving way to a hint of blackcurrant, liquorice and toffee.

Silent Slasher (OG 1051, ABV 5.1%)
Blonde continental-style beer. Light with a floral aroma and flavour and a refreshing dry bitter finish.

Little Willy (OG 1060, ABV 5.9%)

Double Top SIBA

Double Top Brewery, Unit 4, Kilton Terrace, Worksop, Nottinghamshire, S80 2DQ
☎ 07973 521824
Tours by arrangement

☺Double Top began brewing in 2011 on a 100-litre brew kit. This was replaced in 2012 with a 2.5 barrel plant. It caters for its brewery tap, the Mallard, on platform 1 of Worksop railway station plus regional beer festivals and local free houses. There are plans for further expansion.

Shanghai Bitter (OG 1041, ABV 4.2%)

Tungsten (OG 1044, ABV 4.5%)

Serendipity (OG 1046, ABV 4.6%)

Dove Street

Dove Street Brewery Ltd, 82 St Helens Street, Ipswich, Suffolk, IP4 2LB
☎ (01473) 211270 ☎ 07880 707077
⊕ dovestreetbrewery.co.uk
Shop 12-10pm daily
Tours by arrangement

⊗ Dove Street began brewing in 2011 using a 2.5-barrel plant in a garage opposite the Dove Street Inn. The pub and beer festivals are supplied.

Underwood Mild (ABV 3.2%)

DSB (Dove Street Bitter) (ABV 3.7%)

ITFC (ABV 4.1%)

Thirsty Walker (ABV 4.6%)

OIL (Old Ipswich Liquor) (ABV 5.5%)

Dow Bridge SIBA ◉

Dow Bridge Brewery, 2-3 Rugby Road, Catthorpe, Leicestershire, LE17 6DA
☎ (01788) 869121
⊠ dowbridge.brewery@virgin.net
⊕ dowbridgebrewery.co.uk
Tours by arrangement

Dow Bridge commenced brewing in 2001 and takes its name from a local bridge where Watling Street spans the River Avon. The brewery uses English whole hops and malt with no adjuncts or additives. It expanded in 2006 but is looking to relocate as extra capacity is needed. Over 50 outlets are supplied direct. Seasonal and bottle-conditioned beers are also available.

Bonum Mild (OG 1035, ABV 3.5%) ◄
Complex dark brown, full-flavoured mild, with strong malt and roast flavours to the fore and continuing into the aftertaste, leading to a long, satisfying finish.

Acris (OG 1037, ABV 3.8%)

Legion (OG 1038, ABV 3.9%)

Centurion (OG 1039, ABV 4%)

Ratae'd (OG 1041, ABV 4.3%) ◄
Tawny-coloured, bitter beer in which bitter and hop flavours dominate, to the detriment of balance, leading to a long, bitter and astringent aftertaste.

Dow Bridge Dark (DBD) (OG 1042, ABV 4.4%)

Decimus (OG 1046, ABV 4.6%)

Fosse Ale (OG 1046, ABV 4.8%)

Praetorian Porter (OG 1048, ABV 5%) ⌑

Downton SIBA

Downton Brewery Co Ltd, Unit 11, Batten Road, Downton Industrial Estate, Downton, Wiltshire, SP5 3HU
☎ (01725) 513313 ⊠ sales@downtonbrewery.com
⊕ downtonbrewery.com
Shop Mon-Fri 9am-5pm

⊗ Downton was set up in 2003 with equipment leased from the Hop Back Brewery (qv). The brewery has a 20-barrel brew length and three fermenting vessels producing around 1500 barrels a year. Speciality and experimental beers are available as monthly and seasonal offerings alongside six regular beers. Around 100 outlets are supplied direct. Bottle-conditioned beers are also available.

New Forest Ale (OG 1037, ABV 3.8%)

Quadhop (OG 1038, ABV 3.9%)

Elderquad (OG 1039, ABV 4%)

Honey Blonde (OG 1041, ABV 4.3%)

Dark Delight (OG 1053, ABV 5.5%)

IPA (OG 1063, ABV 6.8%)

Draycott EAB

Draycott Brewery, Low Farm, 30 Mill Road, Buckden, Cambridgeshire, PE19 5SS
☎ (01480) 812404 ☎ 07740 374710
⊠ sales@draycottbrewery.co.uk
⊕ draycottbrewery.co.uk

The brewery is in an old farm complex and was set up in 2009 by Jon and Jane Draycott. Only bottle-conditioned beers are produced. These are available in the local area and in a shop catering to holiday makers at Dunster Beach in Somerset.

Driftwood

⊟ Driftwood Brewery, Driftwood Spars Hotel, Trevaunance Cove, St Agnes, Cornwall, TR5 0RT
☎ (01872) 552428 ⊠ driftwoodspars@hotmail.com
⊕ driftwoodspars.com
Shop 10am-5pm daily (Apr-Oct); Sat & Sun 10am-5pm (Oct-Mar)
Tours by arrangement

⊗ Brewing commenced in 2000 in the famous 17th-century pub, Driftwood Spars. The brewery, a custom built five-barrel plant, is located across from the pub. The brews continuously rotate through the range and are available mainly at the Driftwood Spars but are also supplied to other outlets. The full range of bottle-conditioned beers is available in the adjacent brewery shop along with other local bottled ales and produce.

Blackheads Mild (OG 1037, ABV 3.8%) ▨ ◄

Initial burst of cherry, damson and liquorice in the mouth following a brief roast malt and fruit aroma. Malt and sweet caramel run throughout with faint bitterness and dryness at the end.

Dek (OG 1038, ABV 3.8%) ◀
Fruity, grassy hops on the nose lead to bitter, resinous, citrus hops and pronounced dryness in the mouth all the way through. Amber beer in the golden ale style.

Trouble & Strife (OG 1036, ABV 3.8%) ◀
Light-drinking amber session bitter with aroma of hop fruit. Fuggles and Goldings hops provide a dominant bitter flavour balanced by gentle sweetness, hop fruit, malt and astringency.

Blue Hills Bitter (OG 1039, ABV 4%) ◀
Medium-bodied, refreshing amber bitter, with a light, hoppy aroma. Hops dominate the flavour with gentle biscuity malt and a trace of fresh grass. The long finish is bittersweet, malty and dry.

Red Mission (OG 1040, ABV 4%) ◀
Tawny best bitter with fruity hops and light malt on the nose. Malt and hops create a balanced taste with bitterness running through to a dry, hoppy finish.

Montol (OG 1040, ABV 4.1%)
A copper-coloured beer with a rich malt base with hints of chocolate. A strong citrus hop bite and aroma.

Badlands Bitter (OG 1047, ABV 4.8%)
A strong, malty bitter.

Lou's Brew (OG 1049, ABV 5%) ◀
Light aroma of apples and pears. Moderate fruity and hoppy bitterness with a trace of malt in this golden ale. Bitterness and hops persist in the long finish.

Alfie's Revenge (OG 1060, ABV 6.5%) ◀
Rich Old Ale, smooth and clean tasting. Roasted malt aroma leads into smoky malt, coffee and sweet fudge. Fruit esters and bitter hops run through into a long finish. Champion Winter Beer of Britain 2012.

DT

DT Ales, Royal Standard, 700 Dorchester Road, Upwey, Dorset, DT3 5LA
☎ (01305) 812558
✉ info@theroyalstandardupwey.co.uk
⊕ theroyalstandardupwey.co.uk

Brewing began in 2010 using a one-barrel plant.

3 (ABV 3.5%)

4 (ABV 4.5%)

Dunham Massey

Dunham Massey Brewing Co, 100 Oldfield Lane, Dunham Massey, WA14 4PE
☎ (0161) 929 0663
✉ info@dunhammasseybrewing.co.uk
⊕ dunhammasseybrewing.co.uk
Shop Mon-Fri 10am-5pm; Sat-Sun 11am-4pm

☺Dunham Massey commenced in 2007, brewing traditional North-western ales using only English ingredients and no added sugars. The beer range is also available bottle conditioned, which is suitable for vegetarians and vegans. A brewery tap, Costello's Bar in Altrincham, opened recently.

Around 30 outlets are supplied direct. Seasonal beers are available.

Little Bollington Bitter (OG 1037, ABV 3.7%)
A pale, light, easy-drinking bitter.

Chocolate Cherry Mild (OG 1040, ABV 3.8%)
A blend of dark chocolate, coffee and liquorice flavours of a dark mild with dry, bittersweet cherry flavours.

Dunham Dark (OG 1040, ABV 3.8%)
A smooth, easy-drinking dark mild.

Dunham Light (OG 1040, ABV 3.8%)
A creamy, malty, easy-drinking light mild.

Big Tree Bitter (OG 1040, ABV 3.9%)
Golden bitter, full-bodied with a good balance of hops and malt.

Obelisk (OG 1040, ABV 3.9%)
Light and hoppy but not bitter. Hints of citrus and grapefruit on the hop.

Dunham Milk Stout (OG 1051, ABV 4%)
A classic, full-bodied sweet stout with a creamy, roast malt character.

Dunham Stout (OG 1046, ABV 4.2%)
A creamy, full-bodied English dry stout with a classic bitter, burnt, dark roast flavour.

Stamford Bitter (OG 1045, ABV 4.2%)
A golden, full-bodied bitter with a complex blend of hops with a slightly dry finish.

Deer Beer (OG 1047, ABV 4.5%)
A strong, malty bitter; clean and full-bodied with a slight hint of toffee.

Cheshire IPA (OG 1047, ABV 4.7%)
A strong, pale, hoppy beer.

Altrincham Pilsner (OG 1048, ABV 4.8%)
A real lager. Light, refreshing and full of flavour.

Dunham Porter (OG 1056, ABV 5.2%)
A classic old-style English porter; creamy, full-bodied and packed with flavour.

East India Pale Ale (OG 1062, ABV 6%)
A strong, light, hoppy, bitter ale.

Dunham Gold (OG 1070, ABV 7.2%)
Belgium-style English ale. Strong, light and fruity with a hoppy finish.

Dunscar Bridge SIBA

Dunscar Bridge Brewing Co, The Brewery, Dunscar Business Park, Blackburn Road, Bolton, BL7 9PQ
☎ (01204) 600713
✉ hello@dunscarbridgebrewery.co.uk
⊕ dunscarbridgebrewery.co.uk
Tours by arrangement

☺Dunscar Bridge began brewing in 2009 on a four-barrel plant, visible to customers behind a large glazed panel. Beer is available at the Brewhouse and the Thomas Egerton in Bolton as well as many other local pubs both in Bolton and the surrounding areas. The brewery has recently been refurbished and expanded to a 25-barrel plant.

Bombshell (ABV 3.7%)
A light blonde beer with a citrus taste.

Steeplejack (ABV 3.8%)
A light golden ale with a fruity/hoppy taste.

Rialto 47 (ABV 3.9%)

Golden beer brewed with US hops. Grapefruit and orange taste.

Wicketkeeper (ABV 4%)
Amber best bitter. Well-balanced and moreish.

Lofthouse (ABV 4.1%)
Golden, smooth and well-balanced ale with subtle orange and floral notes.

Clockin Off (ABV 4.2%)
Golden-coloured beer with malt/vanilla flavours and a bitter aftertaste.

Lion of Vienna (ABV 4.4%)
Mahogany-coloured with a full-flavoured taste.

Durham SIBA

Durham Brewery Ltd, Unit 6a, Bowburn North Industrial Estate, Bowburn, Co Durham, DH6 5PF
☎ (0191) 377 1991 ✉ steve@durham-brewery.co.uk
⊕ durhambrewery.co.uk
Shop Mon-Fri 8am-4pm; Sat 10am-2pm
Tours by arrangement

☺Established in 1994, Durham now has a portfolio of around 40 beers. These are not all available as regular beers – please see website for full list. A shop and visitor centre is available for tours and tastings every Saturday. Bottles and five litre mini-casks can be purchased and an own label/special message service is available. Seasonal beers are brewed. Bottle-conditioned beers are also available and suitable for vegans.

Magus (OG 1036, ABV 3.8%) ◀
Pale malt gives this brew its straw colour but the hops define its character, with a fruity aroma, a clean bitter mouthfeel, and a lingering dry, citrus-like finish.

White Amarillo (ABV 4.1%)

Earl Soham SIBA

Earl Soham Brewery, The Street, Earl Soham, Suffolk, IP13 7RT
☎ (01728) 684097 ✉ info@earlsohambrewery.co.uk
⊕ earlsohambrewery.co.uk
Shop Mon-Thu 8.30am-5pm; Fri 8.30am-6pm; Sat 9am-4.30pm; closed Sun
Tours by arrangement

Earl Soham was set up behind the Victoria pub in 1984 and continued there until 2001 when the brewery moved 100 yards down the road. The Victoria and the Station in Framlingham both sell the beers on a regular basis, as does the Brewery Tap in Ipswich. When there is spare stock, beer is supplied to local free houses and as many beer festivals as possible. 30 outlets are supplied and three pubs are owned. Seasonal beer is also brewed. Most of the beers are bottle conditioned for the shop next door and other selected outlets.

Gannet Mild (OG 1034, ABV 3.3%) ◀
A beautifully balanced mild, sweet and fruity flavour with a lingering, coffee aftertaste.

Victoria Bitter (OG 1037, ABV 3.6%) ◀
A light, fruity, amber session beer with a clean taste and a long, lingering hoppy aftertaste.

Sir Roger's Porter (OG 1042, ABV 4.2%) ◀
Roast/coffee aroma and berry fruit introduce a full-bodied porter with roast/coffee flavours. Dry roast finish.

Albert Ale (OG 1045, ABV 4.4%)

Hops dominate every aspect of this beer, but especially the finish. A fruity, astringent beer.

Brandeston Gold (OG 1045, ABV 4.5%) ◀
Beer brewed with local ingredients. Lovely sharp, clean flavour, malty/hoppy and heavily laden with citrus fruit. Malty finish.

For Cliff Quay Brewery:

Bitter (OG 1035, ABV 3.4%) ◀
Well-balanced malty sweet bitter with a hint of caramel, followed by a sweet/malty aftertaste. A good flavour for such a low gravity beer.

East Coast SIBA

East Coast Brewing Co, 3 Clay House Yard, Rear of Mitford Street, Filey, North Yorkshire, YO14 9DX
☎ (01723) 514865
✉ eastcoastbrewing@hotmail.co.uk
⊕ eastcoastbrewingcompany.co.uk
Tours by arrangement

⊠ The brewery is housed in a converted stable and coach house. Six regular beers are produced plus at least one special per month. 20 outlets are supplied direct.

Bonhomme Richard (ABV 3.7%)

Mary Rose (ABV 3.8%)

Tucks Tipple (ABV 4.1%)

John Paul Jones (ABV 4.3%)

Alfred Moodies Mild (ABV 6%)

Empress of India (ABV 6%)

East London (NEW) SIBA

East London Brewing Co, Unit 45, Fairways Business Centre, Lammas Road, London, E10 7QB
☎ 07900 288873 ✉ stu@eastlondonbrewing.com
⊕ eastlondonbrewing.com

East London began brewing in 2011 using a 10-barrel plant.

Pale Ale (OG 1042, ABV 4%) ◀
Dark gold beer with a fruity aroma and a slightly orange marmalade character in the flavour. Lingering bitter finish.

Foundation Bitter (OG 1044, ABV 4.2%) ◀
A hoppy brown best bitter with pronounced bitterness. It is balanced by a little maltiness and a touch of blackcurrant.

Nightwatchman (OG 1046, ABV 4.5%)
A well-hopped beer with a smooth mouthfeel.

Eastwood

Eastwood the Brewer, Barge & Barrel, 10-12 Park Road, Elland, West Yorkshire, HX5 9HP
☎ 07949 148476 ✉ taggartkeith@yahoo.co.uk
Tours by arrangement

☺The brewery was founded by John Eastwood at the Barge & Barrel pub. 50-70 outlets are supplied direct. Seasonal beers are also available.

Stirling (ABV 3.8%)
An amber-coloured session beer with a pleasant, long-lasting, fruity finish.

Best Bitter (ABV 4%) ◀
Creamy, yellow, hoppy bitter with hints of citrus fruits. Pleasantly strong bitter aftertaste.

Gold Award (ABV 4.4%) ◄
Complex copper-coloured beer with malt, roast and caramel flavours. It has a hoppy and bitter aftertaste.

Black Prince (ABV 5%)
A distinctive strong black porter with a blend of pale and chocolate malts and roasted barley.

Eccleshall

See Slater's

Eden (NEW) SIBA

Eden Brewery Ltd, Brougham Hall, Brougham, Cumbria, CA10 2DE
☎ (01768) 210565 ☎ 07729 677692
✉ info@edenbrewery.com ⊕ edenbrewery.com

Eden began brewing in 2012 and was set up by enthusiastic home brewers Jason Hill and Stephen Mitchell using a five-barrel brewery located at the Old Brewery at Brougham Hall (previously used by Tirril Brewery).

Best (ABV 3.8%)

Gold (OG 1042, ABV 4.2%)

Edge

See Franklin's

Edinburgh

See Greene King in New Nationals section

Elgood's SIBA IFBB ◉

Elgood & Sons Ltd, North Brink Brewery, Wisbech, Cambridgeshire, PE13 1LW
☎ (01945) 583160 ✉ info@elgoods-brewery.co.uk
⊕ elgoods-brewery.co.uk
Shop Tue-Thu 11.30am-4.30pm (May-Sep)
Tours by arrangement

⊠ The North Brink Brewery was established in 1795 and was one of the first classic Georgian breweries to be built outside London. In 1878 it came under the control of the Elgood family and is still run today as one of the few remaining independent family breweries, with the fifth generation of the family now helping to run the company. The beers go to 42 Elgood's pubs within a 50-mile radius of Wisbech and free trade outlets throughout East Anglia, while wholesalers distribute nationally. Elgood's has a visitor centre, offering a tour of the brewery and the gardens. Seasonal beers: see website.

Black Dog (OG 1036.8, ABV 3.6%) ◄
A black-red mild that comprises a blend of malt, roast and caramel throughout. Pleasantly bittersweet on the palate, it concludes with a roast malt bitterness.

Cambridge Bitter (OG 1037.8, ABV 3.8%) 🗂 ◄
An archetypal English bitter. Excellent malt character all the way through with a good balance of hops and fruit to complement. Some caramel notes. Bittersweet aftertaste.

Golden Newt (OG 1041.5, ABV 4.1%) ◄

Golden ale with floral hops and sulphur aroma. Floral hops and a fruity presence on a bittersweet background lead to a short, muted hoppy and fruity finish.

Pageant Ale (OG 1043.8, ABV 4.3%)
A premium ale with an aroma of hops and malt giving a well-balanced bittersweet flavour and a satisfying finish.

Elland SIBA ◉

Elland Brewery Ltd, Units 3-5, Heathfield Industrial Estate, Heathfield Street, Elland, West Yorkshire, HX5 9AE
☎ (01422) 377677 ✉ brewery@ellandbrewery.co.uk
⊕ ellandbrewery.co.uk
Tours by arrangement

☺The brewery was originally formed as Eastwood & Sanders in 2002 by the amalgamation of the Barge & Barrel Brewery and West Yorkshire Brewery. The company was renamed Elland in 2006 to reinforce its links with the town. The brewery has a capacity to brew 50 barrels a week and supplies more than 150 outlets. In addition to the six regular beers there are at least four seasonal specials and a Head Brewer's Reserve available every month. Bottle-conditioned beers are also available.

Bargee (OG 1038, ABV 3.8%) 🗂 ◄
Amber, creamy session bitter. Fruity, hoppy aroma and taste complemented by a bitter edge in the finish.

Best Bitter (OG 1041, ABV 4%) ◄
Creamy, yellow, hoppy ale with hints of citrus fruits. Pleasantly strong bitter aftertaste.

Beyond the Pale (OG 1042, ABV 4.2%) ◄
Gold-coloured, robust, creamy beer with ripe aromas of hops and fruit. Bitterness predominates in the mouth and leads to a dry, fruity and hoppy aftertaste.

Eden (OG 1042, ABV 4.2%) ◄
A yellow, fruity, hoppy, creamy bitter. Citrus fruit with assertively bitter taste to finish.

Nettlethrasher (OG 1044, ABV 4.4%) ◄
Grainy amber-coloured beer. A rounded nose with some fragrant hops notes followed by a mellow nutty and fruity taste and a dry finish.

1872 Porter (OG 1065, ABV 6.5%) 🗂 ◄
Creamy, full-flavoured porter. Rich liquorice flavours with a hint of chocolate from roast malt. A soft but satisfying aftertaste of bittersweet roast and malt.

Elmtree SIBA EAB

Elmtree Beers, Snetterton Brewery, Unit 10, Oakwood Industrial Estate, Harling Road, Snetterton, Norfolk, NR16 2JU
☎ (01953) 887065 ✉ sales@elmtreebeers.co.uk
⊕ elmtreebeers.co.uk
Shop Mon-Wed & Sat 11am-4pm

⊠ Elmtree was established in 2007 using a five-barrel plant and moved in 2008 to new premises. 120 outlets are supplied direct. Bottle-conditioned beers are available and are suitable for vegetarians and vegans.

Burston's Cuckoo (OG 1038, ABV 3.8%)

An aroma of floral hops with a hint of citrus rounding off into a long, dry finish.

Bitter (OG 1041, ABV 4.2%)
A well-balanced, copper-coloured crisp beer. The early malt notes give way to a complex hop finish.

Dark Horse (OG 1048, ABV 5%) ◄
A roast, slightly salty aroma and matching initial taste introduce this coal black stout. The roast notes are aided by a fruity, prune-like background. Increasingly malty finish.

Golden Pale Ale (OG 1048, ABV 5%)
A pale ale in the traditional style that is initially malty and delicately bittered. The long, dry biscuit finish is enhanced by subtle citrus aromas.

Nightlight Mild (OG 1057, ABV 5.7%) ◄
A heavy mix of liquorice, roast and malt infuses aroma and taste. The heavy character is lightened by a sweet, spicy, slowly-developing aftertaste.

Elveden EAB

Elveden Ales, The Courtyard, Elveden Estate, Elveden, Thetford, Norfolk, IP24 3TA
☎ (01842) 878922

Elveden is a five-barrel brewery based on the estate of Lord Iveagh, a member of the ennobled branch of the Guinness family. The brewery is run by Frances Moore, daughter of Brendan Moore at Iceni Brewery (qv) and produces three ales: Elveden Stout (ABV 5%) and Elveden Ale (ABV 5.2%), which are mainly bottled in stoneware bottles. The third is Charter Ale (ABV 10%) to mark the celebrations for the award of a Royal Charter for Harwich in 1604. The beer is available in cask and bottle-conditioned versions. The phone number listed is shared with Iceni. The majority of sales take place through the farm shop, adjacent to the brewery. During 2007 the brewery building was restored as part of the development of the outbuilding of the Elveden estate as a tourist attraction. The visitor centre re-opened in 2008, giving regular tours – please phone for details.

Empire SIBA

Empire Brewing, The Old Boiler House, Unit 33, Upper Mills, Slaithwaite, Huddersfield, West Yorkshire, HD7 5HA
☎ (01484) 847343 ☎ 07966 592276
⊕ empirebrewing.com
Tours by arrangement

☺Empire Brewing was set up 2006 in a mill on the bank of the scenic Huddersfield Narrow Canal, close to the centre of Slaithwaite. In 2011 the brewery upgraded from a five-barrel to a 10-barrel plant. Beers are supplied to local free houses and through independent specialist beer agencies and wholesalers. Seasonal and bottle-conditioned beers are also available

Golden Warrior (OG 1039.5, ABV 3.8%)
Pale bitter, quite fruity with a sherbet aftertaste, moderate bitterness.

Strikes Back (OG 1041, ABV 4%)
Pale golden bitter with a hoppy aroma and good hop and malt balance with a citrus flavour, very light on the palate. Good session beer.

Valour (OG 1042.5, ABV 4.2%)

Imperium (OG 1050, ABV 5.1%)

Emsworth (NEW)

Emsworth Brewery, rear of 16 West Street, Emsworth, Hampshire, PO10 7DY
☎ 07717 510294 ✉ room_101@messages.co.uk

Michael and Hilary Bolt began brewing in 2012 on a 2.5-barrel plant in a shed behind an antiques shop in Emsworth. Seasonal beer is also available.

Slipper (ABV 3.9%)

Wayfarer (ABV 3.9%)

Fairfield (ABV 4.1%)

Ennerdale SIBA

Ennerdale Brewery Ltd, The Brewery, Croasdale Farm, Ennerdale, Cleator, Cumbria, CA23 3AT
☎ (01946) 861755 ☎ 07918 626652
✉ info@ennerdalebrewery.co.uk
⊕ ennerdalebrewery.co.uk
Tours by arrangement

☺Ennerdale first brewed in 2010 using a 10-barrel plant following a split in the ownership of Whitehaven Brewing Co Ltd (established 2007).

Blonde (OG 1039, ABV 3.8%)

Copper (ABV 3.8%)

Liquidator (OG 1039, ABV 3.9%)

Darkest Ennerdale (OG 1044, ABV 4.2%)

Enville SIBA

Enville Ales Ltd, Enville Brewery, Coxgreen, Hollies Lane, Enville, Stourbridge, West Midlands, DY7 5LG
☎ (01384) 873728 ✉ info@envilleales.com
⊕ envilleales.com
Tours by arrangement for groups of 12-20 (evenings or weekends)

Enville Brewery is sited on a picturesque Victorian, Grade II-listed farm complex, using natural well water, traditional steam brewing and a reed and willow effluent plant. Enville Ale is infused with honey and is from a 19th-century recipe for beekeeper's ale passed down from the former proprietor's great-great aunt. Seasonal beers: see website.

LPA (Light Pale Ale) (OG 1039, ABV 4%)
Traditional session bitter; dry and golden with a mellow, hoppy flavour.

Nailmaker Mild (OG 1041, ABV 4%)
A well-defined hop aroma and underlying sweetness give way to a dry finish.

Simpkiss Bitter (OG 1040, ABV 4%)

Cherry Blonde (OG 1042, ABV 4.2%)
A light blonde bitter infused with essence of cherry to produce a Belgian-style fruit flavoured beer. The bitter finish is dry, hoppy and refreshing.

Saaz (OG 1042, ABV 4.2%) ◄
Golden lager-style beer. Lager bite but with more taste and lasting bitterness. The malty aroma is late arriving but the bitter finish, balanced by fruit and hops, compensates.

White (OG 1041, ABV 4.2%) ◄
Yellow with a malt, hops and fruit aroma. Hoppy but sweet finish.

Ale (OG 1044, ABV 4.5%) ◄
Sweet malty aroma and taste, honey becomes apparent before bitterness finally dominates.

Old Porter (OG 1044, ABV 4.5%) ◆
Black with a creamy head and sulphurous aroma. Sweet and fruity start with touches of spice. Good balance between sweet and bitter, but hops dominate the finish.

Ginger (OG 1045, ABV 4.6%) ◆
Golden bright with gently gingered tangs. A drinkable beer with no acute flavours but a satisfying aftertaste of sweet hoppiness.

Gothic (OG 1051, ABV 5.2%)
A black beer with lurking hints of honey adding to the roundness of the flavour.

Epping

See Pitfield

Evan Evans SIBA

Evan Evans Brewery, The New Brewery, 1 Rhosmaen Street, Llandeilo, Carmarthenshire, SA19 6LU
☎ (01558) 824455 ✉ company@evan-evans.com
⊕ evan-evans.com
Shop Mon-Fri 10am-4pm
Tours by arrangement

☺Evan Evans opened in 2004 with a brand new Canadian brewing plant. Additional fermenting capacity was added in 2009, taking brewing capacity to 8,000 barrels per annum. Eight pubs are owned. It is Wales' first Soil Association organic-approved brewery. A large range of seasonal ales is available. In 2009 the brewery bought Archers Brewery of Swindon's brands and now brew all of Archers' regular and seasonal ales.

BB/Best Bitter (OG 1038, ABV 3.8%)
An easy-drinking best bitter. Malty with a clean hop palate.

Cwrw (OG 1043, ABV 4.2%)

Warrior (OG 1046, ABV 4.6%)

Under Archers Brewery name:

Village (ABV 3.6%)

Best Bitter (ABV 4%)

Golden (ABV 4.7%)

Everards SIBA IFBB ◉

Everards Brewery Ltd, Castle Acres, Narborough, Leicestershire, LE19 1BY
☎ (0116) 201 4100 ✉ mail@everards.co.uk
⊕ everards.co.uk
Shop Mon-Fri 10am-5pm; Sat 10am-2pm
Tours by arrangement for parties of 8-12

Established by William Everard in 1849, Everards brewery remains an independent family-owned brewery. Four core ales are brewed as well as a range of seasonal beers – see website for more details. Everards owns a pub estate of more than 170 tenanted houses throughout the Midlands.

Beacon Bitter (OG 1036, ABV 3.8%) ◆
Light, refreshing, well-balanced pale amber bitter in the Burton style.

Sunchaser Blonde (OG 1038, ABV 4%) ◆
A golden brew with a sweet, lightly-hopped character. Some citrus notes to the fore in a quick finish that becomes increasingly bitter.

Tiger Best Bitter (OG 1041, ABV 4.2%) ◆

A mid-brown, well-balanced best bitter crafted for broad appeal, benefiting from a long, bittersweet finish.

Original (OG 1050, ABV 5.2%) ◆
Full-bodied, mid-brown strong bitter with a pleasant rich, grainy mouthfeel. Well-balanced flavours, with malt slightly to the fore, merging into a long, satisfying finish.

Exeter SIBA

Exeter Brewery Ltd, 5-6 Lions Rest, Station Road, Exminster, Exeter, Devon, EX6 8DZ
☎ (01392) 823013 ✉ sales@exeterbrewery.co.uk
⊕ exeterbrewery.co.uk

The Exeter Brewery, formerly named the Topsham & Exminster, remains on the same site amid the beautiful Exminster marshes, where it has brewed since 2003. The brewery has been completely refurbished and re-equipped, providing much greater production capacity and enabling a greater range of ales.

Avocet (OG 1038.5, ABV 3.9%)
An organic beer.

Fraid Not (OG 1040, ABV 4%)
A golden, hoppy beer.

Ferryman (OG 1041, ABV 4.2%)

County Best (OG 1045, ABV 4.6%)

Exe Valley SIBA ◉

Exe Valley Brewery, Land Farm, Silverton, Exeter, Devon, EX5 4HF
☎ (01392) 860406 ✉ info@exevalleybrewery.co.uk
⊕ exevalleybrewery.co.uk
Tours for groups by arrangement (charge made)

Exe Valley was established as Barron's Brewery in 1984. The brewery is located in a converted barn overlooking the Exe Valley and Dartmoor hills. Locally sourced malt and English hops are used, along with the brewery's own spring water. Around 100 outlets are supplied within a 45-mile radius of the brewery. Beers are also available nationally via wholesalers. Seasonal beers: see website.

Bitter (OG 1036, ABV 3.7%) ◆
Mid-brown bitter, pleasantly fruity with underlying malt through the aroma, taste and finish.

Barron's Hopsit (OG 1040, ABV 4.1%) ◆
Straw-coloured beer with strong hop aroma, hop and fruit flavour and a bitter hop finish.

Dob's Best Bitter (OG 1040, ABV 4.1%) ◆
Light brown bitter. Malt and fruit predominate in the aroma and taste with a dry, bitter, fruity finish.

Devon Glory (OG 1046, ABV 4.7%)
Mid-brown, fruity-tasting pint with a sweet, fruity finish.

Mr Sheppard's Crook (OG 1046, ABV 4.7%) ◆
Smooth, full-bodied, mid brown beer with a malty-fruit nose and a sweetish palate leading to a bitter, dry finish.

Exmoor SIBA ◉

Exmoor Ales Ltd, Golden Hill Brewery, Wiveliscombe, Somerset, TA4 2NY

☎ (01984) 623798 ⊠ info@exmoorales.co.uk
⊕ exmoorales.co.uk
Tours by arrangement

Somerset's largest brewery was founded in 1980 in the old Hancock's brewery, which closed in 1959. Around 250 outlets in the South-west are supplied and others nationwide via wholesalers and pub chains. Seasonal beers: see website.

Ale (OG 1039, ABV 3.8%) ◄
A pale to mid-brown, medium-bodied session bitter. A mixture of malt and hops in the aroma and taste lead to a hoppy, bitter aftertaste.

Fox (OG 1043, ABV 4.2%)
A mid-brown beer; the slight maltiness on the tongue is followed by a burst of hops with a lingering bittersweet aftertaste.

Gold (OG 1045, ABV 4.5%) ◄
A yellow/golden best bitter with a good balance of malt and fruity hop on the nose and the palate. The sweetness follows through an ultimately more bitter finish.

Stag (OG 1050, ABV 5.2%) ◄
A pale brown beer, with a malty taste and aroma, and a bitter finish.

Beast (OG 1066, ABV 6.6%) ⑤
A dark beer brewed with chocolate and crystal malts.

Facer's

Facer's Flintshire Brewery, A8-9, Ashmount Enterprise Park, Aber Road, Flint, North Wales, CH6 5YL
☎ 07713 566370 ⊠ dave@facers.co.uk
⊕ facers.co.uk
Tours by arrangement for CAMRA groups only

Bragdy Sir y Fflint Facer's (Facer's Flintshire Brewery) is the oldest existing brewery in Flintshire, having moved west from Salford in 2006. Ex-Boddington's head brewer Dave Facer ran the brewery single-handed from its launch in 2003 until 2007, when the first employee was recruited. The brewery was expanded to twice the floor space in early 2008. Around 70 outlets are supplied.

Clwyd Gold (OG 1034, ABV 3.5%) ◄
Clean tasting session bitter, mid-brown in colour with a full mouthfeel. The malty flavours are accompanied by increasing hoppiness in the bitter finish.

Flintshire Bitter (OG 1036, ABV 3.7%) ◄
Well-balanced session bitter with a full mouthfeel. Some fruitiness in aroma and taste with increasing hoppy bitterness in the dry finish.

North Star Porter (OG 1040, ABV 4%) ◄
Dark, smooth, porter-style beer with good roast notes and hints of coffee and chocolate. Some initial sweetness and caramel flavours followed by a hoppy bitter aftertaste.

Sunny Bitter (OG 1040, ABV 4.2%) ◄
An amber beer with a dry taste. The hop aroma continues into the taste where some faint fruit notes are also present. Lasting dry finish.

DHB (Dave's Hoppy Beer)
(OG 1041, ABV 4.3%) ⑤ ◄
A dry-hopped version of Splendid Ale with some sweet flavours also coming through in the mainly hoppy, bitter taste.

This Splendid Ale (OG 1041, ABV 4.3%) ◄
Refreshing tangy best bitter, yellow in colour with a sharp hoppy, bitter taste. Good citrus fruit undertones with hints of grapefruit throughout.

Landslide (OG 1047, ABV 4.9%) ◄
Full-flavoured, complex premium bitter with tangy orange marmalade fruitiness in aroma and taste. Long-lasting hoppy flavours throughout.

Fach

See Celt Experience

Fakir (NEW)

Fakir Brewing Co Ltd, c/o 30 Harford Street, Norwich, NR1 3AY
☎ 07713 789085 ⊠ info@fakirbrewery.com
⊕ fakirbrewery.com

Fakir began brewing in 2010 using spare capacity at several breweries based in Norfolk. Bottle-conditioned beer is also available. Further beers are planned.

Old Fakir's Gold (ABV 5%)

Fallen Angel

Fallen Angel Microbrewery Ltd, 14 Carriers Way, East Hoathly, East Sussex, BN8 6AG
☎ (01825) 841307
⊠ sales@fallenangelbrewery.com
⊕ fallenangelbrewery.com

The brewery was launched in 2004 and in 2009 moved from Battle to its present address. Bottle-conditioned beers are produced for outlets around Kent, Sussex, Surrey and Hampshire. Investment in 2011 meant that output tripled with some beers now being available in casks. Bottle-conditioned beers: see website.

Fallons SIBA

Fallons Exquisite Ales, Unit 15, Darwen Enterprise Centre, Railway Road, Darwen, Lancashire, BB3 3EH
☎ 07905 246810 ⊠ info@fallonsales.com
⊕ fallonsales.com
Tours by arrangement

☺Fallons is a small family brewery established in 2008 with a 10-barrel plant in a unit on railway sidings. Beers are supplied to local pubs and festivals. Dark Prince is suitable for vegans.

Lancastrian Gold (OG 1038.8, ABV 4%)

Tattooers Arms (OG 1039.7, ABV 4.1%)

Jax Best (OG 1047.7, ABV 4.2%)

Goblin (OG 1041.7, ABV 4.3%)

Dark Prince (OG 1047.1, ABV 4.8%)

Falstaff

▤ Falstaff Brewery, 24 Society Place, Normanton, Derby, DE23 6UH
☎ 07947 242710 ⊠ info@falstaffbrewery.co.uk
⊕ falstaffbrewery.co.uk

⊠ Attached to the Falstaff freehouse, the brewery dates from 1999 but was refurbished and reopened in 2003 under new management and has since doubled capacity to 15 barrels. Since 2005 Falstaff has also brewed themed monthly specials for the Babington Arms in Derby. More than 140 outlets are supplied.

3 Faze (OG 1040, ABV 3.8%)
Light gold in colour with a malt and honey nose. Smooth malt flavours lead to a clean, balanced malt and hop finish.

Fist Full of Hops (OG 1044, ABV 4.5%)
An amber ale with lots of hop.

Phoenix (OG 1045, ABV 4.7%) ◆
A smooth, tawny ale with fruit and hop, joined by plenty of malt in the mouth. A subtle sweetness produces a drinkable ale.

Smiling Assassin (OG 1050, ABV 5.2%)
A copper-coloured beer with sweet malt flavours.

Famous Railway Tavern

⧮ Famous Railway Tavern Brewing Co, 58 Station Road, Brightlingsea, Essex, CO7 0DT
Tours by arrangement

The brewery started life as a kitchen-sink affair in 1998. In 2012 the brewery was completely refurbished; a two-barrel plant is used.

Crab & Winkle Mild (OG 1036, ABV 3.6%) ◆
Thin-bodied mild with a pear drop aroma and a rather roasty taste. The aftertaste is slightly ash-like with suggestions of bitter chocolate.

Bladderwrack Stout (OG 1047, ABV 4.7%) ◆
Full-bodied stout with an intense roast grain character that is initially underpinned by subtle sweetness, which subsides to leave a drier finish.

Faringdon (NEW)

⧮ Faringdon Brewery, Swan, 1 Park Road, Faringdon, Oxfordshire, SN7 7BP
☎ (01367) 241480 ☎ 07831 705687
✉ alanwatkins89@yahoo.com
⊕ faringdonbrewerytap.co.uk
Tours by arrangement

Opened in 2010 the brewery moved to a new level in 2011 when taken over by Alan Watkins, owner of Halfpenny and Old Forge breweries. The one-barrel plant has been replaced by a new two-barrel plant as a result of the high demand from the on-site brewery tap, the Swan.

Folly Ale (OG 1039.5, ABV 4%)
A traditional English bitter. Burnt gold in colour with a sweet aroma.

Farmer's Ales ⬚ EAB

Farmer's Ales, Stable Brewery, Silver Street, Maldon, Essex, CM9 4QE
☎ (01621) 851000 ✉ info@maldonbrewing.co.uk
⊕ maldonbrewing.co.uk
Shop Mon-Fri 9am-4pm; Sat 10am-2pm
Tours by arrangement

⊠ Situated in a restored stable block behind the historic Blue Boar Hotel, this eight-barrel brewery started in 2002. In 2011 fermenter capacity was doubled increasing production to 600 barrels a year. All beers are available in the Blue Boar taproom, an increasing number of Gray & Sons houses as well as in a number of local pubs. Bottle-conditioned beers are available. Seasonal beers: see website.

Maldon Mild (OG 1033, ABV 3.3%)
A dark, lightly-hopped traditional mild with a residual sweetness.

Farmer's IPA (OG 1036, ABV 3.6%)
A crisp, traditional amber IPA.

Drop of Nelson's Blood (OG 1038, ABV 3.8%) ◆
Red-brown session bitter. Initially quite sweet and fruity, with a pleasing bite to the aftertaste.

Hotel Porter (OG 1041, ABV 4.1%) ◆
Roast grain dominates this oatmeal stout, but an unusual fresh hop character is evident.

Pucks Folly (OG 1038, ABV 4.2%) ◆
Pale golden ale with spicy notes and sweet fruit. Biscuity malt in the taste fades and the finish is dominated by bitterness.

Captain Ann (OG 1045, ABV 4.5%)
A traditional premium bitter with malt notes. Lightly hopped.

Golden Boar (OG 1050, ABV 5%) ◆
Powerful, deep-golden ale. The hop character is initially full and citrus, but becomes more spicy in the aftertaste.

Dark Horse (OG 1064, ABV 6.6%)
A chestnut bitter with a smooth taste and long finish.

Farnham

⧮ Farnham Brewery, Claverton Marketing Ltd t/a Ball & Wicket Public House, 102-104 Upper Hale Road, Farnham, Surrey, GU9 0PB
☎ (01252) 735278 ✉ ballwick@ntlworld.com

⊠ The Farnham Brewery opened in 2006 and supplies the Ball & Wicket pub as well as around 10 other local outlets. Seasonal beers are also available.

Bishop Sumner (OG 1040, ABV 3.8%)

William Cobbett (OG 1045, ABV 4.3%) ◆
Malt slightly dominates this fruity best bitter, but balancing hop leads to a bitter finish, with some residual sweetness.

Mike Hawthorn (OG 1055, ABV 5.3%) ◆
Fruity and sweet throughout, with some balancing hop bitterness.

Farriers Arms

⧮ Farriers Arms Kent Ltd (FAKL), Farriers Arms, The Forstal, Mersham, Kent, TN25 6NU
☎ (01233) 720444
✉ farriersarmskentltd@gmail.com
⊕ thefarriersarms.com
Tours by arrangement

Brewing commenced in late 2010 using a five-barrel brew plant. The brewery was designed by shareholders and constructed by local engineers, largely from parts from the Black Dog Brewery in Whitby. Seasonal and occasional beers are also available.

Farriers 1606 (OG 1038, ABV 3.7%)

Fat Cat

⧮ Fat Cat Brewing Co, Fat Cat Brewery Tap, 98-100 Lawson Road, Norwich, NR3 4LF
☎ (01603) 788508 ☎ 07795 633368

THE BREWERIES

Office: 49 West End Street, Norwich, NR2 4NA
✉ chris@fatcatpub.co.uk ⊕ fatcatpub.co.uk/brewery
Tours by arrangement

Fat Cat Brewery was founded by the owner of the Fat Cat free house in Norwich. Brewing started in 2005 at the Fat Cat's sister pub, the Fat Cat Brewery Tap, under the supervision of former Woodforde's owner Ray Ashworth. Locally-sourced malt from Norfolk-grown barley is used when possible. Seasonal beers, bottle-conditioned beers and occasional one-off brews are also available.

Bitter (OG 1038, ABV 3.8%) ◆
Gold coloured with a grapefruit and sulphur aroma. A well-balanced citrus and hop beginning is underpinned by malt and then an increasingly dry bitterness.

Hell Cat (ABV 4.1%)
A well-balanced, pale session ale with citrus hop flavours.

Honey Cat (OG 1043, ABV 4.3%) ◆
A malty/hoppy brew with a taste of honey. A pleasant, low key mix of malt and hops bound together with a sweetish honey background. Gold coloured with a grainy mouthfeel.

Stout Cat (OG 1046, ABV 4.6%) ◆
Well-balanced, long-lasting, roasty stout with a malty, sweet aroma and deep red-brown hue. Malt and prunes provide depth and balance. Rich, creamy and satisfying.

Cougar (ABV 4.7%)
Extra pale, heavily-hopped American pale ale.

Wild Cat (OG 1050, ABV 5%) ◆
Pale gold with hoppy citrus airs. Initially sweet and lemony, a growing bitterness becomes apparent. Long finish with a mix of sweetness and a biscuity dryness.

Marmalade Cat (OG 1055, ABV 5.5%) 🍺 ◆
A complex beer with a growing malt influence over a dry hoppy beginning. Sweet fruity notes in the nose continue into the taste. A heavy grainy feel for such a complex, well-balanced brew.

Felinfoel SIBA

Felinfoel Brewery Co Ltd, Farmers Row, Felinfoel, Llanelli, Carmarthenshire, SA14 8LB
☎ (01554) 773357 ✉ info@felinfoel-brewery.com
⊕ felinfoel-brewery.com
Shop 9am-4pm
Tours by arrangement

Founded in the 1830s, the company is still family-owned and is now the oldest brewery in Wales. The present buildings are Grade II* listed and were built in the 1870s. It supplies cask ale to half its 84 houses, though some use top pressure dispense, and to approximately 350 free trade outlets.

Best Bitter (OG 1038, ABV 3.8%) ◆
A well-balanced beer, with a low aroma. Bittersweet initially with an increasing moderate bitterness.

Cambrian Best Bitter (OG 1039, ABV 3.9%)
A full-hopped and refreshing session beer.

Stout (OG 1041, ABV 4.1%)
A Welsh stout created with a subtle blend of chocolate malt giving a predominantly roast barley flavour and a rich, creamy head.

Double Dragon (OG 1042, ABV 4.2%) ◆
This pale brown beer has a malty, fruity aroma. The taste is also malt and fruit with a background hop presence throughout. A malty and fruity finish.

Celtic Pride (OG 1045, ABV 4.5%)
A light, golden premium ale with a bright, clean flavour and citrus overtones.

Fellows

Fellows Brewery Ltd, 2 Leopold Walk, Cottenham, Cambridgeshire, CB24 8XS
☎ (01954) 250262 ✉ ales@fellowsbrewery.co.uk
⊕ fellowsbrewery.co.uk

Mark Burton began test brewing in 2009 before going into full production in 2010. The village of Cottenham once had seven breweries and the villagers were known as the Gulpers because of their appetite for good ale. Beers are increasingly found in the local free trade and at beer festivals.

Cambridge Fellow (ABV 3.8%)
A golden session ale; light and clean tasting.

Gulping Fellow (ABV 4.2%)
A dry, bitter finish complements the spicy hop character of this well-balanced best bitter.

Burton Snatch (ABV 4.8%)
A blonde ale with a citrus aroma and refreshing mouthfeel. A hint of wet leather completes the finish.

Jolly Fellows (ABV 5%)
Full-bodied, clean-tasting premium bitter.

Clever Fellow (ABV 5.2%)
Malt loaf and toffee flavours combine with back of the tongue bitterness to achieve a balanced richness.

Felstar EAB

Felstar Brewery, Felsted Vineyards, Crix Green, Felsted, Essex, CM6 3JT
☎ (01245) 361504 ☎ 07546 096374
✉ sales@felstarbrewery.co.uk
⊕ felstarbrewery.co.uk
Shop 10am-dusk daily
Tours by arrangement

⊠ The Felstar Brewery opened in 2001 with a five-barrel plant based in the old bonded warehouse of the Felsted Vineyard. A small number of outlets are supplied. Seasonal and bottle-conditioned beers are also available.

Felstar (OG 1034, ABV 3.4%)

Best (OG 1040, ABV 4%)

Crix Forest (OG 1040, ABV 4%)

Sunburst (OG 1040, ABV 4%)

Good Knight (OG 1050, ABV 5%)

Hoppy Hen (OG 1050, ABV 5%)

Peckin' Order (OG 1050, ABV 5%)

Fernandes

Fernandes Brewery, 5 Avison Yard, Kirkgate, Wakefield, West Yorkshire, WF1 1UA
☎ (01924) 291709 ✉ brewery@ossett-brewery.co.uk ⊕ ossett-brewery.co.uk
Tours by arrangement

⊛The brewery opened in 1997 and is housed in a 19th-century malthouse. Ossett Brewing Company purchased the brewery and tap in 2007 but independent brewing continues. The former home-brew shop has been turned into a Bavarian-style Bier Keller and sells continental beers as well as real ale. The tap sells Fernandes and Ossett beer as well as guest ales. Fernandes beers are more widely available through Ossett's supply chain.

Malt Shovel Mild (OG 1038, ABV 3.8%)
A dark, full-bodied, malty mild with roast malt and chocolate flavours, leading to a lingering, dry, malty finish.

Triple O (OG 1041, ABV 3.9%)
A light, refreshing, hoppy session beer with a lingering fruity finish.

Ale to the Tsar (OG 1042, ABV 4.1%)
A pale, smooth, well-balanced beer with some sweetness leading to a nutty, malty and satisfying aftertaste.

Centennial (OG 1043, ABV 4.1%)
Light-coloured extremely hoppy beer with a long, lingering aftertaste.

Great Northern (OG 1050, ABV 5.1%)
Pale, citrussy and extremely hoppy.

Double Six (OG 1062, ABV 6%)
A powerful, dark and rich strong beer with an array of malt, roast malt and chocolate flavours and a strong, lasting malty finish, with some hoppiness.

Festival

See Cotswold Lion

FILO SIBA

FILO Brewing Co Ltd, The Old Town Brewery, Torfield Cottage, 8 Old London Road, Hastings, East Sussex, TN34 3HA
☎ (01424) 420212 ✉ info@filobrewing.co.uk
⊕ filobrewing.co.uk
Tours by arrangement

⊠ The brewery at the First In Last Out was established in 1985, with the current owners taking over in 1988. In 2011 the brewery relocated two minutes' walk away, remaining in the Old Town, to a barn at the Torfield Cottage site. One outlet, the First In Last Out, is supplied direct and the brewery sell out to the trade in Sussex and Kent.

Mike's Mild (OG 1035, ABV 3.4%)

Crofters (OG 1037, ABV 3.8%)

Churches Pale Ale (OG 1042, ABV 4.2%)

Old Town Tom (OG 1044, ABV 4.5%)

Gold (OG 1050, ABV 4.8%)

Firefly (NEW)

🔋 Firefly Brewing, Firefly, 54 Lowesmoor, Worcester, WR1 2SE
☎ (01905) 616996 ☎ 07525 445988
✉ thefirefly@hotmail.co.uk

Firefly Brewing was established in 2012 using a 0.5-barrel plant. At present only the pub is supplied. Further beers are planned.

American Pale Ale (ABV 4.2%)

Five Towns

Five Towns Brewery, 651 Leeds Road, Outwood, Wakefield, West Yorkshire, WF1 2LU
☎ (01924) 781887
✉ malcolmbastow@googlemail.com

☺Five Towns began production on a 2.5-barrel plant in 2008 and mostly supplies outlets in Yorkshire. Seasonal and bottle-conditioned beers are also available.

Outwood Bound (OG 1040, ABV 4.2%)
A chestnut beer with a toffee nose and strong, dry, bitter finish.

Yorker (OG 1042, ABV 4.4%)
A dry, pale, strong session beer with a floral aroma and zesty finish.

Niamh's Nemesis (OG 1053, ABV 5.7%)
A full-bodied IPA with hints of grapefruit before a dry finish.

Peculiar Blue (OG 1057, ABV 6%)
A powerful IPA loaded with hops with grapefruit and gooseberry notes in a bitter finish.

Flack Manor SIBA

Flack Manor Brewery Ltd, 8 Romsey Industrial Estate, Greatbridge Road, Romsey, Hampshire, SO51 0HR
☎ (01794) 518520 ✉ info@flackmanor.co.uk
⊕ flackmanor.co.uk
Shop Mon-Fri 9.30am-5pm; Sat 9.30am-12pm
Tours by arrangement

⊠ Flack Manor was established in 2010 using a 20-barrel plant purchased from Canada. The brewery employs the 'double drop' method of brewing. Beers are supplied to local outlets within a 30-mile radius of Romsey. Seasonal beers are available.

Flack's Double Drop (ABV 3.7%)

Flack Catcher (ABV 4.4%)

Flash (NEW)

Flash Brewery, Moss Top Farm, Moss Top Lane, Flash, Staffordshire, SK17 0TA
✉ flashbrewery@hotmail.com

The brewery is located high in the Peak District and was founded by two friends who brew on a part-time basis. All natural ingredients are used including spring water and seawood finings, which makes the beer suitable for vegans. Due to the altitude a brick boiler was found and is used in the brewing process rather than electrical equipment. Three bottle-conditioned beers are produced and sold at Leek market, which is the only sales outlet.

Flipside SIBA

Flipside Brewery, The Brewhouse, East Link Trade Estate, Private Road No. 2, Colwick, Nottinghamshire, NG4 2JR
☎ (0115) 987 7500 ☎ 07970 025863
✉ andrew.dunkin@flipsidebrewery.co.uk
⊕ flipsidebrewery.co.uk
Shop Mon-Fri 9am-6pm; Sat 10am-1pm (extended hours in Dec)
Tours by arrangement

Andrew Dunkin, with the help of his wife Maggie, established a six-barrel brewery in an industrial unit in Colwick in 2010.

THE BREWERIES

Sterling Pale (OG 1039, ABV 3.9%)
A fairly hoppy pale ale. Easy-drinking with a bitter, spicy hop flavour.

Dark Denomination (OG 1040, ABV 4%)
A well-rounded, mildly hopped beer. Chocolate and caramel malt flavours combine with delicate blackcurrant hop flavours.

Copper Penny (OG 1043, ABV 4.2%)
An easy-drinking session bitter. Light brown, moderately bitter but with good hop flavours, ending with a hint of tangerine.

Golden Sovereign (OG 1043, ABV 4.2%)
A golden session ale, refreshingly bitter with dry biscuit flavours and pleasant citrus and grapefruit in the finish.

Random Toss (OG 1044, ABV 4.4%)
A refreshing pale ale with lemon and lime tropical fruit flavours.

Flipping Best (OG 1046, ABV 4.6%)
A traditional dark brown best bitter. Strong malt flavours complemented with good bitterness and gentle hop flavours.

Dusty Penny (OG 1049, ABV 5%)
A full-bodied black porter bursting with chocolate, caramel and vanilla malt flavours, rounded off with bitterness provided by traditional English hops.

Clippings IPA (OG 1062, ABV 6.5%)
A traditional strong IPA, golden in colour with crushed gooseberry and bitter hop flavours.

Florence

▪ Florence Brewery (A Head in a Hat), Florence Public House, 131-133 Dulwich Road, Herne Hill, London, SE24 0NG
☎ 07973 465081 ✉ brewery@florencehernehill.com ⊕ florencebrewery.co.uk

⊠ The Florence has been brewing since opening in 2007. Purchased by beer historian Peter Haydon from Greene King following the acquisition of Capital Pubs, the Florence brews for Capital Pub Co pubs and produces 'A Head in a Hat' beers, specialising in London beer recipes, for the London free trade. Seasonal beer is also available.

Bonobo (OG 1044.8, ABV 4.5%) ◄
A well-balanced brown beer with a strong citrus hop character, some butterscotch and a dry aftertaste.

Weasel (OG 1044.8, ABV 4.5%) ◄
Citrus hops dominate this light-drinking, straw-coloured beer, including the finish, which is dry and bitter.

Beaver (OG 1047.2, ABV 4.8%)
Brewed with wheat malt and orange peel essence to produce a cloudy, aromatic beer.

Flowerpots SIBA

▪ Flowerpots Brewery, Brandy Mount, Cheriton, Hampshire, SO24 0QQ
☎ (01962) 771534 ⊕ flowerpots-inn.co.uk

⊠ Flowerpots began production in 2006. Brewster Catherine Bate succeeded Iain McIntosh in 2011 and continues his award-winning tradition with both established recipes and her own innovations. Many local outlets are supplied direct. Seasonal beers: see website.

Perridge Pale (OG 1035.5, ABV 3.6%) ◄
Very pale, easy-drinking session beer. Honey-scented with high hops and bitterness throughout. Some citrus notes; extremely tasty for its strength.

Bitter (OG 1038, ABV 3.8%) 🍴 ◄
Dry, earthy hop flavours balanced by malt and toffee. Good bitterness with a hoppy aroma and a sharp finish. A refreshing, easy-going bitter.

Goodens Gold (OG 1046, ABV 4.8%) ◄
A yellow-coloured, full-bodied golden ale. More complex than many of its style, but still bursting with hops and citrus fruit in the aroma and taste and a snatch of sweetness, leading to a long, dry finish.

Forge SIBA

Forge Brewery, Ford Hill Forge, Hartland, Devon, EX39 6EE
☎ (01237) 440015 ☎ 07971 388084
✉ dave@forgebrewery.co.uk ⊕ forgebrewery.co.uk

Forge is situated in a coastal village near Bideford in North Devon and began brewing in 2008 on a five-barrel plant. More than 40 outlets are supplied direct. Bottle-conditioned and seasonal beer is also available.

Ambrosia (OG 1036.5, ABV 3.6%)
A light brown, full-flavoured beer.

Discovery (OG 1039, ABV 3.8%)
A golden, hoppy ale.

Hartland Blonde (OG 1040, ABV 4%)
A light, hoppy beer with citrus notes.

Dark Horse (OG 1042, ABV 4.1%)
A rich oat beer, dark copper-coloured with a fruity aroma and smooth finish.

Lite House (OG 1042, ABV 4.3%)
A golden-coloured best bitter with hints of elderflower and a citrus bite.

IPA (OG 1044, ABV 4.5%)
A light, hoppy beer with grapefruit and citrus notes.

Ascension (OG 1046, ABV 4.6%)

Dreckly (OG 1046, ABV 4.8%)
A warm, ruby-coloured strong premium ale fortified with gorse and heather, rich in malt with a spicy aroma and a malty aftertaste.

Handsome (OG 1048, ABV 5.1%)
A light brown, well-balanced, hoppy beer.

Four Alls

▪ Four Alls Brewery, Ovington, North Yorkshire, DL11 7BP
☎ (01833) 627302 ✉ john.stroud@virgin.net
⊕ thefouralls-teesdale.co.uk
Tours by arrangement

☺The one-barrel brewery was launched in 2003 by John Stroud, one of the founders of Ales of Kent, using that name. In 2004 it became Four Alls, named after the pub where it is based, the only outlet for the beers.

Iggy Pop (OG 1036, ABV 3.6%)
A honey-coloured beer.

30 Shillings (OG 1039, ABV 3.8%)
A dark session ale.

Red Admiral (OG 1039, ABV 3.9%)

A deep red, malty ale.

Fowler's

See DemonBrew

Fox Beer

See Burley Street

Fox EAB

■ Fox Brewery, 22 Station Road, Heacham, Norfolk, PE31 7EX
☎ (01485) 570345 ✉ info@foxbrewery.co.uk
⊕ foxbrewery.co.uk
Tours by arrangement

Based in an old cottage adjacent to the Fox & Hounds pub, Fox brewery was established in 2002 and now supplies around 50 outlets as well as the pub. All the Branthill beers are brewed from barley grown on Branthill Farm and malted at Crisps in Great Ryburgh. A hop garden next to the brewery, trialled during 2009, has been enlarged. All cask beers are also available bottle conditioned. Seasonal beers: see website.

Branthill Best (OG 1037, ABV 3.9%)

Heacham Gold (OG 1037, ABV 3.9%) ◆
A gentle beer with light citrus airs. A low but increasing bitterness is the major flavour as some initial sweet hoppiness quickly declines.

Red Knocker (OG 1037, ABV 3.9%)
Copper coloured and malty.

LJB (OG 1040, ABV 4%) ◆
A well-balanced malty brew with a hoppy, bitter background. The long finish holds up well, as a sultana-like fruitiness develops. Mid brown with a slightly thin mouthfeel.

Bullet (OG 1042, ABV 4.2%)
Pale golden yellow beer with resinous hop aroma and tropical fruit flavours.

Branthill Norfolk Nectar (OG 1043, ABV 4.3%)
Slightly sweet. Brewed only with Maris Otter pale malt.

Warrior (OG 1043, ABV 4.4%)

Grizzly Beer (OG 1048, ABV 4.8%)
Honey wheat beer brewed from an American recipe.

Cascade (OG 1051, ABV 5%)
A very light beer with a hoppy flavour.

Nelson's Blood (OG 1049, ABV 5.1%)
A liquor of beers. Red, full-bodied; made with Nelson's Blood Rum.

IPA (OG 1051, ABV 5.2%)
Based on a 19th-century recipe. Easy drinking for its strength.

Foxfield SIBA

■ Foxfield Brewery, Prince of Wales, Foxfield, Broughton in Furness, Cumbria, LA20 6BX
☎ (01229) 716238 ⊕ princeofwalesfoxfield.co.uk
Tours by arrangement

☺Foxfield is a three-barrel plant in old stables attached to the Prince of Wales inn. A few other outlets are supplied. Tigertops in Wakefield is also owned. The beer range constantly changes so the beers listed here may not necessarily be available. There are many occasional and seasonal beers. Dark Mild is suitable for vegetarians and vegans.

Dark Mild (OG 1040, ABV 3.7%)

Brief Encounter (OG 1040, ABV 3.8%)
A fruity beer with a long, bitter finish.

Franklin's

Franklin's Brewing Co, Pebsham Farm, Pebsham Lane, Bexhill-on-Sea, East Sussex, TN40 2RZ
☎ (01424) 731066 ✉ info@franklinsbrewery.co.uk
⊕ franklinsbrewery.co.uk
Tours by arrangement

Formerly White Brewery, in 2011 the Franklin's name was purchased from Sean Franklin of Roosters, who originally set up the brewery in 1980. The original brew plant from Harrogate was also to be used but part of this was stolen so the equipment is made up of parts from the old kit and that of White Brewing Co. The brewery also contract brews for other wholesalers.

Dry Hop (OG 1038, ABV 3.6%)
A ruby-coloured light bitter with a fruity aroma combined with a subtle malty sweetness and a longer, bitter aftertaste.

IPA (OG 1038, ABV 3.6%)

Bitter (OG 1040, ABV 3.8%)

Brighton Rocks (OG 1042, ABV 4%)

EXP (OG 1045, ABV 4.2%)
A crisp bitter, rich in flowery aroma with a dry finish and balanced malty sweetness and bitterness.

Freedom SIBA ◉

Freedom Brewery Ltd, 1 Park Lodge House, Bagots Park, Abbots Bromley, Staffordshire, WS15 3ES
☎ (01283) 840721
✉ freedom@freedombrewery.com
⊕ freedomlager.com
Shop Mon-Fri 9am-5pm
Tours by arrangement

No real ale. Freedom specialises in producing hand-crafted English lagers, all brewed in accordance with the German Reinheitsgebot purity law. It is situated on top of a natural underground lake of Burton brewing water. Water is drawn from this sustainable source and used in the brewing process. Six beers are currently produced; Freedom Four Lager (ABV 4%), Freedom Stout (ABV 4%), Pioneer (ABV 4.6%), Freedom Organic Dark Lager (ABV 4.7%), Freedom Organic Lager (ABV 4.8%), Freedom Pilsner (ABV 5%). All are suitable for vegetarians and vegans.

Freeminer SIBA

Freeminer Ltd, Whimsey Road, Steam Mills, Cinderford, Gloucestershire, Gl14 3JA
☎ (01594) 827989 ✉ sales@freeminer.co.uk

⊠ Founded by Don Burgess in 1992, Freeminer – previously Freeminer Brewery – changed hands in 2006 but Don Burgess remained in post. Bottle-conditioned beers are available (brewed for the Co-op). Co-op beers are now brewed with barley grown on Co-op farms and malted at Warminster.

THE BREWERIES

Fairtrade and organic beers are also produced, with limited edition cask versions available for Fairtrade fortnight.

Bitter (OG 1038, ABV 4%) ◀
A light, hoppy session bitter with an intense hop aroma and a dry, hoppy finish.

Strip & At It (OG 1035, ABV 4%)

Slaughter Porter (OG 1047, ABV 4.8%)

Speculation (OG 1047, ABV 4.8%) ◀
An aromatic, chestnut-brown, full-bodied beer with a smooth, well-balanced mix of malt and hops, and a predominately hoppy aftertaste.

Friends Arms (NEW)

≣ Friends Arms Brewery, Old St Clears Road, Johnstown, Carmerthenshire, SA31 3HH
☎ (01267) 234073 ✉ thefriendsarms@gmail.com
⊕ thefriendsarms.co.uk

The Friends Arms brewery opened in 2011 on the premises of the Friends Arms, a traditional local community pub, which acts as the brewery tap.

Cwrw Cyfeillion (OG 1044, ABV 4.4%)

Carnival Ale (OG 1052, ABV 5.4%)

Frodsham SIBA

Frodsham Brewery, Lady Heyes Craft Centre, Kingsley Road, Frodsham, Cheshire, WA6 6SU
☎ (01928) 787917
✉ enquire@frodshambrewery.co.uk
⊕ frodshambrewery.co.uk
Shop 10am-4pm daily
Tours by arrangement

☺ Frodsham has been brewing since 2005 (initially as Stationhouse Brewery in Ellesmere Port). A 5-barrel electric and propane powered unit is used to produce the core range as well as seasonal and celebration brews: see website. Most beer are also available bottle conditioned.

1'st Lite (OG 1037.8, ABV 3.8%) ◀
Light, hoppy bitter with clean lemon/grapefruit hop flavours and the trademark Station House bitterness and dry aftertaste. Clean and refreshing.

Devil's Garden (OG 1037, ABV 3.9%)
An amber bronze traditional beer with biscuit flavour and raisin aftertaste.

Splash! (OG 1038, ABV 3.9%)
A blonde, refreshing summer beer. Crisp and citrus with hoppy flavours.

Buzzin' (OG 1042, ABV 4.3%) ◀
Golden fruity bitter dominated by a honey sweetness. Good hop flavours in initial taste and a long, lasting dry finish.

Iron Man (OG 1043, ABV 4.5%)
An amber, hop-rich beer with fruity aftertones.

800 Ale (OG 1045.5, ABV 4.7%)
A golden bitter. Floral with late wine flavours.

Aonach (OG 1049, ABV 4.9%)
A typical Scottish style 80/- beer. Dark amber in colour.

Frog Island SIBA

Frog Island Brewery, The Maltings, Westbridge, St James Road, Northampton, Northamptonshire, NN5 5HS
☎ (01604) 587772 ✉ beer@frogislandbrewery.co.uk
⊕ frogislandbrewery.co.uk
Tours by arrangement to licensed trade only

Started in 1994 by home-brewer Bruce Littler and business partner Graham Cherry in a malt house built by the long-defunct Thomas Manning brewery, Frog Island expanded by doubling its brew length to 10 barrels in 1998. It specialises in beers with personalised bottle labels, available by mail order. Some 40 free trade outlets are supplied, with the beer occasionally available through other micro-brewers. Seasonal and bottle-conditioned beers are available.

Best Bitter (OG 1038, ABV 3.8%) ◀
Blackcurrant and gooseberry enhance the full malty aroma with pineapple and papaya joining on the tongue. Bitterness develops in the fairly long Target/Fuggles finish.

Shoemaker (OG 1043, ABV 4.2%) ◀
An orangey aroma of fruity Cascade hops is balanced by malt. Citrus and hoppy bitterness last into a long, dry finish. Amber colour.

That Old Chestnut (OG 1044, ABV 4.4%)
A smooth, easy-drinking beer with subtle roasted notes. Cascade hops bring a sweet spiciness to the beer while Target hops contribute bitterness to the dry, malty finish.

Natterjack (OG 1048, ABV 4.8%) ◀
Deceptively robust, golden and smooth. Fruit and hop aromas fight for dominance before the grainy astringency and floral palate give way to a long, dry aftertaste.

Fire Bellied Toad (OG 1048, ABV 5%) ◀
Amber-gold brew with an extraordinary long bitter/fruity finish. Huge malt and Phoenix hop flavours have a hint of apples.

Croak & Stagger (OG 1056, ABV 5.6%) ◀
The initial honey/fruit aroma is quickly overpowered by roast malt then bitter chocolate and pale malt sweetness on the tongue. Gentle, bittersweet finish.

Front Row (NEW)

Front Row Brewing, Unit 1, Hopkins Close, Congleton, Cheshire, CW12 4TR
☎ 07861 718673 ✉ nick@frontrowbrewing.co.uk
⊕ frontrowbrewing.co.uk

After a few trial brews were seen at various local beer festivals in 2011, Front Row started operating in 2012 using a 2.5-barrel plant. As well as supplying a number of local outlets arrangements with other breweries mean the beers can also be found wider afield.

Crouch (ABV 3.8%)

Touch (ABV 4%)

Pause (ABV 4.5%)

Engage (ABV 4.8%)

Front Street SIBA

≣ Front Street Brewery, 45 Front Street, Binham, Fakenham, Norfolk, NR21 0AL

☎ (01328) 830297
✉ steve@frontstreetbrewery.co.uk
🌐 frontstreetbrewery.co.uk
Tours by arrangement

The brewery is based at the Chequers Inn and is probably Britain's smallest five-barrel plant. Brewing started in 2005 and three regular beers are produced as well as seasonal and occasional brews. Both cask and bottled beers are delivered to the free trade and retail outlets throughout East Anglia. Seasonal beers: see website. Bottle-conditioned beers are also available.

Binham Cheer (OG 1039, ABV 3.9%)

Callums Ale (OG 1043, ABV 4.3%)

Unity Strong (OG 1051, ABV 5%)

Frys SIBA

Frys Brewery Ltd, Trerice, Boyton, Cornwall, PL15 8NU
☎ (01566) 785840 ✉ beer@frysbrewery.co.uk
🌐 frysbrewery.co.uk

⊠ Frys began brewing in 2011 on a 2.5-barrel plant previously used by Forgotten Corner Brewery. Further beers including seasonals may be available – contact brewery for further details.

Frydeal (OG 1037, ABV 3.7%)

Haven (OG 1043, ABV 4.2%)

Golden Chough (OG 1047, ABV 4.7%)

Fugelestou

See Fulstow

Fulflood Arms (NEW)

⚑ Fulflood Arms Brewery, Fulflood Arms, 28 Cheriton Road, Winchester, Hampshire, SO22 5EF
☎ (01962) 842996
✉ thefulfloodarms@hotmail.co.uk

Established in 2012 using a one-barrel plant supplying the pub and other local outlets. Further beers are planned.

Bitter (ABV 3.8%)

Golden Jet (ABV 4.6%)

Fuller's SIBA IFBB 👁

Fuller, Smith & Turner plc, Griffin Brewery, Chiswick Lane South, London, W4 2QB
☎ (020) 8996 2000 ✉ fullers@fullers.co.uk
🌐 fullers.co.uk
Shop Mon-Fri 10am-8pm; Sat 10am-6pm
Tours by arrangement

⊠ Fuller, Smith & Turner's Griffin Brewery has stood on the same site in Chiswick for more than 350 years. The partnership from which the company now takes its name was formed in 1845 and members of the founding families are still involved in running the company today. Three different Fuller's beers have won the Champion Beer of Britain title, Chiswick Bitter, London Pride and ESB. At the end of 2005 Fuller's announced the acquisition of Hampshire brewer George Gale. The company now operates over 360 pubs and hotels. Fuller's stopped brewing at the Gale's Horndean site in 2006 and all of the brands, including some seasonals, are now brewed at Chiswick. Seasonal

beers: see website. Bottle-conditioned beers are also available.

Chiswick Bitter (OG 1034.5, ABV 3.5%) ◀
Refreshing pale brown bitter with some citrus notes on the palate fading in the aftertaste, which is hoppy and slightly dry. Aroma is of hops with a trace of biscuit.

Discovery (OG 1039.5, ABV 3.9%) ◀
Golden ale served cold, which results in a low aroma. Fruit throughout with a sweet malt that becomes more prominent as the beer warms. Finish has a trace of dryness.

London Pride (OG 1040.5, ABV 4.1%) ◀
Well-balanced smooth best bitter with orange citrus fruit, malt and hops in aroma and flavour, which linger into a slightly bitter aftertaste. Honey and toffee develop as the beer matures.

Bengal Lancer (OG 1049.5, ABV 5%) ◀
Rich, creamy and well-balanced IPA with a gold hue. Hops with a dryish bitterness harmonise with the fruit and malty sweetness that linger into the aftertaste.

ESB (OG 1054, ABV 5.5%) ◀
Bitter orange marmalade with hops, creamy toffee and some raisins are all present in this multi-faceted strong brown bitter. A satisfying long, bitter, dry finish balanced by a malty sweetness.

Under the Gale's brand name:

Seafarers Ale (OG 1036.8, ABV 3.6%) 🍺 ◀
A pale brown bitter, predominantly malty, with a refreshing balance of fruit and hops that lingers into the aftertaste where a dry bitterness unfolds.

HSB (OG 1050, ABV 4.8%) 🍺 ◀
Dates and dried fruit with some spicy hops on the nose adding to the caramelised orange and treacle in the flavour of this smooth brown beer. Malty throughout with a bittersweet finish.

Full Mash SIBA

Full Mash Brewery, 17 Lower Park Street, Stapleford, Nottinghamshire, NG9 8EW
☎ (0115) 949 9262 ✉ fullmashbrewery@yahoo.com
🌐 fullmash.net

⊙ Full Mash started brewing in 2003 with a quarter-barrel plant. The brewery has now expanded to four barrels and, with the addition of extra fermenters, 12 barrels a week are now produced.

Seance (OG 1041, ABV 4%) ◀
Predominantly hoppy golden beer, with a refreshing, bitter finish.

Spiritualist (OG 1044, ABV 4.3%) ◀
A reddish-brown traditional malty best bitter with delicate hop flavours.

Warlord (OG 1045, ABV 4.4%)
A rich-flavoured malty ale with an intense hop bite.

Apparition (OG 1046, ABV 4.5%) ◀
A pale hoppy bitter brewed with Brewers Gold hops.

Full Moon SIBA

Full Moon Brewery Ltd, Sharpes Farm, Henley Down, Catsfield, Battle, East Sussex, TN33 9BN
☎ 07832 220745 🌐 fullmoonbrewery.co.uk

Full Moon was established in 2008 by James Pryke and Professor Philip Parsons. They were joined in 2012 by Roger Massey, an experienced craft brewer. Significant investment has also increased capacity to a four-barrel plant resulting in the supply of increasing numbers of local pubs.

Hopdance (OG 1037, ABV 3.9%)
A dry golden ale with a fresh fruit and citrus aroma.

Celestial Blonde (OG 1039, ABV 4.3%)
A pale ale, light golden in colour, fairly dry and slightly bitter with a pine and lemon aroma and a crisp hop and peppery taste.

Fulstow SIBA

Fulstow Brewery, 13 Thames Street, Louth, Lincolnshire, LN11 7AD
☎ (01507) 608202 ✉ fulstow.brewery@virgin.net
⊕ fulstowbrewery.com
Shop: at brewery tap
Tours by arrangement

Fulstow operates on a 2.5-barrel plant and started brewing in Fulstow in 2004. The brewery then moved to Louth in 2006. 'Fugelstou Ales' are distributed throughout Britain and one-off brews are produced on a regular basis. The brewery tap, the Gas Lamp Lounge, opened in Louth in 2010.

Fulstow Common (OG 1038, ABV 3.8%) 🍺
A copper-coloured, medium-bodied beer with a strong hop character and malt discernable in the taste.

Marsh Mild (OG 1039, ABV 3.8%)
Traditional mild with a malty aroma. Chocolate malt on the palate with toffee and caramel overtones.

Village Life (OG 1040, ABV 4%)
Ruby red ale with great depth of malt and hop balance.

Northway IPA (OG 1042, ABV 4.2%)
A clean, crisp ale with a citrus aroma; very hoppy with a dry finish.

Imperial Stout (OG 1044.5, ABV 4.4%)
A full-flavoured stout with rich liquorice flavours with fruit and raisins. A satisfying, bitter aftertaste.

Pride of Fulstow (OG 1045, ABV 4.5%)
Copper-coloured bitter with a ripe malt taste in the mouth and a good hop balance. A dry finish with blackcurrant fruit notes.

Sledgehammer Stout (OG 1077, ABV 8%)
A strong, dark stout with raisin, liquorice and roast barley notes balanced by a strong hop flavour.

Funfair SIBA

Funfair Brewing Co, Chequers Inn, Toad Lane, Elston, Nottinghamshire, NG23 5NS
☎ (01636) 525257
✉ sales@funfairbrewingcompany.co.uk
⊕ funfairbrewingcompany.co.uk
Tours by arrangement

⊗ Funfair was launched in 2004 at the Wheel Inn in Holbrook. The brewery relocated to Ilkeston, Derbyshire, and in 2011 relocated again to its present site at the Chequers Inn in Elston with a new 15-barrel plant. The Chequers also serves as the brewery tap. More than 40 outlets are supplied. Seasonal beers: see website. Bottle-conditioned beers are also available.

Big Wheel (ABV 3.9%)
A straw-coloured, hoppy session bitter.

Waltzer (OG 1045, ABV 4.5%)
A copper-coloured traditional premium bitter.

Dive Bomber (OG 1047, ABV 4.6%)
A straw-coloured, hoppy premium ale.

Dodgem (OG 1047, ABV 4.7%)
A golden, well-balanced bitter.

Tunnel of Love (ABV 5%)
A deep chestnut-coloured aromatic bitter.

Cake Walk (OG 1060, ABV 6%)
A dark ruby beer, full-bodied and fruity.

Fuzzy Duck SIBA

Fuzzy Duck Brewery Ltd, 18 Wood Street, Poulton Industrial Estate, Poulton-le-Fylde, Lancashire, FY6 8JY
☎ 07904 343729 or 07973 154505
✉ ben@fuzzyduckbrewery.co.uk
⊕ fuzzyduckbrewery.co.uk
Tours by arrangement

Fuzzy Duck was established on a half-barrel plant at the owner's home in 2006. It relocated to an industrial unit and expanded capacity to eight barrels. Bottle-conditioned beers are planned. The brewery will relocate to its brewery tap, the Strawberry Gardens in Fleetwood, in the near future.

Golden Cascade (OG 1038, ABV 3.8%)

Mucky Duck (OG 1042, ABV 4%)

Cunning Stunt (OG 1044, ABV 4.3%)

Pheasant Plucker (OG 1044, ABV 4.3%)

Fyfe

🍺 Fyfe Brewing Co, 469 High Street, Kirkcaldy, Fife, KY1 2SN
☎ (01592) 646211/264270
✉ fyfebrew@btinternet.com
Tours by arrangement

⊗ Fyfe was established in an old sailmakers behind the Harbour Bar in 1995 on a 2.5-barrel plant. Most of the output is taken by the pub, the remainder being sold direct to around 30 local outlets. Seasonal beers and monthly specials are also available.

Auld Alliance (OG 1040, ABV 4%) ◈
A bitter beer with a lingering, dry, hoppy finish. Malt and hop, with fruit, are present throughout, fading in the finish.

Lion Slayer (OG 1042, ABV 4.2%)
Amber-coloured ale with malt and fruit on the nose. Fruit predominates on the palate. A slightly dry finish.

First Lyte (ABV 4.3%)

Weiss Squad (OG 1045, ABV 4.5%)
Hoppy, bitter wheat beer with bags of citrus in the taste and finish.

Fyre (OG 1048, ABV 4.8%)
Pale golden best bitter, full-bodied and balanced with malt, hops and fruit. Hoppy bitterness grows in an increasingly dry aftertaste.

Fyne [SIBA]

Fyne Ales Ltd, Achadunan, Cairndow, Argyll, PA26 8BJ
☎ (01499) 600120 ✉ jamie@fyneales.com
⊕ fyneales.com
Shop Mon-Sat 10am-5pm; Sun 12.30-5pm
Tours by arrangement

☺Fyne Ales has been brewing since 2001. The 10-barrel plant was installed in a redundant milking parlour on a farm in Argyll, set in a beautiful glen at the head of Loch Fyne. Around 430 outlets are supplied nationally. In 2012 an on-site brewery tap was added. The range of beers is supplemented by one-off brews for special events. Seasonal beers are also available.

Jarl (OG 1038, ABV 3.8%)

Piper's Gold (OG 1037.5, ABV 3.8%) ◆
Fresh, golden session ale. Well bittered but balanced with fruit and malt. Long, dry, bitter finish.

Maverick (OG 1040.5, ABV 4.2%) ▮ ◆
Full-bodied, roasty, tawny best bitter. It is balanced, fruity and well hopped.

Hurricane Jack (OG 1042.5, ABV 4.4%)
A smooth, golden ale with deep citrus flavours mellowing to a lingering citrus bitter finish.

Vital Spark (OG 1042.5, ABV 4.4%)
A rich, dark beer that shows glints of red. The taste is clean and slightly sharp with a hint of blackcurrant.

Avalanche (OG 1043.5, ABV 4.5%) ◆
This true golden ale starts with stunning citrus hops on the nose. Well-balanced with good body and fruit balancing a refreshing hoppy taste, it finishes with a long bittersweet aftertaste.

Highlander (OG 1046, ABV 4.8%) ▯ ◆
Full-bodied, bittersweet ale with a good dry hop finish. In the style of a Heavy although the malt is less pronounced and the sweetness ebbs away to leave a bitter, hoppy finish.

Sublime Stout (OG 1062, ABV 6.8%)

Gadds

See Ramsgate

Gale's

See Fuller's

Gambling Man (NEW)

Gambling Man Brewing Co, 61 Low Willington, Willington, County Durham, DL15 0BG
☎ 07545 464968

Correspondence: 21 Buchanan Street, Hebburn, Tyne & Wear, NE31 1NB
✉ brewery@gamblingmanbrewco.com
⊕ gamblingmanbrewco.com

☺Gambling Man was established in 2011 by avid home brewers Paul Armstrong and Dave Walls. All ales have gambling/casino related names, the brewery name itself being thought up by the brewers during a game of five card draw. Bi-monthly specials are also available.

Pit Boss (OG 1040, ABV 4.4%)

Jack O' Clubs (OG 1056, ABV 4.7%)

Garage (NEW)

Garage Brewery, c/o London Inn, 8 Church Road, Plympton St Maurice, Devon, PL7 1NH
☎ (01752) 337025 ☎ 07789 437021
✉ garagebrewery@hotmail.co.uk
⊕ garagebrewery.co.uk

Garage was established in 2011 by Russ Gibbs, a keen home brewer, in an outbuilding of the London Inn. It uses a one-barrel, self-constructed brew plant. The brewery is separate to the pub.

Stout Sam (OG 1039, ABV 3.9%)
Full-flavoured with a hint of toasted malt.

Firkin Folly (OG 1044, ABV 4.4%)
Amber-coloured and refreshing with a clean palate and a dry, hoppy finish.

Radiator Spring (OG 1046, ABV 4.5%)
A ruby-red beer with complex flavours and a long-lasting finish.

Young Bob (OG 1064, ABV 6.2%)
Named after the brewer's terrier dog. A strong tasting, malty beer with a hoppy finish.

Gargoyles

See Isca

Garthela

Garthela Brewhouse, Garthela, Beardwood Brow, Blackburn, Lancashire, BB2 7AT
☎ 07515 648630 ✉ garthelabrewhouse@gmail.com
⊕ garthelabrewhouse.co.uk
Tours by arrangement

☺Garthela Brewhouse began production in late 2008 on a 2.5-barrel plant. All beers are also available bottle conditioned. Seasonal beers are also brewed.

Barm Cake Bitter (OG 1038, ABV 3.8%)
Golden-coloured with a malty nose and a clean bitterness through to the finish.

Oven Bottom Blonde (OG 1040, ABV 4%)
A classic blonde with a fresh taste of citrus throughout.

Black Pudding Porter (OG 1045, ABV 4.2%)
Dark with a velvety sweetness and creaminess.

Eccles Cake Ale (OG 1041, ABV 4.2%)
Rich in colour with a hint of ruby. A touch of roast with a clean-tasting, delicate hoppiness throughout.

Gates Burton (NEW)

Gates Burton Brewery, 7 Reservoir Road, Burton upon Trent, Staffordshire, DE14 2BP
☎ (01283) 532567
✉ gatesburtonbrewery@talktalk.net

The Gates Burton Brewery was established in 2011 using a one-barrel plant.

Reservoir Premium (OG 1046, ABV 4.5%)
Amber-coloured with malty aromas. A dry start with a sweet, fruity aftertaste and a lingering malt flavour.

Reservoir Gold (OG 1080, ABV 8%)

THE BREWERIES

Geeves (NEW) SIBA

Geeves Brewery, Unit 12, Grange Lane Industrial Estate, Carrwood Road, Stairfoot, Barnsley, S71 5AS
☎ 07859 039259 ✉ geevesbrewery@msn.com
⊕ geevesbrewery.co.uk
Tours by arrangement

Geeves began brewing in 2011 using a 5.5-barrel plant. Seasonal beers are also available.

No. 1 (OG 1038, ABV 3.8%)
A traditional bitter with a well-rounded, malty base and a hoppy finish.

Bow Hauler (OG 1041, ABV 4.1%)

Red Diesel (OG 1041, ABV 4.1%)

Gunwale Dance (OG 1043, ABV 4.2%)
A pale ale with a dry, citrus bitterness coupled with a zingy aftertaste and aroma.

Smokey Joe Stout (OG 1050, ABV 5%)
A strong stout made with several different malts. Rich and robust.

Fully Laden (OG 1060, ABV 6%)
A strong IPA with a juicy, citrus, sweet floral taste and aroma and a satisfying bitterness.

Geltsdale SIBA

Geltsdale Brewery Ltd, Unit 6, Old Brewery Yard, Craw Hall, Brampton, Cumbria, CA8 1TR
☎ (016977) 41541 ✉ geltsdale@mac.com
⊕ geltsdalebrewery.com
Shop Mon-Fri 10am-5pm; Sat 9am-5pm
Tours by arrangement

☺Geltsdale Brewery was established in 2006 by Fiona Deal and originally operated from a unit in Brampton's Old Brewery, dating back to 1785. A new 15-barrel plant was installed in a larger unit on the same site in 2010. Some of the beers are named after local landmarks within Geltsdale. Around 100 outlets are supplied direct.

Black Dub (OG 1036, ABV 3.6%)

Copper (ABV 3.8%)

Cold Fell (ABV 3.9%)

Bewcastle Brown Ale (ABV 4%)

Brampton Bitter (ABV 4%) ◆
Sweet, fruity, well-balanced hoppy bitter with a clean bitter aftertaste.

Tarn (OG 1040, ABV 4%)

Gold (ABV 4.1%)

Hell Beck (OG 1042, ABV 4.2%)

Lager (ABV 4.5%)

George Wright

See under Wright

George's

See Hop Monster

Gertie Sweet

See New Plassey

Gidley's SIBA

Gidley's Brewery, 5 Gidley's Meadow, Christow, Exeter, Devon, EX6 7QB
☎ (01647) 252120 ✉ beer@gidleysbrewery.co.uk
⊕ gidleysbrewery.co.uk

Gidley's started brewing in 2009 using a five-barrel plant after taking over and rebranding the former Scattor Rock Brewery. The unofficial brewery tap is the Teign House Inn in Christow. Around 50 outlets are supplied direct.

Dartmoor Meadow (OG 1043, ABV 4.5%)
A golden, hoppy ale.

Glastonbury SIBA

Glastonbury Ales, Unit 11, Wessex Park, Somerton Business Park, Somerton, Somerset, TA11 6SB
☎ (01458) 272244 ✉ pnash@glastonbury.com
⊕ glastonburyales.com
Shop Mon-Fri 10am-4pm; Sat 10am-12.30pm
Tours by arrangement

⊗ Glastonbury Ales was established in 2002 on a five-barrel plant. In 2006 the brewery changed ownership and has recently grown to 20-barrels in size. A shop opened in late 2009. Seasonal beers: see website.

Mystery Tor (OG 1040, ABV 3.8%) ◆
A golden bitter with plenty of floral hop and fruit on the nose and palate, the sweetness giving way to a bitter hop finish. Full-bodied for a session bitter.

Lady of the Lake (OG 1042, ABV 4.2%) ◆
A full-bodied amber best bitter with plenty of hops to the fore balanced by a fruity malt flavour and a subtle hint of vanilla, leading to a clean, bitter hop aftertaste.

Love Monkey (OG 1042, ABV 4.2%)
Light medium amber bitter.

Hedge Monkey (OG 1048, ABV 4.6%)
A well-rounded deep amber bitter. Malty, rich and hoppy.

Golden Chalice (OG 1048, ABV 4.8%)
Light and golden best bitter with a robust malt character.

Glenfinnan

Glenfinnan Brewery Co Ltd, Sruth A Mhuilinn, Glenfinnan, PH37 4LT
☎ (01397) 704309 ☎ 07999 261010
✉ info@glenfinnanbrewery.co.uk
⊕ glenfinnanbrewery.co.uk

☺Glenfinnan opened in 2007 and operates on a four-barrel plant. It produces around 600 litres per week during the tourist season. Further expansion is planned. Seasonal beer: see website.

Gold Ale (OG 1040, ABV 3.8%)

Standard Ale (OG 1044, ABV 4.2%)

Glentworth

Glentworth Brewery, Glentworth House, Crossfield Lane, Skellow, Doncaster, South Yorkshire, DN6 8PL
☎ (01302) 725555

☺The brewery was founded in 1996 and is housed in former dairy buildings. The five-barrel plant supplies more than 80 pubs. Production is concentrated on mainly light-coloured, hoppy ales. Seasonal beers are available and are brewed to order.

Lightyear (OG 1037, ABV 3.9%)

Globe

▤ **Globe Brewpub, 144 High Street West, Glossop, Derbyshire, SK13 8HJ**
☎ **(01457) 852417** ⊕ **globemusic.org**

⊠ Globe was established in 2006 on a 2.5-barrel plant in an old stable behind the Globe pub. The beers are mainly for the pub but special one-off brews are produced for beer festivals.

Amber (OG 1040, ABV 3.9%)

Blondie (OG 1039, ABV 3.9%)

Stout (OG 1040, ABV 3.9%)

Comet (OG 1043, ABV 4.3%)

Gloucester (NEW) SIBA

Gloucester Brewery Ltd, Llanthony Warehouse, The Docks, Gloucester, GL1 2EH
☎ **(01452) 690541**
✉ **gloucesterbrewery@yahoo.co.uk**
⊕ **gloucesterbrewery.co.uk**
Shop Fri-Sun 9am-5pm
Tours by arrangement

⊠ Gloucester began brewing in 2011 in an old warehouse in the historic Gloucester Docks. All ales are also available bottle conditioned.

Gold (OG 1040, ABV 3.9%)

Mariner (OG 1043, ABV 4.2%)

Dockside Dark (OG 1053, ABV 5.2%)

Goacher's

P & DJ Goacher, Unit 8, Tovil Green Business Park, Burial Ground Lane, Tovil, Maidstone, Kent, ME15 6TA
☎ **(01622) 682112** ⊕ **goachers.com**
Tours by arrangement

⊠ A traditional brewery that uses only malt and Kentish hops for all its beers. Phil and Debbie Goacher have concentrated on brewing good wholesome beers without gimmicks. Two tied houses and around 30 free trade outlets in the mid-Kent area are supplied. Special is brewed for sale under house names. Seasonal beers are also available.

Real Mild Ale (OG 1033, ABV 3.4%) ⬡ ◄
A rich, flavourful mild with moderate roast barley and a generous helping of chocolate malt.

Fine Light Ale (OG 1036, ABV 3.7%) ◄
A pale, golden brown bitter with a strong, floral, hoppy aroma and aftertaste. A hoppy and moderately malty session beer.

Special/House Ale (OG 1037, ABV 3.8%)

Best Dark Ale (OG 1040, ABV 4.1%) ◄
Dark in colour but light and quaffable in body, this ale features hints of caramel and chocolate malt throughout.

Crown Imperial Stout (OG 1044, ABV 4.5%) ◄

A good, well-balanced roasty stout, dark and bitter with just a hint of caramel and a lingering creamy head.

Gold Star Strong Ale (OG 1050, ABV 5.1%) ◄
A strong pale ale brewed from 100% Maris Otter malt and East Kent Goldings hops.

Old 1066 (OG 1066, ABV 6.7%) ⬡ 🍺

Goddards SIBA ◉

Goddards Brewery Ltd, Barnsley Farm, Bullen Road, Ryde, Isle of Wight, PO33 1QF
☎ **(01983) 611011** ✉ **office@goddardsbrewery.com**
⊕ **goddardsbrewery.com**

⊠ Goddards was established in 1993 on a farmstead on the Isle of Wight. Originally occupying an 18th-century barn, expansion has meant that a new brewery was built in 2008. Seasonal beers: see website.

Ale of Wight (OG 1037, ABV 3.7%)
An aromatic, fresh and zesty pale beer.

Scrumdiggity Bitter (ABV 4%)

Fuggle-Dee-Dum (OG 1047, ABV 4.8%) ◄
Copper-coloured strong ale with plenty of malt and hops.

Goff's SIBA

Goff's Brewery Ltd, 9 Isbourne Way, Winchcombe, Cheltenham, Gloucestershire, GL54 5NS
☎ **(01242) 603383** ✉ **brewery@goffsbrewery.com**
⊕ **goffsbrewery.com**

⊠ Goff's is a family concern that has been brewing cask-conditioned ales since 1994. The ales are available regionally in more than 200 outlets and nationally through wholesalers. The addition of the seasonal Ales of the Round Table provides a range of 12 beers of which four or five are always available: see website for details.

Jouster (OG 1040, ABV 4%) ◄
A drinkable, tawny-coloured ale, with a light hoppiness in the aroma. It has a good balance of malt and bitterness in the mouth, underscored by fruitiness, with a clean, hoppy aftertaste.

Tournament (OG 1038, ABV 4%) ◄
Dark golden in colour, with a pleasant hop aroma. A clean, light and refreshing session bitter with a good hop aftertaste.

White Knight (OG 1046, ABV 4.7%) ◄
A well-hopped bitter with a light colour and full-bodied taste. Bitterness predominates in the mouth and leads to a dry, hoppy aftertaste.

Black Knight (OG 1053, ABV 5.3%)
A very dark, ruby red porter with powerful chocolate aromas and a hint of vanilla. It has smooth, rich, dry malt flavours with a subtle hoppiness.

Golcar

Golcar Brewery Ltd, 60a Swallow Lane, Golcar, Huddersfield, West Yorkshire, HD7 4NB
☎ **(01484) 644241** ☎ **07970 267555**
✉ **golcarbrewrey@btconnect.com**
Tours by arrangement

☺Golcar started brewing in 2001 and production has increased from 2.5 barrels to five barrels a

THE BREWERIES

week. The brewery owns one pub, the Rose &
Crown at Golcar, and supplies other outlets in the
local area.

Dark Mild (OG 1034, ABV 3.4%) ◀
Dark mild with a light roasted malt and liquorice
taste. Smooth and satisfying.

Bitter (OG 1039, ABV 3.9%) ◀
Amber bitter with a hoppy, citrus taste, with fruity
overtones and a bitter finish.

Pennine Gold (OG 1038, ABV 4%)
A hoppy and fruity session beer.

Weavers Delight (OG 1045, ABV 4.8%)
Malty best bitter with fruity overtones.

Guthlac's Porter (OG 1047, ABV 5%)
A robust all grain and malty working man's porter.

Golden Duck (NEW)

Golden Duck Brewery, Unit 2, Redhill Farm, Top
Street, Appleby Magna, Leicestershire, DE12 7AH
☎ 07846 295179
✉ andylunn@goldenduckbrewery.com
⊕ goldenduckbrewery.com

Golden Duck began brewing in 2012 using a five-
barrel plant.

LFB (ABV 4.3%)

Wristy Fitzy (ABV 4.6%)

Nosey Parker (ABV 5%)

Golden Triangle

Golden Triangle Brewery, Unit 9, Watton Road,
Norwich, NR9 4BG
☎ (01603) 757763 ☎ 07976 281132
✉ kevin@trianglebrewery.co.uk
⊕ goldentrianglebrewery.co.uk

Golden Triangle began brewing in 2011 using spare
capacity at Ufford Brewery. The brewery soon
expanded, purchasing Ufford's old 10-barrel plant
when the latter relocated and installing it in new
premises in Norwich. Further beers are planned.

City Gold (ABV 3.8%) ◀
Yellow hued with a grassy hop aroma. A swirling
mix of citrus, hop and bitterness with a gentle
smoky background slowly turns into a dry, bitter
finish.

City Pale (ABV 4.2%)
A hoppy, pale ale.

Golden Valley SIBA

Golden Valley Ales, Old Forge Industrial Estate,
Peterchurch, Herefordshire, HR2 0SD
☎ 07733 891314 ✉ beer@goldenvalleyales.co.uk
Tours by arrangement

☺Golden Valley was set up in 2009 at the Bull Ring
Pub, Kingstone, with equipment from the Dunn
Plowman Brewery. After a year of rapid growth the
brewery moved to an industrial unit in 2010 with a
35-barrel capacity and delivers direct to over 50
outlets. Seasonal beers are also available. Bottle-
conditioned beers are planned.

Hay Bluff (OG 1037, ABV 3.7%)
A pale session bitter.

.410 (OG 1041, ABV 4.1%)
A traditional ale with a rounded finish.

Brewers Choice (OG 1045, ABV 4.5%)
A premium, full-flavoured ale, full of character with
fruity aromas.

**Kenyons Original Oatmeal Stout
(OG 1047, ABV 4.7%)**
A smooth stout with hints of chocolate and
espresso coffee.

Goodall's

▤ Goodall's Brewery, The Lodge, 88 Crewe Road,
Alsager, Staffordshire, ST7 2JA
☎ (01270) 873669
✉ goodalls.brewery@hotmail.co.uk
Tours by arrangement

⊗ Goodall's began brewing in 2010 at the Lodge in
Alsager using a 2.5-barrel plant.

Datum (OG 1039, ABV 4%)

Fur Stoat (ABV 4.5%)

Freight (ABV 4.8%)

Snoweater (OG 1049, ABV 4.9%)

Goody (NEW)

Goody Ales Ltd, Bleangate Brewery, Braggs Lane,
Herne, Kent, CT6 7NP
☎ (01227) 361555 ✉ karen@goodyales.co.uk
⊕ goodyales.co.uk

Goody began brewing in 2012 using local
ingredients.

Genesis (ABV 3.5%)
A ruby-coloured hoppy ale with a lasting bitter
finish.

Good Health (ABV 3.6%)
A deep golden-coloured, floral bitter.

Good Heavens (ABV 4%)
An amber-coloured, hoppy ale.

Good Lord (ABV 4.4%)
A dark, spicy porter.

Goose Eye SIBA

Goose Eye Brewery Ltd, Ingrow Bridge, South Street,
Keighley, West Yorkshire, BD21 5AX
☎ (01535) 605807
✉ gooseeyebrewery@btconnect.com
⊕ goose-eye-brewery.co.uk

☺Goose Eye is a family-run brewery supplying 60-
70 regular outlets, mainly in Yorkshire and
Lancashire. The beers are available through
national wholesalers and pub chains. It produces
monthly occasional and seasonal beers with
entertaining names.

Barm Pot Bitter (OG 1038, ABV 3.8%) ◀
The bitter hop and citrus flavours that dominate
this amber session bitter are balanced by a malty
base. The finish is increasingly dry and bitter.

Bitter (OG 1039, ABV 3.9%)
A tawny brown bitter with a pleasant balance of
hops and bitterness.

Bronte Bitter (OG 1040, ABV 4%) ◀
A brown, malty and hoppy best bitter. Bitterness
increases to give a lingering, dry finish.

Chinook Blonde (OG 1042, ABV 4.2%) ▤ ◀

An increasingly tart, bitter finish follows an assertive grapefruit hoppiness in both the aroma and taste of this satisfying blonde brew.

Golden Goose (OG 1045, ABV 4.5%)
A straw-coloured beer light on the palate with a smooth and refreshing hoppy finish.

Over and Stout (OG 1052, ABV 5.2%) ◆
A full-bodied stout with roast and malt flavours mingling with hops, dark fruit and liquorice on the palate. Look also for tart fruit on the nose and a growing bitter finish.

Pommies Revenge (OG 1052, ABV 5.2%) ◆
This golden yellow, strong bitter combines grassy hops with a cocktail of fruit flavours and a hint of honey leading to a hoppy, bitter finish.

Gower (NEW) SIBA

▤ Gower Brewery Co Ltd, Greyhound Inn, Oldwalls, SA3 1HA
☎ 07967 484356 ✉ chris@gowerbrewery.com
⊕ gowerbrewery.com

Gower began brewing in 2011 using a five-barrel plant.

Sampson's Jack (ABV 4.2%)
A traditional, copper-coloured British ale.

Best Bitter (OG 1045, ABV 4.5%)
Honey-coloured ale with a full-bodied flavour and crisp, lingering bite of hop.

Gold (OG 1045, ABV 4.5%)
A golden ale with refreshing citrus flavours.

Lighthouse (OG 1046, ABV 4.5%)
A continental-style lager.

Power (OG 1052, ABV 5.5%)
A traditional IPA with a full, hoppy flavour.

Grafters SIBA

▤ Grafters Brewery, Half Moon, 23 High Street, Willingham by Stow, Lincolnshire, DN21 5JZ
☎ (01427) 788340 ✉ phil@graftersbrewery.com
⊕ graftersbrewery.com
Tours by arrangement

☺Brewing started on a 2.5-barrel plant in 2007 in a converted garage adjacent to the owner's freehouse, the Half Moon. Seasonal and occasional beers are also produced.

Moonlight (OG 1038, ABV 3.6%)

Traditional Bitter (OG 1040, ABV 3.8%)

Over the Moon (OG 1041.5, ABV 4%)

Brewers Troop (OG 1043, ABV 4.2%)

Darker Side of the Moon (OG 1045, ABV 4.2%)

Golden (OG 1046, ABV 4.3%)

Wobble Gob (OG 1050, ABV 4.9%)

Grafton SIBA

Grafton Brewing Co Ltd, Unit 5, Peppers Warehouse, Blyth Road, Worksop, Nottinghamshire, S81 0TP
☎ (01909) 476121 ☎ 07837 962688

Head Office: 8 Oak Close, Worksop, Nottinghamshire, S80 1GH ✉ allbeers@oakclose.orangehome.co.uk
Tours by arrangement

☺Grafton began brewing in 2007 in a converted stable block at the Packet Inn in Retford. The recipes for the re-named beers were purchased from Broadstone Brewery when that closed in 2006. Due to expansion it moved to its current location in 2010. Around 200 outlets are supplied. Seasonal beers are also available. Beers are also brewed under the Green Duck Beer Co. name.

Lady Julia (OG 1042, ABV 4.3%)

Blondie (OG 1046, ABV 4.8%)

Brewed under Green Duck Beer Co name:

Drunkun Duck (ABV 3.9%)

Duck Blond (ABV 4.2%)

Grain SIBA EAB

Grain Brewery, South Farm, Tunbeck Road, Alburgh, Harleston, Norfolk, IP20 0BS
☎ (01986) 788884 ✉ info@grainbrewery.co.uk
⊕ grainbrewery.co.uk
Shop Mon-Sat 10am-4pm
Tours by arrangement

⊗ Grain Brewery was launched in 2006 by Geoff Wright and Phil Halls. Originally a five-barrel brewery it upgraded to a 15-barrel plant in 2012. Situated in a converted dairy on a farm in the Waveney Valley, it supplies around 40 outlets. In 2010 Grain purchased their first pub, the Plough in Norwich. Seasonal beers: see website. Bottle-conditioned beers are also available.

Tap Room Bitter (OG 1034, ABV 3.4%)
Lightly bitter and dark amber in colour with a chocolatey and nutty lingering taste.

Oak (OG 1038, ABV 3.8%) ◆
A superbly balanced mix of malt and hops with bitter overtones. A lingering hint of molasses develops in the long, uplifting finish. Tawny hued with gentle malt airs.

Blonde Ash Wheat Beer (OG 1040, ABV 4%) ◆
A wheat beer with a lemon, clove, and banana nose. This flows through to a sweet fruity beginning, ably supported by a hoppy bitterness. Caramel appears in a strong finish.

Best Bitter (OG 1042, ABV 4.2%) ◆
A rich malty aroma introduces a well-balanced, full-bodied bitter. A complex mix of flavours dominated by malt and dried fruit ably supported by hops, toffee and bitterness.

Harvest Moon (OG 1045, ABV 4.5%) ◆
An aroma of coffee and vanilla introduces this complex but well-balanced amber-hued brew. Malt and hops vie with a bitter citrus fruitiness for dominance. Mandarins make a late appearance.

Redwood (OG 1049, ABV 4.8%)
A malty, traditional ale. Richly red in colour, well-balanced with light bitterness.

Blackwood Stout (OG 1050, ABV 5%) ◆
Based on a 1790 Whitbread recipe. Black and brooding with roast dominating from the initial aroma to the long, lingering ending. A bittersweet chocolate undercurrent adds depth.

Porter (OG 1052, ABV 5.2%) ◆
A creamy, vanilla-enhanced brew. Well-rounded maltiness flows through both bouquet and taste and gives depth to the creamy, coffee-like roast character. A big, warming finish.

THE BREWERIES

India Pale Ale (OG 1062, ABV 6.5%) ◈
Copper coloured with a brooding vinous character. Malt joins forces with dried fruit and hops to begin a sustained attack on the palate. A long-lasting finish, growing in bitterness.

Grainstore SIBA ◉

Davis'es Brewing Co Ltd, The Grainstore Brewery, Station Approach, Oakham, Rutland, LE15 6RE
☎ (01572) 770065 ✉ info@grainstorebrewery.com
⊕ grainstorebrewery.com
Tours by arrangement

Grainstore, the smallest county's largest brewery, has been in production since 1995. The company's curious name comes from the fact that it was founded by Tony Davis and Mike Davies. After 30 years in the industry Tony decided to set up his own business after finding a derelict Victorian railway grainstore building. 80 outlets are supplied.

Rutland Bitter (OG 1032, ABV 3.4%)
Light in colour and taste but a well-balanced session beer.

Rutland Panther (OG 1034, ABV 3.4%) ◈
This superb reddish-black mild punches above its weight with malt and roast flavours combining to deliver a brew that can match the average stout for intensity of flavour.

Cooking (OG 1036, ABV 3.6%) ◈
Tawny-coloured beer with malt and hops on the nose and a pleasant grainy mouthfeel. Hops and fruit flavours combine to give a bitterness that continues into a long finish.

Triple B (OG 1042, ABV 4.2%) ◈
Initially hops dominate over malt in both the aroma and taste, but fruit is there, too. All three linger in varying degrees in the sweetish aftertaste of this brown brew.

Silly Billy (OG 1043, ABV 4.3%)
A light beer with a pronounced floral aroma and flavour.

Gold (OG 1045, ABV 4.5%)
A refreshing, light golden brew with a complex flavour combining mellow malt sweetness, smooth bitterness and floral aromas.

Ten Fifty (OG 1050, ABV 5%) ◈
Pungent banana and malt notes on the nose. On the palate, rich malt and fruit are joined by subtle hop on a bittersweet base. A dry malt aftertaste with some fruit.

For Phipps Northampton Brewery Co:

Red Star (OG 1038, ABV 3.8%)
A malty, sweet beer.

India Pale Ale (OG 1042, ABV 4.2%)
A pale amber beer with a residual malt sweetness coupled with grapefruit notes from the hops to give a fine, fresh, crisp finish.

For Steamin' Billy Brewing Co (qv):

Bitter (OG 1043, ABV 4.3%) ◈
Brown-coloured best bitter. Initial malt and hops aromas are superseded by fruit and hop taste and aftertaste, accompanied by a refreshing bitterness.

Skydiver (OG 1050, ABV 5%) ◈
Full-bodied, strong, mahogany-coloured beer in which an initial malty aroma is followed by a characteristic malty sweetness that is balanced by a hoppy bitterness.

Great Gable

Great Gable Brewing Co Ltd, Unit 2G, Bridge End Industrial Estate, Egremont, Cumbria, CA22 2RD
☎ (01946) 823846 ✉ thegreatgable@btconnect.com
⊕ greatgablebrewing.com
Tours by arrangement

Great Gable began brewing in 2002 using a five-barrel plant at the Wasdale Head Inn in Gosforth. It moved to its current location in 2010, which also saw the acquisition of its first pub, the Horse & Groom at Gosforth. Seasonal and bottle-conditioned beers are available.

Iron Awe (OG 1039.5, ABV 3.8%) ◈
Well-balanced, full-flavoured, red-style beer with a fruity hoppy nose and a bitter finish.

Wastwater Gold (OG 1041, ABV 3.9%) ◈
Hoppy, fruity session beer with a dry, bitter finish.

Burnmoor Pale Ale (OG 1040, ABV 4.2%) ◈
A dry, hoppy bitter, refreshing and clean-tasting. Straw-coloured with a fruity taste and grapefruit overtones. Long, bitter finish.

Yewbarrow (OG 1054, ABV 5.5%) ◈
Strong, mild dark ale with robust roast flavours, rich and malty. Satisfying with hints of spice and fruit. Smooth chocolate and coffee aromas.

Great Heck SIBA

Great Heck Brewing Co Ltd, Rosebank Cottage, Main Street, Great Heck, North Yorkshire, DN14 0BQ
☎ (01977) 661430 ☎ 07723 381002
✉ denzil@greatheckbrewery.co.uk
⊕ greatheckbrewery.co.uk

☺Great Heck began production in 2008 on a four-barrel plant in a converted slaughterhouse. The brewery moved to a new site across the road in a converted cottage in 2012 and now operates a 15-barrel plant with capacity for 45 barrels per week. Seasonal beers are also available.

Dave (OG 1039, ABV 3.8%)

Heck's Angel (OG 1038, ABV 3.9%)
A dry pale ale with American hops.

Yorkshire Navigator (OG 1038, ABV 3.9%)

Yorkshire Pale Ale (OG 1043, ABV 4.3%)
A premium pale ale with a complex malt character and zesty finish.

Slaughterhouse Porter (OG 1046, ABV 4.5%)
Dark black, full-bodied porter with a smooth malt character.

Amish Mash (OG 1045, ABV 4.7%)
A cloudy, Germany-style weizen. Suitable for vegans.

Famous Five (OG 1049, ABV 5%)

Hequinox (OG 1049, ABV 5%)
A zesty, strong pale ale.

For Bull & Fairhouse, Wakefield:

Golden Bull (OG 1036, ABV 3.8%)
A very hoppy pale ale.

Great Newsome SIBA ◉

Great Newsome Brewery Ltd, Great Newsome Farm, South Frodingham, Winestead, East Yorkshire, HU12 0NR

☎ (01964) 612201 ☎ 07808 367386
✉ enquiries@greatnewsomebrewery.co.uk
⊕ greatnewsomebrewery.co.uk
Shop Mon-Fri 9am-4pm

😊Nestled in the Holderness countryside, Great Newsome began production in 2007 on a 10-barrel plant, brewing in renovated farm buildings. Beer is distributed throughout Yorkshire as well as North Lincolnshire. Seasonal beers: see website.

Sleck Dust (OG 1037, ABV 3.8%)
Straw-coloured, refreshingly bitter session beer with floral aroma and subtle dry finish.

Pricky Back Otchan (OG 1042, ABV 4.2%)
Hoppy golden bitter with fresh citrus aroma.

Frothingham Best (OG 1042, ABV 4.3%)
Dark amber best bitter with subtle dry finish.

Jem's Stout (OG 1044, ABV 4.3%)
Dark, smooth beer with smoky, roasted malt flavours and aroma.

Great Oakley SIBA 👁

Great Oakley Brewery, Ark Farm, High Street South, Tiffield, Northamptonshire, NN12 8AB
☎ (01327) 351759 ☎ 07850 327658
✉ sales@greatoakleybrewery.co.uk
⊕ greatoakleybrewery.co.uk
Tours by arrangement

The brewery started production in 2005 where it was housed in converted stables on a former working farm in Great Oakley. It moved to Tiffield in 2012. It is run by husband and wife team Phil and Hazel Greenway. More than 60 outlets are supplied, including the Malt Shovel Tavern in Northampton, which is the brewery tap. Seasonal beers: see website. Bottle-conditioned beers are also available.

Welland Valley Mild (OG 1037, ABV 3.6%)
A dark, traditional mild. Full of flavour.

Eleanor Cross (OG 1039, ABV 3.8%)
An amber-gold, easy-drinking ale.

Wagtail (OG 1040, ABV 3.9%)
Light coloured with a unique bitterness derived from New Zealand hops.

Wot's Occurring (OG 1040, ABV 3.9%)
Amber-gold session bitter with a subtle hop finish.

Marching In (OG 1041, ABV 4.1%)
A golden, clean-tasting beer.

Harpers (OG 1044, ABV 4.3%)
Traditional mid-brown bitter with a malty taste and slight hints of chocolate and citrus in the finish.

Gobble (OG 1045, ABV 4.5%)
Straw-coloured with a pleasant hop aftertaste.

Delapre Dark (OG 1047, ABV 4.6%)
A dark, full-bodied ale made from five different malts.

Abbey Stout (OG 1051, ABV 5%)
A dark, rich stout.

Tailshaker (OG 1051, ABV 5%)
A complex golden ale with a great depth of flavour.

Great Orme SIBA

Great Orme Brewery Ltd, Nant y Cywarch, Glan Conwy, Conwy, LL28 5PP

☎ (01492) 580548 ✉ info@greatormebrewery.co.uk
⊕ greatormebrewery.co.uk

😊Great Orme is a five-barrel micro-brewery situated on a hillside in the Conwy Valley between Llandudno and Betws-y-Coed, with views of the Conwy Estuary and the Great Orme. Established in 2005, it is housed in a number of converted farm buildings. Around 50 outlets are supplied.

Cambria (OG 1038, ABV 3.8%)
A modern IPA with a full hop flavour and dry finish.

Welsh Black (OG 1042, ABV 4%)
Smooth-tasting dark beer with roast coffee notes in aroma and taste. Sweetish in flavour and having some characteristics of a mild ale with hoppiness also present in the aftertaste.

Orme (OG 1043, ABV 4.2%)
Malty best bitter with a dry finish. Faint hop and fruit notes in aroma and taste, but malt dominates throughout.

Celtica (OG 1045, ABV 4.5%)
Yellow in colour with a zesty taste full of citrus fruit flavours. Some initial sweetness followed by peppery hops and a bitter finish.

Merlyn (OG 1051, ABV 5%)
A strong ale with balanced hop bitterness and sweet malt.

Great Western SIBA

Great Western Brewing Co Ltd, Stream Bakery, Bristol Road, Hambrook, Bristol, BS16 1RF
☎ (0117) 957 2842
✉ contact@greatwesternbrewingcompany.co.uk
⊕ greatwesternbrewingcompany.co.uk
Shop Mon, Wed-Thu 10am-5pm; Fri 10am-5pm; Sat 10am-2pm
Tours by arrangement

Great Western is a 12-barrel brewery set up in 2008 by Kevin Stone in a former bakery. The property has been renovated resulting in a bespoke showpiece brewery retaining many of the building's original features. 200 outlets are supplied and one pub is owned. Seasonal beers are also available.

Maiden Voyage (OG 1040, ABV 4%)
An amber bitter with a strong aroma of malt and fruit. The taste is initially sweet and fruity (damson notes) but the slightly astringent finish is dry and biscuity.

Bees Knees (OG 1041, ABV 4.2%)
A powerful aroma of honey with hints of malt and meadow flowers leads to a taste of honey and malt developing in bitterness through a slightly astringent but finely balanced aftertaste.

Classic Gold (OG 1044, ABV 4.6%)
Golden ale with subtle aroma of malt and pale fruits – pears, melons and golden plums. The taste is fruity with balancing hop character rapidly fading into a slightly astringent finish.

Great Yorkshire

Great Yorkshire Brewery, Cropton, North Yorkshire, YO18 8HH
☎ (01751) 417330
⊕ thegreatyorkshirebrewery.co.uk
Tours by arrangement

☺Established in the cellars of the New Inn in 1984 and originally called the Cropton Brewery, in 2012 it changed its name to the Great Yorkshire Brewery, concentrating on the production of keg lager. Cropton remains in use as a brand name. The cask beer range will be limited.

Green Duck

See Grafton

Green Dragon

▇ Green Dragon Brewery, Green Dragon, 29 Broad Street, Bungay, Suffolk, NR35 1EF
☎ (01986) 892681
Tours by arrangement

⊠ The Green Dragon pub was purchased in 1991 and the buildings at the rear converted to a brewery. In 1994 the plant was expanded and moved into a converted barn. The doubling of capacity allowed the production of a larger range of ales, including seasonal and occasional brews. The beers are available at the pub and beer festivals.

Chaucer Ale (OG 1037, ABV 3.8%)

Gold (OG 1045, ABV 4.4%)

Bridge Street Bitter (OG 1045, ABV 4.5%)

Strong Mild (OG 1054, ABV 5.4%)

Greene King

See under New Nationals section

Greenfield SIBA ◉

Greenfield Real Ale Brewery, Unit 8 Waterside Mills, Greenfield, Saddleworth, Greater Manchester, OL3 7NH
☎ (01457) 879789 ⊠ info@greenfieldrealale.co.uk
⊕ greenfieldrealale.co.uk
Shop 9am-5pm daily
Tours by arrangement

☺ Greenfield was launched in 2002 using a five-barrel plant. The brewery is in an old spinning mill next to the River Chew on the edge of the Peak District National Park. Spring water from the National Park is used for brewing. Floor area doubled in 2008 to provide additional space for cask storage and bottling facilities. The brewery is open to the public. More than 200 outlets are supplied in the north-west and further afield via distributors. Seasonal beers are also available.

Black Five (OG 1040, ABV 4%) ◖
A dark brown beer in which malt, roast, toffee, fruit and chocolate can all be found in aroma and taste. Smooth, malty aftertaste.

Delph Donkey (OG 1041, ABV 4.1%)

Thirst Born (OG 1041, ABV 4.1%)

Dobcross Bitter (OG 1041, ABV 4.2%)

Summer Ice (OG 1042, ABV 4.2%)

Icicle (OG 1044, ABV 4.4%)

Uppermill Ale (OG 1044, ABV 4.4%)

Green Jack SIBA ◉

Green Jack Brewing Co Ltd, Argyle Place, Love Road, Lowestoft, Suffolk, NR32 2NZ
☎ (01502) 562863 ⊠ info@green-jack.co.uk
⊕ green-jack.com
Tours by arrangement

⊠ Green Jack started brewing in 2003 at the Triangle Tavern in Lowestoft and in 2009 moved to a 35-barrel brew house built in a refurbished fish smoking house. The plant at the Triangle closed in 2011. More than 150 outlets are supplied and three pubs are owned. Seasonal beers: see website. Bottle-conditioned beers are available. Beers are also brewed for Hektors Brewery Ltd.

Excelsior (OG 1037, ABV 3.7%) ◖ ◖
Amber ale with sweetish aroma and caramel flavours and a bitter malty aftertaste.

Orange Wheat Beer (OG 1041, ABV 4.2%) ◖
Marmalade aroma with a hint of hops, leading to a well-balanced blend of sweetness, hops and citrus with a malt background. Mixed fruit flavours in the aftertaste.

Trawlerboys Best Bitter
(OG 1045, ABV 4.6%) ◖ ◖
Tawny beer with an aroma of apple, sultana and malt plus hints of caramel and hops. Rich fig and plum base with malt and roast overtones. Strong finish with a sticky mouthfeel.

Lurcher Stout (OG 1046, ABV 4.8%) ◖
Pleasant malt, roast and fruit aromas. Blackberry, raisin and port flavours. Long, dry, bitter roast finish.

Mahseer IPA (OG 1048, ABV 5%)

Red Herring (OG 1048, ABV 5.1%)

Gone Fishing ESB (OG 1052, ABV 5.5%)

Ripper Tripel (OG 1074, ABV 8.5%)

Baltic Trader Export Stout (OG 1092, ABV 10.5%)

Green Mill SIBA

▇ Green Mill Brewery, Cask & Feather, 1 Oldham Road, Rochdale, OL16 1UA
☎ 07967 656887 ⊠ greenmillbrewery@msn.com
⊕ greenmillbrewery.co.uk

☺Green Mill started brewing in 2007 on a 2.5-barrel plant. The brewery moved in 2010 to the rear of the Cask & Feather with plans for further expansion. A number of seasonal and occasional ales are brewed. Around 30 outlets are supplied either directly or through wholesalers.

Gold (OG 1035, ABV 3.6%)

A Bitter T'ale (OG 1039, ABV 4%)

Chief (OG 1041, ABV 4.2%)

Northern Lights (OG 1045, ABV 4.5%)

Greenodd

▇ Greenodd Brewery, Ship Inn, Main Street, Greenodd, Cumbria, LA12 7QZ
☎ 07782 655294
Tours by arrangement

Greenodd was established in 2010 in a building behind the Ship Inn using a two-barrel plant. There is a viewing window from the street behind the pub.

Blonde (OG 1040, ABV 4%)

Best Bitter (OG 1041, ABV 4.1%)

Roundabout (OG 1043, ABV 4.3%)

Brunette (OG 1045, ABV 4.5%)

Green Room

Green Room Ales Ltd, c/o St Stephen Road, Sticker, St Austell, Cornwall, PL26 7HA
☎ 07843 010950 ✉ letstalk@greenroomales.co.uk
⊕ greenroomales.co.uk

Stephen Burton started brewing in 2009 on a 2.5-barrel plant at the listed address. Due to increased demand he started using spare capacity at Keltek Brewery (qv), along with its bottling facilities. Production was relocated from early 2010, with the original plant subsequently moved to Keltek to increase flexibility. Cask beers are occasionally produced but much of the output is bottled, although at present only some of the special brews are bottle conditioned.

Green Tye EAB

Green Tye Brewery, Green Tye, Much Hadham, Hertfordshire, SG10 6JP
☎ (01279) 841041 ☎ 07770 766376
✉ info@gtbrewery.co.uk
Tours by arrangement for small groups

⊠Established in 1999 near Much Hadham, on the edge of the Ash Valley. Green Tye supplies the local free trade, neighbouring counties and further afield via beer agencies and swaps with other microbreweries. Bottle-conditioned beers are available.

Union Jack (OG 1036, ABV 3.6%)
A copper-coloured bitter, fruity with a citrus taste and a hoppy, citrus aroma, with a balanced, bitter finish.

Hadham Gold (OG 1040, ABV 4%)
A pale straw-coloured bitter with a light and fruity body and a dominant fruity aroma.

Grey Trees (NEW)

⌘ Grey Trees Brewery, Red Cow Inn, 6 Merthyr Road, Llwydcoed, CF44 0YE
☎ (01685) 873924

Grey Trees was established in 2011 and uses a one-barrel plant in a converted container at the Red Cow Inn.

Diggers Gold (ABV 4%)

Rechabites Bitter (ABV 4%)

Drummer Boy (ABV 4.2%)
Brewed in memory of the late Stuart Cable, ex-drummer for the Stereophonics. A dark amber bitter with smooth, rounded roast malt.

Gribble

⌘ Gribble Brewery Ltd, Gribble Inn, Oving, West Sussex, PO20 2BP
☎ (01243) 786893 ✉ info@gribbleinn.co.uk
⊕ gribbleinn.co.uk

⊠ The Gribble Brewery was established in 1980. Until 2005 it was run as a managed house operation by Hall & Woodhouse (qv) but is now an independent micro-brewery owned by the publicans of the inn on the same site. Around 20 outlets are supplied direct. Seasonal beer is also available.

CHI P A (ABV 3.8%)

Ale (ABV 4.1%)

Fuzzy Duck (ABV 4.3%)

Reg's Tipple (ABV 4.8%)
Reg's Tipple was named after a customer from the early days of the brewery. It has a smooth nutty flavour with a pleasant afterbite.

Plucking Pheasant (ABV 5%)

Pig's Ear (ABV 6%)

Griffin

⌘ Griffin Brewery, Church Road, Shustoke, Warwickshire, B46 2LB
☎ (01675) 481205
Tours by arrangement

☺Brewing started in 2008 in the old coffin shop premises adjacent to the pub (formerly occupied by Church End Brewery). The brewery is a venture between Griffin licensee Mick Pugh and his son Oliver. In 2012 the capacity was doubled to five barrels so that the free trade are supplied as well as the Griffin Inn. A number of seasonal ales and specials are brewed throughout the year including experimental brews for sale in the pub.

Ramblers Ruin (OG 1041, ABV 4.1%)
A light refreshing session beer with a citrus aftertaste.

BMW (Black Magic Woman) (OG 1051, ABV 5%)
A strong dark bitter with a blackcurrant aftertaste.

Pale Ale (OG 1059, ABV 5.9%)
A light-coloured beer with citrus and grapefruit flavours.

Gun Dog Ales (NEW) SIBA

Gun Dog Ales, Unit 5b, Great Central Way, Woodford Halse, NN11 3PZ
☎ (01327) 264095 ☎ 07834 374751
✉ info@gundogales.co.uk ⊕ gundogales.co.uk

Gun Dog Ales began brewing in 2012 using a six-barrel plant. Bottle-conditioned beer is also available.

Jack's Spaniels (ABV 3.8%)

Old Booze Hound (ABV 4.2%)

Top Dog (ABV 4.2%)

Bad To The Bone (ABV 4.5%)

Gundog (NEW)

Gundog Brewery Ltd, 2 Castle Island Way, North Seaton, Northumberland, NE63 0XL
☎ 07707 703182 ✉ nra.wholesales@hotmail.co.uk

Brewing began in 2011 using a 10-barrel plant.

Magnificent 7 (ABV 3.8%)
A pale, golden, hoppy ale.

Falling Pheasant (ABV 4%)
A pale amber, well-balanced session ale.

THE BREWERIES

Gwaun Valley

Gwaun Valley Brewery, Kilkiffeth Farm, Pontfaen, Fishguard, SA65 9TP
☎ (01348) 881304
✉ enquiries@gwaunvalleybrewery.co.uk
⊕ gwaunvalleybrewery.co.uk
Shop & Vistor Centre 10am-6pm daily
Tours by arrangement

⊠ Gwaun Valley began brewing in 2009 on a four-barrel plant in a converted granary. The brewery also has a campsite and pitches for five caravans.

Bitter Ale (ABV 4%)
A rich, smooth bitter with a lasting hoppy flavour.

Farmhouse Ale (ABV 4%)

Light Ale (ABV 4%)
An easy-drinking ale with fruity undertones and a clean aftertaste.

Dark Ale (ABV 4.2%)
A smooth, mild dark ale with a hint of chocolate.

St Davids Special (ABV 4.2%)

Pembrokeshire Best Bitter (ABV 4.5%)

Gwynant

⋕ Bragdy Gwynant, Tynllidiart Arms, Capel Bangor, Aberystwyth, Ceredigion, SY23 3LR
☎ (01970) 880248 ⊕ tynllidiartarms.com
Tours by arrangement

⊠ Brewing started in 2004 in a 4' 6" x 4' former men's toilet at the front of the pub, with a brew length of nine gallons. Beer is sold only in the pub. The brewery has now been recognised as the smallest commercial brewery in the world by the Guinness Book of Records. Brewing recommenced in late 2009 after a period of suspension. Bottled beers are planned.

Cwrw Gwynant (ABV 4.5%)

Hackney (NEW) SIBA

Hackney Brewery Ltd, Arch 358, Laburnum Street, Hackney, London, E2 8BB
☎ (020) 3489 9595 ✉ info@hackneybrewery.co.uk
⊕ hackneybrewery.co.uk
Tours by arrangement

⊠ Having met eight years ago while working at the Eagle on Farringdon Road, home brewers and good friends Jon Swain and Peter Hills decided to turn their pastime to profession and brew craft beer in the heart of Hackney. They are committed to giving a penny from every pint sold to local community charities. Bottle-conditioned beers are also available.

Golden Ale (OG 1041, ABV 4%)

Best Bitter (OG 1044, ABV 4.4%)

American Pale Ale (OG 1045, ABV 4.5%)

Hadrian Border SIBA

Alnwick Ales Ltd t/a Hadrian Border Brewery, Unit 5, The Preserving Works, Newburn Industrial Estate, Shelley Road, Newburn, Newcastle upon Tyne, Tyne & Wear, NE15 9RT
☎ (0191) 264 9000 ✉ hadrianborder@yahoo.co.uk
⊕ hadrian-border-brewery.co.uk
Tours by arrangement

Originally based at the Four Rivers site in Newcastle, the brewery relocated to Newburn in 2011 with a new 30-barrel brew plant to meet increased demand. The company's products are popular on Tyneside and its customer base extends through Northumberland to Edinburgh and Glasgow and down to Yorkshire. The brands are also available nationally via wholesalers. Seasonal beers: see website.

Tyneside Blonde (OG 1037, ABV 3.9%) ◀
Refreshing blonde ale with zesty notes and a clean, fruity finish.

Farne Island Pale Ale (OG 1038, ABV 4%) ◀
A copper-coloured bitter with a refreshing malt/ hop balance.

Flotsam (OG 1038, ABV 4%)
Bronze coloured with a citrus bitterness and a distinctive floral aroma.

Secret Kingdom (OG 1042, ABV 4.3%)
Dark, rich and full-bodied, slightly roasted with a malty palate ending with a pleasant bitterness.

Reiver's IPA (OG 1042, ABV 4.4%)
Golden bitter with a clean citrus palate and aroma with subtle malt flavours breaking through at the end.

Jetsam (OG 1043, ABV 4.5%)

Northumbrian Gold (OG 1044, ABV 4.5%)

Grainger Ale (OG 1045, ABV 4.6%)
A pale ale with a well-balanced, bitter finish.

Hafod (NEW)

Hafod Brewing Co Ltd, c/o Hafod Road, Pant Glas, Gwernaffield, Flintshire, CH7 5ES
☎ 07901 386638 ✉ sales@welshbeer.com
⊕ welshbeer.com

⊠ Hafod began brewing in 2011 on a small scale supplying local outlets with a number of one-off specials in addition to the core range. There are plans for expansion in 2013.

Classic (ABV 3.8%)
A well-rounded session bitter.

Dark (ABV 4.1%)
A traditional rich, dark porter.

Hopper (ABV 4.3%)

Moel Fammau (ABV 4.5%)
Brewed with local heather.

Light (ABV 4.6%)
Refreshing, light and fruity.

Hammer (ABV 6.6%)

Halfpenny SIBA

⋕ Halfpenny Brewery, Crown Inn, High Street, Lechlade, Gloucestershire, GL7 3AE
☎ (01367) 252198 ☎ 07740 932933
✉ info@crownlechlade.co.uk
⊕ halfpennybrewery.co.uk
Shop (at pub)
Tours by arrangement

⊠ Halfpenny was established in 2008 on a four-barrel plant at the rear of the Crown in Lechlade and is visible in an outbuilding. A further fermentation vessel has been added to keep up with demand making three in total. 20 local outlets are supplied direct. Bottle-conditioned beers are available.

Ha'penny Ale (OG 1039, ABV 4%)

Thames Tickler (OG 1040, ABV 4%)

Anniversary Ale (OG 1042, ABV 4.2%)

Four Seasons' Ale (OG 1042, ABV 4.3%)

Old Lech (OG 1045, ABV 4.5%)

Halifax Steam

▤ Halifax Steam Brewing Co Ltd, The Conclave, Southedge Works, Brighouse Road, Hipperholme, West Yorkshire, HX3 8EF
☎ 07974 544980 ✉ david@halifax-steam.co.uk
⊕ halifax-steam.co.uk

☺Halifax Steam was established in 2001 on a five-barrel plant and supplies only its brewery tap, the Cock o' the North, which is adjacent to the brewery. Approximately 150 different rotating beers are produced, three of which are permanent. The brewery also produces the only rice beers in the country. 10-12 Halifax Steam beers are available at any one time, plus occasional guests on a fair trade basis.

Jamaican Ginger (ABV 4%) ◈
Refreshing, yellow, grainy speciality beer. The ginger predominates but is not too fiery. It finishes sweet with the ginger receding on the palate.

Lily Fogg (ABV 4%)

Uncle John (ABV 4.3%) ◈
Roast predominates in this creamy dark brown stout. The finish is smooth with no harsh edges.

Child Catcher (ABV 4.8%)

Cock o' the North (ABV 5%) ◈
Amber-coloured, grainy strong bitter. Predominantly malty nose and taste, with a dry and astringent finish.

Hall & Woodhouse (Badger) IFBB ◉

Hall & Woodhouse Ltd, Blandford St Mary, Blandford Forum, Dorset, DT11 9LS
☎ (01258) 452141 ✉ info@hall-woodhouse.co.uk
⊕ hall-woodhouse.co.uk
Shop Mon-Sat 9am-6pm; Sun 11am-3pm (Easter-Oct)
Tours by arrangement (call to book)

⊠ Founded by Charles Hall in 1777, Hall & Woodhouse is a major independent family brewer, today run by the seventh generation of the founding family. The Badger logo was adopted in 1875. The company moved from Ansty to its present site in 1900 and a new brewery has been built on part of the existing site. Cask beer is sold in all 220 pubs. Seasonal beers: see website.

K&B Sussex Bitter (OG 1036, ABV 3.5%) ◈
Lightly-hopped, easy-drinking session bitter with hints of malt and caramel and the traditional Badger fruit flavour dominating the lingering bitter aftertaste.

Badger First Gold (OG 1041, ABV 4%) ⊟ ◈
Good example of a best bitter with good, but not over powering, hop aromas and flavours and a bittersweet aftertaste.

Tanglefoot (OG 1047, ABV 4.9%) ◈

Relatively sweet-tasting and deceptive, given its strength. Pale malt provides caramel overtones and bittersweet finish.

Hambleton SIBA ◉

Nick Stafford's Hambleton Ales, Melmerby Green Road, Melmerby, North Yorkshire, HG4 5NB
☎ (01765) 640108 ✉ sales@hambletonales.co.uk
⊕ hambletonales.co.uk
Shop Mon-Fri 7.30am-5pm
Tours by arrangement

☺Hambleton Ales was established in 1991 on the banks of the River Swale in the heart of the Vale of York. Expansion over the years has resulted in relocation to larger premises on several occasions, the last being in 2007. Capacity in the custom-built brewery is 100 barrels a week and a bottling line caters for micros and larger brewers, handling more than 50 brands. Four core ales are brewed constantly along with a monthly special and are supplied to more than 100 outlets throughout Yorkshire and north-east England. The company also contract brew for the Village Brewer and Black Dog Brewery.

Bitter (OG 1038.5, ABV 3.8%)
A golden bitter with a good balance of malty and refreshing citrus notes leading to a mellow, tangy finish.

Goldfield (OG 1041, ABV 4.2%)

Stallion (OG 1041, ABV 4.2%) ◈
A premium bitter, moderately hoppy throughout and richly balanced in malt and fruit, developing a sound and robust bitterness, with earthy hops drying the aftertaste.

Stud (OG 1042.5, ABV 4.3%) ◈
A strongly bitter beer, with rich hop and fruit. It ends dry and spicy.

Nightmare (OG 1050, ABV 5%) ◈
This impressively flavoured beer satisfies all parts of the palate. Strong roast malts dominate, but hoppiness rears out of this complex blend.

For Black Dog Brewery, Whitby:

Whitby Abbey Ale (OG 1037.5, ABV 3.8%)
A light-coloured, hoppy bitter.

Schooner (OG 1041.5, ABV 4.2%)

Rhatas (OG 1045, ABV 4.6%)
A dark, rich bitter. Creamy and smooth to the palate.

For Village Brewer:

White Boar (OG 1037.5, ABV 3.8%) ◈
A light, flowery and fruity ale; crisp, clean and refreshing, with a dry-hopped, powerful but not aggressive bitter finish.

Bull (OG 1039, ABV 4%)

Hammerpot SIBA

Hammerpot Brewery Ltd, Unit 30, The Vinery, Arundel Road, Poling, West Sussex, BN18 9PY
☎ (01903) 883338 ✉ sales@hammerpot-brewery.co.uk ⊕ hammerpot-brewery.co.uk

⊠ Hammerpot started brewing in 2005 using a five-barrel plant, which was upgraded to a 10-barrel plant in 2011. The brewery supplies as far north as Berkshire and into London and from Eastbourne to Southampton. Seasonal and occasional beers: see website. Bottle-conditioned beers are also available.

Shooting Star (OG 1038, ABV 3.8%)

HPA (OG 1044, ABV 4.1%)
A light, golden, tangy pale ale with a full, fresh hop flavour.

Red Hunter (OG 1046, ABV 4.3%)
A ruby-red bitter with a full-bodied, rich character.

Woodcote (OG 1047, ABV 4.5%)
A tangy amber bitter with a pleasant, dry finish.

Bottle Wreck Porter (OG 1047, ABV 4.7%) ⊡ 🍴
A traditional pitch black porter with coffee, chocolate and rich roast malt flavours.

Madgwick Gold (OG 1050, ABV 5%)
A golden ale with a fresh citrus spicy hop aroma.

Handley's (NEW)

🗏 Handley's Brewery, Willow Tree, Front Street, Barnby in the Willows, Nottinghamshire, NG24 2SA
☎ (01636) 629003 ✉ info@willowtreebarnby.co.uk
⊕ willowtreebarnby.co.uk

Handley's began brewing in 2011 on a 0.5-barrel plant installed behind the Willow Tree pub by owner Brett Handley. Beer is mostly sold in the pub but can be found at beer festivals if stocks permit.

Idiot Proof (ABV 3.5%)

Barnby Pale Ale (ABV 3.7%)

Willow Tree Gold (ABV 3.8%)

Wash Sparky (ABV 4%)

FSB (Front Street Bitter) (ABV 4.2%)

Ha'penny SIBA

Ha'penny Brewing Co Ltd, Cuckoo Hall Brewery, Unit 8, Aldborough Hall Farm, Aldborough Hatch, Ilford, Essex, IG2 7TD
☎ (020) 8599 1338 ☎ 07961 161869
✉ info@hapenny-brewing.co.uk
⊕ hapenny-brewing.co.uk
Tours by arrangement

⊠ Ha'penny was established in 2009 by two CAMRA members in a disused stable block that had a former life as a pub and beer house for the Aldborough Hall estate workers.

Sixteen-String Jack IPA (ABV 3.8%) ◥
A fruity pale brown bitter with hops and malt throughout. The bitterness builds on drinking and lingers in the dry aftertaste, which has a hint of toffee.

London Particular Ruby Ale (ABV 4%)

Spring-Heeled Jack Porter (ABV 4%)

London Stone Bitter (ABV 4.5%)

Gog Magog Golden Ale (ABV 5%) ◥
A dark gold beer with a little sulphur on the nose with floral parma violets and vanilla. The flavour is sweet and fruity. The finish short and dry.

Mrs Lovett's Most Efficacious Stout Porter (ABV 5%) ◥
A light-drinking, black, dry stout with a chocolate aroma. Roast notes and molasses dominate the flavour with a lingering sweetness balanced by the dryness.

Happy Valley

Happy Valley Brewery, 8 Hazelhurst Drive, Bollington, Cheshire, SK10 5QT
☎ 07758 512080
✉ dave@happyvalleybrewery.co.uk
⊕ happyvalleybrewery.co.uk
Tours by arrangement

⊠ Happy Valley was established in 2010 by David and Nicola Hughes using a 2.5-barrel plant. Pubs are supplied across Cheshire, Derbyshire, Greater Manchester and Staffordshire.

Sworn Secret (OG 1038, ABV 3.8%)
A pale, straw-coloured session ale with strong hop character and a crisp citrus finish.

Little Rascal (OG 1039, ABV 3.9%)
A light, golden session ale, well-balanced with a lingering citrus and grapefruit aftertaste.

Lazy Daze (OG 1042, ABV 4.2%)
A golden ale with a hoppy finish.

Black Magic (OG 1046, ABV 4.6%)
A full-bodied ale with a malt taste and bitter finish.

Tie the Knot (OG 1050, ABV 5%)
A straw-coloured strong bitter brewed in the IPA style with malty tastes and a big hop character.

Bollywood IPA (OG 1056, ABV 5.9%)
A full-bodied, straw-coloured strong bitter brewed in the IPA style. Rounded malt flavours blended with bitterness and a big hop character. Deep and intensely rich taste.

Harbour (NEW) SIBA

Harbour Brewing Co, Trekillick Farm, Kirland, Bodmin, Cornwall, PL30 5BB
☎ (01208) 832131 ✉ eddie@harbourbrewing.com
⊕ harbourbrewing.com

Harbour Brewing is a 10-barrel brewery founded in 2012 on the outskirts of Bodmin by brewer Rhys Powell.

Light (ABV 3.7%)

Amber (ABV 4%)

Hefeweiss (ABV 4.5%)

Golden Ale (ABV 5%)

IPA (ABV 5%)

Pilsner (ABV 5.5%)

Porter (ABV 5.6%)

Hardknott SIBA

Hardknott Brewery, Unit 10, Devonshire Road Industrial Estate, Millom, Cumbria, LA18 4JS
☎ (01229) 779309 ✉ beer@hardknott.com
⊕ hardknott.com
Tours by arrangement

☺ Hardknott Brewery opened in 2005 using a two-barrel plant at the Woolpack Inn in Boot. The brewery relocated to Millom and expanded in 2010. Since the purchase of two dual purpose fermenters it is now a 12-barrel plant. It specialises in limited edition bottle-conditioned and regular cask-conditioned beers. All bottled beers are suitable for vegans.

Light Cascade (OG 1036, ABV 3.4%) ◥
A well-hopped light ale. The hoppy bitter taste diminishes into an intense bitter finish.

Katalyst (OG 1040, ABV 3.8%)

Continuum (OG 1042, ABV 4%) ◀
An amber-coloured beer with pronounced hops and bitterness through to the aftertaste. Some maltiness in the aroma and taste.

Atomic Narcissus (OG 1045, ABV 4.2%)

Cool Fusion (OG 1044, ABV 4.4%)

Code Black (ABV 5.6%)

Infra Red (OG 1065, ABV 6.2%)

For Woolpack Inn, Boot

Woolpacker (OG 1038, ABV 3.9%)

Hardys & Hansons

See Greene King in New Nationals section

Hart of Preston SIBA

Hart of Preston Brewing Co Ltd, Unit 5, Oxhey Industrial Estate, Greenbank Street, Preston, Lancashire, PR2 6YW
☎ (01772) 437651
✉ johnsmith@hartbreweryltd.co.uk
⊕ hartbreweryltd.co.uk
Shop – Please ring for opening hours
Tours by arrangement

Formerly the Hart Brewery, it opened in 1995 behind the Cartford Hotel in Little Eccleston. In 2010 the brewery was renamed and relocated to Preston. It supplies a number of local outlets and exchanges with other micro-breweries. Seasonal beers are also available.

Golden Guild (ABV 3.7%)

Lancashire Best Bitter (ABV 3.9%)

Dishy Debbie (OG 1040, ABV 4%)

Ice Maiden (OG 1040, ABV 4%) ◀
Hoppy, crisp, straw-coloured bitter with floral notes and a dry finish.

Pinches IPA (ABV 4.3%)

Hart of Stebbing EAB

▤ Hart of Stebbing Brewery, White Hart, High Street, Stebbing, Essex, CM6 3SQ
☎ (01371) 856383
✉ nick@hartofstebbingbrewery.co.uk
⊕ hartofstebbingbrewery.co.uk

⊠ The brewery was established in 2007 by Bob Dovey and Nick Eldred, who is also the owner of the White Hart pub where the brewery is based. At present only the White Hart and local beer festivals are supplied. Occasional specials are also brewed.

Hart IPA (OG 1035, ABV 3.5%)

Hartshorns (NEW)

Hartshorns Brewery, Unit 4, Tomlinsons Industrial Estate, Alfreton Road, Derby, DE21 4ED
☎ 07830 367125 ✉ darren@hartshornsbrewery.com
⊕ hartshornsbrewery.com

Hartshorns began brewing in 2012 using a six-barrel plant installed by brothers Darren and Lindsey Hartshorn.

Highgate (ABV 4.3%)

A copper-coloured, fruity best bitter.

Harveys IFBB 👁

Harvey & Son (Lewes) Ltd, Bridge Wharf Brewery, 6 Cliffe High Street, Lewes, East Sussex, BN7 2AH
☎ (01273) 480209 ✉ maj@harveys.org.uk
⊕ harveys.org.uk
Shop Mon-Sat 9.30am-5.30pm
Tours by arrangement (currently two year waiting list)

⊠ Established in 1790, this independent family brewery operates from the banks of the River Ouse in Lewes. A major development in 1985 doubled the brewhouse capacity and subsequent additional fermenting capacity has seen production rise to more than 45,000 barrels a year. There is also a microbrewery on site used to brew special beers including replicating old Lewes Brewery recipes using the 'County Town Beers' name. Harveys supplies real ale to all its 47 pubs and 450 free trade outlets in the south-east. Seasonal beers: see website. Bottle-conditioned beer is also available.

Sussex XX Mild Ale (OG 1030, ABV 3%) ◀
A dark copper-brown colour. Roast malt dominates the aroma and palate leading to a sweet, caramel finish.

Hadlow Bitter (OG 1033, ABV 3.5%)
Formerly Sussex Pale Ale

Sussex Best Bitter (OG 1040, ABV 4%) ◀
Full-bodied brown bitter. A hoppy aroma leads to a good malt and hop balance, and a dry aftertaste.

Old Ale (OG 1043, ABV 4.3%)

Olympia (OG 1042, ABV 4.3%)

Armada Ale (OG 1045, ABV 4.5%) ◀
Hoppy amber best bitter. Well-balanced fruit and hops dominate throughout with a fruity palate.

Harviestoun SIBA 👁

Harviestoun Brewery Ltd, Alva Industrial Estate, Alva, Clackmannanshire, FK12 5DQ
☎ (01259) 769100 ✉ info@harviestoun.com
⊕ harviestoun.com
Tours by arrangement

☺Harviestoun started in a barn in the village of Dollar in 1985 with a five-barrel brew plant, but now operate on a state-of-the-art 60-barrel brewery in Alva. The brewery supplies local outlets direct and nationwide via wholesalers. It was bought by Caledonian Brewing Co in 2006 but is now independent following the takeover of Caledonian by Scottish & Newcastle in 2008. Further expansion is planned. Seasonal beers: see website.

Bitter & Twisted (OG 1036, ABV 3.8%) ◀
Refreshingly hoppy beer with fruit throughout. A bittersweet taste with a long, bitter finish. A golden session beer.

Natural Blonde (OG 1040, ABV 4%)
A hoppy, crisp, zesty and sharp beer.

Schiehallion (OG 1048, ABV 4.8%) ◀
A Scottish cask lager, brewed using a lager yeast and Hersbrucker hops. A hoppy aroma, with fruit and malt, leads to a malty, bitter taste with floral hoppiness and a bitter finish.

THE BREWERIES

Harwich Town EAB

Harwich Town Brewing Co, Station Approach, Harwich, Essex, CO12 3NA
☎ (01255) 551155 ✉ info@harwichtown.co.uk
⊕ harwichtown.co.uk
Shop – see website
Tours by arrangement

Brewing started in 2007 on a five-barrel plant next to Harwich Town railway station. The brewer is a CAMRA member and former customs officer. Beers are named after local landmarks, characters or events. 50 outlets are supplied. The brewery holds an annual beer festival in July and a festival special is brewed for the Harwich & Dovercourt Bay Winter Ale Festival in December. Seasonal and bottle-conditioned beers are also available.

Bay Bitter (OG 1036, ABV 3.6%)

Ha'Penny Mild (OG 1036, ABV 3.6%)

EPA 100 (OG 1038, ABV 3.8%)

Leading Lights (OG 1038, ABV 3.8%)

Ganges (OG 1040, ABV 4%)

Misleading Lights (OG 1040, ABV 4%)

Bathside Battery Bitter (OG 1042, ABV 4.2%)

Redoubt Stout (OG 1042, ABV 4.2%)

Parkeston Porter (OG 1045, ABV 4.5%)

Lighthouse Bitter (OG 1048, ABV 4.8%)

Phoenix APA (OG 1052, ABV 5.1%)

Hastings SIBA

Hastings Brewery Ltd, Unit 12, Conqueror Industrial Estate, Moorhurst Road, St Leonards, East Sussex, TN38 9NB
☎ (01424) 850961 ☎ 07708 259342
✉ info@hastingsbrewery.co.uk
⊕ hastingsbrewery.co.uk
Tours by arrangement

⊠ The brewery was founded in 2010 by Brett Ross, alongside father and son Andy and Pete Mason. It exclusively produces vegan-friendly beers. The initial brewery had a one-barrel brew length, which was replaced in 2011 by a 5.25-barrel system.

Blonde (OG 1040, ABV 3.9%)

Best (OG 1042, ABV 4.1%)

HPA (OG 1046, ABV 4.7%)

Special Bitter (OG 1053, ABV 5.5%)

Havant SIBA ◁◎▷

Havant Brewery, c/o 29 Gladys Avenue, Cowplain, Waterlooville, Hampshire, PO8 8HT
☎ (02392) 252118
✉ mike@thehavantbrewery.co.uk
⊕ thehavantbrewery.co.uk

⊠ Havant began brewing in 2009 on a one-barrel plant and upgraded in 2011 to a bespoke three-barrel brewery. Seasonal and special beers: see website. Bottle-conditioned beer is available.

Time (OG 1036, ABV 3.6%)

Started (OG 1040, ABV 4%)

Finished (OG 1051, ABV 5%)

Hawkshead SIBA ◁◎▷

Hawkshead Brewery Ltd, Mill Yard, Staveley, Cumbria, LA8 9LR
☎ (01539) 822644
✉ info@hawksheadbrewery.co.uk
⊕ hawksheadbrewery.co.uk
Shop 12–5pm daily

⊛Hawkshead brewery complex is a showcase for real ale. The brewery expanded in 2006, having outgrown its original site (opened in 2002) in a barn at Hawkshead. Further expansion in 2010 added a second bar to the Beer Hall, which is the visitor centre and brewery tap. A kitchen serves 'beer tapas' to complement the beer. Windows throughout look into the cellar, specialist beer shop, brew house and the new fermentation room, which is in the main bar. Pubs are supplied throughout the north west.

Windermere Pale (OG 1036, ABV 3.5%) ◆
Crisp and fruity yellow beer with hints of melon and grapefruit and a strong bitter aftertaste.

Bitter (OG 1037, ABV 3.7%) 🍷 🍺 ◆
Well-balanced, thirst-quenching beer with fruit and hops aroma, leading to a lasting bitter finish.

Lakeland Gold (OG 1043, ABV 4.4%) ◆
Fresh, well-balanced fruity, hoppy beer with a clean bitter aftertaste.

Brodie's Prime (OG 1048, ABV 4.9%) 🍺 ◆
Complex, dark brown beer with plenty of malt, fruit and roast taste. Satisfying full body with clean finish.

Haworth Steam SIBA

Haworth Steam Brewing Co, Rear 98 Main Street, Haworth, West Yorkshire, BD22 0HB
☎ (01535) 646059
✉ haworthsteambrew@gmail.com
⊕ haworthsteambrewery.co.uk
Shop 10am–6pm daily
Tours by arrangement

Haworth Steam was established in 2011 using a five-barrel plant, bringing brewing back to Haworth for the first time in over 70 years. The brewery now has online sales and a café, bar and bistro.

Austerity (ABV 3.8%)

True Tyke (ABV 3.8%)

Rascal (ABV 4.1%)

Ironclad 957 (ABV 4.3%)

Fallwood XXXX (ABV 5.2%)

Haywood Bad Ram SIBA

Haywood Bad Ram Brewery, Callow Top Farm Holiday Park, Sandybrook, Ashbourne, Derbyshire, DE6 2AQ
☎ (01335) 344020 ☎ 07974 948427
✉ acphaywood@aol.com ⊕ callowtop.co.uk
Shop 8.30am-9.30pm daily (peak season); 9.30am-5pm daily (low season)
Tours by arrangement

⊠ Established in 2003, the brewery was based in a converted barn but a new brewery and bottling plant became operational in 2012. One pub is owned (on site) and several other outlets are supplied. Bottle-conditioned beers are available.

Dr Samuel Johnson (ABV 4.5%)

Bad Ram (ABV 5%)

Lone Soldier (ABV 5%)

Woggle Dance (ABV 5%)

Callow Top IPA (OG 1050, ABV 5.2%)

Heart of Wales

▤ Neuadd Arms Brewing Co t/a Heart of Wales Brewery, Stables Yard, Zion Street, Llanwrtyd Wells, Powys, LD5 4RD
☎ (01591) 610236
✉ Lindsay@heartofwalesbrewery.co.uk
⊕ heartofwalesbrewery.co.uk
Shop 10am-6pm daily
Tours by arrangement

The brewery was set up with a six-barrel plant in 2006 in old stables at the rear of the Neuadd Arms Hotel. Beers are brewed using water from the brewery's own borehole. Seasonal brews celebrate local events such as the World Bogsnorkelling Championships. Seasonal and bottle-conditioned beers are available. All bottle-conditioned beers are suitable for vegetarians and vegans. Cambrian Heart was commissioned by and is brewed for the Cambrian Mountains Initiative, inspired by the Prince of Wales, which aims to promote and support rural producers and communities in the region.

Irfon Valley Bitter (OG 1038, ABV 3.6%)

Aur Cymru (OG 1040, ABV 3.8%)

Bitter (OG 1042, ABV 4.1%)

Welsh Black (OG 1045, ABV 4.4%) 🗗 🍺

Cambrian Heart Ale/Noble Eden Ale (OG 1046, ABV 4.5%)

Inn-stable (OG 1065, ABV 6.8%)

High as a Kite (OG 1095, ABV 10.5%) 🗗 🍺

Hebridean

Hebridean Brewing Co, 18a Bells Road, Stornoway, Isle of Lewis, HS1 2RA
☎ (01851) 700123 ✉ info@hebridean-brewery.co.uk ⊕ hebridean-brewery.co.uk
Shop open in summer months only

☺The company was set up in 2001 on a steam powered plant with a 14-barrel brew length. A shop is attached to the brewery. Seasonal beers are produced for Mods, Gaelic festivals that are the Scottish equivalent of the Welsh Eisteddfod.

Celtic Black Ale (OG 1036, ABV 3.9%)
A dark ale full of flavour, balancing an aromatic hop combined with a subtle bite and a pleasantly smooth caramel aftertaste.

Clansman Ale (OG 1036, ABV 3.9%)
A light Hebridean beer, brewed with Scottish malts and lightly hopped to give a subtle bittering.

Seaforth Ale (ABV 4.2%) 🍺
A light, quaffable beer with a delicate nose. A complex mixture of biscuity malt and fruit in the taste leads to a lasting, bittersweet finish.

Islander Strong Premium Ale (OG 1044, ABV 4.8%) 🍺
A malty, fruity strong bitter drinking dangerously below its ABV.

Berserker Export Pale Ale (OG 1068, ABV 7.5%) 🍺

This malty, fruity winter warmer is packed full of flavour, with toffee apple and caramel notes right through to the long, satisfying aftertaste.

Heddon Valley (NEW)

Heddon Valley Ales, Hunters Inn, Heddon Valley, Devon, EX31 4PY
☎ (01598) 763230 ✉ info@thehuntersinn.net
⊕ thehuntersinn.net

Heddon Valley began brewing in 2012 using spare capacity at Country Life Brewery. Beers are available at the Hunters Inn and other local outlets.

Dr Heale (ABV 3.8%)

Miss Loosemoor (ABV 4.5%)

Mr Sluggett (ABV 5.2%)

Hektors

Hektors Brewery Ltd, The Office, Henham Park, Southwold, Suffolk, NR34 8AN
☎ 07900 553426 ✉ hektor@henhampark.com
⊕ hektorsbrewery.com

⊗ Beers are currently brewed by the owner on the equipment of other breweries, including Green Jack and Oakham. However, there are plans to install a brewery in a converted barn at Henham Park in the future. Hektor's beers are provided to Henham Park's 65,000 annual visitors in addition to five other outlets and local events.

Pure (OG 1038, ABV 3.8%)

House (OG 1042, ABV 4.2%)

Scarecrow (OG 1050, ABV 5%)

Hellhound

Hellhound Brewing Ltd, 6 Seager Court, Crockatt Road, Hadleigh, Suffolk, IP7 6RL
☎ 07850 076202 ✉ jack@hellhound.co.uk
⊕ hellhound.co.uk

Hellhound began brewing in 2010 using a six-barrel plant. Seasonal beer is available.

Dirty Blond (ABV 3.9%)

Soul Survivor IPA (ABV 4.2%)

Thunderstruck (ABV 4.2%)
A wheat beer.

Hen House (NEW)

Hen House Brewery, The Old Dairy, Walliscote Farm, High Street, Whitchurch-on-Thames, Oxfordshire, RG8 7EP
☎ 07845 929197 ⊕ henhousebrewery.co.uk
Shop Tue & Fri 2-6pm; Sat 2-4pm

Hen House began brewing in 2012 using a 30-litre plant. Only bottle-conditioned beers are produced. Seasonal and special beers: see website.

Hensting SIBA

Hensting Brewery Ltd, Hill View Farm, Hensting Lane, Owslebury, Hampshire, SO21 1LE
☎ 07775 601827 ✉ rebecca@henstingbrewery.co.uk
⊕ henstingbrewery.co.uk

THE BREWERIES

Hensting Brewery was established in 2010 on the owner's farm using a 0.5-barrel plant. Brewing is currently suspended.

Hepworth SIBA

Hepworth & Co (Brewers) Ltd, The Beer Station, Railway Yard, Horsham, West Sussex, RH12 2NW
☎ (01403) 269696 ✉ mail@hepworthbrewery.co.uk
⊕ hepworthbrewery.co.uk
Sales 9am-6pm daily
Tours by arrangement

⊠ Hepworth's was established in 2001, initially bottling beer only. In 2003 draught beer brewing was started with Sussex malt and hops. In 2004 an organic lager was introduced in bottle and on draught. 274 outlets are supplied. Seasonal beers are also available.

Traditional Sussex Bitter (OG 1035, ABV 3.5%) ◆
A fine, clean-tasting amber session beer. A bitter beer with a pleasant fruity and hoppy aroma that leads to a crisp, tangy taste. A long, dry finish.

Pullman First Class Ale (OG 1041, ABV 4.2%) ◆
A sweet, nutty maltiness and fruitiness are balanced by hops and bitterness in this easy-drinking, pale brown best bitter. A subtle bitter aftertaste.

Prospect Organic (ABV 4.5%)
A well-balanced and traditional brew.

Classic Old Ale (OG 1046, ABV 4.8%)
A traditional winter brew, rich with a variety of roasted malts balanced with sweetness and the bitterness of Admiral hops.

Iron Horse (OG 1048, ABV 4.8%) ◆
There's a fruity, toffee aroma to this light brown, full-bodied bitter. A citrus flavour balanced by caramel and malt leads to a clean, dry finish.

Blonde (ABV 5%)
Organic lager. Suitable for vegans.

Hereford SIBA 👁

▤ Hereford Brewery, 88 St Owen Street, Hereford, HR1 2QD
☎ (01432) 342125 ✉ jfkenyon@aol.com
Tours by arrangement

The brewery was built in a room of the Victory in 2000 by Jim Kenyon, following the purchase of the pub. Initially only serving the pub, it has steadily grown from a four-barrel to a 10-barrel plant. In 2010 the brewery changed its name from Spinning Dog to Hereford Brewery. Around 300 other outlets are supplied. Seasonal and bottle-conditioned beers are also available.

Herefordshire Owd Bull (OG 1039, ABV 3.9%)
A good session beer with an abundance of hops and bitterness. Dry, with a citrus aftertaste.

Dark (OG 1040, ABV 4%)
A dark, malty mild with a hint of bitterness and a touch of roast caramel. A smooth drinkable ale.

Herefordshire Light Ale (OG 1040, ABV 4%)
Brewed along the lines of the award-winning Mutleys Pitstop. Light and refreshing.

Original Bitter (OG 1041, ABV 4.1%)
Light in colour with a distinctive fruitiness from start to finish.

Best Bitter (ABV 4.2%)

A full-bodied, amber-coloured best bitter, rich in malt undertones with a fresh, fruity aroma.

Celtic Gold (OG 1045, ABV 4.5%)
A bright gold best bitter, full of fruit and blackcurrant flavours.

Mutleys Revenge (OG 1048, ABV 4.8%)
A strong, smooth, hoppy beer, amber in colour. Full-bodied with a dry, citrus aftertaste.

Mutts Nuts (OG 1050, ABV 5%)
A dark, strong ale, full bodied with a hint of a chocolate aftertaste.

Hereward

Hereward Brewery, 50 Fleetwood, Ely, Cambridgeshire, CB6 1BH
☎ (01353) 666441
✉ michael.czarnobaj@ntlworld.com

A small home-based brewery launched in 2003 on a 10-gallon kit. The brewery supplies mainly beer festivals and also brews festival specials (brewed to order). Real cider is sometimes produced. Seasonal beers are also available.

Michael's Mild (ABV 3.4%)

Bitter (ABV 3.8%)

St Ethelreda's Golden Bitter (ABV 4%)

Porta Porter (ABV 4.2%)

Oatmeal Stout (ABV 4.5%)

Hesket Newmarket SIBA

Hesket Newmarket Brewery Ltd, Old Crown Barn, Back Green, Hesket Newmarket, Cumbria, CA7 8JG
☎ (01697) 478066 ✉ info@hesketbrewery.co.uk
⊕ hesketbrewery.co.uk
Shop Mon-Fri 8.30am-5pm; Sat 10am-2pm (summer)
Tours by arrangement

☺The brewery was established in 1988 and was bought by a co-operative of villagers in 1999, anxious to preserve a community resource. Most of the original recipes have been retained, all named after local fells except for Doris's 90th Birthday Ale. An 11-barrel plant was installed in 2005 followed by a small-scale bottling plant in 2006. Around 50 regular outlets are supplied. Bottle-conditioned beers are available.

Blencathra Bitter (OG 1035, ABV 3.2%) ◆
A malty, tawny ale, mild and mellow for a bitter, with a dominant caramel flavour.

Haystacks (OG 1037, ABV 3.7%) ◆
Light, easy-drinking, thirst-quenching blond beer; very pleasant for its strength.

Skiddaw Special Bitter (OG 1037, ABV 3.7%)
An amber session beer, malty throughout, well-balanced with a dryish finish.

Black Sail (OG 1042.1, ABV 4%) ◆
A sweet stout with roast flavours.

Helvellyn Gold (OG 1039, ABV 4%)
A smooth, golden bitter. light in colour but full-flavoured.

High Pike (OG 1042, ABV 4.2%) ◆
A traditional style bitter; fruity with a dry finish.

Doris's 90th Birthday Ale (OG 1045, ABV 4.3%)

A fruity premium beer.

Scaféll Blonde (OG 1043, ABV 4.4%)
Pale with bags of hop flavour, not too bitter. A good introduction to real ale for lager drinkers.

Catbells Pale Ale (OG 1050, ABV 5%) 🍷 🍺
Golden ale with a nice balance of fruity sweetness and bitterness, almost syrupy but with an unexpectedly dry finish.

Old Carrock (OG 1060, ABV 6%) 🍾 🍺
Reddy brown strong ale, vine-fruity in flavour with slightly astringent finish.

Hexhamshire SIBA 👁

Hexhamshire Brewery, Leafields, Ordley, Hexham, Northumberland, NE46 1SX
☎ (01434) 606577 ✉ ghb@hexhamshire.co.uk
🌐 hexhamshire.co.uk

⊠ Hexhamshire was founded in 1993 and is run by one of the founding partners and his family. A relocation to the Dipton Mill Inn is planned. 30 outlets are supplied direct and many others through the SIBA scheme.

Devil's Elbow (OG 1036, ABV 3.6%) 🍺
Amber brew full of hops and fruit, leading to a bitter finish.

Shire Bitter (OG 1037, ABV 3.8%) 🍺
A good balance of hops with fruity overtones, this amber beer makes an easy-drinking session bitter.

Blackhall English Stout (ABV 4%)
A pleasant bitter beer with a strong roast malt flavour.

Devil's Water (OG 1041, ABV 4.1%) 🍺
Copper-coloured best bitter, well-balanced with a slightly fruity, hoppy finish.

Whapweasel (OG 1048, ABV 4.8%) 🍺
An interesting smooth, hoppy beer with a fruity flavour. Amber in colour, the bitter finish brings out the fruit and hops.

Old Humbug (OG 1055, ABV 5.5%)

Highgate SIBA

Highgate & Walsall Brewing Co Ltd, Sandymount Road, Walsall, West Midlands, WS1 3AP
☎ (01922) 644453 ✉ info@HWBC-ltd.co.uk
🌐 davenportsbeer.co.uk
Tours by arrangement

☺Built in 1898, Highgate was an independent brewery until 1938 when it was taken over by Mitchells & Butlers subsequently becoming the smallest in the Bass group. It was brought back into the independent sector in 1995 as the result of a management buy-out. It was then bought by Aston Manor in 2000. In 2007 Highgate was bought by Global Star, a pub group. The brewery closed during 2010 and reopened later the same year as the Highgate & Walsall Brewery Company. The brewery supply Molson Coors with Dark Mild as well as having a contract to brew Smiles beers. Beers are brewed at unnamed sites. Seasonal beers are available.

Davenports Fat Catz (OG 1040, ABV 4%)

Davenports IPA (OG 1040.8, ABV 4%)

Davenports Original (OG 1040, ABV 4%)

Davenports England Glory (OG 1044, ABV 4.4%)

Davenports Fox's Nob (OG 1044, ABV 4.4%)

Davenports Highland Whisky Ale (OG 1044, ABV 4.4%)

Davenports Irish Whiskey Ale (OG 1044, ABV 4.4%)

For Coors:

M&B Mild (OG 1034.8, ABV 3.2%)

For Smiles:

Blonde (OG 1038.8, ABV 3.8%)

Best (OG 1041, ABV 4.1%)

Bristol IPA (OG 1044, ABV 4.4%)

Heritage (OG 1052, ABV 5.2%)

High House Farm SIBA

High House Farm Brewery, Matfen, Newcastle upon Tyne, Tyne & Wear, NE20 0RG
☎ (01661) 886192/886769 (Sales line)
✉ info@highhousefarmbrewery.co.uk
🌐 highhousefarmbrewery.co.uk
Shop Sun-Tue 10.30am-5pm, Thu-Sat 10.30am-9pm, closed Wed
Tours by arrangement

⊠ The brewery was founded in 2003 on a working farm with visitor centre, brewery shop and exhibition and function room. Over 350 outlets are supplied. Seasonal beers: see website.

Sundancer (OG 1036, ABV 3.6%)

Pullet Please (OG 1037, ABV 3.7%)
An easy-drinking pale golden ale with a delicate grapefruit nose and a crisp, dry finish.

Auld Hemp (OG 1038, ABV 3.8%) 🍾 🍺
Tawny coloured ale with hop, malt and fruit flavours and a good bitter finish.

Nel's Best (OG 1041, ABV 4.2%) 🍺
Golden hoppy ale full of flavour with a clean, bitter finish.

Matfen Magic (OG 1046.5, ABV 4.8%) 🍺
Well-hopped brown ale with a fruity aroma. Malt and chocolate overtones with a rich, bitter finish.

Highland SIBA

Highland Brewing Co Ltd, Swannay Brewery, by Evie, Swannay, Orkney, KW17 2NP
☎ (01856) 721700
✉ info@highlandbrewingcompany.co.uk
🌐 highlandbrewingcompany.co.uk
Tours by arrangement

☺Brewing began in 2006 and bigger plant was installed a year later. A visitor centre, café and 20-barrel plant are planned. Around 300 outlets are supplied. Seasonal beers are also available.

Orkney Best (OG 1038, ABV 3.6%) 🍾 🍺
A refreshing, light-bodied, low gravity golden beer bursting with hop, peach and sweet malt flavours. The long, hoppy finish leaves a dry bitterness.

Island Hopping (OG 1039, ABV 3.9%) 🍺
Fruity hoppiness with some caramel. Dry aftertaste.

Dark Munro (OG 1040, ABV 4%) 🍷 🍾 🍺
The nose presents an intense roast hit which is followed by summer fruits in the mouth. The strong roast malt continues into the aftertaste.

Scapa Special (OG 1042, ABV 4.2%) 🍺

A good copy of a typical Lancashire bitter, full of bitterness and background hops, leaving your mouth tingling in the lingering aftertaste.

Orkney IPA (OG 1048, ABV 4.8%) 🍷 ◈
A traditional bitter, with light hop and fruit flavour throughout.

St Magnus Ale (OG 1049, ABV 5.2%) ◈
A complex, tawny bitter with a stunning balance of malt and hop and some soft roast. Full-bodied.

Orkney Blast (OG 1058, ABV 6%) ◈
Plenty of alcohol in this warming strong bitter/ barley wine. A mushroom and woody aroma blossoms into a well-balanced smack of malt and hop in the taste.

Highlands & Islands

See Orkney

Highwood (Chelmsford) SIBA

Cann Do Beers Ltd t/a The Highwood Brewery, Pool's Lane, Highwood, Essex, CM1 3QL
☎ (01245) 249300 ✉ canndobeers@btconnect.com

Brewing began in 2011 using a five-barrel plant. Further beers are planned.

Essex IPA (ABV 3.6%)

Highwood

See Tom Wood (under W)

Higsons

See Liverpool Organic

Hilden SIBA

Hilden Brewing Co, Hilden House, Hilden, Lisburn, Co Antrim, BT27 4TY
☎ (02892) 660800
✉ irishbeers@hildenbrewery.co.uk
⊕ hildenbrewery.co.uk
Shop Tue-Sun 12-2.30pm (3pm Sun) – Taproom Restaurant
Tours by arrangement (Tue-Sat 11.30am & 6.30pm)

☺Set up in 1981, Hilden is Ireland's oldest independent brewery. Now in the second generation of the family-owned business, the beers are widely distributed across the UK. Occasional brews plus seasonals are also produced. Beers are regularly available in Wetherspoons in Northern Ireland.

Ale (OG 1038, ABV 4%) ◈
An amber-coloured beer with an aroma of malt, hops and fruit. The balanced taste is slightly slanted towards hops, and hops are also prominent in the full, malty finish.

Silver (OG 1042, ABV 4.2%)
A pale ale, light and refreshing on the palate but with a satisfying mellow hop character.

Molly Malone (OG 1045, ABV 4.6%)
Dark ruby-red porter with complex flavours of hop bitterness and chocolate malt.

Scullion's Irish (OG 1045, ABV 4.6%)

A bright amber ale, initially smooth with a slight taste of honey that is balanced by a long, dry aftertaste.

Halt (OG 1058, ABV 6.1%)
A premium traditional Irish red ale with a malty, mild hop flavour.

For College Green Brewery:

Molly's Chocolate Stout (OG 1042, ABV 4.2%)
A dark chocolate-coloured beer with a full-bodied character.

Headless Dog (OG 1042, ABV 4.3%)
A well-hopped bright amber ale.

Hill Island SIBA

Michael Griffin t/a Hill Island Brewery, Unit 7, Fowlers Yard, Back Silver Street, Durham, DH1 3RA
☎ 07740 932584 ✉ mike@hillisland.freeserve.co.uk
⊕ myspace.com/hillisland
Shop at Durham Indoor Market 10am-4pm Sat
Tours by arrangement

☺The brewery is in the Fowlers Yard complex by the banks of the Wear and 2012 saw the 10th anniversary of brewing on the site. Seasonal beers are available and brews can also be crafted exclusively for individual pubs. Around 40 outlets are supplied. The brewery is open to visitors one weekend most months.

Peninsula Pint (OG 1036.5, ABV 3.7%)
Blonde and hoppy with a zesty aroma.

Bitter (OG 1038, ABV 3.9%)
Red-gold in colour with pronounced caramel notes, balanced with grassy hop aromas.

Dun Cow Bitter (OG 1041, ABV 4.2%)
Golden ale with hints of caramel and citrus hop flavours.

Cathedral Ale (OG 1042, ABV 4.3%)
Ruby red with hints of roast malts and crisp bitterness.

Griffin's Irish Stout (OG 1045, ABV 4.5%)
Black and bitter. Traditional Irish-style stout.

Hillside

See Deeside

Hobden's

See Wessex

Hobsons SIBA ◉

Hobsons Brewery & Co Ltd, Newhouse Farm, Tenbury Road, Cleobury Mortimer, Shropshire, DY14 8RD
☎ (01299) 270837 ✉ beer@hobsons-brewery.co.uk
⊕ hobsons-brewery.co.uk
Shop Mon-Fri 9am-5pm
Tours by arrangement

☺ Established in 1993 in a former sawmill, Hobsons relocated to a farm site with more space in 1995. A second brewery, bottling plant and a warehouse have been added along with significant expansion to the first brewery. Beers are supplied within a radius of 50 miles. The brewery has an onsite wind turbine and utilises environmental sustainable technologies where possible. Seasonal beer is also available.

Mild (OG 1034, ABV 3.2%)
A classic mild. Complex layers of taste come from roasted malts that predominate and give lots of flavour.

Twisted Spire (OG 1036, ABV 3.6%)
A blond beer with a sweet, floral aroma. The initial sweetness gives way to a burst of hop flavour which lingers through to a crisp, dry finish.

Best Bitter (OG 1038.5, ABV 3.8%)
A pale brown to amber, medium-bodied beer with strong hop character throughout. It is consequently bitter, but with malt discernible in the taste.

Town Crier (OG 1044, ABV 4.5%)
An elegant straw-coloured bitter. The hint of sweetness is complemented by subtle hop flavours, leading to a dry finish.

Hoggleys SIBA

Hoggleys Brewery, Unit 12, Litchborough Industrial Estate, Northampton Road, Litchborough, Northamptonshire, NN12 8JB
☎ (01327) 831308 ☎ 07717 078402
✉ enquiries@hoggleys.co.uk ⊕ hoggleys.co.uk
Tours by arrangement

Hoggleys was established in 2002 as a part-time brewery. It expanded to an eight-barrel plant in 2006, became full-time and moved to larger premises. Seasonal and bottle-conditioned beers are also available. Solstice Stout and Mill Lane Mild are suitable for vegans as are all bottle-conditioned beers.

Kislingbury Bitter (OG 1040, ABV 4%)

Mill Lane Mild (OG 1040, ABV 4%)

Northamptonshire Bitter (OG 1040, ABV 4%)

Reservoir Hogs (OG 1042, ABV 4.3%)

Pump Fiction (OG 1045, ABV 4.5%)

Indian Pale Ale (OG 1050, ABV 5%)

Solstice Stout (OG 1050, ABV 5%)

Hogs Back SIBA

Hogs Back Brewery Ltd, Manor Farm, The Street, Tongham, Surrey, GU10 1DE
☎ (01252) 783000 ✉ info@hogsback.co.uk
⊕ hogsback.co.uk
Shop & Visitors' Centre – see website
Tours by arrangement

This traditionally-styled brewery, established in 1992, boasts an extensive range of award-winning ales, brewed from the finest malted barley and whole English hops. The shop sells all the brewery's beers and related merchandise plus over 400 beers and ciders from around the world. Fully guided tours with tastings are available. Over half a million bottles are produced annually for home and export. Seasonal beers: see website.

HBB/Hogs Back Bitter (OG 1039, ABV 3.7%)
An aromatic session beer. Biscuity aroma with some hops and lemon notes. Well-balanced, plenty of hop impact in the mouth with a long-lasting dry, hoppy, bitter aftertaste.

TEA/Traditional English Ale (OG 1044, ABV 4.2%)

A tawny-coloured best bitter with both malt and hops present in the nose. These carry through into a well-rounded flavour with malt slightly dominant and more fruity sweetness than bitterness.

Hop Garden Gold (OG 1048, ABV 4.6%)
Pale golden best bitter. Full-bodied and well-balanced with an aroma of malt, hops and fruit. Hoppy bitterness grows in an increasingly dry aftertaste with a hint of sweetness.

A Over T/Aromas Over Tongham (OG 1094, ABV 9%)
A full-bodied, tawny-coloured barley wine. The malty aroma with hints of vanilla lead to a well-balanced taste where the hops cut through the underlying sweetness and dominate in the finish.

Hogswood SIBA

Hogswood Brewing Co, Higher Goshen, Mithian, St Agnes, Cornwall, TR5 0QE
☎ (01872) 554224 ☎ 07980 275897
✉ vaughan@hogswood.com ⊕ hogswood.com

Hogswood is a small family business set up in 2009 by Vaughan Haynes, a local CAMRA member. Currently with a production capacity of 2.5 barrels, on-site production of a bottle-conditioned range commenced in 2011. Seasonal beers are also available.

Broken Piston (OG 1044, ABV 4.2%)
Rich malt dominates this copper beer from start to finish. Sweet caramel is balanced by bitterness.

Black Boar (OG 1047, ABV 4.6%)
Robust dark brown stout with an aroma of roast malt. Rich flavour initially of grapes but turning to roast malt and sweetness. The finish is long, gaining caramel and nutty bitterness.

Holden's SIBA IFBB

Holden's Brewery Ltd, Hopden Brewery, George Street, Woodsetton, Dudley, West Midlands, DY1 4LW
☎ (01902) 880051 ✉ holdens.brewery@virgin.net
⊕ holdensbrewery.co.uk
Shop Mon-Fri 9am-5pm
Tours by arrangement

A family brewery spanning four generations, Holden's began life as a brew-pub in the 1920s. The company continues to expand with 20 tied pubs and supplies around 70 other outlets. Plans are in place for the construction of a new brewhouse to cope with demand. Seasonal beers: see website.

Black Country Mild (OG 1037, ABV 3.7%)
A good, red/brown mild; a refreshing, light blend of roast malt, hops and fruit, dominated by malt throughout.

Black Country Bitter (OG 1039, ABV 3.9%)
A medium-bodied, golden ale; a light, well-balanced bitter with a subtle, dry, hoppy finish.

Golden Glow (OG 1045, ABV 4.4%)
A pale golden beer with a subtle hop aroma plus gentle sweetness and a light hoppiness.

Special (OG 1052, ABV 5.1%)
A sweet, malty, full-bodied amber ale with hops to balance in the taste and in the good, bittersweet finish.

Holland

Holland Brewery, 5 Browns Flats, Brewery Street, Kimberley, Nottinghamshire, NG16 2JU
✉ hollandbrew@btopenworld.com

Holland Brewery began commercial production in 2000. Brewing is currently suspended.

Holsworthy SIBA

Holsworthy Ales, Unit 5, Circuit Business Park, Clawton, Holsworthy, Devon, EX22 6RR
☎ (01566) 783678 ☎ 07879 401073
✉ dave@holsworthyales.co.uk
⊕ holsworthyales.co.uk
Shop open Sat afternoon
Tours by arrangement

Holsworthy began brewing in 2011 using a six-barrel plant.

Tamar Sauce (ABV 4.1%)
A light, refreshing pale ale with strong fruity notes balanced by hop bitterness.

Muck and Straw (ABV 4.4%)
A traditional English bitter with delicate flavours in the finish.

Tamar Black (ABV 4.8%)
A rich, deep-roasted stout, well-balanced with a pleasant finish.

Holt IFBB ◉

Joseph Holt Ltd, The Brewery, Empire Street, Cheetham, Manchester, M3 1JD
☎ (0161) 834 3285 ⊕ joseph-holt.com
Shop Mon-Fri 9am-4pm

The brewery was established in 1849 by Joseph Holt and his wife Catherine. It is still a family-run business in the hands of the great, great-grandson of the founder. Joseph Holt supplies approximately 100 outlets as well as its own estate of 129 tied pubs. A dedicated 30-barrel brew plant is used for seasonal beers: see website. Fewer and fewer Holts pubs are dispensing cask Mild since the introduction of Keg Black.

Mild (OG 1033, ABV 3.2%) ◄
A dark brown/red beer with a fruity, malty nose. Roast, malt, fruit and hops in the taste, with strong bitterness for a mild, and a dry malt and hops finish.

IPA (ABV 3.8%)
A fresh-tasting, traditional golden IPA with a good floral hop aroma.

Bitter (OG 1040, ABV 4%) ◄
Copper-coloured beer with malt and hops in the aroma. Malt, hops and fruit in the taste with a bitter and hoppy finish.

Hook Norton SIBA IFBB ◉

Hook Norton Brewery Co Ltd, The Brewery, Brewery Lane, Scotland End, Hook Norton, Oxfordshire, OX15 5NY
☎ (01608) 737210 ✉ info@hook-norton-brewery.co.uk ⊕ hooknortonbrewery.co.uk
Visitor Centre & Shop Mon-Sat 9.30am-4.30pm
Tours by arrangement (01608 730384)

⊗ Hook Norton was founded in 1849 by John Harris, a farmer and maltster. The current premises were built in 1900 and Hook Norton is one of the finest examples of a Victorian tower brewery. It is the oldest independent brewery in Oxfordshire. A 25hp steam engine, which is still installed in the original building, was used for most of the brewery's motive power but now only operates occasionally. Hook Norton owns 45 pubs and supplies approximately 300 free trade accounts. Seasonal beers: see website. Bottle-conditioned beers are also available.

Hooky Dark (OG 1033, ABV 3.2%) ◄
A chestnut brown, easy-drinking mild. A complex malt and hop aroma give way to a well-balanced taste, leading to a long, hoppy finish that is unusual for a mild.

Hooky Bitter (OG 1035, ABV 3.5%) ◄
A classic golden session bitter. Hoppy and fruity aroma followed by a malt and hops taste and a continuing hoppy finish.

Hooky Gold (OG 1042, ABV 4.1%)
A golden, crisp beer with a citrus aroma and a fruity, rounded body.

Old Hooky (OG 1048, ABV 4.6%) ◄
A strong bitter, tawny in colour. A well-rounded fruity taste with a balanced bitter finish.

Double Stout (ABV 4.8%)

Hop Back SIBA ◉

Hop Back Brewery plc, Units 22-24, Batten Road Industrial Estate, Downton, Salisbury, Wiltshire, SP5 3HU
☎ (01725) 510986 ✉ info@hopback.co.uk
⊕ hopback.co.uk
Tours by arrangement

Started by John Gilbert in 1987 at the Wyndham Arms in Salisbury, the brewery has expanded steadily ever since. It went public via a Business Expansion Scheme in 1993 and has enjoyed rapid continued growth. The brewery has 10 tied houses and also sells to some 500 other outlets. Seasonal beers are produced on a monthly basis. Entire Stout is suitable for vegans. Bottle-conditioned beers are also produced and bottled on site.

Heracles (OG 1028, ABV 2.8%)
Very clean, malty palate with plenty of aroma. Refreshing, slightly citrus and tasting of a stronger ABV.

GFB/Gilbert's First Brew (OG 1035, ABV 3.5%) ◄
A golden beer, with a light, clean quality that makes it an ideal session ale. A hoppy aroma and taste lead to a good, dry finish.

Odyssey (OG 1040, ABV 4%)
A darker bitter with toasted malty overtones from the use of three dark malts in the recipe.

Crop Circle (OG 1041, ABV 4.2%) ◄
A refreshingly sharp and hoppy summer beer. Gold-coloured with a slight citrus taste. The crisp, dry aftertaste lingers. A dry hopped version is called Spring Zing.

Spring Zing (OG 1041, ABV 4.2%)
A dry-hopped version of Crop Circle which gives it a flowery, more rounded palate.

Taiphoon (OG 1041, ABV 4.2%)
A light gold speciality beer flavoured with lemongrass.

Entire Stout (OG 1044, ABV 4.5%) ⬚ ◄

A rich, dark stout with a strong roasted malt flavour and a long, sweet and malty aftertaste.

Summer Lightning (OG 1048, ABV 5%) ◆
A pleasurable pale bitter with a good, fresh, hoppy aroma and a malty, hoppy flavour. Finely balanced, it has an intense bitterness leading to a long, dry finish.

Hop Me Up

See Sleaford

Hopdaemon SIBA

Hopdaemon Brewery Co Ltd, Unit 1, Parsonage Farm, Seed Road, Newnham, Kent, ME9 0NA
☎ (01795) 892078 ✉ info@hopdaemon.com
⊕ hopdaemon.com
Tours by arrangement

⊗ Hopdaemon began brewing on the edge of the historic city of Canterbury in 2000 and moved to the heart of the hop gardens of East Kent at Newnham in 2005.

Golden Braid (OG 1039, ABV 3.7%) ⬒ ◆
A refreshing golden session bitter with a good blend of bittering and aroma hops underpinned by pale malt.

Incubus (OG 1041, ABV 4%) ◆
A well-balanced, copper-hued best bitter. Pale malt and a hint of crystal malt are blended with bitter and slightly floral hops to give a lingering hoppy finish.

Skrimshander IPA (OG 1045, ABV 4.5%)
An aromatic copper-coloured pale ale with a fruity finish.

Green Daemon (OG 1048, ABV 5%)
A golden beer with tropical fruit aromas and a crisp, clean finish. Brewed in the style of a Bavarian Helles.

Dominator (OG 1050, ABV 5.1%)
A rich, smooth Kentish Bock beer with hints of strawberry and vanilla giving way to a hoppy, citrus finish.

Leviathan (OG 1057, ABV 6%)
A strong ruby ale with spicy hop aromas and a rich, malty finish.

Hope Valley

Hope Valley Brewing Company Ltd, Castleton Youth Hostel, Castle Street, Castleton, Derbyshire, S33 8WG

Brewing started in 2009. The location is a brewing school and it does not produce beer commercially. However beers sometimes appear at beer festivals. The two-barrel plant was formerly used by Edale.

Hop Fuzz (NEW)

Hop Fuzz Brewery, Unit 8, Riverside Industrial Estate, West Hythe, Kent, CT21 4NB
☎ (01303) 230304 ☎ 07850 441267
✉ info@hopfuzz.co.uk ⊕ hopfuzz.co.uk

Hop Fuzz was started by two friends in 2011 and is situated on an industrial estate next to the Royal Military Canal (and a major cycle route) at West Hythe. The brewery is environmentally friendly, using solar power, recovering and reusing heat and supplying feed to the local animal park.

The American (ABV 4%)
A pale ale with a hoppy, zesty flavour.

The English (ABV 4%)
A golden bitter; malty and biscuity.

The Chocolatier (ABV 4.2%)
A dark stout.

Hop Kettle (NEW)

🝴 Hop Kettle Brewing Co, Red Lion, 74 High Street, Cricklade, Wiltshire, SN6 6DD
☎ (01793) 750776
✉ info@theredlioncricklade.co.uk
⊕ theredlioncricklade.co.uk

Brewing began in 2012 using a four-barrel plant. No beer list was available at the time of going to print.

Hop Monster SIBA

Hop Monster Brewery, Millbarn, Common Road, Great Wakering, Essex, SS3 0AG
☎ 07771 871255 ✉ headbrewer@hopmonster.co.uk
⊕ hopmonster.co.uk
Tours by arrangement

Hop Monster and George's Brewery are owned by the same brewer, brewing on the same plant. George's concentrates on traditional beer styles and Hop Monster on the more unusual. Brewing began in 2011 using a five-barrel plant from the Old Ferret & Firkin (via Ramsgate Brewery).

Trout Ale (OG 1036, ABV 3.6%)

Wallasea Wench (OG 1036, ABV 3.6%)
Pale copper, easy-drinking beer with low bitterness.

Wakering Pale (OG 1036, ABV 3.7%)
A copper-coloured Belgian Saison-style beer.

Freak Show (OG 1042, ABV 4.2%)
Copper-coloured beer full of malt and complex hop flavour. Different hops are used for each brew.

Long Shadows (OG 1042, ABV 4.2%)

Rochford Banshee (OG 1044, ABV 4.4%)
A complex smoked beer.

Howler (OG 1046, ABV 4.6%)
A well-balanced, copper-coloured beer with a hint of fruit.

Broadsword (OG 1047, ABV 4.7%)
Ruby/copper-coloured with a malty smooth start and well-balanced dry finish.

Excalibur (OG 1054, ABV 5.4%)

Hopping Mad SIBA

Hopping Mad Brewers Ltd, 42 Yardley Road, Olney, Buckinghamshire, MK46 5ED
☎ (01234) 919200 ✉ info@hoppingmad.com
⊕ hoppingmad.com
Tours by arrangement

☺Hopping Mad began brewing in 2010 using an 11-barrel plant.

Hopnotch (OG 1034, ABV 3.6%)
A malty amber ale with a spicy and fruity hop finish.

Hoppiness (OG 1034, ABV 3.7%)
A traditionally-hopped, well-balanced English ale.

Balmy Days (OG 1036, ABV 3.9%)
A zesty, crisp and dry pale ale with strong hop aromas and a dry finish.

Brainstorm (OG 1040, ABV 4.3%)
A full-bodied yet crisp traditional best bitter with a hoppy finish.

Fruitcase (OG 1041, ABV 4.5%)
A well-balanced golden ale with a fruity citrus hoppiness.

Hopshackle SIBA

Hopshackle Brewery Ltd, Unit F, Bentley Business Park, Blenheim Way, Northfields Industrial Estate, Market Deeping, Lincolnshire, PE6 8LD
☎ (01778) 348542
✉ nigel@hopshacklebrewery.co.uk
⊕ hopshacklebrewery.co.uk

☺ Hopshackle was established in 2006 on a five-barrel brew plant. Monthly seasonals are brewed providing variety in styles and ABVs. More than 40 outlets are supplied direct. Bottle-conditioned beers are also available.

Marillo (OG 1035, ABV 3.8%)

Red Ale (OG 1041, ABV 4.3%)

Historic Porter (OG 1048, ABV 4.8%)

Hopnosis (OG 1050, ABV 5.2%)

Smoked Porter (OG 1050, ABV 5.2%)

Double Momentum (OG 1065, ABV 7%)

Resination (OG 1065, ABV 7%)

Hop & Stagger (NEW)

▤ Hop & Stagger Brewery, 3 West Castle Street, Bridgnorth, Shropshire, WV16 4AB
☎ (01746) 763962 ✉ info@hopandstagger.com
⊕ hopandstagger.com
Shop Sat & Sun 11am-4pm

Hop & Stagger began brewing in 2012 using a 2.5-barrel plant at the White Lion Inn in Bridgnorth, initially brewing a range of bitters with occasional seasonal beers brewed exclusively for the pub.

A Bit on the Dark Side (OG 1040, ABV 3.6%)
A dark, malty ale with strong caramel notes. Porterish with a light hop finish.

Golden Wander (OG 1041, ABV 3.6%)
A crisp, pale golden ale with fruity notes and a light hopped finish.

Guillotine (OG 1040, ABV 4.1%)
A sharp pale golden ale with a good head and extreme hoppy taste.

Hopstar SIBA

Hopstar Brewery, Unit 9, Rinus Business Park, Grimshaw Street, Darwen, Lancashire, BB3 2QX
☎ 07933 590159 ✉ hopstarbrewery@hotmail.com
⊕ hopstarbrewery.co.uk
Tours by arrangement

☺ Hopstar first brewed in 2004 on a 2.5-barrel kit and expanded in 2010 to a new unit with a six-barrel plant. More than 100 outlets are supplied around Lancashire and the Greater Manchester area. A brewery tap recently opened, Number 39 in Darwen.

Chilli (OG 1039, ABV 3.8%)

Dizzy Danny Ale (OG 1039, ABV 3.8%)

Dark Knight (OG 1041, ABV 4%)

JC (OG 1041, ABV 4%)

Lancashire Gold (OG 1041, ABV 4%)

Lush (OG 1041, ABV 4%)

Smokey Joe's Black Beer (OG 1041, ABV 4%) ⊖

Hop Studio (NEW)

The Hop Studio, 3 Handley Park, York Road, Elvington, North Yorkshire, YO41 4AR
☎ (01904) 608029 ✉ hello@thehopstudio.com
⊕ thehopstudio.com

The Hop Studio began brewing in 2012 using a 10-barrel plant.

Blonde (ABV 3.5%)

Pilsner (ABV 4%)

Gold (ABV 4.5%)

XS (ABV 5.5%)

Hornbeam SIBA

Hornbeam Brewery, 1-1c Grey Street, Denton, Manchester, M34 3RU
☎ (0161) 320 5627 ☎ 07984 443383
✉ kevin@hornbeambrewery.com
⊕ hornbeambrewery.com
Tours by arrangement

☺ Hornbeam began brewing in 2007 on an eight-barrel plant. Regular monthly special beers are brewed. Seasonal beers: see website. Bottle-conditioned beers are also available.

Lemon Blossom (OG 1037, ABV 3.7%)
Golden, citrussy and light in colour.

Mary Rose (OG 1037, ABV 3.8%)
A chestnut bitter with an initial citrus taste with floral and grassy notes in the finish.

Top Hop Best Bitter (OG 1041, ABV 4.2%)
Full-bodied with malt appeal and ample bitterness.

Black Coral Stout (OG 1043, ABV 4.5%)
A smooth, dry roast malt. Dark and full-bodied with a rich, creamy head. Satisfying with a subtle bitterness.

Hoskins

Hoskins Brothers Ales, The Ale Wagon, 27 Rutland Street, Leicester, LE1 1RE
☎ (0116) 262 3330 ✉ mail@alewagon.com
⊕ alewagon.co.uk

The Hoskins and Oldfield brewery closed in 2001 and the portfolio of beers is now mainly brewed at the Belvoir Brewery, Old Dalby, using the Hoskins Brothers name. See Belvoir for beer list.

Houston SIBA ◉

▤ Houston Brewing Co, South Street, Houston, Renfrewshire, PA6 7EN
☎ (01505) 612620 ✉ houstonbrewery@gmail.com
⊕ houston-brewing.co.uk
Shop open pub hours, daily
Tours by arrangement

⊗ Established by Carl Wengel in 1997, the brewery is attached to the Fox & Hounds pub and restaurant. Houston deliver throughout Britain either direct or via a network of distributors. Seasonal and monthly beers: see website.

APA (American Pale Ale) (OG 1037, ABV 3.7%)
A pale, refreshing citrus ale. Zingy and fresh with an intense fruit taste.

Killellan (OG 1037, ABV 3.7%) ◆
A light session ale, with a floral hop and fruity taste. The finish of this amber beer is dry and quenching.

Blonde Bombshell (OG 1040, ABV 4%)
A pale ale with a hop aroma with fruit zest. Clean and refreshing with a light, hoppy and satisfying taste of passionfruit.

Peter's Well (OG 1042, ABV 4.2%) ⬚ ◆
Well-balanced fruity taste with sweet hop, leading to an increasingly bittersweet finish.

Slainte (OG 1043, ABV 4.3%)
A chestnut-coloured premium ale with a long, deep taste with mature notes that linger and an aroma of malt and hops.

Tartan Terror (OG 1045, ABV 4.5%)
A dark, smooth and creamy beer with a delicate hint of roasted coffee and a soft bittersweet taste that lingers.

Warlock (OG 1047, ABV 4.7%)
A well-balanced, dark, full-bodied stout. Strong, smooth and bursting with flavour.

Crystal (OG 1050, ABV 5%)
A smooth premium ale.

Howard Town SIBA

Howard Town Brewery Ltd, Hawkshead Mill, Hope Street, Glossop, Derbyshire, SK13 7SS
☎ (01457) 869800
✉ beer@howardtownbrewery.co.uk
⊕ howardtownbrewery.co.uk
Tours by arrangement

Howard Town was established in 2005 and is the Midlands most northerly brewery. More than 100 outlets are supplied. In 2012 a nine-gallon pilot plant was installed aimed at 'Brewer for a Day' sessions. Seasonal beers and bottle-conditioned beers are available.

Mill Town Mild (OG 1038, ABV 3.5%)

Bleaklow (OG 1038, ABV 3.8%)

Longdendale Light (OG 1039, ABV 3.9%)

Monks Gold (OG 1040, ABV 4%)

Wrens Nest (OG 1042, ABV 4.2%)

Dinting Arches (OG 1045, ABV 4.5%)

Glotts Hop (OG 1049, ABV 5%)

Dark Peak (OG 1062, ABV 6.4%)

Sarah Hughes

▤ Sarah Hughes Brewery, Beacon Hotel, 129 Bilston Street, Sedgley, Dudley, West Midlands, DY3 1JE
☎ (01902) 883381
✉ sarahhughesbrewery@btconnect.com
⊕ sarahhughesbrewery.co.uk
Tours by arrangement

☺ A traditional Black Country tower brewery, established in 1921. Brewing ceased in the 1950s and recommenced in 1987. The original grist case and rare open-topped copper add to the ambience of the Victorian brewhouse and give a unique character to the brews. The Beacon Hotel is the brewery tap and the full range of beers is available there. Seasonal beers are also brewed.

Pale Amber (OG 1038, ABV 4%)
A well-balanced beer, initially slightly sweet but with hops close behind.

Sedgley Surprise (OG 1048, ABV 5%) ◆
A bittersweet, medium-bodied, hoppy ale with some malt.

Dark Ruby Mild (OG 1058, ABV 6%) ◆
A dark ruby strong ale with a good balance of fruit and hops, leading to a pleasant, lingering hops and malt finish.

Humpty Dumpty SIBA

Norfolk Broads Brewing LLP t/a Humpty Dumpty Brewery, Church Road, Reedham, Norfolk, NR13 3TZ
☎ (01493) 701818 ☎ 07843 248865
✉ sales@humptydumptybrewery.co.uk
⊕ humptydumptybrewery.co.uk
Shop 12-5 daily (Easter-end Oct); Sat 12.30-4pm (Nov-Xmas); closed Jan-Easter
Tours by arrangement

Established in 1998, this 11-barrel, award-winning brewery moved to its present site in 2001. Local ingredients are used and many regional outlets supplied. The on-site shop sells bottled beer from the brewery as well as from other East Anglian micros and local cider. Seasonal beers: see website.

Nord Atlantic (OG 1039, ABV 3.7%) ◆
Copper-coloured, full-bodied, with a grainy character and a mix of malt, caramel and apple fruitiness. Hops and liquorice bitterness appear at the end.

Little Sharpie (OG 1040, ABV 3.8%) ◆
A well-balanced golden beer with lemon and grapefruit notes. A light, hoppy nose introduces a lively initial taste with hops again to the fore. Citrus flavours mix well with malt to give depth.

Lemon and Ginger (OG 1041, ABV 4%)
An amber, crisp ale with a ginger and lemon tang.

Swallowtail (OG 1041, ABV 4%) ◆
Pineapple and pear on the nose introduce this amber-gold ale. Hops reinforce the citrus backbone and grainy mouthfeel. A pleasant, slowly drying finish.

Ale (OG 1043, ABV 4.1%) ◆
A hoppy vanilla fudge bouquet develops through the initial taste to become the signature flavour. Malt provides balance as a gentle bitterness quickly recedes. Long, sweet, sticky finish.

Broadland Sunrise (OG 1044, ABV 4.2%) ◆
Beautifully smooth almost vinous ale. Swirling malt, hop and fruit aroma. The sweet, hoppy, well-balanced first impression develops into a smooth malty finish.

Reedcutter (OG 1045, ABV 4.4%) ◆
A sweet, malty beer, golden hued with a gentle malt background. Smooth and full-bodied with a quick, gentle finish.

Cheltenham Flyer (OG 1048, ABV 4.6%) ◆

THE BREWERIES

A full-flavoured golden, earthy bitter with a long, grainy finish. A strong hop bitterness dominates throughout. Little evidence of malt.

East Anglian Pale Ale (OG 1046, ABV 4.6%) ◆
A heavy sulphurous nose is lightened by hints of rhubarb. This carries into the flavour where a fruity sweetness contrasts with a grainy hoppiness. A long finish.

Norfolk Nectar (OG 1048, ABV 4.6%) ◆
A sweet honeyed note wraps around other flavours and aromas. Hops and caramel maintain a presence throughout to give a counterpoint to the rich, sweet base.

Hunsbury Craft (NEW)

Hunsbury Craft Brewery, 23 Limefields Way, East Hunsbury, Northampton, NN4 0SA
☎ (01604) 766228
✉ johngeorgemargetts@tiscali.co.uk

⊗ Hunsbury Craft was established in 2010 using a 0.5-barrel plant, increasing to 2.25-barrels to meet demand.

Best Bitter (OG 1039, ABV 3.8%)

Copper (OG 1043, ABV 4.2%)

Alchemy (OG 1041, ABV 4.3%)

Mel's Mild (OG 1051, ABV 5%)

JD's Robust Porter (OG 1061, ABV 5.9%)

IPA (OG 1062, ABV 6%)

Hunter's SIBA

Hunter's Brewery Ltd, Bulleigh Barton Farm, Ipplepen, Devon, TQ12 5UE
☎ (01803) 814399 ☎ 07540 657115

Office: Glebe Acres, Orley Road, Ipplepen, Devon, TQ12 5SA ⊕ thehuntersbrewery.co.uk

Hunters began brewing in 2008 on a five-barrel brew plant. Expansion means the brewery now has six fermenters and is capable of a 60-barrel brew length. Seasonal and bottle-conditioned beers are also available.

Crack Shot (ABV 3.8%)

Butchers Best (ABV 4%)

Half Bore (ABV 4%)

Albion Ale (ABV 4.2%)

Denbury Dreamer (ABV 4.2%)

Pheasant Plucker (ABV 4.3%)

Gold (ABV 4.8%)

Black Jack (ABV 6%)

Full Bore (ABV 8%)

Hurns

See Tomos Watkin (under W)

Hydes IFBB ⊙

Hydes Brewery Ltd, 46 Moss Lane West, Moss Side, Manchester, M15 5PH
☎ (0161) 226 1317 ✉ mail@hydesbrewery.com
⊕ hydesbrewery.com

⊙Hydes is a family-owned brewer dating from 1863. It has been on the same site for more than 120 years but in June 2012 it announced it planned to move to a new site by the end of the year. No information has been given about the possible location but it's believed it will be within Greater Manchester. All Hydes' free-trade business has been sold to Thwaites of Blackburn. Hydes will retain ownership of its 70 pubs. The beers listed below are liable to change. Hydes no longer brew cask Boddingtons for AB InBev.

Light Mild/1863 (OG 1033.5, ABV 3.5%) ◆
Lightly hopped, pale brown session beer with some hops, malt and fruit in the taste and a short, dry finish.

Owd Oak (OG 1033.5, ABV 3.5%) ◆
Dark brown/red in colour, with a fruit and malt nose. Taste includes biscuity malt and green fruits, with a satisfying aftertaste.

Original Bitter (OG 1036.5, ABV 3.8%) ◆
Pale brown beer with a malty nose, malt and an earthy hoppiness in the taste, and a good bitterness through to the finish.

Manchester's Finest (OG 1044, ABV 4.5%)
A full-bodied and slightly sweet beer.

Iceni SIBA EAB

Iceni Brewery, 3 Foulden Road, Ickburgh, Norfolk, IP26 5HB
☎ 07949 488113 ✉ icenibrewe@aol.com
⊕ icenibrewery.co.uk / extraordinaryales.co.uk
Shop Mon-Fri 10am-3pm
Beer Experience events by arrangement

⊗ Iceni was launched in 1995 by Brendan Moore. The brewery is also the headquarters of the East Anglian Brewers Co-op (EAB).

Elveden Forest Gold (OG 1040, ABV 3.9%) ◆
Forest fruits on the nose give way to strong hop bitterness in the initial taste. Residual maltiness provides balance at first but is swamped by a long, dry, bitter finish.

Celtic Queen (OG 1038, ABV 4%) ◆
A golden brew with a light hoppy nose giving way to distinctly bitter characteristics throughout. A shallow mix of malt and hops adds some depth. A long, lingering finish.

Fine Soft Day (OG 1038, ABV 4%) ◆
Toffee tickles both the nostrils and tastebuds as it hovers over a creamy, lightly-hopped backdrop in this golden brew. A gentle mix of flavours softly sinks into a pleasant sweetness.

Fen Tiger (OG 1040, ABV 4.2%)

It's A Grand Day (OG 1044, ABV 4.5%) ◆
Gentle hop and citrus aroma introduces this pale brown brew. An orange sweetness contrasts with the underlying hoppy bitterness. Long-lasting and creamy but undemanding.

Raspberry Wheat (OG 1048, ABV 5%)

Men of Norfolk (OG 1060, ABV 6.2%) ◆
Chocolatey stout with roast overtones from initial aroma to strong finish. Malt and vine fruits counterbalance the initial roast character while a caramel undertone remains to the end.

Idle SIBA

🏚 Idle Brewery, White Hart Inn, Main Street, West Stockwith, South Yorkshire, DN10 4EY
☎ (01427) 753226 ☎ 07949 137174
✉ theidlebrewery@btinternet.com
Tours by arrangement

☺The brewery began production in 2007 and is situated in a converted stable at the back of the White Hart Inn alongside the River Idle. Seasonal beers are also available.

Boggin (OG 1039, ABV 3.8%)
Tawny with a bitter finish.

Dog (OG 1041, ABV 4.2%)
A copper-coloured ale, moderately hoppy with a good balance of malt and hops leading to a bitter finish.

Grunter (OG 1041, ABV 4.2%)

Sod (OG 1041, ABV 4.2%)

Tongue (OG 1041, ABV 4.2%)

Grunter (OG 1041, ABV 4.4%)

Black Abbot (OG 1044, ABV 4.6%)

Idle Landlord (OG 1044, ABV 4.6%)
A dark brown ale with plenty of body, a malty flavour and a caramel/coffee finish.

Ilkley SIBA 👁

Ilkley Brewery Co Ltd, The New Brewery, 40 Ashlands Road, Ilkley, West Yorkshire, LS29 8JT
☎ (01943) 604604 ✉ info@ilkleybrewery.co.uk
🌐 ilkleybrewery.co.uk
Tours by arrangement

☺Ilkley began brewing in 2009 on an eight-barrel plant, bringing brewing back to the town after a gap of some 80 years. In 2011 the brewery moved to new premises and upgraded to a 20-barrel plant. Beers are brewed traditionally using only the highest quality home-grown malted barley and whole hops with soft Yorkshire water. There are plans for expansion. Seasonal and bottle-conditioned beers are also available.

Mary Jane (OG 1036, ABV 3.5%)
A crisp, pale ale with citrus aromas.

Black (OG 1040, ABV 3.7%)
A mellow, easy-drinking dark mild with a hint of liquorice in the finish.

Gold (OG 1040, ABV 3.9%) 🍴
An easy-drinking, golden-coloured ale with a light floral aroma leading to a soft citrus fruit flavour and a gentle bitter aftertaste.

Best (OG 1041, ABV 4%)
A highly hopped golden ale with a strong, bitter finish.

Pale (OG 1042, ABV 4.2%)
A dry, crisp pale ale, strongly hopped to give a strong but mellow citrus finish.

Lotus IPA (OG 1055, ABV 5.6%)
A golden-coloured IPA with strong aromas and flavours of mango, grapefruit and citrus.

Imperial

🏚 Imperial Club & Brewery Ltd, Arcadia Hall, Cliff Street, Mexborough, South Yorkshire, S64 9HU
☎ 07765 857312

Tours by arrangement

☺Imperial started brewing in 2011 using a five-barrel plant providing beers for the club and other outlets in the local area.

Bitter (OG 1038, ABV 3.9%)

Blonde (OG 1040, ABV 4%)

Stout (OG 1047, ABV 4.6%)

Darkness (ABV 5%)

Indian Summer (NEW)

Indian Summer Brewing Co Ltd, Unit 3, Ashdon Road Commercial Centre, Saffron Walden, Essex, CB10 2NH
☎ 07986 637826 ✉ sales@bombayblonde.co.uk
🌐 bombayblonde.co.uk

Indian Summer began brewing in 2012.

Hop & Soul (ABV 4.5%)

Inishmacsaint

Inishmacsaint Brewery, 7 Drumadown Road, Drumskimly, Derrygonnelly, County Fermanagh, BT93 6DN
☎ (028) 6864 1031 ✉ gordyfallis@hotmail.com

Inishmacsaint is a small-scale brewery that has been in production since 2009 brewing mainly bottle-conditioned beers. A larger brew plant is currently under construction.

Innis & Gunn

Innis & Gunn Brewing Co Ltd, Canning Street, Edinburgh, EH3 8EG
☎ (0131) 272 2782
✉ gregg.imlah@innisandgunn.com
🌐 innisandgunn.com

Innis & Gunn does not brew but Tennents produces one regular bottled (not bottle-conditioned) beer for the company, Oak Aged Beer (ABV 6.6%). There are three further beers in the permanent range: Original (ABV 6.6%), Blonde (ABV 6%) and Rum Cask (ABV 7.4%). A range of limited edition beers is also produced each year.

Inveralmond SIBA 👁

Inveralmond Brewery Ltd, 22 Inveralmond Place, Inveralmond, Perth, PH1 3TS
☎ (01738) 449448 ✉ info@inveralmond-brewery.co.uk 🌐 inveralmond-brewery.co.uk
Shop Mon-Fri 10am-7pm
Tours by arrangement

☺Established in 1997, Inveralmond was the first brewery in Perth for more than 30 years. The brewery has expanded from a 10-barrel to a 30-barrel plant and there are plans for further growth. Around 250 outlets are supplied. Seasonal beers: see website.

Independence (OG 1040, ABV 3.8%) 🍴
A well-balanced Scottish ale with fruit and malt tones. Hop provides an increasing bitterness in the finish.

Ossian (OG 1042, ABV 4.1%) 🍴
Well-balanced best bitter with a dry finish. This full-bodied amber ale is dominated by fruit and hop with a bittersweet character although excessive caramel can distract from this.

THE BREWERIES

Thrappledouser (OG 1043, ABV 4.3%) ◆
A refreshing amber beer with reddish hues. The crisp, hoppy aroma is finely balanced with a tangy but quenching taste.

Lia Fail (OG 1048, ABV 4.7%) ◆
The Gaelic name means Stone of Destiny. A dark, robust, full-bodied beer with a deep malty taste. Smooth texture and balanced finish.

Sunburst Pilsner (OG 1045, ABV 4.8%)

Ironbridge

Ironbridge Brewery Ltd, Unit 7, Merrythought, The Wharfage, Ironbridge, Telford, Shropshire, TF8 7NJ
☎ (01952) 433910
✉ david@ironbridgebrewery.co.uk
⊕ ironbridgebrewery.co.uk
Shop & Bar Mon-Wed closed; Thu 12-4pm; Fri & Sat 12-6pm; Sun 12-4pm
Tours by arrangement

☺Ironbridge was established in 2008 and operates on a 12-barrel brewery in an old Victorian warehouse alongside the River Severn in the heart of the Ironbridge Gorge. A visitor centre and shop were opened in 2009.

Blond (OG 1037, ABV 3.6%)

Ironbridge Pale Ale (IPA) (OG 1040, ABV 4%)

Gold (OG 1045, ABV 4.4%)

Wenlock Stout (OG 1052, ABV 5.1%)

Irving SIBA ◉

Irving & Co Brewers Ltd, Unit G1, Railway Triangle, Walton Road, Portsmouth, Hampshire, PO6 1TQ
☎ (023) 9238 9988 ✉ sales@irvingbrewers.co.uk
⊕ irvingbrewers.co.uk
Shop Thu & Fri 3-6pm
Tours by arrangement

⊠ Irving's was set up by former Gale's brewer Malcolm Irving and a small team of ex-Gales employees using a 15-barrel plant. Around 60 outlets are supplied direct. Seasonal beers: see website.

Frigate (OG 1039, ABV 3.8%)
A golden bitter with a citrus hop flavour complemented by background sweetness.

Type 42 (OG 1042, ABV 4.2%)
A robust best bitter with a deep ruby red hue balancing sweet hedgerow berry notes with a long roasted malt finish and a deep bitterness.

Admiral Stout (OG 1042.5, ABV 4.3%)
A classic dark oatmeal stout with a rounded malt flavour balanced with strong bitterness.

Invincible (OG 1048, ABV 4.6%) ◆
A tawny-coloured strong bitter. Sweet and fruity with an underlying maltiness throughout and a dryness that increases gradually, contrasting well with the sweetness of the finish.

Irwell Works SIBA

Irwell Works Brewery Ltd, Irwell Street, Ramsbottom, Lancashire, BL0 9YQ
☎ (01706) 825019
✉ beer@irwellworksbrewery.co.uk
⊕ irwellworksbrewery.co.uk
Shop & Visitor Centre 10am-11pm daily

Tours by arrangement

☺Irwell Works started brewing in 2010 in a building dating from 1888 that once housed the Irwell Steam, Tin, Copper & Iron Works. It was used as an engineering works until a few years ago. It now houses a six-barrel brewery supplied and built by Porter Brewing. A bar opened on the first floor in 2011 and a small kitchen in 2012.

Lightweights & Gentleman (ABV 3.2%)
A refreshing light session ale.

Tin Plate (ABV 3.6%)
A rich, roasted dark mild.

Copper Plate (OG 1037, ABV 3.8%)
A traditional copper-coloured bitter. Complex bitterness with a strong hop character.

Richard Mason 1888 (OG 1039, ABV 4%)
A refreshing, light-coloured pale ale.

Steam Plate (ABV 4.3%)
A traditional golden-coloured best bitter. Mild bitterness and a refreshing hop aroma.

Iron Plate (OG 1042, ABV 4.4%)
A Lancashire stout. A sweet stout with roasted barley aromas with a dark chocolate aftertaste.

Mad Dogs & Englishmen (ABV 5.5%)
An easy-drinking IPA with lots of taste.

Isca SIBA

Isca Ales Ltd, Gargoyles Brewery, Court Farm, Holcombe Village, Dawlish, Devon, EX7 0JT
☎ 07773 444501 ✉ iscaales@yahoo.co.uk

⊠ Two CAMRA members took over Gargoyles Brewery in late 2009 under the name Isca Ales. The original brewery was established in 2005. The Gargoyles name will continue alongside Isca Ales. 10 outlets are supplied.

Gargoyles Citra (ABV 3.8%)
A light, refreshing beer with grapefruit aroma leading to a dry, bitter finish.

Gargoyles Golden Ale (ABV 3.8%)
A golden bitter with a hoppy aroma.

Gargoyles Summer Ale (ABV 3.8%)
A refreshing golden ale.

Gargoyles Dawlish Ale (ABV 3.9%)

Gargoyles Best Bitter (ABV 4.2%)
An amber-coloured beer with a fresh, hoppy aftertaste.

Gargoyles Dawlish Bitter (ABV 4.2%)

Glorious Devon (ABV 4.4%)
A grassy hop aroma with a hoppy aftertaste.

Achilles Ale (ABV 5%)
A dark, malty, strong ale.

Gargoyles Dawlish Pale (ABV 5%)
A grassy hop aroma with an intense hoppy aftertaste.

Gargoyles Wheat (ABV 5%)
A cloudy wheat beer with hints of banana, oranges and spice.

Gargoyles Napier (ABV 5.2%)

Gargoyles Milk Maid Mild (ABV 6%)
A strong, dark ruby ale.

Isfield (NEW)

Isfield Brewing Co Ltd, Imperial Cottage, Station Road, Isfield, East Sussex, TN22 5UJ
☎ (01825) 750633
✉ enquiries@isfieldbrewing.co.uk

⊠ Isfield began brewing in 2012 using a five-barrel plant.

Straw Blond (OG 1042, ABV 4.1%)
A pale, hoppy beer.

Imperial Pale Ale (IPA) (OG 1043, ABV 4.2%)
A malty best bitter with caramel and toffee notes.

Toad in the Ale (OG 1050, ABV 4.8%)
A complex strong ale.

Island SIBA

Island Brewery (Isle of Wight Brewery Ltd), Dinglers Farm, Yarmouth Road, Newport, Isle of Wight, PO30 4LZ
☎ (01983) 821731 ✉ sales@islandales.co.uk
⊕ islandbrewery.co.uk
Tours by arrangement

⊠ Island Brewery is the realisation of Tom Minshull's ambition to brew real ales to complement the existing family-owned drinks distribution business called Island Ales. Brewing commenced in 2010 using a 12-barrel brewery. More than 100 outlets are supplied direct.

Nipper Bitter (OG 1038, ABV 3.8%)
Straw-coloured, light and refreshing with a distinguishable balance of malt and hops and a satisfying afterbite.

Wight Gold (OG 1040, ABV 4%)
Golden brown in colour with rounded malt and hops throughout.

Yachtsman's Ale (OG 1042, ABV 4.2%)
Chestnut-coloured ale with a rich, malty mouthfeel and hop aroma.

Wight Knight (OG 1045, ABV 4.5%)
Strong, full-bodied beer.

Vectis Venom (OG 1048, ABV 4.8%)
A ruby-tinted dark brown ale. Easy-drinking with an underlying smoothness.

Earl's RDA (OG 1050, ABV 5%)
A rich dark ale.

Islay SIBA

Islay Ales Co Ltd, The Brewery, Islay House Square, Bridgend, Isle of Islay, PA44 7NZ
☎ (01496) 810014 ✉ info@islayales.com
⊕ islayales.com
Shop Mon-Sat 10.30am-5pm
Tours by arrangement

☺Brewing started on a four-barrel plant in a converted tractor shed in 2004. The brewery shop is next door. The island is more famous for its whisky, but the brewery has established itself as a must-see place for those visiting the eight working distilleries. Bottle-conditioned beers are available.

Finlaggan Ale (OG 1039, ABV 3.7%)
A mid brown beer with a gentle, rounded bitterness and a fresh, fruity and hoppy flavour.

Black Rock Ale (OG 1040, ABV 4.2%)
A reddish beer with a soft, nutty flavour, a robust body and a floral, grassy and herbal nose.

Angus Og Ale (OG 1045, ABV 4.5%)
A bitter beer; similar to an IPA but without the strength.

Ardnave Ale (OG 1048, ABV 4.6%)
A dry, thirst-quenching, hoppy bitter.

Isle of Arran

See Arran

Isle of Avalon

Isle of Avalon Brewery, c/o Stagman Lane, Ashcott, Somerset, TA7 9QW
☎ (01458) 210050 ✉ avalonwholesale@gmail.com
⊕ avalonbeerfestsandbrewing.com

⊠ Isle of Avalon has brewed since 2009 using spare capacity at Wessex Brewery.

Isle of Mull

See Argyll

Isle of Purbeck SIBA

☰ Isle of Purbeck Brewery, Manor Road, Studland, Dorset, BH19 3AU
☎ (01929) 450227
✉ info@isleofpurbeckbrewery.com
⊕ isleofpurbeckbrewery.com
Tours by arrangement

⊠ The Isle of Purbeck Brewery was founded in 2002, bringing Dorset ales back to the Purbecks following the closure of Poole Brewery. The 10-barrel plant is situated in the grounds of the Bankes Arms Hotel, overlooking Studland Bay on the Jurassic Coast. The beers can be found all over Dorset and Hampshire and are now available in London and further afield. Seasonal and bottle-conditioned beers are available.

Best Bitter (OG 1036, ABV 3.6%) ◀
A classic best bitter with rich malt aroma and taste and smooth, malty, bitter finish.

Force Four (ABV 4%)
A blonde beer with a dry, lingering finish.

Fossil Fuel (OG 1040, ABV 4.1%) ◀
Amber bitter with a complex aroma with a hint of pepper; rich malt dominates the taste, leading to a smooth dry finish.

Solar Power (OG 1043, ABV 4.3%) ◀
Light golden ale brewed using Continental hops to provide a refreshing mouthfeel; hop aromas dominate the taste leading to a smooth, bittersweet finish.

Studland Bay Wrecked (OG 1044, ABV 4.5%) ◀
Deep red ale with a slightly sweet aroma reflecting the mixture of caramel, malt and hops that provide the unique flavour and dry, rich finish.

IPA (OG 1047, ABV 4.8%) ◀
A novel twist on an old style of ale, the complex balance of malt and several hops offer well-balanced taste and aroma leading to a dry bitter, hoppy finish.

Isle of Skye

Isle of Skye Brewing Co (Leann an Eilein) Ltd, The Pier, Uig, Isle of Skye, IV51 9XP
☎ (01470) 542477 ✉ info@skyebrewery.co.uk
🌐 skyebrewery.co.uk
Shop Mon-Sat 10am-6pm; Sun 12.30-4.30pm (Apr-Oct)

☺ The Isle of Skye Brewery was established in 1995, the first commercial brewery in the Hebrides. Originally a 10-barrel plant, it was upgraded to 20-barrels in 2004. Fermenting capacity now stands at 80 barrels, with plans to further increase this and upgrade bottling facilities. Seasonal beers: see website.

Tarasgeir (OG 1040, ABV 4%) ◆
The peat-roasted barley dominates, giving a mellow peaty whisky taste.

Young Pretender (OG 1039, ABV 4%) ◆
A fruity, full-bodied golden ale, predominantly hoppy and fruity. The bitterness in the mouth is also balanced by summer fruits and hops, continuing into the lingering bitter finish.

Red Cuillin (OG 1041, ABV 4.2%) ◆
A light, fruity nose with a hint of caramel leads to a full-bodied malty flavour and a long, dry, bittersweet finish.

Hebridean Gold (OG 1041.5, ABV 4.3%) ◆
Porridge oats are used to produce this delicious speciality beer. Nicely balanced. it has a refreshingly soft fruity, bitter flavour with an oaty background.

Black Cuillin (OG 1044, ABV 4.5%) 🍶 ◆
A complex, tasty brew worthy of its many awards. Full-bodied with a malty richness. Malt holds sway but there are plenty of hops and fruit to be discovered in its varied character. A delicious Scottish Old Ale.

Blaven (OG 1047, ABV 5%) ◆
A well-balanced strong amber bitter with kiwi fruit and caramel in the nose and a lingering sharp bitterness.

Cuillin Beast (OG 1066, ABV 7%) 🍶 ◆
A winter warmer; sweet and fruity and more drinkable that the strength would suggest. Plenty of caramel throughout with a variety of fruit on the nose.

Itchen Valley [SIBA] ◉

Itchen Valley Brewery Ltd, Unit 4, Prospect Commercial Park, Prospect Road, New Alresford, Hampshire, SO24 9QF
☎ (01962) 735111/736429
✉ info@itchenvalley.com 🌐 itchenvalley.com
Shop Mon-Fri 9am-5pm
Tours by arrangement

⊗ Established in 1997, Itchen Valley moved to new premises in 2006 with a 20-barrel plant. The brewery has a gift shop and offers brewery tours and mini conferencing facilities. More than 350 pubs are supplied, with wholesalers used for further distribution. Seasonal beers and monthly specials are also available.

Godfathers (OG 1038, ABV 3.8%) ◆
A pale brown bitter, with a malty aroma and taste and a light body, leading to a bittersweet finish.

Fagin's (OG 1041, ABV 4.1%) ◆
Enjoyable copper-coloured best bitter with a hint of crystal malt and a pleasant bitter aftertaste.

Hampshire Rose (OG 1042, ABV 4.2%)
A golden amber ale. Fruit and hops dominate the taste throughout, with a good mouth feel.

Winchester Ale (OG 1042, ABV 4.5%)
Traditional English bitter, nut brown with a sweet, malty flavour and a good hoppy nose.

Pure Gold (OG 1046, ABV 4.8%) ◆
An aromatic hoppy, golden bitter. Initial maltiness and grapefruit flavours lead to a dry finish.

Jacobi

Jacobi Brewery of Caio, Penlanwen Farm, Pumsaint, Carmarthenshire, SA19 8RR
☎ (01558) 650605 ✉ justin@jacobibrewery.co.uk
🌐 jacobibrewery.co.uk

⊗ Brewing started in 2006 on an eight-barrel plant in a converted barn. Brewer Justin Jacobi is also the owner of the Brunant Arms in Caio, which is a regular outlet for the beers. The brewery is located 50 yards from the Dolaucothi mines where the Romans dug for gold. A visitor centre and bottling line are planned.

Light Ale (OG 1040, ABV 3.8%)

Bee Keepers Delight (OG 1039, ABV 4%)

Red Squirrel (OG 1040, ABV 4%)

Original (OG 1044, ABV 4.4%)

Dark Ale (OG 1052, ABV 5%)

James & Kirkman (NEW)

🍺 **James & Kirkman Brewery, Rear of Robin Hood, 4 Wakefield Road, Pontefract, West Yorkshire, WF8 4HN**
☎ (01977) 702231
✉ eastcoastbrewing@hotmail.co.uk

Brewing began in 2012 behind the Robin Hood pub using a 2.5-barrel plant previously at Hesket Newmarket Brewery. Beers were previously brewed at East Coast Brewing (qv), owned by the same brewers. Further beers are planned.

Little John (ABV 3.7%)

Top Of The Hops (ABV 4.1%)

Jarrow [SIBA]

🍺 **Jarrow Brewery, The Maltings, 9 Claypath Lane, South Shields, Tyne & Wear, NE33 4PG**
☎ (0191) 483 6792
✉ jarrowbrewery@btconnect.com
🌐 jarrowbrewery.co.uk
Tours by arrangement

☺ Real ale enthusiasts Jess and Alison McConnell commenced brewing at the Robin Hood, Jarrow, in 2002. In 2008 all brewing was transferred to the Maltings in South Shields. Seasonal and bottle-conditioned beers are also available.

Bitter (OG 1037.5, ABV 3.8%)
A light golden session bitter with a delicate hop aroma and a lingering fruity finish.

Rivet Catcher (OG 1039, ABV 4%) ◆
A light, smooth, satisfying gold bitter. Subtle fruity hops give the taste profile on the tongue and nose.

Joblings Swinging Gibbet (OG 1041, ABV 4.1%) 🍶

A copper-coloured, evenly balanced beer with a good hop aroma and a fruity finish.

Red Ellen (OG 1042.5, ABV 4.4%)
A rich ruby-red, full-bodied ale with a citrus hop aroma.

McConnells Irish Stout (OG 1045, ABV 4.6%) ◈
A rich, creamy stout with a long, lingering liquorice and pale chocolate finish.

Westoe IPA (OG 1044.5, ABV 4.6%)
A pale gold ale with a soft malt character and a refreshingly complex hop aroma.

Isis (OG 1049, ABV 5%)
A touch of dryness balances the rounded, sweetish malt flavour of this golden strong bitter.

Jennings

See Marston's in the New Nationals section

Jersey

See Liberation

Jollyboat SIBA

Jollyboat Brewery (Bideford) Ltd, The Coach House, Buttgarden Street, Bideford, Devon, EX39 2AU
☎ (01237) 424343
Tours by arrangement

⊗ Established in 1995, the brewery is named after a sailor's leave vessel and all the beers have a nautical theme. Most outlets supplied are in Devon but a trade route to Bristol has been added. Seasonal and bottle-conditioned beers are also available.

Grenville's Renown (OG 1037, ABV 3.8%)
A dark brown session bitter with a full, long taste.

Hart of Oak (OG 1044, ABV 4.4%)
Amber-coloured with a lacy white head. Fruity malt aroma followed by more malt in the flavour. Finish has some chocolate malt with moderate bitterness.

Joseph Herbert Smith

Joseph Herbert Smith Traditional Brewers, Fox Inn, Hanley Broadheath, Nr Tenbury Wells, Worcestershire, WR15 8QS
☎ (01886) 853189 ☎ 07527 066474
✉ jhsbrewery@yahoo.co.uk
⊕ jhstraditionalbrewery.com
Tours by arrangement

☺The brewery was established in 2007 by Jonathan Smith in memory of his grandfather using a 2.5-barrel plant from Danelaw Brewery. In 2008 it relocated from Wombourne in Staffordshire to barns adjacent to the Fox Inn in Tenbury Wells. Now a four-barrel plant with a 12-barrel capacity, all equipment is gas fired and ingredients are sourced locally where possible. Seasonal and monthly beers: see website.

Amy's Rose (OG 1040, ABV 4%)
A traditionally brewed mild ale.

Snooty Fox (OG 1042, ABV 4.1%)
A copper-coloured, English-style best bitter.

Foxy Lady (OG 1043, ABV 4.3%)
A premium light bitter.

Joules

Joules Brewery, The Brewery, Great Hales Street, Market Drayton, Shropshire, TF9 1JP
☎ (01630) 654400 ✉ info@joulesbrewery.co.uk
⊕ joulesbrewery.co.uk
Tours by arrangement

The new Joules Brewery opened in 2010 after a break of 40 years. It is situated in Market Drayton in order to source the purest mineral water which, as before, is the essential foundation for Joule's ales.

Blonde (OG 1038, ABV 3.8%)

Original Pale Ale (OG 1042, ABV 4.1%)
Made from the original Joules' recipe from 1779.

Slumbering Monk (OG 1045, ABV 4.5%)

Junction

See Urban

Just A Minute (NEW)

Just A Minute Brewery, c/o Deerness Rubber Co Ltd, Coulson Street, Spennymoor, County Durham, DL16 7RS
☎ 07586 896091
✉ justaminutebrew@btinternet.com
⊕ justaminutebrewery.co.uk

Just A Minute was established by two friends in 2010, initially with experimental brews for local festivals and pubs. A 2.5-barrel plant came into operation in 2011. Seasonal beers are also available.

Ruby Tuesday (OG 1039, ABV 3.9%)

Darkest Moment (OG 1043, ABV 4.3%)

Golden Dawn (OG 1043, ABV 4.3%)

IPA (OG 1046, ABV 4.6%)

Kelburn SIBA 👁

Kelburn Brewing Co Ltd, 10 Muriel Street, Barrhead, East Renfrewshire, G78 1QB
☎ (0141) 881 2138 ✉ info@kelburnbrewery.com
⊕ kelburnbrewery.com
Tours by arrangement

⊗ Kelburn is an award-winning family business established in 2002. Beers are available bottled and in take-away polypins. Seasonal beers: see website.

Goldihops (OG 1038, ABV 3.8%) ◈
Well-hopped session ale with a fruity taste and a bitter finish.

Pivo Estivo (OG 1038, ABV 3.9%)

Misty Law (OG 1040, ABV 4%)
A dry, hoppy amber ale with a long-lasting bitter finish.

Red Smiddy (OG 1040, ABV 4.1%) ⬓ ◈
This bittersweet ale predominantly features an intense citrus hop character that assaults the nose and continues into the flavour, balanced perfectly with fruity malt.

Dark Moor (OG 1044, ABV 4.5%)
A dark, fruity ale with undertones of liquorice and blackcurrant.

Cart Noir (OG 1046, ABV 4.8%)

Cart Blanche (OG 1048, ABV 5%) ◆
A golden, full-bodied ale. The assault of fruit and hop camouflages the strength of this easy-drinking ale.

Kelham Island SIBA ◉

Kelham Island Brewery Ltd, 23 Alma Street, Sheffield, South Yorkshire, S3 8SA
☎ (0114) 249 4804 ✉ sales@kelhambrewery.co.uk
⊕ kelhambrewery.co.uk
Shop Mon-Fri 9am-4pm (some weekends)
Tours by arrangement

☺The brewery opened in 1990 behind the Fat Cat public house. Due to its success, the brewery moved to new purpose-built premises in 1999 (adjacent to the pub), with five times the capacity of the original brewery. The old building is now used as a visitor centre. Since surviving a flood in 2007, the brewery has gone from strength to strength, installing a new, larger brew plant in 2009 and, more recently, has opened a brewery shop. Five regular beers are brewed as well as monthly themed specials and more than 200 outlets are supplied. Bottle-conditioned beers are also available and are suitable for vegetarians.

Best Bitter (OG 1038, ABV 3.8%) ◆
A clean, characterful, crisp, pale brown beer. The nose and palate are dominated by refreshing hoppiness and fruitiness, which, with a good bitter dryness, lasts in the aftertaste.

Pride of Sheffield (OG 1040.5, ABV 4%) 🍺
A full-flavoured, amber-coloured bitter.

Easy Rider (OG 1041.8, ABV 4.3%) ◆
A pale, straw-coloured beer with a sweetish flavour and delicate hints of citrus fruits. A beer with hints of flavour rather than full-bodied.

Riders on the Storm (OG 1045, ABV 4.5%)
A robust golden pale ale with berry notes and slight roasted notes.

Pale Rider (OG 1050, ABV 5.2%) ◆
A full-bodied, straw pale ale, with a good fruity aroma and a strong fruit and hop taste. Its well-balanced sweetness and bitterness continue in the finish.

Keltek SIBA

OMC (UK) Ltd t/a Keltek Brewery, Candela House, Cardrew Way, Redruth, Cornwall, TR15 1SS
☎ (01209) 313620 ✉ sales@keltekbrewery.co.uk
⊕ keltekbrewery.co.uk
Shop Mon-Fri 9am-5pm
Tours by arrangement

⊗ Keltek Brewery moved to Lostwithiel in 1999 and in 2006 moved again to Redruth and installed a new 25-barrel plant. In 2009 expansion continued with new bottling facilities, labelling equipment and five 50-barrel tanks. Keltek is now a major force in Cornwall with its beers available as far afield as Hong Kong. Bottle-conditioned beer is available and bottling is carried out for several other Cornish breweries. CAMRA members are welcome (by appointment) to try their hand at brewing.

4K Mild (OG 1038, ABV 3.8%)

Golden Lance (OG 1038, ABV 4%) ◆

Golden bitter promising fruit and hops. Refreshing citrus and sweetness fills the mouth with bitterness coming through in the finish.

Magik (OG 1040, ABV 4.2%) ◆
Tawny best bitter with malt and complex fruit on the nose. On the tongue there is perfumed malt, sweetness and bitterness, followed by a long bitter finish, becoming dry.

Mr Murdoch's Golden IPA (OG 1043, ABV 4.5%)

Trevithick's Revenge (OG 1043, ABV 4.5%)

King (OG 1049, ABV 5.1%)

Kemptown

🍺 Kemptown Brewery, 33 Upper St James's Street, Kemptown, Brighton, East Sussex, BN2 1JN
☎ (01273) 699595
Tours by arrangement

☺Kemptown was established in 1989 and built in the tower tradition behind the Hand in Hand, which is possibly the smallest brewpub in England. It takes its name and logo from the former Charrington's Kemptown Brewery, which closed in 1964. In 2011 work was undertaken to restore the brewery and upgrade all facilities. Beer is only available at the Hand in Hand. Quarterly seasonal beers are also brewed.

Gold (ABV 4%)

Red (ABV 4.5%)

Kendal (NEW)

🍺 Kendal Brewing Co, Brewhouse at Burgundy's, 19 Lowther Street, Kendal, Cumbria, LA9 4DH
☎ (01539) 733803

Kendal began brewing in 2011.

Eleven Bells (OG 1039, ABV 3.9%)
A creamy golden beer with a rich hop flavour.

Silver Tanner (OG 1044, ABV 4.4%)
A tan-coloured ale with a malt flavour, citrus aroma and crisp hop bitterness.

Kent SIBA ◉

Kent Brewery Ltd, Birling Place Farm, Stangate Road, Birling, Kent, ME19 5JN
☎ (01634) 780037 ✉ info@kentbrewery.com
⊕ kentbrewery.com
Tours by arrangement.

⊗ Kent Brewery was founded in 2010 by Toby Simmonds (ex-brewer from Dark Star) and Paul Herbert. Originally brewing at Larkins, a ten-barrel plant is now used at the Birling site. More than 50 outlets are supplied direct, mainly throughout Kent and London. Seasonal and bottle-conditioned beers are also available.

Black Gold (OG 1040, ABV 4%)
A rich dark ale.

Pale (OG 1040, ABV 4%)
A golden pale ale; full-flavoured and aromatic.

Cobnut (OG 1041, ABV 4.1%)
A generously-hopped ruby ale; dark and nutty.

KGB (Kent Golding Bitter) (OG 1041, ABV 4.1%)

Zingiber (OG 1041, ABV 4.1%)
A ginger golden ale; refreshing and light.

Beyond the Pale (OG 1050, ABV 5%)
A light and refreshing, highly hopped pale ale with a well-rounded mouthfeel and aromatic aftertaste.

Porter (OG 1055, ABV 5.5%)
An easy-drinking, full, rich porter with subtle coffee and chocolate undertones.

Pocohontas (OG 1060, ABV 6%)

Kernel SIBA

Kernel Brewery, 01 Spa Terminus, Spa Road, London, SE16 4QT
☎ (020) 7231 4516 ☎ 07757 552636
✉ evin@thekernelbrewery.com
⊕ thekernelbrewery.com
Shop (Arch 11, Dockley Rd Ind. Est., SE16) Sat 9am-3pm

Kernel was established in 2010 by Evin O'Riordain and moved to new, larger premises in 2012. It produces bottle-conditioned beers, as well as the occasional cask.

Keswick SIBA

Keswick Brewing Co, The Old Brewery, Brewery Lane, Keswick, Cumbria, CA12 5BY
☎ (01768) 780700 ✉ info@keswickbrewery.co.uk
⊕ keswickbrewery.co.uk
Shop – call for details (usually Mon-Fri 9am-5pm)
Tours by arrangement

Keswick began brewing in 2006 using a 10-barrel plant. It is located on the site of a brewery that closed in 1897. The beer is always available in the Queen's Head Hotel and Dog & Gun in Keswick and many other Lakeland pubs are supplied. Seasonal beers: see website.

Thirst Gold (OG 1035, ABV 3.6%)
Golden-coloured and full of flavour.

Keystone SIBA

Keystone Brewery, Old Carpenters Workshop, Berwick St Leonard, Salisbury, Wiltshire, SP3 5SN
☎ (01747) 820426 ✉ info@keystonebrewery.co.uk
⊕ keystonebrewery.co.uk
Shop Mon, Tue & Fri 10am-5pm
Tours by arrangement

⊗ Keystone Brewery was set up in 2006 with a 10-barrel plant. The beers have low food miles to help support a sustainable local community. The brewery also use an award-winning solar heating system, which reduces carbon emissions. Around 150 outlets are supplied. Seasonal beers: see website. Bottle-conditioned beers are also available.

Bedrock (OG 1035, ABV 3.6%)
A well-balanced beer with sweet citrus flavours.

Gold Spice (OG 1039, ABV 4%)
Light-coloured beer, well-hopped with stem ginger added to the cask.

Gold Standard (OG 1039, ABV 4%)
Gold-coloured beer full of citrus flavours with a hoppy aroma.

Large One (OG 1041, ABV 4.2%)
Distinct malty flavour and a delicate addition of bittering hops with hints of fruit and spice in the aftertaste.

Very Pale Ale (OG 1045, ABV 4.6%)

Light in colour with subtle malt flavours and medium bitterness leading to crisp hop flavours and aromas.

Cornerstone (OG 1047, ABV 4.8%)
A dark, strong beer with plenty of hops. Well-balanced with a long, satisfying finish.

King SIBA ◉

W J King & Co (Brewers), 3-5 Jubilee Estate, Foundry Lane, Horsham, West Sussex, RH13 5UE
☎ (01403) 272102 ✉ sales@kingbeer.co.uk
⊕ kingbeer.co.uk
Shop Mon-Fri 9am-5pm; Sat 10am-2pm
Tours by arrangement (limited to 25)

Launched in 2001 on a 20-barrel plant, the brewery expanded rapidly and in 2004 premises next door were added to give more cellar space and to enable room to stock more bottle-conditioned beers. The brewery was purchased by Ian Burgess and Nigel Lambe in 2010 and continues to expand. Around 200 outlets are supplied direct. Seasonal beers: see website.

Horsham Best Bitter (OG 1038, ABV 3.8%) ◀
A predominantly malty best bitter, brown in colour. The nutty flavours have some sweetness with a little bitterness that grows in the aftertaste.

Brighton Blond (OG 1039, ABV 3.9%)
A crisp, refreshing pale blonde ale with a distinctive hoppy aroma.

Brighton Best (OG 1040, ABV 4%)
A light, golden beer with a complex floral hop aroma.

Red River (OG 1048, ABV 4.8%) ◀
A full-flavoured, mid-brown beer. It is malty with some berry fruitiness in the aroma and taste. The finish is reasonably balanced with a sharp bitterness coming through.

Kings Head

▮ Kings Head Brewery, Kings Head, 132 High Street, Bildeston, Ipswich, Suffolk, IP7 7ED
☎ (01449) 741434
✉ kingshead.bildeston@tiscali.co.uk
⊕ bildestonkingshead.co.uk
Tours by arrangement

⊗ Kings Head has been brewing since 1996 in an old cart lodge at the back of the pub. Under new ownership since 2008, the three-barrel plant brews weekly. Local pubs and beer festivals are supplied. Seasonal beers are also available.

Bildeston Best (OG 1036, ABV 3.6%)
A traditional best bitter. Well-hopped with a malty sweetness and dry finish.

Landlady (OG 1040, ABV 4%)
Pale ale, hoppy and fruity with a dry finish.

Blondie (OG 1040, ABV 4.1%) ◀
Drinkable light summer beer, a good example of a cask lager. Light and refreshing, with fruity notes in the aroma and flavour.

Crowdie (OG 1042, ABV 4.2%)
An oatmeal stout.

Bildeston Porter (OG 1045, ABV 4.4%)
Dark ale with complex maltiness and smooth, hoppy finish.

Brettvale Ale (OG 1044, ABV 4.4%)

Pale ale with balanced malty sweetness and hops.

Hop Baby (OG 1044, ABV 4.4%)

Kingstone SIBA

Kingstone Brewery, Meadow Farm, Tintern, Monmouthshire, NP16 7NX
☎ **(01291) 680111/680101**
✉ **shop@kingstonebrewery.co.uk**
⊕ **kingstonebrewery.co.uk**

Kingstone Brewery is located in the Wye Valley where brewing began on a four-barrel plant in 2005. All cask ales are also available bottle conditioned.

Challenger (ABV 4%)

Gold (ABV 4%)

Classic (ABV 4.5%)

1503 (ABV 4.8%)

Kinneil (NEW)

Kinneil Brew Hoose LLP, Corbie Inn, 84 Corbiehall, Bo'ness, West Lothian, EH51 0AS
☎ **(01506) 824574** ✉ **stuart@kinneilbrew.co.uk**
⊕ **kinneilbrew.co.uk**
Tours by arrangement

Kinneil began brewing in 2011 using a 2.5-barrel plant. The brewery is adjacent to the Corbie Inn but separately owned.

Pennvael Amber (OG 1040, ABV 4%)

Caer Edin Dark Ale (OG 1042, ABV 4.2%)

Kinver SIBA ⊚

Kinver Brewery, Unit 2, Fairfield Drive, Kinver, Staffordshire, DY7 6EW
☎ **07715 842679/07906 146777**
✉ **kinvercave@aol.com** ⊕ **kinverbrewery.co.uk**
Tours by arrangement

⊚Established in 2004, Kinver Brewery consists of a five-barrel plant, producing a wide range of different beer styles, including one-off specials. Around 30 outlets are supplied direct. There are plans to move to a new, larger site. Seasonal beers are available.

Edge (OG 1041, ABV 4.2%) 🍴 ◆
Amber with a malty aroma. Sweet fruity start with a hint of citrus marmalade in the spicy-edged malt; lasting hoppy finish that is satisfyingly bitter.

Noble 600 (ABV 4.5%) ◆
Fruity hop aroma. Fruity start, then the grassy hops give a sharp bitter finish with malt support.

Half Centurion (OG 1048, ABV 5%) 🍴 ◆
A golden best bitter; malty before the American Chinook hop takes command to give a balanced hoppy finish and provides the great aftertaste.

Khyber (OG 1054, ABV 5.8%) ◆
Golden strong bitter with a Centennial hop bite that overwhelms the fleeting malty sweetness and drives through to the long dry finish.

Over The Edge (OG 1076, ABV 7.6%) 🍷

Kirkby Lonsdale SIBA

Kirkby Lonsdale Brewery Co Ltd, Unit 2F, Old Station Yard, Kirkby Lonsdale, Lancashire, LA6 2HP

☎ **(01524) 272221** ☎ **07793 149999**
✉ **info@kirkbylonsdalebrewery.com**
⊕ **kirkbylonsdalebrewery.com**

⊚Kirkby Lonsdale is a family-run business established in 2009 on a six-barrel plant. Seasonal beers are also available.

Tiffin Gold (OG 1036, ABV 3.6%) ◆
A full-flavoured hoppy and bitter beer with grapefruit notes and a dry finish.

Ruskin's Bitter (OG 1039, ABV 3.9%) ◆
A tawny bitter with a distinctive aroma of fruit and malt. The clean, hoppy flavour is well-balanced with fruity sweetness leading to a sustained bittersweet finish.

Radical Red (OG 1042, ABV 4.2%) ◆
Malty beer with a caramel sweetness that is balanced by a bitter finish.

Monumental Blonde (OG 1045, ABV 4.5%)
A floral golden ale.

Jubilee Stout (OG 1055, ABV 5.5%) ◆
Rich, well-balanced stout with malt. A long aftertaste retains this complexity and is surprisingly refreshing.

Westmorland Pale Ale (OG 1060, ABV 6.2%)
A pale ale with fruity, spicy hop flavours and aroma together with a delicate hint of chocolate malt.

Kirkstall SIBA

Kirkstall Brewery Co, Unit 6, Canal Wharf, Wyther Lane, Kirkstall, Leeds, West Yorkshire, LS5 3BT
☎ **(0113) 345 8835**
✉ **info@kirkstallbrewerycompany.com**
⊕ **kirkstallbrewerycompany.com**
Tours by arrangement

⊚Kirkstall began brewing in 2011 using an eight-barrel plant, which is set to expand, and is located within yards of the original Kirstall Brewery. The site is shared with beer importer Vertical Drinks, who are responsible for Kirkstall's sales and marketing. Many of the beer names are derived from the local area or have links with Yorkshire breweries of old. Occasional special one-off brews are created, often in conjunction with other, sometimes International, brewers. The nearby refurbished Old Bridge Inn offers the full range of beers.

BYB (Best Yorkshire Bitter) (ABV 3.5%)

Pale Ale (OG 1040, ABV 4%) ◆
Light in colour but not in taste, this is a feast of hop and grapefruit flavours. There is a tangy bitterness throughout but it is still a well-balanced beer.

Three Swords (OG 1045, ABV 4.5%) ◆
Extremely drinkable and supremely fruity golden-yellow beer with good quantities of hops and fruit in the aroma, satsuma fruitiness in the bittersweet taste and an almost marmalade dry finish.

Dissolution IPA (OG 1050, ABV 5%) ◆
Hops define this amber beer in the massive aroma, through the citrus fruit taste lasts right to the end, which is lingering and satisfyingly bitter.

Black Band Porter (OG 1055, ABV 5.5%) ◆
Smooth, rich, warming Porter with a fulsome aroma and even bigger flavour. A generous fruity, roasty taste featuring port, treacle and liquorice ends with a dry and satisfying finish.

Kissingate

Kissingate Brewery, Pole Barn, Church Lane Farm Estate, Church Lane, Lower Beeding, West Sussex, RH13 6LU
☎ (01293) 882198 ☎ 07909 975664
✉ gary@kissingate.co.uk ⊕ kissingate.co.uk
Tours by arrangement

⊗ Kissingate began brewing commercially in 2010. Inspiration for the beers is drawn from the cottage brewing styles and cultures from the late middle ages. Local outlets and beer festivals are supplied. A purpose-built, larger brew house opposite the old one housing a 10-barrel plant is now used and will have a shop and meeting room.

Best (OG 1040, ABV 4%)

Old Tale Porter (OG 1052, ABV 4.5%)
A classic London porter with full flavours.

Moon (OG 1050, ABV 4.8%)
A bright, golden ale tasting of lightly roasted malts and late autumn apples with a lingering bitterness.

Chennai (OG 1050, ABV 5%)

Smelter's Stout (OG 1052, ABV 5.2%)

Mary's Ruby Mild (OG 1072, ABV 6.5%)
Deep ruby in colour with gentle aromas of well-aged port. Intense, rounded malt flavours and a light, floral hop aftertaste.

Kitchen Garden (NEW)

Kitchen Garden Brewery, Old Walled Garden, Sheffield Park, East Sussex, TN22 3QX
☎ (01825) 790775
✉ admin@kitchengardenbrewery.co.uk
Shop Mon 1-5pm; Tue-Sun 10am-5pm

Kitchen Garden is a small one-barrel plant producing only bottle-conditioned ales, all suitable for vegetarians. It is situated in a Victorian walled kitchen garden at Sheffield Park. Occasional seasonal beers are produced. The beers are available from the brewery shop and at several outlets in Sussex including Middle Farm at Firle.

Kite SIBA

Kite Brewery, Cwmcerrig Farm, Gorslas, Carmarthenshire, SA14 7HU
☎ (01269) 842300 ⊕ thekitebrewery.com
Tours by arrangement

Kite began brewing in 2011 using a 10-barrel plant. Seasonal beers are available.

Gorslas Ale (ABV 4%)

Carmarthen Pale Ale (CPA) (ABV 4.1%)

Thunderbird (ABV 4.5%)

Knops

Knops Beer Co Ltd, c/o 32 Abbotsford Court, Edinburgh, EH10 5EJ
☎ (0131) 447 8104 ✉ info@knopsbeer.co.uk
⊕ knopsbeer.co.uk

☺Knops began brewing in 2010. Beers are based on modern interpretations of traditional beers styles. Beers are currently brewed at Traditional Scottish Ales: see entry for beer list.

Lancaster SIBA ◉

Lancaster Brewery Co Ltd, Heartwick Brewery, Lancaster Leisure Park, Wyresdale Road, Lancaster, LA1 3LA
☎ (01524) 848537 ✉ info@lancasterbrewery.co.uk
⊕ lancasterbrewery.co.uk
Shop 10am-5pm daily
Tours by arrangement

☺Lancaster began brewing in 2005. The brewery moved to new premises in Lancaster in 2010 and installed a larger brewing plant. Seasonal beers are also available.

Straw (OG 1035, ABV 3.5%)

Amber (OG 1038, ABV 3.7%)
Dark gold session beer with a hoppy bouquet and subtle floral and citrus aromas.

Blonde (OG 1042, ABV 4.1%) ◈
A crisp, hoppy flavour with a touch of caramel and a hint of citrus. Golden hued with a smooth, easy-drinking feel. Hops follow through to dominate in the aftertaste.

Black (OG 1046, ABV 4.6%)
Traditional stout; rich and full-bodied.

Red (OG 1048, ABV 4.9%)
Robust ale with a malt-dominated body.

Landlord's Friend

Landlord's Friend Brewery, Unit 1, Kershaw House, Luddenden Lane, Halifax, West Yorkshire, HX2 6NW
☎ (01422) 882222 ✉ landfriendbeers@aol.co.uk
Tours by arrangement

Landlord's Friend began brewing in 2010 using a 2.5-barrel plant with a weekly capacity of 10 barrels, which has since expanded to 20. Around 30 outlets are supplied direct. Seasonal beers are also available.

Mr Smith (OG 1037, ABV 3.6%)

Mr Marshall (OG 1038, ABV 3.8%)

Local Joes Perfect Pitch (OG 1038, ABV 4%)

Frank's 3rd Leg (OG 1044, ABV 4.3%)

Mr Hough (OG 1043, ABV 4.4%)

Mr JK's Irish Stout (ABV 4.4%)

Langham SIBA

Langham Brewery LLP, The Granary, Langham Lane, Lodsworth, West Sussex, GU28 9BU
☎ (01798) 860861 ✉ office@langhambrewery.co.uk
⊕ langhambrewery.co.uk
Shop Mon & Tue 9am-6pm; Thu 9am-2pm; Sat 10am-5pm
Tours by arrangement

⊗ Langham Brewery was established in 2006 in an 18th-century granary barn and is set in the heart of West Sussex with fine views to the rolling South Downs. It is owned by Steve Mansley, Lesley Foulkes and James Berrow who all brew and run the business. The brewery is a 10-barrel steam-heated plant and more than 100 outlets are supplied.

Halfway to Heaven (OG 1035, ABV 3.5%)
A chestnut-coloured beer with a balanced biscuit maltiness and citrus and fruit hop character with a hint of spice.

Hip Hop (OG 1040, ABV 4%)
A blonde beer – clean and crisp. The nose is loaded with floral hop aroma while the pale malt flavour is overtaken by a dry and bitter finish.

Sundowner (OG 1042, ABV 4.2%)
A deep golden beer. The nose has tropical fruit, pineapple and citrus notes with a smooth maltiness in the background. There is a balanced dry and bitter finish with floral hop aroma.

Best (OG 1042, ABV 4.5%)
A tawny-coloured classic best with well-balanced malt flavours and bitterness.

**Langham Special Draught/LSD
(OG 1049, ABV 5.2%)**
An auburn beer with rich, complex flavours and a deep red glow. The sweet maltiness is balanced with spicy hop aromas and a dry finish.

Langton SIBA ◉

Langton Brewery, Grange Farm, Welham Road, Thorpe Langton, Leicestershire, LE16 7TU
☎ 07840 532826 ⊕ langtonbrewery.co.uk
Tours by arrangement

The Langton Brewery started in 1999 in buildings behind the Bell Inn, East Langton. Due to demand, the brewery relocated in 2005 to a converted barn in Thorpe Langton, where a four-barrel plant was installed. Further expansion in 2010 significantly increased capacity. All beers are available to take away in casks, polypins or bottles. Seasonal beers are available.

Caudle Bitter (OG 1039, ABV 3.9%) ◆
Copper-coloured session bitter that is close to pale ale in style. Flavours are relatively well-balanced throughout with hops slightly to the fore.

Inclined Plane Bitter (OG 1042, ABV 4.2%)
A straw-coloured bitter with a citrus nose and long, hoppy finish.

Hop On (OG 1044, ABV 4.4%)
A premium bitter, deep chestnut colour with a good balance of flavours and aroma.

Bowler Strong Ale (OG 1048, ABV 4.8%)
A strong traditional ale with a deep red colour and a hoppy nose.

Larkins SIBA

Larkins Brewery Ltd, Larkins Farm, Hampkins Hill Road, Chiddingstone, Kent, TN8 7BB
☎ (01892) 870328
Tours by arrangement (Nov-Feb)

⊠ Larkins Brewery was founded in 1986 by the Dockerty family, who bought the plant from the former Royal Tunbridge Wells Brewery and moved it to Larkins Farm in 1987. Since then the production of three regular brews and two seasonal ales has steadily increased. All beers now use hops grown on Larkins Farm itself. Larkins supplies around 70 free houses within a radius of 30 miles.

Traditional Ale (OG 1035, ABV 3.4%)
Tawny in colour, a full-tasting hoppy ale with plenty of character for its strength.

Chiddingstone (OG 1040, ABV 4%)
Named after the village where the brewery is based, Chiddingstone is a mid-strength, hoppy, fruity ale with a long, bittersweet aftertaste.

Best (OG 1045, ABV 4.4%) ◆
Full-bodied, slightly fruity and unusually bitter for its gravity.

Leadmill

Leadmill Brewery Ltd, Unit 3, Small Business Centre, Adams Close, Heanor Gate Industrial Estate, Heanor, Derbyshire, DE75 7SW
☎ 07971 189915 ⊠ leadmill@fsmail.net

⊠ Originally set up in a pig sty in Selston, Leadmill moved to Denby in 2001 and again in 2010 to Heanor where it shares a site with Coppice Side Brewery (qv). A sister brewery to Bottle Brook (qv), many of the brews are one-offs using rare hop varieties. The brewery tap is the Butchers Arms in Langley and the Old Oak in Horsley Woodhouse also permanently feature the beers. Seasonal beers are also available.

Langley Best (OG 1036, ABV 3.6%)

Mash Tun Bitter (OG 1036, ABV 3.6%)

Old Oak Bitter (OG 1037, ABV 3.7%)

B52 (OG 1050, ABV 5.2%)

Slumdog (OG 1058, ABV 5.9%)

Leamside (NEW)

▤ Leamside Ale Co Ltd, Three Horseshoes, Pit House Lane, Leamside, County Durham, DH4 6QQ
☎ (0191) 584 2394
⊠ info@threehorseshoesleamside.co.uk
⊕ threehorseshoesleamside.co.uk

Brewing began in 2012 using a 2.5-barrel plant.

Adventure (ABV 3.8%)

Alexandrina (ABV 4%)

Meadows (ABV 4%)

Five Quarter (ABV 4.5%)

Leatherbritches

Leatherbritches Brewery, Tap House, Annwell Lane, Smisby, Derbyshire, LE65 2TA
☎ 07976 279253 ⊠ leatherbritches@btconnect.com
Tours by arrangement

⊕ The brewery, founded in 1993 in Fenny Bentley as a five-barrel plant, moved to the Green Man & Blacks Head Hotel in Ashbourne in 2008 and upgraded to a 24-barrel plant. In 2011 the brewery relocated again to its present address. Both the Tap House Brewery and Leatherbritches brew on the same plant but the two businesses are separate. Seasonal and bottle-conditioned beers are also available.

Goldings (OG 1036, ABV 3.6%)
A light golden beer with a flowery hoppy aroma and a bitter finish.

Lemongrass and Ginger (OG 1036, ABV 3.8%)

Ashbourne Ale (OG 1040, ABV 4%)
A pale bitter brewed with Goldings hops for a crisp lasting taste.

Doctor Johnsons (OG 1040, ABV 4%)
A mid-brown ale, not heavily hopped but full-bodied with some caramel flavour.

Scoundrel (OG 1040, ABV 4.1%)

Dovedale (OG 1044, ABV 4.4%)

A copper bitter with a crisp finish.

Ginger Helmet (OG 1047, ABV 4.7%)

Hairy Helmet (OG 1047, ABV 4.7%)
Pale bitter, well hopped but with a sweet finish. Ginger Helmet is the same beer with ginger.

Bespoke (OG 1050, ABV 5%)
Full-bodied, well-rounded premium bitter.

Porter (OG 1055, ABV 5.5%)

Scary Hairy (ABV 5.9%)

Leeds SIBA IFBB ◉

Leeds Brewery Co Ltd, 3 Sydenham Road, Leeds, West Yorkshire, LS11 9RU
☎ (0113) 244 5866 ✉ sales@leedsbrewery.co.uk
⊕ leedsbrewery.co.uk

◉Leeds Brewery began production in 2007 using a 20-barrel plant. It is the largest independent brewer in the city and uses a unique strain of yeast originally used by another, now defunct, West Yorkshire brewery. Five pubs are owned and around 300 outlets are supplied direct. Seasonal beers: see website. See also Brewery Tap.

Pale (OG 1037.5, ABV 3.8%) ◆
Well-balanced light ale, citrusy with some lemon in both aroma and flavour. Gold in colour with a refreshing bitter, hoppy finish.

Yorkshire Gold (ABV 4%)
A golden ale with a well-balanced, bitter finish.

Best (OG 1041, ABV 4.3%) ◆
Full-flavoured, smooth amber beer. The initial caramel does not detract from the underlying malt character; hops come through later, resulting in a drinkable, bittersweet beer.

Midnight Bell (OG 1047.5, ABV 4.8%) 🍸 ◆
A full-bodied, strong mild, deep red/brown in colour. The malty, rich fruit aroma carries through in the taste along with a hint of chocolate.

Leek SIBA

Staffordshire Brewing Ltd t/a Leek Brewery, 12 Churnet Court, Cheddleton, Staffordshire, ST13 7EF
☎ (01538) 361919 ☎ 07971 808370
✉ leekbrewery@hotmail.com
⊕ beersandcheese.co.uk
Tours by arrangement

Brewing started in 2002 with a 4.5-barrel plant located behind the owner's house, before moving to Cheddleton in 2004. The brewery upgraded to a six-barrel plant in 2007 and to a 20-barrel plant in 2011. In recent years the brewery has concentrated on producing bottle-conditioned beers but the new upgrade means that cask-conditioned beers will be regularly available again. The company also acts as an equipment supplier and bottles beers for many independent brewers.

Staffordshire Gold (OG 1035, ABV 3.8%) ◆
Light, straw-coloured with a pleasing hoppy aroma and a hint of malt. Bitter finish from the hops, making it easily drunk and thirst-quenching.

Danebridge IPA (OG 1038, ABV 4.1%) ◆
Full fruit and hop aroma. Flowery hop start with a bitter taste. Finish of hops and flowers.

Staffordshire Bitter (OG 1040, ABV 4.2%) ◆
Amber with a fruity aroma. Malty and hoppy start with the hoppy finish diminishing quickly.

Black Grouse (OG 1042, ABV 4.5%)

Hen Cloud (OG 1042, ABV 4.5%)

St Edwards (OG 1043, ABV 4.7%)

Rudyard Ruby (OG 1044, ABV 4.8%)

Double Sunset (OG 1050, ABV 5.2%)

Rocheberg Blonde (OG 1052, ABV 5.6%)

Lees IFBB ◉

J W Lees & Co (Brewers) Ltd, Greengate Brewery, Middleton Junction, Manchester, M24 2AX
☎ (0161) 643 2487 ✉ mail@jwlees.co.uk
⊕ jwlees.co.uk

◉ Lees is a family-owned brewery founded in 1828 by John Lees and run by the sixth generation of the family. Brewing takes place in the 1876 brewhouse designed and built by John Willie Lees, the grandson of the founder. The current head brewer is a family member. The brewhouse has been completely modernised in recent years to give greater flexibility. The company has a tied estate of around 170 pubs, mostly in north-west England, with 30 in North Wales; almost all serve cask beer. Seasonal beers are brewed four times a year.

Brewer's Dark (OG 1032, ABV 3.5%) ◆
Formerly GB Mild, this is a dark brown beer with a malt and caramel aroma. Creamy mouthfeel, with malt, caramel and fruit flavours and a malty finish. Becoming rare.

The Governor (OG 1039, ABV 3.8%)
Brewed with Marco Pierre White this crisp, amber ale has a hoppy, malty finish. Named after Marco's family greyhound.

Bitter (OG 1037, ABV 4%) ◆
Copper-coloured beer with malt and fruit in aroma, taste and finish.

Coronation Street (OG 1042, ABV 4.2%)
First brewed in 2009, the name is licensed to Lees by ITV.

John Willie's (OG 1041, ABV 4.5%)
A well-balanced, full-bodied premium bitter.

Moonraker (OG 1073, ABV 7.5%) ◆
A reddish-brown beer with a strong, malty, fruity aroma. The flavour is rich and sweet, with roast malt, and the finish is fruity yet dry. Available only in a handful of outlets.

Leila Cottage SIBA

▤ Leila Cottage Brewery, Countryman, Chapel Road, Ingoldmells, Skegness, Lincolnshire, PE25 1ND
☎ (01754) 872268
✉ countryman_inn@btconnect.com
⊕ countryman-ingoldmells.co.uk
Tours by arrangement

Leila Cottage started brewing in 2007 using a 0.5-barrel plant, which was upgraded in 2009 to a 2.5-barrel one. The brewery is situated at the Countryman pub – Leila Cottage was the original name of the building before it became a licensed club and more recently a pub. The brewery now owns its own bottling line meaning that all beers are also available bottle conditioned, including seasonals.

Ace Ale (OG 1040, ABV 3.8%)

Lincolnshire Life (OG 1040, ABV 4.2%)

One Off (OG 1045, ABV 5.1%)

Leith Hill

▤ Leith Hill Brewery, c/o Plough Inn, Coldharbour Lane, Coldharbour, Surrey, RH5 6HD
☎ (01306) 711793 ✉ theploughinn@btinternet.com
⊕ ploughinn.com
Tours by arrangement

Leith Hill was established in 1996 using home-made equipment to produce nine-gallon brews in a room at the front of the pub. The brewery moved to converted storerooms at the rear of the Plough Inn in 2001 and increased capacity to 2.5-barrels in 2005. All beers brewed are sold only on the premises.

Beautiful South (OG 1036, ABV 3.6%)
Yellowish in colour, a hoppy session beer with a little malt character.

Crooked Furrow (OG 1040, ABV 4%) ◣
A malty beer, with some balancing hop bitterness. Pale brown in colour with an earthy, malty aroma and a long, dry and bittersweet aftertaste. Some fruit is also present throughout.

Tallywhacker (OG 1048, ABV 4.8%) ◣
Dark, sweet and fruity old ale with a good roast malt character.

Leyden SIBA

▤ Leyden Brewing Ltd, Lord Raglan, Walmersley Old Road, Nangreaves, Greater Manchester, BL9 6SP
☎ (0161) 764 6680 ⊕ lordraglannangreaves.co.uk
Tours by arrangement

☺ The brewery was built by Brian Farnworth and started production in 1999. Additional fermenting vessels have been installed, allowing a maximum production of 12 barrels a week. One pub is owned and 30 outlets are supplied. In addition to the permanent beers, a number of seasonal and occasional beers are brewed.

Black Pudding (OG 1040, ABV 3.8%)
A dark brown, creamy mild with a malty flavour, followed by a balanced finish.

Nanny Flyer (OG 1040, ABV 3.8%)
A drinkable session bitter with an initial dryness, and a hint of citrus, followed by a strong, malty finish.

Balaclava (OG 1040, ABV 4.2%)
A brown-coloured session bitter with malty and hoppy flavours.

Rammy Rocket (OG 1042, ABV 4.2%)
A smooth, straw-coloured ale.

Forever Bury (OG 1047, ABV 4.5%)
A dark brown bitter with a distinct fruity aroma and smooth, malty finish.

Light Brigade (OG 1047, ABV 4.6%) ◣
Copper in colour with a citrus aroma. The flavour is a balance of malt, hops and fruit, with a bitter finish.

Raglan Sleeve (OG 1047, ABV 4.6%) ◣
Dark red/brown beer with a hoppy aroma and a dry, roasty, hoppy taste and finish.

Crowning Glory (OG 1068, ABV 6.8%)
A smooth-tasting beer for its strength.

Liberation ⊚

Liberation Brewery, Tregear House, Longueville Road, St Saviour, Jersey, JE2 7WF
☎ (01534) 764089 ✉ paulhurley@victor-hugo-ltd.com ⊕ liberationgroup.com
Tours by arrangement

Following the closure of the original brewery in Ann Street in 2004, the brewery is now located in an old soft drinks factory using a 40-barrel plant. Formerly known as the Jersey Brewery it was renamed in 2010 to the Liberation Brewery following its sale to the Liberation Group. Its flagship beer, Liberation Ale, is now regularly seen on the mainland. 66 pubs are owned with around two-thirds of these serving cask ale. Seasonal beers are brewed on the five-barrel plant formerly at the Tipsy Toad Brewery.

Liberation Ale (OG 1039, ABV 4%)
Golden beer with a hint of citrus on the nose.

Lincoln Green (NEW) SIBA

Lincoln Green Brewing, Unit 5, Enterprise Park, Wigwam Lane, Hucknall, NG15 7SZ
☎ (0115) 963 4233 ☎ 07748 111457
✉ anthony@lincolngreenbrewing.co.uk
⊕ lincolngreenbrewing.co.uk

Anthony Hughes established the Lincoln Green Brewing Company in 2012 using a 10-barrel plant. The brewery takes its name from the colour of dyed woollen cloth associated with the legend of Robin Hood. Seasonal and special beers are available.

Marion (ABV 3.8%)
A full-bodied pale ale packed with citrus hop and a hint of grapefruit.

Hood (ABV 4.2%)
A classic English best bitter with full-rounded bitterness and a gentle floral aroma.

Tuck (ABV 4.7%)
A well-rounded porter with a hint of bitter chocolate and blackcurrant aroma.

Scarlett (ABV 4.8%)
An amber ale with a bitter toffee malt flavour and a mild fruit hop finish.

Linfit

▤ Linfit Brewery, Sair Inn, 139 Lane Top, Linthwaite, Huddersfield, West Yorkshire, HD7 5SG
☎ (01484) 842370

A 19th-century brew-pub that started brewing again in 1982. The beer is only available at the Sair Inn. English Guineas is suitable for vegetarians and vegans.

Bitter (OG 1035, ABV 3.7%) ◣
A refreshing session beer. A dry-hopped aroma leads to a clean-tasting, hoppy bitterness, then a long, bitter finish with a hint of malt.

Gold Medal (OG 1040, ABV 4.2%)
Very pale and hoppy. Use of the dwarf variety of English hops, First Gold, gives an aromatic and fruity character.

Special (OG 1041, ABV 4.3%) ◣
Dry-hopping provides the aroma for this rich and mellow bitter, which has a very soft profile and

character: it fills the mouth with texture rather than taste. Clean, rounded finish.

Swift (OG 1041, ABV 4.3%)

Autumn Gold (OG 1045, ABV 4.7%) ◈
Straw-coloured best bitter with hop and fruit aromas, then the bittersweetness of autumn fruit in the taste and the finish.

English Guineas (OG 1045, ABV 4.7%)

Old Eli (OG 1050, ABV 5.3%)
A well-balanced premium bitter with a dry-hop aroma and a fruity, bitter finish.

Leadboiler (OG 1063, ABV 6.6%)

Lion's Tale SIBA

▤ Lion's Tale Brewery, Red Lion, High Street, Cheswardine, Shropshire, TF9 2RS
☎ (01630) 661234 ✉ cheslion96@yahoo.co.uk

The building that houses the brewery was purpose-built in 2005 and houses a 2.5-barrel plant. Jon Morris and his wife have owned the Red Lion pub since 1996. Seasonal beers are also available.

Blooming Blonde (OG 1041, ABV 4.1%)

Lionbru (OG 1041, ABV 4.1%)

Chesbrewnette (OG 1045, ABV 4.5%)

Little Ale Cart

▤ Little Ale Cart Brewing Co, c/o The Wellington, 1 Henry Street, Sheffield, South Yorkshire, S3 7EQ
☎ (0114) 249 2295

⊗ Brewing started in 2001, as Port Mahon, in a purpose-built brewery behind the Cask & Cutler. In 2007 the brewery and pub were taken over and the names of both changed to Little Ale Cart Brewing and the Wellington. Beer is only brewed for the Wellington and the Dragon pub in Worcester. The beer range varies as the brewer trials new recipes, but tends to include a 4%, 4.3% and a 5% ABV beer.

Little Valley SIBA

Little Valley Brewery Ltd, Unit 3, Turkey Lodge Farm, New Road, Cragg Vale, Hebden Bridge, West Yorkshire, HX7 5TT
☎ (01422) 883888
✉ info@littlevalleybrewery.co.uk
⊕ littlevalleybrewery.co.uk
Shop Mon-Fri 9am-5pm
Tours by arrangement

Little Valley Brewery opened in 2005 and is situated in the Upper Calder Valley, high above Cragg Vale in Hebden Bridge, West Yorkshire. The 10-barrel plant is in a converted chicken and pig farm. It is a wholly organic brewery and is approved by the Soil Association. It does not use isinglass in the beers and is approved by the Vegan Society. The brewery is also a licensee of the Fairtrade Foundation for one of its beers, Ginger Pale Ale. All cask beers are also available in bottle-conditioned form. Around 100 outlets are supplied. Several beers are also contract brewed for Suma Wholefoods. A range of monthly specials was introduced in 2007. In 2012 the brewery was contracted by the Benedictine Order of Ampleforth Abbey to brew and bottle their Ampleforth Double (ABV 7%).

Withens Pale Ale (OG 1037, ABV 3.9%) ◈
Creamy, gold-coloured, refreshingly light ale. Floral, spicy hop aroma, lightly-flavoured with hints of lemon and grapefruit. Clean, bitter aftertaste.

Fairtrade Ginger Pale Ale (OG 1037, ABV 4%) ◈
Full-bodied speciality ale. Ginger predominates in the aroma and taste. It has a pleasantly powerful, fiery and spicy finish.

Cragg Vale Bitter (OG 1039, ABV 4.2%) ◈
Grainy, pale brown-coloured session bitter. Light on the palate with a delicate flavour of malt and fruit and a bitter finish.

Hebden's Wheat (OG 1043, ABV 4.5%) 🍴 🍽 ◈
A pale yellow, creamy wheat beer with a good balance of bitterness and fruit. A hint of sweetness but with a lasting, dry finish.

Stoodley Stout (OG 1044, ABV 4.8%) ◈
Dark brown creamy stout with a rich roast aroma and luscious fruity, chocolate, roast flavours. Well-balanced with a clean, bitter finish.

Tod's Blonde (OG 1045, ABV 5%) ◈
Bright yellow, grainy, speciality beer with a citrus hop start and a dry finish. Fruity with a hint of spice, similar in style to Belgian blonde beer.

Moor Ale (OG 1051, ABV 5.5%) ◈
Tawny in colour with a full-bodied taste. It has a strong malty nose and palate with hints of heather and peat-smoked malt. Well-balanced with a bitter finish.

Python IPA (OG 1055, ABV 6%) ◈
Amber-coloured, grainy beer with a complex bitter fruit palate subtly balance by a malty sweetness, leading to a strongly lingering bitter afterftaste.

Little Brew (NEW)

Little Brew, Unit 21, 43 Carol Street, Camden, London, NW1 0HT
☎ 07817 001376 ✉ stu@littlebrew.co.uk
⊕ littlebrew.co.uk

Brewing began in 2012 using a one-barrel plant. At present only bottle-conditioned ales are produced plus one-off bespoke brews for special events. Bottle-conditioned beers: Pale (ABV 5.6%), Porter (ABV 5.6%). Little Brew concentrate on supplying outlets in the Camden area and deliver the beer in a handcart.

Litton

▤ Litton Ale Brewery, Queens Arms, Litton, North Yorkshire, BD23 5QJ
☎ (01756) 770096 ☎ 07801 657346
✉ info@thequeensarmslitton.co.uk
⊕ thequeensarmslitton.co.uk
Tours by arrangement

⊛Brewing started in 2003 in a purpose-built stone extension at the rear of the pub. Brewing liquor is sourced from a spring that provides the pub with its own water supply.

Ale (OG 1038, ABV 3.8%) ◈
An easy-drinking, traditional bitter with a good malt/hop balance and a bitter finish.

Leading Light (OG 1038, ABV 3.8%) ◈
A long, bitter aftertaste follows a malty flavour with tart fruit and a rising hop bitterness in this light-coloured beer. Low aroma.

Gold Crest (OG 1039, ABV 3.9%)

THE BREWERIES

A very pale beer with a smooth, creamy head. Heavy, fruity hoppiness with no lingering bitterness.

Dark Star (OG 1040, ABV 4%) ◄
A smooth, creamy dark mild, full-bodied for its strength. The taste is quite bitter with roast coffee and tart dark fruit flavours, complemented by a bitter, roast finish.

Potts Beck (OG 1043, ABV 4.2%) ◄
Malt and hops fight for control in this copper-coloured best bitter with a fruity aroma.

Liverpool Craft SIBA

Liverpool Craft Beer Co Ltd, Unit 10, Love Lane, The Railway Arches, Liverpool, L3 7DD
☎ (0151) 236 9400
✉ sales@liverpoolcraftbeer.co.uk
⊕ liverpoolcraftbeer.co.uk

☺Liverpool Craft began brewing in 2011 using a 10-barrel plant. Seasonal and speciality beers are also available.

Icon (OG 1037, ABV 3.8%)
A very pale ale with a long, dry finish with citrus undertones.

Hop Beast (OG 1039, ABV 4%)
Strong hop flavours and bitterness.

Viking Bitter (OG 1041, ABV 4.2%)
A refreshing, light-coloured bitter with some fruity tones.

Icon Dark (OG 1047, ABV 4.8%)
A complex traditional porter; rich and warming.

American Red (OG 1047, ABV 5%)
An American ale packed with hop flavour balanced with a subtle sweetness.

IPA (OG 1047, ABV 5%)
A strong, hoppy beer.

Liverpool One SIBA

Liverpool One Brewery Ltd, 82-84 Vauxhall Road, Liverpool, Merseyside, L3 6DL
☎ 07948 918740
✉ info@liverpoolonebrewery.co.uk
⊕ liverpoolonebrewery.co.uk
Tours by arrangement

☺Liverpool One started brewing in 2010 using a five-barrel plant. Its own pub, Liverpool 1 in Bridewell, opened in 2011. Seasonal and occasional beers are also available.

Kings Regiment (ABV 3.8%)
A dark-coloured malty bitter, smooth and rich.

Light (ABV 4.1%)
Light, hoppy and fruity.

Mersey Mist (ABV 4.1%)
A cloudy wheat beer brewed to the Belgian style flavoured with fresh oranges and lemons with a touch of coriander.

Three Graces (ABV 4.2%)
Straw-coloured with an intense bitter bite.

Dark (ABV 5%)
A full-flavoured classic porter. Roasted and toasted flavours with a smoky finish.

Maharaja IPA (ABV 5.3%)
A classic IPA with a deep golden colour. Packed full of bitterness.

Liverpool Organic SIBA 👁

Liverpool Organic Brewery Ltd, Unit 39, Brasenose Road, Liverpool, Merseyside, L20 8HL
☎ (0151) 933 9660
✉ info@liverpoolorganicbrewery.com
⊕ liverpoolorganicbrewery.com
Tours by arrangement

⊗ Liverpool Organic started brewing in 2009 and has since increased capacity to cope with demand. Outlets are supplied around the extended Merseyside area with its cask range and bespoke food outlets with its bottle-conditioned beers. Seasonal beers are also available. Beers are also brewed under the names of the now defunct Higsons and Cambrinus breweries.

Cascade (ABV 3.8%)

Joseph Williamson (ABV 4%)

Liverpool Pale Ale (OG 1039, ABV 4%)

24 Carat (OG 1041, ABV 4.2%)

Best Bitter (OG 1042, ABV 4.2%)

William Roscoe (ABV 4.3%)

Josephine Butler (OG 1043, ABV 4.5%)

Kitty Wilkinson Chocolate & Vanilla Stout (OG 1047, ABV 4.5%)

Empire Ale (ABV 5.3%)

Shipwreck IPA (OG 1059, ABV 6.5%)

Imperial IPA (ABV 7.6%)

Imperial Russian Stout (ABV 7.9%)

Brewed under Cambrinus Brewery name:

Herald (OG 1036, ABV 3.7%)

Deliverance (OG 1040, ABV 4.2%)

Endurance (OG 1045, ABV 4.3%)

Brewed under Higsons Brewery name:

Mild (ABV 3.5%)

Best Bitter (ABV 4.1%)

Stout (ABV 4.3%)

Lizard

Lizard Ales Ltd, The Old Nuclear Bunker, Pednavounder, Cornwall, TR12 6SE
☎ (01326) 281135 ✉ lizardales@msn.com
⊕ lizardales.co.uk
Tours by arrangement

Launched in 2004 in St Keverne, Lizard Ales supplies mainly west Cornwall. Delivery beyond is by distributor. Bottle-conditioned beers are a speciality. The brewery moved in 2008 into a part of the former RAF Treleaver – a massive disused nuclear bunker in the depths of the Cornish countryside.

Helford River (OG 1036, ABV 3.6%)

Kernow Gold (OG 1035, ABV 3.7%)

Bitter (OG 1040, ABV 4.2%)

Frenchmans Creek (OG 1044, ABV 4.8%)

An Gof (OG 1048, ABV 5.2%)

Llangollen SIBA

Llangollen Brewery, Abbey Grange Brewing Ltd, Horseshoe Pass Road, Llantysilio, Llangollen, LL20 8DD
☎ (01978) 861916 ✉ info@llangollenbrewery.com
⊕ llangollenbrewery.com
Shop open daily in summer; the hotel sells bottles throughout the year
Tours by arrangement

The brewery began in 2010 using a 2.5-barrel plant. All beers are also available bottle-conditioned.

Grange No 1 (ABV 3.2%)
A pale bitter with a fruity aroma and slightly hoppy finish.

Wrexham Borders Bitter (ABV 3.9%)
A pale ale, fruity notes, haylike and distinctively hoppy.

Bitter (ABV 4.2%)
A best bitter with a fruity aroma and distinctive hoppy finish.

Welsh Black (ABV 5.5%)
A black beer with chocolate and toffee notes and a hoppy finish.

Llangorse (NEW)

Llangorse Brewery, Red Lion, Llangors, Powys, LD3 7TY
☎ (01874) 658825 ✉ sales@llangorsebrewery.co.uk
⊕ llangorsebrewery.co.uk
Tours by arrangement

Llangorse began brewing in 2012 and is owned by Howard Marlow who also owns the Breconshire Brewery.

Maid for the Darkside (OG 1037, ABV 3.7%)

Maid in Llangorse (OG 1042, ABV 4.2%)

Maid for Horsin' Around (OG 1044, ABV 4.4%)

Maid for The High Life (OG 1048, ABV 4.8%)

Llŷn (NEW)

Cwrw Llŷn, Unit 6, Ffordd Dewi Sant, Nefyn, Gwynedd, LL53 6EG
☎ 07792 050134 ⊕ cwrwllyn.com

The brewery is a co-operative of 12 friends that began brewing in 2011 producing 44 barrels per week.

Brenin Enlli (ABV 4%)

Seithenyn (ABV 4.2%)

Loch Leven

Loch Leven Brewery, Criochan House, Maryburgh, Blairadam, KY4 0JE
☎ (01383) 831751 ☎ 07592 575329
✉ info@lochlevenbrewery.com
⊕ lochlevenbrewery.com

Loch Leven was established in 2009 on a four-barrel brewery. It supplies beer to most Scottish beer festivals and trades mostly with pubs in Fife and Perthshire. Seasonal beers are also available.

Golden Goose (OG 1037, ABV 3.7%)
A golden ale, light and crisp with a dry aftertaste.

Cock Robin (OG 1041, ABV 4.1%)
A Scottish-style ale; full-bodied with a malty aftertaste.

Nightjar (OG 1042, ABV 4.2%)
A malty ale with a taste of chocolate; lightly hopped with a floral finish.

Loch Lomond (NEW) SIBA

Loch Lomond Brewery, Block 1, Unit 5, Lomond Industrial Estate, Alexandria, G83 0TL
☎ (01389) 755698 ☎ 07891 920213
✉ info@lochlomondbrewery.com
⊕ lochlomondbrewery.com
Shop Sat & Sun 10am-4pm
Tour by arrangement

Loch Lomond was established in 2011 by Fiona and Euan MacEachern and is the only brewery in the Loch Lomond area.

Bonnie & Bitter (ABV 3.6%)
A blonde bitter, easy-drinking with citrus flavours and a full, rounded bitterness.

The West Highland Way (ABV 3.8%)
A light ale with fruity flavours.

Bonnie & Blonde (ABV 4%)
A light, refreshing ale with a well-rounded citrus flavour.

The Ale of Leven (ABV 4.5%)
An amber, easy-drinking beer with a slight sweetness and a spicy bitterness.

Kessog Dark Ale (ABV 5.2%)
Dark with warm, spicy flavours.

Loch Ness SIBA

Loch Ness Brewing Co Ltd, Benleva Hotel, Kilmore Road, Drumnadrochit, IV63 6HH
☎ (01456) 450080 ✉ beer@lochnessbrewery.com
⊕ lochnessbrewery.com
Tours by arrangement

☺Loch Ness began brewing in 2011 using a two-barrel brewplant built in an old bothy in the grounds of the Benleva Hotel. The hotel is the main outlet with any surplus going to a few local outlets and beer festivals.

Light Ness (OG 1040, ABV 3.9%) ✇
Golden, refreshing, hoppy bitter.

Wilder Ness (OG 1040, ABV 3.9%) ✇
Fruity, hoppy brew with a slight malt background. Bittersweet turning to a more bitter finish.

Red Ness (OG 1042, ABV 4.2%) ✇
Reddy brown with a good mix of fruit, malt and hops.

Loch Ness (OG 1044, ABV 4.4%)

Dark Ness (OG 1052, ABV 4.5%) ✇
Roasted chocolate malt with a blackcurrant background. Thick brown head all the way to the bottom.

Hoppy Ness (OG 1050, ABV 5%)

Loddon SIBA ◉

Loddon Brewery Ltd, Dunsden Green Farm, Church Lane, Dunsden, Oxfordshire, RG4 9QD
☎ (0118) 948 1111 ✉ sales@loddonbrewery.com
⊕ loddonbrewery.com
Shop Mon-Fri 9am-5pm; Sat 9.30am-3pm

THE BREWERIES

Tours by arrangement

⊗ Loddon was established in 2002 in a brick and flint barn that houses a 17-barrel brewery able to produce 120 barrels a week. More than 500 outlets are supplied. 2012 saw a comprehensive re-branding across the board. Seasonal beers and monthly specials: see website.

Hoppit (OG 1036.2, ABV 3.5%) ◆
Hops dominate the aroma of this drinkable, light-coloured session beer. Malt and hops create a balanced taste and a pleasant bitterness carries through to the aftertaste.

Hullabaloo (OG 1043.8, ABV 4.2%) ◆
A hint of fruit in the initial taste develops into a balance of hops and malt in this well-rounded, medium-bodied bitter with a bitter aftertaste.

Ferryman's Gold (OG 1045.8, ABV 4.4%) ◆
Golden coloured with a strong hoppy character throughout, accompanied by fruit in the taste and aftertaste.

Bamboozle (OG 1049.5, ABV 4.8%) ◆
Full-bodied and well balanced. Distinctive bittersweet flavour with hop and caramel to accompany.

Forbury Lion (OG 1056.5, ABV 5.5%)
A malty IPA with a strong complex hop finish.

London (NEW) SIBA

⊟ London Brewing Co, Bull, 13 North Hill, Highgate, London, N6 4AB
☎ (020) 8341 0510 ✉ dan@londonbrewing.com
⊕ londonbrewing.com

London Brewing Co began brewing in 2011 at the Bull in Highgate using a 2.5-barrel plant. Seasonal and special beers are also brewed.

Beer Street (ABV 4%)

London Fields (NEW) SIBA

London Fields Brewery, 365-366 Warburton Street, Hackney, London, E8 3RR
☎ (020) 7254 7174 ☎ 07982 367051
✉ sales.londonfieldsbrewery@gmail.com
⊕ londonfieldsbrewery.co.uk

London Fields was first established in 2011 as a 2.5-barrel brewery operating from a railway arch close to London Fields railway station. In 2012 the brewery moved a few arches south and upgraded to a 10-barrel plant. Sales are generally to pubs within the London area. A series of events are organised at weekends at the brewery premises. Seasonal beers are also available.

Session Ale (ABV 3.9%)
A classic, light, pale session ale with light malt and fruity hop flavours.

Love Not War (ABV 4.7%) ◆
Tawny-coloured best bitter with apple and citrus fruit notes with some peppery hops on nose and palate. The citrus dominates the dry, bitter aftertaste.

Hackney Hopster (ABV 4.9%)
A bright, citrussy, tropical fruit-filled pale ale.

Longdog (NEW) SIBA

Longdog Brewery, Unit A1, Moniton Trading Estate, West Ham Lane, Worting, Basingstoke, Hampshire, RG22 6NQ
☎ (01256) 324286 ☎ 07827 618733
✉ contact@longdogbrewery.co.uk
⊕ longdogbrewery.co.uk
Tours by arrangement

Longdog was established in 2011 by Phil Robins using a six-barrel plant. Seasonal beers are available. More than 40 outlets are supplied.

Bunny Chaser (OG 1036, ABV 3.6%)
A dark copper-coloured session bitter with plenty of malt in the mouth and a good whack of bitterness from the English hops.

Golden Poacher (OG 1038, ABV 3.9%)
A very hoppy beer with a crisp, citrus aroma.

Brindle Bitter (OG 1041, ABV 4.2%) ◆
A well-crafted best bitter. Malt nose with hints of caramel and berry fruits. An initial balanced maltiness leads into a moderate hop flavour with bitterness building on the aftertaste.

Lamplight Porter (OG 1048, ABV 5%)
Chocolate and coffee flavours come through together with a robust bitterness from English hops.

Longhill (NEW)

Longhill Brewery, Longhill Cottage, Whitstone, Cornwall, EX22 6UG
☎ (01288) 341466

Longhill began brewing in 2011 using a 0.5-barrel plant, upgraded in 2012 to a four-barrel plant to meet demand. Eight outlets are supplied direct. Seasonal beers are available.

Whistler (ABV 3.8%)

Westerly (ABV 4%)

Gale Force (ABV 4.8%)

Hurricane (ABV 4.8%)

Long Lane

Long Lane Brewery, Matchless Home Brewing, 32 Belvoir Road, Coalville, Leicestershire, LE67 3PN
☎ (01530) 813800

This small 100-litre brewery was established in 2010 and is based in the Matchless Homebrew shop. Beers are mostly bottle-conditioned but cask beers can be produced to order.

Long Man (NEW) SIBA

Long Man Brewery, Church Farm, Litlington, East Sussex, BN26 5RA
☎ (01323) 871850 ☎ 07976 777992
✉ info@longmanbrewery.com
⊕ longmanbrewery.com
Tours by arrangement

Long Man began brewing in 2012 using a 20-barrel plant by Johnson Brewery Design Ltd. Hops and grain are sourced locally with a view to using its own barley currently being grown on the farm as well as a traditional strain of Sussex yeast.

Long Blonde (OG 1040, ABV 3.8%)

A light-coloured golden ale with a distinctive hoppy aroma and crisp, clean bitterness on the finish. Smooth, light and refreshing.

Best Bitter (OG 1040, ABV 4%)
Well-balanced with a complex bittersweet malty taste, fragrant hops and a characteristic long deep finish.

Sussex Pride (OG 1044, ABV 4.5%)
A strong, complex IPA. Bronze in colour with a fruity nose and full, round flavours.

Loose Cannon SIBA

Loose Cannon Brewery, Unit 6, Suffolk Way, Abingdon, Oxfordshire, OX14 5JX
☎ (01235) 531141 ✉ will@lcbeers.co.uk
⊕ lcbeers.co.uk
Shop Mon-Sat 9am-5pm
Tours by arrangement

Loose Cannon began production in 2010 using a 15-barrel brew plant, reviving Abingdon's brewing history after the Morland Brewery closed in 2000. Seasonal beer are also available.

Abingdon Bridge (OG 1041, ABV 4.1%)
Full-flavoured and smooth with well-rounded bitterness and a light citrus and floral finish.

Lord Conrad's

Lord Conrad's Brewery, Unit 21, Dry Drayton Industrial Estate, Scotland Road, Dry Drayton, Cambridgeshire, CB23 8AT
☎ 07736 739700 ✉ lordconrads@gmail.com
⊕ lordconradsbrewery.co.uk

⊠ Lord Conrad's began commercial brewing in 2011 using a 2.5-barrel plant. One permanent outlet is supplied along with other local freehouses and beer festivals. Seasonal beers are also available.

Lickety Spit (OG 1038, ABV 3.8%)
A sweet, malty brown ale; light but not overly hoppy.

Conkerwood (OG 1044, ARV 4%)
A dark porter with hints of liquorice.

Gubbins (OG 1040, ABV 4%)

Pheasant's Rise (OG 1050, ABV 5%)
Smoky, woody, traditional strong ale commemorating the brewer's gamekeeper grandfather.

Stubble Burner (OG 1050, ABV 5%)
A good earthy nose and well-balanced fruity bitterness.

Lovibonds

Lovibonds Brewery Ltd, Rear of 19-21 Market Place, Henley-on-Thames, Oxfordshire, RG9 2AA
☎ (01491) 576596 ✉ info@lovibonds.com
⊕ lovibonds.com
Shop Fri 3-8pm; Sat 11am-5pm; Sun 11am-4pm
Tours by arrangement

Lovibonds Brewery was founded by Jeff Rosenmeier in 2005 and is named after Joseph William Lovibond, who invented the Tintometer to measure beer colour. Brewing takes place on the Old Luxters Brewery plant, five miles from Henley-on-Thames. Only test brewing takes place in

Henley. Beers are available only bottled or in mini kegs.

Loweswater

See Cumbrian Legendary Ales

Luckie

Luckie Ales, c/o 14 Kingsmill Drive, Kennoway, Fife, KY8 5LX
☎ (01333) 352801 ✉ info@luckie-ales.com
⊕ luckie-ales.com

Luckie Ales was established in 2009. Beer is brewed on a one-barrel plant in Markinch.

Midnycht Myld (OG 1037, ABV 3.4%)

Amber Ale (OG 1040, ABV 3.7%)

80/- (OG 1056, ABV 5%)

Ludlow SIBA ◉

Ludlow Brewing Co Ltd, The Railway Shed, Station Drive, Ludlow, Shropshire, SY8 2PQ
☎ (01584) 873291
✉ gary@theludlowbrewingcompany.co.uk
⊕ theludlowbrewingcompany.co.uk
Shop Mon-Fri 10am-5pm; Sat 10am-2pm
Tours by arrangement

The brewery opened in 2006 in a renovated malthouse. During 2010 a move to larger premises, a former railway sidings shed on the same site, took place. In addition a new 20-barrel plant was installed. The premises also functions as the brewery tap and a visitor centre. Bottle-conditioned beer is available.

Best (OG 1037, ABV 3.7%)

Gold (OG 1041, ABV 4.2%)

Black Knight (OG 1045, ABV 4.5%)

Boiling Well (OG 1045.5, ABV 4.7%)

Stairway (OG 1047, ABV 5%)

Lymestone SIBA ◉

Lymestone Brewery Ltd, The Old Brewery, Unit 5 Mount Road Industrial Estate, Mount Road, Stone, Staffordshire, ST15 8LL
☎ (01785) 817796 ☎ 07891 782652
✉ brad@lymestonebrewery.co.uk
⊕ lymestonebrewery.co.uk
Shop Mon-Fri 8am-5pm, Sat & Sun by appointment
Tours by arrangement

Lymestone commenced brewing in 2008 on a 10-barrel brew plant and has since doubled fermenting capacity. The brewery recently took on a neighbouring unit to enable further expansion. Its first pub was opened in 2012, the Lymestone Vaults in Newcastle Under Lyme.

Stone Cutter (OG 1038, ABV 3.7%) ◈
Sulphurous aroma gives way to a caramel sweet start and pleasing hop and fruit balance. The mouth-watering hoppy promise is fulfilled in to the finish.

Stone Faced (OG 1042, ABV 4%)
Subtle citrus and toffee flavours balanced by a hoppy aroma and bitter finish.

Foundation Stone (OG 1047, ABV 4.5%) ◈

An IPA-style beer with pale and crystal malts. Faint biscuit and chewy, juicy fruits burst on to the palate then the spicy Boadicea and Pilot hops pepper the taste buds to leave a dry bitter finish.

Ein Stein (OG 1052, ABV 5%)
A continental-style blonde ale. Biscuit malts give way to a fresh hop aftertaste.

Stone The Crows (OG 1056, ABV 5.4%) ◆
A rich dark beer from chocolate malts. Fruit, roasts and hops abound to leave a deep lingering bitterness from the Styrian Goldings and Millennium hop mix.

Lytham SIBA ⊚

Lytham Brewery Ltd, Unit 8, Campbells Court, Lord Street, Lytham St Annes, Lancashire, FY8 2DF
☎ (01253) 737707 ✉ info@lythambrewery.co.uk
⊕ lythambrewery.co.uk
Tours by arrangement

⊚Lytham started brewing in 2008 at the Hastings Club in Lytham but moved to larger premises soon after due to demand. The brewery originally used a 2.5-barrel plant which was upgraded to a 10-barrel plant in 2010. The brewery burnt down in 2011 and has moved to its present address. The 2.5-barrel plant was salvaged and brewing has recommenced with eight new fermenters and six new conditioning tanks. The 10-barrel plant is also now in use again.

Amber (OG 1037, ABV 3.6%)
A traditional malty beer using English hops.

Blonde (OG 1038, ABV 3.8%)
A pale golden beer with a subtle hop aroma and a smooth, dry finish.

Gold (OG 1042, ABV 4.2%)
A golden beer with a fruity aroma and lasting bitter finish.

Royal (OG 1044, ABV 4.4%)
A full-bodied English ale with a crisp fruity aroma and a smooth, dry finish.

Dark (OG 1047, ABV 5%)
Dark chocolate malt with a hint of vanilla and a smooth, dry finish.

IPA (OG 1054, ABV 5.6%)
A pale bitter with a fresh, sweet, hoppy flavour leading to a long, dry finish.

McGivern

▦ McGivern Ales, c/o The Bridge End Inn, 5 Bridge Street, Ruabon, LL14 6DA
☎ (01978) 810881 ☎ 07891 676614
✉ mcgivernmatt@hotmail.com
⊕ mcgivernales.co.uk
Tours by arrangement

The brewery was established in early 2008 and was originally based at the brewer's home in Wrexham but moved in 2011 to the Bridge End Inn in Ruabon using a 2.5-barrel plant.

Enigma (OG 1040, ABV 3.8%)

Under The Bridge Bitter (OG 1041, ABV 4%)

Amber Ale (OG 1040, ABV 4.2%)

Cascade Pale (OG 1042, ABV 4.2%)

Stout (OG 1044, ABV 4.2%)

McGuinness

See Offa's Dyke

McMullen SIBA IFBB ⊚

McMullen & Sons Ltd, 26 Old Cross, Hertford, Hertfordshire, SG14 1RD
☎ (01992) 584911 ✉ contact@mcmullens.co.uk
⊕ mcmullens.co.uk

⊠ McMullen is Hertfordshire's oldest independent brewery, celebrating 185 years of brewing in 2012. A new brewhouse opened in 2006, giving the company greater flexibility to produce its regular cask beers and up to eight seasonal beers a year. Cask beer is served in all 140 pubs.

AK (OG 1035, ABV 3.7%) ◆
A pleasant mix of malt and hops leads to a distinctive, dry aftertaste that isn't always as pronounced as it used to be.

Cask Ale (OG 1039, ABV 3.8%)
A light and refreshing beer marked by the use of Styrian Goldings and English Fuggle hops.

Country Bitter (OG 1042, ABV 4.3%) ⎚ ◆
A full-bodied beer with a well-balanced mix of malt, hops and fruit throughout.

IPA (OG 1047, ABV 4.8%)
A strong bitter with deep rich flavours created with specially kilned amber malts.

Maclay

See Greene King in New Nationals section

Madcap SIBA

Madcap Brewery Ltd, Unit 3, Broadmeadow Industrial Estate, Ecclefechan, Annan, Dumfriesshire, DG11 3LG
☎ (01461) 203495 ☎ 07801 699161

Registered Office: Greenknowe Avenue, Annan, Dumfriesshire, DG12 6ER
✉ john@madcapbrewery.com
⊕ madcapbrewery.com
Tours by arrangement

⊚Madcap Brewery started production in 2009 using a one-barrel plant in a small outbuilding at the rear of the family home. In 2011 the brewery moved to its present address with a new five-barrel plant. Seasonal and bottle-conditioned beers are available. All bottle-conditioned beers are also available cask-conditioned upon request: see website for details.

Magic Rock SIBA

Magic Rock Brewing Co Ltd, Unit 1, Quarmby Mills, Tanyard Road, Oakes, Huddersfield, West Yorkshire, HD3 4YP
☎ (01484) 649823 ✉ sales@magicrockbrewing.com
⊕ magicrockbrewing.com
Tours by arrangement

⊚Magic Rock began brewing in 2011 in the Old Bed Factory attached to the Rockshop Wholesale Company in Huddersfield. Bottle-conditioned and special beers are available.

Curious (ABV 3.9%)

Rapture (ABV 4.6%)

Highwire (ABV 5.5%)

Dark Arts (ABV 6%)

Magpie SIBA 👁

Magpie Brewery, Unit 4, Ashling Court, Ashling Street, Nottingham, NG2 3JA
☎ 07738 762897 ✉ info@magpiebrewery.com
⊕ magpiebrewery.com

😊Magpie is a six-barrel brewery launched in 2006. It is located a few feet from the perimeter of the Meadow Lane Stadium, home of Notts County FC (the Magpies) from which the brewery name naturally derived. Seasonal and occasional beers: see website.

Hoppit (OG 1035, ABV 3.8%)

Best (OG 1040.7, ABV 4.2%) ◥
A malty, traditional pale brown best bitter, with balancing hops giving a bitter finish.

Blonde (OG 1039.9, ABV 4.2%)
A smooth, blonde bitter.

Raven Stout (OG 1044, ABV 4.4%)

Thieving Rogue (OG 1042, ABV 4.5%) ◥
A hoppy golden ale with a long-lasting, bitter finish.

Midnight Porter (OG 1049.4, ABV 5%)

Home IPA (OG 1047.5, ABV 5.2%)

Maldon

See Farmer's Ales

Mallard SIBA

Mallard Brewery, Unit A, Maythorne, Nottinghamshire, NG25 0RS
☎ (01636) 812365 ☎ 07811 193930
Tours by arrangement

Phil Mallard built and installed a two-barrel plant in a shed at his home and started brewing in 1995. The brewery was taken over in 2010 and moved to its current address. There are plans to expand the plant, increase the range of beers and introduce bottle-conditioned ales. Beers are brewed for the Hearty Goodfellow pub in Southwell, Notts.

Duck 'n' Dive (OG 1037, ABV 3.7%) ◥
A bitter, pale golden beer, with a dry finish. Brewed with First Gold hops.

Greet (OG 1037, ABV 3.7%)

Golden Duck (OG 1039, ABV 3.9%)

Duckling (OG 1041, ABV 4.1%) ◥
A dry-hopped, golden ale. Very bitter; hops dominate in the aroma and aftertaste.

Feather Light (OG 1040, ABV 4.1%) ◥
A straw-coloured lager style beer with a hoppy taste and aroma.

Speckduckular (OG 1042, ABV 4.2%)

Decoy (OG 1045, ABV 4.5%)

Mallinsons

Mallinsons Brewing Co, Plover Road Garage, Plover Road, Huddersfield, West Yorkshire, HD3 3HS
☎ (01484) 654301 ✉ info@drinkmallinsons.co.uk
⊕ drinkmallinsons.co.uk

😊The brewery was set up in 2008 on a six-barrel plant by CAMRA members Tara Mallinson and Elaine Yendall. A range of one-off specials is also brewed along with bottle-conditioned beers.

Emley Moor Mild (ABV 3.4%)
Black with a ruby hint. A full-bodied mild with a nutty taste and slightly bitter finish.

Stadium Bitter (ABV 3.8%)
Straw-coloured with a clean, bitter taste and dry, fruity finish.

Station Best Bitter (ABV 4.2%)
An amber-coloured best bitter with a balance of malt and fruity hops.

Castle Hill Premium (ABV 4.6%)
A golden-coloured premium bitter, hoppy with citrus tones.

Malvern Hills SIBA

Malvern Hills Brewery Ltd, 15 West Malvern Road, Malvern, Worcestershire, WR14 4ND
☎ (01684) 560165 ✉ beer@tiscali.co.uk
⊕ malvernhillsbrewery.co.uk
Tours by arrangement

Founded in 1998 in an old quarrying dynamite store and now an established presence in the Three Counties, Birmingham and the Black Country. Limited use of wholesalers can spread the ales further afield. The core beers are supplemented by a rolling programme of monthly specials.

Cyneweard (OG 1038, ABV 3.8%)
Pale blond and very hoppy.

Feelgood (OG 1037, ABV 3.8%)

Swedish Nightingale (OG 1039, ABV 4%)

Priessnitz Plzen (OG 1040, ABV 4.3%) ◥
A mix of soft fruit and citrus give this straw-coloured brew its quaffability, making it ideal for quenching summer thirsts.

Black Pear (OG 1042, ABV 4.4%) ◥
A sharp citrus hoppiness is the main constituent of this golden brew that has a long, dry aftertaste.

Mansfield

See Marston's in New Nationals section

Marble SIBA

🛢 Marble Beers Ltd, 73 Rochdale Road, Manchester, M4 4HY
☎ (0161) 819 2694
✉ thebrewers_marblebeers@msn.com
Tours by arrangement

😊 Marble opened at the Marble Arch Inn in 1997 and produces organic and vegan beers as well as some non-organic ales. It is registered with the Soil Association and the Vegetarian Society. Marble currently owns three pubs and supplies around 70 outlets. In 2009 a second, 12-barrel plant was installed at Unit 41, Williamson Street, Manchester. All brewing now takes place at this site. A number of bottle-conditioned beers are available as well as regular seasonals.

Draft (OG 1039, ABV 3.9%)

Pint (OG 1038.5, ABV 3.9%)
A very hoppy, pale golden, dry session beer.

Manchester Bitter (OG 1041.7, ABV 4.2%) ◈
Yellow beer with a fruity and hoppy aroma. Hops, fruit and bitterness on the palate and in the finish.

Ginger Marble (OG 1046, ABV 4.5%)
Intense and complex. Full-bodied and fiery with a sharp, snappy bite.

Lagonda IPA (OG 1048, ABV 5%) ◈
Golden yellow beer with a spicy, fruity nose. Fruit, hops and malt in the mouth, with a dry fruitiness continuing into the bitter aftertaste.

Chocolate Marble (OG 1054.5, ABV 5.5%) 🏳
A strong, stout-like ale. Malty flavours are paired with a long-lasting, sweet bitterness.

Dobber (OG 1055.5, ABV 5.9%)
A dark golden ale with big hop character balanced by a pleasant yet noticeable malt base.

Marlpool

Marlpool Brewing Co Ltd, 5 Breach Road, Marlpool, Heanor, Derbyshire, DE75 7NJ
☎ (01773) 711285
✉ enquiries@marlpoolbrewing.co.uk
⊕ marlpoolbrewing.co.uk
Shop Fri 3-9pm; Sat & Sun 12-9pm
Tours by arrangement

Marlpool was set up by brothers Andy and Chris McAuley in 2010 using a 2.5-barrel plant situated in an old slaughterhouse. The majority of the beer is sold through its own ale house, attached to the brewery. The remainder is supplied to pubs within a 10-mile radius.

Otters Pocket (OG 1040, ABV 4%)
An easy-drinking, smooth amber ale.

Stratty Ratty (OG 1044, ABV 4.4%)
A pale ale, lightly hopped with a bitter, dry finish.

Marston Moor ◉

Marston Moor Brewery Ltd, PO Box 9, York, North Yorkshire, YO26 7XW
☎ (01423) 359641
✉ info@marstonmoorbrewery.co.uk
⊕ rudgatebrewery.co.uk

☺ Established in 1983 in Kirk Hammerton, the brewery had a re-investment programme in 2005, moving brewing operations to nearby Tockwith, where it shares the site with Rudgate Brewery (qv). Two special beers are available each month. Around 250 outlets are supplied.

Cromwell's Pale (OG 1036, ABV 3.8%) ◈
A golden beer with hops and fruit in strong evidence on the nose. Bitterness as well as fruit and hops dominate the taste and long aftertaste.

Matchlock Mild (OG 1038, ABV 4%)
Traditional, full-flavoured dark mild.

Mongrel (OG 1038, ABV 4%)
A balanced bitter with plenty of fruit character.

Fairfax Special (OG 1039, ABV 4.2%)
A full-bodied premium bitter, pale in colour with a well-balanced slightly citrus aroma.

Merriemaker (OG 1042, ABV 4.5%)
A premium straw-coloured ale with a typical Yorkshire taste.

Brewers Droop (OG 1045.5, ABV 5%)
A powerful golden ale with a sweet taste.

Marston's

See Marston's in New Nationals section

Masters (NEW)

Masters Brewery, Greenham Business Park, 8 Greenham Park, Greenham, Somerset, TA21 0LR
☎ (01823) 674444
✉ richard@mastersbrewery.co.uk
⊕ mastersbrewery.co.uk

The brewery first started life in 2006 but had to close in 2009. In 2011 it was reopened using a 2.5-barrel plant. It is also the site of the Blackdown Brewery with beers under that name to be launched soon.

Arthurs Ale (ABV 3.8%)

Spypost Bitter (ABV 4%)

Carnival (ABV 4.3%)

Waterloo (ABV 4.3%)

Duke (ABV 4.5%)

Thunderbridge (ABV 4.7%)

Matthews

See Dawkins

Mauldons [SIBA] EAB ◉

Mauldons Ltd, Black Adder Brewery, 13 Church Field Road, Sudbury, Suffolk, CO10 2YA
☎ (01787) 311055 ✉ sims@mauldons.co.uk
⊕ mauldons.co.uk
Shop Mon-Fri 9.30am-4pm
Tours by arrangement

⊠ The Mauldon family started brewing in Sudbury in 1795. The brewery with 26 pubs was bought by Greene King in the 1960s. The current business, established in 1982, was bought by Steve and Alison Sims – both former employees of Adnams – in 2000. They relocated to a new brewery in 2005, with a 30-barrel plant that has doubled production. The brewery tap was bought in 2008 and a second pub in 2010. Around 150 outlets are supplied. There is a rolling programme of seasonal beers: see website.

Micawber's Mild (OG 1035, ABV 3.5%) ◈
Fruit and roast flavours dominate the nose, with vine fruit and caramel on the tongue and a short, dry, coffeeish aftertaste. Full-bodied and satisfying.

Moletrap Bitter (OG 1038, ABV 3.8%) ◈
Delicate hop aroma leading to a refreshing bitter hoppiness, finishing with a citrus aftertaste with hints of orange peel and grapefruit. An excellent session beer, which belies its strength.

Silver Adder (OG 1042, ABV 4.2%)
A light-coloured bitter with five hop and malt combinations giving a refreshing, crisp finish.

Suffolk Pride (OG 1048, ABV 4.8%) ◈
A full-bodied, copper-coloured beer with a good balance of malt, hops and fruit in the taste.

Black Adder (OG 1053, ABV 5.3%) ◈

Superbly balanced dark, sweet ale, but with rich vine fruit throughout. The brewery's flagship beer.

Maxim SIBA 👁

Maxim Brewery, 1 Gadwall Road, Rainton Bridge South, Houghton le Spring, County Durham, DH4 5NL
☎ **(0191) 584 8844** ✉ **admin@dmbc.org.uk**
🌐 **maximbrewery.co.uk**
Tours by arrangement

😊Rising from the ashes of the former Sunderland brewer Vaux, Double Maxim set up a 20-barrel plant in Houghton le Spring in 2007. In 2010 two former brewers from the now defunct Federation Brewery joined the team. More than 100 outlets are supplied direct and four pubs are owned. Seasonal beers are also available.

Lambton's (OG 1037, ABV 3.8%)

Samson (OG 1039, ABV 4%)
A distinctive, well-balanced beer with a lingering, smooth flavour.

Ward's Best Bitter (OG 1039, ABV 4%)
A subtle aroma with hop overtones complements the taste of this malty, full-flavoured traditional Yorkshire Bitter.

Swedish Blonde (OG 1041, ABV 4.2%)

Double Maxim (OG 1046, ABV 4.7%)
A brown ale with a well-balanced, smooth flavour leaving a pleasant, slightly sweet aftertaste.

Maximus (OG 1058, ABV 6%)
A strong premium ale, dark ruby in colour, with a sweet liquorice taste. Warming and easy to drink.

Mayfields SIBA 👁

Mayfields Brewery, No. 8 Croft Business Park, Leominster, Herefordshire, HR6 0QF
☎ **(01568) 611197** ✉ **info@mayfieldsbrewery.co.uk**
🌐 **mayfieldsbrewery.co.uk**
Shop Wed-Fri 10am-4pm (other times by appt)

Established in 2005, Mayfields is a small family brewery located in the heart of one of England's major hop growing regions. 2008 saw a change of location and ownership. Since then the range of core beers has been changed and updated. Around 50 outlets are supplied. Seasonal beers are brewed on a monthly basis: see website. The brewery also distributes draught and bottled traditional local cider.

Copper Fox (OG 1037, ABV 3.8%)
A copper-coloured ale with a fresh malt body and lots of hop character.

Priory Pale Ale (OG 1039, ABV 4%)
A light golden ale with a refreshing malt body and plenty of hops in the aroma, leading to a gentle bitter finish.

Ducking Stool (OG 1041, ABV 4.2%)
A refreshing golden amber-coloured ale with plenty of hop character throughout.

Aunty Myrtle's (OG 1044, ABV 4.5%)
A dark copper-coloured ale with gentle malt flavours and strong hop finish.

Mayflower

Mayflower Brewery, Unit 2, 15-17 Sandbrook Road, Orrell, Lancashire, WN5 8UB

☎ **07984 404567** ✉ **info@mayflowerbeer.co.uk**
🌐 **mayflowerbeer.co.uk**

😊Mayflower is an award-winning 2.5-barrel, family-run microbrewery established in 2001, still using the original vessels and casks. A number of real ale pubs throughout the north-west are supplied regularly as well as beer festivals and private parties.

Tower Hill (OG 1039, ABV 3.8%)
Lightly-hopped and made with three types of grain for added body.

Douglas Valley (OG 1041, ABV 4%)
A distinctive dry, hoppy beer.

Lancashire Stout (OG 1040, ABV 4%)
A traditional English stout; dark, smoky and dry.

MB Gold (OG 1042.5, ABV 4.2%)
A light-coloured, strong bitter.

Wigan Bier (OG 1042, ABV 4.2%)
A golden ale with strong Goldings hops notes.

May Hill (NEW) SIBA

May Hill Brewery, Holly Bush Farm, Ross Road, Longhope, Gloucestershire, GL17 0NG
☎ **(01452) 830222** ✉ **info@mayhillbrewery.com**
🌐 **mayhillbrewery.com**
Shop Mon, Wed, Fri & Sat 9am-2pm; other times by arrangement
Tours by arrangement

Brewing commenced in 2011 using a six-barrel plant housed in a reconstructed farm dairy. A 200-foot bore hole gives the brewery its water supply. Local freehouses are supplied and bottle-conditioned beer is also available via farm shops and specialist outlets. Seasonal beers: see website.

Admiral May (OG 1036, ABV 3.8%)
A full-flavoured light bitter.

Legend (OG 1040, ABV 4.5%)
A rich pale ale with a strong hop finish.

Legless Cow (OG 1044, ABV 4.8%)
A distinctive fruity ale with a palate-cleansing hop finish.

Summit (OG 1045, ABV 4.9%)
A full-flavoured dark ale with a malty aroma and subtle bitter aftertaste.

Maypole

Maypole Brewery Ltd, North Laithes Farm, Wellow Road, Eakring, Newark, Nottinghamshire, NG22 0AN
☎ **07971 277598/07971 277592**
✉ **maypolebrewery@aol.com**
🌐 **maypolebrewery.co.uk**

😊 The brewery opened in 1995 in a converted 18th-century farm building. After changing hands in 2001 it was bought by the former head brewer, Rob Neil, in 2005. Seasonal beers can be ordered at any time for beer festivals: see website for details and list.

Little Weed (OG 1038, ABV 3.8%)

Mayfly Bitter (OG 1038, ABV 3.8%)

Celebration (OG 1040, ABV 4%)

Gate Hopper (OG 1040, ABV 4%)

Mayfair (OG 1040, ABV 4.1%)

Maybee (OG 1041, ABV 4.3%)

THE BREWERIES

Major Oak (OG 1042, ABV 4.4%)

Flanagan's Extra Stout (OG 1044, ABV 4.5%)

Wellow Gold (OG 1044, ABV 4.6%)

Kiwi IPA (OG 1046, ABV 4.8%)

Mayhem (OG 1048, ABV 5%)

Platinum Blonde (OG 1048, ABV 5%)

For Olde Red Lion, Wellow:

Olde Lions Ale (ABV 3.9%)

Meantime SIBA ⊙

Meantime Brewing Co Ltd, Units 4 & 5, Lawrence Trading Estate, Blackwall Lane, London, SE10 0AR
☎ (020) 8293 1111 ✉ info@meantimebrewing.com
⊕ meantimebrewing.com
Tours by arrangement

⊗ Founded in 2000, Meantime brews a wide range of continental style beer and traditional English bottle-conditioned ales. Two pubs are owned. In 2010 the brewery relocated to larger premises in Greenwich. Bottle-conditioned beers are produced, all suitable for vegetarians and vegans. A six-barrel brewery is also owned at the Old Brewery, the Old Royal Naval College in Greenwich and is used to brew limited edition beers.

London Pale Ale (OG 1043, ABV 4.3%) ◆
Amber-coloured best bitter with a citrus hop aroma. The malty sweetness is balanced by strong bitter hops on the palate that fade in the slightly dry finish.

Medieval (NEW)

Medieval Beers, c/o Moot, 27c Carlton Road, Nottingham, NG3 2DG
☎ 07552 798027
✉ james.mansfield14@yahoo.co.uk

Medieval began brewing in 2012 in a garage using a home-made 4.5-barrel plant. It is hoped to relocate the brewery nearer to or within the Moot pub in Nottingham, which is leased and run by the brewer and his wife.

Chivalry (ABV 3.8%)
A pale session ale with a balanced combination of malt and hop.

Knight Hood (ABV 4.2%)
An amber ale with a deep, hoppy taste.

Excalibur (ABV 4.3%)
A pale ale infused with oak chippings.

Crusader (ABV 4.4%)
Pale ale that is slightly sweet with a refreshing citrus finish.

Meesons

See Old Bog

Melbourn

Melbourn Bros Brewery, All Saints Brewery, All Saints Street, Stamford, Lincolnshire, PE9 2PA
☎ (01780) 752186
Tours by arrangement (minimum 10 people, £6 per head including tastings)

A famous Stamford brewery that opened in 1825 and closed in 1974. It re-opened in 1994 and is owned by Samuel Smith of Tadcaster (qv). Melbourn brews three handcrafted, organic fruit beers (Cherry, Strawberry and Raspberry) using the antique steam-driven brewing equipment. The beers are all suitable for vegans and are organic. The beers are only available bottled (not bottle-conditioned).

Merlin SIBA

Merlin Brewing Co Ltd, 3 Springbank Farm, Congleton Road, Arclid, Cheshire, CW11 2UD
☎ (01477) 500893
✉ brewing@merlinbrewing.co.uk
⊕ merlinbrewing.co.uk
Tours by arrangement

⊠ In 2010 David and Sue Peart started brewing in rural Cheshire using an eight-barrel plant. Beers are principally supplied to outlets within a 30-mile radius. All beers are also available bottle conditioned.

King's Ale (OG 1036, ABV 3.6%)
An easy-drinking, tawny-coloured ale, full of taste and flavour.

Merlin's Gold (OG 1038, ABV 3.8%)
A light golden ale with a floral, rounded, citrus flavour.

Spellbound (OG 1040, ABV 4%)
A premium English ale, full-flavoured and bitter with a dry finish. Light chestnut in colour.

The Wizard (OG 1042, ABV 4.2%)
Light amber in colour and bursting with citrus hop aromas and flavour.

Dragonslayer (OG 1054, ABV 5.6%)
A dark brew with a complex depth of flavour with blackcurrant afternotes.

Merry Miner

Merry Miner Brewery Ltd, Grendon House Farm, Warton Lane, Grendon, Warwickshire, CV9 3DT
☎ 07811 932721 ✉ merryminerbrewer@aol.co.uk
⊕ merryminerbrewery.com
Tours by arrangement

☺Merry Miner began brewing in 2010 using a 2.5-barrel plant previously used by Discovery Ales and is based in farm buildings on the outskirts of the village of Grendon. The brewer, Alan Wood, is a former coal miner and played for the Merry Miner football team, hence the name. Seasonal beers are also available.

Warwickshire's Finest (OG 1036, ABV 3.8%)
A light amber session bitter.

Davy's Lamp (OG 1038, ABV 4%)
A pale barley, full-flavoured bitter.

Cap Lamp (OG 1039, ABV 4.2%)
A golden beer with a refreshing, crisp bitterness.

Deputy Drop (OG 1040, ABV 4.3%)

Going Underground (OG 1041, ABV 4.4%)
A refreshing amber bitter.

Pit Pony (OG 1041, ABV 4.5%)
A deep golden smooth bitter.

Methane (OG 1045, ABV 5%)
A light golden bitter with a citrus finish.

Mersea Island

Mersea Island Brewery, Rewsalls Lane, East Mersea, Essex, CO5 8SX
☎ (01206) 385900 ✉ beers@merseawine.com
⊕ merseawine.com
Shop Wed-Sun 10.30am-4pm, closed Mon & Tue

The brewery was established at Mersea Island Vineyard in 2005, producing cask and bottle-conditioned beers. The brewery supplies several local pubs on a guest beer basis as well as most local beer festivals. The brewery holds its own festival of Essex-produced ales over the four-day Easter weekend.

Yo Boy! (OG 1038, ABV 3.8%) ◀
Pale session beer. Peach and orange on the aroma and taste, leading to a pleasantly bitter finish.

Lion Bitter (OG 1038, ABV 3.9%)
A pale amber bitter with nutty and caramel flavours.

Gold (OG 1043, ABV 4.5%)
A refreshing, golden Pilsner-style ale.

Skippers Bitter (OG 1047, ABV 4.8%) ◀
Strong bitter, whose full character is dominated by pear drops and juicy malt. A raspberry tartness follows.

Oyster (OG 1048, ABV 5%)
Traditional dark oyster ale using local Mersea Island oysters to give it a distinct, unique flavour.

Middle Earth (NEW)

Middle Earth Brewing Co, Rowditch Inn, 246 Uttoxeter Road, Derby, DE22 3LL
☎ 07905 604230 ✉ enquiries@mebrewco.com
⊕ mebrewco.com

Formed in 2011, Middle Earth uses the four-barrel plant based at the Rowditch Inn in Derby (also used by the Rowditch Brewery). Bottle-conditioned beers are also available.

Prancing Pony (OG 1041, ABV 3.9%)

Rivendale (OG 1043, ABV 4%)

Dragons Gold (OG 1043, ABV 4.1%)

Honey Dragon (OG 1045, ABV 4.2%)

Witan (ABV 4.5%)

Black Rose (OG 1048, ABV 4.6%)

Mighty Hop SIBA

Mighty Hop Brewery Ltd, Silverdale, Woodmead Road, Lyme Regis, Dorset, DT7 3AD
☎ (01297) 445358
✉ enquiries@mightyhopbrewery.co.uk
⊕ mightyhopbrewery.co.uk

Mighty Hop began brewing in 2010 using a one-barrel plant and only produces bottle-conditioned ales for the licensed trade.

Mighty Oak

Mighty Oak Brewing Co Ltd, 14b West Station Yard, Spital Road, Maldon, Essex, CM9 6TW
☎ (01621) 843713
✉ sales@mightyoakbrewing.co.uk
⊕ mightyoakbrewing.co.uk
Tours by arrangement

⊗ Mighty Oak was formed in 1996 and moved in 2001 to Maldon, where capacity was increased. Around 350 outlets are supplied. Twelve monthly ales are brewed based on a theme.

IPA (OG 1035.6, ABV 3.5%) ◀
Light-bodied, pale session bitter. Hop notes are initially suppressed by a delicate sweetness but the aftertaste is more assertive.

Oscar Wilde (OG 1039.5, ABV 3.7%) ⬚ ◀
Roasty dark mild with suggestions of forest fruits and dark chocolate. A sweet taste yields to a more bitter finish.

Captain Bob (OG 1039.5, ABV 3.8%)
A traditional deep amber bitter with a fruity and hoppy aroma. A slight sweet maltiness balances an easy-going bitterness followed by hints of gooseberry, elderflower and grape in the finish.

Maldon Gold (OG 1039.5, ABV 3.8%) ◀
Pale golden ale with a sharp citrus note moderated by honey and biscuity malt.

Simply The Best (OG 1044.1, ABV 4.4%) ◀
Well-balanced, mid-strength bitter with a sweet start and a dry, bitter finish.

English Oak (OG 1047.9, ABV 4.8%) ◀
Strong tawny, fruity bitter with caramel, butterscotch and vanilla. A gentle hop character is present throughout.

Milestone SIBA ◉

Milestone Brewing Co Ltd, Great North Road, Cromwell, Newark, Nottinghamshire, NG23 6JE
☎ (01636) 822255 ✉ info@milestonebrewery.co.uk
⊕ milestonebrewery.co.uk
Shop Mon-Fri 8am-5pm
Tours by arrangement

☺ The brewery has been in production since 2005 on a 12-barrel plant. Around 150 outlets are supplied. Seasonal and bottle-conditioned beers are also available.

Lions Pride (OG 1038, ABV 3.8%)

Shine On (OG 1039, ABV 4%)

Loxley Ale (OG 1042, ABV 4.2%)

Black Pearl (OG 1043, ABV 4.3%)

Crusader (OG 1044, ABV 4.4%)

Rich Ruby (OG 1044, ABV 4.5%)

American Pale Ale (OG 1046, ABV 4.6%)

Olde English (OG 1049, ABV 4.9%)

Game Keeper (OG 1052, ABV 5.2%)

Raspberry Wheat Beer (OG 1055, ABV 5.6%) ▣

Milk Street SIBA

▤ **Milk Street Brewery Ltd (MSB Ltd), The Griffin, 25 Milk Street, Frome, Somerset, BA11 3DL**
☎ (01373) 467766 ✉ rjlyall@hotmail.com
⊕ milkstreetbrewery.co.uk
Tours by arrangement

⊗ Milk Street was established in 1999 in a former porn cinema situated behind a pub. The cinema is long gone and now houses the brewery, which expanded in 2005 and is now capable of producing 30 barrels per week. It mainly produces for its own estate of three outlets with direct delivery to pubs in a 30-mile radius. Wholesalers are used to distribute the beers further afield.

Mermaid (OG 1041, ABV 3.8%)
Amber-coloured ale with a rich hop character on the nose, plenty of citrus fruit on the palate and a lasting bitter and hoppy finish.

Funky Monkey (OG 1040, ABV 4%) 🍷
Copper-coloured summer ale with fruity flavours and aromas. A dry finish with developing bitterness and an undertone of citrus fruit.

The Usual (OG 1045, ABV 4.4%)

Zig-Zag Stout (OG 1046, ABV 4.5%) 🍷
A dark ruby stout with characteristic roastiness and dryness with bitter chocolate and citrus fruit in the background.

Beer (OG 1049, ABV 5%)
A blonde beer with musky hoppiness and citrus fruit on the nose, while more fruit surges through on the palate before the bittersweet finish.

Mill Green SIBA

📠 Mill Green Brewery, White Horse, Edwardstone, Sudbury, Suffolk, CO10 5PX
☎ (01787) 211118
✉ enquiries@millgreenbrewery.co.uk
⊕ millgreenbrewery.co.uk

⊠ Mill Green started brewing in 2008 in a new complex behind the White Horse pub in Edwardstone. It has won awards for environmental innovation. Brewing liquor is heated by solar panels and a wood-fired boiler whilst a wind turbine supplements power on site. Seasonal beers and one-off brews are also available.

Mawkin Mild (OG 1028, ABV 2.9%) 🍸
A superb complex mild, with a strong aroma and flavour for such a low gravity beer. Bitter coffee notes in the taste and aftertaste.

White Horse Bitter (OG 1036, ABV 3.6%)
A traditional session bitter with a spicy, bitter, lasting finish.

Loveleys Fair (OG 1040, ABV 4%)
A modern-style pale ale, golden in colour and heavily hopped with a tangy, citrus bite.

Tornado Smith (OG 1042, ABV 4.3%)
A fruity pale ale, fashionably strong on hop.

Good Ship Arbella (OG 1054, ABV 5.4%)
An American pale ale style, strong on hop.

Millis

Millis Brewing Co Ltd, St Margaret's Farm, St Margaret's Road, South Darenth, Dartford, Kent, DA4 9LB
☎ (01322) 866233 ⊕ millisbrewing.com
Shop Mon-Fri 12-5pm; Sat 10am-2pm

☺ John and Miriam Millis started with a half-barrel plant at their home in Gravesend. Demand outstripped the facility and Millis moved in 2003 to its current location – a former farm cold store – with a 10-barrel plant. They now supply around 40 outlets within a 50-mile radius. Wetherspoon's pubs are supplied within a 30-mile radius with Kentish Gold (ABV 4.8%). Seasonal and bottle-conditioned beers are also available.

Kentish Dark (OG 1035, ABV 3.5%)
Well-balanced, easy-drinking dark mild.

Gravesend Guzzler (OG 1037, ABV 3.7%)
Pale, easy-drinking, fruity session beer.

Kentish Best (OG 1040, ABV 4%)
A copper-coloured best bitter; tangy, fruity and dry.

Dartford Wobbler (OG 1043, ABV 4.3%)
A tawny-coloured, full-bodied best bitter with complex malt and hop flavours and a long, clean, slightly roasted finish.

Kentish Red Ale (OG 1043, ABV 4.3%)
A traditional red ale with complex malt, hops and fruit notes.

Millstone SIBA 👁

Millstone Brewery Ltd, Unit 4, Vale Mill, Micklehurst Road, Mossley, nr Oldham, OL5 9JL
☎ (01457) 835835 ✉ info@millstonebrewery.co.uk
⊕ millstonebrewery.co.uk

Established in 2003 by Nick Broughton and Jon Hunt, the brewery is located in an 18th-century textile mill. The eight-barrel plant produces a range of pale, hoppy beers including three regular and a range of seasonal/occasional beers (including the 'pub name' series). More than 30 regular outlets are supplied.

Vale Mill (OG 1039, ABV 3.9%)
A pale gold session bitter with a floral and spicy aroma building on a crisp and refreshing taste.

Tiger Rut (OG 1040, ABV 4%)
A pale, hoppy ale with a distinctive citrus/grapefruit aroma.

True Grit (OG 1049, ABV 5%)
A well-hopped strong ale with a mellow bitterness and a citrus/grapefruit aroma.

Milltown (NEW) SIBA

Milltown Brewing Co, The Brewery, The Old Railway Goods Yard, Scar Lane, Milnsbridge, Huddersfield, West Yorkshire, HD3 4PE
☎ 07946 589645 ✉ neil@milltownbrewing.co.uk
⊕ milltownbrewing.co.uk

Milltown began brewing in 2011 using a four-barrel plant. Seasonal and special beers are brewed. Bottle-conditioned beers are planned.

Golden Hop (ABV 3.8%)

Platinum Blonde (ABV 4%)

Slubbers Gold (ABV 4.2%)

Milton SIBA

Milton Brewery Cambridge Ltd, Pegasus House, Pembroke Avenue, Waterbeach, Cambridgeshire, CB25 9PY
☎ (01223) 226198
✉ enquiries@miltonbrewery.co.uk
⊕ miltonbrewery.co.uk
Tours by arrangement

⊠ The brewery has grown steadily since it was founded in 1999 and now operates pubs in Cambridge, London, Peterborough and Norwich through a sister company, Individual Pubs Ltd. The brewery moved from Milton to much larger premises in the neighbouring village of Waterbeach in 2012. Regular seasonal beers are brewed. Nero is suitable for vegetarians and vegans.

Minotaur (OG 1035, ABV 3.3%) ◀
Red/brown mild with a defined malt and roast nose, then a sweetish malt and fruit balance with roast adding depth. The malt and sweetness remain in the aftertaste with little bitterness.

Dionysus (OG 1037, ABV 3.6%)
A straw-coloured bitter; powerfully hoppy with a fine citrus finish.

Tiki (ABV 3.8%) ◀
Good fruity hop character in this golden ale with suggestions of mango and passion fruit. Bitterness in the taste carries through to give a refreshing, fruity hop finish.

Justinian (OG 1039, ABV 3.9%)
A crisp, pale gold-coloured bitter. Bitter orange flavours persist into a satisfying lasting finish.

Pegasus (OG 1043, ABV 4.1%) 🗂 🍴 ◀
A malty red/brown beer with hints of butterscotch and raisins. Smooth malt, caramel and fruit flavours. Bitterness builds, leaving a dry aftertaste with a little malt and fruit.

Sparta (OG 1043, ABV 4.3%) ◀
A light golden beer with a subtle blend of malt and hops on the aroma. The hops subside to allow fruit to balance the malt on the palate; some bitterness. Dry, malty finish.

Nero (OG 1050, ABV 5%) 🗂 ◀
A creamy, mouth-filling black beer with a rich blend of milk chocolate, raisins and liquorice flavours.The aftertaste is full of roast malt bitterness and fruity sweetness.

Cyclops (OG 1055, ABV 5.3%)
Deep copper-coloured ale, with a rich hoppy aroma and full body; fruit and malt notes develop in the finish.

Marcus Aurelius (OG 1075, ABV 7.4%)
A velvety stout bursting with dark, roasty flavours with an underlying vanilla richness.

Minster (NEW)

Minster Ales, 2a Rozel Avenue, Kidderminster, Worcestershire, DY10 2UZ ⊕ mlnsterales.co.uk

Minster Ales began brewing in 2012 using a 2.5-barrel plant. Beers are named on a Kidderminster theme and are only available bottle-conditioned at present.

Mitchell Krause

Mitchell Krause Brewing Ltd, PO Box 86, Workington, Cumbria, CA14 9BD
☎ 07825 580694 ✉ graeme@mkbrewing.co.uk
⊕ mkbrewing.co.uk

Mitchell Krause was set up in 2009 and produces three bottled beers, all brewed at Hardknott Brewery in Millom.

Mithril

Mithril Ales, Mithril, Aldbrough St John, Richmond, North Yorkshire, DL11 7TL
☎ (01325) 374817 ☎ 07889 167128
✉ mithril58@btinternet.com ⊕ mithrilales.co.uk

☉Mithril started brewing in 2010 in an old stables opposite the brewer's house on a 2.5-barrel plant. Owner/brewer Pete Fenwick is a well-known craft brewer who brews twice a week to supply the local area of Darlington and Richmond. Weekly specials are available.

Dere Street (OG 1039, ABV 3.8%)
Amber-coloured bitter with a fruity, malty sweetness and a smooth, hoppy finish.

Route A66 (OG 1041, ABV 4%)
A crisp, refreshing, satisfying golden beer. A dry bitterness with a lingering citrus and spicy hop taste and aroma.

Flower Power (OG 1043, ABV 4.3%)
A pale ale with a massive citrus, fruity hop flavour. Hints of grapefruit and floral notes on the tongue from the late addition of elderflowers.

Mobberley (NEW) SIBA

Mobberley Fine Ales Limited, Kell House Farm, Broad Oak Lane, Mobberley, Cheshire, WA16 6JN
☎ 07879 771209 ✉ phil@mobberleyfineales.co.uk
⊕ mobberleyfineales.co.uk
Tours by arrangement

Mobberley began brewing in 2011 in an old milking parlour on a working farm in the heart of the Cheshire countryside.

HedgeHopper (OG 1038, ABV 3.8%)
A golden ale with a hint of hoppiness and a pleasant, lingering, mildly bitter but malty aftertaste.

RoadRunner (OG 1038, ABV 3.8%)
A pale yellow ale, refreshing with a delicate, lightly spicy finish. Sweet to the taste and smooth with a delicate, refreshing hop aroma.

WhirlyBird (OG 1040, ABV 4%)
Amber-coloured and well-balanced with a mellow, citrus fruitiness to finish.

BarnBuster (OG 1042, ABV 4.2%)
A rich amber ale, full-bodied yet smooth, rich in taste, mildly bitter with a distant hint of spiciness. A real bitter beer with a malty, mildly bitter yet slightly spicy/citrus finish.

Moles ⊚

Moles Brewery (Cascade Drinks Ltd), 5 Merlin Way, Bowerhill, Melksham, Wiltshire, SN12 6TJ
☎ (01225) 704734/708842 ✉ sales@moles-cascade.co.uk ⊕ molesbrewery.com
Shop Mon-Fri 9am-5pm; Sat 9am-12pm
Tours by arrangement

⊗ Moles was established in 1982 by Roger Catte, a former Ushers brewer, using his nickname to name the brewery. 10 pubs are owned, all serving cask beer. Over 200 outlets are supplied direct. Seasonal beers: see website.

Tap Bitter (OG 1035, ABV 3.5%)
A session bitter with a smooth, malty flavour and clean bitter finish.

Double MM Mild (OG 1036, ABV 3.6%)
A light-bodied dark mild with fruit and toasted toffee flavours and a smooth bitterness.

Best Bitter (OG 1040, ABV 4%)
A well-balanced, amber-coloured bitter, clean, dry and malty with some bitterness, and delicate floral hop flavour.

Elmo's Fire (OG 1044, ABV 4.4%)
A medium-bodied pale ale. Refreshingly bitter with a fruity, spicy aroma.

Landlords Choice (OG 1045, ABV 4.5%)
A dark, strong, smooth porter, with a rich fruity palate and malty finish.

Rucking Mole (OG 1045, ABV 4.5%)
A chestnut-coloured premium ale, fruity and malty with a smooth bitter finish.

Mole Catcher (OG 1050, ABV 5%) 🍺
A copper-coloured ale with a delightfully spicy hop aroma and taste, and a long bitter finish.

Moncada (NEW)

Moncada Brewery Ltd, Unit 5, Grand Union Centre, West Row, London, W10 5AS
☎ (020) 8964 0829 ✉ julio@moncadabrewery.co.uk
⊕ moncadabrewery.co.uk
Tours by arrangement

Moncada began brewing in 2011 using a six-barrel plant. Bottle-conditioned beers are available and seasonal beers are planned.

Blonde (ABV 4.2%) ◥
Continental style golden beer with a smooth mouthfeel, sweetish with a touch of honey. Floral hops on nose and palate fade in the aftertaste, leaving a dry, bitter character with a little spiciness.

Bitter (ABV 4.3%) ◥
Brown-coloured beer that has a sweet biscuit taste complemented by a dry, bitter flavour and finish with a little fruitiness.

Amber (ABV 4.4%) ◥
Full-bodied, creamy, amber-coloured beer with the citrus aroma and flavour well balanced by the sweet, slightly toffee maltiness and a bitter dryness that lingers. There is a little flowery hop throughout.

Monty's SIBA

Monty's Brewery Ltd, Unit 1, Castle Works, Hendomen, Montgomery, Powys, SY15 6HA
☎ (01686) 668933 ✉ info@montysbrewery.co.uk
⊕ montysbrewery.co.uk
Tours by arrangement

Monty's began brewing in 2009 and was the first brewery in Montgomeryshire since the Eagle brewery in Newtown closed in 1990. Pump clips are available in English and Welsh. Two pubs are owned, the Sportsman in Newtown and the Red Lion in Caersws with a third joint venture planned in Abermule. Seasonal beers: see website.

Manjana (OG 1039.5, ABV 3.9%)
A well-balanced chestnut bitter.

Midnight (OG 1043, ABV 4%)
A dark, smooth, creamy stout.

Sunshine (OG 1041, ABV 4.2%)
A golden, hoppy, floral/citrus ale with a pleasantly dry finish.

Mischief (OG 1050, ABV 5%)
A strong golden ale with a good balance of malt and hop bitterness.

Moodley's

Moodley's Ltd, Bowen's Farm, Poundsbridge Lane, Penshurst, Kent, TN11 8AJ
☎ (01892) 821366 ☎ 07788 889877
✉ yudhistra@moodleys.co.uk ⊕ moodleys.co.uk
Tours by arrangement

Moodleys was established in 2008, moving to its current site in 2010. At present only bottle-conditioned beers are produced, all approved by the Vegetarian Society. Seasonal beers are also available. Cask-conditioned ale is planned. The beers are available at local pubs, farm shops and online.

Moonstone

⬛ Moonstone Brewery (Gem Taverns Ltd), Ministry of Ale, 9 Trafalgar Street, Burnley, Lancashire, BB11 1TQ
☎ (01282) 830909 ✉ meet@ministryofale.co.uk
⊕ moonstonebrewery.co.uk
Tours by arrangement

⊚ A small, 2.5-barrel brewery, based in the Ministry of Ale pub. Brewing started in 2001 and beer is generally only available in the pub. Seasonal beers are also brewed.

Black Star (OG 1037, ABV 3.4%)

Blue John (ABV 3.6%)

Tigers Eye (OG 1037, ABV 3.8%)

White Sapphire (OG 1037, ABV 3.9%)

Trafalgar Stout (OG 1050, ABV 4.9%)

Moor SIBA ⊚

Moor Beer Co Ltd, c/o Chapel Court, Pitney, Somerset, TA10 9AE
☎ 07887 556521 ✉ justin@moorbeer.co.uk
⊕ moorbeer.co.uk
Tours by arrangement

⊗ Moor Beer was founded in 1996 and rescued from oblivion by award-winning brewer Justin Hawke in 2006. The brewery's capacity was quadrupled in 2011 to meet demand. Special, seasonal and bottle-conditioned beers are also available.

Revival (OG 1038, ABV 3.8%)
An immensely hoppy and refreshing pale ale.

Nor'Hop (OG 1041, ABV 4.1%)
Ultra pale ale showcasing Northern Hemisphere hops.

So'Hop (OG 1041, ABV 4.1%)
Ultra pale ale showcasing Southern Hemisphere hops.

Merlin's Magic (OG 1045, ABV 4.3%) ◥
Dark amber-coloured, complex, full-bodied beer, with fruity notes.

Amoor (OG 1047, ABV 4.5%) ◥
Dark brown/black beer with an initially fruity taste leading to roast malt with a little bitterness. A slightly sweet malty finish.

Illusion (OG 1045, ABV 4.5%)
A session strength black IPA with powerful hop flavours.

Ported Amoor (OG 1049, ABV 4.7%)
Amoor with added Reserve Port.

Somerland Gold (OG 1050, ABV 5%)
Hoppy blonde ale with hints of honey and a long, hoppy finish.

Hoppiness (ABV 6.5%)
Rich malt and fruit flavours of a barley wine with the hoppy crispness of a pale ale.

Old Freddy Walker (OG 1075, ABV 7.3%) 🍴 ◆
Rich, dark, strong ale with a fruity complex taste, leaving a fruitcake finish.

JJJ IPA (OG 1085, ABV 9%)
Copper-coloured, new world IPA. Immensely hoppy and malty.

Moorhouse's SIBA 👁

Moorhouse's Brewery (Burnley) Ltd, The Brewery, Moorhouse Street, Accrington Road, Burnley, Lancashire, BB11 5ZN
☎ (01282) 422864 ✉ info@moorhouses.co.uk
⊕ moorhouses.co.uk
Shop & visitor centre – ring for details
Tours by arrangement

☺ Established in 1865 as a drinks manufacturer, the brewery started producing cask-conditioned ale in 1978 and has achieved recognition by winning more international and CAMRA awards than any other brewery of its size. A new brewhouse, visitors centre and training school were completed in 2010. The company owns six pubs, all serving cask-conditioned beer. Seasonal beers: see website.

Black Cat (OG 1036, ABV 3.4%) ◆
A dark mild-style beer with delicate chocolate and coffee roast flavours and a crisp, bitter finish.

Premier Bitter (OG 1036, ABV 3.7%) ◆
A clean and satisfying bitter aftertaste rounds off this well-balanced hoppy, amber session bitter.

Pride of Pendle (OG 1040, ABV 4.1%) ◆
Well-balanced amber best bitter with a fresh initial hoppiness and a mellow, malt-driven body.

Blond Witch (OG 1045, ABV 4.5%) ◆
Light ale, fruity with a lasting finish.

Pendle Witches Brew (OG 1050, ABV 5.1%) 🍴 ◆
Well-balanced, full-bodied, malty beer with a long, complex finish.

Mordue SIBA 👁

Mordue Brewery, Units D1 & D2, Narvic Way, Tyne Tunnel Estate, North Shields, Tyne & Wear, NE29 7XJ
☎ (0191) 296 1879
✉ enquiries@morduebrewery.com
⊕ morduebrewery.com
Shop: see website for opening times
Tours by arrangement

☺ In 1995 the Fawson brothers revived the Mordue Brewery name (the original closed in 1879). High demand required moves to larger premises and replacing the original five-barrel plant with a 20-barrel one. The beers are distributed nationally and 300 outlets are supplied direct. Seasonal beers: see website.

Five Bridge Bitter (OG 1038, ABV 3.8%) ◆
Crisp, golden beer with a good hint of hops, the bitterness carries on in the finish. A good session bitter.

Northumbrian Blonde (OG 1040, ABV 4%)
A blonde beer with a citrus aroma and hoppy finish.

Geordie Pride (OG 1042, ABV 4.2%) ◆
Well-balanced and hoppy copper-coloured brew with a long, bitter finish.

Workie Ticket (OG 1045, ABV 4.5%) ◆
Complex tasty bitter with plenty of malt and hops, long, satisfying bitter finish.

Radgie Gadgie (OG 1048, ABV 4.8%) 🍴 ◆
Strong, easy-drinking bitter with plenty of fruit and hops.

IPA (OG 1051, ABV 5.1%) ◆
Easy-drinking golden ale with plenty of hops, the bitterness carries on in the finish.

MòR (NEW) SIBA

MòR Brewing Ltd, Old Mill, Kellas, DD5 3PD
☎ 07884 346351 / 07593 245000
✉ jim@morbrewing.com ⊕ morbrewing.com
Tours by arrangement

⊠ Retired lifeboat coxswain Jim Hughan teamed up with CAMRA enthusiast Ross Niven to establish the 2.5-barrel brewery in 2012. Seasonal, special and bottle-conditioned ales are also available.

1 MòR (OG 1038, ABV 3.8%)
A refreshingly hoppy beer with citrus notes and a bitter finish.

Please! (OG 1041, ABV 4.1%)
Golden brown in colour, a full-bodied best bitter.

Morrissey Fox

Morrissey Fox Breweries Ltd, Tickton Hall, Tickton, Beverley, East Yorkshire, HU17 9RX

☺ Morrissey Fox Breweries was developed in 2008 and filmed by Channel 4. The brewery was initially based at the Olde Punchbowl in Marton cum Grafton, North Yorkshire, but the company left the pub in 2009. Beers are contract brewed elsewhere reportedly including Cropton Brewery and Celt Experience.

Bitter (OG 1040, ABV 3.9%)

Blonde (OG 1043, ABV 4.2%)

Morton

Morton Brewery, Unit 10, Essington Light Industrial Estate, Essington, Wolverhampton, WV11 2BH
☎ 07988 069647

Office: 96 Brewood Road, Coven, Staffordshire, WV9 5EF ✉ mortonbrewery@aol.com
⊕ mortonbrewery.co.uk
Tours by arrangement

Morton was established in 2007 on a three-barrel plant by Gary and Angela Morton, both CAMRA members. The brewery moved to Essington in 2008 to increase production. Essington Ale was introduced to celebrate the move and became so popular with the locals that a full range of Essington beers is brewed regularly. 30 outlets are supplied direct plus various beer festivals. Seasonal and special beers: see website. Bottle-conditioned beers are also available.

Essington Bitter (OG 1037, ABV 3.8%)

Merry Mount (OG 1037, ABV 3.8%)

Essington Blonde (OG 1039, ABV 4%)

Essington Ale (OG 1041, ABV 4.2%)

Jelly Roll (OG 1041, ABV 4.2%)

Essington Gold (OG 1044, ABV 4.4%)

Scottish Maiden (OG 1045, ABV 4.6%)

Essington IPA (OG 1047, ABV 4.8%)

Moulin

🍺 Moulin Hotel & Brewery, 2 Baledmund Road, Moulin, Pitlochry, Perthshire, PH16 5EL
☎ (01796) 472196 ✉ enquiries@moulinhotel.co.uk
⊕ moulinhotel.co.uk
Tours by arrangement

☺ The brewery opened in 1995 to celebrate the Moulin Hotel's 300th anniversary. Two pubs are owned and four outlets are supplied. Bottle-conditioned beer is available.

Light (OG 1036, ABV 3.7%) ◀
Thirst-quenching, straw-coloured session beer, with a light, hoppy, fruity balance, ending with a gentle, hoppy sweetness.

Braveheart (OG 1039, ABV 4%) ◀
An amber bitter, with a delicate balance of malt and fruit and a Scottish-style sweetness.

Ale of Atholl (OG 1043.5, ABV 4.5%) ◀
A reddish, quaffable, malty ale, with a solid body and a mellow finish.

Old Remedial (OG 1050.5, ABV 5.2%) ◀
A distinctive and satisfying dark brown old ale, with roast malt to the fore and tannin in a robust taste.

Mr Grundys SIBA

🍺 Mr Grundys Tavern & Brewery, Georgian House Hotel, 34 Ashbourne Road, Derby, DE22 3AD
☎ (01332) 349806 ✉ info@georgianhousehotel.info
⊕ georgianhousehotel.info

The brewery opened in 2010 using a four-barrel plant constructed from 'made to measure' vessels to fit into a converted bedroom. Beers are produced for the company's own tavern (Mr Grundys) and hotels.

Trench Foot (ABV 3.8%)
Darkish in colour with strong malt flavours with some bittering using traditional hops.

Passchendaele (ABV 3.9%)
An all-English, straw-coloured, pale, sharp bitter with citrus overtones.

Over The Top (ABV 4.1%)
A pale, hoppy bitter.

No Man's Land (ABV 4.5%)
Dark in colour yet hoppy retaining the soft malty flavours of a traditional bitter.

Coffin Nail (ABV 5%)

Muirhouse

🍺 Muirhouse Brewery, Unit 1, Enterprise Court, Manners Avenue, Manners Industrial Estate, Ilkeston, Derbyshire, DE7 8EW
☎ 07916 590525 ✉ rmuir@muirhousebrewery.co.uk
⊕ muirhousebrewery.co.uk
Tours by arrangement

Muirhouse Brewery was established in 2009 by keen home brewer Richard Muir initially in a domestic garage in Long Eaton. Expansion in 2011 saw the purchase of a two-barrel plant from Three B's Brewery in Blackburn, which is now located in the former Blue Monkey Brewery unit in Ilkeston. Most beers are also available bottle-conditioned with some being bottled for the Great Central Preserved Railway at Loughborough. One-off brews are also produced.

Shunters Pole (OG 1040, ABV 3.8%)
A pale, refreshing, hoppy beer with a Styrian hop finish and aroma.

Ruby Jewel (OG 1040, ABV 3.9%)
A ruby-coloured session ale, quite malty.

Fully Fitted Freight (OG 1041, ABV 4%)
A refreshing light ale with good balance of malt and hops.

Jurgen's Jungle Juice (OG 1041, ABV 4%)
A light brown bitter with a biscuity and bitter finish.

Last Post (OG 1041, ABV 4%)
A pale, strongly-hopped beer.

Magnum Mild (OG 1045, ABV 4.5%)
A strong mild with burnt roast flavours.

Pirate's Gold (OG 1045, ABV 4.5%)
Pale golden beer with a hint of caramel.

Belly's Beverage (OG 1048, ABV 5%)
A pale and hoppy beer.

Coffee Porter (OG 1048, ABV 5%)
A dark porter with a hint of coffee.

Lurch's Liquor (OG 1050, ABV 5%)
A sweet, smooth stout packed with dark malts.

Stumbling About (OG 1050, ABV 5.2%)
A dark red, strong, malty beer.

Nailsworth SIBA

🍺 Nailsworth Brewery Ltd, Village Inn, The Cross, Nailsworth, Gloucestershire, GL6 0HH
☎ 07878 448377 ✉ jonk@nailsworth-brewery.co.uk
⊕ nailsworth-brewery.co.uk
Tours by arrangement

⊗ The original Nailsworth Brewery closed in 1908. In 2004, after a gap of 98 years, commercial brewing returned in the form of a six-barrel micro-brewery. This is the brainchild of Messrs Hawes and Kemp, whose aim is to make the town of Nailsworth once again synonymous with quality beer. Around 30 outlets are supplied direct. Seasonal and bottle-conditioned beers are also available.

Alestock (ABV 3.6%)

Artist's Ale (OG 1040, ABV 3.8%)
A light-coloured bitter full of citrus flavours.

Dudbridge Donkey (ABV 4%)

Mayor's Bitter (OG 1042, ABV 4.3%)
A best bitter with malt textures complemented by a long-lasting taste of blackcurrant.

Town Crier (OG 1046, ABV 4.5%)
A premium ale with delicate grassy and floral overtones.

Vicar's Stout (ABV 4.5%)

Naked

🍺 Naked Brewer, Corner Pin, Palmerston Street, Westwood, Nottinghamshire, NG16 5HY
☎ 07908 531901
Tours by arrangement

The brewery was set up in 2010 in a skittle alley behind the Corner Pin pub and can be viewed from the function room. Beer is mainly brewed for the Corner Pin but is occasionally supplied to beer festivals and to other local pubs.

Scary's Mild (ABV 3.6%)

Hopsession (OG 1038, ABV 3.8%)

Kiss Me (ABV 3.8%)

Oracle RWB (OG 1040, ABV 4%)

Anniversary (ABV 4.2%)

Blush (OG 1045, ABV 4.5%)

Palindrome Porter (OG 1048, ABV 4.7%)

Maiden Over (ABV 5.9%)

Nant SIBA

Bragdy'r Nant, Penrhwylfa, Maenan, Llanrwst, Conwy, LL26 0UA
☎ 07723 036862
✉ postmaster@jonesgw2.demon.co.uk
⊕ cwrwnant.co.uk

Nant commenced brewing in 2007 with a plant purchased from the Yorkshire Dales Brewery. Capacity is currently 10-15 nine gallon firkins a week. Seasonal and one-off beers are also produced.

Mochyn Hapus (ABV 3.7%)

Cwrw Coryn (ABV 4.2%)

Pen Dafad (ABV 4.2%)

Chawden Aur (ABV 4.3%)

Grans's Lamb (ABV 4.5%)

Mwnci Nell (ABV 5.3%) 🍴 🍷

Natural

Natural Brewing Co, 39 Westgate, Chichester, West Sussex, PO19 3EZ
☎ (01243) 605485
✉ mark@naturalbrewingcompany.co.uk
⊕ naturalbrewingcompany.co.uk

The brewery was launched in 2009 and only produces bottled beer. Beers are brewed under contract by Hook Norton Brewery under the supervision of Natural's brewmaster Julian Herrington. One beer is available at present, Irresistible Premium Ale (ABV 4.2%).

Navigation (NEW) SIBA

🏢 Navigation Brewery Ltd, Trent Navigation Inn, 17 Meadow Lane, Nottingham, NG2 3HS
☎ (0115) 986 9877
✉ enquiries@navigationbrewery.com
⊕ navigationbrewery.com
Shop Mon-Fri 10am-5pm; Sat & Sun 11am-3pm
Tours by arrangement

☺Navigation began brewing in 2012 using a 20-barrel brewery located in the old stable block of the Trent Navigation Inn. The brewery is situated by the Nottingham Canal and the stables were originally built to house canal horses and their horsemen. It is owned by a sister company to Great Northern Inns and will supply all of the cask beers to pubs in their estate with guest beers being provided by brewery swaps.

Traditional (ABV 3.8%)
An amber-coloured, smooth, malty beer; well-balanced with a mellow finish.

Pale Ale (ABV 3.9%)
Pale straw in colour with a distinctive fruity nose, well-hopped, which blends itself to a refreshing, sharp finish.

Golden (ABV 4.3%)
Medium-bodied and clean-tasting, refreshing ale with fruit and malt on the nose and satisfying biscuit flavours with a lasting malty aftertaste.

Stout (ABV 4.4%)
Traditional, robust stout with liquorice, roast almonds and chocolate flavours perfectly balanced with a tight, creamy head.

Classic IPA (ABV 5.2%)
Straw-coloured with powerful citrus fruit balanced with malty sweetness and robust bitter flavours.

Naylor's SIBA 👁

Naylor's Brewery, Unit 1, Midland Mills, Crosshills, Keighley, BD20 7DT
☎ (01535) 637451 ⊕ naylorsbrewery.com
Shop Mon-Thu 9am-5pm; Fri 3-11pm
Tours by arrangement

☺ Naylors started brewing early in 2005, based at the Old White Bear pub in Crosshills. Expansion required a move to the current site in 2006 and included a rebranding of the beers. Further expansion in 2009 gave better facilities for bottling as well as a shop and bar. Around 200 outlets are supplied. Bottle-conditioned ales are also produced. All bottled beers are suitable for vegetarians.

Pinnacle Bitter (OG 1039, ABV 3.9%) 🍴
Predominantly malty, this traditional mid-brown bitter also has subtle fruit and hops in the nose and taste and growing bitterness in the finish.

Velvet (OG 1039, ABV 4%)
Dark, rich and smooth.

Pinnacle Blonde (OG 1041.5, ABV 4.3%) 🍴
This pale-coloured beer has a citrus twang over a sweet malty base followed by a strong grassy hoppiness. The finish remains hoppy with a bitter edge.

Black & Tan (OG 1043, ABV 4.4%)
A blend of porter and bitter recipes.

Pinnacle Porter (OG 1046, ABV 4.8%) 🍴
A roast bitterness characterises this full-bodied black beer. There are also hints of sweetness, chocolate and coffee against a fruity background. Roast and bitterness combine in the lingering aftertaste.

Old Ale (OG 1056, ABV 6.2%)
A strong, malty, amber-coloured ale.

Neath

Neath Ales, Endeavour Close, Port Talbot, SA12 7PT
☎ 07772 468436 ✉ enquiries@neathales.co.uk
⊕ neathales.co.uk

Neath Ales was established in 2009. The brewery also releases small batches of strong, heavily-hopped beers under the Black Falls – Beers for Aficionados brand, available to order online. One-off monthly specials and vegan-friendly bottle-conditioned beers are also available.

Firebrick (ABV 4.2%)
Amber-coloured best bitter with refreshing citrus hop flavour and aroma.

Witch Hunter (ABV 4.2%)
A well-balanced ruby ale with roasted malt and hop fruit flavours.

Gold (ABV 5%)
A citrus/grapefruit hop aroma and flavour dominate this golden ale.

Black (ABV 5.5%)
A strong, black ale with dark malt flavours balanced by aggressive hopping rates.

Nelson SIBA

Nelson Brewing Co UK Ltd, Unit 2, Building 64, The Historic Dockyard, Chatham, Kent, ME4 4TE
☎ (01634) 832828
✉ sales@nelsonbrewingcompany.co.uk
⊕ nelsonbrewery.co.uk
Shop Mon-Fri 11am-4pm
Tours by arrangement

☺Nelson started out in 1995 as the Flagship Brewery but changed its name in 2004. The present owner, Piers MacDonald, acquired the brewery in 2006. The brewery is based in Chatham's preserved Georgian dockyard, where Nelson's flagship, HMS Victory, was built. More than 200 outlets are supplied direct. Most cask beers are also available bottle conditioned. Seasonal and occasional beers: see website.

Admiral IPA (OG 1040, ABV 4%)
A traditional IPA with citrus flavours on the palate.

Midshipman Dark Mild (OG 1040, ABV 4%)
A dark mild leaving a roasted aftertaste on the palate.

Thunderer (OG 1040, ABV 4.2%)
A well-balanced golden ale with a citrus and floral aroma and a soft, bitter aftertaste.

Powder Monkey (OG 1043, ABV 4.3%)
A golden ale with a smooth aftertaste which leaves a sweetness on the palate.

Core Commander (OG 1045, ABV 4.4%)
A golden-coloured ale with a unique combination of flavours.

Dogwatch Stout (OG 1044, ABV 4.5%)
A smooth, creamy stout with a strong hop taste leaving a smoky, chocolate aftertaste.

Friggin' in the Riggin' (OG 1046, ABV 4.5%)
Premium bitter with smooth malt flavour and bittersweet aftertaste.

Purser's Pussy Porter (OG 1051, ABV 4.8%)
A traditional porter brewed with amber malt.

Nelson's Blood (OG 1062, ABV 6%)
A strong, malty ale with mellow roast tones, slightly nutty and fruity with a warm aftertaste.

Nene Valley (NEW) SIBA

Nene Valley Brewery, Oundle Wharf, Station Road, Oundle, Northamptonshire, PE8 4DB
☎ 07950 234497 ✉ sales@nenevalleybrewery.com
⊕ nenevalleybrewery.com

Nene Valley began brewing in 2011 with a 2.5-barrel plant previously used by Cherwell Valley Brewery. As sales quickly outstripped supply larger premises and new vessels were bought to increase capacity.

BSA (Blonde Session Ale) (ABV 3.8%)

NVB (Nene Valley Bitter) (ABV 4.1%)

Nethergate SIBA EAB

Nethergate Brewery Ltd, Growler Brewery, The Street, Pentlow, Essex, CO10 7JJ
☎ (01787) 283220 ✉ orders@nethergate.co.uk
⊕ nethergatebrewery.co.uk
Tours by arrangement

⊠ Nethergate Brewery was established in 1986 at Clare, Suffolk. The plant was doubled in 1993 and the brewery moved over the border into Pentlow, Essex in 2005, where it doubled in size again. The brewery, which is now under new ownership, has won many awards. A large range of individual monthly beers are brewed and most of the permanent and some monthly beers are also available bottle conditioned.

IPA (OG 1036, ABV 3.5%) ◆
Bitter-tasting session beer with some fruit and malt balancing the predominate hop character. Very dry aftertaste.

Priory Mild (OG 1036, ABV 3.5%) ◆
A 'black bitter' rather than a true mild. Strong roast and bitter tastes dominate throughout.

Umbel Ale (OG 1039, ABV 3.8%) ◆
Pleasant, easy-drinking bitter, infused with coriander, which dominates.

Three Point Nine (OG 1040, ABV 3.9%) ◆
Light tasting, sweetish and fruity session beer.

Suffolk County Best Bitter (OG 1041, ABV 4%) ◆
Dark bitter with roast grain tones off-setting biscuity malt and powerful hoppy, bitter notes.

Augustinian Ale (OG 1046, ABV 4.5%) ◆
A pale, refreshing, complex best bitter. A fruity aroma leads to a bittersweet flavour and aftertaste with a predominance of citrus tones.

Essex Border (OG 1049, ABV 4.8%)
A pale golden summer ale, fruity and spicy with a pleasant malty finish; an easy drinking beer.

Old Growler (OG 1051, ABV 5%) 🍺 ◆
Well-balanced porter in which roast grain is complemented by fruit and bubblegum.

Umbel Magna (OG 1051, ABV 5%) 🍺 ◆
Old Growler flavoured with coriander. The spice is less dominant than in Umbel Ale, with some of the weight and body of the beer coming through.

Essex Beast (OG 1062, ABV 6.2%)
Strong, dark, complex and robust ale with chocolate and rich toffee flavours. Brewed in memory of Essex CAMRA stalwart Andrew Clifton.

For Truman's Beer:

Runner (OG 1040, ABV 4%)

Newby Wyke SIBA

Newby Wyke Brewery, Unit 24, Limesquare Business Park, Alma Park Road, Grantham, Lincolnshire, NG31 9SN
☎ (01476) 565682 ✉ sales@newbywyke.co.uk
⊕ newbywyke.co.uk
Tours by arrangement

✕ The brewery is named after a Hull trawler skippered by brewer Rob March's grandfather. It started life in 1998 as a 2.5-barrel plant in a converted garage then moved to premises behind the Willoughby Arms at Little Bytham. In 2009 it moved back to Grantham with a brew length of 10 barrels. Seasonal beers: see website.

Kingston Topaz (OG 1039, ABV 4.2%)
A single-hopped ale with floral undertones.

Bear Island (OG 1043, ABV 4.6%)
A blonde beer with a hoppy aroma and a crisp, dry finish.

White Squall (OG 1044, ABV 4.8%) ◆
Amber-hued with a hoppy aroma. Generous amounts of hop are well-supported by a solid malty undercurrent. An increasingly bittersweet tang makes itself known towards the finish.

Newmans

See Celt Experience

New Plassey SIBA

New Plassey Brewery, Eyton, Wrexham, LL13 0SP
☎ (01978) 781111 ☎ 07050 327127

Originally known as Plassey, the brewery was founded in 1985 on the 250-acre Plassey Estate, which also incorporates a touring caravan park, craft centres, a golf course, three licensed outlets for the ales, and a brewery shop. Following the merger of Plassey and the Gertie Sweet Brewery in 2012 the New Plassey Brewery was formed.

New World Pale (ABV 3.9%)
A very pale beer, well-balanced with a hoppy bite.

Bitter (OG 1041, ABV 4%)
A tawny-coloured, traditional session bitter.

Midnight Mild (ABV 4.2%)
A medium-strength mild, dark and subtle with a fullness of character and flavour.

Offa's Dyke (OG 1043, ABV 4.3%) ◆
Sweetish and fruity refreshing best bitter with caramel undertones. Some bitterness in the finish.

Dusky Maiden Stout (ABV 4.4%)
A very dark, complex flavoured stout.

Deep Porter (ABV 4.5%)
A smooth, deep brown porter.

Cherry Diva (ABV 4.7%)
A pale beer with a subtle flavour of Maraschino cherry.

Cwrw Tudno (OG 1048, ABV 5%) ◆
A mellow, sweetish premium beer with classic Plassey flavours of fruit and hops.

Dragon's Breath (OG 1060, ABV 6%)
A strong, full-bodied tawny bitter, well-balanced between the hops and malt.

Nine Standards SIBA

▤ Nine Standards Brewery, Croglin Castle Hotel, South Road, Kirkby Stephen, Cumbria, CA17 4SY
☎ (01768) 371389
✉ info@ninestandardsbrewery.co.uk
⊕ ninestandardsbrewery.co.uk
Tours by arrangement

☺Established in 2010, the brewery previously operated as the Croglin Brewery and is situated in the cellar of the Croglin Castle Hotel. It now has a new brewer, has been extensively refurbished and renamed after a famous local landmark visible from the brewery. Further beers are planned.

Original Standard (OG 1037, ABV 3.7%)
A dark amber beer with a fruity, spicy nose.

Gold Standard (OG 1040, ABV 4.1%)
A golden ale with a hint of blackcurrant.

Silver Standard (ABV 4.3%)

Double Standard (ABV 4.7%)
A robust porter.

Royal Standard (ABV 5.5%)
A golden ale brewed with five hops.

Nobby's SIBA

▤ Nobby's Brewery, c/o Ward Arms, High Street, Guilsborough, Northamptonshire, NN6 8PY
☎ (01604) 740785 ✉ info@nobbysbrewery.co.uk
⊕ nobbysbrewery.co.uk
Shop Mon-Fri 9am-5pm
Tours by arrangement

Paul 'Nobby' Mulliner started commercial brewing in 2004 on a 2.5-barrel plant at the rear of the Alexandra Arms in Kettering, which also served as the brewery tap. In 2007 a 14-barrel plant was also set up at the Ward Arms, Guilsborough, to where Nobby's Brewery moved. In 2011 the brewery expanded with an additional fermenter and bottle storage. Seasonal beers: see website. The original plant at the Alexandra was sold in 2009 and now brews as J.Church Brewery.

Claridges Crystal (OG 1036, ABV 3.6%)

Guilsborough Guzzler (OG 1036, ABV 3.6%)
A light mild with a soft palate.

Best (OG 1037, ABV 3.8%)

Guilsborough Gold (OG 1041, ABV 4%)

Wild West (OG 1046, ABV 4.6%)

T'owd Navigation (OG 1061, ABV 6.1%)

Nook SIBA

▤ The Nook Brewhouse, 7b Victoria Square, Holmfirth, West Yorkshire, HD9 2DN
☎ (01484) 682373
✉ office@thenookbrewhouse.co.uk
⊕ thenookbrewhouse.co.uk
Tours by arrangement

☺The Nook Brewhouse is the natural progression for the owners of the Nook public house, with a real ale pedigree including 30 consecutive years in the Good Beer Guide. It supplies two brewery taps and is built on the foundations of a previous brewhouse dating back to 1752, next to the River Ribble. A history room with renovated archives dating back to the 1700s and a brewery shop are planned once brewing is consolidated.

Yorks (OG 1037, ABV 3.7%) ◆
A well-balanced bitter with light malt and hop aroma and hop and fruit in the taste, developing in strength. A good session beer.

Bee's Knees (ABV 3.9%)
A well-hopped bitter brewed with Yorkshire honey.

Best (OG 1040.5, ABV 4.2%) ◆

An easy-drinking best bitter with hints of malt and floral hops in the aroma. The taste has an abundance of hops and fruit and a pleasant, crisp, malty aftertaste.

Berry Blond (ABV 4.5%)
A refreshing blonde beer with raspberry notes and a biscuity palate.

Blonde (OG 1042.5, ABV 4.5%) ◆
A golden ale with intense fruit and hop tastes, which decline in the aftertaste.

Fiery Red (ABV 4.5%)
A rich, malty red ale with subtle notes of invigorating ginger and a fruity aroma.

Red (OG 1044, ABV 4.5%) ◆
Complex tastes of fruit and roasted malt throughout, enhanced by a strong, fruity aroma.

Cherry Stout (ABV 5.2%)
An oat stout with notes of cherry and a distinct liquorice palate as well as roasted flavours.

Oat Stout (ABV 5.2%)
A full-flavoured oat stout with distinct liquorice on the palate as well as some burnt flavours.

Norfolk (NEW) SIBA

Norfolk Brewhouse, Moon Gazer Barn, Harvest Lane, Hindringham, Norfolk, NR21 0PW
☎ (01328) 878495 ✉ info@norfolkbrewhouse.co.uk
⊕ norfolkbrewhouse.co.uk

Brewing began in 2012 using a 10-barrel plant.

Moon Gazer Amber Ale (ABV 4%)

Moon Gazer Golden Ale (ABV 4%)

Moon Gazer Ruby Ale (ABV 4%)

Norfolk Square

Norfolk Square Brewery LLP, PO Box 325, Great Yarmouth, Norfolk, NR30 9EX
☎ (01493) 751975
✉ beer@norfolksquarebrewery.co.uk
⊕ norfolksquarebrewery.co.uk

Norfolk Square began brewing in 2008 on a 2.5-barrel plant and only produce bottle-conditioned beers. 'Extreme' one-off beers are also brewed: see website.

North Cotswold SIBA

North Cotswold Brewery Ltd, Unit 3, Ditchford Farm, Stretton-on-Fosse, Warwickshire, GL56 9RD
☎ (01608) 663947
✉ mail@northcotswoldbrewery.co.uk
⊕ northcotswoldbrewery.co.uk
Shop Mon-Thu 9am-5pm; Fri 9am-12pm

⊚North Cotswold started in 1999 as a 2.5-barrel plant, which was upgraded in 2000 to 10 barrels. Bottle-conditioned and seasonal beers are also available.

Windrush Ale (OG 1036, ABV 3.6%)
A traditional session bitter.

Cotswold Best (OG 1040, ABV 4%)
An easy-drinking, chestnut-coloured best bitter.

Shagweaver (OG 1045, ABV 4.5%)
A pale, hoppy bitter.

Hung, Drawn 'n' Portered (OG 1050, ABV 5%)
A strong, dark-coloured porter with a malty finish.

North Curry SIBA

North Curry Brewery Co, The Old Coach House, Gwyon House, Church Road, North Curry, Somerset, TA3 6LH
☎ 07928 815053
✉ thenorthcurrybreweryco@hotmail.co.uk
⊕ thenorthcurrybreweryco.com

⊠ The brewery opened in summer 2006 and is attached to one of the oldest properties in North Curry where brewing last took place in the village in the 1920s. Three outlets are supplied direct. Beers are also sold at farmers markets in Taunton and Minehead and in local shops. All beers are also available bottle conditioned. Seasonal beer: see website.

Howzat (OG 1036, ABV 3.7%)
A golden-coloured ale with fruity hops and a smooth aftertaste.

Curry Gold (OG 1038, ABV 3.9%)
A golden ale with a fruity aroma.

Red Heron (OG 1041, ABV 4.3%)

The Withyman (OG 1042, ABV 4.6%)

Level Headed (OG 1043, ABV 4.7%)
A traditional old English ale, dark ruby in colour, rich and full-flavoured.

Alfred's Stout (OG 1047, ABV 5.1%)
A black, dry stout with a robust flavour and rounded body.

Northern SIBA ◉

Northern Brewing Ltd, Blakemere Brewery, Blakemere Craft Centre, Chester Road, Sandiway, Northwich, Cheshire, CW8 2EB
☎ (01606) 301000 ☎ 07768 790300
✉ sales@norbrew.co.uk ⊕ norbrew.co.uk
Shop Mon-Fri 10am-4pm; Sat & Sun 12-4pm

⊚ Northern first brewed in 2003 on a five-barrel plant located in Runcorn. It relocated to a larger unit at Blakemere Craft Centre in 2005. Some beer names are Northern Soul-themed and at least two specials per month are produced under both the Northern and Blakemere brand names.

Casino (OG 1038, ABV 3.6%)

Blakemere Freshly Squeezed (OG 1039, ABV 3.8%)

Navajo (OG 1039, ABV 3.9%)

Blakemere Bronze (OG 1046, ABV 4.4%)

Blakemere Brown Ale (OG 1046, ABV 4.4%)

Blakemere Gold (OG 1044, ABV 4.5%)

Blakemere Hit & Run (OG 1044, ABV 4.5%)

Jewel IPA (OG 1046, ABV 4.6%)

One-Der-Ful Wheat (OG 1046, ABV 4.7%)

North Riding

⊟ North Riding Brewpub, 161-163 North Marine Road, Scarborough, North Yorkshire, YO12 7HU
☎ (01723) 370004
✉ northridingbrewpub@btconnect.com
⊕ northridingbrewpub.com

Brewing commenced in 2011 with the former Bull Box Brewery two-barrel plant, situated in the cellar of the pub. Seasonal beers and monthly specials are also available.

Neilsons Sauvin (OG 1039, ABV 3.7%)
A pale, hoppy session beer imparting a wine-like finish and taste of crushed gooseberries.

Peasholm Pale Ale (PPA) (OG 1042, ABV 4.3%)
A pale and hoppy single-hopped beer with a citrus bitterness and long, smooth finish.

Fat Lads Mild (OG 1044, ABV 4.5%)
A strong, dark mild with roast and chocolate undertones.

North Star (NEW) SIBA

North Star Brewing Co, Unit 6, Gallows Industrial Park, off Furnace Road, Ilkeston, Derbyshire, DE7 5EP
☎ 07521 961881 ✉ richard@northstarbeers.co.uk
⊕ northstarbeers.co.uk

Brewing began in 2012 on a 10-barrel plant. Seasonal beers are available.

Helmsman (ABV 4.2%)

Molly's Pride (ABV 4.2%)

Astronomer (ABV 4.8%)

Polaris (ABV 5%)

Pathfinder (ABV 5.4%)

Northumberland SIBA ◉

Northumberland Brewery Ltd, Accessory House, Barrington Road, Bedlington, Northumberland, NE22 7AP
☎ (01670) 822112
✉ dave@northumberlandbrewery.co.uk
⊕ northumberlandbrewery.co.uk
Tours by arrangement

☺ The brewery has been in operation for 12 years using a 10-barrel brew plant. More than 400 outlets are supplied. The Legends of the Tyne and Legends of the Wear series of beers are also produced as regulars. Seasonal beers: see website.

Pit Pony (OG 1039, ABV 3.8%)

St James' Park Bitter (OG 1039, ABV 4%)

Fog on the Tyne (OG 1040.5, ABV 4.1%)

North Wales

North Wales Brewery, Ty Tan-y-Mynydd, Moelfre, Abergele, Conwy, LL22 9RF
☎ (01745) 832966
✉ northwalesbrewery@uwclub.net
⊕ northwalesbrewery.net
Shop – ring for opening times

☺ John Wood established his brewery in 2007 on the hillside of the Moelfre mountain overlooking Abergele. In 2012 a well was drilled for beer production. Bottle-conditioned beers are also available.

Bodelwyddan Bitter (ABV 3.8%)

Moelfre IPA (ABV 4%)

Abergele Ale (ABV 5%)

Arthurs Ale (ABV 5.5%)

North Yorkshire SIBA

North Yorkshire Brewing Co, Pinchinthorpe Hall, Pinchinthorpe, North Yorkshire, TS14 8HG
☎ (01287) 630200 ✉ sales@nybrewery.co.uk
⊕ nybrewery.co.uk
Shop 10am-5pm daily
Tours by arrangement (inc 3 course meal)

☺ The brewery was founded in Middlesbrough in 1989 and moved in 1998 to Pinchinthorpe Hall, a moated and listed medieval estate near Guisborough that has its own spring water. More than 100 free trade outlets are supplied. All beers are organic and bottle-conditioned beers are available.

Best (OG 1036, ABV 3.6%)

Golden Ginseng (ABV 3.6%)

Prior's Ale (OG 1036, ABV 3.6%) ◆
Light, refreshing and surprisingly full-flavoured for a pale, low gravity beer, with a complex, bittersweet mixture of malt, hops and fruit carrying through into the aftertaste.

Archbishop Lee's Ruby Ale (OG 1040, ABV 4%)

Boro Best (OG 1040, ABV 4%)

Crystal Tips (OG 1040, ABV 4%)

Love Muscle (OG 1040, ABV 4%)

Honey Bunny (OG 1042, ABV 4.2%)

Mayhem (ABV 4.3%)

Cereal Killer (OG 1045, ABV 4.5%)

Blond (ABV 4.6%)

Fools Gold (OG 1046, ABV 4.6%)

Golden Ale (OG 1046, ABV 4.6%) ◆
A well-hopped, lightly-malted, golden premium bitter, using Styrian Goldings and Goldings hops.

Flying Herbert (OG 1047, ABV 4.7%)

Lord Lee's (OG 1047, ABV 4.7%) ◆
A refreshing, red/brown beer with a hoppy aroma. The flavour is a pleasant balance of roast malt and sweetness that predominates over hops. The malty, bitter finish develops slowly.

White Lady (OG 1047, ABV 4.7%)

Dizzy Dick (OG 1048, ABV 4.8%)

Rocket Fuel (OG 1050, ABV 5%)

Norton

Norton Brewing Co, Norton Priory Museum & Gardens, Tudor Road, Manor Park, Runcorn, Cheshire, WA7 1SX
☎ 07767 354674

Norton Brewing was developed in 2009 to provide employment opportunities for people with learning disabilities, autism and other disabilities. It is situated in the grounds of Norton Priory. The brewery was officially opened by John Bishop in 2011.

Priory Citrus (ABV 3.5%)
A refreshing, fruity, light ale.

Priory Golden (ABV 3.7%)
A crisp, fresh, smooth golden ale.

Priory Ale (ABV 4%)
A refreshingly crisp amber ale.

THE BREWERIES

Norwich Bear

Norwich Bear Brewing Co, Ketts Tavern, 29 Ketts Hill, Norwich, NR1 4EX

☎ (01603) 449654 ✉ norwichbear@hotmail.co.uk
⊕ norwichbear.co.uk

Norwich Bear Brewing Co started in 2010 and is a collaboration between Kevin and Dawn Hopkins and award-winning brewer Carlos Branquinho. Beers are brewed exclusively for Kevin and Dawn's freehouses, the Ketts Tavern and the Rose in Norwich. A micro-brewery is planned at the Rose to increase the range and to involve other brewers and enthusiastic amateurs with the new brews. Seasonal beers are available.

Classic (ABV 3.8%) ◕
Gentle citrus airs introduce this amber-gold, easy-drinking bitter. A dry hoppiness is the main flavour as a curious saltiness adds contrast to the long, slowly drying finish.

Pooh Bear (ABV 4.2%)
A distinct citrus aroma complements the honey in this beer. The orange flavour comes from 20 whole oranges in every brew.

Legend (ABV 4.3%) ◕
A copper-coloured beer with a swirling malty and hoppy nose. A blackberry fruitiness melds with the inherent malt character but quickly fades. The finish is short and increasingly bitter.

NPA (Norwich Pale Ale) (ABV 4.7%) ◕
A smooth drinking amber beer with a well-balanced banana/toffee backbone. Equal amounts of hop, malt and bitterness join in before a short, sharp finish.

Platinum Blonde (ABV 5%) ◕
Light, crisp, and refreshing with a miasma of interlinked flavours. Elderflower, grapefruit and hops mix well against a gentle sweet, malty background. Fragrant aroma.

Nottingham SIBA ◉

⊟ Nottingham Brewing Co Ltd, Plough Inn, 17 St Peter's Street, Radford, Nottingham, NG7 3EN
☎ (0115) 942 2649 ☎ 07815 073447
✉ philip.darby@nottinghambrewery.com
⊕ nottinghambrewery.com
Tours by arrangement

The former owners of the Bramcote and Castle Rock Breweries re-established the Nottingham Brewery in 2000 in a purpose-built brewhouse behind the Plough Inn. Philip Darby and Niven Balfour set out to revive the brands of the original Nottingham Brewery, closed by Whitbread in the 1950s, with a view to supplying local outlets within the LocAle ethos.

James Fellow's Legacy (OG 1038, ABV 3.8%)

Rock Ale Bitter Beer (OG 1038, ABV 3.8%) ⬒ ◕
A pale and bitter, thirst-quenching hoppy beer with a dry finish.

Rock Ale Mild Beer (OG 1038, ABV 3.8%) ◕
A reddish-black, malty mild with some refreshing bitterness in the finish.

Legend (OG 1040, ABV 4%) ◕
A fruity and malty pale brown bitter with a touch of sweetness and bitterness.

Extra Pale Ale (OG 1042, ABV 4.2%) ◕

A hoppy and fruity golden ale with a hint of sweetness and a long-lasting bitter finish.

Broadway Reel Ale (OG 1044, ABV 4.4%)

Dreadnought (OG 1045, ABV 4.5%) ◕
Well-balanced best bitter. Blend of malt and hops give a rounded fruity finish.

Bullion (OG 1047, ABV 4.7%) ◕
A refreshing premium golden ale. Brewed with a single malt variety, it is triple-hopped and exceptionally bitter.

Nutbrook SIBA ◉

Nutbrook Brewery Ltd, 6 Hallam Way, West Hallam, Derbyshire, DE7 6LA

☎ 0800 458 2460 ✉ chris@nutbrookbrewery.com
⊕ nutbrookbrewery.com
Shop Mon-Fri 10am-6pm (by invite only); Sat 9am-5pm at Oakfield Farm (open to all)
Tours by arrangement

Nutbrook was established in 2007 on a one-barrel brewery in the owner's garage. This was supplemented in 2010 with a six-barrel plant at Oakfield Farm, Stanley Common. Beers are brewed to order for domestic and corporate clients, and customers can design their own recipes. All beers are available bottle conditioned.

Or8 (OG 1041.4, ABV 3.8%)

Bitlyke (OG 1040.6, ABV 4.2%)

Monty Revenge (OG 1039, ABV 4.3%)

Banter (OG 1040.8, ABV 4.5%)

Midnight (OG 1048.4, ABV 4.5%)

Mongrel (OG 1046.9, ABV 4.5%)

Same Again (ABV 4.5%)

O'Hanlon's ◉

O'Hanlon's Brewing Co Ltd, Great Barton Farm, Whimple, Devon, EX5 2NY

☎ (01404) 822412 ✉ info@ohanlonsbrewery.com

Since moving to Whimple in 2000, the brewery has continued to expand to cope with increasing demand. More than 100 outlets are regularly supplied, with wholesalers distributing nationwide. Seasonal and bottle-conditioned beers are also available.

Dry Stout (OG 1043, ABV 4.2%) ◕
A dark malty, well-balanced stout with a dry, bitter finish and plenty of roast and fruit flavours up front.

Flagship IPA (OG 1044, ABV 4.2%)
Dark chestnut-coloured beer with subtle malty undertones in the taste. The hops supply a fresh, crisp bitterness.

Original Port Stout (OG 1041, ABV 4.8%) ⬒ ◕
A black beer with roast malt in the aroma that remains in the taste but gives way to hoppy bitterness in the aftertaste.

Stormstay (OG 1048, ABV 5%) ⬒
A ruby-coloured complex ale with a toffee and floral hop aroma and a surprisingly clean and citrusy finish after the malt toffee and biscuit flavours.

Oakham SIBA EAB 👁

Oakham Ales, 2 Maxwell Road, Woodston,
Peterborough, Cambridgeshire, PE2 7JB
☎ (01733) 370500 ✉ info@oakhamales.com
⊕ oakhamales.com
Shop Mon-Fri 9am-5pm
Tours by arrangement

⊗ The brewery started in 1993 in Oakham,
Rutland and moved to Peterborough in 1998. The
brewery's head office and main production site is a
75-barrel plant. An additional six-barrel plant is
located at its brew pub central to the city, which
allows special and one-off brews including beers
made especially for its elite customers as members
of the 'Oakademy of Excellence', which was
launched in late 2008. Around 350 outlets are
supplied and three pubs are owned. Seasonal
beers: see website.

Jeffrey Hudson Bitter/JHB
(OG 1038, ABV 3.8%) ◆
This golden ale is dominated by citrus hop
throughout. Fruit comes through as lemons and
grapefruit. Refreshing aftertaste.

Inferno (OG 1039, ABV 4%) 🗇 ◆
The citrus hop character of this straw-coloured
brew begins on the nose and builds in intensity on
the palate. Clean, dry, citrus finish.

Citra (OG 1042, ABV 4.2%) ◆
Overwhelmingly hoppy, this golden ale is bursting
with intense pink grapefruit and tropical fruit all
the way through to the long dry end.

Scarlet Macaw (OG 1043, ABV 4.4%)

Bishops Farewell (OG 1046, ABV 4.6%) ◆
Powerful citrus character: the hops and fruit on the
aroma of this golden/yellow beer become
bittersweet on the palate. Zesty citrus aftertaste.

Attila (ABV 7.5%) 🍷
Fruit notes and elder flower on aroma. Taste of ripe
red berries and citrus fruit, with a long, bitter, fruity
finish.

Oakleaf SIBA 👁

Oakleaf Brewing Co Ltd, Unit 7, Clarence Wharf
Industrial Estate, Mumby Road, Gosport, Hampshire,
PO12 1AJ
☎ (023) 9251 3222 ✉ info@oakleafbrewing.co.uk
⊕ oakleafbrewing.co.uk
Shop Mon-Fri 9am-5pm; Sat 10am-1pm
Tours by arrangement

⊗ Ed Anderson set up Oakleaf with his father-in-
law, Dave Pickersgill, in 2000. The brewery stands
on the side of Portsmouth Harbour. Some 350
outlets are supplied direct with national deliveries
via wholesalers. Seasonal beers: see website/
facebook. Bottle-conditioned beers are also
available.

Some Are Drinking (OG 1039, ABV 3.9%)
An easy-drinking light summer ale, pale and
refreshing with a zesty hop finish.

Quercus Folium (OG 1040, ABV 4%)
A traditional mid-brown bitter with an inital malty
flavour leading to a long hoppy finish.

Nuptu'ale (OG 1042, ABV 4.2%) ◆
A full-bodied pale ale, strongly hopped with an
uncompromising bitterness. An intense hoppy,
spicy, floral aroma leads to a complex hoppy taste.

Well-balanced with malts and citrus flavours and a
hint of sweetness making for a refreshing bitter.

Pompey Royal (OG 1046, ABV 4.5%)
A traditional mid-brown malty ale with a delicate
hop balance.

Hole Hearted (OG 1048, ABV 4.7%) ◆
An amber-coloured strong bitter with strong floral
hop and citrus notes in the aroma. These continue
to dominate the flavour and lead to a long,
bittersweet finish.

I Can't Believe It's Not Bitter
(OG 1048, ABV 4.9%) 🗇

India Pale Ale (OG 1053, ABV 5.5%)

For Suthwyk Ales:

Old Dick (OG 1038, ABV 3.8%) ◆
Formerly known as Bloomfield Bitter, this is a
pleasant, clean-tasting pale brown bitter. An easy-
drinking and well-balanced. Beer is brewed by
Oakleaf for Suthwyk using ingredients grown on
the farm.

Liberation (OG 1042, ABV 4.2%)
Light-coloured with a soft, berry fruit flavour.

Skew Sunshine Ale (OG 1046, ABV 4.6%) ◆
An amber-coloured beer. Initial hoppiness leads to
a fruity taste and finish. A slightly cloying
mouthfeel.

Palmerston's Folly (OG 1050, ABV 5%)

Oakwell SIBA

Oakwell Brewery, PO Box 87, Pontefract Road,
Barnsley, South Yorkshire, S71 1EZ
☎ (01226) 296161
Tours by arrangement

⊙ Based on the site of the famous Barnsley
Brewery, the present owners purchased the land
and buildings from Courage Group in 1994.
Brewing on site had ceased in 1976 and began
again in 1997 with the new brewery being
established in Courage's former distribution
warehouse. Oakwell supplies around 30 outlets
direct.

Dark Mild (OG 1033.5, ABV 3.4%) ◆
A malty mild with sweet fruit and caramel flavours.
A smooth, clean finish.

Barnsley Bitter (OG 1036, ABV 3.8%) ◆
A fruity and malty bitter with a hoppy, clean, bitter
and mellow finish.

Senior (OG 1043, ABV 4.3%) 🍷 ◆
A golden best bitter with a sharp initial crisp, fruity
flavour of mixed fruits. Sweetness lasts throughout
and finishes with a lingering, dry bitterness.

Oates (NEW)

Oates Brewery, 4C Ladyship Business Park, Mill Lane,
Halifax, West Yorkshire, HX3 6TA
☎ (01422) 320100 ☎ 07770 572055
✉ oates@easy.com

Oates began brewing in 2012 using a six-barrel
plant.

OMT (ABV 3.8%)

Golden Oates (ABV 4.1%)

Wild Oates (ABV 4.3%)

THE BREWERIES

Oban Bay

See Argyll

Odcombe

▤ Odcombe Brewery, Masons Arms, 41 Lower Odcombe, Odcombe, Somerset, BA22 8TX
☎ (01935) 862591
✉ paula@masonsarmsodcombe.co.uk
⊕ masonsarmsodcombe.co.uk
Tours by arrangement

Odcombe Brewery opened in 2000 and closed a few years later. It re-opened in 2005 with assistance from Shepherd Neame. Brewing takes place once a week and beers are only available at the pub. Seasonal beers are also available.

No 1 (OG 1040, ABV 4%)

Spring (OG 1041, ABV 4.1%)

Roly Poly (OG 1042, ABV 4.2%)

Offa's Dyke SIBA

▤ Offa's Dyke Brewery, Barley Mow Inn, Chapel Lane, Trefonen, Oswestry, Shropshire, SY10 9DX
☎ (01691) 656889 ⊕ offasdykebrewery.com
Tours by arrangement

⊗ Offa's Dyke was established in 2007. The brewery and adjoining pub straddle the old England/Wales border, Offa's Dyke. The owner grows barley locally and is experimenting with small-scale hop cultivation. An Oswestry brewery tap opened in 2010, Olde Vaults. Bottle-conditioned beers are available.

Barley Gold (OG 1038, ABV 3.6%)

Offa's Pride (OG 1040, ABV 3.8%)

Thirst Brew (OG 1042, ABV 4%)

Grim Reaper (OG 1050, ABV 5%)

Offbeat SIBA

Offbeat Brewery Ltd, Unit 6, Thomas Street, Crewe, Cheshire, CW1 2BD
☎ 07502 096438 ✉ beer@offbeatbrewery.com
⊕ offbeatbrewery.com
Tours by arrangement

☺Offbeat began brewing at the Borough Arms in Crewe before quickly expanding to a six-barrel plant at the current address. Monthly specials and bottle-conditioned beers are also available.

Outlandish Pale (ABV 3.9%)
A session ale with a big, hoppy hit.

Kooky Gold (ABV 4.1%)
A lightly-hopped, golden session ale.

Odd Ball Red (ABV 4.2%)
A ruby red ale with a spicy flavour and finish.

Out Of Step IPA (ABV 5.8%)
A generously-hopped IPA with abundant citrus flavours leading to a dry, bitter finish.

Okells SIBA ◉

Okell & Son Ltd, Kewaigue, Douglas, Isle of Man, IM2 1QG
☎ (01624) 699400 ✉ mac@okells.co.uk
⊕ okells.co.uk

Tours by arrangement

☺ Founded in 1874 by Dr Okell and formerly trading as Isle of Man Breweries, this is the main brewery on the island, having taken over and closed the rival Castletown Brewery in 1986. The brewery moved in 1994 to a new, purpose-built plant at Kewaigue to replace the Falcon Brewery in Douglas. All the beers are produced under the Manx Brewers' Act 1874 (permitted ingredients: water, malt, sugar and hops only – amended in 1998 to allow the brewing of wheat and fruit beers). 35 of the company's 48 Isle of Man pubs and 19 of the 20 pubs in England and Wales sell cask beer and 60 free trade outlets are also supplied. Seasonal beers: see website.

Mild (OG 1034, ABV 3.4%) ◆
Sweet dark brown mild, easy-drinking.

Bitter (OG 1035, ABV 3.7%) ◆
Well-balanced malt and hops with some fruitiness leading to a short, bitter finish.

Dr Okell's IPA (OG 1044, ABV 4.5%)
A light-coloured beer with a full-bodied taste. The sweetness is offset by strong hopping that gives the beer an overall roundness with spicy lemon notes and a fine dry finish.

Red (OG 1047, ABV 4.8%)
A ruby red ale with a spicy citrus hop aroma. An initial sweetness leads to a smooth, easy-drinking beer.

Alt (OG 1050, ABV 4.9%) ⊓
A beer brewed in the true Altbier manner; burnished copper in colour with a crisp, elegant and fresh flavour with hints of gooseberry and citrus.

Old Bear SIBA

Old Bear Brewery, Unit 1, Aireworth Mills, Aireworth Road, Keighley, West Yorkshire, BD21 4DH
☎ (01535) 601222 ✉ sales@oldbearbrewery.co.uk
⊕ oldbearbrewery.co.uk
Shop Mon-Fri 9am-4pm
Tours by arrangement

☺Old Bear is a family business founded in 1993 at the Old White Bear in Crosshills. The brewery moved to Keighley in 2004 to accommodate increased production and bottle recycling. The original 10-barrel plant was retained and refurbished and there is also a one-barrel plant for special brews. All cask beers are also available bottle conditioned.

Bruin (OG 1037, ABV 3.7%)
The combination of hops gives off a sharp wild blackcurrant taste with a smoothness to follow.

Estivator (OG 1037, ABV 3.8%) ◆
This straw-coloured bitter has a grassy hop character in the aroma and taste with marmalade fruitiness. The finish is dry and bitter.

Great Bear (OG 1039, ABV 3.9%)

Black Mari'a (OG 1043, ABV 4.2%)
A black stout, smooth on the palate with a strong roast malt flavour and fruity finish.

Honeypot (OG 1044, ABV 4.4%)
Straw-coloured beer enhanced with golden honey.

Goldilocks (OG 1047, ABV 4.5%) ◆
A fruity, straw-coloured golden ale, well-hopped and assertively bitter through to the finish.

Hibernator (OG 1055, ABV 5%) ◆
A complex rich dark ale dominated by roast and bitter flavours against a background sweetness. Look for roast coffee, hints of caramel and dark vine fruit on the nose. The finish is distinctly bitter and quite astringent.

Old Bog

◉ Old Bog Brewery, Masons Arms, 2 Quarry School Place, Oxford, OX3 8LH
☎ (01865) 764579 ✉ theoldbog@hotmail.co.uk

Brewing started in 2005 on a one-barrel plant at the Masons Arms. Andy Meeson, brother of the landlord, brews at weekends and produces one brew a fortnight. The beers, when available, are sold at the pub and occasionally at beer festivals. A number of one-off brews appear throughout the year.

Quarry Gold (OG 1041, ABV 4.1%)
Clean-tasting golden bitter with well-balanced sweet and bitter characteristics.

Quarry Goldish (ABV 4.6%)
A golden ale with mild fruit notes and a sweet finish.

Wheat Beer (ABV 5%)
Pale gold with a light citrus hoppiness.

Half Wit (ABV 5.5%)
A malty, dark amber wheat beer.

Monstrous Mild (ABV 5.6%)
Strong, smooth dark mild with fruity and malty tastes.

Old Brewery

See Meantime

Old Cannon

◉ Old Cannon Brewery Ltd, 86 Cannon Street, Bury St Edmunds, Suffolk, IP33 1JR
☎ (01284) 768769
✉ drink@oldcannonbrewery.co.uk
⊕ oldcannonbrewery.co.uk

⊗ The St Edmunds Head pub opened in 1845 with its own brewery. Brewing ceased in 1917, and Greene King closed the pub in 1995. It re-opened in 1999 as the Old Cannon Brewery complete with a unique state-of-the-art brewery housed in the bar area. A growing number of local outlets are supplied. Seasonal beers are also available.

Best Bitter (OG 1037, ABV 3.8%) ◆
Traditional East Anglian bitter. Rich hoppy aroma and bitterness dominate throughout with just a hint of sweetness in the aftertaste.

Hornblower (OG 1038, ABV 4%)
Light in colour with an IPA hoppiness.

Gunner's Daughter (OG 1052, ABV 5.5%) ◆
A well-balanced strong ale with a complexity of hop, fruit, sweetness and bitterness in the flavour, and a lingering hoppy, bitter aftertaste.

Old Chimneys

Old Chimneys Brewery, Hopton End Farm, Church Road, Market Weston, Diss, IP22 2NX
☎ (01359) 221411/221013
⊕ oldchimneysbrewery.com
Shop Fri 2-7pm; Sat 11am-2pm
Tours by arrangement

Old Chimneys opened in 1995. It moved to larger premises in a converted farm building in 2001 and despite the postal address is situated in Suffolk. Most of the beers are named after rare species found nearby. Seasonal, special and bottle-conditioned beers are also available, along with a small quantity of cider.

Military Mild (OG 1035, ABV 3.3%) ◆
A rich, dark mild with good body for its gravity. Sweetish toffee and light roast bitterness dominate, leading to a dry aftertaste.

Ragged Robin (ABV 3.5%)
A refreshing pale mild with subtle hints of toffee, fruit, vanilla and hop.

Great Raft Bitter (OG 1040, ABV 4%)
Pale copper bitter bursting with fruit. Malt and hops add to the sweetish fruity flavour, which is rounded off with hoppy bitterness in the aftertaste.

Black Rat Stout (OG 1048, ABV 4.4%)
Roast malt and coffee flavours with body and sweetness from added lactose.

Golden Pheasant (OG 1044, ABV 4.5%)
Pale, dry bitter with citrus, apple and malt balanced with robust hop bitterness.

Scarlet Tiger (OG 1047, ABV 4.7%)
A premium ruby-coloured beer, full-bodied, malty and fruity.

Barbastelle (ABV 6.2%)
Dark, mellow, bitter chocolate and sourdough balancing creamy toffee flavours.

Good King Henry (OG 1107, ABV 9%)

Old Cross

◉ Old Cross Tavern Brewery, Old Cross Tavern, 8 St Andrew Street, Hertford, Hertfordshire, SG14 1JA
☎ (01992) 583133

⊗ The micro-brewery was set up in 2008 and is located within the pub. Owner Nigel Beviss brews solely for the Old Cross Tavern. There are currently two beers, with one usually available at the bar.

Laugh and Titter (OG 1037, ABV 3.7%)

OXT'ale (OG 1041, ABV 4.1%)

Old Dairy SIBA ◉

Old Dairy Brewery Ltd, The Old Parlour, Rawlinson Farm, Rolvenden, Kent, TN17 4JD
☎ (01580) 243185 ✉ fineale@olddairybrewery.com
⊕ olddairybrewery.com
Tours by arrangement

Old Dairy was founded in 2009. Sales expanded rapidly across pubs in Kent and new staff were taken on after only three months to help cope with the demand. 50 outlets are supplied direct. Bottle-conditioned beers are available.

Red Top (OG 1038, ABV 3.8%) ◆
A sweetish, copper-coloured bitter with hints of caramel and a subtle hop character.

Copper Top (OG 1041, ABV 4.1%)
A rich, dark bitter with a chewy toffee caramel body with chocolate undertones.

Gold Top (OG 1043, ABV 4.3%) ◣
A well-balanced golden ale with a good blend of malt and hops followed by a long, bittersweet finish.

Silver Top (OG 1046, ABV 4.5%) ◣
A well crafted complex stout with a good balance of dark malts, roast barley and caramel, and a long finish.

Blue Top (OG 1048, ABV 4.8%) ◣
Rich and full bodied, this pale brown ale has a long, bittersweet finish and a hint of aroma hop.

Oldershaw SIBA ◉

Oldershaw Brewery, 12 Harrowby Hall Estate, Harrowby, Grantham, Lincolnshire, NG31 9HB
☎ (01476) 572135 ✉ info@oldershawbrewery.com
⊕ oldershawbrewery.com
Shop Mon-Fri 10am-4pm
Tours by arrangement

⊗ Established in 1997, Oldershaw Brewery now supplies more than 100 local freehouses. Under new ownership since 2010, demand has continued to grow for its products and many new beers have been introduced. Seasonal and bottle-conditioned beers are available.

Mowbray's Mash (OG 1037, ABV 3.7%)
A hoppy session beer.

Heavenly Blonde (OG 1038, ABV 3.8%)
A pale blonde beer, packed with zesty tropical fruits with a crisp, dry finish.

Harrowby Pale Ale (OG 1039, ABV 3.9%)
A light, hoppy and moderately bitter pale ale.

Flag Fen Ale (OG 1040, ABV 4%)

Newton's Drop (OG 1041, ABV 4.1%) ◣
Balanced malt and hops but with a strong bitter, lingering taste in this mid-brown beer.

Byard's Leap (OG 1042, ABV 4.2%)
A golden best bitter, fruity and aromatic.

Caskade (OG 1042, ABV 4.2%) ◣
A gentle blend of flavours combine into a smooth, undemanding pint. Malt vies with a hoppy bitterness for initial recognition. Traces of caramel and sulphur appear before the short, sharp finish.

Best Bitter (OG 1043, ABV 4.3%)

Grantham Stout (OG 1043, ABV 4.3%)
Dark brown and smooth with rich roast malt flavour, supported by some fruit and bitterness. A long, moderately dry finish.

Regal Blonde (OG 1042, ABV 4.4%) ◣
Straw-coloured, lager-style beer with a good malt/hop balance throughout; strong bitterness on the taste lingers.

Old Boy (OG 1047, ABV 4.8%) ◣
A full-bodied amber ale, fruity and bitter with a hop/fruit aroma. The malt that backs the taste dies in the long finish.

Blonde Volupta (OG 1050, ABV 5%)
Straw-coloured, zesty premium beer with intense tropical fruit flavours leading to a crisp, dry finish.

Alchemy (OG 1052, ABV 5.3%)
A golden, premium hoppy beer brewed with First Gold hops.

Olde Swan

≣ Olde Swan Brewery, 89 Halesowen Road, Netherton, Dudley, West Midlands, DY2 9PY
☎ (01384) 253075
Tours by arrangement

⊛ A famous brew-pub best known as 'Ma Pardoe's' after the matriarch who ruled it for years. The pub has been licensed since 1835 and the present brewery and pub were built in 1863. Brewing continued until 1988 and restarted in 2001. The plant brews primarily for the on-site pub with some beer available to the trade. Seasonal beer and monthly specials are available together with various commemorative beers for sporting events.

Original (OG 1034, ABV 3.5%) ◣
Straw-coloured light mild, smooth but tangy, and sweetly refreshing with a faint hoppiness.

Dark Swan (OG 1041, ABV 4.2%) ◣
Smooth, sweet dark mild with late roast malt in the finish.

Entire (OG 1043, ABV 4.4%) ◣
Faintly hoppy, amber premium bitter with sweetness persistent throughout.

Bumble Hole Bitter (OG 1052, ABV 5.2%) ◣
Sweet, smooth amber ale with hints of astringency in the finish.

Old Forge

≣ Old Forge Brewery, Radnor Arms, Coleshill, Oxfordshire, SN6 7PR
☎ (01793) 873915 ☎ 07771 613556
✉ sales@oldforgebrewery.co.uk
⊕ oldforgebrewery.co.uk
Tours by arrangement

Old Forge began brewing at the Radnor Arms in 2010 using a four-barrel plant. Alan Watkins (brewer at the Halfpenny and Faringdon breweries) is head brewer, assisted by Gordie Moreing. Visitors can view the plant through several glass windows opposite the entrance to the Radnor Arms.

Anvil Ale (OG 1037, ABV 3.8%)
Light session ale, amber-coloured with traditional bitterness.

Blacksmiths Gold (OG 1042, ABV 4%)
Refreshing straw-coloured ale with citrus notes and a hoppy, floral finish.

Hammer & Tongs (OG 1043, ABV 4.2%)
Ruby chestnut in colour, bitter yet mellow in taste.

Sledgehammer (OG 1048, ABV 5%)
Deep red, full-bodied premium ale with hints of chocolate and caramel.

Old Inn

≣ Old Inn Brewery, Old Inn, Gairloch, IV21 2BD
☎ (01445) 712006 ✉ enquiries@theoldinn.net
⊕ theoldinn.net

Brewing began in 2010 using a 150-litre plant. Seasonal beers are also available.

Mike's Mild (ABV 3.6%)

The Blind Piper (ABV 4.6%)

Old Laxey

▤ **Old Laxey Brewing Co Ltd, Shore Hotel Brew Pub, Old Laxey, Isle of Man, IM4 7DA**
☎ (01624) 863214 ✉ shore@manx.net
⊕ shorehotel.im
Tours by arrangement

Beer brewed on the Isle of Man is brewed to a strict Beer Purity Act. Additives are not permitted to extend shelf life, nor are chemicals allowed to assist with head retention. Most of Old Laxey's beer is sold through the Shore Hotel alongside the brewery. Bosun is also usually available in the HQ Bar in Douglas, which is owned by the co-owner of the brewery.

Bosun Bitter (OG 1038, ABV 3.8%)
Crisp and fresh with a hoppy aftertaste.

Old Luxters

Old Luxters Farm Brewery, Hambleden, Oxfordshire, RG9 6JW
☎ (01491) 638330 ✉ enquiries@chilternvalley.co.uk
⊕ chilternvalley.co.uk/brewery
Cellar Shop Mon-Fri 9am-6pm; Sat- Sun 11am-6pm (5pm winter)
Tours by arrangement

⊗ A traditional, full-mash farm brewery established in 1990 and now with the 'By Royal Appointment' accolade. It is situated in a 17th-century barn alongside the Chiltern Valley Vineyard. The brewery is in Buckinghamshire despite the postal address. Several bottle-conditioned beers are brewed under contract and are also available at the Windsor farm shop. Three winter warmers are brewed for Christmas.

Barn Ale Bitter (OG 1038, ABV 4%)
A fruity, aromatic, fairly hoppy, bitter beer.

Barn Ale Special (OG 1042.5, ABV 4.5%) ◆
Predominantly malty, fruity and hoppy in taste and nose, and tawny/amber in colour. Fairly strong in flavour: the initial, sharp, malty and fruity taste leaves a dry, bittersweet, fruity aftertaste. It can be slightly sulphurous.

Dark Roast Ale (OG 1048, ABV 5%)
The use of chocolate and crystal malts give this ale a nutty, roasty bitter flavour.

Old Mill SIBA ◉

Old Mill Brewery, Mill Street, Snaith, East Yorkshire, DN14 9HU
☎ (01405) 861813 ✉ sales@oldmillbrewery.co.uk
⊕ oldmillbrewery.co.uk
Tours by arrangement

◉Old Mill is a craft brewery opened in 1983 in a 200-year-old former malt kiln and corn mill. The brew-length is 60 barrels. The brewery is building a tied estate, now standing at 19 houses. Beers can be found nationwide through wholesalers and around 80 free trade outlets are supplied direct. There is a rolling programme of seasonal beers (see website) and monthly specials.

Traditional Mild (OG 1034, ABV 3.4%) ◆
A satisfying roast malt flavour dominates this easy-drinking dark mild.

Traditional Bitter (OG 1038.5, ABV 3.8%) ◆
A malty nose is carried through to the initial flavour. Bitterness runs throughout.

Blonde Bombshell (OG 1042, ABV 4%)
A straw-coloured beer. Easy-drinking due to delicate and refreshing fruity flavours.

Red Goose (ABV 4.2%)
A rich, ruby, malty beer.

Yorkshire Porter (OG 1044, ABV 4.4%)
Sweet, roasted and chocolate flavours and a pleasant hop aroma.

Bullion (OG 1047.5, ABV 4.7%) ◆
The malty and hoppy aroma is followed by a neat mix of hop and fruit tastes within an enveloping maltiness. Dark brown/amber in colour.

Old Pie Factory (NEW)

Old Pie Factory Brewery Ltd, Montague Road, Warwick, CV34 5LW
☎ (01926) 402100

Old Pie Factory began brewing in 2011 using a 5.5-barrel plant. The brewery is located at Underwood Wines and is a joint venture between Underwood Wines, the Old Fourpenny Shop Hotel in Warwick and the Case is Altered in nearby Five Ways. More beers are planned.

Bitter (OG 1038.5, ABV 3.9%)

Pale (OG 1039, ABV 4%)

Old Poet's

See Ashover

Old Spot

Old Spot Brewery Ltd, Manor Farm, Station Road, Cullingworth, Bradford, West Yorkshire, BD13 5HN
☎ (01535) 691144 ✉ sales@oldspotbrewery.co.uk
⊕ oldspotbrewery.co.uk
Tours by arrangement

◉ Old Spot started brewing in 2005 and is named after a retired sheepdog on Manor Farm. The brewery has five constant beers and also brews seasonal and one-off beers. The main outlet is the George Hotel in Cullingworth, which acts as the brewery tap.

Light But Dark (OG 1043, ABV 4%) ◆
This ideal session beer is a deep chestnut brown bitter with a malty aroma and taste and hop flavour developing in the finish and aftertaste.

Spot Light (OG 1040, ABV 4.2%) ◆
This smooth-drinking golden ale has a slightly fruity, hoppy aroma leading to a well-balanced fruit and hop flavour with hints of pineapple and a long bittersweet finish.

Inn-Spired (OG 1043, ABV 4.3%)
Light-coloured bitter with a light, hoppy taste and a slight, fruity finish.

OSB (OG 1042, ABV 4.5%) ◆
This malty-flavoured dark golden ale is balanced with fruit and hop bitterness with a slightly sweet finish.

Spot O'Bother (OG 1060, ABV 5.5%)
Porter with a chocolate ice cream taste and slight liquorice bitterness to finish. A complex brew.

Ole Slewfoot SIBA

Ole Slewfoot Brewing Co Ltd, 3 Pollard Road,
Hainford, Norwich, NR10 3BE
☎ (01603) 279927 ☎ 07909 636966
✉ john@oleslewfootbrewery.co.uk
⊕ oleslewfootbrewery.co.uk

⊠ Ole Slewfoot was established in 2009. Five
outlets are supplied direct.

White Dove (OG 1039, ABV 3.7%)

January 8th (OG 1040, ABV 4.2%)

Orange Blossom Special (OG 1042, ABV 4.4%)

Fox on the Run (OG 1046, ABV 4.8%)

Devils Dream (OG 1048, ABV 5%)

Opa Hay's

Opa Hay's Brewery, Glencot, Wood Lane, Aldeby,
Norfolk, NR34 0DA
☎ (01502) 679144 ☎ 07916 282729
✉ mail@engelfineales.com ⊕ engelfineales.com

Opa Hay's began brewing in late 2008. Seasonal
beers are available.

Fruity Little Number (ABV 3.9%) ◄
Powerful citrus/grapefruit aroma with malt and
hops. Smoky sweetish flavours with fruit notes and
a fruity, hoppy aftertaste.

Orkney SIBA

Sinclair Breweries Ltd t/a Orkney Brewery, Quoyloo,
Stromness, Orkney, KW16 3LT
☎ (01667) 404555 ☎ 07721 013227
✉ info@sinclairbreweries.co.uk
⊕ orkneybrewery.co.uk
Tours by arrangement

☺Orkney was set up in 1988 in an old school
building in the remote hamlet of Quoyloo. All beer
is brewed along strict ecological lines from the
brewery's own water supply with all waste water
treated through two lakes on its land, which in turn
support fish and several dozen Mallard ducks.
Development was completed in 2010 to double
the capacity of the brewery on an adjacent site
with plans to convert the original building into a
visitor centre with a shop and an events venue.
After eight years based at Kinlochleven, 2010 saw
the transfer of sister brewery Atlas (qv), part of
Sinclair Breweries, to Quoyloo; the combined
business distributes to some 600 outlets across
Scotland and via wholesalers to the rest of Britain.
Seasonal beers are available.

Raven (OG 1038, ABV 3.8%) 🍷 🍴 ◄
A well-balanced, quaffable bitter. Malty fruitiness
and bitter hops last through to the long, dry
aftertaste.

Dragonhead (OG 1040, ABV 4%) ◄
A strong, dark malt aroma flows into the taste in
this superb Scottish stout. The roast malt continues
to dominate the aftertaste, and blends with
chocolate to develop a strong, dry finish.

Northern Light (OG 1040, ABV 4%) ◄
A well-balanced golden ale with a real smack of
fruit and hops in the taste and an increasingly bitter
aftertaste.

Red MacGregor (OG 1040, ABV 4%) ◄

This tawny red ale has a powerful smack of fruit
and a clean, fresh mouthfeel. A well-balanced
bitter.

Corncrake (OG 1042, ABV 4.1%) ◄
A straw-coloured beer with soft citrus fruits and a
floral aroma.

Dark Island (OG 1045, ABV 4.6%) ◄
The roast malt and chocolate character varies,
making the beer hard to categorise as a stout or an
old ale. A sweetish roast malt taste leads to a long-
lasting roasted, slightly bitter, dry finish.

Skull Splitter (OG 1080, ABV 8.5%) ◄
An intense velvet malt nose with hints of apple,
prune and plum. The hoppy taste is balanced by
satiny smooth malt with fruity spicy edges, leading
to a long, dry finish with a hint of nut.

For Atlas Brewery:

Latitude (OG 1036, ABV 3.6%) ◄
This straw-coloured ale has a light citrus taste with
a smack of hops and grapefruit in the light bitter
finish.

Three Sisters (OG 1043, ABV 4.2%) ◄
Malt, summer fruits and caramel in the nose and
blackcurrant in the taste, followed by a short,
hoppy, bitter finish.

Wayfarer (OG 1044, ABV 4.4%) 🍷 🍴 ◄
Full of citrus fruits and hops

Nimbus (OG 1050, ABV 5%) ◄
A full-bodied golden beer using some wheat malt
and three types of hops. Sweet and fruity at the
front, it becomes slightly astringent with lasting
fruit and a pleasant, dry finish.

Ossett SIBA ⊙

Ossett Brewing Co Ltd, Kings Yard, Low Mill Road,
Ossett, West Yorkshire, WF5 8ND
☎ (01924) 261333 ✉ brewery@ossett-
brewery.co.uk ⊕ ossett-brewery.co.uk
Shop Mon-Fri 9am-4.30pm
Tours by arrangement

☺Brewing began in 1998 but the brewery soon
outgrew the premises, moving to a new site 30
yards away in 2005. A new 2,500 square feet cold
store was added in 2008 and brewing capacity
currently stands at 200 barrels per week. Ossett
delivers between Newcastle and Peterborough and
beer is available through wholesalers. The brewery
owns 18 pubs and three micro-breweries. The
Riverhead Brewery was purchased in 2006,
Fernandes Brewery in 2007 and brewing
commenced at the Rat Brewery in 2011. Seasonal
and special beers: see website.

Pale Gold (OG 1038, ABV 3.8%)
A light, refreshing pale ale with a light, hoppy
aroma.

Yorkshire Blonde (OG 1040, ABV 3.9%)
A pale, full-bodied and well-rounded ale. Slightly
sweet on the palate, with a generous late addition
of Mount Hood hops for aroma.

Big Red Bitter (OG 1042, ABV 4%)
Deep red, malty Yorkshire bitter.

Silver King (OG 1041, ABV 4.3%)
A lager-style beer with a crisp, dry flavour and
citrus fruity aroma.

Excelsior (OG 1051, ABV 5.2%)

A strong pale ale with a full, mellow flavour and a fresh, hoppy aroma with citrus/floral characteristics.

Otley SIBA IFBB ◉

Otley Brewing Co Ltd, Unit 42, Albion Industrial Estate, Pontypridd, Mid Glamorgan, CF37 4NX
☎ (01443) 480555 ✉ info@otleybrewing.co.uk
⊕ otleybrewing.co.uk
Tours by arrangement

☺ Otley Brewing was established in 2005 and since then the brewery has almost tripled in size. Seasonal beers: see website. Bottle-conditioned beers are also available.

Columbo (OG 1040, ABV 4%) 🍺

O1 (OG 1038, ABV 4%) 🍺
A pale golden beer with a hoppy aroma. The taste has hops, malt, fruit and a thirst-quenching bitterness. A satisfying finish completes this beer.

Boss (OG 1042.6, ABV 4.4%)

O-Garden (OG 1046.5, ABV 4.8%) 🍺🍺

Otter SIBA ◉

Otter Brewery Ltd, Mathayes, Luppitt, Honiton, Devon, EX14 4SA
☎ (01404) 891285 ✉ info@otterbrewery.com
⊕ otterbrewery.com
Tours by arrangement

▨ Otter Brewery was set up in 1990 by the McCaig family and has grown into one of the West Country's major producers of beers. The brewery is located in the Blackdown Hills, between Taunton and Honiton. Environmental responsibility lies at the heart of the brewery's ethos. Otter's 'eco cellar' has been built underground and naturally chills the cellar. The beers are made from the brewery's own springs and are delivered to more than 500 pubs across the south-west including the family's first pub, the Holt, in Honiton. Seasonal beers: see website.

Ritter (OG 1036, ABV 3.6%) 🍺
Well-balanced amber session bitter with a fruity nose and bitter taste and aftertaste.

Amber (OG 1038.5, ABV 4%) 🍺🍺🍺
Amber-coloured as the name suggests, with a fruity nose and fruit and hop taste. Well-balanced with a lingering bitter finish.

Bright (OG 1039, ABV 4.3%) 🍺
Pale yellow/golden ale with a strong fruit aroma, sweet fruity taste and a bittersweet finish.

Ale (OG 1043, ABV 4.5%) 🍺
A full-bodied best bitter. A malty aroma predominates with a fruity taste and finish.

Head (OG 1054, ABV 5.8%)
Fruity aroma and taste with a pleasant bitter finish. Dark brown and full-bodied.

Ouseburn Valley SIBA

🍺 Ouseburn Valley Brewery, c/o Brandling Villa, Haddricks Mill Road, South Gosforth, South Gosforth, Tyne & Wear, NE3 1QL
☎ 07932 677899
✉ nige@ouseburnvalleybrewery.co.uk
⊕ ouseburnvalleybrewery.co.uk

Ouseburn Valley started in the owner's garage but has now moved to the cellar of the Brandling Villa pub where both capacity and beer range have increased.

Armstrong Bitter (OG 1042, ABV 4.1%)
A yellow-coloured beer with a light, spicy aroma with soft caramel overtones and a long, bitter finish.

Golden Ale (OG 1044, ABV 4.4%)
Dark gold in colour with a light hop aroma, sweet malty taste and a smooth finish.

Milk Stout (OG 1047, ABV 43.4%)
Traditionally dark in colour with a liquorice aroma, sweet liquorice and slightly coffee taste.

India Pale Ale (OG 1047, ABV 437%)
Pale gold in colour with a strong hop aroma and long, dry finish.

Outlaw

See Roosters

Outstanding

Outstanding Brewing Co Ltd, Britannia Mill, Cobden Street, Bury, Lancashire, BL9 6AW
☎ (0161) 764 7723 ✉ info@outstandingbeers.co.uk
⊕ outstandingbeers.com

The brewery was set up in 2008 as a collaboration between Paul Sandiford, Glen Woodcock, David Porter and Alex Lord. It operates a dual system, brewing on a 15-barrel plant and utilising a 2.5-barrel plant for special and experimental brews. Selective free trade accounts are supplied nationally.

Selling Out (OG 1037, ABV 3.9%)
Pale, smooth and fruity.

Red (OG 1042, ABV 4.4%)
A copper-coloured ale with a distinctive hop finish.

Blond (OG 1044, ABV 4.5%)
Pale and lightly bittered with citrus flavours and a floral nose.

SOS (OG 1044, ABV 4.5%)
Light brown beer, dry and intensely bitter.

White (OG 1048, ABV 5%)
A cloudy wheat beer with earthy, spicy, lemony flavours.

Standing Out (OG 1053, ABV 5.5%)
A pale golden ale, dry and bitter with lots of hop aroma.

Stout (OG 1057, ABV 5.5%)
Thick, jet black and bitter with liquorice overtones.

Pushing Out (OG 1065, ABV 7.4%)
A pale golden ale with a strong, distinctive dry, bitter flavour and hop aroma.

Owenshaw Mill

Owenshaw Mill Brewery Ltd, Owenshaw Works, Old Cawsey, Sowerby Bridge, West Yorkshire, HX6 2AJ
☎ (01422) 839010
✉ info@owenshawmillbrewery.co.uk
⊕ owenshawmillbrewery.co.uk

Owenshaw Mill began production in 2011 using an eight-barrel plant.

Katy's Blonde (OG 1037, ABV 3.6%)

THE BREWERIES

A pale, fruity session beer.

Oxfordshire Ales SIBA

Oxfordshire Ales Ltd, 12 Pear Tree Farm Industrial Units, Bicester Road, Marsh Gibbon, Bicester, Oxfordshire, OX27 0GB
☎ (01869) 278765 ✉ john@oxfordshireales.co.uk
⊕ oxfordshireales.co.uk
Tours by arrangement

The company first brewed in 2005. The five-barrel plant was previously at Picks Brewery but has now been upgraded to a 15-barrel plant. It supplies more than 100 outlets as well as several wholesalers. Seasonal beers are produced.

Triple B (OG 1037, ABV 3.7%) ◀
This pale amber beer has a huge caramel aroma. The caramel diminishes in the initial taste, which changes to a fruit/bitter balance. This in turn leads to a long, refreshing, bitter aftertaste.

Pride of Oxford (OG 1042, ABV 4.1%) ◀
An amber beer, the aroma is butterscotch/caramel, which carries on into the initial taste. The taste then becomes bitter with sweetish/malty overtones. There is a long, dry, bitter finish.

Blenheim (ABV 4.2%)
A refreshing golden ale with a fresh, zesty, spicy hop aroma, biscuity malt taste and pleasant, dry finish.

Marshmellow (OG 1047, ABV 4.7%) ◀
The slightly fruity aroma in this golden-amber beer leads to a hoppy but thin taste, with slight caramel notes. The aftertaste is short and bitter.

Palmers SIBA IFBB ◉

JC & RH Palmer Ltd, The Old Brewery, West Bay Road, Bridport, Dorset, DT6 4JA
☎ (01308) 422396
✉ enquiries@palmersbrewery.com
⊕ palmersbrewery.com
Shop Mon-Sat 9am-6pm
Tours by arrangement (Please ring 01308 427500)

Palmers is Britain's only thatched brewery and dates from 1794. It is situated in Bridport, the heart of the Jurassic Coast in south-west Dorset. The company continues to make substantial investment in its 53 tenanted pubs, all serving cask ale. Around 400 outlets are supplied.

Copper Ale (OG 1036, ABV 3.7%) ◀
Beautifully balanced, copper-coloured light bitter with a hoppy aroma.

Best Bitter (OG 1040, ABV 4.2%) ◀
Hop aroma and bitterness stay in the background in this predominately malty best bitter, with some fruit on the aroma.

Dorset Gold (OG 1046, ABV 4.5%) ◀
More complex than many golden ales thanks to a pleasant banana and mango fruitiness on the aroma that carries on into the taste and aftertaste.

200 (OG 1052, ABV 5%) ◀
This is a big beer with a touch of caramel sweetness adding to a complex hoppy, fruit taste that lasts from the aroma well into the aftertaste.

Tally Ho! (OG 1057, ABV 5.5%) 🍺 ◀
A complex dark old ale. Roast malts and treacle toffee on the palate lead in to a long, lingering finish with more than a hint of coffee.

Panther EAB

Panther Brewery, Unit 1, Collers Way, Reepham, Norfolk, NR10 4SW
☎ 07766 558215 ✉ martin@pantherbrewery.co.uk
⊕ pantherbrewery.co.uk
Shop Mon-Fri 9am-6pm; Sat 10am-3pm
Tours by arrangement

Panther began brewing in 2010 on an industrial estate near the old railway station, formerly the home of Reepham Brewery. The entrance incorporates a small shop selling its bottle-conditioned ales and other merchandise.

Cub (OG 1036, ABV 2.5%)
An amber-coloured beer with floral notes; deceptive in flavour and strong in body.

Ginger Panther (OG 1036, ABV 3.7%)
A ginger wheat beer with a fiery and distinct flavour and subtle lemon notes.

Golden Panther (OG 1037, ABV 3.7%)
A light and refreshing golden ale with a citrus flavour and floral aroma.

Pink Panther (OG 1039, ABV 4%)
A pink ale with a range of fruit flavours and aromas. A balanced wheat beer with a bittersweet, fruity finish.

Red Panther (OG 1041, ABV 4.1%) ◀
A nutty, full-flavoured brew. There's plenty of roasted malt in both aroma and taste. Hops and a residual sweetness provide balance.

Black Panther (OG 1047, ABV 4.5%)
A dark, rich, smooth ale with a complex full flavour and a bittersweet balance leading to a dry finish.

Paradise

🍺 Paradise Coach House Ltd (Paradise Brewery), Bird in Hand, Trelissick Road, Hayle, Cornwall, TR27 4HY
☎ (01736) 753974
✉ birdinhand@paradisepark.org.uk
Tours by arrangement

⊗ Brewing first started in 1981 under the name Paradise Brewery, named after its location, the Paradise Bird Park. The name was changed to Wheal Ale in 1995. Brewing ceased in 2004 but re-started in 2009 under the original Paradise name.

Bitter (OG 1043, ABV 4.3%)

Artist (OG 1055, ABV 5.2%) ◀
Full-bodied tawny ale with a faint aroma of malt. Heavy sweet malt and bubblegum esters in the mouth with a balance of hops. Dryness and bitterness in the finish.

Parish

🍺 Parish Brewery, 6 Main Street, Burrough on the Hill, Leicestershire, LE14 2JQ
☎ (01664) 454801 ☎ 07715 369410
✉ trudygrants@yahoo.co.uk
Tours by arrangement

Parish began in 1983 and operates on a 20-barrel plant located in a 400-year-old building and former stables next to Grant's Freehouse, which is the main outlet for the full range of beers. In addition to the regular range, Poacher's Ale (ABV 6%), a blended ale comprising one part Baz's Bonce Blower and two parts PSB, is also available. Other local outlets are also supplied and special one-off brews are produced for beer festivals held across Leicestershire, Rutland and Cambridgeshire. Baz's Bonce Blower is also available bottle conditioned.

PSB (OG 1039, ABV 3.9%)
Hoppy session beer with malty aftertaste.

Farm Gold (OG 1042, ABV 4.2%)
Light-coloured beer with distinctive hoppy taste and powerful aroma.

Burrough Bitter (OG 1047, ABV 4.8%)
Darker version of PSB with medium to strong bitterness and more pronounced malty aftertaste.

Poacher's Ale (OG 1060, ABV 6%)
Deep ruby-red, full-bodied malty blended beer. Not to be underestimated in strength.

Baz's Bonce Blower (OG 1120, ABV 12%)
Strong, dark beer with a rich, malty character. A Christmas pudding ale.

Partners SIBA ⊚

Partners Brewery Ltd, Unit 12, Saville Bridge Mill, Mill Street East, Dewsbury, West Yorkshire, WF12 9AG
☎ (01924) 457772 ✉ sales@partnersbrewery.co.uk
Tours by arrangement

⊚Partners Brewery, formerly called Anglo Dutch, was bought in 2011 by Paul Horne, landlord of the Spotted Cow in Drighlington, and his business partner Richard Sharp. A full refurbishment of the brewery has been undertaken. Some of the new range is based on original Anglo Dutch beers. Seasonal beers are available.

Pure Gold (ABV 3.5%)
An easy-drinking session beer with a complex character.

Blond (ABV 3.9%)
A blonde, crisp, aromatic session beer.

Spike's (OG 1040.5, ABV 4.2%)
A refreshing ale with slight citrus and orange notes leading to a dry, fruity finish.

Ghost (OG 1043, ABV 4.5%)
A pale, full-bodied bitter with a fresh, gentle nose, taken over by a smooth hop and citrus finish.

Patriot

Patriot Brewery Ltd, Norman Knight, Whichford, Shipston-on-Stour, Warwickshire, CV36 5PE
☎ (01608) 684621 ✉ timbuzzyoung@aol.com
⊕ thepatriotbrewery.co.uk
Tours by arrangement

⊠ Patriot began in 2010 using a four-barrel brew plant. It is located next to the Norman Knight pub, where the beers are regularly available. Seasonal specials are also produced.

Morris (OG 1038, ABV 3.8%)

Kiwi (OG 1041, ABV 4.1%)

Pug IPA (OG 1057, ABV 5.6%)

Peak Ales

Peak Ales, Barn Brewery, Cunnery Barn, Chatsworth, Derbyshire, DE45 1EX
☎ (01246) 583737 ✉ info@peakales.co.uk
⊕ peakales.co.uk
Tours by arrangement

⊚Peak Ales opened in 2005 in converted, former derelict farm buildings on the Chatsworth estate, with the aid of a DEFRA Rural Enterprise Scheme grant, with support from trustees of Chatsworth Settlement. The brewery supplies around 90 local outlets and selected distributors. Seasonal beers are also available.

Swift Nick (OG 1038, ABV 3.8%) ◣
Surprisingly complex for its strength. Easy-drinking, copper-coloured beer with initial flavours of caramel and malt, giving way to bitterness in the finish and aftertaste.

Bakewell Best Bitter (OG 1041, ABV 4.2%) ◣
Full bodied, easy-drinking bitter. Well-balanced with an initial sweetness, which leads to a pleasantly dry finish.

Chatsworth Gold (OG 1045, ABV 4.6%) ◣
Interesting speciality beer made with honey, which comes through in the taste and aroma, giving a pleasant sweetness balanced by a hop and malt finish.

DPA (OG 1045, ABV 4.6%) ◣
Subtle best bitter that is deceptively strong. Flavours of fruit, hops and malt build slowly towards a well-balanced bittersweet finish.

Peakstones Rock SIBA ⊚

Peakstones Rock Brewery, Peakstones Farm, Cheadle Road, Alton, Staffordshire, ST10 4DH
☎ 07891 350908
✉ dedwards@peakstonesrock.co.uk
⊕ peakstonesrock.co.uk
Tours by arrangement

⊠ Peakstones Rock was established in 2006 with a five-barrel plant located on a farm in the Peak District park. The plant was expanded to 10-barrel capacity in 2009 to keep pace with demand. The brewery supplies an expanding free trade market in the North Midlands and surrounding areas.

Nemesis (OG 1042, ABV 3.8%) ◣
Gentle caramel and hop aroma from the pale brown body; sweet start then hops and a touch of roast. Gentle finish.

Chained Oak (OG 1045, ABV 4.2%)
A copper-coloured beer with a bitter finish and hop aroma.

Alton Abbey (OG 1051, ABV 4.5%)

Oblivion (OG 1055, ABV 5.5%)

Peerless SIBA ⊚

Peerless Brewing Co Ltd, The Brewery, 8 Pool Street, Birkenhead, Merseyside, CH41 3NL
☎ (0151) 647 7688
✉ brewer@peerlessbrewing.co.uk
⊕ peerlessbrewing.co.uk
Tours by arrangement (groups only)

Peerless began brewing in 2009 and is under the directorship of Steve Briscoe. Beers are sold through festivals, local pubs and the free trade. Seasonal beers are available.

Dark Arts (ABV 4.1%)
A complex black beer with hints of coffee and chocolate.

Hilbre Gold (ABV 4.5%)
A hoppy golden ale.

THE BREWERIES

Storr Lager (OG 1048, ABV 4.8%)
A pale and hoppy cask lager.

Red Rocks (OG 1050, ABV 5%)
A strong ruby ale.

Full Whack (ABV 6%)
A strong pale ale with a fruity hop finish.

Penlon Cottage

Penlon Cottage Brewery, Penlon Farm, Pencae,
Llanarth, Ceredigion, SA47 0QN
☎ (01545) 580022 ✉ beer@penlon.biz ⊕ penlon.biz

Penlon opened in 2004 and is located on a working
smallholding in the Ceredigion coastal region of
West Wales. Hops and malting barley are part of a
programme of self-sufficiency, with grain, yeast
and beer fed to pigs, sheep and chickens on the
holding. It is the only Welsh brewery to have won
the prestigious Wales True Taste awards twice for
the best alcoholic drinks category. Only bottle-
conditioned beers are produced and are suitable
for vegetarians and vegans.

Pennine SIBA

Pennine Brewery Co Ltd, Unit 8a, Grange Road
Industrial Estate, Batley, West Yorkshire, WF17 6LL
☎ (01924) 440446 ☎ 07725 432652
✉ sales@penninebrewery.com
⊕ penninebrewery.com
Tours by arrangement

Pennine began brewing in 2012 using an 18-barrel
plant from Meantime Brewery. Head brewer Peter
Goldsbrough previously worked at Moorhouses.

Amber Necker (ABV 3.5%)
A session beer with a smooth and creamy texture
and hoppy aftertaste.

Real Blonde (ABV 4%)
A finely-balanced blonde ale with a fruity
aftertaste.

Penpont SIBA

Penpont Brewery, Inner Trenarrett, Altarnun,
Launceston, Cornwall, PL15 7SY
☎ (01566) 86069 ✉ info@penpontbrewery.co.uk
⊕ penpontbrewery.co.uk
Shop – at brewery (please ring first)
Tours by arrangement

⊗ Penpont opened in 2008 and has steadily
increased the range and production since then.
Beers are available in outlets across Cornwall and
at beer festivals. Seasonal and bottle-conditioned
beers: see website.

St Nonna's (OG 1037, ABV 3.7%) ◀
Malt and apple fruitiness dominate the initial
aroma of this brown beer. Hop bitterness is quickly
apparent in the taste and lingers in the long
aftertaste.

Cornish Arvor (OG 1040, ABV 4%)

Shipwreck Coast (OG 1044, ABV 4.4%) ◀
Amber/golden ale with light aroma of orange
citrus hops. Hops dominate with marmalade,
melon and other tropical fruits. Faint malt emerges
as marmalade fades in the finish, becoming dry.

Roughtor (OG 1047, ABV 4.7%) ◀

Malt dominates the nose and follows into the taste
balanced by rising hop bitterness. Strong flavour
slowly fades in the dry finish.

Penzance

▤ Penzance Brewing Co, Star Inn, Crowlas, Penzance,
Cornwall, TR20 8DX
☎ (01736) 740375
Tours by arrangement

⊗ Penzance began brewing in 2008 on a five-
barrel plant. The brewery is situated in the yard of
the Star Inn. The beers are produced by owner
Peter Elvin, who was head brewer for Cotleigh
Brewery for 16 years. To increase production,
fermentation capacity recently expanded. Beer is
mostly produced for the pub though a few selected
outlets are also supplied as well as beer festivals.
The range of beers brewed continues to expand
and includes seasonal specials.

Crowlas Bitter (OG 1037, ABV 3.8%) ◀
Perfectly balanced, tawny session bitter. Clean
fresh taste with balance of malt, hops, bitterness
and a hint of fruit reminiscent of apricots, while the
gentle finish carries malty bitterness.

Jolly Farmer (OG 1036, ABV 3.9%)
Very hoppy golden ale with a citrus finish.

Potion No 9 (OG 1039, ABV 4%) ◀
Citrus marmalade hops dominate the nose and
taste of this smooth golden ale. Bitterness rises in
taste and dominates the finish, which is balanced
by sweetness and astringency.

Brisons Bitter (OG 1043, ABV 4.5%) ◀
Malt is strong in the aroma and taste of this smooth
tawny beer. The flavour is balanced by fruity hops,
sweetness and bitterness. A long, clean finish with
bitter hoppiness and more malt.

Trink (OG 1048, ABV 5.2%)
Well-balanced golden ale, tropical fruit flavour with
citrus bitter finish.

Mellow (OG 1050, ABV 5.5%)
Fruity nose, full fruit flavour in the mouth with
well-rounded smooth finish.

IPA (OG 1058, ABV 6%)
A strong, traditional IPA.

Scilly Stout (OG 1067, ABV 7%)
Strong stout with a hint of chocolate.

Pheasantry (NEW) SIBA

Pheasantry Brewery, High Brecks Farm, Lincoln Road,
East Markham, Nottinghamshire, NG22 0SN
☎ (01777) 872728
✉ email@pheasantrybrewery.co.uk
⊕ pheasantrybrewery.co.uk
Shop Wed-Sun 9am-5pm

Pheasantry began brewing in 2012 using a new
10-barrel plant from Canada. Situated in a listed
barn on a farm, the brewery and visitor centre
incorporates a restaurant, tearooms and bar with
the brewery visible through glass partitions.
Further beers are planned.

Best Bitter (ABV 3.8%)

Phipps NBC

See Grainstore

Phoenix SIBA 👁

Oak Brewing Co Ltd t/a Phoenix Brewery, Green Lane, Heywood, Lancashire, OL10 2EP
☎ (01706) 627009 ✉ tony@phoenixbrewery.co.uk

☺ A company established as Oak Brewery in 1982 at Ellesmere Port, it moved in 1991 to the old Phoenix Brewery and adopted the name. It now supplies 400-500 outlets with additional deliveries via wholesalers. Many seasonal beers are produced throughout the year. Restoration of the old brewery, built in 1897, is ongoing.

Hopsack (OG 1038, ABV 3.8%)
A light-drinking, hoppy session beer.

Navvy (OG 1039, ABV 3.8%) 🍺 ◆
Amber beer with a citrus fruit and malt nose. Good balance of citrus fruit, malt and hops with bitterness coming through in the aftertaste.

Monkeytown Mild (OG 1039, ABV 3.9%)
A traditional creamy dark mild.

Arizona (OG 1040, ABV 4.1%) ◆
Yellow in colour with a fruity and hoppy aroma. A refreshing beer with citrus, hops and good bitterness, and a shortish dry aftertaste.

Pale Moonlight (OG 1042, ABV 4.2%)
A dry and bitter pale ale.

Spotland Gold (OG 1041, ABV 4.4%)
A pale, hoppy beer with a lingering bitter finish.

Black Bee (OG 1045, ABV 4.5%)
Brewed with honey. Rich and creamy.

White Monk (OG 1045, ABV 4.5%) ◆
Yellow beer with a citrus fruit aroma, plenty of fruit, hops and bitterness in the taste, and a hoppy, bitter finish.

Thirsty Moon (OG 1046, ABV 4.6%) ◆
Tawny beer with a fresh citrus aroma. Hoppy, fruity and malty with a dry, hoppy finish.

West Coast IPA (OG 1046, ABV 4.6%) ◆
Golden in colour with a hoppy, fruity nose. Strong hoppy and fruity taste and aftertaste with good bitterness throughout.

Double Gold (OG 1050, ABV 5%)
A full-bodied premium bitter.

Wobbly Bob (OG 1060, ABV 6%) ◆
A red/brown beer with malty, fruity aroma and creamy mouthfeel. Strongly malty and fruity in flavour, with hops and a hint of herbs. Both sweetness and bitterness are evident throughout.

For Brunning & Price pubco:

Brunning & Price Original (ABV 3.8%)

Pictish

Pictish Brewing Co Ltd, Unit 9, Canalside Industrial Estate, Rochdale, Greater Manchester, OL16 5LB
☎ (01706) 522227 ✉ mail@pictish-brewing.co.uk
⊕ pictish-brewing.co.uk

☺ The brewery was established in 2000 by Richard Sutton and supplies 60 free trade outlets in the north-west and west Yorkshire. Seasonal beers: see website.

Brewers Gold (OG 1038, ABV 3.8%) ◆
Yellow in colour, with a hoppy, fruity nose. Soft maltiness and a strong hop/citrus flavour lead to a dry, bitter finish.

Alchemists Ale (OG 1043, ABV 4.3%) ◆
Yellow beer with generous hop and fruit on the nose and palate. Good bitter hop finish.

Pied Bull

Pied Bull Brewery, Pied Bull Hotel, 57 Northgate Street, Chester, CH1 1HQ
☎ (01244) 325829 ✉ contact@piedbull.co.uk
⊕ piedbull.co.uk

☺Pied Bull began brewing in 2011 using a one-barrel plant. Beer is mainly for in-house consumption but local beer festivals are supplied and occasional brewery swaps occur. Seasonal and special ales are also available.

Pied Eyed (OG 1040, ABV 4%)

Bull's Hit (OG 1055, ABV 4.3%)

Black Bull Porter (OG 1060, ABV 5.2%)

Pilgrim SIBA

Pilgrim Brewery, 11 West Street, Reigate, Surrey, RH2 9BL
☎ (01737) 222651
✉ pilgrimbrewery@googlemail.com ⊕ pilgrim.co.uk
Tours by arrangement

☒ Pilgrim was set up in 1982 in Woldingham, Surrey, and moved to Reigate in 1985. The original owner, Dave Roberts, is still in charge. Seasonal beers: see website.

Surrey Bitter (OG 1037, ABV 3.7%) ◆
Pineapple, grapefruit and spicy aromas in this well-balanced quaffing beer. Initial biscuity maltiness with a hint of vanilla give way to a hoppy bitterness that becomes more pronounced in a refreshing bittersweet finish.

Weald Ale (OG 1038, ABV 3.7%)

Moild (OG 1038, ABV 3.8%)

Progress (OG 1041.5, ABV 4%) ◆
A well-rounded, tawny-coloured bitter, predominantly sweet and malty with an underlying fruitiness and a hint of toffee. The flavour is balanced overall with a subdued bitterness. Little aroma and the aftertaste dissipates quickly.

Porter (OG 1042, ABV 4.1%) ◆
Black beer with a good balance of dark malts plus berry fruit flavours. Roast character present throughout to give a bitter finish.

Quest (ABV 4.3%)

Pin-Up

Pin-Up Beers Ltd, Unit 2, Rocks Farm Business Centre, Burnt Oak Road, Stone Cross, East Sussex, TN6 3SJ
☎ (01892) 611411 ✉ info@pinupbeers.com
⊕ pinupbeers.com

Pin-up began brewing in 2011. Beers were initially contract brewed at an unnamed Essex brewer, but the brewery began brewing on its own premises in 2012.

Natural Blonde (ABV 3.8%)

The Brunette (ABV 4%)

Red Head (ABV 4.2%)

Milk Stout (ABV 4.5%)

Pitfield SIBA

Pitfield Brewery, Ashlyns Farm, Epping Road, North
Weald, Epping, Essex, CM16 6RZ
☎ (01787) 282360 ☎ 07999 517231
✉ sales@pitfieldbeershop.co.uk
⊕ pitfieldbeershop.co.uk
Shop daily 10am-4pm
Tours by arrangement

⊗ After 24 years in London, Pitfield Brewery left
the capital in 2006 and moved to new premises in
Essex. It has since moved again to an organic farm
with 25 acres of organic barley for the brewery's
use. The beers are sold at farmers' and organic
markets in the south-east of England. Pitfield also
produces organic fruit wines, cider and perry. The
beers are on sale in the brewery shop (at North
Weald) but the brewery itself is located further
afield on the farm. Seasonal beers are also
available. All beers are organically produced to Soil
Association standards and are vegan-friendly. Two
further beers are produced using non-organic
ingredients under the Epping Brewery name.

Dark Mild (OG 1036, ABV 3.4%)

Bitter (OG 1036, ABV 3.7%)

Lager (OG 1036, ABV 3.7%)

Pure Gold (OG 1039, ABV 3.9%)
A golden ale, initially malty with a complex bitter
finish.

Shoreditch Stout (OG 1038, ABV 4%) ◄
Chocolate and a raisin fruitiness on the nose lead to
a fruity roast flavour and a sweetish finish with a
little bitterness.

Eco Warrior (OG 1043, ABV 4.5%) ◄
Golden ale with a vivid, citrus hop aroma. The hop
character is balanced with a delicate sweetness in
the taste, followed by an increasingly bitter finish.

Red Ale (OG 1046, ABV 4.8%) ◄
Complex beer with a full, malty body and strong
hop character.

1850 London Porter (OG 1048, ABV 5%) ◄
Big-tasting dark ale dominated by coffee and forest
fruits. The finish is dry but not acrid.

N1 Wheat Beer (OG 1048, ABV 5%)

1837 India Pale Ale (OG 1065, ABV 7%)

1792 Imperial Chocolate Stout
(OG 1070, ABV 7.3%)

For Epping Brewery:

Forest Bitter (OG 1036, ABV 3.7%)

Essex Pale Ale (ABV 4.6%)

Plain Ales SIBA

Plain Ales Brewery, Unit 17 b & c, Deverill Road
Trading Estate, Sutton Veny, Wiltshire, BA12 0LG
☎ (01985) 841481 ✉ james@plainales.co.uk
⊕ plainales.co.uk
Tours by arrangement

Plain Ales started production in 2008 on a 2.5-
barrel plant in a garage and expanded to a 10-
barrel plant at the current location in 2009. The
brewery expanded again in 2011 to a 20-barrel
plant.

Sheep Dip (ABV 3.8%)

Arty Farty (OG 1039, ABV 3.9%)

Innocence (OG 1039, ABV 4%)
A straw-coloured, fragrant bitter.

Innspiration (OG 1040, ABV 4%)

Inntrigue (ABV 4.2%)

Plassey

See New Plassey

Plockton

Plockton Brewery, 5 Bank Street, Plockton, Ross-
shire, IV52 8TP
☎ (01599) 544276
✉ andy@theplocktonbrewery.com
⊕ theplocktonbrewery.com
Tours by arrangement

The brewery started trading in 2007 and expanded
to a 2.5-barrel plant in 2009. Bottle-conditioned
beers are available and are suitable for
vegetarians.

Ciste Dhubh (OG 1040, ABV 3.9%) ◄
Excellent mix of malts and hops in this dark brew.
The initial bitterness turns bittersweet.

Plockton Bay (OG 1047, ABV 4.6%) ◄
A well-balanced, tawny coloured best bitter with
plenty of hops and malt that give a bittersweet,
fruity flavour.

Plymouth (NEW) SIBA

Plymouth Beer Co, HQ Business Centre, 237 Union
Street, Stonehouse, Plymouth, Devon, PL1 3HQ
☎ (01752) 660837
✉ info@plymouthbeercompany.com
⊕ plymouthbeercompany.co.uk

Plymouth has been set up in the old Point's West
Brewery at City College by Millfields Trust as a
community brewery. The concept is to put the
profits back into local youth projects in Stonehouse.
The five-barrel plant was bought by college
lecturer Roger Pengelly from the Bitter End
Brewery in Cockermouth, Cumbria.

Fresher Ale (OG 1044, ABV 4.2%)
A light amber ale with a combination of malts
giving a refreshing taste.

Pilgrim Ale (OG 1046, ABV 4.4%)
A dark ruby ale with a twist.

Poachers SIBA

Poachers Brewery, 439 Newark Road, North
Hykeham, Lincolnshire, LN6 9SP
☎ (01522) 807404 ☎ 07954 131972
✉ george@poachersbrewery.co.uk
⊕ poachersbrewery.co.uk
Tours by arrangement

☺Brewing started in 2001 on a five-barrel plant. In
2006 it was reduced to a 2.5-barrel plant and
relocated by brewer George Batterbee to the rear
of his house. In 2011 capacity was increased back
to the original five-barrels. Regular outlets are
supplied throughout Lincolnshire and surrounding
counties; outlets further afield are supplied via
wholesalers. Seasonal and bottle-conditioned
beers are also available.

Shy Talk Bitter (OG 1037, ABV 3.7%)

Clean-tasting session beer, pale gold in colour; slightly bitter finish, dry hopped.

Pride (OG 1040, ABV 4%)
An amber bitter with a fine flavour and lingering aroma.

Bog Trotter (OG 1042, ABV 4.2%)
An amber, full-flavoured, malty beer with a bitter aftertaste.

Lincoln Best (OG 1042, ABV 4.2%)
A flowery hop-nosed, brown beer with a well-balanced but bitter taste that stays with the malt, becoming more apparent in the drying finish.

Billy Boy (OG 1044, ABV 4.4%)
A rich, full-flavoured brown beer named after the brewery dog, a Border Collie.

Imp Ale (OG 1044, ABV 4.4%)

Hykeham Gold (OG 1045, ABV 4.5%)
A cask-conditioned lager.

Monkey Hanger (OG 1045, ABV 4.5%)
A ruby red bitter with a smooth, fruity flavour balanced by bitter hops.

Jock's Trap (OG 1050, ABV 5%)
A strong, pale brown bitter; hoppy and well-balanced with a slightly dry fruit finish.

Trout Tickler (OG 1055, ABV 5.5%)
A strong ruby bitter with intense flavour and character, sweet undertones with a hint of chocolate. A rich, malty beer.

Pocket (NEW)

Pocket Brewery, La Croix, La Rue de la Croix, St Ouen, Jersey, JE3 2HA
☎ 07797 771931 ✉ jerseybeer@jerseymail.co.uk

⊗ Pocket began brewing in 2011 on a small scale. Beer is currently available at beer festivals with several beers brewed to order. There are plans to supply local outlets.

Lady Hamilton (OG 1046, ABV 4.6%)

Porter

See Outstanding

Port Mahon

See Little Ale Cart

Potbelly SIBA ⊙

Potbelly Brewery Ltd, 25-31 Durban Road, Kettering, Northamptonshire, NN16 0JA
☎ (01536) 410818 ☎ 07834 867825
✉ toni@potbelly-brewery.co.uk
⊕ potbelly-brewery.co.uk
Tours by arrangement

Potbelly started brewing in 2005 on a 10-barrel plant and supplies some 200 outlets. The brewery has won more than 30 awards for its beers in only six years of brewing. Seasonal beers: see website. Bottle-conditioned beers are also available.

Best (OG 1036.9, ABV 3.8%)
A traditional chestnut-coloured bitter.

Aisling (OG 1038.5, ABV 4.4%)

A smooth pale bitter with a good balance of hops and malt.

Beijing Black (OG 1045, ABV 4.4%)
A strong dark mild.

Pigs Do Fly (OG 1041, ABV 4.4%)
A light and golden ale.

Bellowhead (OG 1045, ABV 4.5%)
A light-coloured bitter with a citrus hoppy finish. Brewed with the help of Bellowhead, a local band.

Crazy Daze (OG 1050, ABV 5.5%)
A light golden bitter with hidden strength.

Potton SIBA ⊙

Potton Brewery Co Ltd, 10 Shannon Place, Potton, Bedfordshire, SG19 2SP
☎ (01767) 261042 ✉ info@potton-brewery.co.uk
⊕ potton-brewery.co.uk
Tours by arrangement

Set up by the late Clive Towner and Bob Hearson in 1998, it was Potton's first brewery since 1922. The brewery expanded from 20 barrels a week to 50 in 2004 and further expansion is now taking place. Around 150 outlets are supplied. Seasonal and bottle-conditioned beers are also available.

Shannon IPA (OG 1034, ABV 3.6%) 🍺
A well-balanced session bitter with good bitterness and fruity late-hop character.

Shambles Bitter (OG 1043, ABV 4.3%)
A robust pale and heavily hopped beer with a subtle dry hop character imparted by Styrian Goldings.

Village Bike (OG 1043, ABV 4.3%) ⬥
Classic English premium bitter, amber in colour, heavily late-hopped.

Prescott SIBA

Prescott Brewery LLP, Unit 1, The Bramery Business Park, Alstone Lane, Cheltenham, Gloucestershire, GL51 8HE
☎ 07526 934866 ✉ info@prescottales.co.uk
⊕ prescottales.co.uk
Tours by arrangement

Prescott started brewing in 2009 on a 10-barrel plant. Seasonal beers are available.

Hill Climb (OG 1039.5, ABV 3.8%)

Track Record (OG 1044, ABV 4.4%)

Grand Prix (OG 1050, ABV 5.2%)

Preseli

Preseli Brewery, Unit 15, The Salterns, Tenby, Pembrokeshire, SA70 8EQ
☎ 07824 512103 ✉ preseli-brewery@hotmail.com
⊕ preseli-brewery.co.uk

⊗ Preseli began brewing in 2009 on a six-barrel plant. Seasonal beers are also available.

Old Mariners (OG 1040, ABV 4%)

Baggywrinkle (OG 1045, ABV 4.5%)

Powder Monkey (OG 1045, ABV 4.5%)

Rocky Bottom (OG 1045, ABV 4.5%)

Skuttlebutt (OG 1043, ABV 4.5%)

Prestonpans

See DemonBrew

Prior's Well

Prior's Well Brewery, The Old Kennels, Clumber Park, Hardwick Village, Nottinghamshire, S80 3PB
☎ 07971 277598 ✉ priorswell@aol.com
⊕ priorswell.co.uk

⊠ A sister brewery to Maypole, it was established in early 2010 on the Clumber Park Estate. It's housed in the former estate kennels, built in 1891 for the then duchess, which were abandoned in the mid-1960s and have now been sympathetically restored by the National Trust, which owns the property. The five-barrel plant was previously used at Tydd Steam and before that Oldershaws Brewery. Natural Clumber water from the estate is used in the brewing process. Bottle-conditioned beers are planned. Seasonal beers are also available.

Gardener's Tap (OG 1037, ABV 3.8%)

Silver Chalice (OG 1040, ABV 4.1%)

Father Hawkins (OG 1044, ABV 4.5%)

Priors Gold (OG 1045, ABV 4.7%)

Prospect SIBA ◉

Prospect Brewery Ltd, Unit 11, Bradley Hall Trading Estate, Bradley Lane, Standish, Wigan, Lancashire, WN6 0XQ
☎ (01257) 421329 ✉ sales@prospectbrewery.com
⊕ prospectbrewery.com
Tours by arrangement

☺Brewing commenced in 2007 on a five-barrel plant from Bank Top Brewery. The brewery was originally situated at the top of Prospect Hill – hence the name – but moved to new premises in 2010 using a 12-barrel plant. Most of the beers are named along prospecting/mining themes. Seasonal beers are available. A brewery bar is open to the public (Thu 4-7pm; Fri 4-7.30pm). In 2012 the brewery opened the Silver Tally pub (formerly the Foresters Arms) at Shevington Moor in collaboration with Thwaites Brewery.

Silver Tally (OG 1037, ABV 3.7%)
A clean, pale golden bitter with citrus aromas and a full hop flavour with a dry bitter finish.

Whatever! (OG 1040, ABV 3.8%)
A pale bitter packed with hop flavour and aroma.

Nutty Slack (OG 1039, ABV 3.9%) ◆
Dark brown mild ale with malt and fruit in the aroma. Creamy and chocolatey on the palate, with both malt and fruit in evidence. Malty and moderately bitter finish.

Hopper (OG 1040, ABV 4%)
A pale golden beer with citrus hops and a satisfying sweet balance.

One Twenty (OG 1040, ABV 4%)
A yellow/gold beer with zesty citrus notes; clean tasting and refreshing.

Pioneer (OG 1040, ABV 4%)
A light-bodied amber beer with aromas of dry pale malt and earthy hops.

Blinding Light (OG 1042, ABV 4.2%)
A pale refreshing beer with citrus and spicy notes.

Gold Rush (OG 1045, ABV 4.5%)
A deep golden ale with hoppy and bitter flavours, light fruity notes and a grassy, floral finish.

Big John (OG 1047, ABV 4.8%)
A dark stout bursting with smoky liquorice flavour with a satisfying bitter aftertaste.

Purity SIBA ◉

Purity Brewing Co Ltd, The Brewery, Upper Spernall Farm, Great Alne, Warwickshire, B49 6JF
☎ (01789) 488007 ✉ sales@puritybrewing.com
⊕ puritybrewing.com
Shop Mon-Fri 8am-5pm; Sat 10am-1pm
Tours by arrangement

☺ Brewing began in 2005 in a purpose-designed plant housed in converted barns in the heart of Warwickshire. The brewery incorporates an environmentally-friendly effluent treatment system. It supplies the free trade within a 70-mile radius and delivers to more than 500 outlets. It also has contracts with a number of leased and tenanted groups and major retailers.

Pure Gold (OG 1039.5, ABV 3.8%) ▮
An easy-drinking beer with a dry, bitter finish.

Mad Goose (OG 1042.5, ABV 4.2%)
Light copper in colour with a zesty hop character and citrus overtones.

Pure Ubu (OG 1044.8, ABV 4.5%)
An amber-coloured beer, well-balanced and full-flavoured.

Purple Moose SIBA ◉

Bragdy Mws Piws Cyf/Purple Moose Brewery Ltd, Madoc Street, Porthmadog, Gwynedd, LL49 9DB
☎ (01766) 515571 ✉ beer@purplemoose.co.uk
⊕ purplemoose.co.uk
Shop Mon-Fri 9am-5pm
Tours by arrangement

A 10-barrel plant opened in 2005 by Lawrence Washington in a former saw mill and farmers' warehouse in the coastal town of Porthmadog. The names of the beers reflect local history and geography. The brewery now supplies around 250 outlets. Seasonal and monthly special beers: see website.

Cwrw Eryri/Snowdonia Ale
(OG 1035.3, ABV 3.6%) 🍴 ▮ ◆
Golden, refreshing bitter with citrus fruit hoppiness in aroma and taste. The full mouthfeel leads to a long-lasting, dry, bitter finish.

Cwrw Madog/Madog's Ale
(OG 1037, ABV 3.7%) ◆
Full-bodied session bitter. Malty nose and an initial nutty flavour but bitterness dominates. Well balanced and refreshing with a dry roastiness on the taste and a good dry finish.

Cwrw Glaslyn/Glaslyn Ale
(OG 1040.5, ABV 4.2%) 🍴 ▮ ◆
Refreshing light and malty amber-coloured ale. Plenty of hop in the aroma and taste. Good smooth mouthfeel leading to a slightly chewy finish.

Ochr Tywyll y Mws/Dark Side of the Moose
(OG 1045, ABV 4.6%)
A delicious dark ale with a deep malt flavour and a fruity bitterness.

Quantock SIBA 👁

Quantock Brewery, Unit E, Monument View, Summerfield Avenue, Chelston Business Park, Wellington, Somerset, TA21 9ND
☎ (01823) 662669 ✉ rob@quantockbrewery.co.uk
🌐 quantockbrewery.co.uk

Quantock is a family-run microbrewery that began in 2008 using an eight-barrel plant. The philosophy is to brew using traditional craft brewing techniques with natural ingredients sourced locally where possible. Seasonal and bottle-conditioned beers are available. The brewery supplies pubs throughout Somerset and Devon and further afield via wholesalers.

Ale (OG 1036, ABV 3.8%)
An amber-coloured beer with a fruity, full-bodied flavour and dry finish to the palate.

Sunraker (OG 1039, ABV 4.2%)

Wills Neck (OG 1040, ABV 4.3%)
A bright golden ale with a rich, malty flavour. Late-hopped to produce a prominent aroma with hints of grapefruit and cherries and a lasting bitterness on the palate.

Stout (OG 1044, ABV 4.5%)
A full-bodied, traditional dry stout, dark ebony in colour. The blend of hops gives an aroma of liquorice and citrus fruits.

White Hind (OG 1042, ABV 4.5%)
A chestnut-coloured best bitter with a full-bodied, malty flavour with the roast malt coming through to a dry finish. Generously hopped to produce a biscuity, spicy aroma.

Royal Stag IPA (OG 1056, ABV 6%)
Copper-coloured with a malty and fruity flavour, giving a smoky aroma with hints of banana and toffee.

UXB (OG 1088, ABV 9%)
A seriously strong beer, slightly sweet with a full malty flavour.

Quantum

Quantum Brewery, Unit 4, Victoria Works, Hempshaw Lane, Stockport, Greater Manchester, SK1 4LG
☎ 07976 032465
✉ contact@quantumbrewingcompany.co.uk
🌐 quantumbrewingcompany.co.uk

The brewery was established in 2011 using a five-barrel plant on the site of the former Shaws Brewery. A number of seasonal beers, one-offs and specials are brewed: see website. Bottle-conditioned beers are also available.

Bitter (ABV 3.8%)
A dry-hopped amber session bitter.

Pale Ale (ABV 4.5%)

Stout (ABV 4.8%)
A black beer with masses of mocha flavours and a thick mouthfeel.

American Amber Ale (ABV 5.3%)

Quartz SIBA 👁

Quartz Brewing Ltd, Archers, Alrewas Road, Kings Bromley, Staffordshire, DE13 7HW
☎ (01543) 473965 ✉ scott@quartzbrewing.co.uk
🌐 quartzbrewing.co.uk

Shop Mon, Wed & Fri 9.30am-4.30pm; Sat 10am-1.30pm
Tours by arrangement

👁 Quartz was established in 2005 by Scott and Julia Barnett. There are four regular beers produced in cask, bottle and mini-cask, supplemented with seasonal specials. Around 50 outlets are supplied direct.

Blonde (OG 1038, ABV 3.8%) 🍺
Little aroma, gentle hop and background malt. Sweet with unsophisticated sweetshop tastes.

Crystal (OG 1040, ABV 4.2%) 🍺
Sweet aroma with some fruit and yeasty Marmite hints. Hoppiness begins but dwindles to a bittersweet finish.

Extra Blonde (OG 1042, ABV 4.4%) 🍺
Sweet malty aroma with a touch of fruit. Sweet start, smooth with a hint of hops in the sugary finish.

Heart (OG 1045, ABV 4.6%) 🍺
Pale brown with some aroma of fruit and malt. Gentle tastes of fruit and hops eventually clear to leave a bitter finish.

Quay

See Dorset

Quercus SIBA

Quercus Brewery & Beer House, Unit 2M, South Hams Business Park, Churchstow, Kingsbridge, Devon, TQ7 3QH
☎ (01548) 854888 ✉ info@quercusdevonales.com
🌐 quercusdevonales.com
Shop Fri 10am-5pm, Sat 10am-3pm (winter Fri & Sat 10am-5pm)

Quercus began trading in 2007 using an eight-barrel brew plant. The brewery was sold in 2011 to Mike George and Mike Tiner. The Kings Arms Hotel in Kingsbridge is a local outlet for the beers. Seasonal beers: see website.

Origin (OG 1039, ABV 3.9%)
A smooth, easy-drinking amber ale with the sweetness of the malt balanced by the refreshing aroma and taste of Fuggles hops.

Prospect (OG 1039, ABV 4%)
Subtle bitterness and sweet malt flavour with a rich aroma and colour.

Shingle Bay (OG 1041, ABV 4.2%)
A light, golden, easy-drinking ale with fruity citrus aroma and taste giving a subtle, crisp bite to refresh the palate.

QB (Quercus Bitter) (OG 1044, ABV 4.5%)
A full-bodied best bitter with a hint of oak-smoked aroma and taste.

Ramsbury SIBA

Ramsbury Brewery, Stockclose Farm, Mildenhall, Wiltshire, SN8 2NN
☎ (01672) 541407
✉ dgolding@ramsburyestates.com
🌐 ramsburybrewery.com
Shop Mon-Fri 8am-4.30pm
Tours by arrangement

⊗ Ramsbury started brewing in 2004 and is situated high on the Marlborough Downs in Wiltshire. The brewery uses home-grown barley from the Ramsbury Estate. At present a 10-barrel plant is used but there are plans to increase capacity and build a visitor centre and distillery.

Bitter (OG 1036, ABV 3.6%)
Amber-coloured beer with a smooth, delicate aroma and flavour.

Kennet Valley (OG 1040, ABV 4.1%)
A light amber, hoppy bitter with a long, dry finish.

Flint Knapper (OG 1042, ABV 4.2%)
Rich amber in colour with a malty taste.

Gold (OG 1045, ABV 4.5%)
A rich golden-coloured beer with a light hoppy aroma and taste.

Chalk Stream (OG 1050, ABV 5%)

Rum Truffle (OG 1056, ABV 5.6%)

Ramsgate SIBA ◉

Ramsgate Brewery Ltd, Unit 1, Hornet Close, Pyson's Road Industrial Estate, Broadstairs, Kent, CT10 2YD
☎ (01843) 868453 ✉ beer@ramsgatebrewery.co.uk
⊕ ramsgatebrewery.co.uk
Shop Mon-Fri 10am-5pm; Sat 10am-1pm
Tours by arrangement

⊗ Ramsgate was established in 2002 at the back of a Ramsgate pub. In 2006 the brewery moved to its current location, allowing for increased capacity and bottling. Bottle-conditioned beers are available. Seasonal and monthly specials: see website.

Gadds' No. 7 (OG 1037, ABV 3.8%)

Gadds' Seasider (OG 1042, ABV 4.3%)

Gadds' No. 5 (OG 1043, ABV 4.4%)

Gadds' No. 3 (OG 1047, ABV 5%)

Gadds' Dogbolter (OG 1054, ABV 5.6%)

Randalls SIBA

RW Randall Ltd, La Piette Brewery, St Georges Esplanade, St Peter Port, Guernsey, GY1 2BH
☎ (01481) 720134 ✉ tours@rwrandall.co.uk
⊕ randallsbrewery.co.uk
Tours by arrangement

Randalls has been brewing since 1868 and is the only brewery operating in the Bailiwick of Guernsey. A new 36-barrel brewhouse was installed in 2008. 18 pubs are owned and a further 50 outlets are supplied.

Golden Guernsey Ale (OG 1041, ABV 3.9%)

Patois Best Bitter (OG 1045, ABV 4.5%)

Hanois Island Stout (OG 1055, ABV 5.1%)

Rat (NEW)

☷ **Rat Brewery, 40 Chapel Hill, Huddersfield, West Yorkshire, HD1 3EB**
☎ (01484) 542400 ☎ 07906 279038
✉ ratandratchet@ossett-brewery.co.uk

The Rat & Ratchet was originally established as a brew pub in 1994, but brewing ceased before it was purchased by the Ossett Brewery in 2004.

Brewing started again in 2011 with an initial capacity of 18 barrels per week. All beers have a rat-themed name. Occasional beers are also produced.

Dirty Rat (OG 1038, ABV 3.5%)
A velvety dark brown mild. Low bitterness with a sweet, malty finish.

Brown Rat (OG 1040, ABV 3.8%)
A traditional malty ale. Bitterness is moderate while English hops give a fruity/spicy hop aroma.

Golden Rat (OG 1038, ABV 3.8%)
This golden, easy-drinking session bitter has a slightly sweet maltiness. However, due to a generous addition of hops throughout the boil, bitterness and spicy hop aromas dominate.

White Rat (OG 1040, ABV 4%)
A pale, hoppy ale with an intensely aromatic and resinous finish.

Rattus Rattus (OG 1045, ABV 4.3%)
A hazy wheat beer with flavours of bananas and cloves. Fresh coriander gives a herbal, spicy aroma.

Black Rat (OG 1047, ABV 4.5%)
A porter with coffee and chocolate malt character. Slightly sweet on the palate but with moderate bitterness and a fruity/spicy aroma.

King Rat (OG 1050, ABV 5%)
A bitter beer balanced by a residual malty sweetness.

Raw SIBA

Raw Brewing Co Ltd, Units 3 & 4, Silver House, Adelphi Way, Staveley, Derbyshire, S43 3LJ
☎ (01246) 475445 ✉ contact@rawbrew.com
⊕ rawbrew.com
Tours by arrangement

Raw began brewing in 2010 using a five-barrel plant from Prospect Brewery of Wigan. Three core beers are available with plans to extend the range and produce seasonal specials.

Blonde Pale (OG 1039, ABV 3.9%)

JR Best (OG 1042, ABV 4.2%)

Dark Peak (OG 1045, ABV 4.5%)

Edge Pale (OG 1045, ABV 4.5%)

Anubis (OG 1051, ABV 5.2%)

Grey Ghost (OG 1056, ABV 5.9%)

RCH SIBA ◉

RCH Brewery, West Hewish, Weston-Super-Mare, Somerset, BS24 6RR
☎ (01934) 834447 ✉ rchbrew@aol.com
⊕ rchbrewery.com

⊗ The brewery was originally installed in the early 1980s behind the Royal Clarence Hotel at Burnham-on-Sea. Since 1993 brewing has taken place in a former cider mill at West Hewish. A 30-barrel plant was installed in 2000. RCH supplies 150 outlets and the award-winning beers are available nationwide through its own wholesaling company, which also distributes beers from other small independent breweries. Seasonal and bottle-conditioned beers are also available.

Hewish IPA (OG 1036, ABV 3.6%) ◆

Light, hoppy bitter with some malt and fruit, though slightly less fruit in the finish. Floral citrus hop aroma; pale brown/amber colour.

Hewish Mild (ABV 3.6%)

PG Steam (OG 1039, ABV 3.9%) 🍺 ◆
Powerful hop and malt flavour with just a hint of fruit. Bitter aftertaste with the merest suggestion of roast.

Pitchfork (OG 1043, ABV 4.3%) ◆
Yellow best bitter with a citrus hop aroma with pale malt. Hops predominate in a taste whose underlying sweetness becomes slightly astringent before ending with bitter hops.

Old Slug Porter (OG 1046, ABV 4.5%) ◆
Smoky, roast malt and hops with lots of body and dark fruit. Complex, dark-brown slightly sour porter. Sweetness fades leaving a smoky, bitter-sour aftertaste.

East Street Cream (OG 1050, ABV 5%) ◆
Robust tawny-coloured strong bitter. Sweet-and-sour fruit flavours fill the mouth, some balancing hop leading to a slightly astringent finish.

Double Header (OG 1053, ABV 5.3%) ◆
Light brown, full-bodied strong bitter. Nicely balanced flavours of malt, hops and tropical fruits are followed by a long, bittersweet finish. Refreshing and easy-drinking for its strength.

Firebox (OG 1060, ABV 6%) ◆
Full-bodied pale-brown strong bitter; faint aroma of malt and hops with banana notes. Sweet malt and fruit in the mouth soon turn to a bitter astringency; bittersweet aftertaste.

Reality

Reality Brewery, 127 High Road, Chilwell, Nottingham, NG9 4AT
☎ 07801 539523

Reality began brewing in 2010 in the unused space of an IT business. Its relation to this and real ale formed the name. The brewery relocated to nearby premises in 2011 and fermentation capacity was increased. Beers are usually themed around the brewery name.

Virtuale (OG 1039, ABV 3.8%)

No Escape (OG 1043, ABV 4.2%)

Bitter (OG 1044, ABV 4.3%)

Stark (OG 1046, ABV 4.5%)

Czech (OG 1047, ABV 4.6%)

Rebel (NEW) SIBA

Rebel Brewing Co, West End Industrial Estate, Penryn, Cornwall, TR10 8RT
☎ (01326) 378517 ✉ rebelbrewing@hotmail.co.uk
Shop Mon-Sat 10am-6pm
Tours by arrangement

⊗ Rebel began brewing in 2011. In 2012 expansion to a 15-barrel plant with a visitor centre, shop and museum was undertaken.

Barrowboys Bitter (OG 1041, ABV 4%) ◆
Tawny session ale with faint aroma of malt and fruit. Hop bitterness dominates the palate, balanced by malt and sweetness. Malt fades in the finish, leaving a crisp bitterness.

Cornish Sunset Golden Ale (OG 1041, ABV 4%)

An Gwella Best Bitter (OG 1047, ABV 4.8%)

80 Shilling Scotch Ale (OG 1049, ABV 5%)
Dark, malty and sweet.

Rebellion SIBA

Rebellion Beer Co, Marlow Brewery, Bencombe Farm, Marlow Bottom, Buckinghamshire, SL7 3LT
☎ (01628) 476594 ✉ info@rebellionbeer.co.uk
🌐 rebellionbeer.co.uk
Shop Mon-Fri 8am-6pm; Sat 9am-6pm
Tours by arrangement

⊗ Established in 1993, Rebellion filled the void left when Wethereds ceased brewing in 1987 in Marlow. Steady growth led to larger premises being sought and a relocation in 1999. Rebellion's nearby Three Horseshoes pub is the brewery tap. Rebellion Mild is only available in this pub and a few other locals. Around 500 other outlets are supplied. Seasonal beers: see website. Bottle-conditioned beer is also available.

IPA (OG 1039, ABV 3.7%) ◆
Copper-coloured bitter, sweet and malty, with resinous and red apple flavours. Caramel and fruit decline to leave a dry, bitter and malty finish.

Smuggler (OG 1042, ABV 4.1%) ◆
A red-brown beer, well-bodied and bitter with an uncompromisingly dry, bitter finish.

Mutiny (OG 1046, ABV 4.5%) ◆
Tawny in colour, this full-bodied best bitter is predominantly fruity and moderately bitter with crystal malt continuing to a dry finish.

Rectory SIBA

Rectory Ales Ltd, Streat Hill Farm, Streat Hill, Streat, Hassocks, East Sussex, BN6 8RP
☎ (01273) 890570 ✉ rectoryales@hotmail.com
Tours by arrangement (Easter-Sep)

⊗ Rectory was founded in 1995 by the Rector of Plumpton, the Rev Godfrey Broster, to generate funds for the maintenance of his three parish churches. 107 parishioners are shareholders. The brewing capacity is now 20 barrels a week. All outlets are supplied from the brewery. A different seasonal beer is produced each month – please ring for details.

All Saints Tipple (OG 1041, ABV 4.1%)
A traditional bitter, mid-brown in colour.

Red (NEW) SIBA

Red Brewery Co, Unit 1, The Orchard, Garden Farm, The Town, Great Staughton, Cambridgeshire, PE19 5BE
☎ 07827 294229 ✉ john.kearney@redbrewery.com
🌐 redbrewery.com

Red Brewery was established in 2012 in a converted farm building in the village of Great Staughton. A four-barrel plant is used.

Georgic's Pebble (OG 1035, ABV 3.5%)
A dark mild, lightly hopped, with blackcurrant and chocolate notes.

All Saints Ale (OG 1043, ABV 4%)
A garnet-coloured ale. Well-balanced with a fruity taste with blackcurrant flavours.

Staughton Bitter (OG 1040, ABV 4%)

A copper-coloured session bitter with a light, fruity taste and a pleasing hop balance.

Sundial Gold (OG 1044, ABV 4%)
An amber ale with a deep, hoppy character and citrus notes on the palate.

Redchurch (NEW)

Redchurch Brewery, 273 Poyser Street, Bethnal Green, London, E2 9RF
☎ 07968 173097
✉ enquiries@theredchurchbrewery.com
⊕ theredchurchbrewery.com

Redchurch was established in 2011 by Gary Ward using an eight-barrel plant and is situated in a unit under the railway arches in Bethnal Green. Beer is primarily bottle-conditioned but occasional casks are produced for festivals; Hackney Gold (ABV 4.5%), Hoxton Stout (ABV 5.5%), Bethnal Pale Ale (ABV 5.5%), Shoreditch Blonde (ABV 6%), Great Eastern IPA (ABV 7.4%).

Redemption SIBA

Redemption Brewing Co Ltd, Unit 2, Compass West Industrial Estate, 33 West Road, Tottenham, London, N17 0XL
☎ (020) 8885 5227 ☎ 07919 416046
✉ andy.moffat@redemptionbrewing.co.uk
⊕ redemptionbrewing.co.uk
Tours by arrangement for local organisations and CAMRA groups

⊗ Redemption began brewing in 2010 on a 12-barrel plant. Most of the beer is supplied to pubs in north and central London.

Pale Ale (OG 1037.5, ABV 3.8%) ◄
A well-balanced, amber bitter with hops and citrus orange throughout. The sweet maltiness fades in the aftertaste leaving a slightly dry bitter finish. Orange and peach on the nose.

Hopspur (OG 1044.5, ABV 4.5%) ◄
Hoppy bitter notes are present in this tawny brown best bitter, which has a hint of coffee roast throughout and some caramelised citrus notes.

Urban Dusk (OG 1044, ABV 4.6%) ◄
Full-bodied brown best bitter; chocolate and some toffee in the aroma. Citrus, creamy fudge and dark roast chocolate on the palate, drying to leave a slightly dry bitter finish.

Friendship Porter (OG 1052.5, ABV 5.1%) ◄
Sweetish, smooth porter with a mix of liquorice, caramel and roast notes. A pleasant burnt roast gives dry bitter overtones.

Red Fox SIBA

Red Fox Brewery Ltd, The Chicken Sheds, Upp Hall Farm, Salmons Lane, Coggeshall, Essex, CO6 1RY
☎ (01376) 563123 ✉ info@redfoxbrewery.co.uk
⊕ redfoxbrewery.co.uk
Tours by arrangement

Red Fox began brewing in 2008 using a five-barrel plant and has continued to grow in line with increasing demand. Around 35 outlets are supplied direct. Bottle-conditioned beer is available as are seasonal and one-off beers.

Mild (OG 1037, ABV 3.6%)
A dark, full-flavoured mild with hints of chocolate and a deep roast barley flavour.

IPA (OG 1038, ABV 3.7%)
A copper-coloured beer with a delicate flavour.

Bitter (OG 1039, ABV 3.8%)
A traditional-style bitter with well-balanced malt and fruit flavours.

Hunter's Gold (OG 1040, ABV 3.9%)
A golden beer with a delicate citrus aroma.

Coggeshall Gold (OG 1044, ABV 4%)
An aromatic golden beer packed full of citrus and exotic fruit flavours. Unusually for a beer of this style it does not have a bitter finish.

Black Fox Porter (OG 1046, ABV 4.8%)
A rich-flavoured black beer packed with malty flavour and undertones of chocolate.

Wily Ol' Fox (OG 1050, ABV 5.2%)
An aromatic amber beer with a soft, fruity palate.

Red Rat

Red Rat Craft Brewery, Pickering, North Yorkshire

Red Rat started brewing in 2007. The brewery moved to Pickering, North Yorkshire, in the summer of 2012. Contact details were not known at time of going to press.

Crazy Dog Blonde (ABV 4%)

Hadley's (ABV 4.2%)

Hot Stuff Chilli Beer (ABV 4.3%)

Crazy Dog IPA (ABV 5%)

Hadley's Gold (ABV 5%)

The Same Again (ABV 5.2%)

Crazy Dog Stout (ABV 6%)

Jimmy's Flying Pig (ABV 6%)

Jimmy's Large Black Pig (ABV 6%)

Red Rock SIBA

Red Rock Brewery Ltd, Higher Humber Farm, Bishopsteignton, Devon, TQ14 9TD
☎ (01626) 879738 ☎ 07894 035094
✉ john@redrockbrewery.co.uk
⊕ redrockbrewery.co.uk
Shop Mon-Fri 9am-4pm (phone for weekend hours)
Tours by arrangement

Red Rock first started brewing in 2006 with a four-barrel plant and upgraded in 2011 to a 7.5-barrel one. It is based in a converted barn on a working farm using locally-sourced malt, fresh hops and the farm's own spring water. Bottle-conditioned and seasonal beers are also available. The brewery now has a bar, a shop and is able to accommodate private functions.

Red Rock (OG 1041, ABV 4.2%)

Redscar SIBA

🏳 **Redscar Brewery Ltd, c/o The Cleveland Hotel, 9-11 High Street West, Redcar, TS10 1SQ**
☎ 07528 557661 ✉ chris.appleby@ntlworld.com
⊕ redscar-brewery.co.uk
Tours by arrangement

⊕Redscar first brewed in 2008 on a 2.5-barrel plant. The brewery supplies the hotel, local pubs and beer festivals. Occasional specials and seasonal beers are also brewed.

Jazz (OG 1042, ABV 3.8%)

Sands (OG 1042, ABV 3.8%)

Poison (OG 1043, ABV 4%)

Rocks (OG 1042, ABV 4%)

Pier (OG 1045, ABV 4.5%)

Beach (OG 1050, ABV 5%)

Red Shoot

Red Shoot Inn & Brewery, Toms Lane, Linwood, Ringwood, Hampshire, BH24 3QT
☎ (01425) 475792 ✉ redshoot@wadworth.co.uk
⊕ redshoot.co.uk

⊗ The 2.5-barrel brewery was commissioned in 1998. In summer the brewery works to capacity, half the output going to the pub and half to other local outlets, being distributed by Wadworth. There is a part-time brewer, John Sherwood, and the whole process is directed and monitored very closely by Wadworth.

New Forest Gold (ABV 3.8%)

Red, White & Brew (ABV 4%)

Muddy Boot (ABV 4.2%)

Tom's Tipple (ABV 4.8%)

Red Squirrel SIBA ◉

Red Squirrel Brewery Ltd, Unit 24, Boxted Farm, Berkhamsted Road, Potten End, Hertfordshire, HP1 2SQ
☎ (01442) 256970
✉ sales@cellarmasterwines.co.uk
⊕ redsquirrelbrewery.co.uk

⊗ Red Squirrel started brewing in Hertford in 2004 using a 10-barrel plant. In 2011, after a merger with Cellarmaster Wines, it moved to new premises near Hemel Hempstead. There are currently seven core beers complemented by seasonal brews and occasional specials.

Red Tail (OG 1036, ABV 3.6%)
A pale, crisp beer balanced with floral and citrus notes.

Red Dawn (OG 1038, ABV 3.7%)
Dark red in colour, moreish and satisfying with mellow and nutty overtones and a smooth, rounded palate.

Hopfest (OG 1037, ABV 3.8%)
Pale, golden ale with a floral/citrus aroma and elderflower notes.

RSX (OG 1037, ABV 3.9%)
A chestnut-coloured ale showing succulent dried fruit and hoppy aromas.

Conservation Bitter (OG 1040, ABV 4.1%)
A chestnut-brown traditional bitter with a hoppy, fruity bitterness and satisfying biscuit flavours with hints of spice and chocolate.

London Porter (OG 1048, ABV 5%) 🍷
Dark brown/black in colour with a good balance of chocolate and roasted barley. Full-bodied on the palate with bittersweet liquorice and rich chocolate flavours.

Redwood American IPA (OG 1051, ABV 5.4%)
Based on a secret Michigan recipe. Golden orange in colour with complex hoppy aromas, floral and citrus tones and a long, lingering finish.

RedWillow SIBA

RedWillow Brewery Ltd, Sutton Mill, Gunco Lane, Macclesfield, Cheshire, SK11 7JL
☎ (01625) 502315 ✉ sales@redwillowbrewery.com
⊕ redwillowbrewery.com

⊛ RedWillow began brewing in 2010 from a unit within Sutton Mill 100 yards from the site of Stancliffe's Sutton Brewery which, when it closed in 1920, was one of the biggest breweries in Macclesfield. Beers are distributed across the north-west and into Yorkshire. Additional fermenting vessels are expected to double capacity and allow more opportunity for owner and brewer Toby McKenzie's popular experimental beers. Bottle-conditioned beers are available.

Headless (OG 1038, ABV 3.9%)

Feckless (OG 1041, ABV 4.1%)

Directionless (OG 1041, ABV 4.2%)

Wreckless (OG 1046, ABV 4.8%)

Smokeless (OG 1055, ABV 5.7%)

Ageless (OG 1067, ABV 7.2%)

Reedley Hallows (NEW) SIBA

Reedley Hallows Brewing Co, Unit 12, Farrington Court, Burnley, Lancashire, BB11 5SS
☎ 07749 414513 ✉ info@reedley-hallows-brewery.co.uk ⊕ reedley-hallows-brewery.co.uk

Brewing began in 2012 using a five-barrel plant.

Old Laund Bitter (ABV 3.6%)
A session beer, smooth and creamy with a distinctive hoppy aftertaste.

Filly Close Blonde (ABV 3.9%)
A well-balanced ale, fruity and bitter with a spicy finish.

Monkholme Premium (ABV 4.3%)
A premium golden ale with a hoppy taste throughout.

Revolutions SIBA

Revolutions Brewing Co Ltd, Unit B7, Whitwood Enterprise Park, Speedwell Road, Whitwood, Castleford, West Yorkshire, WF10 5PX
☎ (01977) 552649
✉ info@revolutionsbrewing.co.uk
⊕ revolutionsbrewing.co.uk
Tours by arrangement

Revolutions began brewing in 2010 and moved to its own premises in 2011. Beers are inspired by and pay homage to music from the analogue era and are typically brewed to 3.3%, 4.5% and 7.8%, to reflect the speeds at which music used to revolve (33, 45 and 78 rpm). The brewery produces a monthly 4.5% special referencing music from 33 years ago as part of the 'Rewind 33' series.

Beat Red (OG 1044, ABV 4.5%)
A red ale with a big late-hop addition. Medium levels of bitterness give a refreshing, hoppy finish.

Clash London Porter (OG 1045, ABV 4.5%)
A complex dark malty beer rounded off with a smooth hop finish.

Devolution Amber Ale (OG 1043, ABV 4.5%)
A classic American-style amber ale, rich gold in colour.

Kraftwerk Braun Ale (OG 1044, ABV 4.5%)
A brown-coloured beer with a balanced malt and hop character.

Rhymney SIBA 👁

Rhymney Brewery Ltd, Gilchrist Thomas Industrial Estate, Blaenavon, NP4 9RL
☎ (01685) 722253
✉ enquiries@rhymneybreweryltd.com
🌐 rhymneybreweryltd.com
Tours by arrangement

☺ Rhymney first brewed in 2005. The 75-hl plant, sourced from Canada, is capable of producing both cask and keg beers. Around 220 outlets are supplied. In 2012 the brewery relocated to Blaenavon with a new brewing centre and visitor facility.

Best (OG 1037, ABV 3.7%)

Hobby Horse (OG 1038, ABV 3.8%)

Dark (OG 1040, ABV 4%) 🍴

Bevans Bitter (OG 1042, ABV 4.2%)

Bitter (OG 1043, ABV 4.3%)

General Picton (OG 1043, ABV 4.3%)

Export Ale (OG 1050, ABV 5%) 🍴 🍴

Richmond

Richmond Brewing Co Ltd, The Station Brewery, Station Yard, Richmond, North Yorkshire, DL10 4LD
☎ (01748) 828266 ✉ andy@richmondbrewing.co.uk
🌐 richmondbrewing.co.uk
Shop Tue-Sun 12-4pm (may be open outside these hours)
Tours by arrangement

☺Richmond opened in 2008 in the redeveloped Victorian station complex beside the River Swale. The brewery concentrates on bottled ales (some bottle conditioned) with around 20% of output being cask conditioned and available in the local area (often in the Ralph Fitz Randal in Richmond).

SwAle (OG 1035, ABV 3.7%)
A dark mild brewed using chocolate malt with slightly more bitterness than a traditional mild.

Station Ale (OG 1039, ABV 4%)

Happiness (OG 1039, ABV 4.2%)

Pale Ale (OG 1044, ABV 4.6%)

Ridgeside SIBA

Ridgeside Brewing Co Ltd, Unit 24, Penraevon 2 Industrial Estate, Meanwood, Leeds, West Yorkshire, LS7 2AW
☎ 07595 380568
✉ simon.bolderson@ridgesidebrewery.co.uk
🌐 ridgesidebrewery.co.uk
Tours by arrangement

☺Ridgeside began brewing in 2010 using a four-barrel plant. Seasonal special beers are produced each month. Regular outlets are supplied in the Leeds area and beyond.

Jailbreak (OG 1038, ABV 3.8%)

Cascade (OG 1041, ABV 4.1%)

Snakecharmer (OG 1041, ABV 4.1%)

Rushmore (OG 1043, ABV 4.3%) 🍴

Generous hops and citrus fruit take this smooth, golden ale right through from initial aroma to the long, dry finish. Bittersweet and refreshing.

Best (OG 1045, ABV 4.5%)

Desert Aire (OG 1048, ABV 4.8%)

Stargazer (OG 1049, ABV 4.9%)

Black Night (OG 1050, ABV 5%) 🍴
Smooth and dark with an intriguing smoked malt, bitter coffee flavour and a smoky aftertaste with a hint of hop in the strong bitterness.

Eliminator (OG 1060, ABV 6%)

Ridgeway

Ridgeway Brewing, Beer Counter Ltd, South Stoke, Oxfordshire, RG8 0JW
☎ (01491) 873474
✉ peter.scholey@beercounter.co.uk

Ridgeway was set up by ex-Brakspear head brewer Peter Scholey. It specialises in bottle-conditioned beers but equivalent cask beers are also available (usually only available in South Oxfordshire). At present Ridgeway beers are brewed by Peter using his own ingredients on the plants at Hepworth's of Horsham (qv) and Cotswold Brewery (qv). All beers listed are available cask and bottle-conditioned. Bottle-conditioned Christmas beers are produced annually, principally for export to the U.S.

Bitter (OG 1040, ABV 4%)

Organic Beer/ROB (OG 1043, ABV 4.3%)

Ivanhoe (OG 1050, ABV 5.2%)

IPA (OG 1055, ABV 5.5%)

For Coniston Brewing:

Bluebird (ABV 4.2%)

XB (ABV 4.4%)

Old Man (ABV 4.8%)

Ridleys

See Greene King in New Nationals section

Ringmore

Ringmore Craft Brewery Ltd, Higher Ringmore Road, Shaldon, Devon, TQ14 0HG
☎ (01626) 873114
✉ geoff@ringmorecraftbrewery.co.uk

☺Ringmore was established in 2007 on a one-barrel plant and is the first brewery in Shaldon since 1920. It expanded to a 2.5-barrel plant in 2009 to keep up with demand. Bottle-conditioned beers are also available, including seasonals.

Oarsome Ale (OG 1046, ABV 4.6%)

Ringwood

See Marston's in New Nationals section

Ripple Steam (NEW) SIBA

Ripple Steam Brewery Ltd, Parsonage Farm, Vale Road, Sutton, Kent, CT15 5DH

☎ 07917 037611
✉ wheresmyale@ripplesteambrewery.co.uk
⊕ ripplesteambrewery.co.uk

Ripple Steam began brewing commercially in 2012. Seasonal beers: see website.

Milk Stout (ABV 3.5%)

Best Bitter (ABV 4.1%)

IPA (ABV 4.5%)

Riverhead

▤ Riverhead Brewery Ltd, 2 Peel Street, Marsden, Huddersfield, West Yorkshire, HD7 6BR
☎ (01484) 841270 (Pub) ☎ (01924) 261333 (Brewery) ✉ brewery@ossett-brewery.co.uk
⊕ ossett-brewery.co.uk
Tours by arrangement (through Ossett Brewing Co)

☺ Riverhead is a brew-pub that opened in 1995 after conversion from an old grocery shop. Ossett Brewing Co purchased the site in 2006 but runs it as a separate brewery. It has since opened The Dining Room on the first floor, which uses Riverhead beers in its dishes. All original recipes have been retained with new beers also being added. The core range of beers are named after local reservoirs, with the height of the reservoir relating to the strength of the beer. There are many rotating beers produced as well as seasonals.

Sparth Mild (ABV 3.6%)

Butterley Bitter (OG 1038, ABV 3.8%) ◖
A dry, amber-coloured, hoppy session beer.

March Haigh (OG 1046, ABV 4.6%)
A golden-brown premium bitter. Malty and full-bodied with moderate bitterness.

Redbrook Premium (ABV 5.5%)

River Leven (NEW)

R.J. Heskey t/a River Leven Ales, Lab Road, Kinlochleven, PH50 4SG
☎ 07901 873773 ✉ info@riverlevenales.co.uk
⊕ riverlevenales.co.uk

River Leven was established in 2011 in a former aluminium factory building in Kinlochleven. Only pure malt cask-conditioned ale is produced.

Blonde (OG 1040, ABV 4%)

Dark (OG 1040, ABV 4%)

Traditional IPA (OG 1040, ABV 4%)

Riverside

Riverside Brewery, Bee's Farm, Wainfleet, Lincolnshire, PE24 4LX
☎ (01754) 881288 ☎ 07779 280996

☺ Riverside started brewing in 2003 using a five-barrel plant. In 2008 the brewery moved to its present site where around eight barrels a week are produced, with some 15-20 outlets supplied. Seasonal beers are also available.

Dixon's Major (OG 1038, ABV 3.9%)

Dixon's Old Diabolical (OG 1043, ABV 4.4%)

John Roberts

See Three Tuns

Robinson's IFBB 👁

Frederic Robinson Ltd, Unicorn Brewery, Lower Hillgate, Stockport, Cheshire, SK1 1JJ
☎ (0161) 612 4061 ✉ brewery@frederic-robinson.co.uk ⊕ frederic-robinson.com
Tours by arrangement

☺ Robinson's has been brewing since 1838 and the business is still owned and run by the family. It has an estate of just under 400 pubs. A new brewhouse came on stream in 2012, which enables it to produce a wider range of seasonal and one-off beers. Contract beers are also brewed. Seasonal beers: see website.

Dizzy Blonde (OG 1037, ABV 3.8%)
A straw-coloured summer ale with a distinctive hop aroma. A light, refreshing beer with a clean, zesty, hop-dominated palate complemented by a crisp, dry finish.

1892 (OG 1032, ABV 4%) ◖
A light mild with a malty, fruity aroma. Biscuity malt with some hop and fruit in the taste and finish.

1892 Dark (OG 1032, ABV 4%)

Hartleys XB (OG 1040, ABV 4%) ◖
An overly sweet and malty bitter with a bitter citrus peel fruitiness and a hint of liquorice in the finish.

Cumbria Way (OG 1040, ABV 4.1%)
A pronounced malt aroma with rich fruit notes. Rounded malt and hops in the mouth, long dry finish with citrus fruit notes. Brewed for the Hartley's pub estate in Cumbria.

Unicorn (OG 1041, ABV 4.2%) ◖
Amber beer with a fruity aroma. Malt, hops and fruit in the taste with a bitter, malty finish.

Double Hop (OG 1050, ABV 5%) ◖
Pale brown beer with malt and fruit on the nose. Full hoppy taste with malt and fruit, leading to a hoppy, bitter finish.

Old Tom (OG 1079, ABV 8.5%) 🍷 ◖
A full-bodied, dark beer with malt, fruit and chocolate on the aroma. A complex range of flavours includes dark chocolate, full maltiness, port and fruits and lead to a long, bittersweet aftertaste.

Rock & Roll (NEW) SIBA

Rock & Roll Brewhouse, c/o Old Pie Factory Brewery Ltd, Montague Road, Warwick, CV34 5LW
☎ 07922 554181

The Rock & Roll Brewhouse was set up in 2011 in Shirley, Solihull, using a 0.25-barrel plant by Dave Shepherd and Dave Bennett, ex-brewers at Wetheroak Hill. Pubs are supplied in the Birmingham area. In 2012 the brewery moved to temporary quarters at the Old Pie Factory Brewery in Warwick. A further move to Birmingham is planned.

Instant Calmer (ABV 3.8%)

Misty Mountain Hop (ABV 4%)

Bee Hop Deluxe (ABV 4.2%)

Black Dog Porter (ABV 4.7%)

THE BREWERIES

Rockingham SIBA

Rockingham Ales, c/o 25 Wansford Road, Elton, Cambridgeshire, PE8 6RZ
☎ (01832) 280722 ✉ brian@rockinghamales.co.uk
⊕ rockinghamales.co.uk

⊠ A part-time brewery established in 1997 that operates from a converted farm building near Blatherwycke, Northamptonshire (business address as above). The two-barrel plant produces a prolific range of beers and supplies several local outlets. The regular beers are brewed on a rota basis, with special beers brewed to order. Seasonal beers are also available.

Forest Gold (OG 1039, ABV 3.9%)
A hoppy blonde ale with citrus flavours. Well-balanced and clean finishing.

Hop Devil (OG 1040, ABV 3.9%)
Six hop varieties give this golden ale a bitter start and spicy finish.

A1 Amber Ale (OG 1041, ABV 4%)
A hoppy session beer with fruit and blackcurrant undertones.

Saxon Cross (OG 1041, ABV 4.1%)
A golden-red ale with nut and coffee aromas. Citrus hop flavours predominate.

Fruits of the Forest (OG 1043, ABV 4.2%)
A multi-layered beer in which summer fruits and several spices compete with a big hop presence.

Dark Forest (OG 1050, ABV 5%)
A dark and complex beer, similar to a Belgian Dubbel, with malty/smoky flavours that give way to a fruity bitter finish.

Rockin Robin (NEW)

Rockin Robin Brewery, 6 Pickering Street, Maidstone, Kent, ME15 9RS
☎ 07779 986087

Brewing began in 2011 using a one-barrel plant. Local outlets are supplied.

Hoppin Robin (ABV 3.7%)

Mildly Rockin (ABV 3.7%)

Golden Rock (ABV 4%)

Reliant Robin (ABV 4.2%)

Rodham's

Rodham's Brewery, 74 Albion Street, Otley, West Yorkshire, LS21 1BZ
☎ (01943) 464530

Michael Rodham began brewing in 2005 on a one-barrel plant in the cellar of his house. Capacity has gradually increased and is now 2.5 barrels. All beers produced are malt-only, using whole hops. Occasional seasonal and bottle-conditioned beers are available.

Relish (OG 1035, ABV 3.7%)
A pale ale with creamy malt and citrus fruit flavours and a lasting hoppy bitterness.

Rubicon (OG 1039, ABV 4.1%)
Amber-coloured with a nutty, malt and light fruit taste. A dry, peppery and bitter aftertaste.

Wheat Beer (OG 1039, ABV 4.1%)
Naturally cloudy, sharp and refreshing.

Royale (OG 1042, ABV 4.4%)
A golden beer with a citrus, hoppy taste, underlying malt with a bitter finish.

Old Albion (OG 1048, ABV 5%)
A dark garnet-coloured porter with a complex taste of roast malt and tart fruit with a balancing bitterness.

IPA (OG 1053, ABV 5.7%)
Rich malt combines with tart citrus hops giving a long, bitter finish.

Rooster's SIBA ⊙

Rooster's Brewing Co Ltd, Unit 3, Grimbald Park, Wetherby Road, Knaresborough, North Yorkshire, HG5 8LJ
☎ (01423) 865959 ✉ tom@roosters.co.uk
⊕ roosters.co.uk
Tours by arrangement

☺Rooster's was opened in 1993 by Sean and Alison Franklin. From 1996 one-off and seasonal specials were brewed under the Outlaw Brewing Co name. The brewery moved to larger premises in 2001. In 2011 the brewery was bought by Ian Fozard of Market Town Taverns. Sean and Alison ran the brewery until they retired at the end of 2011, when Ian's sons Tom and Oliver took over. All beers are currently brewed under the Roosters name although the Outlaw branding may be used in future for more cutting edge, experimental brews.

Buckeye (OG 1035.5, ABV 3.5%)
An easy-drinking, well-hopped pale ale producing an orange-citrus aroma with moderate bitterness.

Wild Mule (OG 1037, ABV 3.9%)
A pale ale brewed using New Zealand's Nelson Sauvin hop to create a white wine fruitiness with pronounced grapefruit bitterness.

YPA (Yorkshire Pale Ale) (OG 1039.5, ABV 4.1%)
A pale-coloured beer with pronounced raspberry and flower aromas.

Leghorn (OG 1041, ABV 4.3%)
A creamy pale ale with a cocktail of fruit aromas.

Yankee (OG 1041, ABV 4.3%) ◆
A straw-coloured beer with a delicate, fruity aroma leading to a well-balanced taste of malt and hops with a slight evidence of sweetness, followed by a refreshing, fruity/bitter finish.

Roseland

⬙ Roseland Brewery, c/o Roseland Inn, Philleigh, nr St Mawes, Truro, Cornwall, TR2 5NB
☎ (01872) 580254 ☎ 07977 472484

⊠ Roseland was established in 2009 by Phil Heslip at his pub, the Roseland Inn. The beers are mainly named after local birds and are generally only available in the Roseland Inn or its sister pub, the Victory Inn at St Mawes, though beers can be found at local beer festivals.

Cornish Shag (OG 1037, ABV 3.8%)
A copper-coloured session bitter.

Rossendale SIBA

⬙ Rossendale Brewery Ltd, Griffin Inn, 84 Hud Rake, Haslingden, Lancashire, BB4 5AF
☎ (01706) 214021 ⊕ rossendalebrewery.co.uk

⊛Formerly known as Pennine Ales, the brewery acquired the brew plant previously used by Porter Brewing Co in 2007 and is based in the cellar of the Griffin Inn in Haslingden. It produces seven regular cask ales.

Floral Dance (OG 1035, ABV 3.6%)
A pale and fruity session beer.

Hameldon Bitter (OG 1040, ABV 3.8%)
A dark traditional bitter with a dry and assertive character that develops in the finish.

Glen Top (OG 1045, ABV 4%)

Ale (OG 1045, ABV 4.2%)
A malty aroma leads to a complex, malt-dominated flavour, supported by a dry, increasingly bitter finish.

Halo Pail (OG 1045, ABV 4.5%)

Pitch Porter (OG 1050, ABV 5%)
A full-bodied, rich beer with a slightly sweet, malty start, counter balanced with sharp bitterness and a roast barley dominance.

Sunshine (OG 1055, ABV 5.3%)
A hoppy and bitter golden beer with a citrus character. The lingering finish is dry and spicy.

Rother Valley SIBA

Rother Valley Brewing Co, Gate Court Farm, Station Road, Northiam, East Sussex, TN31 6QT
☎ (01797) 252922 ☎ 07798 877551
Tours by arrangement

⊗ Rother Valley Brewery was established in Northiam in 1993 overlooking the Rother Levels and the Kent and East Sussex Railway. Established and new hop varieties are grown on the farm and also sourced locally. Brewing is split between cask and an ever-increasing range of filtered bottled beers. A monthly seasonal ale is available.

Honeyfuzz (OG 1038, ABV 3.8%)
A pale bitter flavoured with Sussex honey, subtle but not sweet with a citrus twang on the finish.

Smild (OG 1038, ABV 3.8%)
A full-bodied, dark, creamy mild with hints of chocolate.

Level Best (OG 1040, ABV 4%) ◈
Full-bodied tawny session bitter with a malt and fruit aroma, malty taste and a dry, hoppy finish.

Hoppers Ale (OG 1044, ABV 4.4%)
A copper-coloured ale. The initial burst of hop is followed by a pleasant caramel taste.

Boadicea (OG 1045, ABV 4.5%)
A straw-coloured beer with a delicate, fruity flavour.

Rotters

Rotters Brewery, Tower Hotel, Talgarth, Powys, LD3 0BW
☎ (01874) 711253 ✉ rottersbrewery@gmail.com
⊕ rottersbrewery.co.uk
Tours by arrangement

⊛Rotters Brewery opened in 2010. Seasonal beer is also available.

Utter Rotter (OG 1040, ABV 3.9%)

Grounds For Divorce (OG 1048, ABV 4.7%)
A premium ruby ale.

Rowditch

Rowditch Inn Brewery, Rowditch Inn, 246 Uttoxeter New Road, Derby, DE22 3LL
☎ (01332) 343123

Rowditch began brewing in 2010 using a four-barrel plant on the premises of the Rowditch pub.

St Stephens (OG 1038, ABV 3.6%)

BSB (Bog Standard Beer) (OG 1040, ABV 3.8%)

RSB (Rowditch Strong Bitter) (OG 1050, ABV 5%)

Rowton SIBA

Rowton Brewery Ltd, Stone House, Rowton, Telford, Shropshire, TF6 6QX
☎ 07746 290995 ✉ rowton.brewery@live.co.uk

Rowton was established in 2008 on a four-barrel plant in an old cow shed on the owner's farm. Barley grown on the farm is sent for malting and returned for use in the brews while water is from a borehole on site. The brewer is experimenting with cider made from locally-pressed apples.

Bitter (OG 1040, ABV 3.9%)

Galaxy (OG 1044, ABV 4.3%)

Dark Side Stout (OG 1045, ABV 4.5%)

Royal Tunbridge Wells SIBA

Royal Tunbridge Wells Brewing Co Ltd, Spa Brewery, 18H Chapman Way, Royal Tunbridge Wells, Kent, TN2 3EF
☎ (01892) 618140
✉ info@royaltunbridgewellsbrewing.co.uk
⊕ royaltunbridgewellsbrewing.co.uk
Tours by arrangement

⊗ Brewing began in 2010 using a 10-barrel plant. Around 250 outlets are supplied direct. Seasonal and bottle-conditioned beers are also available.

Dipper (OG 1038, ABV 3.7%)
An easy-drinking golden brown session ale with a medium body, malty, biscuit and fruity notes and a gentle hop finish.

Royal (OG 1041, ABV 4.1%) ◈
This typically Kentish best bitter has a strong bitter hop character tempered by malt, with hints of fruit in the mouth and a long finish.

Beau (OG 1050, ABV 4.8%)
Dark, rich and full of flavour with hints of coffee, dark chocolate and liquorice. The malt flavours, finely balanced by the hop bitterness, lead to a long, complex finish.

Golden Ticket (OG 1052, ABV 5%)
Full-bodied and full-flavoured with a crisp, citrus aroma on the nose and a long, bitter, refreshing hop finish.

Helles (OG 1052, ABV 5%)
A British golden ale brewed with German Hallertau hops. Rich yet refreshing with light caramel malts and distinctive herbal hop aromas.

Rudgate SIBA ◉

Rudgate Brewery Ltd, 2 Centre Park, Marston Moor Business Park, Tockwith, York, North Yorkshire, YO26 7QF
☎ (01423) 358382 ✉ sales@rudgatebrewery.co.uk
⊕ rudgatebrewery.co.uk

Tours by arrangement

☺Rudgate Brewery was founded in 1992. In 2011 the brewery moved to a new 30-barrel plant capable of brewing twice daily. Several free trade and tied houses are supplied. Three seasonal beers are also produced each month.

Jorvik Blonde (OG 1036, ABV 3.8%)
Flaxen blonde ale with a balanced hoppy bitterness and a crisp, fruity finish.

Viking Bitter (OG 1036, ABV 3.8%) ◆
An initially warming and malty, full-bodied beer, with hops and fruit lingering into the aftertaste.

Battleaxe Bitter (OG 1040, ABV 4.2%) ◆
A well-hopped bitter with slightly sweet initial taste and light bitterness. Complex fruit character gives a memorable aftertaste.

Ruby Mild (OG 1041, ABV 4.4%) 🍷 🍴 ◆
Nutty, rich ruby ale, stronger than usual for a mild.

Nordic Storm (OG 1046, ABV 5%)
A premium ale, pale amber and full-bodied with distinctive citrus on the nose.

IPA (OG 1049, ABV 5.2%)
Initially bittersweet with well-balanced complex fruit, hints of citrus and a bitter, hoppy finish.

Rugby

See Wood Farm

Saddleworth

🍺 **Church Inn & Saddleworth Brewery, Church Lane, Uppermill, Oldham, Greater Manchester, OL3 6LW**
☎ (01457) 820902/872415
Tours by arrangement

☺ Saddleworth started brewing in 1997 in a brewhouse that had been closed for around 120 years. Brewery and inn are set in a historic location at the top of a valley overlooking Saddleworth Moor and next to St Chads Church, which dates from 1215. Brewing capacity was significantly expanded with a new 13-barrel plant in 2011. Seasonal beers are also available.

Mild (OG 1038, ABV 3.6%)

More (OG 1038, ABV 3.8%)

St George's Bitter (OG 1038, ABV 3.8%)

Blue Tree Bitter (OG 1040, ABV 4%)

Honey Smacker (OG 1042, ABV 4.1%)

Hop Smacker (OG 1042, ABV 4.1%)

Slap & Tickle (OG 1045, ABV 4.3%)

Shaftbender (OG 1060, ABV 5.4%)

Sadler's SIBA ◉

Sadler's Ales Brewery, 7 Stourbridge Road, Lye, Stourbridge, West Midlands, DY9 7DG
☎ (01384) 895230 ✉ enquiries@sadlersales.co.uk
⊕ sadlersales.co.uk
Tours by arrangement

☺Thomas Alexander Sadler founded the original brewery in 1900 adjacent to the Windsor Castle Inn, Oldbury. Third and fourth generation brewers John and Chris Sadler re-opened the brewery in its new location in 2004. The brewery tap house was

built and opened in 2006 next to the brewery. Around 250 outlets are supplied.

JPA (OG 1038, ABV 3.8%)
A pale, hoppy bitter with a crisp and zesty lemon undertone.

Red House Mild (OG 1040, ABV 4%)
A Black Country dark mild with hints of chocolate and a dry finish.

Mellow Yellow (OG 1041, ABV 4.1%)
A pale ale brewed with plenty of hop and honey.

Worcester Sorcerer (OG 1043, ABV 4.3%)
Brewed with English hops and barley with hints of mint and lemon, creating a floral aroma and crisp bitterness.

Thin Ice (OG 1045, ABV 4.5%)
A pale ale. Bitter but with an orange and lemon finish.

Hop Bomb (OG 1050, ABV 5%)
A powerful IPA with a balanced malt sweetness supported by large hop aroma and flavour explosion.

Red IPA (OG 1057, ABV 5.7%)

Mud City Stout (OG 1066, ABV 6.6%)
Rich, full-bodied strong stout brewed with raw cocoa, fresh vanilla pods, oats, wheat and dark malts.

Saffron SIBA

Saffron Brewery, The Cartshed, Parsonage Farm, Henham, Essex, CM22 6AN
☎ (01279) 850923 ☎ 07747 696901
✉ dh@saffronbrewery.co.uk ⊕ saffronbrewery.co.uk
Tours by arrangement

⊠ Founded in 2005, Saffron is situated near the historic East Anglian town of Saffron Walden, famous for its malting industry in the 18th century. The brewery was upgraded to a 15-barrel plant in early 2008 and re-located to a converted barn at Parsonage Farm by Henham church, with a purpose-built reed bed for environmentally friendly disposal of waste products. 40 outlets are supplied direct. Seasonal and bottle-conditioned beers are also available.

Ramblers Tipple (OG 1040, ABV 3.9%)
A rich, copper-coloured bitter with toffee and caramel flavours.

Littlebury Lighthouse (ABV 4.2%)

Blonde (OG 1044, ABV 4.3%)
A light golden ale with a delicate balance of citrus and smooth, malty flavours and a crisp finish.

St Andrews (NEW)

St Andrews Brewing Co, Unit 4, Food Resource Base, Faraday Road, Glenrothes, KY6 2RU
☎ 07879 399441
✉ standrewsbrewingco@gmail.com
⊕ standrewsbrewingcompany.com

St Andrews was established in 2012 concentrating initially on bottle-conditioned beers. There are plans for an extensive list of seasonal brews as well as cask-conditioned regulars. A wide selection of shops, hotels, restaurants and golf clubs are supplied within Fife as well as initial outlets in Edinburgh, Glasgow and Aberdeen.

St Austell SIBA IFBB 👁

St Austell Brewery Co Ltd, 63 Trevarthian Road, St Austell, Cornwall, PL25 4BY
☎ (01726) 74444 ✉ info@staustellbrewery.co.uk
🌐 staustellbrewery.co.uk
Shop & Visitor Centre Mon-Fri 9am-5pm; Sat 10am-4pm
Tours by arrangement

⊗ St Austell Brewery celebrated 160 years of brewing in 2010. Founded by Walter Hicks in 1851, the company is still family owned, with a powerful commitment to cask beer, available in all 170 licensed houses, as well as in the free trade. A visitor centre offers guided tours and souvenirs from the brewery. Seasonal and bottle-conditioned beers are also available: see website.

Dartmoor Best Bitter (OG 1035, ABV 3.5%)
An easy-drinking ale with a touch of bitterness complemented by a smooth, malty finish.

Trelawny (OG 1039, ABV 3.8%) ◆
Refreshing copper-coloured bitter with a light aroma of fruit reminiscent of nectarines. Hop bitterness with a touch of citrus develops into malt sweetness. Gentle bitter finish with a lingering maltiness.

Tribute (OG 1043, ABV 4.2%) ◆
Gold/amber ale with a complex flowery aroma with a trace of tangy ester. Citrus maltiness dominates the flavour balanced by bitter hops reminiscent of elderflower, ending refreshingly bitter with a hint of astringency.

Proper Job (OG 1046, ABV 4.5%) ◆
Golden ale with a perfumed aroma of resinous hops. Copious marmalade in the mouth with characteristic bitterness leading to a long citrus fruit yet bitter finish, becoming dry.

Hicks Special Draught/HSD (OG 1052, ABV 5%) ◆
Rich malt and ripe fruit aroma of this tawny premium ale leads into an intense malt flavour balanced by sweetness and bitterness that lasts into the long finish.

St George's SIBA

St George's Brewery Ltd, The Old Bakery, Bush Lane, Callow End, Worcestershire, WR2 4TF
☎ (01905) 831316 ✉ info@stgeorgesbrewery.co.uk
🌐 stgeorgesbrewery.co.uk
Tours by arrangement

The brewery was established in 1998 in old village bakery premises. It was acquired in 2006 by Duncan Ironmonger. Andrew Sankey has been the brewer and brewery manager for a number of years. The brewery supplies local freehouses and wholesalers for a wider distribution. At least two monthly specials are usually available.

Friar Tuck (OG 1040, ABV 4%)
A smooth, refreshing golden bitter with a citrus character.

Lazy Days (OG 1041, ABV 4.1%)
A straw-coloured beer with a fruity taste to start and a bitter edge to finish.

Keep Calm & Carry On (OG 1044, ABV 4.4%)
A smooth beer with a long-lasting bitterness to finish. Amber in colour.

Charger (OG 1046, ABV 4.6%)

A light golden beer with a citrus blast and a hint of grapefruit.

Dragons Blood (OG 1048, ABV 4.8%)
A ruby red beer with a hint of chocolate and an earthy, slightly spicy aroma.

St Peter's SIBA EAB 👁

St Peter's Brewery Co Ltd, St Peter's Hall, St Peter South Elmham, Suffolk, NR35 1NQ
☎ (01986) 782322 ✉ beers@stpetersbrewery.co.uk
🌐 stpetersbrewery.co.uk
Shop Mon-Fri 9am-5pm; Sat & Sun 11am-5pm
Tours by arrangement

⊗ St Peter's Brewery is based adjacent to a moated medieval hall near Bungay, Suffolk. Established in 1996 it concentrates in the main on bottled/keg beer (85% of capacity) but has a rapidly increasing cask market. Two pubs are owned. 40% of production is exported to 32 countries worldwide. Seasonal beers are also available.

Best Bitter (OG 1038, ABV 3.7%) ◆
A complex but well-balanced hoppy brew. A gentle hop nose introduces a singular hoppiness with supporting malt notes and underlying bitterness. Other flavours fade to leave a long, dry, hoppy finish.

Mild (OG 1037, ABV 3.7%) ◆
Heady aroma of caramelised blackberries and black toffee. Complex flavours, with caramel, blackberries, hops and an astringent bitterness. Long, sustained finish with a roast coffee bitterness; increasingly dry.

Organic Best (OG 1041, ABV 4.1%) ◆
A very dry and bitter beer with a growing astringency. Pale brown in colour, it has a gentle hop aroma which makes the definitive bitterness surprising. One for the committed.

Ruby Red (OG 1043, ABV 4.3%)
A tawny red ale with subtle malt undertones and a distinctive spicy hop aroma.

Organic Ale (OG 1045, ABV 4.5%) ◆
A rich toffee apple aroma and a smooth grainy feel. Malt and caramel initially match the dry hoppy bitterness. As the flavours mature, liquorice dryness develops. Full-bodied.

Golden Ale (OG 1047, ABV 4.7%) ◆
Amber-coloured, full-bodied, robust ale. A strong hop bouquet leads to a mix of malt and hops combined with a dry, fruity hoppiness. The malt quickly subsides, leaving creamy bitterness.

Grapefruit Beer (OG 1047, ABV 4.7%) 📖 ◆
With a strong aroma and taste of grapefruit, this refreshing beer is exactly what it says on the tin. A superb example of a fruit beer.

IPA (OG 1055, ABV 5.5%)
A full-bodied, highly-hopped pale ale with a zesty character.

Salamander SIBA

Salamander Brewing Co Ltd, 22 Harry Street, Dudley Hill, Bradford, West Yorkshire, BD4 9PH
☎ (01274) 652323 ✉ salbrewcom@gmail.com
🌐 salamanderbrewing.co.uk
Tours by arrangement

⊗ Salamander first brewed in 2000 in a former pork pie factory. Expansion in 2004 took the brewery to 40-barrel capacity. There are direct deliveries to more widespread areas such as Cumbria, East Yorkshire and Lancashire in addition to the established trade of about 100 outlets throughout Lancashire, Manchester, North Yorkshire and Derbyshire.

Axolotl (OG 1038, ABV 3.9%)

Mudpuppy (OG 1042, ABV 4.2%) ◆
A well-balanced, copper-coloured best bitter with a fruity, hoppy nose and a bitter finish.

Golden Salamander (OG 1045, ABV 4.5%) 🛇 ◆
Citrus hops characterise the aroma and taste of this golden premium bitter, which has malt undertones throughout. The aftertaste is dry, hoppy and bitter.

Salisbury SIBA

Salisbury Brewery, 1 Oakley Business Park, Wylye Valley, Dinton, Wiltshire, SP3 5EU
☎ (01722) 716440 ✉ sales@salisburybrewery.com
⊕ salisburybrewery.com

Salisbury Brewery was established in 2010 brewing deep in the heart of the ancient Wylye Valley. Formerly known as West Country Brewery.

Somer (ABV 3.9%)
A light golden-coloured, fruity beer complemented by a citrus hop note and smooth finish.

English Ale (ABV 4.1%)
A traditional best bitter with malt notes and a subtle depth of hop character.

Salopian SIBA ◉

Salopian Brewery, 67 Mytton Oak Road, Shrewsbury, Shropshire, SY3 8UQ
☎ (01743) 248414
✉ enquiries@salopianbrewery.co.uk
⊕ salopianbrewery.co.uk
Shop Mon-Fri 9am-4pm
Tours by arrangement

⊗ The brewery was established in 1995 in an old dairy on the outskirts of Shrewsbury and, having grown steadily, now produces more than 130 barrels a week. Salopian also brews under the Blackwater Brewery name.

Shropshire Gold (OG 1037, ABV 3.8%) 🛇 🍺
Golden with a floral aroma and a full, hoppy flavour balanced by a crisp, dry maltiness and a rich finish.

Oracle (OG 1040, ABV 4%)
A crisp golden ale with a striking hop profile. Dry and refreshing with a long citrus aromatic finish.

Darwins Origin (OG 1042, ABV 4.3%)
A copper-coloured beer with pronounced hop character leading to a refined malt finish.

Hop Twister (OG 1044, ABV 4.5%) 🍺
The palate is fresh with soft malt overtones and pronounced citrus flavours. Lemon and grapefruit on the finish is balanced by a dry bitterness.

Lemon Dream (OG 1044, ABV 4.5%) 🛇
A golden ale brewed using organic lemons which adds subtle zesty aromas and a citrus-filled fruity finish.

Golden Thread (OG 1048, ABV 5%) 🍺
A bright gold ale; clean and crisp to the palate with a hint of sweetness and a long, fruit-filled finish.

Saltaire SIBA ◉

Saltaire Brewery Ltd, Unit 6, County Works, Dockfield Road, Shipley, West Yorkshire, BD17 7AR
☎ (01274) 594959 ✉ info@saltairebrewery.co.uk
⊕ saltairebrewery.co.uk
Tours by arrangement

☺ Launched in 2006, Saltaire Brewery is an award-winning brewery based in a former Victorian power station. A mezzanine bar gives visitors views of the brewing plant and the chance to taste the beers. More than 300 pubs are supplied across West Yorkshire and the north of England.

South Island Pale (OG 1037, ABV 3.5%) ◆
This low strength, golden-coloured bitter has an intensely hoppy aroma that follows through to a well-balanced fruity, citrus, hop flavour and a long hoppy finish.

Blonde (OG 1042, ABV 4%) ◆
Thirst-quenching and quaffable, this straw-coloured beer is slightly sweet and well-rounded, with fruit, malt and hops in the taste and a fruity, hoppy finish.

Raspberry Blonde (OG 1042, ABV 4%)
Blonde beer infused with a hint of raspberries.

Cascade Pale Ale (OG 1050, ABV 4.8%) ◆
A well-balanced golden bitter with smooth mouth feel, floral hop aromas and pronounced bitterness, culminating in a long, dry finish and dry aftertaste.

Triple Chocoholic (OG 1050, ABV 4.8%) ◆
A creamy, dark brown, roast, chocolate stout with a dry bitter finish and a rich chocolate aroma.

Stateside IPA (OG 1062, ABV 6%)
Full-bodied IPA with good bitterness.

Sambrook's SIBA ◉

Sambrook's Brewery Ltd, Units 1-3, Yelverton Road, Battersea, London, SW11 3QG
☎ (020) 7228 0598
✉ sales@sambrooksbrewery.co.uk
⊕ sambrooksbrewery.co.uk
Shop Mon-Fri 10am-6pm; Sat 10am-1pm
Tours by arrangement

⊗ Sambrooks was established in 2008 by Duncan Sambrook (a former city accountant) and David Welsh (a veteran brewer and former director of Ringwoods) using a 20-barrel plant. Seasonal beers are available.

Wandle Ale (OG 1038, ABV 3.8%) ◆
A touch of dryness balances the rounded sweetish malt flavour of this fruity, quaffable pale brown bitter. Some peach and citrus notes and hops are noticeable when fresh.

Pump House Pale (OG 1041, ABV 4.2%) ◆
A refreshing golden beer with a mellow hint of citrus on the nose becoming more pronounced on the palate and lingering into the finish with a bitterness that develops on drinking.

Junction Ale (OG 1045, ABV 4.5%) ◆
Soft fruit and figs on the nose of this well-balanced best bitter. The fruit on the palate is a little more citrussy plus creamy toffee. Sweetish dry aftertaste.

Powerhouse Porter (OG 1050, ABV 4.9%) ◆
Dark brown Porter with a pleasant roasted malt nose and some sultana and blackcurrant character.

The flavour is of caramelised fruit, treacle and a hint of citrus. Dry roasted finish.

Sandstone SIBA

Sandstone Brewery LLP, Unit 5, Wrexham Enterprise Park, Preston Road, off Ash Road North, Wrexham Industrial Estate, Wrexham, LL13 9JT
☎ 07851 001118 ✉ info@sandstonebrewery.co.uk
⊕ sandstonebrewery.co.uk
Tours by arrangement

☺Sandstone Brewery was established in 2008 using a four-barrel brew plant. More than 60 regular outlets are supplied direct.

Edge (OG 1039, ABV 3.8%) ◆
A satisfying session ale, this pale, dry, bitter beer has a full mouthfeel and a lingering hoppy finish that belies its modest strength.

Sleeping Policeman (OG 1043, ABV 4.2%) ◆
Clean-tasting best bitter, chestnut in colour with a fruity aroma continuing into the taste. Peppery hops are increasingly evident in the aftertaste and dry, bitter finish.

Poacher's Pale (OG 1046, ABV 4.4%)
A bitter beer with a light and refreshing taste.

Post Mistress (OG 1046, ABV 4.4%) ❦ ◆
A full-bodied, smooth premium bitter, ruby-red in colour, with a rich, mellow taste. Good combination of malt, hops and fruit in aroma and initial taste lead to a lasting satisfying finish.

Sarah Hughes

See under Hughes

Sawbridgeworth SIBA

目 Sawbridgeworth Brewery, 81 London Road, Sawbridgeworth, Hertfordshire, CM21 9JJ
☎ (01279) 722313 ✉ thegatepub@talktalk.net
⊕ thegatepub.net
Tours by arrangement

Set up in 2000 by owners Tom and Gary Barnett, the brewery is situated behind the Gate Inn. Tom is a former professional footballer whose clubs included Crystal Palace. Brewing is carried out by ex-Nethergate brewer Bob Renvoise. Special or one-off beers are regularly brewed.

Manor Mild (OG 1034, ABV 3.4%)

Selhurst Park Flyer (OG 1038, ABV 3.7%)

IPA (OG 1038, ABV 3.8%)

Gold (OG 1040, ABV 4%)

Is It Yourself (OG 1042, ABV 4.2%)

Dragon's Blood (OG 1043, ABV 4.3%)

Malt Shovel Porter (OG 1060, ABV 6%)

Saxon City SIBA

Saxon City Ales, Glebe Farm Industrial Estate, Stoke Edith, Herefordshire, HR1 4HG
☎ (01432) 890602 ✉ cstrangehcasks@yahoo.co.uk
⊕ herefordcasks.co.uk

☺Chris Strange, owner of cask manufacturing business Hereford Casks Ltd, diversified into

brewing in 2010. A six-barrel plant is used, housed in a unit adjoining the cask factory.

Dubonni (ABV 3.8%)
Dark and fruity.

Strange Brew (ABV 3.8%)
A light, hoppy session beer.

Scarborough (NEW) SIBA

Scarborough Brewery Ltd, Unit 1b, Barry's Lane, Scarborough, North Yorkshire, YO12 4AA
☎ (01723) 241495
✉ scarboroughbrewery@yahoo.co.uk

Scarborough Brewery was established in 2010 using a one-barrel plant. In 2011 commercial brewing began using a 10-barrel plant from Wold Top Brewery. Beers can be found at its brewery tap, Valley Bar in Scarborough, and nationwide via wholesalers. One-off and seasonal beers are also available.

Blonde (ABV 4.2%)

Zest (ABV 4.2%)

IPA (ABV 4.4%)

Stout (ABV 4.6%)

Strong Gold (ABV 5.8%)

Scattor Rock

See Gidley's

Scottish Borders SIBA

Scottish Borders Brewery Ltd, Lanton Mill, Jedburgh, TD8 6ST
☎ (01835) 830387
✉ info@scottishbordersbrewery.com
⊕ scottishbordersbrewery.com

⊗ Scottish Borders started brewing in 2011 and is a farm development using its own barley.

Wee Beastie (OG 1037, ABV 3.6%)
A hint of dark malt and an unusual mash technique create an extremely light session ale with real body and a surprisingly rich taste.

Foxy Blonde (OG 1037.5, ABV 3.8%)
A golden ale bursting with citrus and floral flavours.

Game Bird (OG 1039.5, ABV 4%)
An amber ale with a balance of malty sweetness and late summer fruit with a long, easy finish.

Holy Cow (OG 1041, ABV 4.2%)
Hints of dark malt combine with a long, floral finish.

Dark Horse (OG 1044, ABV 4.5%)
A classic dark ale with overtones of coffee and chocolate with a spicy finish that lingers on the tongue.

Severn Vale SIBA ◉

Severn Vale Brewing Co, Woodend Lane, Cam, Dursley, Gloucestershire, GL11 5HS
☎ (01453) 547550 ☎ 07971 640244
✉ steve@severnvalebrewing.co.uk
⊕ severnvalebrewing.co.uk
Shop: Please ring first
Tours by arrangement

⊠ Severn Vale started brewing in 2005 in an old milking parlour using a new five-barrel plant. Warminster malted barley is used and mainly Herefordshire hops. Around 50 outlets are supplied. Seasonal beers are also available.

Session (OG 1035, ABV 3.4%)
A classic bitter that belies its low strength. It has a full-bodied malty flavour with a bitter, hoppy finish that lingers on the palate.

Vale Ale (OG 1039, ABV 3.8%)
A rich amber beer with full-bodied malt flavours and complex nose and taste.

Dursley Steam Bitter (OG 1043, ABV 4.2%)
A refreshing golden ale full of flowery hops.

Severn Bells (OG 1048, ABV 4.7%)

Severn Sins (OG 1053, ABV 5.2%)
A jet-black stout with a dry roast malt flavour with hints of chocolate and liquorice.

Shalford SIBA

Shalford Brewery, c/o PO Box 10411, Braintree, Essex, CM7 5WP
☎ (01371) 850925 ☎ 07749 658512
✉ nigel@shalfordbrewery.co.uk
⊕ shalfordbrewery.co.uk

⊠ Shalford began brewing in 2007 on a five-barrel plant at Hyde Farm in the Pant Valley in Essex. Over 50 outlets are supplied direct. Bottle-conditioned beers are available.

1319 Mild (OG 1037, ABV 3.7%)
Roast malt and chocolate sweetness with a slight bitter finish.

Barnfield Bitter (OG 1038, ABV 3.8%) ◆
Pale-coloured but full-flavoured, this is a traditional, hoppy bitter rather than a golden ale. Malt persists throughout, with bitterness becoming more dominant towards the end.

Braintree Market Ale (OG 1040, ABV 4%)
Traditional, easy-drinking session ale with a hoppy, lingering, dry finish.

Levelly Gold (OG 1040, ABV 4%)
Golden, summery bitter with a pleasant finish.

Stoneley Bitter (OG 1042, ABV 4.2%) ◆
Dark amber session beer whose vivid hop character is supported by a juicy, malty body. A dry finish makes this beer very drinkable.

Hyde Bitter (OG 1047, ABV 4.7%) ◆
Stronger version of Barnfield, with a similar but more assertive character.

Levelly Black (ABV 4.8%)
A dark, heavy, well-hopped ale with grainy toffee taste topped with a thick, creamy head.

Springfield (ABV 6%)
Crisp, clean bitter made with wheat and barley malt.

Rotten End (OG 1065, ABV 6.5%)
Strong beer with slightly sweet, nutty undertones and a bitter edge to finish.

Shardlow

Shardlow Brewing Co Ltd, The Old Brewery Stables, British Waterways Yard, Cavendish Bridge, Leicestershire, DE72 2HL
☎ (01332) 799188 ✉ nev@shardlowbrewing.co.uk

Tours by arrangement

☺ On a site associated with brewing since 1819, Shardlow delivers to more than 100 outlets throughout the East Midlands and is also one of the largest UK cider distributors. Reverend Eaton is named after a scion of the Eaton brewing family, Rector of Shardlow for 40 years. The brewery tap is the Blue Bell Inn at Melbourne, Derbyshire. Seasonal and bottle-conditioned beers are also available.

Chancellors Revenge (OG 1036, ABV 3.6%)
A light-coloured, refreshing, full-flavoured and well-hopped session bitter.

Cavendish Dark (OG 1037, ABV 3.7%)

Golden Hop (OG 1041, ABV 4.1%)

Kiln House (OG 1041, ABV 4.1%)

Narrow Boat (OG 1043, ABV 4.3%)
A pale amber bitter, with a short, crisp hoppy aftertaste.

Cavendish Bridge (OG 1045, ABV 4.5%)

Cavendish Gold (OG 1045, ABV 4.5%)

Reverend Eaton (OG 1045, ABV 4.5%)
A smooth, medium-strong bitter, full of malt and hop flavours with a sweet aftertaste.

Mayfly (OG 1048, ABV 4.8%)

Five Bells (OG 1050, ABV 5%)

Whistlestop (OG 1050, ABV 5%)
Maris Otter pale malt and two hops produce this smooth and surprisingly strong pale beer.

Sharp's

See under Molson Coors in Global Giants section

Shaws

See Quantum

Shed (NEW)

Shed Ales, Broadfields, Pewsey, Wiltshire, SN9 5DT
☎ 07554 361701 ✉ shed_ales@hotmail.com
⊕ shed-ales.com

Shed is a small brewery producing bespoke ales from the back garden.

GJE (ABV 4.1%)

Pail Ale (ABV 4.7%)

Sheffield SIBA

Sheffield Brewery Co Ltd, Unit 111, JC Albyn Complex, Burton Road, Sheffield, South Yorkshire, S3 8BT
☎ (0114) 272 7256 ✉ sales@sheffieldbrewery.com
⊕ sheffieldbrewery.com
Tours by arrangement

☺ Sheffield began brewing in 2007 in the former Blanco polish works on a 10-barrel plant. The brewery operates on the tower principle, and also acts as a venue for corporate or social events, catering for up to 40 people. The brewery tap is the nearby Gardeners Rest. More than 50 outlets are supplied direct. Seasonal beers: see website.

Bottle-conditioned beers are also available.

Crucible Best (OG 1038, ABV 3.8%)
A complex traditional bitter.

Five Rivers (OG 1038, ABV 3.8%)
An easy-drinking, straw-coloured session ale with a hoppy aroma.

Blanco Blonde (OG 1042, ABV 4.2%)
A continental lager-style beer.

Seven Hills (OG 1041, ABV 4.2%)

Porter (OG 1045, ABV 4.4%)
A rich, chocolatey, malty porter with caramel flavours.

IPA (OG 1048, ABV 5%)

Shepherd Neame IFBB ⟨◉⟩

Shepherd Neame Ltd, 17 Court Street, Faversham, Kent, ME13 7AX
☎ (01795) 532206 ⊕ shepherd-neame.co.uk
Shop Mon-Sat 10am-4.30pm
Tours by arrangement

Kent's major independent brewery is believed to be the oldest continuous brewer in the country (since 1698), but records show brewing began on the site as far back as the 12th century. The same water source is still used today and 1914 oak mash tuns are still operational. In 2004/2005 investment increased production to more than 200,000 barrels a year. The company has 360 tied houses in the South-east, nearly all selling cask ale. More than 2,000 other outlets are also supplied. All Shepherd Neame ales use locally-sourced ingredients. The cask beers are made with Kentish hops, local malted barley and water from the brewery's own artesian well. In 2007 a micro-plant was installed inside the main brewery to brew speciality ales in small quantities for special occasions. These brews are available for a limited time in selected pubs. A programme of monthly seasonal beers is available: see website for details. Bottle-conditioned beer is also available.

Canterbury Jack (OG 1033, ABV 3.5%)
A full-bodied, pale beer with a grapefruit aroma. Malty, citrus notes on the palate lead to a crisp, refreshing, bitter aftertaste.

Master Brew Bitter (OG 1032, ABV 3.7%) ◆
A distinctive bitter, mid-brown in colour, with a hoppy aroma. Well-balanced, with a nicely aggressive bitter taste from its hops, it leaves a hoppy/bitter finish, tinged with sweetness.

Kent's Best (OG 1036, ABV 4.1%)
A mellow bitter that merges the biscuity sweetness of English malt with the fruity, floral bitterness of locally-grown hops.

Spitfire Premium Ale (OG 1036, ABV 4.2%)
A classic, well-rounded Kentish ale, softly bitter with a deep fruity tang.

Late Red (OG 1042, ABV 4.3%)
A strong bitter with a deep sweetness, toffee and honey characteristics. The Cascade hops give a resinous note reminiscent of autumn leaves.

Bishops Finger (OG 1046, ABV 5%)
A strong ale with a complex hop aroma reminiscent of lemons, oranges and bananas combined with malt, molasses and toffee.

Refreshing with a good malt character tinged with a lingering bitterness.

Sherborne

⊟ Sherborne Brewery Ltd, 257 Westbury, Sherborne, Dorset, DT9 3EH
☎ (01935) 812094 ⊕ sherbornebrewery.co.uk

☺Sherborne Brewery started in late 2005 on a 2.5-barrel plant. It moved in 2006 to new premises at the rear of the brewery's pub, Docherty's Bar. Beer is supplied to the pub and to 15-20 other local outlets as a guest beer.

257 (OG 1039, ABV 3.9%) ◆
Light-coloured best bitter with fruit-hop aromas and flavour with burnt astringent undertones.

Cheap Street (OG 1044, ABV 4.4%) ◆
Faint hop fruit aromas lead to strong astringent flavours and a lingering dry burnt aftertaste; reminiscent of a German Rauch (smoked) beer but with a thinner body.

Sherfield Village SIBA

Sherfield Village Brewery, Goddards Farm, Goddards Lane, Sherfield on Loddon, Hampshire, RG27 0EL
☎ 07906 060429
✉ pete@sherfieldvillagebrewery.co.uk
⊕ sherfieldvillagebrewery.co.uk

Sherfield Village started brewing in 2011. Using a five-barrel plant they make extensive use of New World hops, particularly those from New Zealand. Dry-hopped versions of single-hop beers are usually available.

Threesome (ABV 3%)

SOLO Single Hop (ABV 4.3%)
Ever-changing, highly-hopped golden bitter.

Hoppy Harrington (ABV 4.7%)

Pioneer Stout (ABV 5%)
Black and chocolaty with a hint of vanilla.

IPA (ABV 5.6%)

Ship Inn

⊟ Ship Inn Brewery, Ship Inn, Newton Square, Low Newton by the Sea, Northumberland, NE66 3EL
☎ (01665) 576262 ⊕ shipinnnewton.co.uk

The Ship Inn commenced brewing in 2008 on a 2.5-barrel plant. The brewery now produces 7.5 barrels per week and all regular beers are brewed in constant rotation, brewing three times per week. The beers are only available at the Ship Inn. Seasonal and bottle-conditioned beers are also available. A special beer (4.2% ABV) is brewed for every 100 brews.

Red Herring (ABV 3.8%)

Sandcastles at Dawn (ABV 3.8%)

Sea Coal (ABV 4%)

Sea Wheat (ABV 4%)

Ship Hop Ale (ABV 4%)

White Horses (ABV 4%)

Autumn Rye (ABV 4.1%)

Rye P.A. (ABV 4.1%)

Newton Stout (ABV 4.2%)

THE BREWERIES

Sea Dog (ABV 4.2%)

The Emblestones (ABV 4.2%)

Dolly Daydream (ABV 4.3%)

Pilgrim (ABV 4.3%)

Indian Summer (ABV 4.4%)

Shires

Shires Brewery, All Nations Brewhouse, 20 Coalport Road, Madeley, Shropshire, TF7 5DP
☎ (01952) 580570 (Brewery) ☎ (01746) 769606 (Office) ☎ 07977 900212
✉ info@shiresbrewery.co.uk ⊕ shiresbrewery.co.uk

⊕Shires Brewery (formerly Worfield) was launched in 2009 and is based at the historic All Nations Brewhouse in Madeley near Telford, which has a brewing tradition stretching back to 1831. Mike Handley supervises the 10-barrel plant. The brewery supply the All Nations tap house next door as well as other outlets. Seasonal beers: see website.

Best Bitter (OG 1039, ABV 3.8%)
Pale in colour with fruity undertones and a hint of citrus. A tasty session beer. Sold in the All Nations as Dabley Ale.

Ginger Cob (OG 1043, ABV 4.2%)
Straw-coloured bitter with a hint of fresh ginger.

OBJ (Oh Be Joyful!) (OG 1043, ABV 4.2%) ◆
A light and sweet bitter; delicate flavour belies the strength.

Shropshire Pride (OG 1045, ABV 4.5%)
A mid-coloured bitter, full-bodied and malty with a pleasant bittersweet balance.

Severn Gorgeous (OG 1048, ABV 4.8%)
A light-bodied ale with full hop bitterness accompanying pine and citrus aromas.

Dabley Gold (OG 1050, ABV 5%)
The big brother of Dabley Ale, produced from the same recipe but brewed to a higher gravity giving a sweeter, fuller flavour.

Shoes SIBA

Shoes Brewery, Three Horseshoes Inn, Norton Canon, Hereford, HR4 7BH
☎ (01544) 318375
Tours by arrangement

Landlord Frank Goodwin was a keen home brewer who decided in 1994 to brew on a commercial basis for his pub. The beers are brewed from malt extract and are normally only available at the Three Horseshoes. Each September Canon Bitter is brewed with 'green' hops fresh from the harvest. All beers are also available bottle conditioned.

Norton Ale (OG 1038, ABV 3.6%)

Canon Bitter (OG 1040, ABV 4.1%)

Peploe's Tipple (OG 1060, ABV 6%)

Farriers Ale (OG 1114, ABV 15%)

Shotover SIBA

Shotover Brewing Co Ltd, Coopers Yard, Manor Farm Road, Horspath, Oxfordshire, OX33 1SD
☎ (01865) 876770 ☎ 07801 570444
✉ ed@shotoverbrewing.com
⊕ shotoverbrewing.com

Shop: please ring or email first
Tours by arrangement

⊠ Shotover is a family-run craft brewery four miles from Oxford city centre. It began brewing in 2009. 10 outlets are supplied direct. Bottle-conditioned beers are available and are suitable for vegetarians and vegans. Vegetarian cask ale can be supplied on request.

Prospect (OG 1040, ABV 3.7%)
A pale copper, hoppy session bitter with a big mouthfeel and striking dry hoppiness.

Scholar (OG 1046, ABV 4.5%)
A copper-coloured classic English bitter. It combines a silky malt base with a mixture of oranges, grapefruit and spiciness across the palate and delivers a satisfying bitter finish at the back of the throat.

Shottle Farm (NEW)

Shottle Farm Brewery, School House Farm, Lodge Lane, Shottle, Derbyshire, DE56 2DS
☎ (01773) 550056 ⊕ shottlefarmbrewery.co.uk

Based on a farm in Shottle since 2010, which is part of the Chatsworth Estate. Shottle Farm produces three core beers and a range of seasonals using its own spring water. The brewery tap is the George & Dragon in Belper. Bottle-conditioned beers are also available.

Shottle Pale Ale (SPA) (ABV 3.9%)
A mid-bodied pale ale with a soft, hoppy hit and a hint of citrus and tangerine.

8/- Ale (ABV 4.3%)
A rich, dark beer; smooth and malty with a pleasant aftertaste of treacle and caramel.

Shottle Gold (ABV 4.3%)
Floral aroma with a fruity hint of citrus. Easy-drinking, crisp with a clean, white head.

Shugborough SIBA

Shugborough Brewery, Shugborough Estate, Milford, Staffordshire, ST17 0XB
☎ (01782) 823447 ⊕ shugborough.org.uk
Tours daily Mar-Oct

Brewing in the original brewhouse at Shugborough, home of the Earls of Lichfield, restarted in 1990 but a lack of expertise led to the brewery being a static museum piece until Titanic Brewery of Stoke-on-Trent (qv) began helping in 1996. Brewing takes place every weekend during the visitor season with museum guides in period costume.

Miladys Fancy (OG 1048, ABV 4.6%)

Lordships Own (OG 1052, ABV 5%)

Silhill SIBA

Silhill Brewery Ltd, PO Box 15739, Solihull, West Midlands, B93 3FW
☎ 07977 444564 ✉ info@silhillbrewery.co.uk
⊕ silhillbrewery.co.uk

⊕Silhill began brewing in 2010 using a five-barrel plant, and upgraded in 2012 to 10 barrels.

LDA (Light Dry Ale) (OG 1037, ABV 3.7%)
A light, dry smooth amber ale with a dry, crisp taste.

Session (ABV 3.8%)
A dark, easy-drinking ale with a classic bitter taste and caramel overtones.

SPA (Silhill Pale Ale) (ABV 4%)
A pale, slightly smoky ale.

Progress (ABV 4.3%)

Silverstone

Silverstone Brewing Co Ltd, Kingshill Farm, Syresham, nr Silverstone, Northamptonshire, NN13 5TH
☎ (01280) 850629
✉ services@silverstonebrewingcompany.com
⊕ silverstonebrewingcompany.com
Tours by arrangement

⊠ The brewery, which is located near the celebrated motor racing circuit, opened in 2008. In keeping with its motor racing theme, the brewery is the proud sponsor of Formula V10. 60 outlets are supplied direct. Seasonal and bottle-conditioned beers are also available.

Pitstop Bitter (OG 1038, ABV 3.8%)

Pole Position (ABV 4.1%)

High Octane (ABV 5.5%)

Sinclair

See Orkney

Six Bells SIBA

⧳ Six Bells Brewery, Church Street, Bishop's Castle, Shropshire, SY9 5AA
☎ (01588) 638930 ✉ info@sixbellsbrewery.co.uk
⊕ sixbellsbrewery.co.uk
Tours by arrangement

Neville Richards – 'Big Nev' – started brewing in 1997 with a five-barrel plant and two fermenters. Alterations in 1999 included two more fermenters, a new grain store and mashing equipment. He supplies a number of customers both within the county and over the border in Wales. A new 12-barrel plant opened in 2010. In addition to the core beer range, 12 monthly specials are produced.

Supper (OG 1037, ABV 3.6%)
A light, refreshing ale with a delicate fruity aroma and a hint of spice.

Big Nev's (OG 1037, ABV 3.8%)
A pleasing, faintly grassy aroma leads to a dry, fruity hop flavour and a refreshing dry finish.

Ow Do! (OG 1042, ABV 4%)
A rich amber beer brewed with Goldings hops to give a spicy, fruity character.

Cloud Nine (OG 1043, ABV 4.2%)
A robust, well-hopped beer with citrus notes throughout its aroma, flavour and dry, lingering finish.

Sixpenny SIBA

Wayland's Sixpenny Brewery, The Dairy Building, Manor Farm, Sixpenny Handley, Dorset, SP5 5NU
☎ (01725) 762006 ☎ 07760 802402
✉ mail@sixpennybrewery.co.uk
⊕ sixpennybrewery.co.uk
Shop Wed & Thu 4.30-5.30pm; Fri 4-6pm; Sat 11am-12.30pm

Tours by arrangement

⊠ Established in 2007 on a 2.5-barrel plant and formerly known as Waylands Brewery, Wayland's Sixpenny relocated to Dorset from Surrey in 2009 and expanded to a five-barrel plant. In 2011 it expanded again to a 20-barrel plant. Seasonal beers: see website. Occasional beers are also brewed.

Original (OG 1040, ABV 3.6%)
Refreshing, malty and well-hopped.

Best Bitter (OG 1044, ABV 4%)
A well-balanced session ale with a full-bodied flavour and matching hop bitterness that leads to a long, dry finish.

Gold (OG 1044, ABV 4.2%)
A golden ale, slightly citrus, with a distinctive hoppy floral aroma. Easy-drinking with a soft bittersweet finish.

Special (OG 1051, ABV 5%)
A traditional strong best bitter. Rich and full-bodied with a rounded malt flavour and long finish.

IPA (ABV 5.2%)
Powerfully hopped leading to a long, rounded finish.

Six Trees (NEW) SIBA

Six Trees Brewing Co, Triscombe House, Triscombe, Somerset, TA4 3HG
☎ (01984) 617000 ✉ info@6trees.co.uk
⊕ 6trees.co.uk
Shop Mon-Sat 9am-5.30pm; Sun 12-5pm
Tours by arrangement

⊠ Six Trees began brewing in 2012 operating out of the old apple store of an Edwardian country house. Bottle-conditioned beers are also available.

High Noon (ABV 3.2%)

Bitter Memories (ABV 4.3%)

Jardeeling (ABV 4.3%)

Burnished Brass (ABV 4.8%)

Skinner's SIBA ◉

Skinner's Brewing Co Ltd, Riverside, Newham Road, Truro, Cornwall, TR1 2SU
☎ (01872) 271885 ✉ info@skinnersbrewery.com
⊕ skinnersbrewery.com
Shop & Visitor Centre open daily 9am-5pm
Tours by arrangement (ring 01872 245689)

⊠ Skinner's brewery was founded in 1997. To increase production the brewery moved to bigger premises in 2003, opening a brewery shop and visitor centre. The brewery is now a 25-barrel plant with production capacity of 375 barrels a week. Since opening, the brewery has won numerous awards. Merchandise and beer are available to purchase online. Recently the brewery produced special edition beers under the brand The Cornish Beer & Surf Co. Seasonal beers: see website.

Ginger Tosser (OG 1038, ABV 3.8%)
Hoppy golden ale fused with Cornish honey. The rounded finish has a hint of ginger.

Spriggan Ale (OG 1038, ABV 3.8%) ✎
A light golden, hoppy bitter. Well-balanced with a smooth bitter finish.

Betty Stogs (OG 1040, ABV 4%) ✎

Refreshing copper ale with balance of citrus hops and apple fruit, sweet malt and bitterness. Faint aroma of malt and hops. Bitter finish is slow to develop but long to fade.

Heligan Honey (OG 1040, ABV 4%) 🍴 ◈
Copper-coloured beer with added Cornish honey detectable in the aroma and taste. Sweet in the mouth balanced by bitterness and a little hop. Lingering, bittersweet and dry aftertaste.

Keel Over (OG 1041, ABV 4.2%)
A classic Cornish bitter, amber in colour, beautifully balanced with a smooth finish.

Cornish Knocker Ale (OG 1044, ABV 4.5%) 🍴 ◈
Refreshing golden ale with citrus hops all the way through. Spice and fruit in the mouth are balanced by bitter and faint malt undertones, with a clean and lasting bitter finish.

Figgy's Brew (OG 1044, ABV 4.5%) ◈
With subdued fruit and malt on the nose, a pale brown beer that is gently malty and sweet in the mouth, leading to bitterness that becomes dry in the finish.

Hunny Bunny (OG 1045, ABV 4.5%)
A premium strength golden ale with subtle hints of Cornish honey. Clean-tasting with a hoppy aroma.

Porthleven (OG 1048, ABV 4.8%)
Zingy yellow citrus ale with bite. Very refreshing and smooth with bitter grapefruit on the tongue and a hoppy, bitter aftertaste.

Cornish Blonde (OG 1048, ABV 5%)
A combination of wheat malt and English and American hops makes this light-coloured wheat beer deceptively easy to drink.

Slater's SIBA ◉

Eccleshall Brewing Co Ltd, Slater's Brewery, St Albans Road, Common Road Industrial Estate, Stafford, ST16 3DR
☎ (01785) 257976 ✉ sales@slatersales.co.uk
⊕ slatersales.co.uk
Shop Mon-Fri 9am-5pm, Sat 10am-12pm
Tours by arrangement

☺ The brewery was opened in 1995 and in 2006 moved to new, larger premises, resulting in a tripling of capacity. It has won numerous awards from CAMRA and SIBA. One pub is owned, the George at Eccleshall, which serves as the brewery tap.

Bitter (OG 1035.5, ABV 3.6%)
A pale bitter with an earthy, spicy hop character allied to juicy malt and tart fruit.

Original (OG 1040, ABV 4%) ◈
Amber bitter. Malty aroma with caramel notes, hoppy taste develops into a dry hoppy finish with a touch of sweetness.

Top Totty (OG 1040, ABV 4%) ◈
A yellow colour with a fruit and hop nose. A hop and fruit balanced taste leads to citrus hints with mouth-watering edges. Dry finish with tangs of lemon.

Queen Bee (OG 1042, ABV 4.2%) ◈
Golden with a sweet and spicy aroma and hop background. Honey sweet taste followed by a gentle bitter finish on the tongue.

Premium (OG 1044, ABV 4.4%) ◈

Pale brown bitter with malt and caramel aroma. Malt and caramel taste supported by hops and some fruit provide a warming descent and satisfyingly bitter mouthfeel.

Slaughterhouse SIBA

Slaughterhouse Brewery Ltd, Bridge Street, Warwick, CV34 5PD
☎ (01926) 490986
✉ enquiries@slaughterhousebrewery.com
⊕ slaughterhousebrewery.com
Tours by arrangement

Production began in 2003 on a four-barrel plant in a former slaughterhouse. Due to its success, beer production now consists mainly of Saddleback, supplemented by monthly special and seasonal beers. Around 30 outlets are supplied. The brewery premises are licensed for off-sales direct to the public. In 2010 the brewery opened its first pub, the Wild Boar in Warwick. The pub has a microbrewery attached, brewing regular specials for the pub, other outlets and beer swaps with other breweries.

Saddleback Best Bitter (OG 1038, ABV 3.8%)
Amber-coloured session bitter with a distinctive Challenger hop flavour.

Pacific Pale Ale (OG 1042, ABV 4.2%)
A golden bitter brewed using New Zealand hops, inspired by the 2011 Rugby World Cup.

Boar D'eau (OG 1045, ABV 4.5%)
Blond bitter brewed with lager malt to produce a clean taste, and bright pale colour.

Wild Boar (OG 1052, ABV 5.2%)
A robust dark beer produced using both dark crystal and chocolate malts.

Sleaford SIBA

Hop Me Up Ltd – Sleaford Brewery, 21 Pride Court, Enterprise Park, Sleaford, Lincolnshire, NG34 8GL
☎ 07885 811157 ✉ hopmeup@hotmail.co.uk
⊕ sleafordbrewery.co.uk
Shop hours vary – please ring in advance
Tours by arrangement

Sleaford began brewing in 2010 using a five-barrel brew plant. All beers are also available bottle-conditioned. Over 20 regular beers are produced.

Cool Runnings (ABV 2.5%)

Royal Ruby Mild (ABV 3.5%)

Cats Eyes IPA (ABV 3.7%)

Hedgerow Seville (ABV 3.9%)

Pale Partridge (OG 1039, ABV 3.9%)

Hedgerow Silver (OG 1041, ABV 4%)

Crazy Kiwi (ABV 4.1%)

Go West (ABV 4.1%)

Pleasant Pheasant (OG 1044, ABV 4.2%)

Stout (OG 1044, ABV 4.2%)

Layla Lager (ABV 4.3%)

Hedgerow Gold (OG 1046, ABV 4.4%)

Golden Goose (OG 1047, ABV 4.5%)

Rock It Red (ABV 5%)

Snow Goose (ABV 5%)

Midnight Runner (OG 1055, ABV 5.2%)

Route 17 (OG 1056, ABV 5.3%)

Espresso Stout (ABV 5.5%)

Vanilla Stout (ABV 5.5%)

Stone the Crows (ABV 8%)

Slightly Foxed (NEW) SIBA

Slightly Foxed Brewing Co, Higher Underbank House, Charlestown, West Yorkshire, HX7 6PS
☎ 07412 008221
✉ simon@slightlyfoxedbrewery.co.uk
⊕ slightlyfoxedbrewery.co.uk

☺Slightly Foxed launched in 2011 as a venture between an award-winning landlord and a local businessman. The brewery uses spare capacity at Brass Monkey Brewery. Seasonal and special beers are also available.

Slightly Foxed (ABV 3.8%)

Fox Glove (ABV 4.3%)

Bengal Fox (ABV 5.2%)

Prairie Fox (ABV 5.2%)

Small Paul's

Small Paul's Brewery, 27 Briar Close, Gillingham, Dorset, SP8 4SS
☎ (01747) 823574 ✉ smallbrewer@btinternet.com
Tours by arrangement

⊠ Launched in 2006, this half-barrel brewery is located in the owner's garage. There are usually two brews a month but consideration is being given to increasing capacity following success at beer festivals. A small number of local pubs and clubs are supplied direct and beers can be designed and brewed to order. Seasonal beers are also available.

Gylla's Gold (OG 1039, ABV 3.8%) ◄
Drinkable session ale. Mild fruit/hop aromas lead to bitter hop flavours and a lingering dry hop aftertaste.

Challenger II (OG 1045, ABV 4.3%)
A copper-coloured malty bitter.

Wyvern (OG 1044, ABV 4.4%) ◄
Red-brown, well-balanced best bitter with malt and caramel flavours and a short, bittersweet finish.

Gillingham Pale (OG 1045, ABV 4.5%) ◄
Fruity, caramel aromas lead to complex bittersweet flavours and a short, dry finish.

Elder Sarum (OG 1048, ABV 4.7%)
A pale gold fruity bitter with subtle elderflower flavours and aroma.

Smiles

See Highgate

Samuel Smith

Samuel Smith Old Brewery (Tadcaster), High Street, Tadcaster, North Yorkshire, LS24 9SB
☎ (01937) 832225 ⊕ samuelsmithsbrewery.co.uk

☺ A fiercely independent, family-owned company. Tradition, quality and value are important, resulting in brewing without any artificial additives. All real ale is supplied in wooden casks, though nitrokeg has replaced cask beer in some pubs in recent years. An unfiltered draught wheat beer is a recent addition. Around 200 pubs are owned. A bottle-conditioned beer was introduced in 2008 (Yorkshire Stingo, ABV 8%) but is only available in specialist off-licences.

Old Brewery Bitter/OBB (OG 1040, ABV 4%) ◄
Malt dominates the aroma, with an initial burst of malt, hops and fruit in the taste, which is sustained in the aftertaste.

Snowdonia

🕱 Snowdonia Brewery, Snowdonia Parc Brewpub & Campsite, Waunfawr, Caernarfon, Gwynedd, LL55 4AQ
☎ (01286) 650409 ✉ info@snowdonia-park.co.uk
⊕ snowdonia-park.co.uk

Snowdonia started brewing in 1998 in a two-barrel brewhouse. The brewing is now carried out by the owner, Carmen Pierce. The beer is brewed solely for the Snowdonia Park pub and campsite.

Gwyrfai (OG 1037.4, ABV 3.8%)

Snowdonia Gold (OG 1040, ABV 4%)

Carmen Sutra (OG 1043, ABV 4.4%)

Cais (OG 1046, ABV 5.2%)

Welsh Highland Bitter (OG 1048, ABV 5.2%)

Son of Sid

🕱 Son of Sid Brewery, The Chequers, 71 Main Road, Little Gransden, Bedfordshire, SG19 3DW
☎ (01767) 677348
✉ chequersgransden@btinternet.com
Tours by arrangement

⊠ Son of Sid was established in 2007 on a 2.5-barrel plant in a separate room of the pub. The brewery can be viewed from the lounge bar. It is named after the father of the current landlord, who ran the pub for 42 years. His son has carried the business on for the past 19 years as a family-run enterprise. Beer is sold in the pub and at local beer festivals.

English Ale (OG 1035, ABV 3.5%)
Traditional English ale with a clean, malty taste and good hop character.

Muck Cart Mild (OG 1035, ABV 3.5%) 🍺 ◄
Black mild with a resounding roast malt presence and a caramel background in aroma and taste. There is some sweetness but the balance is predominantly dry and bitter, with increasing bitterness in the aftertaste.

Golden Shower (OG 1041, ABV 4.1%)
Full-bodied golden beer with a light hop character and a defined maltiness.

SouthDowns (NEW)

SouthDowns Brewery Ltd, c/o Shepherd & Dog, The Street, Fulking, East Sussex, BN3 9LU
☎ 07775 743518 ✉ info@southdownsbrewery.com
⊕ southdownsbrewery.com

SouthDowns began brewing in 2011. Beer are distributed mainly in the Sussex and Surrey areas and to local pubs and CAMRA beer festivals. The

THE BREWERIES

brewery is currently using spare capacity at Kent Brewery until a move to its own premises.

Truleigh Gold (OG 1036, ABV 3.7%)
A crisp, clean, refreshing pale golden ale with apricot, orange and citrus aromas and a dab of sweetness.

Ruskin's Ram (OG 1041, ABV 4%)
Traditional English ale with a sharp, clean, malty taste complemented by a subtle aroma with hints of vanilla and elderflower.

Devils Dyke Porter (OG 1050, ABV 5%)
Toffee, chocolate and smoky flavours are complemented by a subtle hint of marmalade.

South Hams SIBA

South Hams Brewery Ltd, Stokeley Barton, Stokenham, Kingsbridge, Devon, TQ7 2SE
☎ (01548) 581151
✉ info@southhamsbrewery.co.uk
⊕ southhamsbrewery.co.uk
Tours by arrangement

⊠ The brewery moved to its present site, a milking parlour, in 2003, with a 10-barrel plant and plenty of room to expand. It supplies more than 60 outlets in Plymouth and south Devon. Wholesalers are used to distribute to other areas. Three pubs are owned. Seasonal beers: see website. Bottle-conditioned beers are also available.

Devon Pride (OG 1039, ABV 3.8%)
A dark amber session ale.

XSB (OG 1043, ABV 4.2%) ◈
Amber nectar with a fruity nose and a bitter finish.

Wild Blond (OG 1045, ABV 4.4%)
A straw-coloured beer with a citrus flavour.

Eddystone (OG 1050, ABV 4.8%)
A golden beer with fruit and citrus flavours.

Southport SIBA

Southport Brewery, Unit 3, Enterprise Business Park, Russell Road, Southport, Merseyside, PR9 7RF
☎ 07748 387652 ✉ southportbrewery@fsmail.net
⊕ southportbrewery.co.uk

☺ The Southport brewery opened in 2004 as a 2.5-barrel plant but moved to a five-barrel plant due to demand. Around 30 pubs are supplied in the North-west. It also supplies the free trade via Boggart Brewery (qv). Seasonal beers: see website.

Cyclone (OG 1039.5, ABV 3.8%)
A bronze-coloured bitter with a fruity blackcurrant aftertaste.

Sandgrounder Bitter (OG 1039.5, ABV 3.8%)
Pale, hoppy session bitter with a floral character.

Carousel (OG 1041.5, ABV 4%)
A refreshing, floral, hoppy best bitter.

Golden Sands (OG 1041.5, ABV 4%)
A golden-coloured, triple hopped bitter with citrus flavour.

Natterjack (OG 1043.5, ABV 4.3%)
A premium bitter with fruit notes and a hint of coffee.

Sperrin (NEW)

⬚ Sperrin Brewery Ltd/Victory Beers, Lord Nelson Inn, Birmingham Road, Ansley, Warwickshire, CV10 9PQ
☎ (02476) 392305
Tours by arrangement

Sperrin began brewing in 2012 using a six-barrel plant. The brewery is owned and run by three brothers, Craig, Warren and Treeve Sperrin.

Band of Brothers (ABV 4.2%)
A blonde, hoppy, full-flavoured bitter.

Spey Valley (NEW)

Spey Valley Brewery, Mains of Mulben, Mulben, Keith, AB55 6YH
✉ finestbreweryofspeyside@hotmail.com

Spey Valley began brewing in 2012 making 13.5-18 gallons per brew and operates on a part-time basis. Most of the beer goes to the Mash Tun in Aberlour, the Craigellachie Hotel and beer festivals.

Stefan's Blueberry Beauty (ABV 3.7%)
A ruby-coloured blueberry ale style mead. Made with honey, barley, blueberries, hops and lavender, it is balanced so that the blueberries and lavender are subtly noticeable on the nose but not the palate, where the honey and hops take over. Also brewed to ABV 6% dependent on batch.

Baby Spey (ABV 4.2%)
Spey Stout's little brother.

David's Not So Bitter (ABV 4.4%)
A simple, well-balanced light brown ale with a good body and plenty of hoppy aroma.

Roystons Hoppy Handful (ABV 4.6%)
Bright, citrusy and hoppy.

Spey Stout (ABV 5.4%)
A subtly bitter, lightly floral, sweet and chocolatey stout.

Spinning Dog

See Hereford

Spire SIBA

Spire Brewery Ltd, Unit 4, Deepdale Close, Hartington Industrial Estate, Staveley, Derbyshire, S43 3YF
☎ (01246) 476005 ☎ 07904 638550
✉ info@spirebrewery.co.uk ⊕ spirebrewery.co.uk
Shop Mon-Fri 9am-4.30pm
Tours by arrangement

☺The brewery was set up by ex-Scots Guards musician and teacher David McLaren in 2006. The brewery moved to larger premises in 2011 with an increased brewing and bottling capacity. More than 100 outlets are supplied direct. Seasonal beers: see website.

Brassed Off! (OG 1036, ABV 3.7%)
Easy drinking session bitter combining malt and fruit flavours, balanced by a long, bitter finish.

Whiter Shade of Pale (OG 1039, ABV 4%)
Pale, straw-coloured session bitter with a subtle lemon hop finish. Refreshingly smooth with a well-balanced malt flavour.

Dark Side of the Moon (OG 1043, ABV 4.3%) ◈

Complex and satisfying ruby mild with coffee aroma and toffee flavours. Dark and sweet but not too strong.

Chesterfield Best Bitter (OG 1044, ABV 4.5%) ◆
Classic brown strong bitter with malt and fruit flavours and a hint of caramel and chocolate in the finish. There is a little bitterness in the aftertaste.

Coal Porter (OG 1045, ABV 4.5%)
A smooth, dark beer combining coffee and bitter chocolate, becoming increasingly dry leading to a bitter finish and aftertaste.

Land of Hop & Glory (OG 1044, ABV 4.5%) ◆
An excellent example of a clean, crisp-tasting golden ale. Easy to drink with grapefruit and lemon flavours developing. These complex citrus hop flavours lead to a bitter, dry aftertaste.

Twist & Stout (OG 1044, ABV 4.5%) ◆
Creamy and dark with flavours of bitter chocolate and coffee. Easy drinking.

Sovereigns Escort IPA (OG 1051, ABV 5.2%)
Strong, amber-coloured IPA with a delicate orange flavour leading to a bitter finish. Full-bodied and easy to drink despite its strength.

Sgt Pepper Stout (OG 1053, ABV 5.5%) ◆
Unique full-flavoured stout brewed with ground black pepper. Liquorice and pepper flavours dominate on both aroma and taste in this original, complex dark and delicious beer.

Enigma (OG 1061, ABV 6.4%) ◆
Strong, complex beer to be savoured and appreciated. Full bodied, with hints of marmalade tartness and fruit, leading to a dry, slightly bitter finish.

Spitting Feathers SIBA ◉

Spitting Feathers Brewery, Common Farm, Waverton, Chester, CH3 7QT
☎ (01244) 332052 ✉ info@spittingfeathers.org
⊕ spittingfeathers.org
Tours by arrangement

Spitting Feathers was established in 2005 at Common Farm on the outskirts of Chester. The brewery and visitors' bar are in traditional sandstone buildings around a cobbled yard, which is also the setting for the West Cheshire Brewers' Beer Festival in July. Beehives provide honey for the brewery and spent grains are fed to livestock. The brewery opened its first pub in Chester in 2008. Around 200 outlets are supplied. Seasonal beers: see website. Bottle-conditioned beers are also available. All bottled beers are suitable for vegetarians and vegans.

Farmhouse Ale (OG 1035, ABV 3.6%)
A golden session bitter.

Thirstquencher (OG 1038, ABV 3.9%) ◆
Powerful hop aroma leads into the taste. Bitterness and a fruity citrus hop flavour fight for attention. A sharp, clean golden beer with a long, dry, bitter aftertaste.

Special Ale (OG 1041, ABV 4.2%) ◆
Complex tawny-coloured beer with a sharp, grainy mouthfeel. Malty with good hop coming through in the aroma and taste. Hints of nuttiness and a touch of acidity. Dry, astringent finish.

Old Wavertonian (OG 1043, ABV 4.4%) ◆
Creamy and smooth stout. Full-flavoured with coffee notes in aroma and taste. Roast and nut

flavours throughout, leading to a hoppy, bitter finish.

Basket Case (OG 1046, ABV 4.8%) ◆
Reddish, complex beer. Sweetness and fruit dominate taste, offset by hops and bitterness that follow through into the aftertaste.

Sportsman

▤ **Sportsman Brewing Co, 1-3 St John's Road, Huddersfield, West Yorkshire, HD1 5AY**
☎ 07766 131123
✉ the.sportsman.hudds@googlemail.com

☺The Sportsman began brewing in 2011 on a two-barrel brew plant housed in the cellar of the pub.

Town Mild (OG 1033, ABV 3.5%)
A light, pleasant-drinking dark mild with a chocolate start and biscuit finish.

Hopscotch (OG 1036, ABV 3.9%)
A pale session ale.

Pigeon Bridge Porter (OG 1050, ABV 4.7%)
A liquorice-tasting porter with a blackberry finish.

Deco IPA (OG 1046, ABV 5%)
An easy-drinking IPA. Blackberry notes to begin and a citrus strawberry hop to finish.

Springhead SIBA ◉

Springhead Brewery, Main Street, Laneham, Nottinghamshire, DN22 0NA
☎ (01636) 821000 ✉ angie@springhead.co.uk
⊕ springhead.co.uk
Shop open daily 9am-6pm
Tours by arrangement

☺ Springhead Brewery opened in 1990, moving to bigger premises three years later and, to meet increased demand, expanded to a brew length of 50 barrels in 2003. In 2011 the brewery relocated to its current address. Around 500 outlets are supplied direct and the brewery owns two pubs. Many of the beer names have a Civil War theme. Drop O' The Black Stuff (seasonal) is suitable for vegans.

Bramley Apple (OG 1036, ABV 3.8%)
A pale, straw-coloured beer with hints of lemon and a dry, biscuity finish.

Robin Hood Bitter (OG 1041, ABV 4%)
A dark traditional bitter with a good head and plenty of hops.

Springhead (OG 1041, ABV 4%)
A clean-tasting, easy-drinking, amber-coloured bitter with a dry, hoppy finish.

Charlie's Angel (OG 1045, ABV 4.5%)
A light, golden beer with a deeply fruity nose from the addition of fresh oranges, well-balanced bitterness and a dry finish from the hint of coriander.

Maid Marian Blonde (OG 1045, ABV 4.5%)
A pale golden beer with a fruity orange aroma and a dry, peppery finish.

The Leveller (OG 1047, ABV 4.8%)
A dark, smoky intense flavour with a burnt toffee finish. Brewed in the style of Belgian Trappist ale.

Roaring Meg (OG 1052, ABV 5.5%)
A smooth golden beer with a sweet, citrus honey aroma and a long dry finish.

THE BREWERIES

Stables

▤ Stables Brewing Co, The Stables, Beamish Hall Country House Hotel, Beamish, County Durham, DH9 0YB
☎ (01207) 288750 ✉ info@beamish-hall.co.uk
⊕ beamish-hall.co.uk/stables
Tours by arrangement

☺Stables was established as part of a £1 million development of an old stable block, converting a disused building to a pub and eight-barrel micro-brewery. Seven regular beers are produced. Seasonal and special beers are also available.

Beamish Hall Best Bitter (OG 1038, ABV 3.8%)

Old Miner Tommy (OG 1037, ABV 3.8%)

Bobby Dazzler (OG 1042, ABV 4.2%)

Coppy Lane (OG 1043, ABV 4.2%)

Silver Buckles (OG 1044, ABV 4.4%)

Beamish Burn (OG 1045, ABV 4.5%)

Bell Tower (OG 1052, ABV 5%)

Staithes (NEW)

Staithes Brewery, Captain Cook Inn, 60 Staithes Lane, Staithes, TS13 5AD
☎ (01947) 840200 ✉ info@captaincookinn.co.uk
⊕ captaincookinn.co.uk

Beers have been brewed since 2011 using spare capacity at various Yorkshire brewers. A brewing plant is currently being installed at the pub.

Boulby Blonde (ABV 3.5%)

Boulby Bronze (ABV 3.6%)

Whitby Golden Beach (ABV 3.8%)

Boulby Dark (ABV 4%)

Stanway

Stanway Brewery, Stanway, Cheltenham, Gloucestershire, GL54 5PQ
☎ (01386) 584320 ⊕ stanwaybrewery.co.uk

☺ Stanway is a small brewery founded in 1993 with a five-barrel plant that confines its sales to the Cotswolds area (15 to 20 outlets). The brewery is the only known plant in the country to use wood-fired coppers for all its production. Seasonal beers: see website.

Stanney Bitter (OG 1042, ABV 4.5%) ◆
A light, refreshing, amber-coloured beer, dominated by hops in the aroma, with a bitter taste and a hoppy, bitter finish.

Star Inn

▤ Star Inn Brewery, Star Inn, Starcliff Ltd, 2 Back Hope Street, Higher Broughton, Salford, Greater Manchester, M7 2PD
☎ (0161) 792 4184 ☎ 07789 175219
✉ starinnbrewery@gmail.com/
bar@staronthecliff.co.uk ⊕ wix.com/
starinnbrewery/brewery

☺Formerly known as Bazens' Brewery, it moved to an outhouse on the premises of the Star Inn on The Cliff in Salford in 2010. The four-barrel plant is now under the wing of the owners of the Star Inn, namely a large group of customers who bought the

pub in 2009, making it Britain's first urban pub cooperative.

Golden Crown (OG 1039, ABV 3.8%)

Starry Night (OG 1040, ABV 4%)

Stationhouse

See Frodsham

Steamin' Billy

Steamin' Billy Brewing Co Ltd, Registered Office: 5 The Oval, Oadby, Leicestershire, LE2 5JB
☎ (0116) 271 2616 ✉ info@steamin-billy.co.uk
⊕ steamin-billy.co.uk
Tours by arrangement

☺ Steamin' Billy was formed in 1995 by licensee Barry Lount and brewer Bill Allingham. Bill originally brewed in Derbyshire but after outgrowing the plant the beers have since been contracted out and are currently brewed at Grainstore Brewery (qv). Seven pubs are owned. Seasonal beers: see website. See Grainstore for regular beers.

Steel City

Steel City Brewing Ltd, c/o The Wellington, 1 Henry Street, Sheffield, South Yorkshire, S3 7EQ
✉ hops@steelcitybrewing.co.uk
⊕ steelcitybrewing.co.uk

⊗ Steel City was established in 2009 and makes use of the brewing facilities at the Little Ale Cart Brewery in Sheffield. Beer is brewed once a month, a different beer each time. A nine-gallon mini-plant is used to brew one-off beers, often extreme with an emphasis on pale and hoppy brews.

Stewart SIBA

Stewart Brewing Ltd, Unit 5, 42 Dryden Road, Bilston Glen Industrial Estate, Loanhead, Midlothian, EH20 9LZ
☎ (0131) 440 2442 ✉ stewartbrewing@gmail.com
⊕ stewartbrewing.co.uk
Shop Mon-Thu 10am-5pm; Fri 10am-6pm; Sat 10am-4pm
Tours by arrangement

☺Established in 2004 by Steve Stewart, a qualified master brewer, and specialising in high-quality cask ales, all made from natural ingredients. Seasonal and bottle-conditioned beers supplement the regular range. Beer in mini-casks and bottles can be purchased direct from the brewery. There are plans to move to a new, larger site (24 Dryden Road, Loanhead, EH20 9HX).

Pentland IPA (OG 1040, ABV 3.9%) ◆
A pleasing, hoppy, golden session ale. The dry bitter taste is well balanced by sweetness from the malt, and fruit flavours. The aftertaste is dry with a lingering bitterness.

Copper Cascade (OG 1041, ABV 4.1%) ◆
This tawny-coloured beer is born from American hops and Scottish malt. The hop character overlays a solid malt base. Hints of roast and substantial fruitiness give a complex character. A bittersweet taste leads to a dry bitter finish.

Edinburgh No.3 Premium Scotch Ale (OG 1043, ABV 4.3%) ◆
An excellent example of a Scottish heavy ale. Full-bodied and dark with a predominantly malt character, fruit notes and a gentle infusion of hop. A bittersweet beer with a dry finish.

80/- (OG 1044, ABV 4.4%) ◆
Superb traditional Scottish heavy. The complex profile is dominated by malt with fruit flavours giving the sweetish character typical of this beer style. Hops provide a gentle balancing bitterness that intensifies in the dry finish.

Edinburgh Gold (OG 1048, ABV 4.8%) ◆
A full-bodied but easy-drinking Continental-style golden ale. Bitterness from the hop character is strong in the finish and complemented in the taste by a little sweetness from malt, and fruit flavours.

Sticklegs

Sticklegs Brewery, Unit 7, Old Forge Court, Colchester Road, Elmstead Market, Essex, CO7 7EA
☎ 07962 012906 ✉ tom@sticklegs.co.uk
⊕ sticklegs.co.uk
Shop Mon-Sat 9.30am-4.30pm; closed Sun
Tours by arrangement

⊠ Sticklegs was established in 2008 at the Cross Inn, Great Bromley. It moved twice in 2009 to Clacton-on-Sea then to its present site in Elmstead and has expanded over the years to use both a two-barrel and six-barrel plant . Bottle-conditioned beers are also available.

Malt Shovel Mild (OG 1032, ABV 3.4%)

Old Forge Bitter (OG 1037, ABV 3.8%)

Tendring 100 (OG 1039, ABV 4%)

Innkeeper Gold (OG 1041, ABV 4.2%)

Elmstead Stout (OG 1043, ABV 4.8%)

Nemesis (OG 1049, ABV 5%)

Stirling

See Traditional Scottish Ales

Stokesley

See Wainstones

Stonehenge SIBA ⊚

Stonehenge Ales Ltd, The Old Mill, Mill Road, Netheravon, Salisbury, Wiltshire, SP4 9QB
☎ (01980) 670631 ✉ info@stonehengeales.co.uk
⊕ stonehengeales.co.uk
Tours by arrangement

The beer is brewed in a mill built in 1914 to generate electricity from the River Avon. The site was converted to a gravity-fed brewery in 1984 (Bunce's Brewery) and in 1994 the company was bought by Danish master brewer Stig Anker Andersen. More than 300 outlets in the south of England and several wholesalers are supplied. Seasonal beers: see website.

Spire Ale (OG 1037, ABV 3.8%)
A light, golden, hoppy bitter.

Pigswill (OG 1039, ABV 4%)

A full-bodied beer, rich in hop aroma, with a warm amber colour.

Heel Stone (OG 1042, ABV 4.3%)
A crisp, clean, refreshing bitter, deep amber in colour, well balanced with a fruity blackcurrant nose.

Great Bustard (OG 1046, ABV 4.8%)
A strong, fruity, malty bitter.

Danish Dynamite (OG 1048, ABV 5%)
A strong, dry ale, slightly fruity with a well-balanced, bitter hop flavour.

Stonehouse SIBA

Stonehouse Brewery, Stonehouse, Weston, Oswestry, Shropshire, SY10 9ES
☎ (01691) 676457
✉ info@stonehousebrewery.co.uk
⊕ stonehousebrewery.co.uk
Shop Mon-Fri 9am-5pm; Sat 10am-2pm
Tours by arrangement

Stonehouse was established in 2007 by Shane and Alison Parr on a 15-barrel plant. The brewery is based in former chicken sheds and is next to the old Cambrian railway line. A new building is currently being planned to expand brewery capacity. More than 120 local outlets are supplied direct. Bottle-conditioned beers are available.

Sunlander (OG 1037, ABV 3.7%)
Light and hoppy.

Station Bitter (OG 1041, ABV 3.9%)
A traditional amber bitter. Full-bodied session beer with a good balance of fruity hops and roasted malt.

Cambrian Gold (OG 1042, ABV 4.2%)
A deep golden fruity beer with a subtle dry finish.

Wheeltapper's Wheat Beer (OG 1045, ABV 4.5%)
Refreshing golden wheat beer with hints of coriander and lemon zest.

Kingston Flyer KPA (OG 1047, ABV 4.6%)
A crisp, pale ale.

Off The Rails (OG 1048, ABV 4.8%)
A rich and malty premium bitter with a classic British hop flavour.

Storm SIBA

Storm Brewing Co Ltd, 2 Waterside, Macclesfield, Cheshire, SK11 7HJ
☎ (01625) 431234 ✉ stormbrewing@dsl.pipex.com
⊕ stormbrewing.co.uk

Storm Brewing was founded in 1998 and operated from an old ICI boiler room until 2001 when the brewing operation moved to the current location, which until 1937 was a public house known as the Mechanics Arms. More than 60 outlets are supplied in Cheshire, Manchester and the Peak District. Seasonal and bottle-conditioned beers are also available.

Beauforts Ale (OG 1038, ABV 3.8%)
Golden brown, full-flavoured session bitter with a lingering hoppy taste.

Desert Storm (OG 1040, ABV 3.9%)
Amber-coloured beer with a smoky flavour of fruit and malt.

Bitter Experience (OG 1040, ABV 4%)

THE BREWERIES

A distinctive hop aroma draws you into this amber-coloured bitter. The palate has a mineral dryness that accentuates the crisp hop flavour and clean bitter finish.

Twister (OG 1041, ABV 4%)
A light golden bitter with a smooth fruity hop aroma complemented by a subtle bitter aftertaste.

Bosley Cloud (OG 1041, ABV 4.1%) ◆
Dry, golden bitter with peppery hop notes throughout. Some initial sweetness and a mainly bitter aftertaste. Soft, well-balanced and quaffable.

Brainstorm (OG 1041, ABV 4.1%)
Light gold in colour and strong in citrus fruit flavours.

Ale Force (OG 1042, ABV 4.2%) ◆
Amber, smooth-tasting, complex beer that balances malt, hop and fruit on the taste, leading to a roasty, slightly sweet aftertaste.

Downpour (OG 1043, ABV 4.3%)
A combination of Pearl and lager malts produces this pale ale with a full, fruity flavour with a hint of apple and sightly hoppy aftertaste.

PGA (OG 1044, ABV 4.4%) ◆
Light, crisp, lager-style beer with a balance of malt, hops and fruit. Moderately bitter and slight dry aftertaste.

Tornado (OG 1044, ABV 4.4%) ◆
Fruity premium bitter with some graininess. Dry, satisfying finish.

Hurricane Hubert (OG 1045, ABV 4.5%)
A dark beer with a refreshing full, fruity hop aroma and a subtle bitter aftertaste.

Windgather (OG 1045, ABV 4.5%)
A gold-coloured beer with a distinctive crisp, fruity flavour right through to the aftertaste.

Silk of Amnesia (OG 1047, ABV 4.7%) ◆
Smooth premium, easy-drinking bitter. Fruit and hops dominate throughout. Not too sweet, with a good lasting finish.

Storm Damage (OG 1047, ABV 4.7%)
A light-coloured, well-hopped and fruity beer balanced by a clean bitterness and smooth full palate.

Typhoon (OG 1050, ABV 5%) ◆
Copper-coloured, smooth strong bitter. Roast overtones and a hint of caramel and marzipan.

Stowey

Stowey Brewery Ltd, Old Cider House, 25 Castle Street, Nether Stowey, Somerset, TA5 1LN
☎ (01278) 732228 ✉ info@stoweybrewery.co.uk
⊕ stoweybrewery.co.uk
Tours by arrangement (small groups only)

⊗ Stowey was established in 2006, primarily to supply the owners' guesthouse and to provide beer to participants on 'real ale walks' run from the accommodation. The brewery also runs brewery workshop courses and supplies seasonal brews to the village pubs on a guest beer basis.

Strands

≣ **Strands Brewery Ltd, Strands Inn, Nether Wasdale, Cumbria, CA20 1ET**

☎ (01946) 26900 ✉ info@thestrandsinn.com
⊕ thestrandsinn.com
Tours by arrangement

☺Strands began brewing in 2007 on a three-barrel plant with a 12-barrel fermenting capacity. In 2011 the brewery expanded to a six-barrel plant with 30-barrel fermentation capability. The majority of beers are also available bottle-conditioned.

Pied Piper (OG 1033, ABV 2.7%)
A dark mild full of roasted malts, with a hint of Dandelion & Burdock.

Zingibeer (OG 1034, ABV 3.4%)
A refreshing, light, crisp ale with a good nose and a background hint of fresh root ginger.

Responsibly (OG 1038, ABV 3.7%)
A light, dry, heavily hopped and slightly smoked beer.

Brown Bitter (OG 1039, ABV 3.8%) ◆
A complex-tasting brown beer with a lingering bitter aftertaste.

Errmmm... (OG 1042, ABV 3.8%) ◆
A complex, traditional bitter.

Dickies Dunkel (OG 1042, ABV 4%)
Bavarian style malty, dark amber creamy beer with a good long finish.

Green Bullet (OG 1030, ABV 4%)
A light & creamy wheat beer heavily hopped with the eponymous high alpha acid hops.

Orange Blossom Special (OG 1039, ABV 4%)
A light, refreshing hoppy ale made with real oranges and orange zest.

T'Errmmm-inator (OG 1056, ABV 4%) ◆
A smooth, full-bodied, well-balanced roasty beer.

Tete a Tete (OG 1040, ABV 4%) ◆
A refreshing melon-fruit taste, with a sweet, gentle bitterness and a clean finish.

Corr'sberg (OG 1044, ABV 4.1%)

Dafydd Ale (OG 1044, ABV 4.2%) ◆
Clean-tasting and gently bittered, initially malty but with a hoppy bitter finish.

Angry Bee (OG 1042, ABV 4.5%)
A very popular golden honeyed beer, full bodied with a clean and spicy finish.

Bersteinale (OG 1047, ABV 4.5%)

Red Screes (OG 1047, ABV 4.5%) ◆
Rich-tasting, smooth, strong bitter; full-flavoured with plenty of roast and malt tastes.

Galaxy Cream (OG 1048, ABV 4.8%)
Dark, rich chocolate stout using traditional English hops giving a rich creamy head.

Irresponsibly (OG 1050, ABV 5%)

Fruit De La Lune (OG 1056, ABV 5.5%)

Russian Imperial Stout (OG 1082, ABV 7.9%)
Cappuccino headed stout, with a massive depth of complex flavours.

Tres Piste (OG 1082, ABV 8%)
Modeled on Trappist beers, strong, winey with a hint of honey on the finish.

Framboisen Bier (OG 1090, ABV 8.5%)
Full bodied, slightly sweetish cloudy raspberry wheat beer.

Barley Wine (OG 1100, ABV 10.5%)

Multi award-winning, rich, warming, full bodied strong mature ale.

Strangford Lough

Strangford Lough Brewing Co, 22 Shore Road, Killyleagh, Downpatrick, Northern Ireland, BT30 9UE
☎ (028) 4482 1461 ✉ contact@slbc.ie ⊕ slbc.ie

Beers for the company are contract brewed by an unnamed brewery in the EU, though there has been talk of a plant opening in Northern Ireland. Only bottled beer (not bottle-conditioned) is available at present.

Strathaven SIBA ◉

Strathaven Ales, Craigmill Brewery, Strathaven, ML10 6PB
☎ (01357) 520419 ✉ info@strathavenales.co.uk
⊕ strathavenales.co.uk
Shop Mon-Fri 9am-5pm (phone at weekend)
Tours by arrangement

Strathaven Ales is a 10-barrel brewery on the River Avon close to Strathaven and was converted from the remains of a 16th-century mill. The range is distributed throughout Scotland and the north of England. Seasonal beers: see website.

Clydesdale (OG 1038, ABV 3.8%)

Avondale (OG 1048, ABV 4%)

Old Mortality (OG 1046, ABV 4.2%)

Claverhouse (OG 1046, ABV 4.5%)

Strathbraan (NEW)

Strathbraan Brewery, Deanshaugh, Amulree, PH8 0EB
☎ (01350) 725264
✉ strathbraan.bry@btinternet.com

Straathbraan began brewing in 2012 using a 10-barrel plant.

Due South (OG 1037.5, ABV 3.8%)

Head East (OG 1041, ABV 4.2%)

Stringers SIBA

Stringers Beer, Unit 3, Low Mill Business Park, Ulverston, Cumbria, LA12 9EE
☎ (01229) 581387 ✉ info@stringersbeer.co.uk
⊕ stringersbeer.co.uk

Stringers is a family-run, small craft brewery. Brewing started in 2008 on a five-barrel plant run on 100% renewable energy. A small number of seasonal beers are produced. No. 2 Stout and Dark Country are suitable for vegans.

No. 2 Stout (OG 1042, ABV 4%)
A jet black stout with a roasty nose. Firmly bitter with some grain and dark toast.

Best Bitter (OG 1041, ABV 4.2%) ◗
Well-crafted and well-balanced with a clean hoppy bitterness.

West Coast Blond (OG 1042, ABV 4.4%) ◗
A golden beer with a hoppy, fruity aroma and taste that fades to a bitter, slightly astringent aftertaste.

Victoria IPA (OG 1053, ABV 5.5%)
Spicy, tropical fruit from the hops then some bitter marmalade with a definite bitter finish.

Stroud SIBA ◉

Stroud Brewery Ltd, Unit 11, Phoenix Works, London Road, Thrupp, Stroud, Gloucestershire, GL5 2BU
☎ (01453) 887122 ☎ 07891 995878
✉ info@stroudbrewery.co.uk ⊕ stroudbrewery.co.uk
Shop Mon-Thu 9am-3pm; Fri 9am-5pm
Tours by arrangement

The brewery commenced brewing in 2006 on a five-barrel plant. A new 20-barrel plant was installed in 2011 allowing the brewery to develop its range of organic bottled beers. Stroud supports the local economy and does not sell any beer through supermarkets, delivering to 40-50 pubs, independent retailers and direct to the public. Seasonal and bottle-conditioned beers are also available.

Tom Long (OG 1039, ABV 3.8%)
An amber-coloured bitter with a spicy citrus aroma.

Organic Ale (OG 1041, ABV 4%)
A fresh, hoppy, golden organic ale.

Budding (OG 1046, ABV 4.5%)
A pale ale with a grassy bitterness, sweet malt and floral aroma.

Stumpy's

See Yates'

Suddaby's

Suddaby's Ltd, Crown Hotel, 12 Wheelgate, Malton, North Yorkshire, YO17 7HP
☎ (01653) 692038 ✉ enquiries@suddabys.co.uk
⊕ suddabys.co.uk

Suddabys no longer brews on site. The beers are contract brewed by Brown Cow (qv) at Selby and are only sold in bottled form in the Malt'on Hops Beer & Wine Shop located within the Crown Hotel and a few other selected outlets. Suddabys draught beers are also available in the Crown Hotel.

Sulwath SIBA

Sulwath Brewers Ltd, The Brewery, 209 King Street, Castle Douglas, Dumfries & Galloway, DG7 1DT
☎ (01556) 504525 ✉ info@sulwathbrewers.co.uk
⊕ sulwathbrewers.co.uk
Shop Mon-Sat 10am-6pm
Tours by arrangement

Sulwath started brewing in 1995. The beers are supplied to markets as far away as Devon in the south and Aberdeen in the north. The brewery has a fully licensed brewery tap and off sales open 10am-6pm Mon-Sat. Cask ales are sold to around 100 outlets and four wholesalers. Seasonal and occasional beers are also available.

The Grace (OG 1044, ABV 4.3%)
A refreshing, rich ale with a full-bodied flavour that balances the caramel undertones.

Black Galloway (OG 1046, ABV 4.4%) 🗇 🍷
A robust porter/stout that derives its colour from the abundance of Maris Otter barley and chocolate malts used in the brewing process.

Criffel (OG 1044, ABV 4.6%) ◗

THE BREWERIES

Full-bodied beer with a distinctive bitterness. Fruit is to the fore of the taste with hops becoming increasingly dominant in the taste and finish.

Galloway Gold (OG 1049, ABV 5%) ◆
A cask-conditioned lager that will be too sweet for many despite being heavily hopped.

Summerskills SIBA ◉

Summerskills Brewery, Unit 15, Pomphlett Farm Industrial Estate, Broxton Drive, Billacombe, Plymouth, Devon, PL9 7BG
☎ (01752) 481283 ✉ info@summerskills.co.uk
⊕ summerskills.co.uk

Originally established in a vineyard in 1983 at Bigbury-on-Sea, Summerskills moved to its present site in 1985. Production has expanded to meet demand from wholesalers, who carry out nationwide distribution, and from national pub companies. Seasonal, occasional and bottle-conditioned beers are also available.

Cellar Vee (OG 1037, ABV 3.7%)

Hopscotch (OG 1041, ABV 4.1%)

Best Bitter (OG 1043, ABV 4.3%) ◆
A mid-brown beer, with plenty of malt and hops through the aroma, taste and finish. A good session beer.

Tamar (OG 1043, ABV 4.3%)
A tawny-coloured bitter with a fruity aroma and a hop taste and finish.

Devon Dew (OG 1047, ABV 4.7%)

Summer Wine SIBA

Summer Wine Brewery Ltd, The Old Furnace, Unit 15, Crossley Mills, New Mill Road, Honley, Holmfirth, West Yorkshire, HD9 6QB
☎ (01484) 665466
✉ info@summerwinebrewery.co.uk
⊕ summerwinebrewery.co.uk

⊛Brewing commenced in 2006 on a 10-gallon kit with an emphasis on bottle-conditioned beer. A 2007 upgrade saw a 0.5-barrel plant installed and in 2008 the brewery expanded to a six-barrel plant. Over 500 outlets are supplied direct. Two differing specials are available each month.

Resistance (ABV 3.7%)

Zenith (ABV 4%)

Gambit (ABV 4.2%)

Barista (ABV 4.8%)

Teleporter (ABV 5%)

Diablo (ABV 6%)

Sunny Republic (NEW) SIBA

Sunny Republic Brewing Co, The Old Grain Barns, North West Farm, West Street, Winterborne Kingston, Dorset, DT11 9AT
☎ (01929) 471600 ✉ info@sunnyrepublic.com
⊕ sunnyrepublic.com

Brewing began in 2012 using a 30-barrel plant.

Beach Blonde (ABV 3.7%)
A refreshing and hoppy pale ale with aromas of grapefruit and lychees.

Huna Red (ABV 4.2%)
A red ale brewed with hibiscus with a light malt body, an earthy fruitiness and hedgerow aromas of blackberries with a hint of citrus.

Surrey Hills SIBA

Surrey Hills Brewery Ltd, Denbies Wine Estate, London Road, Dorking, Surrey, RH5 6AA
☎ (01306) 883603 ✉ info@surreyhills.co.uk
⊕ surreyhills.co.uk
Shop Mon-Wed 10am-3pm; Thu-Sat 10am-5pm
Tours by arrangement

Surrey Hills started in 2005 and was originally based in an old milking parlour in the Surrey Hills. 2011 saw the brewery relocate to its present address. The brewery is an independent concern and not part of Denbies. Nearly 95% of production is sold within 15 miles of the brewery. Seasonal beers: see website.

Ranmore Ale (OG 1039, ABV 3.8%) ◆
A light session beer with plenty of flavour. An earthy hoppy nose leads into a grapefruit and hoppy taste and a clean, bitter finish.

Shere Drop (OG 1043, ABV 4.2%) 🍷 🍺 ◆
A golden amber ale, hoppy with some balancing malt. There is a pleasant citrus aroma and a noticeable fruitiness in the taste, with some sweetness also present. The finish is dry, hoppy and bitter.

Gilt Complex (OG 1047, ABV 4.6%)

Greensand IPA (OG 1047, ABV 4.6%)

Suthwyk

Suthwyk Ales, Offwell Farm, Southwick, Fareham, Hampshire, PO17 6DX
☎ (02392) 325252 ✉ mjbazeley@suthwykales.com
⊕ suthwykales.com/southwickbrewhouse.co.uk

Martin Bazeley farms award-winning malted barley in the fields along the top of Portsdown Hill, which is then brewed by the Oakleaf Brewing Co (qv) in Gosport. Free houses are supplied across Hampshire and into West Sussex. Bottle-conditioned beers are also available. For beer range see Oakleaf entry.

Sutton

See South Hams

Swan

🍺 Swan Microbrewery, Swan on the Green, West Peckham, Maidstone, Kent, ME18 5JW
☎ (01622) 812271 ✉ info@swan-on-the-green.co.uk ⊕ swan-on-the-green.co.uk
Tours by arrangement

The brewery was established in 2000 in an old coal shed behind the pub using a two-barrel plant. The beers are not filtered and no artificial ingredients are used. One pub is owned and other outlets and beer festivals are occasionally supplied. Seasonal beers are also available.

Fuggles Pale (OG 1037, ABV 3.6%)

Trumpeter Best (OG 1041, ABV 4%)

Cygnet (OG 1048, ABV 4.2%)

Bewick (OG 1052, ABV 5.3%)

Swansea SIBA

▤ Swansea Brewing Co, Joiners Arms, 50 Bishopston Road, Bishopston, Swansea, SA3 3EJ
☎ (01792) 232658/290197 (Office)

Office: 74 Hawthorne Avenue, Uplands, Swansea, SA2 0LY ✉ rory@swansea_brewing.co.uk
Tours by arrangement

☺Opened in 1996, Swansea was the first commercial brewery in the area for almost 30 years and is the city's only brew-pub. It doubled its capacity within the first year and now produces four regular beers and occasional experimental ones. Two regular outlets are supplied along with other pubs in the South Wales area. Seasonal beers are also available.

Deep Slade Dark Mild (ABV 4%) 🍺
A dark brown-coloured beer with a reddish hue. The aroma is malty with a little roast. The taste is nutty, malty and very mild.

Bishopswood Bitter (OG 1038, ABV 4.3%) ◆
A delicate aroma of hops and malt in this pale brown colour. The taste is a balanced mix of hops and malt with a growing hoppy bitterness ending in a lasting bitter finish.

Three Cliffs Gold (OG 1042, ABV 4.7%) ◆
A golden beer with a hoppy and fruity aroma, a hoppy taste with fruit and malt, and a quenching bitterness. The pleasant finish has a good hop flavour and bitterness.

Original Wood (ABV 5.2%)
Full-bodied, pale brown beer. Complex blend with increasing bitterness.

Swaton

Swaton Brewery, North End Farm, Swaton, Sleaford, Lincolnshire, NG34 0JP
☎ (01529) 421241
✉ swatonbrewery@hotmail.co.uk
⊕ swatonbrewery.com
Tours by arrangement

Swaton commenced brewing in 2007 on a five-barrel plant and is sited in the outbuildings of the owner's farm. It supplies beer festivals and local pubs. All beers are also available bottle conditioned.

Happy Jack (OG 1040, ABV 4.2%)

Dozy Bull (OG 1041.8, ABV 4.5%)

Three Degrees (OG 1043.5, ABV 4.7%)

Sweet William

See Brodie's

Taddington

Taddington Brewery Ltd, Blackwell Hall, Blackwell, Buxton, SK17 9TQ
☎ (01298) 85734

No real ale. Taddington started brewing in 2007, and brews one Czech-style unpasteurised lager in two different strengths: Moravka (ABV 4.4% and 5%), which is available on draught.

Tap East (NEW)

▤ Tap East Pub & Brewery, Great Eastern Market, Lower Ground Floor, Westfield Stratford City, Stratford, E20 1EE
☎ (020) 8555 4467 ✉ joe@tapeast.co.uk
⊕ tapeast.co.uk

Tap East began brewing in 2011 and is located in the Westfield shopping centre next to the Olympic Park.

East End Mild (OG 1037, ABV 3.5%)

JWB (James Wilson Bitter) (OG 1040, ABV 3.8%)

Tap House

▤ Tap House Brewery, The Tap House, 5 Annwell Lane, Smisby, Derbyshire, LE65 2TA
☎ (01530) 413604 ☎ 07792 548274
✉ info@taphouse-smisby.co.uk
⊕ taphouse-smisby.co.uk
Tours by arrangement

⊠ Established in 2010 this purpose-built brewery was recently upgraded to a 20-barrel plant. The brewery supplies its beers to its two pubs; the Tap House, Smisby and the Kings Arms, Coleorton, as well as pubs across Derbyshire and Leicestershire. The Tap House and Leatherbritches share the same brewery plant and brewer, but the two businesses are run independently.

Ashby Pride (OG 1038, ABV 3.8%)
A light, quaffable session beer.

Gold (OG 1042, ABV 4%)
A light, hoppy golden ale.

Kingdom (OG 1046, ABV 4.5%)
A chestnut-coloured beer with a hint of caramel.

Dark & Dangerous (OG 1048, ABV 5%)
A dark and complex porter with subtle chocolate flavours.

Tatton SIBA

Tatton Brewery Ltd, Unit 7, Longridge Trading Estate, Knutsford, Cheshire, WA16 8PR
☎ (01565) 750747 ☎ 07738 150898
✉ beer@tattonbrewery.co.uk
⊕ tattonbrewery.co.uk
Shop Mon-Fri 9am-4pm (other times by arrangement)
Tours by arrangement

☺Tatton is a family-run business based in the heart of Cheshire. Brewing commenced in 2010 using a steam-fired, custom-built 15-barrel brewhouse. Seasonal and occasional beers are also available. It supplies pubs throughout Cheshire and the north-west as well as events such as the Tatton Park RHS Flower Show.

Ale (OG 1036, ABV 3.7%)
An easy-drinking session ale with a rich copper colour. It has a full malty/toffee flavour balanced by a soft bitterness and hoppy, fruity taste and aroma.

Blonde (OG 1039, ABV 4%)
A clean-tasting, smooth pale ale with a fine New World hop aroma.

Best (OG 1040.5, ABV 4.2%)
A classic light amber-coloured best bitter with a clean malt flavour and fine hop character derived from a blend of aroma hops.

THE BREWERIES

Gold (OG 1046, ABV 4.8%)
A golden special ale with a maltiness backed by a robust hop character.

Timothy Taylor IFBB ⊙

Timothy Taylor & Co Ltd, Knowle Spring Brewery, Keighley, West Yorkshire, BD21 1AW
☎ (01535) 603139 ✉ tim@timtaylors.co.uk
⊕ timothy-taylor.co.uk

☺ Timothy Taylor is an independent, family-owned company established in 1858. It moved to the site of the Knowle Spring in 1863. Its prize-winning ales, which use Pennine spring water, are served in the brewery's 26 tied pubs as well as more than 300 other outlets. Expanded brewing facilities opened on the main site in 2011.

Dark Mild (OG 1034, ABV 3.5%) ◆
Malt and caramel dominate throughout in this sweetish beer with background hop and fruit notes.

Golden Best (OG 1033, ABV 3.5%) ◆
This clean-tasting, refreshing, amber-coloured traditional Pennine light mild is malty throughout. Fruit in the nose increases to complement the delicate hoppy taste. A good session beer.

Best Bitter (OG 1038, ABV 4%) ◆
Hops and fruit combine well with a nutty malt character in this drinkable bitter. Bitterness increases down the glass and lingers in the aftertaste.

Landlord (OG 1042, ABV 4.3%) ⊟ ◆
A hoppy, increasingly bitter finish complements the background malt and citrus character of this full-flavoured and well-balanced amber beer.

Ram Tam (OG 1043, ABV 4.3%) ◆
A black beer with red highlights topped by a coffee-coloured head. Roast coffee bitterness is balanced by fruit and malt with burnt caramel coming through in the dry and bitter finish.

Teignworthy SIBA

Teignworthy Brewery Ltd, The Maltings, Teign Road, Teignworthy, Newton Abbot, Devon, TQ12 4AA
☎ (01626) 332066
✉ sales@teignworthybreweryltd.co.uk
⊕ teignworthybrewery.com
Shop 10am-5pm weekdays at Tuckers Maltings
Tours available for trade customers only

Teignworthy Brewery was established in 1994 and is located in part of the historic Tuckers Maltings building. The brewery is a 20-barrel plant and production is now up to 100 barrels a week, using malt from Tuckers. It supplies around 300 outlets in Devon and Somerset. A large range of seasonal ales is available: see website. Bottle-conditioned beers are also produced. Martha's Mild is suitable for vegans in bottle-conditioned form.

Neap Tide (OG 1038, ABV 3.8%)
A pale, fruity bitter.

Reel Ale (OG 1039.5, ABV 4%) ⊟ ◆
Clean, sharp-tasting bitter with lasting hoppiness; predominantly malty aroma.

Gun Dog (OG 1043.5, ABV 4.3%)
A light, bronze-coloured ale. Goldings hops give it a flowery, fruity aromatic finish.

Springtide (OG 1043.5, ABV 4.3%) ◆

A full and well-rounded, mid-brown beer with a dry, bitter taste and aftertaste.

Old Moggie (OG 1044.5, ABV 4.4%)
A golden, hoppy and fruity ale.

Beachcomber (OG 1045.5, ABV 4.5%) ◆
A pale brown beer with a light, refreshing fruit and hop nose, grapefruit taste and a dry, hoppy finish.

Teme Valley SIBA ⊙

🏭 Teme Valley Brewery, The Talbot, Bromyard Road, Knightwick, Worcestershire, WR6 5PH
☎ (01886) 821235
✉ chris@temevalleybrewery.co.uk
⊕ temevalleybrewery.co.uk
Tours by arrangement

☺ Teme Valley Brewery opened in 1997. In 2005, new investment enabled the brewery to expand to a 15-barrel brew-length. It maintains strong ties with local hop farming, using only Worcestershire-grown hops. Some 30 outlets are supplied. Seasonal beers: see website. Bottle-conditioned beers are also available.

T'Other (OG 1035, ABV 3.5%) ◆
Refreshing amber beer offering an abundance of flavour in the fruity aroma, followed by a short, dry bitterness.

This (OG 1037, ABV 3.7%) ◆
Dark gold brew with a mellow array of flavours in a malty balance.

That (OG 1041, ABV 4.1%) ◆
A rich fruity nose and a wide range of hoppy and malty flavours in this copper-coloured best bitter.

Talbot Blond (OG 1042, ABV 4.4%)
A smooth, rich, pale beer.

Tempest

Tempest Brewing Co, Winchester Row, Kelso, TD5 7DT
☎ (01573) 229664 ✉ brewmeik@gmail.com
⊕ tempestbrewingco.com
Tours by arrangement

Based in a former dairy, Tempest was set up in 2010 by Gavin Meiklejohn, craft brewer and proprietor of the Cobbles Inn in Kelso, which is the brewery tap. The focus is on bold flavours and ingredients to produce interesting styles based on classic and New World beers.

Into the Light Blonde (OG 1041, ABV 4.1%)
A golden ale with light and refreshing fruit salad overtones.

Emanation Pale Ale (OG 1044, ABV 4.5%)
An easy-drinking, copper-coloured ale with a light caramel sweetness and a rich hop and citrus character.

Elemental Porter (OG 1049, ABV 5.1%)
A smooth black porter with a controlled roast character with a hint of coffee and chocolate on the side.

Thame

🏭 Thame Brewery, 1 East Street, Thame, Oxfordshire, OX9 3HP
☎ (01844) 218202
✉ thamebrewery@btinternet.com
⊕ thamebrewery.co.uk
Tours by arrangement

⊠ The brewery was set up by Peter Lambert and Oak Taverns in the old stables at the rear of the Cross Keys in 2009 as a one-barrel plant (the original brew plant of the Goldfinch Brewery in Dorchester). Beer is produced for the Cross Keys and beer festivals. Many one-off brews are also produced.

Mr Splodge's Mild (OG 1040, ABV 4%)
A dark mild named after the pub cat.

Hoppiness (OG 1042, ABV 4.2%)

Theakston ◉

T&R Theakston Ltd, The Brewery, Masham, Ripon, North Yorkshire, HG4 4YD
☎ (01765) 680000 ✉ info@theakstons.co.uk
⊕ theakstons.co.uk
Tours by arrangement

☺In 2009 the brewery welcomed back the production of cask Best Bitter after a 35-year absence. The brewery's flagship brand had been brewed in Carlisle, Workington, Tyne Brewery and then by John Smith's in Tadcaster. All Theakston's cask beers are now brewed at Masham. Theakstons returned to the independent sector in 2003 when the family bought the company back from S&N. It's now owned by four Theakston brothers. The brewery is one of the oldest in Yorkshire, built in 1875 by the brothers' great-grandfather, Thomas Theakston, the son of the company's founder. In 2004 a new fermentation room was added to provide additional flexibility and capacity. Further new capacity was added in 2006, with additional investment in 2009 to allow for the return of cask Best Bitter. Seasonal beers: see website.

Best Bitter (OG 1038, ABV 3.8%)
A golden-coloured beer with a full flavour that lingers pleasantly on the palate. With a good bitter/sweet balance, this beer has a robust hop character, citrus and spicy.

Black Bull Bitter (OG 1037, ABV 3.9%) ◥
A distinctively hoppy aroma leads to a light, hoppy taste with some fruitiness and a short bitter finish.

Lightfoot (OG 1041, ABV 4.1%)
A pale, straw-coloured ale.

XB (OG 1044, ABV 4.5%)
A sweet-tasting bitter with background fruit and spicy hop. Some caramel character gives this ale a malty dominance.

Old Peculier (OG 1057, ABV 5.6%) ▨ ◥
A full-bodied, dark brown, strong ale. Slightly malty but with hints of roast coffee and liquorice. A smooth caramel overlay and a complex fruitiness leads to a bitter chocolate finish.

Thomas Guest

See Black Country

Abraham Thompson

Abraham Thompson's Brewing Co, Flass Lane, Barrow-in-Furness, Cumbria, LA13 0AD
☎ 07708 191437
✉ abraham.thompson@btinternet.com

Abraham Thompson was set up in 2004 to return Barrow-brewed beers to local pubs. This was achieved in 2005 after an absence of more than 30 years following the demise of Case's Brewery in 1972. With a half-barrel plant, this nano-brewery has concentrated almost exclusively on dark beers, reflecting the tastes of the brewer. Distribution is limited to a few outlets in the Low Furness area but beers are always supplied to Ulverston beer festival.

Lickerish Stout (ABV 3.8%)
A black, full-bodied stout with heavy roast flavours and good bitterness.

Oatmeal Stout (ABV 4.5%)
A smooth stout with a sweeter finish.

Porter (ABV 4.8%)
A deep, dark porter with good body and a smooth chocolate finish.

Letargion (ABV 9%)
Black, bitter and heavily roast but still very drinkable. A meal in a glass.

John Thompson

⊟ John Thompson Inn & Brewery, Ingleby, Melbourne, Derbyshire, DE73 7HW
☎ (01332) 862469 ⊕ johnthompsoninn.com
Tours by arrangement

John Thompson set up the brewery in 1977. The pub and brewery are now run by his son, Nick. Seasonal beers are also available.

JTS XXX (OG 1041, ABV 4.1%)

Thornbridge ⟨SIBA⟩ ◉

Thornbridge Brewery, Riverside Business Park, Buxton Road, Bakewell, Derbyshire, DE45 1GS
☎ (01629) 641000
✉ alex@thornbridgebrewery.co.uk
⊕ thornbridgebrewery.co.uk
Shop Mon-Fri 9am-4pm
Tours by arrangement (prior booking essential)

☺The first Thornbridge craft beers were produced in 2005 using a 10-barrel brewery, in the grounds of Thornbridge Hall. The beers have had much success with over 190 CAMRA and SIBA awards won. A 30-barrel brewery opened in Bakewell in 2009. The original site continues to develop new, seasonal and speciality beers. 200 outlets are supplied direct. 12 pubs are managed. Unfiltered and bottle-conditioned beers are available.

Wild Swan (OG 1035, ABV 3.5%) ◥
Extremely pale yet flavoursome and refreshing beer. Plenty of lemony citrus hop flavour, becoming increasingly dry and bitter in the finish and aftertaste.

Black Harry (OG 1038, ABV 3.9%)
A fruity aroma with notes of raspberry, a light, creamy body and a long, nutty finish. Dark, refreshing and very drinkable.

Lord Marples (OG 1041, ABV 4%) ◥
Smooth, traditional, easy-drinking bitter. Caramel, malt and coffee flavours fall away to leave a long, bitter finish.

Ashford (OG 1043, ABV 4.2%)
A brown ale with a floral hoppiness, a smooth, malty kick and a delicate coffee finish.

Kipling (OG 1050, ABV 5.2%) ◥
Golden pale bitter with aromas of grapefruit and passion fruit. Intense fruit flavours continue throughout, leading to a long bitter aftertaste.

Jaipur IPA (OG 1055, ABV 5.9%) 🍺 🍴 ◆
Flavoursome IPA packed with citrus hoppiness that's nicely counterbalanced by malt and underlying sweetness and robust fruit flavours.

Halcyon (OG 1071, ABV 7.7%) 🍴
Rich fruit and hop aroma. Chewy, juicy malts and intense hoppiness with a hint of tangerine and pear drops. Ends will a well-balanced bitterness.

Saint Petersburg (Imperial Russian Stout) (OG 1072.4, ABV 7.7%) 🍺 ◆
Good example of an imperial stout. Smooth and easy to drink with raisins, bitter chocolate and hops throughout, leading to a lingering coffee and chocolate aftertaste.

Three B's ⒮ⒾⒷⒶ ◉

🏳 Three B's Brewery, Black Bull, Brokenstone Road, Tockholes, Blackburn, Lancashire, BB3 0LL
☎ (01254) 581381 ✉ robert@threebsbrewery.co.uk
⊕ threebsbrewery.co.uk
Tours by arrangement

Robert Bell designed and built his original two-barrel brewery in 1998 and in 1999 moved to larger premises in Blackburn. In 2011 the derelict Black Bull pub in Tockholes was bought and the brewery relocated there. More than 50 regular outlets are supplied. Seasonal beers: see website. Bottle-conditioned beers are also available.

Bee Thrifty (OG 1036, ABV 3.4%)
A light and refreshing amber-coloured beer.

Stoker's Slake (OG 1038, ABV 3.6%) ◆
Lightly roasted coffee flavours are in the aroma and the initial taste. A well-rounded, dark brown mild with dried fruit flavours in the long finish.

Honey Bee (OG 1039, ABV 3.7%)
A golden honey beer with honey apparent in both aroma and taste.

Bobbin's Bitter (OG 1038, ABV 3.8%)
A golden bitter with warm aromas of nutty grain and a full, fruity flavour with a light, dry finish.

Bee Blonde (OG 1041, ABV 4%)
A pale bitter with a light, dry, balance of grain and hops and a delicate finish with citrus fruits.

Black Bull (OG 1042, ABV 4%)

Tackler's Tipple (OG 1044, ABV 4.3%)
A dark best bitter with full hop flavour, biscuit tones on the tongue and a deep, dry finish.

Doff Cocker (OG 1045, ABV 4.5%) ◆
Yellow with a hoppy aroma and initial taste giving way to subtle malt notes and orchard fruit flavours. Crisp, dry finish.

Pinch Noggin (OG 1046, ABV 4.6%)
A dark, strong best bitter with full hop flavour and a long aftertaste.

Knocker Up (OG 1047, ABV 4.8%) ◆
A smooth, rich, creamy porter. The roast flavour is foremost without dominating and is balanced by fruit and hop notes.

Shuttle Ale (OG 1050, ABV 5.2%)
A rustic-coloured traditional strong pale ale.

Three Castles ⒮ⒾⒷⒶ ◉

Three Castles Brewery Ltd, Unit 12, Salisbury Road Business Park, Pewsey, Wiltshire, SN9 5PZ

☎ (01672) 564433
✉ sales@threecastlesbrewery.co.uk
⊕ threecastlesbrewery.co.uk
Shop Mon-Fri 9am-4pm; Sat 9am-1pm
Tours by arrangement (May-Sep)

⊗ Three Castles is an independent, family-run brewery, established in 2006. Seasonal beers: see website. Bottle-conditioned beers are available.

Barbury Castle (OG 1039, ABV 3.9%)
A balanced, easy-drinking pale ale with a hoppy, spicy palate.

Saxon Archer (OG 1041, ABV 4%)

Heritage (OG 1042, ABV 4.2%)

Vale Ale (OG 1043, ABV 4.3%)
Golden-coloured with a fruity palate and strong floral aroma.

Corn Dolly (OG 1048, ABV 4.7%)

Three Kings (NEW)

Three Kings Brewery, 14 Prospect Terrace, North Shields, Tyne & Wear, NE30 1DX
☎ 07580 004565 ✉ ewan@threekingsbrewery.co.uk
⊕ threekingsbrewery.co.uk

Three Kings began brewing in 2012 using a 2.5-barrel plant. Further beers are planned.

Broon Ale (ABV 4%)

Three Peaks

Three Peaks Brewery, 7 Craven Terrace, Settle, North Yorkshire, BD24 9DB
☎ (01729) 822939

⊗ Formed in 2006, Three Peaks is run by husband and wife team Colin and Susan Ashwell. The brewery is located in the cellar of their home. Two beers are brewed at present on their 1.25-barrel plant but more are planned.

Pen-y-Ghent Bitter (OG 1040, ABV 3.8%) ◆
The malty character of this mid-brown session bitter is balanced by fruit in the aroma and taste. The finish is malty and hoppy.

Ingleborough Gold (OG 1041, ABV 4%) ◆
This golden-coloured best bitter is hoppy throughout with fruit in the aroma and taste and a hoppy, bitter finish.

Three Tuns ⒮ⒾⒷⒶ ◉

Three Tuns Brewery, 16 Market Square, Bishop's Castle, Shropshire, SY9 5BN
☎ (01588) 638392 ✉ tunsbrewery@aol.com
⊕ threetunsbrewery.co.uk
Shop Mon-Fri 9am-5pm
Tours by arrangement

Brewing started on the site sometime in the 16th century. The brewery was licensed in 1642 and is the oldest licensed brewery in the country. Recent refurbishment has resulted in a significant increase in capacity and styles of beers. Seasonal beers: see website.

1642 Bitter (OG 1042, ABV 3.8%)
A golden ale with a light, nutty maltiness and spicy bitterness.

XXX (OG 1046, ABV 4.3%) ◆

A pale, sweetish bitter with a light hop aftertaste that has a honey finish.

Stout (ABV 4.4%)

Cleric's Cure (OG 1059, ABV 5%)
A light tan-coloured ale with a malty sweetness. Strong and spicy with a floral bitterness.

Thwaites IFBB 👁

Daniel Thwaites plc, Star Brewery, PO Box 50, Blackburn, Lancashire, BB1 5BU
☎ (01254) 686868
✉ marketing@danielthwaites.com
⊕ danielthwaites.com
Tours by arrangement

☺ Established in 1807, Thwaites is still controlled by the Yerburgh family, descendants of the founder, Daniel Thwaites. The company owns around 350 pubs. Real ale is available in more than 60% of these but Nutty Black is hard to find. A monthly Signature range beer is produced and a Quarterly Favourites range beer is available for each season of the year. Three bottle-conditioned beers are also available. In 2012 a 20-barrel plant became operational within the current brewery.

Nutty Black (OG 1036, ABV 3.3%) ◆
A tasty traditional dark mild presenting a malty flavour with caramel notes and a slightly bitter finish.

Original (OG 1036, ABV 3.6%) ◆
Hop driven, yet well-balanced amber session bitter. Hops continue through to the long finish.

Indus IPA (OG 1039, ABV 3.9%)
A well-hopped amber ale.

Wainwright (OG 1042, ABV 4.1%)
A straw-coloured bitter with soft fruit flavours and a hint of malty sweetness.

Lancaster Bomber (OG 1044, ABV 4.4%) 🍴 ◆
Well-balanced, copper-coloured best bitter with firm malt flavours, a fruity background and a long, dry finish.

Tigertops

Tigertops Brewery, 22 Oakes Street, Flanshaw, Wakefield, West Yorkshire, WF2 9LN
☎ (01229) 716238 ☎ 07951 812986
✉ tigertopsbrewery@hotmail.com

☺Tigertops was established in 1995 by Stuart Johnson and his wife Lynda. They own the brewery as well as running the Foxfield brew-pub in Cumbria (qv) but Tigertops is run on their behalf by Barry Smith. Five outlets are supplied. Seasonal and experimental beers are also brewed.

Axeman's Block (OG 1036, ABV 3.6%)
A malty beer with a good hop finish.

Busy Lizzy (ABV 3.6%)

Dark Wheat Mild (OG 1036, ABV 3.6%)
An unusual mild made primarily with wheat malt.

Tom Tom Mild (ABV 3.7%)
Dark rye mild.

Blanche de Newland (OG 1044, ABV 4.5%)
A cloudy Belgian-style wheat beer.

Ginger Fix (OG 1044, ABV 4.6%)
A mid-amber ginger beer.

White Max (OG 1044, ABV 4.6%)

A light, German-style wheat beer.

Uber Weiss (OG 1046, ABV 4.8%)
A dark, German-style wheat beer.

Big Ginger (OG 1058, ABV 6%)
A strong, amber ginger beer.

Tillingbourne (NEW) SIBA

Tillingbourne Brewery, Old Scotland Farm, Staple Lane, Shere, Surrey, GU5 9TE
☎ (01483) 222228 ✉ info@tillybeer.co.uk
⊕ tillybeer.co.uk
Shop Fri 1-6.30pm; Sat 10am-3.30pm
Tours by arrangement

⊗Tillingbourne began brewing in 2011 on a farm site previously used by Surrey Hills Brewery using its old 17-barrel plant. Around 25 local outlets are supplied.

Spring Ale (ABV 3.3%)

Falls Gold (ABV 4.2%)

Tinpot

Tinpot Brewery, Queens Lane, Bridge of Allan, Stirlingshire, FK9 4NY
☎ (01786) 834555 ✉ tinpot@bridgeofallan.co.uk
⊕ tinpotbrewery.co.uk
Shop 12-5pm daily
Tours by arrangement

☺Tinpot opened in 2009 using a one-barrel plant designed to brew speciality beers. Bottle-conditioned beers are available. The beer range varies depending on season and demand.

Gold Pot 70/- (OG 1040, ABV 4%)
A pale golden best bitter.

Thai Pot (OG 1042, ABV 4%)

Choc Pot 80/- (OG 1044, ABV 4.2%)

Marmalade Pot (OG 1046, ABV 4.4%)

Pot Black Stout (OG 1046, ABV 4.4%)

Pot of Gold (OG 1048, ABV 4.5%)

Tintagel SIBA

Tintagel Brewery Ltd, Condolden Farm, Tintagel, Cornwall, PL34 0HJ
☎ (01840) 213371 ✉ tintagelbrewery@gmail.com
⊕ tintagelbrewery.co.uk

⊗ This 7.5-barrel brewery was established in 2009 in a redundant milking parlour on the highest farm in Cornwall. 80 outlets are supplied direct. Bottle-conditioned and seasonal beers are available.

Castle Gold (OG 1038, ABV 3.8%) 🍴

Cornwall's Pride (OG 1040, ABV 4%) ◆

Castle Gold Extra (OG 1042, ABV 4.2%) ◆
Medium-bodied golden ale with a light fruity aroma. Powerful hoppy bitterness on the tongue is balanced by fruit sweetness. Long, bitter and dry finish with some citrus hop fruit.

Gull Rock (OG 1042.6, ABV 4.2%) ◆
A tawny-coloured best bitter with a malt aroma and some berry fruit. The taste is malt sweetness with traces of hop bitterness and caramel, finishing the same but with a little dryness.

Harbour Special (OG 1048.9, ABV 4.8%) ◆

Brown strong ale with a ripe fruit and malt nose. Rich malt, prunes and esters in the mouth are balanced by hops, finishing with a blend of bitterness, malt and dryness.

Tiny Rebel (NEW) SIBA

Tiny Rebel Brewery, Unit 12a, Maesglas Industrial Estate, Greenwich Road, Newport, NP20 2NN
☎ 07980 798268 ✉ info@tinyrebel.co.uk
⊕ tinyrebel.co.uk
Tours by arrangement

Tiny Rebel was set up in 2012 by two enthusiastic home brewers.

Fubar (OG 1044, ABV 4.4%)

Urban IPA (OG 1055, ABV 5.5%)

Tipples SIBA EAB

Tipples Brewery, Units 5 & 6, Damgate Lane Industrial Estate, Acle, Norwich, Norfolk, NR13 3DJ
☎ (01493) 741007 ✉ brewery@tipplesbrewery.com
⊕ tipplesbrewery.com

⊗ Tipples was established by Jason Tipple in 2004 on a six-barrel brew plant and produces both cask and bottle-conditioned ales. The brewery expanded in 2007 and there are plans for further expansion with an increase in the product range and diversity. Seasonal beers are also available.

Hanged Monk (OG 1038, ABV 4%) ◆
Strong roast and malt notes dominate the aroma and follow through to the taste. A slightly grainy mouthfeel is softened by a hint of caramel and a growing vinous finish.

Redhead (OG 1042, ABV 4.2%) ◆
Malt and hops are well matched in both nose and palate. Toffee in the nose and initial taste soon gives way to an increasing bitterness. A fine finale retains the mix of flavours.

Topper (OG 1045, ABV 4.5%) ◆
Black-hued stout. Coffee and dark chocolate to the fore in all aspects. A roast-flavoured beer with just enough malt sweetness and bitterness to provide a counterpoint. Strong, big-hearted fiinish.

Brewers Progress (OG 1046, ABV 4.6%) ◆
A solid malty, tawny beer with strong caramel and vanilla support. The smooth creamy character is given added depth by a blackcurrant fruitiness. Some bitterness in the finish.

Moonrocket (OG 1050, ABV 5%) ◆
A complex golden brew with an earthy aroma. Malt hop bitterness and a fruity sweetness swirl round in an ever-changing kaleidoscope of flavours. A satisfying finish with hops finally emerging on top.

Jacks' Revenge (OG 1058, ABV 5.8%) ◆
An explosion of malt, chocolate, roast and plum pudding fruitiness. Full-bodied with a deep red hue and a strong solid finish that develops into a vinous fruitiness.

Tipsy Toad

See Liberation

Tipsy Angel

▤ Tipsy Angel Brewery, Lower Angel, 27 Buttermarket Street, Warrington, Cheshire, WA1 2LY
☎ (01925) 653326 ⊕ lowerangel.co.uk
Tours by arrangement

☺Tipsy Angel began brewing in 2011 using a one-barrel plant. Beers are produced for the pub and occasionally for beer festivals. The brewery was founded to recreate the recipes of Walkers of Warrington and aims to have at least one of its brews on sale at all times in the Lower Angel pub.

As Mild as an Angel (OG 1039, ABV 3.9%)

Tawny Angel (OG 1040, ABV 4.1%)

Birth of an Angel (OG 1042, ABV 4.4%)

Angel's Folly (OG 1051, ABV 5.2%)

Tír Dhá Ghlas (NEW)

▤ Tír Dhá Ghlas Brewing Co, Cullins Yard, 11 Cambridge Road, Dover, Kent, CT17 9BY
☎ (01304) 211666 ✉ jim@cullinsyard.co.uk
⊕ cullinsyard.co.uk

Brewing began in 2012 using a two-barrel plant. Beers is available only in the restaurant.

Jimmy's Riddle (ABV 4.7%)

MDS (ABV 4.7%)

Tirril

Tirril Brewery Ltd, Red House, Long Marton, Appleby-in-Westmorland, Cumbria, CA16 6BN
☎ (01768) 361846
Tours by arrangement

☺Tirril Brewery was established in 1999 in an abandoned toilet block behind the Queen's Head in Tirril. Since then it has relocated to the 1823 gothic brewing rooms at Brougham Hall and is now at the Red House Barn in Long Marton beneath the Pennines. Capacity has grown from 2.25 barrels to 60 barrels over the years. Around 120 outlets are supplied and one pub is owned. Seasonal beers are also available.

Bewsher's Bitter (OG 1038.5, ABV 3.8%)
A lightly-hopped, golden brown session beer, named after the landlord and brewer at the Queen's Head in the 1830s.

Nameless Ale (OG 1038.5, ABV 3.8%)
A golden, easy-drinking session beer.

Brougham Ale (OG 1039, ABV 3.9%)
A gently hopped, amber bitter.

Old Faithful (OG 1040, ABV 4%) ◆
Initially bitter, gold-coloured ale with an astringent finish.

Pennine Pilsner (OG 1037, ABV 4%)
A top fermented, cask-conditioned lager flavoured with Czech Saaz hops.

1823 (OG 1041, ABV 4.1%)
A full-bodied session bitter with a gentle bitterness.

Academy Ale (OG 1041.5, ABV 4.2%)
A dark, full-bodied, traditional rich and malty ale.

Amber's Ale (OG 1041.5, ABV 4.2%)
Rosy golden ale. Light and hoppy.

Red Barn Ale (OG 1043, ABV 4.4%)

A ruby red ale with a strong hop finish.

Titanic ◉

Titanic Brewery Ltd, Unit 5, Callender Place, Burslem, Stoke-on-Trent, Staffordshire, ST6 1JL
☎ (01782) 823447 ✉ titanic@titanicbrewery.co.uk
⊕ titanicbrewery.co.uk
Tours by arrangement

☺Founded in 1985, the brewery is named in honour of Captain Smith who hailed from the Potteries and had the misfortune to captain the Titanic. A monthly seasonal beer provides the opportunity to offer distinctive beers of many styles, each with a link to the liner. Titanic supplies 300 free trade outlets throughout the country. The brewery has a small, constantly expanding tied house estate. Bottle-conditioned beer is also available.

Mild (OG 1036, ABV 3.5%) ◀
Fresh fruity hop aroma leads to a caramel start then a rush of bitter hoppiness ending with a lingering, dry finish.

Steerage (OG 1036, ABV 3.5%) ◀
Pale yellow bitter. Flavours start with hops and fruit but become zesty and refreshing in this light session beer with a long, dry finish.

Lifeboat (OG 1040, ABV 4%) ◀
Dark brown with fruit, malt and caramel aromas. Sweet start, malty and caramel middle, with hoppiness developing into a fruity and dry, lingering finish.

Anchor Bitter (OG 1042, ABV 4.1%) ◀
Amber beer with a spicy hint to the fruity start, followed by a rush of hops in the dry, bitter finish.

Iceberg (OG 1042, ABV 4.1%) ◀
Yellow/gold sparkling wheat beer with a flowery start leading to a massively hoppy, zesty finish.

Chocolate & Vanilla Stout (OG 1047, ABV 4.5%) ◀
Chocoholic paradise with real coffee and vanilla support. Cocoa, sherry and almonds lend depth to this creamy, drinkable stout.

Stout (OG 1046, ABV 4.5%) 🍷 🍺 ◀
Roasty, toasty with tobacco, autumn bonfires, chocolate and hints of liquorice; perfectly balanced with a bitter, dry finish reminiscent of real coffee.

White Star (OG 1050, ABV 4.8%) ◀
Hints of cinnamon apple pie are found before the hops take over to give a bitter edge to this well-balanced refreshing, fruity beer.

Plum Porter (OG 1051, ABV 4.9%) ◀
Dark brown with a powerful fruity aroma. A sweet plum fruitiness gives way to a gentle bitter finish.

**Captain Smith's Strong Ale
(OG 1054, ABV 5.2%)** ◀
Red/brown and full-bodied, lots of malt and roast with a hint of honey but a strong, bittersweet finish.

Toft

Toft Brewing, 6 Tuscan Close, Cheadle, Staffordshire, ST10 1HS
☎ (01538) 755639 ✉ toftbrewing@yahoo.co.uk

Toft began brewing in 2009 in the owner's garage on a one-barrel plant. Several local pubs and beer festivals are supplied.

Full Toss (OG 1040, ABV 4%)

Inn Swinger (OG 1043, ABV 4.4%)

Nightwatchman (OG 1045, ABV 4.5%)

Stumped (OG 1045, ABV 4.5%)

Toll End

🏭 **KM Darby Ltd t/a Toll End Brewery, c/o Waggon & Horses, 131 Toll End Road, Tipton, West Midlands, DY4 0ET**
☎ 07903 725574
Tours by arrangement

⊗ The four-barrel brewery opened in 2004. With the exception of Phoebe's Ale, named after the brewer's daughter, all brews commemorate local landmarks, events and people. Toll End is brewing to full capacity and produces around 300 gallons a week. Four outlets are supplied. Several specials are also brewed throughout the year.

Ocker Ale (OG 1042, ABV 4%)

William Perry (OG 1044, ABV 4.3%)

Black Bridge (OG 1046, ABV 4.6%)

Tipton Pride (OG 1048, ABV 4.6%)

Phoebe's Ale (OG 1048, ABV 4.7%)

Little Devil Stout (OG 1054, ABV 5.4%)

Retribution (OG 1054, ABV 5.4%)

Tollgate SIBA ◉

Tollgate Brewery, Unit 1, Southwood House Farm, Staunton Lane, Calke, Derbyshire, LE65 1RG
☎ (01283) 229194 ✉ info@tollgatebrewery.com
⊕ tollgatebrewery.com
Tours by arrangement

⊗ This six-barrel brewery was founded in 2005 on the site of the old Brunt & Bucknall Brewery in Woodville, which was taken over by Thomas Salts Brewery in 1919 and then bought and closed by Bass in 1927. It relocated to new premises on the National Trust's Calke Park Estate in 2012. More than 100 outlets are supplied. Seasonal and bottle-conditioned beers are available, the latter now constituting nearly 40% of production.

Bitter (TGB) (OG 1045, ABV 4.3%)

Red Star IPA (OG 1047, ABV 4.5%)

Billy's Best Bitter (OG 1048, ABV 4.6%)

High Street Bitter (OG 1048, ABV 4.7%)

Red McAdy (OG 1052, ABV 5%)

For Harrington Arms, Thulston:

Earl's Ale (OG 1042, ABV 4%)

Tomos Watkin

See under Watkin

Tonbridge SIBA

Tonbridge Brewery, Whiteoaks, Tudeley Road, Tudeley, Tonbridge, Kent, TN11 0NW
☎ (01732) 366770 ✉ mail@tonbridgebrewery.co.uk
⊕ tonbridgebrewery.co.uk
Tours by arrangement

Tonbridge Brewery was launched in 2010 using a four-barrel plant and is run by Paul and Lynne Bournazian. It produces ales using only Kent-grown hops and supplies pubs within a 25-mile radius of Tonbridge.

Copper Nob (OG 1039, ABV 3.8%)
A fairly dry summer ale with light maltiness, delicate bitterness and fruity taste.

Rustic (OG 1042, ABV 4%)
Deep bronze-coloured, rich-tasting country ale. Lightly-hopped giving a delicate, spicy taste and aroma.

Auburn Myth (OG 1038, ABV 4.2%)
A traditional bitter with a mild maltiness and distinctive taste and aroma with a hint of blackcurrants.

Blonde Ambition (OG 1041, ABV 4.2%)
A crisp, clean-tasting blonde ale with a refreshing bitterness. Full-flavoured with a combination of spicy and citrus notes.

Ebony Moon (OG 1043, ABV 4.2%)
A rich porter with a pronouced maltiness balanced with a mild bitterness.

Topsham SIBA

Topsham Ales, Globe Hotel, Fore Street, Topsham, Exeter, Devon, EX3 0HR
☎ (01392) 873471 ✉ info@topsham-ales.co.uk
⊕ topsham-ales.co.uk
Tours by arrangement

Topsham Ales has been in operation since 2010 and is a co-operative, one of only two in the country. All members live in the town of Topsham. Beer is made with local ingredients and at present is only sold locally.

River (ABV 4%)

The Mythe (ABV 4.5%)

Topsham & Exminster

See Exeter

Tower

Tower Brewery, Old Water Tower, Walsitch Maltings, Glensyl Way, Burton upon Trent, Staffordshire, DE14 1LX
☎ (01283) 530695 ✉ towerbrewery@aol.com
Tours by arrangement

⊗ Tower was established in 2001 by John Mills in a converted derelict water tower of Thomas Salt's Brewery. The conversion was given a Civic Society award for the restoration of a historic building in 2001. Tower has 20 regular outlets. Seasonal beers are also available.

Salt's Burton Ale (OG 1035, ABV 3.5%)
A deep amber beer.

Bitter (OG 1042, ABV 4.2%) ◆
Gold coloured with a malty, caramel and hoppy aroma. A full hop and fruit taste with the fruit lingering. A bitter and astringent finish.

Malty Towers (OG 1044, ABV 4.4%)
Straw-coloured beer with initial sweet malt flavour followed by a long, dry, hoppy finish.

Gone For A Burton (OG 1046, ABV 4.6%)

Amber beer with a malt/hop aroma.

Imperial (OG 1050, ABV 5%)
Light gold IPA with rich citrus fruit and floral hops.

Towles' (NEW) SIBA

Towles' Fine Ales Ltd, Unit 11, Circuit 32, Easton Road, Easton, Bristol, BS5 0DB
☎ (0117) 321 3188 ⊕ towlesfineales.co.uk
Shop Mon-Fri 9.30am-2pm (other times by arrangement)
Tours by arrangement

⊗ Towles' is a 10-barrel brewery built in the tower style and run by Andrew and Anna Towle. They purchased Berrow Brewery in 2011 and brewing commenced on the site in Easton in 2012. The brewery includes a shop and tasting room. Bottle-conditioned beer is also available.

Berrow 4B (OG 1038, ABV 3.9%)
A pale brown session beer with a fruity flavour and bitterness in the palate and finish.

Old Smiler (OG 1041, ABV 4.1%)
A dark amber ale traditionally brewed with malty undertones and a refreshingly bitter finish.

Berrow Topsy Turvy (OG 1055, ABV 5.9%)
A gold-coloured beer with an aroma of malt and hops. Well-balanced malt and hops taste is followed by a hoppy, bitter finish with some fruit notes.

Townes

🬀 **Townes Brewery, Speedwell Inn, Lowgates, Staveley, Chesterfield, Derbyshire, S43 3TT**
☎ (01246) 472252
✉ curly@townes48.wanadoo.co.uk
Tours by arrangement

Townes Brewery started in 1994 in an old bakery on the outskirts of Chesterfield using a five-barrel plant. It was the first brewery in the town for more than 40 years. In 1997, the Speedwell Inn at Staveley was bought and the plant was moved to the rear of the pub, becoming the first brew-pub in north Derbyshire in the 20th century. Seasonal beers are also available.

Speedwell Bitter (OG 1039, ABV 3.9%) ◆
Straw-coloured session bitter with little aroma. Initially quite sweet leading to a bitterness developing in the long, slightly astringent aftertaste.

Staveley Cross (OG 1043, ABV 4.3%) ◆
Amber gold best bitter with a faint banana aroma. Hoppy with bitterness present throughout, culminating in a short, dry, slightly astringent aftertaste.

IPA (OG 1045, ABV 4.5%) ◆
Pleasant, hoppy bitter with little aroma and a good balanced flavour. This leads to a lingering bitter, hoppy aftertaste.

Pynot Porter (OG 1045, ABV 4.5%) ◆
Red-brown porter with a faint malt and roast coffee aroma. Roast malt flavours combine with vine fruit, becoming increasingly bitter towards the finish.

Townhouse

Townhouse Brewery, Units 1-4, Townhouse Studios, Townhouse Farm, Alsager Road, Audley, Staffordshire, ST7 8JQ
☎ 07976 209437/07812 035143
✉ j.nixon2@btinternet.com
Tours by arrangement

Townhouse was set up in 2002 with a 2.5-barrel plant. In 2004 the brewery scaled up to five-barrels. Demand is growing rapidly and in early 2006 two additional fermenting vessels were added. Bottling is planned.

Audley Bitter (OG 1038, ABV 3.8%)
A pale, well-balanced session bitter with a citrus hop character.

Flowerdew (OG 1039, ABV 4%) ◈
Golden with a floral aroma. Fabulous flavour of flowery hops delivering a hoppy bite and a lingering taste of flowery citrus notes.

Dark Horse (OG 1042, ABV 4.3%)
A dark ruby ale with malt character and late hoppy finish.

A'dleyweisse (OG 1043, ABV 4.5%)
An English-style wheat beer, full-bodied and golden with a strongly defined fruity hop character and a dry finish.

Audley Gold (OG 1043, ABV 4.5%) ◈
Gold colour with a flowery hop aroma hinting at lime and grapefruit. Spicy citrus hops hit the palate and become mouth-watering at first but then give a dry touch. Fruit increases but the hops give a slightly astringent finish.

Barney's Stout (OG 1043, ABV 4.5%) ◈
Roast chocolate and toffee nose atop this black stout. Sweet start becoming bitter at the end, with roast throughout.

Armstrong Ale (OG 1045, ABV 4.8%)
A rich, fruity ruby red beer with a hoppy, dry finish.

Monument Ale (OG 1048, ABV 5%)
A copper-coloured, well-balanced strong ale with a pronounced malt character.

Town Mill SIBA

Town Mill Brewery, Mill Lane, Lyme Regis, Dorset, DT7 3PU
☎ (01297) 444354 ✉ office@townmillbrewery.com
⊕ townmillbrewery.com
Shop Mon-Fri 9am-5pm; Sat & Sun 11am-5pm

⊠ Town Mill began brewing in 2010 using a four-barrel plant in a part of the town mill that at one time had been the home of Lyme Regis' electricity generator, although historic use of the building was as a brewer's malthouse. There are plans to expand to a ten-barrel plant. Seasonal and bottle-conditioned beers are also available.

Cobb (OG 1041.2, ABV 3.9%)

Lyme Gold (OG 1042.5, ABV 4.2%)

Best (ABV 4.5%)

Black Ven (OG 1049.5, ABV 5%)

Traditional Scottish Ales SIBA

Traditional Scottish Ales Ltd, Unit 7c, Bandeath Industrial Estate, Throsk, Stirling, FK7 7NP

☎ (01786) 817000
✉ info@traditionalscottishales.com
⊕ traditionalscottishales.co.uk

⊛Established in 2005, and now owned by VC2 Brands, the brewery is located in a former torpedo factory on the shores of the River Forth. A large range of beers is available including many seasonals.

Stirling Bitter (OG 1044, ABV 3.7%)
A session ale, full-flavoured with a nutty, fruity taste and a dry finish.

Red Torpedo (OG 1040, ABV 3.8%)
Lightly-hopped ruby red IPA, full-bodied, rich and malty.

Ben Nevis (OG 1041, ABV 4%) ◈
A traditional Scottish 80/-, with a distinctive roast and caramel character. Bittersweet fruit throughout provides the sweetness typical of a Scottish Heavy.

Silver Mist (OG 1044, ABV 4%)
Clean, sharp and fresh traditional golden bitter. Nutty, fruity and dry aftertaste.

Sporran Warmer Blonde (OG 1044, ABV 4%)
Classic pale golden ale from a Scottish recipe. Warming and refreshing with a hoppy aftertaste.

Stirling Silver (OG 1042, ABV 4%)

Stirling IPA (OG 1041, ABV 4.1%)
A ruby red, malty, slightly-hopped light and refreshing ale.

Bannockburn Ale (OG 1044, ABV 4.2%)
Pale golden and refreshing with a complex hoppy and fruity aroma.

Mountain Dew (OG 1044, ABV 4.2%)
A pale golden-coloured beer with a complex hoppy and fruity aroma

Ruby Red IPA (OG 1041, ABV 4.2%)
A ruby beer brewed for a rich, malty flavour and lightly-hopped aftertaste.

Glencoe Wild Oat Stout (OG 1050, ABV 4.5%) ◈
A sweetish stout, surprisingly not dark in colour. Plenty of malt and roast balanced by fruit and finished with a hint of hop.

Golden Thistle (OG 1048, ABV 4.5%)
A sharp tasting, golden-coloured beer with a hoppy aftertaste.

Sherrifmuir (OG 1048, ABV 4.5%)
A rub red ale, clean, sharp and fresh-tasting. Heavily hopped with a strong aroma.

William Wallace (OG 1048, ABV 4.5%)
A classic ruby strong ale recipe, hoppy and fruity with a hint of treacle.

Double Espresso Wild Oat Stout (OG 1050, ABV 4.8%)
Stout brewed with double strength coffee beans with a hint of treacle and coffee bite.

Amber Monarch (OG 1052, ABV 5%)
Tawny strong beer full of malty flavours.

Ginger Explosion (OG 1052, ABV 5%)
Smooth, full-bodied blonde ale with a ginger flavour and creamy head.

Gold Torpedo (OG 1054, ABV 5%)

Lomond Gold (OG 1052, ABV 5%) ◈
A malty, bittersweet golden ale with plenty of fruity hop character.

Red Mist (OG 1052, ABV 5%)

A raspberry fruit wheat beer, light and full of fruity flavour.

Scotch Mist (OG 1052, ABV 5%)
Clean, sharp and brewed with fruity hop and a hint of citrus.

1488 (OG 1070, ABV 7%)
Brewed from the first waters of the Tullibardine whisky mash tun and matured in oak casks.

For Knops Beer Co Ltd:

Musselburgh Broke (OG 1047, ABV 4.5%)

California Common (OG 1048, ABV 4.6%)

India Pale Ale (ABV 5%)

Black Cork (ABV 6.6%)

For Trossach's Craft Brewery:

Waylade (OG 1040, ABV 3.9%)

LadeBack (OG 1048, ABV 4.5%)

LadeOut (OG 1055, ABV 5.1%)

Traquair SIBA

Traquair House Brewery, Traquair House, Innerleithen, Peeblesshire, EH44 6PW
☎ (01896) 830323 ✉ enquiries@traquair.co.uk
⊕ traquair.co.uk/brewery
Shop Easter-Oct 12-5pm daily (Jun-Aug 10.30am-5pm)
Tours by arrangement

The 18th-century brewhouse is based in one of the wings of the 1,000-year-old Traquair House, Scotland's oldest inhabited house. The brewhouse was rediscovered by the 20th Laird, the late Peter Maxwell Stuart, in 1965. He began brewing again using all the original equipment, which remained intact, despite having lain idle for more than 100 years. The brewery has been run by Peter's daughter, Catherine Maxwell Stuart, since his death in 1990. The Maxwell Stuarts are members of the Stuart clan, and the main Bear Gates will remain shut until a Stuart returns to the throne. All the beers are oak-fermented and 60 per cent of production is exported. Seasonal and occasional beers are also available.

Traquair House Ale (OG 1069, ABV 7%)

Treboom (NEW) SIBA

Treboom Brewery, Millstone Yard, Main Street, Shipton-by-Beningbrough, North Yorkshire, YO30 1AA
☎ (01904) 471569 ☎ 07761 608662

Office: c/o Nova Scotia Cottage, Acaster Malbis, York, YO23 2PY ✉ info@treboom.co.uk ⊕ treboom.co.uk

Treboom began brewing in 2011 using a 10-barrel plant.

Drum Beat (OG 1038, ABV 3.8%)
A copper-coloured, easy-drinking session bitter.

Yorkshire Sparkle (OG 1039, ABV 4%)
A really pale ale with a fresh citrus taste.

Kettle Drum (OG 1042, ABV 4.3%)
Robust hop flavours and a clean finish.

Baron Saturday (OG 1049, ABV 5.2%)
A porter with hints of coffee and liquorice.

Tring SIBA

Tring Brewery Co Ltd, Dunsley Farm, London Road, Tring, Hertfordshire, HP23 6HA
☎ (01442) 890721 ✉ info@tringbrewery.co.uk
⊕ tringbrewery.co.uk
Shop Mon-Tue 11am-5pm, Wed-Fri 9am-6pm, Sat 9am-5pm, closed Sun
Tours by arrangement

Founded in 1992, Tring Brewery brews more than 90 barrels a week. Most of the beers take their names from local myths and legends. In addition to the core beers, the brewery also produces a range of seasonal and monthly specials. The brewery relocated to larger premises in 2010. Seasonal beers: see website.

Navigator (OG 1034, ABV 3.4%)
A chestnut brown ale with a fruity hop character and a lingering bittersweet finish.

Side Pocket For A Toad (OG 1035, ABV 3.6%)
Citrus notes from American Cascade hops balanced with a floral aroma and a crisp, dry finish in a straw-coloured ale.

Mansion Mild (OG 1036, ABV 3.7%)
Smooth and creamy dark ruby mild with a fruity palate and gentle late hop.

Blonde (OG 1039, ABV 4%)
A refreshing blonde beer with a fruity palate, balanced with a lingering hop aroma.

Ridgeway (OG 1039, ABV 4%)
Balanced malt and hop flavours with a dry, flowery hop aftertaste.

Jack O'Legs (OG 1041, ABV 4.2%)
A combination of four types of malt and two types of aroma hops provide a copper-coloured premium ale with full fruit and a distinctive hoppy bitterness.

Tea Kettle Stout (OG 1047, ABV 4.7%)
Rich and complex traditional stout with a hint of liquorice and moderate bitterness.

Colley's Dog (OG 1051, ABV 5.2%)
Dark but not over-rich, strong yet drinkable, this premium ale has a long dry finish with overtones of malt and walnuts.

Death or Glory (OG 1074, ABV 7.2%)
A strong, dark, aromatic barley wine.

Trinity EAB

Trinity Ales, Church Road, Gisleham, Suffolk, NR33 8DS
☎ (01502) 743121 ✉ graham@trinityales.co.uk
⊕ trinityales.co.uk

⊠ Trinity Ales was launched in 2009 using a four-barrel plant. Pure spring water is used from an ancient well along with Suffolk hops and barley from local farms. Outlets are supplied within a 30-mile radius of the brewery. Bottle-conditioned beers are also available.

Wishing Well (OG 1039, ABV 3.8%)

High Light (OG 1040, ABV 4%)

Black Street Smithy (OG 1045, ABV 4.5%)

Gisleham Gold (OG 1045, ABV 4.5%)

Triple fff SIBA ⊚

Triple fff Brewing Co, Magpie Works, Station Approach, Four Marks, Alton, Hampshire, GU34 5HN
☎ (01420) 561422 ✉ sales@triplefff.com
⊕ triplefff.com
Shop Mon-Thu 9am-5pm, Fri 9am-6pm; Sat 10am-4pm
Tours by arrangement

⊠ The brewery was established in 1997 with a five-barrel plant and through various stages of expansion has been brewing on a 50-barrel plant since 2006. Two pubs are owned; the Railway Arms in Alton and the White Lion in Aldershot. Seasonals, monthly specials and bottle-conditioned ales are also available.

Alton's Pride (OG 1039, ABV 3.8%) ⏷ ◆
An excellent, clean-tasting brown session beer. Full-bodied for its strength with a glorious aroma of lemony hops. An initially malty flavour fades as citrus notes and hoppiness take over, leading to a lasting hoppy/bitter finish.

**Pressed Rat & Warthog
(OG 1039, ABV 3.8%)** ⏷ ◆
Complex hoppy and bitter mild, not in the classic style. Ruby in colour, a toffee aroma with hints of blackcurrant and chocolate lead to a well-balanced flavour with roast, fruit and malt vying with the hoppy bitterness and a dry, bitter finish.

Moondance (OG 1045, ABV 4.2%) ◆
A golden ale, well-hopped, with an aromatic citrus hop nose, balanced by bitterness and a noticeable sweetness in the mouth. Bitterness increases in the finish as the fruit declines, leading to a bittersweet finish.

Trossach's Craft

See Traditional Scottish Ales

Truefitt (NEW)

Truefitt Brewing Co Ltd, 3 Carcutt Road, Lawson Industrial Estate, Middlesbrough, TS3 6QL
☎ 07883 072389 ✉ matt@truefittbrewing.co.uk
⊕ truefittbrewing.co.uk

Brewing began in 2012 using a four-barrel plant purchased from the now closed Cleveland Brewery. The owner and brewer is Matthew Power, formerly with North Yorkshire Brewing Co, Captain Cook Brewery and Lion's Den (Camerons).

Erimus Pale Ale (OG 1039, ABV 3.9%)

North Riding Bitter (OG 1040, ABV 4%)

Ironopolis Stout (OG 1047, ABV 4.7%)

Mydilsburgh IPA (OG 1050, ABV 5%)

Truman's

Truman's Beer, Top Floor, 8 Elder Street, London, E1 6BT
☎ (020) 7247 1147 ✉ trumans@trumansbeer.co.uk
⊕ trumansbeer.co.uk

Founded in 1666, Truman's was brewed for over 300 years until its closure in 1989. In 2010 it was re-established and the owners plan to build a new brewery in East London. The one beer is currently brewed by Nethergate (qv).

Tryst SIBA

Tryst Brewery, Lorne Road, Larbert, Stirlingshire, FK5 4AT
☎ (01324) 554000 ✉ john@trystbrewery.co.uk
⊕ trystbrewery.co.uk
Shop Mon-Fri office hours; Sat am
Tours by arrangement

John McGarva, a member of Scottish Craft Brewers, started brewing in 2003 in an industrial unit near Larbert town. Monthly specials are brewed and all beers are also available bottle conditioned.

Brockville Dark (OG 1039, ABV 3.8%)
A full-tasting session ale with hints of liquorice and roasted grains.

Brockville Pale (OG 1039, ABV 3.9%)
A pale golden session ale, smooth on the palate.

Hop Trial (OG 1040, ABV 3.9%)

Bla'than (OG 1041, ABV 4%)
A strong floral nose and refreshing taste enhanced with elderflower and pale malts.

Drovers 80/- (OG 1041, ABV 4%)
A traditional, well-malted 80/- with an element of sweetness. A gentle nose complements a smooth finish.

VIP (OG 1046, ABV 4.5%)
A light brown best bitter with a deep hop taste and floral nose.

RAJ IPA (OG 1055, ABV 5.5%) ⏷
Exclusively English hopped with balanced flavours, with a hoppy aroma and palate.

Tudor (NEW)

Tudor Brewery, Unit 2, Castle Meadows Park, Merthyr Road, Abergavenny, NP7 7RZ
☎ (01873) 851696 ☎ 07716 284064 ✉ info@tudor-brewery.co.uk ⊕ tudor-brewery.co.uk
Tours by arrangement

Tudor is a two-barrel brewery located at the rear of a unit used by a catering company. Seasonal beer is also available.

Blorenge (OG 1038, ABV 3.8%)
A light pale ale with a fresh citrus undertone.

Skirrid (OG 1042, ABV 4.2%)
A full-flavoured dark beer with a hoppy taste.

Sugarloaf (OG 1047, ABV 4.7%)
A rounded, full-bodied ale with smooth caramelised undertones.

Tunnel SIBA ⊚

Tunnel Brewery Ltd, Old Stable Block, Red House Farm, Nuneaton Road, Ansley, Warwickshire, CV10 0QU
☎ (02476) 394386 ✉ info@tunnelbrewery.co.uk
⊕ tunnelbrewery.co.uk
Shop Mon-Fri 9am-3pm
Tours by arrangement

This five-barrel brewery, established in 2005, originally brewed at the Lord Nelson Inn but relocated in 2011 to a picturesque stable block at Red House Farm. Battlefield Brewery beers are produced for a visitor centre in Bosworth. One pub is owned in conjunction with the Everards' Project William scheme, the Horseshoes in Nuneaton.

THE BREWERIES

Seasonal and bottle-conditioned beers are also available.

Percheron (OG 1037, ABV 3.7%)
A refreshing, pale golden ale with citrus notes.

East India Pale Ale (OG 1058, ABV 5.9%)
A true, robust IPA.

For Battlefield Brewery:

Let Battle Commence (OG 1038, ABV 3.8%)
A sweet vanilla, amber session beer.

Turners (NEW)

Turners Brewery, Highfield Farm, The Broyle, Ringmer, East Sussex, BN8 5AR
☎ 07896 598172 ✉ kestravers@turnersbrewery.com
⊕ turnersbrewery.com

Turners began brewing in early 2012. Initially guest brewing in Hampshire, brewing moved to the current site later in the year. Seasonal beers: see website.

Golden (ABV 3.5%)
A light, refreshing, well-balanced session beer.

Best (ABV 4.1%)
A light brown bitter with a hop nose. Initially sweetish and malty leading to a dry, notably bitter, lingering finish.

Twickenham SIBA ◉

Twickenham Fine Ales Ltd, Unit 6, 18 Mereway, Twickenham, Middlesex, TW2 6RG
☎ (020) 8241 1825 ✉ info@twickenham-fine-ales.co.uk ⊕ twickenham-fine-ales.co.uk
Tours by arrangement

The brewery was set up in 2004 using a 10-barrel brew kit and was the first brewery in Twickenham since the 1920s. It expanded to a 25-barrel plant in larger premises in 2012. Pubs and clubs are supplied within 25 miles of the brewery, including central London. Seasonal beers: see website.

Sundancer (OG 1035, ABV 3.7%) ◆
A light, zesty, golden ale with citrus notes dominating from beginning to end. The finish is bitter but balanced by biscuity sweetness that stops the aftertaste being too intense.

Grandstand Bitter (OG 1037, ABV 3.8%)
A well-hopped, well-balanced brownish amber session beer. Refreshing with light citrus hoppy notes and a fresh, clean finish.

Original (OG 1040.5, ABV 4.2%) ◆
A malty, honey sweetness is balanced by hops and fruit throughout this pale brown best bitter with a creamy mouthfeel . Dryish, slightly bitter aftertaste.

Naked Ladies (OG 1042.5, ABV 4.4%) ◆
Dark golden ale with a perfumed nose and a touch of spicy hop, which is in the initial flavour but fruit dominates. There is a lasting bitterness with some dryness.

Two Bridges SIBA

▤ Two Bridges Brewery, 51 Gosbrook Road, Caversham, Reading, Berkshire, RG4 8BN
☎ (0118) 375 9205 ☎ 07915 540926
✉ kevin.durkan@twobridgesbrewery.co.uk
⊕ twobridgesbrewery.co.uk

Two Bridges Brewery was founded in 2009 by husband and wife Kevin and Kerri Durkan, with help from Kerri's mum. The Two Bridges are those over the Thames between Caversham and Reading. Brewing is currently suspended pending the planned move of the 2.5-barrel plant to the Fox & Hounds pub in Caversham. It is hoped that this will occur during the currency of this Guide.

Two Cocks (NEW) SIBA

Two Cocks Brewery, Christmas Farm, Church Lane, Enborne, Newbury, Berkshire, RG20 0HB
☎ (01635) 47351 ☎ 07836 795961
✉ info@twococksbrewery.com
⊕ christmas-farm.com

The brewery was established in 2011 at Christmas Farm after the owners, Michael and Phil, discovered wild hops growing in the hedgerows surrounding the farm. A 180-feet deep borehole has been drilled to supply water for both the farm and brewery. There are plans for further beers as well as a brewery tap and shop.

1643 Cavalier (ABV 3.8%)
A light, refreshing golden ale with a crisp combination of hops.

1643 Roundhead (ABV 4.2%)
A full-bodied, smooth best bitter.

1643 Puritan (ABV 4.5%)
A dark stout with notes of caramel and chocolate.

Two Roses SIBA

Two Roses Brewery, Unit 9, Darton Business Park, Barnsley Road, Darton, South Yorkshire, S75 5QX
☎ 07780 701254
✉ enquiries@tworosesbrewery.co.uk
⊕ tworosesbrewery.co.uk
Tours by arrangement

⊗ Two Roses commenced brewing in 2011 on an eight-barrel plant and is situated in a former carpet factory. Special beers are also brewed throughout the year.

First Edition (OG 1040, ABV 4%)
A light, hoppy ale with a citrus fruit finish.

Barnsley Pride (OG 1045, ABV 4.5%)
A beer with hints of chocolate and vanilla in the finish.

Black Beauty (OG 1050, ABV 5%)

Two Towers SIBA

Two Towers Brewery Ltd, Unit 1, Mott Street Industrial Estate, 51 Mott Street, Hockley, Birmingham, West Midlands, B19 3HE
☎ (0121) 439 7253
✉ trevorharris@twotowersbrewery.co.uk
⊕ twotowersbrewery.co.uk
Tours by arrangement

The brewery is based in the heart of Birmingham and produces ales using predominantly English ingredients. The two founders have spent in excess of 20 years developing recipes on a non-commercial basis prior to establishing the brewery in 2010. The Brown Lion, located in Birmingham's jewellery quarter, is the brewery tap. Bottle-conditioned beers are available.

Baskerville Bitter (OG 1038, ABV 3.8%)

A full-bodied bitter with a blend of four hops, providing a complex but well-balanced ale.

Chamberlain Pale Ale (OG 1042, ABV 4.5%)
A crisp, light ale loaded with grapefruit flavours with a long, hoppy finish.

Jewellery Porter (OG 1049, ABV 5%)
A wholesome stout with a slick and slightly chocolate texture.

Birmingham Special Ale (BSA) (OG 1048, ABV 5.4%)
A malty, strong bitter with a full body.

Tydd Steam SIBA

Tydd Steam Brewery, Manor Barn, Kirkgate, Tydd Saint Giles, Cambridgeshire, PE13 5NE
☎ (01945) 871020 ☎ 07932 726552
✉ info@tyddsteam.co.uk ⊕ tyddsteam.co.uk
Tours by arrangement

⊠ Tydd Steam opened in 2007 in a converted agricultural barn using a 5.5-barrel plant. The brewery is named after two farm steam engines that were formerly kept in the barn now used for brewing. The steam engines have since been moved to the Museum of Lincolnshire Life. Continued sales growth led to the installation of a new 15-barrel plant and improvement of the brewery facilities in 2009. Around 70 outlets are supplied direct. Seasonal/occasional beers are brewed and bottle-conditioned beers are available on an occasional basis.

Barn Ale (OG 1038, ABV 3.9%) ◀
A golden bitter that has a good biscuity malt aroma and flavour, balanced by spicy hops. Long, dry, fairly astringent finish.

Golden Kiwi (OG 1040, ABV 4.1%)

Piston Bob (OG 1044, ABV 4.6%) ◀
Malt and faint hops on the aroma progress through to a malty flavour complemented by a balance of hops and fruit. A long, dry finish rounds off this amber strong bitter.

Tyne Bank SIBA

Tyne Bank Brewery, Unit 11 Hawick, St Lawrence Road, Newcastle upon Tyne, NE6 1AS
☎ (0191) 265 2828 ☎ 07989 426604
✉ enquiries@tynebankbrewery.co.uk
⊕ tynebankbrewery.co.uk
Tours by arrangement

Tyne Bank began brewing in 2011. It has three fermenters and seven conditioning tanks, meaning that it can produce 20 barrels per brew and attain 60 barrels or 17,000 pints per week. Monthly special beers are also available.

Single Blonde (OG 1037, ABV 3.5%)
A light ale with a pleasing slight dry bitterness. Vanilla and herbal flavours complement the delicate floral aroma.

Castle Gold (OG 1041, ABV 3.9%)
Brewed with English hops giving a mellow bitterness and a subtle fruity aroma with a citrus twist.

Monument Bitter (OG 1042, ABV 4.1%)
A hop mix gives it a berry fruit character with berry aromas and a balanced bitterness, while the malt blend gives a slight caramel undertone.

Silver Dollar (OG 1051, ABV 4.9%)

Southern Star (OG 1051, ABV 5%)

Uffa (NEW)

🍺 Uffa Brewery, White Lion, Lower Street, Lower Ufford, Suffolk, IP13 6DW
☎ (01394) 460770 ✉ stephen-thurlow@hotmail.com ⊕ uffordwhitelion.co.uk
Tours by arrangement

⊠ Uffa Brewery is situated next to the White Lion pub in a converted coach house. Seasonal beers are available.

Tipple (ABV 3.5%)

Gold (ABV 3.7%)

Uley

Uley Brewery Ltd, The Old Brewery, 31 The Street, Uley, Gloucestershire, GL11 5TB
☎ (01453) 860120 ✉ chas@uleybrewery.com
⊕ uleybrewery.com

⊠ Brewing at Uley began in 1833 as Price's Brewery. After a long gap, the premises were restored and Uley Brewery opened in 1985. It has its own spring water, which is used to mash Tucker's Maris Otter malt and boiled with Herefordshire hops. Uley serves 40-50 free trade outlets in the Cotswold area and is brewing to capacity. Seasonal beers are also available.

Hogshead Cotswold Pale Ale (OG 1035, ABV 3.5%) ◀
A pale-coloured, hoppy session bitter with a good hop aroma and a full flavour for its strength, ending in a bittersweet aftertaste.

Bitter (OG 1040, ABV 4%) ◀
A copper-coloured beer with hops and fruit in the aroma and a malty, fruity taste, underscored by a hoppy bitterness. The finish is dry, with a balance of hops and malt.

Laurie Lee's Bitter (OG 1045, ABV 4.5%)
A copper-coloured, full-flavoured, hoppy bitter with some fruitiness and a smooth, balanced finish.

Old Ric (OG 1045, ABV 4.5%) ◀
A full-flavoured, hoppy bitter with some fruitiness and a smooth, balanced finish. Distinctively copper-coloured, this is the house beer for the Old Spot Inn, Dursley.

Old Spot Prize Strong Ale (OG 1050, ABV 5%) ◀
A distinctive full-bodied, red/brown ale with a fruity aroma, a malty, fruity taste, with a hoppy bitterness, and a strong, balanced aftertaste.

Pig's Ear Strong Beer (OG 1050, ABV 5%) ◀
A pale-coloured beer, deceptively strong. Notably bitter in flavour, with a hoppy, fruity aroma and a bitter finish.

Ulverston

Ulverston Brewing Co, Lightburn Road, Ulverston, Cumbria, LA12 0AX
☎ (01229) 584280 ☎ 07840 192022
✉ info.ubc@tiscali.co.uk ⊕ ulverstonbrewing.co.uk
Shop Mon-Sat 11am-3pm (ring for winter opening times)
Tours by arrangement

☺The brewery was established in 2006 on a five-barrel plant situated in the old engine house of the long extinct Lindal Moor Mining Company. In 2010

857

it moved to new premises with a bespoke 12-barrel plant occupying the octagonal bull ring of the old livestock market on the outskirts of Ulverston. There is a shop on site selling local products and craftwork and a bar with a viewing area overlooking the brew plant. Seasonal beers are also available. The beers have a Laurel and Hardy theme: Stan Laurel was born in Ulverston.

Flying Elephants (OG 1037, ABV 3.7%) ◆
Clean, refreshing yellow bitter, sweet and fruity with a dry citrus finish.

Celebration Ale (OG 1039, ABV 3.9%) ◆
Yellow fruity bitter with hints of tangerine and a notably sustained dry finish.

Another Fine Mess (OG 1040, ABV 4%) ◆
A refreshing gold-coloured bitter. Initially fruity but with a rising bitterness.

Laughing Gravy (OG 1040, ABV 4%) ◆
Brown beer with a good mix of flavours.

Lonesome Pine (OG 1042, ABV 4.2%) ◆
A fresh and fruity pale gold beer; honeyed, lemony and resiny with an increasingly bitter finish.

Fra Diavolo (OG 1043, ABV 4.3%)

Uncle Stuarts

Uncle Stuarts Brewery, Wroxham Barns, Tunstead Road, Hoveton, Norwich, NR12 8QU
☎ (01603) 783888
✉ unclestuartsbrewery@btconnect.com
⊕ wroxhambarns.co.uk
Shop open Mon-Sat 10.30am-4.30pm; Sun 11am-4.30pm
Tours by arrangement

⊠ The brewery started in 2002 and in 2009 moved to Wroxham Barns Craft Centre. It recently expanded with the opening of licensed café to complement its existing brewery shop. Beers are available in nine-gallon casks as well as bottle-conditioned from the shop and other outlets.

North Norfolk Beauty (OG 1039, ABV 3.8%)

Pack Lane Mild (OG 1042, ABV 4%)

Broadland Bitter (ABV 4.1%)

Nut Brown Ale (ABV 4.1%)

Stout (ABV 4.4%)

Excelsior (OG 1044, ABV 4.5%)

Local Hero (OG 1047, ABV 4.7%)

Wroxham Barns Bitter (OG 1044, ABV 4.8%)

Ginger (OG 1048, ABV 5%)

Norwich Castle (OG 1048, ABV 5%)

Porter (OG 1053, ABV 5%)

Buckenham Woods (OG 1054, ABV 5.6%) ◆
Spicy with more than a hint of raisin and sultana. Heavy aroma translates into a richly-flavoured ale with a surprisingly light and creamy mouthfeel.

Strumpshaw Fen (OG 1057, ABV 5.7%)

Norwich Cathedral (OG 1059, ABV 6.5%)

Winter Ale (OG 1060, ABV 7%)

Union

⬚ Union Brewery, Unit 7, Brent Mill Industrial Estate, Long Meadow, South Brent, Devon, TQ10 9YT

☎ (01392) 580706 ☎ 07548 578153
✉ info@unionbrewery.co.uk ⊕ unionbrewery.co.uk

The Union Brewery is a small craft brewery originally founded in 2005 at the back of the Dartmoor Union Inn in Holbeton. The brewery fell into disuse when the pub fell on hard times. In 2012 a new company was formed and purchased the four-barrel brew plant, moving it to its new home on the edge of Dartmoor.

Gold (OG 1040, ABV 3.9%)

Jacks (OG 1045, ABV 4.5%)
Golden, hoppy IPA.

Untapped

Untapped Brewing Co, Correspondence: 80 Carlisle Street, Cardiff, CF24 2PF
☎ 07988 199794 ✉ enquiries@untappedbrew.com
⊕ untappedbrew.com

The Untapped Brewing Company was established in 2009 and is owned and run by Owen Davies and Martyn Darby. They are currently brewing at Whittingtons Brewery in Newent, Gloucestershire, where they have an arrangement to use the equipment. Bottle-conditioned beers are also available.

Border (ABV 3.8%)

Sundown (ABV 4%)

Eclipse (ABV 4.4%)

U.P.A. (ABV 4.5%)

Triple S (ABV 4.9%)

Ember (ABV 5.2%)

Crystal (ABV 6%)

Upham SIBA

Upham Brewery llp, Stakes Farm, Cross Lane, Upham, Hampshire, SO32 1FL
☎ (01489) 861383 ✉ info@uphambrewery.co.uk
⊕ uphambrewery.co.uk
Shop Mon, Wed & Fri 10am-2pm; Sat 10.30am-12pm
Tours by arrangement

⊠ Upham began brewing in 2009 using a 3.5-barrel plant. More than 30 outlets are supplied direct.

Classic (OG 1035, ABV 3.6%) ◆
An easy-drinking and light golden ale. Initial hoppiness and fruit is balanced by a maltiness that lasts into the finish.

Punter (OG 1039, ABV 4%)
Rich ochre in colour. Delicate yet structured with hints of syrup and toasted grain. The earthy richness on the palate brings with it a hoppy, dry finish.

Stakes (OG 1045, ABV 4.8%)
Strong, rich and smoky flavour with aromas of caramel.

Urban

⬚ Urban Brewhouse, Junction, Leeman Road, York, YO26 4XH
☎ (01904) 633449
Tours by arrangement

Formerly known as Junction Brewhouse, the brewery is situated to the rear of the train station and the National Railway Museum Junction is York's only brewpub. Production commenced in 2010 using a three-barrel plant. 2012 saw a new brewer, David Kerr, take over plus changes to the brewery name and beer range. Monthly specials and seasonal beers are also brewed.

New Zealand Pale Ale (ABV 3.8%)

Smokestack Lightning (ABV 4.5%)

IPA (ABV 5.4%)

Vale SIBA 👁

Vale Brewery Co, Tramway Business Park, Ludgershall Road, Brill, Buckinghamshire, HP18 9TY
☎ (01844) 239237 ✉ info@valebrewery.co.uk
⊕ valebrewery.co.uk
Shop Mon-Fri 9am-5pm; Sat 9.30-11.30am; Closed Sun & bank hols
Tours by arrangement

⊠ Established in 1994 and initially based in Haddenham, Vale moved to Brill in 2007. Capacity was expanded in 2009 and then doubled to 20 barrel length in 2010. Three pubs are owned, including a flagship outlet, the Hop Pole in Aylesbury. Monthly specials and occasional brews: see website. A wide range of bottle-conditioned beers is available. A sister brewery, the Aylesbury Brewhouse based in the Hop Pole, opened in 2011.

Best Bitter (OG 1036, ABV 3.7%) ◄
This pale amber beer starts with a slight fruit aroma. This leads to a clean, bitter taste where hops and fruit dominate. The finish is long and bitter with a slight hop note.

Black Swan Mild (OG 1038, ABV 3.9%)
Dark and smooth with hints of chocolate and coffee on the nose and a malty, dry finish.

Wychert Ale (OG 1038, ABV 3.9%)
A traditional Thames Valley beer. Woody flavours are notable in this malty beer with a finish of port and berries on the nose.

Red Kite (OG 1040, ABV 4%)
Refreshing chestnut beer with a bitter finish.

VPA/Vale Pale Ale (OG 1042, ABV 4.2%)
An assertive, dry, hoppy ale with a citrus nose, combined with a pronounced malt background.

Special (OG 1046, ABV 4.5%)
Premium ale with a rich, complex and satisfying finish.

Grumpling Premium Ale (OG 1046, ABV 4.6%)
A rich, warming ruby brown traditional English bitter with mellow fruity malt flavours accompanied by a subtle dry, hoppy finish.

Gravitas (OG 1047, ABV 4.8%)
A strong pale ale packed with hop and citrus flavours, rounded off by a dry, malty, biscuit finish. A pronounced hop aroma throughout.

Vale of Glamorgan SIBA

Vale of Glamorgan Brewery Ltd, Unit 8a, Atlantic Trading Estate, Barry, Vale of Glamorgan, CF63 3RF
☎ (01446) 730757 ✉ info@vogbrewery.co.uk
⊕ vogbrewery.co.uk
Tours by arrangement (max. 15 people)

☺Vale of Glamorgan Brewery started brewing in 2005 on a 10-barrel plant. More than 40 local outlets are supplied. Occasional and seasonal beers are brewed and bottle-conditioned beers are available.

Cwrw Haf (OG 1042, ABV 4.2%)

Original No. 1 (OG 1042, ABV 4.2%)

Cwrw Dewi (OG 1050, ABV 5%)

Valhalla

Valhalla Brewery, Shetland Refreshments Ltd, Baltasound, Unst, Shetland, ZE2 9DX
☎ (01957) 711658 ✉ mail@valhallabrewery.co.uk
⊕ valhallabrewery.co.uk
Tours by arrangement

The brewery started production in 1997, set up by husband and wife team Sonny and Sylvia Priest. A bottling plant was installed in 1999. One outlet is supplied direct. A new brewery building is currently being converted.

White Wife (OG 1038, ABV 3.8%) ◄
Predominantly malty aroma with hop and fruit, which remain on the palate. The aftertaste is increasingly bitter.

Old Scatness (OG 1038, ABV 4%)
A light bitter, named after an archaeological dig at the south end of Shetland where early evidence of malting and brewing was found. One of the ingredients is an ancient strain of barley called Bere which used to be common in Shetland until the middle of the last century.

Simmer Dim (OG 1039, ABV 4%) ◄
A light golden ale, named after the long Shetland twilight. The sulphur features do not mask the fruits and hops of this well-balanced beer.

Auld Rock (OG 1043, ABV 4.5%) ◄
A full-bodied, dark Scottish-style best bitter, it has a rich malty nose but does not lack bitterness in the long dry finish.

Sjolmet Stout (OG 1048, ABV 5%) ◄
Full of malt and roast barley, especially in the taste. Smooth, creamy, fruity finish, not as dry as some stouts.

Vens (NEW)

Vens Brewing Co Ltd, Unit 3, Clovelly Works, Chelmsford Road, Rawreth, Essex, SS11 8SY
☎ (01268) 574477 ☎ 07805 634595
✉ info@vensbrewing.co.uk ⊕ vensbrewing.co.uk

Founder Richard Venour commenced brewing in 2010 having previously brewed for the nearby Crouch Vale Brewery. Local outlets and beer festivals are supplied.

Mild (OG 1038, ABV 3.8%)
A smooth, malty dark mild bursting with roasted flavours with a satisfying finish.

Gold (OG 1040, ABV 4%)
A refreshing pale golden beer with a balanced hop aroma.

Best (OG 1042, ABV 4.2%)
Classic best bitter with balanced malt flavours and bitterness.

Verulam

▤ Verulam Brewery, Farmers Boy, 134 London Road, St Albans, Hertfordshire, AL1 1PQ
☎ (01727) 860535 ☎ 07799 137395
✉ douglaskintu@yahoo.co.uk ⊕ farmersboy.co.uk
Tours by arrangement

⊠ Established in 1997 and formerly known as Alehouse Brewery, Verulam is situated at the rear of the Farmer's Boy and reverted to its original name in 2010. It currently brews its regular beers for the pub but also produces regular monthly specials, which can be found in other free trade outlets.

Farmers Delight (OG 1036, ABV 3.9%)
Straw-coloured beer with distinct New World hop aroma and flavour.

Farmers Joy (OG 1043, ABV 4.5%)
Ruby, almost black beer with a good combination of dark malt roast and citrus hop flavours.

Citra (OG 1046, ABV 4.6%)
Pale ale with big US West Coast hop character throughout.

Vibrant Forest (NEW) SIBA

Vibrant Forest Brewery, Moonscross Bungalow, Jacobs Gutter Lane, Totton, Hampshire, SO40 9FR
☎ (02380) 669204 ✉ kevin@vibrantforest.co.uk
⊕ vibrantforest.co.uk

Vibrant Forest is a small, award-winning microbrewery that began brewing commercially in 2011 having crafted ales on a non-commercial level for many years.

Ginja Ninja (OG 1041, ABV 4%)
An amber-coloured beer with stem ginger giving a pleasant ginger zing balanced through the use of delicately spicy English hops.

Stormbrew (OG 1050, ABV 4.7%)
A dark amber beer with strong malt character and hints of toffee and chocolate. The maltiness is finely balanced with a high level of bitterness and fruity hop character.

Wheatwave (OG 1048, ABV 4.8%)
An easy-drinking hazy blond wheat beer with pronounced banana and clove character and a careful balance of malts.

Village Brewer

See Hambleton

Violet Cottage (NEW)

▤ Violet Cottage Brewery, Gwaelod y Garth Inn, Main Road, Gwaelod-y-Garth, CF15 9HH
☎ (02920) 810408

Violet Cottage began brewing in 2012 using a two-barrel plant. The brewery is located in a converted garage within the grounds of the Gwaelod y Garth Inn. No beer list was available at the time of going to print.

VIP (NEW)

VIP Brewery, Village Inn Pub Co, Unit E, Hawkshill, Lesbury, Northumberland, NE66 3PG

☎ 07545 885352 ✉ phil@thevillageinnpub.co.uk
⊕ thevillageinnpub.co.uk

Brewing began in 2012 using a five-barrel plant to serve the owner's pub, the Village Inn in Longframlington, and the local free trade.

The Village Bike (ABV 4%)
A full-bodied, complex best bitter.

The Village Lite (ABV 4%)
A light, hoppy, refreshing beer.

Wadworth SIBA IFBB ⊚

Wadworth & Co Ltd, Northgate Brewery, Devizes, Wiltshire, SN10 1JW
☎ (01380) 723361 ✉ sales@wadworth.co.uk
⊕ wadworth.co.uk
Shop Mon-Sat 10am-5.30pm (4.30pm winter); Sun 11-4pm (summer only)
Tours by arrangement

⊠ A market town brewery set up in 1885 by Henry Wadworth, and still proudly independent. Wadworth is one of few remaining producers to sell beer locally in oak casks; the brewery still employs a cooper. Though solidly traditional, with its own dray horses and sign writers, it continues to invest in the future and to expand, producing up to 2,000 barrels a week to supply a wide-ranging free trade, around 300 outlets in the south of England, as well as its own 250 pubs. All tied houses serve cask beer. Wadworth also has a 2.5-barrel micro-brewery used for brewing trials and speciality brews, as well as a new environmentally-friendly brewhouse. Seasonal beers: see website. Bottle-conditioned beer is also available.

Henry's IPA (OG 1035, ABV 3.6%)
A classic, well-balanced session beer with malt-led flavours.

Boundary (OG 1039.5, ABV 4%)
A distinctive bitter defined by its punchy hop kick and spicy overtones with uplifting hop aroma.

Horizon (OG 1039, ABV 4%)
A pale golden beer with zesty citrus and hop aromas and a crisp, refreshing finish.

6X (OG 1041, ABV 4.3%) ◣
Copper-coloured ale with a malty and fruity nose, and some balancing hop character. The flavour is similar, with some bitterness and a lingering malty, but bitter finish.

Bishops Tipple (OG 1048, ABV 5%)
A golden bitter giving well-balanced bitterness and a clean hop finish.

Waen SIBA

Waen Brewery Ltd, Unit 7, Maesyllan Enterprise Estate, Llanidloes, Powys, SY18 6YU
☎ (01686) 627042 ✉ info@thewaenbrewery.co.uk
⊕ thewaenbrewery.co.uk
Shop Fri-Sat 10am-5pm
Tours by arrangement

⊠ Waen began brewing in 2009 on a five-barrel plant in Penstrowed. Increased demand saw the brewery move to its current address. 100 outlets are supplied direct. Seasonal beers are also available.

Blackberry Stout (OG 1036, ABV 3.8%)
A rich, dark, hoppy stout with subtle flavours of autumn fruit.

Festival Gold (OG 1040, ABV 4.2%)
A hoppy, citrussy session ale.

Janner's Pride (OG 1044, ABV 4.6%)
A smooth, fruity best bitter with hints of ginger and aged malt whisky.

Landmark (OG 1054, ABV 5.5%)
Light-coloured beer with an aroma of sunkissed hops and lemon balm.

Wagtail

Wagtail Brewery, New Barn Farm, Wilby Warrens, Old Buckenham, Norfolk, NR17 1PF
☎ (01953) 887133
✉ wagtailbrewery@btinternet.com
⊕ wagtailbrewery.com

Wagtail brewery went into full-time production in 2006. All beers are now only available bottle-conditioned and are suitable for vegetarians and vegans: see website for full range.

Wainstones SIBA

Wainstones Brewery, Unit 9, Terry Dicken Industrial Estate, Station Road, Stokesley, North Yorkshire, TS9 7AE
☎ 07885 240226 ✉ john@stokesleybrewing.co.uk
⊕ stokesleybrewing.co.uk
Tours by arrangement

⊗ Wainstones, formerly known as Stokesley Brewery, began brewing in 2010 using a 2.5-barrel plant. Local pubs, restaurants and hotels are supplied.

Amber (ABV 3.8%)

Sandstone (ABV 4%)

Ironstone (ABV 4.2%)

Copper (ABV 4.3%)

Steel River (ABV 4.3%)

Jet (ABV 4.5%)

Transporter (ABV 4.5%)

Wall's

Wall's Brewing Co Ltd, County Town Brewery, 1 Binks Close, Standard Way Business Park, Northallerton, North Yorkshire, DL6 2YB
☎ (01609) 258226 ☎ 07810 123084
✉ info@wallsbrewery.co.uk ⊕ wallsbrewery.co.uk

Brewing began in 2011 on a 5.5-barrel plant. Beers can be found in more than 100 local outlets along with a range of bottle-conditioned ales. Seasonal beers: see website.

County Best (OG 1034, ABV 3.2%)

Mild & Easy (OG 1034, ABV 3.2%)

Summer Gold (OG 1036, ABV 3.6%)

Gun Dog Bitter (OG 1041, ABV 3.8%)

Keepers Gold (OG 1039, ABV 3.9%)

Northallerton Dark (OG 1040, ABV 4.4%)

Beaters Choice (OG 1050, ABV 4.6%)

Explorer IPA (OG 1050, ABV 4.7%)

Wantsum SIBA

Wantsum Brewery Ltd, Units 22 & 23, Sparrow Way, Lakesview International Business Park, Hersden, Kent, CT3 4AL
☎ (0845) 040 5980
✉ wantsumbrewery@googlemail.com
⊕ wantsumbrewery.co.uk
Tours by arrangement

⊗ Wantsum Brewery is a six-barrel plant and was established in 2009. It is located about seven miles from the city of Canterbury and close to the Wantsum channel, from which it takes its name. The beers are named after historic events and people in Kent. Around 45 outlets are supplied direct, mainly in East Kent. Seasonal and bottle-conditioned beers are also available. Additional space has been secured by leasing the adjacent unit and a shop has recently opened within the brewery.

More's Head (OG 1034, ABV 3.5%)
A chestnut-coloured bitter with malt and roasted grains balanced against fruit and floral hops with a hint of citrus.

1381 (OG 1036, ABV 3.8%)
A golden IPA with delicate citrus and herbal aromas.

Imperium (OG 1039, ABV 4%)
A deep amber best bitter; smooth biscuit malts and rich, hoppy nose balance this beer perfectly.

Fortitude (OG 1039, ABV 4.2%)
A bitter combining four types of malt to give depth of body with English and American hops for a pronounced finish.

Miller's Mirth (OG 1041, ABV 4.2%)
A copper-coloured floral and spicy best bitter.

Turbulent Priest (OG 1042, ABV 4.4%)
A full-bodied best bitter offering chocolate and coffee notes on top of a sweet malt base.

One Hop (OG 1042, ABV 4.5%)
A single hop beer; the hop will be changed every two months.

Dynamo (OG 1043, ABV 4.6%)
A crisp, light, golden ale, fruity and floral with an orange citrus twist.

Hengist (OG 1046, ABV 5%)
A golden pale ale with flavours of biscuit malt balancing a long, fruity hop profile.

Ravening Wolf (OG 1054, ABV 5.9%)
A light amber strong pale ale; toasted biscuit and rye malt flavours support a pine lemon hop crispness with a hint of vanilla.

Wapping

☱ Wapping Beers Ltd, Baltic Fleet, 33a Wapping, Liverpool, Merseyside, L1 8DQ
☎ (0151) 709 3116 ✉ simon@wappingbeers.co.uk
⊕ wappingbeers.co.uk / balticfleet.co.uk
Merchandise available at bar
Tours by arrangement

☺ Wapping Beers was established in 2002 in the cellars of the pub on the waterfront in Liverpool using the old Passageway Brewery plant. Around half a dozen regular house beers are produced with specials and seasonal brews appearing throughout the year. All cask beers are also available bottle conditioned.

THE BREWERIES

Bitter (OG 1036, ABV 3.6%)

Baltic Gold (OG 1039, ABV 3.9%) ◈
Hoppy golden ale with plenty of citrus hop flavour. Refreshing with good body and mouthfeel.

Bow Sprit (OG 1036, ABV 4%)

Magna 800 (OG 1037, ABV 4%)

Summer Ale (OG 1042, ABV 4.2%) ◈
Refreshing golden beer with floral hops dominating the nose and taste. Some fruit also on the aroma and in the taste. Good bitterness throughout, leading to a dry, bitter aftertaste.

Blonde (OG 1045, ABV 4.5%)

Smoked Porter (OG 1050, ABV 5%) 🍴

Stout (OG 1050, ABV 5%) ◈
Classic dry roasty stout with strong bitterness balanced by fruit and hop flavours. The flavours follow through to a pleasantly dry finish.

Golden Promise IPA (OG 1052, ABV 5.5%)

Warcop

Warcop Ales, c/o 9 Nellive Park, St Brides Wentlooge, Gwent, NP10 8SE
☎ (01633) 680058 ✉ wiliam.picton@tesco.net
⊕ warcopales.com

A small brewery at Newhouse Farm, Saint Brides Wentlooge, based in a converted milking parlour. Cask ales are also available bottle conditioned. The brewery has a portfolio of 28 beers that are made on a cyclical basis, with five to six beers normally in stock at any one time: see website for full range. Seasonal beers: see website.

Warwickshire SIBA

Warwickshire Beer Co Ltd, The Bakehouse Brewery, Queen Street, Cubbington, Warwickshire, CV32 7NA
☎ (01926) 450747 ✉ info@warwickshirebeer.co.uk
⊕ warwickshirebeer.co.uk
Shop open most days inc. Sat am (please ring first)

Warwickshire is a six-barrel brewery operating in a former village bakery since 1998. Brewing takes place four times a week. The cask beers are available in more than 100 outlets as well as the brewery's four pubs. Seasonal beers are also available.

Castle Mild (OG 1034, ABV 3.4%)
Dark in colour with fruit overtones with a hoppy finish.

Shakespeare's County (OG 1034, ABV 3.4%)
A low gravity golden ale.

Best Bitter (OG 1039, ABV 3.9%)
An easy-drinking golden brown session ale with a malty flavour and gentle bitterness, which becomes more assertive in the aftertaste.

Darling Buds (OG 1041, ABV 4%)

Golden Bear (OG 1049, ABV 4.9%)
A golden brown beer with a long-lasting, slightly resiny bitterness. The finish is fruity and warming with hints of spice and orange.

Kingmaker (OG 1055, ABV 5.5%)
A rich, fruity beer. A grainy, spirity aroma leads on to a palate with overtones of whisky, orange and dark chocolate. A warming alcoholic finish.

Watermill SIBA

▤ Watermill Brewing Co, Ings, Cumbria, LA8 9PY
☎ (01539) 821309 ☎ 07831 873300
✉ info@lakelandpub.co.uk ⊕ lakelandpub.co.uk
Tours by arrangement

☺Watermill was established in 2006 in a purpose-built extension to the inn. The five-barrel plant and equipment were originally at the Hops Bar & Grill opposite Daytona International Speedway in Florida. The beers have a doggie theme; dogs are allowed in the main bar of the pub and usually get served with biscuits before their owners. The brewery was extended in 2008. A new brewery is planned within the grounds of the pub, which will double production.

Collie Wobbles (OG 1037.5, ABV 3.7%)
A pale gold bitter with a slight citrus taste. A good hop and malt balance gives way to a dry finish.

Black Beard (OG 1038, ABV 3.8%)
A dark mild with bags of fruit and malt flavours.

A Bit'er Ruff (OG 1041.5, ABV 4.1%) ◈
Copper-coloured, balanced fruity beer with a lingering, bitter aftertaste.

Ruff Justice (OG 1041, ABV 4.2%)
A malty golden ale, well-balanced with caramel, light floral hops and a fresh, dry finish.

Isle of Dogs (OG 1044, ABV 4.5%)
A golden bitter with a fresh, malty aroma and a distinctive citrus fruity flavour with an intense, dry aftertaste.

Wruff Night (OG 1047.5, ABV 5%) ◈
Straw-coloured, sweet and fruity, uncomplicated beer with bitterness in a short-lived aftertaste.

Dogth Vader (OG 1050, ABV 5.1%)
A dark, hoppy ale with a refreshing, dry finish.

Tomos Watkin SIBA

Hurns Brewing Co Ltd t/a Tomos Watkin, Unit 3, Alberto Road, Century Park, Valley Way, Swansea Enterprise Park, Swansea, SA6 8RP
☎ (01792) 797300 ✉ phillparry@tomoswatkin.co.uk
⊕ hurns.co.uk
Shop Mon-Fri 9am-5pm
Tours by arrangement

☺Brewing started in 1995 in converted garages in Llandeilo using a 10-barrel plant. The brewery moved to bigger premises in Swansea in 2000 and the plant increased to a 50-barrel capacity. HBC Ltd was formed in 2002 when the brewery was purchased from Tomos Watkin. Over 60% of production is now bottled beers (not bottle conditioned) and a bottling line was installed in 2010. More than 600 outlets are supplied. Seasonal beers: see website.

Cwrw Braf (OG 1038, ABV 3.7%)
A clean-drinking, amber-coloured ale with a light bitterness and gentle hop aroma.

Blodwens Beer (OG 1045, ABV 4.5%)
Light blond beer with a delicate creamy finish with a hint of citrus.

Old Style Bitter/OSB (OG 1045, ABV 4.5%) ◈
Amber-coloured with an inviting aroma of hops and malt. Full bodied; hops, fruit, malt and bitterness combine to give a balanced flavour continuing into the finish.

Waveney

≣ Waveney Brewing Co, Queen's Head, Station Road, Earsham, Norfolk, NR35 2TS
☎ (01986) 892623 ✉ hampsoid@aol.com

⊗ Established at the Queens Head in 2004, the five-barrel brewery produces three beers, regularly available at the pub along with free trade outlets. Occasional and seasonal beers are also brewed.

East Coast Mild (OG 1037, ABV 3.8%) ◆
A traditional mild with distinctive roast malt aroma and red-brown colouring. A sweet, plummy malt beginning quickly fades as a dry roasted bitterness begins to make its presence felt.

Lightweight (OG 1039, ABV 3.9%) ◆
A gentle beer with a light but well-balanced hop and malt character. A light body is reflected in the quick, bitter finish. Golden hued with a distinctive strawberry and cream nose.

Welterweight (OG 1042, ABV 4.2%)

Wayland's Sixpenny

See Sixpenny

Weard'Ale

≣ Weard'Ale Brewery, Hare & Hounds, 24 Front Street, Westgate, DL13 1RX
☎ (01388) 517212

Weard'Ale began brewing in 2010. The beers are mainly sold on the premises but some has found its way to nearby beer festivals and other local outlets.

Colin's Bitter & Twisty (OG 1038, ABV 3.8%)

Hare O' The Dog (OG 1038, ABV 3.8%)

Weatheroak SIBA

Weatheroak Brewery Ltd, Unit 7, Victoria Works, Birmingham Road, Studley, Warwickshire, B80 7AP
☎ (0121) 445 4411 (eve) ☎ 07798 773894 (day)

Office: Victoria Works, 33 Redditch Road, Studley, Warwickshire, B80 7AU ⊕ weatheroakales.co.uk

The brewery was set up in 1997 in an outhouse at the Coach & Horses, Weatheroak Hill. The first brew was produced in 1998. In 2008 it moved to Alvechurch and then to a spacious factory unit in Studley. Weatheroak supplies 40 outlets. Seasonal beers are brewed on a regular basis. In 2012 the brewery took over the Nags Head in Studley and renamed it Victoria Works for use as its brewery tap.

Light Oak (ABV 3.6%) ◆
This straw-coloured quaffing ale has lots of hoppy notes on the tongue and nose, and a fleetingly sweet aftertaste.

Ale (ABV 4.1%) ◆
The aroma is dominated by hops in this golden-coloured brew. Hops also feature in the mouth and there is a rapidly fading dry aftertaste.

Victoria Works (ABV 4.3%)
A pale, hoppy bitter with a citrus finish.

Keystone Hops (ABV 5%) ◆
A golden yellow beer that is surprisingly easy to quaff given the strength. Fruity hops are the

dominant flavour without the commonly associated astringency.

For Weighbridge, Alvechurch:

Tillerman's Tipple (ABV 3.9%)
A pleasant, pale session beer with hops throughout.

Weatheroak Hill SIBA

≣ Weatheroak Hill Brewery, Coach & Horses, Weatheroak Hill, Warwickshire, B48 7EA
☎ (01564) 823386 (pub)
Tours by arrangement

Weatheroak Hill started brewing in 2008. At present only the pub and beer festivals are supplied. Since the departure of the previous brewer beers are currently brewed on site by an independent contract brewer until a permanent replacement is found.

Icknield Pale Ale (OG 1038, ABV 3.8%)

Bitter (WHB) (OG 1042, ABV 4.2%)

Weetwood SIBA

Weetwood Ales Ltd, The Brewery, Common Lane, Kelsall, Cheshire, CW6 0PY
☎ (01829) 752377 ✉ sales@weetwoodales.co.uk
⊕ weetwoodales.co.uk

☺One of the original Cheshire microbreweries set up at an equestrian centre in 1993. Five years later a 10-barrel brewhouse was installed, tripling capacity. In 2011 a new brewery was built on a site around the corner. A 30-barrel brewhouse was installed and brewing commenced in early 2012. More than 300 outlets are supplied regularly.

Best Bitter (OG 1038.5, ABV 3.8%) ◆
Pale brown beer with an assertive bitterness and a lingering dry finish. Despite initial sweetness, peppery hops dominate throughout.

Mad Hatter (OG 1038.5, ABV 3.9%)
A red-brown beer with fruity and malty flavours throughout. Brewed with American Amarillo hops to give spicy and floral notes.

Cheshire Cat (ABV 4%) ◆
Pale, dry bitter with a spritzy lemon zest and a grapy aroma. Hoppy aroma leads through to the initial taste before fruitiness takes over. Smooth creamy mouthfeel and a short, dry finish.

Eastgate Ale (OG 1043.5, ABV 4.2%) ◆
Well-balanced and refreshing clean amber beer. Citrus fruit flavours predominate in the taste and there is a short, dry aftertaste.

Old Dog Bitter (OG 1045, ABV 4.5%) ◆
Robust, well-balanced amber beer with a slightly fruity aroma. Rich malt and fruit flavours are balanced by bitterness. Some sweetness and a hint of sulphur on nose and taste.

Ambush Ale (OG 1047.5, ABV 4.8%) ◆
Full-bodied malty, premium bitter with initial sweetness balanced by bitterness and leading to a long-lasting dry finish. Blackberries and bitterness predominate alongside the hops.

Oasthouse Gold (OG 1050, ABV 5%) ◆
Straw-coloured, crisp, full-bodied and fruity golden ale with a good dry finish.

Weighbridge (NEW) SIBA

Weighbridge Brewery, Penzance Drive, Swindon, Wiltshire, SN5 7JL
☎ (01793) 881500
✉ weighbridgebrewhouse@hotmail.co.uk
⊕ weighbridgebrewhouse.co.uk

Weighbridge is a family-owned microbrewery based within the Weighbridge Brewhouse restaurant and bar, formerly home to Archers Brewery. Established in 2011 it is under the stewardship of Mark Wallington (former Archer's owner). The beers are also available at the Three Crowns in Brinkworth.

English Ale (OG 1040, ABV 3.9%)
Rounded, refreshing pale ale with a delicate, slightly fruity aroma on the finish.

Best (OG 1044, ABV 4.3%)
A good bitter ale with a malty aftertaste and spicy aroma.

Pooley's Golden (OG 1048, ABV 4.7%)
A robust golden ale, full-bodied with plenty of bitterness with an unusual gooseberry aroma. The aftertaste is a balance of malt and hop.

Welbeck Abbey SIBA

Welbeck Abbey, Lower Motor Yard, Welbeck, Nottinghamshire, S80 3LT
☎ (01909) 512539 ✉ claire.monk@welbeck.co.uk
⊕ welbeckabbeybrewery.co.uk
Tours by arrangement

☺A joint venture between Kelham Island Brewery and Welbeck Estates, which started brewing in 2011. The brewery is housed in a listed barn in the centre of the Welbeck Estate. The 10-barrel plant was originally used at Kelham Island.

Henrietta (OG 1036, ABV 3.6%)

Red Feather (OG 1040, ABV 3.9%)

Ernest George (OG 1040.6, ABV 4.2%)

Portland Black (OG 1043, ABV 4.5%)

Cavendish (OG 1046, ABV 5%)

Wellington Inn (NEW)

▤ **Wellington Inn Brewery, 55 Russell Street, Hull, HU2 9AB**
☎ (01482) 329486 ✉ richardgg51@yahoo.co.uk

☺Launched in 2011, the Wellington Inn Brewery is run by Richard and Janette Gant and is located at their public house in Hull. Regular beers are brewed along with some specials on the 2.5-barrel plant. The beer names all relate in some way to Arthur Wellesley, the first Duke of Wellington.

1st Duke (ABV 3.7%)
A copper-coloured best bitter with a dry hop finish.

Waterloo Porter (ABV 4%)
A rich, dark roast beer.

Beau Douro (ABV 4.5%)
A crisp, pale blond beer.

Leipzig (ABV 5.8%)
A big blonde beer with a light, malty finish.

Wellington

See Wood Street

Wells & Young's

See New Nationals section

Welton's SIBA

Welton's North Downs Brewery Ltd, 1 Mulberry Trading Estate, Foundry Lane, Horsham, West Sussex, RH13 5PX
☎ (01403) 242901/251873 ✉ sales@weltons.co.uk
⊕ weltonsbeer.com
Tours by arrangement

⊗ Ray Welton moved his brewery to a factory unit in Horsham in 2003, which has given him space to expand. Over 100 different beers were brewed during the past year. Around 400 outlets are supplied. Bottle-conditioned beers are also available.

Old Cocky (OG 1043, ABV 4.3%)

Old Harry (OG 1051, ABV 5.2%)

Wensleydale SIBA

Wensleydale Brewery Ltd, Manor Road, Bellerby, North Yorkshire, DL8 5QH
☎ (01969) 622463 ☎ 07900 264235
✉ enquiries@wensleydalebrewery.co.uk
⊕ wensleydalebrewery.co.uk
Shop Mon-Fri 9am-5pm
Tours by arrangement

Wensleydale Brewery (formerly Lidstone's) was set up in 2003 on a two-barrel plant in Yorkshire Dales National Park. A year later the brewery relocated to larger premises six miles away and is now operating on a 4.5-barrel plant. Most beers are available in bottles – some bottle conditioned. Around 100 outlets are supplied. Seasonal beers are also available.

Lidstone's Rowley Mild (OG 1032, ABV 3.2%) ◆
Chocolate and toffee aromas lead into what, for its strength, is an impressively rich and flavoursome taste. The finish is pleasantly bittersweet.

Bitter (OG 1036, ABV 3.7%) ◆
Intensely aromatic, straw-coloured ale offering a superb balance of malt and hops on the tongue.

Falconer Session Bitter (OG 1038, ABV 3.9%)
A fruity, malt-based session ale, copper-coloured with a long, bitter, dry finish.

Semerwater Summer Ale (OG 1040, ABV 4.1%)
A pale ale with citrus aromas. A clean, hoppy nose is balanced by a light, malty sweetness.

Coverdale Gamekeeper (OG 1042, ABV 4.3%)
A copper-coloured best bitter with spicy hop flavours and juicy malt flavour.

Black Dub Oat Stout (OG 1043, ABV 4.4%)
Black and silky, enriched with roast barley, chocolate malt and malted oats. Named after a deep, dark pool (or Dub) in the River Cover to the rear of Middleham Castle.

Sheep Rustler Nut Brown Ale (OG 1043, ABV 4.4%)
A dark, reddish brown beer with a sweetish roast malt taste leading to a long-lasting, roasted, slightly bitter finish.

Gold (OG 1044, ABV 4.5%)

Aromatic and spicy hop flavours combine with light malt to make this a highly quaffable, light golden best bitter.

Coverdale Poacher IPA (OG 1048, ABV 5%) ◥
Citrus flavours dominate both aroma and taste in this pale, smooth, refreshing beer; the aftertaste is quite dry.

Wentwell

Wentwell Brewery, 15 Wingfield Drive, Derby, DE21 4PW
☎ 07900 475755 ✉ contact@wentwellbrewery.com
⊕ wentwellbrewery.com

Wentwell began commercial brewing in early 2011 using a one-barrel plant, upgrading to a three-barrel plant soon after. The brewery is a member of the Derbyshire Brewers' Collective. Several local outlets are supplied. Seasonal and bottle-conditioned beers are also available.

Derbyshire Gold (OG 1039, ABV 3.9%)
A light, hoppy, zesty session beer.

Little Tick (OG 1040, ABV 4%)
Straw-coloured bitter, triple hopped for a fuller flavour.

Farm Hands' Bitter (OG 1042, ABV 4.1%)
A rich, copper-coloured best bitter with a smooth, rounded flavour and nicely balanced bitterness.

Barrel Organ Blues (OG 1046, ABV 4.5%)
A golden-brown, full-bodied premium bitter with a rich, malty flavour and aroma.

Wentworth SIBA

Wentworth Brewery Ltd, Power House, Gun Park, Wentworth, South Yorkshire, S62 7TF
☎ (01226) 747070
✉ info@wentworthbrewery.co.uk
⊕ wentworthbrewery.co.uk
Tours by arrangement

The brewery was founded in 1999 in the power house in the grounds of Wentworth Woodhouse. A new custom-built 30-barrel brewery was commissioned in 2006 with production now around 7,000hl. Wentworth produces around 20 core bottled beers under both the Wentworth brand and the Barnsley Beer Company. Two monthly specials are also produced in addition to the seasonal range.

WPA (OG 1039.5, ABV 4%) ◥
An extremely well-hopped IPA-style beer that leads to some astringency. A very bitter beer.

Wessex

CF Hobden t/a Wessex Brewery, Rye Hill Farm, Longbridge Deverill, Wiltshire, BA12 7DE
☎ (01985) 844532
✉ wessexbrewery@tinyworld.co.uk

⊠ The brewery went into production in 2001 and moved to its current location in 2004. 15 local outlets are supplied. Beers are also available through selected wholesalers. Seasonal beers are also produced.

Potter's Ale (OG 1038, ABV 3.8%)

Mild (OG 1038, ABV 3.9%)

Longleat Pride (OG 1040, ABV 4%)

A pale, hoppy bitter.

Crockerton Classic (OG 1041, ABV 4.1%)
A full-bodied, tawny, full-flavoured bitter; fruity and malty.

Merrie Mink (OG 1041, ABV 4.2%)
A full-flavoured best bitter with a strong hop aroma.

Deverill's Advocate (OG 1046, ABV 4.5%)
A well-balanced golden premium ale.

Warminster Warrior (OG 1045, ABV 4.5%)
Full-flavoured premium bitter.

Golden Apostle (OG 1048, ABV 4.8%)

Russian Stoat (OG 1080, ABV 9%) ▦
Dark, strong stout.

For Isle of Avalon Brewery:

Isle Ale (OG 1038, ABV 3.8%)

Jake's Mild (OG 1039, ABV 4%)

Sunset (OG 1043, ABV 4.3%)

Sunrise (OG 1050, ABV 5%)

Arthur's Ale (OG 1071, ABV 7%)

West SIBA

▤ West Brewery, Bar & Restaurant, Binnie Place, Glasgow Green, Glasgow, G40 1AW
☎ (0141) 550 0135 ✉ info@westbeer.com
⊕ westbeer.com
Tours by arrangement

No real ale. West opened in 2006 and produces a full range of European-style beers. The brewery's copper-clad system, visible from the 300-seat bar and restaurant, is a fully-automated German one with an annual capacity of 1.5 million litres. Brewing is in strict accordance with the Reinheitsgebot, the German purity law, importing all malt, hops and yeast from Germany. Five regular beers are produced along with a range of seasonals. Beers: Hefeweizen (ABV 4.9%), St Mungo (ABV 4.9%), Helles Light (ABV 3.9%), Dunkel (ABV 4.9%), Munich Red (ABV 4.9%).

West Berkshire SIBA

West Berkshire Brewery Co Ltd, The Flour Barn, Frilsham House Farm Units, Yattendon, Berkshire, RG18 0XT
☎ (01635) 202968 ✉ info@wbbrew.co.uk
⊕ wbbrew.com
Shop Mon-Fri 10am-4pm; Sat 10am-1pm
Tours by arrangement

⊠ The brewery, established in 1995 at the Potkiln pub in Frilsham, moved its main site to Yattendon and in 2006 extended the brewhouse and installed a new plant; the original five-barrel plant at the Potkiln pub in Frilsham is now closed. In 2011 a new brewery was built 600 yards down the road, which more than doubled the brewing capacity. Around 150 outlets are supplied and one pub is owned. A monthly beer is also brewed – the beer names follow an annual theme.

Old Father Thames (OG 1038, ABV 3.4%)
A traditional pale ale with a full flavour despite its low strength.

**Mr Chubb's Lunchtime Bitter
(OG 1040, ABV 3.7%)** ◥

A drinkable, balanced, session bitter. A malty caramel note dominates aroma and taste and is accompanied by a nutty bittersweetness and a hoppy aftertaste.

Maggs' Magnificent Mild (OG 1041, ABV 3.8%) ◆
Silky, full-bodied, dark mild with a creamy head. Roast malt aroma is joined in the taste by caramel, sweetness and mild, fruity hoppiness. Aftertaste of roast malt with balancing bitterness.

Good Old Boy (OG 1043, ABV 4%) ◆
Well-rounded, tawny bitter with malt and hops dominating throughout. A balancing bitterness accompanies the taste and aftertaste.

Dr Hexter's Wedding Ale (OG 1044, ABV 4.1%) ◆
Fruit and hops dominate the aroma and are joined in the taste by a hint of malt. The aftertaste has a pleasant bitter hoppiness.

Full Circle (OG 1047, ABV 4.5%) ◆
A golden ale with a pleasing aroma and taste of bitter hops with a hint of malt. The aftertaste is hoppy and bitter with a rounding note of malt.

Dr Hexter's Healer (OG 1052, ABV 5%) ◆
An amber strong bitter with malt, caramel and hops in the aroma. Taste is a balance of malt, caramel, fruit, hops and bittersweetness. Caramel, fruit and bittersweetness dominate the aftertaste.

Westbury

See Wessex

West Country

See Salisbury

Westerham SIBA ◉

Westerham Brewery Co Ltd, Grange Farm, Pootings Road, Crockham Hill, Kent, TN8 6SA
☎ (01732) 864427
✉ sales@westerhambrewery.co.uk
⊕ westerhambrewery.co.uk
Shop Mon-Fri 10am-5pm
Tours by arrangement (min 30 people, charge made)

⊠ The brewery was established in 2004 and restored a brewing tradition to Westerham that was lost when the Black Eagle Brewery was taken over by Ind Coope in 1959 and closed in 1965. Two of Black Eagle's yeast strains were deposited at the National Collection of Yeast Cultures and are used to recreate the true flavour of Westerham beers. The new brewery is based at the National Trust's Grange Farm in a former dairy and uses the same water supply as Black Eagle. Around 200 outlets are supplied in Kent, Surrey, Sussex and South London. Monthly specials: see website. Bottle-conditioned beers are also available.

Finchcocks Original (OG 1036.2, ABV 3.5%)
Mid-gold session beer. Citrus notes on the palate with a hint of biscuit and resiny hoppiness.

Grasshopper Kentish Bitter (OG 1039, ABV 3.8%)
A dark, malty bitter with nutty, roasted notes from the chocolate malt.

Spirit of Kent (OG 1039.5, ABV 4%)
Crisp golden ale with floral and fruity notes. Complex tropical fruit and citrus flavours blend with

the sweet malt. Assertive dry hop notes on the finish.

William Wilberforce Freedom Ale (OG 1040, ABV 4%)
Deep golden ale with a mellow bitterness and long, hoppy finish.

British Bulldog (OG 1043.5, ABV 4.3%)
A rich, full-bodied best bitter with a massive aroma and palate of jammy fruit, biscuity malt and bitter hop resins.

1965 – Special Bitter Ale (OG 1047.5, ABV 4.8%)
A clean, refreshing bitter with a full-bodied flavour.

Audit Ale (OG 1061, ABV 6.2%)
A hoppy ale; strong and bitter.

Whalebone

🍺 Whalebone Brewery, 163 Wincolmlee, Hull, East Yorkshire, HU2 0PA
☎ (01482) 226648
Tours by arrangement

◉ The Whalebone pub, which dates from 1796, was bought by Hull CAMRA founding member Alex Craig in 2002. He opened the brewery the following year and his beers have names connected with the former whaling industry on the adjoining River Hull. Two or three outlets are supplied as well as the pub.

Diana Mild (OG 1037, ABV 3.5%)

Neckoil Bitter (OG 1039, ABV 3.9%)

WharfeBank SIBA ◉

WharfeBank Brewery Ltd, Unit 4, Pool Business Park, Pool Road, Pool in Wharfedale, West Yorkshire, LS21 1FD
☎ (0113) 284 2392
✉ info@wharfebankbrewery.co.uk
⊕ wharfebankbrewery.co.uk
Tours by arrangement

◉ WharfeBank commenced brewing in 2010 using a 20-barrel plant in a converted paper mill on the banks of the River Wharfe. The team is led by Martin Kellaway, ex sales director at Caledonian Brewery, with brewing headed by Ian Smith, former Tetley's head brewer. Beers are available across the north, with flagship brand Tether Blond available regionally through Enterprise and Punch. Seasonal beers are also available.

VPA (Verbeia Pale Ale) (OG 1035, ABV 3.6%)
A pale golden session ale with a citrus, fruity taste. Light and refreshing.

Slingers Gold (OG 1036, ABV 3.7%) ◆
Golden-coloured session ale with fruit and hops carrying bitterness all the way through to the finish.

Tether Blond (OG 1040, ABV 4.1%) ◆
A moderately hopped light ale with some sweetness, smooth and easy to drink, the gentle fruit flavours continue to the short, more bitter finish.

CamFell Flame (OG 1044, ABV 4.4%) ◆
Dark ruby/red, bittersweet and malty ale with a smooth mouthfeel. Some caramel roastiness is present throughout.

WISPA (WharfeBank India Strong Pale Ale) (OG 1050, ABV 5.1%) ◆

Amber-coloured strong bitter. A fruity aroma carries through to the taste along with a balance of sweetness and bitterness.

Wharfedale

See Dark Horse

Whim ⒮ⒾⒷⒶ

Whim Ales Ltd, Whim Farm, Hartington, Derbyshire, SK17 0AX
☎ (01298) 84991 ✉ info@whimales.co.uk

The brewery opened in 1993 in outbuildings at Whim Farm. Whim's beers are available in 50-70 outlets and the brewery's tied house, the Wilkes Head in Leek, Staffs. Some one-off brews are produced. Occasional/seasonal beers are also available.

Arbor Light (OG 1035, ABV 3.6%)
Light-coloured bitter, sharp and clean with good hop character and a delicate light aroma.

Hartington Bitter (OG 1039, ABV 4%) 🍺
A light, golden-coloured, well-hopped session beer. A dry finish with a spicy, floral aroma.

Hartington IPA (OG 1045, ABV 4.5%)
Pale and light-coloured, smooth on the palate allowing malt to predominate. Slightly sweet finish combined with distinctive light hop bitterness. Well rounded.

Flower Power (OG 1053, ABV 5.3%)
Light, golden-coloured beer with a flowery hop aroma, citrus with mild spice on the palate and a dry, bitter finish.

Whitehaven

See Ennerdale

White Horse ⒮ⒾⒷⒶ ◉

White Horse Brewery Co Ltd, 3 Ware Road, White Horse Business Park, Stanford-in-the-Vale, Oxfordshire, SN7 8NY
☎ (01367) 718700 ✉ info@whitehorsebrewery.com
🌐 breweryoxfordshire.co.uk
Shop Mon-Fri 9am-5pm; Sat 8am-12pm

⊠ White Horse was founded on a modern industrial estate in 2004. The brewing plant was manufactured in Belgium and has a brew-length of 6.5 barrels. It uses the continental method of brewing with a lauter tun rather than an infusion mash tun. The brewery now has its own pubs in Oxford and Banbury as well as supplying more than 150 outlets. Seasonal beers are available.

Bitter (OG 1038.7, ABV 3.7%)
Golden bitter, well-hopped with a clean, fruity finish.

Village Idiot (OG 1041.8, ABV 4.1%)
A blonde ale with a complex hop aroma and taste.

Wayland Smithy (OG 1047.1, ABV 4.4%)
A red-brown ale with a nice biscuit flavour that is balanced with a spicy hop finish.

Guv'nor (OG 1063.1, ABV 6.5%)
A light golden strong ale with a fruity finish.

White Park ⒮ⒾⒷⒶ

White Park Brewery, Perry Hill Farm, Bourne End Road, Cranfield, Bedfordshire, MK43 0BA
☎ (01223) 911357 ✉ info@whiteparkbrewery.co.uk
🌐 whiteparkbrewery.co.uk

White Park is a family business established in 2007 on a five-barrel plant. Spent malt is recycled as feed for rare breed cattle. 60 outlets are supplied direct. In 2009 the brewery began bottling and supplies pubs and local stores including Budgens. Seasonal beers: see website.

White Gold (OG 1037, ABV 3.8%)

Bedford Best (OG 1040.5, ABV 4.1%)

Cranfield Bitter (OG 1042.5, ABV 4.4%)

Kellyhopter (OG 1045, ABV 4.8%)

GB (OG 1047, ABV 5%)

Moonshine (OG 1050, ABV 5.2%)

White Rose ⒮ⒾⒷⒶ

White Rose Brewery Ltd, 119 Chapel Road, Burncross, Chapeltown, Sheffield, South Yorkshire, S35 1QL
☎ (0114) 297 6150
✉ whiterose.brewery@btinternet.com
Tours by arrangement

☺Gary Sheriff, former head brewer at Wentworth Brewery, set up White Rose in 2007. The brewery premises are behind the Wellington in Sheffield and are shared with Little Ale Cart Brewery. Some equipment is used jointly but White Rose uses its own fermenters. 100 outlets are supplied direct.

Honey Blonde (OG 1040, ABV 4%)

Original Blonde (OG 1040, ABV 4%)

Stairway to Heaven (OG 1044, ABV 4.3%)

Raven (ABV 4.6%)

Whitewater

Whitewater Brewing Co, 40 Tullyframe Road, Kilkeel, Co Down, Northern Ireland, BT34 4RZ
☎ (028) 4176 9449
✉ info@whitewaterbrewing.com
🌐 whitewaterbrewing.co.uk
Tours by arrangement

Set up in 1996, Whitewater is now the biggest brewery in Northern Ireland. One pub is owned, the White Horse in Saintfield, Co. Down. A range of occasional and seasonal beers is also available.

Copperhead (OG 1037, ABV 3.7%)
An Irish pale ale; well-flavoured with spicy hops.

Crown & Glory (OG 1038, ABV 3.8%)
A grassy, hoppy nose with mild floral tones.

Belfast Black (OG 1042, ABV 4.2%)
A dry, nutty stout with sweet coffee and roasted malt flavours.

Belfast Ale (OG 1046, ABV 4.5%)
A smooth russet ale with a good hoppy flavour.

Clotworthy Dobbin (OG 1050, ABV 5%)
A rich ruby porter with lashings of hoppiness and plenty of fruit and toffee on the palate.

Whitstable SIBA

Whitstable Brewery, Little Telpits Farm, Woodcock Lane, Grafty Green, Kent, ME17 2AY
☎ (01622) 851007
✉ whitstablebrewer@btconnect.com
⊕ whitstablebrewery.info

Whitstable was launched in 2003 when the Green family purchased the Swale and North Weald Brewery to supply their own outlets (a hotel and three restaurants) in Whitstable, and beer festival orders. In 2006 they opened a bar in East Quay. The brewery supplies more than 75 outlets in Kent, Surrey and London. Seasonal beers are also available.

Native Bitter (OG 1036, ABV 3.7%) ◆
A classic copper-coloured Kentish session bitter with hoppy aroma and a long, dry bitter hop finish.

Renaissance Ruby Mild (OG 1038, ABV 3.8%)

East India Pale Ale (OG 1040, ABV 4.1%) ◆
A well-hopped golden IPA with good grapefruit aroma hop character and lingering bitter finish.

Oyster Stout (OG 1045, ABV 4.5%)
Rich, dry deep chocolate and mocha flavours.

Pearl of Kent (OG 1043, ABV 4.5%)
A light-coloured, well-rounded premium beer with tropical fruit flavours.

Winkle Picker (OG 1042, ABV 4.5%)
Amber-coloured best bitter with some fruit on the finish.

Kentish Reserve (OG 1047, ABV 5%)
A copper ale with warm plum pudding flavours and a ruby port finish.

Whittington's SIBA ◉

Whittington's Brewery, Three Choirs Vineyards Ltd, Newent, Gloucestershire, GL18 1LS
☎ (01531) 890555 ✉ brewery@threechoirs.com
⊕ whittingtonbrewery.co.uk
Shop 9am-5pm daily (later during summer)
Tours by arrangement (for a charge)

⊗ Whittington's started in 2003 using a purpose-built five-barrel plant producing 20 barrels a week. The legendary Dick Whittington came from nearby Pauntley, hence the name and feline theme. The beers are available in casks, party 9's and bottle conditioned from the onsite shop, online and from local outlets.

Nine Lives (ABV 3.7%)

Cats Whiskers (ABV 4.6%)

Whittlebury SIBA

Whittlebury Brewery Ltd, Stable Store, Home Farm Business Park, Whittlebury, Northamptonshire, NN12 8XS
☎ 07812 366369
✉ john.evans@whittleburybrewery.com
⊕ whittleburybrewery.com

⊗ Whittlebury was established in 2010 using a 5.5-barrel plant in an old dairy. Beers can be found throughout Northamptonshire and surrounding counties.

Whittlewood (OG 1038, ABV 3.6%)
A traditional, malty session ale.

Nomad Oasis (OG 1039, ABV 3.7%)

A blond beer with citrus aromas.

Special (OG 1039, ABV 3.7%)
A pale golden ale, distinctly hoppy.

Hill Fort (OG 1040, ABV 3.9%)
An amber bitter.

Old Tun (OG 1042, ABV 4.1%)
A chestnut bitter with a crisp, straw-like finish.

Green Dragon (OG 1045, ABV 4.4%)
A traditional amber bitter with a crisp, straw-like finish.

Nomad Dusk (OG 1046, ABV 4.6%)
A dark ruby ale with toffee and spice notes.

Whitworth (NEW) SIBA

Whitworth Brewing Co, c/o 34 Dunard Road, Shirley, West Midlands, B90 2HR
☎ (0121) 347 6450 ⊕ whitworthbrewing.co.uk

Whitworth is a family-run company that began as a 15 year hobby but started brewing commercially in 2012 using a five-barrel plant. It was inspired by CAMRA's LocAle scheme and supplies several local pubs and clubs. Further beers are planned.

Sobriety (OG 1039, ABV 4%)
A golden, well-balanced, mildy hoppy ale.

Why Not

Why Not Brewery, 17 Cavalier Close, Thorpe St Andrew, Norwich, NR7 0TE
☎ (01603) 300786
✉ colin@thewhynotbrewery.co.uk
⊕ thewhynotbrewery.co.uk

Why Not opened in 2006 with equipment located in a custom-built wooden unit. The brewery can produce up to two barrels per brew. All beers are available in bottle-conditioned form and are occasionally put into casks to order.

Wally's Revenge (OG 1040, ABV 4%) ◆
An overtly bitter beer with a hoppy background. The bitterness holds on to the end as an increasing astringent dryness develops.

Hare of the Dog (OG 1045, ABV 4.5%)
A fruity amber ale with a strong, hoppy aftertaste.

Roundhead Porter (OG 1045, ABV 4.5%)
A traditional old-style London porter.

Cavalier Red (OG 1047, ABV 4.7%) ◆
Explosive fruity nose belies the gentleness of the taste. The summer fruit aroma dominates this red-gold brew. A sweet, fruity start disappears under a quick, bitter ending.

Norfolk Honey Ale (OG 1050, ABV 5%)
A golden beer with a honey nose. A definitive hop edge leaves a honey aftertaste.

Chocolate Nutter (OG 1056, ABV 5.5%)
A rich, dark beer with hints of liquorice and chocolate.

Wibblers SIBA

Wibblers Brewery Ltd, Joyces Farm, Southminster Road, Mayland, Essex, CM3 6EB
☎ (01621) 772044 ✉ info@wibblers.com
⊕ wibblers.com
Shop Mon-Fri 9am-4pm
Tours by arrangement

⊠ Wibblers was established in 2007 and expanded in 2009. Production is currently 45 barrels per week with its flagship beer, Apprentice, accounting for 50% of that. Seasonal beers: see website. Bottle-conditioned beers are also available.

Dengie Best (OG 1036, ABV 3.6%)

Apprentice (OG 1039, ABV 3.9%)

Hoppy Helper (OG 1041, ABV 4%)

Crafty Stoat (OG 1056, ABV 5.3%)

Wicked Hathern

Wicked Hathern Brewery Ltd, 17 Nixon Walk, East Leake, Leicestershire, LE12 6HL
☎ (01509) 559308 ✉ sean.oneill@escapade-rs.com
⊕ wicked-hathern.co.uk

☺Opened in 2000, the brewery generally supplies beer on a guest basis to many local pubs and beer festivals, and brews commissioned beers for special occasions. All beers are available bottled from selected off-licences (see website) and from Hathern Stores. Special cask beer is brewed for the Albion Inn, Loughborough, and special bottled beers for Hathern Stores. The brewery itself is not currently operating and the beers are being produced by the Wicked Hathern brewers at Leek Brewery (qv). Seasonal beers are also available.

Dobles' Dog (OG 1035, ABV 3.5%)
A full-bodied, stout-like dark mild with fruit and nut flavours on the palate. Gently bitter, malty finish with a lingering hint of roasted malts.

Hathern Cross (OG 1037, ABV 3.7%)
A golden ale with spicy hops in the aroma. The taste is well-balanced and bittersweet with a lemon note from the hops contrasting with malt sweetness.

St George's Gold (OG 1039, ABV 3.8%)
A light golden ale with a good balance of malt and hops and a hop and citrus aftertaste.

WHB/Wicked Hathern Bitter (OG 1038, ABV 3.8%)
A light-lasting session bitter with a dry palate and good hop aroma.

Cockfighter (OG 1043, ABV 4.2%)
A copper-coloured beer with an aroma of fruit, creamy malt and hop resins.

Hawthorn Gold (OG 1045, ABV 4.5%)
A pale golden ale with delicate malt and spicy hop in the aroma. The taste is hoppy and mostly bitter but with good malt support and body. Dry malt and hops aftertaste.

Derby Porter (OG 1048, ABV 4.8%)
A deep ruby porter with a creamy nose of lightly smoky, chocolatey, nutty dark malts.

Soar Head (OG 1048, ABV 4.8%)
A dark ruby-coloured strong bitter with a cocktail of distinctive flavours.

Swift 'Un (OG 1048, ABV 4.8%)
A light-golden mellow beer with fruity overtones.

For Albion, Canal Bank, Loughborough:

Albion Special (OG 1041, ABV 4%)
A light, copper-coloured bitter with a nutty aroma and smoky malt taste, hops leading through.

For Burleigh Court, Loughborough University Campus:

Burleigh Court Gold (OG 1045, ABV 4.5%)

Wickwar SIBA ◉

Wickwar Brewing Co, Old Brewery, Station Road, Wickwar, Gloucestershire, GL12 8NB
☎ (01454) 292000
✉ brew.crew@wickwarbrewing.com
⊕ wickwarbrewing.com
Shop Mon-Fri 9am-6pm; Sat 10am-4pm (Tel 01454 299592)
Tours by arrangement

Wickwar was established as a 10-barrel brewery in 1990 in the cooper's shop of the former Arnold Perrett Brewery. In 2004 it was expanded to 50 barrels and moved into the original 19th-century brewery. 400 local outlets are supplied on a regular basis and the beers are available nationally through most distributors and SIBA. Seasonal beers are also brewed.

Coopers WPA (OG 1036, ABV 3.5%) ◆
Golden-coloured, this well-balanced beer is light and refreshing, with hops, citrus fruit, apple/pear flavour and notable pale malt character. Bitter, dry finish.

Banker$ Draft (OG 1040, ABV 4%)
An amber-coloured beer with a fruity, citrus aroma. A biscuit malt flavour leads to a floral, crisp and clean finish.

BOB/Brand Oak Bitter (OG 1040, ABV 4%) ◆
Amber-coloured, this has a distinctive blend of hop, malt and apple/pear citrus fruits. The slightly sweet taste turns into a fine, dry bitterness, with a similar malty-lasting finish.

Cotswold Way (OG 1042, ABV 4.2%) ◆
Amber-coloured, it has a pleasant aroma of pale malt, hop and fruit. Good dry bitterness in the taste with some sweetness. Similar though less sweet in the finish, with good hop content.

Rite Flanker (OG 1043, ABV 4.3%)
A powerful fruity body is supported by a hoppy nose.

Station Porter (OG 1062, ABV 6.1%) 🍺 🍫 ◆
A rich, smooth, dark ruby brown ale. Starts with roast malt; coffee, chocolate and dark fruit then develops a complex, spicy, bittersweet taste and a long roast finish

Willey

See Wood Farm

Williams SIBA

Williams Bros Brewing Co (Heather Ale Ltd), New Alloa Brewery, Kelliebank, Alloa, FK10 1NT
☎ (01259) 725511 ☎ 07739 323962
✉ info@williamsbrosbrew.com
⊕ williamsbrosbrew.com
Tours by arrangement

☺Bruce and Scott Williams started brewing Heather Ale in the West Highlands in 1993. A range of indigenous, historic ales were added over the following 10 years before the brothers invested in a 40-barrel brewery and bottling line in 2003. New beers are branded as Williams Bros of which there are many hoppy and esoteric styles to choose from. Hundreds of cask ale outlets are supplied worldwide. Seasonal beers: see website.

Gold (OG 1040, ABV 3.9%)

Golden session beer with a crisp mouthfeel and lemony hop aromas suggesting grapefruit and orange.

Harvest Sun (OG 1038, ABV 3.9%)
Straw-coloured ale with a pleasant citrus aroma giving way to a balanced and satisfyingly bitter finish.

Fraoch Heather Ale (OG 1041, ABV 4.1%) ◄
The unique taste of heather flowers is noticeable in this beer. A fine floral aroma and spicy taste give character to this drinkable speciality beer.

80/- (OG 1039, ABV 4.2%)
A rich mahogany ale with malt and butter aroma, biscuit texture, orange peel infusion and a clean, satisfyingly sweet finish.

Black (OG 1039, ABV 4.2%)
A light-bodied, rich dark ale in the style of Czech dark lagers. Aromatic and full-flavoured with coffee and chocolate undertones and a lovely blackcurrant aroma.

Roisin-Tayberry (OG 1040, ABV 4.2%)
A sweetish, fruity, light pink beer from the tayberries used, giving a distinct soft, fruity aroma and flavour.

Birds & Bees (OG 1040, ABV 4.3%)
A bright, golden ale with a late infusion of fresh elderflowers and lemon zest. Fruity, aromatic and refreshing.

Cock O' The Walk (OG 1046, ABV 4.3%)
A classic red ale with an eclectic blend of hops.

Kelpie (OG 1036, ABV 4.4%)
A rich, dark chocolate ale with a distinctive malty texture. Fresh seaweed is included in the mash tun.

Good Times (OG 1045, ABV 4.5%)
Refreshing, fruity, malty and aromatic.

Red (OG 1045, ABV 4.5%)
A rich amber-coloured beer with a bouquet of caramel, amber malts and sweet berries giving way to a palate of biscuit malts, woody and fruity hops that deliver a medium dry finish.

Ceilidh (OG 1048, ABV 4.7%)
A crisp, citrussy lager.

Grozet (OG 1050, ABV 5%)
A lagered gooseberry beer. Crisp, fresh and clean-tasting.

Joker IPA (OG 1050, ABV 5%)
A well-balanced IPA. Golden-coloured and fruity on the nose with hints of cedar.

Seven Giraffes (OG 1047, ABV 5.1%)
Classic IPA with late infusion of elderflower and lemon. A deep gold colour with an elderflower and citrus aroma followed by sweet caramel. Biscuity malts on the tongue balanced with hoppy bitterness, lemon freshness and floral elderflower aftertaste.

Midnight Sun (OG 1056, ABV 5.6%)
A rich, black, smooth porter with an afterbite of fresh root ginger.

Ebulum (OG 1060, ABV 6.5%)
A dark, rich, fruity beer with a bitter conclusion. Brewed from a 16th-century Scottish recipe.

Alba Scots Pine Ale (OG 1097, ABV 7.5%)
A rich, tawny beer with a complex wood flavour and a lingering finish. From a traditional Highland recipe popular until the end of the 19th-century.

Willy Good

Willy Good Ale, The Old Forge, Hartley's Farm, Winsley, Wiltshire, BA15 2JB
☎ 07711 364202 ⊕ willygoodale.com

Willy Good Ale was established in 2010 on a farm with its own shop. It quickly reached maximum production levels and upgraded to a six-barrel plant in 2011. Bottle-conditioned beers are available.

Willy Hop! (ABV 4%)
A full-flavoured pale ale.

High Five (ABV 5%)
A strong IPA.

Wheat a Minute (ABV 5.7%)
Wheat beer with a hint of orange and coriander.

Willy's

⬛ **Willy's Wine Bar Ltd, 17 High Cliff Road, Cleethorpes, Lincolnshire, DN35 8RQ**
☎ (01472) 602145
Tours by arrangement

The brewery opened in 1989 to provide beer for its then two pubs in Grimsby and Cleethorpes. It has a five-barrel plant with maximum capacity of 15 barrels a week. The brewery can be viewed at any time from pub or street. The second outlet, Swigs, was sold in 2011 leading to reduced capacity brewing.

Original (OG 1039, ABV 3.9%) ◄
A light brown 'sea air' beer with a fruity, tangy hop on the nose and taste, giving a strong bitterness tempered by the underlying malt.

Wilson Potter (NEW)

Wilson Potter Brewery, Unit E2, Hanson Close, Middleton, M24 2QZ
☎ (0161) 654 6446 ☎ 07761 055567
✉ enquiries@wilsonpotterbrewery.co.uk
⊕ wilsonpotterbrewery.co.uk

Wilson Potter began brewing in 2011 using a six-barrel plant and was established by two former home brewers, Kathryn Harrison and Amanda Seddon. The brewery is named after their respective grandmothers. Bottle-conditioned beers are also available.

Cascale (OG 1039, ABV 3.7%)
A pale golden beer with a citrus aroma and a full-balanced bitterness with a clean, tangy finish.

Tandle Hill (OG 1040, ABV 3.9%)
A blonde beer with strong citrus flavours and aroma.

Triple Gem (OG 1040, ABV 3.9%)
A pale ale with oaken flavours and distinct notes of blackberry.

In the Black (OG 1048, ABV 4.2%)
Fruity with roast malt and liquorice notes with a sweet liquorice and roast finish.

Wincle SIBA

Wincle Beer Co Ltd, Tolls Farm, Danebridge, Wincle, Cheshire, SK11 0QE
☎ (01260) 227777 ✉ sales@winclebeer.co.uk
⊕ winclebeer.co.uk
Shop 10am-4.30pm daily
Tours by arrangement

⊕Wincle began brewing in 2008 on a five-barrel plant in an old milking parlour in Rushton Spencer. The brewery relocated in 2011 to the Dane Valley using a 12-barrel plant. 150 outlets are supplied direct. Occasional and bottle-conditioned beers are also available.

Waller (OG 1038, ABV 3.8%)

Rambler (OG 1039, ABV 4%)

Sir Phillip (OG 1041, ABV 4.2%)

Wibbly Wallaby (OG 1044, ABV 4.4%)

Undertaker (OG 1045, ABV 4.5%)

Windsor Castle

See Sadler's

Windsor & Eton SIBA

Windsor & Eton Brewery, Unit 1, Vansittart Estate, Duke Street, Windsor, Berkshire, SL4 1SE
☎ (01753) 854075 ✉ sampleroom@webrew.co.uk
⊕ webrew.co.uk
Shop Mon-Fri 8am-5pm; Sat 10am-2pm
(sometimes later, check website)
Tours by arrangement

⊗ Windsor & Eton Brewery was established in 2010 on an 18-barrel plant, bringing brewing back to Windsor 79 years after the closure of both Noakes and Burge & Co. Around 250 outlets are supplied direct. Special beers are also available throughout the year: see website.

Knight of the Garter (OG 1036.5, ABV 3.8%)
A straw-coloured golden ale with a distinctive fresh citrus hop aroma.

Windsor Knot (OG 1039, ABV 4%)
An amber ale with a grapefruit aroma. Initially has a sweet malt and fruit taste followed by a mild, bittering finish.

Guardsman (OG 1041, ABV 4.2%)
A tangy best bitter, tawny-coloured with a fresh, hoppy finish mellowed with the use of oak during conditioning.

Kohinoor (OG 1043, ABV 4.5%)
A well-balanced golden ale. A classic IPA; hoppy but with a smooth finish.

Conqueror (OG 1049, ABV 5%) 🗂
A complex black IPA with a full, roasted taste and intense hop aroma and flavour.

Windy (NEW)

⧉ Windy Brewery, Volunteer Inn, New Road, Seavington St Michael, Somerset, TA19 0QE
☎ (01460) 240126 ✉ info@thevolly.co.uk
⊕ thevolly.co.uk

The Windy Brewery was established in 2011. The name stems from the time when alterations were carried out to the back of the pub and the workmen suffered extremes of varying weather conditions.

Tornado (OG 1040, ABV 3.9%)

Flurry (OG 1042, ABV 4.1%)

Winster Valley

⧉ Winster Valley Brewery, Brown Horse Inn, Winster, Cumbria, LA23 3NR
☎ (01539) 443443
✉ craig@winstervalleybrewery.co.uk
⊕ winstervalleybrewery.co.uk
Tours by arrangement

⊕Winster Valley was established in 2009 using a 2.5-barrel plant at the Brown Horse Inn in Winster.

Best Bitter (OG 1036, ABV 3.7%)
A full-bodied beer with a roasted malt flavour with a hint of caramel.

Old School (OG 1037, ABV 3.9%)
A pale ale, full-tasting with floral aromas.

Winter's

Winter's Brewery, 8 Keelan Close, Norwich, NR6 6QZ
☎ (01603) 787820 ✉ sales@wintersbrewery.com
⊕ wintersbrewery.com

⊗ Winter's was established in 2001 by David Winter, who had previous award-winning success as brewer for both Woodforde's and Chalk Hill breweries. He purchased the brewing plant from the now defunct Scott's Brewery in Lowestoft. Winter's ales have won many awards with David now passing his brewing knowledge to his son, Mark, an award-winning brewer in his own right. Seasonal beer is also available.

Mild (OG 1036.5, ABV 3.6%) 🌿
Classic dark mild, red-brown with a nutty roast character. A good balance of malt, caramel and roast abetted by both sweetness and a light, hoppy bitterness. Lingering finish develops a plummy feel.

Cloud Burst (OG 1037.5, ABV 3.7%) 🌿
Tawny-coloured with a malty nose. Initial balance of malt and hops tinged with bitterness drops off to a long, dry, bitter ending.

Bitter (OG 1038.5, ABV 3.8%) 🌿
A well-balanced amber bitter. Hops and malt are balanced by a crisp citrus fruitiness. A pleasant hoppy nose with a hint of grapefruit. Long, sustained, dry, grapefruit finish.

Geniuss (OG 1041.5, ABV 4.1%)
A full-bodied stout with a roasted flavour and hints of liquorice.

Golden (OG 1041, ABV 4.1%) 🌿
Just a hint of hops in the aroma. The initial taste combines a dry bitterness with a fruity apple buttress. The finish slowly subsides into a long, dry bitterness.

Revenge (OG 1047, ABV 4.7%) 🌿
Blackcurrant notes give depth to the inherent maltiness of this pale brown beer. A bittersweet background becomes more pronounced as the fruitiness gently wanes.

Storm Force (OG 1053, ABV 5.3%) 🌿
A well-defined, sweetish brew. Hops and vine fruit give depth to the malty backbone of this pale brown strong beer. All flavours hold up well as the finish develops a warming softness.

Wirksworth SIBA

Wirksworth Brewery, 25 St John Street, Wirksworth, Derbyshire, DE4 4DR

THE BREWERIES

☎ (01629) 824011
✉ wirksworthbrewery@hotmail.co.uk
⊕ wirksworthbrewery.co.uk
Off sales: Fri & Sat 9am-5pm

⊗ Jeff Green started brewing in 2007 with a 2.5-barrel plant in a converted stone workshop. Wirksworth supplies Derbyshire pubs with its core beers and supplements these with at least one seasonal offering. Every September there is a brew house open weekend giving visitors the opportunity to gain an insight into the brewing process and taste the real ales.

Cruckbeam (OG 1038, ABV 3.9%)

Sunbeam (OG 1039, ABV 4%)

First Brew (OG 1041, ABV 4.2%)

T'owd Man (OG 1048, ABV 4.9%)

Snowfield (OG 1049, ABV 5%)

Wissey Valley

Wissey Valley Brewery, 1 High Street, Downham Market, Norfolk, PE38 9DA
☎ (01366) 386658
✉ thehopandhog@btconnect.com
⊕ norfolkfoodanddrink.co.uk
Shop Wed-Sun 9am-5pm
Tours by arrangement

⊗ After several moves since starting up in 2002 (as Captain Grumpy's), the brewery is now located at the rear of the local produce store, team room and restaurant, the Hop & Hog.

Captain Grumpy's Best Bitter (OG 1039, ABV 3.9%)

Khaki Sergeant Strong Stout (OG 1059, ABV 6%)

Wizard SIBA

Wizard Ales, Unit 4, Lundy View, Mullacott Cross Industrial Estate, Ilfracombe, Devon, EX34 8PY
☎ (01271) 865350 ✉ mike@wizardales.co.uk
⊕ wizardales.co.uk
Tours by arrangement

⊗ Brewing started in 2003 on a 1.25-barrel plant, since upgraded to five barrels. The brewery moved from Warwickshire to Devon in 2007. Around 20 local outlets are supplied. Bottle-conditioned beers are also available.

Apprentice (OG 1038, ABV 3.6%)

Lundy Gold (OG 1042, ABV 4.1%)

Old Combe (OG 1043, ABV 4.2%)

Druid's Fluid (OG 1048, ABV 5%)

Wold Top SIBA ◉

Wold Top Brewery, Hunmanby Grange, Wold Newton, Driffield, East Yorkshire, YO25 3HS
☎ (01723) 892222
✉ enquiries@woldtopbrewery.co.uk
⊕ woldtopbrewery.co.uk

☺ Wold Top commenced brewing in 2003 in a converted barn and is an integral part of Hunmanby Grange, a family farm. It uses Wold-grown malting barley and chalk-filtered water from the farm's own borehole. The brewery installed a bottling line in 2008 and contract bottles for other breweries. Seasonal beers: see website.

Bitter (OG 1036, ABV 3.7%)
A crisp, clean, aromatic session bitter. Full-flavoured with a long, hoppy finish.

Anglers Reward (OG 1039, ABV 4%)
A refreshing golden pale ale with a fruity bitterness and lingering aftertaste.

Headland Red (OG 1042, ABV 4.3%)
A red beer with a mellow, malty flavour.

Wold Gold (OG 1046, ABV 4.8%)
A light-coloured summer beer with a soft, fruity flavour and a hint of spice.

Wolf SIBA ◉

WBC (Norfolk) Ltd t/a The Wolf Brewery, Rookery Farm, Silver Street, Besthorpe, Attleborough, Norfolk, NR17 2LD
☎ (01953) 457775 ✉ info@wolfbrewery.com
⊕ wolfbrewery.com
Shop Mon-Fri 9am-5pm
Tours by arrangement

⊗ The brewery was founded in 1996 on a 20-barrel plant, which was upgraded to a 30-barrel one in 2006. Over 300 outlets are supplied. Seasonal beers: see website.

Golden Jackal (OG 1039, ABV 3.7%) ◀
A hoppy, citrus nose carries through to the initial taste. The citrus notes remain right to the end as the initial hoppiness is replaced by a dry bitterness.

Lavender Honey (OG 1037, ABV 3.7%)
Lavender honey is added during the brewing process to give this beer a delicate flavour.

Wolf in Sheep's Clothing (OG 1039, ABV 3.7%) ◀
A malty aroma with fruity undertones introduce this reddish-hued mild. Malt, with a bitter background that remains throughout, is the dominant flavour of this clean-tasting beer.

RAF Collection Battle of Britain (ABV 3.9%)
Copper-coloured, full-bodied ale brewed to commemorate 'The Few'. A donation is made to the RAF Association Wings Appeal for every pint sold.

Lupus Lupus (ABV 4.2%)
Unique flavoured blonde ale using fruity hops.

Poppy Ale (ABV 4.2%)
Pale golden ale infused with honey and fruity hops to give a delicate flavour. Brewed to support the Royal British Legion's work. A 10p donation is made to the RBL for every pint sold.

Coyote Bitter (OG 1044, ABV 4.3%) ◀
A well-balanced golden brew with a hop and citrus aroma. The dominant hoppy bitterness is countered by a malty, slightly sweet backdrop. Complex flavours continue to mix as the dry, bitter ending slowly fades.

Straw Dog (OG 1045, ABV 4.5%) ◀
A delicately-flavoured brew with a fruity nuance. An aroma reminiscent of redcurrants gives way to a low key marmalade and hop beginning. A stronger finish with increasing bitterness.

Granny Wouldn't Like It (OG 1049, ABV 4.8%) ◀
Red-brown with a pronounced malty bouquet. Bitterness increases throughout but is softened by a smoky malt background. Some roast notes and a gentle, fruity sweetness add depth.

Woild Moild (OG 1048, ABV 4.8%)

A rich and fruity traditional Norfolk mild. Good balance of malt with liquorice bitterness and lots of chocolate malt. Dark ruby-red with a long, lasting finish.

For City of Cambridge Brewery:

Hobson's Choice (ABV 4.1%) ◆
This golden ale has a predominantly spicy hop aroma. Bittersweet on the palate with plenty of hops leading through to a dry, hoppy finish.

Atom Splitter (ABV 4.5%) ◆
Robust copper-coloured strong bitter with a hop aroma and taste, and a distinct sulphury edge.

Parkers (ABV 5%) ◆
Impressive reddish brew with a defined roast character throughout, and a short, fruity, bittersweet palate

Wolverhampton & Dudley

See Marston's in the New Nationals section

Tom Wood

Tom Wood's Beer Ltd, Melton High Wood Farm, Melton High Wood, Melton Ross, Lincolnshire, DN38 6AA
☎ (01652) 680001 ✉ info@tom-wood.com
⊕ tom-wood.com

Tom Wood's Beers was established as a company in 2011 to take over the former Highwood brew plant and to continue to brew the Tom Wood range of beers. The new venture has no other connection with the former business and is not involved in wholesaling. The brewery intially started in a converted Victorian granary on a family farm in 1995 and the brew-length was increased from 10 barrels to 30 in 2001 using a plant from the Ash Vine brewery and further increased to a 60-barrel plant in 2008.

Best Bitter (OG 1035.5, ABV 3.5%) ◆
A good citrus, passion fruit hop dominates the nose and taste, with background malt. A lingering hoppy and bitter finish.

Lincoln Gold (OG 1041, ABV 4%)
A pale bitter with a fruity aroma and slightly zesty flavour but retaining malt characteristics.

Bomber County (OG 1046, ABV 4.8%) ◆
An earthy malt aroma but with a complex underlying mix of coffee, hops, caramel and apple fruit. The beer starts bitter and intensifies to the end.

Wood SIBA ⟨⊙⟩

Wood Brewery Ltd, Wistanstow, Craven Arms, Shropshire, SY7 8DG
☎ (01588) 672523 ✉ mail@woodbrewery.co.uk
⊕ woodbrewery.co.uk
Shop 9am-4pm Mon-Fri
Tours by arrangement

The brewery opened in 1980 in buildings next to the Plough Inn, still the brewery's only tied house. Steady growth over the years included the acquisition of the Sam Powell Brewery and its beers in 1991. Around 200 outlets are supplied. Seasonal beers: see website. A monthly beer is also brewed.

Quaff (ABV 3.7%)

A pale and refreshing light bitter with a clean, hoppy finish.

Craven Ale (ABV 3.8%)
An attractively coloured beer with a pleasant hop aroma and a refreshing taste.

Parish Bitter (OG 1040, ABV 4%) ◆
A blend of malt and hops with a bitter aftertaste. Pale brown in colour.

Shropshire Lass (OG 1041, ABV 4.1%)
A golden ale with zesty bitterness.

Special Bitter (OG 1042, ABV 4.2%) ◆
A tawny brown bitter with malt, hops and some fruitiness.

Pot O' Gold (OG 1044, ABV 4.4%)

Shropshire Lad (OG 1045, ABV 4.5%)
A strong, well-rounded bitter, drawing flavour from a fine blend of selected English malted barley and Fuggles and Golding hops.

Old Sam (OG 1047, ABV 4.6%)
A dark copper ale with a ripe, rounded flavour and hop bitterness.

Wonderful (OG 1048, ABV 4.8%) ◆
A mid-brown, fruity beer, with a roast and malt taste.

Wooden Hand SIBA ⟨⊙⟩

Wooden Hand Brewery, Unit 3, Grampound Road Industrial Estate, Grampound Road, Truro, Cornwall, TR2 4TB
☎ (01726) 884596 ✉ chris@woodenhand.co.uk
⊕ woodenhand.co.uk

Wooden Hand was founded in 2004. The brewery is named after the Black Hand of John Carew of Penwarne, in the parish of Mevagissey – Carew lost his hand fighting at the siege of Ostend in the reign of Elizabeth I. The brewery supplies around 50 outlets with a high percentage being sold further afield via wholesalers. A bottling line was installed in 2005, which also bottles for other breweries.

Cornish Gribben (ABV 4.1%)
A distinctive, well-hopped beer with citrus and fruit notes. Well-balanced, bittersweet finish.

Wood Farm

Wood Farm Brewery, Coalpit Lane, Willey, Warwickshire, CV23 0SL
☎ (01788) 833469 ⊕ woodfarmbrewery.co.uk
Tours by arrangement

⊙Wood Farm opened in 2011 and previously traded as both Rugby Brewery (until 2010) and Willey Brewing Company. Its visitor centre is on two floors with the brewery viewable from the downstairs bar.

1823 Mild (ABV 3.5%)

Twickers (ABV 3.7%)

Webb Ellis (ABV 3.8%)

Best Bitter (ABV 4.2%)

Victorious (ABV 4.2%)

Union (ABV 4.6%)

No. 8 (ABV 5%)

THE BREWERIES

Woodforde's SIBA 👁

Woodforde's Norfolk Ales, Broadland Brewery, Woodbastwick, Norwich, NR13 6SW
☎ (01603) 720353 ✉ info@woodfordes.co.uk
⊕ woodfordes.co.uk
Shop Mon-Fri 10.30am-4.30pm; Sat & Sun 11.30am-4.30pm (01603 722218)
Tours by arrangement (Tue & Thu evenings)

Founded in 1981 in Drayton, Woodforde's moved to Erpingham in 1982, and then moved again to a converted farm complex in Woodbastwick, with greatly increased production capacity, in 1989. Major expansion took place in 2001 and 2008 to more than double production and included a new brewery shop and visitor centre. Woodforde's runs two tied houses with around 600 outlets supplied on a regular basis. Seasonal, occasional and bottle-conditioned beers are also available. The Woodforde's Club now has over 15,000 members and is free to join: see website for details.

Mardler's (OG 1036, ABV 3.5%) 🍺
Chocolate and roast aromas introduce this well-balanced dark mild. Swathes of vanilla, caramel and malt boost the dominant roast and chocolate flavours. A fine, flavoursome finish.

Wherry (OG 1037.5, ABV 3.8%) 🍺
Amber-coloured with an orange citrus nose. Complex, well-balanced but easy-drinking, the swirling mix of malt, hops, citrus and bitterness combine into a tangy marmalade dryness.

Once Bittern (OG 1040, ABV 4%) 🍺
A light malty nose with a hint of sulphur. A dark marmalade tang gives an edge to the dominant malt character. Complex, grainy, but easily drinkable with a bittersweet ending.

Sundew (OG 1039, ABV 4.1%) 🍺
Hops emerge from a competing fusion of malt, fruit and bitterness to provide a cutting edge to both taste and aroma. Smooth-drinking with a long ending.

Nelson's Revenge (OG 1045, ABV 4.5%) 🍺
An infusion of vine fruit, malt and hops provide a rich, rewarding experience. The aromas and flavours bounce merrily along to a sweet, Madeira-like finale.

Norfolk Nog (OG 1047, ABV 4.6%) 🍺
Echoes of Pontefract cake in all aspects of this red-hued, roast-dominated brew. A plummy sweetness aided by a dry bitterness and a hint of caramel all provide rallying points to counter the main roast character.

Admiral's Reserve (OG 1049, ABV 5%) 🍺
Tawny-coloured strong ale with a gentle malty aroma. A smooth sultana and malt introduction with more than a hint of hop-induced bitterness. Balanced finish with fruit making a noticeably quick retreat.

Headcracker (OG 1069, ABV 7%) 🍺
Malty, sweet-tasting tawny ale with a satisfyingly sticky mouthfeel. Initially the malt matches the heavy fruity aura. Initial traces of hop and caramel soon disappear as the malty influence recedes.

Woodlands SIBA

Woodlands Brewing Co Ltd, Unit 3, Meadow Lane Farm, London Road, Stapeley, Cheshire, CW5 7JU
☎ (01270) 841511

Office: Wayside, Dairy Lane, Nantwich, Cheshire, CW5 6DS ☎ (01270) 620101
✉ enquiries@woodlandsbrewery.co.uk
⊕ woodlandsbrewery.co.uk
Shop Mon-Fri 9am-4.30pm
Tours by arrangement

☺The brewery opened in 2004 with a five-barrel plant from the former Khean Brewery and moved to larger premises in 2008. An extension in 2010 allows for increased production. The beers are brewed using water from a spring that surfaces on a nearby peat field at Woodlands Farm. More than 100 outlets are supplied including the brewery's three tied houses. Bottle-conditioned beers are also available.

Mild (OG 1035, ABV 3.5%)
A dark mild ale.

Old Faithful (OG 1036, ABV 3.6%)
A pale session bitter.

Hop as Hell (OG 1040, ABV 4%)
A pale beer with a long-lasting, bitter finish.

Light Oak (OG 1040, ABV 4%)
A malty pale ale with a crisp, dry aftertaste.

Old Willow (OG 1041, ABV 4.1%)
Fruity and hoppy.

Oak Beauty (OG 1042, ABV 4.2%) 🍺
Malty, sweetish copper-coloured bitter with toffee and caramel flavours. Long-lasting and satisfying bitter finish.

Bitter (OG 1044, ABV 4.4%)

Midnight Stout (OG 1044, ABV 4.4%) 🍺
Classic creamy dry stout with roast flavours to the fore. Well-balanced with bitterness and good hops on the taste and a good dry, roasty aftertaste. Some sweetness.

Redwood (OG 1049, ABV 4.9%)
A dark bitter with a sharp aftertaste.

Wood Street

▤ Wood Street Brewery, Hillsborough, 54-58 Langsett Road, Sheffield, South Yorkshire, S6 2UB
☎ (0114) 234 8307
✉ info@woodstreetbrewery.co.uk
⊕ woodstreetbrewery.co.uk
Tours by arrangement

Formerly the Crown Brewery, Wood Street opened in March 2012 under new ownership at the renamed 'Hillsborough' in Sheffield. Monthly specials are also brewed.

Pale Ale (OG 1038, ABV 3.9%)
A session beer with citrus notes and a fresh, hoppy taste with a crisp, refreshing aftertaste.

Bitter (OG 1039, ABV 4%)
A traditional amber-coloured bitter. Very smooth on the palate.

Golden Larch (OG 1043, ABV 4.5%)
A full-bodied, well-rounded golden ale with a crisp fruitiness.

Ebony Stout (OG 1050, ABV 5%)
A dark stout with a ruby edge with coffee and chocolate undertones and a big, deep aroma.

Yellow Wood IPA (OG 1049, ABV 5.1%)
A well-balanced, strong pale bitter. Smooth-tasting with a distinct hoppy flavour and a long, refreshing finish.

Worfield

See Shires

World's End

World's End Ales, Crown Inn, 60 Wilcot Road, Pewsey, Wiltshire, SN9 5EL
☎ (01672) 562653 ✉ vauni57@hotmail.com
⊕ thecrownatpewsey.com
Tours by arrangement

⊗ World's End Ales was established in 2009 on a one-barrel plant at the rear of the Crown Inn in Pewsey. World's End is the 18th-century name for the area in which the brewery is located.

Bitter End (ABV 4.2%)

Dark World (ABV 4.2%)

Gold Ale (ABV 4.4%)

Worsthorne SIBA

Worsthorne Brewing Co Ltd, Unit 4, Oxford Mill, Burnley Road, Briercliffe, Burnley, Lancashire, BB10 2HQ
☎ 07815 708289
✉ info@worsthornebrewingcompany.co.uk
⊕ worsthornebrewingcompany.co.uk

Worsthorne began brewing in 2011 using a 5.5-barrel plant. 20 outlets are supplied direct. Seasonal beers are available.

Chestnut Mare (OG 1038, ABV 3.5%)
Chestnut-coloured mild with liquorice undertones and a dry blackcurrant finish.

Worsthorne Gold (OG 1036, ABV 3.6%)
Lightly bittered golden ale with a spicy aroma.

Packhorse (OG 1039, ABV 3.7%)
Pale amber ale with subtle earthy bitterness and floral spicy finish.

Some Like It Blond (OG 1041, ABV 3.9%)
A blond beer with a lingering, dry aftertaste.

Old Trout (OG 1047, ABV 4.5%)
A well-flavoured reddish brown ale.

Worth SIBA

Worth Brewing Co, Royal British Legion Club, St Georges Road West, Poynton, Cheshire, SK12 1JY
☎ (01625) 873120 ✉ paul.worthbr@gmail.com
⊕ poyntonlegionclub.co.uk
Tours by arrangement

Brewing began in 2011 on a five-barrel plant. The beer names and pump clips celebrate Poynton's history and mining heritage.

Coppice (ABV 3.5%)
A dark mild session beer.

Blythe's Spirit (ABV 3.8%)
A traditional, slightly sweet bitter.

Anson (ABV 4%)
An intense blond beer, floral and hoppy in character with a bitter finish.

Redacre (ABV 4%)
A full-bodied deep ruby red beer with a rich, creamy head and fruity overtones.

Seam Cutter (ABV 4.2%)
A full-flavoured black beer.

'Bout Time (ABV 4.5%)
An old-fashioned bitter with strong malty flavours.

George Wright SIBA

George Wright Brewing Co, Unit 11, Diamond Business Park, Sandwash Close, Rainford, Merseyside, WA11 8LY
☎ (01744) 886686 ✉ sales@georgewrights.com
⊕ georgewrightbrewing.co.uk
Shop Tue-Fri 10am-5pm
Tours by arrangement

George Wright started production in 2003. The original 2.5-barrel plant was replaced by a five-barrel one, which has since been upgraded again to 25 barrels with production of 200 casks a week.

Black Swan (ABV 3.8%)
A dark, distinctive beer. Creamy and full of malty flavour.

Drunken Duck (ABV 3.9%) ◀
Fruity gold-coloured bitter beer with good hop and a dry aftertaste. Some acidity.

Longboat (ABV 3.9%) ◀
Good hoppy bitter with grapefruit and an almost tart bitterness throughout. Some astringency in the aftertaste. Well-balanced, light and refreshing with a good mouthfeel and long, dry finish.

Pipe Dream (ABV 4.3%) ⬚ ◀
Refreshing hoppy best bitter with a fruity nose and grapefruit to the fore in the taste. Lasting dry, bitter finish.

Pure Blonde (ABV 4.6%)
A premium blond beer, light in colour with a herbal nose, floral taste and sweet finish.

Cheeky Pheasant (ABV 4.7%)
Strong, malty bitter. Highly hopped to give a distinctive dry aftertaste.

Roman Black (ABV 4.8%)
A black bitter. Strong, smooth and creamy.

Blue Moon (ABV 5%) ◀
Easy-drinking strong, gold-coloured beer. Good malt/bitter balance and well hopped.

Wychwood

See Marston's in New Nationals section

Wye Valley SIBA ◉

Wye Valley Brewery Ltd, Stoke Lacy, Herefordshire, HR7 4HG
☎ (01885) 490505
✉ sales@wyevalleybrewery.co.uk
⊕ wyevalleybrewery.co.uk
Shop Mon-Fri 9.30am-4.30pm
Tours by arrangement (for CAMRA groups and customers only)

⊗ Founded in 1985 in Canon Pyon in Herefordshire, the brewery now occupies the historic Symonds Cider site at Stoke Lacy. Growth and investment continue and Wye Valley is now a successful regional brewery. Bottle-conditioned beers are available and are bottled on site.

Bitter (OG 1037, ABV 3.7%) ◀
A beer whose aroma gives little hint of the bitter hoppiness that follows right through to the aftertaste.

HPA (OG 1040, ABV 4%) ◈
A pale, hoppy, malty brew with a hint of sweetness before a dry finish.

Dorothy Goodbody's Golden Ale (OG 1042, ABV 4.2%)
A light, gold-coloured ale with a good hop character throughout.

Butty Bach (OG 1046, ABV 4.5%)
A burnished gold, full-bodied premium ale.

Dorothy Goodbody's Wholesome Stout (OG 1046, ABV 4.6%) ◈
A smooth and satisfying stout with a bitter edge to its roast flavours. The finish combines roast grain and malt.

Wylam SIBA

Wylam Brewery Ltd, South Houghton Farm, Heddon on the Wall, Northumberland, NE15 0EZ
☎ (01661) 853377 ✉ admin@wylambrewery.co.uk
⊕ wylambrewery.co.uk
Shop Mon-Fri 9am-5pm; Sat 11am-3pm
Tours by arrangement

☺Wylam started in 2000 on a 4.5-barrel plant, which increased to nine barrels in 2002. New premises and brew plant (20 barrel) were installed on the same site in 2006 and expansion is continuing. The brewery delivers to more than 200 local outlets and beers are available through wholesalers around the country. Seasonal beers: see website. A visitor reception area was added in 2010 along with a small shop.

Bitter (OG 1039, ABV 3.8%) ◈
A refreshing, copper-coloured, hoppy bitter with a clean, bitter finish.

Gold Tankard (OG 1040, ABV 4%) ◈
Fresh clean flavour, full of hops. This golden ale has a hint of citrus in the finish.

Collingwood Festival Ale (OG 1041, ABV 4.1%)
Honey-soaked in colour with a sweet tangerine aroma. Light and soft-bodied with a citrus zest/fresh pinewood flavour and a dry and bitter finish.

Angel (OG 1044, ABV 4.3%)
A bitter, pale copper ale; well-balanced with a citrus character in the aroma and finish.

Northern Kite (OG 1046.5, ABV 4.5%)
A ruby ale with a subtle hop character and rich palate.

Locomotion No. 1 (OG 1050, ABV 5%)
A continental-style beer, traditionally lagered for three weeks to give a distinctive lager style with the flavour of a classic hop.

Wyre Piddle SIBA

Wyre Piddle Brewery Ltd, Highgrove Farm, Pinvin, nr Pershore, Worcestershire, WR10 2LF
☎ (01905) 841853 ✉ strongbow1@btinternet.com

☺Wyre Piddle was established in the early 1990s and following a relocation and equipment upgrade in 1997 it settled in its current location in 2002. It also brews for the Green Dragon, Malvern: Dragon's Downfall (ABV 3.9%) and for the Severn Valley Railway: Royal Piddle (ABV 4.2%). Seasonal beers are available.

Piddle in the Hole (OG 1039, ABV 3.9%) ◈

Copper-coloured and quite dry, with lots of hops and fruitiness throughout.

Piddle in the Dark (OG 1045, ABV 4.5%)
A rich ruby-red bitter with a smooth flavour.

Piddle in the Wind (OG 1045, ABV 4.5%)
A pale beer with a hoppy nose through to a lasting aftertaste.

XT (NEW) SIBA

XT Brewing Company, Notley Farm, Chearsley Road, Long Crendon, Buckinghamshire, HP18 9ER
☎ (01844) 208310 ✉ xt@xtbrewing.com
⊕ xtbrewing.com
Shop Sat 9.30am-12pm; Mon-Fri please ring first
Tours by arrangement

XT began brewing in 2011 using a 15-barrel plant. Pubs are supplied direct in Buckinghamshire, Oxfordshire and the Midlands. Seasonal beers are available.

Four (ABV 3.8%)
An amber beer with a special Belgian malt and a fruity mix of American and European hops.

Two (ABV 4.2%)
A refreshing golden ale.

Eight (ABV 4.5%)
A smooth, rich, dark beer.

Yard of Ale SIBA

🍺 Yard of Ale Brewing Co Ltd, Surtees Arms, Chilton Lane, Ferryhill, County Durham, DL17 0DH
☎ (01740) 655724 ☎ 07540 733513
✉ surteesarms@btconnect.com
⊕ thesurteesarms.co.uk
Tours by arrangement

Established in 2008, the 2.5-barrel micro supplies ales to its brewery tap, the Surtees Arms, beer festivals and to a growing number of pubs from North Tyne to South Tees. Seasonal specials are available as are bottle-conditioned beers.

One Foot In The Yard (OG 1044, ABV 4.5%)
A premium golden ale. Fruity on the nose and palate with a sweet finish.

Yates SIBA

Yates (Westnewton) Brewery Ltd, Ghyll Farm, Westnewton, Cumbria, CA7 3NX
☎ (01697) 321081 ✉ enquiry@yatesbrewery.co.uk
⊕ yatesbrewery.co.uk
Tours by arrangement

☺Cumbria's oldest micro-brewery, established in 1986. The brewery was bought in 1998 by Graeme and Caroline Baxter, who had previously owned High Force Brewery in Teesdale. A 20-barrel brewhouse and reed bed effluent system have been added on the same site. Deliveries are mainly to its Cumbrian stronghold and the A69 corridor as far as Hexham. Around 40 outlets are supplied. Seasonal beers: see website.

Bitter (OG 1036, ABV 3.7%) ◈
A well-balanced, full-bodied bitter, golden in colour with complex hop bitterness. Good aroma and distinctive flavour.

Golden Ale (OG 1038, ABV 3.9%) ◈

Skilful use of lager malt and hops results in a pale beer with a light bitterness; melon fruit and a clean, refreshing finish.

Sun Goddess (OG 1041, ABV 4.2%) ◄
A complex, full-bodied beer, packed with tropical fruit.

Yates' SIBA

Yates' Brewery, Unit 4C, Langbridge Business Centre, Newchurch, Isle of Wight, PO36 0NP
☎ (01983) 867878 ✉ info@yates-brewery.co.uk
⊕ yates-brewery.co.uk
Tours by arrangement

⊗ Brewing started in 2000 on a five-barrel plant at the Inn at St Lawrence. In 2009 the brewery moved to Newchurch and upgraded to a 10-barrel plant. Stumpy's Brewery was bought out by Yates' in 2009 and Old Stumpy (ABV 4.5%) and Tumbledown (ABV 5%) are now produced by Yates' on request. Seasonal and bottle-conditioned beers are also available.

Golden Bitter (OG 1039, ABV 4%)
A light, refreshing beer with fruity aftertones finished with a well-balanced bitter taste.

Undercliff Experience (OG 1040, ABV 4.1%)
An amber ale with a bittersweet malt and hop taste with a dry, lemon edge that dominates the bitter finish.

Wight Old Knees Up (OG 1045, ABV 4.5%)
A golden beer laced with citrus and elderflower tastes. Hoppy and bitter to start with a smooth finish.

Holy Joe (OG 1050, ABV 4.9%) ◄
Strongly bittered golden ale with pronounced spice and citrus character, and underlying light hint of malt.

Wight Winter (ABV 5%)
A ruby ale with malty milk chocolate in the nose at first then plenty of orange fruit. Bitter, malty and roasted to taste with perfumed bitter orange notes.

YSD/Special Draught (OG 1056, ABV 5.5%) ◄
Easy-drinking strong, amber ale with pronounced tart bitterness and a refreshing bite in the aftertaste.

Yule Be Sorry (ABV 7.2%)
A rich, full-bodied beer.

For Ventnor Botanical Gardens:

Tropicale (OG 1052, ABV 5%)
A hoppy taste to start with plenty of fruit in the aftertaste.

Yeovil SIBA ◉

Yeovil Ales Ltd, Unit 5, Bofors Park, Artillery Road, Lufton Trading Estate, Yeovil, Somerset, BA22 8YH
☎ (01935) 414888 ✉ enquiries@yeovilales.com
⊕ yeovilales.com
Tours by arrangement

⊗ Yeovil Ales was established in 2006 using an 18-barrel plant. Seasonal beers: see website. Bottle-conditioned beers are also available.

Glory (OG 1039, ABV 3.8%)
A well-balanced bitter with citrus hop notes.

Star Gazer (OG 1042, ABV 4%)
Dark copper bitter with late-hopped floral bouquet.

Summerset (OG 1042, ABV 4.1%)
Blond ale with fruity hop finish.

Lynx Wildcat (OG 1045, ABV 4.3%)

Stout Hearted (OG 1045, ABV 4.3%)

Ruby (OG 1047, ABV 4.5%)
Red bitter with rich malt depth.

POSH IPA (OG 1054, ABV 5.4%)
A strong IPA with a fruity body and hoppy finish.

Yetman's

Yetman's Brewery, Bayfield Farm Barns, Bayfield Brecks Farm, Bayfield, Norfolk, BR25 7DZ
☎ 07774 809016 ✉ peter@yetmans.net
⊕ yetmans.net

A 2.5-barrel plant built by Moss Brew was installed in restored medieval barns in 2005. The brewery supplies local free trade outlets. Bottle-conditioned beers are available.

Yellow (OG 1035, ABV 3.5%)

Red (OG 1036, ABV 3.8%)

Orange (OG 1040, ABV 4.2%) ◄
Well-balanced and smooth-drinking. A light fruity aroma leads into a stirring mix of malt and hops supported by a bittersweet background. A big finish combines malt and a vinous fruitiness.

Green (OG 1044, ABV 4.8%)

York SIBA ◉

York Brewery Ltd, 12 Toft Green, York, North Yorkshire, YO1 6JT
☎ (01904) 621162 ✉ enquiries@york-brewery.co.uk
⊕ york-brewery.co.uk
Shop Mon-Sat 12-6pm
Tours by arrangement

York started production in 1996, the first brewery in the city for 40 years and still the only brewery based within the city walls. It rebranded its portfolio in 2011 and has consolidated its range into three regular beers and a varied range of monthly seasonal beers. Five pubs are owned (four in York, one in Leeds) and more than 400 other outlets are supplied. The 20-barrel plant has a viewing platform and is open for guided tours. The brewery also houses the Brewery Tap Room and hosts an annual charity beer festival. The brewery was acquired by Mitchell's of Lancaster in 2008. Seasonal beers: see website.

Guzzler (OG 1036, ABV 3.6%) 🏳 ◄
Refreshing golden ale with dominant hop and fruit flavours developing throughout.

Yorkshire Terrier (OG 1041, ABV 4.2%) ◄
Refreshing and distinctive amber/gold brew where fruit and hops dominate the aroma and taste. Hoppy bitterness remains assertive in the aftertaste.

Centurion's Ghost Ale (OG 1051, ABV 5.4%) ◄
Dark ruby in colour, full tasting with mellow roast malt character balanced by light bitterness and autumn fruit flavours that linger into the aftertaste.

Yorkshire Dales

Yorkshire Dales Brewing Co Ltd, Seata Barn, Elm Hill, Askrigg, North Yorkshire, DL8 3HG

☎ (01969) 622027 ☎ 07818 035592
✉ rob@yorkshiredalesbrewery.com
⊕ yorkshiredalesbrewery.com

☺Situated in the heart of the Yorkshire Dales, brewing started in 2005. Installation of a five-barrel plant and additional fermenters at the converted milking parlour increased capacity to 20 barrels a week. Over 150 pubs are supplied throughout the North of England. Four monthly special are always available, including a dark mild. Bottle-conditioned beers are also available.

Butter Tubs (OG 1037, ABV 3.7%)
A pale golden beer with a dry bitterness complemented by strong citrus flavours and aroma.

Leyburn Shawl (OG 1038, ABV 3.8%)
A crisp, dry, pale ale with an underlying sharpness.

Buckden Pike (OG 1040, ABV 3.9%)
A refreshing blond beer with a crisp, fruity finish.

Nappa Scar (OG 1041, ABV 4%)
A golden ale brewed with a trio of American hops for citrus and peach flavours throughout.

Muker Silver (OG 1041, ABV 4.1%)
A blond lager-style ale, very crisp with a sharp, hoppy finish.

Askrigg Ale (OG 1043, ABV 4.3%)
A pale golden ale with an intense aroma that generates a crisp, dry flavour with a long, bitter finish.

Garsdale Smokebox (OG 1057, ABV 5.6%)
A complex ale created by smoked and dark malts. Deep, rich chocolate and coffee flavours are complemented by the smokiness.

Yorkshire Heart SIBA

Yorkshire Heart Brewery Ltd, The Vineyard, Pool Lane, Nun Monkton, York, YO26 8EL
☎ (01423) 330716 ✉ chris.spak1@gmail.com
⊕ yorkshireheart.com
Tours by arrangement

⊗ Yorkshire Heart began brewing in 2011 and is situated adjacent to the Yorkshire Heart Vineyard and Winery, not far from York. Seasonal beers are available.

Traditional Mild (OG 1036, ABV 3.5%)
A traditional mild, smooth with lots of character.

Hearty Bitter (OG 1037, ABV 3.7%)
A traditional chestnut brown bitter with a long aftertaste.

JRT Best Bitter (OG 1041, ABV 4.2%)
A golden ale with a refreshing taste and flavours.

Yorkshire (NEW)

Yorkshire Brewing Co, 70 Humber Street, Hull, HU1 1TU
☎ (01482) 329999 ☎ 07850 494990
✉ info@yorkshirebrewing.co.uk

Brewing started in 2012 on a six-barrel plant. A bottling plant, tours and a retail outlet are to be established as production grows.

Holy Trinity (OG 1045, ABV 4.5%)
A refreshing light and hoppy beer with a slight citrus aftertaste.

True North (OG 1048, ABV 4.8%)
A classic amber-coloured Yorkshire bitter.

Young's

See Wells & Young's in New Nationals section

Zerodegrees

☰ Blackheath: Zerodegrees Microbrewery, 29-31 Montpelier Vale, Blackheath, London, SE3 0TJ
☎ (020) 8852 5619

Bristol: Zerodegrees, 53 Colston Street, Bristol, BS1 5BA ☎ (0117) 925 2706

Cardiff: 27 Westgate Street, Cardiff, CF10 1DD
☎ (029) 2022 9494

Reading: 9 Bridge Street, Reading, Berkshire, RG1 2LR ☎ (0118) 959 7959

✉ info@zerodegrees.co.uk ⊕ zerodegrees.co.uk
Tours by arrangement

Brewing started in 2000 in Greenwich, London and incorporates a state-of-the-art, computer-controlled German plant, producing unfiltered and unfined ales and lagers, served from tanks using air pressure (not CO2). Four pubs are owned. All beers are suitable for vegetarians and vegans. All branches of Zerodegrees follow the same concept of beers with natural ingredients. There are regular seasonal specials including fruit beers.

Mango Wheat Ale (OG 1040, ABV 4%) ◗
Mango flavoured wheat beer with plenty of sweetness throughout, bitterness and some lingering astringency. Pale in colour, served cold and cloudy, fruit and yeast lead the aroma.

Wheat Ale (OG 1045, ABV 4.2%) ◗
Authentic Munich-style wheat beer with Hallertau hops and Munich wheat malt. Strong aroma of wheat malt, a flavour of cloves and lemons lasts in a sweetish aftertaste.

Black Lager (OG 1048, ABV 4.6%) ◗
A Czech-style beer based on wheat malt and Continental hops. Strong roast and burnt malt flavours with hints of prunes and fresh coriander.

Pale Ale (OG 1046, ABV 4.6%) ◗
Malt and fruit on the nose of the American-style pale ale lead to an increasingly bitter taste and finish.

Pilsner (OG 1048, ABV 4.8%) ◗
Spicy, zesty Continental lager with sweetish lemony taste and bitter, slightly astringent aftertaste. The peppery malt aroma has hints of camomile and rosemary.

REPUBLIC OF IRELAND BREWERIES
Beoir Chorca Dhuibhne/West Kerry

Beoir Chorca Dhuibhne/West Kerry Brewery, Tig Bhric, nr Ballyferriter, Co Kerry
☎ 00353 66 915 6325 ✉ info@tigbhric.com
⊕ tigbhric.com/grudlann.html

Beer is brewed on a 400-litre plant in a remote area where Irish is the main language. The beers are available on draught in two pubs: Tig Bhric (adjacent to the brewery) and Tig Ui Chathain in nearby Ballyferriter village. Bottle-conditioned beers are also produced.

Beal Ban (ABV 4.1%)

Cul Dhorca (ABV 4.1%)

Carraig Dubh (ABV 6%)

Brew-Eyed

Brew-Eyed Beers, Unit 5, Enterprise Centre, Banagher, Co Offaly
☎ 00353 86 125 0283 ✉ info@brewed.com
⊕ breweyed.com

Established in 2011 in Banagher in County Offaly. Primarily brews lager, including Carrig Lager under contract, but cask-conditioned ales are also produced from time to time.

Blond (ABV 4.5%)

Burren

Burren Brewery, Roadside Tavern, Kincora Road, Lisdoonvarna, Co Clare
☎ 00353 65 707 4084 ✉ roadsidetavern@gmail.com

Brew-pub run by the owners of the Burren Smokehouse, specialising in local food, drink and music. The in-house brewery produces three keg beers for day-to-day sale, but cask editions are also available at the pub several times a year during festivals.

Carlow

Carlow Brewing Co, Muine Bhaeg Business Park, Royal Oak Road, Carlow, Co Carlow
☎ 00353 59 972 0509 ✉ info@carlowbrewing.com
⊕ carlowbrewing.com

One of the bigger Irish independents with a good range of cask beers.

O'Hara's Irish Stout (ABV 4.3%)

O'Hara's Red Ale (ABV 4.3%)

Curim Gold Wheat Beer (ABV 4.7%)

O'Hara's Pale Ale (ABV 5.2%)

Leann Follain Stout (ABV 6%)

Dingle

Dingle Brewing Co, Spa Road, Dingle, Co Kerry
✉ hello@thedinglebrewingco.com
⊕ thedinglebrewingco.com

Launched in the summer of 2011 with a lager commemorating Antarctic explorer Tom Crean, former proprietor of the South Pole Inn in Annascaul on the Dingle Peninsula.

Dungarvan

Dungarvan Brewing Co, Westgate Business Park, Dungarvan, Co Waterford
☎ 00353 58 24000
✉ info@dungarvanbrewingcompany.com
⊕ dungarvanbrewingcompany.com

Established in 2010 and producing three beers and several seasonals in bottle-conditioned format, increasingly available cask-conditioned.

Comeragh Challenger (ABV 3.8%)

Black Rock (ABV 4.3%)

Coffee & Oatmeal Stout (ABV 4.3%)

Copper Coast (ABV 4.3%)

Helvick Gold (ABV 4.9%)

Eight Degrees

Eight Degrees Brewing Co, Unit 3, Coolnanave, Dublin Road, Mitchelstown, Co Cork
☎ 00353 86 159 4855 ✉ scott@eightdegrees.ie
⊕ eightdegrees.ie

Founded by two Antipodean entrepreneurs. All beers are bottle-conditioned. Cask and unpasteurised keg versions also available.

Barefoot Bohemian Pilsner (ABV 4%)

Howling Gale (ABV 5%)

Knockmealdown Porter (ABV 5%)

Sunburnt Irish Red (ABV 5%)

Elbow Lane (NEW)

Elbow Lane Brewhouse, 5-6 Oliver Plunkett Street, Cork City, Co Cork ✉ info@elbowlane.ie
⊕ elbowlane.ie

A new Cork brew-pub with local distribution. Produces a lager, ale and stout brewed specifically to match with food.

Franciscan Well

Franciscan Well Brewery, 14 North Mall, Cork City, Co Cork
☎ 00353 59 913 4356
✉ info@franciscanwellbrewery.com
⊕ franciscanwellbrewery.com

Multi-award-winning brew-pub that brings choice to a city dominated by Heineken-owned Beamish and Murphy. Cask versions of its range regularly appear on guest pumps around the country, while a series of special edition bottle-conditioned beers was launched in 2011.

Blarney Blonde (ABV 4.2%)

Shandon Stout (ABV 4.2%)

Rebel Red (ABV 4.3%)

Purgatory Pale Ale (ABV 4.5%)

Friar Weisse (ABV 4.7%)

Galway Bay (NEW)

Galway Bay Brewery, Oslo, Upper Salthill Road, Salthill, Co Galway
☎ 00353 91 448390 ⊕ winefoodbeer.com/brewery

Based at the Oslo Bar & Restaurant in Salthill, just outside Galway City, Galway Bay produces two ales and a porter. Sold on key at the owners' other pubs in Galway and Dublin, both are served from the conditioning tanks in the Oslo.

Bay Ale (ABV 4.2%)

Full Sail Pale Ale (ABV 4.2%)

Stormy Port Porter (ABV 4.2%)

Galway Hooker

Galway Hooker Brewery, Roscommon Business Park, Racecourse Road, Roscommon, Co Roscommon
☎ 00353 87 77 62823 ✉ aidan@galwayhooker.ie
⊕ galwayhooker.ie

Galway Hooker brews unpasteurised keg beer for the Irish market but also produces occasional casks for festivals in both Britain and Ireland.

THE BREWERIES

Irish Pale Ale (ABV 4.4%)

Nectar (ABV 4.5%)

Opus II (ABV 4.5%)

Kinnegar (NEW)

Kinnegar Brewing, Aughavennon, Rathmullan, Co Donegal ⊕ kinnegarbrewing.com

New nano-brewery in Donegal. Three bottle-conditioned ales are brewed: Devil's Backbone (ABV 4.5%), Lime Burner (ABV 4.5%), Scraggy Bay (ABV 5.3%).

Messrs Maguire

Messrs Maguire Brewing Co, 1-2 Burgh Quay, Dublin 2
☎ 00353 1 670 5777 ✉ info@messrsmaguire.ie
⊕ messrsmaguire.ie

Pub, brewery and restaurant in the historic O'Connell Bridge area of the city. It brews a range of unpasteurised keg beers, including porter, red ale and wheat beer. Revitalised in 2010 with a new brewer, a new menu and a new range of seasonals.

Metalman

Metalman Brewing Co Ltd, 14 Tycor Business Park, Tycor, Co Waterford ✉ info@metalmanbrewing.com
⊕ metalmanbrewing.com

Up-and-coming Waterford microbrewery known for its hop-dominated ales. Occasional casks are produced for festivals and pubs with real ale taps.

Pale Ale (ABV 4.3%)

Windjammer (ABV 4.8%)

Porterhouse

Porterhouse Brewing Co, Unit 6D, Rosemount, Park Road, Ballycoolin, Blanchardstown, Dublin 15
☎ 00353 1 822 7417 ⊕ theporterhouse.ie

The oldest surviving craft brewery in the Republic of Ireland. It has three pubs in Dublin: 16-18 Parliament Street, Temple Bar, Dublin 2; Porterhouse North, Cross Guns Bridge, Glasnevin, Dublin 9; Porterhouse Central, 45-47 Nassau Street, City Centre South, Dublin 2 plus Porterhouse Bray, Strand Road, Co Wicklow. There are also branches in Covent Garden, London and Pearl Street, New York City. Only one permanent cask ale is produced, but a number of other stouts and ales are produced regularly in cask form for sale in the Temple Bar flagship and as guest ales in other pubs.

TSB (ABV 3.7%)

Plain Porter (ABV 4.3%)

Porterhouse Red (ABV 4.4%)

Oyster Stout (ABV 4.8%)

Hophead (ABV 5%)

Wrassler's XXXX (ABV 5%)

Brainblasta (ABV 7%)

Celebration (ABV 7%)

Trouble

Trouble Brewing, Allenwood, Co Kildare
☎ 00353 87 908 6658 ✉ info@troublebrewing.ie
⊕ troublebrewing.ie

Small craft brewery producing two regular beers. Also hosts an annual competition for home brewers in association with beer consumer group Beoir.org where the winning recipe becomes that summer's seasonal.

Or (ABV 4.3%)
A golden ale.

Dark Arts Porter (ABV 4.4%)

White Gypsy

White Gypsy, Railway Road, Templemore, Co Tipperary
☎ 00353 86 17 24520 ✉ info@whitegypsy.ie
⊕ whitegypsy.ie

Produces a wide range of cask and keg ales and lagers, plus a range of bottle-conditioned strong beers. The brewery features Ireland's only commercial hop garden and produces the only beer made from 100% Irish ingredients.

Emerald IPA (ABV 5%)
Made from all-Irish ingredients.

Bock (ABV 7%)

Scottish Ale (ABV 7%)

Imperial Porter (ABV 7.5%)

India Pale Ale (ABV 7.5%)

The closed brewery

To be sure, it was a deserted place, down to the pigeon-house in the brewery-yard, which had been blown crooked on its pole by some high wind, and would have made the pigeons think themselves at sea, if there had been any pigeons there to be rocked by it. But, there were no pigeons in the dove-cot, no horses in the stable, no pigs in the sty, no malt in the store-house, no smells of grains and beer in the copper or the vat. All the uses and scents of the brewery might have evaporated with its last reek of smoke. In a by-yard, there was a wilderness of empty casks, which had a certain sour remembrance of better days lingering about them; but it was too sour to be accepted as a sample of the beer that was gone.
Charles Dickens, Great Expectations, 1861

R.I.P.

The following breweries have closed, gone out of business or suspended operations since the 2012 Guide was published:

Alexandra Ales, Rugby, Warwickshire
Berrow, Berrow, Somerset
Best Mates, Ardington, Oxfordshire
Blackwater, Stourbridge, West Midlands
Cambrinus, Knowsley, Merseyside
Cherwell, Middleton Cheney, Oxfordshire
Chester, Chester, Cheshire
Cleveland, Stockton-on-Tees, Durham
Compasses, Littley Green, Essex
Crondall, Crondall, Hampshire
Dolphin, Shrewsbury, Shropshire
Festival, Cheltenham,
   Gloucestershire & Bristol
Hetty Pegler, Nailsworth,
   Gloucestershire & Bristol
Highgate, Walsall, West Midlands
Jolly Brewer, Wrexham, North-East Wales
Malt B, Maltby le Marsh, Lincolnshire
Moorview, Leeds, West Yorkshire
Northcote, Norwich, Norfolk
Oban Ales, Oban, Argyll & the Isles
St Judes, Ipswich, Suffolk
Spectrum, Norwich, Norfolk
Storyteller, Terrington, North Yorkshire
Thorne, Thorne, South Yorkshire
Ufford, Ufford, Cambridgeshire

FUTURE

The following new breweries have been notified to the Guide and will start to produce beer during 2012/2013. In a few cases, they were in production during the summer of 2012 but were too late for a full listing:

Aardvark, Sheffield, South Yorkshire
Abbeyford, Chertsey, Surrey
Adventure, Chessington, Greater London
Alfred's, Winchester, Hampshire
All Hallows, Goodmanham, East Yorkshire
Barlick, Barnoldswick, Lancashire
Bedlam, Alborne, West Sussex
Blackhill, Stanley, Durham
Blackjack, Manchester, Greater Manchester
Brighton, Brighton, East Sussex
Bumpmill, Shirland, Derbyshire
Cellar Rat, Stockport, Greater Manchester
Clarence & Fredericks, Sutton,
   Greater London
Cronx, Croydon, Greater London
Duchess of Cambridge, London,
   Greater London
Evesham, Evesham, Worcestershire
Four Thorns, Heslington, North Yorkshire
Friday Beer Co, Malvern, Worcestershire
Furnace, Derby, Derbyshire
Hart Family Brewers, Northamptonshire
Hearsall, Coventry, Warwickshire
Hurst, Hurstpierpoint, West Sussex
Jo C's, East Rudham, Norfolk
Jubilee Tower, Darwen, Lancashire
Knaresborough, Knaresborough,
   North Yorkshire
Latimer, Kettering, Northants
Ledbury, Ledbury, Herefordshire
Lion & Key, Hull, East Yorkshire
Little Beer, Guildford, Surrey
Moray, Forres, Aberdeen & Grampian
Nag's Head, Abercych, West Wales
Newark, Newark, Nottinghamshire
Old School, Warton, Lancashire
Problem Child, Parbold, Lancashire
Putney Bridge, London, Greater London
Robin Hood, Nottingham,
   Nottinghamshire
Rocky Head, London, Greater London
Rosebud, Brightlingsea, Essex
Rye Lane, London, Greater London
Tom Smith, Kettering,
   Northamptonshire
Swifty's, Chester, Cheshire
Temptation, Houghton-le-Spring,
   Tyne & Wear
Unsworth's Yard, Cartmel, Cumbria
Weird Beard, London, Greater London

New nationals

Greene King, Marston's and Wells & Young's are such a major force in British brewing that they have outstripped their status as 'super regionals' and become fully national producers. This is a result of the volumes of beer they produce and their national reach to consumers through their substantial pub estates and the free trade. These 'new nationals' do not match the size of the global brewers (see next section) but unlike the globals they have a powerful commitment to cask beer. Greene King's IPA, Marston's Pedigree and Wells & Young's Young's Bitter, Courage Best and Bombardier are among the best-selling cask beers in Britain. The nationals have reached their status by different routes: Greene King has a track record of buying and closing breweries, such as Ridley's and Hardy & Hanson, and concentrating production at its Suffolk plant. Marston's, on the other hand, has bought the likes of Brakspear/Wychwood, Jennings and Ringwood and kept those breweries in operation; though it did close the Mansfield Brewery. Wells & Young's is a result of a merger in 2006 between Charles Wells of Bedford and Young's of Wandsworth in London, but Young's had signalled its intention to leave brewing and the merger was more of an arranged marriage. All production is now based at the Bedford brewery. As a result of low interest in cask beer among the global producers, the nationals have picked up contracts to brew such once-revered brands as Draught Bass and Tetley Bitter. In the case of Wells & Young's, it now owns the former S&N/Heineken brands Courage Best and Directors.

GREENE KING

Greene King ◉

Greene King plc, Westgate Brewery, Bury St Edmunds, Suffolk, IP33 1QT
☎ (01284) 763222 ✉ solutions@greeneking.co.uk
⊕ greeneking.co.uk
Shop and Visitor Centre Mon-Fri 10.30am-4.30pm; Sat 10.30am-5.30pm
Tours everyday and Thu eves in summer

⊠ Greene King has been brewing in the market town of Bury St Edmunds since 1799. In the 1990s it bought the brands of the former Morland and Ruddles breweries and has given a massive promotion to Old Speckled Hen, which in bottled form is now the biggest ale brand in Britain. As a result of buying the former Morland pub estate, the company acquired a major presence in the Thames Valley region. But it has not confined itself to East Anglia or the Home Counties. Its tenanted and managed pubs, which include Old English Inns and Hungry Horse, total more than 2,400 while the development of its free trade sales, totalling more than 3,000 outlets, means its beers can be found as far from its home base as Wales and the north of England. In 2005 Greene King bought and closed Ridley's of Essex. Also in 2005, the group bought Belhaven of Dunbar in Scotland. Belhaven has a large pub estate that has enabled Greene King to build sales north of the border. In 2006 the group bought and closed Hardys & Hansons in Nottingham. In 2012, it launched two stronger versions of IPA, Gold and Reserve, and has introduced several new cask beers. Seasonal beers change monthly with sporting or topical names. Bottle-conditioned beer: Hen's Tooth (ABV 6.5%).

Tolly English Ale (ABV 2.8%)
Amber ale brewed using a complex mix of hops to offer balanced bitterness with strong tropical notes.

XX Mild (OG 1035, ABV 3%)
A dark mild with a sweet and roast flavour.

IPA (OG 1036, ABV 3.6%) ◈
Hop-infused fruit cake aromas. Complex flavours of malt, caramel and hop with both sweetness and bitterness. A lingering mellow aftertaste with blackberries.

Ruddles Best Bitter (OG 1037, ABV 3.7%) ◈
An amber/brown beer, strong on bitterness but with some initial sweetness, fruit and subtle, distinctive Bramling Cross hop. Dryness lingers in the aftertaste.

H&H Bitter (OG 1038, ABV 3.9%)
A balance of sweetness and bitterness with subtle hop character. A distinctive beer with a full finish.

London Glory (ABV 4%)
Rich and fruity brew that combines crystal malt with Challenger and Goldings hops.

Morland Original Bitter (OG 1039, ABV 4%)
A subtle malt and fruit character and a pronounced bitter finish.

IPA Gold (ABV 4.1%)
A deep golden ale brewed with Savinsjki Goldings hops which creates a blend of tropical fruits, mango and spicy notes.

Old Golden Hen (ABV 4.1%)
Light golden beer brewed using the Galaxy hop to give tropical fruit notes.

H&H Olde Trip (OG 1043, ABV 4.3%)
A rich toffee flavoured beer with a fruity character and a clean, bitter finish.

Ruddles County (OG 1048, ABV 4.3%) ◈
Sweet, malty and bitter, with a dry and bitter aftertaste.

Old Speckled Hen (OG 1045, ABV 4.5%) ◈
Smooth, malty and fruity, with a short finish.

Abbot Ale (OG 1049, ABV 5%)
A full-bodied, distinctive beer with a bittersweet aftertaste.

IPA Reserve (ABV 5.4%)
A full-bodied amber ale. Grapefruit and orange citrus tones combine with floral and herbal notes from the Styrian Goldings hops and lead to a dry bitter finish.

Belhaven

Belhaven Brewing Co, Spott Road, Dunbar, East Lothian, EH42 1RS
☎ (01368) 862734 ✉ info@belhaven.co.uk
⊕ belhaven.co.uk
Shop open during tours
Tours by arrangement

☺Belhaven is located in Dunbar, some 30 miles east of Edinburgh on the East Lothian coast. The company claimed to be the oldest independent brewery in Scotland but it lost that independence when it was acquired by Greene King. Belhaven owns 300 tied pubs and has around 2,500 direct free trade accounts. Only 3% of production is cask beer: the company concentrates on its Belhaven Best keg beer. 70/- has been discontinued and Belhaven no longer conrtact brews for Edinburgh Brewing Co and Maclays pub group. Seasonal beers: see website.

60/- Ale (OG 1030, ABV 2.9%) ◆
A fine but virtually unavailable example of a Scottish light. This bittersweet, reddish-brown beer is dominated by fruit and malt with a hint of roast and caramel, and increasing bitterness in the aftertaste.

IPA (OG 1038, ABV 3.8%)
A golden ale with refreshing floral and citrus tones produced by a well-balanced fusion of malt and hops giving a clean, crisp flavour.

80/- Ale (OG 1040, ABV 4.2%) ◆
One of the last remaining original Scottish 80 Shillings. Malt is the predominant flavour characteristic, though it is balanced by fruit and a little hop. A complex ale, true to the 80/- style.

Black (OG 1041, ABV 4.2%)
A roasty stout, a new addition to the Belhaven portfolio.

St Andrew's Ale (OG 1046, ABV 4.9%)
A bittersweet beer with lots of body. The malt, fruit and roast mingle throughout with hints of hop and caramel.

MARSTON'S SIBA

Marston's plc, Marston's House, Wolverhampton, West Midlands, WV1 4JT
☎ (01902) 711811 ✉ enquiries@marstons.co.uk
⊕ marstons.co.uk

Marston's, formerly Wolverhampton & Dudley, has grown with spectacular speed in recent years. It became a 'super regional' in 1999 when it bought both Mansfield and Marston's breweries, though it quickly closed Mansfield. In 2005 it bought Jennings of Cockermouth and has invested £250,000 in Cumbria to expand fermenting and cask racking capacity. In total, Marston's owns 2,150 pubs and supplies some 3,000 free trade pubs and clubs throughout the country. It no longer has a stake in Burtonwood Brewery (qv) but brews Burtonwood Bitter for the pub estate, which is owned by Marston's. It added a further 70 pubs in 2006 when it bought Celtic Inns for £43.6 million. In 2007 it paid £155 million for the 158-strong Eldridge Pope pub estate. In the same year it bought Ringwood in Hampshire and added Brakspear and Wychwood in Witney, Oxfordshire.

Banks's

Banks's Brewery, Park Brewery, Wolverhampton, West Midlands, WV1 4NY
☎ (01922) 711811 ✉ enquiries@marstons.co.uk
⊕ bankssbeer.co.uk
Shop Mon-Fri 10am-5pm; Sat 9.30am-12pm (excluding Bank Holidays)
Tours can be booked online or phone (01902) 329653

Banks's was formed in 1890 by the amalgamation of three local companies. Hanson's was acquired in 1943 but its Dudley brewery was closed in 1991. Hanson's beers are now brewed in

Wolverhampton, though its pubs retain the Hanson's livery. Banks's Original, the biggest-selling brand, is a fine example of West Midlands mild ale and in 2010 the group decided to return to the traditional name of Mild to keep pace with growing demand for the style. Beers from the closed Mansfield Brewery are now brewed at Wolverhampton. Hanson's Mild has been discontinued.

Mild (OG 1036, ABV 3.5%) ◆
An amber-coloured, well-balanced, refreshing session beer.

Bitter (OG 1038, ABV 3.8%) ◆
A pale brown bitter with a pleasant balance of hops and malt. Hops continue from the taste through to a bittersweet aftertaste.

Mansfield Cask Ale (OG 1038, ABV 3.9%)
A full bodied session bitter with a smooth finish.

Brewed at Banks's for the Marston's estate

EPA (OG 1036, ABV 3.6%)

Sunbeam (OG 1042, ABV 4.2%)

Brakspear

Brakspear Brewing Co, Eagle Maltings, The Crofts, Witney, Oxfordshire, OX28 4DP
☎ (01993) 890800 ✉ info@brakspear-beers.co.uk
⊕ brakspear-beers.co.uk
Merchandise available online or in Brewery store Mon-Sat 10am-5pm (excluding Bank Holidays)
Tours by Saturdays and Sundays: booking essential

Brakspear, along with Wychwood (see below) was bought by Marston's in 2007. Brakspear was originally based in Henley-on-Thames and is one of Britain's oldest breweries, founded before 1700 and run by the Brakspear family since 1779. In 2002, the brewery closed and became a pub company. Refresh UK, a company based in Witney and owners of Wychwood, bought the rights to the Brakspear brands and brewed them again from 2004 after moving the Henley equipment, including the famous 'double drop' fermenters, to Witney. NB Pubs that carry the Brakspear name belong to a separate company that has no connection with Brakspear Brewing Co, though the brewery does supply the pub company with beer. Bottle-conditioned beers are available.

Bitter (OG 1035, ABV 3.4%)
A classic copper-coloured pale ale with big hop resins, juicy malt and orange fruit aroma, intense hop bitterness in the mouth and finish, and a firm maltiness and tangy fruitiness throughout.

Oxford Gold (OG 1040, ABV 4%)
English Target hops give this beer a remarkable aroma. Late hopping with Goldings and fermentation with Brakspear yeast create a zesty aroma, a full, fruity flavour and golden colour.

Jennings ◎

Jennings Bros plc, Castle Brewery, Cockermouth, Cumbria, CA13 9NE
☎ 0845 129 7185 ⊕ jenningsbrewery.co.uk
Shop Mon-Sat 10am-4pm, Sun 10am-4pm (Jul & Aug)
Tours daily (except Sun); 7 days a week Jul & Aug. Booking advised. Other tours by arrangement.
Book online or call 0845 129 7190

⊕Jennings Brewery was established as a family concern in 1828 in the village of Lorton. The company moved to its present location in 1874. Pure Lakeland water is still used for brewing, drawn from the brewery's own well, along with Maris Otter barley malt and Fuggles and Goldings hops. The brewery was badly damaged in the Cumbrian floods of 2009 and was out of operation for three months. Marston's commitment to the plant was shown by the rapid repairs at a cost of several million pounds. Regular specials reflect the Cumbrian heritage of Jennings and include Crag Rat (ABV 4.3%) and Tom Fool (4%).

Dark Mild (OG 1031, ABV 3.1%) ◄
A well-balanced, dark brown mild with a malty aroma, strong roast taste, not over-sweet, with some hops and a slightly bitter finish.

Bitter (OG 1035, ABV 3.5%) ◄
A malty beer with a good mouthfeel that combines with roast flavour and a hoppy finish.

Cumberland Ale (OG 1039, ABV 4%) ◄
A light, creamy, hoppy beer with a dry aftertaste.

Cocker Hoop (OG 1044, ABV 4.6%)
A rich, creamy, copper-coloured beer with raisiny maltiness balanced with a resiny hoppiness, with a developing bitterness towards the end.

Sneck Lifter (OG 1051, ABV 5.1%) ◄
A strong, dark brown ale with a complex balance of fruit, malt and roast flavours through to the finish.

Marston's ⊙

Marston, Thompson & Evershed, Marston's Brewery, Shobnall Road, Burton upon Trent, Staffordshire, DE14 2BW
☎ (01283) 531131 ✉ enquiries@marstons.co.uk
⊕ marstons.co.uk
Shop Mon-Fri 10am-5pm; Sat 9.30am-12pm (excluding Bank Holidays)
Tours can be booked on (01283) 507391

⊕Marston's has been brewing cask beer in Burton since 1834 and the current site is the home of the only working 'Burton Union' fermenters, housed in rooms known as the 'Cathedral of Brewing'. Burton Unions were developed in the 19th century to cleanse the new style of pale ale of yeast. Only Pedigree is fermented in the unions but yeast from the system is used to ferment the other beers. Pedigree celebrated its 60th anniversary in 2012.

Burton Bitter (OG 1037, ABV 3.8%) ◄
Overwhelming sulphurous aroma supports a scattering of hops and fruit with an easy-drinking sweetness. The taste develops from the sweet middle to a satisfyingly hoppy finish.

Pedigree (OG 1043, ABV 4.5%) ◄
Pale brown with a gentle aroma of sweet malt and a dash of hops. Light in taste with no dominant flavours but a sweet aftertaste.

Old Empire (OG 1057, ABV 5.7%) ◄
Sulphur dominates the gentle malt aroma. Malty and sweet to start but developing bitterness with fruit and a touch of sweetness. A balanced aftertaste of hops and fruit leads to a lingering bitterness.

For AB InBev:

Draught Bass (OG 1043, ABV 4.4%) ◄
Hints of caramel on aroma and taste, lightly hopped for a short bitter finish.

Ringwood ⊙

Ringwood Brewery Ltd, Christchurch Road, Ringwood, Hampshire, BH24 3AP
☎ (01425) 471177
✉ enquiries@ringwoodbrewery.co.uk
⊕ ringwoodbrewery.co.uk
Shop Mon-Sat 9.30am-5pm
Tours Sat & Sun afternoon

Ringwood was bought in 2007 by Marston's for £19 million. The group plans to increase production to 50,000 barrels a year. Some 750 outlets are supplied and seven pubs are owned. Seasonal beers are available.

Best Bitter (OG 1038, ABV 3.8%) ◄
A malty session bitter with strong toffee notes in the aroma, leading to a short, bittersweet finish. Malt tends to dominate throughout.

Boondoggle (OG 1043, ABV 4.2%)

Fortyniner (OG 1049, ABV 4.9%) ◄
This robust bitter has a caramel, biscuity aroma with hints of damson, leading to a sweet but well-balanced taste with malt, fruit and hop flavours all present. The finish is bittersweet with some fruit.

Brewery organisations

There are three organisations mentioned in this Guide to which breweries can belong. The Independent Families Brewers of Britain (IFBB) represents around 35 regional companies still owned by families. As many regional breweries closed in the 1990s, the IFBB represents the interests of the survivors, staging events such as the annual Cask Ale Week to emphasise the important role played by the independent sector.

The Society of Independent Brewers (SIBA) represents the growing number of small craft or micro brewers: some smaller regionals are also members. SIBA is an effective lobbying organisation and played a leading role in persuading the government to introduce Progressive Beer Duty. It has also campaigned to get large pub companies to take beers from smaller breweries and has had considerable success with Enterprise Inns.

The East Anglian Brewers' Co-operative (EAB) was the brainchild of Brendan Moore at Iceni Brewery. Finding it impossible to get their beers into pub companies and faced by the giant power of Greene King in the region, the co-op makes bulk deliveries to the genuine free trade and also sells beer at farmers' markets and specialist beer shops. EAB also buys malt and hops in bulk for its members, thus reducing costs.

Old Thumper (OG 1055, ABV 5.6%) ◆
A powerful, sweet, copper-coloured beer. A fruity aroma preludes a strong, sweet, malty taste with soft fruit and caramel, which is not cloying and leads to a surprisingly bittersweet aftertaste.

Wychwood 👁

Wychwood Brewery Ltd, Eagle Maltings, The Crofts, Witney, Oxfordshire, OX28 4DP
☎ (01993) 890800 ✉ info@wychwood.co.uk
⊕ wychwood.co.uk
Shop 10am-5pm Mon-Sat (not bank holidays)
Tours on Saturdays and Sundays: booking essential

Wychwood Brewery is located on the fringes of the ancient medieval forest, the Wychwood. The brewery was founded in 1983 on a site dating back to the 1880s, which was once the original maltings for the town's brewery, Clinch's. Monthly seasonal beers are produced and bottle-conditioned beers are available.

Hobgoblin (OG 1045, ABV 4.5%)
The beer was reduced in strength early in 2008 by the previous owner, Refresh UK.

WELLS & YOUNG'S
Wells & Young's IFBB 👁

Wells & Young's Brewing Co, Bedford Brewery, Havelock Street, Bedford, MK40 4LU
☎ (01234) 272766
✉ postmaster@wellsandyoungs.co.uk
⊕ wellsandyoungs.co.uk
Tours by arrangement

Wells & Young's was created following the merger of the brewing and brands divisions of Charles Wells of Bedford and Young & Co of Wandsworth in 2006, creating Britain's largest private brewery. Brewing has been synonymous with Bedford since 1876 when the founder, Charles Wells, established a brewery on the banks of the Great Ouse River.

Since then the company has thrived, to become a major force in the brewing industry. Wells and Young's run separate pub estates. In 2007, Wells & Young's acquired the Courage brands from Scottish & Newcastle (now Heineken UK). Seasonal beers include Young's Waggle Dance. Bottle-conditioned beers are also available.

Eagle IPA (OG 1035, ABV 3.6%) ◆
A refreshing, amber session bitter with pronounced citrus hop aroma and palate, faint malt in the mouth, and a lasting dry, bitter finish.

Young's Bitter (OG 1036, ABV 3.7%) ◆
This light drinking amber bitter has citrus initially on the palate with sweet malt and a hint of hops that linger into a slightly dry and bitter finish.

Courage Best Bitter (OG 1038, ABV 4%)
Malt and hops on the nose, with a full palate of malt, fruit and hops, and a dry and bitter finish.

Wells Bombardier (OG 1042, ABV 4.1%)

Young's Special (OG 1044, ABV 4.5%) ◆
Pale brown in colour, this rounded best bitter has citrus throughout plus some slight creamy toffee, which balances the bitterness that grows in the aftertaste.

Courage Directors Bitter (OG 1045.5, ABV 4.8%)
A chestnut-coloured beer with a rich, malty aroma, fruit and hops in the mouth and a long, malty, fruity and hoppy finish.

Young's London Gold (ABV 4.8%) ◆
A dark gold beer with a smooth mouthfeel. Citrus and malt in the low aroma, coming through more strongly on the palate and aftertaste with a little peach. Dry finish.

Young's Winter Warmer (OG 1055, ABV 5%) ◆
Rich malt and raisins are the main flavours in this ruby-brown beer that is complemented by roast and a little burnt bitter dryness. Blackberry, citrus and toffee overtones.

Greene King Westgate Brewery, Bury St Edmunds

THE BREWERIES

Global giants

Eight out of ten pints of beer brewed in Britain come from the international groups listed below. They concentrate their production and marketing budgets on promoting processed beers – lagers and 'smooth-flow' keg ales – but they are slowly starting to grasp the reality of a changing beer scene in which the only small growth comes from the cask beer sector. Heineken UK, Britain's biggest brewer, who took over the Scottish & Newcastle pub and brewing operations, announced in June 2011 a scheme called Cask Orders that offers its free trade customers a portfolio of 42 regional and seasonal ales sourced from 20 smaller brewers. Cask Orders initially was for the 2011 summer season but it could become a permanent feature of Heineken's operation. June 2011 saw the end of brewing at the historic Tetley plant in Leeds, a cause for sorrow well beyond Yorkshire. The Tetley cask brands are now brewed for Carlsberg by Marston's and they are being given some much-needed promotion by their owner, with the promise of seasonal beers to follow. The most dramatic sign of the globals interest in the cask sector came in 2011 when Molson Coors bought the successful Sharp's brewery in Cornwall, best known for its Doom Bar bitter, while it invested £1 million in a new craft beer plant, the William Worthington's Brewery, in Burton-on-Trent. The penny has yet to drop at AB InBev, the world's biggest brewer, who still believes the future lies with American Budweiser and Stella Artois and has put up for sale such legendary cask beers as Draught Bass, Boddingtons and Flowers. We list only those breweries that produce real ale.

AB INBEV

AB InBev

AB InBev UK Ltd, Porter Tun House, 500 Capability Green, Luton, Bedfordshire, LU1 3LS
☎ (01582) 391166
✉ name.surname@interbrew.co.uk ⊕ inbev.com

The biggest merger in brewing history in 2008 created AB InBev, when InBev of Belgium and Brazil bought American giant Anheuser-Busch, best-known for the world's biggest (but not best) beer brand, Budweiser. The giant is a major player in the European market with such lager brands as Stella Artois and Jupiler. It has a slight interest in ale brewing with the cask- and bottle-conditioned wheat beer, Hoegaarden, and the Abbey beer Leffe. It has a ruthless track record of closing plants and disposing of brands: it has already announced the closure of the historic Stag Brewery in Mortlake, London, formerly Watney's, where the British version of Budweiser is brewed. It's not known where the brand will be produced following the closure of the Mortlake plant but it's unlikely that many readers of the Good Beer Guide will care. In 2000 Interbrew, as it was then known, bought both Bass's and Whitbread's brewing operations, giving it a 32 per cent market share. The British government told Interbrew to dispose of parts of the Bass brewing group, which were bought by Coors, now Molson Coors (qv). Draught Bass has declined to around 37,000 barrels a year: it once sold close to one million barrels a year, but was sidelined by the Bass empire. It is now brewed under licence by Marston's (see New Nationals section). Caks conditioned Boddingtons was brewed for AB InBev by Hydes but the contract expired in 2012 and the beer is currently not being brewed. AB InBev has put Draught Bass, Boddingtons and Flowers cask beers up for sale for £15 million.

Brewed for AB InBev by Brains of Cardiff:

Flowers IPA (ABV 3.6%)

Flowers Original (ABV 4.5%)

CARLSBERG

Carlsberg UK

Carlsberg Brewing Ltd, Bridge Street, Northampton, NN1 1PZ
☎ (01604) 668866 ⊕ carlsberg.com

Tetley, the historic Leeds brewery, closed in June 2011. The two Tetley Milds are produced by Marston's at its Burton-on-Trent site and cask Tetley Bitter moved to Banks's Brewery in by Wolverhampton. Carlsberg UK is a wholly-owned subsidiary of Carlsberg Breweries of Copenhagen, Denmark.

Brewed for Carlsberg by JW Lees:

Draught Burton Ale (OG 1047, ABV 4.8%) ◆
A beer with hops, fruit and malt present throughout, and a lingering complex aftertaste, but lacking some hoppiness compared to its Burton original.

Brewed for Carlsberg by Marston's:

Tetley Dark Mild (OG 1031, ABV 3.2%)

Tetley Mild (OG 1034, ABV 3.3%) ◆
A mid-brown beer with a light malt and caramel aroma. A well-balanced taste of malt and caramel follows, with good bitterness and a satisfying finish.

Tetley Bitter (OG 1035, ABV 3.7%) ◆
A smooth, creamy bitter with a hoppy nose. Hops are joined by a good dose of balancing malt until both give way to the long, bitter finish.

MOLSON COORS

Molson Coors SIBA

Molson Coors Brewers Ltd, 137 High Street, Burton upon Trent, Staffordshire, DE14 1JZ
☎ (01283) 511000 ⊕ molsoncoorsbrewers.com

Molson Coors is the result of a merger between Molson of Canada and Coors of Colorado, U.S. Coors established itself in Europe in 2002 by buying part of the former Bass brewing empire, when Interbrew (now AB InBev) was instructed by the British government to divest itself of some of its interests in Bass. Coors owns several cask ale brands. It brews 110,000 barrels of cask beer a year (under licensing arrangements with other brewers) and also provides a further 50,000 barrels of cask beer from other breweries. In February 2011 Molson Coors bought Sharp's brewery in Cornwall in a bid to increase its stake in the cask beer sector.

Stones Bitter (OG 1037, ABV 3.7%)
Brewed under contract by Everards.

Worthington's White Shield (ABV 5.6%)

Bottle-conditioned: Sweet aroma, woody tastes with angelica, nettles and sharp apples. Ever-changing tastes but a long hoppy finish. Due to the success of the beer since it returned to Burton, production has moved to the main Coors brewery where more than 100,000 barrels a year are produced. The beer has been a major success in Sainsbury's stores and increased production has allowed the beer to go on sale in Asda, Morrisons and Waitrose outlets.

Brewed for Molson Coors by Brains of Cardiff:

Hancock's HB (OG 1038, ABV 3.6%) 🍺
A pale brown, slightly malty beer whose initial sweetness is balanced by bitterness but lacks a noticeable finish. A consistent if inoffensive Welsh beer.

Worthington's Bitter (OG 1038, ABV 3.6%)
A pale brown bitter of thin and unremarkable character.

M&B Brew XI (OG 1039.5, ABV 3.8%)
A sweet, malty beer with a hoppy, bitter aftertaste.

Sharp's 👁

Sharp's Brewery, Pityme Business Centre, Rock, Cornwall, PL27 6NU
☎ (01208) 862121
✉ enquiries@sharpsbrewery.co.uk
⊕ sharpsbrewery.co.uk
Shop Mon-Fri 9am-5pm
Tours by arrangement

Sharp's was bought for £20 million by Molson Coors in February 2011. The brewery was founded in 1994. Within 15 years it had grown from producing 1,500 barrels a year to 60,000. A £7.5 million investment by Molson Coors over 24 months has brought capacity up to 200,000 barrels a year. The company owns no pubs and delivers beer to more than 1,200 outlets across the south of England via temperature-controlled depots in Bristol and London. Molson Coors has stressed that it will maintain production in Cornwall . Seasonal beer: see website. Bottle-conditioned beer is also available.

Cornish Coaster (OG 1035.2, ABV 3.6%) 🍺
Refeshing light session bitter with delicate fruit aroma. Gentle balance of hops, fruit, malt and bitterness in the mouth. Fruit persists in the finish with a little bitterness and dryness.

Doom Bar (OG 1038, ABV 4%) 🍺
Rich spicy hop and malt aroma to this pale brown bitter. Refreshing fruity bitterness is perfectly balanced by sweet malt all the way through to a peppery and dry finish.

Own (OG 1042, ABV 4.4%) 🍺
Full-bodied, deep golden brown beer, rich in nutty malt and hops on the tongue. Bitterness develops, persisting in the finish, together with some hoppy dryness and malt.

Special (OG 1048.5, ABV 5%) 🍺
Deep golden brown with a fresh hop aroma. Dry malt and hops in the mouth; the finish is malty but becomes dry and hoppy.

William Worthington's Brewery

National Brewery Centre, Horninglow Street, Burton upon Trent, Staffordshire, DE14 1YQ
☎ (01283) 532880 ⊕ nationalbrewerycentre.co.uk

Molson Coors invested £1 million on this brewing plant in 2011, set within the brewery centre; the brewery is named after one of the famous Burton brewers from the 18th and 19th centuries who developed the pale ale style that transformed brewing in Britain. The brewery is open for visitors as part of the brewery centre tours. There's a shop and also a restaurant and bar where beers from the brewery can be sampled. There are regular monthly and seasonal beers, including Spring, Summer, Autumn and Winter Shields. The new brewery has replaced the on-site White Shield Brewery, but this can still be visited and beers from the Worthington plant are pumped to the old site where fermentation takes place.

M&B Mild (OG 1033, ABV 2.8%)
A former Birmingham classic mild that was contracted out; the beer has been brought back to Burton with four times the previous volumes.

Allowance Ale (OG 1033, ABV 3.5%)

Worthington's Red Shield (OG 1038, ABV 4.2%)

Brewery Tap (OG 1042, ABV 4.5%)

Worthington E (OG 1044, ABV 4.8%)
Cask version of one of the infamous keg beers of the 1970s.

SIBA Direct Delivery Scheme

In 2003 the Society of Independent Brewers (SIBA) launched a Direct Delivery Scheme (DDS) that enables its members to deliver beer to individual pubs rather than to the warehouses of pub companies. Before the scheme came into operation, small craft brewers could only sell beer to the national pubcos if they delivered beer to their depots. In one case, a brewer in Sheffield was told by Punch Taverns that the pubco would only take his beer if he delivered it to a warehouse in Liverpool and then returned to pick up the empty casks. In the time between delivery and pick-up, some of the beer would have been delivered by Punch to...Sheffield.
Now SIBA has struck agreements with Admiral Taverns, Edinburgh Woollen Mills, Enterprise Inns, New Century Inns, Orchard Pubs, and Punch, as well as off-licence chains Asda and Thresher to deliver direct to their pubs or shops. The scheme has been such a success that DDS is now a separate but wholly-owned subsidiary of SIBA.

See **www.siba.co.uk/dds_site** for more information.

Worthington's White Shield (OG 1049, ABV 5.6%)
A draught version of the celebrated bottle-conditioned India Pale Ale.

Czar's Imperial Stout (OG 1078, ABV 8%) ◆
A library of tastes, from a full roast, liquorice beginning, dark toffee, brown sugar, molasses, Christmas pudding, rum, dark chocolate to name but a few. Fruit emerges, blackberry changing to blackcurrant jam, then liquorice root.

No 1 Barley Wine (OG 1105, ABV 10.5%)
This classic strong Burton Ale was not brewed in 2011, due to changes in the brewing plant, but it remains part of the portfolio.

HEINEKEN
Heineken UK

Heineken UK, 2-4 Broadway Park, South Gyle Broadway, Edinburgh, EH12 9JZ
☎ (0131) 528 1000 ⊕ heineken.com

Heineken UK, formerly Scottish & Newcastle, is Britain's biggest brewing group with close to 30% of the market. Scottish & Newcastle was formed in 1960, a merger between Scottish Brewers (Younger and McEwan) and Newcastle Breweries. In 1995 it bought Courage from its Australian owners, Foster's/Carlton & United. Since the merger that formed Scottish Courage, the group rationalised by closing its breweries in Edinburgh, Newcastle, Nottingham, Halifax and George's Brewery in Bristol. The remaining beers were transferred to John Smith's in Tadcaster. It bought the financially stricken Bulmer's Cider group. Heineken continues to own Bulmer's and the S&N 2,000-strong pub estate (including the ex-Globe Pub Co), though the pub estate is also being whittled down. In 2003, S&N sold the Theakston's Brewery in Yorkshire back to the original family (see Theakston's entry in Independents section). In 2008 S&N bought Caledonian Brewing Co, which is now a subsidiary of Heineken. S&N's sole Scottish cask beer, McEwan's 80/-, has been discontinued. The Courage brands are now brewed by Wells & Young's.

Caledonian SIBA ⊙

Caledonian Brewing Co Ltd, 42 Slateford Road, Edinburgh, EH11 1PH

☎ (0131) 337 1286 ✉ info@caledonian-brewery.co.uk ⊕ caledonian-brewery.co.uk
Tours by arrangement

The brewery was founded by Lorimer & Clark in 1869 and was sold to Vaux of Sunderland in 1919. In 1987 the brewery was saved from closure by a management buy-out. The brewery site was purchased by S&N in 2004 and became a wholly-owned subsidiary of S&N/Heineken in 2008. Monthly guest beers are produced that are sometimes of an unusual style, as well as a rolling programme of special beers covering each of the seasons. The Harviestoun Brewery (qv), which was a subsidiary of Caledonian, is now independent.

Deuchars IPA (OG 1039, ABV 3.8%) ◆
Refreshing golden session ale with hop aroma and dry bittersweet finish. Although a hoppy beer, there is sufficient malt to give a pleasing body. Fruit and a hint of diacetyl (butterscotch) add sweetness and balance.

Flying Scotsman (ABV 4%)

80 (OG 1042, ABV 4.1%) ◆
A predominantly malty, brown beer with caramel and hints of roast throughout. Fruit provides the sweetness typical of a Scottish 80/- while a little hop gives a gentle bitterness to the finish.

John Smith (Heineken UK Tadcaster)

John Smith's Brewery, Tadcaster, North Yorkshire, LS24 9SA

☎ (01937) 832091 ⊕ heineken.com
Tours by arrangement

The brewery was built in 1879 by a relative of Samuel Smith (qv). John Smith's became part of the Courage group in 1970 before being taken over by S&N. Major expansion has taken place, with 11 new fermenting vessels installed. Traditional Yorkshire Square fermenters have been replaced by conical vessels. John Smith's cask Magnet has been discontinued.

John Smith's Bitter (OG 1035.8, ABV 3.8%) ◆
A copper-coloured beer, well-balanced but with no dominating features. It has a short hoppy finish. It is brewed under contract by Cameron's in Hartlepool.

What is real ale?

Real ale is also known as cask-conditioned beer or simply cask beer. In the brewery, the beer is neither filtered nor pasteurised. It still contains sufficient yeast and sugar for it to continue to ferment and mature in the cask. Once it has reached the pub cellar, it has to be laid down for maturation to continue, and for yeast and protein to settle at the bottom of the cask. Some real ale also has extra hops added as the cask is filled, a process known as 'dry hopping' for increased flavour and aroma. Cask beer is best served at a cellar temperature of 11-12 degrees C, although some stronger ales can benefit from being served a little warmer. Each cask has two holes, in one of which a tap is inserted and is connected to tubes or 'lines' that enable the beer to be drawn to the bar. The other hole, on top of the cask, enables some carbon dioxide produced during secondary fermentation to escape. It is vital that some gas, which gives the beer its natural sparkle or condition, is kept within the cask: the escape of gas is controlled by inserting porous wooden pegs called spiles into the spile hole. Real ale is a living product and must be consumed within three or four days of a cask being tapped as oxidation develops.

Indexes & Further Information

Places index

Watford 209
Wath upon Dearne 546
Wath 535
Watnall 382
Watton 359
Waunfawr 600
Wavertree, Liverpool 341
Waytown 139
Weatheroak 511
Wedmore 414
Wednesbury 492
Wednesfield 492
Weeley 166
Welcombe 130
Weldon 367
Wellesbourne 479
Welling 301
Wellingborough 367
Wellington, Telford 400
Wells 414
Wells-next-the-Sea 359
Wendens Ambo 166
Wendover 57
Wendron 87
Wennington 248
Wensley 535
Wentworth 546
West Acre 359
West Boldon 471
West Bridgford 382
West Bromwich 493
West Chiltington 463
West Chinnock 414
West Derby, Liverpool 341
West Dulwich 296
West Ealing 311
West End 194
West Haddlesey 535
West Hanney 393
West Herrington 471
West Huntspill 414
West Itchenor 464
West Kensington 311
West Linton 626
West Lulworth 139
West Malling 232
West Malvern 511
West Monkseaton 472
West Norwood 297
West Parley 139
West Peckham 232
West Stockwith 383
West Stour 139
West Tytherley 194
West Wickham 301
West Witton 535
Westcliff-on-Sea 166
Westcote Barton 393
Wester Balgedie 658
Westerham 232
Westfield Stratford City 286
Westgate 150
Westgate-on-Sea 232
Westhoughton 334
Westminster 302
Weston by Welland 367
Weston 427
Weston-super-Mare 414
Westport 414
Westwood 383
Westwoodside 274

Wetheral 99
Weybourne 359
Weybridge 446
Weymouth 139
Whaley Bridge 112
Whalley Range 334
Whalley 249
Wheathampstead 209
Whichford 479
Whimple 130
Whipsnade 42
Whiston
  Staffordshire 427
  Yorkshire (South) 547
Whitbourne 200
Whitby 535
Whitchurch
  Hampshire 195
  Shropshire 400
Whitebridge 646
Whitecroft 180
Whitehall 302
Whitehaven 99
Whitehill 195
Whitehough 112
Whiteparish 504
Whiteshill 180
Whitley Bay 472
Whitminster 180
Whitstable 233
Whittlesey 67
Whittlesford 67
Whitton 314
Whitwick 259
Wibsey 564
Wick 646
Wickhambreaux 233
Wicklewood 360
Wickwar 180
Widdington 166
Widecombe in the Moor 130
Widnes 77
Wigan 334
Wigginton 209
Wigston Magna 259
Wigtown 629
Wildhill 209
Wildmoor 511
Willenhall 493
Willey 479
Willingham by Stow 275
Willington
  Derbyshire 112
  Durham 151
Williton 415
Willoughton 275
Wilmslow 77
Wilnecote 427
Wilpshire 249
Wilton 504
Wimbledon 305
Wincanton 415
Winchester 195
Winchfield 196
Winchmore Hill 290
Windermere 99
Windsor 49
Wing 58
Wingfield 42
Winkfield 50
Winkton 140
Winmarleigh 249
Winsford 77

Winsley 504
Winslow 58
Winsor 196
Winster 99
Wintersett 564
Winterton 275
Winterton-on-Sea 360
Wirksworth 112
Wisbech 67
Wishaw 641
Wistow 67
Witherslack 99
Withington 200
Withyham 456
Witney 393
Witton Gilbert 151
Witton le Wear 151
Wiveliscombe 415
Wivelsfield Green 456
Wivenhoe 166
Woburn Sands 58
Woking 446
Wokingham 50
Wollaston 493
Wolsingham 151
Wolverhampton 493
Wombourne 427
Wombwell 547
Wooburn Common 58
Wood Street 447
Woodbastwick 360
Woodbridge 436
Woodchester 180
Woodchurch 233
Woodford Green 286
Woodford
  Greater Manchester 335
  Northamptonshire 367
Woodham Mortimer 166
Woodsetton 495
Woodside 50
Woodstock 393
Woodthorpe 112
Wookey Hole 415
Woolaston Common 180
Woolmer Green 209
Woolpit 437
Woolton, Liverpool 342
Woolwich 296
Wootton 42
Worcester 511
Wordsley 495
Worksop 383
Wormadale, Shetland 654
Wormshill 233
Worsley 335
Worth Matravers 140
Worthing 464
Worthington 335
Wortley 547
Wortwell 360
Wotton-under-Edge 180
Wrantage 415
Wray 249
Wreay 99
Wrexham 594
Wrightington 249
Writtle 166
Wrotham 233

Wycombe Marsh 58
Wylam 373
Wymeswold 259
Wymondham 360
Wysall 383

Y
Yapton 464
Yarde Down 131
Yardley Hastings 367
Yarm 536
Yarmouth 212
Yattendon 50
Yaxley 437
Yealmpton 131
Yeovil 415
Ynystawe 577
York 536
Yoxall 427
Ysceifiog 594
Ystalyfera 577

Z
Zeals 504

Beers index

These beers refer to those in bold type in the breweries section (beers in regular production) and so therefore do not include seasonal, special or occasional beers that may be mentioned elsewhere in the text.

CB1 Best Bitter Cambridge
Moonshine 713
Ceilidh Williams 870
Celebration Ale Conwy 720
Ulverston 858
Celebration Maypole 791
Porterhouse 880
Celestial Blonde Full Moon 746
Cellar Vee Summerskills 844
Celt Bleddyn Celt Experience 715
Celt Bronze Celt Experience 715
Celt Cryf Celt Experience 715
Celt Dark Age Celt Experience 715
Celt Golden Celt Experience 715
Celt Iron Age Celt Experience 715
Celt Native Storm Celt
Experience 715
Celt Red Castle Cream Celt
Experience 715
Celtic Black Ale Hebridean 761
Celtic Gold Hereford 762
Celtic Pride Felinfoel 740
Celtic Queen Iceni 770
Celtica Great Orme 753
Centennial Fernandes 741
Centurion Dow Bridge 732
Centurion's Ghost Ale York 877
Cereal Killer North Yorkshire 803
Chained Oak Peakstones
Rock 813
Chalk Stream Ramsbury 820
Challenger II Small Paul's 837
Challenger Copper Dragon 721
Kingstone 778
Chamberlain Pale Ale Two
Towers 857
Chancellors Revenge
Shardlow 832
Chardonnayle Bob's 699
Charger St George's 829
Charlie's Angel Springhead 839
Chase Bitter Blythe 698
Chasewater Bitter Beowulf 692
Chatsworth Gold Peak Ales 813
Chaucer Ale Green Dragon 754
Chawden Aur Nant 799
CHB Chalk Hill 716
Cheap Street Sherborne 833
Cheeky Pheasant George
Wright 875
Cheltenham Flyer Humpty
Dumpty 769
Chennai Kissingate 779
Cherry Blonde Enville 736
Cherry Diva New Plassey 801
Cherry Porter Copthorne 721
Cherry Stout Bartrams 688
Nook 802
Chesbrewnette Lion's Tale 783
Cheshire Cat Weetwood 863
Cheshire Gold Coach House 718
Cheshire IPA Dunham
Massey 733
Chesterfield Best Bitter Spire 839
Chestnut Mare Worsthorne 875
Chestnut Burton Old Cottage 710
Chevin Light Briscoe's 706
CHH Bryncelyn 708
CHI P A Gribble 755
Chiddingstone Larkins 780
Chief Green Mill 754
Child Catcher Halifax Steam 757
Chilli Hopstar 768
Chiltern Ale Chiltern 716
Chinook Blonde Goose Eye 750

Chiswick Bitter Fuller's 745
Chivalry Medieval 792
Choc Pot 80/- Tinpot 849
Chocolate Cherry Mild Dunham
Massey 733
Chocolate Marble Marble 790
Chocolate Nutter Why Not 868
Chocolate Orange Stout
Amber 680
Cambridge Moonshine 713
Chocolate & Vanilla Stout
Titanic 851
Chocolate Wheat Artisan 683
The Chocolatier Hop Fuzz 767
Chorlton Pale Ale Bootleg 699
Chuffin Ale Box Steam 701
Churches Pale Ale FILO 741
Ciste Dhubh Plockton 816
Citadel Clun 718
Citra Brodie's 707
Oakham 805
Verulam 860
City Gold Golden Triangle 750
City Pale Golden Triangle 750
Clansman Ale Hebridean 761
Claridges Crystal Nobby's 801
Clash London Porter
Revolutions 823
Classic Blonde Clark's 717
Classic Gold Great Western 753
Classic IPA Navigation 799
Classic Old Ale Hepworth 762
Classic Caythorpe 715
Copthorne 721
Hafod 756
Kingstone 778
Norwich Bear 804
Upham 858
Claverhouse Strathaven 843
Cleopatra Derventio 729
Cleric's Cure Three Tuns 849
Clever Fellow Fellows 740
Cliffhanger Brass Castle 703
Clipper IPA Broughton 707
Clippings IPA Flipside 742
Clockin Off Dunscar Bridge 734
Clotworthy Dobbin
Whitewater 867
Cloud Burst Winter's 871
Cloud Nine Six Bells 835
Cloven Hoof Concrete Cow 720
Club Bitter Concertina 719
Clwyd Gold Facer's 738
Clyde Puffer Arran 683
Clydesdale Strathaven 843
Coachman's Best Bitter Coach
House 718
Coal Porter Spire 839
Cobb Town Mill 853
Cobblers Thomas Guest (Black
Country) 695
Cobbydale Bitter Barley
Bottom 687
Cobbydale Blonde Barley
Bottom 687
Cobbydale Gold Barley
Bottom 687
Cobdens Hotel Bitter/Cwrw
Gwesty Cobdens Conwy 721
Cobnut Kent 774
Cock 'n' Bull Story Concrete
Cow 720
Cock o' the North Halifax
Steam 757
Cock O' The Walk Williams 870

Cock Robin Loch Leven 785
Cocker Hoop Jennings 884
Cockfighter Wicked Hathern 869
Cockleroy Alechemy 679
Cockpit (Cadlas Ceiliog)
Denbigh 729
Code Black Hardknott 759
Codger Cotswold Spring 723
Coff-Stout-ee 4Ts 677
Coffee & Oatmeal Stout
Dungarvan 879
Coffee Porter Muirhouse 798
Coffee Stout Binghams 693
Coffin Lane Stout Ashover 684
Coffin Nail Mr Grundys 798
Coggeshall Gold Red Fox 822
Cold Fell Geltsdale 748
Colin's Bitter & Twisty
Weard'Ale 863
Colley's Dog Tring 854
Collie Wobbles Watermill 862
Collingwood Festival Ale
Wylam 876
Columbo Otley 811
Columbus Bottle Brook 700
Comanche Copthorne 721
Comeragh Challenger
Dungarvan 879
Comet Globe 749
Commando Hoofing Cotleigh 722
Comrade Bill Bartram's
Egalitarian Anti-Imperialist
Soviet Stout Bartrams 688
Conkerwood Lord Conrad's 787
Conqueror Windsor & Eton 871
Conservation Bitter Red
Squirrel 823
Continuum Hardknott 759
Cooking Grainstore 752
Cool Fusion Hardknott 759
Cool Runnings Sleaford 836
Coopers WPA Wickwar 869
Copper Ale Palmers 812
Copper Cascade Stewart 840
Copper Coast Dungarvan 879
Copper Fox Mayfields 791
Copper Nob Tonbridge 852
Copper Penny Flipside 742
Copper Plate Irwell Works 772
Copper Top Old Dairy 807
Copper Ennerdale 736
Geltsdale 748
Hunsbury Craft 770
Wainstones 861
Copperhead Whitewater 867
Coppice Light Coppice Side 721
Coppice Worth 875
Coppy Lane Stables 840
Corby Ale Cumberland 725
Corby Blonde Cumberland 725
Core Commander Nelson 800
Corn Dolly Three Castles 848
Corncrake Orkney 810
Cornerstone Keystone 777
Cornish Arvor Penpont 814
Cornish Blonde Skinner's 836
Cornish Coaster Sharp's 887
Cornish Gribben Wooden
Hand 873
Cornish Knocker Ale
Skinner's 836
Cornish Riviera Coastal 718
Cornish Shag Roseland 826
Cornish Sunset Golden Ale
Rebel 821

Deeside Pale Ale
Brewmeister *704*
Dek Driftwood *733*
Delapre Dark Great Oakley *753*
Deliverance Cambrinus (Liverpool Organic) *784*
Delph Donkey Greenfield *754*
Demon Black DemonBrew *728*
Denbury Dreamer Hunter's *770*
Dengie Best Wibblers *869*
Deputy Drop Merry Miner *792*
Derail Ale Box Steam *701*
Derby Porter Wicked Hathern *869*
Derbyshire Gold Wentwell *865*
Dere Street Mithril *795*
Derwent Blonde Derwent *729*
Desert Aire Ridgeside *824*
Desert Storm Storm *841*
Deuchars IPA Caledonian *888*
Deux Citra AllGates *680*
Deverill's Advocate Wessex *865*
Devil Best Devilfish *730*
Devil's Elbow Hexhamshire *763*
Devil's Garden Frodsham *744*
Devil's Nightmare Cathedral Heights *715*
Devils Dream Ole Slewfoot *810*
Devils Dyke Porter SouthDowns *838*
Devil's Water Hexhamshire *763*
Devolution Amber Ale Revolutions *823*
Devon Darter Clearwater *717*
Devon Dew Summerskills *844*
Devon Dumpling Bays *690*
Devon Dympsy Clearwater *717*
Devon Earth Devon Earth *730*
Devon Glory Exe Valley *737*
Devon Pride South Hams *838*
Devonshire Cat Pale Ale Brew Company *704*
DHB (Dave's Hoppy Beer) Facer's *738*
Diablo Summer Wine *844*
Diamond Geezer By the Horns *712*
Diamond Nine Copthorne *721*
Diana Mild Whalebone *866*
Dick Turpin Coach House *718*
Dickies Dunkel Strands *842*
Dictators Concertina *719*
Diesel Colchester *719*
Diggers Gold Grey Trees *755*
Dinner Ale Bollington *699*
Dinting Arches Howard Town *769*
Dionysus Milton *795*
Dipper Royal Tunbridge Wells *827*
Directionless RedWillow *823*
Dirty Blond Hellhound *761*
Dirty Rat Rat *820*
Discovery Captain Cook *714*
Forge *742*
Fuller's *745*
Dishy Debbie Hart of Preston *759*
Dissolution IPA Kirkstall *778*
Dive Bomber Funfair *746*
Dixie's Bollards DarkTribe *727*
Dixie's Mild DarkTribe *727*
Dixon's Major Riverside *825*
Dixon's Old Diabolical Riverside *825*
Dizzy Blonde ABC *678*
Robinson's *825*
Dizzy Danny Ale Hopstar *768*
Dizzy Dick North Yorkshire *803*

DNA (Dark Nomadic Ale) Dancing Man *726*
Dobber Marble *790*
Dob's Best Bitter Exe Valley *737*
Dobcross Bitter Greenfield *754*
Dobles' Dog Wicked Hathern *869*
Dockside Dark Gloucester *749*
Doctor Johnsons Leatherbritches *780*
Dodgem Funfair *746*
Doff Cocker Three B's *848*
Dog Idle *771*
Dogth Vader Watermill *862*
Dogwatch Stout Nelson *800*
Dolly Daydream Ship Inn *834*
Dominator Hopdaemon *767*
Doodle Stout Binghams *694*
Doom Bar Sharp's *887*
Doris's 90th Birthday Ale Hesket Newmarket *762*
Dorothy Goodbody's Golden Ale Wye Valley *876*
Dorothy Goodbody's Wholesome Stout Wye Valley *876*
Dorset Gold Palmers *812*
Double Dragon Felinfoel *740*
Double Espresso Wild Oat Stout Traditional Scottish Ales *853*
Double Gold Phoenix *815*
Double Header RCH *821*
Double Hop Robinson's *825*
Double Mash Derby *729*
Double Maxim Maxim *791*
Double MM Mild Moles *795*
Double Momentum Hopshackle *768*
Double Six Fernandes *741*
Double Standard Nine Standards *801*
Double Stout Hook Norton *766*
Double Sunset Leek *781*
Douglas Valley Mayflower *791*
Dovedale Leatherbritches *780*
Dover Beck Caythorpe *715*
Dow Bridge Dark (DBD) Dow Bridge *732*
Downpour Storm *842*
Dozy Bull Swaton *845*
DPA Peak Ales *813*
Dr Heale Heddon Valley *761*
Dr Hexter's Healer West Berkshire *866*
Dr Hexter's Wedding Ale West Berkshire *866*
Dr Okell's IPA Okells *806*
Dr Samuel Johnson Haywood Bad Ram *760*
Draft Marble *789*
Dragon Slayer B&T *685*
Dragon Smoke Stout Beowulf *692*
Dragon Bowland *700*
Dragon's Blood Sawbridgeworth *831*
Dragon's Breath New Plassey *801*
Dragonhead Orkney *810*
Dragons Blood St George's *829*
Dragons Gold Middle Earth *793*
Dragonslayer Merlin *792*
Draught Bass Marston's *884*
Draught Burton Ale Lees (Carlsberg UK) *886*

Draymans Best Bitter Branscombe Vale *703*
Dreadnought Chalk Hill *716*
Nottingham *804*
Dreckly Forge *742*
Driver's Bitter Attwood *685*
Drop of Nelson's Blood Farmer's Ales *739*
Drovers 80/- Tryst *855*
Druid's Fluid Wizard *872*
Drum Beat Treboom *854*
Drummer Boy Grey Trees *755*
Drunken Duck George Wright *875*
Drunkun Duck Green Duck (Grafton) *751*
Dry Hop Franklin's *743*
Dry Stout O'Hanlon's *804*
DSB (Dove Street Bitter) Dove Street *732*
Dubonni Saxon City *831*
Duck 'n' Dive Mallard *789*
Duck Blond Green Duck (Grafton) *751*
Ducking Stool Mayfields *791*
Duckling Mallard *789*
Dudbridge Donkey Nailsworth *798*
Due South Strathbraan *843*
Duke Masters *790*
Dun Cow Bitter Hill Island *764*
Dunham Dark Dunham Massey *733*
Dunham Gold Dunham Massey *733*
Dunham Light Dunham Massey *733*
Dunham Milk Stout Dunham Massey *733*
Dunham Porter Dunham Massey *733*
Dunham Stout Dunham Massey *733*
Dunstable Giant B&T *685*
Durdle Door Dorset *731*
Dursley Steam Bitter Severn Vale *832*
Dusk Ruby Bitter Cross Bay *724*
Dusky Maiden Stout New Plassey *801*
Dusty Penny Flipside *742*
Dynamo Wantsum *861*

E

Eagle IPA Wells & Young's *885*
Earl's Ale Tollgate *851*
Earl's RDA Island *773*
East Anglian Pale Ale Cox & Holbrook *724*
Humpty Dumpty *770*
East Coast Mild Waveney *863*
East End Mild Tap East *845*
East India Pale Ale Dunham Massey *733*
Tunnel *856*
Whitstable *868*
East Street Cream RCH *821*
Eastgate Ale Weetwood *863*
Easy Rider Kelham Island *776*
Ebony Moon Tonbridge *852*
Ebony Stout Wood Street *874*
Ebulum Williams *870*
Eccles Cake Ale Garthela *747*
Eclipse Blue Buzzard *698*
Untapped *858*

Formidable Ale/FA Robert
Cain *712*
Fortitude Wantsum *861*
Fortyniner Ringwood *884*
Fosse Ale Dow Bridge *732*
Fossil Fuel Isle of Purbeck *773*
Foundation Bitter East
London *734*
Foundation Stone
Lymestone *787*
Foundryman's Gold Canterbury
Brewers *714*
Four Seasons' Ale Halfpenny *757*
Four XT *876*
Fox Glove Slightly Foxed *837*
Fox on the Run Ole Slewfoot *810*
Fox Exmoor *738*
Foxtale Ale Alcazar *679*
Foxy Blonde Scottish Borders *831*
Foxy Lady Joseph Herbert
Smith *775*
Fra Diavolo Ulverston *858*
Fraid Not Exeter *737*
Framboisen Bier Strands *842*
Frank's 3rd Leg Landlord's
Friend *779*
Fraoch Heather Ale Williams *870*
Freak Show Hop Monster *767*
Freight Goodall's *750*
Frenchmans Creek Lizard *784*
Fresher Ale Plymouth *816*
Friar Tuck St George's *829*
Friar Weisse Franciscan Well *879*
Friendship Porter
Redemption *822*
Frigate Irving *772*
Friggin' in the Riggin'
Nelson *800*
Frightened Pheasant Blue
Bell *698*
Frothingham Best Great
Newsome *753*
Fruit Bat B&T *685*
Fruit De La Lune Strands *842*
Fruitcase Hopping Mad *768*
Fruiterer's Mild Cannon
Royall *713*
Fruits of the Forest
Rockingham *826*
Fruity Little Number Opa
Hay's *810*
Frydeal Frys *745*
FSB (Front Street Bitter)
Handley's *758*
Fubar Tiny Rebel *850*
Fuggle-Dee-Dum Goddards *749*
Fuggles Pale Swan *844*
Full Ahead DarkTribe *727*
Full Bore Hunter's *770*
Full Circle West Berkshire *866*
Full Monty Barlow *687*
Full Sail Pale Ale Galway Bay *879*
Full Toss Toft *851*
Full Whack Peerless *814*
Fully Fitted Freight
Muirhouse *798*
Fully Laden Geeves *748*
Fulstow Common Fulstow *746*
Funky Monkey Milk Street *794*
Funnel Blower Box Steam *701*
Fur Stoat Goodall's *750*
Fuzzy Duck Gribble *755*
Fyre Fyfe *746*

G

Gadds' Dogbolter Ramsgate *820*
Gadds' No. 3 Ramsgate *820*
Gadds' No. 5 Ramsgate *820*
Gadds' No. 7 Ramsgate *820*
Gadds' Seasider Ramsgate *820*
Galapagos Stout Darwin *727*
Galaxy Cream Strands *842*
Galaxy Rowton *827*
Gale Force Longhill *786*
Galleon Gold Argyll *682*
Galloway Gold Sulwath *844*
Gambit Summer Wine *844*
Game Bird Scottish Borders *831*
Game Keeper Milestone *793*
Ganges Harwich Town *760*
Gannet Mild Earl Soham *734*
Gardener's Tap Prior's Well *818*
Gargoyles Best Bitter Isca *772*
Gargoyles Citra Isca *772*
Gargoyles Dawlish Ale Isca *772*
Gargoyles Dawlish Bitter
Isca *772*
Gargoyles Dawlish Pale Isca *772*
Gargoyles Golden Ale Isca *772*
Gargoyles Milk Maid Mild
Isca *772*
Gargoyles Napier Isca *772*
Gargoyles Summer Ale Isca *772*
Gargoyles Wheat Isca *772*
Garsdale Smokebox Yorkshire
Dales *878*
Gate Hopper Maypole *791*
GB White Park *867*
Geek Unique Beer Geek *691*
Gem Bath Ales *689*
General Picton Rhymney *824*
Genesis Goody *750*
Geniuss Winter's *871*
Geordie Pride Mordue *797*
Georgie's Pebble Red *821*
GFB/Gilbert's First Brew Hop
Back *766*
Ghost Ship Adnams *679*
Ghost Partners *813*
Gillingham Pale Small Paul's *837*
Gilt Complex Surrey Hills *844*
Ginger Bear Beartown *690*
Ginger Cob Shires *834*
Ginger Doodle Stout
Binghams *694*
Ginger Explosion Traditional
Scottish Ales *853*
Ginger Fix Tigertops *849*
Ginger Helmet
Leatherbritches *781*
Ginger Jakey Argyll *682*
Ginger Marble Marble *790*
Ginger Panther Panther *812*
Ginger Tom Hoskins Bros
(Belvoir) *692*
Ginger Tosser Skinner's *835*
Ginger Enville *737*
Uncle Stuarts *858*
Gingernut Premium Coach
House *718*
Ginja Ninja Vibrant Forest *860*
Gisleham Gold Trinity *854*
GJE Shed *832*
Glamaig Cuillin *725*
Glen Top Rossendale *827*
Glencoe Wild Oat Stout
Traditional Scottish Ales *853*
Gloriette Corfe Castle *721*
Glorious Devon Isca *772*

Glory Yeovil *877*
Glotts Hop Howard Town *769*
Go West Sleaford *836*
Goat's Leap IPA Cheddar Ales *716*
Goat's Milk Church End *717*
Gobble Great Oakley *753*
Goblin Fallons *738*
Godfathers Itchen Valley *774*
An Gof Lizard *784*
Gog Magog Golden Ale
Ha'penny *758*
Going Underground Merry
Miner *792*
Gold Ale Glenfinnan *748*
World's End *875*
Gold Award Eastwood *735*
Gold Beacons Brecon *703*
Gold Crest Litton *783*
Gold Digger Bank Top *686*
Blue Ball *697*
Gold Medal Linfit *782*
Gold Muddler Andwell *681*
Gold Pot 70/- Tinpot *849*
Gold Rush Prospect *818*
Gold Spice Keystone *777*
Gold Standard Keystone *777*
Nine Standards *801*
Gold Star Strong Ale
Goacher's *749*
Gold Tankard Wylam *876*
Gold Top Old Dairy *808*
Gold Torpedo Traditional Scottish
Ales *853*
Gold Bays *690*
Bowland *700*
Brentwood *704*
Britannia *706*
Butcombe *711*
Buxton *711*
Cairngorm *712*
Cap House *714*
Chalk Hill *716*
Copthorne *721*
Cuerden *725*
Dancing Duck *726*
Doghouse *731*
Eden *735*
Exmoor *738*
Festival (Cotswold Lion) *723*
FILO *741*
Geltsdale *748*
Gloucester *749*
Gower *751*
Grainstore *752*
Green Dragon *754*
Green Mill *754*
Hop Studio *768*
Hunter's *770*
Ilkley *771*
Ironbridge *772*
Kemptown *776*
Kingstone *778*
Ludlow *787*
Lytham *788*
Mersea Island *793*
Neath *800*
Ramsbury *820*
Sawbridgeworth *831*
Sixpenny *835*
Tap House *845*
Tatton *846*
Uffa *857*
Union *858*
Vens *859*

Hampshire Rose Itchen Valley *774*
Hancock's HB Brains (Molson Coors) *887*
Handliner Coastal *718*
Handsome Forge *742*
Hanged Monk Tipples *850*
Hanois Island Stout Randalls *820*
Happiness Richmond *824*
Happy Chappy Cromarty *724*
Happy Jack Swaton *845*
Harbour Special Tintagel *849*
Hare O' The Dog Weard'Ale *863*
Hare of the Dog Why Not *868*
Harlequin Best Bitter Brew Company *704*
Harlequin Blonde Brew Company *704*
Harpers Great Oakley *753*
Harrier Cotleigh *722*
Harrowby Pale Ale Oldershaw *808*
Hart IPA Hart of Stebbing *759*
Hart of Oak Jollyboat *775*
Hartington Bitter Whim *867*
Hartington IPA Whim *867*
Hartland Blonde Forge *742*
Hartlebury Tipple Cannon Royall *714*
Hartleys XB Robinson's *825*
Harvest Moon Mild Cambridge Moonshine *713*
Harvest Moon Grain *751*
Harvest Pale Castle Rock *714*
Harvest Sun Williams *870*
Hathern Cross Wicked Hathern *869*
Haven Frys *745*
Hawthorn Gold Wicked Hathern *869*
Hay Bluff Golden Valley *750*
Haystacks Hesket Newmarket *762*
Hazy Daze Ginger Clockwork *718*
HBB/Hogs Back Bitter Hogs Back *765*
Heacham Gold Fox *743*
Head East Strathbraan *843*
Head Otter *811*
Headcracker Woodforde's *874*
Headland Red Wold Top *872*
Headless Dog College Green (Hilden) *764*
Headless RedWillow *823*
Heanor Pale Ale Bottle Brook *700*
Heart Quartz *819*
Hearty Bitter Yorkshire Heart *878*
Heath Robinson Barlow *687*
Heavenly Blonde Oldershaw *808*
Hebden's Wheat Little Valley *783*
Hebridean Gold Isle of Skye *774*
Heck's Angel Great Heck *752*
Hedge Monkey Glastonbury *748*
HedgeHopper Mobberley *795*
Hedgerow Gold Sleaford *836*
Hedgerow Seville Sleaford *836*
Hedgerow Silver Sleaford *836*
Heel Stone Stonehenge *841*
Hefeweiss Harbour *758*
Helford River Lizard *784*
Heligan Honey Skinner's *836*
Hell Beck Geltsdale *748*
Hell Cat Fat Cat *740*
Helles Style Lager Artisan *683*

Helles Canterbury Brewers *714*
Royal Tunbridge Wells *827*
Hells Lager Camden Town *713*
Helmsman North Star *803*
Helvellyn Gold Hesket Newmarket *762*
Helvick Gold Dungarvan *879*
Hen Cloud Leek *781*
Hen Harrier Bowland *700*
Hengist Wantsum *861*
Henrietta Welbeck Abbey *864*
Henry's IPA Wadworth *860*
Hequinox Great Heck *752*
Heracles Hop Back *766*
Herald Cambrinus (Liverpool Organic) *784*
Herefordshire Light Ale Hereford *762*
Herefordshire Owd Bull Hereford *762*
Heresy Bishop Nick *694*
Heritage Smiles (Highgate) *763*
Three Castles *848*
Hetton Pale Ale Dark Horse *726*
Hewish IPA RCH *820*
Hewish Mild RCH *821*
Hibernator Old Bear *807*
Hicks Special Draught/HSD St Austell *829*
High as a Kite Heart of Wales *761*
High Five Willy Good *870*
High Light Trinity *854*
High Noon Six Trees *835*
High Octane Silverstone *835*
High Pike Hesket Newmarket *762*
High Street Bitter Tollgate *851*
High Tor Buxton *711*
Highgate Hartshorns *759*
Highlander Fyne *747*
Highwayman Buntingford *709*
Highwire Magic Rock *789*
Hilbre Gold Peerless *813*
Hill Climb Prescott *817*
Hill Fort Whittlebury *871*
Hip Hop Green Bullet Art Brew *683*
Hip Hop Langham *780*
Historic Porter Hopshackle *768*
The Hoard Backyard *686*
Hobby Horse Rhymney *824*
Hobgoblin Wychwood *885*
Hobs Best Mild Hoskins Bros (Belvoir) *692*
Hobs Bitter Hoskins Bros (Belvoir) *692*
Hobson's Choice City of Cambridge (Wolf) *873*
Hogshead Cotswold Pale Ale Uley *857*
Hole Hearted Oakleaf *805*
Holly Hop Bryncelyn *708*
Holy Cow Scottish Borders *831*
Holy Joe Yates' *877*
Holy Trinity Yorkshire *878*
Home IPA Magpie *789*
Honey Bear Cannon Royall *713*
Honey Bee Three B's *848*
Honey Blonde Downton *732*
White Rose *867*
Honey Bunny North Yorkshire *803*
Honey Buzzard Cotleigh *722*
Honey Cat Fat Cat *740*
Honey Dragon Middle Earth *793*

Honey Fayre/Cwrw Mel Conwy *720*
Honey Mild DarkTribe *727*
Honey Smacker Saddleworth *828*
Honey Bees *691*
Honeyfuzz Rother Valley *827*
Honeypot Bitter Coach House *718*
Honeypot Old Bear *806*
Hood Cannon Royall *714*
Lincoln Green *782*
Hooky Bitter Hook Norton *766*
Hooky Dark Hook Norton *766*
Hooky Gold Hook Norton *766*
Hop A Doodle Doo Brewster's *705*
Hop as Hell Woodlands *874*
Hop Baby Kings Head *778*
Hop Beast Liverpool Craft *784*
Hop Bomb Sadler's *828*
Hop Devil Rockingham *826*
Hop Garden Gold Hogs Back *765*
Hop Gear Barrowden *688*
Hop Monster Brew Company *704*
Coastal *718*
Hop Ripper IPA Brew Company *704*
Hop Smacker Saddleworth *828*
Hop & Soul Indian Summer *771*
Hop Till You Drop Derby *729*
Hop Token: Amarillo Adur *679*
Hop Token: Summit Adur *679*
Hop Trial Tryst *855*
Hop Twister Salopian *830*
Hop Blackedge *695*
Hop On Langton *780*
Hopdance Full Moon *746*
Hope & Glory Brentwood *704*
Hopfest Red Squirrel *823*
Hophead Brewster's *705*
Dark Star *727*
Porterhouse *880*
Hopleaf Buffy's *708*
Hopnosis Hopshackle *768*
Hopnotch Hopping Mad *767*
Hopper Hafod *756*
Prospect *818*
Hoppers Ale Rother Valley *827*
Hoppin Robin Rockin Robin *826*
Hoppiness Hopping Mad *767*
Moor *796*
Thame *847*
Hoppit Loddon *786*
Magpie *789*
Hoppy Gold ABC *678*
Hoppy Harrington Sherfield Village *833*
Hoppy Helper Wibblers *869*
Hoppy Hen Felstar *740*
Hoppy Ness Loch Ness *785*
Hops 4 Heroes 8 Sail *677*
Hopsack Phoenix *815*
Hopscotch Sportsman *839*
Summerskills *844*
Hopsession Naked *799*
Hopspur Redemption *822*
Horizon Wadworth *860*
Hornblower Old Cannon *807*
Horsham Best Bitter King *777*
Hot Dog Chilli Stout Binghams *694*
Hot Stuff Chilli Beer Red Rat *822*
Hotel Porter Farmer's Ales *739*
House Hektors *761*
Howden Bittern Bird Brain *694*

Jolly Fellows Fellows 740
Jorvik Blonde Rudgate 828
Joseph Williamson Liverpool Organic 784
Josephine Butler Liverpool Organic 784
Jouster Goff's 749
Joyces Choice Bridgetown 706
JPA Sadler's 828
JR Best Raw 820
JRT Best Bitter Yorkshire Heart 878
JTS XXX John Thompson 847
Jubilee IPA Blue Anchor 697
Jubilee Stout Kirkby Lonsdale 778
Junction Ale Sambrook's 830
Jurassic Dorset 731
Jurgen's Jungle Juice Muirhouse 798
Just Married Cathedral Heights 715
Justinian Milton 795
JWB (James Wilson Bitter) Tap East 845

K

K&B Sussex Bitter Hall & Woodhouse (Badger) 757
Kamikaze Dent 729
Katalyst Hardknott 759
Katie's Pride Corvedale 722
Katy's Blonde Owenshaw Mill 811
Keel Over Skinner's 836
Keelman Brown Big Lamp 693
Keep Calm & Carry On St George's 829
Keepers Gold Wall's 861
Kellyhopter White Park 867
Kelpie Williams 870
Kennet Valley Ramsbury 820
Kent's Best Shepherd Neame 833
Kentish Best Millis 794
Kentish Dark Millis 794
Kentish Red Ale Millis 794
Kentish Reserve Whitstable 868
Kenyons Original Oatmeal Stout Golden Valley 750
Kernow Gold Lizard 784
Kernow Imperial Stout Coastal 718
Kessog Dark Ale Loch Lomond 785
Kettle Drum Treboom 854
Kew Green Botanist 699
Keystone Hops Weatheroak 863
KGB (Kent Golding Bitter) Kent 776
Khaki Sergeant Strong Stout Wissey Valley 872
Khyber Kinver 778
Kildonan An Teallach 681
Killellan Houston 769
Killer Bee Darwin 727
Kiln House Shardlow 832
Kilt Lifter Argyll 682
Kinder Downfall Buxton 711
Kinder Stout Buxton 711
Kinder Sunset Buxton 711
King John Andwell 681
King Rat Rat 820
King Keltek 776
King's Ale Merlin 792
Kingdom Tap House 845

Kingmaker Warwickshire 862
Kings Regiment Liverpool One 784
Kingsdown Special Ale Arkell's 682
King's Shilling Cannon Royall 713
King's Shipment IPA Compass 719
Kingston Flyer KPA Stonehouse 841
Kingston Topaz Newby Wyke 801
Kipling Thornbridge 847
Kislingbury Bitter Hoggleys 765
Kiss Me Naked 799
Kitty Wilkinson Chocolate & Vanilla Stout Liverpool Organic 784
Kiwi IPA Maypole 792
Kiwi Patriot 813
Knight Hood Medieval 792
Knight of the Garter Windsor & Eton 871
Knocker Up Three B's 848
Knockmealdown Porter Eight Degrees 879
Kodiak Gold Beartown 690
Kohinoor Windsor & Eton 871
Kooky Gold Offbeat 806
Kraftwerk Braun Ale Revolutions 824
Kynance Blonde Cornish Chough 722

L

LA Gold Anchor Springs 680
Lacey's Ale Country Life 723
LadeBack Trossach's Craft (Traditional Scottish Ales) 854
LadeOut Trossach's Craft (Traditional Scottish Ales) 854
Lady Hamilton Pocket 817
Lady Julia Grafton 751
Lady of the Lake Glastonbury 748
Laf Deeside 728
Lager Clockwork 718
Cotswold 723
Geltsdale 748
Pitfield 816
Lagonda IPA Marble 790
Laguna Seca Burley Street 709
Laid Back Lucille Blue Ball 697
Lakeland Gold Hawkshead 760
Lambeth Walk By the Horns 712
Lambton's Maxim 791
Lamp Light Big Lamp 693
Lamplight Porter Longdog 786
Lancashire Best Bitter Hart of Preston 759
Lancashire Gold Hopstar 768
Lancashire Stout Mayflower 791
Lancaster Bomber Thwaites 849
Lancastrian Gold Fallons 738
Land of Hop & Glory Spire 839
Landlady Kings Head 777
Landlord Timothy Taylor 846
Landlords Choice Moles 796
Landmark Waen 861
Landslide Facer's 738
Langdale Cumbrian Legendary 725
Langham Special Draught/LSD Langham 780
Langley Best Leadmill 780
Large One Keystone 777

Last Post Muirhouse 798
Last Waltz Dancing Man 726
Late Red Shepherd Neame 833
Latitude Atlas (Orkney) 810
Laugh and Titter Old Cross 807
Laughing Gravy Ulverston 858
Laurie Lee's Bitter Uley 857
Lavender Honey Wolf 872
Lawless Bootleg 699
Laycock DB 728
Layla Lager Sleaford 836
Lazy Days St George's 829
Lazy Daze Happy Valley 758
LDA (Light Dry Ale) Silhill 834
Leadboiler Linfit 783
Leading Light Litton 783
Leading Lights Harwich Town 760
Leann Follain Stout Carlow 879
Leezie Lundie Ayr 685
Legend of the Golden Geek Beer Geek 691
Legend Dartmoor 727
May Hill 791
Norwich Bear 804
Nottingham 804
Leghorn Rooster's 826
Legion Dow Bridge 732
Legless Cow May Hill 791
Legless Rambler Beachy Head 690
Leipzig Wellington Inn 864
Lemon Blossom Hornbeam 768
Lemon Dream Salopian 830
Lemon and Ginger Humpty Dumpty 769
Lemongrass and Ginger Leatherbritches 780
Leprechaun Stout Bank Top 686
Let Battle Commence Battlefield (Tunnel) 856
Letargion Abraham Thompson 847
Level Best Rother Valley 827
Level Headed North Curry 802
The Leveller Springhead 839
Levelly Black Shalford 832
Levelly Gold Shalford 832
Leviathan Hopdaemon 767
Leyburn Shawl Yorkshire Dales 878
LFB Golden Duck 750
Lia Fail Inveralmond 772
Liberation Ale Liberation 782
Liberation Suthwyk (Oakleaf) 805
Lickerish Stout Abraham Thompson 847
Lickety Spit Lord Conrad's 787
Lidstone's Rowley Mild Wensleydale 864
Lifeboat Titanic 851
Light Ale Gwaun Valley 756
Jacobi 774
Light Brigade Leyden 782
Light But Dark Old Spot 809
Light Cascade Hardknott 758
Light Mild/1863 Hydes 770
Light Nancy Bollington 699
Light Ness Loch Ness 785
Light Oak Weatheroak 863
Woodlands 874
Light Rale Ashover 684
Light Hafod 756
Harbour 758
Liverpool One 784
Moulin 798

Merry Maidens Mild Coastal 718
Merry Miller 8 Sail 677
Merry Mount Morton 797
Mersey Mist Liverpool One 784
Mersey Porter DB 728
Methane Merry Miner 792
Metropolis Colchester 719
Micawber's Mild Mauldons 790
Michael's Mild Hereward 762
Midhurst Mild Ballard's 686
Midnight Bell Leeds 781
Midnight Mass Julian Church 716
Midnight Mild New Plassey 801
Midnight Owl Castle Rock 715
Midnight Porter Magpie 789
Midnight Runner Sleaford 837
Midnight Stout Woodlands 874
Midnight Sun Williams 870
Midnight Monty's 796
  Nutbrook 804
Midnycht Myld Luckie 787
Midshipman Dark Mild
  Nelson 800
Mike Hawthorn Farnham 739
Mike's Mild FILO 741
  Old Inn 808
Miladys Fancy Shugborough 834
Mild Ale Batham 689
Mild & Easy Wall's 861
Mild Mannered Mae Blue
  Ball 697
Mild Banks's 883
  Branscombe Vale 703
  Buckingham 708
  Buffy's 708
  Cuerden 725
  Higsons (Liverpool
  Organic) 784
  Hobsons 765
  Holt 766
  Okells 806
  Red Fox 822
  Saddleworth 828
  St Peter's 829
  Titanic 851
  Vens 859
  Wessex 865
  Winter's 871
  Woodlands 874
Mildly Rockin Rockin Robin 826
Military Mild Old Chimneys 807
Milk Stout Ouseburn Valley 811
  Pin-Up 815
  Ripple Steam 825
Milky Way Black Hole 696
Mill Lane Mild Hoggleys 765
Mill Town Mild Howard Town 769
Mill Botley 700
The Miller's Ale Canterbury
  Ales 714
Miller's Mirth Wantsum 861
Millwright Mild 8 Sail 677
Miners A Pint Cap House 714
Minion of the Moon Cambridge
  Moonshine 713
Minotaur Milton 795
Mischief Monty's 796
Misleading Lights Harwich
  Town 760
Miss Loosemoor Heddon
  Valley 761
Misty Law Kelburn 775
Misty Mountain Hop Rock &
  Roll 825
Mochyn Hapus Nant 799

Moel Fammau Hafod 756
Moelfre IPA North Wales 803
Moild Pilgrim 815
Mole Catcher Moles 796
Moletrap Bitter Mauldons 790
Molly Malone Hilden 764
Molly's Chocolate Stout College
  Green (Hilden) 764
Molly's Pride North Star 803
Molly's Secret Brandon 702
Money for Old Rope Bespoke 692
Mongrel Marston Moor 790
  Nutbrook 804
Monkey Hanger Poachers 817
Monkey IPA Art Brew 683
Monkey Wrench Daleside 726
Monkeytown Mild Phoenix 815
Monkholme Premium Reedley
  Hallows 823
Monks Gold Howard Town 769
Monstrous Mild Old Bog 807
Montol Driftwood 733
Monty Revenge Nutbrook 804
Monument Ale Townhouse 853
Monument Bitter Tyne Bank 857
Monumental Blonde Kirkby
  Lonsdale 778
Moon Gazer Amber Ale
  Norfolk 802
Moon Gazer Golden Ale
  Norfolk 802
Moon Gazer Ruby Ale
  Norfolk 802
Moon Kissingate 779
Moondance Triple fff 855
Moonlight Arkell's 682
  Grafters 751
Moonraker Lees 781
Moonrocket Tipples 850
Moonshine Abbeydale 678
  White Park 867
Moor Ale Little Valley 783
Moor Top Buxton 711
Moorland Bitter Bridgehouse 705
More Tea Vicar Julian Church 716
More Saddleworth 828
More's Head Wantsum 861
Morland Original Bitter Greene
  King 882
Morocco Ale Daleside 726
Morris Patriot 813
Mountain Dew Traditional
  Scottish Ales 853
Mowbray's Mash Oldershaw 808
Mr Chubb's Lunchtime Bitter
  West Berkshire 865
Mr Hough Landlord's Friend 779
Mr JK's Irish Stout Landlord's
  Friend 779
Mr Marshall Landlord's Friend 779
Mr Murdoch's Golden IPA
  Keltek 776
Mr Sheppard's Crook Exe
  Valley 737
Mr Sluggett Heddon Valley 761
Mr Smith Landlord's Friend 779
Mr Splodge's Mild Thame 847
Mrs Lovett's Most Efficacious
  Stout Porter Ha'penny 758
Mrs Simpson's Thriller in Vanilla
  Porter Brown Cow 707
Muck Cart Mild Son of Sid 837
Muck and Straw Holsworthy 766
Mucky Duck Buffy's 708
  Fuzzy Duck 746

Mud City Stout Sadler's 828
Muddy Boot Red Shoot 823
Mudpuppy Salamander 830
Mug Billy Burscough 709
Muker Silver Yorkshire Dales 878
Munich Cuerden 725
Musselburgh Broke Knops
  (Traditional Scottish Ales) 854
Mutineer Derwent 729
Mutiny Rebellion 821
Mutleys Revenge Hereford 762
Mutts Nuts Hereford 762
Mwnci Nell Nant 799
Mydilsburgh IPA Truefitt 855
Mystery Tor Glastonbury 748
The Mythe Topsham 852

N
N1 Wheat Beer Pitfield 816
Nailbourne Abigale 678
Nailmaker Mild Enville 736
Naked Ladies Twickenham 856
Nameless Ale Tirril 850
Nanny Flyer Leyden 782
Napoleon's Retreat AllGates 680
Nappa Scar Yorkshire Dales 878
Nappertandy Brandon 702
Narrow Boat Shardlow 832
Native Bitter Whitstable 868
Natterjack Frog Island 744
  Southport 838
Natural Blonde Birds 694
  Harviestoun 759
  Pin-Up 815
Natural Selection
  Battledown 689
Navajo Northern 802
Navigator Bees 691
  Tring 854
Navvy Phoenix 815
Neap Tide Teignworthy 846
Nebula Blue Buzzard 698
Nechtan Deeside 728
Neck Oil Beavertown 690
Neckoil Bitter Whalebone 866
Nectar Bitter Attwood 685
Nectar Pale Blue Bee 697
Nectar Galway Hooker 880
Neilsons Sauvin North Riding 803
Nel's Best High House Farm 763
Nelson's Blood Fox 743
  Nelson 800
Nelson's Revenge
  Woodforde's 874
Nemesis Peakstones Rock 813
  Sticklegs 841
Nero Milton 795
Nessies Monster Mash
  Cairngorm 712
Nettle Ale Coles 719
Nettlethrasher Elland 735
New Dawn Alcazar 679
New Forest Ale Downton 732
New Forest Gold Red Shoot 823
New World Pale New Plassey 801
New Zealand Pale Ale Urban 859
Newton Stout Ship Inn 833
Newton's Drop Oldershaw 808
Niamh's Nemesis Five Towns 741
Nice Weather Dancing Duck 726
Nightfall Pale Bitter Cross
  Bay 724
Nightjar Loch Leven 785
Nightlight Mild Elmtree 736

Organic Beer/ROB Ridgeway 824
Organic Best St Peter's 829
Origin Quercus 819
Original (70/-) Devon Ales 730
Original Bitter Bellingers 692
  Hereford 762
  Hydes 770
Original Black Stout Amber 680
Original Blonde White Rose 867
Original No. 1 Vale of
  Glamorgan 859
Original Pale Ale Joules 775
Original Port Stout
  O'Hanlon's 804
Original Standard Nine
  Standards 801
Original Wood Swansea 845
Original Barum 688
  Black Cat 695
  Blue Monkey 698
  Dark Star 727
  Everards 737
  Jacobi 774
  Olde Swan 808
  Sixpenny 835
  Slater's 836
  Thwaites 849
  Twickenham 856
  Willy's 870
Orkney Best Highland 763
Orkney Blast Highland 764
Orkney IPA Highland 764
Orme Great Orme 753
OSB Old Spot 809
Oscar Wilde Mighty Oak 793
Ossian Inveralmond 771
Otters Pocket Marlpool 790
Out Of Step IPA Offbeat 806
Outlandish Pale Offbeat 806
Outwood Bound Five Towns 741
Oven Bottom Blonde
  Garthela 747
Over a Barrel Bespoke 692
Over The Edge Kinver 778
Over the Moon Grafters 751
Over and Stout Goose Eye 751
Over The Top Mr Grundys 798
Ow Do! Six Bells 835
Owd Miner Coppice Side 721
Owd Oak Hydes 770
Own Gear Barrowden 688
Own Sharp's 887
Oxford Gold Brakspear 883
Oxfordshire Black Porter
  Complete Pig 719
OXT'ale Old Cross 807
Oyster Catcher Brancaster
  (Beeston) 691
Oyster Stout Arbor 682
  Porterhouse 880
  Whitstable 868
Oyster Mersea Island 793
Oystercatcher Stout
  Brimstage 706

P

Pacific Pale Ale
  Slaughterhouse 836
Pack Lane Mild Uncle Stuarts 858
Packhorse Worsthorne 875
Paddys Pride Brandon 702
Pageant Ale Elgood's 735
Pail Ale Concrete Cow 720
  Shed 832

Pale Ale Ashley Down 684
  Brewshed 705
  Broughs 707
  Camden Town 713
  Clun 718
  Devon Brewing 730
  East London 734
  Griffin 755
  Kirkstall 778
  Metalman 880
  Navigation 799
  Quantum 819
  Redemption 822
  Richmond 824
  Wood Street 874
  Zerodegrees 878
Pale Amber Sarah Hughes 769
Pale Gold Ossett 810
Pale Moonlight Phoenix 815
Pale Partridge Sleaford 836
Pale Rider Botley 700
  Kelham Island 776
Pale Sunlight Coastal 718
Pale Blackmore 696
  Britannia 706
  Cuerden 725
  Ilkley 771
  Kent 776
  Leeds 781
  Old Pie Factory 809
Palindrome Porter Naked 799
Palmer's Poison Blythe 698
Palmerston's Folly Suthwyk
  (Oakleaf) 805
Paragon Ale Black Paw 696
Parish Bitter Wood 873
Park Life Bollington 699
Parkers City of Cambridge
  (Wolf) 873
Parkeston Porter Harwich
  Town 760
Parson's Nose Julian Church 716
Parsons Pledge Derwent 729
Partridge Best Bitter Dark
  Star 727
Passchendaele Mr Grundys 798
Pastiche Burton Old Cottage 710
Pathfinder North Star 803
Patois Best Bitter Randalls 820
Pause Front Row 744
Pavilion Pale Ale Bank Top 686
Paw's Gold Black Paw 696
Pearl of Kent Whitstable 868
Peasholm Pale Ale (PPA) North
  Riding 803
Peckin' Order Felstar 740
Peculiar Blue Five Towns 741
Pedigree Marston's 884
Pegasus Milton 795
Pembrokeshire Best Bitter
  Gwaun Valley 756
Pen Dafad Nant 799
Pen-y-Ghent Bitter Three
  Peaks 848
Pendle Witches Brew
  Moorhouse's 797
Peninsula Pint Hill Island 764
Pennine Gold Bridestones 705
  Golcar 750
Pennine Pilsner Tirril 850
Pennvael Amber Kinneil 778
Penny's Porter Derby 729
Pentland IPA Stewart 840
Peploe's Tipple Shoes 834
Percheron Tunnel 856

Peregrine Pale Black Iris 696
Perfecta Porcus Complete
  Pig 719
Perridge Pale Flowerpots 742
Peter's Well Houston 769
PG Steam RCH 821
PGA Storm 842
Pheasant Plucker Bowland 700
  Fuzzy Duck 746
  Hunter's 770
Pheasant's Rise Lord
  Conrad's 787
Phoebe's Ale Toll End 851
Phoenix APA Harwich Town 760
Phoenix Gold Byatt's 711
Phoenix Falstaff 739
Piddle in the Dark Wyre
  Piddle 876
Piddle in the Hole Wyre
  Piddle 876
Piddle in the Wind Wyre
  Piddle 876
Piddle Dorset Piddle 731
Pied Eyed Pied Bull 815
Pied Piper Strands 842
Pier Redscar 823
Pig on the Wall Black Country 695
Pig's Ear Strong Beer Uley 857
Pig's Ear Gribble 755
Pigeon Bridge Porter
  Sportsman 839
Pigs Do Fly Potbelly 817
Pigswill Stonehenge 841
Pilgrim Ale Plymouth 816
Pilgrim Ship Inn 834
Pilgrim's Pale Ale Dancing
  Man 726
Pilot Barrowden 688
Pilsner Harbour 758
  Hop Studio 768
  Zerodegrees 878
Pinch Noggin Three B's 848
Pinches IPA Hart of Preston 759
Pink Panther Panther 812
Pinnacle Bitter Naylor's 799
Pinnacle Blonde Naylor's 799
Pinnacle Porter Naylor's 799
Pinnacle Cuillin 725
Pint Marble 790
Pioneer Stout Sherfield
  Village 833
Pioneer Prospect 818
Pipe Dream George Wright 875
Piper's Gold Fyne 747
Pirate's Gold Muirhouse 798
Piston Bitter Beer Engine 691
Piston Bob Tydd Steam 857
Piston Broke Box Steam 701
Pit Boss Gambling Man 747
Pit Pony Merry Miner 792
  Northumberland 803
Pitch Porter Rossendale 827
Pitchfork RCH 821
Pitstop Bitter Silverstone 835
Pivo Estivo Kelburn 775
Plain Porter Porterhouse 880
Platinum Blonde Maypole 792
  Milltown 794
  Norwich Bear 804
Pleasant Pheasant Sleaford 836
Please! MòR 797
Plockton Bay Plockton 816
Plucking Pheasant Gribble 755
Plum Porter Titanic 851
Poacher's Ale Parish 813

Red Mission Driftwood 733
Red Mist Traditional Scottish
   Ales 853
Red Monk of Iona Argyll 682
Red Ness Loch Ness 785
Red Panther Panther 812
Red Queen Bartrams 688
Red River King 777
Red Rock DarkTribe 727
   Red Rock 822
Red Rocker Cromarty 724
Red Rocks Peerless 814
Red Rye Barney's 687
   Canterbury Brewers 714
Red Screes Strands 842
Red Smiddy Kelburn 775
Red Squirrel Arran 683
   Jacobi 774
Red Star IPA Tollgate 851
Red Star Phipps (Grainstore) 752
Red Tail Red Squirrel 823
Red Top Old Dairy 807
Red Torpedo Traditional Scottish
   Ales 853
Red Watch Blueberry Ale
   Cambridge Moonshine 713
Red, White & Brew Red
   Shoot 823
Red Kemptown 776
   Lancaster 779
   Nook 802
   Okells 806
   Outstanding 811
   Williams 870
   Yetman's 877
Redacre Worth 875
Redbrook Premium
   Riverhead 825
Redemption Deverells 730
Redhead Tipples 850
Redoubt Stout Harwich Town 760
Redwood American IPA Red
   Squirrel 823
Redwood Grain 751
   Woodlands 874
Reedcutter Humpty Dumpty 769
Reel Ale Cambridge
   Moonshine 713
   Teignworthy 846
The Reeve's Ale Canterbury
   Ales 714
Regal Blond Byatt's 711
Regal Blonde Oldershaw 808
Reg's Tipple Gribble 755
The Reiver Broughton 707
Reiver's IPA Hadrian Border 756
Reliant Robin Rockin Robin 826
Relish Rodham's 826
Remus Cox & Holbrook 724
Renaissance Ruby Mild
   Whitstable 868
Reservoir Gold Gates Burton 747
Reservoir Hogs Hoggleys 765
Reservoir Premium Gates
   Burton 747
Resination Hopshackle 768
Resistance Summer Wine 844
Resolute Bitter Andwell 681
Resolution Captain Cook 714
Responsibly Strands 842
Retribution Toll End 851
Rev James Brains 701
Rev Rob Beckstones 690
Revelation Dark Star 727
Revenge Winter's 871

Reverend Eaton Shardlow 832
Revival Moor 796
Rhatas Black Dog
   (Hambleton) 757
Rhode Island Red Bitter
   Brimstage 706
Rialto 47 Dunscar Bridge 733
Rich Ruby Milestone 793
Richard Mason 1888 Irwell
   Works 772
Richmond Ale Darwin 727
Riders on the Storm Kelham
   Island 776
Ridgeway Abigale 678
   Tring 854
Ridley's Rite Bishop Nick 694
Ridware Pale Blythe 698
Riggwelter Black Sheep 696
Rip Tide Anchor Springs 680
Ripper Tripel Green Jack 754
Rite Flanker Wickwar 869
Rivendale Middle Earth 793
River Topsham 852
Riverside Pale Ale Brew
   Company 704
Rivet Catcher Jarrow 774
Roadrunner Bottle Brook 700
RoadRunner Mobberley 795
Roaring Meg Springhead 839
Robbie's Red Adur 679
Robin Hood Bitter
   Springhead 839
Rocheberg Blonde Leek 781
Rochford Banshee Hop
   Monster 767
Rock Ale Bitter Beer
   Nottingham 804
Rock Ale Mild Beer
   Nottingham 804
Rock It Red Sleaford 836
Rocket Fuel North Yorkshire 803
Rocks Redscar 823
Rocky Bottom Preseli 817
Roisin-Tayberry Williams 870
Rolling Hitch Darwin 727
Roly Poly Odcombe 806
Roman Black George Wright 875
Roman Gold Castor 715
Ropetackle Golden Ale Adur 679
Ropewalk Big River 693
Rotten End Shalford 832
Rotunda Red ABC 678
Rougham Ready Bartrams 688
Roughtor Penpont 814
Roundabout Greenodd 755
Roundhead Porter Why Not 868
Route 17 Sleaford 837
Route A66 Mithril 795
Royal Ginger Brandon 702
Royal Ruby Mild Sleaford 836
Royal Stag IPA Quantock 819
Royal Standard Nine
   Standards 801
Royal Lytham 788
   Royal Tunbridge Wells 827
Royale Rodham's 826
Roystons Hoppy Handful Spey
   Valley 838
RSB (Rowditch Strong Bitter)
   Rowditch 827
RSX Red Squirrel 823
Rubicon Rodham's 826
Ruby (1874) Mild Bushy's 710
Ruby Jewel Muirhouse 798
Ruby Mild Rudgate 828

Ruby Red IPA Traditional Scottish
   Ales 853
Ruby Red St Peter's 829
Ruby Tuesday Just A Minute 775
Ruby Cap House 714
   Festival (Cotswold Lion) 723
   Yeovil 877
Rucking Mole Moles 796
Ruddles Best Bitter Greene
   King 882
Ruddles County Greene King 882
Ruddy Darter Andwell 681
Rudyard Ruby Leek 781
Ruff Justice Watermill 862
Rum Porter Boggart Hole
   Clough 699
Rum Truffle Ramsbury 820
Run of the Mill Arkwright's 682
Runner Truman's
   (Nethergate) 800
Running the Gauntlet
   Bespoke 692
Rushmore Ridgeside 824
Ruskin's Bitter Kirkby
   Lonsdale 778
Ruskin's Ram SouthDowns 838
Russian Imperial Stout
   Strands 842
Russian Stoat Wessex 865
Rustic Tonbridge 852
Rusty Bucket Brandon 702
Rutland Bitter Grainstore 752
Rutland Panther Grainstore 752
Rutterkin Brewster's 705
RWB (Royal Wootton Bassett)
   Braydon 703
Rye P.A. Ship Inn 833
Ryhope Tug Bull Lane 709

S

SA Gold Brains 701
SA Brains 701
Saaz Enville 736
Saddleback Best Bitter
   Slaughterhouse 836
Sailmakers Porter Big River 693
St Ambrose Allsaints
   (Coastal) 718
St Andrew's Ale Belhaven 883
St Arnold Allsaints (Coastal) 718
St Davids Special Gwaun
   Valley 756
St Edwards Leek 781
St Ethelreda's Golden Bitter
   Hereward 762
St George's Bitter
   Saddleworth 828
St George's Gold Wicked
   Hathern 869
St George's Stout Corvedale 722
St James' Park Bitter
   Northumberland 803
St Magnus Ale Highland 764
St Moses the Black Allsaints
   (Coastal) 718
St Nonna's Penpont 814
Saint Petersburg (Imperial
   Russian Stout)
   Thornbridge 848
St Petrus Brew Company 704
St Piran Cornish Best Bitter
   Allsaints (Coastal) 718
St Pirans Porter Coastal 718
St Stephens Rowditch 827

Traditional Butts 711
Navigation 799
Trafalgar Stout Moonstone 796
Trafalgar Copthorne 721
Traitor DB 728
Transporter DB 728
Wainstones 861
Trappers Hat Bitter
Brimstage 706
Traquair House Ale Traquair 854
Trawlerboys Best Bitter Green
Jack 754
Trelawny St Austell 829
Trench Foot Mr Grundys 798
Tres Piste Strands 842
Trevithick's Revenge Keltek 776
Trial Run Blackbeck 694
Tribute St Austell 829
Trident Arundel 683
Trink Penzance 814
Triple B Grainstore 752
Oxfordshire Ales 812
Triple Champion 1648 677
Triple Chocoholic Saltaire 830
Triple Gem Wilson Potter 870
Triple Hop Brunswick 707
Derby 729
Triple S Untapped 858
Triple O Fernandes 741
Troll Craddock's 724
Trophy Special Camerons 713
Tropicale Yates' 877
Troubadour Dancing Man 726
Trouble at Mill Arkwright's 682
Trouble & Strife Driftwood 733
Trout Ale Hop Monster 767
Trout Tickler Poachers 817
True Grit Millstone 794
True North Yorkshire 878
True Tyke Haworth Steam 760
Truleigh Gold SouthDowns 838
Trumpeter Best Swan 844
TSB Porterhouse 880
Tuck Lincoln Green 782
Tucks Tipple East Coast 734
Tungsten Double Top 732
Tunnel of Love Funfair 746
Tunnel Vision Box Steam 701
Turbulent Priest Wantsum 861
Twickers Wood Farm 873
Twilight Beacons Brecon 703
Twin Screw DarkTribe 727
Twist & Stout Spire 839
Twisted Spire Hobsons 765
Twister Storm 842
Twitchell Buntingford 709
Two Brewers Bitter B&T 685
Two Llocks Church End 717
Two XT 876
Twyford Tipple Binghams 693
Tyneside Blonde Hadrian
Border 756
Type 42 Irving 772
Typhoon Storm 842

U

U.P.A. Untapped 858
Uber Weiss Tigertops 849
Ugly Australian DB 728
Umbel Ale Nethergate 800
Umbel Magna Nethergate 800
Uncle John Halifax Steam 757
Uncle Stan Single Brown Stout
Cox & Holbrook 724

Under The Bridge Bitter
McGivern 788
Undercliff Experience Yates' 877
Undercurrent Anchor Springs 680
Undertaker Wincle 871
Underwood Mild Dove Street 732
Unicorn Robinson's 825
Union Jack Green Tye 755
Union Wood Farm 873
Unit 3 IPA Coppice Side 721
Unity Strong Front Street 745
Uppermill Ale Greenfield 754
Urban Dusk Redemption 822
Urban IPA Tiny Rebel 850
Urban Red Byatt's 711
The Usual Brunswick 707
Milk Street 794
Utter Rotter Rotters 827
UXB Quantock 819

V

Vale Ale Severn Vale 832
Three Castles 848
Vale Mill Millstone 794
Valour Empire 736
Vanguard Ashley Down 684
Vanilla Stout Binghams 694
Sleaford 837
Vectis Venom Island 773
Velocity Adur 679
Velvet Naylor's 799
Very Pale Ale Keystone 777
Vicar's Ruin Church End 717
Vicar's Stout Nailsworth 798
Victoria Bitter Earl Soham 734
Victoria IPA Stringers 843
Victoria Works Weatheroak 863
Victorian Porter 8 Sail 677
Victorious Wood Farm 873
Vienna Lager Artisan 683
Viking Bitter Liverpool Craft 784
Rudgate 828
Village Bike Potton 817
The Village Bike VIP 860
Village Idiot White Horse 867
Village Life Beeston 691
Fulstow 746
The Village Lite VIP 860
Village Archers (Evan Evans) 737
VIP Tryst 855
Virtuale Reality 821
Vital Spark Fyne 747
Vixen's Vice Alcazar 679
Volcano IPA Barney's 687
VPA (Verbeia Pale Ale)
WharfeBank 866
VPA/Vale Pale Ale Vale 859

W

W&M Dark Mild Derwent 729
W&M Pale Ale Derwent 729
Wagtail Best Bitter Allendale 680
Wagtail Great Oakley 753
Wainwright Thwaites 849
Wakering Pale Hop Monster 767
Wallasea Wench Hop
Monster 767
Waller Wincle 871
Wallops Wood Bowman 700
Wally's Revenge Why Not 868
Waltzer Funfair 746
Wandering Beacons Brecon 703
Wandle Ale Sambrook's 830
Wantage Bells Betjeman 693

Warbler Bowman 700
Ward's Best Bitter Maxim 791
Warlock Houston 769
Warlord Full Mash 745
Warminster Warrior Wessex 865
Warrior Evan Evans 737
Fox 743
Warwickshire's Finest Merry
Miner 792
Wash Sparky Handley's 758
Washington Old Hall Honey Beer
Delavals 728
Wasp Nest Brampton 702
Wassail Ballard's 686
Wastwater Gold Great Gable 752
Waterloo Porter Wellington
Inn 864
Waterloo Masters 790
Waxies Dargle Brandon 702
Wayfarer Atlas (Orkney) 810
Emsworth 736
Waylade Trossach's Craft
(Traditional Scottish Ales) 854
Wayland Smithy White Horse 867
Weald Ale Pilgrim 815
Weasel Florence 742
Weavers Delight Golcar 750
Webb Ellis Wood Farm 873
Wee Beastie Scottish Borders 831
Wee Drop of Mischief
Brandon 702
Weiss Squad Fyfe 746
Welland Valley Mild Great
Oakley 753
Wellow Gold Maypole 792
Wells Bombardier Wells &
Young's 885
Welsh Black Bullmastiff 709
Great Orme 753
Heart of Wales 761
Llangollen 785
Welsh Gold Bullmastiff 709
Welsh Highland Bitter
Snowdonia 837
Welsh Pale Ale Breconshire 704
Welsh Pride/Balchder Cymru
Conwy 720
Welsh Red Bullmastiff 709
Welterweight Waveney 863
Wenlock Stout Ironbridge 772
West Coast Blond Stringers 843
West Coast IPA Black Iris 696
Phoenix 815
The West Highland Way Loch
Lomond 785
Westerly Longhill 786
Westgate Gold Clark's 717
Westmorland Gold
Barngates 687
Westmorland Pale Ale Kirkby
Lonsdale 778
Westoe IPA Jarrow 775
Weymouth Best Bitter
Dorset 731
Weymouth Harbour Master
Dorset 731
Whaler Bridgetown 706
Whapweasel Hexhamshire 763
What the Fox's Hat Church
End 717
Whatever! Prospect 818
WHB/Wicked Hathern Bitter
Wicked Hathern 869
Wheat a Minute Willy Good 870
Wheat Ale Zerodegrees 878

Pubs transport guide
Leave the car behind and travel to the pub by bus, train or tram

Using public transport is an excellent way to get to the pub, but many people use it irregularly, and systems can be slightly different from place to place. This guide is designed to help you.

Information

You should find route and timetable information at bus stop or platform timetable cases, which usually give contact telephone numbers and details of text messaging services. You can also get information from information centres run nationally, regionally or locally. Remember that many operators will not tell you about other operators' services.

Information by phone

The national **Traveline** system (0871 200 22 33) gives information on all bus and local rail services throughout England, Scotland and Wales. Calls are put through to a local call centre and if necessary your call will be switched through to a more relevant centre. Mobile phone users will be given a series of menu options to locate the relevant centre. In London use Traveline or the **Transport for London** information line, 020 7222 1234. For **National Rail Enquiries** telephone 08457 48 49 50.

On the net

Try Transport Direct, **www.transportdirect.info**, or Traveline, **www.traveline.org.uk**. For London try **www.tfl.gov.uk**. National Rail Enquiries are at **www.nationalrail.co.uk/ times_fares**. Scotland has its own planner at **www.travelinescotland.com**, with a link from Traveline. Just a tip – it can help to know the postcode of the pub(s) you want to visit!

Coach

The two main UK coach sites are: National Express, 08717 818181, **www.nationalexpress.com** Scottish Citylink, 08705 505050, **www.citylink.co.uk**.

National Express has kindly teamed up with CAMRA to offer members a 15% discounted rate on coach travel until 1st June 2013. National Express coaches operate to more than 1,000 UK destinations and carry over 18 million customers a year. For further details and to take up this offer, simply sign in to your CAMRA account at **www.camra.org.uk**.

Using the bus

If there are a number of bus stops in an area, make sure the service you want is listed on the bus stop plate or timetable case. If no services are listed then all buses should stop there, apart perhaps from some 'express' buses.

Some routes operate on a 'hail and ride' principle where the bus will stop anywhere it is safe to do so. Ask the enquiry service or operator, or, if you use a stop on the outward journey, ask the driver. If you don't know where to get off, ask the driver to let you know. It's often worth asking where your return stop is, as sometimes it's not too obvious.

Some buses run 'on demand' so you'll have to telephone in advance. The information centre should know, and give you the contact number.

Paying your fare

Have some small change ready to pay the driver as some companies operate a 'fast fare' system and don't give change. In central London and on many tram systems you need to buy a ticket in advance from a nearby machine.

The most economical and convenient way to travel around in London, on buses, trams, underground and most trains, is with an Oyster card which can be obtained from Oyster ticket shops, Underground and some rail stations. There is a refundable £3 deposit for one.

Special fares

Where available, return tickets are often cheaper than two singles. Many operators, and some local authorities, offer 'network' tickets for a number of journeys. If buying an operator's multi-journey ticket check that you can use it on other operators' services – important if more than one company operates the route.

On trains, standard and 'saver' return tickets allow you to break your journey, so if you are visiting a number of pubs by train, book to the furthest station. This may not apply to other types of rail ticket – ask in advance.

Concessionary fares

There are concessionary fares schemes for seniors and people with certain disabilities. The English national concessionary fares scheme provides free travel for pass-holders on buses anywhere in England between 09:30 and 23:00, and at any time at weekends or on bank holidays. It does not provide free bus travel outside England, nor is it generally valid on trains, trams or ferries. However, there are local exceptions where the scheme is enhanced, either for local residents or for everyone. It is worth checking locally.

The Scottish, Welsh and Northern Irish schemes are slightly different. Eligible people should enquire locally. As in England, there are local enhancements.

National Express offer half fare discounts for people over 60 or with certain disabilities on most of their services throughout the United Kingdom. If you think you are eligible, ask before you book. If you have a concessionary fares card, this will generally give proof of entitlement. Scottish passes are valid on long distance coaches within Scotland, such as those operated by Scottish CityLink. This entitlement is only for Scottish residents.

National Rail sell a range of rail cards, including ones for people over 60, with certain disabilities, or between the ages of 16 and 25. These give a discount of 34% on most tickets, and there can be other advantages. Either ask at your nearest staffed station, telephone National Rail Enquiries, or look on the National Rail web site.

Complaints, problems & lost property

If you have any complaints, problems or lose anything when using public transport, please contact the operator running the service as soon as possible. Keep your ticket. The information is important. If you feel your complaint is not dealt with satisfactorily, contact the relevant Transport Authority who may be able to help. Service reliability is improving rapidly but occasionally things do go wrong and the bus doesn't turn up. If, because of this, you need get a taxi, ask for a receipt and send it in with your complaint. You may get reimbursed.

Outside Mainland UK, but within the area of this Guide, information services are:

NORTHERN IRELAND

Translink, 02890 666630, **www.translink.co.uk** or **www.traveline.org.uk**

ISLE OF MAN

Isle of Man Transport, 01624 662525, **www.iombusandrail.info**

JERSEY

Telephone 01534 877772, **www.thisisjersey.com**

GUERNSEY

Island Coachways 01481 720210, **www.buses.gg**

NOTE: All information was correct at the time of writing, however CAMRA cannot be held responsible for any changes made since that date.

Award winning pubs
Local CAMRA Pubs of the Year

The Pub of the Year competition is judged by CAMRA members. Each of the CAMRA branches votes for its favourite pub. They are judged on criteria including the quality and choice of real ale, atmosphere, décor, customer service and value. The pubs listed below are current winners of the title; look out for the ♔ symbol next to the entries in the Guide.

England

♔ **Bedfordshire**
Albion, Ampthill
Cricketers Arms, Bedford
Engineers Arms, Henlow

Engineers Arms, Henlow, Bedfordshire

♔ **Berkshire**
Old Manor, Bracknell
Nag's Head, Reading
Royal Oak, Yattendon

♔ **Buckinghamshire**
Watts Arms, Hanslope
White Horse, Hedgerley

♔ **Cambridgeshire**
Pig & Abbot, Abington Pigotts
Devonshire Arms, Cambridge
Letter B, Whittlesey

Brewery Tap, Chester, Cheshire

♔ **Cheshire**
Lodge, Alsager
Egerton Arms, Chelford
Brewery Tap, Chester
Penny Black, Northwich
Prospect, Runcorn

♔ **Cornwall**
Front, Falmouth

♔ **Cumbria**
King's Head, Carlisle
Brook, Cleator
Black Swan Inn, Ravenstonedale
Swan Inn, Ulverston

♔ **Derbyshire**
Chesterfield Arms, Chesterfield
Five Lamps, Derby
Admiral Rodney Inn, Hartshorne

Dewdrop Inn, Ilkeston, Derbyshire

Front, Falmouth, Cornwall

Tom Cobley Tavern, Spreyton, Devon

Dewdrop Inn, Ilkeston
Hunter Arms, Kilburn
Angler's Rest, Miller's Dale
Devonshire Arms, South Normanton
Flying Childers, Stanton in Peak
Old Hall Inn, Whitehough

🏆 **Devon**
Foxhound, Brixton
Old Market Inn, Holsworthy
Tom Cobley Tavern, Spreyton
Rugglestone Inn, Widecombe in the Moor

🏆 **Dorset**
Tiger Inn, Bridport
Castle Inn, West Lulworth

🏆 **Durham**
Quakerhouse, Darlington
Victoria Inn, Durham

🏆 **Essex**
Old Lifeboat House, Clacton-on-Sea
Crooked Billet, Leigh-on-Sea
Compasses, Littley Green
Thatchers Arms, Mount Bures
Old English Gentleman, Saffron Walden
Rising Sun, Stanford-le-Hope
Prince of Wales, Stow Maries

🏆 **Gloucestershire & Bristol**
Three Tuns, Bristol: Central
Craven Arms, Brockhampton
Salutation, Ham

Thatchers Arms, Mount Bures, Essex

🏆 **Hampshire**
Railway Arms, Alton
Prince of Wales, Farnborough
Waggon & Horses, Hartley Wintney
Hole in the Wall, Portsmouth
Guide Dog, Southampton

🏆 **Herefordshire**
Sun Inn, Leintwardine

🏆 **Hertfordshire**
Queen's Head, Allens Green
Rising Sun, Berkhamsted
Land of Liberty, Peace & Plenty, Heronsgate
Old Cross Tavern, Hertford
Red Lion, Preston

Land of Liberty, Peace & Plenty, Heronsgate, Hertfordshire

🏆 **Isle of Wight**
Crown Inn, Shorwell

🏆 **Kent**
Halfway House, Brenchley
Dolphin, Canterbury
Elephant, Faversham
Jolly Drayman, Gravesend
Bowl Inn, Hastingleigh
Stile Bridge, Marden
Conqueror Alehouse, Ramsgate
King's Arms, Upper Upnor
Berry, Walmer

Railway Arms, Alton, Hampshire

Red Lion, Bromley, Greater London

♈ Lancashire
Bridge Bier Huis, Burnley
White Cross, Lancaster
Old Black Bull, Preston
Fifteens of St Annes, St Annes on the Sea

♈ Leicestershire & Rutland
Wheel, Branston
Plough, Greetham
New Plough Inn, Hinckley
Salmon, Leicester
Generous Briton, Loughborough
Boat, Melton Mowbray

♈ Lincolnshire
Five Bells, Claypole
No. 2 Refreshment Rooms, Cleethorpes
Strugglers Inn, Lincoln
Gas Lamp Lounge, Louth
Half Moon, Willingham by Stow

♈ Greater London
Robin Hood & Little John, Bexleyheath
Red Lion, Bromley
Hope, Carshalton
Red Lion, E11: Leytonstone
Bar, Gants Hill
Olde Mitre Inn, High Barnet

Olde Mitre Inn, High Barnet, Greater London

Prince of Wales, Twickenham, Greater London

Pineapple, NW5: Kentish Town
Blythe Hill Tavern, SE23: Forest Hill
Lamb, Surbiton
Trafalgar, SW19: South Wimbledon
Prince of Wales, Twickenham
Fox, W7: Hanwell
Harp, WC2: Charing Cross

Harp, WC2: Charing Cross, Greater London

♈ Greater Manchester
Costello's Bar, Altrincham
Victoria & Albert, Horwich
White Lion, Leigh
Baum, Rochdale
New Oxford, Salford
Sportsman, Strines
Royal Oak, Wigan

♈ Merseyside
Gallaghers Pub & Barbers Shop, Birkenhead
Roscoe Head, Liverpool: City Centre
Duke of Cambridge, St Helens
Guest House, Southport

Pineapple, NW5: Kentish Town, Greater London

Sportsman, Strines, Greater Manchester

Norfolk
Fat Cat, Norwich
Union Jack, Roydon

Northamptonshire
Alexandra Arms, Kettering

Northumberland
Boathouse Inn, Wylam

Nottinghamshire
Horse & Plough, Bingham
Just Beer Micropub, Newark
Hand & Heart, Nottingham: Central
Horse & Jockey, Selston
Mallard, Worksop

Oxfordshire
Red Lion, Brightwell-cum-Sotwell
Far from the Madding Crowd, Oxford
Cross Keys, Thame
Shoulder of Mutton, Wantage
Fox Inn, Westcote Barton

Shropshire
Salopian Bar, Shrewsbury
Fighting Cocks, Stottesdon

Somerset
Castle Green Inn, Taunton
Nog Inn, Wincanton

Roscoe Head, Liverpool: City Centre, Merseyside

Fat Cat, Norwich, Norfolk

Staffordshire
Royal Oak, Barton-under-Needwood
Swan Hotel, Brewood
Cross Keys Hotel, Hednesford
George & Dragon, Lichfield
Sun, Stafford
Congress, Stoke-on-Trent
New Inn, Wombourne

Suffolk
Fat Cat, Ipswich
Buck, Rumburgh
Brewery Tap, Sudbury

Surrey
Thyme at the Tavern, Chertsey
Jolly Coopers, Epsom
Row Barge, Guildford
Surrey Oaks, Newdigate

East Sussex
Robin Hood, Icklesham
Brewers Arms, Lewes

West Sussex
Sportsman, Amberley
Swan, Crawley

Beacon Hotel, Sedgeley, West Midlands

Kelham Island Tavern, Sheffield: Central, South Yorkshire

♟ Tyne & Wear
Bacchus, Newcastle: City Centre
Fitzgerald's, Sunderland

♟ Warwickshire
New Dolphin Inn, Atherstone
Bull & Butcher, Corley Moor
Somerville Arms, Leamington Spa
Victoria Inn, Rugby
Norman Knight, Whichford

♟ West Midlands
Bull's Head, Barston
Wellington, Birmingham: City Centre
Greyhound Inn, Coventry
Beacon Hotel, Sedgley
Duke William, Stourbridge
Bishop Vesey, Sutton Coldfield
Black Country Arms, Walsall
Vine, Wednesfield

♟ Wiltshire
Barge Inn, Honeystreet
Bell Inn, Lacock
Victoria & Albert, Netherhampton
Fox & Hounds, Warminster

♟ Worcestershire
Weighbridge, Alvechurch
Crown & Trumpet, Broadway

Anchor Inn, Caunsall
Firefly, Worcester

♟ East Yorkshire
Rose & Crown, Driffield
Goodmanham Arms, Goodmanham
Lion & Key, Hull
Jemmy Hirst at the Rose & Crown, Rawcliffe

♟ North Yorkshire
Duke of Wellington, Danby
White Swan, Danby Wiske
North Riding Brew Pub, Scarborough
Waggon & Horses, York

♟ South Yorkshire
Old No. 7, Barnsley
Cask Corner, Doncaster
Black Lion, Firbeck
Kelham Island Tavern, Sheffield: Central

♟ West Yorkshire
Sparrow Bier Cafe, Bradford
West Riding Licensed Refreshment Rooms,
    Dewsbury
Cricketers Arms, Horbury
Sportsman, Huddersfield
Old Cock, Otley
King's Arms, Silsden
Jubilee Refreshment Rooms, Sowerby Bridge

City Arms, Cardiff, Glamorgan

Wales
♟ Glamorgan
Red Cow, Aberdare
City Arms, Cardiff
Vale of Glamorgan Inn, Cowbridge
Village Inn, Killay

West Riding Refreshment Rooms, Dewsbury, West Yorkshire

Bridge End Inn, Ruabon, North-East Wales

Blue Peter Hotel, Kirkcolm, Dumfries & Galloway

🏆 Gwent
Coach & Horses, Chepstow
Star Inn, Llanfihangel Tor-y-Mynydd

🏆 Mid-Wales
Ancient Briton, Pen-y-Cae
Star Inn, Talybont on Usk

🏆 North-East Wales
North-East Wales
Y Dderwen (The Oak), Hendre
Bridge End Inn, Ruabon

🏆 North-West Wales
Pen-y-Bryn, Colwyn Bay
Snowdonia Park, Waunfawr

🏆 West Wales
Taberna Inn, Herbrandston
Plash, Llanfallteg
Y Talbot, Tregaron

🏆 Greater Glasgow & Clyde Valley
Drum & Monkey, Glasgow
Fox & Hounds, Houston

🏆 Highlands & Western Isles
Benleva Hotel, Drumnadrochit

🏆 Kingdom Of Fife
Central Bar, St Andrews

🏆 Loch Lomond, Stirling & The Trossachs
Woolpack Inn, Tillicoultry

🏆 Tayside
Ericht Alehouse, Blairgowrie

Fox & Hounds, Houston, Greater Glasgow & Clyde Valley

Grill, Aberdeen, Aberdeen & Grampian

Scotland
🏆 Aberdeen & Grampian
Grill, Aberdeen

🏆 Borders
Cobbles Inn, Kelso

🏆 Dumfries & Galloway
Cavens Arms, Dumfries
Blue Peter Hotel, Kirkcolm

Northern Ireland
🏆 Spinning Mill, Ballymena

Channel Islands

🏆 Guernsey
Cornerstone Café Bar, St Peter Port

🏆 Jersey
Forum, St Helier

🏆 Isle of Man
Sidings, Castletown

Readers' recommendations

Suggestions for pubs to be included or excluded

All pubs are regularly surveyed by local branches of the Campaign for Real Ale to ensure they meet the standards required by the *Good Beer Guide*. If you would like to comment on a pub already featured, or on any you think should be featured, please fill in the form below (or a copy of it), and send it to the address indicated. Alternatively, email **gbgeditor@camra.org.uk**. Your views will be passed on to the branch concerned. Please mark your envelope/email with the county where the pub is, which will help us to direct your comments efficiently.

Pub name:

Address:

Reason for recommendation/criticism:

Pub name:

Address:

Reason for recommendation/criticism:

Pub name:

Address:

Reason for recommendation/criticism:

Your name and address:

Please send to: [Name of county] Section, Good Beer Guide,
230 Hatfield Road, St Albans, Hertfordshire AL1 4LW

Pub name:

Address:

Reason for recommendation/criticism:

Pub name:

Address:

Reason for recommendation/criticism:

Pub name:

Address:

Reason for recommendation/criticism:

Pub name:

Address:

Reason for recommendation/criticism:

Your name and address:

Please send to: [Name of county] Section, Good Beer Guide,
230 Hatfield Road, St Albans, Hertfordshire AL1 4LW

Have your say

Feedback on the Good Beer Guide

We are always trying to improve the *Good Beer Guide* for our readers and we welcome your feedback. If you have any suggestions for how the *Good Beer Guide*, Good Beer Guide Mobile Edition or sat-nav POI could be improved, please let us know. Simply fill out the form below (or a copy of it) and send it to the address indicated, or make your comments on our website at: **www.camra.org.uk/gbgfeedback**. Thank you.

Colour sections:

_____

_____

_____

_____

Pubs section:

_____

_____

_____

_____

Brewery section:

_____

_____

_____

_____

Good Beer Guide e-book:

_____

_____

_____

_____

Good Beer Guide Mobile:

_____

_____

_____

_____

Good Beer Guide sat-nav POI:

_____

_____

_____

_____

What other suggestions do you have?

_____

_____

_____

Please send to: Good Beer Guide – Have your say,
230 Hatfield Road, St Albans, Hertfordshire, AL1 4LW

Noble Beers Get the Bullet

How much loved ales are being killed

The first popular edition of the *Good Beer Guide* in 1974 described Boddingtons Bitter succinctly as 'one of the best'. In the early days of CAMRA and the Guide, it was a beer that enjoyed iconic status, an unusually pale, golden version of bitter, with a distinctive bittersweet malt and hops character.

It was also a highly successful beer, at one time reaching the status of the fourth biggest cask ale in the country, with volumes of around 850,000 barrels a year. And yet, in the hands of the world's biggest brewer, AB InBev, it's on the point of extinction.

How could such a beer, popular and best-selling, face oblivion at a time when real ale is the only success story in town? The answer lies in the distorted values of global brewers such as AB InBev. It's interested only in mass volume brands such as 'American' Budweiser – brewed in London – and 'Belgian' Stella Artois – brewed in Wales. To companies of this size, with global stretch, Boddingtons represents the small change of brewing and it will be consigned to the rubbish heap of history, regardless of its legion of devoted drinkers. Smaller brewers can only rub their eyes in disbelief when they see a beer with sales they would die for being sidelined.

The history of Boddingtons goes back to 1778. In the 19th century it was brewing 100,000 barrels a year, a remarkable amount at a time when Manchester was packed with rival brewers. In the late 1960s it fought off a takeover bid by the national group Allied Breweries but it went on the takeover trail itself in the 1980s when it bought the Oldham Brewery and Higsons of Liverpool. This brought it to the attention of the fast-growing Whitbread group, which in 1989 made a successful bid worth £50.7 million for Boddingtons and its subsidiaries.

Whitbread boosted sales of the beer but did little for its reputation by producing canned and keg versions with the slogan 'the Cream of Manchester'. Then in 2000 Whitbread quit brewing and ownership of its plants passed to the Belgian company Interbrew. In a series of rapid amalgamations, Interbrew merged with the Brazilian Ambev to form InBev and then in 2008 the biggest merger in brewing history saw the creation of AB InBev when it bought Anheuser-Busch of the United States, producer of the world's biggest beer brand, Budweiser.

The writing was on the wall for what the global giant deemed to be 'small volume' brands. In 2011 it put up for sale Draught Bass, Boddingtons and Flowers IPA and Original for £15 million. Sales

Even iconic, national ale brands are not safe from global beer forces

of Bass, once the biggest-selling premium cask beer in Britain, have dwindled to around 30,000 barrels a year. It's currently brewed for AB InBev by Marston's, while the Flowers beers are produced by Brains in Cardiff.

The cask version of Boddingtons was brewed for several years by Hydes in Manchester but the contract expired in spring 2012 and was not renewed. Hydes plans to move to a new brewing site and will concentrate on its own core brands. AB InBev says it will offer the production of Boddingtons to other breweries but the volumes are now so small that they are of little interest to regional brewers.

The sad fact is that Boddingtons is likely to disappear. Like spoilt milk, the Cream of Manchester will be poured down the drain.

Another once famous and popular beer, Ansells Mild, disappeared for good in 2012. Ansells was a giant Birmingham brewery that became the Midlands arm of Allied Breweries, which included Ind Coope and Tetley. When Allied split up in the 1990s, the brands passed to Carlsberg. Nothing is left of the three breweries. Tetley's milds and bitter are brewed under licence by Marston's while Ansells Mild was brewed by JW Lees in Manchester.

The mild was a delicious example of a style that has seen an encouraging revival in recent years, to such an extent that the 2011 Champion Beer of Britain was Mighty Oak's Oscar Wilde Mild. Yet Carlsberg, lacking the wit or the wisdom to promote the Ansells version, said volumes had become so small that it was not worth continuing with production. We can expect Ind Coope Draught Burton Ale, also brewed by Lees, to follow suit.

It's a sad reflection on the priorities of global giants such as AB InBev and Carlsberg that see no future in the likes of Boddingtons and Ansells, enjoyed by generations of drinkers. But then if your roots are in Belgium, Brazil, the U.S. and Denmark, you cannot be expected to care too much for the proud history and traditions of British brewing.

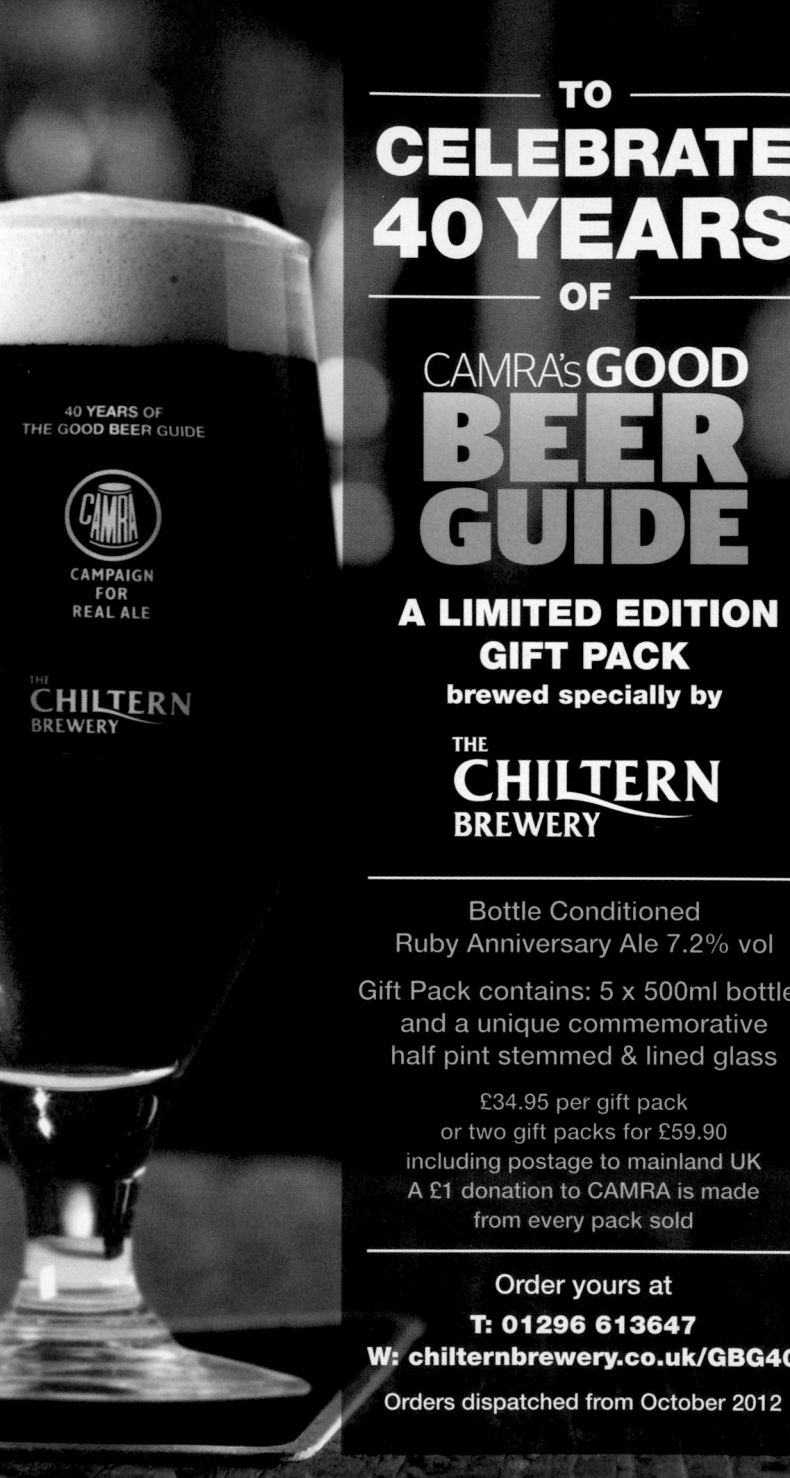

Good Beer Guide digital editions

The *Good Beer Guide* is also available in digital formats, including an e-book, mobile app and sat-nav download. Together, these offer the perfect solution to pub-finding on the move. To discover more, scan the QR code or visit **www.camra.org.uk/gbgdigital.**

Good Beer Guide e-book

The *Good Beer Guide* 2013 e-book will be available from autumn 2012 in the widely compatible ePUB and Kindle formats. The e-book provides all the benefits of portable, searchable and adaptable digital content while also making the Guide fully interactive, taking advantage of GPS, mobile and Internet connectivity to bring exciting new features.

- Portable, electronic version of the printed Guide
- Fully interactive, searchable content in ePUB and Kindle formats, compatible with iPad, Kindle and many other e-readers
- Includes full colour features and images from the printed book as well as complete pubs and breweries listings*
- Active e-mail and web links within entries*
- Postcode links to Google maps to help you navigate*

Visit **www.camra.org.uk/gbg** for further information and for details of where to buy.

*Where e-reader allows.

Good Beer Guide Mobile

Available from 13th September 2012, the new Good Beer Guide Mobile app for Apple and Android™ devices provides detailed information on local *Good Beer Guide* pubs, breweries and beers wherever you are or wherever you are going. Features include:†

- Search results with full pub descriptions and detailed visitor information
- Detailed information on all UK real-ale breweries and their beers
- CAMRA tasting notes for hundreds of regular beers
- Interactive maps help you find your way
- Search by postcode, pub or place name, or auto-locate
- Custom functions allow you to mark your favourite pubs and write your own personal reviews

To download, visit the Apple **App Store** or **Google Play** store. For more information visit: **www.camra.org.uk/gbgmobile**

†App is free to download with an in-app suscription required for full features. Subscription-free use allows for sinlge, auto-locate search results only. NOTE: Standard network charges apply when using the app.

Good Beer Guide sat-nav download

Priced at just £5, the Good Beer Guide POI (Points of Interest) file allows users of TomTom, Garmin and Navman sat-nav systems to see the locations of all the 4,500 current *Good Beer Guide* pubs and all the UK's real-ale breweries and plan routes to them. So, no more wasting time getting lost down country lanes – now, wherever you are, there is no excuse for not finding your nearest *Good Beer Guide* pub.

- For more information and to download visit: **www.camra.org.uk/gbgpoi**

Books for beer lovers

Great British Pubs

Adrian Tierney-Jones

Great British Pubs is a practical guide that takes you around the very best public houses in Britain and celebrates the pub as a national institution. Every kind of pub is represented in these pages with categorised listings featuring full-colour photography illustrating a host of excellent pubs from the seaside to the city and from the historic to the ultra-modern. Articles on beer brewing, cider making, classic pub food recipes and traditional pub games are included to help the reader fully understand what makes a pub 'Great'.

£14.99 ISBN 987-1-85249-265-6   CAMRA members' price £12.99

101 Beers Days Out

Tim Hampson

101 Beer Days Out is the perfect handbook for the beer tourist wanting to explore beer and brewing culture in their local area and around the UK. From historic city pubs to beer festivals; idyllic country pub walks to rail ale trails; tourist brewery tours to serious brewing courses – Britain has beer and brewing experiences to rival any in the world. 101 Beer Days Out brings together for the first time the best of these experiences, ordered geographically and with full visitor information, maps and colour photography – the best way to celebrate Britain's national drink.

£12.99 ISBN 978-1-85249-288-5   CAMRA members' price £10.99

South East Pub Walks

Bob Steel

South East Pub Walks is a pocket-sized, traveller's guide to some of the best walking and best pubs in South East England. It features 30 walks of varying lengths, all accessible by public transport and aimed at both the casual walker and more serious hiker. Each route has been selected for its unique and varied landscape, and its beer, with the walks taking you on a tour of the best real ale pubs the area has to offer. The essential guide for anyone wanting to see and taste the best of South East England.

£9.99 ISBN 978-1-85249-287-8   CAMRA members' price £7.99

Peak District Pub Walks

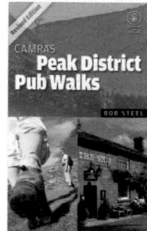

Bob Steel

CAMRA's Peak District Pub Walks helps you to see the best of Britain's oldest national park whilst never straying too far from a decent pint. A practical, pocket-sized guide to some of the best pubs and best walking in the Peak District, this recently revised guide features 25 walks, as well as cycle routes and local attractions. Full-colour Ordnance Survey maps and detailed route information make CAMRA's Peak District Pub Walks the essential guide for anyone wanting a taste of the Peak.

£9.99 ISBN 978-1-85249-303-5   CAMRA members' price £7.99

London's Best Beer, Pubs & Bars

Des de Moor

London's Best Beer, Pubs & Bars is the essential guide to beer drinking in London. This practical book is packed with detailed maps and easy-to-use listings to help you find the best places to enjoy perfect pints in the capital. Laid out by area, find the best pubs serving the best British and international beers wherever you are. Features tell you more about London's rich history of brewing and the city's vibrant modern brewing scene. The venue listings include a variety of real ale pubs, bars and other outlets with detailed information on opening hours, local landmarks, and public transport links to make planning any excursion quick and easy.

£12.99 ISBN 978-1-85249-285-4   CAMRA members' price £10.99

300 Beers to Try Before You Die!

Roger Protz

300 beers from around the world, handpicked by award-winning journalist and author Roger Protz for you to try before you die! This revised edition presents a comprehensive portfolio of top beers from the smallest micro-breweries in the US through family-run British breweries to the world's largest brands. This book is indispensible for both beer novices and aficionados.

£12.99 ISBN 978-1-85249-273-1   CAMRA members' price £10.99

An Appetite for Ale

Fiona Beckett & Will Beckett

A beer and food revolution is under way in Britain and award-winning food writer Fiona Beckett and her publican son, Will, have joined forces to explore this exciting new food phenomenon. This collection of more than 100 simple and approachable recipes has been specially created to show the versatility and fantastic flavour that ale has to offer. With sections on Spreads and Dips, Meat Feasts, Spicy Foods and Sweet Treats it provides countless ideas for using beer from around the world. With an open mind, a bottle opener and a well-stocked larder, this exciting book will allow you to enjoy real food, real beer and real flavour.

£19.99 ISBN 978-1-85249-234-2   Sale price £6.00   CAMRA members' price £5.00

Good Bottled Beer Guide

Jeff Evans

The seventh edition of this pocket-sized guide is a must for all real ale fans who enjoy a fresh glass of their favourite real ales at home. The book is a comprehensive guide to all bottle conditioned real ales brewed in the UK, and includes a special section highlighting the best 500 bottle conditioned beers. The guide lists beers by style, with information about the range of styles available, recommendations for matching beers with food, and a section on the best examples of foreign bottled beers.

£12.99 ISBN 978-1-85249-262-5   CAMRA members' price £10.99

CAMRA at 40

Edited by Roger Protz

With contributions from respected beer writers, journalists, public figures and prominent CAMRA members, *CAMRA at 40* is a celebration of the Campaign, reflecting both its breadth and the variety of views about its work, and an assessment of how it might need to evolve to be relevant for another forty years. CAMRA will always campaign as the champion of the beer drinker, so let's raise a glass and toast the remarkable achievements of the past forty years that has seen real ale revive beyond the wildest dreams of its founders.

£7.99 ISBN 978-1-85249-300-4   CAMRA members' price £6.99

The Book of Beer Knowledge

Jeff Evans

This absorbing, pocket-sized book is packed with beer facts, feats, records, stats and anecdotes so you'll never be lost for words at the pub again. More than 200 entries cover the serious, the silly and the downright bizarre from the world of beer. Inside this pint-sized compendium you'll find everything from the biggest brewer in the world to the beers with the daftest names. A quick skim before a night out and you'll always have enough beery wisdom to impress your friends.

£7.99 ISBN 978-1-85249-292-2   CAMRA members' price £6.99

Order these and other CAMRA books online at **www.camra.org.uk/books**, ask your local bookstore, or contact: CAMRA, 230 Hatfield Road, St Albans, AL1 4LW. Telephone 01727 867201.

An offer for CAMRA members
Good Beer Guide annual subscription

Being a CAMRA member brings many benefits, not least a big discount on the *Good Beer Guide*. Now you can take advantage of an even bigger discount on the Guide by taking out an annual subscription.

Simply fill in the form below and the Direct Debit form on p943 (photocopies will do if you don't want to spoil your book), and send them to CAMRA at 230 Hatfield Road, St Albans, Hertfordshire AL1 4LW. You will then receive the **Good Beer Guide** automatically every year. It will be posted to you before the official publication date and before any other postal sales are processed. You won't have to bother with filling in cheques every year

and you will receive the book at a lower price than other CAMRA members (for instance, the **2013** Guide was sold to annual subscribers **for just £10** including postage & packing). So sign up now and be sure of receiving your copy early every year.

Note: This offer is open only to CAMRA members and is only available through using a Direct Debit instruction to a U.K. bank. This offer applies to the **Good Beer Guide 2014** onwards.

Name
_____

CAMRA Membership No.
_____

Address and Postcode
_____

_____

_____

_____

_____

I wish to purchase the *Good Beer Guide* annually by Direct Debit and I have completed the Direct Debit instructions to my bank which are enclosed.

Signature _____   Date _____

✂ detached and retained this section

CAMPAIGN FOR REAL ALE

Instruction to your Bank or Building Society to pay by Direct Debit

DIRECT Debit

Please fill in the form and send to: Campaign for Real Ale Ltd. 230 Hatfield Road, St. Albans, Herts. AL1 4LW

Name and full postal address of your Bank or Building Society

To The Manager   Bank or Building Society

Address

Postcode

Originator's Identification Number

| 9 | 2 | 6 | 1 | 2 | 9 |

Name (s) of Account Holder (s)

FOR CAMRA OFFICIAL USE ONLY
This is not part of the instruction to your Bank or Building Society

Membership Number

Name

Postcode

Bank or Building Society account number

Branch Sort Code

Reference Number

Instruction to your Bank or Building Society

Please pay CAMRA Direct Debits from the account detailed on this Instruction subject to the safeguards assured by the Direct Debit Guarantee. I understand that this instruction may remain with CAMRA and, if so, will be passed electronically to my Bank/Building Society

Signature(s)

Date

Banks and Building Societies may not accept Direct Debit Instructions for some types of account

Join the Campaign!

CAMRA, the Campaign for Real Ale, is an independent not-for-profit, volunteer-led consumer group. We promote good-quality real ale and pubs, as well as lobbying government to champion drinkers' rights and protect local pubs as centres of community life.

CAMRA has over 140,000 members from all ages and backgrounds, brought together by a common belief in the issues that CAMRA deals with and their love of good quality British beer. From just £23 a year – that's less than a pint a month – you can join CAMRA and enjoy the following benefits:

- A monthly colour newspaper and quarterly magazine informing you about beer and pub news and detailing events and beer festivals around the country.
- Free or reduced entry to over 160 national, regional and local beer festivals.
- Money off many of our publications including the *Good Beer Guide* and the *Good Bottled Beer Guide*.
- A 10% discount on all holidays booked with Cottages4you and Hoseasons, and a 15% discount with UK Boat Hire and National Express.
- £20-worth of JD Wetherspoon real ale vouchers (40 x 50 pence off a pint).

Do you feel passionately about your pint? Then why not join CAMRA

Just fill in the application form (or a photocopy of it) and the Direct Debit form on the previous page to receive 15 months membership for the price of 12!*

If you wish to join but do not want to pay by Direct Debit, please fill in the application form below and send a cheque, payable to CAMRA, to: CAMRA, 230 Hatfield Road, St Albans, Hertfordshire, AL1 4LW. Please note than non Direct Debit payments will incur a £2 surcharge. Figures are given below.

Please tick appropriate box	Direct Debit		Non Direct Debit	
Single membership (UK & EU)	£23.00	☐	£25.00	☐
Concessionary membership (under 26 or 60 and over)	£15.50	☐	£17.50	☐
Joint membership	£28.00	☐	£30.00	☐
Concessionary joint membership	£18.50	☐	£20.50	☐

Life membership information is available on request.

Title _____ Surname _____

Forename(s) _____

Address _____

_____ Postcode _____

Date of Birth _____ Email address _____

Signature _____

Partner's details (for Joint Membership)

Title _____ Surname _____

Forename(s) _____

Date of Birth _____ Email address _____

CAMRA will occasionally send you e-mails related to your membership. We will also allow your local branch access to your email. If you would like to opt-out of contact from your local branch please tick here ☐ (at no point will your details be released to a third party).

Find out more at **www.camra.org.uk/joinus** or telephone **01727 867201**

*15 months membership for the price of 12 is only available the first time a member pays by Direct Debit.

NOTE: Membership benefits are subject to change.

REF: GBG2013